LAYOUT OF MAP PAGES 2-89

Scale 1:4 500 000

0   20   40   60   80   100 Kilometres

0   20   40   60   Miles

Dedicated
by gracious permission to
Her Royal Highness
The Princess Anne

Bartholomew

Gazetteer of Britain

Compiled by Oliver Mason M.A.

John Bartholomew & Son Ltd.

First Edition 1977
ISBN 0 85152 771X

PRINTED AND PUBLISHED IN SCOTLAND BY
JOHN BARTHOLOMEW AND SON LTD
EDINBURGH EH9 1TA

6189

Gazetteer computer set in Eterna by Computaprint Ltd., London
Printed by offset lithography in Scotland by John Bartholomew & Son Ltd., Edinburgh.

CONTENTS

ENDPAPERS
Layout to Road Maps

INTRODUCTORY AND STATISTICAL
Introduction   vii
General Abbreviations   viii
Etymology   ix-xiii
Rainfall   xiv
Temperature   xv

POPULATION AND RELATED STATISTICS
Population of England, Scotland and Wales   xvii-xxi
Population of Places   xxii-xxxii
Population of Standard Regions and Metropolitan Counties   xxxiii
New Towns in Britain   xxxiii-xxxiv
Population change in the United Kingdom   xxxv-xxxvi
Population : age and sex structure   xxxvii
Migration   xxxviii-xxxix
Marriage and Divorce trends   xl
Family   xli
Health   xlii-xliii
Leisure   xliv
Work   xlv
Trade   xlvi-xlvii

The National Grid   xlviii

GAZETTEER OF BRITAIN   1-272

ATLAS SECTION
Road Maps
1 : 300 000 maps of Gt Britain, 1 : 1 250 000 Route Planning maps;
Town plans   2-112

Thematic Maps
Comparative Heights and Depths in Britain   113
1 : 1 250 000 maps of Counties, Regions and Districts   114-119
Weather   120-121
Land Use   122
Food   123
Population   124
Energy   125
Manufacturing Industries   126-127
Famous Places   128

INTRODUCTION

This book has been compiled to meet the insistent demand for an up-to-date reference gazetteer of Britain, the need for which has become more urgent as a result of the changes brought about by local government reorganisation, in England and Wales in 1974, and in Scotland in 1975. The area covered consists of England, Scotland, Wales, and the Isle of Man.

In order to provide a precise and convenient system of locating the places and features listed, a set of maps has been included, and map references are given in the body of the work. Each entry includes a reference to these map pages (and, where applicable, the map squares). An asterisk at the end of the map reference denotes that the place or feature is not named on the map itself; it can, however, easily be located, since its distance and direction from another place is also given. At the end of the entry the National Grid reference is shown, in all cases where such reference is considered meaningful. The reference given for a river is that of its mouth.

Wherever practicable, measurements are given in both imperial and metric units (except distances of one mile, one kilometre or two kilometres, which are given in accordance with one system of measurement only). However, where two measurements are given it cannot be assumed that the one is necessarily an accurate conversion of the other. For instance, a distance of about five miles may be given as 5m/7km, 5m/8km, or 5m/9km, that is, to the nearest kilometre; and areas given in acres and hectares, or in square miles and square kilometres, may be in round figures only. Particular caution should be exercised in interpreting the conversions of mountain heights, since in some cases the latest available survey material has been expressed in feet and in other cases in metres.

The gazetteer is arranged in alphabetical order, on the letter-by-letter system, in accordance with the English alphabet. It is hoped that Welsh users will forgive the placing of Chwitfford before Cydweli, for example, and of Ffontygari before Forlan, Y. Place names incorporating the word 'Saint', abbreviated to 'St', are arranged in the order in which they would appear if they were spelt out in full.

Human settlements are described as cities, towns, villages, hamlets, or localities. It is, however, hardly possible, and perhaps not even desirable, to define these terms; one merges into the other, and the choice of which term to use depends upon the area in which the particular place is located and other factors; it is largely a matter of subjective judgement. (The term 'hamlet' is not generally used in Scotland, and is not employed in this gazetteer to describe places in that country.)

For the sake of economy, care has been taken to keep the entries as short as possible, without omitting information of importance or outstanding interest. The temptation to write a guide book rather than a reference book has been resisted. Whilst every effort has been made to ensure accuracy, it must be appreciated that the face of Britain is continuously and rapidly changing, so that what is correct 'at time of going to press' may well be less than wholly so on the day of publication. Nevertheless, the publishers will always be grateful to readers who point out any inaccuracies or significant omissions.

GENERAL ABBREVIATIONS

admin	administrative	m	mile (s)
A.M.	Ancient Monument	mkt	market
	(in care of Department of	mnfg	manufacturing
	the Environment)	mnfre	manufacture
b	born	monmt	monument
bldg	building	mt	mountain
br	bridge	N	north
c	century (e.g. 14c)	NT	National Trust
c.	*circa*	NTS	National Trust for
cas	castle		Scotland
ch	church	opp	opposite
d	died	par	parish
Dec	Decorated	Perp	Perpendicular
dist	district	pop.	population
E	east	Pt	Point
EE	Early English	qv	*quod vide*
Elizn	Elizabethan	r	river
esp	especially	RAF	Royal Air Force
etc.	*et cetera*	RC	Roman Catholic
ft	feet	rd	road
Ggn	Georgian	resr	reservoir
grnds	grounds	rly	railway
Gt (r)	Great (er)	RN	Royal Navy, Royal Naval
ham	hamlet	S	south
Hd	Head	sq	square
HQ	headquarters	St	Saint
Hr	Higher	stn	station
hse	house	tn	town
I., Is.	Island, Islands	TV	television
incl	including	Upr	Upper
Jacbn	Jacobean	Victn	Victorian
km	kilometre (s)	vil	village
Lit	Little	W	west
loc	locality	wd	wood
Lr	Lower	WT	wireless telegraphy

ABBREVIATIONS
used in the gazetteer
for counties of England and Wales
and regions of Scotland

Beds	Bedfordshire	Lancs	Lancashire
Berks	Berkshire	Leics	Leicestershire
Bucks	Buckinghamshire	Lincs	Lincolnshire
Cambs	Cambridgeshire	Northants	Northamptonshire
Ches	Cheshire	Notts	Nottinghamshire
D & G	Dumfries and Galloway	Nthmb	Northumberland
Derbys	Derbyshire	Oxon	Oxfordshire
Glam	Glamorgan (Mid, S, W)	S'clyde	Strathclyde
Glos	Gloucestershire	Som	Somerset
H & W	Hereford and Worcester	Staffs	Staffordshire
Hants	Hampshire	Warwicks	Warwickshire
Herts	Hertfordshire	Wilts	Wiltshire
H'land	Highland	Yorks	Yorkshire (N, S, W)

Western Isles (Islands Area) is abbreviated to W Isles.

Etymology of British place names

The following Glossary contains the principal components of the place-names in the British Isles, and with its aid the derivation of many names may be acertained, while something of the physical conditions of various localities in early times may also be learned. In Scotland, Ireland and Wales, where most of the names are Gaelic, Irish and Welsh respectively, derivations tend to be less complex than in parts of England where Celts, Romans, Scandinavians, Anglo-Saxons and Normans have all had a share in forming the present nomenclature. Many names, however, in all four countries, have been changed to the extent that their original forms are no longer recognisable, and some words of different origin and meaning have become identical in form. In such cases, the true derivation of a name can often only be ascertained by finding its earlier forms in old records. It should be emphasised, therefore, that this glossary is merely a general guide, and in case of doubt, more comprehensive works on place-names should be consulted.

Note: In Gaelic, both Scottish and Irish, **aspiration** denotes the change that an initial consonant may undergo in various changes of syntax; it is used to denote gender, number, case or tense. Thus in Knockvaddy, the original form is **Cnoc a' Mhadaidh**, where **madadh**, dog, is here the possessive mhadaidh. This gives a **v** sound, which when Anglicised becomes -vaddy. Similarly, adjectives like **mór**, big, become **mhór** after feminine nouns and are sometimes transcribed as **-vore**. This aspiration affects all letters in the Gaelic alphabet, with the exception of l, n, r and vowels.

ABBREVIATIONS -

A.S., Anglo Saxon; G., Gaelic; I., Irish; Lat., Latin; O.N., Old Norse; Scand., Scandinavian.

A (Norse), a river, as in Greta. Also an island in the sea (**a** and **ay**) e.g. Rona, Mingulay. **Ea** and **ey** are generally A.S. forms. Plurals: **eyre, ayre** and **aire** e.g. Saltaire, Eye, Sheppey.

Ab, Abb (Lat. **abbas**, abbot, G., aba). Ballinab, Milnab.

Aber (Welsh, Cymric), a confluence, or river-mouth, e.g. Aberford, Aberdeen, Barmouth.

Abh, Abhain, Abhainn (Celtic), water, river. Avonmore, Awn, Owenbeg, Abhuinnsuidhe.

Abhall (Celtic) apple.

-Ach, -agh, -lach, -nach, -och, -rach, -tach, -trach, -seach, (G.) suffixes denoting 'full of, abounding in', e.g. Keppoch,Mortlach.

Achadh (G.), field. Ardagh, Aghadoe, Auchinleck, Achnasheen.

Acker (O.N.), open country, untilled land.

Aebhinn (G.), delightful. Rathevin, Drumeevin.

Aik (Scots), oak.

Ail, Fail (O. Gaelic), rock. Allagower, Alleen, Alloa.

Airigh (G.), also anglicised **Airie**, shieling, mountain pasture. Airieglassan, Aringour.

Airne (I.), sloe. Killarney, Magherarny.

Ait (G.), a house site. Attidermot, Attivally, Aith.

Alainn, Aluinn (G.), bright, beautiful. Moyallan, Derraulin.

All (O. Gaelic), white. Aln, Ellen.

Allt- (G.), anglicised to **Ald-, Auld-, Ault-**, stream, burn. Garvald Altaggart Burn, Old Water of Cluden.

Alltan-. Diminutive of **allt**, little stream.

Alt (I.), **Allt** (Welsh), a height, cliff. Altavilla, Tonanilt, Builth.

An (G.), Contracted form of **abhainn** q.v.

An (G.), the.

An, een, og, oc, net, can. Diminutive G and I suffixes. Lochan, Killasnet, Briancan.

Aonach (G.), assembly, cattle-fair. Enagh, Nenagh, Ballineanig, Eantybeg.

Ar (G.), sloe. Aire, Arre.

Arbhar (G. & I.), corn. Knockanaroor, Clonarrow.

Ard (G. & I.), high, a height. Also **Aird**. Ardmore, Armagh, Airdrie, Ardrossan.

Arn, Ern (Teutonic), place, dwelling, house. Arn, Chiltern, Whithorn.

Aros (G.), house, dwelling, abode. Aros (Mull).

Asc (Norse **askr**) ash tree. Ascaig, Ascog.

Ath (G.), a ford. Athnagar, Aghanlugha, Athole.

Atta (G.), from 'fada', long.

Auchter (G.), from **Uachdar**, q.v., the summit, upper. Auchterarder. Other form; Ochter.

Ault. See **Allt**

Avon. See **Abhainn**, Welsh **afon**.

Ay (Scand.) an island. See **A**.

Ayr (Scand.) from **eyrr**, beach. Eoropie.

Bach, Bychan (Welsh), little. Fem., fach, fechan.

Bad (G.), grove, clump, thicket. Diminutive **badan**. Badcall, Badachro.

Badhun (I.), a fenced enclosure. Bawn, Bavan.

Baile (G. & I.). Anglicised to **Bal-, Bally-**, farm, town. Balquidder, Ballyleague, Ballaboy, Ballabtrae.

Ban (G. & I.), white, fair. Loughbawn, Carrickbaun, Edinbane.

Barr (G.), hill-top. Burglass, Barr.

Bard (Norse), extremity, point.

Barrow (A.S.), from **beorh**, a hill. Other forms: borough, berg, berry; e.g. Ingleborough, Queensberry.

Bass (G.), from **bathais**, forehead.

Battle. See **Botl**.

Bealach (G.), pass. (Irish-road). Ballaghboy, Ballinvally, Balloch.

Beann, beinn (G. & I.), mountain. Anglicised to **Ben**. Akin to Welsh **pen.** Ben Nevis, Bengore, Bannagh.

Bearn (G. & I.), gap, breach. Ballynabearny.

Beck (Scand.), a brook. Another form : batch.

Bedd (Welsh), a grave.

Beg. From Gaelic **beag**, little. Awbeg, Drumbeg, Carrickbeg.

Beith (G. & I.), birch-tree. Behagh, Aghaveagh, Kilbaha, Dalbeattie, Largvey; Welsh, **Bedw**; Penbeddw.

Bettws (Welsh), corruption of English bede-house.

Beul (G.). Anglicised to **Bel**, mouth, entrance; sometimes a ford (I.). Belfast, Belleek, Belnahua.

Big (Norse) from **bygg**, barley.

Bigging (A.S.), from **byggan**, to build, hence a dwelling.

Bile (G. & I.), sacred tree. Ringville, Altavilla.

Bior (O. Gaelic), well, water, fountain. Bere, Bervie.

Blaen (Welsh), a summit. Plural, **Blaenau.**

Blair (G.), a field. Blairgowan, Blawrainy. In Ireland found only in the diminutive, **Blarney.**

Bó (G.), a cow. Aghaboe, Annamoe, Bowling.

Bo, Bol, Bold (Norse from **boldstadr**, dwelling. Skibo, Leurbost, Newbold.

Bod (Cymric), a house. Another form: bos. Bodmin, Hafod, Bosher.

Bog (G.), soft, miry, damp.

Bon, Bonn (G.), from **Bun**, q.v.

Bor, Bore (O.E. and Swedish), from **bord**, a table, board.

Borg (Danish), a fort, shelter-place, burgh.

Borough (A.S.), from **beorgan**, to shelter, An earthwork, and hence a fortified town. Other forms: bury, brough, burgh and barrow.

Bost (Norse). See **Bo, Bol**, etc.

Both (G.), hut, house, bothy. Diminutive **bothan**. Bochastle, Bohuntin.

Botl (A.S.), a dwelling. Newbottle, Newbattle, Bootle.

Bradan (G.), a salmon. Loughbraddan.

Braghad (G.), throat, gorge. Braid, Bradoge.

Braich (Welsh), an arm.

Braigh, Bread, Brae (G.), the top, summit, upper part. Breadalbane. Braid Hills.

Bran (G.), from braon, a drop, drizzling rain.

Bre (Celtic), a promontory; e.g. Bredon.

Breac (G.), speckled; hence trout, Bealanbrack, Altnabreac.

Bri (Celtic), hill. Brigown, Bray; Akin to Braigh.

Bro (Celtic), a district; e.g. Pembroke.

Broc (A.S.), a badger. Clonbrock, Brockra, Broxburn.

Bron (Welsh), a breast, a slope.

Broom (G.), from braon, drizzling rain. Also (O.E.), brom=broom.

Brugh (I.), a palace, or important house. Bruree, Bruce, Bryan, Bruff, Brough. Akin to Borg and Burgh.

Bryn (Welsh), a brow, a ridge; e.g. Brandon, Birnwood, Braintree, Brinton.

Buachaille (G. & I.), cowherd. Bowhill, Buachaille Etive.

Buidhe (G. & I.), yellow. Athboy, Benwee, Loch Buie, Achiltibuie.

Buinne (G.), a wave, flood. Boyne, Cloonabunny.

Bun (G. & I.), foot or mouth. Bundoran, Bunessan, Buncrana.

Burgh (Teutonic), a fortified town, a town.

Bwlch (Welsh), a mountain pass.

By, Byr, (Scand.), a dwelling-place. Other forms; bere, beer, and bear; e.g. Aylesbere, Bere Alston, Beardon, Bearhaven, Whitby, Duncansby.

Cabhan (G.), a hollow. Cavan, Cavens, Cowan; sometimes a round bare hill. Cavanaleck, Cavanagh.

Cader (Welsh), a seat.

Caein (I.), beautiful. Killykeen, Drumquin.

Caer (Welsh), a fortress. Another form: car; e.g. Caernarvon, the fort opposité Mon (Anglesey), Carlisle, Carstairs.

Cailleach (G.), a nun, old woman. Calliaghstown.

Cairn See Carn.

Caiseal (I.), circular stone fort. Cashel, Ballycastle.

Caisle (I.), a small inlet. Cashla Bay, Cashleen.

Caladh (G.), harbour, landing-place.

Cam (G. & I.), crooked. Roscam, Camelon.

Camas (G.), bay, creek, sometimes anglicised to Cambus, indicating a meander in a river. Camusterach, Cambusnethan.

Caol (G.), narrow, a strait. Angl. form Kyle. Caolisport, Caolas, Kyle of Lachalsh, Kyles of Bute.

Capall (G. & I., form Lat. caballus), horse. Gortnacapul, Portincaple, Capplegill.

Car (G.), a turn, twist; crooked, bending.

Carcach (I.), a marsh. Cork, Curkish.

Careg (Welsh), a rock or stone. Another form: cerrig.

Carn (G.), Cairn (angl. form), heap of stones, rocky mound, akin to Carn, Carnedd (Welsh). Carnlea, Carnoch, Cairntoul.

Carrach (G. & I.), rough. Slieve Corragh.

Carraig (G. & I.) headland, cliff, crag, rock. Also Carra and Carrick. Carrigafoyle, Carrickfergus, Carrick.

Carse (Norse), low alluvial land along a river.

Cathair (I. & G.), seat, fortress. Carlow, see Caer.

Cau (Welsh), a hollow.

Cauld (Norse), cold.

Ceanannus (G.), head, abode. Modified by the English to Kenlis and then contracted to Kells.

Ceann (G. & I.), head, top. Cannafahy, Kanturk, Kinsale, Kenbane, Kenmare, Kintyre, Kencot.

Ceapach (G. & I.), plot of ground. Cappoquin, Cappamore, Keppoch,

Cefn (Welsh), a ridge; e.g. Chevin, Keynton, Chevy Chase, Cheviot.

Ceum (G. & I.), step, pass. Caim, Keam, Cushcam.

-Char, -Chor, (G.). Suffix denoting collective form. Cranagher.

Chart, a dense part of a forest. Another form: Kart.

Chester (Saxon), from the Lat. castra, a camp. It occurs also as cester and caster, and in Wroxeter, Exeter, etc.

Chipping (A.S.), from ceapian, to buy; e.g. Chepstow, Chippingham.

Cill (G. & I.), cell, burial-ground, church. Anglicised to Kill- q.v.

Cil (Welsh), a cell, recess.

Clach, Cloch (G. & I.), stone. (I. clogh). See Cloch, Clough.

Clachan (G.), hamlet, church with burial ground.

Clais (G. & I.), a trench. Clashanaffrin, Classagh, Clashmock, Cleish.

Clar (I.), a board, plain. Clare, Clarbane, Claragh.

Clere (A.N.), a royal or episcopal residence on a high hill.

Cloch and Clough (G. & I.), stone. Cloghabally, Cloughmore, Aughnacloy. See Clach.

Cluain (G. & I.), a meadow. Clonmel, Clintycracken, Clane, Cloncaird, Clunes.

Cnoc (G. & I.), hill, knoll, eminence, mound.

Coat (Welsh), from coed, a wood.

Coch (Welsh), red. Fem., Goch.

Coed (Welsh), a wood. This word occurs in Cotswold, Chat Moss, Catlow, etc.

Coileach-greigh (I.); coileach-fraoich (G.), cock of the heath, grouse; cearc-fraoich, grouse hen. Cronacarkfree, Coolkirky.

Coille (G. & I.), a wood. Cullycapple, Cuiltybo, Killiecrankie, Killiehuntly.

Colonia (Lat.), a colony; e.g. Colne, Lincoln.

Comar, Com, Cum, Cumber (G.), confluence, meeting-place; Cymmer (Welsh). See also Comhrac.

Combe (Celto-Saxon), a bowl-shaped valley. In Welsh, cwm; e.g. Compton, Gomshall, Commaun, Cummeen.

Comhrac (I.), a meeting of rivers, roads, men in battle, etc. Cloncorick, Carrigahorig.

Cong (I.), a narrow neck, narrows of a river, small channel. Nancung, Cungmore.

Cop (Saxon), a head.

Cor (Welsh), a choir, church.

Corran (G.), a sickle, hence a curved sand-spit. Corran.

Corrie (from G. coire), a cauldron, ravine. Corrour, Corra Linn. Similar to Welsh cwm.

Cors (Welsh), a bog.

Cote (A.S.), a mud cottage.

Craig (G.), a rock. Anglicised form of Creag; creagach, rocky. Craigellachie, Craignure, Kennacraig.

Craobh (G. & I.), a tree, branch. Derrycreevy, Crevagh, Corncravie.

Creag (G.), rock. Anglicised to Craig; creagach, rocky. Craigellachie, Craignure, Kennacraig.

Cri (G.), from crioch, a boundary, frontier.

Crib (Welsh), a crest.

Crioch (G.), boundary, frontier, march. Achnacree.

Croft (A.S.), an enclosed field.

Crois (G.), Croes (Welsh), a cross. Dalcross, Ardnacross.

Crom (G. & I.), bent, crooked. Bencrom, Croome, Cromdale.

Cron (I.), swarthy, dark brown. Cronkill.

Cron (Celtic), a round hollow. Cronebane, Cronroe.

Cruach (G.) and Croagh (I.), stack, hill, haunch. Croagh, Crohane, Cruachan, Cruachlussa.

Cu (G. & I.), a dog.

Cuan (I.), harbour, (G.), ocean, Cooneen, Tincoon, Cuan Sound.

Cuil (G. & I.), back, a nook. Coleraine, Culrain, Culloden.

Cuirreagh (I.), marsh, plain. Curragh, Curraheen.

Cum See Combe.

Cwm See Combe.

Daingean (I.), strong, a stronghold. Dangan, Dundanion, Dingle, Ballindine.

Dail (G. & I.), field, meadow. Dalkeith, Dalintart, Deloraine.

Dair (O. Gaelic & I.), oak. Daar, Adare, Darrach.

Dairt (I.), a heifer. Slieve Dart, Glandarta.

Dal (Norse dalr), valley. Also Dale (q.v.); in Scotland, Glendale, Laudale, Glenborrowdale, Swordale; in England, Kendal, Arundel, Oundle.

Dale (Norse), a valley. Sometimes contracted to dal; e.g. Kendal, Arundel, Oundle.

Damh (G. & I.), an ox. Dawros Head, Inchnadamph.

Dau (Welsh), two. Fem., dwy.

Dealg (I.), a thorn. Moneydollig, Kildellig.

Dearg (G. & I.), red. Derg, Darrig, Ratherrig, Beinn Dearg.

Deas, Deasceart (G. & I.), right hand, south. Ratass, Deskart, Diskirt.

Den(A.S.), a deep-wooded valley, a swine pasture.

Den, Dean, Dene (A.S.), wooded hollow or valley.

Derry From Gaelic doire, thicket, q.v.

Dian (G. & I.), strong. Dinin, Deenagh.

Dodd (Norse), a limb; one of the lower peaks of a mountain.

Doire (G. & I.), thicket, clump, grove. Londonderry, Dernagree, Glen Derry.

Donn (G. & I.), brown, dun. Barnadown.

Dover (Celtic), water. G. & I., dobhar, Welsh dŵr, dyffryn. Doory,

Dooragh, Bundoran, Deveron.

Droichead (G. & I.), bridge. Drogheda, Beladrihid, Kildrought, Kildrochat.

Drui (I.), a Druid. Tobernadree, Killadroy.

Druim (G. & I.), ridge, back. Rathdrum, Dromore, Drumderg, Drumnadrochit.

Dubh (G. & I.), black. Carrickduff, Doolough, Douglas, Blardubh, Dowlas.

Dun (G. & I.), a fort. Downpatrick, Donegal, Dundrum, Dunbar, etc.

Dur (from O.C. **dwr**, water).

Dyffryn (Welsh), a valley. See Dover.

Each (G. & I.), from Lat. equus, a horse. Aughinish, Russagh, Dunecht.

Eadar (G.), middle, between. Craigadder, Dunadry, Eddrachillis, Benderloch.

Eaglais (G. & I.), Eglws (Welsh), from Lat. **ecclesia**, a church. Hence **Eccles**, Eaglesfield, Ecclefechan, Terregles.

Eala (G. & I.), a swan. Doonvinalla, Monalla.

Eanach (I.), a watery place. Annaduff, Inchenny, Rathanny.

Eas (G. & I.), waterfall. Doonass, Ballysadare, Askeaton, Fetteresso.

Easpog (I.), **Easbuig** (G.) from Lat. episcopus, a bishop. Killaspy, Killaspugbrone, Gillespie, Ernespie.

Eigil (A.S.), a mythical archer and hero; e.g. Aylesbury.

Eilean (G.), island. Angl. **Ellan.**

Eo, Eochaill (I.), a yew, yew-wood. Mayo, Gleno, Youghal, Aughall, Oghilly, Donohill.

Eofer (A.S.), a wild boar; e.g. Evershot, Eversley.

Eorna (I. & G.), barley. Coolnahorna.

Esk. From an early Celtic word meaning water. The word is found in a large variety of forms, such as Esk, Usk, Ash, Exe, Axe, Ock, Ouse, Ose, Wash, Ease, and Es (Thames).

Eudan (I.), forehead, face. Edenderry, Edinkillie. Also Gaelic **Aodann.**

Ey (Scand.), island. Lambay, Dalkey, Ireland's Eye, Lundy, Walney. See **A.**

Fach. See **Bach.**

Fada (G. & I.), long. Knockfadda, Killyfad, Banada, Inchfad.

Fair (Norse), from faers (ligature ae), sheep. Other form: **far.**

Fal (Scots), from **faw** or **fauch**, dun, pale red.

Fawr. See **Mawr.**

Fearna (G. & I.), alder. Fernagh, Glenfarne, Gortnavern.

Fearsad (Old Irish), a sandbank. Belfast, Calanafersy, Fersit.

Fell (Scand), fjall, mountain.

Fetter from G. **foithir**, field, portion of land. Fetteresso.

Feur (G.), grass. Fearglass, Ferbane, Lissanair.

Ffordd (Welsh), a road; e.g. Minffordd.

Fiadh (G. & I.), deer. Clonea, Knockaneag, Gortnavea.

Field (A.S.), a forest clearing where trees have been felled; e.g. Dryfield, Scafell.

Fiodh, Fothair (I. & G.), wood, forest. Fecbane, Finnis, Fiddown, Fews, Gortnafira, Wheery.

Fionn, Finn (I. & G.), white. Tullaghfin, Finaway, Fancroft; sometimes clear, Finglas, Rosenallis, Phoenix Park, Finlass.

Fiord (Scand, **fjord**), fiord or firth. Wexford, Carlingford, Sunart, Gruinard, Pentland Firth.

Fleet (Scand.), a flowing stream.

Flegg (Norse), flat. Corrupted into **fleck**; e.g. Fleckney.

Fòd (I. & G.), a sod, soil, land. Fodagh, Mullanavode.

Fold (Norse), an enclosure formed by **felled** trees.

Folk (A.S.), people. Norfolk, Suffolk.

Force (from Norse **fors**), waterfall. Glenforsa, Forsinard.

Ford (A.S.), a ford.

Forrach (I.), a meeting-place. Farrow, Gortnafurra.

Fors. See **Force.**

Fraoch (G. & I.), heather. Freaghillaun, Inishfree.

Frea (A.S.), name of a goddess; e.g. Frathorpe, Freasley.

Gabhar (G. & I.), goat. Glenagower, Ballynagore, Ardgour.

Gair (from Gaelic **gearr**), short. Gairloch, Loch Gair.

Gall (G. & I.), a foreigner, stranger.

Garbh (G. & I.), rough, rugged. Garven, Garvellachs.

Garn, Gart (G. & I.) from **garadh**, enclosure, garden. Gartnavel, Gartmain.

Garran (I.), shrubbery. Garranamanagh, Ballygarrane.

Garrdha (I.), a garden. Garryowen, Ballingarry.

Garth (O.N.), from **gardr**, enclosed place, farm.

Gate (Scand.), a road; e.g. Reigate, Gatton, Jervis Gut.

Gate (Norse), from **geit**, a goat; sometimes A.S., a door.

Gay (A.S.), a forest clearing, a settlement.

Geal (G. & I.), white. Galvone, Galcussagh.

Gearr (G.), short. See **Gair.** Castlegar.

Gill (Norse), a ravine.

Glac (G.), hollow. Glack.

Glais (I.), a small stream. Glashaboy, Douglas, Glasnevin.

Glan (Welsh), a bank, shore; e.g. Rhuddlan.

Glas (G. & I.) green, greyish. Glaslough, Kilmaglush.

Gleann (G. & I.), glen, valley. Glenmaddy, Glandine, Glencoe, Finglen.

Glen. See **Gleann.**

Gleoir (I.), brightness, clearness. Glore, Lough Glore.

Glor (I.), a voice, noise. Gloreen, Glashnagloragh.

Gluair (I.), pure, clear. Glooria, Glowria.

Glyn (Welsh), a glen.

Gobha (G. & I.), a smith. Ballygow, Ardgivna, Balgown.

Gobhar. See **Gabhar.**

Goe (O.N.), from **gjó**, creek, cleft.

Goirtean, diminutive of **Gort** (q.v.)

Gorm (G. & I.), blue.

Gort (G.), a tilled field. Gortnaclogh, Gartsherrie.

Gower (G.), from gabhar, goat.

Graigh, Groigh (G. & I.), flock, herd. Garrymagree, Slievenagry.

Graineog (I.), hedgehog.

Grange (Scots), a corn farm, or storehouse for grain.

Grian (G.), the sun.

Grianan (G. & I.), sunny spot, bower, balcony, palace. Greenane, Clogrennan, Greenoge.

Guala (G. & I.), shoulder of a hill.

Guard. See **Garth.**

Gwent (British). Latinised into **Venta**, a plain; e.g. Winchester, Daventry.

Gwy. See **Wy.**

Gwyn (Welsh), white. Also **wyn.** Fem., **gwen** and **wen.**

Hafod (Welsh), a summer dwelling.

Hal (Celtic), salt; e.g. Haling, Pwllheli.

Ham (A.S.), an enclosure, a home. Other forms: am, ym and ome.

Har, Her (O.E.), a boundary mark.

Hatch (A.S.), a hitch-gate at the edge of a forest.

Haugh. See **How.**

Haugh, Heugh (Scots), a low-lying meadow on the banks of a stream, or between hills.

Hause, the neck or summit ridge of a pass = **col.**

Hay (A.S.), place surrounded by hedge. Older form: **haigh.**

Helga (A.S.), goddess of the under-world. Perhaps in Hellifield, Healey, Helagh, and Halliford.

Hithe (A.S.), a wharf.

Hop, Hope, How (Norse), a recess among hills, a shelter.

Holm (Scand.), island, usually small. In Outer Hebrides often becomes a suffix -am.

Holm (A.S.), a river island, a plain near a river.

Holt (A.S.), a copse. Often corrupted into hot; e.g. Bagshot, Aldershot.

Hoved (Scand.), a head. Howth.

How (Norse), a sepulchral mound, from haugr. Another form: **haugh.** Also applied to a gentle eminence.

Hurst (A.S.), a thick wood.

I, Inch, Innis, Inish (Celtic), an island, pasture land near water. Inishimacsaint, Enniskeen, Inchcolm, Inches.

Iar, Iarach (G. & I.), west. Ardaneer, Baurearagh, Clonshire.

Inbhir (G. & I.), mouth of a river. Anglicised to **Inver.** Dromineer, Ennereilly, Inverness, Inverurie.

Inch, Innis, Inish (G. & I.), island, pasture land near water. Inishmacsaint, Enniskeen, Inchcolm, Inches.

Ing (Scand.), a patronymic ending, equivalent to **mac** in Scotland. Used as a prefix it denotes a meadow. Ingham.

Iochdar (G. & I.), lower. Carroweighter, Broighter.

Iseal (G. & I.), low. Gorteeshall, Athassel. **Isel** (Welsh), low; **is**, lower; **isaf** lowest.

Iubhar (G. & I.), yew tree. Uregare, Ballynure, Newry, Glenure.

Keld (Norse), a spring. Another form; Kell; e.g. Threlkeld.

Ken, Kin (G. & I.). See **Ceann.**

Kerry (G. & I.) from **Cill** and **Coille** (q.v.). **Cill** from Lat. **cella**, church. Kildare, Kildellig, KImacolm, Killin, etc.

Kip (G.), from **ceap**, stump, block, and diminutive **ceapan.** Kippen, Kippendavie.

Kirk (Scots), a church. Also Scand., e.g. Kirkwall, Kirkibost, Kirkby Stephen.

Knock (from G. **cnoc** (q.v.)).

Kyle. Anglicised form of **Caol** (q.v.).

Lad (Norse), a pile or heap. Laid, Ledaig.

Lag (G. & I.), a hollow. Hence Logie, Logan. Diminutive **laggan.** Logierait, Lugton, Laggan, Lagg.

Lagh (I.), a hill. Portlaw, Ballinla, Law.

Lang (Scots), long.

Lann (G. & I.), **Llan** (Welsh), enclosure, house, church. Llanbedr (St. Peter), Lampeter, Lamlash, Long Newton, Lumphanan.

Lax (Scand.), a salmon. Leixlip, Laxweir, Laxford.

Leathann (G. & I.), broad. Ardlahan, Gortlane.

Legio (Lat.), a legion; e.g. Leicester, Lexdon, Caerleon.

Leim, Leum (G. & I.), a leap. Leam, Lemnaroy, Limavady.

Leiter (G. & I.), a hill-side. Lettermullen, Latteragh, Lettreen, Letterfinlay, Letters.

Leithead (I.) and **Leathad** (G.), breadth. Moyhelid, Carrighead.

Leth (G. & I.), half. Letham, Lavally, Leighlin.

Leven, Lomond (G.), from **leamhan**, an elm.

Ley (A.S.), a clearing in a wood. Another form: leigh.

Liagh (I., Welsh form, **Llach**), a flat stone. Leag, Leek, Ballyleague, Lickmolassy, Harlech, Lecroft, Leadburn, Auchinleck.

Liath (G. & I.), grey. Leafin. Rosslea.

Lín (G. & I.), flax. Coolaleen, Curraghaleen, Linshart.

Linn (G. & I.), and **Llyn** (Welsh), a deep pool. Lindores, Linton, Dublin.

Lios, Lis (I.), a fort, garden. Listowel, Lissaniska.

Llam (Welsh), a stride, step.

Lleyn (Welsh), a tongue of land.

Llwyd (Welsh), grey.

Llwyn (Welsh), a grove.

Llyn, Welsh form of **Linn,** q.v.

Loch (G.), **Lough** (I.), lake, arm of the sea.

Lod (G.), and diminutive **lodan,** wet place, swamp.

Low (A.S.), from **Hlaw**, a mound. Another form: law.

Lund (Norse), a sacred grove.

Madadh (G. & I.), dog, fox, wolf. Ballinamaddy, Knockavaddy, Drummodie, Lochmaddy, Maddiston.

Mael (I.), **Maol** (G.), **Moel** (Welsh), bald, bare, a bare hill. Lismoyle, Mweelahorna, Melrose, Mull.

Maen (Welsh), a stone. Another form; man; e.g. Old Man, Dodman, Manuel.

Maes (Welsh), a field.

Magh (O.G.), a level field, plain. Macosquin, Malton, Mogeely, Armagh, Maghera, The Mearns.

Màm (G.), large round hill, waste. Mam Rattachan, Mamlorn.

Manach (G. & I.) from Lat. **monacus**, monk. Knocknamanagh, Farramanny, Milmannoch.

Mark (A.S.), a boundary; e.g. Marbury, Merkbury, March, Marchmont.

Mawr (Welsh), great. Another form: fawr.

Meadhon (G. & I.), middle. Inishmaan, Kilmaine, Drummenagh, Maidenhead (Wigtown).

Meall (G. & I.), a heap, hillock. Manlanimirish, Milleenahorna, Mollance.

Mere (A.S.), a lake. Windermere.

Milui (I.), low, marshy ground. Meelick.

Mín (G. & I.), smooth, fine. Meeniska, Clomneen, Menlough, Mindrim.

Minster (A.S.), a monastery.

Moin, Moine (G. & I.), a bog or moor. Monabraher, Mindork, Moniaive, Monifieth. From diminutive **Mointin.** Moanteen.

Molt (G. & I.), a wether. Annamult.

Mon (G.), from **monadh**, a hill. Moncrieff, Moneymore.

Mór (G. & I.), great. (See Welsh **mawr**). Dromore, Benmore, Dunmore.

Muc (G. & I.), pig, sow. Muckross, Muckloon, Auchtermuchty.

Muine (I.), a brake, shrubbery. Monaghan, Moneydorragh, Bunnyconellan, Leaffony. Allied to **Moin.**

Muir (Scots), a moor. Boroughmuir, Menmuir.

Muir (G. & I.), the sea. Connemara, Kenmare, Murree, Glamorgan, Morecambe.

Murbhach (I.), a marsh by the sea, a salt marsh. Murvagh, Murrey, Kilmurvey.

Mynydd (Welsh), a bald head, bare mountain, moor.

Nab (O.N. **nappi**), a point, headland.

Nant (Welsh), a valley, stream.

Nas (I.), a meeting-place. Naas, Nash, Ballynaas.

Naze. See **Ness.**

Ness (Scand.) from **nes**, headland. Durness, Waternish, Girdle Ness, Orford Ness.

Newydd (Welsh), new.

Noup (Scand.), a lofty headland.

Ochter (G.). Another form of **Auchter**, q.v.

Odhar (G. & I.), dun-coloured, light brown. Ardore, Derroar, Odder, Corrour.

Oe, O (Norse), an island.

Oillean. See Eilean.

Oir, Oirthear (G. & I.). Also **Ear**, east. Tullahar, Orior, Oristown.

Or (Scand.), sand point. Carnsore.

Or (A.S.), from **ora**, a bank or shore; e.g. Windsor, Oare.

Ord (G.), high, hammer-shaped hill. Muir of Ord, Kirkurd.

Pab, Pap (Norse), priest. Papa Westray, Pabbay.

Pant (Welsh), a hollow.

Peel, from Lat. **Palus**, stake. A small tower.

Pen (Welsh), a head, hence a mountain. Akin to **Ken** in G. names.

Pit, Pitten (Pictish), a farmstead, portion. Pitlochty, Pittenweem.

Plas (Welsh), a palace.

Pol, another name for **Balder**, q.v.; e.g. Polstead.

Poll (G. & I.), **Pwll** (Welsh), a pool, small inlet. Pollanass, Poolbeg, Pouldine, Ballinphuill, Polmont.

Pont (Welsh), from Lat. **pons.** Another form: bont.

Porth (Welsh), a port. Another form: borth.

Prest (O.E.), from preost, a priest.

Quoich (from G. cuach), a cup, cup-shaped hollow.

Rath, Rait (G. & I.), fort, town. Rathfarnham, Rathcool, Rothiemay, Rothiemurchus.

Re, aire, cumulative suffixes. Craigera, Fodre, Machaire.

Rea. Anglicised form of G. **reidh**, smooth, flat plain.

Reamhar (G. & I.), thick, fat. Killyrover, Reenrour.

Reithe (G. & I.), a ram. Leamareha, Ralny Hill.

Rhaidar (Welsh), a waterfall.

Rhiw (Welsh), a brow or slope; e.g. Ruabon (Rhiwafon).

Rhudd (Welsh), red; e.g. Ruthin = **Rhudd-din** (Redfort), Rutland.

Rhu, Rhuda (alternative form **Ruhba**, see below), (G.), a cape, headland.

Rhyd (Celtic), a ford.

Rhyn (Welsh), a promontory. See **Rinn** or **Roinn.**

Riabhach (G. & I.), greyish, brindled. Aghareagh, Carrickrevagh, Braeriach.

Ridire (G. & I.), from Teuronic **Ritter**) a knight. Kilruddery, Ballyruther.

Rigg (Scots), a ridge, furrow. Harperrig, Riggend.

Righ (G. & I.), a king. Athenry, Rye Water, Monaree, Dalry.

Rinn, Roinn (G. & I.), a point. Rinanagh, Ringville, Randoon, Rineen, Ringford, Rinns of Islay.

Rioghan (I.), a queen. Bellarena, Tagharina.

Rithe (A.S.), running water; e.g. Meldreth.

Ron (G.), a seal. Roaninish, Carrignarona, Roundstone Bay.

Ros (G. & I.), a promontory, wood. Muckross, Roscam, Portrush, Roseneath, Roslin, Ardrossan.

Royd (Teutonic), a place that has beed **ridded** of trees.

Ruadh (G. & I.), reddish, ruddy. Ruan, Rown, Cloghroe, Mulroy, Roughan, Rothes, Roy Bridge, Rutherglen.

Rubha (G.). point, promontory. Rowardennan.

Rudge (A.S.), from **hrvch**, a ridge or back. Another form: rigge; e.g. Reigate, Rugeley.

S. A termination for abstract nouns.

Sagart (G. & I., from Lat. **sacerdos**), a priest. Kylenasaggart, Taggartsland, Dumhaggart, Glentaggart.

Sail, Sealach (G. & I.), **Sealh** (A.S.), a willow, osier. Corsillagh. Solloghod, Cloonsellan, Kiltallaghan, Loch Salachie, Sauchie, Achnashellach.

Sal, Sail (G. & I.), brine. Kinsale, Rossalia, Salen.

Sall (A.S.), a stone house, hall; e.g. Kensal.

Samh (G. & I.), clover, sorrel. Inishmacsaint, Savoch.

Scadan, sgadan (G. & I.), a herring. Balscaddan, Coolscuddan.

Scairbh (I.), a rough, shallow ford. Scarva, Ballinascarry, Enniskerry.

Scaur, Scuir (G.), from **sgor**, sharp-pointed rock.

Sceilig (I.), a rock in the sea. The Skelligs.

Sceir (Scand. **skjer**), a rock in the sea. Scar, Skerry, The Skerries, Scarborough.

Scoil (G. & I., from Lat. **schola**, a school. Tinascolly, Scullen, Attinaskollia.

Scolb (I.), a twig used in thatching. Scullaboge.

Scornach (I.), the windpipe. Scornagh, Ballinascorney.

Sean (G. & I.), old. Shandon, Bawnatanavoher, Shambellie.

Set (A.S.), from **seta**, a settlement. Another form: Shiel.

Shaw (A.S.), from **sceaga**, a wood.

Sheal, Shealing (Scand.), a hut, or shed. Other form: Shiel.

Shee (G.). Another form of **sith** or **sidh**, q.v.

Sidh (G. & I.), a fairy. Mullaghshee, Sheerevagh, Shane, Cheek Point, Ballintine, Sidlaw Hills.

Sidhean (G.), a fairy hill. Strontian.

Siol (G. & I.), seed, progeny. Shillelagh (sons of Elaigh).

Sliebh (I.), **Sliabh** (G.), **Slieu** (Manx), a mountain moor. Slievemore, Slamannan.

Sneaght (I.), snow. Slieve Sneaght, Drumsnat.

Soke (A.S.), a local court; e.g. Thorp le Soken, Soke of Peterborough.

Spital (Norman French), from Lat. **hospitium**, hospital, or place of entertainment.

Srath (G. & I.), soft level meadow land, wide valley. Strabane, Straness, Strathmore, Yester.

Sron, Stron (G.). a nose, nose-like hill or promontory. Stronachlachar, Strontian.

Sruth, Sruthair (G.), a stream. Abbeyshrule, Struell, Struan.

Stack (Norse), a columnar rock. Other forms: stake, stick, stickle.

Stadr (Scand.), territory, estate, place. Ulster, Minster, Scrabster.

Staf (Norse), a perpendicular or pillar-like rock.

Staple (old English) **stapol**, pillar or post; Stapleford (i.e. ford indicated by post). Often corrupted into stable.

Sten (Icelandic), a stone. Stennis, Stenton.

Stoke (A.S.), a stockaded place. Another form: stow.

Stone (A.S.), **Stan** (Norse), a stone; e.g. Thurston.

Strath. See **Srath**.

Stuc (G. & I.), a pinnacle, rocky point, stack. Cloghastucan, Stuc a Chroin.

Sych (Welsh), dry; e.g. Sychnant (dry valley).

Tairbeart (G.), a narrow isthmus. Tarbet, Tarbert..

Tal (Welsh), a headland, front.

Tan (Welsh), under.

Tarbh (G.), a bull. Tarf.

Teach (G. & I.), house, dwelling. Also **Tigh** (G.). Tincoon, Tiglin, Teebane, Timahoe, Tighnabruaich, Taynuilt.

Teamhar (I.), pleasant, a hill commanding a wide view. Tara, Towermore, Tawran.

Thing (Norse), a provincial parliament; Dingley, Tinwell, Dinsdale, Dengewell, Tinwald.

Thor (Scand.), **Thunor** (A.S.), name of a god; e.g. Thurscross, Thurlow, Tursdale, Thurso, Torboll.

Thorpe (Danish), a village. Other forms: throp, trop, trope.

Thwaite (Norse), a forest clearing.

Tigh. See **Teach**.

Tilly, Tully, from G. **tulach**, a knoll. Tillycoultry, Tulloch.

Tin, Tinny, Tyn (G.), from **teine**, fire. Ardentinny.

Tír (G. & I.), country, land. Tyrone, Tyrawley, Teernacreeve.

Tiw (A.S.), name of a god; e.g. Tewin, Dewerstone.

Tobar (G. & I.), a spring. Tobar, Tipperkevin, Tipperlinn, Tobermory.

Tod, a fox; e.g. Todburn, Todfield.

Toft (Scand.), homestead, field. Another form: tot.

Toin (G. & I.), rump, hill, lowland. Tonduff, Toneel.

Tom (G.), a little hill, mound. Tomatin, Tomnahurich.

Ton (A.S.), a place surrounded by a hedge or palisade, a town, village.

Tonn (G. & I.), wave, billow. Townlough, Loughannadown.

Tor, Torr (G. & I.), a tower, pinnacle of rock. Toralt, Tory Island, Torquay, Dunster, Torphichen.

Torc (G. & I.), a wild boar. Torc Mountain, Kanturk, Drumhirk, Edendurk.

Towyn (Welsh), a strand. Another form: **tywyn**.

Traigh (G.), **Tracht** (I.), **Traeth** (Welsh), a strand.

Tre (Cymric), a village, a house; e.g. Trefriw, Treton.

Tri (Cymric), three; e.g. Tryfan (three-headed), Truro.

Tromm (I.), elder-tree. Trim, Trummery, Tromman.

Tuaim (I.), a tumulus. Tuam, Toone, Tomgrany. See also **Tom**.

Tuath, Tuaith (G. & I.), left hand, north. Rattoo, Kiltoy, Tievetooey.

Tulach (G. & I.), a hillock. Tullaroan, Tullyallen, Tulloch. See also **Tilly, Tully.**

Twistle (Old English), twisla; (O.N.), **kvisel,** a junction of two rivers; fork of a river.

Ty (Cymric), a house. In Cornwall **chy** and **ky.**

Uachdar (G. & I.), upper. Kiloughter, Clowater, Watree, Moy Otra, Auchterarder, Ochtertyre.

Uaine (G. & I.), green.

Uamh (G. & I.), a cave.

Uan (G. & I.), a lamb. Strananoon.

Uchel (Welsh), high; **uch,** higher; **uchaf,** highest. Ochil, Ogilivie. Welsh form of **uachdar.**

Uisge (G. & I.), water. Eask, Lissaniska, Phoenix Park. See **Esk.**

Ulv (Danish), a wolf. Ulva.

Ve (Norse), a sacred place; e.g. Wyndale, Weighton.

Ville, Well (French), an abode.

Voe (Norse) a little bay, inlet. See **Goe.**

Vrack. Anglicised form of **Breac,** q.v.

Ware (Teutonic), inhabitants, people of. Worcester, **Hwic-wara-ceaster;** Canterbury, **Cant-wara-burig.**

Wark (Norse), a fortress.

Wath (A.S.), a ford. Another form: wash.

Weald (A.S.), woodland. Another form: **wold, wald**; e.g. Waltham.

Well (Norse), an abode. Identical with Ger. **weiler** and Nor. Fr. **ville.** Another form: will; e.g. Kettlewell. In some names well means a spring of water.

Wen. See **Gwyn.**

Wheal (Cymric), **huel,** a tin mine; e.g. Brown Willy **(Brynhuel).**

Wick (A.S.), a village, and also a marsh; (Norse), a bay. Salt was obtained by evaporation in bays, and hence the name **wick** or **wich** was given to inland places where there was salt; e.g. Droitwich, Wickham, Wicklow.

Woden (A.S.), the name of a god. Wednesbury, Wanborough, Wanstead,

Worth (A.S.), a warded or protected place.

Wrath (Norse), from **hvarf,** a turning-point. Cape Wrath.

Wy (Welsh) water. It also takes the form **way.**

Y (Welsh), the.

Yard (A.S.), a place guarded or girded round.

Ynys (Welsh), an island.

Monthly and annual averages of rainfall
(in millimetres) over the 30 year period 1941-1971

Station	Height (m)	Grid Ref.	Jan	Feb	Mar	Apr	May	Jun	Jul	Aug	Sep	Oct	Nov	Dec	Year
Aberdeen/Craibstone	91	NJ 8710	80	57	51	48	70	58	83	86	68	82	88	76	847
Aberporth (Dyfed)	133	SN 2452	92	62	60	59	64	56	66	77	95	99	114	102	946
Achnashellach (H'land)	67	NH 0349	210	173	160	157	113	127	149	157	205	252	204	254	2161
Ambleside (Cumbria)	46	NY 3704	202	140	122	116	108	109	123	164	201	197	204	216	1902
Auchincruive (S'clyde)	45	NS 3823	83	55	51	52	57	62	81	92	103	98	90	94	918
Belper (Derbys)	60	SK 3446	69	55	501	49	55	53	59	70	62	60	75	67	724
Benbecula (W. Isles)	6	NF 7855	130	90	82	71	63	78	81	89	123	141	119	137	1204
Bexhill (E Sussex)	4	TQ 7307	73	54	47	43	45	41	53	66	66	76	95	75	734
Birmingham/Edgbaston	163	SP 0486	67	54	55	54	69	54	66	78	65	62	79	71	774
Bognor Regis (W Sussex)	7	SZ 9399	78	55	50	44	51	44	53	67	63	68	87	78	738
Boscombe Down (Wilts)	126	SU 1740	72	46	48	45	57	47	47	67	64	74	82	75	724
Bournemouth (Dorset)	40	SZ 0791	86	53	56	49	56	48	50	65	76	86	94	83	802
Bradford (W Yorks)	134	SE 1435	85	72	57	59	63	53	66	89	74	72	90	87	867
Braemar (Grampian)	339	NO 1591	82	67	52	55	69	55	61	83	81	87	89	98	879
Buxton (Derbys)	314	SK 0672	133	100	84	89	86	85	103	114	111	111	128	140	1284
Cambridge	12	TL 4557	46	35	36	36	45	47	59	62	46	47	51	46	556
Cape Wrath (H'land)	112	NC 2574	109	84	78	72	61	81	90	98	111	132	118	122	1156
Cardiff	62	ST 1979	107	72	68	66	77	68	82	108	104	104	115	114	1085
Douglas (I of Man)	87	SC 3877	117	78	76	70	75	69	77	102	112	116	120	125	1137
Dover (Kent)	6	TR 3241	71	60	49	44	47	43	68	69	66	82	105	74	778
Dumfries	49	NX 9874	99	67	67	64	77	68	85	99	112	106	105	103	1052
Dundee	45	NO 4231	64	48	45	45	65	57	76	83	68	65	70	69	755
Duntulm (H'land)	90	NG 3971	127	92	91	83	73	94	107	110	141	162	138	148	1366
Durham	102	NZ 2641	58	51	37	40	51	46	57	74	59	53	71	53	650
East Malling (Kent)	37	TQ 7156	59	47	41	44	49	45	56	64	60	66	75	65	671
Edinburgh/Blackford Hill	134	NT 2570	54	41	36	38	58	47	75	86	63	57	64	54	673
Eskdalemuir (D & G)	242	NT 2302	155	106	100	100	99	102	114	133	151	144	147	155	1506
Fochabers/Gordon Castle	32	NJ 3559	59	50	43	40	52	57	78	98	69	66	74	69	755
Glasgow/Abbotsinch	5	NS 4866	96	92	61	61	68	60	75	89	104	105	94	106	991
Glentee (D & G)	55	NX 6080	163	110	102	91	91	81	98	126	153	158	158	176	1507
Gorleston (Norfolk)	4	TG 5303	51	42	37	38	39	43	55	62	52	61	68	56	604
Huddersfield/Oakes	232	SE 1117	76	64	56	56	62	49	64	84	66	66	87	76	806
Ilfracombe (Devon)	8	SS 5247	103	69	67	63	68	60	78	99	95	109	119	117	1047
Isles of Scilly/St Mary's	48	SV 9112	92	77	69	47	65	49	62	71	72	78	99	100	881
Kingston upon Hull	2	TA 0830	58	48	41	46	48	50	58	72	54	48	68	54	645
Kirkwall (Orkney)	26	HY 4807	105	80	74	59	59	55	65	75	98	113	119	124	1026
Lake Vyrnwy (Powys)	303	SJ 0119	177	134	109	107	111	92	107	133	142	160	170	191	1633
Lerwick (Shetland)	82	HU 4539	130	101	85	79	58	62	67	72	111	133	130	144	1172
London/Regent's Park	39	TQ 2882	53	43	41	42	49	51	60	65	56	57	65	56	638
Long Ashton (Avon)	51	ST 5470	79	58	54	54	69	58	70	95	82	79	93	85	876
Manchester/Ringway	75	SJ 8284	71	53	48	53	60	61	76	91	76	75	78	77	819
Morecambe	7	SD 4364	87	61	55	61	66	69	80	100	107	102	96	98	982
Nairn (H'land)	6	NH 8656	45	38	33	37	48	51	61	81	53	57	55	54	613
Nelson (Lancs)	165	SD 8738	104	82	67	73	71	73	96	120	110	108	113	121	1138
Newquay	54	SW 8161	94	65	60	49	62	48	67	74	76	83	99	104	881
Nottingham	59	SK 5639	54	40	41	41	49	46	55	70	50	49	59	48	602
Onich (H'land)	15	NN 0363	191	152	142	137	107	130	149	166	208	232	179	236	2029
Oxford	63	SP 5007	59	41	43	42	56	50	59	68	60	58	63	60	659
Penzance	19	SW 4730	127	90	85	61	75	56	71	83	91	101	128	130	1098
Perth	23	NO 1023	70	53	46	45	64	56	74	81	73	69	68	79	778
Plymouth/Mount Batten	27	SX 4952	108	75	74	57	68	56	70	85	86	92	109	110	990
Pontefract	78	SE 4521	48	40	38	41	50	47	56	71	50	47	62	43	593
Raunds (Notts)	59	SP 9972	54	40	43	40	50	49	53	57	49	48	59	51	593
Redcar (Cleveland)	8	NZ 5924	51	42	32	36	43	46	57	69	51	49	69	49	594
Rhyl (Clwyd)	9	SJ 0080	60	45	40	39	50	43	49	63	60	62	69	62	642
Ross-on-Wye	68	SO 5923	66	49	49	48	63	47	47	64	64	61	81	69	708
Rothamsted (Herts)	128	TL 1313	60	48	45	47	53	54	62	68	60	64	72	64	697
St Abb's Head	75	NT 9169	54	40	37	37	49	42	55	81	54	53	65	50	617
Sandown (I of Wight)	4	SZ 6084	83	54	52	45	49	42	54	66	70	75	92	89	771
Scarborough	36	TA 0488	60	48	38	41	50	47	56	71	50	47	62	43	593
Sheffield	131	SK 3387	81	67	58	54	65	52	60	74	64	65	88	74	802
Shoeburyness (Essex)	2	TQ 9485	43	35	35	33	41	41	48	61	53	49	55	45	539
Shrewsbury	56	SJ 5113	53	41	41	41	57	46	55	67	58	52	61	55	627
Skegness	5	TF 5663	52	40	38	40	44	48	57	66	51	48	61	51	596
Southampton	3	SU 4111	81	55	54	47	58	50	54	74	74	82	91	81	801
Stornoway	3	NB 4533	111	84	76	72	57	66	75	83	106	122	112	130	1094
Stratford on Avon	49	SP 1654	52	37	41	42	54	49	56	71	53	53	62	53	623
Swansea	8	SS 6492	116	76	76	70	77	71	85	105	112	113	128	129	1158
Tiree (S'clyde)	9	NL 9944	115	74	70	65	58	70	85	88	127	133	114	130	1129
Torbay	8	SX 9063	103	72	70	52	69	46	57	70	75	83	102	99	898
Tredegar (Gwent)	313	SO 1408	167	120	106	100	108	93	98	131	135	149	172	180	1559
Valley (Gwyn)	10	SH 2979	90	60	51	52	58	55	61	77	89	87	97	94	871
Weston-super-Mare	9	ST 3160	72	50	49	49	65	50	63	85	78	76	90	79	806
Wick	36	ND 3652	82	60	53	44	47	50	63	76	70	74	83	86	788
Wisley (Surrey)	35	TQ 0658	56	43	42	42	50	44	64	61	55	59	70	62	648

Source: Meteorological Office.

Monthly and annual values of air temperature

(°C) over the 30 year period 1941-1971

Station	Height(m)	Grid Ref.	Jan	Feb	Mar	Apr	May	Jun	Jul	Aug	Sep	Oct	Nov	Dec	Year
Aberdeen/Craibstone	91	NJ 8710	2.4	2.6	4.4	6.5	8.7	11.9	13.3	13.1	11.7	9.1	5.3	3.5	7.7
Aberporth (Dyfed)	133	SN 2452	4.7	4.6	6.3	8.2	10.7	13.3	14.7	14.9	13.7	11.2	7.9	5.9	9.7
Achnashellach (H'land)	67	NH 0349	2.6	2.7	5.0	6.9	9.7	12.4	13.3	13.3	11.7	9.0	5.3	3.7	7.9
Ambleside (Cumbria)	46	NY 3704	3.0	3.3	5.2	7.8	10.9	13.7	14.9	14.7	12.9	9.9	6.1	3.9	8.9
Auchincruive (S'clyde)	45	NS 3823	3.4	3.5	5.5	7.7	10.3	13.1	14.3	14.2	12.7	9.9	6.1	4.5	8.8
Belper (Derbys)	60	SK 3446	2.9	3.3	5.4	8.1	11.2	14.3	15.7	15.4	13.4	10.0	6.3	4.1	9.2
Benbecula (W. Isles)	6	NF 7855	4.6	4.5	5.9	7.5	9.7	12.3	13.2	13.4	12.1	10.1	7.0	5.7	8.9
Bexhill (E Sussex)	4	TQ 7307	4.2	4.3	6.1	8.7	11.7	14.7	16.5	16.5	15.1	12.1	8.1	5.5	10.3
Birmingham/Edgbaston	163	SP 0486	3.3	3.5	5.7	8.5	11.4	14.5	16.0	15.7	13.0	10.7	6.5	4.5	9.5
Bognor Regis (W Sussex)	7	SZ 9399	4.3	4.3	6.0	8.7	11.7	14.7	16.3	16.5	14.9	11.9	7.9	5.7	10.3
Boscombe Down (Wilts)	126	SU 1740	3.3	3.7	5.9	8.6	11.3	14.5	16.1	15.9	13.9	10.7	6.7	4.5	9.6
Bournemouth (Dorset)	40	SZ 0791	4.3	4.5	6.5	9.1	11.8	14.9	16.6	16.5	14.6	11.7	7.7	5.5	10.3
Bradford (W Yorks)	134	SE 1435	2.7	2.9	4.9	7.7	10.5	13.7	15.2	14.9	13.1	9.9	5.9	3.9	8.8
Braemar (Grampian)	339	NO 1591	0.4	0.5	2.7	5.2	8.2	11.5	12.7	12.3	10.3	7.5	3.4	1.7	6.4
Buxton (Derbys)	314	SK 0672	1.7	1.7	3.8	6.5	9.4	12.5	13.9	13.7	11.9	8.7	5.0	2.9	7.6
Cambridge	12	TL 4557	3.2	3.7	5.9	8.9	11.9	15.1	16.7	16.4	14.4	10.9	6.5	4.2	9.8
Cape Wrath (H'land)	112	NC 2574	4.3	3.9	5.1	6.3	8.3	10.7	11.8	12.3	11.3	9.5	6.7	5.3	7.9
Cardiff	62	ST 1979	4.1	4.2	6.4	9.1	11.9	14.9	16.3	16.2	14.3	11.3	7.5	5.3	10.1
Douglas (I of Man)	87	SC 3877	4.6	4.3	5.7	7.7	10.3	13.0	14.3	14.3	13.0	10.7	7.5	5.9	9.3
Dover (Kent)	6	TR 3241	4.1	4.3	6.1	8.9	11.9	14.7	16.7	16.9	15.4	12.2	8.1	5.5	10.4
Dumfries	49	NX 9874	2.8	3.1	5.1	7.5	10.3	13.3	14.5	14.3	12.5	9.7	5.8	3.9	8.5
Dundee	45	NO 4231	2.6	3.1	5.0	7.5	10.1	13.3	14.8	14.3	12.5	9.5	5.5	3.6	8.5
Duntulm (H'land)	90	NG 3971	4.2	4.0	5.5	6.9	9.3	11.6	12.6	12.9	11.7	9.7	6.7	5.2	8.3
Durham	102	NZ 2641	2.7	2.9	4.9	7.5	10.1	13.2	14.9	14.6	12.8	9.8	5.8	3.7	8.5
East Malling (Kent)	37	TQ 7156	3.3	3.7	5.9	8.7	11.5	14.7	16.5	16.1	14.2	10.7	6.7	4.5	9.7
Edinburgh/Blackford Hill	134	NT 2570	3.1	3.2	5.1	7.5	9.9	12.9	14.5	14.2	12.6	9.8	6.0	4.3	8.6
Eskdalemuir (D & G)	242	NT 2302	1.4	1.5	3.7	6.1	8.9	11.9	13.1	12.9	11.1	8.3	4.5	2.5	7.2
Fochabers/Gordon Castle	32	NJ 3559	2.9	3.2	5.2	7.4	9.7	12.9	14.1	13.9	12.3	9.5	5.7	4.0	8.4
Glasgow/Abbotsinch	5	NS 4866	3.1	3.5	5.5	7.9	10.7	13.6	14.7	14.5	12.7	9.9	6.0	4.2	8.9
Glentee (D & G)	55	NX 6080	2.5	2.9	4.8	7.3	10.1	13.1	14.4	14.1	12.1	9.3	5.5	3.7	8.3
Gorleston (Norfolk)	4	TG 5303	3.7	3.9	5.4	8.1	10.9	14.1	16.1	16.2	14.7	11.7	7.5	5.1	9.8
Huddersfield/Oakes	232	SE 1117	2.5	2.6	4.7	7.4	10.4	13.7	15.1	14.7	12.9	9.8	5.7	3.7	8.5
Ilfracombe (Devon)	8	SS 5247	6.1	5.7	7.3	9.3	11.9	14.6	16.2	16.5	15.2	12.7	9.3	7.3	11.0
Isles of Scilly/St Mary's	48	SV 9112	7.7	7.3	8.5	9.9	11.9	14.4	16.0	16.3	15.1	12.9	10.2	8.7	11.6
Kingston upon Hull	2	TA 0830	3.5	3.9	5.7	8.7	11.4	14.6	16.3	16.1	14.3	11.0	6.7	4.5	9.7
Kirkwall (Orkney)	26	HY 4807	3.6	3.4	4.7	6.3	8.5	11.0	12.3	12.7	11.4	9.2	6.2	4.3	7.8
Lake Vyrnwy (Powys)	303	SJ 0119	2.3	2.3	4.3	6.7	9.7	12.7	14.0	13.7	12.0	9.1	5.3	3.5	7.9
Lerwick (Shetland)	82	HU 4539	3.0	2.8	3.8	5.4	7.6	10.1	11.7	11.9	10.6	8.5	5.6	4.0	7.1
London/Regent's Park	39	TQ 2882	4.1	4.5	6.7	9.7	12.9	16.1	17.7	17.1	15.3	11.9	7.5	5.2	10.7
Long Ashton (Avon)	51	ST 5470	4.1	4.3	6.3	8.9	11.7	14.8	16.3	16.0	14.1	11.1	7.1	5.2	10.0
Manchester/Ringway	75	SJ 8284	3.3	3.7	5.7	8.3	11.3	14.3	15.7	15.5	13.7	10.5	6.5	4.3	9.4
Morecambe	7	SD 4364	3.6	3.7	5.7	8.3	11.5	14.4	15.7	15.7	13.9	10.9	6.9	4.7	9.5
Nairn (H'land)	6	NH 8656	2.8	3.3	5.2	7.2	9.5	12.5	14.1	13.7	12.1	9.5	5.6	3.9	8.3
Nelson (Lancs)	165	SD 8738	2.5	2.6	4.6	7.1	10.2	13.2	14.6	14.4	12.6	9.6	5.7	3.6	8.4
Newquay	54	SW 8161	6.1	5.7	7.4	9.3	11.5	14.1	15.7	15.8	14.5	12.1	8.9	7.3	10.7
Nottingham	59	SK 5639	3.3	3.7	5.8	8.5	11.7	14.9	16.5	16.1	14.1	10.7	6.7	4.5	9.7
Onich (H'land)	15	NN 0363	3.5	3.6	5.5	7.3	10.3	12.5	13.5	13.7	12.1	9.7	6.1	4.5	8.6
Oxford	63	SP 5007	3.5	4.0	6.2	9.1	12.1	15.3	16.9	16.5	14.4	10.9	6.9	4.6	10.1
Penzance	19	SW 4730	6.9	6.5	8.1	9.8	12.1	14.7	16.1	16.2	14.9	12.6	9.5	8.0	11.3
Perth	23	NO 1023	2.2	2.8	5.0	7.7	10.4	13.7	14.7	14.3	12.3	9.3	5.2	3.3	8.4
Plymouth/Mount Batten	27	SX 4952	5.9	5.5	7.1	9.2	11.5	14.3	15.9	15.9	14.5	12.1	8.7	7.1	10.7
Pontefract	78	SE 4521	3.0	3.3	5.2	8.1	10.9	14.1	15.5	15.3	13.5	10.3	6.3	4.1	9.1
Raunds (Notts)	59	SP 9972	2.7	3.3	5.5	8.3	11.5	14.7	16.3	16.0	13.9	10.3	6.1	3.8	9.3
Redcar (Cleveland)	8	NZ 5924	3.9	4.1	5.8	8.3	10.5	13.7	15.5	15.3	13.9	10.9	7.1	4.9	9.5
Rhyl (Clwyd)	9	SJ 0080	4.6	4.5	6.5	8.7	11.3	14.1	15.6	15.5	14.2	11.3	7.7	5.7	10.0
Ross-on-Wye	68	SO 5923	4.0	4.2	6.2	8.9	11.7	14.8	16.3	15.9	14.0	10.9	7.0	5.0	9.9
Rothamsted (Herts)	128	TL 1313	2.7	3.0	5.2	8.2	11.2	14.2	15.9	15.7	13.7	10.3	5.9	3.7	9.1
St Abb's Head	75	NT 9169	3.6	3.5	4.9	6.9	8.9	12.0	13.8	13.7	12.3	9.9	6.7	4.8	8.5
Sandown (I of Wight)	4	SZ 6084	4.9	5.0	6.7	9.3	12.1	15.1	17.0	17.1	15.5	12.6	8.6	6.3	10.9
Scarborough	36	TA 0488	3.9	4.2	5.8	8.3	10.6	13.8	15.5	15.5	13.9	11.1	7.1	4.9	9.5
Sheffield	131	SK 3387	3.4	3.5	5.5	8.3	11.3	14.5	16.0	15.7	13.9	10.7	6.6	4.6	9.5
Shoeburyness (Essex)	2	TQ 9485	3.9	4.2	6.0	8.9	11.9	15.2	17.1	17.1	15.1	11.8	7.5	5.1	10.3
Shrewsbury	56	SJ 5113	3.3	3.7	5.9	8.5	11.4	14.7	16.1	15.7	13.7	10.5	6.5	4.5	9.5
Skegness	5	TF 5663	3.2	3.5	5.3	8.1	10.8	14.0	15.9	15.7	14.1	11.0	6.7	4.4	9.5
Southampton	3	SU 4111	4.5	4.9	6.9	9.7	12.6	15.7	17.3	17.1	15.1	11.9	7.8	5.5	10.7
Stornoway	3	NB 4533	4.1	4.1	5.6	6.9	9.1	11.7	12.9	12.9	11.6	9.5	6.4	4.9	8.3
Stratford on Avon	49	SP 1654	3.0	3.5	5.6	8.4	11.3	14.5	16.1	15.9	13.7	10.4	6.3	4.0	9.4
Swansea	8	SS 6492	5.1	5.1	6.9	9.5	12.3	15.2	16.5	16.5	14.9	12.1	8.4	6.3	10.7
Tiree (S'clyde)	9	NL 9944	5.1	4.9	6.2	7.7	9.9	12.2	13.4	13.6	12.5	10.5	7.6	6.2	9.1
Torbay	8	SX 9063	5.7	5.6	7.1	9.5	11.9	15.0	16.5	16.5	14.9	12.2	8.7	6.9	10.9
Tredegar (Gwent)	313	SO 1408	2.6	2.6	4.7	7.3	10.1	13.2	14.5	14.3	12.4	9.5	5.7	3.7	8.4
Valley (Gwyn)	10	SH 2979	5.2	5.0	6.5	8.5	11.0	13.6	15.1	15.3	14.1	11.5	8.3	6.5	10.1
Weston-super-Mare	9	ST 3160	4.5	4.7	6.7	9.3	12.1	15.3	16.9	16.7	15.0	11.9	7.9	5.7	10.5
Wick	36	ND 3652	3.1	3.3	4.7	6.4	8.3	11.0	12.5	12.6	11.5	9.3	5.9	4.1	7.7
Wisley (Surrey)	35	TQ 0658	3.5	4.0	6.3	9.1	12.1	15.2	16.9	16.5	14.4	10.9	6.8	4.5	10.0

Source: Meteorological Office.

Location of climatic stations

POPULATION OF ENGLAND, WALES & SCOTLAND

England - Estimated population as at 30 June 1975 (Provisional)

	Population	Approximate Area in sq km
ENGLAND	46 453 700	130 356.78
WALES	2 765 000	20 761.36
SCOTLAND	5 206 200	77 205.27
GREATER LONDON	7 111 500	1579.50
GREATER MANCHESTER COUNTY[1]	2 708 900	1289.15
Districts		
Wigan	309 600	208.25
Bolton	263 300	142.27
Bury	180 400	99.17
Rochdale	211 500	159.06
Oldham	228 400	141.05
Tameside	222 800	103.27
Stockport	293 400	126.07
Manchester	506 300	110.30
Salford	266 500	96.89
Trafford	226 700	105.74
MERSEYSIDE COUNTY[1]	1 588 400	647.50
Districts		
Wirral	348 200	155.48
Sefton	305 300	151.86
Liverpool	548 800	112.58
Knowsley	191 400	97.39
St Helens	194 700	130.31
SOUTH YORKSHIRE COUNTY[1]	1 317 500	1561.12
Districts		
Barnsley	224 000	328.93
Doncaster	285 000	562.50
Rotherham	248 700	282.79
Sheffield	559 800	368.26
TYNE & WEAR COUNTY[1]	1 192 600	535.12
Districts		
Newcastle upon Tyne	295 700	105.22
North Tyneside	205 700	85.46
South Tyneside	171 800	63.58
Gateshead	221 400	143.35
Sunderland	298 000	137.50
WEST MIDLANDS COUNTY[1]	2 777 500	899.42
Districts		
Walsall	271 000	106.29
Wolverhampton	269 000	68.80
Dudley	300 700	97.94
Sandwell	315 500	85.89
Birmingham	1 084 600	264.21
Solihull	199 700	180.06
Coventry	337 000	96.54
WEST YORKSHIRE COUNTY[1]	2 082 600	2039.06
Districts		
Calderdale	192 400	363.77
Bradford	460 600	370.06
Leeds	749 000	545.98
Wakefield	305 500	333.20
Kirklees	375 100	409.91
AVON COUNTY	919 600	1345.97
Districts		
Northavon	114 100	463.39
Bristol	420 100	109.54
Kingswood	78 900	48.00
Woodspring	148 700	375.02
Wansdyke	73 500	317.33
Bath	84 300	28.70

[1] Metropolitan counties.

	Population	Approximate Area in sq km
BEDFORDSHIRE COUNTY	489 500	1234.89
Districts		
North Bedfordshire	130 500	475.89
Mid Bedfordshire	95 600	501.81
South Bedfordshire	97 300	212.00
Luton	166 100	43.13
BERKSHIRE COUNTY	658 300	1255.25
Districts		
Newbury	112 900	692.64
Reading	132 900	36.85
Wokingham	111 200	179.00
Bracknell	71 400	109.40
Windsor & Maidenhead	127 100	197.72
Slough	102 800	27.77
BUCKINGHAMSHIRE COUNTY	501 800	1877.74
Districts		
Milton Keynes	82 100	308.25
Aylesbury Vale	117 200	903.60
Wycombe	150 500	323.70
Chiltern	89 900	201.21
Beaconsfield	62 100	
CAMBRIDGESHIRE COUNTY	551 100	3409.21
Districts		
Peterborough	115 000	333.55
Fenland	65 700	556.58
Huntingdon	115 800	924.46
East Cambridgeshire	51 900	655.38
South Cambridgeshire	98 800	906.12
Cambridge	103 900	40.71
CHESHIRE COUNTY	910 900	2328.46
Districts		
Warrington	164 800	176.11
Halton	110 700	67.41
Ellesmere Port	85 100	75.24
Vale Royal	110 200	384.25
Macclesfield	147 600	522.69
Chester	117 200	448.20
Crewe & Nantwich	98 100	430.78
Congleton	77 200	211.17
CLEVELAND COUNTY	565 400	852.87
Districts		
Hartlepool	97 300	94.29
Stockton-on-Tees	164 000	194.53
Middlesbrough	153 300	47.06
Langbaurgh	150 800	247.10
CORNWALL AND ISLES OF SCILLY COUNTY	403 500	3542.20
Districts		
North Cornwall	60 400	1194.82
Caradon	60 500	644.11
Restormel	74 800	454.03
Carrick	72 400	459.96
Kerrier	80 400	473.14
Penwith	53 000	302.98
Isles of Scilly	2000	16.83
CUMBRIA COUNTY	473 800	6885.55
Districts		
Carlisle	99 700	1031.77
Allerdale	94 800	1255.09
Eden	41 700	2158.02
Copeland	70 600	737.09
South Lakeland	93 100	1549.43
Barrow-in-Furness	73 900	122.81

	Population	Approximate Area in sq km		Population	Approximate Area in sq km
DERBYSHIRE COUNTY	887 400	2631.05	**GLOUCESTERSHIRE COUNTY**	487 600	2641.53
Districts			Districts		
High Peak	80 200	540.78	Forest of Dean	69 800	526.63
West Derbyshire	66 200	795.48	Gloucester	90 700	33.35
North East Derbyshire	91 300	276.94	Tewkesbury	79 500	450.34
Chesterfield	93 700	65.78	Cheltenham	86 500	38.68
Bolsover	70 400	161.38	Cotswold	67 100	1142.44
Amber Valley	106 300	265.38	Stroud	94 000	454.26
Erewash	101 000	109.24			
Derby	215 200	78.03	**HAMPSHIRE COUNTY**	1 449 700	3781.69
South Derbyshire	63 100	339.15	Districts		
			Basingstoke	117 900	637.21
DEVON COUNTY	936 300	6710.82	Hartley Wintney	69 900	218.34
Districts			Rushmoor	80 700	36.19
North Devon	72 600	1086.16	Test Valley	86 800	637.22
Torridge	47 100	398.58	Winchester	88 700	659.34
Tiverton	55 800	915.59	East Hampshire	84 200	514.82
East Devon	101 700	816.52	New Forest	137 900	748.86
Exeter	94 100	44.67	Southampton	215 400	56.34
Teignbridge	93 600	676.10	Eastleigh	80 900	79.67
West Devon	40 200	1159.73	Fareham	85 700	74.27
Plymouth	257 900	80.68	Gosport	84 800	27.40
South Hams	63 500	886.92	Portsmouth	200 900	37.43
Torbay	109 800	62.67	Havant	115 900	55.25
DORSET COUNTY	572 900	2687.58	**HEREFORD & WORCESTER COUNTY**		
Districts				585 600	3926.28
North Dorset	47 200	608.71	Districts		
Wimborne	57 600	354.79	Wyre Forest	92 600	195.72
Christchurch	45 800	51.70	Bromsgrove	77 900	219.76
Bournemouth	146 400	47.05	Redditch	48 000	54.32
Poole	112 800	63.99	Wychavon	85 800	666.10
Purbeck	38 800	391.42	Worcester	74 300	31.87
West Dorset	77 800	1080.17	Malvern Hills	80 000	902.47
Weymouth & Portland	56 500	40.15	Leominster	34 900	931.55
			Hereford	47 300	20.36
DURHAM COUNTY	607 600	2435.96	South Herefordshire	44 800	904.56
Districts					
Chester-le-Street	47 000	65.75	**HERTFORDSHIRE COUNTY**	938 100	1634.11
Derwentside	91 200	270.91	Districts		
Durham	86 500	189.69	North Hertfordshire	104 200	373.65
Easington	105 700	143.00	Stevenage	73 300	25.32
Sedgefield	91 700	219.77	East Hertfordshire	104 300	477.14
Wear Valley	63 600	505.04	Broxbourne	75 000	52.22
Teesdale	24 100	843.01	Welwyn Hatfield	93 900	126.98
Darlington	97 800	199.81	St Albans	123 500	161.26
			Dacorum	120 400	210.01
EAST SUSSEX COUNTY	657 300	1795.30	Three Rivers	78 300	87.53
Districts			Watford	77 800	21.35
Hove	88 700	23.86	Hertsmere	87 400	75.80
Brighton	159 000	59.14			
Lewes	76 400	292.41	**HUMBERSIDE COUNTY**	848 200	3513.19
Wealden	112 200	452.48	Districts		
Eastbourne	72 700	45.96	North Wolds	69 000	422.49
Rother	73 700	510.67	Holderness	42 800	540.90
Hastings	74 600	31.44	Kingston upon Hull	279 700	71.20
			Beverley	106 800	404.57
ESSEX COUNTY	1 410 900	3672.77	Boothferry	56 000	643.44
Districts			Scunthorpe	67 800	31.95
Uttlesford	56 100	641.54	Glanford	61 500	582.40
Braintree	102 100	611.32	Grimsby	94 200	30.48
Colchester	129 200	335.07	Cleethorpes	70 400	164.23
Tendring	107 300	336.51			
Maldon	42 900	358.71	**ISLE OF WIGHT COUNTY**	110 700	381.00
Chelmsford	127 800	342.35	Districts		
Epping Forest	115 600	344.57	Medina	65 000	117.15
Harlow	80 300	25.58	South Wight	45 700	263.84
Brentwood	74 000	148.92			
Basildon	138 100	110.98	**KENT COUNTY**	1 445 400	3734.77
Rochford	69 100	169.21	Districts		
Southend-on-Sea	159 400	41.62	Dartford	83 900	69.88
Castle Point	81 400	43.67	Gravesham	96 500	100.06
Thurrock	127 600	184.34	Medway	145 300	160.00
			Gillingham	93 400	45.01

	Population	Approximate Area in sq km
Swale	106 500	373.86
Canterbury	115 100	312.44
Thanet	118 200	103.56
Dover	101 700	311.83
Shepway	86 300	357.19
Ashford	81 200	580.55
Maidstone	125 300	394.50
Tonbridge & Malling	94 700	240.18
Sevenoaks	102 100	370.63
Tunbridge Wells	95 200	330.38
LANCASHIRE COUNTY	1 369 200	3039.45
Districts		
Lancaster	125 500	565.65
Wyre	98 800	279.98
Blackpool	147 100	43.37
Fylde	70 100	161.52
Preston	131 900	142.39
Ribble Valley	53 900	579.17
Pendle	86 100	168.21
Burnley	92 700	133.90
Rossendale	62 200	138.11
Hyndburn	81 000	73.15
Blackburn	142 200	137.53
Chorley	82 600	205.00
South Ribble	89 700	111.10
West Lancashire	105 400	326.61
LEICESTERSHIRE COUNTY	836 500	2552.93
Districts		
North West Leicestershire	74 200	280.33
Charnwood	132 400	279.29
Melton	41 000	481.65
Rutland	30 800	393.64
Harborough	57 800	593.04
Oadby & Wigston	52 500	23.73
Leicester	290 600	73.41
Blaby	76 600	130.36
Hinckley & Bosworth	80 600	297.59
LINCOLNSHIRE COUNTY	521 300	5885.24
Districts		
West Lindsey	74 200	1153.34
Lincoln	73 200	35.71
East Lindsey	100 100	1748.99
North Kesteven	76 600	923.01
Boston	49 800	354.73
South Kesteven	89 200	942.98
South Holland	58 200	729.19
NORFOLK COUNTY	659 300	9562.33
Districts		
West Norfolk	115 100	1477.08
North Norfolk	79 700	963.14
Great Yarmouth	76 100	177.12
Broadland	92 000	549.37
Norwich	121 800	39.07
South Norfolk	87 100	906.92
Breckland	87 500	1305.00
NORTHAMPTONSHIRE COUNTY	500 100	2367.45
Districts		
East Northamptonshire	59 800	510.12
Corby	55 300	80.31
Kettering	70 200	233.65
Daventry	53 000	665.70
Wellingborough	62 200	162.64
Northampton	139 900	80.64
South Northamptonshire	59 700	633.49
NORTHUMBERLAND COUNTY	286 700	5032.13
Districts		
Berwick-upon-Tweed	25 700	976.02
Alnwick	28 900	1080.06

	Population	Approximate Area in sq km
Castle Morpeth	47 900	619.11
Wansbeck	62 500	68.47
Blyth Valley	66 300	71.42
Tynedale	55 400	2220.99
NORTH YORKSHIRE	646 000	8316.30
Districts		
Scarborough	97 900	818.45
Ryedale	76 200	1598.19
Hambleton	72 300	1311.56
Richmondshire	46 800	1317.18
Craven	46 400	1176.24
Harrogate	133 500	532.45
York	102 700	29.52
Selby	70 300	736.52
NOTTINGHAMSHIRE COUNTY	982 700	2212.16
Districts		
Bassetlaw	99 500	641.51
Mansfield	96 900	76.92
Newark	102 200	661.66
Ashfield	102 800	110.11
Gedling	101 900	112.36
Broxtowe	102 600	81.07
Nottingham	287 800	74.32
Rushcliffe	89 000	409.51
OXFORDSHIRE COUNTY	539 100	2611.50
Districts		
Cherwell	103 800	589.81
West Oxfordshire	81 500	714.90
Oxford	116 600	35.55
Vale of White Horse	96 600	580.93
South Oxfordshire	140 600	690.18
SALOP COUNTY	354 800	3490.36
Districts		
Oswestry	31 000	256.18
North Shropshire	48 400	679.54
Shrewsbury & Atcham	83 900	602.68
The Wrekin	109 700	291.37
South Shropshire	33 300	825.22
Bridgnorth	48 506	633.69
SOMERSET COUNTY	401 700	3457.99
Districts		
West Somerset	29 400	726.72
Taunton Deane	82 600	458.30
Sedgemoor	84 200	566.15
Mendip	82 700	747.42
Yeovil	122 800	959.05
STAFFORDSHIRE COUNTY	988 400	2716.19
Districts		
Newcastle-under-Lyme	121 200	211.08
Stoke-on-Trent	255 800	92.74
Staffordshire Moorlands	93 300	576.24
Stafford	114 300	595.70
East Staffordshire	95 600	388.17
South Staffordshire	87 500	408.57
Cannock Chase	83 800	78.90
Lichfield	87 700	329.99
Tamworth	49 200	30.95
SUFFOLK COUNTY	570 000	3807.29
Districts		
Forest Heath	46 600	373.96
St Edmundsbury	80 400	656.80
Mid Suffolk	63 500	870.80
Waveney	94 900	370.99
Suffolk Coastal	94 300	892.10
Ipswich	122 600	40.16
Babergh	67 700	594.81

	Population	Approximate Area in sq km		Population	Approximate Area in sq km
SURREY COUNTY	1 000 700	1679.11	**WEST SUSSEX**	623 100	2016.64
Districts			Districts		
Spelthorne	97 300	56.17	Chichester	95 000	788.51
Runnymede	74 600	78.24	Horsham	91 200	535.86
Surrey Heath	70 500	96.52	Crawley	71 600	36.27
Woking	78 200	63.58	Mid Sussex	106 400	338.04
Elmbridge	111 800	96.68	Adur	56 700	41.56
Epsom & Ewell	71 100	34.10	Worthing	92 800	34.45
Reigate & Banstead	113 800	129.55	Arun	109 400	220.15
Tandridge	79 400	249.87			
Mole Valley	76 600	250.22			
Guildford	120 000	271.00			
Waverley	107 400	345.43			
WARWICKSHIRE COUNTY	471 800	1980.55	**WILTSHIRE COUNTY**	511 600	3480.70
Districts			Districts		
North Warwickshire	61 700	285.81	Thamesdown	142 400	221.70
Nuneaton	112 600	79.26	North Wiltshire	102 400	778.40
Rugby	86 400	355.91	Kennet	68 600	958.03
Warwick	111 700	282.43	West Wiltshire	93 500	518.93
Stratford-on-Avon	99 400	971.23	Salisbury	164 700	1004.99

Wales - Estimated population as at 30 June 1975 (Provisional)

	Population	Approximate Area in sq km		Population	Approximate Area in sq km
WALES	2 765 000	20 761.36	Dwyfor	26 100	619.95
			Aberconwy	50 200	605.98
CLWYD COUNTY	374 800	2475.94	Meirionnydd	30 700	1517.21
Districts					
Colwyn	46 400	552.66			
Rhuddlan	49 800	94.02	**MID GLAMORGAN COUNTY**	540 100	1018.72
Delyn	61 400	277.06	Districts		
Alyn & Deeside	70 100	153.35	Ogwr	128 200	285.17
Wrexham-Maelor	108 100	363.89	Rhondda	86 400	96.66
Glyndŵr	39 000	965.94	Cynon Valley	69 600	180.63
			Merthyr Tydfil	60 600	111.62
DYFED COUNTY	321 700	5766.78	Rhymney Valley	105 700	176.12
Districts			Taff-Ely	89 600	169.39
Ceredigion	57 400	1793.52			
Preseli	63 500	1044.16			
South Pembrokeshire	38 000	550.57	**POWYS COUNTY**	100 800	5077.42
Carmarthen	49 900	1177.66	Districts		
Llanelli	76 800	257.63	Montgomery	44 200	2064.34
Dinefwr	36 100	970.70	Radnor	19 300	1219.29
			Brecknock	37 300	1794.30
GWENT COUNTY	440 100	1375.66			
Districts			**SOUTH GLAMORGAN COUNTY**	391 600	416.05
Blaenau Gwent	83 700	126.75	Districts		
Islwyn	66 000	98.61	Vale of Glamorgan	107 200	296.36
Torfaen	89 800	117.50	Cardiff	284 400	120.09
Monmouth	67 100	920.04			
Newport	133 500	200.46	**WEST GLAMORGAN COUNTY**	371 700	815.35
			Districts		
GWYNEDD COUNTY	224 200	4059.84	Swansea	190 500	244.87
Districts			Lliw	57 800	213.51
Ynys Môn - Isle of Anglesey	63 900	715.05	Neath	65 200	230.11
Arfon	53 300	460.12	Afan	58 200	151.25

Scotland - Estimated population as at 30 June 1975

	Population	Approximate Area in sq km		Population	Approximate Area in sq km
SCOTLAND	5 206 200	77 205.27	Berwickshire	17 513	875.42
BORDERS REGION	99 409	4671.05	**CENTRAL REGION**	269 281	2621.85
Districts			Districts		
Tweeddale	13 877	899.24	Clackmannan	47 610	161.10
Ettrick and Lauderdale	32 164	1356.12	Stirling	78 892	2169.89
Roxburgh	35 855	1540.27	Falkirk	142 779	290.86

	Population	Approximate Area in sq km
DUMFRIES AND GALLOWAY REGION	143 667	6369.82
Districts		
Wigtown	30 030	1712.76
Stewartry	22 348	1670.54
Nithsdale	56 141	1433.04
Annandale and Eskdale	35 148	1553.48
FIFE REGION	336 339	1306.65
Districts		
Kirkcaldy	147 876	235.95
North East Fife	64 951	757.57
Dunfermline	123 512	313.13
GRAMPIAN REGION	448 772	8702.88
Districts		
Moray	80 590	2230.50
Banff and Buchan	75 331	1526.02
Gordon	47 939	2214.18
Aberdeen City	210 362	184.41
Kincardine and Deeside	34 550	2547.77
HIGHLAND REGION	182 044	25 123.69
Districts		
Caithness	29 604	3152.28
Sutherland	11 877	4481.46
Ross and Cromarty	39 200	4999.46
Skye and Lochalsh	9672	2481.99
Lochaber	19 827	4467.47
Inverness	53 179	2800.04
Badenoch and Strathspey	9380	2319.08
Nairn	9305	421.91
LOTHIAN REGION	754 008	1754.71
Districts		
West Lothian	121 224	418.28
Edinburgh City	470 085	265.21
Midlothian	83 841	357.94
East Lothian	78 858	713.28

	Population	Approximate Area in sq km
STRATHCLYDE REGION	2 504 909	13 849.97
Districts		
Argyll and Bute	64 613	6756.25
Dumbarton	80 105	476.82
Renfrew	208 862	308.73
Inverclyde	105 801	157.73
Clydebank	56 529	51.28
Bearsden and Milngavie	37 572	20.20
Glasgow City	880 617	197.36
Strathkelvin	80 354	164.46
Eastwood	50 573	115.51
Cumbernauld & Kilsyth	54 063	103.86
Monklands	108 689	157.99
Motherwell	159 640	177.93
Lanark	55 017	1324.78
Hamilton	106 780	131.31
East Kilbride	81 299	284.64
Cunninghame	131 362	878.52
Kilmarnock and Loudoun	83 117	373.22
Kyle and Carrick	111 316	1290.59
Cumnock and Doon Valley	48 600	878.78
TAYSIDE REGION	401 987	7502.42
Districts		
Angus	88 086	2032.88
Dundee City	194 732	234.65
Perth and Kinross	119 169	5234.89
ORKNEY (Islands Council)	17 675	975.65
SHETLAND (Islands Council)	18 494	1429.16
WESTERN ISLES (Islands Council)	29 615	2897.42

POPULATION OF PLACES

England

Places included in this list are inhabited settlements with a population of 5000 or more. The figures have been taken from the 1971 Census of England and Wales, although the County and District names included in each reference are from the subsequent local government re-organisation of 1974. Entries are laid out, in alphabetical order, with the name of the place first, followed by the District name and then the County name. In cases where places fall into parts of more than one County or District, these constituent parts are indicated after the place name. The population figure completes the entry.

Abingdon	Vale of White Horse, Oxfordshire	18 610
Accrington	Hyndburn, Lancashire	36 894
Aireborough	Leeds, W Yorkshire	28 170
Aldershot	Rushmoor, Hampshire	33 390
Alfreton	Amber Valley, Derbyshire	8910
Alnwick	Alnwick, Northumberland	7190
Alton	East Hampshire, Hampshire	9920
Altrincham	Trafford, Gtr Manchester	40 787
Alvechurch	Bromsgrove, Hereford and Worcester	5120
Amesbury	Salisbury, Wiltshire	5540
Andover	Test Valley, Hampshire	25 881
Annfield Plain	Derwentside, Durham	8690
Ascot	Windsor and Maidenhead; Bracknell, Berkshire	15 630
Ashbourne	West Derbyshire, Derbyshire	5560
Ashby de la Zouch	North West Leicestershire, Leicestershire	7490
Ashby Woulds	North West Leicestershire, Leicestershire	5190
Ashford	Ashford, Kent	31 240
Ashington	Wansbeck, Northumberland	25 950
Ashton-in-Makerfield		
	Wigan, Gtr.Manchester	21 120
Ashton-under-Lyne	Tameside, Gtr Manchester	48 952
Askern	Doncaster, S Yorkshire	8440
Aspull	Wigan, Gtr Manchester	5040
Aston	Rotherham, S Yorkshire	8580
Atherstone	North Warwickshire, Warwickshire	10 170
Audley	Newcastle-under-Lyme, Staffordhsire	7830
Aveley	Thurrock, Essex	10 570
Aylesbury	Aylesbury Vale, Buckinghamshire	40 569
Aylesford	Tonbridge and Malling, Kent	17 720
Backworth (including Shiremoor)		
	North Tyneside, Tyne and Wear	7130
Bacup	Rossendale, Lancashire	15 118
Baldock	North Hertfordshire, Hertfordshire	6420
Banbury	Cherwell, Oxfordshire	29 387
Barnard Castle	Teesdale, Durham	5270
Barnoldswick	Pendle, Lancashire	9620
Barnsley	Barnsley, S Yorkshire	75 395
Barnstaple	North Devon, Devon	17 317
Barrow-in-Furness	Barrow-in-Furness, Cumbria	64 034
Barton-upon-Humber		
	Glanford, Humberside	5940
Basildon	Basildon, Essex	88 000
Basingstoke	Basingstoke, Hampshire	52 587
Bath	Bath, Avon	84 670
Batley	Kirklees, W Yorkshire	42 006
Beaconsfield	Beaconsfield, Buckinghamshire	12 640
Bebington	Wirral, Merseyside	61 582
Beccles	Waveney, Suffolk	8015
Bedford	Bedford, Bedfordshire	73 229

Bedlington	Wansbeck, Northumberland	14 460
Belper	Amber Valley, Derbyshire	16 110
Berkhamsted	Dacorum, Hertfordshire	14 280
Berwick-upon-Tweed		
	Berwick-upon-Tweed, Northumberland	11 647
Beverley	Beverley, Humberside	17 132
Bewdley	Wyre Forest, Hereford and Worcester	7237
Bexhill	Rother, E Sussex	32 898
Bicester	Cherwell, Oxfordshire	7530
Biddulph	Staffordshire Moors, Staffordshire	16 100
Bideford	Torridge, Devon	11 802
Biggleswade	Mid Bedfordshire, Bedfordshire	8740
Billericay	Basildon, Essex	22 880
Billington	Ribble Valley, Lancashire	9240
Bingley	Bradford, W Yorkshire	20 420
Birkenhead	Wirral, Merseyside	137 852
Birmingham	Birmingham, W Midlands	1 014 670
Birstall	Charnwood, Leicestershire	12 670
Birtley	Gateshead, Tyne and Wear	13 310
Bishop Auckland	Wear Valley, Durham	25 350
Bishop's Cleeve	Tewkesbury, Gloucestershire	7790
Bishop's Stortford	East Hertfordshire, Hertfordshire	20 750
Blackburn	Blackburn, Lancashire	101 816
Blackhall Colliery	Easington, Durham	5430
Blackpool	Blackpool, Lancashire	151 860
Bletchley	Milton Keynes, Buckinghamshire	23 110
Blidworth	Newark, Nottinghamshire	5120
Blyth	Blyth Valley, Northumberland	34 653
Bodmin	North Cornwall, Cornwall	9207
Bognor Regis	Arun, W Sussex	39 150
Boldon	South Tyneside, Tyne and Wear	18 740
Bollington	Macclesfield, Cheshire	6190
Bolsover	Hinckley and Bolsover, Derbyshire	13 880
Bolton	Bolton, Gtr Manchester	154 199
Bolton-le-Sands	Lancaster, Lancashire	6400
Bootle	Sefton, Merseyside	74 294
Bordon	East Hampshire, Hampshire	7470
Boston	Boston, Lincolnshire	26 025
Bourne	South Kesteven, Lincolnshire	5420
Bournemouth	Bournemouth, Dorset	153 869
Bowburn	Durham, Durham	5060
Bracknell	Bracknell, Berkshire	42 600
Bradford	Bradford, W Yorkshire	294 177
Bradford-on-Avon	West Wiltshire, Wiltshire	6910
Braintree	Braintree, Essex	22 310
Braunton	North Devon, Devon	5350
Breaston	Erewash, Derbyshire	5850
Breedsall	Erewash, Derbyshire	5230
Brentwood	Brentwood, Essex	51 330
Bricket Wood	St. Albans, Hertfordshire	9570
Bridgnorth	Bridgnorth, Salop	9400
Bridgwater	Sedgemoor, Somerset	26 642
Bridlington	North Wolds, Humberside	26 776
Bridport	West Dorset, Dorset	6369
Brighouse	Calderdale, W Yorkshire	34 141

Brightlingsea	Tendring, Essex	5950
Brighton	Brighton, E Sussex	161 351
Bristol	Bristol, Avon	426 657
Brixham	Torbay, Devon	12 000
Bromsgrove	Bromsgrove, Hereford and Worcester	30 210
Buckingham	Aylesbury Vale, Buckinghamshire	5076
Bulkington	Nuneaton, Warwickshire	6190
Burgess Hill	Mid Sussex, W Sussex	16 280
Burley	Bradford, W Yorkshire	9030
Burnham-on-Sea	Sedgemoor, Somerset	11 010
Burnley	Burnley, Lancashire	76 513
Burntwood	Lichfield, Staffordshire	18 070
Burscough	West Lancashire, Lancashire	7380
Burton-upon-Trent	East Staffordshire, Staffordshire	50 201
Bury	Bury, Gtr Manchester	67 849
Bury St. Edmunds	St. Edmundsbury, Suffolk	25 661
Buxton	High Peak, Derbyshire	20 324
Calne	North Wiltshire, Wiltshire	9688
Calverton	Gedling, Nottinghamshire	6090
Cambourne (including Redruth)		
	Kerrier, Cornwall	36 180
Cambridge	Cambridge, Cambridgeshire	98 840
Cannock	Cannock Chase, Staffordshire	66 980
Canterbury	Canterbury, Kent	33 176
Canvey Island	Castle Point, Essex	20 820
Carlisle	Carlisle, Cumbria	71 582
Carnforth	Lancaster, Lancashire	5160
Castleford	Wakefield, W Yorkshire	38 234
Chalfont St. Giles	Chiltern, Buckinghamshire	8500
Chalfont St. Peter	Chiltern, Buckinghamshire	18 760
Chard	Yeovil, Somerset	7908
Chatham	Medway, Kent	57 153
Cheadle	Staffordshire Moors, Staffordshire	6750
Chelmsford	Chelmsford, Essex	58 194
Cheltenham	Cheltenham, Gloucestershire	74 356
Chesham	Chiltern, Buckinghamshire	37 270
Chester	Chester, Cheshire	62 911
Chesterfield	Chesterfield, Derbyshire	70 169
Chester-le-Street	Chester-le-Street, Durham	21 320
Chichester	Chichester, W Sussex	20 649
Chippenham	North Wiltshire, Wiltshire	18 696
Chopwell	Gateshead, Tyne and Wear	5020
Chorley	Chorley, Lancashire	31 659
Christchurch	Christchurch, Dorset	31 463
Cinderford	Forest of Dean, Gloucestershire	6640
Cirencester	Cotswold, Gloucestershire	11 990
Clacton	Tendring, Essex	33 040
Clay Cross	North East Derbyshire, Derbyshire	25 600
Cleator Moor	Copeland, Cumbria	6980
Cleethorpes	Cleethorpes, Humberside	35 837
Clevedon	Woodspring, Avon	13 070
Clitheroe	Ribble Valley, Lancashire	13 194
Clowne	Bolsover, Derbyshire	5810
Coalville	North West Leicestershire, Leicestershire	27 960
Cobham	Elmbridge, Surrey	14 580
Cockermouth	Allerdale, Cumbria	5750
Codsall	South Staffordshire, Staffordshire	12 120
Colchester	Colchester, Essex	76 531
Coleshill	North Warwickshire, Warwickshire	7590
Colne	Pendle, Lancashire	18 940
Congleton	Congleton, Cheshire	20 341
Consett	Derwentside, Durham	36 790
Cookham	Windsor and Maidenhead, Berkshire	5500
Coppull	Chorley, Lancashire	6980
Corby	Corby, Northamptonshire	53 500
Corsham	North Wiltshire, Wiltshire	6360
Coventry	Coventry, W Midlands	335 238
Cowes	Medina, Isle of Wight	17 260
Cramlington	Blyth Valley, Northumberland	6500
Crawley	Crawley, W Sussex	73 000
Creswell	Bolsover, Derbyshire	6680
Crewe	Crewe and Nantwich, Cheshire	51 421
Cromer (including Sheringham)		
	North Norfolk, Norfolk	12 540
Crook	Wear Valley, Durham	11 900
Crosby	Sefton, Merseyside	57 497
Crowborough	Wealden, E Sussex	11 540
Crowthorne	Bracknell; Wokingham, Berkshire	10 400
Cudworth	Barnsley, S Yorkshire	11 470
Cuffley	Welwyn Hatfield, Hertfordshire	5600
Culcheth	Warrington, Cheshire	7260
Dalton	Barrow-in-Furness, Cumbria	7440
Darenth	Dartford, Kent	5920
Darfield	Barnsley, S Yorkshire	6650
Darlington	Darlington, Durham	85 938
Dartford	Dartford, Kent	45 705
Dartmouth	South Hams, Devon	5707
Darwen	Blackburn, Lancashire	28 926
Daventry	Daventry, Northamptonshire	11 815
Dawlish (including Teignmouth)		
	Teignbridge, Devon	19 880
Deal	Dover, Kent	25 432
Derby	Derby, Derbyshire	219 582
Devizes	Kennet, Wiltshire	10 179
Dewsbury	Kirklees, W Yorkshire	51 326
Didcot	South Oxfordshire, Oxfordshire	12 990
Dinnington	Rotherham, S Yorkshire	15 380
Doncaster	Doncaster, S Yorkshire	82 668
Dorchester	West Dorset, Dorset	13 736
Dorking	Mole Valley, Surrey	22 530
Dover	Dover, Kent	34 395
Driffield	North Wolds, Humberside	7040
Droitwich	Wychavon, Hereford and Worcester	12 748
Dronfield	North East Derbyshire, Derbyshire	13 980
Dudley	North Tyneside, Tyne and Wear	5060
Dudley	Dudley, W Midlands	185 581
Dukinfield	Tameside, Gtr Manchester	17 315
Dunstable	South Bedfordshire, Bedfordshire	31 828
Durham	Durham, Durham	24 776
Durrington	Salisbury, Wiltshire	5120
Dursley	Stroud, Gloucestershire	9370
Eaglescliffe	Stockton-on-Tees, Cleveland	8140
Earl Shilton	Hinckley and Bosworth, Leicestershire	12 280
Easington	Easington, Durham	9430
Eastbourne	Eastbourne, E Sussex	70 921
East Dereham	Breckland, Norfolk	8060
East Grinstead	Mid Sussex, W Sussex	16 560
Eastleigh	Eastleigh, Hampshire	45 361
East Retford	Bassetlaw, Nottinghamshire	18 413
Eccles	Salford, Gtr Manchester	38 505
Edenbridge	Sevenoaks, Kent	5620
Egremont	Copeland, Cumbria	6790
Elland	Calderdale, W Yorkshire	18 850
Ellesmere Port	Ellesmere Port, Cheshire	61 637
Elloughton	Beverley, Humberside	8400
Elstree	Hertsmere, Hertfordshire	28 840
Ely	East Cambridgeshire, Cambridgeshire	9020
Emsworth	Havant, Hampshire; Chichester, W Sussex	14 510
Epping	Epping Forest, Essex	10 830
Epsom and Ewell	Epsom and Ewell, Surrey	72 301
Evesham	Wychavon, Hereford and Worcester	13 855
Exeter	Exeter, Devon	95 729
Exmouth	East Devon, Devon	21 030

Falmouth	Carrick, Cornwall	18 041
Farnham	Waverley, Surrey	21 110
Farnworth	Bolton, Gtr Manchester	26 862
Faversham	Swale, Kent	14 818
Fawley	New Forest, Hampshire	9740
Featherstone	Wakefield, W Yorkshire	11 530
Felixstowe	Suffolk Coastal, Suffolk	17 980
Ferryhill	Sedgefield, Durham	11 530
Fleet	Hartley Wintney, Hampshire	17 260
Fleetwood	Wyre, Lancashire	28 599
Folkestone	Shepway, Kent	43 801
Formby	Sefton, Merseyside	17 330
Frampton Cotterell	Northavon, Avon	7570
Freckleton	Fylde, Lancashire	6750
Freshwater	South Wight, Isle of Wight	5570
Frinton and Walton	Tendring, Essex	8130
Frodsham	Vale Royal, Cheshire	7540
Frome	Mendip, Somerset	12 310

Gainsborough	West Lindsey, Lincolnshire	18 110
Garforth	Leeds, W Yorkshire	9420
Gateshead	Gateshead, Tyne and Wear	94 469
Gillingham	Gillingham, Kent	86 862
Glastonbury	Mendip, Somerset	6558
Glossop	High Peak, Derbyshire	24 272
Gloucester	Gloucester, Gloucestershire	90 232
Glusburn	Craven, N Yorkshire	5650
Godalming	Waverley, Surrey	18 669
Goffs Oak	Broxbourne, Hertfordshire	5620
Golbourne	Wigan, Gtr Manchester	16 950
Goole	Boothferry, Humberside	18 072
Gosport	Gosport, Hampshire	76 116
Grantham	South Kesteven, Lincolnshire	27 943
Gravesend	Gravesham, Kent	54 106
Great Harwood	Hyndburn, Lancashire	11 280
Great Malvern	Malvern Hills, Hereford and Worcester	26 460
Great Shelford	South Cambridgeshire, Cambridgeshire	5770
Great Yarmouth	Great Yarmouth, Norfolk	50 236
Grimethorpe	Barnsley, S Yorkshire	8310
Grimsby	Grimsby, Humberside	95 540
Guildford	Guildford, Surrey	57 213
Guisborough	Langbaurgh, Cleveland	8860

Hagley	Bromsgrove, Hereford and Worcester	5760
Hailsham	Wealden, E Sussex	11 660
Halesowen	Dudley, W Midlands	53 980
Halifax	Calderdale, W Yorkshire	91 272
Halstead	Braintree, Essex	6590
Hampreston	Wimbourne, Dorset	11 120
Harlow	Harlow, Essex	83 500
Harpenden	St. Albans, Hertfordshire	21 230
Harrogate	Harrogate, N Yorkshire	62 427
Hartlepool	Hartlepool, Cleveland	97 094
Hartley	Dartford, Kent	6610
Harwich	Tendring, Essex	14 926
Harworth	Bassetlaw, Nottingham	6890
Haslemere	Waverley, Surrey	10 920
Haslingden	Rossendale, Lancashire	14 924
Hastings	Hastings, E Sussex	72 410
Hatfield	Welwyn Hatfield, Hertfordshire	26 000
Hatfield	Doncaster, S Yorkshire	20 140
Haverhill	St. Edmundsbury, Suffolk	8870
Hayling	Havant, Hampshire	10 560
Haywards Heath	Mid Sussex, W Sussex	23 090
Heanor	Amber Valley, Derbyshire; Broxtowe, Nottinghamshire	36 230
Hebden Royal	Calderdale, W Yorkshire	9280
Hedge End	Eastleigh, Hampshire	6240

Helston	Kerrier, Cornwall	9978
Hemel Hempstead	Dacorum, Hertfordshire	76 000
Hemsworth	Wakefield, W Yorkshire	14 680
Henley-on-Thames	South Oxfordshire, Oxfordshire	11 431
Hereford	Hereford, Hereford and Worcester	46 503
Herne Bay	Canterbury, Kent	24 350
Hertford	East Hertfordshire, Hertfordshire	20 362
Hexham	Tynedale, Northumberland	9270
Heywood	Rochdale, Gtr Manchester	30 440
High Wycombe	Wycombe, Buckinghamshire	59 340
Hinckley	Hinckley and Bosworth, Leicestershire	29 000
Hitchin	North Hertfordshire, Hertfordshire	25 610
Hockley	Rochford, Essex	18 120
Hoddesdon	Broxbourne, Hertfordshire	20 500
Holmfirth	Kirklees, W Yorkshire	17 650
Honiton	East Devon, Devon	5072
Hoo	Medway, Kent	6910
Horley	Reigate and Banstead, Surrey	13 700
Hornsea	Holderness, Humberside	6610
Horsham	Horsham, W Sussex	25 800
Horsley	Guildford, Surrey	6350
Horwich	Bolton, Gtr Manchester	15 940
Houghton (including Hetton)		
	Sunderland, Tyne and Wear	47 850
Hove	Hove, E Sussex	73 086
Hoylake	Wirral, Merseyside	25 700
Hoyland Nether	Barnsley, S Yorkshire	19 700
Hucknall	Ashfield, Nottinghamshire	25 500
Huddersfield	Kirklees, W Yorkshire	131 190
Humberston	Cleethorpes, Humberside	7860
Huntingdon and Godmanchester		
	Huntingdon, Cambridgeshire	16 557
Hurstpierpoint	Mid Sussex, W Sussex	11 700
Hyde	Tameside, Gtr Manchester	37 095
Hythe	New Forest, Hampshire	14 710
Hythe	Shepway, Kent	11 959

Ilfracombe	North Devon, Devon	8360
Ilkeston	Erewash, Derbyshire	34 134
Ilkley	Bradford, W Yorkshire	10 930
Immingham	Grimsby, Humberside	6030
Ingatestone	Brentwood, Essex	5420
Ipswich	Ispwich, Suffolk	123 312
Irthlingborough	East Northamptonshire, Northamptonshire	5270
Iver	Beaconsfield, Buckinghamshire	10 970

Jarrow	South Tyneside, Tyne and Wear	28 907

Keighley	Bradford, W Yorkshire	55 345
Kemsing	Sevenoaks, Kent	7650
Kendal	South Lakeland, Cumbria	21 596
Kenilworth	Warwick, Warwickshire	19 670
Kettering	Kettering, Northamptonshire	42 668
Keynsham	Wansdyke, Avon	13 370
Keyworth	Rushcliffe, Nottinghamshire	6130
Kidderminster	Wyre Forest, Hereford and Worcester	47 326
Kidlington	Cherwell, Oxfordshire	9070
Kidsgrove	Congleton, Cheshire	35 170
Kimberley	Broxtowe, Nottinghamshire	9230
Kingsbury	North Warwickshire, Warwickshire	5480
King's Lynn	West Norfolk, Norfolk	30 107
Kingsteignton	Teignbridge, Devon	5080
Kingston upon Hull	Kingston upon Hull, Humberside	285 970

Kippax	Leeds, W Yorkshire	10 940
Kirkby	Knowsley, Merseyside	58 360
Kirkby in Ashfield	Ashfield, Nottinghamshire	22 890
Kirkham	Fylde, Lancashire	8000
Knaresborough	Harrogate, N Yorkshire	10 640
Knottingley	Wakefield, W Yorkshire	13 740
Knutsford	Macclesfield, Cheshire	10 050
Lakenheath	Forest Heath, Suffolk	6530
Lancaster	Lancaster, Lancashire	49 584
Lancing	Adur, W Sussex	21 380
Leatherhead	Mole Valley, Surrey	37 550
Leeds	Leeds, W Yorkshire	496 009
Leek	Staffordshire Moors, Staffordshire	19 230
Leicester	Leicester, Leicestershire	284 208
Leigh	Wigan, Gtr Manchester	46 181
Leighton-Linslade	South Bedfordshire, Bedfordshire	17 580
Leominster	Leominster, Hereford and Worcester	7079
Letchworth	North Hertfordshire, Hertfordshire	27 150
Lewes	Lewes, E Sussex	14 159
Leyland	South Ribble, Lancashire	26 100
Lichfield	Lichfield, Staffordshire	22 660
Lincoln	Lincoln, Lincolnshire	74 269
Liskeard	Caradon, Cornwall	5264
Littlehampton	Arun, W Sussex	29 660
Liverpool	Liverpool, Merseyside	610 113
Loftus	Langbaurgh, Cleveland	6850
London	Greater London	7 452 346
London Boroughs		
Barking		157 600
Barnet		297 200
Bexley		216 900
Brent		268 900
Bromley		301 500
Camden		191 600
City of London		5500
City of Westminster		218 500
Croydon		329 300
Ealing		294 200
Enfield		263 700
Greenwich		212 800
Hackney		208 000
Hammersmith		169 900
Haringey		228 800
Harrow		204 400
Havering		243 200
Hillingdon		232 500
Hounslow		203 300
Islington		178 800
Kensington and Chelsea		167 400
Kingston upon Thames		136 500
Lambeth		295 300
Lewisham		253 100
Merton		175 000
Newham		230 600
Redbridge		235 200
Richmond upon Thames		169 500
Southwark		241 700
Sutton		167 200
Tower Hamlets		150 000
Waltham Forest		230 700
Wandsworth		291 000
Long Eaton	Erewash, Derbyshire	30 910
Longridge	Ribble Valley, Lancashire	5600
Longton	South Ribble, Lancashire	8550
Loughborough	Charnwood, Leicestershire	45 875
Louth	East Lindsey, Lincolnshire	11 170
Lowestoft	Waveney, Suffolk	52 267
Ludlow	South Shropshire, Salop	6780
Luton	Luton, Bedfordshire	161 405
Lydney	Forest of Dean, Gloucestershire	5990
Lymington	New Forest, Hampshire	35 733
Lymm	Warrington, Cheshire	8450
Lytham St. Annes	Fylde, Lancashire	40 299

Macclesfield	Macclesfield, Cheshire	44 401
Maghull	Sefton, Merseyside	26 640
Maidenhead	Windsor and Maidenhead, Berkshire	45 288
Maidstone	Maidstone, Kent	70 987
Maldon	Maldon, Essex	13 891
Maltby	Rotherham, S Yorkshire	13 750
Manchester	Manchester, Gtr Manchester	543 650
Mansfield	Mansfield, Nottinghamshire	57 644
March	Fenland, Cambridgeshire	13 110
Margate	Thanet, Kent	50 347
Market Drayton	North Shropshire, Salop	5890
Market Harborough	Harborough, Leicestershire	13 130
Marlborough	Kennet, Wiltshire	6108
Marlow	Wycombe, Buckinghamshire	10 350
Marple	Stockport, Gtr Manchester	17 170
Marske	Langbaurgh, Cleveland	6760
Maryport	Allerdale, Cumbria	11 670
Matlock	West Derbyshire, Derbyshire	12 860
Melksham	West Wiltshire, Wiltshire	9540
Meltham	Kirklees, W Yorkshire	5950
Melton Mowbray	Melton, Leicestershire	17 810
Meopham	Gravesham, Kent	5660
Middleton	Rochdale, Gtr Manchester	53 512
Middlewich	Congleton, Cheshire	8070
Mildenhall	Forest Heath, Suffolk	6780
Milford	Waverley, Surrey	5750
Millom	Copeland, Cumbria	7430
Milnrow	Rochdale, Gtr Manchester	9270
Milton Keynes	Milton Keynes, Buckinghamshire	70 000
Minehead	West Somerset, Somerset	7370
Minster-in-Sheppey	Swale, Kent	10 230
Morecambe and Heysham		
	Lancaster, Lancashire	41 908
Morley	Leeds, W Yorkshire	44 345
Morpeth	Castle Morpeth, Northumberland	14 054
Mossley	Tameside, Gtr Manchester	10 086
Murton	Easington, Durham	8160
Nailsea	Woodspring, Avon	5900
Nantwich	Crewe and Nantwich, Cheshire	11 210
Narborough	Blaby, Leicestershire	9110
Nelson	Pendle, Lancashire	31 249
Neston	Ellesmere Port, Cheshire	11 780
Netley	Eastleigh, Hampshire	5100
Newark	Newark, Nottinghamshire	24 646
Newbiggin	Wansbeck, Northumberland	8480
Newbury	Newbury, Berkshire	23 634
Newcastle-under-Lyme		
	Newcastle-under-Lyme, Staffordshire	77 126
Newcastle upon Tyne		
	Newcastle upon Tyne, Tyne and Wear	222 209
Newhaven	Lewes, E Sussex	9710
Newmarket	Forest Heath, Suffolk	9900
New Mills	High Peak, Derbyshire	17 160
Newport	Medina, Isle of Wight	22 309
Newport	The Wrekin, Salop	5230
Newport Pagnell	Milton Keynes, Buckinghamshire	5120
Newquay	Restormel, Cornwall	12 240
Newton Abbot	Teignbridge, Devon	19 130
Newton Aycliffe	Sedgefield, Durham	26 000
Newton-le-Willows	St. Helens, Merseyside	21 490
New Windsor	Windsor and Maidenhead, Berkshire	30 114
Normanton	Wakefield, W Yorkshire	13 560
Northallerton	Hambleton, N Yorkshire	9300
Northam	North Devon, Devon	5580
Northampton	Northampton, Northamptonshire	151 000
North Walsham	North Norfolk, Norfolk	5540
Northwich	Vale Royal, Cheshire	42 820
Norton (including Radstock)		
	Wansdyke, Avon	14 150
Norton	Ryedale, N Yorkshire	8900
Norwich	Norwich, Norfolk	122 083
Nottingham	Nottingham, Nottinghamshire	300 630
Nuneaton	Nuneaton, Warwickshire	67 027

Ockbrook	Erewash, Derbyshire	5090
Oldham	Oldham, Gtr Manchester	105 913
Oldland	Kingswood, Avon	13 440
Old Windsor	Windsor and Maidenhead, Berkshire	8570
Ollerton	Newark, Nottinghamshire	9170
Ongar	Epping Forest, Essex	5600
Ormskirk	West Lancashire, Lancashire	21 410
Ossett	Wakefield, W Yorkshire	17 183
Oswestry	Oswestry, Salop	13 000
Otley	Leeds, W Yorkshire	12 910
Oxford	Oxford, Oxfordshire	108 805
Oxted	Tandridge, Surrey	12 410

Peacehaven	Lewes, E Sussex	8350
Pelton	Chester-le-Street, Durham	6020
Penrith	Eden, Cumbria	10 590
Penryn	Carrick, Cornwall	5135
Penzance	Penwith, Cornwall	19 415
Pershore	Wychavon, Hereford and Worcester	5530
Peterborough	Peterborough, Cambridgeshire	102 500
Peterlee	Easington, Durham	26 500
Petersfield	East Hampshire, Hampshire	8060
Pill	Woodspring, Avon	5220
Plymouth	Plymouth, Devon	239 452
Poole	Poole, Dorset	107 161
Pontefract	Wakefield, W Yorkshire	31 364
Portishead	Woodspring, Avon	8820
Portland	Weymouth and Portland, Dorset	9990
Portsmouth	Portsmouth, Hampshire	197 431
Potters Bar	Hertsmere; Welwyn Hatfield, Hertfordshire	26 990
Poynton	Macclesfield, Cheshire	12 240
Prescot	Knowsley, Merseyside	39 040
Preston	Preston, Lancashire	98 088
Prestwich	Bury, Gtr Manchester	32 911
Princes Risborough	Wycombe, Buckinghamshire	7520
Prudhoe	Tynedale, Northumberland	9400
Pudsey	Leeds, W Yorkshire	38 143

Queenborough-in-Sheppey		
	Swale, Kent	31 590
Queensbury	Bradford, W Yorkshire	6070

Radcliffe	Bury, Gtr Manchester	29 278
Radcliffe on Trent	Rushcliffe, Nottinghamshire	7550
Radlett	Hertsmere, Hertfordshire	8180
Rainford	St. Helens, Merseyside	5010
Ramsbottom	Bury, Gtr Manchester	15 390
Ramsgate	Thanet, Kent	39 561
Rawtenstall	Rossendale, Lancashire	21 432
Reading	Reading, Berkshire	132 939
Redditch	Redditch, Hereford and Worcester	51 800
Reigate	Reigate and Banstead, Surrey	56 223
Richmond	Richmondside, N Yorkshire	7245
Rickmansworth	Chiltern, Buckinghamshire; Three Rivers, Hertfordshire	19 320
Ringwood	New Forest, Hampshire	7850
Ripley	Amber Valley, Derbyshire	16 090
Ripon	Harrogate, N Yorkshire	10 989
Rishton	Hyndburn, Lancashire	5120
Rochdale	Rochdale, Gtr Manchester	91 454
Rochester	Medway, Kent	55 519
Romsey	Test Valley, Hampshire	10 043
Rossington	Doncaster, S Yorkshire	10 570

Ross-on-Wye	South Herefordshire, Hereford and Worcester	6390
Rotherham	Rotherham, S Yorkshire	84 801
Rothwell	Leeds, W Yorkshire	16 170
Rowlands Gill (including High Spen)		
	Gateshead, Tyne and Wear	7830
Royal Leamington Spa		
	Warwick, Warwickshire	45 064
Royal Tunbridge Wells		
	Tunbridge Wells, Kent	44 612
Royston	North Hertfordshire, Hertfordshire	6490
Royston	Barnsley, S Yorkshire	8640
Ruddington	Rushcliffe, Nottinghamshire	5450
Rugby	Rugby, Warwickshire	59 396
Rugeley	Cannock Chase, Staffordshire	17 240
Runcorn	Halton, Cheshire	51 698
Ryde	Medina, Isle of Wight	23 204
Ryehill	Wakefield, W Yorkshire	6650

St. Albans	St. Albans, Hertfordshire	52 174
St. Austell and Fowey		
	Restormel, Cornwall	32 265
St. Blazey	Restormel, Cornwall	6170
St. Helens	St. Helens, Merseyside	104 341
St. Ives	Huntingdon, Cambridgeshire	7148
St. Ives	Penwith, Cornwall	9839
St. Neots	Huntingdon, Cambridgeshire	10 110
St. Stephen	Restormel, Cornwall	6780
Saffron Walden	Uttlesford, Essex	9971
Sale	Trafford, Gtr Manchester	55 769
Salford	Salford, Gtr Manchester	130 976
Salisbury	Salisbury, Wiltshire	35 302
Saltash	Caradon, Cornwall	9926
Saltburn	Langbaurgh, Cleveland	6160
Sandbach	Congleton, Cheshire	10 920
Sandown (including Shanklin)		
	South Wight, Isle of Wight	13 890
Sarisbury	Fareham, Hampshire	13 060
Sawbridgeworth	East Hertfordshire, Hertfordshire	5460
Scarborough	Scarborough, N Yorkshire	44 440
Scunthorpe	Scunthorpe, Humberside	70 907
Seaford	Lewes, E Sussex	12 470
Seaham	Easington, Durham	25 870
Seaton Burn	North Tyneside, Tyne and Wear	8720
Seaton Delaval	Blyth Valley, Northumberland	7460
Selby	Selby, N Yorkshire	13 200
Selsey	Chichester, W Sussex	5650
Selston	Amber Valley, Derbyshire; Ashfield, Nottinghamshire	13 760
Sevenoaks	Sevenoaks, Kent	24 750
Sheerness	Swale, Kent	13 860
Sheffield	Sheffield, S Yorkshire	520 327
Shepshed	Charnwood, Leicestershire	7510
Shepton Mallet	Mendip, Somerset	5030
Sherbourne	West Dorset, Dorset	5880
Shevington	Wigan, Gtr Manchester	7650
Shildon	Sedgefield, Durham	13 620
Shirebrook	Bolsover, Derbyshire	16 340
Shotton Colliery	Easington, Durham	5560
Shrewsbury	Shrewsbury and Atcham, Salop	56 188
Sidmouth	East Devon, Devon	9740
Sileby	Charnwood, Leicestershire	5280
Silsden	Bradford, W Yorkshire	5390
Sittingbourne	Swale, Kent	26 450
Skegness	East Lindsey, Lincolnshire	12 680
Skelmanthorpe	Kirklees, W Yorkshire	6000
Skelmersdale	West Lancashire, Lancashire	40 700
Skipton	Craven, N Yorkshire	13 220
Sleaford	North Kesteven, Lincolnshire	7880
Slough	Slough, Berkshire	87 075
Solihull	Solihull, W Midlands	107 095
Somercotes	Amber Valley, Derbyshire	7930
Southampton	Southampton, Hampshire	215 118

Southend-on-Sea	Southend-on-Sea, Essex	162 770
South Kirkby	Wakefield, W Yorkshire	19 710
South Ockendon	Thurrock, Essex	20 800
South Normantown	Bolsover, Derbyshire	11 560
Southport	Sefton, Merseyside	84 574
South Shields	South Tyneside, Tyne and Wear	100 659
Spalding	South Holland, Lincolnshire	15 850
Spenborough	Kirklees, W Yorkshire	40 690
Spennymoor	Sedgefield, Durham	17 380
Stafford	Stafford, Staffordshire	55 001
Stakeford	Wansbeck, Northumberland	11 800
Stalybridge	Tameside, Gtr Manchester	22 805
Stamford	South Kesteven, Lincolnshire	14 662
Stanford	Thurrock, Essex	21 810
Stanley	Derwentside, Durham	24 020
Stevenage	Stevenage, Hertfordshire	76 000
Steyning	Horsham, W Sussex	7060
Stockport	Stockport, Gtr Manchester	139 644
Stocksbridge	Sheffield, S Yorkshire	10 800
Stoke-on-Trent	Stoke-on-Trent, Staffordshire	265 258
Stone	Stafford, Staffordshire	10 210
Stonehouse	Stroud, Gloucestershire	8490
Stotfold	Mid Bedfordshire, Bedfordshire	5900
Stourbridge	Dudley, West Midlands	54 344
Stourport-on-Severn	Wyre Forest, Hereford and Worcester	14 230
Stowmarket	Mid Suffolk, Suffolk	7560
Stratford-on-Avon	Stratford-on-Avon, Warwickshire	19 452
Street	Mendip, Somerset	7550
Stretford	Trafford, Gtr Manchester	54 297
Stroud	Stroud, Gloucestershire	25 580
Studley	Stratford-on-Avon, Warwickshire	6150
Sudbury	Babergh, Suffolk	8166
Sunderland	Sunderland, Tyne and Wear	217 079
Sutton-at-Hone	Dartford, Kent	5030
Sutton Coldfield	Birmingham, W Midlands	83 291
Sutton in Ashfield	Ashfield, Nottinghamshire	38 610
Swadlincote	South Derbyshire, Derbyshire	29 170
Swanage	Purbeck, Dorset	7860
Swanley	Sevenoaks, Kent	15 210
Swindon	Thamesdown, Wiltshire	91 033
Swinton and Pendlebury	Salford, Gtr Manchester	40 167
Syston	Charnwood, Leicestershire	6750
Tadley	Basingstoke, Hampshire	7200
Tamworth	Tamworth, Staffordshire	40 285
Taunton	Taunton Deane, Somerset	37 444
Taverham (including Drayton)	Broadland, Norfolk	5050
Tavistock	West Devon, Devon	6720
Teesside	Stockton-on-Tees; Middlesbrough; Langbaurgh, Cleveland	396 230
Telford	The Wrekin, Salop	96 700
Tenterden	Ashford, Kent	5930
Tewkesbury	Tewkesbury, Gloucestershire	8749
Thame	South Oxfordshire, Oxfordshire	5450
Thatcham	Newbury, Berkshire	8560
Thetford	Breckland, Norfolk	13 727
Thirsk	Hambleton, N Yorkshire	5820
Thornbury	Northavon, Avon	6340
Thorne	Doncaster, S Yorkshire	14 890
Thurcroft	Rotherham, S Yorkshire	5760
Thurmaston	Charnwood, Leicestershire	7710
Thurrock	Thurrock, Essex	47 020
Tidworth	Test Valley, Hampshire; Kennet, Wiltshire	9990
Tilbury	Thurrock, Essex	11 130
Tiverton	Tiverton, Devon	15 566
Todmorden	Calderdale, W Yorkshire	15 163
Tonbridge	Tonbridge and Malling, Kent	32 890
Torbay	Torbay, Devon	109 257
Totnes	South Hams, Devon	5772
Tring	Dacorum, Hertfordshire	7790
Trowbridge	West Wiltshire, Wiltshire	19 420
Truro	Carrick, Cornwall	14 849
Tynemouth	North Tyneside, Tyne and Wear	69 338
Ulverston	South Lakeland, Cumbria	10 710
Up Holland	West Lancashire, Lancashire	8630
Upton	Wakefield, W Yorkshire	5500
Ushaw Moor	Durham, Durham	7590
Uttoxeter	East Staffordshire, Staffordshire	8430
Ventnor	South Wight, Isle of Wight	5360
Virginia Water	Runnymede, Surrey	6980
Wakefield	Wakefield, W Yorkshire	59 590
Wales	Rotherham, S Yorkshire	6220
Wallasey	Wirral, Merseyside	97 215
Wallingford	South Oxfordshire, Oxfordshire	6182
Wallsend	North Tyneside, Tyne and Wear	45 797
Walsall	Walsall, W Midlands	184 734
Wantage	Newbury, Berkshire	7200
Ware	East Hertfordshire, Hertfordshire	13 740
Warley	Sandwell, W Midlands	163 567
Warminster	West Wiltshire, Wiltshire	11 040
Warrington	Warrington, Cheshire	133 400
Warsop	Mansfield, Nottinghamshire	8170
Warwick	Warwick, Warwickshire	18 296
Washington	Sunderland, Tyne and Wear	41 000
Watford	Watford, Hertfordshire	78 465
Wellingborough	Wellingborough, Northamptonshire	27 540
Wellington (including Dawley and Oakengates)	The Wrekin, Salop	67 600
Wellington	Taunton Deane, Somerset	7620
Wells	Mendip, Somerset	8604
Welwyn	Welwyn Hatfield, Hertfordshire	6890
Welwyn Garden City	Welwyn Hatfield, Hertfordshire	40 000
Wendover	Aylesbury Vale, Buckinghamshire	8660
West Bromwich	Sandwell, W Midlands	166 593
Westbury	West Wiltshire, Wiltshire	6800
Westhoughton	Bolton, Gtr Manchester	14 180
Weston-super-Mare	Woodspring, Avon	50 894
Wetherby	Leeds, W Yorkshire	5900
Weymouth and Melcombe Regis	Weymouth and Portland, Dorset	42 349
Whaley Bridge	High Peak, Derbyshire	5120
Wheatley Hill	Easington, Durham	5110
Whitburn	South Tyneside, Tyne and Wear	7150
Whitby	Scarborough, N Yorkshire	12 150
Whitchurch	North Shropshire, Salop	7360
Whitehaven	Copeland, Cumbria	26 724
Whitley Bay	North Tyneside, Tyne and Wear	37 817
Whitstable	Canterbury, Kent	21 950
Whittle-le-Woods	Chorley, Lancashire	6120
Whittlesey	Fenland, Cambridgeshire	8010
Whitworth	Rossendale, Lancashire	7300
Wickford	Basildon, Essex	21 110
Widnes	Halton, Cheshire	56 949
Wigan	Wigan, Gtr Manchester	81 147
Willington	Wear Valley, Durham	7380
Wilmslow	Macclesfield, Cheshire	27 220
Wimbourne Minster	Wimbourne, Dorset	7400
Winchester	Winchester, Hampshire	31 107

Windermere	South Lakeland, Cumbria	7140	Worksop	Bassetlaw, Nottinghamshire	36 098
Wingate	Easington, Durham	5760	Worthing	Worthing, W Sussex	88 407
Winsford	Vale Royal, Cheshire	16 490	Writtle	Chelmsford, Essex	5030
Wisbech	Fenland, Cambridgeshire	17 016	Wroughton	Thamesdown, Wiltshire	6810
Witham	Braintree, Essex	8060	Wymondham	South Norfolk, Norfolk	5260
Withernsea	Holderness, Humberside	5790	Wythall	Bromsgrove, Hereford and Worcester	5050
Witney	West Oxfordshire, Oxfordshire	9800			
Wokingham	Wokingham, Berkshire	21 069			
Wolverhampton	Wolverhampton, W Midlands	269 112			
Wolverton	Milton Keynes, Buckinghamshire	9920			
Wombourne	South Staffordshire, Staffordshire	11 610			
Wooburn	Wycombe, Buckinghamshire	8510	Yate	Northavon, Avon	10 370
Woodbridge	Suffolk Coastal, Suffolk	8660	Yateley	Hartley Wintney, Hampshire	8300
Wootton Bassett	North Wiltshire, Wiltshire	5140	Yeovil	Yeovil, Somerset	25 503
Worcester	Worcester, Hereford and Worcester	73 452	York	York, N Yorkshire	104 782
Workington	Allerdale, Cumbria	28 431	Yorkley	Forest of Dean, Gloucestershire	5760

Wales

Places included in this list are inhabited settlements with a population of 2000 or more. The figures have been taken from the 1971 Census of England and Wales, although the County and District names included in each reference are from the subsequent local government re-organisation of 1974. Entries are laid out, in alphabetical order, with the name of the place first, followed by the District name and then the County name. In cases where places fall into parts of more than one County or District, these constituent parts are indicated after the place name. The population figure completes the entry.

Aberbargoed	Rhymney Valley, Mid Glamorgan	4550	Caerleon	Newport, Gwent	4700
Abercarn	Islwyn, Gwent	19 090	Caernarfon	Arfon, Gwynedd	9260
Aberdare	Cynon Valley, Mid Glamorgan	40 220	Caerphilly	Rhymney Valley, Mid Glamorgan	29 400
Abergavenny	Monmouth, Gwent	9401	Caldicot	Monmouth, Gwent	6390
Abergele	Colwyn, Clwyd	7800	Cardiff	Cardiff, South Glamorgan	279 111
Abertillery	Blaenau Gwent, Gwent	19 980	Cardigan	Ceredigion, Dyfed	3810
Aberystwyth	Ceredigion, Dyfed	10 688	Carmarthen	Carmarthen, Dyfed	13 081
Amlwch	Ynys Môn - Isle of Anglesey, Gwynedd	2970	Cefn Cribbwr	Ogwr, Mid Glamorgan	2090
Ammanford	Dinefwr, Dyfed	6060	Cefn-Mawr	Wrexham-Maelor, Clwyd	8820
			Chepstow	Monmouth, Gwent	8480
			Chirk	Glyndŵr, Clwyd	3440
			Clydach	Lliw Valley, West Glamorgan	7090
			Colwyn Bay	Colwyn, Clwyd	25 564
			Connah's Quay	Alyn and Deeside, Clwyd	34 340
			Conwy	Aberconwy, Gwynedd	12 206
Bangor	Arfon, Gwynedd	14 558	Cwm	Blaenau Gwent, Gwent	3610
Bargoed	Rhymney Valley, Mid Glamorgan	8850	Cwmbran	Torfaen, Gwent	45 000
Barmouth	Meirionnydd, Gwynedd	2150	Cymmer	Afan, West Glamorgan	4830
Barry	Vale of Glamorgan, South Glamorgan	41 681			
Beaumaris	Ynys Môn - Isle of Anglesey, Gwynedd	2102			
Beddau	Taff-Ely, Mid Glamorgan	8260			
Bedwas	Rhymney Valley, Mid Glamorgan	6590			
Bersham	Wrexham-Maelor, Clwyd	4200	Denbigh	Glyndŵr, Clwyd	8101
Bethesda	Arfon, Gwynedd	4190	Dolgellau	Meirionnydd, Gwynedd	2340
Bishopston	Swansea, West Glamorgan	4050			
Blackwood	Islwyn, Gwent	12 700			
Blaenau-Ffestiniog	Meirionnydd, Gwynedd	3120			
Blaenavon	Torfaen, Gwent	7980			
Blaengwrach	Neath, West Glamorgan	6470			
Blaen-gwynfi	Afan, West Glamorgan	2650	Ebbw Vale	Blaenau Gwent, Gwent	22 490
Blaina	Blaenau Gwent, Gwent	17 380			
Brecknock	Brecknock, Powys	6304			
Bridgend	Ogwr, Mid Glamorgan	27 140			
Broughton	Wrexham-Maelor, Clwyd	10 210			
Bryncethin	Ogwr, Mid Glamorgan	4640			
Buckley	Alyn and Deeside, Clwyd	8080	Fishguard	Preseli, Dyfed	2810
Burry Port	Llanelli, Dyfed	5540	Flint	Delyn, Clwyd	14 662

Place	Area	Population
Gelligaer	Rhymney Valley, Mid Glamorgan	14 830
Gilfach Goch	Ogwr, Mid Glamorgan	5400
Gilwern	Blaenau Gwent, Gwent	4090
Glanamman	Dinefwr, Dyfed	3870
Goodwick	Preseli, Dyfed	2070
Gorseinon	Lliw Valley, West Glamorgan	13 840
Gowerton	Lliw Valley, West Glamorgan	3300
Gresford	Wrexham-Maelor, Clwyd	2250
Gwaun-Cae-Gurwan	Lliw Valley, West Glamorgan	4120
Gwersyllt	Wrexham-Maelor, Clwyd	6070
Haverfordwest	Preseli, Dyfed	9104
Holyhead	Ynys Môn - Isle of Anglesey, Gwŷnedd	11 530
Hope	Alyn and Deeside, Clwyd	5810
Kidwelly	Llanelli, Dyfed	3084
Kinmel Bay	Colwyn, Clwyd	2300
Lampeter	Dyfed, Ceredigion	2189
Langstone	Newport, Gwent	2660
Llandovery	Dinefwr, Dyfed	2002
Llandrindod Wells	Radnor, Powys	2970
Llandudno	Aberconwy, Gwŷnedd	15 890
Llanelli	Llanelli, Dyfed	26 383
Llanfairfechan	Aberconwy, Gwŷnedd	3000
Llanfair-yn-Neubwll	Ynys Môn - Isle of Anglesey, Gwŷnedd	2050
Llangefni	Ynys Môn - Isle of Anglesey, Gwŷnedd	3520
Llangennech	Llanelli, Dyfed	3410
Llangollen	Glyndŵr, Clwyd	3080
Llangyfelach	Lliw Valley, West Glamorgan	3330
Llanharan	Taff-Ely, Mid Glamorgan	3780
Llanharry	Taff-Ely, Mid Glamorgan	2710
Llanidloes	Montgomery, Powys	2335
Llanrwst	Aberconwy, Gwŷnedd	2610
Llantrisant	Taff-Ely, Mid Glamorgan	6480
Llantwit Major	Vale of Glamorgan, South Glamorgan	8740
Llay	Wrexham-Maelor, Clwyd	3550
Machan	Rhymney Valley, Mid Glamorgan	2100
Machynlleth	Montgomery, Powys	2030
Maesteg	Ogwr, Mid Glamorgan	21 420
Markham	Islwyn, Gwent	3420
Menai Bridge	Ynys Môn - Isle of Anglesey, Gwŷnedd	2340
Merthyr Tydfil	Merthyr Tydfil, Mid Glamorgan	55 317
Milford Haven	Preseli, Dyfed	13 960
Mold	Delyn, Clwyd	7490
Monmouth	Monmouth, Gwent	6570
Mountain Ash	Cynon Valley, Mid Glamorgan	24 040
Nant-y-moel	Ogwr, Mid Glamorgan	3080
Neath	Neath, West Glamorgan	28 619
Nelson	Rhymney Valley, Mid Glamorgan	3800
Newport	Newport, Gwent	112 286
Newtown	Montgomery, Powys	5450
New Tredegar	Rhymney Valley, Mid Glamorgan	7230
Neyland	Preseli, Dyfed	2130
Oakdale	Islwyn, Gwent	3830
Ogmore Valley	Ogwr, Mid Glamorgan	5000
Pembroke	South Pembrokeshire, Dyfed	14 197
Penarth	Vale of Glamorgan, South Glamorgan	22 570
Pencoed	Ogwr, Mid Glamorgan	4920
Penmaenmawr	Aberconwy, Gwŷnedd	3040
Penrhyn	Aberconwy, Gwŷnedd	2530
Penrhyndeudraeth	Meirionnydd, Gwŷnedd	2230
Penycae	Wrexham-Maelor, Clwyd	3010
Pen-y-Fai	Ogwr, Mid Glamorgan	3780
Pontardawe (including Alltwen)	Lliw Valley, West Glamorgan	7860
Pontardulais	Llanelli, Dyfed	
	Lliw Valley, West Glamorgan	7910
Pont-Llan-Fraith	Islwyn, Gwent	7870
Pontyberem	Llanelli, Dyfed	2770
Pontycymmer	Ogwr, Mid Glamorgan	9980
Pontypool	Torfaen, Gwent	37 580
Porthcawl	Ogwr, Mid Glamorgan	12 520
Porthkerry	Vale of Glamorgan, South Glamorgan	2810
Porthmadog	Dwyfor, Gwŷnedd	3840
Port Talbot	Afan, West Glamorgan	50 729
Pwllheli	Dwyfor, Gwŷnedd	4180
Pyle	Ogwr, Mid Glamorgan	10 910
Resolven	Neath, West Glamorgan	2890
Rhondda	Rhondda, Mid Glamorgan	88 994
Rhosllanerchrugog	Wrexham-Maelor, Clwyd	8970
Rhostyllen	Wrexham-Maelor, Clwyd	2580
Rhuddlan	Rhuddlan, Clwyd	2530
Rhyl (including Prestatyn)	Rhuddlan, Clwyd	34 150
Rhymney	Rhymney Valley, Mid Glamorgan	8990
Risca	Islwyn, Gwent	19 270
Ruabon	Wrexham-Maelor, Clwyd	3290
Ruthin	Glyndŵr, Clwyd	4338
St Andrews Major	Vale of Glamorgan, South Glamorgan	5530
St Asaph	Rhuddlan, Clwyd	2910
Seven Sisters	Neath, West Glamorgan	5510
Skewen	Neath, West Glamorgan	11 610
Swansea	Swansea, West Glamorgan	173 413
Tenby	South Pembrokeshire, Dyfed	4994
Tondu	Ogwr, Mid Glamorgan	2380
Tonyrefail	Taff-Ely, Mid Glamorgan	6870
Tredegar	Blaenau Gwent, Gwent	19 460
Tywyn	Meirionnydd, Gwŷnedd	2060
Usk	Monmouth, Gwent	2060
Welshpool	Montgomery, Powys	7030
Wrexham	Wrexham-Maelor, Clwyd	39 052
Ynysddu	Islwyn, Gwent	3880
Ynysybwl	Cynon Valley, Mid Glamorgan	4070
Ystradgynlais (including Ystalyfera)	Brecknock, Powys	12 340

Scotland

Places included in this list are inhabited settlements with a population of 2000 or more. The figures have been taken from the 1971 Census of Scotland, although the Region and District names included in each reference are from the subsequent local government re-organisation of 1975. Entries are laid out, in alphabetical order, with the name of the place first, followed by the District name and then the Region name. In cases where places fall into parts of more than one Region or District, these constituent parts are indicated after the place name. The population figure completes the entry.

Aberdeen	City of Aberdeen, Grampian	182 071
Airdrie	Monklands, Strathclyde	37 951
Alexandria	Dumbarton, Strathclyde	9758
Alloa	Clackmannan, Central	14 100
Alness	Ross & Crom., Highland	2560
Alva	Clackmannan, Central	4180
Annan	Annandale & Eskdale, Dumfries & Galloway	7754
Annbank Station	Kyle & Carrick, Strathclyde	2530
Arbroath	Angus, Tayside	22 586
Ardrossan	Cunninghame, Strathclyde	10 562
Armadale	West Lothian, Lothian	9510
Arniston	Midlothian, Lothian	2020
Auchinleck	Cumnock & Doon Valley, Strathclyde	4883
Auchterarder	Perth & Kinross, Tayside	2446
Ayr	Kyle & Carrick, Strathclyde	47 896
Balerno	City of Edinburgh, Lothian	3576
Ballingry	Dunfermline; Kirkcaldy, Fife	4332
Banchory	Kincardine & Deeside, Grampian	2355
Banff	Banff & Buchan, Grampian	3723
Bankhead	City of Glasgow, Strathclyde	2564
Bannockburn	Stirling, Central	5889
Bargeddie	Monklands, Strathclyde	2891
Barrhead	Renfrew, Strathclyde	18 289
Bathgate	West Lothian, Lothian	14 224
Bearsden	Bearsden & Milngavie, Strathclyde	25 013
Beith	Cunninghame, Strathclyde	5859
Bellsbank	Cumnock & Doon Valley, Strathclyde	3066
Bellshill	Motherwell, Strathclyde	18 166
Bishopbriggs	Strathkelvin, Strathclyde	21 684
Bishopton	Renfrew, Strathclyde	2931
Blackburn	West Lothian, Lothian	7636
Blairgowrie & Rattray		
	Perth & Kinross, Tayside	5960
Blantyre	Hamilton, Strathclyde	13 992
Bo'ness	Falkirk, Central	12 853
Bonhill	Dumbarton, Strathclyde	4385
Bonnybridge	Falkirk, Central	5701
Bonnyrigg & Lasswade		
	Midlothian, Lothian	7102
Bothwell	Hamilton, Strathclyde	4840
Branderburgh	see Lossiemouth	
Brechin	Angus, Tayside	6578
Bridge of Allan	Stirling, Central	4314
Bridge of Don	City of Aberdeen, Grampian	4086
Bridge of Weir	Renfrew, Strathlcyde	4724
Brightons	Falkirk, Central	3106
Broxburn	West Lothian, Lothian	7776
Buckhaven & Methil		
	Kirkcaldy, Fife	18 396
Buckie	Moray, Grampian	7919
Bucksburn	City of Aberdeen, Grampian	6567
Burnside	City of Glasgow, Strathclyde	3487
Burntisland	Kirkcaldy, Fife	5699
Busby	East Kilbride; Eastwood, Strathclyde	2925
Calderbank	Monklands, Strathclyde	2116
Caldercruix	Monklands, Strathclyde	2251
Cambuslang	City of Glasgow, Strathclyde	14 607
Campbeltown	Argyll & Bute, Strathclyde	5960
Caol	Lochaber, Highland	3719
Cardenden	Kirkcaldy, Fife	6802
Carluke	Lanark, Strathclyde	8864
Carmyle	City of Glasgow, Strathclyde	3568
Carnoustie	Angus, Tayside	6232
Carron	Falkirk, Central	2626
Castle Douglas	Stewartry, Dumfries & Galloway	3331
Cathkin	City of Glasgow, Strathclyde	3235
Catrine	Cumnock & Doon Valley, Strathclyde	2681
Chapelhall	Motherwell, Strathclyde	3928
Chryston	Strathkelvin, Strathlcyde	8322
Clackmannan	Clackmannan, Central	3248
Clarkston	Eastwood, Strathclyde	8404
Cleland	Motherwell, Strathclyde	3117
Clydebank	Clydebank, Strathclyde	48 300
Coatbridge	Monklands, Strathclyde	52 145
Cockenzie & Port Seton		
	East Lothian, Lothian	3580
Cowdenbeath	Dunfermline, Fife	10 464
Cowie	Stirling, Central	2751
Crieff	Perth & Kinross, Tayside	5603
Crosshouse	Kilmarnock & Loudoun, Strathclyde	2034
Cults	City of Aberdeen, Grampian	3336
Cumbernauld	Cumbernauld & Kilsyth, Strathclyde	43 000
Cumnock & Holmhead		
	Cumnock & Doon Valley, Strathclyde	5714
Cupar	North East Fife, Fife	6603
Currie	City of Edinburgh, Lothian	6764
Dalbeattie	Stewartry, Dumfries & Galloway	3412
Dalkeith	Midlothian, Lothian	9688
Dalry	Cunninghame, Strathclyde	5833
Danderhall	Midlothian, Lothian	3130
Darvel	Kilmarnock & Loudoun, Strathclyde	3209
Denny & Dunipace	Falkirk, Central	9841
Dingwall	Ross & Cromarty, Highland	4232
Dollar	Clackmannan, Central	2280
Drongan	Cumnock & Doon Valley, Strathclyde	3609
Dumbarton	Dumbarton, Strathclyde	25 640
Dumfries	Nithsdale, Dumfries & Galloway	29 382
Dunbar	East Lothian, Lothian	4611
Dunblane	Stirling, Central	4693
Dundee	City of Dundee, Tayside	182 204
Dundonald	Kyle & Carrick, Strathclyde	2256
Dunfermline	Dunfermline, Fife	49 897
Dunipace	see Denny	
Dunoon	Argyll & Bute, Strathclyde	9718
Duntocher	Dumbarton, Strathclyde	3532
Dyce	City of Aberdeen, Grampian	2733

Eaglesham	Eastwood, Strathclyde	2788
East Calder	West Lothian, Lothian	2690
East Kilbride	East Kilbride, Strathclyde	73 800
East Wemyss	Kirkcaldy, Fife	2004
Eastfield	City of Glasgow, Strathclyde	2733
Eddlewood	Hamilton, Strathclyde	4227
Edinburgh	City of Edinburgh, Lothian	453 584
Elderslie	Renfrew, Strathclyde	5204
Elgin	Moray, Grampian	16 407
Ellon	Gordon, Grampian	2263
Eyemouth	Berwickshire, Borders	2530
Falkirk	Falkirk, Central	37 579
Fallin	Stirling, Central	3159
Fauldhouse	West Lothian, Lothian	5247
Forfar	Angus, Tayside	10 499
Forres	Moray, Grampian	4718
Fort William	Lochaber, Highland	4214
Forth	Lanark, Strathclyde	2929
Fraserburgh	Banff & Buchan, Grampian	10 606
Galashiels	Ettrick & Lauderdale, Borders	12 609
Galston	Kilmarnock & Loudoun, Strathclyde	4859
Garrowhill	City of Glasgow, Strathclyde	6159
Giffnock	Eastwood, Strathclyde	10 987
Girvan	Kyle & Carrick, Strathclyde	7410
Glasgow	City of Glasgow, Strathclyde	897 483
Glenboig	Monklands, Strathclyde	2352
Glenrothes	Kirkcaldy, Fife	32 000
Gorebridge	Midlothian, Lothian	3426
Gourock	Inverclyde, Strathclyde	10 922
Grangemouth	Falkirk, Central	24 569
Greenholm	see Newmilns	
Greenock	Inverclyde, Strathclyde	69 502
Haddington	East Lothian, Lothian	6502
Hamilton	Hamilton, Strathclyde	46 349
Hardgate	Clydebank, Strathclyde	3729
Harthill	Motherwell, Strathclyde Lothian, W Lothian	4712
Hawick	Roxburgh, Borders	16 286
Helensburgh	Dumbarton, Strathclyde	12 870
High Blantyre	Hamilton, Strathclyde	3590
High Valleyfield	Dunfermline, Fife	2766
Holmhead	see Cumnock	
Holytown	Motherwell, Strathclyde	4436
Huntly	Gordon, Grampian	3645
Hurlford	Kilmarnock & Loudoun, Strathclyde	4294
Inchinnan	Renfrew, Strathclyde	2143
Innerleithen	Tweeddale, Borders	2128
Invergordon	Ross & Cromarty, Highland	2350
Inverkeithing	Dunfermline, Fife	5861
Inverness	Inverness, Highland	34 839
Inverurie	Gordon, Grampian	5437
Irvine	Cunninghame, Strathclyde	52 600
Jedburgh	Roxburgh, Borders	3874
Johnstone	Renfrew, Strathclyde	22 617

Keith	Moray, Grampian	4177
Kelso	Roxburgh, Borders	4852
Kelty	Dunfermline, Fife	6573
Kennoway	Kirkcaldy, Fife	4703
Kilbarchan	Renfrew, Strathclyde	2669
Kilbirnie	Cunninghame, Strathclyde	8259
Kilmacolm	Renfrew; Inverclyde, Strathclyde	3448
Kilmarnock	Kilmarnock & Loudoun, Strathclyde	48 787
Kilmaurs	Kilmarnock & Loudoun, Strathclyde	2518
Kilrenny, Anstruther E & W	North East Fife, Fife	3037
Kilsyth	Cumbernauld & Kilsyth, Strathclyde	10 165
Kilwinning	Cunninghame, Strathclyde	8290
Kincardine	Dunfermline, Fife	3278
Kinghorn	Kirkcaldy, Fife	2146
Kinloss	Moray, Grampian	2378
Kinross	Perth & Kinross, Tayside	2418
Kirkcaldy	Kirkcaldy, Fife	50 360
Kirkconnel	Nithsdale, Dumfries & Galloway	3318
Kirkcudbright	Stewartry, Dumfries & Galloway	2502
Kirkhill	Midlothian, Lothian	2409
Kirkhill	Eastwood, Strathclyde	2230
Kirkintilloch	Strathkelvin, Strathclyde	25 206
Kirkliston	West Lothian, Lothian	2200
Kirkmuirhill	Lanark, Strathclyde	2575
Kirkwall	Orkney	4617
Kirriemuir	Angus, Tayside	4138
Lanark	Lanark, Strathclyde	8700
Langholm	Annandale & Eskdale, Dumfries & Galloway	2344
Larbert	Falkirk, Central	4922
Largs	Cunninghame, Strathclyde	9771
Larkhall	Hamilton, Strathclyde	15 926
Lasswade	see Bonnyrigg	
Laurieston	Falkirk, Central	3300
Law	Lanark, Strathclyde	2038
Lennoxtown	Strathkelvin, Strathclyde	3070
Lerwick	Shetland	6127
Leslie	Kirkcaldy, Fife	3342
Lesmahagow	Lanark, Strathclyde	3906
Leuchars	North East Fife, Fife	2482
Leven	Kirkcaldy, Fife	9472
Linlithgow	West Lothian, Lothian	5684
Linwood	Renfrew, Strathclyde	10 510
Livingston	West Lothian, Lothian	24 860
Loanhead	Midlothian, Lothian	5963
Locharbriggs	Nithsdale, Dumfries & Galloway	2561
Lochgelly	Dunfermline, Fife	7980
Lochore	Dunfermline, Fife	2994
Lochwinnoch	Renfrew, Strathclyde	2064
Lockerbie	Annandale & Eskdale, Dumfries & Galloway	2999
Lossiemouth & Branderburgh	Moray, Grampian	5678
Macduff	Banff & Buchan, Grampian	3709
Maddiston	Falkirk, Central	2418
Markinch	Kirkcaldy, Fife	2225
Mauchline	Cumnock & Doon Valley, Strathclyde	3612
Maybole	Kyle & Carrick, Strathclyde	4523
Mayfield	Midlothian, Lothian	8232
Melrose	Ettrick & Lauderdale, Borders	2185
Methil	see Buckhaven	
Methilhill	Kirkcaldy, Fife	2221
Mill of Haldane	Dumbarton, Strathclyde	4626
Milngavie	Bearsden & Milngavie, Strathclyde	10 741
Moffat	Annandale & Eskdale, Dumfries & Galloway	2031

Motherwell & Wishaw		
	Motherwell, Strathlcyde	73 658
Muirkirk	Cumnock & Doon Valley, Strathclyde	2607
Musselburgh	East Lothian, Lothian	16 849
Monifieth	City of Dundee, Tayside	6338
Montrose	Angus, Tayside	9959
Mossend	Motherwell, Strathclyde	4428

Nairn	Nairn, Highland	8037
Neilston	Renfrew, Strathclyde	4358
Netherlee	Eastwood, Strathclyde	2907
New Cumnock	Cumnock & Doon Valley, Strathclyde	5077
New Scone	Perth & Kinross, Tayside	3830
New Stevenson	Motherwell, Strathclyde	3778
Newarthill	Motherwell, Strathclyde	7003
Newburgh	North East Fife, Fife	2062
Newmains	Motherwell, Strathclyde	6847
Newmilns & Greenholm		
	Kilmarnock & Loudoun, Strathclyde	3406
Newport-on-Tay	North East Fife, Fife	3719
Newton Mearns	Eastwood, Strathclyde	6901
Newtongrange	Midlothian, Lothian	4555
North Berwick	East Lothian, Lothian	4414
North Mount Vernon		
	City of Glasgow, Strathclyde	2287

Oakley	Dunfermline, Fife	3499
Oban	Argyll & Bute, Strathclyde	6897
Old Kilpatrick	Clydebank, Strathclyde	3256
Ormiston	West Lothian, Lothian	2027

Paisley	Renfrew, Strathclyde	95 357
Patna	Cumnock & Doon Valley, Strathclyde	2867
Peebles	Tweeddale, Borders	5884
Penicuik	Midlothian, Lothian	10 066
Perth	Perth & Kinross, Tayside	43 030
Peterhead	Banff & Buchan, Grampian	14 160
Pitlochry	Perth & Kinross, Tayside	2599
Plains	Monklands, Strathclyde	3374
Polmont	Falkirk, Central	2153
Poltonhall	Midlothian, Lothian	4699
Port Glasgow	Inverclyde, Strathclyde	22 398
Port Seton	see **Cockenzie**	
Prestonpans	East Lothian, Lothian	8436
Prestwick	Kyle & Carrick, Strathclyde	13 437

Queensferry	City of Edinburgh, Lothian	5172

Ralston	Renfrew, Strathclyde	4052
Rattray	see **Blairgowrie**	
Renfrew	Renfrew, Strathclyde	18 595

Renton	Dumbarton, Strathclyde	3443
Rothesay	Argyll & Bute, Strathclyde	6595
Rutherglen	City of Glasgow, Strathclyde	24 732

St. Andrews	North East Fife, Fife	11 630
Saltcoats	Cunninghame, Strathclyde	14 904
Sauchie	Clackmannan, Central	6082
Selkirk	Ettrick & Lauderdale, Borders	5684
Shotts	Motherwell, Strathclyde	9512
Springboig	City of Glasgow, Strathclyde	4058
Springhall	City of Glasgow, Strathclyde	2524
Stamperland	Eastwood, Strathclyde	3803
Stenhousemuir	Falkirk, Central	8203
Stepps	Strathkelvin, Strathclyde	2916
Stevenston	Cunninghame, Strathclyde	12 047
Stewarton	Kilmarnock & Loudoun, Strathclyde	4492
Stirling	Stirling, Central	29 776
Stonehaven	Kincardine & Deeside, Grampian	4730
Stonehouse	Annandale & Eskdale	8100
Stornoway	Western Isles	5152
Stranraer	Wigtown, Dumfries & Galloway	9853
Strathaven	East Kilbride, Strathclyde	5464

Tannochside	Motherwell, Strathclyde	3535
Tarbolton	Kyle & Carrick, Strathclyde	2224
Tayport	North East Fife, Fife	2897
Thornliebank	Eastwood, Strathclyde	3560
Thurso	Caithness, Highland	9087
Tillicoultry	Clackmannan, Central	4026
Tranent	East Lothian, Lothian	6773
Troon	Kyle & Carrick, Strathclyde	11 318
Tullibody	Clackmannan, Central	6082
Turriff	Banff & Buchan, Grampian	2858

Uddingston	Lanark, Strathclyde	5278

Viewpark	Motherwell, Strathclyde	9812

Wallyford	East Lothian, Lothian	2475
West Calder	West Lothian, Lothian	2005
West Kilbride	Cunninghame, Strathclyde	3883
Whitburn	West Lothian, Lothian	10 176
Wick	Caithness, Highland	7842
Winchburgh	West Lothian, Lothian	2409
Wishaw	see **Motherwell**	

Populations of standard regions and metropolitan counties

Millions

	Mid-year estimates							Projections (1973-based)			
	1961	1966	1971	1972	1973	1974	1975	1976	1981	1986	1991
Northern	3.1	3.1	3.1	3.1	3.1	3.1	3.1	3.1	3.1	3.1	3.1
Tyne and Wear[1]	1.2	1.2	1.2	1.2	1.2	1.2	1.2				
Yorkshire and Humberside	4.7	4.8	4.9	4.9	4.9	4.9	4.9	4.9	4.8	4.8	4.8
South Yorks[1]	1.3	1.3	1.3	1.3	1.3	1.3	1.3	1.3			
West Yorks[1]	2.0	2.1	2.1	2.1	2.1	2.1	2.1				
North West	6.4	6.5	6.6	6.6	6.6	6.6	6.6	6.6	6.6	6.5	6.5
Greater Manchester[1]	2.7	2.7	2.7	2.7	2.7	2.7	2.7				
Merseyside[1]	1.7	1.7	1.7	1.6	1.6	1.6	1.6				
East Midlands	3.3	3.5	3.6	3.7	3.7	3.7	3.7	3.8	3.9	4.0	4.2
West Midlands	4.8	4.9	5.1	5.2	5.2	5.2	5.2	5.2	5.2	5.2	5.3
West Midlands[1]	2.7	2.8	2.8	2.8	2.8	2.8	2.8				
South East	16.1	16.7	17.0	17.0	17.0	17.0	17.0	17.0	17.0	17.2	17.4
Greater London Council	8.0	7.8	7.4	7.3	7.3	7.2	7.1	7.0	6.6	6.3	6.0
Outer Metropolitan area[2]	4.5	5.0	5.3	5.4	5.4	5.4	5.5	5.5	5.7	5.9	6.2
Outer South East[2]	3.6	3.9	4.2	4.3	4.3	4.3	4.3	4.5	4.7	5.0	5.2
East Anglia	1.5	1.6	1.7	1.7	1.7	1.8	1.8	1.8	2.0	2.1	2.2
South West	3.7	3.9	4.1	4.1	4.2	4.2	4.2	4.2	4.4	4.5	4.7
Wales	2.6	2.7	2.7	2.7	2.7	2.8	2.8	2.8	2.8	2.8	2.9
England and Wales	46.2	47.8	48.9	49.0	49.2	49.2	49.2	49.4	49.6	50.2	51.1
Scotland	5.2	5.2	5.2	5.2	5.2	5.2	5.2	5.2	5.2	5.2	5.3
Clydeside	1.9	1.9	1.9	1.9	1.9	1.8	1.8				
Great Britain	51.4	53.0	54.1	54.2	54.4	54.4	54.4	54.6	54.7	55.5	56.3
Northern Ireland	1.4	1.5	1.5	1.5	1.5	1.5	1.5	1.5	1.6	1.6	1.6
United Kingdom	52.8	54.5	55.6	55.8	55.9	56.0	56.0	56.1	56.3	57.7	58.0

[1] Metropolitan counties.   [2] Based on pre-April 1974 local authority areas.   *Source: Office of Population Censuses and Surveys.*

New Towns in Great Britain

Among the earliest towns consciously founded and built to a specific plan were the thirteenth century 'bastides' or fortified towns built by Edward I in North Wales; Flint, Conwy, Beaumaris, Harlech and Caernarfon are among the best examples. Six hundred years later enlightened employers such as William Lever and George Cadbury built their factories and housing for their workers in rural areas; the best known of these exist today at Bournville near Birmingham, and Port Sunlight on the Mersey.

Garden Cities, the forerunner of 'new towns' as we know them today, were originally conceived by Ebenezer Howard towards the end of the nineteenth century. Reacting against the overcrowding and poor living conditions in the industrial towns of Great Britain, he advocated the growth of new self-contained communities in the countryside where housing, industry and all the other necessary related facilities would be provided, and where people would be able to lead fuller and more satisfying lives. Letchworth (est. 1903) and Welwyn Garden City (est. 1920) were the first towns to be established on these principles.

The Barlow Report, published in 1940, drew on the experiences of these early pioneers in town planning and contained recommendations for the dispersal of industry and population away from congested urban areas, in particular London and south east England to new rural locations. This and the recommendations of the New Towns Committee, set up in 1945 under the chairmanship of Lord Reith, were embodied in the first New Towns Act of 1946; this and most of the subsequent legislation relating to new towns has since been consolidated in the New Towns Act of 1975. Since 1946, 28 new towns have been designated in Britain, 23 in England and Wales and 5 in Scotland, most of these having as their nucleus an existing village or town.

The New Towns in Great Britain

	Name	Date of Designation	Area in sq km	Original Population	Population at 31.12.75	Ultimate Planned Population
ENGLAND	Aycliffe	19 April 1947	12.56	60	26 000	45 000
	Basildon	4 Jan. 1949	31.64	25 000	88 000	134 000
	Bracknell	17 June 1949	13.37	5149	42 600	55-60 000
	Central Lancashire	26 March 1970	142.67	234 500	243 900	not estimated
	Corby	1 April 1950	17.90	15 700	53 500	83 000
	Crawley	9 Jan. 1947	23.96	9100	73 000	77 000
	Harlow	25 March 1947	25.88	4500	83 500	undecided
	Hatfield	20 May 1948	9.47	8500	26 000	29 000
	Hemel Hempstead	4 Feb. 1947	23.92	21 000	76 000	85 000
	Milton Keynes	23 Jan. 1967	89.03	40 000	70 000	250 000
	Northampton	14 Feb. 1968	80.80	131 120	151 000	240 000
	Peterborough	1 Aug. 1967	64.51	81 000	102 500	not available
	Peterlee	10 March 1948	11.33	200	26 500	30 000
	Redditch	10 April 1964	29.06	32 000	51 800	90 000
	Runcorn	10 April 1964	29.27	28 500	51 698	100 000
	Skelmersdale	9 Oct. 1961	16.69	10 000	40 700	80 000
	Stevenage	11 Nov. 1946	25.32	6700	76 000	100-105 000
	Telford	12 Dec. 1968	78.10	70 000	96 700	250 000
	Warrington	26 April 1968	75.32	122 300	133 400	201 500
	Washington	26 July 1964	22.70	20 000	41 000	80 000
	Welwyn Garden City	20 May 1948	17.47	18 500	40 000	50 000
WALES	Cwmbran	4 Nov. 1949	12.79	12 000	45 000	not estimated
	Mid-Wales (Newtown)	18 Dec. 1967	6.06	5000	7200	13 000
SCOTLAND	Cumbernauld	9 Dec. 1955	31.52	3000	43 000	100 000
	East Kilbride	6 May 1947	41.48	2400	73 800	90 000
	Glenrothes	30 June 1948	23.33	1100	32 000	70 000
	Irvine	9 Nov. 1966	50.34	34 600	52 600	120 000
	Livingston	17 April 1962	27.10	2000	24 860	100 000

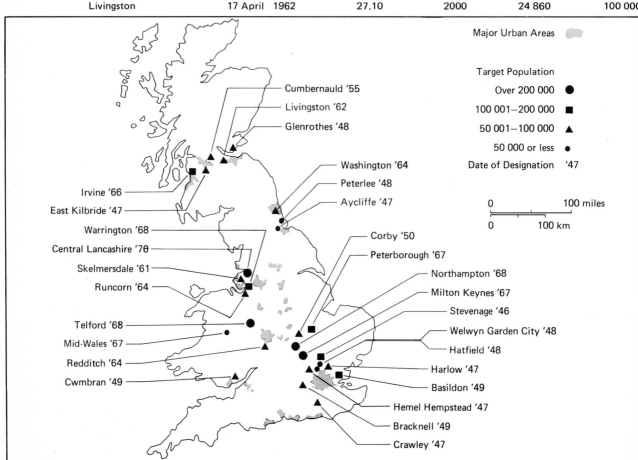

Source: Annual Reports of the New Town Development Corporations.

Population change in the United Kingdom

Census results since 1801[1]

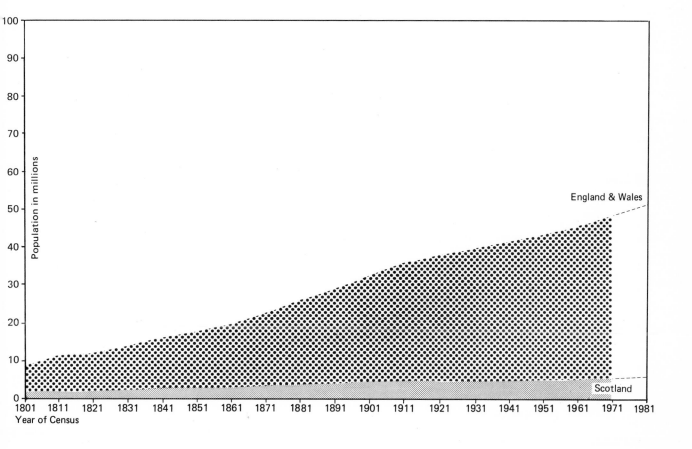

ENGLAND AND WALES			SCOTLAND		
Date of Census	Population	Per sq km	Date of Census	Population	Per sq km
1801 March 10	8 892 536	58.86	1801 March 10	1 608 420	20.43
1811 May 27	10 164 256	67.28	1811 May 27	1 805 864	22.94
1821 May 28	12 000 236	79.43	1821 May 28	2 091 521	26.56
1831 May 29	13 896 797	91.99	1831 May 29	2 364 386	30.03
1841 June 7	15 914 609	105.35	1841 June 7	2 620 184	33.28
1851 March 31	17 927 609	118.67	1851 March 31	2 888 742	36.69
1861 April 8	20 066 224	132.83	1861 April 8	3 062 294	38.90
1871 April 3	22 712 266	150.35	1871 April 3	3 360 018	42.68
1881 April 4	25 974 439	171.94	1881 April 4	3 735 573	47.45
1891 April 6	29 002 525	191.99	1891 April 6	4 025 647	51.13
1901 April 1	32 527 843	215.33	1901 April 1	4 472 103	56 81
1911 April 2	36 070 492	238.78	1911 April 2	4 760 904	60.48
1921 June 19	37 886 899	250.80	1921 June 19	4 882 479	62.02
1931 April 26	39 947 931	264.45	1931 April 26	4 842 554	61.50
1951 April 8	43 744 924	289.58	1951 April 8	5 095 969	64.73
1961 April 23	46 071 604	304.98	1961 April 23	5 178 490	65.78
1971 April 25	48 593 658	321.68	1971 April 25	5 228 963	66.42

[1] Relates to Great Britain only.

Source: Office of Population Censuses and Surveys.

Population change in the United Kingdom

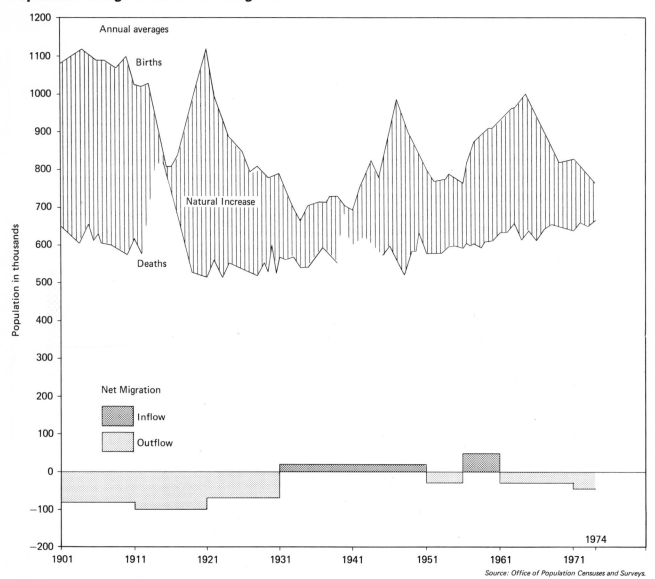

Source: Office of Population Censuses and Surveys.

Birth and death rates in the United Kingdom

	1901	1911	1921	1931	1951	1961	1971	1973	1974
Births									
Live births per 1000 population	29	25	23	16	16	18	16	14	13
Illegitimate as % of all live births	4	5	5	5	5	6	8	8	9
Premarital conceptions as % of legitimate live births[1]									
Mother aged: under 20					55	57	57	55	53
20-24					12	11	10	9	8
Death rates									
Males									
Infant mortality (deaths per 1000 live births)	161	138	94	78	35	25	20	19	19
Crude death rates (per 1000 population - all ages)	18	16	13	13	13	13	12	12	12
Females									
Infant mortality (deaths per 1000 live births)	133	114	73	59	27	19	16	15	14
Crude death rates (per 1000 population - all ages)	16	14	12	12	12	11	11	12	12

[1] relates to Great Britain only.

Source: Office of Population Censuses and Surveys.

Population of Great Britain: age and sex structure

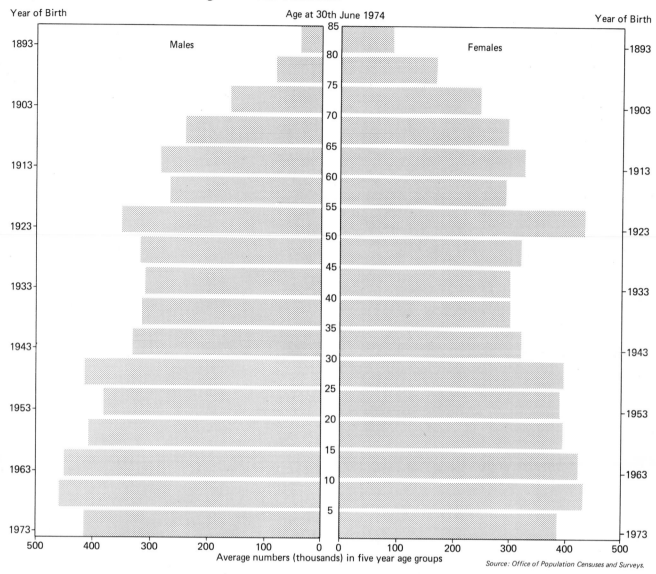

Year of Birth · Age at 30th June 1974 · Year of Birth

Average numbers (thousands) in five year age groups

Source: Office of Population Censuses and Surveys.

Age structure of the population in Great Britain of New Commonwealth descent 1971

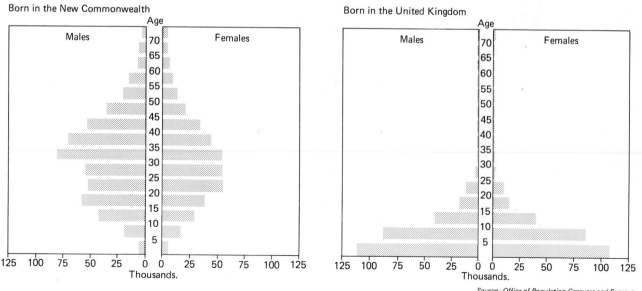

Born in the New Commonwealth

Born in the United Kingdom

Thousands.

Source: Office of Population Censuses and Surveys.

Immigrants to the United Kingdom 1964-1973

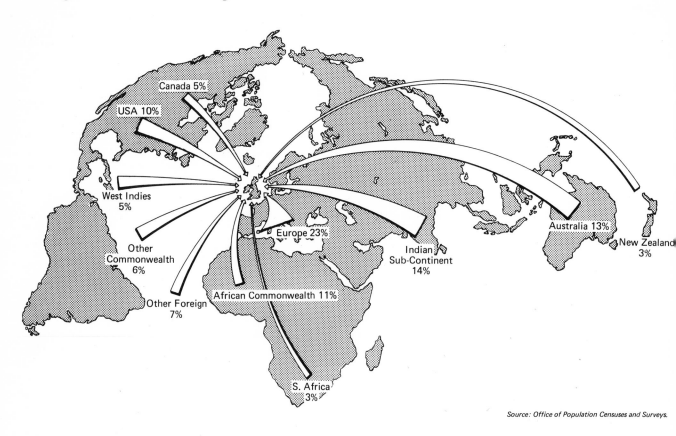

Canada 5%

USA 10%

West Indies
5%

Other
Commonwealth
6%

Other Foreign
7%

Europe 23%

African Commonwealth 11%

Indian
Sub-Continent
14%

Australia 13%

New Zealand
3%

S. Africa
3%

Source: Office of Population Censuses and Surveys.

Emigrants from the United Kingdom 1964-1973

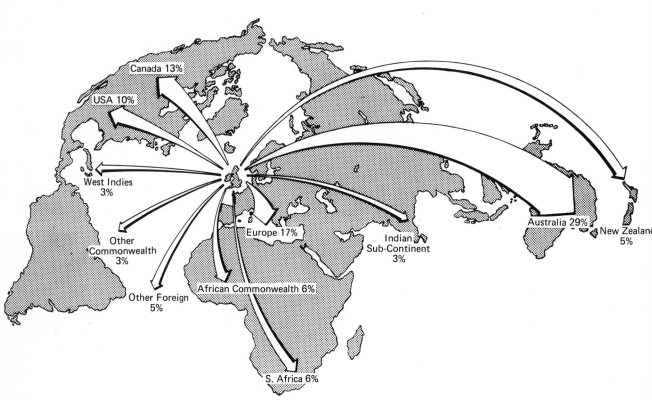

Canada 13%

USA 10%

West Indies
3%

Other
Commonwealth
3%

Other Foreign
5%

Europe 17%

African Commonwealth 6%

Indian
Sub-Continent
3%

Australia 29%

New Zealand
5%

S. Africa 6%

Source: Office of Population Censuses and Surveys.

Distribution of international migrants within the United Kingdom 1971-1973

Area of origin/destination	Immigrants %	Emigrants %	Area of origin/destination	Migration Index Immigrants	Migration Index Emigrants
United Kingdom	100	100	United Kingdom	100	100
England	91	87	England	110	104
North	2	4	North	39	61
Yorkshire and Humberside	5	6	Yorkshire and Humberside	59	69
North West	8	10	North West	65	83
East Midlands	4	4	East Midlands	69	69
West Midlands	7	6	West Midlands	74	61
East Anglia	2	3	East Anglia	74	87
South East	58	49	South East	189	158
South West	4	5	South West	64	74
Wales	2	2	Wales	45	49
Scotland	6	9	Scotland	62	96
Northern Ireland	1	2	Northern Ireland	21	79

Source: Office of Population Censuses and Surveys.

Migration to and from the United Kingdom (thousands)

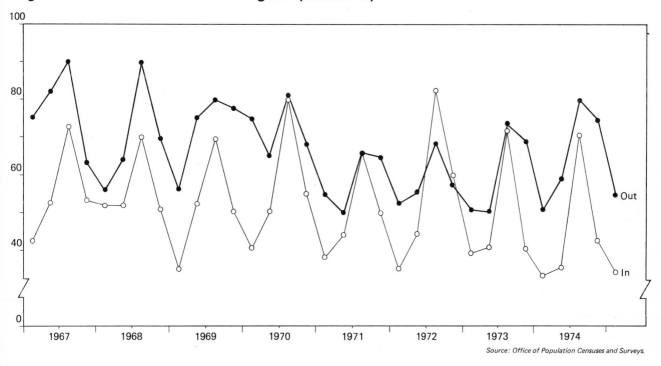

Source: Office of Population Censuses and Surveys.

Population movements within Great Britain by standard regions [1]

Area of former residence	North	Yorkshire and H'side	North West	East Midlands	West Midlands	East Anglia	South East	South West	Wales	Scotland
North	*	246	2188	1446	1325	648	4753	1066	385	1482
Yorkshire and Humberside	3630	*	4022	4046	1876	1081	6257	1736	703	1127
North West	1874	3485	*	1906	2958	854	8427	2710	3362	1471
East Midlands	957	3501	1628	*	2585	1618	5737	1932	604	845
West Midlands	1023	1523	3211	3566	*	854	7635	4072	2112	978
East Anglia	339	782	522	1282	551	*	5337	1002	312	403
South East	3372	4760	6489	7343	6275	10 992	*	19 399	3654	4614
South West	801	1025	1493	1224	2284	917	13 395	*	1429	1080
Wales	361	559	1779	674	1845	347	4279	2040	*	434
Scotland	1611	1360	2164	1415	1382	587	6415	1326	399	*

[1] based on a 10% sample of the period 1966-71.

Source: Office of Population Censuses and Surveys.

Marital condition 1951 and 1971 in Great Britain

1951

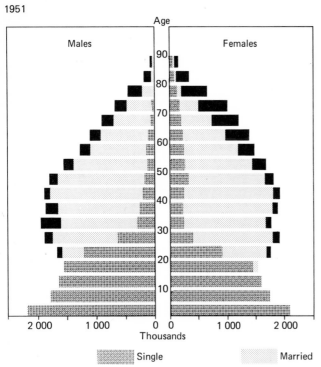

1971

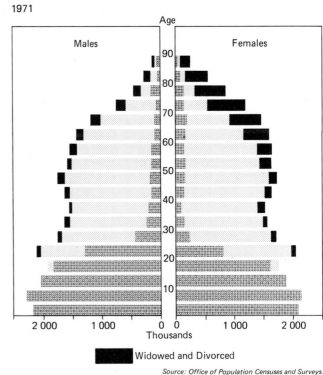

Single   Married   Widowed and Divorced

Source: Office of Population Censuses and Surveys.

Marriages United Kingdom

	Thousands		
	1964	1969	1973
Total marriages	410	452	454
Age at marriage			
Males			
Under 18 years	3	4	5
18 and under 21	56	67	70
21-24	166	206	166
25-29	95	89	102
30-34	31	29	35
35-44	27	25	33
45-54	13	14	21
55 and over	17	18	23
Females			
Under 18 years	28	27	30
18 and under 21	138	143	138
21-24	136	173	138
25-29	46	48	65
30-34	18	17	24
35-44	20	18	25
45-54	12	13	18
55 and over	11	12	15
Previous marital status			
Males	410	452	454
Single	365	397	366
Widowed	20	20	21
Divorced	26	34	66
Females	410	452	454
Single	380	401	369
Widowed	17	19	21
Divorced	25	32	63

Source: Office of Population Censuses and Surveys.

Divorce trends United Kingdom

	Thousands		
	1964	1969	1973
Total divorces	34.9	51.3	106.0
Age at marriage			
Males			
Under 20 years	2.8	5.8	12.5
20-24	18.5	28.2	58.5
25-29	8.6	20.9	21.8
30-39	3.7	4.8	9.8
40-49	0.9	1.1	2.4
50 and over	0.4	0.5	1.0
Females			
Under 20 years	11.8	20.1	40.5
20-24	16.3	23.1	48.0
25-29	4.0	4.8	10.1
30-39	2.1	2.4	5.2
40-49	0.5	0.7	1.6
50 and over	0.2	0.3	0.7
Duration of marriage at divorce (years)			
0-4 years	3.9	6.9	16.1
5-9	11.4	16.9	31.1
10-14	7.1	10.8	20.0
15-19	5.3	6.7	13.9
20 and over	7.2	10.0	24.8

Source: Office of Population Censuses and Surveys.

Mean ultimate family size in the United Kingdom 1860-1970

Year of marriage

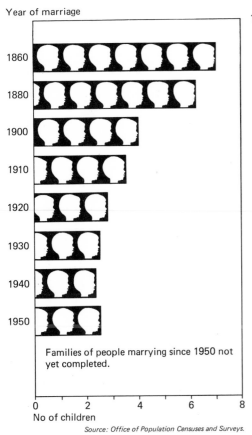

Families of people marrying since 1950 not yet completed.

No of children

Source: Office of Population Censuses and Surveys.

Economic activity of married women[1] by duration of marriage

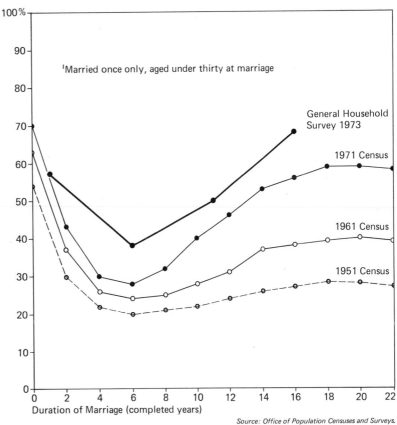

[1]Married once only, aged under thirty at marriage

General Household Survey 1973

1971 Census

1961 Census

1951 Census

Duration of Marriage (completed years)

Source: Office of Population Censuses and Surveys.

Family expenditure in the United Kingdom 1973

All Households
Average £39.43

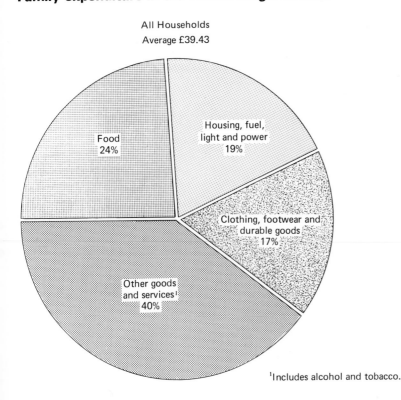

Food 24%

Housing, fuel, light and power 19%

Clothing, footwear and durable goods 17%

Other goods and services[1] 40%

[1]Includes alcohol and tobacco.

Households with head aged 65 or over

Average £21.95

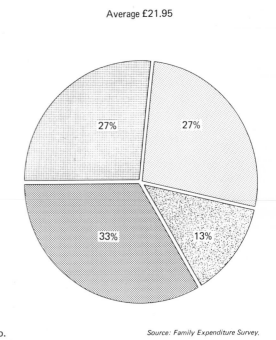

27%

27%

33%

13%

Source: Family Expenditure Survey.

Alcoholism in the United Kingdom (thousands)

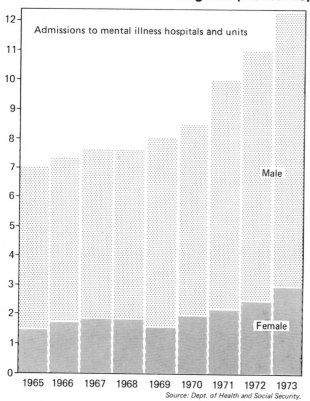

Admissions to mental illness hospitals and units

Male

Female

1965 1966 1967 1968 1969 1970 1971 1972 1973

Source: Dept. of Health and Social Security.

United Kingdom smoking habits 1972

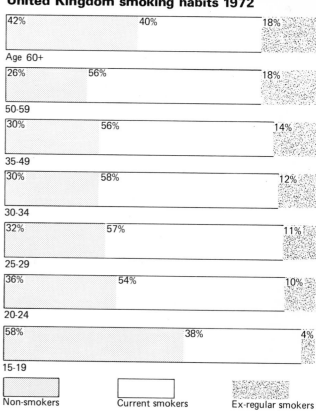

| 42% | 40% | 18% |
Age 60+

| 26% | 56% | 18% |
50-59

| 30% | 56% | 14% |
35-49

| 30% | 58% | 12% |
30-34

| 32% | 57% | 11% |
25-29

| 36% | 54% | 10% |
20-24

| 58% | 38% | 4% |
15-19

Non-smokers   Current smokers   Ex-regular smokers

Source: General Household Survey.

Car Licences in the United Kingdom (millions)

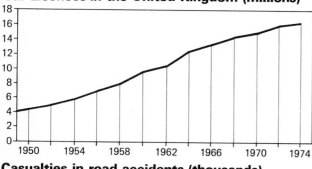

1950 1954 1958 1962 1966 1970 1974

Casualties in road accidents (thousands)

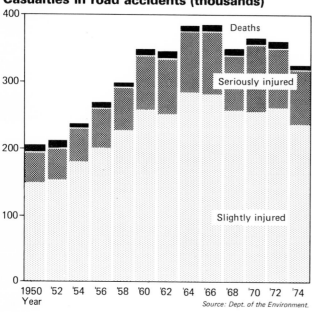

Deaths

Seriously injured

Slightly injured

1950 '52 '54 '56 '58 '60 '62 '64 '66 '68 '70 '72 '74
Year

Source: Dept. of the Environment.

Dangerous drugs addicts in the United Kingdom

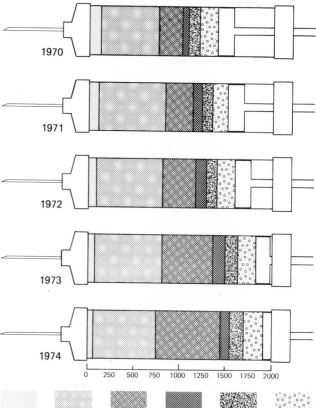

1970

1971

1972

1973

1974

0   250   500   750   1000   1250   1500   1750   2000

Under 20   20-25   25-30   30-35   35-50   Over 50
years of age

Source: Home Office.

Expectation of life in Great Britain

Further number of years which a person can expect to live	Males						Females					
	1901	1931	1961	1966	1971	1973	1901	1931	1961	1966	1971	1973
at birth	48.1	58.4	67.9	68.5	68.6	68.9	51.8	62.5	73.8	74.7	74.9	75.2
at age 1 year	55.1	62.1	68.6	68.9	69.1	69.2	57.6	65.2	74.2	74.9	75.2	75.3
5 years	55.5	60.0	64.9	65.2	65.2	65.5	58.0	63.0	70.5	71.1	71.2	71.5
30	34.5	38.1	40.9	41.2	41.2	40.9	37.1	41.0	46.1	46.7	46.8	47.0
45	23.1	25.5	26.9	27.2	27.2	27.4	25.4	28.2	31.9	32.6	32.7	32.8
60	13.4	14.4	15.0	15.2	15.1	15.4	14.9	16.4	19.0	19.7	19.7	19.9
70	8.4	8.6	9.3	9.5	9.4	9.4	9.2	10.0	11.7	12.3	12.4	12.6
80	4.9	4.7	5.2	5.5	5.5	5.5	5.3	5.5	6.3	6.9	6.9	7.0

Source: Government Actuary Department.

Principal causes of death in Great Britain 1973

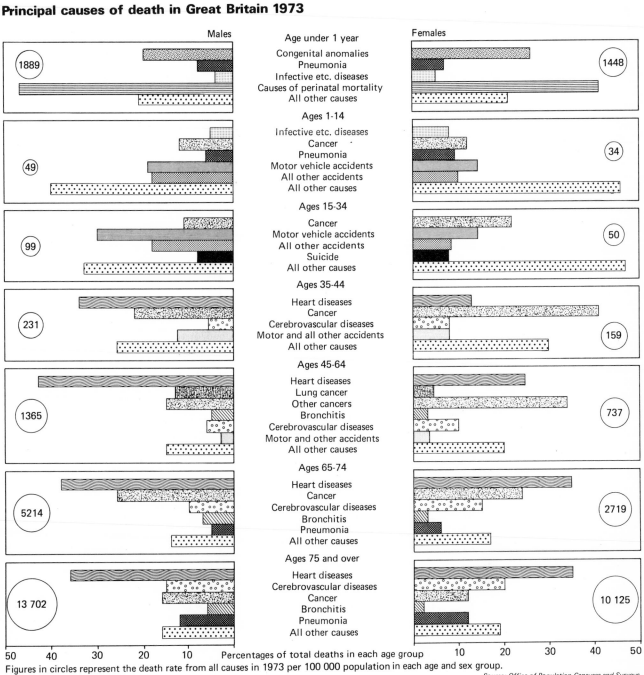

Percentages of total deaths in each age group

Figures in circles represent the death rate from all causes in 1973 per 100 000 population in each age and sex group.

Source: Office of Population Censuses and Surveys.

Leisure Activities (1973) Great Britain

KEY

	Outdoor sports/games
	Indoor sports/games
	Watching sports/games
	Open air outings
	Visits to buildings/museums
	Cultural outings
	Out for a meal
	Out for a drink
	Gardening
	Hobbies
	TV, radio, records
	Clubs
	Social and voluntary work
	Leisure classes

Percentage of sample in each area following activity

	🎾	🏓	👁	☁	🏛	🎭	🍴	🍺	🌹	✏	📺	🎰	✔	★
Conurbations	14.3	8.5	8.8	21.5	9.3	20.4	28.6	37.9	24.5	42.5	95.7	10.9	6.6	1.8
Other urban areas	17.7	10.4	10.8	21.4	8.6	17.4	28.5	39.7	29.3	49.2	95.2	12.3	7.1	1.8
Semi rural areas	22.8	11.0	9.6	23.0	9.0	15.5	32.5	36.9	28.6	56.9	94.8	11.9	9.0	2.1
Rural areas	19.6	8.3	11.8	15.2	7.3	12.1	25.2	32.4	38.1	57.0	93.8	12.8	8.8	2.8

Population breakdown (millions)
Total population = 23 437

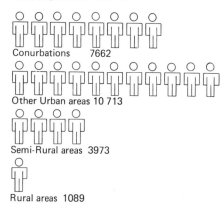

Conurbations 7662

Other Urban areas 10 713

Semi-Rural areas 3973

Rural areas 1089

Average percentage of total sample following each activity

Source: General Household Survey.

Destination of holidays in Europe (average %) Years 1966, 1969-1974

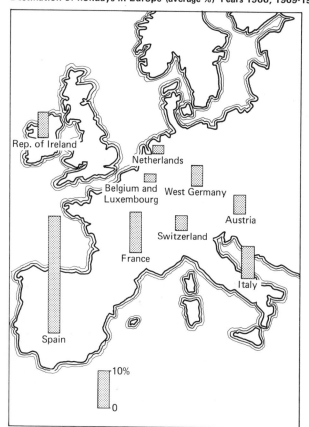

Rep. of Ireland

Netherlands

Belgium and Luxembourg

West Germany

Austria

Switzerland

France

Italy

Spain

10%

0

Source: British National Travel Survey.

Holidays taken by residents of Great Britain (millions)

	1966	1969	1970	1971	1972	1973	1974
in Great Britain	31.00	30.50	34.50	34.00	37.50	40.50	40.50
Abroad	5.50	5.75	5.75	7.25	8.50	8.25	6.75
TOTAL	36.50	36.25	40.25	41.25	46.00	48.75	47.25

Destinations of holidays abroad (Percent)

	1966	1969	1970	1971	1972	1973	1974
All in Europe	94	90	88	89	86	86	86
All other countries	5	8	10	9	11	13	12

Source: British National Travel Survey.

Annual paid holidays (year ending December)
Full-time adult male manual workers

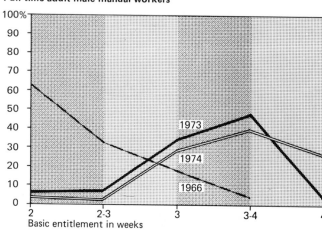

Basic entitlement in weeks

Source: Department of Employment.

Economically active population 1971

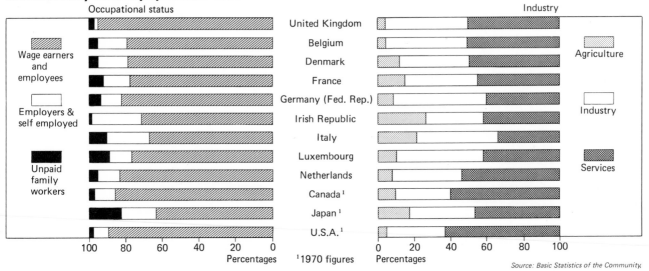

Occupational status · Industry

Wage earners and employees · Employers & self employed · Unpaid family workers

United Kingdom · Belgium · Denmark · France · Germany (Fed. Rep.) · Irish Republic · Italy · Luxembourg · Netherlands · Canada[1] · Japan[1] · U.S.A.[1]

Agriculture · Industry · Services

Percentages   [1]1970 figures   Percentages

Source: Basic Statistics of the Community.

Distribution of total working population in Great Britain

	1961	1966	1971	1972	1973	1974
Employment structure (thousands)						
Employees in employment	21 788	22 788	21 648	21 650	22 183	22 296
Employers and self-employed	1672	1614	1843	1872	1916	1916
HM forces and women's services	474	417	368	371	361	345
Employed labour force	23 934	24 819	23 859	23 893	24 460	24 557
Unemployed registered for employment	255	253	687	767	546	516
Total working population	24 189	25 072	24 546	24 660	25 006	25 073
Industrial structure (percentage of total employees in employment)						
Agriculture, forestry and fishing	3.2	2.5	1.9	1.9	1.9	1.8
Mining and quarrying	3.3	2.5	1.8	1.7	1.6	1.6
Manufacturing	38.4	36.9	36.4	35.2	34.6	34.6
of which textiles, leather, clothing and footwear	6.3	5.5	4.9	4.8	4.6	4.4
Construction	6.6	7.0	5.6	5.8	6.0	5.8
Gas, electricity and water	1.7	1.9	1.7	1.6	1.5	1.5
Transport and communication	7.6	7.0	7.1	7.0	6.8	6.7
Distributive trades	12.4	12.5	11.8	12.0	12.1	12.1
Financial, professional and scientific services	12.6	14.7	17.9	18.5	19.0	19.7
Miscellaneous services (incl. catering and hotels)	8.2	8.9	8.8	9.2	9.5	9.4
Public administration	5.9	6.1	6.8	7.0	7.0	7.0

Source: Department of Employment.

Destination of school leavers England & Wales[1]

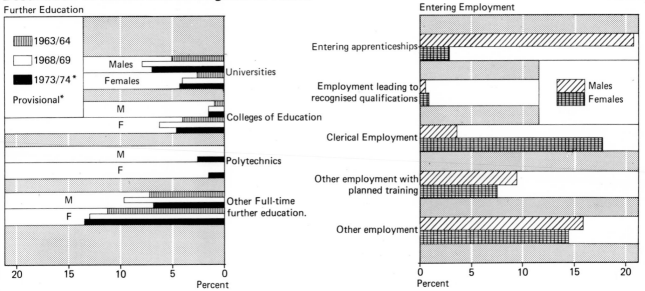

Further Education

1963/64 · 1968/69 · 1973/74* · Provisional*

Males · Females · Universities
M · F · Colleges of Education
M · F · Polytechnics
M · F · Other Full-time further education.

Percent

Entering Employment

Entering apprenticeships
Employment leading to recognised qualifications
Clerical Employment
Other employment with planned training
Other employment

Males · Females

Percent

[1] comparable figures for Scotland not available.

Source: Statistics of Education and Department of Employment.

Balance of Payments Current Account (United Kingdom)

Imports	1964	1974	Exports	1964	1974
Non-manufactures			Non-manufactures	654	2409
Food, Beverages and Tobacco	1771	3779	Manufactures		
Basic materials	1118	2580	Chemicals	418	2146
Fuel	584	4627	Textiles	283	746
All non-manufactures	3474	10 986	Metals	510	1713
Manufactures	2161	11 938	Machinery and Transport equipment	1865	6052
Other commodities	62	203	Other	697	3027
			All manufactures	3773	13 684
Total on overseas Trade Statistics basis	5696	23 117	Other commodities	138	401
Valuation and coverage adjustments	−675	−1997	**Total on overseas Trade Statistics basis**	4565	16 494
			Coverage adjustments	−44	−608
Total on balance of payments basis	5021	21 120	**Total on balance of payments basis**	4521	15 886

Source: Central Statistical Office.

Value of external trade in the United Kingdom Balance of Payments

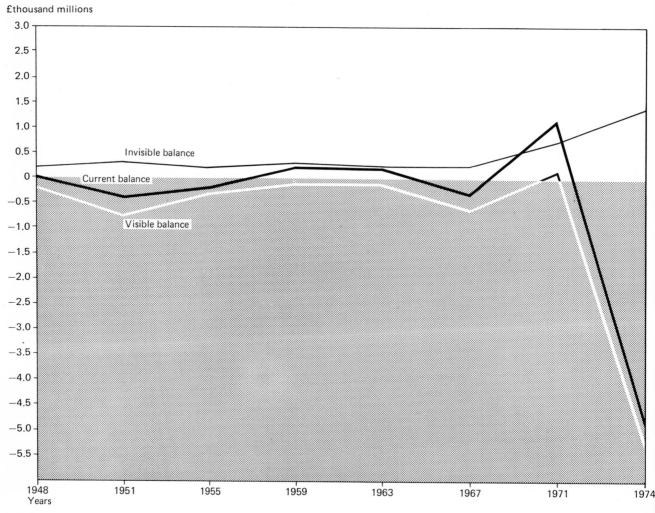

Source: Central Statistical Office.

Overseas visitors to the United Kingdom 1974 (thousands)

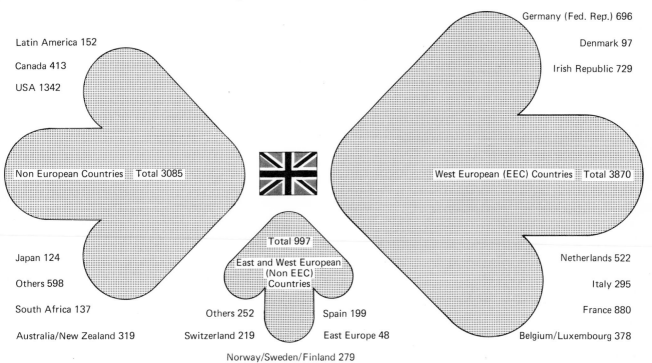

Latin America 152
Canada 413
USA 1342

Germany (Fed. Rep.) 696
Denmark 97
Irish Republic 729

Non European Countries   Total 3085

West European (EEC) Countries   Total 3870

Total 997
East and West European (Non EEC) Countries

Japan 124
Others 598
South Africa 137
Australia/New Zealand 319

Netherlands 522
Italy 295
France 880
Belgium/Luxembourg 378

Others 252   Spain 199
Switzerland 219   East Europe 48
Norway/Sweden/Finland 279

Source: British Tourist Authority.

The trade of British ports [1]

Port		Value in £million	Commodities by rank value
LONDON	Exports	2616	Diamonds, motor cars and parts, medicines, distillate fuels, alcoholic beverages, cigarettes.
	Imports	2638	Crude petroleum, meat (beef and lamb), diamonds, lumber, raw sugar, copper, newsprint paper, wood pulp, wheat, soya beans.
SOUTHAMPTON	Exports	988	Motor cars and parts, alcoholic beverages, woollen fabrics, chemicals, textile machinery.
	Imports	1352	Crude petroleum, clothing, tobacco, motor cars and parts.
LIVERPOOL	Exports	1183	Motor cars and parts, lorries and trucks, electric power machinery, alcoholic beverages.
	Imports	1081	Crude petroleum, copper, raw sugar, tobacco, wool, raw cotton.
DOVER	Exports	745	Office machinery, motor cars and parts, meat (beef).
	Imports	945	Motor cars, wine.
HARWICH	Exports	648	Motor cars and parts, silver, nickel and alloys.
	Imports	801	Motor cars, bacon and other pig meats.
FELIXSTOWE	Exports	601	Motor cars and parts, photographic equipment, furs.
	Imports	796	Television broadcast receivers, motor cars and parts, chemicals, raisins, photographic equipment, machine tools.
HULL	Exports	558	Tin and tin alloys, synthetic fibre yarns, synthetic dye stuffs, carpets, textile machinery, woollen fabrics.
	Imports	717	Lumber, bacon and other pig meats, wheat, butter, cocoa butter, cocoa beans.
IMMINGHAM	Exports	272	Motor cars and parts, distillate fuels, textile yarns.
	Imports	435	Crude petroleum, iron-ore, processed iron.
MANCHESTER	Exports	257	Copper and tin products, woollen fabrics, household ceramics.
	Imports	352	Copper, raw cotton, maize.
MIDDLESBROUGH	Exports	240	Chemicals, iron and steel, distillate fuels.
	Imports	342	Crude petroleum, motor cars.
BRISTOL	Exports	51	Motor cars, lead and lead alloys, agricultural machinery.
	Imports	373	Tea, coffee, oilseed cake and meal, meat (lamb), cocoa, newsprint paper, wheat, tin and zinc ores, tobacco.
GREENOCK	Exports	212	Alcoholic beverages, motor cars, ships and boats, internal combustion engines, textile yarns, office machinery.
	Imports	202	Crude petroleum, tobacco, raw sugar.
GRANGEMOUTH	Exports	149	Alcoholic beverages, distillate fuels, tractors.
	Imports	133	Lumber, lorries, crude petroleum, wood pulp.

1 compiled from Annual Statement of Overseas Trade 1973.

Source: HM Customs and Excise.

The National Grid

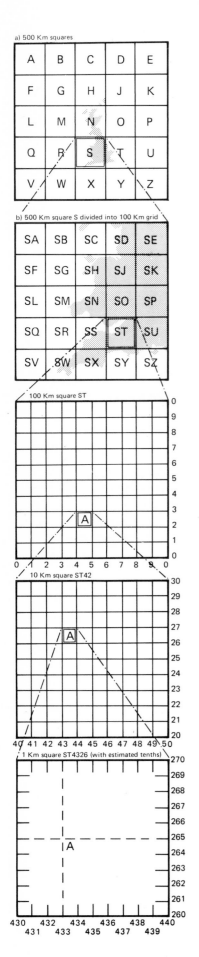

The Ordnance Survey have devised a grid system to cover Britain whereby any point may be located on any of their maps. The grid, known as the 'National Grid', originates from a position south-west of the Isles of Scilly and is a systematic breakdown of progressively smaller squares identified by letters and then by numbers. The largest units are 500 km squares, each designated by a letter, the first letter to be quoted in the full National Grid reference — see fig. a.

The 500 km squares are then broken down into twenty-five 100 km squares. These are also designated by a letter, the second letter of the full National Grid Reference. Fig. b represents the grid of 100 km squares covering part of Britain and shows the 500 km square S broken down into its 100 km squares SA, SB, etc. It can be seen that no two 100 km squares can have the same combination of letters.

Within the 100 km squares each smaller grid of 10 km, 1 km or 100 m side is numbered, firstly by the distance of its lower left-hand corner eastwards (eastings) and secondly, northwards (northings). To enable these distances or 'co-ordinates' to be easily found their values are printed in the map margins against the grid lines concerned. These provide the numbers which identify each particular grid square. A point within one of the smallest grid squares can be indicated still more closely by estimating the tenths eastwards and northwards of that square.

To give a grid reference correct to 100 metres.

Example: Point A.   Grid Letters: ST

Eastings: Take the west edge of the kilometre square in which the point lies and read along the line of figures printed in the top and bottom margins.   43
                                        Estimate the tenths eastwards.   3
                                                                          433

Northings: Take the south edge of the kilometre square in which the point lies and read along the line to the figures printed opposite this line in the side margins.   26
                                        Estimate the tenths northwards.   5
                                                                          265

Then the full 100 metre reference for point A will be the 100 km square letters combined with the easting and the northing, that is ST 433265. Note that the easting is always given before the northing. If the estimated tenths are omitted the resulting 'four figure reference' ST 4326 will be correct to 1000 metres.

GAZETTEER OF BRITAIN

A

Abaty Cwmhir Welsh form of Abbeycwmhir, qv.
Abbas Combe Som 9 E2 vil 4m/6km S of Wincanton. ST 7022
Abberley H & W 26 C1 vil 5m/7km SW of Stourport. Victn Gothic clocktower on A. Hill to S. SO 7567
Abberley Common H & W 26 C1 vil 5m/8km SW of Stourport. SO 7467
Abberton Essex 30 D6 vil 4m/6km S of Colchester. **Abberton Resr** large resr to W. TM 0019
Abberton H & W 27 E2 vil 6m/9km NE of Pershore. SO 9953
Abberwick Nthmb 67 G6* loc 4m/6km W of Alnwick. NU 1213
Abbess End Essex 20 C1* loc just SW of Abbess Roding, 2m/4km SW of Leaden Roding. TL 5611
Abbess Roding Essex 20 C1 vil 2m/3km SW of Leaden Roding. TL 5711
Abbey Devon 7 H4 loc 6m/10km N of Honiton. Site of ruined 13c Dunkeswell Abbey. ST 1410
Abbey 6 B3* r rising 3m/4km E of Hartland, Devon, and flowing W past Hartland Abbey into the Atlantic Ocean between Hartland Pt and Hartland Quay. SS 2225
Abbeycwmhir (Abaty Cwmhir) Powys 25 E1/F1 ham in valley of Clywedog Brook 6m/10km N of Llandrindod Wells. Site of ruined 12c abbey. SO 0571
Abbeydale H & W 27 E1* dist of Redditch E of tn centre. SP 0467
Abbeydale S Yorks 43 G3 loc in Sheffield 4m/6km SE of city centre. SK 3282
Abbey Dore H & W 25 H5 vil 2m/3km N of Pontrilas. SO 3830
Abbey Gate Kent 20 D5* loc 2m/3km N of Maidstone. Remains of medieval Boxley Abbey on E side. TQ 7558
Abbey Green S'clyde. Alternative name for Lesmahagow.
Abbey Head D & G 58 C6 headland 3m/4km S of Dundrennan. NX 7343
Abbeyhill Lothian 66 A2* dist of Edinburgh 2km E of city centre. NT 2774
Abbey Hulton Staffs 43 E6* loc in Stoke-on-Trent 3m/5km NE of city centre. SJ 9148
Abbeylands Isle of Man 46 B5 loc 3m/5km N of Douglas. SC 3779
Abbey St Bathans Borders 67 E3 vil on R Whiteadder 5m/8km N of Duns. Ch incorporates fragments of 13c nunnery. NT 7562
Abbeystead Lancs 47 F3 ham in R Wyre valley 7m/11km SE of Lancaster. SD 5654
Abbey Town Cumbria 59 F6 vil 4m/7km SE of Silloth. Ch comprises most of the nave of Holme Cultram Abbey, 12c. NY 1750
Abbey Trading Estate H & W 27 E1* dist of Redditch N of tn centre. SP 0468
Abbey Village Lancs 47 G5* vil 1km E of Withnell. SD 6422
Abbey Wood London 20 B4 loc in borough of Greenwich 2m/3km E of Woolwich and 10m/17km E of Charing Cross. TQ 4678
Abbots Bickington Devon 6 C4* vil 7m/11km NE of Holsworthy. SS 3813
Abbots Bromley Staffs 35 G2 vil 6m/9km W of Uttoxeter. SK 0824
Abbotsbury Dorset 8 D5 vil 8m/13km NW of Weymouth. Ruined abbey (A.M.). 15c tithe barn. Swannery. SY 5785
Abbotsfield Merseyside 42 B2* loc 3m/5km SE of St Helens. SJ 5492
Abbotsford Borders 66 C5 mansion erected by Sir Walter Scott on S bank of R Tweed 2m/4km W of Melrose. Scott lived and died here. NT 5034
Abbot's Hall Saltings Essex 30 D6* marshes to N of Salcott Channel 7m/12km S of Colchester. TL 9713
Abbotsham Devon 6 C3 vil 2m/3km W of Bideford. SS 4226
Abbotsinch S'clyde 64 C2 Glasgow Airport, 2m/3km N of Paisley and W of Renfrew. NS 4766
Abbotskerswell Devon 5 E4 vil 2m/3km S of Newton Abbot. SX 8568
Abbots Langley Herts 19 E2 suburb 3m/5km N of Watford. TL 0902
Abbots Leigh Avon 16 B4 vil 3m/4km W of Bristol. ST 5473
Abbotsleigh Devon 4 D5* loc 5m/8km W of Dartmouth. SX 8048
Abbotsley Cambs 29 F2 vil 4m/6km SE of St Neots. TL 2256
Abbots Morton H & W 27 E2 vil 7m/11km N of Evesham. SP 0355
Abbots Ripton Cambs 37 G6 vil 4m/6km N of Huntingdon. TL 2378
Abbot's Salford Warwicks 27 E3* ham 5m/7km NW of Evesham. SP 0650
Abbotstone Hants 10 C2* loc 2m/3km NW of New Alresford. SU 5634
Abbot's Way Devon 4 C4* old trackway on southern Dartmoor, between Princetown and Buckfastleigh. SX 66
Abbotswood Surrey 19 E6* NE dist of Guildford. TQ 0151
Abbots Worthy Hants 10 C2* ham on R Itchen 2m/4km N of Winchester. SU 4932
Abbotts Ann Hants 10 A1 vil 3m/4km SW of Andover. SU 3243
Abbott's Barton Hants 10 B2* loc in N part of Winchester. SU 4830
Abdon Salop 34 C5 vil 8m/13km NE of Ludlow. SO 5786
Abdy S Yorks 44 A2* loc 4m/6km N of Rotherham. SK 4398
Abel 33 H3* stream running E to join R Fyllon at Llanfyllin, Powys, and form R Cain. SJ 1419
Abenhall Glos 26 B5* loc 2m/4km NE of Cinderford. SO 6717
Aber Gwynedd 40 D4 vil 2m/3km SW of Llanfairfechan. Mound marks site of motte and bailey cas. **A. Falls** or **Rhaeadr Fawr** is high vertical waterfall 2m/3km S in course of R Goch. SH 6572
Aberaeron Dyfed 24 A2 small tn and former port on Cardigan Bay 14m/23km SW of Aberystwyth. SN 4562
Aberafan Welsh form of Aberavon, qv.
Aberaman Mid Glam 15 E2 loc adjoining Aberdare to SE. SO 0101
Aberangell Gwynedd 33 F3 vil at confluence of R Angell and R Dovey 2m/3km SW of Mallwyd. SH 8410
Aberarad Dyfed 23 E2 loc 1km SE of Newcastle Emlyn. SN 3140
Aberargie Tayside 73 E3 vil 2m/3km W of Abernethy. NO 1615
Aberarth Dyfed 24 B2 coastal vil on Cardigan Bay 2km NE of Aberaeron. SN 4763
Aberavon (Aberafan) W Glam 14 D3 dist of Port Talbot on W side of R Afan. **A. Sands** on coast. SS 7590
Aber-banc Dyfed 23 E2 loc 3m/5km E of Newcastle Emlyn. SN 3541
Aberbargod Welsh form of Aberbargoed, qv.
Aberbargoed (Aberbargod) Mid Glam 15 F2 loc on E side of Bargoed. ST 1599
Aberbechan Powys 33 H5* loc at confluence of Bechan Brook and R Severn 3m/4km NE of Newtown. SO 1493
Aberbeeg (Aberbig) Gwent 15 G2 loc 2km S of Abertillery. SO 2101
Aberbig Welsh form of Aberbeeg, qv.
Aberbran Powys 25 E5* loc 4m/6km W of Brecon. SN 9829
Abercanaid Mid Glam 15 F1 vil 2m/3km S of Merthyr Tydfil. SO 0503

Abercarn Gwent 15 G2 tn on Ebbw R 7m/11km NW of Newport. Coal-mining, tinplate mnfre. ST 2195
Abercastell Welsh form of Abercastle, qv.
Abercastle (Abercastell) Dyfed 22 B3 coastal hamlet 2m/3km NW of Mathry. SM 8533
Abercegin Gwynedd 40 C4* loc 1m E of Bangor. SH 5972
Abercegir Powys 33 E4* ham 2m/3km SW of Cemmaes Rd. SH 8001
Aberchirder Grampian 83 E2 vil 8m/13km SW of Banff. NJ 6252
Aberconwy 116 admin dist of Gwynedd.
Abercorn Lothian 65 G1 loc on S side of Firth of Forth 3m/5km W of Forth Rd Br. NT 0879
Abercraf Powys 14 D1 vil 4m/6km NE of Ystalyfera. SN 8112
Abercregan W Glam 14 D2* vil 3m/5km N of Maesteg. SS 8496
Abercrombie Fife 73 G4 loc 1m NW of St Monance. NO 5102
Abercwmboi Mid Glam 15 E2* vil 2m/3km SE of Aberdare. ST 0299
Abercych Dyfed 22 D2/23 E2 vil 4m/6km W of Newcastle Emlyn. SN 2440
Abercynffig Welsh form of Aberkenfig, qv.
Abercynon Mid Glam 15 F2* vil at confluence of Rs Cynon and Taff 3m/5km N of Pontypridd. ST 0894
Aber Cywarch Gwynedd 33 F3 loc 1m NE of Dinas Mawddwy. SH 8514
Aberdalgie Tayside 72 D3 loc 3m/5km SW of Perth. NO 0720
Aberdare Mid Glam 15 E2 tn on R Cynon 20m/32km NW of Cardiff. Coal-mining, brick mnfre. SO 0002
Aberdaron Gwynedd 32 A2 vil on **Aberdaron Bay** near tip of Lleyn peninsula. The bay extends from Pen y Cil NE to Trwyn y Penrhyn. SH 1726
Aberdaugleddyf Welsh form of Milford Haven, qv.
Aberddawan Welsh form of Aberthaw, qv.
Aberdeen Grampian 77 H1 cathedral and university city and commercial centre on E coast 57m/92km NE of Dundee. Known as 'The Granite City', the local stone having been used in many of its bldgs. Centre of North Sea oil industry. Third largest fishing port in Britain. Other industries include canning and refrigeration, electronics, plastics, shipbuilding and engineering, mechanical handling equipment, paper and packaging. Airport at Dyce, 6m/9km NW. Provost Ross's House (NTS) in the Shiprow, built 1593, is HQ of the British Council in the North of Scotland. NJ 9406
Aberdene Tarn N Yorks 53 H5* small lake on Whiteside Moor 2m/3km S of Low Row. SD 9894
Aberdesach Gwynedd 40 B6* loc on Caernarvon Bay at mouth of R Desach 8m/12km SW of Caernarvon. SH 4251
Aberdinas Dyfed 22 A3* small bay 4m/6km E of St David's Hd. SM 7730
Aberdour Fife 73 E5 small tn and resort on N shore of Firth of Forth 3m/4km W of Burntisland. Remains of 17c cas (A.M.). NT 1985
Aberdour Bay Grampian 83 G1 bay on N coast, N of New Aberdour. NJ 8965
Aberdovey (Aberdyfi) Gwynedd 32 D5 small resort on N shore of R Dovey estuary near mouth, 9m/14km W of Machynlleth. **A. Bar** is sandbank opp mouth of r about 2km W. SN 6196
Aberdulais W Glam 14 D2 vil 2m/3km NE of Neath. SS 7799
Aberdyfi Welsh form of Aberdovey, qv.
Aberedw Powys 25 F3 vil 3m/5km SE of Builth Wells across R Wye. Slight remains of baronial cas to W. To S, **A. Rocks**, terraced outcrop of Silurian rock above R Wye. SO 0747
Abereiddy (Abereiddi) Dyfed 22 A3 ham on **Abereiddy Bay** 5m/7km NE of St David's. SM 7931
Abererch Gwynedd 32 B1 vil on R Erch 2m/3km NE of Pwllheli. See also Morfa Abererch. SH 3936
Aberfan Mid Glam 15 F2 vil on R Taff 4m/6km S of Merthyr Tydfil. SO 0700
Aberfeldy Tayside 75 H6 small tn astride Urlar Burn near its confluence with R Tay, 8m/13km SW of Pitlochry. Distillery. NN 8549
Aberffraw Gwynedd 40 B4 vil on Anglesey at head of R Ffraw estuary 12m/20km W of Menai Br. Barclodiad y Gawres Burial-chamber (A.M.) on coast 2m/3km NW; Din Dryfol Burial-chamber (A.M.) 3m/5km NE. SH 3568
Aberffraw Bay Gwynedd 40 B4 bay at mouth of R Ffraw, W coast of Anglesey. SH 3567
Aberffrwd Dyfed 24 C1* loc 4m/6km W of Devil's Br. SN 6878
Aberford W Yorks 49 F4 vil 5m/8km NE of Garforth. SE 4337
Aberfoyle Central 71 F4 vil 8m/13km SW of Callander. Situated on R Forth between Achray and Loch Ard Forests and below SW end of Menteith Hills. NN 5201
Abergarw Mid Glam 15 E3 loc 3m/5km N of Bridgend. SS 9184
Abergarwed W Glam 14 D2* loc 1m W of Resolven across R Neath. SN 8102
Abergavenny (Fenni, Y) Gwent 15 G1 mkt tn at S end of Black Mts at confluence of Rs Gavenny and Usk, 9m/14km NW of Pontypool. Light engineering, printing. The Roman *Gobannium*. Slight remains of medieval cas. SO 2914
Abergeldie Castle Grampian 76 D2 16c cas with 19c additions, on S bank of R Dee 2m/3km E of Balmoral Castle. NO 2895
Abergele Clwyd 41 F4 resort near N Wales coast 5m/7km SW of Rhyl. Castell Cawr is ancient British hill camp 1m SW. Gwrych Castle, 19c hse in Gothic style, 1m W. SH 9477
Abergiar Dyfed 24 B4 loc 2m/4km SW of Llanybydder. SN 5041
Aberglaslyn Pass Gwynedd 40 C6 narrow part of R Glaslyn valley below Beddgelert. SH 5946
Abergorlech Dyfed 24 B4 ham 3m/4km SW of Llansawel. SN 5833
Abergwaun Welsh form of Fishguard, qv.
Abergwesyn Powys 24 D3 ham 4m/7km N of Llanwrtyd Wells. SN 8552
Abergwili Dyfed 23 F3/F4 vil 2m/3km E of Carmarthen. Palace of Bishop of St David's is here. SN 4321
Abergwydol Powys 33 E4 loc 3m/5km E of Machynlleth. SH 7903
Abergwynfi W Glam 14 D2/15 E2 vil 5m/8km W of Rhondda. SS 8996
Abergynolwyn Gwynedd 32 D4 vil at confluence of Rs Dysynni and Gwernol 7m/11km NE of Tywyn. SH 6707
Aberhafesp Powys 33 G5 loc 3m/4km W of Newtown. SO 0792
Aberhirnant Forest Gwynedd 33 F2* afforested area about 4m/6km SE of Bala. SH 93
Aberhonddu Welsh form of Brecon, qv.
Aberhosan Powys 33 E4* loc 5m/7km SE of Machynlleth. SN 8197
Aberkenfig (Abercynffig) Mid Glam 15 E3 vil 3m/4km N of Bridgend. SS 8983
Aberlady Lothian 66 C1 vil on **A. Bay**, a nature reserve, on Firth of Forth 6m/10km SW of N Berwick. NT 4679
Aberlemno Tayside 77 E5 vil 5m/8km NE of Forfar. Two 8c stones (A.M.) display reliefs of combats. NO 5255
Aberllefenni Gwynedd 33 E3 vil 6m/9km N of Machynlleth. Slate quarries. SH 7709

Aberllynfi Welsh form of Three Cocks, qv.
Aberlour Grampian 82 B3 small distillery tn on right bank of R Spey 4m/6km S of Rothes. Also known as Charlestown of Aberlour. NJ 2643
Abermenai Point Gwynedd 40 B5 headland on Anglesey at SW end of Menai Strait. SH 4461
Abermeurig Dyfed 24 B3* loc 5m/8km N of Lampeter. SN 5656
Abermiwl Welsh form of Abermule, qv.
Abermo Welsh form of Barmouth, qv.
Abermorddu Clwyd 41 H5* loc nearly 1m S of Caergwrle. SJ 3056
Abermule (Abermiwl) Powys 33 H5* ham on R Severn 4m/6km NE of Newtown. SO 1694
Abernant Dyfed 23 E3 ham 5m/8km W of Carmarthen. SN 3323
Aber-nant Mid Glam 15 E1/E2 loc adjoining Aberdare to NE. SO 0103
Abernant Lake Powys 24 D3* small lake beside N bank of R Irfon nearly 1m E of Llanwrtyd Wells. SN 8946
Abernethy Tayside 73 E3 vil 3m/5km W of Newburgh. Round tower (A.M.) may date from 9c; height 74 ft or nearly 23 metres. Remains of Roman fortress and naval base to NE in grnds of Carpow, near S bank of R Tay. NO 1916
Abernethy Forest H'land 82 A5 coniferous forest 6m/10km S of Grantown-on-Spey in Badenoch and Strathspey dist. NJ 9917
Abernyte Tayside 73 F2 vil 9m/14km W of Dundee. NO 2531
Aberogwr Welsh form of Ogmore-by-Sea, qv.
Aberpennar Welsh form of Mountain Ash, qv.
Aberporth Dyfed 23 E1 fishing vil 6m/10km NE of Cardigan. SN 2651
Aberriw Welsh form of Berriew, qv.
Abersoch Gwynedd 32 B2 small resort on St Tudwal's Bay at mouth of R Soch, 6m/9km SW of Pwllheli across bay. SH 3128
Abersychan Gwent 15 G1 tn 2m/3km NW of Pontypool. SO 2603
Abertawe Welsh form of Swansea, qv.
Aberteifi Welsh form of Cardigan, qv.
Aberthaw, East S Glam 15 F4 vil 5m/8km W of Barry. Cement works. See also Aberddawan. ST 0366
Aberthaw, West S Glam 15 E4* loc 1km E of Gileston. Power stn to S. See also Aberddawan. ST 0266
Aberthin S Glam 15 E4* vil 1m NE of Cowbridge. ST 0075
Abertillery (Abertyleri) Gwent 15 G1 tn 12m/19km NW of Newport. Coal-mining, brewing, tinplate works. SO 2104
Abertridwr Mid Glam 15 F3 vil 3m/5km NW of Caerphilly. ST 1289
Abertridwr Powys 33 G3 vil 1m E of Lake Vyrnwy dam. SJ 0319
Abertyleri Welsh form of Abertillery, qv.
Abertysswg Mid Glam 15 F1* loc 2km SE of Rhymney. SO 1305
Aberuthven Tayside 72 D3 vil on Ruthven Water 3m/4km NE of Auchterarder. NN 9715
Aber Village Powys 25 F5* ham 1m S of Talybont. SO 1021
Aberyscir Powys 25 E5 loc 3m/5km W of Brecon. Remains of Roman fort of *Bannium* (A.M.) across R Yscir. SO 0029
Aberystwyth Dyfed 32 D6 resort and small port at mouth of Rs Rheidol and Ystwyth on Cardigan Bay 82m/132km NW of Cardiff. Commercial capital of Mid-Wales. University College of Wales, the senior constituent college of University of Wales. National Library of Wales. Remains of 13c cas on sea front. SN 5881
Abhainn an t-Srathain H'land 84 C2* stream in Sutherland dist running into Sandwood Loch – see Strath Shinary. NC 2363
Abhainn Dalach 70 C1 stream in S'clyde region running SE into Loch Etive, Argyll, 5m/8km NE of narrows at Bonawe. NN 0538
Abhainn Duibhe 75 E5 r in Tayside region running NE down Gleann Duibhe to R Gaur below Loch Eigheach. NN 4656
Abhainn Gaoire 75 F5 r in Tayside region running E from Loch Eigheach to head of Loch Rannoch. Anglicised form: (R) Gaur. NN 5056
Abhainn na Coinnich H'land 68 F3* stream in Lochaber dist running SE from Loch Uisge to Loch a' Choire. NM 8452
Abhainn Righ H'land 74 B5 r in Lochaber dist running W down Glen Righ to Loch Linnhe 1m NW of Onich. Series of waterfalls nearly 1m above mouth. NN 0162
A' Bhuidheanach H'land 75 E2* mt in Badenoch and Strathspey dist 3m/5km W of head of Loch Laggan. Height 3171 ft or 967 metres. NN 4890
A' Bhuidheanach H'land 75 G3* mt in Badenoch and Strathspey dist, close to border with Tayside region, 4m/6km S of Dalwhinnie. Height 2867 ft or 874 metres. **A' Bhuidheanach Bheag** is mt 1m S, on border of the two regions. Height 3064 ft or 934 metres. NN 6579
Abingdon Oxon 17 H2 tn on R Thames 6m/9km S of Oxford. SU 4997
Abinger Common Surrey 19 E6 ham 4m/6km SW of Dorking. TQ 1145
Abinger Hammer Surrey 19 E6* vil 5m/7km W of Dorking. Site of Roman bldg 1km E. TQ 0947
Abington Northants 28 C2 NE dist of Northampton. **A. Vale** dist to S. SP 7762
Abington S'clyde 65 F6 vil on R Clyde 11m/18km SW of Biggar. NS 9323
Abington, Great Cambs 30 A3 vil 4m/7km NE of Gt Chesterford. TL 5348
Abington, Little Cambs 30 A3 vil 5m/7km NE of Gt Chesterford. TL 5349
Abington Pigotts Cambs 29 G3 vil 4m/6km NW of Royston. TL 3044
Ab Kettleby Leics 36 C2 vil 3m/5km NW of Melton Mowbray. SK 7223
Ab Lench H & W 27 E3* loc 5m/8km N of Evesham. SP 0151
Ablington Glos 17 E1 vil 1m NW of Bibury. SP 1007
Ablington Wilts 17 F6* loc just SE of Figheldean and 4m/6km N of Amesbury. SU 1546
Abney Derbys 43 G3 ham 2m/4km SW of Hathersage. SK 1979
Above Church Staffs 43 E6* loc adjoining Ipstones to NW. SK 0150
Aboyne Grampian 77 E2 vil on N bank of R Dee 10m/16km E of Ballater. Highland gathering held in September. See also Loch of A. NO 5298
Abram Gtr Manchester 42 B2 tn 3m/5km SE of Wigan. Coal-mining. SD 6001
Abriachan H'land 81 E4 locality on W side of Loch Ness, Inverness dist, 3m/5km from NE end of loch. NH 5535
Abridge Essex 20 B2 vil 3m/5km S of Epping. Site of Roman settlement 1m W. TQ 4696
Abronhill S'clyde 65 E2* residential area of Cumbernauld 2km NE of tn centre. NS 7875
Abson Avon 16 C4 ham 5m/8km S of Chipping Sodbury. ST 7074
Abthorpe Northants 28 B3 vil 3m/5km SW of Towcester. SP 6546
Aby Lincs 45 G3 vil 3m/5km NW of Alford. TF 4178
Acaster Malbis N Yorks 49 G4 vil on W bank of R Ouse 4m/7km S of York. SE 5845
Acaster Selby N Yorks 49 G4 vil on W bank of R Ouse 6m/9km E of Tadcaster. SE 5741
Accrington Lancs 48 A5 tn 5m/8km E of Blackburn. Textiles, textile and general engineering, brick mnfg. SD 7528
Acha Coll, S'clyde 68 A3 loc 3m/5km SW of Arinagour. NM 1854
Achadophris H'land 85 F5* locality on E side of Loch Shin in Sutherland dist 4m/6km N of Lairg. NC 5611
Achadun S'clyde 70 A1* small bay and remains of cas on N coast of Lismore in Loch Linnhe, 3m/5km W of Achnacroish. NM 8039
Achahoish S'clyde 63 E1 vil in Knapdale, Argyll, at head of Loch Caolisport and 7m/11km SW of Ardrishaig. NR 7877
A' Chailleach H'land 75 G1 mt in Monadhliath range, in Badenoch and Strathspey dist, 5m/8km NW of Kingussie. NH 6804
A' Chailleach H'land 85 B8 mt in Ross and Cromarty dist 2m/3km S of Loch a' Bhraoin. Height 3276 ft or 999 metres. NH 1371
Achaleven S'clyde 70 B2* locality on S shore of Loch Etive, Argyll, 1km E of Connel. NM 9234
Achallader Castle S'clyde 71 E1 ruined cas in Argyll 1m E of NE corner of Loch Tulla. Ancient stronghold of the Fletchers and later of the Campbells; here the massacre of Glencoe is said to have been planned. NN 3244
Achanalt H'land 80 C2 locality in Ross and Cromarty dist 4m/6km W of head of Loch Luichart. See also Loch A. NH 2561
Achanamara S'clyde 69 F8 locality on inlet on E side of Loch Sween in Knapdale, Argyll, 5m/7km S of Crinan. NR 7787
Acharacle H'land 68 E2 vil in Lochaber dist 2m/4km N of Salen. NM 6767
Acharn Tayside 71 H1 vil on S shore of Loch Tay at foot of **A. Burn** 2m/3km SW of Kenmore. Falls of A., cascade nearly 1km S. NN 7543
Achateny H'land 68 D2 loc near N coast of Ardnamurchan peninsula in Lochaber dist, 7m/12km E of Ardnamurchan Pt. NM 5270
Achavanich H'land 86 E3 loc in Caithness dist 6m/10km NW of Lybster. ND 1742
Achddu Dyfed 23 F5* loc in N part of Burry Port. SN 4401
Achentoul H'land 86 B4 loc in Sutherland dist 2km N of Kinbrace. NC 8733
Achentoul Forest H'land 86 B3 tract in Sutherland dist N of Kinbrace. NC 83
Achfary H'land 84 C4 locality in Sutherland dist at lower end of Loch More. NC 2939
Achiltibuie H'land 85 A6 vil on NW coast of Ross and Cromarty dist 10m/16km NW of Ullapool. NC 0208
Achina H'land 86 A2* loc near N coast of Caithness dist 1km S of Bettyhill. NC 7060
Achinhoan Head S'clyde 63 E6* headland on E coast of Kintyre 4m/6km SE of Campbeltown. NR 7617
Achintee H'land 80 A3 locality in Ross and Cromarty dist at head of Loch Carron. NG 9441
Achintraid H'land 79 F5 locality at head of Loch Kishorn, Ross and Cromarty dist. NG 8438
A' Chleit H'land 85 A5 rocky islet 2m/3km off Kirkaig Pt on W coast of Sutherland dist. NC 0320
Achluachrach H'land 74 D3 loc in Glen Spean, Lochaber dist, 2m/4km E of Roy Br. NN 3081
Achlyness H'land 84 C3 locality 1km NW of Rhiconich at head of Loch Inchard, W coast of Sutherland dist. NC 2452
Achmelvich H'land 85 A5 loc on W coast of Sutherland dist 2m/4km NW of Lochinver. **Achmelvich Bay** to NW. NC 0624
Achmore H'land 79 F5 loc in Skye and Lochalsh dist 1m SW of Stromeferry. NG 8533
Achmore W Isles 88 B2* vil on Lewis 8m/12km W of Stornoway. NB 3029
Achnabreck S'clyde. See Cairnbaan.
Achnacarry H'land 74 C3 locality in Lochaber dist between Loch Lochy and foot of Loch Arkaig. Home of the Camerons of Lochiel. NN 1787
Achnacloich Skye, H'land 79 D7 loc near W coast of Sleat peninsula, 1km S of Tarskavaig. NG 5908
Achnacroish S'clyde 70 A1 vil with landing stage halfway along E coast of island of Lismore in Loch Linnhe. NM 8540
Achnagarron H'land 87 A8 loc in Ross and Cromarty dist 2m/3km NW of Invergordon. NH 6870
Achnahaird Bay H'land 85 A5 inlet in Enard Bay, NW coast of Ross and Cromarty dist 4m/6km SE of Rubha Coigeach. See also Brae of Achnahaird. NC 0114
Achnahanat H'land 85 E6 loc in Sutherland dist 7m/12km NW of Bonar Br. NH 5198
Achnanearnan H'land 84 A4 loc 3m/4km SE of Pt of Stoer, W coast of Sutherland dist. NC 0431
Achnanerain H'land 85 E5* locality on E side of Loch Shin in Sutherland dist, 4m/7km N of Lairg. NC 5512
Achnasheen H'land 80 B2 vil at head of Strath Bran in Ross and Cromarty dist. NH 1658
Achnashellach H'land 80 A3 lodge and rly stn in Glen Carron, Ross and Cromarty dist, at NE end of Loch Dhughaill or Doule. **A. Forest** is deer forest astride glen. NH 0048
A' Chràlaig H'land 80 B6 mt on border of Inverness and Skye & Lochalsh dists 3m/5km NE of head of Loch Cluanie. Height 3673 ft or 1120 metres. Also known as Garbh Leac. Anglicised form: Cralic. NH 0914
Achranich H'land 68 E4* locality in Lochaber dist near mouth of Rannock R at head of Loch Aline. NM 7047
Achray Forest Central 71 F4 state forest surrounding Loch Achray, W of Loch Venachar. Forms part of Queen Elizabeth Forest Park. NN 5104
Achreamie H'land 86 C1 loc near N coast of Caithness dist 2m/3km E of Dounreay atomic energy establishment. ND 0166
Achriesgill H'land 84 C3 locality 2km N of Rhiconich at head of Loch Inchard, W coast of Sutherland dist. NC 2554
A' Chrois S'clyde 71 E4 mt in Argyll 2m/3km N of head of Loch Long. Height 2785 ft or 849 metres. NN 2807
A' Chruach 75 E5 mt ridge on border of Highland and Tayside regions between Blackwater Resr and Loch Laidon. Summit is Stob na Cruaiche, 2420 ft or 738 metres. NN 3657
Achterneed H'land 81 E2 loc in Ross and Cromarty dist 1m N of Strathpeffer. NH 4859
Achtoty H'land 86 A2 loc near N coast of Caithness dist 2m/4km W of Bettyhill across Torrisdale Bay. NC 6762
A' Chùli S'clyde 69 E6 one of the Garvellachs group of islands in Firth of Lorn. Lies between Eileach an Naoimh and Garbh Eileach. NM 6511
Achurch Northants 37 E6* vil 4m/6km S of Oundle. TL 0283
Ackenthwaite Cumbria 53 E6* loc 1km E of Milnthorpe. SD 5081
Ackergill H'land 86 F2 loc in Caithness dist 2km N of Wick. Airport to E. ND 3553
Acklam Cleveland 54 D3* dist of Middlesbrough 2m/3km S of tn centre. NZ 4817
Acklam N Yorks 50 C2 vil 6m/10km NE of Stamford Br. SE 7861
Ackleton Salop 34 D4 vil 5m/8km NE of Bridgnorth. SO 7798
Acklington Nthmb 61 G2 vil 3m/4km SW of Amble. Airfield to S. NU 2201
Ackton W Yorks 49 F5* ham 1km W of Featherstone. SE 4121
Ackworth W Yorks 49 F6 par and group of vils: **High Ackworth, Low Ackworth,** and **Ackworth Moor Top,** 3m/5km to 4m/6km S of Pontefract. SE 4417
Acle Norfolk 39 G4 small tn 8m/13km W of Gt Yarmouth. TG 4010
Acocks Green W Midlands 35 G5 loc in Birmingham 4m/7km SE of city centre. SP 1283
Acol Kent 13 H1 vil on Isle of Thanet 4m/6km SW of Margate. TR 3067
Acomb Nthmb 61 E5 vil 2km N of Hexham across R Tyne. NY 9266
Acomb N Yorks 50 B3 dist of York 2m/3km W of city centre. SE 5751
Acombe Som 8 A3* loc 5m/8km SE of Wellington. ST 1913
Aconbury H & W 26 A4* vil 4m/7km S of Hereford. SO 5133
Acorn Bank Cumbria 53 E2* hse (NT), partly 16c but mainly 18c, on Crowdundle Beck 1km NE of Temple Sowerby. NY 6128
Acre Lancs 47 H5 loc 1m N of Haslingden. SD 7824
Acrefair Clwyd 41 H6 loc 2m/3km W of Ruabon. SJ 2743
Acreknowe Reservoir Borders 60 B1* small resr 2m/3km S of Hawick. NT 4910
Acre, North Norfolk 38 D5 loc 3m/5km SE of Watton. TL 9598
Acre, South Norfolk 38 C3 ham 4m/6km N of Swaffham. TF 8114
Acre, West Norfolk 38 C3 vil 5m/7km NW of Swaffham. Remains of 12c priory. TF 7715

Acrise Kent 13 G3 loc 4m/7km N of Folkestone. TR 1942

Acton Ches 42 C5 vil 2km W of Nantwich. SJ 6353

Acton Clwyd 41 H6* N dist of Wrexham. SJ 3451

Acton Dorset 9 G6* loc 1km W of Langton Matravers and 3m/4km W of Swanage. SY 9878

Acton H & W 26 D1 ham 3m/5km SE of Stourport. SO 8467

Acton London 19 F3 dist in borough of Ealing 6m/10km W of Charing Cross. Includes locs of **N, S, E, W Acton** and **Acton Green.** TQ 2080

Acton Salop 34 A5* loc 3m/4km S of Bishop's Castle. SO 3184

Acton Staffs 35 E1 ham 1m NE of Whitmore. SJ 8241

Acton Suffolk 30 D3 vil 3m/4km NE of Sudbury. Ch contains brass of Sir Robert de Bures, 1302. TL 8944

Acton Beauchamp H & W 26 C3* vil 3m/5km SE of Bromyard. SO 6750

Acton Bridge Ches 42 B4 vil 4m/6km W of Northwich. SJ 5975

Acton Burnell Salop 34 C4 vil 7m/11km S of Shrewsbury. Remains of 13c fortified manor hse (A.M.). Langley Chapel, 2km S, 16c chapel (A.M.) with 17c furnishings. SJ 5302

Acton Green H & W 26 C3 ham 4m/7km SE of Bromyard. SO 6950

Acton Pigott Salop 34 C4* loc 1m NE of Acton Burnell. SJ 5402

Acton Round Salop 34 C4 vil 3m/5km S of Much Wenlock. SO 6395

Acton Scott Salop 34 B5 vil 3m/4km S of Church Stretton. Site of Roman villa. SO 4589

Acton Trussell Staffs 35 F3 vil 3m/5km S of Stafford. SJ 9318

Acton Turville Avon 16 C3 vil 5m/8km E of Chipping Sodbury. ST 8080

Adabrock W Isles 88 C1* loc near N end of Lewis 1m S of Port of Ness. NB 5362

Adbaston Staffs 34 D2 vil 6m/9km N of Newport. SJ 7627

Adber Dorset 8 D2* ham 4m/6km NE of Yeovil. ST 5920

Add S'clyde 70 A5 r in Argyll rising 4m/7km NW of Furnace on W shore of Loch Fyne and flowing SW to Crinan Loch, Sound of Jura. NR 7994

Adderbury, East Oxon 27 H4 vil 3m/5km S of Banbury. SP 4735

Adderbury, West Oxon 27 H4 vil adjoining E Adderbury 3m/5km S of Banbury. SP 4635

Adderley Salop 34 D1 vil 4m/6km N of Mkt Drayton. SJ 6639

Adderley Green Staffs 35 E1 loc in Stoke-on-Trent 3m/5km E of city centre. SJ 9244

Adderstone Nthmb 67 G5 loc 3m/5km SE of Belford. NU 1330

Addiewell Lothian 65 F3 vil 4m/7km S of Bathgate. NS 9862

Addingham W Yorks 48 D3 vil 3m/5km NW of Ilkley. SE 0749

Addington Bucks 28 C4/C5* vil 2m/3km W of Winslow. SP 7428

Addington Cornwall 3 G2* E dist of Liskeard. SX 2565

Addington Kent 20 C5 vil 2m/3km E of Wrotham Heath. Prehistoric burial chambers to NW. TQ 6559

Addington London 20 A5 loc in borough of Croydon 3m/5km E of Croydon tn centre. TQ 3764

Addington, Great Northants 28 D1 vil 6m/10km SE of Kettering. Vil of **Lit Addington** to S. SP 9575

Addiscombe London 19 G5 dist of Croydon 1m E of tn centre. TQ 3466

Addlestone Surrey 19 E5 suburban loc 2m/3km W of Weybridge. TQ 0464

Addlethorpe Lincs 45 H4 ham 4m/6km N of Skegness. TF 5468

Adel W Yorks 49 E4 loc in Leeds 4m/7km N of city centre. SE 2740

Adeney Salop 34 D3* loc 3m/5km W of Newport. SJ 7018

Adeyfield Herts 19 E1* E dist of Hemel Hempstead. TL 0707

Adfa Powys 33 G4* ham 2km W of Llanwyddelan. SJ 0601

Ad Fines Nthmb. See Chew Green.

Adforton H & W 25 H1 vil 7m/12km E of Knighton. SO 4071

Adgestone Isle of Wight 10 C6* loc 1m SW of Brading. SZ 5986

Adisham Kent 13 G2 vil 3m/4km SW of Wingham. TR 2253

Adlestrop Glos 27 F5 vil 4m/6km E of Stow-on-the-Wold. SP 2427

Adlingfleet Humberside 50 D6 vil 7m/11km E of Goole. SE 8420

Adlington Ches 43 E3 loc 2m/4km NW of Bollington. **A. Hall,** 15c-18c hse to W. SJ 9180

Adlington Lancs 47 F6 tn 7m/12km NW of Bolton. SD 6013

Admaston Salop 34 C3 vil 2m/3km NW of Wellington. SJ 6313

Admaston Staffs 35 F2 ham on W side of Blithfield Resr 4m/6km N of Rugeley. SK 0523

Admington Warwicks 27 F3 vil 5m/8km NW of Shipston on Stour. SP 2046

Adsborough Som 8 B2 ham 4m/7km NE of Taunton. ST 2729

Adscombe Som 8 A1* ham on Quantock Hills 2km SW of Nether Stowey. ST 1837

Adstock Bucks 28 C4 vil 3m/4km NW of Winslow. SP 7330

Adstone Northants 28 B3 vil 6m/10km W of Towcester. SP 5951

Adswood Gtr Manchester 42 D3* loc 2km E of Cheadle. SJ 8887

Adur 11 H4 r rising W of Horsham in W Sussex and flowing S into English Channel at Shoreham-by-Sea. Another branch rises near Burgess Hill and joins the former branch 2km W of Henfield. TQ 2304

Adur 119 admin dist of W Sussex.

Advent Cornwall 3 F1 loc to SE of Camelford. SX 1081

Adversane W Sussex 11 G3 ham 2m/3km SW of Billingshurst. TQ 0723

Advie H'land 82 A4 loc in Badenoch and Strathspey dist 7m/12km NE of Grantown-on-Spey. Distillery. NJ 1234

Adwalton W Yorks 49 E5 loc 2m/3km W of Morley. To W is site of Battle of A. Moor, Royalist victory in Civil War, 1643. SE 2328

Adwell Oxon 18 B2 loc 3m/5km N of Watlington. SU 6999

Adwick le Street S Yorks 44 A1 colliery tn 4m/6km NW of Doncaster. SE 5307

Adwick upon Dearne S Yorks 44 A1 vil 1m N of Mexborough. SE 4701

Adziel Grampian 83 G2* loc 2km S of Strichen. NJ 9453

Aeron 24 A2 r rising W of Blaenpenal, Dyfed, and flowing, in a wide loop to the S, into Cardigan Bay at Aberaeron. SN 4563

Ae Village D & G 59 E3 vil 8m/13km N of Dumfries, on S side of **Forest of Ae,** a state forest. **Water of Ae** is r rising on E side of Queensberry and flowing S through forest and vil, then SE to Kinnel Water 2m/4km N of Lochmaben. NX 9889

Afan 118 admin dist of W Glam.

Afan 14 D3 r rising E of Blaengwynfi, W Glam, and flowing W into Bristol Channel at Port Talbot. SS 7488

Affcot, Upper Salop 34 B5 ham 3m/4km N of Craven Arms. SO 4486

Affetside Gtr Manchester 47 G6* loc 4m/6km NE of Bolton. SD 7513

Affleck Grampian 83 G4* loc 1km E of Whiterashes. NJ 8623

Affleck Tayside 73 G1 loc adjoining Monikie, 5m/8km NW of Carnoustie. **A. Castle** (A.M.) is well-preserved 15c tower hse. NO 4938

Affpuddle Dorset 9 E5 vil on R Piddle or Trent 3m/5km E of Puddletown. SY 8093

Affric H'land 80 D4 r in Inverness dist running E through Glenaffric Forest, Loch Affric and Loch Beneveian to Fasnakyle. NH 3028

Affric Forest H'land 80 C4, D4* state forest about lower part of Glen Affric in Inverness dist. NH 2828

Afon Eitha Clwyd 41 H6* loc 2km NW of Ruabon. Named after stream on which it is situated (see Eitha). SJ 2845

Afon-wen Clwyd 41 G4* loc nearly 1m S of Caerwys. SJ 1371

Afon Wen Gwynedd 32 C1* loc at mouth of r of same name 4m/6km W of Criccieth. SH 4437

Afton Isle of Wight 10 A6* loc 1m S of Freshwater. SZ 3586

Afton Bridgend S'clyde 56 F3 loc opp New Cumnock near mouth of Afton Water. NS 6213

Afton Reservoir S'clyde 56 F3 resr in course of Afton Water, 6m/10km S of New Cumnock. NS 6304

Afton Water 56 F3 r in Strathclyde region rising 2km S of Afton Resr and flowing N through the resr to R Nith at New Cumnock. NS 6214

Agden Reservoir S Yorks 43 G2* resr on W side of Bradfield. SK 2692

Aggborough H & W 35 E6* S dist of Kidderminster. SO 8375

Agglethorpe N Yorks 54 A6* ham 2m/3km S of Wensley. SE 0886

A' Ghlas-bheinn H'land 80 A5/B5 mt 4m/7km E of head of Loch Duich in Skye and Lochalsh dist. Height 3006 ft or 916 metres. NH 0023

Aglionby Cumbria 60 A5 loc 3m/5km E of Carlisle. NY 4456

Agneash Isle of Man 46 C4/C5* loc 2km N of Laxey. SC 4386

Aigas Forest H'land 80 D3, 81 E3* state forest around Crask of Aigas, qv. Also dam and hydro-electric power stn. NH 4642

Aigburth Merseyside 42 A3 dist of Liverpool 4m/6km SE of city centre. SJ 3886

Aignish W Isles 88 C2* loc on Eye Peninsula, Lewis, 2m/3km W of Garrabost. NB 4832

Aike Humberside 51 E4 ham 4m/7km N of Beverley. TA 0445

Aikerness Orkney 89 B5 loc on northern peninsula on island of Westray running out to Bow Hd. Headland of **Aiker Ness** on E side of peninsula opp small island, **Holm of Aikerness.** HY 4552

Aiker Ness Orkney 89 B6* headland on NE coast of Mainland 2m/3km N of Woodwick. See also Broch of Gurness. HY 3826

Aiketgate Cumbria 60 A6/B6* ham 1m E of Low Hesket. NY 4846

Aikhead Cumbria 52 C1* loc 2km NW of Wigton. NY 2349

Aikrigg End Cumbria 53 E5* loc in N part of Kendal. SD 5193

Aikton Cumbria 59 G6 ham 4m/6km SE of Kirkbride. NY 2753

Ailby Lincs 45 H4* loc 2km NW of Alford. TF 4376

Ailnack Water 82 B5*. See Water of Ailnack.

Ailsa Craig S'clyde 56 A4 bleak granite island and prominent seamark, some 2m/3km in circumference, lying 10m/16km W of Girvan. Haunt of sea birds. Lighthouse on E side. Granite quarries produce material for curling stones. NX 0199

Ailstone Warwicks 27 F3* loc 3m/4km S of Stratford-upon-Avon. SP 2051

Ailsworth Cambs 37 F4 vil in Peterborough 5m/8km W of city centre. **A. Heath Nature Reserve** to N. TL 1199

Aimes Green Essex 20 A2* loc 2m/3km NE of Waltham Abbey. TL 3902

Ainderby Quernhow N Yorks 54 C6 vil 5m/8km W of Thirsk across R Swale. SE 3480

Ainderby Steeple N Yorks 54 C5 vil 2m/4km SW of Northallerton. SE 3392

Aingers Green Essex 31 E6 ham 5m/8km NW of Clacton-on-Sea. TM 1120

Ainleys W Yorks 48 D6* loc 3m/4km NW of Huddersfield. SE 1119

Ainsdale Merseyside 41 H1 dist of Southport 4m/6km SW of tn centre. **Ainsdale-on-Sea** loc 2km W. SD 3112

Ainstable Cumbria 60 B6 vil 10m/16km SE of Carlisle. NY 5346

Ainsworth Gtr Manchester 47 H6 loc 3m/4km W of Bury. SD 7610

Ainthorpe N Yorks 55 E4 vil on S bank of R Esk opp Danby. NZ 7008

Aintree Merseyside 42 A2 loc 6m/9km NE of Liverpool. Racecourses. SJ 3798

Aira Force Cumbria 52 D3 waterfall in Aira Beck 1m SE of Dockray. NY 4020

Aird W Isles 88 C2* vil on Eye Peninsula, Lewis, 2km SW of Tiumpan Hd. NB 5536

Aird W Isles 88 D1/D2 loc on NW coast of Benbecula. NF 7654

Aird an Rùnair W Isles 88 D1 headland at westernmost point of N Uist. NF 6870

Aird Barvas W Isles 88 B1* headland on NW coast of Lewis 2m/4km N of Barvas. NB 3553

Aird Brenish W Isles 88 A2* headland on W coast of Lewis 1m NW of vil of Brenish. NA 9226

Aird Castle Kintyre, S'clyde. See Carradale.

Aird Fenish W Isles 88 A2* headland on W coast of Lewis 7m/12km SW of Gallan Hd. NA 9929

Aird Kilfinichen S'clyde 69 D5* low-lying headland on E side of Kilfinichen Bay on Loch Scridain, Mull. NM 4924

Aird Laimishader W Isles 88 B2* headland on W coast of Lewis 2m/4km W of Carloway. Lighthouse. NB 1742

Aird Linn D & G 58 D3* waterfall in course of Shinnel Water, 1km below Tynron. NX 8192

Aird of Kinloch S'clyde 69 D5 low-lying promontory almost enclosing Loch Beg, at head of Loch Scridain, Mull. NM 5228

Aird of Kinuachdrach S'clyde 69 D7* headland on NE coast of Jura 2m/3km from northern point of island. NR 7098

Aird of Sleat Skye, H'land 79 D7 vil at S end of Sleat peninsula 2m/4km E of Pt of Sleat. NG 5900

Aird Point Skye, H'land 78 A4/B4* headland on Loch Snizort Beag on E side of entrance to Loch Treaslane. NG 3952

Airdrie S'clyde 65 E2 tn 11m/17km E of Glasgow. Industries include light engineering, pharmaceutical products, distilling. NS 7665

Airdriehead S'clyde 65 E2* loc in Cumbernauld 1m NW of tn centre. NS 7475

Airds Bay S'clyde 70 B1 bay on N side of entrance to Loch Creran, Argyll. NM 9044

Airds Moss S'clyde 56 F2 desolate area NE of Cumnock. Scene of skirmish in 1680 between Royalists and Covenanters. NS 5924

Airds Point S'clyde 70 B2 headland on S side of Loch Etive, Argyll, 2m/4km NW of Taynuilt. **A. Bay** 2km SE. NM 9834

Aird, The H'land 81 E3 fertile dist in Inverness dist S of Beauly. NH 5543

Aird Tunga W Isles 88 C2* headland on E coast of Lewis 4m/6km NE of Stornoway across Melbost Sands. NB 4636

Aire 49 H5 r whose source lies underground in limestone country in vicinity of Malham Tarn, N Yorks, and which issues above ground at foot of Malham Cove. The r then flows SE by Skipton, Keighley, Bingley, Shipley, and Leeds to Knottingley, then E to join R Ouse 1km above Boothferry Br, Humberside. SE 7226

Aire and Calder Canal 49 E5-H5 canal connecting Leeds, W Yorks, and Goole, Humberside. With the Leeds and Liverpool Canal it provides a waterway link between the Irish Sea and the North Sea.

Aire Point Cornwall 2 A5* headland at N end of Whitesand Bay 2m/3km N of Land's End. SW 3528

Aire View N Yorks 48 C3* loc 3m/5km S of Skipton. SD 9946

Airies D & G 57 A6* loc 7m/11km NW of Stranraer. NW 9767

Airlie Castle Tayside 76 D5 remains of historic Ogilvy residence, sacked by the Campbells in 1640. NO 2952

Airmyn Humberside 50 C5 vil on right bank of R Aire near its confluence with R Ouse and 2m/3km NW of Goole. **Lit Airmyn** ham on opp bank, in N Yorks. SE 7225

Airntully Tayside 72 D1 vil 2m/3km N of Stanley. NO 0935

Airor H'land 79 E7 loc with jetty on coast of Knoydart, Lochaber dist, and 4m/7km E of Kilbeg, Skye, across Sound of Sleat. **Airor I.** is islet near coast here. NG 7105

Air, Point of (Y Parlwr Du) Clwyd 41 G3 promontory at W end of R Dee estuary 4m/6km E of Prestatyn. Also spelt Point of Ayr. SJ 1285

Airth Central 72 C5 vil 5m/7km N of Falkirk. **A. Castle** to S is modernised 16c mansion. NS 8987

Airthrey Central 72 B5/C5 cas and estate on SE side of Br of Allan. Site of University of Stirling. NS 8196

Airton N Yorks 48 B2 vil on R Aire 4m/6km NW of Gargrave. SD 9059

Aisby Lincs 37 E1 ham 6m/9km SW of Sleaford. TF 0138

Aisby Lincs 44 D2* ham 1m N of Corringham. SK 8792
Aisgill Cumbria 53 G5 loc 7m/11km S of Kirkby Stephen. SD 7797
Aish Devon 4 D4* ham just NW of S Brent. To S, ham of **Gt Aish.** SX 6960
Aish Devon 5 E4* ham 3m/4km SE of Totnes. SX 8458
Aisholt Som 8 A1* ham on E slopes of Quantock Hills 3m/4km S of Nether Stowey. 1 km SE, ham of **Lr Aisholt.** ST 1935
Aiskew N Yorks 54 B5 vil adjoining Bedale to NE. SE 2788
Aislaby Cleveland 54 C4 ham 1m W of Yarm across R Tees. NZ 4012
Aislaby N Yorks 55 F6 ham 2m/3km NW of Pickering. SE 7785
Aislaby N Yorks 55 G4 vil 3m/5km SW of Whitby. NZ 8508
Aisthorpe Lincs 44 D3* vil between Brattleby and Scampton 6m/9km N of Lincoln. SK 9480
Aith Orkney 89 C6 loc at centre of island of Stronsay. HY 6525
Aith Shetland 89 E7 vil on Mainland at head of **A. Voe,** large inlet S of Papa Little. HU 3455
Aith Shetland 89 F6* loc near S coast of Fetlar. **A. Ness** headland on coast to S, on N shore of Wick of Tresta. **Wick of A.** is small bay to E. HU 6390
Aith Ness Shetland 89 E7 headland at N end of island of Bressay, S of Score Head. HU 5144
Aith Ness Shetland 89 E7* headland on Mainland on W side of entrance to Aith Voe. **Loch of Aithness** to SW. HU 3359
Aithsetter Shetland 89 E8* loc on Mainland 2km S of Fladdabister. HU 4430
Aithsting and Sandsting Shetland 89 E7* dist of Mainland lying between Aith Voe and Bixter Voe. HU 35
Aith Voe Shetland 89 E7* large inlet on N coast of island of Bressay. HU 5043
Akebar N Yorks 54 B5* loc 1m S of Hunton. SE 1990
Akeld Nthmb 67 F5 ham 2m/4km W of Wooler. NT 9529
Akeley Bucks 28 C4 vil 3m/4km N of Buckingham. SP 7037
Akenham Suffolk 31 F3* vil 3m/5km N of Ipswich. TM 1448
Aketon N Yorks 49 F3* loc 1m NW of Spofforth. SE 3552
Alan 33 H3 r running E into R Fyllon 1km W of Llanfyllin, Powys. SJ 1319
A la Ronde Devon. See Hulham.
Alaw 40 A3* r on Anglesey running SW through Llyn Alaw resr to Llanfachraeth and the channel between Holy I. and the main island of Anglesey. SH 2981
Albany Tyne & Wear 61 G5* dist of Washington to N of tn centre. NZ 2957
Alberbury Salop 34 B3 vil 8m/13km W of Shrewsbury. Remains of cas beside ch. Remains of medieval priory 1m NE, incorporated in farmhouse. SJ 3514
Albert Town Dyfed 22 B4* loc adjoining Haverfordwest to W. SM 9415
Albourne W Sussex 11 H3 vil 1m W of Hurstpierpoint. Loc of **A. Green** at N end of vil. TQ 2616
Albrighton Salop 34 B3 vil 4m/6km N of Shrewsbury. **Albright Hussey** is 16c hse 1km SE. SJ 4918
Albrighton Salop 35 E4 vil 7m/11km NW of Wolverhampton. SJ 8104
Albro Castle Dyfed 22 D1/D2* loc adjoining St Dogmaels to N. SN 1646
Alburgh Norfolk 39 F6 vil 3m/5km NE of Harleston. Vil of **A. Street** adjoins to NW. TM 2786
Albury Herts 29 H5 vil 3m/5km E of Puckeridge. Loc of **A. End** 1km SW. TL 4324
Albury Oxon 18 B1 loc 4m/6km W of Thame. SP 6505
Albury Surrey 19 E6 vil 4m/6km E of Guildford. TQ 0447
Albyfield Cumbria 60 B6* loc 2m/3km S of Castle Carrock. NY 5452
Alby Hill Norfolk 39 F2* loc 1km E of Aldborough. TG 1934
Alcaig H'land 81 E2 vil in Ross and Cromarty dist 2km SE of Dingwall across head of Cromarty Firth. NH 5657
Alcester Warwicks 27 E2 tn on site of Roman settlement at confluence of R Alne and R Arrow 7m/11km W of Stratford-upon-Avon. See also Ragley Hall. SP 0857
Alcester Lane's End W Midlands 35 G6* loc in Birmingham 4m/7km S of city centre. SP 0780
Alciston E Sussex 12 B6 vil below S Downs 2m/3km N of Alfriston. TQ 5005
Alcombe Som 7 G1 loc adjoining Minehead to S. SS 9745
Alconbury Cambs 29 F1 vil 4m/7km NW of Huntingdon. **A. Airfield** to E. TL 1875
Alconbury Brook 29 F1* stream rising W of Hemington, Northants, and flowing SE through Alconbury and into R Ouse on SW side of Huntingdon, Cambs. TL 2271
Alconbury Weston Cambs 37 F6 vil 5m/8km NW of Huntingdon. TL 1776
Aldborough Norfolk 39 F2 vil 5m/8km N of Aylsham. TG 1834
Aldborough N Yorks 49 F2 vil 1km SE of Boroughbridge on site of Roman tn of *Isurium* (A.M.). SE 4066
Aldborough Hatch London 20 B3* loc in borough of Redbridge 2m/3km NE of Ilford. TQ 4589
Aldbourne Wilts 17 G4 vil 6m/10km NE of Marlborough. SU 2675
Aldbrough Humberside 51 F4 vil 6m/10km SE of Hornsea. TA 2438
Aldbrough N Yorks 54 B4 vil 4m/6km N of Scotch Corner. NZ 2011
Aldbury Herts 18 D1 vil 3m/5km NW of Berkhamsted. SP 9612
Aldcliffe Lancs 47 E2* SW dist of Lancaster. SD 4760
Alde 31 H3 r rising in par of Tannington, Suffolk, and flowing SE to Snape Maltings, where it forms estuary which runs to Slaughden, S of Aldeburgh. It then runs SW parallel to coast and flows into North Sea 2km E of Hollesley. From Orford Ness to mouth the r is known as R Ore. TM 4249
Aldeburgh Suffolk 31 H3 E coast tn 6m/10km SE of Saxmundham. Sea encroachment; medieval Moot Hall now on beach. Annual music festival at Snape Maltings at head of R Alde estuary to W. TM 4656
Aldeby Norfolk 39 H5 vil 2m/4km S of Haddiscoe. TM 4493
Aldenham Herts 19 F2 vil 2m/4km NE of Watford. TQ 1398
Aldenham Reservoir Herts 19 F2* resr 3m/4km SE of Aldenham, and 1km W of Elstree. TQ 1695
Alder Bay 75 F4* inlet on W shore of Loch Ericht, 3m/5km N of dam at S end. **Alder Burn** runs SE into bay and here forms border of Highland and Tayside regions. NN 5067
Alderbury Wilts 9 H2 vil 3m/5km SE of Salisbury. SU 1827
Aldercar Derbys 43 H6* loc 1m NE of Heanor. SK 4447
Aldercarr Green Norfolk 39 G5* loc 2m/3km NW of Bungay across R Waveney. TM 3191
Alderfen Broad Norfolk 39 G3* small broad or lake 2m/3km NE of Horning. TG 3519
Alderford Norfolk 39 E3 vil 9m/15km NW of Norwich. TG 1218
Alder Forest Gtr Manchester 42 C2* loc 1m N of Eccles. SJ 7599
Alderholt Dorset 9 H3 vil 2m/3km SW of Fordingbridge. SU 1212
Alderley Glos 16 C3 vil 2m/3km S of Wotton-under-Edge. ST 7690
Alderley Edge Ches 42 D3 residential tn 2m/3km S of Wilmslow. Wooded sandstone escarpment (NT) of same name to E, commanding wide views. SJ 8478
Alderley, Nether Ches 42 D4 vil 2m/3km S of Alderley Edge. Restored 15c corn mill (NT). SJ 8476
Alderman's Green W Midlands 36 A5 loc in Coventry 3m/5km NE of city centre. SP 3583
Aldermaston Berks 18 B5 vil 8m/12km E of Newbury. Atomic Energy Research Establishment to S. Vil of **A. Wharf** on Kennet and Avon Canal 2km N. SU 5965
Alderminster Warwicks 27 F3 vil 4m/7km SE of Stratford-upon-Avon. SP 2348
Alder Moor Staffs 35 H2* loc 3m/4km N of Burton upon Trent. SK 2227
Aldersbrook London 20 B3* loc 1m S of Wanstead in borough of Redbridge. Site of Roman bldg in Wanstead Park to N. TQ 4186
Alder's End H & W 26 B4* loc 7m/11km E of Hereford. SO 6239
Aldersey Green Ches 42 A5 loc 7m/11km SE of Chester. SJ 4656
Aldershot Hants 18 D6 garrison tn 8m/13km W of Guildford. Both military and civilian parts redeveloped in 1960s and 1970s. SU 8650
Aldersyde N Yorks 49 G3* loc in York 2m/4km SW of city centre. SE 5849
Alderton Glos 27 E4 vil 4m/6km NW of Winchcombe. SP 0033
Alderton Northants 28 C3 vil 3m/5km E of Towcester. SP 7446
Alderton Salop 34 B2 loc 7m/11km N of Shrewsbury. SJ 4923
Alderton Suffolk 31 G4 vil 7m/11km SE of Woodbridge. TM 3441
Alderton Wilts 16 D3 vil 7m/11km W of Malmesbury. ST 8482
Alderwasley Derbys 43 G5 vil 2m/3km E of Wirksworth. SK 3153
Aldfield N Yorks 49 E2 vil 3m/5km W of Ripon. SE 2669
Aldford Ches 42 A5 vil 5m/7km S of Chester. SJ 4159
Aldham Essex 30 D5 vil 5m/8km W of Colchester. TL 9125
Aldham Suffolk 31 E3/E4 ham 2km NE of Hadleigh. Ham of **A. Street** 1km NE. TM 0444
Aldingbourne W Sussex 11 E4 vil 4m/7km E of Chichester. SU 9205
Aldingham Cumbria 46 D1 ham on Morecambe Bay 4m/6km SE of Dalton-in-Furness. SD 2871
Aldin Grange Durham 54 B1* loc 2m/3km W of Durham. NZ 2442
Aldington H & W 27 E3* vil 2m/3km E of Evesham. SP 0644
Aldington Kent 13 F3 vil 6m/9km W of Hythe. Hams of **A. Corner** 1m, and **A. Frith** 2m/4km, to W. TR 0736
Aldinna Loch S'clyde 56 D4* small loch 3m/5km NW of Shalloch on Minnoch. NX 3693
Aldon Salop 34 B6* loc 2m/3km S of Craven Arms. SO 4379
Aldoth Cumbria 52 B1* loc 2m/4km SW of Abbey Town. NY 1448
Aldourie Castle H'land 81 F4 cas near NE end of Loch Ness 2m/3km N of Dores, Inverness dist. NH 6037
Aldous's Corner Suffolk 31 G1* loc 3m/5km NW of Halesworth. TM 3681
Aldreth Cambs 30 A1 vil 7m/11km SW of Ely. TL 4473
Aldridge W Midlands 35 F4 tn 3m/5km NE of Walsall. Industries include brick and plastics mnfre, engineering. SK 0500
Aldringham Suffolk 31 H2 vil 1m S of Leiston. TM 4461
Aldrington E Sussex 11 H4* W dist of Hove. TQ 2705
Aldsworth Glos 17 F1 vil 6m/10km W of Burford. SP 1510
Aldsworth W Sussex 10 D4* loc 2m/3km NE of Emsworth. SU 7608
Aldwark Derbys 43 G5 ham 4m/7km NW of Wirksworth. SK 2257
Aldwark N Yorks 50 A2 vil on R Ouse 6m/9km SW of Easingwold. 1m S, Aldwark Br, toll br over R Ouse. SE 4663
Aldwarke S Yorks 44 A2* loc 2m/3km NE of Rotherham. SK 4494
Aldwick W Sussex 11 E5 W dist of Bognor Regis. SZ 9198
Aldwincle Northants 37 E6 vil 4m/7km SW of Oundle. TL 0081
Aldworth Berks 18 A3 vil 3m/4km W of Streatley. SU 5579
Aled 41 F4 r rising in Llyn Aled, Clwyd, and flowing N through Aled Isaf Resr and Llansannan to R Elwy 2m/3km E of Llanfair Talhaiarn. SH 9571
Aled Isaf Reservoir Clwyd 41 E5* resr in course of R Aled 4m/7km S of Llansannan. SH 9159
Alemoor Loch Borders 66 B6 loch and resr 7m/11km W of Hawick. NT 3914
Ale Water 66 D6 r in Borders region running NE through Alemoor Loch to Ashkirk and Lilliesleaf. R then flows E to Ancrum, where it turns briefly S to run into R Teviot. NT 6223
Alexandra Palace London 19 G3 TV relay stn 1m W of Wood Green in borough of Haringey. TQ 2990
Alexandria S'clyde 64 B1 tn on R Leven 3m/5km N of Dumbarton. Industries include textile dyeing and bleaching, distilling. NS 3979
Aley Som 8 A1* ham on lower slopes of Quantock Hills 2km S of Nether Stowey. ST 1838
Aley Green Beds 29 E5* ham 3m/4km SW of Luton. TL 0618
Alfardisworthy Devon 6 B4* loc 6m/9km NW of Holsworthy. SS 2911
Alfington Devon 7 H5 vil 2m/3km NE of Ottery St Mary. SY 1197
Alfold Surrey 11 F2 vil 4m/6km SW of Cranleigh. TQ 0334
Alfold Bars W Sussex 11 F2* loc 6m/9km NW of Billingshurst. TQ 0333
Alfold Crossways Surrey 11 F2 ham 3m/4km SW of Cranleigh. TQ 0435
Alford Grampian 83 E5 small tn and agricultural centre 23m/37km W of Aberdeen. Site of defeat of Covenanters by Montrose in 1645. See also Bridge of A., Howe of A. NJ 5715
Alford Lincs 45 H4 small tn 11m/17km SE of Louth. TF 4575
Alford Som 8 D1 vil 2m/4km W of Castle Cary. ST 6032
Alfred's Castle Oxon 17 G3* Iron Age fort to W of Ashdown Park 4m/7km N of Aldbourne. SU 2782
Alfreton Derbys 43 H5 tn 10m/15km S of Chesterfield. Coal-mining, engineering, textiles. SK 4155
Alfrick H & W 26 C2 vil 7m/11km W of Worcester. SO 7453
Alfrick Pound H & W 26 C2* ham 7m/11km W of Worcester. SO 7452
Alfriston E Sussex 12 B6 S Downs vil on Cuckmere R, 4m/6km NE of Newhaven. **Clergy Hse** (NT), 14c; first property acquired by the Trust, 1896. TQ 5103
Algarkirk Lincs 37 G1 vil 6m/10km SW of Boston. TF 2935
Alham 8 D1* r rising 4m/6km E of Shepton Mallet, Som, and flowing S then SW into R Brue 5m/8km W of Bruton. ST 6033
Alham, Higher Som 9 E1 loc 4m/6km N of Bruton. ST 6741
Alhampton Som 8 D1 vil 2m/3km NW of Castle Cary. ST 6234
Alice Holt Forest Hants 11 E1* wooded area some 3m/5km SW of Farnham. SU 8042
Aline H'land 68 E4* r in Lochaber dist running S to head of Loch Aline. NM 6947
Alkborough Humberside 50 D6 vil 7m/11km N of Scunthorpe. SE 8821
Alkerton Oxon 27 G3 vil 5m/8km W of Banbury. SP 3742
Alkham Kent 13 G3 vil 4m/6km W of Dover. Ham of **S Alkham** 1km SW. TR 2542
Alkington Salop 34 C1 loc 2m/3km SW of Whitchurch. SJ 5238
Alkmondpark Pool Salop 34 B3 lake 2m/4km N of Shrewsbury. SJ 4816
Alkmonton Derbys 35 G1 ham 4m/7km NE of Sudbury. SK 1838
Allaleigh Devon 5 E5* loc 5m/8km W of Dartmouth. SX 8053
Allandale Central 65 E1* loc on SW side of Bonnybridge. NS 8078
Allanfearn H'land 81 F3* loc in Inverness dist 4m/6km E of Inverness. NH 7147
Allan Tarn Cumbria 52 C5* wide stretch of R Crake below S end of Coniston Water. SD 2989
Allanton Borders 67 F3 vil 2km S of Chirnside, at confluence of Blackadder Water and Whiteadder Water. NT 8654
Allanton S'clyde 64 D5* loc 3m/4km E of Darvel. Site of Roman fort. NS 6037
Allanton S'clyde 65 E3 vil 4m/6km NE of Wishaw. NS 8557
Allan Water 60 A1 r in Borders region running N to R Teviot at Newmill, SW of Hawick. NT 4510
Allan Water 72 B5 r rising near Blackford in Tayside region and running SW down Strath Allan to Dunblane in Central region, then continuing S to R Forth 2m/3km N of Stirling. NS 7896
Allaston Glos 16 B1* suburban loc 2km N of Lydney. SO 6304
Allbrook Hants 10 B3 loc 2km N of Eastleigh. SU 4521
All Cannings Wilts 17 E5 vil 4m/7km E of Devizes. SU 0761
Allean Forest Tayside 75 H5* state forest on N side of Loch Tummel, 3m/4km S of Blair Atholl. NN 8561
Allen 2 D4* r rising to S of Newlyn Downs, Cornwall, and flowing S through Truro to join R Kenwyn and form Truro R. SW 8244
Allen 3 E1 r rising S of Delabole, Cornwall, and flowing SW into R Camel 1m SE of Wadebridge. SX 0071
Allen 60 D5 r formed by confluence of Rs East Allen and West Allen 3m/5km NW

of Allendale Tn, Nthmb, and flowing thence N through deep wooded valley into R South Tyne 2km E of Bardon Br. NY 8064
Allen 9 G4* r rising S of Sixpenny Handley in Dorset and flowing S into R Stour at Wimborne. SZ 0199
Allen 9 H3* upper reach of Ashford Water, rising at Martin, Hants. See Ashford Water. SU 1413
Allendale Cottages Durham 61 F5* loc 1m E of Ebchester. NZ 1155
Allendale Town Nthmb 60 D5 small tn on R East Allen 5m/9km S of Haydon Br. NY 8355
Allen, East 60 D5 r rising 2m/3km S of Allenheads, Nthmb, and flowing N to Allendale Tn, then NW to join R West Allen and form R Allen. NY 8058
Allenheads Nthmb 53 G1 vil 4m/6km N of Wearhead. NY 8545
Allensford 61 F6 loc on R Derwent on border of Durham and Nthmb 2m/3km W of Consett. NZ 0750
Allen's Green Herts 29 H6 ham 4m/6km SW of Bishop's Stortford. TL 4516
Allensmore H & W 26 A4 vil 4m/6km SW of Hereford. SO 4635
Allenton Derbys 36 A1 dist of Derby 3m/4km SE of tn centre. SK 3732
Allen, West 60 D5 r rising on Coalcleugh Moor, near Coalcleugh, Nthmb, and flowing N to join R East Allen and form R Allen 3m/5km NW of Allendale Tn. NY 8058
Aller Devon 7 F3* ham 3m/5km E of S Molton. SS 7625
Aller Som 8 C2 vil 2m/3km NW of Langport. ST 4029
Allerby Cumbria 52 B1 ham 4m/6km NE of Maryport. NY 0839
Allercombe Devon 7 H5* ham 3m/5km W of Ottery St Mary. SY 0494
Allerdale 116 admin dist of Cumbria.
Allerdean, West Nthmb 67 F4 loc 5m/8km SW of Berwick-upon-Tweed. NT 9646
Allerford Som 7 G1 vil 2km E of Porlock. SS 9046
Allerston N Yorks 55 G6 vil 5m/8km E of Pickering. SE 8782
Allerthorpe Humberside 50 C3 vil 2m/3km SW of Pocklington. SE 7847
Allerthorpe N Yorks 54 C6* loc 3m/5km SE of Leeming. SE 3386
Allerton Merseyside 42 A3* dist of Liverpool 5m/8km SE of city centre. SJ 4086
Allerton W Yorks 48 D4 dist of Bradford 3m/5km W of city centre. SE 1234
Allerton Bywater W Yorks 49 F5 coal-mining loc on R Aire 2m/3km NW of Castleford. SE 4127
Allerton Mauleverer N Yorks 50 A2 ham 6m/9km S of Boroughbridge. **Allerton Park** is 19c mansion in large park with lakes. SE 4158
Allesley W Midlands 35 H6 loc in Coventry 3m/5km W of city centre. Also par adjoining Coventry to NW. SP 2980
Allestree Derbys 35 H1 N suburb of Derby. SK 3539
Allet Common Cornwall 2 D3* loc 3m/5km NW of Truro. SW 7948
Allexton Leics 36 D4 vil 3m/5km W of Uppingham. SK 8100
Alley, The Berks 18 A4* ham 3m/5km NE of Newbury. SU 5170
Allgreave Ches 43 E4 ham in Peak Dist National Park 6m/9km SE of Macclesfield. SJ 9766
Allhallows Kent 20 D4 vil 8m/13km NE of Rochester. TQ 8377
Alligin H'land. See Inver Alligin.
Allimore Green Staffs 35 E3* loc 1m SW of Haughton. SJ 8519
Allington Dorset 8 C5* NW dist of Bridport. SY 4693
Allington Kent 20 D5* loc in N part of Maidstone beside R Medway. Restored medieval cas. TQ 7457
Allington Lincs 36 D1 vil 5m/7km NW of Grantham. SK 8540
Allington Wilts 16 D4* ham 2m/3km NW of Chippenham. ST 8975
Allington Wilts 17 E5 vil 4m/7km E of Devizes. SU 0663
Allington Wilts 9 H1 vil on R Bourne 7m/11km NE of Salisbury. SU 2039
Allington, East Devon 4 D5 vil 3m/5km NE of Kingsbridge. SX 7748
Allington, South Devon 4 D6* ham 3m/4km NE of Prawle Pt. SX 7938
Allison Lane End Humberside 51 F3* loc just NE of Lissett. TA 1458
Allithwaite Cumbria 47 E1 vil 2km S of Cartmel. SD 3876
Alloa Central 72 C5 tn on N side of R Forth 6m/9km E of Stirling. Industries include wool spinning, glass mnfre, brewing. Distillery at Carsebridge, qv. Small harbour. **S Alloa** is loc on S bank of r. NS 8892
Allonby Cumbria 52 B1 vil on Solway Firth 5m/8km NE of Maryport across **Allonby Bay**, which extends from Maryport northwards to Dubmill Pt. NY 0842
Allotment, West Tyne & Wear 61 G4* loc 5m/8km NE of Newcastle. NZ 3070
Alloway S'clyde 56 D2 vil 2m/4km S of Ayr. Birthplace of Robert Burns, 1759; cottage is Burns museum. Auld Brig o' Doon, with Burns associations, spans R Doon to S. NS 3318
Allowenshay Som 8 C3* ham 2m/4km SE of Ilminster. ST 3913
All Saints South Elmham Suffolk 31 G1 ham 4m/7km NW of Halesworth. TM 3482
Allscott Salop 34 C3* loc 3m/4km NW of Wellington. SJ 6113
All Stretton Salop 34 B4/B5 vil 2km NE of Church Stretton. SO 4695
Allt a' Chràisg H'land 84 F4* r in Caithness dist running NE down Strath Vagastie to head of Loch Naver. NC 5734
Allt a' Gheallaidh 82 B3* r running SE down Glen Gheallaidh and through Scootmore Forest to R Spey nearly 1km N of confluence of R Spey and R Avon in Grampian region. NJ 1737
Alltami Clwyd 41 H5* loc 2m/3km NE of Mold. SJ 2665
Alltan Dubh H'land 85 A5 loc on NW coast of Ross and Cromarty dist 4m/6km S of Rubha Coigeach. NB 9812
Allt Bail a' Mhuilinn 71 F1* stream in Tayside region running N into R Lyon at Milton Eonan, qv. NN 5746
Allt Breinag H'land 81 E5 r in Inverness dist rising on Glendoe Forest and running N down Glen Brein to R Feehlin at White Br, 3m/5km S of Foyers. NH 4815
Alltcailleach Forest Grampian 76 D2* state forest 3m/5km SW of Ballater. NO 3392
Allt Chomraidh 75 F5* r in Tayside region running NE down Gleann Chomraidh to R Gaur above Loch Rannoch. NN 5056
Allt Chonoghlais S'clyde 71 E1* r in Argyll rising on S side of Beinn a' Dothaidh and running in a wide loop round Beinn Dorain to R Orchy 1km S of Br of Orchy. NN 2938
Allt Dearg Mór H'land 79 C6 r rising on Cuillin Hills, Skye, and running NE to join R Sligachan about 1km above head of Loch Sligachan. NG 4829
Allt Doe H'land 80 D6. See Glen Doe.
Allt Easach 70 C1* stream in S'clyde region running S into Loch Etive, Argyll, 5m/7km from head of loch. NN 0639
Allt Eigheach 75 E5* r in Tayside region running S into Loch Eigheach. NN 4457
Allt Fearnach 76 B4 r in Tayside region running S down Gleann Fearnach to join Brerachan Water and form R Ardle 3m/5km NW of Kirkmichael. NO 0463
Allt Girnaig 76 A4 r in Tayside region running SW down Glen Girnaig to R Garry at Killiecrankie. NN 9162
Allt Gleann Da-Eig 71 G1* stream in Tayside region running N into R Lyon 2m/4km E of Br of Balgie. Waterfalls 1km from mouth. NN 6147
Allt Goibhre H'land 81 E2 stream running E into R Orrin 3m/5km W of Muir of Ord, Ross and Cromarty dist. NH 4751
Alltmawr Powys 25 F3 ham on R Wye 3m/5km SE of Builth Wells. SO 0746
Allt Melyd Welsh form of Meliden, qv.
Allt Mheuran S'clyde 70 D1* stream in Argyll rising between Stob Coir' an Albannaich and Glas Beinn Mhór, and running NW to R Etive 2km E of Loch Etive. See also Eas nam Meirleach. NN 1346
Allt Mór H'land 81 H6 stream rising on Cairngorms and running N then W to head of Loch Morlich in Glen More Forest Park, Badenoch and Strathspey dist. NH 9709
Allt na Caillich H'land 84 E3 stream in Sutherland dist rising on S side of Ben Hope and running SW to Strathmore R, 3m/5km S of Loch Hope. High waterfall in course of stream at top of steep descent to mouth. NC 4545
Allt na h-Airbhe H'land 85 B7 locality on W shore of Loch Broom, Ross and Cromarty dist, opp Ullapool. Ferry for pedestrians. NH 1193
Allt na Lairige H'land 74 D4* r in Lochaber dist running S to head of Loch Treig. NN 3069
Allt Tolaghan S'clyde 70 D1 r in Argyll running NE to join Linne nam Beathach at W end of Loch Tulla. NN 2742
Alltwalis Dyfed 24 A5 ham 8m/12km N of Carmarthen. SN 4431
Alltwen W Glam 14 C2 vil 1km SE of Pontardawe. SN 7203
Alltyblaca Dyfed 24 B3 vil 2km N of Llanybydder. SN 5245
Allt-yr-yn Gwent 15 G3* loc 1m NW of Newport. ST 2988
Allweston Dorset 9 D3 vil 2m/4km SE of Sherborne. ST 6614
Allwood Green Suffolk 31 E1* loc 2m/3km W of Gislingham. TM 0471
Almeley H & W 25 H3 vil 4m/6km SE of Kington. Ham of **A. Wooton** 1km N. SO 3351
Almer Dorset 9 F4 ham 5m/8km S of Blandford Forum. SY 9198
Almholme S Yorks 44 B1 ham 3m/5km NE of Doncaster. SE 5908
Almington Staffs 34 D1 ham 2m/3km E of Mkt Drayton. SJ 7034
Almiston Cross Devon 6 C3 ham 8m/12km SW of Bideford. SS 3420
Almodington W Sussex 11 E5* loc 3m/5km NW of Selsey. SZ 8297
Almondbank Tayside 72 D2 vil on R Almond 4m/6km NW of Perth. NO 0626
Almondbury W Yorks 48 D6 dist of Huddersfield 2m/3km SE of tn centre. SE 1615
Almondsbury Avon 16 B3 vil 7m/12km N of Bristol. Four-level motorway interchange 1m E. ST 6084
Aln 61 G1 r rising at Alnham, Nthmb, and flowing E by Alnwick into North Sea at Alnmouth. NU 2410
Alne N Yorks 49 G2 vil 3m/5km SW of Easingwold. SE 4965
Alne 27 E2* r rising on borders of H & W and Warwicks, E of Redditch, and flowing in a loop, E then S then SW, into R Arrow at Alcester, Warwicks. SP 0957
Alne, Great Warwicks 27 F2 vil 2m/4km NE of Alcester. SP 1159
Alne, Little Warwicks 27 F2 ham 3m/5km S of Henley-in-Arden. SP 1361
Alness H'land 81 F1 small tn on N side of Cromarty Firth, Ross and Cromarty dist, 3m/5km W of Invergordon. Expansion in connection with North Sea oil developments. Distillery. Airfield to S on shore of firth. **R Alness** runs from NW through tn to firth. NH 6569
Alney Island Glos 26 C5* loc between branches of R Severn in W part of Gloucester. SO 8219
Alnham Nthmb 61 E1 ham 5m/8km W of Whittingham. NT 9910
Alnmouth Nthmb 61 G1 small resort with wide sands at mouth of R Aln 4m/7km SE of Alnwick. **Alnmouth Bay** extends from Seaton Pt (N) to Amble (S). NU 2410
Alnwick Nthmb 61 F1 tn on R Aln 17m/28km N of Morpeth. Norman cas, stronghold of the Percys, much enlarged and restored. NU 1813
Alperton London 19 F3 loc in borough of Brent 8m/12km W of Charing Cross. TQ 1883
Alphamstone Essex 30 D4 vil 4m/6km S of Sudbury. TL 8735
Alpheton Suffolk 30 D3 vil 3m/5km N of Long Melford. TL 8851
Alphington Devon 7 G6 S dist of Exeter 2m/3km from city centre. Par of same name lies to W and S of city. SX 9190
Alpington Norfolk 39 G4 loc 6m/10km SW of Norwich. TG 2901
Alport Derbys 43 G4 vil on R Lathkill in former lead-mining area 3m/4km S of Bakewell. SK 2264
Alport 43 F3/G3 r rising on Bleaklow Hill, Derbys, 5m/8km E of Glossop, and flowing SE into R Derwent in Ladybower Resr. SK 1986
Alpraham Ches 42 B5 vil 3m/5km SE of Tarporley. SJ 5859
Alre 10 C6 r rising 2m/3km E of New Alresford in Hampshire and flowing into R Itchen 1m W of the tn. SU 5732
Alresford Essex 31 E5 vil 2m/3km E of Wivenhoe. TM 0621
Alresford Creek Essex 31 E6* inlet of R Colne 2m/3km below Wivenhoe. Sites of Roman villas on both sides of creek near mouth. TM 0619
Alrewas Staffs 35 G3 vil 5m/8km NE of Lichfield. SK 1715
Alsager Ches 42 D5 tn 6m/10km E of Crewe. **A. Heath** loc 2km NW. SJ 7955
Alsagers Bank Staffs 42 D6 loc 3m/5km NW of Newcastle-under-Lyme. SJ 8048
Alsop en le Dale Derbys 43 F5 ham 6m/9km N of Ashbourne. SK 1655
Alston Cumbria 53 F1 small mkt tn above R South Tyne 16m/26km NE of Penrith. NY 7146
Alston Devon 8 B4* ham 2km S of Chardstock. ST 3002
Alstone Glos 26 D5* W dist of Cheltenham. SO 9322
Alstone Glos 27 E4 vil 4m/6km NW of Winchcombe. SO 9832
Alstone Som 15 H6* loc 1km SW of Highbridge. ST 3146
Alstone Staffs 35 E3* loc 2km NW of Bradley. SJ 8518
Alstonefield Staffs 43 F5 vil 6m/10km NW of Ashbourne. SK 1355
Alston Sutton Som 15 H6* ham 3m/4km NW of Wedmore. ST 4151
Alswear Devon 7 E3 vil 3m/4km S of S Molton. SS 7222
Alt Gtr Manchester 43 E1* loc in Oldham 2m/3km SE of tn centre. SD 9403
Alt 41 H1 r rising at Roby, Merseyside, and flowing NW into Crosby Channel 3m/4km S of Formby. SD 2903
Altarnun Cornwall 6 B6 vil below NE side of Bodmin Moor 7m/11km W of Launceston. SX 2281
Altassmore H'land 85 E6 loc in Sutherland dist on edge of Oykel Forest 7m/11km SW of Lairg. NC 4900
Altcar, Great Lancs 41 H1 vil 2m/3km E of Formby. SD 3206
Altcar, Little Merseyside 41 H1 SE dist of Formby. SD 3006
Altgaltraig S'clyde 63 G1 loc in Argyll on E shore of Kyles of Bute, 1m SE of Colintraive. NS 0473
Altham Lancs 48 A5 vil 2m/3km W of Padiham. SD 7732
Alt Hill Gtr Manchester 43 E1* loc 2m/3km SE of Oldham. SD 9401
Althorne Essex 21 E2 vil 3m/5km NW of Burnham-on-Crouch. TQ 9199
Althorp Northants 28 C2 par and seat 5m/9km NW of Northampton. SP 6865
Althorpe Humberside 44 C1 vil on W bank of R Trent 4m/6km W of Scunthorpe. SE 8309
Altnabreac H'land 86 C3 loc and rly stn in Caithness dist 12m/19km SW of Halkirk. ND 0045
Altnaharra H'land 84 F4 vil in Caithness dist at W end of Loch Naver, 13m/22km S of Tongue. NC 5635
Altofts W Yorks 49 F5 loc 1m NW of Normanton. **Lr Altofts** loc adjoining to NE. SE 3723
Alton Derbys 43 H4 vil 2m/3km W of Clay Cross. SK 3664
Alton Hants 10 D1 tn 10m/16km SE of Basingstoke. Breweries. Hospital and school for disabled. Curtis Museum in main street – agricultural and domestic. SU 7139
Alton Staffs 35 G1 vil 4m/7km E of Cheadle. Remains of Norman cas beside R Churnet. To N across r, **A. Towers**, ruined 19c hse by Pugin. SK 0742
Alton Barnes Wilts 17 E5* vil adjoining Alton Priors to W and 4m/6km NW of Pewsey. SU 1062
Altonhill S'clyde 64 B5* N dist of Kilmarnock. NS 4239
Alton Pancras Dorset 9 E4 vil 2m/3km N of Piddletrenthide. ST 6902
Alton Priors Wilts 17 E5 vil adjoining Alton Barnes to E and 4m/6km NW of Pewsey. SU 1162
Altrincham Gtr Manchester 42 D3 tn 8m/13km SW of Manchester. Machine tools, printing machines. SJ 7687

Alturlie Point H'land 81 F3 headland in Inverness dist on S side of Inner Moray Firth or Inverness Firth, 4m/7km NE of Inverness. **Alturlie Bay** to E. NH 7149
Alum Bay Isle of Wight 10 A6 bay to NE of The Needles, noted for variegated sand. SZ 3085
Alum Pot N Yorks 48 B1* limestone cavern 1km W of Selside. SD 7875
Alum Rock W Midlands 35 G5* loc in Birmingham 4m/6km E of city centre. SP 1287
Alun 22 A3 r rising 4m/6km NE of St David's, Dyfed, and flowing SW by St David's into St Brides Bay 1m SW of vil. SM 7423
Alun 42 A5 r rising on N slopes of Maesyrychen Mt, N of Llangollen, Clwyd. It flows N to Rhyd-y-mwyn, then SE to Bradley, N of Wrexham, then NE by Gresford to Rossett, and finally E into R Dee 2m/4km E of Rossett. SJ 3956
Alva Central 72 C5 tn 3m/4km N of Alloa. Woollen and knitwear mnfg; coal-mining in vicinity. Waterfalls in **A. Glen** to N. NS 8896
Alvanley Ches 42 B4 vil 2km S of Helsby. SJ 4974
Alvaston Derbys 36 A1 dist of Derby 3m/4km SE of Derby. SK 3833
Alvechurch H & W 27 E1 vil 3m/5km N of Redditch. SP 0272
Alvecote Warwicks 35 H4* ham 3m/4km E of Tamworth. SK 2404
Alvediston Wilts 9 G2 vil 4m/7km W of Broad Chalke. ST 9723
Alveley Salop 34 D5 vil 6m/10km SE of Bridgnorth. SO 7684
Alverdiscott Devon 6 D3 ham 4m/7km E of Bideford. SS 5225
Alverstoke Hants 10 C5 S dist of Gosport. SZ 6098
Alverstone Isle of Wight 10 C6 vil 2m/3km NW of Sandown. SZ 5785
Alverthorpe W Yorks 49 E5* dist of Wakefield 2m/3km NW of city centre. SE 3021
Alverton Notts 44 C6 ham 7m/12km S of Newark-on-Trent. SK 7942
Alves Grampian 82 A1 loc including that of Crook of Alves, 5m/9km W of Elgin. NJ 1362
Alvescot Oxon 17 G1 vil 5m/8km NE of Lechlade. SP 2704
Alveston Avon 16 B3 vil 2km S of Thornbury. ST 6388
Alveston Warwicks 27 F2 vil 2m/4km E of Stratford-upon-Avon. SP 2356
Alvie H'land 75 H1 locality in Badenoch and Strathspey dist, on shore of Loch A., 3m/4km SW of Aviemore. NH 8609
Alvingham Lincs 45 G2 vil 3m/5km NE of Louth. TF 3691
Alvington Glos 16 B2 vil 2m/4km SW of Lydney. SO 6000
Alvington, West Devon 4 D6 vil 1km W of Kingsbridge. SX 7243
Alwalton Cambs 37 F5 vil 4m/7km SW of Peterborough. Manor hse of *c.* 1700. East of England Showground to E. TL 1395
Alway Gwent 15 H3* loc in Newport 2m/3km E of tn centre. ST 3488
Alwen 41 F6/G6 r rising in Llyn Alwen, Clwyd, and running E into Alwen Resr, then SE into R Dee 2km SW of Corwen. SJ 0642
Alwen Reservoir Clwyd 41 F5, F6 large resr 3m/4km N of Cerrigydrudion. SH 9552
Alwhat 56 F3 mt on border of Strathclyde and Dumfries & Galloway regions 1m S of Afton Resr. Height 2063 ft or 629 metres. NS 6402
Alwin 61 E1 r rising near Cushat Law in the Cheviot Hills, Nthmb, and flowing S into R Coquet at Low Alwinton, near Alwinton. NT 9205
Alwington Devon 6 C3* loc 4m/6km SW of Bideford. SS 4023
Alwinton Nthmb 61 E1 vil in Upr Coquetdale 9m/14km W of Rothbury. Loc of **Low Alwinton** to S beside R Coquet. NT 9206
Alwoodley W Yorks 49 E4* dist of Leeds 4m/7km N of city centre. **A. Gates** loc 2km E. **A. Old Hall,** gabled 17c hse on S side of Eccup Resr. SE 2940
Alyn and Deeside 116 admin dist of Clwyd.
Alyth Tayside 76 C6 small tn 5m/8km NE of Blairgowrie. NO 2448
Amalebra Cornwall 2 B4 loc 3m/5km SW of St Ives. SW 4936
Aman Welsh form of Amman (r) qv.
Amat Forest H'land 85 E7 deer forest at head of Strath Carron 8m/13km W of Bonar Br. Woods on left bank of R Carron above its confluence with Abhainn an t-Strath Chuilionaich. NH 4690
Am Balg H'land 84 B2 group of islets 2km NW of Rubh' a' Bhuachaille, headland on NW coast of Sutherland dist. NC 1866
Ambaston Derbys 36 A1/A2* ham 2km E of Elvaston. SK 4232
Amber 43 H5* r rising SW of Chesterfield, Derbys, and flowing S into R Derwent at Ambergate. SK 3451
Ambergate Derbys 43 H5 loc 3m/4km N of Belper. SK 3451
Amber Hill Lincs 45 F6 loc 6m/10km W of Boston. TF 2346
Amberley Glos 16 D2* vil 2km N of Nailsworth. SO 8501
Amberley W Sussex 11 F4 vil 4m/6km N of Arundel. Medieval cas. TQ 0313
Amber Row Derbys 43 H5* loc 1km NE of S Wingfield. SK 3856
Ambersham, South W Sussex 11 E3 ham 2m/3km E of Midhurst. SU 9120
Amberstone E Sussex 12 C5 loc adjoining Hailsham to N. TQ 5911
Amber Valley 117 admin dist of Derbys.
Amble Nthmb 61 G2 small tn on S side of R Coquet estuary 7m/12km SE of Alnwick. NU 2604
Amblecote W Midlands 35 E5 N dist of Stourbridge. SO 8985
Ambler Thorn W Yorks 48 D5* vil 3m/4km N of Halifax. SE 0929
Ambleside Cumbria 52 D4 small tn and holiday centre in Lake Dist 4m/7km NW of Windermere. NY 3704
Ambleston (Treamlod) Dyfed 22 C3 vil 7m/11km NE of Haverfordwest. SN 0025
Am Bodach H'land 74 C5* mt on Mamore Forest in Lochaber dist, 2m/3km N of Kinlochleven. Height 3391 ft or 1034 metres. NN 1765
Ambrosden Oxon 28 B5 vil 2m/4km SE of Bicester. SP 6019
Amcotts Humberside 50 D6 vil on W bank of R Trent 5m/8km E of Crowle. SE 8514
Amen Corner Berks 18 C4* loc 2m/3km E of Wokingham. SU 8469
America Salop 34 B3* loc 2m/3km NW of Shrawardine. SJ 3716
Amersham Bucks 18 D2 tn 3m/4km S of Chesham. SU 9597
Amersham on the Hill Bucks 18 D2* loc 1km N of Amersham. SU 9698
Amerton Staffs 35 F2* loc 5m/9km NE of Stafford. SJ 9927
Amesbury Wilts 9 H1 tn on R Avon at SE corner of Salisbury Plain, 7m/11km N of Salisbury. Army camps and training areas to N. 1m W, loc of W Amesbury. 2m/3km W, Stonehenge, Neolithic – Bronze Age earthwork and stone circle (A.M.). SU 1541
Ameysford Dorset 9 G4* loc 1m SW of W Moors. SU 0702
Am Faochagach H'land 85 D8* mt in Ross and Cromarty dist 3m/5km W of head of Loch Vaich. Height 3130 ft or 954 metres. NH 3079
Am Fiar Loch H'land 80 C3 small loch in course of R Orrin, Ross and Cromarty dist, 5m/8km W of head of Orrin Resr. NH 2446
Am Fraoch Eilean S'clyde 62 C2 offshore island at S end of Jura, at entrance to Sound of Islay. NR 4662
Amhainn a' Ghlinne H'land 68 E4* r in Lochaber dist, running W to R Aline 4m/6km N of Lochaline. NM 6950
Amhainn a' Ghlinne Bhig H'land 79 F6* r in Lochaber dist running W into Sound of Sleat 1m SW of Glenelg. NG 8018
Amhainn Inbhir Ghuiserein H'land. See Glen Guseran.
Amhainn Rath H'land 74 D4* r in Lochaber dist running E to head of Loch Treig. NN 3168
A' Mhòine H'land 84 E2 upland tract on borders of Caithness and Sutherland dists between Kyle of Tongue and Loch Eriboll. NC 56
Amhuinn Mhór Ceann Resort W Isles 88 A2* r rising in Forest of Harris and flowing N into head of Loch Resort. NB 1017
Amhuinnsuidhe W Isles 88 A3* loc on coast of Harris on N side of W Loch Tarbert 2m/3km E of Govick. NB 0408
Amington Staffs 35 H4 loc 2m/3km E of Tamworth. SK 2304
Amisfield Town D & G 59 E3 vil 5m/7km NE of Dumfries. **Amisfield Tower,** 1m NW, is well-preserved stronghold of *c.* 1600. NY 0082
Amlwch Gwynedd 40 B2 small port on N coast of Anglesey 15m/24km NW of Menai Br. Loc of **Amlwch Port** E of tn centre. Plant for extracting bromine from sea water. SH 4492
Amman (Aman) 23 G4 r rising on Black Mt, Dyfed, as two streams, **Aman Fawr** and **Aman Fach** which join 1m NE of Rhosaman and then flow W into R Loughor on S side of Ammanford. SN 6210
Ammanford (Rhydaman) Dyfed 23 G4 tn on edge of S Wales coalfield 12m/20km N of Swansea. Coal-mining, hosiery, furniture, precision tools. SN 6212
Amotherby N Yorks 50 C1 vil 3m/4km NW of Malton. SE 7473
Ampfield Hants 10 B3 vil 3m/5km E of Romsey. SU 4023
Ample Burn Central. See Burn of Ample.
Ampleforth N Yorks 50 B1 vil 10m/16km E of Thirsk. RC boarding school for boys 1m E. SE 5878
Ampney Crucis Glos 17 E2 vil 3m/4km E of Cirencester. SP 0601
Ampney St Mary Glos 17 E2 vil 4m/7km E of Cirencester. SP 0802
Ampney St Peter Glos 17 E2 vil 4m/6km E of Cirencester. SP 0801
Amport Hants 10 A1 vil 4m/7km W of Andover. SU 2944
Ampthill Beds 29 E4 tn 8m/12km S of Bedford. Houghton Hse, ruined 16c hse (A.M.) 1m N. TL 0338
Ampton Suffolk 30 D1 vil 4m/7km N of Bury St Edmunds. TL 8671
Amroth Dyfed 22 D5 vil on Saundersfoot Bay 2m/4km NE of Saundersfoot. **A. Castle** has 14c gateway. Submerged forest visible at low tide. SN 1607
Amulree Tayside 72 C1 vil on R Quaich 9m/14km SW of Dunkeld. NN 9036
Amwell, Great Herts 20 A1 vil 2km SE of Ware. TL 3612
Amwell, Little Herts 20 A1 vil 2m/3km S of Ware. TL 3511
Anafon 40 D4 r rising S of Llyn Anafon, Gwynedd, and running through the tarn then NW into R Rhaeadr Fawr 2m/3km SW of Llanfairfechan. SH 6671
An Caisteal Central 71 E3* mt 4m/6km S of Crianlarich. Height 3265 ft or 995 metres. NN 3719
An Caisteal H'land 84 F3* summit of Ben Loyal, Caithness dist. Height 2506 ft or 764 metres. NC 5748
Ancaster Lincs 37 E1 vil 5m/9km W of Sleaford, on site of Roman tn of *Causennae.* Airfield on Barkston Heath to SW. SK 9843
Ancholme 51 E6 r rising near Spridlington, Lincs, and flowing N into R Humber at Ferriby Sluice. From Bishopbridge the New R Ancholme has been artificially created and follows a straight course, almost entirely separate from the mostly circuitous course of the Old R. SE 9721
Anchor Salop 33 H5 ham 6m/10km SE of Newcastle. SO 1785
Anchor Corner Norfolk 39 E5* loc 3m/5km NW of Attleborough. TM 0098
Anchorsholme Lancs 46 D4/47 E4* loc on W side of Thornton. SD 3342
Anchor Street Norfolk 39 G3* loc 4m/7km SE of N Walsham. TG 3124
Ancoats Gtr Manchester 42 D2* dist of Manchester 1m E of city centre. SJ 8598
An Coileachan H'land 80 C1 mt in Ross and Cromarty dist 2m/3km NW of lower end of Loch Fannich. Height 3027 ft or 923 metres. NH 2468
Ancroft Nthmb 67 F4 ham 5m/8km S of Berwick-upon-Tweed. NU 0045
Ancrum Borders 66 D6 vil 3m/5km NW of Jedburgh. On **A. Moor** to N is site of battle of 1545 in which Scots defeated English. NT 6224
Ancton W Sussex 11 F5* loc in Middleton-on-Sea, 3m/5km E of Bognor Regis. SU 9800
Anderby Lincs 45 H4 vil 4m/7km E of Alford. **A. Creek** on coast at outfall of stream known as Main Drain. TF 5275
Anderita E Sussex. See Pevensey.
Andersea Som 8 B1* loc 3m/5km SE of Bridgwater. ST 3333
Andersfield Som 8 B1* loc 1km W of Goathurst and 4m/6km SW of Bridgwater. ST 2434
Anderson Dorset 9 F4 ham 3m/4km NE of Bere Regis. SY 8897
Anderton Ches 42 C4* loc 2km NW of Northwich. Boat lift forms junction between R Weaver and Trent and Mersey Canal. SJ 6475
Andover Hants 10 B1 tn on R Anton 13m/21km NW of Winchester. New tn development. SU 3645
Andoversford Glos 27 E5 vil 5m/8km E of Cheltenham. SP 0219
Andreas Isle of Man 46 B3 vil 4m/7km NW of Ramsey. SC 4199
An Dubh-sgeir H'land 84 E2* rock island on E side of Eilean Hoan at mouth of Loch Eriboll, N coast of Sutherland dist. NC 4568
An Dubh-sgeir S'clyde 62 D3* group of rocks nearly 1km N of N end of island of Gigha. NR 6655
An Dubh-sgeir Skye, H'land 79 B6 island rock nearly 1km off SW coast at S side of entrance to Loch Eynort. NG 3422
An Dun 75 G3* mt on border of Highland and Tayside regions 6m/10km SE of Dalwhinnie. Height 2707 ft or 825 metres. NN 7180
Anerley London 19 G4* loc in borough of Bromley 2km S of Crystal Palace. TQ 3469
Anfield Merseyside 42 A2* dist of Liverpool 3m/4km NE of city centre. SJ 3793
An Garbh-eilean H'land 84 D1 islet lying off Cleit Dhubh, headland on N coast of Sutherland dist 4m/7km E of Cape Wrath. Also known as Garve I. NC 3373
Angarrack Cornwall 2 B4 vil 2m/3km E of Hayle. SW 5838
Angarrick Cornwall 2 D4* loc 2m/3km N of Penryn. SW 7937
An Gearanach H'land 74 C4* mt in Lochaber dist, on Mamore Forest 3m/5km N of Kinlochleven. Height 3230 ft or 985 metres. **An Garbhanach** is peak along ridge to S, 3206 ft or 977 metres. NN 1867
Angelbank Salop 34 C6 ham 4m/6km E of Ludlow. SO 5776
Angel Corner Suffolk. See Bury St Edmunds.
Angell 33 F3* r running SE through Dovey Forest into R Dovey at Aberangell, Gwynedd. For the last part of its course it marks border between Gwynedd and Powys. SH 8409
Angell Town London 19 G4* loc in borough of Lambeth 3m/4km S of Charing Cross. TQ 3176
Angersleigh Som 8 A3 ham 4m/6km SE of Wellington. ST 1919
Angerton Cumbria 59 G5 loc adjoining Kirkbride to N. NY 2257
Angerton, High Nthmb 61 F3* loc just S of Hartburn. **A. Hall,** 1823. NZ 0985
Angerton, Low Nthmb 61 F3* loc 1km S of High Angerton. NZ 0984
Angle Dyfed 22 B5 fishing vil at W end of **Angle Bay** on S side of Milford Haven. 1m W across peninsula is **W Angle Bay,** at entrance to Milford Haven. **Angle Pt** is headland on W side of entrance to Angle Bay. SM 8602
Anglesey (Môn) Gwynedd 40 island, known to the Romans as *Mona,* about 26m/42km E to W and 21m/33km N to S, off NW coast of Welsh mainland, separated from it by Menai Strait. To W of main island lies Holy I., qv, which administratively forms part of Anglesey and on which Holyhead, the principal tn, is situated. Anglesey is connected to Welsh mainland, and Holy I. to main island, by rd and rly brs. SH 47
Anglesey Hants 10 C5* S dist of Gosport. SZ 6098
Anglesey Abbey Cambs. See Lode.
Angle Tarn Cumbria 52 C4* small lake 1km N of Bow Fell. NY 2407
Angle Tarn Cumbria 52 D3 small lake 2m/3km SE of Patterdale. NY 4114
Anglezarke Lancs 47 G6* moorland par N of Horwich. **Anglezarke Resr** 2m/3km NW of Horwich. SD 6217
Angmering W Sussex 11 F4 built-up area 3m/5km NE of Littlehampton. 2m/3km S is resort of **Angmering-on-Sea.** TQ 0604
An Gorm-loch H'land 80 C3 small loch on E Monar Forest, Ross and Cromarty dist. NH 2244
Angram N Yorks 49 G3 ham 4m/6km NE of Tadcaster. SE 5148
Angram N Yorks 53 G5 loc 2m/3km NW of Muker. SD 8899

Angram Grange N Yorks 50 A1* loc 2km N of Husthwaite. SE 5176

Angram Reservoir N Yorks 48 C1 resr near source of R Nidd 10m/16km NW of Pateley Br. SE 0476

Angus 115 admin dist of Tayside region.

Angus Folk Museum Tayside. See Glamis.

Anick Nthmb 61 E5* loc 2km NE of Hexham. NY 9565

Anker 35 G4 r rising near Wolvey, Warwicks, and flowing NW into R Tame at Tamworth, Staffs. SK 2003

Ankerville H'land 87 B8 loc in Ross and Cromarty dist 3m/5km W of Balintore on E coast. Loc of **A. Corner** adjoins to E. NH 8174

Ankle Hill Leics 36 C3* loc in Melton Mowbray 1km S of tn centre. SK 7518

Anlaby Humberside 51 E5 suburb 4m/7km W of Hull. TA 0328

Anmer Norfolk 38 C2 vil 10m/15km NE of King's Lynn. TF 7429

Anmore Hants 10 D4* ham 1km E of Denmead and 3m/4km W of Horndean. SU 6711

Annan D & G 59 G4 tn near mouth of R Annan, 15m/24km E of Dumfries, and the same distance NW of Carlisle across Solway Firth. Industries include engineering, fishing, hosiery and woollens. R rises on Devil's Beef Tub, N of Moffat, and flows S past Moffat, Lochmaben, and Annan, to Solway Firth 2km S of Annan. NY 1966

Annandale and Eskdale 116 admin dist of D & G region.

Annaside Cumbria 52 B6 loc 2km SW of Bootle. SD 0986

Annat H'land 74 C4 locality at head of Loch Linnhe, 2m/4km NW of Fort William across head of loch. Pulp mill. NN 0877

Annat H'land 80 A2 at head of Upr Loch Torridon, Ross and Cromarty dist, 1m S of Torridon. NG 8954

Annat Bay H'land 85 A7, B7 gently curving bay on SW side of entrance to Loch Broom on W coast of Ross and Cromarty dist. NH 0496

Annathill S'clyde 64 D2* loc 3m/5km N of Coatbridge. NS 7270

Anna Valley Hants 10 B1* vil 2m/3km SW of Andover. SU 3443

Annbank S'clyde 64 B6 vil in colliery dist 5m/7km E of Ayr. **Annbank Stn** is vil 1m N. NS 4023

Anne Hathaway's Cottage Warwicks. See Shottery.

Annell 24 C4 r rising at NE corner of Dolaucothi Estate, NE of Pumsaint, Dyfed, and flowing SW into R Cothi 2m/3km E of Llansawel. SN 6435

Annesley Woodhouse Notts 44 A5 loc 2m/3km S of Kirkby in Ashfield. SK 4953

Annet Isles of Scilly 2 A1 second largest of the uninhabited islands, lying W of St Agnes. SV 8608

Annfield Plain Durham 61 F6 tn 2m/3km SW of Stanley. Coal-mining, brick mnfre. NZ 1751

Annick Water 64 B5 r in Strathclyde region running SW past Stewarton to R Irvine on S side of tn of Irvine. Also gives its name to a dist of Irvine New Tn through which it flows, 2km E of original tn. NS 3237

Anniesland S'clyde 64 C2* loc in Glasgow 4m/6km NW of city centre. NS 5468

Annitsford Tyne & Wear 61 G4* loc 6m/10km N of Newcastle. NZ 2674

Ann, Little Hants 10 A1* loc 2m/3km SW of Andover. SU 3343

Annscroft Salop 34 B3 loc 4m/6km SW of Shrewsbury. SJ 4507

An Riabhachan H'land 80 B4 mt mass in Skye and Lochalsh dist N of N Lungard or head of Loch Mullardoch. Summit 3702 ft or 1129 metres. NH 1334

An Ruadh-stac H'land 80 A3 peak on Ben-damph Forest, Ross and Cromarty dist, 4m/6km N of head of Loch Carron. Height 2919 ft or 890 metres. NG 9248

An Rubha S'clyde 69 C7* headland on W coast of Colonsay 3m/4km W of Scalasaig. NR 3595

Ansdell Lancs 47 E5 dist of Lytham St Anne's N of tn centre. SD 3428

Ansford Som 8 D1 vil adjoining Castle Cary to N. ST 6333

An Sgarsoch 76 A3 mt on border of Grampian and Tayside regions 12m/19km N of Blair Atholl. Height 3300 ft or 1006 metres. NN 9383

An Sgurr H'land 68 C1 basaltic peak on island of Eigg, 1291 ft or 393 metres. Highest point on island. Also known as Scuir of Eigg. NM 4684

An Sidhean H'land 80 C3* mt on E Monar Forest, Ross and Cromarty dist. Height 2661 ft or 811 metres. NH 1745

Ansley Warwicks 35 H5 vil 4m/6km W of Nuneaton. SP 2991

Anslow Staffs 35 H2 vil 2m/3km NW of Burton upon Trent. **A. Gate** ham 1m W. **A. Leys** loc 1km SW. SK 2125

An Socach Grampian 76 B3 mt ridge 6m/9km S of Inverey. Summit 3097 ft or 944 metres. NO 0879

An Stac H'land 74 A3 peak in Lochaber dist 1km S of head of Loch Morar. Height 2350 ft or 716 metres. NM 8688

Ansteadbrook Surrey 11 F2* loc 2m/3km E of Haslemere. SU 9332

Anstey Herts 29 G4 vil 4m/6km NE of Buntingford. TL 4033

Anstey Leics 36 B3 vil 4m/6km NW of Leicester. SK 5408

Anstey, East Devon 7 F3 vil on S edge of Exmoor 3m/5km SW of Dulverton. SS 8626

Anstey, West Devon 7 F3 vil on S slopes of Exmoor 4m/6km W of Dulverton. SS 8527

Anston, North S Yorks 44 A3 vil 5m/8km NW of Worksop. **S Anston** vil adjoining to S. SK 5284

Anstruther Fife 73 H4 resort and fishing port on Firth of Forth 9m/14km SE of St Andrews. Consists of adjoining tns of **A. Easter** and **A. Wester** (see also Kilrenny). Industries include mnfre of oilskins and woollen goods. Formerly port for herring fishing industry. Scottish Fisheries Museum. NO 5603

Ansty Dorset 9 E4 hams of **Hr** and **Lr Ansty** and locs of **Lit Ansty** and **Ansty Cross**, all in par of Hilton 6m/10km N of Puddletown. ST 7603

Ansty Warwicks 36 A5 vil 5m/8km NE of Coventry. SP 3983

Ansty Wilts 9 F2 vil 2m/3km S of Tisbury. ST 9526

Ansty W Sussex 11 H3 vil 2km SW of Cuckfield. TQ 2923

Ansty Coombe Wilts 9 F2* ham adjoining Ansty and 2m/3km S of Tisbury. ST 9526

Ant 39 G3 r rising at Antingham, Norfolk, and flowing S through Barton Broad to R Bure 2m/3km E of Horning. TG 3716

An Teallach H'land 85 B7 mt in W part of Ross and Cromarty dist 3m/4km SW of Lit Loch Broom. Height 3483 ft or 1062 metres. NH 0684

An t-Eilean Meadhoin H'land 79 E8* wooded islet in Loch Morar, Lochaber dist, 1m E of dam. NM 7092

Antermony Loch S'clyde 64 D2* small loch 2m/3km NE of Kirkintilloch. NS 6676

Anthill Common Hants 10 D3* loc 2km S of Hambledon. SU 6412

Anthorn Cumbria 59 G5 ham on N shore of R Wampool estuary 3m/4km W of Kirkbride across r. NY 1958

Antingham Norfolk 39 F2 vil 3m/4km NW of N Walsham. TG 2532

Anton 10 B1* r in Hampshire rising 1m S of Enham Alamein and flowing S through Andover and into R Test 3m/5km NE of Stockbridge. SU 3838

Anton, East Hants 10 B1* loc 2m/3km N of Andover. SU 3747

Antonine Wall 64 C2-65 F1 Roman fortification dating from 1c, now only intermittently visible, extending 37m/60km from Old Kirkpatrick on N bank of R Clyde to Carriden, E of Bo'ness on S bank of R Forth.

Antony Cornwall 3 H3 vil 3m/4km W of Torpoint. Antony Hse (NT), 18c, to NE with grounds running down to St Germans R. SX 3954

Antrobus Ches 42 C3* ham 2m/3km NW of Gt Budworth. SJ 6479

Anvil Green Kent 13 F2* loc 6m/9km SW of Canterbury. TR 1049

Anwick Lincs 45 E6 vil 4m/7km NE of Sleaford. TF 1150

Anwoth D & G 58 B5 vil 1m W of Gatehouse of Fleet. 8c cross in churchyard of former, ruined, ch. NX 5856

Aonach air Chrith H'land 74 B1 peak towards E end of Maol Chinn-dearg, qv, and summit of the ridge, on border of Lochaber and Skye & Lochalsh dists. Height 3350 ft or 1021 metres. NH 0508

Aonach Beag H'land 74 C4 mt in Lochaber dist 2m/3km E of Ben Nevis. Height 4054 ft or 1236 metres. Aonach Mór, 1m along ridge to N, 3999 ft or 1219 metres. NN 1971

Aonach Beag H'land 75 E4* mt in Badenoch and Strathspey dist 2m/3km W of Loch An Sgòir. Height 3656 ft or 1114 metres. NN 4574

Aonach Buidhe H'land 80 B4 mt on Killilan Forest, Skye and Lochalsh dist. Height 2949 ft or 899 metres. NH 0532

Aonach Dubh H'land. See Three Sisters of Glen Coe.

Aonach Eagach H'land 74 C5 mt ridge on N side of Glen Coe. Summit is Sgorr nam Fiannaidh at W end of ridge; height 3173 ft or 967 metres. NN 1458

Aonach Mór H'land. See Aonach Beag.

Aonach Mór S'clyde 70 D1 mt ridge in Argyll to W of Clach Leathad. Summit 2839 ft or 865 metres. NN 2247

Aonach Shasuinn H'land 80 C5 mt in Inverness dist 5m/8km N of dam of Loch Cluanie. Height 2901 ft or 884 metres. NH 1718

Ape Dale Salop 34 B5* valley on W side of Wenlock Edge watered by Byne Brook, NE of Craven Arms. SO 4889

Apes Dale H & W 27 E1 loc 3m/4km NE of Bromsgrove. SO 9972

Apethorpe Northants 37 E5 vil 4m/6km SW of Wansford. Site of Roman villa in park of mainly 16c and 17c hall. TL 0295

Apeton Staffs 35 E3* loc 1km NE of Ch Eaton. SJ 8518

Apley Lincs 45 E4 vil 2m/4km SW of Wragby. TF 1075

Apperknowle Derbys 43 H3 vil 2m/3km E of Dronfield. SK 3878

Apperley Glos 26 D4 vil 7m/11km NW of Cheltenham. SO 8628

Apperley Bridge W Yorks 48 D4* loc on R Aire in NE part of Bradford. SE 1937

Apperley Dene Nthmb 61 F5* loc 4m/6km NW of Ebchester. Site of small Roman fort to S. NZ 0558

Apperley, Lower Glos 26 D5 ham 6m/9km NE of Gloucester. SO 8627

Appersett N Yorks 53 G5 loc at confluence of Widdale Beck and R Ure 1m NW of Hawes. SD 8590

Appin 74 B6-C5 mountainous area bounded by Loch Linnhe, Glen Creran, and Glen Coe, partly in Strathclyde and partly in Highland region. See also Strath of Appin. NN 05

Appin of Dull Tayside. See Strath of Appin.

Appleby Cumbria 53 F3 small tn on R Eden 12m/19km SE of Penrith. Cas with 12c keep. NY 6820

Appleby Humberside 50 D6 vil 5m/8km NE of Scunthorpe. SE 9514

Appleby Som 7 H3 ham 4m/7km W of Wellington. ST 0721

Appleby Magna Leics 35 H3 vil 5m/8km SW of Ashby de la Zouch. **Appleby Parva** vil 1km SW. SK 3109

Appleby Street Herts 19 G2* loc 2m/4km NW of Cheshunt. TL 3304

Applecross H'land 78 E4 vil at S end of **A. Bay** on W coast of Ross and Cromarty dist, opp Raasay across Inner Sound. **R Applecross** runs SW into bay. **A. Forest** is deer forest to E. NG 7144

Appledore Devon 6 D2 large vil on W side of R Torridge estuary at its confluence with R Taw 3m/4km N of Bideford. Ferry for pedestrians to Instow. SS 4630

Appledore Devon 7 H4 ham 7m/11km SW of W Wellington. ST 0614

Appledore Kent 13 E4 vil on W side of Romney Marsh 5m/8km SE of Tenterden. Loc of **A. Heath** adjoins it to N. TQ 9529

Appledram W Sussex. See Apuldram.

Appleford Oxon 18 A2 vil 2m/4km N of Didcot. SU 5293

Applegarth Town D & G 59 F3 loc 3m/4km NW of Lockerbie. NY 1084

Appleshaw Hants 17 G6 vil 4m/7km NW of Andover. SU 3048

Applethwaite Cumbria 52 C3 loc 2km N of Keswick. NY 2625

Appleton Ches 42 B3 dist of Widnes 1m N of tn centre. SJ 5186

Appleton Ches 42 C3 vil in SE part of Warrington. **Appleton Resr**, small resr 2m/4km W. SJ 6383

Appleton Norfolk 38 C2* loc 2km SE of Sandringham. Site of Roman villa 1km E. TF 7027

Appleton Oxon 17 H2 vil 4m/7km NW of Abingdon. SP 4401

Appleton, East N Yorks 54 B5 ham 2km S of Catterick. SE 2395

Appleton-le-Moors N Yorks 55 F6 vil 5m/7km NW of Pickering. SE 7387

Appleton-le-Street N Yorks 50 C1 vil 4m/6km W of Malton. SE 7373

Appleton Roebuck N Yorks 49 G4 vil 4m/7km E of Tadcaster. SE 5542

Appleton, West N Yorks 54 B5* ham 3m/4km SW of Catterick. SE 2294

Appleton Wiske N Yorks 54 C4 vil 6m/9km SW of Yarm. NZ 3904

Appletreehall Borders 66 C6* loc 2m/4km NE of Hawick. NT 5117

Appletreewick N Yorks 48 C2 vil in Wharfedale 2m/3km SE of Burnsall. SE 0560

Appley Isle of Wight 10 C5* loc on NE coast adjoining Ryde to E. SZ 6092

Appley Bridge Lancs 42 B1* loc 2km NW of Shevington. SD 5209

Appuldurcombe House Isle of Wight 10 C6 ruined early 18c home (A.M.) of Worsley family. SZ 5480

Apse Heath Isle of Wight 10 C6* vil 2m/3km W of Sandown. SZ 5683

Apsey Green Suffolk 31 G2* loc 1km W of Framlingham. TM 2763

Apsley Herts 19 E1 S dist of Hemel Hempstead. Partly industrial. TL 0605

Apsley End Beds 29 F4 ham 5m/8km NW of Hitchin. TL 1233

Apuldram W Sussex 11 E4 vil 2km SW of Chichester. Medieval manor hse. Name of vil sometimes spelt Appledram. SU 8403

Aquae Arnemetiae Derbys. See Buxton.

Aquae Sulis Avon. See Bath.

Aqualate Mere Staffs 34 D3 large lake in park 2m/3km NE of Newport. SJ 7720

Aquhorthies, East Grampian. See Easter Aquhorthies.

Aquhythie Grampian 83 F5* loc 2m/3km N of Kemnay. NJ 7418

Arabella H'land 87 B8* loc in Ross and Cromarty dist 4m/7km S of Tain. NH 8075

Aran 25 F2 r rising about 4m/6km NE of Llanbister, Powys, and flowing S into R Ithon nearly 1m N of Penybont. SO 1165

Aray S'clyde 70 C4 r in Argyll running S down Glen Aray to Loch Fyne at Inveraray. NN 0908

Arbeadie Grampian 77 F2* loc adjoining Banchory to NE. NO 7096

Arberth Welsh form of Narberth, qv.

Arberth 22 D2 r rising 2km S of Aberporth, Dyfed, and flowing S into R Teifi at Llechryd. SN 2143

Arbigland D & G 59 E5 loc on Solway Firth 2km SE of Kirkbean. Birthplace of John Paul, later known as Paul Jones, 1747-92, founder of the American navy. NX 9857

Arbirlot Tayside 77 F6 vil 3m/4km W of Arbroath. To SE is Kellie Castle, 16c and earlier, former seat of the Auchterlonies. NO 6040

Arborfield Berks 18 C4 vil 5m/7km SE of Reading. 1km SE, vil of **A. Cross.** SU 7567

Arbor Low Derbys 43 F4 ancient stone circle (A.M.) 3m/5km W of Youlgreave. SK 1663

Arbourthorne S Yorks 43 H3* loc in Sheffield 2m/3km SE of city centre. SK 3784

Arbroath Tayside 73 H1 industrial tn, port with small harbour, and resort, 15m/25km NE of Dundee. Engineering, fishing, jute and linen mnfre, boat-building. Smoked haddock ('smokies') a speciality. Remains (A.M.) of 12c abbey. NO 6440

Arbury Ches 42 B2* loc 1km E of Winwick. SJ 6192

Arbury Warwicks 35 H5 17c-18c Gothic Revival mansion in park, 2m/4km SW of Nuneaton. SP 3389

Arbuthnott Grampian 77 G3 vil 2m/4km NW of Inverbervie. NO 8074

Arcadia Kent 13 E3 loc 2m/3km N of Tenterden. TQ 8736
Archdeacon Newton Durham 54 B3 ham on site of former vil 3m/4km NW of Darlington. NZ 2517
Archiestown Grampian 82 B3 vil 4m/6km W of Craigellachie. NJ 2344
Arcuil H'land. Gaelic form of Arkle, qv.
Ardachadail H'land 85 B6/B7 locality on NE shore of Loch Broom 3m/5km NW of Ullapool. NH 0997
Ardalanish S'clyde 69 C6 loc on Ross of Mull 2m/3km S of Bunessan, a short distance inland from **A. Bay** on S coast. **Ardalanish Pt** (or Rubh' Ardalanish) is headland 2km S of bay. NM 3719
Ard a' Mhòrain W Isles 88 E1* promontory on N coast of N Uist reaching to within 1m of island of Boreray. NF 8379
Ardarroch H'land 79 F5* locality in Ross and Cromarty dist at head of Loch Kishorn. NG 8339
Ardbeg S'clyde 62 B3 small fishing vil on S coast of Islay 3m/5km E of Port Ellen. Distillery. NR 4146
Ardbeg S'clyde 70 D6 locality in Argyll at head of Holy Loch. NS 1583
Ardbeg Point S'clyde 63 G1 headland on E coast of Bute between Kames Bay to N and Rothesay Bay to S. Loc of **Ardbeg** to S forms part of Port Bannatyne, large vil and resort extending along coast on both sides of headland. NS 0867
Ardcharnich H'land 85 B7 locality in Ross and Cromarty dist on E side of Loch Broom, 5m/7km SE of Ullapool. NH 1888
Ardchattan Priory S'clyde 70 B2 13c ruin (A.M.) on N side of Loch Etive, Argyll, opp Airds Pt. NM 9835
Ardchonnell Castle S'clyde. See Innis Chonnell.
Ardchronie, Upper H'land 85 F7 loc on S shore of Dornoch Firth 2km SE of Ardgay, Sutherland dist. NH 6188
Ardchyle Central 71 F2 loc in Glen Dochart 4m/7km SW of Killin. NN 5229
Ardclach Bell Tower Grampian 81 H3 fortified 17c belfry (A.M.) above R Findhorn, 8m/13km SE of Nairn. NH 9545
Ardd-lin Powys 34 A3* ham 6m/9km NE of Welshpool. SJ 2515
Ardeer S'clyde 64 A4/A5* loc adjoining Stevenston to SE. Mnfre of chemicals and explosives. NS 2740
Ardeley Herts 29 G5 vil 5m/8km E of Stevenage. TL 3027
Ardelve H'land 79 F6 locality on N side of Loch Alsh, Skye and Lochalsh dist, 1km W of Dornie across entrance to Loch Long. **Ardelve Pt** is promontory opp Dornie. NG 8726
Ardens Grafton Warwicks 27 F2* vil 5m/9km W of Stratford-upon-Avon. SP 1154
Ardentinny S'clyde 70 D5/D6 vil on W shore of Loch Long 4m/7km N of Strone Pt. NS 1887
Ardeonaig Central 71 G2 vil on S side of Loch Tay 6m/10km NE of Killin. NN 6635
Ardersier H'land 81 G2 vil in Inverness dist on E shore of Inner Moray Firth or Inverness Firth 2m/3km SE of Fort George. Formerly known as Campbelltown. NH 7855
Ardessie H'land 85 A7 loc in Ross and Cromarty dist on S shore of Lit Loch Broom, 5m/8km SE of Badluchrach. **A. Falls,** high waterfall to S. NH 0589
Ardestie Tayside 73 G1/G2* loc 2km N of Monifieth. Ancient souterrain or earth-house (A.M.). NO 5034
Ard Fada S'clyde 69 C5* headland on S side of Loch Scridain 5m/7km E of Bunessan, Mull. NM 4424
Ardfern S'clyde 70 A4 locality on W side of Loch Craignish in Argyll 2km SW of head of loch. NM 8004
Ardgartan S'clyde 70 D4 locality on W shore of Loch Long at foot of Glen Croe in Argyll. **A. Forest** is state forest to N and S along side of loch, forming part of Argyll Forest Park. NN 2702
Ardgay H'land 85 F7 vil in Sutherland dist 1m SW of Bonar Br. Location of Bonar Br rly stn. NH 5990
Ard Ghunel Skye, H'land 79 E7* headland on E coast of Sleat peninsula 1km SE of Isle Ornsay. NG 7011
Ardgoil Estate S'clyde 70 D5 mountainous area between Loch Long and Loch Goil forming part of Argyll Forest Park. NN 2200
Ardgoil Forest S'clyde 70 D5* state forest running along E side of Loch Goil in Argyll. NS 2198
Ardgour H'land 74 A4-B5 area of Lochaber dist between Sunart and Loch Linnhe. NM 96
Ardhasaig W Isles 88 B3 loc on Harris 2m/4km NW of Tarbert. NB 1202
Ardheslaig H'land 78 F4 locality on SW side of Loch Torridon, Ross and Cromarty dist, 3m/4km NW of Shieldaig. NG 7856
Ardindrean H'land 85 B7 locality on W shore of Loch Broom, Ross and Cromarty dist, 2m/4km from head of loch. NH 1588
Ardingly W Sussex 11 H2 vil 4m/6km N of Haywards Heath. Agricultural showground to N. TQ 3429
Ardington Oxon 17 H3 vil 2m/4km E of Wantage. SU 4388
Ardington Wick Oxon 17 H3* loc 3m/4km NE of Wantage. SU 4389
Ardintigh Point H'land 79 F8 promontory on S shore of Loch Nevis, Lochaber dist, 1m NW of Tarbet. **A. Bay** is small bay on W side of point. NM 7793
Ardintoul Point H'land 79 F6 promontory on S shore of Loch Alsh, Skye and Lochalsh dist, 2m/3km E of entrance to Kyle Rhea. NG 8324
Ardivachar Point W Isles 88 D2 headland at NW corner of S Uist. Loc of **Ardivachar** to S. NF 7445
Ardlamont Point S'clyde 63 F2 headland in Argyll on N side of Sound of Bute, at junction of Kyles of Bute and Loch Fyne. **A. Bay** 2km NW. NR 9963
Ardlaw, Mid Grampian 83 G1 loc near N coast 4m/6km SW of Fraserburgh. NJ 9463
Ardle 76 C5 r in Tayside region running SE down Strath A. to join Black Water below Br of Cally and form R Ericht. NO 1451
Ardleigh Essex 31 E5 vil 5m/7km NE of Colchester. Ham of **A. Heath** 1km N. TM 0529
Ardleigh Green London 20 B3 loc in borough of Havering 2km E of Romford. TQ 5389
Ardler Tayside 76 C6 vil 3m/5km E of Coupar Angus. NO 2641
Ardley Oxon 28 A5 vil 4m/7km NW of Bicester. SP 5427
Ardley End Essex 20 B1 loc 3m/5km E of Sawbridgeworth. TL 5214
Ardlui S'clyde 71 E3 locality at head of Loch Lomond, on W shore. NN 3115
Ardlussa S'clyde 69 E8 loc on E coast of Jura nearly 1m NE of Inverlussa at mouth of Lussa R. Small bay and landing stage. NR 6487
Ardmaddy S'clyde 70 C2 hse and bay on E side of Loch Etive, Argyll, 5m/9km from head of loch. NN 0737
Ardmaddy Castle S'clyde 70 A3 ancient seat of Marquess of Breadalbane, on **A. Bay,** Seil Sound, 4m/7km SW of Kilninver in Argyll. NM 7816
Ardmair H'land 85 B6 loc on W coast of Ross and Cromarty dist 3m/5km NW of Ullapool. NH 1198
Ardmaleish Point S'clyde 63 G1 headland on Bute at entrance to E arm of Kyles of Bute. NS 0769
Ardmeanach S'clyde 69 C5 dist on W coast of Mull, N of Loch Scridain. Its SW corner is NTS property – see Burg. NM 4428
Ardmhór W Isles 88 D3* loc on peninsula of **Àrd Mhór,** NE coast of Barra. NF 7103
Ardmillan S'clyde 56 B4 mansion dating from 16c and 18c, near coast 2m/4km S of Girvan. NX 1694
Ardminish S'clyde 62 D3 vil with jetty on **A. Bay** on E side of island of Gigha. **A. Point** is headland 2km NE. NR 6448
Ardmore H'land 87 A7 loc on S shore of Dornoch Firth 6m/9km NW of Tain, Ross and Cromarty dist. To N, the low-lying promontory of **Ardmore Pt** protrudes into the firth. NH 7086
Ard More Mangersta W Isles 88 A2* headland on W coast of Lewis 4m/6km W of Uig. NA 9932
Ardmore Point H'land 84 B3 headland on W coast of Sutherland dist on E side of entrance to Loch Laxford. NC 1851
Ardmore Point H'land 86 A2 headland on N coast of Caithness dist 2m/3km NW of Armadale. NC 7666
Ardmore Point Mull, S'clyde 68 C3 headland at E end of **A. Bay,** on N coast of island 3m/5km NW of Tobermory. NM 4759
Ardmore Point S'clyde 62 C3 headland on SE coast of Islay 5m/8km NE of Ardbeg. NR 4750
Ardmore Point Skye, H'land 78 A8 headland on NW coast 5m/8km S of Vaternish Pt. NG 2159
Ardmucknish Bay S'clyde 70 B2 bay on S side of Benderloch, qv, between Rubha Garbh-àird and Ledaig Pt, Argyll. NM 8937
Ardnacross Bay S'clyde 63 E5 bay on E coast of Kintyre 4m/7km NE of Campbeltown. NR 7625
Ardnadam S'clyde 70 D6 vil on S side of Holy Loch in Argyll, 2m/4km N of Dunoon. NS 1780
Ardnagrask H'land 81 E3* loc in Ross and Cromarty dist 1m SW of Muir of Ord. NH 5149
Ardnahoe Loch S'clyde 62 B1 small loch 2km N of Port Askaig, Islay. NR 4271
Ardnameacan Skye, H'land 79 E6 headland on SE coast on E side of entrance to Loch na Dal. NG 7114
Ard nam Madadh W Isles 88 E1* headland on S side of entrance to Loch Maddy, E coast of N Uist. Junction of land and submarine cables. NF 9567
Ardnamurchan H'land 68 C2-E3 peninsula on W coast in Lochaber dist, running W from Salen to **Ardnamurchan Pt,** the most westerly point of British mainland. Lighthouse. NM 5766
Ardnarff H'land 80 A4 locality on SE shore of Loch Carron, Skye and Lochalsh dist. NG 8935
Ardnastang H'land 68 F3 locality on N side of Loch Sunart in Lochaber dist, 1m W of Strontian. NM 8161
Ardnave Point S'clyde 62 A1 headland on N coast of Islay, on W side of entrance to Loch Gruinart. NR 2975
Ard Neackie H'land 84 D2* promontory on E bank of Loch Eriboll, Sutherland dist, 4m/7km from head of loch. NC 4459
Ardneil Bay S'clyde 64 A4* bay on Firth of Clyde on E side of Farland Hd. NS 1848
Ardnish H'land 68 E1 peninsula on coast of Lochaber dist between Loch Ailort and Loch nan Uamh, the southern and northern arms respectively of Sound of Arisaig. NM 7281
Ardoch Tayside 72 C4 site of Roman fort to N of Braco, qv. NN 8309
Ardoch Burn 72 B4 r in Central region running S to R Teith on S side of Doune. NN 7300
Ardochu H'land 85 F6* loc in Sutherland dist 6m/10km E of Lairg. NC 6703
Ardpatrick Point S'clyde 63 E2 headland at S end of Knapdale, Argyll, at entrance to W Loch Tarbert. NR 7357
Ardrishaig S'clyde 70 B6 tn in Argyll on W shore of Loch Gilp 2m/3km S of Lochgilphead. TV and radio transmitting stn. SE terminus of Crinan Canal – see Crinan. NR 8585
Ardross H'land 85 F8 loc in Ross and Cromarty dist 3m/4km N of Alness. **Ardross Castle** is mansion 2m/3km W. **Ardross Forest,** state forest to N. NH 6473
Ardrossan S'clyde 64 A4 port on Firth of Clyde 12m/20km W of Kilmarnock. Passenger boat services to Arran and Northern Ireland. NS 2342
Ardross Castle Fife 73 G4 ruined 14c cas on N coast of Firth of Forth between Elie and St Monance. NO 5000
Ardscalpsie Point S'clyde 63 G2* headland on W coast of island of Bute, on W side of Scalpsie Bay. NS 0457
Ardsley S Yorks 43 H1 loc in Barnsley 3m/4km E of tn centre. SE 3805
Ardsley East W Yorks 49 E5 vil 3m/5km SE of Morley. **Ardsley Resr** 1km W. SE 3025
Ardslignish H'land 68 D3 loc on S side of Ardnamurchan peninsula in Lochaber dist, 8m/13km W of Salen. NM 5661
Ardtalnaig Tayside 71 G1 vil on S side of Loch Tay 6m/10km SW of Kenmore. Old copper and lead mines in vicinity. NN 7039
Ard Thurinish Skye, H'land 79 D8 headland at S end of Sleat peninsula 2m/4km E of Pt of Sleat. NM 5999
Ardtoe H'land 68 D2 loc in Lochaber dist on N side of entrance to Kentra Bay, 3m/5km NW of Acharacle. NM 6370
Ardtornish Point H'land 68 E4 headland on Sound of Mull 2km SE of entrance to Loch Aline, Lochaber dist. Ruins of 14c cas, stronghold of the Lords of the Isles. **Ardtornish Bay** on E side of headland. NM 6942
Ardtreck Point Skye, H'land 79 B5 headland in Loch Bracadale at entrance to Loch Harport. NG 3336
Ardtun S'clyde 69 E6 scattered loc on Ross of Mull NE of Bunessan. NM 4022
Arduaine S'clyde 70 A4 loc on Asknish Bay on coast of Argyll, 4m/6km SW of Kilmelford. NM 8010
Ardvasar Skye, H'land 79 E7 vil on E coast of Sleat peninsula, 5m/8km NE of Pt of Sleat. NG 6303
Ardveenish W Isles 88 D3* loc on peninsula of **Àrd Veenish,** at head of North Bay, Barra. NF 7103
Ardverikie Forest H'land 75 E3, F3* deer forest in Badenoch and Strathspey dist, S of Lochan na h-Earba. NN 5081
Ardvourlie Castle W Isles 88 B3* locality on W shore of Loch Seaforth, Harris, opp Seaforth I. NB 1810
Ardwall Island D & G 58 B6 one of the Islands of Fleet, off E shore of Wigtown Bay. Foundations of several early Christian churches have been uncovered. NX 5749
Ardwell D & G 57 B7 vil on E coast of Rinns of Galloway, 3m/5km S of Sandhead. **A. Bay** on W coast 2m/4km W. **A. Point** on S side of bay. NX 1045
Ardwick Gtr Manchester 42 D2 dist of Manchester 2km SE of city centre. SJ 8597
Ardyne Point S'clyde 63 G1 headland in Argyll 3m/4km W of Toward Pt. NS 0968
Arecleoch Forest S'clyde 57 B5* state forest 4m/6km SW of Barrhill. NX 1879
Areley Kings H & W 26 C1* loc 1km SW of Stourport across R Severn. SO 8070
Arenig Fawr Gwynedd 33 E1 mt 6m/10km E of Trawsfynydd. Height 2800 ft or 854 metres. SH 8236
Arfon 116 admin dist of Gwynedd.
Arford Hants 11 E2 vil 4m/6km W of Hindhead. SU 8236
Argoed Gwent 15 F2 ham 2m/3km N of Blackwood. SO 1700
Argoed Salop 34 A2* loc 1km W of Kinnerley. SJ 3320
Argoed Mill Powys 25 E2* loc on R Wye 4m/6km S of Rhayader. SN 9962
Argos Hill E Sussex 12 C4* loc 2km SE of Rotherfield. Windmill at top of hill. TQ 5628
Argyll S'clyde 114,116 former county on W side of Scotland including the mainland between Loch Linnhe in the NW and Loch Long in the SE; the peninsulas of Cowal, Kintyre, Knapdale, and the area (now administratively in Highland region) enclosed by Loch Shiel, Loch Linnhe, the Sound of Mull, and the sea; and the islands of Coll, Tiree, Mull and Iona, Colonsay, Jura, and Islay. The

whole area is noted for its outstanding scenery of sea, loch, and mountain. The principal tns, none large, are, from N to S, Oban, Inveraray, Lochgilphead, Dunoon, and Campbeltown.
Argyll and Bute 114, 116 admin dist of Strathclyde region.
Argyll Forest Park S'clyde 70 C5, D5 forest and mt area in Argyll between Loch Long and Loch Fyne, occupying much of northern part of peninsula of Cowal. NS 19
Argyll's Bowling Green S'clyde 70 D5 mountainous area in Argyll between Loch Goil and Loch Long. NS 2298
Aribruach W Isles 88 B2* vil on Lewis at N end of Loch Seaforth, 4m/6km SW of Balallan. NB 2417
Ariconium H & W 26 B5* Roman settlement 1m E of Weston under Penyard. SO 6423
Arinacrinachd H'land 78 F3 locality in Ross and Cromarty dist on SW coast of Loch Torridon, 6m/9km NW of Shieldaig. NG 7458
Arinagour Coll, S'clyde 68 A3 sole vil and port of the island, situated on SE coast 5m/8km from NE end, at head of Loch Eatharna. NM 2256
Arisaig H'land 68 E1 vil and surrounding area on coast of Lochaber dist. Vil is 7m/11km S of Mallaig, at head of Loch nan Ceall. See also Rubh' Arisaig, Sound of Arisaig. NM 6586
Aris Dale Shetland 89 E6* valley in S part of Yell. **Burn of Arisdale** is stream running S down valley to Hamna Voe. **Hill of Arisdale** is ridge to E of valley, running SW to NE and culminating in Ward of Otterswick – see Otters Wick. HU 4882
Arkendale N Yorks 49 F2 vil 4m/6km S of Boroughbridge. SE 3860
Arkengarthdale N Yorks. See Arkle Beck.
Arkesden Essex 29 H4 vil 5m/7km SW of Saffron Walden. TL 4834
Arkholme Lancs 47 F1 vil 4m/7km SW of Kirkby Lonsdale. SD 5872
Arkle H'land 84 C3 mt ridge in Sutherland dist 5m/8km SE of Rhiconich. Summit 2580 ft or 786 metres. Gaelic form: Arcuil. NC 3046
Arkle Beck 53 H4/H5 r rising on Arkengarthdale Moor, N Yorks, and flowing first NE then SE through Langthwaite into R Swale at Grinton 1km SE of Reeth. Valley of Arkle Beck is known as Arkengarthdale. SE 0498
Arkleby Cumbria 52 B1 loc 2m/3km S of Aspatria. NY 1439
Arkleside N Yorks 54 A6 loc 7m/11km SW of Middleham. SE 0480
Arkle Town N Yorks 54 A4* loc in Arkengarthdale 3m/4km NW of Reeth. NZ 0001
Arkley London 19 F2 loc in borough of Barnet 11m/17km NW of Charing Cross. TQ 2295
Arksey S Yorks 44 B1 suburb 2m/4km N of Doncaster. SE 5706
Arkwright Town Derbys 43 H4* vil 3m/5km E of Chesterfield. SK 4270
Arle Glos 26 D5* loc in NW part of Cheltenham. SO 9223
Arlecdon Cumbria 52 A3/B3 vil 5m/8km E of Whitehaven. NY 0419
Arle Court Glos 26 D5* W dist of Cheltenham. SO 9121
Arlesey Beds 29 F4 elongated vil 5m/7km N of Hitchin. TL 1936
Arleston Salop 34 D3* SE suburb of Wellington. SJ 6610
Arley Ches 42 C3 ham 4m/7km N of Northwich. SJ 6780
Arley Warwicks 35 H5 vil 5m/8km W of Nuneaton. Colliery, and loc of **New Arley,** to SE. SP 2890
Arley, Upper H & W 34 D6 vil on E bank of R Severn 3m/5km NW of Bewdley. Ferry for pedestrians. SO 7680
Arlingham Glos 26 C6 vil in loop of R Severn 9m/15km NW of Stroud. SO 7010
Arlington Devon 7 E1 ham 6m/9km NE of Barnstaple. **A. Beccott,** loc in N part of par. **A. Court,** hse and grounds (NT), to W of ch. SS 6140
Arlington E Sussex 12 B5 vil in valley of Cuckmere R below S Downs 3m/5km W of Hailsham. TQ 5407
Arlington Glos 17 E1 loc adjoining Bibury to W. SP 1106
Armadale H'land 86 A2 vil near N coast of Caithness dist 6m/10km W of Melvich. **A. Bay** to E. **A. Burn** is stream running N into bay. NC 7864
Armadale Lothian 65 F2 tn 7m/11km SW of Linlithgow. Industries in vicinity include coal, iron, steel; hosiery and brick mnfre. NS 9368
Armadale Skye, H'land 79 E5. **A. Bay** and pier, 1km NE of Ardvasar on E coast of Sleat peninsula; vehicle ferry to Mallaig across Sound of Sleat. **A. Castle,** 1km N of bay, estate and site of former cas of the Lords Macdonald, Barons of Sleat. NG 6303
Armathwaite Cumbria 60 B6 vil on R Eden 9m/15km SE of Carlisle. **Armathwaite Castle,** peel tower beside r. NY 5046
Arminghall Norfolk 39 F4 vil 3m/5km SE of Norwich. TG 2504
Armitage Staffs 35 G3 vil 3m/4km SE of Rugeley. SK 0716
Armitage Bridge W Yorks 48 D6* loc in Huddersfield 2m/3km S of tn centre. SE 1313
Armley W Yorks 49 E5* dist of Leeds 2m/3km W of city centre. HM prison. SE 2733
Armscote Warwicks 27 F3 vil 3m/4km N of Shipston on Stour. SP 2444
Armshead Staffs 43 E6* loc 1km N of Werrington. SJ 9348
Armston Northants 37 F5 ham 2m/3km SE of Oundle. TL 0685
Armstrong Tyne & Wear 61 G5* industrial estate in NW part of Washington. NZ 2957
Armthorpe S Yorks 44 B1 coal-mining loc and suburb 3m/5km E of Doncaster. SE 6205
Arnaby Cumbria 52 B6/C6* loc just E of The Green. SD 1884
Arncliffe N Yorks 48 C1 vil in Littondale 7m/11km NW of Grassington. **Arncliffe Cote** loc 2km SE. SD 9371
Arncott, Lower Oxon 28 B5* loc 3m/5km SE of Bicester. SP 6018
Arncott, Upper Oxon 28 B5* loc 4m/6km SE of Bicester. SP 6117
Arncroach Fife 73 G4 vil 2m/4km N of St Monance. NO 5105
Arne Dorset 9 G5 ham 3m/5km E of Wareham, in area of heath and marsh at W end of Poole Harbour. SY 9788
Arnesby Leics 36 C5 vil 5m/8km N of Husbands Bosworth. SP 6192
Arnfield Derbys 43 E2* loc 1km NW of Tintwistle. **Arnfield Resr** to S. SK 0198
Arngill Force Durham 53 G3* waterfall in Arngill Beck above Fish Lake on Lune Forest. NY 8423
Arnisdale H'land 79 F7 vil in Lochaber dist on N shore of Loch Hourn, some 5m/8km E of entrance to loch from Sound of Sleat. Also r running W down Glen A. to Loch Hourn 1m SE of vil. NG 8410
Arnish Skye, H'land 78 D4 loc on Raasay 3m/5km from N end of island. NG 5948
Arnish Point W Isles 88 C2* headland on W side of entrance to Stornoway Harbour, Lewis. Lighthouse. NB 4330
Arnol W Isles 88 B1 vil near NW coast of Lewis 3m/5km W of Barvas. Contains The Black House (A.M.), former dwelling house, now museum and national monmt. **R Arnol** rises among lochs to S and flows N between A. and Bragar into Loch A. and thence into bay of Port A. NB 3148
Arnold Humberside 51 F4* vil adjoining Long Riston to S. TA 1241
Arnold Notts 44 B6 tn adjoining Nottingham to NE and 4m/6km from city centre. SK 5845
Arno's Vale Avon 16 B4* dist of Bristol 2m/3km SE of city centre. ST 6071
Arnot Reservoir Tayside 73 E4 small resr 3m/4km W of Leslie. NO 2002
Arnprior Central 71 G5 vil 12m/19km W of Stirling. NS 6194
Arnside Cumbria 47 E1 tn on left bank of R Kent estuary 6m/9km N of Carnforth. SD 4578
Aros S'clyde 68 C4, D4 dist of Mull S of Tobermory. **Aros R** runs E down Glen Aros to Sound of Mull 1m N of Salen. **A. Castle,** formerly stronghold of the Lords of the Isles, at mouth of r. NM 5051
Aros Bay S'clyde 62 C3* small bay on E coast of Islay 1m N of Ardmore Pt. NR 4652
Arowry Clwyd 34 B1 loc 5m/8km W of Whitchurch. SJ 4539
Arrad Foot Cumbria 52 C6 ham 2km S of Penny Br. SD 3080
Arram Humberside 51 E4 vil 3m/5km N of Beverley. See also New Arram. TA 0344
Arran S'clyde 63 mountainous island, with mild though wet climate and fertile valleys, on W side of Firth of Clyde and separated from Kintyre by Kilbrannan Sound. Measures 20m/32km N to S and about 9m/15km E to W; area 166 sq miles or 430 sq km. Main industries are tourism, sheep and cattle grazing, fishing. Highest point is Goat Fell, 2866 ft or 874 metres. Brodick, on E coast, is chief tn. NR 93
Arras Humberside 50 D4 loc 3m/5km E of Mkt Weighton. SE 8241
Arrathorne N Yorks 54 B5 ham 5m/8km NW of Bedale. SE 2093
Arreton Isle of Wight 10 C6 vil 3m/5km SE of Newport. SZ 5486
Arrington Cambs 29 G3 vil 6m/10km N of Royston. TL 3250
Arrochar S'clyde 71 E4 vil at head of Loch Long on E side of loch, 2km W of Tarbert on Loch Lomond and 13m/21km N of Helensburgh. NN 2904
Arrow Warwicks 27 E2 vil on r of same name 1m SW of Alcester. SP 0856
Arrow 26 A2 r rising near Glascwm, Powys, and flowing E through Kington into R Lugg 2m/3km SE of Leominster, H & W. SO 5156
Arrow 27 E3* r rising 8m/13km SW of Birmingham and flowing S into R Avon 5m/8km NE of Evesham. SP 0850
Arrowe Hill Merseyside 41 H3* loc in Birkenhead 3m/5km W of tn centre. SJ 2787
Arrowfield Top H & W 27 E1* loc 4m/7km N of Redditch. SP 0274
Arscott Salop 34 B3* ham 1m S of Gt Hanwood. SJ 4307
Arth 24 B2* r rising 3m/5km W of Llangeitho, Dyfed, and flowing W into Cardigan Bay at Aberarth. SN 4764
Arthington W Yorks 49 E4* vil 5m/7km E of Otley. SE 2744
Arthingworth Northants 36 C6 vil 4m/6km S of Mkt Harborough. SP 7581
Arthog Gwynedd 32 D3 loc 5m/7km NE of Llwyngwril. SH 6414
Arthrath Grampian 83 G3* loc 4m/6km N of Ellon. NJ 9636
Arthursdale W Yorks 49 F4* loc 1km N of Scholes. SE 3737
Arthur's Point Grampian 82 C1* headland on N coast at W end of Buckie. NJ 4065
Arthur's Round Table Cumbria. See Eamont Bridge.
Arthur's Seat Lothian 66 A2 hill of volcanic origin in E part of Edinburgh 2km SE of city centre. Height 823 ft or 251 metres. NT 2772
Arthur's Stone H & W. See Dorstone.
Arthur's Stone W Glam. See Cefn Bryn.
Artle Beck 47 F2* r rising on N slopes of Forest of Bowland, Lancs, and flowing NW into R Lune 4m/7km NE of Lancaster. SD 5365
Artro 32 D2 r in Gwynedd running SW into Tremadoc Bay on S side of Llandanwg. SH 5627
Arun 11 F5 r rising in St Leonard's Forest E of Horsham, W Sussex, and flowing W and then S into English Channel at Littlehampton. TQ 0201
Arun 119 admin dist of W Sussex.
Arundel W Sussex 11 F4 tn on hill above R Arun 3m/5km N of Littlehampton. Cas originally Norman but mainly Victn, in spacious A. Park, which contains site of Romano-British settlement N of Swanbourne Lake. TQ 0107
Aryg, Yr Gwynedd 40 D4 mt 4m/6km E of Bethesda. Height 2875 ft or 876 metres. SH 6867
Asby Cumbria 52 B3* ham 2km NE of Arlecdon. NY 0620
Asby, Great Cumbria 53 F3 vil 5m/7km S of Appleby. **Lit Asby** ham 2m/4km SE. NY 6813
Ascog S'clyde 63 G2 vil on E coast of Bute 2km SE of Rothesay, extending N and S of **Ascog Pt.** **A. Bay** is small bay on N side of headland. See also Loch Ascog. NS 1063
Ascot Berks 10 D4 residential loc 6m/10km SW of Windsor across Windsor Gt Park. Famous racecourse. **S Ascot** loc to S. SU 9268
Ascott Bucks 28 D5 loc 2m/4km SW of Leighton Buzzard. Hse and garden (NT). SP 8922
Ascott Warwicks 27 G4 loc 5m/8km N of Chipping Norton. SP 3236
Ascott d'Oyley Oxon 27 G5* loc adjoining vil of Ascott-under-Wychwood to E. SP 3018
Ascott Earl Oxon 27 G5* loc adjoining vil of Ascott-under-Wychwood to SW. SP 2918
Ascott-under-Wychwood Oxon 27 G5 vil 4m/6km W of Charlbury. SP 3018
Ascreavie Tayside 76 D5 loc 4m/6km NW of Kirriemuir. NO 3357
Ascrib Islands H'land 78 B3 group of small uninhabited islands at entrance to Loch Snizort, Skye. The named islands, from N to S, are Eilean Iosal, Eilean Creagach, Sgeir na Capaill, Eilean Garave (or Geary), and S Ascrib. NG 3064
Ascrib, South H'land 78 B3 one of the Ascrib Is., qv.
Asenby N Yorks 49 F1 vil 5m/8km SW of Thirsk on far bank of R Swale. SE 3975
As Fawr, Yr Welsh form of Monknash, qv.
Asfordby Leics 36 C3 vil 3m/5km W of Melton Mowbray. **A. Hill** loc 1m E. SK 7068
Asgarby Lincs 45 E6 ham 3m/5km E of Sleaford. TF 1145
Asgarby Lincs 45 G4 ham 4m/7km W of Spilsby. TF 3366
Asgog Bay S'clyde 63 F1/F2 bay on E side of Loch Fyne, Argyll, 4m/6km NW of Ardlamont Pt. **A. Loch** is small loch 2m/3km N. NR 9367
Ash Devon 6 D4 loc 3m/5km NW of Hatherleigh. SS 5108
Ash Dorset 9 F3* loc at SW end of Cranborne Chase 3m/5km NW of Blandford Forum. ST 8610
Ash Kent 13 H2 vil 3m/5km W of Sandwich. TR 2858
Ash Kent 20 C5 vil 3m/5km S of Longfield. TQ 6064
Ash Som 8 C2 vil 1m NE of Martock. ST 4720
Ash Surrey 18 D6 urban loc 2m/3km E of Aldershot. **A. Green** small loc to E. SU 8950
Ash 20 A1* r rising about 3m/5km E of Buntingford, Herts, and flowing S into R Lea 2km SE of Ware. TL 3713
Ashampstead Berks 18 B4 vil 3m/5km SW of Streatley. Loc of **A. Green** adjoins to N. SU 5676
Ashbocking Suffolk 31 F3 ham 6m/10km N of Ipswich. Vil of **A. Green** 1m E. TM 1754
Ashbourne Derbys 43 F6 tn on R Henmore near its junction with R Dove 13m/20km NW of Derby. SK 1846
Ash Bourne 12 C5* one of the streams feeding Waller's Haven (qv) in E Sussex. TQ 6712
Ashbrittle Som 7 H3 vil 6m/9km W of Wellington. ST 0521
Ashburnham E Sussex 12 C5 loc 4m/6km W of Battle. TQ 6814
Ashburton Devon 4 D4 mkt tn close to E side of Dartmoor, 7m/11km W of Newton Abbot. SX 7569
Ashbury Devon 6 D5* ham 5m/9km NW of Okehampton. SX 5098
Ashbury Oxon 17 G3 vil 7m/11km E of Swindon. SU 2685
Ashby Humberside 44 D1 dist of Scunthorpe 2m/3km SE of tn centre. SE 9008
Ashby Suffolk 39 H5 loc 5m/8km NW of Lowestoft. Loc of **Ashby Dell** to N. TM 4899
Ashby by Partney Lincs 45 G4 vil 2m/3km E of Spilsby. TF 4266
Ashby Canal 36 A5-A3 canal running N from Coventry Canal at Marston Junction towards Ashby de la Zouch, Leics. Navigable to Illott Wharf, near Snarestone. There are no locks on this canal.

Ashby cum Fenby Humberside 45 F2 vil 5m/9km S of Grimsby. Wray Almshouses, 1641. TA 2500
Ashby de la Launde Lincs 45 E5 vil 6m/9km N of Sleaford. Site of Roman bldg to E of A. Hall. WT stn to N. TF 0555
Ashby de la Zouch Leics 36 A3 mkt tn 16m/26km NW of Leicester. Remains of cas (A.M.). SK 3516
Ashby Folville Leics 36 C3 vil 5m/8km SW of Melton Mowbray. SK 7012
Ashby Hill Humberside 45 F2* loc 1m SW of Brigsley. TA 2400
Ashby Magna Leics 36 B5 vil 4m/7km N of Lutterworth. SP 5690
Ashby Mere Norfolk 39 E5* small lake 1m E of Snetterton. TM 0090
Ashby Parva Leics 36 B5 vil 3m/4km N of Lutterworth. SP 5288
Ashby Puerorum Lincs 45 G4 vil 5m/7km E of Horncastle. TF 3271
Ashby St Ledgers Northants 28 B1 vil 4m/6km N of Daventry. Ancient manor hse was seat of the Catesbys. SP 5768
Ashby St Mary Norfolk 39 G4 vil 3m/5km NW of Loddon. TG 3202
Ashby, West Lincs 45 F4 vil 2m/3km N of Horncastle. TF 2672
Ashchurch Glos 26 D4* vil 2m/3km E of Tewkesbury. SO 9233
Ashclyst Forest Devon. See Broad Clyst.
Ashcombe Avon 15 H5* E dist of Weston-super-Mare. ST 3361
Ashcombe Devon 5 E3 vil 3m/5km E of Chudleigh. SX 9179
Ashcott Som 8 C1 vil 3m/5km W of Street. ST 4337
Ashdale Falls S'clyde. See Glenashdale Burn.
Ashdon Essex 30 B4 vil 4m/6km NE of Saffron Walden. Site of Roman bldg 1m NW. TL 5842
Ashdown Forest E Sussex 12 B4 ancient forest now mainly heath, extending from Coleman's Hatch (N) to Fairwarp (S) and from Crowborough (E) to Chelwood Gate (W). TQ 4530
Ashdown House Oxon 17 G3 17c house (NT) in park 4m/7km N of Aldbourne. SU 2881
Ashe Hants 17 H6 ham 2km E of Overton at source of R Test. SU 5349
Asheldham Essex 21 E2 vil 4m/6km NE of Burnham-on-Crouch. TL 9701
Ashen Essex 30 C4 vil 5m/8km SE of Haverhill. TL 7442
Ashendon Bucks 28 C6 vil 5m/8km N of Thame. SP 7014
Ashfield Central 72 B4* loc 2m/3km N of Dunblane. NN 7803
Ashfield Hants 10 B3* loc 1m SE of Romsey. SU 3619
Ashfield H & W 26 B5 loc in S part of Ross-on-Wye. SO 5923
Ashfield Suffolk 31 F2 vil 2m/4km E of Debenham. TM 2162
Ashfield 117 admin dist of Notts.
Ashfield, Great Suffolk 31 E2 vil 4m/7km SE of Ixworth. TL 9967
Ashfield Green Suffolk 30 C3* loc 8m/12km SW of Bury St Edmunds. TL 7655
Ashfield Green Suffolk 31 F1* ham 2m/3km E of Stradbroke. TM 2673
Ashfields Salop 34 D2* loc 1km E of Hinstock. SJ 7026
Ashford Derbys 43 G4 vil 2m/3km NW of Bakewell. SK 1969
Ashford Devon 4 D5 ham 1km N of Aveton Gifford and 3m/5km SE of Modbury. SX 6848
Ashford Devon 6 D2 vil 2m/3km NW of Barnstaple. **W Ashford** loc 1km W. SS 5335
Ashford Kent 13 F3 mkt, industrial and dormitory tn on Gt Stour R 13m/21km SW of Canterbury. TR 0142
Ashford Surrey 19 E4 urban loc 2m/3km E of Staines. TQ 0671
Ashford Bowdler Salop 26 A1* vil on R Teme 3m/4km S of Ludlow. SO 5170
Ashford Carbonel Salop 26 A1 vil on R Teme 3m/4km S of Ludlow. SO 5270
Ashford Hill Hants 18 A5 vil 3m/5km NE of Kingsclere. SU 5562
Ashford Water 9 H3* r rising as Allen R at Martin, Hants, and flowing SE into R Avon on S side of Fordingbridge. SU 1413
Ashgill S'clyde 65 E4* loc 2m/3km SE of Larkhall. NS 7850
Ash Green Warwicks 36 A5* loc 2m/3km SW of Bedworth. SP 3384
Ashgrove Grampian 82 B1* SE dist of Elgin. NJ 2262
Ashill Devon 7 H4 vil 5m/8km NE of Cullompton. ST 0811
Ashill Norfolk 38 D4 vil 5m/8km SE of Swaffham. Site of Roman bldg 2m/3km NE. TF 8804
Ashill Som 8 B3 vil 3m/5km NW of Ilminster. ST 3217
Ashingdon Essex 21 E3 suburb 2m/3km N of Rochford. TQ 8693
Ashington Nthmb 61 G3 coal-mining tn 5m/8km E of Morpeth. NZ 2787
Ashington Som 8 D2 ham 4m/6km N of Yeovil. ST 5621
Ashington W Sussex 11 G3 vil 3m/3km N of Washington. Site of Roman bldg to W. TQ 1316
Ashkirk Borders 66 C6 vil on Ale Water 4m/6km S of Selkirk. NT 4722
Ashlett Hants 10 B4 loc on shores of Southampton Water between Fawley oil refinery and power stn. SU 4603
Ashleworth Glos 26 C5 vil 5m/7km N of Gloucester. SO 8125
Ashleworth Quay Glos 26 C5* ham on W bank of R Severn 4m/7km N of Gloucester across r. 15c tithe barn (NT). SO 8125
Ashley Cambs 30 C2 vil 4m/6km E of Newmarket. TL 6961
Ashley Ches 42 D3 vil 2m/4km S of Altrincham. SJ 7784
Ashley Devon 7 E4* ham 3m/5km SW of Chulmleigh. SS 6411
Ashley Hants 10 A5 suburban loc adjoining New Milton to E. SZ 2595
Ashley Hants 10 B2 vil 3m/5km SE of Stockbridge. Remains of old cas. SU 3831
Ashley Kent 13 H2* vil 5m/7km N of Dover. TR 3048
Ashley Northants 36 D5 vil 5m/7km NE of Mkt Harborough. SP 7990
Ashley Staffs 34 D1 vil 6m/10km NW of Eccleshall. **A. Dale** loc 1km SW. **A. Heath** loc 1m W. SJ 7636
Ashley Wilts 16 C4 vil 5m/8km NE of Bath. ST 8168
Ashley Wilts 16 C5* hams of **Gt** and **Lit Ashley** about 1m NW of Bradford-on-Avon. ST 8162
Ashley Down Avon 16 B4* dist of Bristol 2m/3km NE of city centre. ST 5975
Ashley Green Bucks D1 vil 2m/3km SW of Berkhamsted. SP 9705
Ashley Park Surrey 19 E5* loc adjoining Walton-on-Thames to S. TQ 1065
Ashling, East W Sussex 11 E4 vil 3m/5km NW of Chichester. SU 8207
Ashling, West W Sussex 11 E4 vil 4m/6km NW of Chichester. SU 8107
Ash Magna Salop 34 C1 vil 2m/4km SE of Whitchurch. Ham of **A. Parva** adjoins to SE. SJ 5739
Ashmanhaugh Norfolk 39 G3 ham 3m/4km NE of Wroxham. TG 3121
Ashmansworth Hants 17 H5 vil 4m/7km NE of Hurstbourne Tarrant. SU 4157
Ashmansworthy Devon 6 C3 ham 9m/14km SW of Bideford. SS 3318
Ashmill Devon 6 C5* loc 6m/10km SE of Holsworthy. SX 3995
Ash Mill Devon 7 F3 vil 5m/8km SE of S Molton. SS 7823
Ashmore Dorset 9 F3 vil on Cranborne Chase 5m/8km SE of Shaftesbury. ST 9117
Ashmore Green Berks 18 A4* vil 3m/4km NE of Newbury. SU 5069
Ashop 43 F2 r rising 3m/5km SE of Glossop, Derbys, and flowing E into R Alport at head of Woodlands Valley. SK 1489
Ashorne Warwicks 27 G2 vil 5m/8km S of Leamington. SP 3057
Ashover Derbys 43 H4 vil 3m/5km W of Clay Cross. SK 3463
Ashover Hay Derbys 43 H5* loc 3m/4km SW of Clay Cross. SK 3560
Ashow Warwicks 27 G1 vil on R Avon 2m/3km SE of Kenilworth. SP 3170
Ashperton H & W 26 B3 vil 5m/8km NW of Ledbury. SO 6441
Ashprington Devon 5 E5 vil 2m/4km SE of Totnes. SX 8157
Ash Priors Som 8 A2 vil 3m/5km NE of Milverton. ST 1529
Ashreigney Devon 7 E4 vil 4m/6km W of Chulmleigh. SS 6213
Ashridge Park Herts 19 E1 estate, partly NT, 3m/4km N of Berkhamsted. Hse occupied by Ashridge Management College. SP 9912
Ash Street Suffolk 31 E3* ham 3m/5km N of Hadleigh. TM 0146
Ashtead Surrey 19 F5 suburban loc 2m/3km NE of Leatherhead. Loc of **Lr Ashtead** 1m W. Site of Roman villa beyond A. Common to N. TQ 1858
Ash Thomas Devon 7 G4 ham 3m/5km SE of Tiverton. ST 0010
Ashton Cambs 37 F4* loc 5m/8km E of Stamford. TF 1005
Ashton Cornwall 2 B5 vil 4m/6km W of Helston. SW 6038
Ashton Cornwall 3 H2 loc 2m/3km SE of Callington. SX 3868
Ashton Devon 5 E2 par 3m/5km N of Chudleigh, containing hams of **Hr** and **Lr Ashton.** SX 8584
Ashton Hants 10 C3* loc 2km N of Bishop's Waltham. SU 5419
Ashton H & W 26 A2* ham 4m/6km N of Leominster. SO 5164
Ashton Lancs 47 E3* loc to E of R Lune estuary 3m/5km SW of Lancaster. The hall dates partly from 14c. SD 4657
Ashton Northants 28 C3 vil 5m/8km E of Towcester. SP 7649
Ashton Northants 37 F5 vil 2km E of Oundle. TL 0588
Ashton S'clyde 64 A2 SW dist of Gourock. NS 2377
Ashton Canal Gtr Manchester. See Ashton-under-Lyne.
Ashton Common Wilts 16 D5* ham 3m/4km E of Trowbridge. ST 8958
Ashton-in-Makerfield Gtr Manchester 42 B2 tn 4m/6km S of Wigan. Coal-mining, light engineering (esp locks and hinges). SJ 5799
Ashton Keynes Wilts 17 E2 vil 4m/6km W of Cricklade. SU 0494
Ashton, North Gtr Manchester 42 B2* loc 2m/3km NW of Ashton-in-Makerfield. SD 5500
Ashton on Ribble Lancs 47 F5 dist of Preston 2m/4km W of tn centre. SD 5030
Ashton under Hill H & W 27 E4 vil 4m/7km SW of Evesham. SO 9938
Ashton-under-Lyne Gtr Manchester 43 E2 tn 6m/10km E of Manchester. Engineering, textiles, brewing, tobacco. **Ashton Canal** runs from its junction here with the Peak Forest Canal into Manchester. SJ 9399
Ashton upon Mersey Gtr Manchester 42 D2 loc in Sale 1m NW of tn centre. SJ 7792
Ashton Watering Avon 16 A4* loc 5m/7km W of Bristol. ST 5269
Ashton, West Wilts 16 D5 vil 2m/3km SE of Trowbridge. ST 8755
Ashurst Hants 10 A4 residential loc 3m/5km NE of Lyndhurst. SU 3310
Ashurst Kent 12 B3 vil 5m/8km W of Tunbridge Wells. TQ 5138
Ashurst Lancs 42 A1* N dist of Skelmersdale. SD 4907
Ashurst W Sussex 11 G3 vil 3m/5km N of Steyning. TQ 1716
Ashurst Bridge Hants 10 A3* loc 2km SW of Totton. SU 3412
Ashurstwood W Sussex 12 B3 vil 2m/3km SE of E Grinstead. TQ 4236
Ash Vale Surrey 18 D6 urban loc 2m/3km NE of Aldershot. SU 0952
Ashwater Devon 6 C5 vil 6m/10km SE of Holsworthy. SX 3895
Ashway Gap Gtr Manchester 43 E1* location of Mountain Rescue Post beside Dove Stone Resr 6m/10km E of Oldham. SE 0204
Ashwell Herts 29 G4 vil 4m/6km NE of Baldock. TL 2639
Ashwell Leics 36 D3 vil 3m/5km N of Oakham. SK 8613
Ashwell End Herts 29 F4* loc 1m NW of Ashwell and 4m/7km N of Baldock. TL 2540
Ashwellthorpe Norfolk 39 E5 vil 3m/5km SE of Wymondham. TM 1497
Ash Wharf Surrey 18 D6* loc beside Basingstoke Canal 2m/3km NE of Aldershot. SU 8951
Ashwick Som 16 B6* vil 3m/5km N of Shepton Mallet. ST 6348
Ashwicken Norfolk 38 B3/C3* ham 5m/8km E of King's Lynn. TF 7018
Ashworth Moor Reservoir Gtr Manchester 47 H6* resr 4m/7km NW of Rochdale. SD 8315
Askam in Furness Cumbria 46 D1 vil 3m/4km N of Dalton-in-Furness. SD 2177
Aske Hall N Yorks 54 B4 hse with 15c peel tower 2km N of Richmond. NZ 1703
Askern S Yorks 49 G6 coal-mining tn 7m/11km N of Doncaster. SE 5613
Askerswell Dorset 8 D5 vil 4m/7km E of Bridport. SY 5292
Askerton Castle Cumbria 60 B4 hse dating from 15c, 5m/8km N of Brampton. NY 5569
Askett Bucks 18 C1 vil 2km NE of Princes Risborough. SP 8105
Askham Cumbria 53 E3 vil 4m/7km S of Penrith. NY 5123
Askham Notts 44 C4 vil 3m/4km N of Tuxford. SK 7474
Askham Bryan N Yorks 49 G3 vil 4m/6km SW of York. Yorkshire Institute of Agriculture to S. SE 5548
Askham Richard N Yorks 49 G3 vil 5m/8km SW of York. HM prison (Askham Grange). SE 5347
Askival H'land 79 C8 highest point on island of Rum, 3m/5km S of Kinloch. Height 2663 ft or 812 metres. NM 3995
Asknish S'clyde 70 B5 hse on Loch Gair in Argyll, on W side of Loch Fyne. **A. Forest** is state forest to NW and SW. NR 9391
Asknish Bay S'clyde 70 A4 small bay on coast of Argyll 4m/6km SW of Kilmelford. NM 7910
Askrigg N Yorks 53 H5 vil in Wensleydale 4m/6km NW of Aysgarth. SD 9491
Askwith N Yorks 48 D3 vil in Wharfedale 3m/4km NW of Otley across R Wharfe. SE 1648
Aslackby Lincs 37 F2 vil 7m/11km N of Bourne. TF 0830
Aslacton Norfolk 39 F5* vil 7m/12km NE of Harleston. TM 1590
Asland Lancs 47 E5 alternative name for lower reaches of R Douglas, qv. SD 4326
Aslockton Notts 36 C1 vil 2m/4km E of Bingham. Birthplace of Thomas Cranmer, 1489. SK 7440
Aspall Suffolk 31 F2 loc 2km N of Debenham. TM 1765
Asparagus Island Cornwall 2 C6* rock island lying off Kynance Cove, qv. SW 6813
Aspatria Cumbria 52 B1 small tn 8m/12km NE of Maryport. NY 1441
Aspenden Herts 29 G5 vil 1km S of Buntingford. TL 3528
Asperton Lincs 37 G1* loc 1m N of Wigtoft. TF 2637
Aspley Staffs 35 E1* loc 1m W of Millmeece. SJ 8133
Aspley Guise Beds 28 D4 vil 2m/3km N of Woburn. SP 9435
Aspley Hall Notts 36 B1* loc in Nottingham 2m/3km NV of city centre. SK 5441
Aspley Heath Beds 28 D4* vil 2m/3km NW of Woburn. SP 9235
Aspley Heath Warwicks 27 E1* loc 4m/7km NW of Henley-in-Arden. SP 0970
Aspull Gtr Manchester 42 B1 tn 3m/4km NE of Wigan. SD 6108
Aspull Common Gtr Manchester 42 C2* loc 2km SW of Leigh. SJ 6498
Asselby Humberside 50 C5 vil 2m/3km W of Howden. SE 7127
Assendon, Lower Oxon 18 C3 vil 2m/3km NW of Henley-on-Thames. SU 7484
Assendon, Middle Oxon 18 C3 loc 3m/4km NW of Henley-on-Thames. SU 7385
Asserby Lincs 45 H3* loc 1m SE of Markby. **A. Turn** loc 1m W. TF 4977
Assich Forest H'land 81 G3 state forest in Nairn dist S and SW of Cawdor. NH 8146
Assington Suffolk 30 D4 vil 4m/7km SE of Sudbury. TL 9338
Assington Green Suffolk 30 C3* ham 4m/6km N of Clare. TL 7751
Astbury Ches 42 D5 vil 2km SW of Congleton. SJ 8461
Astcote Northants 28 B2* vil 3m/5km N of Towcester. SP 6753
Asterby Lincs 45 F3 ham 6m/10km N of Horncastle. TF 2679
Asterleigh Oxon 27 G5/H5* loc 2m/4km SE of Enstone. SP 4022
Asterley Salop 34 B4 ham 2m/3km W of Pontesbury. SJ 3707
Asterton Salop 34 B5 ham 4m/6km SW of Church Stretton across Long Mynd. Gliding on hilltop. SO 3991
Asthall Oxon 27 G6 vil 2m/4km E of Burford. Site of Romano-British settlement. Site of Roman villa 1m E. SP 2811
Asthall Leigh Oxon 27 G6 vil 4m/6km E of Burford. SP 3012
Astle Ches 42 D4* loc 1m E of Chelford. SJ 8373
Astley H & W 26 C1 vil 3m/5km SW of Stourport. SO 7867
Astley Salop 34 C3 vil 5m/8km NE of Shrewsbury. **A. Lodge** and **Upr Astley** locs 1km NW and S respectively. SJ 5218

Astley Warwicks 35 H5 vil 4m/6km SW of Nuneaton. **A. Castle,** mainly Elizn with parts dating from 13c. SP 3189
Astley W Yorks 49 F5* loc 7m/11km SE of Leeds. SE 3828
Astley Abbotts Salop 34 D4 vil 2m/4km N of Bridgnorth. SO 7096
Astley Bridge Gtr Manchester 47 G6 dist of Bolton 2km N of tn centre. SD 7111
Astley Cross H & W 26 C1 loc 2km S of Stourport. SO 8069
Astley Green Gtr Manchester 42 C2 loc 2m/3km SE of Tyldesley. SJ 7099
Astley Hall Lancs 47 F6 hse of 16c and later, 1km NW of Chorley tn centre. SD 5718
Astley Town H & W 26 C1* loc 3m/4km SW of Stourport. SO 7968
Astmoor Ches 42 B3* industrial area in N part of Runcorn. SJ 5383
Aston Berks 18 C3 vil 2m/3km NE of Henley-on-Thames across r. SU 7884
Aston Ches 42 B3 ham 4m/6km SE of Runcorn. **A. Heath** loc 1km NE. SJ 5578
Aston Ches 42 B6/C6 vil 4m/7km SW of Nantwich. SJ 6146
Aston Clwyd 41 H4 S suburb of Shotton, 6m/10km W of Chester. SJ 3067
Aston Derbys 35 G2* loc 1km E of Sudbury. SK 1631
Aston Derbys 43 F3 vil 3m/5km NW of Hathersage. SK 1883
Aston Herts 29 G5 vil 3m/4km SE of Stevenage. TL 2722
Aston H & W 26 A2* loc 3m/5km NW of Leominster. SO 4662
Aston H & W 26 A1 ham 4m/6km SW of Ludlow. SO 4671
Aston Oxon 17 G2 vil 4m/7km S of Witney. SP 3403
Aston Salop 34 C2 ham 1m E of Wem. SJ 5228
Aston Salop 34 C3* loc 1m E of Uppington. SJ 6109
Aston Salop 35 E5* ham 6m/10km E of Bridgnorth. SO 8093
Aston Staffs 34 D1 vil 7m/11km SW of Newcastle-under-Lyme. SJ 7541
Aston Staffs 35 E2 vil 2m/3km S of Stone. SJ 9131
Aston Staffs 35 E2* ham 2m/3km W of Stafford. SJ 8923
Aston S Yorks 43 H3 loc 5m/8km SE of Rotherham. **A. Common** loc adjoining to S. SK 4685
Aston W Midlands 35 G5* loc in Birmingham 2m/3km NE of city centre. **A. Hall** is a large 17c hse. SP 0889
Aston Abbotts Bucks 28 D5 vil 4m/7km NE of Aylesbury. SP 8420
Aston Blank Glos 27 F5 vil (formerly known as Cold Aston) 3m/5km NE of Northleach. SP 1219
Aston Botterell Salop 34 C5 ham 6m/10km NW of Cleobury Mortimer. SO 6384
Aston Cantlow Warwicks 27 F2 vil 4m/6km NE of Alcester. SP 1359
Aston Clinton Bucks 18 D1 par and vil, 4m/6km E of Aylesbury. SP 8712
Aston Crews H & W 26 B5 vil 4m/6km SW of Newent. SO 6723
Aston Cross Glos 26 D4 loc 3m/5km E of Tewkesbury. SO 9433
Aston, East Hants 10 B1* loc adjoining Longparish and 2m/4km SW of Whitchurch. SU 4345
Aston End Herts 29 F5/G5 vil 2m/4km E of Stevenage. TL 2724
Aston Eyre Salop 34 D5 vil 4m/7km W of Bridgnorth. SO 6594
Aston Fields H & W 27 E1 SE dist of Bromsgrove. SO 9669
Aston Flamville Leics 36 A5 vil 3m/4km E of Hinckley. SP 4692
Aston Ingham Glos 26 C5 vil 3m/5km SW of Newent. SO 6823
Aston juxta Mondrum Ches 42 C5 loc 4m/6km W of Crewe. SJ 6556
Astonlane Salop 34 D5* loc 5m/7km W of Bridgnorth. SO 6494
Aston le Walls Northants 28 A3 vil 7m/11km NE of Banbury. SP 4950
Aston, Little Staffs 35 G4 vil 3m/5km NW of Sutton Coldfield. SK 0900
Aston Magna Glos 27 F4 vil 2m/3km N of Moreton-in-Marsh. SP 1935
Aston, Middle Oxon 27 H5 vil 3m/5km S of Deddington. SP 4727
Aston, North Oxon 27 H4 vil 2m/3km S of Deddington. SP 4729
Aston on Carrant Glos 26 D4* loc 4m/6km E of Tewkesbury. SO 9434
Aston on Clun Salop 34 B6 vil 3m/4km W of Craven Arms. SO 3981
Aston Pigott Salop 34 A4* ham 1m NE of Worthen. SJ 3305
Aston Rogers Salop 34 A4* ham 2km NE of Worthen. SJ 3406
Aston Rowant Oxon 18 C2 vil 4m/6km NE of Watlington. SU 7299
Aston Sandford Bucks 18 C1 vil 3m/5km E of Thame. SP 7507
Aston Somerville H & W 27 E4 vil 4m/6km S of Evesham. SP 0438
Aston Subedge Glos 27 F3 vil below escarpment of Cotswold Hills 2m/3km N of Chipping Campden. SP 1341
Aston Tirrold Oxon 18 A3 vil 3m/5km SE of Didcot. SU 5585
Aston upon Trent Derbys 36 A2 vil 6m/9km SE of Derby. SK 4129
Aston, Upper Salop 35 E5 ham 6m/10km E of Bridgnorth. SO 8194
Aston Upthorpe Oxon 18 A3 vil 3m/5km SE of Didcot. SU 5586
Astrop Northants 28 A4* loc 4m/7km SE of Banbury. SP 5036
Astrope Herts 28 D6* loc 3m/5km NW of Tring. SP 8914
Astrop, Upper Northants 28 A4* loc 5m/8km W of Brackley. SP 5137
Astwick Beds 29 F4 vil 4m/6km NW of Baldock. TL 2138
Astwith Derbys 43 H4* loc 2m/3km S of Heath. SK 4464
Astwood Bucks 28 D3 vil 6m/10km W of Bedford. SP 9547
Astwood Bank H & W 27 E2 vil 4m/6km S of Redditch. SP 0462
Aswarby Lincs 37 F1 ham 4m/6km S of Sleaford. TF 0639
Aswardby Lincs 45 G4 vil 3m/5km NW of Spilsby. TF 3770
Atcham Salop 34 C3 vil on R Severn 4m/6km SE of Shrewsbury. 18c br. SJ 5409
Atch Lench H & W 27 E3 ham 4m/7km N of Evesham. SP 0350
Athelhampton Dorset 9 E5* ham 1m E of Puddletown. SY 7794
Athelington Suffolk 31 F1 vil 2m/4km SW of Stradbroke. TM 2171
Athelney Som 8 B2 ham 5m/8km W of Langport. Obelisk erected 1801 commemorates King Alfred's having hidden here in 878. ST 3428
Athelstaneford Lothian 66 C1 vil 3m/4km NE of Haddington. NT 5377
Atherfield Green Isle of Wight 10 B6* loc 2m/4km S of Shorwell. SZ 4679
Atherfield, Little Isle of Wight 10 B6 loc 2m/3km S of Shorwell. SZ 4680
Atherfield Point Isle of Wight 10 B6 rocky headland on SW coast between Brighstone Bay and Chale Bay. SZ 4579
Atherington Devon 6 D3 vil 7m/11km S of Barnstaple. SS 5923
Atherington W Sussex 11 F5* loc on coast 5m/8km E of Bognor Regis. TQ 0000
Athersley S Yorks 43 H1* loc in Barnsley 2m/3km N of tn centre. **Athersley North** loc adjoining to NW. SE 3509
Atherstone Som 8 B3* loc 2m/3km NE of Ilminster. ST 3816
Atherstone Warwicks 36 H4 tn 5m/8km NW of Nuneaton. SP 3097
Atherstone on Stour Warwicks 27 F3* vil 3m/4km S of Stratford-upon-Avon. SP 2050
Atherton Gtr Manchester 42 C1 tn 4m/7km SW of Bolton. Textiles, coal-mining, pharmaceutical products. SD 6703
Atholl Tayside 75 G4-H4 mt area of some 450 sq miles or 1200 sq km at S end of Grampians, including **Forest of A.,** deer and game forest N of Glen Garry. NN 77
Atholl Sow Tayside. See Sow of Atholl.
Atlantic Bridge, The S'clyde. See Clachan Bridge.
Atley Hill N Yorks 54 C4 loc 4m/7km NE of Catterick Br. NZ 2802
Atlow Derbys 43 G6 vil 4m/6km E of Ashbourne. SK 2348
Attadale Forest H'land 80 A4, B4 deer forest on borders of Ross & Cromarty and Skye & Lochalsh dists SE of head of Loch Carron. NG 9935
Attenborough Notts 36 B1 loc adjoining Beeston to S. SK 5134
Atterby Lincs 44 D2 ham 5m/8km SE of Kirton in Lindsey. SK 9893
Attercliffe S Yorks 43 H2* dist of Sheffield 2m/3km NE of city centre. Loc of **A. Hill Top** to NE. SK 3788
Atterley Salop 34 C4/D4* loc 2m/3km SE of Much Wenlock. SO 6497
Atterton Leics 35 H4* loc 3m/4km E of Atherstone. SP 3598
Attingham Salop 34 C3. 18c mansion (NT) in large park. SJ 5509
Attleborough Norfolk 39 E5 small tn 14m/23km SW of Norwich. Industries include cider-making, turkey-farming, and general agriculture. TM 0495
Attleborough Warwicks 36 A5 SE dist of Nuneaton. SP 3790
Attlebridge Norfolk 39 E3 vil on R Wensum 8m/13km NW of Norwich. TG 1216
Attleton Green Suffolk 30 C3* ham 7m/12km NE of Haverhill. TL 7454
Atwick Humberside 51 F3 vil near coast 2m/3km NW of Hornsea. TA 1950
Atworth Wilts 16 D5 vil 3m/5km NW of Melksham. Site of Roman villa 1km NW. ST 8635
Auberrow H & W 26 A3* loc 5m/8km N of Hereford. SO 4947
Aubourn Lincs 44 D5 vil 6m/10km SW of Lincoln. SK 9262
Auchagallon S'clyde 63 F4 stone circle (A.M.) on W coast of Arran 4m/7km N of Blackwaterfoot. NR 8934
Auchalick S'clyde 63 F1 r in Argyll running SW to **A. Bay** on E side of Loch Fyne 3m/5km S of Kilfinan. NR 9174
Aucha Lochy S'clyde 63 E5* small loch in Kintyre 2km N of Campbeltown. NR 7222
Auchenback S'clyde 64 C3* loc in SE part of Barrhead. NS 5058
Auchenblae Grampian 77 G3 vil 8m/12km NW of Inverbervie. NO 7278
Auchencairn D & G 58 D6 vil 7m/11km S of Dalbeattie. To E is **A. Bay,** inlet on Solway Firth. NX 7951
Auchencorth Moss 65 H3* upland plateau on borders of Lothian and Borders regions about 3m/5km SW of Penicuik. NT 2055
Auchencrow Borders 67 E3 vil 3m/5km N of Chirnside. NT 8560
Auchendinny Lothian 66 A3 vil 2m/3km NE of Penicuik. NT 2562
Auchendores Reservoir S'clyde 64 B2* small resr 2km N of Kilmacolm. NS 3572
Auchengillan Central 64 C1* loc 3m/5km W of Strathblane. NS 5180
Auchengray S'clyde 65 F3 vil 5m/8km N of Carnwath. NS 9954
Auchenhalrig Grampian 82 C1 loc near N coast 4m/6km SW of Buckie. NJ 3761
Auchenheath S'clyde 65 E4 loc 1m E of Blackwood across R Nethan. NS 8043
Auchenlochan S'clyde 63 F1* loc in Argyll on W shore of Kyles of Bute, 1km S of Tighnabruaich. NR 9772
Auchenmalg Bay D & G 57 C7 southward-facing bay on E side of Luce Bay, 4m/7km SE of Glenluce. NX 2351
Auchenreoch Loch D & G 58 D4 loch 1m SW of Crocketford. NX 8171
Auchenroddan Forest D & G 59 F3* state forest 4m/7km N of Lockerbie. NY 1289
Auchinairn S'clyde 64 D2 loc 1km SE of Bishopbriggs. NS 6169
Auchinbee S'clyde 65 E2* loc in Cumbernauld 2m/3km W of tn centre. NS 7375
Auchincruive S'clyde 64 B6 agricultural college 3m/5km E of Ayr. NS 3823
Auchindoun Castle Grampian. See Dufftown.
Auchindown Grampian 82 C3 loc 2m/3km E of Dufftown. NJ 3539
Auchinleck S'clyde 56 E2 tn in colliery dist 2km NW of Cumnock. NS 5521
Auchintaple Loch Tayside 76 C4* small loch 3m/5km N of Kirkton of Glenisla. NO 1964
Auchintore H'land 74 C4 locality on E shore of Loch Linnhe 1m SW of Fort William. NN 0972
Auchleven Grampian 83 E4 vil 3m/4km S of Insch. NJ 6224
Auchmacoy Grampian 83 G4/H4 loc and estate 2m/4km E of Ellon. NJ 9930
Auchmithie Tayside 73 H1 vil with harbour on coast 3m/5km NE of Arbroath. NO 6844
Auchmore Arran, S'clyde. Alternative name for S Thundergay. See Thundergay.
Auchmuirbridge Fife 73 E4 loc 2m/3km W of Leslie. NO 2101
Auchmuty Fife 73 F4* central dist of Glenrothes. NO 2700
Auchnafree Hill Tayside 72 B2 mt 2m/4km E of Ben Chonzie, S of Glen Almond. Height 2565 ft or 782 metres. NN 8030
Auchnagatt Grampian 83 G3 vil 4m/6km S of Maud. NJ 9341
Auchrannie Tayside 76 C5/D5* loc 3m/5km NE of Alyth. **Slug of A.,** waterfall in R Isla to N. NO 2852
Auchtascailt H'land 85 B7 locality in Ross and Cromarty dist at head of Lit Loch Broom on W coast. NH 0987
Auchterarder Tayside 72 C3 small tn 8m/12km SE of Crieff. Woollen and shirt mnfg. NN 9412
Auchterderran Fife 73 E5 vil in coal-mining area 4m/7km NE of Cowdenbeath. NT 2196
Auchterhouse Hill Tayside 73 F1 hill with ancient fort on Sidlaw Hills 1m W of Craigowl Hill, qv, and 6m/10km NW of Dundee. See also Kirkton of Auchterhouse. NO 3539
Auchterless Grampian. See Kirktown of Auchterless.
Auchtermuchty Fife 73 E3 small tn 4m/7km S of Newburgh. Woollen mnfre, sawmilling, iron founding. Site of Roman camp on E side of tn. NO 2311
Auchtertool Fife 73 E5 vil 4m/6km W of Kirkcaldy. NT 2190
Auchtertyre H'land 79 F6 locality in Skye and Lochalsh dist 3m/4km W of Dornie. NG 8427
Auchtoo Central 71 F3 loc 2km E of Balquidder. NN 5520
Auckengill H'land 86 F2 loc near E coast of Caithness dist 6m/9km S of John o' Groats. ND 3664
Auckland Park Durham 54 B2* loc 2km E of Bishop Auckland. NZ 2228
Auckland, West Durham 54 B2 vil adjoining Bishop Auckland to SW. NZ 1826
Auckley S Yorks 44 B1 vil 5m/8km E of Doncaster. SE 6501
Audenshaw Gtr Manchester 43 E2* tn 5m/8km E of Manchester. **Audenshaw Resrs** to W. Industries include textiles, leather, engineering. SJ 9196
Audlem Ches 34 D1 vil 6m/10km N of Mkt Drayton. SJ 6643
Audley Staffs 42 D6 vil 4m/7km NW of Newcastle-under-Lyme. SJ 7950
Audley End Essex 30 A4 ham 1m W of Saffron Walden. **Audley End Hse** (A.M.) is large 17c hse in park. TL 5237
Audley End Essex 30 C4* S end of Gestingthorpe, 4m/7km N of Halstead. TL 8137
Audley End Suffolk 30 D3* ham 5m/7km N of Long Melford. TL 8553
Audley's Cross Staffs 34 D1* site of battle, 1459, 3m/4km E of Mkt Drayton. SJ 7135
Audmore Staffs 35 E2* loc 1km NE of Gnosall. SJ 8321
Aughton Humberside 50 C4 vil 11m/18km W of Mkt Weighton. Earthworks of motte and bailey cas. SE 7038
Aughton Lancs 42 A1 vil 2m/4km SW of Ormskirk. **A. Park,** S dist of Ormskirk. SD 3905
Aughton Lancs 47 F2 ham 6m/10km NE of Lancaster. SD 5567
Aughton S Yorks 43 H3* loc 4m/7km S of Rotherham. SK 4586
Aughton Wilts 17 F5* ham just N of Collingbourne Kingston and 4m/6km N of Ludgershall. SU 2356
Augill Castle Cumbria 53 G3 early Victn hse 1m SE of Brough. NY 8013
Auld Brig o' Doon S'clyde. See Alloway.
Auldearn H'land 81 H2 vil in Nairn dist 2m/4km E of Nairn. Site of battle in 1645 in which Montrose defeated Covenanters under General Hurry. NH 9155
Aulden H & W 26 A2* ham 3m/5km SW of Leominster. SO 4654
Auldgirth D & G 59 E3* vil on E bank of R Nith, 7m/12km NW of Dumfries. NX 9186
Auldhouse S'clyde 64 D4 loc 3m/4km S of E Kilbride. NS 6250
Auld Wives' Lifts S'clyde. See Craigmaddie Reservoir.
Aultbea H'land 78 F1 vil on E shore of Loch Ewe, W coast of Ross and Cromarty dist, 5m/8km N of Poolewe. NG 8789
Aultgrishan H'land 78 E2 vil on W coast of Ross and Cromarty dist 4m/6km S of Rubha Réidh. NG 7485
Ault Hucknall Derbys 44 A4 ham 5m/8km NW of Mansfield. SK 4665
Aultmore Grampian 82 C2* loc with distillery 2m/4km NW of Keith. Also moorland tract (82 D2) to NE, from which Burn of A. runs S to R Isla. NJ 4053

Aultvaich H'land 81 E3* loc in Ross and Cromarty dist 2km SW of Muir of Ord. NH 5148
Aunby Lincs 37 E3* loc 5m/8km N of Stamford. TF 0214
Aunk Devon 7 H5 loc 5m/7km NW of Ottery St Mary. ST 0400
Aunsby Lincs 37 F1 vil 5m/7km S of Sleaford. TF 0438
Auskerry Orkney 89 C6 uninhabited island 1m N to S and 1km E to W, situated 2m/4km S of Stronsay across **A. Sound.** Lighthouse at S end. HY 6716
Aust Avon 16 B3 vil below E end of Severn Rd Br, 4m/7km W of Thornbury. ST 5789
Austcliffe H & W 35 E6* loc 3m/4km NE of Kidderminster. SO 8480
Austendike Lincs 37 G3* loc 3m/5km E of Spalding. TF 2921
Austerfield S Yorks 44 B2 vil 1m NE of Bawtry. SK 6694
Austerlands Gtr Manchester 43 E1* loc 2m/3km E of Oldham. SD 9505
Austhorpe W Yorks 49 F4/F5* loc 2km NW of W Garforth. **A. Hall** is a stone hse of late 17c in classical style. SE 3733
Austonley W Yorks 43 F1 loc 2m/3km W of Holmfirth. SE 1107
Austrey Warwicks 35 H4 vil 5m/9km N of Atherstone. SK 2906
Austwick N Yorks 48 A2 vil 4m/7km NW of Settle. SD 7668
Autherley Junction W Midlands 35 E4* junction of Staffs & Worcs Canal and Shropshire Union Canal in Wolverhampton 2m/4km N of tn centre. SJ 9002
Authorpe Lincs 45 G3 vil 5m/8km NW of Alford. TF 4080
Authorpe Row Lincs 45 H4 loc 1m N of Hogsthorpe. TF 5373
Avebury Wilts 17 E4 vil (NT) partly enclosed by megalithic stone circle, 6m/9km W of Marlborough. SU 1069
Avebury Trusloe Wilts 17 E4* loc just W of Avebury. SU 0969
Aveley Essex 20 C4 tn 3m/5km NW of Grays. TQ 5680
Avening Glos 16 D2 vil 2m/3km SE of Nailsworth. ST 8897
Averham Notts 44 C5 vil 2m/4km W of Newark-on-Trent across r. SK 7654
Avery Hill London 20 B4* loc 2km E of Eltham in borough of Greenwich. TQ 4474
Aveton Gifford Devon 4 D5 vil at head of R Avon estuary 3m/5km NW of Kingsbridge. SX 6947
Avich S'clyde 70 B3 r in Argyll running from Loch Avich to Loch Awe. NM 9713
Aviemore H'land 81 H6 vil and skiing centre on R Spey in Badenoch and Strathspey dist 11m/18km NE of Kingussie. NH 8912
Avill 7 G1* r in Somerset rising on Exmoor and flowing past Dunster into Blue Anchor Bay. SS 9945
Avington Berks 17 G4* ham 2m/4km E of Hungerford. SU 3768
Avington Hants 10 C2 ham 4m/6km NE of Winchester. **Avington Hse,** 17c hse in park with lake, beside R Itchen. SU 5332
Avoch H'land 81 F2 vil in Ross and Cromarty dist on W shore of Inner Moray Firth or Inverness Firth 2m/3km SW of Fortrose. NH 7055
Avon Hants 9 H4 ham on R Avon 4m/6km N of Christchurch. SZ 1498
Avon 118 western county of England, bounded by Gloucestershire, Wiltshire, Somerset, and the Severn estuary. Mainly composed of the urban complex of Bristol, Bath, and their environs, although there are rural areas around the Chew valley in the S and along the limestone ridge of the Cotswolds bordering its E side. Weston-super-Mare is the only other large tn. R Avon traverses the county from E to W.
Avon 16 A4 r rising W of Sherston, Wilts, and flowing through Bath and Bristol to R Severn estuary at Avonmouth. Navigable to Bristol for large vessels; tidal to Swineford, E of Keynsham. ST 5078
Avon 26 D4 r rising on borders of Leics and Northants near S Kilworth and flowing generally SW by Rugby, Warwick, Stratford, Evesham, and Pershore, and into R Severn at Tewkesbury, Glos. SO 8833
Avon 4 C6 Devon r rising on Dartmoor and flowing generally S into Bigbury Bay 2km NW of Thurlestone. SX 6543
Avon 65 F1 r rising 3m/5km S of Falkirk, Central region, and flowing W towards Cumbernauld, then turning E to Avonbridge, NE to Linlithgow, NW towards Grangemouth, and finally NE to Firth of Forth between Grangemouth and Bo'ness. Between Avonbridge and Linlithgow r forms boundary between Central and Lothian regions. NS 9882
Avon 82 B3 r in Grampian region rising on Cairngorm Mts and running E through Loch Avon and down Glen Avon, then N to Tomintoul and down Strath Avon to R Spey just below Ballindalloch Castle, 7m/11km SW of Charlestown of Aberlour. See also Forest of Glenavon. NJ 1737
Avon 9 H5 r rising in Vale of Pewsey in Wiltshire and flowing S through Amesbury, Salisbury, Fordingbridge, and Ringwood, and thence into Christchurch Harbour, Dorset. SZ 1692
Avonbridge Central 65 F2 vil 5m/8km S of Falkirk. NS 9172
Avoncliff Wilts 16 C5* loc 2km SW of Bradford-on-Avon across r. ST 8059
Avondale Gwent 15 G2* industrial estate in N part of Cwmbran. ST 2996
Avon Dam Reservoir Devon 4 D4 resr on Dartmoor (R Avon) 4m/6km W of Buckfastleigh. SX 6765
Avon Dassett Warwicks 27 H3 vil 7m/11km NW of Banbury. SP 4150
Avon, Little 16 B2 r rising in Cotswold Hills near Wotton-under-Edge, Glos, and flowing into R Severn near Berkeley. SO 6600
Avonmouth Avon 16 A4 port of Bristol, 6m/9km NW of city centre. Large docks. R Avon here spanned by M5 motorway. ST 5178
Avon Water 10 A5* r rising 2km S of Burley, Hants, and flowing SE into the Solent at Keyhaven. SZ 3091
Avon Water 65 E3 r in Strathclyde region rising 6m/10km SE of Galston and flowing NE past Strathaven to Larkhall, then N to R Clyde 1m E of Hamilton. NS 7356
Avonwick Devon 4 D5 vil on R Avon 2m/3km SE of S Brent. SX 7158
Awbridge Hants 10 A2 vil 2m/4km NW of Romsey. SU 3223
Awe 70 C2 r in Argyll, S'clyde, running from Loch Awe through Pass of Brander to Loch Etive at Bonawe. NN 0132
Awliscombe Devon 7 H5 vil 2m/3km NW of Honiton. ST 1301
Awre Glos 16 C1 vil on R Severn estuary 2m/4km E of Blakeney. SO 7008
Awsworth Notts 36 B1 vil 6m/10km NW of Nottingham. SK 4844
Axbridge Som 16 A5 vil 2m/3km W of Cheddar. ST 4354
Axe 15 G5 r rising under Mendip Hills and flowing out above ground at Wookey Hole, Som, thence NW into Bristol Channel at Weston Bay S of Weston-super-Mare. ST 2959
Axe 8 B5 r rising N of Beaminster in Dorset and flowing W and then SW into Lyme Bay to E of Seaton in Devon. SY 2589
Axford Hants 10 C1 vil 1m N of Preston Candover. SU 6143
Axford Wilts 17 F4 vil on R Kennet 3m/5km E of Marlborough. SU 2370
Axholme, Isle of Humberside 44 C1 area of slight elevation above flat and formerly marshy tract bounded by Rs Trent, Torne and Idle. Tns and vils include Belton, Epworth and Haxey on the higher ground, and Owston Ferry and W Butterwick beside R Trent. SE 7080
Axminster Devon 8 B4 small tn on R Axe, 5m/8km NW of Lyme Regis. SY 2998
Axmouth Devon 8 B5 small resort near mouth of R Axe 2km NE of Seaton across r. SY 2591
Axton Clwyd 41 G3* loc 3m/4km SE of Prestatyn. SJ 1080
Axtown Devon 4 B4* loc 5m/8km SE of Tavistock. SX 5167
Aycliffe Durham 54 C3 vil 5m/8km N of Darlington. Adjoins **A. Industrial Estate** in New Tn of Newton Aycliffe, which is itself sometimes referred to as Aycliffe. NZ 2822
Aydon Nthmb 61 E5 ham 2m/3km NE of Corbridge. **A. Castle,** late 13c fortified hse 1km NW. NZ 0066
Aygill N Yorks 53 G4* loc 1km S of Keld. NY 8800
Aylburton Glos 16 B2 vil 1m SW of Lydney. SO 6101
Ayle Nthmb 53 F1* loc 2m/3km N of Alston. NY 7149
Aylesbeare Devon 7 H5 vil 5m/7km SW of Ottery St Mary. SY 0392
Aylesbury Bucks 18 C1 county tn on plain below N escarpment of Chiltern Hills 36m/58km NW of London. Various light industries. Many old bldgs and streets. The King's Head (NT), still an inn, dates partly from 15c. Airport at Haddenham, 6m/10km SW. SP 8113
Aylesby Humberside 45 F1 vil 4m/7km W of Grimsby. TA 2007
Aylesford Kent 20 D5 vil on R Medway 3m/5km NW of Maidstone. 14c br spans r. Industrial and residential development to W. TQ 7258
Aylesham Kent 13 G2 coal-mining vil 7m/11km SE of Canterbury. TR 2352
Aylestone Leics 36 B4 dist of Leicester 2m/4km S of city centre. **A. Park** loc adjoining to NE. SK 5700
Aylmerton Norfolk 39 F1 vil 3m/4km SW of Cromer. TG 1839
Aylsham Norfolk 39 F2 small mkt tn on R Bure 12m/19km N of Norwich. TG 1926
Aylton H & W 26 B4* ham 3m/5km W of Ledbury. SO 6537
Aymestrey H & W 26 A1 vil 6m/9km NW of Leominster. SO 4265
Aynho Northants 28 A4 vil 6m/9km SE of Banbury. SP 5133
Ayot Green Herts 19 F1 ham 2km NW of Welwyn Garden City. TL 2214
Ayot St Lawrence Herts 29 F6 vil 2m/4km W of Welwyn. Shaw's Corner (NT), formerly home of George Bernard Shaw. TL 1916
Ayot St Peter Herts 29 F6 ham 2km SW of Welwyn. TL 2115
Ayr S'clyde 64 B6 tn and resort on Firth of Clyde at mouth of **R Ayr** 12m/19km SW of Kilmarnock. Racecourse. Industries include engineering, mnfre of agricultural implements, carpets, chemicals, electrical equipment, footwear. TV stn to SW. R rises E of Muirkirk and flows W through Sorn and Catrine. NS 3321
Ayre, Point of Isle of Man. See Point of Ayre.
Ayre's Quay Tyne & Wear 61 H5* loc on S bank of R Wear in Sunderland, 1km NW of tn centre. Power stn to S. NZ 3857
Ayres, The Isle of Man 46 B3, C3 flat and barren coastal strip between Rue Pt and Pt of Ayre. NX 40
Ayre, The Orkney 89 A7* narrow neck of land, carrying a rd, linking peninsula of S Walls with S end of Hoy. ND 2889
Ayr, Point of (Y Parlwr Du) Clwyd 41 G3 promontory at W end of R Dee estuary 4m/6km E of Prestatyn. Also spelt Point of Air. SJ 1285
Aysgarth N Yorks 54 A5 vil in Wensleydale 7m/12km W of Leyburn. 1m E, downstream, is **Aysgarth Force,** also known as Aysgarth Falls, waterfall in R Ure descending in series of rock 'steps'. SE 0088
Ayshford Devon 7 H3 ham 2km NE of Sampford Peverell. ST 0317
Ayside Cumbria 52 D6 ham 2m/4km SE of Newby Br. SD 3983
Ayston Leics 36 D4 ham 1m N of Uppingham. SK 8600
Aythorpe Roding Essex 30 B6* par to NE of Leaden Roding. TL 6015
Ayton Borders 67 F3 vil on Eye Water 3m/4km SW of Eyemouth. NT 9261
Ayton Tyne & Wear 61 G5* dist of Washington SW of tn centre. NZ 2855
Ayton, East N Yorks 55 G6 vil 4m/6km SW of Scarborough, on E side of R Derwent. SE 9984
Ayton, Great N Yorks 54 D4/55 E4 vil 5m/8km SW of Guisborough. **Lit Ayton** ham 1m E. Group of Iron Age cairns and hut circles on Gt Ayton Moor 2m/4km E. NZ 5510
Ayton, West N Yorks 55 G6 vil on W bank of R Derwent opp E Ayton and 4m/7km SW of Scarborough. **A. Castle,** ruined 14c tower hse. SE 9884
Aywick Shetland 89 F6* loc on Yell 1m NE of Otterswick. Bay of **Ay Wick** to E. HU 5386
Azerley N Yorks 49 E1* ham 4m/6km NW of Ripon. SE 2574

B

Bà S'clyde 68 D4* r on Mull running N from Loch Bà to head of Loch na Keal. NM 5341
Bà S'clyde 75 E6 r in Argyll rising S of Clach Leathad and running E through Loch Buidhe, Lochan na Stainge, and Loch Bà, to head of Loch Laidon. NN 3551
Babbacombe Devon 5 E4 dist of Torquay giving its name to bay stretching from Hope's Nose in the S to The Parson and Clerk, between Teignmouth and Dawlish, in the N. SX 9265
Babbet Ness Fife 73 H3 headland at SE end of St Andrews Bay 2km N of Kingsbarn. NO 5914
Babbington Notts 36 B1* loc 1km SW of Kimberley. SK 4943
Babbinswood Salop 34 A2 loc 1m SE of Whittington. SJ 3330
Babb's Green Herts 29 G6* ham 3m/4km NE of Ware. TL 3916
Babcary Som 8 D2 vil 3m/5km NW of Sparkford. ST 5628
Babel Dyfed 24 D4* loc 4m/7km E of Llandovery. SN 8335
Babel Green Suffolk 30 C3* loc 4m/7km NE of Haverhill. TL 7348
Babell Clwyd 41 G4 loc 2m/4km SW of Holywell. SJ 1573
Babergh 119 admin dist of Suffolk.
Babingley Norfolk 38 B2* loc 2m/3km SW of Sandringham. TF 6726
Babingley 38 B2 r rising E of Flitcham, Norfolk, and flowing W then SW into R Ouse at its mouth N of King's Lynn. TF 6023
Bablock Hythe Oxon 17 H1 loc on R Thames 3m/5km S of Eynsham. Ferry for pedestrians. SP 4304
Babraham Cambs 30 H3 vil 7m/11km SE of Cambridge. TL 5150
Babworth Notts 44 B3 ham 2km W of E Retford. SK 6880
Babylon Clwyd 41 H5* loc 2m/3km NE of Hope. SJ 3260
Bac an Eich H'land 80 C3 mt on Strathconon Forest, Ross and Cromarty dist. Height 2787 ft or 849 metres. NH 2248
Bac Beag Treshnish Isles, S'clyde 69 A5 island at SW end of group. See also Bac Mór. NM 2337
Bachau Gwynedd 40 B3* loc on Anglesey nearly 1m E of Llanerchymedd. SH 4383
Bachelors' Club S'clyde. See Tarbolton.
Bach Island S'clyde 70 A2 small island off Rubha na Feundain at SW end of Kerrera. NM 7726
Back W Isles 88 C2 vil near E coast of Lewis 6m/10km NE of Stornoway. NB 4840
Backaland Orkney 89 B6 loc near S end of island of Eday. To E is **Bay of B.**, where there is a landing stage. HY 5730
Backaskail Bay Orkney 89 C5* wide bay on S coast of island of Sanday 4m/6km W of Tres Ness. HY 6438
Back Bar Grampian 83 H1 sand dunes between Strathbeg Bay and Loch of Strathbeg on NE coast, 7m/11km SE of Fraserburgh. NK 0759
Backbarrow Cumbria 52 D6 loc 2km SW of Newby Br. SD 3584
Backe Dyfed 23 E4* loc 2km W of St Clears. SN 2615
Backford Ches 42 A4 vil 3m/5km N of Chester. **B. Cross** loc 2km NW. SJ 3971
Backhill Grampian 77 H1 loc in W part of Aberdeen, 3m/5km from city centre. NJ 8905
Backmoor S Yorks 43 H3* loc in Sheffield 3m/5km S of city centre. SK 3682
Backmuir of New Gilston Fife 73 G4 vil 3m/5km N of Largo. NO 4308
Back of Keppoch H'land 68 D1/E1. See Keppoch.
Back o' th' Brook Staffs 43 F5* loc just N of Waterfall. SK 0851

Back's Green Suffolk 39 G6* loc 2km W of Redisham. TM 3884

Back Stream 8 A2* r in Somerset rising on W slopes of Quantock Hills and flowing SE through Bishop's Lydeard into Halse Water just above its confluence with R Tone 2km W of Taunton. ST 2025

Back Street Suffolk 30 C2* loc 7m/11km SE of Newmarket. TL 7458

Backwater Reservoir Tayside 76 C4, C5 resr nearly 4km long N to S, in Glenisla Forest 7m/11km N of Alyth. NO 2559

Backwell Avon 16 A4 vil 6m/10km SW of Bristol. ST 4968

Backworth Tyne & Wear 61 G4 coal-mining loc 3m/5km W of Whitley Bay. NZ 3072

Bac Mór Treshnish Isles, S'clyde 69 A5 island towards SW end of group. Also known as Dutchman's Cap, owing to its shape. Bac Beag, its neighbour to S, is at the extreme SW of group. NM 2438

Bacon End Essex 30 B6* loc 2m/4km SW of Gt Dunmow. Loc of **Baconend Green** 1km N. TL 6018

Bacon Hole W Glam 23 G6* cave at foot of cliffs 1km W of Pwlldu Hd on S coast of Gower peninsula. Here ancient animal remains were discovered in 1850. SS 5586

Bacon's End W Midlands 35 G5 loc 2m/3km SW of Coleshill. SP 1787

Baconsthorpe Norfolk 39 E1 vil 3m/5km SE of Holt. Remains of 15c cas (A.M.) and of 16c hall to NW. TG 1237

Bacton H & W 25 H4 vil 4m/6km NW of Pontrilas. SO 3732

Bacton Norfolk 39 G2 vil on coast 5m/7km NE of N Walsham. **N Bacton** loc adjoining to N. **B. Gas Terminal** 1m NW. TG 3433

Bacton Suffolk 31 E2 vil 5m/9km N of Stowmarket. Loc of **B. Green** 2km SW. TM 0567

Bacup Lancs 48 B5 tn near head of R Irwell valley 6m/10km S of Burnley and N of Rochdale. Textiles, footwear, engineering. Extensive quarries to S. SD 8623

Badachro H'land 78 E2 vil on S shore of Gair Loch, W coast of Ross and Cromarty dist. **R Badachro** runs into loch here from S. NG 7873

Badanloch Forest H'land 86 B4 deer forest in Sutherland dist NW of Kinbrace. NC 83

Badbury Wilts 17 F3 vil 4m/6km SE of Swindon. Loc of **B. Wick** 1m NW. SU 1980

Badbury Hill Oxon 17 G2 NT property with Iron Age fort 2m/3km W of Faringdon. SU 2694

Badbury Rings Dorset 9 G4 Iron Age fort enclosing a wood, 4m/6km NW of Wimborne. ST 9603

Badby Northants 28 B2 vil 3m/4km SW of Daventry. SP 5659

Badcall H'land 84 C2 locality on N side of Loch Inchard 1m E of Kinlochbervie, near W coast of Sutherland dist. NC 2455

Badcall H'land 84 C3 loc on N side of **B. Bay,** W coast of Sutherland dist, 2m/3km S of Scourie. NC 1541

Badcaul H'land 85 A7 vil on SW side of Lit Loch Broom, W coast of Ross and Cromarty dist. NH 0191

Baddeley Edge Staffs 43 E6* loc 3m/5km NE of Hanley. SJ 9150

Baddeley Green Staffs 43 E6* loc 2km SW of Endon. SJ 9151

Baddesley Clinton Warwicks 27 F1* vil 7m/11km NW of Warwick. **B. C. Hall** is a moated medieval manor hse. SP 2072

Baddesley Ensor Warwicks 35 H4 mining vil 2m/3km W of Atherstone. SP 2798

Baddesley, North Hants 10 B3 vil 3m/5km E of Romsey. SU 4020

Baddesley, South Hants 10 A5* ham 2m/3km E of Lymington. SZ 3596

Baddiley Mere Reservoir Ches 42 B6* resr 4m/6km W of Nantwich. SJ 5950

Baddinsgill Reservoir Borders 65 G3* resr on Pentland Hills 3m/4km NW of W Linton. NT 1255

Baddow, Great Essex 20 D2 suburb adjoining Chelmsford to SE. TL 7204

Baddow, Little Essex 20 D1 vil 5m/8km E of Chelmsford. TL 7807

Baden Bay H'land A6 bay on NW coast of Ross and Cromarty dist opp Achiltibuie. Also known as Badentarbat Bay. NC 0108

Badenoch H'land 75 F3-H2 S part of Badenoch and Strathspey dist round about Kingussie, traversed by R Spey, between Monadhliath Mts and the Central Grampians S of the Cairngorms. NN 79

Badenoch and Strathspey 114, 115 admin dist of H'land region.

Badentarbat Bay H'land. See Baden Bay.

Badgall Cornwall 6 B6* loc 6m/10km W of Launceston. SX 2386

Badgeney Cambs 37 H5* loc in E part of March. TL 4296

Badger Salop 34 D4 vil 5m/8km NE of Bridgnorth. SO 7699

Badgers Mount Kent 20 B5* loc and rd junction 3m/5km SE of Orpington. TQ 4962

Badgeworth Glos 26 D5 vil 3m/5km SW of Cheltenham. SO 9019

Badgworth Som 15 H6 vil 3m/4km SW of Axbridge. ST 3952

Badgworthy Water 7 F1* r rising on N Exmoor and flowing into the E Lyn R about 3m/5km SE of Foreland Pt. SS 7948

Badharlick Cornwall 6 B6* loc 4m/7km W of Launceston. SX 2686

Badicaul H'land 79 E5 loc in Skye and Lochalsh dist, on coast 1m N of Kyle of Lochalsh. NG 7529

Badingham Suffolk 31 G2 vil 3m/5km NE of Framlingham. TM 3068

Badlesmere Kent 21 F6* vil 5m/8km S of Faversham. TR 0054

Badley Suffolk 31 E3 par and loc 2m/3km SE of Stowmarket. TM 0655

Badluarach H'land 85 A7 vil on W side of Lit Loch Broom, W coast of Ross and Cromarty dist, nearly 2m/3km SE of Stattic Pt. NG 9994

Badminton, Great Avon 16 C3 vil at S end of B. Park, 5m/8km E of Chipping Sodbury. Ham of **Lit Badminton** 1m N across park. ST 8082

Badrallach H'land 85 B7 locality on NE side of Lit Loch Broom, W coast of Ross and Cromarty dist, 3m/5km from head of loch. NH 0691

Badsey H & W 27 E3 vil 2m/4km E of Evesham. SP 0743

Badshot Lea Surrey 11 E1 vil 2m/3km NE of Farnham. SU 8648

Badsworth W Yorks 49 F6 vil 3m/4km NE of Hemsworth. SE 4614

Badwell Ash Suffolk 31 E2 vil 4m/6km E of Ixworth. TL 9969

Badwell Green Suffolk 31 E2* loc 2m/3km E of Badwell Ash. TM 0169

Badworthy Devon 4 D4* ham 2m/3km NW of S Brent. SX 6861

Baffins Hants 10 D4* E dist of Portsmouth. SU 6601

Bagber Dorset 9 E3* ham 1km E of Lydlinch and 2m/3km W of Sturminster Newton. ST 7513

Bagborough, West Som 8 A1 vil at foot of Quantock Hills 7m/11km NW of Taunton. 1m SE, ham of **E Bagborough.** ST 1733

Bagby N Yorks 54 D6 vil 2m/4km SE of Thirsk. SE 4680

Bag Enderby Lincs 45 G4 vil 5m/8km NW of Spilsby. TF 3472

Bagendon Glos 17 E1 vil 3m/5km N of Cirencester. SP 0106

Bagginswood Salop 34 D6* loc 4m/6km N of Cleobury Mortimer. SO 6881

Baggrow Cumbria 52 B1 loc 2m/3km E of Aspatria. NY 1742

Baggy Point Devon 6 C2 headland (NT) 8m/13km SW of Ilfracombe between Barnstaple (or Bideford) Bay to S and Morte Bay to N. SS 4140

Bagham Kent 21 F6* loc 5m/9km SW of Canterbury. TR 0753

Bàgh Gleann nam Muc S'clyde 69 E7* bay 1km SW of northern point of Jura. NM 6800

Bàgh Gleann Speireig S'clyde 69 E7 bay on NW coast of Jura 1km SW of Glengarrisdale Bay. NR 6396

Bàgh Hirivagh W Isles. See Northbay.

Bàgh nam Faoileann W Isles 88 E2 bay containing numerous islets between Benbecula and S Uist on E side. NF 84

Bàgh an Trailleich Coll, S'clyde 68 A3* bay on NW coast 3m/5km N of Arinagour. NM 2161

Bagillt Clwyd 41 H4 loc on R Dee estuary 2m/3km NW of Flint. Textile works. SJ 2275

Baginton Warwicks 35 H6 vil 3m/4km S of Coventry. Coventry Civil Airport to E. SP 3474

Baglan W Glam 14 D2 tn 2m/3km NW of Port Talbot. Oil refinery to SW, beside **B. Bay,** at mouth of R Neath. SS 7592

Bagley Salop 34 B2* ham 5m/8km S of Ellesmere. SJ 4027

Bagley Som 16 A6* ham 2m/3km SE of Wedmore. ST 4546

Bagley W Yorks 49 E4* loc 2km N of Pudsey. SE 2236

Bagley Green Som 7 H3* ham 2km SW of Wellington. ST 1219

Bagmore Hants 18 B6 ham 5m/8km S of Basingstoke. SU 6644

Bagnall Staffs 43 E6 vil 5m/8km NE of Stoke-on-Trent. SJ 9250

Bagnor Berks 17 H4 loc 2m/3km NW of Newbury. SU 4569

Bagpath Glos 16 C2* loc 3m/5km E of Wotton-under-Edge. ST 8094

Bagshot Surrey 18 D5 tn 4m/6km NE of Camberley. To S, **B. Heath,** former haunt of highwaymen now traversed by M3 motorway. SU 9163

Bagshot Wilts 17 G5* loc 3m/4km SW of Hungerford. SU 3165

Bagslate Moor Gtr Manchester 47 H6* loc in Rochdale 2m/3km W of tn centre. SD 8613

Bagthorpe Norfolk 38 C2 ham 4m/6km SE of Docking. TF 7932

Bagthorpe Notts 44 A5 loc 3m/5km N of Eastwood. SK 4751

Baguley Gtr Manchester 42 D2 loc 2m/4km SE of Altrincham. SJ 8089

Bagworth Leics 36 A3 coal-mining vil 4m/7km S of Coalville. SK 4408

Bagwy Lydiart H & W 26 A5* ham 3m/5km E of Pontrilas. SO 4426

Baildon W Yorks 48 D4 suburb 4m/6km N of Bradford. Spinning, dyeing, galvanising. **B. Green** 1m SW. SE 1539

Baile Mór S'clyde 69 B5* vil on E coast of Iona. Site of 6c monastery; 13c remains. Maclean's Cross (A.M.), 15c. Cathedral to N. Ferry to Fionnphort on Mull across Sound of Iona. NM 2824

Bailey Green Hants 10 D2* loc 3m/4km NE of W Meon. SU 6727

Bailey Grove Notts 44 A6* loc 1km W of Eastwood. SK 4646

Bailey Mill Cumbria 60 B4 loc 6m/10km S of Newcastleton. NY 5178

Bailiff Bridge W Yorks 48 D5 loc 2km N of Brighouse. SE 1425

Bailivanish W Isles. See Balivanish.

Baillieston S'clyde 64 D3 suburb 5m/9km E of Glasgow. NS 6764

Bailrigg Lancs 47 F2* loc 2m/3km S of Lancaster. Site of University of Lancaster. SD 4858

Bain 45 F3 r rising at Ludford Parva, Lincs, and flowing S through Lincolnshire W Wolds into R Witham at Dogdyke. TF 2055

Bain 53 H5 r rising on moors S of Hawes, N Yorks, and flowing NE through Semer Water and Bainbridge into R Ure 1m W of Askrigg. SD 9390

Bainbridge N Yorks 53 H5 vil on R Bain near its confluence with R Ure 4m/6km E of Hawes. Site of Roman fort to E. SD 9390

Bainton Cambs 37 F4 vil 4m/7km E of Stamford. TF 0906

Bainton Humberside 50 D3/51 E3 vil 5m/8km SW of Gt Driffield. SE 9652

Bainton Oxon 28 B5* loc 3m/5km N of Bicester. SP 5826

Baird's Monument Tayside 72 C3 monmt on hill above N bank of R Earn, 3m/4km W of Crieff. Commemorates Sir David Baird, 1757-1829. NN 8221

Baitings Reservoir W Yorks 48 C6* resr on S side of Littleborough-Ripponden rd 2m/3km W of Ripponden. SE 0118

Bait Island Tyne & Wear 61 H4* island rock off North Sea coast, with lighthouse, 2m/3km N of Whitley Bay. Also known as St Mary's. NZ 3575

Baker's Bridge Lincs 37 G1* loc with br over New Hammond Beck 3m/5km W of Boston. TF 2842

Baker's End Herts 29 G6 loc 3m/5km SE of Ware. TL 3917

Baker's Hill Glos 26 B6* loc 1m NE of Coleford. SO 5811

Baker's Island Hants 10 D4* uninhabited island in Langstone Harbour off Farlington Marshes. SU 6903

Baker's Lane Warwicks 35 G6* loc 4m/7km SE of Solihull. SP 1874

Baker Street Essex 20 C3 loc 3m/5km N of Tilbury. TQ 6381

Bakestone Moor Derbys 44 A3* loc adjoining Whitwell to SW. SK 5276

Bakewell Derbys 43 G4 old mkt tn on R Wye 7m/12km NW of Matlock. Saxon cross in churchyard. 15c br spans r. SK 2168

Bala Gwynedd 33 F1 mkt tn on R Tryweryn near its confluence with R Dee near lower, NE, end of **Bala Lake.** The lake runs SW to NE and is the largest natural lake in Wales, being nearly 6km long and 1km wide. SH 9236

Balado Tayside 72 D4* loc 2m/3km W of Kinross. NO 0802

Balallan W Isles 88 B2 vil on N side of Loch Erisort, E coast of Lewis, near head of loch. NB 2920

Balavil H'land 75 G1 loc in Badenoch and Strathspey dist 2m/4km NE of Kingussie. NH 7802

Balbeggie Tayside 73 E2 vil 5m/8km NE of Perth. NO 1629

Balbegno Castle Grampian 77 F4 cas, 16c and later, 1km SW of Fettercairn. NO 6473

Balblair H'land 81 E3* loc in Inverness dist 2km SW of Beauly. NH 5246

Balblair H'land 81 F1 vil on S side of Cromarty Firth, Ross and Cromarty dist, opp Invergordon. NH 7066

Balblair H'land 87 A7* loc with distillery on W side of Edderton, in Ross and Cromarty dist. NH 7084

Balblair Forest H'land 85 F7* state forest astride Kyle of Sutherland, NW of Bonar Br, Sutherland dist. NH 59

Balby S Yorks 44 B1 dist of Doncaster 2m/3km SW of tn centre. SE 5501

Balcary D & G 58 D6 loc on **B. Bay,** 2m/3km SE of Auchencairn. **Balcary Pt** is headland on SE side of bay. NX 8249

Balchreick H'land 84 B2* vil near W coast of Sutherland dist 3m/5km NW of Kinlochbervie. NC 1959

Balcombe W Sussex 11 H2 residential loc 4m/7km N of Haywards Heath. TQ 3030

Balcombe Lane W Sussex 11 H2 loc 2km N of Balcombe and 4m/6km SE of Crawley. TQ 3132

Balcurvie Fife 73 F4* vil adjoining Windygates to N. NO 3400

Balder 53 H3* r rising on Stainmore Common, Cumbria, and flowing E through Balderhead, Blackton, and Hury Resrs into R Tees at Cotherstone, Durham. NZ 0120

Balderhead Reservoir Durham 53 H3* first of three resrs in course of R Balder 5m/8km NW of Bowes. NY 9218

Baldersby N Yorks 49 F1 vil 5m/8km SW of Thirsk. SE 3578

Baldersby St James N Yorks 49 F1* ham 2km SE of Baldersby. SE 3676

Balderstone Gtr Manchester 48 B6* loc in Rochdale 2m/3km SE of tn centre. SD 9011

Balderstone Lancs 47 G5 vil 4m/7km NW of Blackburn. SD 6332

Balderton Ches 42 A5* loc 1m NE of Dodleston. SJ 3762

Balderton Notts 44 C5 suburb adjoining Newark-on-Trent to SE. See also New Balderton. SK 8151

Baldhoon Isle of Man 46 B5* loc 1m W of Laxey. SC 4184

Baldhu Cornwall 2 D4* loc 4m/6km W of Truro. SW 7742

Baldingstone Gtr Manchester 47 H6* loc in Bury 2m/4km N of tn centre. SD 8014

Baldock Herts 29 F4 tn 6m/10km N of Stevenage. Industries include hosiery mnfre. TL 2433

Baldon Row Oxon 18 B2* loc at Toot Baldon 5m/8km SE of Oxford. SP 5600

Baldovan Tayside 73 G1/G2 dist of Dundee 3m/4km N of city centre. NO 3834

Baldrine Isle of Man 46 C5 vil 2m/3km S of Laxey. SC 4281

Baldwin Isle of Man 46 B5 ham 4m/6km NW of Douglas. SC 3581

Baldwin 46 B5* r on Isle of Man running S into R Glass 3m/5km N of Douglas. SC 3680
Baldwinholme Cumbria 59 H6 loc 2m/4km NW of Dalston. NY 3351
Baldwin's Gate Staffs 35 E1* loc 2km SW of Whitmore. SJ 7939
Baldwins Hill Surrey 12 A3* loc adjoining E Grinstead to N. TQ 3839
Bale Norfolk 39 E1 vil 4m/7km W of Holt. TG 0136
Balemartine Tiree, S'clyde 69 A8 vil on Hynish Bay, 4m/7km SW of Scarinish across the bay. NL 9841
Balephetrish Bay Tiree, S'clyde 69 A7 wide bay on N coast 3m/5km NW of Scarinish. NM 0047
Balephuil Bay Tiree, S'clyde 69 A8 wide bay at SW end of island. Loc of **Balephuil** is on E side of bay. NL 9440
Balerno Lothian 65 G2/H2 vil 7m/12km SW of Edinburgh. Malleny, 17c hse; garden (NTS). NT 1666
Baleshare W Isles 88 D1, E1 low-lying island off W coast of N Uist to W of Carinish. NF 7861
Balfour Orkney 89 B6 loc and small harbour on S coast of Shapinsay near its western end. **B. Castle** is baronial-style mansion to W. HY 4716
Balfour Castle Tayside 76 D5. See Kirkton of Kingoldrum.
Balfron Central 71 F5 vil 6m/9km N of Strathblane. NS 5488
Balgavies Loch Tayside 77 E5 small loch 5m/8km E of Forfar. NO 5350
Balgedie Tayside. See Easter B. and Wester B.
Balgillie Reservoir Fife 73 E4/E5* small resr 2km N of Leslie. NO 2403
Balgonie Castle Fife 73 F4 15c tower with later courtyard, on W side of Milton of Balgonie across R Leven. NO 3100
Balgowan H'land 75 F2 loc in Badenoch and Strathspey dist 2km E of Laggan Br. NN 6394
Balgown Skye, H'land 78 B3 loc 4m/6m N of Uig. NG 3868
Balgray Tayside 73 G1 vil 5m/8km N of Dundee. NO 4038
Balgray Reservoir S'clyde 64 C3 resr 2km SE of Barrhead. NS 5157
Balhalgardy Grampian 83 F4* loc 2m/3km NW of Inverurie. NJ 7623
Balham London 19 G4* dist in borough of Wandsworth 1m S of Clapham Common. TQ 2873
Balhinny Grampian 82 D4 loc 2m/4km W of Rhynie. Also known as Belhinnie. NJ 4627
Baliasta Shetland 8 F5* loc on Unst 2km W of Baltasound. HP 6009
Baligill H'land 86 B2 loc on N coast of Caithness dist 3m/5km SE of Strathy Pt. NC 8566
Balintore H'land 87 B8 vil on E coast of Ross and Cromarty dist 7m/11km SE of Tain. NH 8675
Balintore Tayside 76 D5 loc and cas 7m/11km NW of Kirriemuir. NO 2859
Balintraid H'land 87 A8* loc on Cromarty Firth, Ross and Cromarty dist, 2m/4km NE of Invergordon. Developments in connection with North Sea oil. NH 7370
Balivanish W Isles 88 E1* vil on NW coast of Benbecula. Benbecula Airfield on low promontory to N. NF 7855
Balk N Yorks 49 F1 loc 3m/5km E of Thirsk. SE 4780
Balkeerie Tayside 73 F1* loc 3m/5km NE of Newtyle. NO 3244
Balk Field Notts 44 B3* loc adjoining E Retford to E. SK 7181
Balkholme Humberside 50 C5 ham 2m/4km E of Howden. SE 7828
Ball Salop 34 A2 loc 2m/4km SE of Oswestry. SJ 3026
Balla W Isles 88 E3* vil at NW end of island of Eriskay. NF 7811
Ballabeg Isle of Man 46 A6 vil 2m/3km NW of Castletown. SC 2470
Ballacannell Isle of Man 46 C5* loc 1m S of Laxey. SC 4382
Ballachulish H'land 74 B5 locality on S shore of Loch Leven in Lochaber dist. **N. Ballachulish** is vil on N shore. Rd br spans loch. NN 0559
Ballacottier 46 C5* r on Isle of Man running S then SE to sea at Port Groudle at foot of Groudle Glen on E coast. SC 4278
Ballaglasa W Isles 88 E1* loc on island of Grimsay between N Uist and Benbecula. NF 8457
Ballajora Isle of Man 46 C4 loc 3m/5km SE of Ramsey. SC 4790
Ballakilpheric Isle of Man 46 A6 loc nearly 1m NW of Colby. SC 2271
Ballam, Higher Lancs 47 E5 loc 2m/3km NE of Lytham St Anne's. **Lr Ballam** loc 1km NE. SD 3630
Ballantrae S'clyde 57 B5 small fishing port on **B.Bay** 12m/19km SW of Girvan. Not the scene of R. L. Stevenson's *Master of Ballantrae* (see Borgue). NX 0882
Ballantrushal W Isles 88 B1* vil near NW coast of Lewis 3m/4km N of Barvas. NB 3753
Ballaragh Isle of Man 46 C5* loc 2km NE of Laxey. SC 4585
Ballard Point Dorset 9 G6* headland at E end of Purbeck Hills and at N end of Swanage Bay. SZ 0481
Balla Reservoir Fife 73 E4 resr 2m/3km NW of Leslie. NO 2204
Ballasalla Isle of Man 46 B6 vil 2m/3km NE of Castletown. SC 2870
Ballater Grampian 76 D2 vil and resort on R Dee 14m/22km E of Braemar and 17m/28km W of Aberdeen. Pass of B. carries E–W rd 1km N. NO 3695
Ballathona Isle of Man 46 B3 loc 2m/3km NW of Andreas. Also known as The Lhen. NX 3901
Ballaugh Isle of Man 46 B4 vil 7m/11km W of Ramsey. SC 3493
Ballchraggan H'land 87 B8 vil in Ross and Cromarty dist 5m/7km S of Tain. NH 7675
Ballcladdish H'land 84 A4 loc on W coast of Sutherland dist 3m/5km S of Pt of Stoer. NC 0330
Ballencleuch Law S'clyde 59 E1 mt in Lowther Hills 8m/12km S of Elvanfoot. Height 2267 ft or 386 metres. NS 9304
Ball Green Staffs 42 D5* loc 2m/3km NE of Tunstall. SJ 8852
Ball Haye Green Staffs 43 E5 loc 1km NE of Leek. SJ 9957
Ball Hill Hants 17 H5* vil 4m/7km SW of Newbury. SU 4263
Ballidon Derbys 43 G5 ham 5m/8km N of Ashbourne. SK 2054
Ballindalloch Castle Grampian 82 B3 baronial cas, with modern additions and alterations, on right bank of R Avon near its confluence with R Spey 7m/11km SW of Charlestown of Aberlour. NJ 1736
Ballingdon Suffolk 30 D4 loc on R Stour across r from Sudbury. TL 8640
Ballinger Common Bucks 18 D2 vil 3m/5km W of Chesham. SP 9103
Ballingham H & W 26 B4* vil in loop of R Wye 7m/11km SE of Hereford. SO 5731
Ballingry Fife 73 E4 tn 3m/4km N of Cowdenbeath. NT 1797
Ballinluig Tayside 76 A5 vil on R Tummel 4m/7km SE of Pitlochry. **Lit Ballinluig** is loc on R Tay 4m/7km W. NN 9752
Ballintuim Tayside 76 B5 vil in Strath Ardle 3m/5km NW of Br of Cally. NO 1054
Balloch H'land 81 F3 loc in Inverness dist 4m/7km E of Inverness. NH 7347
Balloch S'clyde 64 B1 locality at S end of Loch Lomond, adjoining Alexandria to N. **B. Castle** is early 19c mansion on E side of loch, near moated mound marking site of old cas. NS 3881
Balloch S'clyde 65 E2* loc in Cumbernauld 2km W of tn centre. NS 7374
Ballochbuie Forest Grampian 76 C2 forest on S side of R Dee 3m/5km E of Braemar. NO 1990
Ballochling Loch S'clyde 56 E4* small loch 2m/3km NW of S end of Loch Doon. NX 4594
Ballochmyle House S'clyde. See Catrine.
Balloch, The Grampian 82 C2 hilly tract 3m/5km SE of Keith. NJ 4748
Ballogie Grampian 77 F2 loc and estate 4m/6km SE of Aboyne. NO 5795
Balls Cross W Sussex 11 F3 ham 3m/5km N of Petworth. SU 9826
Balls Green Essex 31 E5* ham 6m/10km E of Colchester. TM 0924
Ball's Green E Sussex 12 B3* ham 1km NE of Withyham and 6m/9km W of Tunbridge Wells. TQ 4936
Ball's Green Glos 16 D2* loc 1m E of Nailsworth. ST 8699
Balls Green W Sussex 11 G3* loc 2m/3km SE of Billingshurst. TQ 1023
Balls Hill W Midlands 35 F5* loc in W Bromwich 2m/3km N of tn centre. SO 9993
Ballygown S'clyde 68 C4 locality on **B. Bay,** on N side of Loch Tuath, Mull. Ruined broch. NM 4343
Ballygrant S'clyde 62 B2 vil on Islay 3m/5km SW of Port Askaig. Loch B. is small loch to E. NR 3966
Balmacaan Forest H'land 80 D5, 81 E5 deer forest in Inverness dist SW of Drumnadrochit. NH 4125
Balmacara H'land 79 F5/F6 locality (NTS) in Skye and Lochalsh dist 3m/5km E of Kyle of Lochalsh. **B. Bay** is small bay on Loch Alsh to S. NG 8028
Balmaclellan D & G 58 C4 vil 2km NE of New Galloway. NX 6579
Balmaha Central 71 E5/F5 vil on E shore of Loch Lomond 3m/5km W of Drymen. NS 4290
Balmanno Castle Tayside 73 E3 restored 16c mansion at Dron, 5m/8km S of Perth. NO 1415
Balmaqueen H'land 78 C2* loc near N end of Skye 2km S of Rubha na h-Aiseig. NG 4474
Balmartin W Isles 88 D1* loc near NW coast of N Uist 2m/3km S of Griminish Pt. NF 7273
Balmeanach Bay Skye, H'land 79 D5* bay on E coast opp S end of Raasay. NG 5334
Balmedie Grampian 83 G5 vil 7m/12km N of Aberdeen. NJ 9617
Balmer Heath Salop 34 B1* loc 3m/5km E of Ellesmere. SJ 4434
Balmerino Fife 73 F2 vil on Firth of Tay 5m/7km SW of Newport-on-Tay. Ruins of 13c abbey (NTS). NO 3524
Balmerlawn Hants 10 A4* loc 1km NE of Brockenhurst. SU 3003
Balm Hill Lancs 47 E2* loc in Morecambe 1m SE of tn centre. SD 4463
Balmoral Castle Grampian 76 C2 royal residence, built in 19c by Prince Albert on site of earlier cas, on S bank of R Dee 7m/11km E of Braemar. **Balmoral Forest** is deer forest to S. NO 2595
Balmore S'clyde 64 D2 vil 3m/5km E of Milngavie. NS 6073
Balmullo Fife 73 G3 vil 2m/3km W of Leuchars. NO 4220
Balnaboth Tayside 76 D4 loc 9m/15km NW of Kirriemuir. NO 3066
Balnacra H'land 80 A3 locality in Glen Carron, Ross and Cromarty dist, at SW end of Loch Dhughaill or Doule. NG 9746
Balnagown H'land 81 G1 r running into Nigg Bay on N side of Cromarty Firth, Ross and Cromarty dist, 5m/9km NE of Invergordon. **B. Castle** 2m/3km NW on right bank of r. NH 7873
Balnaguard Tayside 76 A5 vil in Strath Tay 2m/3km W of confluence of Rs Tay and Tummel. Falls of B., waterfall in **B. Burn** to S. NN 9451
Balnahard S'clyde 69 C5 locality on W coast of Mull, 2km S of entrance to Loch na Keal. NM 4534
Balnakailly Bay S'clyde 63 F1/G1* bay on N coast of Bute 1km E of Buttock Pt. NS 0274
Balnakeil H'land 84 D1/D2 loc on **B. Bay** on N coast of Sutherland dist 1m NW of Durness. NC 3968
Balnatoich H'land 81 F4 loc in Inverness dist 6m/10km S of Inverness. NH 6835
Balornock S'clyde 64 D2* dist of Glasgow 2m/3km NE of city centre. NS 6168
Balquhidder Central 71 F3 vil at foot of Loch Voil, 4m/6km SW of Lochearnhead. Burial place of the outlaw Rob Roy, d 1734. See also Braes of B. NN 5320
Balsall W Midlands 35 H6 vil 5m/7km NW of Kenilworth. SP 2476
Balsall Common W Midlands 35 H6 loc 6m/10km W of Coventry. SP 2377
Balsall Heath W Midlands 35 G5* loc in Birmingham 2m/3km S of city centre. SP 0784
Balsall Street W Midlands 35 H6* loc 5m/9km NW of Kenilworth. SP 2276
Balscote Oxon 27 G3 vil 4m/7km W of Banbury. SP 3941
Balsham Cambs 30 B3 vil 6m/10km NW of Haverhill. TL 5850
Balstonia Essex 20 C3* suburb 1m NE of Stanford le Hope. TQ 6983
Balta Shetland 89 F5 uninhabited island 2km N to S at entrance to Balta Sound, E coast of Unst. HP 6608
Balta Sound Shetland 89 F5 large inlet on E coast of Unst between main island and that of Balta. At head of inlet is vil of **Baltasound,** with airfield to S. HP 6208
Balterley Staffs 42 D6* ham 2m/4km W of Audley. **B. Green** loc to N. **B. Heath** loc to W. SJ 7650
Balthangie Grampian 83 F2* loc 2m/4km NE of Cuminestown. NJ 8050
Baltonsborough Som 8 D1 vil 4m/6km SE of Glastonbury. ST 5434
Balvaird Castle Tayside 73 E3* remains of 15c tower 2m/4km E of Glenfarg. NO 1611
Balvenie Grampian 82 C3 loc 1m N of Dufftown. Distillery. Remains of cas (A.M.), 13c and later. NJ 3241
Balvicar S'clyde 70 A3 vil on **B. Bay** on E coast of Seil 2m/4km S of Clachan Br. Slate quarry. NM 7616
Balwest Cornwall 2 B5* loc 4m/7km W of Helston. SW 5930
Bamber Bridge Lancs 47 F5 loc 3m/5km SE of Preston. Textiles. SD 5625
Bamber's Green Essex A5/B5 ham 3m/5km W of Gt Dunmow. TL 5723
Bamburgh Nthmb 67 H5 vil on North Sea coast opp Farne Is. and 5m/7km E of Belford. Large cas, Norman but much restored. St Aidan died here, 651. Grace Darling buried in churchyard. Grace Darling Museum. NU 1834
Bamford Derbys 43 G3 vil 2m/3km NW of Hathersage. SK 2083
Bamford Gtr Manchester 42 D1* loc in Rochdale 2m/3km W of tn centre. SD 8612
Bamfurling Glos 26 D5* loc 3m/5km W of Cheltenham. SO 8921
Bamfurlong Gtr Manchester 42 B2* loc 2m/4km NE of Ashton-in-Makerfield. SD 5901
Bampton Cumbria 53 E3 ham 3m/5km NW of Shap. NY 5118
Bampton Devon 7 G3 mkt tn on R Batherm 6m/10km N of Tiverton. Annual pony fair in October. SS 9522
Bampton Oxon 17 G2 vil 5m/8km SW of Witney. SP 3103
Bampton Grange Cumbria 53 E3* ham just E of Bampton. NY 5218
Bampton, Little Cumbria 59 G5 ham 3m/5km SE of Kirkbride. NY 2755
Banavie H'land 74 C4 locality, with **Lr Banavie,** in Lochaber dist beside Caledonian Canal 2m/3km N of Fort William. Series of locks on canal. NN 1177
Banbury Oxon 27 H3/H4 tn on R Cherwell 22m/35km N of Oxford. SP 4540
Banbury Reservoir 20 A3* resr in R Lea valley 2km NW of Walthamstow and 7m/12km N of London Br. TQ 3691
Bancffostfelen Dyfed 23 F4 vil 1m NW of Pontyberem. SN 4811
Banchory Grampian 77 F2 small tn on R Dee at its confluence with Water of Feugh, 11m/18km NW of Stonehaven. See also Bridge of Feugh. NO 6995
Banchory-Devenick Grampian 77 H1 loc 3m/5km SW of Aberdeen city centre across R Dee. NJ 9101
Bancycapel Dyfed 23 F4* ham 3m/5km S of Carmarthen. SN 4315
Bancyfelin Dyfed 23 E4 vil 3m/5km NE of St Clears. SN 3218
Bandley Hill Herts 29 F5* E dist of Stevenage. TL 2623
Bandrake Head Cumbria 52 C6* loc 1km N of Colton. SD 3187
Banff Grampian 83 E1 small tn on N coast, on W side of **B. Bay** between Banff and Macduff. Industrial estate adjoining tn centre. Distillery. To S is Duff Hse (A.M.), in Ggn baroque style by William Adam. NJ 6863
Bangor Gwynedd 40 C4 cathedral tn and resort on Menai Strait 51m/82km W of Chester. University College of North Wales, constituent college of University of Wales. **Upr Bangor,** residential quarter to N of tn centre, overlooking strait. SH 5771

Bangor Is-coed Clwyd 42 A6 vil on R Dee 5m/7km SE of Wrexham. Also known as Bangor-on-Dee. SJ 3845

Bangor-on-Dee. See Bangor Is-coed.

Bangor's Green Lancs 42 A1* loc 1km SE of Halsall. SD 3709

Bangor Teifi Dyfed 23 E2 loc 3m/4km W of Llandysul. SN 3740

Bangrove Suffolk 30 D1* loc adjoining Bardwell to S. TL 9472

Banham Norfolk 39 E5 vil 6m/10km NW of Diss. TM 0688

Bank Hants 10 A4 ham 1m SW of Lyndhurst. SU 2807

Bank End Cumbria 52 C6 loc 1m NW of Broughton in Furness. SD 1988

Bankend D & G 59 E4 vil on Lochar Water 6m/10km SE of Dumfries. NY 0268

Bank, Far S Yorks 49 H6* loc adjoining Fishlake to W. SE 6413

Bankfoot Tayside 72 D1 vil 5m/8km SE of Dunkeld. NO 0635

Bankglen S'clyde 56 F3 vil 2km SW of New Cumnock. NS 5912

Bankhead Grampian 83 G5 NW suburb of Aberdeen. NJ 8910

Bankhill, High Cumbria 53 E1* ham 1km NE of Kirkoswald. NY 5642

Bankland Som 8 B2* ham 2km NW of Lyng. ST 3129

Bank Newton N Yorks 48 B3 loc on Leeds and Liverpool Canal 2m/3km SW of Gargrave. SD 9053

Banknock Central 65 E1 loc 4m/6km E of Kilsyth. NS 7779

Banks Cumbria 60 B5 loc 3m/5km NE of Brampton. NY 5664

Banks Lancs 47 E5 loc 4m/7km NE of Southport. **Far B.** loc 2km NE. SD 3920

Bankshill D & G 59 G3 locality 4m/6km E of Lockerbie. NY 1981

Bank Side S Yorks 49 H6* loc on E side of R Don 2m/4km N of Thorne. SE 6716

Bank, South Cleveland 54 D3 urban loc 3m/4km E of Middlesbrough. NZ 5420

Bank, South N Yorks 50 B3* dist of York 1m SW of city centre. SE 5950

Bank Street H & W 26 B2* loc 5m/7km SE of Tenbury Wells. SO 6362

Bank, The Ches 42 D5* loc 2m/3km N of Kidsgrove. SJ 8457

Bank, The Salop 34 C4* loc adjoining Much Wenlock to W. SO 6199

Bank Top Lancs 42 B1* loc 2km W of Shevington. SD 5207

Bank Top Staffs 42 D6* loc 1m E of Tunstall tn centre. SJ 8751

Bank Top W Yorks 48 D4* loc in Bradford 2m/4km NE of city centre. SE 1836

Bank Top W Yorks 48 D5* loc 1m SE of Halifax. SE 1024

Bank, West Ches 42 B3 dist of Widnes 1m S of tn centre beside R Mersey. SJ 5183

Bannau Brycheiniog Welsh form of Brecon Beacons, qv.

Bannaventa Northants. See Norton.

Banners Gate W Midlands 35 G4* loc 3m/4km W of Sutton Coldfield. SP 0895

Banningham Norfolk 39 F2 vil 2m/4km NE of Aylsham. TG 2129

Bannister Green Essex 30 B5 vil 4m/7km W of Braintree. TL 6921

Bannium Powys. See Aberyscir.

Bannock Burn H'land 86 B4 r in Sutherland dist running S from Loch an Ruathair to R Helmsdale 2km SW of Kinbrace. NC 8530

Bannock Burn 72 C5 stream in Central region running E to vil of **Bannockburn,** 2m/4km SE of Stirling, then NE to R Forth 2m/4km E of Stirling. Between tn and burn is site of battle of 1314 in which Scots under Robert Bruce routed English under Edward II. See also Borestone Brae. NS 8393

Banovallum Lincs. See Horncastle.

Banstead Surrey 19 F5 tn 3m/5km S of Sutton. TQ 2559

Bantam Grove W Yorks 49 E5* loc 1m E of Morley. SE 2727

Bantham Devon 4 D6 ham on S side of R Avon estuary near its mouth, 4m/7km W of Kingsbridge. SX 6643

Banton S'clyde 65 E1* vil 2m/4km E of Kilsyth. NS 7479

Banvie Burn 75 H4 stream in Tayside region running SE down Glen Banvie through grnds of Blair Castle to R Garry on W side of Blair Atholl. NN 8665

Banwell Avon 15 H5 vil 5m/8km E of Weston-super-Mare. ST 3959

Banwell 15 H4* r rising at vil of Banwell, Avon, under N slopes of Mendip Hills, and flowing NW into mouth of R Severn 2km NW of Wick St Lawrence. ST 3466

Banwen Pyrddin W Glam 14 D1* loc 3m/4km NW of Glyn-neath. SN 8509

Banwy 33 H3 r rising 5m/9km W of Llangadfan, Powys, and flowing E to join R Einion 2m/3km NW of Llanfair Caereinion. The combined stream, known indifferently as Banwy or Einion, then continues SE to Llanfair Caereinion, then NE into R Vyrnwy 2km SW of Meifod. SJ 1411

Banyard's Green Suffolk 31 G1* loc 1km NE of Laxfield. TM 3072

Baosbheinn H'land 78 F3 mt in W part of Ross and Cromarty dist 5m/8km N of Upr Loch Torridon. Height 2869 ft or 875 metres. NG 8665

Bapchild Kent 21 E5 vil 2m/3km E of Sittingbourne. TQ 9262

Baptist End W Midlands 35 F5* 1m S of Dudley tn centre. SO 9488

Bapton Wilts 9 G1 ham 2km W of Wylye. ST 9938

Barafundle Bay Dyfed 22 C6* small bay 1km N of Stackpole Hd. SR 9995

Barassie S'clyde 64 B5* loc on Firth of Clyde adjoining Troon to N. NS 3232

Baravaig Skye, H'land 79 E7* locality on Camas B., bay on E coast of Sleat peninsula 2m/3km S of Isle Ornsay. Loch B. is small loch to W. NG 6909

Barbaraville H'land 87 A8 vil on Nigg Bay, Cromarty Firth 4m/6km NE of Invergordon, Ross and Cromarty dist. NH 7472

Barber Booth Derbys 43 F3 loc 4m/7km NE of Chapel-en-le-Frith. SK 1184

Barber Green Cumbria 52 D6* loc 3m/4km SE of Newby Br. SD 3982

Barber's Moor Lancs 47 F6* loc 1km NE of Croston. SD 4919

Barbican Devon 4 B5* dist of Plymouth 1km from city centre. SX 4854

Barbon Cumbria 53 F6 vil 3m/4km N of Kirkby Lonsdale. SD 6282

Barbon Beck 53 E6* r rising as Barkin Beck on Barkin Fell, NE of Kirkby Lonsdale, Cumbria, and flowing SW to Barbon and into R Lune 2km W thereof. SD 6081

Barbourne H & W 26 D2 N dist of Worcester. SO 8457

Barbreck S'clyde 70 A4* r in Argyll running SW down Gleann Domhain to head of Loch Craignish. NM 8205

Barbridge Ches 42 B5/C5* loc 4m/6km NW of Nantwich. SJ 6156

Barbrook Devon 7 E1 vil on W Lyn R 1m S of Lynton. SS 7147

Barbrook Reservoir Derbys 43 G3* resr 4m/6km NE of Baslow. SK 2777

Barbury Castle Wilts 17 F4 ancient hill fort on N edge of Marlborough Downs 5m/8km S of Swindon. Probable site of medieval vil to S. SU 1476

Barby Northants 28 B1 vil 4m/6km SE of Rugby. SP 5470

Barcaldine S'clyde 70 B2 locality on Dearg Abhainn on S side of Loch Creran, Argyll. **B. Forest** is state forest to S and E. NM 9641

Barcheston Warwicks 27 G4* vil 1km SE of Shipston on Stour. SP 2639

Barclodiad y Gawres Burial-chamber Gwynedd. See Aberffraw.

Barclose Cumbria 60 A5* loc just SW of Scaleby. NY 4462

Barco Hill Cumbria 53 E2* E dist of Penrith. NY 5230

Barcombe E Sussex 12 A5 vil in R Ouse valley 3m/4km N of Lewes. TQ 4114

Barcombe Cross E Sussex 12 A5 vil 4m/6km N of Lewes. TQ 4215

Barcraigs Reservoir S'clyde 64 B3* western part of resr 2m/3km S of Howwood. Eastern part known as Rowbank Resr. NS 3857

Barden N Yorks 48 C3 moorland area S of Burnsall to W of R Wharfe. On Barden Moor are **Upr** and **Lr Barden Resrs. Barden Br,** 17c rd br over R Wharfe on N side of **Barden Tower,** ruined Tudor hse. SE 0557

Barden N Yorks 54 B5* ham 3m/5km NE of Leyburn. SE 1493

Barden Beck 48 C3/D3* stream rising on Barden Moor, N Yorks, and flowing E through Upr and Lr Barden Resrs into R Wharfe below Barden Br and above The Strid. SE 0556

Barden Park Kent 20 C6* loc in W part of Tonbridge. TQ 5846

Bardfield End Green Essex 30 B4 ham 1m E of Thaxted. TL 6230

Bardfield, Great Essex 30 B5 vil 2m/3km S of Finchingfield. TL 6730

Bardfield, Little Essex 30 B4/B5 vil 3m/5km E of Thaxted. TL 6530

Bardfield Saling Essex 30 B5* ham 5m/8km NE of Gt Dunmow. TL 6826

Bardister Shetland 89 E6 loc on Mainland at head of Gluss Voe, 2m/3km S of Ollaberry. **Ness of B.** is headland on Sullom Voe to E. HU 3577

Bardney Lincs 45 E4 vil 9m/14km W of Horncastle. Sugar beet factory. Slight remains of Saxon abbey to N. TF 1169

Bardon Leics 36 A3 vil 2m/3km SE of Coalville. **B. Hill,** 1m E, is highest point of Charnwood Forest, 916 ft or 279 metres. SK 4412

Bardon Mill Nthmb 60 D5 vil on R South Tyne 4m/6km W of Haydon Br. NY 7764

Bardowie S'clyde 64 C2* vil 2m/3km SE of Milngavie, on E side of **B. Loch,** on whose N shore stands **B. Castle,** 16c. NS 5873

Bardrainney S'clyde 64 B2* loc 2km SE of Port Glasgow. NS 3373

Bardsea Cumbria 46 D1 vil on W bank of R Leven estuary 3m/4km S of Ulverston. **B. Green** loc adjoining to W. SD 3074

Bardsey W Yorks 49 F4 vil 7m/11km NE of Leeds. SE 3643

Bardsey Island (Ynys Enlli) Gwynedd 32 A3 sparsely inhabited island lying 2m/3km off SW tip of Lleyn peninsula, across Bardsey Sound. It is about 3km long N to S and 1km wide E to W. Remains of abbey near N end. Lighthouse near S end. SH 1221

Bardsey Sound 32 A2, A3 sea passage with dangerous currents between Bardsey I. and the SW extremity of Lleyn peninsula, Gwynedd. SH 1323

Bardsley Gtr Manchester 43 E1 loc in Oldham 2m/3km S of tn centre. SD 9201

Bardwell Suffolk 30 D1 vil 2m/4km N of Ixworth. TL 9473

Bare Lancs 47 E2 NE dist of Morecambe. SD 4564

Bar End Hants 10 B2* SE dist of Winchester. SU 4828

Barewood H & W 25 H2 ham 5m/9km E of Kington. SO 3856

Barewood, Lower H & W 25 H2 loc 6m/10km E of Kington. SO 3957

Barfield Tarn Cumbria 52 B6* small lake 1m S of Bootle. SD 1088

Barford Norfolk 39 E4 vil 8m/12km W of Norwich. TG 1107

Barford Warwicks 27 G2 vil 3m/5km S of Warwick. SP 2760

Barford, Great Beds 29 F3 vil 3m/5km NW of Sandy. TL 1352

Barford, Little Beds 29 F2 vil 2m/4km S of St Neots. Power stn 1km N. TL 1856

Barford St John Oxon 27 H4 vil 2m/4km NW of Deddington. SP 4333

Barford St Martin Wilts 9 G2 vil on R Nadder 3m/4km W of Wilton. SU 0531

Barford St Michael Oxon 27 H4 vil 2m/4km W of Deddington. SP 4332

Barforth Durham 54 B3* loc 1km W of Gainford across R Tees. NZ 1616

Barfreston Kent 13 G2 ham with Norman ch 6m/10km NW of Dover. TR 2650

Bargaly Glen D & G 57 E6 valley of Palnure Burn, qv. NX 4666

Bargate Derbys 43 H6* loc 2km SE of Belper. SK 3646

Bargatton D & G 58 C5 small loch 2m/3km S of Laurieston. NX 6961

Bargeddie S'clyde 64 D2 tn 2m/3km W of Coatbridge. NS 6964

Bargod Welsh form of Bargoed, qv.

Bargod 23 E2 r rising 4m/6km S of Llangeler, Dyfed, and flowing N into R Teifi 3m/4km E of Newcastle Emlyn. SN 3440

Bargoed (Bargod) Mid Glam 15 F2 tn in coal-mining valley 8m/12km N of Caerphilly. ST 1599

Bargrennan D & G 58 A4* loc on R Cree 8m/12km NW of Newton Stewart. NX 3576

Barham Cambs 29 F1 vil 7m/11km NW of Huntingdon. TL 1375

Barham Kent 13 G2 vil 6m/10km SE of Canterbury. TR 2050

Barham Suffolk 31 F3* scattered vil 5m/7km N of Ipswich. TM 1451

Barhapple Loch D & G 57 C6* small loch 4m/7km E of Glenluce. NX 2659

Bar Hill Cambs 29 G2* vil with industrial estate 5m/8km NW of Cambridge. TL 3863

Barholm Lincs 37 F3 vil 5m/7km NE of Stamford. TF 0910

Barholm Castle D & G 58 B6 ruined 16c-17c stronghold of the McCullochs, 5m/7km SE of Creetown. NX 5253

Barkby Leics 36 C3 vil 5m/7km NE of Leicester. **B. Thorpe** ham 1km S. SK 6309

Barkers Green Salop 34 C2* loc 1m SE of Wem. SJ 5228

Barkestone Leics 36 D1 vil 8m/13km W of Grantham. SK 7834

Barkham Berks 18 C4 vil 3m/4km SW of Wokingham. SU 7866

Barkin Beck Cumbria. See Barbon Beck.

Barking London 20 B3 borough and tn on N side of R Thames 8m/12km E of London Br. **B. Creek** is formed by R Roding before its confluence with R Thames at **B. Reach.** Borough includes also tn of Dagenham. TQ 4483

Barking Suffolk 31 E3 vil 4m/6km S of Stowmarket. TM 0753

Barkingside London 20 B3 loc in borough of Redbridge 2m/3km N of Ilford. TQ 4489

Barking Tye Suffolk 31 E3* vil 4m/7km S of Stowmarket. TM 0652

Barkin Isles W Isles 88 C2* group of islets at entrance to Loch Leurbost, E coast of Lewis. NB 3923

Barkisland W Yorks 48 C6 vil 1m E of Ripponden. SE 0519

Barkla Shop Cornwall 2 C3* ham 2km E of St Agnes. SW 7350

Barkston Lincs 37 E1 vil 4m/6km N of Grantham. SK 9341

Barkston N Yorks 49 G4 vil 4m/7km S of Tadcaster. **B. Ash** loc adjoining to W. SE 4936

Barkway Herts 29 G4 vil 4m/6km SE of Royston. TL 3835

Barkwith, East Lincs 45 F3 vil 3m/5km NE of Wragby. **W Barkwith** ham 1m SW. TF 1681

Barland Powys 25 G2* loc 3m/4km SW of Presteigne. Motte and bailey cas. SO 2862

Barlaston Staffs 35 E1 vil 3m/5km N of Stone. Wedgwood pottery works. SJ 8938

Barlavington W Sussex 11 F3* ham 4m/6km S of Petworth. SU 9716

Barlborough Derbys 44 A3 vil 7m/11km W of Worksop. Hall is Elizn. SK 4777

Barlby N Yorks 50 B4 loc 2km NE of Selby. SE 6334

Barle 7 G3 r in Somerset rising on Exmoor at Pinkery Pond and flowing SE through Withypool and Dulverton to join R Exe 1km NE of Exebridge. SS 9325

Barlestone Leics 36 A4 vil 2m/3km NE of Mkt Bosworth. SK 4205

Barley Herts 29 G4 vil 3m/5km SE of Royston. TL 3938

Barley Lancs 48 B4 vil 3m/5km NW of Nelson. SD 8240

Barleycroft End Herts 29 H5 E end of vil of Furneux Pelham, 4m/7km NE of Puckeridge. TL 4327

Barley Green Suffolk 31 F1* loc 1km E of Stradbroke. TM 2473

Barley Hole S Yorks 43 H2* loc 1m SW of Wentworth. SK 3797

Barley Mow Tyne & Wear 61 G5/G6* loc 1m S of Birtley. NZ 2754

Barleythorpe Leics 36 D3 vil 1m NW of Oakham. SK 8409

Barling Essex 21 E3 vil 3m/5km N of Shoeburyness. TQ 9389

Barlings Lincs 45 E4 ham 7m/11km E of Lincoln. At loc of **Low B.** 2km SE are remains of 12c abbey. TF 0774

Barlinnie S'clyde 64 D2 HM prison in Riddrie dist of Glasgow. NS 6366

Barlocco Bay D & G 58 D6 small bay 3m/4km E of Dundrennan. NX 7946

Barlocco Isle D & G 58 B6 southernmost of the Islands of Fleet, group of small islands near E side of Wigtown Bay. NX 5748

Barlow Derbys 43 H4 vil 3m/5km NW of Chesterfield. SK 3474

Barlow N Yorks 50 B5 vil 3m/5km SE of Selby. SE 6428

Barlow Tyne & Wear 61 F5* vil 2m/4km SW of Blaydon. NZ 1560

Barlow Moor Gtr Manchester 42 D2* loc in Manchester on R Mersey 4m/6km SW of city centre. SJ 8292

Barmby Moor Humberside 50 C3 vil 2m/3km W of Pocklington. SE 7748

Barmby on the Marsh Humberside 50 C5 vil 4m/6km W of Howden. SE 6928

Barmer Norfolk 38 C3 ham 4m/6km SE of Docking. TF 8133

Barming, East Kent 20 D6 vil on R Medway 3m/4km W of Maidstone. Site of Roman villa to E and to W. TQ 7254

Barming Heath Kent 20 D6* loc adjoining E Barming to N. TQ 7355

Bar Moor Tyne & Wear 61 F5* loc adjoining Ryton to W. NZ 1464

Barmore Island S'clyde 63 E1/F1 peninsula on W side of Loch Fyne, Argyll, 2m/3km N of Tarbert. NR 8771
Barmouth (Abermo) Gwynedd 32 D3 resort on **B. Bay** on N side of mouth of R Mawddach 8m/12km W of Dolgellau. The bay, which forms part of the much larger Cardigan Bay, extends from Morfa Dyffryn (N) to Llwyngwril (S). SH 6115
Barmpton Durham 54 C3 ham 3m/5km NE of Darlington. NZ 3118
Barmston Humberside 51 F3 vil near coast 5m/8km S of Bridlington. TA 1659
Barmston Tyne & Wear 61 G5* E dist of Washington. NZ 3156
Barnaby Green Suffolk 31 H1* loc 1km NE of Wangford. TM 4779
Barnack Cambs 37 F4 vil 3m/4km SE of Stamford. Remains of limestone quarries known as 'Hills and Holes'. TF 0705
Barnacle Warwicks 36 A5* loc 5m/8km NE of Coventry. SP 3884
Barnacre Reservoir Lancs 47 F3* resr 3m/5km NE of Garstang. SD 5247
Barnard Castle Durham 54 A3 tn on R Tees 15m/24km W of Darlington. Chemicals, agriculture. Remains of 12c cas (A.M.). Bowes Museum has large collection of art treasures. NZ 0516
Barnard Gate Oxon 27 H6 ham 3m/5km E of Witney. SP 4010
Barnardiston Suffolk 30 C3 ham 3m/5km NE of Haverhill. TL 7148
Barnard's Green H & W 26 C3 loc in E part of Gt Malvern. SO 7945
Barnburgh S Yorks 44 A1 coal-mining vil 2m/4km N of Mexborough. SE 4803
Barnby Suffolk 39 H5 vil 4m/6km E of Beccles. **B. Broad,** small lake 1km N. TM 4789
Barnby Dun S Yorks 44 B1 vil 5m/8km NE of Doncaster. SE 6109
Barnby, East N Yorks 55 F4 vil 5m/7km W of Whitby. NZ 8212
Barnby in the Willows Notts 44 C5 vil 4m/7km E of Newark-on-Trent. SK 8652
Barnby Moor Notts 44 B3 vil on former Great North Road 4m/6km NW of E Retford. SK 6684
Barnby, West N Yorks 55 F4 vil 5m/8km W of Whitby. NZ 8212
Barne Barton Devon 4 B5* NW dist of Plymouth, 3m/5km from city centre. SX 4457
Barnehurst London 20 B4 loc in borough of Bexley 1m N of Crayford and 12m/21km E of Charing Cross. TQ 5075
Barnes London 19 F4 dist in loop of R Thames in borough of Richmond S of Hammersmith Br. B. Common to S. TQ 2276
Barnes Cray London 20 B4* loc in borough of Bexley in R Cray valley 1km E of Crayford. TQ 5275
Barnes Street Kent 20 C6* vil 4m/6km E of Tonbridge. TQ 6448
Barnet London 19 F2 borough 11m/17km N of Charing Cross, containing dists of Chipping B., East B., Friern B., High B., New B. TQ 2494
Barnetby le Wold Humberside 45 E1 vil 4m/6km E of Brigg. TA 0509
Barnet, East London 19 F2* dist in borough of Barnet 9m/14km N of Charing Cross. TQ 2794
Barnet Gate London 19 F2* loc in borough of Barnet 11m/17km NW of Charing Cross. TQ 2195
Barnet, High London 19 F2* loc in borough of Barnet adjoining Chipping Barnet to NW. TQ 2396
Barnettbrook H & W 35 E6* loc 4m/6km E of Kidderminster. SO 8876
Barney Norfolk 39 E2 vil 5m/8km E of Fakenham. TF 9932
Barnham Suffolk 38 D6 vil 3m/4km S of Thetford. TL 8779
Barnham W Sussex 11 F4 vil 4m/6km NE of Bognor Regis. SU 9604
Barnham Broom Norfolk 39 E4 vil 4m/7km N of Wymondham. TG 0807
Barnham, West W Sussex 11 F4* loc adjoining Barnham, qv.
Barnhead Tayside 77 F5 loc 3m/5km W of Montrose across Montrose Basin. NO 6657
Barnhill Ches 42 B5* loc 2m/3km E of Clutton. SJ 4954
Barnhill Grampian 82 A2/B2 loc 6m/9km SW of Elgin. See also Pluscarden Priory. NJ 1457
Barnhill Tayside 73 G2* dist of Dundee 1m E of Broughty Ferry. NO 4731
Barningham Durham 54 A4 vil 4m/7km SE of Barnard Castle. NZ 0810
Barningham Suffolk 30 D1 vil 5m/8km NE of Ixworth. TL 9676
Barningham, Little Norfolk 39 F2 vil 5m/9km NW of Aylsham. **B. Green** loc 1m W. TG 1433
Barnoldby le Beck Humberside 45 F1 vil 4m/7km SW of Grimsby. TA 2303
Barnoldswick Lancs 48 B3 tn 4m/7km N of Colne. Textiles, engineering. SD 8746
Barnsbury London 19 G3* loc in borough of Islington 2m/4km N of Charing Cross. TQ 3084
Barns Green W Sussex 11 G2 ham 3m/4km E of Billingshurst. TQ 1227
Barnsley Glos 17 E1 vil 4m/6km NW of Cirencester. SP 0705
Barnsley Salop 34 D5* loc 3m/4km E of Bridgnorth. SO 7592
Barnsley S Yorks 43 G1/H1 industrial tn on R Dearne 12m/19km N of Sheffield. Coal-mining and general mnfg. SE 3406
Barns Ness Lothian 66 D1/67 E1* headland with lighthouse 3m/5km E of Dunbar. NT 7277
Barnstaple Devon 6 D2 mkt tn at head of R Taw estuary 34m/55km NW of Exeter. R flows into **B. Bay,** also known as Bideford Bay, which extends from Baggy Pt westwards to Hartland Pt. SS 5533
Barnston Essex 30 B5* vil 2m/3km SE of Gt Dunmow. TL 6419
Barnston Merseyside 41 H3 vil 2km NE of Heswall. SJ 2883
Barnstone Notts 36 C1 vil 3m/5km SE of Bingham. SK 7335
Barns, West Lothian 66 D1 loc 2km W of Dunbar. NT 6578
Barnt Green H & W 27 E1 vil 4m/7km NW of Redditch. SP 0073
Barnton Ches 42 C4 suburb 2km NW of Northwich. SJ 6573
Barnton Lothian 66 A2 dist of Edinburgh 4m/7km W of city centre. NT 1874
Barnwell Cambs 29 H2* E dist of Cambridge. TL 4658
Barnwell Northants 37 F5 par containing adjoining vils of **B. St Andrew** and **B. All Saints** 2m/4km S of Oundle. TL 0484
Barnwood Glos 26 D5 E dist of Gloucester. SO 8518
Barochan Cross S'clyde 64 B2* weathered Celtic cross (A.M.), on hillock 2km N of Houston. NS 4069
Barons' Cross H & W 26 A2* loc 1m W of Leominster. SO 4758
Barons Point S'clyde 64 A1 headland on E side of entrance to Loch Long, between Cove and Kilcreggan. NS 2280
Barpa Langass W Isles. See Cairn of Barpa Langass.
Barr S'clyde 56 C4 vil on R Stinchar 6m/10km SE of Girvan. NX 2794
Barr Som 8 A2* ham 2m/3km W of Taunton. ST 1925
Barra W Isles 88 D3, D4 island of about 20 sq miles or 52 sq km lying S of S Uist across the Sound of Barra, the shortest distance being 5m/7km (Scurrival Pt to Kilbride). The island is hilly, rising to 1260 ft or 384 metres at Heaval. There are silver sands on the much indented coastline. Airfield (Northbay) on Tràigh Mhór. Fishing and crofting are carried on. NF 6801
Barrachan D & G 57 D7 loc 4m/6km NE of Port William. NX 3649
Barrack Hill Gwent 15 G3* loc in N part of Newport. ST 3089
Barracks, The Tayside 75 F5 mansion on S bank of R Gaur 1km above Loch Rannoch. Erected to accommodate government soldiers after the 1745 rising. NN 4956
Barraglom W Isles 88 B2* loc at S end of Gt Bernera, W coast of Lewis, just E of rd br connecting Gt Bernera to main island. NB 1634
Barra Head W Isles 88 D4 headland on S coast of island of Berneray and the most southerly point of the Western Isles or Outer Hebrides. NL 5579
Barrapoll Tiree, S'clyde 69 A7 loc near W end of island 3m/4km SE of Rubha Chraiginis. NL 9542
Barrasford Nthmb 61 E4 vil 6m/10km N of Hexham. NY 9173
Barr Common W Midlands 35 F4* loc 3m/5km E of Walsall. SP 0599
Barrel of Butter Orkney 89 B7* island rock with beacon in Scapa Flow, 2m/3km E of lighthouse at N end of island of Cava. HY 3500
Barrets Green Ches 42 B5* loc 3m/5km SE of Tarporley. SJ 5959
Barr, Great W Midlands 35 F4 loc in NE part of W Bromwich. SP 0495
Barrhead S'clyde 64 C3 tn 4m/6km S of Paisley. Industries include engineering, iron founding, canning, textiles, mnfre of sanitary earthenware. NS 4958
Barrhill S'clyde 57 C5 vil on Duisk R 10m/16km S of Girvan. NX 2382
Barrington Cambs 29 G3 vil 6m/10km NE of Royston. Cement works to N. TL 3949
Barrington Glos 27 F6* par containing vils of **Gt** and **Lit Barrington** to W of Burford. SP 2013
Barrington Som 8 C3 vil 3m/5km NE of Ilminster. B. Court (NT), early 16c hse. ST 3818
Barrington, Great Glos 27 F6 vil 3m/5km W of Burford. Site of Roman bldg 1km SE beside R Windrush. SP 2013
Barrington, Little Glos 27 F6 vil 3m/5km W of Burford. SP 2012
Barriper Cornwall 2 C4* vil 2km SW of Camborne. SW 6338
Barrisdale H'land 74 A1/A2 locality in Lochaber dist, at head of **B. Bay** on S side of Loch Hourn. **R Barrisdale** runs W down **Glen B.,** then N into bay. NG 8704
Barri, Y Welsh form of Barry, qv.
Barr Loch S'clyde 64 B3* loch and bird sanctuary on S side of Lochwinnoch tn. **Barr Castle** to NW of loch has 16c tower. NS 3557
Barrmill S'clyde 64 B4 vil 2m/3km SE of Beith. NS 3651
Barrnacarry Bay S'clyde 70 A3 northward-facing bay on S side of entrance to Loch Feochan in Argyll 1m NW of Kilninver. NM 8122
Barr-nam-boc Bay S'clyde 70 A2 bay on W coast of Kerrera. NM 7928
Barrock H'land 86 E1 loc near N coast of Caithness dist 2m/4km E of Dunnet. ND 2571
Barrow Glos 26 D5* ham 4m/7km NW of Cheltenham. SO 8824
Barrow Lancs 48 A4 vil 2km N of Whalley. SD 7338
Barrow Leics 36 D3 ham 4m/7km NE of Oakham. SK 8915
Barrow Salop 34 D4 loc 2m/4km E of Much Wenlock. SJ 6500
Barrow Som 16 B6* loc 3m/4km S of Wells. ST 5541
Barrow Som 9 E1 vil 4m/6km SE of Bruton. ST 7231
Barrow Suffolk 30 C2 vil 6m/9km W of Bury St Edmunds. TL 7663
Barroway Drove Norfolk 38 A4/B4 loc 3m/4km W of Downham Mkt. TF 5703
Barrow Bridge Gtr Manchester 47 G6* loc in Bolton 2m/4km NW of tn centre. SD 6811
Barrowby Lincs 36 D1 vil 2m/4km W of Grantham. SK 8836
Barrowcliff N Yorks 55 H6 dist of Scarborough 2km NW of tn centre. TA 0289
Barrowden Leics 37 E4 vil 5m/8km E of Uppingham. SK 9400
Barrowford Lancs 48 B4 tn 1m N of Nelson. SD 8539
Barrow, Great Ches 42 A4 vil 4m/7km E of Chester. **Lit Barrow** vil 1m N. SJ 4768
Barrow Green Kent 21 E5* loc adjoining Teynham to N. TQ 9563
Barrow Gurney Avon 16 A4 vil 5m/7km SW of Bristol. Resrs to SE. ST 5367
Barrow Hann Humberside 51 E5/E6* loc 1m NE of Barrow upon Humber. TA 0822
Barrow Haven Humberside 51 E5 vil on S bank of R Humber 2km W of New Holland. Site of motte and bailey cas to S. TA 0622
Barrow Hill Derbys 43 H3 loc 4m/6km NE of Chesterfield. SK 4175
Barrow Hill Hants 10 A3* ham 2m/3km NE of Cadnam. SU 3115
Barrow-in-Furness Cumbria 46 D2 port on Irish Sea 18m/19km NW of Lancaster across Morecambe Bay. Shipbuilding, engineering, iron and steel works. SD 1969
Barrow Mere Humberside 51 E6* loc 1m W of Barrow upon Humber. TA 0521
Barrow Nook Lancs 42 A1/A2 loc 6m/10km NW of St Helens. SD 4402
Barrow, North Som 8 D2 vil 2m/3km N of Sparkford. ST 6029
Barrows Green Ches 42 C5* loc 2m/3km NW of Crewe. SJ 6958
Barrows Green Cumbria 53 E5/E6* ham 3m/5km S of Kendal. SD 5288
Barrow's Green Merseyside 42 B3* loc 2m/3km NE of Widnes. SJ 5288
Barrow, South Som 8 D2 vil 4m/6km SW of Castle Cary. ST 6027
Barrow Street Wilts 9 F2 loc 2m/3km SE of Mere. ST 8330
Barrow upon Humber Humberside 51 E6 vil 3m/4km E of Barton-upon-Humber. TA 0721
Barrow upon Soar Leics 36 B3 vil 3m/5km SE of Loughborough. SK 5717
Barrow upon Trent Derbys 36 A2 vil 5m/8km S of Derby. SK 3528
Barrule, North Isle of Man 46 C4 mt 2m/4km S of Ramsey. Height 1854 ft or 565 metres. SC 4490
Barrule, South Isle of Man 46 A5 mt 5m/9km N of Castletown. Height 1586 ft or 483 metres. SC 2575
Barr Water S'clyde 62 D4 r in Kintyre running SW to Glenbarr and into Atlantic Ocean 1km SW of vil. NR 6635
Barry (Barri, Y) S Glam 15 F4 port and resort 7m/11km SW of Cardiff. Ship-repairing, chemicals, plastics, sheet metal. Gateway of ruined cas to W. **Barry I.,** peninsula to S with bathing and a holiday camp. ST 1168
Barry Tayside 73 G1/H2 vil 2m/3km W of Carnoustie. **B. Sands** extend W and N of Buddon Ness. NO 5334
Barry Hill Tayside 76 C5* hill and Iron Age fort 2m/3km NE of Alyth. NO 2650
Barsalloch Point D & G 57 D8 headland on E side of Luce Bay, 2m/3km S of Port William. **Barsalloch Fort** (A.M.), is Iron Age fort on headland. NX 3441
Barsby Leics 36 C3 ham 6m/9km SW of Melton Mowbray. SK 6911
Barscobe Castle D & G 58 C3 remains of old cas 2m/4km E of Dalry. **Barscobe Hill** to E; **Barscobe Loch** to NE. NX 6680
Barsham Suffolk 39 G5 vil 2m/3km W of Beccles. Loc of **B. Hill** 1m E. TM 3989
Barsham, East Norfolk 38 D2 vil 3m/4km N of Fakenham. Tudor brick manor hse. **N Barsham** ham 1km N. **W Barsham** ham 1m W. TF 9133
Barstable Essex 20 D3* dist of Basildon E of tn centre. TQ 7288
Barston W Midlands 35 G6 vil 4m/6km E of Solihull. SP 2078
Bartestree H & W 26 B3* vil 4m/6km E of Hereford. SO 5640
Barthol Chapel Grampian 83 F3* vil 4m/6km SE of Fyvie. NJ 8134
Bartholomew Green Essex 30 B5* ham 3m/4km SW of Braintree. TL 7221
Barthomley Ches 42 D5 vil 4m/7km SE of Crewe. SJ 7652
Bartle, Higher Lancs 47 F4* ham 1km S of Woodplumpton. **Lr Bartle** ham 1km W. SD 5033
Bartley Hants 10 A3 vil 1m E of Cadnam. SU 3013
Bartley Green W Midlands 35 F6 dist of Birmingham 5m/8km SW of city centre. SP 0081
Bartley Reservoir W Midlands 35 F6* resr to S of Bartley Green 5m/9km SW of Birmingham city centre. SP 0081
Bartlow Cambs 30 B3 vil 5m/9km W of Haverhill. TL 5845
Barton Cambs 29 H2 vil 3m/5km SW of Cambridge. TL 4055
Barton Ches 42 A5 vil 2m/4km E of Holt. SJ 4454
Barton Cumbria 53 E2 loc 3m/5km SW of Penrith. NY 4826
Barton Devon 5 E4 N dist of Torbay, 2m/3km N of Torquay tn centre. SX 9067
Barton Glos 27 E5* loc 6m/9km W of Stow-on-the-Wold. SP 1025
Barton Isle of Wight 10 B5* E dist of Newport. SZ 5088
Barton Lancs 42 A1 ham 4m/7km W of Ormskirk. SD 3509
Barton Lancs 47 F4 vil 5m/8km N of Preston. SD 5139
Barton N Yorks 54 B4 vil 2m/4km NE of Scotch Corner. NZ 2308
Barton Oxon 18 A1* E dist of Oxford. SP 5507
Barton Suffolk 30 D2* loc 2km SE of Gt Barton. TL 9065
Barton Warwicks 27 E3* ham on R Avon 6m/10km NE of Evesham. SP 1051
Barton Bendish Norfolk 38 C4 vil 4m/6km N of Stoke Ferry. TF 7105

Barton Broad Norfolk 39 G3 broad or lake on course of R Ant 5m/8km NE of Wroxham. TG 3621
Barton Common Norfolk 39 G3* vil 5m/8km NE of Wroxham. TG 3522
Barton, East Devon 6 D3* ham 4m/6km E of Bideford. SS 5127
Bartongate Oxon 27 H5* loc 4m/6km SW of Deddington. SP 4425
Barton Gate Staffs 35 G3* loc 1m NW of Barton-under-Needwood. SK 1719
Barton, Great Suffolk 30 D2 vil 3m/5km NE of Bury St Edmunds. TL 8967
Barton Green Staffs 35 G3* loc adjoining Barton-under-Needwood to SW. SK 1818
Barton Hartshorn Bucks 28 B4 ham 4m/7km SW of Buckingham. SP 6430
Barton Hill N Yorks 50 C2 loc 7m/11km SW of Malton. SE 7064
Barton in Fabis Notts 36 B2 vil 5m/8km SW of W Bridgford. Site of Roman villa 1km S. SK 5232
Barton in the Beans Leics 36 A4 vil 7m/11km SE of Ashby de la Zouch. SK 3906
Barton in the Clay Beds 29 E4 vil 6m/10km N of Luton. TL 0832
Barton-le-Street N Yorks 50 C1 vil 4m/7km W of Malton. SE 7274
Barton-le-Willows N Yorks 50 C2* vil 5m/8km N of Stamford Br. SE 7163
Barton, Middle Oxon 27 H5* vil 4m/7km SW of Deddington. SP 4325
Barton Mills Suffolk 30 C1 vil on S bank of R Lark 8m/13km NE of Newmarket. TL 7273
Barton on Sea Hants 10 A5 W dist of Lymington, on Christchurch Bay. SZ 2393
Barton-on-the-Heath Warwicks 27 F4/G4 vil 3m/5km E of Moreton-in-Marsh. SP 2532
Barton St David Som 8 D2 vil 1m NW of Keinton Mandeville. ST 5431
Barton Seagrave Northants 28 D1 loc in SE part of Kettering. SP 8877
Barton Stacey Hants 10 B1 vil 5m/8km SW of Whitchurch. SU 4341
Barton Town Devon 7 E2* ham on W edge of Exmoor 6m/9km W of Simonsbath. Loc of **Barton Gate** 1km NE. SS 6840
Barton Turf Norfolk 39 G3 loc 4m/7km NE of Wroxham. TG 3421
Barton Turn Staffs 35 G3* loc 1km E of Barton-under-Needwood. SK 2018
Barton-under-Needwood Staffs 35 G3 vil 5m/8km SW of Burton upon Trent. SK 1818
Barton-upon-Humber Humberside 51 E5 tn on S bank of R Humber 6m/9km SW of Hull across r. TA 0321
Barton upon Irwell Gtr Manchester 42 C2/D2* loc in Eccles 1km SW of tn centre. SJ 7697
Barton Waterside Humberside 51 E5* loc on S bank of R Humber adjoining Barton-upon-Humber to N. TA 0223
Barton, West Devon 6 D3* loc 4m/6km E of Bideford. SS 5027
Barugh S Yorks 43 G1 loc 3m/4km NW of Barnsley. **Barugh Green** loc adjoining to S. **Low Barugh** loc adjoining to N. SE 3108
Barugh, Great N Yorks 50 C1 vil 5m/8km NW of Malton. SE 7479
Barugh, Little N Yorks 50 C1 ham 5m/8km N of Malton. SE 7679
Barvas W Isles 88 B1 vil near NW coast of Lewis 11m/18km NW of Stornoway. Localities of **Upr** and **Lr Barvas** 1km N and W respectively. See also Aird B., Glen Mór B., Loch Mór B. NB 3649
Barvas W Isles 88 B1* r rising among lochs some 6m/10km S of Barvas vil, Lewis, and flowing N down Glen Mór Barvas to Loch Mór Barvas and thence into Atlantic Ocean 2m/3km SW of Aird Barvas. NB 3450
Barway Cambs 38 A6 ham 3m/5km S of Ely. TL 5475
Barwell Leics 36 A4 large vil 2m/4km NE of Hinckley. SP 4496
Barwick Herts 29 G5* loc 4m/6km NE of Ware. TL 3819
Barwick Norfolk 38 C2 loc 3m/4km E of Docking. TF 8035
Barwick Som 8 D3 vil 2m/3km S of Yeovil. ST 5613
Barwick in Elmet W Yorks 49 F4 vil 7m/11km E of Leeds. SE 3937
Basaleg Welsh form of Bassaleg, qv.
Baschurch Salop 34 B2 vil 7m/11km NW of Shrewsbury. SJ 4221
Base Green Suffolk 31 E2* loc 1km NE of Wetherden. TM 0163
Basford Ches 42 C5* loc 2m/3km S of Crewe. SJ 7152
Basford Notts 36 B1 dist of Nottingham 2m/3km NW of city centre. SK 5543
Basford Staffs 42 D6* loc on borders of Newcastle-under-Lyme and Stoke-on-Trent 1m NE of the former's tn centre. SJ 8646
Basford Green Staffs 43 E5/E6* loc 2km SE of Cheddleton. SJ 9951
Bashall Eaves Lancs 47 G4 ham 4m/6km W of Clitheroe. SD 6943
Bashall Town Lancs 47 G4 loc 2m/3km W of Clitheroe. SD 7142
Bashley Hants 10 A5 loc 5m/8km SW of Brockenhurst. SZ 2497
Basildon Berks 18 B4 vil 2m/4km NW of Pangbourne. Site of Roman bldg beside R Thames to N. SU 6178
Basildon Essex 20 D3 New Tn designated 1949, 26m/42km E of London. Light industry. TQ 7088
Basildon, Upper Berks 18 B4 vil 2m/4km W of Pangbourne. SU 5976
Basing Hants 18 B6 extensive loc 2m/3km E of Basingstoke. Ruins of B. Hse, mansion destroyed in Civil War. SU 6652
Basingstoke Hants 18 B6 tn 17m/27km NE of Winchester. Mnfre of motor vehicle accessories, precision instruments, chemicals, mechanical handling gear; various light industries. Considerable expansion in 1960s and 1970s. SU 6351
Basingwerk Abbey Clwyd. See Greenfield.
Baslow Derbys 43 G4 vil 3m/5km NE of Bakewell. SK 2572
Bason Bridge Som 15 H6 vil on R Brue 2m/3km SE of Highbridge. ST 3445
Bassaleg (Basaleg) Gwent 15 G3 vil 2m/4km W of Newport across Ebbw R. ST 2787
Bassenthwaite Cumbria 52 C2 vil 2m/3km E of N end of B. Lake and 6m/10km N of Keswick. **B. Lake,** northernmost lake of the Lake Dist, runs roughly N and S. Length 4m/6km. Formed by R Derwent. NY 2332
Bassetlaw 117 admin dist of Notts.
Bassett Hants 10 B3 N dist of Southampton. SU 4116
Bassingbourn Cambs 29 G3 vil 3m/4km NW of Royston. Airfield to N. TL 3343
Bassingfield Notts 36 C1* loc 2m/3km SW of Radcliffe on Trent. SK 6137
Bassingham Lincs 44 D5 vil 8m/13km SW of Lincoln. SK 9159
Bassingthorpe Lincs 37 E2 ham 6m/9km SE of Grantham. Small 16c manor hse. SK 9628
Bass Rock Lothian 73 H5 small island of basalt rock in Firth of Forth 2km N of Tantallon Castle. Height 350 ft or 107 metres. Haunt of sea birds, esp gannet. Lighthouse. NT 6087
Basta Shetland 89 E5/F5* loc on Yell on W side of B. Voe. Headland of **B. Ness** on coast 1m SE. HU 5294
Basta Voe Shetland 89 E5/F5* long inlet on E coast of Yell, running up to Dalsetter. HU 5296
Baston Lincs 37 F3 vil 4m/7km S of Bourne. TF 1113
Bastonford H & W 26 C3* loc 4m/6km SW of Worcester. SO 8150
Bastwick Norfolk 39 H3* vil 2m/3km W of Martham. TG 4217
Baswich Staffs 35 F2* loc in Stafford 2m/3km SE of tn centre. SJ 9422
Batch Som 15 H5* loc just S of R Axe and 3m/4km N of Brent Knoll. ST 3255
Batchley H & W 27 E1* W dist of Redditch. SP 0267
Batchworth Herts 19 E2 loc on R Colne adjoining Rickmansworth to SE. Loc of **B. Heath** 1m SE. TQ 0694
Batcombe Dorset 8 D4 vil below the steep B. Hill 4m/6km NW of Cerne Abbas. ST 6104
Batcombe Som 9 E1 vil 3m/4km N of Bruton. ST 6939
Bate Heath Ches 42 C3 loc 4m/7km W of Knutsford. SJ 6879
Batel, Y Welsh form of Battle, qv.
Bateman's E Sussex. See Burwash.
Batesmoor Norfolk 39 E2*loc 1m NE of Foulsham. TG 0425
Batford Herts 29 F6* NE dist of Harpenden. TL 1415
Bath Avon 16 C5 city and spa on R Avon 11m/18km SE of Bristol. The Roman spa of *Aquae Sulis;* hot springs unique in Britain. Roman baths. Abbey ch rebuilt 1501. Many 18c bldgs. University to E above Claverton. ST 7564
Bathampton Avon 16 C4 vil 2m/3km NE of Bath. ST 7766
Bathealton Som 7 H3 vil 4m/7km NW of Wellington. ST 0724
Batheaston Avon 16 C4 suburb 3m/4km NE of Bath. Iron Age fort (NT) at Lit Solsbury Hill, 1km W. ST 7767
Batherm 7 G3 r rising 1km SW of Clatworthy Resr in Somerset and flowing SW into R Exe 1m S of Bampton, Devon. SS 9520
Bathford Avon 16 C4 vil 3m/5km NE of Bath. ST 7866
Bathgate Lothian 65 F2 tn 5m/9km S of Linlithgow. Coal and iron works in vicinity. NS 9768
Bathley Notts 44 C5 vil 4m/6km N of Newark-on-Trent. SK 7759
Bathpool Cornwall 3 G1 vil 6m/9km NW of Callington. SX 2874
Bathpool Som 8 B2 vil 2m/3km E of Taunton. ST 2525
Bathway Som 16 B6* ham 1km SW of Chewton Mendip. ST 5952
Batlers Green Herts 19 F2* loc adjoining Radlett to S. TQ 1598
Batley W Yorks 49 E5 tn 7m/11km SW of Leeds. Wool textiles, carpets, engineering. **Upr Batley** loc 1m N. **Batley Carr** loc adjoining to S. SE 2424
Batsford Glos 27 F4 vil 2km NW of Moreton-in-Marsh. SP 1833
Batson Devon 4 D6* loc at head of creek 1km N of Salcombe. SX 7339
Battersby N Yorks 55 E4 vil 3m/5km SE of Gt Ayton. **B. Junction** loc at former rly junction 1km SW. NZ 5907
Battersea London 19 G4* dist on S side of R Thames in borough of Wandsworth. B. Park between Albert and Chelsea Brs. B. Power Stn at Nine Elms. Heliport beside r on B. Reach. TQ 2876
Battisborough Cross Devon 4 C5* ham near S coast 3m/5km SE of Yealmpton. SX 5948
Battisford Suffolk 31 E3 loc 3m/5km S of Stowmarket. TM 0554
Battisford Tye Suffolk 31 E3* vil 3m/5km SW of Stowmarket. TM 0254
Battle E Sussex 12 D5 tn 6m/9km NW of Hastings. Remains of abbey founded by William I overlooks site of Battle of Hastings, 1066. 14c gatehouse gives on to tn square. TQ 7415
Battle (Batel, Y) Powys 25 E5 ham 3m/4km NW of Brecon. SO 0031
Battledown Glos 26 D5/27 E5* loc 2km E of Cheltenham. SO 9621
Battlefield Salop 34 C3 loc on site of Battle of Shrewsbury, 1403, 3m/5km N of the tn. SJ 5116
Battlefield S'clyde 64 C3* loc in Glasgow 3m/4km S of city centre. NS 5861
Battle of the Standard. See Brompton, N Yorks.
Battlesbridge Essex 20 D2 vil near head of R Crouch estuary 2m/4km E of Wickford. TQ 7794
Battlesden Beds 28 D4 loc 3m/5km SE of Woburn. M1 motorway service area 2km E. SP 9628
Battlesea Green Suffolk 31 F1* loc 1m NW of Stradbroke. TM 2275
Battleton Som 7 G3* ham on R Barle just S of Dulverton. SS 9127
Battlies Green Suffolk 30 E2* loc 3m/5km E of Bury St Edmunds. TL 8964
Battramsley Hants 10 A4* loc 2m/3km S of Brockenhurst. SZ 3099
Batt's Corner Surrey 11 E1 loc 4m/6km SW of Farnham. SU 8141
Battye Ford W Yorks 48 D6* loc adjoining Mirfield to NW. College of Community of the Resurrection is here. SE 1920
Baugh Tiree, S'clyde 69 A7 loc on S coast 2km SW of Scarinish. NM 0243
Baughton H & W 26 D3 ham 6m/9km N of Tewkesbury. SO 8742
Baughurst Hants 18 B5 vil 4m/6km NE of Kingsclere. SU 5861
Baulking Oxon 17 G2 vil 4m/6km SE of Faringdon. SU 3190
Baumber Lincs 45 F4 vil 4m/6km NW of Horncastle. TF 2274
Baunton Glos 17 E1 vil 2m/3km N of Cirencester. SP 0204
Baveney Wood Salop 34 D6 loc 3m/4km NE of Cleobury Mortimer. Roman fort 1km SW. SO 6979
Baverstock Wilts 9 G1 vil 4m/7km W of Wilton. SU 0232
Bavington, Great Nthmb 61 E3 ham 3m/4km S of Kirkwhelpington. NY 9880
Bavington, Little Nthmb 61 E4* ham 4m/6km S of Kirkwhelpington. NY 9878
Bawburgh Norfolk 39 F4 vil on R Yare 5m/7km W of Norwich. TG 1508
Bawden Rocks Cornwall 2 C3* two island rocks, also known as Man and his Man, 2km N of St Agnes Hd. SW 7053
Bawdeswell Norfolk 39 E3 vil 6m/9km NE of E Dereham. TG 0420
Bawdrip Som 8 B1 vil 3m/5km NE of Bridgwater. ST 3439
Bawdsey Suffolk 31 G4 vil near coast 7m/12km SE of Woodbridge. Loc of **B. Manor** 2km SW on coast. TM 3440
Bawn W Yorks 49 E5* loc in Leeds 3m/5km W of city centre. SE 2532
Bawtry S Yorks 44 B2 small tn 8m/13km SE of Doncaster. Site of small Roman fort 1km E across R Idle. SK 6593
Baxenden Lancs 48 A5 vil 2m/3km SE of Accrington. SD 7726
Baxterley Warwicks 35 H4 mining vil 2m/3km SW of Atherstone. SP 2797
Baxter's Green Suffolk 30 C2* loc 2m/4km W of Chedburgh. TL 7558
Bay Dorset 9 E2* loc on E side of Gillingham. ST 8127
Bay H'land 78 A4 r running N into Loch Bay, NW coast of Skye. NG 2654
Bayble, Upper and Lower W Isles 88 C2 adjacent vils on Eye Peninsula, Lewis, 2km SE and S respectively of Garrabost. NB 5231
Baybridge Nthmb 61 E6* loc 1km W of Blanchland. NY 9550
Baycliff Cumbria 46 D1 vil 4m/6km S of Ulverston. SD 2872
Baydon Wilts 17 G4 vil 3m/5km N of Lambourn. SU 2878
Bayford Herts 19 G1 vil 3m/4km S of Hertford. TL 3108
Bayford Som 9 E2 vil 1m E of Wincanton. ST 7229
Bayham Abbey E Sussex 12 C3 ruined medieval abbey (A.M.) by R Teise on Kent border 2m/3km W of Lamberhurst. Also 19c mansion in Jacbn style in park on Kent side of r. TQ 6536
Bayhead W Isles 88 D1* vil near W coast of N Uist 5m/9km S of Griminish Pt. NF 7468
Bayherivagh W Isles. See Northbay. NF 7103
Baylham Suffolk 31 E3 vil 6m/9km NW of Ipswich. TM 1051
Baylis Green H & W 27 E1* loc 3m/5km NE of Redditch. SP 0870
Baynard's Green Oxon 28 A4/B4 loc 5m/8km NW of Bicester. SP 5429
Bay, North Orkney 89 A7* bay on N side of The Ayre, narrow neck of land connecting peninsula of S Walls to S end of island of Hoy. ND 2890
Bay ny Carrickey Isle of Man 46 A6 bay between Port St Mary and Castletown, extending from Kallow Pt eastwards to Scarlett Pt. SC 2268
Bay of Cruden Grampian. See Cruden Bay.
Bay of Firth Orkney 89 B6 bay on coast of Mainland facing NE towards Shapinsay. Vil of Finstown at head of bay. HY 3814
Bay of Holland Orkney 89 C6* large bay on S coast of Stronsay between Greenli Ness and Tor Ness. HY 6422
Bay of Houseby Orkney. See Houseby.
Bay of Howton Orkney 89 A7* small bay on coast of Mainland to E of Howton Hd, 2m/4km NE of coast of Hoy across Bring Deeps. HY 3103
Bay of Ireland Orkney 89 A6* bay on coast of Mainland 2m/3km E of Stromness. HY 2809
Bay of Keisgaig H'land 84 C1/C2 small bay on NW coast of Sutherland dist 4m/6km S of Cape Wrath. NC 2469
Bay of Laig H'land 68 C1 bay on W coast of Eigg. NM 4688
Bay of Meil Orkney 89 B6* bay on coast of Mainland between Hd of Work and Hd of Holland, 2m/3km E of Kirkwall. HY 4812
Bay of Quendale Shetland. See Quendale.

Bay of Skaill Orkney 89 A6* small bay on W coast of Mainland 4m/6km W of Dounby. On S side is Skara Brae, qv, remains of Neolithic settlement. HY 2319
Bay of Tuquoy Orkney 89 B5* large bay on S coast of island of Westray. **Ness of Tuquoy** headland on W side of bay. HY 4644
Bay of Work Orkney 89 B6* small bay on Mainland on S side of Hd of Work, opp Shapinsay and 3m/5km NE of Kirkwall. HY 4813
Baysham H & W 26 B4 ham 3m/5km NW of Ross-on-Wye across loop of r. SO 5727
Bay Stacka Isle of Man 46 A6* southward-facing bay 2m/3km SW of Port St Mary. SC 1966
Baystone Bank Reservoir Cumbria 52 C6* small resr 4m/6km N of Millom. SD 1786
Baystonhill Salop 34 B3 vil 3m/4km S of Shrewsbury. SJ 4808
Bayston, Lower Salop 34 B3* loc 1km SE of Baystonhill. SJ 4908
Bayswater London 19 F3* loc in City of Westminster on N side of Hyde Park. TQ 2580
Baythorn End Essex 30 C4 ham 4m/6km SE of Haverhill. TL 7242
Baythorpe Lincs 37 G1*loc 1m NE of Swineshead. TF 2441
Bayton H & W 26 C1 vil 2m/3km SE of Cleobury Mortimer. SO 6973
Bayton Common H & W 26 C1* loc 3m/5km SE of Cleobury Mortimer. SO 7172
Bayton, Little Warwicks 36 A5* loc 2km S of Bedworth. SP 3585
Bay, West Dorset 8 C5 vil on coast with small harbour 2m/3km S of Bridport. SY 4690
Bay, West 8 D6 bay to W of Portland, Dorset. SY 6773
Bayworth Oxon 18 A2* ham 3m/4km N of Abingdon. SP 5001
Bazil Point Lancs 47 E3* headland on right bank of R Lune estuary 1km S of Overton. SD 4356
Beach Avon 16 C4* loc 5m/8km NW of Bath. ST 7070
Beachampton Bucks 28 C4 vil 2m/4km SW of Stony Stratford. SP 7736
Beachamwell Norfolk 38 C4 vil 5m/8km SW of Swaffham. TF 7502
Beach, High Essex 20 B2 vil on W edge of Epping Forest 2m/4km SE of Waltham Abbey. TQ 4097
Beachley Glos 16 B3 loc below W end of Severn Rd Br. **Beachley Pt** is headland to S at mouth of R Wye. ST 5491
Beachy Head E Sussex 12 C6 chalk headland on coast 3m/5km SW of Eastbourne. Lighthouse at foot. TV 5895
Beacon Devon 8 A3* loc 1km NW of Yarcombe. ST 2308
Beacon Devon 8 A4 ham 3m/5km N of Honiton. ST 1805
Beacon End Essex 30 D5 suburb 3m/4km W of Colchester. TL 9524
Beacon Hill Bucks hill and notable viewpoint (NT), commonly known as Ivinghoe Beacon, 1m E of Ivinghoe on N escarpment of Chiltern Hills. SP 9616
Beacon Hill Bucks 18 D2* loc at Penn 3m/4km E of High Wycombe. SU 9093
Beacon Hill Essex 21 E1* loc 3m/4km SE of Witham. TL 8512
Beacon Hill E Sussex 12 B4* loc on W side of Crowborough. TQ 5030
Beacon Hill Surrey 11 E2* loc 1m NW of Hindhead. SU 8736
Beacon Point Durham 54 D1 headland on North Sea coast on N side of Shippersea Bay, 2m/4km NE of Easington. NZ 4445
Beacon Point Nthmb 61 G3 headland on North Sea coast 1m N of Newbiggin-by-the-Sea. NZ 3189
Beacon Point, West Dyfed 22 D6* headland at SW corner of Caldy I., at S end of Sandtop Bay. SS 1296
Beacon Ring Powys 34 A4* ancient camp on summit of Long Mountain, 3m/4km E of Welshpool. SJ 2605
Beacon's Bottom Bucks 18 C2 vil 5m/8km W of High Wycombe. SU 7895
Beaconsfield Bucks 18 D3 tn 5m/8km SE of High Wycombe. SU 9490
Beacon Tarn Cumbria 52 C5* small lake 1m W of S end of Coniston Water. SD 2790
Beacravik W Isles 88 A3* loc on SE coast of Harris 1m NE of Manish. NG 1190
Beadlam N Yorks 55 E6 ham adjoining Nawton to W, 3m/4km E of Helmsley. SE 6584
Beadlow Beds 29 E4* ham 2km E of Clophill. TL 1038
Beadnell Nthmb 67 H5 fishing vil and resort on North Sea coast 2m/3km S of Seahouses. **B. Bay** to S; foreshore partly NT. 18c lime kilns (NT) by harbour. NU 2329
Beaford Devon 6 D4 vil 5m/7km SE of Torrington. SS 5515
Beaford Brook 6 D3* stream rising on Beaford Moor, Devon, and flowing NW then W into R Torridge 2m/3km SE of Torrington. SS 5116
Beal Nthmb 67 G4 ham 6m/10km NW of Belford. Access to Holy I. along rd to E leading to causeway across **B. Sands,** passable at low tide. NU 0642
Beal N Yorks 49 G5 vil on S bank of R Aire 2m/4km NE of Knottingley. SE 5325
Bealach a' Mhaim Skye, H'land 79 C6 pass on N side of Cuillin Hills between Sligachan and Glen Brittle. NG 4426
Bealings, Great Suffolk 31 F3 vil 3m/4km W of Woodbridge. TM 2348
Bealings, Little Suffolk 31 F3 vil 3m/5km W of Woodbridge. TM 2247
Bealsmill Cornwall 3 H1* ham on R Inny 5m/7km N of Callington. SX 3576
Beam 20 B3 r rising E of Romford in borough of Havering, London, and flowing S into R Thames at Dagenham. TQ 4981
Beambridge Ches 42 C5 ham 1m N of Nantwich. SJ 6453
Beam Hill Staffs 35 H2* loc 2m/3km N of Burton upon Trent. SK 2325
Beamhurst Staffs 35 F1 loc 3m/5km NW of Uttoxeter. SK 0636
Beaminster Dorset 8 C4 small tn 5m/9km N of Bridport. ST 4801
Beamish Durham 61 G6* vil 2m/3km E of Stanley. NZ 2253
Beamish Burn Durham 61 G6* loc 2km NE of Stanley. Situated on stream of same name. NZ 2054
Beamond End Bucks 18 D2* ham 3m/4km W of Amersham. SU 9196
Beamsley N Yorks 48 D3 vil 4m/6km NW of Ilkley. To E is **B. Beacon,** hill topped by cairn and forming notable landmark. SE 0752
Bean Kent 20 C4 loc 2km SW of Swanscombe. TQ 5872
Beanacre Wilts 16 D4* vil 2km N of Melksham. ST 9066
Beane 29 G6 r rising W of Buntingford, Herts, and flowing S into R Lea at Hertford. TL 3212
Bea Ness Orkney 89 C5* headland on S coast of Sanday between Backaskail and Kettletoft Bays. HY 6538
Beanfield Northants 36 D5* W dist of Corby. SP 8688
Beanley Nthmb 67 G6 ham 2m/3km W of Eglingham. NU 0818
Beansburn S'clyde 64 B5/C5* loc adjoining Kilmarnock to NE. NS 4339
Bearasay W Isles 88 A2* small uninhabited island off W coast of Lewis 2m/3km NW of island of Gt Bernera. NB 1242
Bear Cross Dorset 9 G4* N dist of Bournemouth. SZ 0696
Bearded Lake Gwynedd. See Llyn Barfog.
Beardwood Lancs 47 G5* loc in Blackburn 2km NW of tn centre. SD 6629
Beare Devon 7 G5* ham on R Culm 4m/7km SW of Cullompton. SS 9801
Beare Green Surrey 11 G1 ham 4m/7km S of Dorking. TQ 1743
Bearfield Wilts 16 D5* N dist of Bradford-on-Avon. ST 8261
Bearley Warwicks 27 F2 vil 4m/6km N of Stratford-upon-Avon. Loc of **B. Cross** 1km NW. SP 1760
Bearpark Durham 54 B1 vil in coal-mining dist 2m/4km W of Durham. NZ 2343
Bearraich Mull, S'clyde 69 C5. See Burg.
Bearsbridge Nthmb 60 D5 ham 6m/9km SW of Haydon Br. NY 7857
Bearsden S'clyde 64 C2 largely residential tn on line of Antonine Wall 5m/8km NW of Glasgow. NS 5472
Bearsted Kent 20 D6 E suburb of Maidstone. TQ 8055
Bearstone Salop 34 D1* ham 2km NE of Norton in Hales. SJ 7038
Bearwardcote Derbys 35 H1* loc 5m/8km SW of Derby. SK 2833
Bearwood W Midlands 35 F5* loc in Birmingham 3m/4km W of city centre. SP 0286
Bear Wood Lake Berks 18 C4* large lake in grnds of Bearwood. See Sindlesham. SU 7768
Beasdale H'land 68 E1 burn in Lochaber dist running W down Glen Beasdale into Loch nan Uamh, 3m/4km SE of Arisaig. NM 6984
Beasley Cross Devon 6 D5* ham 6m/9km W of Okehampton. SX 5093
Beath Bleachfield Fife 73 E5* loc adjoining Cowdenbeath to W. NT 1590
Beattock D & G 59 F2 vil 2m/3km S of Moffat. Site of Roman camp 1m SE. **B. Summit,** summit of London to Glasgow main rly line, 10m/16km NW; height 1029 ft or 314 metres. NT 0702
Beauchamp Roding Essex 20 C1* ham 2m/4km S of Leaden Roding. TL 5810
Beauclerc Nthmb 61 E5* loc 1km W of Riding Mill. NZ 0061
Beaudesert Warwicks 27 F1 loc adjoining Henley-in-Arden to E. Traces of motte and bailey cas. SP 1566
Beaufort (Cendl) Gwent 25 F6 tn 2m/3km N of Ebbw Vale. SO 1611
Beaufront Castle Nthmb 61 E5 mansion of 1840 in park 2m/3km NE of Hexham. NY 9665
Beaulieu Hants 10 B4 vil at head of Beaulieu R estuary 6m/9km NE of Lymington. Yachting. Remains of 13c abbey, of which Palace Hse is former gatehouse; motor museum in grounds. SU 3802
Beaulieu 10 B5* r rising in New Forest near Lyndhurst, Hants, and flowing SE past the vil of Beaulieu and into the Solent 4m/7km SE thereof. SZ 4498
Beaulieu Hall Northants. See Hemington.
Beauly H'land 81 E3 tn on r of same name in Inverness dist. Tweed mnfre. Ruins of 13c priory (A.M.). R formed by confluence of Rs Farrar and Glass and flowing NE past tn and into head of **B. Firth,** wide inlet giving out into Inner Moray Firth or Inverness Firth. NH 5246
Beaumaris (Biwmares) Gwynedd 40 C4 resort on Anglesey on E side of Conwy Bay. Industries include boat-building and coach-body building. Remains of cas (A.M.) dating in part from late 13c. SH 6076
Beaumont Cumbria 59 H5 vil on R Eden 4m/6km NW of Carlisle. NY 3459
Beaumont Essex 31 F5 vil 6m/10km N of Clacton-on-Sea. TM 1725
Beaumont Hill Durham 54 C3* loc 3m/4km N of Darlington. NZ 2918
Beaupre Castle S Glam 15 E4* 16c bldg on site of fortified hse dating from 13c. Present remains (A.M.) largely incorporated in adjacent farmhouse. ST 0072
Beausale Warwicks 27 F1 vil 5m/7km NW of Warwick. SP 2470
Beauvale Notts 44 A6* E dist of Eastwood. SK 4846
Beauworth Hants 10 C2 ham 4m/7km S of New Alresford. SU 5726
Beaver Dyke Reservoirs N Yorks 49 E3* two resrs 2m/3km E of Fewston. On S bank of upper resr earthwork marks site of **John of Gaunt's Cas.** SE 2254
Beaver Green Kent 13 F3* SW dist of Ashford. TQ 9941
Beaworthy Devon 6 D5 vil 8m/13km NW of Okehampton. SX 4699
Beazley End Essex 30 C5 ham 4m/6km N of Braintree. TL 7429
Bebington Merseyside 41 H3 tn 3m/5km S of Birkenhead. Industries incl mnfre of soaps, detergents, edible oils and fats. SJ 3384
Bebside Nthmb 61 G3 loc 2m/4km W of Blyth. NZ 2881
Beccles Suffolk 39 G5 tn on R Waveney 8m/13km W of Lowestoft. Engineering and printing works. Perp ch has detached tower. TM 4290
Becconsall Lancs 47 E5* vil 2m/3km N of Tarleton. SD 4423
Bechan Brook 33 H5* r rising 2km S of Manafon, Powys, and flowing S into R Severn at Aberbechan. SO 1493
Becka Brook 4 D3* stream in Devon rising on Dartmoor S of Manaton and flowing generally E into R Bovey 1m S of Lustleigh. See Becka Falls. SX 7780
Becka Falls Devon 4 D3 waterfall in wooded valley of Becka Brook, tributary of R Bovey, 4m/6km S of Moretonhampstead. SX 7580
Beck Bottom W Yorks 49 E5* loc 2m/4km NW of Wakefield. SE 3023
Beckbury Salop 34 D4 vil 4m/7km S of Shifnal. SJ 7601
Beckenham London 20 A4 tn in borough of Bromley 8m/13km SE of Charing Cross. TQ 3769
Beckering Lincs 45 E3* ham 1km SE of Holton. TF 1280
Beckermet Cumbria 52 A4 vil 3m/4km S of Egremont. NY 0106
Beckermonds N Yorks 53 G6 loc in Langstrothdale, or upper reaches of R Wharfe, 5m/7km NW of Buckden. SD 8780
Becker's Green Essex 30 C5* loc adjoining Braintree to SE. TL 7722
Beckery Som 8 C1* loc on SW side of Glastonbury. ST 4838
Beckett End Norfolk 38 C4* loc 1km E of Foulden. TL 7798
Beck Foot Cumbria 53 E5 loc 4m/6km NW of Sedbergh. SD 6196
Beckfoot Cumbria 59 F6 vil on Solway Firth 3m/5km S of Silloth. NY 0949
Beck Foot W Yorks 48 D4* loc at confluence of Harden Beck and R Aire on S side of Bingley. SE 1038
Beckford H & W 27 E4 vil 6m/9km E of Tewkesbury. SO 9735
Beckham, East Norfolk 39 F1* vil 2m/3km S of Sheringham. **W Beckham** vil 1m W. TG 1539
Beckhampton Wilts 17 E4 ham and rd junction 1m SW of Avebury. SU 0868
Beckhithe Norfolk 39 F4* loc 1m N of Hethersett. TG 1506
Beck Hole N Yorks 55 F4 loc 2m/3km S of Grosmont. NZ 8202
Beckingham Lincs 44 D5 vil 5m/8km E of Newark-on-Trent. SK 8753
Beckingham Notts 44 C4 vil 3m/4km W of Gainsborough. SK 7790
Beckington Som 16 C6 vil 3m/5km NE of Frome. ST 8051
Beckley E Sussex 12 D4 vil 5m/8km NW of Rye. TQ 8523
Beckley Oxon 28 B6 vil 5m/7km NE of Oxford. Site of Roman bldg to E. SP 5611
Beck Row Suffolk 38 B6 vil 2m/4km NW of Mildenhall. TL 6977
Beck Side Cumbria 52 C6 ham 4m/6km SE of Broughton in Furness. SD 2382
Beck Side Cumbria 52 D6* loc 2km N of Cartmel. SD 3780
Beckside Cumbria 53 F5/F6* loc 4m/6km SW of Sedbergh. SD 6188
Beckton London 20 B3* loc in borough of Newham 2km S of E Ham. TQ 4381
Beckwith N Yorks 49 E3* loc 2m/3km SW of Harrogate. SE 2852
Beckwithshaw N Yorks 49 E3 vil 3m/4km SW of Harrogate. SE 2653
Becontree London 20 B3* dist in borough of Barking 3m/5km E of Barking tn centre. TQ 4885
Bedale N Yorks 54 B5 small tn 7m/11km SW of Northallerton. SE 2688
Bedales Hants 10 D2* coeducational boarding school founded 1893, situated at Steep, 2km N of Petersfield. SU 7425
Bedburn Durham 54 A2 loc on B. Beck 3m/5km W of Witton le Wear. NZ 1031
Bedburn Beck 54 A2/B2 r rising on Eggleston Common, Durham, and flowing E into R Wear 2km NW of Witton le Wear. NZ 1232
Bedchester Dorset 9 F3 ham 3m/5km S of Shaftesbury. ST 8317
Beddau Mid Glam 15 F3 vil 3m/5km S of Pontypridd. ST 0585
Beddgelert Gwynedd 40 C6 vil at confluence of Rs Colwyn and Glaslyn 12m/19km SE of Caernarvon and 4m/7km S of Snowdon. SH 5948
Beddingham E Sussex 12 B5 vil 2m/4km SE of Lewes. TQ 4407
Beddington London 19 G5 dist in borough of Sutton 2m/3km W of Croydon. B. Park 1km NW. Site of Roman bath hse 1m N. Loc of **B. Corner** 2km NW. Loc of **S Beddington** 1km S. TQ 2964
Beddmanarch Bay Gwynedd 40 A3* inlet of Holyhead Bay on N side of rd and rly embankment connecting Holy I. with main island of Anglesey. SH 2780
Bedd Taliesin Dyfed 32 D5 loc nearly 1m E of Tre Taliesin. Traditional burial-place of Taliesin, Welsh bard, perhaps mythical, of 6c. SN 6791
Bedfield Suffolk 31 F2 vil 4m/6km NE of Debenham. Ham of **B. Long Green** adjoins to N. Loc of **B. Lit Green** 2km SE. TM 2266
Bedfont, East London 19 E4 loc in borough of Hounslow on S side of London (Heathrow) Airport. TQ 0873

Bedfont, West Surrey 19 E4* loc on S side of London (Heathrow) Airport and 3m/5km NE of Staines. TQ 0674
Bedford Beds 29 E3 county tn on R Ouse 46m/74km N of London. Industries include engineering and brick-making. TL 0449
Bedford Castle S Glam 15 E4* cas on NE side of Llantwit Major. Site marked by earthworks. SS 9869
Bedford Level 37 G4 large drainage area of the Fens (qv) consisting of **N Level,** between Rs Welland and Nene; **Middle Level,** between R Nene and New Bedford R; and **S Level,** between New Bedford R and Brandon. TF, TL
Bedford Park London 19 F3* dist on borders of Ealing and Hounslow boroughs 6m/9km W of Charing Cross. TQ 2179
Bedfordshire 119 south midland county of England, bounded by Hertfordshire, Buckinghamshire, Northamptonshire, and Cambridgeshire. The northern end of the Chilterns runs through the S and SE of the county, which is otherwise mostly flat. Bedford is the county tn. Luton and Dunstable are industrial centres, mainly of engineering and vehicle mnfre; elsewhere brick mnfre and vegetable growing are carried on. Chief r is the Ouse.
Bedgebury Forest Kent 12 D3 large wooded area some 3m/5km S of Goudhurst. At N edge, **Bedgebury Park,** with 19c château-style mansion now girls' boarding school. S of park, **Bedgebury Pinetum** contains many varieties of trees and shrubs. **Bedgebury Cross** loc 1m E of Kilndown. TQ 7233
Bedgrove Bucks 18 C1* SE dist of Aylesbury. SP 8412
Bedham W Sussex 11 F3* ham 3m/4km E of Petworth. TQ 0121
Bedhampton Hants 10 D4 W dist of Havant. SU 6906
Bedingfield Suffolk 31 F2 vil 4m/6km N of Debenham. Ham of **B. Street** 1km S. Loc of **B. Green** 2km S. TM 1868
Bedingham Green Norfolk 39 G5* ham 4m/6km NW of Bungay. TM 2892
Bedlam Lancs 48 A5* loc 2km S of Accrington. SD 7526
Bedlam N Yorks 49 E2 ham 2km NW of Ripley. SE 2661
Bedlam Som 16 C6* loc 2m/3km NW of Frome. ST 7549
Bedlar's Green Essex 30 A5* ham 3m/4km E of Bishop's Stortford. TL 5220
Bedlington Nthmb 61 G3 tn in coal-mining dist 4m/7km SE of Morpeth. NZ 2581
Bedlinog Mid Glam 15 F2 vil 3m/4km N of Treharris. SO 0901
Bedminster Avon 16 B4* S dist of Bristol. ST 5771
Bedminster Down Avon 16 B4* SW dist of Bristol. ST 5769
Bedmond Herts 19 E2 vil 4m/6km SE of Hemel Hempstead. TL 0903
Bednall Staffs 35 F3 vil 4m/7km SE of Stafford. SJ 9517
Bedrule Borders 66 D6 vil on Rule Water 4m/6km SW of Jedburgh. NT 6018
Bedruthan Steps Cornwall. See St Eval.
Bedstone Salop 34 B6 vil 6m/9km E of Knighton. SO 3675
Bedwas Mid Glam 15 F3 coal-mining tn 2m/3km NE of Caerphilly. Light industry on industrial estate beside Rymney R. ST 1788
Bedwell Herts 29 F5* dist of Stevenage on E side of tn centre. TL 2424
Bedwellty (Bedwellte) Gwent 15 F2 ham 2km E of Bargoed. SO 1600
Bedwellty Pits Gwent 15 F1* loc 2m/3km S of Tredegar. SO 1506
Bedworth Warwicks 36 A5 tn in coal-mining dist 5m/8km N of Coventry. SP 3587
Bedworth Heath Warwicks 35 H5 loc 2km W of Bedworth. Loc of **Bedworth Little Heath** adjoins S. SP 3386
Bedworth Woodlands Warwicks 35 H5* loc 1m W of Bedworth. SP 3487
Bedwyn, Great Wilts 17 G5 vil on Kennet and Avon Canal 5m/8km SW of Hungerford. SU 2764
Bedwyn, Little Wilts 17 G5 vil 4m/6km SW of Hungerford. SU 2966
Beeby Leics 36 C3 ham 5m/9km NE of Leicester. **Lit Beeby** loc to SE. SK 6608
Beech Hants 10 D1 vil 2km W of Alton. SU 6938
Beech Staffs 35 E1* ham 5m/8km S of Newcastle-under-Lyme. SJ 8538
Beech Hedge Tayside 73 E1*. See Meikleour.
Beech Hill Berks 18 B5 vil 6m/9km S of Reading. SU 6964
Beech Hill Gtr Manchester 42 B1* dist of Wigan 2km NW of tn centre. SD 5606
Beechingstoke Wilts 17 E5* vil 5m/8km W of Pewsey. SU 0859
Beech Lane W Midlands 35 F5* loc in Birmingham 3m/5km W of city centre. SP 0185
Beechwood Ches 42 B3* S dist of Runcorn. SJ 5480
Beechwood Gwent 15 H3* loc in Newport 2m/3km E of tn centre. ST 3388
Beeding, Lower W Sussex 11 H2 vil 4m/6km SE of Horsham. TQ 2227
Beeding, Upper W Sussex 11 G4 vil in R Adur valley 4m/6km N of Shoreham-by-Sea. TQ 1910
Beedon Berks 18 A4 vil 7m/11km N of Newbury. Ham of **B. Hill** 1km SE. SU 4878
Beeford Humberside 51 F3 vil 7m/11km E of Gt Driffield. TA 1354
Beeley Derbys 43 G4 vil 5m/8km N of Matlock. SK 2667
Beelsby Humberside 45 F1 vil 6m/10km SW of Grimsby. TA 2001
Beenham Berks 18 B4 vil 9m/14km W of Reading. Locs of **B. Stocks** and **B. Hills** to E. SU 5868
Beenham's Heath Berks 18 C4* loc 4m/6km E of Twyford. SU 8475
Beeny Cornwall 6 A5* loc near coast at **B. Cliff** 2m/3km NE of Boscastle. SX 1192
Beer Devon 8 A5 small resort on Seaton Bay 2km W of Seaton. 1m S, **Beer Hd,** W end of the bay. SY 2289
Beercrocombe (or Beer Crocombe) Som 8 B2 vil 4m/7km NW of Ilminster. ST 3220
Beer Hackett Dorset 8 D3 vil 4m/6km SW of Sherborne. ST 5911
Beesands Devon 5 E6* fishing vil 2m/4km N of Start Pt. SX 8240
Beesby Humberside 45 F2* loc 2m/3km SW of N Thoresby. TF 2696
Beesby Lincs 45 H3 vil 3m/5km N of Alford. TF 4680
Beeson Devon 5 E6* vil 1km from coast and 3m/4km NW of Start Pt. SX 8140
Beeston Beds 29 F3 vil 1km S of Sandy across R Ivel. TL 1748
Beeston Ches 42 B5 ham 3m/4km S of Tarporley. Remains of 13c cas (A.M.) on hill to NW. SJ 5458
Beeston Norfolk 38 D3 vil 5m/9km W of E Dereham. TF 9015
Beeston Notts 36 B1 tn adjoining Nottingham to SW. Industries include pharmaceutical products, hosiery and textiles. **B. Canal** runs from R Trent on S side of tn to Nottingham city centre. SK 5236
Beeston W Yorks 49 E5 dist of Leeds 2m/3km S of city centre. **B. Park Side** loc adjoining to S. **B. Royds** loc adjoining to W. SE 2830
Beeston Regis Norfolk 39 F1 suburb 1m E of Sheringham. TG 1742
Beeston St Lawrence Norfolk 39 G3 loc 4m/6km NE of Wroxham. TG 3222
Beeswing D & G 59 E4 vil 7m/11km SW of Dumfries. NX 8969
Beetham Cumbria 47 F1 vil 6m/9km N of Carnforth. SD 4979
Beetham Som 8 B3* ham 2m/3km W of Combe St Nicholas. ST 2712
Beetley Norfolk 38 D3 vil 4m/6km N of E Dereham. TF 9718
Beezley Falls N Yorks 48 A1* series of waterfalls in R Doe 2km NE of Ingleton. SD 7074
Beffcote Staffs 35 E3* loc 2m/3km SW of Gnosall. SJ 8019
Begbroke Oxon 27 H6 vil 6m/9km NW of Oxford. SP 4713
Begdale Cambs 38 A4* loc 2m/3km S of Wisbech. TF 4506
Begeli Welsh form of Begelly, qv.
Begelly (Begeli) Dyfed 22 D5 vil 4m/7km N of Tenby. SN 1107
Beggarington Hill W Yorks 49 E5* loc 2m/4km SE of Morley. SE 2724
Beggar's Bush Powys 25 G2* loc 3m/5km W of Presteigne. SO 2664
Beggars Pound S Glam 15 E4* loc 3m/5km E of Llantwit Major. ST 0168
Beggearn Huish Som 7 H2* ham on edge of Exmoor National Park 3m/4km SW of Watchet. ST 0439
Beguildy (Bugeildy) Powys 25 F1 vil in R Teme valley 7m/12km NW of Knighton. SO 1979
Beich Burn 71 G3 r running S down Glen Beich to Loch Earn 2m/3km E of Lochearnhead in Central region. NN 6124
Beighton Norfolk 39 G4 vil 2m/3km SW of Acle. TG 3808
Beighton S Yorks 43 H3 dist of Sheffield 6m/10km SE of city centre. SK 4483
Beili-glas Gwent 15 G1* loc 3m/4km S of Abergavenny. SO 3010
Beinn a' Bha'ach Ard H'land 80 D3 mt in Inverness dist 3m/5km NW of Struy Br. Height 2827 ft or 862 metres. NH 3643
Beinn a' Bheithir H'land 74 G5, C5* mt mass in Lochaber dist S of Ballachulish. Anglicised form: Ben Vair. Summit is Sgorr Dhearg, qv. NN 0555
Beinn a' Bhric H'land 74 D5* mt in Lochaber dist 3m/5km S of head of Loch Treig. Height 2863 ft or 873 metres. NN 3164
Beinn a' Bhuic Central 71 F1* mt 4m/6km NW of Killin. Height 2668 ft or 813 metres. NN 5538
Beinn a' Bhùird Grampian 76 B1, B2 mt ridge running N and S about 6m/10km NW of Braemar. Height of N top 3924 ft or 1196 metres; S top 3860 ft or 1177 metres. NJ 0900
Beinn a' Bhùiridh S'clyde 70 C2 peak 2m/3km SE of summit of Ben Cruachan in Argyll. Height 2941 ft or 896 metres. NN 0928
Beinn a' Chàisgein Mór H'land 85 A8 mt in W part of Ross and Cromarty dist 2m/3km N of head of Fionn Loch. Height 2802 ft or 854 metres. 3m/4km N is **Beinn a' Chàisgein Beag,** height 2234 ft or 681 metres. NG 9878
Beinn a' Chaisteil 71 E2 mt on border of Strathclyde and Tayside regions 4m/7km N of Tyndrum. Height 2897 ft or 883 metres. NN 3436
Beinn a' Chait Tayside 75 H4 mt on Forest of Atholl 6m/10km N of Blair Atholl. Height 2942 ft or 897 metres. NN 8674
Beinn Achaladair 71 E1 mt on border of Strathclyde and Tayside regions 2m/4km E of Loch Tulla. Height 3403 ft or 1037 metres. NN 3443
Beinn a' Chaolais S'clyde 62 C1 westernmost of the Paps of Jura, qv, and the third in height: 2407 ft or 734 metres. NR 4873
Beinn a' Chaorainn H'land 75 E3 mt in Lochaber dist 3m/4km NE of W end of Loch Moy. Height 3445 ft or 1050 metres. NN 3884
Beinn a' Chaoruinn Grampian 76 B1 mt in Cairngorms 4m/6km NE of Ben Macdui. Height 3550 ft or 1082 metres. NJ 0401
Beinn a' Chapuill H'land 79 F6 mt in Lochaber dist 3m/4km SE of Glenelg. Height 2421 ft or 738 metres. NG 8215
Beinn a' Chlachair H'land 75 E3 mt in Badenoch and Strathspey dist, 2m/3km S of SW end of Lochan na h-Earba. Height 3565 ft or 1087 metres. NN 4778
Beinn a' Chleibh 70 D2/D3 peak on border of Central and Strathclyde regions 1m SW of summit of Ben Lui. Height 3008 ft or 917 metres. NN 2525
Beinn a' Chonnaich Tayside. Gaelic form of Ben Chonzie, qv.
Beinn a' Chreachain Tayside 71 E1 mt up against border with Strathclyde region 3m/5km N of head of Loch Lyon. Height 3545 ft or 1081 metres. NN 3744
Beinn a' Chroin Central 71 E3 mt 4m/7km S of Crianlarich. Height 3104 ft or 946 metres. NN 3918
Beinn a' Chruinnich Grampian 82 B5 mt 5m/9km SE of Tomintoul. Height 2536 ft or 773 metres. NJ 2313
Beinn a' Chrùlaiste H'land 74 D5 mt in Lochaber dist 5m/8km SE of Kinlochleven. Height 2811 ft or 857 metres. NN 2456
Beinn a' Chuallaich Tayside 75 G5 mt 2m/4km NE of Kinloch Rannoch. NN 6861
Beinn a' Chùirn 71 E1* mt on border of Strathclyde and Tayside regions 4m/6km E of Br of Orchy. Height 3032 ft or 924 metres. NN 3641
Beinn a' Chumhainn 75 E4 mt on border of Tayside region and Lochaber and Badenoch & Strathspey dists of Highland region, 2m/3km W of Ben Alder. Height 2958 ft or 902 metres. NN 4671
Beinn a' Ghlo Tayside 76 A4 mt mass 8m/12km NE of Blair Atholl. Also known as Ben-y-Gloe. Summit is Carn nan Gabhar, 3675 ft or 1120 metres. NN 9773
Beinn Alligin H'land 78 F3 mt in Ross and Cromarty dist 2m/4km N of Upr Loch Torridon. The two peaks of Sgurr Mhór and Tom na Gruagaich are respectively 3232 ft or 985 metres and 3020 ft or 920 metres in height. NG 8660
Beinn a' Mhanaich S'clyde 70 D5* mt 3m/5km NE of Garelochhead. Height 2328 ft or 710 metres. NS 2694
Beinn an Armuinn H'land. Gaelic form of Ben Armine, qv.
Beinn an Dòthaidh S'clyde 71 E1 mt in Argyll 2m/3km E of Br of Orchy. Height 3289 ft or 1002 metres. NN 3240
Beinn an Eóin H'land 80 A2 mt in Ross and Cromarty dist 5m/8km N of head of Upr Loch Torridon. Height 2805 ft or 855 metres. NG 9064
Beinn an Lochain S'clyde 70 D4* mt in Argyll 4m/7km N of Lochgoilhead. Height 2992 ft or 912 metres. NN 2107
Beinn an Oir S'clyde 62 C1 highest of the Paps of Jura, qv. Height 2571 ft or 784 metres. NR 4975
Beinn an t-Seilich S'clyde 70 D4 mt in Argyll 4m/7km N of Lochgoilhead. Height 2359 ft or 719 metres. NN 2007
Beinn Bhàn H'land 74 C3 mt in Lochaber dist 3m/4km W of SW end of Loch Lochy. Height 2613 ft or 796 metres. NN 1485
Beinn Bhàn H'land 78 F4 mt mass in Ross and Cromarty dist 6m/9km S of Shieldaig. Highest point 2938 ft or 396 metres. NG 8045
Beinn Bharrain S'clyde 63 F3 mt on Arran 2m/3km SE of Pirnmill. Height 2366 ft or 721 metres. Anglicised form: Ben Varren. NR 9042
Beinn Bheigeir S'clyde 62 B2/C3 hill on Islay 3m/5km SW of McArthur's Hd. Highest point on Islay: 1609 ft or 490 metres. NR 4256
Beinn Bheòil H'land 75 F4 mt in Badenoch and Strathspey dist between Loch Ericht and Loch a' Bhealaich Bheithe. Height 3343 ft or 1019 metres. NN 5171
Beinn Bheula S'clyde 70 D5 mt in Argyll 4m/6km SW of Lochgoilhead. Height 2557 ft or 779 metres. NS 1598
Beinn Bhreac Central 71 F2* mt 4m/7km W of Killin. Height 2607 ft or 795 metres. NN 5032
Beinn Bhreac H'land 79 C7 hill on island of Soay off S coast of Skye. At 455 ft or 108 metres it is highest point on island. NG 4615
Beinn Bhreac S'clyde 63 F3 mt on Arran 2m/4km E of Pirnmill. Height 2333 ft or 711 metres. Anglicised form: Ben Vrackie. NR 9044
Beinn Bhreac S'clyde 71 E4 mt 3m/5km S of Tarbet on W shore of Loch Lomond. Height 2233 ft or 681 metres. NN 3200
Beinn Bhreac Tayside 71 H1 mt 2m/3km E of Ardtalnaig. Height 2348 ft or 716 metres. NN 7340
Beinn Bhreac Tayside 75 A3* mt 10m/17km N of Blair Atholl. Height 2992 ft or 912 metres. NN 8682
Beinn Bhreac Tayside 76 A4 mt 3m/5km N of Pitlochry. Height 2760 ft or 841 metres. Anglicised form: Ben Vrackie. NN 9563
Beinn Bhreac-liath S'clyde 71 E2 mt in Argyll 3m/5km NW of Tyndrum. Height 2633 ft or 803 metres. NN 3033
Beinn Bhreac Mhór H'land 81 F5 mt in Inverness dist 5m/8km S of E Croachy. Height 2641 ft or 805 metres. NH 6719
Beinn Bhrotain Grampian 76 A2 mt at S end of Cairngorms. Height 3795 ft or 1157 metres. NN 9592
Beinn Bhuidhe H'land 74 A2 mt in Knoydart, in Lochaber dist, 2m/3km NE of Kylesknoydart on Loch Nevis. Height 2803 ft or 854 metres. NM 8296
Beinn Bhuidhe S'clyde 70 D3 mt in Argyll 4m/7km N of head of Loch Fyne. Height 3106 ft or 947 metres. NN 2018
Beinn Ceitlein S'clyde 70 D1 mt in Argyll to E of Glen Etive, 5m/8km NE of head of Loch Etive. Height 2731 ft or 832 metres. NN 1749
Beinn Chabhair Central 71 E3 mt 5m/8km S of Crianlarich. Height 3053 ft or 931 metres. NN 3617

Beinn Chaorach Central 71 E2 mt 2m/4km NE of Tyndrum. Height 2685 ft or 818 metres. NN 3532

Beinn Chaorach S'clyde 71 E5 mt 3m/5km E of Garelochhead. Height 2338 ft or 713 metres. NS 2892

Beinn Cheathaich Central 71 F2 mt 8m/13km W of Killin. Height 3076 ft or 938 metres. NN 4432

Beinn Chorranach S'clyde 70 D4 mt in Argyll 4m/7km NW of Arrochar. Height 2903 ft or 885 metres. NN 2509

Beinn Chuirn 70 D2 mt on border of Central and Strathclyde regions 3m/5km W of Tyndrum. Height 2878 ft or 877 metres. NN 2829

Beinn Cleith Bric H'land. Gaelic form of Ben Klibreck, qv.

Beinn Damh H'land 78 F4 mt in Ross and Cromarty dist 2km E of Loch Damh and 3m/5km S of head of Upr Loch Torridon. Height 2958 ft or 902 metres. Anglicised form: Ben Damph. NG 8950

Beinn Dearg H'land 80 A2 mt in Ross and Cromarty dist 3m/5km N of head of Upr Loch Torridon. Height 2995 ft or 913 metres. NG 8960

Beinn Dearg H'land 85 C8 mt in Ross and Cromarty dist 6m/9km SE of head of Loch Broom. Height 3536 ft or 1078 metres. NH 2581

Beinn Dearg Tayside 75 F6 mt 2m/3km NE of Innerwick in Glen Lyon. Height 2702 ft or 824 metres. NN 6049

Beinn Dearg Tayside 75 H3 mt on Forest of Atholl 8m/12km N of Blair Atholl. Height 3307 ft or 1008 metres. NN 8577

Beinn Dearg Mhór H'land 85 A8 mt in Fisherfield Forest, Ross and Cromarty dist, 4m/6km SW of An Teallach. Height 2974 ft or 906 metres. NH 0379

Beinn Dòrain S'clyde 71 E1 mt in Argyll 2m/3km SE of Br of Orchy. Height 3530 ft or 1076 metres. Anglicised form: Ben Douran. NN 3237

Beinn Dronaig H'land 80 B4 mt in Skye and Lochalsh dist on SW side of Loch Calavie. Height 2612 ft or 796 metres. NH 0338

Beinn Dubh S'clyde 70 D4 mt on W side of Loch Sloy, 3m/5km NW of Inveruglas on W shore of Loch Lomond. Height 2509 ft or 765 metres. NN 2511

Beinn Dubhchraig Central 71 E2 mt 5m/8km W of Crianlarich. Height 3204 ft or 977 metres. NN 3025

Beinn Eibhinn H'land 75 E4 mt on border of Lochaber and Badenoch & Strathspey dists 2m/3km E of Loch Ghuilbinn. Height 3611 ft or 1100 metres. NN 4473

Beinn Eich S'clyde 71 E5 mt 4m/6km W of Luss. Height 2302 ft or 702 metres. NS 3094

Beinn Eighe H'land 80 A2 mt mass and national nature reserve in Ross and Cromarty dist to W of Kinlochewe. Anglicised form: Ben Eay. Highest peak is Ruadh-stac Mór, 3312 ft or 1010 metres. NG 9561

Beinn Eunaich S'clyde 70 C2 mt in Argyll 4m/6km NW of Dalmally. Height 3242 ft or 988 metres. NN 1332

Beinneun Forest H'land 74 D1 deer forest on border of Inverness and Lochaber dists E of Loch Loyne. NH 2208

Beinn Fhada H'land 74 C5. See Three Sisters of Glen Coe.

Beinn Fhada H'land 80 B5 mt on Kintail Forest (NTS), in Skye and Lochalsh dist, 5m/8km E of Shiel Br. Height 3383 ft or 1031 metres. Also known as Ben Attow. NH 0119

Beinn Fhionnlaidh H'land 80 B4* mt on S side of Loch Mullardoch, Skye and Lochalsh dist. Height 3294 ft or 1004 metres. NH 1128

Beinn Fhionnlaidh S'clyde 70 C1 mt in Argyll, 3m/5km N of head of Loch Etive. Height 3145 ft or 959 metres. NN 0949

Beinn Ghlas Tayside 71 G1 SW shoulder (NTS) of Ben Lawers. Height 3657 ft or 1115 metres. Slopes noted for alpine plants. NN 6240

Beinn Heasgarnich Tayside 71 E1 mt 2m/3km S of centre of Loch Lyon. Height 3538 ft or 1078 metres. NN 4138

Beinn Iaruinn H'land 74 D2/D3 mt in Lochaber dist 4m/7km S of head of Loch Lochy. Height 2636 ft or 803 metres. NN 2990

Beinn Iutharn Mhór 76 B3 mt on border of Grampian and Tayside regions, 10m/16km SW of Braemar. Height 3428 ft or 1045 metres. **Beinn Iutharn Bheag** is mt 2km E; height 3127 ft or 953 metres. NO 0679

Beinn Laoghal H'land 84 F3 mt in Caithness dist 5m/8km S of Tongue. Height 2506 ft or 764 metres. Anglicised form: Ben Loyal. NC 5748

Beinn Laoigh. Gaelic form of Ben Lui, qv.

Beinn Liath Mhór H'land 80 A3 mt ridge, Ross and Cromarty dist, 3m/5km NW of Achnashellach Lodge. Summit 3034 ft or 925 metres. NG 9652

Beinn Lochain S'clyde 70 D4* mt in Argyll 3m/4km W of Lochgoilhead. Height 2306 ft or 703 metres. NN 1600

Beinn Luibhean S'clyde 70 D4* mt in Argyll 4m/7km NW of Arrochar. Height 2811 ft or 857 metres. NN 2407

Beinn Lurachan S'clyde 70 D2 mt in Argyll 4m/7km N of Dalmally. Height 2346 ft or 715 metres. NN 1633

Beinn Mhanach Tayside 71 E1 mt 1m N of head of Loch Lyon. Height 3130 ft or 954 metres. Anglicised form: Ben Vannoch. NN 3741

Beinn Mheadhoin Grampian 76 B1 mt in Cairngorms 3m/5km NE of Ben Macdui. Height 3878 ft or 1182 metres. NJ 0201

Beinn Mhic Chasgaig S'clyde 74 D6 mt in Argyll 2km W of Clach Leathad on E side of Glen Etive. Height 2820 ft or 860 metres. NN 2250

Beinn Mhic-Mhonaidh S'clyde 70 D2 mt in Argyll 6m/10km NE of Dalmally. Height 2602 ft or 793 metres. NN 2035

Beinn Mholach Tayside 75 F4 mt 3m/5km SW of S end of Loch Garry. Height 2758 ft or 841 metres. NN 5865

Beinn Mhór S'clyde 70 C5 mt in Argyll 2m/3km W of middle of Loch Eck. NS 1090

Beinn Mhór W Isles 88 B3 mt on Lewis 2m/3km N of head of Loch Claidh. Height 1874 ft or 571 metres. NB 2509

Beinn Mhór W Isles 88 E2 mt on S Uist 2m/4km N of Loch Eynort. Height 2034 ft or 620 metres. NF 8031

Beinn Muic Duibhe Grampian. See Ben Macdui.

Beinn na Caillich H'land 74 C5* mt on N side of Loch Leven in Lochaber dist, 3m/5km W of Kinlochleven. Height 2502 ft or 763 metres. NN 1462

Beinn na Caillich H'land 79 F7 mt in Knoydart, in Lochaber dist, 3m/4km NW of Ladhar Bheinn. Height 2573 ft or 784 metres. NH 7906

Beinn na Caillich Skye, H'land 79 D6 mt 3m/4km W of Broadford. Height 2400 ft or 732 metres. NG 6023

Beinn na Caillich Skye, H'land 79 F6 mt 2m/4km SE of Kyleakin near E end of island. Height 2396 ft or 730 metres. NG 7722

Beinn na Cille H'land 68 F3 mt in Lochaber dist 1m N of Loch a' Choire. Height 2136 ft or 651 metres. NM 8554

Beinn na Croise S'clyde 69 D5 hill on Mull 3m/4km NE of Carsaig. Source of Leidle Water. Height 1649 ft or 503 metres. NM 5625

Beinn na Gainimh Tayside 72 C2* mt 4m/7km W of Amulree. Height 2382 ft or 726 metres. NN 8334

Beinn na h-Eaglaise H'land 80 A3 mt on Ben-damph Forest, Ross and Cromarty dist, 2m/3km S of head of Loch Torridon. Height 2410 ft or 735 metres. NG 9052

Beinn na Lap H'land 75 E4 mt in Lochaber dist 1m N of Loch Ossian. Height 3073 ft or 937 metres. NN 3769

Beinn nam Fuaran 71 E1 mt on border of Strathclyde and Tayside regions 4m/7km E of Br of Orchy. Height 2632 ft or 802 metres. NN 3638

Beinn nan Aighenan S'clyde 70 D1 mt in Argyll 4m/6km SE of head of Loch Etive. Height 3141 ft or 957 metres. NN 1440

Beinn nan Caorach H'land 74 A1 mt in Lochaber dist 2m/3km NE of Arnisdale on Loch Hourn. Height 2536 ft or 773 metres. NG 8712

Beinn nan Imirean Central 71 E2 mt 4m/7km NE of Crianlarich. Height 2769 ft or 844 metres. NN 4130

Beinn nan Lus S'clyde 70 C2 mt in Argyll on N side of Glen Kinglass. Height 2327 ft or 709 metres. NN 1337

Beinn nan Oighreag 71 F1 mt on border of Central and Tayside regions 6m/10km W of Ben Lawers. NN 5843

Beinn Narnain S'clyde 70 D4* mt in Argyll 2m/3km NW of head of Loch Long. Height 3036 ft or 925 metres. NN 2706

Beinn Nuis S'clyde 63 F4 mt on Arran 2m/4km SW of Goat Fell. Height 2597 ft or 792 metres. NR 9539

Beinn Odhar 71 E2 mt on border of Central and Strathclyde regions 2m/4km N of Tyndrum. Height 2948 ft or 899 metres. NN 3333

Beinn Odhar Mhór H'land 74 A3/A4 mt in Moidart, Lochaber dist, 4m/6km W of Glenfinnan. Height 2853 ft or 870 metres. **Beinn Odhar Bheag** is nearly 1m S, height 2895 ft or 882 metres. NM 8579

Beinn Pharlagain Tayside 75 E5 mt on Rannoch Forest 4m/6km N of Loch Eigheach. Height 2836 ft or 864 metres. NN 4464

Beinn Reithe S'clyde 70 D5* mt in Argyll 3m/4km SE of Lochgoilhead. Height 2142 ft or 653 metres. NS 2298

Beinn Sgritheall H'land 74 A1 mt in Lochaber dist 2km N of Arnisdale on Loch Hourn. Height 3196 ft or 974 metres. Also known as Ben Screel. NG 8312

Beinn Sguliaird S'clyde 70 C1 mt ridge 3m/5km E of head of Loch Creran, Argyll. Height of summit 3059 ft or 932 metres. NN 0546

Beinn Shiantaidh S'clyde 62 C1 easternmost of the Paps of Jura, qv, and the second in height: 2477 ft or 755 metres. NR 5174

Beinn Spionnaidh H'land 84 D2 mt in Sutherland dist 3m/4km NW of head of Loch Eriboll. Height 2535 ft or 773 metres. NC 3657

Beinn Suidhe S'clyde 70 D1 mt in Argyll 6m/9km W of Br of Orchy. Height 2215 ft or 675 metres. NN 2140

Beinn Teallach H'land 74 D3/75 E3 mt in Lochaber dist 3m/5km N of W end of Loch Moy. Height 2994 ft or 913 metres. NN 3685

Beinn Tharsuinn H'land 80 B3* mt on W Monar Forest on border of Ross & Cromarty and Skye & Lochalsh dists. Height 2807 ft or 856 metres. NH 0543

Beinn Toaig S'clyde 70 D1 mt in Argyll on SE side of Stob a' Choire Odhair and 2m/3km E of Stob Ghabhar. Height 2712 ft or 827 metres. NN 2645

Beinn Trilleachan S'clyde 70 C1 mt 2m/3km SW of head of Loch Etive, Argyll. Height 2752 ft or 839 metres. NN 0843

Beinn Tulaichean Central 71 E3* mt 4m/6km SE of Crianlarich. Height 3099 ft or 945 metres. NN 4119

Beinn Udlaidh S'clyde 70 D2 mt in Argyll 4m/6km NW of Tyndrum. Height 2759 ft or 841 metres. NN 2833

Beinn Udlamain Tayside 75 F4* mt on border with Highland region on Dalnaspidal Forest to E of Loch Ericht. Height 3306 ft or 1008 metres. NN 5773

Beith S'clyde 64 B3 tn 10m/16km SW of Paisley. Industries include mnfre of furniture, hosiery, textiles. NS 3453

Bekesbourne Kent 13 G2 vil 3m/5km SE of Canterbury. Loc of **B. Hill** 1km N. TR 1955

Bela 53 E6* r rising E of Kendal, Cumbria, and flowing S to Beetham, N to Milnthorpe, and W into R Kent estuary. SD 4881

Belah Cumbria 59 H5* loc in Carlisle 1m N of city centre. NY 3957

Belah 53 G3/G4 r rising on moors E of Kirkby Stephen, Cumbria, and flowing generally NW into R Eden 2m/3km SW of Brough. NY 7612

Belaugh Norfolk 39 G3 vil 1m NW of Wroxham across R Bure. **B. Green** loc 1m NE. **B. Broad** small broad or lake 1m S. TG 2818

Belbroughton H & W 35 E6 vil 5m/8km S of Stourbridge. SO 9176

Belchalwell Dorset 9 E3 ham 3m/5km S of Sturminster Newton. 1km SE, ham of **B. Street.** ST 7909

Belchamp Otten Essex 30 C4 vil 5m/7km W of Sudbury. TL 8041

Belchamp St Paul Essex 30 C4 vil 5m/8km W of Sudbury. TL 7942

Belchamp Walter Essex 30 C4 vil 3m/5km W of Sudbury. TL 8140

Belchford Lincs 45 G4 vil 4m/7km NE of Horncastle. TF 2975

Bele 23 E3* r rising 5m/7km SE of Newcastle Emlyn, Dyfed, and flowing SE into R Duad below Cwmduad, 2m/3km N of Conwil Elvet. SN 3730

Belfield Gtr Manchester 48 C6* loc in Rochdale 2km E of tn centre. SD 9113

Belford Nthmb 67 G5 vil 14m/23km SE of Berwick-upon-Tweed. NU 1033

Belgrano Clwyd 41 F3* loc 2km NE of Abergele. SH 9578

Belgrave Staffs 35 H4* loc 2km SE of Tamworth. SK 2202

Belgravia London 19 F4* area in City of Westminster W of Victoria Stn and S of Knightsbridge. TQ 2879

Belhaven Lothian 66 D1 W dist of Dunbar. NT 6678

Belhaven Bay Lothian 66 D1 bay on W side of Dunbar. NT 6578

Belhelvie Grampian 83 G5 loc 7m/12km N of Aberdeen. NJ 9417

Belhinnie Grampian. See Balhinny.

Bellahouston S'clyde 64 C3* loc in Glasgow 2m/4km SW of city centre. NS 5564

Bellanoch S'clyde 70 A5 locality in Argyll on SW side of Crinan Canal 2m/3km from Crinan vil. Rd br across canal and R Add. NR 8092

Bellart S'clyde 68 C4 r on Mull running NW to Loch na Cuilce, 5m/8km W of Tobermory. NM 4351

Bellasize Humberside 50 C5 loc 5m/8km E of Howden. SE 8227

Bell Bar Herts 19 F1 loc 3m/4km SE of Hatfield. TL 2505

Bell Busk N Yorks 48 B3* vil 3m/4km NW of Gargrave. SD 9056

Belleau Lincs 45 G3 vil 4m/6km NW of Alford. TL 4078

Belle Isle Cumbria 52 D5 island on Windermere about 1km long opp Cockshot Pt. SD 3996

Belle Isle W Yorks 49 E5* dist of Leeds 3m/5km S of city centre. SE 3129

Bell End H & W 35 F6 ham 4m/7km N of Bromsgrove. SO 9377

Bellerby N Yorks 54 A5 vil 2km N of Leyburn. SE 1192

Belle Vale W Midlands 35 F5* loc in Halesowen 1m NW of tn centre. SO 9584

Bellever Devon 4 C3* loc on Dartmoor 2km S of Postbridge. Clapper br over E Dart R. SX 6577

Belle Vue Cumbria 52 B2* loc 1m NW of Cockermouth across R Derwent. NY 1131

Belle Vue Cumbria 59 H5 dist of Carlisle 2m/3km W of city centre. NY 3755

Belle Vue Salop 34 B3 S dist of Shrewsbury. SJ 4911

Belle Vue W Yorks 49 E6* dist of Wakefield 2km SE of city centre across R Calder. SE 3419

Bellfields Surrey 19 E6* N dist of Guildford. SU 9951

Bell Green London 20 A4* loc in borough of Lewisham 2m/3km S of Lewisham tn centre and 7m/11km SE of Charing Cross. TQ 3672

Bell Green Suffolk 31 G1* N part of Cratfield. TM 3175

Bell Green W Midlands 36 A6 loc in Coventry 2m/4km NE of city centre. SP 3581

Bell Hall N Yorks. See Naburn.

Bell Heath H & W 35 F6* loc 4m/7km N of Bromsgrove. SO 9577

Bell Hill Hants 10 D3* loc adjoining Petersfield to NW. SU 7424

Bellingdon Bucks 18 D1* vil 3m/4km N of Chesham. SP 9405

Bellinge Northants 28 C2 E dist of Northampton, containing former vils of Gt and Lit Billing. SP 8062

Bellingham London 20 A4* loc in borough of Lewisham 2m/3km S of Lewisham tn centre and 7m/11km SE of Charing Cross. TQ 3772

Bellingham Nthmb 60 D3 small tn on R North Tyne 14m/23km NW of Hexham. NY 8383

Bellister Shetland 89 E7* loc on Mainland on S side of Dury Voe. **Bight of B.** is small bay to E. HU 4860

Bellister Castle Nthmb 60 C5 17c hse (NT) with ruined tower of former cas attached, 1km SW of Haltwhistle. NY 7063
Bellochantuy S'clyde 62 D4 vil on **B. Bay** on W coast of Kintyre. NR 6632
Bell o' th' Hill Ches 42 B6* ham 3m/5km NW of Whitchurch. SJ 5245
Bellow Water 56 F2* r in Strathclyde region running SW to join Glenmuir Water and form Lugar Water 1km E of vil of Lugar. NS 5921
Bell's Close Tyne & Wear 61 F5* loc on N side of R Tyne 4m/6km W of Newcastle. NZ 1964
Bells Creek Kent. See Harty, Isle of.
Bell's Cross Suffolk 31 F3* loc 5m/8km N of Ipswich. TM 1552
Bellshill Nthmb 67 G5 loc 2m/4km SE of Belford. NU 1230
Bellshill S'clyde 64 D3/65 E3 loc 2m/4km NW of Motherwell. Red sandstone quarry. NS 7360
Bellsquarry Lothian 65 G2 loc in Livingston 2m/3km SW of tn centre. NT 0465
Bells Yew Green E Sussex 12 C3 ham 3m/4km SE of Tunbridge Wells. TQ 6036
Belluton Avon 16 B5 ham 3m/4km E of Chew Magna. ST 6164
Belmesthorpe Leics 37 F3 loc 2m/4km NE of Stamford. TF 0410
Belmont Lancs 47 G6 vil 5m/8km NW of Bolton. **Belmont Resr** to N. SD 6716
Belmont London 19 F3* loc in borough of Harrow 11m/17km NW of Charing Cross. TQ 1690
Belmont London 19 F5 loc in borough of Sutton 2km S of Sutton tn centre. TQ 2562
Belmont S'clyde 64 B6* S dist of Ayr. NS 3420
Belmont Shetland 89 F5 loc at SW end of Unst near bay named **Wick of B.**, whence vehicle ferry plies across Bluemull Sound to Gutcher on island of Yell. HP 5601
Belmont Castle Tayside 76 D6 formerly home of Sir H. Campbell-Bannerman, 1836-1908, prime minister. On S side of Meigle. NO 2843
Belmont Television Transmitter Lincs. See Benniworth.
Belnahua S'clyde 70 A4* small island 2km W of NW coast of Luing. NM 7112
Belnie Lincs 37 G2* loc 1m SE of Gosberton. TF 2430
Belowda Cornwall 3 E2* loc 4m/6km E of St Columb Major. SW 9661
Belper Derbys 43 H6 industrial tn 7m/11km N of Derby: iron, cotton, oil refining. **B. Lane End** ham 2km NW. SK 3447
Belph Derbys 44 A3* loc 2km SE of Whitwell. SK 5475
Belsar's Hill Cambs. See Willingham.
Belsay Nthmb 61 F4 vil 5m/9km NW of Ponteland. 14c cas and 17c hse 1m W. NZ 1078
Belsford Devon 4 D4* ham 2m/4km W of Totnes. SX 7659
Belsize Herts 19 E2* ham 4m/7km N of Rickmansworth. TL 0300
Belstead Suffolk 31 E4 vil 3m/5km SW of Ipswich. TM 1341
Belstone Devon 7 E5 vil on N edge of Dartmoor 2m/4km SE of Okehampton. SX 6103
Belthorn Lancs 48 A5* vil 4m/6km SE of Blackburn. SD 7224
Beltie, Mid Grampian 77 F1* loc 1m S of Torphins. NJ 6200
Beltinge Kent 13 G1 E dist of Herne Bay. TR 1967
Beltingham Nthmb 60 D5* ham 3m/5km W of Haydon Br. NY 7863
Beltoft Humberside 44 C1 vil 3m/4km NE of Epworth. SE 8006
Belton Humberside 44 C1 vil 2m/3km N of Epworth. SE 7806
Belton Leics 36 A2 vil 6m/9km W of Loughborough. SK 4420
Belton Leics 36 D4 vil 3m/5km W of Uppingham. SK 8101
Belton Lincs 37 E1 vil 3m/4km NE of Grantham. **B. Hse,** 17c hse with large park. SK 9339
Belton Norfolk 39 H4 vil 4m/7km SW of Gt Yarmouth. TG 4802
Beltring Kent 20 C6 loc 2m/3km N of Paddock Wd. Large group of oasthouses. TQ 6747
Belvide Reservoir Staffs 35 E3 resr 2km NW of Brewood. SJ 8610
Belvoir Leics 36 D1 ham 6m/10km W of Grantham. **B. Castle,** early 19c edifice on hilltop site of Norman cas. **Vale of B.,** broad valley to W, running NE to SW. SK 8233
Bembridge Isle of Wight 10 D5 resort and yachting centre 4m/7km SE of Ryde. Airport to W. To SW, Bembridge and Culver Downs (NT). SZ 6488
Bemersley Green Staffs 42 D5* loc 3m/4km NE of Tunstall. SJ 8854
Bemersyde Borders 66 D5 loc 4m/6km S of Earlston. **Bemersyde Hse,** seat of the Haigs since 1162; present hse includes 16c tower. NT 5933
Bemerton Wilts 9 H2* loc in W part of Salisbury beside R Nadder. SU 1230
Bempton Humberside 51 F1 vil 3m/5km N of Bridlington. TA 1972
Benacre Suffolk 39 H6 ham 5m/8km N of Southwold. 2km SE is **B. Broad,** small lake behind shingle beach. 2m/3km E is **B. Ness,** headland. TM 5184
Ben Aden H'land 74 A2 peak in Lochaber dist 2m/3km W of head of Loch Quoich. Height 2905 ft or 885 metres. NM 8998
Ben Alder H'land 75 E4/F4 mt in Badenoch and Strathspey dist to W of Loch a' Bhealaich Bheithe. Height 3765 ft or 1148 metres. **Benalder Forest** is mt area extending NE. NN 4971
Ben Armine H'land 86 A4 mt in Sutherland dist 5m/8km SE of Loch Choire. Height 2338 ft or 713 metres. Gaelic form: Beinn an Armuinn. **B.A. Forest** is surrounding deer forest. NC 6924
Ben Arthur S'clyde 70 D4 mt in Argyll 3m/4km W of Arrochar. Height 2891 ft or 881 metres. Also known as The Cobbler. NN 2505
Ben Attow H'land 80 B5 mt on Kintail Forest (NTS), in Skye and Lochalsh dist, 5m/8km E of Shiel Br. Height 3383 ft or 1031 metres. Also known as Beinn Fhada. NH 0119
Ben Avon Grampian 76 B1, C1 mt mass 7m/11km N of Braemar. For individual peaks see Mullach Lochan nan Gabhar, Stob Bac an Fhurain, and the summit, Leabaidh an Daimh Bhuidhe. NJ 1301
Benbecula W Isles 88 E2 low-lying island, 6m/10km by 5m/8km in extent, between N and S Uist, containing innumerable lochs. Sand dunes on W coast; many islets off E coast. Airfield at Bailivanish at NW corner of island. Rd causeways to both N and S Uist. NF 85
Ben Buie S'clyde 69 D5 mt on Mull 2km N of Lochbuie. Height 2354 ft or 717 metres. NM 6027
Ben Challum Central 71 E2* mt 4m/6km E of Tyndrum. Height 3363 ft or 1025 metres. NN 3832
Benchill Gtr Manchester 42 D3* dist of Manchester 2km W of Gatley. SJ 8288
Ben Chonzie Tayside 71 H2 mt 6m/9km N of Comrie. Height 3048 ft or 929 metres. Gaelic form: Beinn a' Chonnaich. NN 7730
Ben Cleuch Central 72 C4 mt 3m/4km NW of Tillicoultry. Summit of Ochil Hills: 2363 ft or 720 metres. NN 9000
Ben Creach S'clyde 69 E5 mt on Mull 3m/4km NE of Lochbuie. Height 2289 ft or 698 metres. Gaelic form: Creach Beinn. NM 6427
Ben Cruachan S'clyde 70 C2 mt in Argyll 4m/6km E of Bonawe. Height 3695 ft or 1126 metres. Hydro-electricity generating stn within mt pumps water from Loch Awe to Cruachan Resr. NN 0630
Ben Damph. H'land. Anglicised form of Beinn Damh, qv.
Ben-damph Forest H'land 80 A3 deer forest in Ross and Cromarty dist to S of Upr Loch Torridon. NG 8852
Benderloch S'clyde 70 B1, C1 peninsular area of Argyll lying between Loch Creran and Loch Etive. NM 9338
Bendish Herts 29 F5 ham 5m/8km E of Luton. TL 1621
Ben Donich S'clyde 70 D4 mt in Argyll 2m/4km N of Lochgoilhead. Height 2774 ft or 846 metres. NN 2104
Ben Douran S'clyde. Anglicised form of Beinn Dòrain, qv.
Ben Eay. H'land. Anglicised form of Beinn Eighe, qv.
Benefield, Lower Northants 37 E5 vil 3m/5km W of Oundle. Vil of **Upr Benefield** 1km NW. SP 9988
Benenden Kent 12 D3 vil 3m/5km SE of Cranbrook. Girls' boarding school. Roman ford to S. TQ 8032
Benfieldside Durham 61 F6 NW dist of Consett. NZ 0952
Benfleet Creek Essex 20 D3* inlet of R Thames estuary on N side of Canvey I. TQ 7885
Benfleet, North Essex 20 D3 vil 3m/5km E of Basildon. TQ 7589
Benfleet, South Essex 20 D3 tn at head of Benfleet Creek 6m/10km W of Southend-on-Sea. TQ 7786
Bengairn D & G 58 D6 hill 5m/8km S of Castle Douglas. Height 1283 ft or 391 metres. NX 7754
Bengate Norfolk 39 G2* loc 1m N of Worstead. TG 3027
Bengeo Herts 19 G1 N dist of Hertford. TL 3213
Bengeworth H & W 27 E3* loc in E part of Evesham. SO 0443
Benhall Glos 26 D5* W dist of Cheltenham. SO 9221
Benhall Suffolk 31 G2* loc 2km SW of Saxmundham. Vil of **B. Green** 1m E. Ham of **B. Street** 1m W. TM 3761
Benhar, West S'clyde 65 F3 loc 2km SW of Harthill. NS 8863
Ben Hee H'land 84 D4 mt in Sutherland dist 9m/14km W of Altnaharra. Height 2864 ft or 873 metres. NC 4233
Ben Hiant H'land 68 D3 mt near S coast of Ardnamurchan peninsula in Lochaber dist, 3m/5km E of Kilchoan. Height 1729 ft or 527 metres. NM 5363
Benhilton London 19 F5 loc in borough of Sutton 1km N of Sutton tn centre. TQ 2565
Benholm Grampian 77 G4 loc near E coast 3m/4km SE of Inverbervie. **B. Castle,** 1km N, is early 15c tower of the Earls Marischal. NO 8069
Ben Hope H'land 84 E3 mt in Sutherland dist 2km E of head of Loch Hope. Height 3042 ft or 927 metres. NC 4750
Ben Ime S'clyde 70 D4 mt in Argyll 4m/6km NW of Arrochar. Height 3318 ft or 1011 metres. NN 2508
Beningbrough N Yorks 50 A3 ham 6m/9km NW of York. Hall is early 18c hse in large park to NW. SE 5257
Benington Herts 29 G5 vil 4m/6km E of Stevenage. TL 2923
Benington Lincs 45 G6 vil 5m/8km E of Boston. **B. Sea End** loc 1km SE. TF 3946
Beninner D & G 56 F4* mt 3m/5km NE of Carsphairn. Height 2329 ft or 710 metres. NX 6097
Ben Killilan H'land 80 A4 mt in Skye and Lochalsh dist 2km NE of Killilan and 2m/3km NE of head of Loch Long. Height 2466 ft or 752 metres. NG 9631
Ben Klibreck H'land 84 F4 mt in Caithness dist 4m/6km S of Altnaharra. Height 3154 ft or 961 metres. Gaelic form: Beinn Cleith Bric. NC 5829
Ben Lair H'land 85 A8 mt in Letterewe Forest, W part of Ross and Cromarty dist, 2m/4km NE of Letterewe on NE shore of Loch Maree. Height 2817 ft or 858 metres. NG 9873
Ben Lawers Tayside 71 G1 mt 3m/5km NW of Lawers on Loch Tay. The peak and southern slopes are in the care of the NTS. Known as 'the echoing mountain', it commands views extending from the Atlantic to the North Sea. Height 3984 ft or 1214 metres. NN 6341
Ben Ledi Central 71 F4 mt 4m/7km NW of Callander. Height 2883 ft or 879 metres. NN 5609
Ben Leoid H'land 84 D4 mt in Sutherland dist 6m/10km NE of Inchnadamph. Height 2597 ft or 791 metres. Also spelt Beinn Leoid. NC 3229
Benlister Burn S'clyde 63 G4 r on Arran running E down **Benlister Glen** to Lamlash Bay on S side of Lamlash. NS 0230
Benllech Gwynedd 40 C3 coastal resort on E side of Anglesey 8m/13km SE of Amlwch. SH 5182
Ben Lomond Central 71 E4 mt 3m/5km N of Rowardennan on E shore of Loch Lomond. Height 3192 ft or 973 metres. NN 3602
Ben Loyal H'land 84 F3 mt in Caithness dist 5m/8km S of Tongue. Height 2506 ft or 764 metres. Gaelic form: Beinn Laoghal. NC 5748
Ben Lui 70 D2 mt on border of Central and Strathclyde regions 7m/11km E of Dalmally. Height 3708 ft or 1130 metres. Gaelic form: Beinn Laoigh. NN 2626
Ben Macdui Grampian 76 A2 mt in Cairngorms 9m/15km SE of Aviemore. Height 4296 ft or 1309 metres; highest mt in Britain after Ben Nevis. NN 9898
Ben More Central 71 F3 mt 3m/5km E of Crianlarich. Height 3843 ft or 1171 metres. NN 4324
Ben More S'clyde 69 D5 mt on Mull 3m/4km NW of head of Loch Scridain. Height 3169 ft or 966 metres – highest point of island. NM 5233
Ben More Assynt H'land 85 D5 mt in Sutherland dist 5m/7km E of Inchnadamph at head of Loch Assynt. Height 3273 ft or 998 metres. NC 3120
Benmore Forest H'land 85 D5* deer forest in Sutherland dist to S of Ben More Assynt. NC 3115
Benmore Forest S'clyde 70 C5* state forest on W side of Loch Eck in Argyll, in Argyll Forest Park. NS 1391
Bennachie Grampian 83 E4 upland area 7m/11km W of Inverurie. Bennachie (or Benanchie) Forest is state forest surrounding it. NJ 6622
Bennacott Cornwall 6 B6 ham 5m/8km NW of Launceston. SX 2992
Bennane Head S'clyde 57 B5 bold headland at N end of Ballantrae Bay. NX 0986
Bennan Head S'clyde 63 F5/G5 headland on S coast of Arran 7m/11km S of Lamlash. NR 9920
Bennan Loch S'clyde 64 C4 loch and resr 4m/6km W of Eaglesham. NS 5250
Bennetland Humberside 50 C5* loc 1km SW of Gilberdyke. SE 8228
Bennett End Bucks 18 C2* loc at Radnage 2m/3km E of Stokenchurch. SU 7897
Bennett Head Cumbria 52 D3* loc 2m/3km W of Pooley Br. NY 4423
Bennetts End Herts 19 E1* SE dist of Hemel Hempstead. TL 0705
Ben Nevis H'land 74 C4 mt in Lochaber dist 4m/7km E of Fort William. Height 4408 ft or 1344 metres. Highest mt in Britain. NN 1671
Benniworth Lincs 45 F3 vil 5m/9km NE of Wragby. Belmont TV transmitter to NE. TF 2081
Ben Oss Central 71 E2 mt 4m/7km SW of Tyndrum. Height 3374 ft or 1028 metres. NN 2825
Benover Kent 20 D6 vil 2km S of Yalding. TQ 7048
Ben Resipol H'land 68 E3 mt in Sunart, in Lochaber dist, 4m/6km W of Scotstown. Height 2774 ft or 845 metres. NM 7665
Ben Rhydding W Yorks 48 D3 E dist of Ilkley, formerly known as Wheatley. SE 1347
Ben Rinnes Grampian 82 B3 mt 5m/8km SW of Dufftown. Height 2755 ft or 840 metres. Distillery to N at foot of mt. NJ 2535
Ben Screel H'land 74 A1 mt in Lochaber dist 2km N of Arnisdale on Loch Hourn. Height 3196 ft or 974 metres. Also known as Beinn Sgritheall. NG 8312
Benson Oxon 18 B2 vil 2m/3km N of Wallingford across R Thames. Airfield to E. SU 6191
Ben Starav S'clyde 70 C1 mt 2m/3km S of foot of Glen Etive, Argyll. Height 3541 ft or 1079 metres. NN 1242
Benston Shetland 89 E7* locality in S Nesting, Mainland, 2m/3km W of Moul of Eswick. **Loch of B.** to S, separated by narrow neck of land from Cat Firth. HU 4653
Ben Tangaval W Isles 88 D4* mt in SW part of Barra 2m/3km W of Castlebay. Height 1092 ft or 333 metres. NL 6399
Ben Tee H'land 74 D2 mt on Glengarry Forest, Lochaber dist, 5m/8km SW of Invergarry. Height 2957 ft or 901 metres. NN 2497
Bentfield Essex 30 A5* loc 3m/5km N of Bishop's Stortford. TL 5025
Bent Gate Lancs 48 B5 loc 1m S of Haslingden. SD 7922

Benthall Salop 34 D4 loc 1m SW of Ironbridge. 1km NW, **B. Hall** (NT), 16c hse. SJ 6602
Bentham Glos 26 D5* loc 4m/7km SW of Cheltenham. SO 9116
Bentham, High N Yorks 47 G2 vil 7m/11km SE of Kirkby Lonsdale. SD 6669
Bentham, Lower N Yorks 47 G2 vil 6m/10km SE of Kirkby Lonsdale. SD 6469
Bentilee Staffs 43 E6* dist of Stoke-on-Trent 2m/4km E of city centre. SJ 9146
Ben Tirran Tayside 76 D3 mt 3m/5km E of Clova. Height 2939 ft or 896 metres. NO 3774
Bent Lanes Gtr Manchester 42 C2* loc 2km NW of Urmston. SJ 7596
Bentlawn Salop 34 A4* loc 1km W of Hope. SJ 3301
Bentley Essex 20 C2* loc 3m/4km NW of Brentwood. TQ 5696
Bentley Hants 11 E1 vil 4m/6km SW of Farnham. Site of Roman bldg 2km NW. SU 7844
Bentley Humberside 51 E4 ham 3m/4km S of Beverley. TA 0235
Bentley Suffolk 31 E4* vil 5m/8km SW of Ipswich. TM 1138
Bentley S Yorks 44 B1 coal-mining loc and suburb adjoining Doncaster to N. SE 5605
Bentley Warwicks 36 H4 ham 2m/4km SW of Atherstone. SP 2895
Bentley W Midlands 35 F4* W dist of Walsall. SO 9899
Bentley W Yorks 49 E4* dist of Leeds 2m/3km N of city centre. SE 2836
Bentley, Great Essex 31 E5 vil 6m/9km NW of Clacton-on-Sea. TM 1121
Bentley Heath Herts 19 F2* loc 1m S of Potters Bar. TQ 2499
Bentley Heath W Midlands 35 G6 loc in Solihull 2m/4km S of tn centre. SP 1676
Bentley, Little Essex 31 E5 vil 4m/6km S of Manningtree. TM 1125
Bentley, Lower H & W 27 E1 ham 3m/5km SE of Bromsgrove. SO 9865
Bentley Rise S Yorks 44 B1* S dist of Bentley, adjoining Doncaster to N. SE 5604
Bentley, Upper H & W 27 E1 vil 4m/6km SE of Bromsgrove. SO 9966
Bentpath D & G 59 G3 vil on R Esk 5m/8km NW of Langholm. NY 3190
Bents Green S Yorks 43 G3* loc in Sheffield 3m/5km SW of city centre. SK 3183
Bents, South Tyne & Wear 61 H5* loc on North Sea coast 1km S of Whitburn. NZ 4060
Bentwaters Airfield Suffolk. See Rendlesham, Wantisden.
Bentworth Hants 10 D1 vil 3m/5km W of Alton. SU 6640
Ben Vair H'land. Anglicised form of Beinn a' Bheithir, qv.
Benvane Central 71 F3 mt 4m/7km S of Balquhidder. Height 2685 ft or 818 metres. NN 5313
Ben Vane S'clyde 70 D4 mt 4m/6km NW of Arrochar. Height 3004 ft or 916 metres. NN 2709
Ben Vannoch Tayside. Anglicised form of Beinn Mhanach, qv.
Ben Varren S'clyde 63 F3. See Beinn Bharrain.
Ben Venue Central 71 F4 mt 4m/7km NW of Aberfoyle. Height 2386 ft or 727 metres. NN 4706
Benville Lane Dorset 8 D4 loc 2m/4km W of Evershot. ST 5403
Ben Vorlich S'clyde 71 E3/E4 mt 3m/4km SW of Ardlui at head of Loch Lomond. Height 3092 ft or 942 metres. NN 2912
Ben Vorlich Tayside 72 A3 mt close to border with Central region 4m/6km SE of Lochearnhead. Height 3231 ft or 985 metres. NN 6218
Ben Vrackie S'clyde 63 F3. See Beinn Bhreac.
Ben Vrackie Tayside 76 A4 mt 3m/5km N of Pitlochry. Height 2760 ft or 841 metres. Gaelic form: Beinn Bhreac. NN 9563
Ben Vrottan Grampian. Anglicised form of Beinn Bhrotain, qv.
Ben Vuirich Tayside 76 B4 mt 8m/13km NE of Blair Atholl. Height 2961 ft or 902 metres. NN 9970
Benwell Tyne & Wear 61 G5* dist of Newcastle 2m/3km W of city centre. NZ 2164
Benwick Cambs 37 H5 vil on R Nene (old course) 4m/7km NW of Chatteris. TL 3490
Ben Wyvis H'land 81 E1 mt in Ross and Cromarty dist 8m/13km NW of Dingwall. Height 3433 ft or 1046 metres. Distillery to S at foot of mt. NH 4668
Benyellary D & G 57 D5 mt in Glentrool Forest Park 2km SW of Merrick. NX 4183
Ben-y-Gloe Tayside 76 A4 mt mass 8m/12km NE of Blair Atholl. Also known as Beinn a' Ghlo. Summit is Carn nan Gabhar, 3675 ft or 1120 metres. NN 9773
Beoley H & W 27 E1 vil 2m/3km NE of Redditch. SP 0669
Beoraidbeg H'land 79 E8* loc in Lochaber dist 2m/3km S of Mallaig. NM 6793
Bepton W Sussex 11 E3 vil under S Downs 3m/4km SW of Midhurst. SU 8618
Berden Essex 29 H5 vil 5m/9km N of Bishop's Stortford. TL 4629
Bere Alston Devon 4 B4 small tn in market-gardening area between Rs Tamar and Tavy 5m/8km SW of Tavistock. SX 4466
Bere Ferrers Devon 4 B4 vil beside R Tavy 7m/11km S of Tavistock. Abandoned silver mines towards R Tamar. SX 4563
Berepper Cornwall 2 C6 ham 3m/5km S of Helston. SW 6522
Bere Regis Dorset 9 F4 vil 7m/11km NW of Wareham. SY 8494
Bergh Apton Norfolk 39 G4 vil 7m/11km SE of Norwich. TG 3001
Bergholt, East Suffolk 31 E4 vil 7m/12km NE of Colchester. Birthplace of Constable, 1776. Flatford Mill and Willy Lott's Cottage (NT) on R Stour to S. Ch bells housed in cage in churchyard. TM 0634
Bergholt, West Essex 30 D5 vil 3m/4km NW of Colchester. TL 9627
Berhill Som 8 C1* loc 3m/4km W of Street. ST 4436
Berinsfield Oxon 18 B2 vil 5m/8km NW of Wallingford. SU 5796
Berkeley Glos 16 C2 vil 5m/8km W of Dursley. **B. Castle**, scene of Edward II's murder in 1327. Nuclear power stn beside R Severn estuary to W. ST 6899
Berkeley, Vale of 16 B2* low-lying area between Cotswold Hills and R Severn estuary in vicinity of Berkeley, Glos. ST 69
Berkhamsted Herts 19 E1 tn in narrow gap of Chiltern Hills 25m/40km NW of London. Industries include clothing and furniture mnfre. Remains of motte and bailey cas (A.M.), with keep of later date. **B. Common** (NT) to N. SP 9907
Berkhamsted, Little Herts 19 G1 vil 4m/6km SW of Hertford. TL 2907
Berkley Som 16 C6 vil 3m/4km E of Frome. To W, loc of **B. Marsh**. ST 8149
Berkshire 119 central southern county of England, bounded by Hampshire, Wiltshire, Oxfordshire, Buckinghamshire, and Surrey. On its W and NW borders rise bare chalk hills (a continuation of the Wiltshire Downs), bearing many prehistoric remains and much used for racehorse training. On the SE side are bare sandy heaths, some being military exercise areas. R Thames forms part of the county's N border and crosses the extreme E; R Kennet traverses it S of the Downs, then flows NE into the Thames at Reading. Residential and industrial developments largely cover the E side of the county. Principal tns are Reading, the county tn; Bracknell, Maidenhead, Newbury, Slough, Windsor, and Wokingham.
Berkswell W Midlands 35 H6 vil 6m/9km W of Coventry. SP 2479
Bermondsey London 19 G4* dist S of R Thames in vicinity of Tower Br and in borough of Southwark. TQ 3379
Bernard's Heath Herts 19 F1* N dist of St Albans. TL 1508
Bernera S'clyde 70 A1 island off W coast of Lismore, in Loch Linnhe. **B. Bay** is southward-facing bay formed by the two islands. NM 7939
Bernera, Great W Isles 88 A2/B2 island in Loch Roag, W coast of Lewis, 6m/9km N to S and from 1m to 2m/4km in width. Connected to main island of Lewis by rd br at S end. NB 13
Bernera, Little W Isles 88 A2* island off W coast of Lewis between entrances to E and W Loch Roag and off N shore of Gt Bernera. Measures about 1m E to W and an average of 1km N to S. NB 1440
Berneray W Isles 88 A4 island on W side of Sound of Harris, lying off N end of N Uist. Nearly 6km NE to SW and 3km across at widest point. NF 9181
Berneray W Isles 88 D4 island of about 450 acres or 180 hectares nearly 1km S of Mingulay. High cliffs, with lighthouse at W end of island. Grazing for sheep. The most southerly of the Western Isles or Outer Hebrides. NL 5580
Berners Roding Essex 20 C1 ham 2m/4km S of Leaden Roding. TL 6009
Berney Arms Mill Norfolk. See Reedham.
Bernisdale Skye, H'land 78 B4/C4 vil on W side of head of Loch Snizort Beag, 7m/11km NW of Portree. NG 4050
Berrick Prior Oxon 18 B2 ham 3m/5km N of Wallingford. SU 6294
Berrick Salome Oxon 18 B2 vil 3m/5km N of Wallingford. SU 6293
Berriedale H'land 87 D5 vil near E coast of Caithness dist 8m/12km NE of Helmsdale. Situated at confluence of Langwell Water and **B. Water,** r rising about 14m/23km NW. ND 1122
Berrier Cumbria 52 D3 ham 7m/11km W of Penrith. NY 4029
Berriew (Aberriw) Powys 33 H4 vil 5m/8km SW of Welshpool. SJ 1800
Berrington H & W 26 B1* ham 2km SW of Tenbury Wells. Ham of **B. Green** 1km SE. SO 5767
Berrington Nthmb 67 F4* loc 2m/4km N of Lowick. NU 0043
Berrington Salop 34 C4 ham 4m/7km SE of Shrewsbury. **B. Pool,** small lake to NW. SJ 5206
Berrington Hall H & W 26 A2 18c hse (NT) in grnds laid out by Capability Brown, 3m/5km N of Leominster. SO 5063
Berriowbridge Cornwall 4 A3* ham 7m/11km SW of Launceston. SX 2775
Berrow H & W 26 C4* loc 6m/10km W of Tewkesbury. SO 7934
Berrow Som 15 G6 loc 2km N of Burnham-on-Sea. ST 3051
Berrow Green H & W 26 C2 ham 7m/11km W of Worcester. SO 7458
Berry Brow W Yorks 48 D6* loc in Huddersfield 2km SW of tn centre. SE 1314
Berry Cross Devon 6 D4* loc 3m/5km SW of Torrington. SS 4714
Berry Down Cross Devon 6 D1* loc 4m/7km SE of Ilfracombe. SS 5743
Berry End, Higher Beds 29 E4* loc on E side of Woburn Park, 4m/7km SW of Ampthill. SP 9834
Berry Head Devon 5 E5 headland at S end of Tor Bay to E of Brixham. Limestone quarries. SX 9456
Berry Hill Bucks 18 D3* loc 2km E of Maidenhead. SU 9081
Berry Hill Dyfed 22 C2 loc 1m NE of Newport. SN 0640
Berry Hill Glos 26 B6 loc 2km N of Coleford. SO 5712
Berry Hill, Lower Glos 26 B6 loc 1km N of Coleford. SO 5711
Berryhillock Grampian 82 D1 loc near N coast 4m/6km S of Cullen. NJ 5060
Berrylands London 19 F4* loc in borough of Kingston 1km E of Surbiton. TQ 1967
Berrynarbor Devon 6 D1 vil 3m/5km E of Ilfracombe. SS 5646
Berry Pomeroy Devon 5 E4 vil 2m/3km E of Totnes. SX 8261
Berry's Green London 20 B5* loc in borough of Bromley 2km E of Biggin Hill. TQ 4359
Bers Welsh form of Bersham, qv.
Bersham (Bers) Clwyd 41 H6* vil 2m/3km W of Wrexham. SJ 3049
Bersted, North W Sussex 11 E5 suburban loc 2km NW of Bognor Regis. SU 9201
Bersted, South W Sussex 11 F5 N dist of Bognor Regis. SU 9300
Berth-ddu Clwyd 41 G4* loc 3m/4km W of Northop. SJ 2069
Berthengam Clwyd 41 G3* loc 4m/6km SE of Prestatyn. SJ 1179
Berthlwyd W Glam 23 G5* loc 2km W of Gowerton. SS 5696
Berth Pool Salop 34 B2* small lake 1m N of Baschurch – one of four in vicinity. Ancient earthwork, **The Berth,** on N side. SJ 4323
Bervie Water 77 G4 r in Grampian region rising in Drumtochty Forest and running SE to E coast at **Bervie Bay,** on E side of Inverbervie. NO 8372
Berwick E Sussex 12 B6 vil below S Downs 2km N of Alfriston. TQ 5105
Berwick Bassett Wilts 17 E4 vil 2m/3km N of Avebury. SU 0973
Berwick Hills Cleveland 54 D3* dist of Middlesbrough 2m/3km SE of tn centre. NZ 5118
Berwick, North Lothian 66 C1 tn and resort on S side of entrance to Firth of Forth 19m/31km E of Edinburgh. **N Berwick Law** to S, hill and ancient fort, height 613 ft or 187 metres, surmounted by ruins of watch-tower built in Napoleonic Wars. NT 5585
Berwick St James Wilts 9 G1 vil on R Till 5m/8km N of Wilton. SU 0739
Berwick St John Wilts 9 F2 vil 6m/10km E of Shaftesbury. ST 9422
Berwick St Leonard Wilts 9 F1* vil 8m/12km NE of Shaftesbury. ST 9233
Berwickshire 115, 117 admin dist of Borders region.
Berwick-upon-Tweed Nthmb 67 F3 border tn at mouth of R Tweed 58m/93km NW of Newcastle and 47m/76km SE of Edinburgh. Medieval tn walls (A.M.); remains of Norman cas (A.M.); 18c barracks and tn hall. Small fishing and shipbuilding industries. NT 9953
Berwick, Upper Salop 34 B3* ham 3m/4km NW of Shrewsbury. 1km S, chapel and almshouses of 17c in grnds of 18c **Berwick Hse.** SJ 4715
Berwyn 24 C2* stream flowing W to join R Groes 1m E of Tregaron, Dyfed. The combined stream then continues SW into R Teifi 1km SW of Tregaron. SN 6959
Berwyn Mountains (Berwyn Y) 33 G1, G2 mt range in Wales running SW from Llangollen. Mainly in Clwyd but also partly in Powys and Gwynedd. Highest peak is Moel Sych, qv. Its twin peak Cadair Berwyn is fractionally lower. SJ 03,13
Bescar Lancs 42 A1* vil 1km E of Scarisbrick. SD 3913
Bescot W Midlands 35 F4* loc in S part of Walsall. SP 0097
Besford H & W 26 D3 vil 2m/4km W of Pershore. SO 9144
Besom Hill Gtr Manchester 43 E1* loc in Oldham 3m/5km NE of tn centre. **Besom Hill Resr,** small resr to NW. SD 9508
Bessacarr S Yorks 44 B1* dist of Doncaster 3m/4km SE of tn centre. SE 6001
Bessborough Reservoir Surrey 19 E4* resr on W side of W Molesey. TQ 1268
Bessels Green Kent 20 B5* W suburb of Sevenoaks. TQ 5055
Bessels Leigh Oxon 17 H2 ham 4m/6km NW of Abingdon. SP 4501
Besses o' th' Barn Gtr Manchester 42 D1 loc 1m SE of Whitefield. SD 8105
Bessingby Humberside 51 F2 vil 2km SW of Bridlington tn centre. TA 1565
Bessingham Norfolk 39 F2 vil 4m/7km S of Sheringham. TG 1636
Besthorpe Norfolk 39 E5* vil 1m E of Attleborough. TM 0695
Besthorpe Notts 44 C4 vil 7m/12km N of Newark-on-Trent. SK 8264
Bestwood Park Notts 44 A6* loc 5m/8km N of Nottingham. SK 5648
Beswick Gtr Manchester 42 D2* dist of Manchester 2km E of city centre. SJ 8598
Beswick Humberside 51 E3 vil 5m/9km N of Beverley. TA 0148
Betchton Heath Ches 42 D5* loc 2km E of Sandbach. SJ 7760
Betchworth Surrey 19 F6 vil 3m/5km E of Dorking. TQ 2149
Bethania Dyfed 24 B2 loc 2m/3km E of Cross Inn. SN 5763
Bethania Gwynedd 40 D6 loc adjoining Blaenau Ffestiniog to S. SH 7045
Bethel Gwynedd 33 F1/G1 loc at rd junction 4m/7km NE of Bala. SH 9839
Bethel Gwynedd 40 B4 ham on Anglesey 5m/8km SW of Llangefni. SH 3970
Bethel Gwynedd 40 C5 vil 3m/5km NE of Caernarvon. SH 5265
Bethersden Kent 13 E3 vil 6m/9km W of Ashford. TQ 9240
Bethesda Dyfed 22 D4* ham 2m/4km NW of Narberth. SN 0917
Bethesda Gwynedd 40 C4 slate-quarrying tn 5m/7km SE of Bangor. Complex of quarries to S and SW, esp **Penrhyn Quarries.** SH 6266
Bethlehem Dyfed 24 C5 ham 3m/4km SW of Llangadog. SN 6825
Bethnal Green London 19 G3* dist in borough of Tower Hamlets 2m/3km NE of London Br. TQ 3482
Betley Staffs 42 C6 vil 6m/10km W of Newcastle-under-Lyme. **B. Common** loc to W. **B. Mere** small lake to SW. SJ 7548
Betsham Kent 20 C4 vil 2m/3km S of Swanscombe. TQ 6071
Betteshanger Kent 13 H2 ham 4m/7km W of Deal. TR 3152
Bettiscombe Dorset 8 C4 vil 4m/6km SW of Broadwindsor. ST 3800

Bettisfield Clwyd 34 B1 vil on Shropshire Union Canal 4m/6km E of Ellesmere. SJ 4535
Betton Salop 34 D1* loc 2m/3km NE of Mkt Drayton. SJ 6936
Betton Abbots Salop 34 C3/C4* loc 3m/5km SE of Shrewsbury. SJ 5107
Betton Alkmere Salop 34 C3* loc 2m/4km SE of Shrewsbury. SJ 5009
Betton Pool Salop 34 C3/C4* small lake 3m/5km S of Shrewsbury. SJ 5107
Betton Strange Salop 34 C3* loc 2m/4km SE of Shrewsbury. SJ 5009
Bettws (Betws) Gwent 15 G2/G3 loc 2m/3km N of Newport. ST 2990
Bettws Bledrws (Betws Bledrws) Dyfed 24 B3 ham 3m/4km NE of Lampeter. SN 5952
Bettws Evan Dyfed 23 E1. See Betws Ifan.
Bettws Newydd Gwent 15 H1 ham 3m/5km W of Raglan. SO 3605
Bettws-y-Crwyn Salop 33 H6 ham 6m/10km W of Clun. SO 2081
Bettyhill H'land 86 A2 vil near N coast of Caithness dist 9m/15km SW of Strathy Pt. NC 7061
Betws Dyfed 23 G4 loc 1km SE of Ammanford. SN 6311
Betws Mid Glam 15 E3 vil 4m/7km N of Bridgend. SS 8986
Betws Welsh form of Bettws, qv.
Betws Cedewain Powys 33 H4 vil on Bechan Brook 4m/6km N of Newtown. See also Dolforwyn Castle. SO 1296
Betws Garmon Gwynedd 40 C5 loc 5m/8km SE of Caernarvon. SH 5357
Betws Gwerful Goch Clwyd 41 F6 ham 4m/6km NW of Corwen. SJ 0346
Betws Ifan Dyfed 23 E1 ham 4m/7km N of Newcastle Emlyn. Also known as Bettws Evan. SN 3047
Betws-y-coed Gwynedd 41 E5 vil and tourist centre among woods and streams 14m/23km S of Colwyn Bay. SH 7956
Betws-yn-Rhos Clwyd 41 E4 vil 4m/6km SW of Abergele. SH 9073
Beulah Dyfed 23 E2 ham 4m/6km N of Newcastle Emlyn. SN 2846
Beulah Powys 25 E3 vil 4m/6km NE of Llanwrtyd Wells. SN 9251
Beul an Toim W Isles 88 E1* channel between island of Baleshare and N coast of Benbecula. NF 7857
Beult 12 C2 r rising SW of Ashford in Kent and flowing W into R Medway at Yalding. TQ 6850
Bevercotes Notts 44 B4* ham 3m/4km NW of Tuxford. SK 6972
Beverley Humberside 51 E4 tn 8m/12km N of Hull. Minster, EE to Perp. TA 0339
Beverley Brook 19 F4 r rising near Morden Park in London borough of Merton and flowing N through Richmond Park and into R Thames above Putney Br. TQ 2376
Beverstone Glos 16 D2 vil 2m/3km W of Tetbury. ST 8693
Bewaldeth Cumbria 52 C2 loc 3m/5km SE of Bothel. Site of Roman fort 2km N. NY 2034
Bewbush W Sussex 11 H2* SW dist of Crawley. TQ 2535
Bewcastle Cumbria 60 B4 ham 9m/14km N of Brampton, on site of Roman fort. Saxon cross, headless, in churchyard. Remains of medieval cas. NY 5674
Bewdley H & W 34 D6/35 E6 mainly 17c and 18c tn on R Severn 3m/5km W of Kidderminster. SO 7875
Bewell Head H & W 26 D1* loc in N part of Bromsgrove. SO 9571
Bewerley N Yorks 48 D2 vil on SW side of Pateley Br across R Nidd. SE 1565
Bewholme Humberside 51 F3 vil 3m/5km NW of Hornsea. TA 1650
Bewick Nthmb 67 G6 par SE of Wooler, containing hams of Old and New Berwick, qv. NU 0621
Bewl 12 C3 r rising near Flimwell, E Sussex, and flowing W then N through Bewl Br Resr and into R Teise to E of Lamberhurst, Kent. TQ 6936
Bewl Bridge Reservoir 12 C3 large resr on border of E Sussex and Kent 2m/3km S of Lamberhurst. TQ 6833
Bewley Castle Cumbria 53 F3* ruined cas 3m/4km W of Appleby. NY 6421
Bewley Common Wilts. See Bowden Hill.
Bexhill E Sussex 12 D6 seaside residential tn and resort 5m/8km W of Hastings. TQ 7407
Bexington, West Dorset 8 D5* vil on coast 3m/5km NW of Abbotsbury. Above vil, **Limekiln Hill** (NT), former stone workings on crest of ridge overlooking Chesil Bank. SY 5386
Bexley London 20 B4 borough on S side of R Thames, with river frontage extending from Barking Reach to mouth of R Darent. The S limit of the borough is at Foots Cray. TQ 4973
Bexleyheath London 20 B4 dist in borough of Bexley 2m/3km SW of Erith and 12m/19km E of Charing Cross. TQ 4875
Bexleyhill W Sussex 11 E3* loc 3m/5km NE of Midhurst. SU 9125
Bexton Ches 42 C3* loc 1m S of Knutsford. SJ 7476
Bexwell Norfolk 38 B4 vil 2km E of Downham Mkt. TF 6303
Beyton Suffolk 30 D2 vil 5m/8km E of Bury St Edmunds. Vil of **B. Green** adjoins to N. TL 9362
Bibra Cumbria. See Newtown.
Bibury Glos 17 F1 vil on R Coln 7m/11km NE of Cirencester. SP 1106
Bicester Oxon 28 B5 tn 11m/18km NE of Oxford. SP 5822
Bickenhall Som 8 B3 scattered vil 5m/9km SE of Taunton. ST 2818
Bickenhill W Midlands 35 G6 vil 3m/5km NE of Solihull. National Exhibition Centre, opened 1976. Loc of **Middle B.** 1m E. SP 1882
Bicker Lincs 37 G1 vil 2m/3km NE of Donington. **B. Bar** loc 1m NE. **B. Friest** loc 1km SW. **B. Gauntlet** loc 1m NW. TF 2237
Bickershaw Gtr Manchester 42 B1* loc 1m NE of Abram. SD 6202
Bickerstaffe Lancs 42 A1 vil 2m/3km SW of Skelmersdale. SK 4404
Bickerton Ches 42 B6* loc 4m/6km NE of Malpas, on SE side of **B. Hill.** See also Maiden Castle. SJ 5052
Bickerton Devon 5 E6* loc 2m/3km NW of Start Pt. SX 8138
Bickerton Nthmb 61 E2* loc 4m/6km W of Rothbury. NT 9900
Bickerton N Yorks 50 A3 vil 3m/5km NE of Wetherby. SE 4550
Bickford Staffs 35 E3 ham 2m/4km W of Penkridge. SJ 8814
Bickham Som 7 G1* ham 3m/4km SW of Dunster. SS 9541
Bickington Devon 4 D3 vil 3m/5km NE of Ashburton. SX 7972
Bickington Devon 6 D2 suburb 2m/3km W of Barnstaple. SS 5332
Bickington, High Devon 6 D3 vil 7m/11km E of Torrington. SS 6030
Bickleigh Devon 4 B4 vil 6m/9km NE of Plymouth. To E, **B. Vale,** wooded stretch of R Plym valley running down to Plym Forest. SX 5262
Bickleigh Devon 7 G4 vil with thatched cottages and br over R Exe 4m/6km S of Tiverton. SS 9407
Bickley London 20 B4 loc in borough of Bromley 2km E of Bromley tn centre. TQ 4269
Bickley N Yorks 55 G5* ham 6m/10km W of Scalby. SE 9191
Bickley Moss Ches 42 B6 vil 5m/8km N of Whitchurch. SJ 5449
Bickmarsh H & W 27 E3* loc 6m/9km NE of Evesham. SP 1049
Bicknacre Essex 20 D2 vil 5m/8km SW of Maldon. TL 7802
Bicknoller Som 7 H2 vil at foot of Quantock Hills 4m/6km SE of Watchet. ST 1139
Bicknor Kent 21 E5* ham 4m/7km SW of Sittingbourne. TQ 8658
Bickton Hants 9 H3* loc on R Avon 2km S of Fordingbridge. SU 1412
Bicton Devon 5 F2 loc 3m/5km N of Budleigh Salterton. The hse, originally 18c, is an agricultural institute; grnds open to public. SY 0686
Bicton H & W 26 A2* loc 4m/6km NW of Leominster. SO 4663
Bicton Salop 34 A6* ham 2km NW of Clun. SO 2882
Bicton Salop 34 B3 vil 3m/5km NW of Shrewsbury. SJ 4415
Bidborough Kent 12 C3* vil 3m/5km SW of Tonbridge. TQ 5643
Biddenden Kent 13 E3 vil 4m/6km S of Headcorn. TQ 8538
Biddenden Green Kent 13 E3* loc 4m/6km E of Headcorn. TQ 8842
Biddenham Beds 29 E3 suburb in loop of R Ouse to W of Bedford. TL 0250
Biddestone Wilts 16 D4 vil 4m/6km W of Chippenham. ST 8673
Biddick Tyne & Wear 61 G5* dist of Washington to SE of tn centre. NZ 3055
Biddisham Som 15 H5* vil 3m/5km W of Axbridge. ST 3853
Biddlesden Bucks 28 B4 ham 4m/6km NE of Brackley. SP 6340
Biddlestone Nthmb 61 E1 loc 3m/4km NE of Alwinton. NT 9508
Biddulph Staffs 42 D5 tn 7m/12km N of Stoke-on-Trent. Industries include coal-mining, engineering, textiles. **B. Moor** loc 2m/3km NE. SJ 8856
Bidean an Eòin Deirg H'land 80 B3* mt in Ross and Cromarty dist 2m/3km NE of head of Loch Monar. Height 3430 ft or 1046 metres. NH 1044
Bidean nam Bian 74 C5 mt on border of H'land and S'clyde regions S of Glen Coe. Height 3766 ft or 1148 metres. NN 1454
Bideford Devon 6 C3 36m/58km NW of Exeter. Small port with quay on R Torridge crossed by 15c br. R flows into **B. Bay,** also known as Barnstaple Bay, which extends from Baggy Pt westwards to Hartland Pt. SS 4562
Bidein a' Choire Sheasgaich H'land 80 B3* peak on W Monar Forest on border of Ross & Cromarty and Skye & Lochalsh dists. Height 3102 ft or 945 metres. NH 0541
Bidein a' Ghlas Thuill H'land 85 B7* summit of An Teallach, qv, in Ross and Cromarty dist. Height 3483 ft or 1062 metres. NH 0684
Bidford-on-Avon Warwicks 27 E3 vil 7m/11km W of Stratford-upon-Avon. SP 1051
Bidlake Devon 6 D6* loc 7m/11km SW of Okehampton. SX 4988
Bidno 33 F6* r running SE through S part of Hafren Forest and into R Wye 1m W of Llangurig, Powys. SN 8980
Bidston Merseyside 41 H3 loc in NW corner of Birkenhead. SJ 2890
Bidwell Beds 29 E5* loc 2m/3km N of Dunstable. TL 0124
Bielby Humberside 50 C4 vil 5m/9km W of Mkt Weighton. SE 7843
Bieldside Grampian 77 H1 SW suburb of Aberdeen, 4m/7km from city centre. NJ 8802
Bierley Isle of Wight 10 B6* ham 1m N of Niton. SZ 5178
Bierley W Yorks 48 D5* dist of Bradford 2m/3km SE of city centre. **E Bierley** loc 2km SE. SE 1730
Bierley, East W Yorks 48 D5 vil 3m/5km SE of Bradford. SE 1929
Bierley, North W Yorks 48 D5 dist of Bradford 2m/3km S of city centre. SE 1429
Bierton Bucks 28 D6 vil 2m/3km NE of Aylesbury. SP 8415
Biga 33 F5* r running E through Hafren Forest into Clywedog Resr, Powys. SN 8889
Big Balcraig D & G 57 D7* site of cup and ring marked rocks, 2m/4km E of Port William. See also Drumtroddan. NX 3744
Bigbury Devon 4 C5 vil on high ground to W of R Avon estuary 3m/5km S of Modbury. SX 6646
Bigbury-on-Sea Devon 4 C6 small resort with extensive sands 5m/8km S of Modbury. Situated on **Bigbury Bay,** which extends from Bolt Tail to Stoke Pt. SX 6544
Bigby Lincs 45 E1 vil 4m/6km E of Brigg. TA 0507
Bigga Shetland 89 E6* uninhabited island of about 235 acres or 95 hectares midway between Mainland and Yell at SE end of Yell Sound. HU 4479
Biggar Cumbria 46 C2/D2 loc on Walney I., 2m/3km S of causeway to Barrow-in-Furness. SD 1966
Biggar S'clyde 65 G5 small tn 13m/21km W of Peebles. Slight remains of Boghall Castle on S side. NT 0437
Biggar Road S'clyde 65 E3* loc adjoining Newarthill to NE, 3m/5km NE of Hamilton. NS 7960
Biggin Derbys 43 F5 vil 8m/13km N of Ashbourne. SK 1559
Biggin Derbys 43 G6* ham 5m/8km E of Ashbourne. SK 2648
Biggin N Yorks 49 G4 ham 2m/4km SE of Ch Fenton. SE 5434
Biggin Hill London 20 B5 loc in borough of Bromley 4m/6km E of Warlingham. Airfield. TQ 4159
Biggins, The Cambs 37 H5* loc 1km SW of Manea. TL 4788
Biggleswade Beds 29 F3 tn on R Ivel in market-gardening area 9m/15km SE of Bedford. Airfield 3m/4km W. TL 1844
Bighton Hants 10 C2 vil 2m/3km NE of New Alresford. SU 6134
Biglands Cumbria 59 G6* ham 3m/4km SE of Kirkbride. NY 2553
Bigland Tarn Cumbria 52 D6* small lake 1m SE of Haverthwaite. SD 3582
Big Mancot Clwyd 41 H4* loc between Hawarden and Queensferry. SJ 3167
Big Mere Ches 42 B6 lake on S side of Marbury. SJ 5645
Bignall End Staffs 42 D6* loc adjoining Audley to E. SJ 8051
Bignell's Corner Herts 19 F2* loc 2m/3km W of Potters Bar. TL 2200
Bignor W Sussex 11 F3 vil below S Downs 5m/7km S of Petworth. Roman villa to E. SU 9814
Bigod's Hill Norfolk 39 G5* loc 3m/5km NW of Beccles. TM 3992
Bigrigg Cumbria 52 A4* vil 2m/3km N of Egremont. NY 0013
Big Sand H'land 78 E2 locality on W coast of Ross and Cromarty dist 3m/5km NW of Gairloch. NG 7578
Bigton Shetland 89 E8* loc on bay of **B. Wick** on W coast of Mainland 9m/14km N of Sumburgh Hd. HU 3721
Bilborough Notts 36 B1 dist of Nottingham 3m/5km NW of city centre. SK 5241
Bilbrook Som 7 G1 ham 3m/5km SE of Dunster. ST 0341
Bilbrook Staffs 35 E4 loc adjoining Codsall to E. SJ 8803
Bilbrough N Yorks 49 G3 vil 4m/6km NE of Tadcaster. SE 5346
Bilby Notts 44 B3* loc 4m/6km NE of Worksop. SK 6383
Bildershaw Durham 54 B3 ham 3m/5km S of Bishop Auckland. NZ 2024
Bildeston Suffolk 30 D3/31 E3 large vil with many timbered hses, 5m/7km N of Hadleigh. TL 9949
Billericay Essex 20 C2 tn 5m/8km E of Brentwood. TQ 6794
Billesdon Leics 36 C4 vil 8m/13km E of Leicester. SK 7102
Billesley Warwicks 27 F2* vil 4m/6km W of Stratford-upon-Avon. **B. Hall,** early 17c. SP 1456
Billesley W Midlands 35 G6* loc in Birmingham 4m/7km SE of city centre. SP 0980
Billing Northants. See Bellinge.
Billingborough Lincs 37 F1/F2 vil 9m/14km N of Bourne. TF 1134
Billinge Merseyside 42 B2 tn 3m/5km NE of St Helens. Coal-mining, brick mnfre. SD 5300
Billingford Norfolk 31 F1 ham 3m/5km E of Diss. TM 1678
Billingford Norfolk 39 E3 vil 5m/8km NE of E Dereham. TG 0120
Billingham Cleveland 54 D3 industrial tn 2m/4km NE of Stockton-on-Tees. Chemical works. NZ 4522
Billinghay Lincs 45 F5 vil 8m/13km NE of Sleaford. TF 1554
Billingley S Yorks 43 H1* vil 2m/3km W of Goldthorpe. **B. Green** loc to S. SE 4304
Billingshurst W Sussex 11 G3 small tn 6m/10km SW of Horsham. TQ 0825
Billingsley Salop 34 D5 vil 5m/8km S of Bridgnorth. SO 7085
Billington Beds 28 D5 vil 2m/3km SE of Leighton Buzzard. SP 9422
Billington Staffs 35 E2/E3* loc 3m/4km SW of Stafford. SJ 8820
Billington, Little Beds 28 D5* ham 2m/3km S of Leighton Buzzard. SP 9322
Billockby Norfolk 39 H3 ham 2m/4km NE of Acle. TG 4213
Bill Quay Tyne & Wear 61 G5 E dist of Felling on S bank of R Tyne. NZ 2962
Bill Street Kent 20 D4* urban loc adjoining Rochester to N. TQ 7470
Billy Mill Tyne & Wear 61 G4* loc 2km W of N Shields. NZ 3369
Billy Row Durham 54 B2 vil 1m N of Crook. NZ 1637
Bilney, East Norfolk 38 D3 vil 5m/7km NW of E Dereham. TF 9519
Bilney, West Norfolk 38 C3 ham 7m/11km SE of King's Lynn. TF 7115
Bilsborrow Lancs 47 F4* vil 2m/3km N of Barton. SD 5139

Bilsby Lincs 45 H4 vil 1m E of Alford. **B. Field** loc 1m SW. TF 4676
Bilsdean Lothian 67 E2 loc near coast 6m/10km SE of Dunbar. **B. Creek** on coast to E. Site of Dunglass Castle above creek. NT 7672
Bilsham W Sussex 11 F4* ham 3m/5km NE of Bognor Regis. SU 9702
Bilsington Kent 13 F3 vil 6m/9km S of Ashford. TR 0434
Bilson Green Glos 26 B6* loc adjoining Cinderford to W. SO 6514
Bilsthorpe Notts 44 B5 coal-mining vil 4m/7km S of Ollerton. **B. Moor** loc 1km S. SK 6460
Bilston Lothian 66 A2 loc 2km SW of Loanhead. Colliery at **B. Glen** to E. NT 2664
Bilston W Midlands 35 F4 SE dist of Wolverhampton. Industries include metal and engineering products, glass, textiles. SO 9596
Bilstone Leics 36 A4 ham 7m/11km S of Ashby de la Zouch. SK 3605
Bilting Kent 13 F2 loc 5m/8km NE of Ashford. TR 0549
Bilton Humberside 51 F5 suburb 5m/8km NE of Hull. TA 1632
Bilton Nthmb 61 G1* loc 2km W of Alnmouth. **B. Banks** loc 2km W. NU 2210
Bilton N Yorks 49 E3 N dist of Harrogate. **B. Dene** loc 1km E. SE 3057
Bilton N Yorks 50 A3 vil 5m/8km E of Wetherby. SE 4750
Bilton Warwicks 27 H1 SW dist of Rugby. SP 4873
Bimbister Orkney 89 A6* loc on Mainland 3m/4km NW of Finstown. HY 3216
Binbrook Lincs 45 F2 vil 7m/11km NE of Mkt Rasen. B. Airfield to NW. TF 2193
Binchester Durham 54 B2 loc 2km N of Bishop Auckland across loop of R Wear, on site of Roman fort of *Vinovium*. NZ 2031
Binchester Blocks Durham 54 B2* loc 2m/3km SW of Spennymoor. NZ 2232
Bincombe Dorset 9 E5 vil 4m/6km S of Dorchester and N of Weymouth. SY 6884
Bindalein Island W Isles 88 B2* rock island on S side of entrance to Loch Carloway on W coast of Lewis, 2m/3km W of Carloway vil. NB 1741
Bindon Som 7 H3* ham 2m/3km SW of Milverton. ST 1024
Binegar Som 16 B6 vil 4m/6km N of Shepton Mallet. ST 6149
Bines Green W Sussex 11 G3 loc beside R Adur 4m/6km N of Steyning. TQ 1817
Binfield Berks 18 C4 vil 2m/3km NW of Bracknell. SU 8471
Binfield Heath Oxon 18 C4 vil 3m/4km S of Henley-on-Thames. SU 7478
Bingfield Nthmb 61 E4 ham 5m/8km N of Corbridge. NY 9772
Bingham Notts 36 C1 vil 8m/13km E of Nottingham. 1m N is site of Roman tn of *Margidunum*. SK 7039
Bingham's Melcombe Dorset 9 E4* ham 5m/8km N of Puddletown. ST 7702
Bingley W Yorks 48 D4 tn on R Aire and on Leeds and Liverpool Canal 5m/8km NW of Bradford. Textiles, light engineering. SE 1039
Bings Salop 34 C3 loc 5m/8km NE of Shrewsbury. SJ 5418
Binham Norfolk 38 D1 vil 5m/8km SE of Wells. Remains of 13c priory (A.M.). TF 9839
Binley Hants 17 H6 vil 3m/4km E of Hurstbourne Tarrant. SU 4253
Binley W Midlands 36 A6 E dist of Coventry. SP 3778
Binnegar Dorset 9 F5* ham 3m/4km W of Wareham. SY 8887
Binnein Mór H'land 74 D4 mt on Mamore Forest in Lochaber dist 3m/5km NE of Kinlochleven. Height 3700 ft or 1128 metres. **Binnein Beag** is peak 1m NE, height 3083 ft or 940 metres. NN 2166
Binness Island, North Hants 10 D4* uninhabited island at N end of Langstone Harbour off Farlington Marshes. 1m SE in Langstone Harbour, **S Binness I.** SU 6904
Binns, The Lothian 65 G1 hse (NTS), dating in parts from 15c but mainly from 17c, 4m/6km E of Linlithgow. NT 0578
Bin of Cullen Grampian 82 D1 hill 3m/5km SW of Cullen, commanding wide views. Height 1053 ft or 321 metres. NJ 4764
Binscombe Surrey 11 F1* N suburb of Godalming. SU 9745
Binsoe N Yorks 49 E1 ham 2km NW of W Tanfield. SE 2579
Binstead Isle of Wight 10 C5 loc 2km W of Ryde. SZ 5792
Binsted Hants 11 E1 vil 4m/6km NE of Alton. SU 7741
Binsted W Sussex 11 F4 ham 2m/4km W of Arundel. SU 9806
Bin, The Grampian 82 D2* hill and surrounding state forest (**The Bin Forest**) 3m/5km NW of Huntly. NJ 5043
Binton Warwicks 27 F2 vil 4m/6km W of Stratford-upon-Avon. SP 1454
Bintree Norfolk 39 E3 vil 7m/12km SE of Fakenham. TG 0123
Binweston Salop 34 A4* loc 2m/3km W of Worthen. SJ 3004
Biod Ruadh Skye, H'land 79 B6 headland on W coast 4m/7km SW of Carbost. NG 3128
Birch Essex 30 D6 vil 5m/8km SW of Colchester. TL 9419
Birch Gtr Manchester 42 D1 loc 1m NW of Middleton. SD 8507
Bircham, Great Norfolk 38 C2 vil 3m/5km S of Docking. **B. Newton** vil 1km N. **B. Tofts** vil 1km E. TF 7632
Birchanger Essex 30 A5 vil 2m/3km NE of Bishop's Stortford. TL 5022
Birch Cross Staffs 35 G2* ham 1m W of Marchington. SK 1230
Birchencliffe W Yorks 48 D6* loc in Huddersfield 2m/4km NW of tn centre. SE 1118
Bircher H & W 26 A1 ham 4m/7km N of Leominster. SO 4765
Bircher Common H & W 26 A1* loc, partly NT, 5m/8km NW of Leominster. SO 4666
Birches Staffs 35 F3* loc 2km S of Rugeley. SK 0316
Birches Green W Midlands 35 G5* loc in Birmingham 4m/7km NE of city centre. SP 1190
Birches Head Staffs 42 D6* loc 1m NE of Hanley. SJ 8948
Birchett's Green E Sussex 12 C4* loc 2m/3km NW of Ticehurst. TQ 6631
Birchfield W Midlands 35 G5* loc in Birmingham 3m/4km N of city centre. SP 0790
Birch Green Essex 30 D6 vil 5m/8km SW of Colchester. TM 9418
Birch Green Herts 19 G1* loc 2m/4km W of Hertford. TL 2911
Birch Green Lancs 42 B1* dist of Skelmersdale N of tn centre. SD 4906
Birchgrove S Glam 15 F3* dist of Cardiff 3m/4km N of city centre. Brick works. ST 1680
Birchgrove W Glam 14 C2 vil 3m/5km W of Neath. SS 7098
Birch Grove W Sussex 12 A4* ham 2m/3km NE of Horsted Keynes. TQ 4029
Birchgrove Pool Salop 34 B2* small lake 1m NE of Baschurch – one of four in vicinity. SJ 4323
Birch Heath Ches 42 B5 loc 1km SW of Tarporley. SJ 5461
Birch Hill Berks 18 D4* S dist of Bracknell. SU 8766
Birchington Kent 13 H1 W dist of Margate. N coast resort. TR 3069
Birchley Heath Warwicks 35 H5 vil 3m/4km SW of Atherstone. SP 2894
Birch, Little H & W 26 A4* vil 6m/9km S of Hereford. SO 5131
Birchmoor Warwicks 35 H4* loc 1m SW of Polesworth. SK 2501
Birchover Derbys 43 G5 vil 4m/6km NW of Matlock. SK 2362
Birch Vale Derbys 43 E3 vil 1m W of Hayfield. SK 0286
Birchwood Herts 19 F1* N dist of Hatfield. TL 2209
Birch Wood Som 8 B3* ham 2m/3km W of Buckland St Mary. ST 2414
Birchwood, Upper Derbys 43 H5* loc 2m/3km E of Alfreton. **Lr Birchwood** loc 1km SW. SK 4355
Bircotes Notts 44 B2* coal-mining loc 2m/3km SW of Bawtry. SK 6291
Birdbrook Essex 30 C4 vil 4m/6km SE of Haverhill. TL 7041
Birdbush Wilts 9 F2 loc 4m/6km E of Shaftesbury. ST 9123
Bird Dyke Cumbria 52 B3* loc just N of Lamplugh. NY 0921
Bird End W Midlands 35 F5* loc 2m/3km NE of W Bromwich tn centre. SP 0193
Birdforth N Yorks 49 F1* ham 1km NW of Thormanby. SE 4875
Birdham W Sussex 11 E5 vil 4m/6km SW of Chichester. 1km N, Chichester Yacht Basin. SU 8200
Birdingbury Warwicks 27 H1 vil 4m/7km N of Southam. SP 4368
Birdlip Glos 26 D6 vil at top of steep hill on escarpment of Cotswold Hills 6m/10km SE of Gloucester; and 5m/8km SW of Cheltenham. SO 9214
Birdoswald Cumbria 60 B5 loc 2km W of Gilsland, on site of Roman fort of *Camboglanna* (A.M.). NY 6166
Birdsall N Yorks 50 C2 vil 4m/7km SE of Malton. SE 8165
Birds Green Essex 20 C1* ham 3m/5km S of Leaden Roding. TL 5808
Birdsgreen Salop 34 D5 ham 6m/10km SE of Bridgnorth. SO 7684
Birdsmoor Gate Dorset 8 C4 ham 3m/5km W of Broadwindsor. ST 3900
Birdston S'clyde 64 D2* loc 1m N of Kirkintilloch. NS 6575
Bird Street Suffolk 31 E3* loc 5m/8km SW of Stowmarket. TM 0052
Birdwell S Yorks 43 H1 loc 3m/5km S of Barnsley. SE 3401
Birdwood Glos 26 C5 loc 6m/9km W of Gloucester. SO 7418
Birgham Borders 67 E4 vil 3m/5km W of Coldstream. NT 7939
Birichin H'land 87 A7 loc in Sutherland dist 3m/5km NW of Dornoch. NH 7592
Birkacre Lancs 47 F6* loc adjoining Coppull to NE. SD 5714
Birk Beck 53 E4 r rising on Shap Fells, Cumbria, and flowing SE into R Lune at Tebay. NY 6105
Birkby Cumbria 52 B2* loc 2m/3km NE of Maryport. NY 0537
Birkby N Yorks 54 C4 ham 6m/9km N of Northallerton. NZ 3302
Birkdale Merseyside 46 D6 SW dist of Southport. Golf course. SD 3214
Birkdale Tarn N Yorks 53 G4 small lake 3m/4km W of Keld. NY 8501
Birkenburn Reservoir S'clyde 64 D1* small resr 3m/5km NE of Lennoxtown. NS 6780
Birkenhead Merseyside 41 H3 industrial tn and port on Wirral peninsula near mouth of R Mersey, 2km SW of Liverpool across r. Connected with Liverpool by two rd tunnels and one rly tunnel. Industries include ship building and repairing. SJ 3288
Birkenshaw W Yorks 49 E5 loc 4m/6km SE of Bradford. **B. Bottoms** loc adjoining to SE. SE 2028
Birker Force Cumbria 52 B5/C5* waterfall on Low Birker Pool 1m SE of Boot. SD 1899
Birkhill Tayside 73 F2 loc 4m/6km NW of Dundee. NO 3534
Birkholme Lincs 37 E2* loc 3m/4km E of Colsterworth. SK 9723
Birkin N Yorks 49 G5 vil 3m/4km NE of Knottingley across R Aire. SE 5326
Birks W Yorks 48 D5* loc in Bradford 2m/3km W of city centre. SE 1332
Birks W Yorks 49 E5* loc adjoining Morley to S. SE 2626
Birkshaw Nthmb 60 D5* loc 1m NW of Bardon Mill. NY 7765
Birkshaw Forest D & G 59 F4* state forest 3m/4km S of Lockerbie. NY 1177
Birks Tarn N Yorks 48 C1* small lake on Birks Fell 2km SW of Buckden. SD 9276
Birley H & W 26 A2* vil 4m/7km SW of Leominster. SO 4553
Birley S Yorks 43 H3* loc in Sheffield 4m/6km SE of city centre. SK 3983
Birley Carr S Yorks 43 G2 dist of Sheffield 4m/6km NW of city centre. SK 3392
Birley Edge S Yorks 43 G2* loc 1km S of Grenoside. SK 3392
Birling Kent 20 C5 vil 2m/3km N of W Malling. TQ 6860
Birling Nthmb 61 G1 loc just N of Warkworth. NU 2406
Birling Gap E Sussex 12 B6 loc on coast 2m/3km W of Beachy Hd, at E end of Seven Sisters cliffs. TV 5596
Birlingham H & W 26 D3 vil 2m/3km SW of Pershore across loop of R Avon. SO 9343
Birmingham W Midlands 35 G5 mnfg and commercial city and communications centre 100m/116km NW of London. Cathedral, former par ch, in baroque style. University. City centre re-developed in 1960s and 1970s. International airport at Elmdon, 7m/11km E. SP 0686
Birmingham and Fazeley Canal 35 G5-G4 canal connecting Birmingham with the Coventry Canal at Fazeley Junction, Staffs.
Birnam Tayside 72 D1 vil on S side of R Tay 1km SE of Dunkeld. **Birnam Wd,** famous from Shakespeare's *Macbeth*, 2m/3km SE. NO 0341
Birnbeck Island Avon 15 G5* rock island at N end of Weston Bay connected to mainland by a pier. ST 3062
Birnie Grampian 82 B2 loc with 12c ch 3m/4km S of Elgin. NJ 2058
Birns Water 66 C2 r in Lothian region rising on Lammermuir Hills and flowing NE then N into R Tyne 4m/6km SE of Tranent. NT 4568
Birrenswark D & G 59 F3 hill 3m/4km N of Ecclefechan. Earthworks of Roman and earlier settlements. Also known as Burnswark. NY 1878
Birsay Orkney 89 A6 loc near NW end of Mainland 2km E of Brough Hd. Earl's Palace, ruined 16c palace of the Earls of Orkney. HY 2527
Birse Grampian 77 E2 loc 2m/3km SE of Aboyne. See also Forest of Birse. NO 5597
Birsemore Grampian 77 E2 loc 1km S of Aboyne, across R Dee. NO 5297
Birstall Leics 36 B3 suburb 3m/5km N of Leicester. SK 5909
Birstall W Yorks 49 E5 loc 2m/3km NW of Batley. **B. Smithies** loc adjoining to S. SE 2226
Birstwith N Yorks 49 E2 vil 5m/8km NW of Harrogate. SE 2359
Birthorpe Lincs 37 F2 loc 1m W of Billingborough. TF 1134
Birtle Gtr Manchester 47 H6* loc 3m/4km NE of Bury. SD 8313
Birtley H & W 25 H1 scattered ham 4m/7km NE of Presteigne. SO 3669
Birtley Nthmb 60 D4 vil 4m/7km SE of Bellingham. NY 8778
Birtley Tyne & Wear 61 G5 tn 5m/8km S of Gateshead. Coal-mining. NZ 2755
Birtsmorton H & W 26 C4* loc 6m/10km W of Tewkesbury. **B. Court** is moated hse of all periods 13c-20c. SO 8035
Birts Street H & W 26 C4 vil 5m/8km E of Ledbury. SO 7836
Biruaslum W Isles 88 D4* small uninhabited island off W coast of Vatersay. NL 6096
Bisbrooke Leics 36 D4 vil 2km E of Uppingham. SP 8899
Biscathorpe Lincs 45 F3* ham 2km N of Donington on Bain. TF 2284
Biscot Beds 29 E5* N dist of Luton. TL 0723
Bisham Berks 18 D3 vil 1km S of Marlow across R Thames. SU 8585
Bishampton H & W 27 E3 vil 5m/7km NE of Pershore. SO 9851
Bish Mill Devon 7 E3* ham 2m/3km E of S Molton. SS 7425
Bishop Auckland Durham 54 B2 tn on right bank of R Wear 9m/15km SW of Durham. Coal-mining, engineering, textiles. Cas, of various dates, is residence of Bishops of Durham. NZ 2029
Bishopbridge Lincs 45 E2 ham at rd crossing of R Ancholme 5m/8km W of Mkt Rasen. TF 0391
Bishopbriggs S'clyde 64 D2 suburb 3m/5km N of Glasgow. NS 6070
Bishop Burton Humberside 51 E4 vil 3m/5km W of Beverley. SE 9839
Bishopdale Beck 53 H5/H6 r rising N of Buckden Pike, N Yorks, and flowing NE into R Ure 2m/3km E of Aysgarth. SE 0289
Bishopdown Wilts 9 H2* NE dist of Salisbury. SU 1531
Bishop Hill Tayside 73 E4 hill noted for gliding, 4m/7km E of Milnathort. NO 1804
Bishop Loch S'clyde 64 D2 small loch in Glasgow 6m/10km E of city centre. NS 6866
Bishop Middleham Durham 54 C2 vil 2m/4km NW of Sedgefield. NZ 3231
Bishopmill Grampian 82 B1 N dist of Elgin. NJ 2665
Bishop Monkton N Yorks 49 E2 vil 3m/5km S of Ripon. SE 3266
Bishop, North Dyfed 22 A3* rocky island 3m/5km W of St David's Hd. One of the larger islands in the group known as Bishops and Clerks, qv. SM 6728
Bishop Norton Lincs 44 D2 vil 5m/8km SE of Kirton in Lindsey. SK 9892
Bishop Rock Isles of Scilly 2 A1* rock with lighthouse at W extremity of Scillies, 5m/7km W of St Agnes. SV 8006
Bishops and Clerks Dyfed 22 A3 group of over twenty small rocky islands lying off St David's Hd, the largest being N Bishop, Carreg Rhoson, Daufraich, and Em-sger or S Bishop, the last having a lighthouse. SM 62

Bishopsbourne Kent 13 G2 vil 4m/7km SE of Canterbury. TR 1852
Bishops Cannings Wilts 17 E5 vil 3m/4km NE of Devizes. SU 0364
Bishop's Castle Salop 34 A5 small tn in hills on Welsh border 8m/12km NW of Craven Arms. Scanty remains of cas. Small brewery and clothing factory. SO 3288
Bishop's Caundle Dorset 8 E3 vil in Blackmoor Vale 4m/7km SE of Sherborne. ST 6913
Bishop's Cleeve Glos 26 D4 vil 4m/6km N of Cheltenham. SO 9527
Bishop's Clyst Devon 7 G5* loc adjacent to Clyst St Mary 4m/6km E of Exeter. SX 9791
Bishopsdale Kent 12 D3* loc 3m/5km W of Tenterden. TQ 8434
Bishop's Fonthill Wilts. See Fonthill Bishop.
Bishop's Frome H & W 26 B3 vil 4m/7km S of Bromyard. SO 6648
Bishops Gate Surrey 18 D4 loc in Windsor Gt Park 4m/6km W of Staines. SU 9871
Bishop's Green Essex 30 B6 ham 3m/4km S of Gt Dunmow. TL 6317
Bishop's Green 17 H5* loc on Berks/Hants border 3m/5km SE of Newbury. SU 5063
Bishop's Hull Som 8 A2 W suburb of Taunton. ST 2024
Bishopside N Yorks 48 D2 moorland area consisting of **High** and **Low Bishopside** to NE of Pateley Br. SE 1766
Bishop's Itchington Warwicks 27 G2 vil 3m/5km SW of Southam. SP 3857
Bishop's Lydeard Som 8 A2 vil 5m/8km NW of Taunton. ST 1629
Bishop's Norton Glos 26 D5* ham 4m/6km N of Gloucester. SO 8424
Bishop's Nympton Devon 7 F3 vil 3m/5km SE of S Molton. SS 7523
Bishop's Offley Staffs 34 D2 ham 3m/5km W of Eccleshall. SJ 7829
Bishop, South Dyfed 22 to W of sq A4. Rocky island 3m/4km W of Ramsey I. One of the larger islands in the group known as Bishops and Clerks, qv, and the southernmost. Lighthouse. Also known as Em-sger. SM 6522
Bishop's Stortford Herts 29 H5 tn on R Stort 8m/13km N of Harlow. Birthplace of Cecil Rhodes. Industries include malting, light engineering. TL 4821
Bishops Sutton Hants 10 C2 vil 2m/3km SE of New Alresford. SU 6031
Bishop's Tachbrook Warwicks 27 G2 vil 3m/5km S of Leamington. SP 3161
Bishop's Tawton Devon 6 D2 vil 2m/3km S of Barnstaple. SS 5630
Bishopsteignton Devon 5 E3 vil on N side of R Teign estuary 2m/3km W of Teignmouth. Remains of medieval Bishop's Palace to NE. SX 9173
Bishopstoke Hants 10 B3 E suburb of Eastleigh. SU 4619
Bishopston Avon 16 B4* dist of Bristol 2m/3km N of city centre. ST 5975
Bishopston (Llandeilo Ferwallt) W Glam 23 G6 vil 5m/9km SW of Swansea. SS 5789
Bishopstone Bucks 18 C1 vil 3m/4km S of Aylesbury. SP 8010
Bishopstone E Sussex 12 B6 vil 2km N of Seaford. TQ 4701
Bishopstone H & W 26 A3* vil 7m/11km W of Hereford. SO 4143
Bishopstone Kent 13 G1* loc 2m/3km E of Herne Bay tn centre. TR 2068
Bishopstone Wilts 17 F3 vil 6m/10km E of Swindon. Site of Roman bldg to SE. SU 2483
Bishopstone Wilts 9 G2 vil on R Ebble 4m/6km SW of Wilton. SU 0725
Bishopstrow Wilts 16 D6 vil 2m/3km SE of Warminster. ST 8943
Bishop Sutton Avon 16 B5 vil 2m/4km S of Chew Magna. ST 5859
Bishop's Waltham Hants 10 C3 small tn 7m/11km N of Fareham. Remains of 13c Bishop's Palace (A.M.). SU 5517
Bishopswood (or Bishops Wood) Som 8 B3 vil 5m/8km NW of Chard. ST 2512
Bishop's Wood Staffs 35 E3 vil 8m/13km NW of Wolverhampton. SJ 8309
Bishopsworth Avon 16 B4 SW dist of Bristol. ST 5668
Bishop Thornton N Yorks 49 E2 vil 2m/4km NW of Ripley. SE 2663
Bishopthorpe N Yorks 49 G3 vil 3m/4km S of York. Archbishop's palace on E side on banks of R Ouse. SE 5947
Bishopton Durham 54 C3 vil 5m/8km W of Stockton-on-Tees. NZ 3621
Bishopton N Yorks 49 E1 loc adjoining Ripon to W. SE 2971
Bishopton S'clyde 64 B2 vil 6m/9km NW of Paisley. Ordnance factory adjoining rly stn. NS 4371
Bishopton Warwicks 27 F2* loc in NW part of Stratford-upon-Avon. SP 1856
Bishop Wilton Humberside 50 C3 vil 5m/8km E of Stamford Br. SE 7955
Bishpool Gwent 15 H3* loc in Newport 3m/4km E of tn centre. ST 3488
Bishton (Trefesgob) Gwent 15 H3 vil 5m/8km E of Newport. Steel works to S. ST 3987
Bishton Staffs 35 F2/F3* ham adjoining Colwich to SE. SK 0120
Bisley Glos 16 D1 vil 4m/6km E of Stroud. SO 9006
Bisley Surrey 18 D5 vil 4m/6km W of Woking. **B. Camp** and rifle ranges to SW. SU 9559
Bispham Lancs 46 D4 coastal loc in Blackpool 3m/4km N of tn centre. **Lit Bispham** loc 1m N along shore. SD 3140
Bispham Green Lancs 42 B1 ham 2m/3km N of Parbold. SD 4813
Biss 16 D5* r rising S of Westbury in Wiltshire and flowing N, to W of the tn and through Trowbridge, to join R Avon 1m N of Trowbridge. ST 8559
Bissoe Cornwall 2 D4* vil 4m/6km SW of Truro. SW 7741
Bisterne Hants 9 H4 ham 3m/4km S of Ringwood. SU 1401
Bisterne Close Hants 9 H4* loc 2km E of Burley and 6m/9km E of Ringwood. SU 2203
Bitchburn, North Durham 54 B2* loc 2m/3km S of Crook. NZ 1732
Bitchet Green Kent 20 C6* loc 3m/4km E of Sevenoaks. TQ 5654
Bitchfield Lincs 37 E2 vil 6m/10km SE of Grantham. SK 9828
Bittadon Devon 6 D1 ham 4m/7km SE of Ilfracombe. SS 5441
Bittaford Devon 4 C5* vil on S edge of Dartmoor 2m/3km E of Ivybridge. SX 6657
Bittel Reservoirs H & W 27 E1* two resrs, **Upr** and **Lr Bittel**, 5m/8km N of Redditch. SP 0275
Bittering Norfolk 38 D3* loc 4m/7km NW of E Dereham. **B. Street** ham 2km E. TF 9317
Bitterley Salop 34 C6 vil 4m/6km NE of Ludlow. SO 5677
Bitterne Hants 10 B3 E dist of Southampton to E of R Itchen. Includes Roman riverside settlement of *Clausentum*. SU 4413
Bitterne Pari Hants 10 B3* dist of Southampton 2m/3km NE of city centre across R Itchen. SU 4414
Bitterscote Staffs 35 G4* loc in Tamworth 1km SW of tn centre. SK 2003
Bittesby Leics 36 B5* loc 3m/4km W of Lutterworth. SP 5085
Bitteswell Leics 36 B5 vil 1m N of Lutterworth. Airfield to W. SP 5385
Bitton Avon 16 B4 vil 2m/3km E of Keynsham. ST 6869
Biwmares Welsh form of Beaumaris, qv.
Bix Oxon 18 C3 vil 3m/4km NW of Henley-on-Thames. Site of Roman bldg to E. SU 7285
Bixter Shetland 89 E7 loc on Mainland on E side of **B. Voe,** 6m/10km E of Walls. **Ness of B.** is headland on The Firth, to E. HU 3352
Bla Bheinn Skye, H'land 79 D6 mt 2m/4km W of head of Loch Slapin. Height 3042 ft or 927 metres. Also known as Blaven. NG 5221
Blaby Leics 36 B4 suburb 5m/7km S of Leicester. SP 5697
Blackaburn Nthmb 60 D4* loc on Blacka Burn, Wark Forest, 4m/7km W of Wark. **B. Lough** small lake 2m/3km NW. NY 7977
Blackadder Water 67 E3 r in Borders region rising on Lammermuir and running SE to Greenlaw, then NE to Whiteadder Water at Allanton. NT 8654
Blackaton Brooks 4 D2* stream in Devon rising at Raybarrow Pool on Dartmoor and flowing first NE then S into N Teign R 2km W of Chagford. SX 6888
Blackaton Reservoir Devon 6 D3* small resr 2m/3km NE of Torrington. SS 5121
Blackawton Devon 4 D5 vil 5m/7km W of Dartmouth. SX 8050
Black Bank Warwicks 36 A5* loc in S part of Bedworth. SP 3586
Blackbeck Cumbria 52 A4* loc 1km E of Beckermet. NY 0206
Blackbeck Tarn Cumbria 52 C4* small lake 2m/3km SE of Buttermere lake. NY 2012
Blackborough Devon 7 H4 5m/8km E of Cullompton. ST 0909
Blackborough Norfolk 38 B3* loc 5m/8km SE of King's Lynn. Faint remains of 12c priory. **B. End** loc 1km NW. TF 6714
Black Bourn 30 D1* r rising SE of Bury St Edmunds, Suffolk, and flowing N through Ixworth into Lit Ouse R 2m/4km SE of Thetford. TL 8880
Black Bourton Oxon 17 G1 vil 6m/9km SW of Witney. SP 2804
Blackboys E Sussex 12 B4 vil 3m/5km E of Uckfield. TQ 5220
Black Bridge Dyfed 22 B5* loc 1km E of Milford Haven. SM 9106
Blackbridge Brook 10 C5* stream in Isle of Wight rising 2km N of Newchurch and flowing N into Wootton Creek below Wootton Br and thence into the Solent. SZ 5593
Blackbrook Derbys 43 H6* ham 2km W of Belper. SK 3347
Blackbrook Leics 36 A3* loc 5m/8km W of Loughborough. **Blackbrook Resr** to S. SK 4618
Blackbrook Merseyside 42 B2 urban loc 2m/3km E of St Helens. SJ 5496
Blackbrook Staffs 34 D1 ham 6m/10km NE of Mkt Drayton. SJ 7639
Blackbrook 4 C3 r in Devon rising at Blackbrook Head on Dartmoor and flowing S past Princetown prison then E into W Dart R 1m SE of Two Bridges. SX 6174
Black Brook 41 H5* stream rising on SW side of Buckley, Clwyd, and running S into R Alun 1m NW of Hope. SJ 2959
Black Brook 41 H6* stream rising near Ruabon, Clwyd, and running N into R Clywedog on S side of Wrexham. SJ 3248
Blackburn Grampian 83 F5 vil 8m/13km NW of Aberdeen. NJ 8212
Blackburn Lancs 47 G5 industrial tn on R Darwen and on Leeds and Liverpool Canal 21m/34km NW of Manchester. Cathedral is former par ch. Industries include textiles, textile machinery and general engineering. SD 6828
Blackburn Lothian 65 F2 tn 2m/3km S of Bathgate. NS 9865
Black Burn r in Cumbria. See Shield Water. NY 7143
Blackburn S Yorks 43 H2* loc 2m/4km W of Rotherham tn centre. SK 3892
Black Burn 57 D6 stream in Dumfries & Galloway region running W into R Bladnoch 3m/5km N of Kirkcowan. NX 3365
Blackburn Lake Nthmb 61 F2 small lake 2m/3km E of Rothbury. NU 0801
Blackbushe Airport Hants 18 C5* airfield 2km SW of Yateley. SU 8059
Black Callerton Tyne & Wear 61 F4* ham 6m/9km NW of Newcastle. NZ 1769
Black Car Norfolk 39 E5* loc 3m/5km E of Attleborough. TM 0995
Black Carr W Yorks 48 D5* loc 2m/3km NW of Queensbury. SE 0831
Black Cart Water 64 C2 r in Strathclyde region running NE from Castle Semple Loch to join White Cart Water 3m/4km N of Paisley and flow into R Clyde 1km farther N. NS 4968
Blackcraig S'clyde 56 F3 mt 5m/8km S of New Cumnock. Height 2298 ft or 700 metres. NS 6406
Blackcraig Forest Tayside 76 B5* state forest on W side of Strath Ardle and Br of Cally. **Blackcraig Castle** is a hse beside r at N end of forest. NO 1151
Black Crofts S'clyde 70 B2* locality on N shore of Loch Etive, Argyll, 2km E of Ledaig Pt. NM 9234
Black Cross Cornwall 2 D2 loc 2m/3km S of St Columb Major. SW 9060
Blackden Heath Ches 42 D4* loc 3m/4km NE of Holmes Chapel. SJ 7871
Black Devon 72 C5 r running W to Clackmannan in Central region, then SW to R Forth at Clackmannan Pow, 2km below Alloa. NS 8990
Black Dod 65 G6 hill on border of Strathclyde and Borders regions 5m/8km E of Elvanfoot. Height 1797 ft or 548 metres. NT 0319
Black Dog Devon 7 F4 ham 6m/10km NW of Crediton. SS 8009
Blackdown Dorset 8 C4 ham 3m/4km W of Broadwindsor. ST 3903
Black Down W Sussex 11 E2 viewpoint (NT) surrounded by sandy heaths and wds. Highest point in Sussex at 919 ft or 280 metres. SU 9129
Blackdown Hill Warwicks 27 G1* loc 2m/3km N of Leamington. SP 3168
Blackdown Hills 8 A3 hill ridge running E and W on borders of Somerset and Devon. Wellington Monmt (NT) is prominent landmark (see Wellington). ST 1121
Blackdyke Cumbria 59 F6* loc 2m/4km E. NY 1452
Blackeley Reservoir W Yorks 43 E1* narrow resr in steep-sided valley 2km S of Marsden. SE 0509
Blacker S Yorks 43 G1* loc adjoining Staincross to E. SE 3309
Blacker Hill S Yorks 43 H1* vil 1m N of Hoyland Nether. SE 3602
Black Esk 59 G2/G3 r in Dumfries & Galloway region running S through **Black Esk Resr** and Castle O'er Forest to join R White Esk and form R Esk 8m/13km NW of Langholm. NY 2590
Blackfell Tyne & Wear 61 G5* W dist of Washington. NZ 2956
Blackfen London 20 B4* loc in borough of Bexley 1m N of Sidcup and 11m/17km SE of Charing Cross. TQ 4674
Blackfield Hants 10 B4 suburban loc 2km SW of Fawley. SU 4402
Blackfleet Broad Norfolk 39 H3* small broad or lake 2km SW of Horsey, draining by Eelfleet Dike into R Thurne. TG 4421
Blackford Cumbria 59 H5 loc 4m/6km N of Carlisle. NY 3962
Blackford Som 16 A6* vil 2m/3km W of Wedmore. ST 4147
Blackford Som 8 D2 vil 4m/6km W of Wincanton. ST 6526
Blackford Tayside 72 C4 vil 4m/6km SW of Auchterarder. NN 8909
Blackford Bridge Gtr Manchester 42 D1 loc in Bury 2m/3km S of tn centre. SD 8007
Blackfordby Leics 35 H3 vil 2m/3km NW of Ashby de la Zouch. SK 3217
Blackford Hill Lothian 66 A2* hill in Edinburgh 2m/3km S of city centre. Royal Observatory. NT 2670
Blackgang Isle of Wight 10 B6 vil above coast and B. Chine, 1km SE of Chale. SZ 4876
Blackgate Lancs 47 E6* loc 2km E of Mere Brow. SD 4319
Blackhall Lothian 66 A2 dist of Edinburgh 2m/4km W of city centre. NT 2174
Blackhall S'clyde 64 C3* SE dist of Paisley. NS 4963
Blackhall Colliery Durham 54 D1 large coal-mining loc 2km SE of Peterlee. NZ 4539
Blackhall Forest Grampian 77 F2 afforested estate to W of Banchory across R Dee. NO 6795
Blackhall Mill Tyne & Wear 61 F5* vil on R Derwent 4m/6km N of Consett. NZ 1256
Black Halls Durham 54 D1* loc near coast 3m/4km SE of Peterlee. **Blackhalls Rocks** on coast to NE. NZ 4738
Blackhall Wood Cumbria 59 H6 loc 2km NE of Dalston. NY 3851
Blackham E Sussex 12 B3 loc 6m/9km W of Tunbridge Wells. TQ 4940
Blackhammer Orkney 89 B6* prehistoric cairn (A.M.) on island of Rousay, 2km W of Brinyan. HY 4127
Blackhaugh Borders 66 B4* loc on Caddon Water 2m/3km NW of Clovenfords. NT 4238
Black Head Cornwall 2 D6 headland on E coast of Lizard peninsula 6m/9km NE of Lizard Pt across bay. SW 7716
Black Head Cornwall 3 E3 headland at W end of St Austell Bay and N end of Mevagissey Bay. SX 0447
Black Head D & G 57 A7 headland with lighthouse at S end of the small Killantringan Bay on coast of Rinns of Galloway, 2m/3km NW of Portpatrick. Lighthouse is known as Killantringan Lighthouse. NW 9856
Black Head Isle of Man 46 A6* headland (Manx NT) on SW promontory of island to E of Spanish Hd. SC 1865

Black Head Ponds Humberside 44 D1* group of three small lakes 2m/3km W of Scawby. SE 9305

Blackheath Essex 30 D5 loc in S part of Colchester. TM 0021

Blackheath London 20 A4 dist in borough of Lewisham 1m NE of Lewisham tn centre and 7m/11km SE of Charing Cross. The heath itself is large open space, although traversed by roads. TQ 3976

Blackheath Suffolk 31 H1* ham 1km S of Wenhaston. TM 4274

Blackheath Surrey 19 E6 vil 3m/5km SE of Guildford. TQ 0346

Blackheath W Midlands 35 F5 dist of Warley 2m/3km W of tn centre. SO 9786

Black Heddon Nthmb 61 F4 loc 2m/4km SW of Belsay. NZ 0776

Black Hill D & G 58 D1* hill in Lowther Hills 2km N of Durisdeer. Height 1741 ft or 531 metres. NS 8905

Blackhill Durham 61 F6 dist of Consett 1km W of tn centre. NZ 0951

Blackhill S'clyde 64 D2* loc in Glasgow 2m/4km E of city centre. NS 6266

Blackhill S'clyde 65 E4* hill and viewpoint (NTS) 3m/5km W of Lanark. NS 8343

Black Hill Tyne & Wear 61 G5* dist of Gateshead 3m/5km SE of tn centre. NZ 2859

Black Hill Warwicks 27 F2 loc 3m/5km NE of Stratford-upon-Avon. SP 2359

Blackhillock Grampian 82 C2 loc 5m/8km W of Keith. Distillery 1m E. NJ 3550

Blackhillock Grampian 82 D2 loc 2m/3km S of Keith. NJ 4348

Blackhills Grampian 82 B2 loc 4m/7km SE of Elgin. NJ 2758

Blackhills Grampian 83 H3* loc near E coast 1km W of Murdoch Hd. NK 1139

Blackhills W Glam 23 G6* loc 1m E of Swansea (Fairwood Common) Airport. SS 5891

Black Holm Orkney 89 C7* islet 1m NW of Copinsay and 2km S of Pt of Ayre at E end of Mainland. HY 5902

Blackhope Scar 66 B4 hill on Moorfoot range on border of Lothian and Borders regions 6m/10km NE of Peebles. Height 2136 ft or 651 metres; summit of Moorfoot Hills. NT 3148

Blackhorse Devon 7 G5* ham 4m/6km E of Exeter. SX 9793

Black House, The W Isles. See Arnol.

Black Isle H'land 81 F2 peninsula in Ross and Cromarty dist between Cromarty Firth and Inverness Firth running out to Cromarty and S Sutor. NH 6557

Blackjack Lincs 37 G1* loc 2m/3km E of Swineshead. TF 2639

Black Lake W Midlands 35 F5* loc in W Bromwich 1m N of tn centre. SO 9992

Blackland Som 7 F2* Exmoor ham 2km NW of Withypool. SS 8336

Blackland Wilts 17 E4* loc 2m/3km SE of Calne. SU 0168

Black Lane Gtr Manchester 42 D1 loc adjoining Radcliffe to NW. SD 7708

Black Law Borders 65 H5 mt on Ettrick Forest 3m/5km NW of St Mary's Loch. Height 2285 ft or 696 metres. NT 2127

Blackleach Lancs 47 E4/F4* loc 1km W of Swillbrook. SD 4734

Blackley Gtr Manchester 42 D1* dist of Manchester 3m/5km NE of city centre. **Hr Blackley** dist 2km NW. SD 8502

Blackley W Yorks 48 D6* loc 3m/5km NW of Huddersfield. SE 1019

Black Linn Reservoir S'clyde 64 C2* small resr 3m/5km NE of Dumbarton. NS 4477

Black Loch D & G 57 C6* small loch 1m NE of Loch Ronald and 4m/7km NW of Kirkcowan. NX 2865

Black Loch D & G. See Lochinch Castle.

Black Loch D & G 57 D5* small narrow loch at N end of Loch Ochiltree, 7m/11km SE of Barrhill. NX 3175

Black Loch 65 E2 small loch on border of Central and Strathclyde regions 2m/3km S of Slamannan. NS 8670

Black Lochs of Kilquhockadale D & G 57 C6* two small lochs or tarns 6m/10km NW of Kirkcowan. NX 2769

Blacklorg 56 F3 mt on border of Strathclyde and Dumfries & Galloway regions 2km E of Afton Resr. Height 2231 ft or 680 metres. NS 6504

Black Lough Nthmb 61 F1* small lake 2km E of Edlingham. NU 1308

Blacklunans Tayside 76 C5 vil on Black Water 9m/15km N of Blairgowrie. NO 1460

Black Lyne 60 B4 r rising on Kershope Forest, Cumbria, and flowing SW to join R White Lyne and form R Lyne 5m/7km W of Bewcastle. NY 4973

Blackmill (Melin Ifan Ddu) Mid Glam 15 E3 ham 5m/8km N of Bridgend. SS 9386

Black Mixen Powys 25 F2/G2 hill on Radnor Forest with WT stn. Height 2133 ft or 650 metres. SO 1964

Blackmoor Gtr Manchester 42 C2* loc 1m S of Tyldesley. SD 6900

Blackmoor Hants 11 E2 vil 4m/6km W of Liphook. SU 7833

Black Moor Lancs 47 F6* loc 1m W of Mawdesley. SD 4814

Black Moor W Yorks 49 E4* loc in Leeds 4m/6km N of city centre. SE 2939

Blackmoorfoot W Yorks 48 D6 ham 4m/6km SW of Huddersfield. **Blackmoorfoot Resr** to S. SE 0913

Blackmoor Vale 9 E2, E3 fertile stretch of country extending roughly from Wincanton in Somerset S to Haselbury Bryan (or Hazelbury Bryan) in Dorset and thence W to Yetminster. ST 7315

Blackmore Essex 20 C2 vil 3m/5km NW of Ingatestone. TL 6001

Blackmore Salop 34 A3* loc 3m/4km W of Westbury. SJ 3109

Blackmore End Essex 30 C5 vil 5m/8km N of Braintree. TL 7430

Blackmore End Herts 29 F6 loc 3m/5km NE of Harpenden. TL 1616

Blackmoss Pool Cumbria 60 B6* small lake 2m/3km NW of Armathwaite. NY 4847

Black Moss Reservoir W Yorks 43 E1* small resr 2m/3km SW of Marsden. SE 0308

Black Moss Reservoirs Lancs 48 B4* two small resrs on E side of Pendle Hill 3m/5km NW of Nelson. SD 8241

Black Moss Tarn Cumbria 53 E5* small lake 2m/3km W of Grayrigg. SD 5497

Black Mount S'clyde 70 D1-71 E1 moorland area in Argyll containing several small lochs, traversed by rd running N from Br of Orchy towards Glen Coe. R Bà flows through centre of area from W to E. NN 24

Black Mountain (Mynydd Du, Y) 24 C6, D5 mt range running roughly E and W between Brynamman, Dyfed, and Trecastle, Powys, culminating in Carmarthen Van (Bannau Brycheiniog), qv. SN 7182

Black Mountains 25 G5 hill range of Old Red Sandstone, intersected by deep valleys, mainly in Wales but partly in England, extending from Hay-on-Wye (N) to Abergavenny (S) and from Longtown (E) to Llangorse Lake (W). SO 2223

Blackness Central 65 G1 vil on **B. Bay** on S side of Firth of Forth 4m/6km E of Bo'ness. **B. Castle** (A.M.) dates from 15c. NT 0580

Blackness Tayside 73 F2* dist of Dundee 2m/3km W of city centre. NO 3730

Blacknest Berks 18 D4 ham at W end of lake of Virginia Water 1km NE of Sunningdale. SU 9568

Blacknest Hants 11 E1 ham 4m/7km SW of Farnham. SU 7941

Black Neuk S'clyde 56 B4 headland 2m/3km SW of Girvan. NX 1695

Blackney Dorset 8 C4* ham 3m/5km SW of Beaminster. SY 4399

Black Nore Avon 16 A4* headland on mouth of R Severn 2km W of Portishead. ST 4476

Black Notley Essex 30 C5 vil 2m/3km S of Braintree. TL 7620

Blacko Lancs 48 B4 vil 2m/4km N of Nelson. SD 8541

Black Pill W Glam 23 G6 loc in Swansea 3m/4km SW of tn centre. SS 6190

Black Point Dyfed 22 B4* headland on E side of St Brides Bay 2m/4km S of Rickets Hd. SM 8515

Black Point Essex 21 E2* headland on S bank of R Crouch estuary 2m/4km W of Burnham-on-Crouch. TQ 9196

Blackpole H & W 26 D2* loc in NE part of Worcester. SO 8657

Black Pole Lancs 47 F4* loc 2km NW of Woodplumpton. SD 4836

Blackpool Devon 5 E5* loc on S coast 3m/5km SW of Dartmouth. SX 8547

Blackpool Dyfed 22 C4* loc 1km SW of Canaston Br. SN 0614

Blackpool Lancs 46 D4 large coastal resort and conference centre on Irish Sea 15m/24km W of Preston. **B. Tower** is notable landmark. Industries include light engineering, confectionery. Airport 3m/5km S. SD 3035

Black Pool Powys 25 F1* tarn 2m/3km SE of Llanbister. SO 1270

Blackpool Corner Devon 8 B4* loc on Dorset border 3m/4km E of Axminster. SY 3398

Blackridge Lothian 65 F2 vil 3m/5km W of Armadale. NS 8967

Blackrock Cornwall 2 C5* loc 3m/5km SE of Camborne. SW 6634

Blackrock Gwent 25 G6 loc 2m/3km E of Brynmawr. SO 2112

Blackrod Gtr Manchester 47 F6/G6 tn 7m/11km W of Bolton. Coal-mining, textiles. SD 6110

Black Scar Dyfed 22 A4* rock island on W side of Green Scar, 1m W of Dinas-fawr. SM 7922

Blackshaw D & G 59 F5* loc near shore of Solway Firth 8m/13km SE of Dumfries. **B. Bank,** sandbank to S. NY 0465

Blackshaw Head W Yorks 48 C5 vil 2m/4km W of Hebden Br. SD 9527

Blackshawmoor Reservoirs Staffs 43 E5 two small resrs 1km SE of Upr Hulme. SK 0160

Blackside S'clyde 64 D5* hill ridge 3m/5km NE of Sorn, culminating in Wedder Hill, 1411 ft or 430 metres. NS 5930

Black's Memorial Lighthouse S'clyde 70 A2 lighthouse on E coast of Mull 1km S of Duart Pt, built in memory of William Black, 19c novelist. NM 7534

Blacksmith's Green Suffolk 31 F2* loc 1m SE of Wetheringsett. TM 1465

Blacksnape Lancs 48 A5* ham 2km E of Darwen. SD 7121

Black Spout Tayside 76 A5* waterfall in wds 1km SE of Pitlochry. NN 9557

Blackstone W Sussex 11 H3* ham 2m/3km E of Henfield. TQ 2416

Blackstone Edge 48 C6* moorland ridge 2m/4km E of Littleborough on borders of Gtr Manchester and W Yorks. Section of paved Roman rd traverses ridge. **Blackstone Edge Resr** below N end of ridge. SD 9717

Blackstone Point Cumbria 47 E1* headland on left bank of R Kent estuary opp Grange-over-Sands. SD 4377

Black Street Suffolk 39 H6* ham 1m W of Kessingland. TM 5186

Black Tar Dyfed 22 C5* loc on W bank of Daugleddau R above **Blacktar Pt,** to E of Llangwm. SM 9909

Blackthorn Oxon 28 B5 vil 3m/5km SE of Bicester. SP 6219

Blackthorpe Suffolk 30 D2* vil 3m/5km E of Bury St Edmunds. TL 9063

Blacktoft Humberside 50 D5 vil on N bank of R Ouse 3m/5km S of Gilberdyke. SE 8329

Blackton Reservoir Durham 53 H3* middle resr of three in Baldersdale, 7m/11km W of Barnard Castle. NY 9418

Blacktop Grampian 77 H1 loc 5m/8km W of Aberdeen. NJ 8604

Black Torrington Devon 6 D4 vil 5m/8km W of Hatherleigh. SS 4605

Blacktown Gwent 15 G3 loc 5m/8km SW of Newport. ST 2581

Black Vein Gwent 15 G2* loc on S side of Crosskeys across Ebbw R. ST 2291

Black Ven Dorset. See Golden Cap.

Blackwall London 20 A3* loc in borough of Tower Hamlets 4m/6km E of London Br . Rd tunnels under R Thames. **B. Reach** is stretch of r above Blackwall. TQ 3880

Blackwater Cornwall 2 C4 vil 4m/6km NE of Redruth. SW 7346

Blackwater Dorset 9 H4* loc on R Stour 3m/4km NW of Christchurch. SZ 1396

Blackwater Hants 18 C5/D5 suburban loc 2km W of Camberley. SU 8559

Black Water H'land 75 E5 stream in Lochaber dist running W to head of Blackwater Resr. NN 3760

Black Water H'land 81 E2 r in Ross and Cromarty dist running S down Strath Garve to Loch Garve, then SE through Contin to R Conon, 2m/3km S of Strathpeffer. NH 4754

Black Water H'land 87 B5 r in Sutherland dist running SE from Ben Armine Forest to R Brora 8m/12km NW of Brora vil. NC 8011

Blackwater Isle of Wight 10 C6 vil 2m/3km S of Newport. SZ 5086

Blackwater Norfolk 39 E3* loc 2km E of Sparham. TG 0920

Blackwater Som 8 B3* ham 2km N of Buckland St Mary and 6m/9km NW of Chard. ST 2615

Blackwater Suffolk 31 H1* N suburb of Southwold across Buss Creek. TM 5077

Blackwater 18 C5 r rising at Aldershot, Hants, and flowing N to Sandhurst, then W into R Loddon at Swallowfield S of Reading. SU 7265

Blackwater 21 F1 r rising N of Braintree, Essex, and flowing via Coggeshall, Kelvedon, and Witham to Maldon and thence E into North Sea to S of Mersea I. TM 0010

Blackwater 39 E4* r rising 2km W of Shipdham, Norfolk, and flowing E to R Yare 5m/8km NW of Wymondham. TG 0406

Black Water 58 B3/C3 r in Dumfries & Galloway region running W into Water of Ken 5m/8km N of Dalry. NX 6188

Black Water 71 F4* r in Central region running from Loch Achray to Loch Venachar, W of Callander. NN 5405

Black Water 76 C5 r in Tayside region originating in Shee Water and running S down Glen Shee to join R Ardle and form R Ericht nearly 1km E of Br of Cally. NO 1451

Black Water 82 C4 r rising 5m/7km SW of Cabrach in Grampian region and running NE to R Deveron 3m/4km N of the vil. NJ 3830

Blackwaterfoot S'clyde 63 F5 vil on Drumadoon Bay, W coast of Arran, at mouth of **Black Water,** 9m/14km SW of Brodick. NR 8928

Blackwater Forest Grampian 82 C4 deer forest astride upper reaches of Black Water, 8m/13km S of Dufftown. NJ 3126

Blackwater Reservoir H'land 74 D5 resr in Lochaber dist, 8m/12km long E to W. Dam is 4m/6km E of Kinlochleven. Supplies water for aluminium works there. NN 3059

Blackwaters Staffs 34 D2/35 E2* loc 4m/6km NW of Eccleshall. SJ 7832

Blackwell Derbys 43 F4 ham 4m/7km E of Buxton. SK 1272

Blackwell Derbys 43 H5 vil 3m/4km NE of Alfreton. SK 4458

Blackwell Durham 54 B3/B4 loc in Darlington 2km SW of tn centre. NZ 2712

Blackwell H & W 27 E1* loc 2m/3km NE of Bromsgrove. SO 9872

Blackwell Warwicks 27 F3 vil 2m/3km NW of Shipston on Stour. SP 2443

Blackwell W Sussex 12 A3* N dist of E Grinstead. TQ 3939

Blackwell End Glos 26 C5 ham 5m/9km NW of Gloucester. SO 7825

Blackwood (Coed-duon) Gwent 15 F2 tn in coal-mining dist 7m/11km N of Caerphilly. ST 1797

Blackwood S'clyde 65 E4 vil 6m/9km W of Lanark and adjoining vil of Kirkmuirhill to N. NS 7943

Blackwood Hill Staffs 43 E5* loc 4m/6km W of Leek. SJ 9255

Black Wood of Rannoch Tayside 75 F5* wood of ancient firs on S side of Loch Rannoch, 6m/10km W of Kinloch Rannoch. NN 5656

Blacon Ches 42 A4 NW dist of Chester. SJ 3868

Bladnoch D & G 57 D7 vil on N bank of R Bladnoch 1m SW of Wigtown. Distillery, the most southerly in Scotland. R issues from Loch Maberry on border with Strathclyde region, and flows SE to Wigtown Bay on S side of Wigtown. NX 4254

Bladon Oxon 27 H6 vil 2km S of Woodstock across park of Blenheim Palace. SP 4414

Blaenafon Welsh form of Blaenavon, qv.

Blaenannerch Dyfed 22 D1/23 E1 ham 2m/3km SW of Aberporth. SN 2449

Blaenau Welsh form of Blaina, qv.

Blaenau Ffestiniog Gwynedd 40 D6 slate-quarrying tn 3m/4km N of Ffestiniog and 17m/27km SE of Caernarvon. Llechwedd Quarries, with underground shafts, 1km N. SH 7045
Blaenau-Gwent Gwent 15 G1* loc adjoining Abertillery to NW. SO 2104
Blaenau Gwent 118 admin dist of Gwent.
Blaenavon (Blaenafon) Gwent 15 G1 tn 5m/8km N of Pontypool. Coal-mining, iron and steel works. SO 2508
Blaenawey Gwent 25 G5 ham 3m/5km N of Abergavenny. SO 2919
Blaen Bran Reservoirs Gwent 15 G2* two small resrs 2m/3km NW of Cwmbran. ST 2697
Blaen Celyn Dyfed 23 E1* loc 3m/4km E of Llangranog. SN 3554
Blaen Clydach Mid Glam 15 E2* loc 2m/3km SE of Rhondda. SS 9893
Blaen-cwm Mid Glam 15 E2* ham 4m/6km NW of Rhondda. SS 9298
Blaen-Dyryn Powys 25 E4 loc 2m/3km N of Llanfihangel Nant Bran. SN 9336
Blaenffos Dyfed 22 D2 ham 6m/9km S of Cardigan. SN 1937
Blaengarw Mid Glam 15 E2 coal-mining vil 8m/13km N of Bridgend. SS 9092
Blaen-geuffordd Dyfed 32 D6* loc 1km W of Capel Bangor. SN 6480
Blaengwawr Mid Glam 15 E2* loc adjoining Aberdare to SE. SO 0001
Blaengwrach W Glam 14 D1 vil 2m/3km SW of Glyn-neath. SN 8605
Blaengwynfi W Glam 15 E2 vil 5m/8km W of Rhondda. SS 8996
Blaenhafren Powys 33 E5 source of R Severn on NE slopes of Plynlimon. SN 8289
Blaenllechau Mid Glam 15 E2* loc in valley of Lit Rhondda R (Afon Rhondda Fach) 2m/3km NE of Rhondda. ST 0097
Blaenpenal Dyfed 24 C2 ham 4m/7km NW of Tregaron. SN 6364
Blaenplwyf Dyfed 24 B1 ham 4m/6km S of Aberystwyth. SN 5775
Blaenporth Dyfed 23 E1 vil 2m/3km S of Aberporth. SN 2648
Blaenrhondda Mid Glam 15 E2 coal-mining vil at head of Rhondda valley 4m/6km NW of Rhondda. SS 9299
Blaenwaun Dyfed 22 D3 ham 7m/11km N of Whitland. SN 2327
Blaen-y-coed Dyfed 23 E3 ham 6m/9km NW of Carmarthen. SN 3026
Blagdon Avon 16 A5 vil below N slopes of Mendip Hills 5m/8km SE of Congresbury. To NE, **B. Lake** (or Yeo Resr), large resr in valley of R Yeo. ST 5058
Blagdon Devon 5 E4* loc 2m/4km W of Paignton. SX 8561
Blagdon Devon 6 C5* loc 5m/7km SE of Holsworthy. 1km S, **B. Lake,** small lake in side valley of Henford Water, tributary of R Carey. SX 3697
Blagdon Hill Som 8 A3 ham 4m/7km S of Taunton. ST 2118
Blaguegate Lancs 42 A1* loc adjoining Skelmersdale to W. SD 4506
Blaich H'land 74 B4 vil in Lochaber dist on S side of Loch Eil. NN 0376
Blaina (Blaenau) Gwent 15 G1 coal-mining loc 2m/4km S of Brynmawr. SO 1908
Blainslie Borders 66 C4* loc 3m/4km S of Lauder. NT 5443
Blairadam Forest 73 E5* state forest on W side of Kelty, Fife. NT 1195
Blair Atholl Tayside 76 A4 vil at confluence of R Tilt and R Garry 6m/10km NW of Pitlochry. To NW is **Blair Castle,** large mansion in Scottish baronial style dating in part from 13c, seat of the Dukes of Atholl. NN 8765
Blair Castle S'clyde 64 B4 cas mainly of 17c, with later additions, 2km SE of Dalry. NS 3047
Blair Drummond Central 72 B4 estate with safari park 5m/8km NW of Stirling. **Blairdrummond Moss** is low-lying area to SW. NS 7398
Blairgowrie Tayside 73 E1 tn on R Ericht 17m/27km NW of Dundee. Fruit growing and canning; jute and rayon, agricultural machinery, and stationery mnfre. Ski school. NO 1745
Blairhall Fife 72 D5 loc in Fife coalfield 6m/9km W of Dunfermline. NT 0089
Blairingone Tayside 72 D5 vil 4m/6km NW of Saline. NS 9896
Blairlinn S'clyde 65 E2* industrial area of Cumbernauld 2km S of tn centre. NS 7572
Blairlogie Central 72 C5 vil 3m/5km NE of Stirling. NS 8296
Blairmore H'land 84 B2 loc near W coast of Sutherland dist 3m/4km NW of Kinlochbervie. NC 1959
Blairmore S'clyde 70 D6 vil and resort in Argyll 1m N of Strone Pt at entrance to Loch Long. NS 1981
Blairs College Grampian 77 H1 RC seminary, founded in 1827, 5m/8km SW of Aberdeen. Present bldg dates from 1908. NJ 8800
Blaisdon Glos 26 C5 vil 4m/6km NE of Cinderford. SO 7016
Blaise Hamlet Avon 16 B4* loc in NW Bristol. Ancient hill forts to SE. ST 5578
Blakebrook H & W 35 E6 W dist of Kidderminster. SO 8176
Blakedown H & W 35 E6 vil 3m/5km E of Kidderminster. SO 8878
Blake End Essex 30 B5* ham 4m/6km W of Braintree. TL 7022
Blakelaw Tyne & Wear 61 G5* dist of Newcastle 2m/4km NW of city centre. NZ 2166
Blakeley Staffs 35 E5* loc adjoining Wombourn to SW, 5m/8km SW of Wolverhampton. SO 8692
Blakeley Lane Staffs 43 E6* loc 2m/3km E of Werrington. SJ 9747
Blakelow Ches 42 C6* loc 2m/3km E of Nantwich. SJ 6851
Blakemere Ches 42 B4* ham 7m/11km W of Northwich. SJ 5571
Blakemere H & W 25 H4 vil 9m/15km W of Hereford. SO 3641
Blake Mere Salop 34 B1* lake, one of several in dist, 2km SE of Ellesmere. SJ 4133
Blake Mere Salop 34 C1* small lake 2km NE of Whitchurch. SJ 5542
Blakemere Pool Staffs 34 D2/35 E2* small lake beside Shropshire Union Canal 1km N of Norbury. SJ 7824
Blakenall Heath W Midlands 35 F4* loc in Walsall 2m/3km N of tn centre. SK 0001
Blakeney Glos 16 B1 vil near R Severn estuary 4m/6km NE of Lydney. SO 6707
Blakeney Norfolk 39 E1 vil near coast 5m/7km NW of Holt. Yachting centre. Remains of 15c guildhall (A.M.). **Blakeney Pt** (NT), nature reserve on spit of land to N. TG 0343
Blakenhall Ches 42 C6 ham 6m/9km SE of Nantwich. SJ 7247
Blakenhall W Midlands 35 E4/F4 S dist of Wolverhampton. SO 9297
Blakenham, Great Suffolk 31 E3 vil 5m/8km NW of Ipswich. TM 1150
Blakenham, Little Suffolk 31 E3* vil 5m/7km NW of Ipswich. TM 1048
Blakeshall H & W 35 E6* loc 3m/5km N of Kidderminster. SO 8381
Blakesley Northants 28 B3 vil 4m/7km W of Towcester. SP 6250
Blanchland Nthmb 61 E6 stone vil with large square in upper valley of R Derwent 9m/14km S of Hexham. Remains of medieval monastery. NY 9650
Blandford Camp Dorset 9 F3* military camp 3m/5km NE of Blandford Forum. ST 9208
Blandford Forum Dorset 9 F4 tn on R Stour 16m/26km NW of Bournemouth. Usually known simply as Blandford. ST 8806
Blandford St Mary Dorset 9 F4 vil 1km S of Blandford Forum across R Stour. ST 8905
Bland Hill N Yorks 49 E3 ham 5m/8km N of Otley. SE 2053
Blanefield Central 64 C1 vil 1km NW of Strathblane. Printing works. NS 5579
Blanerne Borders 67 E3* loc on Whiteadder Water 3m/5km E of Preston. NT 8356
Blane Water 64 C1* r in Central region running NW down Strath Blane to Endrick Water 2km W of Killearn. NS 5085
Blankney Lincs 45 E5 vil 9m/15km SE of Lincoln. TF 0660
Blantyre S'clyde 64 D3 tn adjoining Hamilton to NW. Birthplace of David Livingstone, 19c explorer. **High** and **Low Blantyre** are parts of the tn lying to SW and E respectively. NS 6857
Blarmachfoldach H'land 74 C4 locality in Lochaber dist 3m/5km S of Fort William. NN 0969
Blasford Hill Essex 20 D1* loc 3m/4km N of Chelmsford. TL 7011
Blashford Hants 9 H3 loc 1m N of Ringwood. SU 1506
Blaston Leics 36 D5 vil 5m/8km SW of Uppingham. SP 8095
Blatchington, East E Sussex 12 B6 N suburb of Newhaven. TQ 4800
Blatchington, West E Sussex 11 H4 N dist of Hove. TQ 2807
Blatherwycke Northants 37 E5 vil 6m/10km NW of Oundle. **B. Lake** to N. SP 9795
Blatobulgium D & G. See Middlebie.
Blaven Skye, H'land 79 D6 mt 2m/4km W of head of Loch Slapin. Height 3042 ft or 927 metres. Also known as Bla Bheinn. NG 5221
Blawith Cumbria 47 E1* loc 1m NE of Grange-over-Sands. SD 4178
Blawith Cumbria 52 C6* ham 6m/10km N of Ulverston. SD 2888
Blaxhall Suffolk 31 G3 vil at N end of Tunstall Forest 4m/7km S of Saxmundham. TM 3657
Blaxton S Yorks 44 B1 vil 5m/8km N of Bawtry. SE 6700
Blaydon Tyne & Wear 61 F5 tn on S side of R Tyne 5m/7km W of Gateshead. Coal-mining, engineering, chemicals. **B. Burn** loc 2km SW. NZ 1863
Bleaberry Tarn Cumbria 52 B3* small lake 2km SW of Buttermere ham. NY 1615
Bleadney Som 16 A6* ham 4m/7km W of Wells. ST 4845
Bleadon Avon 15 H5 vil 3m/5km SE of Weston-super-Mare and below S slope of **B. Hill.** ST 3456
Blea Gill Waterfall N Yorks 48 C2* waterfall in Blea Beck on Hebden Moor 1m NW of Grimwith Resr. SE 0466
Bleak Hey Nook Gtr Manchester 43 E1 loc 6m/10km NE of Oldham. SE 0009
Bleaklow Hill Derbys 43 F2 ridge on High Peak extending from Bleaklow Hd to Bleaklow Stones (each 2060 ft or 628 metres above sea level), and forming the watershed for the head waters of Rs Derwent, Westend, Alport, and Ashop, as well as several streams feeding R Etherow to N and W. SK 1096
Blean Kent 13 F1 vil 3m/4km NW of Canterbury. TR 1260
Bleasby Lincs 45 E3* loc 3m/5km SE of Mkt Rasen. **B. Moor** loc 1m SW. TF 1283
Bleasby Notts 44 B6 vil 3m/5km S of Southwell. SK 7149
Blea Tarn Cumbria 52 C3 small lake 2m/3km E of Rosthwaite. NY 2914
Blea Tarn Cumbria 52 C4 small lake 3m/5km W of Skelwith Br. NY 2904
Bleatarn Cumbria 53 F3 loc 2m/3km SW of Warcop. NY 7313
Blea Tarn Reservoir Lancs 47 F2* small resr 2m/3km SE of Lancaster. SD 4958
Bleathwood Common H & W 26 B1* loc 3m/5km NW of Tenbury Wells. SO 5570
Blea Water Cumbria 52 D4 small lake 1m W of S end of Haweswater Resr. NY 4410
Blea Wyke Point N Yorks 55 G5* headland on North Sea coast 1km E of Ravenscar. NZ 9901
Blebocraigs Fife 73 G3* loc 5m/8km W of St Andrews. NO 4315
Bleddfa Powys 25 G2 vil 6m/9km SW of Knighton. Earthworks mark site of former cas. SO 2068
Bledington Glos 27 F5 vil 4m/6km SE of Stow-on-the-Wold. SP 2422
Bledlow Bucks 18 C2 vil 2m/3km SW of Princes Risborough. Site of Roman bldg 1km SW. SP 7702
Bledlow Ridge Bucks 18 C2 vil 5m/8km NW of High Wycombe. SU 7997
Bleet Wilts 16 D5* ham 3m/4km E of Trowbridge. ST 8958
Blelham Tarn Cumbria 52 D5* lake (NT) 2m/3km NE of Hawkshead. NY 3600
Blencarn Cumbria 53 F2 vil 2m/3km NW of Milburn. NY 6331
Blencathra Cumbria 52 C2 mt in Lake Dist 4m/7km NE of Keswick. Height 2847 ft or 868 metres. Also known as Saddleback. NY 3227
Blencogo Cumbria 52 B1/C1 vil 4m/6km W of Wigton. NY 1948
Blencow, Great Cumbria 52 D2 ham 4m/6km NW of Penrith. **Lit Blencow** ham adjoining to NW. NY 4532
Blendworth Hants 10 D3 vil 1km NE of Horndean. SU 7113
Bleng 52 B4 r rising in Cumbrian Mts 2m/4km S of head of Ennerdale Water, Cumbria, and flowing SW to Wellington, near Gosforth, then E into R Irt NW of Santon Br. NY 1003
Blenheim Oxon 27 H6 par to S and W of Woodstock, containing **B. Palace,** huge hse built by Vanbrugh for Duke of Marlborough, early 18c, in large park with lake. SP 4416
Blenkinsopp Castle Nthmb 60 C5 mainly 19c hse incorporating fragments of 14c cas. NY 6664
Blennerhasset Cumbria 52 B1 ham 2m/3km E of Aspatria. NY 1741
Blestium Gwent. See Monmouth.
Bletchingdon Oxon 28 A5 vil 7m/11km N of Oxford. SP 5017
Bletchingley Surrey 19 G6 vil 3m/5km E of Redhill. Site of Roman bldg 1m N. TQ 3250
Bletchley Bucks 28 D4 tn at S end of Milton Keynes, 43m/70km NW of London. Brick works. Light engineering and various industries. SP 8733
Bletchley Salop 34 C1 ham 4m/6km W of Mkt Drayton. SJ 6233
Bletchley, Far Bucks 28 D4* W dist of Bletchley. SP 8533
Bletherston (Trefelen) Dyfed 22 C4 ham 5m/8km NW of Narberth. SN 0621
Bletsoe Beds 29 E2 vil 6m/9km N of Bedford. Site of Roman bldg to W. Remains of original cas moat E of ch. TL 0258
Blewbury Oxon 18 A3 vil 3m/5km S of Didcot. Prehistoric fort to E. SU 5385
Blickling Norfolk 39 F2 vil 2km NW of Aylsham. **B. Hall** (NT), mainly 17c hse in large grnds. TG 1728
Blidworth Notts 44 B5 coal-mining vil 5m/7km SE of Mansfield. **B. Bottoms** ham 1m S. SK 5956
Blindcrake Cumbria 52 B2 vil 3m/5km NE of Cockermouth. NY 1434
Blindley Heath Surrey 12 A2 vil 5m/8km N of E Grinstead. TQ 3645
Blindman's Bay S'clyde 63 F2 bay on W side of Kyles of Bute 2km N of Ardlamont Pt, Argyll. NR 9965
Blisland Cornwall 3 F1 moorland vil 4m/7km NE of Bodmin. SX 1073
Blissford Hants 9 H3* loc on edge of New Forest 2m/3km E of Fordingbridge. SU 1713
Bliss Gate H & W 26 C1 ham 3m/5km SW of Bewdley. SO 7472
Blisworth Northants 28 C2/C3 vil at N end of long tunnel on Grand Union Canal 4m/6km NE of Towcester. SP 7253
Blithbury Staffs 35 G3 ham 3m/4km NE of Rugeley. SK 0820
Blithe 35 G3 r rising E of Stoke-on-Trent, Staffs, and flowing SE through Blithfield Resr and into R Trent 1km NW of King's Bromley. SK 1117
Blithfield Staffs 35 F2 loc 4m/6km N of Rugeley. **B. Hall,** seat of Bagots since 1086. **Blithfield Resr,** large resr to E. SK 0424
Blitterlees Cumbria 59 F6 loc adjoining Silloth to S. NY 1052
Blockley Glos 27 F4 vil 3m/5km NW of Moreton-in-Marsh. SP 1635
Blofield Norfolk 39 G4 vil 7m/11km E of Norwich. TG 3309
Blo' Norton Norfolk 31 E1 vil 7m/11km W of Diss. TM 0179
Bloomfield W Midlands 35 F5* loc in W part of W Bromwich. SO 9593
Bloomsbury London 19 G3* dist of Central London in borough of Camden about 1m N of Charing Cross. Contains London University bldgs and British Museum. TQ 2982
Blore Staffs 43 F6 ham 3m/5km NW of Ashbourne. SK 1349
Blount's Green Staffs 35 G2 loc 1m SW of Uttoxeter. SK 0832
Blowick Merseyside 47 E6 loc in Southport 2m/3km E of tn centre. SD 3616
Blowing Sands Lancs 46 D5* loc in Blackpool 2m/4km SE of tn centre. SD 3232
Blowup Nose Grampian 77 H1/H2* headland on E coast between Hare Ness and Findon Ness, 5m/8km S of Aberdeen. NO 9498
Bloxham Oxon 27 H4 vil 4m/6km SW of Banbury. SP 4235
Bloxholm Lincs 45 E5 ham 5m/8km N of Sleaford. TF 0653

Bloxwich W Midlands 35 F4 dist of Walsall 3m/4km NW of tn centre. **Lit Bloxwich** loc adjoining to NE. SJ 9902
Bloxworth Dorset 9 F4 vil 2m/4km E of Bere Regis. 1km E, loc of **E Bloxworth.** SY 8894
Blubberhouses N Yorks 48 D3 ham 7m/11km N of Otley. SE 1655
Blue Anchor Som 7 G1 ham on coast (**Blue Anchor Bay**), 2m/4km W of Watchet. More bldgs located at former rly stn to W. ST 0343
Blue Anchor W Glam 23 G6* vil 7m/11km W of Swansea. SS 5495
Blue Bell Hill Kent 20 D5 vil 4m/6km S of Rochester. TQ 7462
Blue John Mine Derbys 43 F3* cavern 2km W of Castleton, containing deposits of amethystine spar or *bleu-jaune.* SK 1382
Blue Lins Brook 33 G6* stream running E into R Ithon 2m/3km N of Llanbadarn Fynydd. SO 0880
Blue Mull Shetland 89 F5 headland on W coast of Unst, at N end of **Bluemull Sound,** strait separating Unst and Yell. HP 5504
Blundellsands Merseyside 41 H2 NW dist of Crosby. SJ 3099
Blundeston Suffolk 39 H5 vil 4m/6km NW of Lowestoft. TM 5197
Blunham Beds 29 F3 vil 2m/3km NW of Sandy. TL 1551
Blunsdon St Andrew Wilts 17 F3 vil 4m/6km N of Swindon. SU 1389
Bluntington H & W 26 D1* vil 4m/7km E of Kidderminster. SO 8974
Bluntisham Cambs 37 H6 vil 7m/12km S of Chatteris. TL 3674
Blunts Cornwall 3 H2 loc 6m/10km E of Liskeard. SX 3462
Blurton Staffs 35 E1 loc in Stoke-on-Trent SW of Longton. SJ 8941
Blyborough Lincs 44 D2 ham 3m/5km S of Kirton in Lindsey. SK 9394
Blyford Suffolk 31 H1 ham 3m/4km E of Halesworth. TM 4276
Blymhill Staffs 35 E3 vil 6m/10km SE of Newport. **B. Common** loc 2km W. **B. Lawn** loc 1m SE. SJ 8012
Blyth Notts 44 B3 vil in loop of R Ryton 6m/10km NW of E Retford. Ch, mainly Norman, incorporates remains of former priory. SK 6287
Blyth Nthmb 61 G3 port and resort on North Sea coast at mouth of R Blyth 8m/13km N of Tynemouth. Coal-mining area. **N Blyth** loc across r to N. NZ 3181
Blyth 31 H1 r rising near Laxfield, Suffolk, and flowing E through Blythburgh into North Sea between Southwold and Walberswick. Tidal to a point 1km below Blyford. TM 5074
Blyth 35 H5 r rising at Shirley Heath, Solihull, W Midlands, and flowing into R Cole at B. End, 2km NE of Coleshill, Warwicks. SP 2191
Blyth 61 G3 r rising W of Kirkheaton, Nthmb, and flowing E across open country to Bedlington and the North Sea at Blyth. NZ 3280
Blyth Bridge Borders 65 G4 vil 6m/10km N of Broughton. NT 1345
Blythburgh Suffolk 31 H1 vil on R Blyth 4m/6km W of Southwold. TM 4575
Blythe Bridge Staffs 35 F1 loc 5m/9km SE of Stoke-on-Trent. SJ 9541
Blythebridge Staffs 35 F2* loc 4m/7km SW of Uttoxeter. SK 0428
Blythe End Warwicks 35 H5* loc 2m/3km NE of Coleshill. **Blythe Hall** is a 17c hse, re-fronted 18c. SP 2190
Blythe Marsh Staffs 35 F1 loc 4m/6km SW of Cheadle. SJ 9641
Blyth Valley 117 admin dist of Nthmb.
Blyton Lincs 44 C2 vil 4m/7km NE of Gainsborough. SK 8594
Boardhouse, Loch of Orkney 89 A6* large loch in NW Mainland 2m/3km SE of Brough Hd. Named after locality at its NW end. HY 2625
Boarhills Fife 73 H3 vil 4m/7km SE of St Andrews. NO 5714
Boarhunt Hants 10 C4 ham 2m/3km NE of Fareham. SU 6008
Boarhunt, North Hants 10 C4 vil 2m/3km SE of Wickham. SU 6010
Boar of Badenoch 75 F3/F4 mt on border of Highland and Tayside regions on W side of Pass of Drumochter, qv, and 6m/9km S of Dalwhinnie. Height 2422 ft or 738 metres. NN 6276
Boarsgreave Lancs 48 B6* loc 2m/3km SE of Rawtenstall. SD 8320
Boarshead E Sussex 12 B3 loc 2m/3km NE of Crowborough. TQ 5332
Boar's Head Gtr Manchester 42 B1* loc 2m/3km N of Wigan. SD 5708
Boars Hill Oxon 18 A2 loc 3m/5km SW of Oxford. SP 4802
Boars of Duncansby 86 F1 sea passage between Island of Stroma and Ness of Duncansby on N coast of Caithness dist, H'land. ND 3775
Boarstall Bucks 28 B6 ham 6m/9km SE of Bicester. SP 6214
Boath of Toft Shetland. See Toft.
Boat of Garten H'land 81 H5 vil on R Spey in Badenoch and Strathspey dist, 5m/8km NE of Aviemore. NH 9418
Boat, Upper (Glan-bad) Mid Glam 15 F3 loc 3m/5km SE of Pontypridd. ST 1087
Bobbing Kent 21 E5 vil 2km NW of Sittingbourne. TQ 8865
Bobbington Staffs 35 E5 vil 6m/10km E of Bridgnorth. SO 8090
Bobbingworth Essex 20 B2 loc 2m/3km NW of Chipping Ongar. TL 5305
Bobby Hill Suffolk 31 E1 loc adjoining Wattisfield to N. TM 0074
Boblainy Forest H'land 81 E4* state forest and deer forest in Inverness dist 6m/10km S of Beauly. NH 4837
Bocaddon Cornwall 3 F3* loc 6m/9km NW of Looe. SX 1758
Bockhampton Dorset 9 H4* locs of **Middle, N,** and **S Bockhampton,** about 3m/4km NE of Bournemouth. SZ 1796
Bockhampton, Higher Dorset 9 E5* ham 2m/4km NE of Dorchester. Birthplace, in small thatched hse (NT), of Thomas Hardy, 1840. ST 7292
Bockhampton, Lower Dorset 9 E5 loc beside R Frome 2m/4km E of Dorchester. SY 7290
Bocking Essex 30 C5 NW part of Braintree. For administrative purposes the two places are treated as one place referred to as Braintree and Bocking. TL 7523
Bocking Churchstreet Essex 30 C5 suburban loc adjoining Braintree to N. TL 7525
Bockleton H & W 26 B2 loc 4m/7km S of Tenbury Wells. SO 5961
Bockmer End Bucks 18 C3* loc 3m/4km W of Marlow. SU 8186
Boconnoc Cornwall 3 F2 loc 3m/4km E of Lostwithiel. SX 1460
Bodach Mór H'land 85 D7 mt in Freevater Forest, Sutherland dist, 7m/11km W of head of Strath Carron. Height 2689 ft or 820 metres. NH 3689
Boddam Grampian 83 H3 fishing vil on E coast 2m/4km S of Peterhead. **B. Castle** is ruin to S. NK 1342
Boddam Shetland 89 E8 loc at head of inlet on E coast of Mainland 5m/8km N of Sumburgh Hd. HU 3915
Boddam, Upper Grampian 83 E4* loc 1m SE of Largie and 8m/13km SE of Huntly. NJ 6230
Bodden Som 16 B6* loc 2km E of Shepton Mallet. ST 6444
Boddington Glos 26 D5* vil 4m/6km NW of Cheltenham. SO 8925
Boddington, Lower Northants 28 A3 vil 8m/12km N of Banbury. SP 4852
Boddington, Upper Northants 28 A2 vil 8m/13km N of Banbury. SP 4853
Boddin Point Tayside 77 G5 headland on E coast at N end of Lunan Bay 3m/5km S of Montrose. NO 7153
Bodedern Gwynedd 40 A3 vil on Anglesey 3m/4km E of Valley. SH 3380
Bodelwyddan Clwyd 41 F4 vil 2m/4km W of St Asaph. 19c ch has arcades of marble. SJ 0075
Bodendun Hill Tayside 76 C4 mt to E of Glen Isla 5m/8km N of Kirkton of Glenisla. Height 2429 ft or 740 metres. NO 2067
Bodenham H & W 26 A3 vil 7m/11km N of Hereford. Vil of **B. Moor** 1m SE. SO 5351
Bodenham Wilts 9 H2 vil on R Avon 3m/5km SE of Salisbury. SU 1626
Bodewryd Gwynedd 40 B3 ham on Anglesey 3m/4km SE of Cemaes. SH 3990
Bodfari Clwyd 41 G4 vil 4m/6km NE of Denbigh. SJ 0970
Bodffordd Gwynedd 40 B4 vil at W end of Cefni Resr, Anglesey, and 2m/4km W of Llangefni. SH 4276
Bodfuan Gwynedd 32 B1 ham 4m/6km NW of Pwllheli. SH 3237
Bodham Street Norfolk 39 E1/F1 vil 3m/5km E of Holt. TG 1240
Bodiam E Sussex 12 D4 vil 2m/3km SW of Sandhurst. **B. Castle** (NT), 14c moated cas on rising ground above R Rother valley. TQ 7825
Bodicote Oxon 27 H4 vil 2m/3km S of Banbury. SP 4637
Bodieve Cornwall 3 E1* loc 1km N of Wadebridge. SW 9973
Bodinnick Cornwall 3 F3 vil on R Fowey connected with tn of Fowey by car ferry. SX 1352
Bodle Street Green E Sussex 12 C5 vil 5m/8km NE of Hailsham. TQ 6514
Bodmin Cornwall 3 F2 old county tn below SW edge of B. Moor, 26m/42km W of Plymouth. **B. Moor** is a large expanse of granite moorland attaining a height of 1375 ft or 419 metres at Brown Willy. SX 0767
Bodnant Gardens Gwynedd. See Graig.
Bodney Norfolk 38 C4 loc 4m/6km NE of Mundford. **B. Camp** 2km E. TL 8398
Bodorgan Gwynedd 40 B4* loc on Anglesey on W side of R Cefni estuary, 2km S of Llangadwaladr. SH 3867
Bodorgan Gwynedd 40 B4* loc on Anglesey beside rly 4m/6km S of Gwalchmai. SH 3870
Bodowyr Burial-chamber Gwynedd. See Llanidan.
Bodrane Cornwall 3 G2* loc 3m/5km SW of Liskeard. SX 2061
Bodsham Green Kent 13 F3 ham 6m/10km E of Ashford. TR 1045
Bodwen Cornwall 3 E2* ham 5m/8km N of St Austell. SX 0360
Bodymoor Heath Warwicks 35 G4* loc 5m/7km N of Coleshill. SP 1996
Bogany Point S'clyde 63 G2 headland on E coast of Bute, at E end of Rothesay Bay. NS 1065
Bogha-cloiche H'land 75 G3 mt on Gaick Forest, in Badenoch and Strathspey dist, 7m/11km E of Dalwhinnie. Height 2945 ft or 898 metres. NN 7486
Boghall Lothian 65 F2* loc 2km E of Bathgate. NS 9968
Boghall Castle S'clyde. See Biggar.
Boghead S'clyde 65 E4 loc 1m SW of Kirkmuirhill. NS 7741
Bogie 82 D3 r in Grampian region rising on E side of The Buck and running NE to Rhynie and N to R Deveron 1m NE of Huntly. NJ 5341
Bognor, Little W Sussex 11 F3 ham 2m/3km SE of Petworth. TQ 0020
Bognor Regis W Sussex 11 F5 seaside resort 6m/10km SE of Chichester. SZ 9399
Bog, The Salop 34 B4 loc 6m/10km N of Bishop's Castle. SO 3597
Bogthorn W Yorks 48 C4* loc 2m/3km SW of Keighley. SE 0439
Bogton Loch S'clyde 56 E3 small loch in course of R Doon 1m W of Dalmellington. NS 4605
Bohemia Wilts 9 H2* loc 5m/9km NE of Fordingbridge. SU 2019
Bohetherick Cornwall 4 B4* loc above R Tamar 4m/6km SE of Callington. SX 4167
Bohortha Cornwall 2 D5* ham 2m/4km SW of Porthscatho. SW 8632
Bohuntine H'land 74 D3* loc in Lochaber dist, 2m/3km NE of Roy Br. NN 2883
Boisdale, North W Isles 88 E3* vil on S Uist 2m/3km S of Daliburgh. **S Boisdale** vil 1m SE. NF 7418
Bojewyan Cornwall 2 A5* loc 2m/4km NE of St Just. SW 3934
Bokiddick Cornwall 3 E2* loc 3m/5km S of Bodmin. SX 0562
Bolam Durham 54 B3 vil 4m/7km S of Bishop Auckland. NZ 1922
Bolam Nthmb 61 F3 loc 3m/4km N of Belsay. **B. Lake** 1m SW. NZ 0982
Bolas, Great Salop 34 D2 vil 6m/10km N of Wellington. **Bolas, Little** loc 1km NW across R Tern. SJ 6421
Bolberry Devon 4 D6 loc 3m/5km W of Salcombe. SX 6939
Bolder Mere Surrey 19 E5* lake beside A3 rd 2m/3km NE of Ripley. TQ 0758
Bold Heath Merseyside 42 B3* loc 3m/5km NE of Widnes. SJ 5389
Boldmere W Midlands 35 G5 S dist of Sutton Coldfield. SP 1194
Boldon Tyne & Wear 61 H5 coal-mining tn in S Tyneside dist between S Shields and Sunderland, consisting of **E** and **W Boldon. B. Colliery** to W. NZ 3561
Boldre Hants 10 A5 vil 2m/3km N of Lymington. SZ 3298
Boldre, East Hants 10 B4 vil 2km SW of Beaulieu. SU 3700
Boldron Durham 54 A3 ham 2m/3km SW of Barnard Castle. NZ 0314
Bole Notts 44 C3 vil 2m/3km S of Beckingham. SK 7987
Bolehall Staffs 35 H4* loc in Tamworth 1km E of tn centre. SK 2103
Bolehill Derbys 43 G5 vil 1km NE of Wirksworth. SK 2955
Bolehill S Yorks 43 H3* loc in Norton Woodseats dist of Sheffield 3m/5km S of city centre. SK 3582
Bolenowe Cornwall 2 C4* loc 2m/3km SE of Camborne. SW 6737
Bolesbridge Water 6 B6* stream in Cornwall rising 3m/4km S of Whitstone and flowing S into R Ottery 3m/5km NW of Launceston. SX 2987
Bolham Devon 7 G4 ham 2m/3km N of Tiverton. SS 9514
Bolham Notts 44 B3* loc adjoining E Retford to N. SK 7082
Bolham Water Devon 8 A3* ham 6m/10km SE of Wellington. ST 1612
Bolingey Cornwall 2 C3* vil on SE side of Perranporth. SW 7653
Bollihope Burn 53 H3* r rising on Bollihope Common, SW of Stanhope, Durham, and flowing E into R Wear 1m E of Frosterley. NZ 0336
Bollin 42 C3 r rising 3m/5km SE of Macclesfield, Ches, and flowing NW through Macclesfield and Wilmslow into R Mersey 5m/8km E of Warrington. SJ 6888
Bollington Ches 42 C3 vil 3m/5km E of Lymm. SJ 7286
Bollington Ches 43 E3 tn 3m/4km NE of Macclesfield. **B. Cross** loc adjoining to SW. SJ 9377
Bolney W Sussex 11 H3 vil 3m/5km W of Cuckfield. TQ 2622
Bolnhurst Beds 29 E2 vil 7m/11km NE of Bedford. TL 0859
Bolsover Derbys 44 A4 tn 6m/9km E of Chesterfield. Industries include coal-mining, chemical products, oil refining. Cas (A.M.), Norman, rebuilt in 17c. **B. Woodhouse** loc 2km NW. See also New Bolsover. SK 4770
Bolster Moor W Yorks 48 D6* loc 1m N of Slaithwaite. SE 0815
Bolsterstone S Yorks 43 G2* vil 1m S of Stocksbridge. SK 2796
Bolstone H & W 26 B4* ham 5m/8km SE of Hereford. SO 5532
Boltby N Yorks 54 D6 vil 5m/8km NE of Thirsk. SE 4986
Bolter End Bucks 18 C2 loc 4m/7km W of High Wycombe. SU 7992
Bolt Head Devon 4 D6 headland at mouth of Kingsbridge Estuary 2m/3km S of Salcombe. Cliffs from here to Bolt Tail are NT property. SX 7235
Bolton Cumbria 53 F3 vil 4m/6km NW of Appleby. NY 6323
Bolton Gtr Manchester 42 C1 tn on R Croal 10m/17km NW of Manchester. Textiles, aero-engineering, tanning. SD 7109
Bolton Humberside 50 C3 ham 4m/7km SE of Stamford Br. SE 7752
Bolton Lothian 66 C2 vil 3m/4km S of Haddington. NT 5070
Bolton Nthmb 67 G6 ham 5m/8km W of Alnwick. NU 1013
Bolton W Yorks 48 D4* dist of Bradford 2km N of city centre. SE 1735
Bolton Abbey N Yorks 48 D3 ham 5m/8km NW of Ilkley. **Bolton Priory,** remains of 12c priory beside R Wharfe. **Bolton Hall** consists of priory gatehouse of 14c with later additions. SE 0753
Bolton by Bowland Lancs vil 3m/5km W of Gisburn. SD 7849
Boltonfellhead Cumbria 60 A4 ham 6m/9km NW of Brampton. NY 4768
Boltongate Cumbria 52 C1 ham 5m/8km S of Wigton. NY 2240
Bolton Green Lancs 47 F6* loc 2m/3km W of Chorley. SD 5517
Bolton Houses Lancs 47 E4* loc just N of Treales. SD 4433
Bolton-le-Sands Lancs 47 F2 tn 4m/7km N of Lancaster. SD 4867
Bolton, Little Gtr Manchester 42 D2* loc in Salford 3m/4km W of tn centre. SJ 7898
Bolton Low Houses Cumbria 52 C1 ham 3m/5km SW of Wigton. NY 2344
Bolton New Houses Cumbria 52 C1* loc 3m/4km S of Wigton. NY 2444
Bolton-on-Swale N Yorks 54 B5 vil 5m/8km E of Richmond. SE 2599
Bolton Percy N Yorks 49 G4 vil 3m/5km SE of Tadcaster. SE 5341
Bolton Town End Lancs 47 E2/F2 loc adjoining Bolton-le-Sands to S. SD 4867

Bolton upon Dearne S Yorks 43 H1 colliery tn 2m/4km NW of Mexborough. SE 4502
Boltonwood Lane Cumbria 52 C1* loc 3m/4km S of Wigton. NY 2544
Bolton Woods W Yorks 48 D4* loc in Bradford 2m/3km N of city centre. SE 1536
Bolt Tail Devon 4 C6 headland at SE end of Bigbury Bay, 5m/7km W of Salcombe. Cliffs from here to Bolt Hd are NT property. SX 6639
Bolventor Cornwall 3 F1 vil on Bodmin Moor 9m/15km NE of Bodmin. SX 1876
Bomarsund Nthmb 61 G3* loc 2m/3km S of Ashington. NZ 2784
Bomby Cumbria 53 E3* loc 1km SE of Bampton. NY 5217
Bomere Heath Salop 34 B3 vil 5m/7km N of Shrewsbury. SJ 4719
Bomere Pool Salop 34 B3/C3 lake 3m/5km S of Shrewsbury. SJ 4908
Bonahaven S'clyde 62 B1 vil on bay of same name on NE coast of Islay, 3m/4km N of Port Askaig. Distillery. Gaelic form: Bunnahabhainn. NR 4273
Bonaly Reservoir Lothian 66 A2 small resr in Edinburgh 6m/9km SW of city centre. NT 2166
Bonar Bridge H'land 85 F7 vil in Sutherland dist at head of Dornoch Firth, 14m/23km W of Dornoch. Rly stn at Ardgay, 1m SW. NH 6191
Bonawe S'clyde 70 C2 locality in Argyll at mouth of R Awe on S side of Loch Etive. On N side is locality of **B. Quarries,** with granite quarries to E. NN 0131
Bonbusk Notts 44 A4* loc 1m SE of Creswell. SK 5373
Bonby Humberside 51 E6 vil 5m/7km SW of Barton-upon-Humber. TA 0015
Boncath Dyfed 22 D2 ham 5m/8km S of Cardigan. SN 2038
Bonchester Bridge Borders 60 B1 vil on Rule Water 6m/9km E of Hawick. To E is **Bonchester Hill,** surmounted by ancient earthworks. NT 5812
Bonchurch Isle of Wight 10 C6 loc 1m NE of Ventnor. SZ 5778
Bondend Glos 26 D5* loc 3m/5km SE of Gloucester. SO 8615
Bond End Staffs 35 G3* loc adjoining Yoxall to S. SK 1418
Bondgate N Yorks 50 B4/B5* loc adjoining Selby to NW. SE 6033
Bondleigh Devon 7 E4 vil 3m/4km SE of Winkleigh. SS 6504
Bonds Lancs 47 F4* ham adjoining Garstang to SE. SD 4944
Bond's Green H & W 25 H3* loc 4m/7km E of Kington. SO 3654
Bonehill Staffs 35 G4 loc 2km SW of Tamworth. SK 1902
Bo'ness Central 65 F1 tn on S side of Firth of Forth 17m/27km W of Edinburgh. Name contracted from Borrowstounness. Kinneil Hse, 1m SW, is 16c-17c mansion. NS 9981
Boney Hay Staffs 35 F3 loc 3m/5km N of Brownhills. SK 0510
Bonfire Hill Dorset 9 H3* loc adjoining Alderholt to NE and 2m/3km SW of Fordingbridge. SU 1213
Bonhill S'clyde 64 B1 tn on E bank of R Leven 3m/5km N of Dumbarton. NS 3979
Boningale Salop 35 E4 vil 5m/8km SE of Shifnal. SJ 8102
Bonjedward Borders 66 D6 loc 2m/3km N of Jedburgh. NT 6523
Bonkle S'clyde 65 E3 vil 3m/5km NE of Wishaw. NS 8356
Bonner's Cottages Norfolk. See Dereham, East.
Bonning Gate Cumbria 53 E5* loc 3m/4km NW of Kendal. SD 4895
Bonnington Kent 13 F3* vil 5m/8km SE of Ashford. TR 0535
Bonnington Lothian 65 G2* loc 2km SW of Ratho. NT 1269
Bonnington Linn S'clyde 65 F4 waterfall on R Clyde 2m/3km S of Lanark. NS 8840
Bonnybank Fife 73 F4 loc 1m NE of Kennoway. NO 3503
Bonnybridge Central 65 E1 industrial loc on Bonny Water 4m/6km W of Falkirk. To E is well-preserved section of Antonine Wall, with Roman fort of Rough Castle (NTS). **High B.** is loc to SE across rly. NS 8280
Bonnykelly Grampian 83 G2 loc 2m/3km SW of New Pitsligo. NJ 8653
Bonnyrigg Lothian 66 B2 tn 2m/3km SW of Dalkeith. Industries include mnfre of carpets, industrial overalls, kitchen equipment. NT 3065
Bonnyton S'clyde 64 B5* W dist of Kilmarnock. NS 4138
Bonny Water 65 E1 stream in Central region running E through Bonnybridge to R Carron, 3m/5km W of Falkirk. NS 8481
Bonsall Derbys 43 G5 vil 2m/3km SW of Matlock. SK 2758
Bontddu Gwynedd 32 D3 loc 4m/6km NE of Barmouth. SH 6618
Bont Dolgadfan Powys 33 F4* ham on R Twymyn 5m/8km N of head of Clywedog Resr. SH 8800
Bont-faen, Y Welsh form of Cowbridge, qv; also of Pontfaen, qv.
Bontgoch Dyfed. Alternative name of Elerch, qv.
Bonthorpe Lincs 45 H4* loc 1m NE of Willoughby. TF 4872
Bont-newydd Clwyd 41 F4* loc at rd br across R Elwy 2m/3km E of Llannefydd. SJ 0170
Bontnewydd Dyfed 24 B2* ham 4m/6km S of Llangwyryfon and 1m SE of Llyn Eiddwen. SN 6165
Bontnewydd Gwynedd 40 B5 vil on R Gwyrfai 2m/3km S of Caernarvon. SH 4859
Bontuchel Clwyd 41 G5 ham on R Clywedog 3m/4km W of Ruthin. SJ 0857
Bonvilston (Tresimwn) S Glam 15 F4 vil 4m/7km E of Cowbridge. ST 0674
Bon-y-maen W Glam 23 H5/H6 loc in Swansea 2m/3km NE of tn centre across R Tawe. SS 6795
Boode Devon 6 D2* ham 5m/7km NW of Barnstaple. SS 5038
Booker Bucks 18 D3 SW dist of High Wycombe. SU 8391
Bookham, Great Surrey 19 E6 suburban loc 2m/3km SW of Leatherhead. To N, **Gt B. Common** (NT). TQ 1354
Bookham, Little Surrey 19 E6 suburban loc 3m/5km W of Leatherhead. TQ 1254
Boon Hill Staffs 42 D6* loc 1km E of Audley. SJ 8150
Boorley Green Hants 10 C3* loc 1km N of Botley. SU 5014
Boosbeck Cleveland 55 E3 vil 3m/5km S of Saltburn. NZ 6516
Boose's Green Essex 30 C5* ham 2m/3km E of Halstead. TL 8430
Boot Cumbria 52 B4 ham 6m/10km NE of Ravenglass. NY 1701
Booth Humberside 50 C5 ham on N bank of R Ouse 2m/3km N of Goole. **Boothferry Br** here carries A614 rd over r. SE 7326
Booth W Yorks 48 C5* ham 2m/3km NE of Mytholmroyd. SE 0427
Booth Bank W Yorks 48 C6/D6* loc 2km SW of Slaithwaite. SE 0613
Boothby Graffoe Lincs 44 D5 vil 8m/12km S of Lincoln. SK 9859
Boothby Pagnell Lincs 37 E2 vil 5m/7km SE of Grantham. Moated Norman manor hse in grnds of hall. SK 9730
Boothen Staffs 35 E1 dist of Stoke-on-Trent 1km S of city centre. SJ 8744
Boothgate Derbys 43 H6* loc 1km S of Heage. SK 3749
Booth Green Ches 43 E3* loc 2km S of Poynton. SJ 9281
Boothlane Head Ches 42 C5 loc 2km W of Sandbach. SJ 7361
Boothorpe Leics 35 H3* loc 2m/4km W of Ashby de la Zouch. SK 3117
Boothroyd W Yorks 49 E5* dist of Dewsbury 1m W of tn centre. SE 2321
Booths Mere Ches 42 D3* small lake 1m E of Knutsford. SJ 7578
Boothstown Gtr Manchester 42 C2 loc 2m/3km SE of Tyldesley. SD 7100
Boothtown W Yorks 48 D5 loc in Halifax 1m N of tn centre. SE 0826
Boothville Northants 28 C2* loc in NE part of Northampton. Site of Roman bldg. Also known as Buttock's Booth. SP 7864
Booth Wood W Yorks 48 C6 loc 2m/3km S of Ripponden. **Booth Wood Resr,** narrow resr between M62 motorway and A672 rd 1km SW. SE 0316
Bootle Cumbria 52 B6 vil 7m/11km NW of Millom. SD 1088
Bootle Merseyside 41 H2 tn on R Mersey estuary adjoining Liverpool to N. Docks and general industry. Large tin plant. SJ 3494
Booton Norfolk 39 E3 loc 2km E of Reepham. B. Street loc 1km W. TG 1222
Boots Green Ches 42 C4* loc 3m/5km N of Holmes Chapel. SJ 7572
Boot Street Suffolk 31 F3* loc adjoining Gt Bealings to W, 3m/5km W of Woodbridge. TM 2248
Booze N Yorks 54 A4* loc 1km E of Langthwaite. NZ 0102
Boquhan Burn 72 B5 stream in Central region, rising on Fintry Hills and running N into R Forth 2km NE of Kippen. NS 6696
Boraston Salop 26 B1 vil 2m/3km NE of Tenbury Wells. SO 6170
Borden Kent 21 E5 vil 2m/3km W of Sittingbourne. TQ 8862
Borden W Sussex 11 E3* loc 4m/7km NW of Midhurst. SU 8224
Border Cumbria 59 F5* loc 4m/6km E of Silloth. NY 1654
Border Forest Park 60 large area of hills and conifer forests covering parts of Cumbria and Northumberland in England, and of Borders and Dumfries & Galloway regions in Scotland. NY
Borders 115–117 admin region of SE Scotland, comprising the former counties of Berwick, Peebles, Roxburgh, Selkirk, and part of Midlothian. It extends from the Tweedsmuir Hills in the W to the North Sea on either side of St Abb's Hd in the E, and from the Pentland, Moorfoot and Lammermuir Hills in the N to the Cheviots and the English border in the S. R Tweed rises in the extreme W and flows between the N and S ranges of hills, forming the border with England from between Kelso and Coldstream, and finally passing into England 4m/6km W of Berwick-upon-Tweed. The fertile area of rich farmland between the hills to N and S is known as The Merse. The area around Peebles and Galashiels is noted for woollen mnfre.
Bordesley H & W 27 E1* N dist of Redditch. SP 0469
Bordesley Green W Midlands 35 G5* loc in Birmingham 2m/4km E of city centre. SP 1086
Bordley N Yorks 48 C2* loc 3m/5km W of Threshfield. SD 9464
Bordon Hants 11 E2* loc adjoining B. Camp to SE, 5m/9km W of Hindhead. SU 8035
Bordon Camp Hants 11 E2 military camp 6m/9km W of Hindhead. SU 7936
Boreham Essex 20 D1 vil 4m/6km NE of Chelmsford. TL 7509
Boreham Wilts 16 D6 vil 2km SE of Warminster. ST 8844
Boreham Street E Sussex 12 C5 vil 5m/8km NW of Bexhill. TQ 6611
Borehamwood Herts 19 F2 suburb 3m/4km N of Edgware. Film studios. TQ 1996
Boreland D & G 59 F2/F3 vil 6m/10km N of Lockerbie. NY 1791
Boreley H & W 26 D1* loc 4m/7km S of Stourport. SO 8265
Boreraig Skye, H'land 78 A4 locality on W shore of Loch Dunvegan, 2m/3km S of Dunvegan Hd. NG 1853
Boreraig Skye, H'land 79 D6* locality on N shore of Loch Eishort, 2m/3km E of Rubha Suisnish. NG 6116
Boreray W Isles (W of 88 A3) rocky island (NTS) with steep cliffs about 52m/83km W of Harris. One of the St Kilda group. Area about 190 acres or 77 hectares. Haunt of sea birds. See also Stac an Armin and Stac Lee. NA 1505
Boreray W Isles 88 E1 uninhabited island off N coast of N Uist. Measures 2km by 1km. NF 8581
Borestone Brae Central 72 B5* loc 2km S of Stirling. Site of Bannockburn Monmt (NTS), including rotunda, and equestrian statue of Robert the Bruce. See Bannock Burn. NS 7990
Boretree Tarn Cumbria 52 D6* small lake 2km NW of Newby Br. SD 3587
Borgadelmore Point S'clyde 62 D6 headland on S coast of Kintyre 2m/3km E of Mull of Kintyre. NR 6305
Borgie H'land 84 F2 r in Caithness dist running NE through Lochs Loyal and Craggie to Torrisdale Bay on N coast. NC 6862
Borgie Forest H'land 84 F2* afforested area astride R Borgie 3m/5km S of Torrisdale Bay, N coast of Caithness dist. **Borgie Br** carries A836 rd over r at N end of forest. NC 65
Borgue D & G 58 C6 vil 4m/6km SW of Kirkcudbright. Scene of R.L. Stevenson's *Master of Ballantrae.* NX 6348
Borgue H'land 86 D4 loc near E coast of Caithness dist 3m/5km SW of Dunbeath. ND 1325
Borle Brook 34 D6* r rising 4m/7km W of Bridgnorth, Salop, and flowing SE into R Severn 6m/10km NW of Kidderminster, H & W. SO 7581
Borley Essex 30 D4 ham 2m/3km NW of Sudbury. Ham of **B. Green** 1km W. TL 8443
Borley Green Suffolk 31 E2* loc 4m/6km NW of Stowmarket. TL 9960
Bornaskitaig Skye, H'land 78 B3 loc on N coast, inland from Ru Bornaskitaig and 5m/8km N of Uig. NG 3771
Bornish W Isles 88 D2* locality on S Uist on N side of **Loch B.,** 2km E of Rubha Ardvule. NF 7329
Borough London 19 G4* dist in borough of Southwark on S side of R Thames between Southwark and London Brs. On E side of High Street, George Inn (NT), only remaining galleried inn in London, built in 1677. TQ 3279
Boroughbridge N Yorks 49 F2 small tn on S bank of R Ure 6m/10km SE of Ripon. On E side of tn are The Devil's Arrows, three monoliths, probably Neolithic. SE 3966
Borough Green Kent 20 C5 vil 5m/8km E of Sevenoaks. TQ 6057
Borough Head Dyfed 22 B4* headland on S side of St Brides Bay 1km N of Talbenny. SM 8312
Borrans, High Cumbria 52 D4* loc 2m/3km NE of Windermere. **Borrans Resr** is a small resr to W. NY 4300
Borras Head Clwyd 42 A5* loc 3m/4km NE of Wrexham. SJ 3653
Borrobol Forest H'land 86 A4, B4 deer forest in Sutherland dist to SW of Kinbrace. NC 7726
Borrowash Derbys 36 A1 suburb 4m/7km E of Derby. SK 4134
Borrow Beck 53 E4 r rising on Borrowdale Moss, 7m/11km W of Tebay, Cumbria, and flowing SE into R Lune 2m/3km S of Tebay. NY 6101
Borrowby N Yorks 54 D5 vil 5m/7km N of Thirsk. SE 4289
Borrowby N Yorks 55 F3 loc 2m/3km S of Staithes. NZ 7715
Borrowdale Cumbria 52 C3 valley of R Derwent above, or S of, Derwent Water. Loc of same name towards upper end of valley, below **B. Fells,** which rise steeply to S. NY 2514
Borrowstounness Central. See Bo'ness.
Borstal Kent 20 D5 S dist of Rochester. TQ 7366
Borth Dyfed 32 D5 resort on Cardigan Bay 5m/8km N of Aberystwyth. **Upr Borth** coastal locality adjoining to S. SN 6089
Borthwen Gwynedd 40 A4* small bay on S coast of Holy I., Anglesey, to SE of Rhoscolyn. SH 2774
Borthwick Lothian 66 B3 loc 2m/3km SE of Gorebridge. **B. Castle** is massive 15c edifice. NT 3659
Borthwick Water 59 H1 r in Borders region running NE along SE side of Craik Forest to Roberton, then E to R Teviot 2m/3km SW of Hawick. NT 4713
Borth-y-gest Gwynedd 32 D1 small resort on R Glaslyn estuary 1m S of Portmadoc. SH 5637
Borve W Isles 88 A4* vil on SE coast of island of Berneray in the Sound of Harris. NF 9281
Borve W Isles 88 B1* r in N part of Lewis running NW into Atlantic Ocean 1km N of High Borve. NB 4057
Borve W Isles 88 D3* vil on Barra 2m/3km N of Castlebay. **Borve Pt** is headland 1m W. Ancient burial ground between. Chambered cairn 2km E. NF 6501
Borve, High W Isles 88 B1 loc near NW coast of Lewis 5m/9km NE of Barvas. See also Five Penny Borve, Melbost Borve. NB 4156
Borvemore W Isles 88 A3 loc on W coast of Harris 5m/7km N of Leverburgh. NG 0294
Borwick Lancs 47 F1 vil 2m/4km NE of Carnforth. Hall has 14c peel tower. SD 5273
Borwick Rails Cumbria 46 C1 loc adjoining Millom to SE. SD 1879
Bosbury H & W 26 C3 vil 4m/6km N of Ledbury. SO 6943

Boscarne Cornwall 3 E2* loc 3m/4km W of Bodmin. SX 0367

Boscastle Cornwall 6 A6 vil 5m/7km N of Camelford. Coast to N is NT. SX 0990

Boscaswell, Higher Cornwall 2 A5* loc 2m/3km NE of St Just. SW 3834

Boscaswell, Lower Cornwall 2 A5 loc near coast 2m/3km N of St Just. SW 3734

Boscobel House Salop 35 E4* early 17c hse (A.M.), preserving hiding-place of Charles II. SJ 8308

Boscombe Dorset 9 H5 seaside dist of Bournemouth, with pier, 2m/3km E of tn centre. SZ 1191

Boscombe Wilts 9 H1 vil on R Bourne just S of Allington and 7m/11km NE of Salisbury. To W, **B. Down Airfield.** SU 2038

Boscoppa Cornwall 3 E3 loc on NE outskirts of St Austell. SX 0353

Bosham W Sussex 11 E4 vil at head of Chichester Harbour (B. Channel), 4m/6km W of Chichester. Yachting centre. SU 8004

Bosham Hoe W Sussex 11 E4* loc on N side of Chichester Channel 2m/3km S of Bosham. SU 8101

Bosherston Dyfed 22 C6 vil 4m/7km S of Pembroke. SR 9694

Bosleake Cornwall 2 C4* loc 2m/3km E of Camborne. SW 6740

Bosley Ches 43 E4 vil 5m/8km S of Macclesfield. **Bosley Resr** to E. SJ 9165

Bosquoy, Loch of Orkney 89 A6* small loch 2km SE of Dounby, Mainland. HY 3018

Bossall N Yorks 50 C2* ham 3m/5km N of Stamford Br. SE 7160

Bossiney Cornwall 6 A6* vil near N coast 4m/7km NW of Camelford. **B. Haven** bay just N of vil. SX 0688

Bossingham Kent 13 G2 vil 6m/9km S of Canterbury. TR 1549

Bossington Hants 10 A2 loc 3m/5km S of Stockbridge. SU 3330

Bossington Som 7 F1 vil near coast, 2km NE of Porlock, below **B. Hill.** SS 8947

Bostock Green Ches 42 C4 ham 3m/5km NW of Middlewich. SJ 6769

Boston Lincs 37 H1 tn and port on R Witham near mouth, 28m/45km SE of Lincoln. Industries include agricultural products, shipping, canning, timber milling. Pilgrim Fathers sailed from here, 1620. Medieval ch has tower known as The Stump, 272 ft or 83 metres high. TF 3244

Boston Spa W Yorks 49 F4 vil 4m/6km W of Tadcaster. SE 4245

Boswarthan Cornwall 2 A5* loc 3m/4km NW of Penzance. SW 4433

Boswinger Cornwall 3 E4 vil above Veryan Bay 3m/5km SW of Mevagissey. SW 9941

Bosworth Field Leics. See Mkt Bosworth.

Botallack Cornwall 2 A5* vil to N of St Just. SW 3632

Botallack Head Cornwall 2 A5* headland 2m/3km N of St Just. SW 3633

Botany Bay Avon 16 B4* N dist of Bristol. ST 5679

Botany Bay Kent 13 H1* bay 2km NW of N Foreland. TR 3971

Botany Bay London 19 G2 vil in borough of Enfield 3m/4km NW of Enfield. TQ 2999

Botcherby Cumbria 60 A5* dist of Carlisle 2km E of city centre. NY 4255

Botcheston Leics 36 B4* loc to W of Leicester 1m N of Desford. SK 4804

Botesdale Suffolk 31 E1 vil adjoining Rickinghall Superior, 5m/8km SW of Diss. TM 0475

Bothal Nthmb 61 G3 vil 3m/4km E of Morpeth. **B. Castle** dates from 14c. NZ 2386

Bothamsall Notts 44 B4 vil 4m/7km NE of Ollerton. Earthwork marks site of former cas. SK 6773

Bothel Cumbria 52 B1 vil 3m/5km SE of Aspatria. NY 1838

Bothenhampton Dorset 8 C5 vil 1m SE of Bridport. SY 4791

Bothwell S'clyde 64 D3 tn 2m/3km NW of Hamilton across R Clyde. Industries include coal, iron and steel. **B. Castle** (A.M.)is ruined cas standing in wds above r. To SE is **B. Bridge,** site of battle of 1679 in which Covenanters were heavily defeated by Monmouth and Claverhouse. NS 7058

Bothwell Castle S'clyde. See Uddingston.

Botley Bucks 18 D2* vil 2km E of Chesham. SP 9802

Botley Hants 10 C3 small tn on R Hamble 6m/10km E of Southampton. To S, Steeple Court, 17c hse. SU 5113

Botley Oxon 18 H1 suburb 2m/3km W of Oxford. Loc of **B. Pound** adjoins to W. SP 4806

Botloe's Green Glos 26 C4 ham 2m/3km N of Newent. SO 7228

Botolph Claydon Bucks 28 C5 vil 3m/5km SW of Winslow. SP 7324

Botolph's Bridge Kent 13 F4* loc 3m/4km W of Hythe. TR 1233

Bottesford Humberside 44 D1 vil 2m/4km S of Scunthorpe. SE 8907

Bottesford Leics 36 D1 vil 7m/11km W of Grantham. SK 8038

Bottisham Cambs 30 A2 vil 6m/10km E of Cambridge. TL 5460

Bottle Island H'land 85 A6 small island in group known as the Summer Isles, qv. Lies 1m SW of Eilean Dubh. NB 9501

Bottlesford Wilts 17 F5* ham just S of Woodborough and 3m/5km W of Pewsey. SU 1159

Bottom Boat W Yorks 49 F5* loc 2m/3km SW of Methley. SE 3624

Bottom Flash Ches 42 C4 lake formed by R Weaver on S side of Winsford. See also Top Flash. SJ 6565

Bottom of Hutton Lancs 47 F5* loc 2km W of Hutton. SD 4827

Bottom o' th' Moor Gtr Manchester 47 G6* loc 2km E of Horwich. SD 6511

Bottoms W Yorks 48 C5 ham 2m/3km S of Todmorden. SD 9321

Bottoms Reservoir Derbys 43 E2* lowest of chain of five resrs in R Etherow valley, 2m/3km N of Glossop. SK 0297

Botts Green Warwicks 35 H5* loc 4m/6km NE of Coleshill. SP 2492

Botusfleming Cornwall 4 B4 vil 2m/3km NW of Saltash. SX 4061

Botwnnog Gwynedd 32 A2* vil 4m/6km NW of Abersoch. Elizn grammar school (restored). SH 2631

Bough Beech Kent 20 B6 vil 3m/5km E of Edenbridge. **B.B. Resr** to N. TQ 4846

Boughrood (Bochrwyd) Powys 25 F4 ham 4m/6km NW of Talgarth across R Wye. **Boughrood Brest** ham 2km E. SO 1239

Boughspring Glos 16 B2* loc 3m/4km NE of Chepstow. Site of Roman bldg. ST 5597

Boughton Norfolk 38 B4* vil 2km N of Stoke Ferry. TF 6902

Boughton Northants 28 C1 vil 4m/6km N of Northampton. SP 7565

Boughton Notts 44 B4 vil 2m/3km E of Ollerton. SK 6768

Boughton Aluph Kent 13 F2 loc 4m/6km NE of Ashford. TR 0348

Boughton Green Kent 20 D6 vil in par of Boughton Monchelsea 3m/5km S of Maidstone. Site of Roman bldg to E. TQ 7651

Boughton Heath Ches 42 A4 suburb adjoining Chester to E. SJ 4265

Boughton Lees Kent 13 F2 vil 3m/5km N of Ashford. TR 0247

Boughton Malherbe Kent 13 E2 ham 2m/3km SW of Lenham. TQ 8849

Boughton Monchelsea Kent. See Boughton Green.

Boughton Street Kent 21 F5 vil 3m/5km E of Faversham. TR 0559

Boulby Cleveland 55 F3 loc at E end of steep, high cliffs on North Sea coast 2km W of Staithes. NZ 7618

Boulder Clough W Yorks 48 C5* loc 2m/3km W of Sowerby Br. SE 0323

Bouldnor Isle of Wight 10 B5* loc 2km E of Yarmouth. SZ 3789

Bouldon Salop 34 C5 ham 7m/11km N of Ludlow. SO 5485

Boulge Suffolk 31 F3 loc 2m/4km N of Woodbridge. TM 2552

Boulmer Nthmb 61 G1 vil on North Sea coast 3m/4km NE of Alnmouth. **B. Haven** bay to S. NU 2614

Boulston Dyfed 22 C4* loc 2m/4km SE of Haverfordwest.

Boultham Lincs 44 D4 SW dist of Lincoln 2m/3km from city centre. See also New Boultham. SK 9569

Boulton Derbys 36 A1 dist of Derby 3m/5km SE of tn centre. SK 3832

Boundary Derbys 36 A3* loc on border with Leics 2m/4km E of Swadlincote. SK 3318

Boundary Staffs 35 F1* ham 2m/3km W of Cheadle. SJ 9842

Bound Skerry Shetland. See Out Skerries.

Bourn Cambs 29 G2 vil 8m/13km W of Cambridge. Hall stands within earthworks of 11c cas. TL 3256

Bournbrook W Midlands 35 F5 dist of Birmingham 3m/5km SW of city centre. SP 0482

Bourne Lincs 37 F3 tn 10m/15km W of Spalding. Agricultural produce and engineering. TF 0920

Bourne 9 H2* r rising in par of Burbage to E of Pewsey in Wiltshire and flowing S through Tidworth into R Avon on SE side of Salisbury. SU 1529

Bournebridge Essex 20 B2* vil 4m/6km N of Romford. TQ 5094

Bourne Brook 30 C5* stream rising 2m/3km E of Finchingfield, Essex, and flowing E into R Colne 2m/3km E of Halstead. TL 8429

Bourne End Beds 28 D3 ham 6m/10km SW of Bedford. SP 9644

Bourne End Beds 29 E2* loc 2m/3km E of Sharnbrook. TL 0160

Bourne End Bucks 18 D3 residential loc and resort on R Thames 3m/5km E of Marlow. SU 8987

Bourne End Herts 19 E1 vil on W edge of Hemel Hempstead. TL 0206

Bournemouth Dorset 9 G5 large seaside resort with mild climate 24m/39km SW of Southampton. Conference centre. Light industries. Symphony orchestra. Airport (Hurn) 5m/8km NE of tn centre. SZ 0891

Bourne Rivulet 17 H6* stream in Hampshire rising at Upton, 2m/3km NW of Hurstbourne Tarrant, and flowing SE into R Test 1m SE of Hurstbourne Priors. SU 4445

Bournes Green Essex 21 E3 E dist of Southend-on-Sea. TQ 9186

Bournes Green Glos 16 D1* loc 4m/6km E of Stroud. Site of Roman villa. SO 9104

Bournes Green H & W 26 D1* loc 4m/7km NW of Bromsgrove. SO 9174

Bourne, The Surrey 11 E1* S dist of Farnham. SU 8444

Bournheath H & W 26 D1* vil 2m/4km N of Bromsgrove. SO 9473

Bournmoor Durham 61 G6 loc in coal-mining area 2m/4km E of Chester-le-Street. NZ 3151

Bournville W Midlands 35 F6 dist of Birmingham 4m/6km SW of city centre. Originated as estate developed late 19c for housing people employed in chocolate factory. SP 0481

Bourton Avon 15 H5 loc 5m/7km NE of Weston-super-Mare. ST 3864

Bourton Bucks 28 C4* loc on E side of Buckingham. SP 7033

Bourton Dorset 9 E2 vil 4m/6km E of Wincanton. 1km S, ham of **W Bourton.** ST 3935

Bourton Oxon 17 F3 vil 5m/8km E of Swindon. SU 2387

Bourton Salop 34 C4 vil 3m/5km SW of Much Wenlock. SO 5996

Bourton Wilts 17 E5* ham 3m/5km NE of Devizes. SU 0464

Bourton, Great Oxon 27 H3 vil 3m/5km N of Banbury. SP 4545

Bourton, Little Oxon 27 H3 ham 3m/4km N of Banbury. SP 4544

Bourton on Dunsmore Warwicks 27 H1 vil 5m/9km SW of Rugby. SP 4370

Bourton-on-the-Hill Glos 27 F4 vil 2m/3km W of Moreton-in-Marsh. SP 1732

Bourton-on-the-Water Glos 27 F5 small tn on R Windrush 4m/6km SW of Stow-on-the-Wold. SP 1620

Bourtonville Bucks 28 C4* loc in E part of Buckingham. SP 7033

Boustead Hill Cumbria 59 G5* loc 2m/3km W of Burgh by Sands. NY 2959

Bouth Cumbria 52 C6/D6 vil 2m/3km NE of Greenodd. SD 3285

Bouthwaite N Yorks 48 D1 ham 4m/7km NW of Pateley Br. SE 1271

Bovehill W Glam 23 F6* loc on Gower peninsula 1m E of Cheriton. SS 4693

Boveney Bucks 18 D4 loc 3m/4km SW of Slough. SU 9377

Boveridge Dorset 9 G3 ham 2km NE of Cranborne. SU 1014

Boverton (Trebeferad) S Glam 15 E4 loc on E side of Llantwit Major. SS 9868

Bovey 5 E3 Devon r rising on N Dartmoor and flowing first NE and then SE past Bovey Tracey and into R Teign 2km S of Chudleigh Knighton. SX 8475

Bovey, North Devon 4 D2 vil on R Bovey 2m/3km SW of Moretonhampstead. SX 7483

Bovey Tracey Devon 4 D3 small tn on R Bovey 5m/9km NW of Newton Abbot. SX 8178

Bovingdon Green Bucks 18 C3* loc adjoining Marlow to W. SU 8387

Bovington Herts 19 E2 vil 3m/5km SW of Hemel Hempstead. Airfield to W. TL 0103

Bovington Camp Dorset 9 F5 military camp on heathland 6m/10km W of Wareham. SY 8389

Bow Cumbria 59 H5* loc 4m/7km W of Carlisle. NY 3356

Bow Devon 5 E5* ham 3m/4km S of Totnes at head of **B. Creek** running into R Dart estuary. SX 8156

Bow Devon 7 E5 vil 7m/12km W of Crediton. SS 7201

Bow London 20 A3* dist in borough of Tower Hamlets 3m/5km NE of London Br. Loc of **B. Common** 1m S. TQ 3783

Bowbank Durham 53 H3 loc 1m S of Middleton in Teesdale. NY 9423

Bowbeat Hill 66 A4/B4* hill on Moorfoot range on border of Lothian and Borders regions, 3m/5km E of Eddleston. Height 2050 ft or 623 metres. NT 2946

Bow Brickhill Bucks 28 D4* vil 2m/3km E of Bletchley. SP 9034

Bow Brook 26 D3* r rising E of Worcester and flowing S into R Avon near Defford, SW of Pershore, H & W. SO 9142

Bowburn Durham 54 C1* vil 4m/6km SE of Durham. NZ 3038

Bowcombe Isle of Wight 10 B6 ham 3m/4km SW of Newport. SZ 4686

Bowden Borders 66 C5 vil 2m/4km S of Melrose beyond Eildon Hills. NT 5530

Bowden Devon 5 E5 loc 3m/4km SW of Dartmouth. SX 8449

Bowden Close Durham 54 B2* loc 1m W of Willington. NZ 1835

Bowden, Great Leics 36 C5 vil adjoining Mkt Harborough to NE. SP 7488

Bowden Hill Wilts 16 D4* vil 4m/6km S of Chippenham. Bewley Common to NW is partly NT property. ST 9367

Bowden, Little Leics 36 C5 loc adjoining Mkt Harborough to E. SP 7487

Bowdon Gtr Manchester 42 C3 tn 2km SW of Altrincham. SJ 7586

Bowdun Head Grampian 77 H3* headland on E coast 1m SE of Stonehaven. NO 8884

Bower Ashton Avon 16 B4* loc in W part of Bristol. ST 5671

Bowerchalke Wilts 9 G2 vil 2m/3km SW of Broad Chalke. SU 0123

Bower, East Som 8 B1* loc 2km E of Bridgwater. ST 3237

Bower Fold Gtr Manchester 43 E2* loc 1m SE of Stalybridge. SJ 9797

Bowerhill Wilts 16 D5* loc 2m/3km SE of Melksham. ST 9262

Bower Hinton Som 8 C3 loc at S end of Martock. ST 4518

Bower House Tye Suffolk 30 D4* loc 3m/4km SW of Hadleigh. TL 9840

Bowermadden H'land 86 E2 loc in Caithness dist 4m/6km SE of Castletown. ND 2364

Bowers Staffs 35 E1* ham 4m/7km N of Eccleshall. SJ 8135

Bowers Gifford Essex 20 D3 vil 3m/4km E of Basildon. TQ 7588

Bowes Durham 53 H3 small tn on site of Roman tn of *Lavatrae* 4m/6km SW of Barnard Castle. Remains of Norman keep of cas (A.M.). **B. Moor** to W. NY 9913

Bowes Museum Durham. See Barnard Castle.

Bowes Park London 19 G3* loc on borders of Enfield and Haringey boroughs, 7m/11km N of Charing Cross. TQ 3091

Bow Fell Cumbria 52 C4 mt in Lake Dist 5m/8km W of Chapel Stile. Height 2960 ft or 902 metres. NY 2406

Bowgreave Lancs 47 F4 vil 1km S of Garstang. SD 4944

Bowgreen Gtr Manchester 42 C3* loc adjoining Bowdon to S. SJ 7586

Bow Head Orkney 89 B5 headland at N end of island of Westray. HY 4553

Bowhill Borders 66 B5 hse and estate 3m/5km W of Selkirk. NT 4227

Bowhousebog (or Liquo) S'clyde 65 E3* loc 2m/3km SW of Shotts. NS 8558

Bowithick Cornwall 3 F1* loc 5m/8km E of Camelford. SX 1882
Bowker's Green Lancs 42 A1* loc 3m/4km S of Ormskirk. SD 4004
Bowland Borders 66 C4 loc on Gala Water 3m/5km NW of Galashiels. NT 4540
Bowland Bridge Cumbria 52 D5 loc at crossing of R Winster 4m/6km NE of Newby Br. SD 4189
Bowland Forest Lancs. See Forest of Bowland.
Bowlee Gtr Manchester 42 D1* loc 2km W of Middleton. SD 8406
Bowley H & W 26 B2* ham 5m/8km SE of Leominster. Loc of **B. Town** to N. SO 5452
Bowlhead Green Surrey 11 E2 ham 3m/4km NE of Hindhead. SU 9138
Bowling S'clyde 64 B2/C2 vil on N bank of R Clyde 3m/5km E of Dumbarton. Shipbuilding, distilling. W terminus of Forth and Clyde Canal (disused). NS 4474
Bowling W Yorks 48 D5* dist of Bradford 2km SE of city centre. (Bradford annual holiday is known as Bowling Tide.) **W. Bowling** dist of Bradford 2km W, 1m S of city centre. SE 1831
Bowling Bank Clwyd 42 A6 loc 4m/7km E of Wrexham. SJ 3948
Bowling Green H & W 26 C3 loc 3m/5km SW of Worcester. SO 8151
Bowmanstead Cumbria 52 C5 ham 1km S of Coniston. SD 2996
Bowmont Water border r of Scotland and England. See Glen.
Bowmore S'clyde 62 B2 vil and fishing port on E side of Loch Indaal, Islay, 4m/6km NE of Laggan Pt. Distillery. NR 3159
Bowness-on-Solway Cumbria 59 G5 vil on Solway Firth 4m/6km N of Kirkbride. Roman sites in vicinity, at W end of Hadrian's Wall. NY 2262
Bowness-on-Windermere Cumbria 52 D5 loc on E shore of Windermere adjoining Windermere tn to S. SD 4096
Bow of Fife Fife 73 F3 loc 4m/6km W of Cupar. NO 3213
Bowood, North Dorset 8 C4* loc 3m/4km SW of Beaminster. SY 4499
Bowood, South Dorset 8 C4 loc 3m/5km SW of Beaminster. SY 4498
Bowscale Cumbria 52 D2* loc 1m N of Mungrisdale. **B. Tarn** small lake 2km W below steep crags on **B. Fell.** NY 3531
Bowsden Nthmb 67 F4 ham 2m/3km NW of Lowick. NT 9941
Bowston Cumbria 53 E5* loc 3m/5km N of Kendal. SD 4996
Bow Street Dyfed 32 D5/D6 vil 3m/5km NE of Aberystwyth. SN 6284
Bow Street Norfolk 39 E5* loc 3m/5km NW of Attleborough. TM 0197
Bowthorpe Norfolk 39 F4 loc in Norwich 3m/5km W of city centre. TG 1709
Box Glos 16 D2* vil 1m NE of Nailsworth. SO 8500
Box Wilts 16 D4 vil 5m/8km NE of Bath. Site of Roman villa. ST 8268
Box 31 E4 r rising 2m/3km S of Lavenham, Suffolk, and flowing SE into R Stour 1m SW of Higham. TM 0234
Boxbush Glos 26 B5* loc 5m/7km SW of Newent. SO 6720
Box End Beds 29 E3 loc 3m/4km W of Bedford across R Ouse. TL 0049
Boxford Berks 17 H4 vil 4m/6km NW of Newbury. Site of Roman bldg 1m E. SU 4271
Boxford Suffolk 30 D4 vil 4m/7km W of Hadleigh. TL 9640
Boxgrove W Sussex 11 E4 vil 3m/5km NE of Chichester. Benedictine priory ch, with fragments of monastic bldgs. SU 9007
Box Hill Surrey 19 F6 steep chalk hill (NT) forming part of N Downs 2km NE of Dorking. Loc of same name 2km E. TQ 1751
Boxley Kent 20 D5 vil 2m/4km N of Maidstone, in conservation area on edge of N Downs. Remains of medieval **B. Abbey** to W. TQ 7759
Boxmoor Herts 19 E1 SW dist of Hemel Hempstead. TL 0406
Box's Shop Cornwall 6 B5* loc 3m/5km S of Bude. SS 2101
Boxted Essex 30 D4 ham 5m/8km N of Colchester. Ham of **B. Cross** 1km SE. Ham of **B. Heath** 1m S. TL 9933
Boxted Suffolk 30 C3 vil 4m/6km NW of Long Melford. TL 8250
Boxwell Glos 16 C2 loc 5m/8km W of Tetbury. ST 8192
Boxworth Cambs 29 G2 vil 7m/11km NW of Cambridge. TL 3464
Boxworth End Cambs 29 G1 S end of Swavesey. TL 3667
Boyd 16 C4 r rising S of Chipping Sodbury and flowing into R Avon 2m/3km above Keynsham, Avon. ST 6868
Boyden Gate Kent 13 G1* vil 3m/5km SE of Herne Bay. TR 2265
Boylestone Derbys 35 G1 vil 3m/4km NE of Sudbury. SK 1835
Boyndie Grampian 83 E1 vil 3m/5km W of Banff. **B. Bay** is sandy bay extending westwards from Banff to Knock Hd. NJ 6463
Boyndie Grampian 83 G1 loc, with **Upr** and **Nether B.**, near N coast 5m/9km SW of Fraserburgh. NJ 9162
Boyne Bay Grampian 83 E1 small bay on N coast 2m/3km E of Portsoy. Burn of Boyne runs N into bay. Remains of **Boyne Castle** on burn nearly 1km from bay. NJ 6166
Boyne Water Salop 34 C5* small lake 2km S of summit of Brown Clee Hill. SO 5984
Boynton Humberside 51 F2 vil 3m/5km W of Bridlington. Hall dates from 16c. TA 1368
Boys Heath, Little Bucks 18 D2* loc 4m/6km W of Amersham. SU 9099
Boys Hill Dorset 8 D3* loc 5m/7km SE of Sherborne. ST 6710
Boys Village S Glam 15 E4* loc 1km E of Gileston. ST 0167
Boythorpe Derbys 43 H4* loc in Chesterfield 2km SW of tn centre. SK 3669
Boyton Cornwall 6 C6 vil 5m/8km N of Launceston. SX 3292
Boyton Suffolk 31 G3 vil 7m/11km E of Woodbridge. TM 3747
Boyton Wilts 9 F1 vil on R Wylye 3m/4km SE of Heytesbury. ST 9539
Boyton Cross Essex 20 C1* ham 4m/6km NW of Chelmsford. TL 6409
Boyton End Suffolk 30 C3* ham 3m/5km E of Haverhill. TL 7144
Bozeat Northants 28 D2 vil 6m/9km S of Wellingborough. SP 9059
Braaid Isle of Man 46 B5 ham 4m/6km W of Douglas. SC 3276
Braal H'land 86 D2 ancient cas on left bank of R Thurso on NE side of Halkirk, Caithness dist. Also spelt Brawl. ND 1360
Braan 72 D1 r in Tayside region running NE down Strath Braan to R Tay at Dunkeld. NO 0242
Brabling Green Suffolk 31 G2* loc 1m NE of Framlingham. TM 2964
Brabourne Kent 13 F3 vil 6m/9km E of Ashford. TR 1041
Brabourne Lees Kent 13 F3 vil 5m/8km SE of Ashford. TR 0740
Brabourne, West Kent 13 F3* ham 4m/7km E of Ashford. TR 0842
Brabstermire H'land 86 F1 loc in Caithness dist 4m/6km S of St John's Pt on Pentland Firth. ND 3269
Bracadale Skye, H'land 79 B5 vil near SW coast 10m/16km NW of Sligachan. Loch B. is large inlet to W. **Bracadale Pt** is headland 1m SW. NG 3438
Braceborough Lincs 37 F3 vil 5m/8km NE of Stamford. TF 0813
Bracebridge Lincs 44 D4 dist of Lincoln 2m/3km S of city centre. **B. Low Fields** loc 1m S. SK 9668
Bracebridge Heath Lincs 44 D4 suburb 3m/4km S of Lincoln. SK 9867
Braceby Lincs 37 E1 ham 6m/10km E of Grantham. TF 0135
Bracewell Lancs 48 B3 ham 2km NW of Barnoldswick. SD 8746
Bracken Bank W Yorks 48 C4* loc in Keighley 2m/3km SW of tn centre. SE 0439
Bracken Bay S'clyde 56 C2* bay on W side of Heads of Ayr, at S end of Firth of Clyde. NS 2718
Brackenber Cumbria 53 E3* loc 1km S of Shap. NY 5614
Brackenber Cumbria 53 F3 loc 3m/4km E of Appleby. NY 7219
Brackenberry Wykes N Yorks 55 F3* bay on North Sea coast 1m E of Staithes. NZ 7918
Brackenborough Lincs 45 G2* loc 2m/3km N of Louth. TF 3290
Brackenbottom N Yorks 48 B1* loc just E of Horton in Ribblesdale. SD 8172
Brackenfield Derbys 43 H5 ham 5m/8km E of Matlock. **B. Green** loc to SW. SK 3759
Brackenhall W Yorks 48 D6* loc in Huddersfield 2m/4km N of tn centre. SE 1519
Bracken Hill S Yorks 43 G2 loc 2km N of Grenoside. SK 3396
Bracken Hill W Yorks 48 D6* loc 2km NW of Mirfield. SE 1821
Brackenhill W Yorks 49 F6* loc adjoining Ackworth Moor Top to W. SE 4216
Brackenthwaite Cumbria 52 B3 loc 2km NE of Loweswater ham. NY 1522
Brackenthwaite Cumbria 52 C1* loc 3m/4km SE of Wigton. NY 2946
Brackenthwaite N Yorks 49 E3 loc 3m/5km SW of Harrogate. SE 2851
Brackla H'land 81 G2 loc and distillery in Nairn dist 4m/6km SW of Nairn. NH 8651
Bracklesham W Sussex 11 E5* coastal loc adjoining E Wittering to SE. **B. Bay** is formed by gently curving coast extending from Chichester Harbour to Selsey Bill. SZ 8096
Brackley Northants 28 B4 tn 8m/13km E of Banbury. SP 5837
Brackley Gate Derbys 36 A1* loc 5m/7km NE of Derby. SK 3842
Brackley Hatch Northants 28 B3* loc 5m/8km NE of Brackley. SP 6441
Bracklinn Falls Central 72 A4 waterfall in course of Keltie Water 2km E of Callander. NN 6408
Bracknell Berks 18 D4 New Tn designated 1949, 4m/6km E of Wokingham. Light industry. Home of Meteorological Office. SU 8769
Brack, The S'clyde 70 D4 mt in Argyll 2m/3km W of Ardgartan on W shore of Loch Long. Height 2580 ft or 786 metres. NN 2403
Braco Tayside 72 C4 vil on R Knaik 6m/10km NE of Dunblane. In grnds of Ardoch Hse to N is well-preserved site of Roman fort; site of Roman camp 1km N of fort. **B. Castle** 2km NW. NN 8309
Bracon Humberside 44 C1 loc 2m/3km N of Epworth. SE 7807
Bracon Ash Norfolk 39 F4/F5 vil 6m/10km SW of Norwich. TM 1899
Bracora H'land 79 E8 locality on N shore of Loch Morar in Lochaber dist 4m/6km SE of Mallaig. NM 7192
Bracorina H'land 79 E8 loc in Lochaber dist 1km E of Bracora, qv. NM 7292
Bradbourne Derbys 43 G5 vil 4m/7km NE of Ashbourne. SK 2052
Bradbourne Brook 43 F6* r rising near vil of Bradbourne to NE of Ashbourne, Derbys, and flowing SW into R Dove 2km W of the tn. SK 1646
Bradbury Durham 54 C2 vil 3m/4km W of Sedgefield. NZ 3128
Bradda Isle of Man 46 A6* loc consisting of **Bradda E** and **Bradda W** 1km N of Port Erin. **Bradda Hd** is headland 1km W of Bradda W. SC 1970
Bradda Hill Isle of Man 46 A6* hill above cliffs at S end of Niarbyl Bay 1m NE of Bradda Hd. SC 1971
Bradden Northants 28 B3 vil 3m/5km W of Towcester. SP 6448
Braddock Cornwall 3 F2* loc 4m/6km NE of Lostwithiel. Site of Civil War battle, 1643. Also known as Broadoak. SX 1662
Braddocks Hay Staffs 42 D5* loc adjoining Biddulph to E. SJ 8857
Bradeley Staffs 42 D6* loc 2km NE of Burslem. SJ 8851
Bradenham Bucks 18 C2 vil 4m/6km NW of High Wycombe. SU 8297
Bradenham, East Norfolk 38 D4 vil 5m/8km SW of E Dereham. **W Bradenham** vil adjoins to W. TF 9208
Bradenstoke Wilts 17 E3 vil 5m/7km W of Wootton Bassett. SU 0079
Brades Village W Midlands 35 F5* loc 1km NW of Oldbury. SO 9890
Bradfield Berks 18 B4 vil 3m/5km SW of Pangbourne. Boys' public school. SU 6072
Bradfield Essex 31 E5/F5 vil 3m/4km E of Manningtree. TM 1430
Bradfield Norfolk 39 F2* ham 1m E of Antingham. TG 2633
Bradfield S Yorks 43 G2 vil on moors 6m/10km NW of Sheffield. Remains of motte and bailey cas. Vil of **Low Bradfield** in valley 1km SW. SK 2692
Bradfield Combust Suffolk 30 D2 vil 5m/8km SE of Bury St Edmunds. Name recalls burning of hall during 14c riots. TL 8957
Bradfield Green Ches 42 C5 ham 3m/5km NW of Crewe. SJ 6859
Bradfield Grove Oxon 17 H2* loc 3m/4km N of Wantage. SU 4091
Bradfield Heath Essex 31 E5 vil 2m/4km SE of Manningtree. TM 1329
Bradfield St Clare Suffolk 30 D2* vil 1m E of Bradfield Combust. TL 9057
Bradfield St George Suffolk 30 D2 vil 4m/7km SE of Bury St Edmunds. TL 9160
Bradford Cornwall 3 F1* loc 6m/10km NE of Bodmin. SX 1175
Bradford Derbys 43 G4* loc adjoining Youlgreave to E. SK 2164
Bradford Devon 6 C4 ham 5m/9km NE of Holsworthy. SS 4207
Bradford Gtr Manchester 42 D2* dist of Manchester 2m/3km E of city centre. Chemical and iron works. SJ 8698
Bradford Nthmb 61 F3* loc 2m/4km W of Belsay. NZ 0679
Bradford Nthmb 67 H5 loc 3m/4km SW of Bamburgh. NU 1532
Bradford W Yorks 48 D5 industrial city 8m/13km W of Leeds. Centre of wool industry; various other industries include mechanical and electrical engineering. Cathedral is former par ch. University. Leeds and Bradford Airport at Yeadon, 6m/10km NE. SE 1633
Bradford Abbas Dorset 8 D3 vil on R Yeo 3m/4km SE of Yeovil. ST 5814
Bradford Leigh Wilts 16 D5* ham 2km NE of Bradford-on-Avon. ST 8362
Bradford-on-Avon Wilts 16 D5 hillside tn of Bath stone 3m/5km NW of Trowbridge. ST 8260
Bradford-on-Tone Som 8 A2 vil 3m/4km NE of Wellington. ST 1722
Bradford Peverell Dorset 8 D5 vil on R Frome 3m/4km NW of Dorchester. SY 6593
Bradford, West Lancs 48 A4 vil on R Ribble 2m/3km N of Clitheroe. SD 7444
Bradgate Leics 36 B3 ruins of 15c–16c brick mansion in deer park, 5m/8km NW of Leicester. Birthplace of Lady Jane Grey, 1537. SK 5310
Bradgate S Yorks 43 H2 dist of Rotherham 2km W of tn centre. SK 4093
Bradiford Devon 6 D2* loc on NW outskirts of Barnstaple. SS 5434
Bradiford Water 6 D2* r rising near Bittadon, Devon, and flowing S into R Taw estuary 2km W of Barnstaple. SS 5333
Brading Isle of Wight 10 C6 vil 2m/3km N of Sandown. To SW, remains of Roman villa. 2m/3km NE, **B. Harbour**, at mouth of R Yar. SZ 6087
Bradley Ches 42 B3/B4* loc 1m SE of Frodsham. SJ 5377
Bradley Clwyd 41 H5* loc 2m/4km N of Wrexham. SJ 3253
Bradley Cumbria 53 E2* loc adjoining Ousby to NW, 2km N of Skirwith. NY 6135
Bradley Derbys 43 G6 vil 3m/5km E of Ashbourne. SK 2245
Bradley Hants 10 D1 vil 5m/9km NW of Alton. SU 6341
Bradley Humberside 45 F1 vil 3m/4km SW of Grimsby. TA 2406
Bradley H & W 27 E2 vil 6m/10km E of Droitwich. SO 9860
Bradley N Yorks 48 C1 loc 6m/10km NE of Kettlewell. SE 0380
Bradley Staffs 35 E3 vil 4m/7km SW of Stafford. SJ 8717
Bradley W Midlands 35 F5 SE dist of Wolverhampton. SO 9595
Bradley W Yorks 48 D6* loc 3m/5km NE of Huddersfield. To E, junction of Huddersfield Canal and Calder and Hebble Navigation. SE 1720
Bradley Common Ches 42 B6* loc 2m/3km SE of Malpas. SJ 5145
Bradley Fold Gtr Manchester 42 C1* loc 3m/4km E of Bolton. SD 7508
Bradley, Great Som 7 F2* Exmoor ham 2km SE of Withypool. SS 8534
Bradley, Great Suffolk 30 B3 vil 5m/8km N of Haverhill. TL 6653
Bradley Green H & W 27 E1 ham 5m/9km E of Droitwich. SO 9861
Bradley Green Warwicks 35 H4* loc just SW of Grendon. SK 2800
Bradley, High N Yorks 48 C3* loc 2km SE of Skipton. SE 0049
Bradley in the Moors Staffs 35 F1 vil 4m/6km E of Cheadle. SK 0641
Bradley, Little Suffolk 30 B3 vil 4m/7km N of Haverhill. TL 6852
Bradley, Low N Yorks 48 C3 vil 2m/3km SE of Skipton. SE 0048
Bradley Mills W Yorks 48 D6* loc in Huddersfield 1m NE of tn centre. SE 1517
Bradley Mount Ches 43 E3* loc 1km E of Prestbury. SJ 9177
Bradley, North Wilts 16 D5 vil 2m/3km S of Trowbridge. ST 8555
Bradley, West Som 8 D1* vil 4m/6km SE of Glastonbury. ST 5536

Bradmore Notts 36 B2 vil 6m/9km S of Nottingham. SK 5831
Bradmore W Midlands 35 E4 W dist of Wolverhampton. SO 8997
Bradney Som 8 B1* loc 3m/4km NE of Bridgwater. ST 3338
Bradninch Devon 7 G4 small tn 8m/12km NE of Exeter. SS 9903
Bradnop Staffs 43 E5* vil 2m/3km SE of Leek. SK 0155
Bradnor Green H & W 25 G2* loc 1km NW of Kington. Golf course running up to **Bradnor Hill** (NT). SO 2957
Bradpole Dorset 8 C5 vil adjoining Bridport to NE. SY 4394
Bradshaw Gtr Manchester 47 G6 loc 2m/4km N of Bolton. SD 7312
Bradshaw W Yorks 48 C6* loc 2m/3km N of Marsden. SE 0514
Bradshaw W Yorks 48 D5* vil 3m/5km N of Halifax. SE 0730
Bradstone Devon 6 C6* ham 4m/6km SE of Launceston. SX 3880
Bradwall Green Ches 42 C5* ham 2m/3km N of Sandbach. SJ 7563
Bradway S Yorks 43 G3 dist of Sheffield 5m/7km SW of city centre, comprising Bradway, Upr Bradway, and Lr Bradway. SK 3380
Bradwell Bucks 28 C4/D4 vil in Milton Keynes 2km SE of Wolverton. Remains of medieval priory to W across rly. Vil also known as Old Bradwell. SP 8339
Bradwell Derbys 43 F3 vil 4m/6km W of Hathersage. SK 1781
Bradwell Devon 6 D1* loc 3m/5km SW of Ilfracombe. SS 4942
Bradwell Essex 30 C5 vil 3m/5km E of Braintree. TL 8023
Bradwell Norfolk 39 H4 suburb 2km W of Gorleston. TG 5003
Bradwell Staffs 42 D6* loc in Newcastle-under-Lyme 2m/3km N of tn centre. SJ 8449
Bradwell-on-Sea Essex 21 F2 vil 2m/3km from E coast and 7m/12km NE of Burnham-on-Crouch. On coast to E is *Othona* (qv), remains of Roman fort of the Saxon shore. Nuclear power stn 1m N. TM 0006
Bradwell Waterside Essex 21 F1 vil near right bank of R Blackwater estuary 8m/12km NE of Burnham-on-Crouch. Marina. Nuclear power stn 1km NE. TL 9907
Bradworthy Devon 6 C4 vil 7m/11km N of Holsworthy. SS 3214
Brae Shetland 89 E6 vil on Mainland at head of Busta Voe. To W is the narrow neck of land separating Busta Voe from Sullom Voe. HU 3567
Braehead D & G 57 D7* loc 1km N of Kirkinner, S of Wigtown. NX 4252
Braehead Orkney 89 B5* loc on island of Westray 1km SE of Pierowall. HY 4447
Braehead S'clyde 64 B6* NE dist of Ayr. NS 3522
Braehead S'clyde 65 F4 vil 3m/5km NW of Carnwath. NS 9550
Braemar Grampian 76 C2 vil in dist of same name, on Clunie Water near its confluence with R Dee. Tourist centre. B. Gathering (Highland Games) held in September. Cas dates from 17c. NO 1591
Braemore H'land 86 D4 loc in Caithness dist 5m/8km W of Dunbeath. ND 0730
Braemore Forest H'land 85 C8 deer forest astride head of Strath More, S of Loch Broom in Ross and Cromarty dist. NH 1876
Brae of Achnahaird H'land 85 A5 loc near NW coast of Ross and Cromarty dist 3m/5km SE of Rubha Coigeach. See also Achnahaird Bay. NC 0013
Braeriach 76 A1 mt in Cairngorms on border of Grampian and Highland regions 4m/7km SW of Cairn Gorm. Height 4252 ft or 1296 metres. NN 9599
Braeroddach Loch Grampian 77 E1* lochan or tarn 3m/4km NW of Aboyne. NJ 4800
Braeside S'clyde 64 A2* loc 2km S of Gourock. NS 2375
Braes of Abernethy H'land 82 A5 upland area E of Abernethy Forest in Badenoch and Strathspey dist. NJ 0615
Braes of Balquhidder Central 71 F3 upland area W of Balquhidder and N of Loch Doine and Loch Voil. NN 4921
Braes of Doune Central 71 G4, H4 upland area 3m/5km NW of Doune. NN 6905
Braes of Glenlivet Grampian 82 B4 upland area S of Glen Livet and 5m/8km E of Tomintoul. NJ 2421
Braes of the Carse Tayside 73 E2, F2* foothills of Sidlaw Hills above Carse of Gowrie between Perth and Dundee. NO 2530
Braes of Ullapool H'land 85 B7 locality on E shore of Loch Broom, Ross and Cromarty dist, 1m SE of Ullapool. NH 1493
Braes o' Lochaber H'land 74 D3 part of Glen Spean in Lochaber dist between Roy Br and confluence of Rs Spean and Treig. NN 3280
Braeswick Orkney 89 C5 loc on small bay of **Braes Wick** on W coast of Sanday, 2m/4km N of Spur Ness. HY 6137
Brae Wick Shetland 89 D6* bay on N shore of St Magnus Bay 2km E of Esha Ness. Loc of **Braewick** at head of bay. HU 2478
Brafferton Durham 54 C3 vil 4m/7km N of Darlington. NZ 2921
Brafferton N Yorks 49 F2 vil on R Swale 6m/9km W of Easingwold. SE 4370
Brafield-on-the-Green Northants 28 C2/D2 vil 4m/7km E of Northampton. SP 8258
Braga Ness Shetland 89 D7* headland on W coast of Mainland 2m/3km SE of Wats Ness. HU 1948
Bragar W Isles 88 B1 vil near NW coast of Lewis 5m/7km W of Barvas. See also Port Mhór B. NB 2947
Bragbury End Herts 29 F5* ham 3m/4km SE of Luton. TL 2621
Bragenham Bucks 28 D5 loc 3m/4km NW of Leighton Buzzard. SP 9028
Brahan Castle H'land 81 E2* ruined cas in Ross and Cromarty dist 4m/6km SW of Dingwall. Formerly stronghold of Earls of Seaforth, chiefs of Clan Mackenzie. NH 5154
Braichmelyn Gwynedd 40 C5 loc 1km S of Bethesda. SH 6265
Braich y Pwll Gwynedd 32 A2* W extremity (NT) of Lleyn peninsula, where once Celtic pilgrims embarked for Bardsey I. Holy well and site of St Mary's Chapel. SH 1325
Braid Lothian 66 A2 dist of Edinburgh 2m/4km S of city centre. **B. Hills** to SE. NT 2470
Braid Cairn 77 E2 mt on border of Grampian and Tayside regions 6m/10km SE of Ballater. Height 2907 ft or 886 metres. NO 4287
Braidford S'clyde 64 D3* loc in Glasgow 3m/5km SE of city centre. NS 6363
Braidwood S'clyde 65 E4 vil 2m/3km S of Carluke. NS 8447
Bràigh a' Choire Bhig H'land 80 C4 mt ridge in Ross and Cromarty dist 1m S of Sgurr na Lapaich. Height 3322 ft or 1013 metres. NH 1533
Braigh Sròn Ghorm Tayside 76 A3* mt 3m/5km E of Beinn Dearg, N of Blair Atholl. Height 2882 ft or 878 metres. NN 9078
Brailes, Lower Warwicks 27 G4 vil 4m/6km E of Shipston on Stour. SP 3139
Brailes, Upper Warwicks 27 G4 vil 3m/5km E of Shipston on Stour. SP 3039
Brailsford Derbys 35 H1 vil 7m/11km NW of Derby. **B. Green** loc adjoining to W. SK 2541
Brain 30 C6 r rising near Braintree, Essex, and flowing SE into R Blackwater 2km SE of Witham. TL 8313
Brain's Green Glos 16 B1* loc 1km NW of Blakeney. SO 6608
Braint 40 B5 r on Anglesey rising E of Pentraeth and flowing SW into Menai Strait on E side of Newborough Warren. SH 4363
Braintree Essex 30 C5 tn 11m/17km NE of Chelmsford. Industries include mnfre of rayon and of prefabricated bldgs. TL 7523
Braiseworth Suffolk 31 F1 ham 2m/3km SW of Eye. TM 1371
Braishfield Hants 10 B2 vil 3m/5km NE of Romsey. SU 3725
Braithwaite Cumbria 52 C3 vil 2m/4km W of Keswick. NY 2323
Braithwaite S Yorks 49 G6 vil 3m/5km NW of Hatfield. SE 6112
Braithwaite W Yorks 48 C4* loc on W side of Keighley. SE 0341
Braithwaite Hall N Yorks 54 A6* 17c hse, now a farmhouse, 2km SW of Middleham (NT, with Braithwaite Moor to S). SE 1185
Braithwaite, Low Cumbria 60 A6* loc 1m SE of Ivegill. NY 4242
Braithwell S Yorks 44 A2 vil 2m/3km N of Maltby. SK 5292
Brakefield Green Norfolk 39 E4* loc 4m/6km SE of E Dereham. TG 0309
Bramber W Sussex 11 G4 vil in R Adur valley 4m/6km NW of Shoreham-by-Sea. Ruins of Norman cas (NT). TQ 1810
Brambridge Hants 10 B3* ham 2m/3km NE of Eastleigh. SU 4721
Bramcote Notts 36 B1 loc 2km NW of Beeston. SK 5037
Bramcote Mains Warwicks 36 A5* loc 4m/6km SE of Nuneaton. SP 4087
Bramdean Hants 10 C2 vil 3m/5km SE of New Alresford. 1m E, site of Roman villa. SU 6128
Bramerton Norfolk 39 G4 vil 5m/8km SE of Norwich. TG 2904
Bramfield Herts 29 G6 vil 3m/5km NW of Hertford. TL 2915
Bramfield Suffolk 31 G1 vil 3m/4km S of Halesworth. TM 3973
Bramford Suffolk 31 E3 vil 3m/4km NW of Ipswich. TM 1246
Bramhall Gtr Manchester 42 D3 tn 4m/6km S of Stockport. SJ 8984
Bramham W Yorks 49 F4 vil 4m/6km S of Wetherby. To SW is **B. Park,** 18c classical mansion in grnds modelled on those of Versailles. To SE is **B. Moor,** where the Earl of Northumberland was defeated by the army of Henry IV in 1408. SE 4242
Bramhope W Yorks 49 E4 suburb 7m/11km NW of Leeds. See also Old Bramhope. SE 2543
Bramley Derbys 43 H3* loc 2m/3km W of Eckington. SK 4079
Bramley Hants 18 B5 vil 5m/7km N of Basingstoke. SU 6458
Bramley Surrey 11 F1 long vil 3m/5km S of Guildford. TQ 0044
Bramley S Yorks 44 A2 suburb 4m/6km E of Rotherham. SK 4992
Bramley W Yorks 49 E4 dist of Leeds 3m/5km W of city centre. SE 2435
Bramley Corner Hants 18 B5* ham 5m/7km N of Basingstoke. SU 6359
Bramley Green Hants 18 B5* loc 5m/8km NE of Basingstoke. SU 6659
Bramley Head N Yorks 48 D2/D3* loc 3m/5km NW of Blubberhouses. SE 1258
Bramley Meade Lancs 48 A4* loc 1km NE of Whalley. SD 7336
Bramley Vale Derbys 44 A4* loc 6m/9km NW of Mansfield. SK 4666
Brampford Speke Devon 7 G5 vil on R Exe 4m/6km N of Exeter. SX 9298
Brampton Cambs 29 F1 vil 2m/3km W of Huntingdon. TL 2170
Brampton Cumbria 53 F3 vil 2m/3km S of Appleby. NY 6823
Brampton Cumbria 60 B5 small tn 9m/14km NE of Carlisle. NY 5361
Brampton Lincs 44 C3 ham 7m/11km S of Gainsborough. SK 8479
Brampton Norfolk 39 F3 vil 3m/4km SE of Aylsham. TG 2224
Brampton Suffolk 31 H1 ham 4m/6km NE of Halesworth. Loc of **B. Street** 1km W. TM 4381
Brampton S Yorks 43 H1* coal-mining loc 2km SE of Wombwell. SE 3903
Brampton Abbotts H & W 26 B5* vil 2m/3km N of Ross-on-Wye. SO 6027
Brampton Ash Northants 36 D5 vil 4m/6km E of Mkt Harborough. SP 7987
Brampton Bryan H & W 25 H1 vil 5m/8km E of Knighton. SO 3772
Brampton en le Morthen S Yorks 44 A2 vil 5m/9km SE of Rotherham. SK 4888
Brampton, Little H & W 25 G2* medieval farmhouse 2m/3km S of Presteigne. SO 3061
Brampton, Little Salop 34 B6 ham 4m/7km W of Craven Arms. SO 3681
Brampton, The Staffs 42 D6* dist of Newcastle-under-Lyme 1km NE of tn centre. SJ 8546
Bramshall Staffs 35 F1 vil 2m/3km W of Uttoxeter. SK 0633
Bramshaw Hants 10 A3 vil in New Forest 2m/3km NW of Cadnam. **B. Common** (NT). SU 2715
Bramshill Hants 18 C5 loc 2m/3km SE of Riseley. 2km SE, Bramshill Hse, Jacbn hse now police college. SU 7461
Bramshott Hants 11 E2 vil 1m N of Liphook. SU 8432
Bramstead Heath Staffs 35 E3 vil 4m/6km SE of Newport. SJ 7917
Bramwell Som 8 C2 ham 2m/3km N of Langport. ST 4329
Bramwith, South S Yorks 49 G6 ham on S side of Kirk Bramwith across R Don. SE 6211
Bran H'land 80 D2 r in Ross and Cromarty dist running E from Achnasheen down Strath Bran to Loch Luichart. NH 3162
Bran 24 C5 r rising 2m/3km SE of Myddfai, Dyfed, and flowing W into R Towy 1km W of Llangadog. SN 6928
Bran 24 D4 r rising E of Llyn Brianne Resr on borders of Dyfed and Powys and flowing S into R Towy 2km SW of Llandovery. SN 7532
Bran 25 E5 r rising on Mynydd Epynt, Powys, and flowing SE into R Usk at Aberbran, 4m/6km W of Brecon. SN 9829
Branahuie W Isles 88 C2* locality adjoining Melbost 2m/4km E of Stornoway, Lewis. **Loch B.** is lakelet to E on spit of land connecting Eye Peninsula to rest of Lewis. **B. Banks** is bay to S. NB 4632
Brancaster Norfolk 38 C1 vil near coast 4m/6km W of Burnham Mkt. **B. Bay** to N. Slight remains of Roman fort of *Branodunum* to E. **B. Staithe** vil 2km E. TF 7743
Brancepeth Durham 54 B1 vil 4m/7km SW of Durham. Cas dates partly from 14c though mainly 19c. **B. Camp** 1km S. See also New Brancepeth. NZ 2237
Branch End Nthmb 61 F5* loc 2m/4km SW of Prudhoe. NZ 0661
Brand End Lincs 45 G6* loc 1km W of Butterwick. TF 3745
Branderburgh Grampian 82 B1 tn on N coast adjoining, and forming N part of, Lossiemouth. NJ 2371
Brandesburton Humberside 51 F3 vil 6m/9km W of Hornsea. TA 1147
Brandeston Suffolk 31 F2 vil 5m/7km NW of Wickham Mkt. TM 2460
Brand Green Glos 26 C4 loc 2m/3km NE of Newent. SO 7428
Brandhill Salop 34 B6* loc 3m/4km S of Craven Arms. SO 4278
Brandis Corner Devon 6 C4 ham 4m/7km E of Holsworthy. SS 4103
Brandish Street Som 7 G1* ham 2km E of Porlock. SS 9046
Brandiston Norfolk 39 F3 vil 3m/5km SE of Reepham. TG 1421
Brandon Durham 54 B1 coal-mining tn 3m/4km SW of Durham. NZ 2440
Brandon Lincs 44 D6 vil 8m/12km N of Grantham. SK 9048
Brandon Nthmb 67 G6 loc on R Breamish 2m/4km NW of Glanton. NU 0417
Brandon Suffolk 38 C5 tn on Lit Ouse R, former centre of flint-knapping industry. TL 7886
Brandon Warwicks 36 A6 vil 5m/8km E of Coventry. Faint traces of 13c cas. SP 4076
Brandon Bank Norfolk 38 B5* loc on E bank of Lit Ouse R 4m/6km S of Southery. TL 6288
Brandon Creek Norfolk 38 B5 loc at confluence of Rs Gt and Lit Ouse 4m/7km NE of Littleport. TL 6091
Brandon Parva Norfolk 39 E4 ham 5m/8km NW of Wymondham. TG 0708
Brands Bay Dorset 9 G5* inlet on S side of Poole Harbour. SZ 0185
Brandsbutt Stone Grampian. See Inverurie.
Brandsby N Yorks 50 B1 vil 4m/6km NE of Easingwold. SE 5872
Brands Hatch Kent 20 C5 motor-racing circuit 3m/4km SE of Farningham. TQ 5764
Brands Hill Berks 19 E4* loc 3m/5km SE of Slough. TQ 0177
Brandwood End W Midlands 35 F6/G6* loc in Birmingham 5m/7km S of city centre. SP 0679
Brandy Brook 22 B4* r rising 2m/3km S of Mathry, Dyfed, and flowing S to Roch Br, then W into St Brides Bay at Newgale. SM 8422
Brane Cornwall 2 A5* loc 3m/5km SE of St Just. SW 4028
Bran End Essex 30 B5 vil 3m/4km NE of Gt Dunmow. TL 6525
Brankfleet Essex 21 F2 reach of R Roach at its confluence with R Crouch W of Foulness I. TQ 9894
Branksome Dorset 9 G5 E dist of Poole on N side of B. Park. Stream runs down to B. Chine. SZ 0592
Branksome Durham 54 B3* loc in Darlington 2m/3km NW of tn centre. NZ 2615
Branodunum Norfolk. See Brancaster.
Bransbury Hants 10 B1* ham 2km NW of Barton Stacey. SU 4242

Bransby Lincs 44 D3 ham 3m/4km N of Saxilby. SK 8979
Branscombe Devon 5 G2 vil in combe above S coast 5m/7km E of Sidmouth. Coast is NT property. SY 1988
Bransdale N Yorks 55 E5 loc 9m/15km N of Helmsley, at head of valley of same name. SE 6298
Bransford H & W 26 C2* vil 4m/7km W of Worcester. Bransford Br carries rd over R Teme 1km NE. SO 7952
Bransgore Hants 9 H4 vil 4m/6km NE of Christchurch. SZ 1897
Branson's Cross H & W 27 E1 loc 4m/6km NE of Redditch. SP 0970
Branston Leics 36 D2 vil 7m/12km NE of Melton Mowbray. SK 8129
Branston Lincs 45 E4 vil 4m/6km SE of Lincoln. **B. Booths** ham 3m/5km E. TF 0267
Branston Staffs 35 H2 vil 2m/3km SW of Burton upon Trent. SK 2221
Branstone Isle of Wight 10 C6* ham 3m/4km W of Sandown. SZ 5583
Bransty Cumbria 53 A3* loc in Whitehaven 1km N of tn centre. NX 9719
Brant 44 D5 r rising at Gelston, Lincs, and flowing N into R Witham 5m/8km S of Lincoln. SK 9563
Brant Broughton Lincs 44 D5 vil 7m/12km E of Newark-on-Trent. SK 9154
Brantham Suffolk 31 E4 vil 7m/12km SW of Ipswich. TM 1134
Branthwaite Cumbria 52 B3 vil 5m/7km SE of Workington. NY 0524
Branthwaite Cumbria 52 C2* loc 2m/3km SW of Caldbeck. NY 2937
Brantingham Humberside 50 D5 vil 2m/3km N of Brough. Site of Roman villa 1km SW. SE 9429
Branton Nthmb 67 G6 ham 2m/3km NW of Glanton. NU 0416
Branton S Yorks 44 B1 vil 4m/7km E of Doncaster. SE 6401
Branton Green N Yorks 50 A2* ham 1km NW of Gt Ouseburn. SE 4462
Branxholm Borders 60 A1 locality and cas in Teviotdale 3m/5km SW of Hawick. Old cas blown up in 1570; present hse dates in part from 1571–6. **B. Easter Loch** and **B. Wester Loch** are two small lochs, respectively 3km and 4km W. NT 4611
Branxton Nthmb 67 F4/F5 vil 2m/4km SE of Cornhill on Tweed. Site of Battle of Flodden Field, 1513, in which English defeated Scots. NT 8937
Brassey Green Ches 42 B5* loc 2m/3km SW of Tarporley. SJ 5260
Brassington Derbys 43 G5 vil 4m/6km W of Wirksworth. SK 2354
Brasted Kent 20 B6 vil 2m/3km E of Westerham. **B. Place,** 18c mansion where Napoleon III resided in 1840. Vil of **B. Chart** 1m S. TQ 4755
Bratch, The Staffs 35 E5 loc 4m/7km SW of Wolverhampton. SO 8693
Brathay 52 D4 r rising on Wrynose Pass, Cumbria, and flowing E into the head of Windermere. SD 3703
Brathens Grampian 77 F2* loc 2m/4km NW of Banchory. NO 6798
Bratoft Lincs 45 H4 vil 6m/9km W of Skegness. TF 4764
Brattleby Lincs 44 D3 vil 6m/10km N of Lincoln. SK 9480
Bratton Salop 34 C3* loc 2m/3km NW of Wellington. **Bratton Rd** loc to S. SJ 6314
Bratton Som 7 G1* ham on edge of Exmoor National Park 2km W of Minehead. SS 9446
Bratton Wilts 16 D6 vil 3m/4km E of Westbury. Iron Age camp (A.M.) on hill to W. ST 9152
Bratton Clovelly Devon 6 D5 vil 8m/13km W of Okehampton. SX 4691
Bratton Fleming Devon 7 E2 vil 6m/10km NE of Barnstaple. SS 6437
Bratton Seymour Som 8 D2/9 E2 vil 3m/4km W of Wincanton. ST 6729
Braughing Herts 29 G5 vil 2km N of Puckeridge. TL 3925
Braughing Friars Herts 29 H5* loc 2m/4km NE of Puckeridge. TL 4124
Brauncewell Lincs 45 E5 loc 4m/7km N of Sleaford. TF 0452
Braunston Leics 36 D4 vil 2m/3km SW of Oakham. SK 8306
Braunston Northants 28 B1 vil at junction of Oxford and Grand Union Canals 3m/5km NW of Daventry. Canal basin, locks and tunnel. Boat-building. SP 5366
Braunstone Leics 36 B4 suburb 2m/4km SW of Leicester city centre. SK 5502
Braunton Devon 6 D2 tn near N coast 5m/8km NW of Barnstaple. To W on coast behind Saunton Sands, **B. Burrows:** dunes, nature reserve. Chivenor Airfield to S of tn – see Chivenor. SS 4836
Bravoniacum Cumbria. See Kirkby Thore.
Brawby N Yorks 50 C1 vil 5m/8km NW of Malton. SE 7378
Brawdy (Breudeth) Dyfed 22 B3 loc 4m/6km E of Solva. Airfield to NW. SM 8524
Brawl H'land 86 D2 ancient cas on left bank of R Thurso on NE side of Halkirk, Caithness dist. Also spelt Braal. ND 1360
Brawlbin H'land 86 D2 locality in Caithness dist 1m S of Loch Calder. ND 0757
Braworth N Yorks 54 D4* loc 2km W of Stokesley. NZ 5007
Braxted, Great Essex 30 C6 ham 3m/4km E of Witham. TL 8614
Braxted, Little Essex 30 C6 ham 1m E of Witham. TL 8314
Bray Berks 18 D3 vil on R Thames 2km SE of Maidenhead. Loc of **B. Wick** 1km W. SU 9079
Bray 7 E3 r rising on Exmoor and running S into R Mole 3m/5km SW of S Molton, Devon. SS 6722
Braybrooke Northants 36 D5* vil 3m/4km SE of Mkt Harborough. SP 7684
Braydon Wilts 17 E3 loc 4m/6km N of Wootton Bassett. SU 0588
Braydon Pond Wilts 17 E3 lake 4m/7km E of Malmesbury. ST 9987
Braydon Side Wilts 17 E3* loc 5m/9km E of Malmesbury. SU 0185
Brayford Devon 7 E2 vil 6m/10km NW of S Molton below Exmoor. SS 6834
Bray, High Devon 7 E2 ham on W Exmoor 6m/9km NW of S Molton. SS 6934
Brays Grove Essex 20 B1* SE dist of Harlow. TL 4608
Bray Shop Cornwall 3 G1* vil 4m/6km NW of Callington. SX 3374
Braystones Cumbria 52 A4 loc 3m/5km S of Egremont. NY 0005
Braythorn N Yorks 49 E3* ham 4m/6km NE of Otley. SE 2449
Brayton N Yorks 50 B5 vil 2km SW of Selby. SE 6030
Braytown Dorset 9 F5* loc adjoining Wool to W. SY 8386
Braywoodside Berks 18 D4* loc 4m/6km S of Maidenhead. SU 8775
Brazacott Cornwall 6 B6 loc 6m/9km NW of Launceston. SX 2691
Brea Cornwall 2 C4* loc 1m E of Camborne. SW 6640
Breach Kent 21 E5* loc 1m NW of Newington. TQ 8465
Breach W Sussex 10 D4* N part of Southbourne, 2km E of Emsworth. SU 7606
Breachacha Castle Coll, S'clyde 68 A4 14c stronghold of the Macleans at head of Loch Breachacha on S coast, 5m/7km SW of Arinagour. 18c mansion that succeeded it is nearby. NM 1553
Breachwood Green Herts 29 F5 vil 4m/6km E of Luton. TL 1522
Breackerie Water S'clyde 62 D6 r in Kintyre running S down Glen Breackerie to Carskey Bay on S coast of the peninsula. NR 6507
Breaclete W Isles 88 A2/B2* vil at centre of Gt Bernera, W coast of Lewis. NB 1536
Breadalbane 71 E2-H1 area of Grampian Mts between Glen Lyon and Strathearn, and between Br of Orchy and Dunkeld. NN 4735
Breaden Heath Salop 34 B1* loc 3m/5km E of Ellesmere. SJ 4436
Breadsall Derbys 36 A1 vil 2m/4km NE of Derby. **B. Hilltop** loc 1km S. SK 3739
Breadstone Glos 16 C2 ham 2m/3km NE of Berkeley. SO 7000
Bread Street Glos 16 D1* loc 2km NW of Stroud. SO 8306
Breage Cornwall 2 B5 vil 3m/4km W of Helston. SW 6128
Breakish, Upper Skye, H'land 79 E6 loc 2m/3km E of Broadford. Loc of **Lr Breakish** to N on inlet of Ob Breakish. NG 6823
Breaksea Point S Glam 15 E5 headland on Bristol Channel coast 1m S of Gileston. ST 0265
Bream Glos 16 B1 vil 2m/4km NW of Lydney. SO 6005
Breamish r in Nthmb. See Till.
Breamore Hants 9 H3 vil 3m/4km N of Fordingbridge. SU 1518
Brean Som 15 G5 loc on Bristol Channel coast 4m/7km N of Burnham-on-Sea. ST 2956
Brean Down Som 15 G5 promontory (NT) protruding into Bristol Channel at S end of Weston Bay and SW of Weston-super-Mare. Can be reached by ferry from Uphill. ST 2859
Brearley W Yorks 48 C5* loc 1m E of Mytholmroyd. SE 0225
Brearton N Yorks 49 E2 vil 2m/4km E of Ripley. SE 3260
Breasclete W Isles 88 B2 vil on E Loch Roag, W coast of Lewis, 13m/21km W of Stornoway. NB 2135
Breaston Derbys 36 A1 suburb 2m/3km W of Long Eaton. SK 4633
Breawick Shetland 89 E7* loc on Mainland on W side of Aith Voe, 2km N of Aith. HU 3357
Brechfa Dyfed 24 B5 vil at centre of large state forest (Forest of Brechfa) 10m/15km NE of Carmarthen. SN 5230
Brechin Tayside 77 F5 market and mnfg tn on R South Esk 7m/12km W of Montrose. Mnfre of linen, jute, cotton goods. Distilling. 12c cathedral with 11c round tower attached. **Lit Brechin** is vil 2m/3km NW. NO 5960
Brechta Pool Powys 25 F4* small lake or tarn 1m W of Llyswen. SO 1137
Breckenbrough N Yorks 54 C6* loc 1m S of Kirby Wiske. SE 3883
Breckland 38 C5, D5 area of sandy heaths, much of it planted with conifers, around Thetford and Brandon on borders of Norfolk and Suffolk. TL 8090
Breckles Norfolk 38 D5 ham 5m/8km SE of Watton. **B. Hall** is Elizn. TL 9594
Breck Ness Orkney 89 A6* headland on W coast of Mainland 2m/3km W of Stromness. HY 2209
Brecknock 118 admin dist of Powys.
Brecon (Aberhonddu) Powys 25 F5 mkt tn at confluence of Rs Honddu and Usk 14m/22km N of Merthyr Tydfil. Cathedral is former priory ch. Remains of medieval cas. Canal navigable to Pontypool. Remains of ancient British camps on Pen-y-crug, 2km NW, and Slwch Tump, 1km E. SO 0428
Brecon Beacons (Bannau Brycheiniog) Powys 25 E5 mt range, largely NT, to S and SW of Brecon. The two chief peaks are Pen y Fan, 2907 ft or 886 metres, and Corn Du, 2863 ft or 873 metres. SO 02
Bredbury Gtr Manchester 43 E2* tn 3m/4km E of Stockport. **Lr Bredbury** loc 1km W. SJ 9391
Brede E Sussex 13 D3 vil 6m/9km N of Hastings. **B. Place** is Tudor hse 1km E. TQ 8218
Brede 13 E5 r rising near Battle, E Sussex, and flowing E into R Rother at Rye. TQ 9220
Bredenbury H & W 26 B2 vil 3m/5km NW of Bromyard. SO 6056
Bredfield Suffolk 31 F3 vil 3m/4km N of Woodbridge. TM 2653
Bredgar Kent 21 E5 vil 3m/4km SW of Sittingbourne. Site of Roman bldg 1m N. TQ 8860
Bredhurst Kent 20 D5 vil 3m/5km S of Gillingham. TQ 7962
Bredicot H & W 26 D2 loc 4m/6km E of Worcester. SO 9054
Bredon H & W 26 D4* vil on E bank of R Avon 3m/5km NE of Tewkesbury. 14c tithe barn (NT). SO 9236
Bredon's Hardwick H & W 26 D4* ham 2m/3km NE of Tewkesbury. SO 9135
Bredon's Norton H & W 26 D4 vil 5m/8km NE of Tewkesbury. SO 9339
Bredwardine H & W 25 G3 vil on R Wye 11m/18km W of Hereford. SO 3344
Bredy, Little (or Littlebredy) Dorset 8 D5 vil 6m/10km W of Dorchester. SY 5889
Breedon on the Hill Leics 36 A2 vil 5m/8km NE of Ashby de la Zouch. Ch is within ramparts of Iron Age fort. SK 4022
Brefi 24 C3* stream flowing W to Llandewi Brefi, Dyfed, and continuing W to join R Teifi 2km W of the vil. SN 6454
Breich Lothian 65 F3 loc 3m/5km S of Whitburn. **B. Water** is stream running NE to R Almond 5m/7km NE. NS 9660
Breidden Hills Powys 34 A3 isolated group of three peaks above right bank of R Severn about 6m/9km NE of Welshpool. The northernmost, **Breidden Hill,** 1202 ft or 366 metres, largely wooded, bears monmt commemorating naval victory of 1782 (Rodney's Pillar). There are ancient earthworks of uncertain origin. See also Middletown Hill, Moel y Golfa. SJ 21,31
Breightmet Gtr Manchester 42 C1* E dist of Bolton. SD 7409
Breighton Humberside 50 C4/C5* vil 2km S of Bubwith. SE 7034
Breinton H & W 26 A4* vil on N bank of R Wye 3m/4km W of Hereford. **B. Springs** (NT), farm and woodland incl site of deserted medieval vil. SO 4739
Breinton Common H & W 26 A4* loc 4m/6km W of Hereford. SO 4539
Breinton, Upper H & W 26 A3 loc 3m/5km W of Hereford. SO 4640
Breivig W Isles 88 C2* loc near E coast of Lewis 1km S of Back. NB 4839
Brelston Green H & W 26 B5* loc 4m/6km SW of Ross-on-Wye. SO 5520
Bremenium Nthmb. See Rochester.
Bremetennacum Lancs. See Ribchester.
Bremhill Wilts 17 E4 vil 2m/3km NW of Calne. Loc of **B. Wick** 1m NW. ST 9873
Brenchley Kent 12 C3 vil 2m/3km S of Paddock Wd. TQ 6741
Brendon Devon 6 C4* loc 3m/4km NE of Holsworthy. SS 3607
Brendon Devon 7 F1 vil on E Lyn R 3m/5km SE of Lynton. SS 7648
Brendon Hills Som 7 G2, H2 eastward extension of Exmoor Forest, qv. Included in Exmoor National Park. SS 93, ST 03
Brenfield Point S'clyde 70 B6 headland on W side of Loch Fyne 2m/3km S of Ardrishaig, Argyll. NR 8582
Brenig 41 F6 r rising in Llyn Bran, Clwyd, and flowing S through Brenig Resr to R Alwen 2km E of Alwen Resr. SH 9752
Brenig Reservoir Clwyd 41 F5* resr 4m/7km S of Bylchau. SH 9756
Brenish W Isles 88 A2* vil near W coast of Lewis 6m/10km SW of Uig. NA 9926
Brenkley Tyne & Wear 61 G4 loc 7m/11km N of Newcastle. NZ 2175
Brent London 19 F3* borough lying some 7m/12km NW of Charing Cross. Contains dists of Wembley and Willesden. TQ 1984
Brent 19 F4 r rising as Dollis Brook in borough of Barnet in N London, flowing S through borough of Brent (and forming Brent Resr), and running into R Thames at Brentford above Kew Br. TQ 1877
Brent, East Som 15 H6 vil 3m/5km NE of Burnham-on-Sea. ST 3452
Brent Eleigh Suffolk 30 D3 vil 2m/3km SE of Lavenham. TL 9447
Brentford London 19 F4 dist in borough of Hounslow 8m/13km W of Charing Cross. TQ 1777
Brentingby Leics 36 D3 ham 2m/3km E of Melton Mowbray. SK 7818
Brent Knoll Som 15 H6 vil at W foot of hill of same name and 2m/3km NE of Burnham-on-Sea. ST 3350
Brentor, North Devon 4 B3 vil 5m/7km N of Tavistock. Loc of S Brentor 1m S. **Brent Tor** itself, 1m SW, is conical hill of 1100 ft or 335 metres, topped by medieval ch. SX 4881
Brent Pelham Herts 29 H4 vil 5m/7km E of Buntingford. TL 4330
Brent Reservoir London 19 F3 resr 7m/11km NW of Charing Cross, lying partly in borough of Barnet and partly in borough of Brent. TQ 2187
Brent, South Devon 4 D4 vil below S edge of Dartmoor 5m/7km SW of Buckfastleigh. SX 6960
Brentwood Essex 20 C2 tn 11m/17km SW of Chelmsford. TQ 5993
Brenzett Kent 13 F4 vil on Romney Marsh 3m/5km SE of Appledore. Ham of **B. Green** 1m NE. TR 0027
Brerachan Water 76 B4 r in Tayside region running E down Glen Brerachan to join Allt Fearnach and form R Ardle 3m/5km NW of Kirkmichael. NO 0463
Brereton Staffs 35 F3 loc 2m/3km SE of Rugeley. SK 0516
Brereton Cross Staffs 35 G3* vil 2m/4km SE of Rugeley. SK 0615
Brereton Green Ches 42 D4 vil 2m/3km S of Holmes Chapel. SJ 7764
Brereton Heath Ches 42 D4* loc 4m/6km W of Congleton. SJ 8064
Breretonhill Staffs 35 F3* loc 2m/3km SE of Rugeley. SK 0515

Brereton Pool Ches 42 D4* small lake 1m N of Brereton Green and 2km SE of Holmes Chapel. SJ 7765
Bressay Shetland 89 E7 island of 11 sq miles or 28 sq km off E coast of Mainland, from which it is separated by **B. Sound.** The sound affords protection to shipping and the harbour of Lerwick. Fishing and fish-processing are carried on. Island attains height of 743 ft or 226 metres in **Ward of B.**, conical hill 2m/3km N of Bard Hd. HU 44, 53
Bressingham Norfolk 39 E6 vil 3m/4km W of Diss. Loc of **B. Common** 2km NE. TM 0780
Bretabister Shetland. Alternative spelling of Brettabister, qv.
Bretby Derbys 35 H2 vil 4m/6km E of Burton upon Trent. Earthworks mark site of former cas. **B. Park** is early 19c castellated mansion. SK 2923
Bretford Warwicks 36 A6 vil 5m/8km W of Rugby. SP 4277
Bretforton H & W 27 E3 vil 4m/6km E of Evesham. SP 0943
Bretherton Lancs 47 F6 vil 5m/7km W of Leyland. SD 4720
Brett 31 E4 r rising 1m N of Brettenham, Suffolk, and flowing S into R Stour just S of Higham. TM 0335
Brettabister Shetland 89 E7* loc on Mainland on S Nesting Bay 2m/3km NE of Skellister. Also spelt Bretabister. HU 4857
Brettenham Norfolk 38 D6 ham 4m/6km E of Thetford on N bank of R Thet. Site of Romano-British settlement to NE. TL 9383
Brettenham Suffolk 30 D3 vil 5m/7km NE of Lavenham. TL 9654
Bretton Cambs 37 F4* NW dist of Peterborough. TF 1601
Bretton Clwyd 42 A5* ham 4m/6km SW of Chester across R Dee. SJ 3563
Bretton Derbys 43 G3* loc 2km E of Gt Hucklow. SK 2077
Bretton, West W Yorks 49 E6 vil 5m/9km SW of Wakefield. To S, **Bretton Hall,** hse dating partly from early 18c, in large park with lake. SE 2813
Breudeth Welsh form of Brawdy, qv.
Brevig W Isles 88 D4* loc on **B. Bay** on Barra, 2m/3km E of Castlebay. NL 6998
Brewers Green Norfolk 39 E6* loc 1m NW of Diss. TM 1080
Brewer Street Surrey 19 G6* loc 2m/3km W of Godstone. TQ 3251
Brewham Som 9 E1 par 3m/4km E of Bruton, containing vils of **N** and **S Brewham.** ST 7236
Brewood Staffs 35 E3 vil on Shropshire Union Canal 7m/11km N of Wolverhampton. SJ 8808
Breydon Water Norfolk 39 H4 wide part of R Yare estuary to W of Gt Yarmouth, 3m/5km long and about 1km wide. TG 4907
Briantspuddle Dorset 9 E5 vil on R Piddle or Trent 2m/4km SW of Bere Regis. SY 8193
Bricett, Great Suffolk 31 E3 vil 5m/8km N of Hadleigh. TM 0350
Bricett, Little Suffolk 31 E3* loc 5m/8km N of Hadleigh. TM 0549
Brick End Essex 30 A5* ham 4m/7km NW of Gt Dunmow. TL 5725
Bricket Wood Herts 19 E2* suburban loc 4m/6km NE of Watford. TL 1302
Brickfields H & W 26 D2* NE dist of Worcester. SO 8656
Brickhill, Great Bucks 28 D4 vil 3m/5km SE of Bletchley. SP 9030
Brickhill, Little Bucks 28 D4 vil 2m/4km SE of Bletchley. SP 9132
Brickkiln Green Essex 30 C4* loc 3m/5km E of Finchingfield. TL 7331
Bricklehampton H & W 27 E3 vil 4m/6km W of Evesham. SO 9842
Bride Isle of Man 46 C3 vil 4m/7km N of Ramsey. NX 4401
Bride 8 C5 r rising at Lit Bredy in Dorset and flowing W into Lyme Bay 1km W of Burton Bradstock. SY 4789
Bridekirk Cumbria 52 B2 vil 2m/3km N of Cockermouth. NY 1133
Bridell Dyfed 22 D2 loc 3m/4km S of Cardigan. SN 1742
Bridestowe Devon 6 D6 vil 6m/10km SW of Okehampton. SX 5189
Brideswell Grampian 83 E3* loc 3m/5km E of Huntly. NJ 5739
Bridford Devon 4 D2 vil 4m/6km E of Moretonhampstead. SX 8186
Bridge Cornwall 2 C4* ham 2m/3km NW of Redruth. SW 6744
Bridge Kent 13 G2 vil 3m/5km SE of Canterbury. TR 1854
Bridge, East Suffolk 31 H2 ham 2m/4km N of Leiston. TM 4566
Bridge End Beds 29 E3 loc adjoining Bromham to S, 3m/5km W of Bedford. TL 0050
Bridge End Clwyd 41 H5* loc at S end of Hope. SJ 3057
Bridge End Cumbria 52 B6/C6* loc just SE of The Green. SD 1884
Bridge End Cumbria 52 C5* loc 3m/5km NE of Broughton in Furness. SD 2490
Bridge End Cumbria 53 F2* loc adjoining Kirkby Thore to S. NY 6325
Bridge End Cumbria 59 H6* loc 1m S of Dalston. NY 3748
Bridge End Devon 4 D5* loc on S side of R Avon opp Aveton Gifford, 3m/5km NW of Kingsbridge. SX 6946
Bridge End Durham 54 A2* loc just W of Frosterley across R Wear. NY 0236
Bridge End Essex 30 B4/B5 N end of Gt Bardfield, 2km SW of Finchingfield. TL 6730
Bridge End Lincs 37 F1 loc 4m/7km W of Donington. TF 1436
Bridge End Nthmb 61 E5* loc at N end of br over R South Tyne 2m/3km NW of Hexham. NY 9166
Bridge End Nthmb 61 E5* loc at N end of rd br across R Tyne at Hexham. NY 9464
Bridge End Shetland 89 E8* loc on W Burra I. at br connection with E Burra I. HU 3733
Bridge End Surrey 19 E5* loc adjoining Ockham to NE, 5m/8km E of Woking. TQ 0756
Bridge End Warwicks 27 G2 loc in S part of Warwick. SP 2864
Bridgefoot Cumbria 52 B2* loc adjoining Lit Clifton to N. NY 0529
Bridgeford, Great Staffs 35 E2 vil 4m/6km NW of Stafford. **Lit Bridgeford** loc 1km NW. SJ 8826
Bridge, Great W Midlands 35 F5 loc in W Bromwich 2m/3km NW of tn centre. SO 9792
Bridge Green Essex 29 H4* loc 5m/8km W of Saffron Walden. TL 4637
Bridge Green Norfolk 39 E6* loc 3m/5km NE of Diss. TM 1483
Bridgehampton Som 8 D2 ham 3m/5km E of Ilchester, beyond Yeovilton airfield. ST 5624
Bridge Hewick N Yorks 49 E2 ham 2m/3km E of Ripon. SE 3370
Bridge, High Cumbria 59 H6* loc on Roe Beck 4m/7km S of Dalston. NY 3943
Bridgehill Durham 61 F6* W dist of Consett. NZ 0951
Bridgemarsh Island Essex 21 E2 marshy island in R Crouch estuary 3m/5km W of Burnham-on-Crouch. **Bridgemarsh Creek** separates it from mainland on N side. TQ 8996
Bridgemary Hants 10 C4* NW dist of Gosport. SU 5803
Bridgend Cornwall 3 F2 dist of Lostwithiel E of R Fowey. SX 1159
Bridgend Cumbria 52 D3 loc 1m S of Patterdale. NY 3914
Bridgend Dyfed 22 D2* loc at S end of br across R Teifi at Cardigan. SN 1745
Bridgend Glos 16 C1* loc 3m/5km W of Stroud. SO 8004
Bridgend Grampian 82 C4 loc 6m/10km SE of Dufftown. NJ 3731
Bridgend Grampian 83 F2* loc on S side of Turriff across Idoch Water. NJ 7249
Bridgend Lothian 65 G2* vil 3m/5km E of Linlithgow. NT 0475
Bridgend Mid Glam 15 E3 tn on Ogmore R 18m/28km W of Cardiff. Iron works. Industrial estate to SE. SS 9079
Bridgend S'clyde 62 B2 vil on Islay at NE end of Loch Indaal. NR 3362
Bridgend Tayside 73 E2 E dist of Perth across R Tay. NO 1223
Bridgend Tayside 77 E4* loc on West Water 4m/6km W of Edzell. NO 5368
Bridgend of Lintrathen Tayside 76 D5 vil on E side of Loch of Lintrathen. NO 2854
Bridgeness Central 65 F1* loc on S side of Firth of Forth, adjoining Bo'ness to E. NT 0181
Bridge, North Surrey 11 F2 loc 4m/6km S of Milford. SU 9636
Bridge of Alford Grampian 82 D5 loc at rd br across R Don 2km NW of Alford. NJ 5617
Bridge of Allan Central 72 B5 residential tn with light industry 3m/4km N of Stirling. See also Airthrey. NS 7997
Bridge of Avon Grampian 82 B3 rd br over R Avon 1km above Ballindalloch Castle, 7m/11km SW of Charlestown of Aberlour. NJ 1835
Bridge of Balgie Tayside 71 G1 loc in Glen Lyon 10m/16km W of Fortingall. NN 5746
Bridge of Brewlands Tayside 76 C4* loc with rd br across R Isla 2m/3km NW of Kirkton of Glenisla. NO 1961
Bridge of Brown 82 A5. See Glen Brown.
Bridge of Cally Tayside 76 C5 vil at rd crossing of R Ardle 5m/7km NW of Blairgowrie. NO 1451
Bridge of Canny Grampian 77 F2 vil and rd br over Burn of Canny 3m/5km W of Banchory. NO 6597
Bridge of Coe H'land 74 C5 rd br across R Coe at foot of Glen Coe, Lochaber dist. NN 1058
Bridge of Craigisla Tayside 76 C5* loc on R Isla 4m/6km N of Alyth. See also Reekie Linn. NO 2553
Bridge of Dee D & G 58 C5 vil, and rd br across R Dee, 3m/4km SW of Castle Douglas. NX 7360
Bridge of Don Grampian 77 H1 vil on N bank of R Don 2m/4km N of centre of Aberdeen. Rd br spans r. NJ 9409
Bridge of Dye Grampian 77 F3 loc in Glen Dye 4m/6km S of Strachan. NO 6586
Bridge of Earn Tayside 73 E3 vil on R Earn 4m/6km S of Perth. NO 1318
Bridge of Ericht Tayside 75 F5* locality and rd br near mouth of R Ericht on N side of Loch Rannoch. NN 5258
Bridge of Feugh Grampian 77 F2 rd br over Water of Feugh 1km S of Banchory. Incorporates platform for observing salmon-leap. NO 7095
Bridge of Forss H'land 86 C1 loc and br in Caithness dist carrying A836 rd over Forss Water 5m/8km W of Thurso. ND 0368
Bridge of Gaur Tayside 75 F5* locality on R Gaur 1km above Loch Rannoch. See also (The) Barracks. NN 5056
Bridge of Muchalls Grampian. See Muchalls.
Bridge of Orchy S'clyde 71 E1 vil on R Orchy 2m/3km S of Loch Tulla, Argyll. NN 2939
Bridge of Walls Shetland 89 D7* loc on Mainland at head of Gruting Voe. HU 2651
Bridge of Weir S'clyde 64 B2/B3 small tn and golfing resort on R Gryfe 6m/10km W of Paisley. Tanneries. NS 3865
Bridge Reach 20 D4* stretch of R Medway at Rochester, Kent, spanned by a rd and a rly br connecting the city with Strood on the left bank. TQ 7468
Bridge Reeve Devon 7 E4* loc on R Taw 2m/3km W of Chulmleigh. SS 6613
Bridgerule Devon 3 B5 vil 4m/7km W of Holsworthy. SS 2702
Bridges Salop 34 B4* loc 6m/10km NE of Bishop's Castle. SO 3996
Bridge Sollers H & W 26 A3 vil on R Wye 6m/10km W of Hereford. SO 4142
Bridge Street Suffolk 30 D3 ham 2m/4km W of Lavenham. TL 8749
Bridgeton S'clyde 64 D3* dist of Glasgow 1m SE of city centre. NS 6064
Bridgetown Cornwall 6 C6 ham 3m/5km N of Launceston. SX 3489
Bridgetown Som 7 G2 vil on R Exe just S of Exton and 3m/5km N of Dulverton. SS 9233
Bridge Trafford Ches 42 A4 vil on R Gowy 4m/7km NE of Chester. SJ 4471
Bridgewater Canal 42 C2-B3 canal linking Leeds and Liverpool Canal at Leigh, Gtr Manchester, with Trent and Mersey Canal at Preston Brook, Ches.
Bridgeyate Avon 16 C4* loc 6m/10km E of Bristol. ST 6873
Bridgford, East Notts 36 C1 vil 8m/13km E of Nottingham. SK 6943
Bridgford, West Notts 36 B1 tn on S side of Nottingham across R Trent. Industries include coach-building, light engineering. SK 5837
Bridgham Norfolk 38 D6 vil 6m/10km E of Thetford. TL 9585
Bridgnorth Salop 34 D5 tn on cliff above R Severn. Remains of Norman cas. Half-timbered tn hall of 17c. SO 7193
Bridgtown Staffs 35 F3 urban loc 1m S of Cannock. SJ 9808
Bridgwater Som 8 B1 industrial tn and small port on R Parrett 9m/15km NE of Taunton. **B. and Taunton Canal** connects the two tns. ST 2937
Bridgwater Bay Som 15 F6, G6 wide bay in Bristol Channel extending from Brean Down W of Weston-super-Mare to Greenaleigh Pt NW of Minehead. ST 1852
Bridlington Humberside 51 F2 old port and fishing tn, also modern North Sea coastal resort, 24m/39km N of Hull. **B. Bay** extends from Flamborough Hd to Hornsea. TA 1766
Bridport Dorset 8 C5 mkt tn 14m/23km W of Dorchester. SY 4692
Bridstow H & W 26 B5* vil 1m W of Ross-on-Wye across r. SO 5824
Briercliffe Lancs 48 B4* loc 3m/4km SE of Nelson. SD 8834
Brierfield Lancs 48 B4 textile tn adjoining Nelson to SW. SD 8436
Brierley Glos 26 B5* vil 2m/3km NW of Cinderford. SO 6215
Brierley H & W 26 A2 loc 2m/3km S of Leominster. SO 4956
Brierley S Yorks 49 F6 vil 2m/3km SW of Hemsworth. SE 4110
Brierley Hill W Midlands 35 E5 SW dist of Dudley. SO 9186
Brierton Cleveland 54 D2 loc 3m/4km SW of Hartlepool. NZ 4730
Briery Cumbria 52 C3* loc 2km E of Keswick. NY 2824
Briery Hill Gwent 15 F1* loc on W side of Ebbw Vale. SO 1608
Briestfield W Yorks 49 E6* loc 2m/3km N of Flockton. SE 2217
Brigflatts Cumbria 53 F5* loc 2km W of Sedbergh. SD 6491
Brigg Humberside 45 E1 small tn 7m/12km E of Scunthorpe. Agricultural products; mnfre of agricultural implements. TA 0007
Briggate Norfolk 39 G2* ham 3m/5km SE of N Walsham. TG 3127
Briggswath N Yorks 55 G4* vil on N bank of R Esk opp Sleights. NZ 8608
Brigham Cumbria 52 B2 vil 2m/4km W of Cockermouth. NY 0830
Brigham Humberside 51 E3 ham 4m/7km SE of Gt Driffield. TA 0753
Brighouse W Yorks 48 D5 tn on R Calder 4m/7km N of Huddersfield. Textiles, carpets, engineering. SE 1423
Brighouse Bay D & G 58 C6 inlet on E side of Wigtown Bay, 2m/3km S of Borgue. NX 6345
Brighstone Isle of Wight 10 B6 vil 2m/3km W of Shorwell. To S, **B. Bay,** extending from Chilton Chine south-eastwards to Atherfield Pt. SZ 4282
Brightgate Derbys 43 G5* loc 2m/4km W of Matlock. SK 2659
Brighthampton Oxon 17 G2 ham 4m/7km SE of Witney. SP 3803
Brightholmlee S Yorks 43 G2* loc 1km NW of Wharncliffe Side. SK 2995
Brightling E Sussex 12 C4 vil 5m/8km NW of Battle. Obelisk and observatory on B. Down to E. TQ 6821
Brightlingsea Essex 31 E6 tn on **B. Creek** near mouth of R Colne 8m/12km SE of Colchester. Yachting and boat-building centre; oyster fisheries. TM 0816
Brighton Cornwall 2 D3 loc 7m/12km SE of Newquay. SW 9054
Brighton E Sussex 11 H4 seaside resort and commercial centre 48m/77km S of London. Regency squares at Kemp Town. Pavilion built in Oriental style for Prince Regent. University of Sussex at Stanmer Park (see Stanmer). TQ 3104
Brighton le Sands Merseyside 41 H2* dist of Crosby on coast 2km NW of tn centre. SJ 3099
Brightons Central 65 F1 vil 3m/5km SE of Falkirk. NS 9277
Brightside S Yorks 43 H2* dist of Sheffield 3m/5km NE of city centre. SK 3890
Brightwalton Berks 17 H4 vil 8m/13km N of Newbury. Hams of **B. Green** and **B. Holt** 1km S and 2km SE respectively. SU 4279
Brightwell Oxon 18 B3 vil 2m/3km NW of Wallingford. SU 5790
Brightwell Suffolk 31 F4 vil 6m/9km E of Ipswich. TM 2543
Brightwell Baldwin Oxon 18 B2 vil 2m/4km W of Watlington. SU 6595

Brightwell Upperton Oxon 18 B2* ham 2m/3km W of Watlington. SU 6594
Brigmerston Wilts 17 F6* loc adjoining Milston, 3m/4km N of Amesbury. SU 1645
Brignall Durham 54 A3/A4 vil above **B. Banks** beside R Greta 3m/5km SE of Barnard Castle. NZ 0712
Brig o' Turk Central 71 F4 vil 6m/10km W of Callander. NN 5306
Brigsley Humberside 45 F1 vil 5m/8km S of Grimsby. TA 2501
Brigsteer Cumbria 53 E5 vil 2m/4km N of Levens. SD 4889
Brigstock Northants 37 E5 vil 4m/6km SE of Corby. Manor hse medieval and later. SP 9485
Brill Bucks 28 B6 vil 6m/10km NW of Thame. SP 6513
Brill Cornwall 2 C5* ham 5m/8km SW of Penryn. SW 7229
Brilley H & W 25 G3 vil 5m/8km NE of Hay-on-Wye. SO 2649
Brimaston (Treowman) Dyfed 22 B3 loc 2km E of Hayscastle Cross. SM 9325
Brimfield H & W 26 A1 vil 4m/7km W of Tenbury Wells. SO 5267
Brimfieldcross H & W 26 B1* ham 3m/5km W of Tenbury Wells. SO 5468
Brimham Rocks N Yorks 49 E2 large group of rocks (NT) fantastically shaped by erosion, 3m/5km E of Pateley Br. SE 2064
Brimington Derbys 43 H4 loc 2m/3km NE of Chesterfield. See also New Brimington. **B. Common** loc 1m S. SK 4073
Brimley Devon 4 D3 loc 5m/8km NE of Ashburton. SX 7977
Brimpsfield Glos 26 D6 vil 6m/9km S of Cheltenham. SO 9312
Brimpton Berks 18 B5 vil 4m/7km NE of Kingsclere. SU 5564
Brims Orkney 89 A7* loc at S end of Hoy 1m SE of Melsetter. To E is headland of **B. Ness.** ND 2888
Brimscombe Glos 16 D2* vil 2m/3km SE of Stroud. SO 8602
Brimsdown London 20 A2* loc in R Lea valley 3m/4km E of Enfield in borough of Enfield. TQ 3697
Brims Ness H'land 86 D1 headland on N coast of Caithness dist 5m/8km W of Thurso. ND 0471
Brimstage Merseyside 41 H3 ham 4m/7km SW of Birkenhead. Oratory of 14c–15c. SJ 3082
Brinacory H'land 79 F8 locality on N shore of Loch Morar, in Lochaber dist, 4m/7km E of foot of loch. **Brinacory I.** is islet in loch. NM 7591
Brincliffe S Yorks 43 G3* dist of Sheffield 2m/3km SW of city centre. SK 3385
Brind Humberside 50 C5 ham 2m/3km N of Howden. SE 7430
Brindham Som 8 C1* loc 2km NE of Glastonbury. ST 5140
Brindister Shetland 89 D7* loc on Mainland on W shore of **B. Voe,** narrow inlet off St Magnus Bay, S of island of Vementry. HU 2857
Brindister Shetland 89 E8* locality on Mainland 1m N of Easter Quarff. **Loch of Brindister** to W. HU 4336
Brindle Lancs 47 F5 vil 6m/9km SW of Blackburn. SD 5924
Brindle Heath Gtr Manchester 42 D2* dist of Salford 2m/3km NW of tn centre. SJ 8099
Brindley Ford Staffs 42 D5 loc 2m/4km NE of Tunstall. SJ 8754
Brineton Staffs 35 E3 ham 5m/9km SE of Newport. SJ 8013
Bring Deeps Orkney 89 A7 sea passage between Bring Hd on island of Hoy and Howton Hd on island of Mainland. HY 2902
Bring Head Orkney 89 A7* headland at N end of island of Hoy 3m/4km E of Ward Hill. HY 2702
Bringhurst Leics 36 D5 vil 4m/7km NW of Corby. SP 8492
Brington Cambs 29 E1 vil 6m/9km E of Thrapston. TL 0875
Brington Northants 28 B2 par containing vils of **Gt** and **Lit Brington,** 6m/10km NW of Northampton. SP 6664
Briningham Norfolk 39 E2 vil 4m/6km SW of Holt. TG 0334
Brinkburn Priory Nthmb 61 F2 priory of *c.* 1200 restored in 1858, in loop of R Coquet 4m/7km SE of Rothbury. NZ 1198
Brinkhill Lincs 45 G4 vil 5m/8km N of Spilsby. TF 3773
Brinkley Cambs 30 B3 vil 6m/9km S of Newmarket. TL 6254
Brinkley Notts 44 B5* loc 2km SE of Southwell. SK 7152
Brinklow Warwicks 36 A6 vil 6m/10km E of Coventry. Remains of motte and bailey cas. SP 4379
Brinkworth Wilts 17 E3 vil 5m/9km E of Malmesbury. SU 0184
Brinnington Gtr Manchester 43 E2* loc in Stockport 2m/3km NE of tn centre. SJ 9192
Brinscall Lancs 47 G5 vil 6m/9km SW of Blackburn. SD 6221
Brinscombe Som 15 H6* loc 3m/5km N of Wedmore. ST 4252
Brinsea Avon 16 A5* loc 2km S of Congresbury. ST 4462
Brinsford Staffs 35 E4* loc 1m SE of Coven. SJ 9105
Brinsley Notts 44 A6 vil 2km N of Eastwood. SK 4648
Brinsop H & W 26 A3 loc 5m/9km NW of Hereford. SO 4444
Brinsworth S Yorks 43 H2 loc 2m/3km S of Rotherham. SK 4189
Brinton Norfolk 39 E2 vil 3m/5km SW of Holt. TG 0335
Brinyan Orkney 89 B6 loc at SE end of island of Rousay. There is a pier or landing stage. HY 4327
Brisco Cumbria 60 A6 ham 3m/5km SE of Carlisle. NY 4251
Briscoe, East Durham 53 H3* loc 2m/3km SW of Romaldkirk. **W Briscoe** loc 1km W, at S end of Hury Resr dam. NY 9719
Brisley Norfolk 38 D3 vil 6m/9km NW of E Dereham. TF 9521
Brislington Avon 16 B4 dist of Bristol 3m/4km SE of city centre. ST 6270
Brisons, The Cornwall 2 A5 two island rocks off Cape Cornwall to SW. SW 3431
Brissenden Green Kent 13 E3* ham 1m SE of Bethersden. TQ 9339
Bristnall Fields W Midlands 35 F5* loc in Warley 1m W of tn centre. SO 9986
Bristol Avon 16 B4 city 106m/171km W of London. Port on R Avon with docks in the city itself and at Avonmouth and Portishead. Commercial, industrial, university and cathedral city. Industries include food, tobacco, aircraft manufacture. Historical links with N America. Airport at Lulsgate, 7m/11km SW. ST 5872
Bristol Channel 14, 15 extension of mouth of R Severn separating S Wales from the English counties of Avon, Somerset, and Devon. SS 76
Bristol, Little Avon 16 C3* loc adjoining Charfield to S, 2m/4km SW of Wotton-under-Edge. ST 7291
Briston Norfolk 39 E2 vil 4m/6km S of Holt. TG 0632
Brit 8 C5 r rising N of Beaminster, Dorset, and flowing S through Bridport into Lyme Bay at W Bay. SY 4690
Britannia Lancs 48 B5 loc 2km SE of Bacup. SD 8821
Britannia Bridge Gwynedd 40 C4 rly br across Menai Strait 2m/4km W of Bangor. Original design by Robert Stevenson modified after fire in 1970. SH 5471
Britford Wilts 9 H2 vil in R Avon valley 2km SE of Salisbury. SU 1628
Brithdir Gwynedd 33 E3* ham 3m/4km E of Dolgellau. SH 7618
Brithdir Mid Glam 15 F2* vil 2km N of Bargoed. SO 1502
Brithem Bottom Devon 7 G4* loc 2m/3km NW of Cullompton. ST 0110
British Legion Village Kent 20 D5* rehabilitation centre 3m/4km NW of Maidstone. TQ 7257
Briton Ferry (Llansawel) W Glam 14 C2 tn at mouth of R Neath on E bank, 2m/3km S of Neath. Docks, steel works. SS 7494
Brittle H'land 79 C6 r in S part of Skye rising in Cuillin Hills and running down to head of Loch B. NG 4020
Britwell Bucks 18 D3* suburban loc 2m/3km N of Slough. SU 9582
Britwell Salome Oxon 18 B2. Par (Britwell) and vil 2km SW of Watlington. SU 6393
Brixham Devon 5 E5 tn on coast 5m/8km S of Torquay across Tor Bay. Fishing, tourism. William of Orange landed here in 1688. SX 9256
Brixton Devon 4 C5 vil 5m/8km E of Plymouth. SX 5552
Brixton London 19 G4* dist in borough of Lambeth 3m/5km S of Charing Cross. TQ 3175
Brixton Deverill Wilts 9 F1 vil 4m/7km S of Warminster and 5m/8km NE of Mere. ST 8638
Brixworth Northants 28 C1 vil 7m/11km N of Northampton. Kennels of Pytchley foxhounds 1km NW. SP 7470
Brize Norton Oxon 17 G1 vil 4m/6km W of Witney. Airfield to SW. SP 3007
Broad Alley H & W 26 D1* ham 3m/5km N of Droitwich. SO 8867
Broad Bay W Isles 88 C2 large bay on E coast of Lewis extending from Tolsta Hd to Tiumpan Hd on Eye Peninsula, and south-westwards to Laxdale, N of Stornoway. Also known as Loch a' Tuath. NB 43
Broad Blunsdon Wilts 17 F3 vil 4m/6km N of Swindon. SU 1590
Broadbottom Gtr Manchester 43 E2 loc 3m/5km E of Hyde. SJ 9993
Broadbridge W Sussex 11 E4* vil 3m/5km W of Chichester. Site of Roman bldg. SU 8105
Broadbridge Heath W Sussex 11 G2 suburban loc 2m/3km W of Horsham. Field Place to N is birthplace of Shelley. TQ 1431
Broadbury Devon 6 C5, D5 upland area 8m/13km W of Okehampton. SX 4596
Broad Cairn 76 C3 mt on border of Grampian and Tayside regions 2m/3km W of head of Loch Muick. Height 3274 ft or 998 metres. NO 2481
Broad Campden Glos 27 F4 vil 1m SE of Chipping Campden. SP 1537
Broad Carr W Yorks 48 D6* ham adjoining Holywell Green to E. SE 0919
Broad Chalke Wilts 9 G2 vil on R Ebble 5m/8km SW of Wilton. SU 0325
Broad Clough Lancs 48 B5* loc 1km N of Bacup. SD 8624
Broad Clyst Devon 7 G5 vil 5m/8km NE of Exeter. Most of vil is NT property, as is Killerton Park, Danes Wd, and Ashclyst Forest, all within par. SX 9897
Broad Colney Herts 19 F2* loc 3m/5km SE of St Albans. TL 1703
Broadfield Dyfed 22 D5* loc 2m/3km N of Tenby. SN 1303
Broadfield Gtr Manchester 42 D1* loc in Heywood 1m W of tn centre. SD 8410
Broadfield Lancs 47 F5* loc adjoining Leyland to W. SD 5222
Broadfield Lancs 48 A5* loc adjoining Accrington to S. SD 7527
Broadfield S'clyde 64 B2* loc 2km SE of Port Glasgow. NS 3473
Broadfield W Sussex 11 H2* SW dist of Crawley. TQ 2635
Broad Ford Kent 12 D3* loc 1m SE of Horsmonden. TQ 7139
Broadford Skye, H'land 79 E6 vil on **B. Bay** 7m/11km SW of Kyleakin. NG 6423
Broadford Bridge W Sussex 11 G3 ham 3m/5km S of Billingshurst. TQ 0921
Broadgate Lincs 37 H3* loc 2m/4km S of Sutton St Edmund. TF 3609
Broadgrass Green Suffolk 30 D2* loc 1km NW of Woolpit. TL 9663
Broad Green Beds 28 D3 loc adjoining Cranfield to N, 7m/11km SW of Bedford. SP 9543
Broad Green Cambs 30 B2* loc 4m/6km SE of Newmarket. TL 6859
Broad Green Essex 29 H4* loc adjoining Chrishall to W, 5m/9km E of Royston. TL 4439
Broad Green Essex 30 D5 ham 2m/3km E of Coggeshall. TL 8723
Broad Green H & W 27 E1* loc 2m/4km E of Bromsgrove. SO 9970
Broad Green H & W 26 C2 ham 5m/8km W of Worcester. SO 7655
Broad Green London 19 G5* loc in borough of Croydon 1m N of Croydon tn centre. TQ 3166
Broad Green Merseyside 42 A2 dist of Liverpool 4m/7km E of city centre. SJ 4090
Broad Green Suffolk 30 C2* ham 1km SW of Chevington. TL 7859
Broad Green Suffolk 31 E2* loc 1km SW of Forward Green. TM 0859
Broad Green Suffolk 31 F2* loc 2m/3km NW of Debenham. TM 1464
Broadhaigh Gtr Manchester 42 D1* loc in Rochdale 2km W of tn centre. SD 8713
Broad Haven Dyfed 22 B4 vil on St Brides Bay 6m/9km W of Haverfordwest. SM 8613
Broad Haven Dyfed 22 C6 inlet 1m N of St Govan's Hd. SR 9794
Broadhaven H'land 86 F2/F3 loc on small bay of Broad Haven on E coast of Caithness dist, on E side of Wick. ND 3751
Broadheath Gtr Manchester 42 D2* dist of Altrincham 1m N of tn centre. SJ 7689
Broadheath H & W 26 B1 loc 5m/8km SE of Tenbury Wells. SO 6665
Broadheath, Lower H & W 26 C2 vil 3m/4km NW of Worcester. SO 8157
Broadheath, Upper H & W 26 C2 vil 3m/5km W of Worcester. SO 8055
Broadhembury Devon 7 H4 vil 5m/7km NW of Honiton. ST 1004
Broadhempston Devon 4 D4 vil 4m/6km SE of Ashburton. SX 8066
Broad Hill Cambs 38 B6* loc 2m/4km N of Soham. TL 5976
Broad Hinton Wilts 17 E4 vil 4m/7km N of Avebury. SU 1076
Broadholme Notts 44 D4 loc 5m/9km NW of Lincoln. SK 8974
Broadland 119 admin dist of Norfolk.
Broadland Row E Sussex 12 D5 ham 1m NE of Brede. TQ 8319
Broadlands Devon 5 E3* W dist of Newton Abbot. SX 8571
Broadlands Hants. See Romsey.
Broad Lanes Salop 34 D5/35 E5* loc 5m/8km SE of Bridgnorth. SO 7788
Broad Law Borders 65 G6 mt 3m/5km E of Tweedsmuir. Height 2756 ft or 840 metres. NT 1423
Broadlay Dyfed 23 E4 loc 1km SE of Ferryside. SN 3709
Broad Laying Hants 17 H5 vil 4m/6km SW of Newbury. SU 4362
Broadley Grampian 82 C1* loc near N coast 3m/5km SW of Buckie. NJ 3961
Broadley Gtr Manchester 47 H6 loc in Rochdale 2m/4km NW of tn centre. SD 8716
Broadley Common Essex 20 B1* loc 2m/3km SW of Harlow. TL 4207
Broad Marston H & W 27 F3 ham 5m/7km N of Chipping Campden. SP 1446
Broadmayne Dorset 9 E5 vil 4m/6km SE of Dorchester. SY 7386
Broad Meadow Staffs 42 D6* loc in Newcastle-under-Lyme 2m/3km N of tn centre. SJ 8348
Broadmere Hants 18 B6* loc 1km NW of Farleigh Wallop and 3m/5km SW of Basingstoke. SU 6247
Broadmoor Dyfed 22 D5* ham 4m/6km NW of Tenby. SN 0905
Broadmoor Glos 26 B5* loc 1m NW of Cinderford. SO 6515
Broadmoor Hospital Berks. See Crowthorne.
Broadmore Green H & W 26 C2* loc 2m/4km W of Worcester. SO 8153
Broadoak Clwyd 42 A5* loc 1m N of Rossett. SJ 3658
Broadoak Cornwall 3 F2* loc 4m/6km NE of Lostwithiel. Site of Civil War battle, 1643. Also known as Braddock. SX 1662
Broad Oak Cumbria 52 B5* loc 4m/7km N of Bootle. SD 1194
Broad Oak Devon 7 H5 loc 3m/4km SW of Ottery St Mary. SY 0693
Broadoak Dorset 8 C4* ham 3m/5km NW of Bridport. SY 4396
Broad Oak (Derwen-fawr) Dyfed 23 G3 loc 3m/5km W of Llandeilo. SN 5722
Broadoak E Sussex 12 C4 ham 2km E of Heathfield. TQ 6022
Broad Oak E Sussex 12 D5 vil 6m/10km W of Rye. TQ 8219
Broadoak Glos 26 C6* loc on right bank of R Severn 3m/4km E of Cinderford. SO 6912
Broadoak Hants 10 C3* loc 1km W of Botley. SU 5013
Broad Oak H & W 26 A5 vil 6m/9km N of Monmouth. SO 4821
Broadoak Kent 13 G1 vil 1m NW of Sturry. TR 1661
Broad Oak Merseyside 42 B2 dist of St Helens 2km E of tn centre. SJ 5395
Broadoak End Herts 19 G1* loc in W part of Hertford. TL 3013
Broad Piece Cambs 38 A6/B6* loc 1km NW of Soham. TL 5874
Broad Road Suffolk 31 G1* loc 1km SE of Fressingfield. TM 2776
Broadsea Grampian 83 G1 NW dist of Fraserburgh. NJ 9967
Broad's Green Essex 20 D1* ham 4m/6km N of Chelmsford. TL 6912
Broadshard Som 8 C3* N dist of Crewkerne. ST 4410

Broad Sound 22 A5 sea channel between islands of Skomer and Skokholm off SW coast of Wales. SM 7206

Broadstairs Kent 13 H1 resort on E coast of Isle of Thanet 2m/3km N of Ramsgate. TR 3967

Broads, The Norfolk 39 G3/H3 series of shallow lakes in E part of county (except Oulton Broad, which is in Suffolk), surrounded by reedy marshes abounding in waterfowl, and for the most part connected by channels with Rs Bure, Waveney, or Yare, the whole system forming a popular boating area. TG 31, 41

Broadstone Dorset 9 G4 suburban locality 3m/5km N of Poole. SZ 0095

Broadstone Salop 34 C5 ham 8m/13km NE of Craven Arms. SO 5489

Broadstone Reservoir S Yorks 43 F1* resr 4m/6km NW of Penistone. SE 1906

Broad Street Essex 30 A6* NE end of vil of Hatfield Broad Oak, 5m/8km SE of Bishop's Stortford. TL 5516

Broad Street E Sussex 13 E5* ham adjoining Icklesham to W. TQ 8616

Broad Street Kent 13 F3* ham 5m/7km NW of Hythe. TR 1140

Broad Street Kent 20 D5 vil 5m/7km E of Maidstone. TQ 8256

Broad Street Wilts 17 E5* loc 4m/6km W of Pewsey. SU 1059

Broad Street Green Essex 21 E1 loc 2m/3km N of Maldon. TL 8609

Broad, The H & W 26 A2* loc 1m N of Leominster. SO 4960

Broad Town Wilts 17 E4 vil 3m/5km SE of Wootton Bassett. SU 0977

Broadwas H & W 26 C2 vil 6m/9km W of Worcester. SO 7555

Broad Water Gwynedd 32 D4 wide part of R Dyfynni estuary to N of Tywyn. SH 5702

Broadwater Herts 29 F5* S dist of Stevenage. TL 2422

Broadwater Lincs 37 E1* loc 2m/4km SW of Sleaford. TF 0344

Broadwater W Sussex 11 G4 dist of Worthing 1m N of tn centre. TQ 1404

Broadwater Down Kent 12 C3* SW dist of Tunbridge Wells. TQ 5737

Broadwaters H & W 35 E6* loc in NE part of Kidderminster. SO 8478

Broadwath Cumbria 60 B5* loc 2m/3km SW of Hayton. NY 4755

Broadway Dyfed 22 B4 loc 5m/8km W of Haverfordwest. SM 8713

Broadway Dyfed 23 E4 loc adjoining Laugharne to SW. SN 2910

Broadway H & W 27 E4 small tn below escarpment of Cotswold Hills 5m/9km SE of Evesham. Tourism. SP 0937

Broadway Som 16 B6* loc adjoining Chilcompton to S, 3m/4km SW of Midsomer Norton. ST 6451

Broadway Som 8 B3 vil 3m/4km W of Ilminster. ST 3215

Broadway Suffolk 31 G1 loc 1m N of Halesworth. TM 3978

Broadwell Glos 27 F5 vil 2km NE of Stow-on-the-Wold. Site of Roman bldg to NW. SP 2027

Broadwell Oxon 17 F1 vil 4m/6km NE of Lechlade. SP 2503

Broadwell Warwicks 27 H1 vil 4m/6km NE of Southam. SP 4565

Broadwell Lane End Glos 26 B6* loc 1m E of Coleford. SO 5811

Broadwey Dorset 8 D5 loc 3m/5km N of Weymouth. SY 6683

Broadwindsor Dorset 8 C4 vil 3m/5km W of Beaminster. 1m S, Lewesdon Hill (NT), wooded summit commanding wide views. ST 4302

Broadwood Kelly Devon 7 E4 vil 2m/3km SW of Winkleigh. SS 6105

Broadwoodwidger Devon 6 C6 vil 6m/9km NE of Launceston. SX 4189

Brobury H & W 25 H3 loc 11m/17km W of Hereford. SO 3444

Brocastle 15 E4* loc on borders of Mid and S Glam 3m/4km SE of Bridgend. SS 9377

Brochan 33 F5/F6 stream running NE into R Dulas on SW side of Llanidloes, Powys. SN 9483

Brochel Skye, H'land 78 D4 loc near E coast of Raasay 5m/7km from N end of island. Ruined cas of the Macleods of Raasay. NG 5846

Broch of Gurness Orkney 89 B6* prehistoric cas and domestic settlement on Aiker Ness, Mainland. HY 3826

Broch of Mousa Shetland 89 E8* ancient Pictish *broch* or cas (A.M.) on W coast of island of Mousa. It is 45 ft or 14 metres high, and thought to be nearly 2000 years old. HU 4523

Brock Lancs 47 F4* loc on r of same name adjoining Bilsborrow to N, 2m/3km N of Barton. SD 5140

Brock 47 E4 r rising on Forest of Bowland and flowing W into R Wyre at St Michael's on Wyre, Lancs. SD 4641

Brockamin H & W 26 C2* loc 5m/8km W of Worcester. SO 7753

Brockbridge Hants 10 C3* ham just E of Droxford across R Meon. SU 6118

Brockdish Norfolk 31 F1 vil 3m/5km SW of Harleston. TM 2179

Brockencote H & W 26 D1* loc adjoining Chaddesley Corbett to W, 4m/6km SE of Kidderminster. SO 8873

Brockenhurst Hants 10 A4 vil on S edge of New Forest, 4m/6km S of Lyndhurst. SU 3002

Brockey 7 G3* stream in Somerset rising near E Anstey, Devon, and flowing E into R Exe 1km SW of Exebridge. SS 9223

Brockford Green Suffolk 31 E2/F2* loc 1m S of Wetheringsett. TM 1265

Brockford Street Suffolk 31 E2 ham 4m/7km NW of Debenham. TM 1166

Brockhall Northants 28 B2 vil 4m/6km E of Daventry. SP 6362

Brockham Surrey 19 F6 vil 2m/3km E of Dorking. TQ 1949

Brockhampton Glos 26 D5* loc 3m/4km N of Cheltenham. SO 9426

Brockhampton Glos 27 E5 ham 4m/6km S of Winchcombe. SP 0322

Brockhampton Hants 11 D4* SW dist of Havant. SU 7106

Brockhampton H & W 26 C2 ham 2m/3km E of Bromyard. Par contains area of farmland and woods (NT) which includes **Brockhampton,** modernised early Ggn hse, and **Lr Brockhampton,** late 14c moated manor hse. SO 6855

Brockhampton H & W 26 B4 vil 5m/8km N of Ross-on-Wye across loop of r. SO 5931

Brockhampton Green Dorset 9 E4* ham 2km W of Mappowder and 7m/11km SW of Sturminster Newton. ST 7106

Brock Hill Essex 20 D2* ham 2m/3km N of Wickford. TQ 7396

Brockholes W Yorks 48 D6 vil 4m/6km S of Huddersfield. SE 1511

Brockholes, Upper W Yorks 48 D5* ham 3m/5km NW of Halifax. SE 0629

Brockhurst Hants 10 C4 dist of Gosport 2km NW of tn centre. SU 6001

Brocklebank Cumbria 52 C1 loc 5m/7km SE of Wigton. NY 3043

Brocklesby Humberside 45 F1 vil 9m/14km W of Grimsby. Estate vil at gates of **B. Park.** TA 1411

Brockley Avon 16 A4 vil 3m/5km NE of Congresbury. ST 4767

Brockley London 20 A4* loc in borough of Lewisham 5m/8km SE of Charing Cross. TQ 3675

Brockley Suffolk 30 C1/D1* loc 1km N of Culford. TL 8371

Brockley Suffolk 30 C3* loc 6m/9km S of Bury St Edmunds. TL 8255

Brockley Green Suffolk 30 C3 vil 6m/9km NW of Long Melford. TL 8254

Brockley Green Suffolk 30 C3* ham 3m/5km E of Haverhill. TL 7247

Brockleymoor Cumbria 53 E2* loc adjoining Plumpton Wall to W. NY 4936

Brockmoor W Midlands 35 E5* loc in Dudley 3m/5km SW of tn centre. SO 9087

Brock's Green Hants 17 H5* loc 2m/4km NW of Kingsclere. SU 5061

Brockton Salop 34 A4 ham 6m/10km E of Welshpool. SJ 3104

Brockton Salop 34 A5* vil 2m/3km S of Bishop's Castle. SO 3285

Brockton Salop 34 C5 vil 5m/8km SW of Much Wenlock. SO 5793

Brockton Salop 34 D3* ham 2m/3km SW of Newport. SJ 7216

Brockton Salop 34 D4* loc 1m SW of Kemberton. SJ 7203

Brockton Staffs 35 E2* ham 2m/3km N of Eccleshall. SJ 8131

Brockweir Glos 16 B2 vil on R Wye 5m/8km N of Chepstow. SO 5301

Brockworth Glos 26 D5 tn 4m/6km SE of Gloucester. Industrial estate. SO 8916

Brocolitia Nthmb 60 D4 remains of Roman fort on Hadrian's Wall 4m/6km W of Humshaugh. Site of Mithraic temple (A.M.) at Carrawbrough to E. NY 8571

Brocton Staffs 35 F3 vil 4m/6km SE of Stafford. SJ 9619

Brodgar, Ness of Orkney 89 A6* narrow tongue of land, carrying a rd, between Loch of Harray and Loch of Stenness, on Mainland 4m/6km W of Finstown. HY 3012

Brodick S'clyde 63 G4 small port and resort on **B. Bay** on E coast of Arran. Passenger ferry to Ardrossan on mainland. **B. Castle** (NTS) 2km N. NS 0136

Brodie Castle Grampian 82 A2* ancient cas, seat of Brodie of Brodie, 4m/6km W of Forres. Park contains notable Pictish stone. NH 9757

Brodsworth S Yorks 44 A1 vil 5m/8km NW of Doncaster. SE 5007

Brogan, The 33 H2* r running NE into R Cain 1m W of Llansanffraid-ym-Mechain, Powys. SJ 2020

Brogborough Beds 28 D4* loc 5m/7km W of Ampthill. Brick works to SE. SP 9638

Brogden Lancs 48 B3* loc 2m/3km W of Barnoldswick. SD 8547

Brokenborough Wilts 16 D3 vil 2m/3km NW of Malmesbury. ST 9189

Broken Cross Ches 42 C4 loc 2m/3km E of Northwich. SJ 6873

Broken Cross Ches 42 D4 loc 2m/3km W of Macclesfield. SJ 8973

Broker W Isles 88 C2* loc on Eye Peninsula, Lewis, 1m SW of Tiumpan Hd. NB 5536

Brokerswood Wilts 16 D6* ham 3m/4km W of Westbury. ST 8352

Brokes N Yorks 54 B5* loc 2km SW of Richmond. SE 1599

Brolass S'clyde 69 D5, D6 tract on Ross of Mull between Pennyghael (N) and Malcolm's Pt (S). NM 5022

Bromborough Merseyside 42 A3 dist of Bebington 2m/3km SE of tn centre. SJ 3482

Brome Suffolk 31 F1 vil 2m/3km N of Eye. Ham of **B. Street** 1m E. TM 1376

Bromeswell Suffolk 31 G3 vil 2m/3km NE of Woodbridge across R Deben. TM 3050

Bromfield Cumbria 52 B1 vil 4m/6km NE of Aspatria. NY 1746

Bromfield Salop 34 B6 vil at confluence of R Onny and R Teme 3m/4km NW of Ludlow. Site of Roman camp to N. SO 4876

Bromford W Midlands 35 G5* loc in Birmingham 4m/7km NE of city centre. SP 1289

Bromham Beds 29 E3 vil 3m/4km W of Bedford. Site of Roman bldg 1km S. TL 0051

Bromham Wilts 16 D5 vil 4m/6km NW of Devizes. ST 9665

Bromley London 20 A3* dist in borough of Tower Hamlets 3m/5km NE of London Br. Sometimes known as Bromley-by-Bow. Loc of **S Bromley** 2km SE. TQ 3782

Bromley London 20 A4 borough and tn 9m/15km SE of Charing Cross. The borough is large, extending about 11m/17km from N to S and from E to W. TQ 4069

Bromley S Yorks 43 G2* loc 2km E of Wortley. SK 3298

Bromley W Midlands 35 E5* loc in Dudley 3m/4km SW of tn centre. SP 9088

Bromley Common London 20 B5 loc in borough of Bromley 2m/3km SE of Bromley tn centre. TQ 4266

Bromley Cross Gtr Manchester 47 G6* loc 3m/5km N of Bolton. SD 7213

Bromley, Great Essex 31 E5 vil 6m/9km E of Colchester. TM 0826

Bromley Green Kent 13 F3 loc 4m/6km S of Ashford. TQ 9936

Bromley Hurst Staffs 35 G2* loc 2km S of Abbots Bromley. SK 0922

Bromley, Little Essex 31 E5 vil 2m/3km SW of Manningtree. TM 0928

Brompton Kent 20 D5 N dist of Gillingham. TQ 7768

Brompton N Yorks 54 C5 suburb 2km N of Northallerton. 2km NW is site of Battle of the Standard, 1138, in which army of King Stephen of England defeated army of King David of Scotland. SE 3796

Brompton N Yorks 55 G6 vil 7m/11km SW of Scarborough. SE 9482

Brompton Salop 34 C3/C4* loc 1km NE of Cross Hses and 5m/7km SE of Shrewsbury. SJ 5407

Brompton Som 7 H2 vil 3m/5km N of Wiveliscombe. SS 0832

Brompton-on-Swale N Yorks 54 B5 vil 3m/5km E of Richmond. SE 2199

Brompton Ralph Som 7 H2 vil 3m/5km N of Wiveliscombe. ST 0832

Brompton Regis Som 7 G2 vil on Exmoor 3m/5km NE of Dulverton. SS 9531

Bromsash H & W 26 B5 vil 3m/5km E of Ross-on-Wye. SO 6424

Bromsberrow Glos 26 C4* ham 3m/5km SE of Ledbury. SO 7434

Bromsberrow Heath Glos 26 C4 vil 3m/5km SE of Ledbury. SO 7333

Bromsgrove H & W 26 D1 tn 12m/20km SW of Birmingham. SO 9570

Bromwich, Little W Midlands 35 G5* loc in Birmingham 3m/5km E of city centre. SP 1186

Bromwich, West W Midlands 35 F5 tn 5m/8km NW of Birmingham. Various industries. SP 0091

Bromyard H & W 26 B2 old mkt tn 12m/9km W of Worcester. SO 6554

Bronaber Gwynedd 33 E2* loc 3m/4km S of Trawsfynydd. SH 7131

Brondesbury London 19 F3* loc in borough of Brent 4m/7km NW of Charing Cross. Loc of **B. Park** to SW. TQ 2484

Brongest Dyfed 23 E2 ham 3m/5km N of Newcastle Emlyn. SN 3245

Bronington Clwyd 34 B1* vil 4m/6km SW of Whitchurch. SJ 4839

Bronllys Powys 25 F4 vil 1m NW of Talgarth. Remains of 12c–13c cas (A.M.) to SE. SO 1434

Bronnant Dyfed 24 C2 ham 2m/3km S of Lledrod. SN 6467

Bronwydd Arms Dyfed 23 F3* vil 2m/4km N of Carmarthen. SN 4123

Bronydd Powys 25 G3 loc 2km NE of Clyro. SO 2245

Bronygarth Salop 34 A1* ham 2m/3km W of Chirk. SJ 2637

Bron-y-Mor Gwynedd 32 D4* loc on coast on W side of Tywyn. SH 5700

Brook Dyfed 23 E4 loc 2m/3km W of Laugharne. SN 2609

Brook Hants 10 A3 ham in New Forest 2m/3km NW of Cadnam. To N, ham of **B. Hill.** SU 2714

Brook Isle of Wight 10 B6 vil near S coast 4m/7km W of Shorwell. **B. Bay** to SW. **B. Chine** and strip of coast at bay NT. SZ 3983

Brook Kent 13 F3 vil 4m/6km E of Ashford. TR 0644

Brook Surrey 11 F2 vil 3m/5km SW of Milford. SU 9238

Brook Surrey 19 E6* loc 5m/7km SE of Guildford. TQ 0646

Brook Wilts 16 D6 loc 2km W of Westbury. ST 8551

Brook Bottom Gtr Manchester 43 E1* loc adjoining Mossley to NW. SD 9602

Brooke Leics 36 D4 ham 2m/3km S of Oakham. SK 8405

Brooke Norfolk 39 G5 vil 7m/11km SE of Norwich. TM 2999

Brook End Beds 29 E2 N end of vil of Keysoe, 3m/5km SE of Kimbolton. TL 0763

Brook End Beds 29 F3* loc 2km SW of Sandy. TL 1647

Brook End Beds 29 F4* W end of Stotfold, 3m/5km NW of Baldock. TL 2136

Brook End Bucks 28 D3* loc 3m/4km E of Newport Pagnell. SP 9144

Brook End Cambs 29 E1* loc just W of vil of Catworth. TL 0873

Brookend Essex 20 D1* loc 2m/3km E of Chelmsford. TL 7307

Brookend Glos 16 B2 ham 3m/5km SW of Lydney. Site of Roman villa 1km S beside R Severn estuary. ST 5999

Brookend Glos 16 C2* loc 2m/3km N of Berkeley. SO 6802

Brook End Herts 29 G5* ham 3m/4km W of Buntingford. TL 3229

Brook End H & W 26 D3* loc 3m/5km S of Worcester. SO 8649

Brookend Oxon 27 G5* loc 3m/4km NW of Charlbury. SP 3221

Brook End Staffs 35 G3* loc adjoining Longdon to N. SK 0814

Brook End, North Cambs 29 G3* loc 5m/7km NW of Royston. TL 2944

Brookfield Derbys 43 E2* loc 2m/3km NW of Glossop. SK 0195

Brookfield Glos 26 D5* loc 4m/6km E of Gloucester. SO 8920

Brookfield S'clyde 64 B3* loc 2km NW of Johnstone. NS 4164

Brookfoot W Yorks 48 D5* loc 1km W of Brighouse. SE 1323

Brookgreen Isle of Wight 10 B6* loc just S of Brook and 5m/7km W of Shorwell. SZ 3883

Brook Green London 19 F3* dist in borough of Hammersmith 4m/7km W of Charing Cross. TQ 2379
Brookhampton Oxon 18 B2* loc at Stadhampton 6m/9km N of Wallingford. SU 6098
Brookhouse Ches 43 E4 loc 3m/4km NE of Macclesfield. SJ 9475
Brook House Clwyd 41 G4* loc 2km E of Denbigh. SJ 0566
Brookhouse Lancs 47 F2 vil 5m/7km NE of Lancaster. SD 5464
Brookhouse S Yorks 44 A2* vil 2km E of Thurcroft. SK 5189
Brookhouse Green Ches 42 D5* ham 3m/5km W of Congleton. SJ 8161
Brook Houses Derbys 43 E3* ham 2m/3km SW of Chapel-en-le-Frith. SK 0478
Brookhouses Staffs 35 F1* loc 1m W of Cheadle. SJ 9943
Brookland Kent 13 E4 vil 5m/8km W of New Romney. TQ 9825
Brooklands Gtr Manchester 42 D2* dist of Manchester 2m/3km NE of Altrincham. SJ 7989
Brooklands Gtr Manchester 42 D2* dist of Sale to S of tn centre. SJ 7891
Brooklands Salop 34 C1* loc 1m NW of Whitchurch. SJ 5342
Brooklands Surrey 19 E5 former motor-racing circuit now an industrial site, on N side of Byfleet. TQ 0662
Brookmans Park Herts 19 F2 residential loc 2m/3km N of Potters Bar. TL 2404
Brooks Powys 33 H4 loc 3m/5km W of Berriew. SO 1499
Brooksby Leics 36 C3 loc 5m/8km W of Melton Mowbray. SK 6716
Brooks Green W Sussex 11 G3 loc 3m/4km E of Billingshurst. TQ 1224
Brookside Salop 34 D4* dist of Telford SE of Dawley. SJ 7005
Brook, South 29 F2* stream rising W of Keysoe Row, Beds, and flowing SE to Wilden, then E into R Ouse 2m/3km S of Eaton Socon. TL 1655
Brook Street Essex 20 C2 W suburb of Brentwood. TQ 5792
Brook Street Kent 13 E3 ham 3m/5km E of Tenterden. TQ 9233
Brook Street W Sussex 11 H3 ham 2km N of Cuckfield. TQ 3026
Brookthorpe Glos 26 D6 vil 4m/7km S of Gloucester. SO 8312
Brookvale Ches 42 B3* SE dist of Runcorn. SJ 5580
Brookville Norfolk 38 C5* loc 1m N of Methwold. Site of Roman bldg to SW. TL 7396
Brookwood Surrey 18 D5 vil beside Basingstoke Canal 4m/6km W of Woking. To S across rly, **B. Cemetery,** largest in England. SU 9457
Broom Beds 29 F3 vil 2m/3km SW of Biggleswade. TL 1742
Broom Durham 54 B1 vil 2m/3km W of Durham. NZ 2441
Broom Dyfed 22 D5* 1km NW of Begelly. SN 1108
Broom Fife 73 F4* NW dist of Leven. NO 3701
Broom H'land 85 C7 r running N down Strath More to head of Loch Broom, Ross and Cromarty dist. NH 1785
Broom S Yorks 43 H2* dist of Rotherham 1m SE of tn centre. SK 4391
Broom Warwicks 27 E2 vil 7m/11km W of Stratford-upon-Avon. SP 0953
Broomage, North Central 65 E1* loc on N side of Larbert. **S Broomage** is loc on E side of Larbert. NS 8583
Broome H & W 35 E6 vil 4m/6km S of Stourbridge. SO 9078
Broome Norfolk 39 G5 vil 2km NE of Bungay. Ham of **B. Street** 1km N. TM 3591
Broome Salop 34 B6 ham 2m/4km SW of Craven Arms. SO 4080
Broomedge Ches 42 C3 vil 2m/3km E of Lymm. SJ 7085
Broomer's Corner W Sussex 11 G3 loc 2km S of Coolham. TQ 1221
Broomfield Essex 21 D1 suburb 2m/4km N of Chelmsford. TL 7010
Broomfield Grampian 83 G4* loc 1m N of Ellon. NJ 9532
Broomfield Kent 13 G1 SE dist of Herne Bay. TR 1966
Broomfield Kent 20 D6 vil 5m/9km E of Maidstone. TQ 8352
Broomfield Som 8 A2* ham on E slopes of Quantock Hills 4m/7km W of N Petherton. ST 2232
Broomfields W Yorks 49 E4* dist of Leeds 2km NW of city centre. SE 2735
Broomfleet Humberside 50 D5 vil 4m/6km SW of S Cave. SE 8827
Broom Green Norfolk 39 E2/E3* loc 1m SW of Guist. TF 9824
Broomhall Surrey 18 D5* loc on N edge of Chobham Common 1km S of Sunningdale. SU 9566
Broomhall Green Ches 42 C6* loc 3m/5km NW of Audlem. SJ 6247
Broomhaugh Nthmb 61 E5* vil adjoining Riding Mill to SE. NZ 0161
Broomhaugh Island Nthmb 61 E5 island in R Tyne below br across r at Hexham. NY 9464
Broomhead Reservoir S Yorks 43 G2* resr below Broomhead Moor 2m/3km S of Stocksbridge. SK 2695
Broomhill Avon 16 B4* NE dist of Bristol. ST 6276
Broom Hill Dorset 9 G4* loc 3m/4km NE of Wimborne. SU 0302
Broom Hill Durham 61 F5/F6* loc 1km SE of Ebchester. NZ 1054
Broom Hill Gtr Manchester 42 D1* loc 2m/3km SW of Heywood. SD 8408
Broom Hill H & W 35 E6* ham 4m/7km NW of Bromsgrove. SO 9175
Broom Hill London 20 B5* loc in borough of Bromley between Petts Wd and Orpington. TQ 4566
Broomhill Norfolk 38 B4* loc adjoining Downham Mkt to NE. TF 6104
Broomhill Nthmb 61 G2 vil 2m/3km SW of Amble. **S Broomhill** vil 1m S. NU 2401
Broomhill S'clyde 64 C2* loc in Partick dist of Glasgow. NS 5467
Broom Hill S Yorks 43 H1* ham 2m/3km E of Wombwell. SE 4102
Broomholm Norfolk 39 G2* loc adjoining Bacton to S. TG 3433
Broomhouse Lothian 66 A2* dist of Edinburgh 4m/6km SW of city centre. NT 2071
Broomielaw Durham 54 A3 loc 2m/4km E of Barnard Castle. NZ 0818
Broomlee Lough Nthmb 60 D4 lake to E of Greenlee Lough and 3m/5km N of Bardon Mill. NY 7969
Broomley Nthmb 61 E5 loc 4m/7km SE of Corbridge. NZ 0360
Broom's Green Glos 26 C4 ham 3m/5km S of Ledbury. SO 7132
Brooms, High Kent 12 C3 N dist of Tunbridge Wells. TQ 5941
Broomside Durham 54 C1* loc adjoining Carrville to E. NZ 3043
Broomsthorpe Norfolk 38 D2 loc 2km E of E Rudham. TF 8428
Brora H'land 87 C6 vil on E coast of Sutherland dist at mouth of R Brora, 10m/17km SW of Helmsdale. Tweed mnfre. Distillery to N. R flows SE down Strath Brora and through Loch Brora to coast. NC 9004
Brosdale Island S'clyde 62 C2 small island off S coast of Jura, 4m/6km SW of Craighouse. NR 4962
Broseley Salop 34 D4 urban loc 1m S of Ironbridge. **Broseley Wd** loc to N. SJ 6701
Brotherhouse Bar Lincs 37 G3* loc 2m/3km S of Cowbit. TF 2614
Brotheridge Green H & W 26 C3* loc 3m/5km E of Malvern Wells. SO 8241
Brother Isle Shetland 89 E6* uninhabited island in Yell Sound 1m N of Mio Ness on Mainland. HU 4281
Brotherlee Durham 53 H1 ham 3m/4km E of St John's Chapel. NY 9237
Brother Loch S'clyde 64 C3* small loch 4m/6km S of Barrhead. NS 5052
Brothers Water Cumbria 52 D4 small lake 2m/3km S of Patterdale. NY 4012
Brothertoft Lincs 45 F6 loc 4m/6km W of Boston. TF 2746
Brotherton Lothian 65 G2* loc in Livingston 2m/4km SW of tn centre. NT 0465
Brotherton N Yorks 49 F5 vil on R Aire 1km N of Ferrybridge across r. SE 4825
Brothybeck Cumbria 59 H6* loc 2m/3km NW of Sebergham. NY 3343
Brotton Cleveland 55 E3 tn 2m/3km SE of Saltburn. See also New Brotton. NZ 6819
Brough Cumbria 53 G3 vil 4m/6km N of Kirkby Stephen. Remains of medieval cas (A.M.), restored in 17c, on site of Roman tn. NY 7914
Brough Derbys 43 F3 loc 3m/5km W of Hathersage. Site of Roman fort of *Navio* beside R Noe. SK 1882
Brough H'land 86 E1 loc 2m/4km SE of Easter Hd, N coast of Caithness dist. ND 2273
Brough Humberside 50 D5 loc on N bank of R Humber on site of Roman *Petuaria* 10m/16km W of Hull. Airfield to SE. SE 9326
Brough Notts 44 C5 ham on Foss Way on site of Roman settlement of *Crococalana*, 4m/7km NE of Newark-on-Trent. SK 8358
Brough Orkney 89 A6* loc on Mainland 2m/3km SE of Dounby. HY 3118
Brough Shetland 89 E6 loc on NE coast of Mainland opp SW end of Yell. HU 4377
Brough Shetland 89 E7* loc near E coast of Mainland 2m/3km W of Moul of Eswick. HU 4754
Brough Shetland 89 F7 vil near N coast of island of Whalsay. **Brough Hd** is headland 1km W. HU 5565
Broughall Salop 34 C1 vil 2m/3km E of Whitchurch. SJ 5641
Brougham Cumbria 53 E2 loc 2m/3km SE of Penrith. Cas (A.M.) dates from 12c. To SE of cas is site of Roman fort of *Erocavum*. NY 5328
Brough Head H'land 86 F2 headland on E coast of Caithness dist 6m/10km S of John o' Groats. ND 3763
Brough Head Orkney 89 A6 headland with beacon at W end of islet of Brough of Birsay, off NW coast of Mainland, accessible on foot at low tide. St Peter's Chapel (A.M.), at other end of islet. HY 2328
Brough Ness Orkney 89 B7 headland at S end of S Ronaldsay. ND 4482
Brough of Birsay Orkney. See Brough Hd.
Brough Sowerby Cumbria 53 G3 ham 2km S of Brough. NY 7912
Broughton Borders 65 G5 vil 4m/7km E of Biggar. NT 1136
Broughton Bucks 28 D4 vil 3m/4km SE of Newport Pagnell. SP 8940
Broughton Bucks 28 D6* loc 2m/3km E of Aylesbury. SP 8413
Broughton Cambs 37 G6 vil 5m/7km NE of Huntingdon. TL 2877
Broughton Clwyd 41 H5 vil 2m/3km SE of Hawarden. SJ 3363
Broughton Hants 10 A2 vil 3m/5km SW of Stockbridge. SU 3032
Broughton Humberside 44 D1 vil 3m/5km NW of Brigg. SE 9608
Broughton Lancs 47 F4 vil 4m/6km N of Preston. SD 5235
Broughton Mid Glam 15 E4 ham 6m/9km S of Bridgend. SS 9270
Broughton Northants 28 D1 vil 3m/4km SW of Kettering. SP 8375
Broughton N Yorks 48 C3 ham 3m/5km W of Skipton. Hall dates from mid-18c. SD 9451
Broughton N Yorks 50 C1* vil 2m/3km NW of Malton. SE 7673
Broughton Oxon 27 H4 vil 3m/5km SW of Banbury. SP 4238
Broughton Astley Leics 36 B5 vil 5m/8km N of Lutterworth. SP 5292
Broughton Bay W Glam 23 F6 bay 2km W of Llanmadog SS 4293
Broughton Beck Cumbria 52 C6 loc 3m/4km N of Ulverston. SD 2882
Broughton Common Wilts 16 D5* loc 2m/3km W of Melksham. ST 8764
Broughton Cross Cumbria 52 B2* loc 3m/5km W of Cockermouth, adjoining Brigham to W. NY 0730
Broughton Gifford Wilts 16 D5 vil 2m/3km W of Melksham. ST 8763
Broughton, Great Cumbria 52 B2 vil 3m/5km W of Cockermouth. NY 0731
Broughton, Great N Yorks 54 D4 vil 2m/3km SE of Stokesley. NZ 5406
Broughton Green H & W 26 D2* ham 4m/6km SE of Droitwich. SO 9461
Broughton Hackett H & W 26 D2 vil 5m/8km E of Worcester. SO 9254
Broughton, Higher Gtr Manchester 42 D2* dist of Salford 2km N of tn centre. **Lr Broughton** loc 1km SE. SD 8200
Broughton in Furness Cumbria 52 C6 vil 8m/12km NW of Ulverston. SD 2187
Broughton, Little Cumbria 52 B2* vil adjoining Gt Broughton to N, 3m/5km W of Cockermouth. NY 0731
Broughton Mills Cumbria 52 B5 ham 2m/3km N of Broughton in Furness. SD 2290
Broughton Moor Cumbria 52 B2 vil 2m/3km SE of Maryport. NY 0533
Broughton, Nether Leics 36 C2 vil 6m/9km NW of Melton Mowbray. SK 6925
Broughton Park Gtr Manchester 42 D1* loc in Salford 2m/3km N of tn centre. SD 8302
Broughton Poggs Oxon 17 F1 vil 3m/5km NE of Lechlade. SP 2303
Broughton, Upper Notts 36 C2 vil 6m/10km NW of Melton Mowbray. SK 6826
Broughtown Orkney 89 C5* loc on island of Sanday 1km SW of head of Otters Wick. HY 6641
Broughty Ferry Tayside 73 G2 dist of Dundee 4m/6km E of city centre. Docks. **Broughty Castle,** (A.M.), built in 15c. NO 4631
Browland Shetland 89 D7* loc on Mainland on E side of **Voe of B.**, inlet at head of main inlet of Gruting Voe. HU 2650
Brownber Cumbria 53 F4* loc 6m/9km E of Tebay. NY 7005
Brownbread Street E Sussex 12 C5* loc 5m/7km W of Battle. TQ 6715
Brown Candover Hants 10 C1 vil 4m/7km N of New Alresford. SU 5739
Brown Carrick Hill S'clyde 56 C2 hill commanding wide views, 2m/3km E of Dunure. NS 2815
Brown Caterthun Tayside 77 E4. See Caterthun.
Brown Clee Hill Salop 34 C5 prominent hill and landmark 9m/15km NE of Ludlow, rising to 1772 ft or 540 metres. SO 5986
Browndown Hants 10 C5* loc 3m/5km W of Gosport. Rifle ranges. SZ 5899
Brown Edge Lancs 47 E6* loc 2m/4km SE of Southport. SD 3614
Brownedge Lancs 47 F5 loc 2m/4km SE of Preston. SD 5526
Brown Edge Merseyside 42 B2* loc in St Helens 2m/3km SW of tn centre. SJ 4993
Brown Edge Staffs 43 E5 vil 3m/5km SE of Biddulph. SJ 9053
Browney 54 C1 r rising S of Consett, Durham, and flowing E into R Wear 3m/4km S of Durham. NZ 2738
Brown Head S'clyde 63 F5 headland on SW coast of Arran 2m/3km S of Blackwaterfoot. NR 9025
Brown Heath Ches 42 A5* loc 4m/6km E of Chester. SJ 4564
Brown Heath Hants 10 C3* loc 2m/3km NE of Botley. SU 5216
Brownheath Salop 34 B2* loc 3m/5km W of Wem. SJ 4629
Brownhill Lancs 47 G5* dist of Blackburn 2m/3km N of tn centre. SD 6830
Brownhill Reservoir W Yorks 43 F1* resr 1km SW of Holmbridge. SE 1106
Brownhills W Midlands 35 F4 tn in coal-mining area 5m/8km NE of Walsall. SK 0405
Browninghill Green Hants 18 B5* ham 4m/6km E of Kingsclere. SU 5859
Brown Lees Staffs 42 D5* loc 1km SW of Biddulph. SJ 8756
Brownlow Ches 42 D5* loc 2m/4km SW of Congleton. **B. Heath** loc 1km S. SJ 8361
Brown Moss Salop 34 C1* marshy area with lakes and pools 2m/3km SE of Whitchurch. SJ 5639
Brown's Bank Ches 34 D1* loc 1m SW of Audlem. SJ 6443
Brownsea Island Dorset 9 G5 largest (about 2km by 1km) island (NT) in Poole Harbour. Nature reserve. Remains of Tudor cas at E end. SZ 0288
Brown's Green W Midlands 35 F5* loc in Birmingham 3m/5km NW of city centre. SP 0491
Brownshill Glos 16 D2* vil 3m/5km SE of Stroud. SO 8802
Brownshill Green W Midlands 35 H6 loc in Coventry 3m/5km NW of city centre. SP 3082
Brownside Lancs 48 B5* loc 2m/3km E of Burnley. SD 8632
Brownsover Warwicks 36 B6* loc on N edge of Rugby. SP 5077
Brownston Devon 4 D5 vil 3m/4km E of Modbury. SX 6952
Brownstone Devon 5 E5* loc 2m/3km E of Dartmouth across R Dart estuary. SX 9050
Brown Street Suffolk 31 E2* loc 3m/5km N of Stowmarket. TM 0663

Brown Willy Cornwall 3 F1 granite tor on Bodmin Moor 4m/7km SE of Camelford. Highest point in county, 1375 ft or 419 metres. SX 1579
Brow of the Hill Norfolk 38 B3* loc 4m/7km E of King's Lynn. TF 6819
Browston Green Norfolk 39 H4* loc 4m/7km SW of Gt Yarmouth. TG 4901
Broxa N Yorks 55 G5 ham 6m/10km W of Scarborough. SE 9491
Broxbourne Herts 20 A1 S suburb of Hoddesdon. TL 3707
Broxburn Lothian 65 G2 tn 11m/18km W of Edinburgh. Light industry. NT 0872
Broxholme Lincs 44 D3 loc 6m/9km NW of Lincoln. SK 9177
Broxted Essex 30 A5/B5 vil 3m/5km SW of Thaxted. TL 5727
Broxton Ches 42 B5* loc 8m/13km N of Whitchurch. SJ 4953
Broxtowe 117 admin dist of Notts.
Broxwood H & W 25 H3 vil 5m/7km E of Kington. SO 3654
Broyle Side E Sussex 12 B5* loc 1m NE of Ringmer and 4m/6km NE of Lewes. TQ 4613
Bruan H'land 86 F3 loc on E coast of Caithness dist 5m/8km NE of Lybster. ND 3139
Bruar Water 75 H4 r in Tayside region running S down Glen Bruar to R Garry 3m/5km W of Blair Atholl. See also Falls of the Bruar. NN 8265
Brucefield Lothian 65 G2* loc 3m/4km SW of Livingston. NT 0464
Brucehill S'clyde 64 B2* W dist of Dumbarton. NS 3875
Bruce's Cave D & G 59 G4* man-made cave in cliff face in valley of Kirtle Water, 1km W of Kirkpatrick-Fleming. Here Robert Bruce lay hidden for about three months in 1306. NY 2670
Bruce's Stone D & G. See Clatteringshaws Loch.
Brucklay Grampian 83 G2 loc 3m/5km S of Strichen. **B. Castle** is ruined bldg to W. NJ 9250
Brue W Isles 88 B1* vil near NW coast of Lewis 2km W of Barvas across R Barvas. NB 3449
Brue 15 G6 r rising about 5m/8km E of Bruton in Somerset and flowing W into R Parrett estuary 1m S of Burnham-on-Sea. ST 3047
Bruern Oxon 27 G5* loc 5m/8km N of Burford. SP 2620
Bruernish W Isles 88 D3* loc on NE coast of Barra. To SE, peninsula runs out to **Bruernish Pt** on E coast. NF 7202
Bruichladdich S'clyde 62 A2 vil on W side of Loch Indaal, Islay, 2m/3km N of Port Charlotte. Distillery. NR 6126
Bruisyard Suffolk 31 G2 vil 3m/5km NE of Framlingham. Vil of **B. Street** 1m E. TM 3266
Brumby Humberside 44 D1 dist of Scunthorpe 1m S of tn centre. SE 8909
Brumstead Norfolk 39 G2 loc 1m N of Stalham. TG 3626
Brunach na Frithe Skye, H'land 79 C6 a peak of the Cuillin Hills. Height 3143 ft or 958 metres. NG 4625
Brundall Norfolk 39 G4 vil 6m/10km E of Norwich. TG 3208
Brundish Norfolk 39 G5* loc 1km S of Raveningham. TM 3995
Brundish Suffolk 31 G2 vil 4m/6km N of Framlingham. Ham of **B. Street** 2km NW. TM 2769
Brunerican Bay S'clyde 62 D6 bay on S coast of Kintyre, 1km S of vil of Southend. NR 6907
Brunshaw Lancs 48 B5* loc in Burnley 2km E of tn centre. SD 8532
Brunstock Cumbria 60 A5* loc 2m/4km NE of Carlisle. NY 4159
Brunswick Village Tyne & Wear 61 G4* loc 5m/8km N of Newcastle. NZ 2372
Bruntcliffe W Yorks 49 E5* loc 1m W of Morley. SE 2427
Bruntingthorpe Leics 36 B5 vil 4m/7km NW of Husbands Bosworth. Airfield to S. SP 6089
Brunton Fife 73 F3* vil 5m/8km NW of Cupar. NO 3220
Brunton Nthmb 61 E4* loc on line of Hadrian's Wall 1km NE of vil of Wall. NY 9269
Brunton Nthmb 67 H5 ham 2m/3km NW of Embleton. NU 2024
Brunton Tyne & Wear 61 G4* loc adjoining Gosforth to N. NZ 2370
Brunton Wilts 17 F5 ham 1km NE of Collingbourne Kingston and 4m/6km N of Ludgershall. SU 2456
Bruntsfield Lothian 66 A2* dist of Edinburgh 1m SW of city centre. NT 2472
Bruray Shetland. See Out Skerries.
Brushes Gtr Manchester 43 E2* loc 1m E of Stalybridge. SJ 9799
Brushes Clough Reservoir Gtr Manchester 43 E1* small resr 4m/6km NE of Oldham. SD 9509
Brushes, The Derbys 43 H3* loc 3m/4km N of Chesterfield. SK 3775
Brushfield Derbys 43 F4* loc 1m E of Taddington. SK 1571
Brushford Devon 7 E4 par on E side of Winkleigh. Ch at **B. Barton.** SS 6707
Brushford Som 7 G3 vil 2m/3km SE of Dulverton. SS 9225
Bruton Som 9 E1 small tn 7m/11km SE of Shepton Mallet. Many bldgs made of Doulting stone. ST 6834
Bryan's Green H & W 26 D1 ham 3m/5km N of Droitwich. SO 8968
Bryanston Dorset 9 F4 vil 1m W of Blandford Forum across R Stour. Boys' school in landscaped park. ST 8607
Bryant's Bottom Bucks 18 D2* ham 4m/7km N of High Wycombe. SU 8599
Brydekirk D & G 59 F4 vil 3m/4km N of Annan. NY 1870
Bryher Isles of Scilly 2 A1 the smallest of the five populated islands. SV 8714
Brymbo Clwyd 41 H5 industrial loc 3m/5km NW of Wrexham. Steel-mnfg. SJ 2953
Brympton Som 8 C3* ham 2m/4km W of Yeovil. ST 5115
Bryn Ches 42 B4* loc 4m/6km W of Northwich. SJ 6072
Bryn Dyfed 23 G5 loc 3m/4km E of Llanelli. SN 5400
Bryn Gtr Manchester 42 B2 loc adjoining Ashton-in-Makerfield to N. SD 5700
Bryn Gwent 15 F2* loc 2km S of Blackwood. ST 1795
Bryn Salop 34 A5 loc 3m/5km N of Clun. SO 2985
Bryn W Glam 14 D2* vil 4m/6km NE of Port Talbot. SS 8192
Brynamman Dyfed 14 C1 loc 6m/9km E of Ammanford. **Upr** and **Lr Brynamman,** locs adjoining to NE and SW respectively. SN 7114
Brynawel Gwent 15 G2 loc 2m/4km W of Risca. ST 2091
Brynberian Dyfed 22 D2 ham 4m/6km SE of Newport. SN 1035
Brynbryddan W Glam 14 D2* loc 2m/3km N of Port Talbot. SS 7792
Brynbuga Welsh form of Usk, qv.
Bryn-bwbach Gwynedd 32 D1* loc 3m/5km SW of Maentwrog. SH 6237
Bryncae Mid Glam 15 E3* loc 1km W of Llanharan. SS 9982
Bryn Celin Clwyd 41 G4* loc 1km N of Holywell. SJ 1876
Bryncelli Ddu Gwynedd 40 C4* ancient stone circles and burial-chamber (A.M.) on Anglesey 3m/5km W of Menai Br. SH 5170
Bryncethin Mid Glam 15 E3* loc 3m/5km N of Bridgend. SS 9184
Bryncir Gwynedd 32 C1 ham 4m/7km N of Criccieth. SH 4844
Bryncoch Mid Glam 15 E3* loc 3m/4km N of Bridgend. SS 9183
Bryn-coch W Glam 14 C2 vil 2m/3km NW of Neath. SS 7399
Bryncroes Gwynedd 32 A2 ham 5m/7km NE of Aberdaron. SH 2231
Bryncrug Gwynedd 32 D4 vil 2m/4km NE of Tywyn. SH 6003
Bryn Eden Gwynedd 33 E2* loc 4m/6km S of Trawsfynydd. SH 7129
Bryneglwys Clwyd 41 G6 vil 5m/8km NE of Corwen. SJ 1447
Bryn Eglwys Gwynedd 40 C4* vil 1m W of Bethesda. SH 6166
Brynffordd Clwyd 41 G4 vil 1m SW of Holywell. SJ 1774
Brynfields Clwyd 41 H6* housing estate on E side of Ruabon. SJ 3044
Bryn Gates Gtr Manchester 42 B2* vil 2m/3km NE of Ashton-in-Makerfield. SD 5901
Brynglas Gwent 15 G3* loc in N part of Newport. ST 3089
Bryn Golau Mid Glam 15 E3* loc adjoining Tonyrefail to W. ST 0088
Bryngwran Gwynedd 40 A4/B4 vil on Anglesey 4m/6km E of Valley. SH 3577
Bryngwyn Gwent 15 H1 ham 2m/3km NW of Raglan. SO 3909
Bryngwyn Powys 25 F3/G3 ham 5m/8km NW of Hay-on-Wye. SO 1849
Bryn-henllan Dyfed 22 C2* vil 2km S of Dinas Hd. SN 0039
Brynhoffnant Dyfed 23 E1 ham 2m/3km S of Llangranog. SN 3351
Bryning Lancs 47 E5* loc 1m S of Wrea Green. SD 4029
Brynithel Gwent 15 G2* loc 2m/3km S of Abertillery. SO 2101
Brynmawr Gwent 15 G1 tn on N edge of S Wales coalfield, 7m/11km W of Abergavenny. SO 1911
Bryn-mawr Gwynedd 32 A2* ham 2m/3km S of Tudweiliog. SH 2433
Brynmenyn Mid Glam 15 E3* loc 3m/5km N of Bridgend. SS 9084
Bryn Meurig Gwynedd 40 C4* loc on Anglesey 2m/3km NE of Menai Br. SH 5874
Brynmill W Glam 23 G6* loc in Swansea 2km W of tn centre. University College of Swansea to W. SS 6392
Bryn-minceg Gwynedd 40 C4 loc on Anglesey 2m/3km NE of Menai Br. SH 5774
Brynna Mid Glam 15 E3* vil 5m/9km E of Bridgend. SS 9883
Brynnau Gwynion Mid Glam 15 E3* loc 5m/8km E of Bridgend. SS 9782
Brynowen Dyfed 32 D5* loc 1m S of Borth. SN 6088
Bryn-penarth Powys 33 G4* loc 2km S of Llanfair Caereinion. Site of small Roman fort to SE of Gibbet Hill. SJ 1004
Bryn Pen-y-lan Clwyd 41 H6* loc 2m/3km E of Ruabon. SJ 3342
Brynrefail Gwynedd 40 B3* loc on Anglesey 5m/7km SE of Amlwch. SH 4886
Brynrefail Gwynedd 40 C5* vil 2m/3km NW of Llanberis at N end of Llyn Padarn. SH 5562
Brynrodyn Dyfed 32 D5* loc 2km S of Borth. SN 6088
Brynsadler Mid Glam 15 E3* vil 2m/3km SW of Llantrisant. ST 0280
Brynsaithmarchog Clwyd 41 G6* ham 4m/7km N of Corwen. SJ 0750
Brynsiencyn Gwynedd 40 B4 vil on Anglesey 6m/9km SW of Menai Br. SH 4867
Brynteg Clwyd 41 H5/H6* loc 2m/4km NW of Wrexham. SJ 3052
Brynteg Gwynedd 40 B3/C3 loc on Anglesey 5m/8km NE of Llangefni. SH 4582
Brynteg Mid Glam 15 F3* loc 1m NE of Llantrisant. ST 0683
Bryn, The Gwent. Alternative name for Llangattock nigh Usk, qv.
Bryn y Castell. See Knighton, Powys.
Bryn-y-cochin Salop 34 B1* loc 2m/4km W of Ellesmere. SJ 3635
Brynygwenin Gwent 25 H6* loc 2m/4km NE of Abergavenny. SO 3316
Bryn-y-maen Clwyd 41 E4* ham 2m/3km S of Colwyn Bay. SH 8376
Bryn-yr-Eos Clwyd 34 A1* loc 2m/3km N of Chirk. SJ 2840
Buachaille Etive Beag S'clyde 74 C5 mt ridge in Argyll, to S of Glen Coe and W of Buachaille Etive Mór. Summit is Stob Dubh at SW end of ridge; height 3142 ft or 958 metres. NN 1753
Buachaille Etive Mór S'clyde 74 C6-D5 mt mass (NTS) on Royal Forest on N side of Glen Etive, Argyll. Summit is Stob Dearg, at NE end; height 3352 ft or 1022 metres. NN 2254
Buaile an Ochd W Isles 88 C2* loc on E coast of Lewis on S side of Back. NB 4839
Buailnaluib H'land 78 F1 locality on E shore of Loch Ewe, Ross and Cromarty dist, 1m NW of Aultbea. NG 8690
Bualadubh W Isles 88 E2* loc at N end of S Uist, 3m/5km E of Ardivachar Pt. NF 7846
Bualintur Skye, H'land 79 C6 locality in SW part of island at head of Loch Brittle. NG 4020
Bubbenhall Warwicks 27 G1 vil 5m/8km NE of Leamington. SP 3672
Bubbleton Dyfed 22 C5* loc 2m/4km SW of Tenby. SS 0998
Bubnell Derbys 43 G4* loc 1km NW of Baslow. SK 2472
Bubwith Humberside 50 C4 vil on E bank of R Derwent 5m/9km NW of Howden. SE 7136
Buccleuch Borders 66 B6 loc on Rankle Burn 11m/18km W of Hawick. NT 3214
Buchan Grampian 83 G2, H2 stretch of country in NE of region, lying roughly NE of a line drawn from Banff on N coast to Newburgh on E. NJ 94
Buchanan Castle Central 71 F5. See Drymen.
Buchanhaven Grampian 83 H2 N dist of Peterhead. NK 1247
Buchan Ness Grampian 83 H3 headland with lighthouse on E coast 3m/4km S of Peterhead. NK 1342
Buchlyvie Central 71 G5 vil 14m/22km W of Stirling. NS 5793
Bucinch Central 71 E5* wooded islet (NTS) in Loch Lomond 2m/4km W of Balmaha. NS 3891
Buckabank Cumbria 59 H6 ham 1m S of Dalston. NY 3749
Buckby Wharf Northants 28 B1 loc on Grand Union Canal 3m/5km NE of Daventry. SP 6165
Buckden Cambs 29 F1 vil 4m/6km SW of Huntingdon. Remains of **B. Palace,** ancient palace of Bishops of Lincoln and scene of Catherine of Aragon's virtual imprisonment. TL 1967
Buckden N Yorks 48 C1 vil in Upper Wharfedale 4m/6km N of Kettlewell. To NE is **B. Pike,** mt of 2302 ft or 702 metres. SD 9477
Buckenham Norfolk 39 G4 ham 4m/6km SW of Acle. TG 3506
Buckenhill H & W 26 B2* loc 2km N of Bromyard. SO 6556
Buckerell Devon 7 H5 par and vil 3m/4km W of Honiton. ST 1200
Buckfast Devon 4 D4 vil 1m N of Buckfastleigh. 20c abbey. SX 7467
Buckfastleigh Devon 4 D4 mkt and mnfg tn 5m/8km NW of Totnes. SX 7366
Buckhaven Fife 73 F4 tn and port on N coast of Firth of Forth 7m/11km NE of Kirkcaldy. Formerly a joint burgh with Methil. NT 3698
Buckholm Borders 66 C4* loc 2m/3km NW of Galashiels. NT 4838
Buckholt 26 A5* ham on border of England and Wales 2m/3km N of Monmouth. SO 5016
Buckhorn Weston Dorset 9 E2 vil 4m/6km W of Gillingham. ST 7524
Buckhurst Hill Essex 20 B2 large residential area to S of Epping Forest 11m/17km NE of London. TQ 4193
Buckie Grampian 82 C1 fishing tn and resort on Spey Bay 13m/21km E of Elgin. NJ 4265
Buckingham Bucks 28 C4 tn on R Ouse 11m/18km W of Bletchley. Industries include milk and cream processing; light industry. Chantry chapel with Norman doorway (NT) on Market Hill. University college. SP 6933
Buckinghamshire 119 south midland county of England, bounded by Surrey, Berkshire, Oxfordshire, Northamptonshire, Bedfordshire, Hertfordshire, and Gtr London. The chalk downs of the Chilterns traverse the S part of the county, which is otherwise mostly flat. R Thames flows along its S border. Chief tns are Aylesbury, the county tn; Beaconsfield, and High Wycombe, around which, and other smaller tns, is a variety of light industry, as well as extensive residential areas.
Buckland Bucks 18 D1 vil 2m/4km W of Tring. SP 8812
Buckland Devon 4 D6 ham just N of Thurlestone and 4m/6km W of Kingsbridge. SX 6743
Buckland Devon 5 E3* E dist of Newton Abbot. SX 8771
Buckland Glos 27 E4 vil 2km SW of Broadway. SP 0836
Buckland Hants 10 A5* loc 1km NW of Lymington. To E, loc of **Lr Buckland.** SZ 3196
Buckland Herts 29 G4 vil 3m/5km N of Buntingford. TL 3533
Buckland H & W 26 B2* loc 4m/7km E of Leominster. SO 5556
Buckland Oxon 17 G2 vil 4m/6km NE of Faringdon. SU 3498
Buckland Surrey 19 F6 vil 2m/3km W of Reigate. TQ 2250
Buckland Abbey (NT). See Buckland Monachorum.
Buckland Brewer Devon 6 C3 vil 4m/7km SW of Bideford. SS 4120
Buckland Common Bucks 18 D1* vil 4m/7km NW of Chesham. SP 9206
Buckland Dinham Som 16 C6 vil 3m/4km NW of Frome. ST 7551
Buckland, East Devon 7 E2 vil 4m/7km NW of S Molton. SS 6731

Buckland End W Midlands 35 G5* loc in Birmingham 5m/8km E of city centre. SP 1588
Buckland Filleigh Devon 6 D4 ham 6m/9km NW of Hatherleigh. SS 4609
Buckland, Great Kent 20 C5* ham 6m/9km SW of Rochester. TQ 6664
Buckland in the Moor Devon 4 D3 ham on E edge of Dartmoor 3m/5km NW of Ashburton. SX 7273
Buckland Monachorum Devon 4 B4 vil 4m/6km S of Tavistock. 1m S, **Buckland Abbey** (NT), former home of Drake family. SX 4968
Buckland Newton Dorset 9 E4 vil 8m/13km NW of Puddletown. ST 6905
Buckland, North Devon 6 D2* ham 5m/8km SW of Ilfracombe. SS 4840
Buckland Ripers Dorset 8 D6* ham 3m/5km NW of Weymouth. SY 6582
Buckland St Mary Som 8 B3 vil 5m/7km NW of Chard. ST 2713
Buckland-tout-Saints Devon 4 D6* ham 2m/3km NE of Kingsbridge. SX 7546
Buckland Valley Kent 13 H3* N dist of Dover. TR 3143
Buckland, West Devon 7 E2 vil 5m/8km NW of S Molton. SS 6531
Buckland, West Som A2 vil 2m/4km E of Wellington. ST 1720
Bucklandwharf Bucks 18 D1* loc on old canal 2m/3km W of Tring. SP 8911
Bucklebury Berks 18 A4 vil 6m/9km NE of Newbury. Vil of **Upr Bucklebury** 2m/3km SW. SU 5570
Bucklegate Lincs 37 H1* loc 3m/4km SE of Kirton. TF 3335
Bucklers Hard Hants 10 B4 vil with quay on Beaulieu R 2m/3km SE of Beaulieu. Maritime museum. SU 4000
Bucklesham Suffolk 31 F4 vil 5m/9km E of Ipswich. TM 2441
Buckley (Bwcle) Clwyd 41 H5 tn 9m/15km N of Wrexham. Brick and cement mnfre. **B. Mountain** loc to N. SJ 2864
Buckley Gtr Manchester 48 B6 loc in Rochdale 2km NE of tn centre. SD 9015
Buckley Green Warwicks 27 F1* loc 1m NE of Henley-in-Arden. SP 1567
Buckley Hill Merseyside 42 A2* dist of Bootle 2m/3km N of tn centre. SJ 3499
Bucklow Hill Ches 42 C3* vil 3m/5km NW of Knutsford. SJ 7383
Buckminster Leics 36 D2 vil 3m/5km W of Colsterworth. SK 8722
Bucknall Lincs 45 F4 vil 3m/5km E of Bardney. TF 1668
Bucknall Staffs 43 E6 dist of Stoke-on-Trent 2km E of Hanley. SJ 9047
Bucknell Oxon 28 B5 vil 3m/4km NW of Bicester. SP 5525
Bucknell Salop 25 H1 vil 4m/7km E of Knighton. SO 3573
Buckpool Grampian 82 C1* W dist of Buckie, on N coast. NJ 4165
Buckpool W Midlands 35 E5* loc in Dudley 4m/6km SW of tn centre. SO 8986
Buckquoy Point Orkney. See Point of Buckquoy.
Buckridge H & W 26 C1* ham 4m/7km W of Bewdley. SO 7274
Bucksburn Grampian 77 H1 NW suburb of Aberdeen. NJ 8909
Buck's Cross Devon 6 C3 ham 2m/4km SE of Clovelly. SS 3422
Bucks Green W Sussex 11 G2 ham 3m/5km SE of Alfold Crossways. TQ 0832
Bucks Hill Herts 19 E2 loc 4m/6km NW of Watford. TL 0500
Bucks Horn Oak Hants 11 E1 ham in Alice Holt Forest 4m/6km SW of Farnham. SU 8041
Buckskin Hants 18 B6* W dist of Basingstoke. SU 6051
Buck's Mills Devon 6 C3 ham in steeply descending coombe above Barnstaple (or Bideford) Bay 3m/4km SE of Clovelly. SS 3523
Buckton Humberside 51 F1 ham 4m/6km N of Bridlington. TA 1872
Buckton H & W 25 H1 loc 6m/10km E of Knighton. SO 3873
Buckton Vale Gtr Manchester 43 E1/E2* loc 2m/3km NE of Stalybridge. SD 9800
Buckworth Cambs 29 F1 vil 6m/10km NW of Huntingdon. TL 1476
Budbrooke Warwicks 27 G2 vil 2m/3km W of Warwick. SP 2565
Budby Notts 44 B4 ham 3m/5km NW of Ollerton. SK 6170
Buddon Ness Tayside 73 H2 low headland on N side of entrance to Firth of Tay, 3m/5km S of Carnoustie. NO 5430
Budd's Titson Cornwall 6 B5 ham 4m/6km SE of Bude. Also known as Titson. SS 2401
Bude Cornwall 6 B4 resort (Bude-Stratton) on N coast 15m/24km NW of Launceston. SS 2006
Bude 6 B4 r in Cornwall rising near Jacobstow and flowing N into B. Bay. SS 2006
Budge's Shop Cornwall 3 G2* ham 6m/9km SE of Liskeard. SX 3259
Budlake Devon 7 G5* loc 5m/8km SW of Cullompton. SS 9800
Budle Nthmb 67 H5 loc on S side of B. Bay. NU 1535
Budle Bay Nthmb 67 H5 bay on North Sea coast 2m/3km NW of Bamburgh. NU 1536
Budleigh, East Devon 5 F2 vil 2m/3km N of Budleigh Salterton. SY 0684
Budleigh Salterton Devon 5 F3 resort on S coast 4m/7km E of Exmouth. SY 0682
Budle Point Nthmb 67 H5 headland on North Sea coast on E side of mouth of Budle Bay. NU 1636
Budlett's Common E Sussex 12 B4* loc 1km SE of Maresfield. TQ 4723
Budock Water Cornwall 2 D5* vil 2m/3km W of Falmouth. SW 7832
Budworth, Great Ches 42 C3 vil 2m/4km N of Northwich. **B. Heath** loc 1km N. **B. Mere**, lake to SW. SJ 6677
Budworth, Little Ches 42 B4 vil 3m/4km NE of Tarporley. SJ 5965
Buersil Gtr Manchester 42 D1 loc in Rochdale 2km S of tn centre. **Buersil Hd** loc 1m SE. SD 8911
Buerton Ches 42 C6 vil 2m/3km E of Audlem. **B. Moss** loc 1km N. SJ 6843
Buffler's Holt Bucks 28 B4* loc 2m/3km NW of Buckingham. SP 6635
Bugbrooke Northants 28 B2 vil 5m/9km SW of Northampton. SP 6757
Bugeildy Welsh form of Beguildy, qv.
Bugeilyn Powys 33 E5 lake 4m/7km W of head of Clywedog Resr. SN 8292
Buglawton Ches 42 D5* loc in Congleton 1km NE of tn centre. SJ 8763
Bugle Cornwall 3 E3 vil in china clay dist 4m/7km N of St Austell. SX 0158
Bugsbyns Reach 20 A4* stretch of R Thames in London below Blackwall, 6m/10km E of Charing Cross in a straight line. TQ 3979
Bugthorpe Humberside 50 C3 vil 4m/7km E of Stamford Br. SE 7757
Buidhe Bheinn H'land 74 B1 mt in Lochaber dist 2km N of Kinloch Hourn. Height 2884 ft or 879 metres. NG 9508
Building End Essex 29 H4* loc 6m/9km SE of Royston. TL 4337
Buildwas Salop 34 C4/D4 vil 3m/5km NE of Much Wenlock. Remains of 12c abbey (A.M.) across R Severn to SE. SJ 6304
Builg Burn 76 C1 stream in Grampian region running N from Loch Builg to R Avon 5m/8km W of Cock Br. NJ 1707
Builth Road Powys 25 E3 loc and rly stn 2m/3km NW of Builth Wells. SO 0253
Builth Wells (Llanfair-ym-Muallt) Powys 25 E3 tn on R Wye 14m/23km N of Brecon. Agricultural centre; crystal glass mnfre. Remains of cas consist almost entirely of Norman motte and bailey. SO 0451
Bulbourne Herts 28 D6* loc 2km N of Tring. SP 9313
Bulbourne 19 E3 r rising in Chiltern Hills NW of Berkhamsted, Herts, and flowing SE into R Gade at Hemel Hempstead. TL 0506
Bulby Lincs 37 F2 loc 5m/8km NW of Bourne. TF 0526
Bulcote Notts 36 C1 vil 6m/10km NE of Nottingham. SK 6544
Bulford Wilts 17 F6 vil and large military barracks 2m/3km NE of Amesbury. SU 1643
Bulgham Bay Isle of Man 46 C5 bay 2m/3km NE of Laxey. SC 4585
Bulkeley Ches 42 B5 vil 8m/12km W of Nantwich. SJ 5354
Bulkington Warwicks 36 A5 vil 2m/3km E of Bedworth. SP 3986
Bulkington Wilts 16 D5 vil 4m/7km SE of Melksham. ST 9458
Bulkworthy Devon 6 C4 vil 7m/11km SW of Torrington. SS 3914
Bullamoor N Yorks 54 C5* loc 2m/3km E of Northallerton. SE 3994
Bull Bay Gwynedd 40 B2 bay on N coast of Anglesey to N of Amlwch. Name also applied to the small resort on W side of bay. SH 4393
Bullbridge Derbys 43 H5* loc 3m/5km N of Belper. SK 3552
Bullbrook Berks 18 D4 E dist of Bracknell. SU 8869
Bullen, High Devon 6 D3 loc 3m/4km E of Torrington. SS 5120
Bullen's Green Herts 19 F1* loc 2m/3km SW of Hatfield. TL 2105
Bullers of Buchan Grampian 83 H3 huge circular cavern on E coast 2m/3km NE of Cruden Bay. The sea enters the cavern at its base, the top being open to the sky. In stormy weather the sea climbs to the top of the vertical walls of rock. NK 1038
Bulley Glos 26 C5 loc 4m/7km W of Gloucester. SO 7619
Bullgill Cumbria 52 B2 loc 4m/6km E of Maryport. NY 0938
Bull Green Suffolk 30 D2* loc 3m/5km S of Bury St Edmunds. TL 8459
Bull Hill Hants 10 A5* loc 2m/3km NE of Lymington. SZ 3498
Bull Hole S'clyde 69 B5* narrow strait in Sound of Iona separating Eilean nam Ban from Ross of Mull. NM 3024
Bullingham, Lower H & W 26 A4 SE suburb of Hereford. SO 5238
Bullinghope H & W 26 A4* loc 2m/3km S of Hereford. SO 5137
Bullington Hants 10 B1 ham 4m/7km S of Whitchurch. SU 4541
Bullington Lincs 45 E3* ham 3m/4km W of Wragby. TF 0977
Bullington, East Hants 10 B1* loc 1km E of Bullington and 4m/7km S of Whitchurch. SU 4641
Bullow Brook 7 E4* stream rising 1m SW of Winkleigh, Devon, and flowing E into R Taw 3m/4km E of Winkleigh. SS 6707
Bull Point Devon 6 C1 headland on N coast 4m/6km W of Ilfracombe. SS 4646
Bulls Cross Herts 19 G2* 2km SW of Waltham Cross. TQ 3499
Bull's Green Herts 29 G6 ham 3m/4km E of Welwyn. TL 2717
Bull's Green Norfolk 39 G5* loc 3m/4km N of Beccles. TM 4194
Bullslaughter Bay Dyfed 22 B6/C6* small bay 2m/4km W of St Govan's Hd, displaying contorted rock strata. SR 9494
Bulmer Essex 30 C4 vil 2m/3km W of Sudbury. TL 8440
Bulmer N Yorks 50 C2 vil 6m/10km W of Malton. SE 6967
Bulmer Tye Essex 30 D4 vil 2m/4km SW of Sudbury. TL 8438
Bulphan Essex 20 C3 vil 5m/8km SW of Basildon. TQ 6385
Bulstone Devon 5 G2* loc 4m/6km NE of Sidmouth. SY 1789
Bulverhythe E Sussex 12 D5* loc on coast 3m/4km W of Hastings tn centre. TQ 7708
Bulwark Grampian 83 G2/G3 loc 2km S of Maud. NJ 9345
Bulwark, The W Glam 23 F6* hill fort S of Llanmadog, qv. SS 4492
Bulwell Notts 36 B1 dist of Nottingham 4m/6km NW of city centre. SK 5344
Bulwick Northants 37 E5 vil 6m/10km NW of Oundle. SP 9693
Bumble Hole W Midlands 35 F5 loc in Dudley 2km S of tn centre. SO 9488
Bumble's Green Essex 20 B1* vil 4m/6km SW of Harlow. TL 4005
Bunacaimb H'land 68 E1* loc on W coast of Lochaber dist 2km N of Arisaig. NM 6588
Bunarkaig H'land 74 C3 locality in Lochaber dist on NW shore of Loch Lochy, 2m/3km N of foot of loch. NN 1887
Bunavoneader W Isles 88 A3/B3* locality in Harris at head of Loch Bun Abhainn-eadar, inlet of W Loch Tarbert. NB 1304
Bunbury Ches 42 B5 vil 3m/5km S of Tarporley. **Lr Bunbury** vil adjoining to SW. **B. Heath** loc 1km W. **B. Locks** on Shropshire Union Canal 1km NE. SJ 5658
Bunchrew H'land 81 F3* loc in Inverness dist on S side of Beauly Firth, 3m/5km W of Inverness. Camping and caravan site. NH 6145
Buncton W Sussex 11 G4* loc below S Downs 2m/3km E of Washington. Site of Roman bldg to S. TQ 1413
Bundalloch H'land 80 A5 locality on shore of Loch Long, Skye and Lochalsh dist, 1m NE of Dornie. NG 8927
Bunessan S'clyde 69 C6 vil on Ross of Mull at SE corner of Loch na Lathaich. NM 3821
Bungay Suffolk 39 G5 tn above R Waveney valley 14m/21km SE of Norwich. Remains of 12c cas of the Bigods. 17c mkt cross. Printing works. TM 3389
Bunker's Hill Gwent 15 G1* loc on N side of Blaenavon. SO 2509
Bunkers Hill Lancs 48 B4* loc 1m W of Colne. SD 8739
Bunker's Hill Lincs 45 F5* loc 2km SE of New York. TF 2653
Bunker's Hill Norfolk 39 F4* loc in Norwich 3m/4km W of city centre. TG 1809
Bunkers Hill Norfolk 39 F4* loc 3m/5km NW of Norwich. TG 1810
Bunkers Hill W Midlands 35 F4* E dist of Wolverhampton. SO 9597
Bunloinn Forest H'land 80 C6 deer forest in Inverness dist between Lochs Cluanie and Loyne. NH 1608
Bunloit H'land 81 E5 locality on NW side of Loch Ness, 3m/5km S of Drumnadrochit, Inverness dist. NH 5025
Bunmhullin W Isles 88 E3* loc on N coast of island of Eriskay. NF 7912
Bunnahabhainn S'clyde 62 B1 vil on bay of same name on NE coast of Islay, 3m/4km N of Port Askaig. Distillery. Anglicised form: Bonahaven. NR 4273
Bunny Notts 36 B2 vil 7m/11km S of Nottingham. SK 5829
Buntingford Herts 29 G5 small tn 10m/15km N of Ware. TN 3629
Bunting's Green Essex 30 C5* ham 2m/3km E of Halstead. TL 8330
Bunwell Norfolk 39 E5 ham 6m/9km S of Wymondham. Vil of **B. Street** 1m NW. Loc of **B. Hill** 1km S. TM 1292
Bunzeach Forest Grampian 76 D1* deer forest 7m/11km N of Ballater. NJ 3707
Burbage Derbys 43 E4/F4 loc in Buxton 1m W of tn centre. SK 0472
Burbage Leics 36 A5 SE suburb of Hinckley. SP 4492
Burbage Wilts 17 F5 vil 4m/7km E of Pewsey. SU 2361
Burchett's Green Berks 18 C3* vil 3m/5km W of Maidenhead. SU 8481
Burcombe Wilts 9 G2 vil on R Nadder 2m/3km W of Wilton. SU 0730
Burcot H & W 27 E1 loc 2m/3km E of Bromsgrove. SO 9871
Burcote Salop 34 D5* loc 2m/4km NE of Bridgnorth. SO 7494
Burcott Bucks 28 D5 ham 3m/5km W of Leighton Buzzard. SP 8723
Burdale N Yorks 50 D2 loc 2m/3km N of Fridaythorpe. SE 8762
Burdiehouse Lothian 66 A2 dist of Edinburgh 4m/7km S of city centre. NT 2767
Burdon Tyne & Wear 61 H6* loc 2m/3km SW of Ryhope. See also Old Burdon. NZ 3851
Burdon, Great Durham 54 C3 ham 2m/4km NE of Darlington. **Lit Burdon** ham 1m E. NZ 3116
Burdrop Oxon 27 G4* loc adjoining Sibford Gower to E, 6m/10km W of Banbury. SP 3537
Bure 39 H4 r rising near Melton Constable, Norfolk, and flowing SE into R Yare at Gt Yarmouth. TG 5107
Bures 30 D4 vil astride R Stour 5m/8km SE of Sudbury, partly in Essex and partly in Suffolk. St Edmund was crowned here in 855. TL 9034
Burfa Powys 25 G2* loc 3m/5km SW of Presteigne. Ancient British camp in woods to SE. SO 2761
Burford Oxon 27 F6 small Cotswold tn on R Windrush 7m/11km W of Witney. SP 2512
Burford Salop 26 B1* vil 1km W of Tenbury Wells across R Teme. SO 5868
Burford Som 8 D1* loc 2m/3km SW of Shepton Mallet. ST 5941
Burf, The H & W 26 C1 ham on W bank of R Severn 3m/4km S of Stourport. SO 8167
Burg S'clyde 68 C4 loc near W coast of Mull, 3m/5km E of Rubh' a' Chaoil. **Port B.** is small bay on Loch Tuath to S. Dùn Bàn is 1c galleried fort to SE on shore of loch. NM 3845
Burg S'clyde 69 C5* area (NTS) at SW end of Ardmeanach, Mull, rising steeply from Loch Scridain and culminating in hill of Bearraich, 1416 ft or 432 metres. NM 4124

Burgate Suffolk 31 E1 ham 4m/6km SW of Diss. Hams of **B. Great Green** and **B. Little Green** 1km N and 1km SW respectively. TM 0875
Burgate, Lower Hants 9 H3 ham in R Avon valley 1m N of Fordingbridge. SU 1515
Burgates Hants 10 D2* ham adjoining Liss to N. SU 7728
Burgate, Upper Hants 9 H3 ham in R Avon valley 2m/3km N of Fordingbridge. SU 1516
Burge End Herts 29 F4* loc at N end of Pirton, 3m/5km NW of Hitchin. TL 1432
Burgess Hill W Sussex 11 H3 tn 9m/15km N of Brighton. TQ 3119
Burgh Suffolk 31 F3 vil 3m/5km NW of Woodbridge. Site of Roman bldg near ch. TM 2351
Burgh by Sands Cumbria 59 G5 vil on line of Hadrian's Wall 5m/9km NW of Carlisle. NY 3259
Burgh Castle Norfolk 39 H4 vil 3m/5km SW of Gt Yarmouth. Remains of 3c Roman fort of *Gariannonum* (A.M.) on R Waveney. TG 4805
Burghclere Hants 17 H5 vil 4m/6km NW of Kingsclere. SU 4761
Burghead Grampian 82 A1 large fishing vil 8m/12km NW of Elgin. Radio transmitting stn. Well, or early Christian baptistry, (A.M.), within remains of Iron Age fort. **B. Bay** extends W to mouth of R Findhorn. NJ 1168
Burghfield Berks 18 B4 vil 4m/7km SW of Reading. Royal Ordnance Factory to E. SU 6668
Burghfield Common Berks 18 B4 vil 6m/9km SW of Reading. SU 6566
Burghfield Hill Berks 18 B4* loc 1m SW of Burghfield and 5m/8km SW of Reading. SU 6567
Burgh, Great Surrey 19 F5* urban loc to E of Epsom Racecourse, 2m/3km SE of Epsom. TQ 2358
Burgh Head Orkney 89 C6 headland on E coast of Stronsay. HY 6923
Burgh Heath Surrey 19 F5 suburban loc 2km SW of Banstead. TQ 2457
Burghill H & W 26 A3 vil 4m/6km NW of Hereford. SO 4744
Burgh Island Devon 4 C6 island in Bigbury Bay opp Bigbury-on-Sea, from which it is accessible on foot at low tide. SX 6443
Burgh le Marsh Lincs 45 H4 vil 5m/7km W of Skegness. TF 5065
Burghley House Cambs 37 E4 Elizn mansion in large park on SE side of Stamford, Lincs. Built by William Cecil, Lord High Treasurer to Elizabeth I. TF 0406
Burghmarsh Point Cumbria 59 G5* spit of land 2m/3km N of Burgh by Sands, on S bank of R Eden estuary opp Rockcliffe Marsh. NY 3161
Burgh next Aylsham Norfolk 39 F2 vil on R Bure 2m/3km SE of Aylsham. TG 2125
Burgh on Bain Lincs 45 F3 vil 7m/11km W of Louth. TF 2286
Burgh St Margaret Norfolk 39 H3 vil 4m/6km NE of Acle. TG 4414
Burgh St Peter Norfolk 39 H5 vil 3m/4km SE of Haddiscoe. TM 4693
Burghwallis S Yorks 49 G6 vil 6m/10km N of Doncaster. SE 5311
Burham Kent 20 D5 vil above R Medway valley 4m/7km S of Rochester. Several Roman sites in vicinity. TQ 7262
Buriton Hants 10 D3 vil 2m/3km S of Petersfield. SU 7320
Burland Ches 42 B5/C5 vil 2m/4km W of Nantwich. SJ 6153
Burlawn Cornwall 3 E2 vil 2km S of Wadebridge. SW 9970
Burleigh Berks 18 D4* suburb 1m NW of Ascot. SU 9170
Burleigh Castle Tayside 73 E4 ruined 15c-16c cas (A.M.) on E side of Milnathort. NO 1204
Burlescombe Devon 7 H3 ham 5m/8km SW of Wellington. ST 0716
Burleston Dorset 9 E5 ham 2km E of Puddletown. SY 7794
Burley Hants 9 H4 vil 4m/7km SE of Ringwood. SU 2103
Burley Leics 36 D3 vil 2m/3km NE of Oakham. **Burley on the Hill,** large early 18c hse. SK 8810
Burley W Yorks 49 E4* dist of Leeds 2km NW of city centre. SE 2734
Burleydam Ches 34 C1 vil 4m/6km W of Audlem. SJ 6042
Burley Gate H & W 26 B3 ham 7m/11km NE of Hereford. SO 5947
Burley in Wharfedale W Yorks 48 D3 vil 3m/5km E of Ilkley. SE 1646
Burley Lawn Hants 9 H4 loc 1km NE of Burley and 5m/8km E of Ringwood. SU 2103
Burley Street Hants 9 H4 vil 4m/6km E of Ringwood. SU 2004
Burley Woodhead W Yorks 48 D4* vil 2km SW of Burley in Wharfedale. SE 1544
Burlingham, North Norfolk 39 G4 vil 2m/4km W of Acle. **S Burlingham** vil 2m/3km S. **B. Green** ham 1km N. TG 3610
Burlingjobb Powys 25 G2* loc 3m/5km SE of New Radnor. SO 2558
Burlton Salop 34 B2 ham 4m/6km SW of Wem. SJ 4526
Burmantofts W Yorks 49 E4* dist of Leeds 2km E of city centre. SE 3134
Burmarsh Kent 13 F4 vil at E corner of Romney Marsh 4m/7km W of Hythe. TR 1032
Burmington Warwicks 27 G4 vil 2m/3km S of Shipston on Stour. SP 2637
Burn N Yorks 49 G5 vil 3m/4km SW of Selby. SE 5928
Burn 38 D1* r rising 2km S of S Creake, Norfolk, and flowing N to North Sea at Burnham Harbour. TF 8445
Burn 4 B3* r rising S of Brent Tor in Devon and flowing S into R Tavy 2km NE of Tavistock. SX 4976
Burn 54 B6 r rising on Masham Moor, N Yorks, and flowing E into R Ure 1m SE of Masham. SE 2379
Burnage Gtr Manchester 42 D2 dist of Manchester 4m/6km SE of city centre. SJ 8692
Burnaston Derbys 35 H2 vil 5m/8km SW of Derby. SK 2832
Burnbank S'clyde 64 D3* NW dist of Hamilton. NS 7056
Burnbanks Cumbria 53 E3* loc 2km S of Bampton. NY 5016
Burnbrae S'clyde 65 E3/F3* loc on W side of Stane. NS 8859
Burnbrae Reservoir S'clyde 64 C2* small resr 3m/5km NW of Clydebank. NS 4774
Burnby Humberside 50 D4 vil 3m/4km SE of Pocklington. SE 8346
Burncrooks Reservoir 64 C1* resr on borders of Central and Strathclyde regions 5m/8km W of Strathblane. NS 4879
Burncross S Yorks 43 H2* vil adjoining Chapeltown to W. SK 3496
Burnden Gtr Manchester 42 C1* loc in Bolton 2km SE of tn centre. SD 7207
Burnedge Gtr Manchester 48 C6* loc 3m/4km SE of Rochdale. SD 9210
Burneside Cumbria 53 E5 vil 2m/3km N of Kendal. SD 5095
Burness Orkney 89 C5* loc in NW part of island of Sanday. HY 6644
Burneston N Yorks 54 C6 vil 3m/5km SE of Bedale. SE 3085
Burnett Avon 16 B5 ham 2m/4km S of Keynsham. ST 6665
Burnfoot Borders 66 C6* loc adjoining Hawick to N. NT 5116
Burnham Bucks 18 D3 suburb 3m/5km NW of Slough. SU 9382
Burnham Humberside 51 E6 loc 4m/6km SE of Barton-upon-Humber. TA 0517
Burnham Abbey Bucks 18 D3* loc 3m/4km W of Slough. Remains of medieval abbey. SU 9280
Burnham Beeches Bucks 18 D3 woodland area containing beech and other trees 3m/5km NW of Slough. Name also applied to residential loc on E side of area. SU 9585
Burnham Deepdale Norfolk 38 C1 ham 2m/4km NW of Burnham Mkt. TF 8044
Burnham, East Bucks 18 D3* loc 3m/5km N of Slough. SU 9584
Burnham Green Herts 29 F6 suburban loc 2m/4km E of Welwyn. TL 2616
Burnham, Low Humberside 44 C1 ham 1m S of Epworth. SE 7802
Burnham Market Norfolk 38 C1/D1 vil 5m/8km W of Wells. TF 8342
Burnham Norton Norfolk 38 C1* ham 1m N of Burnham Mkt. TF 8243
Burnham-on-Crouch Essex 21 E2 tn on R Crouch estuary 9m/14km SE of Maldon. Yachting centre. Oyster fisheries. TQ 9496
Burnham-on-Sea Som 15 G6 small resort on Bristol Channel 8m/12km N of Bridgwater. Industrial development inland. ST 3049
Burnham Overy Norfolk 38 D1 ham 1m NE of Burnham Mkt. TF 8442
Burnham Sutton and Ulph Norfolk 38 D1* loc adjoining Burnham Mkt to S. TF 8341
Burnham Thorpe Norfolk 38 D1 vil 2m/3km SE of Burnham Mkt. Birthplace of Nelson, 1758. TF 8541
Burnham Westgate Norfolk 38 C1* W end of Burnham Mkt. TF 8342
Burnhaven Grampian 83 H2 vil 2km S of Peterhead across Peterhead Bay. NK 1244
Burnhervie Grampian 83 F5 loc on R Don 3m/5km W of Inverurie. NJ 7319
Burnhill Green Staffs 35 E4* ham 3m/4km SW of Albrighton. SJ 7800
Burnhope Durham 54 B1 vil 2m/3km E of Lanchester. NZ 1948
Burnhope Burn 53 G1* r rising on Burnhope Moor, Durham, and flowing E through Burnhope Resr to join Killhope Burn and form R Wear, at Wearhead. NY 8539
Burnhope Burn 61 E6* r rising on Stanhope Common, N of Stanhope, Durham, and flowing NE into R Derwent below Derwent Resr. NZ 0351
Burnhope Reservoir Durham 53 G1 resr in course of Burnhope Burn 1m W of Wearhead. NY 8539
Burnhope Seat Durham 53 G1/G2 mt 5m/7km W of Wearhead. Height 2449 ft or 746 metres. NY 7837
Burnlee W Yorks 43 F1* loc 1m SW of Holmfirth. SE 1307
Burnley Lancs 48 B5 industrial tn 22m/36km N of Manchester. Engineering, tyre mnfg, textiles, coal-mining. **B. Lane** loc 2km N of tn centre. SD 8332
Burnmoor Tarn Cumbria 52 B4 lake (NT) 2m/3km N of Boot. NY 1804
Burnmouth Borders 67 F3 vil on coast 2m/3km S of Eyemouth. NT 9560
Burn Naze Lancs 46 D4/47 E4 loc 2km E of Cleveleys. SD 3343
Burnock Water 56 E2 r in Strathclyde region running N to Lugar Water at Ochiltree. NS 5121
Burn of Ample 71 G3 r in Central region running N down Glen Ample to Loch Earn 1m E of Lochearnhead. See also Falls of Edinample. NN 6023
Burn of Aultmore 82 D2 stream in Grampian region running S to R Isla 2m/3km E of Keith. See also Aultmore. NJ 4551
Burn of Boyne Grampian 83 E1. See Boyne Bay.
Burn of Brown 82 A5*. See Glen Brown.
Burn of Cairnie 82 D2 stream in Grampian region running E to Cairnie then NE by Ruthven to R Isla 5m/8km N of Huntly. NJ 5147
Burn of Canny 77 F2* stream in Grampian region running S into R Dee 2m/3km W of Banchory. NO 6796
Burn of Forgue 83 E2* stream in Grampian region running N to R Deveron at Inverkeithny. NJ 6247
Burn of Kergord Shetland. See Weisdale.
Burn of Lochy 82 B4 stream running NE down Glen Lochy to R Avon 4m/7km N of Tomintoul, Grampian. NJ 1424
Burn of Lyth H'land 86 F2 r in Caithness dist running SE from Loch Heilen to Sinclair's Bay, N of Wick. ND 3357
Burn of Maitland Shetland 89 F5* stream on island of Unst running N through Loch of Cliff to head of Burra Firth. HP 6014
Burn of Pettawater Shetland. See Sand Water.
Burn of Setter 89 E6* stream on island of Yell, Shetland, running N into Whale Firth. HU 4891
Burn of Sheeoch 77 G2 stream in Grampian region running NE to R Dee 5m/8km E of Banchory. NO 7796
Burn of Tulchan H'land 82 A3 stream in Badenoch and Strathspey dist running SE down Glen Tulchan to R Spey 8m/12km NE of Grantown-on-Spey. NJ 1235
Burnopfield Durham 61 F5 vil 3m/5km NW of Stanley. NZ 1756
Burnrigg Cumbria 60 A5/B5* loc 1km S of Warwick Br. NY 4755
Burnsall N Yorks 48 C2 vil in Wharfedale 3m/4km SE of Grassington. SE 0361
Burn's Green Herts 29 G5* ham 5m/7km E of Stevenage. TL 3022
Burnside Fife 73 E4 loc 4m/6km SW of Strathmiglo. NO 1608
Burnside S'clyde 56 F3* loc 3m/4km SW of New Cumnock. NS 5811
Burnside Shetland 89 D6* loc on Mainland 2km W of head of Ura Firth. HU 2778
Burnswark D & G. Alternative spelling of Birrenswark, qv.
Burntfen Broad Norfolk 39 G3* small broad or lake 1m N of Horning. TG 3318
Burnt Hill Berks 18 B4* loc 4m/7km W of Pangbourne. SU 5674
Burnt Houses Durham 54 A3 loc 1km S of Cockfield. NZ 1223
Burntisland Fife 73 E5 shipbuilding tn on N bank of Firth of Forth 4m/7km SW of Kirkcaldy. See also Rossend Castle. NT 2385
Burnt Islands S'clyde 63 F1/G1 group of small islands in Kyles of Bute on E side of Buttock Pt, at N end of Bute. NS 0175
Burnt Mill Essex 20 B1* N dist of Harlow. TL 4410
Burnt Mills Essex 20 D3* industrial estate in NE part of Basildon. TQ 7390
Burnt Oak E Sussex 12 B4* loc 3m/4km S of Crowborough. TQ 5127
Burnt Oak London 19 F3* loc in borough of Barnet 2m/3km NW of Hendon and 9m/15km NW of Charing Cross. TQ 2091
Burntwick Island Kent 21 E4 island in estuary of R Medway S of Isle of Grain. TQ 8572
Burntwood Staffs 35 F3 loc 3m/4km N of Brownhills. **B. Green** loc 1km SE. SK 0609
Burnt Yates N Yorks 49 E2 vil 2m/4km W of Ripley. SE 2561
Burnworthy Som 8 A3* ham 1m N of Churchstanton. ST 1815
Burpham Surrey 19 E6* NE dist of Guildford. TQ 0151
Burpham W Sussex 11 F4 vil on R Arun 4m/7km N of Littlehampton. TQ 0408
Burradon Nthmb 61 E1 ham 6m/9km NW of Rothbury. NT 9806
Burradon Tyne & Wear 61 G4* coal-mining loc 5m/8km N of Newcastle. NZ 2772
Burra, East and **West** Shetland 89 E8 two long, narrow, adjacent islands S of Scalloway, Mainland, beyond island of Trondra, at either end of which rd brs afford a connection with Mainland. Another br connects the two islands with each other across the narrow strait between them. Fishing industry centred on vil of Hamnavoe, W Burra. HU 3733
Burra Firth Shetland 89 F5 deep inlet on N coast of Unst. At its head is loc of **Burrafirth.** HP 6114
Burra Firth, East Shetland 89 E7* inlet on E side of Aith Voe, Mainland. Loc of **E Burrafirth** at head of inlet. HU 3557
Burra Firth, West Shetland 89 D7* inlet on Mainland on S shore of St Magnus Bay, 4m/6km E of Melby. Loc of **W Burrafirth** to W near head of inlet. HU 2557
Burra Ness Shetland 89 E6* headland on S coast of Yell 1km SW of Burravoe. HU 5178
Burra Ness Shetland 89 F5 headland at easternmost point of Yell. HU 5595
Burras Cornwall 2 C5* loc 5m/7km S of Redruth. SW 6734
Burra Sound Orkney 89 A7* narrow sea channel between islands of Graemsay and Hoy. HY 2404
Burraton Cornwall 4 B4* loc 4m/6km SE of Callington. SX 4167
Burraton Cornwall 4 B4* W dist of Saltash. To S, dist of **B. Coombe.** SX 4159
Burrator Reservoir Devon 4 C4 resr on W side of Dartmoor 4m/6km SW of Princetown. SX 5568
Burravoe Shetland 89 E6 loc on Mainland on E shore of Busta Voe. HU 3667
Burravoe Shetland 89 E6 vil on inlet of Burra Voe at SE end of Yell. HU 5179
Burra Voe Shetland 89 E6 bay on NE coast of Mainland on Yell Sound 4m/6km S of Pt of Fethaland. 1m NE is the headland **Ness of Burravoe.** HU 3689
Burray Orkney 89 B7 inhabited island between S Ronaldsay and Mainland and linked to both by Churchill Barrier, qv. Measures some 4m/6km E to W and 2m/4km N to S. Boat-building is carried on. ND 49
Burray Haas Orkney 89 B7* headland at NE end of island of Burray. ND 4998

Burray Ness Orkney 89 B7* headland at E end of Burray. ND 5096
Burrelton Tayside 73 E1 vil adjoining Woodside to S, 2m/4km SW of Coupar Angus. NO 2037
Burrian Broch Orkney 89 C5* remains of Iron Age fortification or cas at S end of island of N Ronaldsay. HY 7651
Burridge Devon 6 D2* loc 2m/3km NE of Barnstaple. SS 5635
Burridge Devon 8 B4* ham 2m/3km SW of Chard. ST 3106
Burridge Hants 10 C4* vil 2km N of Park Gate. SU 5110
Burrier Wick Shetland 89 E6* sound between Uyea and Mainland. HU 3192
Burrigill H'land 86 E4* loc near E coast of Caithness dist 2km W of Lybster. ND 2234
Burrill N Yorks 54 B6* ham 2m/3km W of Bedale. SE 2387
Burringham Humberside 44 C1 vil on E bank of R Trent 4m/6km W of Scunthorpe. SE 8309
Burrington Avon 16 A5 vil below N slopes of Mendip Hills 2km W of Blagdon. ST 4759
Burrington Devon 7 E3 vil 4m/6km NW of Chulmleigh. SS 6316
Burrington H & W 26 A1 vil 5m/8km W of Ludlow. SO 4472
Burrium Gwent. See Usk.
Burrough End Cambs 30 B2/B3 E end of Westley Waterless. TL 6255
Burrough Green Cambs 30 B2/B3 vil 5m/8km S of Newmarket. The Hall is Elizn. TL 6355
Burrough on the Hill Leics 36 D3 vil 5m/9km S of Melton Mowbray. SK 7510
Burrow Devon 5 F2* vil adjoining Newton Poppleford and 5m/8km N of Budleigh Salterton. SY 0789
Burrow Som 7 G1* ham on slopes of Exmoor 4m/6km W of Dunster. SS 9342
Burrow Som 8 C2* ham 3m/5km W of Martock. Also ham of **Hr Burrow** to W and of **Lr Burrow** to N. ST 4120
Burrow Bridge Som 8 B2 vil on R Parrett 4m/7km NW of Langport. See also Burrow Mump. ST 3629
Burrow Head D & G 57 E8 headland 2m/3km SW of Isle of Whithorn, at W end of Wigtown Bay. NX 4534
Burrowhill Surrey 18 D5 vil adjoining Chobham to N. SU 9763
Burrow Mump Som 8 B2* isolated hill (NT) beside Burrow Br, with all-round views; crowned by unfinished 18c chapel joined to ruined medieval one. ST 3530
Burrow, Nether Lancs 47 F1 ham 2m/4km S of Kirkby Lonsdale. SD 6175
Burrow, Over Lancs 47 F1* ham 2m/3km S of Kirkby Lonsdale. Site of Roman fort. SD 6176
Burrows Cross Surrey 19 E6 loc 5m/7km N of Cranleigh. TQ 0846
Burry W Glam 23 F6* loc on Gower peninsula 2m/3km W of Reynoldston. SS 4590
Burrygreen W Glam 23 F6* ham on Gower peninsula 2m/3km E of Llangennith. SS 4691
Burry Holms W Glam 23 F6 detached headland and bird sanctuary at N end of Rhosili Bay at W end of Gower peninsula. SS 4092
Burry Inlet 23 F5 arm of Carmarthen Bay formed by estuary of R Loughor, S Wales. SS 49
Burry Port Dyfed 23 F5 tn and small port on N bank of Burry Inlet 4m/6km W of Llanelli. Chemical works. Large power stn. Tinplate mnfre. SN 4400
Burscough Lancs 42 A1 loc 2m/3km NE of Ormskirk. **Burscough Br** loc on Leeds and Liverpool Canal 1m NE. SD 4310
Bursea Humberside 50 C5 ham 5m/8km NE of Howden. **B. Lane Ends** loc 1m NW. SE 8033
Burshill Humberside 51 E3 loc 7m/11km NE of Beverley. TA 0948
Bursledon Hants 10 B4 vil on W bank of R Hamble 2m/3km NW of Park Gate. SU 4809
Burslem Staffs 42 D6 one of the tns of Stoke-on-Trent: Burslem, Fenton, Hanley, Longton, Stoke, Tunstall. Burslem lies 3m/5km N of city centre. SJ 8745
Burstall Suffolk 31 E4 vil 4m/7km W of Ipswich. TM 0944
Burstead, Great Essex 20 C3 suburban loc 2km S of Billericay. TQ 6892
Burstead, Little Essex 20 C3 vil 2m/3km S of Billericay. TQ 6692
Burstock Dorset 8 C4 vil 1m W of Broadwindsor. ST 4202
Burston Norfolk 39 E6 vil 3m/4km NE of Diss. TM 1383
Burston Staffs 35 F2* loc 4m/6km SE of Stone. SJ 9330
Burstow Surrey 11 H1 vil 2m/3km SE of Horley. TQ 3141
Burstwick Humberside 51 F5 vil 3m/4km E of Hedon. TA 2227
Burtersett N Yorks 53 G5 ham 2km E of Hawes. SD 8989
Burthorpe Green Suffolk 30 C2* ham adjoining Barrow to NE. TL 7764
Burthwaite Cumbria 60 A6* loc 4m/6km S of Carlisle. NY 4149
Burtle Hill Som 15 H6 loc 8m/12km NW of Glastonbury. ST 3943
Burton Ches 41 H4 vil 3m/4km SE of Neston. **Burton Wd** (NT), area covered with Scots pines. SJ 3174
Burton Ches 42 B5 ham 3m/5km W of Tarporley. SJ 5063
Burton Clwyd 42 A5* loc 1km W of Rossett. SJ 3557
Burton Cumbria 47 F1 vil 4m/7km NE of Carnforth. M6 motorway service area to W. SD 5376
Burton Dorset 9 E5 loc 1km N of Dorchester. SY 6891
Burton Dorset 9 H4 suburb 2km NE of Christchurch. SZ 1694
Burton Dyfed 22 C5 vil 3m/4km S of Llangwm. **B. Ferry** loc on estuary to SW. SM 9805
Burton Lincs 44 D4 vil 2m/4km N of Lincoln. SK 9674
Burton Nthmb 67 H5* loc 2km S of Bamburgh. NU 1733
Burton Som 15 G6 ham 3m/4km N of Nether Stowey. ST 1944
Burton Wilts 16 C3 vil 1m SE of Acton Turville. ST 8179
Burton Wilts 9 F1* loc 1km E of Mere. ST 8232
Burton Agnes Humberside 51 E2 vil 5m/8km SW of Bridlington. Hall, brick bldg of early 17c. Norman Manor Hse (A.M.) dates from 1170. TA 1063
Burton Bradstock Dorset 8 C5 vil near coast 3m/4km SE of Bridport. To SW, **Burton Cliff** (NT), high bluff on coast. SY 4889
Burton Coggles Lincs 37 E2 vil 3m/5km NE of Colsterworth. SK 9725
Burton Constable Humberside 51 F4 par containing **B.C. Hall,** Tudor hse with 18c state rooms, and gardens laid out by Capability Brown. TA 1836
Burton Dassett Warwicks 27 G3* ham 4m/6km E of Kineton. SP 3951
Burton, East Dorset 9 F5* loc 1m W of Wool. SY 8387
Burton End Essex 30 A5* ham 3m/5km NE of Bishop's Stortford, on N side of Stansted Airport. TL 5323
Burton Fleming Humberside 51 E1 vil 7m/11km NW of Bridlington. Also known as N Burton. TA 0872
Burton Green Clwyd 42 A5* loc 2km NW of Rossett. SJ 3458
Burton Green 35 H6* ham on borders of Warwicks and W Midlands 3m/5km NW of Kenilworth. SP 2675
Burton Hastings Warwicks 36 A5 vil 3m/5km E of Nuneaton. SP 4189
Burton in Lonsdale N Yorks 47 G1 vil on R Greta 3m/5km W of Ingleton. SD 6572
Burton Joyce Notts 36 C1 suburb 5m/9km NE of Nottingham. SK 6443
Burton Latimer Northants 28 D1 tn 3m/5km SE of Kettering. Footwear and other industries. SP 9074
Burton Lazars Leics 36 D3 vil 2m/3km SE of Melton Mowbray. SK 7616
Burton Leonard N Yorks 49 E2 vil 5m/8km S of Ripon. SE 3263
Burton, Lower H & W 26 A2* loc 5m/8km W of Leominster. SO 4256
Burton, North Humberside 51 E1 vil 7m/11km NW of Bridlington. Also known as Burton Fleming. TA 0872
Burton on the Wolds Leics 36 B2 vil 4m/6km E of Loughborough. SK 5921
Burton on Trent Staffs. See Burton upon Trent.
Burton Overy Leics 36 C4 vil 7m/11km SE of Leicester. SP 6798
Burton Pedwardine Lincs 37 F1 vil 2m/3km SW of Heckington. TF 1142
Burton Pidsea Humberside 51 F4 vil 4m/7km NE of Hedon. TA 2431
Burton Salmon N Yorks 49 G5 vil 2m/3km N of Ferrybridge. SE 4927
Burton's Green Essex 30 C5 ham 3m/4km S of Halstead. TL 8226
Burton Stather Humberside 50 D6* ham on E bank of R Trent 1km NW of Burton upon Stather. SE 8618
Burton upon Stather Humberside 50 D6 vil 5m/7km N of Scunthorpe. SE 8717
Burton upon Trent Staffs 35 H2 industrial tn 11m/17km SW of Derby. Chief industry is brewing, but others include engineering, rubber mnfre. SK 2423
Burton, West N Yorks 54 A6 vil 2km SE of Aysgarth. SE 0186
Burton, West W Sussex 11 F4 vil 4m/7km N of Arundel. SU 9913
Burtonwood Ches 42 B2 vil 4m/6km NW of Warrington. Airfield to S. SJ 5692
Burtree Ford Durham 53 G1 loc 1km N of Wearhead. NY 8540
Burwardsley Ches 42 B5 vil 5m/7km SW of Tarporley. **Hr Burwardsley** loc to E. SJ 5156
Burwarton Salop 34 C5 vil 8m/13km SW of Bridgnorth. SO 6185
Burwash E Sussex 12 C4 vil on ridge between valleys of Rs Rother and Dudwell 6m/10km E of Heathfield. Vil of **B. Weald** 2m/3km SW, and of **B. Common** 2m/4km W. Bateman's, 17c ironmaster's hse (NT), once home of Rudyard Kipling, is 1km S. TQ 6724
Burwell Cambs 30 B2 large vil 4m/7km NW of Newmarket. Site of 12c cas W of ch. TL 5866
Burwell Lincs 45 G3 vil 5m/9km S of Louth. TF 3579
Burwen Gwynedd 40 B2 ham near N coast of Anglesey 2m/3km W of Amlwch. SH 4193
Burwen Castle N Yorks 48 C3* site of Roman fort just W of Elslack. SD 9249
Bur Wick Shetland 89 E7* bay on coast of Mainland 1km NW of Scalloway. **Ness of Burwick** is headland on N coast of bay. **Burwick Holm** is tiny island at entrance to bay. HU 3940
Bury Cambs 37 G6 vil 1m S of Ramsey. TL 2883
Bury Gtr Manchester 42 D1 tn on R Irwell 8m/13km N of Manchester. Textiles, engineering, paper mnfre. SD 8010
Bury Som 7 G3 vil on R Haddeo 2m/3km E of Dulverton. SS 9427
Bury W Sussex 11 F4 vil in R Arun valley 4m/6km N of Arundel. TQ 0113
Buryas Bridge Cornwall 2 A5 ham on W side of Penzance. SW 4429
Bury End Beds 29 F4* loc at N end of Shillington, 3m/5km SW of Shefford. TL 1235
Bury End Bucks 18 D2* loc at S end of Amersham. SU 9697
Bury End H & W 27 E4* ham 1km S of Broadway. SP 0936
Bury Green Herts 19 G2* loc 1m W of Cheshunt tn centre. TL 3401
Bury Green Herts 29 H5 ham 2m/4km W of Bishop's Stortford. TL 4521
Bury St Edmunds Suffolk 30 D2 tn on R Lark 23m/37km NW of Ipswich. Many old bldgs, esp Ggn. Remains of abbey (A.M.). St James's ch now cathedral. Moyse's Hall, 12c, E Anglian museum. Angel Corner (NT), 18c hse, with collection of clocks and watches. Industries include agriculture and agricultural machinery, brewing. TL 8564
Burythorpe N Yorks 50 C2 vil 4m/7km S of Malton. SE 7964
Bury Walls Salop 34 C2* large Iron Age fort 2m/3km E of Lee Brockhurst. SJ 5727
Busbie Muir Reservoir S'clyde 64 A4* small resr 3m/4km N of Ardrossan. NS 2446
Busby S'clyde 64 C3 suburb 6m/9km S of Glasgow. NS 5756
Busby, Great N Yorks 54 D4 vil 2m/3km S of Stokesley. NZ 5205
Buscot Oxon 17 F2 vil 2m/3km SE of Lechlade. NT property, together with **Buscot Hse.** Loc of **B. Wick** 1m W. SU 2397
Bush Cornwall 6 B4* loc 1m N of Stratton. SS 2307
Bush Dyfed 22 D5* loc 2m/3km W of Saundersfoot. SN 1005
Bush Bank H & W 26 A3 vil 8m/13km NW of Hereford. SO 4551
Bushbridge Surrey 11 F1 loc 1m SE of Godalming. SU 9742
Bushbury W Midlands 35 E4 dist of Wolverhampton 2m/4km N of tn centre. SJ 9202
Bushby Leics 36 C4 loc 4m/7km E of Leicester. SK 6504
Bush Estate Norfolk 39 G2* loc on coast 2m/3km SE of Happisburgh. TG 4029
Bushey Herts 19 E2 residential tn 3m/4km SE of Watford. **B. Heath** loc adjoining to SE. TQ 1395
Bushey Heath Herts 19 F2 SE dist of Bushey. TQ 1594
Bushey, Little Herts 19 F2* E dist of Bushey. TQ 1594
Bushey Mead London 19 F4* loc in borough of Merton 2km S of Wimbledon. TQ 2468
Bush Fair Essex 20 B1* SE dist of Harlow. TL 4608
Bush Green Norfolk 39 E5* loc 2m/4km NW of Attleborough. TM 0298
Bush Green Norfolk 39 F5/F6* loc 2km NE of Pulham Mkt. TM 2187
Bush Green Suffolk 30 D2/D3* loc 2km E of Bradfield Combust. TL 9157
Bush Hill London 19 G2* loc in borough of Enfield 1km S of Enfield tn centre and 9m/14km N of Charing Cross. Locality of **B.H. Park** adjoins to E. TQ 3295
Bush House Lothian 66 A2 University of Edinburgh agricultural research station, 2m/4km N of Penicuik. NT 2463
Bushley H & W 26 D4 vil 2km NW of Tewkesbury across R Severn and R Avon. SO 8734
Bushley Green H & W 26 D4* loc 2m/4km NW of Tewkesbury. SO 8634
Bush, Lower and Bush, Upper Kent 20 D5* adjoining locs 1m W of Cuxton and 3m/5km W of Rochester. TQ 6967
Bushmead Beds 29 F2 loc 4m/7km W of St Neots. Remains of 12c priory. TL 1160
Bushton Wilts 17 E4* ham 3m/5km S of Wootton Bassett. SU 0677
Bushy Common Norfolk 38 D3* loc 2m/4km W of E Dereham. TF 9513
Bushy Park London 19 F4 large deer park in borough of Richmond opp Kingston across R Thames. Hampton Court Palace is at SW corner. TQ 1569
Busk Cumbria 53 E1* loc 2km SE of Renwick. NY 6042
Busk Gtr Manchester 43 E1* loc in Oldham 1m E of tn centre. SD 9105
Buslingthorpe Lincs 45 E3* loc 1m E of Faldingworth. TF 0785
Bussage Glos 16 D1 loc 2m/4km SE of Stroud. SO 8803
Buss Creek Suffolk 31 H1 tidal arm of R Blyth on N side of Southwold. TM 4975
Bustard's Green Norfolk 39 F5* loc 1km NW of Wacton. TM 1792
Busta Voe Shetland 89 E6* inlet on W side of Mainland, E of Muckle Roe. HU 3566
Buston, High Nthmb 61 G1 loc 2m/4km E of Shilbottle. **Low Buston** loc 1m SW. NU 2308
Butcher Hill W Yorks 48 C5* loc 1m SW of Todmorden. SD 9323
Butcherlawn Pond Derbys 44 A3* small lake in grnds of Barlborough Hall. See Barlborough. SK 4878
Butcher's Common Norfolk 39 G3* loc 3m/5km NE of Wroxham. TG 3320
Butcher's Cross E Sussex 12 B4 loc at N end of Five Ashes, 2m/3km W of Mayfield. TQ 5525
Butcher's Pasture Essex 30 B5* vil 2m/3km NW of Gt Dunmow. TL 6024
Butcher's Row W Sussex 11 G3* loc across R Adur from W Grinstead, 6m/10km S of Horsham. TQ 1720
Butcombe Avon 16 A5 vil 2m/3km NE of Blagdon. ST 5161
Bute S'clyde 63 F1-G3 island in Firth of Clyde separated from mainland of Argyll by narrow channel, the Kyles of B. The E coast, S of the Kyles of B., is about 5m/8km from Strathclyde mainland across Firth of Clyde, and the SW coast about 6m/10km from Arran. Area nearly 50 sq miles or 130 sq km. Chief tn and port is Rothesay. Mild climate. Chief industries are tourism and farming, esp dairy

farming. Car ferry services from Colintraive and Wemyss Bay. See also Maids of B., Sound of B. NS 06
Bute Town Mid Glam 15 F1* loc 2m/3km NW of Rhymney. SO 1009
Butetown S Glam 15 G4* dockland area of Cardiff 1m S of city centre. ST 1875
Butleigh Som 8 C1 vil 3m/5km SE of Street. ST 5233
Butleigh Wootton Som 8 C1* ham 2m/3km SE of Street. ST 5035
Butler Green Gtr Manchester 42 D1* loc 2m/3km SW of Oldham. SD 9003
Butlersbank Salop 34 C2* loc 2m/3km NE of Shawbury. SJ 5822
Butler's Cross Bucks 18 C1 loc 2m/3km W of Wendover. SP 8407
Butler's Cross Bucks 18 D2* loc adjoining Chalfont St Giles to SW. SU 9792
Butlers Marston Warwicks 27 G3 vil 2km SW of Kineton. SP 3150
Butley Suffolk 31 G3 vil 4m/6km W of Orford. To E is **Butley R** or **Creek,** running from ham of **B. Mills** down to R Ore. To S is loc of **B. Abbey,** with remains of priory. TM 3651
Butley Corner Suffolk 31 G3* loc 2km SE of vil of Butley and 3m/4km W of Orford across Butley R or Creek. TM 3849
Butleylow Corner Suffolk 31 G3* loc 2km SE of vil of Butley and 3m/4km W of Orford across Butley R or Creek. TM 3849
Butley Town Ches 43 E3* loc 2km W of Bollington. SJ 9177
Butlocks Heath Hants 10 B4* loc 1km NE of Netley. SU 4609
Butsa Shetland 89 F6* headland at SE end of Fetlar 2km S of Funzie. (See also The Snap, to SW.) HU 6688
Butser Hill Hants 10 D3 3m/4km SW of Petersfield. Highest point of S Downs, on which is a WT stn, as well as many prehistoric barrows, banks, and field systems. SU 7120
Butsfield, East Durham 61 F6* loc 4m/6km S of Consett. **W Butsfield** loc 1m W. NZ 1145
Buttercrambe N Yorks 50 C3 ham on R Derwent 2m/3km NE of Stamford Br. SE 7358
Butterknowle Durham 54 A2 vil 4m/6km N of Staindrop. NZ 1025
Butterleigh Devon 7 G4 vil 3m/5km SE of Tiverton. 1m NE, ham of **E Butterleigh.** SS 9708
Butterley Derbys 43 H5 loc 1m N of Ripley. SK 4051
Butterley Reservoir W Yorks 43 E1* resr 1km S of Marsden. SE 0410
Buttermere Cumbria 52 B3 lake (NT) formed by R Cocker above, or S of, Crummock Water. Ham of Buttermere at N end. **B. Fell,** hillside, rises steeply on NE side of lake. NY 1815
Buttermere Wilts 17 G5 loc 2m/4km SE of Shalbourne. SU 3461
Butters Green Staffs 42 D6 loc 4m/6km NW of Newcastle-under-Lyme. SJ 8150
Buttershaw W Yorks 48 D5 dist of Bradford 3m/5km SW of city centre. SE 1329
Butterstone Tayside 72 D1 vil 3m/5km NE of Dunkeld. Loch of Butterstone is small loch to SW. NO 0645
Butterton Staffs 42 D6* ham 2m/4km SW of Newcastle-under-Lyme. SJ 8242
Butterton Staffs 43 F5 vil 6m/9km E of Leek. SK 0756
Buttertubs N Yorks 53 G5 deeply eroded limestone rocks forming pillars resembling buttertubs on N slope of Buttertubs Pass between Hawes and Muker. SD 8796
Butterwick Durham 54 C2 loc 2m/3km E of Sedgefield. NZ 3829
Butterwick Lincs 45 G6 vil 4m/6km E of Boston. TF 3845
Butterwick N Yorks 50 C1 ham 5m/8km NW of Malton. SE 7377
Butterwick N Yorks 51 E1 vil 9m/14km N of Gt Driffield. SE 9971
Butterwick, East and **West** Humberside 44 C1 vils on opp banks of R Trent 5m/8km SW of Scunthorpe. Nearest br at Keadby, 3m/5km N. SE 8305
Butt Green Ches 42 C6* loc 2km SE of Nantwich. SJ 6651
Buttington Powys 34 A3 ham 2m/3km NE of Welshpool across R Severn. SJ 2408
Butt Lane Staffs 42 D5 loc adjoining Kidsgrove to W. SJ 8254
Buttock Point S'clyde 63 F1 headland on Kyles of Bute at N end of island of Bute. NS 0175
Buttock's Booth Northants 28 C2* loc in NE part of Northampton. Site of Roman bldg. Also known as Boothville. SP 7864
Butt of Lewis W Isles 88 C1 headland with lighthouse at N end of Lewis. NB 5166
Buttonbridge Salop 34 D6* loc 4m/7km NE of Cleobury Mortimer. SO 7379
Buttonoak Salop 34 D6 ham 3m/5km NW of Bewdley. SO 7577
Buttons' Green Suffolk 30 D3* loc 3m/4km N of Lavenham. TL 9153
Button Street Kent 20 B4* loc 2km E of Swanley. TQ 5368
Butts Devon 4 D2* loc adjoining Dunsford and 4m/6km NE of Moretonhampstead. SX 8089
Buttsash Hants 10 B4* loc at S end of suburban extension of Hythe and 3m/4km NW of Fawley. SU 4205
Butt's Green Essex 20 D2* ham 4m/7km SE of Chelmsford. TL 7603
Butt's Green Hants 10 A2* ham 1km SE of Lockerley and 4m/7km NW of Romsey. SU 3026
Butts, The Glos 26 D5* suburban loc 4m/7km SE of Gloucester. SO 8916
Butts, The Som 16 C6* SW dist of Frome. ST 7647
Buxhall Suffolk 31 E2 vil 3m/5km W of Stowmarket. Loc of **B. Fen Street** 1m N. TM 0057
Buxted E Sussex 12 B4 vil 2m/3km NE of Uckfield. TQ 4923
Buxton Derbys 43 F4 elevated inland spa (the Roman *Aquae Arnemetiae*) and resort 21m/34km SE of Manchester. Limestone quarrying in vicinity. SK 0573
Buxton Norfolk 39 F3 vil 4m/6km SE of Aylsham. **B. Heath** loc 1m S. TG 2322
Buxton Heath Norfolk 39 F3* vil 2km W of Hevingham. TG 1821
Buxworth Derbys 43 E3* vil 1m NE of Whaley Br. SK 0282
Bwcle Welsh form of Buckley, qv.
Bwlch Powys 25 F5 vil 5m/8km NW of Crickhowell. SO 1422
Bwlch-derwin Gwynedd 40 B6* loc 1m W of Pant-glas. SH 4646
Bwlch-gwyn Clwyd 41 H5 vil 5m/8km NW of Wrexham. SJ 2653
Bwlchllan Dyfed 24 B2 ham 6m/10km W of Tregaron. SN 5758
Bwlchtocyn Gwynedd 32 B2* ham 2km S of Abersoch. SH 3026
Bwlch-y-cibau Powys 33 H3 ham 3m/4km SE of Llanfyllin. SJ 1717
Bwlchyddar Clwyd 33 H2 loc 2m/4km NE of Llanfyllin. SJ 1722
Bwlchyfadfa Dyfed 24 A3* loc 2km SE of Talgarreg. SN 4349
Bwlch-y-ffridd Powys 33 G4 ham 4m/6km NW of Newtown. SO 0695
Bwlch-y-groes Dyfed 22 D2/23 E2 ham 5m/8km SW of Newcastle Emlyn. SN 2436
Bwlchyllyn Gwynedd 40 C5* loc 5m/8km S of Caernarvon. SH 5055
Bwlchymynydd W Glam 23 G5* loc adjoining Gorseinon to W. SS 5798
Bwlch-y-Rhiw (also known as Rhiw or Y Rhiw) Gwynedd 32 A2 ham 4m/6km E of Aberdaron. To E is Plas yn Rhiw (NT), medieval and later manor hse. SH 2227
Bwlch-y-sarnau Powys 25 E1 ham 6m/9km NE of Rhayader. SO 0274
Bwrd Arthur Clwyd 41 F4* ancient British amphitheatre 2m/3km NE of Llansannan. SH 9667
By Brook 16 C4 r rising on borders of Avon and Wilts near Tormarton, SE of Chipping Sodbury, and flowing through Castle Combe into R Avon near Bathford. ST 7867
Bycastwood Mid Glam 15 E3* loc on E side of Coity 2m/3km NE of Bridgend. SS 9281
Bye Green Bucks 18 D1* loc adjoining Weston Turville to E, 3m/5km SE of Aylesbury. SP 8611
Byerhope Reservoir Nthmb 53 G1* small resr 1km N of Allenheads. NY 8546
Byermoor Tyne & Wear 61 F5* loc 1m NE of Burnopfield. NZ 1857
Byers Green Durham 54 B2 vil 2m/3km W of Spennymoor. NZ 2234
Byfield Northants 28 A2 vil 7m/11km SW of Daventry. SP 5153
Byfleet Surrey 19 E5 suburban loc 4m/6km NE of Woking. Loc of **W Byfleet** 2km W. TQ 0661
Byford H & W 25 H4* vil on N side of R Wye 7m/12km W of Hereford. SO 3942
Bygrave Herts 29 F4/G4 vil 2m/3km NE of Baldock. TL 2636
Byker Tyne & Wear 61 G5* dist of Newcastle 2m/3km E of city centre. NZ 2764
Byland Abbey N Yorks 50 B1 ham 2m/4km W of Ampleforth. Ruins of 12c monastery (A.M.). SE 5478
Bylaugh Norfolk 39 E3 loc on R Wensum 4m/7km NE of E Dereham. TG 0318
Bylchau Clwyd 41 F5 ham 5m/8km SW of Denbigh. SH 9763
Byley Ches 42 C4 ham 2m/4km NE of Middlewich. SJ 7269
Bynack Burn 76 B3 stream in Grampian region running NE to Geldie Burn 5m/8km W of Inverey. NO 0086
Bynack More H'land 76 B1 mt in Cairngorms, in Badenoch and Strathspey dist, 3m/4km NE of Cairn Gorm. Height 3574 ft or 1090 metres. Formerly known as Caiplich. NJ 0406
Bynea Dyfed 23 G5 loc 3m/5km E of Llanelli. SS 5599
Byram N Yorks 49 F5/G5 loc 1km N of Ferrybridge across R Aire. SE 4825
Byrness Nthmb 60 D2 ham in upper Redesdale 2km SE of Catcleugh Resr. NT 7602
Bystock Devon 5 F2* ham 2m/4km NE of Exmouth. SY 0283
Bytham, Little Lincs 37 E3 vil 7m/11km N of Stamford. TF 0118
Bythorn Cambs 29 E1 vil 4m/7km SE of Thrapston. TL 0575
Byton H & W 25 H2 vil 4m/6km E of Presteigne. SO 3764
Bywell Nthmb 61 E5 ham on N bank of R Tyne 4m/7km SE of Corbridge. **B. Castle,** 15c tower hse. **B. Hall,** 18c. NZ 0461
Byworth W Sussex 11 F3 vil 1m SE of Petworth. SU 9821

C

Caaf Reservoir S'clyde 64 A4* small resr 2m/4km W of Dalry. NS 2550
Cabaan Forest H'land 80 D3 deer forest in Ross and Cromarty dist N of Orrin Resr. NH 3650
Caban Coch Reservoir Powys 24 D2/25 E2 large resr at junction of R Elan and R Claerwen valleys 4m/6km SW of Rhayader. SN 9264
Cabourne Lincs 45 E1 vil 2m/3km E of Caistor. **C. Parva** loc 1m NE. TA 1401
Cabrach Grampian 82 C4 vil on R Deveron 7m/11km W of Rhynie. NJ 3826
Cac Carn Beag Grampian. Summit of Lochnagar, qv.
Cackle Street E Sussex 12 C5 loc 1m SE of Brightling. TQ 6919
Cackle Street E Sussex 12 B4* loc 2km SE of Nutley. TQ 4526
Cacra Hill Borders 66 B6* hill on E side of Ettrick Water at its confluence with Rankle Burn, and 2m/3km N of Buccleuch. Height 1546 ft or 471 metres. NT 3117
Cadair Berwyn Clwyd 33 G2 a peak of the Berwyn Mts 1km NE of Moel Sych. Height 2712 ft or 827 metres. SJ 0732
Cadair Fronwen Clwyd 33 G1 a peak of the Berwyn Mts 3m/5km SE of Llandrillo. Height 2572 ft or 784 metres. SJ 0734
Cadbury Devon 7 G4 vil 6m/9km NE of Crediton. On hill to NE is **C. Castle,** Iron Age fort. SS 9104
Cadbury Castle Som 8 D2 extensive Iron Age camp 2m/3km SE of Sparkford. Possible site of King Arthur's legendary Camelot. ST 6225
Cadbury Heath Avon 16 B4* loc 5m/8km E of Bristol. ST 6672
Cadbury, North Som 8 D2 vil 5m/8km W of Wincanton. ST 6327
Cadbury, South Som 8 D2 vil 2m/3km E of Sparkford. See also Cadbury Castle. ST 6315
Caddam Wood Tayside 76 D5* wood 1m N of Kirriemuir. Here is most northerly known Roman rd. NO 3755
Caddington Beds 29 E5 vil 2m/3km SW of Luton. TL 0619
Caddonfoot Borders 66 C5 loc at mouth of Caddon Water, 3m/5km W of Galashiels. NT 4434
Caddon Water 66 C5 r in Borders region rising on N side of Windlestraw Law and flowing SE to R Tweed at Caddonfoot, 3m/5km W of Galashiels. NT 4434
Cadeby Leics 36 A4 vil 2km SE of Mkt Bosworth. SK 4202
Cadeby S Yorks 44 A1 vil in coal-mining area 3m/4km E of Mexborough. SE 5100
Cadeleigh Devon 7 G4 vil 4m/6km SW of Tiverton. SS 9108
Cader Clwyd 41 F5* loc 4m/7km SW of Denbigh. SJ 0060
Cader 32 D4* r rising on W slope of Cader Idris, Gwynedd, and running SW into R Dysynni 4m/7km NE of Llanegryn. SH 6508
Cader Idris Gwynedd 33 E3 precipitous ridge 3m/5km SW of Dolgellau whose central peak and summit, **Pen y Gadair,** attains height of 2927 ft or 893 metres. See also Tyrau Mawr and Mynydd Moel. SH 7113
Cade Street E Sussex 12 C4 ham 2km E of Heathfield. TQ 6020
Cadgwith Cornwall 2 C6* vil on E coast of Lizard peninsula 3m/4km NE of Lizard Pt. To S, rock ring known as The Devil's Frying Pan. Surrounding cliffs NT. SW 7214
Cadham Fife 73 F4 NE dist of Glenrothes. NO 2702
Cadishead Gtr Manchester 42 C2 loc on N side of Manchester Ship Canal 2m/3km SW of Irlam. SJ 7091
Cadle W Glam 23 G5* loc in Swansea 3m/5km NW of tn centre. SS 6297
Cadley Lancs 47 F5* suburb 2m/3km NW of Preston. SD 5231
Cadley Wilts 17 F4 ham 2m/3km SE of Marlborough. SU 2066
Cadley Wilts 17 F5* ham adjoining Collingbourne Ducis to NE and 2m/4km NW of Ludgershall. SU 2454
Cadmore End Bucks 18 C2 vil 3m/5km SE of Stokenchurch. SU 7892
Cadnam Hants 10 A3 vil on edge of New Forest 4m/7km W of Totton. To NW, **C. Common** (partly NT). SU 2913
Cadnant 40 C4* r on Anglesey running S into Menai Strait on NE side of Menai Br. SH 5672
Cadney Humberside 45 E1 vil 3m/4km SE of Brigg. TA 0103
Cadole Clwyd 41 G5 loc 2m/4km SW of Mold. SJ 2062
Cadoxton (Tregatwg) S Glam 15 F4 NE dist of Barry. ST 1269
Cadoxton-juxta-Neath (Llangatwg) W Glam 14 D2 vil on N side of Neath across R Neath. SS 7598
Cadson Bury Cornwall 3 H2* ancient British camp (NT) 2m/3km SW of Callington. SX 3467
Cadwell Herts 29 F4* loc 2m/3km N of Hitchin. TL 1832
Cadwell Lincs 45 G3* loc 2m/3km SW of Tathwell. TF 3283
Cadwst Clwyd 33 G1* loc 1m S of Llandrillo. SJ 0335
Cadzow S'clyde 64 D3/65 E3 S dist of Hamilton. **C. Castle,** remains of 13c royal residence beside Avon Water to E. NS 7153
Caeathro Gwynedd 40 C5 ham 2m/3km SE of Caernarvon. SH 5061
Caebitra 34 A5* stream rising 3m/5km E of Kerry, Powys, and running NE into R Camlad at Church Stoke. SO 2794
Cae-gaer Powys 33 E6* site of Roman fort 4m/6km SE of Plynlimon. SN 8281
Caehopkin Powys 14 D1* loc 4m/7km NE of Ystalyfera. SN 8212
Cae Llwyd Reservoir Clwyd 41 H6* small resr 3m/5km NW of Ruabon. SJ 2747
Caenby Lincs 44 D2/45 E2 vil 7m/11km W of Mkt Rasen. **C. Corner** loc and cross rds 2m/3km W. TF 0089
Caenlochan Forest Tayside 76 C3, C4* deer forest to S of Glas Maol. National nature reserve. NO 1775

Caeo Dyfed 24 C4 vil 2km E of Pumsaint. **C. Forest,** area of wooded hills to E. SN 6739

Caerau Mid Glam 14 D2 vil 2m/3km N of Maesteg. SS 8594

Caerau Powys 25 E3* site of Roman fort, 1m W of Llanlleonfel, between Beulah and Garth. SN 9250

Caerau S Glam 15 F4 loc in Cardiff 3m/5km W of city centre. ST 1375

Cae'r-bont Powys 14 D1* loc 3m/4km NE of Ystalyfera. SN 8011

Cae'rbryn Dyfed 23 G4* loc 2km SW of Llandybie. SN 5913

Caerdeon Gwynedd 32 D3 loc 3m/5km NE of Barmouth. SH 6518

Caer Drewyn Clwyd 33 G1* stone rampart on hill 1m NE of Corwen across R Dee. Probably dates from about 5c. SJ 0844

Caerdydd Welsh form of Cardiff, qv.

Caerestyn Clwyd 41 H5* loc 1m SE of Hope. SJ 3157

Caerfanell 25 F5* r rising 3m/5km E of Brecon Beacons, Powys, and flowing S then NE through Talybont Resr into R Usk at Llansanffraid, 6m/9km SE of Brecon. SO 1223

Caer-Farchell Dyfed 22 A3 ham 3m/5km NE of St David's. SM 7927

Caerffili Welsh form of Caerphilly, qv.

Caerfyrddin Welsh form of Carmarthen, qv.

Caergeiliog Gwynedd 40 A4 vil on Anglesey 1m SE of Valley. SH 3078

Caergwrle Clwyd 41 H5 vil on R Alun 5m/8km N of Wrexham. Once a Roman military stn. Remains of medieval cas. SJ 3057

Caergybi Welsh form of Holyhead, qv.

Caerhun Gwynedd 40 C4* loc 2m/3km S of Bangor. SH 5769

Caerhun Gwynedd 40 D4 loc 4m/7km S of Conwy. Ch stands on site of Roman fort of *Canovium*. SH 7770

Caeriw Welsh form of Carew, qv.

Cae'r Lan Powys 14 D1 loc 3m/5km NE of Ystalfera. SN 8012

Caerlaverock Castle D & G 59 E5 ruined late 13c cas (A.M.) near shore of Solway Firth 7m/12km SE of Dumfries. NY 0265

Caer Leb Gwynedd. See Llanidan.

Caerleon (or **Caerilion**) Gwent 15 H2 small tn on N bank of R Usk, on site of Roman tn of *Isca*, 3m/4km NE of Newport. Remains of Roman amphitheatre and legionary fortress (A.M.). ST 3390

Caernarvon (Caernarfon) Gwynedd 40 B5 tn and small port near SW end of Menai Strait at mouth of R Seiont, 8m/13km SW of Bangor. Medieval cas and remains of tn walls (A.M.). Site of Roman fort of *Segontium* (NT) in SE part of tn. SH 4762

Caernarvon Bay 40 A5 bay opp Caernarvon, Gwynedd, extending from Holy I., Anglesey, southwards to the Lleyn peninsula. SH 3536

Caerphilly (Caerffili) Mid Glam 15 F3 tn 6m/10km N of Cardiff. Engineering, light industry; coal-mining. Remains of large 13c cas (A.M.), much restored in 20c, on site of Roman fort. ST 1586

Caersws Powys 33 G5 vil on R Severn 5m/8km W of Newtown. Site of Roman military stn. 'New tn' extends from here to Newtown along R Severn valley. SO 0391

Caerwedros Dyfed 24 A3* ham 3m/4km S of New Quay. SN 3755

Caerwent Gwent 16 A3 vil 5m/8km SW of Chepstow, on site of Roman tn of *Venta Silurum* (A.M.). Parts of the Roman walls are visible. Traces of early British fort 2km N at Llanmellin. ST 4690

Caerwent Brook Gwent 16 A3* ham 1km S of Caerwent. Limestone quarries to S. ST 4789

Caerwys Clwyd 41 G4 vil 4m/6km SW of Holywell. SJ 1272

Caer y Twr Gwynedd 40 A3* ancient British fort on Holyhead Mt, qv. SH 2182

Cage Green Kent 20 C6* loc in Tonbridge 1km NE of tn centre. TQ 5947

Caggle Street Gwent 25 H6* loc just NE of Llanvetherine. SO 3617

Caigher Point Calf of Man 46 A6 headland at SW corner of island. SC 1564

Cailleach Head H'land 85 A6 headland on NE side of entrance to Lit Loch Broom, W coast of Ross and Cromarty dist. NG 9898

Cailliness Point D & G 57 B8 headland on E side of Rinns of Galloway, 3m/5km N of Mull of Galloway. NX 1535

Caim Gwynedd 40 C3* loc on Anglesey 2km NE to Llangoed. SH 6280

Cain 33 H2/H3* r formed by confluence of Rs Abel and Fyllon at Llanfyllin, Powys, and flowing E into R Vyrnwy on E side of Llansanffraid-ym-Mechain. SJ 2220

Caiplich H'land. Former name of Bynack More, qv.

Caiplich Water 82 A5. See Water of Ailnack.

Cairnbaan S'clyde 70 A5 locality on Crinan Loch in Argyll 2m/4km NW of Lochgilphead. Cup and ring marked rocks (A.M.); also at Achnabreck, 2km E. NR 8390

Cairnbulg Grampian 83 H1 loc on NE coast adjoining Inverallochy to W. **Cairnbulg Pt** is headland to NW, at E end of Fraserburgh Bay. NK 0365

Cairndow S'clyde 70 D4 vil at mouth of Kinglas Water on Loch Fyne in Argyll, near head of loch. NN 1711

Cairn Edward Forest D & G 58 B4, C4 state forest to S and SW of New Galloway, astride R Dee valley and enclosing **Cairn Edward Hill.** NX 6171

Cairness Grampian 83 H1 loc 5m/7km SE of Fraserburgh. NK 0360

Cairneyhill Fife 72 D5 vil 3m/5km W of Dunfermline. NT 0486

Cairngarroch Bay D & G 57 A7 bay on coast of Rinns of Galloway, 4m/6km SE of Portpatrick. NX 0449

Cairn Gorm 76 B1 mt in Cairngorms, on border of Grampian and Highland regions, 8m/13km SE of Aviemore. Height 4084 ft or 1245 metres. Ski slopes on NW side. NJ 0004

Cairn Gorm of Derry Grampian 76 82 mt in Cairngorms 2m/3km E of Ben Macdui. Height 3788 ft or 1155 metres. Also known as Derry Cairngorm. NO 0198

Cairngorms, The 76 A2, B1 granite mt mass between Aviemore in Highland region and Braemar in Grampian region. Popular with walkers, climbers, skiers. Deep defile of Lairig Ghru divides range into its E and W parts. Summit is Ben Macdui, 4296 ft or 1309 metres. NJ 0103

Cairnharrow D & G 58 B5 hill 4m/7km W of Gatehouse of Fleet. Height 1497 ft or 456 metres. NX 5355

Cairn Holy D & G 58 B6* chambered cairns (A.M.), 4m/6km SE of Creetown. NX 5154

Cairnie Grampian 82 D3 loc 4m/7km NW of Huntly. See also Burn of Cairnie. NJ 4844

Cairn Lochan 81 H6* SW peak of Cairn Gorm, on border of Grampian and Highland regions. Height 3896 ft or 1215 metres. NH 9802

Cairn na Burgh Treshnish Isles, S'clyde 68 B4 two islands, **Cairn na Burgh More** and **Cairn na Burgh Beg,** at NE end of group. On former is the ruin of an ancient cas, and on latter the remains of an old fort. NM 3044

Cairn of Barpa Langass W Isles 88 E1* ancient communal burial-chamber on N Uist, on N side of Loch Langass at head of Loch Eport, 5m/9km W of Lochmaddy. NF 8365

Cairn of Claise 76 C3 mt on border of Grampian and Tayside regions 7m/12km NE of Spittal of Glenshee. Height 3491 ft or 1064 metres. NO 1878

Cairn of Get H'land. See Ulbster.

Cairnorrie Grampian 83 G3 loc 4m/6km S of New Deer. NJ 8641

Cairnryan D & G 57 B6 small port on E side of Loch Ryan. Car ferry service to Larne in Northern Ireland. NX 0668

Cairnsmore of Carsphairn D & G 56 F4 mt 4m/6km NE of Carsphairn. Height 2612 ft or 796 metres. Also known as **Cairnsmore of Deugh.** NX 5998

Cairnsmore of Fleet D & G 57 E6 mt mass 6m/9km E of Newton Stewart. Summit 2331 ft or 710 metres. NX 5067

Cairns of Coll Coll, S'clyde 68 B3* two island rocks lying nearly 2m/3km NE of main island. NM 2766

Cairn Table S'clyde 64 D6/65 E6 hill 3m/5km SE of Muirkirk. Height 1944 ft or 593 metres. NS 7224

Cairn Taggart Grampian 76 C3 mt 6m/9km SE of Braemar. Height 3435 ft or 1047 metres. Also known as Carn an t-Sagairt Mór. NO 2084

Cairn Toul Grampian 76 A2 mt in Cairngorms 2m/3km SW of Ben Macdui. Height 4241 ft or 1293 metres. NN 9697

Cairntrodlie Grampian 83 H2* W dist of Peterhead. NK 1246

Cairn Water 58 D3 r in Dumfries & Galloway region flowing SE from near Moniaive to join Old Cluden Water and form Cluden Water 6m/10km NW of Dumfries. NX 8879

Cairnwell, The 76 C3 mt on border of Grampian and Tayside regions 5m/8km N of Spittal of Glenshee. Height 3059 ft or 933 metres. **Cairnwell Pass** to E, carrying rd from Braemar to Spittal of Glenshee, is highest main rd pass in Britain (2199 ft or 670 metres). NO 1377

Caisteal Dubh Tayside 76 A5*. See Moulin.

Caister-on-Sea Norfolk 39 H4 coastal resort 3m/5km N of Gt Yarmouth. Site of Roman tn (A.M.). Remains of 15c cas 1m W. TG 5212

Caister, West Norfolk 39 H4* ham 1m W of Caister-on-Sea. TG 5011

Caistor Lincs 45 E2 small tn on site of Roman stn 8m/12km N of Mkt Rasen. TA 1101

Caistor St Edmund Norfolk 39 F4 vil 3m/5km S of Norwich. Site of Roman tn of *Venta Icenorum* to SW. TG 2303

Caithness 114, 115 admin dist of H'land region.

Cakebole H & W 26 D1* loc 4m/6km E of Stourport. SO 8772

Cake Street Norfolk 39 E5 loc 3m/5km SE of Attleborough. TM 0790

Cake Street Suffolk 38 B6 S end of vil of Beck Row 2m/3km NW of Mildenhall. TL 6977

Calabrie Island W Isles 88 B2* islet at entrance to Loch Erisort, E coast of Lewis. NB 3822

Calais Street Suffolk 30 D4* ham 4m/6km W of Hadleigh. TL 9739

Calbost W Isles 88 C2* locality on E coast of Lewis 2m/4km N of Kebock Hd across mouth of Loch Ouirn. NB 4117

Calbourne Isle of Wight vil 5m/8km W of Newport. SZ 4286

Calcaria N Yorks. See Tadcaster.

Calceby Lincs 45 G4* loc 2m/3km NW of Ulceby Cross. TF 3975

Calcoed Clwyd 41 G4* loc 1m SW of Holywell. SJ 1774

Calcot Row Berks 18 B4 suburban vil 3m/5km W of Reading. SU 6672

Calcott Kent 13 G1 loc 2m/3km N of Sturry. TR 1762

Calcott Salop 34 B3* loc 3m/5km W of Shrewsbury. SJ 4413

Calcott Green Glos 26 C5* ham 3m/5km W of Gloucester. SO 7817

Calcutt Wilts 17 E2 loc 1km E of Cricklade. SU 1193

Caldarvan Loch S'clyde 64 B1 small loch 3m/5km NE of Alexandria. NS 4283

Caldbeck Cumbria 52 C1 vil 7m/11km SE of Wigton. NY 3239

Caldbergh N Yorks 54 A6* loc 3m/4km SW of Middleham. SE 0985

Caldecote Cambs 29 G2 vil 6m/10km W of Cambridge. TL 3456

Caldecote Cambs 37 F5* vil 2km SW of Stilton. TL 1488

Caldecote Herts 29 F4 ham 3m/5km N of Baldock. TL 2338

Caldecote Northants 28 C3 loc 2m/3km N of Towcester. SP 6851

Caldecote Warwicks 36 A4/A5 ham 2m/3km NW of Nuneaton. SP 3594

Caldecote, Lower Beds 29 F3* ham 2km S of Sandy. TL 1746

Caldecote, Upper Beds 29 F3 vil 2m/3km NW of Biggleswade. TL 1645

Caldecott Leics 36 D5 vil in R Welland valley 4m/6km S of Uppingham. SP 8693

Caldecott Northants 29 E1 vil 2m/3km W of Higham Ferrers. SP 9868

Caldecott Oxon 18 A2* S dist of Abingdon. SU 4996

Caldecotte Bucks 28 D4 loc 2m/3km NE of Bletchley. SP 8935

Calder Cumbria 52 A4 loc 2m/3km N of Seascale. Calder Hall Atomic Power Stn to W. NY 0303

Calder H'land 75 G2 r in Badenoch and Strathspey dist running E to R Spey 1m SW of Newtonmore. NN 7097

Calder 47 F4 r rising on Calder Fell on W side of Forest of Bowland, Lancs, and flowing SW into R Wyre at Catterall. SD 4943

Calder 48 A4 r rising 4m/7km SE of Burnley, Lancs, and flowing NW through Burnley, Padiham, and Whalley, to join R Ribble 2m/3km W of Whalley. SD 7037

Calder 49 F5 r rising near Todmorden, W Yorks, and flowing E by Hebden Br, Sowerby Br, Brighouse, Dewsbury and Wakefield to join R Aire at Castleford. SE 4226

Calder 52 A4 r rising at W end of Ennerdale Fell, Cumbria, and flowing SW past Calder Hall Atomic Power Stn into Irish Sea 2km NW of Seascale. SD 0102

Calder and Hebble Navigation 48 C5-49 E5 canal running from Sowerby Br, W Yorks, to Wakefield, where it connects with the Wakefield branch of the Aire and Calder Navigation from Wakefield to Castleford.

Calderbank S'clyde 65 E3 vil 2m/3km S of Airdrie. NS 7763

Calder Bridge Cumbria 52 A4/B4 vil 4m/6km SE of Egremont. NY 0406

Calderbrook Gtr Manchester 48 C6 vil 2km N of Littleborough. SD 9418

Caldercruix S'clyde 65 E2 vil 4m/7km NE of Airdrie. NS 8267

Calderdale 117 admin dist of W Yorks metropolitan county.

Calder Dam S'clyde 64 A3 small resr 5m/8km SW of Kilmacolm. NS 2965

Calder, East Lothian 65 G2 vil 2m/3km E of Livingston. NT 0867

Calder Grove W Yorks 49 E6* vil 3m/5km SW of Wakefield. SE 3016

Calder, Mid Lothian 65 G2 vil 2km SE of Livingston. NT 0767

Caldermill S'clyde 64 D4 loc on Calder Water 3m/5km SW of Strathaven. NS 6641

Caldermoor Gtr Manchester 48 C6 loc adjoining Littleborough to W. SD 9316

Calderstones Merseyside 42 A3* dist of Liverpool 4m/7km SE of city centre. SJ 4087

Calder Vale Lancs 47 F3* ham 3m/4km E of Garstang. SD 5345

Calder Water 64 D3 r in Strathclyde region rising S of E Kilbride and running NE into R Clyde 4m/6km E of Rutherglen. Also known as Rotten Calder. NS 6761

Calder Water 64 D4* stream in Strathclyde region rising as Calder Burn and running E into Avon Water 1km below Caldermill and 3m/5km SW of Strathaven. NS 6741

Calder Water, South 65 E3 r in Strathclyde region flowing W into R Clyde on W side of Motherwell, after passing to N of tn. NS 7257

Calder, West Lothian 65 F3/G3 vil 4m/7km SE of Bathgate. NT 0163

Calderwood S'clyde 64 D3* dist of E Kilbride to E of tn centre. NS 6555

Caldew 59 H5 r rising on E slopes of Skiddaw, Cumbria, and flowing N into R Eden on N side of Carlisle. NY 3956

Caldey Island. See Caldy Island.

Caldicot Gwent 16 A3 tn 5m/8km SW of Chepstow. Cas has round 13c-14c keep. ST 4888

Caldon Canal 42 D6-43 E6 canal running from the Trent and Mersey Canal at Etruria, Staffs, to Froghall.

Caldron Snout 53 G2 waterfall in R Tees below Cow Green Resr on border of Cumbria and Durham. NY 8128

Caldwell N Yorks 54 B3 vil 4m/6km SW of Piercebridge. NZ 1613

Caldy Merseyside 41 H3 loc 1m SE of W Kirby. **C. Hill** (NT) affords view across R Dee estuary. SJ 2285

Caldy Island (Ynys Byr) Dyfed 22 D6 island at SW end of Carmarthen Bay about 2km E to W and 1km N to S, separated from mainland at Giltar Pt by **Caldy Sound,** strait about 1km wide. Old Priory, 13c-15c. Abbey, early 20c, houses community of Trappist monks. Lighthouse at SE corner of island. SS 1496

Cale 9 E2 r rising N of Wincanton, Som, and flowing S through the tn and into R Stour to W of Marnhull in Dorset. ST 7519

Calebrack Cumbria 52 D2* loc 2m/3km S of Hesket Newmarket. NY 3435

Caledfwlch Dyfed 24 C5* loc 2m/3km NE of Llandeilo. SN 6525
Caledonian Canal H'land 114 ship canal connecting Moray Firth to Loch Linnhe, through Lochs Ness, Oich, Lochy, and the mouth of Loch Eil. Nowadays used by small cargo boats and pleasure craft.
Caletwr 33 F1 r running NW into R Dee 2km SW of Llandderfel, Gwynedd. SH 9735
Calf Hey Reservoir Lancs 48 A5* resr 2m/4km W of Haslingden. SD 7522
Calf of Eday Orkney 89 B5* uninhabited island of about 750 acres or 300 hectares lying off NE coast of Eday, separated from it by narrow strait of **Calf Sound.** HY 5839
Calf of Flotta Orkney 89 B7* small uninhabited island off NE end of island of Flotta across narrow strait of Calf Sound. ND 3896
Calf of Man 46 A6 island (Manx NT), about 2km across, off SW extremity of Isle of Man, separated from main island by Calf Sound, qv. Noted for bird life. SC 1565
Calford Green Suffolk 30 B3* loc 2m/3km E of Haverhill. TL 6945
Calf Sound Isle of Man 46 A6 strait separating Calf of Man from main island. Width nearly 1km. SC 1766
Calfsound Orkney 89 B5* loc at NE end of island of Eday on Calf Sound. See Calf of Eday. HY 5738
Calgary Mull, S'clyde 68 B4 vil near W coast of island at **C. Bay.** Emigrants from here gave its name to Calgary in Alberta, Canada. NM 3751
Calgary Point Coll, S'clyde 69 B7 headland at SW end of island. NM 0152
Caliach Point Mull, S'clyde 68 B3 headland on W coast of island 10m/16km W of Tobermory. NM 3454
California Central 65 F2* vil 3m/5km SE of Falkirk. NS 9076
California Derbys 35 H1 dist of Derby 1m SW of tn centre. SK 3435
California Norfolk 39 H3* coastal resort 5m/7km N of Gt Yarmouth. TG 5114
California Suffolk 31 F4 E dist of Ipswich. TM 1844
Calke Derbys 36 A2 vil 4m/6km N of Ashby de la Zouch. In park to W is **C. Abbey,** large 18c hse on site of former priory. SK 3722
Calkin Rig D & G. Alternative spelling of Cauldkine Rig, qv.
Callaly Nthmb 61 E1/F1 loc 2m/3km SW of Whittingham. **C. Castle** is a 17c–19c hse. NU 0509
Callander Central 71 G4 tn and tourist centre 14m/22km NW of Stirling. NN 6207
Callanish W Isles 88 B2 vil on W coast of Lewis 13m/21km W of Stornoway, and 2km S of Breasclete. Standing stones, (A.M.), thirty-nine in number, are ancient gravestones of uncertain date. NB 2133
Callater Burn 76 C2 r in Grampian region running N through Loch Callater and down Glen Callater to join Clunie Water 2m/3km S of Braemar. NO 1588
Callaughton Salop 34 C4* loc 2m/3km S of Much Wenlock. SO 6197
Callerton Tyne & Wear 61 F4* loc 1m E of loc of **C. Lane End** and 5m/8km NW of Newcastle. NZ 1768
Callerton, High Nthmb 61 F4 loc 2m/3km S of Ponteland. NZ 1670
Callestick Cornwall 2 D3 ham 3m/4km SE of Perranporth. SW 7750
Calleva Hants. See Silchester.
Calligarry Skye, H'land 79 E7 loc 1km W of Ardvasar, on E side of Sleat peninsula. NG 6203
Callington Cornwall 3 H2 tn standing on high ground above R Lynher 8m/13km NW of Saltash. SX 3669
Callingwood Staffs 35 G2* loc 3m/5km W of Burton upon Trent. SK 1923
Callow H & W 26 A4 vil 4m/6km S of Hereford. SO 4934
Callowell Glos 16 D1* N dist of Stroud. SO 8406
Callow End H & W 26 D3 vil 4m/6km S of Worcester. SO 8349
Callow Hill H & W 27 E2* loc on SW edge of Redditch. SP 0164
Callow Hill H & W 26 C1* loc 3m/4km SW of Bewdley. SO 7473
Callow Hill Wilts 17 E3 ham 3m/4km NW of Wootton Bassett. SU 0384
Callows Grave H & W 26 B1* loc 1m S of Tenbury Wells. SO 5966
Calmore Hants 10 A3 vil 2m/3km NW of Totton. SU 3314
Calmsden Glos 17 E1 ham 4m/7km N of Cirencester. SP 0408
Calne Wilts 17 E4 tn 5m/8km E of Chippenham. Bacon mnfre. ST 9971
Calow Derbys 43 H4 loc 2m/3km E of Chesterfield. SK 4070
Calpa Mór H'land 81 F6 mt on Coignafearn Forest in Inverness dist. Height 2668 ft or 813 metres. NH 6610
Calshot Hants 10 B4 loc 2m/3km SW of Fawley. 1m NW on spit of land jutting into Southampton Water, **C. Castle,** built by Henry VIII for defence against the French. SU 4701
Calstock Cornwall 4 B4 former port on R Tamar 5m/8km E of Callington. 1m W, Cotehele Hse (NT) above r. SX 4368
Calstone Wellington Wilts 17 E4 vil 3m/4km SE of Calne. SU 0268
Calternish W Isles 88 E2* loc on E coast of S Uist 5m/9km NE of Howmore. NF 8341
Calthorpe Norfolk 39 F2 vil 3m/5km N of Aylsham. TG 1831
Calthorpe Street Norfolk 39 G2/G3* ham 1m SE of Ingham. TG 4025
Calthwaite Cumbria 52 D1 vil 7m/11km N of Penrith. NY 4640
Calton N Yorks 48 B2 ham 7m/11km NW of Skipton. SD 9059
Calton S'clyde 64 D3* loc in Glasgow 1m SE of city centre. NS 6064
Calton Staffs 43 F6 vil 5m/9km NW of Ashbourne. **C. Green** loc adjoining to E. SK 1050
Calton Hill Lothian 66 A2* hill in Edinburgh to E of city centre. National Monmt, Nelson's Monmt, City Observatory. NT 2674
Calva Mór and **Calva Beg** H'land 84 B4 two small uninhabited islands in Eddrachillis Bay 3m/5km S of Badcall, W coast of Sutherland dist. Alternative spelling: Calbha Mór and Calbha Beag. NC 1636, 1536
Calvay W Isles 88 E3* islet in Sound of Eriskay off NE point of island of Eriskay. NF 8112
Calvay W Isles 88 E3* small island with lighthouse on S side of entrance to Loch Boisdale, S Uist. NF 8218
Calve Island S'clyde 68 D3 uninhabited island at entrance to Tobermory Bay, island of Mull. NM 5254
Calver Derbys 43 G4 vil 4m/7km N of Bakewell. **C. Sough** loc adjoining to N. SK 2374
Calverhall Salop 34 C1 vil 5m/8km SE of Whitchurch. SJ 6037
Calver Hill H & W 25 H3* loc 4m/6km E of Willersley. SO 3748
Calverleigh Devon 7 G4 ham 2m/4km NW of Tiverton. SS 9214
Calverley W Yorks 48 D4/49 E4 loc 4m/6km NE of Bradford. **C. Carr** loc adjoining to W. SE 2037
Calvert Bucks 28 B5* loc 6m/10km S of Buckingham. Brick works. SP 6824
Calverton Bucks 28 C4 vil 1m S of Stony Stratford. SP 7938
Calverton Notts 44 B6 vil 7m/11km NE of Nottingham. SK 6149
Calvine Tayside 75 H4 vil near confluence of Errochty Water and R Garry 4m/7km W of Blair Atholl. NN 8065
Calvo Cumbria 59 F5/F6 ham 2m/4km E of Silloth. NY 1453
Calzeat Borders 65 G5* loc, part of Broughton vil. NT 1135
Cam Glos 16 C2 vil 1m N of Dursley. Vil of **Lr Cam** 1m N. ST 7599
Cam 30 A1 r of two branches: R Cam or Granta rises in Essex 3m/5km W of Thaxted; R Cam or Rhee rises at Ashwell, Herts. The two branches join S of Grantchester, Cambs, and flow NE as R Cam or Granta through Cambridge and into R Ouse 4m/6km S of Ely. TL 5374
Camas Baravaig Skye, H'land 79 E7*. See Baravaig.
Camascross Skye, H'land 79 E7 loc on bay of same name on E coast of Sleat peninsula 1km S of Isle Ornsay. NG 6911
Camas Cuil ant-Saimh S'clyde 69 B6* wide bay on W coast of Iona. NM 2623
Camas Fhionnairidh Skye, H'land 79 D6 inlet of Loch Scavaig on S coast 3m/5km N of Elgol. NG 5118
Camas Luinge H'land 79 F8* small bay with landing stage on S side of Loch Morar, Lochaber dist, at mouth of R Meoble. NM 7889
Camas nan Gall H'land 79 C7 bay on S coast of Soay, island off S coast of Skye. NG 4514
Camas Sgiotaig H'land 68 C1* bay on W coast of Eigg, N of Bay of Laig. NM 4689
Camas Shallachain H'land 74 B5* bay on W side of Sallachan Pt, Lochaber dist, on W side of Loch Linnhe. NM 9862
Camastianavaig Skye, H'land 79 C5 locality on E coast 3m/5km SE of Loch Portree. NG 5039
Camas Uig W Isles 88 A2* bay on W coast of Lewis 2m/3km W of Uig. NB 0233
Camault Muir H'land 81 E3* loc in Inverness dist 4m/7km S of Beauly. NH 5040
Camb Shetland 89 E6* loc on Yell on N side of Mid Yell Voe. HU 5092
Cambeak Cornwall 6 A5 headland (NT) 4m/7km NE of Boscastle. SX 1296
Camber E Sussex 13 E5 seaside resort on Rye Bay 3m/5km E of Rye. TQ 9618
Camberley Surrey 18 D5 residential and military tn 6m/9km S of Bracknell. Royal Staff College on N side. SU 8660
Camberwell London 19 G4* dist in borough of Southwark 3m/4km SE of Charing Cross. TQ 3276
Camblesforth N Yorks 50 B5 vil 3m/4km N of Snaith. SE 6426
Cambo Nthmb 61 E3 vil 11m/17km W of Morpeth. Wallington Hall, qv, 1m S. Vil is largely estate vil of hall. NZ 0285
Camboglanna Cumbria. See Birdoswald.
Cambois Nthmb 61 G3 loc on North Sea coast 2km N of Blyth across R Blyth. Power stn on N bank of estuary. NZ 3083
Camborne Cornwall 2 C4 industrial tn 11m/18km W of Truro. Formerly a centre of tin-mining industry. **C. Beacon** loc 1km S. SW 6440
Cambrian Mountains 118 mt range of central Wales, extending from Cader Idris in the NW to Brecon Beacons in the SE. Consist largely of remote, bare hills, although there is extensive afforestation in places. SH 80
Cambridge Cambs 29 H2 city on R Cam 49m/79km N of London. University founded 13c; many notable bldgs. Industries include preserves, fertilisers, dairy equipment, electronic equipment, radios. Airport at Teversham 3m/4km E. TL 4458
Cambridge Glos 16 C1 vil 4m/6km N of Dursley. SO 7403
Cambridgeshire 119 eastern county of England, bounded by Essex, Hertfordshire, Bedfordshire, Northamptonshire, Lincolnshire, Norfolk, and Suffolk. Flat country, with fenland to N and E, although there are low chalk hills in the S and SE. Sugar beet, potatoes, and corn are grown; soft fruit and vegetable cultivation and canning are also important rural industries. Brick mnfre is carried on S of Peterborough. Chief tns are the city of Cambridge, the county tn; the cathedral cities of Ely and Peterborough; and Huntingdon and Wisbech. Rs include the Cam, Nene, and Ouse.
Cambridge Town Essex 21 E2 E dist of Southend-on-Sea, 1km W of Shoeburyness. TQ 9284
Cam Brook 16 C5* r rising at Hinton Blewett, Avon, and flowing E into Wellow Brook at Midford, 3m/4km S of Bath. ST 7660
Cambrose Cornwall 2 C4* ham 2m/3km E of Portreath. SW 6845
Cambus Central 72 C5 vil 2m/3km W of Alloa. Distilleries. NS 8593
Cambusbarron Central 72 B5 suburb 2km W of Stirling. NS 7792
Cambuscurrie Bay H'land 87 A7 bay on S side of Dornoch Firth, Ross and Cromarty dist, on E side of vil of Edderton. NH 7285
Cambuskenneth Central 72 C5 loc with remains of medieval abbey (A.M.) 1km NE of Stirling across R Forth (footbridge). NS 8094
Cambuslang S'clyde 64 D3 tn on S bank of R Clyde 5m/8km SE of Glasgow. NS 6460
Cambusnethan S'clyde 65 E3 loc adjoining Wishaw to E. NS 8155
Cam Chreag Tayside 71 F1 mt 3m/5km NW of Br of Balgie. Height 2823 ft or 860 metres. NN 5949
Cam Creag 71 E2* mt at meeting point of Central, Strathclyde, and Tayside regions 4m/6km NE of Tyndrum. Height 2887 ft or 880 metres. NN 3734
Camddwr 24 D3 r rising about 6m/9km E of Tregaron, Dyfed, and flowing SE to join R Towy in Llyn Brianne Resr. SN 8050
Camddwr 25 F1* r rising about 3m/5km NE of Llanbister, Powys, and flowing S then SW into R Ithon 1m N of Llanddewi Ystradenni. SO 1070
Camden London 19 G3* borough and loc (**C. Town**) 2m/4km N of Charing Cross. Borough includes dists of Hampstead, Holborn, St Pancras. TQ 2883
Camdentown Hants 10 C4 dist of Gosport 1m NW of tn centre. SU 6000
Camel 3 E1 r rising near Davidstow, Cornwall, and flowing S then NW past Wadebridge and Padstow into the sea at Padstow Bay. SW 9278
Cameley Avon 16 B5* vil 4m/6km NW of Midsomer Norton. ST 6157
Camelford Cornwall 6 A6 small tn 11m/17km N of Bodmin and 4m/7km E of coast at Port Isaac Bay. Slate quarries in vicinity. Bodmin Moor extends SE. SX 1083
Camel Hill Som 8 D2* loc 1km N of Queen Camel. ST 5825
Camelon Central 65 E1 industrial suburb W of Falkirk. NS 8680
Camelsdale W Sussex 11 E2 loc 2km W of Haslemere. SU 8832
Camel, West Som 8 D2 vil 2m/3km SW of Sparkford. ST 5724
Camer Kent 20 C5 loc 1km NE of Meopham and 5m/7km S of Gravesend. TQ 6567
Camer's Green H & W 26 C4 ham to E of S end of Malvern Hills 8m/12km W of Tewkesbury. SO 7735
Camerton Avon 16 C5 vil 2m/3km N of Radstock. ST 6857
Camerton Cumbria 52 A2 vil 3m/5km NE of Workington. NY 0330
Camlachie S'clyde 64 D2/D3* dist of Glasgow 2m/3km E of city centre. NS 6164
Camlad 33 H4 r rising near More, Salop, and flowing W to Church Stoke, then N to Hockleton Br, then W into R Severn 4m/7km S of Welshpool, Powys. SJ 2000
Cam Loch H'land 85 C5 loch in Sutherland dist 6m/9km S of Inchnadamph. NC 2113
Cammachmore Grampian 77 H2 vil 7m/12km S of Aberdeen. NO 9094
Cammarch 25 E3* r running S into R Irfon at Llangammarch Wells, Powys. SN 9347
Cammeringham Lincs 44 D3 vil 7m/11km N of Lincoln. SK 9482
Camnant 33 G6* stream running E into R Ithon 3m/5km N of Llanbadarn Fynydd. SO 0882
Camore H'land 87 B7* loc in Sutherland dist 2km W of Dornoch. NH 7790
Campay W Isles 88 A2* small uninhabited island off W coast of Lewis 2km N of island of Gt Bernera. NB 1442
Campbelltown H'land 81 G2. Former name of Ardersier, vil in Inverness dist on E shore of Inner Moray Firth or Inverness Firth 2m/3km SE of Fort George. NH 7855
Campbeltown S'clyde 63 E5 chief tn and port of Kintyre, at head of **C. Loch** 30m/48km S of Tarbert. Fishing, distilling; oil storage depot. NR 7120
Camperdown Tyne & Wear 61 G4* loc 5m/8km N of Newcastle. NZ 2771
Camp Hill Dyfed 22 D4* loc 1km S of Narberth. SN 1113
Camp Hill Warwicks 36 A5* NW dist of Nuneaton. SP 3493
Camphill Reservoir S'clyde 64 A3 resr 3m/5km W of Kilbirnie. NS 2755
Cample Water 58 D2 r in Dumfries & Galloway region running S then W to R Nith on S side of Thornhill. NX 8693
Campmuir Tayside 73 E1* loc 2m/3km S of Coupar Angus. Site of Roman camp to SE. NO 2137
Camps Lothian 65 G2* loc 1km N of Kirknewton. NT 1068

Campsall S Yorks 49 G6 vil 7m/11km N of Doncaster. SE 5413

Campsea Ash Suffolk 31 G3 vil 2m/3km E of Wickham Mkt. Sometimes spelt Campsea Ashe. TM 3255

Camps End Cambs 30 B3/B4* ham 4m/7km SW of Haverhill. TL 6142

Camps Heath Suffolk 39 H5 loc 3m/4km W of Lowestoft. TM 5194

Campsie (or Clachan of Campsie) S'clyde 64 D1 vil 2m/3km NW of Lennoxtown. NS 6179

Campsie Fells 64 C1, D1 range of hills on borders of Central and Strathclyde regions E of Killearn. Summit is Earl's Seat, qv. NS 58

Camps Reservoir S'clyde 65 F6/G6 resr 3m/5km E of Crawford. NT 0022

Camp, The Glos 16 D1* loc 5m/8km NE of Stroud. SO 9109

Camp, The Herts 19 F1* SE dist of St Albans. TL 1606

Campton Beds 29 F4 vil 1m SW of Shefford. TL 1338

Camptown Borders 66 D6 loc on Jed Water 5m/8km S of Jedburgh. NT 6713

Camp Town W Yorks 49 E4* dist of Leeds 4m/6km N of city centre. SE 2939

Camros Welsh form of Camrose, qv.

Camrose (Camros) Dyfed 22 B4 vil 3m/5km NW of Haverfordwest. Remains of motte and bailey cas. SM 9220

Camserney Tayside 75 H6* vil 2m/4km W of Aberfeldy. NN 8149

Camster H'land 86 E3 loc in Caithness dist 4m/6km N of Lybster. Grey Cairns of C. (A.M.), 2km N, are Stone to Bronze Age burial cairns. ND 2641

Camulodunum Essex. See Colchester.

Camus Castle Skye, H'land. Former name of Knock Castle. See Knock.

Camusdarrach H'land 79 E8 loc on coast of Lochaber dist 3m/5km N of Arisaig. NM 6691

Camusnagaul H'land 85 B7 locality on S shore of Lit Loch Broom, Ross and Cromarty dist, 2m/3km from head of loch. NH 0689

Camusteel H'land 78 E5 loc on W coast of Ross and Cromarty dist 2km S of Applecross. NG 7042

Camusterrach H'land 78 E5 loc on W coast of Ross and Cromarty dist 2m/3km S of Applecross. NG 7141

Camusvrachan Tayside 75 F6 loc in Glen Lyon 3m/5km E of Br of Balgie. NN 6247

Can 20 D1 r rising near High Roding S of Gt Dunmow, Essex, and flowing SE into R Chelmer at Chelmsford. TL 7106

Canada Avon 16 H5* two locs of **Lr** and **Upr Canada** on N slope of Bleadon Hill, 3m/5km SE of Weston-super-Mare. ST 3658

Canada Hants 10 A3 vil 3m/5km N of Cadnam. **C. Common,** partly NT, to SW. SU 2818

Canal Side S Yorks 49 H6* loc on SW side of Thorne across Stainforth and Keadby Canal. SE 6812

Canaston Bridge Dyfed 22 C4 loc at crossing of Eastern Cleddau R 3m/5km W of Narberth. SN 0615

Candlesby Lincs 45 H4 vil 4m/6km E of Spilsby. TF 4567

Candle Street Suffolk 31 E1* loc 1km S of Rickinghall Inferior. TM 0474

Candyburn 65 G4* loc on border of Strathclyde and Borders regions 3m/5km NE of Biggar. NT 0741

Cane End Oxon 18 B3 ham 5m/7km NW of Reading. SU 6779

Canewdon Essex 21 E2 vil 3m/5km NE of Rochford. TQ 8994

Canfield End Essex 30 B5* ham 3m/4km W of Gt Dunmow. TL 5821

Canfield, Great Essex 30 B6 ham 3m/5km SW of Gt Dunmow. TL 5918

Canford Bottom Dorset 9 G4 loc 2m/3km E of Wimborne. SU 0400

Canford Heath Dorset. See Canford Magna.

Canford, Little Dorset 9 G4* loc beside R Stour 3m/4km E of Wimborne. SZ 0499

Canford Magna Dorset 9 G4 ham 2m/3km SE of Wimborne. Canford School beside R Stour in Canford Park. To S, **Canford Heath,** large open space 4m/7km NW of Bournemouth tn centre. SZ 0398

Cangate Common Norfolk 39 G3* loc 3m/4km NE of Wroxham. TG 3219

Canham's Green Suffolk 31 E2* loc 2km S of Bacton. TM 0565

Canisbay, East H'land 86 F1 vil near N coast of Caithness dist 4m/6km W of Duncansby Hd. **W Canisbay** loc to W. ND 3472

Canisp H'land 85 C5 mt in Sutherland dist 4m/6km SW of Inchnadamph. Height 2779 ft or 847 metres. NC 2018

Canklow S Yorks 43 H2* loc in Rotherham 2km S of tn centre. SK 4292

Canley W Midlands 35 H6* loc in Coventry 2m/4km SW of city centre. SP 3076

Cann Dorset 9 F2 ham 1m S of Shaftesbury. ST 8521

Canna H'land 79 A7, B7 island in Inner Hebrides 4m/6km NW of island of Rum. Is nearly 5m/8km E to W and from 1km to 1m N to S. Crofting, lobster fishing. Harbour at E end. See also Sanday. NG 2405

Cannich H'land 80 D4 vil in Inverness dist at confluence of Rs Cannich and Glass 7m/11km SW of Struy Br. **R Cannich** runs here from Loch Mullardoch, which is 7m/11km W of vil. NH 3431

Cannington Som 8 B1 vil 3m/5km NW of Bridgwater. ST 2539

Canning Town London 20 B3 loc in borough of Newham 4m/7km E of London Br. TQ 3981

Cannock Staffs 35 F3 tn of coal-mining and other industries 8m/13km NE of Wolverhampton. To N, **C. Chase,** elevated and wooded mining area with tracts of moorland; former hunting forest. SJ 9810

Cannock Wood Staffs 35 F3* loc 4m/7km E of Cannock. SK 0412

Cannon 33 F4* stream running SE into R Gam 4m/6km SW of Llangadfan, Powys. SH 9606

Cannop Glos 26 B6* loc in Forest of Dean 2m/3km E of Coleford. SO 6011

Canonbie D & G 59 H4 vil on R Esk 6m/9km S of Langholm. NY 3976

Canon Bridge H & W 26 A3* ham on S side of R Wye 5m/8km W of Hereford. No br over r despite name. SO 4340

Canonbury London 19 G3* loc in borough of Islington 3m/5km NE of Charing Cross. TQ 3284

Canon Frome H & W 26 B3 vil 6m/9km NW of Ledbury. SO 6543

Canon Pyon H & W 26 A3 vil 6m/10km NW of Hereford. SO 4648

Canons Ashby Northants 28 B3 vil 10m/16km NE of Banbury. SP 5750

Canons Town Cornwall 2 B5 vil 2m/3km SW of Hayle. SW 5335

Canovium Gwynedd. See Caerhun.

Cant Clough Reservoir Lancs 48 B5* resr 4m/7km E of Burnley. SD 8930

Canterbury Kent 13 G2 premier cathedral city on R Gt Stour 54m/88km E of London. University on hill to N. Roman and medieval remains, incl city walls. Modern shopping centre; industrial development on outskirts. TR 1457

Cantick Head Orkney 89 B7 headland at E end of S Walls, peninsula at SE end of Hoy. Lighthouse on S side and beacon on N. **Cantick Sound** is strait between headland and island of Switha. ND 3489

Cantley Norfolk 39 G4 vil 4m/7km SW of Acle. TG 3804

Cantley S Yorks 44 B1 vil 4m/6km E of Doncaster. Site of Roman pottery kilns on **C. Estate** to W. SE 6202

Cantlop Salop 34 C4* loc 2m/3km E of Condover. SJ 5205

Canton (Cantwn) S Glam 15 F4 dist of Cardiff 2km W of city centre. ST 1676

Cantref Reservoir Powys 15 E1 resr in valley of Taf fawr R, 6m/10km N of Merthyr Tydfil. SW corner of resr is in Mid Glam. SN 9915

Cantsfield Lancs 47 F1 vil 4m/6km S of Kirkby Lonsdale. SD 6272

Cantwn Welsh form of Canton, qv.

Canvey Island Essex 20 D3 island on N bank of R Thames estuary bounded by R Thames, and Holehaven, E Haven, and Benfleet Creeks, the last spanned by rd br opp S Benfleet. Island contains tn of same name, a resort with bungalow and industrial development. TQ 7883

Canvey Point Essex 20 D3* headland at E end of Canvey I. TQ 8383

Canwick Lincs 44 D4 vil 2km SE of Lincoln. SK 9869

Canworthy Water Cornwall 6 B6 vil on R Ottery 8m/13km NW of Launceston. SX 2291

Caol H'land 74 C4 vil in Lochaber dist at head of Loch Linnhe 2km N of Fort William. NN 1076

Caolard Rubha S'clyde 70 B6 headland on Loch Fyne 3m/5km SE of Lochgilphead in Argyll. NR 8783

Caolas an Eilein S'clyde 62 B3 strait between S coast of Islay and island of Texa. NR 3944

Caolas Mór S'clyde 69 C8 sea strait separating island of Oronsay from Eilean Ghaoideamal and rocks to SW thereof. NR 3687

Caolas Port na Lice S'clyde 62 C3* strait between Eilean Craobhach and SE coast of Islay to S of Ardmore Pt. NR 4649

Caoles Tiree, S'clyde 69 B7 loc near E end of island 1km W of Rubha Dubh. NM 0848

Caol Fladda Skye, H'land 78 D4* narrow channel separating Fladday, qv, from Raasay. NG 5950

Caol Ila S'clyde 62 B1* distillery at Ruadh-phort Mór to N of Port Askaig, Islay. NR 4269

Caolis an Scarp W Isles 88 A3* narrow strait between island of Scarp and W coast of Harris. NA 9913

Caol Mór Skye, H'land 79 D5 sea channel between islands of Raasay and Scalpay. Also known as Kyle More. NG 5833

Caol Rona Skye, H'land 78 D4 strait separating islands of Raasay and Rona. Also known as Kyle Rona. NG 6154

Caol Scotnish S'clyde 69 F8 long narrow arm of Loch Sween in Knapdale, Argyll, at N end of loch. NR 7689

Capel Kent 12 C3 ham 3m/5km E of Tonbridge. TQ 6344

Capel Surrey 11 G1 vil 6m/9km S of Dorking. TQ 1740

Capel Bangor Dyfed 32 D6 ham 4m/7km E of Aberystwyth. SN 6580

Capel Betws Leucu Dyfed 24 B2 loc 5m/7km W of Tregaron. SN 6058

Capel Coch Gwynedd 40 B3 ham on Anglesey 4m/7km N of Llangefni. SH 4582

Capel Colman Dyfed 22 D2* loc 1m E of Boncath. SN 2138

Capel Curig Gwynedd 40 D5 ham at confluence of Rs Gwryd and Llugwy 5m/8km W of Betws-y-coed. SH 7258

Capel Cynon Dyfed 23 E1* loc 7m/11km NE of Newcastle Emlyn. SN 3849

Capel Dewi Dyfed 23 F4 ham 4m/6km E of Carmarthen. SN 4720

Capel Dewi Dyfed 24 A4 ham on R Clettwr 2m/4km NE of Llandyssul. SN 4542

Capel Dewi Dyfed 32 D6 ham 3m/5km E of Aberystwyth. SN 6382

Capel Fell 59 F1 mt on border of Dumfries & Galloway and Borders regions 5m/8km E of Moffat. Height 2223 ft or 678 metres. NT 1606

Capel Fleet Kent. See Harty, Isle of.

Capel Garmon Gwynedd 41 E5 vil 4m/7km S of Llanrwst. 1km S is large Bronze Age burial-chamber (A.M.). SH 8155

Capel Gwyn Dyfed 23 F3* loc 4m/6km NE of Carmarthen. SN 4622

Capel Gwyn Gwynedd 40 A4/B4* loc on Anglesey 2km S of Bryngwran. SH 3475

Capel Gwynfe Dyfed 24 C5 ham 4m/6km S of Llangadog. SN 7222

Capel Hendre Dyfed 23 vil 2m/4km W of Ammanford. SN 5911

Capel Isaac Dyfed 24 B5* loc 2m/3km E of Llanfynydd. SN 5826

Capel Iwan Dyfed 23 E2 vil 3m/5km S of Newcastle Emlyn. SN 2936

Capel le Ferne Kent 13 G3* vil 3m/4km NE of Folkestone. TR 2539

Capel Llanilltern (Llanilltern) Mid Glam 15 F3 loc 6m/9km W of Cardiff. ST 0979

Capel Lligwy Gwynedd 40 B3* small medieval chapel (A.M.) near E coast of Anglesey, 1m W of Moelfre. See also Din Lligwy, Lligwy Bay. SH 4986

Capel Mawr Gwynedd 40 B4* ham on Anglesey 4m/6km SW of Llangefni. SH 4171

Capel St Andrew Suffolk 31 G3 ham 7m/11km E of Woodbridge. TM 3748

Capel St Mary Suffolk 31 E4 vil 5m/8km SE of Hadleigh. TM 0838

Capel Seion Dyfed 24 C1 ham 3m/5km SE of Aberystwyth. SN 6379

Capel-St Silin Dyfed 24 B3 loc 4m/7km NW of Lampeter. SN 5251

Capel Trisant Dyfed 24 C1* loc 2m/3km SW of Devil's Br. SN 7175

Capel Tygwydd Dyfed 23 E2* loc 3m/5km NW of Newcastle Emlyn. SN 2743

Capeluchaf Gwynedd 40 B6 loc 1m E of Clynnog-fawr. SH 4349

Capel Uchaf Welsh form of Upr Chapel. See Chapel, Upper.

Capelulo Gwynedd 40 D4 vil 2m/4km W of Conwy. SH 7476

Capel Vicar Dyfed 24 A3* loc 1m NW of Mydroilyn. SN 4556

Capel Water 59 E2 r in Dumfries & Galloway region running S to Water of Ae in Forest of Ae, 3m/5km N of Ae Village. NX 9893

Capel-y-ffin Powys 25 G4 loc in Vale of Ewyas 3m/5km NW of Llanthony, Gwent. SO 2531

Capel-y-graig Gwynedd 40 C4* loc 3m/4km SW of Bangor. SH 5469

Capenhurst Ches 42 A4 vil 5m/8km NW of Chester. Atomic energy plant to N. SJ 3673

Capernwray Lancs 47 F1* loc 2m/4km E of Carnforth. SD 5371

Cape Wrath H'land 84 C1 headland with lighthouse at NW point of Sutherland dist. NC 2574

Capheaton Nthmb 61 E3 ham 4m/6km SE of Kirkwhelpington. Hall, 1668. Grnds, landscaped in 18c, include large lake known as Sir Edward's Lake. NZ 0380

Caplaw Dam S'clyde 64 B3* small resr 4m/6km W of Barrhead. NS 4358

Capon's Green Suffolk 31 G2* loc 1km E of Dennington. TM 2967

Cappercleuch Borders 66 A6 locality on W shore of St Mary's Loch in Ettrick Forest. NT 2423

Capplegill D & G 59 F1 loc 5m/8km NE of Moffat. NT 1409

Capster Hill Gtr Manchester 43 E1* loc in Oldham 2km S of tn centre. SD 9203

Capstone Kent 20 D5 loc 2m/4km SE of Chatham tn centre. TQ 7865

Captain Cook's Monument N Yorks 55 E4 obelisk on Easby Moor, 2km NE of Easby, commemorating the 18c explorer. NZ 5910

Captain Fold Gtr Manchester 42 D1* loc in Heywood 1km E of tn centre. SD 8610

Capton Devon 5 E5* ham 3m/4km NW of Dartmouth. SX 8353

Capton Som 7 H2* ham 3m/4km S of Watchet. ST 0839

Caputh Tayside 72 D1 vil 4m/7km E of Dunkeld. NO 0840

Cara S'clyde 62 D3 island 1km S of Gigha. NR 6344

Caradon 118 admin dist of Cornwall.

Caradon Hill Cornwall 3 G2* hill on SE side of Bodmin Moor. Height 1213 ft or 370 metres. TV stn. SX 2770

Caradon Town Cornwall 3 G1* loc 4m/7km NW of Callington. SX 2971

Carberry Tower Lothian 66 B2* enlarged 16c hse, now a Church of Scotland training centre, 2m/4km SE of Musselburgh. NT 3669

Carbeth, West Central 64 C1 locality 2m/4km W of Strathblane. **Carbeth Loch** is small loch 1km E. NS 5279

Carbis Bay Cornwall 2 B4 bay to SE of St Ives; gives name also to suburb of the tn. SW 5238

Carbisdale Castle H'land 85 F7 youth hostel in Kyle of Sutherland 3m/5km NW of Bonar Br, Sutherland dist. NH 5795

Carbost Skye, H'land 78 C4 loc 5m/8km NW of Portree. NG 4248

Carbost Skye, H'land 79 B5 vil on SW shore of Loch Harport, 10m/16km SW of Portree. Talisker Distillery at NW end of vil. NG 3731

Carbrain S'clyde 65 E2* residential area of Cumbernauld near tn centre. **S Carbrain** is industrial area to S. NS 7674

Carbrook S Yorks 43 H2 dist of Sheffield 3m/4km NE of city centre. SK 3889

Carbrooke Norfolk 38 D4 vil 2m/4km E of Watton. TF 9402

Carburton Notts 44 B4 loc in Dukeries of S side of Clumber Park. SK 6173

Carclew Cornwall 2 D4* loc 3m/4km N of Penryn. SW 7838

Car Colston Notts 36 C1 vil 2m/4km NE of Bingham. SK 7142
Carcroft S Yorks 44 A1 coal-mining loc 5m/8km NW of Doncaster. SE 5410
Cardenden Fife 73 E5 vil in coal-mining area 4m/7km NE of Cowdenbeath. NT 2195
Cardeston Salop 34 B3 loc 6m/10km W of Shrewsbury. SJ 3912
Cardew Cumbria 59 H6* loc 2m/3km SW of Dalston. NY 3449
Cardewlees Cumbria 59 H6* loc 2km NW of Dalston. NY 3551
Cardiff (Caerdydd) S Glam 15 G4 city and port at mouth of R Taff 130m/209km W of London. Capital of Wales. Various industries incl engineering; iron, steel, vehicle, and paper mnfre; shipbuilding. University of Wales (University College of S Wales). National Museum of Wales. Remains of medieval cas. Cathedral (Llandaff). Airport (Rhoose). 9m/15km SW. ST 1876
Cardigan (Aberteifi) Dyfed 22 D2 tn on R Teifi estuary 34m/54km SW of Aberystwyth across Cardigan Bay. Remains of 12c cas.
Cardigan Island Dyfed 22 D1 uninhabited offshore island at mouth of R Teifi 4m/6km N of Cardigan. Area 35 acres or 14 hectares. SN 1651
Cardinal's Green Cambs 30 B3* ham 4m/6km W of Haverhill. TL 6146
Cardington Beds 29 E3 vil 3m/4km SE of Bedford. Airship mnfre. TL 0847
Cardington Salop 34 C4/C5 vil 4m/6km E of Church Stretton. SO 5095
Cardinham Cornwall 3 F2 vil 4m/6km NE of Bodmin. Earthwork remains of medieval **C. Castle** to S. SX 1268
Cardonald S'clyde 64 C3* dist of Glasgow on S side of R Clyde 4m/6km W of city centre. **S Cardonald** adjoins to S. NS 5264
Cardoness Castle D & G 58 B5 ruined 15c tower of the McCullochs (A.M.), 1m SW of Gatehouse of Fleet. NX 5955
Cardow Grampian 82 B3 loc with distillery 6m/10km W of Craigellachie. NJ 1942
Cardrona Forest Borders 66 B5 state forest 2m/3km W of Innerleithen across R Tweed. Ruined tower of Cardrona on NE edge of forest. NT 3036
Cardross S'clyde 64 B2 vil on N side of Firth of Clyde 3m/5km NW of Dumbarton. NS 3477
Cardurnock Cumbria 59 F5 ham near coast of Solway Firth 4m/6km W of Kirkbride across R Wampool estuary. Sites of small Roman forts in vicinity. NY 1758
Careby Lincs 37 E3 vil 6m/10km N of Stamford. TF 0216
Careless Green W Midlands 35 F5* loc in Stourbridge 2m/3km E of tn centre. SO 9283
Careston Tayside 77 E4 loc 4m/7km W of Brechin. **C. Castle** is mainly 15c. NO 5260
Carew (Caeriw) Dyfed 22 C5 vil on r of same name 4m/7km E of Pembroke. Remains of medieval cas. SN 0403
Carew 22 C5* r rising W of Saundersfoot, Dyfed, and flowing W to vil of Carew, where it forms an estuary which continues NW to join Cresswell R and flow into Daugleddau R at Jenkins Pt. SN 0106
Carew Cheriton Dyfed 22 C5 ham 4m/6km E of Pembroke. SN 0402
Carew Newton Dyfed 22 C5* ham 1km N of Carew. SN 0404
Carey H & W 26 B4 ham in R Wye valley 6m/10km SE of Hereford. SO 5631
Carey 4 A2* r rising near Halwill, Devon, and flowing SW into R Tamar 2km NE of Launceston. SX 3584
Carfan 33 F4* r rising 4m/6km NE of Cemmaes, Powys, and flowing S to join R Cwm and form R Rhiw Saeson 2km N of Llanbrynmair. SH 9004
Carfin S'clyde 65 E3 loc 2m/3km NE of Motherwell. NS 7758
Cargate Common Norfolk 39 E5* loc 2km S of Bunwell. TM 1390
Cargate Green Norfolk 39 G3* ham just NW of Upton. TG 3912
Cargenbridge D & G 59 E4* loc on Cargen Water 2km SW of Dumfries. NX 9574
Cargen Water D & G 59 E4 stream in Dumfries & Galloway region flowing E then SE to R Nith 2m/4km S of Dumfries. NX 9772
Cargill Tayside 73 E1 loc on R Tay 5m/8km W of Coupar Angus. NO 1536
Cargo Cumbria 59 H5 vil 3m/5km NW of Carlisle. NY 3659
Cargo Fleet Cleveland 54 D3 loc on R Tees 2km E of Middlesbrough. NZ 5120
Cargreen Cornwall 4 B4 vil beside R Tamar 7m/11km SE of Callington. SX 4362
Carham Nthmb 67 E4 ham on R Tweed 4m/6km W of Cornhill. 2m/4km E beyond Wark is site of battle of 1018 in which Scots defeated English. NT 7938
Carhampton Som 7 G1 vil 2km SE of Dunster. ST 0142
Carharrack Cornwall 2 C4* vil among former tin and copper mines, 2m/3km E of Redruth. SW 7341
Carhouse Humberside 44 C1* loc 1km W of Belton. SE 7806
Carinish W Isles 88 E1 vil at S end of N Uist 8m/13km SW of Lochmaddy. NF 8159
Carisbrooke Isle of Wight 10 B5 vil adjoining Newport to SW. **C. Castle** (A.M.), mainly Tudor. Charles I was imprisoned there. SZ 4888
Carishader W Isles 88 A2* vil on Lewis 2km SE of Miavaig. NB 0933
Cark Cumbria 47 E1 vil 2m/3km SW of Cartmel. Hall of 16c-17c on N side of vil. SD 3676
Carkeel Cornwall 4 B4 vil 2m/3km NW of Saltash. SX 4160
Carland Cross Cornwall 2 D3 loc 5m/8km SE of Newquay. SW 8454
Carlatton Cumbria 60 B6 loc 6m/10km S of Brampton. NY 5251
Carlbury Durham 54 B3 ham adjoining Piercebridge to E. **Low C.** loc adjoining to E. NZ 2115
Carlby Lincs 37 F3 vil 5m/7km N of Stamford. TF 0513
Carlecotes S Yorks 43 F1* loc 4m/7km W of Penistone. SE 1703
Carleen Cornwall 2 B5* ham 3m/5km NW of Helston. SW 6130
Carleton Cumbria 52 A4* loc 1m SE of Egremont. NY 0109
Carleton Cumbria 52 B5* loc 2km SE of Drigg. SD 0898
Carleton Cumbria 53 E2 loc 1m E of Penrith. NY 5329
Carleton Cumbria 60 A6* loc 3m/5km SE of Carlisle. NY 4252
Carleton Lancs 46 D4 loc 3m/4km NE of Blackpool. **Lit Carleton** loc 1m S. SD 3339
Carleton N Yorks 48 C3 vil 2m/3km SW of Skipton. SD 9749
Carleton W Yorks 49 F6 loc 2km SE of Pontefract. SE 4620
Carleton Castle S'clyde 56 B4 ruined medieval cas on S side of Lendalfoot. NX 1389
Carleton, East Norfolk 39 F4 vil 5m/9km SW of Norwich. TG 1701
Carleton Forehoe Norfolk 39 E4 vil 3m/5km N of Wymondham. TG 0905
Carleton Rode Norfolk 39 E5 vil 5m/7km SE of Attleborough. TM 1192
Carleton St Peter Norfolk 39 G4* ham 3m/5km N of Loddon. TG 3402
Carley Hill Tyne & Wear 61 H5* dist of Sunderland 2m/3km N of tn centre. Quarries. NZ 3859
Carlidnack Cornwall 2 D5* loc 3m/4km SW of Falmouth, adjoining Mawnan Smith. SW 7729
Carlingcott Avon 16 C5* ham 2m/4km N of Radstock. ST 6958
Carlingheugh Bay Tayside 77 F6 small bay 2m/3km NE of Arbroath. NO 6742
Carlingwark Loch D & G 58 D5 loch on S side of Castle Douglas. Haunt of wildfowl. NX 7661
Carlin How Cleveland 55 E3/F3 loc 2km E of Brotton. NZ 7019
Carlisle Cumbria 59 H5 cathedral city and industrial tn at confluence of R Eden and R Caldew 54m/87km W of Newcastle upon Tyne. Engineering equipment mnfre, biscuits, textiles. Rly marshalling yards at Kingmoor, qv. Airport 6m/9km NE. Racecourse 2m/4km S. Remains of Norman cas (A.M.) above R Eden. Line of Hadrian's Wall runs through N suburbs. NY 4056
Carloggas Cornwall 2 D2* loc 4m/7km NE of Newquay. SW 8765
Carlops Borders 65 G3/H3 vil on E side of Pentland Hills 3m/5km N of W Linton. NT 1655
Carloway W Isles 88 B2 vil near W coast of Lewis at head of estuary of **Carloway R**, which rises among lochs to S. See also Dun C., Loch C. NB 2042
Carlton Beds 28 D2 vil 7m/11km NW of Bedford, adjoining vil of Chellington. SP 9555
Carlton Cambs 30 B3 vil 5m/8km N of Haverhill. TL 6453
Carlton Cleveland 54 C3 vil 4m/6km NW of Stockton-on-Tees. NZ 3921
Carlton Leics 36 A4 vil 2km NW of Mkt Bosworth. **C. Gate** ham to W. SK 3905
Carlton Notts 36 C1 tn adjoining Nottingham to E. SK 6141
Carlton N Yorks 50 B5 vil 2km N of Snaith. SE 6423
Carlton N Yorks 54 A6 vil 4m/6km SW of Wensley. SE 0684
Carlton N Yorks 54 D4 vil 3m/5km SW of Stokesley. NZ 5004
Carlton N Yorks 55 E6 ham 2m/3km N of Helmsley. SE 6186
Carlton Suffolk 31 G2* vil 1m N of Saxmundham. TM 3864
Carlton S Yorks 43 H1 dist of Barnsley 3m/4km NE of tn centre. SE 3610
Carlton W Yorks 49 E5 vil 4m/6km N of Wakefield. SE 3327
Carlton Colville Suffolk 39 H5 vil 3m/5km SW of Lowestoft. TM 5190
Carlton Curlieu Leics 36 C4 vil 7m/11km NW of Mkt Harborough. SP 6997
Carlton, East Northants 36 D5 vil 4m/7km W of Corby. SP 8389
Carlton, East W Yorks 49 E4* ham 2m/3km SE of Otley. **W Carlton** loc 1m W. SE 2243
Carlton, Great Lincs 45 G3 vil 6m/9km E of Louth. **Lit Carlton** vil 1km W. TF 4185
Carlton Green Cambs 30 B3 ham 4m/7km N of Haverhill. TL 6451
Carlton Husthwaite N Yorks 49 G1 vil 5m/8km N of Easingwold. SE 4976
Carlton in Lindrick Notts 44 B3 vil 3m/4km N of Worksop. SK 5984
Carlton Lake Notts 44 B3* lake on SW side of Carlton in Lindrick. SK 5883
Carlton-le-Moorland Lincs 44 D5 vil 9m/15km SW of Lincoln. SK 9057
Carlton, Little Notts 44 C5* loc 3m/4km NW of Newark-on-Trent. SK 7757
Carlton Miniott N Yorks 54 C6 vil 2m/4km W of Thirsk. SE 3981
Carlton, North Lincs 44 D3 vil 4m/7km NW of Lincoln. **S Carlton** vil 1km S. SK 9477
Carlton, North Notts 44 B3 N part of vil of Carlton in Lindrick. SK 5984
Carlton-on-Trent Notts 44 C4 vil 6m/10km N of Newark-on-Trent. SK 7963
Carlton Scroop Lincs 44 D6 vil 6m/10km NE of Grantham. SK 9445
Carlton, South Notts 44 B3 S part of vil of Carlton in Lindrick. SK 5983
Carluke S'clyde 65 E4 tn 5m/8km NW of Lanark. NS 8450
Carlungie Tayside 73 G1* loc 2m/4km N of Monifieth. Ancient souterrain or earth-house (A.M.). NO 5135
Carlyon Bay Cornwall 3 E3 coastal resort 2m/4km E of St Austell. SX 0552
Carman Reservoir S'clyde 64 B1* small resr 1km W of Renton, N of Dumbarton. NS 3778
Carmarthen (Caerfyrddin) Dyfed 23 F4 tn on R Towy, on site of Roman fort of *Moridunum*, 22m/36km NW of Swansea. Cattle mkt. Industries include milk processing, mnfre of agricultural implements. SN 4120
Carmarthen Bay 22 D5/23 E5 large bay off coast of S Wales extending from Worms Hd, W Glam, westwards to Caldy I. Receives the waters of Rs Loughor, Towy, and Taf, and of several lesser streams. SS 29
Carmarthen Van Powys 24 D5 mt above W side of Llyn y Fan fawr, 4m/6km SE of Llanddeusant. Height 2632 ft or 802 metres. SN 8221
Carmel Clwyd 41 G4 loc adjoining Holywell to NW. SJ 1776
Carmel Dyfed 23 G4 vil 4m/7km SW of Llandeilo. SN 5816
Carmel Gwynedd 40 C5 vil 5m/8km S of Caernarvon. SH 4955
Carmel Head (Trwyn y Gader) Gwynedd 40 A2 headland on N coast of Anglesey 5m/7km W of Cemaes Bay. SH 2993
Carmichael S'clyde 65 F5 loc 3m/5km W of Thankerton. NS 9238
Carminish Islands W Isles 88 A4* group of islets off SW coast of Harris about 3m/5km up the coast from Renish Pt. NG 0185
Carmunnock S'clyde 64 D3 vil 3m/5km NW of E Kilbride. NS 5957
Carmyle S'clyde 64 D3 loc on N bank of R Clyde 4m/7km SE of Glasgow. NS 6561
Carmyllie Tayside 73 H1 loc 6m/10km W of Arbroath. NO 5442
Carna H'land 68 D3 island at entrance to Loch Teacuis, Lochaber dist. NM 6158
Carnaby Humberside 51 F2 vil 2m/3km SW of Bridlington. TA 1465
Carnach H'land 74 A2 r in Lochaber dist running SW to head of Loch Nevis. NM 8696
Carn a' Choire Bhuidhe H'land 80 C5 mt in Inverness dist 4m/7km N of dam of Loch Cluanie. Height 2778 ft or 847 metres. NH 1817
Carn a' Choire Ghairbh H'land 80 B5* mt on Glenaffric Forest, Inverness dist, 2m/3km S of head of Loch Affric. Height 2827 ft or 862 metres. NH 1318
Carn a' Choire Ghlaise H'land 75 F1 mt in Inverness dist 11m/17km E of Fort Augustus. Height 2555 ft or 779 metres. NH 5408
Carn a' Chuilinn H'land 75 E1 mt on Glendoe Forest, Inverness dist, 4m/6km SE of Fort Augustus. Height 2677 ft or 816 metres. NH 4103
Carn a' Mhaim Grampian 76 B2 mt in Cairngorms 2m/4km S of Ben Macdui. Height 3402 ft or 1037 metres. NN 9995
Carn an Fhidhleir 76 A3 mt on border of Grampian, Highland, and Tayside regions, 12m/19km N of Blair Atholl. Height 3261 ft or 994 metres. Anglicised form: Carn Ealar. NN 9084
Carn an Fhidhleir Lorgaidh H'land 75 H3 mt on Glenfeshie Forest in Badenoch and Strathspey dist 10m/16km SE of Kingussie. Height 2786 ft or 849 metres. NN 8587
Carn an Fhreiceadain H'land 75 G1 mt in Monadhliath range in Badenoch and Strathspey dist, 5m/7km NW of Kingussie. Height 2879 ft or 878 metres. NH 7207
Carnan Mór Tiree, S'clyde 69 A8* hill near SW end of island, to E of Balephuil Bay. Highest point of Tiree, 460 ft or 140 metres. NL 9640
Carn an Righ Tayside 76 B3* mt 7m/11km NW of Spittal of Glenshee. Height 3377 ft or 1029 metres. NO 0277
Carn an t-Sagairt Mór Grampian 76 C3 mt 6m/9km SE of Braemar. Height 3435 ft or 1047 metres. Also known as Cairn Taggart. NO 2084
Carn an t-Suidhe Grampian 82 B4* mt 6m/10km SE of foot of Glen Livet. Height 2401 ft or 732 metres. NJ 2626
Carn an Tuirc Grampian 76 C3 mt 7m/11km S of Braemar. Height 3343 ft or 1019 metres. NO 1780
Carn Aosda Grampian 76 C3 mt 8m/12km S of Braemar. Height 3009 ft or 917 metres. NO 1379
Carnassarie Castle S'clyde 70 A4 16c cas (A.M.) in Argyll, 3m/5km S of head of Loch Craignish. NM 8300
Carn Bàn H'land 75 F1* mt in Monadhliath range, on border of Inverness and Badenoch & Strathspey dists, 6m/9km NW of Newtonmore. NH 6303
Carn Ban S'clyde 63 F5* long cairn (A.M.) on Arran 4m/6km W of Whiting Bay. NR 9926
Carnbane Castle Tayside 75 G6* ruined stronghold of the Macnaughtons in Glen Lyon 1m E of Invervar. NN 6748
Carn Bàn Mór H'land 75 H2 mt in Badenoch and Strathspey dist in W part of Cairngorms 7m/11km SE of Kincraig. Height 3451 ft or 1052 metres. NN 8997
Carn Beag Dearg H'land. See Carn Mór Dearg.
Carnbee Fife 73 G4/H4 vil 3m/5km NW of Anstruther. NO 5306
Carn Bhac 76 B3 mt on border of Grampian and Tayside regions 5m/8km SW of Inverey. Height 3018 ft or 920 metres. NO 0482
Carnbo Tayside 72 D4 vil 4m/7km W of Kinross. NO 0503
Carnbrae Cornwall 2 C4* ham, with **Carnbrae Ch Tn**, 1km SW of Redruth. To SW, granite tor, **Carn Brae**, commanding wide views and topped by monmt of 1836 commemorating Lord de Dunstanville. SW 6840
Carn Brea Cornwall 2 A5* hill (NT) 3m/5km NE of Land's End, with wide sea view. Two Bronze Age barrows. SW 3828

Carn Chòis Tayside 72 B2* mt on W side of Loch Turret. Height 2578 ft or 786 metres. NN 7927
Carn Chuinneag H'land 85 E7 mt in Diebidale Forest on border of Ross & Cromarty and Sutherland dists 5m/7km NW of head of Loch Morie. Height 2749 ft or 838 metres. NH 4883
Carn Coire na h-Easgainn H'land 81 G5/G6 mt in Monadhliath range, on border of Inverness and Badenoch & Strathspey dists, 8m/13km N of Kingussie. Height 2591 ft or 790 metres. NH 7313
Carn Dearg H'land 74 C4 NW and SW peaks of Ben Nevis, in Lochaber dist. Height of NW peak 3975 ft or 1212 metres; height of SW peak 3348 ft or 1020 metres. NN 1572
Carn Dearg H'land 74 D2 mt in Lochaber dist 4m/6km E of NE end of Loch Lochy. Height 2677 ft or 816 metres. (Another mt of same name 2km to S; height 2523 ft or 769 metres.) NN 3496
Carn Dearg H'land 74 D3 mt in Lochaber dist 7m/11km NE of Roy Br. Height 2736 ft or 834 metres. NN 3488
Carn Dearg H'land 75 F1 mt in Monadhliath range, in Badenoch and Strathspey dist 8m/12km W of Kingussie. Height 3100 ft or 945 metres, the summit of the range. NH 6302
Carn Dearg H'land 75 F4 mt in Badenoch and Strathspey dist, 10m/16km SW of Dalwhinnie. Height 3391 ft or 1034 metres. NN 5076
Carn Dearg 75 E4 mt on border of Highland and Tayside regions 3m/5km E of head of Loch Ossian. Height 3088 ft or 941 metres. NN 4166
Carn Dearg Mór H'land 75 H2 mt in Badenoch and Strathspey dist 7m/11km SE of Kingussie. Height 2813 ft or 857 metres. NN 8291
Carn Deas H'land 85 A6 small island in group known as the Summer Isles, qv. Adjacent to and E of Carn Iar, Carn Deas lies less than 1km SW of Eilean Dubh. NB 9602
Carndu H'land 80 A5 locality in Skye and Lochalsh dist on shore of Loch Long 1km NE of Dornie. NG 8927
Carne Cornwall 3 E3* loc 6m/9km NW of St Austell. SW 9558
Carn Ealar 76 A3 mt on border of Grampian, Highland, and Tayside regions, 12m/19km N of Blair Atholl. Height 3261 ft or 994 metres. Gaelic form: Carn an Fhidhleir. NN 9084
Carnedd Dafydd Gwynedd 40 D5 mt 3m/5km SE of Bethesda. Height 3426 ft or 1044 metres. SH 6663
Carnedd Llywelyn Gwynedd 40 D5 mt 5m/7km NW of Capel Curig. Height 3484 ft or 1062 metres. SH 6864
Carn Eige H'land 80 B5 mt on border of Inverness and Skye & Lochalsh dists, 3m/5km N of Loch Affric. Height 3880 ft or 1182 metres. NH 1226
Carn Eiteige H'land 80 C3 peak on E Monar Forest, Ross and Cromarty dist, 2m/4km N of dam of Loch Monar. Height 2894 ft or 882 metres. NH 2143
Car Ness Orkney 89 B6* headland on Mainland 2m/4km NE of Kirkwall. **Bay of Carness** to E. Oil service base. HY 4614
Carnetown Mid Glam 15 F2* vil 3m/5km N of Pontypridd. ST 0794
Carnforth Lancs 47 F1 tn and rly junction 6m/9km N of Lancaster. SD 4970
Carn Ghluasaid H'land 80 B6/C6* peak on border of Inverness and Skye & Lochalsh dists 3m/5km NW of dam of Loch Cluanie. Height 3140 ft or 957 metres. NH 1412
Carnglas W Glam 23 G6* loc in Swansea 2m/4km W of tn centre. SS 6293
Carn Gorm H'land 80 B3 mt on Glencarron Forest, Ross and Cromarty dist, 6m/9km S of Achnasheen. Height 2866 ft or 874 metres. NH 1350
Càrn Gorm Tayside 75 G6 mt 6m/9km S of Kinloch Rannoch. Height 3370 ft or 1027 metres. NN 6350
Carnhedryn Uchaf Dyfed 22 A3 loc 3m/5km NE of St David's. SM 8027
Carnhell Green Cornwall 2 B4 ham 2m/4km SW of Camborne. SW 6137
Carn Iar H'land 85 A6 small island in group known as the Summer Isles, qv. Lies 1km SW of Eilean Dubh. NB 9206
Carn Icean Duibhe H'land 81 F6 mt in Monadhliath range, on border of Inverness and Badenoch & Strathspey dists, 7m/12km NW of Kingussie. Height 2652 ft or 808 metres. NH 7111
Carnkie Cornwall 2 C4* former mining vil 2km SW of Redruth. SW 6839
Carnkie Cornwall 2 C5* vil 4m/7km W of Penryn. SW 7134
Carn Leac H'land 75 E2 mt on border of Inverness, Lochaber, and Badenoch & Strathspey dists, 7m/12km S of Fort Augustus. Height 2889 ft or 881 metres. NN 4097
Carn Liath H'land 75 E2 mt in Badenoch and Strathspey dist 4m/6km W of head of Loch Laggan. Height 3301 ft or 1006 metres. NN 4790
Carn Liath Tayside 76 A4 SW shoulder of Beinn a' Ghlo, 7m/12km N of Pitlochry. Height 3197 ft or 975 metres. NN 9369
Càrn Mairg Tayside 75 G5 mt 5m/8km S of Kinloch Rannoch. Height 3419 ft or 1042 metres. NN 6851
Carn Mór Grampian 82 B5 highest point of Ladder Hills, 6m/10km E of Tomintoul. Height 2636 ft or 804 metres. NJ 2618
Carn Mór Dearg H'land 74 C4 mt in Lochaber dist 1m NE of Ben Nevis. Height 4012 ft or 1223 metres. Carn Beag Dearg, 1m along ridge to NW, 3265 ft or 995 metres. NN 1772
Carn na Caim 75 G3 mt on border of Highland and Tayside regions 3m/5km SE of Dalwhinnie. Height 3087 ft or 941 metres. NN 6782
Carn nan Coireachan Cruaidh H'land 80 C5* mt in Inverness dist 5m/8km N of dam of Loch Cluanie. Height 2830 ft or 863 metres. NH 1818
Carn nan Gabhar Tayside 76 A4* summit of Beinn a' Ghlo, 8m/12km NE of Blair Atholl. Height 3675 ft or 1120 metres. NN 9773
Carn nan Gobhar H'land 80 C4* mt in Inverness dist 3m/5km NW of dam of Loch Mullardoch. Height 3253 ft or 992 metres. NH 1834
Carn Naun Point Cornwall 2 A4 headland on N coast 3m/4km W of St Ives. SW 4741
Carno Powys 33 F4 vil 5m/8km NW of Caersws. Site of Roman fort. SN 9696
Carnoch H'land 74 A5* r in Lochaber dist running W from top of Glen Tarbert to head of Loch Sunart. NM 8360
Carnock Fife 72 D5 vil 3m/5km W of Dunfermline. NT 0489
Carnon Downs Cornwall 2 D4* vil 3m/5km SW of Truro. SW 7940
Carnoustie Tayside 73 H1 coastal resort 6m/10km SW of Arbroath. Golf-courses, incl one of championship status. NO 5634
Carn Sgùlain H'land 75 G1 mt in Monadhliath range on border of Inverness and Badenoch & Strathspey dists, 6m/9km NW of Kingussie. Height 3020 ft or 920 metres. NH 6805
Carntyne S'clyde 64 D2* dist of Glasgow 2m/4km E of city centre. **C. Industrial Estate** to S. NS 6365
Carnwadric S'clyde 64 C3* dist of Glasgow 5m/7km SW of city centre. NS 5459
Carnwath S'clyde 65 F4 vil 7m/11km E of Lanark. NS 9846
Carnyorth Cornwall 2 A5* loc on N side of St Just. SW 3733
Carol Green W Midlands 35 H6* ham 5m/9km W of Coventry. SP 2577
Carperby N Yorks 54 A5 vil 1m N of Aysgarth across R Ure. SE 0089
Carpow Tayside 73 E3. See Abernethy.
Carr Gtr Manchester 47 H6* loc adjoining Ramsbottom to W. SD 7817
Carr S Yorks 44 A2* loc 2m/3km SW of Maltby. SE 5190
Carracks, The Cornwall 2 A4* two small islands off N coast 1km W of Carn Naun Pt. SW 4640
Carradale S'clyde 63 E4 fishing vil on E coast of Kintyre 2km E of Dippen. Ruins of Aird Castle on cliff to S of pier. Remains of ancient fort on **C. Point,** headland to S, on E side of **C. Bay.** **C. Water** is r running S into bay. **C. Forest** is state forest astride r. NR 8138
Carraig Fhada S'clyde 62 B3* headland with lighthouse on E coast of The Oa, Islay, 2km SW of Port Ellen across bay. NR 3444
Carrant Brook 26 D4* r rising near Ashton under Hill, H & W, and flowing W into R Avon at Tewkesbury, Glos. SO 8933
Carrawbrough Nthmb. See *Brocolitia.*
Carrbridge H'land 81 H5 vil on R Dulnain in Badenoch and Strathspey dist 7m/11km N of Aviemore. Landmark Visitor Centre has exhibition explaining history of local environment. NH 9022
Carrbrook Gtr Manchester 43 E1* loc 2km SE of Mossley. SD 9801
Carr Cross Lancs 42 A1* loc just N of Scarisbrick. SD 3713
Carreg Cennen Dyfed 23 G4* ruined 13c cas on limestone cliff above R Cennen 3m/5km SE of Llandeilo. SN 6619
Carreg Cennen Dyfed 23 G4* ruined medieval cas (A.M.) above R Cennen 3m/5km SE of Llandeilo. SN 6619
Carreg-fran Dyfed 22 A3/A4* rocky headland (NT) at E end of Porthlysgi Bay 2m/3km SW of St David's. SM 7322
Carreg-gwylan-fach Dyfed 22 A3* small island off Aberdinas, 2km W of Abereiddy. SM 7730
Carreglefn Gwynedd 40 B3* vil on Anglesey 3m/5km S of Cemaes Bay. SH 3889
Carreg-lydan Dyfed 22 D1* headland on mainland opp Cardigan I. SN 1651
Carregonnen Dyfed 22 B2* group of three small islands off **C. Bay,** on W side of Strumble Hd. SM 8841
Carreg Rhoson Dyfed 22 A3 rocky island 3m/5km W of Pt St John. One of the larger islands in the group known as Bishops and Clerks, qv. SM 6625
Carreg Wastad Point Dyfed 22 B2 headland 3m/5km NW of Fishguard. French invasion force of 1,400 convicts landed here in 1797 and surrendered two days later. SM 9340
Carregwen Dyfed 22 D2* loc 4m/6km SE of Cardigan. SN 2241
Carreg y Defaid Gwynedd 32 B2* headland 1m NE of Llanbedrog. SH 3432
Carreg-yr-esgob Dyfed 22 A4* rock island at entrance to Porthlysgi Bay 2m/3km SW of St David's. SM 7223
Carr Gate W Yorks 49 E5* vil 2m/4km NW of Wakefield. SE 3124
Carr Hill Notts 44 B2* loc 1km NW of Everton. SK 6892
Carr Houses Merseyside 41 H1* loc adjoining Ince Blundell to E. SD 3203
Carrick S'clyde 56 C4, D4 that part of the region lying S of R Doon, qv, S of Ayr. The Prince of Wales, as Steward of Scotland, bears the title of Earl of Carrick. NX 39
Carrick S'clyde 70 D5 vil on W shore of Loch Goil 2m/3km NW of its junction with Loch Long. **C. Castle** is keep dating mainly from 15c. NS 1994
Carrick 118 admin dist of Cornwall.
Carrick Forest S'clyde 56 D4* state forest forming part of Glen Trool Forest Park, 5m/8km S of Straiton. NX 49
Carrick Lane 56 E4* r in Strathclyde region formed by confluence of Eglin Lane and Whitespout Lane and running E into Loch Doon. NX 4794
Carrickowel Point Cornwall 3 E3* headland on W side of St Austell Bay 2m/3km SE of St Austell. SX 0350
Carrick Roads Cornwall 2 D4, D5 estuary of R Fal, running from Turnaware Pt past Falmouth into English Channel at Pendennis Pt. SW 8334
Carrickstone S'clyde 65 E2* loc in Cumbernauld 1m NW of tn centre. NS 7576
Carriden Central 65 F1* vil on S side of Firth of Forth 2km E of Bo'ness. Site of Roman fort, most easterly fort of Antonine Wall, 1km SE. NT 0181
Carrington Gtr Manchester 42 C2 vil on R Mersey 3m/5km W of Sale. Oil refinery to S. SJ 7392
Carrington Lincs 45 G5 loc 3m/5km SE of Coningsby. TF 3155
Carrington Lothian 66 B3 vil 2m/3km W of Gorebridge across R South Esk. NT 3160
Carrington Notts 36 B1* dist of Nottingham 2km N of city centre. SK 5642
Carr Mill Merseyside 42 B2 NE dist of St Helens. Lake to N. SJ 5297
Carrog Clwyd 33 G1 vil 2m/4km E of Corwen. SJ 1143
Carrog Gwynedd 40 D6* loc 4m/7km E of Blaenau Ffestiniog. SH 7647
Carrog 24 B2* r running into R Wyre at Llanrhystud, Dyfed. SN 5469
Carrog 40 B5* r running from near Rhostryfan, Gwynedd, into Foryd Bay. SH 4458
Carron Central 65 F1 loc adjoining Falkirk to N. Iron works founded in 1760. Site of Roman temple. NS 8882
Carron Grampian 82 B3 loc with distillery on left bank of R Spey 5m/8km SW of Craigellachie. NJ 2241
Carron H'land 80 A3 r in Ross and Cromarty dist rising above Loch Sgamhain or Scaven and running SW down Glen Carron to head of Loch Carron. NG 9341
Carron H'land 85 F7 r in Sutherland dist running E down Strath Carron to Kyle of Sutherland at Bonar Br. NH 6091
Carron 65 F1 r rising on Campsie Fells on borders of Central and Strathclyde regions, and flowing E through C. Valley Resr and into Firth of Forth on N side of Grangemouth in Central region. NS 9484
Carronbridge D & G 58 D2 vil at confluence of R Nith and Carron Water, qv. Site of Roman fort. NX 8698
Carronshore Central 65 F1 loc 2m/3km N of Falkirk. NS 8983
Carron Valley Reservoir 64 D1 resr on borders of Central and Strathclyde regions 5m/8km NE of Lennoxtown, almost surrounded by Carron Valley state forest. NS 6983
Carron Water 58 D2* r in Dumfries & Galloway region rising on Lowther Hills and running S to R Nith at Carronbridge, 2m/3km N of Thornhill. NX 8697
Carrow Hill Gwent 16 A3* loc 2m/3km W of Caerwent. ST 4390
Carr Shield Nthmb 53 G1 vil 5m/9km E of Alston. NY 8047
Carrugh an t-Sruith S'clyde 62 C1* headland on W coast of Jura 2m/3km N of Feolin Ferry. NR 4371
Carrutherstown D & G 59 F4 vil 7m/11km NW of Annan. NY 1071
Carr Vale Derbys 44 A4* loc adjoining Bolsover to SW. SK 4669
Carrville Durham 54 C1 vil 2m/4km E of Durham. NZ 3043
Carr, West Humberside 44 C1* loc 3m/5km NW of Epworth. **W Carr Hses** loc 1km S. SE 7306
Carsaig S'clyde 69 D6 locality on **C. Bay** on S coast of Mull 2m/3km W of entrance to Loch Buie. **C. Arches,** 3m/5km SW, are large tunnels carved out of the rocks by the sea. NM 5321
Carsaig Bay S'clyde 69 F8 bay on W coast of Knapdale 1km NW of Tayvallich in Argyll. Carsaig I. is narrow island nearly 1km long N to S, lying off shore to N. NR 7387
Carsebridge Central 72 C5* loc 1m NE of Alloa. Distillery. NS 8993
Carse of Gowrie Tayside 73 E2, F2 fertile tract on N side of Firth of Tay between Perth and Dundee. Strawberry-growing. NO 22
Carse of Stirling Central 71 G5-H5* wide, level, fertile area to W of Stirling, extending N and S of R Forth from the foothills of the Highlands to the Gargunnock Hills. NS 69, 79
Carsethorn D & G 59 E5 fishing vil on Solway Firth at mouth of R Nith, 10m/16km S of Dumfries. NX 9959
Carsfad Loch D & G 58 B3* loch and resr in course of Water of Ken 3m/5km N of Dalry. NX 6086
Carshalton London 19 F5 dist in borough of Sutton 2km E of Sutton tn centre. Locs of **C. Beeches** and **C. on the Hill** 1m S. TQ 2764
Carsie Tayside 73 E1* loc 2m/3km S of Blairgowrie. NO 1742
Carsington Derbys 43 G5 vil 2m/4km W of Wirksworth. SK 2553
Carskey Bay S'clyde 62 D6 bay on S coast of Kintyre 4m/7km E of Mull of Kintyre. NR 6607
Carsluith D & G 57 E7 loc on E shore of Wigtown Bay 2m/4km S of Creetown. Remains of **C. Castle** (A.M.), 16c tower hse, 1km SE. NX 4854

Carsphairn D & G 56 E4 vil 9m/14km SE of Dalmellington. **C. Forest** is state forest to N. **C. Lane** is r running SE into Water of Deugh 1km W of vil. See also Cairnsmore of C. NX 5693
Carstairs S'clyde 65 F4 vil 4m/6km E of Lanark. **C. Junction** is vil and rly junction 1m SE. NS 9346
Carter Bar 60 C1 point in Cheviot Hills at which A68 rd crosses border between England and Scotland. NT 6906
Carter's Clay Hants 10 A2* loc 2km SE of Lockerley. SU 3024
Carter's Green Essex 20 B1* loc 4m/7km E of Harlow. TL 5110
Carter's Hill Berks 18 C4* loc 2km SW of Winnersh. SU 7769
Carter's Rocks Cornwall 2 C3* alternative name for Gull Rocks, two rock islands off Penhale Pt, 4m/6km SW of Newquay. SW 7559
Carterton Oxon 17 G1 large loc adjacent to Brize Norton Airfield, 4m/6km SE of Burford. SP 2706
Carterway Heads Nthmb 61 E6* loc at crossroads 4m/6km W of Consett. NZ 0451
Carthew Cornwall 3 E3 vil in china clay dist 3m/4km N of St Austell. SX 0056
Carthorpe N Yorks 54 C6 vil 4m/6km SE of Bedale. SE 3083
Cartington Nthmb 61 E1 loc 2m/4km NW of Rothbury. Remains of cas dating from 14c. NU 0304
Cartland S'clyde 65 E4* loc 2m/3km NW of Lanark. NS 8646
Cartledge Derbys 43 G3* loc adjoining Holmesfield to S. SK 3277
Cartmel Cumbria 52 D6 vil 4m/7km S of Newby Br. SD 3778
Cartmel Fell Cumbria 52 D6* loc 5m/8km N of Lindale. SD 4188
Cartworth W Yorks 43 F1* loc 1km S of Holmfirth. SE 1407
Carway (Carwe) Dyfed 23 F5* vil 5m/7km NW of Llanelli. SN 4606
Carwe Welsh form of Carway, qv.
Cary 8 B1 r rising near Castle Cary in Somerset and flowing W to Henley where it becomes the King's Sedgemoor Drain, flowing NW into R Parrett at Dunball. ST 3140
Cas-bach Welsh form of Castleton, qv.
Cas-blaidd Welsh form of Wolf's Castle, qv.
Cascob Powys 25 G2 loc 5m/8km SW of Knighton. SO 2366
Caseg 40 C5/D5* r running W into R Llafar 1km SE of Bethesda, Gwynedd. SH 6366
Cas-fuwch Welsh form of Castlebythe, qv.
Cas-gwent Welsh form of Chepstow, qv.
Cashes Green Glos 16 D1* W dist of Stroud. SO 8205
Cashmoor Dorset 9 G3 loc 3m/5km SE of Tollard Royal. ST 9713
Caskieberran Fife 73 F4* W dist of Glenrothes. NO 2500
Cas-lai Welsh form of Hayscastle, qv.
Cas-mael Welsh form of Puncheston, qv.
Casmorys Welsh form of Castle Morris, qv.
Casnewydd-ar-Wysg Welsh form of Newport (Gwent), qv.
Casnewydd-bach Welsh form of Lit Newcastle. See Newcastle, Little.
Cassington Oxon 27 H6 vil 5m/8km NW of Oxford. SP 4510
Cassley H'land 85 E6 r in Sutherland dist running SE down Glen Cassley into R Oykel 8m/12km SW of Lairg. NC 4700
Cassop Colliery Durham 54 C1 vil 5m/8km SE of Durham. See also Old Cassop. NZ 3438
Castell Gwynedd 40 D4* loc 2km N of Dolgarrog. SH 7669
Castell 33 E6* r running W into R Rheidol at Ponterwyd, Dyfed. SN 7480
Castell Bryn-Gwyn Gwynedd. See Llanidan.
Castell Caereinion Powys 33 H4 vil 4m/6km W of Welshpool. SJ 1605
Castell Cawr Clwyd. See Abergele.
Castell Coch S Glam 15 F3* medieval fortified hse (A.M.), restored in 19c, on steep wooded slope overlooking R Taff 5m/8km NW of Cardiff. ST 1382
Castellcollen Powys 25 F2* remains of Roman camp 1m N of Llandrindod Wells. SO 0562
Castell Dinas Powys 25 F5* slight remains of motte and bailey cas on eminence 3m/4km SE of Talgarth. SO 1730
Castell du Powys. See Sennybridge.
Castelldwyran Dyfed 22 D4 loc 4m/6km W of Whitland. SN 1418
Castell Fflemish Welsh form of Castle Flemish, qv.
Castell Gwalchmai Welsh form of Walwyn's Castle, qv.
Castellhenllys Dyfed 22 D2* ancient fort 2m/3km W of Eglwyswrw. SN 1139
Castellhenri Welsh form of Henry's Moat, qv.
Castellmartin Welsh form of Castlemartin, qv.
Castell-mawr Dyfed 22 D2 ancient fort 2m/3km W of Eglwyswrw. SN 1137
Castell-nedd Welsh form of Neath, qv.
Castellnewydd Emlyn Welsh form of Newcastle Emlyn, qv.
Castellnewydd, Y Welsh form of Newcastle, qv.
Castell-paen Welsh form of Painscastle, qv.
Castell Pictwn Welsh form of Picton Castle. See Picton Park.
Castell y Bere Gwynedd 32 D4* ruined cas (A.M.) of uncertain date, to SW of Llanfihangel-y-Pennant. SH 6608
Casterton Cumbria 47 F1/G1 vil 1m NE of Kirkby Lonsdale across R Lune. **High C.** ham 1km S. SD 6279
Casterton, Great Leics 37 E3 vil 2m/4km NW of Stamford, on site of Roman tn. TF 0008
Casterton, Little Leics 37 E3 ham 2m/3km N of Stamford. Site of Roman villa 1km W. TF 0009
Castle Acre Norfolk 38 C3 vil 4m/6km N of Swaffham. Remains of 11c–13c cas (A.M.), and of 12c priory (A.M.). TF 8115
Castle-an-Dinas Cornwall 3 E3 ancient hill fort on Castle Downs, 703 ft or 214 metres. SW 9462
Castle Ashby Northants 28 D2 vil 6m/10km SW of Wellingborough. **C. A. House,** Elizn and later, seat of Earl of Northampton. SP 8659
Castle Bank Staffs 35 E2* loc 2km SW of Stafford. SJ 9021
Castlebay W Isles 88 D4 small tn at head of **Castle Bay** on S coast of Barra. Chief port and settlement of island, although airfield is at N end. NL 6698
Castlebeach Bay Dyfed 22 B5* bay at W end of Milford Haven on S side of Dale Pt. SM 8204
Castle Bolton N Yorks 54 A5 vil above Wensleydale to N, 5m/8km W of Leyburn. Ruins of 14c cas. SE 0391
Castle Bromwich W Midlands 35 G5 suburb 5m/9km E of Birmingham. Remains of motte-and-bailey cas beside M6 motorway. Hall of 17c. SP 1489
Castle Bytham Lincs 37 E3 vil 8m/12km N of Stamford. Earthwork remains of Norman cas. SK 9818
Castlebythe (Cas-fuwch) Dyfed 22 C3 ham 7m/11km SE of Fishguard. Remains of motte to E. SN 0228
Castle Caereinion. See Castell Caereinion.
Castle Campbell Central 72 D4 late 15c cas (A.M.), once known as Castle Gloom, in glen (NTS) nearly 1m N of Dollar. NS 9699
Castle Camps Cambs 30 B3* vil 3m/5km SW of Haverhill. Ch stands in outer moat of former cas built in 12c. TL 6343
Castle Carrock Cumbria 60 B5 vil 4m/6km S of Brampton. NY 5455
Castlecary Central 65 E2 loc 3m/5km SW of Bonnybridge. Site of Roman camp, traversed by rly. NS 7878
Castle Cary Som 8 D2 small tn 3m/5km SW of Bruton. ST 6332
Castle Combe Wilts 16 D4 vil 5m/9km NW of Chippenham. ST 8477
Castlecroft Staffs 35 E4* loc 3m/5km W of Wolverhampton. SO 8697
Castle Dhu Tayside 76 A5*. See Moulin.
Castle Dikes N Yorks 49 E1* site of Roman villa 1m S of N Stainley. SE 2975
Castle Donan H'land. See Eilean Donan.
Castle Donington Leics 36 A2 vil 7m/12km NW of Loughborough. E Midlands Airport 1m SE. SK 4427
Castle Douglas D & G 58 D6 mkt tn at N end of Carlingwark Loch 9m/14km NE of Kirkcudbright. NX 7662
Castledykes D & G. See Kirkcudbright.
Castle, East Durham 61 F6* loc 3m/4km E of Consett. NZ 1452
Castle Eaton Wilts 17 F2 vil on R Thames 3m/5km E of Cricklade. SU 1495
Castle Eden Durham 54 D1 vil 2m/3km S of Peterlee. The cas is a hse of 18c. NZ 4238
Castle Eden Burn 54 D1* stream rising near Shotton Colliery, Durham, and flowing S then E down wooded dene into North Sea at Dene Mouth N of Blackhall Colliery. NZ 4540
Castle End Cambs 37 F4* loc adjoining Maxey to N. TF 1208
Castlefairn Water 58 D3 r in Dumfries & Galloway region running NE to join Dalwhat Water and form Cairn Water, 1km SE of Moniaive. NX 7890
Castle Flemish (Castell Fflemish) Dyfed 22 C3* remains of small Roman fort 2m/3km S of Puncheston. SN 0026
Castleford W Yorks 49 F5 tn on R Aire at its confluence with R Calder 10m/15km SE of Leeds. Coal-mining. Tn stands on site of Roman *Lagentium.* **C. Ings** loc adjoining to NE. SE 4225
Castle Frome H & W 26 B3* vil 6m/9km S of Bromyard. SO 6645
Castle Gate Cornwall 2 B5* loc 3m/4km NE of Penzance. SW 4934
Castle Gloom Central. See Castle Campbell.
Castle Goring W Sussex 11 G4* loc 3m/5km NW of Worthing. TQ 1005
Castle Grant H'land. See Grantown-on-Spey.
Castle Grant H'land 82 A4 former seat of the chiefs of Grant, Earls of Seafield, in Badenock and Strathspey dist 2m/3km N of Grantown-on-Spey. NJ 0430
Castle Green Cumbria 53 E5* loc on E side of Kendal. SD 5392
Castle Green London 20 B3* loc in borough of Barking 2m/3km E of Barking tn centre. TQ 4783
Castle Green Powys 25 F4* loc to NW of Talgarth, opp Bronllys Castle across R Llynfi. SO 1534
Castle Green Surrey 18 D5* loc adjoining Chobham to S. SU 9761
Castle Green S Yorks 43 G1* loc adjoining Penistone to SE. SE 2502
Castle Gresley Derbys 35 H3 loc 2m/3km SW of Swadlincote. SK 2718
Castlehead S'clyde 64 C3* dist of Paisley 1km SW of tn centre. NS 4763
Castle Head, Great Dyfed 22 A5* headland 2m/3km N of St Ann's Hd. Cliff cas or fort. SM 7905
Castle Head, Great Dyfed 22 B5* headland on N shore of Milford Haven 2km SE of St Ishmael's, topped by cliff cas or fort. Lighthouse. SM 8405
Castle Head, Little Dyfed 22 A5* headland (NT) 1m NW of St Ann's Hd. SM 7903
Castle Head, Little Dyfed 22 B5* headland on N shore of Milford Haven 1km S of Sandy Haven. SM 8506
Castlehead Rocks Nthmb 67 G4* two rocks off N coast of Holy I. NU 1344
Castle Heaton Nthmb 67 F4 loc 3m/5km NE of Cornhill on Tweed. NT 9041
Castle Hedingham Essex 30 C4 vil 4m/6km NW of Halstead. Old mkt tn. 12c cross in churchyard. Remains of Norman cas. TL 7835
Castle Hill Kent 12 C3* loc 2m/4km SE of Paddock Wd. TQ 6942
Castlehill S'clyde 64 B2* NW dist of Dumbarton. NS 3876
Castle Hill Suffolk 31 F3* N dist of Ipswich. TM 1547
Castle Hill Wilts 9 H1* loc at entrance to Old Sarum, 2m/3km N of Salisbury. SU 1432
Castle Hill W Yorks 48 D6* loc in Huddersfield 2km S of tn centre. Ancient hill fort. SE 1514
Castle Howard N Yorks 50 C2 baroque mansion by Vanbrugh in large formal grnds 5m/7km W of Malton. SE 7170
Castle Huntly Tayside 73 F2 cas dating from 15c, 1m SW of Longforgan. NO 3029
Castle Island S'clyde 63 G3 small island off E coast of island of Lit Cumbrae. Remains of medieval tower. NS 1551
Castle Island Tayside 73 E4 island in Loch Leven 2km E of Kinross. Remains of cas dating from 15c, where Mary, Queen of Scots was held prisoner 1567–8. NO 1301
Castle Kennedy D & G 57 B6 vil 3m/5km E of Stranraer. Ruins of late 16c cas to N – see Lochinch Castle. NX 1059
Castle Lachlan S'clyde 70 C5 hse in Argyll near mouth of Strathlachlan R. Ruined 16c tower of the Maclachlans on shore of Loch Fyne to W. NN 0195
Castlelaw Fort Lothian. See Glencorse.
Castle Levington Cleveland 54 D4* loc on R Leven 2m/3km E of Kirklevington. Cas consists of Norman motte surrounded by ditch. NZ 4610
Castle Loch D & G. See Lochmaben.
Castle Loch D & G 57 C7 loch 6m/10km E of Glenluce. Remains of cas on islet near E end of loch. NX 2853
Castlemartin (Castellmartin) Dyfed 22 B5 vil 5m/8km SW of Pembroke. Army training area to S. SR 9198
Castle Menzies Tayside 75 H6 Scottish mansion of 16c 2km W of Aberfeldy across R Tay. NN 8349
Castlemilk S'clyde 64 D3 loc 2m/3km SW of Rutherglen. NS 6059
Castle Morpeth 117 admin dist of Nthmb.
Castle Morris (Casmorys) Dyfed 22 B3 vil 5m/8km SW of Fishguard. SM 9031
Castlemorton H & W 26 C4 vil 4m/6km SE of Malvern Wells. SO 7937
Castle Moy S'clyde 69 D5/E5 ruined keep at Lochbuie, Mull. Former stronghold of Maclaines of Loch Buie. NM 6124
Castle O'er D & G 59 G2 ancient earthwork surrounded by large state forest known as **Castle O'er Forest,** S of Eskdalemuir. NY 2492
Castle of Dunnideer Grampian 83 E4* remains of ancient hill fort 2km W of Insch. NJ 6128
Castle of Fiddes Grampian 77 G3 tower of late 16c, restored 1965. NO 8281
Castle of Old Wick H'land. See Old Man of Wick.
Castle of Park D & G 57 C7 castellated late 16c tower hse, 1km W of Glenluce across Water of Luce. NX 1857
Castle Park N Yorks 55 G4* W dist of Whitby. NZ 8810
Castle Point Dyfed 22 C2* headland on E side of entrance to the old harbour at Fishguard, an inlet at S end of Fishguard Bay at mouth of R Gwaun. SM 9637
Castle Point Nthmb 67 G4* headland at SE corner of Holy I. near cas. NU 1441
Castle Point Nthmb 67 H6 headland at S end of Embleton Bay on which Dunstanburgh Castle stands. NU 2522
Castle Point 119 admin dist of Essex.
Castle Pulverbatch Salop 34 B4* ham 1km SW of Ch Pulverbatch. SJ 4202
Castlerigg Cumbria 52 C3* loc 1m SE of Keswick. 1m NE, **C. Stone Circle** (A.M.), megalithic circle of thirty-eight stones, some 100 ft or 30 metres in diameter, with another ten stones set in a rectangle within. NY 2822
Castle Rising Norfolk 38 B2 vil 4m/7km NE of King's Lynn. Remains of Norman cas (A.M.). Trinity Hospital, 17c almshouses. TF 6624
Castle Rushen Isle of Man. See Castletown.
Castles Bay Dyfed 22 B5* bay on N side of Sheep I. at entrance to Milford Haven. SM 8401
Castlesea Bay Tayside 77 F6* small bay 3m/5km NE of Arbroath. NO 6843
Castle Semple Loch S'clyde 64 B3 loch on E side of Lochwinnoch. **Castle Semple Water Park** and bird sanctuary. At NE end of loch are remains of **Castle Semple Collegiate Ch** (A.M.), founded 1504.

Castleshaw Reservoirs Gtr Manchester 43 E1* two resrs 5m/9km NW of Oldham. Site of Roman fort on E side of S resr. SD 9909
Castleside Durham 61 F6 suburb 2m/3km SW of Consett. NZ 0748
Castle Sowerby Cumbria 52 D2* loc 2km N of Hutton Roof. NY 3836
Castle Stalker S'clyde 70 B1* cas on islet at entrance to Loch Laich, Argyll, S of Shuna I. Originally built for James IV, late 15c. NM 9247
Castlesteads Cumbria 53 E1* loc 1m N of Plumpton Wall, at site of Roman fort of *Voreda*. NY 4938
Castlesteads Cumbria 60 B5 site of Roman fort of *Uxellodunum*, 1m SW of Walton. NY 5163
Castle Street W Yorks 48 C5* ham 1m E of Todmorden. SD 9524
Castle Sween S'clyde 69 E8 ruined cas (A.M.) of the MacNeils, dating from 11c, on E side of Loch Sween in Argyll, opp Danna I. NR 7178
Castlethorpe Bucks 28 C3 vil 3m/4km N of Stony Stratford. Loc of **C. Wharf** is 1m SW on Grand Union Canal. SP 7944
Castlethorpe Humberside 44 D1* loc 1m W of Brigg. SE 9807
Castleton Borders 60 B3 loc in Liddesdale 3m/4km NE of Newcastleton. NY 5190
Castleton Derbys 43 F3 vil 5m/8km W of Hathersage. Remains of Norman Peveril Castle (A.M.) on limestone hill to S. Various caves in vicinity. SK 1582
Castleton Gtr Manchester 42 D1 dist of Rochdale 2m/3km S of tn centre. SD 8810
Castleton (Cas-bach) Gwent 15 G3 vil 5m/7km SW of Newport. ST 2583
Castleton N Yorks 55 E4 vil on R Esk in N Yorks Moors National Park 8m/12km W of Egton. NZ 6808
Castletown Cumbria 53 E2* W dist of Penrith. NY 5030
Castletown Dorset 9 E6* loc at N end of Portland. Helicopter stn to W. SY 6874
Castletown H'land 86 E1 vil with small harbour on Dunnet Bay, N coast of Caithness dist 5m/8km E of Thurso. ND 1968
Castletown Isle of Man 46 A6 small tn with harbour on **C. Bay**, 9m/14km SW of Douglas. Remains of Castle Rushen, dating from 13c. The bay extends from Langness Pt westwards to Scarlett Pt. SC 2667
Castletown Staffs 35 E2* loc in Stafford to W of tn centre. SJ 9123
Castletown Tyne & Wear 61 H5 dist of Sunderland 2m/4km W of tn centre across R Wear. NZ 3558
Castley N Yorks 49 E4 vil on N side of R Wharfe 6m/10km S of Harrogate. SE 2645
Caston Norfolk 38 D5 vil 3m/5km SE of Watton. TL 9597
Castor Cambs 37 F4 W dist of Peterborough. TL 1298
Castra Exploratum Cumbria. See Netherby.
Caswell W Glam 23 G6* loc 3m/5km W of Mumbles Hd, above **C. Bay**, which extends SE to Whiteshell Pt. SS 5987
Cas-wis Welsh form of Wiston, qv.
Catacol S'clyde 63 F3 loc on N side of **C. Bay** on NW coast of Arran. See also Glen Catacol. NR 9149
Cat and Fiddle Inn Ches 43 E4 on Macclesfield–Buxton rd 4m/6km W of Buxton. Stands at height of 1690 ft or 515 metres above sea level. SK 0071
Cataractonium N Yorks. See Catterick.
Catbrain Avon 16 B3* loc at W end of Filton Airfield, 5m/8km N of Bristol. ST 5780
Catbrook Gwent 16 A2* loc 2m/3km S of Trelleck. SO 5102
Catchall Cornwall 2 A5 ham 3m/4km SW of Penzance. SW 4328
Catchems Corner W Midlands 35 H6* loc adjoining Balsall to E, 4m/7km NW of Kenilworth. SP 2476
Catchems End H & W 35 E6* loc 3m/4km W of Kidderminster. SO 7976
Catchgate Durham 61 F6* loc adjoining Annfield Plain to NW, 2m/3km W of Stanley. NZ 1652
Catcleugh Reservoir Nthmb 60 C2 resr in upper Redesdale 3m/5km SE of Carter Bar. NT 7403
Catcliffe S Yorks 43 H2 vil 5m/9km E of Sheffield. SK 4288
Catcott Som 8 C1 vil on N side of Polden Hills 7m/11km W of Glastonbury. 3m/4km N across C Heath, ham of **C. Burtle.** ST 3939
Caterham Surrey 19 G5 tn on N Downs 6m/10km S of Croydon. TQ 3455
Caterthun Tayside 77 E4. **Brown C.** is an Iron Age fort with four concentric entrenchments, 5m/8km NW of Brechin. **White C.** is another Iron Age fort nearly 1m SW. NO 5566
Catesby Northants 28 A2 par containing hams of **Upr** and **Lr Catesby** some 4m/6km SW of Daventry. SP 5259
Catfield Norfolk 39 G3 vil 2m/4km SE of Stalham. **C. Common** loc 1m E. TG 3821
Cat Firth Shetland 89 E7 inlet on Mainland N of Lambgarth Hd on E coast. **Catfirth** is loc at head of inlet. HU 4453
Catford London 20 A4* dist in borough of Lewisham 2km S of Lewisham tn centre and 7m/11km SE of Charing Cross. TQ 3873
Catforth Lancs 47 F4 vil 6m/9km NW of Preston. SD 4735
Catfoss Humberside 51 F3* loc 2m/3km NE of Brandesburton. Airfield to W. TA 1448
Catharine Slack W Yorks 48 D5* loc 2m/3km N of Halifax. SE 0928
Cathays S Glam 15 G4* dist of Cardiff to N of city centre. C. Park to W of city centre. ST 1877
Cathcart S'clyde 64 C3/D3* dist of Glasgow 4m/6km S of city centre. NS 5860
Cathedine (Cathedin) Powys 25 F5 ham 2m/3km S of Llangorse. SO 1425
Catherine de Barnes Heath W Midlands 35 G6* loc in Solihull 2m/3km E of tn centre. SP 1780
Catherington Hants 10 D3 suburban loc 1m NW of Horndean. SU 6914
Catherston Leweston Dorset 8 B5* 2m/4km NE of Lyme Regis. SY 3794
Cat Hill S Yorks 43 G1* loc 2km N of Penistone. SE 2405
Cathkin S'clyde 64 D3 loc in E Kilbride 3m/4km N of tn centre. NS 6258
Catholes Cumbria 53 F5* loc 1m S of Sedbergh. SD 6590
Catisfield Hants 10 C4 suburban loc 2m/3km W of Fareham. SU 5406
Cat Law Tayside 76 D5 mt 6m/9km NW of Kirriemuir. Height 2193 ft or 668 metres. NO 3161
Catley Lane Head Gtr Manchester 47 H6* loc in Rochdale 2m/3km NW of tn centre. SD 8715
Catlodge H'land 75 F2 loc in Badenoch and Strathspey dist 5m/8km N of Dalwhinnie. NN 6392
Catlow Lancs 48 B4 loc 2m/3km SE of Nelson. SD 8836
Catmere End Essex 29 H4* ham 3m/5km W of Saffron Walden. TL 4939
Catmore Berks 17 H3 vil 8m/13km N of Newbury. SU 4580
Catmose, Vale of Leics 36 D3/D4 dist surrounding Oakham, levelled by weathering of Upper Lias. SK 8709
Caton Lancs 47 F2 vil 4m/6km NE of Lancaster. SD 5364
Caton Green Lancs 47 F2* ham 2km E of Caton. SD 5465
Catrake Force N Yorks 53 G4* waterfall to NE of Keld. NY 8901
Catrine S'clyde 56 E2 vil on R Ayr 2m/3km SE of Mauchline. Ballochmyle Hse, 1km NW, is subject of two songs by Burns. NS 5225
Cat's Ash Gwent 15 H2/H3* ham 2m/3km E of Caerleon across R Usk. ST 3790
Catsfield E Sussex 12 D5 vil 2m/3km SW of Battle. Loc of **C. Stream** 1km SW. TQ 7213
Catsham Som 8 D1* loc 2m/3km N of Keinton Mandeville. ST 5533
Catshaw S Yorks 43 G1* loc 3m/4km W of Penistone. SE 2003
Catshill H & W 26 D1* loc 2m/3km N of Bromsgrove. Loc of **Upr Catshill** adjoins to NE. SO 9573
Catshill W Midlands 35 F4* loc in Brownhills S of tn centre. SK 0505
Cattal N Yorks 50 A3 vil on R Nidd 3m/4km S of Whixley. SE 4454
Cattawade Suffolk 31 E4 vil at head of R Stour estuary 8m/13km SW of Ipswich. Xylonite works. TM 1033
Cattedown Devon 4 B5* dist of Plymouth 2km SE of city centre. SX 4953
Catterall Lancs 47 F4 vil 2m/3km S of Garstang. SD 4942
Catteralslane Salop 34 C1* loc 2km E of Whitchurch. SJ 5640
Catterick N Yorks 54 B5 vil 5m/7km SE of Richmond. Airfield to SE. Racecourse at **Catterick Br**, vil on R Swale 2km NW, on site of Roman tn of *Cataractonium*. SE 2397
Catterick Camp N Yorks 54 B5 large permanent military establishment 2m/3km S of Richmond. SE 1897
Catterlen Cumbria 52 D2/53 E3* ham 3m/4km NW of Penrith. Hall, 1m S, dates from 16c. NY 4833
Catterline Grampian 77 H3 fishing vil on E coast 5m/8km S of Stonehaven. NO 8678
Catterton N Yorks 49 G3/G4 ham 2m/4km NE of Tadcaster. SE 5145
Catteshall Surrey 11 F1 E suburb of Godalming. SU 9844
Cattewater 4 B5* stretch of R Plym estuary off Cattedown, SE dist of Plymouth. SX 4953
Catthorpe Leics 36 B6 vil 4m/6km NE of Rugby. SP 5578
Cattishall Suffolk 30 D2* loc 2m/3km E of Bury St Edmunds. TL 8865
Cattistock Dorset 8 D4 vil 2km N of Maiden Newton. SY 5999
Cattle End Northants 28 B3 loc adjoining Silverstone to SW, 4m/6km SW of Towcester. SP 6643
Catto N Yorks 54 D5* loc 4m/6km E of Northallerton. SE 4292
Catton Norfolk 39 F3/F4 suburb 3m/4km N of Norwich. See also New Catton. TG 2312
Catton Nthmb 60 D5 vil 2km N of Allendale Tn. NY 8257
Catton N Yorks 49 F1* vil 2m/4km NW of Topcliffe. SE 3678
Catton, High Humberside 50 C3 vil 2km S of Stamford Br. **Low Catton** vil 1m W. SE 7153
Catwick Humberside 51 F4 vil 5m/8km W of Hornsea. **Lit Catwick** loc adjoining to S. TA 1245
Catworth Cambs 29 E1 vil 10m/15km W of Huntingdon. Loc of **Lit Catworth** 1m SE. TL 0873
Caudle Green Glos 26 D6 ham 6m/10km NE of Stroud. SO 9410
Caudworthy Water 6 B6* r in Cornwall rising S of Whitstone and flowing S into R Carey near N Petherwin. SX 2688
Caulcott Beds 29 E3* loc 4m/6km NW of Ampthill. TL 0042
Caulcott Oxon 28 A5* ham 5m/8km W of Bicester. SP 5024
Cauldcleuch Head Borders 60 A2 hill 5m/7km SE of Teviothead. Height 1996 ft or 608 metres. NT 4600
Cauldhame Central 71 G5 vil adjoining Kippen to SW, 9m/15km W of Stirling. NS 6494
Cauldkine Rig D & G 59 G3 hill 5m/8km NW of Langholm. Height 1478 ft or 450 metres. Also known as Calkin Rig. NY 2987
Cauldon Staffs 43 F6 ham among quarries 6m/9km NE of Cheadle. **C. Lowe** 1m S. SK 0749
Cauldshiels Loch Borders 66 C5 small loch 2m/4km SW of Melrose. NT 5132
Cauldwell Derbys 35 H3 ham 3m/5km SW of Swadlincote. SK 2517
Caulkerbush D & G 59 E5* loc 7m/11km SE of Dalbeattie. See also Southwick. NX 9257
Caundle Brook 9 E3* r rising to W of Buckland Newton in Dorset and flowing N and then NE into R Lydden N of Lydlinch. ST 7414
Caundle Marsh Dorset 8 E3* ham 3m/5km SE of Sherborne. ST 6713
Caundle Wake Dorset 8 E3* ham 1km SE of Bishop's Caundle and 5m/8km SE of Sherborne. ST 7012
Caunsall H & W 35 E6 loc 3m/5km NE of Kidderminster. SO 8581
Caunton Notts 44 C5 vil 5m/8km NW of Newark-on-Trent. SK 7460
Causamul W Isles 88 D1* group of rocks nearly 2m/3km W of Aird an Rùnair, W coast of N Uist. NF 6670
Causennae Lincs. See Ancaster.
Causeway End Cumbria 53 E6* loc at S end of Levens. SD 4885
Causeway End Essex 30 B5/B6* ham 4m/6km SE of Gt Dunmow. TL 6819
Causeway End Lancs 47 E6* loc 1m S of Rufford. SD 4514
Causeway Foot W Yorks 48 D5* ham 2m/3km S of Denholme. SE 0630
Causeway Green W Midlands 35 F5* loc 1m NW of Warley tn centre. SO 9987
Causewayhead Central 72 B5/C5 loc 2km N of Stirling. NS 8095
Causey Durham 61 G5* loc 2m/3km N of Stanley. NZ 2056
Cautley Cumbria 53 F5* loc 3m/5km NE of Sedbergh. **C. Spout** waterfall below C. Crag 2km N. SD 6995
Cava Orkney 89 A7 uninhabited island of about 180 acres or 70 hectares lying 2km off E coast of Hoy at SE end of Bring Deeps. Lighthouse at N end of island. ND 3299
Cavendish Suffolk 30 C3 vil on R Stour 4m/6km W of Long Melford. TL 8046
Cavendish Bridge Leics 36 A2* loc on R Trent 2m/3km N of Castle Donington. SK 4429
Cavenham Suffolk 30 C1 vil 7m/11km NW of Bury St Edmunds. TL 7669
Cave, North Humberside 50 D5 vil 6m/10km S of Mkt Weighton. **S Cave** vil 2m/3km SE. SE 8932
Cavers Borders 66 C6 loc 2m/4km NE of Hawick. NT 5315
Caversfield Oxon 28 B5 loc 2m/3km N of Bicester. Site of Roman bldg 1m E. SP 5825
Caversham Berks 18 C4 N dist of Reading, across R Thames. Dist of **C. Heights** 2km W. SU 7274
Caversta W Isles 88 B2* locality on S side of Loch Erisort, Lewis, 2m/4km SE of Laxay across the loch. NB 3620
Caverswall Staffs 35 F1 vil 4m/6km W of Cheadle. SJ 9542
Cavil Humberside 50 C5* loc 2m/3km NE of Howden. SE 7730
Cawdor H'land 81 G3 vil in Nairn dist 5m/8km SW of Nairn. Remains of cas dating from 15c and later. NH 8449
Cawkeld Humberside 51 E3* loc 1km N of Kilnwick. SE 9950
Cawkwell Lincs 45 F3 loc 6m/9km SW of Louth. TF 2879
Cawood N Yorks 49 G4 vil on R Ouse 4m/7km NW of Selby. Gatehouse of former cas dates from 15c. SE 5737
Cawsand Cornwall 4 B5 vil 2km SE of Millbrook, adjoining Kingsand on **C. Bay,** which stretches from Picklecombe Pt in the N to Penlee Pt in the S. SX 4350
Cawston Norfolk 39 F3 vil 4m/7km SW of Aylsham. TG 1323
Cawston Warwicks 27 H1* loc 3m/4km SW of Rugby. SP 4773
Cawthorn N Yorks 55 F5/F6* loc 4m/6km NW of Pickering. Earthworks of Roman camps to NE. SE 7789
Cawthorne S Yorks 43 G1 vil 4m/6km W of Barnsley. SE 2808
Cawthorpe Lincs 37 F2 ham 2km N of Bourne. TF 0922
Cawthorpe, Little Lincs 45 G3 vil 3m/5km SE of Louth. TF 3583
Cawton N Yorks 50 B1 ham 2m/3km W of Hovingham. SE 6476
Caxton Cambs 29 G2 vil 9m/15km W of Cambridge. **C. Gibbet,** loc and crossroads 2m/3km N. TL 3058
Caxton End Cambs 29 G2* NW end of vil of Bourn. TL 3157
Caxton End Cambs 29 G2* E end of vil of Eltisley. TL 2759
Caynham Salop 26 B1 vil 3m/5km E of Ludlow. SO 5573
Caythorpe Lincs 44 D6 vil 8m/13km N of Grantham. Agricultural college to E. SK 9348
Caythorpe Notts 44 B6 vil 2km SE of Lowdham. SK 6845
Cayton N Yorks 49 E2* loc 2m/3km N of Ripley. SE 2863

Cayton N Yorks 55 H6 vil 3m/5km S of Scarborough. **C. Bay** on North Sea coast 1m NE. TA 0583
Ceannacroc Forest H'land 80 C6 deer forest in Inverness dist N of Loch Cluanie. Also state forest in Glen Moriston to E. Power stn for hydro-electricity scheme at Ceannacroc Br. NH 1713
Ceanna Mór H'land 74 A6 headland on S side of entrance to Loch a' Choire, Lochaber dist. NM 8551
Ceann an t-Sàilein S'clyde 69 E8 narrow inlet of Loch Sween, Argyll, running up to N end of Danna I. NR 7079
Ceann Ear W Isles 88 D1* one of the Monach Isles, qv. Sands between Ceann Ear and adjoining island of Ceann Iar to W are fordable at low tide. NF 6462
Ceann Garbh S'clyde 70 D3 peak in Argyll to NE of summit of Beinn Bhuidhe and 6m/9km SE of Dalmally. Height 2635 ft or 803 metres. NN 2220
Ceann Iar W Isles 88 D1* one of the Monach Isles, qv. See also Ceann Ear. NF 6162
Ceardach Central 71 E5* wooded islet (NTS) in Loch Lomond 2m/3km W of Balmaha. NS 3991
Cedar House Surrey. See Cobham.
Cedig 33 G2 r rising in Gwynedd 6m/10km SE of Bala and flowing S into Lake Vyrnwy, Powys. SH 9921
Cefn Clwyd 41 F4* ham 2m/4km SW of St Asaph. Prehistoric caves beside R Elwy to S. SJ 0171
Cefn Berain Clwyd 41 F4* loc 4m/6km NW of Denbigh. SH 9969
Cefn-brith Clwyd 41 F6 ham 2m/3km NW of Cerrigydrudion. SH 9350
Cefn Bryn W Glam 23 F6 moorland ridge on Gower peninsula, running W from Penmaen for about 4m/6km. To N, 1m S of Llanrhidian, is **Arthur's Stone,** large dolmen of millstone grit. SS 5089
Cefn-bryn-brain Dyfed 14 C1* loc 2m/3km E of Brynamman. SN 7114
Cefn Byrle Powys 14 D1* loc 5m/8km NE of Ystalyfera. SN 8311
Cefn Canol Clwyd 33 H2* loc 1km NW of Rhydycroesau. SJ 2331
Cefn Coch Powys 33 G4* loc 1km NW of Llanllugan. SJ 0402
Cefn-coed-y-cymmer Mid Glam 15 E1 loc 2m/3km NW of Merthyr Tydfil. SO 0308
Cefn Coleshill Clwyd 41 H4* hill 2m/3km W of Flint. Remains of medieval fortress. SJ 2173
Cefn-crib Gwent 15 G2* loc 3m/5km W of Pontypool. ST 2399
Cefn Cribwr Mid Glam 14 D3 vil 4m/6km NW of Bridgend. SS 8582
Cefn Cross Mid Glam 14 D3* loc on E side of Cefn Cribwr. SS 8682
Cefn-ddwysarn Gwynedd 33 F1 loc 3m/5km NE of Bala. SH 9638
Cefn Einion Salop 34 A5 loc 4m/6km N of Clun. SO 2886
Cefneithen Dyfed 23 G4 loc 1m NW of Cross Hands. SN 5513
Cefn Fforest Gwent 15 F2* loc in Blackwood. ST 1697
Cefn Glas Mid Glam 15 E3* loc adjoining Bridgend to NW. SS 8980
Cefngorwydd Powys 25 E3 ham 2m/3km E of Llanwrtyd Wells. SN 9045
Cefn Hengoed W Glam 23 H5* loc in Swansea 2m/4km NE of tn centre across R Tawe. SS 6875
Cefni 40 B5 r on Anglesey running S through Cefni Resr and Llangefni, then SW through Malltraeth Marsh and Malltraeth Sands into Caernarvon Bay. SH 3765
Cefni Reservoir Gwynedd 40 B4 resr in course of R Cefni on Anglesey, 2m/3km NW of Llangefni. SH 4477
Cefn-llwyd Dyfed 32 D6* loc 4m/7km E of Aberystwyth. SN 6583
Cefnllys Castle Powys 25 F2* motte and bailey on which the 13c cas once stood, 2m/3km E of Llandrindod Wells. SO 0861
Cefn-mawr Clwyd 41 H6 vil 2km SW of Ruabon. SJ 2842
Cefnpennar Mid Glam 15 E2/F2* vil 1m NW of Mountain Ash. SO 0300
Cefn Rhigos Mid Glam 15 E1* loc 1m N of Rhigos.
Cefn-y-bedd Clwyd 41 H5 loc 4m/6km N of Wrexham. SJ 3156
Cefn-y-bedd. Former name of Cilmery (Cilmeri), Powys, qv.
Cefn-y-Castell Powys 34 A3 remains of ancient camp on Middletown Hill, qv. See also Breidden Hills. SJ 3013
Cefn y Garth W Glam 14 C2* loc 2km SE of Clydach towards Neath. SN 7000
Cefn-y-pant Dyfed 22 D3* ham 2m/3km NW of Llanboidy. SN 1925
Cegidfa Welsh form of Guilsfield, qv.
Cegidog 41 H5* r running E into R Alun on S side of Cefn-y-bedd, Clwyd, 4m/6km N of Wrexham. SJ 3155
Cegin 40 C4* r rising S of Pentir, near Bangor, Gwynedd, and flowing N into Menai Strait on E side of Bangor. SH 5972
Ceibwr Bay Dyfed 22 D2 small bay 1m NW of Moylgrove. SN 1045
Ceidiog 33 G1 r originating in various streams in Berwyn Mts S of Llandrillo, Clwyd, and flowing N through Llandrillo into R Dee 1m NW of the vil. SJ 0238
Ceinewydd Welsh form of New Quay, qv.
Ceiriog 34 A1 r rising in Berwyn Mts SE of Corwen, Clwyd, and running E by Glyn Ceiriog and Chirk into R Dee 2m/3km NE of Chirk. SJ 3139
Ceirw 41 F6* r rising 3m/5km S of Pentrefoelas, Clwyd, and flowing E into R Alwen on SE side of Maerdy. SJ 0244
Cellan Dyfed 24 B3/C3 loc 2m/4km E of Lampeter. SN 6149
Cellarhead Staffs 43 E6 ham 5m/8km E of Stoke-on-Trent. SJ 9547
Cellar Head W Isles 88 C1 headland on NE coast of Lewis 6m/9km N of Tolsta Hd. NB 5656
Celleron Cumbria 53 E2 loc 4m/6km S of Penrith. NY 4925
Celynog 33 E3* r running W into R Wnion 4m/7km E of Dolgellau, Gwynedd. SH 7920
Cemaes Bay Gwynedd 40 B2 wide bay on N coast of Anglesey 5m/8km W of Amlwch. E coast of bay, NT. Name also applied to fishing vil and resort on S shore of bay. SH 3793
Cemaes Head Dyfed 22 D1 headland on W side of mouth of R Teifi, 4m/6km NW of Cardigan. SN 1350
Cemais Welsh form of Kemeys (qv) and Cemaes.
Cemais Comawndwr Welsh form of Kemeys Commander, qv.
Cemmaes Powys 33 F4 vil 7m/11km NE of Machynlleth. SH 8306
Cemmaes Road Powys 33 E4 ham 5m/8km NE of Machynlleth. SH 8204
Cenarth Dyfed 23 E2 vil 3m/4km W of Newcastle Emlyn. Salmon-leap, where coracle fishing formerly prospered. SN 2641
Cendl Welsh form of Beaufort, qv.
Cennen 23 G3* r rising on Black Mountain SE of Llandeilo, Dyfed, and flowing W then N into R Towy on S side of Llandeilo. SN 6321
Central 114 admin region of Scotland bounded by Strathclyde to S and W, Tayside to N, and Fife and Lothian astride Firth of Forth to E; it comprises the former counties of Clackmannan and Stirling, and the SW part of Perth. The terrain and scenery are varied: the northern part is in the Highlands, reaching the S shore of Loch Tay, and including Glen Lochay; it also includes Loch Katrine and the Trossachs. The southern part encloses the fertile basin of R Forth, which flows E to Stirling and the Firth of Forth. The western border runs down the middle of Loch Lomond, whilst in the extreme SE the region includes the industrial area around Falkirk and Grangemouth.
Central Lancashire New Town 42 F5*. Designated 1970. Area of 55 sq miles or 142 sq km includes Preston in the N and Chorley in the S. SD 52
Centre Vale Park W Yorks 48 C5* loc adjoining Todmorden to W. SD 9324
Ceredigion 118 admin dist of Dyfed.
Ceres Fife 73 G3 vil 3m/4km SE of Cupar. NO 4011
Ceri 23 E2 r rising SE of Llangranog, Dyfed, and flowing S into R Teifi at Cwmcoy. SN 2941
Cerist Powys 33 F5* loc on r of same name 2m/4km N of Llanidloes. SN 9688
Cerist 33 F3* r running E into R Dovey at Dinas Mawddwy, Gwynedd. SH 8614
Cerist 33 G5* r rising near Van, Powys, and flowing E into R Trannon 2km W of Caersws. SO 0190
Cerne 9 D5, E5 r rising near Up Cerne in Dorset and flowing S into R Frome on N side of Dorchester. SY 6991
Cerne Abbas Dorset 8 D4 vil on R Cerne 7m/11km N of Dorchester. To N on Giant Hill is **The Cerne Giant** (NT), Romano-British figure of a man cut in the chalk, 180 ft or 55 metres in length. ST 6601
Cerne, Nether Dorset 9 D4 ham 2m/3km S of Cerne Abbas. SY 6798
Cerney, North Glos 17 E1 vil 4m/6km N of Cirencester. SP 0107
Cerney, South Glos 17 E2 vil 4m/6km SE of Cirencester. Airfield to N. SU 0497
Cerney Wick Glos 17 E2 vil 2m/3km NW of Cricklade. SU 0796
Cerrigceinwen Gwynedd 40 B4 vil on Anglesey 2m/4km SW of Llangefni. SH 4273
Cerrig-gwylan Dyfed 22 A3* two small islands 1km N of Abereiddy Bay. SM 7932
Cerrigydrudion Clwyd 41 F6 vil 12m/20km SW of Ruthin. SJ 9548
Cess Norfolk 39 H3* loc 1km W of Martham. TG 4417
Cessford Borders 67 E6 loc 3m/4km W of Morebattle. **C. Castle,** ruined 14c stronghold of the Kers. NT 7323
Cessnock Castle S'clyde 64 C5 early 15c tower with 16c-17c hse attached, 1m SE of Galston. NS 5135
Cessnock Water 64 C5 r in Strathclyde region rising 3m/5km S of Darvel and running circuitously NW to R Irvine between Galston and Kilmarnock. NS 4737
Ceunant Gwynedd 40 C5* ham 3m/5km E of Caernarvon. SH 5361
Chaceley Glos 26 D4 vil 3m/5km SW of Tewkesbury across R Severn. SO 8530
Chace Terrace Staffs 35 F3 loc 3m/4km N of Brownhills. SK 0409
Chacewater Cornwall 2 C4 vil 4m/6km NE of Redruth. SW 7544
Chackmore Bucks 28 B4/C4 vil 2km NW of Buckingham. SP 6835
Chacombe Northants 28 A3 vil 3m/5km NE of Banbury. SP 4943
Chad Brook 30 D3* r rising N of Rede, Suffolk, and flowing generally SE into R Stour on SW side of Long Melford. TL 8545
Chadderton Gtr Manchester 42 D1 tn 6m/10km NE of Manchester. Textiles, general and textile engineering. **C. Fold** and **C. Heights** locs 1m NW and 2km N respectively. SD 9005
Chaddesden Derbys 36 A1 dist of Derby 2m/3km E of tn centre. SK 3837
Chaddesley Corbett H & W 26 D1* vil 4m/7km SE of Kidderminster. SO 8973
Chaddleworth Berks 17 H4 vil 7m/11km NW of Newbury. SU 4177
Chadlington Oxon 27 G5 vil 3m/4km NW of Charlbury. SP 3221
Chadshunt Warwicks 27 G2/G3* ham 2m/3km NE of Kineton. SP 3452
Chadstone Northants 28 D2* loc 1km SW of Castle Ashby and 7m/11km SW of Wellingborough. SP 8558
Chad Valley W Midlands 35 F5 loc in Birmingham 2m/3km SW of city centre. Botanical gardens. SP 0485
Chadwell Leics 36 D2 ham 4m/6km NE of Melton Mowbray. SK 7824
Chadwell Salop 34 D3/35 E3* loc 4m/7km SE of Newport. SJ 7814
Chadwell End Beds 29 E2 loc adjoining vil of Pertenhall to W, 2m/3km SW of Kimbolton. TL 0865
Chadwell Heath London 20 B3 loc in borough of Barking 2m/3km W of Romford. TQ 4888
Chadwell St Mary Essex 20 C4 urban loc 2m/3km N of Tilbury. TQ 6478
Chadwick End W Midlands 27 F1 ham 4m/6km E of Hockley Heath. SP 2073
Chadwick Green Merseyside 42 B2* loc 1m SW of Billinge. SJ 5299
Chaffcombe Som 8 B3 vil 2m/4km NE of Chard. ST 3510
Chagford Devon 7 E6 small tn on E edge of Dartmoor 4m/6km NW of Moretonhampstead. SX 7087
Chailey E Sussex 12 A4 vil 6m/10km N of Lewes. **C. Heritage** is rehabilitation centre for handicapped children, to N. TQ 3919
Chainbridge Cambs 37 H4* loc 3m/4km SE of Guyhirn. TF 4200
Chain Bridge Lincs 37 G1* loc with br over New Hammond Beck 2m/3km SW of Boston. TF 3043
Chainhurst Kent 20 D6* vil 2m/4km N of Marden. TQ 7347
Chalbury Dorset 9 G4* ham 4m/7km N of Wimborne. SU 0106
Chalbury Common Dorset 9 G4* loc 4m/7km N of Wimborne. SU 0206
Chaldon Surrey 19 G5 vil 2m/3km W of Caterham. TQ 3155
Chaldon, East Dorset. Alternative name for Chaldon Herring, qv. SY 7983
Chaldon Herring Dorset 9 E5 vil 4m/7km SW of Wool. Also known as E Chaldon. SY 7983
Chaldon, West Dorset 9 E5* ham 2km N of coast 5m/8km SW of Wool. SY 7782
Chale Isle of Wight 10 B6 vil near S coast 5m/8km W of Ventnor, and just inland from **C. Bay,** which extends from Atherfield Pt (NW) to Rocken End (SE). 2km N, vil of **C. Green.** SZ 4877
Chalfield, Great Wilts 16 D5* ham 3m/5km W of Melksham. Moated 15c manor hse (NT). 1km W, loc of **Lit Chalfield.** ST 8663
Chalfont Common Bucks 19 E2* suburb 1m N of Chalfont St Peter. TQ 0092
Chalfont, Little Bucks 18 D2* suburb 2m/4km E of Amersham. SU 9997
Chalfont St Giles Bucks 18 D2 tn 3m/5km SE of Amersham. SU 9893
Chalfont St Peter Bucks 19 E3 tn 6m/9km NW of Uxbridge. TQ 0090
Chalford Glos 16 D2 vil 4m/6km SE of Stroud. SO 8902
Chalford Wilts 16 D6* loc in S part of Westbury. ST 8650
Chalgrave Beds 29 E5 loc 4m/6km N of Dunstable. TL 0027
Chalgrove Oxon 18 B2 vil 4m/6km NW of Watlington. Airfield to N. Site of Civil War battle (1643) to E. SU 6396
Chalk Kent 20 C4 E dist of Gravesend. TQ 6772
Chalk End Essex 20 C1* loc 3m/5km SE of Leaden Roding. TL 6310
Chalk Farm London 19 G3* loc in borough of Camden 3m/4km NW of Charing Cross. TQ 2884
Chalk Hill Herts 19 F1* SW dist of St Albans. TL 1305
Chalk Hill Humberside 45 E1* loc 1m E of Melton Ross. TA 0811
Chalkhouse Green Oxon 18 C4* loc 3m/5km N of Reading. SU 7178
Chalkshire Bucks 18 C1* loc 2m/3km W of Wendover. SP 8407
Chalkstone Suffolk 30 B3* loc adjoining Haverhill to NE. TL 6746
Chalkwell Essex 21 E3* W dist of Southend-on-Sea. TQ 8585
Chalkwell Kent 21 E5* W dist of Sittingbourne. TQ 8964
Challacombe Devon 7 E1 vil on W side of Exmoor 5m/8km W of Simonsbath. To N of vil, **Challacombe Resr.** SS 6941
Challister Shetland 89 F6/F7* loc on island of Whalsay 1km E of Brough. **C. Ness** is headland on N coast of island, 2km NE. HU 5665
Challoch D & G 58 A5 loc 2m/3km NW of Newton Stewart. NX 3867
Challock Lees Kent 21 F6 vil 4m/6km E of Charing. TR 0050
Challow, East Oxon 17 G3 vil 2km W of Wantage. SU 3888
Challow, West Oxon 17 G3 vil 2m/3km W of Wantage. SU 3688
Chalmington Dorset 8 D4 loc, with **Hr Chalmington** to N, 2m/3km N of Maiden Newton. ST 5901
Chalton Beds 29 E5 vil 5m/8km NW of Luton. TL 0326
Chalton Hants 10 D3 vil 3m/4km NE of Horndean. Sites of Roman bldgs 1m E and 2km NW. SU 7316
Chalvey Berks 18 D3 SW dist of Slough. SU 9679
Chalvington E Sussex 12 B5 vil 5m/7km W of Hailsham. TQ 5209
Chancery Dyfed 24 B1* loc 3m/5km S of Aberystwyth. SN 5876
Chanctonbury Ring W Sussex 11 G4 site of Iron Age fort on N edge of South Downs 2km E of Washington surmounted by beech clump, a well-known landmark. TQ 1412
Chandler's Cross Herts 19 E2* ham 3m/4km W of Watford. TQ 0698
Chandler's Ford Hants 10 B3 NW suburb of Eastleigh. SU 4320

Changue Forest S'clyde 56 C4, D4* state forest in Glentrool Forest Park, 2m/3km E of Barr. NX 3193
Channel's End Beds 29 E2* loc 6m/10km NE of Bedford. TL 1156
Channer Wick Shetland 89 E8* inlet on E coast of Mainland 12m/20km S of Lerwick. Loc of **Channerwick** at head of inlet. HU 4023
Chanonry Point H'land 81 G2 headland with lighthouse in Ross and Cromarty dist at entrance to Inner Moray Firth or Inverness Firth opp Fort George. NH 7455
Chantry Som 16 C6 vil 4m/6km W of Frome. ST 7147
Chantry Suffolk 31 F4 SW dist of Ipswich. TM 1443
Chantry Point Suffolk 31 H3* headland on right bank of R Ore 1m S of Orford. TM 4248
Chaoruinn H'land 75 G3 mt in Badenoch and Strathspey dist close to border with Tayside region, 5m/7km S of Dalwhinnie. Height 3004 ft or 916 metres. NN 6477
Chapel Cumbria 52 C2* loc just S of Bassenthwaite. NY 2231
Chapel Fife 73 F5 NW dist of Kirkcaldy. NT 2593
Chapel Allerton Som 15 H6 vil 2m/4km NW of Wedmore. ST 4050
Chapel Allerton W Yorks 49 E4 dist of Leeds 2m/3km N of city centre. SE 3037
Chapel Amble Cornwall 3 E1 vil 2m/3km N of Wadebridge. SW 9975
Chapel Brampton Northants 28 C1 vil 4m/7km NW of Northampton. SP 7266
Chapel Chorlton Staffs 35 E1 vil 6m/10km NW of Stone. SJ 8137
Chapel Cleeve Som 7 G1* ham just S of Blue Anchor and 2m/4km W of Watchet. ST 0342
Chapelcross D & G 59 G4 nuclear power stn, the first in Scotland, 3m/4km NE of Annan. NY 2269
Chapel Cross E Sussex 12 C4 loc adjoining Punnett's Tn to W, 2m/4km E of Heathfield. TQ 6120
Chapel End Beds 29 E2* S end of vil of Colmworth. TL 1058
Chapel End Beds 29 E3* E end of Wilshamstead, 4m/7km SE of Bedford. TL 0743
Chapel End Beds 29 E3* E end of Cardington, 3m/5km SE of Bedford. TL 0948
Chapel End Beds 29 E3/E4* E end of Houghton Conquest, 3m/4km NE of Ampthill. TL 0541
Chapel End Cambs 37 F6 S end of vil of Gt Gidding, 5m/8km SW of Stilton. TL 1182
Chapel End Ches 34 D1* loc 1m E of Audlem. SJ 6743
Chapel End Northants 37 F5* E end of vil of Lutton, 5m/8km E of Oundle. TL 1187
Chapel End Warwicks 35 H5 loc adjoining Hartshill to S, 3m/4km W of Nuneaton. SP 3293
Chapelend Way Essex 30 C4* vil 4m/7km NE of Finchingfield. TL 7038
Chapel-en-le-Frith Derbys 43 F3 mnfg tn 5m/8km N of Buxton. SK 0580
Chapel Field Gtr Manchester 42 D1* loc 1m SE of Radcliffe. SD 7906
Chapel Field Norfolk 39 G3* loc 1km SW of Stalham. TG 3624
Chapel Finian D & G 57 C7 traces of 10c-11c chapel (A.M.) on E shore of Luce Bay, 5m/8km NW of Port William. NX 2748
Chapelgate Lincs 37 H2* loc adjoining Gedney to E. TF 4124
Chapelgill Hill Borders 65 G5* hill 5m/8km S of Biggar. Height 2282 ft or 696 metres. NT 0630
Chapel Green Northants 28 B3/C3* loc on E edge of Silverstone Motor-racing Circuit 4m/7km S of Towcester. SP 6842
Chapel Green Warwicks 28 A2* ham adjoining Napton on the Hill to S, 3m/5km SE of Southam. SP 4660
Chapel Green Warwicks 35 H5* loc 6m/10km NW of Coventry. SP 2685
Chapel Haddlesey N Yorks 49 G5 vil 4m/7km SW of Selby. SE 5826
Chapelhall S'clyde 65 E3 vil 2m/3km SE of Airdrie. NS 7862
Chapel Hill Grampian 83 H3* loc near E coast 2m/3km E of vil of Cruden Bay. NK 0635
Chapel Hill Gwent 16 A2 vil 4m/6km N of Chepstow. SO 5300
Chapel Hill Lincs 45 F5* vil 3m/5km E of Billinghay. TF 2054
Chapel Hill N Yorks 49 F6* loc 2km N of Fenwick. SE 5818
Chapel Hill N Yorks 49 E3* ham 6m/10km SE of Harrogate. SE 3446
Chapelhill Tayside 72 D2* loc 3m/4km N of Methven. NO 0030
Chapelhill Tayside 73 E3* loc 3m/5km W of Errol. NO 2021
Chapelhouse Cumbria 59 H5* loc 2m/4km NW of Carlisle. NY 3759
Chapel House Lancs 42 A1 loc in W part of Skelmersdale. SD 4706
Chapelhouse Reservoir Cumbria 52 C2* small resr 1m SE of Uldale. NY 2635
Chapel Island Cumbria 46 D1* small island in R Leven estuary 1m SE of Hammerside Pt. SD 3275
Chapel Knapp Wilts 16 D4* loc adjoining vil of Gastard to S, 4m/7km SW of Chippenham. ST 8868
Chapelknowe D & G 59 G4 vil 3m/5km NE of Kirkpatrick-Fleming. NY 3173
Chapel Lawn Salop 34 A6 ham 3m/5km S of Clun. SO 3176
Chapel le Dale N Yorks 48 A1 ham 4m/7km NE of Ingleton. SD 7477
Chapel Leigh Som 7 H2* ham 2m/4km N of Milverton. ST 1229
Chapel, Lower Powys 25 E4 vil 5m/7km N of Brecon. SO 0235
Chapel Milton Derbys 43 F3* loc 1km N of Chapel-en-le-Frith. SK 0581
Chapel Ness Fife 73 G4 headland at W end of bay enclosing Elie harbour. NT 4899
Chapel of Garioch Grampian 83 F4 vil 4m/6km NW of Inverurie. The Maiden Stone (A.M.) 1m NW, 9c inscribed Celtic cross. NJ 7124
Chapel Point Cornwall 3 E4 headland at S end of Mevagissey Bay 2km SE of Mevagissey. SX 0243
Chapel Point Dyfed 22 D6* headland at SE end of Caldy I. Lighthouse. SS 1495
Chapel Point Lincs 45 H4 headland 1m N of Chapel St Leonards. TF 5673
Chapel Row Berks 18 B4 vil 6m/10km E of Newbury. SU 5669
Chapel Row Essex 20 D2* loc adjoining Woodham Ferrers to NW 7m/11km SE of Chelmsford. TL 7900
Chapels Cumbria 52 C6 loc 3m/5km SE of Broughton in Furness. SD 2383
Chapel St Leonards Lincs 45 H4 coastal vil 6m/9km N of Skegness. TF 5572
Chapel Stile Cumbria 52 C4 vil 4m/6km W of Ambleside. NY 3205
Chapelthorpe W Yorks 49 E6* loc in Wakefield 3m/5km S of city centre. SE 3215
Chapelton Devon 6 D3 ham 5m/8km SE of Barnstaple. SS 5726
Chapelton H'land 81 H5* loc in Badenoch and Strathspey dist 2m/3km W of Boat of Garten. NH 9119
Chapelton S'clyde 64 D4 vil 3m/5km NW of Strathaven. NS 6848
Chapel Town Cornwall 2 D3* ham 6m/9km SE of Newquay. SW 8855
Chapeltown Grampian 82 B5 loc 5m/8km E of Tomintoul. NJ 2421
Chapeltown Lancs 47 G6 vil 4m/7km N of Bolton. SD 7315
Chapeltown S Yorks 43 H2 loc 6m/9km N of Sheffield. SK 3596
Chapel, Upper (Capel Uchaf) Powys 25 E4 ham 8m/13km N of Brecon. SO 0040
Chapmanslade Wilts 16 D6 vil 4m/6km SW of Westbury. ST 8247
Chapman's Pool Dorset 9 F6* small bay 2km N of St Alban's Hd. SY 9577
Chapmans Well Devon 6 C5* ham 6m/9km N of Launceston. SX 3593
Chapmore End Herts 29 G6 ham 3m/4km N of Hertford. TL 3216
Chappel Essex 30 D5 vil 5m/7km E of Halstead. TL 8928
Char 8 B5* r flowing through Marshwood Vale in Dorset and into Lyme Bay at Charmouth. SY 3693
Charaton Cornwall 3 G2* loc 4m/6km W of Callington. SX 3069
Chard Som 8 B3 mkt tn in elevated position 12m/19km SE of Taunton. Light industries include lace, twine, pencils, shirts. **Chard Resr** to N. ST 3208
Chardleigh Green Som 8 B3* ham 2km N of Chard. ST 3110
Chard, South Som 8 B4* vil 2m/3km S of Chard. ST 3205
Chardstock Devon 8 B4 vil 3m/5km S of Chard. ST 3104
Charfield Avon 16 C2 vil 3m/4km W of Wotton-under-Edge. ST 7292
Charford H & W 26 D1* S dist of Bromsgrove. SO 9569
Charford, North Hants 9 H2 ham 5m/8km NE of Fordingbridge. SU 1919
Charing Kent 13 E2 small tn on hillside below Pilgrims' Way 6m/9km NW of Ashford. Scant remains of former Archbishop's Palace. Loc of **C. Heath** 2m/3km W. TQ 9549
Charing Cross Dorset 9 H3* loc adjoining Alderholt and 2m/4km SW of Fordingbridge. SU 1112
Charing Cross London 19 G3 cross-roads at N end of Whitehall in City of Westminster. Rd distances from London are measured from this point. Rly stn of same name is in Strand nearby. TQ 3080
Charingworth Glos 27 F4* ham 3m/5km E of Chipping Campden. SP 2039
Charlbury Oxon 27 G5 par and small tn 6m/9km SE of Chipping Norton. SP 3519
Charlcombe Avon 16 C4 vil 2m/3km N of Bath. ST 7567
Charlcutt Wilts 17 E4 ham 3m/5km N of Calne. ST 9875
Charlecote Warwicks 27 G2 vil 4m/7km E of Stratford-upon-Avon. **C. Park** (NT), 16c hse in deer park. SP 2656
Charles Devon 7 E2 ham 5m/8km N of S Molton. SS 6832
Charleshill Surrey 11 E1 loc 4m/6km SE of Farnham. SU 8944
Charleston S'clyde 64 C3 dist of Paisley 1m S of tn centre. NS 4862
Charleston Tayside 73 F1 vil 1km S of Glamis. NO 3845
Charlestown Cornwall 3 E3 dist to SE of St Austell. China clay port. SX 0351
Charlestown Derbys 43 E2* loc adjoining Glossop to S. SK 0392
Charlestown Dorset 8 D6* loc 2m/3km W of Weymouth. SY 6579
Charlestown Fife 65 G1 vil and small port on N side of Firth of Forth 3m/5km SW of Dunfermline. NT 0683
Charlestown Grampian 77 H1 loc 4m/6km S of Aberdeen. NJ 9300
Charlestown Grampian 83 H1 loc on NE coast at N end of St Combs. NK 0563
Charlestown Gtr Manchester 42 D2* dist of Salford 2km NW of tn centre. SD 8100
Charlestown Gtr Manchester 42 D1* dist of Manchester 4m/6km NE of city centre. SD 8703
Charlestown H'land 78 F2 vil at head of Gair Loch, W coast of Ross and Cromarty dist, 2km S of Gairloch vil. NG 8074
Charlestown H'land 81 F3 loc in Ross and Cromarty dist on N shore of Beauly Firth 1m W of N Kessock. NH 6448
Charlestown Lincs 37 E1* loc 1km N of Ancaster. SK 9844
Charlestown W Yorks 48 D4* S dist of Baildon. SE 1538
Charlestown W Yorks 48 C5* vil on R Calder 2km W of Hebden Br. SD 9726
Charlestown of Aberlour Grampian 82 B3 small distillery tn on right bank of R Spey 4m/6km S of Rothes. Also known as Aberlour. NJ 2643
Charles Tye Suffolk 31 E3* ham 4m/7km SW of Stowmarket. TM 0252
Charlesworth Derbys 43 E2 vil 2m/3km W of Glossop. SK 0092
Charleton, East and **West** Devon 4 D6 vils in par of Charleton 2m/3km SE of Kingsbridge. SX 7542
Charlinch Som 8 A1* ham 4m/6km W of Bridgwater. 1km SE, loc of **Lit Charlinch.** ST 2337
Charlotteville Surrey 11 F1* SE dist of Guildford. TQ 0049
Charlton Cleveland 55 E3* ham 2m/4km E of Guisborough. NZ 6415
Charlton Hants 10 B1 loc in NW part of Andover. SU 3547
Charlton Herts 29 F5 loc in SW part of Hitchin. TL 1728
Charlton H & W 26 D1* loc 2km E of Stourport. SO 8371
Charlton H & W 27 E3 vil 2m/3km NW of Evesham. SP 0145
Charlton London 20 B4 loc in borough of Greenwich 7m/12km E of Charing Cross. Community centre and library at **Charlton Hse,** Jacobean manor hse. TQ 4177
Charlton Northants 28 A4 vil 4m/6km W of Brackley. SP 5236
Charlton Oxon 17 H3 E dist of Wantage. SU 4088
Charlton Salop 34 C3* ham 4m/6km W of Wellington. Mound of medieval cas. SJ 5911
Charlton Som 16 B6* loc on E side of Shepton Mallet. ST 6343
Charlton Som 16 C6 ham 2m/3km S of Radstock. ST 6852
Charlton Som 8 B2* ham astride Bridgwater and Taunton Canal 4m/7km E of Taunton. ST 2926
Charlton Surrey 19 E4 loc on E edge of Queen Mary Resr 2m/3km W of Sunbury. TQ 0869
Charlton Wilts 16 D3 vil 2m/3km NE of Malmesbury. ST 9688
Charlton Wilts 17 F5* vil 2km NW of Upavon. SU 1156
Charlton Wilts 9 H2 vil in R Avon valley 5m/7km S of Salisbury. SU 1723
Charlton W Sussex 11 E4 vil below S Downs 1km E of Singleton. SU 8812
Charlton Abbots Glos 27 E5 ham 3m/4km S of Winchcombe. SP 0324
Charlton Adam Som 8 D2 vil 4m/7km NE of Ilchester. ST 5328
Charlton Hill Salop 34 C4* loc and hill 2m/3km SE of Wroxeter. SJ 5807
Charlton Kings Glos 26 D5/27 E5* tn adjoining Cheltenham to E. SO 9620
Charlton Mackrell Som 8 C2 vil 3m/5km E of Somerton. ST 5228
Charlton Marshall Dorset 9 F4 vil on R Stour 2m/3km SE of Blandford Forum. ST 8806
Charlton Musgrove Som 9 E2* vil 1m NE of Wincanton. ST 7229
Charlton, North Nthmb 67 H6 ham 6m/10km N of Alnwick. NU 1622
Charlton-on-Otmoor Oxon 28 B6 vil 4m/7km S of Bicester. SP 5615
Charlton on the Hill Dorset 9 F4* ham adjoining Charlton Marshall SW of Blandford Forum. ST 8904
Charlton, South Nthmb 67 H6 ham 5m/7km N of Alnwick. NU 1620
Charlwood E Sussex 12 A3* loc 2m/3km W of Forest Row. TQ 3934
Charlwood W Sussex 11 H1 vil on W side of London (Gatwick) Airport 3m/5km NW of Crawley. TQ 2441
Charlynch Som. See Charlinch.
Charminster Dorset 9 E5 vil 2km N of Dorchester. SY 6892
Charminster Dorset 9 G4* dist of Bournemouth 2m/3km NE of tn centre. SZ 0994
Charmouth Dorset 8 B5 small resort on coast 2m/3km NE of Lyme Regis. SY 3693
Charndon Bucks 28 B5 vil 6m/9km E of Bicester. SP 6724
Charney Bassett Oxon 17 G2 vil 4m/7km N of Wantage. SU 3894
Charnock Green Lancs 47 F6* loc 2m/3km W of Chorley. SD 5516
Charnock Richard Lancs 47 F6 vil 2m/4km SW of Chorley. SD 5515
Charnwood 119 admin dist of Leics.
Charnwood Forest Leics 36 B3 elevated area, former hunting ground, SW of Loughborough, composed of pre-Cambrian rocks which obtrude above ground at various points. Quarrying is carried on. The area attains height of 916 ft or 279 metres at Bardon Hill, 2m/4km E of Coalville. SK 4914
Charsfield Suffolk 31 F3 vil 3m/5km W of Wickham Mkt. TM 2556
Chart Corner Kent 20 D6* loc 4m/7km SE of Maidstone. TQ 7950
Charter Alley Hants 18 B5 ham 5m/7km NW of Basingstoke. SU 5957
Charterhall Borders 67 E4 motor-racing circuit 4m/6km E of Greenlaw. NT 7646
Charterhouse Som 16 A5 ham on Mendip Hills 3m/5km NE of Cheddar. ST 5055
Charterhouse Surrey 11 F1 boys' school on NW outskirts of Godalming. Founded in London in 1611, removed to Godalming in 1872. SU 9645
Charterville Allotments Oxon 27 G6 loc 3m/5km W of Witney. SP 3110
Chart, Great Kent 13 E3 vil 2m/3km W of Ashford. TQ 9842
Chartham Kent 13 F2 vil on R Gt Stour 3m/5km SW of Canterbury. TR 1055
Chartham Hatch Kent 21 F6 vil 3m/5km W of Canterbury. TR 1056

Chart, Little Kent 13 E2 vil 3m/4km S of Charing. Site of Roman bath hse to W. TQ 9445

Chartridge Bucks 18 D2 vil 2m/4km NW of Chesham. SP 9303

Chart Sutton Kent 12 D2 vil 4m/6km NW of Headcorn. Roman bldg to N. TQ 8049

Chart, The Kent 20 B6• loc 2m/3km S of Brasted. TQ 4652

Chart, The Surrey 20 B6• vil 2m/3km SW of Westerham. TQ 4251

Chartway Street Kent 12 D2• loc 4m/6km N of Headcorn. TQ 8350

Chartwell Kent 20 B6• hse and grnds (NT) 2m/3km S of Westerham. Formerly home of Sir Winston Churchill. TQ 4551

Charvil Berks 18 C4• vil 1m W of Twyford. SU 7775

Charwelton Northants 28 A2 vil 5m/8km SW of Daventry. SP 5356

Chase Cross London 20 B3• N dist of Romford, borough of Havering. TQ 5191

Chase End Street H & W 26 C4 loc 4m/6km SE of Ledbury, below E slope of **Chase End Hill,** at S end of Malvern Hills. SO 7635

Chase Side London 19 G2• loc in borough of Enfield 1km N of Enfield tn centre and 11m/17km N of Charing Cross. TQ 3297

Chase, The Hants 17 H5• small woodland nature reserve (NT) threaded by chalk stream 1km NE of vil of Broad Laying. SU 4462

Chasetown Staffs 35 F3 urban loc 2m/3km N of Brownhills. SK 0408

Chasewater W Midlands 35 F3/F4• lake 2km NW of Brownhills. Small part of lake is in Staffs. SK 0307

Chastleton Oxon 27 F4 vil 4m/7km NW of Chipping Norton. Early 17c Cotswold manor hse. SP 2429

Chasty Devon 6 C5 ham just S of Holsworthy. SS 3402

Chatburn Lancs 48 A4 vil 2m/3km NE of Clitheroe. Extensive quarries between here and Clitheroe. SD 7644

Chatcull Staffs 35 E1• ham 2km W of Standon. SJ 7934

Chater 37 E4 r rising S of Whatborough Hill, E of Tilton, Leics, and flowing E into R Welland 2m/3km W of Stamford. TF 0005

Chatham Kent 20 D5 tn on R Medway between Rochester and Gillingham, 28m/45km E of London. Naval and military base. Light industry. TQ 7567

Chatham Mid Glam 15 G3• loc adjoining Machen to E. ST 2188

Chatham Green Essex 30 B6• ham 5m/8km N of Chelmsford. TL 7115

Chathill Nthmb 67 H5 ham 4m/6km SW of Seahouses. NU 1826

Chat Hill W Yorks 48 D5• loc in Bradford 3m/5km W of city centre. SE 1132

Chat Moss Gtr Manchester 42 C2 extensive area of peat bog, now largely reclaimed, to W of Eccles. Traversed by Liverpool and Manchester rly (George Stephenson, 1829). SJ 7097

Chatsworth House Derbys 43 G4 mansion of 17c–19c, seat of Duke of Devonshire, in R Derwent valley 7m/12km W of Chesterfield. Large formal grnds. SK 2670

Chatter End Essex 29 H5• loc 3m/4km N of Bishop's Stortford. TL 4725

Chatteris Cambs 37 H5 small tn 7m/11km S of March. TL 3985

Chatterley Staffs 42 D6• loc 3m/5km N of Newcastle-under-Lyme. SJ 8451

Chattern Hill Surrey 19 E4• urban loc adjoining Ashford to E, 3m/5km E of Staines. TQ 0871

Chattisham Suffolk 31 E4 vil 4m/7km E of Hadleigh. TM 0942

Chattle Hill Warwicks 35 G5• loc 1m N of Coleshill. SP 1990

Chatton Nthmb 67 G5 vil 4m/6km E of Wooler. NT 0528

Chatwell, Great Staffs 35 E3 ham 4m/7km SE of Newport. SJ 7914

Chaulden Herts 19 E1• W dist of Hemel Hempstead. TL 0306

Chaul End Beds 29 E5• loc 2m/4km W of Luton. TL 0521

Chawleigh Devon 7 E4 vil 2m/3km SE of Chulmleigh. SS 6814

Chawley Oxon 17 H1 loc 3m/5km W of Oxford. SP 4604

Chawston Beds 29 F2 loc 3m/5km SW of St Neots. TL 1556

Chawton Hants 10 D1 vil 2km SW of Alton. Jane Austen's hse now a museum. SU 7037

Chazey Heath Oxon 18 B4• loc 3m/5km NW of Reading. SU 6977

Cheadle Gtr Manchester 42 D3 tn 3m/4km W of Stockport. **C. Heath** loc 1m NE. **C. Hulme** loc 2km S. SJ 8588

Cheadle Staffs 43 E6 tn 8m/13km E of Stoke-on-Trent. SK 0043

Cheam London 19 F5 dist in borough of Sutton 1m W of Sutton tn centre. Loc of **N Cheam** 1m N. TQ 2463

Cheapside Berks 18 D4• loc on SW edge of Windsor Gt Park 1m E of Ascot. SU 9469

Chearsley Bucks 18 C1 vil 3m/5km N of Thame. SP 7110

Chebsey Staffs 35 E2• vil 2m/3km E of Eccleshall. SJ 8628

Checkendon Oxon 18 B3 vil 4m/7km E of Goring. SU 6682

Checkley Ches 42 C6 loc 2m/4km N of Woore. **C. Hall,** late 17c. **C. Green** loc to SW. SJ 7346

Checkley H & W 26 B4 ham 5m/8km E of Hereford. SO 5938

Checkley Staffs 35 F1 vil 5m/8km NW of Uttoxeter. SK 0237

Chedburgh Suffolk 30 C2 vil 6m/10km SW of Bury St Edmunds. TL 7957

Cheddar Som 16 A6 tn on S slopes of Mendip Hills 8m/12km NW of Wells, at foot of **C. Gorge,** deep limestone gorge with large caves much visited by tourists. Cliffs on N side of gorge (NT). ST 4553

Cheddington Bucks 28 D5 vil 4m/6km N of Tring. SP 9217

Cheddleton Staffs 43 E5 vil 3m/5km S of Leek. **C. Heath** loc 1m NE. SJ 9752

Cheddon Fitzpaine Som 8 A2 vil 2m/4km NE of Taunton. 1m NW, vil of **Upr Cheddon.** ST 2427

Chedglow Wilts 16 D2 loc 4m/6km N of Malmesbury. ST 9493

Chedgrave Norfolk 39 G5 vil adjoining Loddon to N across R Chet, 7m/11km NW of Beccles. TM 3699

Chedington Dorset 8 C4 vil 4m/6km SE of Crewkerne. Above vil, **Winyard's Gap** (NT), area of woodland. ST 4805

Chediston Suffolk 31 G1• vil 2m/3km W of Halesworth. Loc of **C. Green** 1km NW. TM 3577

Chedworth Glos 27 E6 vil 4m/7km SW of Northleach. SP 0511

Chedzoy Som 8 B1 vil 3m/5km E of Bridgwater. ST 3437

Cheek, North N Yorks 55 G4• headland on North Sea coast 1m NE of Robin Hood's Bay. Also known as Ness Pt. NZ 9506

Cheek, South N Yorks 55 G4• headland at S end of Robin Hood's Bay on North Sea coast 1km N of Ravenscar. Also known as Old Peak. NZ 9802

Cheesden Gtr Manchester 47 H6 loc 2m/4km SE of Edenfield. SD 8216

Cheesman's Green Kent 13 F3• loc 3m/4km SE of Ashford. TR 0238

Cheetham Gtr Manchester 42 D2• dist of Manchester 2km N of city centre. SD 8300

Cheetham Hill Gtr Manchester 42 D1 dist of Manchester 2m/4km N of city centre. SD 8401

Cheetwood Gtr Manchester 42 D2 dist of Manchester 2km N of city centre. SD 8300

Cheglinch Devon 6 D1• loc 3m/5km S of Ilfracombe. SS 5143

Chelborough, East Dorset 8 D4• ham 2m/3km NW of Evershot. ST 5505

Chelborough, West Dorset 8 D4 ham 2m/3km W of Evershot. ST 5405

Chelburn Reservoirs Gtr Manchester 48 C6• two resrs on Chelburn Moor 2km NE of Littleborough. SD 9518

Cheldon Devon 7 E4• ham 3m/5km E of Chulmleigh. SS 7313

Chelford Ches 42 D4 vil 6m/10km W of Macclesfield. SJ 8174

Chelker Reservoir N Yorks 48 C3• resr 2km NW of Addingham. SE 0551

Chellaston Derbys 36 A2 dist of Derby 4m/7km SE of tn centre. SK 3730

Chell, Great Staffs 42 D5• loc 1m NE of Tunstall. SJ 8652

Chellington Beds 28 D2 vil 7m/11km NW of Bedford, adjoining vil of Carlton. TL 9555

Chells Herts 29 F5 loc in NE part of Stevenage. TL 2624

Chelmarsh Salop 34 D5 vil 3m/5km S of Bridgnorth. Resr to E. SO 7287

Chelmer 21 E1 r rising near Thaxted, Essex, and flowing S to Chelmsford and thence E to join R Blackwater at Maldon. TL 8507

Chelmondiston Suffolk 31 F4 vil 4m/6km NW of Shotley Gate. TM 2037

Chelmorton Derbys 43 F4 vil 4m/7km SE of Buxton. SK 1170

Chelmsford Essex 20 D1 cathedral and county tn on R Chelmer 30m/48km NE of London. Industries include electrical and radio equipment. TL 7006

Chelmsley Wood W Midlands 35 G5• suburb 7m/12km E of Birmingham. SP 1886

Chelsea London 19 F4• dist SW of Central London and royal borough (Kensington and Chelsea). Situated on N bank of R Thames, crossed here by Battersea, Albert, and Chelsea Brs. Royal C. Hospital, by Wren, houses pensioners. Barracks. TQ 2778

Chelsfield London 20 B5 vil 2m/3km SE of Orpington. TQ 4864

Chelsham Surrey 20 A5 loc 1m E of Warlingham. TQ 3759

Chelston Heath Som 8 A2• ham 2km E of Wellington. ST 1621

Chelsworth Suffolk 30 D3 vil 4m/7km NW of Hadleigh. TL 9848

Chelt 26 D5 r rising to E of Cheltenham and flowing W through the tn and into R Severn 5m/8km N of Gloucester. SO 8426

Cheltenham Glos 26 D5 largely residential tn, formerly a spa, 8m/12km E of Gloucester. Industries include mnfre of aircraft components. Many Regency and Victn bldgs. SO 9422

Cheltenham Gwent 25 G6• loc between Blackrock and Clydach, E of Brynmawr. SO 2212

Chelveston Northants 29 E1 vil 2m/3km E of Higham Ferrers. SP 9969

Chelvey Avon 16 A4 ham 4m/7km SE of Clevedon. ST 4668

Chelwood Avon 16 B5 vil 4m/7km S of Keynsham. ST 6361

Chelwood Common E Sussex 12 B4• loc 2m/3km E of Horsted Keynes. TQ 4129

Chelwood Gate E Sussex 12 B4 ham 3m/5km S of Forest Row. TQ 4130

Chelworth Wilts 16 D2 loc 5m/8km NE of Malmesbury. ST 9794

Chelworth Lower Green Wilts 17 E2• ham 2km SW of Cricklade. SU 0892

Chelworth Upper Green Wilts 17 E2• ham 2km W of Cricklade. SU 0892

Cheney Longville Salop 34 B5• ham 2m/3km NW of Craven Arms. SO 4284

Chenies Bucks 19 E2 vil 4m/6km E of Amersham. Site of Roman villa 2km W beside R Chess. TQ 0198

Chepstow (Cas-gwent) Gwent 16 A2 tn on R Wye 15m/24km E of Newport. Remains of cas (A.M.), partly Norman but mainly of 14c. ST 5393

Chequerbent Gtr Manchester 42 C1• loc 2km E of Westhoughton. SD 6706

Chequerfield W Yorks 49 F6• loc adjoining Pontefract to SE. SE 4621

Chequers Bucks 18 C1 Prime Minister's country residence 3m/4km NE of Princes Risborough. Part dates from 16c. SP 8405

Chequers Corner Norfolk 38 A4• loc 3m/4km E of Wisbech. TF 4908

Chequer, The Clwyd 34 B1 loc 3m/5km W of Whitchurch. SJ 4940

Cherbury Camp Oxon 17 G2 ancient earthwork 1m N of Charney Bassett. SU 3796

Cherhill Wilts 17 E4 vil 3m/5km E of Calne. SU 0370

Cherington Glos 16 D2 vil 4m/6km E of Nailsworth. ST 9098

Cherington Warwicks 27 G4 vil 3m/5km SE of Shipston on Stour. SP 2936

Cheriton Devon 7 E1• loc 2m/3km SE of Lynton. SS 7346

Cheriton Dyfed 22 C6 ham 3m/4km S of Pembroke. Also known as Stackpole Elidor. SR 9897

Cheriton Hants 10 C2 vil 3m/4km S of New Alresford. 1m NE, site of Civil War battle, 1644. SU 5828

Cheriton Kent 13 G3 W dist of Folkestone. TR 2036

Cheriton W Glam 23 F6 vil near W end of Gower peninsula 2m/4km S of Whitford Pt and 13m/20km W of Swansea. SS 4593

Cheriton Bishop Devon 7 F5 vil 6m/10km SW of Crediton. SX 7793

Cheriton Cross Devon 7 F5 ham adjoining Cheriton Bishop, 6m/10km SW of Crediton. SX 7793

Cheriton Fitzpaine Devon 7 F4 vil 4m/7km NE of Crediton. SS 8606

Cheriton, Higher Devon 7 H5• loc 4m/6km W of Honiton. **Lr Cheriton** loc adjacent to N. ST 1000

Cheriton, North Som 9 E2 vil 2m/4km SW of Wincanton. ST 6925

Cheriton, South Som 9 E2 vil 3m/4km SW of Wincanton. ST 6924

Cherrington Salop 34 D3 vil 5m/8km W of Newport. SJ 6619

Cherry Brook 4 C3• stream in Devon rising N of Two Bridges on Dartmoor and flowing S into W Dart R 2m/3km below Two Bridges. SX 6373

Cherry Burton Humberside 51 E4 vil 3m/5km NW of Beverley. SE 9842

Cherry Green Essex 30 A5• ham 3m/4km W of Thaxted. TL 5729

Cherry Hinton Cambs 30 A2 SE dist of Cambridge. TL 4856

Cherry Orchard H & W 26 D2 S dist of Worcester. SO 8553

Cherry Tree Gtr Manchester 43 E2• loc 1m E of Romiley. SJ 9590

Cherry Tree Lancs 47 G5• loc 2m/3km SW of Blackburn. SD 6526

Cherry Trees Herts 19 F1• loc 2m/3km E of Harpenden. TL 1614

Cherry Willingham Lincs 45 E4 vil 4m/6km E of Lincoln. SK 0372

Chertsey Surrey 19 E5 tn on right bank of R Thames 3m/5km S of Staines. Seven-arched 18c br spans r. Scant remains of 7c abbey. TQ 0466

Cherwell 119 admin dist of Oxon.

Cherwell 18 A1 r rising N of Woodford Halse, Northants, and flowing S through Banbury into R Thames at Oxford. SP 5105

Cheselbourne Dorset 9 E4 vil 4m/6km N of Puddletown. SY 7699

Chesham Bucks 18 D2 tn on S side of Chiltern Hills 25m/40km NW of London. SP 9601

Chesham Gtr Manchester 42 D1• dist of Bury 1m N of tn centre. SD 8012

Chesham Bois Bucks 18 D2 suburb between Chesham and Amersham. SU 9699

Cheshire 116,117 north-western county of England, bounded by Merseyside, Gtr Manchester, Derbyshire, Staffordshire, Salop, and the Welsh county of Clwyd. In the NW it reaches the estuaries of Rs Dee and Mersey. The country is mainly flat, except in the NE, where the foothills of the Pennines enter the county. The rural areas, which are mostly in the S and W, are noted for dairy products. Much of the county is industrialised; there are coal mines, large salt mines with an associated chemicals industry, silk and cotton mills, and engineering. Chief tns are the cathedral city of Chester; Congleton, Crewe, Ellesmere Port, Macclesfield, Northwich, Warrington, and Wilmslow. Chief rs are the Dane, Dee, and Weaver.

Cheshunt Herts 20 A2 tn in R Lea valley 14m/22km N of London. Fruit and vegetables grown under glass. TL 3502

Cheshunt Field Essex 30 D5• loc 3m/4km SW of Colchester containing sites of a Roman temple and a Roman theatre. TL 9622

Chesil Bank (or Chesil Beach) Dorset 8 D6 shingle bank stretching from Abbotsbury to Isle of Portland. SY 5882

Cheslyn Hay Staffs 35 F4 loc 2m/3km S of Cannock. SJ 9707

Chess 19 E2 r rising at Chesham in Bucks and flowing SE into R Colne to E of Rickmansworth, Herts. TQ 0694

Chessetts Wood Warwicks 27 F1• ham 2m/4km E of Hockley Heath. SP 1873

Chessington London 19 F5 loc in borough of Kingston 4m/6km S of Kingston tn centre. Zoological Gardens to S. TQ 1863

Chestall Staffs 35 F3• loc 4m/6km S of Rugeley. SK 0512

Chester Ches 42 A4 county tn and cathedral city on R Dee 34m/54km SW of Manchester and 15m/24km SE of Birkenhead, on site of Roman tn of *Deva.* Medieval walls (A.M.) well preserved. Various industries incl light engineering, electrical components. SJ 4066

Chesterblade Som 8 D1 vil 3m/5km SE of Shepton Mallet. ST 6641

Chesterfield Derbys 43 H4 mkt and industrial tn 10m/16km S of Sheffield. Industries include coal, iron, engineering. Ch has famous twisted spire. SK 3871
Chesterfield Canal 44 C2-B3 canal formerly linking Chesterfield, Derbys, with R Trent at Stockwith. Now navigable only from Stockwith to Worksop, Notts.
Chesterford, Great Essex 30 A3 vil on R Cam 3m/5km NW of Saffron Walden. Site of Roman tn. TL 5042
Chesterford, Little Essex 30 A4 vil 3m/4km NW of Saffron Walden. TL 5141
Chesterhill Lothian 66 B2* loc 3m/5km SE of Dalkeith. NT 3765
Chesterholme Nthmb 60 D5 loc on site of Roman fort of *Vindolanda*, 2km NW of Bardon Mill. NY 7766
Chesterhope Nthmb 60 D3* loc 5m/8km S of Otterburn. NY 8985
Chester-le-Street Durham 61 G6 tn on site of Roman military stn of *Concangium* beside R Wear 6m/9km N of Durham. Coal-mining, light industry. See also Lambton Castle; Lumley Castle. NZ 2751
Chester, Little Derbys 36 A1* loc in Derby 1km N of tn centre. Site of Roman fort of *Derventio*. SK 3537
Chester Moor Durham 61 G6* vil 2km S of Chester-le-Street. NZ 2649
Chesters Borders 60 C1 vil 5m/9km NW of Carter Bar. NT 6210
Chesters Nthmb 60 D4 remains (A.M.) of Roman fort of *Cilurnum* on Hadrian's Wall, 1km W of Chollerford and 2m/3km NE of Fourstones. NY 9170
Chesters, The Lothian 66 C1* earthworks of ancient fort (A.M.), nearly 1m S of Drem. Similar site of same name 3m/5km S of Dunbar. NT 5078
Chesterton Cambs 29 H2 NE dist of Cambridge. TL 4660
Chesterton Cambs 37 F5 vil 5m/7km SW of Peterborough. TL 1295
Chesterton Oxon 28 B5 vil 2m/3km W of Bicester. SP 5621
Chesterton Salop 34 D4/35 E4 ham 5m/8km NE of Bridgnorth. SO 7897
Chesterton Staffs 42 D6 loc 3m/4km N of Newcastle-under-Lyme tn centre, on site of Roman settlement. SJ 8349
Chesterton Warwicks 27 G2* loc 5m/9km SE of Leamington. Site of Roman bldg to W. SP 3558
Chesterton Green Warwicks 27 G2* ham 5m/8km SE of Leamington. SP 3458
Chesterton, Little Oxon 28 B5* ham 2m/4km SW of Bicester. SP 5520
Chesterwood Nthmb 60 D5 ham 1m NW of Haydon Br. 1Y 8365
Chestfield Kent 13 G1* SE suburb of Whitstable. TR 1365
Chestnut Street Kent 20 D5* loc 2m/3km W of Sittingbourne. TQ 8763
Cheston Devon 4 C5* ham 2m/3km SW of S Brent. SX 6858
Cheswardine Salop 34 D2 vil 4m/6km SE of Mkt Drayton. SJ 7129
Cheswell Salop 34 D3* loc 2m/4km SW of Newport. SJ 7117
Cheswick Nthmb 67 G4 ham 5m/7km SE of Berwick-upon-Tweed. **C. Buildings** loc to SW. **C. Sands** on coast to E. NU 0346
Cheswick Green W Midlands 35 G6* loc 3m/4km NW of Hockley Heath. SP 1375
Chet 39 G4 r rising NW of E Poringland, Norfolk, and flowing E into R Yare 3m/5km NE of Loddon. TG 4001
Chetney Kent 21 E4* loc on marshland 2m/3km NW of Iwade. TQ 8870
Chetnole Dorset 8 D3 vil 6m/9km SE of Yeovil. ST 6008
Chettiscombe Devon 7 G4* loc 2m/3km NE of Tiverton. SS 9614
Chettisham Cambs 38 A6 ham 2m/3km N of Ely. TL 5483
Chettle Dorset 9 F3 vil 3m/5km S of Tollard Royal. ST 9513
Chetton Salop 34 D5* vil 4m/6km SW of Bridgnorth. SO 6690
Chetwode Bucks 28 B4 ham 5m/7km SW of Buckingham. SP 6429
Chetwynd Aston Salop 34 D3 vil 2km SE of Newport. SJ 7517
Chetwynd End Salop 34 D3* loc in N part of Newport. **C. Park** loc 2km N. SJ 7419
Cheveley Cambs 30 B2 vil 3m/5km SE of Newmarket. TL 6860
Chevening Kent 20 B5 ham 3m/5km NW of Sevenoaks. TQ 4857
Cheverell, Great Wilts 17 E5 vil 5m/8km SW of Devizes. ST 9854
Cheverell, Little Wilts 17 E6 vil 5m/8km S of Devizes. ST 9853
Cheverell's Green Herts 29 E6 loc at SW end of Markyate, 4m/7km SW of Luton. TL 0515
Chevet W Yorks 49 E6* loc 4m/6km S of Wakefield. SE 3415
Chevington Suffolk 30 C2 vil 5m/8km SW of Bury St Edmunds. TL 7859
Chevington Drift Nthmb 61 G2 vil 3m/5km S of Amble. NZ 2699
Chevington, East Nthmb 61 G2* loc adjoining Chevington Drift to S, 3m/5km S of Amble. NZ 2699
Chevington, West Nthmb 61 G2 ham 2m/3km NW of Widdrington. NZ 2297
Chevinside Derbys 43 H6* loc 1km SW of Belper across R Derwent. SK 3446
Chevin, The W Yorks 49 E4 steep ridge S of Otley. SE 2044
Cheviot Hills 67 F6 range of hills extending along border of England and Scotland and attaining in **The Cheviot** a height of 2676 ft or 816 metres. Hills provide pasturage for sheep, esp breed known as Cheviots. Part of area on English side is used as artillery ranges. NT 9020
Chevithorne Devon 7 G3 vil 2m/4km NE of Tiverton. SS 9715
Chevy Chase, Battle of. See Otterburn.
Chew 16 B4* r rising at Chewton Mendip, Som, and flowing through Chew Valley Lake into R Avon at Keynsham, Avon. ST 6568
Chew Green Nthmb 60 D1* site of Roman camps, *Ad Fines*, at head of Coquetdale 6m/9km E of Carter Bar. NT 7808
Chew Magna Avon 16 B5 vil 6m/10km S of Bristol. ST 5763
Chew Moor Gtr Manchester 42 C1* loc in Bolton 3m/5km W of tn centre. SD 6607
Chew Reservoir Gtr Manchester 43 E1 resr near head of Chew Brook valley 5m/7km E of Mossley. SE 0301
Chew Stoke Avon 16 B5 vil 7m/11km S of Bristol. ST 5561
Chewton Keynsham Avon 16 B4 ham 2km S of Keynsham. ST 6566
Chewton Mendip Som 16 B6 vil below N slopes of Mendip Hills 6m/9km NE of Wells. ST 5953
Chew Valley Lake Avon 16 B5 large resr in valley of R Chew 8m/13km S of Bristol. ST 5760
Cheylesmore W Midlands 35 H6* loc in Coventry 1m S of city centre. SP 3377
Cheynies Shetland 89 E7* uninhabited island of 24 acres or 10 hectares 4m/6km W of Scalloway, Mainland. HU 3438
Chichacott Devon 7 E5* loc 2m/3km NE of Okehampton. SX 6096
Chicheley Bucks 28 D3 vil 2m/4km NE of Newport Pagnell. SP 9045
Chichester W Sussex 11 E4 county tn, the Roman *Noviomagus*, 9m/14km E of Havant, near head of **C. Harbour** (C. Channel), large inlet of sea with four main arms, or channels, E of Hayling I. Tn has cathedral, mainly Norman; 16c mkt cross; Festival Theatre of 1962. SU 8604
Chicken Head W Isles 88 C2 headland at S end of Eye Peninsula, Lewis. Offshore is **Chicken Rock,** with beacon. NB 4929
Chickenley W Yorks 49 E6* loc 2m/3km E of Dewsbury. **C. Heath** loc adjoining to N. SE 2721
Chicken Rock 46 A6 rock with lighthouse 1km SW of Caigher Pt, Calf of Man. SC 1463
Chickerell Dorset 8 D6 vil 3m/4km NW of Weymouth. SY 6480
Chickering Suffolk 31 F1 loc 2m/3km NW of Stradbroke. TM 2176
Chicklade Wilts 9 F1 vil 8m/12km NE of Shaftesbury. ST 9134
Chickney Essex 30 A5/B5 loc 3m/5km SW of Thaxted. TL 5728
Chicksands Beds 29 F4 par containing **C. Priory** 2km W of Shefford. TL 1239
Chicksgrove, Lower Wilts 9 G2 ham on R Nadder 2m/3km E of Tisbury. ST 9730
Chicksgrove, Upper Wilts 9 G2* ham on R Nadder 2km E of Tisbury. ST 9629
Chick, The Cornwall 2 C2* island (NT) off Kelsey Hd 3m/5km W of Newquay. SW 7661
Chidden Hants 10 D3 ham 4m/7km NW of Horndean. SU 6517
Chidden Holt Hants 10 D3* loc 1km SW of Chidden and 2km NE of Hambledon. SU 6516
Chiddingfold Surrey 11 F2 vil 5m/7km S of Milford. Site of Roman villa 2km E. SU 9635
Chiddingly E Sussex 12 B5 ham 4m/7km NW of Hailsham. TQ 5414
Chiddingstone Kent 12 B2 vil (partly NT) 4m/6km E of Edenbridge. Cas is 17c hse castellated in 19c Gothic revival. **C. Causeway** vil 2km NE. **C. Hoath** ham 2m/3km S. TQ 5045
Chideock Dorset 8 C5 vil near coast 3m/5km W of Bridport. 1km N, ham of **N Chideock.** SY 4292
Chidham W Sussex 11 E4 vil opp Bosham near head of Chichester Harbour (Bosham Channel). SU 7403
Chidswell W Yorks 49 E5 dist of Dewsbury 2km NE of tn centre. SE 2623
Chieflowman, Higher Devon 7 G3* ham 4m/6km NE of Tiverton. ST 0015
Chieveley Berks 17 H4 vil 4m/6km N of Newbury. SU 4773
Chignall St James Essex 20 C1 ham 3m/4km NW of Chelmsford. TL 6709
Chignall Smealy Essex 20 C1 ham 4m/6km NW of Chelmsford. TL 6611
Chigwell Essex 20 B2 tn 12m/19km NE of London. Loc of **C. Row** 2m/3km E. TQ 4493
Chilbolton Hants 10 B1 vil in R Test valley 4m/6km NE of Stockbridge. SU 3940
Chilcomb Hants 10 C2 ham 2m/3km SE of Winchester. SU 5028
Chilcombe Dorset 8 C5* ham 4m/7km E of Bridport. SY 5291
Chilcompton Som 16 B6 vil 2m/3km SW of Midsomer Norton. ST 6452
Chilcote Leics 35 H3 vil 6m/9km SW of Ashby de la Zouch. SK 2811
Childerditch Essex 20 C3 loc 3m/4km SE of Brentwood. TQ 6089
Childerley Cambs 29 G2 par with 19c hall on site of earlier bldg 6m/10km NW of Cambridge. TL 3561
Childer Thornton Ches 42 A3 vil 2m/4km W of Ellesmere Port. SJ 3677
Child Okeford Dorset 9 F3 vil in R Stour valley at SW end of Cranborne Chase 3m/5km E of Sturminster Newton. ST 8312
Childrey Oxon 17 G3 vil 2m/4km W of Wantage. SU 3687
Child's Ercall Salop 34 D2 vil 6m/10km NW of Newport. SJ 6625
Child's Hill London 19 F3* loc in borough of Barnet 5m/8km NW of Charing Cross. TQ 2486
Childswickham H & W 27 E4 vil 2m/3km NW of Broadway. SP 0738
Childwall Merseyside 42 A3 dist of Liverpool 5m/7km E of city centre. SJ 4189
Childwick Green Herts 19 F1 ham 2m/4km N of St Albans. TL 1410
Chilfrome Dorset 8 D4 vil 1m NW of Maiden Newton. SY 5898
Chilgrove W Sussex 11 E3 ham 3m/5km W of Singleton. SU 8214
Chilham Kent 21 F6 vil 6m/9km SW of Canterbury. Remains of medieval cas. TR 0653
Chilhampton Wilts 9 G1* loc beside R Wylye 2km N of Wilton. SU 0933
Chilla Devon 6 C5* loc 6m/10km E of Holsworthy. SS 4402
Chilland Hants 10 C2* loc 1km W of Itchen Abbas and 3m/5km NE of Winchester. SU 5232
Chillaton Devon 4 B3 vil 6m/9km NW of Tavistock. SX 4381
Chillenden Kent 13 G2 vil 3m/5km SE of Wingham. TR 2653
Chillerton Isle of Wight 10 B6 vil 3m/5km S of Newport. SZ 4984
Chillesford Suffolk 31 G3 vil 3m/4km NW of Orford. TM 3852
Chilley Devon 4 D5* loc 4m/7km NE of Kingsbridge. SX 7650
Chillingham Nthmb 67 G5 vil 4m/7km E of Wooler. Cas, 14c–19c. Chillingham herd of cattle in park. On far side of park, Ross Castle (NT), ancient hill fort. NU 0625
Chillington Devon 4 D6 4m/6km E of Kingsbridge. SX 7942
Chillington Som 8 C3 vil 4m/6km W of Crewkerne. To S, ham of **Hr Chillington.** ST 3811
Chillington Hall Staffs 35 E4 18c hse in spacious grnds laid out by Capability Brown. SJ 8606
Chilmark Wilts 9 G1 vil 8m/12km W of Wilton. ST 9732
Chilson Oxon 27 G5 vil 3m/4km W of Charlbury. SP 3119
Chilson Som 8 B4 ham 3m/5km S of Chard. **C. Common** loc 1km N. ST 3203
Chilsworthy Cornwall 4 B3* vil 1m W of Gunnislake. SX 4172
Chilsworthy Devon 6 C4 vil 2m/3km NW of Holsworthy. SS 3206
Chiltern 119 admin dist of Bucks.
Chiltern Hills 18 C2 range of chalk hills extending NE from R Thames valley in vicinity of Goring, Oxon, to N Herts. **Chiltern Hundreds:** area comprising Burnham, Desborough, and Stoke in Bucks, the Stewardship of which was formerly an office of profit under the Crown, now purely nominal but retained to enable a Member of Parliament voluntarily to resign his seat. SU 79
Chilthorne Domer Som 8 C3 vil 3m/5km NW of Yeovil. ST 5219
Chiltington, East E Sussex 12 A5* ham 4m/7km NW of Lewes. TQ 3715
Chiltington, West W Sussex 11 G3 vil 3m/5km E of Pulborough. TQ 0918
Chilton Bucks 18 B1 vil 4m/6km N of Thame. SP 6811
Chilton Devon 7 F4 loc 3m/5km NE of Crediton. SS 8604
Chilton Durham 54 C2 loc adjoining Ferryhill to SE. **Chilton Bldgs** loc 2km SW. NZ 3031
Chilton Oxon 18 A3 vil 4m/6km SW of Didcot. SU 4885
Chilton Suffolk 30 D4* loc 2km NE of Sudbury. TL 8942
Chilton Candover Hants 10 C1 ham 5m/8km N of New Alresford. SU 5940
Chilton Cantelo Som 8 D2* vil 4m/7km N of Yeovil. ST 5722
Chilton Foliat Wilts 17 G4 vil on R Kennet 2m/3km NW of Hungerford. SU 3270
Chilton Moor Tyne & Wear 61 G6* loc 1m SW of Houghton-le-Spring. NZ 3249
Chilton Polden Som 8 B1 vil on N side of Polden Hills 5m/8km NE of Bridgwater. ST 3739
Chilton Street Suffolk 30 C3 vil 2km NW of Clare. TL 7546
Chilton Trinity Som 8 B1 vil 2km N of Bridgwater. ST 2939
Chilvers Cotton Warwicks 36 A5 S dist of Nuneaton. SP 3690
Chilwell Notts 36 B1 loc adjoining Beeston to SW. SK 5135
Chilworth Hants 10 B3 vil 4m/6km N of Southampton. 1m S in built-up area, **C. Ring,** prehistoric fort. SU 4018
Chilworth Surrey 11 F1 loc 2m/4km SE of Guildford. TQ 0247
Chimney Street Suffolk 30 C3* loc 4m/6km NE of Haverhill. TL 7248
Chineham Hants 18 B5 vil adjoining Basingstoke to NE. SU 6554
Chingford London 20 A2 tn in borough of Waltham Forest 9m/15km NE of London Br. Dists of **C. Green** and **C. Hatch** are N and S respectively of tn centre. TQ 3894
Chinley Derbys 43 E3 vil 2m/3km NW of Chapel-en-le-Frith. SK 0482
Chinnock, East Som 8 C3 vil 4m/6km W of Yeovil. 2m/3km W, vil of **W Chinnock.** Just E of W Chinnock is the ham of **Middle Chinnock.** ST 4913
Chinnor Oxon 18 C2 vil 4m/7km SE of Thame. Cement works to S. SP 7500
Chipchase Castle Nthmb 60 D4 14c tower hse and Jacbn manor hse above banks of R North Tyne 2m/3km SE of Wark across r. NY 8875
Chipley Som 7 H3 ham 2m/4km NW of Wellington. ST 1123
Chipnall Salop 34 D2 ham 4m/6km SE of Mkt Drayton. SJ 7231
Chippenhall Green Suffolk 31 G1 loc 2m/3km W of Cratfield. TM 2875
Chippenham Cambs 30 B1 vil 4m/7km N of Newmarket. TL 6669
Chippenham Wilts 16 D4 tn on R Avon 12m/19km NE of Bath. Industries include brakes and food products. ST 9173
Chipperfield Herts 19 E2 vil 4m/6km S of Hemel Hempstead. TL 0401
Chipping Herts 29 G4 vil 2m/3km N of Buntingford. TL 3532
Chipping Lancs 47 G4 vil 4m/6km NE of Longridge. SD 6243
Chipping Barnet London 19 F2* dist in borough of Barnet 11m/17km N of Charing Cross. TQ 2496

Chipping Campden Glos 27 F4 small tn of Cotswold stone 8m/12km SE of Evesham. Former centre of wool trade. Arcaded Jacbn mkt hall (NT). SP 1539
Chipping Norton Oxon 27 G5 Cotswold tn 18m/29km NW of Oxford. Brewing. Tweed mill to W. SP 3127
Chipping Ongar Essex 20 C2 small tn 6m/10km NW of Brentwood. TL 5502
Chipping Sodbury Avon 16 C3 tn 11m/17km NE of Bristol. ST 7282
Chipping Warden Northants 28 A3 vil 6m/9km NE of Banbury. Site of Roman villa 1m SE. SP 4948
Chipstable Som 7 H3 ham 3m/4km W of Wiveliscombe. ST 0427
Chipstead Kent 20 B5 NW suburb of Sevenoaks. TQ 5056
Chipstead Surrey 19 F5 vil 2m/4km SE of Banstead. TQ 2757
Chirbury Salop 34 A4 vil 3m/5km N of Church Stoke. SO 2698
Chirdon Burn 60 D3 r rising on Wark Forest, Nthmb, near Cumbrian border, and flowing NE into R North Tyne 4m/6km W of Bellingham, below mouth of Tarset Burn. NY 7885
Chirk (Waun, Y) Clwyd 34 A1 small tn above R Ceiriog 5m/8km N of Oswestry. Motte near ch marks site of 11c cas. Present cas, 2km W, dates in part from early 14c. SJ 2937
Chirk Green Clwyd 34 A1 N part of Chirk. SJ 2938
Chirnside Borders 67 F3 vil 6m/9km E of Duns. **Chirnsidebridge** is vil 2km W on Whiteadder Water. NT 8656
Chirton Tyne & Wear 61 H4* dist of N Shields 1m W of tn centre. **W Chirton** loc adjoining to W. NZ 3468
Chirton Wilts 17 E5 vil 5m/8km SE of Devizes. SU 0757
Chisbury Wilts 17 G4 ham 4m/7km SW of Hungerford. **C. Camp**, ancient earthwork, to SE. SU 2766
Chiselborough Som 8 C3 vil 6m/9km W of Yeovil. ST 4614
Chiseldon Wilts 17 F3 vil 4m/6km SE of Swindon. SU 1879
Chisenbury, East Wilts 17 F6 vil on R Avon 2m/3km S of Upavon. SU 1452
Chisenbury, West Wilts 17 F6 loc 2km S of Upavon. SU 1352
Chishill, Great Cambs 29 H4 vil 4m/7km E of Royston. TL 4238
Chishill, Little Cambs 29 H4 ham 5m/7km SE of Royston. TL 4137
Chislehampton Oxon 18 B2 ham 7m/11km SE of Oxford. SU 5999
Chislehurst London 20 B4 dist in borough of Bromley 11m/18km SE of Charing Cross. **C. West** loc 2km NW. Caves to W. TQ 4469
Chislet Kent 13 G1 vil 4m/6km SE of Herne Bay. TR 2264
Chisley W Yorks 48 C5* vil 1m NE of Hebden Br. SE 0028
Chiswellgreen Herts 19 E2* suburb 2m/3km SW of St Albans. TL 1304
Chiswick London 19 F4 dist N of R Thames in borough of Hounslow 6m/10km W of Charing Cross. Chiswick Br over r. Chiswick Hse (A.M.), 18c Italianate hse. **C. Eyot**, island in R Thames. TQ 2078
Chiswick End Cambs 29 G3* loc adjoining Meldreth to S, 3m/5km N of Royston. TL 3745
Chisworth Derbys 43 E2* vil 3m/4km SW of Glossop. SJ 9992
Chithurst W Sussex 11 E3 ham 3m/5km W of Midhurst. SU 8423
Chittening Worth Avon 16 A3* loc 2m/3km S of Severn Beach. Gas and chemical works. Chittening Trading Estate. ST 5382
Chittering Cambs 30 A1 ham 8m/13km NE of Cambridge. TL 4970
Chitterne Wilts 17 E6 vil on Salisbury Plain 8m/12km E of Warminster. ST 9944
Chittlehamholt Devon 7 E3 vil 5m/8km SW of S Molton. SS 6421
Chittlehampton Devon 7 E3 vil 5m/8km W of S Molton. SS 6325
Chittoe Wilts 16 D4* vil 5m/8km SE of Chippenham. ST 9566
Chivelstone Devon 4 D6 ham 3m/4km N of Prawle Pt. SX 7838
Chivenor Devon 6 D2* loc and airfield to S of Braunton. SS 5034
Chno Dearg H'land 75 E4 mt in Lochaber dist 3m/5km SE of foot of Loch Treig. Height 3433 ft or 1046 metres. NN 3774
Chobham Surrey 18 D5 vil 3m/5km NW of Woking, on S side of **C. Common**, expanse of fairly open heath to S of Windsor Gt Park. SU 9761
Choinneachain Hill Tayside 72 C2* mt on E side of Loch Turret. Height 2535 ft or 773 metres. NN 8228
Cholderton Wilts 17 F6 vil 5m/7km E of Amesbury. SU 2242
Cholderton, East Hants 10 A1* loc adjoining Thruxton to E and 4m/7km W of Andover. SU 2945
Cholesbury Bucks 18 D1 vil 4m/6km NW of Chesham. SP 9307
Chollerford Nthmb 61 E4* loc at rd crossing of R North Tyne 4m/6km N of Hexham. NY 9170
Chollerton Nthmb 61 E4 vil 5m/8km N of Hexham. NY 9371
Cholmondeley Castle Ches 42 B6 large early 19c castellated mansion in park with lakes, 6m/10km N of Whitchurch. SJ 5351
Cholsey Oxon 18 B3 vil 2m/4km SW of Wallingford. SU 5886
Cholstrey H & W 26 A2 loc 2m/3km W of Leominster. SO 4659
Cholwell Avon 16 B5 ham 4m/7km NW of Midsomer Norton. ST 6158
Chop Gate N Yorks 54 D5 ham 6m/10km S of Stokesley. SE 5599
Choppington Nthmb 61 G3* vil 2km N of Bedlington. NZ 2583
Chopwell Tyne & Wear 61 F5 vil 3m/5km SE of Prudhoe. NZ 1158
Chorley Ches 42 B6 vil 5m/9km W of Nantwich. **C. Green** loc to N. SJ 5751
Chorley Ches 42 D3* loc on SW side of Alderley Edge. **C. Hall** is a 14c–17c hse with moat. SJ 8378
Chorley Lancs 47 F6 tn 10m/16km NW of Bolton. Engineering, textiles. See also Astley Hall. SD 5817
Chorley Salop 34 D5 vil 5m/8km N of Cleobury Mortimer. SO 6983
Chorley Staffs 35 G3* loc 3m/5km NW of Lichfield. SK 0711
Chorleywood Herts 19 E2 residential tn 2m/3km NW of Rickmansworth. **C. Bottom** and **C. West** are W suburbs. TQ 0396
Chorlton Ches 42 C6* ham 4m/6km SE of Crewe. SJ 7250
Chorlton cum Hardy Gtr Manchester 42 D2 dist of Manchester 3m/4km SW of city centre. SJ 8293
Chorlton Lane Ches 42 A6* ham 2m/3km W of Malpas. SJ 4547
Chorlton on Medlock Gtr Manchester 42 D2* dist of Manchester 2km SE of city centre. Royal Infirmary. Manchester University. SJ 8496
Chorrie Island H'land 84 D2 island nearly 1m in length in Loch Eriboll, in Sutherland dist, 2m/4km from head of loch. Also known as Eilean Choraidh. NC 4258
Chourdon Point Durham B1 H6 headland on North Sea coast 2m/3km S of Seaham. NZ 4446
Chrishall Essex 29 H4 vil 6m/9km E of Royston. TL 4439
Christchurch (Eglwys y Drindod) Gwent suburb 3m/4km E of Newport. ST 3489
Christchurch Cambs 38 A5 vil 3m/4km NW of Welney. TL 4996
Christchurch Dorset 9 H5 residential tn near coast 5m/8km E of Bournemouth, at confluence of Rs Avon and Stour. Yachting based on **C. Harbour**, with outlet into **C. Bay.** Large priory ch. Ruins of Norman hse (A.M.) within bailey of Norman cas (A.M.). SZ 1592
Christchurch Glos 26 B6* loc 2m/3km N of Coleford. SO 5713
Christian Malford Wilts 16 D3 vil 4m/7km NE of Chippenham. ST 9678
Christleton Ches 42 A4 suburb 3m/4km E of Chester. SJ 4465
Christmas Common Oxon 18 C2 ham 2m/3km SE of Watlington. SU 7193
Christon Avon 15 H5 vil 5m/7km SE of Weston-super-Mare. ST 3757
Christon Bank Nthmb 67 H6 ham 2km W of Embleton. NU 2123
Christow Devon 5 E2 vil 4m/6km NW of Chudleigh. SX 8384
Christ's Hospital W Sussex 11 G2 boys' boarding school 2m/3km SW of Horsham, moved from London in 1902. TQ 1428
Christ's Kirk Grampian 83 E4 loc 2m/3km SW of Insch. **Hill of C. K.** to N. NJ 6026
Chrona Island H'land 84 A4/B4 small uninhabited island 1m W of Oldany I. off W coast of Sutherland dist. Also known as Eilean Chrona. NC 0633
Chryston S'clyde 64 D2 vil adjoining Muirhead to N, 4m/7km NW of Coatbridge. NS 6870
Chuckery, The W Midlands 35 F4* dist of Walsall to E of tn centre. SP 0298
Chuck Hatch E Sussex 12 B3* loc on N slope of Ashdown Forest 2m/3km S of Hartfield. TQ 4733
Chudleigh Devon 5 E3 small tn 5m/8km N of Newton Abbot. SX 8679
Chudleigh Knighton Devon 5 E3 vil by R Teign 4m/6km N of Newton Abbot. SX 8477
Chulmleigh Devon 7 E4 small tn 8m/12km S of S Molton. SS 6814
Chunal Derbys 43 E2* loc 2km S of Glossop. SK 0391
Church Lancs 48 A5 textile tn adjoining Accrington to W. SD 7429
Churcham Glos 26 C5 vil 4m/7km W of Gloucester. SO 7618
Church Aston Salop 34 D3 vil 1m S of Newport. SJ 7417
Church Bay Gwynedd 40 A3 bay on NW coast of Anglesey 3m/5km S of Carmel Hd. SH 2988
Church Brampton Northants 28 C1 vil 4m/7km NW of Northampton. SP 7165
Churchbridge Staffs 35 F3* loc 2km S of Cannock. SJ 9808
Church Brough Cumbria 53 G3* loc adjoining Brough to S. NY 7913
Church Broughton Derbys 35 G1 vil 3m/5km NE of Sudbury. SK 2033
Church Charwelton Northants 28 B2* loc to SE of Charwelton, 5m/8km SW of Daventry. SP 5455
Church Clough Lancs 48 B4* loc adjoining Colne to S. SD 8939
Church Common Hants 10 D3* loc 2km N of Petersfield. SU 7325
Church Crookham Hants 18 C6 loc 2km S of Fleet. SU 8152
Churchdown Glos 26 D5 suburb 4m/6km E of Gloucester. SO 8819
Church Eaton Staffs 35 E3 vil 6m/9km SW of Stafford. SJ 8417
Churchend Avon 16 C3* loc 3m/5km SW of Wotton-under-Edge. ST 7191
Church End Beds 28 D4* N end of Husborne Crawley, 2m/3km N of Woburn. SP 9536
Church End Beds 29 E2* N end of vil of Colmworth. TL 1058
Church End Beds 29 E2* W end of vil of Thurleigh. TL 0558
Church End Beds 29 E3* W end of Renhold vil, 3m/5km NE of Bedford. TL 0852
Church End Beds 29 E3* W end of Biddenham, 2m/4km W of Bedford. TL 0149
Church End Beds 29 E4* SW end of Eversholt, 2m/4km E of Woburn. SP 9832
Church End Beds 29 E5 SE end of Totternhoe, 2m/3km W of Dunstable. Site of Roman villa across rd from ch. SP 9921
Church End Beds 29 F4 vil at N end of Arlesey, 5m/8km N of Hitchin. TL 1937
Church End Bucks 18 B1* loc round the ch at Long Crendon. SP 6909
Church End Bucks 28 D6* loc at Pitstone, 3m/4km NE of Tring. SP 9415
Church End Cambs 29 E1* NE part of vil of Catworth. TL 0873
Church End Cambs 29 G1* NW end of vil of Over. TL 3770
Church End Cambs 29 G1* N end of Swavesey. TL 3669
Church End Cambs 29 G2* S end of Comberton. TL 3855
Church End Cambs 30 A2 N end of Cherry Hinton. TL 4857
Church End Cambs 37 G6* NW end of vil of Pidley 2m/3km SE of Warboys. TL 3278
Church End Cambs 37 G6* loc in vicinity of Wood Walton ch, 1m N of vil and 7m/11km N of Huntingdon. TL 2082
Church End Cambs 37 H4 loc 2km E of Parson Drove. TF 3909
Churchend Essex 21 F3* vil on Foulness I., 9m/14km NE of Southend-on-Sea. TR 0093
Church End Essex 30 B4* SW end of vil of Ashdon, 3m/5km NE of Saffron Walden. TL 5841
Churchend Essex 30 B5 loc 1km N of Gt Dunmow. TL 6222
Church End Essex 30 C5 ham 4m/6km NW of Braintree. TL 7228
Church End Essex 30 C6* loc 5m/7km S of Braintree. TL 7316
Church End Glos 16 C1* 1km NE of Eastington. SO 7805
Church End Hants 18 B5 ham 4m/6km NE of Basingstoke. SU 6756
Church End Herts 19 E1 loc adjoining Redbourn to SW, 4m/6km NE of Hemel Hempstead. TL 1011
Church End Herts 19 E2* ham 3m/4km NW of Rickmansworth. TQ 0398
Church End Herts 29 F4* E end of vil of Weston, 3m/5km SE of Baldock. TL 2630
Church End Herts 29 H5* ham 3m/4km W of Bishop's Stortford. TL 4422
Church End Humberside 51 E3 loc 1km W of N Frodingham. TA 0953
Church End Lincs 37 G2 ham 1km N of Quadring. TF 2234
Church End Lincs 45 G2 loc 1km S of N Somercotes. TF 4295
Church End London 19 F3* loc at Finchley in borough of Barnet 7m/11km NW of Charing Cross. TQ 2490
Church End Norfolk 38 A3* loc adjoining Walpole St Peter to S. TF 5115
Church End Surrey 19 E5* loc adjoining Ockham to W, 4m/7km E of Woking. TQ 0656
Church End Warwicks 35 H5 loc 5m/7km W of Nuneaton. SP 2992
Church End Warwicks 35 H5* E end of vil of Shustoke and 3m/5km NE of Coleshill. SP 2490
Church Enstone Oxon 27 G5 vil 4m/7km E of Chipping Norton. SP 3725
Church Fenton N Yorks 49 G4 vil 2m/4km NE of Sherburn in Elmet. Airfield to NE. SE 5136
Churchfield W Midlands 35 F5* dist of W Bromwich 1m NE of tn centre. SP 0192
Churchgate Herts 19 G2 loc 1km W of Cheshunt tn centre. TL 3402
Church Green Devon 8 A4* ham 3m/5km S of Honiton. SY 1796
Church Gresley Derbys 35 H3 loc 1m SW of Swadlincote. SK 2918
Church Hanborough Oxon 27 H6 vil 5m/8km NE of Witney. SP 4212
Church, High Nthmb 61 F3* SW dist of Morpeth. NZ 1985
Church Hill Ches 42 C4* ham adjoining Winsford to S. SJ 6565
Church Hill Derbys 43 H4* loc adjoining N Wingfield to SW. SK 4064
Church Hill H & W 27 E1* NE dist of Redditch. SP 0668
Churchhill Lothian 66 A2* dist of Edinburgh 2km SW of city centre. NT 2471
Church Hill Staffs 35 F3* loc 2m/3km NE of Cannock. SK 0011
Church Honeybourne H & W 27 F3* vil 4m/7km N of Broadway. SP 1144
Church Hougham Kent 13 H3 ham 3m/4km W of Dover. TR 2740
Church Houses N Yorks 55 E5 ham 7m/11km N of Kirkbymoorside. SE 6697
Churchill Avon 16 A5 vil below N slopes of Mendip Hills 3m/4km S of Congresbury. ST 4459
Churchill Devon 6 D6* loc 5m/9km NE of Barnstaple. SS 5940
Churchill Devon 8 B4* ham 3m/4km N of Axminster. ST 2902
Churchill H & W 26 D2 vil 5m/8km E of Worcester. SO 9253
Churchill H & W 35 E6 vil 3m/5km S of Stourbridge. SO 8879
Churchill Oxon 27 G5 vil 3m/4km SW of Chipping Norton. SP 2824
Churchill Barrier Orkney 89 B7* series of causeways carrying rd and linking islands of Mainland, Lamb Holm, Glims Holm, Burray, and S Ronaldsay. Built in World War II to block eastern approaches to anchorage of Scapa Flow. ND 49
Churchingford Som 8 A3 vil 8m/12km S of Taunton. ST 2112
Church Knowle Dorset 9 F6 vil 2km W of Corfe Castle. SY 9481
Church Langton Leics 36 C5 vil 4m/6km N of Mkt Harborough. SP 7293
Church Lawford Warwicks 36 A6 vil 4m/6km W of Rugby. SP 4476
Church Lawton Ches 42 D5* vil 2km NW of Kidsgrove. SJ 8255
Church Leigh Staffs 35 F1 vil 5m/7km NW of Uttoxeter. SK 0235
Church Lench H & W 27 E3 vil 5m/8km N of Evesham. SP 0251
Church Minshull Ches 42 C5 vil on R Weaver 4m/7km NW of Crewe. SJ 6660
Church Norton W Sussex 11 E5* ham 2m/3km NE of Selsey. SZ 8695

Church Oakley Hants 18 B6 alternative name for vil of Oakley, qv.
Churchover Warwicks 36 B6 vil 4m/6km N of Rugby. SP 5180
Church Preen Salop 34 C4* vil 5m/8km W of Much Wenlock. SO 5498
Church Pulverbatch Salop 34 B4 vil 7m/12km SW of Shrewsbury. SJ 4302
Church, South Durham 54 B2* vil 1m SE of Bishop Auckland. NZ 2128
Churchstanton Som 8 A3 vil 5m/8km SE of Wellington. ST 1914
Church Stoke Powys 34 A5 vil on R Camlad 3m/5km SE of Montgomery. SO 2794
Churchstow Devon 4 D6 vil 2m/3km NW of Kingsbridge. SX 7145
Church Stowe Northants 28 B2 vil 5m/8km SE of Daventry. SP 6357
Church Street Essex 30 C4 ham in vicinity of ch of Belchamp St Paul, 2m/4km SE of Clare. TL 7943
Church Street Kent 20 D4* ham 4m/6km N of Rochester. TQ 7174
Church Street Suffolk 39 H6* loc 1km W of Wrentham. TM 4883
Church Stretton Salop 34 B5 tn under E slope of Long Mynd 12m/19km S of Shrewsbury. SO 4593
Churchthorpe Lincs 45 G2 loc adjoining Fulstow to N. TF 3297
Churchtown Derbys 43 G5* ham 3m/4km NW of Matlock. SK 3662
Church Town Humberside 44 C1* part of vil of Belton in which ch is situated. SE 7806
Churchtown Isle of Man 46 B4* ham 2m/3km W of Ramsey. Also known as Lezayre. SC 4294
Churchtown Lancs 46 D4* loc in Blackpool 3m/5km N of tn centre. SD 3140
Churchtown Lancs 47 F4 vil 2km SW of Garstang. SD 4842
Church Town Leics 36 A3* loc 1km W of Coleorton. SK 3917
Churchtown Merseyside 47 E6 loc in Southport 2m/3km NE of tn centre. SD 3618
Churchtown Salop 34 A5* ham 5m/8km NW of Clun. SO 2687
Church Town Surrey 20 A6* ham 1km E of Godstone. TQ 3551
Church Village Mid Glam 15 F3 vil 3m/5km S of Pontypridd. **Upr Church Village** adjoins to NW. ST 0885
Church Warsop Notts 44 A4 vil 1km N of Warsop and 5m/8km NE of Mansfield. SK 5668
Church Wilne Derbys 36 A2* loc 3m/5km SW of Long Eaton. SK 4431
Churn 17 E2 r rising at Seven Springs, 4m/6km S of Cheltenham, Glos, and flowing S into R Thames at Cricklade, Wilts. SU 0994
Churn Clough Reservoir Lancs 48 B4* small resr 1km NE of Sabden. SD 7838
Churnet 35 G1 r rising NE of Upr Hulme, Staffs, and flowing SW of Leek, then in a loop to W thereof, then SE into R Dove 2km S of Rocester. SK 1037
Churston Ferrers Devon 5 E5 vil on W outskirts of Brixham. SX 9056
Churt Surrey 11 E1 vil 3m/4km NW of Hindhead. SU 8538
Churton Ches 42 A5 vil 6m/10km S of Chester. SJ 4156
Churwell W Yorks 49 E5 vil 2km NE of Morley. SE 2729
Chute Wilts 17 G5 par 7m/11km NW of Andover containing vil of **Upr Chute,** hams of **C. Cadley** and **C. Standen,** and part of ham of **Lr Chute.** SU 3053
Chute Forest Wilts 17 G6* par 5m/8km NW of Andover containing part of ham of **Lr Chute.** SU 3151
Chwefri 25 E3 r rising some 2m/3km SE of Caban Coch Resr, Powys, and flowing SE into R Irfon just above its junction with R Wye near Builth Wells. SO 0351
Chwiler Welsh form of (R) Wheeler, qv.
Chwilog Gwynedd 32 C1 vil 4m/7km W of Criccieth. SH 4338
Chwitffordd Welsh form of Whitford, qv.
Chwythlyn Gwynedd 41 E5 small lake 3m/5km NE of Llanrwst. SH 8364
Chyandour Cornwall 2 B5* loc to NE of Penzance. SW 4730
Chynhalls Point Cornwall 2 D6* headland on E coast of Lizard peninsula on S side of Coverack. SW 7817
Chysauster Cornwall 2 A5* loc 3m/4km N of Penzance. To N, **C. Ancient Village** (A.M.). SW 4734
Cil Powys 33 H4 loc 1km NW of Berriew. SJ 1801
Cilcain Clwyd 41 G4/G5 vil 4m/6km W of Mold. SJ 1765
Cilcennin Dyfed 24 B2 vil 4m/7km E of Aberaeron. SN 5260
Cilcewydd Powys 34 A4* loc on R Severn 2m/3km S of Welshpool. SJ 2203
Cilfrew W Glam 14 D2* vil 2m/3km NE of Neath. SN 7700
Cilfynydd Mid Glam 15 F2 vil 2km NE of Pontypridd. ST 0891
Cilgerran Dyfed 22 D2 vil on left bank of R Teifi 2m/3km SE of Cardigan. Quarries to E and N. Ruins of 13c cas (NT) on cliff above r. SN 1943
Cilgeti Welsh form of Kilgetty, qv.
Cilgwyn Dyfed 22 C2 loc 2m/4km SE of Newport. SN 0736
Ciliau Aeron Dyfed 24 B2 loc 4m/6km SE of Aberaeron. SN 5058
Cilieni 25 E5* r rising on Mynydd Epynt, Powys, and flowing S into R Usk 2km NW of Sennybridge. SN 9329
Cilmaengwyn W Glam 14 C1* vil 2m/3km NE of Pontardawe. SN 7405
Cilmery (Cilmeri) Powys 25 E3 ham 2m/4km W of Builth Wells. Formerly known as Cefn-y-bedd. SO 0051
Cilrhedyn Dyfed 23 E2 ham 4m/6km SW of Newcastle Emlyn. SN 2734
Cilsan Dyfed 23 G3* ham 2m/3km W of Llandeilo. SN 5922
Cilurnum Nthmb 60 D4 Roman fort on Hadrian's Wall. See Chesters. NY 9170
Cilybebyll W Glam 14 C1 vil 2km E of Pontardawe. SN 7404
Cilycwm Dyfed 24 C4 vil on R Gwenlas 4m/6km N of Llandovery. SN 7540
Cimla W Glam 14 D2 SE dist of Neath. SS 7696
Cinderford Glos 26 B6 colliery tn in Forest of Dean 11m/18km W of Gloucester. SO 6514
Cinderhill Derbys 43 H6* loc 2m/3km E of Belper. SK 3746
Cinderhill Notts 36 B1* loc in Nottingham 3m/4km NW of city centre. SK 5443
Cinder Hill W Midlands 35 F5* loc on borders of Dudley and Wolverhampton, 3m/5km N of Dudley tn centre. SO 9294
Cindery Island Essex 31 E6* uninhabited island in Brightlingsea Creek. TM 0915
Cinnamon Brow Ches 42 C2* loc in NE part of Warrington. SJ 6291
Cinque Ports 12, 13 tns on coast of English Channel which in former times combined for defence. The original five members were Hastings, Romney, Hythe, Dover, and Sandwich, although other places were added later. The Cinque Ports are under the jurisdiction of a Lord Warden, who is admiral of the ports and governor of Dover Castle. See also Walmer.
Cippenham Berks 18 D3 W dist of Slough. SU 9480
Cippyn Dyfed 22 D1* loc 2m/3km NW of St Dogmaels. SN 1448
Cirencester Glos 17 E2 country tn on site of Roman *Corinium* 14m/22km NW of Swindon. SP 0202
Cir Mhór S'clyde 63 F3 mt (NTS) on Arran 3m/5km W of Corrie. Height 2618 ft or 798 metres. NR 9743
Cissbury Ring W Sussex 11 G4 Iron Age fort (NT) on S Downs 2km E of Findon, on site of flint-mining industry of early Neolithic period. Views to Beachy Hd and Isle of Wight. TQ 1408
Ciste Diubh H'land 80 B5 mt on border of Inverness and Skye & Lochalsh dists 3m/5km N of head of Loch Cluanie. Height 3218 ft or 981 metres. NH 0616
Citadel H'land 81 F3* dist of Inverness 1km N of tn centre. NH 6646
Citadilla N Yorks 54 B5* loc 1km N of Catterick Br. NZ 2200
City S Glam 15 E4* loc 2m/4km N of Cowbridge. SS 9978
City Dulas Gwynedd 40 B3* loc on Anglesey 4m/6km NE of Llanerchymedd. SH 4787
City of London See London, City of.
City of Westminster London. See Westminster. TQ 3079
City, The Beds 29 E2* loc at N end of vil of Colmworth. TL 1159
City, The Bucks 18 C2 vil 2m/3km E of Stokenchurch. SU 7896
City, The Suffolk 39 G5* loc 2m/3km SW of Beccles. TM 3988
Clabhach Coll, S'clyde 68 A3 loc near NW coast 3m/5km NW of Arinagour. NM 1858
Clachaig S'clyde 69 D5* r on Mull running N to Loch Bà 2km NW of head of loch. NM 5737
Clachaig S'clyde 70 C6 loc on Lit Eachaig R in Argyll, 5m/8km NW of Dunoon. NS 1181
Clachan S'clyde 63 E2 vil in Kintyre, Argyll, 10m/16km SW of Tarbert. NR 7656
Clachan S'clyde 70 D3 locality with power stn at head of Loch Fyne in Argyll. NN 1812
Clachan Skye, H'land 79 D5 loc on W coast of Raasay, 2m/3km NW of S end of island. NG 5436
Clachan W Isles 88 E1* loc near W coast of N Uist 3m/5km N of Carinish. NF 8163
Clachan Bridge S'clyde 70 A3 hump-backed rd br connecting island of Seil with mainland of Argyll. Commonly known as The Atlantic Bridge. NM 7819
Clachan Mór Tiree, S'clyde 69 A7* loc on N coast 5m/7km NW of Scarinish. NL 9747
Clachan of Campsie S'clyde. See Campsie.
Clachan of Glendaruel S'clyde 70 C6 vil in Argyll, on R Ruel 4m/6km N of head of Loch Riddon. NR 9984
Clachan-Seil S'clyde 70 A3 loc on island of Seil nearly 1m S of Clachan Br. NM 7818
Clach Leathad S'clyde 70 D1 mt in Argyll 7m/11km NW of Br of Orchy. Height 3602 ft or 1098 metres. Also known as Clachlet. Skiing facilities. NN 2449
Clachlet S'clyde. See Clach Leathad.
Clachnaharry H'land 81 F3* loc in Inverness dist at N terminus of Caledonian Canal on NW side of Inverness. NH 6446
Clackmannan Central 72 C5 tn 2m/3km E of Alloa. Wool spinning. **C. Tower** (A.M.) is tall 15c tower to W. **C. Pow** is small harbour at mouth of Black Devon R, 2km SW. NS 9191
Clackmarras Grampian 82 B2* loc 3m/5km SE of Elgin. NJ 2458
Clackriach Grampian 83 G2/G3 loc 1m S of Maud. Remains of cas. NJ 9246
Clacton, Great Essex 31 F6 N dist of Clacton-on-Sea. TM 1716
Clacton, Little Essex 31 F6 vil 3m/4km N of Clacton-on-Sea. TM 1618
Clacton-on-Sea Essex 31 F6 North Sea resort 13m/21km SE of Colchester. TM 1714
Cladich S'clyde 70 C3 locality in Argyll near E side of Loch Awe 5m/9km SW of Dalmally. NN 0921
Cladswell H & W 27 E2* vil 3m/4km NW of Alcester. SP 0558
Claerddu 24 D2* stream running SE from W side of Llyn Fyrddon-Fach, Dyfed, to the head of Claerwen Resr. SN 8167
Claerwen 24 D2/25 E2 r rising on borders of Dyfed and Powys SE of Cwmystwyth, Dyfed, and flowing S to the head of Claerwen Resr, then SE through the resr, and on to the head of Caban Coch Resr, where it turns NE to join R Elan in the resr. SN 9163
Claerwen Reservoir Powys 24 D2 large resr in R Claerwen valley 7m/11km W of Rhayader. A small part of the W end of the resr is in Dyfed. SN 8663
Claggain Bay S'clyde 62 C3 bay on E coast of Islay 4m/6km S of McArthur's Hd. NR 4653
Claggan H'land 68 E4 locality in Lochaber dist 4m/6km N of Lochaline. NM 6949
Claines H & W 26 D2 ham 3m/4km N of Worcester. SO 8558
Clairinch Central 71 E5* island in Loch Lomond 1km SW of Balmaha. Part of nature reserve comprising also Inchcailloch and Torrinch. NS 4189
Clandon, East Surrey 19 E6 vil 4m/7km E of Guildford. TQ 0651
Clandon Park Surrey 19 E6 18c hse and grnds (NT), 3m/4km E of Guildford. TQ 0451
Clandon, West Surrey 19 E6 vil 4m/6km NE of Guildford. TQ 0452
Clandown Avon 16 C5* loc on N side of Radstock. ST 6855
Clanfield Hants 10 D3 suburban vil 3m/4km N of Horndean. SU 6916
Clanfield Oxon 17 G2 vil 4m/7km N of Faringdon. SP 2802
Clanfield, Little Oxon 17 G2 loc 4m/6km E of Lechlade. SP 2701
Clannaborough Devon 7 E5* loc 6m/10km W of Crediton. SS 7402
Clanville Hants 17 G6 vil 4m/6km NW of Andover. Site of Roman villa to W. SU 3148
Clanyard Bay D & G 57 B8 bay on W coast of Rinns of Galloway, 2m/3km S of Port Logan. NX 0938
Claonaig S'clyde 63 F2 loc in Kintyre, Argyll, 2m/3km W of Skipness. **C. Water** is r running S through loc to **C. Bay.** NR 8756
Clapgate Dorset 9 G4 loc 2m/3km N of Wimborne. SU 0102
Clapgate Herts 29 H5* ham 4m/6km NW of Bishop's Stortford. TL 4425
Clap Gate N Yorks 49 E3 loc 4m/6km W of Wetherby. SE 3447
Clapham Beds 29 E3 vil on R Ouse 2m/3km NW of Bedford. TL 0352
Clapham Devon 5 E2* loc 4m/6km SW of Exeter. SX 8987
Clapham London 19 G4* dist in borough of Lambeth 3m/5km S of Charing Cross. C. Common is large open space to W; to W again is C. Junction, well-known rly junction. TQ 2975
Clapham N Yorks 48 A2 vil 6m/9km NW of Settle. SD 7469
Clapham W Sussex 11 G4 vil 4m/7km NW of Worthing. TQ 0906
Clapham Folly Beds 29 E3* suburban loc adjoining Clapham to NW, 3m/4km NW of Bedford. TL 0253
Clapham Green Beds 29 E3* loc adjoining Clapham to NE, 2m/3km NW of Bedford. TL 0352
Clapham Green N Yorks 49 E2/E3* ham 1km S of Birstwith. SE 2458
Clapham Hill Kent 13 F1 loc in S part of Whitstable. TR 1064
Clappersgate Cumbria 52 D4* loc 1km SW of Ambleside. Site of Roman fort of *Galava.* NY 3603
Clappers, The Beds 29 E4* NT property to S of Sharpenhoe, qv. TL 0630
Clapton Glos 27 F5 vil 4m/6km NE of Northleach. SP 1617
Clapton Som 16 B6* ham 2m/3km SW of Midsomer Norton. ST 6453
Clapton Som 8 C4 vil 3m/4km SW of Crewkerne. ST 4106
Clapton-in-Gordano Avon 16 A4 vil 3m/4km SE of Portishead. ST 4774
Clapton, Lower London 20 A3* loc in borough of Hackney 1km NE of H. tn centre. TQ 3585
Clapton Park London 20 A3* loc in borough of Hackney to S of H. Marshes and 1m NE of H. tn centre. TQ 3685
Clapton, Upper London 19 G3* loc in borough of Hackney 5m/8km NE of Charing Cross. TQ 3486
Clapworthy Devon 7 E3 ham 3m/4km SW of S Molton. **C. Cross** loc 2km NW. SS 6724
Clarach Dyfed 32 D6* loc on N side of Llangorwen, 2m/3km NE of Aberystwyth. **C. Bay** at mouth of R Stewy 1m W. SN 6083
Clara Vale Tyne & Wear 61 F5* vil 2km W of Ryton. NZ 1364
Clarbeston Dyfed 22 C4 vil 7m/11km NE of Haverfordwest. **Clarbeston Rd** vil 2m/3km W. SN 0421
Clarborough Notts 44 C3 vil 2m/4km NE of E Retford. SK 7383
Clardon Head H'land 86 D1 headland on N coast of Caithness dist 3m/4km NE of Thurso. ND 1570
Clare Suffolk 30 C3 tn on R Stour 7m/11km NW of Sudbury. Many pargeted hses. Faint remains of medieval cas and priory. TL 7645
Clareland H & W 26 C1/D1* loc 2km SE of Stourport. SO 8269
Claremont Park Surrey 19 E5 park containing Claremont, 18c hse now a school, and C. Woods (NT), 1m S of Esher. TQ 1363
Clarencefield D & G 59 F4 vil 7m/11km W of Annan. NY 0968
Clarendon Park Leics 36 B4* loc in Leicester 2km S of city centre. SK 5902

Clarendon Park Wilts 9 H2 par 3m/5km E of Salisbury, containing the classical mansion, Clarendon Hse, and the remains of the medieval Clarendon Palace. SU 1830
Clareton N Yorks 49 F2 loc 3m/5km NE of Knaresborough. SE 3959
Clarilaw Borders 66 C6 loc 3m/5km NE of Hawick. NT 5218
Clarken Green Hants 18 B6* loc 5m/8km W of Basingstoke. SU 5650
Clark Green Ches 43 E3* loc 1m N of Bollington. SJ 9379
Clark's Green Surrey 11 G1* loc 6m/9km N of Horsham. TQ 1739
Clarkston S'clyde 64 C3 suburb 5m/8km S of Glasgow. NS 5757
Clas-ar-Wy, Y Welsh form of Glasbury, qv.
Clashdorran H'land 81 E3* loc in Ross and Cromarty dist 2km SW of Muir of Ord. NH 5148
Clashindarroch Forest Grampian 82 D4 state forest 6m/9km SW of Huntly. NJ 4633
Clashmore H'land 84 A4 loc 3m/5km S of Pt of Stoer, W coast of Sutherland dist. NC 0331
Clashmore H'land 87 A7 vil in Sutherland dist 3m/5km W of Dornoch. NH 7489
Clashnessie H'land 84 A4 loc on **C. Bay**, W coast of Sutherland dist 4m/6km SE of Pt of Stoer. NC 0530
Clashnoir Grampian 82 B4/B5* loc 5m/7km NE of Tomintoul. NJ 2222
Clatford Wilts 17 F4* loc 2m/3km W of Marlborough. SU 1568
Clatford Oakcuts Hants 10 A1* loc 3m/5km NW of Stockbridge. SU 3339
Clatford, Upper Hants 10 B1 vil 2km S of Andover. SU 3543
Clatt Grampian 82 D4 vil 3m/5km E of Rhynie. Also known as Kirktown of Clatt. NJ 5325
Clatter Powys 33 G5 ham 3m/4km NW of Caersws. SN 9994
Clattercote Oxon 27 H3* loc 5m/8km N of Banbury. Resr to SW. SP 4549
Clatterford Isle of Wight 10 B5* ham adjoining Newport to SW. SZ 4887
Clatterford End Essex 20 B2* ham 2m/3km W of Chipping Ongar. TL 5202
Clatterford End Essex 20 C1* loc 2m/3km E of Leaden Roding. TL 6113
Clatterford End Essex 20 C1 loc adjoining Fyfield to SW, 3m/4km N of Chipping Ongar. TL 5606
Clatteringshaws Loch D & G 58 B4 large loch and resr (Galloway Hydro-electricity Scheme) 5m/9km W of New Galloway. Bruce's Stone (NTS), or The King's Stone, granite boulder on E shore, marks site of battle of 1307 in which Robert Bruce defeated the English. Galloway Deer Museum on E shore 1km S of Bruce's Stone. NX 5476
Clatto Reservoir Tayside 73 F2* small resr in NW part of Dundee. NO 3634
Clatworthy Som 7 H2 ham 3m/4km NW of Wiveliscombe. To W, Clatworthy Resr, in upper valley of R Tone. ST 0530
Clauchlands Point S'clyde 63 G4 headland on E coast of Arran, at N end of Lamlash Bay. NS 0532
Claughton Lancs 47 F2 vil 6m/10km NE of Lancaster. SD 5666
Claughton Lancs 47 F4 ham 3m/5km SE of Garstang. SD 5242
Claughton Merseyside 41 H3* dist of Birkenhead 2km W of tn centre. SJ 3088
Clausentum Hants. See Bitterne.
Clava Cairns H'land 81 G3* group of Stone Age-Bronze Age burial cairns (A.M.), 6m/9km E of Inverness beyond Culloden. NH 7544
Clavelshay Som 8 B2* loc 3m/4km SW of N Petherton. ST 2531
Claverdon Warwicks 27 F2 vil 3m/5km E of Henley-in-Arden. SP 1964
Claverham Avon 16 A4 vil 2m/3km N of Congresbury. ST 4466
Clavering Essex 29 H4 vil 7m/11km N of Bishop's Stortford. TL 4731
Claverley Salop 35 E5 vil 5m/8km E of Bridgnorth. SO 7993
Claverton Avon 16 C5 vil above R Avon and Kennet and Avon Canal 3m/4km E of Bath. Museum of American domestic life. 1m SW, loc of **C. Down.** ST 7864
Claw 6 C5 r in Devon rising 2m/3km E of Hollacombe and flowing SW through Clawton to R Tamar W of Tetcott. SX 3296
Clawdd-coch S Glam 15 F4* ham 4m/7km NE of Cowbridge. ST 0577
Clawdd Newydd Clwyd 41 G6 ham 5m/7km SW of Ruthin. SJ 0852
Clawthorpe Cumbria 47 F1 loc 1km N of Burton. SD 5377
Clawton Devon 6 C5 vil 3m/5km S of Holsworthy. SX 3599
Claxby Lincs 45 E2 vil 4m/6km N of Mkt Rasen. TF 1194
Claxby Lincs 45 H4 loc 3m/5km S of Alford. TF 4571
Claxby Pluckacre Lincs 45 G4 loc 4m/7km SE of Horncastle. TF 3065
Claxton Cleveland 54 D2* loc 2km W of Greatham. NZ 4728
Claxton Norfolk 39 G4* vil 2m/3km E of Rockland St Mary. TG 3303
Claxton N Yorks 50 C2 vil 3m/5km N of Stamford Br. SE 6960
Claybrooke Magna Leics 36 B5 vil 4m/7km NW of Lutterworth. SP 4988
Claybrooke Parva Leics 36 B5 vil 4m/6km NW of Lutterworth. SP 4987
Clay Common Suffolk 31 H1* loc 4m/6km NW of Southwold. TM 4780
Clay Coton Northants 36 B6 vil 6m/9km E of Rugby. SP 5977
Clay Cross Derbys 43 H4 tn 5m/8km S of Chesterfield. Coal and iron. SK 3963
Claydon Oxon 27 H3 vil 6m/10km N of Banbury. SP 4550
Claydon Suffolk 31 E3/F3 vil 4m/6km NW of Ipswich. TM 1349
Claydon Brook 28 C4* r flowing into R Ouse 2m/3km E of Buckingham. One branch rises E of Winslow, Bucks and one N of Bicester, Oxon, the two joining 3m/5km S of Buckingham. SP 7234
Claydon, East Bucks 28 C5 vil 2m/4km SW of Winslow. SP 7325
Claydon, Middle Bucks 28 C5 vil 4m/6km SW of Winslow. **Claydon Hse,** 18c (NT). SP 7225
Clay End Herts 29 G5* ham 4m/7km E of Stevenage. TL 3025
Claygate Kent 12 D3 ham 3m/5km E of Paddock Wd. TQ 7144
Claygate Surrey 19 F5 residential loc 2km SE of Esher. TQ 1563
Claygate Cross Kent 20 C6 loc 2km S of Borough Green. TQ 6155
Clay Gates Staffs 35 E3* loc 2km NE of Brewood. SJ 9009
Clayhall London 20 B3* loc in borough of Redbridge 2m/4km NW of Ilford. TQ 4289
Clayhanger Devon 7 G3 vil 4m/7km E of Bampton. ST 0222
Clayhanger Som 8 B3* ham 2m/3km N of Chard. ST 3111
Clayhanger W Midlands 35 F4 loc 1km SW of Brownhills. SK 0404
Clay Head Isle of Man 46 C5 headland at S end of Laxey Bay, 5m/8km NE of Douglas. SC 4480
Clayhidon Devon 8 A3 ham 4m/6km SE of Wellington. ST 1615
Clay Hill Avon 16 B4 dist of Bristol 3m/5km NE of city centre. ST 6274
Clayhill E Sussex 12 D4* ham 2km W of Beckley. TQ 8423
Clayhill Hants 10 A4 loc 1km S of Lyndhurst. SU 3007
Clay Hill London 19 G2* loc in borough of Enfield 2km N of Enfield tn centre. TQ 3298
Clayhythe Cambs 30 A2* loc on E bank of R Cam 5m/8km NE of Cambridge. TL 5064
Clay Lake Lincs 37 G3* loc 1km SE of Spalding. TF 2521
Clayland Cross Devon 5 E4* loc on SW side of Paignton. SX 8759
Clay Mills Staffs 35 H2* loc 2m/4km NE of Burton upon Trent. SK 2526
Claypit Hill Cambs 29 G3* ham 6m/10km SW of Cambridge. TL 3554
Claypits Glos 16 C1* vil 5m/8km W of Stroud. SO 7606
Claypole Lincs 44 C6 vil 5m/7km SE of Newark-on-Trent. SK 8449
Claypotts Castle Tayside 73 G2* 16c cas (A.M.) 1km NW of Broughty Ferry. NO 4531
Clay Street Suffolk 31 E1* loc 1km W of Thornham Magna. TM 0970
Claythorn S'clyde 64 C2* loc in Glasgow 3m/5km NW of city centre. NS 5468
Claythorpe Lincs 45 G3 loc 3m/5km NW of Alford. TF 4179
Clayton Gtr Manchester 42 D2* dist of Manchester 3m/5km E of city centre. Steel, iron, chemical works. **Clayton Br** loc 1km NE. SJ 8898
Clayton Staffs 42 D6 S dist of Newcastle-under-Lyme. SJ 8543
Clayton S Yorks 44 A1 vil 3m/4km SW of S Elmsall. SE 4507
Clayton W Sussex 11 H4 vil 6m/10km N of Brighton. On S Downs above vil are two windmills known as Jack and Jill. TQ 2914
Clayton W Yorks 48 D5 dist of Bradford 3m/5km W of city centre. **C. Heights** loc 1km S. SE 1131
Clayton Brook Lancs 47 F5* loc 1km N of Clayton Green. SD 5724
Clayton Green Lancs 47 F5 vil 2m/4km E of Leyland. SD 5723
Clayton-le-Dale Lancs 47 G5* loc 2km NE of Osbaldeston. SD 6633
Clayton-le-Moors Lancs 48 A5 tn 2m/3km NW of Accrington. Textiles, engineering, brick mnfre. SD 7431
Clayton-le-Woods Lancs 47 F5* loc 2km E of Leyland. SD 5622
Clayton West W Yorks 43 G1 vil 6m/10km NW of Barnsley. SE 2510
Clayworth Notts 44 C2/C3 vil 5m/8km N of E Retford. SK 7288
Cleadale H'land 68 C1 loc at NW end of Eigg. NM 4788
Cleadon Tyne & Wear 61 H5 loc in S Tyneside dist 3m/5km S of S Shields. NZ 3862
Clearbrook Devon 4 B4 ham on R Meavy 7m/12km NE of Plymouth. SX 5265
Clearwell Glos 16 B1 vil 2m/3km S of Coleford. Loc of **C. Meend** 1m E. SO 5708
Cleasby N Yorks 54 B3 vil 3m/4km W of Darlington across R Tees. NZ 2513
Cleat Orkney 89 B7* loc near S end of S Ronaldsay 2km NE of Brough Ness. ND 4584
Cleat W Isles 88 D3* loc on N coast of Barra 2km E of Greian Hd. NF 6604
Cleatham Humberside 44 D1 loc 2km N of Kirton in Lindsey. Extensive quarries. SE 9300
Cleatlam Durham 54 A3 vil 2km S of Staindrop. **S Cleatlam** loc 1km SE. NZ 1118
Cleator Cumbria 52 A4 mining vil 2m/3km N of Egremont. **C. Moor** loc 1m N. NY 0113
Cleaves N Yorks 54 D6 loc 5m/7km E of Thirsk. SE 4882
Cleckheaton W Yorks 48 D5 tn 4m/7km NW of Dewsbury. SE 1925
Cledan 33 F4* stream running E into R Garno 1km NW of Carno, Powys. SN 9697
Cledan 33 G4* stream running N into R Gam 2m/3km S of Llangadfan, Powys. SJ 0007
Cledlyn 24 B4* r rising NW of Cwrt-newydd, Dyfed, and flowing by Cwrt-newydd and Drefach into R Teifi at Rhyddlan, 2m/3km W of Llanybydder. SN 4943
Cledwen 41 E4 r running N by Gwytherin, Clwyd, to join R Gallen at Llangernyw and form R Elwy. SH 8767
Cleedownton Salop 34 C6* loc 6m/9km NE of Ludlow. SO 5880
Cleehill Salop 34 C6 vil 5m/8km E of Ludlow. SO 5975
Clee Hill Salop 34 C6 prominent hill and landmark 5m/8km W of Cleobury Mortimer, rising to 1750 ft or 533 metres. Extensively quarried on S slope. Known also as Titterstone Clee Hill. SO 5977
Cleers Cornwall 3 E3* loc 5m/7km NW of St Austell. SW 9758
Clee St Margaret Salop 34 C5 vil 7m/11km NE of Ludlow. SO 5684
Cleestanton Salop 34 C6* loc 5m/8km NE of Ludlow. SO 5779
Cleethorpes Humberside 45 G1 tn and resort at mouth of R Humber adjoining Grimsby to E. TA 3008
Cleeton St Mary Salop 34 C6 vil 5m/7km NW of Cleobury Mortimer. SO 6178
Cleeve Avon 16 A5 vil 2m/3km NE of Congresbury. ST 4666
Cleeve Hill Glos 27 E5* vil 4m/6km NE of Cheltenham. SO 9826
Cleeve Prior H & W 27 E3 vil 5m/8km NE of Evesham. SP 0849
Clegg, Little Gtr Manchester 48 C6* loc 2km SW of Littleborough. SD 9215
Clehonger H & W 26 A4 vil 3m/5km SW of Hereford. SO 4637
Cleigh S'clyde 70 B2/B3 loc in Argyll 3m/5km S of Oban. NM 8725
Cleish Tayside 72 D4 vil 3m/5km SW of Kinross at foot of **C. Hills,** which extend from Saline to Kelty. **C. Castle** is restored 16c–17c cas to W. NT 0998
Cléit Dhubh H'land 84 C1 headland on N coast of Sutherland dist 4m/7km E of Cape Wrath. NC 3273
Cleland S'clyde 65 E3 vil 3m/5km E of Motherwell. NS 7958
Clement's End Beds 29 E6* loc 6m/9km SW of Luton. TL 0215
Clementsgreen Creek Essex 20 D2* inlet of R Crouch estuary 2m/3km SE of S Woodham Ferrers. TQ 8296
Clement Street Kent 20 B4* loc 2m/3km NE of Swanley. TQ 5370
Clenchwarton Norfolk 38 B3 vil 2m/3km W of King's Lynn across R Ouse. TF 5820
Clennell Nthmb 61 E1 loc 1km NE of Alwinton. NT 9207
Clent H & W 35 F6 vil to S of **C. Hills** (NT), 4m/6km SE of Stourbridge. Ham of **Lr Clent** 1km NW. SO 9279
Cleobury Mortimer Salop 34 D6 vil 10m/16km E of Ludlow. SO 6775
Cleobury North Salop 34 C5 vil 7m/11km SW of Bridgnorth. SO 6286
Clerkenwell London 19 G3* loc in boroughs of Camden and Islington 2km NE of Charing Cross. TQ 3182
Clerk Green W Yorks 49 E5* loc 1m W of Batley. SE 2223
Clermiston Lothian 66 A2* dist of Edinburgh 4m/6km W of city centre. NT 1974
Clestran Sound Orkney 89 A7* sea passage between islands of Mainland and Graemsay. Named after loc on Mainland to E. HY 2706
Clett H'land 86 D1 islet on W side of Holborn Hd, Caithness dist, 2m/3km N of Thurso. ND 1071
Clett Skye, H'land 78 A4 islet off NW coast 1m S of Ardmore Pt. NG 2258
Clettack Skerry Orkney 89 B8* one of the Pentland Skerries, qv. Clettack Skerry is the most easterly of the group. ND 4877
Clett Head Shetland 89 F7 headland at S end of island of Whalsay. HU 5560
Clettwr 24 A4 r rising as **C. fawr** and **C. fach** S of Llanarth, Dyfed. The two streams converge at Pontshaen to form R Clettwr, which continues S to join R Teifi 1m W of Llanfihangel-ar-Arth. SN 4440
Clettwr 32 D5 r rising 4m/6km NE of Talybont, Dyfed, and flowing W to Tre'r-ddol, then NW into R Dovey 2m/3km above Aberdovey. SN 6495
Clevancy Wilts 17 E4 ham 4m/7km NE of Calne. SU 0575
Clevedon Avon 16 A4 residential tn on R Severn estuary 8m/13km NE of Weston-super-Mare. Shingle beach, small pier 2km E. C. Court (NT), manor hse of many periods. **E Clevedon** loc adjoining to E. ST 4071
Cleveland 117 north-eastern county of England, bounded by N Yorkshire, Durham, and the North Sea. A small county, largely composed of the urban complex of the Teesside tns: Billingham, Middlesbrough, Stockton, Thornaby, and, on the coast, Hartlepool, Redcar, and Saltburn. Industries include iron and steel, light and heavy engineering, oil, chemicals, and shipbuilding. The Cleveland Hills penetrate into the rural SE of the county, while lofty cliffs characterise the coast E of Saltburn.
Cleveley Oxon 27 G5* vil 1m E of Enstone and 4m/6km NE of Charlbury. SP 3923
Cleveleys Lancs 46 D4 coastal tn 5m/7km N of Blackpool. SD 3143
Clevelode H & W 26 D3 loc on W bank of R Severn 4m/6km E of Gt Malvern. SO 8346
Cleverton Wilts 17 E3 ham 3m/5km E of Malmesbury. ST 9785
Cleves Cross Durham 54 C2* loc on E side of Ferryhill. NZ 2932
Clewer Som 16 A6 ham 2m/3km SW of Cheddar. ST 4451
Clewer Green Berks 18 D4* SW dist of Windsor. SU 9475
Clewer New Town Berks 18 D4 southward expansion of Clewer Village in W part of Windsor. SU 9576
Clewer Village Berks 18 D4 W dist of Windsor. SU 9576
Cley (or Cley next the Sea) Norfolk 39 E1 vil 4m/6km NW of Holt. Bird sanctuary on marshes to N. TG 0443
Cley Hill Wilts 16 D6* chalk hill (NT) on which is an Iron Age fort, 2m/4km W of Warminster. ST 8344

Cliad Bay Coll, S'clyde 68 A3 bay on NW coast of island, 3m/4km NW of Arinagour. NM 1960
Cliatasay W Isles 88 A2* islet in Loch Roag, W coast of Lewis, opp entrance to Lit Loch Roag. NB 1333
Cliburn Cumbria 53 E2 vil 6m/9km SE of Penrith. Hall of 16c. NY 5824
Clickhimin Broch Shetland 89 E7* ancient *broch* or cas (A.M.) at end of causeway running out into Loch of Clickhimin on W side of Lerwick. HU 4640
Cliddesden Hants 18 B6 vil 2m/3km S of Basingstoke. SU 6349
Clieves Hills Lancs 42 A1* loc 2m/3km W of Ormskirk. SD 3808
Cliffe Kent 20 D4 vil 5m/8km N of Rochester. To N, C. Marshes on S bank of R Thames estuary. TQ 7376
Cliffe Lancs 48 A5* loc adjoining Gt Harwood to N. SD 7332
Cliffe N Yorks 50 B5 vil 3m/5km E of Selby. SE 6631
Cliffe N Yorks 54 B3 ham on S bank of R Tees opp Piercebridge. NZ 2115
Cliffe Hill W Yorks 48 D5* loc 2km N of Brighouse. SE 1425
Cliff End E Sussex 13 E5 coastal vil 5m/8km E of Hastings. TQ 8813
Cliff End Isle of Wight 10 A5* headland between Totland and Yarmouth opp Hurst Castle on the English mainland, at W end of Solent. SZ 3289
Cliff End W Yorks 48 D6 loc in Huddersfield 2km W of tn centre. SE 1216
Cliffe, North Humberside 50 D4 ham 3m/4km S of Mkt Weighton. **S Cliffe** ham 1km S. SE 8737
Cliffe, West Kent 13 H3 ham 3m/5km NE of Dover and 2km inland from S Foreland. TR 3444
Cliffe Woods Kent 20 D4* loc 2m/3km S of Cliffe and 3m/5km N of Rochester. TQ 7373
Cliff Grange Salop 34 D2* loc 2m/3km SW of Mkt Drayton. SJ 6532
Cliff, Great W Yorks 49 E6* vil 4m/6km SW of Wakefield. SE 3015
Clifford H & W 25 G3 vil on R Wye 2m/4km NE of Hay-on-Wye. Remains of 13c cas. SO 2445
Clifford W Yorks 49 F4 vil 3m/5km SE of Wetherby. SE 4244
Clifford Chambers Warwicks 27 F3 vil 2m/3km S of Stratford-upon-Avon. SP 1952
Clifford's Mesne Glos 26 C5 vil 2m/4km SW of Newent. SO 7023
Cliff Reach Essex 21 E2* reach of R Crouch estuary 2m/3km W of Burnham-on-Crouch. TQ 9296
Cliffsend Kent 13 H1 loc on Pegwell Bay, Ramsgate. TR 3464
Clifftown Essex 21 E3* dist of Southend-on-Sea S of tn centre. TQ 8785
Cliff, West N Yorks 55 G4* W dist of Whitby. NZ 8811
Clift Hills Shetland 89 E8 line of hills running N and S on Mainland on E side of Clift Sound. HU 3930
Clifton Avon 16 B4 W dist of Bristol, largely residential. Suspension br by I.K. Brunel spans Avon Gorge. ST 5673
Clifton Beds 29 F4 vil 2km E of Shefford. TL 1638
Clifton Central 71 E2 vil on NW side of Tyndrum. NN 3230
Clifton Ches 42 B3 loc 1m S of Runcorn. SJ 5280
Clifton Cumbria 53 E2 vil 3m/4km SE of Penrith. **C. Dykes** loc 1km E. NY 5326
Clifton Derbys 43 F6 vil 2km SW of Ashbourne. SK 1644
Clifton Devon 6 D1* ham 6m/10km NE of Barnstaple. SS 6041
Clifton Gtr Manchester 42 D1 loc 1m N of Swinton. **C. Junction** loc 1m E. SD 7903
Clifton H & W 26 D3 ham 6m/9km S of Worcester. SO 8446
Clifton Lancs 47 E5 vil 5m/8km W of Preston. SD 4630
Clifton Notts 36 B1 suburb 3m/4km SW of W Bridgford. SK 5534
Clifton Nthmb 61 G3 loc 2m/3km S of Morpeth. NZ 2082
Clifton N Yorks 48 D3* ham 2m/3km N of Otley. SE 1948
Clifton N Yorks 50 B3 dist of York 1m NW of city centre. SE 5953
Clifton Oxon 28 A4 vil on R Cherwell 2km E of Deddington. SP 4931
Clifton S Yorks 43 H2 central dist of Rotherham. SK 4392
Clifton S Yorks 44 A2* vil 2km S of Conisbrough. SK 5196
Clifton W Yorks 48 D5* vil 2km E of Brighouse. SE 1622
Clifton Campville Staffs 35 H3 vil 5m/8km NE of Tamworth. SK 2510
Clifton Castle N Yorks 54 B6 mansion of early 19c above R Ure, 2m/4km N of Masham. SE 2184
Clifton Gardens Humberside 50 C5* NW dist of Goole. SE 7324
Clifton, Great Cumbria 52 A2 vil 3m/5km E of Workington. NY 0429
Clifton Green Cumbria 52 B2* loc adjoining Lit Clifton to S. NY 0528
Clifton Hampden Oxon 18 A2 vil 3m/5km E of Abingdon. SU 5495
Clifton, Little Cumbria 52 B2 vil 4m/6km E of Workington. NY 0528
Clifton Maybank Dorset 8 D3* ham 2m/3km SE of Yeovil. ST 5713
Clifton, North Notts 44 C4 vil 9m/15km W of Lincoln. **S Clifton** vil 2km S. SK 8272
Clifton Reynes Bucks 28 D3 vil 5m/8km N of Newport Pagnell. SP 9051
Clifton upon Dunsmore Warwicks 36 B6 vil 2m/3km NE of Rugby. SP 5376
Clifton upon Teme H & W 26 C2 vil 6m/9km NE of Bromyard. SO 7161
Cliftonville Kent 13 H1* E dist of Margate. TR 3671
Clift Sound Shetland 89 E8* sea channel S of Scalloway between Mainland and islands of Trondra and E Burra. HU 3934
Cligga Head Cornwall 2 C3* headland at S end of Perran Bay to W of Perranporth. SW 7353
Climping W Sussex 11 F4 vil 2m/3km W of Littlehampton. TQ 0002
Clink Som 16 C6* NE dist of Frome. ST 7948
Clint N Yorks 49 E2 vil 4m/7km NW of Harrogate. SE 2559
Clint Green Norfolk 39 E4 vil 3m/4km SE of E Dereham. TG 0210
Clippesby Norfolk 39 H3* ham 3m/5km NE of Acle. TG 4214
Clippings Green Norfolk 39 E3* loc 4m/6km E of E Dereham. TG 0412
Clipsham Leics 37 E3 vil 7m/11km NW of Stamford. Limestone quarries to SE. SK 9716
Clipston Northants 36 C6 vil 4m/6km SW of Mkt Harborough. SP 7181
Clipston Notts 36 C1 ham 6m/9km SE of Nottingham. SK 6334
Clipstone Notts 44 B4 vil 5m/8km NE of Mansfield. Remains of medieval royal hunting lodge for Sherwood Forest. See also New Clipstone. SK 6064
Clisham W Isles 88 B3 mt in N Harris 5m/7km N of Tarbert. Highest point on Isle of Lewis, at 2622 ft or 799 metres. NB 1507
Clitheroe Lancs 48 A4 tn above R Ribble valley 10m/15km NE of Blackburn. Textiles, light engineering, limestone quarrying and cement, agricultural chemicals. Remains of 12c cas. SD 7441
Clive Salop 34 C2 vil 3m/5km S of Wem. SJ 5124
Clivocast Shetland 89 F5* loc on S coast of Unst 1km E of Uyeasound across bay. HP 6000
Clixby Lincs 45 E1 ham 2m/4km N of Caistor. TA 1004
Clocaenog Clwyd 41 G5 vil 4m/6km SW of Ruthin. **C. Forest,** afforested area to W. SJ 0854
Clochan Grampian 82 C1 vil near N coast 3m/5km S of Buckie. NJ 4060
Cloch Point S'clyde 64 A2 headland with lighthouse on Firth of Clyde opp Dunoon and 3m/4km SW of Gourock. NS 2075
Clock Face Merseyside 42 B2 loc 3m/4km SE of St Helens. SJ 5291
Cloddiau Powys 33 H3* loc 2m/3km NW of Welshpool. SJ 2009
Clodgy Point Cornwall 2 B4* headland on N coast 1m NW of St Ives. SW 5041
Clodock H & W 25 H5 ham 4m/7km W of Pontrilas. SO 3227
Cloford Som 16 C6* loc 4m/6km SW of Frome. ST 7243
Cloigyn Dyfed 23 F4* loc 4m/6km S of Carmarthen. SN 4314
Clola Grampian 83 H3 vil 8m/13km W of Peterhead. NK 0043
Clophill Beds 29 E4 vil 3m/5km E of Ampthill. TL 0837
Clopton Northants 37 F6 vil 4m/7km E of Thrapston. TL 0680
Clopton Suffolk 31 F3 ham 4m/6km NW of Woodbridge. Hams of **C. Corner** and **C. Green** 2km N. TM 2252
Clopton Warwicks 27 F2* N dist of Stratford-upon-Avon. SP 1956
Clopton Green Suffolk 30 C3* ham 6m/9km N of Clare. TL 7654
Clopton Green Suffolk 30 D2 loc 1km N of Rattlesden. TL 9760
Closeburn D & G 58 D2/D3 vil 2m/4km SE of Thornhill. To E is **C. Castle,** 14c tower hse. NX 8992
Close, High Durham 54 B3* loc 2km S of Gainford across R Tees. NZ 1715
Close Houses Cumbria 53 F2* loc 2m/3km SE of Milburn. NY 6727
Close, North Durham 54 B2* loc 1m S of Spennymoor. NZ 2632
Closworth Som 8 D3 vil 4m/6km S of Yeovil. ST 5610
Clothall Herts 29 G4 vil 2m/3km SE of Baldock. TL 2731
Clotton Ches 42 B5 ham 2m/3km NW of Tarporley. SJ 5263
Cloud, The 43 E5* hill (NT) on Ches–Staffs border 3m/5km E of Congleton, commanding wide views. SJ 9063
Clough Gtr Manchester 43 E1* loc adjoining Shaw to E. SD 9408
Clough Gtr Manchester 48 C6 loc 1km NW of Littleborough. SD 9317
Clough W Yorks 48 D6* vil 3m/5km SW of Huddersfield. SE 0914
Clough 53 F5* r rising near Garsdale Head, N Yorks, and flowing W into R Rawthey 2km E of Sedbergh, Cumbria. SD 6792
Clough Bottom Reservoir Lancs 48 B5* resr on Forest of Rossendale 4m/6km S of Burnley. SD 8426
Clough Dene Durham 61 F5* loc 2km S of Burnopfield. NZ 1755
Clough Field S Yorks 43 G3* loc in Sheffield 2m/3km W of city centre. SK 3187
Clough Fold Lancs 48 B5* loc 1km E of Rawtenstall. SD 8222
Clough Foot W Yorks 48 B5* ham 2m/3km W of Todmorden. SD 9023
Clough Head W Yorks 48 D5* ham 1km S of Sowerby Br. SE 0622
Cloughton N Yorks 55 H5 vil 4m/7km N of Scarborough. TA 0094
Cloughton Newlands N Yorks 55 H5 loc 1km N of Cloughton. TA 0195
Cloughton Wyke N Yorks 55 H5* bay on North Sea coast 1km E of Cloughton and 4m/7km N of Scarborough. TA 0295
Clousta Shetland 89 E7* loc on Mainland at head of **Voe of C.**, inlet S of island of Vementry. HU 3057
Clova Tayside 76 D4 vil in Glen C., 12m/19km N of Kirriemuir. Fragment of **C. Castle** overlooks vil. NO 3273
Clovelly Devon 6 C3 vil on N coast 9m/14km W of Bideford, built on steep cliffside with small harbour at foot. Cobbled main street with steps. SS 3124
Clovenfords Borders 66 C5 vil 3m/4km W of Galashiels. NT 4436
Cloverley Salop. Alternative name for Calverhall, qv.
Clovulin H'land 74 B5 locality on W shore of Loch Linnhe in Lochaber dist, 2km NE of Sallachan Pt. NN 0063
Clow Bridge Lancs 48 B5* ham 3m/5km S of Burnley. **Clowbridge Resr** to E. SD 8228
Clown Welsh form of Clun (r), qv.
Clowne Derbys 44 A3 small tn 3m/5km NE of Bolsover. SK 4975
Clows Top H & W 26 C1 vil 4m/6km SE of Cleobury Mortimer. SO 7171
Cluanie Forest H'land 74 B1* deer forest in Skye and Lochalsh dist to S and W of head of Loch Cluanie. NH 0409
Clubbie Craig Grampian 83 G1* headland on N coast at Fraserburgh, 1km W of Kinnairds Hd. NJ 9967
Clubbiedean Reservoir Lothian 65 H2* small resr 2m/4km E of Balerno. NT 2066
Clubmoor Merseyside 42 A2* dist of Liverpool 3m/5km NE of city centre. SJ 3893
Cluddley Salop 34 C3* loc 2km SW of Wellington. SJ 6310
Cluden Water 59 E4 r in Dumfries & Galloway region running E to R Nith 1m N of Dumfries. NX 9677
Clugston Loch D & G 57 D7 small loch 3m/4km SE of Kirkcowan. NX 3457
Clumber Park Notts 44 B4 late 18c landscape design (NT) created out of heathland bordering Sherwood Forest 4m/6km SE of Worksop. SK 6274
Clun Salop 34 A6 vil 5m/9km N of Knighton and 8m/13km W of Craven Arms. Remains of 12c cas overlooking R Clun. SO 3080
Clun (Clown) 15 F3* r rising N of Llantwit Fardre, Mid Glam, and flowing SW into Ely R at Pontyclun. ST 0381
Clun 34 B6 r rising at Anchor, Salop, near Welsh border, and flowing E to Aston on Clun, then S to join R Teme at Leintwardine. SO 4073
Clunas H'land 81 G3* loc 3m/5km SE of Cawdor. **Clunas Resr,** small resr 2km W. NH 8545
Clunbury Salop 34 B6 vil 4m/7km W of Craven Arms. SO 3780
Clunderwen Welsh form of Clynderwen, qv.
Clunes H'land 74 C3 locality in Lochaber dist on NW shore of Loch Lochy, 3m/5km NE of foot of loch. **C. Forest** is state forest round shore of this part of loch. NN 2088
Clun Forest Salop 34 A5 area of hill country some 6m/10km NW of Clun. SO 2186
Clungunford Salop 34 B6 vil on R Clun 4m/6km SW of Craven Arms. SO 3978
Clunie Tayside 72 D1/73 E1 locality on W shore of Loch of C., qv, 4m/7km W of Blairgowrie. See also Forest of C. NO 1143
Clunie Water 76 C2 r in Grampian region running N down Glen Clunie to R Dee on N side of Braemar. NO 1492
Clunton Salop 34 A6 vil 2m/4km E of Clun. SO 3381
Cluny Fife 73 F5* loc 3m/5km NW of Kirkcaldy. NT 2495
Cluny Grampian 77 F1* loc and cas 3m/4km N of Banchory. NO 6899
Clutton Avon 16 B5 vil 4m/6km NW of Midsomer Norton. 1m NE, ham of **C. Hill.** ST 6259
Clutton Ches 42 A5 vil 4m/6km E of Holt. SJ 4654
Clwt-y-bont Gwynedd 40 C5* loc adjoining Deiniolen to W. SH 5763
Clwyd 116, 118 northern county of Wales, bounded by Gwynedd, Powys, the English counties of Salop and Cheshire, and the sea. The E side has coal mines and associated industries; the N and W are largely rural. Resorts line the coast. Apart from Deeside and the Vale of C., the county is mountainous, with large stretches of open moorland. Tns include Colwyn Bay, Denbigh, Llangollen, Rhyl, Ruthin, Wrexham, and Mold, the county tn. Chief rs are the Clwyd and the Dee.
Clwyd 41 F3 r rising in Clogaenog Forest, Clwyd, and flowing S to Melin-y-wig, then NE to Ruthin, then N to coast on W side of Rhyl. Between Ruthin and St Asaph valley is known as **Vale of Clwyd.** SH 9980
Clwydian Range (or Hills) Clwyd 41 G4, G5 line of hills extending N from Llantysilio Mt to Prestatyn, punctuated by a series of high passes. Highest point is Moel Fammau, qv. SJ 16
Clwyd-y-fagwyr Mid Glam 15 E1* 2km W of Merthyr Tydfil. SO 0206
Clydach Gwent 25 G6 vil 2m/3km E of Brynmawr. SO 2213
Clydach W Glam 23 H5 tn 6m/10km NE of Swansea. Nickel-refining, chemicals. SN 6901
Clydach 24 B5* r rising some 4m/6km S of Llanybydder, Dyfed, and flowing S through Gwernogle in Forest of Brechfa and into R Cothi 1m E of Brechfa. SN 5430
Clydach, Lower 23 H5 r rising on borders of Dyfed and W Glam about 4m/6km SE of Ammanford, Dyfed, and flowing S into R Tawe at Clydach, W Glam. SN 6801
Clydach Terrace Gwent 25 G6* loc 1m N of Brynmawr. SO 1813
Clydach, Upper 23 H5* r rising near Gwaun-cae-Gurwen, W Glam, and flowing S into R Tawe at Pontardawe. SN 7203
Clydach Vale Mid Glam 15 E2 vil 2km S of Rhondda. SS 9793
Clydan 24 B2* r rising E of Nebo, Dyfed, and flowing NW into Cardigan Bay on W side of Llanon. SN 5066

Clydau Welsh form of Clydey, qv.
Clyde 64 B2 r in Strathclyde region rising S of Abington and W of Moffat, and flowing NW through Glasgow to Firth of Clyde at Dumbarton. See also Falls of C., Firth of C. NS 3974
Clydebank S'clyde 64 C2 industrial tn on N bank of R Clyde 6m/10km NW of Glasgow. Industries include shipbuilding, marine engineering, chemicals. NS 5069
Clydebank 114 admin dist of S'clyde region.
Clyde Law 65 G6 hill on border of Strathclyde and Borders regions 5m/8km E of Elvanfoot. Height 1789 ft or 545 metres. NT 0217
Clydey (Clydau) Dyfed 23 E2* ham 5m/8km SW of Newcastle Emlyn. SN 2535
Clyffe Pypard Wilts 17 E4 vil 4m/6km S of Wootton Bassett. SU 0776
Clynder S'clyde 64 A1 vil on W shore of Gare Loch 3m/4km N of Kilcreggan. NS 2484
Clynderwen (Clunderwen) Dyfed 22 D4 vil 3m/5km N of Narberth. SN 1219
Clyne W Glam 14 D2* loc 4m/6km NE of Neath. SN 8000
Clynekirkton H'land 87 B6/C6. **Easter** and **Wester C.** are two locs in Sutherland dist, respectively 2km N and 3km NW of Brora on E coast. NC 9006
Clynelish H'land 86 B6* loc in Sutherland dist 1m NW of Brora. Distillery. NC 8905
Clyn-gwyn Powys 15 E1* farm above valley of R Mellte in vicinity of which are three waterfalls, **Upr, Middle,** and **Lr Clyn-gwyn Falls.** SN 9210
Clyn-gwyn Falls Powys 15 E1* three waterfalls in course of R Mellte near its confluence with R Hepste, S of Ystradfellte. SN 9210
Clynnog-fawr Gwynedd 40 B6 vil near coast of Caernarvon Bay 9m/14km SW of Caernarvon. SH 4149
Clynnog, Upper Gwynedd 40 B6* loc 4m/6km S of Llanllyfni. SH 4746
Clyro (Cleirwy) Powys 25 G3 vil 2km NW of Hay-on-Wye across r. Traces of Roman fort 1m E. Remains of motte and bailey cas. SO 2143
Clyst 7 G6 r in Devon rising at Clyst William 1m E of Plymtree and flowing SW to Broad Clyst then S into R Exe estuary opp Exton. SX 9785
Clyst Honiton Devon 7 G5 vil 5m/7km E of Exeter. Exeter Airport to E of vil. SX 9893
Clyst Hydon Devon 7 H5 vil 4m/6km S of Cullompton. 2km W, Paradise Copse (NT). ST 0301
Clyst St George Devon 5 F2 vil 5m/8km SE of Exeter. SX 9888
Clyst St Lawrence Devon 7 H5 vil 5m/8km NW of Ottery St Mary. ST 0200
Clyst St Mary Devon 5 F2 vil 4m/6km E of Exeter. SX 9790
Clyst William Devon 7 H4* ham 4m/7km SE of Cullompton. ST 0702
Clyth H'land 86 E4 loc near E coast of Caithness dist 2m/3km E of Lybster. Locs of **Upr** and **Mid C.** 1km and 2km NE respectively. ND 2736
Clyth, Mid H'land 86 F3 loc in Caithness dist 1m N of Clyth Ness. To N on small hill, Hill o' Many Stanes (A.M.), prehistoric arrangement of about 200 stones in parallel rows. ND 2937
Clyth Ness H'land 86 F4 headland with lighthouse on E coast of Caithness dist 3m/4km E of Lybster. ND 2936
Clywedog 24 C3* stream with tributaries **Nant Clywedog-uchaf** and **Nant Clywedog-ganol** flowing W into R Teifi at Llanfair Clydogau, Dyfed. SN 6251
Clywedog 33 E3 r rising on E slopes of Cader Idris and flowing N into R Wnion about 2km E of Dolgellau, Gwynedd. SH 7418
Clywedog 33 F3* r running S into R Dugoed 3m/4km E of Mallwyd, Gwynedd. SH 9012
Clywedog 33 F5 r rising 3m/5km SW of Pennant, Powys, and flowing SE through Clywedog Resr to join R Severn at Llanidloes. SN 9584
Clywedog 41 G5* r rising in N part of Clocaenog Forest, Clwyd, and flowing E to Bontuchel, then N to join R Clwyd 3m/4km E of Denbigh. SJ 0865
Clywedog 42 A6 r rising in hills W of Wrexham, Clwyd, and flowing E, by the S side of Wrexham, into R Dee 5m/8km E of Wrexham. SJ 4047
Clywedog Brook 25 F2* r rising NE of Bwlch-y-sarnau, Powys, and flowing S by Abbeycwmhir to R Ithon 3m/4km NE of Llandrindod Wells. SO 0764
Clywedog Reservoir Powys 33 F5 large resr in R Clywedog valley 3m/5km NW of Llanidloes. SN 9187
Cnap Coire na Spreidhe H'land 76 B1* NE peak of Cairn Gorm, in Badenoch and Strathspey dist. Height 3776 ft or 1151 metres. NJ 0104
Cnoc Coinnich S'clyde 70 D5* mt in Argyll in area known as Argyll's Bowling Green, between Loch Goil and Loch Long. Height 2497 ft or 761 metres. NN 2300
Cnoc Freiceadain H'land. See Reay.
Cnwch Coch Dyfed 24 C1 ham 4m/6km W of Devil's Br. SN 6775
Coad's Green Cornwall 4 A3 vil 5m/9km SW of Launceston. SX 2976
Coal Aston Derbys 43 H3 loc adjoining Dronfield to NE. SK 3679
Coalbournbrook W Midlands 35 E5 loc in NW part of Stourbridge. SO 8985
Coalbrookdale Salop 34 D4 loc in gorge of R Severn 2m/3km SW of Dawley, Telford. Cradle of iron industry. SJ 6604
Coalbrookvale Gwent 15 G1 loc in coal-mining dist 2m/3km S of Brynmawr. SO 1909
Coalburn S'clyde 65 E5 vil in colliery dist 3m/5km S of Lesmahagow. NS 8134
Coalburns Tyne & Wear 61 F5 ham 3m/4km SW of Ryton. NZ 1260
Coalcleugh Nthmb 60 D6 loc 2m/3km NE of Nenthead. To S is **C. Moor,** source of R West Allen. NY 8045
Coaley Glos 16 C2 vil 3m/4km N of Dursley. SO 7701
Coalfell Cumbria 60 B5 loc 4m/7km E of Brampton. NY 5960
Coalhill Essex 20 D2* ham 3m/5km N of Wickford. TQ 7597
Coalhouse Point Essex 20 C4* E point of E Tilbury Marshes on N bank of R Thames, 3m/5km E of Tilbury. TQ 6876
Coalmoor Salop 34 D4* loc 2m/3km W of Dawley. SJ 6607
Coalpit Heath Avon 16 B3 loc adjoining Frampton Cotterell to S. ST 6780
Coalpit Hill Staffs 42 D5* loc adjoining Kidsgrove to SW. SJ 8253
Coal Pool W Midlands 35 F4* loc in Walsall 2km N of tn centre. SK 0100
Coalport Salop 34 D4* vil on R Severn 2km S of Madeley, Telford. SJ 6902
Coalsnaughton Central 72 C5 vil 1km S of Tillicoultry across R Devon. Coal-mining. NS 9295
Coal Street Suffolk 31 F1* loc 2m/3km S of Stradbroke. TM 2370
Coaltown of Balgonie Fife 73 F4 vil 2km S of Markinch. NT 3099
Coaltown of Wemyss Fife 73 F5 vil 1km N of W Wemyss and 4m/7km NE of Kirkcaldy. NT 3295
Coalville Leics 36 A3 coal-mining tn on W edge of Charnwood Forest 12m/19km NW of Leicester. SK 4214
Coalway Lane End Glos 26 B6* loc 1m SE of Coleford. SO 5810
Coanwood Nthmb 60 C5* ham 3m/5km SW of Haltwhistle. NY 6859
Coat Som 8 C2 ham 1m NW of Martock. ST 4520
Coatbridge S'clyde 64 D2 tn 9m/14km E of Glasgow. Industries include coal, iron, steel, paper, clothing, hosiery. NS 7265
Coate Wilts 17 E5 vil 2m/4km E of Devizes. SU 0461
Coates Cambs 37 G4 vil 3m/4km E of Whittlesey. TL 3097
Coates Glos 17 E2 vil 3m/5km W of Cirencester. SO 9700
Coates Lancs 48 B3* loc adjoining Barnoldswick to E. SD 8847
Coates Lincs 44 D3* loc 2m/3km NE of Stow. SK 9083
Coates Notts 44 C3* loc 1m N of Cottam. SK 8281
Coates W Sussex 11 F3 ham 3m/4km SE of Petworth. SU 9917
Coates, Great Humberside 45 F1 vil 2m/4km W of Grimsby. **Lit Coates** loc in Grimsby 1m SE. TA 2310
Coates, North Lincs 45 G2 vil 7m/12km SE of Grimsby. Airfield on coast 2m/3km NE. See also Northcoates Pt. TA 3400
Coate Water Wilts 17 F3 resr 2m/3km SE of Swindon. SU 1782
Coatham Cleveland 55 E3 loc on North Sea coast adjoining Redcar to W. **C. Sands** along coast to W. **W Coatham** industrial loc to SW; chemical works. NZ 5925
Coatham Mundeville Durham 54 C3 loc 4m/6km N of Darlington. NZ 2820
Cobbaton Devon 7 E3 ham 6m/km SE of Barnstaple. SS 6127
Cobbie Row, Castle of Orkney 89 B6* remains of 12c Norse cas (A.M.) on island of Wyre. 'Cobbie Row' is corruption of 'Kolbein Hruga', name of chieftain who built it. HY 4426
Cobbinshaw Reservoir Lothian 65 F3/G3 resr 3m/5km S of W Calder. NT 0158
Cobbler's City Berks 18 C4* loc 4m/6km E of Reading. SU 7773
Cobbler's Green Norfolk 39 G5* loc 4m/6km NW of Bungay. TM 2892
Cobbler's Plain Gwent 16 A2* loc 2km N of Devauden. SO 4700
Cobbler, The S'clyde 70 D4 mt in Argyll 3m/4km W of Arrochar. Height 2891 ft or 881 metres. Also known as Ben Arthur. NN 2505
Cobby Syke N Yorks 48 D3* loc 1km N of Fewston. SE 1955
Cobden Devon 7 H5* loc 4m/7km W of Ottery St Mary. SY 0396
Cober 2 C5* r, also known as Looe or Loe, rising 3m/5km SE of Camborne, Cornwall, and flowing into Looe Pool, qv. SW 6424
Coberley Glos 26 D5 vil 4m/6km S of Cheltenham. SO 9616
Coberley, Upper Glos 27 E5 ham 4m/7km SE of Cheltenham. SO 9715
Cobhall Common H & W 26 A4* loc 5m/7km SW of Hereford. SO 4535
Cobham Kent 20 C5 vil 4m/6km SE of Gravesend. **C. Hall** (NT), 16c–17c hse, 18c alterations; girls' boarding school. Owletts (NT), 17c hse. Ch has well-known collection of brasses. TQ 6768
Cobham Surrey 19 E5 enlarged vil on R Mole 4m/7km NW of Leatherhead. Cedar Hse (NT), 15c hse with later alterations and additions. TQ 1060
Cob Island, Great Essex 21 F1 island at mouth of Tollesbury Fleet 2m/3km E of Tollesbury. TL 9810
Cobler's Green Essex 30 B5/B6 ham 4m/7km SE of Gt Dunmow. TL 6819
Cobley Hill H & W 27 E1* loc 3m/5km NW of Redditch. SP 0171
Cobmarsh Island Essex 21 F1 island off W end of Mersea I. TM 0012
Cobnash H & W 26 A2 ham 3m/5km W of Leominster. SO 4560
Cobridge Staffs 42 D6* loc in Stoke-on-Trent between Burslem and Hanley. SJ 8748
Cochill Burn 72 C1 r in Tayside region running S down Glen Cochill to join R Quaich and form R Braan 2m/3km NE of Amulree. NN 9238
Cochno Loch S'clyde 64 C2* small loch on Kilpatrick Hills 4m/6km W of Milngavie. NS 4976
Cochran Grampian 77 F1/F2* loc adjoining Kincardine O'Neil to SE. NO 5999
Cock Alley Derbys 43 H4 loc 2m/3km E of Chesterfield. SK 4170
Cock and End Suffolk 30 C3* loc 6m/9km NE of Haverhill. TL 7253
Cockayne Hatley Beds 29 F3 vil in fruit-growing area 2m/4km E of Potton. TL 2549
Cock Bank Clwyd 42 A6* loc 3m/5km SE of Wrexham. SJ 3545
Cock Bevington Warwicks 27 E3* loc 6m/9km N of Evesham. SP 0552
Cock Bridge Grampian 82 B6 rd br over R Don 8m/12km SE of Tomintoul. See also Corgarff Castle. NJ 2509
Cockburnspath Borders 67 E2 vil near coast 8m/12km SE of Dunbar. NT 7771
Cock Clarks Essex 20 D2 vil 4m/6km SW of Maldon. TL 8102
Cockden Lancs 48 B4* loc 2m/3km SE of Nelson. SD 8734
Cockenzie and Port Seton Lothian 66 B1 tn on Firth of Forth 4m/6km NE of Musselburgh. Fishing port. Power stn to W. NT 4075
Cocker 52 B2* r rising in Cumbrian Mts N of Gt Gable, Cumbria, and flowing N through Buttermere and Crummock Water into R Derwent at Cockermouth. NY 1230
Cocker Bar Lancs 47 F5* loc 3m/4km W of Leyland. SD 5022
Cocker Brook Lancs 48 A5* loc 2m/4km SW of Accrington. SD 7325
Cockerham Lancs 47 E3 vil 6m/10km S of Lancaster. SD 4652
Cocker Hill D & G 58 C1 hill 3m/4km NE of Kirkconnel. Height 1651 ft or 503 metres. NS 7515
Cockerington, North Lincs 45 G2 vil 4m/6km NE of Louth. **S Cockerington** vil 2km S. TF 3790
Cockermouth Cumbria 52 B2 tn at confluence of Rs Cocker and Derwent 8m/13km E of Workington. Industries include clothing and footwear mnfre. Remains of 13c–14c cas. In Main Street, 18c hse (NT), birthplace of Wordsworth, 1770. NY 1230
Cockernhoe Green Herts 29 E5* ham 3m/4km NE of Luton. TL 1223
Cockersdale W Yorks 49 E5* loc 2m/4km NW of Morley. SE 2329
Cockerton Durham 54 B3 dist of Darlington 1m W of tn centre. NZ 2715
Cockett W Glam 23 G6 loc in Swansea 2m/3km NW of tn centre. SS 6394
Cockfield Durham 54 A3 vil 2m/4km N of Staindrop. NZ 1224
Cockfield Suffolk 30 D3 vil 4m/6km N of Lavenham. TL 9054
Cockfosters London 19 F2* dist on borders of Barnet and Enfield boroughs 10m/16km N of Charing Cross. TQ 2796
Cock Gate H & W 26 A1* ham 5m/7km NW of Leominster. SO 4665
Cock Green Essex 30 B5/B6* ham 5m/7km SW of Braintree. TL 6919
Cocking W Sussex 11 E3 vil 3m/4km S of Midhurst. SU 8717
Cocking Causeway W Sussex 11 E3* ham 1m S of Midhurst. SU 8819
Cockington Devon 5 E4 vil of cob and thatch on W side of Torbay 2km W of Torquay tn centre. SX 8963
Cocklake Som 15 H6* vil 1m N of Wedmore. ST 4349
Cocklaw Nthmb 61 E4 loc 4m/7km N of Hexham. **C. Tower,** probably 15c. NY 9371
Cockleford Glos 26 D6/27 E6* loc 5m/8km S of Cheltenham. SO 9614
Cockle Park Nthmb 61 G3 loc 3m/5km N of Morpeth. 16c tower. NZ 2091
Cockley Cley Norfolk 38 C4 vil of N Breckland 4m/6km SW of Swaffham. Remains of 7c Saxon ch. TF 7904
Cockmuir Grampian 83 G2* loc 3m/4km E of Strichen. NJ 9855
Cock of Arran S'clyde 63 F3 headland at N end of island of Arran. NR 9552
Cockpen Lothian 66 B2* loc 2m/3km S of Dalkeith. NT 3264
Cockpole Green Berks 18 C3* vil 3m/5km E of Henley-on-Thames across r. SU 7981
Cockshead Dyfed 24 C3* loc 4m/6km SW of Tregaron. SN 6355
Cockshot Point Cumbria 52 D5* headland (NT) on E shore of Windermere 1km SW of Bowness. SD 3996
Cockshut Hill W Midlands 35 G5* loc in Birmingham 5m/8km E of city centre. SP 1485
Cockshutt Salop 34 B2 vil 4m/7km SE of Ellesmere. SJ 4329
Cockthorpe Norfolk 39 E1 ham 4m/7km E of Wells. TF 9842
Cockwood Devon 5 F3 vil on W side of R Exe estuary opp Exmouth. SX 9780
Cockwood Som 16 G6* loc 2km E of Stogursey. ST 2242
Cockyard Derbys 43 E3 ham 2km SW of Chapel-en-le-Frith. SK 0479
Cod Beck 49 F1 r rising on Cleveland Hills near Osmotherley, N Yorks, and flowing S through Thirsk into R Swale 2km SE of Topcliffe. SE 4174
Coddenham Suffolk 31 F3 vil 6m/10km N of Ipswich. Site of Romano-British settlement by R Gipping 2km SW. TM 1354
Coddington Ches 42 A5 vil 8m/12km SE of Chester. SJ 4555
Coddington H & W 26 C3* vil 3m/5km N of Ledbury. SO 7142
Coddington Notts 44 C5 vil 3m/4km E of Newark-on-Trent. SK 8354
Codford St Mary Wilts 9 G1 vil 4m/6km SE of Heytesbury. ST 9739
Codford St Peter Wilts 9 G1 vil 3m/4km SE of Heytesbury. ST 9640
Codicote Herts 29 F5/F6 vil 2m/3km NW of Welwyn. TL 2118
Codmore Hill W Sussex 11 F3 ham 2km NE of Pulborough. Site of Roman villa 1km E. TQ 0520

Codnor Derbys 43 H6 vil 2m/3km SE of Ripley. **C. Gate** loc 1km NW. SK 4249
Codrington Avon 16 C3 ham 2m/3km S of Chipping Sodbury. ST 7278
Codsall Staffs 35 E4 urban loc 4m/7km NW of Wolverhampton. **Codsall Wd** vil 2m/3km NW. SJ 8603
Coedcae-Caradoc Gwent 15 G1* loc on NE side of Blaenavon. SO 2509
Coedcae, Upper Gwent 15 G1 loc on E side of Blaenavon. SO 2508
Coedcernyw Welsh form of Coedkernew, qv.
Coed Cwnwr Gwent 15 H2* loc 2m/4km E of Usk. ST 4199
Coed-duon Welsh form of Blackwood, qv.
Coedely Mid Glam 15 E3* loc 2m/3km S of Tonyrefail. ST 0185
Coed Eva Gwent 15 G2* loc in SW part of Cwmbran. ST 2793
Coedkernew (Coedcernyw) Gwent 15 G3* loc 4m/6km SW of Newport. ST 2783
Coed-llai Welsh form of Leeswood, qv.
Coed Mawr Gwynedd 40 C4* loc 1m SW of Bangor. SH 5670
Coed Morgan Gwent 25 H6 loc 4m/6km SE of Abergavenny. SO 3511
Coedpoeth Clwyd 41 H6 loc 3m/5km W of Wrexham. SJ 2851
Coedty Reservoir Gwynedd 40 D4* resr in course of R Porth-llwyd 1m W of Dolgarrog. SH 7566
Coedway Powys 34 A3* loc 2km E of Crew Green. SJ 3414
Coed y Brenin Forest Gwynedd 33 E2* large wooded area 3m/5km to 6m/10km N of Dolgellau. SH 7326
Coed-y-bryn Dyfed 23 E2* ham 4m/7km NE of Newcastle Emlyn. SN 3545
Coed-y-Bwnydd Gwent 15 H1* ancient hilltop fort (NT) 3m/5km W of Raglan. SO 3606
Coed-y-caerau Gwent 15 H2* loc 3m/5km E of Caerleon across R Usk. ST 3891
Coedylade Powys 34 A3* loc 1m N of Welshpool. SJ 2209
Coed-y-paen (Coed-y-paun) Gwent 15 H2 vil 3m/5km SW of Usk. ST 3398
Coed-y-parc Gwynedd 40 C4* loc 1km W of Bethesda. SH 6166
Coed-y-paun Welsh form of Coed-y-paen, qv.
Coed-yr-ynys Powys 25 F5 loc on R Usk 4m/7km W of Crickhowell. SO 1520
Coed Ystumgwern Gwynedd 32 D2* loc adjoining Dyffryn or Dyffryn Ardudwy to N. SH 5823
Coelbren Powys 14 D1 vil 3m/4km NE of Seven Sisters. SN 8511
Coffinswell Devon 5 E4 vil 3m/5km SE of Newton Abbot. SX 8968
Coffle End Beds 29 E2* loc at E end of vil of Sharnbrook. TL 0059
Cofflete Creek Devon 4 C5* creek running S into R Yealm 2m/3km NE of Wembury. Sometimes spelt Coffleet. SX 5449
Cofton Devon 5 F3* loc 2m/4km N of Dawlish. SX 9680
Cofton Hackett H & W 27 E1* vil 6m/9km NW of Redditch. SP 0075
Cogan S Glam 15 G4 NW dist of Penarth. ST 1772
Cogenhoe Northants 28 D2 vil 5m/8km E of Northampton. SP 8360
Cogges Oxon 17 G1* loc just E of Witney across R Windrush. Loc of **High C.** 2km E. SP 3609
Coggeshall Essex 30 C5 vil 6m/9km E of Braintree. Paycocke's (NT), dating from c 1500, is one of several old hses. Ham of **C. Hamlet** 1km S. TL 8522
Coigach H'land 85 B6 upland area in Ross and Cromarty dist N of Ullapool and SE of Achiltibuie. NC 00, 10
Coignafearn Forest H'land 81 F6 deer forest on Monadhliath Mts in Inverness dist, astride upper reaches of R Findhorn. NH 6412
Coilleag a' Phrionnsa W Isles 88 E3* 'The Prince's Beach' on W coast of island of Eriskay where Prince Charles Edward first landed on Scottish soil in 1744. NF 7810
Coillemore Point S'clyde 63 F3* headland at N end of Arran, on W side of entrance to Loch Ranza. NR 9251
Coiltie H'land 81 E4 r in Inverness dist running NE to Urquhart Bay on NW side of Loch Ness. NH 5229
Coiltry H'land 80 D6 loc in Inverness dist 3m/4km SW of Fort Augustus. NH 3506
Coire Cas H'land 76 B1* corrie in Badenoch and Strathspey dist. Main skiing area on NW slope of Cairn Gorm. NH 9904
Coire Fhionn Lochan S'clyde 63 F3* tarn below N slope of Beinn Bhreac on island of Arran. NR 9045
Coire Làgan Skye, H'land 79 C6* corrie and noted climbing area in Cuillin Hills W of Sgurr Alasdair. NG 4320
Coire na Ciste H'land 76 B1* corrie and skiing area in Badenoch and Strathspey dist 2km N of summit of Cairn Gorm. NJ 0006
Coire Odhar Tayside 71 G1* SW slope (NTS) of Ben Lawers. HQ of Scottish Ski Club. NN 6140
Coity Mid Glam 15 E3* vil 2m/3km NE of Bridgend. Site of ancient burial-chamber to N. Ruins of Norman cas (A.M.), abandoned in 16c. SS 9281
Cokeham, Lower W Sussex 11 G4* loc 2m/3km E of Worthing. TQ 1704
Cokeham, Upper W Sussex 11 G4* urban loc 3m/4km NE of Worthing. TQ 1705
Coker, East Som 8 D3 vil 3m/4km SW of Yeovil. **N Coker** vil 1km N. **W Coker** vil 2m/3km NW. ST 5412
Cokhay Green Derbys 35 H2* loc 1m SW of Repton. SK 2926
Coladoir S'clyde 69 D5* r on Mull running W down Glen More to head of Loch Scridain. NM 5328
Colan Cornwall 2 D2 ham 4m/6km E of Newquay. SW 8661
Colaton Raleigh Devon 5 F2 vil 4m/6km N of Budleigh Salterton. SY 0787
Colburn N Yorks 54 B5* vil 3m/5km W of Catterick. SE 1999
Colbury Hants 10 A4 ham 2m/3km SW of Totton. SU 3410
Colby Cumbria 53 F3 vil 2km W of Appleby. NY 6620
Colby Isle of Man 46 A6 vil 2m/4km E of Port Erin. SC 2370
Colby Norfolk 39 F2 vil 3m/5km NE of Aylsham. TG 2231
Colby 46 A6* r on Isle of Man running S into Bay ny Carrickey. SC 2268
Colchester Essex 30 D5/31 E5 tn on R Colne 51m/82km NE of London, dating from Iron Age. Was first Roman capital of Britain (*Camulodunum*); many Roman remains. Remains of Norman cas now museum. Many old bldgs, but also modern tn with engineering works and general industry. University of Essex 2m/4km SE. TL 9925
Colchester Green Suffolk 30 D3* ham 7m/11km SE of Bury St Edmunds. TL 9255
Colcot S Glam 15 F4* loc 1m N of Barry. ST 1069
Cold Ash Berks 18 A4 vil 3m/5km NE of Newbury. SU 5169
Cold Ashby Northants 36 C6 vil 5m/8km S of Husbands Bosworth. SP 6576
Cold Ashton Avon 16 C4 vil 5m/8km N of Bath. ST 7472
Cold Aston Glos. Former name of Aston Blank, qv.
Coldbackie H'land 84 F2 vil to S of Tongue Bay, N coast of Caithness dist 2m/4km NE of Tongue. NC 6160
Cold Blow Dyfed 22 D4 loc 2km SE of Narberth. SN 1212
Coldblow London 20 B4* loc in borough of Bexley 2m/4km W of Dartford. TQ 5073
Cold Brayfield Bucks 28 D3 vil in loop of R Ouse 3m/4km E of Olney. SP 9352
Cold Cotes N Yorks 48 A1* loc 2m/3km SE of Ingleton. SE 7171
Coldean E Sussex 12 A5* NE dist of Brighton. TQ 3308
Coldeast Devon 5 E3* ham 3m/5km NW of Newton Abbot. SX 8174
Coldeaton Derbys 43 F5* loc 3m/4km SE of Hartington. SK 1456
Colden W Yorks 48 C5 ham 2m/3km NW of Hebden Br. SD 9628
Colden Common Hants 10 B3 vil 3m/5km NE of Eastleigh. SU 4822
Coldermeadow Northants 36 D5* SW dist of Corby. SP 8687
Coldfair Green Suffolk 31 H2 vil 1m SW of Leiston. TM 4361
Cold Green H & W 26 C3* loc 4m/6km NW of Ledbury. SO 6842
Coldham Cambs 37 H4 loc 5m/8km SW of Wisbech. TF 4302
Cold Hanworth Lincs 45 E3* ham 2m/4km W of Faldingworth. TF 0383
Coldharbour Dorset 8 D6* loc 2m/4km N of Weymouth. SY 6581
Coldharbour Glos 16 B1* loc 1km S of St Briavels. SO 5503
Coldharbour London 20 B4* loc on N bank of R Thames on Aveley Marshes in borough of Havering, 14m/22km E of Charing Cross. TQ 5278
Cold Harbour Oxon 18 B3* loc 2m/4km E of Goring. SU 6379
Coldharbour Surrey 11 G1 vil 4m/6km S of Dorking. TQ 1443
Cold Hatton Salop 34 C2 loc 6m/10km N of Wellington. **C. H. Heath** loc 1km E. SJ 6221
Cold Hesledon Durham 61 H6 vil 2m/3km SW of Seaham. NZ 4047
Cold Hiendley W Yorks 49 F6* ham 2m/3km NE of Royston. **Cold Hiendley Resr** to N, adjoining Wintersett Resr to W. SE 3714
Cold Higham Northants 28 B2 vil 4m/6km NW of Towcester. SP 6653
Coldingham Borders 67 F2 vil 3m/5km NW of Eyemouth. Ruins of 12c priory. **C. Bay** on coast 1m E. NT 9066
Cold Inn Dyfed 22 D5* loc 2m/3km W of Saundersfoot. SN 1005
Cold Kirby N Yorks 54 D6 vil 5m/8km W of Helmsley. SE 5384
Cold Knap Point S Glam 15 F4* headland at S end of Barry, W of Barry I. ST 1066
Coldmartin Loughs Nthmb 67 G5* two small lakes 2km E of Wooler. NU 0127
Cold Newton Leics 36 C4 loc 8m/13km E of Leicester, near site of former vil. SK 7106
Cold Northcott Cornwall 6 B6* loc 7m/11km E of Camelford. SX 2086
Cold Norton Essex 21 E2 vil 4m/7km S of Maldon. TL 8400
Cold Overton Leics 36 D3 vil 3m/5km W of Oakham. SK 8110
Coldred Kent 13 G3 vil 5m/7km NW of Dover. TR 2746
Coldridge Devon 7 E4 vil 4m/7km E of Winkleigh. SS 6907
Cold Row Lancs 47 E4* loc 2m/3km S of Preesall. SD 3744
Coldstream Borders 67 E4 small tn on R Tweed 9m/14km NE of Kelso. C. Guards raised here by General Monk, 1660. NT 8439
Coldwaltham W Sussex 11 F3 vil 2m/3km SW of Pulborough. TQ 0216
Coldwell Reservoirs Lancs 48 B4* two small resrs 3m/4km S of Colne. SD 9036
Coldwells Grampian 83 H3* loc near E coast 1m W of Murdoch Hd. NK 1039
Cold Weston Salop 34 C5/C6* loc 6m/9km NE of Ludlow. SO 5583
Coldyreath Cornwall 3 E3* loc 4m/7km NW of St Austell. SW 9858
Cole Som 8 D1* vil 2km SW of Bruton. ST 6633
Cole 17 F2 r rising at Swindon, Wilts, and flowing N into R Thames 1km below Lechlade, Glos. SU 2299
Cole 35 H5 r rising near Portway about 9m/14km S of Birmingham, and flowing N and NE into R Tame 2m/3km NE of Coleshill, Warwicks. SP 2191
Colebatch Salop 34 A5 ham 2km S of Bishop's Castle. SO 3187
Colebrook Devon 7 G4* loc 2km SW of Cullompton. ST 0006
Colebrooke Devon 7 F5 vil 4m/7km W of Crediton. SS 7700
Coleburn Grampian 82 B2 loc with distillery 4m/7km S of Elgin. NJ 2455
Coleby Humberside 50 D6 vil 6m/9km N of Scunthorpe. SE 8919
Coleby Lincs 44 D5 vil 7m/11km S of Lincoln. SK 9760
Cole End Warwicks 35 G5* N end of Coleshill. SP 1989
Coleford Devon 7 F5 vil 4m/7km W of Crediton. SS 7701
Coleford Glos 26 B6 tn in Forest of Dean 4m/7km SE of Monmouth. SO 5710
Coleford Som 16 C6 vil 6m/9km W of Frome. ST 6848
Coleford Water Som 7 H2* ham 4m/7km NE of Wiveliscombe. ST 1133
Colegate End Norfolk 39 F5* ham 2km N of Pulham Mkt. TM 1987
Cole Green Herts 19 G1 ham 3m/5km E of Welwyn Garden City. TL 2811
Cole Green Herts 29 H4* NW end of Brent Pelham, 5m/7km E of Buntingford. TL 4331
Cole Henley Hants 17 H6* loc 2m/3km N of Whitchurch. SU 4751
Colerne Wilts 16 C4 vil 6m/10km W of Chippenham. Airfield to W. Site of Roman villa on N side of airfield. ST 8271
Colehill Dorset 9 G4 vil adjoining Wimborne to NE. SU 0201
Coleman Green Herts 19 F1* loc 3m/5km W of Welwyn Garden City. TL 1812
Coleman's Hatch E Sussex 12 B3 ham on N edge of Ashdown Forest 2m/3km SE of Forest Row. TQ 4533
Cole Mere Salop 34 B1 lake, one of several in dist, 2m/4km SE of Ellesmere. SJ 4333
Colemere Salop 34 B2 vil 3m/4km SE of Ellesmere. SJ 4332
Colemore Hants 10 D2 ham 5m/8km S of Alton. SU 7030
Colemore Green Salop 34 D4* loc 3m/5km N of Bridgnorth. SO 7097
Coleorton Leics 36 A3 loc 3m/4km NW of Coalville. **C. Moor** loc 1km S. SK 4017
Colesbourne Glos 27 E6 vil 6m/10km SE of Cheltenham. SO 9913
Colesbrook Dorset 9 E2* loc 1m N of Gillingham. ST 8027
Cole's Common Norfolk 39 F5* loc 2km N of Pulham Mkt. TM 2088
Colesden Beds 29 F2* loc 6m/10km NE of Bedford. TL 1255
Coles Green H & W 26 C3* loc 4m/6km N of Gt Malvern. SO 7751
Coles Green Suffolk 31 E4* ham 4m/7km W of Ipswich. TM 1041
Cole's Green Suffolk 31 G2* loc 1km SE of Framlingham. TM 2862
Coleshill Bucks 18 D2 vil 2km SW of Amersham. SU 9495
Coleshill Oxon 17 F2 vil (NT) 4m/6km W of Faringdon. SU 2393
Coleshill Warwicks 35 G5 tn 9m/14km E of Birmingham. SP 1989
Colestocks Devon 7 H5* loc 3m/5km N of Ottery St Mary. ST 0900
Coleton Devon 5 E5* loc 2m/3km E of Dartmouth across R Dart. SX 9051
Coley Avon 16 B5* ham 1m E of E Harptree. ST 5855
Coley Staffs 35 F2* loc 4m/6km NW of Rugeley. SK 0122
Coley W Yorks 48 D5* loc 2m/4km NE of Halifax. SE 1226
Colfa Welsh form of Colva, qv.
Colgate W Sussex 11 H2 ham 4m/6km E of Horsham. TQ 2332
Colgrave Sound Shetland 89 F6 sea passage between Yell and Fetlar S of Hascosay. HU 5789
Colham Green London 19 E3* loc in borough of Hillingdon 2m/3km SE of Uxbridge. TQ 0781
Colindale London 19 F3* loc in borough of Barnet 1m NW of Hendon. TQ 2189
Colinsburgh Fife 73 G4 vil built in 18c, 2m/4km NW of Elie. NO 4703
Colinton Lothian 66 A2 dist of Edinburgh 4m/6km SW of city centre. NT 2168
Colintraive S'clyde 63 G1 vil in Argyll on E shore of Kyles of Bute, 2m/3km SE of entrance to Loch Riddon. Car and pedestrian ferry service to Rhubodach on island of Bute. NS 0374
Colkirk Norfolk 38 D2 vil 2m/3km S of Fakenham. TF 9126
Coll S'clyde 68 A3 sparsely populated island of Inner Hebrides, measuring 12m/20km NE to SW and nearly 4m/6km at greatest width. Its NE point is 9m/15km W of Ardnamurchan Pt on mainland and its SW point is 2m/3km NE of neighbouring island of Tiree. Coll is fairly low-lying, and somewhat bleak and windswept. Lochs noted for trout fishing. NM 15
Coll W Isles 88 C2* r on Lewis flowing SE into Broad Bay or Loch a' Tuath between Coll and Upr Coll vils. NB 4639
Coll W Isles 88 C2* vil near E coast of Lewis 5m/8km NE of Stornoway. Vil of **Upr Coll** 1km SW across R Coll. NB 4640
Collace Tayside 73 E2 loc 8m/12km NE of Perth. See also Kirkton of C. NO 2032
Colla Firth Shetland 89 E6* inlet on E coast of Mainland 4m/6km N of Laxo and the head of Dury Voe. HU 4369
Colla Firth Shetland 89 E6 inlet of Yell Sound on NE coast of Mainland. Locs of **N** and **S Collafirth** at head of inlet, 6m/10km N of Sullom. HU 3583
Collaton St Mary Devon 5 E4 vil on W edge of Paignton. SX 8660
College Burn 67 F5 r rising on the Cheviot, Nthmb, and flowing N to Westnewton, where it joins Bowmont Water to form R Glen. NT 9030
College Green Som 8 D1* loc 1km E of Parbrook and 5m/8km SE of Glastonbury. ST 5636

College Milton S'clyde 64 D3* dist and industrial estate in E Kilbride 2km W of tn centre. NS 6154
College Town Berks 18 D5* military tn adjoining Royal Military Academy at Sandhurst. SU 8561
College, Upper Salop 34 C1* loc 5m/8km SE of Whitchurch. SJ 5734
Collessie Fife 73 F3 vil 6m/9km W of Cupar. NO 2813
Collett's Green H & W 26 C3* loc 3m/5km SW of Worcester. SO 8251
Collie Head Grampian 83 F1* headland on N coast 1km SW of Troup Hd. NJ 8167
Collier Row London 20 B3 NW dist of Romford, borough of Havering. TQ 4990
Collier's End Herts 29 G5 vil 4m/7km N of Ware. TL 3720
Collier's Green E Sussex 12 D4* loc 1km E of Staple Cross. TQ 7922
Collier's Reach Essex 21 E1* channel of R Blackwater 2m/3km E of Maldon, passing N of Northey I. TL 8807
Collier Street Kent 12 D2 vil 3m/5km S of Yalding. TQ 7145
Colliers Wood London 19 F4* loc in borough of Merton 2km E of Wimbledon. Running S from High Street on W side of rly stn is Merton Abbey Wall (NT). TQ 2670
Colliery Row Tyne & Wear 61 G6* loc adjoining Houghton-le-Spring to W. NZ 3249
Collieston Grampian 83 H4 vil on E coast 3m/5km NE of Newburgh across R Ythan and Sands of Forvie. NK 0328
Collin D & G 59 E4 vil 4m/6km E of Dumfries. NY 0276
Collingbourne Ducis Wilts 17 F5 vil 2m/4km NW of Ludgershall. SU 2453
Collingbourne Kingston Wilts 17 F5 vil 4m/6km NW of Ludgershall. SU 2355
Collingham W Yorks 49 F3/F4 vil 2m/3km SW of Wetherby. SE 3845
Collingham, North Notts 44 C5 vil 6m/9km NE of Newark-on-Trent. **S Collingham** vil adjoining to S. SK 8361
Collington H & W 26 B2* ham 4m/6km N of Bromyard. SO 6460
Collingtree Northants 28 C2 vil at S end of Northampton. SP 7555
Collins End Oxon 18 B4* loc 2m/3km NE of Pangbourne. SU 6678
Collins Green Ches 42 B2 vil 5m/8km NW of Warrington. SJ 5594
Collins Green H & W 26 C2* loc 6m/9km E of Bromyard. SO 7457
Colliston Tayside 77 F6 former name of Gowanbank, vil 4m/6km NW of Arbroath. Colliston Hse, 16c. NO 6045
Collum Green Bucks 18 D3* loc 2m/4km S of Beaconsfield. SU 9596
Collycroft Warwicks 36 A5 N dist of Bedworth. SP 3587
Collyhurst Gtr Manchester 42 D2* dist of Manchester 2m/3km NE of city centre. SD 8500
Collyweston Northants 37 E4 vil 3m/5km SW of Stamford. SK 9902
Colmonell S'clyde 57 B5 vil in R Stinchar valley 5m/7km NE of Ballantrae. NX 1486
Colmworth Beds 29 E2 vil 7m/11km NE of Bedford. TL 1058
Coln 17 F2 r rising near Brockhampton, Glos, and flowing SW into R Thames 1m above Lechlade. SU 2199
Colnbrook Bucks 19 E4 loc 4m/6km SE of Slough. TQ 0277
Colne Cambs 37 H6 vil 6m/10km S of Chatteris. TL 3775
Colne Lancs 48 B4 tn 6m/9km NE of Burnley. Textiles, leather, engineering. **C. Edge** loc 1km N. SD 8840
Colne 31 E6 r rising in NW Essex and flowing SE through Colchester into North Sea between Brightlingsea and Mersea I. TM 0715
Colne 48 D6 r rising W of Marsden, W Yorks, and flowing NE through Marsden, Slaithwaite, and Huddersfield, into R Calder W of Mirfield. SE 1720
Colne Bridge W Yorks 48 D6* loc on R Colne 2m/3km W of Mirfield. SE 1720
Colne Engaine Essex 30 C5 vil 2m/4km E of Halstead. TL 8530
Colney Norfolk 39 F4 vil on R Yare 3m/5km W of Norwich. TG 1807
Colney Hatch London 19 G3* loc in borough of Barnet 7m/12km N of Charing Cross. TQ 2791
Colney Heath Herts 19 F1 vil 3m/4km SW of Hatfield. TL 2005
Colney Street Herts 19 F2 loc 3m/5km N of St Albans. Site of Roman villa 1km NW. TL 1502
Coln Rogers Glos 17 E1 vil 4m/6km SW of Northleach. SP 0809
Coln St Aldwyns Glos 17 F1 vil 2m/3km SE of Bibury. SP 1405
Coln St Dennis Glos 27 E6 vil 3m/5km SW of Northleach. SP 0810
Colonsay S'clyde 69 C7, C8 island of some 16 sq miles or 40 sq km lying 8m/13km NW of Jura in Inner Hebrides. Has rocky coastline interspersed with sandy beaches. Chief settlement is Scalasaig on E coast. Sea birds abound. Joined to Oronsay, qv, to S at low tide. NR 39
Colonsay, Little S'clyde 69 C5 uninhabited island of about 200 acres or 80 hectares lying 1m off SW coast of Ulva. NM 3736
Colpy Grampian 83 E4 loc 9m/14km SE of Huntly. NJ 6432
Colsay Shetland 89 E8* uninhabited island of 54 acres or 22 hectares lying off W coast of Mainland opp Bay of Scousburgh. HU 3618
Colscott Devon 6 C4* loc 7m/11km N of Holsworthy. SS 3614
Colsterdale N Yorks 54 A6* loc 4m/7km S of Middleham. SE 1381
Colsterworth Lincs 37 E2 vil 7m/12km S of Grantham. SK 9324
Colston S'clyde 64 D2* loc in Glasgow 3m/4km N of city centre. NS 6069
Colston Bassett Notts 36 C1/C2 vil 4m/7km S of Bingham. Old mkt cross (NT). SK 7033
Colt Crag Reservoir Nthmb 61 E4 resr 9m/14km N of Hexham. NY 9378
Colthouse Cumbria 52 D5* loc just E of Hawkshead. SD 3598
Coltishall Norfolk 39 F3 vil 8m/12km NE of Norwich. **C. Airfield** to N. TG 2719
Coltness S'clyde 65 E3* loc 1m N of Wishaw. NS 7956
Colton Cumbria 52 C6 ham 2m/3km N of Greenodd. SD 3186
Colton Norfolk 39 E4 vil 5m/8km N of Wymondham. TG 1009
Colton N Yorks 49 G4 vil 4m/6km E of Tadcaster. SE 5444
Colton Staffs 35 F2/F3 vil 2m/3km N of Rugeley. SK 0520
Colton W Yorks 49 F5* vil in Leeds 4m/7km E of city centre. SE 3632
Columbia Tyne & Wear 61 G5* dist of Washington SE of tn centre. NZ 3155
Colwall H & W 26 C3 vil 3m/5km NE of Ledbury. SO 7342
Colwall Green H & W 26 C3* vil 3m/5km NE of Ledbury. SO 7541
Colwall Stone H & W 26 C3 vil 3m/5km SW of Gt Malvern. SO 7542
Colwell Nthmb 61 E4 vil 7m/11km N of Hexham. NY 9575
Colwell Bay Isle of Wight 10 A5 bay N of Totland extending from Warden Pt (S) to Cliff End (N). SU 3288
Colwich Staffs 35 F2 vil on R Trent 3m/5km NW of Rugeley. SK 0121
Colwick Notts 36 C1 loc 3m/5km E of Nottingham. SK 6140
Colwinston (Tregolwyn) S Glam 15 E4 vil 4m/6km W of Cowbridge. SS 9475
Colworth W Sussex 11 E4* vil 3m/5km NW of Bognor Regis. SU 9102
Colwyn 40 C6* r rising on SW slopes of Snowdon, Gwynedd, and flowing S into R Glaslyn at Beddgelert. SH 5948
Colwyn Bay Clwyd 41 E3 bay on SE side of Rhos-on-Sea. Also tn and resort situated on it, 10m/16km W of Rhyl. See also Old Colwyn. SH 8479
Colwyn Brook 33 G5 stream running SE into R Trannon 2m/3km W of Caersws, Powys. SO 0191
Colwyn Brook 33 H3* stream running E into R Vyrnwy 4m/6km SE of Llanfyllin, Powys. SJ 1916
Coly 8 B5 r rising S of Honiton, Devon and flowing into R Axe to E of Colyford. SY 2592
Colyford Devon 8 B5 2m/3km N of Seaton. SY 2592
Colyton Devon 8 B5 vil 3m/4km N of Seaton. SY 2493
Combe Berks 17 G5 ham 5m/8km N of Hurstbourne Tarrant. SU 3760
Combe Devon 4 D4* ham below E side of Dartmoor 3m/4km NW of Buckfastleigh. SX 7068
Combe Devon 4 D6* loc just W of S Pool and 4m/6km N of Prawle Pt. SX 7640
Combe Devon 7 G3* ham 2m/3km E of Morebath. SS 9825
Combe H & W 25 H2* ham 2m/4km E of Presteigne. SO 3463
Combe Oxon 27 G6* vil 5m/9km NE of Witney. SP 4115
Combe Som 8 C2* ham 1m N of Langport. ST 4128
Combe Abbey Warwicks 36 A6 hse in park with lake, 4m/7km E of Coventry. Originally a Cistercian monastery, founded in 12c. SP 4079
Combe Common Surrey 11 F2* loc adjoining Chiddingfold to NW and 4m/6km S of Milford. SU 9536
Combe Down Avon 16 C5 SE dist of Bath. ST 7662
Combe, East Som 8 A2* ham 1km E of Combe Florey. ST 1631
Combe Florey Som 8 A2 vil 6m/10km NW of Taunton. ST 1531
Combe Hay Avon 16 C5 vil 3m/5km S of Bath. ST 7359
Combe, Higher Som 7 G2* ham 2m/3km NW of Dulverton. SS 9030
Combeinteignhead Devon 5 E3 vil 3m/4km E of Newton Abbot. SX 9071
Combe Martin Devon 6 D1 vil running down to **C. M. Bay** on N coast 4m/6km E of Ilfracombe. SS 5846
Combe Moor H & W 25 H2* vil 4m/6km E of Presteigne. SO 3663
Combe Pafford Devon 5 E4* N dist of Torbay, 2km N of Torquay tn centre. SX 9166
Combe Raleigh Devon 8 A4 vil 1m N of Honiton. ST 1502
Comberbach Ches 43 C3 vil 3m/4km NW of Northwich. SJ 6477
Comberford Staffs 35 G3/G4 ham 2m/4km N of Tamworth. SK 1907
Comber Mere Ches 34 C1 large natural lake set in park of 19c hse which embodies remains of 12c abbey, 3m/5km NE of Whitchurch. SJ 5844
Comberton Cambs 29 G2 vil 4m/7km W of Cambridge. TL 3856
Comberton H & W 26 A1 ham 5m/9km N of Leominster. SO 4967
Comberton, Great H & W 26 D3 vil on R Avon 3m/4km S of Pershore. SO 9542
Comberton, Little H & W 26 D3/27 E3 vil 2m/4km SE of Pershore. SO 9642
Combe St Nicholas Som 8 B3 vil 2m/4km NW of Chard. ST 3011
Combpyne Devon 8 B5 ham in par of **Combpyne Rousdon** 3m/5km W of Lyme Regis. SY 2992
Combridge Staffs 35 G1* loc 3m/4km N of Uttoxeter. SK 0937
Combrook Warwicks 27 G3 vil 7m/11km E of Stratford-upon-Avon. SP 3051
Combs Derbys 43 E3* ham 2m/3km SW of Chapel-en-le-Frith. **Combs Resr** 1km N. SK 0478
Combs Suffolk 31 E3 vil 2m/3km S of Stowmarket. TM 0456
Combs Ford Suffolk 31 E2* S dist of Stowmarket. TM 0557
Combwich Som 15 G6 vil on tidal reach of R Parrett 4m/7km NW of Bridgwater. ST 2542
Comely Bank Lothian 66 A1/A2* dist of Edinburgh 1m NW of city centre. NT 2374
Comers Grampian 83 E6 loc 8m/12km N of Banchory. NJ 6707
Come-to-Good Cornwall 2 D4* loc 3m/5km S of Truro. SW 8140
Comfort Cornwall 2 D4* loc 2m/3km NE of Penryn adjoining Mylor Br. SW 8036
Comfort, Little Cornwall 4 A3* loc 3m/4km S of Launceston. SX 3480
Comhampton H & W 26 D1* vil 3m/5km SE of Stourport. SO 8366
Comin Capel Betws Dyfed 24 C2* loc 4m/7km W of Tregaron. SN 6157
Comins Coch Dyfed 32 D6* loc 2m/3km E of Aberystwyth. SN 6182
Comiston Lothian 66 A2* dist of Edinburgh 3m/5km S of city centre. NT 2469
Commando Memorial H'land. See Spean Bridge.
Commercial End Cambs 30 B2 loc at N end of Swaffham Bulbeck 6m/9km W of Newmarket. TL 5563
Commins-coch Powys 33 F4 ham 2m/3km SE of Cemmaes Rd. SH 8403
Commondale N Yorks 55 E4 vil 2m/4km NW of Castleton. NZ 6610
Common, East N Yorks 50 B5* SE dist of Selby. SE 6231
Common Edge Lancs 46 D5* loc in Blackpool 2m/3km SE of tn centre. SD 3232
Common End Cumbria 52 A3* loc adjoining Distington to S. NY 0022
Common, High Norfolk 31 F1* loc 4m/6km E of Diss. TM 1781
Common, High Norfolk 38 D4/39 E4* loc 1km NW of Southburgh. TF 9905
Common, Little E Sussex 12 D5 W dist of Bexhill. TQ 7108
Common, Little S Yorks 43 G3* loc in Sheffield 3m/5km SW of city centre. SK 3283
Common, Low Norfolk 38 F5* loc 6m/10km S of Wymondham. TM 1461
Common, Lower Hants 18 C5* ham 1km W of Eversley. SU 7662
Common Marsh Hants. See Stockbridge.
Common Moor Cornwall 3 G2* vil 3m/5km N of Liskeard. SX 2469
Common, North Avon 16 B4* loc 6m/9km E of Bristol. ST 6772
Common, North E Sussex 12 A4* ham 2m/3km W of Newick. TQ 3921
Common, North Suffolk 31 E1* loc 1km NW of Hepworth. TL 9775
Common Platt Wilts 17 E3* loc 3m/5km NW of Swindon. SU 1086
Common Side Ches 42 B4* loc 1m SE of Helsby. SJ 5074
Commonside Derbys 35 H1 loc 8m/12km NW of Derby. SK 2441
Common Side Derbys 43 G4/H4* loc 1km NW of Barlow. SK 3375
Commonside Notts 44 A5* loc adjoining Huthwaite to S. SK 4658
Common Side S Yorks 43 H3* loc in Sheffield 3m/4km SE of city centre. SK 3884
Common Square Lincs 45 E4* loc 2m/3km E of Washingborough. TF 0470
Common, The Wilts 17 E3* loc 1m NE of Brinkworth and 3m/5km NW of Wootton Bassett. SU 0285
Common, The Wilts 9 H1* vil in par of Winterslow 7m/11km E of Salisbury. SU 2432
Commonty, North Grampian 83 G2* loc 2km NW of New Deer. NJ 8648
Commonwood Clwyd 42 A5* loc 2m/3km W of Holt. SJ 3753
Compstall Gtr Manchester 43 E2* vil 2m/3km E of Romiley. SJ 9690
Compton Berks 18 A3 vil 5m/7km W of Streatley. SU 5279
Compton Devon 4 B5* dist of Plymouth 2m/3km NE of city centre. SX 4956
Compton Devon 5 E4 ham 3m/5km W of Torquay. C. Castle (NT) is a restored medieval manor hse. SX 8664
Compton Hants 10 A2* ham 4m/6km S of Stockbridge. SU 3429
Compton Hants 10 B2 vil 3m/4km S of Winchester. SU 4625
Compton Som 8 C1 vil at E end of Sedgemoor 3m/4km S of Street. ST 4832
Compton Staffs 35 E5* ham 5m/8km W of Stourbridge. SO 8284
Compton Surrey 11 E1* loc adjoining Farnham to E. SU 8546
Compton Surrey 11 F1 vil 3m/5km SW of Guildford. Watts Picture Gallery. Norman sanctuary of ch has upper chamber unique in Europe. SU 9547
Compton Wilts 17 F6 ham on R Avon 2m/3km S of Upavon. SU 1352
Compton W Sussex 10 D3 vil 7m/11km NE of Havant. SU 7714
Compton W Yorks 49 F4* loc 2m/4km S of Wetherby. SE 3944
Compton Abbas Dorset. See Compton, West.
Compton Abbas Dorset 9 F3 vil on W edge of Cranborne Chase 3m/5km S of Shaftesbury. ST 8618
Compton Abdale Glos 27 E5 vil 4m/6km NW of Northleach. SP 0616
Compton Bassett Wilts 17 E4 vil 3m/4km E of Calne. SU 0372
Compton Bay Isle of Wight 10 B6 bay extending SE from Freshwater Bay to Hanover Pt on SW coast. SZ 3684
Compton Beauchamp Oxon 17 G3 vil 5m/9km S of Faringdon. SU 2887
Compton Bishop Som 15 H5* vil 2m/3km W of Axbridge. ST 4055
Compton Chamberlayne Wilts 9 G2 vil 5m/7km W of Wilton. SU 0229
Compton Common Avon 16 B5* loc 1km SW of Compton Dando. ST 6464
Compton Dando Avon 16 B5 vil 7m/11km W of Bath. ST 6464
Compton Durville Som 8 C3* ham 4m/7km NE of Ilminster. ST 4117
Compton, East Dorset 9 F3* ham 1km NE of Compton Abbas and 2m/4km S of Shaftesbury. ST 8718

Compton, East Som 8 D1* ham 2km S of Shepton Mallet. ST 6141
Compton, Little Warwicks 27 G4 vil 4m/6km NW of Chipping Norton. SP 2630
Compton Martin Avon 16 B5 vil below N slopes of Mendip Hills 3m/5km S of Chew Stoke. ST 5457
Compton, Nether Dorset 8 D3 vil 3m/5km E of Yeovil. ST 5917
Compton, Over Dorset. See Over Compton.
Compton Pauncefoot Som 8 D2* vil 3m/4km E of Sparkford. ST 6426
Compton Valence Dorset 8 D5 vil 3m/5km S of Maiden Newton. SY 5993
Compton Verney Warwicks 27 G2 loc 7m/11km E of Stratford-upon-Avon. SP 3152
Compton, West Dorset 8 D5* ham 3m/5km SW of Maiden Newton. Also known as Compton Abbas. SY 5694
Compton, West Som 16 B6* ham 2m/3km SW of Shepton Mallet. ST 5942
Compton Wynyates Warwicks 27 G3 loc 5m/7km E of Shipston on Stour. Brick Tudor hse surrounded by low hills. SP 3341
Comrie Fife 72 D5* vil 5m/7km W of Dunfermline. Colliery. NT 0189
Comrie Tayside 72 B3 vil and resort at junction of Glen Artney, Glen Lednock, and Strathearn, 6m/10km W of Crieff. NN 7722
Cona H'land 74 B4 r in Lochaber dist running E down Cona Glen to R Scaddle. NN 0169
Conachair W Isles (W of 88 A3) summit of island of St Kilda, qv. Height 1411 ft or 430 metres. NA 0900
Cona Glen H'land 74 A4, B4 valley of Cona R in Lochaber dist, running E to R Scaddle, W of Loch Linnhe. NM 9472
Conamheall H'land. Gaelic form of Conival, qv.
Concangium Durham. See Chester-le-Street.
Concord Tyne & Wear 61 G5* N dist of Washington. NZ 3057
Concwest 41 F5* r running E to R Clywedog 1m W of Cyffylliog, Clwyd. SJ 0458
Condate Ches. See Northwich.
Conder 47 E2* r rising E of Lancaster and flowing SW into R Lune at Conder Green, Lancs, to E of Glasson. SD 4556
Conder Green Lancs 47 E3 loc 4m/6km S of Lancaster. SD 4556
Conderton H & W 26 D4 vil 5m/9km NE of Tewkesbury. SO 9637
Condicote Glos 27 F4 vil 3m/5km NW of Stow-on-the-Wold. SP 1528
Condorrat S'clyde 64 D2/65 E2 residential area of Cumbernauld 2m/3km SW of tn centre. NS 7373
Condover Salop 34 B4 vil 4m/7km S of Shrewsbury. **C. Green** loc 1m SE. SJ 4905
Coney Hall London 20 A5* loc in borough of Bromley 4m/6km N of Biggin Hill. TQ 3964
Coney Hill Glos 26 D5* SE dist of Gloucester. SO 8517
Coneyhurst Common W Sussex 11 G3 ham 2m/3km SE of Billingshurst. TQ 1023
Coney Island H'land 84 C2* small uninhabited island off W coast of Sutherland dist 2km NW of Kinlochbervie. Also known as Eilean a' Chonnaidh. NC 2057
Coneysthorpe N Yorks 50 C1 estate vil of Castle Howard 5m/8km W of Malton. SE 7171
Coneythorpe N Yorks 49 F2 loc 3m/5km NE of Knaresborough. SE 3958
Coney Weston Suffolk 30 D1 vil 5m/8km N of Ixworth. TL 9578
Conford Hants 11 E2 loc 2km NW of Liphook. SU 8233
Congdon's Shop Cornwall 4 A3* ham 5m/8km SE of Launceston. SX 2878
Congerstone Leics 36 A4 vil 7m/11km S of Ashby de la Zouch. SK 3605
Congham Norfolk 38 C2* vil 7m/11km E of King's Lynn. TF 7123
Conglass Water 82 B4, B5 r in Grampian region running NW into R Avon 3m/5km NW of Tomintoul. NJ 1422
Congleton Ches 42 D5 tn on R Dane 11m/18km N of Stoke-on-Trent. Industries include yarn mnfre, light engineering. SJ 8562
Congl-y-wal Gwynedd 33 E1* loc 1m S of Blaenau Ffestiniog. SH 7044
Congra Moss Cumbria 52 B3* lake 1m S of Lamplugh. NY 0919
Congresbury Avon 16 A5 vil 5m/9km S of Clevedon. ST 4363
Congreve Staffs 35 E3* loc 2km SW of Penkridge. SJ 9013
Conieglen Water S'clyde 62 D6 r in Kintyre running S down **Conie Glen** to Brunerican Bay on S coast of the peninsula. NR 6907
Coningsby Lincs 45 F5 vil 4m/6km SE of Woodhall Spa. Airfield to S. TF 2258
Conington Cambs 29 G2 vil 9m/15km NW of Cambridge. 18c hall. TL 3266
Conington Cambs 37 F5 vil 2m/4km SE of Stilton. TL 1785
Coninish 71 E2 r in Central region rising on slopes of Ben Lui and running E to R Fillan 2km SE of Tyndrum. NN 3428
Conisbrough S Yorks 44 A2 tn in coal-mining area 5m/8km SW of Doncaster. Remains of Norman cas (A.M.) above R Don. **C. Parks** loc adjoining to S. SK 5198
Conisby S'clyde 62 A2* loc on Islay 1km N of Bruichladdich. NR 2661
Coniscliffe, High Durham 54 B3 vil on R Tees 4m/6km W of Darlington. **Low Coniscliffe** loc 2m/3km SE. NZ 2215
Conisholme Lincs 45 G2 vil 7m/11km NE of Louth. TF 4095
Coniston Cumbria 52 C5 vil 6m/10km SW of Ambleside at N end of **C. Water,** lake 5m/9km long but less than 1km wide. See also Old Man of Coniston. SD 3097
Coniston Humberside 51 F4 vil 5m/9km NE of Hull. TA 1535
Coniston Cold N Yorks 48 B3 vil 6m/10km NW of Skipton. SD 9055
Conistone N Yorks 48 C2 vil in Wharfedale 2m/4km NW of Grassington. SD 9867
Conival H'land 85 C5 mt in Sutherland dist 4m/6km E of Inchnadamph. Height 3234 ft or 986 metres. Gaelic form: Conamheall. NC 3019
Conlach Mhór Tayside 76 A3* mt 8m/12km N of Blair Atholl. Height 2818 ft or 859 metres. NN 9376
Connah's Quay Clwyd 41 H4 industrial tn and port on R Dee 7m/12km W of Chester and 4m/6km SE of Flint. Power stn. SJ 2969
Connel S'clyde 70 B2 vil on S side of entrance to Loch Etive, Argyll. Cantilever br with span of some 500 ft or 150 metres carries rd (formerly rly) across loch. **N Connel Airfield** on N side, at S end of Ardmucknish Bay. See also Falls of Lora. NM 9134
Connel Park S'clyde 56 F3 colliery vil 1m SW of New Cumnock. NS 6012
Connor Downs Cornwall 2 B4 vil 2m/4km NE of Hayle. SW 5939
Conock Wilts 17 E5* ham 5m/8km SE of Devizes. 18c manor hse. SU 0657
Conon H'land 78 B3 r in Skye running W into Uig Bay. NG 3963
Conon H'land 81 E2 r in Ross and Cromarty dist running E from Loch Luichart to head of Cromarty Firth. See also Falls of Conon. NH 5658
Conon Bridge H'land 81 E2 vil in Ross and Cromarty dist on R Conon near head of Cromarty Firth. NH 5455
Cononley N Yorks 48 C3 vil 3m/5km S of Skipton. SD 9846
Consall Staffs 43 E6 ham 7m/11km E of Stoke-on-Trent. SJ 9848
Consett Durham 61 F6 industrial tn 12m/19km SW of Newcastle upon Tyne. Iron and steel works. Coal mines in vicinity. NZ 1051
Constable Burton N Yorks 54 B5 vil 3m/5km E of Leyburn. SE 1690
Constable Lee Lancs 48 B5* loc 1km N of Rawtenstall. SD 8123
Constantine Cornwall 2 C5 vil 5m/8km SW of Falmouth. SW 7329
Constantine Bay Cornwall vil near bay of same name; 3m/5km W of Padstow. SW 8674
Contin H'land 81 E2 vil in Ross and Cromarty dist 2m/3km SW of Strathpeffer. NH 4556
Contrary Head Isle of Man 46 A5 headland on W coast 2km SW of Peel. SC 2282
Conway Gwynedd. See Conwy.
Conwil Elvet (Cynwyl Elfed) Dyfed 23 E3 vil 5m/8km NW of Carmarthen. SN 3727
Conwy Gwynedd 40 D4 resort and small port on W bank of R Conwy estuary 3m/5km S of Llandudno across r. 13c cas and tn walls (A.M.). Rd and rly brs by Telford and Robert Stevenson respectively (the former NT). **Plas Mawr,** Elizn hse in High Street. **C. Mountain** (Mynydd y Dref) 2km W, with remains of ancient British fort on summit. **C. Bay** extends from Gt Ormes Hd westwards to Puffin I. or Priestholm. SH 7877
Conwy 40 D3 r rising at Llyn Conwy, Gwynedd, 5m/9km NE of Ffestiniog, and flowing N by Betws-y-coed and Llanrwst into Conwy Bay on N side of tn of Conwy. Tidal to Trefriw, near Llanrwst. SH 7779
Conwy Falls Gwynedd 41 E6 waterfall in course of R Conwy 5m/8km S of Llanrwst. SH 8053
Conyer Kent 21 E5 loc at head of creek running into The Swale 4m/6km NW of Faversham. TQ 9664
Conyer's Green Suffolk 30 D2* ham adjoining Gt Barton to N. TL 8868
Cooden E Sussex 12 D6 W dist of Bexhill. TQ 7107
Cooil Isle of Man 46 B5 ham 2m/4km W of Douglas. SC 3476
Cookbury Devon 6 C4 vil 5m/7km NE of Holsworthy. **C. Wick** is loc in SW part of par. SS 4006
Cookham Berks 18 D3 riverside resort on R Thames 3m/4km N of Maidenhead. Locs of **C. Rise** and **C. Dean** to W. Much NT property in vicinity. SU 8985
Cookhill H & W 27 E2 vil 2m/4km W of Alcester. SP 0558
Cookley H & W 35 E6 vil 2m/4km N of Kidderminster. SO 8480
Cookley Suffolk 31 G1 ham 3m/4km SW of Halesworth. Locs of **C. Green** and **C. Street** 1m W and E respectively. TM 3475
Cookley Green Oxon 18 B3 vil 2m/4km N of Nettlebed. SU 6990
Cooksbridge E Sussex 12 A5 loc 2m/4km NW of Lewes. TQ 4013
Cooksey Green H & W 26 D1* loc 3m/5km W of Bromsgrove. SO 9069
Cook's Green Suffolk 30 D3 ham 6m/9km SW of Stowmarket. TL 9753
Cookshill Staffs 35 F1 loc 4m/7km W of Cheadle. SJ 9443
Cooksland Cornwall 3 F2* loc 1m E of Bodmin. SX 0867
Cooksmill Green Essex 20 C1 vil 4m/7km W of Chelmsford. TL 6306
Cookson Green Ches 42 B4* loc just W of Crowton. SJ 5774
Cookson's Green Durham 54 C2* loc 1m N of Ferryhill. NZ 2934
Coolham W Sussex 11 G3 vil 3m/5km SE of Billingshurst. TQ 1222
Cooling Kent 20 D4 vil on edge of **C. Marshes** 5m/8km N of Rochester. Ruins of 14c cas. TQ 7576
Cooling Street Kent 20 D4 loc 2km SW of Cooling. TQ 7474
Coomb Dod 65 G6 mt on border of Strathclyde and Borders regions 7m/11km S of Coulter. Height 2082 ft or 634 metres. NT 0423
Coombe Cornwall 2 D4* loc 3m/4km S of Truro. SW 8340
Coombe Cornwall 3 E3* vil 4m/6km W of St Austell. SW 9551
Coombe Cornwall 6 B4 loc near coast 4m/6km N of Bude. NT property to E and W. SS 2111
Coombe Devon 7 H5* ham adjacent to Tipton St John and 2m/3km S of Ottery St Mary. SY 0992
Coombe Som 8 B2* ham 1km NE of W Monkton. ST 2729
Coombe Som 8 C3* ham 2m/3km W of Crewkerne. ST 4109
Coombe Wilts 17 F6* loc on R Avon 3m/5km S of Upavon. SU 1550
Coombe Bissett Wilts 9 H2 vil on R Ebble 3m/5km SW of Salisbury. SU 1026
Coombe, East Devon 7 G4* loc 4m/7km NE of Crediton. SS 8803
Coombe End Som 7 G2* ham 4m/6km NW of Wiveliscombe. ST 0229
Coombe Hill Glos 26 D5 ham 5m/8km NW of Cheltenham. SO 8827
Coombe Keynes Dorset 9 F5 vil 2m/3km S of Wool. SY 8484
Coombe, North Devon 7 F4* loc 4m/6km NE of Crediton. SS 8704
Coombes W Sussex 11 G4 loc 2m/3km SE of Steyning. TQ 1908
Coombe Street Som 9 E2* ham adjoining Penselwood to E and 4m/6km NE of Wincanton. ST 7631
Coombeswood W Midlands 35 F5* loc in NE part of Halesowen. SO 9785
Coombe Throop Som 9 E2* loc 4m/6km S of Wincanton. ST 7123
Coomb Island H'land 84 F2 small uninhabited island off N coast of Caithness dist opp Skerray. Also known as Neave I. NC 6664
Coombs Dyfed 22 B5* E dist of Milford Haven. SM 9106
Coom Burn D & G. See Garroch Burn. NX 6180
Cooperhill Grampian 82 A2* vil 4m/7km SW of Forres across R Findhorn. NH 9953
Coopersale Common Essex 20 B2* vil 1m E of Epping. Ham of **Coopersale Street** 1km S. TL 4702
Cooper's Corner Kent 20 B6* loc 2km S of Ide Hill. TQ 4849
Cooper's Creek Essex 21 E2* inlet of R Blackwater estuary S of Osea I. TL 9005
Cooper's Green E Sussex 12 B4* loc 2km N of Uckfield. TQ 4823
Cooper's Green Herts 19 F1* loc 3m/4km W of Hatfield. TL 1909
Cooper Street Kent 13 H1* loc 2m/3km NW of Sandwich. TR 3059
Cooper Turning Gtr Manchester 42 C1* loc 5m/8km W of Bolton. SD 6308
Cootham W Sussex 11 G3 loc adjoining Storrington to W. TQ 0714
Copcut H & W 26 D2* loc 2m/3km SW of Droitwich. SO 8861
Copdock Suffolk 31 E4 vil 3m/5km SW of Ipswich. TM 1142
Copeland 116 admin dist of Cumbria.
Copeland Forest Cumbria 52 B4 area of fells N of West Water. NY 10
Copford Green Essex 30 D5 vil 5m/7km W of Colchester. TL 9222
Copgrove N Yorks 49 F2 ham 4m/6km SW of Boroughbridge. SE 3463
Copinsay Orkney 89 C7 uninhabited island of about 200 acres or 80 hectares 2m/3km SE of Pt of Ayre, Mainland. Steep cliffs on E side, with lighthouse. Bird sanctuary. HY 6101
Copister Shetland 89 E6* loc at S end of Yell, W of Hamna Voe. **Ness of C.** is headland to E. **Wick of C.** and **Wester Wick of C.** are two small bays to S and SW respectively. HU 4879
Cople Beds 29 E3 vil 4m/6km E of Bedford. TL 1048
Copley Durham 54 A2 vil 6m/10km NE of Barnard Castle. NZ 0825
Copley Gtr Manchester 43 E2* loc 1km E of Stalybridge. SJ 9798
Copley W Yorks 48 D5* loc in Halifax on R Calder 2m/3km S of tn centre. SE 0822
Copley Hill W Yorks 49 E5* loc 1km E of Birstall. SE 2326
Coplow Dale Derbys 43 F3* loc just N of Lit Hucklow. SK 1679
Copmanthorpe N Yorks 49 G3 vil 4m/7km SW of York. SE 5646
Cop Mere Staffs 35 E2 lake 2m/3km W of Eccleshall. **Copmere End** ham on S side of lake. SJ 8029
Copner Hants 10 D4* dist of Portsmouth 2km NE of city centre. SU 6501
Copp Lancs 47 E4 ham 5m/8km N of Kirkham. SD 4239
Coppathorne Cornwall 6 B5* ham 4m/6km S of Bude. SS 2000
Coppay W Isles 88 A3* small uninhabited island 2km W of Toe Hd, W coast of Harris. NF 9393
Coppenhall Staffs 35 E3 vil 2m/4km S of Stafford. SJ 9019
Coppenhall Moss Ches 42 C5 loc in Crewe 2m/3km N of tn centre. SJ 7058
Copperas Bay Essex 31 F5* bay on S side of R Stour estuary NE of Wrabness. TM 1932
Copperhouse Cornwall 2 B4* loc 1m E of Hayle. SW 5738
Coppicegate Salop 34 D6* loc 5m/8km NE of Cleobury Mortimer. SO 7380
Coppingford Cambs 37 F6 loc 7m/11km NW of Huntingdon. TL 1680
Coppleridge Dorset 9 F2 ham 3m/4km NW of Shaftesbury. ST 8426
Copplestone Devon 7 F5 vil 5m/8km NW of Crediton. SS 7702
Coppull Lancs 42 B1 loc 6m/9km N of Wigan. **C. Moor** loc adjoining to S. SD 5614

Copsale W Sussex 11 G3 vil 4m/6km S of Horsham. TQ 1724
Copse Hill London 19 F4* loc at S end of Wimbledon Common in borough of Merton 8m/13km SW of Charing Cross. TQ 2270
Copster Green Lancs 47 G4* vil 4m/6km N of Blackburn. SD 6734
Copston Magna Warwicks 36 A5 ham 4m/6km SE of Hinckley. SP 4588
Cop Street Kent 13 H1 ham 1m N of Ash. TR 2959
Copt Green Warwicks 27 F1* loc 3m/4km SE of Hockley Heath. SP 1769
Copthall Green Essex 20 B2* ham 3m/4km W of Epping. TL 4200
Copthall Saltings Essex 30 D6* marshes to N of Salcott Channel 7m/12km S of Colchester. TL 9813
Copt Hewick N Yorks 49 E1 vil 2m/3km E of Ripon. SE 3371
Copthill Durham 53 G1* loc 1m N of Wearhead. NY 8540
Copthorne Ches 34 D1* loc 1m SW of Audlem. SJ 6543
Copthorne 11 H2 vil on border of Surrey and W Sussex 3m/5km NE of Crawley. TQ 3139
Copt Oak Leics 36 B3 loc beside M1 motorway 4m/6km E of Coalville. SK 4812
Copt Point Kent 13 G3 headland on E side of Folkestone. TR 2436
Copy's Green Norfolk 38 D1* ham just SE of Wighton across R Stiffkey. Site of Roman fort 1km E. TF 9439
Copythorne Hants 10 A3 vil 1m NE of Cadnam. SU 3014
Coquet 61 G1 r rising on border of England and Scotland in the Cheviot Hills 4m/6km N of Byrness, Nthmb, and flowing E into North Sea at Amble, opp Coquet I. NU 2705
Coquet Island Nthmb 61 G1/G2 island in North Sea 2km E of mouth of R Coquet and 2m/3km E of Amble. Lighthouse on SW side. NU 2904
Corbets Tey London 20 C3 loc in borough of Havering 1km S of Upminster. TQ 5685
Corbet Tower Borders. See Morebattle.
Corbie Head Shetland 89 F6* headland on W coast of Fetlar 3m/4km W of Houbie. HU 5891
Corbridge Nthmb 61 E5 small tn on N bank of R Tyne 3m/5km E of Hexham. 17c rd br across r. Remains (A.M.) of Roman military tn of *Corstopitum* 1km NW. NY 9864
Corby Northants 36 D5 steel-mnfg tn 7m/11km N of Kettering. New Tn designated 1950. SP 8988
Corby Glen Lincs 37 E2 vil 7m/11km NW of Bourne. SK 9924
Corby, Great Cumbria 60 A5/A6 vil on E bank of R Eden 6m/9km SW of Brampton. **Corby Castle,** hse incorporating part of medieval peel tower. NY 4754
Corby Hill Cumbria 60 B5* loc 4m/7km SW of Brampton. NY 4757
Corby, Little Cumbria 60 A5/B5 loc 5m/8km E of Carlisle. NY 4757
Corby Loch Grampian 83 G5 small loch 5m/8km N of Aberdeen. NJ 9214
Cordon Hill Borders 65 G5 hill 4m/7km S of Biggar. Height 2218 ft or 676 metres. NT 0631
Cordwell Derbys 43 G3* loc 1m SW of Holmesfield. SK 3176
Cordwell Norfolk 39 E5* loc adjoining Bunwell to E, 5m/9km S of Wymondham. TM 1393
Coreley Salop 26 B1* ham 4m/6km N of Tenbury Wells. SO 6173
Cores End Bucks 18 D3* loc 1km E of Bourne End. SU 9087
Corfe Som 8 A3 vil 3m/5km S of Taunton. ST 2319
Corfe 9 G5* r rising S of Purbeck Hills in Dorset 2km NW of Kimmeridge and flowing E and then N through gap in hills at C. Castle and into Poole Harbour. SY 9886
Corfe Castle Dorset 9 G6 vil 4m/6km SE of Wareham, in gap of Purbeck Hills. Remains of Norman cas (A.M.). SY 9682
Corfe Mullen Dorset 9 G4 vil 3m/4km SW of Wimborne. SY 9798
Corfton Salop 34 B5 vil 4m/7km E of Craven Arms. SO 4984
Corgarff Grampian 76 C1 loc 2km E of Cock Br. To W across R Don is **C. Castle;** derelict tower hse dates from 16c or early 17c. NJ 2708
Corgarff Castle Grampian 82 B6 remains of 16c cas (A.M.) 1km SW of Cock Br. NJ 2508
Corgrain Point H'land 81 F3 headland in Ross and Cromarty dist on N shore of Beauly Firth 4m/6km W of N Kessock. NH 5948
Corhampton Hants 10 C3 vil adjoining Meonstoke to N. SU 6120
Corkerhill S'clyde 64 C3* loc in Glasgow on W side of Pollok Grnds – see Pollok. NS 5462
Corlarach Forest S'clyde 63 G1 state forest in Argyll between Dunoon and Ardyne Pt. NS 1271
Corley Warwicks 35 H5 vil 5m/7km NW of Coventry. Vils of **C. Ash** 1km NW and **C. Moor** 2km W respectively. SP 3085
Cormiston S'clyde 65 G5* loc 2m/3km W of Biggar. NT 0037
Cornaa Isle of Man 46 C4* loc 3m/5km S of Ramsey. Situated on stream running out to sea at Port Cornaa, qv. SC 4689
Cornard, Great Suffolk 30 D4 SE suburb of Sudbury. TL 8840
Cornard, Little Suffolk 30 D4 ham 2m/4km SE of Sudbury. TL 9039
Cornard Tye Suffolk 30 D4* ham 2m/3km E of Sudbury. TL 9041
Corndon Devon 7 E6* loc 4m/6km W of Moretonhampstead. SX 6985
Corndon Hill Powys 34 A4 rounded hill close to English border 3m/5km NE of Church Stoke. Height 1684 ft or 513 metres. SO 3096
Corn Du Powys 25 E5 one of the two chief peaks of Brecon Beacons, qv. SO 0021
Corneli Welsh form of Cornelly, qv.
Cornelian Bay N Yorks 55 H6* small bay 2m/3km SE of Scarborough. TA 0686
Cornelly, North Mid Glam 14 D3 vil 3m/5km N of Porthcawl. See also Corneli. SS 8181
Cornelly, South Mid Glam 14 D3 vil 2m/3km N of Porthcawl. See also Corneli. SS 8180
Corner, North Avon 16 B3* loc adjoining Frampton Cotterell to W. ST 6582
Corner, The Salop 34 B5* ham 3m/5km N of Craven Arms. SO 4387
Corney Cumbria 52 B5 loc 2m/3km N of Bootle. SD 1191
Cornforth Durham 54 C2 vil 4m/7km NW of Sedgefield. **W Cornforth** loc adjoining to SE. NZ 3134
Cornhill Grampian 83 E2 vil 5m/8km S of Portsoy. NJ 5858
Cornhill Staffs 42 D5* loc 2m/3km NE of Burslem. SJ 8952
Cornhill Cross Staffs 43 E5* loc 1km S of Leek. SJ 9855
Cornhill on Tweed Nthmb 67 E4 vil opp Coldstream across r and 12m/20km SW of Berwick-upon-Tweed. NT 8539
Corn Holm Orkney 89 C7* small uninhabited island 1km W of Copinsay, qv. HY 5901
Cornholme W Yorks 48 B5 vil 2m/4km NW of Todmorden. SD 9026
Cornish Hall End Essex 30 B4 vil 2m/4km N of Finchingfield. TL 6836
Cornish Loch S'clyde 56 D4* small loch 2m/3km N of Shalloch on Minnoch. NX 4094
Cornmeadow Green H & W 26 D2* loc 2m/3km N of Worcester. SO 8558
Cornriggs Durham 53 G1 loc 2km N of Wearhead. NY 8441
Cornsay Durham 54 B1 vil 3m/5km SW of Lanchester. **C. Colliery** vil 2m/3km E. NZ 1443
Corntown (Corntwn) Mid Glam 15 E5 ham 2m/3km SE of Bridgend across Ewenny R. SS 9177
Cornwall 118 south-westernmost county of England, bounded by Devon and the sea. The coast is wild and rocky, headlands and cliffs interspersed with large sandy beaches in the N, and deeply indented with river estuaries in the S. Inland are areas of moorland, notably the granite mass of Bodmin Moor in the NE, farmlands providing rich cattle-grazing, and deep river valleys. The climate is mild, and flower cultivation is carried on extensively. The many derelict tin mines witness to the former importance of this industry, which has been partly revived. The chief industry is tourism. China clay is produced in large quantities in the St Austell area, and there is some fishing. Chief tns are the cathedral city and admin centre of Truro; Bodmin, Camborne-Redruth, Falmouth, Penzance, and St Austell. Rs include the Tamar, forming the boundary with Devon; Fowey, E and W Looe, Fal, Camel, and Lynher.
Cornwell Oxon 27 G5* ham 3m/4km W of Chipping Norton. SP 2727
Cornwood Devon 4 C4 vil on S edge of Dartmoor 3m/5km NW of Ivybridge. SX 6059
Cornworthy Devon 5 E5 vil 4m/6km SE of Totnes. 2km E, ham of **E Cornworthy.** SX 8255
Corodale Bay W Isles 88 E2* small bay on E coast of S Uist 3m/4km N of Loch Eynort. Here Charles Edward Stuart sought refuge after Battle of Culloden, 1746. NF 8331
Corpach H'land 74 C4 vil in Lochaber dist at entrance to Caledonian Canal from head of Loch Linnhe. Pulp mill at Annat, qv, to W. NN 0976
Corpach Bay S'clyde 69 D8 bay on NW coast of Jura 7m/11km NW of entrance to Loch Tarbert. NR 5691
Corpusty Norfolk 39 E2 vil opp Saxthorpe across R Bure, 5m/9km NW of Aylsham. TG 1130
Corra Linn S'clyde 65 F4 waterfall on R Clyde 2km S of Lanark. NS 8841
Corran H'land 74 A1 locality in Lochaber dist on NE shore of Loch Hourn 1m SE of Arnisdale. NG 8509
Corran H'land 74 B5 locality on W shore of Loch Linnhe in Lochaber dist. Vehicle ferry to opp shore across **C. Narrows.** NN 0163
Corran S'clyde 62 C1 r on Jura rising on slopes of Paps of Jura and running E then S to Loch na Mile, on E side of Leargybreck. NR 5471
Corrany Isle of Man 46 C4 loc 4m/6km N of Laxey. SC 4589
Correen Hills Grampian 82 D4 small range of hills between Alford and Rhynie. NJ 5122
Corrennie Forest Grampian 83 E5 state forest 6m/9km SE of Alford. **Corrennie Moor** is upland area to W. NJ 6410
Corribeg H'land 74 B3/B4* locality in Lochaber dist, on N shore of Loch Eil 2km E of Kinlocheil. NM 9978
Corrie S'clyde 63 G3 vil on E coast of Arran 4m/7km N of Brodick. NS 0243
Corrie Common D & G 59 G3 vil 5m/9km NE of Lockerbie. NY 2086
Corriecravie S'clyde 63 F5 loc near SW coast of Arran 3m/5km SE of Blackwaterfoot. See also Torr a' Chaisteil. NR 9223
Corriehallie Forest H'land 80 D3 deer forest in Ross and Cromarty dist S of Orrin Resr. NH 3748
Corriemoillie Forest H'land 80 D1 deer forest in Ross and Cromarty dist SE of Loch Glascarnoch. NH 3567
Corriemulzie H'land 85 D6 r in Sutherland dist running NE down Strath Mulzie into R Einig 4m/6km SW of Oykel Br. NH 3397
Corriemulzie Burn 76 B2* stream in Grampian region running N to R Dee 3m/5km SW of Braemar. See also Linn of Corriemulzie. NO 1189
Corrie na Urisgean Central 71 F4 cave near E end of Loch Katrine. Commonly known as Goblin's Cave. NN 4807
Corrieshalloch Gorge H'land 85 C8 spectacular gorge (NTS) in Ross and Cromarty dist, 5m/8km S of head of Loch Broom. Contains Falls of Measach, qv. NH 2077
Corrieyairack Forest H'land 75 E2 deer forest in Badenoch and Strathspey dist, running up to border with Inverness and Lochaber dists 7m/11km SE of Fort Augustus. **C. Pass** carries General Wade's Military Rd over to Culachy Forest and Glen Tarff. **C. Hill,** on border with Inverness dist, attains height of 2922 ft or 891 metres. NN 4497
Corrimony H'land 80 D4* loc in Inverness dist 8m/12km W of Drumnadrochit. Prehistoric chambered cairn (A.M.). NH 3830
Corringham Essex 20 D3 tn 4m/6km S of Basildon. Oil refinery to SE beside R Thames. TQ 7083
Corringham Lincs 44 D2 vil 4m/6km E of Gainsborough. SK 8791
Corris Gwynedd 33 E4 vil 4m/7km N of Machynlleth. Ham of **Corris Uchaf,** or **Upr Corris,** 1m NW. SH 7507
Corris 41 G5 r running NE to R Clywedog at Cyffylliog, Clwyd. SJ 0557
Corrour Forest H'land 75 E4 state forest bordering Loch Ossian in Lochaber dist. Also deer forest to SE of loch. NN 4167
Corrwg 14 D2* r rising N of Glyncorrwg, W Glam, and flowing SW through Glyncorrwg into R Afan at Cymmer. SS 8696
Corrygills Point S'clyde 63 G4 headland on E coast of Arran 2m/3km SE of Brodick Bay. NS 0435
Corryhabbie Hill Grampian 82 C4 mt 6m/10km E of foot of Glen Livet. Height 2563 ft or 781 metres. NJ 2828
Corryvreckan. See Strait of Corryvreckan.
Corsback H'land 86 E1 loc near N coast of Caithness dist 2km E of Dunnet. ND 2372
Corscombe Dorset 8 C4 vil 6m/9km SE of Crewkerne. ST 5105
Cors Ddyga Welsh form of Malltraeth Marsh, qv.
Corse Glos 26 C4* loc 7m/11km N of Gloucester. SO 7827
Corse Grampian 83 E3 loc 5m/7km E of Huntly. NJ 6040
Corse Castle Grampian 77 E1 ruined cas, bearing date 1581, 3m/5km NW of Lumphanan. NJ 5507
Corsegight Grampian 83 F2/G2 loc 3m/5km NW of New Deer. NJ 8450
Corse Lawn H & W 26 D4 ham 7m/11km N of Gloucester. SO 8330
Corserine D & G 56 E4 mt 4m/6km S of S end of Loch Doon. Height 2669 ft or 814 metres. Summit of Rinns of Kells. NX 4987
Corsewall Point D & G 57 A6 headland with lighthouse 4m/6km NW of Kirkcolm. Ruins of **Corsewall Castle** 1m SE. NW 9872
Cors Fochno Dyfed 32 D5 large marsh on E side of Borth and S of R Dovey estuary. SN 6391
Corsham Wilts 16 D4 tn 4m/6km SW of Chippenham. ST 8670
Corsley Wilts 16 D6 vil 3m/5km NW of Warminster. 1m SW, vil of **C. Heath.** ST 8246
Corsock D & G 58 D4 vil 8m/13km E of New Galloway. **C. Loch** is small loch 1km SW. NX 7576
Corston Avon 16 C5 vil 4m/6km W of Bath. Site of Roman villa 2km E. ST 6965
Corston Wilts 16 D3 vil 2m/3km S of Malmesbury. ST 9284
Corstopitum Nthmb. See Corbridge.
Corstorphine Lothian 65 H2 dist of Edinburgh 4m/6km W of city centre. **C. Hill** to NE. NT 1972
Cortachy Tayside 76 D5 loc and cas near foot of Glen Clova 4m/6km N of Kirriemuir. Noted for breeding of Aberdeen Angus cattle. NO 3959
Corton Suffolk 39 H5 vil and coastal resort 3m/4km N of Lowestoft. TM 5497
Corton Wilts 9 F1 vil 2m/3km SE of Heytesbury. ST 9340
Corton Denham Som 8 D2 vil 3m/5km SE of Sparkford. ST 6322
Corve 34 C3 r rising 3m/4km SW of Much Wenlock, Salop, and flowing SW through Corve Dale E of Wenlock Edge to join R Teme on W side of Ludlow. SO 5075
Corve Dale Salop 34 C5 valley of R Corve below E slope of Wenlock Edge. SO 58
Corwen Clwyd 33 G1 small mkt tn on R Dee 8m/13km W of Llangollen. SJ 0743
Coryton Devon 4 B3 ham 6m/10km N of Tavistock. SX 4583
Coryton Essex 20 D3 oil refinery tn beside R Thames 5m/8km S of Basildon. TQ 7382
Cosby Leics 36 B5 vil 7m/11km SW of Leicester. SP 5494
Coscote Oxon 18 A3* loc 2km S of Didcot. SU 5188

Coseley W Midlands 35 F5 N dist of Dudley. SO 9494

Cosford Warwicks 36 B6* loc 2m/4km N of Rugby. SP 4979

Cosgrove Northants 28 C3 vil on Grand Union Canal 2km N of Stony Stratford across canal and R Ouse. SP 7942

Cosham Hants 10 D4 N dist of Portsmouth below Portsdown. SU 6505

Cosheston Dyfed 22 C5 vil 2m/3km NE of Pembroke. 2km W is **Cosheston Pt**, headland at mouth of creek running into estuary of Daugleddau R. SN 0003

Coskills Humberside 45 E1* loc 1m NW of Barnetby le Wold. TA 0410

Cosmeston S Glam 15 G4* loc 4m/6km E of Barry. ST 1769

Cossall Notts 36 B1 vil 6m/9km W of Nottingham. **C. Marsh** loc to N. SK 4842

Cossington Leics 36 B3 vil 6m/10km N of Leicester. SK 6013

Cossington Som 8 B1 vil 5m/7km NE of Bridgwater. ST 3540

Costa Orkney 89 A6* loc at N end of Mainland 1m E of Loch of Swannay. HY 3328

Costessey Norfolk 39 F4 vil 4m/6km NW of Norwich. See also New Costessey. TG 1711

Costock Notts 36 B2 vil 5m/8km NE of Loughborough. SK 5726

Coston Leics 36 D2 ham 5m/8km W of Colsterworth. SK 8422

Coston Norfolk 39 E4 ham 4m/7km NW of Wymondham. TG 0606

Cote Oxon 17 G2 ham 4m/7km S of Witney. SP 3504

Cote Som 15 H6 loc 3m/4km SE of Highbridge. ST 3444

Cotebrook Ches 42 B4 vil 2m/3km NE of Tarporley. SJ 5765

Cote, East Cumbria 59 F5* loc on Solway Firth 2km NE of Silloth. Site of small Roman fort. NY 1155

Cotehele House (NT). See Calstock.

Cotehill Cumbria 60 A6 vil 6m/9km SE of Carlisle. **Low Cotehill** to E. NY 4650

Cote Houses Lincs 44 C1* loc 1km E of Susworth. SE 8401

Cotes Cumbria 53 E6 loc 1km N of Levens. SD 4886

Cotes Leics 36 B2* ham 2km NE of Loughborough. SK 5520

Cotes Staffs 35 E1* loc 1km SW of Swynnerton. SJ 8434

Cotesbach Leics 36 B6 vil 2km S of Lutterworth. SP 5382

Cote Wall W Yorks 49 E6* loc 1km S of Ravensthorpe across R Calder. SE 2119

Cotgrave Notts 36 C1 vil 6m/9km SE of Nottingham. SK 6435

Cotham Avon 16 B4* dist of Bristol to N of city centre. ST 5874

Cotham Notts 44 C6 vil 4m/7km S of Newark-on-Trent. SK 7947

Cothelstone Som 8 A2 ham at foot of Quantock Hills 6m/9km NW of Taunton. ST 1831

Cotheridge H & W 26 C2 ham 4m/7km W of Worcester. SO 7855

Cotherstone Durham 54 A3 vil 3m/5km NW of Barnard Castle. Scant remains of Norman cas to N. NZ 0119

Cothi 23 F4 r rising about 8m/13km E of Lampeter, Dyfed, and flowing SW into R Towy 5m/9km E of Carmarthen. SN 4920

Cothill Oxon 17 H2 ham 3m/4km NW of Abingdon. SU 4699

Cotleigh Devon 8 A4 vil 3m/5km NE of Honiton. ST 2002

Cotmanhay Derbys 36 A1/B1 urban loc adjoining Ilkeston to N. SK 4643

Coton Cambs 29 H2 vil 3m/4km W of Cambridge. TL 4058

Coton Northants 28 B1 vil 9m/14km NW of Northampton. SP 6771

Coton Salop 34 C1 loc 4m/7km S of Whitchurch. SJ 5234

Coton Staffs 35 E3 ham 4m/7km E of Newport. SJ 8120

Coton Staffs 35 F2 ham 5m/9km E of Stone. **Coton Hill, Coton Hayes,** locs 1km and 1m NE respectively. SJ 9732

Coton Staffs 35 G4 ham 2m/3km NW of Tamworth. SK 1805

Coton Clanford Staffs 35 E2* ham 3m/5km W of Stafford. SJ 8723

Coton Hill Salop 34 B3* N dist of Shrewsbury. SJ 4813

Coton in the Clay Staffs 35 G2 vil 6m/9km NW of Burton upon Trent. SK 1629

Coton in the Elms Derbys 35 H3 vil 5m/8km S of Burton upon Trent. SK 2415

Coton Park Derbys 35 H3* loc 2m/4km SW of Swadlincote. SK 2717

Cotonwood Salop 34 C1* loc 4m/6km S of Whitchurch. SJ 5335

Cotonwood Staffs 35 E2* loc 2m/3km W of Gnosall. SJ 8020

Cotswold 118, 119 admin dist of Glos.

Cotswold Hills 16 D1 limestone heights extending from Edge Hill, NW of Banbury, Oxon, to R Avon valley at Bath, Avon. SO 90

Cott Devon 4 D4 vil 2km NW of Totnes. SX 7861

Cottage End Hants 10 B1* ham 1km W of Forton and 3m/5km E of Andover. SU 4143

Cottam Humberside 51 E2 loc 5m/8km N of Gt Driffield. Site of former vil to N. SE 9964

Cottam Lancs 47 F5 vil 3m/5km NW of Preston. SD 5032

Cottam Notts 44 C3 ham 7m/12km E of E Retford. SK 8179

Cottarville Northants 28 C2* dist of Northampton 2m/4km NE of tn centre. SP 7862

Cottenham Cambs 30 A1 vil 6m/9km N of Cambridge. TL 4567

Cottenham Park London 19 F4* loc at S end of Wimbledon Common 2km W of Wimbledon. TQ 2270

Cotterdale N Yorks 53 G5 loc 4m/6km NW of Hawes. SD 8393

Cottered Herts 29 G5 vil 3m/4km W of Buntingford. TL 3129

Cotteridge W Midlands 35 F6 loc in Birmingham 4m/7km S of city centre. SP 0480

Cotterstock Northants 37 F5 vil on R Nene 2m/3km NE of Oundle. TL 0490

Cottesbrooke Northants 28 C1 vil 9m/14km N of Northampton. SP 7073

Cottesmore Leics 37 E3 vil 4m/6km NE of Oakham. SK 9013

Cottingham Humberside 51 E5 tn adjoining Hull to NW. TA 0432

Cottingham Northants 36 D5 vil 3m/5km W of Corby. SP 8490

Cottingley W Yorks 48 D4 residential dist 2km S of Bingley. SE 1137

Cottingwith, East Humberside 50 C4 vil 11m/18km W of Mkt Weighton. Junction of Pocklington Canal and R Derwent. SE 7042

Cottisford Oxon 28 B4 ham 5m/8km S of Bicester. SP 5831

Cotton Suffolk 31 E2 vil 5m/9km N of Stowmarket. TM 0766

Cotton End Beds 29 E3 loc 4m/6km SE of Bedford. TL 0845

Cotton End Northants 28 C2* loc in Northampton to S of tn centre. SP 7559

Cotton, Far Northants 28 C2 S dist of Northampton. SP 7459

Cotton, Near Staffs 43 F6 ham 4m/7km NE of Cheadle. **Upr Cotton** loc 1m NW. SK 0646

Cotton Tree Lancs 48 B4 loc 2km E of Colne. SD 9040

Cottonworth Hants 10 B1* loc 1m SW of Wherwell. SU 3739

Cot-town Grampian 83 F3* loc 4m/6km NE of Fyvie. NJ 8240

Cotts Devon 4 B4* ham 6m/9km W of Yelverton. SX 4365

Cottwood Devon 7 E4* loc 5m/8km W of Chulmleigh. SS 6114

Cotwall Salop 34 C3* loc 1km E of High Ercall. SJ 6017

Cotwalton Staffs 35 F1* loc 2km W of Hilderstone. SJ 9234

Couch Green Hants 10 C2* loc 1m W of Itchen Abbas and 3m/5km NE of Winchester. SU 5233

Couchsmill Cornwall 3 F2 loc 3m/5km E of Lostwithiel. SX 1459

Coughton H & W 26 B5 loc 2m/3km S of Ross-on-Wye. SO 5921

Coughton Warwicks 27 E2 vil 2m/3km N of Alcester. **C. Court** (NT), Tudor hse of the Throckmortons. SP 0860

Coulderton Cumbria 52 A4* loc 2m/3km SW of Egremont. NX 9808

Coulin Forest H'land 80 A2 deer forest in Ross and Cromarty dist SW of Kinlochewe beyond Loch Clair. NG 9954

Coull Grampian 77 E1 loc 3m/4km N of Aboyne. Site of medieval cas. NJ 5102

Coul Point S'clyde 62 A2 headland on W coast of Islay 2m/3km W of Loch Gorm. NR 1864

Coulregrain W Isles 88 C2* loc on Lewis 1m NE of Stornoway. WT stn. NB 4334

Coulsdon London 19 G5 dist in borough of Croydon 5m/8km S of Croydon tn centre. Loc of **Old C.** to SE. TQ 3158

Coulston, East Wilts 16 D5* vil 6m/9km SW of Devizes. ST 9554

Coulter S'clyde 65 G5 vil 3m/4km S of Biggar. **C. Motte Hill** (A.M.) 2m/3km N. NT 0233

Coultings Som 8 A1 loc 2m/3km SE of Stogursey. ST 2241

Coulton N Yorks 50 B1 ham 2m/3km SW of Hovingham. SE 6374

Cound Salop 34 C4 ham 6m/10km SE of Shrewsbury. **Upr Cound** ham 1km W. **Coundlane** loc 1km E. SJ 5504

Cound Brook 34 C4 r rising on the Long Mynd, Salop, and flowing N to Condover, then E into R Severn 2km below Wroxeter. SJ 5606

Coundmoor Salop 34 C4* loc 2m/3km S of Cound. SJ 5502

Coundon Durham 54 B2 vil 2m/3km E of Bishop Auckland. **Coundongate** loc 1m W. **C. Grange** loc 2km SW. See also New C. NZ 2329

Coundon W Midlands 35 H6* loc in Coventry 2m/4km NW of city centre. SP 3181

Counters End Herts 19 E1* W dist of Hemel Hempstead. TL 0407

Countersett N Yorks 53 H6 ham at N end of Semer Water 2m/3km SW of Bainbridge. SD 9187

Countess Wilts 17 F6 loc 1km N of Amesbury. SU 1542

Countess Pillar Cumbria 53 E2 commemorative stone pillar erected in 1656 by Lady Anne Clifford, 2m/4km E of Penrith. NY 5428

Countess Wear Devon 5 E2 SE dist of Exeter. SX 9490

Countesthorpe Leics 36 B4 vil 6m/9km S of Leicester. SP 5895

Counthorpe Lincs 37 E3 loc 6m/9km W of Bourne. TF 0020

Countisbury Devon 7 E1 ham on N coast 2m/3km E of Lynton. SS 7449

Country, North Cornwall 2 C4* loc 2km N of Redruth. SW 6944

County Oak W Sussex 11 H2 N dist of Crawley. TQ 2738

Coupall 74 D5* r rising between Buachaille Etive Mór and Buachaille Etive Beag in Argyll, S'clyde region, and running NE, then E along border of H'land and S'clyde regions to R Etive at head of Glen Etive. NN 2454

Coupar Angus Tayside 73 E1 small tn 4m/7km SE of Blairgowrie. Printing, mnfre of agricultural implements. Fragment of 12c abbey. 18c tollbooth. NO 2240

Coup Green Lancs 47 F5* loc 4m/6km E of Preston. SD 5927

Coupland Cumbria 53 F3 loc 2m/3km SE of Appleby. NY 7118

Coupland Nthmb 67 F5 ham 4m/6km NW of Wooler. 17c cas. NT 9331

Cour Bay S'clyde 63 E3 bay on E coast of Kintyre, Argyll, 3m/5km N of Grogport. NR 8248

Court-at-Street Kent 13 F3 loc 4m/7km W of Hythe. TR 0935

Court Colman Mid Glam 14 D3* loc 2m/3km NW of Bridgend. SS 8881

Courteachan H'land 79 E8* loc in Lochaber dist to E of Mallaig across harbour. NM 6897

Courteenhall Northants 28 C2/C3 vil 4m/7km S of Northampton. SP 7653

Court Henry Dyfed 23 G3* vil 5m/7km W of Llandeilo. SN 5522

Court Herbert W Glam 14 C2/D2* loc adjoining Neath to W. SS 7497

Court Hey Merseyside 42 A3* loc 1m W of Roby. SJ 4190

Court House Green W Midlands 36 A6* loc in Coventry 2m/4km NE of city centre. SP 3581

Courtsend Essex 21 F3 vil on Foulness I., 2m/3km SW of Foulness Pt. TR 0293

Courtway Som 8 A1* ham at foot of Quantock Hills 4m/6km S of Nether Stowey. ST 2034

Cousland Lothian 66 B2* vil 3m/5km E of Dalkeith. NT 3768

Cousley Wood E Sussex 12 C3 vil 2km NE of Wadhurst. TQ 6533

Cove Devon 7 G3 vil on R Exe 2m/3km S of Bampton. SS 9519

Cove Hants 18 D5 suburban loc 2m/3km NW of Farnborough. SU 8455

Cove H'land 78 F1 vil on W shore of Loch Ewe, Ross and Cromarty dist, 7m/11km NW of Poolewe. NG 8090

Cove S'clyde 64 A1 vil on **C. Bay** on E shore of Loch Long, 2km NW of Kilcreggan. NS 2282

Cove Bay Grampian 77 H1 vil on E coast 3m/5km S of Aberdeen. NJ 9501

Cove Bottom Suffolk 31 H1* loc 1km S of S Cove. TM 4979

Covehithe Suffolk 31 H1 ham near coast 4m/6km NE of Southwold. TM 5281

Coven Staffs 35 E4 vil 5m/8km N of Wolverhampton. **C. Lawn** loc 1km S. SJ 9006

Coveney Cambs 38 A6 vil 4m/6km NW of Ely. TL 4882

Covenham St Bartholomew Lincs 45 G2 vil adjoining vil of **Covenham St Mary** to N, 5m/7km N of Louth. TF 3394

Cove, North Suffolk 39 H5 vil 3m/5km E of Beccles. TM 4689

Coventry W Midlands 35 H6 industrial city 17m/27km E of Birmingham. Various industries, esp motor car mnfre. Cathedral built 1954–62 beside ruins of medieval cathedral destroyed in air raid in 1940. University of Warwick in SW part of city. Civil airport at Baginton to S. **C. Canal** runs N to Trent and Mersey Canal at Fradley Junction near Lichfield, Staffs. SP 3379

Cover 54 B6 r rising on moors N of Kettlewell, N Yorks, and flowing SE down Coverdale into R Ure 2km E of Middleham. SE 1487

Coverack Cornwall 2 D6 vil on E coast of Lizard peninsula 10m/15km SE of Helston. SW 7818

Coverack Bridges Cornwall 2 C5* ham 2m/3km N of Helston. SW 6630

Coverham N Yorks 54 A6 ham on R Cover 2m/3km SW of Middleham. Remains of 13c abbey, partly absorbed into Ggn hse. SE 1086

Covesea Grampian 82 B1 loc near N coast of region, 3m/5km W of Lossiemouth. Lighthouse (C. Skerries) 2km E. NJ 1870

Coves Haven Nthmb 67 G4* bay on N coast of Holy I. NU 1243

Cove, South Suffolk 31 H1 ham 3m/5km N of Southwold. TM 4980

Coves Reservoir S'clyde 64 A2* small resr 1m SE of Gourock. NS 2476

Covingham Wilts 17 F3* E dist of Swindon. SU 1885

Covington Cambs 29 E1 vil 6m/10km E of Higham Ferrers. TL 0570

Cowal S'clyde 70 C6, C5 peninsula in Argyll between Loch Fyne and Loch Long. C. Hydro-electricity Scheme at head of Loch Striven. NS 0888

Cowan Bridge Lancs 47 G1 vil 2m/3km SE of Kirkby Lonsdale. SD 6376

Cow and Calf W Yorks 48 D3* outcrop of millstone grit rocks on edge of Ilkley Moor above Ben Rhydding. SE 1346

Cowarne, Little H & W 26 B3 vil 4m/6km SW of Bromyard. SO 6051

Cowbar Cleveland 55 F3* loc at mouth of Roxby Beck opp Staithes on North Sea coast. NZ 7818

Cowbeech E Sussex 12 C5 ham 4m/6km NE of Hailsham. TQ 6114

Cowbit Lincs 37 G3 vil 3m/5km S of Spalding. TF 2618

Cowbridge (Bont-faen, Y) S Glam 15 E4 mkt tn 12m/19km W of Cardiff. SS 9974

Cowbridge Som 7 G1* ham just N of Timberscombe and 2m/4km W of Dunster. SS 9542

Cowburn Tunnel Derbys 43 F3 rly tunnel on Manchester-Sheffield line between Chinley and Edale, 2m/3km long. SK 0883

Cowcliffe W Yorks 48 D6* loc in Huddersfield 2m/3km N of tn centre. SE 1318

Cowden Kent 12 B3 vil 5m/8km E of E Grinstead. Loc of **C. Pound** 2km N. TQ 4640

Cowdenbeath Fife 73 E5 tn 5m/8km NE of Dunfermline. Centre of Fife coalfield. NT 1691

Cowdenburn Borders 66 A3 loc 4m/7km NW of Eddleston. NT 2052

Cowden, Great Humberside 51 F4 ham 4m/6km SE of Hornsea. TA 2242

Cowdenknowes Borders 66 D5 16c tower on E bank of Leader Water 1m S of Earlston; formerly a stronghold of the Homes, now incorporated in modern hse. NT 5736

Cowdray Park W Sussex. See Midhurst.

Cowen Head Cumbria 53 E5* loc 3m/5km N of Kendal. SD 4997

Cowers Lane Derbys 43 G6 ham 3m/4km W of Belper. SK 3046
Cowes Isle of Wight 10 B5/C5 tn at mouth of R Medina opp **E Cowes** (vehicle ferry), 4m/7km N of Newport and 9m/15km W of Portsmouth across Solent. Headquarters of Royal Yacht Squadron. Yachting centre with yearly regatta dating from 1814. SZ 4995
Cowesby N Yorks 54 D5 vil 5m/9km NE of Thirsk. SE 4689
Cowesfield Green Wilts 10 A3* loc 6m/10km W of Romsey. SU 2523
Cowes Roads 10 C5* that part of the Solent immediately N of Cowes in the Isle of Wight. SZ 5097
Cowey Green Essex 31 E5* loc 4m/6km S of Manningtree. TM 0925
Cowfold W Sussex 11 H3 vil 6m/9km SE of Horsham. TQ 2022
Cowgill Cumbria 53 F6 loc in Dentdale 3m/5km E of Dent. SD 7586
Cowgill Reservoirs S'clyde 65 F5* two small resrs, **Cowgill Upr** and **Cowgill Lr**, about 2m/4km SE of Lamington. NT 0128
Cowglen S'clyde 64 C3* loc in Glasgow 4m/6km SW of city centre. NS 5361
Cow Green Suffolk 31 E2* loc 1m S of Bacton. TM 0565
Cow Green Reservoir 53 G2 large resr in upper Teesdale on borders of Cumbria and Durham 9m/14km NW of Middleton in Teesdale. NY 8129
Cowhill Derbys 43 H6* loc adjoining Belper to S. SK 3546
Cow Honeybourne H & W 27 F3 vil 4m/6km N of Broadway. SP 1143
Cowhythe Head Grampian 83 E1* headland on N coast 2m/3km E of Portsoy. Boyne Bay to S and E. NJ 6166
Cowick, East Humberside 50 B5 vil 2km E of Snaith. **W Cowick** vil 1m W. SE 6621
Cowie Central 72 C5 mining vil 4m/6km SE of Stirling. NS 8489
Cowie Grampian 77 H2 vil adjoining Stonehaven to N, at mouth of **C. Water**, r rising on hills to W and running E through Fetteresso Forest. 1km from mouth of r is Glenury Viaduct, with distillery below. NO 8786
Cowlairs S'clyde 64 D2* loc in Glasgow 2m/3km NE of city centre. NS 6067
Cowlam Humberside 51 E2 loc 2m/3km E of Sledmere. Former vil no longer exists. SE 9665
Cowlands Cornwall 2 D4* loc at head of C. Creek, 3m/4km S of Truro. SW 8340
Cowley Derbys 43 G3/H3* loc 2km SW of Dronfield. SK 3377
Cowley Devon 7 G5 ham at confluence of Rs Exe and Yeo 2m/3km N of Exeter. SX 9095
Cowley Glos 26 D6 vil 5m/8km S of Cirencester. SO 9614
Cowley London 19 E3 loc in borough of Hillingdon 2km S of Uxbridge. Loc of **C. Peachey** adjoins to S. TQ 0582
Cowley Oxon 18 A1 SE dist of Oxford. Car factory. SP 5403
Cowling Lancs 47 F6* loc in SE part of Chorley. SD 5916
Cowling N Yorks 48 C4 vil 5m/9km E of Colne. SD 9642
Cowling N Yorks 54 B6* ham 2m/3km W of Bedale. SE 2387
Cowlinge Suffolk 30 C3 vil 6m/10km NE of Haverhill. TL 7154
Cowmes W Yorks 48 D6 loc 2m/4km E of Huddersfield. SE 1716
Cowm Reservoir Lancs 47 H6* resr just W of Whitworth. SD 8818
Cownwy 33 G3 r rising in Powys 3m/4km E of Llanymawddwy, Gwynedd, and running E into R Vyrnwy 2km S of Lake Vyrnwy dam. SJ 0217
Cowpe Lancs 48 B6* loc 2m/4km SW of Bacup. **Cowpe Resr** to S. SD 8420
Cowpen Nthmb 61 G3 W dist of Blyth. NZ 2981
Cowpen Bewley Cleveland 54 D3 loc 2m/3km NE of Billingham. NZ 4824
Cowplain Hants 10 D4 urban loc 2km NE of Waterlooville. SU 6911
Cowpren Point Cumbria 47 E1* headland at outfall of R Leven estuary into Morecambe Bay 2m/3km SW of Flookburgh. SD 3474
Cowsden H & W 26 D2* loc 5m/8km N of Pershore. SO 9453
Cowshill Durham 53 G1 vil 1km N of Wearhead. NY 8540
Cowsic 4 C3 r in Devon rising at Cowsic Head on Dartmoor and flowing S into W Dart R at Two Bridges. SX 6075
Cowthorpe N Yorks 50 A3 vil 3m/5km NE of Wetherby. SE 4252
Cowton Castle N Yorks 54 C4* tower hse of late 15c in par of S Cowton 2km SE of N Cowton. NZ 2902
Cowton, East N Yorks 54 C4 vil 7m/11km NW of Northallerton. NZ 3003
Cowton, North N Yorks 54 C4 vil 7m/11km S of Darlington. NZ 2803
Cowton, South N Yorks 54 C4* loc 1m SE of N Cowton. Par contains **C. Castle**, qv. NZ 2902
Coxall H & W 34 B6* loc 6m/9km E of Knighton. SO 3774
Coxbank Ches 34 D1* vil 2km S of Audlem. SJ 6541
Coxbench Derbys 36 A1 vil 5m/8km N of Derby. SK 3743
Coxbridge Som 8 D1* loc 3m/5km SE of Glastonbury. ST 5436
Cox Common Suffolk 31 G1* loc 3m/5km N of Halesworth. TM 4082
Coxford Norfolk 38 D2 loc adjoining Tattersett to S. Remains of 13c priory. TF 8429
Cox Green Essex 20 D2* loc 2m/4km NW of Wickford. TQ 7195
Cox Green Tyne & Wear 61 G5* loc on S bank of R Wear 5m/7km W of Sunderland. NZ 3255
Coxheath Kent 20 D6* suburb 3m/5km SW of Maidstone. TQ 7451
Coxhoe Durham 54 C2 vil 5m/8km SE of Durham. Coal-mining, quarrying. NZ 3235
Coxley Som 16 A6 vil 2m/3km SW of Wells. To NW, ham of **C. Wick**. ST 5343
Coxley W Yorks 49 E6* loc 1km E of Middlestown. SE 2717
Coxlodge Tyne & Wear 61 G4* loc in Gosforth 3m/4km N of Newcastle city centre. NZ 2368
Coxpark Cornwall 4 B3* loc 2m/3km W of Gunnislake. SX 4072
Coxtie Green Essex 20 C2 ham 3m/4km NW of Brentwood. TQ 5695
Coxwell, Great Oxon 17 G2 vil 2m/3km SW of Faringdon. Huge 13c monastic barn (NT). SU 2693
Coxwell, Little Oxon 17 G2 vil 2m/3km S of Faringdon. SU 2893
Coxwold N Yorks 50 B1 vil 5m/8km N of Easingwold. Laurence Sterne, author of *Tristram Shandy*, was vicar here, and lived at Shandy Hall from 1760 to 1768. SE 5377
Coychurch (Llangrallo) Mid Glam 15 E3 vil 2m/3km E of Bridgend. SS 9379
Coyle, Water of S'clyde. See Water of Coyle.
Coylton S'clyde 56 D2 vil 5m/8km E of Ayr, on W edge of coal-mining dist. NS 4119
Coylumbridge H'land 81 H6 loc in Badenoch and Strathspey dist 2m/3km SE of Aviemore. NH 9110
Coytrahen (Goetre-hen, Y) Mid Glam 14 D3 vil 4m/6km N of Bridgend. SS 8985
Crabbs Cross H & W 27 E2 S dist of Redditch. SP 0464
Crabgate Norfolk 39 E2* loc 3m/5km N of Reepham. TG 0927
Crab Orchard Dorset 9 G3* loc 2km S of Verwood. SU 0806
Crabtree Devon 4 B5 dist of Plymouth on R Plym 3m/4km NE of city centre. SX 5156
Crabtree S Yorks 43 H2* dist of Sheffield 2km N of city centre. SK 3589
Crabtree W Sussex 11 H3 vil 2m/3km N of Cowfold. TQ 2225
Crabtree Green Clwyd 41 H6* loc 4m/6km S of Wrexham. SJ 3344
Crabtree, Upper S Yorks 43 H2* loc in Sheffield 2m/3km N of city centre. SK 3590
Cracaval W Isles 88 A2* mt near W coast of Lewis 2km S of Mealisval. Height 1682 ft or 513 metres. NB 0225
Crackenedge W Yorks 49 E5* loc in Dewsbury to N of tn centre. SE 2422
Crackenthorpe Cumbria 53 F3 vil 2m/3km NW of Appleby. NY 6622
Crackington Haven Cornwall 6 A5 vil and coastal resort 5m/8km NE of Boscastle. SX 1496
Crackington, Higher Cornwall 6 A5 ham 5m/8km NE of Boscastle. SX 1595
Crackley Staffs 42 D6* loc in Newcastle-under-Lyme 3m/5km N of tn centre. SJ 8350
Crackley Warwicks 27 G1* loc 1m NE of Kenilworth. SP 2973
Crackleybank Salop 34 D3 ham 3m/5km E of Oakengates. SJ 7510
Crackpot N Yorks 53 H5* loc 1m SW of Low Row. SD 9796
Crackthorn Corner Suffolk 31 E1* loc 1km E of Thelnetham. TM 0278
Cracoe N Yorks 48 C2 vil 3m/5km SW of Grassington. SD 9760
Craddock Devon 7 H4 vil 2km E of Uffculme and 5m/8km NE of Cullompton. ST 0812
Cradley H & W 26 C3 vil 3m/4km W of Gt Malvern. SO 7347
Cradley W Midlands 35 F5 NW dist of Halesowen. SO 9485
Cradley Heath W Midlands 35 F5* loc in Warley 4m/6km W of tn centre. SO 9486
Cradoc Powys 25 E5* ham 2m/3km NW of Brecon. SO 0130
Crafnant 41 E5* r running NE through Llyn Crafnant Resr, Gwynedd, into R Conwy on N side of Trefriw. SH 7863
Crafthole Cornwall 3 H3 vil 5m/8km W of Torpoint. SX 3654
Crafton Bucks 28 D5* ham 4m/6km SW of Leighton Buzzard. SP 8819
Crag Foot Lancs 47 E1* loc 3m/4km NW of Carnforth. SD 4873
Cragg W Yorks 48 C5 ham 2m/3km S of Mytholmroyd. SE 0023
Craggan H'land 82 A4 loc in Badenoch and Strathspey dist 2km SW of Grantown-on-Spey. NJ 0126
Craggan More Grampian 82 B4* hill 9m/14km SW of Charlestown of Aberlour. Distillery to N at foot of hill. NJ 1634
Cragg Hill W Yorks 49 E4* loc in Horsforth 4m/7km NW of Leeds. SE 2437
Craggiemore H'land 81 G3* loc in Inverness dist 5m/9km SE of Inverness. NH 7339
Craghead Durham 61 G6 vil 2m/3km SE of Stanley. NZ 2150
Crag Hill Cumbria 52 C3* mt in Lake Dist 2m/4km NE of Buttermere ham. Height 2753 ft or 839 metres. NY 1920
Crag Houses Cumbria 52 B3 loc adjoining ham of Buttermere to NW. NY 1717
Crag Lough Nthmb 60 C4/D4 lake on N side of Hadrian's Wall 2m/4km NW of Bardon Mill. NY 7668
Crag Point Nthmb 61 H4* headland on North Sea coast on S side of Seaton Sluice. NZ 3476
Cragside Nthmb 61 F2 19c mansion by Norman Shaw 2km E of Rothbury. NU 0702
Crai Welsh form of Cray, qv.
Craibstone Grampian 83 G5 loc 6m/9km NW of Aberdeen. Site of agricultural college. NJ 8611
Craichie Tayside 77 E6 loc 4m/6km SE of Forfar. NO 5047
Craig Tayside. Par S of Montrose. See Kirkton of C.
Craigallian Loch S'clyde 64 C1* small loch 3m/4km NW of Milngavie. NS 5378
Craiganour Forest Tayside 75 F4 mt area and game forest in Atholl SW of Loch Garry. NN 6068
Craig Berthlwyd Mid Glam 15 F2* loc 1km S of Treharris. ST 0996
Craigcaffie Castle D & G 57 B6 16c keep near E side of Loch Ryan, 3m/4km NE of Stranraer across head of loch. NX 0864
Craig Castle Grampian 82 D4 16c cas with 18c portal and wing, overlooking wooded glen 2m/3km N of Lumsden. NJ 4724
Craig-cefn-parc W Glam 23 H5 loc 2km NW of Clydach. SN 6703
Craigdam Grampian 83 F4/G4 loc 3m/5km NE of Oldmeldrum. NJ 8430
Craigdow Loch S'clyde 56 C3* small loch 3m/5km SW of Maybole. NS 2606
Craigeam W Isles 88 B2* rock island off W coast of Lewis 2m/4km W of Carloway. NB 1643
Craigearn Grampian 83 F5 loc 2km SW of Kemnay. Lang Stane o' C. is antiquity to N. NJ 7214
Craigellachie Grampian 82 C3 vil with distilleries at confluence of R Fiddich and R Spey 3m/5km S of Rothes. NJ 2845
Craigend Tayside 73 E3 loc 2m/3km S of Perth. NO 1220
Craigendoran S'clyde 64 B1 suburb at E end of Helensburgh. Terminus for passenger boat services. NS 3081
Craigendunton Reservoir S'clyde 64 C4* resr 5m/8km SW of Eaglesham. NS 5245
Craigenloch Hill Tayside 76 C4* mt 4m/6km E of Spittal of Glenshee. Height 2419 ft or 737 metres. NO 1669
Craigenreoch S'clyde 56 D4* hill in Glentrool Forest Park 4m/7km SE of Barr. Height 1854 ft or 565 metres. NX 3391
Craigens S'clyde 56 F2* vil 2km SE of Cumnock. NS 5818
Craig Goch Reservoir Powys 24 D1 highest in series of large resrs in R Elan valley, 5m/8km W of Rhayader. SN 8968
Craig Head Grampian 82 D1* headland on N coast W of Findochty. NJ 4667
Craighouse S'clyde 62 C2 vil and small port on E coast of Jura 3m/5km N of S end of island. Distillery. NR 5267
Craigie S'clyde 64 B5 vil 4m/6km S of Kilmarnock. NS 4232
Craigie S'clyde 64 B6 E dist of Ayr. NS 3521
Craigie Tayside 73 E1 vil on SE side of Loch of Clunie 4m/6km W of Blairgowrie. NO 1143
Craigie Tayside 73 E2/E3* SW dist of Perth. NO 1122
Craigie Tayside 73 G2* dist of Dundee 2m/3km NE of city centre. Industrial estate. NO 4331
Craigielaw Lothian 66 C1 loc 1km W of Aberlady. To W is **C. Point**, headland on Firth of Forth at SW end of Aberlady Bay. NT 4579
Craigievar Castle Grampian 83 E5 early 17c cas (NTS) 4m/6km S of Alford. Noble example of Scottish baronial architecture. NJ 5609
Craigleith Lothian 66 A2* dist of Edinburgh 2m/3km W of city centre. NT 2274
Craigleith Lothian 73 H5 small island 1m N of N Berwick. Haunt of puffins. NT 5587
Craiglockhart Lothian 66 A2* dist of Edinburgh 3m/5km SW of city centre. NT 2270
Craigluscar Reservoirs Fife 72 D5* two small resrs below Craigluscar Hill 2m/4km NW of Dunfermline. NT 0690
Craiglyn Dyfi Gwynedd 33 F2 tarn 5m/8km S of Llanuwchllyn. SH 8622
Craigmaddie Reservoir S'clyde 64 C2* small resr on NE side of Milngavie. **C. Castle**, with moated tower, 1m NE. On **C. Muir** to E are boulders known as Auld Wives' Lifts. NS 5675
Craigmillar Lothian 66 A2 dist of Edinburgh 3m/4km SE of city centre. **C. Castle** (A.M.), ruined cas to S. NT 2871
Craignant Salop 34 A1* loc 1m NW of Sellatyn. SJ 2535
Craigneil Castle S'clyde 57 B5 13c stronghold of the Kennedys, opp Colmonell across R Stinchar. NX 1485
Craignethan Castle S'clyde 65 E4 restored tower hse (A.M.) dating from 15c, 1km W of Crossford. NS 8146
Craigneuk S'clyde 65 E3* loc 2km E of Motherwell. Steel works. NS 7756
Craignish Castle S'clyde 69 F7 cas dating from 16c near S end of peninsula (par of **Craignish**) W of Loch Craignish in Argyll. **Craignish Pt** is headland at S end of peninsula. NM 7701
Craignure S'clyde 68 E4 fishing vil on **C. Bay** on E coast of Mull opp entrance to Loch Linnhe. Car ferry to Oban. NM 7137
Craigo Tayside 77 F4 vil on R North Esk 5m/7km N of Montrose. NO 6864
Craigower Tayside 76 A5 hill (NTS) 2km NW of Pitlochry, commanding extensive views. NN 9260
Craigowl Hill Tayside 73 F1 summit of Sidlaw Hills 6m/10km N of Dundee. Height 1492 ft or 455 metres. Radio stn. NO 3740

Craig Rostan Central 71 E4 slopes of Ptarmigan above E shore of Loch Lomond opp Tarbet. NN 3404
Craigrothie Fife 73 F3 vil 2m/4km S of Cupar. NO 3710
Craig's End Essex 30 C4* loc 4m/6km NE of Finchingfield. TL 7137
Craigshill Lothian 65 G2* residential area of Livingston near tn centre. NT 0668
Craigside Durham 54 A2* loc 2m/3km S of Tow Law. NZ 1235
Craigs, The H'land 85 E7 loc in Sutherland dist at foot of Strath Chuilionaich 8m/13km W of Bonar Br. NH 4791
Craigston Castle Grampian 83 F2 17c cas 4m/7km NE of Turriff. NJ 7655
Craigton H'land 81 F3 loc in Ross and Cromarty dist at entrance to Beauly Firth opp Inverness. **Craigton Pt,** headland with beacon. NH 6648
Craigton S'clyde 64 C3* loc in Glasgow 3m/5km W of city centre, across R Clyde. NS 5464
Craigton Tayside 73 G1 vil 4m/6km NW of Carnoustie. NO 5138
Craigton Tayside 76 D5 vil 4m/7km SW of Kirriemuir. NO 3250
Craigvinean Forest Tayside 76 A6, B6* state forest on W side of Strath Tay above Dunkeld. NN 9943
Craig-y-don Gwynedd 41 E3* loc adjoining Llandudno to E. SH 7981
Craig-y-nos Powys 24 D6 loc in R Tawe valley 6m/10km NE of Ystalyfera. Geriatric hospital. SN 8315
Craik Cross Hill 59 G1* hill on border of Dumfries & Galloway and Borders regions 5m/9km NE of Eskdalemuir. Site of Roman signal stn. NT 3004
Craik Forest Borders 59 G1, H1* state forest 10m/16km W of Hawick. Encloses Crib Law, with fire tower; height 1389 ft or 423 metres. NT 3309
Crail Fife 73 H4 small fishing tn and resort 2m/4km SW of Fife Ness. Specialises in crab and lobster fishing. 16c tolbooth. Several old hses restored by NTS. NO 6107
Crailing Borders 66 D6 vil 4m/6km NE of Jedburgh. NT 6824
Craiselound Humberside 44 C2 vil 1m S of Haxey. SK 7798
Crake 52 C6* r flowing from foot of Coniston Water, Cumbria, southwards to join R Leven at Greenodd. SD 3182
Crakehall, Great N Yorks 54 B5 vil 2m/3km NW of Bedale. **Lit Crakehall** ham adjoining to NW. SE 2490
Crakehill N Yorks 49 F1* loc 2m/4km SE of Topcliffe. SE 4273
Crakemarsh Staffs 35 G1* loc 2m/3km N of Uttoxeter. SK 0936
Cralic H'land. Anglicised form of A'Chràlaig, qv.
Crambe N Yorks 50 C2 vil 6m/9km SW of Malton. SE 7364
Cramlington Nthmb 61 G4 tn 8m/12km N of Newcastle upon Tyne. Light industry. Industrial estate to NW. NZ 2676
Cramlington, East Nthmb 61 G4* loc adjoining Cramlington to E. NZ 2876
Crammag Head D & G 57 B8 headland with lighthouse on W coast of Rinns of Galloway, 5m/8km NW of Mull of Galloway. NX 0834
Crammers Devon 5 E3* loc 2km NE of Chudleigh. SX 8880
Cramond Lothian 65 H1 dist of Edinburgh 5m/7km W of city centre. **C. Bridge** is loc 1m SW at rd crossing of R Almond. Site of Roman fort to N. **C. Island,** small island 1m N in Firth of Forth, accessible across sands at low tide. NT 1876
Cranage Ches 42 C4 vil 1m NW of Holmes Chapel. SJ 7568
Cranberry Staffs 35 E1* ham 5m/8km W of Stone. SJ 8236
Cranborne Dorset 9 G3 vil 8m/12km NW of Ringwood. Jacbn manor hse. SU 0513
Cranborne Chase 9 F3 hilly, partly wooded, area on borders of Dorset and Wiltshire, formerly a forest and hunting preserve. ST 91
Cranbourne Berks 18 D4* vil 3m/4km N of Ascot. To E in Windsor Forest, wooded area of **C. Chase.** SU 9272
Cranbrook Kent 12 D3 small tn 7m/11km W of Tenterden. Ham of **C. Common** 2m/3km NE. TQ 7736
Cranbrook London 20 B3* NW dist of Ilford in borough of Redbridge. TQ 4287
Crane 19 F4 r rising as Yeading Brook at Harrow and flowing in a long loop through Hounslow and into R Thames at Isleworth. TQ 1675
Crane 9 G4* r rising 2m/4km NW of Cranborne in Dorset and flowing SE through the vil and thence S into Moors R, to SE of Verwood. SU 1006
Crane Islands Cornwall 2 B4* group of small islands off N coast 2m/3km SW of Portreath. SW 6344
Crane Moor S Yorks 43 G1* vil 1m E of Thurgoland. SE 3001
Crane's Corner Norfolk 38 D3* loc 2km E of Gt Fransham. TF 9113
Cranes Industrial Estate Essex 20 D3* area in NE part of Basildon. TQ 7290
Cranfield Beds 28 D3 vil 8m/12km SW of Bedford. Airfield to W. SP 9542
Cranford London 19 E4 loc in borough of Hounslow on E side of London (Heathrow) Airport and 12m/19km W of Charing Cross. C. Park is 1km NW across Grand Union Canal, in borough of Hillingdon. TQ 1077
Cranford Northants 28 D1 par containing vils of **C. St Andrew** and **C. St John,** 4m/6km E of Kettering. SP 9277
Cranham Glos 26 D6 vil 5m/9km SE of Gloucester. SO 8912
Crank Merseyside 42 B2 vil 3m/4km N of St Helens. SJ 5099
Crankwood Gtr Manchester 42 B2* loc 1m SE of Abram. SD 6100
Cranleigh Surrey 11 F1 tn 8m/12km SE of Guildford. TQ 0639
Cranley Suffolk 31 F1* loc 1m SE of Eye. TM 1572
Cranley Gardens London 19 G3* loc in borough of Haringey 6m/9km N of Charing Cross. TQ 2989
Cran Loch H'land 81 H2 small loch in Nairn dist 4m/7km E of Nairn. NH 9459
Cranmere Pool Devon 7 E6 hollow in a bog at the heart of Dartmoor 6m/10km S of Okehampton. SX 6085
Cranmer Green Suffolk 31 E1 loc 1m E of Walsham le Willows. TM 0171
Cranmore Isle of Wight 10 B5* loc 3m/4km E of Yarmouth. SZ 3990
Cranmore Som 16 B6 par 4m/6km E of Shepton Mallet, containing vil of **W Cranmore** and ham of **E Cranmore.** ST 6743
Cranoe Leics 36 D5 vil 5m/9km N of Mkt Harborough. SP 7695
Cransford Suffolk 31 G2 vil 2m/4km E of Framlingham. TM 3164
Cranshaws Borders 66 D3 vil on Whiteadder Water 8m/12km NW of Duns. NT 6961
Cransley Northants 36 D6 par containing vil of **Gt Cransley** and loc of **Lit Cransley,** 3m/4km SW of Kettering. SP 8376
Cranstackie H'land 84 D2 mt in Sutherland dist 3m/4km W of head of Loch Eriboll. Height 2630 ft or 801 metres. NC 3555
Cranstal Isle of Man 46 C3 loc 2m/3km S of Pt of Ayre. See also Point Cranstal. NX 4602
Cranswick Humberside 51 E3 loc at S end of Hutton Cranswick, 4m/6km S of Gt Driffield. TA 0252
Crantock Cornwall 2 D2 vil near coast 2m/3km SW of Newquay across R Gannel. SW 7960
Cranwell Lincs 45 E6 vil 4m/6km NW of Sleaford. RAF college and airfield to W. TF 0349
Cranwich Norfolk 38 C5 ham 2m/3km NW of Mundford. TL 7894
Cranworth Norfolk 38 D4 vil 6m/9km S of E Dereham. TF 9804
Crapstone Devon 4 B4 loc 5m/7km SE of Tavistock. SX 5067
Craro Island S'clyde 62 D3 small island off W coast of Gigha, 2km from S end of it. NR 6247
Crask of Aigas H'land 81 E3 loc in wooded area beside R Beauly 4m/7km SW of Beauly tn in Inverness dist. NH 4642
Craster Nthmb 67 H6 fishing vil on North Sea coast 6m/10km NE of Alnwick. NU 2519
Craswall H & W 25 G4 ham 5m/8km SE of Hay-on-Wye. Remains of **C. Priory** 1m N. SO 2736
Crateford Staffs 35 E3* loc 2m/3km E of Brewood. SJ 9009
Cratfield Suffolk 31 G1 vil 5m/8km W of Halesworth. TM 3175
Crathes Grampian 77 G2 vil on N side of R Dee 3m/5km E of Banchory. 1m W is **C. Castle** (NTS), 16c with later additions; gardens. NO 7596
Crathie Grampian 76 C2 vil on R Dee 1km E of Balmoral Castle. NO 2695
Crathie Point Grampian 82 D1* headland on N coast 2m/4km E of Cullen. NJ 5467
Crathorne N Yorks 54 D4 vil 4m/6km S of Yarm. NZ 4407
Craufurdland Water 64 B5/C5 r in Strathclyde region running SW to confluence with Fenwick Water 2km NE of Kilmarnock. The combined stream, known as Kilmarnock Water, flows through Kilmarnock to R Irvine on S side of tn. NS 4339
Craven 117 admin dist of N Yorks.
Craven Arms Salop 34 B6 small tn and rly junction 7m/11km NW of Ludlow. SO 4382
Crawcrook Tyne & Wear 61 F5 loc 2km W of Ryton. NZ 1363
Crawcwellt 32 D2/33 E2 r running E into R Eden 2m/3km S of Trawsfynydd, Gwynedd. SH 7032
Crawcwellt 33 E2* r running E into R Eden 4m/7km S of Trawsfynydd, Gwynedd. SH 7128
Crawford Lancs 42 B1 loc 3m/5km SE of Skelmersdale. SD 4902
Crawford S'clyde 65 F6 vil on R Clyde 2m/4km SE of Abington. Site of Roman fort and fragment of old cas to N across r. NS 9520
Crawfordjohn S'clyde 65 F6 vil 3m/5km W of Abington. NS 8823
Crawhin Reservoir S'clyde 64 A2* small resr 4m/6km SW of Greenock. NS 2470
Crawick D & G 58 D1 vil 1m NW of Sanquhar. **C. Water** is r running SW through vil to R Nith 1km S. NS 7711
Crawley Hants 10 B2 vil 5m/8km NW of Winchester. SU 4234
Crawley Oxon 27 G6 vil 2m/3km NW of Witney. SP 3412
Crawley W Sussex 11 H2 tn 27m/43km S of London. Designated New Tn 1947. Light industry. Pedestrian precinct at tn centre. London (Gatwick) Airport to N. TQ 2736
Crawley Down W Sussex 11 H2* residential loc 5m/7km E of Crawley. TQ 3437
Crawley, Little Bucks 28 D3* ham 3m/5km E of Newport Pagnell. SP 9245
Crawley, North Bucks 28 D3 vil 3m/5km E of Newport Pagnell. SP 9244
Crawley Side Durham 53 H1 loc 1km N of Stanhope. NY 9940
Crawnon 25 F5 r rising S of Talybont Resr, Powys, and flowing NE down Dyffryn Crawnon into R Usk at Cwm Crawnon, W of Llangynidr. SO 1419
Crawshaw Booth Lancs 48 B5 vil 2m/3km N of Rawtenstall. SD 8125
Crawyn Isle of Man 46 B4 ham 4m/6km NE of Kirk Michael. SC 3496
Craxe's Green Essex 30 D6* loc 5m/8km SW of Colchester. TL 9519
Cray N Yorks 48 C1 ham 2km N of Buckden. SD 9479
Cray (Crai) Powys 24 D5 ham 3m/5km SW of Sennybridge. **Cray Resr** 2m/3km S. SN 8924
Cray 20 B4 r rising at St Mary Cray in the London borough of Bromley and flowing NE into R Darent 2km N of Dartford, Kent. TQ 5376
Crayford London 20 B4 dist in borough of Bexley in R Cray valley 2m/3km W of Dartford. **C. Ness** on S bank of R Thames to NE beyond **C. Marshes.** TQ 5174
Crayke N Yorks 50 B1/B2 vil 2m/3km E of Easingwold. 15c cas, part ruined, part incorporated in 19c hse. SE 5670
Cray, North London 20 B4 loc in borough of Bexley 2m/3km E of Sidcup. TQ 4872
Crays Hill Essex 20 D3 vil 2m/3km N of Basildon. TQ 7192
Cray's Pond Oxon 18 B3 loc 2m/4km E of Goring. SU 6380
Crazies Hill Berks 18 C3 ham 3m/5km N of Twyford. SU 7980
Creachan Mór S'clyde 70 D5 mt in Argyll 2m/3km W of junction of Loch Goil with Loch Long. Height 2156 ft or 657 metres. NS 1891
Creach Beinn S'clyde 69 E5 mt on Mull 3m/4km NE of Lochbuie. Height 2289 ft or 698 metres. Anglicised form: Ben Creach. NM 6427
Creach Bheinn H'land 74 A5 mt in Lochaber dist 3m/5km SE of head of Loch Sunart. Height 2798 ft or 853 metres. NM 8757
Creach Bheinn S'clyde 70 C1 mt in Argyll, 2m/4km SE of Loch Creran. Height 2657 ft or 810 metres. NN 0242
Creacombe Devon 7 F3 ham 3m/5km N of Witheridge. SS 8119
Creagan S'clyde 70 B1* locality on N shore of Loch Creran, Argyll, 3m/5km E of Portnacroish. NM 9744
Creag an Fheadain Tayside 71 F1* peak 1m SW of dam of Loch an Daimh. Height 2909 ft or 887 metres. NN 4945
Creag an Loch Tayside 72 C1* mt 3m/5km NW of Amulree, on S side of Loch Fender. Height 2163 ft or 659 metres. NN 8740
Creag an Lochain Tayside 71 G1* mt on W side of Lochan na Lairige. Height 2742 ft or 836 metres. NN 5940
Creag an Sgliata Tayside 71 H1 mt 3m/4km S of Acharn. Height 2288 ft or 697 metres. NN 7639
Creag Dubh H'land 80 C4 peak in Inverness dist 3m/4km NW of dam of Loch Mullardoch. Height 3102 ft or 946 metres. NH 1935
Creag Ghorm a' Bhealaich H'land 80 C3* peak on border of Inverness and Ross & Cromarty dists 4m/6km NE of dam of Loch Monar, on E side of Sgurr Fhuar-thuill. Height 3378 ft or 1030 metres. NH 2443
Creag Ghreusaiche H'land 81 H6* hill and TV transmitting stn in Badenoch and Strathspey dist 3m/5km E of Aviemore. NH 9412
Creag Island S'clyde 70 A2* islet off S coast of Lismore, nearly 1km S of Eilean Dubh and on W side of Pladda I. NM 8337
Creag Meagaidh H'land 75 E3 mt on border of Lochaber and Badenoch & Strathspey dists 3m/5km N of E end of Loch Moy. Height 3708 ft or 1130 metres. NN 4187
Creag Mhór Central 71 F2 mt 4m/6km W of Killin. Height 2359 ft or 719 metres. NN 5134
Creag Mhór 71 E2 mt on border of Central and Tayside regions 5m/8km NE of Tyndrum. Height 3437 ft or 1048 metres. NN 3936
Creag na Caillich Central 71 F2* mt 3m/5km N of Killin. Height 2990 ft or 911 metres. NN 5637
Creag nan Damh H'land 80 A6 peak on border of Lochaber and Skye & Lochalsh dists 4m/6km NE of Kinloch Hourn. Height 3012 ft or 918 metres. NG 9811
Creagnaneun Forest H'land 81 E5* state forest in Inverness dist on NW shore of Loch Ness, NE of Invermoriston. NH 4418
Creagorry W Isles 88 E2 loc on S coast of Benbecula 4m/7km S of Benbecula Airfield. NF 7948
Creag Pitridh H'land 75 E3* mt in Badenoch and Strathspey dist 2km E of SW end of Lochan na h-Earba. Height 3031 ft or 924 metres. NN 4881
Creag Uchdag 71 G2 mt on border of Central and Tayside regions 3m/5km SE of Ardeonaig on S shore of Loch Tay. NN 7032
Creake, North Norfolk 38 D1 vil 7m/11km NW of Fakenham. **S Creake** vil 2km S. To N are remains of Creake Abbey (A.M.), mainly 13c. TF 8538
Creamore Bank Salop 34 C2* loc 1m N of Wem. SJ 5130
Creaton Northants 28 C1 vil 8m/13km NW of Northampton. Ham of **Lit Creaton** to SE. SP 7071
Creca D & G 59 G4 loc 3m/5km NE of Annan. NY 2270
Credenhill H & W 26 A3 vil 4m/7km NW of Hereford. SO 4543
Crediton Devon 7 F5 ancient small tn, formerly seat of bishops of the South West. Cider-making. SS 8300
Cree 57 E7 r in Dumfries & Galloway region, whose headwaters are in Glentrool Forest Park on borders with Strathclyde region. R then flows S to Newton Stewart and Wigtown Bay. NX 4655
Creebridge D & G 57 D6 loc opp Newton Stewart across R Cree. NX 4165
Creech Dorset 9 F5 ham 3m/4km S of Wareham. SY 9183

Creech, East Dorset 9 F5* ham 3m/5km S of Wareham. SY 9282
Creech Heathfield Som 8 B2* vil 4m/6km NE of Taunton. ST 2727
Creech St Michael Som 8 B2 vil 3m/5km E of Taunton. ST 2725
Creed Cornwall 3 E3 ham 6m/9km SW of St Austell. SW 9347
Creed W Isles 88 C2* r on Lewis rising among lochs some 6m/10km NW of Stornoway and flowing SE into Stornoway Harbour. Also known as Greeta R. NB 4131
Creedy 7 F5* r in Devon rising NE of Morchard Bishop and flowing SE to join R Yeo 2km SE of Crediton. SX 8599
Creedy, Lower Devon 7 F5* loc on R Creedy 2m/3km N of Crediton. SS 8402
Creekmouth London 20 B3* loc on R Thames on E side of Barking Creek in borough of Barking. TQ 4581
Creeting Green, West Suffolk 31 E2* vil 2m/3km E of Stowmarket. TM 0758
Creeting St Mary Suffolk 31 E3 vil 3m/5km SE of Stowmarket. TM 0956
Creeton Lincs 37 E3 ham 5m/8km W of Bourne. TF 0119
Creetown D & G 57 E6 vil on E side of R Cree estuary at mouth of Moneypool Burn, 6m/10km SE of Newton Stewart. Granite quarries to S. NX 4758
Creggan a' Chaise Cairn Grampian 82 A4* summit of Hills of Cromdale, 5m/8km SE of Grantown-on-Spey. Height 2368 ft or 722 metres. NJ 1024
Creggans S'clyde 70 C4 locality in Argyll, on E shore of Loch Fyne 1m NW of Strachur. NN 0802
Cregneish Isle of Man 46 A6 ham 2km W of Port St Mary. SC 1867
Cregrina Powys 25 F3 loc 5m/8km E of Builth Wells. SO 1252
Creich Fife 73 F3 loc 5m/8km NW of Cupar. NO 3221
Creich S'clyde 69 B5* tract at NW end of Ross of Mull. NM 3124
Creich, Little H'land 85 F7 loc in Sutherland dist on N shore of Dornoch Firth 2m/4km SE of Bonar Br. NH 6389
Creigau Gwent 16 A2* loc 1km N of Devauden. ST 4899
Creigiau Mid Glam 15 F3* vil 3m/4km E of Llantrisant. ST 0881
Creinch S'clyde 71 E5 small island in Loch Lomond 2m/3km E of Rossdhu. NS 3988
Crelly Cornwall 2 C5* loc 3m/5km N of Helston. SW 6732
Cremyll Cornwall 4 B5 vil beside R Tamar estuary opp Stonehouse dist of Plymouth. To S, Mt hse and park; 16c hse rebuilt after World War II fire. SX 4553
Crendell Dorset 9 G3* loc 2m/3km E of Cranborne. SU 0813
Creran 70 C1 r rising S of Sgorr na h-Ulaidh, H'land region, and running W along border with S'clyde region, then SW down Glen C., S'clyde, to head of Loch C. NM 9945
Cressage Salop 34 C4 vil 3m/5km NW of Much Wenlock. SJ 5904
Cressbrook Derbys 43 F4* ham on R Wye 4m/7km NW of Bakewell. SK 1773
Cresselly Dyfed 22 C5 vil 6m/9km NE of Pembroke. SN 0606
Cressex Bucks 18 D2* SW dist of High Wycombe. SU 8591
Cressing Essex 30 C5 vil 3m/4km SE of Braintree. TL 7920
Cressingham, Great Norfolk 38 C4 vil 5m/8km SE of Swaffham. Vil of **Lit Cressingham** 2m/3km SE. TF 8501
Cresswell Dyfed 22 C5 vil at head of R Cresswell estuary 6m/10km NW of Tenby. SN 0506
Cresswell Nthmb 61 G2 vil on coast 4m/6km N of Ashington. NZ 2993
Cresswell Staffs 35 F1 vil 3m/5km SW of Cheadle. SJ 9739
Cresswell 22 C5 r rising NW of Saundersfoot, Dyfed, and flowing W to vil of Cresswell, where it forms an estuary which continues W to join Carew R and flow into Daugleddau R at Jenkins Pt. SN 0106
Creswell Derbys 43 A4 vil 4m/7km NE of Bolsover. Model vil adjoins to W. SK 5274
Creswell Green Staffs 35 G3* loc 3m/5km W of Lichfield. SK 0710
Cretingham Suffolk 31 F2 vil 4m/6km SE of Debenham. TM 2260
Creuddyn 24 B3 r rising near Temple Bar, Dyfed, and flowing S into R Teifi on SW side of Lampeter. SN 5747
Crewe Ches 42 B5 vil 1m E of Holt across R Dee. SJ 4253
Crewe Ches 42 C5 tn with important rly stn, junction, and works, 12m/20km NW of Stoke-on-Trent. **C. Green** ham 2m/3km E. **C. Hall,** 17c mansion restored 19c, 2m/3km SE. SJ 7055
Crew Green Powys 34 A3 vil 8m/13km NE of Welshpool. SJ 3215
Crewi 33 E4* r running into R Dulas 1m E of Machynlleth, Powys. SH 7600
Crewkerne Som 8 C3 tn 8m/13km SW of Yeovil. Largely stone-built, with long-established sail-making industry. ST 4409
Crews Hill H & W 26 B5* ham 4m/7km SW of Newent. SO 6722
Crew's Hole Avon 16 B4* loc on N bank of R Avon in E part of Bristol. ST 6273
Crewton Derbys 36 A1 dist of Derby 2m/4km SE of tn centre. SK 3733
Crianlarich Central 71 E2 vil on R Fillan 12m/20km SW of Killin. Rly junction of Oban and Fort William lines. NN 3825
Cribach Bay Dyfed 23 E1* bay 1km NW of Aberporth. SN 2552
Cribden Side Lancs 48 B5* loc below Cribden Hill 1km NE of Haslingden. SD 7924
Crib Law Borders. See Craik Forest.
Cribyn Dyfed 24 B3 ham 4m/6km NW of Lampeter. SN 5251
Criccieth Gwynedd 32 C1 resort on Tremadoc Bay 15m/24km S of Caernarvon. Remains of 13c cas (A.M.). SH 5038
Crich Derbys 43 H5 vil 4m/7km N of Belper. **C. Carr** loc 1km W. **C. Common** loc 7km S. SK 3554
Crichope Linn D & G 59 E2* waterfall in Crichope Linn, valley of Crichope Burn, 2m/3km E of Thornhill. NX 9195
Crichton Lothian 66 B3 loc 2m/3km S of Pathhead. **C. Castle** (A.M.), 14c and later. NT 3862
Crick Gwent 16 A3 loc 4m/7km SW of Chepstow. ST 4890
Crick Northants 28 B1 vil 6m/9km E of Rugby. Loc of **C. Wharf** 1km E across Grand Union Canal. SP 5872
Crickadarn Powys 25 F3 ham 6m/10km SE of Builth Wells. SO 0942
Cricket Hill Hants 18 C5* loc 1km SE of Yateley. SU 8260
Cricket Malherbie Som 8 B3 ham 3m/5km NE of Chard. ST 3611
Cricket St Thomas Som 8 B3 ham 3m/5km E of Chard, grouped round small mansion in grnds now wildlife park. ST 3708
Crickham Som 15 H6* ham 2km N of Wedmore. ST 4349
Crickheath Salop 34 A2* loc 4m/7km S of Oswestry. Loc of **C. Wharf** to N on Shropshire Union Canal. SJ 2922
Crickhowell (Crucywel) Powys 25 G6 vil on R Usk 6m/9km NW of Abergavenny. Faint remains of old cas. SO 2118
Cricklade Wilts 17 E2 vil on R Thames 7m/11km NW of Swindon. Site of Roman bldg to N. SU 1093
Cricklewood London 19 F3* dist in borough of Brent 5m/9km NW of Charing Cross. TQ 2385
Crickley Hill Glos 26 D5* hill, partly NT, with Iron Age fort on escarpment of Cotswold Hills 4m/6km S of Cheltenham. SO 9216
Crick's Green H & W 26 B3* loc 2m/4km SW of Bromyard. SO 6351
Criddlestyle Hants 9 H3* loc 1m E of Fordingbridge. SU 1614
Cridling Stubbs N Yorks 49 G5 vil 2m/3km SE of Knottingley. SE 5221
Crieff Tayside 72 C3 tn and resort above left bank of R Earn 16m/25km W of Perth. NN 8621
Criffell D & G 59 E5 hill and prominent landmark, commanding extensive views, 3m/4km S of New Abbey. Height 1866 ft or 569 metres. NX 9561
Criggan Cornwall 3 E2* loc 5m/8km N of St Austell. SX 0160
Criggion (Crugion) Powys 34 A3 vil 6m/10km NE of Welshpool. SJ 2914
Crigglestone W Yorks 49 E6 vil 3m/5km SW of Wakefield. SE 3116
Crigyll 40 A4* r on Anglesey flowing S into Caernarvon Bay on N side of Rhosneigr. SH 3173
Crimble Gtr Manchester 42 D1* loc 2m/3km W of Rochdale. SD 8611
Crimchard Som 8 B3* NW dist of Chard. ST 3109
Crimdon Beck 54 D2* stream rising near Hutton Henry, Durham, and flowing E down wooded dene into North Sea 3m/5km N of Hartlepool, Cleveland. NZ 4936
Crime Rigg Durham 54 C1* loc 1km SE of Sherburn Hill. NZ 3441
Crimond Grampian 83 H2 vil near NE coast 8m/13km NW of Peterhead. NK 0556
Crimple Beck 49 F3* r rising SW of Harrogate, N Yorks, and flowing generally E by Pannal and Spofforth to join R Nidd 1km W of Walshford. SE 4053
Crimplesham Norfolk 38 B4 vil 3m/4km E of Downham Mkt. TF 6503
Crinan S'clyde 70 A5 vil on **C. Loch** in Argyll 6m/10km NW of Lochgilphead. **C. Canal** connects C. Loch with Ardrishaig and Loch Fyne. Lighthouse at entrance to canal. **C. Ferry** is locality to E across R Add; ferry for pedestrians across r. NR 7894
Crincoed Point Dyfed 22 B2 headland on W side of Fishguard Bay 2m/3km N of Fishguard. SM 9540
Crindai Welsh form of Crindau, qv.
Crindau (Crindai) Gwent loc in N part of Newport. ST 3089
Crindledyke S'clyde 65 E3* loc 1m E of Newmains. NS 8356
Cringae 33 G3* stream running E into R Vyrnwy 1m NW of Dolanog, Powys. SJ 0513
Cringleford Norfolk 39 F4 vil 3m/4km SW of Norwich. TG 1905
Crinkle Crags Cumbria 52 C4 fell in Lake Dist S of Bow Fell. Attains height of 2816 ft or 858 metres. NY 2404
Crinow (Crynwedd) Dyfed 22 D4 ham 2km E of Narberth. SN 1214
Cripple's Ease Cornwall 2 B4* loc 2m/4km SE of St Ives. SW 5036
Cripplesty Dorset 9 G3* loc 3m/4km E of Cranborne. SU 0912
Cripp's Corner E Sussex 12 D4 loc 4m/6km NE of Battle. TQ 7721
Critchell's Green Hants. See Lockerley.
Crizeley H & W 26 A4* loc 7m/11km SW of Hereford. SO 4432
Croachy H'land 81 F4 two locs, **E** and **W Croachy,** in Inverness dist 5m/9km SE of Dores. NH 6427
Croal 42 C1* r rising on Turton Moor, Lancs, and flowing S through Bolton, Gtr Manchester, into R Irwell on E side of Farnworth. SD 7406
Crockenhill Kent 20 B5 vil 2km SW of Swanley. TQ 5067
Crocker End Oxon 18 C3* ham 1km E of Nettlebed. SU 7086
Crockerhill Hants 10 C4* loc 2m/3km N of Fareham. SU 5709
Crockerhill W Sussex 11 E4* ham 4m/7km E of Chichester. SU 9207
Crockernwell Devon 7 F5 vil 4m/7km N of Moretonhampstead. SX 7592
Crockerton Wilts 16 D6 vil 2m/3km S of Warminster. To NE, ham of **C. Green.** ST 8642
Crocketford D & G 58 D4 vil 8m/13km NE of Castle Douglas. Also known as Nine Mile Bar. NX 8372
Crockey Hill N Yorks 50 B3 loc 4m/6km S of York, on rd to Selby. SE 6246
Crockham Hill Kent 20 B6 vil 2m/3km S of Westerham. NT property to NE. TQ 4450
Crockhurst Street Kent 12 C2 loc 2m/4km SE of Tonbridge. TQ 6244
Crockleford Heath Essex 31 E5* loc 3m/5km E of Colchester. TM 0326
Crock Ness Orkney 89 A7* headland on E coast of Hoy opp island of Flotta. ND 3293
Crock Street Som 8 B3 loc 1m S of Broadway. ST 3213
Crococalana Notts. See Brough.
Croe H'land 80 A5 r running NW to head of Loch Duich in Skye and Lochalsh dist. NG 9521
Croeserw W Glam 14 D2* vil 3m/4km N of Maesteg. SS 8695
Croesgoch Dyfed 22 B3 ham 6m/9km NE of St David's. SM 8230
Croes-lan Dyfed 23 E2* ham 3m/5km NW of Llandyssul. SN 3844
Croesor Gwynedd 32 D1* ham 4m/6km N of Penrhyndeudraeth. SH 6344
Croesor 32 D1* r rising W of Blaenau Ffestiniog, Gwynedd, and running SW into R Glaslyn 3m/5km NE of Tremadoc. SH 5943
Croespenmaen Gwent 15 G2* loc 1m NW of Newbridge. ST 1998
Croesyceiliog Dyfed 23 F4 ham 2m/4km S of Carmarthen. SN 4016
Croesyceiliog Gwent 15 G2 loc in NE part of Cwmbran. ST 3096
Croes-y-mwyalch Gwent 15 G2 loc 3m/4km N of Newport. ST 3092
Croes y pant Gwent 15 G1 loc 3m/5km NE of Pontypool. SO 3104
Croesywaun Gwynedd 40 C5* loc 3m/5km SE of Caernarvon. SH 5259
Croford Som 7 H2* loc 2m/3km E of Wiveliscombe. ST 1027
Croft Ches 42 C2 vil 4m/6km NE of Warrington. SJ 6393
Croft Dyfed 22 D2* loc 2m/4km SW of Cardigan. SN 1542
Croft H & W 26 A1 loc 5m/8km NW of Leominster. Par contains **Croft Castle** (NT), medieval bldg with later modifications. Estate includes **Croft Ambrey,** Iron Age hill fort. SO 4465
Croft Leics 36 B4 vil 6m/9km E of Hinckley. Syenite quarries to N. SP 5195
Croft Lincs 45 H5 vil 2m/3km NE of Wainfleet. TF 5061
Croft N Yorks 54 C4 vil on R Tees 3m/5km S of Darlington. NZ 2809
Croftamie S'clyde 71 F6 vil 2m/3km S of Drymen. NS 4786
Croft, East Cumbria 52 A3* loc adjoining High Harrington to N, 2m/3km S of Workington tn centre. NY 0025
Croftfoot S'clyde 64 D3* dist of Glasgow 3m/5km S of city centre. NS 6060
Croft Head D & G 59 F1 mt 4m/7km E of Moffat. Height 2085 ft or 636 metres. NT 1505
Croftmoraig Tayside 71 H1* loc with triple stone circle on S side of R Tay near its confluence with R Lyon. NN 7947
Crofton Cumbria 52 C1 loc 3m/5km E of Wigton. NY 3049
Crofton Wilts 17 G5 loc on Kennet and Avon Canal, and on line of Roman rd, 6m/10km SW of Hungerford. SU 2662
Crofton W Yorks 49 F6 vil 4m/6km SE of Wakefield. See also New Crofton. SE 3717
Crofts Bank Gtr Manchester 42 C2* loc to N of Urmston tn centre. SJ 7695
Crofts End Avon 16 B4* dist of Bristol 3m/5km NE of city centre. ST 6274
Crofty W Glam 23 G6* vil 1m SE of Salthouse Pt. SS 5294
Crogga 46 B6* stream on Isle of Man running out to sea at Port Soderick on E coast. SC 3472
Croggan Mull, S'clyde 68 E5 vil on S side of entrance to Loch Spelve. NM 7027
Croglin Cumbria 60 B6 vil 9m/15km S of Brampton. NY 5747
Croglin Water 53 E1 r rising on Gilderdale Forest, W of Alston, Cumbria, and flowing generally W past Croglin and into R Eden 2m/3km N of Lazonby. NY 5342
Croick H'land 85 E7 loc in Sutherland dist at foot of Strath Chuilionaich, 10m/15km W of Bonar Br. NH 4591
Croitecaley Isle of Man 46 A6 loc 2km NE of Port St Mary. SC 2269
Cromalt Hills H'land 85 C6 upland area on border of Ross & Cromarty and Sutherland dists S of Elphin. NC 2106
Cromar Grampian 77 E1 area or dist between Aboyne and Tarland. NJ 40
Cromarty H'land 81 G1 small tn with harbour, Ross and Cromarty dist, on S side of entrance to **C. Firth,** 15m/24km NE of Inverness. Hugh Miller's Cottage (NTS), birthplace of eminent geologist etc, dates from 1650; contains small museum. The firth is arm of sea extending 18m/29km hence to beyond Dingwall; industrial developments mainly in connection with North Sea oil. NH 7867
Cromarty Bay H'land 81 F1/G1 bay on S side of Cromarty Firth, Ross and Cromarty dist, between Balblair and Cromarty. NH 7466
Cromarty Firth H'land 81 F1 long inlet of Moray Firth extending past Nigg Bay and Invergordon to Dingwall, Ross and Cromarty dist. NH 6667

Crombie Fife 72 D5/D6* loc 3m/5km SW of Dunfermline. NT 0485
Crombie Castle Grampian 83 E2 medieval cas 2m/4km W of Aberchirder. NJ 5952
Crombie Reservoir Tayside 73 G1 small resr 4m/7km NW of Carnoustie. NO 5240
Cromdale H'land 82 A4 vil in Badenoch and Strathspey dist 3m/5km E of Grantown-on-Spey. Distillery 1m S. Hills of C. is hill ridge to SE, running SW to NE on border of Highland and Grampian regions. Haughs of C. is tract between vil and hills. NJ 0728
Cromer Herts 29 G5 vil 4m/7km W of Buntingford. TL 2928
Cromer Norfolk 39 F1 coastal resort 21m/33km N of Norwich. TG 2142
Cromer Hyde Herts 19 F1 loc 2m/3km W of Welwyn Garden City. TL 2012
Cromer Point N Yorks 55 H5* headland 3m/5km N of Scarborough. TA 0392
Cromford Derbys 43 G5 vil 2m/3km N of Wirksworth. SK 2956
Cromhall Avon 16 C3 vil 4m/6km E of Thornbury. Site of Roman villa 1km SW. Loc of **C. Common** 1m S. ST 6990
Cromore W Isles 88 C2* vil on S side of entrance to Loch Erisort, E coast of Lewis. Loch C. is small loch to S. NB 4021
Crompton Gtr Manchester 43 E1 urban area incl locs of **High C.** and **C. Fold,** 3m/5km N of Oldham. Electric lamps, light engineering, textiles. SD 9309
Cromwell Notts 44 C5 vil 5m/8km N of Newark-on-Trent. 1km E is site of Roman br across R Trent. SK 7961
Cromwell Bottom W Yorks 48 D5* loc 2km W of Brighouse. SE 1222
Cronberry S'clyde 56 F2 vil 3m/5km NE of Cumnock. NS 6022
Crondall Hants 11 E1 vil 3m/5km NW of Farnham. Site of Roman villa 1m S. SU 7948
Cronk, The Isle of Man 46 B4 vil near W coast 4m/6km NE of Kirk Michael. SC 3495
Cronk-y-Voddy Isle of Man 46 B5* loc 3m/5km N of St John's. SC 3085
Cronton Merseyside 42 B3 vil 2m/4km NW of Widnes. SJ 4988
Cronwern Welsh form of Crunwear, qv.
Crook Cumbria 52 D5 vil 4m/6km W of Kendal. SD 4695
Crook Durham 54 B2 tn 5m/8km NW of Bishop Auckland. Coal-mining, engineering. NZ 1635
Crook Aldersey Ches 42 A5* loc adjoining Coddington to E. SJ 4555
Crookdale Cumbria 52 B1/C1 loc 3m/5km E of Aspatria. NY 1943
Crooke Gtr Manchester 42 B1* loc 3m/4km NW of Wigan. SD 5507
Crooked End Glos 26 B5* loc adjoining vil of Ruardean to E, 3m/5km NW of Cinderford. SO 6217
Crookedholm S'clyde 64 C5 loc 2m/3km E of Kilmarnock tn centre. NS 4537
Crooked Oak 7 E3 r rising on S foothills of Exmoor and flowing W through Ash Mill into R Mole at Alswear, 3m/4km S of S Molton, Devon. SS 7222
Crooked Soley Wilts 17 G4* loc 3m/5km NW of Hungerford. See also Straight Soley. SU 3172
Crookes S Yorks 43 G3 dist of Sheffield 2m/3km W of city centre. SK 3287
Crookesmoor S Yorks 43 G3* dist of Sheffield 1m W of city centre. SK 3387
Crookfoot Reservoir 54 D2* resr on border of Cleveland and Durham 5m/8km W of Hartlepool. NZ 4331
Crook Gate Lancs 47 E4* loc 2m/3km E of Hambleton. SD 4042
Crookgate Bank Durham 61 F5* loc just SE of Burnopfield. NZ 1856
Crook Gate Reservoir Gtr Manchester 48 C6* small resr 4m/6km E of Milnrow. SD 9811
Crookhall Durham 61 F6* loc adjoining Consett to SE. NZ 1150
Crookham Berks 18 A5* ham 4m/6km NE of Kingsclere. SU 5464
Crookham Nthmb 67 F4 ham on R Till 4m/6km E of Cornhill on Tweed. **C. Eastfield** loc 1m NW. NT 9138
Crookham Village Hants 18 C6 vil 2m/3km SW of Fleet. SU 7952
Crookhill Tyne & Wear 61 F5* loc adjoining Ryton to E. NZ 1663
Crooklands Cumbria 53 E6 ham 6m/9km S of Kendal. SD 5383
Crook of Alves Grampian 81 A1. See Alves.
Crook of Devon Tayside 72 D4 vil on bend of R Devon 5m/9km W of Kinross. NO 0300
Crookston S'clyde 64 C3 loc in Glasgow 2m/4km E of Paisley. **C. Castle** (A.M.), early 15c cas surrounded by 12c earthworks. NS 5263
Croome D'Abitot H & W 26 D3* loc 7m/11km S of Worcester. SO 8844
Cropredy Oxon 27 H3 vil 4m/6km N of Banbury. Site of Civil War battle, 1644. SP 4646
Cropston Leics 36 B3 vil 5m/7km NW of Leicester. **Cropston Resr** to W. SK 5510
Cropthorne H & W 27 E3 vil on S bank of R Avon 3m/4km W of Evesham. SO 9944
Cropton N Yorks 55 F5/F6 vil 4m/7km NW of Pickering. SE 7589
Cropwell Bishop Notts 36 C1 vil 8m/12km SE of Nottingham. SK 6835
Cropwell Butler Notts 36 C1 vil 8m/12km SE of Nottingham. SK 6837
Crosby Cumbria 52 B2 vil 3m/4km NE of Maryport. NY 0738
Crosby Humberside 50 D6 NW dist of Scunthorpe. SE 8711
Crosby Isle of Man 46 B5 vil 4m/7km NW of Douglas. SC 3279
Crosby Merseyside 41 H2 tn on coast opp **C. Channel** at mouth of R Mersey 6m/9km N of Liverpool. **Gt Crosby** NE dist of tn. **Lit Crosby** vil to N. SJ 3198
Crosby Garrett Cumbria 53 F4 vil 3m/5km W of Kirkby Stephen. NY 7209
Crosby, High Cumbria 60 A5* ham 4m/6km NE of Carlisle and 1km E of Low Crosby. NY 4559
Crosby, Low Cumbria 60 A5 vil 4m/6km NE of Carlisle. NY 4459
Crosbymoor Cumbria 60 A5* loc 4m/7km W of Brampton. NY 4659
Crosby Ravensworth Cumbria 53 E3/F3 vil 5m/9km SW of Appleby. See also Ewe Close. NY 6214
Crosby Villa Cumbria 52 B1* loc 4m/6km NE of Maryport. NY 0939
Croscombe Som 16 B6 vil 3m/5km E of Wells. ST 5944
Crosemere Salop 34 B2* loc adjoining Cockshutt to N. SJ 4329
Crosland Edge W Yorks 48 D6* loc 1m NE of Meltham. SE 1012
Crosland Hill W Yorks 48 D6* loc in Huddersfield 2m/3km SW of tn centre. SE 1114
Crosland, South W Yorks 48 D6* loc in Huddersfield 3m/5km SW of tn centre. SE 1112
Cross Som 15 H5 vil 2km W of Axbridge. ST 4154
Cross W Isles 88 C1 vil near N end of Lewis 2m/4km SW of Port of Ness. NB 5062
Cross W Yorks 48 D5* loc 2km SW of Cleckheaton. SE 1723
Crossaig, North and **South** S'clyde 63 E3 two adjoining locs S of **C. Glen,** on rd running beside E coast of Kintyre, Argyll, 4m/7km SW of Claonaig. NR 8351
Crossapol Bay Coll, S'clyde 69 B7 wide bay on S coast near SW end of island. NM 1352
Crossapoll Tiree, S'clyde 69 A7 loc on S coast 3m/5km W of Scarinish. **C. Point** is headland to S. NL 9943
Cross Ash Gwent 25 H5 ham 3m/5km W of Skenfrith. SO 4019
Cross-at-Hand Kent 12 D2 ham 2m/3km N of Staplehurst. TQ 7846
Cross Bank H & W 26 C1* loc 3m/4km SW of Bewdley. SO 7573
Crossbarrow Cumbria 52 A2/B2* loc 3m/5km E of Workington. NY 0428
Crossbost W Isles 88 C2 vil on E coast of Lewis on N side of entrance to Loch Leurbost. NB 3924
Crossbush W Sussex 11 F4 loc 1m SE of Arundel. TQ 0306
Crosscanonby Cumbria 52 B1 ham 3m/4km NE of Maryport. NY 0639
Crossdale Street Norfolk 39 F1* vil 2m/3km S of Cromer. TG 2239
Cross End Beds 29 E2* loc 1km E of vil of Thurleigh. TL 0658
Cross End Bucks 28 D4* ham adjoining Wavendon to E, 4m/6km NW of Woburn. SP 9137
Cross End Essex 30 D4* loc adjoining Pebmarsh to NE, 4m/6km NE of Halstead. TL 8533
Crossens Merseyside 47 E6 loc in Southport 3m/4km NE of tn centre. SD 3719
Cross Fell Cumbria 53 F2 mt 4m/6km NE of Milburn. Height 2930 ft or 893 metres, summit of Pennine Range. NY 6834
Crossflatts W Yorks 48 D4* N dist of Bingley. SE 1040
Crossford Fife 72 D5 vil 2m/3km W of Dunfermline. NT 0686
Crossford S'clyde 65 E4 vil near confluence of Rs Nethan and Clyde, 3m/4km SW of Carluke. NS 8246
Crossgate Lincs 37 G2 loc 1km N of Pinchbeck. TF 2426
Crossgate Staffs 35 F1* loc 4m/6km NE of Stone. SJ 9437
Crossgates Cumbria 52 B3* loc 1m W of Lamplugh. NY 0721
Crossgates Fife 73 E5 vil 2m/3km SW of Cowdenbeath. NT 1488
Crossgates N Yorks 55 H6* loc 3m/4km S of Scarborough. TA 0384
Crossgates Powys 25 F2 loc at crossroads 3m/5km NE of Llandrindod Wells. SO 0864
Cross Gates W Yorks 49 F4 dist of Leeds 4m/6km E of city centre. SE 3534
Crossgill Cumbria 53 F1* loc at confluence of Cross Gill and R South Tyne 1km SE of Garrigill. NY 7440
Crossgill Lancs 47 F2* ham 5m/8km E of Lancaster. SD 5562
Cross Green Devon 6 C6* loc 4m/7km NE of Launceston. SX 3888
Cross Green Staffs 35 E4* loc 1km SE of Coven. SJ 9106
Cross Green Suffolk 30 C3* ham just N of vil of Hartest, 5m/7km NW of Long Melford. TL 8353
Cross Green Suffolk 30 D3* ham 6m/9km SE of Bury St Edmunds. TL 8955
Cross Green Suffolk 30 D3/31 E3 ham 5m/9km SW of Stowmarket. TL 9852
Cross Green W Yorks 49 E5* loc in Leeds 2m/3km SE of city centre. Industrial estate. SE 3232
Cross Hands Dyfed 22 C4* loc 2m/3km S of Canaston Br. SN 0712
Crosshands Dyfed 22 D3* loc 2km W of Llanboidy. SN 1922
Cross Hands Dyfed 23 G4 vil 8m/13km N of Llanelli. SN 5612
Cross, High Cornwall 2 C5* vil 4m/7km SW of Falmouth. SW 7428
Cross, High Gwent 15 G3* loc 2m/3km W of Newport. ST 2888
Cross, High Hants 10 D2 vil 3m/5km NW of Petersfield. SU 7126
Cross, High Herts 29 G5/G6 vil 3m/5km N of Ware. TL 3618
Cross, High Leics 36 A5/B5* loc at intersection of Watling Street and Foss Way, 4m/7km SE of Hinckley, on site of Roman settlement of *Venonae.* SP 4788
Cross, High Warwicks 27 F1* loc 3m/5km E of Henley-in-Arden. SP 1967
Cross, High W Sussex 11 H3* loc 2m/3km W of Hurstpierpoint. TQ 2417
Cross Hill Derbys 43 H6 loc 2m/3km NW of Heanor. SK 4148
Crosshill Fife 73 E5* locality adjoining Lochore to S. NT 1796
Crosshill S'clyde 56 D3 vil 3m/5km SE of Maybole. NS 3206
Crosshill S'clyde 64 C3* loc in Govanhill dist of Glasgow. NS 5862
Crosshill S'clyde 64 D3* loc in suburb of Baillieston, 6m/9km E of Glasgow. NS 6864
Cross Hills N Yorks 48 C4 loc in Airedale 4m/7km NW of Keighley. SE 0045
Crosshouse S'clyde 64 B5 loc 2m/3km W of Kilmarnock. NS 3938
Cross Houses Salop 34 C4 vil 4m/7km SE of Shrewsbury. SJ 5407
Cross Houses Salop 34 D5* loc 2km SW of Bridgnorth. SO 6991
Crossings, Lower Derbys 43 E3/F3* loc adjoining Chapel-en-le-Frith to W. SK 0480
Cross in Hand E Sussex 12 B4 vil 2km W of Heathfield. TQ 5621
Cross Inn Dyfed 24 A3 vil 2m/3km S of New Quay. SN 3857
Cross Inn Dyfed 24 B2 loc 5m/9km E of Aberaeron. SN 5464
Crosskeys Gwent 15 G2 vil 1m NW of Risca. ST 2291
Cross Keys Kent 20 B6* loc in SW part of Sevenoaks. TQ 5253
Cross Keys Wilts 16 D4* loc on N side of Corsham. ST 8771
Cross Kirk Borders. See Peebles.
Crosskirk H'land 86 C1 loc near N coast of Caithness dist 5m/9km W of Thurso. Ruined Chapel of St Mary (A.M.), probably 12c. **C. Bay** is small bay to NW. ND 0369
Crosslands Cumbria 52 D5* ham 3m/4km NW of Newby Br. SD 3489
Cross Lane Isle of Wight 10 C5 NE dist of Newport. SZ 5089
Cross Lane Head Salop 34 D4/D5 vil 2m/3km N of Bridgnorth. SO 7095
Cross Lanes Bucks 18 C2* loc 2m/3km W of Princes Risborough. SP 7702
Cross Lanes Clwyd 42 A6* loc 3m/5km SE of Wrexham. SJ 3746
Cross Lanes Cornwall 2 C6 loc 4m/7km SE of Helston. SW 6921
Cross Lanes N Yorks 49 G2 loc 3m/5km S of Easingwold. SE 5265
Crosslanes Salop 34 A3 ham 7m/12km SE of Oswestry. SJ 3218
Crosslee S'clyde 64 B2 loc 2m/4km NW of Johnstone. NS 4166
Crossley W Yorks 48 D5/49 E5* loc 1m N of Mirfield. SE 2021
Crossley Hall W Yorks 48 D5* loc in Bradford 2m/3km W of city centre. SE 1333
Cross Mere Salop 34 B2 lake, one of several in dist, 3m/5km SE of Ellesmere. SJ 4330
Crossmichael D & G 58 C5 vil 4m/6km NW of Castle Douglas. NX 7366
Cross Moor Cumbria 46 D1* loc 2m/3km SW of Ulverston. SD 2676
Crossmoor Lancs 47 E4 loc 4m/7km N of Kirkham. SD 4438
Crossmyloof S'clyde 64 C3* loc in Glasgow 2m/4km S of city centre. NS 5762
Cross Oak Powys 25 F5* loc 1m NW of Talybont. SO 1023
Cross of Jackson Grampian 83 F4 loc and rd junction 5m/8km NW of Oldmeldrum. NJ 7432
Cross o' th' Hands Derbys 43 G6 ham 4m/7km W of Belper. SK 2846
Crossraguel Abbey S'clyde 56 C3 ruins (A.M.), mainly 15c to 16c, of abbey founded in 1244, 2m/3km SW of Maybole. NS 2708
Crossroads Fife 73 F4* NW dist of Methil. NO 3600
Cross Street Suffolk 31 F1 vil 3m/5km NE of Eye. TM 1876
Cross Town Ches 42 C3* E dist of Knutsford. SJ 7578
Cross Water of Luce 57 B6 r rising in Strathclyde region, in vicinity of Arecleoch Forest, E of Ballantrae, and flowing S into Dumfries & Galloway region to join Main Water of Luce at New Luce, to form Water of Luce, qv. NX 1764
Crossway Gwent 26 A5* loc 1m SW of Skenfrith. SO 4419
Crossway Powys 25 E2/F2 loc 2m/3km S of Llandrindod Wells. SO 0558
Crossway Green Gwent 16 A2* loc 1km NW of Chepstow. ST 5294
Crossway Green H & W 26 D1 vil 3m/4km SE of Stourport. SO 8468
Crossways Dorset 9 E5* loc 6m/9km E of Dorchester. SY 7788
Crossways Glos 26 B6 loc 1km NW of Coleford. SO 5611
Crosswell Dyfed 22 D2* ham 2m/3km SW of Eglwyswrw. SN 1236
Cross, West W Glam 23 G6 loc in Swansea 3m/5km SW of tn centre across Swansea Bay. SS 6189
Crosswood (Trawsgoed) Dyfed 24 C1* loc 3m/5km SE of Llanilar. SN 6672
Crosswood Reservoir Lothian 65 G3 resr 4m/7km SE of W Calder. NT 0557
Crosthwaite Cumbria 52 D5 ham 4m/7km W of Kendal. SD 4491
Crosthwaite, Great Cumbria 53 C3* ham adjoining Keswick to NW. NY 2624
Crosthwaite, Little Cumbria 52 C2* loc on E side of Bassenthwaite Lake 4m/6km NW of Keswick. NY 2327
Croston Lancs 47 F6 vil 6m/10km W of Chorley. SD 4818
Crostwick Norfolk 39 F3 ham 5m/8km NE of Norwich. TG 2516
Crostwight Norfolk 39 G2 loc 3m/5km E of N Walsham. TG 3330
Crouch Kent 20 C6 loc 2km SE of Borough Green. TQ 6155
Crouch 21 F2 r rising W of Basildon, Essex, and flowing E into North Sea to N of Foulness I. Estuary well known for yachting. TR 0396

Crouch End London 19 G3* loc in borough of Haringey 5m/8km N of Charing Cross. TQ 2988
Croucheston Wilts 9 G2* ham adjoining Bishopstone 4m/7km SW of Wilton. SU 0625
Crouch Hill Dorset 9 E3 ham 2m/3km S of Bishop's Caundle. ST 7010
Croughton Northants 28 A4/B4 vil 4m/6km SW of Brackley. SP 5433
Crovie Grampian 83 F1 fishing vil on E side of Gamrie Bay, 6m/10km E of Macduff. **Crovie Hd** is headland to N. NJ 8065
Crow Hants 9 H4 loc 2km SE of Ringwood. SU 1603
Crowan Cornwall 2 C5 vil 3m/5km S of Camborne. SW 6434
Crowborough E Sussex 12 B4 tn in elevated position to E of Ashdown Forest 7m/11km SW of Tunbridge Wells. Loc of **C. Town** 1km NW. TQ 5131
Crowcombe Som 7 H2 vil at foot of Quantock Hills 6m/10km SE of Watchet. ST 1436
Crowden Derbys 43 F2 loc on N shore of Torside Resr 4m/6km E of Tintwistle. Mountain rescue post. SK 0799
Crowden Devon 6 D5* loc 7m/11km NW of Okehampton. SX 4999
Crowdhill Hants 10 B3 loc 2m/4km E of Eastleigh. SU 4919
Crowdicote Derbys 43 F4 ham 1m E of Longnor. SK 1065
Crowdundle Beck 53 E2 r rising on SE slope of Cross Fell, Cumbria, and flowing SW into R Eden between Culgaith and Temple Sowerby. NY 6028
Crow Edge S Yorks 43 F1* ham 4m/6km W of Penistone. SE 1804
Crowell Oxon 18 C2 ham 3m/4km NW of Stokenchurch. SU 7499
Crow End Cambs 29 G2* N end of vil of Bourn. TL 3257
Crowfield Northants 28 B3* loc 4m/6km NE of Brackley. SP 6141
Crowfield Suffolk 31 F3 vil 4m/7km SW of Debenham. Loc of **C. Green** 1km N. TM 1457
Crowgate Street Norfolk 39 G3* loc 3m/5km N of Wroxham. TG 3021
Crow Green Essex 20 C2* ham 2m/3km NW of Brentwood. TQ 5896
Crow Hill H & W 26 B5 vil 3m/5km NE of Ross-on-Wye. SO 6426
Crowhole Derbys 43 H3 loc 4m/7km NW of Chesterfield. **Crowhole Resr** 2km SW. SK 3375
Crowhurst E Sussex 12 D5 vil 4m/7km NW of Hastings. TQ 7512
Crowhurst Surrey 20 A6 ham 3m/5km S of Oxted. TQ 3947
Crowhurst Lane End Surrey 20 A6* ham 3m/5km SE of Godstone. TQ 3748
Crowland Lincs 37 G3 small fenland tn 8m/13km NE of Peterborough. Remains of abbey founded in 8c. Triangular br of 14c. TF 2310
Crowland Suffolk 31 E1 ham 1m SE of Walsham le Willows. TM 0170
Crowlas Cornwall 2 B5 vil 3m/5km NE of Penzance. SW 5133
Crowle Humberside 50 C6 vil 8m/12km W of Scunthorpe across R Trent. SE 7712
Crowle H & W 26 D2 vil 5m/7km E of Worcester. Ham of **C. Green** adjoins to N. SO 9256
Crowlin Islands H'land 79 E5 group of three islands lying close together 1m off W coast of Ross and Cromarty dist on N side of entrance to Loch Carron. Total area 420 acres or 170 hectares. Eilean Mór is the largest and nearest to mainland; Eilean Meadhonach lies to its W; Eilean Beag, the smallest, is immediately N of Eilean Meadhonach. Beacon on Eilean Beag. NG 6934
Crowlista W Isles 88 A2* loc near W coast of Lewis 1m W of Uig. NB 0433
Crowmarsh Gifford Oxon 18 B3 vil across R Thames from Wallingford. SU 6189
Crown Corner Suffolk 31 F2* ham 3m/5km SE of Stradbroke. TM 2570
Crow Nest W Yorks 48 D4* E dist of Bingley. SE 1139
Crownhill Devon 4 B4 N dist of Plymouth, 3m/5km from city centre. SX 4858
Crown Hills Leics 36 C4* loc in Leicester 2m/3km E of city centre. SK 6204
Crownpits Surrey 11 F1* loc in Godalming 1km SE of tn centre. SU 9743
Crownthorpe Norfolk 39 E4 vil 2m/3km NW of Wymondham. TG 0803
Crown Town Cornwall 2 C5 ham 3m/4km NW of Helston. SW 6330
Crown Wood Berks 18 D4* SE dist of Bracknell. SU 8767
Crowpill Som 8 B1* N dist of Bridgwater. ST 2937
Crows-an-wra Cornwall 2 A5 ham 4m/6km NE of Land's End. SW 3927
Crow's Nest Cornwall 3 G2* loc 3m/5km N of Liskeard. SX 2669
Crowsnest Salop 34 B4* loc 1km SW of Snailbeach. SJ 3601
Crowther Tyne & Wear 61 G5* industrial estate in W part of Washington. NZ 2856
Crowthorne Berks 18 C5 tn 4m/6km SW of Bracknell. Wellington College. Broadmoor Hospital. Road Research Laboratory. SU 8464
Crowton Ches 42 B4 vil 5m/8km W of Northwich. SJ 5774
Croxall Staffs 35 G3 ham 6m/10km N of Tamworth. SK 1913
Croxby Lincs 45 F2 loc 3m/5km NW of Binbrook. **C. Top** loc 2km W. TF 1998
Croxdale Durham 54 B2 vil 2m/3km N of Spennymoor. NZ 2636
Croxden Staffs 35 F1 ham 4m/7km SE of Cheadle. Remains of EE abbey (A.M.). SK 0639
Croxley Green Herts 19 E2 loc 1m NE of Rickmansworth. TQ 0695
Croxton Cambs 29 F2 ham on edge of park 4m/6km E of St Neots. TL 2459
Croxton Humberside 45 E1 vil 7m/11km NE of Brigg. TA 0912
Croxton Norfolk 38 D5 vil 2m/4km N of Thetford. TL 8786
Croxton Staffs 35 E2 ham 3m/5km NW of Eccleshall. **Croxtonbank** loc 1km NW. SJ 7831
Croxton Green Ches 42 B5/B6 loc 7m/11km N of Whitchurch. SJ 5452
Croxton Kerrial Leics 36 D2 vil 7m/11km SW of Grantham. SK 8329
Croxton, South Leics 36 C3 vil 7m/12km NE of Leicester. SK 6910
Croy H'land 81 G3 vil in Inverness dist close to border with Nairn dist, 7m/11km SW of Nairn. NH 7649
Croy S'clyde 64 D2/65 E2 vil 2km SE of Kilsyth. NS 7275
Croy Brae S'clyde 56 C3* hillside near coast at N end of Culzean Bay, where by an optical illusion a downward slope appears to be an upward. Known as the 'Electric Brae'. NS 2513
Croyde Devon 6 C2 vil 7m/12km SW of Ilfracombe, on stream running down to **C. Bay,** SE of Baggy Pt. Ham also named **C. Bay** is on coast W of vil. SS 4439
Croydon Cambs 29 G3 vil 6m/10km NW of Royston. TL 3149
Croydon London 19 G5 tn and borough 10m/15km S of Charing Cross. Extensive tn centre development. TQ 3266
Croydon Hill Som 7 G1, G2 afforested upland area of N Exmoor to S of Dunster. SS 9740
Cruachan Reservoir S'clyde 70 C2 resr of North of Scotland Hydro-Electric Board 2km SE of Ben Cruachan, qv, in Argyll. NN 0828
Cruach an t-Sithein S'clyde 70 D5* mt 4m/7km NE of Garelochhead. Height 2244 ft or 684 metres. NS 2796
Cruach Ardrain Central 71 E3 mt 3m/5km SE of Crianlarich. Height 3428 ft or 1045 metres. NN 4021
Crucifixion Cave S'clyde. See Davarr I.
Cruckmeole Salop 34 B3 ham 4m/7km SW of Shrewsbury. SJ 4309
Cruckton Salop 34 B3 ham 4m/7km SW of Shrewsbury. Site of Roman villa. SJ 4310
Crucywel Welsh form of Crickhowell, qv.
Cruden Bay Grampian 83 H3 vil near mouth of Water of Cruden 7m/11km S of Peterhead. See also Port Erroll. **Bay of Cruden** extends S to headland opp The Skares, qv. Firm sands backed by sand dunes. NK 0936
Crudgington Salop 34 C3 vil 4m/7km N of Wellington. **C. Green** ham 1km SE. SJ 6318
Crudwell Wilts 16 D2 vil 4m/6km N of Malmesbury. Loc of **W Crudwell** 1km W. ST 9592
Cruggleton D & G 57 E7 loc and ruined cas of the Comyns on W side of Wigtown Bay, 3m/5km NE of Whithorn. **C. Bay** (or Rigg Bay) to N. NX 4843
Crugion Welsh form of Criggion, qv.
Crugmeer Cornwall 2 D1 loc 2km NW of Padstow. SW 9076
Crugybar Dyfed 24 C4* loc 2m/3km S of Pumsaint. SN 6537
Cruinn a' Bheinn Central 71 E4 peak between Ben Lomond and Loch Arklet. Height 2077 ft or 633 metres. NN 3605
Crulivig W Isles 88 B2* loc on W side of Lewis 1km SE of br connecting Gt Bernera with main island. NB 1733
Crumlin (Crymlyn) Gwent 15 G2 loc adjoining Newbridge to N. ST 2198
Crummock Water Cumbria 52 B3 lake (NT) formed by R Cocker between Loweswater and Buttermere, 4km in length and 1km maximum width. NY 1519
Crumpfield H & W 27 E1* loc 2m/3km SW of Redditch. SP 0165
Crumpsall Gtr Manchester 42 D1* dist of Manchester 3m/4km N of city centre. SD 8402
Crumpsbrook Salop 34 C6* loc 3m/5km NW of Cleobury Mortimer. SO 6278
Crundale Dyfed 22 C4 loc 2m/3km NE of Haverfordwest. SM 9718
Crundale Kent 13 F2 vil 2m/4km NE of Wye. TR 0749
Crunwear (Cronwern) Dyfed 22 D4 ham 4m/6km S of Whitland. SN 1810
Cruwys Morchard Devon 7 F4 loc 5m/8km W of Tiverton. SS 8712
Crux Easton Hants 17 H5 ham 4m/6km NE of Hurstbourne Tarrant. SU 4256
Crwbin Dyfed 23 F4 ham 6m/9km SE of Carmarthen. SN 4713
Crwys, Y Welsh form of Three Crosses, qv.
Crychan Forest 24 D4* large afforested area on borders of Dyfed and Powys NE of Llandovery. SN 8384
Crychddwr 40 B6* stream running NW into R Llyfni 1m SW of Penygroes, Gwynedd. SH 4651
Cryers Hill Bucks 18 D2 vil 3m/4km N of High Wycombe. SU 8796
Crymlyn Welsh form of Crumlin, qv.
Crymmych Dyfed 22 D2/D3 vil 8m/12km S of Cardigan. SN 1833
Crynant W Glam 14 D1 vil 5m/8km NE of Neath. **C. Forest,** afforested area to W and NW. SN 7904
Crynwedd Welsh form of Crinow, qv.
Crystal Palace London 19 G4* site of glass exhibition hall originally erected in Hyde Park for Great Exhibition of 1851, later moved to this site and burnt out in 1936. Site now occupied by TV mast and sports centre. Name is also applied to surrounding dist. TQ 3471
Cuaig H'land 78 E3 loc near W coast of Ross and Cromarty dist 1m S of Rubha na Chuaig. NG 7057
Cubbington Warwicks 27 G1 vil 2m/4km NE of Leamington. Suburb of **New Cubbington** to W. SP 3468
Cubert Cornwall 2 D3 vil 3m/5km SW of Newquay. SW 7857
Cubitt Town London 20 A4* dist of Isle of Dogs, borough of Tower Hamlets, on N bank of R Thames and 5m/8km E of Charing Cross. TQ 3878
Cubley S Yorks 43 G1* loc adjoining Penistone to S. SE 2402
Cubley, Great Derbys 35 G1 vil 4m/6km N of Sudbury. **Lit Cubley** ham 1km SW. SK 1638
Cublington Bucks 28 C5/D5 vil 6m/9km N of Aylesbury. SP 8322
Cublington H & W 26 A4* ham 7m/11km W of Hereford. SO 4038
Cuckfield W Sussex 11 H3 small tn 2m/3km W of Haywards Heath. TQ 3024
Cucklington Som 9 E2 vil 3m/5km E of Wincanton. ST 7527
Cuckmere 12 B6 r in E Sussex rising near Heathfield and flowing S through gap in S Downs at Alfriston and into English Channel at C. Haven. TV 5197
Cuckmere Haven E Sussex 12 B6 bay at mouth of Cuckmere R 3m/4km SE of Seaford. TV 5197
Cuckney Notts 44 A4 vil 7m/11km N of Mansfield. SK 5671
Cuckold's Green Suffolk 31 H1* loc 1m W of Wrentham. TM 4882
Cuckold's Point Suffolk 31 H3* headland at NE end of Havergate I. in R Ore S of Orford. TM 4248
Cuckoo Oak Salop 34 D4 loc 1km E of Madeley. SJ 7004
Cuckoo Bridge Lincs 37 G3* loc with br over N Drove Drain 3m/5km SW of Spalding. TF 2020
Cuckoo's Corner Hants 10 D1 loc adjoinin9 Holybourne to NE, 2m/4km NE of Alton. SU 7441
Cudden Point Cornwall 2 B5 headland on Mount's Bay 5m/8km E of Penzance. SW 5427
Cuddesdon Oxon 18 B2 vil 6m/9km SE of Oxford. Church of England Theological College. SP 6003
Cuddington Bucks 18 C1 vil 4m/6km NE of Tring. SP 7311
Cuddington Ches 42 B4 vil 4m/7km W of Northwich. SJ 5972
Cuddington Heath Ches 42 A6/B6 ham 1m W of Malpas. SJ 4847
Cuddy Hill Lancs 47 F4 loc 6m/10km NW of Preston. SD 4937
Cudham London 20 B5 vil in borough of Bromley 2m/3km E of Biggin Hill. TQ 4459
Cudlipptown Devon 4 B3 ham 4m/6km NE of Tavistock. SX 5279
Cudworth Som 8 B3 vil 4m/6km E of Chard. ST 3810
Cudworth S Yorks 43 H1 colliery tn 3m/5km NE of Barnsley. **Upr Cudworth** loc adjoining to N. **C. Common** loc 1m S. SE 3808
Cuerdale Lancs 47 F5* loc 2km NE of Walton-le-Dale. SD 5729
Cuerden Green Lancs 47 F5* loc 2m/3km N of Leyland. SD 5524
Cuerdley Cross Ches 42 B3* loc 2m/3km NE of Widnes. SJ 5486
Cuffhill Reservoir S'clyde 64 B3* small resr 3m/4km E of Beith. NS 3855
Cuffley Herts 19 G2 residential loc 2m/4km W of Cheshunt. TL 3002
Cuil Bay 74 B5 bay on E side of Loch Linnhe, extending SE from Rubha Mór. Partly in Highland and partly in Strathclyde region. NM 9754
Cuillin Hills Skye, H'land 79 C6 group of gabbroic mts with serrated peaks in S part of island to E and NE of Loch Brittle in dist known as Minginish. There are several peaks of over 3000 ft (914 metres), the highest being Sgurr Alasdair, 3309 ft or 1009 metres. The range is noted for rock climbing. NG 4422
Culachy Forest H'land 75 E2 deer forest in Inverness dist 6m/10km S of Fort Augustus. NN 3999
Culbin Forest 81 H2 state forest on coast extending westwards from Findhorn Bay, Grampian, planted on drifting sands which had buried original farmland. Forest is almost entirely in Grampian region, although its western extremity is in the Nairn dist of Highland region. NH 9861
Culbokie H'land 81 F2 vil on Black Isle, Ross and Cromarty dist, nearly 1m from SE shore of Cromarty Firth and 7m/12km NE of Muir of Ord. NH 6059
Culbone Som 7 F1 loc near coast 3m/5km W of Porlock. To S, **C. Hill,** 1355 ft or 413 metres, on N edge of Exmoor and traversed by main rd. SS 8448
Culburnie H'land 81 E3* loc in Inverness dist 4m/6km SW of Beauly. NH 4941
Culcabock H'land 81 F3 E suburb of Inverness. NH 6844
Culcharry H'land 81 G3 loc in Nairn dist 4m/7km S of Nairn. NH 8650
Culcheth Ches 42 C2 tn 3m/5km S of Leigh. SJ 6595
Culcheth Gtr Manchester 42 D2* loc in Manchester 3m/5km E of city centre. SJ 8899
Culdrose Cornwall 2 B5* loc to SE of Helston. Culdrose RN airfield to S. SW 6626
Culford Suffolk 30 D1 vil 4m/6km N of Bury St Edmunds. 18c hall in park houses a school. TL 8370
Culfordheath Suffolk 30 D1* loc 7m/11km N of Bury St Edmunds. TL 8574
Culgaith Cumbria 53 E2 vil 6m/10km E of Penrith. NY 6129
Culham Oxon 18 A2 vil 2km S of Abingdon. Atomic energy research establishment. SU 5095
Culkein H'land 84 A4 vil 2m/3km SE of Pt of Stoer, W coast of Sutherland dist. NC 0332
Culkerton Glos 16 D2 ham 3m/5km NE of Tetbury. ST 9395
Cullaloe Reservoir Fife 73 E5* small resr 2km N of Aberdour. NT 1985

Cullen Grampian 82 D1 fishing vil on **C. Bay** on N coast 6m/10km E of Buckie. **Cullen Hse,** partly 13c, 1km SW. Bin of C., hill 3m/5km SW, commands wide views. NJ 5066

Cullercoats Tyne & Wear 61 H4 former fishing vil between Tynemouth and Whitley Bay, now adjoining both. NZ 3670

Cullerlie Stone Circle Grampian. See Garlogie. NJ 7804

Cullernose Point Nthmb 67 H6 headland on North Sea coast 1km S of Craster. NU 2618

Cullicudden H'land 81 F1 loc on SE side of Cromarty Firth, Ross and Cromarty dist, 3m/5km SW of Balblair. NH 6564

Culligran H'land 80 D3 power stn on N side of R Farrar in Inverness dist 1m W of Struy Br. **C. Falls,** waterfall in R Farrar 1km SW. NH 3841

Cullingworth W Yorks 48 D4 vil 2m/3km E of Haworth. SE 0636

Cullipool S'clyde 70 A4 vil on NW coast of Luing. NM 7313

Cullivoe Shetland 89 F5 vil on NE coast of Yell at head of inlet of **Culli Voe.** HP 5402

Culloden Moor H'land 81 F3, G3 tract in Inverness dist 4m/7km E of Inverness. Site of battle in 1746 in which the army of Prince Charles Edward was destroyed by the Duke of Cumberland. Various sites, museum, and visitor centre, all owned by NTS. **C. Forest** is state forest to NE and to S. NH 7445

Cullompton Devon 7 G4 small tn on R Culm 5m/9km SE of Tiverton. ST 0207

Cullykhan Bay Grampian 83 F1* small bay 2km SE of Troup Hd. NJ 8366

Culm 7 G5 r rising in Blackdown Hills in Somerset and flowing into R Exe below Stoke Canon in Devon. SX 9396

Culm Davy Devon 7 H3* ham 2m/3km NE of Culmstock. ST 1215

Culmington Salop 34 B6 vil 5m/8km N of Ludlow. SO 4982

Cul Mór H'land 85 B5 mt in Ross and Cromarty dist 8m/13km SW of Inchnadamph. Height 2786 ft or 849 metres. **Cul Beag** is mt 2m/4km SW; height 2523 ft or 769 metres. NC 1611

Culmstock Devon 7 H4 vil below W end of Blackdown Hills 5m/8km SW of Wellington. ST 1013

Culnaknock Skye, H'land 78 C3 loc near NE coast 3m/5km S of Staffin. NG 5162

Culpho Suffolk 31 F3 ham 4m/6km W of Woodbridge. TM 2149

Culrain H'land 85 F7* loc in Sutherland dist 3m/5km NW of Bonar Br. NH 5794

Culross Fife 72 D5 small tn on N side of R Forth 7m/11km W of Dunfermline. Several NTS properties in tn, which displays good examples of 16c and 17c Scottish domestic architecture. **C. Abbey** (A.M.). **C. Palace** (A.M.), 16c-17c. NS 9885

Culsalmond Grampian 83 E4*. See Kirkton of Culsalmond.

Culsh Grampian 82 D6* site of prehistoric earth hse (A.M.) 2m/3km E of Tarland. NJ 5005

Culswick Shetland 89 D7* loc on Mainland 4m/6km W of Garderhouse. HU 2745

Culter Fell 65 G5 mt on border of Strathclyde and Borders regions 6m/9km S of Biggar. Height 2454 ft or 748 metres. NT 0529

Culter Waterhead Reservoir S'clyde 65 G5* resr 4m/7km S of Coulter. NT 0327

Cults Grampian 77 H1 suburb of Aberdeen 3m/5km SW of city centre. NJ 8903

Culver Cliff Isle of Wight 10 C6 cliff between Whitecliff Bay and Sandown Bay on SE coast. SZ 6385

Culver Down Isle of Wight. See Bembridge.

Culverhole Point Devon 8 B5* E end of Seaton Bay (see Seaton). SY 2789

Culverlane Devon 4 D4* loc 3m/4km E of S Brent. SX 7460

Culverstone Green Kent 20 C5 loc 3m/5km N of Wrotham Heath. TQ 6362

Culverthorpe Lincs 37 E1 ham 4m/7km SW of Sleaford. TF 0240

Culwatty Bay S'clyde 64 A1* bay on N side of Rosneath Pt near entrance to Gare Loch. NS 2781

Culworth Northants 28 B3 vil 7m/11km NE of Banbury. SP 5446

Culzean Castle S'clyde 56 C3 late 18c mansion (NTS) built round medieval tower of the Kennedys, on coast 4m/7km W of Maybole. **Culzean Bay** extends northwards towards Dunure. NS 2310

Cumberlow Green Herts 29 G4* loc 4m/6km W of Buntingford. TL 3030

Cumbernauld S'clyde 65 E2 tn 12m/20km NE of Glasgow. New Tn designated 1955. Variety of light industries. Original vil of C. 1m N of tn centre. NS 7674

Cumberworth Lincs 45 H4 vil 4m/6km SE of Alford. TF 5073

Cumberworth, Lower W Yorks 43 G1 vil 1km N of Denby Dale. **Upr Cumberworth** vil 1m SW. SE 2209

Cumbrae, Great S'clyde 63 H2 island in Firth of Clyde lying about 2km off mainland of Strathclyde across Fairlie Roads. Measures about 3m/5km N to S and 2m/3km E to W. See Keppel Pier, Millport. NS 1656

Cumbrae, Little S'clyde 63 G3 island lying 1km S of Gt Cumbrae, qv. Measures nearly 2m/3km N to S by nearly 1m E to W. Lighthouse on W side. NS 1451

Cumbria 116,117 north-western county of England, bounded by Northumberland, Durham, N Yorkshire, and Lancashire; the Scottish regions of Borders and Dumfries & Galloway; and the Solway Firth and Irish Sea. A narrow strip of flat country along the coast widens to a plain in the N and around Carlisle. Otherwise the county is composed of mts, moorland, and lakes, and includes the scenically famous Lake District. Coal is mined at Whitehaven, Workington, and Maryport; there is shipbuilding and other heavy industry at Barrow-in-Furness, and light industry at Carlisle. Calder Hall, N of Seascale, was Britain's first atomic power stn. Otherwise the county is almost entirely rural, much of it uncultivated and used only for sheep-grazing. Apart from those already mentioned, tns include Appleby, Cockermouth, Kendal and Keswick. R Eden is the chief of many rs. The largest of the lakes are Windermere and Ullswater.

Cumdivock Cumbria 59 H6* loc 2m/3km SE of Thursby. NY 3448

Cuminestown Grampian 83 F2 vil 5m/8km E of Turriff. Alternative spellings: Cuminestone, Cummestone, Cumminestown. NJ 8050

Cumlewick Ness Shetland 89 E8* headland on E coast of Mainland 9m/14km N of Sumburgh Hd. Situated on W side of entrance to bay of Sand Wick. HU 4222

Cummersdale Cumbria 59 H5 vil on R Caldew on S outskirts of Carlisle. NY 3953

Cummertrees D & G 59 F4 vil near shore of Solway Firth 4m/6km W of Annan. NY 1366

Cummestone Grampian. See Cuminestown.

Cumminestown Grampian. See Cuminestown.

Cummingstown Grampian 82 A1 vil on N coast 2km E of Burghead. NJ 1368

Cumnock S'clyde 56 E2 tn (C. and Holmhead) on Lugar Water 14m/23km E of Ayr. Industries include coal-mining, engineering, mnfre of bricks, carpets, footwear, textiles. NS 5619

Cumnock and Doon Valley 116 admin dist of S'clyde region.

Cumnor Oxon 17 H2 vil 4m/6km W of Oxford. SP 4604

Cumrew Cumbria 60 B6 vil 7m/11km S of Brampton. NY 5450

Cumwhinton Cumbria 60 A6 vil 4m/6km SE of Carlisle. NY 4452

Cumwhitton Cumbria 60 B6 vil 7m/11km E of Carlisle. NY 5052

Cundall N Yorks 49 F1 vil 4m/7km NE of Boroughbridge. SE 4272

Cunninghame 114, 116 admin dist of S'clyde region.

Cunning Park S'clyde 64 B6* S dist of Ayr. NS 3220

Cunning Point Cumbria 52 A3* headland on Irish Sea 3m/5km N of Whitehaven. NX 9722

Cunningsburgh Shetland 89 E8 loc on E coast of Mainland 8m/13km S of Lerwick. HU 4329

Cunstone Nab N Yorks 55 H6* headland on North Sea coast 2m/3km NW of Filey. TA 1083

Cunswick Tarn Cumbria 53 E5* small lake 2m/3km NW of Kendal. SD 4893

Cupar Fife 73 F3 market tn on R Eden 9m/14km S of Newport-on-Tay and 10m/16km NE of Glenrothes. Agricultural produce, iron founding, textile mnfg, agricultural engineering. NO 3714

Cupid Green Herts 19 E1* loc in NE part of Hemel Hempstead. TL 0709

Cup Nick, High Cumbria 53 F2 cliff at head of High Cup Gill 4m/6km E of Dufton. NY 7426

Cupworthy Som 7 G2* ham 2m/3km S of Luxborough. SS 9734

Curbar Derbys 43 G4 vil 4m/7km NE of Bakewell. SK 2574

Curborough Staffs 35 G3* loc 2m/3km N of Lichfield. SK 1212

Curbridge Hants 10 C4 ham near head of R Hamble estuary 2km SE of Botley. SU 5211

Curbridge Oxon 17 G1 vil 2m/3km SW of Witney. SP 3308

Curdridge Hants 10 C3 vil 2km W of Botley. SU 5213

Curdworth Warwicks 35 G5 vil 3m/5km NW of Coleshill. SP 1892

Curland Som 8 B3 scattered vil 6m/9km SE of Taunton. ST 2717

Curlew Green Suffolk 31 G2* loc 2m/3km N of Saxmundham. TM 3865

Curling Tye Green Essex 21 E1* loc 2m/3km W of Maldon. TL 8207

Curload Som 8 B2* ham 5m/8km W of Langport. ST 3428

Curraghs, The Isle of Man 46 B4* area of marsh and woodland 2m/3km W of Sulby. C. Wildlife Park. SC 3694

Curridge Berks 18 A4 ham 3m/5km N of Newbury. SU 4871

Currie Lothian 65 H2 suburb on Water of Leith 6m/9km SE of Edinburgh. Heriot-Watt University (Riccarton Campus) 1m NW. NT 1866

Curriott Hill Som 8 C3* S dist of Crewkerne. ST 4309

Currock Cumbria 60 A6* dist of Carlisle 2km S of city centre. NY 4054

Curry Mallet Som 8 B2 vil 7m/11km E of Taunton. Vil contains hams of **Hr Street, Lr Street,** and **Silver Street.** ST 3321

Curry, North Som 8 B2 vil 6m/10km E of Taunton. ST 3125

Curry Rivel Som 8 B2 vil 2m/3km SW of Langport. ST 3925

Curry, West Cornwall 6 B5* ham 6m/10km NW of Launceston. SX 2893

Curteis' Corner Kent 13 E3 loc 1km N of Biddenden. TQ 8539

Curthwaite Cumbria 59 H6* loc 2km SE of Thursby. NY 3348

Curthwaite, West Cumbria 52 C1* ham 1m S of Thursby. NY 3248

Curtisden Green Kent 12 D3 ham 2m/3km NE of Goudhurst. TQ 7440

Curtisknowle Devon 4 D5* ham 6m/9km SW of Totnes. SX 7353

Curtismill Green Essex 20 B2* loc 5m/8km N of Romford. TQ 5196

Cury Cornwall 2 C6 ham 4m/6km S of Helston. SW 6721

Curyan Cornwall 3 E3 ham in china clay dist 4m/7km NW of St Austell. SW 9656

Cusgarne Cornwall 2 C4* loc 4m/6km E of Redruth. SW 7640

Cushuish Som 8 A2* ham 4m/7km NW of Taunton. ST 1930

Cusop H & W 25 G4 vil on Welsh border 1m SE of Hay-on-Wye. SO 2341

Custards Hants 10 A4* loc adjoining Lyndhurst to NE. SU 3008

Cusworth S Yorks 44 A1* loc 2m/3km NW of Doncaster. Hall is 18c hse containing museum, in large grnds with lake. SE 5404

Cutcombe Som 7 G2 ham on Exmoor 5m/8km SW of Dunster. SS 9239

Cutgate Gtr Manchester 47 H6* loc in Rochdale 2m/3km W of tn centre. SD 8614

Cutiau Gwynedd 32 D3* loc 2m/3km NE of Barmouth. SH 6317

Cutlers Green Essex 30 B4/B5 ham 1m W of Thaxted. TL 5930

Cutnall H & W 26 D1 vil 3m/5km N of Droitwich. SO 8868

Cutsdean Glos 27 E4 vil 4m/7km E of Winchcombe. SP 0830

Cutsyke W Yorks 49 F5 loc adjoining Castleford to S. SE 4224

Cutthorpe Derbys 43 H4 vil 3m/4km NW of Chesterfield. **C. Green** loc to S. SK 3473

Cuttyhill Grampian 83 H2 loc 6m/10km NW of Peterhead. NK 0650

Cuween Hill Orkney 89 B6* site of communal burial cairn (A.M.) of *c.* 1800 BC, 1km S of Finstown, Mainland. HY 3612

Cuxham Oxon 18 B2 vil 5m/9km NE of Wallingford. SU 6695

Cuxton Kent 20 D5 industrial and residential loc on a ridge overlooking R Medway opp Rochester, 2m/3km SW of Strood. TQ 7066

Cuxwold Lincs 45 F2 vil 4m/6km E of Caistor. TA 1701

Cwm Clwyd 41 F4 ham 3m/5km S of Prestatyn. SJ 0677

Cwm Gwent 15 G1 loc 3m/4km S of Ebbw Vale. SO 1805

Cwm 33 F4* r rising on Mynydd Llyn Coch-hwyad, Powys, and running S to join R Carfan and form R Rhiw Saeson 2km N of Llanbrynmair. SH 9004

Cwmafan Welsh form of Cwmavon, qv.

Cwmafon Welsh form of Cwmavon, qv.

Cwmaman Mid Glam 15 E2 vil 2m/3km S of Aberdare. ST 0099

Cwmann Dyfed 24 B3 loc 1km SE of Lampeter. SN 5847

Cwmavon (Cwmafon) Gwent 15 G1* loc 2m/3km SE of Blaenavon. SO 2706

Cwmavon (Cwmafan) W Glam 14 D2 vil 2m/3km NE of Port Talbot. SS 7892

Cwmbach Dyfed 23 E3 vil 6m/10km N of St Clears. SN 2525

Cwm-bach Dyfed 23 F5* loc 2km NW of Llanelli. SN 4801

Cwmbach Mid Glam 15 E2 loc 2m/3km SE of Aberdare. SO 0201

Cwmbach Powys 25 E3 ham 2m/3km N of Builth Wells. SO 0254

Cwmbach Powys 25 F4 ham 1km W of Glasbury. SO 1639

Cwmbelan Powys 33 F6 loc 2m/3km S of Llanidloes. SN 9481

Cwm Berwyn Plantation Dyfed 24 C3* afforested area some 3km E to W by 2km N to S, 3m/5km SE of Tregaron. SN 7256

Cwmbran (Cwmbrân) Gwent 15 G2 tn 4m/7km N of Newport. New Tn designated 1949. Residential and industrial: coal-mining, iron and steel, engineering; tinplate, brick, and biscuit mnfre. **Upr Cwmbran** loc to N. ST 2894

Cwmbrwyno Dyfed 33 E6 loc 3m/5km NW of Devil's Br. SN 7080

Cwm Capel Dyfed 23 F5* loc 1m N of Burry Port. SN 4502

Cwmcarfan Welsh form of Cwmcarvan, qv.

Cwmcarn Gwent 15 G2 vil 1m S of Abercarn. ST 2193

Cwmcarvan (Cwmcarfan) Gwent 16 A1 ham 4m/6km SW of Monmouth. SO 4707

Cwm-celyn Gwent 15 G1* loc on E side of Blaina. SO 2008

Cwm-Cewydd Gwynedd 33 F3* loc 1m NE of Mallwyd. SH 8713

Cwmcoy (Cwmcou) Dyfed 23 E2 vil 2km NW of Newcastle Emlyn. SN 2942

Cwm Crawnon Powys 25 F5 ham 1km W of Llangynidr. SO 1419

Cwmdare Mid Glam 15 E2 vil 2km NW of Aberdare. SN 9803

Cwm-dows Gwent 15 G2* loc adjoining Newbridge to SW. ST 2096

Cwmdu Dyfed 24 C5* loc 5m/8km N of Llandeilo. SN 6330

Cwmdu Powys 25 G5 ham 4m/7km NW of Crickhowell. SO 1823

Cwmdu W Glam 23 G6* loc in Swansea 2km NW of tn centre. SS 6494

Cwmduad Dyfed 23 E3 ham 6m/10km SW of Llandyssul. SN 3731

Cwmerfyn Dyfed 33 E6* loc 5m/7km NW of Devil's Br. SN 6982

Cwmfelin Mid Glam 14 D3* vil 1m SE of Maesteg. SS 8689

Cwmfelin Mid Glam 15 F2* ham 3m/4km N of Treharris. SO 0900

Cwmfelin Boeth Dyfed 22 D4 vil 2m/3km N of Whitland. SN 1919

Cwmfelinfach Gwent 15 G2 vil 4m/6km S of Blackwood. ST 1891

Cwmfelin Mynach Dyfed 22 D3 vil 5m/9km N of Whitland. SN 2224

Cwmffrwd Dyfed 23 F4 ham 2m/3km S of Carmarthen. SN 4217

Cwm Ffrwd-oer Gwent 15 G2 loc 2km NW of Pontypool. SO 2601

Cwm Gelli Gwent 15 F2* loc 1km N of Blackwood. ST 1798

Cwmgiedd Powys 14 D1 vil 2m/3km NE of Ystalyfera. SN 7811

Cwmgwili Dyfed 23 G4* vil 4m/6km W of Ammanford. SN 5710

Cwmgwrach W Glam 14 D1* loc adjoining Blaengwrach to S. SN 8605

Cwmgwyn W Glam 23 G6* loc in Swansea 2m/3km W of tn centre. SS 6393

Cwm Head Salop 34 B5* loc 4m/6km SW of Church Stretton. SO 4288

Cwmhiraeth Dyfed 23 E2* loc 3m/4km SE of Newcastle Emlyn. SN 3337

Cwmifor Dyfed 24 C5* loc 2m/3km NE of Llandeilo. SN 6525

Cwmisfael Dyfed 23 F4* loc 1m SW of Llandarog. SN 4915

Cwm-llawenog 33 H1 stream rising on S side of Cadair Fronwen in Berwyn Mts and running E into R Ceiriog 2m/3km NW of Llanarmon Dyffryn Ceiriog, Clwyd. SJ 1334

Cwm-llechen 32 D3* r flowing S into R Mawddach estuary at Bontddu, Gwynedd. SH 6718
Cwm Llinau (Cwmlline) Powys 33 F4 ham 3m/5km S of Mallwyd. SH 8407
Cwmllinfell W Glam 14 C1 vil 2m/4km SE of Brynamman. SN 7413
Cwm-llwch 25 E5* r rising on N side of Brecon Beacons, Powys, and flowing N into R Tarell 2m/3km SW of Brecon. SO 0127
Cwm-mawr Dyfed 23 G4* loc adjoining Tumble to NW. SN 5312
Cwmmiles Dyfed 22 D3* loc 1km S of Login. SN 1622
Cwm-Morgan Dyfed 23 E2 ham 4m/6km S of Newcastle Emlyn. SN 2934
Cwm-mynach 32 D3 r flowing S into R Mawddach opp Penmaenpool, Gwynedd. SH 6918
Cwmnantcol 32 D2 r in Gwynedd running W into R Artro 3m/4km SE of Harlech. SH 6027
Cwmnantyrodyn Gwent 15 G2* loc 2m/3km SW of Newbridge. ST 1895
Cwm-parc Mid Glam 15 E2 vil 2m/3km W of Rhondda. SS 9495
Cwmpengraig Dyfed 23 E2 ham 4m/6km SE of Newcastle Emlyn. SN 3436
Cwm Penmachno Gwynedd 40 D6* loc 4m/6km E of Blaenau Ffestiniog. SH 7547
Cwmpennar Mid Glam 15 F2* vil 1km NW of Mountain Ash. SO 0400
Cwm Plysgog Dyfed 22 D2* loc adjoining Cilgerran to N. SN 1943
Cwmrhos Powys 25 G5* loc 4m/7km NW of Crickhowell. SO 1824
Cwmrhydyceirw W Glam 23 H5* loc in N part of Swansea 4m/6km N of tn centre. SS 6699
Cwmsychpant Dyfed 24 B3 ham 6m/10km W of Lampeter. SN 4746
Cwmsyfiog Mid Glam 15 F2* ham 2m/3km N of Bargoed. SO 1502
Cwmsymlog Dyfed 33 E6 loc 5m/8km NW of Devil's Br. SN 6983
Cwmtillery (Cwmtyleri) Gwent 15 G1 loc 1m N of Abertillery. **Cwmtillery Resr** small resr 1m N. SO 2105
Cwmtwrch-isaf Powys 14 D1* loc 2m/3km SE of Cwmllynfell. SN 7610
Cwmtwrch-uchaf Powys 14 D1* loc 2km SE of Cwmllynfell. SN 7510
Cwmtyleri Welsh form of Cwmtillery, qv.
Cwm y Geifr 33 H1* stream running E into R Ceiriog 2km NW of Llanarmon Dyffryn Ceiriog, Clwyd. SJ 1334
Cwm-y-glo Dyfed 23 G4* vil adjoining Cross Hands to N. SN 5513
Cwm-y-glo Gwynedd 40 C5 vil 2m/4km NW of Llanberis. SH 5562
Cwmynyscoy Gwent 15 G2* loc 1km S of Pontypool. ST 2899
Cwmyoy Gwent 25 G5 loc 6m/9km N of Abergavenny. SO 2923
Cwmyrhaiadr 33 E5* valley with waterfalls on borders of Dyfed and Powys 3m/5km S of Machynlleth, Powys. SN 7596
Cwmystwyth Dyfed 24 D1 ham 4m/7km SE of Devil's Br. SN 7873
Cwrt Gwynedd 33 E4 loc 4m/6km W of Machynlleth. SH 6800
Cwrt-newydd Dyfed 24 B3 vil 6m/9km W of Lampeter. SN 4847
Cwrt-y-Cadno Dyfed 24 C4* loc on R Cothi 3m/5km NE of Pumsaint. SN 6944
Cwrt-y-gollen Powys 25 G6* loc 2km SE of Crickhowell. SO 2316
Cwymwysg Powys 24 D5* loc 2m/3km W of Trecastle. SN 8528
Cych 22 D2/23 E2 r rising S of Newcastle Emlyn, Dyfed, and flowing N into R Teifi between Newcastle Emlyn and Cardigan. SN 2441
Cydweli Welsh form of Kidwelly, qv.
Cyffylliog Clwyd 41 F5 vil on R Clywedog 4m/6km W of Ruthin. SJ 0657
Cylinders, The W Sussex 11 E2* loc adjoining Fernhurst to S, 3m/5km S of Haslemere. SU 8928
Cymdda Mid Glam 15 E3* loc 2m/3km N of Bridgend. SS 9083
Cymdu Clwyd 41 H5* ham 4m/7km NW of Wrexham. SJ 2955
Cymer Abbey Gwynedd 33 E3 ruined 13c abbey (A.M.) to E of Llanelltyd across R Mawddach. SH 7219
Cymerig 33 F1* stream running N into Cwm Hirnant at Rhos-y-gwaliau, Gwynedd. SH 9434
Cymmer Mid Glam 15 E3* loc 1km S of Porth. ST 0290
Cymmer W Glam 14 D2 vil 3m/5km N of Maesteg. SS 8696
Cymyran Bay Gwynedd 40 A4 bay on W coast of Anglesey bounded by S coast of Holy I. and adjacent coast of main island on SW side of Valley Airfield. SH 2974
Cyncoed S Glam 15 G3* dist of Cardiff 3m/4km N of city centre. ST 1880
Cyncoed Welsh form of Kingcoed, qv.
Cynfal 32 D1 r running W into R Dwyryd 2km W of Ffestiniog, Gwynedd. SH 6841
Cynffig Welsh form of Kenfig, qv.
Cynghordy Dyfed 24 D4 ham 4m/7km NE of Llandovery. SN 8039
Cynheidre Dyfed 23 F5 coal-mining loc 4m/7km N of Llanelli. SN 4907
Cynin 23 E4 r rising N of Trelech, Dyfed, and flowing S into R Taf at St Clears. SN 2815
Cynllaith 33 H2* r rising 3m/4km S of Glyn Ceiriog, Clwyd, and flowing S into R Tanat on border of Clwyd, Powys, and Salop, on E side of Pen-y-bont. SJ 2123
Cynon 15 F2 r rising N of Hirwaun, Mid Glam, and flowing SE by Aberdare and Mountain Ash into R Taff at Abercynon. ST 0894
Cynon Valley 118 admin dist of Mid Glam.
Cynonville W Glam 14 D2* ham 1m W of Duffryn. SS 8295
Cynrig 25 F5* r rising on E side of Brecon Beacons, Powys, and flowing NE into R Usk 2m/3km E of Brecon. SO 0627
Cyntwell S Glam 15 F4* loc in Cardiff 4m/6km W of city centre. ST 1275
Cynwyd Clwyd 33 G1 vil in R Dee valley 2m/3km SW of Corwen. SJ 541
Cynwyl Elfed Welsh form of Conwil Elvet, qv.
Cyprus London 20 B3* loc in borough of Newham at E end of Royal Albert Dock 2m/3km S of E Ham. TQ 4380
Cywarch 33 F3 r running S into R Dovey at Aber Cywarch, Gwynedd. SH 8615
Cywyn 23 E4 r rising 2m/4km E of Trelech, Dyfed, and flowing S into R Taf 3m/4km SE of St Clears. SN 3012

D

Daaey Shetland 89 F5* small island off N coast of Fetlar opp Urie Ness. HU 6095
Daccombe Devon 5 E4 ham 3m/4km N of Torquay. SX 9068
Dacorum 119 admin dist of Herts.
Dacre Cumbria 52 D2 vil 4m/7km SW of Penrith. **D. Castle** is 14c peel tower. NY 4526
Dacre N Yorks 48 D2 ham 4m/6km SE of Pateley Br. **D. Banks** vil 1m N. SE 1962
Daddry Shield Durham 53 G1 ham 1km E of St John's Chapel. NY 8937
Dadford Bucks 28 B4 ham 3m/5km NW of Buckingham. SP 6638
Dadlington Leics 36 A4 vil 3m/5km NW of Hinckley. SP 4098
Daer Water 59 E1 r in Strathclyde region rising on Lowther Hills and flowing N through the large **Daer Resr** to join Potrail Water and form R Clyde 2m/3km S of Elvanfoot. NS 9513
Dafen Dyfed 23 G5 loc adjoining Llanelli to E. Engineering and rubber works. SN 5201
Daff Reservoir S'clyde 64 A2* resr 4m/7km SW of Greenock. NS 2370
Daffy Green Norfolk 38 D4* loc 3m/5km SW of E Dereham. TF 9609
Dagdale Staffs 35 F1* loc 3m/4km W of Uttoxeter. SK 0534
Dagenham London 20 B3 dist in borough of Barking 3m/5km S of Romford. Motor works to S beside R Thames. TQ 5084
Daglingworth Glos 17 E1 vil 3m/4km NW of Cirencester. Site of Roman bldg 1km SE. SO 9905
Dagnall Bucks 29 E6 vil 4m/6km S of Dunstable. SP 9916
Dagworth Suffolk 31 E2* loc 2m/3km N of Stowmarket. TM 0461
Dailly S'clyde 56 C3/C4 vil on S bank of Water of Girvan, 6m/9km E of Girvan. See also Old Dailly. NS 2701
Dail-na-mine Forest Tayside 75 G3, H3* deer forest on Forest of Atholl 9m/15km NW of Blair Atholl. NN 7777
Dainton Devon 5 E4 ham beside main-line rly 3m/5km S of Newton Abbot near summit of steep incline. SX 8566
Dairsie Fife 73 G3 vil 3m/5km NE of Cupar. Remains of medieval cas 1m S, near 17c br over R Eden. Vil also known as **Dairsiemuir** or Osnaburgh. NO 4117
Dairy Houses Humberside 51 F5* loc 3m/4km E of Hedon. TA 2229
Daisy Bank W Midlands 35 F4* loc in E part of Walsall. SP 0497
Daisy Green Essex 30 D5* loc 4m/7km W of Colchester. TL 9325
Daisy Green Suffolk 31 E2* loc 1m E of Gt Ashfield. TM 0167
Daisy Hill Gtr Manchester 42 C1 loc 1m S of Westhoughton. SD 6504
Daisy Hill W Yorks 48 D4* loc in Bradford 2m/4km NW of city centre. SE 1334
Daisy Hill W Yorks 49 E5* loc 1km NE of Morley. SE 2728
Daisy Nook Gtr Manchester 43 E1 loc 2km NW of Ashton-under-Lyne. SD 9100
Dalavich S'clyde 70 B4 locality on W shore of Loch Awe in Argyll 1km S of mouth of R Avich. NM 9612
Dalbeattie D & G 58 D5 small granite tn on Kirkgunzeon Lane 13m/20km SW of Dumfries. Granite quarries in vicinity. **D. Forest** is state forest to S. NX 8361
Dalbeg Bay W Isles 88 B1* bay on NW coast of Lewis 2m/4km NE of Carloway. NB 2246
Dalbeth S'clyde 64 D3* loc in Tollcross dist of Glasgow, on N bank of R Clyde. NS 6362
Dalbury Derbys 35 H1 ham 6m/9km W of Derby. SK 2634
Dalby Isle of Man 46 A5 ham near W coast 4m/6km S of Peel. **Dalby Pt,** headland 1km W. SC 2178
Dalby Lincs 45 G4* loc 3m/4km N of Spilsby. TF 4070
Dalby N Yorks 50 B1 ham 2m/3km W of Terrington. SE 6471
Dalby, Great Leics 36 C3 vil 3m/5km S of Melton Mowbray. **Lit Dalby** ham 2m/3km E. SK 7414
Dalby Wolds Leics 36 C2* loc 2m/3km SW of Old Dalby. SK 6522
Dalcairnie Linn S'clyde 56 E3* waterfall in course of Dalcairnie Burn, 2km SW of Dalmellington. NS 4604
Dalch 7 E4 r rising on Witheridge Moor 4m/6km E of Witheridge, Devon, and flowing W into R Yeo 1km S of Lapford. SS 7307
Dalchalm H'land 87 C6 loc on E coast of Sutherland dist 1m N of Brora. NC 9105
Dalchreichart H'land 80 C6/D6 loc in Glen Moriston, Inverness dist, 6m/9km NW of Fort Augustus. NH 2912
Dalchuirn H'land 80 A4 locality in Ross and Cromarty dist on NW shore of Loch Carron, adjoining vil of Lochcarron. NG 9039
Dalcross H'land 81 G2 airport on E side of Inner Moray Firth 8m/13km NE of Inverness. NH 7752
Dalderby Lincs 45 F4 loc 2m/4km S of Horncastle. TF 2466
Dalditch Devon 5 F2*ham 2m/3km NW of Budleigh Salterton. SY 0483
Dale Cumbria 53 E1* loc 2m/3km N of Kirkoswald. NY 5444
Dale Derbys 36 A1 ham 3m/4km SW of Ilkeston. Slight remains of Norman abbey. **D. Moor** loc to E. SK 4338
Dale Dyfed 22 B5 vil on **D. Roads,** bay at W end of Milford Haven 2m/3km N of St Ann's Hd. 1m E is **Dale Pt,** headland on which **D. Fort,** now a field study centre, is situated. SM 8005
Dale Gtr Manchester 43 E1* loc adjoining Delph to E. SD 9808
Dalebank Derbys 43 H5* loc 2m/3km SW of Clay Cross. SK 3661
Dale Bottom Cumbria 52 C3* loc 2m/3km SE of Keswick. NY 2921
Dalebrow Ches 42 D3* loc adjoining Prestbury to S. SJ 9076
Dale Dike Reservoir S Yorks 43 G2* resr 2m/3km W of Bradfield. SK 2491
Dale End Derbys 43 G5* loc 1km NW of Elton. SK 2161
Dale End N Yorks 48 C3* loc adjoining Lothersdale to E. SD 9646
Dale Head Cumbria 52 C3* ham 4m/7km SE of Keswick on E side of Thirlmere. NY 3118
Dalehouse N Yorks 55 F3 loc 1km SW of Staithes. NZ 7717
Dalelia H'land 68 E2 locality with pier on N shore of Loch Shiel in Lochaber dist, 3m/4km SE of Kinlochmoidart. NM 7369
Dalemain Cumbria 52 D2 loc 3m/5km SW of Penrith. NY 4726
Dale Pond N Yorks 50 B1* small lake to N of Brandsby. SE 5972
Dales Brow Gtr Manchester 42 D2* loc 1m S of Swinton. SD 7700
Dales Farm Grampian. See Peterhead.
Dales Green Staffs 42 D5* loc 2m/3km NE of Kidsgrove. SJ 8556
Dales Voe Shetland 89 E6* narrow inlet on NE coast of Mainland 2m/4km SE of Scatsta. HU 4270
Dales Voe Shetland 89 E7* inlet on E coast of Mainland 3m/5km N of Lerwick. HU 4546
Dalgarven S'clyde 64 A4 loc on R Garnock 2m/3km N of Kilwinning. NS 2945
Dalgety Bay Fife 65 G1/H1 housing development on bay of same name 3m/4km E of Inverkeithing. Donibristle Industrial Estate adjoins to NW. On shore of bay is ruined ch of St Bridget (A.M.), dating from 1244. NT 1683
Dalginross Tayside 72 B3 vil on S side of R Earn opp Comrie. Roman sites to S. NN 7721
Dalhalvaig H'land 86 B2 vil in Strath Halladale, in Caithness dist, 6m/10km S of Melvich. NC 8954
Dalham Suffolk 30 C2 vil 5m/8km E of Newmarket. TL 7261
Dalhousie Castle Lothian 66 B2 cas dating from mid-15c 1m W of Newtongrange across R South Esk. Formerly seat of the Ramsays. NT 3263
Daliburgh W Isles 88 D3 vil near W coast of S Uist 3m/5km NW of Lochboisdale. NF 7521
Dalkeith Lothian 66 B2 tn astride Rs North and South Esk 6m/10km SE of Edinburgh. Grain mkt. Industries include mnfre of brushes, carpets, textiles; coal-mining in vicinity. **D. House** to N, built *c.* 1700, formerly seat of the Dukes of Buccleuch. NT 3367
Dall Tayside 75 F5 locality on S shore of Loch Rannoch 5m/7km W of Kinloch Rannoch. Hse (1855) is part of Rannoch boys' public school. NN 5956
Dallachoilish S'clyde 70 B1 locality on S side of the narrows of Loch Creran, Argyll. NM 9744
Dallachy, Nether Grampian 82 C1 vil near N coast 4m/6km W of Buckie. Vil of **Upr Dallachy** 1m S on far side of disused airfield. NJ 3663
Dallas Grampian 82 A2 vil on R Lossie 9m/14km SW of Elgin. **D. Forest** is state forest to N. See also Tor Castle, Loch Dallas. NJ 1252
Dalleagles S'clyde 56 F3 loc 4m/6km SW of Cumnock. NS 5710
Dallinghoo Suffolk 31 F3 vil 4m/6km N of Woodbridge. TM 2654
Dallington E Sussex 12 C5 vil 5m/8km E of Heathfield. TQ 6519
Dallington Northants 28 C2 NW dist of Northampton. SP 7362
Dallow N Yorks 48 D1 loc 4m/7km NE of Pateley Br across D. Moor. SE 1971
Dally Castle Nthmb 60 D3 remains of cas dating from 13c. NY 7784
Dalmacallan Forest D & G 58 D3* state forest 2m/4km SE of Moniaive. NX 8087
Dalmahoy Lothian 65 G2 loc 1m SE of Ratho. Golf-course. NT 1469
Dalmally S'clyde 70 D2 vil on R Orchy in Argyll 2m/3km E of NE end of Loch Awe. NN 1627
Dalmarnock S'clyde 64 D3* dist of Glasgow on N bank of R Clyde 2m/3km SE of city centre. NS 6163

Dalmellington S'clyde 56 E3 small colliery tn on tributary of nearby R Doon, 13m/21km SE of Ayr. Site of 13c priory. NS 4805
Dalmeny Lothian 65 G1 vil 2km E of S Queensferry. NT 1477
Dalmilling S'clyde 64 B6* E dist of Ayr. NS 3622
Dalmore H'land 81 F1 loc on N shore of Cromarty Firth, Ross and Cromarty dist, 1m SE of Alness. Distillery. NH 6668
Dalmore W Isles 88 B1/B2* loc near NW coast of Lewis 2m/3km NE of Carloway. D. Bay on coast to NW. NB 2144
Dalmuir S'clyde 64 C2 loc 2km NW of Clydebank. NS 4870
Dalnabreck H'land 68 E2 locality in Lochaber dist 3m/5km N of Salen across head of Loch Shiel. NM 7069
Dalnacardoch Forest Tayside 74 G3, G4* deer forest to N of Dalnacardoch Lodge in Glen Garry. NN 6875
Dalnaspidal Forest Tayside 75 F4* mt area on borders with Highland region NW of Loch Garry. Dalnaspidal Lodge and rly stn near foot of Loch Garry to E. NN 6074
Dalness S'clyde 74 C6 loc in Glen Etive, Argyll, SW of Buachaille Etive Mór. Series of waterfalls in R Etive. Mountainous area to N is property of NTS. NN 1651
Dalquharran S'clyde 56 C3 loc with cas of 15c beside Water of Girvan, and another of late 18c on higher ground to NW. Situated opp Dailly across r. NS 2702
Dalry D & G 58 C3 vil on Water of Ken 2m/4km N of New Galloway. Also known as St John's Tn of D., from a former ch of the Knights Templars. NX 6281
Dalry Lothian 66 A2* dist of Edinburgh 2km SW of city centre. NT 2372
Dalry S'clyde 64 A4 tn on R Garnock 6m/10km NE of Ardrossan. Industries include mnfre of textiles and hosiery, brick works, quarrying. NS 2949
Dalrymple S'clyde 56 D3 vil 5m/8km S of Ayr. NS 3514
Dalscote Northants 28 C2* loc 4m/6km N of Towcester. SP 6854
Dalserf S'clyde 65 E4 vil 2m/4km E of Larkhall. NS 8050
Dalsetter Shetland 89 E5 loc on Yell near head of Basta Voe. HU 5099
Dalston Cumbria 59 H6 vil on R Caldew 4m/7km SW of Carlisle. Hall, mainly late 19c, dates partly from 16c and 17c. NY 3650
Dalston London 19 G3* loc in borough of Hackney 4m/6km NE of Charing Cross. TQ 3384
Dalswinton D & G 59 E3 vil 6m/10km N of Dumfries. Site of Roman fort to SW beside rly. NX 9385
Dalton Cumbria 47 F1* ham 1m E of Burton. SD 5476
Dalton D & G 59 F4 vil 7m/11km NW of Annan. NY 1174
Dalton Lancs 42 B1* loc 2m/3km NE of Skelmersdale. SD 5007
Dalton Nthmb 61 F4* ham 4m/6km W of Ponteland. NZ 1172
Dalton N Yorks 49 F1 vil 2m/3km E of Topcliffe. SE 4376
Dalton N Yorks 54 A4 vil 6m/10km NW of Richmond. NZ 1108
Dalton S Yorks 43 A2 loc adjoining Rotherham to NE. Locs of **D. Magna** and **D. Parva** 1m S and 1km SW respectively. SK 4694
Dalton-in-Furness Cumbria 46 D1 tn 4m/6km NE of Barrow-in-Furness. Felt mnfre, quarrying, textiles. Dalton Castle (NT), restored 14c peel tower in mkt place. SD 2374
Dalton-le-Dale Durham 61 H6 vil 2m/3km SW of Seaham. NZ 4048
Dalton, North Humberside 50 D3 vil 6m/10km SW of Gt Driffield. SE 9352
Dalton-on-Tees N Yorks 54 C4 vil 4m/7km S of Darlington. NZ 2907
Dalton Parlours W Yorks 49 F4* loc 2m/4km S of Wetherby. Site of Roman villa. SE 4044
Dalton Piercy Cleveland 54 D2 ham 3m/5km W of Hartlepool. NZ 4631
Dalton, South Humberside 50 D4/51 E4 vil 6m/10km E of Mkt Weighton. SE 9645
Dalton's Point W Glam 23 G5* headland at end of marshes at head of Burry Inlet, N of Pen-clawdd. SS 5396
Dalwhat Water 58 D3 r in Dumfries & Galloway region running SE to join Castlefairn Water and form Cairn Water, 1km SE of Moniaive. NX 7890
Dalwhinnie H'land 75 F3 vil on R Truim in Badenoch and Strathspey dist 12m/20km SW of Kingussie. Distillery. NN 6384
Dalwood Devon 8 B4 vil 3m/5km NW of Axminster. ST 2400
Dalziel S'clyde 65 E3 par between Motherwell and Wishaw. Contains **Dalzell Hse**, with 15c tower. NS 7555
Damask Green Herts 29 F4/F5* S end of vil of Weston, 3m/4km S of Baldock. TL 2529
Damerham Hants 9 G3 vil 3m/5km NW of Fordingbridge. SU 1015
Damflask Reservoir S Yorks 43 G2* resr 5m/8km NW of Sheffield. SK 2890
Damgate Norfolk 39 G4* vil adjoining Acle to S. TG 4009
Damgate Norfolk 39 H3* loc adjoining Martham to N. TG 4519
Dam Green Norfolk 39 E6* loc 1m SE of Kenninghall. TM 0585
Dam, High Cumbria 52 D5* small lake 2m/3km N of Newby Br. SD 3688
Damsbrook Derbys 44 A4* loc 2km S of Clowne. SK 4973
Dam Side Lancs 47 E3* loc just NE of Pilling. SD 4048
Danaway Kent 21 E5 loc 3m/5km W of Sittingbourne. TQ 8663
Danbury Essex 20 D2 vil 5m/8km E of Chelmsford. **D. Common** (NT) to S; Lingwood Common (NT) to N. TL 7705
Danby N Yorks 55 E4 vil on R Esk 12m/19km W of Whitby. **Danby Castle**, remains of medieval cas 1m SE. NZ 7008
Danby Botton N Yorks 55 E4* loc 2m/4km S of Castleton. NZ 6904
Danby Wiske N Yorks 54 C5 vil 4m/6km NW of Northallerton. SE 3398
Dan Caerlan Mid Glam 15 F3* loc on NE side of Llantrisant. ST 0583
Dancers Hill Herts 19 F2* loc 2m/3km SW of Potters Bar. TQ 2399
Dancing Green H & W 26 B5* loc 3m/5km SE of Ross-on-Wye. SO 6320
Danderhall Lothian 66 B2* loc 2m/3km NW of Dalkeith. NT 3069
Dane 42 C4 r rising on borders of Ches and Derbys SW of Buxton and flowing W to Middlewich, Ches, then NW into R Weaver at Northwich. SJ 6573
Danebank Ches 43 E3* loc adjoining Disley to SE. SJ 9784
Dane Bank Gtr Manchester 42 D2* loc 1m W of Denton. SJ 9095
Danebridge 43 E4* ham on R Dane on Ches–Staffs border 1km SE of Wincle. SJ 9665
Danebury Hill Hants 10 A1 Iron Age hill fort with three lines of ramparts, 2m/4km NW of Stockbridge. SU 3237
Dane End Herts 29 G4* loc 3m/5km S of Royston. TL 3435
Dane End Herts 29 G5 ham 5m/8km N of Ware. TL 3321
Danehill E Sussex 12 A4 vil 5m/8km NE of Haywards Heath. TQ 4027
Dane Hills Leics 36 B4* dist of Leicester 2m/3km W of city centre. SK 5604
Dane in Shaw Ches 42 D5* loc in Congleton 2km SE of tn centre. SJ 8761
Danemoor Green Norfolk 39 E4* loc 4m/7km NW of Wymondham. TG 0505
Dane's Brook 7 F2* stream rising on Exmoor between Twitchen and Withypool and forming for most of its length part of boundary between Devon and Somerset before joining R Barle 2m/4km NW of Dulverton. SS 8829
Daneshill Hants 18 B6* NE dist of Basingstoke. SU 6453
Danesmoor Derbys 43 H4 loc 1km E of Clay Cross. SK 4063
Danes Wood Devon. See Broad Clyst.
Daneway Glos 16 D1* loc 5m/9km W of Cirencester. SO 9303
Dangerous Corner Gtr Manchester 42 C1* loc 2m/3km W of Atherton. SD 6402
Dangerous Corner Lancs 42 B1* loc 5m/8km NW of Wigan. SD 5210
Danhiraeth Dyfed 23 E2* loc 3m/4km SE of Newcastle Emlyn. SN 3438
Daniel's Water Kent 13 E3* loc 3m/5km W of Ashford. TQ 9641
Danna Island S'clyde 69 E8 peninsula in Argyll, joined by an isthmus of a road's width to S end of peninsula between Loch Sween and Sound of Jura. NR 6978
Dan's Castle Durham 54 A1 N part of Tow Law. NZ 1239
Danskine Loch Lothian 66 C2 small loch 2m/3km E of Gifford. NT 5667
Danthorpe Humberside 51 F5* loc 1m N of Burton Pidsea. TA 2432
Danum S Yorks. See Doncaster.
Dan-y-coed W Glam 23 G6* loc in N part of Mumbles. SS 6189
Danygraig Gwent 15 G3* loc opp Risca across Ebbw R. ST 2390
Dan y Graig W Glam 23 H6* loc in Swansea 1m E of tn centre across R Tawe. SS 6793
Dan yr Ogof Powys 24 D6* extensive cave system 2km N of Pen-y-cae, beyond Craig-y-nos. SN 8316
Danzey Green Warwicks 27 F1* loc 3m/5km NW of Henley-in-Arden. SP 1269
Dapple Heath Staffs 35 F2* loc 1km NE of Newton. SK 0426
Darby End W Midlands 35 F5* loc in Dudley 2m/3km S of tn centre. SO 9587
Darby Green Hants 18 C5 loc 1km S of Sandhurst. SU 8360
Darby Green H & W 26 C2* ham 5m/9km E of Bromyard. SO 7456
Darby's Hill W Midlands 35 F5* loc 2km W of Oldbury. SO 9689
Darcy Lever Gtr Manchester 42 C1* loc in Bolton 2km SE of tn centre. SD 7308
Darden Lough Nthmb 61 E2* small lake 3m/5km S of Hepple. NY 9795
Daren Powys 25 G6* loc 2m/3km SW of Crickhowell. SO 2016
Daren-felen Gwent 25 G6* loc 2m/3km E of Brynmawr. SO 2112
Darent 20 B4 r rising near Westerham, Kent, and flowing E then N into R Thames N of Dartford. TQ 5478
Darenth Kent 20 C4 vil on R Darent 2m/3km SE of Dartford. Site of Roman villa to S. TQ 5671
Darenth, South Kent 20 C4 vil on R Darent 2km S of Darenth and 3m/5km SE of Dartford. TQ 5669
Daresbury Ches 42 B3 vil 4m/6km SW of Warrington. SJ 5782
Darfield S Yorks 43 H1 tn 5m/7km E of Barnsley. Coal-mining. SE 4104
Dargate Kent 21 F5 vil 4m/6km SW of Whitstable. TR 0861
Darite Cornwall 3 G2* vil 3m/5km N of Liskeard. SX 2569
Darland Clwyd 42 A5* loc adjoining Lavister to E. SJ 3757
Darland Kent 20 D5 loc in S part of Gillingham. TQ 7865
Darlaston Staffs 35 E1 loc 2km NW of Stone. SJ 8735
Darlaston W Midlands 35 F4 SW dist of Walsall. SO 9796
Darlaston Green W Midlands 35 F4* W dist of Walsall. SO 9897
Darley N Yorks 48 D2 vil 4m/7km SE of Pateley Br. **D. Head** vil adjoining to W. SE 2059
Darley Abbey Derbys 35 H1 dist of Derby 2km N of tn centre. SK 3438
Darley Bridge Derbys 43 G5* vil 2m/3km NW of Matlock. SK 2661
Darley Dale Derbys 43 G4/G5 stretch of R Derwent valley between Rowsley and Darley Br. SK 2762
Darley Ford Cornwall 3 G1* loc 6m/9km N of Liskeard. SX 2773
Darley Hillside Derbys 43 G4* loc 3m/4km NW of Matlock. SK 2763
Darley, North Cornwall 3 G1* loc 6m/10km N of Liskeard. SX 2773
Darlingscott Warwicks 27 F3 vil 2m/3km NW of Shipston on Stour. SP 2342
Darlington Durham 54 C3 industrial tn on R Skerne 31m/50km S of Newcastle upon Tyne. Rly engineering, br bldg, wire mnfre, knitting yarns. NZ 2914
Darliston Salop 34 C1 loc 6m/9km SE of Whitchurch. SJ 5833
Darlton Notts 44 C4 vil 3m/5km NE of Tuxford. SK 7773
Darnall S Yorks 43 H2 dist of Sheffield 3m/4km E of city centre. SK 3988
Darnaway Forest 81 H2 forest mainly in Grampian region, but partly in Nairn dist of Highland region, SW of Forres and E of Nairn. Darnaway Castle is seat of the Earl of Moray. NH 9853
Darn Hill Gtr Manchester 42 D1* loc in Heywood 2km W of tn centre. SD 8310
Darnick Borders 66 C5 vil 1m W of Melrose. 16c peel tower. NT 5334
Daron 32 A2* stream running SW into Aberdaron Bay at Aberdaron, Gwynedd. SH 1726
Darowen Powys 33 E4/F4 ham 2m/3km S of Cemmaes Rd. SH 8301
Darra Grampian 83 F2 loc 2m/3km SE of Turriff. NJ 7447
Darracott Devon 6 B3* ham 8m/12km N of Bude. SS 2317
Darras Hall Nthmb 61 F4 suburb adjoining Ponteland to S. NZ 1571
Darrington W Yorks 49 F6 vil 2m/3km SE of Pontefract. SE 4820
Darrow Green Norfolk 39 F5* loc 4m/6km N of Harleston. Traces of motte and bailey cas to E. TM 2589
Darsham Suffolk 31 H2 vil 2m/3km NE of Yoxford. TM 4170
Dart 5 E5 Devon r rising as E and W Dart on N Dartmoor. The two streams join at Dartmeet and the river then flows generally SE into the sea just below Dartmouth. Tidal from Totnes; estuary opens out opp Stoke Gabriel. SX 8949
Dart 7 G4 r in Devon rising 2m/3km N of Templeton and flowing SE to join R Exe at Bickleigh. SS 9307
Dartford Kent 20 B4 industrial tn on R Darent and 2m/3km from S bank of R Thames where **D. Tunnel** conveys rd traffic across r to Purfleet. TQ 5474
Dartington Devon 4 D4 vil 2m/3km NW of Totnes. **D. Hall** is an educational and commercial establishment; central bldg is medieval. SX 7862
Dart, Little 7 E4 r rising on Rackenford Moor N of Rackenford, Devon, and flowing W into R Taw near Chulmleigh. SS 6613
Dartmeet Devon 4 C3 loc on Dartmoor at confluence of E and W Dart Rs, 6m/9km NW of Ashburton. Clapper br over E Dart beside rd br. SX 6773
Dartmoor Forest Devon 4 C3 extensive bare upland area of granite (generally known simply as Dartmoor) with many rocky summits or *tors* of between 1000 and 2000 ft (300 and 600 metres). Numerous swift streams as well as boggy areas. A national park. Northern part used as artillery range. SX 68
Dartmouth Devon 5 E5 small port and resort on R Dart estuary 7m/12km SE of Totnes. Royal Naval College on hill above tn. Cas (A.M.) at harbour entrance 1m S. Ferries cross r. SX 8751
Dartmouth Park London 19 G3* loc in borough of Camden to E of Highgate Ponds and 4m/7km N of Charing Cross. TQ 2886
Darton S Yorks 43 G1 colliery tn on R Dearne 3m/5km NW of Barnsley. **D. Lane Head** loc 1m NE. SE 3110
Darvel S'clyde 64 C5 tn on R Irvine 9m/14km E of Kilmarnock. Textiles. Birthplace of Sir Alexander Fleming, 1881-1955, discoverer of penicillin. NS 5637
Darvilshill Bucks 18 C2* loc 3m/5km SE of Princes Risborough. SU 8399
Darwell Hole E Sussex 12 C5 loc 4m/6km NW of Battle. TQ 6919
Darwell Reservoir E Sussex 12 D4 resr 4m/6km NW of Battle. TQ 7121
Darwen Lancs 47 G5 industrial tn 4m/6km S of Blackburn. Wallpaper, paint, textiles, plastics. **Lr Darwen** loc 2m/3km N, in Blackburn. SD 6922
Darwen 47 F5 r rising near Darwen, Lancs, and flowing N to Blackburn, then W to R Ribble at Walton-le-Dale. SD 5428
Datchet Berks 19 E4 tn on N bank of R Thames opp Windsor Home Park. SU 9877
Datchworth Herts 29 F5 vil 3m/5km NE of Welwyn. TL 2619
Datchworth Green Herts 29 F6 ham 3m/5km NE of Welwyn. TL 2718
Daubhill Gtr Manchester 42 C1 dist of Bolton 2m/3km SW of tn centre. SD 7007
Daufraich Dyfed 22 A3* rocky island 2m/3km W of Ramsey I. One of the larger islands in the group known as Bishops and Clerks, qv.
Daugleddau 22 C5* estuarial r formed by confluence of Rs Eastern Cleddau and Western Cleddau and flowing S then W into Milford Haven, Dyfed. SM 9704
Dauntsey Wilts 17 E3* ham 4m/7km SE of Malmesbury. Ham of **D. Green** 1m E. ST 9882
Dauntsey Lock Wilts 17 E3* ham on former Wilts and Berks Canal 5m/8km W of Wootton Bassett. ST 9980
Davarr Island S'clyde 63 E5 island opp entrance to Campbeltown Loch on E coast of Kintyre. Lighthouse at N point. On SE side is cave known as Crucifixion Cave. NR 7520
Davenham Ches 42 C4 vil 2m/3km S of Northwich. SJ 6571
Davenport Gtr Manchester 42 D3 loc in Stockport 1m S of tn centre. SJ 8988

Davenport Green Ches 42 D3* loc in Wilmslow 1m SW of tn centre. SJ 8379
Davenport Green Gtr Manchester 42 D3* loc 3m/4km SE of Altrincham. SJ 8086
Daventry Northants 28 B2 tn 12m/19km W of Northampton. Radio transmitting stn to E on Borough Hill: remains of Iron Age fort and site of Roman bldg. Resr to NE. SP 5762
Davidson's Mains Lothian 66 A2 dist of Edinburgh 3m/5km NW of city centre. Formerly known as Muttonhole. NT 2075
Davidstow Cornwall 6 A6 vil 4m/6km NE of Camelford. SX 1587
David Street Kent 20 C5* loc 2km S of Meopham and 4m/6km N of Wrotham Heath. TQ 6464
David's Well Powys 33 G6 loc 8m/13km S of Newtown. SO 0578
Daviot Grampian 83 F4 vil 5m/7km NW of Inverurie. Loanhead Stone Circle (A.M.) to N dates from Bronze Age. NJ 7528
Daviot H'land 81 F3 loc in Inverness dist 5m/8km SE of Inverness. NH 7239
Davoch of Grange Grampian 82 D2* loc 3m/5km E of Keith. NJ 4851
Davyhulme Gtr Manchester 42 C2* loc adjoining Urmston to NW. SJ 7595
Daw Cross N Yorks 49 E3 loc 2m/4km S of Harrogate. SE 2951
Daw End W Midlands 35 F4 loc 2m/3km NE of Walsall. SK 0300
Dawley Salop 34 D3/D4 tn forming central area of Telford and situated 3m/5km SE of Wellington. Industries include engineering, quarrying, brick mnfre. Loc of **D. Bank** to N, and of **Lit Dawley** to S. SJ 6807
Dawley Brook W Midlands 35 E5* loc 3m/5km N of Stourbridge. SO 8889
Dawlish Devon 5 E3 12m/20km S of Exeter. Resort with sands and red cliffs; rly runs between tn and beach. **D. Water** rises on Haldon to E and flows through tn centre. 2m/3km NE, **D. Warren,** sandy spit with chalets and caravans at mouth of R Exe. SX 9676
Dawn Gwynedd 41 E4* ham 4m/6km S of Colwyn Bay. SH 8672
Daw's Green Som 8 A2* loc 3m/4km SW of Taunton. ST 1921
Daws Heath Essex 20 D3 loc 2km S of Rayleigh. TQ 8188
Daw's House Cornwall 4 A3* loc 2m/3km SW of Launceston. SX 3182
Dawsmere Lincs 38 A2 loc 5m/7km N of Long Sutton. TF 4430
Dawyck House Borders 65 H5 hse, park and gardens in R Tweed valley 6m/10km SW of Peebles. NT 1635
Day Green Ches 42 D5* loc 1km S of Hassall Green. SJ 7757
Dayhills Staffs 35 F1/F2* loc 1m NW of Milwich. SJ 9532
Dayhouse Bank H & W 35 F6* loc 4m/6km S of Halesowen. SO 9578
Daylesford Glos 27 F5 ham 4m/6km E of Stow-on-the-Wold. SP 2425
Daywall Salop 34 A1* loc 1km W of Gobowen. SJ 2933
Ddawan Welsh form of Thaw (r), qv.
Ddol Clwyd 41 G4 loc 2km SE of Caerwys. SJ 1471
Ddol Clwyd 41 H6* loc 2km SW of Wrexham. SJ 3149
Ddol Clwyd 42 A6* loc 4m/7km SE of Wrexham. SJ 3845
Ddol Cownwy Powys 33 G3* loc on R Cownwy 2km S of Lake Vyrnwy dam. SJ 0117
Ddraenen Wen, Y Welsh form of Hawthorn, qv.
Ddu 40 D4* r running NW into Conwy Bay at Llanfairfechan, Gwynedd. SH 6775
Ddu 40 D4 r running NE from Llyn Cowlyd Resr into R Conwy SE of Dolgarrog, Gwynedd. SH 7866
Ddwyryd, Y Welsh form of Druid, qv. (The form Druid is a corruption in common use.)
Deacons Som 8 A2* loc 3m/4km NW of Taunton. ST 2028
Deadman's Cross Beds 29 E3/E4* loc 3m/4km NW of Shefford. TL 1141
Deadman's Green Staffs 35 F1* loc 1km E of Checkley. SK 0337
Deadwater Hants 11 E2* loc adjoining Bordon and Bordon Camp to E, 5m/8km W of Hindhead. SU 8035
Deaf Hill Durham 54 C2* vil just S of Trimdon Colliery. NZ 3736
Deal Kent 13 H2 cinque port and resort on E coast 8m/13km NE of Dover. Cas (A.M.) built by Henry VIII. TR 3752
Dean Cumbria 52 B3 vil 5m/7km SW of Cockermouth. NY 0725
Dean Devon 4 D4 vil 1m S of Buckfastleigh. SX 7364
Dean Devon 6 D1* loc 3m/5km S of Ilfracombe. SS 5042
Dean Dorset 9 G3 loc 2m/3km SW of Sixpenny Handley. ST 9715
Dean Hants 10 C3* ham 2km NE of Bishop's Waltham. SU 5619
Dean Lancs 48 B5* loc on Forest of Rossendale. SD 8525
Dean Oxon 27 G5 ham 2m/3km NW of Charlbury. SP 3422
Dean 42 D3 r rising 4m/7km E of Macclesfield, Ches, and flowing NW through Bollington into R Bollin on N side of Wilmslow. SJ 8382
Dean Bank Durham 54 C2 loc adjoining Ferryhill to W. NZ 2832
Dean Clough Reservoir Lancs 48 A4/A5 resr 4m/6km NE of Blackburn. SD 7133
Dean Court Oxon 17 H1* suburban loc 3m/4km W of Oxford. SP 4705
Deane Gtr Manchester 42 C1 dist of Bolton 2km SW of tn centre. SD 6908
Deane Hants 18 A6 ham 6m/9km W of Basingstoke. SU 5450
Dean, East Hants 10 A2 vil on Wilts border 3m/4km NE of Whiteparish. SU 2726
Dean, East W Sussex 11 E4 vil below S Downs 6m/9km NE of Chichester. SU 9013
Deanend Dorset 9 G3* loc 2m/3km W of Sixpenny Handley. ST 9717
Dean Head S Yorks 43 G1* loc 2m/4km SE of Penistone. SE 2600
Deanhead W Yorks 48 C6* ham 3m/4km S of Ripponden. **Deanhead Resr,** small resr 1km SW. SE 0416
Dean Head Reservoirs W Yorks 48 C5* pair of resrs 6m/9km NW of Halifax. SE 0230
Deanland Dorset 9 G3* ham 1m NW of Sixpenny Handley. ST 9918
Deanlane End W Sussex 10 D4* loc on Hampshire border 4m/6km N of Havant. SU 7412
Dean, North, Lower Bucks 18 D2* loc 4m/6km N of High Wycombe. SU 8598
Dean, North, Upper Bucks 18 D2* loc 4m/6km N of High Wycombe. SU 8498
Dean Prior Devon 4 D4 vil on E side of Dartmoor 2m/3km S of Buckfastleigh. SX 7363
Dean Row Ches 42 D3* loc 2m/3km E of Wilmslow. SJ 8681
Deans Lothian 65 G2* W dist of Livingston. **D. Industrial Estate.** NT 0269
Deans Bottom Kent 21 E5* loc 1m W of Bredgar and 3m/5km SW of Sittingbourne. TQ 8660
Deanscales Cumbria 52 B2 ham 3m/5km SW of Cockermouth. NY 0926
Deansgreen Ches 42 C3* loc 2km SE of Lymm. SJ 6985
Deanshanger Northants 28 C4 vil 2m/3km W of Stony Stratford across R Ouse. SP 7639
Deanston Central 72 B4 vil 1m W of Doune across R Teith. Distillery. NN 7101
Dean Street Kent 20 D6 ham 2m/3km SW of Maidstone. TQ 7452
Dean, Upper Beds 29 E1 vil 11m/18km N of Bedford. **Lr Dean** ham 1m NE. TL 0467
Dean Water 76 D6 r in Tayside region running W from Loch Forfar, past Glamis Castle, to R Isla 3m/5km SE of Alyth. NO 2845
Dean, West Wilts 10 A2 vil on Hants border 2m/4km NE of Whiteparish. SU 2527
Dean, West W Sussex 11 E4 vil below S Downs 5m/8km N of Chichester. SU 8612
Deard's End Herts 29 F5* loc adjoining Knebworth to W, 2m/4km S of Stevenage. TL 2420
Dearg Abhainn 70 B1* stream in Argyll, S'clyde region running NW down Gleann Salach to Loch Creran 2m/3km SW of Dallachoilish. NM 9541
Dearham Cumbria 52 B2 suburb 2m/3km E of Maryport. NY 0736
Dearne 44 A1* r rising E of Huddersfield, W Yorks, and flowing SE through Barnsley and into R Don N of Conisbrough, S Yorks. SK 5099
Dearnley Gtr Manchester 48 C6* loc 1m W of Littleborough. SD 9215
Debach Suffolk 31 F3 ham 4m/6km NW of Woodbridge. TM 2454
Debdale Gtr Manchester 42 D2* loc in Manchester 5m/7km SE of city centre. SJ 8995
Debden Essex 30 A4 vil 4m/6km SE of Saffron Walden. Airfield to N. TL 5533
Debden Cross Essex 30 B4 loc 2m/3km W of Thaxted. TL 5832
Debden Green Essex 20 B2* loc at N end of Loughton. TQ 4398
Debden Green Essex 30 B4* loc 2m/4km W of Thaxted. TL 5732
Debdon Lake Nthmb 61 F2* small lake 1m N of Rothbury. NU 0602
Deben 31 G4 r rising to W of Debenham, Suffolk, and flowing SE to Wickham Mkt, then S to Woodbridge, where it forms estuary flowing S into North Sea at Woodbridge Haven 3m/4km NE of Felixstowe. TM 3336
Debenham Suffolk 31 F2 vil on R Deben near its source, 11m/18km N of Ipswich. TM 1763
Deblin's Green H & W 26 C3* ham 4m/6km NE of Gt Malvern. SO 8249
Dechmont Lothian 65 G2* loc 2km SW of Uphall. NT 0470
Decker Hill Salop 34 D3* loc 2km N of Shifnal. SJ 7509
Decoy Broad Norfolk 39 G3* small broad or lake on S side of R Bure 1m N of Woodbastwick. TG 3216
Deddington Oxon 27 H4 vil of Cotswold stone 6m/9km S of Oxford. Remains of cas (A.M.). SP 4631
Dedham Essex 31 E4 vil on R Stour 6m/10km NE of Colchester. TM 0533
Dedham Heath Essex 31 E5* loc 6m/9km NE of Colchester. TM 0631
Dedridge Lothian 65 G2* residential area of Livingston 2km S of tn centre. NT 0666
Dedworth Berks 18 D4* W dist of Windsor. SU 9476
Dee (Dyfrdwy) 41 G3* r flowing from NE end of Bala Lake, Gwynedd, circuitously by Corwen, LLangollen, and Chester into Irish Sea between Pt of Air and Hilbre Pt, Hoylake. Has a long and wide estuary. SJ 1983
Dee 53 F5* r rising on Blea Moor, E of Whernside, N Yorks, and flowing NW to Dent and into R Rawthey 1m SW of Sedbergh, Cumbria. SD 6491
Dee 58 C6 r in Dumfries & Galloway region, issuing from Loch Dee in Glentrool Forest Park, and flowing SE through Clatteringshaws Loch to Loch Ken, then S to Kirkcudbright Bay. NX 6645
Dee 77 H1 r in Grampian region rising at Pools of Dee in the Cairngorms and running E for about 90m/145km to North Sea at Aberdeen. See also Linn of Dee. NJ 9605
Deene Northants 37 E5 vil 4m/6km NE of Corby. **D. Hall,** Tudor home of the Brudenells. SP 9492
Deenethorpe Northants 37 E5 vil 4m/7km NE of Corby. SP 9591
Deepcar S Yorks 43 G2 loc 1m E of Stocksbridge. SK 2897
Deepcut Surrey 18 D5* loc 3m/5km SE of Camberley largely consisting of military barracks. SU 9057
Deepdale Cumbria 53 F6 loc and valley of Deepdale Beck running N into Dentdale SE of Dent. SD 7284
Deepdale N Yorks 48 B1 loc in Langstrothdale 4m/6km NW of Buckden. SD 8979
Deepdale Beck 54 A3 r rising on Bowes Moor, Durham, and flowing E into R Tees at Barnard Castle. NZ 0416
Deepdene Surrey 19 F6 E dist of Dorking. TQ 1749
Deepfields W Midlands 35 F5* loc 3m/5km SE of Wolverhampton tn centre. SO 9394
Deep, Great W Sussex. See Thorney I.
Deepgrove Wyke N Yorks 55 G3* small bay on N side of Sandsend Ness. NZ 8514
Deeping Gate Cambs 37 F3 vil on S bank of R Welland 7m/12km N of Peterborough. TF 1509
Deeping St James Lincs 37 F3 vil on R Welland adjoining Mkt Deeping to E. TF 1509
Deeping St Nicholas Lincs 37 G3 vil 5m/8km SW of Spalding. TF 2116
Deeping, West Lincs 37 F3/F4 vil on R Welland 5m/8km E of Stamford. 17c manor hse. TF 1108
Deep Pit S Yorks 43 H3* loc in Sheffield 2m/3km SE of city centre. SK 3785
Deeps, The Shetland 89 E7 sea area to E of Skelda Ness, Mainland. HU 3241
Deepweir Gwent 16 A3* loc 1km E of Caldicot. ST 4887
Deer 6 C5 r rising N of Chilsworthy, Devon, and flowing S into R Tamar on E side of N Tamerton. SX 3197
Deerdykes S'clyde 64 D2* loc in Cumbernauld 3m/5km SW of tn centre. NS 7172
Deer Hill Reservoir W Yorks 48 D6* resr 2km E of Marsden. SE 0711
Deerhurst Glos 26 D4 vil on E bank of R Severn 7m/11km NW of Cheltenham. Odda's Chapel (A.M.), 11c. SO 8729
Deerhurst Walton Glos 26 D4* loc 3m/5km S of Tewkesbury. SO 8828
Deerness Orkney 89 B7 loc and peninsula at E end of Mainland 8m/13km SE of Kirkwall beyond Deer Sound. HY 5605
Deerness 54 B1 r rising at Tow Law, Durham, and flowing E into R Wear 2m/3km SW of Durham. NZ 2540
Deer Sound Orkney 89 B6 large inlet on N coast of Mainland between Mull Hd (E) and Rerwick Hd (W). HY 50
Deerton Street Kent 21 E5* loc 3m/5km W of Faversham. TQ 9762
Defford H & W 26 D3 vil 3m/4km SW of Pershore. SO 9143
Defynnog Powys 25 E5 vil 1km S of Sennybridge. SN 9227
Deganwy Gwynedd 40 D3 suburb 2m/3km S of Llandudno. Remains of cas on hill. SH 7779
Deighton N Yorks 50 B4 vil 5m/8km S of York. SE 6244
Deighton N Yorks 54 C4 vil 5m/8km N of Northallerton. NZ 3801
Deighton W Yorks 48 D6 loc in Huddersfield 2m/4km NE of tn centre. SE 1619
Deighton, North N Yorks 49 F3 vil 2m/3km N of Wetherby. SE 3951
Deil's Cauldron Tayside 72 B2 chasm containing Falls of Lednock, in course of R Lednock 1m N of Comrie. NN 7623
Deil's Craig Dam Central 64 C1* small resr 1km S of Strathblane. NS 5578
Deil's Dyke D & G 58 C1, D1* series of ancient earthworks of uncertain origin S of Sanquhar. NS 70
Deiniolen Gwynedd 40 C5 vil in slate-quarrying dist 2m/3km N of Llanberis. SH 5763
Delabole Cornwall 3 F1 vil 2m/4km W of Camelford. Old Delabole Slate Quarry on E side of vil. SX 0784
Delamere Ches 42 B4 vil 6m/9km W of Winsford. **D. Forest** is partly wooded area, former hunting reserve, to N and NE. SJ 5668
Delgatie Castle Grampian 83 F2 residence dating from 13c, 2m/3km E of Turriff. **D. Forest** is state forest to SE. Alternative spelling is Delgaty. NJ 7550
Dell W Isles 88 C1* r in N part of Lewis running N into Atlantic Ocean 1km N of S Dell vil and 3m/5km SW of Butt of Lewis. NB 4862
Dell, North W Isles 88 C1* loc between S Dell and Cross, 3m/5km S of Butt of Lewis. NB 4961
Dell Quay W Sussex 11 E4* ham with quay on Chichester Harbour (Chichester Channel), 2m/3km SW of Chichester. SU 8302
Dell, South W Isles 88 C1* vil 4m/6km SW of Butt of Lewis. NB 4861
Delly End Oxon 27 G6* loc 2m/4km N of Witney. SP 3513
Delmonden Green Kent 12 D4* loc 2m/3km W of Hawkhurst. TQ 7330
Delny H'land 87 A8 loc in Ross and Cromarty dist 3m/5km NE of Invergordon. NH 7372
Delph Gtr Manchester 43 E1 loc 4m/7km NE of Oldham. **New D.** loc adjoining to SE. SD 9807
Delph W Midlands 35 F5* loc in Dudley 3m/5km SW of tn centre. SO 9286

Delph 38 B4 artificial branch of R Ouse running from Earith, Cambs, to confluence with New Bedford R, 2m/3km SW of Denver Sluice. TL 5798
Delph Bridge Norfolk 38 A5 rd br spanning R Delph and Old Bedford R at Welney. TL 5293
Delph Reservoir Lancs 47 G6* resr on moors 4m/7km N of Bolton. SD 7015
Delting Shetland 89 E6* dist of Mainland between Dales Voe and Olna Firth. HU 4067
Delves Durham 61 F6* SE suburb of Consett. NZ 1249
Delves, The W Midlands 35 F4* loc 3m/5km NE of W Bromwich tn centre. SP 0295
Delyn 116 admin dist of Clwyd.
Dembleby Lincs 37 F1 ham 5m/9km S of Sleaford. TF 0437
Demelza Cornwall 3 E2* loc 4m/6km E of St Columb Major. SW 9763
Denaby S Yorks 44 A2 vil 5m/9km NE of Rotherham. **D. Main** coal-mining loc 2km E. SK 4899
Denbeath Fife 73 F4* dist of Buckhaven. NT 3598
Denbigh (Dinbych) Clwyd 41 F4 tn on rocky limestone hill above R Clwyd 10m/16km S of Rhyl. Limestone-quarrying, agriculture. Remains of 12c–13c cas (A.M.). SJ 0566
Denbury Devon 5 E4 vil 3m/5km SW of Newton Abbot. SX 8268
Denby Derbys 43 H6 vil 3m/4km S of Ripley. **D. Bottles** loc 1m W. SK 3946
Denby Dale W Yorks 43 G1 tn 8m/12km W of Barnsley. Coal and clay mining, worsted and rug mnfg. SE 2208
Denby, Lower W Yorks 43 G1* loc 1m SE of Denby Dale. SE 2307
Denby, Upper W Yorks 43 G1 vil 1km S of Denby Dale. SE 2207
Denchworth Oxon 17 G2 vil 3m/5km NW of Wantage. SU 3891
Dendron Cumbria 46 D1 vil 3m/5km E of Barrow-in-Furness. SD 2470
Dene 27 G2* r rising on N edge of Cotswold Hills near Edge Hill, Warwicks, and flowing NW into R Avon at Charlecote Park, E of Stratford-upon-Avon. SP 2556
Dene, East S Yorks 43 H2* dist of Rotherham 2km E of tn centre. SK 4493
Denel End Beds 29 E4* N end of Flitwick, 2km S of Ampthill. TL 0335
Deneside Durham 61 H6* W dist of Seaham. NZ 4148
Dene, The Durham 61 F5* loc 2m/3km N of Consett. NZ 1154
Denford Northants 29 E1 vil 2km S of Thrapston. SP 9976
Dengie Essex 21 F2 vil 4m/7km NE of Burnham-on-Crouch. TL 9801
Denham Bucks 19 E3 vil 2m/3km NW of Uxbridge. Suburban loc of **D. Green** 1m N. TQ 0487
Denham Suffolk 30 C2 vil 6m/10km W of Bury St Edmunds. Earthworks of motte and bailey cas 1m NW. Loc of **D. End** 1m N. TL 7561
Denham Suffolk 31 F1 vil 3m/5km E of Eye. Loc of **D. Green** 1km S. Loc of **D. Street** 2km SW. TM 1974
Denhead Fife 73 G3 loc 3m/5km SW of St Andrews. NO 4613
Denhead Grampian 83 G2/H2* loc 2km S of New Leeds. NJ 9952
Denholm Borders 66 C6 vil 5m/8km NE of Hawick. NT 5618
Denholme W Yorks 48 D4 vil 6m/10km W of Bradford. Locs of **D. Clough** and **D. Gate** 1m S. SE 0734
Denio Gwynedd 32 B1* loc adjoining Pwllheli to N. SH 3735
Denmead Hants 10 D4 vil 2m/4km NW of Waterlooville. 1m NW, Rookwood Farm, Tudor and earlier. SU 6512
Dennington Suffolk 31 G2 vil 2m/4km N of Framlingham. TM 2867
Dennis Head Cornwall 2 D5* headland at mouth of Helford R on S side, 8m/13km E of Helston. SW 7825
Dennis Head Orkney 89 C5 headland at E extremity of island of N Ronaldsay, at NE end of Linklet Bay. HY 7955
Dennis Ness Orkney 89 C5* headland at NE end of island of N Ronaldsay. Lighthouse. HY 7855
Dennis Park W Midlands 35 E5 loc 2km N of Stourbridge tn centre. SO 9085
Dennistoun S'clyde 64 D2* dist of Glasgow 2km E of city centre. NS 6165
Denny Central 65 E1 forms one tn with Dunipace, 5m/8km W of Falkirk. Light industries. **Denny Resr** is small resr 1m SW. NS 8182
Denny Hill Glos 26 C5* loc on right bank of R Severn 5m/8km W of Gloucester across r. SO 7516
Denny Island Avon 16 B5* island lying towards N end of Chew Valley Lake. ST 5760
Denny Island 16 A3* rock island in Severn estuary on line of demarcation between Avon (England) and Gwent (Wales). ST 4581
Dennyloanhead Central 65 E1 vil 2m/3km S of Denny. NS 8080
Denny Lodge Hants 10 A4 loc in New Forest 3m/4km SE of Lyndhurst. SU 3305
Denny Priory Cambs. See Waterbeach.
Den of Ogil Reservoir Tayside 77 E4/E5* small resr 3m/5km NW of Tannadice. NO 4361
Denshaw Gtr Manchester 43 E1 loc 5m/8km NE of Oldham. SD 9710
Denside Grampian 77 G2* loc 2m/3km E of Kirkton of Durris. NO 8095
Densole Kent 13 G3* vil 4m/6km N of Folkestone. TR 2141
Denston Suffolk 30 C3 vil 5m/7km N of Clare. TL 7652
Denstone Staffs 35 G1 vil 5m/8km N of Uttoxeter. 1km W, **D. College,** boys' public school. SK 1040
Dent Cumbria 53 F6 small tn in valley of R Dee known as Dentdale, 4m/7km SE of Sedbergh. Cobbled streets. SD 7087
Denton Cambs 37 F5 vil 2km SW of Stilton. TL 1487
Denton E Sussex 12 B6 suburban loc 1m N of Newhaven. TQ 4502
Denton Gtr Manchester 43 E2 tn 4m/6km NE of Stockport. Engineering, storage batteries. SJ 9295
Denton Kent 13 G3 vil 7m/11km N of Folkestone. TR 2147
Denton Kent 20 C4* E dist of Gravesend. TQ 6673
Denton Lincs 36 D2 vil 4m/6km SW of Grantham. **Denton Resr** 1km N. Site of Roman villa 1m SE. SK 8632
Denton Norfolk 39 F5 vil 4m/6km W of Bungay. TM 2788
Denton Northants 28 D2 vil 5m/9km E of Northampton. SP 8357
Denton N Yorks 48 D3* vil 2m/3km NE of Ilkley across R Wharfe. **D. Hall,** 18c hse by Carr of York, in park to SE. SE 1448
Denton Oxon 18 B2 ham 6m/9km SE of Oxford. SP 5902
Denton, East Tyne & Wear 61 G5* suburb 4m/6km W of Newcastle. **W Denton** adjoins to W, **Denton Burn** to S. NZ 1966
Denton Holme Cumbria 59 H5* loc in Carlisle 1km S of city centre. NY 4054
Denton's Green Merseyside 42 B2* NW dist of St Helens. SJ 4996
Denton, Upper Cumbria 60 B5 loc 2km SW of Gilsland. NY 6165
Denver Norfolk 38 B4 vil 1m S of Downham Mkt. **D. Sluice,** 2m/3km W, is control point of fenland drainage system. TF 6101
Denwick Nthmb 67 H6 ham 2km E of Alnwick. NU 2014
Deopham Norfolk 39 E4 vil 4m/6km W of Wymondham. Vil of **D. Green** 1m S. TG 0400
Depden Suffolk 30 C2* loc 6m/10km SW of Bury St Edmunds. TL 7856
Depden Green Suffolk 30 C2* ham 1m W of Chedburgh. TL 7757
Deppers Hill Warwicks 28 A2* loc 2m/3km SW of Southam. SP 3959
Deptford London 20 A4* dist in borough of Lewisham 5m/8km E of Charing Cross. To E is **D. Creek,** stream running into R Thames at Greenwich Reach, opp Isle of Dogs. D. Power Stn is beside mouth of creek to W. TQ 3777
Deptford Tyne & Wear 61 H5* dist of Sunderland on S bank of R Wear 1m NW of tn centre. Contains **D. Industrial Estate.** NZ 3857
Deptford Wilts 9 G1 ham 1km NE of Wylye across r. SU 0138
Derby Derbys 36 A1 industrial city and county tn on R Derwent 35m/56km NE of Birmingham. Cathedral mainly by James Gibbs, 1725. Industries include engineering; aero-engine, rly locomotive and rolling-stock mnfre; pottery. SK 3536
Derbyhaven Isle of Man 46 B6 vil on bay of **Derby Haven,** 2km E of Castletown. SC 2867
Derbyshire 117,119 midland county of England, bounded by Gtr Manchester, Cheshire, Staffordshire, Leicestershire, Nottinghamshire, and S and W Yorkshire. The high steep hills in the N, which include the dramatic scenery of The Peak, are the southern extremities of the Pennines, and provide grazing for sheep and cattle. There is some textile industry in the tns of the N and W. The S of the county is dominated by heavy industry, mining, and quarrying. Chief tns are Derby (the county tn), Ilkeston, and Long Eaton in the S; Chesterfield in the NE; Chapel-en-le-Frith and Glossop in the NW; Bakewell and Matlock in the centre; and Buxton and Ashbourne in the W. Principal rs are the Dove, forming much of the boundary with Staffordshire and noted for scenery and fishing, and the Derwent; the Trent flows through the S corner.
Derby, West Merseyside 42 A2 dist of Liverpool 4m/6km E of city centre. SJ 4092
Dereham, East Norfolk 38 D3 tn 16m/25km W of Norwich. Industries include iron founding, mnfre of agricultural machinery. Large par ch with detached bell tower. Bonner's Cottages, early 16c, pargeted, now museum of local history. TF 9813
Dereham, West Norfolk 38 B4 vil 3m/5km SE of Downham Mkt. TF 6500
Deri Mid Glam 15 F2 vil 2m/3km NW of Bargoed. SO 1201
Dernaglar Loch D & G 57 C6 small loch 4m/7km E of Glenluce. NX 2658
Dernol 25 E1* stream running SE into R Wye 4m/6km S of Llangurig. SN 9274
Derril Devon 6 B5* loc 2m/4km W of Holsworthy. SS 3003
Derrill Water 6 B5* r rising near Pyworthy, Devon, and flowing S into R Tamar 2km NW of N Tamerton. SX 3098
Derringstone Kent 13 G2 vil 6m/10km SE of Canterbury. TR 2049
Derrington Staffs 35 E2 vil 2m/3km W of Stafford. SJ 8922
Derriton Devon 6 C5* loc just SW of Holsworthy. SS 3303
Derry Cairngorm Grampian 76 B2 mt in Cairngorms 2m/3km E of Ben Macdui. Height 3788 ft or 1155 metres. Also known as Cairn Gorm of Derry. NO 0198
Derry Downs London 20 B5* loc in borough of Bromley 1m NE of Orpington. TQ 4767
Derry Hill Wilts 16 D4 ham 3m/4km W of Calne. ST 9570
Derrythorpe Humberside 44 C1* ham on W bank of R Trent 2m/3km S of Keadby. SE 8208
Dersingham Norfolk 38 B2 vil 7m/11km S of Hunstanton. TF 6830
Dervaig S'clyde 68 C4 vil on Mull 5m/8km W of Tobermory. Group of standing stones 1km E. NM 4352
Derventio Cumbria. See Papcastle.
Derventio Derbys. See Chester, Little.
Derwen Clwyd 41 G6 vil 5m/8km N of Corwen. SJ 0750
Derwen Mid Glam 15 E3* loc 2m/3km N of Bridgend. SS 9182
Derwen-fawr Welsh form of Broad Oak, qv.
Derwen-gam Welsh form of Oakford, qv.
Derwen-las Powys 33 E4 ham 2m/3km SW of Machynlleth. SN 7299
Derwent 36 A2 r rising on NE slopes of Bleaklow Hill 6m/10km E of Glossop, Derbys, and flowing S through Derwent and Ladybower Resrs, Baslow, Matlock, Belper, and Derby, and into R Trent at Gt Wilne 3m/5km SW of Long Eaton. SK 4530
Derwent 50 B5 r rising on Fylingdales Moor, S of Whitby, N Yorks, and flowing S to the Vale of Pickering at Ayton, then SW to Malton, then S by Stamford Br to join R Ouse 5m/7km SE of Selby. SE 6728
Derwent 52 A2 r rising in Cumbrian Mts NE of Sca Fell, Cumbria, and flowing N to Derwent Water, then NW to Bassenthwaite Lake, then W by Cockermouth to Solway Firth at Workington. NX 9829
Derwent 61 G5 r formed by confluence of streams about borders of Durham and Nthmb near Hunstanworth and flowing generally NE through Derwent Resr and by Shotley Br and Ebchester to R Tyne at Derwent Haugh, E of Blaydon, county of Tyne & Wear. NZ 2063
Derwent Haugh Tyne & Wear 61 G5* loc at mouth of R Derwent 3m/5km W of Gateshead. NZ 2063
Derwent Reservoir Derbys 43 F2 resr in Derwent Dale between Howden and Ladybower Resrs, 9m/14km E of Glossop across High Peak. SK 1790
Derwent Reservoir 61 E6 large resr in valley of R Derwent on border of Durham and Nthmb 5m/7km W of Consett. NZ 0251
Derwentside 117 admin dist of county of Durham.
Derwent Water Cumbria 52 C3 lake formed by R Derwent SW of Keswick, about 3m/5km long N to S and up to 2km wide E to W. Part owned by NT. NY 2521
Derwydd Dyfed 23 G4 loc 3m/5km S of Llandeilo. SN 6117
Desach 40 B6* stream running N into Caernarvon Bay at Aberdesach, Gwynedd, 8m/12km SW of Caernarvon. SH 4251
Desborough Northants 36 D5/D6 small mnfg tn 5m/8km NW of Kettering. SP 8083
Desford Leics 36 B4 vil 7m/11km E of Leicester. SK 4703
Dessary H'land 74 B3 r in Lochaber dist running E down Glen D. to join R Pean 1km above head of Loch Arkaig. NM 9791
Detchant Nthmb 67 G5 loc 2m/3km NW of Belford. NU 0836
Dethick Derbys 43 H5 loc 2m/4km SE of Matlock. SK 3257
Detling Kent 20 D5 vil 3m/4km NE of Maidstone. County Agricultural Showground 1km NE. TQ 7958
Deuddwr Powys 34 A3* ham 6m/10km N of Welshpool. SJ 2417
Deunant 41 F4* r running N into R Aled 2m/3km NE of Llansannan, Clwyd. SH 9567
Deuxhill Salop 34 D5 loc 4m/6km S of Bridgnorth. SO 6987
Deva Ches. See Chester.
Devauden Gwent 16 A2 vil 4m/7km NW of Chepstow. ST 4898
Deveron 83 E1 r in Grampian region rising S of Cabrach, and flowing generally NE by Huntly and Turriff to Banff Bay on E side of Banff. NJ 6964
Devilla Forest Fife 72 D5* state forest to E of Kincardine-on-Forth. NS 9588
Devil's Arrows, The N Yorks 49 F2* three monoliths, probably Neolithic, at Boroughbridge. SE 3966
Devil's Beef Tub D & G 59 F1 vast semicircular hollow in hills 5m/8km N of Moffat. Source of R Annan. NT 0613
Devil's Bridge (Pontarfynach) Dyfed 24 C1 ham in landscape of crags and wooded glens 10m/16km E of Aberystwyth. SN 7376
Devil's Brook 9 E5 r rising at Lit Ansty in Dorset and flowing S into R Piddle or Trent at Burleston, E of Puddletown. SY 7794
Devil's Chimney Glos 26 D5* rock outcrop on W side of Leckhampton Hill 2m/4km S of Cheltenham. Hill fort at summit. SO 9518
Devil's Ditch or Dyke Cambs 30 B2 ancient military earthwork dating from early Anglo-Saxon times, running from Reach across Newmarket Heath to a point 3m/5km S of Newmarket. TL 6062
Devil's Dyke W Sussex 11 H4 steep declivity in S Downs above vil of Poynings; the subject of legend. Dyke is below a large Iron Age fort. TQ 2611
Devil's Elbow Tayside 76 C3 double hairpin bend, now bypassed, 1km S of Cairnwell Pass on rd from Braemar to Spittal of Glenshee. NO 1476
Devil's Frying Pan, The Cornwall 2 C6*. See Cadgwith.
Devil's Kitchen Gwynedd 40 D5* fissure in rock face on N side of Glyder Fawr. Also known as Twll Du. SH 6358
Devil's Point, The Grampian 76 A2 peak at SE end of Cairn Toul, in Cairngorms. Height 3294 ft or 1004 metres. NN 9795
Devil's Punch Bowl Surrey 11 E2 deep dell, mainly NT, on S side of Hindhead Hill 2m/3km N of Haslemere. SU 8936

Devil's Water 61 E5 r rising on Allendale Common 5m/7km SE of Allendale Tn, Nthmb, and flowing NE into R Tyne 1m W of Corbridge. NY 9764
Devitts Green Warwicks 35 H5* loc 5m/8km E of Coleshill. SP 2790
Devizes Wilts 17 E5 mkt tn 10m/16km SE of Chippenham, on Kennet and Avon Canal at W end of Vale of Pewsey. Large central square. Museum of Wiltshire prehistory. Army barracks to NE at Roundway. SU 0061
Devoke Water Cumbria 52 B5 lake 2m/4km SE of Eskdale Green. SD 1596
Devon 118 large county in SW peninsula of England, bounded by Bristol Channel to N, English Channel to S, Cornwall to W, and Somerset and Dorset to E. Includes western end of Exmoor and the whole of the granite mass of Dartmoor, whose summit, High Willhays, is also the highest point in southern England. Moorland areas apart, the county is largely given over to agriculture, and, on the coast, to fishing and tourism. On Dartmoor there are quarries, and a military training area; and there are china clay workings in the S. Daffodils are grown commercially in R Tamar valley. The chief tns are Exeter, Plymouth, and Torbay in the S, and Barnstaple and Bideford in the N. Chief rs are Exe, Teign, Dart, Avon, Erme, Tamar, and Tavy in the S; and Taw and Torridge in the N. The granite island of Lundy is included in the county for administrative purposes.
Devon 44 C5 r rising near Eaton, Leics, and flowing N into R Trent at Newark-on-Trent, Notts. SK 7853
Devon 72 C5 r rising on borders of Central and Tayside regions and running E down Glen D. to vil of Glendevon, then SE to Crook of D., where it turns sharply to run almost due W to the S side of Menstrie, then S to R Forth 2m/4km W of Alloa. NS 8493
Devonport Devon 4 B5 W dist of Plymouth beside stretch of R Tamar estuary known as the Hamoaze. Naval dockyard. Car ferry to Torpoint. SX 4555
Devonside Central 72 C5 vil on S bank of R Devon opp Tillicoultry. NS 9296
Devoran Cornwall 2 D4 vil at head of Restronguet Creek 4m/6km SW of Truro. SW 7939
Dewchurch, Little H & W 26 A4 vil 5m/9km S of Hereford. SO 5331
Dewi Fawr 23 E4 r rising E of Trelech, Dyfed, and flowing S into R Cynin at St Clears. SN 2816
Dewlish Dorset 9 E4 vil 3m/5km NE of Puddletown. SY 7798
Dewsall H & W 26 A4* loc 4m/7km SW of Hereford. SO 4933
Dewsbury W Yorks 49 E5 tn on R Calder 8m/13km SW of Leeds. Wool textiles, chemicals, engineering. **D. Moor** loc adjoining to W. SE 2421
Dhoo 46 B5* r on Isle of Man rising on Greeba Mt and flowing SE to join R Glass on W side of Douglas, whence the combined stream continues along S side of tn into Douglas harbour. SC 3875
Dhoon Isle of Man 46 C4 loc 2m/3km NE of Laxey. **D. Bay,** small bay at foot of **D. Glen,** 1km SE. SC 4586
Dhoor Isle of Man 46 C4* loc 2km NW of Ramsey. SC 4496
Dhowin Isle of Man 46 B3 loc 1m N of Andreas. NX 4100
Diabaig, Upper and **Lower** H'land 78 F3 two localities on NE side of Loch Torridon, Ross and Cromarty dist. Lr D. is on Loch Diabaig and has a landing stage. Upr D. is 1m E on N shore of Loch Diabaigs Airde. NG 8160
Dial Avon 16 A4* loc 2m/3km NE of Bristol (Lulsgate) Airport and 5m/9km SW of Bristol. ST 5366
Dial Green W Sussex 11 F2* ham 5m/7km NE of Midhurst. SU 9227
Dial Post W Sussex 11 G3 vil 5m/7km NE of Washington. TQ 1519
Dibden Hants 10 B4 vil 2km N of D. Purlieu. SU 4107
Dibden Hill Bucks 19 E2* loc adjoining Chalfont St Giles to S. SU 9992
Dibden Purlieu Hants 10 B4 suburb adjoining Hythe to SW, on edge of New Forest. SU 4106
Dickens' Heath W Midlands 35 G6* loc 3m/5km SW of Solihull. SP 1176
Dicker, Lower E Sussex 12 B5 ham 3m/4km NW of Hailsham. TQ 5311
Dicker, The E Sussex 12 B5 loc 3m/4km W of Hailsham. TQ 5509
Dicker, Upper E Sussex 12 B5 ham 2m/4km W of Hailsham. TQ 5510
Dick Hatteraick's Cave D & G 58 B6 cave on E shore of Wigtown Bay, on NW side of Ravenshall Pt. Largest of several caves in the vicinity. NX 5152
Dickleburgh Norfolk 31 F1 vil 4m/6km NE of Diss. Ham of **D. Moor** 1km N. TM 1682
Didbrook Glos 27 E4 ham 3m/4km NE of Winchcombe. SP 0531
Didcot Oxon 18 A3 tn 10m/16km S of Oxford. SU 5290
Diddington Cambs 29 F2 vil 4m/6km N of St Neots. TL 1965
Diddlebury Salop 34 C5 vil 5m/8km E of Craven Arms. SO 5085
Didley H & W 26 A4* loc 6m/10km SW of Hereford. SO 4532
Didling W Sussex 11 E3 ham 4m/6km SW of Midhurst. SU 8318
Didlington Norfolk 38 C5 par with ch and park 3m/4km NW of Mundford. TL 7796
Didmarton Glos 16 C3 vil 6m/9km SW of Tetbury. ST 8287
Didsbury Gtr Manchester 42 D2 dist of Manchester 5m/8km S of city centre. Locs of **E** and **W Didsbury** to SE and NW respectively. SJ 8490
Diebidale H'land 85 E7 r in Sutherland dist running NE down Glen Diebidale to head of Glen Calvie, qv. **Diebidale Forest** is deer forest extending E and W of r. NH 4686
Digby Lincs 45 E5 vil 6m/9km N of Sleaford. TF 0854
Diggle Gtr Manchester 43 E1 vil 6m/9km E of Oldham. **Diggle Resr,** small resr 1m E. SE 0008
Digley Reservoir W Yorks 43 F1* resr on edge of Peak Dist National Park 2m/4km W of Holmfirth. SE 1007
Digmoor Lancs 42 B1* SE dist of Skelmersdale. SD 4904
Digswell Herts 29 F6 loc at N end of Welwyn Garden City. TL 2315
Digswell Water Herts 19 F1* loc 2km NE of Welwyn Garden City. TL 2414
Dihewyd Dyfed 24 B3 ham 5m/8km SE of Aberaeron. SN 4855
Dikler 27 F5* r rising to NW of Stow-on-the-Wold, Glos, and flowing S into R Windrush 2km SE of Bourton-on-the-Water. SP 1718
Dilham Norfolk 39 G2/G3 vil 5m/7km SE of N Walsham. TG 3325
Dilhorne Staffs 35 F1 vil 2m/4km W of Cheadle. SJ 9743
Dillington Cambs 29 F2* ham 3m/4km SE of Kimbolton. TL 1365
Dilston Nthmb 61 E5 ham 2km SW of Corbridge. **D. Castle** is remains of medieval tower hse with Elizn and later alterations. NY 9763
Dilton Marsh Wilts 16 D6 vil 2m/3km W of Westbury. ST 8449
Diluw 24 D1* r rising 5m/8km W of Llangurig, Powys, and flowing S into R Ystwyth. Throughout its course it forms border between Dyfed and Powys. SN 8475
Dilworth Lancs 47 F4/G4* loc 1m E of Longridge. SD 6137
Dilwyn H & W 26 A2 vil 6m/9km SW of Leominster. SO 4154
Dimple Gtr Manchester 47 G6* loc 1km NW of Egerton. SD 7015
Dimsdale Staffs 42 D6* loc in Newcastle-under-Lyme 2km N of tn centre. SJ 8448
Dinas Dyfed 22 C2 vil 4m/6km E of Fishguard. **Dinas Hd,** headland on coast 2m/3km N, at N end of promontory of **Dinas I.** SN 0138
Dinas Dyfed 23 E3 loc 7m/11km S of Newcastle Emlyn. SN 2730
Dinas Gwynedd 32 B1 ham 2m/3km E of Tudweiliog. SH 2636
Dinas Gwynedd 32 C1* loc at W end of Criccieth. SH 4937
Dinas Mid Glam 15 E2* loc 4m/7km W of Pontypridd. ST 0091
Dinas Dinlle Gwynedd 40 B5* loc on coast 1m W of Llandwrog. Site of ancient British fort at S end. SH 4356
Dinas-fach Dyfed 22 B3/B4* headland on St Brides Bay 5m/8km E of St David's. SM 8222
Dinas-fawr Dyfed 22 B3/B4 headland (NT) on St Brides Bay 4m/6km E of St David's. SM 8122
Dinas Gynfor Gwynedd 40 B2* site of Iron Age fort (NT) on Llanlleiana Hd, at northernmost point of Anglesey (excluding Middle Mouse rock). SH 3895
Dinas Head Cornwall 2 D1* headland on N coast on SW side of Trevose Hd. SW 8476
Dinas Mawddwy Gwynedd 33 F3 ham 8m/13km E of Dolgellau. SH 8514
Dinas Oleu Gwynedd 32 D3* cliffland (NT) at S end of Barmouth, overlooking Barmouth Bay. The first property acquired by the National Trust (1895). SH 6115
Dinas Powis (Dinas Powys) S Glam 15 F4 suburb 2m/3km W of Penarth. Site of ancient hill fort 1km N. Remains of medieval cas. ST 1571
Dinas Reservoir Dyfed 33 E6* resr in course of R Rheidol 3m/5km N of Devil's Br. SN 7482
Dinas Trefni Gwynedd 40 B5* headland at S end of Aberffraw Bay, W coast of Anglesey. SH 3665
Dinbych Welsh form of Denbigh, qv.
Dinbych-y-pysgod Welsh form of Tenby, qv.
Dinchope, Lower Salop 34 B5* loc 2m/3km NE of Craven Arms. SO 4584
Dinchope, Upper Salop 34 B5* loc 2m/3km E of Craven Arms. SO 4583
Dinckley Lancs 47 G4 loc 2m/4km W of Whalley. SD 6936
Dinder Som 16 B6 vil 2m/3km SE of Wells. ST 5744
Din Dryfol Burial-chamber Gwynedd. See Aberffraw.
Dinedor H & W 26 A4 vil 3m/4km SE of Hereford. SO 5376
Dinefwr 118 admin dist of Dyfed.
Dines Green H & W 26 C2* W dist of Worcester. SO 8255
Dingestow (Llanddingad) Gwent 26 A6 vil 4m/6km SW of Monmouth. SO 4510
Dingle Merseyside 42 A3* dist of Liverpool 3m/4km SE of city centre. SJ 3687
Dingle Reservoir Lancs 47 G6* small resr next to Springs Resr 4m/6km NW of Bolton. SD 6914
Dingleton Borders 66 C5* loc adjoining Melrose to S. NT 5433
Dingley Northants 36 D5 vil 2m/4km E of Mkt Harborough. SP 7787
Dingwall H'land 81 E2 chief tn of Ross and Cromarty dist at head of Cromarty Firth, 11m/18km NW of Inverness. NH 5458
Din Lligwy Gwynedd 40 B3* remains of 4c vil (A.M.) near E coast of Anglesey, 1m W of Moelfre. See also Capel Lligwy, Lligwy Bay. SH 4986
Dinmael Clwyd 33 G1* loc nearly 1m W of Maerdy. SJ 0044
Dinmore H & W 26 A3* loc 7m/11km N of Hereford. SO 4850
Dinnet Grampian 77 E2 loc on N side of R Dee 6m/10km E of Ballater. Muir of Dinnet is flat area to W. NO 4598
Dinnington Som 8 C3 vil 3m/5km SE of Ilminster. ST 4012
Dinnington S Yorks 44 A3 coal-mining loc 6m/9km NW of Worksop. SK 5285
Dinnington Tyne & Wear 61 G4 vil 3m/4km E of Ponteland. NZ 2073
Dinorben Clwyd 41 F4* Iron Age hill fort W of St George. SH 9775
Dinorwic Gwynedd 40 C5 vil in slate-quarrying dist 2km SE of Deiniolen. SH 5961
Dinsdale, Low Durham 54 C4 ham on R Tees 4m/7km SE of Darlington. NZ 3411
Dinsdale, Over N Yorks. See Over Dinsdale.
Dinting Vale Derbys 43 E2* loc 2km W of Glossop. **Hr Dinting** loc 1km E. SK 0194
Dinton Bucks 18 C1 vil 4m/6km SW of Aylesbury. SP 7611
Dinton Wilts 9 G1 vil 5m/8km W of Winton. D. Park, Phillipps Hse, and Hyde's Hse are NT properties. SU 0131
Dinworthy Devon 6 C4* ham 2km NW of Holsworthy. SS 3115
Dionard 84 D2 r of Sutherland dist, H'land, rising on Reay Forest and running N down **Strath Dionard** into Kyle of Durness. NC 3661
Dipford Som 8 A2* ham 2m/3km SW of Taunton. ST 2022
Dipley Hants 18 C5* loc 2m/3km W of Hartley Wintney. SU 7457
Dippen S'clyde 63 E4 vil near E coast of Kintyre, 4m/6km N of Saddell. **D. Bay** to S. NR 7937
Dippenhall Surrey 11 E1* loc 2m/3km W of Farnham. SU 8146
Dippin Head S'clyde 63 G5 headland at SE end of Arran 2m/4km S of Whiting Bay. NS 0522
Dipple S'clyde 56 C3* loc on coast 2m/3km S of Turnberry. NS 2002
Diptford Devon 4 D5 vil 3m/5km SE of S Brent. SX 7256
Dipton Durham 61 F6 vil 3m/5km NE of Consett. NZ 1553
Diptonmill Nthmb 61 E5* loc on W Dipton Burn 2m/3km S of Hexham. NY 9260
Dirleton Lothian 66 C1 vil 2m/4km W of N Berwick. Massive ruins of 13c cas (A.M.). NT 5184
Dirrie More H'land 85 C8 pass between Loch Glascarnoch and Strath More, Ross and Cromarty dist, carrying rd from Dingwall to Ullapool. Height 915 ft or 279 metres. NH 2475
Dirrington Great Law Borders 66 D3 conical hill on Lammermuir, 2m/3km S of Longformacus. **Dirrington Little Law,** another conical hill 2km SW. Heights respectively 1309 ft or 399 metres and 1191 ft or 363 metres. NT 6954
Dirt Pot Nthmb 53 G1* ham 1km NW of Allenheads. NY 8546
Discoed Powys 25 G2 loc 2m/4km W of Presteigne. SO 2764
Diserth Welsh form of Dyserth, qv.
Diseworth Leics 36 A2 vil 6m/10km NW of Loughborough. SK 4524
Disgynfa 33 G2* one of the headwaters of R Rhaeadr, rising in Berwyn Mts SW of Moel Sych and flowing E to Pistyll Rhaeadr, 4m/6km NW of Llanrhaeadr-ym-Mochnant, Clwyd. SJ 0729
Dishforth N Yorks 49 F1 vil 4m/7km N of Boroughbridge. Airfield to S. SE 3873
Dishley Leics 36 B2* loc 2m/3km NW of Loughborough. SK 5121
Disley Ches 43 E3 tn 2m/3km W of New Mills. **Hr Disley** loc adjoining to SE. SJ 9784
Diss Norfolk 39 E6 small mkt tn on R Waveney 19m/31km SW of Norwich. Industries include agriculture and agricultural engineering. TM 1180
Disserth Powys 24 E2 loc on R Ithon 2m/4km SW of Llandrindod Wells. SO 0358
Distington Cumbria 52 A3 loc 3m/5km S of Workington. NY 0023
Ditchampton Wilts 9 G1* loc adjoining Wilton to N. SU 0831
Ditcheat Som 8 D1 vil 3m/5km NW of Castle Cary. ST 6236
Ditchend Brook 9 H3* stream rising in New Forest 5m/8km E of Fordingbridge, Hants, and flowing W into R Avon 1km S of the tn. SU 1413
Ditchingham Norfolk 39 G5 vil 2km N of Bungay. TM 3391
Ditchley Oxon 27 G5 loc 3m/4km NE of Charlbury. D. Park, 18c mansion by James Gibbs, now Anglo-American conference and study centre. Sites of Roman villas to SE. SP 3921
Ditchling E Sussex 12 A5 large vil 3m/4km SE of Burgess Hill. 2km S on S Downs, **D. Beacon** (partly NT), noted viewpoint and hill fort. TQ 3215
Ditherington Salop 34 C3* NE dist of Shrewsbury. SJ 5014
Ditteridge Wilts 16 C4 ham 5m/8km NE of Bath. ST 8169
Dittisham Devon 5 E5 vil to S and W of R Dart estuary 3m/4km N of Dartmouth. SX 8655
Ditton Ches 42 B3 dist of Widnes 2km W of tn centre. SJ 4985
Ditton Kent 20 D5 vil forming part of industrial and residential development 3m/5km NW of Maidstone. TQ 7157
Ditton Green Cambs 30 B2 vil 3m/5km S of Newmarket. TL 6558
Ditton, Little Cambs 30 B2* ham 3m/5km SE of Newmarket. TL 6658
Ditton Priors Salop 34 C5 vil 7m/11km S of Much Wenlock. SO 6089
Divach Falls H'land 81 E4 waterfall in course of Divach Burn, Inverness dist, 2m/3km SW of Drumnadrochit. NH 4927
Divelish 9 E3* r rising near Woolland in Dorset and flowing N into R Stour 1m NW of Sturminster Newton. ST 7715
Divie 82 A3 r in Grampian region running N to join Dorback Burn and continue N to R Findhorn 6m/10km S of Forres. NJ 0049
Dixton Glos 27 E4* ham below W slope of D. Hill 3m/5km NW of Winchcombe. SO 9830
Dixton Gwent 16 A6* loc adjoining Monmouth to NE. SO 5113
Dizzard Cornwall 6 A5* loc near N coast 6m/9km SW of Bude. Valley running

down to sea is NT property. 1km NW is **Dizzard Pt,** headland at S end of Bude Bay. SX 1698

Dobcross Gtr Manchester 43 E1* vil 4m/7km E of Oldham. SD 9906

Dobwalls Cornwall 3 G2 vil 3m/4km W of Liskeard. SX 2165

Doccombe Devon 7 F6 ham 2m/3km E of Moretonhampstead. SS 7786

Dochanassie H'land 74 C3* locality on SE shore of Loch Lochy in Lochaber dist, opp Bunarkaig. NN 2085

Dochart 71 G2 r in Central region running NE down Glen Dochart to join R Lochay at head of Loch Tay. NN 5733

Dochgarroch H'land 81 F3 locality on Caledonian Canal 4m/7km SW of Inverness. NH 6140

Dockeney Norfolk 39 G5* loc 1km SW of Geldeston. TM 3891

Dockenfield Surrey 11 E1* loc 4m/7km S of Farnham. SU 8240

Dockens Water 9 H3* stream rising in New Forest and flowing SW into R Avon 1km N of Ringwood, Hants. SU 1406

Docker Cumbria 53 E5* loc 4m/6km NE of Kendal. SD 5695

Docker Lancs 47 F1* ham 4m/6km SW of Kirkby Lonsdale. SD 5774

Docking Norfolk 38 C1 vil 11m/17km NW of Fakenham. TF 7637

Docklow H & W 26 B2 vil 4m/7km E of Leominster. SO 5657

Dockray Cumbria 52 C1* loc 2km NE of Wigton. NY 2649

Dockray Cumbria 52 D3 ham on Aira Beck 4m/6km S of Troutbeck. NY 3921

Dockroyd W Yorks 48 C4* loc 2m/4km SW of Keighley. SE 0338

Dock Tarn Cumbria 52 C3* small lake 1m E of Rosthwaite. NY 2714

Dodbrooke Devon 4 D6* E dist of Kingsbridge. SX 7344

Doddenham H & W 26 C2* ham 6m/10km W of Worcester. SO 7556

Dodd Fell N Yorks 53 G6 mt 4m/6km SW of Hawes. Height 2189 ft or 667 metres. SD 8484

Doddinghurst Essex 20 C2 vil 3m/5km N of Brentwood. TQ 5999

Doddington Cambs 37 H5 vil 3m/5km N of Chatteris. TL 3990

Doddington Ches 42 C6* loc 5m/8km SE of Nantwich. 15c cas and 18c hall. SJ 7046

Doddington Kent 21 E5 vil 4m/7km SE of Sittingbourne. TQ 9357

Doddington Lincs 44 D4 vil 5m/8km W of Lincoln. SK 9070

Doddington Nthmb 67 F5 vil 3m/4km N of Wooler. NT 9932

Doddington Salop 34 C6 vil 4m/6km W of Cleobury Mortimer. SO 6176

Doddington, Great Northants 28 D2 vil 2m/4km SW of Wellingborough. SP 8864

Doddiscombsleigh Devon 5 E2 vil 6m/9km SW of Exeter. SX 8586

Dodd Reservoir Nthmb 53 G1* small resr 1m NW of Allenheads. NY 8446

Doddshill Norfolk 38 C2* loc adjoining Dersingham to E. TF 6930

Doddycross Cornwall 3 G2* loc 4m/6km SE of Liskeard. SX 3062

Dodford H & W 26 D1 vil 2m/3km NW of Bromsgrove. SO 9372

Dodford Northants 28 B2 vil 3m/5km SE of Daventry. SP 6160

Dod, Great Cumbria 52 D3 mt in Lake Dist 6m/9km SE of Keswick. Height 2807 ft or 856 metres. NY 3426

Dodington Avon 16 C3 ham 2m/3km SE of Chipping Sodbury. Loc of **D. Ash** 1m S. ST 7480

Dodington Som 7 H1 ham at foot of Quantock Hills 2km NW of Nether Stowey. ST 1740

Dodleston Ches 42 A5 vil 4m/7km SW of Chester. Remains of motte and bailey cas. SJ 3661

Dodman Point Cornwall 3 E4 headland (NT) on S coast 4m/6km S of Mevagissey, at E end of Veryan Bay. SX 0039

Dodmarsh H & W 26 B3* loc 4m/7km NE of Hereford. SO 5743

Dodscott Devon 6 D3 loc 3m/5km E of Torrington. SS 5419

Dods Leigh Staffs 35 F1* ham 1m SW of Ch Leigh. SK 0134

Dodworth S Yorks 43 G1 colliery tn 2m/3km W of Barnsley. **D. Bottom** loc adjoins to S. **D. Green** loc adjoins to SW. SE 3105

Doe H'land 80 C6 r in Inverness dist rising on Glenaffric Forest and running SE to Glen Moriston 3m/5km E of dam of Loch Cluanie. NH 2211

Doe 47 G1 r rising E of Whernside, N Yorks, and flowing SW, underground in the vicinity of Chapel le Dale, to join Kingsdale Beck at Ingleton and form R Greta. Series of waterfalls at Beezley Falls and Snow Falls. SD 6973

Doe Bank W Midlands 35 D4 loc 1km N of Sutton Coldfield tn centre. SP 1297

Doe Green Ches 42 B3* loc in W part of Warrington. SJ 5587

Doehole Derbys 43 H5* loc 4m/6km E of Matlock. SK 3558

Doe Lea Derbys 44 A4* loc 1km SE of Heath. SK 4566

Doffcocker Gtr Manchester 47 G6* dist of Bolton 2m/3km NW of tn centre. SD 6910

Dogdyke Lincs 45 F5 vil 3m/5km E of Billinghay. TF 2055

Dog Fall H'land 80 C4 waterfall in Glen Affric 1m below Loch Beneveian, Inverness dist. NH 2828

Dog Hill Gtr Manchester 43 E1* loc 3m/5km NE of Oldham. SD 9509

Dog Hillock Tayside 76 D4/77 E4 hill 3m/5km E of Rottal in Glen Clova. Height 2369 ft or 722 metres. NO 4269

Dog Kennel Pond S Yorks 43 H2* small lake 3m/4km NW of Rotherham. SK 4096

Dog Lane Norfolk 39 F3* loc 1km W of Horsford. TG 1815

Dogley Lane W Yorks 48 D6* loc 3m/5km SE of Huddersfield. SE 1814

Dogmersfield Hants 18 C6 vil 3m/5km NE of Odiham. SU 7852

Dogs, Isle of London 20 A4* dist in borough of Tower Hamlets 5m/8km E of Charing Cross. Though not an island, the dist is bounded by R Thames on S, E, and W sides, and contains extensive docks at Millwall. TQ 3878

Dogsthorpe Cambs 37 G4* loc in Peterborough 2m/3km N of city centre. TF 1901

Dogtail End H & W 27 E2* loc adjoining Astwood Bank to N, 3m/5km S of Redditch. SP 0463

Dog Village Devon 7 G5* vil adjacent to Broad Clyst 5m/8km NE of Exeter. SX 9896

Doilinn Head W Isles 88 D4* headland on W coast of Barra 3m/4km W of Castlebay. NL 6299

Dolanog Powys 33 G3 ham on R Vyrnwy 5m/7km NW of Llanfair Caereinion. SJ 0612

Dolau Mid Glam 15 E3 vil adjoining Llanharen to S, 6m/10km E of Bridgend. ST 0082

Dolau Powys 25 F2* loc nearly 1m W of Llanfihangel Rhydieithon. SO 1467

Dolaucothi Estate. See Pumsaint, Dyfed.

Dolbadarn Castle Gwynedd. See Llanberis.

Dolbenmaen Gwynedd 32 C1 ham 5m/7km NW of Portmadoc. Motte marks site of Norman cas. SH 5043

Dolemeads Avon 16 C5* E dist of Bath. ST 7564

Doley Staffs 34 D2* loc 2m/3km NW of Adbaston. SJ 7429

Dolfor Powys 33 G5 ham 3m/5km S of Newtown. SO 1087

Dolforwyn Castle Powys 33 H4/H5* ruined cas (A.M.), probably 13c, above R Severn 2m/3km SE of Betws Cedewain. SO 1595

Dolgarrog Gwynedd 40 D4 vil 6m/10km S of Conwy. Aluminium works. SH 7667

Dolgellau Gwynedd 33 E3 small mkt tn and resort on R Wnion 17m/27km SW of Bala. SH 7217

Dolgoch Gwynedd 32 D4 loc 5m/8km NE of Tywyn. SH 6504

Dol-gran Dyfed 24 A4* loc 2km SW of Pencader. SN 4334

Doll H'land 87 B6 loc 2km W of Brora on E coast of Sutherland dist. NC 8803

Dollar Central 72 D4 small tn at foot of Ochil Hills 6m/10km NE of Alloa. D. Academy is school opened in 1818. Colliery to E. NS 9697

Dollar Law Borders 65 H5 mt 5m/8km SE of Drumelzier. Height 2680 ft or 817 metres. NT 1727

Dolley Green Powys 25 G2* loc 2m/3km W of Presteigne. SO 2865

Dollis Hill London 19 F3* loc in borough of Brent 6m/10km NW of Charing Cross. TQ 2286

Dollywaggon Pike Cumbria 52 D4 mt in Lake Dist 2km S of Helvellyn. Height 2810 ft or 856 metres. NY 3413

Dolor Point Cornwall 2 D6* headland at Coverack on E coast of Lizard peninsula. SW 7818

Dolphin Clwyd 41 G4* vil 2km S of Holywell. SJ 1973

Dolphinholme Lancs 47 F3 ham 6m/9km SE of Lancaster. SD 5153

Dolphinton S'clyde 65 G4 vil 7m/11km NE of Biggar. NT 1046

Dolton Devon 6 D4 vil 7m/11km SE of Torrington. SS 5712

Dolwen Clwyd 41 E4 ham 4m/6km SE of Colwyn Bay. SH 8874

Dolwen Dyfed 33 E6* loc on N side of Goginan, 4m/7km NW of Devil's Br. SN 6881

Dolwen Reservoir Clwyd 41 F4* small resr 1km W of Llannefydd. SH 9770

Dolwyddelan Gwynedd 40 D6 vil on R Lledr 5m/7km SW of Betws-y-coed. Slate-quarrying. To W is keep of Norman cas (A.M.). SH 7352

Dolybont Dyfed 32 D5 loc 2m/3km SE of Borth. SN 6288

Dolywern Clwyd 34 A1 ham on R Ceiriog 4m/7km W of Chirk. SJ 2237

Domgay Powys 34 A3* loc 1m E of Llandysilio. SJ 2819

Dominion Estate Leics 36 B4* housing estate on W edge of Leicester 3m/4km from city centre. SK 5405

Don 48 B5* r rising on Boulsworth Hill, E of Burnley, Lancs, and flowing W into R Calder at Burnley. SD 8432

Don 50 C5 r rising W of Dunford Br, S Yorks, and flowing E to Penistone, then SE to Sheffield, then NE by Rotherham, Mexborough, and Doncaster to join R Ouse at Goole, Humberside. SE 7422

Don 83 G5 r in Grampian region rising 7m/11km S of Tomintoul and running E by Alford and Inverurie to North Sea on N side of Aberdeen. NJ 9509

Donan H'land. Also Castle Donan. See Eilean Donan.

Doncaster S Yorks 44 B1 tn on R Don on site of Roman fort of *Danum,* 17m/27km NE of Sheffield on E edge of S Yorks coalfield. Industries include rly workshops, rayon mnfre, wire rope mnfre, confectionery esp butter-scotch. Racecourse on E side of tn with grandstand by Carr of York, 1776. Airport to SE. SE 5703

Dones Green Ches 42 B3* loc 4m/6km NW of Northwich. SJ 6077

Donhead St Andrew Wilts 9 F2 vil 4m/6km E of Shaftesbury. ST 9124

Donhead St Mary Wilts 9 F2 vil 3m/5km E of Shaftesbury. ST 9024

Donibristle Industrial Estate Fife 65 G1* 2m/3km E of Inverkeithing and 1m N of **D. Bay.** NT 1584

Doniert Stone Cornwall. See St Cleer.

Doniford Som 7 H1 ham on coast 1m E of Watchet. **D. Stream** is r rising on Quantock Hills and flowing NW into Bristol Channel at Doniford. ST 0842

Donington Lincs 37 G1 vil 9m/14km N of Spalding. **Donington S Ings** loc 1m S. TF 2035

Donington Salop 35 E4 loc 8m/12km NW of Wolverhampton. SJ 8004

Donington le Heath Leics 36 A3 loc 2km S of Coalville. SK 4212

Donington on Bain Lincs 45 F3 vil 6m/10km SW of Louth. TF 2382

Donisthorpe Leics 35 H3 vil 3m/5km SW of Ashby de la Zouch. SK 3114

Donkey Street Kent 13 F4* loc just E of Burmarsh. TR 1032

Donkey Town Surrey 18 D5 loc 2m/3km SE of Bagshot. SU 9360

Don, Little 43 G2* r rising on Harden Moor, W of Langsett, S Yorks, and flowing E through Langsett and Underbank Resrs, and through Stocksbridge into R Don on the E side of Stocksbridge. SK 2997

Donna Nook Lincs 45 H2 promontory on North Sea coast 2m/3km NE of N Somercotes. TF 4399

Donnington Berks 17 H4 N suburb of Newbury. **D. Castle** (A.M.) has 14c gatehouse. SU 4668

Donnington Glos 27 F4 vil 2m/3km N of Stow-on-the-Wold. SP 1928

Donnington H & W 26 C4* loc 2m/4km S of Ledbury. SO 7034

Donnington Salop 34 C3/C4* loc 1m E of Wroxeter. SJ 5807

Donnington Salop 34 D3 urban loc 2m/3km N of Oakengates. **D. Wood** loc 1m S. SJ 7013

Donnington W Sussex 11 E4 ham 2m/3km S of Chichester. SU 8502

Donolly Reservoir Lothian 66 D2* small resr 3m/4km E of Gifford. NT 5768

Donwell Tyne & Wear 61 G5* NW dist of Washington. NZ 2958

Donyatt Som 8 B3 vil 2km W of Ilminster. ST 3314

Doon 56 D2 r in Strathclyde region issuing from Loch Doon and flowing NW through Bogton Loch, Patna, and Dalrymple to Firth of Clyde at S end of Ayr. See also Alloway. NS 3219

Doonfoot S'clyde 56 D2* loc on Firth of Clyde at mouth of R Doon, on S side of Ayr. NS 3219

Dorback Burn H'land 82 A5 r in Badenoch and Strathspey dist running NW to R Nethy 2km SE of Nethy Br. NJ 0119

Dorback Burn 81 H3 r in Grampian region running N from Lochindorb to join R Divie and flow into R Findhorn 6m/10km S of Forres. NJ 0047

Dorchester Dorset 9 E5 county tn on R Frome 7m/12km N of Weymouth. SY 6990

Dorchester Oxon 18 B2 vil on R Thame near its confluence with R Thames; 4m/6km NW of Wallingford. Roman tn. Medieval abbey. SU 5794

Dordale H & W 26 D1* loc 3m/5km NW of Bromsgrove. SO 9274

Dordon Warwicks 35 H4 vil 3m/5km NW of Atherstone. SK 2600

Dore S Yorks 43 G3 dist of Sheffield 5m/8km SW of city centre. SK 3081

Dore 25 H5 r rising E of Hay-on-Wye and flowing SE down Golden Valley and into R Monnow S of Pontrilas, H & W. SO 3926

Dore Holm Shetland 89 D6* small island off W coast of Mainland to SE of Stenness. HU 2176

Dores H'land 81 F4 vil in Inverness dist on E side of Loch Ness 2m/3km S of NE end of loch. NH 5934

Dorket Head Notts 44 B6 loc 5m/8km N of Nottingham. SK 5947

Dorking Surrey 19 F6 tn below N Downs 11m/17km E of Guildford. TQ 1649

Dorley's Corner Suffolk 31 G2* loc 2m/3km N of Saxmundham. TM 3865

Dorlin H'land 68 E2* locality on S side of Loch Moidart in Lochaber dist, 5m/8km N of Salen. See also Tioram Castle. NM 6672

Dormans Land Surrey 12 A3 vil 3m/4km N of E Grinstead. TQ 4042

Dormanstown Cleveland 55 E3 loc adjoining Redcar to SW. NZ 5823

Dormer's Wells London 19 F3* loc in borough of Ealing 1m NE of Southall. TQ 1380

Dormington H & W 26 B3 vil 5m/7km E of Hereford. SO 5840

Dormston H & W 27 E2 ham 6m/10km W of Alcester. SO 9857

Dorn Glos 27 F4* loc 1m N of Moreton-in-Marsh. SP 2034

Dorn 27 H5 r rising N of Heythrop, Oxon, and flowing generally SE into R Glyme 2m/3km N of Woodstock. SP 4419

Dornell Loch D & G 58 C5* small loch 4m/7km NW of Castle Douglas. NX 7065

Dorney Bucks 18 D4 vil 3m/4km W of Slough. Loc of **D. Reach** on R Thames 1m W. SU 9279

Dornie H'land 79 F6 vil in Skye and Lochalsh dist on E side of entrance to Loch Long, 8m/12km E of Kyle of Lochalsh. NG 8826

Dornoch H'land 87 B7 small tn in Sutherland dist on N shore of **D. Firth** 12m/19km E of Bonar Br. 13c cathedral, rebuilt 19c. **Dornoch Pt** is headland 2km S. Firth marks border between Ross & Cromarty and Sutherland dists and runs from Bonar Br out to Tarbat Ness, 22m/36km. NH 7989

Dornock D & G 59 G4 vil 3m/4km E of Annan. NY 2366

Dorridge W Midlands 35 G6 dist of Solihull 3m/5km S of tn centre. SP 1675

Dorrington Lincs 45 E5 vil 5m/7km N of Sleaford. TF 0852
Dorrington Salop 34 B4 vil 6m/10km S of Shrewsbury. SJ 4702
Dorset W Yorks 49 E4* loc in Harehills dist of Leeds 2m/3km NE of city centre. SE 3235
Dorset 118, 119 county in SW England, bounded by the English Channel and the counties of Devon, Somerset, Wiltshire and Hampshire. Hilly, with chalk downs. Noted for agricultural and dairy produce. There are quarries on Portland and Purbeck. The chief coastal tns are Christchurch, Bournemouth, Poole, Swanage, Weymouth, and Lyme Regis. Inland are Dorchester, the county tn; and Wimborne, Shaftesbury, Gillingham, Blandford, and the former ports of Bridport and Wareham. Among numerous minor rs are the Stour, Frome, and Piddle or Trent. There are many prehistoric and Roman remains. The county forms the main part of the Wessex of Thomas Hardy.
Dorsington Warwicks 27 F3 vil 6m/9km SW of Stratford-upon-Avon. SP 1349
Dorstone H & W 25 G4 vil 6m/9km E of Hay-on-Wye. Arthur's Stone (A.M.), burial chamber 1km N. SO 3141
Dorton Bucks 28 B6 vil 6m/9km NW of Thame. SP 6814
Doseley Salop 34 D4* loc 1km SW of Dawley. SJ 6706
Dosthill Staffs 35 H4 loc in Tamworth 3m/4km S of tn centre. SK 2100
Dottery Dorset 8 C4 loc 2m/3km N of Bridport. SY 4595
Doublebois Cornwall 3 F2* loc 4m/6km W of Liskeard. SX 1964
Double Dykes D & G 57 B8* earthworks, supposedly Pictish defence works, on neck of land 2km W of Mull of Galloway. NX 1430
Douchary H'land 85 C7 r on borders of Ross & Cromarty and Sutherland dists, running N down **Glen Douchary** into Rhiddoraoh R above Loch Achall, E of Ullapool. NH 2593
Doughton Glos 16 D3* loc 2km SW of Tetbury. ST 8791
Douglas Isle of Man 46 B5 port, resort, seat of government and chief tn of the island, on E coast 19m/30km S of Pt of Ayre and 14m/23km NE of Calf of Man. Situated on **Douglas Bay,** which extends from **Douglas Hd** northwards to Onchan Hd. SC 3875
Douglas S'clyde 65 E5 small tn with industrial estate, 8m/13km S of Lanark. Coal-mining in vicinity. St Bride's Ch (A.M.) is 12c chancel in churchyard. Fragment of **D. Castle** to NE. **D. Water** is r rising 7m/11km SW and flowing past tn, and past vil of D. Water 4m/7km NE, to R Clyde 3m/4km SE of Lanark. NS 8330
Douglas 47 E5 r rising near Wigan, Gtr Manchester, and flowing NW into R Ribble estuary opp Freckleton, Lancs. Lower reaches known also as R Asland. SD 4326
Douglas Hill Gwynedd 40 C5* loc 2km W of Bethesda. SH 6065
Douglastown Tayside 76 D6/77 E6 vil 3m/5km SW of Forfar. NO 4147
Douglas Water S'clyde 70 C4 r in Argyll running E to Loch Fyne 3m/5km S of Inveraray. NN 0704
Douglas Water 71 E5 r in S'clyde region running E down Glen Douglas to Loch Lomond at Inverbeg. NS 3498
Doulting Som 16 B6 vil 2m/3km E of Shepton Mallet. ST 6443
Dounby Orkney 89 A6 vil on Mainland 6m/10km NW of Finstown. HY 2920
Doune Central 72 B4 vil 4m/6km W of Dunblane. **D. Castle** is partially restored 15c cas to S beside R Teith. See also Braes of D. NN 7201
Doune Hill S'clyde 71 E5 mt 5m/7km S of Arrochar. Height 2409 ft or 734 metres. NS 2997
Dounepark S'clyde 56 B4 S dist of Girvan. NX 1897
Dounreay H'land 86 C1 loc on N coast of Caithness dist 8m/13km W of Thurso. Site of Experimental Reactor Establishment of Atomic Energy Authority. NC 9867
Dousland Devon 4 C4 vil on W edge of Dartmoor 5m/8km SW of Tavistock. SX 5368
Dovaston Salop 34 A2 loc 7m/11km SE of Oswestry. SJ 3421
Dove 31 F1 r rising near Mendlesham, Suffolk, and flowing NE past Eye into R Waveney 1km N of Hoxne. TM 1778
Dove 35 H2 r rising on borders of Derbys and Staffs 4m/6km SW of Buxton and flowing S to Uttoxeter then SE into R Trent at Newton Solney, 3m/5km NE of Burton upon Trent. SK 2726
Dove 43 H1* r rising SW of Barnsley, S Yorks, and flowing E into R Dearne on S side of Darfield. SE 4103
Dove 55 F6 r rising on Cleveland Hills 4m/6km SE of Ingleby Greenhow, N Yorks, and flowing S into R Rye 3m/5km E of Nunnington. SE 7178
Dovecot Merseyside 42 A2* dist of Liverpool 5m/8km E of city centre. SJ 4191
Dove Cottage Cumbria. See Grasmere.
Dove Dale 43 F5 stretch of R Dove valley on Derbys–Staffs border between Hartington and Thorpe, in Peak Dist National Park. The river flows between steep limestone cliffs, wooded in parts. Much NT property on both banks. SK 15
Dove Holes Derbys 43 F3 vil 3m/5km N of Buxton. Extensive quarries in Doveholes Dale to SE. SK 0777
Dovenby Cumbria 52 B2 vil 3m/4km NW of Cockermouth. NY 0933
Dovendale Lincs 45 G3* loc 3m/5km SW of Louth. TF 3082
Dover Kent 13 H3 Channel port 15m/24km SE of Canterbury with large modern docks for freight and passengers, dominated by high white cliffs and cas (A.M.). Cinque port and resort. Industries include furniture, paper. See also Strait of Dover. TR 3141
Dovercourt Essex 31 F5 dist of Harwich. Resort. TM 2531
Dovercourt, Upper Essex 31 F5 W dist of Harwich. TM 2430
Doverdale H & W 26 D1 vil 3m/5km NW of Droitwich. SO 8666
Doveridge Derbys 35 G1 vil 2m/3km E of Uttoxeter across R Dove. SK 1134
Dove Stone Reservoir Gtr Manchester 43 E1* resr 6m/10km E of Oldham. SE 0103
Dovey (Dyfi) 32 D5 r rising as several streams N of Llanymawddwy, Gwynedd, and flowing SW by Machynlleth, Powys, into Cardigan Bay to W of Aberdovey. Wide estuary below confluence with R Einion. SN 6095
Dovey Forest 33 E3, E4 afforested area on borders of Gwynedd and Powys to W of Aberangell in R Dovey valley. SH 80,81
Dowanhill S'clyde 64 C2* loc in Glasgow 2m/3km NW of city centre. NS 5667
Doward, Great H & W 26 B5* vil above right bank of R Wye 4m/6km NE of Monmouth across loops of r. SO 5516
Doward, Little H & W 26 A5* ham 3m/5km NE of Monmouth. SO 5316
Dowbridge Lancs 47 E5* loc adjoining Kirkham to E. SD 4331
Dowdeswell Glos 27 E5* loc 3m/5km SE of Cheltenham. Par contains **Dowdeswell Resr.** SO 9919
Dowlais Mid Glam 15 F1 dist of Merthyr Tydfil to NE of tn centre. Industrial estate. SO 0707
Dowland Devon 6 D4 ham 7m/12km SE of Torrington. SS 5610
Dowlands Devon 8 B5 loc 3m/4km E of Seaton. To S above coast, **D. Landslip,** where cliffs partially collapsed in 1839. Now nature reserve. SY 2890
Dowles H & W 34 D6* loc 1m NW of Bewdley. SO 7776
Dowlish Wake Som 8 B3 vil 2m/3km SE of Ilminster. 2km W, ham of **Dowlish Ford.** ST 3712
Down Ampney Glos 17 E2 vil 2m/4km N of Cricklade. Birthplace of Vaughan Williams. **Down Ampney Hse,** Tudor and later. SU 1097
Downan Point S'clyde 57 B5 headland at S end of Ballantrae Bay. NX 0680
Downderry Cornwall 3 G3 small resort on S coast 4m/6km E of Looe. SX 3154
Downe London 20 B5 vil 2m/3km NE of Biggin Hill. Down Hse, once home of Charles Darwin, contains Darwin relics. TQ 4361
Down, East Devon 6 D1 ham 6m/10km NE of Barnstaple. SS 6041
Downend Avon 16 B4 dist of Mangotsfield 5m/8km NE of Bristol. ST 6476
Downend Isle of Wight 10 C5 loc 2m/4km SE of Newport. To E, site of Roman villa. SZ 5387
Down End Som 8 B1 loc adjoining Dunball to N and 3m/5km N of Bridgwater. ST 3141
Downfield Cambs 30 B1* loc 2km SE of Soham. TL 6071
Downfield Tayside 73 F2/G2 NW dist of Dundee. NO 3833
Downgate Cornwall 3 H1 vil 2m/3km NE of Callington. SX 3772
Downham Cambs 38 A6 vil 3m/4km N of Ely. Remains of medieval palace of Bishops of Ely on N side. TL 5283
Downham Essex 20 D2* vil 2m/3km NW of Wickford. TQ 7295
Downham Lancs 48 B4 vil 3m/5km NE of Clitheroe. SD 7844
Downham London 20 A4* loc in borough of Lewisham 2m/3km SE of Lewisham tn centre. TQ 3971
Downham Market Norfolk 38 B4 mkt tn and agricultural centre near E bank of R Ouse 10m/17km S of King's Lynn. Industries include milling, light engineering, electronics. TF 6103
Down Hatherley Glos 26 D5* vil 4m/6km NE of Gloucester. SO 8622
Downhead Som 16 C6 vil 5m/8km E of Shepton Mallet. Quarries. ST 6945
Downhead Som 8 D2* ham 3m/4km W of Sparkford. ST 5625
Downhill Tyne & Wear 61 H5* housing estate in NW part of Sunderland. NZ 3559
Downholland Cross Lancs 42 A1 loc 3m/5km W of Ormskirk. SD 3606
Downholme N Yorks 54 A5 vil 4m/7km SW of Richmond. SE 1197
Down House London. See Downe.
Downie Point Grampian 77 H3* headland on E coast 1km SE of Stonehaven, at N end of Strathlethan Bay. NO 8885
Downies Grampian 77 H2 vil on E coast 7m/11km S of Aberdeen. NO 9295
Downley Bucks 18 D2 suburb 2m/3km NW of High Wycombe. SU 8495
Down, Little Hants 17 G5 loc 4m/6km NW of Hurstbourne Tarrant. SU 3557
Down, Lower Salop 34 A5 ham 3m/5km S of Bishop's Castle. SO 3384
Downs S Glam 15 F4* loc 5m/8km W of Cardiff. TV stn to S. ST 1074
Down St Mary Devon 7 E4 vil 7m/11km NW of Crediton. SS 7404
Downs Banks Staffs 35 E1 area of undulating moorland (NT) 1m SE of Barlaston. SJ 9037
Downs, Higher Cornwall 2 B5* loc 4m/6km S of Hayle. SW 5530
Downside Som 16 B6 loc 1m N of Shepton Mallet. ST 6244
Downside Som 16 B6* ham 4m/7km SW of Radstock. 1m E, D. Abbey, Benedictine monastery and boys' school. ST 6450
Downside Surrey 19 E5* ham 2km S of Cobham. TQ 1058
Downs, North 18, 19, 12, 13 range of chalk hills running E from the vicinity of Basingstoke in Hampshire, above the 'gap' tns of Guildford, Dorking, Sevenoaks, Maidstone, and Ashford, and terminating at S Foreland, E of Dover in Kent. Maximum height 965 ft or 294 metres at Leith Hill near Dorking. With the S Downs they enclose region known as The Weald. SU,TQ,TR
Downs, South 11, 12 range of chalk hills running E from vicinity of Petersfield in Hampshire parallel and close to Sussex coast and terminating at Beachy Hd, W of Eastbourne. Maximum height 888 ft or 271 metres at Butser Hill, 3m/4km SW of Petersfield. With the N Downs they enclose region known as The Weald. SU,TQ,TV
Downs, West Cornwall 3 E2* loc on W side of Lanivet, 3m/4km SW of Bodmin. SX 0364
Down, The Salop 34 D5* ham 3m/4km SW of Bridgnorth. SO 6890
Down Thomas Devon 4 B5 vil 3m/5km SE of Plymouth across R Plym estuary. SX 5050
Downton Hants 10 A5 ham 4m/6km SW of Lymington. SZ 2693
Downton Wilts 9 H2 vil on R Avon 6m/10km S of Salisbury. SU 1821
Downton on the Rock H & W vil 5m/9km W of Ludlow. SO 4273
Down, West Devon 6 D1 vil 4m/6km S of Ilfracombe. SS 5142
Dowry Reservoir Gtr Manchester 43 E1* resr 6m/9km NE of Oldham. SD 9811
Dowsby Lincs 37 F2 vil 6m/10km N of Bourne. **D. Hall** dates partly from 17c. TF 1129
Dowthorpe End Northants 28 D2* E end of Earls Barton, 4m/6km SW of Wellingborough. SP 8563
Doxey Staffs 35 E2* loc in NW part of Stafford. SJ 9023
Doxford Nthmb 67 H6* loc 3m/5km W of Embleton. **D. Hall,** early 19c. NU 1823
Doynton Avon vil 6m/10km N of Bath. ST 7174
Dozmary Pool Cornwall 3 F1 natural lake on Bodmin Moor 9m/15km NE of Bodmin. Subject of legends. SX 1974
Drabblegate Norfolk 39 F2* loc 1m N of Aylsham. TG 2028
Draethen Mid Glam 15 G3* ham 4m/6km E of Caerphilly. ST 2287
Dragley Beck Cumbria 46 D1 S dist of Ulverston. SD 2977
Dragonby Humberside 50 D6* loc 2m/3km N of Scunthorpe. Site of Roman settlement. SE 9014
Dragon Ness Shetland 89 E7* headland on E coast of Mainland opp island of W Linga. HU 5164
Dragons Green W Sussex 11 G3* loc 4m/6km E of Billingshurst. TQ 1423
Drakelow H & W 35 E6* loc 3m/4km N of Kidderminster. SO 8180
Drakemyre S'clyde 64 A4 vil 1km N of Dalry. NS 2950
Drakes Broughton H & W 26 D3 vil 2m/3km NW of Pershore. SO 9248
Drakes Cross H & W 35 G6 loc 7m/11km S of Birmingham. SP 0776
Drake's Island Devon 4 B5 island (NT) in Plymouth Sound, fortified since 15c. SX 4652
Drakewalls Cornwall 4 B6* loc which grew up with tin-mining industry, 1km S of Gunnislake. SX 4270
Draughton Northants 36 C6/D6 vil 7m/11km W of Kettering. SP 7676
Draughton N Yorks 48 C3 vil 3m/5km E of Skipton. SE 0352
Drawdykes Castle Cumbria 60 A5 loc 2m/3km NE of Carlisle. Hse with peel tower on line of Hadrian's Wall. NY 4158
Drax N Yorks 50 B5 vil 5m/9km SE of Selby. Power stn. See also Long Drax. SE 6726
Draycote Warwicks 27 H1 vil 5m/8km SW of Rugby. SP 4470
Draycot Foliat Wilts 17 F4* loc adjoining Chiseldon Camp to W, 5m/7km S of Swindon. SU 1877
Draycott Derbys 36 A1 suburb 3m/5km W of Long Eaton. SK 4433
Draycott Glos 27 F4 vil 3m/4km NW of Moreton-in-Marsh. SP 1835
Draycott H & W 26 D3 loc 4m/7km S of Worcester. SO 8548
Draycott Salop 35 E5 loc 6m/10km E of Bridgnorth. SO 8192
Draycott Som 16 A6 vil below S slopes of Mendip Hills 2m/3km SE of Cheddar. ST 4750
Draycott Cross Staffs 35 F1* loc 2m/3km SW of Cheadle. SJ 9841
Draycott in the Clay Staffs 35 G2 vil 5m/8km SE of Uttoxeter. SK 1528
Draycott in the Moors Staffs 35 F1 vil 3m/5km SW of Cheadle. SJ 9840
Draycott Moor Oxon 17 G2* loc 6m/10km W of Abingdon. SU 4098
Drayford Devon 7 F4* loc 6m/10km E of Chulmleigh. SS 7813
Draynes Cornwall 3 G2* loc 4m/6km NW of Liskeard. SX 2169
Drayton Hants 10 D4* N dist of Portsmouth below E end of Portsdown. SU 6705
Drayton H & W 35 E6 vil 5m/8km E of Kidderminster. SO 9076
Drayton Leics 36 D5 vil 5m/8km NW of Corby. SP 8392
Drayton Lincs 37 G1 loc 1km SE of Swineshead. TF 2439
Drayton Norfolk 39 F3 suburb 5m/7km NW of Norwich. TG 1813
Drayton Oxon 17 H2 vil 2m/3km SW of Abingdon. SU 4794
Drayton Oxon 27 H3 vil 2m/3km NW of Banbury. SP 4241
Drayton Som 8 C2 vil 2m/3km SW of Langport. ST 4024
Drayton Warwicks 27 F2* loc 2m/4km W of Stratford-upon-Avon. SP 1654
Drayton Bassett Staffs 35 G4 vil 3m/4km SW of Tamworth. SK 1900

Drayton Beauchamp Bucks 18 D1 vil 2km W of Tring. SP 9012
Drayton, East Notts 44 C4 vil 4m/6km NE of Tuxford. SK 7775
Drayton, Little Salop 34 D1* W dist of Mkt Drayton. SJ 6633
Drayton Parslow Bucks 28 D5 vil 4m/6km SW of Bletchley. SP 8328
Drayton Reservoir Northants 28 B2 resr 2km N of Daventry. SP 5664
Drayton St Leonard Oxon 18 B2 vil 4m/7km N of Wallingford. SU 5996
Drayton, West London 19 E3 dist of Hillingdon borough 15m/23km W of Charing Cross. TQ 0679
Drayton, West Notts 44 B4 vil 4m/7km S of E Retford. SK 7074
Drebley N Yorks 48 C2 loc above R Wharfe 2m/3km SE of Burnsall. SE 0559
Dreemskerry Isle of Man 41 C4* loc 2m/3km SE of Ramsey. SC 4791
Dreenhill Dyfed 22 B4 ham 2m/4km SW of Haverfordwest. SM 9214
Drefach Dyfed 23 E2 vil 3m/5km E of Newcastle Emlyn. SN 3538
Drefach Dyfed 23 G4 vil 2m/3km W of Cross Hands. SN 5612
Drefach Dyfed 24 B3 ham 5m/8km W of Lampeter. SN 5045
Drefelin Dyfed 23 E2* loc 4m/6km SE of Newcastle Emlyn. SN 3538
Dreghorn S'clyde 64 B5 loc 3m/5km E of Irvine. NS 3538
Drem Lothian 66 C1 vil 4m/6km N of Haddington. NT 5179
Drenewydd Welsh form of Newtown and Newton, qv.
Drenewydd Gelli-farch Welsh form of Shirenewton, qv.
Dresden Staffs 35 E1 loc in S part of Longton, Stoke-on-Trent. SJ 9042
Dreswick Point Isle of Man 46 B6* headland with lighthouse at S end of Langness promontory, on E side of Langness Pt. SC 2865
Drewsteignton Devon 7 E5 vil 3m/5km N of Moretonhampstead. SX 7390
Driby Lincs 45 G4 ham 5m/8km N of Spilsby. TF 3874
Driesh Tayside 76 C4 mt 4m/6km W of Clova. Height 3108 ft or 947 metres. NO 2773
Driffield Glos 17 E2 vil 4m/6km SE of Cirencester. Loc of **D. Cross Roads** 1m SW. SU 0799
Driffield, Great Humberside 51 E3 tn 11m/18km SW of Bridlington. **Lit Driffield** vil 1m W. TA 0257
Drift, Higher Cornwall 2 A5* loc to W of Lr Drift, qv. SW 4328
Drift, Lower Cornwall 2 A5 ham 2m/3km SW of Penzance. SW 4328
Drift, Middle Cornwall 3 F2* loc 4m/6km NE of Lostwithiel. SX 1364
Drift Reservoir Cornwall 2 A5 resr 2m/4km W of Penzance. SW 4329
Drigg Cumbria 52 B5 vil 2m/3km SE of Seascale. SD 0699
Drigg Point Cumbria 52 B5* headland on N side of R Esk estuary at its outfall into Irish Sea 1m SW of Ravenglass. SD 0795
Drighlington W Yorks 49 E5 vil 3m/4km W of Morley. SE 2229
Drimnin H'land 68 D3 vil on E shore of Sound of Mull, 4m/6km E of Tobermory across sound. NM 5554
Drimpton Dorset 8 C4 vil 3m/5km SW of Crewkerne. ST 4105
Dringhouses N Yorks 49 G3 dist of York 2m/3km SW of city centre. SE 5849
Drinishader W Isles 88 B3* locality on inlet of E Loch Tarbert, Harris, 4m/6km SE of Tarbert. NG 1794
Drinkstone Suffolk 30 D2 vil 6m/10km NW of Stowmarket. Vil of **D. Green** 1km S. TL 9561
Driver's End Herts 29 F5* ham 2m/4km N of Welwyn. TL 2219
Drointon Staffs 35 F2 ham 6m/9km N of Rugeley. SK 0226
Droitwich H & W 26 D2 tn 6m/10km NE of Worcester. Former spa status due to saline springs. Site of Roman tn of *Salinae* to N. SO 8963
Dron Tayside 73 E3 vil 5m/8km S of Perth. NO 1415
Dronfield Derbys 43 H3 tn 5m/8km N of Chesterfield. Coal, iron and steel works. **D. Woodhouse** loc 2m/3km W. SK 3578
Drongan S'clyde 56 D2 vil in colliery dist 7m/11km E of Ayr. NS 4418
Droop Dorset 9 E3 ham 1m E of Hazelbury Bryan and 4m/7km SE of Sturminster Newton. ST 7508
Drope S Glam 15 F4* loc 5m/8km W of Cardiff. ST 1075
Droxford Hants 10 C3 vil on R Meon 1m SW of Meonstoke. The Old Rectory (NT), 18c hse next to ch. SU 6018
Droylsden Gtr Manchester 42 D2 tn adjoining Manchester to E. Textiles, engineering, preserves. SJ 9198
Drub W Yorks 48 D5* ham 1m N of Cleckheaton. SE 1926
Druid (Ddwyryd, Y) Clwyd 33 G1 ham 2m/4km W of Corwen. SJ 0443
Druid's Heath W Midlands 35 F4* loc 1km N of Aldridge. SK 0501
Druidston Dyfed 22 B4* ham 1m S of Nolton. SM 8616
Druie H'land 81 H6 r in Badenoch and Strathspey dist running NW into R Spey at Aviemore. NH 8911
Druimarbin H'land 74 C4 locality on E shore of Loch Linnhe 2m/4km SW of Fort William. NN 0771
Druim Chòsaidh H'land 74 A2, B2 mt ridge in Lochaber dist running E and W on N side of head of Loch Quoich, and attaining height of 2994 ft or 913 metres at Sgurr a' Choire-bheithe. NG 9100
Druim Fada H'land 74 A1 mt ridge in Lochaber dist running E and W on N side of narrow part of Loch Hourn, SE of Arnisdale. Highest point 2327 ft or 709 metres. NG 8908
Druim Fada H'land 74 B3, C3 mt ridge on Locheil Forest, Lochaber dist, 5m/8km N of Fort William. Summit, at E end of ridge, is Stob an Ghrianain, 2420 ft or 738 metres. NN 0882
Druim Fiaclach H'land 68 F2 mt ridge in Moidart, Lochaber dist, 3m/4km SE of Lochailort. Height 2852 ft or 869 metres. NM 7979
Druimindarroch H'land 68 E1 locality on N side of Loch nan Uamh, 2m/3km SE of vil of Arisaig in Lochaber dist. NM 6884
Druim Leathad nam Fias H'land 74 B4 mt ridge and watershed between Cona Glen and Glen Scaddle in Lochaber dist. NM 9670
Druim nan Cnamh H'land 74 C1 mt ridge on border of Inverness and Skye & Lochalsh dists, between Lochs Cluanie and Loyne. Summit 2555 ft or 779 metres. NH 1307
Druimyeon Bay S'clyde 62 D3 bay on E side of island of Gigha, N of Ardminish Pt. NR 6550
Drum Gwynedd 40 D4 mt 4m/6km SE of Llanfairfechan. Height 2528 ft or 771 metres. SH 7069
Drum Tayside 72 D4* vil 5m/7km W of Kinross. NO 0400
Drumadoon Bay S'clyde 63 F5 bay on W coast of Arran, extending either side of Blackwaterfoot. **Drumadoon Pt** is headland at NW end of bay. NR 8927
Drumbeg H'land 84 B4 vil on S side of Eddrachillis Bay, W coast of Sutherland dist. NC 1232
Drumblade Grampian 83 E3 loc 4m/6km E of Huntly. NJ 5840
Drumbowie Reservoir Central 65 E1* small resr 2m/3km SW of Denny. NS 7881
Drumbuie H'land 79 F5 locality in Skye and Lochalsh dist 2m/4km NE of Kyle of Lochalsh. NG 7731
Drumburgh Cumbria 59 G5 ham on line of Hadrian's Wall 4m/6km W of Burgh by Sands. Various Roman sites in vicinity. **D. Castle** incorporates wall of 16c cas. NY 2659
Drum Castle Grampian 77 G1 14c cas tower with hse adjoining, 3m/5km W of Peterculter. NJ 7900
Drumchapel S'clyde 64 C2* loc in Glasgow 5m/8km NW of city centre. NS 5270
Drumclog S'clyde 64 D5* vil 5m/8km E of Darvel. Monmt 1m NW commemorates battle of 1679 in which Covenanters defeated Claverhouse (Dundee). NS 6338
Drumcoltran Tower D & G 58 D4* 16c tower (A.M.) 1m N of Kirkgunzeon. NX 8668
Drumelzier Borders 65 G5 vil on **D. Burn** near its confluence with R Tweed, 8m/13km SW of Peebles. Ruins of Tinnis Castle on hillside to NE. Faint remains of **D. Castle** beside R Tweed 1m SW. NT 1334
Drumfearn Skye, H'land 79 E6 loc at head of Sleat peninsula 3m/4km NW of Isle Ornsay. NG 6715
Drumlamford Loch S'clyde 57 C5 small loch 4m/7km SE of Barrhill. NX 2877
Drumlanrig Castle D & G 58 D2 seat of the Duke of Buccleuch, dating from late 17c, in Nithsdale 3m/5km NW of Thornhill. NX 8599
Drumlasie Grampian 77 F1 loc 3m/4km NE of Torphins. NJ 6405
Drumlemble S'clyde 62 D5 vil in Kintyre 4m/6km W of Campbeltown. NR 6619
Drumlithie Grampian 77 G3 vil 6m/10km SW of Stonehaven. NO 7880
Drum Mains S'clyde 64 D2* loc in Cumbernauld 3m/5km W of tn centre. NS 7173
Drummoddie D & G 57 D7* loc 4m/6km E of Port William. NX 3945
Drummond H'land 81 F1 loc on S side of Evanton, Ross and Cromarty dist, across R Skiack. NH 6065
Drummond Castle Tayside 72 C3 cas, founded in 15c, 3m/4km SW of Crieff. Much restored. NN 8418
Drummond Hill Tayside 71 H1 wooded hill to N of Kenmore at foot of Loch Tay. NN 7646
Drummore D & G 57 B8 vil on **D. Bay** on E coast of Rinns of Galloway, 4m/7km N of Mull of Galloway. NX 1336
Drummossie Muir H'land 81 F4-G3 moorland tract in Inverness dist centred on the southern part of Culloden Forest SE of Inverness. NH 7343
Drummuir Castle Grampian 82 C3 cas 4m/7km NE of Dufftown. NJ 3744
Drumnadrochit H'land 81 E4 vil on R Enrick 1m W of Urquhart Bay on Loch Ness, Inverness dist. NH 5029
Drumnagorrach Grampian 82 D2* loc 6m/9km E of Keith. NJ 5252
Drumoak Grampian 77 G2 loc 3m/5km W of Peterculter. NO 7998
Drumochter See Pass of Drumochter.
Drumoyne S'clyde 64 C2* loc in Govan dist of Glasgow. NS 5465
Drumrunie Forest H'land 85 B6 deer forest in Ross and Cromarty dist around Cul Mór, 10m/16km N of Ullapool. NC 1810
Drumry S'clyde 64 C2* loc on N side of Clydebank. NS 5070
Drumtochty Forest Grampian 77 F3 state forest N and S of **Drumtochty Castle,** now a boys' school. NO 6980
Drumtroddan D & G 57 D7* site of Bronze Age cup and ring marked rocks (A.M.), 2m/3km NE of Port William. See also Big Balcraig. NX 3644
Drumuie Skye, H'land 78 C4 loc 3m/4km NW of Portree. NG 4546
Drumuillie H'land 81 H5 loc in Badenoch and Strathspey dist 3m/4km NE of Boat of Garten. NH 9420
Druridge Nthmb 61 G2* loc 2km E of Widdrington. To E is **D. Bay** , extending from Hauxley in the N to Snab Pt in the S. NZ 2796
Drury Clwyd 41 H5 loc 1m E of Buckley. SJ 2964
Drury Square Norfolk 38 D3* loc 1km S of Beeston. TF 9014
Drybeck Cumbria 53 F3 ham 3m/5km S of Appleby. NY 6615
Drybridge Grampian 82 D1* loc near N coast on Burn of Buckie 2m/3km S of Buckie. NJ 4362
Drybrook Glos 26 B5 vil 2m/4km N of Cinderford. SO 6417
Drybrook H & W 26 B5* ham 4m/6km S of Ross-on-Wye. SO 5918
Drybrook, Little Glos 16 B1* loc 3m/4km S of Coleford. SO 5907
Dryburgh Borders 66 D5 vil 1km N of St Boswells across R Tweed. **D. Abbey** (A.M.), remains of abbey founded in 1150, in loop of R Tweed. Burial place of Sir Walter Scott, d 1832, and of Field-Marshal Lord Haig, d 1928 (see Bemersyde). Large statue of William Wallace, erected in 1814, to N of vil. NT 5932
Dry Doddington Lincs 44 C6 vil 6m/9km SE of Newark-on-Trent. SK 8546
Dry Drayton Cambs 29 G2 vil 5m/8km NW of Cambridge. TL 3862
Dryfe Water 59 F3 r in Dumfries & Galloway region rising on S side of Loch Fell and running S to R Annan 2m/3km W of Lockerbie. NY 1082
Drylaw Lothian 66 A2* dist of Edinburgh 2m/3km NW of city centre. NT 2275
Drymen Central 71 F5 vil 7m/11km NE of Balloch. To W is site of Buchanan Castle, formerly seat of Duke of Montrose. NS 4788
Drymuir Grampian 83 G2* loc 2km SW of Maud. NJ 9145
Drynham Wilts 16 D5* loc 2km S of Trowbridge. ST 8656
Drynoch H'land 79 C5 r in Skye running W to head of Loch Harport, on S side of locality of Drynoch. See also Glen Drynoch. NG 4031
Dry Sandford Oxon 17 H2 loc 3m/4km NW of Abingdon. SP 4600
Dryslwyn Dyfed 23 G4 ham on R Towy 5m/8km W of Llandeilo. Ruins of medieval cas. SN 5520
Dry Street Essex 20 D3 loc S of Lee Chapel, Basildon. TQ 6986
Duad 23 E3* r rising 5m/8km S of Llandyssul, Dyfed, and flowing S into R Gwili 4m/7km NW of Carmarthen. SN 3826
Duar 24 B4* r flowing NW into R Teifi at Llanybydder, Dyfed. SN 5244
Duart Point S'clyde 70 A2 headland on E coast of Mull opp entrance to Loch Linnhe. **D. Bay** to W. **D. Castle** on point, seat of the chief of the Macleans. NM 7435
Dubbs Reservoir Cumbria 52 D4* small resr 1m SE of Troutbeck. NY 4201
Dubford Grampian 83 F1* loc 1m S of Gardenstown. NJ 7963
Dubh Loch Grampian 76 C3 small loch 2m/3km W of Loch Muick and 7m/12km SE of Braemar. NO 2382
Dubh Loch H'land 78 F3 upper part of Loch Bad an Sgalaig, qv, Ross and Cromarty dist. NG 8470
Dubh Loch H'land 85 A8 loch in W part of Ross and Cromarty dist adjacent to head of Fionn Loch and 2km S of Beinn a' Chàisgein Mór. NG 9876
Dubh Loch S'clyde 70 C4 small loch in Argyll in course of R Shira, 2m/3km NE of Inveraray. NN 1111
Dubh Lochain H'land 74 A1 small loch in Lochaber dist 3m/5km E of Arnisdale. NG 8809
Dubh Sgeir S'clyde 70 A3* rock island 2km SW of Bach I. in Firth of Lorn. NM 7625
Dubh Sgeirean H'land 84 B3* group of island rocks 1m off W coast of Sutherland dist 4m/6km W of Kinlochbervie. NC 1654
Dublin Suffolk 31 F2* loc 1km N of Rishangles. TM 1669
Dubmill Point Cumbria 52 B1 headland at N end of Allonby Bay. NY 0745
Dubmire, High Tyne & Wear 61 G6* loc adjoining Houghton-le-Spring to W. NZ 3249
Duchray Castle Central 71 F4 former stronghold of the Grahams, on S bank of **D. Water** in Loch Ard Forest W of Aberfoyle. The r flows E through forest to R Forth 1m W of vil. NS 4899
Duchray Hill Tayside 76 C4 mt 4m/6km SE of Spittal of Glenshee. Height 2301 ft or 701 metres. Also known as Mealna Letter. NO 1667
Duck End Beds 29 E3* loc adjoining Stevington to SW, 5m/7km NW of Bedford. SP 9852
Duck End Beds 29 E3* loc 4m/6km S of Bedford. TL 0644
Duck End Bucks 28 C5* loc adjoining Swanbourne to NW, 2m/3km E of Winslow. SP 7927
Duck End Cambs 29 F2* W end of vil of Graveley, 5m/8km S of Huntingdon. TL 2464
Duck End Cambs 29 H2* loc in S part of Girton. TL 4261
Duck End Essex 30 B4* N end of vil of Finchingfield. TL 6833
Duck End Essex 30 B5 loc 3m/5km NE of Gt Dunmow. TL 6526
Duckend Green Essex 30 C5* loc 2m/3km W of Braintree. TL 7223
Duckington Ches 42 B6* loc 3m/5km N of Malpas. SJ 4851
Ducklington Oxon 17 G1 vil 2m/3km S of Witney. SP 3507
Duckmanton Derbys 43 H4 vil 2m/3km S of Staveley. See also Long Duckmanton. SK 4472
Duck's Cross Beds 29 E2* loc 6m/9km NE of Bedford. TL 1156

Ducks Island London 19 F2* loc in borough of Barnet 1m SW of Chipping Barnet and 10m/16km NW of Charing Cross. TQ 2395
Duck Street Hants 17 G6* ham 4m/6km NW of Andover. SU 3249
Duck Street N Yorks 48 D2* loc adjoining Greenhow Hill to S. SE 1163
Duck Street Suffolk 30 D3 ham 4m/7km NE of Lavenham. TL 9554
Duckworth Hall Lancs 48 A5* loc 1m SW of Oswaldtwistle. SD 7626
Dudden Hill London 19 F3* loc N of Willesden in borough of Brent, 6m/9km NW of Charing Cross. TQ 2285
Duddenhoe End Essex 29 H4* ham 5m/8km W of Saffron Walden. TL 4636
Duddingston Lothian 66 A2/B2 dist of Edinburgh 3m/5km E of city centre. **D. Loch** is a bird sanctuary. NT 2972
Duddington Northants 37 E4 vil 5m/8km SW of Stamford. SK 9800
Duddlestone Som 8 A2* ham 2m/4km S of Taunton. ST 2321
Duddleswell E Sussex 12 B4* ham on S side of Ashdown Forest 4m/7km N of Uckfield. TQ 4627
Duddo Nthmb 67 F4 ham 4m/6km SE of Norham. NT 9342
Duddon Ches 42 B5 vil 3m/5km NW of Tarporley. SJ 5164
Duddon 52 C6 r rising at Wrynose Pass, Cumbria, and flowing S into Irish Sea between Haverigg Pt and the Furness peninsula. SD 1575
Duddon Bridge Cumbria 52 C6 loc at rd crossing of R Duddon 1m NW of Broughton in Furness. SD 1988
Dudleston Salop 34 A1* ham 4m/7km NW of Ellesmere. SJ 3438
Dudlestone Heath Salop 34 B1 loc 3m/4km NW of Ellesmere. SJ 3636
Dudley Tyne & Wear 61 G4* loc in coal-mining area 6m/9km N of Newcastle. NZ 2673
Dudley W Midlands 35 F5 industrial tn 8m/12km W of Birmingham, producing metals and metal goods, boilers, leather, clothing, bricks, glass. Freightliner terminal. Remains of cas and 12c priory. Geological nature reserve. Zoo. SO 9490
Dudley Hill W Yorks 48 D5 dist of Bradford 2m/3km SE of city centre. SE 1830
Dudley Port W Midlands 35 F5 W dist of W Bromwich. SO 9691
Dudley Wood W Midlands 35 F5* loc in Dudley 2m/4km S of tn centre. SO 9486
Dudlow's Green Ches 42 B3/C3* loc 3m/5km S of Warrington tn centre. SJ 6284
Dudsbury Dorset 9 G4 residential loc 5m/8km N of Bournemouth. SZ 0798
Dudwell 12 D4 r in E Sussex rising to E of Heathfield and flowing E into R Rother below Etchingham. TQ 7126
Duff House Grampian. See Banff.
Duffield Derbys 35 H1 vil on R Derwent 5m/8km N of Derby. Mound of Norman cas. SK 3443
Duffield, North N Yorks 50 C4 vil 5m/9km NE of Selby. **S Duffield** vil 2m/4km S. SE 6837
Duffryn W Glam 14 D2 vil 3m/5km N of Maesteg. SS 8395
Dufftown Grampian 82 C3 small tn at confluence of Dullan Water and R Fiddich 16m/26km SE of Elgin. Quarries, distilleries. Auchindown Castle (A.M.), ruined 15c cas 2m/3km SE. NJ 3239
Duffus Grampian 82 B1 vil near N coast 5m/8km NW of Elgin. **D. Castle** (A.M.), 2km SE, ruined 14c cas standing on earlier motte. St Peter's Kirk and shaft of 14c cross (A.M.) on E side of vil. NJ 1768
Dufton Cumbria 53 F2 vil 3m/5km N of Appleby. NY 6825
Duggleby N Yorks 50 D2 vil 6m/10km SE of Malton. **D. Howe,** to SE, is large round barrow of Neolithic period. SE 8767
Dugoed 33 F3 r rising on borders of Gwynedd and Powys 4m/7km NE of Mallwyd, Gwynedd, and flowing S then W into R Dovey on W side of Mallwyd. SH 8512
Duhonw 25 F3* r rising about 6m/9km SW of Builth Wells, Powys, and running into R Wye 2km E thereof. SO 0651
Duirinish H'land 79 F5 locality in Skye and Lochalsh dist 3m/5km NE of Kyle of Lochalsh. NG 7831
Duisdalemore Skye, H'land 79 E7 loc on E side of Sleat peninsula 1km N of Isle Ornsay. NG 7013
Duisk 57 C5 r in Strathclyde region running NW past Barrhill to R Stinchar at Pinwherry. NX 1986
Duke End Warwicks 35 H5* loc 2m/4km E of Coleshill. SP 2388
Dukehouse Norfolk 39 E2* loc 2m/3km E of Wood Norton. TG 0327
Dukeries, The Notts. See Sherwood Forest.
Dukesfield Nthmb 61 E5* loc 4m/7km S of Hexham. NY 9457
Duke's Meadows London 19 F4* sports grnd on N bank of R Thames on loop of r between Chiswick Br and Barnes (rly) Br. TQ 2076
Dukestown Gwent 15 F1 industrial locality on N edge of S Wales coalfield, adjoining Tredegar to N. SO 1310
Duke Street Suffolk 31 E4* ham 4m/6km E of Hadleigh. TM 0742
Dukinfield Gtr Manchester 43 E2 tn 6m/10km E of Manchester. Textiles, engineering. SJ 9497
Dulais 14 D2 r rising near Seven Sisters, W Glam, and flowing S into R Neath 2m/3km NE of tn of Neath. SS 7799
Dulais 23 G3 r rising NE of Llanfynydd, Dyfed, and flowing S into R Towy 1km E of Rhosmaen. SN 6423
Dulais 24 C5* r rising on Caeo Forest, Dyfed, and flowing S into R Towy 1km S of Llanwrda. SN 7130
Dulas Gwynedd 40 B3 loc near NE coast of Anglesey 2m/5km SE of Amlwch. **D. Bay** to E, with inlet of Traeth Dulas, qv. SH 4789
Dulas H & W 25 H5* loc 2m/3km NW of Pontrilas. SO 3729
Dulas 23 E1/E2* r rising 2m/4km S of Llangranog, Dyfed, and flowing S into R Ceri 4m/6km N of Newcastle Emlyn. SN 3146
Dulas 23 E2* r rising near Blaenffos, Dyfed, and flowing E into R Cych 4m/6km W of Newcastle Emlyn. SN 2538
Dulas 23 G4 r rising 3m/5km NE of Llanfynydd, Dyfed, and flowing SW into R Towy 1m E of Llanarthney. SN 5420
Dulas 24 B3* r rising 2m/4km S of Llangeitho, Dyfed, and flowing S into R Teifi at Lampeter. SN 5847
Dulas 25 E3 r rising S of Caban Coch Resr, Powys, and flowing S to R Irfon at Garth. SN 9549
Dulas 25 E3 r running NE by Tirabad, Powys, into R Irfon 1m W of Llangammarch Wells. SN 9146
Dulas 25 F2 r rising E of Rhayader, Powys, and running S then SE into R Ithon 2m/3km N of Llandrindod Wells. SO 0663
Dulas 25 F4* r rising N of Brecon, Powys, and flowing E into R Llynfi 1km NW of Talgarth. SO 1434
Dulas 33 E4 r rising in Glaslyn Lake, Powys, and flowing NW into R Dovey 1m NE of Machynlleth. SH 7501
Dulas 33 E4 r running S into R Dovey nearly 1m NE of Machynlleth, Powys. SH 7051
Dulas 33 F5 r rising 2m/3km SE of Llangurig, Powys, and flowing E then NW into R Severn 1km SW of Llanidloes. SN 9483
Dulas 41 E3/E4 r rising about 5m/8km S of Colwyn Bay, Clwyd, and running NE to coast at Llanddulas. SH 9178
Dulcote Som 16 B6 vil 2km SE of Wells. To SE, D. Hill, with quarries. ST 5644
Dulford Devon 7 H4 ham 3m/5km E of Cullompton. ST 0705
Dull Tayside 75 H6 vil 3m/5km W of Aberfeldy. See also Strath Appin. NN 8049
Dullan Water 82 C3 r in Grampian region running NE down Glen Rinnes to R Fiddich at Dufftown. NJ 3339
Dullatur S'clyde 65 E1* vil 2m/3km NW of Cumbernauld. NS 7476
Dullingham Cambs 30 B2 vil 4m/6km S of Newmarket. Ham of **D. Ley** 2km SE. TL 6357
Dulnain H'land 81 H5 r in Badenoch and Strathspey dist rising on Monadhliath Mts and running NE to R Spey 1m SE of Dulnain Br. NJ 0023
Dulnain Bridge H'land 82 A4 vil in Badenoch and Strathspey dist 3m/5km SW of Grantown-on-Spey. NH 9924
Duloe Beds 29 F2 ham 2m/3km W of St Neots. TL 1560
Duloe Cornwall 3 G2 vil 4m/6km S of Liskeard. SX 2358
Dulverton Som 7 G2 small tn on R Barle on S edge of Exmoor 10m/16km N of Tiverton. SS 9127
Dulwich London 19 G4* large dist in borough of Southwark in SE London some 5m/8km SE of Charing Cross. Sub-districts are **E** and **W Dulwich,** the latter being partly in borough of Lambeth; and **D. Village,** which still retains something of a village character. There are considerable open spaces, including D. Common, D. Park, and the grnds of D. College. TQ 3372
Dulyn 40 D4* r rising above Dulyn Resr, Gwynedd, and flowing E into R Conwy 1km E of Tal-y-bont. SH 7768
Dulyn Reservoir Gwynedd 40 D4 resr 4m/7km W of Dolgarrog. SH 7066
Dumbarton S'clyde 64 B2 tn situated at confluence of R Leven and R Clyde 14m/22km NW of Glasgow. Industries include shipbuilding, distilling, mnfre of boilers and tubes. Ancient cas (A.M.) on rocky eminence above R Clyde. **D. Muir** is moorland area to NE. NS 3975
Dumbleton Glos 27 E4 vil 5m/8km N of Winchcombe. SP 0136
Dumbreck S'clyde 64 C3* loc in Glasgow 2m/3km SW of city centre. NS 5563
Dumbrock Loch Central 64 C1* small loch 1m SW of Strathblane. NS 5578
Dumcrieff D & G 59 F1/F2 loc on Moffat Water 2km SE of Moffat. NT 1003
Dumfries D & G 59 E4 mnfg tn on R Nith, 60m/97km SE of Glasgow, and 29m/47km NW of Carlisle across head of Solway Firth. Industries include mnfre of agricultural implements, chemicals, clothing, hosiery, rubber goods. **D. Trading Estate** 2m/3km NE. Burns lived in tn from 1791 to his death in 1796; Burns mausoleum. NX 9776
Dumfries and Galloway 116 admin region of SW Scotland, comprising the former counties of Dumfries, Kirkcudbright, and Wigtown. From the Tweedsmuir and Lowther Hills, the Rinns of Kells and Carrick Forest, strung out E to W along the region's northern border, the Rs Esk, Annan, Nith, Dee and Cree descend southwards to the Solway Firth, past the tns of Langholm, Annan, Dumfries, Kirkcudbright, and Newton Stewart and Wigtown respectively. The hilly areas are largely given over to sheep-grazing and afforestation, while farther S there is some good-quality arable farmland. Galloway is the area comprising the former counties of Kirkcudbright and Wigtown, at the extreme W of which is the peninsula known as the Rinns of Galloway, and the port of Stranraer, which provides passenger and car ferry services to Larne in Northern Ireland.
Dumgoyne Central 64 C1* loc 4m/6km NW of Strathblane. Distillery 1km SE. NS 5283
Dummer Hants 18 B6 vil 5m/8km SW of Basingstoke. SU 5846
Dumpdon Hill Devon 8 A4* hill 2m/4km NE of Honiton, with Iron Age fort near summit. ST 1704
Dumpling Green Norfolk 39 E3* loc 2km SE of E Dereham. TG 0011
Dumplington Gtr Manchester 42 D2* loc 2km N of Urmston. SJ 7796
Dun Tayside 77 F5 loc 3m/5km NW of Montrose. NO 6659
Dùn W Isles (W of 88 A3) steep, rocky, uninhabited island (NTS) in the St Kilda group about 54m/86km W of Harris and 35m/56km W of N Uist, lying off SE end of St Kilda itself. Is a narrow island nearly 1m wide. Haunt of sea birds. NF 1097
Dunadd S'clyde 70 A5* ancient fort (A.M.) of 6c in Argyll 4m/6km N of Lochgilphead. NR 8393
Dunagoil S'clyde 63 G3* remains of Iron Age fort on SW coast of Bute, 2km NW of Garroch Hd. **D. Bay** to N. NS 0853
Dunalastan Reservoir Tayside 75 G5 resr in course of R Tummel below Kinloch Rannoch. NN 6958
Dunan S'clyde 63 G1 loc in Argyll on W shore of Firth of Clyde, adjoining Innellan to NE. NS 1570
Dunan Ruadh W Isles 88 D3* site of ancient burial-chambers on W coast of island of Fuday, off Barra. NF 7208
Dunball Som 8 B1 vil at confluence of King's Sedgemoor Drain and R Parrett, 3m/4km N of Bridgwater. ST 3141
Dùn Bàn Mull, S'clyde. See Burg.
Dunbar Lothian 66 D1 coastal resort with small harbour 27m/43km E of Edinburgh. Industries include fishing, brewing, mnfre of agricultural implements. Scant remains of cas on headland. 2m/3km S is site of battle of 1296 in which English defeated Scots, and 2m/3km SE is site of battle of 1650 in which Cromwell defeated supporters of Charles II under Leslie. NT 6878
Dunbeath H'land 86 E4 vil on E coast of Caithness dist 18m/29km SW of Wick, at mouth of **D. Water,** r rising 11m/17km W. Clifftop cas 1m S. ND 1629
Dunbeg S'clyde 70 B2 vil on Dunstaffnage Bay, 2m/3km W of Connel, Argyll. NM 8733
Dunblane Central 72 B4 small tn on Allan Water 5m/8km N of Stirling. 13c cathedral. Site of Roman camp to SW. NN 7801
Dunbog Fife 73 F3 vil 3m/5km E of Newburgh. NO 2818
Dunbridge Hants 10 A2* loc 1km SW of Mottisfont. SU 3126
Dunburgh Hill Norfolk 39 G5* loc adjoining Gillingham to W. TM 4091
Dùn Caan Skye, H'land 79 D5 highest point on Raasay 4m/6km from S end of island. Height 1456 ft or 444 metres. Caves on S side. NG 5739
Duncansby H'land 86 F1 vil in NE corner of Caithness dist nearly 2m/3km W of **Duncansby Hd,** headland with lighthouse. Stacks of Duncansby is group of rocks off coast to E. Ness of D. is headland to N. ND 3872
Duncanston Grampian 83 E4 vil 4m/6km W of Insch. NJ 5726
Duncanston H'land 81 E2 loc 2m/3km SW of Culbokie on Black Isle, Ross and Cromarty dist. NH 5856
Dun Carloway W Isles 88 B2* loc near W coast of Lewis 2km SW of Carloway vil. Here is an Iron Age *broch* or fort (A.M.). NB 1841
Dunchideock Devon 5 E2 ham 4m/7km SW of Exeter. 1m S, Lawrence Castle, prominent belvedere tower erected 1788. SX 8787
Dun Chonnuill S'clyde 69 E6* most northerly of Garvellachs group of islands in Firth of Lorn. Ruins of 13c cas. Also known as Eileach Chonail. NM 6812
Dunchurch Warwicks 27 H1 vil 3m/4km SW of Rugby. SP 4871
Duncolm S'clyde 64 C2* summit of Kilpatrick Hills, 5m/8km E of Dumbarton. Height 1316 ft or 401 metres. NS 4777
Duncombe Lancs 47 F4 vil 7m/11km N of Preston. SD 5139
Duncombe Park N Yorks 55 E6 mansion, partly 18c, seat of Earls of Feversham, now boarding school for girls, 1m SW of Helmsley. Formal gardens with classical-style temples. SE 6083
Duncote Northants 28 B3 loc 2m/3km NW of Towcester. SP 6750
Duncraig Castle College H'land 78 F5 school of domestic science in Skye and Lochalsh dist, 1km E of Plockton across bay. NG 8133
Dun Creich H'land 85 75 ancient fort on N shore of Dornoch Firth 3m/5km SE of Bonar Br, Sutherland dist. NH 6588
Duncrievie Tayside 73 E3 vil 3m/5km N of Milnathort. NO 1309
Duncton W Sussex 11 F3 vil below S Downs 3m/5km S of Petworth. Site of Roman bath hse to S of vil. SU 9617
Dundale Pond N Yorks 55 F5* small lake 1m N of Levisham. SE 8291
Dundarg Grampian 83 G1* ruined cas on Aberdour Bay on N coast, 3m/5km SW of Rosehearty. NJ 8964
Dundas Castle Lothian 65 G1 large 19c mansion with 15c tower adjoining, 1m S of Forth Rd Br. NT 1176
Dundee Tayside 73 G2 commerical and industrial city and port 18m/29km E of

Perth on N side of Firth of Tay, crossed here by a rd br and a rly br (the latter 2m/3km long and the former over 2km). Jute mnfre was formerly staple industry, but much diversification has taken place. Episcopal cathedral on site of former cas. University. Airfield at Riverside Park. **D. Law,** hill of 571 ft or 174 metres 1m NW of city centre, bears war memorial. NO 4030
Dundeugh Forest D & G 56 E4, F4* state forest to S of Carsphairn. NX 5690
Dundon Som 8 C1 vil on W side of D. Hill and 3m/4km S of Street. 1km NW, locality of **D. Hayes,** overlooking Sedgemoor. ST 4832
Dundonald S'clyde 64 B5 vil 4m/6km NE of Troon. Remains of **D. Castle** (A.M.), mainly 13c. NS 3634
Dundonnell H'land 85 B7 r in W part of Ross and Cromarty dist running N through D. Forest to head of Lit Loch Broom. NH 0888
Dundonnell Forest H'land 85 B8 deer forest in W part of Ross and Cromarty dist between Strath na Sealga and Strath More. NH 1181
Dundraw Cumbria 52 C1 ham 3m/5km W of Wigton. NY 2149
Dundreggan H'land 80 D5 loc in Glen Moriston, Inverness dist, 7m/11km W of Invermoriston. **D. Forest** is deer forest to N. NH 3114
Dundreich Borders 66 A4* hill on Moorfoot range 2m/4km NE of Eddleston. Height 2042 ft or 622 metres. NT 2749
Dundrennan D & G 58 D6 vil 5m/7km SE of Kirkcudbright. Ruined 12c abbey (A.M.). NX 7447
Dundridge Hants 10 C3* loc 2m/3km E of Bishop's Waltham. SU 5718
Dundry Avon 16 B4 vil on **D. Hill** 4m/6km SW of Bristol with extensive view of city. Ch tower built as landmark by Merchant Venturers in 1484. ST 5566
Dundry, East Avon 16 B5* ham 2km SE of Dundry and 4m/7km S of Bristol. ST 5766
Dunduff Castle S'clyde 56 C2 ruins of old baronial fortress 2km E of Dunure. NS 2716
Duneaton Water 65 F6 r in Strathclyde region rising on slopes of Cairn Table and running E to R Clyde 2m/3km N of Abington. NS 9326
Dunecht Grampian 77 G1 vil 2m/4km N of Echt. NJ 7509
Dunfermline Fife 72 D5-73 E5 historic tn 5m/8km NW of Forth rd br. Residence of Scottish kings; burial place of several, incl Robert Bruce. Birthplace of Andrew Carnegie, 1835. Abbey and palace (A.M.). Industries include coal-mining, textiles, engineering. NT 0987
Dunfield Glos 17 F2 ham 2m/4km S of Fairford. SU 1497
Dunford Bridge S Yorks 43 F1 loc on edge of Peak Dist National Park 4m/6km S of Holmfirth. SE 1502
Dungate Kent 21 E5* loc 3m/4km S of Sittingbourne. TQ 9159
Dungavel Hill S'clyde 65 F5 hill 2km N of Roberton. Height 1673 ft or 510 metres. NS 9430
Dungeness Kent 13 F5 loc and headland with lighthouse at SW end of St Mary's Bay, 15m/24km SW across the bay from Folkestone. Atomic power stn. TR 0916
Dungeon Ghyll Force Cumbria 52 C4* waterfall in Dungeon Ghyll 2m/3km NW of Chapel Stile. NY 2906
Dunglass Central 64 C1* outcrop of volcanic rock, incl columnar basalt, 1m E of Strathblane. NS 5778
Dunglass Lothian 67 E2 loc near coast 7m/11km SE of Dunbar. Collegiate ch (A.M.) dates from 15c. **D. Burn** here forms boundary between Lothian and Borders regions. Site of **D. Castle** above Bilsdean Creek – see Bilsdean. NT 7671
Dunglass Point S'clyde 64 B2* headland on N bank of R Clyde at W end of Bowling and 3m/4km E of Dumbarton. Ruins of old cas. NS 4373
Dungworth S Yorks 43 G2* loc 5m/8km NW of Sheffield. SK 2889
Dunham Notts 44 C4 vil on R Trent 5m/8km E of Tuxford. SK 8174
Dunham, Great Norfolk 38 D3 vil 5m/8km NE of Swaffham. **Lit Dunham** vil 2km S. TF 8714
Dunham-on-the-Hill Ches 42 A4 vil 6m/9km NE of Chester. SJ 4772
Dunhampstead H & W 26 D2* loc 2m/4km SE of Droitwich. SO 9160
Dunhampton H & W 26 D1 vil 4m/6km SE of Stourport. SO 8466
Dunham Town Gtr Manchester 42 C3 vil 2m/3km W of Altrincham. SJ 7487
Dunham Woodhouses Gtr Manchester 42 C3* vil 3m/4km W of Altrincham. SJ 7288
Dun Hill Iona, S'clyde. See Dun I.
Dunholme Lincs 45 E3 vil 6m/10km NE of Lincoln. TF 0279
Dun I S'clyde 69 B5 hill on Iona 1km N of Baile Mór. Summit of island, 332 ft or 101 metres. Also known as Dun Hill. NM 2825
Dunino Fife 73 H3 vil 4m/6km SE of St Andrews. Site of Roman camp 2km NE. NO 5311
Dunipace Central 65 E1 tn adjoining Denny and 6m/9km W of Falkirk. NS 8083
Dunkeld Tayside 72 D1 vil on R Tay 10m/15km W of Blairgowrie. D. Cathedral, partly ruined, dates from 12c, though mainly from 14c-15c. Hses (NTS) near cathedral, late 17c, restored. Stanley Hill (NTS), wooded hill to W. **Lit D.** is vil across R Tay to S (rd br by Telford, 1809). NO 0242
Dunkerton Avon 16 C5 vil 4m/7km SW of Bath. ST 7159
Dunkery Hill Som 7 F1 moorland area (NT) on Exmoor 6m/9km SW of Minehead, attaining height of 1705 ft or 520 metres at **Dunkery Beacon,** highest point of Exmoor and of Somerset. SS 8941
Dunkeswell Devon 7 H4 vil 5m/8km N of Honiton. 2m/3km N, ruined 13c D. Abbey; see Abbey. ST 1407
Dunkeswick W Yorks 49 E3 vil 5m/8km S of Harrogate. SE 3046
Dunkirk Ches 42 A4* loc 1m SE of Capenhurst. SJ 3873
Dunkirk Kent 21 F5 vil 5m/8km W of Canterbury. TR 0759
Dunkirk Staffs 42 D5* loc 2m/3km SW of Kidsgrove. SJ 8152
Dunk's Green Kent 20 C6 ham 1m SE of Plaxtol. Site of Roman villa to NE. TQ 6152
Dun Law S'clyde 59 E1* mt in Lowther Hills 2m/3km SE of Leadhills. Height 2216 ft or 675 metres. NS 9113
Dunley Hants 17 H6* loc 1km W of Litchfield. SU 4553
Dunley H & W 26 C1 vil 2m/4km SW of Stourport. SO 7869
Dunlop S'clyde 64 B4 vil 2m/4km N of Stewarton. Gives name to local cheese. Yarn dyeing. NS 4049
Dùn Mór Vaul Tiree, S'Clyde 69 B7* excavated broch of 1c–3c, on N coast to N of Vaul, qv. NM 0449
Dunmow, Great Essex 30 D5 tn on R Chelmer 9m/14km E of Bishop's Stortford. Bacon factory. Ancient 'Dunmow Flitch' ceremony. TL 6222
Dunmow, Little Essex B5 vil 2m/3km E of Gt Dunmow. TL 6521
Dunnet H'land 86 E1 vil on **D. Bay,** N coast of Caithness dist 7m/11km E of Thurso. Loc of **W Dunnet** 1km NW. To N is promontory of **Dunnet Hd.**, culminating in headland of **Easter Hd.** qv. ND 2271
Dunnichen Tayside 77 E6 vil 4m/6km E of Forfar. To E, site of Battle of D. (or Nechtansmere), 685, in which Picts defeated Angles. NO 5048
Dunnideer Grampian. See Castle of D.
Dunning Tayside 72 D3 vil 5m/8km E of Auchterarder. NO 0114
Dunnington Humberside 51 F3 ham 4m/7km NW of Hornsea. TA 1552
Dunnington N Yorks 50 B3 vil 4m/7km E of York. SE 6652
Dunnington Warwicks 27 E2 vil 7m/11km NE of Evesham. SP 0653
Dunnockshaw Lancs 48 B5 vil 3m/5km S of Burnley. SD 8127
Dunnose Isle of Wight 10 C6 headland on SE coast 2km NE of Ventnor. SZ 5878
Dunnottar Grampian 77 H3 loc 2km S of Stonehaven. **D. Castle** is cas on rock on coast to E, dating in part from late 14c. NO 8783
Dunn Street Kent 20 D5* loc adjoining Bredhurst to S, 4m/6km S of Gillingham. TQ 7961
Dunollie Castle S'clyde 70 B2 ruined medieval stronghold on coast 1m N of Oban. NM 8531
Dunoon S'clyde 63 H1 tn and resort in Argyll 4m/7km W of Gourock across Firth of Clyde. Ferry services for vehicles and pedestrians to Gourock and Wemyss Bay. Traces of medieval cas on conical rock above pier. NS 1776
Dunphail Grampian 82 A3* hse and cas on E bank of R Divie 7m/11km S of Forres. NJ 0147
Dunragit D & G 57 B7 vil 3m/5km W of Glenluce. NX 1557
Dunraven Bay Mid Glam 14 D4* small bay on coast 2km S of St Bride's Major. SS 8872
Dun Rig Borders 66 A5 mt 6m/9km S of Peebles. Height 2433 ft or 742 metres. NT 2531
Dunrobin Castle H'land 87 B6 seat of the Sutherland family, on E coast of Sutherland dist 1m NE of Golspie. NC 8500
Dunrossness Shetland 89 E8 dist on Mainland, in par of same name, 5m/8km N of Sumburgh Hd. HU 3915
Duns Borders 67 E3 small tn 13m/21km W of Berwick-upon-Tweed. **D. Law** to N is hill surmounted by earthworks of ancient fort and by Covenanters' Stone, which commemorates encampment of Covenanters' army here in 1639. **D. Castle** is 19c mansion to NW. NT 7853
Dunsa Derbys 43 G4* loc just NW of Edensor. SK 2470
Dunsby Lincs 37 F2 vil 4m/7km N of Bourne. TF 1026
Dunscaith Skye, H'land 79 D7 ruined cas of the Barons of Sleat, on S side of entrance to Loch Eishort. NG 5912
Dunscar Gtr Manchester 47 G6* loc 3m/4km N of Bolton. SD 7113
Dunscore D & G 58 D3 vil 8m/13km NW of Dumfries. NX 8684
Dunscroft S Yorks 44 B1* loc adjoining Hatfield to S. SE 6509
Dunsdale Cleveland 55 E3 ham 2m/3km N of Guisborough. NZ 6018
Dunsden Green Oxon 18 C4* ham 3m/4km NE of Reading. SU 7377
Dun's Dish Tayside 77 F5 small loch 3m/5km E of Brechin. NO 6460
Dunsfold Surrey 11 F2 vil 4m/6km SW of Cranleigh. Airfield to E. TQ 0036
Dunsford Devon 4 D2 vil 4m/7km NE of Moretonhampstead. SX 8189
Dunsforth, Lower N Yorks 49 F2 vil 3m/5km SE of Boroughbridge. SE 4464
Dunsforth, Upper N Yorks 49 F2 ham 4m/6km SE of Boroughbridge. SE 4463
Dunshelt Fife 73 F3 vil 2m/3km N of Falkland. NO 2410
Dunshill H & W 26 D4* ham 4m/6km W of Tewkesbury across R Severn. SO 8331
Dunshillock Grampian 83 G2 vil between Old Deer and Mintlaw. NJ 9848
Dunside Reservoirs S'clyde 65 E5 pair of small resrs 5m/7km SW of Lesmahagow. NS 7437
Dunsinane Hill Tayside 73 E2 hill in Sidlaw range 8m/12km NE of Perth, surmounted by ancient fort identified by Shakespeare with cas of Macbeth. NO 2131
Dunskeath H'land 81 G1 vil in Ross and Cromarty dist on N side of entrance to Cromarty Firth. NH 7968
Dunskeig Bay S'clyde 63 E2* bay on W coast of Kintyre, Argyll, W of Clachan. NR 7556
Dunskey Castle D & G 57 A7 ruined early 16c cas on coast of Rinns of Galloway, 1km S of Portpatrick. NX 0053
Dunsley N Yorks 55 G4 ham 3m/4km W of Whitby. NZ 8511
Dunsley Staffs 35 E5* loc 3m/5km W of Stourbridge. SO 8583
Dunsley, Upper Herts 18 D1* loc on E side of Tring. SP 9311
Dunsmore Bucks 18 D1 vil 2m/3km S of Wendover. SP 8605
Dunsop 47 G3* r rising on Forest of Bowland, Lancs, and flowing S into R Hodder at Dunsop Br. SD 6650
Dunsop Bridge Lancs 47 G3 ham 8m/12km NW of Clitheroe. SD 6650
Dunstable Beds 29 E5 tn at N end of Chiltern Hills 5m/7km W of Luton, at crossing of Roman Watling Street and more ancient Icknield Way, and on site of Roman *Durocobrivae*. Engineering and other industries. Gliding on **D. Downs** (partly NT) to SW. TL 0121
Dunstaffnage Bay S'clyde 70 B2* northward-facing bay 2m/3km W of Connel, Argyll. Remains of **D. Castle** (A.M.), dating from 13c, on W side. NM 8834
Dunstall Staffs 35 G2 ham 4m/6km SW of Burton upon Trent. SK 1820
Dunstall W Midlands 35 E4* loc in Wolverhampton 1m NW of tn centre. **D. Hill** loc adjoining to E. SJ 9000
Dunstall Common H & W 26 D3* loc 6m/10km N of Tewkesbury. SO 8842
Dunstall Green Suffolk 30 C2* loc 7m/11km E of Newmarket. TL 7461
Dunstan Nthmb 67 H6 ham near North Sea coast 3m/5km N of Longhoughton. NU 2419
Dunstanburgh Castle Nthmb 67 H6 ruined 14c cas (NT) on headland at S end of Embleton Bay. NU 2522
Dunstan Steads Nthmb 67 H6* loc 1m E of Embleton. NU 2422
Dunster Som 7 G1 vil below Exmoor and near coast, 2m/3km SE of Minehead. Wide main street with old stone hses; yarn mkt, butter cross (both A.M.). Cas (NT) dates from 11c. SS 9943
Duns Tew Oxon 27 H4/H5 vil 2m/3km S of Deddington. SP 4528
Dunston Lincs 45 E5 vil 8m/12km SE of Lincoln. Beside main rd 4m/6km W, **D. Pillar,** erected in 18c as beacon for travellers. Lamp replaced in 1810 by statue of George III (removed in Second World War as danger to aircraft). TF 0662
Dunston Norfolk 39 F4* ham 4m/6km S of Norwich. TG 2202
Dunston Staffs 35 E3 vil 3m/5km S of Stafford. **D. Heath** loc 2km W. SJ 9217
Dunston Tyne & Wear 61 G5* loc 2m/3km W of Gateshead. **D. Hill** loc adjoining to S. NZ 2262
Dunstone Devon 4 C5 ham 1m E of Yealmpton. SX 5951
Dunstone Devon 4 D3 ham 5m/8km NW of Ashburton. SX 7175
Dunstone Devon 4 D6* loc 4m/6km NE of Prawle Pt. SX 7940
Dunsville S Yorks 44 B1* loc adjoining Hatfield to SW. SE 6407
Dunswell Humberside 51 E4 vil 4m/7km N of Hull. TA 0735
Dunsyre S'clyde 65 F4 vil 6m/9km E of Carnwath. NT 0748
Duntarvie Castle Lothian 65 G1 ruined cas 1m N of Winchburgh. NT 0976
Dunterton Devon 4 A3 ham 5m/7km SE of Launceston. SX 3779
Duntisbourne Abbots Glos 16 D1 vil 5m/8km NW of Cirencester. SO 9707
Duntisbourne Leer Glos 17 E1* ham 5m/7km NW of Cirencester. SO 9707
Duntisbourne, Middle Glos 17 E1* ham 4m/6km NW of Cirencester. SO 9806
Duntisbourne Rouse Glos 17 E1* vil 3m/5km NW of Cirencester. SO 9806
Duntish Dorset 9 E4 ham 1km N of Buckland Newton and 7m/12km SE of Sherborne. ST 6906
Duntocher S'clyde 64 C2 tn on line of Antonine Wall 2m/3km N of Clydebank. Site of Roman fort to E. NS 4972
Dunton Beds 29 F3 vil 3m/5km E of Biggleswade. TL 2344
Dunton Bucks 28 C5 vil 4m/7km SE of Winslow. SP 8224
Dunton Norfolk 38 D2 ham 2m/4km W of Fakenham. **D. Patch** loc to N. TF 8730
Dunton Bassett Leics 36 B5 vil 4m/6km N of Lutterworth. SP 5490
Dunton Green Kent 20 B5 N suburb of Sevenoaks. TQ 5157
Dunton Hills Essex 20 C3* W dist of Basildon. TQ 6688
Dunton Wayletts Essex 20 C3* loc 4m/6km W of Basildon. TQ 6590
Duntreath Castle Central 64 C1 remains of cas, partly 15c, 2m/3km NW of Strathblane. NS 5679
Duntrune Castle S'clyde 70 A5 modernised cas in Argyll on N shore of Crinan Loch. Formerly stronghold of the Campbells, dating from 13c. NR 7995
Duntulm Skye, H'land 78 C2 loc near N coast, 7m/11km N of Uig. **D. Bay** to NW. **D. Castle,** ancient cas restored 1911, at S end of bay. NG 4174
Duntz 6 C3* r rising N of Stibb Cross and flowing N into R Yeo S of Littleham, Devon. SS 4322

Dunure S'clyde 56 C2/C3 vil on coast 5m/8km NW of Maybole. Fragment of old castle. NS 2515
Dunvant (Dynfant) W Glam 23 G6 loc 4m/7km W of Swansea. SS 5893
Dunvegan Skye, H'land 78 A4 vil at head of **Loch D.** on NW coast. **D. Castle** 1m N is ancient stronghold of the Macleods. **Dunvegan Pt** is headland on W side of entrance to loch. NG 2547
Dunwan Dam S'clyde 64 C4 resr 2m/3km SW of Eaglesham. NS 5549
Dunwich Suffolk 31 H2 vil on coast 4m/6km SW of Southwold. Once thriving port submerged by sea. Remains of medieval priory. To S, **D. Common** (NT). TM 4770
Dunwood Staffs 43 E5* loc 3m/4km W of Leek. SJ 9455
Dupplin Castle Tayside 72 D3 mansion of 1832 5m/7km SW of Perth. Stone cross to SW marks site of battle of 1332 in which Balliol defeated Mar. NO 0519
Dupplin Lake Tayside 72 D3 small lake 2m/3km E of Findo Gask and 6m/9km W of Perth. NO 0320
Durdar Cumbria 60 A6* loc 3m/5km S of Carlisle. NY 4051
Durgan Cornwall 2 D5* ham, partly NT, on N bank of Helford R 4m/6km SW of Falmouth. NT property to N includes Glendurgan Hse and grounds. SW 7727
Durgates E Sussex 12 C3 NW part of Wadhurst. TQ 6332
Durham Durham 61 G6 cathedral city on R Wear 14m/22km S of Newcastle upon Tyne. Cathedral is largely Norman. Medieval cas. University. Gulbenkian Museum of Oriental Art. NZ 2742
Durham 117 county of northern England bounded by Tyne and Wear, Northumberland, Cumbria, N Yorkshire, Cleveland, and the North Sea. In the E there is coal-mining and heavy industry; in the W are the open moorlands of the Pennines, which provide rough sheep-grazing, and water for the urban areas from a number of large resrs. Chief tns are the cathedral city of Durham (the county tn) and Peterlee in the E, Darlington, Bishop Auckland and Newton Aycliffe in the S, and the iron and steel tn of Consett in the NW. The principal rs are the Tees and the Wear.
Durisdeer D & G 58 D2 vil 5m/9km N of Thornhill. Sites of Roman camps to S. **Durisdeermill** is loc 1km W. NS 8903
Durkar W Yorks 49 E6* loc 3m/4km SW of Wakefield. SE 3117
Durleigh Som 8 B1 vil below dam of resr 2m/3km W of Bridgwater. ST 2736
Durley Hants 10 C3 vil 2m/4km N of Botley. SU 5116
Durley Wilts 17 F5* vil 5m/8km SE of Marlborough. SU 2364
Durley Street Hants 10 C3 ham 2m/3km W of Bishop's Waltham. SU 5217
Durlow Common H & W 26 B4* loc 8m/12km E of Hereford. SO 6339
Durlston Head Dorset 9 G6 headland 1m S of Swanage at S end of **Durlston Bay**, which extends northwards to Peveril Pt. SZ 0377
Durn Gtr Manchester 48 C6* loc adjoining Littleborough to E. SD 9416
Durnamuck H'land 85 A7 vil on SW side of Lit Loch Broom, W coast of Ross and Cromarty dist. NH 0192
Durness H'land 84 D2 vil near N coast of Sutherland dist 3m/4km S of Far Out Hd. See also Smoo Cave. NC 4067
Durnford, Great Wilts 9 H1 vil on R Avon 5m/8km N of Salisbury. SU 1337
Durnford, Little Wilts 9 H1* ham on R Avon 3m/5km N of Salisbury. SU 1234
Durno Grampian 83 F4 loc 6m/9km NW of Inverurie. NJ 7128
Durobrivae 37 F4* Roman tn on R Nene whose site lies to E of Water Newton, Cambs. TL 1297
Duror 74 B5 r on border of Highland and Strathclyde regions running W into Cuil Bay on E shore of Loch Linnhe. NM 9754
Durranhill, Low Cumbria 60 A5* loc in Carlisle 2m/3km E of city centre. NY 4255
Durrant Green Kent 13 E3* loc 2m/3km N of Tenterden. TQ 8836
Durrants Hants 10 D4* loc 2m/4km N of Havant. SU 7209
Durrington Wilts 17 F6 military vil 2m/3km N of Amesbury. To S, ancient earthwork (A.M.) known as Woodhenge. SU 1544
Durrington W Sussex 11 G4 NW dist of Worthing. TQ 1204
Durris Forest Grampian 77 G2 state forest 6m/9km E of Banchory across R Dee. TV transmitting stn. NO 7892
Dursley Glos 16 C2 Cotswold tn 7m/12km SW of Stroud. ST 7597
Dursley Cross Glos 26 C5* ham 4m/6km S of Newent. SO 7020
Durston Som 8 B2 vil 5m/8km NE of Taunton. Hams of **Hr** and **Lr Durston** to W and E respectively. ST 2928
Durweston Dorset 9 F3 vil on R Stour 2m/4km NW of Blandford Forum. ST 8508
Dury Voe Shetland 89 E7 large inlet on E coast of Mainland opp island of Whalsay. HU 4762
Duston Northants 28 C2 loc in Northampton 2m/3km W of tn centre. Site of Romano-British settlement. SP 7261
Dutchman's Cap Treshnish Isles, S'clyde. See Bac Mór.
Dutch River 50 C5* lowest reach of R Don, flowing E into R Ouse at Goole, Humberside. SE 7422
Duthil H'land 81 H5 vil in Badenoch and Strathspey dist 2m/3km E of Carrbridge. NH 9324
Dutlas Powys 25 G1 loc on R Teme 6m/9km NW of Knighton. SO 2177
Duton Hill Essex 30 B5* vil 3m/5km N of Gt Dunmow. TL 6026
Dutson Cornwall 6 C6* ham 2km NE of Launceston. SX 3485
Dutton Ches 42 B3 vil 4m/6km SE of Runcorn. SJ 5779
Dutton Lancs 47 G4* loc 2m/3km NE of Ribchester. SD 6637
Duxford Cambs 29 H3 vil 3m/4km NW of Gt Chesterford. 13c chapel (A.M.) near Whittlesford rly stn. TL 4746
Dwarfie Stone, The Orkney 89 A7* Neolithic communal burial-chamber on island of Hoy 3m/5km E of Rackwick. HY 2400
Dwyfach 32 C1* r flowing S to join R Dwyfor 2m/4km W of Criccieth, Gwynedd. SH 4637
Dwyfor 116, 118 admin dist of Gwynedd.
Dwyfor 32 C1 r rising in Cwmdwyfor below Trum y Ddysgl, Gwynedd, and flowing S into Tremadoc Bay to W of Criccieth. SH 4737
Dwygyfylchi Gwynedd 40 D4 small resort 2km E of Penmaenmawr. SH 7377
Dwyran Gwynedd 40 B5* vil on Anglesey 2m/3km E of Newborough. SH 4465
Dwyryd 32 D1* r rising near Blaenau Ffestiniog, Gwynedd, and running SW through Vale of Ffestiniog into Traeth Bach, where it joins R Glaslyn off Harlech Pt. SH 5535
Dyce Grampian 83 G5 vil 5m/9km NW of Aberdeen. Aberdeen (Dyce) Airport on W side of vil. **D. Sculptured Stones** (A.M.), 2m/3km N. NJ 8812
Dye House Nthmb 61 E5 ham 4m/6km S of Hexham. NY 9358
Dyer's End Essex 30 C4* S end of vil of Stambourne, 4m/7km NE of Finchingfield. TL 7238
Dyer's Green Cambs 29 G3* loc 3m/5km N of Royston. TL 3545
Dye Water 66 D3 r in Borders region rising on Lammermuir Hills and running E to Whiteadder Water 2m/4km SE of Cranshaws. NT 7159
Dyfatty Dyfed 23 F5* loc on E side of Burry Port, N of power stn. SN 4501
Dyfed 118 large south-western county of Wales, bounded by Powys, W Glamorgan, and the sea. Except for the SW corner and the S coastal area, the county is mountainous, much of it open moorland given over to sheep- and pony-grazing. The SW coast has spectacular cliff scenery and is famed for its bird life. There is coal-mining in the SE coastal area, and other industries which include steel, tinplating, chemicals, and glass mnfre. At Milford Haven there are oil refineries and docks. Tns include Aberystwyth, Carmarthen, Cardigan, Fishguard, which is a port for Ireland, Haverfordwest, Llanelli, Milford Haven, Pembroke, Pembroke Dock, and the resort of Tenby. Carmarthen is the county tn. The many rs include the E and W Cleddau, Taf, Teifi, Towy, and Ystwyth.
Dyffryn Dyfed 22 B2 loc adjoining Goodwick to SW, 1m W of Fishguard. SM 9437
Dyffryn Dyfed 23 E3* loc 2m/3km W of Abernant. SN 3122
Dyffryn Gwynedd 32 D2 vil 5m/8km N of Barmouth. Also known as Dyffryn Ardudwy. Ancient burial-chamber (A.M.) to S. SH 5823
Dyffryn Mid Glam 14 D2 vil 2km N of Maesteg. SS 8593
Dyffryn S Glam 15 F4* loc 3m/4km NW of Barry. ST 0971
Dyffryn Ardudwy Gwynedd 32 D2 vil 5m/8km N of Barmouth. Also known as Dyffryn, qv. SH 5823
Dyffryn Castell Dyfed 33 E6 loc 4m/6km NE of Devil's Br. SN 7781
Dyffryn Cellwen W Glam 14 D1* vil 3m/5km NW of Glyn-neath. Traces of Roman fort to N. SN 8509
Dyffryn Edeirnion (or Vale of Edeyrnion) Clwyd 33 G1 valley of R Dee in vicinity of Corwen. SJ 0743
Dyffryn Meifod Powys 33 H3* valley of R Vyrnwy in vicinity of Meifod. SJ 1512
Dyfi Welsh form of (R) Dovey, qv.
Dyfnant Forest Powys 33 G3 afforested area about 3m/5km S of Lake Vyrnwy. SH 9915
Dyfrdwy Welsh form of (R) Dee, qv.
Dyke Devon 6 B3* loc 1km S of Clovelly. SS 3123
Dyke Grampian 81 H2 vil 6m/10km E of Nairn and 3m/5km W of Forres. NJ 9858
Dyke Lincs 37 F2 vil 2m/3km N of Bourne. TF 1022
Dykehead S'clyde 65 E3 loc 5m/9km NE of Wishaw. NS 8759
Dykehead Tayside 76 D5 vil near foot of Glen Clova 4m/6km N of Kirriemuir. NO 3860
Dyke, High Cumbria 52 D2* loc 3m/5km NW of Penrith. NY 4733
Dyke, Low Cumbria 53 E2* loc 3m/4km NW of Penrith. NY 4833
Dykesfield Cumbria 59 G5* loc 2km W of Burgh by Sands. NY 3059
Dyke Water H'land 86 B3 r running NE into R Halladale 8m/13km S of Melvich. NC 8952
Dylife Powys 33 F5 loc 3m/4km SW of Pennant. SN 8694
Dymchurch Kent 13 F4 small coastal tn at E edge of Romney Marsh 5m/8km SW of Hythe. Holiday camp to NE. TR 1029
Dymock Glos 26 C4 vil 4m/6km NW of Newent. SO 7031
Dynevor Castle Dyfed 23 G3 Victn mansion on site of Elizn hse 1m W of Llandeilo. Used as centre for music and the arts. SN 6122
Dynfant Welsh form of Dunvant, qv.
Dyrham Avon 16 C4 ham 4m/7km S of Chipping Sodbury. **D. Park** (NT), 17c–18c hse with deer park. ST 7375
Dysart Fife 73 F5 loc on Firth of Forth adjoining Kirkcaldy to NE. NT 3093
Dyserth (Diserth) Clwyd 41 F3 vil 3m/4km S of Prestatyn. SJ 0579
Dysynni 32 D4 r rising on S slopes of Cader Idris, Gwynedd, and flowing SW through Tal-y-llyn Lake to Cardigan Bay N of Tywyn. SH 5603

E

Eabost Skye, H'land 79 B5* locality on E side of Loch Bracadale 2m/3km NW of Bracadale. NG 3139
Eachaig S'clyde 70 D6 r in Argyll running S through Loch Eck to head of Holy Loch. NS 1681
Eachaig, Little S'clyde 70 D6* r in Argyll running E down Glen Lean to Clachaig, and continuing E to R Eachaig at head of Holy Loch. NS 1582
Eachwick Nthmb 61 F4* loc 3m/5km SW of Ponteland. NZ 1171
Eagland Hill Lancs 47 E3/E4 ham 4m/6km W of Garstang. SD 4345
Eagle Lincs 44 D4 vil 7m/11km SW of Lincoln. **Eagle Moor** loc 1m NE. **Eagle Barnsdale** loc 1m S. SK 8767
Eaglescliffe Cleveland 54 D3 suburb 3m/5km SW of Stockton-on-Tees. NZ 4215
Eaglesfield Cumbria 52 B2 vil 2m/4km SW of Cockermouth. NY 0928
Eaglesfield D & G 59 G4 vil 3m/5km E of Ecclefechan. NY 2374
Eaglesham S'clyde 64 C4 vil 4m/7km SW of E Kilbride. NS 5751
Eaglethorpe Northants 37 F5* ham adjoining vil of Warmington to N, 3m/5km NE of Oundle. TL 0791
Eag na Maoile Coll, S'clyde 68 B3 group of islets lying nearly 1m off NE end of main island. NM 2765
Eairy Isle of Man 46 B5* loc 3m/5km SE of St John's. SC 2977
Eakring Notts 44 B5 vil 4m/6km S of Ollerton. SK 6762
Ealand Humberside 50 C6 vil 2km SE of Crowle. SE 7811
Ealing London 19 F3 borough and tn 8m/13km W of Charing Cross. Borough contains dists of Acton and Southall and locs of **W Ealing** and **Ealing Common.** TQ 1780
Eamont 53 E2 r flowing from Ullswater in Cumbria and thence NE, passing S of Penrith and running into R Eden 2m/3km SE of Langwathby. NY 5831
Eamont Bridge Cumbria 53 E2 vil at rd crossing of R Eamont, 1m SE of Penrith. Arthur's Round Table (A.M.), ancient earthwork over 90 metres across. See also Mayburgh Henge. NY 5228
Earadale Point S'clyde 62 D5 headland on W coast of Kintyre 4m/6km SW of Machrihanish. NR 5917
Earby Lancs 48 B3 tn 4m/7km N of Colne. Textiles, light engineering. SD 9046
Earcroft Lancs 47 G5* loc adjoining Darwen to N. SD 6824
Eardington Salop 34 D5 vil 2km S of Bridgnorth. SO 7290
Eardisland H & W 26 A2 vil on R Arrow 5m/8km W of Leominster. SO 4168
Eardisley H & W 25 G3 vil 5m/8km S of Kington. SO 3149
Eardiston H & W 26 C1 vil 6m/10km E of Tenbury Wells. SO 6968
Eardiston Salop 34 B2 ham 6m/9km SE of Oswestry. SJ 3625
Earith Cambs 37 H6 vil on R Ouse 7m/11km S of Chatteris. TL 3874
Earle Nthmb 67 F5 loc 2km S of Wooler. NT 9826
Earle's Fields Lincs 37 E1* loc in Grantham 2km W of tn centre. SK 9035
Earlestown Merseyside 42 B2* W dist of Newton-le-Willows. Rly engineering works. SJ 5794
Earley Berks 18 C4 loc 2m/3km E of Reading. SU 7472
Earlham Norfolk 39 F4* loc in Norwich 2m/3km W of city centre. Site of University of E Anglia. **Earlham Hall** dates from 17c. TG 1908
Earlish Skye, H'land 78 B3 loc 2km S of Uig. NG 3861
Earls Barton Northants 28 D2 vil 4m/6km SW of Wellingborough. SP 8563
Earlsburn Reservoirs Central 72 B5* two small resrs 7m/11km SW of Stirling. NS 7089
Earls Colne Essex 30 C5/D5 vil 3m/5km SE of Halstead. TL 8628
Earl's Common H & W 26 D2 ham 5m/7km SE of Droitwich. SO 9559
Earl's Court London 19 F4* dist in borough of Kensington and Chelsea 3m/5km W of Charing Cross. Exhibition hall. TQ 2578
Earl's Croome H & W 26 C3* vil 6m/10km N of Tewkesbury. SO 8742
Earlsdon W Midlands 35 H6 SW dist of Coventry. SP 3177
Earlsferry Fife 73 G4 resort on Firth of Forth adjoining Elie to W. NT 4899
Earlsfield London 19 F4* loc in borough of Wandsworth 5m/8km SW of Charing Cross. TQ 2673
Earl's Green Suffolk 31 E2* loc 2km W of Bacton. TM 0366
Earlsheaton W Yorks 49 E5/E6* dist of Dewsbury 1km E of tn centre. SE 2521
Earl Shilton Leics 36 A4 suburb 4m/6km NE of Hinckley. Hosiery and footwear industries. SP 4697
Earl Soham Suffolk 31 F2 vil 3m/5km W of Framlingham. TM 2363

Earl's Palace Orkney. See Birsay.
Earl's Seat 64 C1 summit of Campsie Fells, on border of Central and Strathclyde regions 3m/5km SE of Killearn. Height 1896 ft or 578 metres. NS 5783
Earl Sterndale Derbys 43 F4 vil 4m/7km SE of Buxton. SK 0967
Earlston Borders 66 C4 small tn in Lauderdale 4m/6km NE of Melrose. NT 5738
Earl Stonham Suffolk 31 E2 vil 4m/6km E of Stowmarket. TM 1058
Earlstoun Loch D & G 58 B3/C3* loch and resr 1m N of Dalry. **Earlstoun Castle**, to E of head of loch, is ruined seat of the Gordons. NX 6183
Earlstrees Northants 36 D5* industrial estate on N side of Corby. SP 8890
Earlswood Surrey 19 F6 SE dist of Reigate. TQ 2749
Earlswood W Midlands 35 G6 vil 4m/7km SW of Solihull. **Earlswood Lakes** are resrs (in Warwicks). SP 1174
Earn 73 E3 r in Tayside region flowing E from Loch Earn down Strath Earn to R Tay 6m/10km SE of Perth. NO 1918
Earncraig 59 E2 hill in Lowther Hills on border of Strathclyde and Dumfries & Galloway regions 7m/11km W of Beattock. Height 2000 ft or 610 metres. NS 9701
Earnley W Sussex 11 E5 vil 3m/5km NW of Selsey. SZ 8196
Earnshaw Bridge Lancs 47 F5* loc adjoining Leyland to NW. SD 5322
Earsdon Tyne & Wear 61 G4 urban loc 2m/3km W of Whitley Bay. NZ 3272
Earshader W Isles 88 B2* loc on W side of Lewis on S side of br connecting Gt Bernera with main island. NB 1633
Earsham Norfolk 39 G5 vil 1m W of Bungay. **Earsham Hall** 17c-19c hse 1m NW. TM 3289
Earsham Street Suffolk 31 F1* ham 2m/3km W of Fressingfield. TM 2378
Earswick N Yorks 50 B3 loc 4m/6km N of York. See also New Earswick. SE 6257
Eartham W Sussex 11 F4 vil 5m/8km W of Arundel. SU 9309
Eas a' Chual Aluinn H'land. Alternative form of Eas Coul Aulin, qv.
Easby N Yorks 54 B5 ham 1m SE of Richmond. Remains of 13c-14c abbey (A.M.) beside R Swale. NZ 1800
Easby N Yorks 55 E4 ham 2m/3km SE of Gt Ayton. See also Captain Cook's Monmt. NZ 5708
Eas Coul Aulin H'land 84 C4 waterfall 1m SE of head of Loch Glencoul. Height 658 ft or 201 metres; highest in Britain. Also known as Eas a' Chual Aluinn. NC 2827
Easdale S'clyde 70 A3 small island off W coast of island of Seil. Former slate quarries. Ferry to Seil across narrow **Easdale Sound.** NM 7317
Easebourne W Sussex 11 E3 estate vil of Cowdray Park 1m NE of Midhurst. SU 8922
Easedale Tarn Cumbria 52 C4* small lake 2m/4km NW of Chapel Stile. NY 3008
Easenhall Warwicks 36 A6 vil 4m/6km NW of Rugby. SP 4679
Eas Fors S'clyde 68 C4* waterfall on Allt an Eas Fors on N side of Loch Tuath, W coast of Mull, 1m NW of Laggan Bay. NM 4442
Eashing Surrey 11 F1 vil 2m/3km W of Godalming. Ham of **Upr Eashing** to E. SU 9443
Easington Bucks 18 B1 ham 3m/5km NW of Thame. SP 6810
Easington Cleveland 55 F3 vil 2km E of Loftus. NZ 7418
Easington Durham 54 D1 2m/4km NW of Peterlee. With **Easington Colliery** to E forms large coal-mining loc near North Sea coast. NZ 4143
Easington Humberside 51 G6/H6 vil near North Sea coast 6m/10km SE of Patrington. TA 3919
Easington Nthmb 67 G5 loc 1m NE of Belford. NU 1234
Easington Oxon 18 B2 loc 3m/4km NW of Watlington. SU 6697
Easington Oxon 27 H4* S dist of Banbury. SP 4538
Easington Lane Tyne & Wear 54 C1 coal-mining loc 2km SE of Hetton-le-Hole. NZ 3646
Easingwold N Yorks 50 A2 small tn 12m/19km NW of York. SE 5269
Eas Mór S'clyde 63 G5* waterfall on Arran 2km NW of Kildonan Castle. NS 0222
Eas nam Meirleach (Robbers' Waterfall) S'clyde 70 C1/D1* waterfall in Argyll in course of Allt Mheuran, qv. NN 1444
Easole Street Kent 13 G2 loc adjoining Nonington to E, 4m/6km S of Wingham. TR 2652
Eassie and Nevay Tayside 73 F1 vil 4m/6km W of Glamis. NO 3345
EAST. For names beginning with this word, see under next word. This also applies to names beginning with North, South, West; Great, Little; Greater, Lesser; High, Low; Higher, Lower; Upper, Nether; Far, Near; Mid, Middle; Isle(s) of; The, Y, Yr.
Eastacott Devon 7 E3 loc 6m/9km W of S Molton. **Eastacott Cross** loc to N. SS 6223
Eastbourne Durham 54 C3 dist of Darlington 2km E of tn centre. NZ 3013
Eastbourne E Sussex 12 C6 coastal resort and conference centre 19m/31km E of Brighton. TV 6199
Eastbrook S Glam 15 F4* loc adjoining Dinas Powis to N. ST 1571
Eastburn Humberside 51 E3 loc 2m/4km SW of Gt Driffield. SE 9955
Eastburn W Yorks 48 C4* vil 1km W of Steeton. SE 0244
Eastbury Berks 17 G4 vil 2m/3km SE of Lambourn. SU 3477
Eastbury Herts 19 E2* loc 3m/5km S of Watford. TQ 0992
Eastby N Yorks 48 C3 vil 3m/5km NE of Skipton. SE 0154
Eastchurch Kent 21 F4 vil on Isle of Sheppey 2m/4km SE of Minster. TQ 9871
Eastcombe Glos 16 D1 vil 3m/5km E of Stroud. SO 8904
Eastcote London 19 E3 loc in borough of Hillingdon 4m/7km NE of Uxbridge. Loc of **Eastcote Village** 1km NW. TQ 1187
Eastcote Northants 28 B2 vil 4m/6km N of Towcester. SP 6854
Eastcote W Midlands 35 G6 ham 3m/5km E of Solihull. SP 1979
Eastcott Cornwall 6 B4* loc 7m/11km NE of Bude. SS 2515
Eastcott Wilts 17 E5 ham 4m/6km S of Devizes. 16c manor hse. SU 0255
Eastcotts Beds 29 E3 loc in SE part of Bedford. TL 0747
Eastcourt Wilts 17 E2 vil 4m/7km NE of Malmesbury. ST 9792
Eastcourt Wilts 17 F5* ham adjoining Burbage to E and 5m/8km E of Pewsey. SU 2361
Eastdean E Sussex 12 B6 vil on S Downs 4m/6km W of Eastbourne. TV 5597
Eastdown Devon 5 E5* loc 3m/5km SW of Dartmouth. SX 8249
Eastend Essex 20 B1* loc 2m/3km W of Harlow. TL 4210
Eastend Essex 21 E3 ham 5m/7km E of Rochford. TQ 9492
Eastend Green Essex 31 E6* E dist of Brightlingsea. TM 0916
Eastend Green Herts 19 G1* loc 2m/4km SW of Hertford. TL 2910
Easter Aquhorthies Grampian 83 F4* site of ancient stone circle (A.M.), 3m/5km W of Inverurie. NJ 7320
Easter Balgedie Tayside 73 E4 vil nearly 1km SE of Wester Balgedie and 3m/5km E of Milnathort. NO 1703
Easter Balmoral Grampian 76 C2 loc on S bank of R Dee 1m SE of Balmoral Castle. Distillery. NO 2693
Easter Bush Lothian 66 A2* veterinary field station 6m/10km S of Edinburgh. NT 2564
Easter Clynekirkton H'land. See Clynekirkton.
Easter Compton Avon 16 B3 vil 6m/10km N of Bristol. ST 5783
Easter Elchies Grampian 82 B3* loc with distillery 1m W of Craigellachie across R Spey. NJ 2744
Easter Fearn Burn H'land 85 F7 stream running NE into Dornoch Firth at **Easter Fearn Pt**, Ross and Cromarty dist, low-lying promontory protruding into the firth 4m/6km SE of Ardgay. See also Wester Fearn Burn. NH 6487
Eastergate W Sussex 11 F4 vil 4m/7km N of Bognor Regis. SU 9405
Easter Head H'land 86 E1 headland with lighthouse at N end of Dunnet Hd, 4m/6km N of Dunnet vil in Caithness dist. Most northerly point of Scottish mainland. ND 2076
Easter, High Essex 20 C1 vil 2m/3km NE of Leaden Roding. TL 6214
Easterhouse S'clyde 64 D2 dist of Glasgow 6m/10km E of city centre. NS 6865
Easter Howgate Lothian 66 A2 loc 3m/5km N of Penicuik. NT 2464
Easter Kinkell H'land 81 E2* loc on Black Isle, Ross and Cromarty dist, 4m/7km NE of Muir of Ord. NH 5755
Easter Lednathie Tayside 76 D4* loc in Glen Prosen 6m/10km NW of Kirriemuir. NO 3363
Eastern Cleddau 22 C4 r rising SW of Crymych Arms, Dyfed, and flowing SW to its confluence with Western Cleddau R to form Daugleddau R. SN 0011
Eastern Green, Lower W Midlands 35 H6* loc in Coventry 3m/5km W of city centre. SP 2979
Eastern Isles Isles of Scilly 2 A1 group of most easterly islands in the Scillies; uninhabited. SV 9414
Easter Pencaitland Lothian. See Pencaitland.
Easter Quarff Shetland 89 E8 loc on Mainland 5m/8km SW of Lerwick at head of bay called **E Voe of Quarff** on E coast. Loc of **Wester Quarff** is 1m W at head of **W Voe of Quarff**, on Lift Sound on W coast. HU 4235
Easter Reach Essex 21 E2* length of R Crouch estuary opp Bridgemarsh I. TQ 8996
Easter Ross H'land 85 C7-F7 eastern part of Ross and Cromarty dist. NH 48
Easterside Cleveland 54 D3* loc in Middlesbrough 2m/3km S of tn centre. NZ 5017
Easter Skeld Shetland 89 E7* loc on Mainland at head of Skelda Voe, to W of Reawick. HU 3144
Easterton Wilts 17 E5 vil 4m/7km S of Devizes. 1km NW, loc of **Easterton Sands.** SU 0255
Eastertown Som 15 H5* loc 1km E of Lympsham. ST 3454
Eastfield Avon 16 B4* dist of Bristol 3m/4km N of city centre. ST 5776
Eastfield Fife 73 F4* dist and industrial estate on SE side of Glenrothes. NT 2999
Eastfield N Yorks 55 H6* loc 3m/4km S of Scarborough. TA 0384
Eastfield S'clyde 65 E2* loc in Cumbernauld 1m W of tn centre. NS 7474
Eastfield S'clyde 65 F3* vil 3m/5km W of Whitburn. NS 8964
Eastgate Durham 53 H1 vil on R Wear 3m/5km W of Stanhope. NY 9538
Eastgate Lincs 37 F3 loc adjoining Bourne to SE. TF 1019
Eastgate Norfolk 39 F3* ham 1m SE of Cawston. TG 1423
Easthall Herts 29 F5* ham 3m/4km W of Stevenage. TL 2022
Eastham H & W 26 B1* ham 4m/6km E of Tenbury Wells. SO 6568
Eastham Merseyside 42 A3 loc in Bebington 3m/5km SE of tn centre. **Eastham Ferry** loc beside R Mersey estuary 1m N. **Eastham Locks**, entrance to Manchester Ship Canal 1m NE. SJ 3680
Easthampstead Berks 18 D4 S dist of Bracknell. SU 8667
Easthampton H & W 26 A2* ham 6m/10km NW of Leominster. SO 4063
Easthaugh Norfolk 39 E3* loc 1m E of Lyng. TG 0817
Easthope Salop 34 C5 vil 5m/8km SW of Much Wenlock. SO 5695
Easthorpe Essex 30 D5 ham 6m/9km W of Colchester. TL 9121
Easthorpe Humberside 50 D4 loc 2m/4km N of Mkt Weighton. Site of former vil to W, partly in Londesborough Park. SE 8845
Easthorpe Leics 36 D1 ham 7m/11km W of Grantham. SK 8138
Easthorpe Notts 44 B5 loc adjoining Southwell to E. SK 7053
Easthorpe N Yorks 50 C1* loc 3m/5km W of Malton. SE 7371
Easthouses Lothian 66 B2 vil 2km SE of Dalkeith. Tweed mnfre. NT 3465
Eastington Devon 7 F4 ham 5m/8km SE of Chulmleigh. SS 7409
Eastington Glos 16 C1 vil 5m/8km W of Stroud. SO 7705
Eastington Glos 27 F6 ham 2km SE of Northleach. SP 1213
Eastleach Glos 17 F1 par 4m/6km N of Lechlade, containing vils of **Eastleach Martin** and **Eastleach Turville**, connected by br over R Leach. SP 1905
Eastleigh Devon 6 D3 ham 2m/4km E of Bideford. SS 4827
Eastling Kent 21 E6 vil 8m/7km SW of Faversham. TQ 9656
Eastmoor Derbys 43 G4* loc 5m/8km W of Chesterfield. SK 3071
Eastmoor Norfolk 38 C4* loc 3m/4km NE of Stoke Ferry. TF 7303
Eastney Hants 10 D5 dist of Portsmouth 2m/3km E of city centre. SZ 6799
Eastnor H & W 26 C4 vil 2km E of Ledbury. SO 7337
Eastoft Humberside 50 C6 vil 3m/4km NE of Crowle. SE 8016
Eastoke Hants 10 D5 loc at E end of S Hayling on Hayling I. **Eastoke Pt** is SE tip of island 1m E. SZ 7398
Easton Berks 17 H4* loc 5m/7km NW of Newbury. SU 4172
Easton Cambs 29 F1 vil 6m/10km W of Huntingdon. TL 1371
Easton Cumbria 59 G5* ham 3m/5km W of Burgh by Sands. NY 2759
Easton Devon 4 D5* loc 3m/5km S of Modbury. SX 6747
Easton Devon 7 E6 ham 3m/5km NW of Moretonhampstead. SX 7188
Easton Dorset 9 E6 vil at centre of Portland. SY 6971
Easton Hants 10 C2 vil in R Itchen valley 2m/4km NE of Winchester. SU 5132
Easton Isle of Wight 10 A5* loc 1km S of Freshwater. SZ 3486
Easton Lincs 37 E2 ham 2m/3km N of Colsterworth. SK 9326
Easton Norfolk 39 E4/F4 vil 6m/10km W of Norwich. TG 1310
Easton Som 16 A6 ham 3m/4km NW of Wells. ST 5147
Easton Suffolk 31 G2 vil 2m/4km NW of Wickham Mkt. TM 2858
Easton Wilts 16 D4 ham 3m/4km SW of Chippenham. ST 8970
Easton Broad Suffolk 31 H1 small broad or lake behind beach 2m/3km NE of Southwold. TM 5179
Easton, Great Essex 30 B5 vil 3m/4km NW of Gt Dunmow. TL 6025
Easton, Great Leics 36 D5 vil 4m/7km NW of Corby. SP 8493
Easton Grey Wilts 16 D3 vil 3m/5km W of Malmesbury. Site of Romano-British settlement to S beside R Avon. ST 8887
Easton-in-Gordano Avon 16 A4 tn 3m/5km E of Portishead. ST 5175
Easton, Little Essex 30 B5 vil 2m/3km NW of Gt Dunmow. TL 6023
Easton Maudit Northants 28 D2 vil 6m/10km S of Wellingborough. SP 8858
Easton Neston Northants 28 C3 loc 1km NE of Towcester. SP 7049
Easton on the Hill Northants 37 E4 vil 2m/3km SW of Stamford. Priest's hse of 15c (NT). TF 0104
Easton Royal Wilts 17 F5 vil 3m/5km E of Pewsey. SU 2060
Eastrea Cambs 37 G4 vil 2m/3km E of Whittlesey. TL 2997
Eastriggs D & G 59 G4 vil 3m/5km E of Annan. NY 2466
Eastrington Humberside 50 C5 vil 3m/5km E of Howden. SE 7930
Eastrop Wilts 17 F2* loc adjoining Highworth to E. SU 2092
Eastry Kent 13 H2 vil 3m/4km SW of Sandwich. TR 3154
East-the-Water Devon 6 D3 dist of Bideford E of R Torridge. SS 4526
Eastville Avon 16 B4* dist of Bristol 2m/4km NE of city centre. ST 6174
Eastville Lincs 45 G5 ham 6m/10km W of Wainfleet. TF 4056
Eastwell Leics 36 D2 vil 6m/10km N of Melton Mowbray. SK 7728
Eastwell Park Kent 13 F2 park with lake in par of Eastwell 3m/4km N of Ashford. Traversed by Pilgrims' Way. TR 0147
Eastwick Herts 20 B1 vil 2km NW of Harlow. TL 4311
Eastwood Essex 21 E3 NW dist of Southend-on-Sea. TQ 8488
Eastwood Notts 44 A6 tn 8m/12km NW of Nottingham. Industries include coal-mining, engineering. Birthplace of D.H. Lawrence, 1885. SK 4646
Eastwood S Yorks 43 H2 dist of Rotherham 1m NE of tn centre. SK 4493
Eastwood W Yorks 48 C5* ham 2m/3km E of Todmorden. SD 9625
Eastwood 116 admin dist of S'clyde region.
Eastwood End Cambs 37 H5* loc adjoining vil of Wimblington to NE. TL 4292
Eathorpe Warwicks 27 G1 vil 5m/8km N of Southam. SP 3969
Eaton Ches 42 B5 vil 2km E of Tarporley. SJ 5763
Eaton Ches 42 D4 vil 2m/3km NE of Congleton. SJ 8765
Eaton H & W 26 A2* loc 1m SE of Leominster across R Lugg. SO 5058

Eaton Leics 36 D2 vil 7m/11km NE of Melton Mowbray. SK 7929
Eaton Norfolk 38 C1* loc 1m W of Sedgeford. TF 6936
Eaton Norfolk 39 F4 dist of Norwich 2m/3km SW of city centre. TG 2006
Eaton Notts 44 B3 vil 2m/3km S of E Retford. SK 7178
Eaton Oxon 17 H2 ham 5m/7km W of Oxford. SP 4403
Eaton Salop 34 B5 loc 3m/5km E of Bishop's Castle. SO 3789
Eaton Salop 34 C5 ham 4m/6km SE of Church Stretton. SO 4990
Eaton Bishop H & W 26 A4 vil 4m/7km W of Hereford. SO 4439
Eaton Bray Beds 28 D5 vil 3m/5km W of Dunstable. SP 9720
Eaton Constantine Salop 34 C4 vil 5m/8km SW of Wellington. SJ 5906
Eaton Ford Cambs 29 F2 loc at N end of Eaton Socon, opp St Neots across R Ouse. TL 1759
Eaton Green Beds 28 D5 ham 3m/5km W of Dunstable. SP 9621
Eaton Hastings Oxon 17 G2 ham on R Thames 3m/5km E of Lechlade. SU 2698
Eaton, Little Derbys 36 A1 vil 3m/5km N of Derby. SK 3641
Eaton Socon Cambs 29 F2 vil 2km SW of St Neots across R Ouse. Traces of medieval cas beside r to E. TL 1658
Eaton upon Tern Salop 34 D2 ham 4m/7km SE of Hodnet. SJ 6523
Eau 44 C1 r rising E of Gainsborough, Lincs, and flowing N and then E into R Trent 2m/3km S of E Butterwick. SE 8303
Eau Brink Norfolk 38 B3* loc 2km NW of Wiggenhall St Germans across R Ouse. TF 5816
Eau, Great 45 H2 r rising S of Driby, Lincs, and flowing NE into North Sea at Saltfleet Haven. The **Long Eau** rises SE of Louth and joins the Gt Eau 1km SE of Saltfleetby All Saints. TF 4793
Eau Withington H & W 26 B3* loc 3m/4km NE of Hereford. SO 5442
Eaval W Isles 88 E1 hill at SE end of N Uist and the highest point on the island, 1138 ft or 347 metres. NF 8960
Eaval W Isles 88 A3* r in Harris rising in Forest of Harris and flowing S into E Loch Tarbert 1km SE of Amhuinnsuidhe. NB 0407
Eaves Brow Ches 42 C2* loc 1km SE of Croft. SJ 6493
Eaves Green Lancs 47 F4* loc 1m NE of Goosnargh. SD 5637
Eaves Green W Midlands 35 H6* vil 5m/8km NW of Coventry. SP 2682
Eaves, The Glos 16 B1* loc 3m/4km NW of Lydney. SO 6006
Eavestone N Yorks 49 E2 loc 4m/7km NE of Pateley Br. **Eavestone Lake** to SE. SE 2268
Ebberston N Yorks 55 G6 vil 6m/10km E of Pickering. SE 8982
Ebbesbourne Wake Wilts 9 G2 vil 4m/7km SE of Tisbury. ST 9924
Ebble 9 H2* r rising to SE of Tisbury, Wilts, and flowing E into R Avon at Bodenham 3m/5km SE of Salisbury. SU 1726
Ebbor Gorge Som 16 A6* 3m/4km NW of Wells. Wooded limestone gorge (NT) in Mendip Hills. Nature reserve. Public access over footpaths. ST 5248
Ebbw (Ebwy) 15 G3 r rising in Powys about 3m/5km N of tn of Ebbw Vale, Gwent, and flowing S into estuary of R Usk S of Newport. ST 3183
Ebbw Vale (Glynebwy) Gwent 15 F1 tn in steep-sided valley 20m/33km N of Cardiff. Coal-mining, steel and brick mnfre. SO 1609
Ebchester Durham 61 F5 vil on R Derwent 3m/4km N of Consett. Site of Roman fort of *Vindomora* in vil. NZ 1055
Ebdon Avon 15 H5* loc just S of Wick St Lawrence and 4m/6km NE of Weston-super-Mare. ST 3664
Ebford Devon 5 F2 vil 5m/8km SE of Exeter. SX 9887
Ebley Glos 16 C1 loc 2m/3km W of Stroud. SO 8204
Ebnal Ches 42 B6* ham 1m NE of Malpas. SJ 4948
Ebnall H & W 26 A2* loc 2km W of Leominster. SO 4758
Eboracum N Yorks. See York.
Ebrington Glos 27 F4 vil 2m/4km E of Chipping Campden. SP 1840
Ebsworthy Town Devon 4 B2* ham 1m NW of Bridestowe. SX 5090
Ebwy Welsh form of Ebbw (R), qv.
Ecchinswell Hants 17 H5 vil 2m/3km W of Kingsclere. SU 4959
Ecclefechan D & G 59 G4 small tn 5m/8km N of Annan. Birthplace of Thomas Carlyle, 1795-1881, in hse (NTS) in main street. NY 1974
Eccles Borders 67 E4 vil 5m/8km W of Coldstream. NT 7641
Eccles Gtr Manchester 42 C2 tn 4m/6km W of Manchester. Textiles, engineering. SJ 7798
Eccles Kent 20 D5 vil 1m N of Aylesford. Site of Roman bldg to N and to W. TQ 7260
Ecclesbourne 43 H6* r rising S of Wirksworth, Derbys, and flowing S into R Derwent at Duffield. SK 3543
Ecclesfield S Yorks 43 H2 suburb in coal-mining area 4m/7km N of Sheffield. SK 3594
Eccles Green H & W 25 H3* loc 4m/7km E of Willersley. SO 3748
Eccleshall Staffs 35 E2 vil 7m/11km NW of Stafford. SJ 8329
Eccleshill Lancs 48 A5* loc 1m NE of Darwen. SD 7023
Eccleshill W Yorks 48 D4 dist of Bradford 2m/4km NE of city centre. SE 1736
Ecclesmachan Lothian 65 G2 vil 3m/5km N of Livingston. NT 0568
Eccles Road Norfolk 39 E5 ham named after rly stn 4m/6km SW of Attleborough. TM 0190
Eccleston Ches 42 A5 vil 3m/4km S of Chester. SJ 4162
Eccleston Lancs 47 F6 tn 4m/7km W of Chorley. SD 5217
Eccleston Merseyside 42 B2 suburb adjoining St Helens to W. **Eccleston Mere** lake to S. SJ 4895
Eccleston, Great Lancs 47 E4 vil 5m/8km E of Poulton-le-Fylde. **Lit Eccleston** loc 1m W. SD 4240
Eccup W Yorks 49 E4 vil 6m/9km N of Leeds. **Eccup Resr,** large resr to SE. SE 2842
Echt Grampian 77 G1 vil 12m/20km W of Aberdeen. NJ 7305
Eckford Borders 66 D5 vil 5m/8km NE of Jedburgh. NT 7026
Eckington Derbys 43 H3 loc 5m/8km E of Dronfield. SK 4379
Eckington H & W 26 D3 vil in loop of R Avon 3m/5km SW of Pershore. SO 9241
Ecton Northants 28 D2 vil 5m/8km E of Northampton. SP 8263
Ecton Staffs 43 F5 loc 1km E of Warslow. SK 0958
Edale Derbys 43 F3 vil 5m/8km NE of Chapel-en-le-Frith, at S end of Pennine Way, in part of R Noe valley known as **Vale of Edale.** SK 1285
Eday Orkney 89 B5, B6 island 8m/12km long N to S and from 4km to under 1km wide, lying between islands of Stronsay and Westray. Peat is plentiful, and is used as fuel on this and other islands in the group. **Eday Sound** is strait between Eday and Sanday to E. See also Calf of Eday. HY 53
Edburton W Sussex 11 H4 ham below Edburton Hill on S Downs 3m/5km S of Henfield. TQ 2311
Edderside Cumbria 52 B1 loc 2m/3km NE of Allonby. NY 1045
Edderthorpe S Yorks 43 H1* loc 1m N of Darfield. SE 4105
Edderton H'land 87 A7 vil on S side of Dornoch Firth, Ross and Cromarty dist, 5m/8km W of Tain. Distillery (Balblair). NH 7084
Eddington Berks 17 G4 loc adjoining Hungerford to N. SU 3469
Eddington Kent 13 G1 loc on S side of Herne Bay. TR 1867
Eddistone Devon 6 B3 loc 5m/8km SW of Clovelly. SS 2421
Eddleston Borders 66 A4 vil 4m/7km N of Peebles. **Eddleston Water** is stream running S through vil to R Tweed at Peebles. NT 2447
Eddlewood S'clyde 64 D3 S dist of Hamilton. NS 7153
Eddrachillis Bay H'land 84 B4 bay on W coast of Sutherland dist extending from Pt of Stoer north-eastwards to Badcall. NC 13
Eddystone Rocks in English Channel (S of 4 A6) about 13m/21km SSW of Rame Hd. Lighthouse. SX 3833
Edeirnion. See Dyffryn Edeirnion.
Eden 116, 117 admin dist of Cumbria.
Eden 12 B3 r rising near Oxted in Surrey and flowing generally SE through Edenbridge, past Hever Castle, and into R Medway at Penshurst, Kent. TQ 5243
Eden 33 E2 r rising S of Trawsfynydd, Gwynedd, and flowing S into R Mawddach 3m/5km N of Llanelltyd. SH 7224
Eden 59 G5 r rising on Black Fell Moss, 6m/10km S of Kirkby Stephen, Cumbria, and flowing SW to Aisgill then N by Kirkby Stephen, Appleby, and Carlisle into Solway Firth W of Bowness-on-Solway. From Burghmarsh Pt forms wide estuary which joins that of R Esk N of Bowness. NY 1763
Eden 73 G3 r rising in Tayside region N of Kinross and flowing E through Fife region to North Sea at St Andrews Bay. NO 4921
Edenbridge Kent 20 B6 small tn 9m/15km W of Tonbridge. TQ 4446
Edenfield Lancs 47 H6 vil 5m/9km N of Bury. SD 7919
Edenhall Cumbria 53 E2 ham 4m/6km NE of Penrith. NY 5632
Edenham Lincs 37 F3 vil 3m/4km NW of Bourne. TF 0621
Eden Mount Cumbria 47 E1* loc adjoining Grange-over-Sands to N. SD 4078
Eden Park London 20 A4* loc in borough of Bromley 1m S of Beckenham. TQ 3768
Edensor Derbys 43 G4 estate vil of Chatsworth Hse 2m/4km E of Bakewell. SK 2569
Edenthorpe S Yorks 44 B1* suburb 4m/6km NE of Doncaster. SE 6206
Edentown Cumbria 59 H5* dist of Carlisle 1km N of city centre. NY 3957
Eden Vale Durham 54 D2 loc 1km S of Castle Eden. NZ 4237
Edern Gwynedd 32 B1 vil 1km SW of Morfa Nefyn. SH 2739
Edeyrnion. See Dyffryn Edeirnion.
Edford Som 16 B6* loc at S end of Holcombe 4m/6km S of Radstock. ST 6749
Edgarley Som 8 C1 loc on SE side of Glastonbury. ST 5138
Edgbaston W Midlands 35 F5 dist of Birmingham 2m/3km SW of city centre. Contains University of Birmingham. SP 0584
Edgcote Northants 28 A3* loc 5m/8km NE of Banbury. SP 5047
Edgcott Bucks 28 B5 vil 6m/10km E of Bicester. SP 6722
Edgcott Som 7 F2* ham on upper reach of R Exe just N of Exford. SS 8438
Edge Durham 54 A2 loc adjoining vil of Woodland to E. NZ 0726
Edge Glos 16 D1 vil 2km W of Painswick. SO 8409
Edge Salop 34 B3 ham 6m/10km SW of Shrewsbury. SJ 3908
Edgebolton Salop 34 C2 loc 5m/8km SW of Hodnet. SJ 5721
Edge End Glos 26 B6* loc 2m/3km NE of Coleford. SO 5913
Edge End Lancs 48 A5* loc adjoining Gt Harwood to W. SD 7232
Edgefield Norfolk 39 E2 vil, with **Edgefield Green,** 3m/5km SE of Holt. TG 0934
Edge Fold Gtr Manchester 42 C1* loc in Bolton 2m/3km SW of tn centre. SD 6906
Edge Green Ches 42 B6* loc 2m/4km N of Malpas. SJ 4850
Edge Green Gtr Manchester 42 B2* loc 2km E of Ashton-in-Makerfield. SJ 5999
Edge Green Norfolk 39 E6* loc 1m S of Kenninghall. TM 0485
Edgehead Lothian 66 B2* vil 3m/5km SE of Dalkeith. NT 3765
Edge Hill Merseyside 42 A3* dist of Liverpool 2m/3km E of city centre. SJ 3689
Edge Hill Warwicks 27 G3 marlstone escarpment of extension of Cotswold Hills 7m/11km NW of Banbury. Site of Civil War battle (1642) in plain 2km NW. Quarries on E side of hill. SP 3747
Edgelaw Reservoir Lothian 66 B3 small resr 4m/6km SW of Gorebridge. NT 3058
Edgeley Salop 34 C1 loc 2km SE of Whitchurch. SJ 5540
Edge, Nether S Yorks 43 H3* loc in Sheffield 2m/3km SW of city centre. SK 3484
Edgerley Salop 34 A3/B3 loc 9m/15km NW of Shrewsbury. SJ 3518
Edgerton W Yorks 48 D6* dist of Huddersfield 1m NW of tn centre. SE 1317
Edgeside Lancs 48 B5* vil 2m/3km N of Bacup. SD 8322
Edgeworth Glos 16 D1 vil 5m/9km NW of Cirencester. SO 9406
Edginswell Devon 5 E4 loc at NW edge of Torbay 2m/3km NW of Torquay tn centre. SX 8866
Edgiock H & W 27 E2* loc 4m/6km NW of Alcester. SP 0360
Edgmond Salop 34 D3 vil 2m/3km W of Newport. **Edgmond Marsh** loc 1m NW. SJ 7219
Edgton Salop 34 B5 vil 4m/6km NW of Craven Arms. SO 3885
Edgware London 19 F3 dist in borough of Barnet 10m/16km NW of Charing Cross. Edgware Rd between here and Central London follows line of Roman 'Watling Street'. Roman settlement of *Sulloniacae* 2km NW. TQ 1992
Edgworth Lancs 47 G6 loc 5m/8km N of Bolton. SD 7416
Edial Staffs 35 G3 loc 3m/4km W of Lichfield. SK 0708
Edinample Central 71 G3 old castellated hse on S side of Loch Earn, 1m SE of Lochearnhead across head of loch. See also Falls of Edinample. NN 6022
Edinbain Skye, H'land 78 B4 vil at head of Loch Greshornish on N coast. Also spelt Edinbane. NG 3450
Edinburgh Lothian 66 A2 historic city and capital of Scotland on S side of Firth of Forth 41m/66km E of Glasgow and 334m/537km NNW of London. Legal, banking, insurance, and cultural centre. Medieval cas (A.M.) on rocky eminence overlooks central area, while Arthur's Seat, qv, guards eastern approaches. Palace of Holyroodhouse (A.M.) is chief royal residence of Scotland. Cathedral. University dating from 1582, and Heriot-Watt University. Port at Leith, qv. Industries include engineering, paper mnfre, printing and publishing, brewing, distilling, tourism. International Festival of Music and Drama held annually. Airport at Turnhouse, 6m/10km W. NT 2573
Edingale Staffs 35 H3 vil 5m/8km N of Tamworth. SK 2112
Edingley Notts 44 B5 vil 3m/4km NW of Southwell. SK 6655
Edingthorpe Norfolk 39 G2 vil 3m/5km NE of N Walsham. **Edingthorpe Green** and **Edingthorpe Street** hams to SW and W respectively. TG 3232
Edington Som 8 B1 vil on N side of Polden Hills 7m/11km W of Glastonbury. 2m/3km N across Edington Heath, vil of **Edington Bugle.** ST 3839
Edington Wilts 16 D6 vil 4m/6km E of Westbury. ST 9253
Edithmead Som 15 H6* ham 2km E of Burnham-on-Sea. ST 3249
Edith Weston Leics 36 E4 vil on S side of Empingham Resr 5m/8km SE of Oakham. SK 9205
Edlaston Derbys 43 F6/G6 ham 3m/4km S of Ashbourne. SK 1842
Edlesborough Bucks 28 D5 vil 4m/6km SW of Dunstable. SP 9719
Edlingham Nthmb 61 F1 vil 5m/8km SW of Alnwick. **Edlingham Castle** is ruined tower hse of 14c. NU 1109
Edlington Lincs 45 F4 vil 2m/3km NW of Horncastle. TF 2371
Edmondbyers Durham 61 E6 vil 5m/8km W of Consett. NZ 0150
Edmondsham Dorset 9 G3 vil 2km S of Cranborne. Manor hse 16c–18c. SU 0611
Edmondsley Durham 54 B1 vil 5m/8km NW of Durham. NZ 2349
Edmondstown Mid Glam 15 E3* loc 2km N of Tonyrefail. ST 0090
Edmondthorpe Leics 36 D3 vil 6m/9km N of Oakham. SK 8517
Edmonton Cornwall 3 E1* loc 2m/3km W of Wadebridge. SW 9672
Edmonton London 19 G2 tn in borough of Enfield 9m/14km N of Charing Cross. Locs of **Lr Edmonton** and **Upr Edmonton** to N and S respectively. TQ 3493
Edmund Hill Som 8 C1* loc on N side of Glastonbury. ST 5039
Ednam Borders 67 E5 vil 2m/3km N of Kelso. NT 7337
Ednaston Derbys 35 H1 loc 8m/13km NW of Derby. SK 2442
Edney Common Essex 20 C2 loc 3m/5km N of Ingatestone. TL 6504
Ednol Powys 25 G2* loc 3m/4km SE of Bleddfa. SO 2364
Edradour Tayside 76 A5* loc 2km E of Pitlochry. Distillery, reputed to be the smallest in Scotland. NN 9557
Edrom Borders 67 E3 vil 3m/5km E of Duns. NT 8255
Edstaston Salop 34 C2 ham 2m/3km N of Wem. SJ 5131

Edstone, Great N Yorks 55 E6 vil 2m/3km SE of Kirkbymoorside. SE 7084
Edstone, Little N Yorks 55 F6* loc 1km NE of Gt Edstone. SE 7184
Edvin Loach H & W 26 B2* loc 2m/4km N of Bromyard. SO 6658
Edw 25 F3* r rising about 4m/7km W of New Radnor, Powys, and flowing S then SW into R Wye near Aberedw, SE of Builth Wells. SO 0747
Edwalton Notts 36 B1 loc adjoining W Bridgford to SE. SK 5935
Edwardstone Suffolk 30 D4 loc 4m/7km E of Sudbury. TL 9442
Edwardsville Mid Glam 15 F2* loc 4m/7km N of Pontypridd. ST 0896
Edwinstowe Notts 44 B4 vil 2m/3km W of Ollerton. SK 6266
Edworth Beds 29 F4 vil 3m/5km SE of Biggleswade. TL 2240
Edwyn Ralph H & W 26 B2* vil 2m/3km N of Bromyard. SO 6457
Edzell Tayside 77 F4 vil on R North Esk 6m/9km N of Brechin. Remains of cas, with 16c tower, 1m W. NO 6068
Eela Water Shetland 89 E6* small but deep loch on Mainland 2m/4km SW of Ollaberry. HU 3378
Eel Pie Island London 19 F4* inhabited island in R Thames in borough of Richmond. Foot br connects island with Twickenham on left bank. TQ 1673
Efail-fach W Glam 14 D2* vil 2m/4km SE of Neath. SS 7895
Efailisaf Mid Glam 15 F3 vil 4m/6km S of Pontypridd. ST 0884
Efailnewydd Gwynedd 32 B1 vil 2m/3km W of Pwllheli. SH 3535
Efailwen Dyfed 22 D3 ham 2m/4km NW of Login. SN 1325
Efenechdyd Clwyd 41 G5 ham 2m/3km S of Ruthin. SH 1155
Effingham Surrey 19 E6 vil 4m/6km SW of Leatherhead. TQ 1153
Effirth Shetland 89 E7* loc on Mainland near head of small inlet of **Effirth Voe**, W of Bixter. HU 3152
Efflinch Staffs 35 G3* loc 1km S of Barton-under-Needwood. SK 1917
Efford Devon 4 B5* dist of Plymouth 2m/4km NE of city centre. SX 5056
Egbury Hants 17 H6 loc 3m/5km NW of Whitchurch. SW 4352
Egdean W Sussex 11 F3 loc 2m/3km SE of Petworth. SU 9920
Egdon H & W 26 D3* loc 5m/8km SE of Worcester. SO 9151
Egel 14 C1 r rising W of Pen Rhiwfawr, W Glam, and flowing S into Upr Clydach R at Rhydyfro. SN 7105
Egerton Gtr Manchester 47 G6 vil 4m/6km N of Bolton. SD 7014
Egerton Kent 13 E2 vil 3m/5km W of Charing. TQ 9047
Egerton Green Ches 42 B5/B6 loc 1m NW of Cholmondeley Castle. SJ 5252
Egerton Park Merseyside 41 H3* dist of Birkenhead 2m/3km S of tn centre. SJ 3286
Eggardon Hill Dorset 8 D4 hill 4m/6km SW of Maiden Newton, crowned by Roman camp. SY 5494
Eggborough, Low N Yorks 49 G5 vil 4m/5km E of Knottingley. Loc of **High Eggborough** 2km SE. SE 5623
Egg Buckland Devon 4 B5 dist of Plymouth 3m/4km NE of city centre. SX 5057
Eggerness Point D & G 57 E7* headland at E end of Garlieston Bay, on W side of Wigtown Bay. NX 4946
Eggesford Devon 7 E4 ham 2m/3km S of Chulmleigh across R Taw. SS 6811
Eggington Beds 28 D5 vil 2m/4km E of Leighton Buzzard. TL 9525
Egginton Derbys 35 H2 vil 4m/6km NE of Burton upon Trent. SK 2628
Egglescliffe Cleveland 54 D3 suburb 4m/6km S of Stockton-on-Tees. NZ 4113
Eggleston Durham 53 H3 vil 4m/6km E of Middleton in Teesdale. NY 9923
Eggleston Burn 53 H3* r rising as Gt Eggleshope Beck on Middleton Common, N of Middleton in Teesdale, Durham, and flowing S into R Tees 1m W of Eggleston. NY 9823
Egglestone Abbey Durham 54 A3 ruined 12c abbey (A.M.) on SW bank of R Tees 2km SE of Barnard Castle. NZ 0615
Egham Surrey 19 E4 mainly residential tn 2m/3km W of Staines. TQ 0171
Egham Wick Surrey 18 D4* loc in Windsor Gt Park 2m/3km W of Egham. SU 9870
Egilsay Orkney 89 B6 sparsely populated island off E coast of Rousay, 3m/5km long N to S, 2km wide near N end, tapering to a point at S end. See also St Magnus's Church. HY 4730
Egilsay Shetland 89 E6* uninhabited island of 54 acres or 22 hectares off W coast of Mainland at entrance to Mangaster Voe. HU 3169
Egleton Leics 36 D4* vil 2km SE of Oakham. SK 8707
Egleton, Lower H & W 26 B3 ham 8m/13km E of Hereford. SO 6245
Egleton, Upper H & W 26 B3* ham 9m/14km E of Hereford. SO 6345
Eglingham Nthmb 67 G6 vil 6m/10km NW of Alnwick. NU 1019
Eglin Lane 56 E4 r running N from Loch Enoch along border of Dumfries & Galloway and Strathclyde regions. R then enters Strathclyde region and continues N to join Whitespout Lane and form Carrick Lane, qv. NX 4693
Eglinton S'clyde 64 B4 loc in Irvine New Tn 2m/3km SE of Kilwinning. NS 3241
Egloshayle Cornwall 3 E1 vil on R Camel opp Wadebridge. SX 0072
Egloskerry Cornwall 6 B6 vil 4m/6km NW of Launceston. SX 2786
Eglwysbach Gwynedd 41 E4 vil 6m/9km N of Llanrwst. SH 8070
Eglwys Brewis S Glam 15 E4* loc 3m/4km E of Llantwit Major. ST 0069
Eglwys Cross Clwyd 34 B1 ham 4m/7km W of Whitchurch. SJ 4741
Eglwyseg River 41 G6* r running S into R Dee at Pentrefelin, 2km NW of Llangollen, Clwyd. SJ 2043
Eglwysfach Dyfed 32 D5/33 E5 loc 5m/8km SW of Machynlleth. SN 6895
Eglwys Fair y Mynydd Welsh form of St Mary Hill, qv.
Eglwys Lwyd, Yr Welsh form of Ludchurch, qv.
Eglwys Newydd ar y Cefn, Yr Gwent. Welsh name of Newchurch, 16 A2, ham 2m/3km W of Devauden. ST 4597
Eglwys Newydd, Yr Welsh form of Whitchurch (S Glam), qv.
Eglwys Newydd, Yr Welsh form of Newchurch, Powys, qv.
Eglwys Nynnid W Glam 14 D3* loc 4m/7km SE of Port Talbot. Resr to W. SS 8084
Eglwys Wen Welsh form of Whitechurch, qv.
Eglwyswrw Dyfed 22 D2 vil 5m/8km SW of Cardigan. Remains of motte and bailey cas. SN 1438
Eglwys Wythwr Welsh form of Monington, qv.
Eglwys y Drindod Welsh form of Christchurch, qv.
Egmanton Notts 44 C4 vil 2km S of Tuxford. SK 7368
Egremont Cumbria 52 A4 small industrial tn 5m/8km SE of Whitehaven. Norman cas on R Ehen. NY 0110
Egremont Merseyside 41 H2 dist of Wallasey to N of tn centre, beside R Mersey estuary. SJ 3192
Egton N Yorks 55 F4 vil 6m/10km SW of Whitby. **Egton Br** vil on R Esk 1km SW. NZ 8006
Egypt Hants 10 B1 loc 5m/8km S of Whitchurch. SU 4640
Egypt S'clyde 64 D3* loc in Tollcross dist of Glasgow. NS 6463
Egypt Point Isle of Wight 10 B5 headland with lighthouse at N end of Cowes. SZ 4896
Ehen 52 A4 r rising as R Liza in Cumbrian Mts on N slopes of Gt Gable, Cumbria, and flowing W into Ennerdale Water, whence it emerges as R Ehen, and flows by Ennerdale Br and Egremont into Irish Sea with R Calder NW of Seascale. NY 0202
Eiddew 33 F2* r rising in Gwynedd and running E into N end of Lake Vyrnwy, Powys. SH 9624
Eiddon 33 E2* stream running S into R Wnion at Rhydymain, 5m/8km NE of Dolgellau, Gwynedd. SH 8021
Eididh nan Clach Geala H'land 85 C7 mt in Ross and Cromarty dist 2m/3km N of Beinn Dearg. Height 3045 ft or 928 metres. NH 2584
Eifl, Yr Welsh form of The Rivals. (Yr Eifl: The Forks.) See Rivals, The.
Eigg H'land 68 C1 island in Inner Hebrides of about 9 sq miles or 23 sq km lying 4m/7km SE of Rum across Sound of Rum. Rises to 1291 ft or 393 metres (An Sgurr or Scuir of Eigg). Sound of Eigg is sea passage between Eigg and Muck. NM 4687
Eight and Forty Humberside 50 D5 loc adjoining Scalby to E. SE 8429
Eight Ash Green Essex 30 D5 vil 3m/5km W of Colchester. TL 9425
Eighton Banks Tyne & Wear 61 G5* loc 3m/5km SE of Gateshead. NZ 2758
Eighton, Low Tyne & Wear 61 G5* loc 2km N of Birtley. NZ 2657
Eildon Borders 66 C5* loc on E side of Eildon Hills, 2m/3km SE of Melrose. NT 5732
Eildon Hills Borders 66 C5 hill with three conspicuous peaks on S side of Melrose. The middle peak rises to 1385 ft or 422 metres; the N peak, 1327 ft or 404 metres, shows traces of prehistoric settlement; the S peak rises to 1216 ft or 371 metres. NT 5432
Eileach an Naoimh S'clyde 69 E6 narrow uninhabited island, 2km long NE to SW, at SW end of Garvellachs group between Jura and Mull. Remains of Celtic monastery (A.M.). Lighthouse at SW end. NM 6409
Eileach Chonail S'clyde 69 E6* alternative name for Dun Chonnuill, qv.
Eilean a' Chalmain S'clyde 69 B6 small island off SW end of Mull, nearly 1m S of island of Erraid. NM 3017
Eilean a' Chaoil H'land 84 F2* islet at entrance to Tongue Bay, 1km E of Midfield, Caithness dist. NC 5965
Eilean a' Chaolais H'land 68 E1* islet off S side of Rubha Chaolais, qv. NM 6980
Eilean a' Char H'land 85 A6* small island in group known as the Summer Isles, qv. Lies 2km W of island of Tanera More and nearly 4m/6km W of Achiltibuie on NW coast of Ross and Cromarty dist. NB 9608
Eilean a' Chleirich H'land 85 A6* uninhabited island, outlier of the Summer Isles group, 4m/7km NE of Greenstone Pt on W coast of Ross and Cromarty dist. Area about 500 acres or 200 hectares. Also known as Priest I. NB 9202
Eilean a' Chonnaidh H'land 84 C2* small uninhabited island off W coast of Sutherland dist 2km NW of Kinlochbervie. Also known as Coney I. NC 2057
Eilean a' Chùirn S'clyde 62 C3 island off SE coast of Islay 2km S of Ardmore Pt. NR 4749
Eilean a' Ghobha W Isles (W of 88 A2) one of the Flannan Isles, qv. Eilean a' Ghobha lies 2m/3km W of the main island, Eilean Mór. NA 6946
Eilean a' Mhuneil H'land. See Poll a' Mhuneil.
Eileanan Diraclett W Isles 88 B3* group of islets in E Loch Tarbert, Harris, 2km SE of Tarbert. NG 1698
Eilean an Eireannaich H'land 84 C3* small uninhabited island at junction of Loch Laxford and Loch a' Chadh-Fi near W coast of Sutherland dist. NC 2050
Eilean an Fhraoich Skye, H'land 78 D4* islet in Kyle Rona, or Caol Rona, between islands of Raasay and Rona. NG 6153
Eileanan Glasa S'clyde 68 D4 group of islets in Sound of Mull 2m/3km NE of Salen. NM 5945
Eileanan Iasgaich W Isles 88 E3* group of islets in Loch Boisdale, S Uist. NF 7818
Eileanan nan Glas Leac H'land 84 D1 group of islets off N coast of Sutherland dist 3m/5km W of Faraid Hd (or Far Out Hd) across entrance to Balnakeil Bay. Also known as Na Glas Leacan. NC 3472
Eilean Annraidh S'clyde 69 B5 islet off NE point of Iona. NM 2926
Eilean an Ròin Mór and **Eilean an Ròin Beag** H'land 84 B2 two uninhabited islands off W coast of Sutherland dist 3m/5km NW of Kinlochbervie. NC 1758
Eilean an Tighe W Isles. See Shiant Is.
Eilean an Tighe W Isles 88 B2* islet at head of E Loch Roag, W coast of Lewis. NB 2230
Eilean a' Phidhir H'land 79 E8 wooded island in Loch Morar, Lochaber dist, 2km E of dam. NH 7092
Eilean a' Phiobaire H'land 74 A1* islet in Lochaber dist off SW shore of Loch Hourn, 2km SW of Corran across loch. NG 8308
Eilean Ard H'land 84 B3* small uninhabited island in Loch Laxford, W coast of Sutherland dist. NC 1850
Eilean Arsa S'clyde 69 F6 small island between island of Shuna and mainland of Argyll. NM 7807
Eilean Balnagowan S'clyde 74 B5/B6 island nearly 1m off E shore of Loch Linnhe at foot of Salachan Glen. NM 9653
Eilean Bàn H'land 79 E8* wooded islet in Loch Morar, Lochaber dist, 1km E of dam. NM 6992
Eilean Beag H'land 79 E5. See Crowlin Is.
Eilean Beag a' Bhaigh W Isles. See Eilean Mór a' Bhaigh.
Eilean Bhride S'clyde 62 C1 most northerly of the Small Isles, qv, off E coast of Jura. NR 5569
Eilean Chalbha S'clyde 69 B5 islet off N coast of Iona 1m W of Eilean Annraidh. NM 2826
Eilean Chaluim Chille W Isles 88 B2/C2* small uninhabited island at entrance to Loch Erisort, E coast of Lewis. Ruins of St Columb's Ch at S end. NB 3821
Eilean Chasgaidh H'land 68 C1 small uninhabited island off Galmisdale at SE end of Eigg. Also known as Eilean Chathastail. NM 4883
Eilean Chathastail H'land 68 C1 small uninhabited island off Galmisdale at SE end of Eigg. Also known as Eilean Chasgaidh. NM 4883
Eilean Choraidh H'land 84 D2 island nearly 1m in length in Loch Eriboll, in Sutherland dist, 2m/4km from head of loch. Also known as Chorrie I. NC 4258
Eilean Chrona H'land 84 A4/B4 small uninhabited island 1m W of Oldany I. off W coast of Sutherland dist. Also known as Chrona I. NC 0633
Eilean Clùimhrig H'land 84 E2 islet at mouth of Loch Eriboll, N coast of Sutherland dist, 2km SE of Eilean Hoan. NC 4665
Eilean Coltair S'clyde 70 A4* islet near N shore of Loch Melfort, 3m/5km W of Kilmelford in Argyll. NM 8012
Eilean Craobhach S'clyde 62 C3* island off SE coast of Islay 1m S of Ardmore Pt. NR 4649
Eilean Creagach H'land 78 B3 one of the Ascrib Is., qv.
Eilean Creagach S'clyde 70 A4* small island between Shuna and mainland. NM 7809
Eilean Dearg H'land 79 E7* one of group of islets off shore of Knoydart, Lochaber dist, off W end of Sandaig Bay. NG 7000
Eilean Dearg S'clyde 63 F1* islet in Loch Riddon, Argyll, with ruins of 17c fort. NS 0077
Eilean Dioghlum S'clyde 68 B4 islet on S side of entrance to Loch Tuath, Mull, off NW coast of Gometra. NM 3542
Eilean Diomhain S'clyde 62 C1* one of the Small Isles, qv, off E coast of Jura. NR 5468
Eilean Donan H'land 80 A5 rocky islet at entrance to Loch Duich, S of Dornie, Skye and Lochalsh dist, with restored cas of the Macraes. NG 8825
Eilean Dubh H'land 85 A6 one of the Summer Isles, qv. Lies 2m/3km S of island of Tanera More. Area about 200 acres or 80 hectares. NB 9703
Eilean Dubh S'clyde 63 F1* small island on W side of entrance to Loch Riddon, Argyll. NS 0075
Eilean Dubh S'clyde 69 B6 small island off SW end of Mull between Eilean a' Chalmain and island of Erraid. Another small island of same name lies off W coast of Erraid. NM 3018
Eilean Dubh S'clyde 69 F7* small island in Loch Craignish 2km E of Craignish Castle. NM 7902
Eilean Dubh S'clyde 70 A2 small island in Loch Linnhe between island of Lismore and mainland to E. NM 8742

Eilean Dubh S'clyde 70 A2 islet off S coast of Lismore, 2m/3km S of Achnacroish. Joined by causeway to Eilean na Cloiche. Other islets in same group are Eilean nan Gamhna, Creag I. and Pladda I. NM 8338

Eilean Dubh Skye, H'land 79 D7* islet near S shore of Loch Eishort, 3m/5km NE of Tarskavaig. NG 6214

Eilean Dubh a' Bhaigh W Isles. See Eilean Mór a' Bhaigh.

Eilean Dubh Mór S'clyde 69 E6 uninhabited island of about 150 acres or 60 hectares lying 2m/3km W of island of Luing. Smaller island, Eilean Dubh Beag, lies across narrow channel to N. NM 6910

Eilean Dùin S'clyde 70 A3 small island off coast of Argyll W of Kilninver. NM 8221

Eilean Fada Mór H'land 85 A6* one of the Summer Isles, qv. Lies between islands of Tanera More and Tanera Beg. Area about 150 acres or 60 hectares. NB 9707

Eilean Fhianain H'land 68 E2* islet in the narrows of Loch Shiel in Lochaber dist. Ruined chapel of St Finnan. NM 7568

Eilean Fladday Skye, H'land 78 D4 uninhabited island of about 360 acres or 145 hectares lying off W coast of Raasay midway between Manish Pt and Eilean Tigh, and separated from Raasay by narrow channel of Caol Fladda. NG 5851

Eilean Flodigarry H'land 78 C3 small uninhabited island 1km off NE coast of Skye 2m/3km N of Staffin. NG 4871

Eilean Fraoch S'clyde 70 C3* islet in Loch Awe opp entrance to arm of loch running NW to Pass of Brander in Argyll. Ruined cas of the Macnaughtons. NN 1025

Eilean Furadh Mór H'land. See Foura.

Eilean Gaineamhach Boreraig Skye, H'land 79 D6* islet in Loch Eishort, opp Boreraig and 2m/4km E of Rubha Suisnish. NG 6215

Eilean Gamhna S'clyde 70 A4 islet at entrance to Loch Melfort, Argyll. NM 7810

Eilean Garave H'land 78 B3 one of the Ascrib Is., qv. Also known as Eilean Geary.

Eilean Garbh S'clyde 62 D3* promontory at N end of W Tarbert Bay, island of Gigha. NR 6553

Eilean Garbh S'clyde 68 C4* islet in Loch Tuath between Ulva and mainland of Mull. NM 4440

Eilean Garbh Skye, H'land 78 D4 small uninhabited island off W coast of Rona. NG 6056

Eilean Geary H'land 78 B3 one of the Ascrib Is., qv. Also known as Eilean Garave.

Eilean Ghaoideamal S'clyde 69 C8 islet off SE coast of Oronsay across Caolas Mór. NR 3787

Eilean Ghòmain S'clyde 69 B6* islet off NW end of Erraid at S end of Sound of Iona. NM 2820

Eilean Glas H'land 79 E7 islet at entrance to Loch Nevis, 1m SW of Sandaig Bay, Knoydart, in Lochaber dist. NG 7000

Eilean Glas W Isles 88 C2* islet at entrance to Loch Erisort, E coast of Lewis. NB 3922

Eilean Heast Skye, H'land 79 E6 small uninhabited island near N shore of Loch Eishort 1km S of locality of Heast. NG 6416

Eilean Hoan H'land 84 D2 small uninhabited island with rocky coast on W side of entrance to Loch Eriboll, N coast of Sutherland dist. Island lies 2m/4km E of Durness and 1km from coast of mainland. NC 4467

Eilean Horrisdale H'land 78 F2 small island in Gair Loch, W coast of Ross and Cromarty dist, opp vil of Badachro. NG 7874

Eilean Iarmain Skye, H'land. See Isle Ornsay.

Eilean Ighe H'land 68 D1 small uninhabited island off coast of Lochaber dist 2m/3km W of Arisaig. NM 6388

Eilean Imersay S'clyde 62 B3* island off S coast of Islay 1km E of Ardbeg across inlet. NR 4246

Eilean Iosal H'land 78 B3 one of the Ascrib Is., qv.

Eilean Iosal H'land 84 F2 small uninhabited island off W coast of Roan I., off N coast of Caithness dist. NC 6365

Eilean Iuyard W Isles 88 B3/C3* uninhabited island at mouth of Loch Shell, E coast of Lewis. NB 3809

Eilean Kearstay W Isles 88 B2* small uninhabited island off W coast of Lewis opp Callanish. NB 1933

Eilean Loain S'clyde 69 F8 island near E shore of Loch Sween in Knapdale, Argyll, 2km SE of Tayvallich across loch. NR 7585

Eilean Meadhonach H'land 79 E5. See Crowlin Is.

Eilean Mhic Chrion S'clyde 70 A4 narrow island, 2km long NE to SW, near W shore of Loch Craignish in Argyll 2km from head of loch. NM 8003

Eilean Mhic Coinnich S'clyde 62 A3* island off S end of Rinns of Islay, 1km S of Rubha na Faing. NR 1652

Eilean Mhuire W Isles. See Shiant Is.

Eilean Mòineseach H'land 85 B5* islet in Enard Bay between Eilean Mór and NW coast of Ross and Cromarty dist. NC 0617

Eilean Molach Central 71 F4 islet at E end of Loch Katrine. Commonly known as Ellen's Isle. NN 4808

Eilean Molach W Isles 88 A2* islet off Ard More Mangersta, headland on W coast of Lewis 4m/6km W of Uig. NA 9932

Eilean Mór Coll, S'clyde 68 B3 small island (but largest of a group) lying 1km off NE end of main island. NM 2764

Eilean Mór H'land 79 E5. See Crowlin Is.

Eilean Mór H'land 85 A5/B5 small uninhabited island in Enard Bay 1km off NW coast of Ross and Cromarty dist. NC 0517

Eilean Mór S'clyde 62 D1 island in Sound of Jura lying 2m/3km SE of Danna I. in Argyll. Remains of St Cormac's Chapel (A.M.), medieval chapel with upper chamber. NR 6675

Eilean Mór S'clyde 69 B6 small island off S shore of Ross of Mull 1m W of Ardalanish Pt. NM 3416

Eilean Mór S'clyde 70 B2 islet opp Dunstaffnage Bay, 2m/3km W of Connel, Argyll. NM 8834

Eilean Mór S'clyde 70 B6 offshore island in Loch Fyne 3m/5km SE of Lochgilphead, Argyll. NR 8883

Eilean Mór W Isles (W of 88 A2) largest of the Flannan Isles, qv, having area of some 30 acres or 12 hectares. Uninhabited except for staff of lighthouse, to S of which are ruins of small chapel dedicated to St Flannan. Island is sometimes used for sheep-grazing. NA 7246

Eilean Mór a' Bhaigh W Isles 88 B3* small uninhabited island off S coast of Lewis 2km SE of entrance to Loch Seaforth. Islets of Eilean Dubh a' Bhaigh and Eilean Beag a' Bhaigh towards coast to N, the last named being the smallest and nearest to coast. NB 2600

Eilean Mór Bayble W Isles 88 C2* islet off Lr Bayble Bay, E coast of Eye Peninsula, Lewis. NB 5330

Eilean Mór Laxay W Isles 88 B2* small uninhabited island near N shore of Loch Erisort, Lewis, S of Laxay. NB 3320

Eilean Mullagrach H'land 85 A6 one of the Summer Isles, qv, nearly 2m/3km off NW coast of Ross and Cromarty dist near Alltan Dubh. Area about 180 acres or 75 hectares. NB 9511

Eilean Musdile S'clyde 70 A2 island with lighthouse off SW end of Lismore, 2m/3km E of Duart Pt on Mull. NM 7735

Eilean na Bà H'land 79 E5 small uninhabited island off W coast of Ross and Cromarty dist 4m/7km S of Applecross. NG 6938

Eilean na Cloiche S'clyde 70 A2* islet off S coast of Lismore, 2m/3km SW of Achnacroish. Joined by causeway to Eilean Dubh to S. Other islets in same group are Eilean nan Gamhna, Creag I. and Pladda I. NM 8338

Eilean na Gàmhna H'land 79 E7* one of group of islets off shore of Knoydart, Lochaber dist, off W end of Sandaig Bay. NG 7001

Eilean na h-Adaig H'land 84 B2 islet off W coast of Sutherland dist 2m/4km NW of Kinlochbervie. NC 1958

Eilean na h-Airde H'land 79 D7 islet off S coast of Skye opp Strathaird Pt or Rubha na h-Easgainne and 2m/3km S of Elgol. NG 5211

Eilean na h-Aon Chaorach S'clyde 69 B6* islet 1km off S coast of Iona. NM 2520

Eilean nam Ban S'clyde 69 B5* small island in Sound of Iona 1km N of Fionnphort. Separated from Ross of Mull by strait of Bull Hole. NM 3024

Eilean nam Breac H'land 79 E8* wooded islet in Loch Morar, on S side of Eilean a' Phidhir, qv. NM 7091

Eilean nam Feannag W Isles 88 A2* islet in Loch Roag, W coast of Lewis, 2km NE of entrance to Lit Loch Roag. NB 1433

Eilean nam Gamhna S'clyde 70 A2 islet off NW coast of island of Kerrera. NM 8130

Eilean nam Muc S'clyde 69 B6* small island off W coast of island of Erraid at SW end of Mull. NM 2819

Eilean nan Coinein S'clyde 62 C1* one of the Small Isles, qv, off E coast of Jura. NR 5468

Eilean nan Each H'land 68 B2/C2 small uninhabited island off NW end of Muck, in Inner Hebrides. NM 3981

Eilean nan Gabhar S'clyde 62 C2 largest and most southerly of the Small Isles, qv, off E coast of Jura. NR 5367

Eilean nan Gamhna S'clyde 70 A2* islet off S coast of Lismore, 1km S of Kilcheran Loch. In same group of islets are Eilean na Cloiche, Eilean Dubh, Creag I. and Pladda I. NM 8338

Eilean nan Gillean H'land 79 E6* small uninhabited island (NTS) 1m NW of Kyle of Lochalsh, Skye and Lochalsh dist. NG 7428

Eilean nan Gobhar H'land 68 E2 islet at entrance to Loch Ailort, Lochaber dist. NM 6979

Eilean nan Ròn H'land 84 F2 fertile island of about 300 acres or 120 hectares, with rocky coast, at entrance to Tongue Bay, N coast of Caithness dist. Also known as Roan I. NC 6465

Eilean na Saille H'land 84 B3* islet off W coast of Sutherland dist 5m/8km W of Rhiconich. NC 1753

Eileann Sionnach Skye, H'land 79 E7* islet with lighthouse in Sound of Sleat, off SE coast of Ornsay. NG 7112

Eilean Ornsay Coll, S'clyde 68 A3 small island lying off SE coast of main island, on W side of entrance to Loch Eatharna. NM 2255

Eilean Ràrsaidh H'land 74 A1* islet off N shore of Loch Hourn in Lochaber dist, 2m/3km W of Arnisdale. NG 8111

Eilean Righ S'clyde 70 A4 narrow island nearly 2m/3km long NE to SW near E shore of Loch Craignish in Argyll. NM 8001

Eilean Ruairidh Skye, H'land 79 D7* islet on S side of entrance to Loch Eishort. NG 5912

Eilean Ruairidh Mór H'land 85 A8* wooded island in Loch Maree, Ross and Cromarty dist. NG 8973

Eilean Rubha an Ridire H'land 68 E4* islet in Sound of Mull lying 1km NW of Rubha an Ridire, Lochaber dist. NM 7240

Eilean Sgòrach Skye, H'land 79 D8 islet lying close to Pt of Sleat on W side. NM 5599

Eilean Shamadalain H'land 79 E7* islet off NW coast of Knoydart, Lochaber dist, 1m NE of Airor. NG 7306

Eilean Shona H'land 68 D2, E2 hilly and partly wooded island at entrance to Loch Moidart in Lochaber dist. E part of island is known as Shona Beag, joined to rest of island by narrow neck of land. NM 6573

Eilean Sneth Dian S'clyde 69 E6 islet off S coast of Mull 2m/4km E of entrance to Loch Buie. Also known as Frank Lockwood's I. NM 6219

Eileans, The S'clyde 63 H2* islets in Millport Bay at S end of island of Gt Cumbrae. NS 1654

Eilean Subhainn H'land 85 A8 island in Loch Maree, Ross and Cromarty dist, nearly 1m NE of Talladale. NG 9272

Eilean Tigh Skye, H'land 78 D4 uninhabited island off N end of Raasay. Area about 180 acres or 75 hectares. NG 6053

Eilean Tighe W Isles (W of 88 A2) second in size of the Flannan Isles, qv, and lying close to, and S of, Eilean Mór, the largest. NA 7246

Eilean Tioram H'land 79 F6 islet at head of Loch Alsh, Skye and Lochalsh dist, opp entrance to Loch Duich. NG 8726

Eilean Traighe S'clyde 63 E2* island at entrance to W Loch Tarbert, Argyll, between Knapdale and Kintyre. NR 7457

Eilean Trodday H'land 78 C2 small uninhabited island 1m N of Rubha na h-Aiseig, headland at northern point of Skye. Used for sheep grazing. NG 4478

Eilean Vow S'clyde 71 E3* islet in Loch Lomond 2m/3km S of Ardlui. Ruined cas of the Macfarlanes. Islet is also known as Island I Vow. NN 3312

Einig H'land 85 D6 r in Sutherland dist running E down Glen Einig into R Oykel 1km SE of Oykel Br. NC 3900

Einion 32 D5 r running NW into R Dovey 1km N of Eglwysfach, Dyfed. SN 6896

Einion 33 H3 r rising in Llyn Hir, Powys, and running E to join R Banwy 2m/3km NW of Llanfair Caereinion. The combined stream, known indifferently as Banwy or Einion, then continues SE to Llanfair Caereinion, then NE into R Vyrnwy 2km SW of Meifod. SJ 1411

Eirth 33 G2 r running SE into R Tanat at Llangynog, Powys. SJ 0525

Eishken W Isles 88 B3 locality on Lewis on N side of Loch Shell 4m/6km W of Lemreway. NB 3211

Eisingrug Gwynedd 32 D1 loc 3m/5km NE of Harlech. SH 6134

Eitha 41 H6* stream rising on Ruabon Mt, Clwyd, and running E through Penycae and the loc of Afon Eitha, then SE to Ruabon, then S into R Dee 2m/3km S of Ruabon. SJ 3041

Elai Welsh form of Ely (R), qv.

Elan 25 E2 r rising 2m/3km E of Cwmystwyth, Dyfed, and flowing E to the Powys border, then SE to Pont ar Elan at head of Craig Coch Resr. It then runs S through Pen-y-garreg and Garreg Ddu Resrs to Caban Coch Resr, where it turns NE and finally SE to join R Wye 2m/3km S of Rhayader. SN 9665

Elan Village Powys 25 E2 ham 3m/5km SW of Rhayader. SN 9365

Elberton Avon 16 B3 ham 3m/4km SW of Thornbury. Quarry to S. ST 6088

Elburton Devon 4 C5 SE dist of Plymouth 4m/6km from city centre. SX 5353

Elchaig H'land 80 A4 r in Skye and Lochalsh dist running NW to head of Loch Long. NG 9330

Elchies Forest Grampian 82 B3* moorland tract W of Rothes. See also Easter Elchies, Wester Elchies. NJ 2246

Elcho Castle Tayside 73 E3 16c stronghold (A.M.) of the Earls of Wemyss. NO 1621

Elcock's Brook H & W 27 E2* loc 3m/5km SW of Redditch. SP 0064

Elcombe Wilts 17 F3* ham 3m/5km SW of Swindon. SU 1380

Eldernell Cambs 37 G4 loc 3m/5km E of Whittlesey. TL 3198

Eldersfield H & W 26 C4* vil 6m/10km W of Tewkesbury. SO 8031

Elderslie S'clyde 64 C3 carpet mnfg tn adjoining Johnstone to E. NS 4462

Elder Street Essex 30 B4* loc 3m/5km SE of Saffron Walden. TL 5734

Eldmire N Yorks 49 F1* loc 2m/3km SE of Topcliffe. Former vil no longer exists. SE 4274

Eldon Durham 54 B2 vil 1m N of Shildon. See also Old Eldon. NZ 2327

Eldridge Essex 29 H4 ham 3m/4km W of Newport. TL 4832

Eldrig Loch D & G 57 C5* small loch or tarn 7m/11km NW of Kirkcowan. NX 1260

Eldroth N Yorks 48 A2* loc 4m/6km W of Settle. SD 7665

Eldwick W Yorks 48 D4* loc 2km NE of Bingley. SE 1240
Electric Brae S'clyde. See Croy Brae.
Elegug Stacks Dyfed 22 B6 two rocks off coast 3m/5km W of St Govan's Hd. Haunt of sea birds (Welsh 'heligog' = guillemot). SR 9294
Elemore Vale Tyne & Wear 54 C1* coal-mining loc adjoining Easington Lane to W. **Elemore Hall** is 18c brick mansion 1m S. NZ 3545
Elerch Dyfed 32 D5/33 E5 vil 3m/4km SE of Talybont. Also known as Bontgoch. SN 6886
Elfhowe Cumbria 52 D5* loc 1m N of Staveley. SD 4699
Elford Nthmb 67 H5 loc 2m/3km W of Seahouses. NU 1831
Elford Staffs 35 G3 vil on R Tame 4m/7km N of Tamworth. SK 1810
Elford Closes Cambs 30 A1* loc 2m/3km SW of Stretham. TL 5072
Elgin Grampian 82 B1 tn and cathedral city mainly on right bank of R Lossie, 5m/8km S of Lossiemouth and 36m/59km E of Inverness. Woollen mfg, distilling. Notable ruins of 13c cathedral (A.M.). Traces of ancient cas. 16c Bishop's Hse (A.M.). NJ 2162
Elgol Skye, H'land 79 D7 vil on E side of Loch Scavaig, on S coast. NG 5214
Elham Kent 13 G3 vil 6m/9km NW of Folkestone. Ham of **N Elham** 1km NE. TR 1743
Elibank Borders 66 B5 loc and ruined stronghold of the Murrays, 4m/7km E of Innerleithen across R Tweed. NT 3936
Elibank and Traquair Forest Borders 66 B5 state forest on S side of R Tweed, to E of Innerleithen. NT 3635
Eliburn Lothian 65 G2* residential area of Livingston 2m/3km W of tn centre. NT 0367
Elie Fife 73 G4 resort on Firth of Forth 5m/8km W of Anstruther. Small harbour. **Elie Ness** is headland with lighthouse at E end of bay enclosing harbour. NO 4900
Elilaw Nthmb 61 E1 loc 4m/6km NE of Alwinton. NT 9708
Elim Gwynedd 40 B3* ham 1km SE of Llanddeusant, Anglesey. SH 3584
Eling Berks 18 A4* loc 6m/9km NE of Newbury. SU 5275
Eling Hants 10 B3 vil adjoining Totton to S. SU 3612
Eliseg's Pillar Clwyd. See Valle Crucis Abbey.
Elishaw Nthmb 60 D2 loc at rd junction 2m/4km NW of Otterburn. NY 8695
Elkesley Notts 44 B3/B4 vil 4m/6km S of E Retford. SK 6975
Elkington Northants 36 C6* loc 8m/12km E of Rugby. SP 6276
Elkington, North Lincs 45 F2 loc 3m/5km NW of Louth. **S Elkington** vil 2km SE. TF 2890
Elkins Green Essex 20 C2* loc just E of Blackmore 3m/5km NW of Ingatestone. TL 6002
Elkstone Glos 26 D6/27 E6 vil 6m/10km S of Cheltenham. Site of Roman villa 2km SE. SO 9612
Elkstone, Upper Staffs 43 F5 ham 5m/8km E of Leek. **Lr Elkstone** loc 1km SE. SK 0559
Ella, East Humberside 51 E5* dist of Hull 3m/4km W of city centre. TA 0529
Ellanbeich S'clyde 69 E6 loc in Argyll adjoining Easdale on W coast of island of Seil. NM 7417
Elland W Yorks 48 D6 tn on S bank of R Calder 4m/6km NW of Huddersfield. Wool textiles. **Elland Lr Edge** and **Elland Upr Edge** locs to E. SE 1021
Ella, South Humberside 51 E5* loc adjoining Kirk Ella to S. TA 0229
Ellastone Staffs 43 F6 vil 4m/7km SW of Ashbourne. **Upr** and **Lr Ellastone** hams adjoining to NW and SE respectively. SK 1143
Ella, West Humberside 51 E5 vil 6m/9km W of Hull. TA 0029
Ellbridge Cornwall 4 B4* loc 3m/5km NW of Saltash. SX 4063
Ellel Lancs 47 F3 vil 4m/6km S of Lancaster. SD 4856
Ellen 52 A2 r rising on Uldale Fells, SE of Uldale, Cumbria, and flowing generally W to Solway Firth at Maryport. NY 0236
Ellenborough Cumbria 52 A2 loc in SE part of Maryport. NY 0435
Ellenbrook Gtr Manchester 42 C1/C2* loc 2m/4km E of Tyldesley. SD 7201
Ellenbrook Herts 19 F1* loc adjoining Hatfield to W. TL 2108
Ellenhall Staffs 35 E2* vil 2m/3km SE of Eccleshall. SJ 8426
Ellen's Green Surrey 11 G2 ham 3m/5km SE of Cranleigh. TQ 0935
Ellen's Isle Central 71 F4 islet at E end of Loch Katrine. Gaelic name: Eilean Molach. NN 4808
Ellenthorpe N Yorks 49 F2* loc 2km E of Boroughbridge across R Ure. SE 4167
Ellerbeck N Yorks 54 D5 ham 4m/7km NE of Northallerton. SE 4396
Ellerburn N Yorks 55 F6 loc 3m/4km E of Pickering. SE 8484
Ellerby Humberside. See Old Ellerby. TA 1637
Ellerby N Yorks 55 F3 ham near North Sea coast 3m/5km S of Staithes. NZ 7914
Ellerdine Salop 34 C2/C3 loc 5m/8km S of Hodnet. **Ellerdine Heath**, ham 1m NE. SJ 6020
Ellergreen Cumbria 53 E5* loc 2m/3km N of Kendal. SD 4995
Ellerhayes Devon 7 G5* loc 5m/7km SW of Cullompton. SS 9702
Eller Keld Cumbria 52 A2* loc 2km E of Workington. NY 0128
Ellerker Humberside 50 D5 vil 2km S of S Cave. SE 9229
Ellers N Yorks 48 C4 loc adjoining Sutton-in-Craven to S. SE 0043
Ellerton Humberside 50 C4 vil 11m/18km W of Mkt Weighton. SE 7039
Ellerton N Yorks 54 B5 vil 1m E of Catterick across R Swale. SE 2597
Ellerton Salop 34 D2* loc 2m/3km E of Hinstock. SJ 7125
Ellerton Abbey N Yorks 54 A5 loc 3m/5km SE of Reeth. Sparse remains of Cistercian nunnery. SE 0797
Ellesborough Bucks 18 C1 vil 2m/4km W of Wendover. SP 8306
Ellesmere Salop 34 B1 small tn 8m/12km NE of Oswestry. The Mere, on E side, one of several in dist, is a large lake used for pleasure boating. SJ 3934
Ellesmere Park Gtr Manchester 42 D2* dist of Eccles 1km N of tn centre. SJ 7799
Ellesmere Port Ches 42 A4 tn at SE end of Wirral peninsula 7m/11km N of Chester. Docks on Manchester Ship Canal. Large oil refinery at Stanlow, 2km E. Other industries include chemicals, paper. SJ 4077
Ellingham Hants 9 H3 loc 2m/3km N of Ringwood. SU 1408
Ellingham Norfolk 39 G5 vil 2m/4km NE of Bungay. TM 3592
Ellingham Nthmb 67 H5 vil 5m/8km SW of Seahouses. NU 1725
Ellingham, Great Norfolk 39 E5 vil 2m/4km NW of Attleborough. Vil of **Lit Ellingham** 2m/3km N. TM 0196
Ellingstring N Yorks 54 B6 vil 4m/6km NW of Masham. SE 1783
Ellington Cambs 29 F1 vil 5m/8km W of Huntingdon. TL 1671
Ellington Nthmb 61 G2/G3 vil 3m/4km N of Ashington. NZ 2791
Ellington, High N Yorks 54 B6 vil 2m/4km NW of Masham. SE 1983
Ellington, Low N Yorks 54 B6 ham 1km NE of High Ellington. SE 2083
Ellington Thorpe Cambs 29 F1* ham 1km S of Ellington and 5m/8km W of Huntingdon. TL 1570
Elliot's Green Som 16 C6* ham 2m/3km SE of Frome. ST 7945
Ellisfield Hants 18 B6 vil 4m/6km S of Basingstoke. SU 6345
Ellisland D & G 59 E3 farm on W bank of R Nith 6m/9km NW of Dumfries, once rented by Burns. NX 9283
Ellistown Leics 36 A3 loc in coal-mining area 2m/3km S of Coalville. SK 4310
Ellon Grampian 83 G4 small tn on R Ythan 15m/24km N of Aberdeen. NJ 9530
Ellonby Cumbria 52 D2 ham 1m W of Skelton. NY 4235
Ellough Suffolk 39 H6* loc 3m/4km SE of Beccles. Loc of **Ellough Moor** 1m N. TM 4486
Elloughton Humberside 50 D5 vil 1m N of Brough. SE 9428
Ellwick Orkney 89 B6* loc and bay on S coast of Shapinsay. Balfour is situated on W side of bay. Elwick is alternative spelling. HY 4816
Ellwood Glos 16 B1* ham 2m/3km SE of Coleford. SO 5908
Elm Cambs 38 A4 vil 2m/3km S of Wisbech. TF 4707
Elmbridge Glos 26 D5* E dist of Gloucester. SO 8519
Elmbridge H & W 26 D1 ham 3m/5km N of Droitwich. SO 8967
Elmbridge 119 admin dist of Surrey.
Elmdon Essex 29 H4 vil 5m/8km W of Saffron Walden. TL 4639
Elmdon W Midlands 35 G5 loc 7m/11km E of Birmingham, on S side of Birmingham Airport. SP 1783
Elmdon Heath W Midlands 35 G6* dist of Solihull 1m NE of tn centre. SP 1680
Elmer W Sussex 11 F5* loc in Middleton-on-Sea, 3m/5km E of Bognor Regis. SU 9800
Elmers End London 20 A4* loc in borough of Bromley 1m SW of Beckenham. **Upr Elmers End** loc 1m SE. TQ 3668
Elmer's Green Lancs 42 B1* loc in NE part of Skelmersdale. SD 4906
Elmesthorpe Leics 36 A4 vil 3m/4km NE of Hinckley. SP 4696
Elmfield Isle of Wight 10 C5* SE dist of Ryde. SZ 6091
Elm, Great Som 16 C6 vil 2m/3km NW of Frome. ST 7449
Elm Green Essex 20 D2* loc adjoining Danbury to W, 4m/7km E of Chelmsford. TL 7705
Elm Grove Norfolk 39 H4* loc adjoining Belton to NE. TG 4803
Elmham, North Norfolk 38 D3 vil 5m/8km N of E Dereham. Remains of Saxon cathedral. TF 9820
Elmhurst Staffs 35 G3* ham 2m/3km N of Lichfield. SK 1112
Elmley Castle H & W 27 E3 vil 4m/6km SW of Evesham. Site of medieval cas 1km S. SO 9841
Elmley Island Kent 21 E5 area of marshland on Isle of Sheppey bounded by The Swale, The Dray, and Windmill Creek. TQ 9468
Elmley Lovett H & W 26 D1* vil 4m/6km E of Stourport. SO 8669
Elm, Little Som 16 C6* ham 4m/7km W of Frome. ST 7146
Elmore Glos 26 C5/C6 vil on left bank of R Severn 4m/6km SW of Gloucester across loop of r. SO 7815
Elmore Back Glos 26 C5 ham on left bank of R Severn 4m/7km W of Gloucester across loop of r. SO 7616
Elm Park London 20 B3* loc in borough of Havering 2m/3km SW of Hornchurch. TQ 5285
Elmsall, North and South W Yorks coal-mining tns 1m apart, respectively 6m/9km and 7m/11km S of Pontefract. SE 4711
Elmscott Devon 6 B3 loc near coast 10m/16km N of Bude. SS 2321
Elmsett Suffolk 31 E3 vil 3m/5km NE of Hadleigh. TM 0546
Elms Green H & W 26 C1* loc 6m/10km SW of Stourport. SO 7267
Elmstead Essex 31 E5 loc 4m/7km E of Colchester. TM 0626
Elmstead London 20 B4* loc in borough of Bromley 2m/3km NE of Bromley tn centre. TQ 4270
Elmstead Heath Essex 31 E5* loc 2m/3km NE of Wivenhoe. TM 0622
Elmstead Market Essex 31 E5 vil 4m/7km E of Colchester. TM 0624
Elmstead Row Essex 31 E5* loc 2m/3km E of Wivenhoe. TM 0621
Elmsted Kent 13 F3 ham 7m/11km E of Ashford. TR 1144
Elmstone Kent 13 G1 ham 2m/4km NE of Wingham. TR 2660
Elmstone Hardwicke Glos 26 D5* ham 3m/5km NW of Cheltenham. SO 9226
Eileanan Gleann Righ S'clyde 69 D8* group of islets in Loch Tarbert, Jura, 1m SE of Rubh' an t-Sàilein. NR 5182
Elmswell Humberside 51 E3 vil 2m/3km W of Gt Driffield. SE 9958
Elmswell Suffolk 31 E2 vil 5m/8km NW of Stowmarket. TL 9863
Elmton Derbys 44 A4 vil 3m/4km NE of Bolsover. SK 5073
Elm Tree Hill S Yorks 43 H3* loc in Sheffield 2m/4km SE of city centre. SK 3885
Elphin H'land 85 C5 vil in Sutherland dist 7m/11km S of Inchnadamph. NC 2111
Elphinstone Lothian 66 B2 vil 2m/3km S of Tranent. NT 3970
Elphinstone Point Kent 21 E4* pt on Isle of Grain at E end of Stoke Saltings. TQ 8574
Elrick Grampian 77 G1 loc 7m/12km W of Aberdeen. NJ 8206
Elrig D & G 57 D7 vil 3m/5km N of Port William. **Elrig Loch** is small loch 1km N. NX 3247
Elsdon Nthmb 61 E2 vil on Elsdon Burn 3m/5km E of Otterburn. Motte and bailey cas. NY 9393
Elsecar S Yorks 43 H1 loc adjoining Hoyland Nether to E. **Elsecar Resr** 1km SW. SE 3800
Elsenham Essex 30 A5 vil 4m/7km NE of Bishop's Stortford. TL 5326
Elsfield Oxon 28 A6 vil 3m/5km NE of Oxford. SP 5310
Elsham Humberside 45 E1 vil 4m/6km NE of Brigg. TA 0312
Elsing Norfolk 39 E3 vil 5m/7km NE of E Dereham. TG 0516
Elslack N Yorks vil 4m/7km W of Skipton. SD 9349
Els Ness Orkney 89 C5* peninsula on S coast of island of Sanday 2m/4km W of Tres Ness. **Holm of Els Ness** is rocky islet to W. HY 6737
Elson Hants 10 C4* N dist of Gosport. SU 6002
Elson Salop 34 B1* loc 1m NW of Ellesmere. SJ 3835
Elsrickle S'clyde 65 G4 vil 3m/5km N of Biggar. NT 0643
Elstead Surrey 11 E1 vil 4m/6km W of Godalming. SU 9043
Elstead Marsh W Sussex 11 E3* loc 3m/5km W of Midhurst. SU 8320
Elsted W Sussex 11 E3 vil 5m/8km W of Midhurst. SU 8119
Elsthorpe Lincs 37 F2 ham 3m/5km NW of Bourne. TF 0523
Elstob Durham 54 C3 loc 4m/6km S of Sedgefield. NZ 3423
Elston Lancs 47 F5 ham 4m/7km NE of Preston. SD 6032
Elston Notts 44 C6 vil 5m/7km SW of Newark-on-Trent. SK 7647
Elston Wilts 17 E6* loc adjoining Shrewton to N and 6m/9km NW of Amesbury. SU 0744
Elstone Devon 7 E3* ham 2m/3km NW of Chulmleigh. SS 6716
Elstow Beds 29 E3 vil 2m/3km S of Bedford. TL 0546
Elstree Herts 19 F2 vil 5m/8km E of Watford. Elstree Airfield 2km NW. Film studios at Borehamwood to E. TQ 1795
Elstronwick Humberside 51 F5 vil 3m/5km NE of Hedon. TA 2232
Elswick Lancs 47 E4 vil 4m/6km N of Kirkham. SD 4238
Elswick Tyne & Wear 61 G5* dist of Newcastle on N bank of R Tyne 2km SW of city centre. NZ 2363
Elsworth Cambs 29 G2 vil 7m/11km SE of Huntingdon. TL 3163
Elterwater Cumbria 52 D4 vil 3m/5km W of Ambleside. To SE is Elter Water lake. NY 3204
Eltham London 20 B4 dist in borough of Greenwich 9m/14km SE of Charing Cross. **Eltham Palace** (A.M.) to S. TQ 4274
Eltisley Cambs 29 G2 vil 6m/9km E of St Neots. TL 2759
Elton Cambs 37 F5 vil 4m/6km S of Wansford. TL 0993
Elton Ches 42 A4 vil 4m/6km E of Ellesmere Port. **Elton Green** loc 1km S. SJ 4575
Elton Cleveland 54 C3 vil 3m/5km W of Stockton-on-Tees. NZ 4017
Elton Derbys 43 G5 vil 5m/8km W of Matlock. SK 2260
Elton Glos 26 C6* loc 2m/3km NE of Newnham. SO 7013
Elton Gtr Manchester 47 H6 loc in Bury 1km NW of tn centre. SD 7911
Elton H & W 26 A1 ham 4m/7km SW of Ludlow. SO 4570
Elton Notts 36 D1 vil 4m/7km E of Bingham. SK 7638
Elton's Marsh H & W 26 A3* loc 3m/5km NW of Hereford. SO 4943
Eltringham Nthmb 61 F5* vil 2km W of Prudhoe. NZ 0762
Eltrington Nthmb 60 D5* loc 2km SE of Haydon Br. NY 8663
Elvanfoot S'clyde 65 F6 vil at confluence of **Elvan Water** and R Clyde 4m/7km S of Abington. Elvan Water rises on Lowther Hills and flows E. NS 9517
Elvaston Derbys 36 A1/A2 vil 4m/7km SE of Derby. SK 4132

Elveden Suffolk 38 C6 vil 4m/6km SW of Thetford. Hall originally Ggn, Indianised 19c, enlarged 20c. TL 8279
Elvet Hill Durham 54 B1* loc 1m SW of Durham. NZ 2641
Elvington Kent 13 H2* vil 6m/10km NW of Dover. Coal mine to E. TR 2750
Elvington N Yorks 50 C3 vil on W bank of R Derwent 7m/11km SE of York. SE 7047
Elwick Cleveland 54 D2 vil 3m/5km W of Hartlepool. NZ 4532
Elwick Nthmb 67 G4/G5 loc 2m/3km N of Belford. NU 1136
Elwick Orkney 89 B6* loc and bay on S coast of Shapinsay. Balfour is situated on W side of bay. Ellwick is alternative spelling. HY 4816
Elworth Ches 42 C5 vil 2km W of Sandbach. SJ 7361
Elworthy Som 7 H2 ham on E edge of Exmoor National Park 5m/8km S of Watchet. ST 0834
Elwy 41 F4 r formed by confluence of Rs Cledwen and Gallen near Llangernyw, Clwyd, and flowing E and finally N into R Clwyd 2km N of St Asaph. SJ 0376
Ely Cambs 30 A1 cathedral city on R Ouse 14m/23km NE of Cambridge. Centre of large fenland agricultural area. TL 5380
Ely (Trelai) S Glam 15 F4 dist of Cardiff S of Ely R 3m/4km W of city centre. Site of Roman villa in Trelai Park to E. ST 1376
Ely (Elai) 15 G4 r rising near Gilfach Goch, Mid Glam, and flowing SE into R Severn estuary at Penarth, S Glam. ST 1972
Emberton Bucks 28 D3 vil 1m S of Olney. SP 8849
Embleton Cumbria 52 B2* vil 3m/5km E of Cockermouth. NY 1730
Embleton Durham 54 D2* loc 4m/7km E of Sedgefield. NZ 4229
Embleton Nthmb 67 H6 vil 7m/11km N of Alnwick. **Embleton Bay** (NT) 1m E on North Sea coast. NU 2322
Embo H'land 87 B7 vil on E coast of Sutherland dist 2m/3km N of Dornoch. **Embo Street** is loc 2km SW. NH 8192
Emborough Som 16 B6 ham 5m/8km N of Shepton Mallet. ST 6151
Embsay N Yorks 48 C3 vil 2m/3km NE of Skipton. **Embsay Moor Resr** 1m NW. SE 0053
Emerson Park London 20 B3* loc in borough of Havering 1km N of Hornchurch. TQ 5488
Emery Down Hants 10 A4 vil 1m W of Lyndhurst. SU 2808
Emley W Yorks 49 E6 vil 3m/5km E of Kirkburton. **Emley Moor** loc 2km W: TV stn. SE 2413
Emmanuel Head Nthmb 67 G4 headland at NE corner of Holy I. NU 1343
Emmer Green Oxon 18 C4 loc 2m/3km N of Reading. SU 7276
Emmets Nest Berks 18 C4* loc adjoining Binfield to S and 2m/3km NW of Bracknell. SU 8470
Emmett Carr Derbys 43 H3* loc 2m/3km SE of Eckington. SK 4577
Emmetts Kent 20 B6* hse and shrub garden (NT) 2m/3km SE of Westerham. TQ 4752
Emmington Oxon 18 C2 ham 3m/5km SE of Thame. SP 7402
Emneth Norfolk 38 A4 vil 2m/4km SE of Wisbech. **Emneth Hungate** loc 2m/3km E. TF 4807
Emorsgate Norfolk 38 A3* loc adjoining Terrington St Clement to W. TF 5320
Empingham Leics 37 E3/E4 vil 5m/8km W of Stamford. **Empingham Resr**, large resr to W. SK 9508
Empshott Hants 10 D2 vil 2m/3km SE of Selborne. Ham of **Empshott Green** to W. SU 7531
Em-sger Dyfed 22 to W of sq A4. Rocky island 3m/4km W of Ramsey I. One of the larger islands in the group known as Bishops and Clerks, qv, and the southernmost. Lighthouse. Also known as S Bishop. SM 6522
Emsworth Hants 10 D4 tn 2m/3km E of Havant. SU 7405
Enard Bay H'land 85 A5 bay on NW coast of Ross and Cromarty dist on E side of Rubha Coigeach. NC 9818
Enborne Berks 17 H5 vil 3m/5km SW of Newbury. SU 4365
Enborne 18 B4 r rising near Inkpen, Berks, and flowing E into R Kennet between Woolhampton and Aldermaston. SU 5866
Enborne Row Berks 17 H3* ham 3m/5km SW of Newbury. SU 4463
Enchmarsh Salop 34 C4 loc 4m/6km NE of Church Stretton. SO 5096
Endcliffe S Yorks 43 G3* loc in Sheffield 2m/3km W of city centre. SK 3286
End, East Beds 28 D3* NE end of Cranfield, 7m/11km SW of Bedford. SP 9642
End, East Beds 29 E2* E end of vil of Wilden. TL 1055
End, East Beds 29 E5* E end of Houghton Regis, 2km N of Dunstable. TL 0224
End, East Bucks 28 C5* loc adjoining Weedon to E, 3m/5km N of Aylesbury. SP 8118
End, East Bucks 28 D3* loc 1m E of N Crawley and 4m/7km E of Newport Pagnell. SP 9444
End, East Cambs 30 B1* E end of vil of Isleham. TL 6574
End, East Cambs 37 H6* E end of vil of Bluntisham. TL 3774
End, East Dorset 9 G4* loc 1km E of Corfe Mullen. SY 9998
End, East Essex 21 F1* loc adjoining Bradwell-on-Sea to E. TM 0007
End, East Hants 10 B5 vil on S edge of Beaulieu Heath in New Forest 3m/5km E of Lymington. SZ 3697
End, East Hants 10 D3* ham 1km E of W Meon. ST 6424
End, East Hants 17 H5 vil 2m/3km W of Highclere. SU 4161
End, East Herts 29 H5* loc 5m/7km NW of Bishop's Stortford. TL 4527
End, East Humberside 51 F3* loc adjoining Ulrome to E. TA 1757
End, East Humberside 51 F5* loc 1km NE of Preston. TA 1930
End, East Humberside 51 G5 loc 1m E of Halsham. TA 2927
End, East Kent 21 E4* loc on N coast of Isle of Sheppey 1m E of Minster. TQ 9673
End, East Oxon 27 G6 ham 4m/7km NE of Witney. Remains of Roman villa (A.M.) to NW. SP 3914
End, East Som 16 B6* ham 4m/6km NE of Shepton Mallet. ST 6746
End, East Som 16 B6* ham 2km S of Chewton Mendip. ST 5951
End, East Suffolk 31 F2* loc 2km E of Stonham Aspal. TM 1559
Enderby Leics 36 B4 vil 5m/8km SW of Leicester. SP 5399
End, Far Cumbria 52 C5* ham adjoining Coniston to N. SD 3098
End Green, West Hants 18 B5* ham 6m/10km NE of Basingstoke. SU 6661
End, Little Cambs 37 G6* NE end of Warboys, 7m/11km NE of Huntingdon. TL 3180
End, Little Essex 20 C2* ham 2m/3km SW of Chipping Ongar. TL 5400
End, Little Humberside 50 C4* loc adjoining Holme upon Spalding Moor to S. SE 8137
End, Lower Beds 28 D5* W end of vil of Totternhoe, 3m/5km W of Dunstable. SP 9722
End, Lower Bucks 18 B1* loc at Long Crendon. SP 6808
End, Lower Bucks 28 D4* ham 3m/5km N of Woburn. SP 9337
End, Lower Northants 28 C2* N end of vil of Brafield-on-the-Green, 4m/7km E of Northampton. SP 8159
End, Lower Northants 28 D2 N end of vil of Grendon, 5m/7km S of Wellingborough. SP 8861
Endmoor Cumbria 53 E6 vil 5m/8km S of Kendal. SD 5384
End, Nether W Yorks 43 G1* loc 2km E of Denby Dale. SE 2407
End, North Avon 16 A4 loc 2m/3km NW of Yatton. ST 4167
End, North Beds 29 E2* loc 1km N of vil of Bletsoe. TL 0259
End, North Cumbria 59 G5/H5* loc adjoining Burgh by Sands to N. NY 3259
End, North Dorset 9 F2* loc 3m/5km NW of Shaftesbury. ST 8427
End, North Essex 30 B6 ham 3m/5km SE of Gt Dunmow. TL 6618
End, North Essex 30 C4* ham 6m/9km W of Sudbury. TL 7839
End, North Hants 10 C2* loc adjoining Cheriton. SU 5829
End, North Hants 10 D4* dist of Portsmouth 2m/3km N of city centre. SU 6502
End, North Hants 9 G3* ham adjoining Damerham and 3m/5km NW of Fordingbridge. SU 1016
End, North Humberside 51 E5* loc adjoining Goxhill to N. TA 1022
End, North Humberside 51 F3* loc 1km N of Bewholme. TA 1650
End, North Humberside 51 F4* loc 1km N of Withernwick. TA 1941
End, North Humberside 51 G5* loc 1km N of Roos. TA 2831
End, North Leics 36 B3* loc adjoining Mountsorrel to NW. SK 5715
End, North Lincs 37 G1* N part of Swineshead. TF 2341
End, North Lincs 45 E2* loc adjoining S Kelsey to N. TF 0499
End, North Lincs 45 G1 loc adjoining Tetney to N. TA 3101
End, North Lincs 45 G2* loc 1km NW of Alvingham. TF 3592
End, North Lincs 45 G2/G3* loc adjoining Saltfleetby St Peter to NW. TF 4289
End, North London 20 B4 loc in borough of Bexley 2km N of Crayford and 14m/22km E of Charing Cross. TQ 5176
End, North Merseyside 41 H1 loc 2km NW of Ince Blundell. SD 3004
End, North Merseyside 42 A3* loc 1m NW of Halewood. SJ 4487
End, North Norfolk 38 D5* loc 1km N of Snetterton. TL 9992
End, North Northants 28 D1* N dist of Higham Ferrers. TL 9669
End, North Nthmb 61 F2* loc 1km N of Longframlington. NU 1301
End, North W Sussex 11 G4* loc 1km N of Findon and 2m/3km S of Washington. TQ 1109
End, North W Sussex 11 F4* ham adjoining Yapton to N, 3m/5km NW of Littlehampton. SU 9804
Endon Staffs 43 E5 vil 4m/7km SW of Leek. **Endon Bank** vil adjoining to NE. SJ 9253
Endrick Water 71 F5 r rising on Fintry Hills in Central region and flowing W into Loch Lomond nearly 1m S of Balmaha. At end of its course it marks border between Central and Strathclyde regions. NS 4289
End, South Beds 29 E3* S dist of Bedford. TL 0448
End, South Berks 18 B4 loc 5m/7km SW of Pangbourne. SU 5970
End, South Hants 9 G3* loc adjoining Damerham to S. SU 1015
End, South Humberside 51 E6 loc 1m SE of Goxhill. TA 1120
End, South Humberside 51 G6 loc 1km S of Easington. TA 3918
End, South Norfolk 38 D5* loc 1km SW of Snetterton. TL 9990
End, Upper Derbys 43 F3* loc just SW of Peak Dale. SK 0876
End, West Avon 16 C3* loc 1km W of Wickwar. ST 7188
End, West Beds 29 E3* ham 1km NW of Stevington, 5m/8km NW of Bedford. TL 9853
End, West Berks 18 C4* ham 2m/3km E of Twyford. SU 8275
End, West Berks 18 D4* loc 2km N of Bracknell. SU 8671
End, West Cambs 29 G1* loc adjoining Fenstanton to W. TL 3168
End, West Cambs 37 H4* NW dist of March. TL 4097
End, West Cumbria 46 D1* loc adjoining Ulverston to S. SD 2977
End, West Cumbria 59 G5 loc adjoining Burgh by Sands to S. NY 3258
End, West Gwent 15 G2* loc in Abercarn on W side of Ebbw R, 2km S of Newbridge. ST 2195
End, West Hants 10 B3 suburb 4m/6km NE of Southampton. SU 4714
End, West Hants 10 C4* SW dist of Fareham. SU 5605
End, West Hants 10 D2* loc 2km SW of Medstead and 4m/6km NE of New Alresford. SU 6335
End, West Herts 19 F1* ham 2m/3km E of Hatfield. TL 2608
End, West Herts 19 G1* ham 3m/4km NW of Cheshunt. TL 3306
End, West Humberside 50 D5* W end of S Cave. SE 9130
End, West Humberside 51 E2 loc adjoining Kilham to W. TA 0564
End, West Humberside 51 F3* loc adjoining Ulrome to W. TA 1656
End, West Humberside 51 F5* loc adjoining Preston to W. TA 1730
End, West Humberside 51 G5 loc at W end of Halsham. TA 2727
End, West Kent 13 G1 loc in SW part of Herne Bay. TR 1565
End, West Lancs 47 E2 SW dist of Morecambe. SD 4263
End, West Lancs 48 A5* loc 2m/3km W of Accrington. SD 7328
End, West Lincs 45 G2 loc 1km S of Marsh Chapel. TF 3598
End, West Norfolk 38 D4* ham 1km NW of W Bradenham. TF 9009
End, West Norfolk 39 H4* ham 2m/3km W of Caister-on-Sea. TG 4911
End, West N Yorks 48 D3 loc on W side of Thruscross Resr 2m/3km NW of Blubberhouses. SE 1457
End, West N Yorks 49 E3* ham 3m/5km NE of Otley. SE 2348
End, West N Yorks 49 G4* loc adjoining Ulleskelf to W. SE 5140
End, West Oxon 17 H1* loc 3m/5km S of Eynsham. SP 4204
End, West Oxon 18 B3* loc adjoining Cholsey to W, 3m/4km SW of Wallingford. SU 5886
End, West S'clyde 65 F4 loc 1m W of Carnwath. NS 9646
End, West Suffolk 39 H6 loc 2m/3km W of Wrentham. TM 4683
End, West Surrey 11 E1 loc 3m/5km S of Farnham. SU 8242
End, West Surrey 18 D5 vil 3m/4km SE of Bagshot. SU 9460
End, West Surrey 19 E5 loc 1km SW of Esher. W End Common to SW. TQ 1263
End, West S Yorks 44 B1* loc 1km S of Hatfield. SE 6608
End, West Wilts 16 D4* loc 4m/7km NE of Chippenham. ST 9777
End, West Wilts 9 F2 loc 4m/6km E of Shaftesbury. ST 9123
End, West Wilts 9 G2* ham 1km W of Ebbesbourne Wake and 4m/6km SE of Tisbury. ST 9824
End, West W Sussex 11 G3* loc adjoining Henfield to W. TQ 2016
End, West W Yorks 48 D5* loc adjoining Cleckheaton to W. SE 1825
End, West W Yorks 49 E4* loc in W part of Horsforth and 5m/8km NW of Leeds. SE 2238
Energlyn Mid Glam 15 F3* loc adjoining Caerphilly to N. Industrial estate. ST 1588
Enfield H & W 27 E1* N dist of Redditch. SP 0368
Enfield London 19 G2 tn and London borough 10m/16km N of Charing Cross. To NW is rural area of **Enfield Chase**, formerly a forest. TQ 3296
Enfield Highway London 20 A2 loc 2m/3km E of Enfield in borough of Enfield. TQ 3597
Enfield Lock London 20 A2* loc on R Lea 3m/5km E of Enfield in borough of Enfield. TQ 3798
Enfield Wash London 20 A2 loc 2m/4km NE of Enfield in borough of Enfield. TQ 3598
Enford Wilts 17 F6 vil on R Avon 2m/4km S of Upavon. SU 1351
Engedi Gwynedd 40 B4* loc on Anglesey 2m/3km W of Gwalchmai. SH 3676
Engine Common Avon 16 C3 vil 2m/4km NW of Chipping Sodbury. ST 6984
Engine, The Lincs 37 G4 loc 2m/3km SE of Crowland. TF 2508
England's Gate H & W 26 B3* loc 7m/12km N of Hereford. SO 5451
Englefield Berks 18 B4 vil 6m/10km W of Reading. SU 6272
Englefield Green Surrey 18 D4* suburban vil 3m/5km W of Staines. SU 9971
Englesea-brook Ches 42 C6 ham 4m/6km SE of Crewe. SJ 7551
English Bicknor Glos 26 B5 vil 3m/5km N of Coleford. SO 5815
Englishcombe Avon 16 C5 vil 3m/4km SW of Bath. ST 7162
English Frankton Salop 34 B2 ham 5m/8km SE of Ellesmere. SJ 4529
Enham Alamein Hants 17 G6 vil 3m/4km N of Andover. Name changed from Knight's Enham in 1945. SU 3649
Enham, Upper Hants 17 G6* loc 3m/5km N of Andover. SU 3649
Enmore Som 8 A1 vil 4m/6km W of Bridgwater. ST 2434
Ennerdale Bridge Cumbria 52 B3 ham astride R Ehen 2km from W end of Ennerdale Water. NY 0615
Ennerdale Water Cumbria 52 B3 lake 4km in length, running E and W in course of

R Liza or Ehen, the W end being 2km E of Ennerdale Br. **Ennerdale Fell** rises steeply to S. **Ennerdale Forest** is area of conifers to E. NY 1015
Enniscaven Cornwall 3 E3* loc 5m/8km NW of Austell. SW 9659
Ennochdhu Tayside 76 B4 loc in Strath Ardle 2m/3km NW of Kirkmichael. Field study centre at Kindrogan, below Kindrogan Hill across R Ardle. NO 0662
Enochdu Tayside. See Ennochdhu.
Enrick H'land 81 E4 r in Inverness dist running E down Glen Urquhart to Urquhart Bay on NW side of Loch Ness. NH 5229
Ensay W Isles 88 A4* barely populated island in Sound of Harris 2m/4km off W coast of Harris at Leverburgh. Measures nearly 3km N to S and 1km E to W. NF 9686
Ensbury Dorset 9 G4 N dist of Bournemouth. SZ 0896
Ensden, Lower Kent 21 F6* loc 5m/8km W of Canterbury. TR 0755
Ensdon Salop 34 B3 ham 2km NE of Shrawardine. SJ 4016
Ensis Devon 6 D3 ham 4m/7km S of Barnstaple. SS 5626
Enson Staffs 35 F2* loc on R Trent 4m/6km NE of Stafford. SJ 9428
Enstone Oxon 27 G5 vil 4m/7km E of Chipping Norton. SP 3724
Enterkinfoot D & G 58 D2 loc at confluence of R Nith and **Enterkin Burn,** 6m/9km N of Thornhill. NS 8504
Enterpen N Yorks 54 D4 loc adjoining Hutton Rudby to S. NZ 4606
Enton Green Surrey 11 F1* loc 2km SE of Milford. SU 9540
Enville Staffs 35 E5 vil 5m/8km W of Stourbridge. SO 8286
Eoligarry W Isles 88 D3* vil on Barra 1m S of Scurrival Pt. NF 7007
Eoropie W Isles 88 C1* vil 1m S of Butt of Lewis. NB 5164
Eorsa S'clyde 68 C4 uninhabited island in Loch na Keal, W coast of Mull. Area about 250 acres or 100 hectares. Provides grazing for sheep. NM 4837
Epney Glos 26 C6* ham on left bank of R Severn 7m/11km SW of Gloucester. SO 7611
Epperstone Notts 44 B6 vil 7m/12km NE of Nottingham. SK 6548
Epping Essex 20 B2 tn at N end of **Epping Forest** and 17m/27km NE of London. Forest is open woodland some 5m/8km long (NE-SW) and 2km wide, traversed by several rds. N and W of tn is par of **Epping Upland,** containing vil of same name and vil of **Epping Green** with loc of **Epping Long Green.** TL 4602
Epping Green Herts 19 G1 ham 4m/6km SW of Hertford. TL 2906
Epple Bay Kent 13 H1* N coast bay at Birchington. TR 3069
Eppleby N Yorks 54 B3 vil 3m/4km SW of Piercebridge. NZ 1713
Eppleton, Great Tyne & Wear 61 H6* loc 1m E of Hetton-le-Hole. NZ 3648
Eppleworth Humberside 51 E5 loc 2m/3km W of Cottingham. TA 0131
Epsom Surrey 19 F5 tn 6m/9km S of Kingston. Racecourse to S. TQ 2060
Epwell Oxon 27 G3 vil 7m/11km W of Banbury. SP 3540
Epworth Humberside 44 C1 small tn on Isle of Axholme 9m/15km N of Gainsborough. Childhood home of John and Charles Wesley. **Epworth Turbary** loc 2km W. SE 7803
Erbistock (Erbistog) Clwyd 42 A6 vil 2km W of Overton across R Dee. SJ 3541
Erbusaig H'land 79 E5/F5 loc in Skye and Lochalsh dist on **Erbusaig Bay** 2km N of Kyle of Lochalsh. NG 7629
Ercall, High Salop 34 C3 vil 5m/8km NW of Wellington. The hall is part of once larger hse of early 17c. SJ 5917
Erch 32 B1/B2 r rising near Llanaelhaearn, Gwynedd, and running S into Pwllheli harbour. SH 3835
Erchless Forest H'land 80 D3 deer forest in Inverness dist W of Beauly and S of Orrin Resr. To S in Strathglass is **Erchless Castle,** 15c seat of The Chisholm, chief of the clan owning Strathglass. NH 4145
Erdington W Midlands 35 G5 loc in Birmingham 5m/7km NE of city centre. SP 1191
Eredine S'clyde 70 B4 hse near N end of **Eredine Forest,** state forest on E side of Loch Awe in Argyll above Portinnisherrich. NM 9609
Erewash 117 admin dist of Derbys.
Erewash 36 B1 r rising S of Kirkby in Ashfield, Notts, and flowing S into R Trent 2m/3km E of Long Eaton. For most of its length it marks boundary between Derbys and Notts. SK 5133
Erewash Canal 43 H6-36 B2 canal running beside R Erewash between Langley Mill, Derbys, and R Trent at Trent Junction near Sawley.
Eriboll H'land 84 D2 locality on E side of Loch Eriboll, Sutherland dist, 2m/4km NE of head of loch. NC 4356
Ericht 75 F5 r in Tayside region issuing from Loch Ericht and flowing S to Loch Rannoch. NN 5257
Ericht 76 C6 r in Tayside region formed by R Ardle and Black Water, and running S to Blairgowrie then SE to R Isla 2m/3km NE of Coupar Angus. NO 2342
Eridge Green E Sussex 12 B3 estate vil on W side of Eridge Park 3m/5km SW of Tunbridge Wells. TQ 5535
Erisey Cornwall 2 C6* loc 4m/7km N of Lizard Pt. SW 7117
Erisgeir S'clyde 69 C5 flat-topped rocky islet 2m/4km NW of Rubha nan Goirteanan on W coast of Mull and 3m/4km S of island of Lit Colonsay. Provides occasional grazing for sheep. NM 3832
Eriska S'clyde 70 B1 island at entrance to Loch Creran. Causeway connection to mainland on S side. NM 9043
Eriskay W Isles 88 E3 island of about 3 sq miles or 8 sq km lying 1m S of S Uist and 5m/8km E of the N point of Barra. Small vil at N end. Lobster-fishing is carried on. Here Prince Charles Edward first landed on Scottish soil in 1744 – see Coilleag a' Phrionnsa. NF 7910
Eriswell Suffolk 38 C6 vil 2m/4km NE of Mildenhall. TL 7278
Erith London 20 B4 dist in borough of Bexley on S bank of R Thames 13m/21km E of Charing Cross. **Erith Marshes** to NW. **Erith Reach** of R Thames to N, and **Erith Rands,** another reach, to E. TQ 5177
Erlestoke Wilts 16 D5 vil 6m/9km E of Westbury. ST 9653
Erme 4 C5 r in Devon rising on Dartmoor and flowing S into Bigbury Bay 2m/3km S of Holbeton. SX 6147
Ermine, East and **West.** Lincs 44 D4* N dists of Lincoln. SK 9773
Ermine Street 29 G1 etc. Roman rd which ran from near Pevensey to York, by London and Lincoln. Another rd of the same name ran from Gloucester to Silchester. Present-day rds follow the line of both for considerable stretches.
Ermington Devon 4 C5 vil on R Erme 2m/3km S of Ivybridge. SX 6353
Ernan Water 82 C5*. See Glen Ernan.
Ernesettle Devon 4 B5* N dist of Plymouth, 4m/6km from city centre. SX 4560
Erocavum Cumbria. See Brougham.
Erpingham Norfolk 39 F2 vil 3m/5km N of Aylsham. TG 1931
Erradale, North H'land 78 E2 vil near W coast of Ross and Cromarty dist 4m/7km NW of Gairloch. NG 7481
Erradale, South H'land 78 E3 loc on W coast of Ross and Cromarty dist 3m/4km N of Red Pt. NG 7471
Erraid S'clyde 69 B6 sparsely populated island of 1 sq mile lying off W end of Ross of Mull across **Erraid Sound,** fordable at low tide. Described in unflattering terms by R.L. Stevenson in *Kidnapped.* NM 2919
Erringden W Yorks 48 C5* loc 1m S of Hebden Br. SD 9826
Erriottwood Kent 21 E5* loc 3m/5km SE of Sittingbourne. TQ 9359
Errochty Water 75 H4 r in Tayside region running E from Loch Errochty down Glen Errochty to R Garry near Calvine. NN 8065
Errogie H'land 81 E5 locality near NE end of Loch Mhór in Inverness dist, 3m/4km E of Inverfarigaig. NH 5622
Errol Tayside 73 F2 vil in Carse of Gowrie 8m/13km E of Perth. NO 2522
Ersary W Isles 88 D3/D4 vil on E coast of Barra 3m/5km E of Castlebay. NL 7099
Erskine Bridge S'clyde 64 C2* rd br across R Clyde at Old Kirkpatrick, 3m/5km below Clydebank. Large housing development in Erskine, on S side of r. NS 4672
Ervie D & G 57 A6 loc 6m/9km NW of Stranraer. NW 9967
Erwarton Suffolk 31 F4 vil 2m/3km W of Shotley Gate. To S on R Stour estuary is **Erwarton Bay,** extending from Shotley Gate to **Erwarton Ness.** TM 2134
Erwood Powys 25 F3 vil 6m/10km SE of Builth Wells. SO 0943
Eryholme N Yorks 54 C4 vil 2m/3km E of Croft across loops of R Tees. NZ 3208
Eryrys Clwyd 41 G5 ham 5m/7km SW of Mold. SJ 2057
Escley Brook 25 H5 r rising SE of Hay-on-Wye and flowing S into R Monnow to E of Longtown, H & W. SO 3228
Escomb Durham 54 B2 ham 2km W of Bishop Auckland. NZ 1830
Escrick N Yorks 50 B4 vil 6m/10km S of York. **Escrick Park** is 18c mansion now girls' boarding school. SE 6243
Esgair Dyfed 23 E3 loc 6m/9km NW of Carmarthen. SN 3728
Esgairgeiliog Powys 33 E4 vil 3m/5km N of Machynlleth. SH 7505
Esgerdawe Dyfed 24 B4/C4* loc 3m/5km N of Llansawel. SN 6140
Esgyryn Gwynedd 41 E3/E4* loc on N side of Llandudno Junction. SH 8078
Esh Durham 54 B1 vil 5m/8km W of Durham. NZ 1944
Esha Ness Shetland 89 D6 peninsula on NW coast of Mainland 5m/8km W of Hillswick Lighthouse. See also Skerry of Eshaness. HU 2178
Esher Surrey 19 F5 residential and shopping tn 4m/6km SW of Kingston. TQ 1364
Esholt W Yorks 48 D4 vil 3m/5km NE of Shipley. Bradford Sewage Works. SE 1840
Eshott Nthmb 61 G2 ham 2m/3km SE of Felton. NZ 2097
Eshton N Yorks 48 C3 ham 2km N of Gargrave. SD 9356
Esh Winning Durham 54 B1* vil 5m/8km W of Durham. NZ 1941
Esk 52 B5 r rising at Esk Hause, Cumbria, to E of Scafell Pikes, and flowing SW into Irish Sea SW of Ravenglass. SD 0694
Esk 55 G4 r rising on Farndale Moor, N Yorks Moors National Park, and flowing N to Castleton, then E into North Sea at Whitby. NZ 9011
Esk 59 G5 r rising in Dumfries & Galloway region as Rs Black Esk and White Esk and flowing SE to Langholm, then S to Canonbie. Continuing S, it passes into England and flows past Longtown to head of Solway Firth, its channel joining that of R Eden SE of Annan. NY 2263
Esk 66 B2, r in Lothian region. **N Esk** rises on Pentland Hills near **N Esk Resr,** 2km N of Carlops, and flows NE to join S Esk 2km N of Dalkeith; the combined r then continues N to Firth of Forth at Musselburgh. **S Esk** rises on Moorfoot Hills and flows N through Gladhouse and Rosebery Resrs to confluence with N Esk. NT 3473
Eskbank Lothian 66 B2 suburb 1km SW of Dalkeith. NT 3266
Eskdale Green Cumbria 52 B5 vil 4m/7km NE of Ravenglass. Outward Bound Mountain School and Mountain Rescue Post. NY 1400
Eskdalemuir D & G 59 G2 loc and ch on White Esk 11m/17km NW of Langholm. Traces of Roman fort nearly 1m N at Raeburnfoot. **Eskdalemuir Observatory,** meteorological stn 3m/5km N. NY 2597
Eskett Cumbria 52 B3* loc 2km E of Frizington. NY 0516
Eskham Lincs 45 G2 loc 1km SE of Marsh Chapel. TF 3698
Esk, North 77 G4 r formed by several streams W of Tarfside, in Tayside region, and running SE down Glen Esk to Edzell, Marykirk, and the North Sea between Montrose and St Cyrus. NO 7462
Eskrigg Tarn Cumbria 53 E5* small lake 2m/4km W of Killington. SD 5788
Esk, South 77 G5 r rising on border of Grampian and Tayside regions SE of Braemar, and running SE down Glen Clova, then E to Brechin and the North Sea at Montrose. NO 7356
Esk Valley N Yorks 55 F4* loc 1km SW of Grosmont. NZ 8204
Esperley Lane Ends Durham 54 B3* loc 2km SW of Evenwood. NZ 1324
Esprick Lancs 47 E4* ham 3m/4km N of Kirkham. SD 4036
Esragan 70 B2 r in S'clyde region running S into Loch Etive, Argyll, opp Airds Pt. NM 9934
Esscroft W Yorks 48 D3* loc on S bank of R Wharfe 2m/4km E of Ilkley. SE 1547
Essendine Leics 37 F3 vil 4m/6km N of Stamford. TF 0412
Essendon Herts 19 F1 vil 3m/4km E of Hatfield. TL 2708
Essex 119 south-eastern county of England, bounded by Gtr London, Hertfordshire, Cambridgeshire, Suffolk, and the Thames estuary and North Sea. The landscape is mostly flat or gently undulating, and the low-lying coast is deeply indented with river estuaries. There is almost continuous urban development along the county's S and W sides, with light industry, power stns, oil refineries, cement works, quarries, and docks. In the N and central parts are farmlands, orchards, mkt and nursery gardens. Chief tns are Chelmsford, the county tn; Basildon, Brentwood, Colchester, Harlow, and the passenger and container port of Harwich. Southend and Clacton are popular resorts. Rs include the Stour, forming part of the boundary with Suffolk, the Lea, forming part of the boundary with Hertfordshire, and the Blackwater, Chelmer, Colne, Crouch and Roding.
Essich H'land 81 F3 loc in Inverness dist 4m/6km S of Inverness. NH 6439
Essington Staffs 35 F4 vil 5m/7km NW of Walsall. SJ 9603
Ess of Glenlatterach Grampian 82 B2* waterfall in course of Leanoch Burn 2km from its confluence with R Lossie and 6m/10km S of Elgin. NJ 1953
Esthwaite Water Cumbria 52 D5 lake extending 2m/3km southwards from Hawkshead. SD 3596
Eston Cleveland 54 D3 tn in Teesside urban complex 4m/6km E of Middlesbrough. NZ 5418
Estover Devon 4 B5* industrial estate 4m/7km NE of Plymouth. SX 5159
Eswick Shetland 89 E7 loc near E coast of Mainland, 1km W of the headland **Moul of Eswick.** Bay of **Es Wick** to N, and **S Bay of Eswick** to S. Lighthouse on Moul of Eswick. HU 4853
Etal Nthmb 67 F4 estate vil on R Till 8m/13km NW of Wooler. 18c hall. Remains of 14c cas. NT 9239
Etchilhampton Wilts 17 E5 vil 3m/5km E of Devizes. SU 0460
Etchingham E Sussex 12 D4 vil 7m/11km N of Battle. TQ 7126
Etchinghill Kent 13 G3 vil 3m/5km N of Hythe. TR 1639
Etchinghill Staffs 35 F3* vil 2km W of Rugeley. SK 0218
Etchingwood E Sussex 12 B4* loc 1m SE of Buxted. TQ 5022
Etherdwick Humberside 51 F4* loc 2km SW of Aldbrough. TA 2337
Etherley Dene Durham 54 B2* ham 1m W of Bishop Auckland. NZ 1928
Etherley, High Durham 54 B2 vil 3m/5km W of Bishop Auckland. **Low Etherley** ham adjoining to N. NZ 1628
Etherow 43 E2 r rising on borders of Derbys and S Yorks SW of Dunford Br and flowing SW into R Goyt N of Marple, Gtr Manchester. SJ 9690
Etive S'clyde 74 C6 r in Argyll running SW down Glen Etive to head of Loch Etive. NN 1145
Etling Green Norfolk 39 E3* loc 2m/3km E of E Dereham. TG 0113
Eton Berks 18 D4 tn on N bank of R Thames opp Windsor. Boys' boarding school founded in 1440. SU 9677
Eton Wick Berks 18 D4* vil 1m W of Eton and 2m/3km SW of Slough. SU 9578
Etrop Green Gtr Manchester 42 D3* loc 3m/5km SE of Altrincham. SJ 8185
Etruria Staffs 42 D6* dist of Stoke-on-Trent 2km NW of city centre, at junction of Caldon Canal and Trent and Mersey Canal. Original site of Wedgwood pottery works, later moved to Barlaston. SJ 8647
Etterby Cumbria 59 H5* loc in Carlisle 2km NW of city centre across R Eden. NY 3857
Ettiley Heath Ches 42 C5* vil 2km W of Sandbach. SJ 7360
Ettingshall W Midlands 35 F4 SE dist of Wolverhampton. SO 9396
Ettington Warwicks 27 G3 vil 6m/9km SE of Stratford-upon-Avon. SP 2649
Etton Cambs 37 F4 vil 6m/10km NW of Peterborough. TF 1406

Etton Humberside 51 E4 vil 4m/6km NW of Beverley. SE 9843
Ettrick Borders 59 G1 vil on Ettrick Water, 15m/24km W of Hawick. Birthplace of James Hogg, poet, 1770–1835. NT 2714
Ettrick and Lauderdale 116, 117 admin dist of Borders region.
Ettrick Bay S'clyde 63 G2 wide bay on W coast of Bute, 3m/5km W of Rothesay. NS 0365
Ettrickbridge End Borders 66 B6 vil on Ettrick Water 6m/9km SW of Selkirk. NT 3824
Ettrick Pen 59 G1 mt on border of Dumfries & Galloway and Borders regions 7m/12km E of Moffat. Height 2269 ft or 692 metres. NT 1907
Ettrick Water 66 C5 r in Borders region rising 6m/9km E of Moffat and flowing NE through **Ettrick Forest** to R Tweed 3m/4km NE of Selkirk. Ettrick Forest is large area of moorland S of Peebles, much used for sheep grazing. NT 4832
Etwall Derbys 35 H2 vil 6m/10km SW of Derby. SK 2631
Euchan Water 58 D1 r in Dumfries & Galloway region running E to R Nith on S side of Sanquhar. NS 7809
Euchar S'clyde 70 A3 r in Argyll running W from Loch Scamadale down Glen Euchar to Loch Feochan N of Kilninver. NM 8222
Eudon George Salop 34 D5* loc 3m/5km SW of Bridgnorth. SO 6889
Eunant 33 F2 r running E into Lake Vyrnwy, Powys, 4m/6km NW of the dam. SH 9622
Eunay Mór W Isles 88 A2* islet in W Loch Roag, W coast of Lewis, close to W shore of Gt Bernera. NB 1336
Euston Suffolk 38 D6 vil 3m/5km SE of Thetford. TL 8979
Euximoor Drove Cambs 38 A4* loc 4m/7km NW of Welney. TL 4798
Euxton Lancs 47 F6 vil 2m/4km NW of Chorley. SD 5519
Evanstown Mid Glam 15 E3* vil on W side of Gilfach Goch. SS 9789
Evanton H'land 81 F1 vil near N shore of Cromarty Firth, Ross and Cromarty dist, 6m/9km NE of Dingwall. NH 6066
Evan Water 59 F2 r in Dumfries & Galloway region rising on Lowther Hills and running S to R Annan 2m/3km S of Moffat. NT 0902
Evedon Lincs 45 E6 vil 2m/3km NE of Sleaford. TF 0947
Eve Hill W Midlands 35 F5 loc 1km W of Dudley tn centre. SO 9390
Evelix H'land 87 A7 r in Sutherland dist running S into Dornoch Firth at Ferrytown, 5m/8km W of Dornoch. NH 7286
Evenjobb Powys 25 G2 vil 4m/6km SW of Presteigne. SO 2662
Evenley Northants 28 B4 vil 2km S of Brackley. SP 5834
Evenlode Glos 27 F4 vil 3m/5km NE of Stow-on-the-Wold. SP 2229
Evenlode 18 A1 r rising near Moreton-in-Marsh, Glos, and flowing into R Thames E of Eynsham, Oxon. SP 4509
Even Swindon Wilts 17 F3* W dist of Swindon. SU 1385
Evenwood Durham 54 B2/B3 vil 2m/3km SW of W Auckland. **Evenwood Gate** loc 1m SE. NZ 1525
Evercreech Som 8 D1 vil 4m/6km SE of Shepton Mallet. ST 6438
Everdon Northants 28 B2 vil 4m/6km SE of Daventry. SP 5957
Everdon, Little Northants 28 B2* ham 3m/5km SE of Daventry. SP 5958
Everingham Humberside 50 C4 vil 5m/8km W of Mkt Weighton. SE 8042
Everleigh Wilts 17 F5 vil 5m/8km NW of Ludgershall. To S, ham of **E Everleigh.** To NW, loc of **Lr Everleigh.** SU 1954
Everley N Yorks 55 G6* loc 4m/7km W of Scarborough. SE 9788
Eversden, Great Cambs 29 G3 vil 6m/10km SW of Cambridge. TL 3653
Eversden, Little Cambs 29 G3 vil 6m/9km SW of Cambridge. TL 3753
Eversholt Beds 29 E4 vil 3m/5km E of Woburn. SP 9932
Evershot Dorset 8 D4 vil 5m/7km N of Maiden Newton. ST 5704
Eversley Hants 18 C5 vil 5m/8km SW of Wokingham. Burial-place of Charles Kingsley, rector 1844–75. Vil of **Eversley Cross** 2km E. SU 7762
Everthorpe Humberside 50 D5 ham 1m SE of N Cave. SE 9031
Everton Beds 29 F3 vil 2m/3km NW of Potton. TL 2051
Everton Hants 10 A5 loc 2m/3km SW of Lymington. Experimental Horticulture Stn 1km E. SZ 2994
Everton Merseyside 42 A2* dist of Liverpool 2km NE of city centre. SJ 3592
Everton Notts 44 B2 vil 3m/5km SE of Bawtry. SK 6991
Everton Shetland 89 E8* loc on Mainland 8m/13km N of Sumburgh Hd. HU 4121
Evertown D & G 59 H4 vil 2m/3km W of Canonbie. NY 3576
Evesbatch H & W 26 C3 vil 5m/7km SE of Bromyard. SO 6848
Eves Corner Essex 20 D2* loc adjoining Danbury to E, 4m/7km W of Maldon. TL 7805
Eves Corner Essex 21 E2* loc 1km N of Burnham-on-Crouch. TQ 9497
Evesham H & W 27 E3 tn on R Avon 13m/21km SE of Worcester. Centre of fruit and vegetable growing area, **Vale of Evesham.** N of tn is site of Battle of Evesham, 1265, marked by obelisk. SP 0344
Evie Orkney 89 B6 loc on Mainland 2m/3km NW of Woodwick. Also known as Georth. HY 3625
Evington Leics 36 C4 dist of Leicester 3m/5km SE of city centre. **N Evington** dist of Leicester 2m/3km E of city centre. SK 6104
Ewden Beck 43 G2 r rising on Margery Hill on moors NW of Sheffield, S Yorks, and flowing E through Broomhead and More Hall Resrs into R Don 1km N of Wharncliffe Side. SK 2995
Ewden Village S Yorks 43 G2* vil 2km S of Stocksbridge. SK 2796
Ewe Close Cumbria 53 E3 site of ancient settlement of uncertain date 2km SW of Crosby Ravensworth. NY 6013
Ewe, Isle of H'land 78 F1 barely inhabited island in Loch Ewe, W coast of Ross and Cromarty dist, opp Aultbea on E shore of loch. Area about 900 acres or 365 hectares. NG 8588
Ewell Surrey 19 F5 tn 5m/8km SE of Kingston. **E** and **W Ewell** locs 2km E and NW respectively. Site of Nonsuch Palace, huge mansion built by Henry VIII, 1km NE in Nonsuch Park. TQ 2162
Ewell Minnis Kent 13 G3* vil 4m/6km NW of Dover. TR 2643
Ewelme Oxon 18 B2 vil 3m/5km SW of Watlington. SU 6491
Ewen Glos 17 E2 vil 3m/5km SW of Cirencester. SU 0097
Ewenni Welsh form of Ewenny, qv.
Ewenny (Ewenni) Mid Glam 15 E4 vil 2m/3km S of Bridgend across Ewenny R. Ruins of 12c priory (A.M.) on river bank. SS 9077
Ewenny (Ewenni) 15 E4* r rising N of Pencoed, Mid Glam, and flowing SW into R Ogmore 3m/4km SW of Bridgend. SS 8776
Ewerby Lincs 45 E6 vil 4m/6km E of Sleaford. **Ewerby Thorpe** loc 1m E. TF 1247
Ewes Water 60 A2 r in Dumfries & Galloway region running S from boundary with Borders region to R Esk at Langholm. NY 3684
Ewhurst E Sussex 12 D4 vil 4m/6km E of Robertsbridge. TQ 7924
Ewhurst Surrey 11 G1 vil 2m/3km E of Cranleigh. TQ 0940
Ewhurst Green Surrey 11 G1 ham 1m S of Ewhurst and 2m/3km E of Cranleigh. TQ 0939
Ewloe Clwyd 41 H4 vil 2km NW of Hawarden. Remains of 13c cas (A.M.) to NW. **Ewloe Green** loc 1km W. SJ 2966
Ewood Lancs 47 G5 loc in Blackburn 2km S of tn centre. SD 6725
Ewood Bridge Lancs 48 B5/B6* loc at crossing of R Irwell 2m/3km S of Haslingden. SD 7920
Eworthy Devon 6 D5* ham 9m/14km W of Okehampton. SS 4495
Ewshot Hants 11 E1 vil 3m/4km NW of Farnham. SU 8149
Ewyas Harold H & W 25 H5 vil 1m NW of Pontrilas. SO 3828
Exbourne Devon 7 E5 vil 4m/7km NE of Okehampton. SS 6002
Exbury Hants 10 B4 vil 3m/5km SW of Fawley. SU 4200
Exceat E Sussex 12 B6 loc on Cuckmere R 1m N of Cuckmere Haven. TV 5199
Exe 7 G6 r rising on Exmoor in Somerset and flowing E to Exton, then S through Tiverton to Exeter. Widens out into estuary at Topsham and flows into English Channel at Exmouth. SX 9980
Exebridge 7 G3 vil on R Exe on border of Devon and Somerset 2m/3km NW of Bampton. SS 9324
Exelby N Yorks 54 C6 vil 2m/3km SE of Bedale. SE 2987
Exe, Nether Devon 7 G5* ham on R Exe 5m/8km N of Exeter. SS 9300
Exeter Devon 7 G5 city and county capital on R Exe 64m/103km SW of Bristol. On site of Roman *Isca Dumnoniorum.* Cathedral: Dec, Norman towers. 15c guildhall. Parts of medieval walls survive. Modern bldgs in centre replace extensive damage from World War II. University 1m N of city centre. Airport 5m/8km E at Clyst Honiton. SX 9292
Exeter Northants 36 D5* S dist of Corby. SP 8887
Exeter Canal Devon 5 E2 canal running from Exeter to R Exe estuary between Exminster and Powderham. SX 98
Exford Som 7 F2 vil on Exmoor and R Exe 9m/15km SW of Dunster. SS 8538
Exfordsgreen Salop 34 B4 ham 5m/8km SW of Shrewsbury. SJ 4506
Exhall Warwicks 27 E2 vil 2m/3km SE of Alcester. SP 1055
Exhall Warwicks 36 A5 loc 2m/3km SW of Bedworth. SP 3485
Exlade Street Oxon 18 B3 ham 4m/6km NE of Pangbourne. SU 6581
Exley W Yorks 48 D5* loc in Halifax 2m/3km S of tn centre. SE 0922
Exminster Devon 5 E2 vil 4m/6km SE of Exeter. SX 9487
Exmoor Forest 7 E1, E2, F1, F2 high moorland area, usually known simply as Exmoor, mainly in Somerset but partly also in Devon, bounded on the N by the Bristol Channel and on the S roughly by a line drawn through Ilfracombe, N Molton, and Dulverton. Once a royal forest, now designated (with Brendon Hills to E) the Exmoor National Park. SS 74
Exmouth Devon 5 F3 resort on E side of mouth of R Exe, 9m/15km SE of Exeter. Ferry to Starcross (foot passengers). SY 0080
Exnaboe Shetland 89 E8* loc on Mainland to N of Sumburgh Airport across Pool of Virkie. HU 3911
Exning Suffolk 30 B2 vil 2m/3km NW of Newmarket. TL 6265
Exted Kent 13 G3 ham 1km NW of Elham. TR 1644
Exton Devon 5 F2 vil on left (E) bank of R Exe estuary 4m/6km N of Exmouth. SX 9886
Exton Hants 10 C3 vil 1km N of Meonstoke. SU 6120
Exton Leics 37 E3 vil 4m/7km E of Oakham. SK 9211
Exton Som 7 G2 vil on R Exe 4m/6km N of Dulverton. SS 9233
Exwick Devon 7 G5 vil beside R Exe, across r opp St David's rly stn and 1m NW of Exeter city centre. SX 9093
Eyam Derbys 43 G3 vil 5m/8km N of Bakewell. Annual well-dressing ceremony. Saxon cross in churchyard. Ancient stone circle (A.M.) on **Eyam Moor** to N. SK 2176
Ey Burn 76 B2* r in Grampian region running N down Glen Ey to R Dee at Inverey, 4m/7km W of Braemar. NO 0889
Eydon Northants 28 B3 vil 8m/13km NE of Banbury. SP 5450
Eye Cambs 37 G4 suburb 4m/6km NE of Peterborough. **Eye Green** loc 1km N. TF 2202
Eye H & W 26 A2* ham 3m/5km N of Leominster. SO 4963
Eye Suffolk 31 F1 small tn 4m/7km SE of Diss. Slight remains of cas. TM 1473
Eye 36 C3 r in Leics. See Wreake.
Eye Brook 36 D5 r rising SW of Tilton, Leics, and flowing SE into Eye Brook Resr and thence into R Welland E of Caldecott. SP 8793
Eyebrook Reservoir Leics 36 D4/D5 large resr nearly 3km long, 1m NW of Caldecott and 5m/8km NW of Corby. SP 8595
Eyebroughty Lothian 73 G5* offshore islet 4m/6km W of N Berwick. Haunt of sea birds. NT 4986
Eye, Little Merseyside 41 G3* small island SE of Hilbre Is. in R Dee estuary opp W Kirby. SJ 1986
Eyemouth Borders 67 F2 fishing tn and resort on coast 8m/13km NW of Berwick-upon-Tweed. Boat-building yards. NT 9464
Eye Peninsula W Isles 88 C2 peninsula on E side of Lewis 4m/6km E of Stornoway, measuring 11km NE to SW and up to 4km NW to SE. Forms SE arm of Broad Bay or Loch a' Tuath. NB 53
Eye Water 67 F2 r rising on Lammermuir Hills 2m/3km SW of Oldhamstocks and running E by Grantshouse and Ayton to North Sea at Eyemouth, Borders. NT 9464
Eyeworth Beds 29 F3 vil 4m/6km E of Biggleswade. TL 2445
Eyhorne Street Kent 20 D6 vil 5m/8km E of Maidstone. TQ 8354
Eyke Suffolk 31 G3 vil 3m/5km NE of Woodbridge, across R Deben. TM 3151
Eynesbury Cambs 29 F2 S dist of St Neots. TL 1859
Eynhallow Orkney 89 B6 uninhabited island, 1km across, in **Eynhallow Sound** between islands of Mainland and Rousay. Faint remains of medieval monastery (A.M.). HY 3529
Eynort H'land 79 B6 r in Skye running S to head of Loch Eynort on SW coast. NG 3826
Eynsford Kent 20 B5 vil on R Darent 3m/4km SE of Swanley. Remains of Norman cas (A.M.). To SW across r, Lullingstone Roman villa (A.M.) and Lullingstone Castle, 18c hse with 16c gateway. TQ 5465
Eynsham Oxon 17 H1 tn 6m/9km NW of Oxford. SP 4309
Eype Dorset 8 C5 vil near coast, 2km SW of Bridport. SY 4491
Eype Mouth Dorset. See Golden Cap.
Eyre Skye, H'land 78 C4 locality on E side of Loch Snizort Beag at entrance to Loch Eyre 7m/11km S of Uig. NG 4152
Eyre Point Skye, H'land 79 D5 headland with lighthouse at SE point of Raasay. NG 5834
Eythorne Kent 13 H2 vil 5m/8km N of Dover. Coal mine to N. Vil of **Lr Eythorne** adjoins to NW. TR 2849
Eyton Clwyd 41 H6* loc nearly 1m S of Stryt-yr-hwch. SJ 3346
Eyton Clwyd 42 A6 loc 2m/3km NW of Overton. SJ 3544
Eyton H & W 26 A2 vil 2m/3km NW of Leominster. SO 4761
Eyton, Little Salop 34 D3* loc in Dawley to N of tn centre. SJ 6807
Eyton on Severn Salop 34 C4* ham 2km SE of Wroxeter. SJ 5706
Eyton upon the Weald Moors Salop 34 D3 vil 2m/3km N of Wellington. SJ 6514

F

Faberstown Hants 17 G6* loc adjoining Ludgershall to E. SU 2750
Faccombe Hants 17 G5 vil 3m/5km N of Hurstbourne Tarrant. SU 3958
Faceby N Yorks 54 D4 vil 4m/6km SW of Stokesley. NZ 4903
Fachwen Gwynedd 40 C5* loc nearly 1m S of Deiniolen. SH 5761
Fachwen Pool Powys 33 G5* small lake 2m/3km NW of Newtown. SO 0893
Facit Lancs 47 H6 loc adjoining Whitworth to N. SD 8819
Fackley Notts 44 A5* loc 2m/3km NW of Sutton in Ashfield. SK 4761
Faddiley Ches 42 B5 vil 4m/6km W of Nantwich. SJ 5953
Fadmoor N Yorks 55 E5/E6 ham 2m/4km NW of Kirkbymoorside. SE 6789
Faenor, Y Welsh form of Vaynor, qv.
Faerdre Welsh form of Vardre, qv.

Fagley W Yorks 48 D4* loc in Bradford 2m/3km NE of city centre. SE 1834
Failand Avon 16 A4* vil 4m/7km W of Bristol. 2km NW, ham of **Lr Failand.** ST 5271
Failsworth Gtr Manchester 42 D1 tn 5m/7km NE of Manchester. Textiles, engineering, chemicals, aircraft components. SD 8901
Fairbourne Gwynedd 32 D3 vil 2m/3km S of Barmouth across R Mawddach estuary. SH 6112
Fairbourne Heath Kent 21 E6* loc 2m/3km S of Harrietsham. TQ 8550
Fairburn N Yorks 49 F5 vil 2m/4km N of Ferrybridge. Lakes to S and W created by coal-mining subsidence. SE 4727
Fair Cross London 20 B3* loc 1m NE of Barking. TQ 4585
Fairfield Cleveland 54 C3/D3* dist of Stockton-on-Tees 2m/3km W of tn centre. NZ 4119
Fairfield Cumbria 52 D3 mt in Lake Dist 2m/4km SE of Helvellyn. Height 2863 ft or 873 metres. NY 3511
Fairfield Derbys 43 F4. E dist of Buxton. SK 0673
Fairfield Gtr Manchester 42 D1* loc in Bury 2m/3km E of tn centre. SD 8211
Fairfield Gtr Manchester 42 D2* loc 4m/6km E of Manchester. SJ 9197
Fairfield H & W 35 F6 vil 3m/5km N of Bromsgrove. SO 9475
Fairfield H & W 27 E3* loc in S part of Evesham. SP 0342
Fairfield Kent 13 E4 loc 2m/3km S of Appledore. TQ 9626
Fairfield Merseyside 41 H3* loc 1km W of Brimstage. SJ 2982
Fairfield Merseyside 42 A2* dist of Liverpool 2m/4km E of city centre. SJ 3791
Fairford Glos 17 F2 small tn 8m/13km E of Cirencester. Airfield to S. SP 1501
Fairham Brook 36 B1 r rising near Old Dalby, Leics, and flowing NW into R Trent at W Bridgford, Notts. SK 5636
Fairhaven Lancs 46 D5* dist of Lytham St Anne's to W of tn centre. **F. Lake** on foreshore. SD 3227
Fair Hill Cumbria 53 E2* loc adjoining Penrith to N. NY 5131
Fairhill S'clyde 64 D3* S dist of Hamilton. NS 7154
Fair Isle Shetland 89 D8 sparsely inhabited island (NTS), about 5km N to S and 2km E to W, lying some 24m/39km SW of Sumburgh Hd. Crofting, mnfre of woollen garments. Bird observatory on **N Haven** on E coast. Harbour at S end of island. HZ 2172
Fairleigh W Yorks 49 F6* loc adjoining Pontefract to SW. SE 4421
Fairlie S'clyde 64 A3 resort on Firth of Clyde 3m/5km S of Largs. Remains of 16c cas inland in F. Glen. **F. Roads,** sea passage between mainland and the Cumbraes. NS 2055
Fairlight E Sussex 13 E5 vil 3m/5km E of Hastings. Coastal loc of **F. Cove** 2km E. TQ 8611
Fairmile Devon 7 H5 ham on R Tale 2km NW of Ottery St Mary. SY 0897
Fairmile Surrey 19 E5 loc 1m NE of Cobham. F. Common to N. TQ 1261
Fairmilehead Lothian 66 A2 dist of Edinburgh 4m/6km S of city centre. NT 2468
Fairmoor Nthmb 61 F3* loc 2km NW of Morpeth. NZ 1887
Fair Oak Devon 7 G3* loc 1km SW of Hockworthy. ST 0318
Fairoak Gwent 15 F2* loc 1m NW of Oakdale. ST 1799
Fair Oak Hants 10 C5 suburb 3m/4km E of Eastleigh. SU 4918
Fairoak Staffs 34 D2 ham 5m/8km NW of Eccleshall. SJ 7632
Fair Oak Green Hants 18 B5 ham 6m/10km NE of Basingstoke. SU 6660
Fairoaks Airport Surrey 19 E5* loc and airfield 2m/3km N of Woking. TQ 0062
Fairseat Kent 20 C5 vil on N Downs 2m/3km NE of Wrotham. TQ 6261
Fairstead Essex 30 C6 ham 4m/6km W of Witham. TL 7616
Fairstead Norfolk 39 G3 ham 4m/7km S of N Walsham. TG 2823
Fairwarp E Sussex 12 B4 ham 4m/6km N of Uckfield. TQ 4626
Fairwater Gwent 15 G2* loc on W side of Cwmbran. ST 2794
Fairwater (Tyllgoed) S Glam 15 F4* dist of Cardiff 3m/4km W of city centre. **F. Grove** loc adjoining to E. ST 1477
Fairwood W Glam 23 G6* loc 5m/9km W of Swansea. Nature reserve. See also F. Common. SS 5693
Fairwood Common W Glam 23 G6 common on which Swansea Airport is situated, 1m S of Fairwood and 5m/9km W of Swansea. SS 5791
Fairy Cross Devon 6 C3 ham 4m/6km SW of Bideford. SS 4024
Faither, The Shetland 89 D6 headland on NW coast of Mainland on W side of entrance to Ronas Voe. HU 2585
Fakenham Norfolk 38 D2 tn on R Wensum 23m/37km NW of Norwich. Agricultural centre. Printing works. TF 9229
Fakenham, Little Suffolk 30 D1 vil 4m/7km N of Ixworth. TL 9076
Fal 2 D5 r rising on Goss Moor N of St Dennis, Cornwall, and flowing S and SW to form estuary of Carrick Rds below Turnaware Pt before flowing past Falmouth into English Channel between Pendennis Pt and Zone Pt. SW 8331
Fala Lothian 66 C3 vil to N of **F. Moor,** 4m/6km SE of Pathhead. NT 4360
Faldingworth Lincs 45 E3 vil 4m/6km SW of Mkt Rasen. TF 0684
Falfield Avon 16 B2 vil 4m/6km NE of Thornbury. ST 9893
Falhouse Green W Yorks 49 E6* loc 2m/3km NW of Flockton. SE 2117
Falkenham Suffolk 31 F4/G4 vil 3m/5km N of Felixstowe. 1m NE is **F. Creek,** running into R Deben. TM 2939
Falkirk Central 65 F1 industrial tn 23m/37km W of Edinburgh. Industries include light castings, light engineering, distilling, mnfre of clothing, electronic components, precast concrete, vehicle bodies. Sections of Antonine Wall visible in tn and vicinity. Scene of battle in 1746 in which Prince Charles Edward defeated government forces. NS 8880
Falkland Fife 73 F4 small tn below NE slope of Lomond Hills 4m/7km N of Glenrothes. Royal Palace (NTS), 16c. NO 2507
Fallgate Derbys 43 H5 loc 3m/4km W of Clay Cross. SK 3562
Fall, High Cumbria 52 D4* waterfall in Rydal Beck just N of Rydal ham. NY 3606
Fallin Central 72 C5 mining vil 3m/4km SE of Stirling. NS 8391
Falling Foss N Yorks 55 G4 waterfall in Lit Beck 5m/8km S of Whitby. NZ 8803
Fallings Heath W Midlands 35 F4* loc on borders of Walsall and W Bromwich, 2m/3km SW of Walsall tn centre. SO 9896
Falloch 71 E3 r rising on W side of Beinn a' Chroin in Central region and running N, then SW down Glen Falloch, then S to head of Loch Lomond in Strathclyde region. See also Falls of Falloch. NN 3115
Fallowfield Gtr Manchester 42 D2* dist of Manchester 3m/4km SE of city centre. SJ 8594
Fallowfield Nthmb 61 E4 loc 1m E of vil of Wall. NY 9268
Fallside S'clyde 64 D3* loc 3m/5km S of Coatbridge. NS 7160
Falls of Acharn Tayside 71 H1. See Acharn.
Falls of Balnaguard Tayside. See Balnaguard.
Falls of Barvick Tayside 72 C2 waterfall in course of Barvick Burn 2m/3km NW of Crieff. NN 8524
Falls of Bracklinn Central 72 A4 waterfall in course of Keltie Water 2km E of Callander. NN 6408
Falls of Clyde S'clyde 65 E4, F4 series of waterfalls in course of R Clyde in vicinity of Lanark. Former impressiveness modified by hydro-electricity schemes. NS 84
Falls of Conon H'land 80 D2 series of cascades in course of R Conon below Loch Luichart, Ross and Cromarty dist. NH 3857
Falls of Cruachan S'clyde 70 B4 waterfall in course of stream in Argyll running from Cruachan Resr into Loch Awe. Diminished since construction of resr. NN 0727
Falls of Damff Tayside 76 D3* waterfall in course of Water of Unich 1m SW of its confluence with Water of Lee. NO 3879
Falls of Divach H'land 81 E4 waterfall in course of Divach Burn, Inverness dist, 2m/3km SW of Drumnadrochit. NH 4927
Falls of Drumly Harry Tayside 77 E4 waterfalls in Noran Water 3m/5km NW of Tannadice. NO 4562
Falls of Edinample Central 71 G3 waterfall in Burn of Ample on S side of Loch Earn, 1m SE of Lochearnhead. NN 6022
Falls of Falloch Central 71 E3 waterfall in Glen Falloch 4m/7km SW of Crianlarich. NN 3320
Falls of Fender Tayside. See Fender Burn.
Falls of Garbh Allt Grampian 76 C2 waterfall in course of stream running N through Ballochbuie Forest to R Dee 3m/5km E of Braemar. NO 1989
Falls of Garry H'land 74 D2* waterfall in Lochaber dist, below dam of Loch Garry. NH 2701
Falls of Glomach H'land 80 B5 waterfall (NTS) in Allt a' Ghlomaich, Skye and Lochalsh dist, 5m/9km SE of Killalan. Height 370 ft or 113 metres. NH 0125
Falls of Keltie Tayside 72 C2 waterfall in course of Keltie Burn 1m W of vil of Monzie. NN 8625
Falls of Keltney Tayside G5/H5*. See Keltney Burn.
Falls of Lednock Tayside 72 B2* waterfall in course of R Lednock passing through chasm of Deil's Cauldron, 1m N of Comrie. NN 7623
Falls of Leny Central 71 G4* waterfall in Pass of Leny, wooded defile below Loch Lubnaig, 2m/4km W of Callander. NN 5908
Falls of Lochay Central 71 F2 waterfall in R Lochay 2m/4km NW of Killin. Hydro-electricity power stn to E. NN 5435
Falls of Lora S'clyde 70 B2* cataract at Connel on Loch Etive, Argyll, formed by reef of rocks stretching two-thirds of way across entrance to loch on E side of rd br. NM 9134
Falls of Measach H'land 85 C8 waterfall (NTS) in Abhainn Droma, headstream of R Broom in Ross and Cromarty dist, where it passes through deep gorge known as Corrieshalloch Gorge. NH 2077
Falls of Moness Tayside 75 H6 series of three waterfalls in Urlar Burn 1m S of Aberfeldy. NN 8547
Falls of Monzie Tayside 72 C2 waterfall 1m N of Monzie vil. NN 8826
Falls of Ness Tayside 72 C3 waterfall in course of Machany Water 2km SE of Muthill. NN 8815
Falls of Rogie H'land 81 E2 waterfall and salmon leap in course of Black Water, Ross and Cromarty dist, 2m/4km W of Strathpeffer. NH 4458
Falls of Tarf Tayside 76 A3 waterfall in course of Tarf Water, 11m/17km NE of Blair Atholl. NN 9879
Falls of the Bruar Tayside 75 H4 waterfall in a fir plantation in course of Bruar Water 1km from its outfall into R Garry E of Calvine. NN 8166
Falls of Truim H'land 75 G2 waterfall in Glen Truim, Badenoch and Strathspey dist, 3m/5km above mouth of R Truim, qv. NN 6792
Falls of Turret Tayside 72 C2 waterfall in Glen Turret 3m/4km NW of Crieff. NN 8324
Falls of Unich Tayside. See Water of Unich.
Falmer E Sussex 12 A5 vil 4m/7km NE of Brighton tn centre. TQ 3508
Falmouth Cornwall 2 D5 10m/16km SE of Redruth; 8m/12km S of Truro in a straight line. Port with large natural anchorage (Carrick Rds); resort. Includes Pendennis Pt, qv. SW 8032
Falmouth Bay Cornwall 2 D5 bay S of Falmouth, extending from Pendennis Pt southwards to Rosemullion Hd. SW 8129
Falsgrave N Yorks 55 H6 SW dist of Scarborough. TA 0387
Falstone Nthmb 60 C3 ham on R North Tyne in Kielder Forest 8m/12km W of Bellingham. NY 7287
Fambridge, North Essex 21 E2 vil on N side of R Crouch estuary 6m/10km W of Burnham-on-Crouch. TQ 8597
Fambridge, South Essex 21 E2 ham on S side of R Crouch estuary 4m/6km N of Rochford. TQ 8595
Fanagmore H'land 84 B3 locality on S side of Loch Laxford 4m/6km N of Scourie, in Sutherland dist. NC 1749
Fancott Beds 29 E5 ham 4m/6km N of Dunstable. TL 0227
Fanellan H'land 81 E3* loc in Inverness dist 4m/6km SW of Beauly. NH 4741
Fan Fawr Powys 25 E5 summit of Fforest Fawr, 2409 ft or 734 metres, 3m/4km SW of Brecon Beacons. SN 9619
Fangdale Beck N Yorks 55 E5* ham 3m/5km S of Chop Gate. SE 5694
Fangfoss Humberside 50 C3 vil 4m/6km SE of Stamford Br. SE 7653
Fan Gyhirych Powys 24 D6 one of the high peaks of Fforest Fawr, qv, 2km S of Cray Resr. Height 2391 ft or 725 metres. SN 8819
Fankerton Central 72 B6* vil 2km W of Denny. NS 7983
Fanmore S'clyde 68 C4 locality on Mull, on N side of Loch Tuath and 5m/8km S of Dervaig. NM 4144
Fanner's Green Essex 20 C1* ham 4m/6km NW of Chelmsford. TL 6812
Fannich Forest H'land 80 C1 deer forest in Ross and Cromarty dist N of Loch Fannich. NH 1969
Fannyside Lochs S'clyde 65 E2 two lochs 2m/4km and 3m/5km E of Cumbernauld. NS 8073
Fan Pool Powys 33 F5* tarn 2m/3km N of Llanidloes. SN 9487
Fans Borders 66 D4 loc 2m/4km SW of Gordon. NT 6240
Fan, Y Welsh form of Van, qv.
FAR. For names beginning with this word, see under next word. This also applies to names beginning with Near, Mid, Middle; High, Low; Higher, Lower; Upper, Nether; Great, Little; Greater, Lesser; Isle(s) of; North, South, East, West; The, Y, Yr.
Fara Orkney. Alternative spelling of Faray, qv.
Fara Orkney 89 A7 barely inhabited island of about 200 acres or 80 hectares off E coast of Hoy between Hoy and Flotta. ND 3295
Faraclett Head Orkney 89 B6* headland at NE end of island of Rousay on E side of Saviskaill Bay. HY 4433
Faraid Head H'land 84 D1 headland on N coast of Sutherland dist 3m/4km N of Durness. Also known as Far Out Hd. NC 3971
Fara, The H'land 75 F3* mt in Badenoch and Strathspey dist 2m/4km W of Dalwhinnie. Height 2986 ft or 910 metres. NN 5984
Faray Orkney 89 B5* narrow uninhabited island less than 2m/3km long N to S lying 1m W of island of Eday across **F. Sound.** Alternative spellings: Fara, Pharay. See also Holm of Faray. HY 5336
Farcet Cambs 37 G5 vil 3m/4km S of Peterborough. Extensive brick works to W. TL 2094
Farden Salop 34 C6* loc 4m/6km E of Ludlow. SO 5775
Fareham Hants 10 C4 6m/9km NW of Portsmouth across Portsmouth Harbour. Old mkt tn and port now part of Portsmouth conurbation. SU 5706
Farewell Staffs 35 G3 ham 3m/4km NW of Lichfield. SK 0811
Farforth Lincs 45 G3 loc 6m/9km S of Louth. TF 3178
Farg 73 E3 r in Tayside region running NE down Glen Farg to R Earn 5m/8km SE of Perth. NO 1717
Farhill Derbys 43 H4* loc 2m/4km W of Clay Cross. SK 3563
Farigaig H'land 81 E5 r running N then W into Loch Ness at Inverfarigaig, 2m/4km NE of Foyers, Inverness dist. NH 5223
Faringdon Oxon 17 G2 tn 11m/17km NE of Swindon. SU 2895
Faringdon, Little Oxon 17 F2 vil 2km NE of Lechlade. SP 2201
Farington Lancs 47 F5* loc adjoining Leyland to N. SD 5423
Farington Lancs 47 F5 loc 2m/3km N of Leyland. SD 5325
Farlam Cumbria 60 B5* loc 3m/4km E of Brampton. NY 5760
Farlam Cumbria 60 B5 ham 2m/4km SE of Brampton. NY 5558
Farland Head S'clyde 64 A4 headland on Firth of Clyde 5m/8km NW of Ardrossan. NS 1748

Farleigh Avon 16 A4 vil 6m/10km SW of Bristol. ST 4969
Farleigh Surrey 20 A5 vil 2m/3km NE of Warlingham. TQ 3760
Farleigh, East Kent 20 D6 vil on R Medway 2m/3km SW of Maidstone. TQ 7353
Farleigh Green Kent 20 D6* vil 3m/5km SW of Maidstone. TQ 7252
Farleigh Hungerford Som 16 C5 vil 4m/6km W of Trowbridge. Remains of 14c cas (A.M.). Site of Roman villa 1km NW. ST 8057
Farleigh Wallop Hants 18 B6 vil 3m/5km S of Basingstoke. SU 6246
Farleigh, West Kent 20 D6 vil above R Medway 3m/5km SW of Maidstone. TQ 7153
Farlesthorpe Lincs 45 H4 vil 2m/3km SE of Alford. TF 4774
Farleton Cumbria 53 E6 ham 5m/8km NW of Kirkby Lonsdale. SD 5381
Farleton Lancs 47 F2* ham 2km SW of Hornby. SD 5868
Farley Derbys 43 G5* loc 1m N of Matlock. SK 2962
Farley Salop 34 C4* loc 2m/3km NE of Much Wenlock. SJ 6302
Farley Staffs 43 F6 ham 4m/6km E of Cheadle. SK 0644
Farley Wilts 9 H2 vil 5m/8km E of Salisbury. SU 2229
Farley Green Suffolk 30 C3* ham 6m/10km NE of Haverhill. TL 7353
Farley Green Surrey 19 E6 ham 4m/6km N of Cranleigh. Site of Roman temple 1km W. TQ 0645
Farley Hill Beds 29 E5* SW dist of Luton. TL 0720
Farley Hill Berks 18 C5* vil 5m/8km SW of Wokingham. SU 7564
Farleys End Glos 26 C6 ham 4m/7km SW of Gloucester across loop of R Severn. SO 7715
Farley Water 7 E1* Exmoor stream flowing N to join E Lyn R at Watersmeet, 3m/5km E of Lynton. SS 7448
Farlington Hants 10 D4 N dist of Portsmouth 2m/3km W of Havant. SU 6805
Farlington N Yorks 50 B2 vil 2m/3km E of Stillington. SE 6167
Farlington Marshes Hants 10 D4 tongue of marshy land at head of Langstone Harbour, between Havant and Portsea I. SU 6804
Farlow Salop 34 C6 ham 4m/6km NW of Cleobury Mortimer. SO 6480
Farmborough Avon 16 B5 vil 4m/6km NW of Radstock. ST 6660
Farmbridge End Essex 20 C1* loc 3m/4km SE of Leaden Roding. TL 6211
Farmcote Glos 27 E4* ham 2m/4km E of Winchcombe. SP 0628
Farmcote Salop 34 D5* loc 4m/7km E of Bridgnorth. Loc of **Upr Farmcote** 1km W. SO 7791
Farmers Dyfed 24 C3/C4 ham 5m/8km SE of Lampeter. SN 6444
Farmington Glos 27 F5/F6 vil 2m/3km E of Northleach. SP 1315
Farmoor Oxon 17 H1* ham beside resr of same name 2m/3km SE of Eynsham. SP 4507
Farm Town Leics 36 A3* loc 1m SE of Coleorton. SK 3916
Farnah Green Derbys 43 H6* loc 1km W of Belper across R Derwent. SK 3346
Farnborough Berks 17 H3 vil 4m/7km SE of Wantage. SU 4381
Farnborough Hants 18 D6 tn in military area 4m/6km S of Camberley. On W side, Royal Aircraft Establishment and airfield; biennial air display. SU 8754
Farnborough London 20 B5 suburban loc in borough of Bromley 2km SW of Orpington. TQ 4464
Farnborough Warwicks 27 H3 vil 6m/10km N of Banbury. **F. Hall** (NT), mid-18c hse. SP 4349
Farnborough Green Hants 18 D5 N suburb of Farnborough. SU 8757
Farnborough Park Hants 18 D5* dist of Farnborough 1km N of tn centre. SU 8755
Farnborough Street Hants 18 D5* N suburb of Farnborough. SU 8756
Farncombe Surrey 11 F1 N suburb of Godalming. SU 9745
Farndish Beds 28 D2* vil 4m/6km SE of Wellingborough. SP 9263
Farndon Ches 42 A5 vil on R Dee 6m/9km NE of Wrexham. SJ 4154
Farndon Notts 44 C5 vil 2m/3km SW of Newark-on-Trent. **F. Field** loc 1m NE. SK 7651
Farndon, East Northants 36 C5 vil 2m/3km SW of Mkt Harborough. SP 7185
Farndon, West Northants 28 A3 ham 8m/13km NE of Banbury. SP 5251
Farne Islands Nthmb 67 H4/H5 about thirty islands (NT) between 2m/3km and 5m/8km offshore opp Bamburgh. St Cuthbert and St Aidan lived here in 7c. Breeding place for seals and some twenty species of sea birds. Lighthouse on Longstone. NU 23
Farnell Tayside 77 F5 vil 3m/5km SE of Brechin. **F. Castle,** now an old people's home, dates from 16c. NO 6255
Farnham Dorset 9 F3 vil 2m/3km SE of Tollard Royal. Pitt-Rivers Museum, established by General Pitt-Rivers in 1880 (see also Tollard Royal). ST 9515
Farnham Essex 29 H5 vil 2m/3km N of Bishop's Stortford. TL 4724
Farnham N Yorks 49 F2 vil 2m/4km N of Knaresborough. SE 3460
Farnham Suffolk 31 G2 vil 2m/4km SW of Saxmundham. TM 3660
Farnham Surrey 11 E1 tn on R Wey 10m/16km W of Guildford. Many Georgian hses at centre. Cas (A.M.) on hill to N: ruined moated keep; domestic bldgs occupied by Centre for International Briefing. Tn is birthplace of William Cobbett, who is buried in St Andrew's churchyard. SU 8446
Farnham Common Bucks 18 D3 suburb 3m/5km N of Slough. SU 9685
Farnham Green Essex 29 H5* loc 3m/4km NW of Bishop's Stortford. TL 4625
Farnham Royal Bucks 18 D3 suburb 2m/3km N of Slough. SU 9683
Farnhill N Yorks 48 C3* loc adjoining Kildwick to NW. SE 0046
Farningham Kent 20 B5 vil on R Darent 5m/7km S of Dartford. Old flour mill. Sites of Roman bldgs. TQ 5466
Farnley N Yorks 49 E3 ham 2m/3km NE of Otley. Hall is 18c hse by Carr of York incorporating Elizn hse. SE 2148
Farnley W Yorks 49 E5* dist of Leeds 3m/5km W of city centre. See also New Farnley. SE 2532
Farnley Tyas W Yorks 48 D6 vil 3m/4km SE of Huddersfield. SE 1612
Farnsfield Notts 44 B5 vil 4m/6km NW of Southwell. SK 6456
Farnworth Ches 42 B3 urban loc 2km N of Widnes. SJ 5187
Farnworth Gtr Manchester 42 C1 tn 2m/4km SE of Bolton. Coal-mining, textiles, engineering. SD 7306
Far Out Head H'land 84 D1 headland on N coast of Sutherland dist 3m/4km N of Durness. Also known as Faraid Hd. NC 3971
Farquhar's Point H'land 68 D2* headland on S side of entrance to Loch Moidart in Lochaber dist, opp W end of Eilean Shona. N1 6272
Farr H'land 81 F4 locality in Inverness dist 8m/12km S of Inverness. Loch F. is small loch to S. NH 6833
Farr H'land 86 A2 vil near N coast of Caithness dist 2km NE of Bettyhill. **Farr Pt** is headland 2km N. **F. Bay** 1km W. NC 7263
Farragon Hill Tayside 75 H5 mt 4m/7km N of Aberfeldy. Height 2559 ft or 780 metres. NN 8455
Farrar H'land 80 D3 r running E from Loch Monar to join R Glass 1km below Struy Br in Inverness dist. NH 4039
Farringdon Devon 7 G5 vil 6m/10km E of Exeter. SY 0191
Farringdon Tyne & Wear 61 H6* dist of Sunderland 3m/5km SW of tn centre. NZ 3653
Farringdon, Lower Hants 10 D2 vil 3m/4km S of Alton. SU 7035
Farringdon, Upper Hants 10 D2 vil 2m/4km S of Alton. SU 7135
Farringford Isle of Wight. See Freshwater.
Farrington Gurney Avon 16 B5 vil 2m/4km W of Midsomer Norton. ST 6255
Farsley W Yorks 49 E4 loc 1m N of Pudsey. **F. Beck Bottom** loc adjoining to E. SE 2135
Farteg, Y Welsh form of Varteg, qv.
Farthing Corner Kent 20 D5* loc 3m/5km SE of Gillingham. TQ 8163
Farthing Green Kent 12 D2* loc 2m/3km NW of Headcorn. TQ 8046
Farthinghoe Northants 28 A4 vil 4m/6km NW of Brackley. SP 5339
Farthingloe Kent 13 H3 loc in W part of Dover. TR 2940
Farthingstone Northants 28 B2 vil 5m/9km SE of Daventry. SP 6155
Farthing Street London 20 B5* loc 3m/4km N of Biggin Hill. TQ 4262
Fartown W Yorks 48 D6* dist of Huddersfield 2km N of tn centre. SE 1418
Farway Devon 8 A4 vil 4m/6km S of Honiton. SY 1895
Faskadale H'land 68 C2 loc on bay of same name 3m/5km W of Ockle Pt, on N coast of Ardnamurchan in Lochaber dist. NM 5070
Faslane Bay S'clyde 70 D5 bay on E side of Gare Loch 1m S of Garelochhead. Polaris submarine base. NS 2489
Fasnakyle H'land 80 D4 loc in Inverness dist where Glen Affric runs into Strathglass. Hydro-electricity power stn. **F. Forest** is deer forest to NW. NH 3128
Fassfern H'land 74 B3/B4 locality on N side of Loch Eil in Lochaber dist, 3m/5km E of Kinlocheil. NN 0278
Fast Castle Borders 67 E2 scanty remains of old cas on cliff 4m/6km NW of St Abb's Hd. NT 8671
Fatfield Tyne & Wear 61 G6 S dist of Washington. NZ 3054
Fathew 32 D4* r rising 2km SW of Abergynolwyn, Gwynedd, and flowing SW into R Dysynni 1km W of Bryncrug. SH 5903
Faugh Cumbria 60 B5* loc 4m/7km S of Brampton. NY 5054
Fauld Staffs 35 G2* loc 2m/3km W of Tutbury. SK 1828
Fauldhouse Lothian 65 F3 vil 3m/4km S of Whitburn. NS 9360
Faulkbourne Essex 30 C6 ham 2m/3km NW of Witham. TL 7917
Faulkland Som 16 C5 vil 3m/5km E of Radstock. ST 7354
Faulsgreen Salop 34 C2* ham 3m/5km NW of Hodnet. SJ 5932
Faulston Wilts 9 G2* loc just SE of Bishopstone and 4m/6km SW of Wilton. SU 0725
Faversham Kent 21 F5 mkt tn and small port at head of creek running into The Swale and thence into Whitstable Bay. Some light industry. TR 0161
Fawdington N Yorks 49 F1 loc 2m/3km N of Brafferton. SE 4372
Fawdon Tyne & Wear 61 G4 dist of Newcastle 3m/5km NW of city centre. NZ 2268
Fawfieldhead Staffs 43 F4 loc 2km SW of Longnor. SK 0763
Fawkham Green Kent 20 C5 vil in par of Fawkham 3m/4km E of Farningham. TQ 5865
Fawler Oxon 27 G5 vil 2m/3km SE of Charlbury. Sites of Roman bldgs. SP 3717
Fawley Berks 17 G3 vil 4m/7km S of Wantage. SU 3981
Fawley Bucks 18 C3 vil 3m/4km N of Henley-on-Thames. Loc of **F. Bottom** to W. SU 7586
Fawley Hants 10 B4 vil on Southampton Water 5m/7km E of Beaulieu. Large oil refinery. Power stn to SE. SU 4503
Fawley Chapel H & W 26 B4* loc beside left bank of R Wye 4m/6km N of Ross-on-Wye across loop of r. SO 5929
Fawley, South Berks 17 G3 ham 4m/7km E of Lambourn. SU 3980
Fawnog 33 E3* stream running SW into Tal-y-llyn lake S of Cader Idris, Gwynedd. SH 7210
Fawsley Northants 28 B2 loc 4m/6km S of Daventry. F. Hall in park dates from Tudor times. SP 5656
Faxfleet Humberside 50 D5 ham on N bank of R Ouse at its confluence with R Trent, which forms R Humber. **F. Ness** headland to W. SE 8624
Faxton Northants 28 C1 deserted vil 6m/9km W of Kettering. SP 7875
Faygate W Sussex 11 H2 ham 4m/6km NE of Horsham. TQ 2134
Fazakerley Merseyside 42 A2* dist of Liverpool 4m/6km NE of city centre. SJ 3795
Fazeley Staffs 35 G4 vil 2m/3km S of Tamworth, at junction of Birmingham and F. Canal and Coventry Canal. SK 2001
Feall Bay Coll, S'clyde 68 A3/A4 bay on NW coast 2m/3km from SW end of island. NM 1354
Fearby N Yorks 54 B6 vil 2m/3km W of Masham. SE 1981
Fearn H'land 87 B8 loc near E coast of Ross and Cromarty dist 2m/3km NW of Balintore. NH 8377
Fearnach Bay S'clyde 70 A3, A4* bay at head of Loch Melfort 1m W of Kilmelford in Argyll. NM 8313
Fearnan Tayside 71 H1 vil on N shore of Loch Tay 3m/5km W of Kenmore. NN 7244
Fearnbeg H'land 78 E3 locality in Ross and Cromarty dist on SW side of Loch Torridon 2km SE of Rubha na Fearn. NG 7359
Fearnhead Ches 42 C2 loc 3m/4km NE of Warrington. SJ 6390
Fearnmore H'land 78 E3 locality on SW side of Loch Torridon, Ross and Cromarty dist, 1km S of Rubha na Fearn. NG 7260
Fearnoch Forest S'clyde 70 B2* state forest 2m/3km W of Taynuilt, Argyll. NM 9631
Featherstone Staffs 35 F4 vil 4m/7km NE of Wolverhampton. SJ 9405
Featherstone W Yorks 49 F5 coal-mining loc 2m/4km W of Pontefract. SE 4222
Featherstone Castle Nthmb 60 C5 hse on R South Tyne 3m/4km SW of Haltwhistle, part dating from 13c but with many later additions and alterations. NY 6761
Feckenham H & W 27 E2 vil 6m/9km NW of Alcester. SP 0061
Feehlin H'land 81 E5 r in Inverness dist running N into R Foyers, 2m/3km S of Foyers on Loch Ness. NH 4917
Feering Essex 30 D5 vil 5m/8km NE of Witham. TL 8720
Feetham N Yorks 53 H5 vil in Swaledale 3m/5km W of Reeth. SD 9898
Feizor N Yorks 47 H2 loc 3m/5km NW of Settle. SD 7867
Felbridge Surrey 12 A3 suburb 2m/3km NW of E Grinstead. TQ 3639
Felbrigg Norfolk 39 F1 vil 2m/3km S of Cromer. To W, **F. Hall** (NT), 17c hse in grnds by Repton. TG 2039
Felcourt Surrey 12 A3* vil 2m/3km N of E Grinstead. TQ 3841
Felden Herts 19 E2* loc in SW part of Hemel Hempstead. TL 0404
Felhampton Salop 34 B5* ham 3m/5km N of Craven Arms. SO 4487
Felindre Dyfed 23 G3 loc 5m/8km W of Llandeilo. SN 5521
Felindre Dyfed 24 B3* loc 2km NE of Temple Bar. SN 5455
Felindre Dyfed 24 C5* loc 2m/3km W of Llanwrda. SN 6830
Felindre Dyfed 24 C5 loc 1km S of Llangadog. SN 7027
Felindre Mid Glam 15 E3* loc 4m/7km E of Bridgend. SS 9781
Felindre Powys 25 G5 loc just S of Cwmdu. SO 1723
Felindre Powys 33 H6 ham on R Teme 8m/12km SE of Newtown. SO 1681
Felindre W Glam 23 G5 ham 3m/5km E of Pontarddulais. SN 6302
Felinfach Dyfed 24 B3* loc 1m NW of Temple Bar. SN 5255
Felinfach Powys 25 F4* loc 4m/7km NE of Brecon. SO 0933
Felinfoel Dyfed 23 F5 loc adjoining Llanelli to NE. Mnfre of radiators and vehicle components. SN 5102
Felingwm Isaf Dyfed 23 F3* ham 6m/10km NE of Carmarthen and 1km S of Felingwm Uchaf. SN 5023
Felingwm Uchaf Dyfed 23 F3 ham 6m/10km NE of Carmarthen. SN 5024
Felin Puleston Clwyd 41 H6* loc 1m SW of Wrexham tn centre. SJ 3249
Felin-wen Welsh form of White Mill, qv.
Felin-Wnda Dyfed 23 E1* loc 4m/7km N of Newcastle Emlyn. SN 3246
Felinwynt Dyfed 22 D1* loc 3m/4km W of Aberporth. SN 2250
Felixkirk N Yorks 54 D6 vil 3m/5km NE of Thirsk. SE 4684
Felixstowe Suffolk 31 G4 resort and port 11m/17km SE of Ipswich. TM 3034
Felixstoweferry Suffolk 31 G4 ham at mouth of R Deben, on W side, 3m/4km NE of Felixstowe. Ferry across r for pedestrians. TM 3237
Felkington Nthmb 67 F4 loc 2km NE of Duddo. NT 9444
Felkirk W Yorks 49 F6* ham 1km W of S Hiendley. SE 3812

Felldyke Cumbria 52 B3* loc 1km S of Lamplugh. NY 0819
Fellgate Tyne & Wear 61 G5* loc in S Tyneside dist 2m/3km S of Hebburn. NZ 3262
Fell, High Tyne & Wear 61 G5* loc in Gateshead 2m/4km SE of tn centre. NZ 2760
Felling Tyne & Wear 61 G5* tn adjoining Gateshead to E. Includes locs of **Gelling Shore** and **High Felling.** NZ 2861
Fell Loch D & G 57 D7 small loch 7m/11km E of Glenluce. NX 3155
Fell, Low Tyne & Wear 61 G5* loc in Gateshead 2m/3km S of tn centre. NZ 2560
Fell Side Cumbria 52 C2* loc 2m/3km SW of Caldbeck. NY 3037
Felmersham Beds 29 E2 vil on R Ouse 6m/10km NW of Bedford. SP 9957
Felmingham Norfolk 39 F2 vil 2m/4km W of N Walsham. TG 2529
Felmore Essex 20 D3* dist of Basildon N of Pitsea. TQ 7389
Felpham W Sussex 11 F5 seaside resort and E dist of Bognor Regis. SZ 9599
Felsham Suffolk 30 D2 vil 7m/12km SE of Bury St Edmunds. TL 9457
Felsted Essex 30 B5 vil 3m/5km E of Gt Dunmow. TL 6720
Feltham London 19 E4 dist in borough of Hounslow 1m SW of Hounslow Heath. TQ 1073
Felthamhill Surrey 19 E4* urban loc 4m/6km E of Staines. TQ 0971
Feltham, Lower London 19 E4* loc in borough of Hounslow 1m SW of Feltham. TQ 0971
Feltham, North London 19 E4* loc in borough of Hounslow on W side of Hounslow Heath, 13m/20km W of Charing Cross. TQ 1074
Felthorpe Norfolk 39 F3 vil 7m/11km NW of Norwich. TG 1618
Felton Avon 16 A5 vil 1m E of Bristol (Lulsgate) Airport and 6m/10km SW of city centre. ST 5265
Felton H & W 26 B3 vil 7m/11km NE of Hereford. SO 5748
Felton Nthmb 61 F2 vil on R Coquet 8m/13km S of Alnwick. NU 1800
Felton Butler Salop 34 B3 ham 2km SE of Nesscliff. SJ 3917
Felton, West Salop 34 A2 vil 4m/7km SE of Oswestry. Earthworks of former cas to W of ch. SJ 3425
Feltwell Norfolk 38 B5/C5 vil 5m/8km NW of Brandon. TL 7190
Fenay Bridge W Yorks 48 D6* loc 3m/4km E of Huddersfield. SE 1815
Fence Lancs 48 B4 vil 2m/4km W of Nelson. SD 8237
Fence S Yorks 43 H3* loc 6m/9km E of Sheffield. SK 4485
Fence Bay S'clyde 64 A3/A4* bay on Fairlie Roads, Firth of Clyde, 2km S of Fairlie. NS 2053
Fence Houses Tyne & Wear 61 G6 loc 2m/3km W of Houghton-le-Spring. NZ 3150
Fencote, Great N Yorks 54 C5* ham 4m/6km SE of Catterick. **Lit Fencote** ham adjoining to S. SE 2893
Fencott Oxon 28 B6 ham 4m/7km S of Bicester. SP 5716
Fender Burn 75 H4 stream in Tayside region running SW down Glen Fender to R Tilt 1m N of Blair Atholl. Falls of Fender near junction with R Tilt. NN 8766
Fendike Corner Lincs 45 H5 ham 3m/5km NW of Wainfleet. TL 4560
Fen Ditton Cambs 30 A2 vil on R Cam 3m/4km NE of Cambridge. TL 4860
Fendoch Tayside 72 C2* site of Roman stn 5m/9km NE of Crieff. NN 9128
Fen Drayton Cambs 29 G1 vil 7m/11km SE of Huntingdon. TL 3368
Fenemere Salop 34 B2* small lake 2km NE of Baschurch – one of four in vicinity. SJ 4422
Fen End Lincs 37 G3* loc 2km S of Spalding. TF 2420
Fen End W Midlands 35 H6 loc 5m/8km NW of Kenilworth. SP 2275
Fengate Norfolk 39 F3* loc adjoining Marsham to NW. TG 1924
Fenham Nthmb 67 G4* loc on coast 5m/7km N of Belford. To S, **F. Burn** runs down to coast and **F. Flats**, mud-flats between mainland and Holy I. NU 0840
Fenham Tyne & Wear 61 G5* dist of Newcastle 2m/3km W of city centre. Site of Roman fort to SW. NZ 2265
Fenhouses Lincs 37 G1 loc 2km E of Swineshead. TF 2540
Feniscliffe Lancs 47 G5* loc 2m/3km SW of Blackburn. SD 6526
Feniscowles Lancs 47 G5* vil 3m/4km SW of Blackburn. SD 6425
Feniton Devon 7 H5 vil 4m/6km W of Honiton. SY 1099
Fenlake Beds 29 E3* loc in SE part of Bedford. TL 0648
Fenland 119 admin dist of Cambs.
Fenn Creek Essex 20 D2* creek running down to R Crouch estuary from N opp Hullbridge. TQ 8095
Fenney Hill Leics 36 A3* loc 1m SW of Shepshed. SK 4718
Fenn Green Salop 34 D5* ham 6m/9km NW of Kidderminster. SO 7783
Fennifach Powys 25 E5* loc 2km W of Brecon. SO 0228
Fenning Island Som 15 G6* peninsula at mouth of R Parrett and 2m/3km W of Highbridge across r. ST 2847
Fenni, Y Welsh form of Abergavenny, qv.
Fenn Street Kent 20 D4* ham 1m E of High Halstow, 5m/9km NE of Strood. TQ 7975
Fenny Bentley Derbys 43 F6 vil 2m/4km N of Ashbourne. SK 1750
Fenny Bridges Devon 7 H5 vil on R Otter 2m/3km NE of Ottery St Mary. SY 1198
Fenny Compton Warwicks 27 H3 vil 8m/12km N of Banbury. SP 4152
Fenny Drayton Leics 36 A4 vil 3m/5km N of Nuneaton. SP 3597
Fenny Stratford Bucks 28 D4 loc in E part of Bletchley beside Grand Union Canal and R Ouzel. Site of Roman settlement of *Magiovinium.* SP 8834
Fenrother Nthmb 61 F3 loc 4m/7km N of Morpeth. NZ 1792
Fenstanton Cambs 29 G1 vil 5m/9km SE of Huntingdon. TL 3168
Fens, The 37, 38 flat, low-lying, fertile part of eastern England draining into the Wash and bounded by the North Sea and, roughly, a line drawn from Skegness through Woodhall Spa, Sleaford, Bourne, Huntingdon, Cambridge, Newmarket, Brandon, Downham Mkt, and King's Lynn. TF, TL
Fen Street Norfolk 38 D5* ham 4m/6km W of Attleborough. TL 9895
Fen Street Norfolk 39 E5* loc 3m/4km S of Attleborough. TM 0591
Fen Street Norfolk 39 E6* loc 1m W of Diss. TM 1079
Fen Street Norfolk 39 E6* loc 4m/6km W of Diss. TM 0680
Fen Street Suffolk 31 E1 loc 7m/11km NE of Ixworth. TL 9879
Fen Street Suffolk 31 E1* loc 1m NE of Redgrave and 4m/6km W of Diss. TM 0579
Fen Street Suffolk 31 F2* loc 1km SE of Debenham. TM 1862
Fenton Cambs 37 G6 ham 1m SE of Warboys. TL 3279
Fenton Cumbria 60 B5* ham 4m/6km SW of Brampton. NY 5056
Fenton Lincs 44 C3 vil 8m/13km S of Gainsborough. SK 8476
Fenton Lincs 44 D6 vil 6m/9km E of Newark-on-Trent. SK 8750
Fenton Notts 44 C3* loc 1km SE of Sturton le Steeple. SK 7983
Fenton Staffs 35 E1 one of the tns of Stoke-on-Trent: Burslem, Fenton, Hanley, Longton, Stoke, Tunstall. Fenton lies to E of city centre. SJ 8944
Fenton Barns Lothian 66 C1 loc 3m/5km SW of N Berwick. NT 5181
Fenton, Little N Yorks 49 G4 vil 2m/3km NE of Sherburn in Elmet. SE 5235
Fenton Tower Lothian 66 C1 ruined 16c stronghold at Kingston, 2m/3km S of N Berwick. NT 5482
Fenton Town Nthmb 67 F5 ham 2m/3km NW of Doddington. NT 9733
Fenwick Nthmb 61 F4 ham 2km W of Stamfordham. NZ 0572
Fenwick Nthmb 67 G4 ham 5m/7km NW of Belford. NU 0640
Fenwick S'clyde 64 C4 vil 4m/7km NE of Kilmarnock. NS 4643
Fenwick S Yorks 49 G6 vil 5m/8km SW of Snaith. SE 5916
Fenwick Water 64 B5/C5 r in Strathclyde region running SW to confluence with Craufurdland Water 2km NE of Kilmarnock. The combined stream, known as Kilmarnock Water, flows through Kilmarnock to R Irvine on S side of tn. NS 4339
Feock Cornwall 2 D4 vil at head of Carrick Rds (R Fal), 4m/6km S of Truro. SW 8238
Feolin Ferry S'clyde 62 C1 loc with pier on W coast of Jura. Ferry across Sound of Islay to Port Askaig, 1km W of Islay. NR 4469
Ferguslie Park S'clyde 64 C3 W dist of Paisley. NS 4664
Ferindonald Skye, H'land 79 E7* loc on E side of Sleat peninsula 1m SW of Teangue. NG 6507
Fern Tayside 77 E4/E5 loc 2m/4km N of Tannadice. NO 4861
Ferndale Mid Glam 15 E2 loc 2m/3km E of Rhondda. SS 9996
Ferndown Dorset 9 G4 suburb 6m/9km N of Bournemouth. SU 0700
Ferness H'land 81 H3 loc in Nairn dist 8m/13km SE of Nairn. NH 9644
Fernham Oxon 17 G2 vil 2m/4km S of Faringdon. SU 2991
Fernhill Gtr Manchester 42 D1* loc in Bury 1m N of tn centre. SD 8011
Fernhill Gate Gtr Manchester 42 C1* loc in Bolton 2m/3km SW of tn centre. SD 6907
Fernhill Gate Hants 10 A5* loc 2km N of New Milton. SZ 2496
Fernhill Heath H & W 26 D2 vil 3m/5km NE of Worcester. SO 8759
Fernhurst W Sussex 11 E2 vil 3m/5km S of Haslemere. SU 8928
Ferniegair S'clyde 65 E3* loc 2km SE of Hamilton. NS 7454
Ferniehill Lothian 66 B2* dist of Edinburgh 4m/6km SE of city centre. NT 2969
Ferniehirst Castle Borders 66 D6 ancient stronghold of the Kers, rebuilt in 1598, now a youth hostel. NT 6518
Fernilea Skye, H'land 79 B5 locality on W side of Loch Harport, 1m NW of Carbost. NG 3732
Fernilee Derbys 43 E3* ham 2m/3km S of Whaley Br. **Fernilee Resr,** long narrow resr to S. SK 0178
Fernworthy Reservoir Devon 4 C2 resr surrounded on three sides by afforestation on E part of Dartmoor, 6m/9km W of Moretonhampstead. SX 6684
Ferny Common H & W 25 H3* loc 5m/8km SE of Kington. SO 3651
Ferrensby N Yorks 49 F2 vil 4m/7km SW of Boroughbridge. SE 3660
Ferriby, North Humberside 51 E5 vil 7m/11km W of Hull. SE 9825
Ferriby Sluice Humberside 51 E6* loc at outfall of R Ancholme into R Humber 1m W of S Ferriby. SE 9721
Ferriby, South Humberside 51 E6 vil 3m/4km W of Barton-upon-Humber. Site of Roman settlement to NE. SE 9820
Ferring W Sussex 11 G4 coastal tn 3m/5km W of Worthing. TQ 0902
Ferriniquarrie Skye, H'land 78 A4 loc near NW coast 4m/7km S of Dunvegan Hd. NG 1850
Ferrybridge W Yorks 49 F5 loc on S bank of R Aire adjoining Knottingley to W. Large power stn. SE 4824
Ferryden Tayside 77 G5 vil on S side of R South Esk opp Montrose. NO 7156
Ferry, East Lincs 44 C2 vil on E bank of R Trent 7m/11km N of Gainsborough. SK 8199
Ferry, High Lincs 45 G6* loc 1m S of Sibsey. TF 3449
Ferry Hill Cambs 37 H6* loc 2km S of Chatteris. TL 3883
Ferryhill Durham 54 C2 tn 6m/10km S of Durham. **Ferryhill Stn** loc 1m SE. NZ 2832
Ferryhill Grampian 77 H1* dist of Aberdeen 1km S of city centre. NJ 9305
Ferry Point H'land 87 A7* promontory on S side of Dornoch Firth, Ross and Cromarty dist, 4m/6km NW of Tain. Former ferry across firth no longer operates. NH 7385
Ferryside Dyfed 23 E4 vil with bathing beach on R Towy estuary opp Llansteffan and 7m/11km S of Carmarthen. Noted for cockles. SN 3610
Ferrytown H'land 87 A7 loc at mouth of R Evelix on N shore of Dornoch Firth, 5m/8km W of Dornoch, Sutherland dist. Former ferry across firth no longer operates. NH 7287
Ferry, West Tayside 73 G2* dist of Dundee 3m/5km E of city centre. NO 4431
Fersfield Norfolk 39 E6 vil 4m/6km NW of Diss. TM 0683
Fers Ness Orkney 89 B5/B6* northward-facing headland on W coast of Eday, on W side of the wide **Fersness Bay.** HY 5334
Feshie H'land 75 H1 r in Badenoch and Strathspey dist, rising on S side of Glenfeshie Forest and running N down Glen Feshie to R Spey 1km below Kincraig. NH 8406
Feshiebridge H'land H1 loc in Badenoch and Strathspey dist 2km SE of Kincraig. NH 8504
Fetcham Surrey 19 F5 suburban loc 2km W of Leatherhead. TQ 1455
Fetlar Shetland 89 F6 large sparsely inhabited island of about 14 sq miles or 36 sq km S of Unst and E of Yell. Nature reserve. HU 6391
Fetterangus Grampian 83 G2 vil 2m/3km N of Mintlaw. NJ 9850
Fettercairn Grampian 77 vil 11m/17km NW of Montrose. Contains shaft of tn cross of Kincardine. Distillery. NO 6573
Fetteresso Forest Grampian 77 G2 state forest 6m/10km W of Stonehaven. See also Kirktown of Fetteresso. NO 7787
Fettes College Lothian 66 A1* boys' public school in Edinburgh, 2km NW of city centre. NT 2375
Fewcott Oxon 28 A4 loc adjoining Ardley to N, 4m/7km NW of Bicester. SP 5427
Fewston N Yorks 48 D3 vil 6m/9km N of Otley. **Fewston Resr** to W. **F. Bents** loc to N. SE 1954
Ffairfach Dyfed 23 G3 vil 1km S of Llandeilo. SN 6221
Ffair Rhos Dyfed 24 C2 ham 6m/10km NE of Tregaron. SN 7368
Ffald-y-Brenin Dyfed 24 C4* loc 3m/4km NW of Pumsaint. SN 6344
Ffawyddog Powys 25 G6 loc 1m W of Crickhowell across R Usk. SO 2018
Ffestiniog Gwynedd 33 E1 vil 9m/14km E of Portmadoc. Slate-quarrying to N. SH 7042
Fflint, Y Welsh form of Flint, qv.
Ffontygari Welsh form of Font-y-gary, qv.
Ffordd-las Clwyd 41 G5* loc 4m/7km N of Ruthin. SJ 1264
Ffordd-las Clwyd 41 H5* loc 1km NW of Hope. SJ 3059
Fforddlas Powys 25 G4* loc 3m/4km SW of Hay-on-Wye. SO 2038
Fforest Dyfed 23 G5 vil 1km NW of Pontarddulais. SN 5804
Fforest-fach W Glam 23 G5 loc in Swansea 3m/4km NW of tn centre. Industrial estate. SS 6295
Fforest Fawr Powys 24 D6/25 E6 range of moorland hills between Black Mountain in the W and Brecon Beacons in the E, attaining height of 2409 ft or 734 metres at Fan Fawr, qv. SN 8191
Fforest Goch W Glam 14 C2* loc 3m/5km N of Neath. SN 7401
Ffostrasol Dyfed 24 A3 ham 5m/8km NW of Llandyssul. SN 3747
Ffos-y-ffin Dyfed 24 A2 vil 2m/3km S of Aberaeron. SN 4460
Ffos-y-go Clwyd 41 H5* loc 3m/5km NW of Wrexham. SJ 3054
Ffraw 40 B4* r on Anglesey running SW into Aberffraw Bay on W coast. SH 3567
Ffrith Clwyd 41 H5 ham 4m/7km NW of Wrexham. SJ 2855
Ffrwd Fawr Powys 33 F5* waterfall in upper Twymyn valley 2m/3km N of head of Clywedog Resr. Height about 140 ft or 43 metres. SN 8794
Ffwl-y-mwn Welsh form of Fonmon, qv.
Ffynnon Dyfed 23 E4* loc 4m/7km SW of Carmarthen. SN 3516
Ffynnon-Ddewi 24 A3* r rising 5m/8km S of Newquay, Dyfed, and flowing NW into Cardigan Bay 3m/4km SW of the tn. SN 3557
Ffynnon Drewi Dyfed 24 B2/C2* chalybeate spring 2km SE of Trefenter. SN 6267
Ffynnongroew Clwyd 41 G3 vil on R Dee estuary 2m/3km NW of Mostyn. SJ 1382
Ffynnon Gynydd Powys 25 F4* ham 2km NW of Glasbury. SO 1641
Ffynnon Lloer Gwynedd 40 D5* tarn 1km S of Carnedd Dafydd. SH 6662

Ffynnon Llugwy Reservoir Gwynedd 40 D5• resr near source of R Llugwy 3m/5km NW of Capel Curig. SH 6962

Ffynnon Taf Welsh form of Taff's Well, qv.

Fiag H'land 85 E5 r in Sutherland dist running S from Loch Fiag to Loch Shin. NC 4620

Fiaray W Isles 88 D3• small uninhabited island off Scurrival Pt at N end of Barra. NF 7010

Fickleshole Surrey 20 A5• ham 3m/4km NE of Warlingham. TQ 3960

Fiddich 82 C3 r in Grampian region rising on Corryhabbie Hill, Glenfiddich Forest, and running NE down Glen Fiddich, then W to Dufftown, then NW to R Spey at Craigellachie. NJ 2945

Fiddich 82 C3 r in Grampian region rising on Corryhabbie Hill, Glenfiddich Forest, and running NE down Glen Fiddich, then W to Dufftown, then NW to R Spey at Craigellachie. NJ 2945

Fiddington Glos 26 D4• ham 2m/3km SE of Tewkesbury. SO 9231

Fiddington Som 8 A1 vil 2m/3km NE of Nether Stowey. ST 2140

Fiddleford Dorset 9 E3• vil 2km SE of Sturminster Newton. ST 8013

Fiddler's Ferry Ches 42 B3• loc on St Helen's Canal 3m/5km E of Widnes. SJ 5686

Fiddler's Green Glos 26 D5• loc in W part of Cheltenham. SO 9122

Fiddler's Green H & W 26 B4 loc 5m/8km SE of Hereford. SO 5735

Fiddler's Green Norfolk 38 C3• loc 1m NE of Castle Acre. TF 8216

Fiddlers' Green Norfolk 39 E5• loc 1m N of Attleborough. TM 0496

Fiddlers Hamlet Essex 20 B2• ham 1m SE of Epping. TL 4701

Fiddler's Reach 20 C4• alternative name for St Clement's Reach, stretch of R Thames extending from Greenhithe, Kent to the N point of Swanscombe Marshes. TQ 5976

Fidra Lothian 73 G5 small island off shore 3m/4km W of N Berwick. Haunt of sea birds. Lighthouse. NT 5186

Field Staffs 35 F1 ham 4m/7km W of Uttoxeter. SK 0233

Field Assarts Oxon 27 G6 loc 4m/6km NW of Witney. SP 3113

Field Broughton Cumbria 52 D6 ham 2m/3km N of Cartmel. SD 3881

Field Dalling Norfolk 39 E1 vil 4m/7km W of Holt. TG 0039

Fieldhead Cumbria 52 D1• loc 1m SW of Calthwaite. NY 4539

Field Head Leics 36 B3• ham 1km E of Markfield. SK 4909

Field Place W Sussex. See Broadbridge Heath.

Field, South Humberside 51 E5• S dist of Hessle. TA 0325

Field, West Humberside 51 F6• loc 1m W of E Halton. TA 1219

Fife 115 admin region of eastern Scotland between Firth of Tay and Firth of Forth, comprising the former county of the same name, known since ancient times as the Kingdom of Fife, and noted for its fine coastline with many distinctive small tns and fishing ports. The historic tn of St Andrews, on the coast between the two firths, is a university tn, and the home of the world's premier golf club. Inland, the region is outstandingly fertile, while in the SW coal-mining is still carried on, although less intensively than in former times.

Fifehead Magdalen Dorset 9 E2 vil 5m/8km W of Shaftesbury. ST 7821

Fifehead Neville Dorset 9 E3 vil 2m/4km SW of Sturminster Newton. ST 7610

Fifehead St Quintin Dorset 9 E3• ham 1km SE of Fifehead Neville and 3m/4km SE of Sturminster Newton. ST 7710

Fife Keith Grampian 82 C2 loc adjoining Keith to W, connected to it by early 17c br. NJ 4250

Fife Ness Fife 73 H3 headland at E extremity of region, 9m/15km SE of St Andrews. NO 6309

Fifield Berks 18 D4 vil 4m/6km W of Windsor. SU 9076

Fifield Oxon 27 F5 vil 4m/7km N of Burford. SP 2318

Fifield Wilts 17 F6• loc 1m S of Enford and 6m/9km N of Amesbury. SU 1450

Fifield Bavant Wilts 9 G2 ham 7m/11km SW of Wilton. SU 0125

Figheldean Wilts 17 F6 vil on R Avon 4m/6km N of Amesbury. SU 1547

Fighting Cocks Durham 54 C3 ham 3m/5km E of Darlington. NZ 3414

Figsbury Ring Wilts 9 H1 Iron Age hill fort 4m/6km NE of Salisbury, commanding views over city. SU 1833

Filby Norfolk 39 H3/H4 vil 5m/8km NW of Gt Yarmouth. **F. Broad** 1km W, broad or lake connected with Rollesby and Ormesby Broads, and with R Bure by Muck Fleet. TG 4613

Filey N Yorks 55 H6 North Sea coast resort on **F. Bay** 7m/11km SE of Scarborough. **F. Brigg** is mile-long reef at N end of bay, covered at high tide; site of Roman signal stn. TA 1180

Filgrave Bucks 28 D3• ham 3m/5km N of Newport Pagnell across loop of R Ouse. SP 8748

Filham Devon 4 C5• ham 1m E of Ivybridge. SX 6455

Filkins Oxon 17 F1 vil 4m/6km NE of Lechlade. SP 2304

Filleigh Devon 7 E2 vil 3m/5km NW of S Molton. SS 6628

Fillingham Lincs 44 D3 vil 9m/15km N of Lincoln. Large lake to W known as **F. Broad.** To E is **F. Castle,** 18c hse in Gothic style. SK 9485

Fillongley Warwicks 35 H5 vil 6m/10km NW of Coventry. SP 2887

Filmore Hill Hants 10 D2 loc 3m/4km NE of W Meon. SU 6627

Filton Avon 16 B3 N suburb of Bristol. Aircraft works and airfield. ST 6079

Fimber Humberside 50 D2 vil 2m/3km NE of Fridaythorpe. SE 8960

Finart Bay S'clyde 71 D5• small bay on W side of Loch Long, on N side of Ardentinny in Argyll. NS 1887

Finavon Tayside 77 E5• loc on R South Esk 5m/8km NE of Forfar. **F. Castle** is ruined 16c stronghold of the Earls of Crawford. NO 4957

Finborough, Great Suffolk 31 E2 vil 3m/4km W of Stowmarket. TM 0157

Finchale Priory Durham 54 C1 remains (A.M.), mainly 13c, of priory founded late 12c, beside R Wear 3m/5km NE of Durham. NZ 2947

Fincham Norfolk 38 B4 vil 5m/8km E of Downham Mkt. TF 6806

Finchampstead Berks 10 C5 vil 4m/6km SW of Wokingham. To E, **F. Ridges** (NT), area of heath and woodland. SU 7963

Fincharn Castle S'clyde 70 B4• remains of former stronghold of the Macdonalds on E shore of Loch Awe in Argyll, 2m/3km E of head of loch. NM 8904

Finchdean Hants 10 D3 vil 4m/7km N of Havant. SU 7312

Finchingfield Essex 30 B4 vil 8m/12km NW of Braintree. Sites of Roman bldgs in vicinity. TL 6832

Finchley London 19 F3 dist in borough of Barnet 7m/11km N of Charing Cross. TQ 2590

Findern Derbys 35 H2 vil 5m/8km SW of Derby. SK 3030

Findhorn Grampian 82 A1 fishing vil on E side of sandy **F. Bay** at mouth of R Findhorn, N of Forres. R rises in Monadhliath Mts, Highland region, W of Kingussie, and flows NE down Strath Dearn to F. Bay and North Sea. NJ 0364

Findlater Castle Grampian 82 D1 ruined cas on cliffs 2m/3km E of Cullen. NJ 5467

Findochty Grampian 82 D1 fishing vil and resort at E end of Spey Bay 3m/5km NE of Buckie. Ruins of **F. Castle** to SW. NJ 4667

Findo Gask Tayside 72 D3 loc surrounded by Roman sites 7m/12km W of Perth. NO 0020

Findon Grampian 77 H2 vil near E coast 5m/9km S of Aberdeen. Also known as Finnan, the form from which smoked haddock takes its name. **F. Ness** is headland on coast here. NO 9397

Findon W Sussex 11 G4 vil in S Downs 4m/7km N of Worthing. TQ 1208

Findon Forest H'land 81 F2 state forest on Black Isle, Ross and Cromarty dist, 5m/8km W of Fortrose. NH 6458

Findon Valley W Sussex 11 G4• N dist of Worthing almost adjoining vil of Findon. TQ 1206

Finedon Northants 28 D1 tn 3m/5km NE of Wellingborough. SP 9272

Fineshade Northants 37 E4 par 6m/10km W of Wansford. Of former **F. Abbey** only stables survive. SP 9797

Fingal's Cave Staffa, S'clyde 69 B5 large cave at S end of island with pillars of basalt at entrance. Dimensions: height 66 ft or 20 metres, depth from entrance to back 227 ft or 69 metres, width of entrance 42 ft or 13 metres. NM 3235

Fingal Street Suffolk 31 F2• ham 2km NW of Worlingworth. TM 2169

Fingask Castle Tayside 73 E2 restored cas, 7m/12km E of Perth, dating from 16c. NO 2227

Fingask Loch Tayside 73 E1• small loch 2m/3km SW of Blairgowrie. NO 1642

Fingerpost H & W 26 C1• loc 3m/5km W of Bewdley. SO 7373

Fingest Bucks 18 C3 vil 5m/9km N of Henley-on-Thames. SU 7791

Finghall N Yorks 54 B5 vil 4m/7km E of Leyburn. SE 1889

Fingland Cumbria 59 G5 loc 2m/3km E of Kirkbride. NY 2557

Finglas Water 71 F4 r in Central region running SE down Glen Finglas, through Glen Finglas Resr, to Black Water between Loch Achray and Loch Venachar, W of Callander. NN 5306

Fingle Bridge Devon 7 F6 br over R Teign in narrow wooded gorge 3m/4km N of Moretonhampstead. SX 7489

Fin Glen S'clyde 64 C1, D1 valley of **Finglen Burn,** stream rising on Campsie Fells and running SE to Glazert Water 2km NW of Lennoxtown. NS 5980

Finglesham Kent 13 H2 ham 3m/4km S of Sandwich. TR 3353

Fingringhoe Essex 31 E6 vil 4m/6km SE of Colchester. Firing ranges on F. Marshes to S. TM 0220

Finham W Midlands 35 H6• loc in Coventry 3m/4km S of city centre. SP 3375

Finkle Street S Yorks 43 G2• loc just SW of Wortley. SK 3098

Finlarig Central 71 G2 loc 1km N of Killin. Power stn to E on shore of Loch Tay. **F. Castle,** remains of former seat of the Earls of Breadalbane. NN 5733

Finlas Water S'clyde 71 E5• r running SE down Glen Finlas into Loch Lomond 1m S of Rossdhu. NS 3687

Finmere Oxon 28 B4 vil 4m/6km W of Buckingham. SP 6332

Finnan Grampian. See Findon.

Finnan H'land 74 A3 r in Lochaber dist running S down Glen Finnan to head of Loch Shiel. NM 9080

Finnart S'clyde 70 D5 locality in Argyll on E side of Loch Long, 3m/4km N of Garelochhead. Oil terminal. NS 2495

Finnart Tayside 75 F5 locality on S side of Loch Rannoch 1km from head of loch. **Loch F.** is small loch 1m S. NN 5157

Finnarts Bay S'clyde 57 A5/A6 small bay near N end of Loch Ryan, at mouth of Water of App. **Finnarts Pt** is headland 1m N. NX 0572

Finney Green Ches 42 D3• loc 2km NE of Wilmslow. SJ 8582

Finnieston S'clyde 64 C2• loc in Glasgow 1m W of city centre. NS 5765

Finningham Suffolk 31 E2 vil 7m/11km N of Stowmarket. TM 0669

Finningley S Yorks 44 B2 vil 4m/7km N of Bawtry. Airfield to SW. SK 6799

Finsbay W Isles 88 A4• locality on loch of same name on SE coast of Harris 2m/4km SW of Manish. NG 0786

Finsbury London 19 G3• dist in borough of Islington about 2km N of Blackfriars Br. TQ 3182

Finsbury Park London 19 G3• loc in boroughs of Haringey and Islington 4m/7km N of Charing Cross. The park itself is to N in borough of Haringey. TQ 3186

Finstall H & W 27 E1 loc 2km E of Bromsgrove. SO 9870

Finsthwaite Cumbria 52 D6 ham 1m N of Newby Br. SD 3687

Finstock Oxon 27 G5 vil 2m/3km S of Charlbury. SP 3616

Finstown Orkney 89 B6 vil on Mainland at head of Bay of Firth 6m/10km W of Kirkwall. HY 3513

Fintry Central 71 G5/G6 vil on Endrick Water 5m/7km E of Balfron. **F. Hills,** range of hills to NE. NS 6186

Fintry Grampian 83 F2 loc 4m/6km NE of Turriff. NJ 7554

Finwood Warwicks 27 F1• ham 3m/5km NE of Henley-in-Arden. SP 1968

Fiola Meadhonach S'clyde 69 E6• small island immediately N of island of Lunga. NM 7109

Fionn Bheinn H'land 80 B2 mt in Ross and Cromarty dist 2m/4km N of Achnasheen. Height 3062 ft or 933 metres. Anglicised form: Foinaven. NH 1462

Fionn Loch H'land 85 A8 loch near W coast of Ross and Cromarty dist 5m/8km E of Poolewe. Length over 5m/8km NW to SE; width about 1km. NG 9478

Fionnphort S'clyde 69 B6 vil on Sound of Iona at W end of Ross of Mull. Ferry to Iona. NM 3023

Firbeck S Yorks 44 A2 vil 3m/5km SE of Maltby. SK 5688

Firby N Yorks 50 C2 ham 4m/7km SW of Malton. SE 7466

Firby N Yorks 54 B6• ham 1m S of Bedale. SE 2686

Firepool Som 8 A2• dist of Taunton to S of rly stn. ST 2225

Firgrove Gtr Manchester 48 C6 loc 2km E of Rochdale. SD 9113

Fir Island Cumbria 52 C5 small wooded island (NT) off E shore of Coniston Water 2m/3km S of Coniston. SD 3094

Firle, West E Sussex 12 B5 vil below S Downs 4m/7km SE of Lewes. **F. Place** is mainly Ggn hse with Tudor core. On ridge of downs 2km SE is **F. Beacon,** viewpoint at 713 ft or 217 metres. TQ 4707

Firrhill Lothian 66 A2• dist of Edinburgh 3m/5km SW of city centre. NT 2369

Firsby Lincs 45 H5 vil 4m/6km NW of Wainfleet. TF 4563

Firsby, East Lincs 45 E3• loc 1km N of Spridlington. **W Firsby** loc 2km W. TF 0085

Firs Lane Gtr Manchester 42 C2 loc in Leigh 1m W of tn centre. SD 6400

Firs Road Wilts 9 H1• loc 5m/8km NE of Salisbury. SU 2133

Firth Shetland 89 E6 loc on NE coast of Mainland 2km S of Mossbank across inlet called Firths Voe. **Firth Ness** is headland 2km E. HU 4473

Firth, Bay of Orkney 89 B6 bay on coast of Mainland facing NE towards Shapinsay. Vil of Finstown at head of bay. HY 3814

Firth of Clyde S'clyde 63, 64 estuary of R Clyde running from Dumbarton past Gourock, then turning S and continuing between the Strathclyde mainland to E and the islands of Bute and Arran to W. NS 15

Firth of Forth 73 estuary of R Forth, running E between Fife and Lothian regions and widening out into North Sea between Fife Ness and N Berwick. At its narrowest point (2km), between N and S Queensferry, firth is spanned by Forth rd and rly brs. NT 38

Firth of Lorn S'clyde 70 A3, A2 sea passage between SE coast of Mull and Scottish mainland. NM 72

Firth of Tay 73 F2 estuary of R Tay extending E from confluence of Rs Tay and Earn past Dundee to Buddon Ness, and dividing regions of Fife and Tayside. Length about 23m/37km; maximum width nearly 3m/5km at Invergowrie, although channel is comparatively narrow owing to presence of sandbanks. NO 3737

Firths Voe Shetland. See Firth.

Firth, The Shetland 89 E7• wide part of inlet SE of Bixter, Mainland. Here Bixter Voe and Tresta Voe join before narrowing again at head of Sandsound Voe. HU 3450

Fir Tree Durham 54 B2 vil 2m/3km SW of Crook. NZ 1434

Fir Vale S Yorks 43 H2 loc in Sheffield 2m/3km N of city centre. SK 3690

Fishbourne Isle of Wight 10 C5 ham 2m/3km W of Ryde. SZ 5692

Fishbourne W Sussex 11 E4 vil 2m/3km W of Chichester. Remains of Roman palace. SU 8304

Fishburn Durham 54 C2 vil 2m/3km N of Sedgefield. NZ 3632

Fishcross Central 72 C5• vil 2m/3km NE of Alloa. Coal-mining. NS 8995

Fisher W Sussex 11 E5 loc just W of S Mundham, 3m/5km S of Chichester. SU 8700

Fisherfield Forest H'land 85 A8 deer forest in Ross and Cromarty dist whose centre is about 8m/13km E of Poolewe. NG 9980

Fisherford Grampian 83 E3 loc 9m/15km E of Huntly. NJ 6635

Fisherrow Lothian 66 B2* loc, W part of Musselburgh. Small harbour. NT 3373

Fishersgate W Sussex 11 H4* E dist of Southwick. TQ 2505

Fishers Green Essex 20 A2* loc on R Lea 2km E of Cheshunt. TL 3802

Fisher's Green Herts 29 F5* loc in NW part of Stevenage. TL 2225

Fisher's Pond Hants 10 C3 vil 5m/8km NW of Bishop's Waltham. SU 4820

Fisher's Row Lancs 47 E3 loc 1km E of Pilling. SD 4148

Fisherstreet W Sussex 11 F2 loc 3m/5km SE of Haslemere. SU 9531

Fisher Tarn Reservoir Cumbria 53 E5* resr 2m/4km E of Kendal. SD 5592

Fisherton H'land 81 G2* loc in Inverness dist on E side of Inner Moray Firth 2km W of Dalcross Airport. NH 7451

Fisherton de la Mere Wilts 9 G1 ham 1m NW of Wylye across r. SU 0038

Fisherwick Staffs 35 G3* loc 4m/6km NW of Tamworth. SK 1709

Fishguard (Abergwaun) Dyfed 22 C2 small tn at S end of **F. Bay,** which extends from Dinas Hd westwards to Crincoed Pt. **F. Harbour,** on W side of bay, is a port, with passenger services to Rosslare, Cork, and Waterford (see Goodwick). SM 9537

Fish Holm Shetland 89 E6* small island off NE coast of Mainland 2m/3km E of Mossbank. HU 4774

Fish Lake Durham 53 G3 small lake on Lune Forest 2km NW of Grains o' th' Beck Br. NY 8620

Fishlake S Yorks 49 H6 vil 3m/4km N of Hatfield. SE 6513

Fishley Norfolk 39 G4* loc 1m N of Acle. TG 4011

Fishley W Midlands 35 F4* loc in Walsall 3m/5km N of tn centre. SK 0003

Fishmere End Lincs 37 G1* loc 2km N of Sutterton. TF 2837

Fishmoor Reservoir Lancs 47 G5* resr in Blackburn 2m/3km SE of tn centre. SD 6926

Fishnet Point Lancs 47 E3* headland on left bank of R Lune estuary to W of Glasson. SD 4456

Fishnish Bay Mull, S'clyde 68 E4 bay on Sound of Mull 4m/7km E of Salen. **Fishnish Pt** is headland on E side of bay. NM 6442

Fishpond Bottom Dorset 8 B4 loc 5m/7km E of Axminster. SY 3698

Fishponds Avon 16 B4* NE dist of Bristol. ST 6376

Fishpool Gtr Manchester 42 D1* loc in Bury 1m SE of tn centre. SD 8109

Fishtoft Lincs 37 H1 vil 2m/4km SE of Boston. TF 3642

Fishtown of Usan Tayside 77 G5 vil on E coast 2m/3km S of Montrose. Also known as Usan. NO 7254

Fishwick Lancs 47 F5 loc in Preston 2km E of tn centre. SD 5629

Fiskavaig Skye, H'land 79 B5 locality and small bay on W coast, on S shore of Loch Bracadale. NG 3334

Fiskerton Lincs 45 E4 vil 5m/8km E of Lincoln. TF 0472

Fiskerton Notts 44 C5 vil on R Trent 3m/5km SE of Southwell. SK 7351

Fistral Bay Cornwall 2 D2* bay between Towan Hd and E Pentire Pt, 2km W of Newquay. SW 7962

Fitful Head Shetland 89 E8 headland on W coast of Mainland 5m/8km NW of Sumburgh Hd. The steep cliffs rise to 929 ft or 283 metres. HU 3413

Fitling Humberside 51 F5/G5* loc 3m/4km S of Aldbrough. TA 2534

Fittleton Wilts 17 F6 vil on R Avon 5m/8km N of Amesbury. SU 1449

Fittleworth W Sussex 11 F3 vil 3m/4km SE of Petworth. TQ 0119

Fittleworth, Lower W Sussex 11 F3* ham on R Rother, adjoining Fittleworth to S. TQ 0118

Fitton End Cambs 37 H3* loc 3m/5km NW of Wisbech. TF 4212

Fitz Salop 34 B3 ham 4m/7km NW of Shrewsbury. SJ 4417

Fitzhead Som 8 A2 vil 3m/3km N of Milverton. ST 1228

Fitzroy Som 8 A2* loc 3m/5km NW of Taunton. ST 1927

Fitzwilliam W Yorks 49 F6* coal-mining vil 2m/3km NW of Hemsworth. SE 4115

Fiunary Forest H'land 68 E4 state forest in Lochaber dist to N and W of Lochaline. NM 6647

Five Acres Glos 26 B6* loc 1m N of Coleford. SO 5712

Five Ash Down E Sussex 12 B4 ham 2m/3km N of Uckfield. TQ 4724

Five Ashes E Sussex 12 B4 vil 2m/3km SW of Mayfield. TQ 5524

Five Bells Som 7 H1* ham 1km S of Watchet. ST 0642

Five Bridges H & W 26 B3 loc 5m/8km S of Bromyard. SO 6547

Fivehead Som 8 B2 vil 5m/8km SW of Langport. ST 3522

Fivehead 8 B2* r rising on E extension of Blackdown Hills in Somerset and flowing E into R Isle 2m/3km SW of Curry Rivel. ST 3722

Five Houses Isle of Wight 10 B5* loc 1m E of Newbridge and 5m/7km W of Newport. SZ 4287

Five Lane Ends W Yorks 48 D4* loc in Eccleshill dist of Bradford. SE 1736

Five Lanes Cornwall 6 B6 ham on NE edge of Bodmin Moor 7m/11km SW of Launceston. SX 2280

Five Lanes Gwent 16 A3* loc 2km W of Caerwent. ST 4490

Five Mile Hill Cross Devon 7 F5* loc 5m/8km W of Exeter. SX 8493

Five Oak Green Kent 12 C2* vil 2km W of Paddock Wd. TQ 6445

Five Oaks W Sussex 11 G2 ham 2m/3km NE of Billingshurst. TQ 0928

Five Penny Borve W Isles 88 B1 vil near NW coast of Lewis adjoining High Borve and 5m/8km NE of Barvas. NB 4056

Five Penny Ness W Isles 88 C1* vil 2km S of Butt of Lewis and 1m NW of Port of Ness. NB 5264

Five Roads Dyfed 23 F5 loc 3m/5km N of Llanelli. SN 4805

Five Sisters of Kintail H'land 80 A5, A6 chain of peaks on Kintail Forest (NTS), Skye and Lochalsh dist: from N to S, Sgurr na Moraich, Sgurr nan Saighead, Sgurr Fhuaran (or Scour Ouran), Sgurr na Carnach, and Sgurr na Ciste Duibhe. NG 91

Five Ways H & W 35 E6* loc 3m/5km NE of Kidderminster. SO 8780

Five Wents Kent 20 D6 loc 1m N of Sutton Valence. TQ 8050

Flackley Ash E Sussex 13 E4* loc adjoining Peasmarsh to NW. TQ 8823

Flack's Green Essex 30 C6* loc 3m/5km W of Witham. TL 7614

Flackwell Heath Bucks 18 D3 suburban loc 3m/5km W of Beaconsfield. SU 8990

Fladbury H & W 26 E3 vil 3m/5km NW of Evesham. SO 9946

Fladbury Cross H & W 27 E3* loc 4m/6km NW of Evesham. SO 9947

Fladda S'clyde 70 A4* islet with lighthouse 1m off NW coast of Luing. NM 7212

Fladda Treshnish Isles, S'clyde 68 B4 one of the larger islands of the group, lying towards NE end. NM 2943

Fladdabister Shetland 89 E8 locality on Mainland 6m/10km S of Lerwick near head of small **Bay of F.** on E coast. **Loch of F.** 1km N. HU 4333

Fladda-chùain H'land 88 C4* narrow uninhabited island, nearly 1m long NW to SE, 4m/6km NW of Rubha Hunish, Skye. NG 3681

Fladday Skye, H'land 78 D4 uninhabited island of about 360 acres or 145 hectares lying off W coast of Raasay midway between Manish Pt and Eilean Tigh, and separated from Raasay by narrow channel of Caol Fladda. NG 5851

Fladday W Isles 88 E1* uninhabited island in Loch Maddy, E coast of N Uist, 2km E of vil of Lochmaddy. NF 9469

Fladday W Isles 88 A3* small uninhabited island off E coast of Scarp opp entrance to Loch Resort, W coast of island of Lewis. NA 9915

Flag Creek Essex 31 E6* creek running into Brightlingsea Creek from NE and thence into Brightlingsea Reach at mouth of R Colne. TM 1016

Flagg Derbys 43 F4 vil 5m/8km W of Bakewell. SK 1368

Flamborough Humberside 51 F2 vil 4m/6km NE of Bridlington. **F. Head** headland on North Sea coast 2m/3km E. TA 2270

Flamstead Herts 19 E1 vil 5m/8km N of Hemel Hempstead. TL 0714

Flamstead End Herts 19 G2 loc 2km NW of Cheshunt. TL 3403

Flanders Green Herts 29 G5* loc 3m/4km W of Buntingford. TL 3228

Flanders Moss Central 71 G5 boggy area between R Forth and Goodie Water, SW of Thornhill. NS 6398

Flannan Isles W Isles (W of 88 A2) group of small uninhabited islands about 21m/34km W of Gallan Hd, Lewis. The main islands, in order of size, are: Eilean Mór, Eilean Tighe, Eilean a' Ghobha, Soray, Roareim, Sgeir Toman, and Sgeir Righinn. There are several smaller islets and rocks. The larger islands are grass-covered and are used for grazing. Birds abound. NA 74

Flansham W Sussex 11 F5 vil 2m/3km NE of Bognor Regis. SU 9601

Flanshaw W Yorks 49 E6* dist of Wakefield 2km W of city centre. SE 3020

Flappit Spring W Yorks 48 C4* loc 2km E of Haworth. SE 0536

Flasby N Yorks 48 C3 loc 4m/7km NW of Skipton. SD 9456

Flash Staffs 43 E4 vil in Peak Dist National Park 4m/7km SW of Buxton. SK 0267

Flashader Skye, H'land 78 B4* locality on E side of Loch Greshornish on N coast. NG 3453

Flash, The Gtr Manchester 42 C2 lake 2km SW of Leigh. SJ 6399

Flatford Mill Suffolk. See Bergholt, East.

Flat Holm S Glam 15 G5 round island about 1m in circumference in Bristol Channel 3m/4km SE of Lavernock Pt. Lighthouse. ST 2264

Flats, High W Yorks 43 G1* loc 4m/6km NW of Penistone. SE 2107

Flatts, High Durham 61 G6* loc 1m NW of Chester-le-Street. NZ 2652

Flaunden Herts 19 E2 vil 4m/6km E of Chesham. TL 0100

Flawborough Notts 36 D1 vil 5m/8km NE of Bingham. SK 7842

Flawith N Yorks 49 F2 ham 4m/7km SW of Easingwold. SE 4865

Flax Bourton Avon 16 A4 vil 5m/8km W of Bristol. ST 5069

Flaxby N Yorks 49 F3 vil 3m/5km E of Knaresborough. SE 3957

Flaxholme Derbys 35 H1* loc 4m/6km N of Derby. SK 3442

Flaxlands Norfolk 39 E5* loc at Carleton Rode, 5m/8km S of Wymondham. TM 1093

Flaxley Glos 26 C5/C6 ham 2m/4km N of Newnham. SO 6916

Flax Moss Lancs 48 B5* loc 1m S of Haslingden. SD 7822

Flaxpool Som 7 H2* ham 7m/11km SE of Watchet. ST 1435

Flaxton N Yorks 50 C2 vil 8m/13km NE of York. SE 6762

Fleckney Leics 36 C5 vil 6m/9km N of Husbands Bosworth. SP 6493

Flecknoe Warwicks 28 A2 vil 4m/6km W of Daventry. SP 5163

Fledborough Notts 44 C4* ham 2km SE of Ragnall. SK 8172

Fleet Dorset 9 D6 ham at SE end of Chesil Bank and 3m/5km W of Weymouth. SY 6380

Fleet Hants 10 D4* loc on Hayling I. just S of Stoke. SU 7201

Fleet Hants 18 C6 tn 4m/6km W of Farnborough. At NE edge, **F. Pond,** lake traversed by rly. To E in par of Hawley, National Gas Turbine Establishment. SU 8154

Fleet H'land 87 B6 r in Sutherland dist rising near Lairg and flowing SE to Loch Fleet and coast 4m/6km N of Dornoch. NH 8195

Fleet Lincs 37 H2 ham 2m/3km E of Holbeach. TF 3823

Fleet Bay D & G 58 B6 inlet of Wigtown Bay at mouth of Water of Fleet. NX 5652

Fleet Dike 39 G3* channel connecting S Walsham Broad, Norfolk, with R Bure 1m NE. TG 4015

Fleet Forest D & G 58 C5, C6* wooded area to S of Gatehouse of Fleet. NX 6055

Fleetham Nthmb 67 H5* ham 3m/5km SW of Seahouses. **E Fleetham** loc 1m NE. NU 1928

Fleet Hargate Lincs 37 H2 vil 2m/3km E of Holbeach. TF 3925

Fleet Moss N Yorks 53 G6 area of bog near summit of pass between Oughtershaw and Hawes. **F. M. Tarn** small lake at E end of bog. SD 8783

Fleetville Herts 19 F1* E dist of St Albans. TL 1607

Fleet, West Dorset 8 D5, D6 freshwater lagoon 5m/8km long behind Chesil Bank W of Weymouth. SY 5982

Fleetwood Lancs 46 D3/47 E3 port at mouth of R Wyre 8m/13km N of Blackpool. Fishing industry. Chemicals, plastics. Radar stn. Computer centre. Passenger ferries to Belfast and Isle of Man. Ferry for pedestrians across r mouth to Knott End-on-Sea. SD 3247

Flemingston (Trefflemin) S Glam 15 E4 vil 3m/5km S of Cowbridge. ST 0170

Flemington S'clyde 64 D3 loc 3m/5km SE of Rutherglen. NS 6659

Flemington S'clyde 64 D4* loc adjoining Strathaven to NE. NS 7044

Flempton Suffolk 30 C1 vil 5m/7km NW of Bury St Edmunds. TL 8169

Flesherin W Isles 88 C2* loc on Eye Peninsula, Lewis, 1km SW of Portnaguiran. NB 5536

Fleshwick Bay Isle of Man 46 A6 inlet at S end of Niarbyl Bay on E side of Bradda Hill. SC 2071

Fletchersbridge Cornwall 3 F2* loc 2m/3km E of Bodmin. SX 1065

Fletchertown Cumbria 52 C1 ham 5m/7km SW of Wigton. NY 2042

Fletching E Sussex 12 B4 vil 3m/5km NW of Uckfield. Burial place of Edward Gibbon, historian. TQ 4223

Fleur-de-lis Gwent 15 F2 loc 2km SW of Blackwood. ST 1596

Flexbury Cornwall 6 B4 N dist of Bude. SS 2107

Flexford Surrey 18 D6* vil 4m/7km W of Guildford. SU 9350

Flexford, East Surrey 18 D6* loc below N side of Hog's Back 1m E of Wanborough. SU 9449

Flimby Cumbria 52 A2 coal-mining vil on coast 2m/3km S of Maryport. Site of Roman signal stn to N. NY 0233

Flimwell E Sussex 12 D4 vil 2m/3km E of Ticehurst. TQ 7131

Flint (Y Fflint) Clwyd 41 H4 tn on R Dee estuary 11m/17km NW of Chester. Paper and rayon mnfre. Chemical works. Remains of 13c cas (A.M.). SJ 2472

Flintham Notts 44 C6 vil 6m/10km SW of Newark-on-Trent. SK 7445

Flint Hill Durham 61 F5/F6* loc 2m/3km N of Annfield Plain. NZ 1654

Flint Mountain Clwyd 41 H4 loc on hill 2m/3km S of Flint. SJ 2370

Flinton Humberside 51 F4 ham 2m/3km SW of Aldbrough. TA 2236

Flint's Green W Midlands 35 H6* loc 4m/7km W of Coventry. SP 2680

Flitcham Norfolk 38 C2 vil 8m/13km NE of King's Lynn. TF 7226

Flitholme Cumbria 53 F3/G3* loc 2m/3km W of Brough. NY 7615

Flitton Beds 29 E4 vil 2m/4km SE of Ampthill. TL 0535

Flitwick Beds 29 E4 vil 2m/3km S of Ampthill. TL 0334

Flixborough Humberside 50 D6 vil 3m/5km NW of Scunthorpe. **F. Stather** ham on E bank of R Trent 1m SW. SE 8715

Flixton Gtr Manchester 42 C2 loc 2km W of Urmston. SJ 7494

Flixton N Yorks 51 E1 vil 5m/8km W of Filey. TA 0479

Flixton Suffolk 39 G6 vil 3m/4km SW of Bungay. TM 3186

Flixton Suffolk 39 H5* loc 3m/5km NW of Lowestoft. **F. Decoy** is a small broad. TM 5196

Flockton W Yorks 49 E6 vil 6m/10km E of Huddersfield. **F. Green** ham 1km E. SE 2314

Floday W Isles 88 A2* small uninhabited island off W coast of Lewis nearly 1m NW of island of Gt Bernera. NB 1241

Floday W Isles 88 A2* small uninhabited island in Loch Roag, W coast of Lewis 2km SE of Miavaig. NB 1033

Flodday W Isles 88 E3* small uninhabited island 3m/5km E of Northbay vil, Barra. NF 7502

Flodday W Isles 88 E1* small low-lying island off N coast of Benbecula 4m/6km E of Benbecula Airfield. NF 8455

Flodday W Isles 88 D4 small uninhabited island 1m W of Sandray and 1m SW of SW point of Vatersay. NL 6192

Floddaymore W Isles 88 E1* uninhabited island off SE coast of N Uist, E of Ronay across narrow strait. NF 9157

Flodden Nthmb 67 F5 loc 2m/4km SE of Branxton. Site of Battle of Flodden Field, 1513, is at Branxton, qv. NT 9235
Flood's Ferry Cambs 37 H5* loc at confluence of Whittlesey Dike and R Nene (old course), 4m/7km SW of March. TL 3593
Flookburgh Cumbria 47 E1 vil 2m/3km S of Cartmel. SD 3675
Floors Castle Borders 66 D5 mansion 1m NW of Kelso. Originally built by Vanbrugh in 1718, but much altered mid-19c. Seat of Duke of Roxburghe. NT 7134
Flordon Norfolk 39 F5 vil 8m/12km SW of Norwich. TM 1897
Flore Northants 28 B2 vil 5m/8km E of Daventry. SP 6460
Florence Staffs 35 E1* loc in SE part of Longton, Stoke-on-Trent. SJ 9142
Flotmanby, West N Yorks 51 E1* loc 2km E of Folkton. TA 0779
Flotta Orkney 89 B7 low-lying island of about 4 sq miles or 10 sq km lying between islands of Hoy and S Ronaldsay. Oil pipeline terminal. Farming and lobster-fishing are carried on. ND 3593
Flotta Shetland 89 E7* small island at entrance to Weisdale Voe, Mainland. HU 3746
Flotterton Nthmb 61 E2 loc 4m/6km W of Rothbury. NU 9902
Floutern Tarn Cumbria 52 B3* small lake 2m/3km N of E end of Ennerdale Water. NY 1217
Flowerdale Forest H'land 78 F3 deer forest in W part of Ross and Cromarty dist about 8m/13km SE of Gairloch. NG 8866
Flowers Green E Sussex 12 C5* loc 1km S of Herstmonceux. TQ 6311
Flowton Suffolk 31 E3 ham 5m/8km W of Ipswich. TM 0846
Flushdyke W Yorks 49 E5* loc 1km NE of Ossett. SE 2821
Flushing Cornwall 2 D5 vil N of Falmouth across estuary. Ferry for pedestrians. SW 8033
Flushing Cornwall 2 D5* ham on S side of Gillan Harbour 8m/12km E of Helston. SW 7825
Fluxton Devon 7 H5* ham 2m/3km SW of Ottery St Mary. SY 0892
Flyford Flavell H & W 27 E2 vil 8m/13km E of Worcester. SO 9854
Foals Green Suffolk 31 F1* loc 2m/4km SE of Stradbroke. TM 2571
Fobbing Essex 20 D3 vil 4m/6km S of Basildon. **F. Marshes** to E. Large oil refinery to S. TQ 7183
Fochabers Grampian 82 C2 vil on E bank of R Spey 8m/13km E of Elgin. Fruit canning. NJ 3458
Fochriw Mid Glam 15 F1* loc 2km SW of Rhymney. SO 1005
Fockerby Humberside 50 D6 vil adjoining Garthorpe to W and 7m/12km SE of Goole. SE 8419
Fodderty H'land 81 E2 vil in Ross and Cromarty dist 2m/4km W of Dingwall. NH 5159
Foddington Som 8 D2* ham 5m/9km NE of Ilchester. ST 5829
Foel Powys 33 G3* ham 2km NW of Llangadfan. SH 9911
Foel Cwm-cerwyn Welsh form of Prescelly Top, qv.
Foel-fras Gwynedd 40 D4 mt 4m/7km S of Llanfairfechan. Height 3091 ft or 942 metres. SH 6968
Foelgastell Dyfed 23 G4* loc 2m/3km NW of Cross Hands. SN 5414
Foel-grach Gwynedd 40 D5 mt 4m/7km E of Bethesda. Height 3195 ft or 974 metres. SH 6865
Foggathorpe Humberside 50 C4 vil 8m/13km W of Mkt Weighton. SE 7537
Foggbrook Gtr Manchester 43 E2* loc in Stockport 2m/4km E. SJ 9389
Foinaven H'land 80 B2 mt in Ross and Cromarty dist 2m/4km N of Achnasheen. Height 3062 ft or 933 metres. Gaelic form: Fionn Bheinn. NH 1462
Foinaven H'land 84 C3 mt ridge running N to S in Sutherland dist at N end of Reay Forest. Highest peak is Ganu Mór, qv. NC 3150
Foindle H'land 84 B3 locality on S side of Loch Laxford near W coast of Sutherland dist. NC 1948
Folda Tayside 76 C4 loc in Glen Isla 3m/5km NW of Kirkton of Glenisla. NO 1864
Fold Head Lancs 47 H6* loc 1km SW of Whitworth. SD 8717
Fold Hill Lincs 45 H5 loc 1km SE of Friskney. TF 4654
Fold, Low W Yorks 49 E4* loc in Horsforth 5m/8km NW of Leeds. SE 2337
Folds, Higher Gtr Manchester 42 C2 loc 2m/3km E of Leigh. SD 6800
Fole Staffs 35 F1 ham 4m/6km NW of Uttoxeter. SK 0437
Foleshill W Midlands 36 A6* N dist of Coventry. SP 3582
Folke Dorset 8 D3* vil 3m/4km SE of Sherborne. ST 6513
Folkestone Kent 13 G3 Channel port and resort 14m/22km E of Ashford. TR 2235
Folkingham Lincs 37 F2 vil 8m/12km S of Sleaford. Remains of 'House of Correction' built in classical style in 1825 on site of former cas. TF 0733
Folkington E Sussex 12 B6 ham on N slope of S Downs 5m/7km NW of Eastbourne. TQ 5503
Folksworth Cambs 37 F5 vil 6m/10km SW of Peterborough. TL 1489
Folkton N Yorks 51 E1 vil 4m/7km W of Filey. TA 0579
Folla Rule Grampian 83 F4* loc 3m/4km NE of Kirktown of Rayne. NJ 7333
Follifoot N Yorks 49 E3 vil 3m/5km SE of Harrogate. SE 3452
Folly Beds 28 D2* loc 1km N of Harrold. SP 9557
Folly Gate Devon 6 D5 vil 2m/3km NW of Okehampton. SX 5797
Folly, The Herts 19 F1 loc 1km NW of Wheathampstead. TL 1614
Fonmon (Ffwl-y-mwn) S Glam 15 F4* loc 4m/6km W of Barry. ST 0467
Font 61 F3 r formed by streams running into Font Resr, S of Rothbury, Nthmb, and flowing from the resr SE by Netherwitton to R Wansbeck at Mitford, above Morpeth. NZ 1785
Fonthill Bishop Wilts 9 F1 vil 2m/4km N of Tisbury. Also known as Bishop's Fonthill. Gateway to Fonthill Park to S dates from 17c. ST 9333
Fonthill Gifford Wilts 9 F2 vil 7m/11km NE of Shaftesbury. ST 3932
Fontmell Brook 9 F3* r rising to E of Fontmell Magna in Dorset and flowing SW into R Stour to E of Hammoon. ST 8214
Fontmell Magna Dorset 9 F3 vil on W edge of Cranborne Chase 4m/6km S of Shaftesbury. ST 8617
Fontmell Parva Dorset 9 F3* ham in R Stour valley 3m/4km E of Sturminster Newton. ST 8214
Font Reservoir Nthmb 61 E2* resr in course of R Font 5m/8km S of Rothbury. NZ 0493
Fontwell W Sussex 11 F4* vil 5m/8km W of Arundel. Racecourse. SU 9407
Font-y-gary (Ffontygari) S Glam 15 F4/F5 loc 4m/6km W of Barry. **Ffontygari Bay** to S. ST 0566
Foolow Derbys 43 F3/G3 ham 3m/4km E of Tideswell. SK 1976
Football Hole Nthmb 67 H5* bay (NT) on North Sea coast between Snook Pt to N and Newton Pt to S, 1km NE of High Newton-by-the-Sea. NU 2425
Footdee Grampian 77 H1* loc on N side of mouth of R Dee at Aberdeen. NJ 9505
Footherley Staffs 35 G4* loc 1m SW of Shenstone. SK 1003
Foots Cray London 20 B4 loc in borough of Bexley 1m SE of Sidcup. TQ 4770
Fora Ness Shetland 89 E6* headland on NE coast of Mainland, almost an island, 2km S of Firth. HU 4571
Fora Ness Shetland 89 E7* long narrow peninsula on Mainland on W side of entrance to Sandsound Voe, 5m/8km NW of Scalloway. HU 3546
Forbestown Grampian 82 C5 loc adjoining vil of Strathdon to E. NJ 3612
Force Green Kent 20 B6* loc 1m N of Westerham. TQ 4455
Force, High Cumbria 52 D3* waterfall in Aira Beck above Aira Force. NY 4020
Force, High Durham 53 G2 waterfall in R Tees 5m/7km NW of Middleton in Teesdale. NY 8828
Force, Low Durham 53 G2/H2* waterfall in R Tees 1m NW of Newbiggin. NY 9027
Forcett N Yorks 54 B4 ham 2m/3km W of Aldbrough. NZ 1712

Ford Bucks 18 C1 vil 4m/6km SW of Aylesbury. SP 7709
Ford Derbys 43 H3 ham 5m/8km SE of Sheffield. SK 4080
Ford Devon 4 B5* dist of Plymouth 2km NW of city centre. SX 4656
Ford Devon 4 C5 ham just N of Holbeton and 2m/4km E of Yealmpton. SX 6150
Ford Devon 4 D6 ham 4m/6km N of Prawle Pt. SX 7840
Ford Devon 6 C3 vil 3m/5km SW of Bideford. SS 4024
Ford Glos 27 E4 ham 4m/7km E of Winchcombe. SP 0829
Ford Lothian 66 B2 loc just W of Pathhead. NT 3864
Ford Merseyside 41 H3* loc in Birkenhead 3m/4km W of tn centre. SJ 2888
Ford Nthmb 67 F4 vil 7m/11km NW of Wooler. Much restored 14c cas. NT 9437
Ford Salop 34 B3 vil 5m/8km W of Shrewsbury. SJ 4113
Ford S'clyde 70 B4 locality nearly 1km SW of head of Loch Awe in Argyll. NM 8603
Ford Som 7 H2 ham 1m NE of Wiveliscombe. ST 0928
Ford Staffs 43 F5 ham on R Hamps 5m/9km E of Leek. SK 0653
Ford Wilts 16 D4* vil 5m/8km W of Chippenham. ST 8474
Ford W Sussex 11 F4 vil 3m/4km SW of Arundel. SU 9903
Forda Devon 6 D5* loc 5m/7km SW of Okehampton. SX 5390
Fordbridge W Midlands 35 G5* suburb 7m/11km E of Birmingham. SP 1787
Fordcombe Kent 12 B3 vil 4m/6km W of Tunbridge Wells. TQ 5240
Forden Powys 34 A4 scattered vil about 4m/6km S of Welshpool. SJ 2201
Ford End Essex 30 B6 vil 3m/5km SE of Gt Dunmow. TL 6716
Forder Cornwall 4 B5* loc 2km W of Saltash. SX 4158
Forder Green Devon 4 D4 ham 3m/4km SE of Ashburton. SX 7867
Fordgate Som 8 B1* loc on Taunton and Bridgwater Canal 2m/3km E of N Petherton. ST 3232
Ford Green Lancs 47 E3* loc 2m/3km NW of Garstang. SD 4746
Fordham Cambs 30 B1 vil 5m/8km N of Newmarket. TL 6370
Fordham Essex 30 D5 vil 5m/8km NW of Colchester. TL 9228
Fordham Norfolk 38 B4 vil 2m/4km S of Downham Mkt. TL 6199
Fordham Heath Essex 30 D5* loc 3m/5km W of Colchester. TL 9426
Ford Heath Salop 34 B3* loc 6m/9km W of Shrewsbury. SJ 4011
Ford Houses W Midlands 35 E4* dist of Wolverhampton 3m/5km N of tn centre. SJ 9103
Fordingbridge Hants 9 H3 tn on R Avon 6m/9km N of Ringwood. SU 1414
Fordon Humberside 51 E1 ham 2km N of Wold Newton. TA 0475
Fordoun Grampian 77 G3 vil 2m/4km SE of Auchenblae. In churchyard (adjoining Auchenblae to S) is fragment of St Palladius' chapel, 'the mother church of the Mearns'. NO 7278
Ford's Green Suffolk 31 E2* loc 1km S of Bacton. TM 0666
Fordstreet Essex 30 D5 vil 5m/8km W of Colchester. TL 9226
Ford Street Som 8 A3* ham 2m/3km SE of Wellington. ST 1518
Fordwells Oxon 27 G6 loc 4m/7km NW of Witney. SP 3013
Fordwich Kent 13 G1 vil on R Gt Stour 2m/4km NE of Canterbury. TR 1859
Fordyce Grampian 82 D1 vil near N coast 3m/4km SW of Portsoy. NJ 5563
Forebridge Staffs 35 F2* SE dist of Stafford. SJ 9222
Foredale N Yorks 48 B2* loc 2km S of Horton in Ribblesdale. SD 8069
Foregate Staffs 35 E2* loc in Stafford to N of tn centre. SJ 9123
Foreland Isle of Wight 10 D5/D6 headland at most easterly point of island. SZ 6687
Foreland, North Kent 13 H1 headland, with lighthouse, at extreme E point of Isle of Thanet 2km N of Broadstairs. TR 4069
Foreland Point Devon 7 E1 headland on N coast near Somerset border. Most northerly point in county, 3m/4km NE of Lynton. SS 7551
Foreland, South Kent 13 H3 headland with lighthouse 3m/5km E of Dover. TR 3643
Foreland, The Dorset 9 G5 headland at SW end of Poole Bay 3m/5km NE of Swanage. Also known as Handfast Pt. SZ 0582
Foremark Derbys 36 A2 ham 2m/3km E of Repton. SK 3326
Foreness Point Kent 13 H1 headland 2m/3km E of Margate. TR 3871
Forest Durham 53 G2* loc 5m/9km NW of Middleton in Teesdale. NY 8629
Forest N Yorks 54 B4/C4* loc 2m/3km E of Scorton. NZ 2700
Forestburn Gate Nthmb 61 F2 loc 3m/5km S of Rothbury. NZ 0696
Forestburn Reservoir S'clyde 65 E2* resr 2m/4km W of Harthill. NS 8664
Forest Coal Pit Gwent 25 G5* ham 4m/7km N of Abergavenny. SO 2820
Forest, Far H & W 34 D6 loc on S side of Wyre Forest 4m/6km W of Bewdley. SO 7275
Forest Gate London 20 B3 loc in borough of Newham 1m N of W Ham. TQ 4085
Forest Green Surrey 11 G1 vil 4m/7km E of Cranleigh. TQ 1241
Forest Head Cumbria 60 B5* loc 4m/6km SE of Brampton. NY 5857
Forest Heath 119 admin dist of Suffolk.
Forest Hill London 20 A4 loc in borough of Lewisham 6m/9km SE of Charing Cross. TQ 3573
Forest Hill Oxon 18 B1 vil 5m/8km E of Oxford. SP 5807
Forest Holme Lancs 48 B5* vil in valley in Forest of Rossendale 3m/4km NE of Rawtenstall. SD 8122
Forest Lane Head N Yorks 49 E3* loc adjoining Harrogate to E. SE 3356
Forest Mill Central 72 D5 vil 3m/5km NE of Clackmannan. NS 9593
Forest of Ae D & G. See Ae Village.
Forest of Alyth Tayside 76 C5 moorland area NW of Alyth. NO 1855
Forest of Atholl Tayside. See Atholl.
Forest of Bere Hants 10 D4 stretch of country, much of it now built up, between Horndean and Portsdown. SU 5042
Forest of Birse Grampian 77 E2 deer forest 4m/7km S of Aboyne. NO 5291
Forest of Bowland Lancs 47 G3 area of wild moorland between Rs Lune and Ribble. **Trough of Bowland** is a pass some 3m/5km NW of Dunsop Br over which the Lancaster-Clitheroe rd is carried. SD 65
Forest of Brechfa. See Brechfa.
Forest of Bunzeach Grampian 76 D1* deer forest 7m/11km N of Ballater. NJ 3707
Forest of Clunie Tayside 76 B5 moorland area W of Br of Cally. NO 0850
Forest of Dean Glos 26 B6 heavily wooded area, formerly a royal hunting-ground, between R Severn and R Wye. Extensive mineral workings. SO 6310
Forest of Deer Grampian 83 G2* state forest N of Old Deer. NJ 9750
Forest of Glenartney Tayside 72 B3 mt area on NW side of Glen Artney. NN 6818
Forest of Glenavon Grampian 76 B1, C1 deer forest on E side of Cairngorms astride Glen Avon. NJ 1005
Forest of Glentanar Grampian. See Glentanar.
Forest of Harris W Isles 88 A3, B3 area of mountains, streams, and lochs in N Harris, Isle of Lewis, between Loch Resort and Loch Seaforth. NB 01, 10
Forest of Mamlorn Central 71 E2 mt area between head of Glen Lochay and that of Glen Lyon. NN 4034
Forest of Pendle, The Lancs. See Pendle Hill.
Forest of Rossendale Lancs 48 B5 moorland area to NE of Rawtenstall. See also Rossendale. SD 82
Forest of Trawden Lancs 48 C4 moorland area SE of Trawden and Colne. SD 9338
Forest Row E Sussex 12 B3 vil 3m/4km SE of E Grinstead, below N edge of Ashdown Forest. TQ 4235
Forest Side Isle of Wight 10 B5* loc 2km W of Newport. SZ 4789
Forestside W Sussex 10 D4 vil 4m/7km N of Emsworth. SU 7512
Forest Town Notts 44 A5* loc 2m/3km E of Mansfield Woodhouse. SK 5662

Forfar Tayside 77 E5 jute mnfg tn 12m/20km N of Dundee. Other industries include fruit processing, agricultural engineering. See also Loch of F. NO 4550

Forgandenny Tayside 72 D3 vil 4m/6km SW of Perth. NO 0818

Forge Powys 33 E4* loc 2km SE of Machynlleth. SN 7699

Forge Hammer Gwent 15 G2* industrial estate in Cwmbran. Iron foundries. ST 2895

Forge, High Durham 61 G6* loc 2m/3km E of Stanley. NZ 2254

Forge Side Gwent 15 G1* loc on W side of Blaenavon. SO 2408

Forge, The H & W 25 H2* loc 4m/6km NE of Kington. SO 3459

Forgewood S'clyde 65 E3* N dist of Motherwell. NS 7458

Forglen Grampian 83 E2 loc 3m/5km NE of Turriff. NJ 6751

Forgue Grampian 83 E3 vil 2m/3km SW of Inverkeithny and 6m/10km NE of Huntly. Distillery 2km SE in Glen Dronach. NJ 6144

Forhill H & W 27 E1 loc 5m/8km N of Redditch. SP 0575

Forlan, Y Welsh form of Vorlan, qv.

Formartine Grampian 83 F4, G4 area or dist N and NE of Inverurie. NJ 8729

Formby Merseyside 41 H1 mainly residential tn 11m/17km N of Liverpool. **Formby Pt** headland 2m/3km W beyond sand dunes. SD 2907

Forncett St Mary Norfolk 39 F5 vil 6m/9km SE of Wymondham. **Forncett St Peter** vil adjoining to S. **Forncett End** vil 2m/3km W. TM 1693

Fornham All Saints Suffolk 30 D2 vil 2m/4km NW of Bury St Edmunds. TL 8367

Fornham St Martin Suffolk 30 D2 vil 2m/3km N of Bury St Edmunds. TL 8567

Forres Grampian 82 A2 tn 4m/6km S of mouth of R Findhorn and 12m/19km W of Elgin. Distilling, agricultural engineering, milling. On NE side of tn is Sueno's Stone (A.M.), ancient obelisk 23ft or 7 metres high, bearing Celtic symbols. NJ 0358

Forsa 68 D4 r on island of Mull, S'clyde, running N down Glen Forsa to Sound of Mull 2m/3km E of Salen. Small airfield at mouth of r on W side. NM 5943

Forsbrook Staffs 35 F1 vil 3m/5km SW of Cheadle. SJ 9641

Forse H'land 86 E4 loc near E coast of Caithness dist 2km E of Latheron. ND 2134

Forsinard H'land 86 B3 loc with rly stn in Caithness dist 14m/22km S of Melvich. NC 8942

Forss Water H'land 86 C1 r in Caithness dist running N from Loch Shurrery to N coast 6m/9km W of Thurso. See also Bridge of Forss. ND 0279

Forstal, The E Sussex loc 4m/6km SW of Tunbridge Wells. TQ 5435

Forstal, The Kent 13 E2 ham 4m/7km SW of Charing. TQ 8946

Forstal, The Kent 13 F3* ham adjoining Mersham 3m/5km SE of Ashford. TR 0439

Forston Dorset 8 D4 loc 4m/6km N of Dorchester. Site of Roman bldg to S. SY 6695

Fort Augustus H'land 80 D6 vil in Inverness dist at entrance to Caledonian Canal from SW end of Loch Ness; lighthouse marks canal entrance. Vil grew up round fort built by General Wade, 1730, now Benedictine monastery and school. NH 3709

Fort Charlotte Shetland. See Lerwick.

Forter Tayside 76 C4 loc in Glen Isla 4m/6km NW of Kirkton of Glenisla. **F. Castle,** ruined cas sacked and burnt in 1640. NO 1864

Forteviot Tayside 72 D3 vil 6m/9km SW of Perth. Site of Roman camp to W. NO 0517

Fort George H'land 81 G2 military depot (A.M.) in Inverness dist at entrance to Inner Moray Firth or Inverness Firth opp Chanonry Pt. Built after rising of 1745. NH 7656

Forth S'clyde 65 F3 vil 7m/12km NE of Lanark. NS 9453

Forth 72 C5 r in Central region formed by two headstreams rising N of Ben Lomond and meeting 1m W of Aberfoyle. It then flows E by Stirling and Alloa to Kincardine, where it widens into the Firth of Forth. NS 9287

Forthampton Glos 26 D4 vil 2m/4km W of Tewkesbury. SO 8532

Forth and Clyde Canal 64, 65 canal traversing Scotland from R Forth at Grangemouth in Central region to R Clyde at Bowling in Strathclyde region. Completed in 1790; closed in 1962.

Forthill Tayside 73 G2* dist of Dundee 1km NE of Broughty Ferry. NO 4631

Forthside Central 72 B5* dist of Stirling on right bank of R Forth E of tn centre. NS 8093

Fortingall Tayside 75 G6 vil in Glen Lyon 7m/12km W of Aberfeldy. NN 7347

Fortis Green London 19 F3* loc on borders of Barnet and Haringey boroughs, 6m/9km N of Charing Cross. TQ 2789

Forton Hants 10 B1 vil on R Test 4m/6km E of Andover. SU 4243

Forton Lancs 47 F3 vil 4m/6km N of Garstang. SD 4851

Forton Salop 34 B3 ham 5m/7km NW of Shrewsbury. Airfield to N. Loc of **F. Heath** 1m NE. SJ 4216

Forton Som 8 B4 ham 2km SE of Chard. ST 3307

Forton Staffs 34 D2 vil 2km N of Newport. SJ 7521

Fortrose H'land 81 F2 small tn and resort in Ross and Cromarty dist on Inner Moray Firth 2m/3km W of Fort George across strait. 15c cathedral, mainly in ruins. NH 7256

Fortune, East Lothian 66 C1 loc 4m/6km S of N Berwick. Former airfield now museum of flight. NT 5579

Fortune Green London 19 F3* loc on borders of Barnet and Camden boroughs 5m/8km NW of Charing Cross. TQ 2485

Fortuneswell Dorset 9 E6 tn at N end of Portland. HM prison to E. SY 6873

Fort William H'land 74 C4 tn in Lochaber dist on E side of Loch Linnhe near head of loch. Distilleries, aluminium works. Pulp mill at Annat, qv. Tourist and mountaineering centre. West Highland Museum. NN 1073

Forty Foot Drain 37 H5 fenland drainage channel connecting R Nene (old course) NE of Ramsey, Cambs, and Old Bedford R at Welches Dam, S of Manea. TL 4785

Forty Foot Drain, South 37 H1 fenland drainage cut running from Guthram Gowt, 5m/8km W of Spalding, to R Witham on S side of Boston, Lincs. Joined by **N Forty Foot Drain** 1m SW of Boston. TF 3242

Forty Green Bucks 18 D2 vil adjoining Beaconsfield to NW. SU 9291

Forty Hill London 19 G2 loc in borough of Enfield 1m NE of Enfield tn centre and 11m/18km N of Charing Cross. TQ 3397

Forvie Ness Grampian 83 H4* headland on seaward side of Sands of Forvie and at S end of Hackley Bay, small bay between Collieston and Newburgh Bar at mouth of R Ythan. Also known as Hackley Hd. NK 0226

Forward Green Suffolk 31 E2 vil 3m/5km E of Stowmarket. TM 0959

Foryd 40 B5* stream rising near Dinas Dinlle, Gwynedd, and flowing N into Foryd Bay. SH 4458

Foryd Bay Gwynedd 40 B5 bay of marsh and mudflats leading into the SW end of Menai Strait to E of Morfa Dinlle. SH 4459

Fosbury Wilts 17 G5 ham 3m/5km S of Shalbourne. SU 3158

Foscote Bucks 28 C4 loc 2m/3km NE of Buckingham. Site of Roman villa 1km SE. SP 7135

Fosdyke Lincs 37 G2 vil 7m/11km S of Boston. **Fosdyke Br** loc 1km S with rd br over R Welland. TF 3133

Foss Cross Glos 17 E1 loc 6m/9km NE of Cirencester. SP 0609

Fossdyke Canal 44 C3-D4 canal of Roman origin running from R Trent at Torksey, Notts, to Lincoln.

Fossebridge Glos 27 E6 ham 3m/5km SW of Northleach. SP 0811

Foss Way (or Fosse Way) 8 D1 etc. Ancient trackway, adapted by the Romans and still largely followed by present-day rds, running from near Sidmouth, Devon, to the Humber, by Ilchester, Leicester and Lincoln, thereafter coinciding with Ermine Street.

Fostall Kent 21 F5 loc 3m/5km E of Faversham. TR 0661

Fosterhouses S Yorks 49 H6* loc 1m N of Fishlake. SE 6514

Foster Street Essex 20 B1 vil 3m/4km E of Harlow. TL 4809

Foston Derbys 35 G2 ham 2m/3km E of Sudbury. SK 1831

Foston Leics 36 B5* ham 6m/10km S of Leicester. SP 6094

Foston Lincs 36 D1 vil 6m/9km NW of Grantham. SK 8542

Foston N Yorks 50 C2* ham 1m E of Thornton-le-Clay. SE 6965

Foston on the Wolds Humberside 51 E3 vil 5m/8km E of Gt Driffield. TA 1055

Fotherby Lincs 45 G2 vil 3m/5km N of Louth. TF 3191

Fothergill Cumbria 52 A2 loc on coast 2m/3km SW of Maryport, adjoining Flimby. NY 0234

Fotheringhay Northants 37 F5 vil on R Nene 4m/6km NE of Oundle. Mound marks site of cas where Mary, Queen of Scots was executed in 1587. TL 0693

Foula Shetland 89 D8 sparsely inhabited island of about 6 sq miles or 15 sq km lying 26m/42km W of Scalloway, Mainland. Foula has high cliffs and is noted as haunt of sea birds. The chief human settlement is Ham, on Ham Voe, on E coast. HT 9639

Foul Anchor Cambs 38 A3* loc at confluence of R Nene and N Level Main Drain 5m/8km N of Wisbech. TF 4617

Foulbridge Cumbria 60 A6* loc 2km W of Wreay. NY 4148

Foulby W Yorks 49 F6* loc 2km E of Crofton. SE 3917

Foulden Borders 67 F3 vil 5m/8km W of Berwick-upon-Tweed. NT 9255

Foulden Norfolk 38 C4 vil 4m/7km E of Stoke Ferry. TL 7699

Foulis Castle H'land 81 E2 residence of chiefs of Clan Munro, nearly 1m NW of **Foulis Pt** on NW shore of Cromarty Firth, 4m/7km NE of Dingwall, Ross and Cromarty dist. NH 5864

Foul Mile E Sussex 12 C5 loc 4m/7km NE of Hailsham. TQ 6215

Foulness 50 D5 r rising near Mkt Weighton, Humberside, and flowing S in a wide westward loop into the Mkt Weighton Canal 2m/3km N of Newport and thence into R Humber 2km NE of Faxfleet. SE 8624

Foulness Island Essex 21 F3 island on E coast bounded by North Sea, R Crouch, R Roach, and The Middleway, 8m/13km NE of Southend-on-Sea. Connected to mainland by rd at SW end. TR 0092

Foulness Point Essex 21 F2 headland at NE end of Foulness I. TR 0495

Foulney Island Cumbria 46 D2 head of narrow peninsula 4m/7km SE of Barrow-in-Furness and 1m E of Piel I. across Piel Channel. SD 2463

Foulride Green E Sussex 12 C6* loc adjoining Polegate to S. TQ 5803

Foulridge Lancs 48 B4 vil 2km N of Colne. SD 8942

Foulsham Norfolk 39 E2 vil 8m/12km SE of Fakenham. TG 0324

Foulstone Cumbria 53 E6 ham 3m/5km NW of Kirkby Lonsdale. SD 5680

Fountainhall Borders 66 B4/C4 vil on Gala Water 3m/5km N of Stow. NT 4349

Fountains Abbey N Yorks 49 E2 remains of medieval abbey (A.M.) beside R Skell 3m/5km SW of Ripon. Fountains Hall, nearby, is 17c hse largely built with materials from ruins of abbey. SE 2768

Fountains Fell Tarn N Yorks 48 B1* small lake on Fountains Fell 4m/6km E of Horton in Ribblesdale. SD 8671

Foura H'land 78 F1 islet off W coast of Ross and Cromarty dist 4m/6km E of Rubha Réidh. Also known as Eilean Furadh Mór. NG 7993

Four Ashes Staffs 35 E3 loc 6m/10km N of Wolverhampton. SJ 9108

Four Ashes Staffs 35 E5* loc 6m/10km SE of Bridgnorth. SO 8087

Four Ashes Suffolk 31 E1 vil adjoining Walsham le Willows to S. TM 0070

Four Ashes W Midlands 35 G6* loc adjoining Dorridge to W, 3m/5km S of Solihull tn centre. SP 1575

Four Crosses Clwyd 33 G1 loc 3m/5km W of Corwen. SJ 0342

Four Crosses Gwynedd 32 B1 vil 3m/5km NE of Pwllheli. Also spelt as one word: Fourcrosses. SH 3939

Four Crosses Powys 34 A3 vil 7m/12km NE of Welshpool. SJ 2718

Four Crosses Staffs 35 F3 loc 2m/3km W of Cannock. SJ 9509

Four Elms Kent 20 B6 vil 2m/3km NE of Edenbridge. TQ 4648

Four Foot Som 8 D1* loc on Fosse Way 3m/5km NE of Keinton Mandeville. ST 5833

Four Forks Som 8 A1 ham 4m/7km W of Bridgwater. ST 2337

Four Gates Gtr Manchester 42 C1 loc 4m/7km NE of Wigan. SD 6407

Four Gotes Cambs 38 A3 vil 4m/7km N of Wisbech. TF 4516

Fourlands Hill N Yorks 47 G1* loc 2m/3km SW of Ingleton. SD 6671

Four Lane End S Yorks 43 G1* loc 2m/3km E of Penistone. SE 2702

Four Lane Ends Ches 42 B5* loc 1m S of Tarporley. SJ 5561

Four Lane Ends Cumbria 46 D2* loc 3m/5km E of Barrow-in-Furness. SD 2468

Four Lane Ends Derbys 43 H4* loc 2m/4km NW of Chesterfield. SK 3573

Fourlane Ends Derbys 43 H5 loc 2m/3km NW of Alfreton. SK 3855

Four Lane Ends Gtr Manchester 47 H6* loc 3m/4km NW of Bury. SD 7612

Four Lane Ends Lancs 47 E4 loc 1km NW of Poulton-le-Fylde. SD 3340

Four Lane Ends Lancs 47 F3* loc just N of Dolphinholme. SD 5153

Four Lane Ends Lancs 47 G5* loc in Blackburn 1m N of tn centre. SD 6729

Four Lane Ends Lancs 48 A5* loc 3m/4km SE of Blackburn. SD 7126

Four Lane Ends N Yorks 50 B3 loc 5m/7km E of York. SE 6751

Four Lane Ends S Yorks 43 H3* loc in Sheffield 2m/4km S of city centre. SK 3483

Four Lane Ends S Yorks 43 H3* loc in Sheffield 3m/5km SE of city centre. SK 3984

Four Lane Ends W Yorks 48 D4* loc in Bradford 2m/3km W of city centre. SE 1333

Four Lanes Cornwall 2 C4 vil 2m/3km S of Redruth. SW 6938

Fourlanes End Ches 42 D5* loc 3m/5km E of Sandbach. SJ 8059

Four Marks Hants 10 D2 vil 4m/6km SW of Alton. SU 6735

Four Mile Bridge Gwynedd 40 A4 rd crossing from main island of Anglesey to Holy I., between Valley and Trearddur Bay. SH 2878

Four Oaks E Sussex 13 E4 loc adjoining Beckley to E. TQ 8624

Four Oaks Glos 26 C4 loc 2m/4km NW of Newent. SO 6928

Four Oaks W Midlands 35 G4 loc 2km N of Sutton Coldfield. Loc of **Four Oaks Common** to NW. **Four Oaks Park** to S. SP 1198

Four Oaks W Midlands 35 H6* ham 6m/9km W of Coventry. SP 2480

Four Points Berks 18 A4* loc 3m/4km SW of Streatley. SU 5578

Four Roads (Pedair-hewl) Dyfed 23 F4 ham 3m/5km NE of Kidwelly. SN 4409

Four Roads Isle of Man 46 A6 loc 1km N of Port St Mary. SC 2068

Fourstones Nthmb 60 D4 vil 4m/6km NW of Hexham. NY 8867

Four Throws Kent 12 D4 ham 1m E of Hawkhurst. TQ 7729

Fovant Wilts 9 G2 vil 4m/6km E of Tisbury. SU 0028

Fowey Cornwall 3 F3 tn on S coast at mouth of R Fowey. Resort; port for export of china clay. R rises in heart of Bodmin Moor and flows through Lostwithiel, where it becomes tidal. SX 1251

Fowley Common Ches 42 C2* loc 1km S of Glazebury. SJ 6796

Fowley Island Hants 10 D4* small uninhabited island in Chichester Harbour near head of Emsworth Channel. SU 7404

Fowley Island Kent 21 E5 island in The Swale off Teynham Level 4m/7km NW of Faversham. TQ 9765

Fowlis (or Fowlis Easter) Tayside 73 F2 vil 6m/9km NW of Dundee. Early 17c cas. NO 3233

Fowlis Wester Tayside 72 C2 vil 4m/7km E of Crieff. 8c cross (A.M.). NN 9224

Fowlmere Cambs 29 H3 vil 5m/9km NE of Royston. TL 4245

Fowl Mere Norfolk 38 D5* lake 4m/7km N of Thetford. TL 8789

Fownhope H & W 26 B4 vil 6m/9km SE of Hereford. SO 5834

Foxcombe Hill Oxon 18 A2* vil 3m/4km N of Abingdon. SP 4901

Fox Corner Surrey 18 D5* loc 4m/6km NW of Guildford. SU 9654

Foxcote Glos 27 E5 loc 5m/8km SE of Cheltenham. SP 0118

Foxcote Som 16 C5* ham 2m/3km E of Radstock. ST 7155
Foxcote Reservoir Bucks 28 C4* resr 2m/3km NE of Buckingham. SP 7136
Foxcotte Hants 10 B1* ham 2m/3km NW of Andover. SU 3447
Foxdale Isle of Man 46 B5 vil 2m/4km S of St John's. **Lr Foxdale** ham 1m N. SC 2778
Foxearth Essex 30 C3 vil 3m/5km NW of Sudbury. TL 8344
Foxfield Cumbria 52 C6 ham 2km S of Broughton in Furness. SD 2185
Foxford W Midlands 36 A5* loc in Coventry 3m/5km N of city centre. SP 3583
Fox Green Derbys 44 A4* loc 1km SE of Creswell. SK 5273
Foxham Wilts 17 E4 ham 4m/7km NE of Chippenham. ST 9777
Fox Hatch Essex 20 C2* loc 3m/5km NW of Brentwood. TQ 5798
Foxhayes Devon 7 G5* loc on W side of Exeter and of R Exe, about 1m W of Exeter city centre. SX 9093
Fox Hill Avon 16 C5* S dist of Bath. ST 7562
Foxhills Hants 10 A3* 2m/3km SW of Totton. SU 3411
Foxhole Cornwall 3 E3* vil 3m/5km NW of St Austell in dist producing china clay. SW 9654
Foxhole W Glam 23 H6* loc in Swansea 1km NE of tn centre across R Tawe. SS 6694
Foxholes N Yorks 51 E1 vil 10m/15km N of Gt Driffield. TA 0173
Foxhunt Green E Sussex 12 B5 loc 3m/5km SW of Heathfield. TQ 5417
Fox Lane Hants 18 D5* suburban loc 3m/4km N of Farnborough. SU 8557
Foxley Norfolk 39 E3 vil 6m/10km NE of E Dereham. TG 0321
Foxley Northants 28 B3 loc 4m/6km NW of Towcester. SP 6451
Foxley Wilts 16 D3 loc 3m/4km W of Malmesbury. Loc of **F. Green** adjoins to E. ST 8986
Foxley Bridge Staffs 43 E6* loc 2m/3km NE of Hanley. SJ 8949
Foxlydiate H & W 27 E1 loc at W edge of Redditch. SP 1067
Fox's Cross Kent 21 F5* loc adjoining Yorkletts to N and 2m/4km SW of Whitstable. TR 0963
Foxstone Dam Derbys 43 H3* small lake 2km S of Eckington. SK 4277
Fox Street Essex 31 E5 loc 3m/4km NE of Colchester. TM 0227
Foxt Staffs 43 E6 vil 2km SE of Ipstones. SK 0348
Foxton Cambs 29 H3 vil 6m/10km NE of Royston. TL 4148
Foxton Durham 54 C3 loc 3m/4km S of Sedgefield. NZ 3624
Foxton Leics 36 C5 vil 3m/5km NW of Mkt Harborough. SP 7090
Foxton N Yorks 54 C5/D5* ham 4m/6km NE of Northallerton. SE 4296
Foxup N Yorks 48 B1 loc 1km W of Halton Gill. SD 8676
Foxwist Green Ches 42 C4* loc 3m/4km NW of Winsford. SJ 6268
Foxwood Salop 34 C6* ham 3m/5km W of Cleobury Mortimer. SO 6276
Foy H & W 26 B4 vil on right bank of R Wye 3m/4km N of Ross-on-Wye across loop of r. SO 5928
Foyers H'land 81 E5 vil on SE side of Loch Ness in Inverness dist, at mouth of **R Foyers.** Aluminium works. **Falls of F.**, two waterfalls in course of r, supply water for hydro-electricity scheme, augmented by pump-storage system from Loch Mhór. NH 4921
Fraddam Cornwall loc 2m/4km SE of Hayle. SW 5934
Fraddon Cornwall 3 E3 vil 3m/5km S of St Columb Major. SW 9158
Fradley Staffs 35 G3 vil 4m/6km NE of Lichfield. **F. Junction,** locality at junction of Coventry and Trent & Mersey Canals 2km W. **Fradley Resr** is small resr 2km NW. SK 1513
Fradswell Staffs 35 F2 vil 7m/11km NE of Stafford. SJ 9931
Fraisthorpe Humberside 51 F2 ham 4m/6km S of Bridlington. TA 1561
Framfield E Sussex 12 B4 vil 2m/3km E of Uckfield. TQ 4920
Framilode, Upper Glos 26 C6 vil on left bank of R Severn 7m/12km SW of Gloucester. SO 7510
Framingham Earl Norfolk 39 F4/G4* vil 5m/8km SE of Norwich. TG 2702
Framingham Pigot Norfolk 39 F4/G4* vil 4m/7km SE of Norwich. TG 2703
Framlingham Suffolk 31 G2 small tn 9m/15km N of Woodbridge. Extensive remains of 12c–13c cas with Tudor chimneys (A.M.). College to N, specialising in agriculture. TM 2863
Frampton Dorset 8 D4 vil 5m/8km NW of Dorchester. SY 6295
Frampton Lincs 37 H1 vil 3m/5km S of Boston. **Frampton W End** loc 2m/3km NW. TF 3239
Frampton Cotterell Avon 16 B3 suburb 4m/7km W of Chipping Sodbury. ST 6682
Frampton Mansell Glos 16 D2 vil 5m/8km E of Stroud. SO 9202
Frampton on Severn Glos vil 7m/11km W of Stroud. SO 7407
Framsden Suffolk 31 F2 vil 3m/5km SE of Debenham. TM 2059
Framwellgate Moor Durham 54 B1 suburb 2km N of Durham. NZ 2644
France, Little Lothian 66 A2/B2 loc in Edinburgh 3m/5km SE of city centre. NT 2870
France Lynch Glos 16 D1* loc adjoining Chalford to E. SO 9003
Frances Green Lancs 47 G4* ham 2m/3km NW of Ribchester. SD 6336
Franche H & W 35 E6 loc in NW part of Kidderminster. SO 8178
Frandley Ches 42 C3* loc 2km E of Hr Whitley. SJ 6379
Frankby Merseyside 41 H3 vil 2m/3km E of W Kirby. SJ 2486
Frankfort Norfolk 39 G3* loc 4m/6km S of N Walsham. TG 3024
Frankley W Midlands 35 F6* vil 6m/10km SW of Birmingham. **Frankley Resr** to E. Ham of **F. Green** to W. SO 9980
Frank Lockwood's Island S'clyde 69 E6 islet off S coast of Mull 2m/4km E of entrance to Loch Buie. Also known as Eilean Sneth Dian. NM 6219
Frank's Bridge Powys 25 F3* loc on R Edw 5m/8km NE of Builth Wells. SO 1156
Frankton Warwicks 27 H1 vil 5m/9km N of Southam. SP 4270
Frankwell Salop 34 B3 W dist of Shrewsbury. SJ 4713
Frans Green Norfolk 39 E3* loc 2km SW of Weston Longville. TG 1014
Fransham, Great Norfolk 38 D3 vil 6m/9km W of E Dereham. **Lit Fransham** vil 1m S. TF 8913
Frant E Sussex 12 C3 vil 3m/4km S of Tunbridge Wells. TQ 5935
Fraoch Bheinn H'land 74 B2 mt in Lochaber dist 2m/3km N of head of Loch Arkaig. Height 2808 ft or 856 metres. NM 9894
Fraochlan H'land 85 A5 islet in Enard Bay 1km off NW coast of Ross and Cromarty dist. Also known as Fraoch Eilean. NC 0518
Fraserburgh Grampian 83 G1 fishing tn and port at W end of **F. Bay** 15m/24km NW of Peterhead. Fish curing and canning. Engineering works. NJ 9966
Frating Essex 31 E5* ham 4m/6km N of Brightlingsea. TM 0822
Frating Green Essex 31 E5 ham 6m/10km E of Colchester. TM 0923
Fratton Hants 10 D4* dist of Portsmouth 1m E of city centre. SU 6500
Freasley Warwicks 35 H4* loc 3m/5km SE of Tamworth. SP 2499
Freathy Cornwall 3 H3* vil 3m/5km SW of Torpoint. SX 3952
Freckenham Suffolk 30 B1 vil 3m/5km SW of Mildenhall. TL 6672
Freckleton Lancs 47 E5 vil 2m/3km S of Kirkham. SD 4228
Freeby Leics 36 D3 vil 3m/5km E of Melton Mowbray. SK 8020
Freefolk Hants 17 G6 ham adjoining Laverstoke 2m/3km E of Whitchurch. To NW across R Test, ham of **F. Priors.** SU 4848
Freehay Staffs 35 F1* loc 2km SE of Cheadle. SK 0141
Freehold Land Gwent 15 G1* loc 2km NW of Pontypool. SO 2702
Freeland Oxon 27 H6 vil 4m/7km NE of Witney. SP 4112
Freemantle Hants 10 B3 dist of Southampton 1m W of city centre. SU 4012
Free Piece Hants 11 E2 loc 1km NW of Bordon Camp. SU 7937
Freester Shetland 89 E7* loc in S Nesting, Mainland, 2km SW of Skellister. HU 4553
Freethorpe Norfolk 39 G4 vil 3m/5km S of Acle. **F. Common** vil adjoining to SW. TG 4004
Free Town Gtr Manchester 42 D1* dist of Bury 1m NE of tn centre. SD 8111
Freevater Forest H'land 85 D7 deer forest in Sutherland dist E of Seana Bhraigh. NH 3588
Freezy Water London 20 A2* loc 3m/5km NE of Enfield in borough of Enfield. TQ 3699
Freiston Lincs 37 H1 vil 3m/5km E of Boston. **F. Shore** loc near coast 2m/3km SE. TF 3743
Fremington Devon 6 D2 vil 3m/5km W of Barnstaple on rd to Bideford. SS 5132
Fremington, High and **Low** N Yorks 54 A5 adjoining hams just E of Reeth. SE 0499
Frenchay Avon 16 B4 loc 5m/8km NE of Bristol. **F. Moor** (NT). ST 6477
Frenchbeer Devon 7 E6 ham on E side of Dartmoor 5m/8km W of Moretonhampstead. SX 6785
Frenches Green Essex 30 B5* loc 4m/6km SW of Braintree. TL 7020
Frenchies, The Hants 10 A3* loc 3m/4km W of Romsey. SU 3022
Frenchman's Bay Tyne & Wear 61 H5* small bay on North Sea coast N of Marsden. NZ 3866
Frenchman's Rocks S'clyde 62 A3* group of rocks off Rubha na Faing, W coast of Rinns of Islay. NR 1553
French Street Kent 20 B6* loc 2km SE of Westerham. TQ 4552
Frensham Surrey 11 E1 vil 4m/6km S of Farnham, on R Wey. To SE, **Fn Common** (NT); to S, **F. Gt Pond** (mostly NT), a lake; to E, **F. Lit Pond.** SU 8441
Frenze Norfolk 39 E6* loc 2km E of Diss. TM 1380
Freshfield Merseyside loc in NW part of Formby. SD 2808
Freshford Avon 16 C5 vil 4m/6km SE of Bath. ST 7860
Freshney 45 F1/G1* r rising SW of Grimsby and flowing through the W part of the tn into R Humber. TA 2711
Freshwater Isle of Wight 10 A5 vil resort 2km E of Totland. To SW, Farringford, formerly home of Tennyson. To S, loc of **F. Bay** on small bay of same name. SZ 3487
Fresh Water Bay Gwynedd 40 B2* eastward-facing bay on coast of Anglesey 3m/4km E of Amlwch. SH 4892
Freshwater East Dyfed 22 C5* loc to NW of bay of same name 3m/5km SE of Pembroke. SS 0198
Fressingfield Suffolk 31 F1/G1 vil 4m/6km S of Harleston. TM 2677
Freston Suffolk 31 F4 vil 4m/6km S of Ipswich. TM 1739
Freswick H'land 86 F1 loc at head of **F. Bay,** on E coast of Caithness dist 4m/6km S of Duncansby Hd. ND 3767
Fretherne Glos 16 C1* vil 8m/12km W of Stroud. SO 7309
Frettenham Norfolk 39 F3 vil 6m/10km N of Norwich. TG 2417
Freuchie Fife 73 F4 vil 4m/6km N of Glenrothes. NO 2806
Freystrop Cross Dyfed 22 C4 ham 3m/4km S of Haverfordwest. **Lr Freystrop** loc 1km N. SM 9511
Friar Houses Durham 53 H2* loc 4m/6km NW of Middleton in Teesdale. NY 8928
Friar Park W Midlands 35 F5* loc in N part of W Bromwich. SP 0094
Friar's Gate E Sussex 12 B3 loc below NE slope of Ashdown Forest 2m/3km NW of Crowborough. TQ 4933
Friarside, High Durham 61 F5* loc 1m W of Burnopfield. NZ 1656
Friar's Point S Glam 15 F4* headland on Barry I. at W end of Whitmore Bay. ST 1165
Friarton Tayside 73 E3 S dist of Perth. **Friarton I.** (or Moncreiffe I.) is island in R Tay to E. NO 1121
Frickley S Yorks 44 A1* loc 1m E of Clayton. SE 4608
Friday Bridge Cambs 38 A4 vil 3m/5km S of Wisbech. TF 4604
Friday Hill London 20 A2* loc in borough of Waltham Forest 1km SE of Chingford tn centre. TQ 3893
Friday Street E Sussex 12 C6 loc 3m/5km N of Eastbourne. TQ 6203
Friday Street Suffolk 31 F2* loc 1m SE of Cretingham. TM 2459
Friday Street Suffolk 31 G2* ham 2m/3km S of Saxmundham. TM 3760
Friday Street Suffolk 31 G3 loc at N edge of Rendlesham Forest, 3m/5km SE of Wickham Mkt. TM 3352
Friday Street Surrey 11 G1 loc 4m/6km SW of Dorking. TQ 1245
Fridaythorpe Humberside 50 D3 vil in the wolds 9m/15km W of Gt Driffield. SE 8759
Friendly W Yorks 48 C5* loc 1m W of Sowerby Br. SE 0623
Friern Barnet London 19 G3 dist in borough of Barnet 8m/12km N of Charing Cross. TQ 2792
Friesland Bay Coll, S'clyde 68 A4 bay on S coast 3m/5km SW of Arinagour. NM 1853
Friesthorpe Lincs 45 E3 vil 4m/7km SW of Mkt Rasen. TF 0783
Frieston Lincs 44 D6 ham adjoining Caythorpe to S. SK 9347
Frieth Bucks 18 C3 vil 4m/7km NW of Marlow. SU 7990
Frieze Hill Som 8 A2* W dist of Taunton. ST 2125
Friezeland Notts 44 A5 loc 3m/4km N of Eastwood. SK 4750
Frilford Oxon 17 H2 vil 4m/6km W of Abingdon. SU 4497
Frilsham Berks 18 A4 vil 5m/9km NE of Newbury. SU 5373
Frimley Surrey 18 D5 tn adjoining Camberley to S. Loc of **F. Green** 1m S. SU 8858
Frindsbury Kent 20 D4 N dist of Rochester across R Medway from tn centre. Site of Roman bldg near river bank at Limehouse Reach. TQ 7469
Fring Norfolk 38 C2 ham 5m/9km SE of Hunstanton. TF 7334
Fringford Oxon 28 B4 vil 4m/7km NE of Bicester. SP 6028
Friningham Kent 20 D5* loc 4m/7km NE of Maidstone. TQ 8158
Frinsted Kent 21 E5 vil 4m/6km S of Sittingbourne. TQ 8957
Frinton-on-Sea Essex 31 F6 resort adjoining Walton on the Naze to SW, 5m/8km NE of Clacton-on-Sea. TM 2319
Friockheim Tayside 77 F5 vil 6m/10km NW of Arbroath. NO 5949
Friog Gwynedd 32 D3 loc on S side of Fairbourne 2m/4km NE of Llwyngwril. SH 6112
Frisby on the Wreake Leics 36 C3 vil 4m/6km W of Melton Mowbray. SK 6917
Friskney Lincs 45 H5 vil 3m/5km SW of Wainfleet. **F. Eaudike** loc 1km NE. **F. Tofts** 1m SE. TF 4655
Friston E Sussex 12 B6 vil 4m/7km W of Eastbourne. TV 5598
Friston Suffolk 31 G2 vil 3m/4km SE of Saxmundham. TM 4160
Fritchley Derbys 43 H5 loc 4m/6km N of Belper. SK 3552
Fritham Hants 10 A3 ham in New Forest 4m/6km W of Cadnam. SU 2314
Frith Bank Lincs 45 G6* loc 2m/3km NW of Boston. TF 3147
Frith Common H & W 26 C1 loc 6m/10km E of Tenbury Wells. SO 6969
Frithelstock Devon 6 D3 vil 2m/3km W of Torrington. Remains of 13c priory. Vil of **F. Stone** 1m SW. SS 4619
Frithsden Herts 19 E1* loc 2m/3km NE of Berkhamsted. TL 0109
Frithville Lincs 45 G6 vil 4m/7km N of Boston. TF 3150
Frittenden Kent 12 D3 vil 3m/4km SW of Headcorn. TQ 8141
Frittiscombe Devon 4 D6* ham 4m/7km E of Kingsbridge. SX 8043
Fritton Norfolk 39 F5 vil 6m/10km N of Harleston. TM 2292
Fritton Norfolk 39 H5 vil 6m/9km SW of Gt Yarmouth. To E is **F. Decoy,** 2m/4km-long lake with wooded banks. TG 4600
Fritwell Oxon 28 A4 vil 3m/4km S of Aynho. SP 5229
Frizinghall W Yorks 48 D4* dist of Bradford 2m/3km NW of city centre. SE 1436
Frizington Cumbria 52 A3 loc 4m/6km E of Whitehaven. NY 0317
Frocester Glos 16 C2 vil 4m/6km NE of Dursley. SO 7803
Frodesley Salop 34 C4 vil 7m/12km S of Shrewsbury. **F. Lane** loc 1m SW. SJ 5101

Frodingham Humberside 50 D6 dist of Scunthorpe E of tn centre. SE 8911
Frodingham Beck 51 E3* r rising as Kelk Beck near Kilham, Humberside, and flowing S into R Hull 2km SW of N Frodingham. TA 0851
Frodingham, North Humberside 51 E3 vil 6m/9km SE of Gt Driffield. TA 0953
Frodsham Ches 42 B3 tn 3m/5km S of Runcorn. SJ 5177
Frog End Cambs 29 G3* ham 5m/7km NE of Royston. TL 3946
Frog End Cambs 30 A2* loc 1km W of Lit Wilbraham. TL 5358
Froggatt Derbys 43 G3 vil 3m/4km N of Baslow. SK 2476
Froghall Staffs 43 E6 ham 3m/4km N of Cheadle. Terminus of Caldon Canal. SK 0247
Frogham Hants 9 H3 loc on edge of New Forest 2m/3km SE of Fordingbridge. SU 1713
Frogham Kent 13 G2* loc 7m/11km NW of Dover. TR 2550
Frogland Cross Avon 16 B3* loc 5m/8km W of Chipping Sodbury. ST 6483
Frogmore Devon 4 D6 vil 3m/5km E of Kingsbridge at head of **F. Creek,** which runs into Kingsbridge Estuary. SX 7742
Frogmore Hants 18 C5* loc 2m/3km W of Camberley. SU 8460
Frogmore Herts 19 F2 loc 2m/4km S of St Albans on W side of Radlett Airfield. TL 1503
Frogpool Cornwall 2 C4* ham 4m/6km E of Redruth. SW 7539
Frog Pool H & W 26 C1 ham 4m/6km S of Stourport. SO 7965
Frogwell Cornwall 3 H2* ham 1m SW of Callington. SX 3468
Frolesworth Leics 36 B5 vil 5m/7km NW of Lutterworth. SP 5090
Frome Som 16 C6 tn 11m/17km S of Bath, with steep medieval streets. 18c wool merchants' hses. Modern industries include textiles, plastics, paint, brewing. ST 7747
Frome 16 C5* r rising 6m/10km S of Frome, Som, and flowing N through the tn and into R Avon 2m/3km W of Bradford-on-Avon. ST 7960
Frome 26 B4 r rising about 6m/10km N of Bromyard and flowing S through that tn and into R Lugg 3m/5km E of Hereford. SO 5638
Frome 9 F5 r rising at Evershot in Dorset and flowing SE to Dorchester, then E to Wareham and thence into Poole Harbour. SY 9487
Fromefield Som 16 C6* NE dist of Frome. ST 7848
Frome St Quintin Dorset 8 D4 vil 3m/5km N of Maiden Newton. ST 5902
Fromes Hill H & W 26 B3 ham 5m/8km S of Bromyard. SO 6746
Frome Vauchurch Dorset 8 D4* loc to S of Maiden Newton. SY 5996
Frome Whitfield Dorset 9 E5* loc 1km N of Dorchester. SY 6991
Fron Clwyd 41 F4* loc adjoining Denbigh to NE. SJ 0566
Fron Gwynedd 40 C5* loc 5m/8km S of Caernarvon. SH 5054
Fron Powys 33 H4 loc 2m/3km S of Berriew. SO 1797
Fron Powys 34 A4 loc 3m/4km S of Welshpool. SJ 2203
Froncysyllte Clwyd 34 A1 vil 3m/4km NW of Chirk. SJ 2741
Fron-goch Gwynedd 33 F1 ham 3m/4km NW of Bala. SH 9039
Fron Isaf Clwyd 34 A1* loc 2m/3km NW of Chirk. SJ 2740
Frostenden Suffolk 31 H1 loc 4m/6km NW of Southwold. TM 4781
Frosterley Durham 54 A2 vil on R Wear 2m/4km SE of Stanhope. NZ 0236
Froxfield Wilts 17 G4 vil 3m/4km W of Hungerford. SU 2968
Froxfield Green Hants 10 D2 vil 3m/5km NW of Petersfield. Site of Romano-British settlement 1km SE. SU 7025
Froyle Hants 10 D1 par containing vils of **Upr** and **Lr Froyle,** about 4m/7km NE of Alton. Site of Roman bldg 1m E of Upr Froyle. SU 7543
Fruid Water 65 G6 r in Borders region running N through **Fruid Resr** to R Tweed 1m SW of Tweedsmuir. NT 0823
Fruin Water 71 E6 r in S'clyde region running SE down Glen Fruin, then E into Loch Lomond 2m/4km N of foot of loch. NS 3685
Fryerning Essex 20 C2 vil 5m/8km NE of Brentwood. TL 6400
Fryerns Essex 20 D3* E dist of Basildon. TQ 7289
Fryton N Yorks 50 C1* loc 1km W of Slingsby. SE 6974
Fuam an Tolla W Isles 88 B3* islet in E Loch Tarbert, Harris, off W coast of Scalpay. NG 2096
Fuar Bheinn H'land 68 F3 mt in Lochaber dist 2m/4km N of Loch a' Choire. NM 8556
Fuar Tholl H'land 80 A3 mt in Ross and Cromarty dist 2m/3km W of Achnashellach Lodge. Height 2975 ft or 907 metres. NG 9748
Fuday W Isles 88 D3/E3* uninhabited island of about 500 acres or 200 hectares 2m/3km E of Scurrival Pt, Barra. Ancient remains at Dunan Ruadh, qv. NF 7308
Fugglestone St Peter Wilts 9 H1 loc 1km E of Wilton. SU 1031
Fuiay W Isles 88 E3* uninhabited island off North Bay, Barra. NF 7402
Fulbeck Lincs 44 D6 vil 9m/15km N of Grantham. SK 9450
Fulbeck Nthmb 61 F3* loc 1m NW of Morpeth. NZ 1987
Fulbourn Cambs 30 A2 vil 5m/7km SE of Cambridge. TL 5156
Fulbrook Oxon 27 F6/G6 vil 1km NE of Burford. SP 2516
Fulflood Hants 10 B2* NW dist of Winchester. SU 4730
Fulford N Yorks 50 B3 vil adjoining York to S, 2m/3km from city centre. Sometimes known as Gate Fulford. SE 6049
Fulford Som 8 A2* ham 3m/5km NW of Taunton. ST 2129
Fulford Staffs 35 F1 vil 4m/7km NE of Stone. SJ 9538
Fulham London 19 F4* dist on N side of R Thames in borough of Hammersmith N of Putney Br. F. Palace, 16c-19c, upstream from Putney Br, is traditional residence of Bishop of London. TQ 2476
Fulking W Sussex 11 H4 vil below N slopes of S Downs 4m/6km SE of Henfield. TQ 2411
Fullaford Devon 7 E2* loc 8m/13km N of S Molton. SS 6838
Fullarton S'clyde 64 B5* S dist of Irvine. NS 3238
Fullarton S'clyde 64 D3* loc 4m/6km E of Glasgow. NS 6462
Fullbrook W Midlands 35 F4* loc in S part of Walsall. SP 0196
Fuller's End Essex 30 A5* S end of vil of Elsenham, 4m/7km NE of Bishop's Stortford. TL 5325
Fuller's Moor Ches 42 B5* loc 2m/4km E of Clutton. SJ 4954
Fuller Street Essex 30 C6 ham 5m/7km W of Witham. TL 7416
Fullerton Hants 10 B1* ham 3m/5km NE of Stockbridge. SU 3739
Fulletby Lincs 45 G4 vil 4m/6km NE of Horncastle. TF 2973
Full Sutton Humberside 50 C3 vil 2m/3km E of Stamford Br. SE 7455
Fullwell Cross London 20 B3* loc in borough of Redbridge 3m/4km N of Ilford. TQ 4490
Fullwood Gtr Manchester 43 E1* loc in Oldham 3m/4km NE of tn centre. SD 9408
Fulmer Bucks 19 E3 vil 4m/7km NE of Slough. SU 9985
Fulmodestone Norfolk 39 E2 ham 5m/8km E of Fakenham. TF 9930
Fulnetby Lincs 45 E3* ham 2m/4km NW of Wragby. TF 0979
Fulney Lincs 37 G2 NE dist of Spalding. **Low F.** loc 1m SE. TF 2523
Fulstone W Yorks 43 F1* loc 2m/4km E of Holmfirth. SE 1709
Fulstow Lincs 45 G2 vil 6m/10km N of Louth. TF 3297
Fulwell Oxon 27 G5 ham 1km S of Enstone. SP 3723
Fulwell Tyne & Wear 61 H5 dist of Sunderland 2km N of tn centre. NZ 3959
Fulwood Lancs 47 F5 suburb adjoining Preston to N. **F. Row** loc 2m/3km E. SD 5331
Fulwood Notts 44 A5* loc adjoining Sutton in Ashfield to SW. SK 4757
Fulwood S Yorks 43 G3 dist of Sheffield 3m/5km W of city centre. SK 3085
Fundenhall Norfolk 39 F5 vil 4m/6km SE of Wymondham. Ham of **F. Street** 1m W. TM 1596
Funlack Burn H'land 81 G4 stream in Inverness dist running SE from Loch Moy to R Findhorn 2m/4km N of Tomatin. NH 8029
Funtington W Sussex 11 E4 vil 5m/7km NW of Chichester. SU 8008
Funtley Hants 10 C4 loc 2m/3km NW of Fareham. SU 5608
Funzie Shetland 89 F6 loc on Fetlar 3m/4km E of Houbie. **F. Bay** to SE. **F. Ness** peninsula to S, at SE corner of island. HU 6690
Furley Devon 8 B4 ham 4m/7km NW of Axminster. ST 2704
Furnace Dyfed 23 F5* dist of Llanelli N of tn centre. SN 5001
Furnace Dyfed 32 D5 loc 4m/6km NE of Talybont. SN 6895
Furnace S'clyde 70 C5 vil on W shore of Loch Fyne in Argyll 7m/11km SW of Inveraray. Large granite quarries. NN 0300
Furnace Green W Sussex 11 H2 SE dist of Crawley. TQ 2835
Furner's Green E Sussex 12 A4* loc 1m S of Danehill. TQ 4026
Furness Cumbria 46 D1* dist lying S of Wrynose Pass between Windermere and R Duddon and narrowing southwards to a peninsula between R Duddon and R Leven estuaries culminating at Barrow-in-Furness, the other principal tns being Dalton-in-Furness and Ulverston. Iron ore abounds. SD 2890
Furness Abbey Cumbria 46 D1 remains of medieval abbey (A.M.), 12c and later, 2m/3km NE of Barrow-in-Furness. NY 2171
Furness Vale Derbys 43 E3 vil 2km SE of New Mills. SK 0083
Furneux Pelham Herts 29 H5 vil 5m/9km NW of Bishop's Stortford. TL 4327
Furnham Som 8 B3 N dist of Chard. ST 3209
Furrah Head Grampian 83 H3* headland on E coast at S end of Sandford Bay, 1km N of Boddam. NK 1243
Furtho Northants 28 C3* ch and farm 2m/3km NW of Stony Stratford. SP 7743
Furzedown London 19 G4* loc in borough of Wandsworth 6m/10km S of Charing Cross. TQ 2871
Furze Green Norfolk 31 F1* loc 2m/4km W of Harleston. TM 2182
Furzehill Devon 7 E1* loc 3m/4km S of Lynton. SS 7245
Furzehill Dorset 9 G4* loc 2km N of Wimborne. SU 0102
Furze Hill Common Dorset 9 E2* ham 3m/5km NW of Gillingham. ST 7830
Furzeley Corner Hants 10 D4* loc 2m/3km W of Waterlooville. SU 6510
Furzey Island Dorset 9 G5* island on S side of Poole Harbour close to Brownsea I. SZ 1087
Furzey Lodge Hants 10 B4* loc in New Forest 2km W of Beaulieu. SU 3602
Furzley Hants 10 A3* ham on edge of New Forest 2m/3km N of Cadnam. To S, **F. Common** (partly NT), with round barrows of late Bronze Age. SU 2816
Fyfet Som 8 A3* loc in par of Otterford 6m/10km S of Taunton. ST 2314
Fyfield Essex 20 C1 vil 3m/4km NE of Chipping Ongar. TL 5706
Fyfield Hants 10 A1 vil 4m/7km W of Andover. SU 2946
Fyfield Oxon 17 H2 vil 5m/8km W of Abingdon. SU 4298
Fyfield Wilts 17 F4* vil 3m/4km W of Marlborough. SU 1468
Fyfield Wilts 17 F5* ham 1m E of Pewsey. SU 1760
Fylde 116 admin dist of Lancs.
Fylingdales Moor N Yorks 55 G5 moorland area SW of Robin Hood's Bay at E end of N Yorks Moors. SE 9299
Fyling Thorpe N Yorks 55 G4 vil 1km SW of Robin Hood's Bay. NZ 9405
Fyllon 33 H3* r rising 2m/3km SE of Hirnant, Powys, and flowing E to its confluence with R Abel at Llanfyllin, below which it becomes R Cain. SJ 1419
Fyne S'clyde 70 D4 r in Argyll running SW down Glen F. to head of Loch F. 6m/10km NE of Inveraray. NN 1810
Fyning W Sussex 11 E3 loc just E of Rogate and 4m/7km E of Petersfield. SU 8123
Fyn Loch S'clyde 64 C2* small loch or tarn on Kilpatrick Hills 4m/7km E of Dumbarton. NS 4577
Fynn 31 F3* stream rising 1m S of Ashbocking, Suffolk, and flowing S then E into Martlesham Creek and thence into R Deben 2km S of Woodbridge. TM 2747
Fyvie Grampian 83 F3 vil on R Ythan 8m/13km S of Turriff. **F. Castle,** 1m N, late 16c. NJ 7637

G

Gabalfa S Glam 15 F3* loc in Cardiff 2m/3km NW of city centre. ST 1678
Gable, Great Cumbria 52 C4 mt in Lake Dist 3m/5km SW of Seatoller. Height 2949 ft or 899 metres. NY 2010
Gable Head Hants 10 D5 loc in S Hayling on Hayling I. SZ 7299
Gabwell Devon 5 E4* two hams, **Hr Gabwell** and **Lr Gabwell,** about 3m/5km N of Torquay. SX 9269
Gaddesby Leics 36 C3 vil 6m/9km SW of Melton Mowbray. SK 6813
Gaddesden, Great Herts 19 E1 vil 3m/5km NE of Berkhamsted. TL 0211
Gaddesden, Little Herts 29 E6 vil 4m/6km N of Berkhamsted. SP 9913
Gaddings Dam W Yorks 48 C5* resr 2km SE of Todmorden. SD 9522
Gade 19 E2 r rising in Chiltern Hills 5m/8km NW of Hemel Hempstead, Herts, and flowing S into R Colne to E of Rickmansworth. TQ 0794
Gadebridge Herts 19 E1* NW dist of Hemel Hempstead. TL 0408
Gadfa Gwynedd 40 B3* loc on Anglesey 2m/4km S of Amlwch. SH 4589
Gadlas Salop 34 B1* loc 2m/4km NW of Ellesmere. SJ 3737
Gadlys Mid Glam 15 E2 loc adjoining Aberdare to W. SN 9902
Gadlys S Glam 15 E4* loc adjoining Llanmaes to N, 2km NE of Llantwit Major. SS 9869
Gads Hill Kent 20 D4 loc on S edge of Higham, 3m/4km NW of Rochester. Home of Charles Dickens, 1857–70. TQ 7170
Gaeilavore Island H'land 78 B2 one of a group of islets 3m/5km NW of Rubha Hunish at northern tip of Skye. See also Gearran I. and Lord Macdonald's Table. NG 3679
Gael-chàrn H'land 75 H1* mt at NW end of Cairngorms in Badenoch and Strathspey dist, 4m/7km SE of Kincraig. NH 8801
Gaer Gwent 15 G3* SW dist of Newport. ST 2986
Gaer-fawr Gwent 16 A2* loc 2km SE of Llangwm. ST 4498
Gaerlwyd Gwent 16 A2* ham 3m/4km NW of Shirenewton. ST 4496
Gaerwen Gwynedd 40 B4 vil on Anglesey 5m/8km W of Menai Br. SH 4871
Gagingwell Oxon 27 H5* loc 6m/10km E of Chipping Norton. SP 4025
Gaick Forest H'land 75 G3 deer forest in Badenoch and Strathspey dist, 7m/11km E of Dalwhinnie. NN 7584
Gailes S'clyde 64 B5* dist of Irvine New Tn 3m/5km S of tn centre. NS 3335
Gailey Staffs 35 E3 ham 2m/4km S of Penkridge. **G. Wharf** loc 1km E on Staffs and Worcs Canal. SJ 9110
Gain 33 E2 r rising E of Trawsfynydd, Gwynedd, and flowing S into R Mawddach in Coed y Brenin Forest 2m/3km N of Ganllwyd. SH 7327
Gainford Durham 54 B3 vil on R Tees 8m/12km W of Darlington. Hall of early 17c. NZ 1716
Gainsborough Lincs 44 C2 inland port on R Trent 15m/25km NW of Lincoln. Engineering, malting, flour milling; timber yards. SK 8189
Gainsford End Essex 30 C4* ham 3m/5km NE of Finchingfield. TL 7235
Gairbeinn H'land 75 E2 mt on Corrieyairack Forest, in Badenoch and Strathspey dist, 8m/13km SE of Fort Augustus. Height 2929 ft or 893 metres. NN 4698
Gairich H'land 74 B2 mt in Lochaber dist 3m/5km SW of dam of Loch Quoich. Height 3015 ft or 919 metres. NN 0299
Gairletter Point S'clyde 70 D6 headland in Argyll, on W side of Loch Long 3m/4km N of Strone Pt. NS 1984
Gairloch H'land 78 F2 vil on W coast of Ross and Cromarty dist at head of Gair Loch. NG 8076

Gairlochy H'land 74 C3 locality on Caledonian Canal at SW end of Loch Lochy in Lochaber dist. NN 1784

Gairn 76 D2 r in Grampian region rising on Invercauld Forest and running E to R Dee 1m NW of Ballater. NO 3596

Gairney Bank Tayside 73 E4* loc 2m/3km S of Kinross. NT 1299

Gairsay Orkney 89 B6 sparsely populated island of about 500 acres or 200 hectares at N end of Wide Firth between Mainland and Shapinsay. HY 4422

Gaisby W Yorks 48 D4* loc in Shipley 1m SE of tn centre. SE 1536

Gaisgill Cumbria 53 F4 loc 2m/3km E of Tebay. NY 6305

Gaitsgill Cumbria 60 A6 ham 3m/4km SE of Dalston. NY 3846

Gala Lane 56 E4 r rising in Dumfries & Galloway region 3m/4km E of Merrick, and running N along border with Strathclyde region into S end of Loch Doon. NX 4892

Galashiels Borders 66 C5 tn on Gala Water 14m/22km N of Hawick. Centre for woollen mnfre. Scottish College of Textiles. Other industries include electronics, light engineering. NT 4936

Galava Cumbria. See Clappersgate.

Gale Gtr Manchester 48 C6* loc 1km NE of Littleborough. SD 9417

Galgate Lancs 47 F3 vil 4m/6km S of Lancaster. SD 4855

Galhampton Som 8 D2 vil 2m/3km S of Castle Cary. ST 6329

Gallachan Bay S'clyde 63 G2* small bay on SW coast of Bute, between Scalpsie Bay and Stravanan Bay. NS 0656

Gallan Head W Isles 88 A2 headland on W coast of Lewis on W side of entrance to W Loch Roag. NB 0539

Gallantry Bank Ches 42 B5* loc at S end of Peckforton Hills 2m/4km SW of Peckforton. SJ 5153

Gallatown Fife 73 F5 loc adjoining Kirkcaldy to N. NT 2994

Gallen 41 E4 r running N to join R Cledwen at Llangernyw, Clwyd, and form R Elwy. SH 8767

Gallery Tayside 77 F4 loc 1m W of Marykirk across R North Esk. NO 6765

Galley Common Warwicks 35 H5* loc 3m/5km W of Nuneaton. SP 3192

Galleyend Essex 20 D2* suburban loc 2m/4km S of Chelmsford. TL 7103

Galley Hill Kent 20 C4 loc 1m W of Northfleet. TQ 6074

Galleywood Essex 20 D2 suburb 3m/4km S of Chelmsford. TL 7002

Gallions Reach 20 B3* stretch of R Thames N of Woolwich between Woolwich Reach and Barking Reach. TQ 4480

Galloway Deer Museum D & G. See Clatteringshaws Loch.

Gallow Hill N Yorks 49 F3* loc 1km S of Knaresborough. SE 3456

Gallowhill S'clyde 64 C2/C3* N dist of Paisley. NS 4965

Gallows Corner London 20 B3* rd junction and loc 2m/3km NE of Romford in borough of Havering. TQ 5390

Gallows Green Essex 30 D5* loc 5m/7km W of Colchester. TL 9226

Gallowsgreen Gwent 15 G1* loc 2m/3km SE of Blaenavon. SO 2606

Gallows Green H & W 26 D2* loc 2m/4km E of Droitwich. SO 9362

Gallows Green Staffs 35 G1* 4m/7km E of Cheadle. SK 0741

Gallows Hill Suffolk 31 E1* loc 1km NE of Redgrave. TM 0378

Gallows Point Gwynedd 40 C4* headland on Menai Strait 1m SW of Beaumaris, Anglesey. SH 5975

Gallowstree Common Oxon 18 B3 loc 5m/7km NW of Reading. SU 6980

Gallowstree Elm Staffs 35 E5 loc adjoining Kinver to N, 4m/7km W of Stourbridge. SO 8384

Gallt-y-foel Gwynedd 40 C5* loc 1km SE of Deiniolen. SH 5862

Gallypot Street E Sussex 12 B3* loc 1km SW of Hartfield. TQ 4735

Galmington Som 8 A2* SW dist of Taunton. ST 2123

Galmisdale H'land 68 C1 loc on SE coast of Eigg. Landing stage. NM 4883

Galmpton Devon 4 D6 vil 3m/5km W of Salcombe. SX 6940

Galmpton Devon 5 E5 loc 3m/5km S of Paignton. Also **G. Warborough.** SX 8856

Galon Uchaf Mid Glam 15 F1* loc in N part of Merthyr Tydfil. SO 0508

Galphay N Yorks 49 E1 vil 4m/6km W of Ripon. SE 2572

Galson, North and **South** W Isles 88 C1 adjacent locs near NW coast of Lewis 7m/11km SW of Port of Ness. **N Galson R** flows into Atlantic Ocean to NE of N Galson; **S Galson R** passes between the two locs and flows out to sea to N of them. NB 4358

Galston S'clyde 64 C5 tn on R Irvine 5m/8km E of Kilmarnock. Mnfre of hosiery, blankets, lace. NS 5036

Galt, The Orkney 89 B6* point at NW extremity of island of Shapinsay, on W side of Veantrow Bay. HY 4821

Gam 33 G3* r rising 2m/4km NE of Llanbrynmair, Powys, and running S then NE into R Banwy on E side of Llangadfan. SJ 0110

Gamble Hill W Yorks 49 E5* loc in Leeds 3m/4km W of city centre. SE 2533

Gamblesby Cumbria 53 E1 vil 8m/13km NE of Penrith. NY 6039

Gamble's Green Essex 30 C6 loc 4m/6km W of Witham. TL 7614

Gamelsby Cumbria 59 G6* loc 3m/4km N of Wigton. NY 2552

Gamesley Derbys 43 E2* loc 2km W of Glossop. Site of Roman fort 1km NW. **Hr Gamesley** loc to S. SK 0194

Gamhnach Mhór S'clyde 69 D6* islet at entrance to Carsaig Bay on S coast of Mull. NM 5420

Gamhna Gigha S'clyde 62 D3* group of rocks lying nearly 2km E of Rubh' a' Chàirn Bhàin near N end of island of Gigha. NR 6854

Gamla Shetland 89 F6* headland with lighthouse on E coast of Yell 3m/5km NE of Otterswick. HU 5489

Gamlan 33 E2 r running E into R Mawddach 3m/5km N of Llanelltyd, Gwynedd. SH 7224

Gamlingay Cambs 29 F3 vil 2m/3km NE of Potton. Hams of **G. Cinques** and **G. Gt Heath** to NW and W respectively. TL 2352

Gammaton Devon 6 D3* loc 2m/3km E of Bideford. To S, **Gammaton Resrs** and loc of **Gammaton Moor.** SS 4825

Gammersgill N Yorks 54 A6 loc 6m/9km SW of Middleham. SE 0583

Gamrie Grampian 83 F1 loc near N coast, 5m/9km E of Macduff. **G. Bay** is 2km N, between Crovie Hd and More Hd. NJ 7962

Gamston Notts 36 B1 ham 3m/5km SE of Nottingham. SK 6037

Gamston Notts 44 B3 vil 3m/5km S of E Retford. SK 7076

Ganarew H & W 26 A5* loc 2m/4km NE of Monmouth. SO 5216

Ganavan Bay S'clyde 70 B2 bay 2m/3km N of Oban, Argyll. NM 8532

Gang Cornwall 3 G2* loc 3m/5km W of Callington. SX 3068

Ganllwyd Gwynedd 33 E2 ham in Coed y Brenin Forest, 4m/7km N of Dolgellau. SH 7224

Gannel 2 D2 r rising at Fraddon, Cornwall, and running out to sea at E Pentire Pt, W of Newquay. Name usually applied to estuary only. SW 7761

Gannochy Tayside 73 E2* NE dist of Perth, on E side of R Tay. NO 1224

Gannow Green H & W 35 F6* loc 3m/5km S of Halesowen. SO 9778

Ganstead Humberside 51 F5* ham 5m/8km NE of Hull. TA 1434

Ganthorpe N Yorks 50 C2 ham 6m/10km W of Malton. SE 6870

Ganton N Yorks 51 E1 vil 8m/13km W of Filey. SE 9877

Gantshill London 20 B3* loc in borough of Redbridge 2km NW of Ilford. TQ 4388

Ganu Mór H'land 84 C3* peak of mt ridge known as Foinaven, in Sutherland dist 5m/9km SW of head of Loch Eriboll. Height 2980 ft or 908 metres. NC 3150

Ganwick Corner Herts 19 F2 loc 2km S of Potters Bar. TQ 2599

Gaor Bheinn H'land 74 B3 mt in Lochaber dist 2m/4km S of head of Loch Arkaig. Height of N summit 3238 ft or 987 metres; S summit 3153 ft or 961 metres. Anglicised form: Gulvain. NM 9986

Gaping Gill Hole N Yorks 48 A1* limestone cavern on SE slope of Ingleborough. Waterfall from mouth to cavern floor. SD 7572

Gappah Devon 5 E3* loc 4m/6km N of Newton Abbot. SX 8677

Garadbhan Forest S'clyde 71 E6, F5* state forest at S end of Loch Lomond in vicinity of Drymen. NS 4790

Garbat Forest H'land 85 E8* deer forest in Ross and Cromarty dist on W side of Ben Wyvis. NH 4368

Garbh Bheinn H'land 74 C5 mt in Lochaber dist 2km SW of Kinlochleven. Height 2835 ft or 864 metres. NN 1760

Garbh-bheinn Skye, H'land 79 D6 mt 2m/4km NW of head of Loch Slapin. Height 2649 ft or 807 metres. NG 5323

Garbh Eileach S'clyde 69 E6 largest of the Garvellachs group of islands in Firth of Lorn. Lies between A' Chùli and Dun Chonnuill. NM 6812

Garbh Eilean Skye, H'land 78 D4 small uninhabited island off S end of island of Rona. NG 6153

Garbh Eilean W Isles. See Shiant Is.

Garbh Eilean W Isles 88 B2* islet in Loch Erisort, Lewis, 1km SE of Keose and 2m/3km E of Laxay. NB 3621

Garbh Ghaoir 75 E5 r in Tayside region running 2m/3km from Loch Laidon to head of Loch Eigheach. NN 4456

Garbh Leac H'land. See A'Chràlaig.

Garbh Rèisa S'clyde 69 F7 small island nearly 1km S of Craignish Pt at entrance to Loch Craignish in Argyll. NR 7597

Garboldisham Norfolk 39 E6 vil 7m/11km W of Diss. TM 0081

Garcrogo Forest D & G 58 C4 state forest 4m/7km E of Balmaclellan. NX 7278

Garden City Clwyd 41 H4 housing estate on N bank of R Dee opp Queensferry. SJ 3269

Gardeners Green Berks 10 C5* ham 2m/3km SE of Wokingham. SU 8266

Gardenstown Grampian 83 F1 fishing vil on Gamrie Bay on N coast, 6m/9km E of Macduff. NJ 8064

Garden Village Clwyd 41 H6* N dist of Wrexham. SJ 3352

Garden Village S Yorks 43 G2* W dist of Stocksbridge. SK 2698

Garderhouse Shetland 89 E7 loc on Mainland at head of Seli Voe 7m/11km NW of Scalloway across entrance to Weisdale Voe. HU 3347

Gardham Humberside 50 D4 loc 5m/8km E of Mkt Weighton. SE 9542

Gardner Street E Sussex 12 C5* loc adjoining Herstmonceux to N. TQ 6312

Gardyne Castle Tayside 77 F6 16c cas 2km SW of Friockheim. NO 5748

Gare Loch S'clyde 70 D5, D6 inlet of R Clyde running S from Garelochhead to Helensburgh. NS 2486

Garelochhead S'clyde 70 D5 vil and resort at head of Gare Loch 7m/11km NW of Helensburgh. **G. Forest** is state forest to S, on W side of loch. NS 2391

Garford Oxon 17 H2 vil 5m/7km W of Abingdon. Site of Roman temple 1km E. SU 4296

Garforth W Yorks 49 F5 tn in coal-mining dist 7m/11km E of Leeds. Locs of **E** and **W Garforth** 1km E and W respectively. SE 4033

Gargrave N Yorks 48 C3 vil on R Aire and on Leeds and Liverpool Canal 4m/7km NW of Skipton. Site of Roman bldg to SE. SD 9354

Gargunnock Central 71 G5 vil 6m/9km W of Stirling. Distillery. **G. Hills,** range of hills to S and SW. NS 7094

Gariannonum Norfolk. See Burgh Castle.

Garioch Grampian 83 E4, F4 area or district around Inverurie. See also Chapel of G. NJ 72

Garlands Cumbria 60 A6* loc 3m/4km SE of Carlisle. NY 4353

Garland Stone Dyfed 22 A5 island rock off N point of Skomer. SM 7210

Garleton Hills Lothian 66 C1 small group of hills 2m/3km N of Haddington, rising to 590 ft or 180 metres. Observation towers. Monmt commemorates Earl of Hopetoun, Peninsular War hero. NT 5076

Garlic Street Norfolk 39 F6* ham 2m/3km W of Harleston. TM 2183

Garlieston D & G 57 E7 vil on **G. Bay,** on W side of Wigtown Bay, 6m/10km SE of Wigtown. NX 4746

Garlinge Green Kent 13 F2* ham 4m/7km SW of Canterbury. TR 1152

Garlogie Grampian 77 G1 loc 3m/5km E of Echt. See also Roadside of G. Nearly 1m S is G. or Cullerlie Stone Circle (A.M.), eight boulders enclosing several small cairns. NJ 7805

Garmelow Staffs 35 E2 loc 3m/4km W of Eccleshall. SJ 7927

Garmond Grampian 83 F2 vil 5m/9km E of Turriff. NJ 8052

Garmondsway Durham 54 C2* loc near site of former vil 2m/3km W of Trimdon. NZ 3434

Garmony Mull, S'clyde 68 E4 loc at W end of Sallastle Bay on Sound of Mull, 7m/11km E of Salen. **Garmony Pt,** headland on sound to E. NM 6740

Garmouth Grampian 82 C1 vil near mouth of R Spey 8m/12km E of Elgin. NJ 3364

Garmston Salop 34 C4* ham 1km NW of Leighton. SJ 6006

Garn Gwynedd 32 B2* loc 4m/6km NW of Llanbedrog. SH 2734

Garnant Dyfed 23 H4 loc adjoining Glanaman to E. SN 6813

Garndiffaith Gwent 15 G1* loc at N end of Abersychan. SO 2605

Garn Dolbenmaen Gwynedd 32 C1 vil 4m/6km N of Criccieth. SH 4944

Garnedd Goch Gwynedd 40 C6 mt 5m/8km W of Beddgelert. Height 2301 ft or 701 metres. SH 5149

Garnett Bridge Cumbria 53 E5* loc at crossing of R Sprint 4m/7km N of Kendal. SD 5299

Garngad S'clyde 64 D2* dist of Glasgow 1m NE of city centre. NS 6066

Garnlydan Gwent 25 F6* loc 2m/3km W of Brynmawr. SO 1612

Garno 33 G5* r rising near Talerddig, Powys, and flowing SE into R Severn at Caersws. SO 0291

Garnock 64 B5 r in Strathclyde region rising about 5m/8km E of Largs and flowing S through Kilbirnie and Dalry to R Irvine, close to Irvine Bay. NS 3038

Garnswllt W Glam 23 G4* loc 2m/3km S of Ammanford. SN 6209

Garn, Y Gwynedd 40 C5 mt 3m/5km E of Llanberis. Height 3104 ft or 946 metres. SH 6359

Garn, Y Welsh form of Roch, qv.

Garn-yr-erw Gwent 25 G6* loc 2km NW of Blaenavon. SO 2310

Garpel Water 64 D6 r in Strathclyde region running NW to R Ayr 1m SW of Muirkirk. NS 6826

Garrabost W Isles 88 C2 vil on Eye Peninsula, Lewis, 4m/7km SW of Tiumpan Hd. NB 5133

Garrachcroit Bàgh S'clyde 63 E3 bay on E coast of Kintyre, Argyll, 4m/7km N of Dippen. NR 0144

Garraries Forest D & G 57 E5 state forest forming part of Glentrool Forest Park, NW of Clatteringshaws Loch. NX 4882

Garras Cornwall 2 C5* ham 4m/6km SE of Helston. SW 7023

Garreg Clwyd 41 G4* loc 1km W of Whitford, under Mynydd-y-garreg. See Whitford. SJ 1377

Garreg Gwynedd 32 D1 ham 2m/3km N of Penrhyndeudraeth. SH 6141

Garreg Ddu Reservoir Powys 25 E2 one of the series of large resrs in R Elan valley. The dam, at S end, is 5m/7km SW of Rhayader. SN 9163

Garrett, High Essex 30 C5 vil 3m/4km NE of Braintree. TL 7726

Garrett's Green W Midlands 35 G5* loc in Birmingham 5m/9km E of city centre. SP 1585

Garrigill Cumbria 53 F1 vil 4m/6km SE of Alston. NY 7441

Garrison of Inversnaid Central. See Inversnaid.

Garriston N Yorks 54 B5* loc 3m/5km NE of Leyburn. SE 1592

Garroch Burn 58 B3 stream in Dumfries & Galloway region running E to confluence with Glenlee Burn, thereafter continuing SE as Coom Burn for about 1km to its confluence with Water of Ken, 1km SW of Dalry. NX 6081

Garroch Head S'clyde 63 G3 headland at S end of island of Bute. NS 0951

Garron Point Grampian 77 H2 headland on E coast 2m/3km NE of Stonehaven. NO 8987

Garron Point Grampian 82 D1* headland on N coast at W end of Sandend Bay, 3m/4km E of Cullen. NJ 5567

Garry 76 A5 r in Tayside region running SE from Loch G. down Glen G. to R Tummel 2m/3km NW of Pitlochry. NN 9159

Garrynamonie W Isles 88 E3* loc near S end of S Uist, 2km N of Kilbride. NF 7516

Garrywhin H'land. See Ulbster.

Gars Bheinn Skye, H'land 79 C6 one of the peaks of the Cuillin Hills, at S end of range. Height 2934 ft or 894 metres. NG 4618

Garscadden S'clyde 64 C2* loc in Glasgow 5m/8km NW of city centre. NS 5268

Garsdale Cumbria 53 F5 loc and valley of R Clough 6m/10km E of Sedbergh. SD 7390

Garsdale Head Cumbria 53 G5* loc 1km SW of Moorcock Inn. SD 7892

Garsdon Wilts 17 E3 vil 2m/4km E of Malmesbury. SU 9687

Garshall Green Staffs 35 F1 ham 4m/7km E of Stone. SJ 9634

Garsington Oxon 18 B2 vil 5m/8km SE of Oxford. SP 5802

Garstang Lancs 47 F4 small tn 10km/17km N of Preston. SD 4945

Garston Merseyside 42 A3 dist of Liverpool 5m/9km SE of city centre. SJ 4084

Garston, East Berks 17 G4 vil 3m/5km SE of Lambourn. SU 3676

Garston Park Herts 19 E2* N dist of Watford. TL 1100

Garswood Gtr Manchester 42 B2* loc 2km W of Ashton-in-Makerfield. SJ 5599

Gartcosh S'clyde 64 D2* loc 3m/4km NW of Coatbridge. NS 6968

Garth Clwyd 41 H6 vil 3m/5km E of Llangollen. SJ 2542

Garth Gwent 15 G3* loc 3m/4km W of Newport. ST 2687

Garth Gwynedd 40 C4 loc on Menai Strait adjoining Bangor to N. SH 5873

Garth Mid Glam 14 D3 loc 1m SE of Maesteg. SS 8690

Garth Powys 25 E3 vil 6m/9km W of Builth Wells. SN 9549

Garth Powys 25 G1* loc on W side of Knighton. SO 2772

Garth Shetland 89 E7* loc in S Nesting, Mainland, 1km SE of Skellister. HU 4754

Garthamlock S'clyde 64 D2* dist of Glasgow 4m/7km E of city centre. NS 6566

Garthbrengy Powys 25 F4 ham 3m/5km N of Brecon. SO 0433

Garth Castle Tayside 75 G5/G6 cas in side valley of Keltney Burn 6m/9km W of Aberfeldy. Built in 14c by the 'Wolf of Badenoch'. NN 7650

Garthdee Grampian 77 H1* dist of Aberdeen 2m/4km SW of city centre. NJ 9103

Gartheli Dyfed 24 B3 loc 5m/9km N of Lampeter. SN 5856

Garthmyl Powys 33 H4 loc 1m S of Berriew. SO 1999

Garthmyn Gwynedd 41 E5* loc 1km NW of Capel Garmon. SH 8055

Garthorpe Humberside 50 D6 vil adjoining Fockerby to E and 7m/12km SE of Goole. SE 8419

Garthorpe Leics 36 D3 vil 6m/9km E of Melton Mowbray. SK 8320

Garth Owen Powys 33 G5* loc adjoining Newtown to S. SO 1090

Garth Penrhyncoch Dyfed 32 D6* ham 4m/7km NE of Aberystwyth. SN 6484

Garth Place Mid Glam 15 G3* loc 2m/3km E of Caerphilly. ST 1887

Garth Row Cumbria 53 E5* ham 3m/5km N of Kendal. SD 5297

Garths Cumbria 53 E5 loc 3m/4km SE of Kendal. SD 5489

Garths Voe Shetland 89 E6* inlet on E side of Sullom Voe 2m/3km W of Firths Voe on E coast of Mainland. HU 4073

Garth Trevor Clwyd 41 H6* vil 3m/4km W of Ruabon. SJ 2642

Gartly Grampian 82 D4* loc 5m/8km S of Huntly. NJ 5232

Gartmore Central 71 F5 vil 3m/4km S of Aberfoyle. NS 5297

Gartmorn Dam Central 72 C5 lake 2m/3km NE of Alloa. NS 9294

Gartocharn S'clyde 71 F6 vil 4m/6km NE of Balloch. NS 4286

Garton Humberside 51 G4 ham 3m/4km SE of Aldbrough. TA 2635

Garton End Cambs 37 G4* loc in Peterborough 2km N of city centre. TF 1900

Garton-on-the-Wolds Humberside 51 E2 vil 3m/5km NW of Gt Driffield. SE 9859

Gartymore H'land 87 C5 loc in Sutherland dist 1m SW of Helmsdale. ND 0114

Garvald Lothian 66 D2 vil 8m/12km SW of Dunbar. NT 5870

Garve H'land 80 D2 locality in Ross and Cromarty dist 10m/15km W of Dingwall. Loch G., qv, 1m SE. NH 3961

Garve Island H'land 84 D1 islet lying off Cléit Dhubh, headland on N coast of Sutherland dist 4m/7km E of Cape Wrath. Also known as An Garbh-eilean. NC 3373

Garvellachs S'clyde 69 E6 chain of small uninhabited islands at SW end of Firth of Lorn some 5m/8km W of island of Luing. See also A' Chùli, Dun Chonnuill, Eileach an Naoimh, Garbh Eileach. NM 6511

Garvellan Rocks D & G 58 B6* group of offshore rocks on W side of entrance to Fleet Bay. NX 5551

Garven. Anglicised form of the Gaelic **Garbh Bheinn,** qv.

Garvestone Norfolk 39 E4 vil 4m/7km SE of E Dereham. TG 0207

Garvock Grampian 77 G4 loc 2m/3km E of Laurencekirk. NO 7470

Garwald Water 59 G2 r in Dumfries & Galloway region running SE to the White Esk 2m/3km N of Eskdalemuir. NT 2400

Garway H & W 25 H5 vil 5m/8km SE of Pontrilas. Circular dovecote survives from Knights Templars' commandery. **G. Hill** loc 2m/3km N. **Lit Garway** loc 2km N. **G. Common** ham 1m E. SO 4522

Garwick Bay Isle of Man 46 C5 inlet of Laxey Bay 1km NW of Clay Hd. SC 4381

Garynahine W Isles 88 B2 loc near W coast of Lewis 3m/5km SE of Breasclete. NB 2331

Garyvard W Isles 88 B2* locality on S side of Loch Erisort, Lewis, 2m/3km SE of Laxay across the loch. NB 3620

Gasker W Isles (W of 88 A3) small uninhabited island 6m/10km W of Husinish Pt, W coast of Harris. **G. Beg** is rock about 1km SE. NA 8711

Gasper Wilts 9 E1* ham 3m/5km W of Mere. ST 7633

Gasstown D & G 59 E4* loc 2m/3km E of Dumfries. NX 9976

Gastard Wilts 16 D4* vil 4m/7km SW of Chippenham. ST 8868

Gasthorpe Norfolk 38 D6 ham 7m/11km E of Thetford. TL 9780

Gaston Green Essex 29 H6* ham 3m/5km S of Bishop's Stortford. TL 4917

Gatcombe Isle of Wight 10 B6 vil 3m/4km S of Newport. SZ 4885

Gateacre Merseyside 42 A3 dist of Liverpool 6m/9km E of city centre. SJ 4388

Gatebeck Cumbria 53 E6* loc 5m/8km SE of Kendal. SD 5485

Gate Burton Lincs 44 C3* ham 1km N of Marton. 18c hall with gazebo temple in park. SK 8382

Gateford Notts 44 B3 loc adjoining Worksop to N. SK 5781

Gateforth N Yorks 49 G5 vil 4m/6km SW of Selby. SE 5628

Gate Fulford N Yorks 50 B3. Alternative name for Fulford, qv. SE 6049

Gatehead S'clyde 64 B5 loc 2m/4km SW of Kilmarnock. NS 3936

Gate Helmsley N Yorks 50 C3 vil 2km W of Stamford Br. SE 6955

Gate, High W Yorks 48 C5 ham 2m/3km NW of Hebden Br. SD 9628

Gateholm Dyfed 22 A5 island off S coast of peninsula at S end of St Brides Bay, 2m/3km SE of Wooltack Pt. Accessible on foot at low tide. SM 7707

Gatehouse of Fleet D & G 58 B5/C5 small tn near mouth of Water of Fleet, 6m/10km NW of Kirkcudbright. NX 6056

Gatelawbridge D & G 59 E2 loc 2m/3km E of Thornhill. NX 9096

Gateley Norfolk 38 D2/D3 ham 4m/7km SE of Fakenham. **G. Hill** loc 1km N. TF 9624

Gate, Middle W Yorks 48 D5* loc 1km W of Liversedge. SE 1923

Gatenby N Yorks 54 C5/C6 ham 4m/6km E of Bedale. SE 3287

Gatesgarth Cumbria 52 C3* loc at SE end of Buttermere lake. NY 1915

Gateshead Tyne & Wear 61 G5 industrial tn on S bank of R Tyne opp Newcastle. Engineering, iron and steel, wire, rope, etc. NZ 2563

Gates Heath Ches 42 A5* loc 2km SE of Hatton Heath. SJ 4760

Gateside Fife 73 E4 vil 2m/3km W of Strathmiglo. NO 1809

Gateside S'clyde 64 B3 loc 1m E of Beith. NS 3855

Gathersnow Hill 65 G6* hill on border of Strathclyde and Borders regions 6m/9km S of Coulter. Height 2263 ft or 690 metres. NT 0525

Gathurst Gtr Manchester 42 B1 loc 1km S of Shevington. SD 5307

Gatley Gtr Manchester 42 D3 tn 3m/5km W of Stockport. SJ 8488

Gattonside Borders 66 C5 loc with housing development on N side of R Tweed opp Melrose. Footbridge across r. NT 5435

Gatwick Airport W Sussex. See London (Gatwick) Airport.

Gaufron Powys 25 E2 loc 2m/3km E of Rhayader. SN 9968

Gaulby Leics 36 C4 vil 7m/11km E of Leicester. SK 6900

Gauldry Fife 73 F2 vil 4m/6km SW of Newport-on-Tay. NO 3723

Gaulkthorn Lancs 48 A5* loc 2km S of Accrington. SD 7526

Gaultree Norfolk 38 A4* loc adjoining Emneth to E. TF 4907

Gaunless 54 B2 r rising 6m/9km N of Barnard Castle, Durham, and flowing E into R Wear on N side of Bishop Auckland. NZ 2130

Gauntons Bank Ches 42 B6* loc 1km E of Norbury. SJ 5647

Gaunt's Common Dorset 9 G4* loc 1m SE of Hinton Martell. SU 0205

Gaunt's Earthcott Avon 16 B3* loc 8m/13km NE of Bristol. ST 6384

Gaunt's End Essex 30 A5* loc 5m/8km NE of Bishop's Stortford. TL 5525

Gaur 75 F5 r in Tayside region running E from Loch Eigheach to head of Loch Rannoch. Gaelic form: (Abhainn) Gaoire. NN 5056

Gautby Lincs 45 F4 ham 4m/6km NE of Bardney. TF 1772

Gavinton Borders 67 E3 vil 2m/3km SW of Duns. NT 7652

Gawber S Yorks 43 G1* loc 2km NW of Barnsley. SE 3207

Gawcott Bucks 28 B4 vil 2km SW of Buckingham. SP 6831

Gawsworth Ches 42 D4 ham 3m/5km SW of Macclesfield. SJ 8969

Gawthorpe W Yorks 48 D6* loc 3m/4km E of Huddersfield. SE 1816

Gawthorpe W Yorks 49 E5* loc 2km E of Dewsbury tn centre. SE 2621

Gawthorpe Hall Lancs 48 B4* early 16c hse on E side of Padiham. SD 8034

Gawthrop Cumbria 53 F6 ham 1m W of Dent. SD 6987

Gawthwaite Cumbria 52 C6 ham 3m/4km NW of Penny Br. SD 2784

Gay Bowers Essex 20 D2* loc 4m/7km W of Maldon. TL 7904

Gaydon Warwicks 27 G2 vil 10m/16km NW of Banbury. Airfield to W. SP 3654

Gayhurst Bucks 28 D3 vil 3m/4km NW of Newport Pagnell. SP 8546

Gayle N Yorks 53 G5 vil just S of Hawes. SD 8789

Gayles N Yorks 54 A4 vil 5m/8km NW of Richmond. NZ 1207

Gay Street W Sussex 11 G3* loc 3m/4km NE of Pulborough. TQ 0820

Gayton Merseyside 41 H3 loc adjoining Heswall to S. SJ 2780

Gayton Norfolk 38 C3 vil 7m/11km E of King's Lynn. Site of Roman bldg 1km N. **G. Thorpe** ham 2km SE. TF 7219

Gayton Northants 28 C2 vil 4m/6km N of Towcester. Site of Roman bldg to SE. SP 7054

Gayton Staffs 35 F2 vil 5m/8km NE of Stafford. SJ 9828

Gayton Engine Lincs 45 H3* loc 1km W of Theddlethorpe All Saints. TF 4588

Gayton le Marsh Lincs 45 G3 vil 6m/9km N of Alford. TF 4284

Gayton le Wold Lincs 45 F3 loc 6m/9km W of Louth. TF 2386

Gazeley Suffolk 30 C2 vil 5m/8km E of Newmarket. TL 7264

Geal Charn H'land 75 E2* mt on Corrieyairack Forest on border of Inverness and Badenoch & Strathspey dists 8m/12km SE of Fort Augustus. Height 2838 ft or 865 metres. NN 4498

Geal Charn H'land 75 F2 mt in Monadhliath range in Badenoch and Strathspey dist 4m/7km NW of Laggan Br. NH 5698

Geal-chàrn H'land 75 F3 mt in Badenoch and Strathspey dist, on E side of Loch Ericht and 5m/8km S of Dalwhinnie. Height 3005 ft or 916 metres. NN 5978

Geal Charn H'land 75 F3 mt on Ardverikie Forest in Badenoch and Strathspey dist, 4m/6km E of SW end of Loch Laggan. Height 3443 ft or 1049 metres. NN 5081

Geal Chàrn H'land 82 A5 mt in Badenoch and Strathspey dist 8m/12km SE of Nethy Br. Height 2692 ft or 821 metres. NJ 0912

Geal Chàrn Tayside 75 G5 mt 3m/5km SE of Kinloch Rannoch. Height 2593 ft or 790 metres. NN 6854

Geal-charn Mór H'land 81 G6 mt in Badenoch and Strathspey dist 4m/6km W of Aviemore. Height 2702 ft or 824 metres. NH 8312

Geal Loch S'clyde 71 E3* small loch on E side of R Falloch near head of Loch Lomond. NN 3116

Gearran Island H'land 78 B2 one of a group of islets 3m/5km NW of Rubha Hunish at northern tip of Skye. See also Gaeilavore I. and Lord Macdonald's Table. NG 3679

Gearr Aonach H'land. See Three Sisters of Glen Coe.

Gear Sands Cornwall 2 C3* sand dunes behind Perran Beach N of Perranporth. Holiday camps. SW 7655

Geary H'land 78 A3 locality on Skye on W side of Loch Snizort, 4m/6km SE of Vaternish Pt. NG 2661

Gedding Suffolk 30 D2 vil 7m/12km SE of Bury St Edmunds. TL 9557

Geddington Northants 36 D6 vil 3m/5km NE of Kettering. In vil square, one of three remaining Eleanor crosses (A.M.); others at Hardingstone and Waltham Cross. To NE, wooded area of **G. Chase.** SP 8983

Gedgrave Suffolk 31 G3 loc 2km SW of Orford. TM 4048

Gedintailor Skye, H'land 79 D5* locality on E coast 5m/8km SE of Loch Portree. NG 5235

Gedling Notts 36 C1 urban loc adjoining Carlton to N. SK 6142

Gedling 117 admin dist of Notts.

Gedney Lincs 37 H2 vil 3m/5km E of Holbeach. **G. Broadgate** ham 1m S. **G. Dyke** ham 2km N. TF 4024

Gedney Drove End Lincs 38 A2 vil 5m/7km NE of Long Sutton. TF 4629

Gedney Hill Lincs 37 H3 vil 6m/10km E of Crowland. TF 3311

Gee Cross Gtr Manchester 43 E2 loc 2km SE of Hyde. SJ 9593

Geedon Creek Essex 31 E6* inlet of R Colne near its mouth, 6m/9km SE of Colchester. To N of creek are **Geedon Saltings.** TM 0417

Gefeiliau Brook 41 H6* stream running N into R Clywedog on S side of Wrexham, Clwyd. SJ 3448

Geilston S'clyde 64 B2* loc adjoining Cardross to N. NS 3478

Geirinish, West W Isles 88 E2* vil towards N end of S Uist, on S side of Loch Bee. Locality of **E Geirinish** 4m/7km E. NF 7741

Gelder Burn 76 C2 stream in Grampian region running N down Glen Gelder to R Dee 1m SW of Balmoral Castle. NO 2494

Geldeston Norfolk 39 G5 vil 3m/4km NW of Beccles. TM 3971

Geldie Burn 76 B2 r in Grampian region running E to R Dee 4m/6km W of Inverey. NO 0288

Gelli Mid Glam 15 E2* loc on S side of Rhondda. SS 9794

Gellideg Mid Glam 15 E1* loc 2km W of Merthyr Tydfil. SO 0207

Gelligaer Mid Glam 15 F2 loc in coal-mining area 6m/10km N of Caerphilly. Remains of small Roman fort of early 2c. ST 1396

Gelligroes Gwent 15 F2* loc 2m/3km S of Blackwood. ST 1794

Gelli-haf Mid Glam 15 F2* loc 1km E of Hengoed across Rhymney Valley. ST 1695

Gellilydan Gwynedd 32 D1* vil 2km E of Maentwrog. SH 6839

Gellinudd W Glam 14 C2* vil 1m E of Pontardawe. SN 7304

Gelli-wen Dyfed 23 E3 ham 5m/7km N of St Clears. SN 2723

Gelli, Y Welsh form of Hay-on-Wye, qv.

Gelly (Gelli) Dyfed 22 C4 loc 4m/6km NW of Narberth. SN 0819

Gelston D & G 58 D5 vil 2m/4km S of Castle Douglas. NX 7758

Gelston Lincs 44 D6 ham 6m/10km N of Grantham. SK 9145

Gelt 60 B5 r rising on Geltsdale, Cumbria, close to Northumbrian border, and flowing NW into R Irthing 3m/4km W of Brampton. NY 4959
Geltbridge Cumbria 60 B5* loc on R Gelt 2km SW of Brampton. NY 5159
Geltsdale Cumbria 60 B6 moorland area E and NE of Cumrew, its full name being King's Forest of Geltsdale. NY 5852
Gelyn 33 E1 stream running SE into N end of Llyn Celyn, Gwynedd. SH 8441
Gembling Humberside 51 F3 ham 6m/9km E of Gt Driffield. TA 1057
Gendros W Glam 23 G6* loc in Swansea 2m/3km NW of tn centre. SS 6395
General Wade's Military Road H'land 74, 75 rd built in 18c and traversing part of the Highlands of Scotland, by Glen More, Fort Augustus, and Corrieyairack Pass, with the object of facilitating the subjugation of the Highlanders after the Jacobite rising of 1715.
Gentlemen's Cave Orkney 89 B5* cave on W coast of island of Westray 1m SE of Noup Hd. Formerly haunt of Jacobites. HY 3948
Gentleshaw Staffs 35 F3 vil 5m/7km E of Cannock. SK 0512
George Green Bucks 19 E3 vil 2m/3km NE of Slough. TQ 0081
Georgeham Devon 6 D2 vil 6m/10km SW of Ilfracombe. SS 4639
George Nympton Devon 7 E3 vil 2m/3km SW of S Molton. SS 7023
Georgetown Gwent 15 F1 loc 1km SE of Tredegar. SO 1408
Georth Orkney 89 B6* loc on Mainland 2m/3km NW of Woodwick. Also known as Evie. HY 3625
Gerard's Bridge Merseyside 42 B2* loc in St Helens 1km NE of tn centre. SJ 5196
Gerlan Gwynedd 40 C4 loc adjoining Bethesda to E. SH 6366
Germansweek Devon 6 C5 vil 9m/15km W of Okehampton. SX 4394
Germoe Cornwall 2 B5 vil 5m/8km W of Helston. SW 5829
Gerniog 33 F4* stream running NE into R Garno at Carno, Powys. SN 9696
Gerrans Cornwall 2 D4* vil on W side of G. Bay adjoining Porthscatho on inland side. SW 8735
Gerrans Bay Cornwall 2 D4, 3 E4 bay on S coast extending from Portscatho eastwards to Nare Hd. SW 9037
Gerrards Cross Bucks 19 E3 suburban loc 4m/7km NW of Uxbridge. TQ 0088
Geshader W Isles 88 A2* loc in W part of Lewis 3m/5km SE of Miavaig. NB 1131
Gestingthorpe Essex 30 C4 vil 4m/7km SW of Sudbury. Site of Roman bldg 1m E. TL 8138
Geuffordd Powys 33 H3 ham 4m/7km N of Welshpool. SJ 2114
Geur Rubha Skye, H'land 79 D7 headland on SW coast of Sleat peninsula 2km N of Pt of Sleat. NG 5501
Ghyllgrove Essex 20 D3* dist of Basildon to N of tn centre. TQ 7089
Gibbet Hill Som 16 C6* W dist of Frome. ST 7647
Gibbet Hill Surrey 11 E2* summit of NT property near Hindhead, overlooking Devil's Punch Bowl. Name refers to murder of a sailor hereabouts in 1786 and fate of the murderers. SU 8935
Gibdale Point Calf of Man 46 A6* headland on N coast of island. SC 1566
Gib Heath W Midlands 35 F5* loc in Birmingham 2km NW of city centre. SP 0588
Gib Hill Ches 42 C3* loc 2km NW of Gt Budworth. SJ 6478
Gibraltar Beds 29 E3* loc 3m/5km SW of Bedford. TL 0046
Gibraltar Lincs 45 H3 S dist of Mablethorpe. TF 5184
Gibraltar Suffolk 31 F3* loc 6m/10km NW of Woodbridge. TM 1954
Gibraltar Point Lincs 45 H5 headland 4m/6km S of Skegness. Nature reserve to N. TF 5657
Gidcott, Higher Devon 6 C4* ham 5m/9km NE of Holsworthy. SS 4009
Giddeahall Wilts 16 D4* loc 4m/6km W of Chippenham. ST 8574
Gidding, Great Cambs 37 F6 vil 5m/8km SW of Stilton. WT stn on E side of vil. TL 1183
Gidding, Little Cambs 37 F6 loc 5m/8km SW of Stilton. TL 1281
Giddy Green Dorset 9 F5* loc 1m W of Wool. SY 8386
Gidea Park London 20 B3 dist of Romford 1m NE of tn centre, borough of Havering. TQ 5290
Gidleigh Devon 7 E6 ham on E edge of Dartmoor 5m/9km NW of Moretonhampstead. SX 6788
Giffnock S'clyde 64 C3 suburb 5m/8km S of Glasgow. NS 5659
Gifford Lothian 66 C2 vil 4m/6km S of Haddington. 1m SE is Yester Hse, 18c mansion, seat of Marquess of Tweeddale, beyond which are ruins of 13c Yester Castle. NT 5368
Giffordtown Fife 73 F3* loc 1m NW of Ladybank. NO 2811
Gigg Gtr Manchester 42 D1* loc in Bury 1m SE of tn centre. SD 8109
Giggleswick N Yorks 48 B2 vil 1km W of Settle across R Ribble. **G. Scar** limestone cliff 2km NW. SD 8164
Gigha S'clyde 62 D3 narrow island of 9 sq miles or 23 sq km, 6m/10km long N to S, lying about 2m/3km off W coast of Kintyre, Argyll, opp Rhunahaorine Pt. Dairy farming, fishing. See also Sound of G. NR 6449
Gight Castle Grampian 83 F3 ruined cas beside left bank of R Ythan, 4m/6km E of Fyvie. NJ 8239
Gigmill W Midlands 35 E5* loc in Stourbridge 1km W of tn centre. SO 8983
Gigolum Island S'clyde 62 D3 small island lying to E of S end of Gigha. NR 6445
Gilbent Gtr Manchester 42 D3* loc 2m/3km W of Bramhall. SJ 8684
Gilberdyke Humberside 50 D5 vil 5m/8km E of Howden. SE 8329
Gilbert's End H & W 26 C3/D3* loc 3m/5km E of Malvern Wells. SO 8242
Gilbertstone W Midlands 35 G5* loc in Birmingham 5m/7km SE of city centre. SP 1384
Gilbert Street Hants 10 D2* loc 1km NE of Ropley and 4m/7km E of New Alresford. SU 6532
Gilchriston Lothian 66 C2* loc 2m/3km S of E Saltoun. NT 4865
Gilcrux Cumbria 52 B2 vil 3m/5km SW of Aspatria. NY 1138
Gilderdale Burn 53 F1* stream rising on **Gilderdale Forest,** wild moorland area W of Alston, Cumbria, and flowing NE into R South Tyne 2m/3km N of Alston. Lower reaches form boundary between Cumbria and Nthmb. NY 7048
Gildersome W Yorks 49 E5 vil 2km NW of Morley. **G. Street** loc 1km to S. SE 2429
Gildingwells S Yorks 44 A3 vil 4m/6km NW of Worksop. SK 5585
Gilesgate Moor Durham 54 C1 suburb adjoining Durham to E. NZ 2942
Gileston (Silstwn) S Glam 15 E4 vil 3m/5km E of Llantwit Major. ST 0167
Gilfach Mid Glam 15 F2 vil adjoining Bargoed to S. ST 1598
Gilfach Goch Mid Glam 15 E3 vil 2m/3km NW of Tonyrefail. SS 9889
Gilfachrheda Dyfed 24 A2* ham 2m/3km SE of Newquay. SN 4058
Gilkicker Point Hants 10 C5 headland at E end of Solent 1m S of Alverstoke. SZ 6097
Gill Cumbria 52 D2* loc 1m SE of Greystoke. NY 4429
Gillamoor N Yorks 55 E5 vil 2m/4km N of Kirkbymoorside. SE 6890
Gillan Cornwall 2 D5* vil on S side of **G. Harbour** at mouth of r running down to Dennis Hd, 8m/12km E of Helston. SW 7825
Gillar's Green Merseyside 42 A2* loc 2m/4km W of St Helens. SJ 4794
Gill Burn H'land 86 F1 r in NE corner of Caithness dist rising near Brabstermire and running E into Freswick Bay 4m/6km S of John o' Groats. ND 3767
Gillerthwaite Cumbria 52 B3* loc 1m E of E end of Ennerdale Water. NY 1414
Gillibrands Lancs 42 A1* industrial estate in SW part of Skelmersdale. SD 4705
Gilling East N Yorks 50 B1 vil 2m/3km S of Oswaldkirk. **Gilling Castle,** 14c–18c hse now preparatory school for Ampleforth College; see Ampleforth. SE 6176
Gillingham Dorset 9 E2 industrial tn on R Stour 4m/7km NW of Shaftesbury. ST 8026
Gillingham Kent 20 D5 large industrial tn adjoining Chatham to E, 30m/48km E of London. TQ 7767
Gillingham Norfolk 39 G5 vil 1m NW of Beccles. TM 4191
Gilling West N Yorks 54 B4 vil 3m/4km N of Richmond. NZ 1805
Gill, Low Cumbria 53 E5/F5* loc 4m/6km NW of Sedbergh. SD 6297
Gillow Heath Staffs 42 D5 loc 1m N of Biddulph. SJ 8858
Gills H'land 86 F1 loc near N coast of Caithness dist 2m/3km S of St John's Pt. **Upr Gills** loc 1km S. **G. Bay** to NE. ND 3272
Gill's Green Kent 12 D4 loc 1m N of Hawkhurst. TQ 7532
Gilman Point Dyfed 22 D5* headland at W end of Pendine Sands 1km SW of Pendine. SN 2207
Gilmerton Lothian 66 B2 dist of Edinburgh 4m/7km SE of city centre. NT 2968
Gilmerton Tayside 72 C2 vil 2m/3km NE of Crieff. NN 8823
Gilmonby Durham 53 H3 ham on S side of Bowes across R Greta. NY 9913
Gilmorton Leics 36 B5 vil 3m/5km NE of Lutterworth. SP 5787
Gilpin 52 D6/53 E6* r rising 2m/3km SE of Windermere tn, Cumbria, and flowing S into R Kent 2km SW of Levens. SD 4784
Gilroyd S Yorks 43 G1* loc in Barnsley 2m/3km SW of tn centre. SE 3204
Gilsay W Isles 88 A4* small uninhabited island in Sound of Harris 2m/3km SW of Renish Pt. NG 0279
Gilslake Avon 16 B3* loc 2m/3km SE of Severn Beach. ST 5683
Gilsland Nthmb 60 C4 vil on R Irthing on Cumbrian border 5m/8km W of Haltwhistle. NY 6366
Gilson Warwicks 35 G5 loc 1m NW of Coleshill. SP 1890
Gilstead W Yorks 48 D4 loc on E side of Bingley. SE 1239
Gilston Herts 20 B1 loc 3m/4km W of Sawbridgeworth. TL 4413
Giltar Point Dyfed 22 D5 headland 2km S of Tenby opp Caldy I. SS 1298
Giltbrook Notts 44 A6* loc adjoining Eastwood to SE. SK 4845
Gilver's Lane H & W 26 C3* loc 3m/4km E of Malvern Wells. SO 8141
Gilwern Gwent 25 G6 vil 3m/5km W of Abergavenny. SO 2414
Gimingham Norfolk 39 G2 vil 4m/7km N of N Walsham. TG 2836
Ginclough Ches 43 E3* loc 3m/5km NE of Macclesfield. SJ 9576
Ginge, East Oxon 17 H3* loc 3m/5km E of Wantage. SU 4486
Ginger's Green E Sussex 12 C5* loc 3m/5km NE of Hailsham. TQ 6212
Ginge, West Oxon 17 H3* loc 3m/5km E of Wantage. SU 4486
Gin Pit Gtr Manchester 42 C2* loc 1km S of Tyldesley. SD 6801
Ginst Point Dyfed 23 E5 headland at mouth of R Taf estuary 2m/4km SE of Laugharne. SN 3208
Gipping Suffolk 31 E2 vil near source of R Gipping and 3m/5km NE of Stowmarket. TM 0763
Gipping 31 F4 r rising some 5m/8km NE of Stowmarket, Suffolk, and flowing S to Ipswich, where it forms estuary known as R Orwell, qv. TM 1544
Gipsey Bridge Lincs 45 F6* ham 5m/7km NW of Boston. TF 2849
Gipton W Yorks 49 E4* loc in Harehills dist of Leeds. SE 3335
Gighay W Isles 88 E3* uninhabited island at S end of Sound of Barra and 4m/6km E of Northbay Airfield, Barra. NF 7604
Girdle Ness Grampian 77 H1* headland with lighthouse 2m/3km E of Aberdeen city centre across R Dee. NJ 9705
Girdle Toll S'clyde 64 B5 loc in Irvine New Tn, NE of tn centre. NS 3440
Girlington W Yorks 48 D4* loc in Bradford 2m/3km NW of city centre. SE 1334
Girlsta Shetland 89 E7 locality on E coast of Mainland at S end of deep freshwater **Loch of G.,** 6m/10km N of Lerwick. HU 4350
Girnock Burn 76 D2 stream in Grampian region running N down Glen Girnock to R Dee 3m/4km W of Ballater. NO 3396
Girsby N Yorks 54 C4 ham on R Tees 5m/8km SW of Yarm. NZ 3508
Girtford Beds 29 F3 loc adjoining Sandy to NW. TL 1649
Girthon D & G 58 C6 loc 2m/3km S of Gatehouse of Fleet. NX 6053
Girton Cambs 29 H2 suburb 3m/5km NW of Cambridge. **G. College,** women's college of Cambridge University, 1m S. TL 4262
Girton Notts 44 C4 vil 8m/13km N of Newark-on-Trent. SK 8266
Girvan S'clyde 56 B4 fishing tn and resort at mouth of Water of Girvan, qv, 17m/28km SW of Ayr. Other industries include alginate processing, boat-building, distilling, mnfre of tweeds and hosiery goods. NX 1897
Gisburn Lancs 48 B3 vil 7m/11km NE of Clitheroe. **G. Cotes** loc 2m/3km W. **G. Forest,** former hunting ground now largely planted with conifers, lies 7m/11km NW, on E side of Forest of Bowland. SD 8248
Gisleham Suffolk 39 H6 ham 4m/6km SW of Lowestoft. TM 5188
Gislingham Suffolk 31 E1 vil 6m/10km SW of Diss. TM 0771
Gissing Norfolk 39 E6 vil 4m/6km NE of Diss. TM 1485
Gittisham Devon 7 H5 vil 2m/3km SW of Honiton. SY 1398
Givendale N Yorks 49 E2* loc 2m/3km SE of Ripon across R Ure. SE 3369
Givendale, Great Humberside 50 C3 ham 3m/5km N of Pocklington. SE 8153
Gladestry (Llanfair Llythynwg) Powys 25 G3 vil 4m/6km W of Kington. SO 2355
Gladhouse Reservoir Lothian 66 B3 large resr 5m/8km SE of Penicuik. NT 2953
Gladsmuir Lothian 66 C2 vil 4m/6km W of Haddington. NT 4573
Glais W Glam 23 H5 loc 1km SE of Clydach across R Tawe. SS 7000
Glaisdale N Yorks 55 F4 vil 2m/4km W of Egton. NZ 7705
Glamaig Skye, H'land 79 D5 mt 2m/3km E of Sligachan. Height 2542 ft or 775 metres. NG 5130
Glamis Tayside 73 F1 vil 10m/16km N of Dundee. Angus Folk Museum (NTS). 1m N is **G. Castle,** mainly 17c but with parts of much earlier date; birthplace of Princess Margaret, 1930. NO 3846
Glamorgan, Mid 118 small county of S Wales, bounded by Gwent, S and W Glamorgan, Powys, and the sea. It comprises the greater part of the S Wales coalfield, and is largely industrial. The county is hilly, and the mining tns and vils spread along steep narrow valleys often dominated by large slag heaps, and interspersed with strips of bare upland.
Glamorgan, South 118 small county of S Wales, bounded by Mid Glamorgan, Gwent, and the sea, and largely comprising the industrial areas radiating from Cardiff. There are large docks at Cardiff and Barry. Industries in the county include coal-mining, iron and steel, and oil-refining. Chief tns are the city and county tn of Cardiff, Barry, Cowbridge, and Penarth.
Glamorgan, West 118 small county of S Wales, bounded by Powys, Mid Glamorgan, Dyfed, and the sea. It is highly industrial, coal, steel, tinplating, and oil-refining being the principal industries. Except along the coast the county is hilly, tns and factories being enclosed in steep narrow valleys. The Gower peninsula, in the extreme SW, is an area of unspoilt natural beauty, much of it NT property. Chief tns are Swansea, the county tn; Neath, and Port Talbot.
Glanaber Terrace Gwynedd 40 D6* loc 3m/5km E of Blaenau Ffestiniog. SH 7547
Glanaman Dyfed 23 G4/H4 tn on edge of S Wales coalfield 3m/5km E of Ammanford. SN 6713
Glanarberth Dyfed 22 D2*loc adjoining Llechryd to E. SN 2243
Glan-bad Welsh form of Upr Boat. See Boat, Upper.
Glan-Denys Dyfed 24 B3* loc 2m/3km N of Lampeter. SN 5750
Glandford Norfolk 39 E1 vil 3m/5km NW of Holt. Museum of shells. TG 0441
Glan-Duar Dyfed 24 B4* loc adjoining Llanybydder to E. SN 5243
Glandwr Dyfed 22 D3 ham 8m/12km N of Whitland. SN 1928
Glandwr Gwent 15 G2 loc 1m W of Llanhilleth. SO 2001
Glan Dwyfach Gwynedd 32 C1* loc in R Dwyfach valley 4m/6km N of Criccieth. SH 4843
Glan-fechan Gwynedd 33 E4* loc 1m N of Machynlleth across R Dovey. SH 7502
Glanford 117 admin dist of Humberside.
Glangrwyne Powys 25 G6 loc 2m/3km SE of Crickhowell. SO 2316

Glan-llyn Mid Glam 15 F3 loc 6m/9km NW of Cardiff. ST 1283
Glanllynfi Mid Glam 14 D3 loc on E side of Maesteg. SS 8691
Glanmerin Lake Powys 33 E4* lake 2km SE of Machynlleth. SN 7599
Glanmule Powys 33 H5* loc 4m/6km E of Newtown. SO 1690
Glannaventa Cumbria. See Ravenglass.
Glanrhyd Dyfed 22 D2 loc 3m/5km SW of Cardigan. SN 1442
Glan-rhyd Powys 14 D1* loc 1km E of Ystalyfera. SN 7809
Glanton Nthmb 61 F1 vil 2m/3km N of Whittingham. **G. Pike** loc 1m W. NU 0714
Glanvilles Wootton Dorset 9 E3 vil 6m/9km SE of Sherborne. ST 6708
Glanwydden Gwynedd 41 E3* loc 2m/3km S of Lit Ormes Hd. SH 8180
Glan-y-don Clwyd 41 G3* vil 1km SE of Mostyn. SJ 1679
Glan-y-nant Powys 33 F5* loc 2km W of Llanidloes. SN 9384
Glan-yr-afon Gwynedd 33 G1* loc 3m/5km W of Corwen. SJ 0242
Glan-yr-afon Gwynedd 40 C3* loc on Anglesey 3m/5km N of Beaumaris. SH 6080
Glanywern Dyfed 32 D5* loc 1m SE of Borth. SN 6188
Glapthorn Northants 37 E5 vil 2m/3km NW of Oundle. Site of Roman villa 1km E. TL 0290
Glapwell Derbys 44 A4* vil 3m/5km S of Bolsover. SK 4766
Glas Bheinn H'land 74 D5 mt in Lochaber dist 2km E of Loch Eilde Mór. Height 2587 ft or 789 metres. NN 2564
Glas Bheinn Mhór S'clyde 70 D1 mt in Argyll 3m/5km SE of head of Loch Etive. Height 3277 ft or 999 metres. NN 1542
Glas Bheinn Mór Skye, H'land 79 D6 mt 1m SE of head of Loch Ainort. Height 1852 ft or 564 metres. NG 5525
Glasbury (Clas-ar-Wy, Y) Powys 25 F4 vil on R Wye 4m/6km SW of Hay-on-Wye. SO 1739
Glascarnoch H'land 84 D8* r in Ross and Cromarty dist running E from Loch G. to join Strath Rannoch at Inchbae Lodge. NH 3969
Glasclune Castle Tayside 73 E1 remains of former stronghold of the Blairs, 2m/3km NW of Blairglowrie. NO 1547
Glascoed Clwyd 41 F4* loc 3m/5km W of St Asaph. SH 9973
Glascoed Clwyd 41 H5* loc 5m/7km NW of Wrexham. SJ 2754
Glascoed (Glasgoed) Gwent 15 H2 loc 3m/5km W of Usk. SO 3301
Glascote Staffs 35 H4 loc in Tamworth 1m SE of tn centre. **G. Heath** loc 1km SE. SK 2203
Glascwm. Alternative spelling of Glasgwm, qv.
Glas Eilean H'land 79 F6 islet in Loch Alsh, Skye and Lochalsh dist, 2m/4km W of Dornie. NG 8425
Glas Eilean S'clyde 62 C2 islet off SW shore of Jura 3m/4km S of Feolin Ferry. NR 4465
Glas Eileanan S'clyde 68 E4* twin islets, the more easterly having a lighthouse, in Sound of Mull 2m/3km E of Scallastle Bay. NM 7139
Glasfryn Clwyd 41 E6 ham 2m/4km NW of Cerrigydrudion. SH 9150
Glasgoed Welsh form of Glascoed, qv.
Glasgow S'clyde 64 C2-D3 city, port, and commercial, industrial, and cultural centre on R Clyde 41m/66km W of Edinburgh and 346m/557km NW of London. Cathedral dates mainly from 13c. G. University on N side of Kelvingrove Park, 2km W of city centre. University of Strathclyde in central area. Industries include shipbuilding, textiles, engineering, and a large variety of light industries. Airport at Abbotsinch, 7m/11km W. NS 5965
Glasgwm (or Glascwm) Powys 25 F3 ham 8m/12km E of Builth Wells. SO 1553
Glasinfryn Gwynedd 40 C4 vil 2m/3km S of Bangor. SH 5868
Glas-leac Beag H'land 85 A6* small uninhabited island, outlier of the Summer Isles group, 6m/9km NE of Greenstone Pt on W coast of Ross and Cromarty dist. NB 9205
Glas-leac Mór H'land 85 A6 one of the Summer Isles, qv. Lies nearly 2m/3km off NW coast of Ross and Cromarty dist near Polbain. Area about 150 acres or 60 hectares. NB 9509
Glasllwch Gwent 15 G3* loc 2km W of Newport. ST 2887
Glaslyn Gwynedd 40 C5 tarn below summit of Snowdon to E. SH 6154
Glaslyn Powys 33 E5 lake 4m/6km SW of Pennant. SN 8294
Glaslyn 32 C1/D1 r in Gwynedd rising on E side of Snowdon summit and running E through Llyn Glaslyn and Llyn Llydaw, then SE through Llyn Gwynant to Beddgelert, then S through Pass of Aberglaslyn to Portmadoc, then SW into Tremadoc Bay off Harlech Pt. SH 5434
Glas Maol Tayside 76 C3 mt 6m/9km NE of Spittal of Glenshee. Height 3502 ft or 1068 metres. NO 1676
Glas Meall Mór Tayside 75 G3 mt 6m/9km SE of Dalwhinnie. Height 3037 ft or 926 metres. **Glas Meall Bheag** 1m SW; height 2859 ft or 871 metres. NN 6876
Glasnacardoch H'land 68 E1 locality on N side of Loch Ailort, on peninsula of Ardnish in Lochaber dist, 1m E of Rubha Chaolais. NM 7080
Glasnacardoch H'land 79 E8 loc on coast of Lochaber dist 1km S of Mallaig, on **G. Bay.** NM 6795
Glasnakille Skye, H'land 79 D7 locality on E side of Strathaird peninsula 2km N of Strathaird Pt. Spar Cave on shore of Loch Slapin here. NG 5313
Glaspwll Powys 33 E4 loc 2m/3km S of Machynlleth. SN 7397
Glass H'land 80 D3 r in Inverness dist running NE down Strathglass to join R Farrar 1km SE of Struy Br. NH 4039
Glass H'land 81 F1 r in Ross and Cromarty dist running SE from Loch Glass to Cromarty Firth E of Evanton. NH 6265
Glass 46 B5* r on Isle of Man rising on central mts and flowing S to join R Dhoo on W side of Douglas, whence the combined stream continues along S side of tn into Douglas harbour. SC 3875
Glassenbury Kent 12 D3 loc 2m/3km W of Goudhurst. **G. Park** is a moated 15c manor hse. TQ 7536
Glasserton D & G 57 D8 loc 2m/3km SW of Whithorn. NX 4238
Glassford S'clyde 64 D4 vil 2m/4km NE of Strathaven. NS 7247
Glass Houghton W Yorks 49 F5 loc 1m SE of Castleford. SE 4424
Glasshouse Glos 26 C5* ham 3m/5km S of Newent. SO 7021
Glasshouse Hill Glos 26 C5 loc 4m/6km S of Newent. SO 7020
Glasshouses N Yorks 48 D2 vil 2km SE of Pateley Br. SE 1764
Glasson Cumbria 59 G5 vil on line of Hadrian's Wall 2km SE of Port Carlisle. NY 2560
Glasson Lancs 47 E3 vil on left bank of R Lune estuary 4m/6km SW of Lancaster. Lighthouse. SD 4456
Glassonby Cumbria 53 E1 vil 7m/11km NE of Penrith. NY 5738
Glaston Leics 36 D4 vil 2m/3km E of Uppingham. SK 8900
Glastonbury Som 8 C1 tn 13m/21km E of Bridgwater. Ancient centre of Christian culture and pilgrimage; also Arthurian legends. Remains of 13c abbey. Tribunal Hse (A.M.). To E, **G. Tor** (NT), conical hill topped by ruined ch. ST 5039
Glas Tulaichean Tayside 76 B3 mt 5m/8km NW of Spittal of Glenshee. Height 3449 ft or 1051 metres. NO 0576
Glasven. Anglicised form of the Gaelic **Glas Bheinn,** qv.
Glatton Cambs 37 F5 vil 2m/4km S of Stilton. TL 1586
Glaven 39 E1 r rising N of Baconsthorpe, Norfolk, and flowing in a southward loop by Hunworth to Letheringsett, then N by Glandford to North Sea 1m N of Cley. TG 0445
Glazebrook Ches 42 C2* loc 1km NW of Cadishead. SJ 6992
Glaze Brook 4 D4* stream in Devon rising on Dartmoor and flowing SE into R Avon 1m S of S Brent. Nature reserve N of Cheston. SX 6958
Glazebury Ches 42 C2 vil 2m/3km SE of Leigh. SJ 6797
Glazeley Salop 34 D5 vil 3m/5km S of Bridgnorth. SO 7088
Gleadless S Yorks 43 H3 loc in Sheffield 3m/4km SE of city centre. **G. Townend** loc adjoining to E. SK 3783
Gleadmoss Ches 42 D4* loc 2m/3km W of Marton. SJ 8268
Gleann an Dubh-lochain H'land 79 F7* upper valley of Inverie R in Knoydart, Lochaber dist, containing Loch an Dubh-lochain. NG 8100
Gleann Beag H'land 79 F6 valley of Amhainn a' Ghlinne Bhig in Lochaber dist, running W into Sound of Sleat 1m SW of Glenelg, qv. NG 8018
Gleann Chomraidh Tayside 75 E5, F5* valley of Allt Chomraidh running NE to R Gaur above Loch Rannoch. NN 4955
Gleann Da-Eig Tayside 71 G1* valley of Allt Gleann Da-Eig, running N into R Lyon 2m/4km E of Br of Balgie. NN 6045
Gleann Domhain S'clyde 70 A4, B4 valley of Barbreck R in Argyll running SW to head of Loch Craignish. NM 8508
Gleann Duibhe Tayside 75 E5 valley of Abhainn Duibhe running NE to R Gaur below Loch Eigheach. NN 4555
Gleann Fearnach Tayside 76 B4 valley of Allt Fearnach running S to head of Strath Ardle. NO 0468
Gleann Geal H'land 68 E4 valley of Amhainn a' Ghlinne in Lochaber dist, running W to R Aline 4m/6km N of Lochaline. NM 7250
Gleann Goibhre H'land 80 D3 valley of Allt Goibhre, qv. Upper part marks boundary between dists of Inverness and Ross & Cromarty. NH 4248
Gleann Lichd H'land 80 A5* upper valley of R Croe in Kintail Forest (NTS), Skye and Lochalsh dist. NG 9818
Gleann Mór Tayside 75 G5. See Keltney Burn.
Gleann na Ghuiserein H'land. See Glen Guseran.
Gleann Oraid Skye, H'land 79 B6 valley of R Talisker running down to Talisker Bay on W coast. NG 3230
Gleann Salach S'clyde 70 B1* valley of Dearg Abhainn in Argyll, running NW to Loch Creran 2m/3km SW of Dallachoilish. NM 9739
Gleaston Cumbria 46 D1 vil 3m/4km SE of Dalton-in-Furness. Remains of medieval Gleaston Castle 1km NE. SD 2570
Glebe Tyne & Wear 61 G5* dist of Washington to E of tn centre. NZ 3056
Gledfield, Lower H'land 85 F7 loc in Sutherland dist 1m W of Bonar Br. NH 5990
Gledhow W Yorks 49 E4 dist of Leeds 2m/4km NE of city centre. SE 3137
Glem 30 D3 r rising SW of Stradishall, Suffolk, and flowing E then S into R Stour 2km W of Long Melford. TL 8446
Glemham, Great Suffolk 31 G2 vil 3m/5km W of Saxmundham. Vil of **Lit Glemham** 2m/4km S, with **Lit Glemham Hall** in park on E side of A12 rd. TM 3461
Glemsford Suffolk 30 C3 vil 3m/4km NW of Long Melford. TL 8348
Glen 37 G2 r rising near Old Somerby, Lincs, and flowing S past Essendine, then NE through Greatford and across Fens to join R Welland 5m/8km NE of Spalding. TF 2829
Glen 67 F5 r rising as Bowmont Water in Scotland near English border SW of the Cheviot and flowing by Town Yetholm and Mindrum to its confluence with College Burn at Westnewton, Nthmb, whence it continues as R Glen to its confluence with R Till 2km W of Doddington, Nthmb. NT 9732
Glenacardoch Point S'clyde 62 D4 headland on W coast of Kintyre 2km NW of Glenbarr. NR 6538
Glen Affric H'land 80 C5 valley of R Affric in Inverness dist. **Glenaffric Forest** is deer forest astride upper reaches of r. NH 1922
Glenaladale H'land 74 A4 r in Lochaber dist running S to Loch Shiel 7m/11km from Glenfinnan. N1 8274
Glen Albyn H'land. See Glen More.
Glen Aldie H'land 87 A8, B8 valley of **Aldie Water,** stream in Ross and Cromarty dist running down to S shore of Dornoch Firth on E side of Tain. NH 7679
Glen Almond Tayside 72 B2, C2 valley of upper part of R Almond, qv. See also Trinity College. NN 9128
Glen Ample Central 71 G3 valley of Burn of Ample running N to Loch Earn 1m E of Lochearnhead. NN 5919
Glenancross H'land 79 E8* loc near coast of Lochaber dist, 3m/5km N of Arisaig. NM 6691
Glen App S'clyde 57 B5 valley of Water of App, running SW to Finnarts Bay near N end of Loch Ryan. NX 0674
Glenapp Castle S'clyde 57 B5 19c mansion 2km S of Ballantrae. NX 0980
Glen Aray S'clyde 70 C3, C4 valley of R Aray in Argyll, running S to Loch Fyne at Inveraray. NN 0812
Glen Aros S'clyde 68 D4 valley of Aros R on island of Mull. See Aros. NM 5345
Glen Artney Tayside 72 B3 valley of Ruchill Water, running NE to Strathearn at Comrie. NN 7217
Glenashdale Burn S'clyde 63 G5 r on Arran running E down **Glen Ashdale** to Whiting Bay. Ashdale Falls, waterfalls just over 2km above mouth. NS 0425
Glenastle Loch S'clyde 62 B3* small loch on The Oa, Islay, 2m/3km S of Rubha Mór. NR 3044
Glen Auldyn Isle of Man 46 C4* ham in valley of same name 2m/3km W of Ramsey. SC 4393
Glen Banvie Tayside 75 H4 valley of Banvie Burn running SE to R Garry on W side of Blair Atholl. NN 8468
Glenbarr S'clyde 62 D4 vil near W coast of Kintyre, 10m/16km N of Machrihanish. NR 6636
Glen Beasdale H'land 68 E1 valley of Beasdale Burn. See Beasdale.
Glen Beich Central 71 G2 valley of Beich Burn running S to Loch Earn 2m/3km E of Lochearnhead. NN 6328
Glenbervie Grampian 77 G3 vil 7m/12km SW of Stonehaven. **Glenbervie Hse** is a fortified mansion. NO 7680
Glenboig S'clyde 64 D2 vil 2m/3km N of Coatbridge. NS 7268
Glen Borrodale H'land 68 D3 valley on Ardnamurchan peninsula in Lochaber dist, running S to **Glenborrodale Bay. Glenborrodale Castle** to W. NM 6061
Glenbranter Forest S'clyde 70 C5* state forest in Argyll round about head of Loch Eck, forming part of Argyll Forest Park. NS 1097
Glen Breackerie S'clyde 62 D6 valley of Breackerie Water in Kintyre, running S to Carskey Bay, on S coast of the peninsula. NR 6510
Glen Brein H'land 81 E6 valley of Allt Breinag in Inverness dist, running N to R Feehlin at White Br, 3m/5km S of Foyers. NH 4809
Glen Brerachan Tayside 76 B4 valley of Brerachan Water, running E to head of Strath Ardle. NO 0263
Glen Brittle Skye, H'land 79 C6 valley of R Brittle – see Brittle. **Glen Brittle Forest** is upland tract and state forest to W of r. NG 4023
Glen Brown 82 A5 valley of Burn of Brown running N into head of Glen Lochy at Bridge of Brown 3m/5km NW of Tomintoul. Glen forms boundary between Grampian and Highland regions. NJ 1219
Glen Bruar Tayside 75 H4 valley of Bruar Water running S to R Garry 3m/5km W of Blair Atholl. See also Falls of the Bruar. NN 8272
Glenbuchat Grampian 82 C5 par and vil 13m/20km W of Alford. Kirkton of G. is vil 1m S, in par. **G. Castle** (A.M.) is a stronghold of the Gordons dating from 1590. NJ 3716
Glenbuck S'clyde 65 E5 vil 6m/9km W of Douglas. **G. Loch** is small loch 1km SE. NS 7429
Glenburn S'clyde 64 C3 suburb 2m/3km S of Paisley. **Glenburn Resr** to S. NS 4761
Glencairn Castle D & G. See Moniaive.
Glen Callater Grampian 76 C3 valley of Callater Burn, running N to join Clunie Water 2m/3km S of Braemar. NO 1685

Glencallum Bay S'clyde 63 G3* small bay on S coast of Bute 1m NE of Garroch Hd. See also Rubha'n Eun. NS 1152
Glen Calvie H'land 85 E7 valley of Water of Glencalvie, Sutherland dist, running N into R Carron at Glencalvie Lodge on S side of Amat Forest. **Glencalvie Forest** is deer forest to W. NH 4687
Glencanisp Forest H'land 85 B5 deer forest SE of Lochinver, Sutherland dist. Includes mt of Canisp, qv. NC 1419
Glencannel S'clyde 69 D5* r on Mull running N down **Glen Cannel** to head of Loch Bà. NM 5836
Glen Cannich H'land 80 C4 valley of R Cannich in Inverness dist. NH 1930
Glencannich Forest H'land 80 C4 deer forest in Inverness dist SE of Loch Monar. NH 2433
Glencaple D & G 59 E4 vil on E bank of R Nith estuary 5m/8km S of Dumfries. NX 9968
Glen Carron H'land 80 A3, B3 valley of R Carron, in Ross and Cromarty dist, running down to Loch Carron from Loch Sgamhain or Scaven. **Glencarron Forest** is deer forest S of the latter. NH 0852
Glencarse Tayside 73 E3 vil 5m/8km E of Perth. NO 1921
Glen Cassley H'land 85 D5, E6 valley of R Cassley in Sutherland dist. See Cassley.
Glen Catacol S'clyde 63 F3 valley running down to Catacol Bay on NW coast of Arran. NR 9248
Glen Chalmadale S'clyde 63 F3 valley on island of Arran running NW to Loch Ranza on NW coast of island. NR 9550
Glen Clova Tayside 76 D3, D4 valley of R South Esk containing vil of Clova, qv. NO 3570
Glen Cochill Tayside 72 C1 valley of Cochill Burn running S to head of Strath Braan. NN 9041
Glen Coe H'land 74 C5 valley of R Coe, Lochaber dist, running W to Loch Leven 3m/5km E of Ballachulish. Scene of notorious massacre in 1692. Vil of **Glencoe** at foot of glen. **Pass of Glencoe** at head of glen, here on border of Highland and Strathclyde regions. See also Bridge of Coe, Pap of Glencoe, Three Sisters of Glen Coe. Much of glen and country to S in care of NTS. NN 1557
Glencorse Lothian 66 A3 loc 2m/3km N of Penicuik. Barracks of Royal Scots Regiment. **Glencorse Resr** on Pentland Hills 2m/3km W. 2km NW, on S side of Castlelaw Hill, is Castlelaw Fort (A.M.), Iron Age fort enclosing an earth hse. NT 2462
Glen Coul H'land 84 C4 steep-sided valley in Sutherland dist running into head of Loch Glencoul 3m/5km SE of Kylesku Ferry. NC 2730
Glencraig Fife 73 E5* vil 1m N of Lochgelly. NT 1895
Glen Creran S'clyde 70 C1 valley of R Creran, running SW to head of Loch Creran, Argyll. NN 0348
Glendaruel S'clyde 70 C6 valley of R Ruel in Argyll, running S to head of Loch Riddon. **G. Forest** is state forest bordering glen. NR 9985
Glendebadel Bay S'clyde 69 E7 bay on NW coast of Jura 2m/3km SW of Glengarrisdale Bay. NR 6295
Glen Dessary H'land 74 B2 valley of R Dessary in Lochaber dist, running E to junction with Glen Pean 1km above head of Loch Arkaig. NM 9592
Glen Devon 72 C4, D4 valley of R Devon on borders of Central and Tayside regions between Dollar and Auchterarder. **Glendevon** vil in glen 6m/10km SE of Auchterarder. **Glendevon Forest** is state forest to NE of vil. **Glendevon Castle** is 15c–16c cas, now a farm, 2km NW of vil. **Upr** and **Lr Glendevon Resrs** near head of glen to W. NN 9505
Glen Dhu H'land 84 C4 steep-sided valley in Sutherland dist running into head of Loch Glendhu 4m/6km E of Kylesku Ferry. Situated in Glendhu Forest, westerly extension of Reay Forest. NC 2833
Glen Diebidale H'land 85 E7 valley of R Diebidale, in Sutherland dist. See Diebidale. NH 4583
Glen Dochart Central 71 F2 valley of R Dochart running NE to join Glen Lochay at head of Loch Tay. NN 4828
Glen Doe H'land 80 D6 valley of Allt Doe in Inverness dist, running N into Loch Ness 2km below head of loch. **Glendoe Forest**, on which stream rises, is deer forest to S. NH 4108
Glen Douglas S'clyde 71 E5 valley of Douglas Water running E to Loch Lomond at Inverbeg. NS 3198
Glen Dronach Grampian. See Forgue.
Glen Drynoch Skye, H'land 79 C5 valley of R Drynoch, running W to head of Loch Harport. NG 4330
Glenduckie Fife 73 F3 loc on S side of **G. Hill** 3m/5km E of Newburgh. NO 2818
Glendurgan House Cornwall. See Durgan.
Glen Duror 74 B5 valley of R Duror on border of Highland and Strathclyde regions, running W to Cuil Bay on E shore of Loch Linnhe. **Glenduror Forest** is state forest astride glen. NN 0154
Glen Dye Grampian 77 F2 valley of Water of Dye running N to Water of Feugh on W side of Strachan. NO 6484
Glen Eagles Tayside 72 C4 valley of upper reaches of Ruthven Water, qv, S of Auchterarder. At foot of glen, remains of **Gleneagles Castle.** To N, **Gleneagles Hotel** is palatial hotel with two well-known golf-courses. NN 9308
Glen Effock Tayside 77 E3 valley of Water of Effock, running NE to Glen Esk 2m/3km W of Tarfside. NO 4477
Glenegedale S'clyde 62 B3 loc on Islay 4m/7km NW of Port Ellen. To W beside Laggan Bay is Islay (Port Ellen) Airport. NR 3351
Glenelg H'land 79 F6 vil in Lochaber dist on **G. Bay,** on mainland at head of Sound of Sleat. **G. Brochs** (A.M.), prehistoric fortifications in Gleann Beag 2m/3km SE. NG 8119
Glen Ernan Grampian 82 C5 valley of Ernan Water, running SE to R Don 5m/8km E of Cock Br. NJ 3310
Glen Errochty Tayside 75 G4, H4 valley of Errochty Water running E from Loch Errochty to R Garry near Calvine. NN 7663
Glen Esk Tayside 77 E3 valley of R North Esk above Edzell. NO 5377
Glen Etive S'clyde 74 C6 valley of R Etive, Argyll, running SW to head of Loch Etive. **Glenetive Forest** is state forest to W. NN 1751
Glen Euchar S'clyde 70 A3, B3 valley of R Euchar in Argyll running W and NW from Loch Scamadale to Loch Feochan. NM 8319
Glen Ey Grampian 76 B3 valley of Ey Burn, running N to R Dee at Inverey, 4m/7km W of Braemar. **Glen Ey Forest** is deer forest astride glen. NO 0886
Glen Eynort Skye, H'land 79 B6 valley of R Eynort running down to head of Loch Eynort. NG 3828
Glen Falloch Central 71 E3 valley of R Falloch running SW towards head of Loch Lomond. See also Falls of Falloch. NN 3421
Glen Farg Tayside 73 E3 valley of R Farg running NE to R Earn 5m/8km SE of Perth. **Glenfarg** is vil on R Farg at head of defile 8m/13km S of Perth. **Glenfarg Resr** is near source of r, 2m/3km W of vil. NO 1513
Glen Fender Tayside 75 H4 valley at Fender Burn running SW to R Tilt 1m N of Blair Atholl. NN 9068
Glen Feochan S'clyde 70 B3 valley in Argyll running W to head of Loch Feochan 4m/6km S of Oban. NM 8924
Glen Feshie H'land 75 H1, H2 valley of R Feshie in Badenoch and Strathspey dist, running N to R Spey 1km below Kincraig. **Glenfeshie Forest** is deer forest astride head of glen. NN 8594
Glen Fiddich Grampian 82 C4 valley of R Fiddich running NE on its way to Dufftown. Distillery at Dufftown named after it. **Glenfiddich Forest** is moorland tract surrounding source of r. NJ 3234
Glenfield Leics 36 B4 suburb 3m/5km NW of Leicester. SK 5406
Glen Finart S'clyde 70 D5 valley of stream in Argyll running SE to Loch Long at Finart Bay on N side of Ardentinny. **Glenfinart Forest** is state forest about glen. NS 1790
Glen Finglas Central 71 F4 valley of Finglas Water running SE to Black Water between Loch Achray and Loch Venachar, W of Callander. Contains **Glen Finglas Resr.** NN 5209
Glen Finlas S'clyde 71 E5* valley of Finlas Water running SE to Loch Lomond 1m S of Rossdhu. Small resr near head of glen. NS 3388
Glen Finnan H'land 74 A3 valley of R Finnan, in Lochaber dist, running S to head of Loch Shiel. At foot of glen is vil of **Glenfinnan,** and Glenfinnan Monmt (NTS), commemorating the raising of Prince Charles Edward's standard here in 1745. Visitor centre, with exposition of the campaign. NM 9083
Glenfintaig H'land 74 C3 locality, hse, and lodge in Lochaber dist 1m S of SE shore of Loch Lochy at Invergloy. NN 2286
Glen Forsa S'clyde 68 D4, E4 valley of R Forsa on island of Mull, running N to Sound of Mull 2m/3km E of Salen. Small airfield at foot of glen on W side. NM 6039
Glen Fruin S'clyde 71 E5, E6 valley of Fruin Water running SE to Loch Lomond 2m/4km N of foot of loch. NS 2987
Glen Fyne S'clyde 63 G1* valley of Ardyne Burn in Argyll, running S to Firth of Clyde 2m/4km W of Toward Pt. NS 1172
Glen Fyne S'clyde 70 D3 valley of R Fyne in Argyll running SW to head of Loch Fyne 6m/10km NE of Inveraray. NN 2215
Glen Gairn Grampian 76 C1, D1 valley of R Gairn, NW of Ballater. NJ 3100
Glengalmadale H'land 68 F3* r in Lochaber dist running S from Creach Bheinn to Loch Linnhe on E side of Loch a' Choire. NM 8652
Glengap Forest D & G 58 C5* state forest 3m/5km NE of Gatehouse of Fleet. NX 6459
Glengarnock S'clyde 64 B3 loc with steel works 1m SE of Kilbirnie across R Garnock. NS 3252
Glengarrisdale Bay S'clyde 69 E7 bay on NW coast of Jura. NR 6497
Glen Garry H'land 74 C2, D2 valley in Lochaber dist running E from Loch Quoich, and containing Gearr Garry, Loch Garry, and R Garry. **Glengarry Forest** is deer forest to S between Lochs Garry and Lochy. NH 1300
Glen Garry Tayside 75 G4 valley of R Garry running SE from Loch Garry to R Tummel 2m/3km NW of Pitlochry. NN 7569
Glengavel Water 64 D5 r issuing from **Glengavel Resr** in Strathclyde region and flowing N to Avon Water 5m/9km E of Darvel. NS 6438
Glen Gelder Grampian 76 C2 valley of Gelder Burn running N to R Dee 1m SW of Balmoral Castle. NO 2689
Glen Gheallaidh 82 A3 valley of Allt a' Gheallaidh, qv, on border of Grampian and Highland regions NE of Grantown-on-Spey. NJ 1238
Glen Girnaig Tayside 76 A4 valley of Allt Girnaig, running SW to R Garry at Killiecrankie. NN 9466
Glen Girnock Grampian 76 D2 valley of Girnock Burn, running N to R Dee 3m/4km W of Ballater. NO 3293
Glen Glass H'land 81 E1 valley of R Glass, Ross and Cromarty dist, W of Evanton. NH 5667
Glen Golly H'land 84 D3 valley and r in Sutherland dist rising on E side of Reay Forest and running SE to head of Strath More. NC 4442
Glen Gour H'land 74 B5 valley of R Gour in Lochaber dist, running E to Camas Shallachain on W side of Sallachan Pt on Loch Linnhe. NM 9464
Glen, Great Leics 36 C4 vil 6m/10km SE of Leicester. SP 6597
Glen Guseran H'land 79 F7 valley of Amhainn Inbhir Ghuiserein, stream in Knoydart, Lochaber dist, running NW to Sound of Sleat at Inverguseran. Also known as Gleann na Ghuiserein. NG 7703
Glengyle Water 71 E3 r in Central region running SE down **Glen Gyle** to head of Loch Katrine. NN 3813
Glen Hurich H'land 74 A4 valley of R Hurich in Lochaber dist, running SW to Loch Doilet. **Glenhurich Forest** is state forest astride glen. NM 8468
Glen Iorsa S'clyde 63 F4 valley of Iorsa Water, on Arran, running SW into Kilbrannan Sound at N end of Machrie Bay. NR 9239
Glen Isla Tayside 76 C4, C5 upper valley of R Isla, from source to Airlie Castle. **Glenisla Forest** is state forest around head of Backwater Resr. See Isla. NO 2563
Glenkens, The D & G 58 B2-C4 N part of Stewartry dist, comprising pars of Balmaclellan, Carsphairn, Dalry, and Kells. NX 5887
Glenkiln Reservoir D & G 58 D4 small resr 3m/5km N of Crocketford. NX 8477
Glen Kin S'clyde 70 C6* valley running N to Lit Eachaig R in Argyll, 2m/3km W of Holy Loch. NS 1380
Glenkinchie Lothian. See Pencaitland.
Glenkindie Grampian 82 D5 vil on R Don 6m/9km SW of Lumsden. NJ 4313
Glen Kingie H'land 74 D2 valley of R Kingie in Lochaber dist, running E into Glen Garry 2m/3km SE of dam of Loch Quoich. NN 0397
Glen Kinglas S'clyde 70 D4 valley of Kinglas Water in Argyll, running W to Loch Fyne at Cairndow, near head of loch. NN 2109
Glen Kinglass S'clyde 70 C2 valley of R Kinglass running W into Loch Etive, Argyll, on S side of Ardmaddy Bay. NN 1235
Glen Lean S'clyde 70 C6* upper valley of Lit Eachaig R, in Argyll. Chalybeate spring on roadside 1m above Clachaig. NS 0982
Glen Lednock Tayside 72 B2 valley of R Lednock running SE to Strathearn at Comrie. Loch Lednock Resr near head of glen. NN 7327
Glen Lee Tayside 76 D3, 77 E3 valley of Water of Lee, running E to join Water of Mark at head of R North Esk 3m/4km W of Tarfside. NO 4079
Glenlee Burn 58 B4* stream in Dumfries & Galloway region running E to confluence with Garroch Burn, qv. At confluence of Coom Burn and Water of Ken is Glenlee Hydro-electric Power Stn. NX 6081
Glen Leidle S'clyde 69 D5* valley of Leidle Water on Mull, running NW to Loch Scridain at Pennyghael. NM 5224
Glen Leirg H'land 84 B4 valley running NW into Loch Nedd and Eddrachillis Bay, W coast of Sutherland dist. NC 12, 13
Glenleith Fell D & G 59 E2* mt in Lowther Hills 2m/3km SE of Durisdeer. NS 9202
Glen Liever S'clyde 70 B4 valley of R Liever in Argyll running S to Loch Awe 2km E of head of loch. NM 8905
Glen Liever S'clyde 70 C2 valley of R Liever, running W into Loch Etive, Argyll, 7m/11km from head of loch. NN 0835
Glen Livet Grampian 82 B4 valley of Livet Water, or R Livet, running NW to R Avon 8m/12km N of Tomintoul. Distilleries. **Glenlivet Forest** is state forest to W. NJ 2126
Glenlochar D & G 58 C5 loc on R Dee 3m/4km NW of Castle Douglas. Site of Roman fort on E bank of r. NX 7364
Glen Lochay Central 71 F2 valley of R Lochay running W to join Glen Dochart at head of Loch Tay. NN 4836
Glen Lochsie Tayside 76 B4 valley of **Glen Lochsie Burn,** stream running SE to head of Glen Shee at Spittal of Glenshee. NO 0472
Glen Lochy Grampian 82 A4, B4 valley of Burn of Lochy, running NE to R Avon 4m/7km N of Tomintoul. NJ 1323
Glen Lochy S'clyde 70 D2, 71 E2 valley of R Lochy in Argyll running W to Glen Orchy 2m/3km E of Dalmally. NN 2428
Glen Loin S'clyde 71 E4* valley of Loin Water running S to head of Loch Long. NN 3006
Glen Lonan S'clyde 70 B2 valley of R Lonan in Argyll running W to head of Loch Nell 3m/5km E of Oban. NM 9427

Glen Loy H'land 74 C3 valley of R Loy in Lochaber dist, running SE into R Lochy 2m/4km SW of Gairlochy. **G. L. Forest** is state forest astride r. NN 1084
Glenluce D & G 57 C7 vil on E side of Water of Luce near its mouth, and 9m/14km E of Stranraer. Remains of **G. Abbey** (A.M.), 2km NW, date in part from 12c; chapter hse of 1470. See also Castle of Park. NX 1957
Glen Lui Grampian 76 B2 valley of Lui Water running SE to R Dee 5m/8km W of Braemar. NO 0592
Glen Luss S'clyde 71 E5 valley of Luss Water running E to Loch Lomond at Luss vil. NS 3193
Glenlussa Water S'clyde 63 E5 r in Kintyre issuing from Lussa Loch and running SE into Ardnacross Bay, 4m/7km NE of Campbeltown. Hydro-electricity power stn 2m/3km above mouth. NR 7625
Glen Lyon Tayside 71 F1-H1 valley of R Lyon, running E from Loch Lyon to R Tay 4m/6km W of Aberfeldy. NN 5646
Glen Mallie H'land 74 B3, C3 valley of R Mallie, in Lochaber dist, running E into S side of Loch Arkaig. NN 0887
Glen Mark Tayside 76 D3, 77 E3 valley of Water of Mark, running first NE then SE to head of R North Esk 3m/4km W of Tarfside. NO 4979
Glen Markie H'land 75 F2 valley of Markie Burn in Badenoch and Strathspey dist, running S to R Spey 2km W of Laggan Br. NN 5893
Glen Massan S'clyde 70 C6 valley of R Massan in Argyll, running SE to R Eachaig 2m/4km NW of head of Holy Loch. NS 1286
Glenmavis S'clyde 65 E2* vil forming part of New Monkland, 2m/3km NW of Airdrie. NS 7467
Glenmaye Isle of Man 46 A5 vil 3m/4km S of Peel. SC 2379
Glen More Bute, S'clyde 63 G1 valley of **Glenmore Burn,** running S to Ettrick Bay. NS 0269
Glen More H'land 74 C3-81 F3 valley extending 60m/97km from Loch Linnhe at Fort William to Moray Firth at Inverness. Contains Lochs Lochy, Oich, and Ness, and is traversed by the Caledonian Canal. Also known as Glen Albyn. NH 3607
Glenmore H'land 79 F6, 80 A5 r in Lochaber dist running NW into Sound of Sleat on N side of vil of Glenelg. **Glen More** is valley of r. NG 8119
Glen More H'land 81 H6 valley of Allt Mór in G. M. Forest Park in Badenoch and Strathspey dist, running N then W into head of Loch Morlich. **G. M. Forest Park** is national park surrounding glen: Scottish Centre of Outdoor Training; ski school; camping. NH 9808
Glen More S'clyde 69 D5, E5 valley of Rs Coladoir and Lussa on island of Mull. NM 6029
Glenmore Bay H'land 68 D3* bay on S side of Ardnamurchan peninsula in Lochaber dist, 6m/10km W of Salen. NM 5961
Glen Moriston H'land 80 C6-D5 valley of R Moriston, Inverness dist, running E from Loch Cluanie to Loch Ness. Power stn for hydro-electricity scheme at Ceannacroc Br. NH 4216
Glen Muick Grampian 76 D2 valley of R Muick, running NE from Loch Muick to R Dee 1km S of Ballater. NO 3187
Glenmuir Water 56 F2 r in Strathclyde region running W to join Bellow Water and form Lugar Water 1km E of vil of Lugar. NS 5921
Glen Nevis H'land 74 C4 valley of Water of Nevis, qv, in Lochaber dist, running down to Loch Linnhe at Fort William. Aluminium works at foot of glen. NN 1468
Glen Noe S'clyde 70 C2 valley of R Noe running NW to Loch Etive, Argyll, 3m/4km E of Bonawe. NN 0733
Glen of Rothes Grampian 82 B2 valley traversed by A941 rd N of Rothes. NJ 2552
Glen of Trool D & G 58 A4 valley of Water of Trool, qv, containing Loch Trool. NX 4180
Glenogil Reservoir Tayside 77 E4* small resr in **Glen Ogil,** valley of Noran Water, 4m/7km NW of Tannadice. NO 4464
Glen Ogle Central 71 F2, G2 valley running SE down to head of Loch Earn. NN 5726
Glen Orchy S'clyde 70 D2 valley of R Orchy in Argyll, running SW to NE end of Loch Awe. NN 2433
Glen Orrin H'land 80 D3 valley of R Orrin. See Orrin. NH 3449
Glen Oykel H'land 85 D5, D6* valley of upper reaches of R Oykel in Sutherland dist. NC 30,31
Glen Parva Leics 36 B4* suburb 4m/7km SW of Leicester. SP 5698
Glen Pean H'land 74 B3 valley of R Pean in Lochaber dist, running E to junction with Glen Dessary 1km above head of Loch Arkaig. NM 9590
Glen Prosen Tayside 76 C4-D5 valley of Prosen Water running SE to R South Esk at foot of Glen Clova 3m/5km NE of Kirriemuir. NO 2967
Glen Quaich Tayside 72 C1 valley of R Quaich running SE then E to head of Strath Braan. NN 8638
Glenquey Reservoir Tayside 72 D4* small resr 2km SW of Glendevon vil. NN 9802
Glen Quoich H'land 74 B1 valley of R Quoich in Lochaber dist, running S into Loch Quoich. **Glenquoich Forest** is deer forest between Loch Quoich and Loch Loyne. NH 0107
Glenridding Cumbria 52 D3 vil on Ullswater 1m NW of Patterdale. NY 3816
Glen Righ H'land 74 B5, C5* valley of Abhainn Righ in Lochaber dist, running W to Loch Linnhe 1m NW of Onich. **Glenrigh Forest** is state forest astride glen. NN 0563
Glen Rinnes Grampian 82 B4-C3 valley of Dullan Water running down to R Fiddich at Dufftown. NJ 3339
Glenrosa Water S'clyde 63 G5 r on Arran running SE down **Glen Rosa** to Brodick Bay. NS 0136
Glenrothes Fife 73 F4 New Tn, designated 1948, 16m/25km NE of Forth rd br. Has variety of light industries. NO 2600
Glen Roy H'land 74 D2, D3 valley of R Roy in Lochaber dist, running down to R Spean at Roy Br. On sides of valley are the Parallel Roads of Glen Roy, shelves or terraces marking successive levels of lake dammed by glaciers during Ice Age. NN 2780
Glen Roy Isle of Man 46 B5, C5 wooded valley with stream running E into Laxey R at Laxey. SC 4284
Glen Sannox S'clyde 63 F3 valley on island of Arran running NE from Cir Mhór to E coast at Sannox Bay. **N Glen Sannox** is valley to N, running E to coast 1km N of Sannox Bay. NR 9944
Glen Scaddle H'land 74 B4 valley of R Scaddle in Lochaber dist, running E to Inverscaddle Bay on Loch Linnhe. NM 9668
Glen Shee Tayside 76 B4, C5 valley of Shee Water and Black Water. See Black Water.
Glen Shiel H'land 80 A6 valley of R Shiel in Skye and Lochalsh dist, running NW down to Shiel Br and head of Loch Duich. 5m/8km SE of Shiel Br is site of skirmish in course of Jacobite rising, 1719. NG 9614
Glenshieldaig Forest H'land 78 F4 deer forest in Ross and Cromarty dist S of Loch Shieldaig. NG 8350
Glen Sligachan Skye, H'land 79 C6 valley of R Sligachan, running down to head of Loch Sligachan on E coast. NG 4927
Glens of Foudland Grampian. See Hill of Foudland.
Glen Spean H'land 74 D3, 75 E3 valley of R Spean in Lochaber dist running W through Loch Moy to Spean Br and R Lochy below Loch Lochy. NN 3479
Glen Strae S'clyde 70 D2 valley of R Strae in Argyll running SW to R Orchy 2m/3km W of Dalmally. NN 1531
Glenstrathfarrar Forest H'land 80 D3, D4 deer forest about valley of R Farrar in Inverness dist. NH 3039
Glentanar Grampian 77 E2 loc near foot of **Glen Tanar,** valley of Water of Tanar, SW of Aboyne. Forest of G. is state forest on either side of glen. NO 4795
Glen Tarbert H'land 74 A5 steep-sided valley in Lochaber dist between Loch Linnhe and head of Loch Sunart. From summit of glen Carnoch R runs W to Loch Sunart, while R Tarbert runs E to Loch Linnhe. NM 8960
Glen Tarff H'land 75 E1 valley of R Tarff in Inverness dist running generally NW to Fort Augustus at head of Loch Ness. NH 3902
Glen Tarsan S'clyde 70 C6* valley in Argyll running S to head of Loch Tarsan, qv. NS 0785
Glentham Lincs 45 E2 vil 7m/11km W of Mkt Rasen. TF 0090
Glen Tilt Tayside 76 A3, A4 valley of R Tilt running SW to R Garry at Blair Atholl. NN 8870
Glen Tolsta W Isles 88 C1* loc near E coast of Lewis, on E side of valley of same name, 3m/4km SW of Tolsta Hd. NB 5244
Glentoo Loch D & G 58 C5 small loch 4m/6km W of Castle Douglas. NX 7062
Glentress Forest Borders 66 A4* state forest 2m/3km E of Peebles. NT 2742
Glen Tromie H'land 75 G2 valley of R Tromie in Badenoch and Strathspey dist, running N to R Spey 2km E of Kingussie. Distillery 4m/6km above confluence. NN 7694
Glentrool Forest D & G 56 D4, 57 D5 state forest 11m/18km N of Newton Stewart. **G. F. Park** is large area enclosing Loch Trool and several other hill lochs, as well as Merrick and part of the Rinns of Kells. Camp sites, picnic areas. **Glentrool Village** is forestry vil 3m/5km W of Loch Trool. Glen of Trool is valley of Water of Trool, qv. NX 3581
Glentrosdale Bay S'clyde 69 E7 small bay 2km SW of northern point of Jura. NM 6700
Glen Truim H'land 75 F3-G2 valley of R Truim in Badenoch and Strathspey dist, running N from Pass of Drumochter to R Spey 5m/8km SW of Kingussie. NN 6789
Glen Tulchan H'land 82 A3 valley of Burn of Tulchan, qv.
Glen Turret Tayside 72 B2, C2 valley of Turret Burn running SE to Strathearn at Crieff. Distillery at Hosh, qv, near foot of glen. See also Falls of Turret. NN 8225
Glentworth Lincs 44 D3 vil 11m/17km N of Lincoln. SK 9488
Glenuig Bay H'land 68 E2 small bay in Lochaber dist on S side of Sound of Arisaig, 2m/4km W of Roshven. NM 6777
Glen Ure S'clyde 70 C1* valley of R Ure, running W into Glen Creran 3m/5km NE of head of Loch Creran, Argyll. NN 0647
Glen Urquhart H'land 80 D4, 81 E4 valley of R Enrick in Inverness dist on W side of Loch Ness above Drumnadrochit. **Glenurquhart Forest** is state forest astride r. NH 4430
Glenury Viaduct Grampian 77 H2* rly viaduct carrying line over Cowie Water, N of Stonehaven. Glenury Royal distillery below. See Cowie. NO 8686
Glen Village Central 65 F1* vil 1m S of Falkirk. NS 8878
Gleouraich H'land 74 B1 peak on Glenquoich Forest, Lochaber dist, 3m/4km NW of dam of Loch Quoich. Height 3392 ft or 1034 metres. NH 0305
Glespin S'clyde 65 E5* loc 3m/4km SW of Douglas. NS 8028
Glet Ness Shetland 89 E7* spit of land on E coast of Mainland, running SW to NE along E side of small inlet, **N Voe of Gletness.** Two small islands, **N** and **S Isle of Gletness** to S of headland. Loc of **Gletness** on **S Voe of Gletness** to SW. HU 4751
Glevum Glos. See Gloucester.
Glewstone H & W 26 B5 vil 3m/5km SW of Ross-on-Wye. SO 5522
Glims Holm Orkney 89 B7* small uninhabited island between islands of Burra and Mainland, linked to both by Churchill Barrier, qv. ND 4799
Glinton Cambs 37 F4 vil 5m/9km NW of Peterborough. TF 1505
Globe Town London 20 A3* loc in borough of Tower Hamlets 2m/4km NE of London Br. TQ 3582
Glodwick Gtr Manchester 43 E1* loc in Oldham 1m SE of tn centre. SD 9304
Glooston Leics 36 C4 vil 6m/9km N of Mkt Harborough. Site of Roman bldg to N. SP 7595
Glororum Nthmb 67 H5 loc 2km SW of Bamburgh. NU 1633
Glossop Derbys 43 E2 tn 13m/22km E of Manchester, on edge of Peak Dist National Park. Industries include textiles, rubber and paper mnfre. See also Old Glossop. SK 0394
Gloucester Glos 26 D5 industrial city on R Severn, on site of Roman *Glevum,* 32m/52km NE of Bristol. Docks on **G. and Sharpness Canal,** navigable to craft up to 350 tons. Norman to Perp cathedral with cloisters. Three Choirs Festival every third year (see also Hereford, Worcester). **Vale of G.** is fertile plain running from NE to SW of city below escarpment of Cotswold Hills. SO 8318
Gloucester and Sharpness Canal connects Gloucester with R Severn estuary at Sharpness. SO 70
Gloucestershire 118,119 western county of England, bounded by Hereford and Worcester, Warwickshire, Oxfordshire, Wiltshire, Avon, and the Welsh county of Gwent. The limestone mass of the Cotswolds dominates the centre of the county, and provides the characteristic pale golden stone of many of its bldgs. R Severn forms a wide valley to the W, ending in a long tidal estuary, beyond which are the hills of the Forest of Dean. Chief tns are the cathedral city and county tn of Gloucester; Cheltenham, and Stroud. Apart from the Severn and the Wye, which forms part of the boundary with Gwent, there are many smaller rs, among them the Chelt, Coln, Evenlode, Leach, Leadon, and Windrush. R Thames rises in the county, and forms part of its S boundary in the vicinity of Lechlade. There is much industry around Gloucester and Stroud, coal-mining in the Forest of Dean, and mkt gardening and orchards in the fertile Severn valley.
Gloup Holm Shetland 89 E5* small island off N coast of Yell. HP 4806
Gloup Ness Shetland 89 E5* headland on N coast of Yell, on E side of entrance to **Gloup Voe,** narrow inlet 2m/3km long. HP 5005
Glover Tyne & Wear 61 G5* industrial estate in E part of Washington. NZ 3157
Glover's Hill Staffs 35 F3* loc 2km SE of Rugeley. SK 0516
Gloy H'land 74 D3 r in Lochaber dist running SW down Glen Gloy, then N into Loch Lochy at Invergloy, 4m/6km NE of foot of loch. NN 2288
Gloyw Lyn Gwynedd 32 D2* tarn 4m/7km E of Harlech. SH 6429
Glumaig Harbour W Isles 88 C2* inlet on S side of Stornoway Harbour, Lewis. NB 4230
Glunimore Island S'clyde 63 E6* islet lying 1km SE of Sheep I. off S coast of Kintyre. NR 7405
Glusburn N Yorks 48 C4 loc 4m/7km NW of Keighley. SE 0044
Gluss Isle Shetland 89 E6* peninsula on NE coast of Mainland on W side of entrance to Sullom Voe. Narrow neck of land joins it to rest of Mainland and separates Sullom Voe from **Gluss Voe,** inlet to W. HU 3778
Glyder Fach Gwynedd 40 D5 mt 4m/7km W of Capel Curig. Height 3262 ft or 994 metres. SH 6558
Glyder Fawr Gwynedd 40 D5 mt 5m/8km W of Capel Curig. Height 3279 ft or 999 metres. SH 6457
Glyme 27 H6 r rising E of Chipping Norton, Oxon, and flowing SE to Wootton, then S through lake in park of Blenheim Palace, Woodstock, and into R Evenlode at S edge of park. SP 4414
Glympton Oxon 27 H5 vil 3m/5km NW of Woodstock. SP 4221
Glyn 33 F2* stream running NW to join Nant Rhyd-wen before flowing into Bala Lake on W side of Llangower, Gwynedd. SH 9032
Glynarthen Dyfed 23 E1 ham 5m/8km N of Newcastle Emlyn. SN 3148
Glyn Ceiriog Clwyd 33 H1 vil on R Ceiriog 3m/4km S of Llangollen. Quarries. SJ 2037
Glyn Collwn Powys 25 F5/F6 valley to S of Talybont enclosing Talybont Resr. SO 1112

Glyncorrwg W Glam 14 D2 vil 5m/8km N of Maesteg. SS 8799
Glynde E Sussex 12 B5 vil below S Downs 3m/5km E of Lewes. **G. Place** is 16c hse built round courtyard. TQ 4509
Glyndebourne E Sussex 12 B5 Elizn hse with 19c and 20c additions 3m/4km E of Lewes. Annual summer opera season in opera hse (1934). TQ 4510
Glynde Reach 12 B5* r in E Sussex originating in numerous streams rising in vicinity of Ripe and flowing W below S Downs through Glynde vil and into R Ouse 2m/4km SE of Lewes. TQ 4307
Glyndŵr 116, 118 admin dist of Clwyd.
Glyndyfrdwy Clwyd 33 H1 vil 4m/6km W of Llangollen. SJ 1542
Glynebwy Welsh form of Ebbw Vale, qv.
Glyn-neath (Glyn-nedd) W Glam 14 D1 vil 10m/16km NE of Neath. SN 8806
Glyn-nedd Welsh form of Glyn-neath, qv.
Glynoch Mid Glam 15 F2* loc 2km N of Pontypridd. ST 0792
Glyntaff Mid Glam 15 F3 loc 2km SE of Pontypridd. ST 0889
Glynteg Dyfed 23 E2* ham 4m/6km SE of Newcastle Emlyn. SN 3637
Gnosall Staffs 35 E2 vil 6m/10km W of Stafford. Loc of **G. Heath** 1km SW. SJ 8220
Goadby Leics 36 C4 vil 7m/12km N of Mkt Harborough. SP 7598
Goadby Marwood Leics 36 D2 vil 5m/8km NE of Melton Mowbray. SK 7826
Goatacre Wilts 17 E4 vil 4m/6km N of Calne. SU 0177
Goat Fell S'clyde 63 F3 mt (NTS) on Arran 4m/6km N of Brodick. Highest point on island: 2866 ft or 874 metres. NR 9941
Goathill Dorset 8 D3* ham 3m/4km E of Sherborne. ST 6717
Goathland N Yorks 55 F5 vil below Goathland Moor 7m/11km SW of Whitby. NZ 8301
Goathurst Som 8 B1 vil 3m/5km SW of Bridgwater. ST 2534
Goathurst Common Kent 20 B6* loc 3m/5km SW of Sevenoaks. TQ 4952
Goat Lees Kent 13 F3 loc adjoining Ashford to N. TR 0145
Goat's Water Cumbria 52 C5 small mountain lake 2m/4km W of Coniston. SD 2697
Gobannium Gwent. See Abergavenny.
Gob Lhiack Isle of Man 46 B6* promontory on E coast 2km NE of Santon Hd. SC 3471
Goblin's Cave Central 71 F4 cave near E end of Loch Katrine. Gaelic name: Corrie na Urisgean. NN 4807
Gob na h-Airde Móire W Isles 88 A2/B2* headland on W coast of Lewis N of Loch Resort opp island of Scarp. NB 0117
Gob ny rona Isle of Man 46 C4* headland (Manx NT) 2km SE of Ramsey. Also known as Tableland Pt. SC 4793
Gobowen Salop 34 A1 vil 3m/4km N of Oswestry. SJ 3033
Goch 40 B3* r rising E of Llanerchymedd, Anglesey, and flowing NE into Dulas Bay. SH 4889
Goch 40 D4* r forming upper reaches of R Rhaeadr Fawr, Gwynedd, incl Aber Falls, the stream continuing N into Conwy Bay 2m/3km W of Llanfairfechan. SH 6670
Godalming Surrey 11 F1 old tn with narrow streets 4m/7km SW of Guildford. Small mkt hse; some half-timbered hses. See also Charterhouse. SU 9643
Goddard's Corner Suffolk 31 G2* loc 1m N of Dennington. TM 2868
Goddard's Green Kent 12 D3* loc adjoining Cranbrook to SW. TQ 7635
Goddard's Green Kent 12 D3* ham 3m/4km E of Cranbrook. TQ 8134
Goddards Green W Sussex 11 H3* loc 2m/3km W of Burgess Hill. TQ 2820
Godden Green Kent 20 C6* loc 2m/3km E of Sevenoaks. TQ 5554
Goddington London 20 B5* loc in borough of Bromley 1m E of Orpington. TQ 4765
Godford Cross Devon 7 H5* loc 2m/4km NW of Honiton. ST 1302
Godington Oxon 28 B5* loc 5m/8km NE of Bicester. SP 6327
Godley Gtr Manchester 43 E2 loc adjoining Hyde to E. SJ 9595
Godleybrook Staffs 35 F2* loc 2m/3km NW of Cheadle. SJ 9744
Godmanchester Cambs 29 F1 small tn on R Ouse opp. and S of, Huntingdon. Charter granted in 1212. 13c br spans r. TL 2470
Godmanstone Dorset 8 D4 vil 4m/7km N of Dorchester. SY 6697
Godmersham Kent 21 F6 vil on Gt Stour R 6m/9km NE of Ashford. TR 0650
Godney Som 8 C1 ham 3m/4km N of Glastonbury. To NW and NE respectively, hams of **Lr** and **Upr Godney.** ST 4842
Godolphin Cross Cornwall 2 B5 ham 4m/6km NW of Helston. SW 6031
Godre'r-graig W Glam 14 C1/D1 loc 2m/3km SW of Ystalyfera. SN 7506
Godrevy Island Cornwall 2 B4 island with lighthouse off N coast opp **Godrevy Pt** (NT), headland 5m/8km NW of Camborne. SW 5743
Godshill Hants 9 H3 loc 2m/3km E of Fordingbridge. SU 1714
Godshill Isle of Wight 10 C6 vil 4m/6km W of Shanklin. SZ 5281
Godstone Staffs 35 F1* loc 1m SW of Ch Leigh. SK 0134
Godstone Surrey 19 G6 vil 5m/7km E of Redhill. TQ 3451
Godwell Devon 4 C5* ham 1km SE of Ivybridge. SX 6455
Godwick Norfolk 38 D3* loc 1m NE of Tittleshall. TF 9022
Goedol 32 D1* r rising near Blaenau Ffestiniog, Gwynedd, and running S to join R Dwyryd NW of Ffestiniog. SH 6943
Goetre Gwent 15 H1* vil 4m/6km NE of Pontypool. SO 3205
Goetre-hen, Y Welsh form of Coytrahen, qv.
Goff's Oak Herts 19 G2 residential loc 3m/4km W of Cheshunt. TL 3203
Gogar Lothian 65 H2 loc 1m SE of Edinburgh Airport. Loc of **Gogarbank** 1m S. NT 1672
Gogarth Gwynedd 40 D3 loc 2km NW of Llandudno. SH 7682
Gogarth Bay Gwynedd 40 A3* westward-facing bay 2m/3km W of Holyhead. SH 2183
Goginan Dyfed 33 E6 ham 4m/7km NW of Devil's Br. SN 6881
Gog Magog Hills Cambs 29 H3 range of low chalk hills 4m/6km SE of Cambridge. See also Wandlebury. TL 4953
Goil S'clyde 70 D4 r in Argyll flowing S to head of Loch Goil. NN 1901
Golan Gwynedd 32 C1* ham 4m/6km NW of Portmadoc. SH 5242
Golant Cornwall 3 F3 vil on right bank of R Fowey 2m/3km N of Fowey. SX 1254
Golberdon Cornwall 3 G1 vil 2m/3km NW of Callington. SX 3271
Golborne Gtr Manchester 42 B2 tn 6m/9km N of Warrington. Coal-mining, textiles, engineering. SJ 6097
Golcar W Yorks 48 D6 vil 3m/5km W of Huddersfield. SE 0915
Goldcliff Gwent 15 H3 vil near coast 5m/8km SE of Newport. **Gold Cliff** headland 1m SE.
Goldenacre Lothian 66 A2* dist of Edinburgh 2km N of city centre. NT 2475
Golden Cap Dorset 8 C5 summit (625 ft or 190 metres) of Wear Cliffs, on coast 4m/7km E of Lyme Regis across Lyme Bay and midway between Black Ven, W of Charmouth, and Eype Mouth, SW of Bridport, a 6m/10km stretch of coast almost entirely NT property. SY 4092
Golden Cross E Sussex 12 B5* loc 4m/6km NW of Hailsham. TQ 5312
Golden Green Kent 20 C6 vil 3m/5km E of Tonbridge. TQ 6348
Golden Grove Dyfed 23 G4* loc 3m/5km SW of Llandeilo. SN 5819
Golden Hill Avon 16 B4* dist of Bristol 2m/4km N of city centre. ST 5876
Golden Hill Dyfed 22 C5* loc 1km N of Pembroke. SM 9802
Golden Hill Staffs 42 D5 loc 2km N of Tunstall. SJ 8553
Golden Pot Hants 10 D1* ham 3m/4km N of Alton. SU 7143
Golden Valley Avon 16 C4* part of R Boyd valley immediately above Bitton, 2m/3km E of Keynsham. ST 6870
Golden Valley Derbys 43 H5* loc 2m/3km E of Ripley. SK 4251
Golden Valley Glos 16 D2* part of R Frome valley SE of Stroud. SO 8802
Golden Valley Glos 26 D5 vil 3m/5km W of Cheltenham. SO 9022
Golden Valley H & W 25 H4 valley of R Dore N and S of Vowchurch. SO 3536
Golden Valley H & W 26 B3* loc 4m/6km S of Bromyard. SO 6549
Golders Green London 19 F3 dist in borough of Barnet 6m/10km NW of Charing Cross. TQ 2488
Goldhanger Essex 21 E1 vil off **G. Creek,** inlet of R Blackwater, and 4m/6km E of Maldon. TL 9008
Gold Hill Bucks 19 E3* loc at Chalfont St Peter SW of tn centre. SU 9990
Gold Hill Dorset 9 F3* loc adjoining Child Okeford to N and 3m/5km E of Sturminster Newton. ST 8313
Gold Hill H & W 26 B3* loc 4m/7km NW of Ledbury. SO 6743
Goldington Beds 29 E3 E dist of Bedford. TL 0750
Goldsborough N Yorks 49 F3 vil 2m/3km E of Knaresborough. Hall dates from early 17c. SE 3856
Goldsborough N Yorks 55 F3 ham near North Sea coast 5m/7km NW of Whitby. NZ 8314
Golds Green W Midlands 35 F5* loc in W Bromwich 2m/3km NW of tn centre. SO 9893
Goldsithney Cornwall 2 B5 vil 4m/7km E of Penzance. SW 5430
Goldstone Salop 34 D2* loc 1m E of Lockleywood. SJ 7028
Goldstone, Lower Kent 13 H1* loc 3m/5km NW of Sandwich. TR 2961
Goldstone, Upper Kent 13 H1* loc 3m/5km NW of Sandwich. TR 2960
Gold Street Kent 20 C5* loc adjoining Sole Street to E and 4m/7km S of Gravesend. TQ 6667
Goldthorn Park W Midlands 35 E4* S dist of Wolverhampton. SO 9196
Goldthorpe S Yorks 44 A1 tn in coal-mining area 7m/12km W of Doncaster. SE 4604
Goldworthy Devon 6 C3 ham 4m/7km SW of Bideford. SS 3922
Golford Kent 12 D3* loc 2km E of Cranbrook. TQ 7936
Gollinglith Foot N Yorks 54 B6* loc 4m/7km W of Masham. SE 1581
Golly Clwyd 41 H5* loc 2m/3km E of Hope. SJ 3358
Golspie H'land 87 B6 vil on E coast of Sutherland dist 15m/24km SW of Helmsdale. NH 8399
Goltho Lincs 45 E3* loc and site of former vil 1m SW of Wragby. TF 1177
Gomeldon Wilts 9 H1* vil 1km SW of Porton and 5m/6km NE of Salisbury. SU 1835
Gomersal W Yorks 49 E5 loc 1m E of Cleckheaton. Worsted and woollen spinning. SE 2026
Gometra S'clyde 68 B4 small sparsely populated island off W end of Ulva. Steep cliffs with columns of basalt in places. Rd br connection with Ulva. NM 3641
Gomshall Surrey 19 E6 vil 6m/9km E of Guildford. TQ 0847
Gonalston Notts 44 B6 vil 1m NE of Lowdham. SK 6747
Gonerby, Great Lincs 36 D1/37 E1 vil 2m/3km NW of Grantham. **Gonerby Hill Foot** loc 1km SE. SK 8938
Gon Firth Shetland 89 E7 inlet on W coast of Mainland. Locality called **Gonfirth** at its head. **Loch of Gonfirth** to E towards vil of Voe. HU 3661
Good Easter Essex 20 C1 vil 2m/3km E of Leaden Roding. TL 6212
Gooderstone Norfolk 38 C4 vil 4m/6km E of Stoke Ferry. TF 7602
Goodleigh Devon 6 D2 vil 3m/5km E of Barnstaple. SS 5934
Goodmanham Humberside 50 D4 vil 2km NE of Mkt Weighton. SE 8943
Goodmayes London 20 B3* loc in borough of Redbridge 2m/3km E of Ilford. TQ 4686
Goodnestone Kent 13 G2 vil 2m/3km S of Wingham. TR 2554
Goodnestone Kent 21 F5 vil 2m/3km E of Faversham. TR 0461
Goodrich H & W 26 B5 vil above R Wye 4m/6km SW of Ross-on-Wye. To N beside r, massive remains of **G. Castle** (A.M.), largely 13c. SO 5719
Goodrington Devon 5 E4 coastal and residential dist to S of Paignton, incl **G. Sands** to S of Roundham Hd. SX 8958
Goodshaw Lancs 48 B5* loc 2m/3km N of Rawtenstall. **G. Fold** ham 1km N. SD 8125
Goodwick (Wdig) Dyfed 22 B2 suburb of Fishguard on W side of Fishguard Bay. Terminal for rail and car ferry services to Ireland. SM 9438
Goodwood House W Sussex 11 E4 18c mansion 3m/5km NE of Chichester. Art collection. Racecourse at N end of Goodwood Park. SU 8808
Goodworth Clatford Hants 10 B1 vil 2m/3km S of Andover. SU 3642
Goodyers End Warwicks 36 A5* loc 2m/3km SW of Bedworth. SP 3385
Goodyhills Cumbria 52 B1* loc adjoining Holme St Cuthbert to SE. NY 1046
Goole Humberside 50 C5 inland port on R Ouse at its confluence with R Don 23m/37km W of Hull. In addition to shipping, industries include shipbuilding, milling, fertiliser mnfre. **G. Fields** loc 2m/3km S. See also Old Goole. SE 7423
Goom's Hill H & W 27 E2* ham 7m/11km N of Evesham. SP 0254
Goonbell Cornwall 2 C3* vil on SE side of St Agnes. SW 7249
Goonhavern Cornwall 2 D3 vil 2m/3km E of Perranporth. SW 7853
Goonhilly Downs Cornwall 2 C6 5m/8km SE of Helston. Barren uplands on Lizard peninsula with many ancient earthworks. Post Office radio stn with prominent aerials. SW 7319
Goon Piper Cornwall 2 D4* loc 4m/6km S of Truro. SW 8139
Goonvrea Cornwall 2 C3* ham 2km SE of St Agnes Hd. SW 7050
Gooseberry Green Essex 20 C2* NW dist of Billericay. TQ 6695
Goose Green Avon 16 B4* ham 6m/9km E of Bristol. ST 6774
Goose Green Avon 16 C3* ham 1m NW of Chipping Sodbury. ST 7183
Goose Green Essex 31 E5* ham 3m/5km NW of Thorpe-le-Soken. TM 1425
Goose Green Essex 31 E5 ham 4m/6km SE of Manningtree. TM 1327
Goose Green Gtr Manchester 42 B1 loc in Wigan 2m/3km SW of tn centre. SD 5603
Goose Green Kent 12 D3* loc 1km SW of Biddenden. TQ 8437
Goose Green Norfolk 38 D4* loc adjoining Ashill to N. TF 8804
Goose Green W Sussex 11 G3 loc 4m/6km N of Washington. TQ 1118
Gooseham Cornwall 3 B4* loc 7m/11km N of Bude. SS 2316
Goosehill W Yorks 49 F6* loc just N of Warmfield. SE 3721
Goosehill Green H & W 26 D2* loc 3m/4km SE of Droitwich. SO 9361
Goosenford Som 8 B2* ham 3m/4km NE of Taunton. ST 2527
Goose Pool H & W 26 A4* loc 4m/6km SW of Hereford. SO 4636
Goose, The Cornwall 2 D2* rock island off E Pentire Pt 2m/4km W of Newquay. SW 7761
Goosewell Devon 4 B5 SE dist of Plymouth 2m/3km beyond R Plym and 4m/6km W of Yealmpton. SX 5252
Goosey Oxon 17 G2 vil 4m/6km NW of Wantage. SU 3591
Goosnargh Lancs 47 F4 vil 3m/5km W of Longridge. SD 5536
Goostrey Ches 42 D4 vil 2m/3km NE of Holmes Chapel. SJ 7770
Gorbals S'clyde 64 D3* dist of Glasgow on S bank of R Clyde 1km S of city centre. NS 5964
Gorcott Hill H & W 27 E1 ham 3m/5km E of Redditch. SP 0968
Gordale Scar N Yorks 48 B2/C2 limestone cliff astride Gordale Beck 2km NE of Malham. The stream cascades over cliff in series of waterfalls. Another waterfall downstream below Gordale Br. SD 9164
Gorddinog Gwynedd 40 D4* loc 1m SW of Llanfairfechan. SH 6773
Gordon Borders 66 D4 vil 8m/13km NW of Kelso. NT 6443
Gordon 115 admin dist of Grampian region.
Gordonbush H'land 87 B5 locality in Sutherland dist near head of Loch Brora, 5m/8km NW of Brora vil on E coast. NC 8409
Gordon Castle Grampian 82 C1/C2 partly ruined cas in valley of R Spey 1km N of Fochabers. NJ 3559
Gordonsburgh Grampian 82 C1/D1* loc on N coast, on E side of Buckie. Harbour and lighthouse. NJ 4366

Gordonstoun Grampian 82 B1 coeducational public school 4m/6km W of Lossiemouth. NJ 1868
Gordonstown Grampian 82 D2 loc 9m/15km SW of Banff. NJ 5656
Gordonstown Grampian 83 F3 vil 7m/12km S of Turriff. NJ 7138
Gorebridge Lothian 66 B3 tn in coal-mining dist 4m/6km S of Dalkeith. Situated on **Gore Water,** stream flowing NW into R South Esk 1m W of tn. NT 3461
Gore End Hants 17 H5 loc 4m/7km SW of Newbury. SU 4163
Gorefield Cambs 37 H3 vil 3m/5km NW of Wisbech. TF 4111
Gore Houses Lancs 42 A1* loc to W of Lydiate across Leeds and Liverpool Canal. SD 3604
Gore Pit Essex 30 D6* loc adjoining Kelvedon to NE, 4m/7km NE of Witham. TL 8719
Gores Wilts 17 E5 ham 4m/6km W of Pewsey. SU 1058
Gore Saltings Essex 21 E1* marsh and mudflats 5m/8km E of Maldon. TL 9308
Gore Street Kent 13 H1 loc 1m E of Sarre. TR 2765
Gorgie Lothian 66 A2* dist of Edinburgh 2m/4km SE of city centre. NT 2271
Gorhambury Herts 19 E1 18c mansion 2m/3km W of St Albans. Ruins of earlier hse in grnds. TL 1107
Goring Oxon 18 B3 tn on R Thames 9m/14km NW of Reading. SU 6081
Goring-by-Sea W Sussex 11 G4 W dist of Worthing. TQ 1102
Goring Heath Oxon 18 B3 loc 2m/4km NE of Pangbourne. SU 6579
Gorlech 24 B4 r rising 4m/6km SE of Llanybydder, Dyfed, and flowing SE through Forest of Brechfa into R Cothi at Abergorlech. SN 5833
Gorleston (or Gorleston-on-Sea) Norfolk 39 H4 S dist of Gt Yarmouth at mouth of R Yare. TG 5203
Gorley, North Hants 9 H3* loc on edge of New Forest 2m/3km SE of Fordingbridge. SU 1611
Gorley, South Hants 9 H3 loc on edge of New Forest 3m/5km N of Ringwood. SU 1610
Gormack Burn 77 G1 stream in Grampian region rising on Hill of Fare and running E to Leuchar Burn 1m W of Peterculter. NJ 8201
Gormire Lake N Yorks 54 D6 lake at foot of escarpment of Hambleton Hills below Sutton Bank, 5m/8km E of Thirsk. SE 5083
Gornal, Lower W Midlands 35 E5 loc in Dudley 2m/3km W of tn centre. SO 9191
Gornal, Upper W Midlands 35 E5 dist of Dudley 2m/3km NW of tn centre. SO 9292
Gornalwood W Midlands 35 E5 dist of Dudley 2m/3km W of tn centre. SO 9190
Gorple Reservoirs W Yorks 48 C5* two resrs on Heptonstall Moor NW of Hebden Br. SD 9231, 9431
Gorpley Reservoir W Yorks 48 B5* resr 2m/3km SW of Todmorden. SD 9122
Gorran Cornwall 3 E4 vil, also known as Gorran Churchtown, 2m/3km SW of Mevagissey. 1m SE on coast, vil of **Gorran Haven.** SW 9942
Gorsedd Clwyd 41 G4 vil 2m/4km W of Holywell. SJ 1576
Gorsedd-y-penrhyn Gwynedd 40 A3 headland on Holy I., Anglesey, 2m/4km SE of Holyhead. SH 2781
Gorse Hill Gtr Manchester 42 D2 dist of Stretford 1m NE of tn centre. SJ 8095
Gorse Hill Wilts 17 F3 dist of Swindon 2km NE of tn centre. SU 1686
Gorseinon W Glam 23 G5 tn 5m/9km NW of Swansea. Garden village to SE. SS 5898
Gorseybank Derbys 43 G5* loc 1km SE of Wirksworth. SK 2953
Gorsey Leys Derbys 35 H3* loc 1km E of Overseal. SK 3015
Gors-goch Dyfed 23 G4* loc 1km SE of Gorslas. SN 5713
Gorsgoch Dyfed 24 B3 ham 6m/10km W of Lampeter. SN 4850
Gorslas Dyfed 23 G4 vil 1m NE of Cross Hands. SN 5713
Gorsley Glos 26 C5* ham 2m/4km W of Newent. SO 6825
Gorsley Common H & W 26 B5 vil 3m/5km W of Newent. SO 6725
Gorsley Green Ches 42 D4* loc 1km NW of Marton. SJ 8469
Gorsley, Little Glos 26 C5 ham 2m/3km SW of Newent. SO 6924
Gorstage Ches 42 B4* loc 3m/5km W of Northwich. SJ 6172
Gorstan H'land 80 D2 loc in Ross and Cromarty dist 10m/15km W of Dingwall. NH 3862
Gorstey Ley Staffs 35 F3* loc 2m/4km N of Brownhills. SK 0609
Gorsty Common H & W 26 A4 vil 4m/7km SW of Hereford. SO 4437
Gorsty Hill Staffs 35 G2* ham 3m/5km S of Uttoxeter. SK 1029
Gortantaoid Point S'clyde 62 B1 headland on N coast of Islay, on E side of wide bay at entrance to Loch Gruinart. NR 3374
Gorton Gtr Manchester 42 D2 dist of Manchester 3m/5km SE of city centre. Resrs to E. Dist of **W Gorton** 1m NW: Belle Vue Zoo and Speedway Stadium; Greyhound Stadium. SJ 8895
Gosbeck Suffolk 31 F3 vil 7m/11km N of Ipswich. TM 1655
Gosberton Lincs 37 G2 vil 6m/9km N of Spalding. TF 2331
Gosberton Cheal Lincs 37 G2* loc 1m SE of Risegate. TF 2228
Gosberton Clough Lincs 37 G2* loc 6m/9km NW of Spalding. TF 1929
Goscote, East Leics 36 C3* loc 1m SW of Rearsby. SK 6413
Goseley Dale Derbys 35 H2/H3 loc 2km E of Swadlincote. SK 3220
Gosfield Essex 30 C5 vil 4m/7km NE of Braintree. TL 7829
Gosford Devon 7 H5* loc 2km N of Ottery St Mary. SY 0997
Gosford H & W 26 A1* loc 4m/6km W of Tenbury Wells. SO 5368
Gosford Oxon 28 A6* loc adjoining Kidlington to SE, 4m/7km N of Oxford. SP 5013
Gosford Bay Lothian 66 C1 westward-facing bay on Firth of Forth 2km SW of Aberlady. NT 4478
Gosford Green W Midlands 36 A6* loc in Coventry 2km E of city centre. SP 3578
Gosforth Cumbria 52 B4 vil 2m/4km NE of Seascale. NY 0603
Gosforth Tyne & Wear 61 G4 tn adjoining Newcastle to N, 2m/3km from city centre. NZ 2468
Gosland Green Ches 42 B5 loc 1km E of Bunbury. SJ 5758
Gosling Street Som 8 D1* loc 2m/3km N of Keinton Mandeville. ST 5433
Gosmore Herts 29 F5 loc 2km S of Hitchin. TL 1827
Gospel End Staffs 35 E5 vil 3m/5km S of Wolverhampton. SO 9093
Gospel Green W Sussex 11 F2 loc 3m/4km SE of Haslemere. SU 9431
Gospel Oak London 19 F3* loc in borough of Camden 4m/6km N of Charing Cross. Name recalls tree where gospel was read during beating of bounds. TQ 2885
Gospel Pass Powys 25 G4* pass in Black Mts carrying rd from Hay-on-Wye to Llanthony between Hay Bluff and Lord Hereford's Knob. SO 2335
Gosport Hants 10 B3* loc just S of Ampfield and 3m/5km E of Romsey. SU 3922
Gosport Hants 10 C4 tn 1m W of Portsmouth across entrance to Portsmouth Harbour (ferry for pedestrians). Submarine base; naval victualling yard and Haslar Hospital (1713). SU 6199
Gossabrough Shetland 89 F6* loc near E coast of Yell 2m/4km N of Burravoe. **Ness of G.** headland to E; **Wick of G.** bay to N. HU 5383
Gossard's Green Beds 28 D3* loc 7m/11km SW of Bedford. SP 9643
Gossa Water Shetland 89 E5* loch in N part of Yell 1m NW of Dalsetter. HU 4899
Gossington Glos 16 C2* ham 3m/5km NW of Dursley. SO 7302
Gossops Green W Sussex 11 H2 W dist of Crawley. TQ 2536
Goswick Nthmb 67 G4 loc near coast 6m/10km SE of Berwick-upon-Tweed. **G. Sands** between here and Holy I. NU 0545
Gotham Notts 36 B2 vil 6m/10km N of Loughborough. SK 5330
Gotherington Glos 26 D4 vil 5m/8km N of Cheltenham. SO 9629
Gothers Cornwall 3 E3* loc 5m/8km NW of St Austell. China clay workings. SW 9658
Gott Bay Tiree, S'clyde 69 B7 wide bay on S coast, NE of Scarinish. NM 0546
Gotton Som 8 B2* ham 1m W of W Monkton. ST 2428
Goudhurst Kent 12 D3 hilltop Wealden vil 4m/6km NW of Cranbrook. TQ 7237
Goulceby Lincs 45 F3 vil 6m/10km N of Horncastle. TF 2579
Gould's Green London 19 E3* loc in borough of Hillingdon 2m/4km SW of Uxbridge. TQ 0731
Gour H'land 74 B5 r in Ardgour, Lochaber dist, running E down Glen Gour to Camas Shallachain, on W side of Sallachan Pt on Loch Linnhe. NM 9862
Gourdon Grampian 77 G4 fishing vil on E coast 1m S of Inverbervie. NO 8270
Gourock S'clyde 64 A2 resort and passenger boat terminus on Firth of Clyde 2m/4km W of Greenock and due S of Kilcreggan across firth. **G. Bay** to E. NS 2477
Gousam W Isles 88 A2* islet in Loch Roag, W coast of Lewis, 2m/3km E of Miavaig. NB 1033
Gouthwaite Reservoir N Yorks 48 D2 large resr in Nidderdale 2m/3km NW of Pateley Br. SE 1468
Govan S'clyde 64 C2 dist of Glasgow on S side of R Clyde 2m/4km W of city centre. Shipbuilding. Car ferry across r. NS 5565
Govanhill S'clyde 64 C3/D3* dist of Glasgow 2m/3km S of city centre. NS 5862
Goverton Notts 44 B6* loc 1km NW of Bleasby. SK 7050
Goveton Devon 4 D5 ham 2m/3km NE of Kingsbridge. SX 7546
Govick W Isles 88 A3 loc on coast of Harris 2m/4km SE of Husinish. NB 0109
Govilon Gwent 25 G6* vil 2m/3km W of Abergavenny. SO 2613
Gowanbank Tayside 77 F6 vil 4m/6km NW of Arbroath. Formerly known as Colliston. Colliston Hse, 16c. NO 6045
Gowanhill Grampian 83 H1* loc 3m/5km SE of Fraserburgh. NK 0363
Gowdall Humberside 50 B5 vil 1m W of Snaith. SE 6222
Gower (Gŵyr) W Glam 23 F6/G6 peninsula of carboniferous limestone, 15m/24km E to W and from 4m to 8m (6km to 13km) N to S, jutting out from W of Swansea westwards into Bristol Channel. Rocky coast, except to N where salt marshes border Burry Inlet. Much of coast owned by NT. SS 4859
Gower Rock Cornwall 6 A6* rock island off N coast 1m W of Boscastle. SX 0890
Gowerton (Tre-gŵyr) W Glam 23 G5 tn 5m/7km NW of Swansea. SS 5896
Gowkhall Fife 72 D5* vil 3m/4km W of Dunfermline. NT 0589
Gowkthrapple S'clyde 65 E3* loc on S side of Wishaw. NS 7853
Gowthams Lincs 45 H4* loc 1km W of Orby. TF 4867
Gowthorpe Humberside 50 C3 loc 3m/5km E of Stamford Br. SE 7654
Gowy 42 A4 r rising SE of Peckforton, Ches, and flowing generally NW into R Mersey at Stanlow, E of Ellesmere Port. SJ 4277
Goxhill Humberside 51 E5/E6 vil 2m/3km SE of New Holland. TA 1021
Goxhill Humberside 51 F4 ham 2m/4km SW of Hornsea. TA 1844
Goyt 42 D2 r rising on the High Peak S of Brown Knoll, Derbys, and flowing W to New Mills, then NW to join R Tame on N side of Stockport and form R Mersey. SJ 8990
Goytre W Glam 14 D3* loc 2m/3km E of Port Talbot. SS 7889
Gozzard's Ford Oxon 17 H2 loc on E side of Abingdon Airfield 2m/3km NW of Abingdon. SU 4698
Graby Lincs 37 F2* loc 6m/10km N of Bourne. TF 0929
Gracemount Lothian 66 A2* dist of Edinburgh 4m/6km SE of city centre. NT 2768
Grade Cornwall 2 C6 ham 2m/3km N of Lizard Pt. SW 7114
Gradeley Green Ches 42 B5/B6* loc 4m/6km W of Nantwich. SJ 5952
Graemsay Orkney 89 A7 sparsely inhabited island of about 250 acres or 100 hectares, situated in Hoy Sound S of Stromness, Mainland. Two lighthouses, at NE and NW ends. HY 2605
Graffham W Sussex 11 F3 vil below S Downs 4m/6km SE of Midhurst. SU 9217
Grafham Cambs 29 F1 vil 5m/8km W of Huntingdon on NE side of large resr, **G. Water.** TL 1669
Grafham Surrey 11 F1 ham 3m/5km NW of Cranleigh. TQ 0241
Grafton H & W 26 A4* loc 2m/4km S of Hereford. SO 4936
Grafton H & W 26 B2* ham 5m/9km W of Leominster. SO 5761
Grafton H & W 27 E4* vil 5m/8km SW of Evesham. SO 9837
Grafton N Yorks 49 F2 vil 2m/4km SE of Boroughbridge. SE 4163
Grafton Oxon 17 G2* ham 4m/6km E of Lechlade. SP 2600
Grafton Salop 34 B3 ham 5m/9km NW of Shrewsbury. SJ 4318
Grafton, East Wilts 17 G5 vil 6m/10km SW of Hungerford. SU 2560
Grafton Flyford H & W 26 D2 vil 7m/11km E of Worcester. SO 9655
Grafton Regis Northants 28 C3 vil 5m/7km NW of Stony Stratford. SP 7546
Grafton Underwood Northants 37 E6 vil 4m/6km E of Kettering. SP 9280
Grafton, West Wilts 17 F5* vil 5m/8km E of Pewsey. SU 2460
Grafty Green Kent 21 E6* vil 5m/8km W of Charing. TQ 8748
Graianrhyd Clwyd 41 H5* loc 3m/4km SW of Treuddyn. SJ 2156
Graig Clwyd 41 G4* ham 1km S of Tremeirchion. SJ 0872
Graig Gwynedd 41 E4 ham 5m/9km SW of Colwyn Bay. Bodnant Gardens (NT) to N. SH 8071
Graig Capel Dyfed 23 F5* loc adjoining Burry Port to N. SN 4401
Graigfechan Clwyd 41 G5 ham 3m/5km SE of Ruthin. SJ 1454
Graig Penllin S Glam 15 E4* loc 1m N of Penllin. SS 9777
Grain Kent 21 E4 loc at E end of Isle of Grain opp Sheerness. TQ 8876
Grain Earth House Orkney 89 B6* prehistoric earth hse (A.M.) opp Kirkwall, Mainland, across head of bay. HY 4411
Grain, Isle of Kent 21 E4 peninsula on W side of mouth of R Medway opp Isle of Sheppey. Extensive oil refinery installations. TQ 8775
Grains Bar Gtr Manchester 43 E1* loc 3m/5km NE of Oldham. SD 9608
Grainsby Lincs 45 F2 vil 6m/10km S of Grimsby. TF 2799
Grains o' th' Beck Bridge Durham 53 G3 br carrying rd from Brough to Middleton in Teesdale across R Lune, 6m/10km NE of Brough. NY 8620
Grainthorpe Lincs 45 G2 vil 7m/11km NE of Louth. **G. Haven,** marshy inlet 3m/4km NE. TF 3897
Gramisdale W Isles 88 E1* loc at N end of Benbecula 2m/3km E of Benbecula Airfield. NF 8155
Grampian 115 admin region of NE Scotland, comprising the former counties of Aberdeen, Banff, Kincardine, and Moray. The coastline extends from 5m/8km E of Nairn on the Moray Firth to the mouth of R North Esk, 3m/5km N of Montrose, and along it are many fishing ports, incl Aberdeen, Fraserburgh, Peterhead, and Stonehaven, as well as several smaller places. The discovery of North Sea oil has made an impact, esp on Aberdeen. The region also contains the great majority of the malt whisky distilleries of Scotland. The Cairngorms are partly in the region, which also includes R Dee and the lower reaches of R Spey and R Findhorn.
Grampian Mountains 74, 75 the great mountain system of Scotland, extending from SW to NE, its southern edge forming the natural boundary between the Highlands and the Lowlands. Includes several smaller chains and groups. NN 88
Grampound Cornwall 3 E3 vil on R Fal 6m/9km SW of St Austell. SW 9348
Grampound Road Cornwall 3 E3* vil beside rly 6m/10km W of St Austell. SW 9150
Granborough Bucks 28 C5 vil 2m/3km S of Winslow. SP 7625
Granby Notts 36 C1/D1 vil 4m/6km SE of Bingham. SK 7536
Grandborough Warwicks 28 A1 vil 5m/8km S of Rugby. SP 4966
Grandhome Grampian 83 G5* loc 4m/7km NW of Aberdeen. NJ 9011
Grandpont Oxon 18 A1* dist of Oxford 1km S of city centre. SP 5105
Grandtully Castle Tayside 75 H5 cas dating from 1560, with later additions, in Strath Tay 3m/4km NE of Aberfeldy. NN 8951
Grand Union Canal 19 G3-36 B2 canal connecting R Thames at London with R Soar S of Leicester and thus with R Trent at Trent Junction N of Kegworth, Leics.

Another branch goes from Norton Junction, SE of Rugby, to Birmingham, by Leamington, Warwick, and Solihull.
Grand Western Canal Devon 7 G4-H3 canal formerly connecting Tiverton and Taunton. Somerset section disused; Devon section still navigable in parts.
Grange Cumbria 52 C3 ham in Borrowdale 1m S of S end of Derwent Water. NY 2517
Grange Cumbria 59 H6* loc 4m/7km SW of Carlisle. NY 3551
Grange Grampian 82 D2 loc 4m/7km E of Keith. Distillery. NJ 4950
Grange Gwent 15 G2* industrial estate in Cwmbran. ST 2995
Grange H'land 80 D4 loc in Inverness dist 8m/13km W of Drumnadrochit. NH 3730
Grange Lothian 66 A2* dist of Edinburgh 2km S of city centre. NT 2571
Grange Merseyside 41 H3 loc 1m E of W Kirby. SJ 2287
Grange S'clyde 64 B5* W dist of Kilmarnock. NS 4137
Grange Tayside 73 F2 loc in Carse of Gowrie 2m/3km NE of Errol. NO 2725
Grange de Lings Lincs 44 D3* loc 4m/7km N of Lincoln. SK 9877
Grange Estate Dorset 9 H4* loc 1m SE of St Leonards and 3m/5km SW of Ringwood. SU 1101
Grange, High Durham 54 B2* loc 2m/4km S of Crook. NZ 1731
Grange Hill Essex 20 B3* S dist of Chigwell. TQ 4492
Grange, Lower W Yorks 48 D5* loc in Bradford 3m/4km W of city centre. SE 1233
Grangemill Derbys 43 G5 ham 4m/6km NW of Wirksworth. SK 2457
Grange Moor W Yorks 49 E6 vil 4m/6km SW of Dewsbury. SE 2216
Grangemouth Central 65 F1 container port on S side of Firth of Forth 3m/5km E of Falkirk. Oil refinery and chemical works. E terminus of Forth and Clyde Canal (disused). NS 9281
Grange-over-Sands Cumbria 47 E1 resort on right bank of R Kent estuary 9m/14km N of Morecambe across Morecambe Bay. SD 4077
Grange Park London 19 G2* loc in borough of Enfield 1m SW of Enfield tn centre and 9m/14km N of Charing Cross. TQ 3195
Grangetown Cleveland 54 D3 urban loc 4m/6km E of Middlesbrough. NZ 5520
Grangetown S Glam 15 G4 dist of Cardiff 2km S of city centre at mouth of R Taff on W bank. Rd br to Butetown and docks. ST 1874
Grangetown Tyne & Wear 61 H5* dist of Sunderland 2km S of tn centre. NZ 4054
Grange View Ches 42 B4* loc 3m/5km W of Northwich. SJ 6074
Grange Villa Durham 61 G6* vil 3m/4km W of Chester-le-Street. NZ 2352
Grannell 24 B3* r rising near Dihewyd, Dyfed, and flowing S into R Teifi 3m/5km W of Lampeter. SN 5346
Gransden, Great Cambs 29 G2 vil 5m/8km NE of Potton. **Lit Gransden** vil adjoining to S. TL 2755
Gransmoor Humberside 51 F3 ham 6m/9km SE of Bridlington. TA 1259
Granston (Treopert) Dyfed 22 B3 ham 5m/7km S of Strumble Hd. SM 8934
Granta 29 H3 r rising near Thaxted, Essex. See (R) Cam.
Grantchester Cambs 29 H2 vil 2m/3km SW of Cambridge. TL 4355
Grantham Lincs 37 E1 tn on R Witham 22m/35km E of Nottingham. Outstanding ch with tall spire. Several old bldgs. **G. Hse** (NT) dates from late 14c. Angel and Royal Hotel, 15c. Industries include agricultural machinery mnfre. SK 9135
Grantley, High N Yorks 49 E2 vil 5m/8km W of Ripon. SE 2370
Grantley, Low N Yorks 49 E2 ham adjoining High Grantley to E. SE 2370
Granton Lothian 66 A1 dist of Edinburgh 2m/4km NW of city centre. Harbour on Firth of Forth. NT 2377
Grantown-on-Spey H'land 82 A4 market tn and resort 19m/31km S of Forres. Castle Grant, 2m/3km N, dating in part from 16c, was formerly home of the chiefs of Grant, Earls of Seafield. NJ 0327
Grantsfield H & W 26 A2* loc 2m/4km E of Leominster. SO 5260
Grantshouse Borders 67 E2 vil on Eye Water 8m/13km W of Eyemouth. NT 8065
Grappenhall Ches 42 C3 loc 3m/4km SE of Warrington tn centre. SJ 6486
Grasby Lincs 45 E1 vil 3m/5km NW of Caistor. TA 0804
Grasmere Cumbria 52 D4 lake 3m/4km NW of Ambleside. Also vil on R Rothay to N of lake. Dove Cottage is former home of Wordsworth. NY 3306
Grasmoor Cumbria 52 B3 mt in Lake Dist 2m/3km N of Buttermere ham. Height 2791 ft or 851 metres. NY 1720
Grasscroft Gtr Manchester 43 E1* loc 3m/5km E of Oldham. SD 9704
Grassendale Merseyside 42 A3 dist of Liverpool 5m/7km SE of city centre. SJ 3985
Grassgarth Cumbria 52 D5* loc 2m/3km E of Windermere. SD 4499
Grassgarth Cumbria 60 A6* loc just W of Welton. NY 3444
Grass Green Essex 30 C4* loc 5m/7km NE of Finchingfield. TL 7338
Grassholm Dyfed 22 to W of sq A5. Small island 8m/12km W of Skomer. Bird sanctuary; breeding place of the gannet. SM 5909
Grass Holm Orkney 89 B6* islet off W coast of Shapinsay opp Salt Ness. HY 4619
Grassholme Reservoir Durham 53 H3 resr in course of R Lune 2m/3km S of Middleton in Teesdale. NY 9422
Grassington N Yorks 48 C2 vil in Wharfedale 8m/13km N of Skipton. SE 0064
Grassmoor Derbys 43 H4 vil 3m/5km SE of Chesterfield. SK 4066
Grass Point S'clyde 70 A2 headland on E coast of Mull, on S side of entrance to Loch Don. NM 7430
Grassthorpe Notts 44 C4 vil 4m/7km SE of Tuxford. SK 7967
Grasswell Tyne & Wear 61 G6/H6* loc in N part of Houghton-le-Spring. NZ 3350
Grateley Hants 10 A1 vil 6m/10km SW of Andover. SU 2741
Gratton Devon 6 C4* loc 5m/8km NE of Holsworthy. SS 3910
Gratton Staffs 43 E5* loc 3m/5km W of Leek. SJ 9356
Gratwich Staffs 35 F2 ham 4m/7km W of Uttoxeter. SK 0231
Graveley Cambs 29 F2 vil 5m/8km S of Huntingdon. TL 2563
Graveley Herts 29 F5 vil 3m/4km N of Stevenage. TL 2327
Gravel Hill Bucks 19 E2* loc in Chalfont St Peter NE of tn centre. TQ 0091
Gravelhill Salop 34 B3* loc in N part of Shrewsbury. SJ 4813
Gravel Hole Gtr Manchester 43 E1* loc 3m/5km N of Oldham. SD 9109
Gravelly Hill W Midlands 35 G5 loc in Birmingham 4m/6km NE of city centre. SP 1090
Gravelly Way Staffs 35 E3* loc 4m/7km W of Cannock. SJ 9109
Graven Shetland 89 E6* loc on Mainland at head of Garths Voe. HU 4173
Graveney Kent 21 F5 vil 3m/4km E of Faversham. **G. Marshes** to N. TR 0562
Gravenhurst, Lower Beds 29 E4* ham 2m/4km SE of Clophill. TL 1135
Gravenhurst, Upper Beds 29 E4 vil 3m/5km SW of Shefford. TL 1136
Gravesend Avon 16 B3* loc 2m/3km SE of Thornbury. Quarries to E. ST 6589
Gravesend Kent 20 C4 industrial tn on R Thames 7m/11km NW of Rochester. Ferry for pedestrians to Tilbury. **G. Reach** is length of r from Tilbury Ness to Coalhouse Pt. TQ 6474
Gravesham 119 admin dist of Kent.
Gravir W Isles 88 B2/C2 vil near E coast of Lewis at head of Loch Ouirn, 3m/5km W of Kebock Hd. NB 3715
Grayingham Lincs 44 D2 vil 2km S of Kirton in Lindsey. SK 9396
Grayrigg Cumbria 53 E5 vil 5m/8km NE of Kendal. **G. Tarn** small lake 2km NE. SD 5797
Grays Essex 20 C4 tn on N bank of R Thames 2m/3km NW of Tilbury. TQ 6177
Grayshott Hants 11 E2 vil 1m W of Hindhead. Much NT property in vicinity. SU 8735
Grays Thurrock Essex. Alternative name for Grays.
Grayston Plain N Yorks 49 E3* loc 1km SW of Hampsthwaite. SE 2557
Grayswood Surrey 11 F2 vil 2km NE of Haslemere. SU 9134
Graythorp Cleveland 54 D2* loc 3m/5km S of Hartlepool. Site of nuclear power stn. NZ 5127
Grazeley Berks 18 B4 ham 4m/7km S of Reading. Royal Ordnance Factory partly in par. SU 6966
Greanamul W Isles 88 D4* islet midway between Pabbay and Sandray. NL 6289
Greanamul W Isles 88 D3/E3* islet 2m/3km E of Northbay Airfield, Barra. NF 7305
Greasbrough S Yorks 43 H2 dist of Rotherham 2m/3km NW of tn centre. SK 4195
Greasby Merseyside 41 H3 suburb 4m/7km W of Birkenhead. SJ 2587
Greasley Notts 44 A6* ham 2m/3km E of Eastwood. Faint remains of 14c cas. SK 4947
GREAT, GREATER. For names beginning with these words, see under next word. This also applies to names beginning with Little, Lesser; High, Low; Higher, Lower; Upper, Nether; Far, Near; Mid, Middle; Isle(s) of; North, South, East, West; The, Y, Yr.
Greatford Lincs 37 F3 vil 5m/8km NE of Stamford. TF 0811
Greatgate Staffs 35 F1 ham 4m/6km SE of Cheadle. SK 0540
Greatham Cleveland 54 D2 vil 3m/5km S of Hartlepool. Steel works to NE. To E, **G. Creek** runs into mouth of R Tees. NZ 4927
Greatham Hants 11 E2 vil 4m/6km W of Liphook. SU 7730
Greatmoor Hill Borders 60 B2 hill 6m/10km SE of Teviothead. Height 1964 ft or 599 metres. NT 4800
Greatness Kent 20 B5* N dist of Sevenoaks. TQ 5356
Greatstone-on-Sea Kent 13 F4 resort on St Mary's Bay 2km SE of New Romney. TR 0823
Greatworth Northants 28 B3 vil 4m/6km NW of Brackley. SP 5542
Greave Gtr Manchester 43 E2* loc 1m NE of Romiley. SJ 9491
Greave Lancs 48 B5* loc adjoining Bacup to E. SD 8723
Greeba 46 B5* r on Isle of Man rising on W side of Greeba Mt and running S to join R Dhoo at Crosby. SC 3279
Greeb Point Cornwall 2 D5 headland 2km S of Porthscatho. SW 8733
Green Clwyd 41 F4* loc 2m/3km N of Denbigh. SJ 0568
Greena Shetland 89 E7* small island at entrance to Weisdale Voe, Mainland. HU 3747
Greenacres Gtr Manchester 43 E1* loc in Oldham 2km E of tn centre. SD 9405
Green Bank Cumbria 52 D6* loc 2km N of Cartmel. SD 3880
Greenbank Lothian 66 A2* dist of Edinburgh 3m/4km S of city centre. NT 2369
Greenbooth Reservoir Gtr Manchester 47 H6* resr in Rochdale 3m/5km NW of tn centre. SD 8515
Green Bottom Cornwall 2 C4* loc 4m/6km W of Truro. SW 7645
Green Bottom Glos 26 B5* loc 2km NE of Cinderford. SO 6715
Greencroft Durham 54 B1 loc 2km NW of Lanchester. NZ 1549
Greencroft Durham 61 F6* loc 1km W of Annfield Plain. NZ 1651
Greencroft Norfolk 39 E1 loc adjoining Blakeney to W. TG 0243
Green Cross Surrey 11 E1* loc 2m/3km NW of Hindhead. SU 8638
Greendale Tarn Cumbria 52 B4* small lake 3m/4km W of Wasdale Hd. NY 1407
Greendykes Nthmb 67 G5* loc 1km E of Chatton. NU 0628
Green, East Suffolk 30 B3* ham 5m/8km N of Haverhill. TL 6853
Green, East Suffolk 31 G2* loc 2m/3km NE of Saxmundham. TM 4065
Green End Beds 29 E2* N end of vil of Lit Staughton 3m/5km S of Kimbolton. TL 1063
Green End Beds 29 E2* S end of vil of Pertenhall, 2m/4km SW of Kimbolton. TL 0864
Green End Beds 29 E3* loc 3m/5km SW of Bedford across R Ouse. TL 0147
Green End Beds 29 F3 NE end of Gt Barford vil, 4m/7km NW of Sandy. TL 1252
Green End Bucks 28 D4* loc adjoining Gt Brickhill to N, 3m/4km SE of Bletchley. SP 9030
Green End Cambs 29 F1 loc on E side of vil of Gt Stukeley, 2m/3km NW of Huntingdon. TL 2274
Green End Cambs 29 G1* N dist of St Ives. TL 3172
Green End Cambs 29 G2 N end of Comberton. TL 3856
Green End Cambs 29 H1* loc 2m/3km E of Cottenham. TL 4768
Green End Cambs 30 A2* loc on E bank of R Cam adjoining Fen Ditton. TL 4860
Green End Cambs 37 F6* S end of vil of Sawtry, 4m/6km S of Stilton. TL 1783
Green End Cambs 38 A6* S end of vil of Stretham. TL 5174
Green End Herts 29 F4* N end of vil of Weston, 2m/4km SE of Baldock. TL 2630
Green End Herts 29 G4* ham 5m/9km E of Baldock. TL 3233
Green End Herts 29 G5 ham 4m/6km W of Puckeridge. TL 3322
Green End Lancs 48 B3* loc adjoining Earby to S. SD 9046
Greenend Oxon 27 G5* loc 2m/4km NW of Charlbury. SP 3221
Green End Warwicks 35 H5* ham 4m/7km SE of Coleshill. SP 2686
Green, Far Glos 16 C2* ham 2m/4km NE of Dursley. SO 7700
Greenfaulds S'clyde 65 E2* residential area of Cumbernauld 1m S of tn centre. NS 7573
Greenfield Beds 29 E4 vil 2m/4km SE of Ampthill. TL 0534
Greenfield Clwyd 41 G4 vil 2km NE of Holywell. Remains of Basingwerk Abbey (A.M.), founded 1131. SJ 1977
Greenfield Gtr Manchester 43 E1* loc 2m/3km NE of Mossley. SD 9904
Greenfield Lincs 45 G3* loc 2m/3km NW of Alford. TF 4377
Greenfield Oxon 18 C2* loc 3m/5km N of Nettlebed. SU 7191
Greenfield Reservoir Gtr Manchester 43 E1* small resr on Saddleworth Moor 6m/10km E of Oldham. SE 0205
Green Field Reservoir Lancs 48 B5* small resr on Forest of Rossendale 2m/4km N of Rawtenstall. SD 8226
Greenfields Derbys 35 H3* loc 2m/3km SW of Swadlincote. SK 2817
Greenford London 19 F3 loc in borough of Ealing 10m/16km W of Charing Cross. Loc of **G. Green** to N. TQ 1482
Greengairs S'clyde 65 E2 vil 3m/5km SE of Cumbernauld. NS 7870
Green Gate Devon 7 G3* ham just NE of Uplowman. ST 0115
Greengate Gtr Manchester 48 B6* loc 2m/3km NE of Rochdale. SD 9115
Greengates W Yorks 48 D4 dist of Bradford 3m/5km NE of city centre. SE 1837
Greengill Cumbria 52 B2* loc 1m SW of Gilcrux. NY 1037
Green, Great and **Little** Norfolk 39 E5* adjoining locs between Bunwell and Bunwell Street. TM 1293
Green, Great Cambs 29 G3* ham 5m/8km NW of Royston. TL 2844
Green, Great Norfolk 39 F5* loc 1m N of Denton. TM 2789
Green, Great Suffolk 30 D2* loc 1m W of Norton. TL 9365
Green, Great Suffolk 30 D3* ham 6m/9km SE of Bury St Edmunds. TL 9155
Green, Great Suffolk 31 F1* ham 2km NW of Wingfield. TM 2178
Green,Great Suffolk 31 F1 loc 2m/3km S of Diss. TM 1277
Green Hailey Bucks 18 C2* loc 2km E of Princes Risborough. SP 8203
Greenhalgh Lancs 47 E4 ham 3m/4km NW of Kirkham. SD 4035
Greenham Berks 18 A5* S suburb of Newbury. SU 4865
Greenham Som 7 H3 ham 4m/6km W of Wellington. ST 0820
Green Hammerton N Yorks 50 A3 vil 7m/12km SE of Boroughbridge. SE 4556
Greenhaugh Nthmb 60 D3 ham 4m/6km NW of Bellingham. NY 7987
Greenhays Gtr Manchester 42 C1* loc 2m/3km SW of Farnworth. SD 7104
Green Head Cumbria 59 H6 loc 1km S of Dalston. NY 3649
Greenhead Nthmb 60 C5 vil on Tipalt Burn 3m/5km W of Haltwhistle. NY 6665
Green Head Orkney 89 A7* headland on E coast of Hoy opp island of Cava. ND 3099
Green Heath Staffs 35 F3* loc 2m/3km NE of Cannock. SJ 9913

Greenheys Gtr Manchester 42 D2* dist of Manchester 2km SE of city centre. Art gallery. Manchester University. SJ 8496
Green, High Cumbria 52 D4* loc adjoining Troutbeck to N. NY 4103
Green, High H & W 26 D3 vil 5m/8km W of Pershore. SO 8745
Green, High Norfolk 38 D3* loc 2km SE of Beeston. TF 9214
Green, High Norfolk 38 D4* loc 2m/3km W of Shipdham. TF 9307
Green, High Norfolk 39 E4* ham 3m/5km NE of Wymondham. TG 1305
Green, High Norfolk 39 F5* vil 1km S of Gt Moulton. TM 1689
Green, High Norfolk 39 F5* W end of Brooke vil. TM 2898
Green, High N Yorks 54 A4* loc adjoining Langthwaite to W. NZ 0002
Green, High Salop 34 D5* loc adjoining vil of Chorley to E, 5m/8km N of Cleobury Mortimer. SO 7083
Green, High Suffolk 30 D2* loc 1km W of Nowton. TL 8560
Green, High S Yorks 43 G2 loc 7m/11km N of Sheffield. SK 3397
Green, High W Yorks 48 D6* loc 4m/6km E of Huddersfield. SE 1915
Green, Higher Gtr Manchester 42 C2 loc 2km SE of Tyldesley. **Lr Green** loc 1km S. SD 7000
Greenhill Central 65 E1* loc 1m S of Bonnybridge. NS 8278
Greenhill Durham 61 H6* loc adjoining Murton to E. NZ 4047
Greenhill H & W 35 E6* NE dist of Kidderminster. SO 8477
Greenhill H & W 26 C3* loc 4m/6km NW of Gt Malvern. SO 7248
Greenhill Kent 13 G1* SW dist of Herne Bay. TR 1666
Greenhill London 19 F3 loc in borough of Harrow 10m/16km NW of Charing Cross. TQ 1588
Greenhill S Yorks 43 H3 loc in Sheffield 4m/6km S of city centre. SK 3481
Green Hill Wilts 17 E3* loc 3m/4km N of Wootton Bassett. SU 0686
Greenhill Bank Salop 34 B1* loc 2m/3km NW of Ellesmere. SJ 3736
Greenhillocks Derbys 43 H6 loc adjoining Ripley to S. SK 4049
Green Hills Cambs 30 B1 loc at SE end of Soham. TL 6072
Greenhills S'clyde 64 D3* dist of E Kilbride 2km SW of tn centre. NS 6252
Greenhithe Kent 20 C4 loc in Thames-side industrial complex 3m/5km E of Dartford. TQ 5875
Greenholm S'clyde. See Newmilns.
Green Holm Shetland 89 E6* island rock off Burra Ness on S coast of Yell. HU 5178
Greenholme Cumbria 53 E4 loc 2m/3km NW of Tebay. NY 5905
Green Holm, Little Orkney 89 B6* islet to S of Muckle Green Holm, qv, across narrow **Sound of the Green Holms.** HY 5226
Greenhow Hill N Yorks 48 D2 vil 3m/5km W of Pateley Br. SE 1164
Green Island Dorset 9 G5* island on S side of Poole Harbour. SZ 0086
Green Island H'land 85 A5 islet in Enard Bay off NW coast of Ross and Cromarty dist 2km S of Eilean Mor. NC 0515
Green Isle Shetland 89 E7* tiny island off E coast of Mainland in Dury Voe. HU 4861
Greenland H'land 86 E1 loc in Caithness dist 3m/4km SE of Dunnet. ND 2467
Greenland S Yorks 43 H2* dist of Sheffield 3m/4km E of city centre. SK 3988
Greenlands H & W 27 E1* S dist of Redditch. SP 0565
Green Lane Devon 4 D3* loc 5m/8km N of Ashburton. SX 7877
Green Lane 27 E2* loc on borders of H & W and Warwicks 3m/4km SE of Redditch. SP 0664
Greenlaw Borders 66 D4 vil on Blackadder Water 7m/11km SW of Duns. NT 7146
Greenlee Lough Nthmb 60 D4 lake 3m/5km N of Bardon Mill. NY 7769
Greenli Ness Orkney 89 C6* headland on S coast of Stronsay on W side of entrance to Bay of Holland. HY 6221
Green, Little Cambs 29 G3* ham 5m/8km NW of Royston. TL 2844
Green, Little Clwyd 34 B1* loc between Eglwys Cross and The Chequer, 4m/6km W of Whitchurch. SJ 4840
Green, Little Notts 36 C1* loc 1km NE of Car Colston. SK 7243
Green, Little Som 16 C6* ham adjoining Mells to S, 3m/5km W of Frome. ST 7248
Green, Little Suffolk 31 E1* loc adjoining Gislingham to W. TM 0671
Greenloaning Tayside 72 C4 loc 5m/8km NE of Dunblane. NN 8307
Green, Long Ches 42 B4* loc 4m/6km S of Helsby. SJ 4770
Green, Low Gtr Manchester 42 B1* loc 1m SW of Hindley. SD 6003
Green, Low N Yorks 49 E2* loc 2m/3km W of Birstwith. SE 2059
Green, Low Suffolk 30 D2* loc 1km NE of Nowton. TL 8661
Green, Lower Essex 29 H4* W part of vil of Langley, 6m/10km SE of Royston. TL 4334
Green, Lower Essex 30 C4* loc 4m/6km E of Finchingfield. TL 7331
Green, Lower Herts 29 F4* loc 2m/3km N of Hitchin. TL 1832
Green, Lower Norfolk 39 E1 ham 1km NE of Hindringham. TF 9937
Green, Lower Norfolk 39 G4* loc adjoining Freethorpe to N. TG 4005
Green, Lower Staffs 35 E4 loc adjoining Coven to N, 5m/9km N of Wolverhampton. SJ 9007
Green, Lower Suffolk 30 C2* N end of Higham, 7m/11km W of Bury St Edmunds. TL 7465
Green, Lower Warwicks 28 A1* loc 5m/7km S of Rugby. SP 4968
Green Lowther S'clyde 58 D1 mt and radar stn 2m/3km SE of Leadhills. Height 2403 ft or 732 metres; highest of Lowther Hills. See also Lowther Hill. NS 9012
Greenmeadow Gwent 15 G2* loc in W part of Cwmbran. ST 2795
Green, Middle Bucks 19 E3* loc 2m/3km E of Slough. TQ 0080
Green, Middle Som 7 H3* ham 1m S of Wellington. ST 1319
Green, Middle Suffolk 30 C2* loc to S of Higham ch, 7m/11km W of Bury St Edmunds. TL 7465
Green Moor S Yorks 43 G2* ham 1m NE of Stocksbridge. SK 2899
Greenmoor Hill Oxon 18 B3* loc 3m/5km E of Goring. SU 6481
Greenmount Gtr Manchester 47 H6 vil 3m/5km SW of Bury. SD 7714
Green, North Norfolk 39 F5 loc 4m/6km NW of Harleston. TM 2288
Green, North Suffolk 31 G1* loc 2km NW of Cratfield. TM 3076
Green, North Suffolk 31 G2* ham 2m/3km SE of Framlingham. TM 3162
Green, North Suffolk 31 G2* loc 2m/3km N of Saxmundham. TM 3966
Greenoak Humberside 50 C5* loc 4m/7km E of Howden. SE 8127
Greenock S'clyde 64 A2 industrial tn and port on S side of Firth of Clyde 2m/3km W of Glasgow. Birthplace of James Watt, 1736-1819. Large harbour and docks; Clydeport container terminal. Industries include shipbuilding, marine engineering, sugar refining, woollen and worsted spinning, mnfre of office equipment. NS 2776
Greenock Water 56 F2 r in Strathclyde region running SW to R Ayr 4m/7km W of Muirkirk. NS 6226
Greenodd Cumbria 52 C6 vil 3m/5km NE of Ulverston. SD 3182
Green Ore Som 16 B6* ham 2m/4km SW of Chewton Mendip. ST 5750
Green Quarter Cumbria 52 D4* ham just E of Kentmere vil. NY 4604
Greenrow Cumbria 59 F6* loc adjoining Silloth to S. NY 1052
Greens Grampian 83 F2/F3* loc 4m/6km W of New Deer. NJ 8245
Green Scar Dyfed 22 A4 rock island lying 1m W of Dinas-fawr, between Black Scar and The Mare. SM 7922
Greensgate Norfolk 39 E3* loc 1km W of Weston Longville. TG 1015
Greenside Tyne & Wear 61 F5 vil 2m/3km SW of Ryton. **Low Greenside** loc to N. NZ 1362
Greenside W Yorks 48 D6* loc in Huddersfield 2m/3km E of tn centre. SE 1716
Green Side W Yorks 49 E5* loc in Wortley dist of Leeds 2m/4km SW of city centre. SE 2632
Greenside Reservoir S'clyde 64 C2* small resr on Kilpatrick Hills 5m/8km E of Dumbarton. NS 4775
Greenside Tarn Cumbria 53 F4* small lake 1km SW of Ravenstonedale. NY 7103
Greens, North Grampian 82 B1* loc near N coast 2m/3km W of Lossiemouth. NJ 2070
Greens Norton Northants 28 B3 vil 2m/3km NW of Towcester. SP 6649
Green, South Essex 20 C3 SE dist of Billericay. TQ 6893
Green, South Essex 31 E6* loc at head of Geedon Creek 5m/7km SE of Colchester. TM 0319
Green, South Kent 20 D5* ham 4m/7km SW of Sittingbourne. TQ 8560
Green, South Norfolk 38 A3* SW part of Terrington St Clement. TF 5319
Green, South Norfolk 39 E3* loc adjoining E Dereham to S. TF 9912
Green, South Norfolk 39 E4 ham just S of Mattishall. TG 0510
Green, South Norfolk 39 F6* loc 1m S of Pulham St Mary. TM 2083
Green, South Suffolk 31 F1* loc 2m/3km NE of Eye. TM 1775
Greenstead Essex 31 E5* E dist of Colchester. TM 0225
Greenstead Green Essex 30 C5 vil 2m/3km S of Halstead. TL 8228
Greensted Essex 20 B2* ham 1m W of Chipping Ongar. Saxon ch with nave walls of oak. TL 5302
Greensted Green Essex 20 B2* ham 2m/3km W of Chipping Ongar. TL 5203
Greenstone Point H'land 78 F1 headland on W coast of Ross and Cromarty dist 11m/18km N of Poolewe. Otherwise known as Rubha na Lice Uaine. NG 8598
Green Street E Sussex 12 D5* loc 1km SE of Crowhurst. TQ 7611
Green Street Glos 26 D5 loc 4m/7km SE of Gloucester. SO 8915
Green Street Herts 19 F2 loc adjoining Borehamwood to N. TQ 1998
Green Street Herts 29 H5* ham 2m/3km W of Bishop's Stortford. TL 4522
Green Street H & W 26 D3* ham 4m/6km S of Worcester. SO 8649
Green Street H & W 26 D3* loc 5m/8km N of Tewkesbury. SO 8740
Green Street Suffolk 31 F1* loc adjoining Hoxne to E. TM 1877
Green Street W Sussex 11 G3* loc 2m/3km E of Coolham. TQ 1422
Green Street Green Kent 20 C4 vil 4m/6km SE of Dartford. TQ 5870
Green Street Green London 20 B5 loc in borough of Bromley 2m/3km S of Orpington. TQ 4563
Greenstreet Green Suffolk 31 E3* loc 5m/8km N of Hadleigh. TM 0450
Green, The Beds 29 E5* loc adjoining Whipsnade to W. TL 0017
Green, The Clwyd 41 H4* loc adjoining Northop to W. SJ 2468
Green, The Cumbria 52 B6 ham 3m/5km N of Millom. SD 1784
Green, The Essex 30 C5* ham 2m/4km SE of Braintree. TL 7719
Green Tye Herts 29 H6 ham 3m/5km SW of Bishop's Stortford. TL 4418
Green, Upper Berks 17 G5 vil 4m/6km SE of Hungerford. SU 3763
Green, Upper Essex 29 H4 E part of vil of Langley, 6m/10km W of Saffron Walden. TL 4435
Green, Upper Essex 30 B4 ham 3m/5km N of Thaxted. TL 5935
Green, Upper Gwent 25 H5* loc 4m/7km W of Skenfrith. SO 3819
Green, Upper Suffolk 30 C2* loc at S end of Higham, 7m/11km W of Bury St Edmunds. TL 7464
Green, Upper W Yorks 49 E5* loc 2m/3km SE of Morley. SE 2825
Greenway Glos 26 C4* loc 3m/5km S of Ledbury. SO 7033
Greenway S Glam 15 F4* ham 4m/6km E of Cowbridge. ST 0574
Greenway Som 8 B2* loc 3m/4km NE of Taunton. ST 2527
Greenway Som 8 B2 ham adjoining N Curry 6m/9km E of Taunton. ST 3124
Greenwell Cumbria 60 B5* loc 3m/5km S of Brampton. NY 5356
Green, West Hants 18 C5* ham 2m/3km NE of Hook. West Green Hse (NT), early 18c. SU 7456
Green, West London 19 G3* loc in borough of Haringey 6m/9km N of Charing Cross. TQ 3289
Green, West W Sussex 11 H2* W dist of Crawley. TQ 2637
Greenwich London 20 A4 tn and borough on S bank of R Thames 6m/9km E of Charing Cross. The borough extends from Plumstead Marshes (N) to New Eltham (S) and from Bostall Woods (E) to Deptford (W). At Greenwich itself is the Royal Naval College on site of former royal palace, the National Maritime Museum, and old Royal Observatory. TQ 3977
Greenwich Reach 20 A4* reach of R Thames at Greenwich, on the S bank. The Isle of Dogs is on the N bank. TQ 3778
Green Withens Reservoir W Yorks 48 C6* resr on Rishworth Moor 3m/5km SW of Rishworth. SD 9816
Greenwood Lee W Yorks 48 C5* loc 2m/3km NW of Hebden Br. SD 9729
Greet Glos 27 E4* ham 1m N of Winchcombe. SP 0230
Greeta W Isles 88 C2* r on Lewis rising among lochs some 6m/10km NW of Stornoway and flowing SE into Stornoway Harbour. Also known as R Creed. NB 4131
Greete Salop 26 B1* vil 2m/3km NW of Tenbury Wells. SO 5770
Greetham Leics 37 E3 vil 6m/9km NE of Oakham. SK 9214
Greetham Lincs 45 G4 vil 3m/5km E of Horncastle. TF 3070
Greetland W Yorks 48 D5 vil 1m W of Elland. **G. Nook** ham 2km W. SE 0921
Greg Ness Grampian 77 H1* headland on E coast at S end of Nigg Bay, Aberdeen. NJ 9704
Gregson Lane Lancs 47 F5* loc 4m/6km SE of Preston. SD 5926
Gregynog Hall Powys 33 G4 former private hse and park now property of University of Wales, containing pictures and printing press, 2km SW of Tregynon. SO 0897
Greian Head W Isles 88 D3 headland on NW coast of Barra 4m/7km SW of Scurrival Pt. NF 6404
Greineim W Isles 88 A2* islet nearly 1km off W coast of Lewis 2km N of Mealasta I. NA 9824
Greine Sgeir W Isles 88 A3* rock island off W coast of island of Lewis opp entrance to Loch Resort. NB 0015
Greinton Som 8 C1 vil on S side of Polden Hills 5m/7km W of Street. ST 4136
Grendon Northants 28 D2 vil 5m/8km S of Wellingborough. SP 8760
Grendon Warwicks 35 H4 ham 2m/4km NW of Atherstone. SK 2800
Grendon Green H & W 26 B2 loc 4m/6km W of Bromyard. SO 5957
Grendon Underwood Bucks 28 B5 vil 6m/10km E of Bicester. SP 6820
Grenetote W Isles 88 E1* loc at N end of N Uist 2km E of Sollas. NF 8275
Grenham Bay Kent 13 H1* N coast bay at Birchington. TR 2970
Grenofen Devon 4 B4* loc 2m/3km SE of Tavistock. SX 4971
Grenoside S Yorks 43 G2 suburb 5m/7km N of Sheffield. SK 3394
Gresffordd Welsh form of Gresford, qv.
Gresford (Gresffordd) Clwyd 42 A5 colliery tn 3m/5km N of Wrexham. SJ 3454
Gresham Norfolk 39 F1 vil 3m/5km S of Sheringham. Faint remains of medieval cas. TG 1638
Gresham's School Norfolk. See Holt.
Greshornish Skye, H'land 78 B4 locality on W side of Loch G., N coast. **Greshornish Pt** is headland 2m/3km NE, at entrance to loch. NG 3353
Greskine Forest D & G 59 E1 state forest 4m/6km NW of Moffat. NT 0307
Gress W Isles 88 C1/C2* r on Lewis rising 6m/9km NW of Gress vil and flowing S into Broad Bay or Loch a' Tuath 1m S of the vil. NB 4941
Gress W Isles 88 C1 vil near E coast of Lewis 7m/12km NE of Stornoway. NB 4942
Gressenhall Norfolk 38 D3 vil 2m/4km NW of E Dereham. **G. Green** vil 1m NE. TF 9615
Gressingham Lancs 47 F2 vil 5m/8km E of Carnforth. SD 5769
Gresty Green Ches 42 C5* loc 2km S of Crewe. SJ 7053
Greta 47 F1 r formed by confluence of R Doe and Kingsdale Beck at Ingleton, N Yorks, and flowing W into R Lune 1m N of Melling, Lancs. SD 5972

Greta 54 A3 r rising on Stainmore Forest, E of Brough, Cumbria, and flowing E past Bowes and Brignall to Greta Br, thence N into R Tees at N end of Rokeby Park, 3m/4km SE of Barnard Castle, Durham. NZ 0814
Greta Bridge Durham 54 A3 ham on R Greta 3m/5km SE of Barnard Castle, on site of Roman fort. Dickens stayed at coaching inn here. NZ 0813
Gretna D & G 59 G4 vil 8m/12km E of Annan. **G. Green** is vil 1km N, famous for runaway marriages in former times. NY 3167
Gretna Green Suffolk 31 F1* loc 1km E of Eye. TM 1573
Gretton Glos 27 E4 vil 2m/3km NW of Winchcombe. SP 0030
Gretton Northants 37 E5 vil 4m/6km N of Corby. Kirby Hall (A.M.), 2m/3km SE, is partly restored 16c–17c mansion. SP 8994
Gretton Salop 34 C5 ham 4m/7km E of Church Stretton. SO 5195
Grewelthorpe N Yorks 49 E1 vil 3m/5km S of Masham. SE 2376
Grey Cairns of Camster H'land. See Camster.
Grey Friar Cumbria 52 C5 mountain in Lake Dist 3m/5km NW of Coniston. Height 2536 ft or 773 metres. NY 2600
Greygarth N Yorks 48 D1* loc 4m/7km N of Pateley Br. SE 1872
Grey Green Humberside 44 C1 ham 2m/4km N of Epworth. SE 7807
Grey Head Orkney 89 B5* headland at N end of Calf of Eday, island off NE coast of Eday. HY 5740
Greylake Som 8 B1 loc on Sedgemoor 2km N of Othery. ST 3833
Greylake Fosse Som 8 C1* loc 3m/5km NE of Othery. ST 4035
Grey Mare's Tail D & G 59 F1 spectacular waterfall (NTS), 200 ft or over 60 metres high, 9m/14km NE of Moffat. NT 1815
Grey Mare's Tail D & G 59 E2* waterfall in upper reaches of Crichope Burn, 3m/5km E of Thornhill. NX 9295
Grey Mare's Tail H'land 74 C5 high waterfall in course of Allt Coire na Bà, to N of Kinlochleven, Lochaber dist. NN 1862
Greymoorhill Cumbria 59 H5* loc in Carlisle 2m/4km N of city centre. NY 3959
Greys Green Oxon 18 C3 ham 3m/4km W of Henley-on-Thames. SU 7282
Greysouthen Cumbria 52 B2 vil 3m/5km W of Cockermouth. NY 0729
Greystead Nthmb 60 D3* loc in valley of R North Tyne 5m/7km NW of Bellingham. NY 7785
Greystoke Cumbria 52 D2 vil 5m/8km W of Penrith. Cas is 19c mansion in Elizn style by Salvin, added to original 14c peel tower. NY 4430
Greystone Tayside 77 E6 vil 7m/11km W of Arbroath. NO 5343
Greystone Heath Ches 42 B3 loc in W part of Warrington. SJ 5687
Greystones S Yorks 43 G3* dist of Sheffield 2m/3km SW of city centre. SK 3285
Greywell Hants 18 C6 vil 2km W of Odiham. SU 7151
Grianan W Isles 88 C2* loc on Lewis 2m/3km N of Stornoway. NB 4135
Gribba Point Cornwall 2 A5* headland 3m/5km N of Land's End. SW 3530
Gribbin Head Cornwall 3 F3 headland (NT) at E limit of St Austell Bay. SX 0949
Gribbin, Little Cornwall 3 F3* headland on E side of St Austell Bay. SX 0950
Gribthorpe Humberside 50 C4 loc 5m/7km N of Howden. SE 7635
Gribun S'clyde 69 C5* locality on W coast of Mull, 2m/3km S of entrance to Loch na Keal. Coast rd passes below **G. Rocks,** range of overhanging cliffs. NM 4533
Grice Ness Orkney 89 C6* headland on E coast of Stronsay at N end of Mill Bay. HY 6728
Gridley Corner Devon 6 C6* ham 4m/6km NE of Launceston. SX 3690
Griffithstown Gwent 15 G2 industrial suburb 2km S of Pontypool. Engineering and steel works. ST 2999
Griffydam Leics 36 A3* loc 3m/5km N of Coalville. SK 4118
Grif Skerry Shetland 89 F7* rock island 1km E of E Linga and 3m/5km SE of Skaw Taing, headland at NE end of island of Whalsay. HU 6362
Grimbister Orkney 89 B6* loc on Mainland on S side of Bay of Firth, 2km SE of Finstown. To NE in bay is small uninhabited island of Holm of G. HY 3712
Grimeford Village Lancs 47 G6* ham 2km NW of Horwich. SD 6112
Grimes Graves Norfolk 38 C5* Neolithic flint mines (A.M.), 3m/5km NE of Brandon. TL 8189
Grimesthorpe S Yorks 43 H2* dist of Sheffield 2m/3km NE of city centre. SK 3790
Grimethorpe S Yorks 43 H1* coal-mining loc 2m/3km E of Cudworth. SE 4109
Griminish W Isles 88 E2* loc near W coast of Benbecula 2m/3km S of Bailivanish. NF 7751
Griminish Point W Isles 88 D1 headland at NW end of N Uist. NF 7276
Grimister Shetland 89 E6 loc on Yell on S side of Whale Firth. HU 4693
Grimley H & W 26 D2 vil 4m/6km N of Worcester. SO 8360
Grim Ness Orkney 89 B7 headland at E extremity of St Margaret's Hope. ND 4992
Grimoldby Lincs 45 G3 vil 4m/7km E of Louth. TF 3987
Grimpo Salop 34 B2 ham 5m/8km E of Oswestry. SJ 3626
Grimsargh Lancs 47 F4 vil 4m/7km NE of Preston. Group of small resrs to N. SD 5834
Grimsay W Isles 88 E1 island of about 3 sq miles or 8 sq km between N Uist and Benbecula, with causeway connection to both. Lobster-fishing is carried on. NF 8656
Grimsbury Oxon 27 H3 loc in E part of Banbury. SP 4641
Grimsbury Castle Berks 18 A4* prehistoric fort 4m/6km NE of Newbury. SU 5172
Grimsby Humberside 45 F1 port at mouth of R Humber 16m/26km SE of Hull across estuary. Important centre for North Sea fishing industry: docks, warehouses, fish mkt. Other industries include timber importing, flour milling, jam mnfre. TA 2709
Grimsby, Little Lincs 45 G2 ham 3m/4km N of Louth. TF 3291
Grimscote Northants 28 B2 vil 4m/6km NW of Towcester. SP 6553
Grimscott Cornwall 6 B4 ham 2m/3km E of Stratton. SS 2606
Grimsetter Orkney 89 B6 airport for Kirkwall, Mainland, situated 3m/4km SE of the tn at head of Inganess Bay. **Point of G.** is headland on bay to N. HY 4808
Grimshader W Isles 88 B2/C2* vil on E coast of Lewis at head of long narrow inlet, Loch G., 5m/8km S of Stornoway. NB 4025
Grimshaw Lancs 48 A5* loc 3m/5km SE of Blackburn. SD 7024
Grimshaw Green Lancs 42 B1* loc 1m N of Parbold. SD 4912
Grimstead Wilts 9 H2 par 6m/9km SE of Salisbury, containing vils of **E** and **W Grimstead.** SU 2227
Grimsthorpe Lincs 37 F2 ham 4m/6km NW of Bourne. **G. Castle,** large mansion by Vanbrugh in huge park. TF 0423
Grimston Humberside 51 G4/G5 coastal loc 3m/5km SE of Aldbrough. TA 2835
Grimston Leics 36 C2 vil 5m/8km NW of Melton Mowbray. SK 6821
Grimston Norfolk 38 C3 vil 7m/11km E of King's Lynn. TF 7221
Grimston N Yorks 49 G4 loc containing **G. Park,** 19c hse by Decimus Burton in park, 2m/3km SE of Tadcaster. SE 4941
Grimston N Yorks 50 B3 loc 3m/5km E of York. SE 6451
Grimstone Dorset 8 D5 ham beside R Frome 4m/6km NW of Dorchester. SY 6494
Grimstone End Suffolk 30 D2* ham 1m S of Ixworth. TL 9369
Grimston, North N Yorks 50 D2 vil 4m/7km SE of Malton. SE 8467
Grimwith Reservoir N Yorks 48 C2/D2 resr 3m/4km NE of Burnsall. SE 0664
Grindale Humberside 51 F2 vil 4m/7km NW of Bridlington. Site of Roman bldg on E side of vil. TA 1371
Grindle Salop 34 D4* loc 1km W of Ryton. SJ 7503
Grindleford Derbys 43 G3 vil on R Derwent 3m/4km S of Hathersage. SK 2477
Grindleton Lancs 48 A4 vil 3m/4km N of Clitheroe. SD 7545
Grindley Staffs 35 F2 loc 5m/8km SW of Uttoxeter. SK 0329
Grindley Brook Salop 34 C1 vil 2m/3km NW of Whitchurch. SJ 5243
Grindlow Derbys 43 F3 ham 2m/4km NE of Tideswell. SK 1877
Grindon Cleveland 54 C2 loc 5m/8km NW of Stockton-on-Tees. NZ 3925
Grindon Nthmb 67 F4 loc 2m/3km SE of Norham. NT 9144
Grindon Staffs 43 F5 vil 8m/12km NW of Ashbourne. SK 0854
Grindon Tyne & Wear 31 H5 dist of Sunderland 3m/5km W of tn centre. NZ 3555
Grindon, High Tyne & Wear 61 H5* dist of Sunderland 2m/4km SW of tn centre. NZ 3655
Grindon Lough Nthmb 60 D4 small lake 3m/5km NW of Haydon Br. NY 8067
Gringley, Little Notts 44 C3* loc 2m/3km E of E Retford. SK 7380
Gringley on the Hill Notts 44 C2 vil 6m/9km E of Bawtry. SK 7390
Grinsdale Cumbria 59 H5 vil on R Eden 2m/4km NW of Carlisle across loop of r. NY 3658
Grinshill Salop 34 C2 vil 7m/11km N of Shrewsbury. SJ 5223
Grinstead, East W Sussex 12 A3 tn 8m/13km E of Crawley. TQ 3938
Grinstead, West W Sussex 11 G3 vil 3m/5km SW of Cowfold. TQ 1720
Grinsty, Lower H & W 27 E1* SW dist of Redditch. SP 0265
Grinton N Yorks 54 A5 vil 1km SE of Reeth. SE 0498
Grisdale Cumbria 53 G5* loc 2km W of Moorcock Inn. SD 7793
Grisedale Beck 52 D3* stream rising in Lake Dist mts of Cumbria 2m/3km S of Helvellyn and flowing NE through **G. Tarn** down Grisedale and into Goldrill Beck between Patterdale and Ullswater lake. NY 3916
Grisedale Pike Cumbria 52 C3 mt in Lake Dist 4m/7km W of Keswick. Height 2593 ft or 790 metres. NY 1922
Grishipoll Coll, S'clyde 68 A3 loc near NW coast at **G. Bay.** **G. Point** is headland at W end of bay. NM 1959
Gristhorpe N Yorks 55 H6 vil 2m/3km NW of Filey. **G. Cliff** on North Sea coast 1m NE. TA 0882
Griston Norfolk 38 D4 vil 2m/3km SE of Watton. TL 9499
Grittenham Wilts 17 E3 ham 2m/4km W of Wootton Bassett. SU 0382
Grittleton Wilts 16 D3 vil 6m/9km NW of Chippenham. ST 8580
Grizebeck Cumbria 52 C6 ham 3m/4km SE of Broughton in Furness. SD 2385
Grizedale Cumbria 52 D5 ham 3m/4km S of Hawkshead in **G. Forest,** extensive area of coniferous woodland between Coniston Water and Windermere. **G. Tarn** small lake in forest 1km E. SD 3394
Grizedale Lea Reservoir Lancs 47 F3* resr 3m/5km NE of Garstang. SD 5348
Groay W Isles 88 E1* small uninhabited island at SE end of Sound of Harris 4m/7km off E coast of N Uist. NG 0079
Groby Leics 36 B4 vil 5m/7km NW of Leicester. SK 5207
Groes Clwyd 41 F5 ham 3m/5km W of Denbigh. SJ 0064
Groes 24 C2* stream flowing W to join R Berwyn 1m E of Tregaron, Dyfed. The combined stream then continues SW into R Teifi 1km SW of Tregaron. SN 6959
Groes-faen Mid Glam 15 F3 ham 2m/3km SE of Llantrisant. ST 0780
Groesffordd Gwynedd 32 B1 ham 1m SW of Morfa Nefyn. SH 2739
Groeslon Gwynedd 40 C5* loc 4m/6km SE of Caernarvon. SH 5260
Groes-llwyd Powys 33 H3 loc 3m/4km N of Welshpool. SJ 2111
Groes-wen Mid Glam 15 F3* ham 2m/3km W of Caerphilly. ST 1286
Grogport S'clyde 63 E3 loc on Garrachcroit Bàgh on E coast of Kintyre, Argyll, 4m/7km N of Dippen. NR 8044
Gronant Clwyd 41 G3 vil 2km E of Prestatyn. SJ 0682
Groombridge 12 B3 vil on border of E Sussex and Kent 4m/6km W of Tunbridge Wells. TQ 5337
Grosebay W Isles 88 B3* locality at head of Loch Grosebay on SE coast of Harris 4m/7km S of Tarbert. NG 1592
Grosmont Gwent 25 H5 vil above right bank of R Monnow 2m/3km S of Pontrilas. Remains of 13c cas (A.M.). SO 4024
Grosmont N Yorks 55 F4 vil 6m/9km SW of Whitby. NZ 8205
Groton Suffolk 30 D4 vil 4m/7km W of Hadleigh. TL 9541
Grotton Gtr Manchester 43 E1* loc 3m/4km E of Oldham. SD 9604
Groudle Glen Isle of Man 46 B5, C5 valley descending to Port Groudle on E coast, 2m/3km SW of Clay Hd. SC 4178
Grove Bucks 28 D5* loc 2m/3km SW of Leighton Buzzard. SP 9122
Grove Dorset 9 E6 loc on E side of Portland. SY 7072
Grove Dyfed 22 C5* loc adjoining Pembroke to E. SM 9900
Grove Notts 44 C3 vil 2m/4km E of E Retford. SK 7379
Grove Oxon 17 H3 vil 2m/3km N of Wantage. SU 4090
Grove Common, Upper H & W 26 B5* vil 3m/5km NW of Ross-on-Wye. SO 5526
Grove End Kent 21 E5* loc 2m/3km S of Sittingbourne. TQ 8961
Grove Green Kent 20 D6* ham 2km E of Maidstone. TQ 7856
Grovehill Herts 19 E1* N dist of Hemel Hempstead. TL 0609
Grove Park London 19 F4* loc in borough of Hounslow on N bank of R Thames above Chiswick Br. TQ 2077
Grove Park London 20 A4* loc in borough of Lewisham 3m/5km SE of Lewisham tn centre and 9m/14km SE of Charing Cross. TQ 4072
Grove Place Hants. Elizn hse at Nursling, qv.
Grove Place W Yorks 48 D6* loc in Huddersfield 2m/3km E of tn centre. SE 1616
Grovesend (Pengelli-ddrain) W Glam 23 G5 vil 2m/3km S of Pontarddulais. SN 5900
Grove, The H & W 26 D3* ham 1m E of Upton upon Severn across r. SO 8640
Grove Town W Yorks 49 F5* SE dist of Pontefract. SE 4621
Grove Vale W Midlands 35 F5* loc 3m/4km NE of W Bromwich tn centre. SP 0394
Grubb Street Kent 20 C4* loc 1m NW of Longfield and 4m/7km SW of Gravesend. TQ 5869
Grub Street Norfolk 39 G2* loc 1km SW of Happisburgh. TG 3730
Grudie H'land 85 F6 r in Sutherland dist rising between Loch Shin and Glen Cassley and running SE into R Shin 3m/5km S of Lairg. NC 5702
Gruids H'land 85 F6 loc in Sutherland dist 2m/3km SW of Lairg. NC 5604
Gruinard Island H'land 85 A7 uninhabited island, property of Ministry of Defence, in **G. Bay,** W coast of Ross and Cromarty dist between Greenstone Pt and Stattic Pt. Area about 520 acres or 210 hectares. **Gruinard R** flows N into bay from Loch na Sealga. **Lit Gruinard R** flows N into bay from Fionn Loch. NG 9494
Gruinart S'clyde 62 A2/B2 locality at head of Loch Gruinart on Islay. Here in 1598 Macdonalds repelled invasion of the Macleans of Mull. NR 2866
Grula Skye, H'land 79 B6* locality at head of Loch Eynort, SW coast. NG 3826
Gruline S'clyde 68 D4 locality at head of Loch na Keal, Mull, 3m/5km SW of Salen. Mausoleum in grnds of Gruline Hse commemorates Lachlan Macquarie, first governor of New South Wales, Australia. NM 5440
Grumbla Cornwall 2 A5* loc 2m/4km SE of St Just. SW 4029
Grunasound Shetland 89 E8* loc on island of W Burra 2km S of Hamnavoe. HU 3733
Gruna Stack Shetland 89 E6* rock island off NW coast of Mainland 1m NE of entrance to Ronas Voe. **Lit Gruna Stacks** group of rocks on S side of Gruna Stack. HU 2886
Grundisburgh Suffolk 31 F3 vil 3m/5km W of Woodbridge. TM 2250
Grune Point Cumbria 59 F5 headland at entrance to Moricambe Bay 2km NE of Skinburness. NY 1456
Gruney Shetland 89 E5* uninhabited island nearly 1m N of Point of Fethaland. HU 3896
Gruting Shetland 89 D7 loc in W part of Mainland, on E side of **G. Voe,** large inlet whose entrance is on E side of island of Vaila. HU 2749
Grwyne Fawr 25 G6 r rising in Black Mts 2m/3km N of Waun Fach, Powys, and

flowing S to its confluence with Grwyne Fechan, then S again into R Usk 2m/3km SE of Crickhowell. SO 2315

Grwyne Fawr Reservoir Powys 25 G4/G5* resr near head of Grwyne Fawr R. SO 2330

Grwyne Fechan 25 G5 r rising on Waun Fach, Powys, and flowing S to join Grwyne Fawr 2m/3km NE of Crickhowell. SO 2419

Gryfe 64 C2 r in Strathclyde region rising on hills S of Greenock and running N to Gryfe Resr, then SE down Strath G. to Br of Weir, then E to Black Cart Water 2m/4km NW of Paisley. NS 4666

Gryfe Reservoirs S'clyde 64 A2 pair of resrs 3m/5km S of Greenock. NS 2871

Guanockgate Lincs 37 H3* loc 2m/4km S of Sutton St Edmund. TF 3609

Guardbridge Fife 73 G3* vil at head of R Eden estuary with modern rd br across r beside old 15c br, 2m/3km S of Leuchars. Large paper mill. NO 4518

Guarlford H & W 26 C3* vil 2m/3km E of Gt Malvern. SO 8145

Gubbion's Green Essex 30 C6* loc 4m/6km SW of Braintree. TL 7317

Gubblecote Herts 28 D6* loc 3m/4km NW of Tring. SP 9015

Guelt Water 56 F2* r in Strathclyde region running NW to Glenmuir Water at Kyle Castle, 5m/8km E of Cumnock. NS 6419

Guestling Green E Sussex 12 D5 vil 4m/7km NE of Hastings. Ham of **G. Thorn** 2km N. TQ 8513

Guestwick Norfolk 39 E2 vil 4m/6km NW of Reepham. **G. Green** ham 1km SW. TG 0627

Gugh Isles of Scilly 2 A1 island joined to island of St Agnes by a sand and rock bar at low tide. SV 8908

Guide Lancs 48 A5 ham 2m/3km SE of Blackburn. SD 7025

Guide Bridge Gtr Manchester 43 E2* loc 2km SW of Ashton-under-Lyne. SJ 9297

Guide Post Nthmb 61 G3 coal-mining loc 4m/6km E of Morpeth. NZ 2585

Guilden Down Salop 34 A6* loc 2km NE of Clun. SO 3082

Guilden Morden Cambs 29 G3 vil 5m/8km NW of Royston. TL 2744

Guilden Sutton Ches 42 A4 vil 3m/5km E of Chester. SJ 4468

Guildford Surrey 11 F1 county tn on R Wey 27m/43km SW of London. Remains of Norman cas keep. Modern cathedral and University of Surrey on Stag Hill to NW of tn centre. SU 9949

Guildtown Tayside 73 E2 vil 5m/8km N of Perth. NO 1331

Guile Point Nthmb 67 G4 headland on mainland opp S end of Holy I. NU 1340

Guillamon Island Skye, H'land 79 E6 islet 1km off SE coast of Scalpay. NG 6327

Guilsborough Northants 28 B1 vil 9m/15km NW of Northampton. SP 6773

Guilsfield (Cegidfa) Powys 33 H3 vil 3m/4km N of Welshpool. SJ 2111

Guilthwaite S Yorks 43 H2* loc 3m/4km SE of Rotherham. SK 4589

Guilton Kent 13 H2* loc adjoining Ash to W. TR 2858

Guineaford Devon 6 D2* ham 3m/4km N of Barnstaple. SS 5437

Guirasdeal S'clyde 69 E6 small island off SW shore of island of Lunga. NM 6907

Guisachan Forest H'land 80 C5 deer forest to S of Glen Affric in Inverness dist. **G. Fall** is waterfall in G. state forest to N. NH 2520

Guisborough Cleveland 55 E3 tn 6m/9km S of Redcar. Remains of 12c priory (A.M.). NZ 6116

Guiseley W Yorks 48 D4 tn 8m/13km NW of Leeds. Engineering, textiles, lamps, perambulators. SE 1941

Guist Norfolk 39 E2 vil 6m/9km SE of Fakenham. **Upr Guist** loc 1km NE. TF 9925

Guiting Power Glos 27 E5 vil 6m/10km W of Stow-on-the-Wold. SP 0924

Gulber Wick Shetland 89 E7/E8* large inlet on coast of Mainland 3m/4km SW of Lerwick, at head of which is loc of **Gulberwick.** HU 4438

Guldeford, East E Sussex 13 E4 vil 2km NE of Rye. TQ 9321

Gulf of Corryvreckan S'clyde. See Strait of Corryvreckan.

Gulland Rock Cornwall 2 D1* island off N coast W of Padstow and 3m/4km NE of Trevose Hd. SW 8779

Gullane Lothian 66 C1 resort on **G. Bay,** on Firth of Forth 4m/7km SW of N Berwick. Championship golf-course (Muirfield) to N. **G. Point** is headland at W end of bay. To S of headland are **G. Sands,** a nature reserve. NT 4882

Gull Point S'clyde 63 G3 headland at S end of island of Lit Cumbrae. NS 1450

Gull Rock Cornwall 2 C4* island rock off N coast opp Portreath. SW 6445

Gull Rock Cornwall 2 C6* rock island lying off Kynance Cove, qv. SW 6813

Gull Rock Cornwall 3 E3* rock island 1km E of Nare Hd. SW 9336

Gull Rock Cornwall 6 A6* island rock off N coast opp S end of Trebarwith Strand 2m/3km SW of Tintagel. SX 0386

Gull Rocks Cornwall 2 C3* alternative name for Carter's Rocks, two rock islands off Penhale Pt, 4m/6km SW of Newquay. SW 7559

Gully W Yorks 43 F1* loc adjoining Holmfirth to SE. SE 1407

Gulvain H'land 74 B3 mt in Lochaber dist 2m/4km S of head of Loch Arkaig. Height of N summit 3238 ft or 987 metres; S summit 3153 ft or 961 metres. Gaelic form: Gaor Bheinn. NM 9986

Gulval Cornwall 2 B5 ham to NE of Penzance. Heliport to S. SW 4831

Gumfreston Dyfed 22 D5 ham 2m/3km W of Tenby. SN 1001

Gumley Leics 36 C5 vil 4m/6km NW of Mkt Harborough. SP 6890

Gunby Humberside 50 C4* loc 1km S of Bubwith. SE 7135

Gunby Lincs 37 E2 vil 2m/3km SW of Colsterworth. SK 9121

Gunby Lincs 45 H4 ham 7m/11km NW of Skegness. **G. Hall** (NT), hse of 1700. TF 4767

Gundleton Hants 10 C2* ham 2m/3km E of New Alresford. SU 6133

Gun Hill Warwicks 35 H5* loc 5m/8km W of Nuneaton. SP 2889

Gunn Devon 7 E2 ham 5m/8km E of Barnstaple. SS 6333

Gunna Coll, S'clyde 69 B7 island, 2km long E to W, lying off SW end of main island across Caolas Ban. NM 1051

Gunnels Wood Herts 29 F5* industrial estate in W part of Stevenage. TL 2323

Gunnersbury London 19 F4* loc in borough of Hounslow N of Kew Br 7m/11km W of Charing Cross. G. Park has recreational facilities and museum. TQ 1978

Gunnerside N Yorks 53 H5 vil in Swaledale 6m/9km W of Reeth. SD 9598

Gunnerton Nthmb 60 D4 vil 3m/5km SE of Wark. Remains of motte and bailey cas to N. NY 9075

Gunness Humberside 50 D6 vil 3m/5km W of Scunthorpe. SE 8411

Gunnislake Cornwall 4 B3 former tin-mining place on steep bank overlooking R Tamar, crossed here by 14c New Bridge. SX 4371

Gunnister Shetland 89 E6* loc in N part of Mainland 2m/4km N of Mangaster, at head of **G. Voe,** inlet on W coast. At entrance to inlet is rock island, **Isle of G.** HU 3274

Gunnister Shetland 89 E7* loc near N coast of island of Bressay opp small island of **Holm of Gunnister.** HU 5043

Gunstone Staffs 35 E4* loc 1m N of Codsall. SJ 8704

Guns Village W Midlands 35 F5* loc in W Bromwich 1km W of tn centre. SO 9991

Gunthorpe Cambs 37 G4* loc in Peterborough 3m/5km N of city centre. TF 1802

Gunthorpe Leics 36 D4* loc 2m/3km S of Oakham. SK 8605

Gunthorpe Norfolk 39 E2 vil 5m/8km SW of Holt. TG 0134

Gunthorpe Notts 36 C1 vil 7m/12km NE of Nottingham. SK 6844

Gunthwaite S Yorks 43 G1* loc 2m/3km N of Penistone. SE 2306

Gunton Norfolk 39 F2 loc consisting of 18c hse and ch in G. Park. Hse partly burnt down, 1882. TG 2234

Gunton Suffolk 39 H5 N dist of Lowestoft. TM 5495

Gunville Isle of Wight 10 B5 loc 2km W of Newport. SZ 4888

Gunwalloe Cornwall 2 C6 ham on coast 3m/5km S of Helston. SW 6522

Gurnal Dubs Cumbria 53 E5* small lake 2m/3km N of Burneside. SD 5099

Gurnard Isle of Wight 10 B5 vil adjoining Cowes to W. G. Bay to NW. SZ 4795

Gurnards Head Cornwall 2 A4 headland on N coast 5m/9km W of St Ives. SW 4338

Gurness Orkney. See Broch of G.

Gurnett Ches 43 E4* loc 2km S of Macclesfield. SJ 9271

Gurney Slade Som 16 B6 vil 4m/6km N of Shepton Mallet. ST 6249

Gurnos Mid Glam 15 F1* loc in N part of Merthyr Tydfil. SO 0408

Gurnos Powys 14 D1 vil 1km NE of Ystalyfera. SN 7709

Gushmere Kent 21 F6* loc 3m/5km SE of Faversham. TR 0457

Gussage All Saints Dorset 9 G3 vil 4m/6km SW of Cranborne. SU 0010

Gussage St Andrew Dorset 9 G3* ham 2m/4km SW of Sixpenny Handley. ST 9714

Gussage St Michael Dorset 9 G3 vil 5m/7km W of Cranborne. ST 9811

Guston Kent 13 H3 vil 2m/3km N of Dover. TR 3244

Gutcher Shetland 89 F5 loc on **Wick of G.,** bay on E coast of Yell at S end of Bluemull Sound. Vehicle ferry to Wick of Belmont, on Unst. HU 5499

Guthram Gowt Lincs 37 F2* loc on R Glen 5m/7km W of Spalding. TF 1722

Guthrie Tayside 77 E5/F5 vil 7m/11km E of Forfar. **G. Castle** has 15c tower and notable gardens. NO 5650

Gutter, The Berks 18 B4* W dist of Reading. SU 6674

Guyhirn Cambs 37 H4 vil 6m/9km SW of Wisbech. **G. Gull** loc 1km NW. TF 3903

Guy's Cliffe Warwicks 27 G1* loc on R Avon 1m N of Warwick. SP 2966

Guy's Marsh Dorset 9 F2* loc 2m/3km SW of Shaftesbury. ST 8420

Guyzance Nthmb 61 G2 ham 3m/5km S of Shilbottle. NU 2103

Gwaelod-y-garth Mid Glam 15 F3 vil 6m/10km NW of Cardiff. ST 1184

Gwaenysgor Clwyd 41 G3* vil 1m S of Prestatyn. SJ 0781

Gwalchmai Gwynedd 40 B4 vil on Anglesey 4m/7km W of Llangefni. SH 3876

Gwared 24 D5* r in Powys. See Gwydderig.

Gwash 37 F4 r rising near Knossington, Leics, and flowing E through Empingham Resr and into R Welland 2km E of Stamford, Lincs. TF 0407

Gwastad Dyfed 22 C3* loc 1km NE of Llys-y-fran. SN 0424

Gwastadnant Gwynedd 40 C5* loc in Pass of Llanberis 3m/4km SE of tn of Llanberis. SH 6157

Gwaum-tre-Oda S Glam 15 F3* loc in Cardiff 2m/3km NW of city centre. ST 1679

Gwaun 22 C2 r rising about 4m/6km S of Newport, Dyfed, and flowing W into Fishguard Bay at Fishguard. SM 9637

Gwaun-cae-Gurwen W Glam 14 C1 coal-mining loc 5m/8km N of Pontardawe. SN 7011

Gwaun-Leision W Glam 14 C1 loc 1m SW of Brynamman. SN 7012

Gwaun Meisgyn Mid Glam 15 F3* loc 2km NE of Llantrisant. ST 0684

Gwavas Lake Cornwall 2 A5* part of Mount's Bay off Newlyn on S coast. SW 4728

Gwbert-on-Sea Dyfed 22 D1 loc on E side of mouth of R Teifi 3m/4km N of Cardigan. SN 1649

Gweek Cornwall 2 C5 vil with quay on Helford R at head of creek, 3m/5km E of Helford. SW 7026

Gwehelog Gwent 15 H1* vil 2m/3km N of Usk. SO 3804

Gwely'r Misgl Mid Glam 14 D3* rock island on edge of Kenfig Sands 3m/5km NW of Porthcawl. SS 7880

Gwenddwr Powys 25 F4 ham 4m/7km S of Builth Wells. SO 0643

Gwendraeth Fach 23 F5 r rising SE of Llanarthney, Dyfed, and flowing SW to Kidwelly, thereafter forming a common estuary with Gwendraeth Fawr R and flowing W into Carmarthen Bay. SN 3906

Gwendraeth Fawr 23 F5 r rising near Gorslas, Dyfed, and flowing SW to join Gwendraeth Fach R in a common estuary flowing W into Carmarthen Bay. SN 3906

Gwendreath Cornwall 2 C6* loc on S edge of Goonhilly Downs 4m/6km N of Lizard Pt. SW 7316

Gwenffrwd 24 B2* stream running S into R Aeron 2m/3km SW of Llangeitho, Dyfed. SN 5958

Gwenfo Welsh form of Wenvoe, qv.

Gwenfro 41 H6* r rising near Bwlch-gwyn, Clwyd, and running E through Wrexham into R Clywedog on SE side of Wrexham. SJ 3449

Gwenlas 24 C4 r rising 3m/5km NW of Cilycwm, Dyfed, and flowing SE to Cilycwm and into R Towy 1m SE of the vil. SN 7538

Gwennap Cornwall 2 C4 vil in former tin and copper-mining area 3m/4km SE of Redruth. 2m/3km NW, **G. Pit,** natural amphitheatre now terraced, where John Wesley used to preach. SW 7340

Gwennap Head Cornwall 2 A6 headland 3m/4km SE of Land's End. SW 3621

Gwent 118 county of S Wales, bounded by S and Mid Glamorgan, Powys, the English counties of Gloucestershire and Hereford & Worcester, and the Bristol Channel. The W side of the county, adjoining S and Mid Glamorgan, has coal mines and much varied industry, with docks at Newport on the Usk estuary. The country is hilly, with mining and industrial tns in steep-sided narrow valleys. To E and N the landscape is of gently rolling hills and wds, almost entirely agricultural; the Black Mts, with sheep-grazing, penetrate the extreme N of the county. Tns include Abergavenny, Chepstow, Cwmbran, Ebbw Vale, Monmouth, Newport, and Pontypool. Chief rs are the Monnow, Usk, and Wye, which, below Monmouth, forms the boundary with Gloucestershire.

Gwenter Cornwall 2 C6* loc on S edge of Goonhilly Downs 5m/8km NE of Lizard Pt. SW 7417

Gwernaffield Clwyd 41 G5 vil 2m/3km W of Mold. SJ 2064

Gwernesney (Gwerneshi) Gwent 15 H2 ham 3m/4km E of Usk. SO 4101

Gwernesni Welsh form of Gwernesney, qv.

Gwernestyn Clwyd 41 H5* loc 1km SE of Hope. SJ 3157

Gwernogle Dyfed 24 B4* ham 2m/4km N of Brechfa. SN 5234

Gwernol 32 D4* stream running NW into R Dysynni at Abergynolwyn, Gwynedd. SH 6707

Gwernymynydd Clwyd 41 H5 vil 2m/3km SW of Mold. SJ 2162

Gwern-y-Steeple S Glam 15 F4* ham 1km SW of Peterston-super-Ely. ST 0775

Gwersyllt Clwyd 41 H5* loc 2m/4km NW of Wrexham. SJ 3153

Gwespyr Clwyd 41 G3* vil 3m/4km E of Prestatyn. SJ 1182

Gwili 23 F4 r rising to E of Llanpumsaint, Dyfed, and flowing W to the vil, then circuitously to join R Towy to E of Carmarthen. SN 4320

Gwili 23 G5 r rising near Cross Hands, Dyfed, and flowing S into R Loughor to W of Pontarddulais, W Glam. SN 5803

Gwinear Cornwall 2 B4 vil 2m/3km E of Hayle. SW 5937

Gwithian Cornwall 2 B4 vil 4m/6km W of Camborne. SW 5841

Gwndy Welsh form of Undy, qv.

Gwngu 24 D1* stream running E into Llyn Gwngu, Dyfed, 3m/5km E of Cwmystwyth, and continuing E to join R Elan 3m/4km NW of head of Craig Goch Resr. From Llyn Gwngu to R Elan it forms border between Dyfed and Powys. SN 8773

Gwredog Gwynedd 40 B3* loc on Anglesey 2m/3km NW of Llanerchymedd. SH 4086

Gwrhay Gwent 15 G2* loc 1km N of Oakdale. ST 1899

Gwril 32 D3 r running W into Barmouth Bay at Llwyngwril, Gwynedd. SH 5810

Gwrych Castle Clwyd. See Abergele.

Gwy Welsh form of (R) Wye, qv.

Gwyddelwern Clwyd 41 G6 vil 3m/4km N of Corwen. SJ 0746

Gwydderig 24 D4 r rising as Nant Gwared, N of Trecastle, Powys, and flowing S to Llywel then NW into R Towy at Llandovery, Dyfed. SN 7734

Gwyddgrug Dyfed 24 A4/B4 ham 6m/10km SW of Llanybydder. SN 4635

Gwydir Castle Gwynedd 41 E5* cas in R Conwy valley opp Llanrwst, of various dates from 14c to 20c. Of **Gwydir Uchaf,** former mansion across rd from cas, only the 17c chapel (A.M.) remains. SH 7961
Gwynedd 116, 118 north-western county of Wales, bounded by Clwyd, Powys, Dyfed (at the Dovey estuary), and the sea. It includes the island of Anglesey, which is linked to the mainland by a rd br and a rly br across the Menai Strait. The whole mainland area except the Lleyn peninsula in the NW is extremely mountainous and contains the scenically famous Snowdonia National Park. There is slate-quarrying in the Ffestiniog valley, otherwise sheep-farming and tourism are the principal occupations, the coastline being much developed for the holiday trade. Tns include Bangor, Caernarvon, the county tn, and Conwy; Holyhead, on Anglesey, is a port for Ireland. Among the many rs are the Conwy, Dee, and Wnion.
Gwynfryn Clwyd 41 H6* loc 5m/8km W of Wrexham. SJ 2552
Gŵyr Welsh form of Gower, qv.
Gwyrfai 40 B5* r rising on W slopes of Snowdon, Gwynedd, and flowing NW through Llyn Cwellyn to Waunfawr, then W by Bontnewydd into Foryd Bay. SH 4559
Gwys 24 D6 r rising as two streams, **Gwys Fawr** and **Gwys Fach,** rising on S foothills of Black Mt, Powys, and joining 2m/4km N of Ystalyfera, then flowing SW into R Twrch at Cwmtwrch-uchaf. SN 7511
Gwystre Powys 25 F2 loc 3m/5km N of Llandrindod Wells. SO 0665
Gwytherin Clwyd 41 E5 vil 4m/6km S of Llangernyw. SH 8761
Gyfarllwyd Falls Dyfed 24 C1* waterfall in Cwm Rheidol 1km N of Devil's Br. SN 7477
Gyfelia Clwyd 41 H6 loc 3m/5km S of Wrexham. SJ 3245
Gyffin Gwynedd 40 D4 suburb on S side of Conwy. SH 7776
Gylen Castle S'clyde 70 A2 ruined cas at S end of Kerrera. Destroyed by Cromwell's troops in 1645. NM 8026
Gyrn-goch Gwynedd 40 B6* loc 2km SW of Clynnog-fawr. SH 4048

H

Haaf Gruney Shetland 89 F5* uninhabited island lying nearly 1m off SE coast of Unst. Area about 50 acres or 20 hectares. Nature reserve. HU 6398
Habberley Salop 34 B4 vil 8m/13km SW of Shrewsbury. SJ 3903
Habberley, High H & W 35 E6* loc on W edge of Kidderminster. SO 8077
Habberley, Low H & W 35 E6 loc 2km/3km NW of Kidderminster. SO 8077
Habergham Lancs 48 B4/B5* dist of Burnley 2m/3km W of tn centre. SD 8033
Habergham Eaves Lancs 48 B5 moorland loc adjoining Burnley to S. SD 8329
Habin W Sussex 11 E3* loc 1m S of Rogate and 4m/7km E of Petersfield. SU 8022
Habitancum Nthmb. See Woodburn, West.
Habost W Isles 88 B2* locality on Lewis on S side of Loch Erisort opp Laxay. NB 3219
Habost W Isles 88 C1 vil near N end of Lewis 1m W of Port of Ness. NB 5263
Habrough Humberside 51 F6 vil 2m/3km W of Immingham. TA 1413
Habton, Great N Yorks 50 C1 vil 3m/5km NW of Malton. SE 7576
Habton, Little N Yorks 50 C1 loc 4m/7km NW of Malton. SE 7477
Haccombe Devon 5 E3* loc 3m/4km E of Newton Abbot. SX 8970
Hacconby Lincs 37 F2 vil 3m/5km N of Bourne. TF 1025
Haceby Lincs 37 E1 ham 7m/12km E of Grantham. Site of Roman villa 1m NW. TF 0236
Hacheston Suffolk 31 G2 vil 2m/4km N of Wickham Mkt. TM 3059
Hacheston, Lower Suffolk 31 G3* loc 1m NE of Wickham Mkt. TM 3156
Hackenthorpe S Yorks 43 H3 dist of Sheffield 5m/8km SE of city centre. SK 4183
Hackford Norfolk 39 E4* vil 3m/5km W of Wymondham. TG 0502
Hackforth N Yorks 54 B5 vil 3m/5km S of Catterick. SE 2493
Hackington Kent 13 G1 loc adjoining Canterbury to N. TR 1560
Hacklete W Isles 88 A2/B2* loc at S end of Gt Bernera, W coast of Lewis, to W of rd br connecting Gt Bernera to main island. NB 1534
Hackleton Northants 28 C2 vil 5m/8km SE of Northampton. SP 8055
Hackley Head Grampian 83 H4* headland at S end of **Hackley Bay,** small bay between Collieston and Newburgh Bar at mouth of R Ythan. Also known as Forvie Ness. NK 0226
Hackman's Gate H & W 35 E6* loc 4m/6km E of Kidderminster. SO 8977
Hackness N Yorks 55 G5 vil 5m/8km W of Scarborough. SE 9690
Hackness Orkney 89 A7/B7* loc at NE end of peninsula of S Walls, Hoy. **Pt of H.** is headland to N. ND 3390
Hackney London 20 A3* borough and tn 3m/5km NE of London Br. **S Hackney** and **H. Wick** are locs 1km SE and 2km E respectively of H. tn centre. **H. Marshes** in R Lea valley to NE. TQ 3484
Hackney, Upper Derbys 43 G5 loc 1m NW of Matlock. SK 2961
Hacksness Orkney 89 B6* headland at SE end of Shapinsay on Shapinsay Sound. HY 5214
Hacks Ness Orkney 89 C5 headland with beacon on S coast of island of Sanday 1km E of Spur Ness. HY 6134
Hackthorn Lincs 44 D3 vil 7m/11km N of Lincoln. SK 9982
Hackthorpe Cumbria 53 E3 vil 5m/8km S of Penrith. NY 5423
Hacton London 20 B3* loc in borough of Havering 2km SW of Upminster. TQ 5485
Haddenham Bucks 18 C1 vil 3m/4km NE of Thame. Aylesbury and Thame Airport to NW. SP 7408
Haddenham Cambs 38 A6 vil 6m/9km SW of Ely. Loc of **H. End** adjoins to N. TL 4674
Haddeo 7 G3* r in Somerset rising 3m/4km W of Clatworthy Resr and flowing SW into R Exe 2km N of Exebridge. SS 9326
Haddington Lincs 44 D5 ham 7m/11km SW of Lincoln. SK 9163
Haddington Lothian 66 C2 historic tn on R Tyne 16m/26km E of Edinburgh. Grain mkt, brewing, hosiery mnfre. Birthplace of John Knox, 1505. Renovated ch of St Mary, 14c–15c. St Martin's Church (A.M.). NT 5173
Haddiscoe Norfolk 39 H5 vil 4m/7km N of Beccles. TM 4496
Haddlesey, West N Yorks 49 G5 vil on N bank of R Aire, 5m/8km SW of Selby and connected to it by Selby Canal. See also Chapel Haddlesey. SE 5626
Haddo House Grampian 83 G3 mansion of 1732 by William Adam, 6m/10km NW of Ellon. Seat of Marquess of Aberdeen. NJ 8634
Haddon Cambs 37 F5 vil 5m/8km SW of Peterborough. TL 1392
Haddon, East Northants 28 B1 vil 8m/12km NW of Northampton. SP 6668
Haddon Hall Derbys 43 G4 medieval hse in R Wye valley 2m/3km SE of Bakewell. SK 2366
Haddon, West Northants 28 B1 vil 7m/11km NE of Daventry. SP 6371
Hade Edge W Yorks 43 F1* loc 2m/3km S of Holmfirth. SE 1405
Hademore Staffs 35 G3* loc 3m/5km NW of Tamworth. SK 1708
Hadfield Derbys 43 E2 loc 2m/3km NW of Glossop. SK 0296
Hadham Cross Herts 29 H6 S end of Much Hadham, 4m/7km SE of Bishop's Stortford. TL 4218
Hadham Ford Herts 29 H5 vil 3m/5km W of Bishop's Stortford. TL 4321
Hadham, Little Herts 29 H5 vil 3m/5km W of Bishop's Stortford. TL 4322
Hadleigh Essex 20 D3 tn 4m/7km W of Southend-on-Sea. Remains of Norman cas (A.M.). TQ 8187
Hadleigh Suffolk 31 E4 tn 8m/13km W of Ipswich. Agricultural machinery. 15c guildhall. TM 0242
Hadleigh Heath Suffolk 31 E4 loc 2m/3km W of Hadleigh. TL 9941
Hadleigh Ray Essex 20 D3* mouth of Benfleet Creek, at E end of Canvey I. TQ 8284
Hadley H & W 26 D2* ham 3m/4km W of Droitwich. SO 8663
Hadley London 19 F2* loc in borough of Barnet 3m/4km S of Potters Bar. TQ 2496
Hadley Salop 34 D3 loc 2km E of Wellington. SJ 6712
Hadley End Staffs 35 G3 vil 7m/11km N of Lichfield. SK 1320
Hadley Wood London 19 F2 loc in borough of Enfield 3m/4km S of Potters Bar and 11m/18km N of Charing Cross. TQ 2697
Hadlow Kent 20 C6 vil 4m/6km NE of Tonbridge. Tower 170 ft or 52 metres high is remains of 19c Gothic cas. TQ 6349
Hadlow Down E Sussex 12 B4 vil 4m/7km NE of Uckfield. TQ 5324
Hadlow Stair Kent 20 C6 loc in NE part of Tonbridge. Also known as The Stair. TQ 6047
Hadnall Salop 34 C3 vil 5m/8km NE of Shrewsbury. SJ 5220
Hadrian's Camp Cumbria 60 A5* suburb 2m/3km NE of Carlisle on line of Hadrian's Wall. NY 4158
Hadspen Som 8 D2* ham 1m E of Castle Cary. ST 6532
Hadstock Essex 30 A3 vil 4m/7km N of Saffron Walden. TL 5544
Hadyhill Derbys 43 H4* loc in Chesterfield 1km E of tn centre. SK 3970
Hadzor H & W 26 D2 vil 2km SE of Droitwich. SO 9162
Haffenden Quarter Kent 13 E3* loc 1m S of Smarden. TQ 8841
Hafhesp 33 F1* stream running S through Llyn Maen Bras, Gwynedd, into R Dee on E side of Llanfor. SH 9436
Hafod Bridge Dyfed 24 C4 loc on R Dulais 3m/5km NW of Llanwrda. SN 7131
Hafod-y-llyn Gwynedd 32 D2* tarn 2m/3km SE of Harlech. SH 5929
Hafodyrynys Gwent 15 G2* loc 2m/3km NE of Newbridge. ST 2298
Hafren Welsh form of (R) Severn, qv.
Hafren Forest Powys 33 F5 state forest between Plynlimon and Clywedog Resr. Traversed by the infant R Severn (Hafren). SN 88
Hagbourne, East Oxon 18 A3 vil 2km SE of Didcot. SU 5388
Hagbourne, West Oxon 18 A3 vil 2m/3km SW of Didcot. SU 5187
Haggate Lancs 48 B4 loc 2m/3km SE of Nelson. SD 8735
Haggersta Shetland 89 E7* locality on Mainland, between Weisdale Voe and Loch of Strom. HU 3848
Haggerston London 19 G3* loc in borough of Hackney 3m/5km NE of Charing Cross. TQ 3483
Haggerston Nthmb 67 G4 ham 3m/5km NE of Lowick. Cas keep of uncertain date. NU 0443
Hagget End Cumbria 52 A4* loc adjoining Egremont to SW. NY 0010
Haggrister Shetland 89 E6* locality on Mainland on W side of Sullom Voe near the head of the inlet. **Bight of H.** is bay on Sullom Voe to S. **Loch of H.** to W. **Ness of H.** headland to E. HU 3470
Haggs Central 72 B6* loc 2m/4km W of Bonnybridge. NS 7979
Hag Hill Derbys 43 H4* loc 2m/3km NE of Clay Cross. SK 4066
Haghill S'clyde 64 D2* loc in Dennistoun dist of Glasgow. NS 6265
Hagley H & W 35 E6 suburb 2m/4km S of Stourbridge. Loc of **W Hagley** to SW. SO 9180
Hagley H & W 26 B3 vil 3m/5km E of Hereford. SO 5641
Hagmore Green Suffolk 30 D4* loc 3m/5km N of Nayland. TL 9539
Hagnaby Lincs 45 G5 loc 4m/7km SW of Spilsby. TF 3462
Hagnaby Lincs 45 H3* loc 3m/5km NE of Alford. TF 4879
Hague Bar Derbys 43 E3* loc 1m W of New Mills. SJ 9885
Hague, The Gtr Manchester 43 E2* loc 1m S of Hollingworth. SK 0095
Hagworthingham Lincs 45 G4 vil 5m/9km E of Horncastle. TF 3469
Haigh Gtr Manchester 42 B1 loc 3m/4km NE of Wigan. SD 6009
Haigh Moor W Yorks 49 E5* loc 3m/4km SE of Morley. SE 2824
Haighton Green Lancs 47 F4* loc 4m/6km NE of Preston. SD 5634
Haile Cumbria 52 A4 ham 2m/3km SE of Egremont. NY 0308
Hailes Glos 27 E4* loc 2m/3km NE of Winchcombe. Ruined Cistercian abbey (NT). SP 0430
Hailes Castle Lothian 66 C1 ruined cas of 13c-15c on S bank of R Tyne 2km SW of E Linton. NT 5775
Hailey Herts 20 A1* suburban loc 2km N of Hoddesdon. TL 3710
Hailey Oxon 18 B3 loc 3m/5km SE of Wallingford. SU 6485
Hailey Oxon 27 G6 vil 2m/3km N of Witney. SP 3512
Haileybury College Herts 20 A1 boys' public school 2km NW of Hoddesdon. TL 3510
Hailsham E Sussex 12 C5 tn 7m/11km N of Eastbourne. TQ 5809
Hail Weston Cambs 29 F2 vil 2m/3km NW of St Neots. TL 1662
Hainault London 20 H3* loc in borough of Redbridge 4m/6km N of Ilford. 2km NE is wooded area of **H. Forest.** TQ 4591
Haine Kent 13 H1 loc in W part of Ramsgate. TR 3566
Haines Hill Som 8 A2* S dist of Taunton. ST 2223
Hainford Norfolk 39 F3 vil 6m/10km N of Norwich. TG 2218
Hainton Lincs 45 F3 vil 6m/9km SE of Mkt Rasen. TF 1884
Hainworth W Yorks 48 C4* loc 2km S of Keighley. SE 0539
Haisthorpe Humberside 51 F2 vil 4m/6km SW of Bridlington. TA 1264
Hakin Dyfed 22 B5* W dist of Milford Haven. SM 8905
Halam Notts 44 B5 vil 2km NW of Southwell. SK 6754
Halbeath Fife 73 E5* loc 2m/4km E of Dunfermline. NT 1288
Halberry Head H'land 86 F3 headland on E coast of Caithness dist 4m/6km E of Lybster. ND 3037
Halberton Devon 7 G4 vil 3m/5km E of Tiverton. ST 0013
Halcro H'land 86 E2 loc in Caithness dist 5m/8km SE of Castletown. ND 2360
Halcro Head Orkney 89 B7* headland on E coast of S Ronaldsay 3m/4km NE of Brough Ness. ND 4785
Halden Herts 19 F1* NE dist of Welwyn Garden City. TL 2414
Haldenby Humberside 50 D6* loc 4m/7km NE of Crowle. SE 8217
Halden, High Kent 13 E3 vil 3m/4km NE of Tenterden. TQ 8937
Haldon, Great Devon 5 E3 wooded ridge running NW to SE between Exeter and Newton Abbot, crossed by two main rds. SX 8983
Hale Ches 42 A3 vil 4m/6km SW of Widnes. **H. Bank** loc 2km N. **H. Head** headland on R Mersey estuary 1m S. SJ 4682
Hale Cumbria 47 F1 loc 5m/8km N of Carnforth. **H. Green** loc adjoining to NE. SD 5078
Hale Gtr Manchester 42 D3 tn adjoining Altrincham to S. **H. Green** loc 2km E. SJ 7786
Hale Hants 9 H3 vil 4m/7km NE of Fordingbridge. To S, **H. Purlieu** (NT), an area of heath and woodland. SU 1918
Hale Kent 20 D5 loc in E part of Chatham. TQ 7765
Hale Surrey 11 E1 loc 1m NE of Farnham. **Upr Hale** loc adjoining to NW. SU 8448
Halebarns Gtr Manchester 42 D3 loc 2km SE of Hale. SJ 7985
Hale End London 20 A3 loc in borough of Waltham Forest 2km NE of Walthamstow tn centre. TQ 3891
Hale, Great Lincs 37 F1 vil 1km S of Heckington. **Lit Hale** vil 1km S. TF 1442
Hale Nook Lancs 47 E4* loc 3m/4km SE of Preesall. SD 3944
Hales Norfolk 39 G5 vil 2m/3km SE of Loddon. TM 3897

Hales Staffs 34 D1 vil 3m/4km E of Mkt Drayton. Site of Roman villa 1km E. SJ 7133
Halesfield Salop 34 D4* industrial estate E of Madeley, Telford. SJ 7104
Halesgate Lincs 37 G2/H2* loc 2m/3km NE of Moulton. TF 3226
Hales Green Derbys 43 F6* loc 3m/5km S of Ashbourne. SK 1841
Halesowen W Midlands 35 F5 tn 7m/11km W of Birmingham. Industries include iron and steel goods. SO 9683
Hales Street Norfolk 39 F6* loc 3m/4km W of Pulham Mkt. TM 1587
Hale Street Kent 20 C6 vil 3m/4km N of Paddock Wd. TQ 6749
Halesworth Suffolk 31 G1 tn 24m/39km NE of Ipswich. Industries include agricultural engineering, malting, milk-processing. TM 3877
Halewood Merseyside 42 A3 loc 4m/6km W of Widnes. Car factory to SW. **H. Green** loc 1m NW. SJ 4585
Half Acre Gtr Manchester 42 D1* loc 1m N of Prestwich. SD 8104
Half Moon Bay Lancs 47 E2 bay to N of Heysham harbour. SD 4060
Halford Devon 4 D3* loc on E edge of Dartmoor National Pk 4m/6km NW of Newton Abbot. SX 8174
Halford Salop 34 B5 ham just E of Craven Arms across R Onny. SO 4383
Halford Warwicks 27 G3 vil 3m/5km N of Shipston on Stour. SP 2645
Halfpenny Cumbria 53 E6* loc 4m/6km S of Kendal. SD 5387
Halfpenny Furze Dyfed 23 E4* loc 2m/3km S of St Clears. SN 2713
Halfpenny Green Staffs 35 E5* ham 7m/11km SW of Wolverhampton. Airfield to S. SO 8291
Halfway Berks 17 H4* loc 4m/7km W of Newbury. SU 4068
Halfway Dyfed 23 G5* loc on E side of Llanelli. SN 5200
Halfway Dyfed 24 C5 loc 5m/9km N of Llandeilo. SN 6430
Halfway S Yorks 43 H3 loc in Sheffield 6m/10km SE of city centre. SK 4381
Halfway 24 D4 ham on border of Dyfed and Powys 4m/7km E of Llandovery. To NE, in Powys, is the wooded area **Halfway Forest.** Earthworks of Roman camps 1m S. SN 8232
Halfway Bridge W Sussex 11 F3* loc midway between Midhurst and Petworth. SU 9321
Halfway House Salop 34 A3* ham 1m SE of Wollaston. SJ 3411
Halfwayhouse S'clyde 64 C3* loc in Cardonald dist of Glasgow. NS 5363
Halfway Houses Kent 21 E4 loc on Isle of Sheppey midway between Queenborough and Minster. TQ 9373
Halfway Houses Lincs 44 D5* ham roughly halfway between Newark and Lincoln on A46 rd (Foss Way). SK 8863
Halfway Reach 20 B3* stretch of R Thames below London between Dagenham to N and Erith Marshes to S. TQ 4981
Halidon Hill Nthmb 67 F3 hill 2m/3km NW of Berwick-upon-Tweed, site of English victory over Scots in 1333. NT 9654
Halifax W Yorks 48 D5 industrial tn 7m/11km SW of Bradford. Textiles and carpets, confectionery, engineering. SE 0925
Halistra, Upper and **Lower** Skye, H'land 78 A4 adjoining locs 5m/8km S of Vaternish Pt. NG 2459
Halket S'clyde 64 B4* loc 1m E of Lugton. NS 4252
Halkin Clwyd. See Halkyn.
Halkirk H'land 86 D2 vil on R Thurso 6m/9km S of Thurso tn, Caithness dist. ND 1359
Halkyn (Helygain) Clwyd 41 G4/H4 vil 3m/5km SE of Holywell. To W, **H. Mountain,** NW-SE ridge with remains of lead mines and quarries. SJ 2171
Halladale H'land 86 B2 r in Caithness dist running N down Strath Halladale to Melvich Bay on N coast. NC 8965
Hallam Head S Yorks 43 G3* dist of Sheffield 3m/5km W of Sheffield. SK 3086
Hallam, Little Derbys 36 B1* dist of Ilkeston 1km S of tn centre. SK 4640
Hallam, West Derbys 36 A1 vil 2m/3km W of Ilkeston. **W Hallam Common** loc 1km NW. SK 4341
Halland E Sussex 12 B5 ham 4m/6km SE of Uckfield. TQ 5016
Halland's Field Humberside 51 E6* loc 1km SW of Goxhill. TA 0920
Hallaton Leics 36 D4 vil 7m/11km NE of Mkt Harborough. Site of motte and bailey cas to W. SP 7896
Hallatrow Avon 16 B5 vil 3m/4km NW of Midsomer Norton. ST 6357
Hallbankgate Cumbria 60 B5 ham 4m/6km E of Brampton. NY 5859
Hallbeck Cumbria 53 F5* loc 3m/5km SW of Sedbergh. SD 6288
Hall Common Norfolk 39 G3* loc 1km S of Ludham. TG 3817
Hall Cross Lancs 47 E5* loc 1m S of Kirkham. SD 4230
Hall Dunnerdale Cumbria 52 C5 ham in R Duddon valley 5m/8km N of Broughton in Furness. SD 2195
Hallen Avon 16 B3 5m/8km NW of Bristol. ST 5580
Hall End Beds 29 E4* W end of Clophill. TL 0737
Hall End Warwicks 35 H4* loc adjoining Dordon to W. SK 2500
Halleypike Lough Nthmb 60 D4 small lake on moors 4m/6km W of Simonburn. NY 8172
Hallfield Gate Derbys 43 H5* loc 2m/3km NW of Alfreton. SK 3957
Hallgarth Durham 54 C1* ham 1km S of Pittington. NZ 3243
Hall Garth Ponds N Yorks 49 E1* two small lakes to W of Nunwick. SE 3174
Hall Green Ches 42 D5* loc adjoining Scholar Green to S. SJ 8356
Hall Green Lancs 42 B1 SE dist of Skelmersdale. SD 5004
Hall Green Lancs 47 E5* loc 1m W of Walmer Br. SD 4624
Hall Green Norfolk 38 D3* loc 4m/6km W of E Dereham. TF 9315
Hall Green Norfolk 39 F6* ham 2km SW of Tivetshall St Mary. TM 1585
Hall Green W Midlands 35 G6* loc in Birmingham 4m/7km SE of city centre. SP 1081
Hall Green W Midlands 36 A5/A6* loc in Coventry 3m/5km NE of city centre. SP 3582
Hall Green W Yorks 49 E6* loc 1km S of Crigglestone. SE 3115
Hall Grove Herts 19 F1* SE dist of Welwyn Garden City. TL 2511
Hallhills Loch D & G 59 F3* small loch 5m/8km N of Lockerbie. NY 1688
Halliford, Lower Surrey 19 E4 loc adjoining Shepperton to E and 2km SW of Sunbury. TQ 0867
Halliford, Upper Surrey 19 E4 loc 1m W of Sunbury. TQ 0968
Hallin Skye, H'land 78 A4 loc near NW coast 5m/8km S of Vaternish Pt. NG 2459
Halling Kent 20 D5 industrial loc on R Medway 4m/6km SW of Rochester. Locs of **N Halling** and **Upr Halling** 1m N and W respectively. TQ 7064
Hallingbury, Great Essex vil 2m/3km SE of Bishop's Stortford. TL 5119
Hallingbury, Little Essex 30 A6 vil 3m/4km S of Bishop's Stortford. TL 5017
Hallington Lincs 45 G3 ham 2m/3km SW of Louth. TF 3085
Hallington Nthmb 61 E4 ham 7m/11km N of Corbridge. To W, **Hallington Resrs,** two adjacent resrs. NY 9875
Hall i' th' Wood Gtr Manchester 42 C1* 16c hse containing a museum, to N of Tonge Moor in Bolton; childhood home of Samuel Crompton, inventor of spinning mule. SD 7211
Halliwell Gtr Manchester 47 G6 dist of Bolton 2km NW of tn centre. SD 7010
Halloughton Notts 44 B5 ham 2km SW of Southwell. SK 6851
Hallow H & W 26 D2 vil 3m/4km NW of Worcester. Loc of **H. Heath** 1km N. SO 8258
Hallsands Devon 5 E6 small fishing vil on S coast 2km NW of Start Pt. SX 8138
Hallsgreen Essex 20 B1* loc 2m/4km SW of Harlow. TL 4108
Hall's Green Herts 29 G5* ham 4m/6km NE of Stevenage. TL 2728
Hallthwaites Cumbria 52 B6* loc 3m/5km N of Millom. SD 1885
Halltoft End Lincs 45 G6 loc 3m/5km E of Boston. TF 3645
Hall, West Cumbria 60 B4* ham 4m/7km W of Gilsland. NY 5667
Hallwood Green Glos 26 B4* loc 4m/6km SW of Ledbury. SO 6733
Hallworthy Cornwall 6 B6 loc 6m/9km NE of Camelford. SX 1887
Hallyburton Forest Tayside 73 E1* state forest 4m/6km S of Coupar Angus. NO 2334
Hallyne Borders 65 H4* loc on Lyne Water 4m/6km W of Peebles. Sites of Roman forts on both sides of r. NT 1940
Halmer End Staffs 42 D6 loc 4m/6km NW of Newcastle-under-Lyme. SJ 8048
Halmond's Frome H & W 26 B3* loc 5m/7km S of Bromyard. SO 6747
Halmore Glos 16 C2 vil 2m/4km NE of Berkeley. SO 6902
Halnaker W Sussex 11 E4 vil 4m/6km NE of Chichester. Halnaker Hse, ruined medieval manor hse to N. SU 9008
Halsall Lancs 42 A1 vil 3m/5km NW of Ormskirk. SD 3710
Halse Northants 28 B3* ham 3m/4km NW of Brackley. SP 5640
Halse Som 8 A2 vil in Vale of Taunton Deane 2m/3km NE of Milverton. On N side of vil, **H. Water,** r rising near Brompton Ralph and flowing SE into R Tone on W side of Taunton. ST 1427
Halse Town Cornwall 2 B4 vil just S of St Ives. Knill Monument to E. SW 5038
Halse Water 8 A2* r in Somerset rising on E slopes of Brendon Hills near Brompton Ralph and flowing SE into R Tone at Bishop's Hull 2km W of Taunton. ST 2055
Halsham Humberside 51 G5 vil 4m/7km W of Withernsea. TA 2726
Halsinger Devon 6 D2* loc 5m/7km NW of Barnstaple. SS 5138
Halstead Essex 30 C5 tn on R Colne 6m/10km NE of Braintree. TL 8130
Halstead Kent 20 B5 vil 4m/6km SE of Orpington. TQ 4861
Halstead Leics 36 C4 ham just E of Tilton and 8m/13km NW of Uppingham. SK 7505
Halstock Dorset 8 D3 vil 5m/8km S of Yeovil. To W, locs of **Hr** and **Lr Halstock Leigh.** ST 5308
Halstow, High Kent 20 D4 vil 5m/8km NE of Strood. Northward Hill Nature Reserve to N on edge of Cooling Marshes. TQ 7875
Halstow, Lower Kent 21 E5 vil on inlet of R Medway estuary 4m/6km NW of Sittingbourne. Brick works. TQ 8567
Halsway Som 7 H2* ham at foot of Quantock Hills 5m/8km SE of Watchet. ST 1237
Haltcliff Bridge Cumbria 52 D2* loc on R Caldew 2m/3km N of Hutton Roof. NY 3636
Haltham Lincs 45 F5 vil 4m/6km S of Horncastle. TF 2463
Halton Bucks 18 D1 vil 2m/3km N of Wendover. SP 8710
Halton Ches 42 B3* loc in Runcorn 2km E of tn centre. Remains of medieval cas. **H. Brook** loc to NW. SJ 5381
Halton Clwyd 34 A1* ham 2m/3km NE of Chirk. SJ 3039
Halton Lancs 47 F2 vil on N bank of R Lune 3m/4km NE of Lancaster. SD 5064
Halton Nthmb 61 E4 ham 2m/4km N of Corbridge. **H. Castle,** 14c tower hse with later hses or wings attached. NY 9967
Halton W Yorks 49 F5 dist of Leeds 3m/5km E of city centre. **H. Moor** loc adjoining to S. SE 3433
Halton 117 admin dist of Ches.
Halton, East Humberside 51 F6 vil 4m/7km NW of Immingham. **E Halton Skitter** loc on R Humber at mouth of E Halton Beck 2m/3km N. TA 1319
Halton East N Yorks 48 C3 vil 4m/6km NE of Skipton. SE 0453
Halton Fenside Lincs 45 G5* loc 2m/4km SE of Spilsby. TF 4263
Halton Gill N Yorks 48 B1 ham near head of Littondale 4m/7km NW of Arncliffe. SD 8876
Halton Green Lancs 47 F2* loc 4m/6km NE of Lancaster. SD 5165
Halton Holegate Lincs 45 G4 vil 2km SE of Spilsby. TF 4165
Halton Lea Gate Nthmb 60 C5 ham 5m/8km SW of Haltwhistle. NY 6558
Halton Park Lancs 47 F2* loc 4m/7km NE of Lancaster. SD 5265
Halton, West Humberside 50 D6 vil 6m/10km N of Scunthorpe. SE 9020
Halton West N Yorks 48 B3 vil 2m/3km SW of Hellifield. SD 8454
Haltwhistle Nthmb 60 C5 mkt tn for former coal-mining area, on R South Tyne 14m/23km W of Hexham. NY 7064
Halvergate Norfolk 39 G4 vil 3m/5km N of Reedham. TG 4206
Halway Som 8 A2* loc 2km SE of Taunton. ST 2423
Halwell Devon 4 D5 vil 5m/8km SW of Totnes. SX 7753
Halwill Devon 6 C5 vil 6m/10km SE of Holsworthy. To S and SE, **H. Forest,** upland area partly wooded. 1m E, **H. Junction,** vil at site of former rly junction. SX 4299
Ham Devon 4 B5* dist of Plymouth 2m/3km NW of city centre. SX 4657
Ham Devon 8 A4* ham 2m/3km S of Stockland. ST 2301
Ham Glos 16 B2 vil 1km S of Berkeley. ST 6798
Ham Glos 27 E5 loc 2m/3km E of Cheltenham. SO 9721
Ham London 19 F4 loc in borough of Richmond between Richmond Park and R Thames. To N beside r is **Ham Hse** (NT), 17c hse and grnds. TQ 1772
Ham Shetland 89 D8 chief settlement of island of Foula, qv. It is situated on E coast on the island's only harbour, **Ham Voe.** HT 9738
Ham Shetland 89 E7* loc on island of Bressay 2km SE of Lerwick across Bressay Sound. HU 4939
Ham Som 8 B2 vil 4m/6km E of Taunton. ST 2825
Ham Som 8 B3* loc 2m/3km SW of Broadway. ST 2913
Ham Wilts 17 G5 vil 4m/6km S of Hungerford. SU 3363
Hamarsay W Isles 88 B3* islet in E Loch Tarbert, Harris, off W coast of Scalpay. NG 2194
Hamars Ness Shetland 89 F5* headland at NW corner of Fetlar. HU 5894
Hamble Hants 10 B4 vil near mouth of R Hamble on E side of Southampton Water opp Fawley. Yachting and boat-building; aircraft factories; air training establishments. SU 4806
Hamble 10 B4 r rising near Bishop's Waltham, Hants, and flowing into Southampton Water between Hamble and Warsash. Site of Roman bldg on NT property at head of estuary near Curbridge. Lower reach noted for yachting. SU 4805
Hambleden Bucks 18 C3 vil 3m/5km NE of Henley-on-Thames. SU 7886
Hambledon Hants 10 D3 vil 4m/6km SE of Meonstoke. Traditionally 'home of cricket', the vil club being founded in 18c. Site of Roman bldg SE of vil. SU 6414
Hambledon Surrey 11 F2 vil 3m/5km SE of Milford. SU 9638
Hambleton Lancs 47 E4 vil 3m/4km S of Preesall. **H. Moss Side** 1km E. SD 3742
Hambleton N Yorks 49 G5 vil 4m/7km W of Selby. SE 5530
Hambleton 117 admin dist of N Yorks.
Hambleton Hills, The N Yorks 54 D5 hills lying between R Rye valley to the E and the A19 rd to the W. SE 49, 58
Hambleton, Upper Leics 37 E4 vil on island in Empingham Resr 3m/4km E of Oakham. Locs of **Middle** and **Nether H.** submerged. SK 9007
Hambridge Som 8 C2 vil 3m/4km S of Curry Rivel. ST 3921
Hambridge Som 8 D1* loc 4m/7km SW of Shepton Mallet. ST 5936
Hambrook Avon 16 B4 loc 5m/8km NE of Bristol. ST 6478
Hambrook W Sussex 11 E4* vil 1km N of Nutbourne and 5m/8km W of Chichester. SU 7807
Ham Common Dorset 9 E2 loc 1m SE of Gillingham. ST 8125
Hamdon Hill Som 8 C3* hill 5m/8km W of Yeovil. Source of famous honey-coloured building stone known as Ham stone. ST 4716
Ham, East London 20 B3 tn in borough of Newham 7m/11km E of London Br. TQ 4283
Hameringham Lincs 45 G4 vil 4m/6km SE of Horncastle. TF 3167
Hamerton Cambs 37 F6 vil 8m/13km NW of Huntingdon. TL 1379

Hamford Water Essex 31 F5* stream draining marshes W of The Naze and flowing out into North Sea at Pennyhole Bay. TM 2426
Ham Green Avon 16 A4* loc 4m/6km NW of Bristol. ST 5375
Ham Green H & W 26 C3* loc 2m/4km W of Gt Malvern. SO 7444
Ham Green H & W 27 E2* ham 3m/5km SW of Redditch. SP 0163
Ham Green Kent 13 E4* loc 1km SW of Wittersham. TQ 8926
Ham Green Kent 21 E5 loc 1m N of Upchurch and 5m/7km E of Gillingham. TQ 8468
Ham, High Som 8 C2 vil on high ground overlooking Sedgemoor, 3m/5km N of Langport. ST 4231
Ham Hill Kent 20 D5 loc 1m SW of Snodland. TQ 6960
Hamilton S'clyde 64 D3 tn 11m/17km SE of Glasgow and 1m W of confluence of Rs Avon and Clyde. Industries include iron and steel, mnfre of electrical equipment, carpets, hosiery and knitwear. Racecourse. NS 7255
Hamiltonhill S'clyde 64 C2* loc in Glasgow 2km N of city centre. NS 5867
Hamilton House Lothian. See Prestonpans.
Hamlet Devon 7 H5 ham 2km W of Honiton. SY 1499
Hamlet Dorset 8 D3* ham adjoining Chetnole to N, 2km S of Yetminster. ST 5908
Ham, Low Som 8 C2 vil 2m/3km NE of Langport. ST 4329
Hammer W Sussex 11 E2* vil 2m/3km W of Haslemere. SU 8732
Hammerpot W Sussex 11 F4 loc 3m/5km NE of Littlehampton. TQ 0605
Hammerside Point Cumbria 52 C6* headland on W bank of R Leven estuary 2m/3km E of Ulverston. SD 3177
Hammersmith Derbys 43 H5* loc 1km N of Ripley. SK 3951
Hammersmith London 19 F4 5m/8km W of Charing Cross. Borough on N side of R Thames, crossed here by Hammersmith, Putney, and Wandsworth Brs. TQ 2278
Hammerwich Staffs 35 G3/G4* vil 2m/3km NE of Brownhills. **Hammerwich Sq** loc adjoining to W. SK 0607
Hammerwood E Sussex 12 B3 loc 3m/5km E of E Grinstead. TQ 4339
Hammond Street Herts 19 G2 loc 2m/3km NW of Cheshunt. TL 3304
Hammoon Dorset 9 E3 vil on R Stour 2m/3km E of Sturminster Newton. ST 8114
Hamna Voe Shetland 89 D6 inlet on NW coast of Mainland, 3m/5km NW of Hillswick. HU 2379
Hamna Voe Shetland 89 E6 inlet on S coast of Yell. Loc of **Hamnavoe** at its head. HU 4980
Hamnavoe Shetland 89 E8 fishing vil at N end of island of W Burra, with natural harbour formed by bay of **Hamna Voe.** Connected to Mainland by rd brs at either end of island of Trondra. HU 3635
Hamnish Clifford H & W 26 A2* loc 2m/4km E of Leominster. SO 5359
Hamoaze 4 B5* anchorage between Devonport, Devon, and Torpoint, Cornwall, forming part of R Tamar estuary. SX 4455
Hamp Som 8 B1* S dist of Bridgwater. ST 3036
Hampden, Great Bucks 18 D2 loc 3m/5km E of Princes Risborough. **Hampden Hse,** rebuilt 1754, is former home of John Hampden who defied Charles I. SP 8402
Hampden, Little Bucks 18 D2 ham 3m/4km S of Wendover. SP 8503
Hampden Park E Sussex 12 C6 N dist of Eastbourne. TQ 6002
Hampden Row Bucks 18 D2 ham 3m/4km SE of Princes Risborough. SP 8401
Hamperden End Essex 30 A4/A5* ham 3m/4km W of Thaxted. TL 5630
Hampnett Glos 27 E5 vil 1m NW of Northleach. SP 1015
Hampnett, East W Sussex 11 E4 loc on N side of Tangmere airfield 4m/6km E of Chichester. SU 9106
Hampole S Yorks 44 A1 vil 6m/10km NW of Doncaster. SE 5010
Hampreston Dorset 9 G4 vil 5m/8km NW of Bournemouth. SZ 0598
Hamps 43 F5 r rising 4m/6km NE of Leek, Staffs and flowing S to Winkhill, E to Waterhouses, then N to its confluence with R Manifold 2km E of Grindon. SK 1045
Hampshire 118, 119 county in southern England bounded by the English Channel and the counties of W Sussex, Surrey, Berkshire, Wiltshire, and Dorset. The centre of the county consists largely of chalk downs interspersed with fertile valleys. In the SW is the New Forest, while in the NE is the military area centred on Aldershot. The much indented coastline borders the Solent and looks across it to the Isle of Wight. The chief tns are Winchester, county tn and ancient capital of Wessex; the port of Southampton and naval base of Portsmouth; and the industrial tns of Basingstoke and Eastleigh. The chief rs are the Itchen and Test, chalk streams flowing into Southampton Water.
Hampson Green Lancs 47 F3* loc 5m/7km S of Lancaster. SD 4954
Hampstead London 19 F3 dist in borough of Camden 4m/6km NW of Charing Cross. Includes locs of **S** and **W Hampstead** and large open space of H. Heath on high ground to N, at N edge of which is Kenwood Hse, 18c hse by Robert Adam. To N again is **H. Garden Suburb.** TQ 2685
Hampstead Marshall Berks 17 H5 vil 4m/6km W of Newbury. SU 4165
Hampstead Norris Berks 18 A4 vil 6m/10km NE of Newbury. Site of Roman villa 1km S. SU 5276
Hampsthwaite N Yorks 49 E2/E3 vil 4m/6km NW of Harrogate. 17c rd br over R Nidd. SE 2558
Hampton Devon 8 B4* loc 3m/4km SW of Axminster. SY 2696
Hampton H & W 27 E3 W dist of Evesham. SP 0243
Hampton Kent 13 G1 W dist of Herne Bay. TR 1668
Hampton London 19 F4 loc to N of R Thames in borough of Richmond, 3m/5km W of Kingston. Loc of **H. Hill** lies 1m NE; that of **H. Wick** 3m/4km E across Bushy Park opp Kingston. H. Court Palace (qv) is 2m/3km SE. TQ 1370
Hampton Salop 34 D5 vil on W bank of R Severn 4m/7km S of Bridgnorth. SO 7486
Hampton Wilts 17 F2 ham 1km W of Highworth. SU 1892
Hampton Bishop H & W 26 B4 vil between R Wye and R Lugg 3m/5km SE of Hereford. SO 5538
Hampton Court Palace London 19 F4 large mansion on left bank of R Thames 2km W of Kingston Br. Built by Cardinal Wolsey in 16c; 17c additions by Wren. TQ 1568
Hampton Fields Glos 16 D2* loc 2m/4km E of Nailsworth. ST 8899
Hampton Gay Oxon 28 A5/A6 ham on R Cherwell 7m/11km N of Oxford. SP 4816
Hampton Green Ches 42 B6* loc 1m E of Hampton Heath. SJ 5149
Hampton Heath Ches 42 B6 ham 2m/3km NE of Malpas. SJ 4949
Hampton in Arden W Midlands 35 G6 vil 3m/5km E of Solihull. SP 2080
Hampton Loade Salop 34 D5 loc on E bank of R Severn opp Hampton, 4m/7km S of Bridgnorth. SO 7486
Hampton Lovett H & W 26 D1 vil 2m/3km N of Droitwich. SO 8865
Hampton Lucy Warwicks 27 F2/G2 vil 4m/6km E of Stratford-upon-Avon. SP 2557
Hampton on the Hill Warwicks 27 F2 vil 2m/3km W of Warwick. SP 2564
Hampton Park Hants 10 B3* N dist of Southampton. SU 4315
Hampton Poyle Oxon 28 A6 vil 6m/10km N of Oxford. SP 5015
Hampton Wafre H & W 26 B2* loc 5m/8km E of Leominster. SO 5757
Hamptworth Wilts 10 A3 ham 7m/12km W of Romsey. SU 2419
Hamra H'land 78 A4* r running NW into Loch Pooltiel on NW coast of Skye. NG 1649
Hamrow Norfolk 38 D2/D3* loc 1km N of Whissonsett. TF 9124
Hamsey E Sussex 12 A5 ham in R Ouse valley 2m/3km N of Lewes. TQ 4012
Hamsey Green Surrey 20 A5* loc adjoining Warlingham to NW. TQ 3559
Hams Hall Power Station Warwicks. See Lea Marston. SP 2091
Ham, South Hants 18 B6* W dist of Basingstoke. SU 6151
Hams, South 118 admin dist of Devon.
Hamstall Ridware Staffs 35 G3 vil 4m/6km E of Rugeley. Elizn manor hse. SK 1019
Hamstead Isle of Wight 10 B5 loc 3m/5km E of Yarmouth. SZ 4091
Hamstead W Midlands 35 F5 loc in NE part of W Bromwich. SP 0493
Hamsteels Durham 54 B1 loc 2m/3km S of Lanchester. NZ 1744
Hamsterley Durham 54 A2 vil 2m/3km W of Witton le Wear. **H. Common,** moorland area to W; to S of it is **H. Forest,** wooded area planted with conifers. NZ 1131
Hamsterley Durham 61 F5* vil 1m NE of Ebchester. **H. Mill** loc 2m/3km E. **H. Hall,** 18c hse, was home of Surtees, author of *Jorrocks.* NZ 1156
Ham Street Kent 13 F4 vil 6m/9km S of Ashford. TR 0033
Ham Street Som 8 D1 vil 4m/7km SE of Glastonbury. ST 5534
Ham, West London 20 A3 tn in borough of Newham 5m/8km E of London Br. TQ 4083
Hamworthy Dorset 9 G5 urban loc 2m/4km W of Poole tn centre across Holes Bay. **Lr Hamworthy** loc to SE on Poole Harb. SY 9991
Hanbury H & W 26 D2 vil 4m/7km S of Bromsgrove. The Hall (NT) is a red-brick hse of 1701. SO 9664
Hanbury Staffs 35 G2 vil 5m/8km NW of Burton upon Trent. **H. Woodend** loc 1m SW. SK 1727
Hanby Lincs 37 E2* loc 2km N of Lenton. TF 0232
Hanchet End Suffolk 30 B3* loc 2km NW of Haverhill. TL 6546
Hanch Reservoir Staffs 35 G3* small resr 3m/5km N of Lichfield. SK 1013
Hanchurch Staffs 35 E1* ham 3m/4km S of Newcastle-under-Lyme. SJ 8441
Handa H'land 84 B3 island and bird sanctuary of about 1 sq mile or 3 sq km off W coast of Sutherland dist opp loc of Tarbet across Sound of Handa. NC 1348
Handale Cleveland 55 F3* loc 1m E of Liverton. NZ 7215
Hand and Pen Devon 7 H5* ham 3m/5km W of Ottery St Mary. SY 0495
Handbridge Ches 42 A4/A5 S dist of Chester S of R Dee. SJ 4065
Handcross W Sussex 11 H2 vil 5m/7km S of Crawley. TQ 2629
Handfast Point Dorset 9 G5 alternative name for The Foreland, headland at SW end of Poole Bay 3m/5km NE of Swanage. SZ 0582
Handforth Ches 42 D3 loc 2km NE of Wilmslow. SJ 8583
Hand Green Ches 42 B5* 1km W of Tiverton. SJ 5460
Handley Ches 42 A5 vil 7m/11km SE of Chester. SJ 4657
Handley Derbys 43 H5* ham 2km SW of Clay Cross. SK 3761
Handley Green Essex 20 C2* loc 2m/3km NE of Ingatestone. TL 6501
Handley, Middle Derbys 43 H3 vil 3m/5km E of Dronfield. Hams of **Nether Handley** and **W Handley** to S and W respectively. SK 4077
Handley's Cross H & W 26 A3* loc 6m/10km W of Hereford. SO 4140
Handsacre Staffs 35 G3 vil 3m/5km SE of Rugeley. SK 0916
Handside Herts 19 F1* W dist of Welwyn Garden City. TL 2212
Handsworth S Yorks 43 H3 coal-mining dist of Sheffield 4m/6km E of city centre. SK 4086
Handsworth W Midlands 35 F5 NW dist of Birmingham. SP 0490
Handy Cross Bucks 18 D3 loc 2m/3km SW of High Wycombe. SU 8590
Hanford Dorset 9 F3* loc 4m/6km NW of Blandford Forum. ST 8411
Hanford Staffs 42 D6 loc in Stoke-on-Trent 2m/3km S of city centre. SJ 8742
Hanford, Little Dorset 9 F3* loc 5m/7km NW of Blandford Forum. ST 8411
Hangersley Hill Hants 9 H4* loc 2m/3km NE of Ringwood. SU 1706
Hanging Bridge Derbys 43 F6 loc on R Dove 2km SW of Ashbourne. SK 1645
Hanging Heaton W Yorks 49 E5* loc 1m SE of Batley. SE 2523
Hanging Houghton Northants 28 C1 ham 8m/13km N of Northampton. SP 7573
Hanging Langford Wilts 9 G1 vil in R Wylye valley 5m/8km NW of Wilton. SU 0336
Hangingshaw S'clyde 64 D3* loc in Glasgow 2m/4km S of city centre. NS 5961
Hanging Walls of Mark Anthony Cumbria 53 F2* loc 2m/4km E of Skirwith. NY 6532
Hangleton E Sussex 11 H4 NW dist of Hove. TQ 2607
Hangleton W Sussex 11 G4* loc 2km SE of Angmering. TQ 0903
Hanham Avon 16 B4 S dist of Kingswood 4m/6km E of Bristol. ST 6472
Hanham Abbots Avon. See Hanham Green.
Hanham Green Avon 16 B4* ham in par of Hanham Abbots 4m/6km E of Bristol. ST 6470
Hankelow Ches 42 C6 vil 2km NE of Audlem. SJ 6745
Hankerton Wilts 17 E3 vil 3m/5km NE of Malmesbury. SU 9690
Hankham E Sussex 12 C6* loc on S side of Pevensey Levels 4m/7km N of Eastbourne. TQ 6105
Hanley Staffs 42 D6 one of the tns of Stoke-on-Trent: Burslem, Fenton, Hanley, Longton, Stoke, Tunstall. Hanley lies 2km N of city centre. SJ 8847
Hanley Castle H & W 26 D3 vil on W bank of R Severn 2km NW of Upton upon Severn. SO 8442
Hanley Childe H & W 26 B2* ham 4m/7km SE of Tenbury Wells. SO 6565
Hanley Swan H & W 26 C3 vil 3m/4km SE of Gt Malvern. SO 8142
Hanley William H & W 26 B1* ham 5m/8km E of Tenbury Wells. SO 6765
Hanlith N Yorks 48 B2 ham just E of Kirkby Malham. SD 9061
Hanmer Clwyd 34 B1 vil 5m/9km W of Whitchurch. **H. Mere** is lake on S side of vil. SJ 4539
Hannafore Point Cornwall 3 G3* headland at SW end of Looe Bay in suburb of W Looe. SX 2552
Hannah Lincs 45 H3 loc 4m/6km NE of Alford and 2m/4km SW of Sutton on Sea. TF 5079
Hanney, East Oxon 17 H2 vil 4m/6km N of Wantage. SU 4193
Hanney, West Oxon 17 H2 vil 3m/5km N of Wantage. SU 4092
Hanningfield, East Essex 20 D2 vil 6m/9km SE of Chelmsford. TL 7701
Hanningfield Reservoir Essex 20 D2* large resr 4m/7km NE of Billericay. TQ 7398
Hanningfields Green Suffolk 30 D3* loc 5m/8km N of Long Melford. TL 8754
Hanningfield, South Essex 20 D2 vil on SE side of Hanningfield Resr 3m/4km N of Wickford. Ham of **S Hanningfield Tye** adjoins vil to E. TQ 7497
Hanningfield, West Essex 20 D2 vil on N side of Hanningfield Resr 5m/8km S of Chelmsford. TQ 7399
Hannington Hants 18 A5 vil 2m/4km SE of Kingsclere. SU 5355
Hannington Northants 28 C1 vil 5m/9km NW of Wellingborough. SP 8171
Hannington Wilts 17 F2 vil 2m/3km W of Highworth. Ham of **H. Wick** 2km N. Site of Roman villa 1km NE of H. Wick. SU 1793
Hanover Point Isle of Wight 10 B6 headland on SW coast between Compton Bay and Brook Bay. SZ 3783
Hanscombe End Beds 29 E4* ham 3m/5km SE of Clophill. TL 1133
Hanslope Bucks 28 C3 vil 5m/8km NW of Newport Pagnell. SP 8046
Hanthorpe Lincs 37 F2 ham 3m/4km N of Bourne. TF 0823
Hanwell London 19 F3 loc in borough of Ealing 9m/15km W of Charing Cross. TQ 1580
Hanwell Oxon 27 H3 vil 2m/4km NW of Banbury. **H. Castle,** Tudor and later. Site of Roman bldg to W. SP 4343
Hanwoodbank Salop 34 B3* loc 3m/5km SW of Shrewsbury. SJ 4410
Hanwood, Great Salop 34 B3 vil 4m/7km SW of Shrewsbury. SJ 4309
Hanworth Berks 18 D4* S dist of Bracknell. SU 8666
Hanworth London 19 E4 loc in borough of Hounslow 3m/5km W of Twickenham. H. Park is large open space to N and E. TQ 1171
Hanworth Norfolk 39 F2 vil 4m/7km S of Cromer. TG 1935
Happisburgh Norfolk 39 G2 coastal resort 6m/10km E of N Walsham. **H. Common** vil 2km S. TG 3731
Hapsford Ches 42 A4 ham 2km SW of Helsby. SJ 4774

Hapsford Som 16 C6* loc 2km NW of Frome. ST 7649

Hapton Lancs 48 B5 vil 2km S of Padiham. See also Shuttleworth Hall. SD 7931

Hapton Norfolk 39 F5 vil 6m/9km SE of Wymondham. TM 1796

Harberton Devon 4 D4 vil 2m/3km SW of Totnes. SX 7758

Harbertonford Devon 4 D5 vil 3m/4km S of Totnes. SX 7856

Harbledown Kent 13 G2 W suburb of Canterbury. Ham of **Upr Harbledown** to W. TR 1358

Harborne W Midlands 35 F5 dist of Birmingham 3m/5km SW of city centre. SP 0284

Harborough 119 admin dist of Leics.

Harborough Magna Warwicks 36 B6 vil 3m/5km NW of Rugby. Loc of **Harborough Parva** adjoins to S. SP 4779

Harbottle Nthmb 61 E2 vil 2km SE of Alwinton. Remains of 12c cas. NT 9304

Harbourne 5 E5* Devon r rising at H. Head on Dartmoor 3m/5km W of Buckfastleigh and flowing generally SE into R Dart at Stoke Pt opp Stoke Gabriel. SX 8356

Harbours Hill H & W 26 D1* loc 3m/5km S of Bromsgrove. SO 9565

Harbridge Hants 9 H3 loc 3m/4km S of Fordingbridge. 1km NW, loc of **H. Green.** SU 1410

Harbury Warwicks 27 G2 vil 3m/5km SW of Southam. SP 3759

Harby Leics 36 C2 vil 8m/12km N of Melton Mowbray. SK 7431

Harby Notts 44 D4 vil 6m/10km W of Lincoln. **N Harby** loc 1m N. SK 8770

Harcombe Bottom Devon 8 B4* ham 2m/4km N of Lyme Regis. SY 3395

Harden Nthmb 61 E1* loc 3m/5km NE of Alwinton. NT 9608

Harden S Yorks loc on edge of Peak Dist National Park 3m/5km S of Holmfirth. Resr in **H. Clough** to W. SE 1503

Harden W Midlands 35 F4* loc in Walsall 2m/3km N of tn centre. SK 0101

Harden W Yorks 48 D4 vil 2km SW of Bingley. SE 0838

Harden Beck 48 D4* stream rising near Denholme, W Yorks, and flowing N into R Aire at Bingley. SE 1038

Hardendale Cumbria 53 A3 loc 2km E of Shap. NY 5814

Hardenhuish Wilts 16 D4 loc adjoining Chippenham to NW. ST 9074

Harden Park Ches 42 D3* loc in Wilmslow 1m S of tn centre. SJ 8479

Hardgate Grampian 77 G1* loc 3m/5km W of Peterculter. NJ 7801

Hardgate N Yorks 49 E2 loc 2m/3km NW of Ripley. SE 2662

Hardham W Sussex 11 F3 ham 1m SW of Pulborough. Remains of 13c priory to SW. TQ 0317

Hardhorn Lancs 47 E4 loc 2km S of Poulton-le-Fylde. SD 3537

Hardingham Norfolk 39 E4 vil 2m/3km NE of Hingham. TG 0403

Hardingstone Northants 28 C2 S dist of Northampton. One of the three remaining Eleanor crosses (A.M.) is here, the other two being at Geddington and Waltham Cross. SP 7657

Hardings Wood Staffs 42 D5* loc adjoining Kidsgrove to W. SJ 8254

Hardington Som 16 C6* vil 4m/6km NW of Frome. ST 7452

Hardington Mandeville Som 8 C3 vil 4m/6km SW of Yeovil. 1m E, ham of **Hardington Moor.** 2km S, ham of **Hardington Marsh.** ST 5111

Hardknott Castle Cumbria 52 C4* site of Roman fort of *Mediobogdum* (A.M.), at W end of Hard Knott Pass. NY 2101

Hard Knott Pass Cumbria 52 C4 steep pass between valleys of R Duddon and R Esk traversed by rd from Skelwith Br to Eskdale Green at height of 1291 ft or 393 metres. NY 2301

Hardley Hants 10 B4 vil adjoining Fawley oil refinery to W. SU 4304

Hardley Street Norfolk 39 G4* ham 2m/3km NE of Loddon. TG 3801

Hardmead Bucks 28 D3 loc 4m/7km NE of Newport Pagnell. SP 9347

Hardown Hill Dorset. See Morcombelake.

Hardres, Lower Kent 13 G2 vil 3m/5km S of Canterbury. TR 1552

Hardres, Upper Kent 13 G2 loc 5m/7km S of Canterbury. TR 1550

Hardrow N Yorks 53 G5 ham 1m N of Hawes across R Ure. **H. Force** waterfall on Fossdale Gill to N. SD 8691

Hardsough Lancs 48 B6* loc on R Irwell 2m/3km S of Haslingden. SD 7920

Hardstoft Derbys 43 H4* ham 3m/5km E of Clay Cross. SK 4363

Hardway Hants 10 C4 loc in Gosport 2km NW of tn centre. SU 6001

Hardway Som 9 E1* ham 3m/4km E of Bruton. ST 7234

Hardwick Bucks 28 C5 vil 4m/6km N of Aylesbury. SP 8019

Hardwick Cambs 29 G2 vil 5m/8km W of Cambridge. TL 3758

Hardwick Lincs 44 D4* loc 2m/3km W of Saxilby. SK 8675

Hardwick Norfolk 38 B3* loc and industrial estate adjoining King's Lynn to SE. TF 6318

Hardwick Norfolk 39 F5 vil 4m/7km N of Harleston. TM 2289

Hardwick Northants 28 D1 vil 3m/5km NW of Wellingborough. Former manor hse once housed Knights Templars. SP 8569

Hardwick Oxon 17 G1 ham 3m/4km SE of Witney. SP 3706

Hardwick Oxon 28 B4 ham 4m/7km N of Bicester. SP 5729

Hardwick S Yorks 44 A3* loc 2m/3km N of Todwick. SK 4886

Hardwick W Midlands 35 G4* loc 3m/5km NW of Sutton Coldfield. SP 0798

Hardwicke Glos 26 C6 vil 5m/8km SW of Gloucester. SO 7912

Hardwicke Glos 26 D5 ham 4m/7km NW of Cheltenham. SO 9127

Hardwicke H & W 25 G3 ham 3m/5km E of Hay-on-Wye. SO 2743

Hardwick, East W Yorks 49 F6 vil 2m/3km S of Pontefract. **W Hardwick** ham 3m/5km W. SE 4618

Hardwick Grange Notts 44 B3* loc in Clumber Park 4m/7km SE of Worksop. SK 6375

Hardwick Hall Derbys 44 A4 Elizn mansion (NT) 5m/8km NW of Mansfield. SK 4663

Hardwick, Lower H & W 26 A2* loc 6m/10km W of Leominster. SO 4056

Hardwick, Upper H & W 26 A2* loc 6m/9km W of Leominster. SO 4057

Hardy Monument Dorset 8 D5* monmt (NT) on Black Down 5m/8km SW of Dorchester, erected 1846 to commemorate the flag-captain of *Victory* at Trafalgar. SY 6187

Hardy's Green Essex 30 D5 ham 5m/8km SW of Colchester. TL 9320

Harebeating E Sussex 12 C5* loc in N part of Hailsham. TQ 5910

Hareby Lincs 45 G4 ham 4m/7km W of Spilsby. TF 3365

Hare Croft W Yorks 48 D4* ham 1km SW of Wilsden. SE 0835

Harefield Hants 10 B3 E dist of Southampton 3m/5km E of city centre across R Itchen. SU 4613

Harefield London 19 E3 loc in borough of Hillingdon 3m/4km S of Rickmansworth. Loc of **S Harefield** 1m S. TQ 0590

Hare Green Essex 31 E5* ham 6m/10km E of Colchester. TM 0924

Hare Hatch Berks 18 C4 vil 2km NE of Twyford. SU 8077

Harehill Derbys 35 G1* ham 2m/4km NE of Sudbury. SK 1735

Harehills W Yorks 49 E4 dist of Leeds 2m/3km NE of city centre. SE 3135

Harehope Nthmb 67 G6* loc 1m NW of Eglingham. NU 0920

Harelaw Durham 61 F6* loc 1m N of Annfield Plain. NZ 1652

Harelaw Dam S'clyde 64 C3 resr 2m/4km S of Neilston. NS 4753

Harelaw Reservoir S'clyde 64 B2* small resr 2km SW of Port Glasgow. NS 3173

Harelaw Reservoir S'clyde 64 C3* small resr 1m NW of Barrhead. NS 4859

Hare Ness Grampian 77 H1 headland on E coast 4m/6km S of Aberdeen. NO 9599

Hare Park Cambs 30 B2* loc 5m/8km SW of Newmarket. TL 5859

Hareplain Kent 12 D3* loc 2km NW of Biddenden. TQ 8339

Haresceugh Cumbria 53 E1 loc 1m E of Renwick. Remains of cas. NY 6142

Harescombe Glos 26 D6 vil 5m/8km S of Gloucester. SO 8310

Haresfield Glos 16 C1 vil 4m/7km NW of Stroud. **Lit Haresfield** ham 1m SW. SO 8110

Hareshaw S'clyde 65 E3* loc 4m/7km SE of Airdrie. NS 8160

Harestock Hants 10 B2* NW dist of Winchester. SU 4631

Hare Street Essex 20 B1* W dist of Harlow. TL 4309

Hare Street Essex 20 C2* ham 2m/3km SE of Chipping Ongar. TL 5300

Hare Street Herts 29 G5 loc 4m/6km W of Buntingford. TL 3128

Hare Street Herts 29 G5 vil 2m/3km E of Buntingford. TL 3929

Harewood H & W 26 A4* loc 5m/8km NW of Ross-on-Wye. SO 5328

Harewood W Yorks 49 E4 estate vil 7m/11km N of Leeds. **Harewood Hse,** 18c–19c mansion with grnds laid out by Capability Brown. Remains of 14c cas overlooking Wharfedale. SE 3245

Harewood End H & W 26 A4 ham 5m/8km NW of Ross-on-Wye. SO 5226

Harewood Forest Hants 10 B1 wooded area E of Andover. SU 3943

Harford Devon 4 C4 vil on R Erme 2m/3km N of Ivybridge. SX 6359

Harford Devon 7 F5* loc 3m/5km SW of Crediton. SX 8196

Hargate Norfolk 39 E5* loc 6m/10km S of Wymondham. TM 1191

Hargatewall Derbys 43 F4* ham 2m/4km W of Tideswell. SK 1175

Hargrave Ches 42 B5 vil 6m/9km SE of Chester. SJ 4862

Hargrave Northants 29 E1 vil 5m/8km E of Higham Ferrers. TL 0370

Hargrave Suffolk 30 C2 loc 6m/9km W of Bury St Edmunds. Vil of **H. Green** 1km S. TL 7760

Haringey London 19 G3* borough some 5m/8km N of Charing Cross. Contains dists of Hornsey, Tottenham, and Wood Green. TQ 3290

Harker Cumbria 59 H5 loc 3m/5km N of Carlisle. NY 3960

Harknett's Gate Essex 20 B1* loc 3m/4km SW of Harlow. TL 4206

Harkstead Suffolk 31 F4 vil 4m/6km W of Shotley Gate. TM 1834

Harlaston Staffs 35 H3 vil 4m/7km N of Tamworth. SK 2110

Harlaw Grampian 83 F4 site of battle of 1411 in which Donald, Lord of the Isles, was defeated by the Earl of Mar. Situated 2m/4km NW of Inverurie. NJ 7524

Harlaw Reservoir Lothian 65 H2 resr 2km SE of Balerno. NT 1864

Harlaxton Lincs 36 D2 vil 3m/5km SW of Grantham. To SE, **H. Manor,** large ornate 19c edifice by Salvin. SK 8832

Harleburn Head S'clyde 65 F6 hill 3m/5km E of Elvanfoot. Height 1783 ft or 543 metres. NT 0017

Harlech Gwynedd 32 D2 small tn at S end of Morfa Harlech on E side of Tremadoc Bay. Ruined 13c cas (A.M.) stands on rocky eminence above marsh. SH 5831

Harlech Point Gwynedd 32 D1 headland at NW end of Morfa Harlech at mouth of Traeth Bach, 3m/5km N of Harlech. SH 5535

Harlequin Notts 36 C1* loc adjoining Radcliffe on Trent to E. SK 6639

Harlescott Salop 34 C3 NE suburb of Shrewsbury. SJ 5015

Harlesden London 19 F3 loc in borough of Brent 6m/9km W of Charing Cross. TQ 2183

Harleston Devon 4 D6* ham 4m/6km E of Kingsbridge. SX 7945

Harleston Norfolk 39 F6 small tn in R Waveney valley 8m/13km E of Diss. TM 2483

Harleston Suffolk 31 E2 vil 3m/4km NW of Stowmarket. TM 0160

Harlestone Northants 28 C2 vil 4m/7km NW of Northampton. SP 7064

Harle Syke Lancs 48 B4 loc 3m/4km NE of Burnley. SD 8635

Harley Salop 34 C4 vil 2m/3km NW of Much Wenlock. SJ 5901

Harley S Yorks 43 H2* vil 1m W of Wentworth. SK 3698

Harley Brook 34 C4 r rising as Hughley Brook NW of Plaish, Salop, and flowing first SE then NE through vil of Hughley and to E of Harley into R Severn 1km S of Leighton. SJ 6004

Harling, East Norfolk 38 D6 vil 6m/10km SW of Attleborough. TL 9986

Harling, Middle Norfolk 38 D6 loc 1m SW of E Harling. TL 9885

Harlington Beds 29 E4 vil 7m/11km NW of Luton. TL 0330

Harlington London 19 E4 dist in borough of Hillingdon 13m/21km W of Charing Cross. TQ 0978

Harlington S Yorks 44 A1* vil adjoining Barnburgh to S. SE 4802

Harlock Reservoir Cumbria 46 D1* resr below SW slope of Harlock Hill 3m/4km W of Ulverston. SD 2479

Harlosh Skye, H'land 79 B5 locality on peninsula protruding southwards into Loch Bracadale, 4m/7km SE of Dunvegan. **Harlosh Pt** is headland at end of peninsula. **Harlosh I.** is small uninhabited island off headland. NG 2841

Harlow Essex 20 B1 New Tn designated 1947, 21m/33km NE of London. TL 4409

Harlow Green Tyne & Wear 61 G5* dist of Gateshead 3m/5km S of tn centre. NZ 2658

Harlow Hill Nthmb 61 F4 ham 4m/6km W of Heddon-on-the-Wall. NZ 0768

Harlsey Castle N Yorks 54 C5 loc 4m/7km NE of Northallerton. There are scant remains of medieval cas. SE 4198

Harlsey, East N Yorks 54 D5 vil 5m/8km NE of Northallerton. SE 4299

Harlthorpe Humberside 50 C4 ham 10m/15km W of Mkt Weighton. SE 7437

Harlton Cambs 29 G3 vil 6m/9km SW of Cambridge. TL 3852

Harlyn Cornwall 2 D1* loc 3m/4km W of Padstow. **H. Bay** to N. SW 8775

Harman's Corner Kent 21 E5* loc 2km SW of Sittingbourne. TQ 8862

Harman's Cross Dorset 9 G6* vil 2m/3km SE of Corfe Castle. SY 9880

Harmans Water Berks 18 D4* S dist of Bracknell. SU 8767

Harmby N Yorks 54 A5 vil 2km E of Leyburn. SE 1289

Harmer Green Herts 29 F6* suburban loc 2m/3km E of Welwyn. TL 2516

Harmerhill Salop 34 B2 ham 6m/10km N of Shrewsbury. SJ 4922

Harmondsworth London 19 E4 loc in borough of Hillingdon on N side of London (Heathrow) Airport and 15m/25km W of Charing Cross. TQ 0577

Harmston Lincs 44 D5 vil 6m/9km S of Lincoln. SK 9762

Harnage Salop 34 C4* ham 1km SE of Cound. SJ 5604

Harnham Nthmb 61 F3* loc 2m/3km NW of Belsay. **H. Hall,** 16c hse, with medieval tower behind. NZ 0780

Harnham, East Wilts 9 H2 S dist of Salisbury. SU 1428

Harnham Hill Wilts 9 H2* SW dist of Salisbury. SU 1328

Harnham, West Wilts 9 H2 SW dist of Salisbury. SU 1329

Harnhill Glos 17 E2* ham 3m/5km E of Cirencester. SP 0600

Harnog 33 E2* r running W into R Wnion 6m/10km NE of Dolgellau, Gwynedd. SH 8122

Harold Hill London 20 B3* loc in borough of Havering 3m/4km NE of Romford. TQ 5492

Harold Park London 20 C3* loc in borough of Havering 3m/5km NE of Romford. TQ 5591

Harold's Stones. See Trelleck.

Haroldston West Dyfed 22 B4 ham near E coast of St Brides Bay 5m/9km W of Haverfordwest. SM 8615

Harold's Wick Shetland 89 F5 inlet on E coast of Unst. At its head is fishing vil of **Haroldswick.** HP 6312

Harold Wood London 20 C3 loc in borough of Havering 3m/4km NE of Romford. TQ 5490

Harome N Yorks 55 E6 vil 3m/4km SE of Helmsley. SE 6482

Harpenden Herts 19 E1 mainly residential tn 5m/7km N of St Albans. Rothamsted (agricultural) Experimental Stn to SW. TL 1314

Harperleas Reservoir Fife 73 E4* small resr 3m/5km NW of Leslie. NO 2105

Harperley Durham 61 F6* loc 1m N of Annfield Plain. NZ 1753

Harperrig Reservoir Lothian 65 G3 resr 4m/7km S of Mid Calder. NT 0961

Harper's Brook 37 E6* stream rising N of Desborough, Northants, and flowing E to Brigstock then SE into R Nene near Aldwincle. TL 0181

Harpers, Higher Lancs 48 B4* vil 2m/3km W of Nelson. SD 8337

Harpford Devon 5 F2 vil 3m/5km NW of Sidmouth. SY 0990

Harpham Humberside 51 E2 vil 5m/8km NE of Gt Driffield. TA 0961
Harpley H & W 26 C2 vil 5m/7km NE of Bromyard. SO 6861
Harpley Norfolk 38 C2 vil 9m/14km W of Fakenham. TF 7825
Harpole Northants 28 C2 vil 4m/7km W of Northampton. Site of Roman bldg 1km SW. SP 6960
Harpsden Oxon 18 C3 ham 1m S of Henley-on-Thames. Site of Roman villa to SW. SU 7680
Harpswell Lincs 44 D2 vil 5m/9km S of Kirton in Lindsey. SK 9390
Harpton, Lower H & W 25 G2* loc 3m/4km NW of Kington. SO 2760
Harptree, East Avon 16 B5 vil 7m/11km N of Wells. ST 5655
Harptree, West Avon 16 B6 vil 7m/11km N of Wells. ST 5656
Harpurhey Gtr Manchester 42 D1* dist of Manchester 3m/4km NE of city centre. SD 8601
Harpur Hill Derbys 43 F4 loc in Buxton 2km S of tn centre. SK 0671
Harrabol Skye, H'land 79 E6 loc on coast adjoining Broadford to E. Also known as Harrapool. NG 6523
Harraby Cumbria 60 A6* dist of Carlisle 2m/3km SE of city centre. NY 4254
Harracott Devon 6 D3* ham 4m/6km S of Barnstaple. SS 5526
Harrapool Skye, H'land 79 E6 loc on coast adjoining Broadford to E. Also known as Harrabol. NG 6523
Harraton Devon 4 D5* ham 2km SE of Modbury. SX 6750
Harray Orkney 89 A6* locality on Mainland 3m/5km NW of Finstown. To W is the large Loch of Harray. HY 3217
Harrietfield Tayside 72 D2 vil on N side of R Almond 9m/15km NE of Crieff. NN 9829
Harrietsham Kent 21 E6 vil 7m/11km E of Maidstone. TQ 8652
Harringay London 19 G3* loc in borough of Haringey 5m/8km N of Charing Cross. TQ 3188
Harrington Cumbria 52 A3 dist of Workington on coast 2m/4km S of tn centre. **High H.** loc 1m E. NX 9825
Harrington Lincs 45 G4 vil 4m/7km NW of Spilsby. TF 3671
Harrington Northants 36 D6 vil 6m/10km W of Kettering. SP 7780
Harringworth Northants 37 E4 vil 6m/9km N of Corby. SP 9197
Harriot's Hayes Salop 35 E4* loc 2m/3km E of Albrighton. SJ 8305
Harris W Isles 88 A3, B3 southern and more mountainous part of Isle of Lewis, S of Loch Resort and W of Loch Seaforth. See also Forest of H. NG 09
Harriseahead Staffs 42 D5* loc 2km W of Biddulph. SJ 8656
Harris Green Norfolk 39 F5 loc 4m/7km N of Harleston. TM 2389
Harriston Cumbria 52 B1* loc 1m E of Aspatria. NY 1641
Harrogate N Yorks 49 E3 spa tn and conference centre 13m/21km N of Leeds. **High H.** dist of tn 1m E of tn centre. SE 3055
Harrold Beds 28 D2 vil 8m/12km NW of Bedford. SP 9456
Harrop Dale Gtr Manchester 43 E1 loc 6m/9km E of Oldham. SE 0008
Harrop Fold Lancs 48 A3* loc 3m/4km W of Bolton by Bowland. SD 7449
Harrop Tarn Cumbria 52 C3* small lake 2km E of Blea Tarn. NY 3113
Harrow London 19 F3 borough 10m/16km NW of Charing Cross. Includes locs of **H. Weald,** and **N, S,** and **W Harrow;** also **H. on the Hill,** where Harrow School, well-known boys' public school, is situated. TQ 1587
Harrowbarrow Cornwall 3 H2* vil 3m/4km E of Callington. SX 3969
Harrowbeer Devon 4 B4* loc 5m/7km SE of Tavistock. SX 5168
Harrowden Beds 29 E3* loc 2m/3km SE of Bedford. TL 0747
Harrowden, Great Northants 28 D1 vil 2m/3km N of Wellingborough. SP 8870
Harrowden, Little Northants 28 D1 vil 3m/4km NW of Wellingborough. SP 8671
Harrowgate Hill and **Harrowgate Village** Durham 54 C3 suburb 2m/3km N of Darlington tn centre. NZ 2917
Harrow Green Suffolk 30 D3* ham 5m/9km N of Long Melford. TL 8554
Harry Crofts S Yorks 44 A3* loc 1km N of Thorpe Salvin. SK 5282
Harry Furlough's Rocks Gwynedd 40 A2* group of rocks lying off N coast of Anglesey opp Trwyn Cemlyn, 2m/4km E of Carmel Hd. Northernmost rock has beacon light. SH 3394
Harry Stoke Avon 16 B4* loc 2km E of Filton. ST 6278
Harsgeir W Isles 88 A2* islet off W coast of Lewis, at entrance to W Loch Roag. NB 1140
Harsington Som 9 E2 vil 3m/5km S of Wincanton. ST 6623
Harston Cambs 29 H3 vil 6m/9km SW of Cambridge. TL 4250
Harston Leics 36 D2 vil 5m/9km SW of Grantham. SK 8331
Harswell Humberside 50 D4 ham 3m/5km W of Mkt Weighton. SE 8240
Hart Cleveland 54 D2 vil 3m/5km NW of Hartlepool. **N Hart** loc adjoining to N. **Hart Stn** loc 2km NE. NZ 4634
Hartamul W Isles 88 E3* islet lying nearly 1m off SE point of S Uist and nearly 2m/3km E of Eriskay. NF 8311
Hartburn Nthmb 61 F3 vil on Hart Burn 7m/11km W of Morpeth. Site of small Roman fort 1km NW. NZ 0886
Hart Burn 61 F3 r rising on moors N of Kirkwhelpington, Nthmb, and flowing E into R Wansbeck 6m/9km W of Morpeth. NZ 1085
Hartburn, East Cleveland 54 D3 dist of Stockton-on-Tees 2km SW of tn centre. NZ 4217
Hart Common Gtr Manchester 42 C1* loc 2km NE of Hindley. SD 6305
Hartest Suffolk 30 C3 vil 4m/7km NW of Long Melford. TL 8352
Hart Fell 59 F1 mt on border of Dumfries & Galloway and Borders regions 6m/9km N of Moffat. NT 1113
Hartfield E Sussex 12 B3 vil 6m/9km SE of E Grinstead. Ham of **Upr. Hartfield** 1m SW below N edge of Ashdown Forest
Hartford Cambs 29 G1 NE dist of Huntingdon. TL 2572
Hartford Ches 42 C4 suburb 2km SW of Northwich. **Hartfordbeach** loc to N. SJ 6372
Hartford Som 7 G2* loc beside R Haddeo 3m/5km E of Dulverton. SS 9529
Hartfordbridge Hants 18 C5 ham 1m NE of Hartley Wintney. SU 7757
Hartford, East Nthmb 61 G3/G4* vil 2m/3km SE of Bedlington. NZ 2679
Hartford End Essex 30 B6 ham on R Chelmer 5m/8km SE of Gt Dunmow. TL 6817
Hartforth N Yorks 54 B4 ham 3m/5km N of Richmond. NZ 1706
Hartgrove Dorset 9 F3* ham 4m/7km NE of Sturminster Newton. ST 8418
Hartham Herts 19 G1* loc in E part of Hertford. TL 3213
Hart Hill Beds 29 E5* E dist of Luton. TL 1021
Harthill Ches 42 B5 vil 9m/15km SE of Chester. SJ 5055
Harthill S'clyde 65 F2/F3 vil 5m/8km SW of Bathgate. Service area on M8 motorway. NS 9064
Harthill S Yorks 44 A3 vil 6m/10km W of Worksop. **Harthill Resr** to W. SK 4980
Harthill Castle Grampian 83 E4* ruined cas 1m SE of Oyne. NJ 6825
Harthope Burn r in Nthmb. See Wooler Water.
Harting W Sussex 11 E3 par 3m/5km SE of Petersfield containing vils of **E** and **S Harting** and ham of **W Harting.** SU 7820
Hartington Derbys 43 F5 vil 9m/15km N of Ashbourne. SK 1260
Hartington, High Nthmb 61 E3 loc 3m/5km NE of Kirkwhelpington. NZ 0288
Hartland Devon 6 B3 vil 4m/6km W of Clovelly. 3m/5km W, **Hartland Pt,** headland with lighthouse at W end of Barnstaple (or Bideford) Bay. SS 2624
Hartlebury H & W 26 D1 vil 2m/3km E of Stourport. **H. Castle,** residence of Bishops of Worcester, mainly medieval with 17c additions. SO 8470
Hartlepool Cleveland 54 D2 port on **H. Bay** 8m/12km N of Middlesbrough. Shipbuilding and marine engineering, steel works. Nuclear power stn at Graythorp, qv. NZ 5032
Hartley Cumbria 53 G4 vil 1km E of Kirkby Stephen. NY 7808
Hartley Devon 4 B5* dist of Plymouth 2m/3km N of city centre. SX 4857
Hartley Kent vil now joined to Longfield to N by suburban development which includes **H. Green,** 5m/8km SW of Gravesend. TQ 6166
Hartley Kent 12 D3 vil 2km SW of Cranbrook. TQ 7534
Hartley Nthmb 61 H4 loc near North Sea coast 3m/4km N of Whitley Bay. NZ 3475
Hartley Green Staffs 35 F2* loc 1m NW of Gayton. SJ 9729
Hartley Ground Cumbria 52 C5* loc 2km N of Broughton in Furness. SD 2187
Hartley Mauditt Hants 10 D2* loc 2m/4km SE of Alton. SU 7436
Hartley's Village Merseyside 42 A2* loc in Liverpool 4m/7km NE of city centre. SJ 3796
Hartley Wespall Hants 18 B5 vil 3m/5km NW of Hook. SU 6958
Hartley Wintney Hants 18 C5 vil 3m/5km NE of Hook. SU 7656
Hartlington N Yorks 48 C2* loc just E of Burnsall across R Wharfe. SE 0361
Hartlip Kent 20 D5 vil 4m/7km W of Sittingbourne. Locs of **H. Hill** and **Lr Hartlip** to N and E respectively. Site of Roman villa to W. TQ 8364
Hartoft End N Yorks 55 F5* loc 2m/3km NE of Lastingham. SE 7592
Harton N Yorks 50 C2* vil 4m/6km N of Stamford Br. SE 7062
Harton Tyne & Wear 61 H5* dist of S Shields 2km S of tn centre. **W Harton** loc 1m W. NZ 3764
Hartpury Glos 26 C5 vil 5m/7km N of Gloucester. SO 7925
Hartshay, Lower Derbys 43 H5* ham 2km NW of Ripley. **Upr Hartshay** loc 1km S. SK 3851
Hartshead W Yorks 48 D5* vil 2km SW of Liversedge. Locs of **H. Moor Side** and **H. Moor Top** 2km and 2m/3km NW respectively. SE 1822
Hartshead Green Gtr Manchester 43 E1* loc 1m W of Mossley. SD 9502
Hartshill Warwicks 35 H5 NW suburb of Nuneaton. SP 3293
Hartshorne Derbys 35 H2 vil 2m/3km NE of Swadlincote. SK 3220
Hartsop Cumbria 52 D3/D4 loc 2m/3km S of Patterdale. NY 4013
Hartswell Som 7 H2* loc adjoining Wiveliscombe to S. ST 0827
Hartwell Bucks 18 C1 par containing ham of **Lr Hartwell,** 2m/3km W of Aylesbury. **Hartwell Hse** is a Jacbn manor hse. SP 7916
Hartwell Northants 28 C3 vil 7m/11km NW of Newport Pagnell. SP 7850
Hartwith N Yorks 49 E2 ham 1m SE of Summer Br. SE 2161
Hartwood S'clyde 65 E3* loc 4m/7km NE of Wishaw. NS 8459
Harty, Isle of Kent 21 F5 SE part of Isle of Sheppey, bounded by The Swale to S, Capel Fleet to N, the sea to E, and mouth of Bells Creek to W. TR 0267
Harvel Kent 20 C5 vil 4m/6km N of Wrotham Heath. TQ 6563
Harvills Hawthorn W Midlands 35 F5* loc in W Bromwich 2km NW of tn centre. SO 9893
Harvington H & W 26 D1 vil 3m/5km E of Kidderminster. SO 8774
Harvington H & W 27 E3 vil 3m/5km NE of Evesham. SP 0548
Harvington Cross H & W 27 E3* vil adjoining Harvington to NW, 4m/6km N of Evesham. SP 0549
Harwell Notts 44 B2* ham 1km NW of Everton. SK 6891
Harwell Oxon 18 A3 vil 2m/3km W of Didcot. Atomic Energy Research Establishment 2m/3km SW. SU 4989
Harwich Essex 31 F5 port for Continental passenger and containerised freight traffic, 16m/26km E of Colchester. TM 2531
Harwood Durham 53 G2 loc 10m/15km NW of Middleton in Teesdale. NY 8133
Harwood Gtr Manchester 47 G6* loc in Bolton 2m/3km NE of tn centre. SD 7410
Harwood Nthmb 61 E3* loc 4m/6km N of Kirkwhelpington. NZ 0090
Harwood Dale N Yorks 55 G5 vil 7m/11km NW of Scarborough. SE 9695
Harwood, Great Lancs 48 A5 tn 4m/7km NE of Blackburn. Aero-engineering, textiles, coal-mining. See also Martholme. SD 7332
Harwood Lee Gtr Manchester 47 G6* loc 3m/4km NE of Bolton. SD 7412
Harworth Notts 44 B2 vil 2m/3km SE of Tickhill. SK 6191
Hasbury W Midlands 35 F5/F6 dist of Halesowen 1km W of tn centre. SO 9583
Hascombe Surrey 11 F1 vil 3m/5km SE of Godalming. SU 9939
Hascosay Shetland 89 F6 island between Yell and Fetlar. **H. Sound** runs between it and Yell. Sea birds abound. HU 5592
Haselbech Northants 36 C6 vil 6m/10km S of Mkt Harborough. SP 7177
Haselbury Bryan Dorset. See Hazelbury Bryan.
Haselbury Plucknett Som 8 C3 vil 2m/3km NE of Crewkerne. ST 4710
Haseley Warwicks 27 F1* vil 4m/6km NW of Warwick. SP 2367
Haseley, Great Oxon 18 B2 vil 5m/8km SW of Thame. SP 6401
Haseley Knob Warwicks 27 F1* ham 4m/6km W of Kenilworth. SP 2371
Haseley, Little Oxon 18 B2 ham 5m/9km SW of Thame. SP 6400
Haselor Warwicks 27 F2 loc 2m/4km E of Alcester. SP 1257
Hasfield Glos 26 C4/D4 vil 6m/9km N of Gloucester across R Severn. SO 8227
Hasguard Dyfed 22 B5 loc 4m/7km NW of Milford Haven. SM 8509
Haskayne Lancs 42 A1* vil 4m/6km W of Ormskirk. SD 3508
Haskeir Island W Isles (W of 88 D1) small rocky uninhabited island 8m/13km NW of Griminish Pt, N Uist. Seal sanctuary. **Haskeir Eagach** is group of rocks about 1m SW. Also known as Heisgeir I. and Heisgeir Eagach. NF 6182
Hasketon Suffolk 31 F3 vil 2m/3km NW of Woodbridge. TM 2450
Hasland Derbys 43 H4 loc in Chesterfield 2km SE of tn centre. **H. Green** loc adjoining to S. SK 3969
Haslemere Surrey 11 E2 tn in wooded and hilly area 8m/13km SW of Godalming. Much NT property in surrounding countryside. SU 9033
Haslingden Lancs 48 B5 tn 4m/6km SE of Accrington. Textiles, footwear, engineering, quarrying. **H. Grane** loc 2km W. SD 7823
Haslingfield Cambs 29 H3 vil 5m/8km SW of Cambridge. TL 4052
Haslington Ches 42 C5 vil 2m/3km E of Crewe. SJ 7355
Hasluck's Green W Midlands 35 G6* loc in Solihull 3m/5km W of tn centre. SP 1078
Hassall Ches 42 D5* loc 2m/4km S of Sandbach. **H. Green** 2km NE. SJ 7657
Hassell Street Kent 13 F2* loc 3m/4km E of Wye. TR 0946
Hassendean Borders 66 C6 loc 5m/7km NE of Hawick. NT 5420
Hassingham Norfolk 39 G4 ham 4m/6km SW of Acle. TG 3605
Hassocks W Sussex 11 H3 loc adjoining Keymer to W below S Downs 2m/4km S of Burgess Hill. TQ 3015
Hassop Derbys 43 G4 ham 2m/4km N of Bakewell. SK 2272
Hasthorpe Lincs 45 H4* loc 1m SW of Sloothby. TF 4869
Hastigrow H'land 86 E2 loc in Caithness dist 6m/10km SE of Castletown. ND 2661
Hastingleigh Kent 13 F3 vil 6m/9km E of Ashford. TR 0944
Hastings E Sussex 12 D5 seaside resort 32m/52km E of Brighton. Cinque port. Remains of Norman cas on cliff top. Battle of 1066 fought at Battle, 6m/9km NW. TQ 8109
Hastings Som 8 B3* loc 3m/5km NW of Ilminster. ST 3116
Hastingwood Essex 20 B1* vil 3m/5km SE of Harlow. TL 4807
Hastoe Herts 18 D1 ham 2km S of Tring. SP 9109
Haswell Durham 54 C1 vil 3m/4km W of Easington. **High H.** loc 1km NW. **Low H.** loc 1m NW. **H. Moor** loc 2km S. **H. Plough** vil 1km S. NZ 3743
Hatch Beds 29 F3* loc 2km SW of Sandy. TL 1547
Hatch Beauchamp Som 8 B2 vil 5m/9km SE of Taunton. ST 3020
Hatch Bottom Hants 10 B3* loc adjoining West End to N and 4m/6km NE of Southampton. SU 4614
Hatch, East Wilts 9 F2 ham 5m/9km NE of Shaftesbury. ST 9228
Hatch End Beds 29 E2* loc at W end of vil of Keysoe Row. TL 0761
Hatch End London 19 E3 loc in borough of Harrow 4m/6km SE of Watford. TQ 1291
Hatchet Green Hants 9 H3* loc adjoining Hale and 4m/7km NE of Fordingbridge. SU 1919

Hatch Green Som 8 B3* ham 1km S of Hatch Beauchamp. ST 3019
Hatching Green Herts 19 E1 loc 1m S of Harpenden. TL 1312
Hatchlands Surrey 19 E6* 18c hse (NT) to E of vil of E Clandon 5m/8km E of Guildford. TQ 0652
Hatchmere Ches 42 B4 ham 7m/11km W of Northwich. SJ 5571
Hatch, West Som 8 B2* vil 1m W of Hatch Beauchamp. ST 2821
Hatch, West Wilts 9 F2 ham 5m/8km NE of Shaftesbury. ST 9227
Hatcliffe Humberside 45 F2 vil 7m/11km SW of Grimsby. TA 2100
Hatfield Herts 19 F1 tn 18m/29km N of London. New Tn, designated 1948, to SW of old. Aircraft factory to W. To E is **Hatfield Hse,** 17c hse in large park. **S Hatfield** is S dist of tn. TL 2308
Hatfield H & W 26 B2 vil 6m/10km E of Leominster. SO 5959
Hatfield S Yorks 44 B1 tn 7m/11km NE of Doncaster. **H. Chase** area of fen 3m/5km E. **H. Woodhouse** vil 2km SE. SE 6609
Hatfield Broad Oak Essex 30 A6 vil 5m/8km SE of Bishop's Stortford. TL 5416
Hatfield Forest Essex 30 A5 wooded area, largely NT, 3m/5km E of Bishop's Stortford. TL 5320
Hatfield Garden Village Herts 19 F1* N suburb of Hatfield. TL 2109
Hatfield, Great Humberside 51 F4 vil 3m/5km S of Hornsea. **Lit Hatfield** loc 1m W. TA 1842
Hatfield Heath Essex 30 A6 vil 5m/8km SE of Bishop's Stortford. TL 5215
Hatfield Hyde Herts 19 F1 SE dist of Welwyn Garden City. TL 2511
Hatfield Peverel Essex 20 D1 vil 3m/5km SW of Witham. TL 7911
Hatford Oxon 17 G2 vil 3m/5km E of Faringdon. SU 3394
Hatherden Hants 17 G6 vil 3m/5km NW of Andover. SU 3450
Hatherleigh Devon 6 D4 vil 7m/11km NW of Okehampton. SS 5404
Hatherlow Gtr Manchester 43 E2* loc adjoining Romiley to W. SJ 9390
Hathern Leics 36 B2 vil 3m/4km NW of Loughborough. SK 5022
Hatherop Glos 17 F1 vil 3m/4km N of Fairford. SP 1505
Hathersage Derbys 43 G3 vil 8m/13km N of Bakewell. **H. Booths** ham 1km SE. SK 2381
Hathershaw Gtr Manchester 43 E1* loc in Oldham 1m S of tn centre. SD 9203
Hatherton Ches 42 C6 ham 3m/5km NE of Audlem. SJ 6847
Hatherton Staffs 35 F3 ham 2km W of Cannock. SJ 9510
Hatherwood Point Isle of Wight 10 A6* headland between Alum Bay and Totland Bay, near W extremity of the island. SZ 3086
Hatley, East Cambs 29 G3 vil 4m/7km E of Potton. TL 2850
Hatley St George Cambs 29 G3 vil 4m/6km E of Potton. TL 2751
Hatt Cornwall 3 H2* vil 3m/4km NW of Saltash. SX 3962
Hattersley Gtr Manchester 43 E2* loc 2m/3km E of Hyde. SJ 9794
Hatt Hill Hants 10 A2* loc just W of Mottisfont. SU 3126
Hattingley Hants 10 D1* loc 1m W of Medstead. SU 6437
Hatton Ches 42 B3 vil 4m/6km S of Warrington. SJ 5982
Hatton Derbys 35 H2 vil 5m/8km N of Burton upon Trent. SK 2130
Hatton Grampian 83 H3 vil near E coast 8m/12km SW of Peterhead. NK 0537
Hatton Lincs 45 F3/F4 ham 3m/5km E of Wragby. TF 1776
Hatton London 19 E4 loc at E end of London (Heathrow) Airport in borough of Hounslow 12m/21km W of Charing Cross. TQ 0975
Hatton Warwicks 27 F1 vil 4m/6km NW of Warwick. SP 2367
Hatton Castle Grampian 83 F2 residence comprising remains of ancient cas of Balquholly, 3m/5km SE of Turriff. NJ 7546
Hatton Heath Ches 42 A5 loc 4m/7km SE of Chester. SJ 4561
Hatton, High Salop 34 C2 ham 3m/4km S of Hodnet. SJ 6124
Hatton, Lower Staffs 35 E1* loc 5m/8km NW of Stone. **Upr Hatton** loc 1km N. SJ 8236
Hatton of Fintray Grampian 83 F5 vil 5m/9km SE of Inverurie. NJ 8416
Haugh Gtr Manchester 48 C6* loc 2km SE of Milnrow. SD 9411
Haugh Lincs 45 G4* loc 3m/4km W of Alford. TF 4175
Haugham Lincs 45 G3 ham 4m/6km S of Louth. TF 3381
Haugh Head Nthmb 67 G5 loc 2km SE of Wooler. NU 0026
Haughley Suffolk 31 E2 vil 3m/4km NW of Stowmarket. Slight remains of Norman cas. Vil of **H. Green** 2km N. Ham of **H. New Street** 1m W. **H. Park** is restored 17c hse. TM 0262
Haughmond Abbey Salop 34 C3* remains of 12c abbey (A.M.) 3m/5km NE of Shrewsbury. SJ 5415
Haugh, Nether S Yorks 43 H2* vil 3m/4km N of Rotherham. SK 4196
Haugh of Glass Grampian 82 C3/D3 loc 7m/11km W of Huntly. NJ 4239
Haugh of Urr D & G 58 D5 vil 4m/6km N of Dalbeattie. NX 8066
Haughs of Cromdale H'land 82 A4. See Cromdale.
Haughton Notts 44 B4 loc 4m/6km NE of Ollerton. SK 6772
Haughton Powys 34 A3* loc 2m/4km E of Four Crosses. SJ 3118
Haughton Salop 34 B2* ham 5m/9km E of Oswestry. SJ 3727
Haughton Salop 34 C3 loc 5m/7km NE of Shrewsbury. SJ 5516
Haughton Salop 34 D3 ham 1km NW of Shifnal. SJ 7408
Haughton Staffs 35 E3 vil 4m/7km SW of Stafford. SJ 8620
Haughton Castle Nthmb 61 E4 medieval tower hse 1m N of Humshaugh. NY 9172
Haughton Green Gtr Manchester 43 E2* loc 1m SE of Denton. SJ 9393
Haughton le Skerne Durham 54 C3 dist of Darlington 2m/3km NE of tn centre. NZ 3116
Haughton Moss Ches 42 B5 vil 6m/9km NW of Nantwich. SJ 5756
Haugh, Upper S Yorks 43 H2* loc 3m/5km N of Rotherham. SK 4297
Haultin H'land 78 C4 r in Skye running W into Loch Eyre 7m/11km NW of Portree. NG 4151
Haultwick Herts 29 G5 ham 3m/5km W of Puckeridge. TL 3323
Haun W Isles 88 E3* loc on bay of same name on N coast of Eriskay. Ferry to Ludac on S Uist. NF 7912
Haunton Staffs 35 H3 vil 5m/7km NE of Tamworth. SK 2310
Hautbois, Little Norfolk 39 F3 loc 2m/3km NW of Coltishall. TG 2521
Hauxley Nthmb 61 G2 vil near North Sea coast 2km SE of Amble. **Low Hauxley** loc 1km E. NU 2703
Hauxton Cambs 29 H3 vil 4m/7km S of Cambridge. TL 4352
Hauxwell, East N Yorks 54 B5 vil 4m/6km NE of Leyburn. SE 1693
Havannah Ches 42 D4* loc 2km NE of Congleton. SJ 8664
Havant Hants 10 D4 tn in Portsmouth conurbation 6m/10km NE of Portsmouth across Langstone Harbour. SU 7106
Haven H & W 26 A2* loc 7m/11km W of Leominster. SO 4054
Haven Bank Lincs 45 F5* loc 2m/3km SW of New York. TF 2352
Haven, East Tayside 73 H1 loc on coast 2m/3km NE of Carnoustie. NO 5836
Havengore Island Essex 21 E3/F3 'island' on E coast 4m/6km NE of Shoeburyness. TQ 9789
Haven, Little Dyfed 22 B4 vil on St Brides Bay 6m/10km W of Haverfordwest. SM 8512
Haven, Little W Sussex 11 G2* NE dist of Horsham. TQ 1832
Haven, North Shetland. See Fair Isle.
Haven Point, South Dorset 9 G5* pt at S side of entrance to Poole Harbour. SZ 0386
Haven Side Humberside 51 F5* loc adjoining Hedon to S, on N bank of Hedon Haven. TA 1828
Haven Side Humberside 51 G6 ham 2km SW of Patrington. TA 3021
Havenstreet Isle of Wight 10 C5 vil 3m/4km SW of Ryde. SZ 5690
Haven, The Lincs 37 H1 estuary of R Witham below Boston. TF 3639
Haven, The W Sussex 11 G2 loc 3m/5km N of Billingshurst. TQ 0830
Havercroft W Yorks 49 F6 coal-mining loc 3m/5km NE of Royston. SE 3914
Haverfordwest (Hwlffordd) Dyfed tn on Western Cleddau R, 28m/45km W of Carmarthen. River navigable for small craft between tn and sea (Milford Haven). Tn is a mkt and agricultural centre. Ruins of 12c cas. Scant remains of 12c priory. SM 9515
Havergate Island Suffolk 31 G3/H3* uninhabited island in R Ore SW of Orford. TM 4147
Haverhill Suffolk 30 B3 industrial tn 16m/26km SE of Cambridge. TL 6745
Haverigg Cumbria 46 C1 vil 2km SW of Millom. **Haverigg Pt** headland 2km W. SD 1678
Havering London 20 B3 borough at E extremity of Greater London; centre of borough is some 15m/24km E of London Br. Contains tns of Hornchurch, Rainham, Romford, Upminster, and vil of Havering-atte-Bower. TQ 5586
Havering-atte-Bower London 20 B2 vil in borough of Havering 3m/4km N of Romford. TQ 5193
Haveringland Norfolk 39 F3 loc 9m/14km NW of Norwich. TG 1520
Havering Park London 20 B3* NW dist of Romford in borough of Havering. TQ 4992
Havering's Grove Essex 20 C2* vil 2m/3km W of Billericay. TQ 6494
Haverscroft Street Norfolk 39 E5 loc 2km SW of Attleborough. TM 0393
Haversham Bucks 28 C3/D3 vil 2km NE of Wolverton. SP 8242
Haverthwaite Cumbria 52 D6 vil 2m/4km SW of Newby Br. SD 3483
Haverton Hill Cleveland 54 D3 loc adjoining Billingham to E. NZ 4822
Haviker Street Kent 20 D6* loc 2m/3km NW of Marden. TQ 7246
Havra, Little Shetland 89 E8* small uninhabited island lying off W coast of island of S Havra. HU 3526
Havra, North Shetland 89 E7* small uninhabited island off S end of peninsula of Strom Ness, Mainland. HU 3642
Havra, South Shetland 89 E8 uninhabited island of about 150 acres or 60 hectares lying 1m W of coast of Mainland and about 1m S of islands of E and W Burra. HU 3627
Havyat Som 8 C1* loc on SE side of Glastonbury. ST 5337
Hawarden (Penarlag) Clwyd 41 H4 tn 2m/3km S of Queensferry and 6m/9km W of Chester. **H. Castle,** formerly home of W.E. Gladstone, 19c statesman; remains of 13c cas in grnds. H. Airport 2m/3km E. SJ 3165
Hawbush Green Essex 30 C5* ham 3m/4km SE of Braintree. TL 7820
Hawcoat Cumbria 46 D1 loc in N part of Barrow-in-Furness. SD 2072
Hawen Dyfed 23 E1 ham 5m/8km NE of Newcastle Emlyn. SN 3446
Hawerby Humberside 45 F2* loc 2m/3km W of N Thoresby. TF 2697
Hawes N Yorks 53 G5 small tn in Wensleydale 14m/22km SE of Kirkby Stephen. SD 8789
Hawe's Green Norfolk 39 F5* ham 1km W of Shotesham. TM 2399
Hawes Side Lancs 46 D4 loc in Blackpool 2km SE of tn centre. SD 3234
Hawes Water Lancs 47 E1* lake 2km NE of Silverdale. SD 4776
Haweswater Reservoir Cumbria 53 E3 one of the lakes of Lake Dist converted into a resr. Dam is 4m/6km W of Shap. Resr runs SW to NE; length about 4m/7km. NY 5015
Hawetown, West Som 7 G2* ham on Exmoor just E of Winsford. SS 9134
Hawick Borders 66 C6 tn on R Teviot noted for tweed and hosiery mnfre, 39m/63km S of Edinburgh and 37m/59km N of Carlisle. NT 5014
Hawkchurch Devon 8 B4 vil 3m/5km NE of Axminster. ST 3400
Hawkcraig Point Fife 65 H1 headland on Firth of Forth on E side of Aberdour. NT 2084
Hawkedon Suffolk 30 C3 vil 6m/10km NW of Long Melford. TL 7953
Hawkehouse Green S Yorks 49 G6* loc 1km SE of Moss. SE 6013
Hawkenbury Kent 12 C3 SE suburb of Tunbridge Wells. TQ 5938
Hawkenbury Kent 12 D2* loc 2m/3km NE of Staplehurst. TQ 8045
Hawkeridge Wilts 16 D5 vil 2m/3km N of Westbury. ST 8653
Hawkerland Devon 5 F2* loc 4m/7km N of Budleigh Salterton. SY 0588
Hawkesbury Avon 16 C3 vil 4m/7km NE of Chipping Sodbury. Vil of **H. Upton** 1m E. ST 7686
Hawkesbury Warwicks 36 A5* loc at junction of Coventry Canal and Oxford Canal 4m/7km N of Coventry. SP 3684
Hawk Green Gtr Manchester 43 E3* loc adjoining Marple to S. SJ 9587
Hawk Hill Cumbria 52 A2* loc 2km NE of Workington across R Derwent. NY 0129
Hawkhill Nthmb 61 G1 loc 3m/4km E of Alnwick. NU 2212
Hawkhurst Kent 12 D4 vil 4m/6km S of Cranbrook. TQ 7630
Hawkinge Kent 13 G3 vil 3m/4km N of Folkestone. TR 2139
Hawkley Hants 10 D2 vil 2m/3km NW of Liss. SU 7429
Hawkridge Som 7 F2 Exmoor vil 4m/6km NW of Dulverton. SS 8630
Hawkridge Reservoir Som 8 A1* small resr at foot of Quantock Hills 1m SW of Spaxton. ST 2036
Hawksdale Cumbria 59 H6* loc 2km S of Dalston. NY 3648
Hawkshaw Lane Gtr Manchester 47 G6* loc 4m/6km NW of Bury. SD 8010
Hawkshead Cumbria 52 D5 vil 4m/7km S of Ambleside. **H. Hill** ham 1m NW. SD 3598
Hawksheads Lancs 47 F2 loc 1km NE of Bolton-le-Sands. SD 4968
Hawksmoor Staffs 43 E6* woodland and open space (NT) 2m/3km NE of Cheadle. SK 0344
Hawks Ness Shetland 89 E7* headland on E coast of Mainland 5m/8km N of Lerwick. HU 4649
Hawkswick N Yorks 48 C1/C2* ham 2m/3km SE of Arncliffe. SD 9570
Hawksworth Notts 36 D1 vil 4m/6km N of Bingham. SK 7543
Hawksworth W Yorks 48 D4* vil 6m/9km N of Bradford. SE 1641
Hawksworth W Yorks 49 E4* dist of Leeds 3m/5km NW of city centre. SE 2537
Hawkwell Essex 21 E3 vil 2km NW of Rochford. TQ 8591
Hawley Hants 18 D5 suburb 3m/4km N of Farnborough. 1m W, **H. Lake,** lake surrounded by wds on H. Common. SU 8558
Hawley Kent 20 B4* loc 2m/3km S of Dartford. TQ 5471
Hawley's Corner London 20 B5* loc at extreme S edge of borough of Bromley 2m/3km SE of Biggin Hill. TQ 4356
Hawling Glos 27 E5 vil 4m/7km SE of Winchmore. SP 0623
Hawnby N Yorks 54 D5 vil on R Rye 6m/10km NW of Helmsley. SE 5489
Haworth W Yorks 48 C4 tn above R Worth valley 2m/4km SW of Keighley. Parsonage is former home of Brontë family and now a museum. SE 0237
Hawsker Bottoms N Yorks 55 G4* loc 1km E of High Hawsker. NZ 9307
Hawsker, High N Yorks 55 G4 vil 3m/5km SE of Whitby. NZ 9207
Hawsker, Low N Yorks 55 G4 loc 3m/4km SE of Whitby. NZ 9207
Hawstead Suffolk 30 D2 vil 3m/5km S of Bury St Edmunds. Loc of **H. Green** 1km S. TL 8559
Hawthorn (Ddraenen Wen, Y) Mid Glam 15 F3* loc 2m/3km SE of Pontypridd. ST 0987
Hawthorn Durham 61 H6 vil 2km N of Easington. NZ 4145
Hawthorn Hants 10 D2* loc 1m S of Four Marks and 4m/7km SW of Alton. SU 6733
Hawthorn S'clyde 64 D2* loc in Glasgow 2m/3km N of city centre. NS 5968
Hawthorn Wilts 16 D4* vil 2m/3km SW of Corsham. ST 8469
Hawthorn Burn 54 D1* stream rising W of Easington, Durham, and flowing NE down wooded dene into North Sea at Hawthorn Hive, S of Seaham. NZ 4445
Hawthorn Hill Berks 18 D4* loc 5m/8km S of Maidenhead. SU 8773
Hawthorn Hill Lincs 45 F5 ham 2m/3km S of Coningsby. TF 2155
Hawthorn Hive Durham 61 H6 small bay on North Sea coast 2m/3km S of Seaham. NZ 4446
Hawthorpe Lincs 37 F2 loc 6m/9km NW of Bourne. TF 0427

Hawthwaite, Lower Cumbria 52 C5 loc 2km N of Broughton in Furness. SD 2189
Hawton Notts 44 C5 ham 2m/3km S of Newark-on-Trent. SK 7851
Haxby N Yorks 50 B3 vil 4m/6km N of York. **H. Gates** loc adjoining to S. **H. Moor End** loc adjoining to N. SE 6058
Haxey Humberside 44 C2 vil 3m/4km S of Epworth. **H. Turbary** loc 2km NW. SK 7699
Haxton Wilts 17 G6* loc adjoining Fittleton and 5m/8km N of Amesbury. SU 1449
Hay Bluff Powys 25 G4 mt at N end of Black Mts 4m/6km S of Hay-on-Wye. Height 2219 ft or 677 metres. SO 2436
Haybridge Salop 34 D3 urban loc 2km E of Wellington. SJ 6711
Haybridge Som 16 A6* loc 1m W of Wells. ST 5346
Hayburn Wyke N Yorks 55 H5 bay on North Sea coast 6m/9km N of Scarborough. TA 0197
Hayden Cross W Midlands 35 F5* loc in Dudley 4m/6km SE of tn centre. SO 9685
Haydock Merseyside 42 B2 tn 4m/6km E of St Helens. Coal-mining, light engineering. **H. Park** racecourse to NE. SJ 5696
Haydon Dorset 8 D3 vil 2m/3km E of Sherborne. ST 6715
Haydon Som 8 B2* ham 2m/3km SE of Taunton. ST 2523
Haydon Wilts 17 F3* loc 3m/5km NW of Swindon. SU 1288
Haydon Bridge Nthmb 60 D5 small tn astride R South Tyne 6m/10km W of Hexham. NY 8464
Haydon Wick Wilts 17 F3 NW suburb of Swindon. SU 1387
Haye Cornwall 3 H2* loc just W of Callington. SX 3469
Hayes London 19 E3 dist in borough of Hillingdon 3m/5km SE of Uxbridge. Includes locs of **H. End** and **H. Town.** TQ 0980
Hayes London 20 A5 dist in borough of Bromley 2m/3km S of Bromley tn centre. **H. Common** is extensive area of heath and woodland to S. TQ 4066
Hayesden, Upper Kent 12 C2* loc 2m/3km SW of Tonbridge. TQ 5644
Hayes Green Warwicks 36 A5* 1m SW of Bedworth. SP 3485
Hayes Point S Glam 15 F4* headland at W end of Sully Bay, E of Barry. ST 1467
Hayeswater Cumbria 52 D4 small lake 3m/5km SE of Patterdale. NY 4312
Hayfield Derbys 43 E3 tn 4m/7km S of Glossop. **Lit Hayfield** vil 1km N. SK 0387
Hayfield Fife 73 F5* N dist of Kirkcaldy. NT 2792
Haygate Salop 34 D3 urban loc 1m SE of Wellington. SJ 6410
Hay Green Herts 29 G4* ham 3m/4km S of Royston. TL 3336
Hay Green Norfolk 38 A3* ham 2km S of Terrington St Clement. TF 5418
Haygrove Som 8 B1* W dist of Bridgwater. ST 2836
Haylands Isle of Wight 10 C5 SW dist of Ryde. SZ 5891
Hayle Cornwall 2 B4 industrial tn with small harbour 3m/5km SE of St Ives across R Hayle estuary. SW 5537
Hayle 2 B4* r rising 3m/5km S of Camborne, Cornwall, and flowing into St Ives Bay. SW 5438
Hayley Green W Midlands 35 F6* loc in SW part of Halesowen. SO 9482
Hayling Bay Hants 10 D5 bay formed by gently curving S coast of Hayling I. SZ 7198
Hayling Island Hants 10 D4 island S of Havant between Langstone and Chichester Harbours, 6km from N to S and nearly 7km from E to W at its southern end although little more than 1km wide at its centre. Connected to mainland by Langstone Br, at N end. Ferry for pedestrians to Portsea I. at SW extremity. SU 7200
Hayling, North Hants 10 D4 vil near N end of Hayling I. Site of Roman bldg to W. SU 7303
Hayling, South Hants 10 D5 tn at S end of Hayling I. stretching across almost the entire width of the island. SZ 7299
Hay, Little Staffs 35 G4 vil 4m/6km N of Sutton Coldfield. SK 1202
Haymarket Lothian 65 H2* loc and rly stn in Edinburgh 1m W of city centre. Whisky distillery. NT 2473
Hay Mills W Midlands 35 G5 loc in Birmingham 3m/5km SE of city centre. SP 1184
Haymoor Green Ches 42 C6* loc 2m/4km E of Nantwich. SJ 6850
Hayne Devon 7 G3* ham 2m/3km N of Tiverton. SS 9515
Haynes Beds 29 E4 vil 4m/7km NW of Shefford. TL 0841
Haynes West End Beds 29 E4 ham 2m/3km NW of Clophill. TL 0640
Hay-on-Wye (Gelli, Y) Powys 25 G4 small mkt tn at N end of Black Mts 15m/24km NE of Brecon. Remains of motte and bailey 2km E. Remains of 12c cas at tn centre. SO 2242
Hay Place Hants 11 E1 loc adjoining Binsted to S, 4m/6km NE of Alton. SU 7740
Hayscastle (Cas-lai) Dyfed 22 B3 ham 8m/13km SW of Fishguard. **H. Cross** ham 1m E. SM 8925
Haysden Kent 12 C2* loc 2km W of Tonbridge. TQ 5645
Hay Street Herts 29 G5 ham 2m/3km N of Puckeridge. TL 3926
Hayton Cumbria 52 B1 vil 3m/4km W of Aspatria. **H. Castle,** hse dating partly from 15c. NY 1041
Hayton Cumbria 60 B5 vil 3m/4km SW of Brampton. NY 5057
Hayton Grampian 77 H1* N dist of Aberdeen. NJ 9208
Hayton Humberside 50 C4 vil 4m/7km NW of Mkt Weighton. SE 8245
Hayton Notts 44 C3 vil 3m/4km NE of E Retford. SK 7284
Hayton, Lower Salop 34 C6 loc 4m/6km N of Ludlow. SO 5080
Hayton's Bent Salop 34 C6* loc 4m/6km N of Ludlow. SO 5180
Hayton, Upper Salop 34 C6 loc 4m/7km N of Ludlow. SO 5181
Haytor Vale Devon 4 D3 vil on E edge of Dartmoor 5m/8km N of Ashburton. 1m W, **Haytor Rocks,** granite outcrop and popular viewpoint. SX 7777
Haytown Devon 6 C4* ham 8m/12km SW of Torrington. SS 3814
Haywards Heath W Sussex 12 A4 largely residential tn 12m/19km N of Brighton. TQ 3323
Hay, West Avon 16 A5* loc 2m/3km E of Congresbury. ST 4663
Haywood H & W 26 A4* loc 4m/6km SW of Hereford. SO 4834
Haywood S Yorks 43 G2* S dist of Stocksbridge. SK 2797
Haywood S Yorks 49 G6 ham 2m/3km E of Askern. SE 5812
Haywood, Great Staffs 35 F2 vil on R Trent 4m/6km NW of Rugeley. Junction of Staffs and Worcs Canal with Trent and Mersey Canal. **Lit Haywood** vil 1m SE. SJ 9922
Haywood Oaks Notts 44 B5* loc 1m SE of Blidworth. SK 6055
Hazard's Green E Sussex 12 C5* loc 5m/8km NW of Bexhill. TQ 6812
Hazelbank S'clyde 65 E4 vil on R Clyde 3m/5km NW of Lanark. NS 8345
Hazelbeach Dyfed 22 C5* loc on estuary, adjoining Llanstadwell to W. SM 9404
Hazeley Hants 18 C5 loc 2m/3km NW of Hook. SU 7459
Hazel Grove Gtr Manchester 43 E3 tn 3m/4km SE of Stockport. SJ 9286
Hazel Head N Yorks 55 F5* loc 2m/3km SW of Goathland. SE 8099
Hazelhurst Gtr Manchester 42 C2 loc 1m W of Swinton. SD 7501
Hazelhurst Gtr Manchester 43 E2* loc in Ashton-under-Lyne 2m/3km NE of tn centre. SD 9600
Hazelhurst Gtr Manchester 47 H6* loc 1m SW of Ramsbottom. SD 7815
Hazel Leys Northants 36 D5* dist of Corby to W of tn centre. SP 8888
Hazelmere Lancs 47 F4* loc 3m/5km N of Preston. SD 5233
Hazelrigg, North Nthmb 67 G5* loc 4m/6km W of Belford. **S Hazelrigg** loc 1m S. NU 0533
Hazelshaw S Yorks 43 G2* loc 2m/3km N of Grenoside. SK 3296
Hazels, High S Yorks 43 H2* loc in Darnall dist of Sheffield 3m/5km E of city centre. SK 3987
Hazelslack Cumbria 47 E1* loc 1m E of Arnside. SD 4778
Hazelslade Staffs 35 F3 loc 3m/5km NE of Cannock. SK 0212
Hazel Street Kent 12 C3* loc 1km SW of Horsmonden. TQ 6939
Hazelwood Derbys 43 G6/H6 vil 2m/3km SW of Belper. SK 3246
Hazelwood London 20 B5* loc 3m/4km NE of Biggin Hill. TQ 4461
Hazelwood S'clyde 64 C3* loc in Glasgow 3m/4km SW of city centre. NS 5563
Hazlehead S Yorks 43 F1* loc on R Don 3m/5km W of Penistone. SE 1902
Hazlemere Bucks 18 D2 suburb 2m/3km NE of High Wycombe. SU 8895
Hazlerigg Tyne & Wear 61 G4* loc 5m/7km N of Newcastle. NZ 2371
Hazles Staffs 43 E6* loc 1m NW of Kingsley. SK 0047
Hazlescross Staffs 43 E6* loc 1km NW of Kingsley. SK 0047
Hazleton Glos 27 E5 vil 3m/5km NW of Northleach. SP 0718
Hazon Nthmb 61 F2* loc 3m/4km N of Felton. NU 1904
Heacham Norfolk 38 B1 vil 2m/4km S of Hunstanton. TF 6737
Headbourne Worthy Hants 10 B2 vil 2m/3km N of Winchester. SU 4832
Headcorn Kent 12 D3 vil 9m/14km SE of Maidstone. TQ 8344
Head, East W Sussex 10 D5 spit of land (NT) on E side of entrance to Chichester Harbour with dunes, saltings, and sandy beaches. SZ 7699
Headingley W Yorks 49 E4* dist of Leeds 2m/3km NW of city centre. Contains Yorkshire County Cricket Ground. SE 2835
Headington Oxon 18 A1 dist of Oxford E of R Cherwell, 2m/4km E of city centre. SP 5407
Headington Hill Oxon 18 A1 dist of Oxford E of R Cherwell, 2km E of city centre. SP 5306
Headlam Durham 54 B3 vil 3m/4km NW of Piercebridge. **H. Hall,** stone manor hse of 17c and 18c. NZ 1818
Headless Cross H & W 27 E1 S dist of Redditch. SP 0365
Headley Hants 11 E2 vil 4m/6km W of Hindhead. SU 8236
Headley Hants 17 H5 vil 3m/4km N of Kingsclere. SW 5162
Headley Surrey 19 F6 vil 3m/4km E of Leatherhead. NT property on H. Heath and in vicinity. TQ 2054
Headley Down Hants 11 E2* loc 3m/5km W of Hindhead. SU 8436
Headley Heath H & W 35 F6* loc 6m/10km S of Birmingham. SP 0676
Headley Park Avon 16 B4* S dist of Bristol. ST 5769
Head, North Cumbria 52 A3* headland at W extremity of the county 1m N of St Bees Hd. NX 9314
Head of Brough Shetland 89 E6* headland on W coast of Yell 2m/3km S of W Sandwick. HU 4485
Head of Garness Grampian 83 F1 headland on N coast 3m/4km E of Macduff. NJ 7464
Head of Hesta Shetland 89 F6* headland at easternmost point of Fetlar. HU 6791
Head of Holland Orkney 89 B6* headland on Mainland 3m/4km E of Kirkwall between Bay of Meil and Inganess Bay. HY 4912
Head of Work Orkney 89 B6* headland on coast of Mainland opp Shapinsay, 3m/5km NE of Kirkwall. Beacon. HY 4813
Headon Devon 6 C5* loc 2m/3km SE of Holsworthy. SS 3602
Headon Notts 44 C3 vil 4m/6km SE of E Retford. Ham of **Nether H.** to N. SK 7076
Head o' th' Lane Staffs 42 D5* loc 2m/3km N of Tunstall. SJ 8553
Heads Nook Cumbria 60 B5* vil 4m/7km SW of Brampton. NY 4955
Heads of Ayr S'clyde 56 C2 headland at S end of Firth of Clyde 4m/7km SW of Ayr. Holiday camp to E. NS 2818
Head, South Cumbria 52 A4 headland on Irish Sea 1m SE of St Bees Hd. NX 9511
Head, The Dyfed 22 A5 headland at W end of island of Skokholm. SM 7204
Head, West Norfolk 38 B4* loc 3m/5km NW of Downham Mkt across R Ouse. TF 5705
Heady Hill Gtr Manchester 42 D1* loc in Heywood 2km W of tn centre. SD 8310
Heage Derbys 43 H5/H6 vil 2m/3km W of Ripley. **Nether H.** vil 1m W. SK 3750
Healaugh N Yorks 49 G3 vil 3m/5km NE of Tadcaster. SE 5047
Healaugh N Yorks 54 A5 vil in Swaledale 2km W of Reeth. SE 0399
Healaval Beg Skye, H'land 79 A5 hill 4m/6km SW of Dunvegan. Also known as Macleod's Table South. Height 1601 ft or 488 metres. NG 2242
Healaval More Skye, H'land 79 A5 hill 3m/5km SW of Dunvegan. Also known as Macleod's Table North. Height 1538 ft or 469 metres. NG 2144
Heald Green Gtr Manchester 42 D3 loc 2m/3km S of Gatley. SJ 8485
Heale Devon 7 E1* loc near N coast 5m/8km SW of Lynton. SS 6446
Heale Som 8 B2* ham 1m NW of Curry Rivel. ST 3825
Healey Lancs 47 H6 loc 2km S of Whitworth. **H. Stones** loc 1km SE. SD 8816
Healey Nthmb 61 E5 loc 2m/3km S of Riding Mill. NZ 0158
Healey N Yorks 54 B6 vil 3m/4km W of Masham. SE 1880
Healey W Yorks 49 E5* W dist of Batley. SE 2224
Healey W Yorks 49 E6* loc on R Calder 1m SW of Ossett. SE 2719
Healing Humberside 45 F1 vil 4m/6km W of Grimsby. TA 2110
Heamoor Cornwall 2 A5 loc to N of Penzance. SW 4631
Heaning Cumbria 52 D5* loc 2km E of Windermere. SD 4399
Heanish Tiree, S'clyde 69 B7 loc on S coast 1km SW of Scarinish. NM 0343
Heanor Derbys 43 H6* coal-mining tn 3m/5km NW of Ilkeston. Also hosiery, pottery. **H. Gate** loc adjoining to W. SK 4346
Heanton Punchardon Devon 6 D2* vil 4m/6km NW of Barnstaple. SS 5035
Heap Bridge Gtr Manchester 42 D1 loc in Heywood 2m/3km W of tn centre. SD 8210
Heapey Lancs 47 F5 loc 3m/4km N of Chorley. SD 6020
Heapham Lincs 44 D2/D3 vil 4m/6km E of Gainsborough. SK 8788
Hearn Hants 11 E2* loc 4m/6km NW of Hindhead. SU 8337
Hearnden Green Kent 12 D2* loc 2m/3km N of Headcorn. TQ 8246
Heart's Delight Kent 21 E5* loc 2m/3km SW of Sittingbourne. TQ 8862
Heasley Mill Devon 7 E2 ham on SW edge of Exmoor National Park 4m/7km N of S Molton. SS 7332
Heasley, North Devon 7 E2* loc 5m/8km N of S Molton. SS 7333
Heast Skye, H'land 79 E6 loc 4m/6km S of Broadford. See also Eilean H. NG 6417
Heath Derbys 43 H4 vil 5m/8km SE of Chesterfield. SK 4466
Heath S Glam 15 F3/G3* dist of Cardiff 2m/3km N of city centre.
Heath W Yorks 49 F6* vil 2m/3km E of Wakefield. SE 3519
Heath and Reach Beds 28 D5 N suburb of Leighton Buzzard. SP 9227
Heathbrook Salop 34 C2* loc 1m E of Hodnet. SJ 6228
Heath Common W Sussex 11 G3* loc 2m/3km E of Storrington. TQ 1114
Heathcote Derbys 43 F5* ham 2km E of Hartington. SK 1460
Heathcote Salop 34 D2 loc 3m/4km E of Hodnet. SJ 6528
Heathencote Northants 28 C3 loc 2km SE of Towcester. SP 7147
Heath End Avon 16 C3* loc 1km S of Cromhall, 2m/3km NW of Wickwar. ST 6989
Heath End Bucks 18 D2* loc 4m/6km N of High Wycombe. SU 8898
Heath End Hants 17 H5* loc 5m/8km SW of Newbury. SU 4162
Heath End Hants 18 B5 extensive loc 7m/11km NW of Basingstoke. SU 5862
Heath End Leics 36 A2* loc 3m/5km N of Ashby de la Zouch. SK 3621
Heath End Surrey 18 C6* urban loc 2km SW of Aldershot. SU 8449
Heath End W Midlands 35 F4* loc 2m/4km N of Walsall. SK 0202
Heathend W Sussex 11 F3* loc 2m/3km S of Petworth. SU 9618
Heather Leics 36 A3 vil 4m/7km SE of Ashby de la Zouch. SK 3910
Heatherstane Law S'clyde 65 G5 mt 4m/6km SE of Lamington. Height 2055 ft or 626 metres. NT 0227
Heathfield Ches 42 C6* loc just N of Hatherton. SJ 6847
Heathfield Devon 5 E3 loc 3m/5km NW of Newton Abbot. SX 8376

Heathfield E Sussex 12 C4 small tn 11m/18km S of Tunbridge Wells. See also Old Heathfield. TQ 5821

Heathfield N Yorks 48 D2* loc 2m/3km NW of Pateley Br. SE 1367

Heathfield S'clyde 64 B6* N dist of Ayr. NS 3423

Heathfield Som 8 A2 ham in Vale of Taunton Deane 4m/7km NW of Taunton. ST 1626

Heath, Great W Midlands 36 A6* loc in Coventry 1m NE of city centre. SP 3480

Heath Hayes Staffs 35 F3 urban loc 2m/3km E of Cannock. SK 0110

Heath, High W Midlands 35 F4* loc 3m/4km NE of Walsall. SK 0202

Heath Hill Salop 34 D3 ham 4m/6km S of Newport. SJ 7614

Heath House Som 16 A6* loc 2km SW of Wedmore. ST 4146

Heathlands Devon 7 H5* loc 3m/4km SW of Ottery St Mary. SY 0692

Heath, Little Ches 34 D1* loc 1km NE of Audlem. SJ 6644

Heath, Little Herts 19 E1* loc (NT) 2m/3km E of Berkhamsted. TL 0108

Heath, Little London 20 B3* loc in borough of Redbridge 3m/4km NE of Ilford. TQ 4688

Heath, Little W Midlands 36 A6* N dist of Coventry. SP 3482

Heath, Lower Ches 42 D4/D5* loc in Congleton 1km N of tn centre. SJ 8664

Heath, North Berks 17 H4* loc 5m/7km N of Newbury. SU 4574

Heath, North W Sussex 11 F3* loc 2m/3km NE of Pulborough. TQ 0621

Heath Park London 20 B3* SE dist of Romford in borough of Havering. TQ 5288

Heathrow London. See London (Heathrow) Airport.

Heath Side Kent 20 B4* loc at S edge of Dartford Heath 2m/3km SW of Dartford. TQ 5172

Heath, South Bucks 18 D2* loc 1m E of Gt Missenden. SP 9101

Heath, The H & W 35 E6* loc 2m/3km W of Kidderminster. SO 8076

Heath, The Staffs 35 G1* NW dist of Uttoxeter. SK 0834

Heath, The Suffolk 31 E4* ham 6m/9km SW of Ipswich. TM 1236

Heathton Salop 35 E5 ham 6m/10km E of Bridgnorth. SO 8192

Heath Town W Midlands 35 F4 E dist of Wolverhampton. SO 9399

Heathwaite Cumbria 52 D5* loc adjoining Windermere to SE. SD 4197

Heath, West Ches 42 D5* loc in Congleton 1m W of tn centre. SJ 8462

Heath, West Hants 18 B5* loc 4m/6km E of Kingsclere. SU 5858

Heath, West Hants 18 D5* NW suburb of Farnborough. SU 8556

Heath, West London 20 B4* loc in borough of Bexley S of Lesnes Abbey Woods, 11m/18km E of Charing Cross. TQ 4777

Heath, West W Midlands 35 F6 dist of Birmingham 6m/10km SW of city centre. SP 0277

Heathy Brow E Sussex 12 A6* loc 1m N of English Channel coast at Peacehaven. TQ 4002

Heatley Ches 42 C3 vil 2m/3km NE of Lymm. SJ 7088

Heaton Gtr Manchester 42 C1* loc in Bolton 2m/3km W of tn centre. SD 6909

Heaton Lancs 47 E2 loc 2m/3km E of Heysham. SD 4460

Heaton Staffs 43 E5* ham 4m/7km NW of Leek. SJ 9562

Heaton Tyne & Wear 61 G5* dist of Newcastle 2m/3km NE of city centre. NZ 2766

Heaton W Yorks 48 D4* dist of Bradford 2m/3km NW of city centre. **H. Royds** loc to N. SE 1335

Heaton Chapel Gtr Manchester 42 D2* loc 2m/3km N of Stockport. SJ 8692

Heaton Mersey Gtr Manchester 42 D2* loc 2m/3km W of Stockport. SJ 8690

Heaton Moor Gtr Manchester 42 D2* loc 2m/3km NW of Stockport. SJ 8791

Heaton Norris Gtr Manchester 42 D2* loc 1m NW of Stockport. SJ 8890

Heaton Park Gtr Manchester 42 D1 park in Manchester 4m/6km N of city centre. **Heaton Park Resr** in NW corner, partly in Prestwich. SD 8304

Heaton's Bridge Lancs 42 A1* ham 2m/4km N of Ormskirk. SD 4011

Heaton, Upper W Yorks 48 D6* ham 1km N of Kirkheaton. SE 1719

Heaval W Isles 88 D4* mt on Barra 1m NE of Castlebay. Height 1260 ft or 384 metres. NL 6799

Heaverham Kent 20 C5 ham 4m/6km NE of Sevenoaks. TQ 5758

Heavitree Devon 7 G5* E dist of Exeter. SX 9492

Hebble Brook 48 D5* r rising on Oxenhope Moor, W Yorks, and flowing S into R Calder at Halifax. SE 0922

Hebburn Tyne & Wear 61 G5 industrial tn on S bank of R Tyne 4m/6km E of Gateshead. Shipbuilding, ship-repairing, paint mnfre, electrical engineering. NZ 3164

Hebden N Yorks C2 vil 2km N of Burnsall. SE 0263

Hebden Bridge W Yorks 48 C5 tn at confluence of Hebden Water and R Calder 7m/11km W of Halifax. Textiles, machine tools. SD 9927

Hebden Green Ches 42 C4* loc 2m/3km SW of Winsford. SJ 6265

Hebing End Herts 29 G5 ham 5m/8km E of Stevenage. TL 3122

Hebron Dyfed 22 D3 ham 7m/11km N of Whitland. SN 1827

Hebron Gwynedd 40 B3* loc on Anglesey 2m/4km E of Llanerchymedd. SH 4584

Hebron Nthmb 61 F3/G3 ham 2m/4km N of Morpeth. NZ 1989

Heck D & G 59 F3 loc 2m/3km SE of Lochmaben, beyond Castle Loch. NY 0980

Heckfield Hants 18 C5 vil 4m/6km N of Hook. SU 7260

Heckfield Green Suffolk 31 F1* vil adjoining Cross Street to E. TM 1875

Heckfordbridge Essex 30 D5 ham 4m/7km SW of Colchester. TL 9421

Heck, Great N Yorks 49 G5/G6 vil 3m/5km W of Snaith. **Lit Heck** loc 1m NE. SE 5922

Heckingham Norfolk 39 G5 loc 2m/3km E of Loddon. TM 3898

Heckington Lincs 37 F1 vil 5m/8km E of Sleaford. **E Heckington** vil 3m/5km E. TF 1444

Heckmondwike W Yorks 48 D5/49 E5 tn 2m/4km NW of Dewsbury. SE 2123

Hecla W Isles 88 E2 mt on S Uist 2m/4km S of Loch Skiport. Height 1988 ft or 606 metres. NF 8234

Heddington Wilts 17 E5 vil 3m/5km S of Calne. ST 9966

Heddon 7 E1* Exmoor r flowing N through Parracombe, Devon, into Bristol Channel at Heddon's Mouth, 4m/7km W of Lynton. SS 6549

Heddon Oak Som 7 H2* loc 5m/8km SE of Watchet. ST 1137

Heddon-on-the-Wall Nthmb 61 F4/F5 vil on line of Hadrian's Wall 7m/12km W of Newcastle. NZ 1366

Hedenham Norfolk 39 G5 vil 3m/5km NW of Bungay. TM 3193

Hedgecourt Pond Surrey 12 A3* lake 2km W of Felbridge. TQ 3540

Hedge End Hants 10 B3 suburb 2m/3km W of Botley. SU 4812

Hedge-end Island Essex 31 F5* uninhabited marshy island 2km W of The Naze. TM 2424

Hedgeley Moor Nthmb 67 G6 site of battle in Wars of the Roses, 1464, in which Yorkists defeated Lancastrians, 1km SE of Wooperton. Percy's Cross monmt marks spot where Lancastrian leader was killed. NU 0419

Hedgerley Bucks 18 D3 vil 3m/4km SE of Beaconsfield. Loc of **H. Green** 1km NE. SU 9687

Hedging Som 8 B2* ham 1m NE of Durston. ST 3029

Hedleyhope, East Durham 54 B1* ham 3m/5km N of Crook. NZ 1540

Hedley on the Hill Nthmb 61 F5 vil 3m/4km S of Prudhoe. NZ 0759

Hednesford Staffs 35 F3 tn in Cannock Chase 2m/3km NE of Cannock. SK 0012

Hedon Humberside 51 F5 tn 6m/9km E of Hull. **H. Haven** stream flows into R Humber 2m/3km W. TA 1828

Hedsor Bucks 18 D3 ham 3m/4km SW of Beaconsfield. SU 9187

Hedworth Tyne & Wear 61 G5/H5* loc in S Tyneside dist 2m/3km S of Jarrow. NZ 3363

Heeley S Yorks 43 H3 dist of Sheffield 2m/3km S of city centre. SK 3584

Heighington Durham 54 B3 vil 2m/4km SW of Newton Aycliffe. NZ 2422

Heighington Lincs 45 H4 vil 4m/6km E of Lincoln. TF 0369

Height End Lancs 48 B5* loc 1m W of Rawtenstall. SD 7923

Heightington H & W 26 C1* ham 3m/5km W of Stourport. SO 7671

Heighton, South E Sussex 12 B6 vil 2km N of Newhaven. TQ 4502

Heisgeir Island W Isles (W of 88 D1) small rocky uninhabited island 8m/13km NW of Griminish Pt, N Uist. Seal sanctuary. **Heisgeir Eagach** is group of rocks about 1m SW. Also known as Haskeir I. and Haskeir Eagach. NF 6182

Heisker W Isles. Alternative name for Monach Is., qv.

Heiton Borders 66 D5 vil 2m/4km S of Kelso. NT 7130

Heldale Water Orkney 89 A7* loch on island of Hoy 2m/4km N of Tor Ness. Length 2km. ND 2592

Hele Devon 4 D3* loc 1km NW of Ashburton. SX 7470

Hele Devon 5 E4* N dist of Torbay 2km N of Torquay tn centre. SX 9166

Hele Devon 6 C6* loc 4m/7km N of Launceston. SX 3391

Hele Devon 6 D1 vil just E of Ilfracombe. SS 5347

Hele Devon 7 G5 vil on R Culm 4m/6km SW of Cullompton. SS 9902

Hele Som 8 A2* ham 3m/4km W of Taunton. ST 1824

Helebridge Cornwall 6 B5 loc 2m/3km S of Bude. SS 2103

Hele, North Devon 7 G3* loc 1km NE of Clayhanger. ST 0223

Helensburgh S'clyde 64 A1 residential tn on N shore of Firth of Clyde 8m/12km NW of Dumbarton. Noted yachting centre. Birthplace of J. L. Baird, 1888–1946, pioneer of television. NS 2982

Helford Cornwall 2 C5 vil on inlet on S side of **Helford R,** 6m/10km E of Helston. Helford R rises near Helston and flows E into English Channel between Mawnan and Dennis Hd. SW 7526

Helford Passage Cornwall 2 D5* ham on N side of Helford R opp Helford. SW 7626

Helhoughton Norfolk 38 D2 vil 4m/6km SW of Fakenham. TF 8626

Helions Bumpstead Essex 30 B4 vil 3m/5km SW of Haverhill. TL 6541

Hellaby S Yorks 44 A2* loc 2m/3km W of Maltby. SK 5092

Helland Cornwall 3 F2 vil 3m/5km N of Bodmin. **Hellandbridge** loc to NW at crossing of R Camel. SX 0771

Helland Som 8 B2* ham adjoining N Curry 6m/10km E of Taunton. ST 3224

Hell Corner Berks 17 G5* loc 2km E of Inkpen. SU 3864

Hellescott Cornwall 6 B6* ham 4m/6km NW of Launceston. SX 2888

Hellesdon Norfolk 39 F4 vil on R Wensum 2m/4km NW of Norwich. **Upr Hellesdon** is dist of Norwich 2m/3km N of city centre. TG 2010

Helliar Holm Orkney 89 B6* small uninhabited island off S coast of Shapinsay opp Balfour. Lighthouse at S end. Hellyar Holm is alternative spelling. HY 4815

Hellidon Northants 28 A2 vil 5m/7km SW of Daventry. SP 5158

Helliers Ness Shetland 89 F6* headland on SW coast of Fetlar 1km NW of Rams Ness. HU 5988

Hellifield N Yorks 48 B3 vil 5m/8km SE of Settle. **H. Green** loc adjoins to S. SD 8556

Helli Ness Shetland 89 E8 headland on E coast of Mainland 8m/13km S of Lerwick. HU 4628

Hellingly E Sussex 12 C5* vil 2m/3km N of Hailsham. TQ 5812

Hellington Norfolk 39 G4 ham 6m/10km SE of Norwich. TG 3103

Hellisay W Isles 88 E3 uninhabited island lying 3m/4km E of Northbay, Barra. NF 7504

Hellister Shetland 89 E7* vil on Mainland, on E side of Weisdale Voe. **Loch of H.** is small loch to E. HU 3849

Hellmoor Loch Borders 66 B6 small loch 7m/12km W of Hawick. NT 3816

Hell's Mouth Gwynedd 32 A2, B2 bay on S side of Lleyn peninsula extending from Trwyn Talfarach eastwards to Trwyn y Fulfran, S of Llanengan. Also known as Porth Neigwl. SH 22

Hell's Mouth Gwynedd 40 B2* small bay on E side of Llanlleiana Hd, Anglesey. Also known as Porth Cynfor. SH 3994

Hellyar Holm Orkney. Alternative spelling of Helliar Holm, qv.

Helman Head H'land 86 F3 headland on E coast of Caithness dist 3m/4km S of Wick. ND 3646

Helm Beck 53 F3* r rising 3m/5km W of Crosby Garrett, Cumbria, and flowing N into R Eden at Lit Ormside, 3m/5km SE of Appleby. NY 7116

Helmdon Northants 28 B3 vil 4m/6km N of Brackley. SP 5843

Helme W Yorks 48 D6 ham 1km N of Meltham. SE 1011

Helmingham Suffolk 31 F3 vil 4m/7km S of Debenham. **H. Hall,** Tudor and later hse in deer park. TM 1857

Helmington Row Durham 54 B2* loc midway between Crook and Willington. NZ 1835

Helmsdale H'land 87 D5 vil on E coast of Sutherland dist at mouth of R Helmsdale 15m/24km NNE of Golspie. R runs SE from Loch Badenloch down Strath Kildonan. ND 0215

Helmshore Lancs 48 B5 loc 1m S of Haslingden. SD 7821

Helmsley N Yorks 55 E6 small tn on R Rye with large cobbled square, 12m/19km E of Thirsk. Remains of 12c cas (A.M.). See also Duncombe Park. SE 6183

Helmsley, Upper N Yorks 50 C3 vil 2km NW of Stamford Br. SE 6956

Helperby N Yorks 49 F2 vil on R Swale adjoining Brafferton to S, 6m/9km W of Easingwold. SE 4369

Helperthorpe N Yorks 50 D2 vil 11m/17km E of Malton. SE 9570

Helpringham Lincs 37 F1 vil 6m/9km SE of Sleaford. TF 1340

Helpston Cambs 37 F4 vil 6m/10km NW of Peterborough. Site of Roman bldg 1m S. TF 1205

Helsby Ches 42 B4 vil 8m/12km NE of Chester. On E side, **H. Hill** (NT), with Iron Age fort. SJ 4875

Helsey Lincs 45 H4* loc 1m NW of Hogsthorpe. TF 5172

Helston Cornwall 2 C5 mkt tn of Lizard peninsula, 15m/24km SW of Truro. SW 6527

Helstone Cornwall 3 F1* vil 2m/3km SW of Camelford. SX 0881

Helton Cumbria 53 E3 ham 5m/9km S of Penrith. NY 5122

Helton Tarn Cumbria 52 D6* small lake formed by R Winster 3m/4km N of Lindale. SD 4184

Helvellyn Cumbria 52 D3 mt in Lake Dist 4m/6km W of Patterdale. Height 3113 ft or 949 metres. NY 3415

Helwith N Yorks 54 A4 loc 3m/5km NE of Reeth. NZ 0702

Helwith Bridge N Yorks 48 B2* loc at crossing of R Ribble 2km N of Stainforth. SD 8169

Helygain Welsh form of Halkyn, qv.

Helygog 33 E3* r running NW into R Wnion 4m/6km E of Dolgellau, Gwynedd. SH 7820

Hem Powys 34 A4* loc 5m/8km S of Welshpool. SJ 2300

Hemblington Norfolk 39 G4 ham 4m/6km W of Acle. **H. Corner** loc 1km W. TG 3411

Hembury Fort Devon 7 H4 Iron Age earthwork 4m/6km NW of Honiton, 884 ft or 269 metres above sea level. ST 1103

Hemel Hempstead Herts 19 E1 tn on R Gade and Grand Union Canal 7m/11km NW of Watford. New Tn, designated 1947, to E of old. Various light industries. TL 0507

Hemerdon Devon 4 C5* vil 6m/10km E of Plymouth. SX 5657

Hemingbrough N Yorks 50 B5 vil 4m/6km E of Selby. SE 6730

Hemingby Lincs 45 F4 vil 3m/5km NW of Horncastle. TF 2374

Hemingfield S Yorks 43 H1* loc 1m S of Wombwell. SE 3901

Hemingford Abbots Cambs 29 G1 vil on R Ouse 3m/5km E of Huntingdon. TL 2870

Hemingford Grey Cambs 29 G1 vil 2km W of St Ives. TL 2970

Hemingstone Suffolk 31 F3* vil 6m/9km N of Ipswich. TM 1453

Hemington Leics 36 A2 vil 7m/11km NW of Loughborough. SK 4528

Hemington Northants 37 F5 vil 4m/6km SE of Oundle. Beaulieu Hall is 17c manor hse. TL 0985
Hemington Som 16 C6 vil 3m/5km SE of Radstock. ST 7253
Hemley Suffolk 31 G4 vil near right bank of R Deben estuary 5m/8km N of Felixstowe. TM 2842
Hemlington Cleveland 54 D3 ham 4m/6km S of Middlesbrough. NZ 5014
Hemp Green Suffolk 31 G2* loc 2km NW of Yoxford. TM 3769
Hempholme Humberside 51 E3 loc 6m/10km SE of Gt Driffield. TA 0850
Hempnall Norfolk 39 F5 vil 9m/14km S of Norwich. Vil of **H. Green** 1m SE. TM 2494
Hempstead Essex 30 B4 vil 5m/8km N of Thaxted. TL 6338
Hempstead Kent 20 D5* loc in S part of Gillingham. TQ 7964
Hempstead Norfolk 39 E1 vil 2m/3km SE of Holt. TG 1037
Hempstead Norfolk 39 G2 ham 2m/4km SE of Happisburgh. TG 4028
Hempsted Glos 26 C5 loc in SW part of Gloucester. SO 8116
Hempton Norfolk 38 D2 vil 1km SW of Fakenham across R Wensum. TF 9129
Hempton Oxon 27 H4 ham 2km W of Deddington. SP 4431
Hems 4 D4* r rising E of Ashburton, Devon, and flowing S into R Dart at Totnes. SX 8061
Hemsby Norfolk 39 H3 vil 2km S of Winterton. TG 4917
Hemswell Lincs 44 D2 vil 5m/8km S of Kirton in Lindsey. SK 9390
Hemsworth W Yorks 49 F6 coal-mining tn 6m/9km S of Pontefract. SE 4213
Hemyock Devon 7 H4 vil under Blackdown Hills 5m/8km S of Wellington. ST 1313
Hen Borth Gwynedd 40 A2* small bay on N coast of Anglesey 2km E of Carmel Hd. SH 3193
Henbrook H & W 26 D1* loc 3m/5km NE of Droitwich. WT stn. SO 9266
Henbury Avon 16 B4 loc in NW Bristol. ST 5678
Henbury Ches 42 D4* vil 3m/4km W of Macclesfield. SJ 8873
Hencott Pool Salop 34 B3 lake 2m/4km N of Shrewsbury. SJ 4916
Hendham Devon 4 D5* loc 4m/7km N of Kingsbridge. SX 7450
Hendomen Powys 33 H4* loc 1m NW of Montgomery. SO 2198
Hendon London 19 F3 dist in borough of Barnet 7m/11km NW of Charing Cross. Loc of **W Hendon** 1m SW. TQ 2289
Hendon Tyne & Wear 61 H5* coastal dist of Sunderland 1m SE of tn centre. NZ 4055
Hendraburnick Cornwall 6 A6* loc 3m/5km NE of Camelford. SX 1287
Hendre Clwyd 41 G4* loc 2m/4km SE of Nannerch. SJ 1967
Hendre Gwynedd 32 B2* loc 4m/6km NW of Llanbedrog. SH 2734
Hendre Mid Glam 15 E3* loc 3m/4km NE of Bridgend. SS 9481
Hendred, East Oxon 17 H3 vil 4m/6km E of Wantage. SU 4588
Hendred, West Oxon 17 H3 vil 3m/5km E of Wantage. SU 4488
Hendreforgan Mid Glam 15 E3* loc 2m/3km W of Tonyrefail. SS 9888
Hendy Dyfed 23 G5 vil on W side of R Loughor opp Pontarddulais. SN 5803
Hendy-gwyn Welsh form of Whitland, qv.
Heneglwys Gwynedd 40 B4 loc on E side of airfield, 2m/4km W of Llangefni, Anglesey. SH 4276
Henfield Avon 16 C4* ham 4m/6km SW of Chipping Sodbury. ST 6779
Henfield W Sussex 11 H3 tn 7m/11km N of Shoreham-by-Sea. TQ 2116
Henford Devon 6 C5 loc 7m/11km NE of Launceston. Also **H. Water,** r rising 3m/4km N and flowing into R Carey 1km SE. SX 3794
Hengastell, Yr Welsh form of Oldcastle, qv.
Hengistbury Head Dorset 9 H5 headland at W end of Christchurch Bay. SZ 1790
Hengoed Mid Glam vil in coal-mining dist 5m/8km N of Caerphilly. ST 1595
Hengoed Salop 34 A1/A2* loc 1m W of Gobowen. Loc of **Upr Hengoed** 1km N. SJ 2833
Hengrave Suffolk 30 C1/C2 vil 3m/5km NW of Bury St Edmunds. **H. Hall,** large Tudor hse in park. TL 8268
Hengrove Avon 16 B4* S dist of Bristol. ST 6069
Hen Gwrt Gwent 25 H6* medieval moated manor hse (A.M.) at Llantilio Crossenny, 6m/10km E of Abergavenny. SO 3915
Henham Essex 30 A5 vil 6m/10km NE of Bishop's Stortford. TL 5428
Henlade Som 8 B2 loc 3m/5km E of Taunton. ST 2724
Henleaze Avon 16 B4* dist of Bristol 3m/4km N of city centre. ST 5876
Henley Dorset 9 E4* ham 1km S of Buckland Newton and 3m/5km N of Piddletrenthide. ST 6904
Henley Glos 26 D5* loc 5m/7km SE of Gloucester. SO 9016
Henley Salop 34 C6* loc 2m/3km NE of Ludlow. SO 5476
Henley Som 8 C1 ham on edge of Sedgemoor 3m/5km E of Othery. ST 4332
Henley Som 8 C3* loc 2km S of Crewkerne. ST 4407
Henley Suffolk 31 F3 vil 4m/7km N of Ipswich. TM 1551
Henley W Sussex 11 E3 vil 3m/4km N of Midhurst. SU 8925
Henley Green W Midlands 36 A6* loc in Coventry 3m/5km NE of city centre. SP 3681
Henley-in-Arden Warwicks 27 F1 vil 7m/12km NW of Stratford-upon-Avon. SP 1565
Henley-on-Thames Oxon 18 C3 tn on R Thames 6m/10km NE of Reading. Annual regatta first week in July. SU 7682
Henley's Down E Sussex 12 D5 ham 3m/5km N of Bexhill. TQ 7312
Henley Street Kent 20 C5* loc 1km SE of Sole Street and 5m/7km S of Gravesend. TQ 6667
Henllan Clwyd 41 F4 vil 2m/3km NW of Denbigh. SJ 0268
Henllan Dyfed 23 E2 ham 3m/5km E of Newcastle Emlyn. SN 3540
Henllan Gwent 25 G5* loc 2km S of Llanthony. SO 2827
Henllan Amgoed Dyfed 22 D4* loc 2m/4km NW of Whitland. SN 1720
Henllys Gwent 15 G2* vil 2km W of Cwmbran. **H. Vale** loc 1m S. ST 2693
Henlow Beds 29 F4 vil 2m/4km E of Shefford. TL 1738
Henmore F6* r rising 2km W of Wirksworth, Derbys, and flowing SW through Ashbourne into R Dove 2m/3km SW of the tn. SK 1644
Hennock Devon 5 E3 vil 2m/3km NE of Bovey Tracey. SX 8380
Henny, Great Essex 30 D4 ham 2m/4km S of Sudbury. TL 8637
Henny, Little Essex 30 D4* loc 2m/3km S of Sudbury. TL 8638
Henny Street Essex 30 D4 ham 2m/3km S of Sudbury. TL 8738
Henrhyd Falls Powys 24 D6* high waterfall (NT) in course of Nant Llech, 2km SE of Pen-y-cae. SN 8511
Henryd Gwynedd 40 D4* ham 2m/3km S of Conwy. SH 7774
Henry's Moat (Castellhenri) Dyfed 22 C3 ham 9m/15km NE of Haverfordwest. SN 0427
Hensall N Yorks 49 G5 vil 3m/5km W of Snaith. SE 5923
Henshaw Nthmb 60 C5 vil 4m/6km E of Haltwhistle. NY 7664
Henshaw W Yorks 49 E4* dist of Yeadon SW of tn centre. SE 2040
Hensingham Cumbria 52 A3 dist of Whitehaven 2km SE of tn centre. NX 9816
Hensington Oxon 27 H5* loc in E part of Woodstock. SP 4516
Hensol Lake S Glam 15 F3* resr 4m/7km NE of Cowbridge. ST 0479
Henstead Suffolk 39 H6 vil 2m/4km W of Kessingland. TM 4985
Hensting Hants 10 C3 ham 3m/5km NE of Eastleigh. SU 4922
Henstridge Som 9 E2 vil 6m/10km S of Wincanton. To N, vil of **H. Ash.** 1m NE, loc of **H. Marsh.** 2m/4km NW, loc of **H. Bowden.** ST 7219
Henton Oxon 18 C2 vil 4m/7km SE of Thame. SP 7602
Henton Som 16 A6 vil 4m/6km W of Wells. ST 4945
Henwick H & W 26 D2* W dist of Worcester. SO 8354
Henwood Cornwall 3 G1* vil 6m/9km N of Liskeard. SX 2673
Henwood Green Kent 12 C3* loc adjoining Pembury to E. TQ 6340
Heogaland, West Shetland 89 D6* loc on Esha Ness, on NW part of Mainland. HU 2278
Heogan Shetland 89 E7* loc on NW coast of island of Bressay on the small **Bay of H.** Fish-meal factory. HU 4743
Heoga Ness Shetland 89 E6/F6* headland at SE end of Yell. HU 5278
Heolgaled (or Salem) Dyfed 24 C5 loc 3m/4km N of Llandeilo. SN 6226
Heolgerrig Mid Glam 15 E1* loc 1km W of Merthyr Tydfil. See also Pen-yr-Heolgerrig. SO 0306
Heol Senni Powys 25 E5 loc 3m/5km S of Sennybridge. SN 9223
Heol-y-cyw Mid Glam 15 E3* vil 4m/6km NE of Bridgend. SS 9484
Hepburn Nthmb 67 G5 loc 3m/4km S of Chatton. **H. Bell** loc 1m W. NU 0624
Hepple Nthmb 61 E2 vil 5m/7km W of Rothbury. NT 9800
Hepscott Nthmb 61 G3 vil 2m/3km SE of Morpeth. NZ 2284
Hepste 25 E6 r rising on S slopes of Fan Fawr, Fforest Fawr, Powys, and flowing SW into R Mellte 2m/4km S of Ystradfellte. SN 9209
Hepste Fall, Upper. See Scwd-yr-Eira.
Hepthorne Lane Derbys 43 loc 2km NE of Clay Cross. SK 4064
Heptonstall W Yorks 48 C5 vil 1km NW of Hebden Br. See also Slack. SD 9828
Hepworth Suffolk 31 E1 vil 5m/7km NE of Ixworth. Loc of **H. South Common** 1km SE. TL 9874
Hepworth W Yorks 43 F1* vil 2m/3km SE of Holmfirth. SE 1606
Herbert's, Little Glos 26 D5/27 E5* loc in S part of Charlton Kings. SO 9620
Herberts, The S Glam 15 E4* loc 2m/3km S of Cowbridge. SS 9971
Herbrandston Dyfed 22 B5 vil 3m/4km W of Milford Haven. Par includes Stack Rock, qv. SM 8707
Hereford H & W 26 A3 cathedral tn on R Wye 45m/72km SW of Birmingham. Many old bldgs. Three Choirs Festival every third year (see also Gloucester, Worcester). Cider factory. SO 5139
Hereford and Worcester 118 west midland county of England, bounded by Gloucestershire, Warwickshire, W Midlands, Staffordshire, Salop, and the Welsh counties of Powys and Gwent. The S and W borders are hilly, and there are isolated ranges of hills, notably the Malverns, throughout the county. It is extremely rural, except in the NE corner, which abuts on to the industrial W Midlands. The Severn valley and Vale of Evesham are noted for orchards, soft fruit and vegetable cultivation, and hop-growing. The farmlands are used predominantly for beef and dairy cattle, and sheep raising. Important tns are the cathedral cities of Hereford and Worcester; Bromsgrove, Evesham, Kidderminster, Malvern, and Redditch. Rs include the Severn, Wye, Avon, Lugg, Monnow, and Teme.
Hereford, Little H & W 26 B1 vil 3m/4km W of Tenbury Wells. SO 5568
Hergest, Lower H & W 25 G3 ham 2m/3km SW of Kington. SO 2755
Hergest, Upper H & W 25 G3 ham 2m/4km SW of Kington. SO 2654
Heriot Borders 66 B3 loc on **H. Water** 7m/11km NW of Stow. R originates in several headstreams on Moorfoot Hills and runs E into Gala Water 2m/3km E of Heriot. NT 3952
Herma Ness Shetland 89 F5 headland at NW end of Unst. **Hermaness** is hill to E. HP 5918
Hermetray W Isles 88 E1* small uninhabited island at S end of Sound of Harris 1km off NE coast of N Uist. NF 9874
Hermitage Berks 18 A4 vil 4m/6km NE of Newbury. SU 5072
Hermitage Dorset 8 D4 vil 6m/9km S of Sherborne. ST 6407
Hermitage W Sussex 10 D4* residential loc adjoining Emsworth to E. SU 7505
Hermitage Castle Borders 60 B2 ruined 13c cas (A.M.) on **Hermitage Water,** 5m/8km N of Newcastleton. R flows E to cas then S to Liddel Water 2m/3km NE of Newcastleton. NY 4996
Hermitage Green Ches 42 B2* loc 1km N of Winwick. SJ 6094
Hermit Hill S Yorks 43 G1* loc 1m W of Pilley. SE 3200
Hermon Dyfed 22 D3 vil 2m/3km SE of Crymmych. SN 2031
Hermon Dyfed 24 C5* loc 2m/4km W of Llangadog. SN 6728
Hermon Gwynedd 40 B4 loc on Anglesey 2m/3km E of Aberffraw. SH 3868
Herne Kent 13 G1 S dist of Herne Bay. Loc of **H. Common** 1km SE. TR 1865
Herne Bay Kent 13 G1 N coast resort on bay of same name 7m/11km N of Canterbury. TR 1768
Herne Hill London 19 G4* loc 4m/6km S of Charing Cross, on borders of Lambeth and Southwark boroughs. TQ 3274
Herne Pound Kent 20 C6* ham 1km N of Mereworth. TQ 6554
Herner Devon 6 D3 ham 5m/7km SE of Barnstaple. SS 5826
Hernhill Kent 21 F5 vil 3m/5km E of Faversham. TR 0660
Hernston Mid Glam 15 E4* loc 1m S of Bridgend. SS 9178
Herodsfoot Cornwall 3 G2* vil 4m/6km SW of Liskeard. SX 2160
Herongate Essex 20 C3 suburban loc 3m/5km SE of Brentwood. TQ 6391
Heronsgate Herts 19 E2* loc 1m S of Chorleywood. TQ 0294
Heron's Ghyll E Sussex 12 B4* loc 4m/6km N of Uckfield. TQ 4827
Herriard Hants 18 B6 ham 4m/7km SE of Basingstoke. SU 6645
Herringfleet Suffolk 39 H5 ham 6m/9km NW of Lowestoft. TM 4797
Herring's Green Beds 29 E3 loc 4m/6km SE of Bedford. TL 0844
Herringswell Suffolk 30 C1 vil 3m/5km S of Mildenhall. TL 7169
Herringthorpe S Yorks 44 A2* dist of Rotherham 2km E of tn centre. SK 4592
Herrington Tyne & Wear 61 H6. **E** and **Middle Herrington** are dists of Sunderland some 3m/5km SW of tn centre. **W** and **New Herrington** are locs some 2m/3km N of Houghton-le-Spring. NZ 3553
Hersden Kent 13 G1 vil on Kent coalfield 5m/8km NE of Canterbury. TR 2062
Hersham Cornwall 6 B4* loc 3m/5km NE of Bude. SS 2507
Hersham Surrey 19 E5 loc on left bank of R Mole 2km W of Esher. TQ 1164
Herstmonceux E Sussex 12 C5 vil 4m/6km NE of Hailsham. Royal Observatory at H. Castle 2m/3km SE. TQ 6312
Herston Dorset 9 G6 loc adjoining Swanage to W. SZ 0178
Hertburn Tyne & Wear 61 G5* loc in E part of Washington. Industrial estate. NZ 3157
Hertford Herts 19 G1 tn on R Lea 20m/32km N of London. TL 3212
Hertford Heath Herts 20 A1 vil 2m/3km NW of Hoddesdon. TL 3511
Hertfordshire 119 south midland county of England, bounded by Gtr London, Buckinghamshire, Bedfordshire, Cambridgeshire, and Essex. The Chilterns rise along the W border, and there are chalk hills in the N around Royston; otherwise the landscape is mostly flat or gently undulating. Many of the vils have large greens or commons. Major rds leading N from London cut through the S part of the county, which is largely urban, with both residential and industrial development. Chief tns, apart from those virtually forming London suburbs, are Hertford, the county tn; Bishop's Stortford, Watford, Hemel Hempstead, Hitchin, Letchworth, St Albans (a cathedral city), Stevenage, Ware, Watford, and Welwyn Garden City. Rs include the Colne, Ivel, and Lea.
Hertingfordbury Herts 19 G1 loc 2km W of Hertford. TL 3012
Hertsmere 119 admin dist of Herts.
Hesgyn 33 F1 stream running S through Llyn Hesgyn into R Tryweryn 1m E of Llyn Celyn dam, Gwynedd. SH 8940
Hesketh Bank Lancs 47 E5 loc 2m/3km N of Tarleton. SD 4423
Hesket, High Cumbria 60 A6 vil 8m/13km SE of Carlisle. **Low Hesket** vil 2km NW; site of Roman signal stn to N. NY 4744
Hesketh Lane Lancs 47 F4/G4 ham 3m/4km NE of Longridge. SD 6141
Hesket Newmarket Cumbria 52 D1 vil 8m/13km SE of Wigton. NY 3438
Heskin Green Lancs 47 F6* loc 4m/6km W of Chorley. SD 5315
Hesleden Durham 54 D1/D2 vil 2m/3km S of Peterlee. **High H.** ham 1km E. See also Monk Hesleden. NZ 4438
Hesleden N Yorks 48 B1 loc 2km S of Halton Gill. SD 8874

Hesledon Moor East Durham 54 C1• loc just S of Murton. **Hesledon Moor West** loc 1km SW. NZ 3946
Heslerton N Yorks 50 D1 vil 9m/15km E of Malton. SE 9276
Heslerton, West N Yorks 50 D1 vil 8m/13km E of Malton. SE 9175
Heslington N Yorks 50 B3 vil 2m/3km SE of York. Location of University of York. SE 6250
Hessary Tor, North Devon 4 C3• Dartmoor tor surmounted by TV mast, 1km NW of Princetown and 6m/10km E of Tavistock. SX 5774
Hessay N Yorks 50 A3 vil 5m/8km W of York. SE 5253
Hessenford Cornwall 3 G3 vil 6m/9km SE of Liskeard. SX 3057
Hessett Suffolk 30 D2 vil 5m/9km E of Bury St Edmunds. TL 9361
Hessle Humberside 51 E5 tn on N bank of R Humber adjoining Hull to W. TA 0326
Hessle W Yorks 49 F6• loc 3m/5km SW of Pontefract. SE 4317
Hest Bank Lancs 47 E2 loc on Morecambe Bay 3m/4km NE of Morecambe. SD 4766
Hester's Way Glos 26 D5• W dist of Cheltenham. SO 9222
Hestley Green Suffolk 31 F2• loc 3m/5km NW of Debenham. TM 1567
Heston London 19 E4 dist in borough of Hounslow 11m/18km W of Charing Cross. TQ 1277
Heston Island D & G 58 D6 small island with lighthouse at entrance to Auchencairn Bay on Solway Firth, S of Dalbeattie. NX 8350
Heswall Merseyside 41 H3 tn on Wirral peninsula 5m/7km SE of W Kirby. SJ 2682
Hethe Oxon 28 B4 vil 5m/7km N of Bicester. SP 5929
Hethelpit Cross Glos 26 C4• loc 8m/12km NW of Gloucester. SO 7729
Hethersett Norfolk 39 F4 vil 5m/8km SW of Norwich. TG 1504
Hethersgill Cumbria 60 A4/B4 ham 5m/8km NW of Brampton. NY 4767
Hetherside Cumbria 60 A5• loc 1m NW of Smithfield. NY 4366
Hethpool Nthmb 67 F5 loc above W bank of College Burn 2m/3km SW of Kirknewton. Ruined 14c peel tower. NT 8928
Hett Durham 54 C2 vil 2m/4km NE of Spennymoor. NZ 2836
Hetton N Yorks 48 C2 vil 5m/8km N of Skipton. SD 9658
Hetton Downs Tyne & Wear 61 H6• coal-mining loc adjoining Hetton-le-Hole to N. NZ 3548
Hetton le Hill Tyne & Wear 54 C1• loc 1m SW of Easington Lane. NZ 3545
Hetton-le-Hole Tyne & Wear 61 H6 coal-mining tn 6m/10km NE of Durham. NZ 3547
Hetton, South Durham 54 C1 coal-mining vil 3m/4km NW of Easington. NZ 3745
Heugh-head Grampian 82 C5 loc 2m/3km SE of vil of Strathdon. NJ 3811
Hevdadale Head Shetland 89 E6• headland on NW coast of Mainland 4m/6km W of Burra Voe. HU 3089
Hevden Ness Shetland 89 E6/E7• headland on Mainland on E side of entrance to Busta Voe. HU 3565
Heveningham Suffolk 31 G1 vil 5m/8km SW of Halesworth. 2km NE, **H. Hall** large Palladian hse in landscaped park. TM 3372
Hever Kent 12 B2 vil 2m/4km SE of Edenbridge. **H. Castle** fortified and moated Tudor manor hse. TQ 4744
Heversham Cumbria 53 E6 vil 2m/3km S of Levens. SD 4983
Hevingham Norfolk 39 F3 vil 8m/13km N of Norwich. TG 2021
Hewas Water Cornwall 3 E3 ham 3m/5km SW of St Austell. SW 9749
Hewelsfield Glos 16 B2 vil 4m/6km W of Lydney. Loc of **H. Common** 2km W. SO 5602
Hewenden W Yorks 48 D4• loc 1km E of Cullingworth. SE 0736
Hewish Avon 15 H5• ham with hams of **E** and **W Hewish,** 6m/9km E of Weston-super-Mare. ST 3964
Hewish Som 8 C3 ham 2m/3km SW of Crewkerne. ST 4208
Hewood Dorset 8 B4• ham 5m/8km NE of Axminster. ST 3502
Heworth N Yorks 50 B3 dist of York 1m E of city centre. SE 6152
Heworth Tyne & Wear 61 G5• central dist of Felling. NZ 2861
Hexham Nthmb 61 E5 mkt tn on S bank of R Tyne 20m/32km W of Newcastle upon Tyne. Medieval priory ch; 19c alterations. Racecourse 2m/3km SW at High Yarridge. NY 9364
Hexham Levels Nthmb 61 E5• on E bank of Devil's Water 2m/3km SE of Hexham. Site of battle in 1464 in which Yorkists defeated Lancastrians. NY 9561
Hextable Kent 20 B4 vil 1m N of Swanley. TQ 5170
Hexthorpe S Yorks 44 A1• dist of Doncaster 1m SW of tn centre. SE 5602
Hexton Herts 29 E4 vil 5m/8km W of Hitchin. TL 1030
Hexworthy Devon 4 C3 ham on Dartmoor 7m/11km W of Ashburton. SX 6572
Hey Gtr Manchester 43 E1• loc 2m/3km E of Oldham. SD 9504
Hey Lancs 48 B4• loc 2m/3km N of Colne. SD 8843
Heybridge Essex 20 C2• vil adjoining Ingatestone to SW. TQ 6498
Heybridge Essex 21 E1 N suburb of Maldon. **H. Basin** loc with timber wharf on Collier Reach 1m SE. TL 8508
Heybrook Bay Devon 4 B5• dist on coast 4m/6km S of Plymouth across R Plym estuary. SX 4949
Heydon Herts 29 H4 vil 5m/8km E of Royston. TL 4340
Heydon Norfolk 39 E2 vil 3m/5km N of Reepham. Hall dates from 16c. TG 1127
Heydour Lincs 37 E1• ham 1km NE of Oasby. TF 0039
Heyford, Lower Oxon 28 A5 vil on R Cherwell and Oxford Canal 6m/10km W of Bicester. SP 4824
Heyford, Nether Northants 28 B2 vil 6m/10km W of Northampton. Site of Roman bldg to E. SP 6658
Heyford, Upper Northants 28 B2 vil 6m/9km W of Northampton. SP 6659
Heyford, Upper Oxon 28 H5 vil 6m/9km NW of Bicester. Airfield to E. SP 4926
Heyheads Gtr Manchester 43 E1• loc 1km SE of Mossley. SD 9701
Hey Houses Lancs 47 E5• loc 1m N of Lytham St Anne's. SD 3429
Heylipoll Tiree, S'clyde 69 A7 loc 4m/7km W of Scarinish. NL 9743
Heylor Shetland 89 E6• loc on Mainland on S shore of Ronas Voe. HU 2980
Heyop Powys 25 G1• loc 3m/5km NW of Knighton. SO 2474
Heyrod Gtr Manchester 43 E2• loc 1m NE of Stalybridge. SJ 9799
Heysham Lancs 47 E2 coastal tn at S end of Morecambe Bay 3m/4km SW of Morecambe, comprising Upr and Lr Heysham. Passenger ferries to Belfast, Dublin, and Londonderry. SD 4161
Heyshaw N Yorks 48 D2 loc 3m/4km S of Pateley Br. SE 1761
Heyshott W Sussex 11 E3 vil 2m/4km S of Midhurst. Ham of **H. Green** to N. SU 8918
Heyside Gtr Manchester 43 E1• loc 2m/3km N of Oldham. SD 9307
Heytesbury Wilts 16 D6 vil on R Wylye 4m/6km SE of Warminster. ST 9242
Heythrop Oxon 27 G4 vil 2m/4km E of Chipping Norton. SP 3527
Heywood Gtr Manchester 42 D1 tn 3m/5km E of Bury. Textiles, engineering, leather. SD 8510
Heywood Wilts 16 D5 vil 2m/3km N of Westbury. ST 8753
Hibaldstow Humberside 44 D1 vil 3m/5km SW of Brigg. Site of Roman settlement 1m NW. SE 9702
Hibb's Green Suffolk 30 D3 ham 5m/8km N of Long Melford. TL 8753
Hickleton S Yorks 44 A1 vil in coal-mining area 6m/10km W of Doncaster. SE 4805
Hickling Norfolk 39 G3 vil 3m/4km E of Stalham. **H. Green** vil adjoining to S. **H. Heath** loc 1m SW. **H. Broad,** large broad or lake 2km S. TG 4124
Hickling Notts 36 C2 vil 7m/12km NW of Melton Mowbray. SK 6929
Hickmans Green Kent 21 F5 loc 3m/5km SE of Faversham. TR 0658
Hicks Forstal Kent 13 G1• loc 3m/4km S of Herne Bay. TR 1863
Hickstead W Sussex 11 H3 ham 4m/6km SW of Cuckfield. TQ 2620
Hidcote Bartrim Glos 27 F3• ham 3m/5km NE of Chipping Campden. Series of formal gardens (NT) at manor hse. SP 1742
Hidcote Boyce Glos 27 F3 ham 3m/4km NE of Chipping Campden. SP 1742
Hiendley, South W Yorks 49 F6 vil 7m/11km SW of Pontefract. SE 3912
Hiendley, Upper W Yorks 49 F6• loc adjoining S Hiendley to N. SE 3913
Higginshaw Gtr Manchester 43 E1• loc 1m N of Oldham. SD 9306
HIGH, HIGHER. For names beginning with these words, see under next word. This also applies to names beginning with Low, Lower; Upper, Nether; Far, Near; Mid, Middle; Great, Little; Greater, Lesser; Isle(s) of; North, South, East, West; The, Y, Yr.
Higham Derbys 43 H5 vil 3m/4km S of Clay Cross. SK 3959
Higham Kent 20 D4 suburban development 3m/5km NW of Rochester. TQ 7171
Higham Lancs 48 B4 vil 2m/3km NE of Padiham. SD 8036
Higham Suffolk 30 C2 vil 7m/11km W of Bury St Edmunds. TL 7465
Higham Suffolk 31 E4 vil 4m/7km S of Hadleigh. TM 0335
Higham S Yorks 43 G1 vil 2m/4km W of Barnsley. **H. Common** loc adjoining to S. SE 3107
Higham Cross Bucks 28 C3• loc 6m/10km NW of Newport Pagnell. SP 7847
Higham Ferrers Northants 28 D1 footwear-mnfg tn 4m/7km E of Wellingborough. SP 9668
Higham Gobion Beds 29 E4 vil 4m/6km S of Clophill. TL 1032
Higham Hill London 20 A3 loc in borough of Waltham Forest 1m W of Walthamstow tn centre. TQ 3690
Higham, Lower Kent 20 D4• loc 1m N of Higham and 3m/5km NW of Rochester. TQ 7172
Higham on the Hill Leics 36 A4 vil 3m/5km NE of Nuneaton. SP 3895
Highampton Devon 6 D4 vil 4m/6km W of Hatherleigh. SS 4804
Highams Park London 20 A3• loc in borough of Waltham Forest 1m N of Walthamstow tn centre. TQ 3791
Higham Wood Kent 20 C6• loc in NE part of Tonbridge. TQ 6048
High and Over E Sussex 12 B6• pass on S Downs between Seaford and Alfriston. TQ 5101
Highbridge Hants 10 B3• loc on R Itchen 2m/3km NE of Eastleigh. SU 4621
Highbridge Som 15 H6 industrial tn on R Brue near its mouth, 2m/3km SE of Burnham-on-Sea. ST 3247
Highbrook W Sussex 12 A4 ham 2m/3km S of W Hoathly. TQ 3630
Highburton W Yorks 48 D6 vil 4m/6km SE of Huddersfield. SE 1913
Highbury London 19 G3• loc in borough of Islington 4m/6km NE of Charing Cross. TQ 3285
Highbury Som 16 C6 vil 4m/6km S of Radstock. ST 6849
Highbury Vale Notts 36 B1 dist of Nottingham 3m/5km NW of city centre. SK 5444
Highclere Hants 17 H5 vil 6m/9km NE of Hurstbourne Tarrant. SU 4360
Highcliffe Dorset 10 A5 seaside dist 4m/6km E of Christchurch tn centre. SZ 2192
Highdown Hill W Sussex 11 G4 hill and archaeological site (NT) 2km E of Angmering. Finds date back to Late Bronze Age. TQ 0904
Higherford Lancs 48 B4• loc adjoining Barrowford to N. SD 8640
Highfield Cleveland 54 D3• loc adjoining Egglescliffe to N. NZ 4214
Highfield Devon 7 E5• loc 7m/11km E of Okehampton. SX 7097
Highfield Gtr Manchester 42 C1• loc adjoining Farnworth to W. SD 7105
Highfield Gtr Manchester 42 B1• loc in Wigan 2km SW of tn centre. SD 5604
Highfield Hants 10 B3• N dist of Southampton. SU 4214
Highfield Herts 19 E1• N dist of Hemel Hempstead. TL 0608
Highfield Humberside 50 C4 loc 5m/8km N of Howden. SE 7236
Highfield Oxon 28 B5• loc in NW part of Bicester. SP 5723
Highfield S'clyde 64 B4• loc 2km E of Dalry. NS 3050
Highfield S Yorks 43 H3• dist of Sheffield 1m S of city centre. SK 3585
Highfield Tyne & Wear 61 F5• vil adjoining Rowlands Gill to W, 4m/6km S of Ryton. NZ 1458
Highfields Cambs 29 G2• vil 6m/10km W of Cambridge. TL 3558
Highfields Derbys 43 H4• loc 2m/3km NE of Clay Cross. SK 4165
Highfields Nthmb 67 F3• N dist of Berwick-upon-Tweed. NT 9954
Highfields S Yorks 44 A1• loc 3m/5km NW of Doncaster. SE 5406
Highgate E Sussex 12 B3• loc adjoining Forest Row to S. TQ 4234
Highgate London 19 F3 loc in borough of Haringey 5m/8km N of Charing Cross. **Highgate Wd** to N. To S in borough of Camden: **H. Ponds,** series of small lakes on E side of Parliament Hill; **H. Cemetery** to W of Waterlow Park. TQ 2887
Highgate N Yorks 49 G6• loc 3m/4km SE of Whitley. SE 5919
Highgate S Yorks 44 A1• loc adjoining Goldthorpe to SW. SE 4503
Highgate Howe N Yorks 55 G4• loc 2km E of Whitby. NZ 9110
Highland 114 admin region of Scotland, covering a large part of the northern half of the country, and comprising the former counties of Caithness, Sutherland, Ross and Cromarty, Nairn, Inverness (incl Skye, and other islands of the Inner Hebrides), and a small portion of Argyll, although excluding the Outer Hebrides (see Western Isles). The region is very sparsely inhabited, being wild and remote, although scenically outstanding, including as it does part of the Cairngorms, and many of the finest sea and inland lochs in Scotland. The discovery of North Sea oil has made an impact on the tns and vils around the Moray Firth.
Highlands, The E Sussex 12 D5• N dist of Bexhill. TQ 7309
Highlane Ches 42 D4• loc 4m/6km SW of Macclesfield. SJ 8868
Highlane Derbys 43 H3 vil 5m/7km SE of Sheffield. SK 4082
Highlanes Staffs 35 E2• loc 2m/3km W of Slindon. SJ 7932
Highlaws Cumbria 52 B1 loc 2m/3km W of Abbey Town. NY 1449
Highleadon Glos 26 C5 ham 5m/8km NW of Gloucester. SO 7723
Highleigh Devon 7 G3• loc 3m/4km W of Bampton. SS 9123
Highleigh W Sussex 11 E5 vil 3m/5km N of Selsey. SZ 8498
Highley Salop 34 D5 colliery vil 6m/10km S of Bridgnorth. SO 7483
Highmoor Cumbria 52 C1 loc 1km SE of Wigton. NY 2647
Highmoor Oxon 18 B3• ham 4m/7km W of Henley-on-Thames. Ham of **H. Cross** to S. SU 7084
Highmoor Hill Gwent 16 A3• loc 1m SW of Caerwent. ST 4689
Highnam Glos 26 C5 scattered vil 3m/4km W of Gloucester. SO 7819
Highnam Green Glos 26 C5• ham 3m/4km W of Gloucester. SO 7920
Highstead Kent 13 G1 loc 3m/4km SE of Herne Bay. TR 2166
Highsted Kent 21 E5• ham 2km S of Sittingbourne. TQ 9061
Highstreet Kent 21 F5• ham 3m/5km SW of Whitstable. TR 0862
Highstreet Green Essex 30 C4 ham 4m/7km NW of Halstead. TL 7634
Highstreet Green Surrey 11 F2• ham 5m/8km E of Haslemere. SU 9835
Hightae D & G 59 F3/F4 vil 3m/4km S of Lochmaben. **H. Mill Loch** is small loch 1m N (see also Lochmaben). NY 0978
Highter's Heath W Midlands 35 G6• loc in Birmingham 5m/8km S of city centre. SP 0879
Hightown Ches 42 D5 loc in Congleton 1m SE of tn centre. SJ 8762
Hightown Hants 10 B4• loc in E part of Southampton 4m/6km E of city centre across R Itchen. SU 4711
Hightown Hants 9 H4• loc 2km E of Ringwood. To E, **H. Common** (NT). ST 1604
Hightown Merseyside 41 H1 loc 2m/4km S of Formby. SD 3003
Hightown W Yorks 48 D5• loc 1m W of Liversedge. SE 1824
Hightown Green Suffolk 30 D3• ham 5m/8km W of Stowmarket. TL 9756
Highway Berks 18 D3• W dist of Maidenhead. SU 8680
Highway Cornwall 2 C4• loc 2km NE of Redruth. SW 7143
Highway H & W 26 A3• loc 7m/11km NW of Hereford. SO 4549
Highway Wilts 17 E4 loc 4m/6km NE of Calne. SU 0474

Highweek Devon 5 E3 NW suburb of Newton Abbot. SX 8472
Highwood H & W 26 B1 ham 4m/6km E of Tenbury Wells. SO 6567
Highwood Hill London 19 F2 loc in borough of Barnet 1m N of Mill Hill and 10m/16km NW of Charing Cross. TQ 2193
Highwood Quarter Essex 20 C2* loc 4m/7km W of Chelmsford. TL 6404
Highworth Wilts 17 F2 tn 6m/9km NE of Swindon. SU 2072
Hilborough Norfolk 38 C4 vil 6m/9km S of Swaffham. TF 8200
Hilbre Islands Merseyside 41 G3 two small islands, Hilbre I. and Lit Hilbre I., at seaward end of R Dee estuary 1m off **Hilbre Pt** at NW tip of Wirral peninsula. See also Lit Eye and Tanskey Rocks. SJ 1887
Hilcott Wilts 17 F5 ham 4m/6km W of Pewsey. SU 1158
Hildasay Shetland 89 E7* uninhabited island of 255 acres or 103 hectares 3m/5km W of Scalloway, Mainland. HU 3540
Hildenborough Kent 20 C6 NW suburb of Tonbridge. TQ 5648
Hildenley N Yorks 50 C1/C2* loc 3m/4km W of Malton. SE 7470
Hildersham Cambs 30 A3 vil 4m/7km NE of Gt Chesterford. TL 5448
Hilderstone Staffs 35 F1 vil 3m/5km E of Stone. SJ 9434
Hilderthorpe Humberside 51 F2 S dist of Bridlington. TA 1765
Hilfield Dorset 9 D4 ham 7m/12km S of Sherborne. ST 6305
Hilfield Park Reservoir Herts 19 F2* resr 3m/5km E of Watford. Elstree Airfield to N. TQ 1596
Hilgay Norfolk 38 B4 vil 3m/5km S of Downham Mkt. TL 6298
Hill Avon 16 B2 vil 3m/5km N of Thornbury. Ham of **Upr Hill** 1m NE. ST 6495
Hill Cumbria 52 D5* loc 2m/3km E of Windermere. SD 4498
Hill Dyfed 22 D5 loc 2km NW of Saundersfoot. SN 1206
Hill H & W 27 E3* loc 3m/5km NE of Pershore. SO 9848
Hill Warwicks 27 H1* ham 4m/7km NE of Southam. SP 4567
Hillam N Yorks 49 G5 vil 3m/5km NE of Ferrybridge. SE 5028
Hillbeck Cumbria 53 G3 loc 1km N of Brough. NY 7915
Hillberry Isle of Man 46 B5 loc 3m/4km N of Douglas. SC 3879
Hillborough Kent 13 G1 loc 2m/3km E of Herne Bay tn centre. TR 2168
Hill Bottom Oxon 18 B3* loc adjoining Whitchurch Hill to N, 2m/3km N of Pangbourne. SU 6479
Hillbourne Dorset 9 G4* suburb 2m/3km N of Poole. SZ 0094
Hill Brow 11 E2* vil on border of Hants and W Sussex 4m/6km NE of Petersfield. SU 7926
Hillbutts Dorset 9 G4 ham 1m NW of Wimborne. ST 9901
Hill Chorlton Staffs 35 E1 vil 5m/8km SW of Newcastle-under-Lyme. SJ 7939
Hillcliffiane Derbys 43 G6* ham 4m/6km W of Belper. SK 2947
Hill Common Norfolk 39 G3* loc at N end of Hickling Broad. TG 4122
Hillcommon Som 8 A2* ham in Vale of Taunton Deane 2m/3km E of Milverton. ST 1426
Hill Cottages N Yorks 55 E5/F5* ham 2km NW of Rosedale Abbey. SE 7295
Hill Crest H & W 35 E6* loc at W edge of Kidderminster. SO 8175
Hill Croome H & W 26 D3 loc 5m/8km N of Tewkesbury. SO 8840
Hill Dale Lancs 42 B1* ham 1m N of Parbold. SD 4912
Hill Deverill Wilts 9 F1* loc adjoining Longbridge Deverill to S and 3m/5km S of Warminster. ST 8640
Hill Dyke Lincs 45 G6* ham 3m/4km NE of Boston. TF 3447
Hill, East Hants 11 E2* loc adjoining Liss to SE, 4m/6km NE of Petersfield. SU 7827
Hill End Durham 54 A2 loc 1m SW of Frosterley. NZ 0136
Hillend Fife 65 G1 vil 2km NE of Inverkeithing. NT 1483
Hill End Glos 26 D4* ham 3m/5km N of Tewkesbury. SO 9037
Hillend Gtr Manchester 43 E2* loc just N of Broadbottom. SJ 9994
Hill End H & W 26 D2* loc in NE part of Droitwich. SO 9063
Hill End London 19 E2* loc in borough of Hillingdon 2m/3km S of Rickmansworth. TQ 0491
Hillend Lothian 66 A2 loc at N end of Pentland Hills, 5m/7km S of Edinburgh. Chair lift to artificial ski-slope. NT 2566
Hillend S'clyde 65 E2 loc 1km SE of Caldercruix, at W end of **Hillend Resr.** NS 8267
Hillend W Glam 23 F6* loc at W end of Gower peninsula, at N end of Rhosili Down. SS 4190
Hill End W Yorks 49 E5* loc in Leeds 3m/4km W of city centre. SE 2533
Hillend Green Glos 26 C4* loc 2m/3km NW of Newent. SO 7028
Hillersland Glos 26 B6* loc 2m/4km N of Coleford. SO 5614
Hillesden Bucks 28 B4/B5 vil 3m/5km S of Buckingham. SP 6828
Hillesley Avon 16 C3 vil 3m/4km S of Wotton-under-Edge. ST 7689
Hillfarance Som 8 A2 vil in Vale of Taunton Deane 4m/6km W of Taunton. ST 1624
Hillfarance Brook 8 A2* r in Somerset rising near Wiveliscombe and flowing E into R Tone 1m NE of Bradford-on-Tone. ST 1724
Hillfoot W Yorks 49 E4/E5* loc adjoining Pudsey to W. SE 2033
Hillfoot End Beds 29 F4* W part of Shillington, 3m/5km SW of Shefford. TL 1234
Hillgreen Berks 17 H4* loc 6m/9km N of Newbury. SU 4576
Hill Green Essex 29 H4* ham adjoining Clavering to NE, 3m/5km W of Newport. TL 4732
Hillhampton H & W 26 C1* loc 4m/7km SW of Stourport. SO 7765
Hillhead Devon 5 E5* loc 2m/3km SW of Brixham. SX 9053
Hill Head Hants 10 C4* suburban locality on shore of the Solent 2km NW of Lee-on-the-Solent. SU 5402
Hillhead S'clyde 56 D2 vil 6m/9km E of Ayr, adjoining Coylton to E. Also known as **Hillhead of New Coylton.** NS 4219
Hillhead S'clyde 64 C2* loc in Glasgow to N of university and 2km NW of city centre. NS 5667
Hill Houses Salop 34 C6* loc 3m/5km NW of Cleobury Mortimer. SO 6379
Hilliard's Cross Staffs 35 G3* loc 3m/4km NE of Lichfield. SK 1412
Hillingdon London 19 E3 borough and loc 14m/23km W of Charing Cross. Locs of **North H.** and **H. Heath** are respectively NE and SW of the loc of Hillingdon. The borough contains the tn of Uxbridge; the dists of Harlington, Harmondsworth, Hayes, Ruislip, W Drayton, and Yiewsley; and London (Heathrow) Airport. TQ 0782
Hillington Norfolk 38 C2 vil 7m/12km NE of King's Lynn. TF 7125
Hillington S'clyde 64 C3 dist of Glasgow on S side of R Clyde 4m/6km W of city centre. **H. Industrial Estate,** outside city boundary, adjoins to N. NS 5264
Hillis Corner Isle of Wight 10 B5* loc 2m/4km SW of Cowes. SZ 4793
Hill, Little Leics 36 B4/C4 loc 4m/7km SE of Leicester. SP 6198
Hillmoor Devon 7 H4* loc just SE of Culmstock 5m/8km SW of Wellington. ST 1013
Hillmorton Warwicks 28 A1 SE dist of Rugby. SP 5374
Hill Mountain Dyfed 22 C5 ham 5m/8km S of Haverfordwest. SM 9708
Hill, North Cornwall 4 A3 vil 6m/10km SW of Launceston. SX 2776
Hill, North Dorset 8 D5 loc between Winterbourne Abbas and Winterbourne Steepleton, and 4m/7km W of Dorchester. SY 6290
Hillock Vale Lancs 48 A5* loc adjoining Accrington to NE. SD 7629
Hill of Beath Fife 73 E5 loc adjoining Cowdenbeath to SW. NT 1590
Hill of Fare Grampian 77 F1 hill 5m/7km N of Banchory. Height 1422 ft or 433 metres. NJ 6803
Hill of Fearn H'land 87 B8 vil near E coast of Ross and Cromarty dist 4m/7km SE of Tain. NH 8377
Hill of Foudland Grampian 83 E3/E4 hill 6m/10km SE of Huntly. Worked-out quarries on N slopes. Glens of Foudland is valley on N side; Skirts of Foudland is S slopes. NJ 6033
Hill of Glansie Tayside 77 E4* hill 4m/6km E of Rottal in Glen Clova. Height 2381 ft or 726 metres. NO 4369
Hill of Rubislaw Grampian 77 H1* hill in W part of Aberdeen 2m/3km from city centre. Rubislaw Quarry is chief source of granite in the area. NJ 9005
Hill of Stake S'clyde 64 A3 summit of hills to NE of Largs. Height 1711 ft or 522 metres. NS 2763
Hill of Tarvit Fife 73 F3/G3 hse (NTS) built late 17c, remodelled early 20c, now used as convalescent home, with farming estate, 2m/3km S of Cupar. Scotstarvit Tower (A.M.) 1km SW, 16c or earlier. NO 3811
Hill of Trusta Grampian 77 G2 hill surrounded by Fetteresso Forest 6m/9km W of Stonehaven. Height 1051 ft or 320 metres. NO 7886
Hill of Wirren Tayside 77 E4 hill ridge 6m/9km NW of Edzell. Height 2220 ft or 677 metres. NO 5273
Hill o' Many Stanes H'land. See Clyth, Mid.
Hillpark S'clyde 64 C3* loc in Pollokshaws dist of Glasgow. NS 5559
Hillpound Hants 10 C3 loc adjoining Swanmore to SE. SU 5815
Hill Ridware Staffs 35 G3 vil 2m/4km E of Rugeley. SK 0817
Hill Row Cambs 38 A6 vil adjoining Haddenham to W. TL 4475
Hills and Holes Cambs. See Barnack.
Hillsborough S Yorks 43 G2* dist of Sheffield 2m/4km NW of city centre. SK 3289
Hill's End Beds 29 E4* ham on E side of Woburn Park, 2m/4km E of Woburn. SP 9833
Hillside Grampian 77 H2 loc near E coast 5m/8km S of Aberdeen. NO 9297
Hillside H & W 26 C2* loc 3m/5km S of Gt Witley. SO 7561
Hillside Tayside 77 F5 vil 2m/4km N of Montrose. Distillery to E. NO 7061
Hill Side W Yorks 48 D6* vil 1km S of Kirkheaton. SE 1717
Hills of Cromdale 82 A4. See Cromdale.
Hill Somersal Derbys 35 G1* loc 1km SE of Somersal Herbert. SK 1434
Hill, South Cornwall 3 G1 ham 3m/4km NW of Callington. SX 3372
Hill, South Som 8 C2* loc 2km SW of Somerton. ST 4726
Hills Town Derbys 44 A4 loc adjoining Bolsover to SE. SK 4769
Hill Street Hants 10 A3* ham 2m/3km NW of Totton. SU 3416
Hillswick Shetland 89 D6 vil on Mainland on W shore of Ura Firth, at neck of peninsula called **Ness of H.** HU 2877
Hill, The Cumbria 52 B6 vil 2m/3km N of Millom. SD 1783
Hill Top Durham 53 H3* loc adjoining Eggleston to N. NY 9924
Hill Top Durham 54 B1* loc adjoining Langley Park to S. NZ 2144
Hill Top Gtr Manchester 42 C1* loc 2km S of Farnworth. SD 7303
Hill Top S Yorks 43 G2* loc 5m/7km W of Sheffield. SK 2889
Hill Top S Yorks 43 H2* loc in Rotherham 2m/3km W of tn centre. SK 3992
Hill Top S Yorks 43 G1* loc 2m/3km NE of Penistone. SE 2705
Hill Top S Yorks 44 A2* loc 2km SW of Conisbrough. SK 4997
Hill Top W Midlands 35 F5 loc in W Bromwich 2km NW of tn centre. SO 9993
Hill Top W Yorks 48 D6* loc 1km SW of Slaithwaite. SE 0713
Hill Top W Yorks 49 E4* loc in Leeds 3m/5km W of city centre. SE 2534
Hill, Upper H & W 26 A2* ham 4m/6km SW of Leominster. SO 4753
Hill View Dorset 9 G4 suburban locality 4m/6km NW of Poole. SY 9895
Hill, West Devon 7 H5 loc 2m/3km W of Ottery St Mary. SY 0794
Hill, West Humberside 51 E5* loc on N bank of R Humber 1km SW of Hessle. TA 0225
Hill, West Humberside 51 F2 W dist of Bridlington. TA 1666
Hill, West London 19 F4* loc in borough of Wandsworth 1m SE of Putney Br and 5m/8km SW of Charing Cross. TQ 2574
Hill, West Wilts 16 D4* loc 2m/4km NW of Melksham. ST 8766
Hill Wootton Warwicks 27 G1* ham 3m/4km SE of Kenilworth. SP 3068
Hillyfields Hants 10 B3* ham 3m/5km NW of Southampton. SU 3715
Hilmarton Wilts 17 E4 vil 3m/5km N of Calne. SU 0175
Hilperton Wilts 16 D5 vil 2km NE of Trowbridge. Adjacent to NW, loc of **H. Marsh.** ST 8759
Hilsea Hants 10 D4 dist of Portsmouth at N end of Portsea I. SU 6503
Hilston Humberside 51 G5 ham 5m/8km NW of Withernsea. TA 2833
Hilton Cambs 29 G2 vil 4m/6km SW of St Ives. TL 2866
Hilton Cleveland 54 D4 vil 5m/8km S of Stockton-on-Tees. NZ 4611
Hilton Cumbria 53 F3 vil at foot of fells 3m/5km E of Appleby. NY 7320
Hilton Derbys 35 H2 vil 8m/12km SW of Derby. SK 2430
Hilton Dorset 9 E4 vil 6m/9km N of Puddletown. ST 7803
Hilton Durham 54 B3 ham 3m/4km E of Staindrop. NZ 1621
Hilton Salop 34 D4 vil 4m/7km E of Bridgnorth. SO 7795
Hilton Staffs 35 G4* loc 2m/3km E of Brownhills. SK 0805
Hilton Beck 53 F3* r rising on Murton Fell, Cumbria, and flowing SW to Hilton and thence into R Eden 2m/3km SE of Appleby. NY 7018
Hilton of Cadboll H'land 87 B8 vil on E coast of Ross and Cromarty dist 1km NE of Balintore. NH 8776
Hilton Park Gtr Manchester 42 D1* loc in SW part of Prestwich. SD 8102
Himbleton H & W 26 D2 vil 4m/7km SE of Droitwich. SO 9458
Himley Staffs 35 E5 vil 5m/8km S of Wolverhampton. SO 8891
Hincaster Cumbria 53 E6* ham 5m/8km S of Kendal. SD 5084
Hinchcliffe Mill W Yorks 43 F1* loc 2km SW of Holmfirth. SE 1207
Hinchingbrooke House Cambs 29 F1 hse of many periods on W side of Huntingdon. Originally a nunnery. TL 2271
Hinchley Wood Surrey 19 F5* loc 1m E of Esher. TQ 1565
Hinckley Leics 36 A5 tn 12m/19km SW of Leicester. Industries include hosiery and footwear. SP 4293
Hindburn 47 F2 r rising on N slopes of Forest of Bowland, Lancs, and flowing NW into R Wenning to E of Hornby. SD 5968
Hinderclay Suffolk 31 E1 vil 6m/10km W of Diss. TM 0276
Hinderton Ches 41 H3/H4* loc 1m E of Neston. SJ 3078
Hinderwell N Yorks 55 F3 vil near North Sea Coast 7m/12km NW of Whitby. NZ 7916
Hindford Salop 34 A1 loc 2km NE of Whittington. SJ 3333
Hindhead Surrey 11 E2 loc in elevated position 2m/3km NW of Haslemere. Much NT property in surrounding countryside. SU 8835
Hindle Fold Lancs 48 A5 loc adjoining Gt Harwood. SD 7332
Hindley Gtr Manchester 42 B1 tn 2m/4km SE of Wigan. Industries include coal-mining, textiles, conveyor belting, paint, paper tubes, rubber. **H. Green** loc adjoining to SE. SD 6104
Hindley Nthmb 61 E5/F5* loc 3m/4km SE of Riding Mill. NZ 0459
Hindlip H & W 26 D2 vil 3m/5km NE of Worcester. SO 8758
Hindlow Hollow Derbys 43 F4* loc 4m/7km SE of Buxton. SK 1068
Hindolveston Norfolk 39 E2 vil 7m/11km SW of Holt. TG 0329
Hindon Som 7 G1* ham 2m/4km W of Minehead. SS 9346
Hindon Wilts 9 F1 vil 7m/11km NE of Shaftesbury. ST 9132
Hindringham Norfolk 39 E1/E2 vil 6m/9km NE of Fakenham. Moated 16c hall. TF 9836
Hindwell Brook 25 H2 r rising on Radnor Forest, Powys, and flowing E into R Lugg 3m/4km E of Presteigne. SO 3563
Hingham Norfolk 39 E4 vil 6m/9km W of Wymondham. TG 0202
Hinksey, North Oxon 18 A1 suburb 2m/3km W of Oxford. SP 4905
Hinksey, South Oxon 18 A1 vil 2km S of Oxford. SP 5004
Hinksford Staffs 35 E5* loc 4m/7km NW of Stourbridge. SO 8689

Hinnisdal H'land 78 B4 r running W into Loch Snizort, N coast of Skye, at entrance to Loch Snizort Beag. NG 3857
Hinstock Salop 34 D2 vil 5m/8km S of Mkt Drayton. SJ 6926
Hintlesham Suffolk 31 E4 vil 4m/7km E of Hadleigh. TM 0843
Hinton Avon 16 C4 ham 4m/6km NW of Marshfield. ST 7376
Hinton Glos 16 C2* loc near R Severn estuary 1km E of Sharpness. SO 6803
Hinton Hants 9 H4 loc 2m/3km W of New Milton. SZ 2095
Hinton H & W 25 H4 ham 8m/13km NW of Pontrilas. SO 3338
Hinton Northants 28 A2/B3 vil 6m/10km SW of Daventry. SP 5352
Hinton Salop 34 B3* ham 6m/9km SW of Shrewsbury. SJ 4008
Hinton Admiral Hants 9 H4 loc 2m/3km W of New Milton. SZ 2195
Hinton Ampner Hants 10 C2 ham 3m/5km S of New Alresford. SU 6027
Hinton Blewett Avon 16 B5 vil 2m/3km E of W Harptree. ST 5956
Hinton Charterhouse Avon 16 C5 vil 4m/7km S of Bath. ST 7758
Hinton, Great Wilts 16 D5 vil 3m/4km E of Trowbridge. ST 9059
Hinton-in-the-Hedges Northants 28 B4 vil 2m/3km W of Brackley. SP 5536
Hinton Marsh Hants 10 C2 loc 3m/5km S of New Alresford. SU 5827
Hinton Martell Dorset 9 G4 vil 4m/6km N of Wimborne. SU 0106
Hinton on the Green H & W 27 E4 vil 3m/4km S of Evesham. SP 0240
Hinton Parva Dorset 9 G4 ham 3m/4km N of Wimborne. SU 0004
Hinton Parva Wilts 17 F3 vil 5m/8km E of Swindon. SU 2283
Hinton St George Som 8 C3 vil 2m/4km NW of Crewkerne. ST 4212
Hinton St Mary Dorset 9 E3 vil 2km N of Sturminster Newton. ST 7812
Hinton Waldrist Oxon 17 G2 vil 6m/10km E of Faringdon. SU 3799
Hints Staffs 35 G4 vil 3m/5km W of Tamworth. SK 1503
Hinwick Beds 28 D2 ham 5m/8km SE of Wellingborough. SP 9361
Hinxhill Kent 13 F3 vil 3m/4km E of Ashford. TR 0442
Hinxton Cambs 29 H3 vil 2m/3km N of Gt Chesterford. TL 4945
Hinxworth Herts 29 F4 vil 4m/7km N of Baldock. TL 2340
Hipperholme W Yorks 48 D5 vil 2m/3km NW of Brighouse. SE 1325
Hipswell N Yorks 54 B5 vil on edge of Catterick Camp 2m/3km SE of Richmond. SE 1898
Hirael Gwynedd 40 C4* NE dist of Bangor. SH 5872
Hiraeth Dyfed 22 D4* loc 3m/5km NW of Whitland. SN 1721
Hirddu 33 F2 r running E into Lake Vyrnwy, Powys, 3m/5km NW of the dam. SH 9721
Hirin 24 D1 stream running from Llyn Cerrigllwydion Uchaf, Powys, through Llyn Cerrigllwydion Isaf to join R Elan 1m NW of head of Craig Goch Resr. SN 8972
Hirnant Powys 33 G2 ham 3m/5km NE of Lake Vyrnwy dam. SJ 0522
Hirnant 33 F1 r running N into R Dee 1km E of Llanfor, Gwynedd. SH 9436
Hirsel, The Borders 67 E4 seat of Douglas-Home family, 1m NW of Coldstream. NT 8240
Hirst Nthmb 61 G3 E dist of Ashington. NZ 2887
Hirst Courtney N Yorks 50 B5 vil 2m/4km NW of Snaith across R Aire. SE 6124
Hirst Head Nthmb 61 G3* loc on N side of Bedlington. NZ 2682
Hirta W Isles. See St Kilda.
Hirwaen Clwyd 41 G5 loc 2m/3km NE of Ruthin. SJ 1361
Hirwaun Mid Glam 15 E1 vil 4m/6km NW of Aberdare. Coal-mining, brick mnfre. Industrial estate 2m/3km W. SN 9505
Hirwaun 23 E2* r rising SE of Aberporth, Dyfed, and flowing S into R Teifi 3m/5km W of Newcastle Emlyn. SN 2542
Hiscott Devon 6 D3 ham 5m/7km S of Barnstaple. SS 5426
Hisehope Reservoir Durham 61 E6* small resr on Muggleswick Common 2m/4km S of Edmondbyers. NZ 0246
Histon Cambs 29 H2 suburb 3m/5km N of Cambridge. TL 4363
Hitcham Suffolk 30 D3/31 E3 vil 6m/10km NW of Hadleigh. Hams of **H. Causeway** and **H. Street** to NE and W respectively. Site of Roman bldg to NW. TL 9851
Hitchin Herts 29 F4/F5 tn 8m/13km NE of Luton. TL 1829
Hither Green London 20 A4* loc in borough of Lewisham 1m SE of Lewisham tn centre and 7m/11km SE of Charing Cross. TQ 3874
Hittisleigh Devon 7 E5 par containing locs of **H. Barton** and **H. Cross,** 7m/12km SW of Crediton. SX 7395
Hive Humberside 50 C5* ham adjoining Sandholme. SE 8230
Hiveland End Humberside 50 C5* loc adjoining Sandholme to W. SE 8230
Hivings, Great Bucks 18 D2* N dist of Chesham. SP 9503
Hixon Staffs 35 F2 vil 6m/9km NW of Rugeley. SK 0025
Hiz 29 F4* r rising on SW side of Hitchin, Herts, and flowing through the tn and northwards into R Ivel at Henlow 4m/6km S of Biggleswade, Beds. TL 1838
Hoaden Kent 13 G1* ham 2km NW of Ash. TR 2659
Hoar Cross Staffs 35 G2 ham 4m/6km E of Abbots Bromley. SK 1323
Hoaroak Water 7 E1* Exmoor stream flowing N to join Farley Water at Hillsford Br. SS 7447
Hoarwithy H & W 26 B4 vil on R Wye 5m/8km NW of Ross-on-Wye. SO 5429
Hoath Kent 13 G1 vil 3m/5km SE of Herne Bay. TR 2064
Hoathly, East E Sussex 12 B5 vil 5m/8km SE of Uckfield. TQ 5216
Hoathly, West W Sussex 12 A3 vil on a ridge 4m/6km SW of E Grinstead. TQ 3632
Hobbins, The Salop 34 D5* loc 2km E of Bridgnorth. SO 7393
Hobbles Green Suffolk 30 C3* loc 5m/8km NE of Haverhill. TL 7053
Hobbs Cross Essex 20 B1* loc 3m/5km E of Harlow. TL 4910
Hobbs Cross Essex 20 B2* loc 2m/3km SE of Epping. TQ 4799
Hobbs Point Dyfed 22 C5* headland on S side of estuary opp Neyland. SM 9604
Hobcarton Crag Cumbria 52 B3* mt escarpment to E of Hopegill Hd summit, N of Buttermere. Part owned by NT. NY 1822
Hobsick Notts 44 A6* loc 1km N of Brinsley. SK 4549
Hobson Durham 61 F5 vil 1km S of Burnopfield. NZ 1755
Hoby Leics 36 C3 vil 5m/9km W of Melton Mowbray. SK 6617
Hockenden London 20 B4* loc 2km W of Swanley. To N is loc of **Upr Hockenden.** TQ 4968
Hockerill Herts 29 H5* E dist of Bishop's Stortford. TL 4920
Hockering Norfolk 39 E3 vil 5m/9km E of E Dereham. **H. Heath** loc 1m NE. TG 0713
Hockerton Notts 44 B5 vil 2m/3km NE of Southwell. SK 7156
Hockham, Great Norfolk 38 D5 vil 6m/10km W of Attleborough. Loc of **Lit Hockham** 1m S. TL 9592
Hockholler Som 8 A2* ham 2m/3km E of Wellington. ST 1621
Hockley Ches 43 E3* loc adjoining Poynton to E. SJ 9283
Hockley Essex 20 D3 suburb 5m/8km NW of Southend-on-Sea. TQ 8492
Hockley Staffs 35 H4* loc in Tamworth 3m/4km SE of tn centre. SK 2200
Hockley W Midlands 35 H6* loc 4m/6km W of Coventry. SP 2780
Hockley Heath W Midlands 27 F2 vil 10m/15km NW of Warwick. SP 1572
Hockliffe Beds 28 D5 vil 4m/7km NW of Dunstable. TL 9726
Hockwold cum Wilton Norfolk 38 C5 vil 4m/6km W of Brandon. TL 7388
Hockworthy Devon 7 H3 vil 7m/11km W of Wellington. ST 0319
Hodbarrow Point Cumbria 46 C1 headland 2m/3km S of Millom. SD 1878
Hoddam Castle D & G 59 F4 ruined 15c stronghold of the Maxwells, in loop of R Annan 3m/4km W of Ecclefechan. NY 1573
Hodder 48 A4 r rising on Forest of Bowland, Lancs, and flowing S through Stocks Resr and Slaidburn into R Ribble 3m/5km SW of Clitheroe. SD 7138
Hoddesdon Herts 20 A1 tn 3m/5km S of Ware. TL 3709
Hoddlesden Lancs 48 A5* vil 2km E of Darwen. SD 7122
Hodge Beck 55 E6 r rising on Cleveland Hills, N Yorks, and flowing S down Bransdale and into R Dove 2m/3km S of Kirkbymoorside. SE 6983
Hodgefield Staffs 43 E5* loc 2km NW of Endon. SJ 9054
Hodgehill Ches 42 D4* loc 2km SW of Siddington. SJ 8369
Hodgehill W Midlands 35 G5* loc in Birmingham 4m/7km E of city centre. SP 1388
Hodgeston Dyfed 22 C5 vil 3m/5km E of Pembroke. SS 0399
Hodley Powys 33 H5 loc 4m/6km E of Newtown. SO 1691
Hodnet Salop 34 C2 vil 5m/9km SW of Mkt Drayton. 19c hall has landscaped gardens. Mound in park marks site of former cas. Loc of **Hodnetheath** 1km S. SJ 6128
Hodsall Street Kent 20 C5 ham 3m/5km N of Wrotham Heath. TQ 6262
Hodsock Notts 44 B3* ham 2km SW of Blyth. SK 6185
Hodson Wilts 17 F3* ham 3m/5km SE of Swindon. SU 1780
Hodthorpe Derbys 44 A3* vil 1m E of Whitwell. SK 5476
Hoe Norfolk 39 E3 ham 2m/3km N of E Dereham. TF 9916
Hoe Gate Hants 10 C3* loc 2km SW of Hambledon. SU 6213
Hoe Point Cornwall 2 B5* headland at W end of Praa Sands 6m/9km W of Helston. SW 5727
Hoe Rape Skye, H'land 79 A5 headland on W coast at S end of Moonen Bay. NG 1543
Hoff Cumbria 53 F3 loc on Hoff Beck 2m/3km S of Appleby. NY 6717
Hoff Beck 53 F3 r rising 2km S of Gt Asby, Cumbria, and flowing N through vil and into R Eden N of Colby. NY 6621
Hoffleet Stow Lincs 37 G1 loc 2km E of Bicker. TF 2437
Hogaland, East Shetland 89 E6* loc on Mainland 2km SW of Ollaberry. HU 3579
Hogaland, West Shetland. See Heogaland, West.
Hogganfield S'clyde 64 D2 locality in Glasgow 3m/5km E of city centre. **H. Loch** in H. Park contains island bird sanctuary. NS 6467
Hoggard's Green Suffolk 30 D3* loc 5m/8km S of Bury St Edmunds. TL 8856
Hoggeston Bucks 28 C5 vil 3m/5km SE of Winslow. SP 8025
Hoggington Wilts 16 D5* loc 2m/4km SW of Trowbridge. ST 8355
Hoggrill's End Warwicks 35 H5* ham 2m/4km NE of Coleshill. SP 2291
Hog Hatch Surrey 11 E1* loc 2km NW of Farnham. SU 8348
Hogh Bay Coll, S'clyde 68 A3 bay on NW coast 4m/6km W of Arinagour. NM 1657
Hoghton Lancs 47 F5 vil 5m/7km W of Blackburn. **H. Bottoms** loc 2km NE. **H. Tower** is hse dating from 16c. SD 6125
Hognaston Derbys 43 G5/G6 vil 4m/7km NE of Ashbourne. SK 2350
Hog's Back 11 F1 narrow chalk ridge in Surrey running W from R Wey valley at Guildford for about 7m/11km. A31 rd runs along top of ridge and Pilgrims' Way below it on S side. Ridge commands long views N and S. SU 9348
Hogsmill 19 F4 r rising near Ewell in Surrey and flowing N into R Thames at Kingston. TQ 1769
Hogspit Bottom Herts 19 E2* loc 4m/6km E of Chesham. TL 0101
Hogsthorpe Lincs 45 H4 vil 6m/10km N of Skegness. TF 5372
Holbeach Lincs 37 H2 small tn 7m/12km E of Spalding. **H. Bank** loc 2m/3km N. **H. Hurn** ham 3m/4km NE. TF 3524
Holbeach Clough Lincs 37 H2 loc 2km NW of Holbeach. TF 3427
Holbeach Drove Lincs 37 H3 vil 6m/9km E of Crowland. TF 3212
Holbeache H & W 34 D6/35 E6* loc 3m/5km NW of Kidderminster. SO 7879
Holbeach St Johns Lincs 37 H3 vil 4m/7km S of Holbeach. TF 3418
Holbeach St Marks Lincs 37 H2 vil 4m/7km N of Holbeach. TF 3731
Holbeach St Matthew Lincs 37 H2 ham 6m/9km NE of Holbeach. TF 4132
Holbeck Notts 44 A4 vil 4m/7km SW of Worksop. **H. Woodhouse** loc 1km SE. SK 5473
Holbeck W Yorks 49 E5* dist of Leeds 2km S of city centre. SE 2931
Holberrow Green H & W 27 E2 ham 4m/7km W of Alcester. SP 0259
Holbeton Devon 4 C5 vil 3m/4km SE of Yealmpton. SX 6150
Holborn London 19 G3* dist at S end of borough of Camden 1m NE of Charing Cross. TQ 3181
Holborn Head H'land 86 D1 headland on N coast of Caithness dist 2m/3km N of Thurso. Lighthouse 1km S at entrance to Thurso Bay. ND 1071
Holbrook Derbys 43 H6 vil 2m/4km SE of Belper. **H. Moor** loc 1km S. SK 3644
Holbrook Suffolk 31 F4 vil 5m/8km S of Ipswich. To S on R Stour estuary is **H. Bay,** extending from S of Harkstead to Stutton Ness. TM 1736
Holbrook S Yorks 43 H3* loc in Sheffield 7m/11km SE of city centre. SK 4481
Holbrook, Lower Suffolk 31 F4 loc 4m/7km W of Shotley Gate. TM 1735
Holbrooks W Midlands 35 H6* N dist of Coventry. SP 3383
Holburn Nthmb 67 G5 loc 3m/5km SE of Lowick. NU 0436
Holbury Hants 10 B4* loc adjoining Fawley oil refinery to W. SU 4303
Holcombe Devon 5 E3 vil 2m/3km NE of Teignmouth. SX 9574
Holcombe Gtr Manchester 47 H6* loc adjoining Ramsbottom to W. SD 7816
Holcombe Som 16 B6* vil 4m/6km S of Radstock. ST 6749
Holcombe Brook Gtr Manchester 47 H6 loc 2km SW of Ramsbottom. SD 7715
Holcombe Burnell Devon 7 F5* loc 4m/6km W of Exeter. SX 8591
Holcombe Rogus Devon 7 H3 vil 5m/9km W of Wellington. ST 0518
Holcot Beds 28 D4* loc 4m/6km N of Woburn. SP 9438
Holcot Northants 28 C1 vil 6m/10km NE of Northampton. SP 7969
Holden Lancs 48 A3/B3 ham 1km W of Bolton by Bowland. SD 7749
Holdenby Northants 28 C1 vil 6m/10km NW of Northampton. SP 6967
Holden Fold Gtr Manchester 42 D1* loc 1km SW of Royton. SD 9106
Holden Gate W Yorks 48 B5* loc on Bacup-Todmorden rd 3m/4km W of Todmorden. SD 8923
Holden Wood Reservoir Lancs 48 A5* resr 1m SW of Haslingden. SD 7722
Holderness Humberside 51 E4/H6 flat, low peninsula extending SE from the Yorkshire Wolds between North Sea and R Humber and terminating in Spurn Hd. TA 22
Holder's Green Essex 30 B5* ham 2m/3km SE of Thaxted. TL 6328
Holders Hill London 19 F3* loc in borough of Barnet 1m NE of Hendon. TQ 2490
Holdfast H & W 26 D4* loc 4m/7km NW of Tewkesbury. SO 8537
Holdgate Salop 34 C5 vil 8m/12km SW of Much Wenlock. SO 5689
Holdingham Lincs 45 E6 ham 1m NW of Sleaford. TF 0547
Holditch Dorset 8 B4 ham 4m/6km NE of Axminster. ST 3402
Holdsworth W Yorks 48 D5* loc 3m/4km N of Halifax. SE 0829
Hole Devon 6 C4* ham 5m/8km E of Holsworthy. SS 4205
Hole Devon 8 A3* loc 6m/10km N of Honiton. ST 1610
Hole Bottom W Yorks 48 C5* loc 1km N of Todmorden. SD 9325
Hole Brook 6 D4* stream rising to S of Sampford Courtenay, Devon, and flowing N past the vil, then NW into R Okement just W of Monkokehampton. SS 5705
Holehaven Creek Essex 20 D3 inlet on W side of Canvey I. TQ 7583
Holehouse Derbys 43 E2* loc 1km SW of Charlesworth. SK 0092
Hole-in-the-Wall H & W 26 B4* ham on left bank of R Wye 3m/5km N of Ross-on-Wye. SO 6128
Holes Bay Dorset 9 G5* inlet off N side of Poole Harbour crossed by rly on causeway. SZ 0091
Hole's Hole Devon 4 B4* ham on banks of R Tamar 6m/10km W of Yelverton. SX 4365
Holes of Scraada Shetland 89 D6* landward end of subterranean cavern to which sea penetrates and from open top of which it may be observed. Situated on Esha Ness, Mainland. HU 2179
Hole, South Devon 6 B3* loc near coast 9m/14km N of Bude. SS 2220
Hole Street W Sussex 11 G3 loc 1m SE of Ashington and 3m/5km NW of Steyning. TQ 1414
Holford Som 7 H1 vil 3m/4km NW of Nether Stowey. ST 1541
Holgate N Yorks 50 B3 dist of York 2km W of city centre. SE 5851

Holker Cumbria 47 E1 vil 1km N of Cark. SD 3677
Holkham Norfolk 38 D1 ham 2m/3km W of Wells. **H. Bay** off coast to N. **H. Hall,** 18c hse by Kent in Palladian style, stands nearly 1m SW in landscaped grnds with lake. TF 8943
Hollacombe Devon 6 C5 vil 2m/4km E of Holsworthy. SS 3703
Hollacombe Devon 7 F5* loc 2m/4km W of Honiton. SS 8000
Hollacombe Hill Devon 4 B5* loc 4m/6km SE of Plymouth across R Plym estuary. SX 5250
Holland Surrey 20 A6* loc adjoining Oxted to S. TQ 4051
Holland Brook 31 F6* stream rising about 2m/3km S of Manningtree, Essex, and flowing SE into North Sea at Holland Haven 3m/5km NE of Clacton. TM 2117
Holland Fen Lincs 45 F6* vil 7m/11km NW of Boston. TF 2349
Holland, Great Essex 31 F6 vil 4m/6km NE of Clacton-on-Sea. TM 2119
Holland Isle D & G 58 C4 island in course of R Dee 2m/3km W of Parton. NX 6669
Holland Lees Lancs 42 B1* loc 2km W of Shevington. SD 5208
Holland Main Drain, South 38 A3* fenland drainage channel running from Cowbit, Lincs, to R Nene 1m S of Sutton Br. TF 2047
Holland-on-Sea Essex 31 F6* NE dist of Clacton-on-Sea. TM 2016
Holland Park London 19 F3* park and dist around it in borough of Kensington and Chelsea, 3m/5km W of Charing Cross. TQ 2479
Hollands, Great Berks 18 D4* SW dist of Bracknell. SU 8567
Holland, South 119 admin dist of Lincs.
Hollandstoun Orkney 89 C5* loc near SW end of island of N Ronaldsay. HY 7553
Hollesley Suffolk 31 G4 vil 6m/9km SE of Woodbridge across R Deben. To SE, **H. Bay** extends from Orford Ness SW to Bawdsey. TM 3544
Hollicombe Devon 5 E4* N dist of Paignton. SX 8962
Hollin Busk S Yorks 43 G2* loc adjoining Stocksbridge to S. SK 2797
Hollingbourne Kent 21 E6 vil 5m/8km E of Maidstone. TQ 8455
Hollingbury E Sussex 12 A5 N dist of Brighton. **H. Camp** is an ancient hill fort. TQ 3108
Hollin Green Ches 42 B5/B6* loc 4m/6km W of Nantwich. SJ 5952
Hollingrove E Sussex 12 C4* loc between Brightling and Darwell Resr. TQ 6920
Hollington Derbys 43 G6 vil 5m/9km SE of Ashbourne. SK 2239
Hollington Staffs 35 F1 vil 4m/6km NW of Uttoxeter. SK 0538
Hollingwood Estate Derbys 43 H4* suburban loc 2km W of Staveley. SK 4174
Hollingworth Gtr Manchester 43 E2 loc 2m/4km NW of Glossop. SK 0096
Hollingworth Lake Gtr Manchester 48 C6 lake 1m S of Littleborough. SD 9314
Hollin Hill N Yorks 54 D4/D5* loc 2km SE of Swainby. NZ 4900
Hollinlane Ches 42 D3* loc 2m/3km N of Wilmslow. SJ 8384
Hollins Derbys 43 G4* loc 4m/6km W of Chesterfield. SK 3271
Hollins Gtr Manchester 42 D1 loc in Bury 2m/3km S of tn centre. SD 8108
Hollins Staffs 42 D5* loc adjoining Kidsgrove to S. SJ 8353
Hollins Staffs 43 E6* loc 3m/4km N of Cheadle. SJ 9947
Hollinsclough Staffs 43 F4 ham 2m/3km NW of Longnor. SK 0666
Hollins End S Yorks 43 H3* loc in Sheffield 3m/5km SE of city centre. SK 3884
Hollins Green Ches 42 C2 vil 6m/10km E of Warrington. SJ 6991
Hollins Lane Lancs 47 F3 loc 4m/6km N of Garstang. SD 4951
Hollinswood Salop 34 D3* loc 2km SW of Oakengates. SJ 6909
Hollinthorpe W Yorks 49 F5* loc 1m N of Swillington. SE 3831
Hollinwood Gtr Manchester 42 D1 loc in Oldham 2m/3km SW of tn centre. SD 9002
Hollinwood Salop 34 C1 loc 4m/6km S of Whitchurch. SJ 5236
Hollocombe Devon 7 E4 vil 4m/6km SW of Chulmleigh. **Hollocombe Tn** ham to NW. SS 6311
Holloway Berks 18 C3* loc 3m/5km W of Maidenhead. SU 8480
Holloway Derbys 43 G5 vil 3m/5km SE of Matlock. SK 3256
Holloway London 19 G3* loc in borough of Islington 3m/5km N of Charing Cross. Women's prison. Loc of **Upr Holloway** 1m NW. TQ 3085
Holloway End W Midlands 35 E5* loc in N part of Stourbridge. SO 8985
Hollowell Northants 28 C1 vil 8m/13km NW of Northampton. **Hollowell Resr** to N. SP 6871
Hollow Meadows S Yorks 43 G2* loc 7m/11km W of Sheffield. SK 2488
Holl Reservoir Fife 73 E4 small resr 2m/3km NW of Leslie. NO 2203
Holly Bank Gtr Manchester 43 E1* loc 1m N of Mossley. SD 9603
Holly Bank W Midlands 35 F4* loc 2km S of Brownhills. SK 0503
Holly Bush Clwyd 42 A6* loc 2km SE of Bangor Is-coed. SJ 4144
Hollybush Gwent 15 F1* vil 4m/6km S of Ebbw Vale. SO 1602
Hollybush H & W 26 C4 vil near S end of Malvern Hills 3m/5km E of Ledbury. SO 7636
Hollybush S'clyde 56 D3 vil 3m/5km NW of Patna. NS 3914
Hollybush Staffs 35 E1* loc in Stoke-on-Trent 1m S of Fenton. SJ 8843
Hollybush Corner Suffolk 30 D2* loc 1km S of Bradfield St George. TL 9159
Holly Cross Berks 18 C3* loc 3m/5km N of Twyford. SU 8080
Holly End Cambs 38 A4* loc 3m/5km SE of Wisbech. TF 4906
Holly Green Bucks 18 C2* loc 2m/4km W of Princes Risborough. SP 7703
Holly Green H & W 26 D3 ham 1km NE of Upton upon Severn across r. SO 8641
Hollyhurst Ches 34 C1* loc 3m/5km NE of Whitchurch. SJ 5744
Hollym Humberside 51 G5 vil 2m/3km S of Withernsea. TA 3425
Hollywater Hants 11 E2* loc 1m SE of Bordon Camp and 3m/4km NW of Liphook. SU 8034
Hollywood H & W 35 G6* loc 6m/10km S of Birmingham. SP 0877
Holm W Isles 88 C2* loc on Lewis 2m/4km SE of Stornoway. **Holm Pt** is headland 1m SW at entrance to Stornoway Harbour. **Holm I.** is small uninhabited island to E of Holm Pt. **H. Bay** is small bay to E of Holm I. NB 4531
Holman Clavel Som 8 A3* loc in Blackdown Hills 2m/3km S of Pitminster. ST 2216
Holmbridge W Yorks 43 F1 vil 2m/3km SW of Holmfirth. SE 1206
Holmbury St Mary Surrey 11 G1 vil in wooded area 5m/8km SW of Dorking. TQ 1144
Holmbush Cornwall 3 E3 loc on E outskirts of St Austell. SX 0452
Holmcroft Staffs 35 E2* N dist of Stafford. SJ 9125
Holme Cambs 37 G5 vil 7m/11km S of Peterborough. **H. Fen Nature Reserve** to NE. TL 1987
Holme Cumbria 47 F1 vil 5m/9km N of Carnforth. SD 5278
Holme Humberside 44 D1* loc 3m/5km SE of Scunthorpe. SE 9206
Holme Lancs 48 B5* loc 1m SE of Haslingden. SD 7922
Holme Notts 44 C5 vil 3m/5km N of Newark-on-Trent. SK 8059
Holme N Yorks 54 C6 ham 1m SE of Pickhill. SE 3582
Holme W Yorks 43 F1 vil 3m/4km SW of Holmfirth. SE 1206
Holme 48 D6* r rising SW of Holmfirth, W Yorks, and flowing NE to Holmfirth, then N into R Colne at Huddersfield. SE 1415
Holmebridge Dorset 9 F5* loc 2m/4km W of Wareham. SY 8987
Holme Chapel Lancs 48 B5 vil 4m/6km SE of Burnley. SD 8728
Holme, East Dorset 9 F5 ham in R Frome valley 2m/3km W of Wareham. SY 8985
Holme Green Berks 18 C4* ham 2km SE of Wokingham. SU 8267
Holme Green N Yorks 49 G4* ham just S of Appleton Roebuck. SE 5541
Holme Hale Norfolk 38 D4 vil 5m/7km E of Swaffham. TF 8807
Holme Island Cumbria 47 E1* peninsula on right bank of R Kent estuary 1m E of Grange-over-Sands. SD 4278
Holme Lacy H & W 26 B4 vil 4m/6km SE of Hereford. SO 5535
Holme Marsh H & W 25 H3 vil 3m/5km SE of Kington. SO 3454
Holme Mills Cumbria 47 F1* loc 1km S of Holme. SD 5278
Holme Moss 43 F1 moorland area on borders of Derbys and W Yorks at top of pass beside Holmfirth-Woodhead rd, with TV transmitting stn. SE 0904
Holme next the Sea Norfolk 38 C1 vil 3m/4km NE of Hunstanton. TF 7043
Holme, North N Yorks 55 E6* loc 3m/5km S of Kirkbymoorside. SE 6981
Holme on the Wolds Humberside 50 D4/51 E4 vil 6m/10km NE of Mkt Weighton. SE 9646
Holme Pierrepont Notts 36 C1 vil 4m/6km E of Nottingham. SK 6239
Holmer H & W 26 A3 N suburb of Hereford. SO 5042
Holmer Green Bucks 18 D2 vil 4m/6km NE of High Wycombe. SU 9097
Holmes Lancs 47 E6* loc adjoining Mere Brow to N. SD 4219
Holme St Cuthbert Cumbria 52 B1 ham 3m/4km NW of Westnewton. NY 1047
Holmescales Cumbria 53 E6* loc 4m/7km SE of Kendal. SD 5587
Holmes Chapel Ches 42 D4 vil 4m/6km E of Middlewich. SJ 7667
Holmesfield Derbys 43 G3 vil 2m/3km W of Dronfield. **H. Common** loc adjoining to W. SK 3277
Holmes House N Yorks 50 C5* 17c brick hse 2km SE of S Duffield. SE 6932
Holme Slack Lancs 47 F5* loc in NE part of Preston. SD 5531
Holme, South N Yorks 50 C1* loc 2m/3km N of Slingsby. SE 7077
Holmes's Hill E Sussex 12 B5 loc 4m/7km NW of Hailsham. TQ 5312
Holmeswood Lancs 47 E6 vil 6m/9km N of Ormskirk. SD 4316
Holme, The N Yorks 49 E2* loc 2km W of Birstwith. SE 2159
Holmethorpe Surrey 19 G6* NE dist of Reigate. TQ 2851
Holme upon Spalding Moor Humberside 50 C4 vil 5m/8km SW of Mkt Weighton. SE 8138
Holme, West Dorset 9 F5 loc 3m/4km W of Wareham. SY 8885
Holmewood Derbys 43 H4* vil 2km W of Heath. SK 4265
Holme Wood S Yorks 44 B1* loc 2m/3km E of Armthorpe. SE 6505
Holmfirth W Yorks 43 F1 tn on R Holme 5m/8km S of Huddersfield. Textiles, engineering. SE 1408
Holmhead S'clyde 56 E2* loc forming part of Cumnock, qv. NS 5620
Holm, Inner and Outer Orkney 89 A6* two islets on E side of Stromness Harbour, Mainland. HY 2508
Holm Island Skye, H'land 78 D4 islet off E coast 6m/9km NE of Portree. NG 5251
Holm, Little Shetland 89 E6* rock island in Yell Sound 3m/4km SE of Burra Voe. HU 4086
Holm of Boray Orkney 89 B6* islet off S coast of island of Gairsay. HY 4520
Holm of Dalry D & G 58 C3/C4* low-lying area in loop of Water of Ken on SW side of vil of Dalry. NX 6180
Holm of Faray Orkney 89 B5* narrow uninhabited island less than 1m in length N to S lying between island of Faray to S and Westray to N. HY 5238
Holm of Grimbister Orkney 89 B6* small uninhabited island in Bay of Firth 2km E of Finstown. HY 3713
Holm of Gunnister Shetland. See Gunnister.
Holm of Heogland Shetland 89 F5* small island at S end of Unst 1m W of Uyea. HU 5799
Holm of Howton Orkney 89 A7* small uninhabited island at entrance to Bay of Howton, 2m/3km NE of coast of Hoy across Bring Deeps. HY 3103
Holm of Huip Orkney 89 C6* small uninhabited island off N coast of island of Stronsay across **Huip Sound.** HY 6231
Holm of Melby Shetland. See Melby.
Holm of Noss Shetland 89 F7* flat-topped turf-covered sheer column of rock off SE coast of Isle of Noss. Height about 160 ft or 50 metres. HU 5539
Holm of Odness Orkney 89 C6* islet off E coast of Stronsay on S side of entrance to Mill Bay. HY 6926
Holm of Papa Orkney 89 B5* small uninhabited island off E coast of Papa Westray. Large chambered cairn (A.M.) with triple central chamber. HY 5051
Holm of Scockness Orkney 89 B6* small uninhabited island at N end of Rousay Sound between islands of Rousay and Egilsay. HY 4531
Holmpton Humberside 51 G5 vil near coast 3m/5km SE of Withernsea. TA 3623
Holmrook Cumbria 52 B5 vil 3m/4km E of Seascale. SD 0799
Holmsey Green Suffolk 38 B6* loc adjoining Beck Row to E. TL 6977
Holmsgarth Shetland 89 E7* loc on Mainland adjoining Lerwick to NW. HU 4642
Holmside Durham 54 B1 loc 6m/9km NW of Durham. NZ 2149
Holmsleigh Green Devon 8 A4* ham 3m/5km NE of Honiton. ST 2002
Holms, North Shetland 89 F5* small rocky island off W coast of Unst. **S Holms** is smaller island 1m S. HP 5711
Holms of Ire Orkney 89 C5* two small islands off Whal Pt at NW end of island of Sanday. HY 6446
Holmwood, North Surrey 19 F6 S dist of Dorking. TQ 1647
Holmwood, South Surrey 19 F6 vil 3m/4km S of Dorking. TQ 1745
Holmwrangle Cumbria 60 B6 loc 2m/3km NW of Ainstable. NY 5148
Holne Devon 4 D4 vil on E side of Dartmoor above R Dart, 3m/5km W of Ashburton. Birthplace of Charles Kingsley, 1819. **Holne Wds** (NT). SX 7069
Holnest Dorset 8 D3 ham 5m/7km SE of Sherborne. ST 6509
Holnicote Som 7 G1* ham to NE of **H. Estate** (NT) and 2m/3km E of Porlock. SS 9146
Holoman Bay Skye, H'land 79 D5 bay on W coast of Raasay 3m/5km from S end of island. **Holoman I.** is islet at N end of bay. NG 5439
Holsworthy Devon 6 C5 tn 9m/14km E of Bude. SS 3403
Holsworthy Beacon Devon 6 C4 ham 3m/5km N of Holsworthy. SS 3508
Holt Clwyd 42 A5 vil on W bank of R Dee 5m/8km E of Wrexham. SJ 4154
Holt Dorset 9 G4 vil 3m/4km NE of Wimborne. SU 0203
Holt H & W 26 D2* ham 5m/8km N of Worcester. SO 8262
Holt Merseyside 42 B2* loc in NW part of Rainhill. SJ 4891
Holt Norfolk 39 E1 small tn 10m/15km W of Cromer. Gresham's School, boys' public school founded as grammar school in 1555. TG 0738
Holt Wilts 16 D5 vil 2m/4km N of Trowbridge. The Courts (NT), 18c hse. ST 8561
Holtby N Yorks 50 B3 vil 5m/8km E of York. SE 6754
Holt End Hants 10 D1 loc 1km SW of Bentworth and 3m/5km W of Alton. SU 6639
Holt End H & W 27 E1 vil 3m/4km NE of Redditch. SP 0769
Holt Fleet H & W 26 C2/D2 loc on R Severn 5m/8km W of Droitwich. SO 8263
Holt Green Lancs 42 A1* loc adjoining Aughton to S. SD 3904
Holt Heath Dorset 9 G4 loc 4m/7km NE of Wimborne. SU 0604
Holt Heath H & W 26 C1 vil on R Severn 5m/9km NW of Worcester. SO 8163
Holton Lincs 45 E3 vil 2m/4km NW of Wragby. TF 1378
Holton Oxon 18 B1 vil 6m/9km E of Oxford. SP 6006
Holton Som 9 E2 vil 2m/3km SW of Wincanton. ST 6826
Holton Suffolk 31 G1 vil 1m E of Halesworth. Loc of **Upr Holton** 1km N. TM 4077
Holton le Clay Humberside 45 G1 vil 4m/7km S of Grimsby. TA 2802
Holton le Moor Lincs 45 E2 vil 3m/5km SW of Caistor. TF 0897
Holton St Mary Suffolk 31 E4 vil 4m/7km SE of Hadleigh. TM 0536
Holt Street Kent 13 G2* loc adjoining Nonington to S, 4m/6km S of Wingham. TR 2551
Holt, The Berks 18 C4* ham 2m/3km NE of Twyford. SU 8078
Holt Town Gtr Manchester 42 D2* loc in Manchester 2km E of city centre. SJ 8698
Holtwood Berks 17 H5* loc 4m/7km SW of Newbury. SU 4164
Holt Wood Dorset 9 G4* loc 1m E of Hinton Martell. SU 0306
Holtye E Sussex 12 B3 loc 4m/7km E of E Grinstead. TQ 4539
Holway Clwyd 41 G4* loc adjoining Holywell to NW. SJ 1776
Holwell Dorset 9 E3 vil in Blackmoor Vale 5m/8km SE of Sherborne. ST 7011

Holwell Herts 29 F4 vil 3m/5km N of Hitchin. TL 1633
Holwell Leics 36 C2 ham 3m/5km N of Melton Mowbray. SK 7323
Holwell Oxon 17 F1 vil 3m/4km SW of Burford. SP 2309
Holwick Durham 53 H2 ham 3m/5km NW of Middleton in Teesdale. NY 9026
Holybourne Hants 10 D1 vil 2m/3km NE of Alton. SU 3741
Holy Cross H & W 35 E6 loc 4m/6km S of Stourbridge. SO 9278
Holy Cross Tyne & Wear 61 G4* loc in N Tyneside dist 1km NE of Wallsend. NZ 3167
Holyfield Essex 20 A2* loc 2m/3km N of Waltham Abbey. TL 3803
Holyhead (Caergybi) Gwynedd 40 A3 port and industrial tn on Holy I., Anglesey, of which it is the principal tn. Industries include engineering, aluminium smelting. Passenger terminal for Republic of Ireland. SH 2482
Holyhead Bay Gwynedd 40 A3 bay on which Holyhead, Anglesey, is situated, extending from North Stack to Carmel Hd. SH 28,29
Holyhead Mountain (Mynydd Twr) Gwynedd 40 A3 granite hill at NW corner of Holy I., Anglesey, 2m/3km W of Holyhead. Quarries. Ancient British fort of Caer y Twr (A.M.). SH 2182
Holy Island (Ynys Gybi) Gwynedd 40 A3, A4 island on which Holyhead is situated, about 12km long from NW to SE and from 1km to 5km wide, lying off W coast of main island of Anglesey. Connected to main island by a rd br and a rd and rly embankment. SH 27,28
Holy Island Nthmb 67 G4 island off coast 5m/8km N of Belford. Rd connection with mainland by causeway passable at low tide. Vil at S end of island (which is 3m/5km E to W and 2km N to S) contains ruins of 11c priory (A.M.). Restored 16c cas (NT) 1km E of vil. NU 1242
Holy Island S'clyde 63 G4 barely inhabited island lying across entrance to Lamlash Bay, E coast of Arran. Measures 2m/3km N to S and about 1km across. Rises to 1030 ft or 314 metres. Lighthouses at S end and on E coast 1km NE. NS 0632
Holy Loch S'clyde 70 D6 inlet in Argyll running up to Ardbeg from between Strone Pt and Hunter's Quay, N of Dunoon. NS 1780
Holymoorside Derbys 43 H4 vil 3m/5km W of Chesterfield. SK 3369
Holyport Berks 18 D4* vil 2m/3km S of Maidenhead. SU 8977
Holyrood Palace Lothian. See Edinburgh.
Holystone Nthmb 61 E2 ham 3m/5km SE of Alwinton. NT 9502
Holytown S'clyde 65 E3 vil 2m/4km NE of Hamilton. Newhouse Industrial Estate 1km NE. NS 7660
Holywell Cambs 29 G1 vil on R Ouse 2m/3km E of St Ives. TL 3370
Holywell (Treffynnon) Clwyd 41 G4 rayon, woollen, and paper mnfg tn near R Dee estuary 14m/23km NW of Chester. Holy well, sacred to the name of St Winefride. SJ 1875
Holywell Cornwall 2 C3* vil near N coast 3m/5km N of Perranporth. To NW, **H. Bay,** extending from Kelsey Hd southwards to Penhale Pt. SW 7658
Holywell Dorset 8 D4 ham 2m/3km E of Evershot. ST 5904
Holywell Nthmb 61 G4 loc adjoining Seaton Delaval to SE. **E** and **W Holywell** locs to S. NZ 3174
Holywell Green W Yorks 48 D6 vil 4m/6km S of Halifax. SE 0819
Holywell Lake Som 7 H3* vil 2m/3km W of Wellington. ST 1020
Holywell Reservoir Devon 7 F2* small resr on Exmoor 5m/7km NE of S Molton. SS 7630
Holywell Row Suffolk 38 B6* vil 2m/3km N of Mildenhall. TL 7077
Holywood D & G 59 E3 vil 4m/6km NW of Dumfries. NX 9480
Home End Cambs 29 H2 SE end of Fulbourn. TL 5255
Home Mere Norfolk 38 D5 small lake 4m/7km NE of Thetford. TL 8989
Homer Salop 34 C4 ham 1m N of Much Wenlock. SJ 6101
Homer Green Merseyside 41 H1* ham 3m/5km NE of Crosby. SD 3402
Homersfield Suffolk 39 F6 vil on R Waveney 4m/7km SW of Bungay. TM 2885
Homerton London 20 A3* loc in borough of Hackney 1km E of Hackney tn centre. TQ 3584
Hom Green H & W 26 B5* loc 2m/3km SW of Ross-on-Wye. SO 5822
Homildon Hill Nthmb 67 F5* site of battle in 1402 in which English defeated Scots, 2m/3km NW of Wooler. NT 9629
Homington Wilts 9 H2 vil on R Ebble 3m/5km SW of Salisbury. SU 1226
Honddu 25 E5/F5 r rising on Mynydd Epynt, Powys, and flowing S into R Usk at Brecon. SO 0428
Honddu 25 H5 r rising in Black Mts on S slope of Hay Bluff, Powys, and flowing S by Llanthony to Llanvihangel Crucorney, then N into R Monnow 1km N of Pandy, Gwent. SO 3323
Honeyborough Dyfed 22 C5 loc 1km N of Neyland. SM 9506
Honeybourne H & W. See Church Honeybourne, Cow Honeybourne.
Honeychurch Devon 7 E5 vil 3m/5km S of Winkleigh. SS 6202
Honey Street Wilts 17 E5* ham astride Kennet and Avon Canal 4m/6km W of Pewsey. SU 1061
Honey Tye Suffolk 30 D4 ham 2m/3km NW of Nayland. TL 9535
Honicknowle Devon 4 B5* N dist of Plymouth, 3m/5km from city centre. SX 4658
Honiley Warwicks 27 F1* ham 3m/5km W of Kenilworth. SP 2472
Honing Norfolk 39 G2 vil 3m/5km NE of N Walsham. TG 3227
Honingham Norfolk 39 E3/E4 vil 8m/13km W of Norwich. **H. Thorpe** loc adjoining Colton 2km S. TG 1011
Honington Lincs 37 E1 vil 5m/8km N of Grantham. SK 9443
Honington Suffolk 30 D1 vil 3m/5km NW of Ixworth. TL 9174
Honington Warwicks 27 G3 vil 2km N of Shipston on Stour. SP 2642
Honister Pass Cumbria 52 C3* pass 2km W of Seatoller carrying rd from Seatoller to Buttermere. NY 2213
Honiton Devon 8 A4 tn on R Otter 16m/24km E of Exeter. ST 1600
Honkley Clwyd 42 A5* loc 2m/3km NW of Rossett. SJ 3459
Honley W Yorks 48 D6 tn 3m/5km S of Huddersfield. SE 1311
Honnington Salop 34 D3 loc 3m/5km SW of Newport. SJ 7215
Honor Oak London 20 A4* loc in borough of Southwark 5m/8km SE of Charing Cross. TQ 3574
Hoo Kent 13 H1* loc 1m W of Minster. TR 2964
Hoo Kent 20 D4 suburban loc 4m/6km NE of Strood. TQ 7872
Hoo Suffolk 31 F2 ham 4m/6km NW of Wickham Mkt. Ham of **Hoo Green** adjoins to S. TM 2558
Hoober S Yorks 43 H2* loc 4m/6km NW of Rotherham. SK 4097
Hoobrook H & W 26 D1* loc 1m S of Kidderminster. SO 8374
Hood Green S Yorks 43 G1* loc 3m/5km SW of Barnsley. SE 3102
Hood Hill S Yorks 43 H2* loc 2km W of Wentworth. SK 3697
Hood Tarn Cumbria 53 E6* small lake 1m SE of Old Hutton across M6 motorway. SD 5787
Hooe Devon 4 B5 S dist of Plymouth to S of R Plym. SX 5052
Hooe E Sussex 12 C5 vil at E edge of Pevensey Levels 4m/6km W of Bexhill. Ham of **H. Common** 1km N. TQ 6809
Hoo Green Ches 42 C3 ham 4m/6km NW of Knutsford. SJ 7182
Hoohill Lancs 46 D4* dist of Blackpool 2km NE of tn centre. SD 3237
Hoo Hole W Yorks 48 C5* loc 1km S of Mytholmroyd. SE 0025
Hook Cambs 37 H5* loc 2m/3km SE of March. TL 4293
Hook Dyfed 22 C4 vil 3m/5km SE of Haverfordwest. **E Hook** loc 1m E. SM 9711
Hook Hants 10 C4* ham 4m/7km W of Fareham. SU 5005
Hook Hants 18 C5 vil 6m/9km E of Basingstoke. SU 7254
Hook Humberside 50 C5 vil 2km NE of Goole. SE 7625
Hook London 19 F5 loc in borough of Kingston 3m/5km S of Kingston tn centre. TQ 1764
Hook Wilts 17 E3 ham 2m/3km NE of Wootton Bassett. SU 0784
Hookagate Salop 34 B3 ham 3m/5km SW of Shrewsbury. SJ 4609
Hooke Dorset 8 D4 vil 4m/7km NW of Maiden Newton. ST 5300
Hook End Oxon 18 B3* loc 4m/6km NE of Pangbourne. SU 6681
Hooker Gate Tyne & Wear 61 F5* loc adjoining High Spen to S, 2km W of Rowlands Gill. NZ 1459
Hookgate Staffs 34 D1 loc 7m/11km NW of Eccleshall. SJ 7435
Hook Green Kent 12 C3 ham 2km W of Lamberhurst. TQ 6535
Hook Green Kent 20 B4* loc 2m/3km SW of Dartford. TQ 5271
Hook Green Kent 20 C4 ham 2m/4km S of Northfleet. TQ 6170
Hook Hill Warwicks 35 G4* loc in Sutton Coldfield 3m/5km NW of tn centre. SK 1000
Hookmoor Brook 6 D5 stream rising to W of Okehampton, Devon, and flowing N into R Lew at Gribbleford Br, 2m/3km SW of Hatherleigh. SS 5201
Hook Norton Oxon 27 G4 vil 5m/8km NE of Chipping Norton. SP 3533
Hook Park Hants 10 C4* loc 1m S of Warsash and 3m/4km SW of Park Gate. SU 4904
Hook Point, South Dyfed 22 B5* headland on N shore of Milford Haven 2m/4km W of Milford Haven tn. Oil refinery to NE, with jetty terminal. SM 8605
Hook's Cross Herts 29 G5* ham 4m/6km SE of Stevenage. TL 2720
Hookway Devon 7 F5 ham 2km SE of Crediton. SX 8598
Hookwood W Sussex 11 H1 loc adjoining Horley to W. TQ 2642
Hoole Ches 42 A4 NE dist of Chester. SJ 4267
Hooley Surrey 19 G5* loc 4m/6km SW of Purley. TQ 2856
Hooley Bridge Gtr Manchester 42 D1 loc on R Roch 3m/5km W of Rochdale. SD 8511
Hooley Brow Gtr Manchester 42 D1* loc adjoining Heywood to N. SD 8511
Hooley Hill Gtr Manchester 43 E2* loc 2km SW of Dukinfield. SJ 9296
Hoo Meavy Devon 4 B4* loc 6m/10km SE of Tavistock. SX 5365
Hoop Gwent 16 A1* loc 3m/5km S of Monmouth. SO 5107
Hooper's Point Dyfed 22 A5 headland at SE end of **Marloes Bay,** extending NW to Gateholm and enclosing Marloes Sands. Headland is 3m/4km N of St Ann's Hd. SM 7806
Hooton Ches 42 A3* loc 3m/4km NW of Ellesmere Port. SJ 3678
Hooton Levitt S Yorks 44 A2* vil 1km SW of Maltby. SK 5191
Hooton Pagnell S Yorks 44 A1 vil 7m/11km NW of Doncaster. Hall has 14c gatehouse. SE 4808
Hooton Roberts S Yorks 44 A2 vil 4m/7km NE of Rotherham. SK 4897
Hopcroft's Holt Oxon 27 H5 loc 4m/7km S of Deddington. SP 4625
Hope Clwyd 41 H5 vil 5m/8km N of Wrexham. SJ 3058
Hope Derbys 43 F3 vil in Hope Valley 4m/6km NW of Hathersage. SK 1783
Hope Devon 4 D6 small resort just N of Bolt Tail, consisting of **Outer H.** and **Inner H.** The cove between the vil and Bolt Tail is known as **H. Cove.** SX 6740
Hope Powys 34 A4* loc 2m/3km E of Welshpool across R Severn. SJ 2507
Hope Salop 34 A4 loc 12m/19km SW of Shrewsbury. SJ 3401
Hope Staffs 43 F5* ham 1km SW of Alstonefield. SK 1255
Hope 84 E2 r in Sutherland dist, H'land, running N from Loch Hope into Loch Eriboll and thence into Atlantic Ocean. NC 4762
Hope Bagot Salop 26 B1 ham 4m/6km N of Tenbury Wells. SO 5873
Hope Bowdler Salop 34 B5 vil 2m/3km SE of Church Stretton. SO 4792
Hope Dale Salop 34 B5 valley below E slope of Wenlock Edge. SO 4887
Hope End Green Essex 30 A5 ham 4m/6km W of Gt Dunmow. TL 5720
Hope Forest Derbys 43 F2* area in High Peak between Derwent Dale and valley of R Ashop to NW of Ladybower Resr. Some conifer afforestation on sides of river valleys. SK 19
Hopegill Head Cumbria 52 B3 mt 3m/5km N of Buttermere. Height 2525 ft or 770 metres. NY 1822
Hope Green Ches 43 E3* loc 1km S of Poynton. SJ 9182
Hope, Lower, The 20 D4 stretch of R Thames extending from E Tilbury Marshes, Essex to **Lr Hope Pt** on Cliffe Marshes, Kent. TQ 7077
Hopeman Grampian 82 B1 fishing vil and resort on N coast 6m/9km W of Lossiemouth. NJ 1469
Hope Mansell H & W 26 B5 vil 3m/5km SE of Ross-on-Wye. SO 6219
Hope, Middle Avon 15 H4* anvil-shaped spit of land protruding into Bristol Channel 3m/5km N of Weston-super-Mare. ST 3366
Hopesay Salop 34 B5 vil 3m/4km W of Craven Arms. To E, **H. Hill** (NT). SO 3983
Hope's Green Essex 20 D3 NW dist of S Benfleet. TQ 7786
Hope's Nose Devon 5 E4 headland at N end of Tor Bay 2m/3km E of Torquay harbour. SX 9563
Hopes Reservoir Lothian 66 C3* small resr on Lammermuir Hills 4m/6km S of Gifford. NT 5462
Hopetoun House Lothian 65 G1 17c mansion on S side of Firth of Forth 2m/4km W of Forth Rd Br. NT 0879
Hopetown W Yorks 49 F5 loc adjoining Normanton to NE. SE 3923
Hope under Dinmore H & W 26 A2 vil 4m/6km S of Leominster. SO 5052
Hopkinstown (Trehopcyn) Mid Glam 15 F3 W dist of Pontypridd. ST 0690
Hopley's Green H & W 25 H3* loc 4m/6km SE of Kington. SO 3452
Hopperton N Yorks 50 A3* ham 5m/9km N of Wetherby. SE 4256
Hopping Hill Northants 28 C2* loc in NW part of Northampton. SP 7262
Hop Pole Lincs 37 G3* loc 3m/4km SW of Deeping St Nicholas. TF 1813
Hopsford Warwicks 36 A5* loc on site of lost vil between Shilton and Withybrook, 6m/10km NE of Coventry. SP 4284
Hopstone Salop 34 D5/35 E5* ham 4m/7km E of Bridgnorth. SO 7894
Hopton Derbys 43 G5 vil 2m/3km W of Wirksworth. SK 2553
Hopton Norfolk 39 H5 vil and coastal resort 5m/8km S of Gt Yarmouth. TG 5200
Hopton Salop 34 B3* loc 1km N of Nesscliff. SJ 3820
Hopton Salop 34 C2* loc 2m/3km SW of Hodnet. SJ 5926
Hopton Staffs 35 F2 ham 2m/4km NE of Stafford. SJ 9426
Hopton Suffolk 31 E1 vil 7m/11km NE of Ixworth. TL 9979
Hopton Cangeford Salop 34 C6 ham 4m/7km NE of Ludlow. SO 5480
Hopton Castle Salop 34 B6 vil 5m/8km SW of Craven Arms. Remains of cas. SO 3678
Hoptonheath Salop 34 B6* ham 5m/8km SW of Craven Arms. SO 3877
Hopton Heath Staffs 35 F2* loc 3m/5km NE of Stafford. Site of Civil War battle, 1643. SJ 9526
Hopton, Lower W Yorks 48 D6/49 E6* S dist of Mirfield. SE 2019
Hopton, Upper W Yorks 48 D6* vil 1m S of Mirfield. SE 1918
Hopton Wafers Salop 34 C6 vil 2m/4km W of Cleobury Mortimer. SO 6376
Hopwas Staffs 35 G4 vil 2m/3km W of Tamworth. SK 1704
Hopwood Gtr Manchester 42 D1* loc 3m/5km SW of Rochdale. SD 8609
Hopwood H & W 27 E1 vil 5m/8km N of Redditch. SP 0275
Hopworthy Devon 6 B5* loc 3m/4km W of Holsworthy. SS 3002
Horam E Sussex 12 C5 vil 3m/4km S of Heathfield. TQ 5717
Horbling Lincs 37 F1 vil 6m/9km W of Donington. TF 1135
Horbury W Yorks 49 E6 mnfg tn 3m/5km SW of Wakefield. Birth and burial place of John Carr ('Carr of York'), 18c architect. **Horbury Br** loc at crossing of R Calder and of Aire and Calder Canal 1m W. SE 2918
Horden Durham 54 D1* loc adjoining Peterlee to E. **H. Hall** to N is early 17c manor hse. **Horden Pt** headland on North Sea coast 2km N. NZ 4441
Horderley Salop 34 B5 loc 3m/5km NW of Craven Arms. SO 4086
Hordle Hants 10 A5 surburban loc 4m/6km W of Lymington. SZ 2795
Hordley Salop 34 B2 ham 3m/5km SW of Ellesmere. Loc of **Lr Hordley** 2km SE. SJ 3830
Horeb Clwyd 41 H5* loc 2km W of Hope. SJ 2857
Horeb Dyfed 23 F2 loc 2m/3km NW of Llandyssul. SN 3942

Horeb Dyfed 23 F5 loc 3m/5km N of Llanelli. SN 4905
Horeb Dyfed 24 B5* loc 2m/3km SW of Brechfa. SN 5128
Horfield Avon 16 B4 dist of Bristol 3m/4km N of city centre. ST 5976
Horham Suffolk 31 F1 vil 2m/3km SW of Stradbroke. TM 2172
Horkesley, Great Essex 30 D5 vil 4m/6km N of Colchester. TL 9730
Horkesley Heath Essex 30 D5 vil 3m/4km N of Colchester. TL 9829
Horkesley, Little Essex 30 D4/D5 vil 5m/8km NW of Colchester. TL 9632
Horkstow Humberside 51 E6 vil 4m/6km SW of Barton-upon-Humber and 7m/11km N of Brigg. SE 9818
Horley Oxon 27 H3 vil 3m/5km NW of Banbury. SP 2743
Horley W Sussex 11 H1 tn 4m/6km N of Crawley. London (Gatwick) Airport 1m S. TQ 2843
Hormead, Great Herts 29 G4/G5 vil 3m/4km E of Buntingford. TL 4029
Hormead, Little Herts 29 G5 ham 3m/4km E of Buntingford. TL 4029
Hornblotton Som 8 D1* ham 3m/5km NE of Keinton Mandeville. 1km S, ham of **H. Green.** ST 5934
Hornby Lancs 47 F2 vil 8m/13km NE of Lancaster. SD 5868
Hornby N Yorks 54 B5 ham 3m/5km S of Catterick. Cas dating partly from 14c. SE 2293
Hornby N Yorks 54 C4 ham 8m/12km N of Northallerton. NZ 3605
Horncastle Lincs 45 F4 tn on R Bain 18m/29km E of Lincoln, on site of Roman tn of *Banovallum*, part of whose walls remain. Industries include agriculture and agricultural engineering, malting. TF 2669
Hornchurch London 20 B3 tn in borough of Havering 2m/4km SE of Romford. **S Hornchurch** loc 3m/4km SW. **H. Marshes** 4m/6km SW on N bank of R Thames. TQ 5487
Horncliffe Nthmb 67 F4 vil on R Tweed 5m/8km SW of Berwick-upon-Tweed. R spanned to N by Union Br, Britain's first suspension br (1820). NT 9249
Horncroft, Lower Sussex 11 F3 loc 3m/4km W of Pulborough. TQ 0017
Horndean Hants 10 D3 tn 5m/7km N of Havant. SU 7013
Horndon Devon 4 B3 ham 4m/7km NE of Tavistock. SX 5280
Horndon, East Essex 20 C3 ham 4m/6km SE of Brentwood. TQ 6389
Horndon on the Hill Essex 20 C3 vil 5m/8km SW of Basildon. TQ 6683
Horndon, West Essex 20 C3 loc 4m/6km SE of Brentwood. TQ 6288
Horne Surrey 19 G6 ham 4m/6km E of Horley. TQ 3344
Horner Som 7 F1* ham, largely NT, 2km SE of Porlock. Ancient packhorse br. SS 8945
Horne Row Essex 20 D2* loc 5m/8km E of Chelmsford. TL 7704
Horner's Green Suffolk 30 D4* loc 4m/6km W of Hadleigh. TL 9641
Horn Hill Bucks and Herts 19 E2 loc 3m/5km SW of Rickmansworth. TQ 0192
Horning Norfolk 39 G3 vil on left bank of R Bure 3m/4km E of Hoveton. TG 3417
Horninghold Leics 36 D4 vil 4m/6km SW of Uppingham. SP 8097
Horninglow Staffs 35 H2 dist of Burton upon Trent 2km N of tn centre. SK 2325
Horningsea Cambs 30 A2 vil on E bank of R Cam 4m/6km NE of Cambridge. TL 4962
Horningsham Wilts 16 C6 vil at S side of Longleat Park 5m/7km SW of Warminster. ST 8141
Horningtoft Norfolk 38 D3 vil 4m/7km S of Fakenham. TF 9323
Horningtops Cornwall 3 G2* loc 3m/5km SE of Liskeard. SX 2760
Hornsbury Som 8 B3* loc 2km N of Chard. ST 3310
Hornsby Cumbria 60 B6* loc 2km S of Cumwhitton. **Hornsbygate** loc to E. NY 5250
Horn's Cross Devon 6 C3 ham 5m/7km SW of Bideford. SS 3823
Horns Cross E Sussex 12 D4* loc 2m/3km S of Northiam. TQ 8222
Horns Cross Kent 20 C4* loc at Stone, 2m/3km E of Dartford. TQ 5774
Hornsea Humberside 51 F3 coastal resort 14m/22km NE of Hull. Large lake, **H. Mere,** on W side of tn. **Hornsea Br** loc adjoining to S. TA 2047
Hornsey London 19 G3 dist in borough of Haringey 6m/9km N of Charing Cross. TQ 3088
Horns Green London 20 B5* loc in borough of Bromley 2m/3km E of Biggin Hill. TQ 4558
Horns, The Kent 12 D4* loc 2km SW of Hawkhurst. TQ 7429
Hornton Oxon 27 G3 vil 5m/8km NW of Banbury. SP 3945
Horpit Wilts 17 F3* loc 4m/6km E of Swindon. SU 2184
Hor Point Cornwall 2 B4* headland (NT) on N coast 2km W of St Ives. SW 4941
Horrabridge Devon 4 B4 vil 4m/6km SE of Tavistock. SX 5169
Horridge Devon 4 D3 loc 3m/4km N of Ashburton. SX 7674
Horringer Suffolk 30 C2 vil 3m/4km SW of Bury St Edmunds. TL 8261
Horringford Isle of Wight 10 C6* loc 1m W of Newchurch and 4m/6km W of Sandown. SZ 5485
Horrington, East Som 16 B6 vil 2m/3km E of Wells. ST 5846
Horrington, West Som 16 B6* ham 2m/3km NE of Wells. ST 5747
Horrocks Fold Gtr Manchester 47 G6* loc in Bolton 3m/4km NW of tn centre. SD 7013
Horrocksford Lancs 48 A4* ham 2km N of Clitheroe. Extensive quarries to E and SE. SD 7443
Horrocks, Great Gtr Manchester 42 D2* loc in Manchester 2km NE of city centre. SJ 8499
Horsea Island Hants 10 C4, D4 island in Portsmouth Harbour, with causeway to Portsea I. SU 6304
Horsebridge Devon 4 B3* ham on R Tamar 5m/8km W of Tavistock. SX 4075
Horsebridge Hants 10 B2 ham on R Test 3m/5km S of Stockbridge. SU 3430
Horse Bridge Staffs 43 E5* loc 2m/4km SW of Leek. SJ 9653
Horsebridge, Lower E Sussex 12 C5 vil on Cuckmere R 2km N of Hailsham. Loc of **Upr Horsebridge** on opp (E) bank. TQ 5711
Horsebrook Staffs 35 E3 loc 3m/5km SW of Penkridge. SJ 8810
Horsecastle Avon 16 A5* loc at N end of Yatton. ST 4266
Horse Green Ches 42 B6* loc just SW of Norbury. SJ 5546
Horsehay Salop 34 D4* loc 1km W of Dawley, Telford. SJ 6707
Horseheath Cambs 30 B3 vil 4m/6km W of Haverhill. Site of Roman settlement to NW. TL 6147
Horsehouse N Yorks 54 A6 vil 7m/11km SW of Middleham. SE 0481
Horse Island H'land 85 A6 one of the Summer Isles, qv. Lies 1m W of NW coast of Ross and Cromarty dist across **Horse Sound.** Area about 350 acres or 140 hectares. NC 0204
Horse Island S'clyde 64 A4 island and bird sanctuary in Firth of Clyde lying 1km out from Ardrossan harbour. NS 2142
Horse Island Shetland 89 E8* rock island lying off S coast of Mainland 2km W of Sumburgh Hd. HU 3807
Horseley Heath W Midlands 35 F5* loc 2m/4km NW of W Bromwich tn centre. SO 9692
Horsell Surrey 18 D5 W suburb of Woking. SU 9959
Horseman's Green Clwyd 42 A6* ham 6m/10km W of Whitchurch. SJ 4441
Horseman Side Essex 20 C2* loc 4m/6km NW of Brentwood. TQ 5496
Horsenden Bucks 18 C2* ham 1m W of Princes Risborough. SP 7902
Horse of Copinsay Orkney 89 C7* rocky but turf-covered islet 1km NE of Copinsay, qv. HY 6202
Horseshoe Common Norfolk 39 E2* loc adjoining Briston to NW. TG 0533
Horseshoe Green Kent 12 B3* ham just SE of Markbeech 3m/5km SE of Edenbridge. TQ 4742
Horseshoes Wilts 16 D5* ham 3m/5km S of Melksham. ST 9159
Horse Sound H'land 85 A6 sea passage between Horse I. and NW coast of Ross and Cromarty dist 2m/3km SE of Achiltibuie. NC 0304

Horsey Norfolk 39 H3 vil near coast 9m/14km NE of Acle. **H. Corner** loc 1km N. **H. Mere** (NT), broad or lake to SW. TG 4622
Horsey Island Devon 6 D2* piece of land on N bank of R Taw estuary 5m/8km W of Barnstaple. SS 4733
Horsey Island Essex 31 F5 island among marshes and creeks 2m/4km W of The Naze. TM 2324
Horsford Norfolk 39 F3 vil 5m/8km NW of Norwich. TG 1916
Horsforth W Yorks 49 E4 suburb 4m/7km NW of Leeds. **H. Woodside** loc adjoining to E. SE 2337
Horsham W Sussex 11 G2 tn 8m/12km SW of Crawley. TQ 1730
Horsham St Faith Norfolk 39 F3 vil 4m/7km N of Norwich. Norwich Airport to S. TG 2115
Horsington Lincs 45 F4 vil 4m/7km W of Horncastle. TF 1968
Horsington Som 9 E2 vil 3m/5km S of Wincanton. **H. Marsh** is loc 1m NE. ST 7023
Horsley Derbys 43 H6 vil 4m/7km S of Ripley. SK 3844
Horsley Glos 16 D2 vil 1m SW of Nailsworth. ST 8398
Horsley Nthmb 60 D2 ham 2km SE of Rochester. NY 8496
Horsley Nthmb 61 F5 vil 2m/4km W of Heddon-on-the-Wall. NZ 0966
Horsley Cross Essex 31 E5 loc 3m/5km SE of Manningtree. TM 1227
Horsleycross Street Essex 31 E5 ham 2m/4km SE of Manningtree. TM 1228
Horsley, East Surrey 19 E6 vil 7m/11km E of Guildford. Suburban development to N. TQ 0952
Horsleygate Derbys 43 G3* loc 1m SW of Holmesfield. SK 3177
Horsleyhill Borders 66 C6 loc 4m/6km NE of Hawick. NT 5319
Horsley Hill Tyne & Wear 61 H5* dist of S Shields 2km SE of tn centre. NZ 3865
Horsleys Green Bucks 18 C2* loc 2m/3km SE of Stokenchurch. SU 7895
Horsley, West Surrey 19 E6 vil 6m/9km E of Guildford. TQ 0752
Horsley Woodhouse Derbys 43 H6 vil 4m/6km S of Ripley. SK 3944
Horsmonden Kent 12 D3 vil 4m/6km SE of Paddock Wd. TQ 7040
Horspath Oxon 18 B1 suburban vil 4m/6km E of Oxford. SP 5704
Horstead Norfolk 39 F3 vil 1km W of Coltishall. TG 2619
Horsted Keynes W Sussex 12 A4 vil 4m/7km NE of Haywards Heath. H.K. rly stn 1m NW is northern terminus of Bluebell Rly (see also Sheffield Park). TQ 3828
Horsted, Little E Sussex 12 B5 ham 2m/3km S of Uckfield. TQ 4718
Horton Avon 16 C3 vil 3m/5km NE of Chipping Sodbury. **H. Court** (NT), Cotswold manor hse. ST 7685
Horton Berks 19 E4 vil 4m/6km SE of Slough. TQ 0175
Horton Bucks 28 D5 ham 4m/6km S of Leighton Buzzard. SP 9219
Horton Dorset 9 G3 vil 5m/8km N of Wimborne. SU 0307
Horton Lancs 48 B3 ham 2m/3km NE of Gisburn. SD 8550
Horton Northants 28 C2/D2 vil 6m/9km SE of Northampton. SP 8154
Horton Oxon 28 B6* vil 6m/10km NE of Oxford. SP 5912
Horton Salop 34 B2* loc 2m/3km NW of Wem. SJ 4930
Horton Salop 34 D3* ham 3m/4km NE of Wellington. SJ 6814
Horton Som 8 B3* vil adjoining Broadway on S side, 3m/4km W of Ilminster. 1m NE, loc of **H. Cross.** ST 3214
Horton Staffs 43 E5 vil 3m/5km W of Leek. SJ 9457
Horton W Glam 23 F6 vil above Port Eynon Bay on S coast of Gower peninsula. SS 4785
Horton Wilts 17 E5 vil 3m/5km NE of Devizes. SU 0563
Horton, Great W Yorks 48 D5 dist of Bradford 2m/3km SW of city centre. **Lit Horton** dist of Bradford adjoining to E. SE 1431
Horton Green Ches 42 A6 ham 3m/4km NW of Malpas. SJ 4549
Horton Heath Hants 10 C3 suburb 3m/5km SE of Eastleigh. SU 4917
Horton in Ribblesdale N Yorks 48 B1 vil 5m/8km N of Settle. Limestone quarries. SD 8172
Horton Kirby Kent 20 C4 vil on R Darent 4m/6km S of Dartford. TQ 5668
Horton, Little Wilts 17 E5* ham 1m SW of Horton and 2m/4km E of Devizes. SU 0462
Horwich Gtr Manchester 47 G6 tn 5m/8km W of Bolton. Rly workshops, leather, paper, textiles. SD 6311
Horwich End Derbys 43 E3* loc adjoining Whaley Br to S. SK 0180
Horwood Devon 6 D3* vil 3m/5km E of Bideford. SS 5027
Horwood, Great Bucks 28 C4 vil 2m/3km N of Winslow. SP 7731
Horwood, Little Bucks 28 C4 vil 2m/4km NE of Winslow. SP 7930
Hoscar Lancs 42 A1 ham 2m/3km E of Burscough Br. SD 4711
Hose Leics 36 C2 vil 7m/11km N of Melton Mowbray. SK 7329
Hoselaw Loch Borders 67 E5* small loch 3m/4km N of Kirk Yetholm. NT 8031
Hosey Hill Kent 20 B6* loc just S of Westerham. TQ 4553
Hosh Tayside 72 C2 vil 2km NW of Crieff. Distillery beside Turret Burn (see Glen Turret). NN 8523
Hosta W Isles 88 D1* loc near NW coast of N Uist 3m/4km S of Griminish Pt. **Loch H.** is small loch to N. NF 7272
Hos Wick Shetland 89 E8 southward-facing bay on E coast of Mainland 12m/20km S of Lerwick. Vil of **Hoswick** at head of bay. HU 4123
Hotham Humberside 50 D4 vil 5m/8km S of Mkt Weighton. SE 8934
Hothersall Lancs 47 G4* loc 2m/3km W of Ribchester. SD 6234
Hothfield Kent 13 E3 vil 3m/5km NW of Ashford. TQ 9644
Hoton Leics 36 B2 vil 3m/5km NE of Loughborough. **H. Hills** loc 1m W. SK 5722
Houbie Shetland 89 F6 loc on S coast of Fetlar at head of bay called **Wick of H.**, an inlet of the much larger Wick of Tresta (see Tresta). HU 6290
Houdston S'clyde 56 B4* loc adjoining Girvan to E. NX 1998
Hough Ches 42 C6 vil 3m/4km S of Crewe. SJ 7151
Hough Ches 42 D3* loc 1m E of Alderley Edge. SJ 8578
Hougham Lincs 36 D1 vil 6m/10km N of Grantham. SK 8844
Hougham, West Kent 13 G3 vil 3m/5km W of Dover. TR 2640
Hougharry W Isles 88 D1* vil on NW coast of N Uist 4m/6km S of Griminish Pt. NF 7071
Hough Bay Tiree, S'clyde 69 A7 bay at W end of island, on N side of Rubha Chraiginis. NL 9346
Hough End W Yorks 49 E5* loc in Leeds 3m/5km W of city centre. SE 2433
Hough Green Ches 42 B3 dist of Widnes 2m/3km W of tn centre. SJ 4886
Hough-on-the-Hill Lincs 44 D6 vil 7m/11km N of Grantham. SK 9246
Hough Side W Yorks 49 E5* loc adjoining Pudsey to E. SE 2333
Hough Skerries Tiree, S'clyde 69 A7* group of island rocks lying 2km NW of Hough Bay at W end of main island. NL 9247
Houghton Cambs 29 G1 vil 3m/4km E of Huntingdon. Timber water-mill (NT) on R Ouse. TL 2872
Houghton Cumbria 60 A5 suburb 2m/3km N of Carlisle. NY 4059
Houghton Dyfed 22 C5 ham 2km S of Llangwm. SM 9807
Houghton Hants 10 A2 vil on R Test 2m/3km S of Stockbridge. SU 3432
Houghton Norfolk 38 C2 par containing **H. Hall,** 18c hse by Kent, in park. See also New H. TF 7928
Houghton W Sussex 11 F4 vil 3m/5km N of Arundel. TQ 0111
Houghton Conquest Beds 29 E4 vil 2m/4km N of Ampthill. TL 0441
Houghton, Great Northants 28 C2 vil in Northampton 3m/4km SE of tn centre. SP 7958
Houghton, Great S Yorks 43 H1 vil 6m/9km E of Barnsley. **Lit Houghton** vil 1km SW. SE 4306
Houghton Green Ches 42 B2* ham on N edge of Warrington. SJ 6291
Houghton Green E Sussex 13 E4* ham 2m/3km N of Rye. TQ 9222
Houghton House Beds. See Ampthill.

Houghton le Side Durham 54 B3 loc 6m/10km NW of Darlington. NZ 2221
Houghton-le-Spring Tyne & Wear 61 H6 tn 6m/9km SW of Sunderland. Coal-mining, light engineering, confectionery. NZ 3450
Houghton, Little Northants 28 C2 vil 3m/5km E of Northampton. SP 8059
Houghton, North Hants 10 A2* loc 1m SW of Stockbridge. SU 3434
Houghton on the Hill Leics 36 C4 vil 6m/9km E of Leicester. SK 6703
Houghton Regis Beds 29 E5 suburb 2km N of Dunstable. TL 0123
Houghton St Giles Norfolk 38 D2 vil 4m/6km N of Fakenham. 14c 'slipper chapel' for shrine at Walsingham. TF 9235
Houlsyke N Yorks 55 F4* ham 5m/8km W of Egton. NZ 7307
Hound Hants 10 B4* vil 1m E of Netley. SU 4708
Hound Green Hants 18 C5* ham 3m/5km N of Hook. SU 7259
Houndmills Hants 18 B6* industrial estate in NW part of Basingstoke. SU 6253
Houndsmoor Som 8 A2* loc just SE of Milverton. ST 1225
Houndwood Borders 67 E2 loc on Eye Water 2m/4km SE of Grantshouse. NT 8463
Hounsdown Hants 10 B3 vil 2km S of Totton. SU 3511
Hounslow London 19 E4 borough of W London extending from Heathrow Airport (W) to Chiswick (E), and from Osterley Park (N) to Kempton Park (S). TQ 1375
Hounslow Green Essex 30 B6 ham 3m/4km SE of Gt Dunmow. TL 6518
Housa Wick Shetland 89 F6* bay on S coast of island of Hascosay. HU 5591
Housay Shetland. See Out Skerries.
Housay W Isles 88 A2* r in Harris rising as Ulladale R in Forest of Harris and flowing NE to head of Loch Resort. NB 1017
Houseby Orkney 89 C6* loc on **Bay of H.** on S coast of Stronsay. HY 6721
House of the Binns Lothian. See Binns, The.
Houses Hill W Yorks 48 D6* ham 2m/3km S of Mirfield. SE 1916
Houses, Lower Essex 30 D6* loc 3m/5km S of Colchester, below dam of Abberton Resr. TL 9820
Houses, Lower Salop 34 C1* loc 1km NE of Whixall. SJ 5235
Houses, Lower W Yorks 48 D6* loc in Huddersfield 1m SE of tn centre. SE 1515
Housesteads Nthmb 60 D4* remains (NT) of Roman fort of *Vercovicium* on Hadrian's Wall 3m/4km N of Bardon Mill. NY 7968
Housetter Shetland 89 E6* loc on Mainland 1km N of Colla Firth. **Loch of H.** small loch to N. HU 3684
Housham Tye Essex 20 B1* loc 4m/6km E of Harlow. TL 5010
Houss Shetland 89 E8* loc on E Burra I. 2km S of br connection with W Burra I. HU 3731
Houston S'clyde 64 B2 vil 3m/5km NW of Johnstone. NS 4066
Houston Industrial Estate Lothian 65 G2* area of Livingston to N of tn centre. NT 0569
Houstry H'land 86 D4/E4 loc in Caithness dist 3m/5km NW of Latheron. ND 1535
Hove E Sussex 11 H4 residential tn and seaside resort adjoining Brighton to W. TQ 2804
Hove Edge W Yorks 48 D5* loc 2km NW of Brighouse. SE 1324
Hoveringham Notts 44 B6 vil 2m/3km E of Lowdham. SK 6946
Hoveton Norfolk 39 G3 vil 8m/12km NE of Norwich. **H. Gt Broad** and **H. Lit Broad** are broads or lakes 2km SE and E respectively. TG 3018
Hovingham N Yorks 50 B1 vil 8m/12km W of Malton. Annual music festival at **H. Hall,** 18c seat of Worsley family. SE 6675
How Cumbria 60 B5* ham 3m/5km SW of Brampton. NY 5056
Howana Geo, Point of Orkney 89 A6* headland on W coast of Mainland 3m/5km S of Marwick Hd. HY 2220
Howarth, Great Gtr Manchester 48 B6* loc 2m/3km NE of Rochdale. SD 9115
Howbrook S Yorks 43 G2* loc 2m/3km SE of Wortley. SK 3298
How Caple H & W 26 B4 vil 4m/7km N of Ross-on-Wye across loop of r. SO 6030
Howden Humberside 50 C5 small tn 3m/5km N of Goole across R Ouse. Partly ruined medieval ch (A.M.). SE 7428
Howden Lothian 65 G2* residential area of Livingston to SW of tn centre. NT 0567
Howden Clough W Yorks 49 E5* vil 1m E of Birstall. SE 2326
Howden Hill N Yorks 54 B3* loc 1km W of Darlington. NZ 2412
Howden-le-Wear Durham 54 B2 vil 2km S of Crook. NZ 1633
Howden Reservoir 43 F2 resr in Derwent Dale 9m/14km E of Glossop across High Peak. The resr is partly in Derbys and partly in S Yorks. SK 1792
Howdon Tyne & Wear 61 G4* loc in N Tyneside dist 2km NE of Wallsend. **H. Pans** loc to SE on N bank of R Tyne. NZ 3267
Howe H'land 86 F2 loc in Caithness dist 8m/13km NW of Wick. Ruthers of H. is loc 1km N. ND 3062
Howe Norfolk 39 F5 ham 6m/10km SE of Norwich. TM 2799
Howe N Yorks 54 C6 ham 1km SE of Ainderby Quernhow. SE 3580
Howe Bridge Gtr Manchester 42 C1* loc adjoining Atherton to SW. SD 6602
Howe, East Dorset 9 G4 N dist of Bournemouth. SZ 0795
Howe Green Essex 20 D2* vil 4m/6km SE of Chelmsford. TL 7403
Howegreen Essex 21 E2* ham 4m/6km S of Maldon. Ham of **Farther H.** to SE. TL 8301
Howell Lincs 45 E6 ham 4m/7km E of Sleaford. TF 1346
Howe, Mid Orkney 89 B6* Neolithic communal burial-chamber, and nearby *broch,* on W coast of island of Rousay. Sometimes spelt as one word, Midhowe. HY 3730
How End Beds 29 E4 loc 2m/3km N of Ampthill. TL 0340
Howe of Alford Grampian 82 D5, 83 E5 valley of R Don in vicinity of Alford. NJ 5716
Howe of Fife Fife 73 F3, F4 fertile area astride R Eden between Strathmiglo and Cupar. NO 2910
Howe of the Mearns Grampian 77 F4 fertile tract E of Fettercairn. NO 6974
Howequoy Head Orkney 89 B7* headland on S coast of Mainland and on E shore of Scapa Flow, 1km W of St Mary's. HY 4600
Howe Street Essex 20 D1 vil 5m/8km N of Chelmsford. TL 6914
Howe Street Essex 30 B4 ham 2km NE of Finchingfield. TL 6934
Howe, West Dorset 9 G4 NW dist of Bournemouth. SZ 0595
Howey Powys 25 F2 vil 2km S of Llandrindod Wells. SO 0558
Howgate Lothian 66 A3 vil 2km SE of Penicuik. NT 2458
Howgill Cumbria 53 F5 loc 3m/5km NW of Sedbergh. SD 6296
Howgill Lancs 48 B3* loc 2m/3km S of Gisburn. SD 8246
Howgill N Yorks 48 D2 loc above R Wharfe 1m SE of Appletreewick. SE 0659
Howgill Castle Cumbria 53 F2 hse dating from 14c, 1km E of Milburn. NY 6629
How Green Herts 29 G5* W end of Buntingford. TL 3529
How Green Kent 20 B6* loc 2m/3km E of Edenbridge. TQ 4746
How Hill Norfolk 39 G3* loc 1m W of Ludham. TG 3719
Howick Nthmb 67 H6 ham on coast 5m/9km NE of Alnwick. **H. Haven** is small inlet to S. NU 2517
Howle Durham 54 A2* ham 1km W of Butterknowle. NZ 0926
Howle Salop 34 D2 ham 4m/7km NW of Newport. SJ 6923
Howle Hill H & W 26 B5* ham 2m/4km S of Ross-on-Wye. SO 6020
Howlett End Essex 30 B4 ham 3m/5km NW of Thaxted. TL 5834
Howley Som 8 B3 ham 4m/6km W of Chard. ST 2609
Howmore W Isles 88 D2/E2 vil near W coast of S Uist 5m/7km NW of Beinn Mhór. NF 7536
Hownam Borders 67 E6 vil on Kale Water 8m/13km E of Jedburgh. NT 7719
Howsell, Lower H & W 26 C3 loc at N end of Gt Malvern. SO 7848
Howsell, Upper H & W 26 C3 loc at N end of Gt Malvern, 1km W of Lr Howsell. SO 7748
Howsham Humberside 45 E1 vil 4m/6km SE of Brigg. TA 0404
Howsham N Yorks 50 C2 vil 7m/11km SW of Malton. Hall has Jacbn exterior. SE 7362
Howt Green Kent 21 E5* loc 2m/3km NW of Sittingbourne. TQ 8965
Howton H & W 25 H5* loc 2m/3km NE of Pontrilas. SO 4129
Howton Head Orkney 89 A7* headland on Mainland 2m/3km NE of Scad Hd, Hoy, across Bring Deeps. To E is the island Holm of Howton at entrance to Bay of Howton. HY 3003
Howtown Cumbria 52 D3 loc close to S shore of Ullswater 4m/6km SW of Pooley Br. NY 4419
Howwood S'clyde 64 B3 vil 3m/4km SW of Johnstone. NS 3960
Hoxa Head Orkney 89 B7 headland at W extremity of S Ronaldsay, opp Flotta across Sound of Hoxa. ND 4092
Hoxne Suffolk 31 F1 vil 3m/5km NE of Eye. TM 1877
Hoxton London 19 G3* loc in borough of Hackney 3m/4km NE of Charing Cross. TQ 3383
Hoy Orkney 89 A7 the second largest, after Mainland, of the Orkney group of islands, lying on W side of Scapa Flow and SW of Mainland across **H. Sound** and Bring Deeps. Island is 14m/22km NW to SE and 6m/10km NE to SW. Rugged, rocky landscape of Old Red Sandstone with steep cliffs to W. See also Old Man of Hoy. ND 29
Hoylake Merseyside 41 H3 coastal resort at NW end of Wirral peninsula 7m/11km W of Birkenhead. SJ 2189
Hoyland, High S Yorks 43 G1 vil 5m/8km NW of Barnsley. SE 2710
Hoyland Nether S Yorks 43 H1 tn 4m/6km S of Barnsley. Coal-mining, textiles. **Upr Hoyland** loc 1km NW. **H. Common** 1m W. SE 3600
Hoyland Swaine S Yorks 43 G1 vil 2km NE of Penistone. SE 2604
Hoyle W Sussex 11 E3* loc 2m/4km SE of Midhurst. SU 9018
Hoyle Green W Yorks 48 C5* loc 1km N of Sowerby Br. SE 0524
Hoyle Mill S Yorks 43 H1* loc in Barnsley 1m E of tn centre. SE 3606
Hoyle Mill Dam W Yorks 49 F6* small lake 1m N of Hemsworth. SE 4314
Hubberholme N Yorks 48 C1 loc at foot of Langstrothdale 2km NW of Buckden. Partly Norman ch has rood loft. SD 9278
Hubberston Dyfed 22 B5 W dist of Milford Haven. SM 8906
Hubbersty Head Cumbria 52 D5* loc 4m/7km S of Windermere. SD 4291
Hubberton Green W Yorks 48 C5* loc 2m/3km W of Sowerby Br. SE 0322
Hubbert's Bridge Lincs 37 G1 loc on S Forty Foot Drain 4m/6km W of Boston. TF 2643
Huby N Yorks 49 E3 vil 5m/8km S of Harrogate. SE 2747
Huby N Yorks 50 B2 vil 8m/13km N of York. SE 5665
Hucclecote Glos 26 D5 E dist of Gloucester; also par to E. Site of Roman villa. SO 8717
Hucclecote Green Glos 26 D5* loc in SE part of Gloucester. SO 8716
Hucking Kent 20 D5/21 E5 ham 5m/8km SW of Sittingbourne. TQ 8458
Huckles Brook 9 H3* stream rising as Latchmore Brook in New Forest 5m/8km E of Fordingbridge, Hants, and flowing SW into R Avon 2m/4km S of the tn. SU 1510
Hucklow, Great Derbys 43 F3 vil 6m/10km NW of Bakewell. **Lit Hucklow** vil 2km NW. SK 1777
Hucknall Notts 44 A6 tn 6m/10km N of Nottingham. Industries include coal-mining, engineering, hosiery. SK 5349
Huddersfield W Yorks 48 D6 industrial tn on R Colne 11m/17km S of Bradford. Textiles, chemicals, engineering. **H. Canal** connects tn to Calder and Hebble Navigation on E side of Bradley. SE 1416
Huddington H & W 26 D2* vil 5m/8km SE of Droitwich. **H. Court** is black and white Tudor hse. SO 9457
Huddlesford Staffs 35 G3* loc 2m/4km E of Lichfield. SK 1509
Huddleston N Yorks 49 F4/F5* loc 2m/3km W of Sherburn in Elmet. **H. Hall** is an Elizn manor hse. Former quarries here supplied stone for York Minster and parts of King's College Chapel, Cambridge. SE 4633
Hudeshope Beck 53 H2* r rising on Middleton Common, Durham, and flowing S into R Tees at Middleton in Teesdale. NY 9425
Hud Hey Lancs 48 B5* loc 1m N of Haslingden. SD 7824
Hudnall Herts 59 E6* vil 4m/6km N of Berkhamsted. To E is H. Common (NT). TL 0013
Hudswell N Yorks 54 B4 vil 2m/3km W of Richmond. SZ 1400
Huggate Humberside 50 D3 vil in the wolds 6m/10km NE of Pocklington. SE 8855
Huggill Force Durham 53 H3* waterfall in Hug Gill 2km SW of Bowes. NY 9712
Hugglescote Leics 36 A3 loc in S part of Coalville. SK 4212
Hughenden Valley Bucks 18 D2* vil 2m/4km N of High Wycombe. 1m S, **Hughenden Manor** (NT), the home of Disraeli from 1847 to 1881. SU 8696
Hughley Salop 34 C4 vil 4m/6km W of Much Wenlock. SO 5697
Hughley Brook Salop 34 C4 upper reaches of Harley Brook, qv. SJ 6004
Hugh Mill Lancs 48 B5* loc 2m/3km E of Rawtenstall. SD 8321
Hugh Town Isles of Scilly 2 A1 capital of the Scillies, situated on the island of St Mary's; harbour. SV 9010
Hugletts Stream 12 C5* one of the streams feeding Waller's Haven (qv) in E Sussex. TQ 6713
Hugus Cornwall 2 D4* ham 3m/5km W of Truro. SW 7743
Huip Orkney. See Holm of Huip.
Huish Devon 6 D4 ham 6m/9km SE of Torrington. SS 5311
Huish Wilts 17 F5* ham 3m/4km N of Pewsey. SU 1463
Huish Champflower Som 7 H2 vil 2m/4km NW of Wiveliscombe. ST 0429
Huish Episcopi Som 8 C2 vil 1km E of Langport. ST 4226
Huish, North Devon 4 D5 ham 3m/4km SE of S Brent. SX 7156
Huish, South Devon 4 D6 loc 3m/5km NW of Salcombe. SX 6941
Hulam Durham 54 D2* loc 1m N of Sheraton. NZ 4436
Hulcott Bucks 28 D6 vil 3m/5km NE of Aylesbury. SP 8516
Hule Moss Borders 66 D4* tarn on Greenlaw Moor 2m/3km N of Greenlaw. NT 7149
Hulham Devon 5 F2* loc 2km N of Exmouth. To NW, A la Ronde, 18c hse of curious construction. SY 0183
Hull Humberside 51 E5 (officially Kingston upon Hull). City and port at confluence of Rs Humber and Hull 50m/80km E of Leeds. Centre of fishing industry; other industries include shipping, flour and saw mills, paint and chemicals. University at Newland. Birthplace of William Wilberforce, slavery abolitionist, 1759. Wilberforce Museum. TA 0928
Hull 51 E5 r rising at Elmswell, Humberside and flowing E on S side of E Driffield to Wansford, then S past Beverley into R Humber at Hull (or Kingston upon Hull). TA 1028
Hulland Derbys 43 G6 vil 4m/7km E of Ashbourne. SK 2446
Hullavington Wilts 16 D3 vil 4m/7km SW of Malmesbury. **H. Airfield** to SE. ST 8982
Hullbridge Essex 20 D2 suburb 3m/4km N of Rayleigh. TQ 8195
Hull Bridge Humberside 51 E4* loc at rd crossing of R Hull 2m/3km NE of Beverley. TA 0541
Hulme Ches 42 B2 loc in Warrington 2m/3km N of tn centre. SJ 6091
Hulme Staffs 43 E6* ham 4m/6km E of Stoke-on-Trent. SJ 9345
Hulme End Staffs 43 F5* ham on R Manifold 2m/3km W of Hartington. SK 1059
Hulme, Upper Staffs 43 E5 vil 3m/5km NE of Leek. SK 0160
Hulme Walfield Ches 42 D4 ham 2m/3km NW of Congleton. SJ 8465

Hulne Priory Nthmb 67 H6 remains of 13c Carmelite priory in park 2m/3km NW of Alnwick. NU 1615
Hulseheath Ches 42 C3* loc 4m/6km NW of Knutsford. SJ 7283
Hulton Lane Ends Gtr Manchester 42 C1* loc 3m/4km SW of Bolton. SD 6905
Hulton, Little Gtr Manchester 42 C1 loc 4m/6km S of Bolton. SD 7203
Hulverstone Isle of Wight 10 B6 ham 4m/6km W of Shorwell. SZ 3984
Hulver Street Norfolk 38 D3* loc 4m/6km W of E Dereham. TF 9312
Hulver Street Suffolk 39 H6 vil 4m/6km SE of Beccles. TM 4686
Humber Devon 5 E3* loc 3m/5km NW of Teignmouth. SX 9075
Humber H & W 26 A2 loc 3m/5km SE of Leominster. SO 5356
Humber 51 G6 estuarial r formed by Rs Trent and Ouse and flowing into North Sea between Spurn Hd, Humberside, and Northcoates Pt, Lincs. The ports of Hull and Grimsby are situated on its left and right banks respectively. TA 3807
Humberside 117 north-eastern county of England, bounded by Lincolnshire, Nottinghamshire, S Yorkshire, N Yorkshire, and the North Sea. R Humber divides the county into N and S parts. A line of chalk hills, the Wolds, runs N and S through the centre, the land on each side being flat. On both sides of the Humber is industrial development, steel, oil, fishing, shipping, and chemicals being predominant. The rest of the county is largely agricultural. Chief tns are Beverley and Hull in the N, and Grimsby, Immingham, and Scunthorpe in the S. Chief rs, in addition to the Humber, are the Hull in the N, with the Derwent forming the boundary with N Yorkshire; and the Trent in the S.
Humberston Humberside 45 G1 suburb 4m/6km SE of Grimsby. **H. Fitties** loc on coast to E. TA 3105
Humberstone Leics 36 C4 dist of Leics 3m/5km E of city centre. See also New Humberstone. SK 6205
Humberton N Yorks 49 F2* loc 2m/3km NE of Boroughbridge across R Ure. SE 4268
Humbie Lothian 66 C2/C3 vil on **H. Water,** 8m/13km SW of Haddington. R flows into Birns Water 2m/4km N. NT 4562
Humbleton Durham 54 A3* loc 3m/4km E of Barnard Castle. NZ 0917
Humbleton Humberside 51 F5 vil 5m/7km NE of Hedon. TA 2234
Humbleton Nthmb 67 F5 loc 1m W of Wooler. NT 9728
Humble, West Surrey 19 F6 vil 2km N of Dorking. Remains of 12c chapel (NT). TQ 1751
Humby Lincs 37 E2 ham 6m/10km E of Grantham. TF 0032
Hume Borders 66 D4 vil 3m/5km S of Greenlaw. Ruins of 13c cas, formerly seat of Earls of Home. NT 7041
Hummer Dorset 8 D2* loc 3m/5km NE of Yeovil. ST 5819
Humphrey Head Point Cumbria 47 E1 headland at outfall of R Kent estuary into Morecambe Bay 2m/4km SE of Flookburgh. SD 3973
Humshaugh Nthmb 61 E4 vil 5m/8km N of Hexham. NY 9171
Huna H'land 86 F1 loc on N coast of Caithness dist 3m/5km W of Duncansby Hd. Ness of Huna is headland to NE. ND 3573
Huncoat Lancs 48 A5/B5* loc 2m/3km NE of Accrington. SD 7730
Huncote Leics 36 B4 vil 6m/10km SW of Leicester. SP 5197
Hunda Orkney 89 B7* barely populated island of about 56 acres or 23 hectares off W end of island of Burray. ND 4396
Hundale Point N Yorks 55 H5* headland on North Sea coast 4m/7km N of Scarborough. TA 0294
Hundall Derbys 43 H3* loc 2m/4km SE of Dronfield. SK 3877
Hunder Holm Shetland 89 E7* small uninhabited island off E coast of Mainland at S end of Lunning Sound and 2m/3km NW of Symbister, Whalsay. HU 5163
Hunderthwaite Durham 53 H3 ham 1m SW of Romaldkirk. NY 9821
Hundland, Loch of Orkney 89 A6* loch at N end of Mainland 3m/5km N of Dounby. HY 2925
Hundleby Lincs 45 G4 vil adjoining Spilsby to W. TF 3866
Hundle Houses Lincs 45 F5* loc 1m S of New York. TF 2553
Hundleton Dyfed 22 C5 vil 2m/3km W of Pembroke. SM 9600
Hundon Suffolk 30 C3 vil 5m/8km NE of Haverhill. TL 7348
Hundred Acres Hants 10 C4* loc 2km E of Wickham. SU 5911
Hundred End Lancs 47 E5* ham 2m/3km SW of Hesketh Bank. SD 4122
Hundred Foot Drain 38 B4. Alternative name for New Bedford River, qv. TF 5800
Hundred House Powys 25 F3 loc on R Edw 5m/8km NE of Builth Wells. SO 1154
Hundred, The H & W 26 A2* loc 4m/6km NE of Leominster. SO 5263
Huney Shetland 89 F5* uninhabited island SW of Balta, off E coast of Unst. HP 6406
Hungarton Leics 36 C4 vil 7m/11km E of Leicester. SK 6907
Hungate End Bucks 28 C3* loc 4m/7km N of Stony Stratford. SP 7846
Hungerford Berks 17 G4 tn on R Kennet and on Kennet and Avon Canal 9m/14km W of Newbury. SU 3368
Hungerford Hants 9 H3 loc on edge of New Forest 2m/3km SE of Fordingbridge. SU 1612
Hungerford Salop 34 C5* ham 8m/12km NE of Craven Arms. SO 5389
Hungerford Som 7 H1* ham 3m/4km SW of Watchet. ST 0440
Hungerford Green Berks 18 A3* loc at Aldworth, 2m/4km W of Streatley. SU 5579
Hungerford, Little Berks 18 A4* loc at Hermitage, 4m/7km NE of Newbury. SU 5173
Hungerford Newtown Berks 17 G4 ham 2m/3km NE of Hungerford. SU 3571
Hunger Hill Gtr Manchester 42 C1* loc in Bolton 3m/4km SW of tn centre. SD 6806
Hunger Hill Lancs 42 B1 loc 5m/8km NW of Wigan. SD 5311
Hungerhill Gardens Notts 36 B1* dist of Nottingham 1m NE of city centre. SK 5841
Hungerton Lincs 36 D2* loc 4m/6km SW of Grantham. SK 8730
Hunglader Skye, H'land 78 B3 loc near N coast 5m/8km N of Uig. Monmt to Flora Macdonald 1m NE. NG 3871
Hungry Hill Norfolk 39 F1* loc 1km E of Northrepps. TG 2539
Hunmanby N Yorks 51 E1 vil 3m/4km SW of Filey. TA 0977
Hunningham Warwicks 27 G1 vil 5m/8km NW of Southam. SP 3768
Hunny Hill Isle of Wight 10 B5 loc 1km N of Newport. SZ 4989
Hunsbury Northants 28 C2* ancient hill fort 2m/3km SW of Northampton. SP 7358
Hunsdon Herts 20 B1 vil 4m/6km E of Ware. TL 4114
Hunsingore N Yorks 50 A3 vil 4m/6km NE of Wetherby. SE 4253
Hunslet W Yorks 49 E5* dist of Leeds 2km S of city centre. **H. Carr** dist adjoining to S. SE 3031
Hunsley, High Humberside 50 D4 loc 6m/10km SW of Beverley. SE 9535
Hunsonby Cumbria 53 E2* ham 1m E of Lit Salkeld. NY 5835
Hunstanton Norfolk 38 B1 coastal resort on the Wash 14m/22km NE of King's Lynn. See also New Hunstanton. TF 6740
Hunstanworth Durham 61 E6 ham 2km SW of Blanchland. NY 9449
Hunston Suffolk 30 D2 vil 5m/8km SE of Ixworth. Loc of **H. Green** 1m S. TL 9768
Hunston W Sussex 11 E4* vil 2m/3km S of Chichester. SU 8602
Hunstrete Avon 16 B5 ham 4m/6km S of Keynsham. ST 6462
Hunsworth W Yorks 48 D5* vil 1m N of Cleckheaton. SE 1826
Hunt End H & W 27 E2 loc on SW edge of Redditch. SP 0363
Huntenhull Green Wilts 16 D6* loc just S of Chapmanslade and 4m/6km NW of Warminster. ST 8247
Hunters Forstal Kent 13 G1 S dist of Herne Bay. TR 1866
Hunter's Quay S'clyde 70 D6 locality with landing stage on W side of Firth of Clyde at entrance to Holy Loch, 2m/3km N of Dunoon,Argyll. NS 1879
Hunterston S'clyde 64 A4 loc on Firth of Clyde opp island of Lit Cumbrae. Atomic power stn. Cas with 16c tower. NS 1851
Huntham Som 8 B2* ham 2km NE of N Curry. ST 3325
Huntingdon Cambs 29 F1 tn on R Ouse 15m/24km NW of Cambridge. See also Hinchingbrooke Hse. TL 2371
Huntingfield Suffolk 31 G1 vil 4m/6km SW of Halesworth. TM 3374
Huntingford Dorset 9 E2 ham 2m/4km N of Gillingham. ST 8030
Huntington H & W 25 G3 vil on Welsh border 4m/6km SW of Kington. SO 2453
Huntington H & W 26 A3* loc in NW part of Hereford. SO 4841
Huntington N Yorks 50 B3 suburb 3m/4km N of York. **E. Huntington** loc adjoining to S. **W. Huntington** loc to SW. SE 6156
Huntington Salop 34 D3 loc 2m/4km S of Wellington. SJ 6507
Huntington Staffs 35 F3 coal-mining vil 2m/3km N of Cannock. SJ 9713
Huntingtower Tayside 72 D2 vil 3m/5km NW of Perth. **H. Castle** (A.M.) dates partly from 16c. NO 0725
Huntley Glos 26 C5 vil 7m/11km W of Gloucester. SO 7219
Huntley Staffs 35 F1* loc 2km S of Cheadle. SK 0041
Huntly Grampian 82 D3 tn near confluence of Rs Deveron and Bogie, 24m/39km SE of Elgin and 33m/53km NW of Aberdeen. Agricultural centre. Mnfre of agricultural implements, bacon curing, brewing, distilling. To N beside R Deveron are remains of **H. Castle** (A.M.), partly 12c but mainly 16c. NJ 5339
Hunton Hants 10 B1 ham 2m/3km W of Micheldever. SU 4839
Hunton Kent 20 D6 vil 5m/8km SW of Maidstone. TQ 7149
Hunton N Yorks 54 B5 vil 5m/8km E of Leyburn. SE 1892
Hunton Bridge Herts 19 E2 loc 3m/5km NW of Watford. TL 0800
Huntscott Som 7 G1* ham 3m/5km SW of Minehead. SS 9243
Hunt's Cross Merseyside 42 A3* loc in Liverpool 6m/10km SE of city centre. SJ 4285
Hunts Green Warwicks 35 G4* loc 4m/7km S of Tamworth. SP 1897
Huntsham Devon 7 G3 vil 3m/5km SE of Bampton. ST 0020
Huntshaw Devon 6 D3* ham 2m/4km N of Torrington. Nearby are locs of **H. Cross, H. Mill Br,** and **H. Water.** SS 5022
Hunt's Hill Bucks 18 D2* loc 3m/4km N of High Wycombe. SU 8596
Huntspill Som 15 G6* vil on flat land known as H. Level, 2km S of Highbridge. To S is the man-made **Huntspill R.** ST 3145
Huntspill 15 G6* r in Somerset, cut through marshes for drainage, rising near Glastonbury and flowing into R Parrett estuary 2km W of Huntspill vil. ST 2945
Huntspill, East Som 15 H6* vil 2m/3km SE of Highbridge. ST 3445
Huntspill, West Som 15 G6* ham 3m/5km S of Burnham-on-Sea. ST 3044
Huntwick Grange W Yorks 49 F6* loc 4m/6km SW of Pontefract. SE 4019
Huntworth Som 8 B1 vil 2m/3km SE of Bridgwater. ST 3134
Hunwick Durham 54 B2 vil 2m/3km S of Willington. NZ 1932
Hunworth Norfolk 39 E2 vil 2m/3km SW of Holt. **H. Green** vil adjoins to SE. TG 0635
Hurcott H & W 35 E6* loc 2m/3km E of Kidderminster. SO 8577
Hurcott Som 8 C2* ham 2km NE of Somerton. ST 5029
Hurcott Som 8 C3* loc 3m/4km E of Ilminster. ST 3916
Hurdley Powys 34 A5* loc 2m/3km E of Church Stoke. SO 2994
Hurdsfield Ches 43 E4 suburb 1km NE of Macclesfield. **Hr Hurdsfield** loc 1km NE. SJ 9274
Hurich H'land 74 A4 r in Lochaber dist running SW from Lochan Dubh down Glen Hurich to Loch Doilet. NM 8167
Hurlers Stone Circle Cornwall. See Minions.
Hurleston Ches 42 C5* par 3m/4km NW of Nantwich, containing **Hurleston Resr,** small resr on W side of **Hurleston Junction,** where Llangollen Branch joins Shropshire Union Canal. SJ 6255
Hurlet S'clyde 64 C3* loc in Nitshill dist of Glasgow. NS 5160
Hurley Berks 18 C3 vil on R Thames 4m/7km NW of Maidenhead. Loc of **H. Bottom** adjoins to S. SU 8283
Hurley Warwicks 35 H4 vil 4m/7km W of Atherstone. Ham of **H. Common** to N. SP 2495
Hurlford S'clyde 64 C5 suburb 2m/3km E of Kilmarnock across R Irvine. NS 4536
Hurliness Orkney 89 A7* loc on Hoy 1km E of Melsetter. ND 2789
Hurlston Lancs 42 A1* loc 2m/3km NW of Ormskirk. **H. Green** loc 1km N. SD 4010
Hurlstone Point Som 7 F1 headland at E end of Porlock Bay. SS 8949
Hurn Dorset 9 H4 vil 5m/8km NE of Bournemouth. 1m NW, Bournemouth (Hurn) Airport. SZ 1297
Hursley Hants 10 B2 vil 4m/7km SW of Winchester. Stretch of country to NW known as **H. Forest.** SU 4225
Hurst Berks 18 C4 vil 5m/8km E of Reading. SU 7973
Hurst Gtr Manchester 43 E2 dist of Ashton-under-Lyne 1m NE of tn centre. SD 9400
Hurst N Yorks 54 A4 loc 2m/3km N of Reeth. NZ 0402
Hurst Som 8 C3* loc on S side of Martock. ST 4518
Hurstbourne Priors Hants 10 B1 vil 2m/3km SW of Whitchurch. SU 4346
Hurstbourne Tarrant Hants 17 G6 vil 5m/8km N of Andover. SU 3853
Hurst Castle Hants 10 A5 cas (A.M.) on spit of land 4m/6km S of Lymington and less than 1m from Cliff End, Isle of Wight; built by Henry VIII for coastal defence. Charles I imprisoned there, 1648. SZ 3189
Hurstead Gtr Manchester 48 B6* loc 2m/3km NE of Rochdale. SD 9115
Hurst Green Essex 31 E6* loc in E part of Brightlingsea. TM 0816
Hurst Green E Sussex 12 D4 vil 7m/11km N of Battle. TQ 7327
Hurst Green Lancs 47 G4 vil 3m/5km NW of Whalley. SD 6838
Hurst Green Surrey 20 A6* loc adjoining Oxted to S. TQ 3951
Hurst Green W Midlands 35 F5* loc in NE part of Halesowen. SO 9885
Hurst Hill W Midlands 35 F5* loc in N part of Dudley. SO 9393
Hurstone Devon 7 E3* loc 5m/7km SW of S Molton. SS 6422
Hurstpierpoint W Sussex 11 H3 tn 3m/5km SW of Burgess Hill. Site of Roman villa 1m S. TQ 2716
Hurst Reservoir Derbys 43 F2* small resr 2km E of Glossop. SK 0593
Hurstway Common H & W 25 G3* loc 2m/3km NW of Willersley. SO 2949
Hurst Wickham W Sussex 11 H3* loc adjoining Hurstpierpoint to E. TQ 2916
Hurstwood Lancs 48 B5 ham 3m/5km E of Burnley. **Hurstwood Resr** to E. SD 8831
Hurstwood, High E Sussex 12 B4 ham 2m/3km N of Buxted. TQ 4926
Hurtmore Surrey 11 F1 loc 2m/3km NW of Godalming. SU 9545
Hurworth Durham 54 C4 vil on R Tees 3m/5km SE of Darlington. NZ 3010
Hurworth Burn Durham 54 C2 loc at S end of **H.B. Resr,** 4m/6km NE of Sedgefield. NZ 4033
Hury Durham 53 H3 loc on N side of **Hury Resr** 3m/4km SW of Romaldkirk. NY 9519
Husbands Bosworth Leics 36 C5 vil 6m/10km W of Mkt Harborough. SP 6484
Husborne Crawley Beds 28 D4 vil 2m/3km N of Woburn. SP 9535
Hushinish W Isles 88 A3 loc on W coast of Harris, on **H. Bay. Hushinish Pt** is headland on W side of bay and 1m S of island of Scarp. **H. Glorigs** is group of rocks 1m S of headland. NA 9811
Husthwaite N Yorks 50 A1 vil 4m/6km N of Easingwold. SE 5175
Hutcherleigh Devon 4 D5* loc 5m/8km NE of Kingsbridge. SX 7850
Hutchesontown S'clyde 64 D3* loc in Glasgow 1m S of city centre. NS 5963
Hutchwns Point Mid Glam 14 D4* headland on W side of Porthcawl. SS 8077
Hut Green N Yorks 49 G5* loc adjoining Low Eggborough to NE. SE 5623
Huthwaite Notts 44 A5 urban loc adjoining Sutton in Ashfield to W. SK 4659
Huthwaite N Yorks 54 D4* loc 1m SE of Swainby. NZ 4801

Huttock Top Lancs 48 B5* loc adjoining Bacup to S. SD 8622
Huttoft Lincs 45 H4 vil 4m/6km S of Sutton on Sea. **H. Grange** loc 1m N. **H. Bank** loc at coast 2m/3km E, comprising part of sea defences built in Roman times. TF 5176
Hutton Avon 15 H5 vil 3m/4km SE of Weston-super-Mare. ST 3558
Hutton Borders 67 F3 vil 6m/9km W of Berwick-upon-Tweed. **H. Castle** 2km NW. NT 9053
Hutton Cumbria 52 D2 ham 6m/9km W of Penrith. **H. John** loc to E. NY 4326
Hutton D & G 59 F3 loc 6m/10km N of Lockerbie. NY 1790
Hutton Essex 20 C2 NE dist of Brentwood. TQ 6295
Hutton Humberside 51 E3 vil adjoining Hutton Cranswick to N. TA 0253
Hutton Lancs 47 F5 vil 3m/5km SW of Preston. **Bottom of Hutton** loc 2km W. SD 4926
Hutton Bonville N Yorks 54 C5 loc 4m/7km N of Northallerton. NZ 3300
Hutton Buscel N Yorks 55 G6 vil 5m/8km SW of Scarborough. TA 9784
Hutton Conyers N Yorks 49 E1 ham 2km NE of Ripon across R Ure. SE 3273
Hutton Cranswick Humberside 51 E3 vil 4m/6km S of Gt Driffield. TA 0252
Hutton End Cumbria 52 D1 ham 2m/3km SW of Calthwaite. NY 4438
Hutton Hang N Yorks 54 B5* loc 2km S of Constable Burton. SE 1788
Hutton Henry Durham 54 D2 vil 6m/10km NW of Hartlepool. NZ 4236
Hutton, High N Yorks 50 C2 vil 3m/5km SW of Malton. Sites of Roman bldgs 2km NE. Vil of **Low Hutton** 1km SE. Par known as Huttons Ambo. SE 7568
Hutton-in-the-Forest Cumbria 52 D2* loc 5m/8km NW of Penrith. NY 4635
Hutton-le-Hole N Yorks 55 E5 vil 2m/4km N of Kirkbymoorside. SE 7089
Hutton, Little N Yorks 49 F1 ham 3m/5km E of Topcliffe. SE 4576
Hutton, Low N Yorks 50 C2 vil on R Derwent 3m/5km SW of Malton. See also Hutton, High. SE 7667
Hutton Lowcross Cleveland 55 E3 ham 2km S of Guisborough. NZ 6013
Hutton Magna Durham 54 A3 vil 6m/9km SE of Barnard Castle. NZ 1212
Hutton Mount Essex 20 C2* E dist of Brentwood. TQ 6194
Hutton Mulgrave N Yorks 55 F4* loc 4m/6km W of Whitby. See also Mulgrave Castle. NZ 8310
Hutton Roof Cumbria 47 F1 vil 3m/4km W of Kirkby Lonsdale. SD 5778
Hutton Roof Cumbria 52 D2 ham 4m/6km SE of Hesket Newmarket. NY 3734
Hutton Rudby N Yorks 54 D4 vil on R Leven 4m/6km W of Stokesley. NZ 4606
Hutton Sessay N Yorks 49 F1 vil 5m/7km SE of Thirsk. SE 4776
Hutton Wandesley N Yorks 50 A3* vil adjoining Long Marston to SE. SE 5050
Huxham Devon 7 G5* ham 4m/6km NE of Exeter. SX 9497
Huxham Green Som 8 D1* loc 5m/8km SW of Shepton Mallet. ST 5936
Huxley Ches 42 B5 vil 3m/5km W of Tarporley. SJ 5061
Huyton Merseyside 42 A2/A3 tn 6m/10km E of Liverpool. SJ 4491
Hwlffordd Welsh form of Haverfordwest, qv.
Hycemoor Cumbria 52 B5 ham at Bootle rly stn 1m NW of Bootle. SD 0989
Hyde Glos 16 D2 loc 2km NE of Minchinhampton. SO 8801
Hyde Glos 27 E4* loc 7m/11km W of Stow-on-the-Wold. SP 0828
Hyde Gtr Manchester 43 E2 tn 5m/7km NE of Stockport. Textiles, engineering, rubber. SJ 9494
Hyde, East Beds 29 E6/F6* ham on R Lea 2m/3km N of Harpenden. TL 1217
Hyde End Berks 18 A5* loc 1m SW of Brimpton and 4m/6km NE of Kingsclere. SU 5563
Hyde End Berks 18 C4* loc 1m E of Spencers Wood and 4m/7km S of Reading. SU 7366
Hyde Heath Bucks 18 D2* vil 2m/3km W of Chesham. SP 9300
Hyde Lea Staffs 35 E3 ham 2m/3km S of Stafford. SJ 9120
Hyde, North London 19 E4* loc in borough of Hounslow 11m/18km W of Charing Cross. M4 motorway service area to S. TQ 1278
Hyde Park S Yorks 44 B1* dist of Doncaster 1km SE of tn centre. SE 5802
Hyde Park Corner Som 8 B1* loc on W side of N Petherton. ST 2832
Hyde's House Wilts. See Dinton.
Hydestile Surrey 11 F1 loc 2m/3km S of Godalming. SU 9740
Hyde, The Essex 30 C4* loc adjoining Gt Yeldham to NE, 6m/10km NW of Halstead. TL 7638
Hyde, The London 19 F3 loc in borough of Barnet 8m/12km NW of Charing Cross. TQ 2188
Hyde, West Herts 19 E2 loc in R Colne valley 3m/4km SW of Rickmansworth. TQ 0391
Hydfer 25 D5 r rising on NE side of Carmarthen Van, Powys, and flowing N into R Usk at Pont ar Hydfer. SN 8627
Hykeham, North Lincs 44 D4 suburb 4m/6km SW of Lincoln. **S Hykeham** ham 1m SW. **Hykeham Moor** loc 1km NW. SK 9466
Hylton Castle Tyne & Wear 61 H5 15c tower hse (A.M.) in NW part of Sunderland. Gives its name to adjacent housing estate. NZ 3558
Hylton, North Tyne & Wear 61 H5* loc in Sunderland 3m/5km W of tn centre across R Wear. NZ 3557
Hylton Red House Tyne & Wear 61 H5* housing estate in NW part of Sunderland. NZ 3659
Hylton, South Tyne & Wear 61 H5 dist of Sunderland 3m/4km W of tn centre. NZ 3556
Hyndburn 117 admin dist of Lancs.
Hyndford Bridge S'clyde 65 F4 rd br over R Clyde 3m/4km SE of Lanark. NS 9141
Hyndland S'clyde 64 C2* loc in Partick dist of Glasgow. NS 5567
Hynish Bay Tiree, S'clyde 69 A7, A8 wide bay on S coast. Loc of **Hynish** is at SW end of bay. NM 0042
Hyskeir H'land. See Oigh-sgeir.
Hyssington Powys 34 A5 ham 3m/4km E of Church Stoke. SO 3194
Hythe Hants 10 B4 vil on W bank of Southampton Water S of Southampton; ferry connection for pedestrians. Urban expansion inland. SU 4207
Hythe Kent 13 G3 cinque port and resort 4m/6km W of Folkestone. Ham of **W Hythe** 2m/4km W. TR 1634
Hythe Surrey 19 E4* loc adjoining Egham to E. TQ 0370
Hythe End Berks 19 E4* loc 1m NE of Egham. TQ 0172
Hythe, The Essex 31 E5 SE dist of Colchester. TM 0024
Hythie Grampian 83 H2 loc 5m/7km SE of Strichen. NK 0051
Hyton Cumbria 52 B6 loc 1m SW of Bootle. SD 0987
Hyvots Bank Lothian 66 A2/B2* dist of Edinburgh 4m/7km SE of city centre. NT 2868

I

Iaen 33 F4* r rising on Mynydd Penypistyll, Powys, and running NE to Talerddig, then NW to join R Twymyn 1km W of Llanbrynmair. SH 8902
Iago 33 E4* stream running W into R Dysynni 1m NE of Abergynolwyn, Gwynedd. SH 6807
Ianstown Grampian 82 D1 E dist of Buckie on N coast. NJ 4366
Ibberton Dorset 9 E3 vil 4m/7km S of Sturminster Newton. ST 7807
Ible Derbys 43 G5* ham 3m/5km NW of Wirksworth. SK 2457
Ibrox S'clyde 64 C3* loc in Govan dist of Glasgow 2m/3km W of city centre. NS 5564
Ibsley Hants 9 H3 loc 3m/4km N of Ringwood. SU 1509
Ibstock Leics 36 A3 large vil 3m/5km SW of Coalville. Coal-mining. Brick works. SK 4010
Ibstone Bucks 18 C2 vil 2m/3km S of Stokenchurch. SU 7593
Ibthorpe Hants 17 G5 vil adjoining Hurstbourne Tarrant to NW. SU 3753
Iburndale N Yorks 55 G4* ham 3m/5km SW of Whitby. NZ 8707
Ibworth Hants 18 B5 ham 5m/8km NW of Basingstoke. SU 5654
Icelton Avon 15 H4* loc just E of Wick St Lawrence and 5m/7km NE of Weston-super-Mare. ST 3765
Ickburgh Norfolk 38 C5 vil 1m NE of Mundford. TL 8194
Ickenham London 19 E3 loc in borough of Hillingdon 2m/3km NE of Uxbridge. TQ 0786
Ickford Bucks 18 B1 vil 4m/6km W of Thame. SP 6407
Ickham Kent 13 G2 vil 5m/7km E of Canterbury. TR 2258
Ickleford Herts 29 F4 vil 2km N of Hitchin. TL 1831
Icklesham E Sussex 13 E5 vil 2m/3km W of Winchelsea. TQ 8716
Ickleton Cambs 29 H3 vil 1m NW of Gt Chesterford. TL 4943
Icklingham Suffolk 30 C1 vil 7m/12km NW of Bury St Edmunds. Site of Roman villa 1m SE. TL 7772
Icknield Way 29 E5 etc. ancient trackway, originally running from the Wash to the S coast of England and later adapted in part by the Romans. Today it can be traced from Thetford to Baldock, below the N escarpment of the Chilterns to Streatley, and thence along the Ridgeway to Avebury.
Ickwell Green Beds 29 F3 vil 3m/4km W of Biggleswade. TL 1545
Ickworth Suffolk 30 C2 hse (NT) of 18c-19c in form of elliptical rotunda, with formal gardens, standing in large park 3m/5km SW of Bury St Edmunds. TL 8161
Icomb Glos 27 F5 vil 2m/4km SE of Stow-on-the-Wold. SP 2122
Idbury Oxon 27 F5 vil 5m/7km SE of Stow-on-the-Wold. SP 2319
Iddesleigh Devon 6 D4 vil 3m/5km NE of Hatherleigh. SS 5708
Iddinshall Ches 42 B5* loc 2km W of Tarporley. SJ 5362
Ide Devon 5 E2 vil 2m/3km SW of Exeter. SX 8990
Ideford Devon 5 E3 vil 4m/7km NE of Newton Abbot. SX 8977
Ide Hill Kent 20 B6 vil 4m/6km SW of Sevenoaks. Wooded hillside (NT) on S side of vil overlooking Weald. TQ 4851
Iden E Sussex 13 E4 vil 2m/4km N of Rye. TQ 9123
Iden Green Kent 12 D3 ham 2km E of Goudhurst. TQ 7437
Iden Green Kent 12 D4 vil 3m/5km E of Hawkhurst. TQ 8031
Idle W Yorks 48 D4 dist of Bradford 3m/5km N of city centre. SE 1737
Idle 44 C2 r formed by confluence of Rs Maun and Polter 4m/6km S of E Retford, Notts, and flowing N through E Retford to Bawtry then E into R Trent at W Stockwith. SK 7894
Idless Cornwall 2 D3* ham 2m/3km N of Truro. SW 8247
Idlicote Warwicks 27 G3 ham 3m/5km NE of Shipston on Stour. SP 2844
Idmiston Wilts 9 H1 vil on R Bourne 6m/9km NE of Salisbury. SU 1937
Idoch Water Grampian 83 F2 r in Grampian region running SW through Cuminestown and turning NW 2m/3km SE of Turriff, then flowing NW into R Deveron on W side of tn. NJ 7150
Idridgehay Derbys 43 G6 vil 3m/5km S of Wirksworth. **I. Green** loc adjoining to NW. SK 2848
Idrigill Point Skye, H'land 79 A5 headland at NW entrance to Loch Bracadale. NG 2536
Idstone Oxon 17 F3 vil 7m/11km E of Swindon. SU 2584
Iffley Oxon 18 A2 S dist of Oxford. SP 5203
Ifield Kent 20 C4 S dist of Gravesend, sometimes known as Singlewell. TQ 6570
Ifield W Sussex 11 H2 W dist of Crawley. TQ 2437
Ifold W Sussex 11 F2* dispersed loc 5m/8km NW of Billingshurst. TQ 0231
Ifold, Upper Surrey 11 F2* loc 7m/11km E of Haslemere. TQ 0033
Iford Dorset 9 H5 dist of Bournemouth beside R Stour 4m/6km E of tn centre. SZ 1393
Iford E Sussex 12 A5 vil 2m/3km S of Lewes. TQ 4007
Ifton Gwent 16 A3 loc 1m W of Caldicot. ST 4687
Ifton Heath Salop 34 A1 loc 5m/8km W of Ellesmere. SJ 3237
Ightenhill Lancs 48 B4* loc lying to E of Padiham. SD 8134
Ightfield Salop 34 C1 vil 4m/6km SE of Whitchurch. Loc of **I. Heath** 1m S. SJ 5938
Ightham Kent 20 C5 vil 4m/7km E of Sevenoaks. 2m/4km S, I. Mote, moated medieval manor hse (NT). TQ 5956
Iken Suffolk 31 G3 vil on S side of R Alde estuary 4m/6km N of Orford. TM 4155
Ilam Staffs 43 F5/F6 vil on R Manifold 1km above its junction with R Dove and 4m/6km NW of Ashbourne. Partly NT property. SK 1350
Ilchester Som 8 C2 vil on Roman Foss Way at crossing of R Yeo 5m/8km NW of Yeovil. ST 5222
Ilderton Nthmb 67 G6 ham 4m/7km SE of Wooler. NU 0121
Ilford London 20 B3 tn in borough of Redbridge 8m/13km NE of London Br. TQ 4386
Ilford Som 8 B3* ham 2m/3km N of Ilminster. ST 3617
Ilfracombe Devon 6 D1 resort on N coast 9m/15km N of Barnstaple. SS 5247
Ilkerton, East Devon 7 E1* loc 2m/3km S of Lynton. SS 7146
Ilkerton, West Devon 7 E1* loc 2m/3km SW of Lynton. SS 7046
Ilkeston Derbys 36 B1 industrial tn 8m/12km NE of Derby and 7m/11km W of Nottingham. Industries include coal-mining, iron and steel, textiles. SK 4641
Ilketshall St Andrew Suffolk 39 G6 ham 3m/5km SE of Bungay. Other hams in vicinity are **Ilketshall St John,** 2km W; **St Lawrence,** 1m SW; **St Margaret,** 2m/4km W. TM 3787
Ilkley W Yorks 48 D3 tn and minor resort in Wharfedale on site of Roman military stn of *Olicana,* 10m/16km N of Bradford. To S, **Ilkley Moor,** forming part of Rombalds Moor, qv. See also **Cow and Calf.** SE 1147
Illand Cornwall 4 A3* ham 5m/7km SW of Launceston. SX 2978
Illey W Midlands 35 F6* ham in SE part of Halesowen. Loc of **Lr Illey** to SW. SO 9881
Illidge Green Ches 42 D5* loc 3m/4km NE of Sandbach. SJ 7963
Illington Norfolk 38 D5 ham 6m/10km NE of Thetford. TL 9490
Illingworth W Yorks 48 D5 loc in Halifax 2m/4km NW of tn centre. **Illingworth Moor** loc to N. SE 0728
Illogan Cornwall 2 C4 vil 2m/3km NW of Redruth. SW 6744
Illogan Highway Cornwall 2 C4* loc 2km W of Redruth. SW 6841
Illshaw Heath W Midlands 35 G6* 2m/3km NW of Hockley Heath. SP 1374
Illston on the Hill Leics 36 C4 vil 8m/13km N of Mkt Harborough. SP 7099
Ilmer Bucks 18 C1 vil 3m/5km NW of Princes Risborough. SP 7605
Ilmington Warwicks 27 F3 vil 4m/6km NW of Shipston on Stour. SP 2143
Ilminster Som 8 B3 mkt tn 10m/16km SE of Taunton. ST 3614
Ilsington Devon 4 D3 vil 4m/7km NE of Ashburton. SX 7876
Ilsington Dorset 9 E5* loc 1m W of Tincleton and 4m/7km E of Dorchester. SY 7591
Ilsley, East Berks 18 A3 vil 9m/14km N of Newbury. SU 4881
Ilsley, West Berks 17 H3 vil 6m/9km SW of Didcot. SU 4782
Ilston (Llanilltud Gŵyr) W Glam 14 B3* vil on W side of Swansea Airport 6m/10km W of Swansea. SS 5590
Ilton N Yorks 48 D1 ham 3m/4km SW of Masham. **Ilton Resr** small resr 1km SW. SE 1978
Ilton Som 8 B3 vil 2m/3km N of Ilminster. ST 3517
Imachar S'clyde 63 F4 loc on W side of Arran 2m/4km S of Pirnmill. **Imachar Pt** is headland to W. NR 8640

Imber Wilts 16 D6 derelict vil on Salisbury Plain 6m/10km NE of Warminster. Situated in Army training area. ST 9648

Immingham Humberside 51 F6 tn 7m/11km NW of Grimsby. To NE on R Humber, **Immingham Docks.** Ship-repairing, oil refinery, chemical works. TA 1714

Impington Cambs 29 H2 vil adjoining Histon to E, 3m/5km N of Cambridge. TL 4463

Ince Ches 42 A4 vil 3m/5km E of Ellesmere Port. SJ 4576

Ince Blundell Merseyside 41 H1 vil 3m/5km SE of Formby. Hall is of 18c. SD 3203

Ince-in-Makerfield Gtr Manchester 42 B1* tn 2km SE of Wigan. Coal-mining, engineering, textiles. SD 5903

Inch Grampian 77 F4 loc 2m/4km SW of Fettercairn. NO 6271

Inch Lothian 66 A2/B2 dist of Edinburgh 3m/4km SE of city centre. NT 2770

Inchaffray Abbey Tayside 72 C3 scanty remains of early 13c abbey 6m/9km E of Crieff. NN 9522

Inchbae Forest H'land 85 D8 deer forest in Ross and Cromarty dist E of Loch Vaich. **Inchbae Lodge** at junction of R Glascarnoch and Strath Rannoch at S end of forest. NH 3778

Inchbare Tayside 77 F4 loc on West Water 2m/3km S of Edzell. NO 6065

Inchberry Grampian 82 C2 loc 7m/12km SE of Elgin. NJ 3155

Inchbraoch Tayside 77 F5/G5 island on S side of Montrose at entrance to Montrose Basin. Connected by rd and rly brs to land on N and S. Also known as Inchbrayock or Rossie. NO 7056

Inchbrayock Tayside 77 F5/G5. See Inchbraoch.

Inch Buie Central 71 F2* lower of two islands in R Dochart at Killin. Former burial place of Clan MacNab. NN 5732

Inchcailloch Central 71 E5 island off E shore of Loch Lomond opp Balmaha. Part of nature reserve comprising also Clairinch and Torrinch. Other spellings include Inchcailleach, Inchcailleoch, and Inchcailliach. NS 4090

Inchcolm Fife 65 H1 island in Firth of Forth 1m E of Dalgety Bay. Ruined medieval abbey (A.M.) NT 1882

Inchconnachan S'clyde 71 E5 island in Loch Lomond 1m SE of Luss. NS 3792

Inchcruin Central 71 E5 island in Loch Lomond 2m/3km W of Balmaha. NS 3891

Inchfad Central 71 E5 island in Loch Lomond 1m W of Balmaha. NS 3990

Inchgalbraith S'clyde 71 E5* islet in Loch Lomond 1km NE of Rossdhu. Remains of cas. NS 3690

Inch Garvie Lothian 65 G1* islet with lighthouse in Firth of Forth beneath Forth rly br. NT 1379

Inchinnan S'clyde 64 C2 vil 3m/5km N of Paisley. Tyre mnfre. NS 4868

Inchkeith Fife 65 H1 narrow island, just over 1km long from N to S, in Firth of Forth 3m/4km SE of Kinghorn. Lighthouse near N end. NT 2982

Inch Kenneth S'clyde 69 C5 island of about 200 acres or 80 hectares at entrance to Loch na Keal, W coast of Mull. Remains of 12c chapel (A.M.). NM 4335

Inchlaggan H'land 74 C2 loc in Glen Garry, Lochaber dist, 8m/13km W of Invergarry. NH 1701

Inchlonaig S'clyde 71 E5 island in Loch Lomond opp vil of Luss. NS 3893

Inchmahome Central 71 G4* island in Lake of Menteith, qv, with remains of medieval priory where Mary, Queen of Scots lay hidden, 1547–8. NN 5700

Inchmarnock S'clyde 63 G2 sparsely populated, low-lying island 1m W of Bute off St Ninian's Pt. Measures about 2m/3km N to S and about 1km across. NS 0259

Inchmickery Lothian 66 A1 islet in Firth of Forth 3m/4km NW of Granton Harbour. NT 2080

Inchmoan S'clyde 71 E5 island in Loch Lomond 1m NE of Rossdhu. NS 3790

Inchmurrin S'clyde 71 E5, E6 largest island in Loch Lomond, 3m/4km N of Balloch. Ruins of old Lennox Castle at SW end of island. NS 3887

Inchnacardoch Forest H'land 74 D1 state forest and deer forest in Inverness dist W of Fort Augustus. NH 3409

Inchnadamph H'land 85 C5 vil in Sutherland dist at head of Loch Assynt. **Inchnadamph Forest** is deer forest to E. Extensive cave system in valley of R Traligill to SE. NC 2521

Inch Talla Central 71 G4* islet in Lake of Menteith, qv, with remains of medieval cas. NN 5700

Inchtavannach S'clyde 71 E5 island close to W shore of Loch Lomond between Luss and Rossdhu. NS 3691

Inchture Tayside 73 F2 vil 8m/12km W of Dundee. NO 2828

Inchtuthill Tayside 73 E1 site of Roman fortress on N side of R Tay 2km SE of Spittalfield, built about AD 83 but soon abandoned. NO 1239

Inchvuilt H'land 80 C4 locality on R Farrar in Inverness dist nearly 2m/3km E of dam of Loch Monar. NH 2238

Inchyra Tayside 73 E3 loc on N bank of R Tay 5m/8km E of Perth. NO 1820

Indian Queens Cornwall 3 E3 vil 3m/5km S of St Columb Major. Origin of name unknown. SW 9159

Ingale Skerry Orkney 89 C6* rock island off S coast of Stronsay 2km SW of Lamb Head, and 2km SE of Tor Ness across **Ingale Sound.** HY 6719

Inga Ness Orkney 89 B5* headland on W coast of island of Westray 4m/7km SE of Noup Hd. HY 4143

Inganess Bay Orkney 89 B6* large bay on N coast of Mainland 2m/3km E of Kirkwall. Grimsetter Airport at head of bay. HY 4808

Ingatestone Essex 20 C2 tn 5m/8km NE of Brentwood. TQ 6499

Ingbirchworth S Yorks 43 G1 vil 2m/3km NW of Penistone. **Ingbirchworth Resr** to W. SE 2205

Ingestre Staffs 35 F2 vil 4m/6km E of Stafford. SJ 9824

Ingham Lincs 44 D3 vil 8m/13km N of Lincoln. SK 9483

Ingham Norfolk 39 G2 vil 2km NE of Stalham. **I. Corner** vil 1km N. TG 3926

Ingham Suffolk 30 D1 vil 4m/7km N of Bury St Edmunds. TL 8570

Ingleborough Norfolk 38 A3 loc 4m/6km N of Wisbech. TF 4715

Ingleborough N Yorks 48 A2* loc adjoining Clapham to E. SD 7469

Ingleborough N Yorks 48 A1 mt 3m/5km NE of Ingleton. Height 2373 ft or 723 metres. Traces of ancient fort at summit. At S skirt of mt is **Ingleborough Cave,** limestone cavern. SD 7474

Ingleby Derbys 36 A2 ham on R Trent 3m/4km NW of Melbourne. SK 3526

Ingleby Lincs 44 D3* loc 2m/3km N of Saxilby. SK 8977

Ingleby Arncliffe N Yorks 54 D4 vil 7m/11km NE of Northallerton. NZ 4400

Ingleby Cross N Yorks 54 D4/D5 loc at crossroads adjoining Ingleby Arncliffe to SE. NZ 4400

Ingleby Greenhow N Yorks 55 E4 vil 4m/6km E of Stokesley. NZ 5806

Ingleigh Green Devon 7 E4* ham 4m/7km NE of Holsworthy. SS 6007

Inglesbatch Avon 16 C5* ham 4m/6km SW of Bath. ST 7061

Inglesham Wilts 17 F2 ham on R Thames 1m SW of Lechlade. Ham of **Upr Inglesham** 2km S. SU 2098

Ingleton Durham 54 B3 vil 3m/5km E of Staindrop. NZ 1720

Ingleton N Yorks 47 G1 vil on R Greta in limestone Craven dist 6m/10km SE of Kirkby Lonsdale. Spelaeological centre. SD 6972

Inglewhite Lancs 47 F4 ham 7m/11km N of Preston. SD 5440

Inglewood Forest Cumbria 52 D1/53 E1* rural area and former hunting district between Penrith and Carlisle. NY 4344

Inglismaldie Forest Grampian 77 F4 state forest midway between Edzell and Marykirk. NO 6467

Ingliston Lothian 65 G2 site of Royal Highland Showground, 7m/11km W of Edinburgh and 1km SW of Edinburgh Airport. Motor-racing circuit. NT 1472

Ingoe Nthmb 61 E4 ham 3m/5km NW of Stamfordham. NZ 0374

Ingol Lancs 47 F5* loc in Preston 2m/4km NW of tn centre. SD 5131

Ingoldisthorpe Norfolk 38 B2 vil 5m/8km S of Hunstanton. TF 6832

Ingoldmells Lincs 45 H4 vil 4m/6km N of Skegness. **Ingoldmells Pt,** headland 1m E. TF 5668

Ingoldsby Lincs 37 E2 vil 7m/11km SE of Grantham. TF 0130

Ingon Warwicks 27 F2 loc 2m/3km NE of Stratford-upon-Avon. SP 2157

Ingram Nthmb 67 G6 vil 4m/7km NW of Whittingham. NU 0116

Ingrave Essex 20 C3 suburban loc 2m/3km SE of Brentwood. TQ 6292

Ingrebourne 20 B3 r rising near Brentwood, Essex, and flowing S into R Thames 1m SW of Rainham, borough of Havering, London. TQ 5180

Ingrow W Yorks 48 C4 S dist of Keighley. SE 0539

Ings Cumbria 52 D5* loc 2m/3km E of Windermere. SD 4498

Ingst Avon 16 B3 ham 3m/5km NE of Severn Beach. ST 5887

Ingstag H'land 86 E1 loc near N coast of Caithness dist 4m/7km E of Castletown. Also spelt Inkstack. ND 2570

Ingworth Norfolk 39 F2 vil 2m/3km N of Aylsham. TG 1929

Inham's End Cambs 37 G4* SE end of Whittlesey. TL 2796

Inhurst Hants 18 B5 loc 4m/6km NE of Kingsclere. SU 5761

Inishail S'clyde 70 C3 island in Loch Awe at entrance to arm of loch running NW to Pass of Brander in Argyll. Ruined ch of St Pindoca. Sometimes spelt Innishail. NN 1024

Inkberrow H & W 27 E2 vil 5m/7km W of Alcester. SP 0157

Inkerman Durham 54 A1* loc 1m NW of Tow Law. NZ 1139

Inkersall Derbys 43 H4* loc 2km S of Staveley. **Inkersall Green** loc 1km NW. SK 4272

Inkpen Berks 17 G5 vil 4m/6km SE of Hungerford. 2km S, **I. Beacon,** viewpoint on chalk downs. SU 3664

Inkstack H'land 86 E1 loc near N coast of Caithness dist 4m/7km E of Castletown. Also spelt Ingstag. ND 2570

Inlands W Sussex 10 D4* loc just NE of Southbourne, 2m/3km E of Emsworth. SU 7706

Inmarsh Wilts 16 D5* loc to S of Seend and 4m/6km W of Devizes. ST 9460

Innellan S'clyde 63 G1 vil and resort in Argyll on W shore of Firth of Clyde, 4m/7km S of Dunoon. NS 1470

Inner Hebrides 114. Group of islands off W coast of Scotland, some in Highland and some in Strathclyde region. The chief islands in Highland region are Skye (with Raasay), Canna, Rum, Eigg, and Muck; and in Strathclyde region Coll, Tiree, Mull (with Iona), Colonsay, Jura, and Islay. See also Western Isles (for Outer Hebrides).

Inner Holm Orkney 89 A6* islet on E side of Stromness Harbour, Mainland, to N of Outer Holm. HY 2508

Innerleithen Borders 66 B5 small tn at confluence of Leithen Water and R Tweed, 6m/9km SE of Peebles. Woollen mnfre. Site of Roman camp on SW side. NT 3336

Innerleven Fife 73 F4 docks area in Methil, at mouth of R Leven. NO 3700

Innerpeffray Tayside 72 C3 loc 3m/5km SE of Crieff. Cas is ruined 17c tower hse. **Innerpeffray Library** is oldest public library in Scotland, founded in 1691 and housed in 18c bldg. Several Roman sites in vicinity. NN 9018

Inner Score Shetland 89 E7* small uninhabited island off N end of island of Bressay, between it and Outer Score. HU 5145

Inner Sound H'land 78, 79 sea channel between W coast of Ross and Cromarty dist and the islands of Raasay and Rona. Width from 4m/7km to 7m/11km. NG 64

Innertown Orkney 89 A6* loc on Mainland just W of Stromness. HY 2409

Innerwick Lothian 67 E2 vil 4m/6km SE of Dunbar. NT 7273

Innerwick Tayside 71 G1 loc in Glen Lyon 1m below Br of Balgie. NN 5847

Inninmore Bay H'land 68 E4 bay on Sound of Mull extending NW from Rubha an Ridire, Lochaber dist. NM 7241

Innis Chonain S'clyde 70 C2* island off W shore of Loch Awe in Argyll 2km SW of vil of Lochawe. Connected to shore by a br. NN 1025

Innis Chonnell S'clyde 70 B4* islet near E shore of Loch Awe in Argyll, opp Dalavich. Ruins of Ardchonnell Castle, 15c stronghold of the Campbells. NM 9711

Innishail S'clyde alternative spelling of Inishail, qv.

Innis Shearraich S'clyde 70 B4* islet off E shore of Loch Awe in Argyll, opp Portinnisherrich. Stepping-stones give access at low water. 13c chapel. NM 9711

Innsworth Glos 26 D5* NE suburb of Gloucester. SO 8621

Inny 3 H1 r rising near Davidstow, Cornwall, and flowing SE into R Tamar S of Dunterton. SX 3877

Insch Grampian 83 E4 vil 10m/16km NW of Inverurie. Picardy Stone (A.M.), 2m/3km NW, dates from 7c or 8c and bears Pictish inscriptions. NJ 6328

Insh H'land 75 H1 vil in Badenoch and Strathspey dist 4m/6km E of Kingussie. **Inshriach Forest** is state forest to NE. NH 8101

Inshegra H'land 84 C2* locality on N side of Loch Inchard, W coast of Sutherland dist. NC 2455

Insh Island S'clyde 69 E6 uninhabited island in Firth of Lorn 1m W of island of Seil, from which it is separated by Sound of Insh. NM 7319

Inskip Lancs 47 E4 vil 7m/12km NW of Preston. **Inskip Moss Side** loc 1m NW. SD 4637

Instoneville S Yorks 49 G6* loc adjoining Askern to S. SE 5512

Instow Devon 6 D2 vil on E side of R Torridge estuary 3m/5km N of Bideford. SS 4730

Intake S Yorks 43 H3 dist of Sheffield 3m/4km SE of city centre. SK 3884

Intake S Yorks 44 B1* dist of Doncaster 2m/3km E of tn centre. SE 6003

Inver H'land 85 B5 r in Sutherland dist flowing W from Loch Assynt to Loch Inver. NC 0923

Inver H'land 87 B7 vil in Ross and Cromarty dist on S shore of Dornoch Firth 5m/8km E of Tain. **Inver Bay** is inlet on N side of vil. NH 8682

Inverailort H'land 68 E1 locality with jetty at head of Loch Ailort, Lochaber dist. NM 7681

Inver Alligin H'land 78 F3 vil in Ross and Cromarty dist on N shore of Upr Loch Torridon. NG 8457

Inverallochy Grampian 83 H1 fishing vil on NE coast 3m/5km E of Fraserburgh. **Castle of Inverallochy,** an old stronghold of the Comyns, 2km S. NK 0465

Inveran H'land 85 F6* location of power stn (Shin Hydro-Electricity Scheme) at confluence of Rs Shin and Oykel in Sutherland dist, 4m/6km NW of Bonar Br. NH 5797

Inveraray S'clyde 70 C4 small tn in Argyll on W shore of Loch Fyne, 6m/10km SW of head of loch and 19m/31km NE of Lochgilphead. **Inveraray Castle** to N, seat of the Dukes of Argyll, dates mainly from 18c; damaged by fire in 1975. NN 0908

Inverarity Tayside 77 E6 loc 4m/6km S of Forfar. NO 4544

Inverarnan Central 71 E3 locality on R Falloch 2m/3km N of Ardlui at head of Loch Lomond. NN 3118

Inverasdale H'land 78 F1/F2 locality on W side of Loch Ewe, W coast of Ross and Cromarty dist, 4m/7km NW of Poolewe. NG 8286

Inverbeg S'clyde 71 E5 locality on W side of Loch Lomond 3m/5km N of Luss. Ferry for pedestrians to Rowardennan. NS 3497

Inverbervie Grampian 77 G4 small tn at mouth of Bervie Water on E coast 9m/14km S of Stonehaven. A royal burgh since 1342. Fish curing, textile mnfre. NO 8372

Inverboyndie Grampian 83 E1* vil 2km W of Banff. NJ 6664

Inverchaolain S'clyde 63 G1 locality on E shore of Loch Striven, Argyll, 4m/7km N of Ardyne Pt. NS 0975

Invercloy S'clyde. Former name of Brodick, Arran.

Inverclyde 114 admin dist of S'clyde region.

Inver Dalavil Skye, H'land 79 D7 bay on W coast of Sleat peninsula 4m/6km N of Pt of Sleat. NG 5705
Inverdruie H'land 81 H6 loc near mouth of R Druie in Badenoch and Strathspey dist, 2km SE of Aviemore. NH 9010
Inveresk Lothian 66 B2 suburb of Musselburgh to S, on site of Roman stn. NT 3472
Inverewe H'land. See Poolewe.
Inverey Grampian 76 B2 loc at foot of Glen Ey 4m/7km W of Braemar. NO 0889
Inverfarigaig H'land 81 E5 locality on SE shore of Loch Ness at mouth of R Farigaig, 2m/4km NE of Foyers, Inverness dist. NH 5223
Invergarry H'land 74 D2 vil at foot of Glen Garry in Lochaber dist. **Invergarry Castle,** ruin on shore of Loch Oich to SE. NH 3001
Invergloy H'land 74 D3 locality in Lochaber dist at mouth of R Gloy on SE shore of Loch Lochy. NN 2288
Invergordon H'land 81 F1 port on N shore of Cromarty Firth, Ross and Cromarty dist, 11m/18km NE of Dingwall. Aluminium works, distillery. Development in connection with North Sea oil. NH 7068
Invergowrie Tayside 73 F2 suburb of Dundee 4m/6km W of city centre, on Firth of Tay. Paper mnfre. Horticultural research institute at Milnefield Farm. NO 3430
Inverguseran H'land 79 E7 loc on NW coast of Knoydart, Lochaber dist, at foot of Glen Guseran. NG 7407
Inverie H'land 79 F7 vil in Lochaber dist, on S side of Knoydart. Vil is situated on **Inverie Bay** on N side of Loch Nevis. **Inverie R** flows W into bay 1m SE of vil. NG 7600
Inverinan Forest S'clyde 70 B3 state forest surrounding locality of **Inverinan** on W side of Loch Awe in Argyll. Information centre and nature trails. See also Inverliever Forest. NM 9917
Inverinate H'land 80 A5 Forestry Commission vil on E bank of Loch Duich, Skye and Lochalsh dist, 2m/3km from head of loch. State forest extends NW and SE. Deer forest to E. NG 9122
Inverkeilor Tayside 77 F5 vil 6m/9km N of Arbroath. NO 6649
Inverkeithing Fife 65 G1 tn on **Inverkeithing Bay** on N side of Firth of Forth, 4m/6km SE of Dunfermline. Paper mnfre, shipbreaking, engineering. NT 1383
Inverkeithny Grampian 83 E2 vil on Burn of Forgue near its confluence with R Deveron, 4m/6km S of Aberchirder. NJ 6246
Inverkip S'clyde 64 A2 vil on Firth of Clyde 5m/8km SW of Greenock. NS 2072
Inverkirkaig H'land 85 B5 locality in Sutherland dist at head of Loch Kirkaig on W coast 2m/3km SW of Lochinver. NC 0719
Inverlael H'land 85 C7 locality at head of Loch Broom, Ross and Cromarty dist. To E is the deer forest of **Inverlael Forest.** NH 1886
Inverleith Lothian 66 A1* dist of Edinburgh 2km NW of city centre. Contains Royal Botanic Garden. NT 2475
Inverliever S'clyde 70 C2 hse and bay on E side of Loch Etive, Argyll, 4m/6km NE of Bonawe. NN 0635
Inverliever Forest S'clyde 70 B4* state forest on W side of Loch Awe in Argyll, to S of Dalavich. Information centre and nature trails. See also Inverinan Forest. NM 9409
Inverlochy H'land 74 C4 locality at mouth of R Lochy in Lochaber dist, 2km NE of Fort William. Distillery. 13c cas (A.M.) near mouth of r; present-day cas 2km NE. NN 1275
Inverlussa S'clyde 69 E8* loc at mouth of Lussa R on E coast of Jura. NR 6486
Invermark Castle Tayside 77 E3* ruined cas, former residence of the Stirlings, at foot of Glen Lee 3m/5km W of Tarfside. NO 4480
Invermoriston H'land 80 D5 vil in Inverness dist on R Moriston 1km above mouth of r. **Invermoriston Forest** is deer forest to N. NH 4216
Invernaver H'land 86 A2 loc near N coast of Caithness dist 1m S of Bettyhill. NC 7060
Inverness H'land 81 F3 tn at mouth of R Ness at entrance to Beauly Firth, 92m/148km W of Peterhead and 113m/181km NW of Edinburgh. Administrative and tourist centre. Industries include distilling, iron founding, saw mills, woollen goods. Airport at Dalcross, qv. Caledonian Canal passes to W of tn. NH 6645
Invernettie Grampian 83 H3 loc 2km S of Peterhead. NK 1244
Inverorar S'clyde 70 D1 locality at SW corner of Loch Tulla in Argyll. NN 2741
Inverpolly Forest H'land 85 B5, B6 nature reserve near NW coast of Ross and Cromarty dist 7m/11km S of Lochinver. NC 0912
Inverroy H'land 74 D3* locality in Lochaber dist between Roy Br and Spean Br. NN 2581
Inversanda H'land 74 B5 locality in Lochaber dist at foot of Glen Tarbert. **Inversanda Bay** to E at mouth of R Tarbert, on Loch Linnhe. NM 9359
Inverscaddle Bay H'land 74 B4 bay of marsh, sand and shingle on W shore of Loch Linnhe, Lochaber dist, at mouth of R Scaddle. NN 0268
Invershiel H'land 80 A5 locality in Skye and Lochalsh dist at head of Loch Duich. NG 9319
Invershin H'land 85 F6 loc in Sutherland dist at confluence of Rs Oykel and Shin, 4m/6km NW of Bonar Br. NH 5796
Invershore H'land 86 E4* loc on E coast of Caithness dist 1km SW of Lybster. Lighthouse. ND 2434
Inversnaid Central 71 E4 locality on E shore of Loch Lomond opp Inveruglas. Garrison of Inversnaid, to NE up glen towards Loch Arklet, is farm incorporating remains of fort built in 1713 as deterrent to the clan Macgregor. NN 3308
Inverugie Grampian 83 H2 loc on R Ugie 2m/4km NW of Peterhead. Ruined cas of the Keiths, Earls Marischal. NK 1048
Inveruglas S'clyde 71 E4 locality on W shore of Loch Lomond 3m/5km N of Tarbet, at mouth of **Inveruglas Water,** stream descending from Loch Sloy. Power stn operated by water conveyed from Loch Sloy by aqueduct. **Inveruglas Isle** is islet in Loch Lomond, with remains of cas. NN 3109
Inverurie Grampian 83 F4 tn near confluence of Rs Don and Urie 14m/22km NW of Aberdeen. On NW outskirts, Brandsbutt Stone (A.M.), with 8c Pictish symbols and oghamic inscriptions. See also Easter Aquhorthies. NJ 7721
Invervar Tayside 76 G6 loc at foot of **Invervar Burn** on N side of Glen Lyon, 5m/8km W of Fortingall. NN 6648
Inverwick Forest H'land 80 D6 deer forest in Inverness dist 3m/5km NW of Fort Augustus. NH 3413
Inwardleigh Devon 6 D5 vil 3m/5km NW of Okehampton. SX 5699
Inworth Essex 30 D6 ham 2km SE of Kelvedon. TL 8817
Inzie Head Grampian 83 H1 headland on NE coast, at NW end of Strathbeg Bay, 2m/3km SE of Inverallochy. NK 0662
Iona S'clyde 69 B5, B6 island about 3m/5km long NE to SW and over 1m wide lying nearly 1m off W end of Ross of Mull across Sound of Iona. Site of monastery founded by St Columba in 6c. Remains of 13c convent. Cathedral, mainly 16c, restored. Tombs of the Kings, where several kings lie buried. Island much visited in summer. Ferry connection with Fionnphort on Mull. NM 2723
Iorsa Water S'clyde 63 F4 r on Arran rising to W of Casteal Abhail and running SW down Glen Iorsa into Kilbrannan Sound at N end of Machrie Bay. NR 8836
Iping W Sussex 11 E3 vil on R Rother 2m/4km NW of Midhurst. SU 8522
Ipplepen Devon 5 E4 vil 3m/5km SW of Newton Abbot. SX 8366
Ippollitts Herts. See St Ippollitts.
Ipsden Oxon 18 B3 vil 3m/5km SE of Wallingford. SU 6385
Ipstones Staffs 43 E6 vil 4m/7km N of Cheadle. SK 0249
Ipswich Suffolk 31 F4 county and industrial tn, and port (R Orwell), 66m/106km NE of London. Airport 3m/4km SE. TM 1644
Irby Merseyside 41 H3 suburb 2m/3km NW of Heswall. **Irby Hill** loc 1km N. **Irby Heath** (NT). SJ 2584
Irby in the Marsh Lincs 45 H5 vil 4m/6km NW of Wainfleet. TF 4763
Irby upon Humber Humberside 45 F1 vil 6m/9km SW of Grimsby. TA 1904
Irchester Northants 28 D2 vil 3m/4km SE of Wellingborough. Vil of **Lit Irchester** to NW. Site of Roman tn to N. SP 9265
Ireby Cumbria 52 C1 vil 6m/10km S of Wigton. **High Ireby** ham 2km S. NY 2338
Ireby Lancs 47 G1 vil 3m/5km NW of Ingleton. SD 6575
Ireland Beds 29 F4* ham 2m/3km N of Shefford. TL 1341
Ireland Orkney 89 A6* loc on Mainland 5m/8km SW of Finstown, on E side of Bay of Ireland. HY 2909
Ireland Shetland 89 E8* loc on W coast of Mainland 9m/14km N of Sumburgh Hd. HU 3721
Ireland's Cross Salop 34 D1* loc 1km SE of Woore. SJ 7341
Ireleth Cumbria 46 D1 vil 2m/4km N of Dalton-in-Furness. SD 2277
Ireshopeburn Durham 53 G1* ham 1m SE of Wearhead. NY 8638
Ireton Houses Derbys 43 H6* loc 2km E of Belper. SK 3747
Irfon 25 E3 r rising 2m/4km SW of Claerwen Resr dam, Powys. It flows S to Llanwrtyd Wells, then E by Llangammarch Wells and Garth to join R Wye on NW side of Builth Wells. SO 0351
Irk 42 D2* r whose head waters join at Middleton, Gtr Manchester, and which then flows S into R Irwell at Manchester. SJ 8398
Irlam Gtr Manchester 42 C2 tn 8m/13km SW of Manchester. Engineering; soap and margarine mnfre. SJ 7193
Irlam o' th' Height Gtr Manchester 42 D2 dist of Salford 2m/4km NW of tn centre. SD 7900
Irnham Lincs 37 E2 vil 6m/10km NW of Bourne. Hall, 16c. Manor hse, 18c. TF 0226
Iron Acton Avon 16 B3 vil 3m/5km W of Chipping Sodbury. ST 6783
Iron Bridge Cambs 38 A4* loc and br over Sixteen Foot Drain 4m/6km NW of Welney. TL 4898
Ironbridge Salop 34 D4 tn in Telford 3m/4km S of Dawley. Situated on side of R Severn gorge and named after br spanning it. Br is world's first cold blast iron br, cast in 1778; still used by pedestrians. SJ 6703
Iron Cross Warwicks 27 E3 loc 6m/9km N of Evesham. SP 0652
Ironmill Bay Fife 65 G1* bay on N side of Firth of Forth to W of Charlestown. Long pier or landing stage on W side of bay. NT 0584
Irons Bottom Surrey 19 F6* loc 2m/4km S of Reigate. TQ 2546
Ironville Derbys 43 H5* vil 3m/4km E of Ripley. SK 4351
Irstead Norfolk 39 G3* ham 3m/4km NE of Horning near S end of Barton Broad. **I. Street** loc 1m SW. TG 3620
Irt 52 B5 r flowing SW from foot of Wast Water, Cumbria, into R Esk estuary at Ravenglass. SD 0896
Irthing 60 A5 r formed by confluence of Gair Burn and Tarn Beck on border of Cumbria and Nthmb on W side of Wark Forest, and flowing generally SW into R Eden 5m/7km E of Carlisle. NY 4657
Irthington Cumbria 60 B5 vil 2m/3km W of Brampton across R Irthing. Carlisle Airport to SW. NY 4961
Irthlingborough Northants 28 D1 tn 4m/7km NE of Wellingborough. Chief industries iron and footwear. SP 9470
Irton N Yorks 55 H6 vil 3m/5km SW of Scarborough. TA 0184
Irvine S'clyde 64 B5 port (and New Tn, designated 1965) on and near mouth of **R Irvine,** 7m/11km W of Kilmarnock. Industries include chemicals, engineering, glass mnfre, plastics. R flows W to Galston, and passes S of Kilmarnock to Irvine and **Irvine Bay** to W. NS 3239
Irwell 42 C2* r rising N of Bacup, Lancs, and flowing S through Ramsbottom and Bury to Manchester and Salford, then W to join R Mersey at Irlam, Gtr Manchester. SJ 7293
Isabella Pit Nthmb 61 G3* loc in SW part of Blyth. NZ 3080
Isauld H'land 86 C2 loc near N coast of Caithness dist 1km E of Reay. NC 9765
Isay W Isles 88 A3* islet in W Loch Tarbert 3m/5km NW of Tarbert, Harris. NB 1002
Isay Island Skye, H'land 78 A4 uninhabited island in Loch Dunvegan 2m/4km E of Dunvegan Hd. NG 2157
Isbister Orkney 89 B6* loc on Mainland at head of **Bay of Isbister,** an inlet of Wide Firth, qv. HY 3918
Isbister Shetland 89 E6 loc on Mainland 3m/4km S of Pt of Fethaland. Northern terminus of rd. HU 3791
Isbister Shetland 89 F7* locality near E coast of island of Whalsay 3m/4km SW of Skaw Taing. **Loch Isbister** to N. **Isbister Holm** small uninhabited island 2km off coast to E. HU 5764
Isbister, Loch of Orkney 89 A6* small loch on Mainland 3m/5km NW of Dounby. HY 2523
Isbourne 27 E3 r rising in Cotswold Hills near Winchcombe, Glos, and flowing N into R Avon at Evesham, H & W. SP 0343
Isca Gwent. See Caerleon.
Isca Dumnoniorum Devon. See Exeter.
Ise 28 D1 r rising N of Naseby, Northants, and flowing E then S past Kettering and into R Nene on SE side of Wellingborough. SP 9067
Isfield E Sussex 12 B5 vil in R Ouse valley 3m/5km SW of Uckfield. TQ 4417
Isham Northants 28 D1 vil 3m/5km S of Kettering. SP 8873
Isington Hants 11 E1* ham 2km SW of Bentley and 5m/8km SW of Farnham. SU 7742
Isla 76 C6 r rising on borders of Grampian and Tayside regions S of Braemar and running S down Glen Isla to Airlie Castle, and on to R Tay 4m/7km W of Coupar Angus. NO 1637
Isla 82 D2 r in Grampian region rising 3m/4km NE of Dufftown and flowing NE to Keith, then E to R Deveron 5m/8km N of Huntly. Noted for trout. NH 5347
Island Barn Reservoir Surrey 19 F4* resr on 'island' formed by Rs Mole and Ember, S of E and W Molesey. TQ 1367
Island Carr Humberside 45 E1* loc adjoining Brigg to W. SE 9907
Island I Vow S'clyde. See Eilean Vow.
Island, Little W Midlands 35 F4* loc in Walsall 3m/4km W of tn centre. SO 9798
Island, Lower Kent 13 F1* W dist of Whitstable. TR 1066
Island Macaskin S'clyde 69 F7 island 2km long NE to SW in Loch Craignish in Argyll, near entrance to loch. NR 7899
Island of Danna S'clyde. See Danna I.
Island of Raasay Skye, H'land. See Raasay.
Island of Rona Skye, H'land. See Rona.
Island of Stroma H'land. See Stroma.
Islandpool H & W 35 E6* loc 3m/4km NE of Kidderminster. SO 8580
Islands of Fleet D & G 58 B6 group of small islands near E side of Wigtown Bay, near entrance to Fleet Bay. See Ardwall I., Barlocco I., and Murray's Is. NX 5749
Island, The Cornwall 2 B4 alternative name for St Ives Hd, N of St Ives. SW 5241
Islay S'clyde 62 most southerly of Inner Hebrides, and third in size, measuring 25m/40km N to S and 20m/32km E to W; lies off SW coast of Jura, from which it is separated by the narrow Sound of Islay. Is mainly low-lying and fertile. Numerous species of birds; large herds of deer in the W. Port Ellen is chief tn and port. Airport at Glenegedale. Port Askaig on Sound of Islay has ferries to Kintyre and Jura. Chief industries are distilling, farming, and fishing. NR 36
Isle 8 C2 r rising N of Chard in Somerset and flowing generally NE into R Parrett 2m/3km S of Langport. ST 4123
Isle Abbotts Som 8 B2 vil 4m/6km N of Ilminster. ST 3520
Isle Brewers Som 8 B2 vil 4m/7km N of Ilminster. ST 3621
Isleham Cambs 38 B6 vil 4m/7km W of Mildenhall. Remains of Norman priory (A.M.). TL 6474

Isle Martin H'land 85 B6 uninhabited island, outlier of the Summer Isles group, off W coast of Ross and Cromarty dist 3m/5km NW of Ullapool. Area about 600 acres or 240 hectares. NH 0999
ISLE OF, ISLES OF. For names beginning with these words, see under next word. This also applies to names beginning with North, South, East, West; Great, Little; Greater, Lesser; High, Low; Higher, Lower; Upper, Nether; Far, Near; Mid, Middle; The, Y, Yr.
Isle Ornsay Skye, H'land 79 E7 vil on E coast of Sleat peninsula, 7m/11km SE of Broadford. Also known as Isleornsay, or Eilean Iarmain. Harbour formed by coast of Sleat and W coast of island of Ornsay, qv. NG 7012
Isle Pool Salop 34 B3* lake in loop of R Severn 4m/6km NW of Shrewsbury. SJ 4617
Isle Ristol H'land. See Ristol.
Islesteps D & G 59 E4* loc 2m/4km S of Dumfries. NX 9672
Isle Tower D & G 59 E3* 16c tower hse on W bank of R Nith, 5m/8km NW of Dumfries. Formerly on an island in r. NX 9383
Isleworth London 19 F4 dist on left bank of R Thames in borough of Hounslow 9m/15km W of Charing Cross. **I. Ait,** an island in the r to E. TQ 1675
Isley Walton Leics 36 A2 ham 7m/11km NE of Ashby de la Zouch. SK 4225
Islington London 19 G3* borough some 3m/4km NE of Charing Cross. TQ 3184
Islington N Yorks 49 G4* loc 1m NE of Tadcaster. SE 5044
Islip Northants 37 E6 vil 1km W of Thrapston. SP 9878
Islip Oxon 28 A6 vil 5m/8km N of Oxford. SP 5214
Islivig W Isles 88 A2* vil near W coast of Lewis 6m/9km SW of Uig. NA 9927
Islwyn 118 admin dist of Gwent.
Istead Rise Kent 20 C4* residential loc 3m/4km S of Northfleet. TQ 6370
Isurium N Yorks. See Aldborough.
Itchen Hants 10 B4 dist of Southampton on E bank of R Itchen 2km E of city centre. Vehicle ferry across r. SU 4311
Itchen 10 B4 r rising 1km W of Hinton Ampner in Hampshire and flowing N to New Alresford, then W to Kings Worthy, then S through Winchester and Eastleigh into Southampton Water at Southampton. A chalk stream famous for trout-fishing in its upper reaches. SU 4209
Itchen Abbas Hants 10 C2 vil on R Itchen 4m/6km NE of Winchester. 1m N, site of Roman villa. SU 5332
Itchenor, West W Sussex 11 E4 vil on S side of Chichester Channel 6m/10km NW of Selsey. SU 7901
Itchen Stoke Hants 10 C2 vil beside R Itchen 2m/3km W of New Alresford. SU 5632
Itchingfield W Sussex 11 G2 vil 3m/5km SW of Horsham. TQ 1328
Itchington Avon 16 B3 loc 3m/4km SE of Thornbury. ST 6587
Ithon 25 E2/E3 r rising 4m/7km S of Newtown, Powys, and flowing S to Llandrindod Wells and into R Wye 2km S of Newbridge on Wye. SO 0156
Itteringham Norfolk 39 F2 vil 4m/6km NW of Aylsham. TG 1430
Itton (Llanddinol) Gwent 16 A2 ham 3m/4km W of Chepstow. ST 4995
Ivegill Cumbria 60 A6 ham 8m/13km S of Carlisle. NY 4143
Ivel 29 F3 r rising near Clothall, SE of Baldock, Herts, and flowing N past Biggleswade and Sandy into R Ouse at Tempsford, Beds. TL 1653
Ivelet N Yorks 53 H5* loc on R Swale 1m W of Gunnerside. SD 9598
Iver Bucks 19 E3 vil in R Colne valley 4m/7km E of Slough. Suburb of **I. Heath** 2km N. TQ 0381
Iveston Durham 61 F6 vil 2m/3km E of Consett. NZ 1350
Ivetsey Bank Staffs 35 E3* loc 2m/3km SE of Blymhill. SJ 8310
Ivinghoe Bucks 28 D6 vil below N escarpment of Chiltern Hills 3m/5km NE of Tring. **I. Beacon** (NT), notable viewpoint, is 1m E. (Also known as Beacon Hill.) SP 9416
Ivinghoe Aston Bucks 28 D5 vil 5m/8km SW of Dunstable. SP 9518
Ivington H & W 26 A2 ham 2m/3km SW of Leominster. SO 4756
Ivington Green H & W 26 A2* ham 3m/4km SW of Leominster. SO 4656
Ivybridge Devon 4 C5 small mnfg tn on R Erme 10m/16km E of Plymouth. SX 6356
Ivychurch Kent 13 F4 vil on Romney Marsh 3m/5km NW of New Romney. TR 0227
Ivy Hatch Kent 20 C6 ham 2m/3km S of Ightham. TQ 5854
Ivythorn Hill Som. See Walton, near Street.
Ivy Todd Norfolk 38 D4 loc 5m/8km E of Swaffham. TF 8909
Iwade Kent 21 E5 vil 3m/4km N of Sittingbourne. TQ 9067
Iwerne 9 F3* r rising at I. Minster in Dorset and flowing S into R Stour between Durweston and Stourpaine, NW of Blandford Forum. ST 8509
Iwerne Courtney Dorset 9 F3 vil at SW end of Cranborne Chase 4m/7km N of Blandford Forum. Also known as Shroton. ST 8512
Iwerne Minster Dorset 9 F3 vil on W edge of Cranborne Chase 5m/8km N of Blandford Forum. ST 8614
Iwerne Stepleton Dorset 9 F3 loc at SW end of Cranborne Chase 4m/6km N of Blandford Forum. ST 8812
Iwrch 33 H2 r rising on Cadair Berwyn, Clwyd, and running SE into R Tanant 2m/3km SE of Llanrhaeadr-ym-Mochnant. SJ 1424
Ixworth Suffolk 30 D1 vil on site of Romano-British settlement 6m/10km NE of Bury St Edmunds. **Ixworth Abbey** is 17c-18c hse with remains of 12c priory. TL 9370
Ixworth Thorpe Suffolk 30 D1 vil 2m/3km NW of Ixworth. TL 9173

J

Jackfield Salop 34 D4* loc 1m SE of Ironbridge. SJ 6802
Jack Green Lancs 47 F5* loc 1m N of Brindle. SD 5925
Jack Hill N Yorks 48 D3/49 E3 loc 1km S of Swinsty Resr. SE 1951
Jackhouse Reservoir Lancs 48 A5* small resr 2m/3km SW of Accrington. SD 7426
Jack-in-the-Green Devon 7 G5* ham 5m/8km W of Ottery St Mary. SY 0195
Jack Key's Reservoir Lancs 48 A6* small resr 2km S of Darwen. SD 7020
Jacksdale Notts 44 A5* loc 2km SW of Selston. SK 4451
Jack's Green Glos 16 D1* loc 2km E of Painswick. SO 8810
Jack's Hatch Essex 20 B1* loc 2m/4km SW of Harlow. TL 4306
Jackson Bridge W Yorks 43 F1* loc 2m/3km E of Holmfirth. SE 1607
Jacobstow Cornwall 6 B5 vil 7m/11km S of Bude. SX 1995
Jacobstowe Devon 6 D5 vil 4m/6km N of Okehampton. SS 5801
Jacobswell Surrey 19 E6* loc 2m/3km N of Guildford. TQ 0053
Jacques Bay Essex 31 F5* bay on S side of R Stour estuary between Mistley and Wrabness. TM 1531
Jagger Green W Yorks 48 D6* loc 2m/3km SW of Elland. SE 0919
Jameston Dyfed 22 C5 ham 4m/7km E of Pembroke. SS 0598
Jamestown H'land 81 E2 loc in Ross and Cromarty dist 2km S of Strathpeffer. NH 4756
Jamestown S'clyde 64 B1 loc 4m/6km N of Dumbarton. NS 3981
Janetstown H'land 86 E4 vil near E coast of Caithness dist 1m SW of Latheron. Also known as **Latheronwheel.** ND 1832
Janetstown H'land 86 F3* loc in Caithness dist adjoining Wick to W. ND 3550
Jarlshof Shetland 89 E8* site of prehistoric settlement (A.M.) on E side of W Voe of Sumburgh. Contains relics of Bronze, Iron, Dark, and Middle Ages. HU 3909
Jarrow Tyne & Wear 61 G5 industrial tn on S bank of R Tyne 5m/8km E of Gateshead. Ship-repairing, iron and steel mnfre, aircraft components. Rd tunnel under r. Light industry developed at Bede Industrial Estate. Par ch incorporates remains (A.M.) of monastery of Venerable Bede (d 735). NZ 3265
Jarvis Brook E Sussex 12 B4 loc in valley on SE side of Crowborough. TQ 5329
Jasper's Green Essex 30 C5 ham 3m/5km NW of Braintree. TL 7226
Jaw Hill W Yorks 49 E5* loc 3m/5km NW of Wakefield. SE 2923
Jaywick Essex 31 E6/F6 coastal suburb 2m/3km SW of Clacton-on-Sea. TM 1513
Jealott's Hill Berks 18 D4* loc 5m/8km S of Maidenhead. SU 8673
Jeater Houses N Yorks 54 D5 loc 4m/7km E of Northallerton. SE 4394
Jedburgh Borders 66 D6 small tn on Jed Water 10m/16km NE of Hawick. Woollen mnfre. Red sandstone ruins (A.M.) of abbey founded in 12c. Site of Roman fort 3m/5km E. NT 6520
Jed Water 66 D6 r in Borders region flowing N through Jedburgh to R Teviot 3m/4km N of the tn. NT 6524
Jeffreyston Dyfed 22 C5/D5 vil 5m/8km NW of Tenby. SN 0806
Jemimaville H'land 81 F1 vil on S side of Cromarty Firth, Ross and Cromarty dist, 4m/7km W of Cromarty. NH 7265
Jenkins' Green E Sussex 12 C6* loc on S side of Pevensey Levels 4m/7km N of Eastbourne. TQ 6205
Jenkins Point Dyfed 22 C5* headland on S side of Cresswell R at its confluence with Daugleddau R. SN 0005
Jennett's Reservoir Devon 6 C3* resr 2km S of Bideford. SS 4425
Jenny Gill Reservoir N Yorks 48 C3* small resr 1km E of Skipton. SE 0051
Jepson's Pond Mid Glam 15 F1* small lake 3m/5km NE of Merthyr Tydfil. SO 0809
Jericho Gtr Manchester 42 D1 loc in Bury 2m/4km E of tn centre. SD 8311
Jersey Marine W Glam 14 C2* loc 4m/7km E of Swansea. SS 7193
Jervaulx Abbey N Yorks 54 B6 remains of 12c Cistercian monastic hse above R Ure 3m/5km SE of Middleham. SE 1785
Jesmond Tyne & Wear 61 G4 dist of Newcastle 1m NE of city centre. **W Jesmond** dist to W. **Jesmond Dene,** wooded glen to E. NZ 2566
Jevington E Sussex 12 B6 vil on S Downs 4m/6km NW of Eastbourne. TQ 5601
Jingle Street Gwent 26 A6 loc 3m/4km SW of Monmouth. SO 4710
Jockey End Herts 19 E1* vil 4m/7km N of Hemel Hempstead. TL 0313
Jodrell Bank Ches 42 D4 loc 3m/5km NE of Holmes Chapel. To N is radio telescope and radio astronomy laboratory of University of Manchester. SJ 7970
Johnby Cumbria 52 D2 ham 2m/3km N of Greystoke. Hall dates from 16c. NY 4333
John of Gaunt's Castle N Yorks. See Beaver Dyke Resrs.
John of Gaunt's Deer Park Hants 10 B2* area of open country on W side of Kings Somborne. SU 3531
John o' Gaunts W Yorks 49 E5/F5* loc 4m/7km SE of Leeds. SE 3529
John o' Groats H'land 86 F1 loc in NE corner of Caithness dist nearly 2m/3km W of Duncansby Hd. ND 3773
John's Cross E Sussex 12 D4 loc 3m/5km N of Battle. TQ 7421
Johnshaven Grampian 77 G4 fishing vil on rocky part of E coast 4m/7km SW of Inverbervie. NO 7967
John's Hole Kent 20 C4* loc 2km E of Dartford. TQ 5673
Johnson's Street Norfolk 39 G3* loc 1m SW of Ludham. TG 3717
Johnston Dyfed 22 B4 vil 4m/6km NE of Milford Haven. **N Johnston** loc 1km N. SM 9310
Johnstone Devon 7 E3* loc 2m/3km E of S Molton. SS 7325
Johnstone S'clyde 64 B3 tn 4m/6km W of Paisley. Industries include textiles, engineering. NS 4263
Johnstonebridge D & G 59 F2 loc, and rd br over R Annan, 7m/11km N of Lockerbie. NY 1092
Johnstown Clwyd 41 H6 loc adjoining Rhosllanerchrugog to E. SJ 3046
Johnstown Dyfed 23 F4 loc 2km W of Carmarthen. SN 3919
Joppa Dyfed 24 B2* loc 3m/4km SE of Llanrhystud. SN 5666
Joppa Lothian 66 B2 dist of Edinburgh adjoining Portobello to SE. NT 3173
Joppa S'clyde 56 D2 loc 1km W of Coylton. NS 4019
Jordanhill S'clyde 64 C2* loc in Glasgow 4m/6km NW of city centre. NS 5368
Jordan Hill Roman Temple Dorset. See Preston.
Jordans Bucks 18 D2 loc 2m/3km E of Beaconsfield. Meeting hse of early Quakers, incl William Penn. SU 9791
Jordans Green Norfolk 39 E3* loc 2m/3km SW of Reepham. TG 0721
Jordanston (Trefwrdan) Dyfed 22 B3 ham 4m/6km SW of Fishguard. SM 9132
Joyford Glos 26 B6* loc 2m/3km N of Coleford. SO 5713
Joy's Green Glos 26 B5* vil 4m/6km NW of Cinderford. SO 6016
Jubilee Cave N Yorks 47 H2* limestone cave on Langcliffe Scar, 1m E of Langcliffe. See also Victoria Cave. SD 8365
Julian Bower Lincs 45 G3* loc adjoining Louth to S. TF 3386
Jumbles Reservoir Lancs 47 G6* resr 3m/5km N of Bolton. SD 7314
Jump S Yorks 43 H1 loc adjoining Hoyland Nether to E. SE 3801
Jumpers Common Dorset 9 H4* urban loc 2km NW of Christchurch tn centre. SZ 1494
Jumper's Town E Sussex 12 B3* loc on N edge of Ashdown Forest 2m/3km SW of Hartfield. TQ 4633
Junction Gtr Manchester 43 E1* loc 5m/8km NE of Oldham. SD 9710
Juniper Green Lothian 66 A2 dist of Edinburgh 5m/8km SW of city centre. NT 1968
Juniper Hall Surrey 19 F6 property of NT used as a field study centre, 2m/3km N of Dorking. TQ 1752
Jura S'clyde 62, 69 fourth in size of the Inner Hebrides, being 28m/45km long NE to SW and 8m/13km at its widest in the S, and situated between Islay and the Scottish mainland. A mt ridge runs almost the entire length, although interrupted by the long inlet of Loch Tarbert on W coast, which nearly bisects the island. Deer are numerous. **J. Forest** is deer forest in S part of island around Paps of Jura, qv. Chief occupation is farming. There is a whisky distillery at Craighouse, the chief port. See also Sound of J. NR 58
Jurby East Isle of Man 46 B4* ham 2m/3km W of Andreas. SC 3899
Jurby Head Isle of Man 46 B4 point on NW coast 4m/6km NW of Sulby. SC 3498
Jurby West Isle of Man 46 B4 ham on W side of Jurby Aerodrome 3m/5km NW of Sulby. SC 3598
Justicetown Cumbria 59 H4 loc 6m/9km N of Carlisle. NY 4056

K

Kaber Cumbria 53 G4 ham 2m/3km S of Brough. NY 7911
Kaimes Lothian 66 A2* loc in Edinburgh 4m/6km S of city centre. NT 2768
Kaimhill Grampian 77 H1* dist of Aberdeen 2m/3km SW of city centre. NJ 9203
Kale Water 66 D5 r in Borders region rising on Cheviot Hills and flowing N to Hownam and Morebattle, where it turns W to run into R Teviot 4m/7km S of Kelso. NT 7027

Kallow Point Isle of Man 46 A6 headland to S of Port St Mary at W end of Bay ny Carrickey. SC 2167
Kalm Dam S'clyde 64 B3* resr 2m/4km N of Lochwinnoch. NS 3462
Kame of Foula Shetland 89 D8* steep cliff on W coast of island of Foula, rising to 1220 ft or 372 metres. HT 9340
Kames S'clyde 56 F2* loc 1km S of Muirkirk. NS 6926
Kames S'clyde 63 F1 vil in Argyll on W side of Kyles of Bute, 5m/8km N of Ardlamont Pt. NR 9771
Kames Bay S'clyde 63 G1 bay on E coast of Bute 2m/3km N of Rothesay. **Kames Castle** at head of bay is medieval cas with tower said to date from 14c. See also Port Bannatyne. NS 0667
Kanaird H'land 85 B6 r running W from Loch a' Chroisg to Loch Kanaird, W coast of Ross and Cromarty dist. NH 1199
Kates Hill W Midlands 35 F5 loc in Dudley 1km E of tn centre. SO 9590
Katherines Essex 20 B1* SW dist of Harlow. TL 4308
Kaye Lane W Yorks 48 D6* loc in Huddersfield 2km SE of tn centre. SE 1514
Kay Holm Shetland 89 E6/F6* small island off E coast of Yell at entrance to Mid Yell Voe. HU 5291
Kea Cornwall 2 D4 vil 2m/3km SW of Truro. SW 8042
Keadby Humberside 50 D6 loc on W bank of R Trent 4m/7km E of Crowle. Rd and rly brs across r to S. Power stn. Junction of Sheffield and S Yorks Navigation with R Trent. SE 8311
Kealasay W Isles 88 A2* small uninhabited island off W coast of Lewis 1m N of island of Gt Bernera, island of Lit Bernera intervening. NB 1441
Keal Cotes Lincs 45 G5 vil 4m/6km SW of Spilsby. TF 3661
Keal, East Lincs 45 G5 vil 2m/3km SW of Spilsby. **W Keal** vil 1m W. TF 3863
Kearby Town End N Yorks 49 E3* loc just S of Clap Gate. SE 3447
Kearsley Gtr Manchester 42 C1 tn 4m/6km SE of Bolton. Textiles, chemicals. SD 7504
Kearstay W Isles 88 A3* small uninhabited island off N coast of Scarp. NA 9617
Kearstwick Cumbria 47 F1 ham 1m N of Kirkby Lonsdale. SD 6079
Kearton N Yorks 53 H5* loc 2km W of Healaugh. SD 9999
Kearvaig 84 C1 r in Sutherland dist, H'land, running N into sea 2m/4km SE of Cape Wrath. NC 2872
Keasden N Yorks 48 A2 loc 2m/4km SW of Clapham. SD 7266
Keava W Isles 88 B2* small uninhabited island in E Loch Roag opp Breasclete on W coast of Lewis. NB 1935
Kebister Ness Shetland 89 E7* headland on E coast of Mainland on E side of entrance to Dales Voe, 4m/6km N of Lerwick. HU 4746
Kebock Head W Isles 88 C3 headland on E coast of Lewis 12m/19km S of Stornoway. NB 4213
Kebroyd W Yorks 48 C5/C6* loc 1m N of Ripponden. SE 0421
Keckwick Ches 42 B3 loc 4m/6km E of Runcorn. SJ 5783
Keddington Lincs 45 G3* loc 2km NE of Louth. **K. Corner** loc 1m NE. TF 3488
Kedington Suffolk 30 C3 vil 2m/4km E of Haverhill. TL 7046
Kedleston Derbys 35 H1 loc 4m/7km NW of Derby. **K. Hall** is Ggn hse in deer park with lake. SK 3041
Keelby Lincs 45 F1 vil 7m/11km W of Grimsby. TA 1609
Keele Staffs 42 D6 vil 3m/4km W of Newcastle-under-Lyme. University of Keele to E. SJ 8045
Keeley Green Beds 29 E3 loc 4m/6km SW of Bedford. TL 0046
Keeley Lane Beds 29 E3* loc 4m/6km SW of Bedford. TL 0046
Keelham W Yorks 48 D5* ham 1m SE of Denholme. SE 0732
Keer 47 E2 r rising SW of Kirkby Lonsdale and flowing SW into Morecambe Bay W of Carnforth, Lancs. SD 4770
Keeres Green Essex 20 C1 ham 1km N of Leaden Roding. TL 5914
Keer Holme Lancs 47 F1* loc 2km E of Priest Hutton. SD 5573
Keeston Dyfed 22 B4 vil 4m/6km NW of Haverfordwest. SM 9019
Keevil Wilts 16 D5 vil 4m/7km E of Trowbridge. ST 9258
Kegworth Leics 36 B2 vil on R Soar 5m/8km NW of Loughborough. SK 4826
Kehelland Cornwall 2 B4* ham 2m/3km NW of Camborne. SW 6241
Keig Grampian 83 E5 vil 3m/5km NE of Alford. NJ 6119
Keighley W Yorks 48 C4/D4 industrial tn on R Worth near its confluence with R Aire, 13m/21km NW of Bradford. Engineering, textiles. SE 0641
Keighton Hill Avon 16 B5* loc 1m W of W Harptree. ST 5456
Keilarsbrae Central 72 C5* loc between Alloa and New Sauchie. NS 8993
Keillour Forest Tayside 72 C3, D3* tract between Crieff and Methven. **Keillour Castle** is seat 3m/5km W of Methven. NN 9523
Keinton Mandeville Som 8 D2 vil 6m/10km SE of Glastonbury. Birthplace of Sir Henry Irving, 1838. ST 5430
Keir Mill D & G 58 D2 vil 2km SE of Penpont. NX 8593
Keirsleywell Row Nthmb 60 D6* loc 5m/8km NE of Alston. NY 7751
Keisby Lincs 37 E2/F2 loc 7m/11km NW of Bourne. TF 0328
Keiss H'land 86 F2 vil on E coast of Caithness dist 6m/10km N of Wick. Ruined cas. ND 3461
Keith Grampian 82 D2 tn on right bank of R Isla 15m/24km SE of Elgin. Distilling, woollen mnfg. NJ 4350
Keith Hall Grampian 83 F4 hse and estate 1m E of Inverurie across R Urie. Hse dates from 16c. NJ 7821
Keith Inch Grampian 83 H2 former island off coast at Peterhead, now connected to the tn by brs and forming part of it. Lies on NE side of Peterhead Bay and is most easterly point of Scotland, excluding Shetland. NK 1345
Kelbrook Lancs 48 B4 vil 3m/5km N of Colne. SD 9044
Kelburn Castle S'clyde 64 A3 16c cas with later additions, 2m/3km S of Largs. NS 2156
Kelby Lincs 37 E1 ham 5m/8km SW of Sleaford. TF 0041
Keld Cumbria 53 E3 loc 1m SW of Shap. **K. Chapel** small pre-Reformation bldg (NT). NY 5514
Keld N Yorks 53 G4 vil 2m/4km NW of Muker. NY 8901
Keld Head N Yorks 55 F6* loc adjoining Pickering to W. SE 7884
Keldholme N Yorks 55 E6 loc 1m E of Kirkbymoorside. SE 7086
Kelfield Humberside 44 C1 loc on W bank of R Trent 3m/5km SE of Epworth. SE 8201
Kelfield N Yorks 49 G4 vil 2km E of Cawood across R Ouse. SE 5938
Kelham Notts 44 C5 vil 2m/3km NW of Newark-on-Trent. K. Hall, red-brick 19c Gothic pile by G.G. Scott. SK 7755
Kelk Beck Humberside. See Frodingham Beck.
Kelk, Great Humberside 51 E3 ham 3m/5km S of Burton Agnes. **Lit Kelk** loc 2km N. TA 1058
Kella Isle of Man 46 B4* loc adjoining Sulby to N. SC 3995
Kellacott Devon 6 C6* loc 5m/8km NE of Launceston. SX 4088
Kellan Head Cornwall 3 E1* headland on N coast at E end of Portquin Bay, 2m/3km W of Port Isaac. SW 9781
Kellas Grampian 82 B2 loc 3m/5km E of Dallas. NJ 1654
Kellas Tayside 73 G1* vil 3m/5km N of Broughty Ferry. NO 4535
Kellaton Devon 4 D6* vil 2m/4km NW of Start Pt. SX 8039
Kellaways Wilts 16 D4* loc 2m/4km NE of Chippenham. ST 9575
Kelleth Cumbria 53 F4 loc 3m/5km E of Tebay. NY 6605
Kellet, Nether Lancs 47 F2 vil 2m/3km S of Carnforth. SD 5068
Kelleythorpe Humberside 51 E3 loc 1m SW of Gt Driffield. TA 0156
Kellie Castle Fife 73 G4 hse of 16c–17c (part dating from 14c) 2m/4km N of St Monance. Restored in 19c. NO 5105
Kellie Castle Tayside. See Arbirlot.
Kellie Reservoir S'clyde 64 A2* small resr in course of Kellie Burn 2m/3km E of Wemyss Bay. NS 2268
Kelling Norfolk 39 E1 vil 3m/4km NE of Holt. TG 0942
Kellingley N Yorks 49 G5* loc 2km E of Knottingley. SE 5223
Kellington N Yorks 49 G5 vil 3m/5km E of Knottingley. SE 5524
Kelloe Durham 54 C2* vil 5m/8km N of Sedgefield. See also Tn Kelloe. NZ 3436
Kello Water 58 C1 r in Dumfries & Galloway region, rising on, and running along, border with Strathclyde region before turning E to join R Nith 1m E of Kirkconnel. NS 7411
Kelly Devon 4 B3 ham 5m/7km SE of Launceston. SX 3981
Kelly Bray Cornwall 3 H1 vil 2km N of Callington. SX 3571
Kelmarsh Northants 36 C6 vil 5m/8km S of Mkt Harborough. SP 7379
Kelmscot Oxon 17 F2 vil on R Thames. Old gabled manor hse once home of William Morris. SU 2599
Kelsale Suffolk 31 G2 vil 2km N of Saxmundham. TM 3865
Kelsall Ches 42 B4 vil 8m/12km E of Chester. SJ 5268
Kelsey Head Cornwall 2 C2 headland 3m/5km W of Newquay. SW 7660
Kelsey, North Lincs 45 E1 vil 5m/8km W of Caistor. **N Kelsey Moor** vil 2m/3km E, with site of Roman bldg to S. TA 0401
Kelsey, South Lincs 45 E2 vil 5m/8km SW of Caistor. TF 0498
Kelshall Herts 29 G4 vil 3m/5km SW of Royston. TL 3236
Kelsick Cumbria 59 G6 ham 2m/3km E of Abbey Tn. NY 1950
Kelso Borders 67 E5 mkt tn opp confluence of Rs Teviot and Tweed, 18m/29km NE of Hawick and 20m/32km SW of Berwick-upon-Tweed. Centre of agricultural area, with corn and livestock mkts. Large Ggn square. Br by Rennie, 1801. Remains of 12c abbey (A.M.). NT 7233
Kelstern Lincs 45 F2 vil 5m/8km W of Louth. TF 2590
Kelsterton Clwyd 41 H4* loc 1m NW of Connah's Quay. SJ 2770
Kelston Avon 16 C4 vil 4m/6km NW of Bath. ST 7067
Keltney Burn 75 G6/H6* stream in Tayside region which rises as Allt Mór and runs down Gleann Mór, then turns S as Keltney Burn to run into R Lyon at **Keltneyburn,** loc 5m/8km W of Aberfeldy. Falls of Keltney, waterfall near mouth. NN 7748
Kelton Hill D & G 58 C5 vil 2m/3km SW of Castle Douglas. NX 7459
Kelty Fife 73 E5 tn at N edge of Fife coalfield 2m/3km N of Cowdenbeath. NT 1494
Kelty Water 71 F5 r in Central region running E through Loch Ard Forest to R Forth 3m/5km SE of Aberfoyle. NS 5596
Kelvedon Essex 30 C6 vil 4m/6km NE of Witham. TL 8518
Kelvedon Hatch Essex 20 C2 vil 3m/4km S of Chipping Ongar. TQ 5798
Kelvin S'clyde 64 D3* industrial estate in S part of E Kilbride. NS 6353
Kelvin 64 C2 r in Strathclyde region rising 3m/5km E of Kilsyth and flowing W, then SW through NW part of Glasgow to R Clyde 2m/3km W of city centre. NS 5565
Kelvindale S'clyde 64 C2* housing estate in Kelvinside dist of Glasgow. NS 5568
Kelvingrove Park S'clyde. See Glasgow.
Kelvinhaugh S'clyde 64 C2* loc in Glasgow 2km W of city centre. NS 5666
Kelvinside S'clyde 64 C2* dist of Glasgow 2m/4km NW of city centre. NS 5668
Kelynack Cornwall 2 A5* ham to S of St Just. SW 3729
Kemacott Devon 7 E1* loc 4m/6km SW of Lynton. SS 6647
Kemback Fife 73 G3 vil 3m/5km E of Cupar. NO 4115
Kemberton Salop 34 D4 vil 2m/4km SW of Shifnal. SJ 7304
Kemble Glos 17 E2 vil 4m/6km SW of Cirencester. Airfield to W. ST 9897
Kemerton H & W 26 D4 vil 4m/7km NE of Tewkesbury. SO 9437
Kemeys (Cemais) **Inferior** Gwent 15 H2 loc 6m/10km NE of Newport. ST 3892
Kemeys Commander (Cemais Comawndwr) Gwent 15 H1 ham 3m/5km NW of Usk. SO 3404
Kemnay Grampian 83 F5 vil on R Don 4m/7km SW of Inverurie. **K. Forest** is state forest to N, forming part of Bennachie Forest. NJ 7316
Kemp 34 B6 r rising near Bishop's Castle, Salop, and flowing SE into R Clun 3m/5km W of Craven Arms. SO 3881
Kempe's Corner Kent 13 F2* loc 3m/5km NE of Ashford. Racecourse 1km E. TR 0346
Kempley Glos 26 B4 vil 4m/6km NW of Newent. Vil of **K. Green** 1km SE. SO 6729
Kempock Point S'clyde 64 A2* headland on Firth of Clyde at Gourock, opp Kilcreggan. NS 2478
Kempsey H & W 26 D3 vil on R Severn 4m/6km S of Worcester. SO 8549
Kempsford Glos 17 F2 vil 3m/5km S of Fairford. SU 1696
Kemps Green Warwicks 27 F1* loc 2km SW of Hockley Heath. SP 1470
Kempshott Hants 18 B6* SW dist of Basingstoke. SU 6050
Kempshott Hants 18 B6* loc 4m/6km SW of Basingstoke. SU 5947
Kempston Beds 29 E3 tn 2m/3km SW of Bedford across R Ouse. Various industries. TL 0347
Kempston Church End Beds 29 E3* loc beside R Ouse 3m/4km SW of Bedford across r. TL 0147
Kempstone Norfolk 38 D3* loc 1m S of Litcham. TF 8816
Kempston Hardwick Beds 29 E3* loc 4m/6km S of Bedford. TL 0244
Kempston West End Beds 29 E3* loc 4m/6km W of Bedford across R Ouse. SP 9948
Kempton Salop 34 B5/B6 ham 5m/7km W of Craven Arms. SO 3582
Kempton Park Surrey 19 E5 park containing racecourse 1m N of Sunbury, 4m/6km W of Kingston. TQ 1170
Kemp Town E Sussex 11 H4 E dist of Brighton on coast, with Regency squares and terraces. TQ 3303
Kemsing Kent 20 B5 vil with suburban development 3m/4km NE of Sevenoaks. TQ 5558
Kemsley Kent 21 E5* loc 2m/3km N of Sittingbourne. Paper mills to E. TQ 9066
Kenardington Kent 13 E4 vil 2m/3km W of Ham Street. TQ 9732
Kenchester H & W 26 A3 ham 5m/8km W of Hereford. To S is site of Roman tn (*Magnis*). SO 4343
Kencot Oxon 17 F1 vil 4m/7km NE of Lechlade. SP 2504
Kendal Cumbria 53 E5 tn on R Kent 19m/31km N of Lancaster. Footwear, carpets, machinery, tobacco. Remains of Norman cas. Abbot Hall, Ggn hse by Carr of York, now art gallery. SD 5192
Kendal End H & W 27 E1 loc 4m/6km NE of Bromsgrove. SP 0074
Kenderchurch H & W 25 H5 loc 1km NE of Pontrilas. SO 4028
Kendleshire Avon 16 B3* loc 7m/11km NE of Bristol. ST 6679
Kendoon Loch D & G 56 F4 loch, and meeting point of several streams running into Water of Ken, in Dundeugh Forest 6m/9km N of Dalry. NX 6090
Kenfig (Cynffig) Mid Glam 14 D3 vil 3m/5km N of Porthcawl. Site of ancient Kenfig tn to N, and remains of **K. Castle. K. Pool** lake to W, with **K. Burrows** and **K. Sands** on coast. **K. Hill** is loc 3m/4km E on far side of Pyle. SS 8081
Kenfig (Cynffig) 14 D3 r rising N of Cefn Cribwr, Mid Glam, and flowing W into Swansea Bay S of Margam. For much of its course it forms boundary between Mid and W Glam. SS 7783
Kenidjack Cornwall 2 A5* loc on NW side of St Just. **K. Castle,** ancient camp on coast to W. SW 3632
Kenilworth Warwicks 35 H6 tn 5m/8km SW of Coventry. Ruins of red sandstone cas (A.M.), Norman and later. SP 2872
Kenley London 19 G5 loc in borough of Croydon 2m/3km SE of Purley. K. Airfield to S. TQ 3259
Kenley Salop 34 C4 vil 4m/7km W of Much Wenlock. SJ 5600

Kenmore H'land 78 E3 locality on Loch a' Chracaich on SW side of Loch Torridon, Ross and Cromarty dist, 4m/7km NW of Shieldaig. NG 7557

Kenmore Tayside 71 H1 vil at foot of Loch Tay 6m/9km SW of Aberfeldy. On islet in loch is a ruined 12c priory. NN 7745

Kenmure Castle D & G 58 C4 cas of 15c-17c, long the seat of the Gordons, 1m S of New Galloway. NX 6376

Kenn Avon 16 A4 vil 2m/3km S of Clevedon. ST 4169

Kenn Devon 5 E2 vil 5m/7km S of Exeter. SX 9285

Kenn 15 H4 r rising near Brockley, Avon, and flowing W into mouth of R Severn 2m/4km SW of Clevedon. ST 3868

Kenn 5 F2* r in Devon rising 1m S of Longdown and flowing SE into the R Exe estuary between Powderham and Starcross. SX 9783

Kennacley W Isles 88 B3* locality on W shore of E Loch Tarbert, Harris, 4m/6km SE of Tarbert. NG 1794

Kennards House Cornwall 6 B6* loc 3m/5km W of Launceston. SX 2883

Kenneggy Downs Cornwall 2 B5* loc 6m/9km W of Helston. Kenneggy is a loc to S. SW 5629

Kennerleigh Devon 7 F4 vil 5m/8km N of Crediton. SS 8207

Kennessee Green Merseyside 42 A2* dist of Maghull S of tn centre. SD 3701

Kennet 118, 119 admin dist of Wilts.

Kennet 18 C4 r rising near Uffcott, Wilts, and running S, at times underground, to Avebury, then E through Marlborough, Hungerford, and Newbury, into R Thames at Reading. **K. and Avon Canal** runs from Reading to R Avon at Bath; navigable in parts. SU 7373

Kennethmont Grampian. Par containing vil of Kirkhill of K., qv. See also Leith Hall. NJ 5328

Kennett Cambs 30 C1 ham 5m/8km NE of Newmarket. TL 6968

Kennett, East Wilts 17 F4 vil 2m/3km SE of Avebury. SU 1167

Kennett, West Wilts 17 F4 ham 2km SE of Avebury. Long barrow, or burial-chamber, (A.M.), dating from 4c BC, 1km SW. The Sanctuary (A.M.), site of ancient stone and timber circles 1km E. SU 1168

Kennford Devon 5 E2 vil 4m/6km S of Exeter. SX 9186

Kennick Reservoir Devon 4 D2* resr on E edge of Dartmoor 3m/5km E of Moretonhampstead. SX 8084

Kenninghall Norfolk 39 E6 vil 6m/9km S of Attleborough. TM 0386

Kennington Kent 13 F3 N dist of Ashford. TR 0245

Kennington London 19 G4* dist in borough of Lambeth SE of Vauxhall Br. The Oval, Test Match cricket ground and HQ of Surrey County Cricket Club. TQ 3177

Kennington Oxon 18 A2 suburb 2m/4km S of Oxford. SP 5202

Kennishead S'clyde 64 C3* loc in Carnwadric dist of Glasgow. NS 5460

Kennoway Fife 73 F4 small tn 2m/4km NW of Leven. NO 3502

Kenny Som 8 B3* ham 1km NW of Ashill and 4m/6km NW of Ilminster. ST 3117

Kennyhill Suffolk 38 B6 ham 4m/7km NW of Mildenhall. TL 6679

Kennythorpe N Yorks 50 C2 ham 4m/6km S of Malton. SE 7865

Kenovay Tiree, S'clyde 69 A7 loc 3m/5km W of Scarinish. NL 9946

Kensaleyre Skye, H'land 78 C4 locality at head of Loch Eyre 7m/11km NW of Portree. NG 4251

Kensal Green London 19 F3* loc in borough of Brent 5m/8km W of Charing Cross. Loc of **K. Rise** to E, and of **K. Town** to SE in borough of Kensington and Chelsea. TQ 2382

Kensey 6 C6* r rising near Treneglos, Cornwall, and flowing E through N part of Launceston and into R Tamar 2m/3km E. SX 3584

Kensham Green Kent 12 D4* loc 2m/3km SW of Rolvenden. TQ 8229

Kensington London 19 F4* dist W of Central London and royal borough (Kensington and Chelsea). Contains Victoria and Albert Museum, and Natural History and Science Museums; K. Palace in K. Palace Gardens. TQ 2579

Kensington, North London 19 F3* dist in borough of Kensington and Chelsea 4m/6km W of Charing Cross. TQ 2382

Kensington, South London 19 F4* area in borough of Kensington and Chelsea running SW from Victoria and Albert Museum. TQ 2678

Kenson S Glam 15 F4* loc on W side of Penmark. ST 0568

Kenstone Salop 34 C2* loc 2km W of Hodnet. SJ 5928

Kensworth Beds 29 E5 vil 2m/3km SE of Dunstable. TL 0319

Kensworth Common Beds 29 E5 vil 3m/4km SE of Dunstable. TL 0318

Kent 119 south-easternmost county of England, bounded by E Sussex, Surrey, Gtr London, the Thames estuary and the Strait of Dover. The chalk ridge of the North Downs runs along the N side, then SE to Folkestone and Dover. R Medway cuts through the chalk in the vicinity of Maidstone, and there are low-lying areas to E of Canterbury and of Tonbridge, on Romney Marsh in the S, and bordering the Thames estuary in the N. Chief tns are Maidstone, the county tn; Ashford, Dover, Folkestone, Margate, Ramsgate, Tonbridge, Tunbridge Wells, the cathedral city of Canterbury, and the Medway tns (Chatham, Gillingham, and the cathedral city of Rochester). Rs include the Medway, Stour, and Beult. Chief industrial areas are around Maidstone, Ashford, Tonbridge, and especially along the Medway estuary. Chatham is a naval base; Dover, Folkestone, and Sheerness are ports; Ramsgate is a hovercraft terminal. There is coal-mining between Canterbury and Dover. The rest is highly productive agricultural land, important crops being fruit and hops, with extensive sheep-grazing on Romney Marsh.

Kent 47 E1 r rising in Lake Dist, Cumbria, 1m S of the summit of High Street and flowing S through Kentmere Resr and Kendal and thence into Morecambe Bay off Humphrey Hd Pt. SD 3973

Kentallen H'land 74 B5 vil at head of the narrow **K. Bay** on Loch Linnhe, Lochaber dist, 3m/5km SW of Ballachulish. NN 0057

Kentchurch H & W 25 H5 ham 2m/3km SE of Pontrilas. SO 4125

Kent Ditch 12 D4 stream rising near Flimwell, E Sussex, and flowing into R Rother 2km E of Bodiam Castle. For almost all its length it marks boundary between counties of Kent and E Sussex. TQ 8025

Kentford Suffolk 30 C2 vil 5m/8km E of Newmarket. TL 7066

Kent Green Ches 42 D5* loc 2m/3km N of Kidsgrove. SJ 8357

Kentisbeare Devon 7 H4 vil 3m/5km E of Cullompton. ST 0608

Kentisbury Devon 7 E1 ham on W edge of Exmoor 7m/11km SW of Lynton. 1m S, loc of **K. Ford.** SS 6243

Kentish Town London 19 G3* loc in borough of Camden 3m/5km N of Charing Cross. TQ 2984

Kentmere Cumbria 52 D4 vil on R Kent 4m/6km N of Staveley. **Kentmere Resr** 3m/4km N. NY 4504

Kenton Devon 5 E2 vil 4m/7km N of Dawlish. SX 9583

Kenton London 19 F3 loc on borders of Brent and Harrow boroughs 9m/15km NW of Charing Cross. TQ 1788

Kenton Suffolk 31 F2 vil 2m/3km NE of Debenham. Loc of **K. Corner** 1m SE. TM 1965

Kenton Tyne & Wear 61 G4* dist of Newcastle 2m/4km NW of city centre. **K. Bar** loc to W. NZ 2267

Kenton Bank Foot Tyne & Wear 61 G4* loc 4m/6km NW of Newcastle. NZ 2068

Kenton Green Glos 26 C6* loc 4m/7km SW of Gloucester across loop of R Severn. SO 7714

Kentra H'land 68 E2 loc in Lochaber dist on E side of **K. Bay** and 4m/6km NW of Salen. NM 6569

Kentrigg Cumbria 53 E5* loc adjoining Kendal to N. SD 5194

Kents Bank Cumbria 47 E1 loc on W bank of R Kent estuary 2km SW of Grange-over-Sands. SD 3976

Kent's Green Glos 26 C5 vil 2m/3km SE of Newent. SO 7423

Kent's Oak Hants 10 A2* vil 3m/5km NW of Romsey. SU 3224

Kent Street Kent 20 C6 loc 1km NE of Mereworth. TQ 6654

Kent Water 12 B3 stream rising E of E Grinstead and marking the E Sussex–Kent border until flowing into R Medway 1km N of Ashurst, to W of Tunbridge Wells. TQ 5140

Kentwell Hall Suffolk. See Long Melford.

Kenwick Salop 34 B2* loc 3m/5km SE of Ellesmere. SJ 4230

Kenwick Bar Lincs 45 G3* loc 2m/3km S of Louth. TF 3384

Kenwood House London 19 F3* 18c hse by Robert Adam at N edge of Hampstead Heath 5m/8km N of Charing Cross. TQ 2787

Kenwyn Cornwall 2 D4 vil on N outskirts of Truro. Also r rising some 4m/6km W and flowing through Truro to join R Allen and form Truro R. SW 8145

Kenyon Gtr Manchester 42 C2* loc 2m/3km W of Culcheth. SJ 6395

Keoldale H'land 84 D2 loc on E side of Kyle of Durness, Sutherland dist, 2m/3km SW of Durness. Ancient cairns and standing stones to E. NC 3866

Keose W Isles 88 B2* vil near E coast of Lewis 2km E of Laxay. **K. Glebe** is loc adjoining to E. **Keose I.** is islet 1km SE in Loch Erisort. NB 3521

Kepnal Wilts 17 F5* ham 1km E of Pewsey. SU 1760

Keppel Pier S'clyde 63 H2 landing stage on SE coast of island of Gt Cumbrae, 1m E of Millport. Scottish Marine Biological Station, with museum and aquarium. NS 1754

Keppoch H'land 68 D1/E1* locality in Lochaber dist on N side of Loch nan Ceall, W of Arisaig. Back of K. is locality to N. NM 6586

Kepwick N Yorks 54 D5 vil 6m/10km N of Thirsk. SE 4690

Kerdiston Norfolk 39 E2/E3* loc 2km NW of Reepham. TG 0824

Keresley W Midlands 35 H5/H6 vil 3m/5km NW of Coventry. Colliery. SP 3183

Kernborough Devon 4 D6* loc 4m/7km SE of Kingsbridge. SX 7941

Kerne Bridge H & W 26 B5 loc 3m/5km S of Ross-on-Wye. SO 5819

Kerrera S'clyde 70 A2 island, 5m/7km long NE to SW and 2m/3km at widest point, lying opp Oban and mainland to SW thereof, from which it is separated by K. Sound. See also Gylen Castle. NM 8128

Kerridge Ches 43 E3* loc 1km S of Bollington. SJ 9376

Kerridge-end Ches 43 E4* loc 2m/3km NE of Macclesfield. SJ 9475

Kerrier 118 admin dist of Cornwall.

Kerris Cornwall 2 A5* ham 2m/3km SW of Penzance. SW 4427

Kerry Powys 33 H5 vil 3m/4km SE of Newtown. To S, **K. Hills,** partly afforested, formerly noted for a breed of sheep. SO 1490

Kerrycroy S'clyde 63 G2 model vil on **K. Bay** on E coast of Bute, 2km S of Ascog and at N entrance to estate of Mountstuart, qv. NS 1061

Kerrytonlia Point S'clyde 63 G2* headland on E coast of Bute, at NE end of Kilchattan Bay. NS 1156

Kersal Gtr Manchester 42 D1* loc in Salford 2m/3km NW of tn centre. **Lr Kersal** loc adjoining to SE. SD 8101

Kersall Notts 44 B5 vil 5m/8km SE of Ollerton. SK 7162

Kersey Suffolk 31 E4 vil 2m/3km NW of Hadleigh. Locs of **K. Tye** and **K. Upland** to SW; **K. Vale** to S. TM 0044

Kershader W Isles 88 B2* vil on S side of Loch Erisort, Lewis, opp Laxay. NB 3420

Kershope Burn 60 A3 r rising on borders of England and Scotland some 5m/8km E of Newcastleton and flowing SW along the border into Liddel Water at Kershopefoot, Cumbria. NY 4782

Kershopefoot Cumbria 60 A3 ham at confluence of Kershope Burn and Liddel Water 3m/5km S of Newcastleton. **Kershope Forest** area to E largely planted with conifers. NY 4782

Kerswell Devon 7 H4 vil 4m/6km E of Cullompton. ST 0806

Kerswell Green H & W 26 D3 vil 5m/9km S of Worcester. SO 8646

Kerthen Wood Cornwall 2 B5* loc 3m/5km SE of Hayle. SW 5833

Kesgrave Suffolk 31 F3 suburb 4m/6km E of Ipswich. TM 2145

Kessingland Suffolk 39 H6 vil 4m/7km SW of Lowestoft. Coastal resort and caravan park of **K. Beach** adjoins to E. TM 5286

Kessock, North H'land 81 F3 vil in Ross and Cromarty dist on N shore of Beauly Firth opp Inverness. **S Kessock** is suburb of Inverness on S bank. NH 6547

Kesteven, North and **South** 117, 119 admin dists of Lincs.

Kestle Cornwall 3 E4* ham 2m/3km W of Mevagissey. SW 9945

Kestle Mill Cornwall 2 D3* ham 3m/5km SE of Newquay. SW 8559

Keston London 20 A5 loc in borough of Bromley 3m/5km S of Bromley tn centre. Loc of **Keston Mark** is 1km NE. Site of Roman villa to S. TQ 4164

Keswick Cumbria 52 C3 tn at NE end of Derwent Water 16m/26km W of Penrith. Tourist centre for Lake Dist. Pencil mnfre; quarrying. NY 2623

Keswick Norfolk 39 F4 vil 3m/5km SW of Norwich. TG 2004

Keswick Norfolk 39 G2 loc on coast 1km SE of Bacton. TG 3533

Keswick, East W Yorks 49 F4 vil 4m/6km SW of Wetherby. SE 3644

Ketley Salop 34 D3* loc 2m/3km E of Wellington. SJ 6710

Ketleybank Salop 34 D3 loc 1m SW of Oakengates. SJ 6910

Ketligill Head Shetland 89 D6* headland on NW coast of Mainland, on E side of Ronas Voe near its entrance. HU 2784

Ketsby Lincs 45 G4 ham 3m/5km NW of Ulceby Cross. TF 3676

Kettering Northants 28 D1 tn 13m/21km NE of Northampton. Industries include footwear, clothing. SP 8678

Ketteringham Norfolk 39 F4 vil 6m/9km SW of Norwich. TG 1602

Kettins Tayside 73 E1 vil 2m/3km SE of Coupar Angus. NO 2339

Kettla Ness Shetland 89 E8* headland at S end of island of W Burra. HU 3429

Kettlebaston Suffolk 30 D3 vil 3m/5km E of Lavenham. TL 9650

Kettlebridge Fife 73 F4 loc 2km S of Ladybank. NO 3007

Kettlebrook Staffs 35 H4 loc in Tamworth 1km SE of tn centre. SK 2103

Kettleburgh Suffolk 31 F2 vil 2m/4km SW of Framlingham. TM 2660

Kettle Corner Kent 20 D6* loc on R Medway 3m/4km SW of Maidstone. TQ 7253

Kettlehill Fife 73 F4* loc 2m/3km SE of Ladybank. NO 3207

Kettleholm D & G 59 F4 loc 3m/5km S of Lockerbie. NY 1476

Kettle Ness N Yorks 55 F3 headland on North Sea coast at E end of Runswick Bay, 5m/8km NW of Whitby. To S is ham of **Kettleness** and site of Roman signal stn. NZ 8316

Kettleshulme Ches 43 E3 vil 6m/9km NE of Macclesfield. SJ 9879

Kettlesing N Yorks 49 E3 ham 5m/8km W of Harrogate. **K. Bottom** vil 1km NE. **K. Head** loc 1km SW. SE 2256

Kettlester Shetland 89 E6* loc near S coast of Yell adjoining Burravoe to NW. **Loch of K.** is small loch to N. HU 5180

Kettlestone Norfolk 38 D2 vil 3m/5km E of Fakenham. TF 9631

Kettlethorpe Lincs 44 C4 vil 3m/5km W of Saxilby. SK 8475

Kettletoft Orkney 89 C5* loc and promontory on S coast of island of Sanday between Backaskail Bay to W and **K. Bay** to E, with a landing stage on the latter. HY 6538

Kettlewell N Yorks 48 C1 vil in Upper Wharfedale 6m/9km N of Grassington. SD 9672

Ketton Leics 37 E4 vil 4m/6km SW of Stamford. Extensive stone quarries to N. SK 9804

Kevingtown London 20 B5* loc in borough of Bromley 2km NE of Orpington. TQ 4767

Kevock Lothian 66 B2* loc in W part of Bonnyrigg and Lasswade. NT 2965

Kew London 19 F4 loc on S side of R Thames, crossed by Kew Br, 7m/11km W of Charing Cross. Royal Botanic Gardens to W, containing K. Palace (A.M.), 17c–18c hse with George III relics. TQ 1977

Kewstoke Avon 15 H5 vil 2m/3km NE of Weston-super-Mare. Viewpoint (NT) known as Monk's Steps or St Kew's Steps. ST 3363

Kexborough S Yorks 43 G1 loc 4m/6km NW of Barnsley. SE 3009
Kexby Lincs 44 D3 vil 4m/7km SE of Gainsborough. SK 8785
Kexby N Yorks 50 C3 vil 6m/10km E of York. SE 7051
Keyford Som 16 C6* SE dist of Frome. To S, ham of **Lit Keyford.** ST 7847
Key Green Ches 42 D4/D5* ham 2m/3km E of Congleton. SJ 8963
Key Green N Yorks 55 F4* loc 1m SW of Egton. NZ 8004
Keyham Leics 36 C4 vil 5m/9km E of Leicester. SK 6706
Keyhaven Hants 10 A5 vil on coast 3m/5km S of Lymington. SZ 3091
Keyingham Humberside 51 F5 vil 4m/7km SE of Hedon. TA 2425
Keymer W Sussex 11 H3 tn below S Downs 2m/4km S of Burgess Hill. TQ 3115
Keynsham Avon 16 B4 tn on R Avon midway between Bristol and Bath. Mnfres include chocolate, paper, soap. Loc of **K. Hams** 1km N. Site of Roman villa 1km NW. ST 6568
Keysers Estate Essex 20 A1* loc on R Lea 2m/3km S of Hoddesdon. TL 3706
Keysoe Beds 29 E2* vil 8m/13km N of Bedford. Vil of **K. Row** 1m SE. TL 0762
Key's Toft Lincs 45 H5 loc 1km S of Wainfleet. TF 4957
Keyston Cambs 29 E1 vil 4m/6km SE of Thrapston. TL 0475
Key Street Kent 21 E5 loc 2km W of Sittingbourne. TQ 8864
Keyworth Notts 36 C2 vil 7m/11km SE of Nottingham. SK 6130
Kiachnish H'land 74 C4* r in Lochaber dist running N from Lochan Lunn Da Bhra then turning W and running into Loch Linnhe 4m/6km SW of Fort William. NN 0669
Kibblesworth Tyne & Wear 61 G5 vil 2m/3km W of Birtley. Coal-mining, brick mnfre. NZ 2456
Kibworth Beauchamp Leics 36 C5 vil 5m/8km NW of Mkt Harborough. SP 6893
Kibworth Harcourt Leics 36 C5 vil 5m/9km NW of Mkt Harborough. SP 6894
Kidbrooke London 20 B4 loc in borough of Greenwich 8m/12km E of Charing Cross. TQ 4176
Kidburngill Cumbria 52 B3* loc 2m/3km SW of Ullock. NY 0621
Kiddal Lane End W Yorks 49 F4 loc 2km N of Barwick in Elmet. SE 4039
Kiddemore Green Staffs 35 E3 loc 7m/12km NW of Wolverhampton. SJ 8508
Kidderminster H & W 35 E6 industrial tn on R Stour 16m/27km W of Birmingham. Developed mainly in 19c but has 1960s tn centre. Industries include carpets, spinning, engineering. SO 8376
Kiddington Oxon 27 H5 loc 3m/4km SE of Enstone. SP 4122
Kiddington, Over Oxon 27 H5 ham 3m/4km SE of Enstone. SP 4022
Kidd's Moor Norfolk 39 E4* loc 2km N of Wymondham. TG 1103
Kidlington Oxon 28 A6 suburb 5m/8km N of Oxford. Oxford Airport to NW. SP 4914
Kidmore End Oxon 18 B3 vil 4m/6km N of Reading. SU 6979
Kidnall Ches 42 B6* loc 2m/3km NW of Malpas. SJ 4749
Kidsgrove Staffs 42 D5 tn 6m/10km NW of Stoke-on-Trent. Industries include chemicals, textiles. SJ 8354
Kidwelly (Cydweli) Dyfed 23 F5 small tn on R Gwendraeth Fach 7m/12km NW of Llanelli. Mnfre of optical glass, silica bricks. Remains of 12c–14c cas (A.M.) on N bank of r. SN 4006
Kielder Nthmb 60 C2 vil in Kielder Forest 7m/11km NW of Falstone. **Kielder Castle** dates in part from 18c. NY 6293
Kielder Burn 60 C2 r rising on Cheviot Hills, Nthmb, 3m/5km SW of Carter Bar, and flowing SW into R North Tyne at Kielder. NY 6393
Kielder Forest Nthmb 60 C3 large area of conifer forest planted by Forestry Commission astride upper valley of R North Tyne, up against Scottish border. NY 68, 69
Kiells S'clyde 62 B2 loc on Islay 1m SW of Port Askaig. NR 4168
Kiessimul W Isles 88 D4* tiny islet in Castle Bay, S coast of Barra, on which stands **K. Castle,** ancient stronghold of the Clan Macneil of Barra. Also spelt Kisimul. NL 6697
Kilantringan Loch S'clyde 57 B5 small loch 2m/4km S of Ballantrae. NX 0979
Kilbagie Central 72 C5 vil 2m/3km N of Kincardine-on-Forth. NS 9290
Kilbarchan S'clyde 64 B3 small tn 2m/3km W of Johnstone, formerly noted for tartan weaving. 18c weaver's cottage (NTS). NS 4063
Kilbeg Skye, H'land 79 E7 loc on E coast of Sleat peninsula 2m/4km NE of Ardvasar. NG 6506
Kilberry S'clyde 62 D2 vil near W coast of Knapdale, Argyll, 4m/6km NW of Ardpatrick Pt. **K. Head** is headland nearly 1m W, to N of **K. Bay.** Collection of medieval gravestones (A.M.) in grnds of **K. Castle.** NR 7164
Kilbirnie S'clyde 64 B3 tn on R Garnock 9m/15km NE of Ardrossan. Mnfre of thread, net, lace, and rubber. **K. Loch** 1m E. NS 3154
Kilbowie S'clyde 64 C2 loc on N side of Clydebank. Sewing-machine factory. NS 4971
Kilbrannan Sound S'clyde 63 E3, E4 sea passage between Arran and Kintyre. Width between 3m/5km and 8m/13km. NR 8441
Kilbride S'clyde 70 A3/B3 loc in Argyll 3m/4km S of Oban. See also Lerags Cross. NM 8525
Kilbride W Isles 88 E3 vil at SW end of S Uist. NF 7514
Kilbride Bay S'clyde 63 F2 bay in Argyll at entrance to Loch Fyne, 2m/4km NW of Ardlamont Pt. NR 9666
Kilbride, East S'clyde 64 D3 tn 7m/11km S of Glasgow. New Tn designated 1947; various industries, incl engineering, textiles, electronics. National Engineering Laboratory is UK research centre for mechanical engineering industry. Electricity research centre. NS 6354
Kilbride Point Skye, H'land 78 B3 headland on E shore of Loch Snizort 2m/4km NW of Uig. NG 3766
Kilbride, West S'clyde 64 A4 tn 4m/7km NW of Ardrossan. Law Castle has late 15c tower. NS 2048
Kilbryde Castle Central 72 B4 cas dating from 15c on Ardoch Burn, 2m/4km NW of Dunblane. NN 7503
Kilbucho Borders 65 G5 loc 3m/5km SW of Broughton. NT 0835
Kilburn Derbys 43 H6 vil 2m/4km SE of Belper. **Lr Kilburn** loc 1km SW. SK 3845
Kilburn London 19 F3* loc in borough of Brent 4m/6km NW of Charing Cross. Loc of **W Kilburn** to SW. TQ 2583
Kilburn N Yorks 50 A1 vil 6m/9km E of Thirsk. **High Kilburn** ham up hill to E. **K. White Horse** is figure of horse cut in chalk of hillside 1m N. SE 5179
Kilby Leics 36 C4/C5 vil 6m/10km S of Leicester. SP 6295
Kilcadzow S'clyde 65 F4 loc 3m/4km SE of Carluke. NS 8848
Kilchattan S'clyde 63 G2 vil on S side of the wide **K. Bay** on E coast of Bute, 2m/4km N of Garroch Hd. NS 1055
Kilchattan, Upper S'clyde 69 C7 loc on Colonsay 2m/3km NW of Scalasaig. Loc of **Lr Kilchattan** adjoins to SW. NR 3795
Kilchenzie S'clyde 62 D5 vil in Kintyre 4m/6km NW of Campbeltown. NR 6724
Kilcheran Loch S'clyde 70 A1 small loch on Lismore, 2m/3km SW of Achnacroish. Port Kilcheran is small bay to S. NM 8239
Kilchiaran S'clyde 62 A2 loc near W coast of Rinns of Islay at **K. Bay.** NR 2060
Kilchoan H'land 68 C3 vil on S side of Ardnamurchan peninsula in Lochaber dist, 5m/8km SE of Ardnamurchan Pt. **K. Bay** to W of vil. NM 4863
Kilchoan Bay S'clyde 70 A4* bay on N side of Loch Melfort, Argyll. **K. Loch** is small loch to N. NM 7913
Kilchoman S'clyde 62 A2 loc 1km inland from Machir Bay on W coast of Islay. NR 2163
Kilchrenan S'clyde 70 C3 vil in Argyll 6m/10km SE of Taynuilt. NN 0322
Kilchurn Castle S'clyde 70 C2 remains of cas (A.M.), dating partly from 15c, at NE end of Loch Awe 2m/3km W of Dalmally, Argyll. NN 1327
Kilconquhar Fife 73 G4 vil 2km N of Elie. **K. Loch** is small circular loch on S side of vil. NO 4802
Kilcot Glos 26 C5* vil 2m/3km W of Newent. SO 6925
Kilcott, Lower Avon 16 C3* loc 2m/4km NW of Didmarton. **Upr Kilcott** loc 1km SE. ST 7889
Kilcoy H'land 81 E2/E3 loc in Ross and Cromarty dist 3m/5km E of Muir of Ord. **K. Castle,** restored. NH 5751
Kilcreggan S'clyde 64 A1 vil at S end of peninsula between Gare Loch and Loch Long, opp Gourock across Firth of Clyde. Ferry for pedestrians to Gourock. NS 2380
Kildale N Yorks 55 E4 vil 5m/8km E of Stokesley. NZ 6009
Kildalton S'clyde 62 B3/C3 loc at SE end of Islay 2km NE of Ardbeg. Graveyard of chapel has 8c carved Celtic cross. NR 4347
Kildavanan Point S'clyde 63 G2* headland on W coast of Bute, at entrance to W arm of Kyles of Bute and at NW end of Ettrick Bay. NS 0266
Kildermorie Forest H'land 85 E8 deer forest in Ross and Cromarty dist to W of Loch Morie. NH 4678
Kildonan H'land 87 C5 loc in Strath K., Sutherland dist, 8m/13km NW of Helmsdale. NC 9120
Kildonan S'clyde 63 G5 loc at S end of Arran 2km SW of Dippin Hd. **K. Castle** is a ruined keep. NS 0321
Kildonan W Isles 88 D2* locality and loch near W coast of S Uist, 2m/3km SE of Rubha Ardvule. Ruined bldg near S end of loch is Flora Macdonald's birthplace (1722). NF 7327
Kildonnan H'land 68 C1 loc on E coast of Eigg. NM 4985
Kildrum S'clyde 65 E2* residential area of Cumbernauld near tn centre. NS 7675
Kildrummy Grampian 82 D5 loc 3m/4km S of Lumsden. **K. Castle** (A.M.) is ruined cas 2km SW, dismantled after Jacobite rising of 1715. NJ 4717
Kildwick 48 C3 vil on borders of N and W Yorks 4m/7km NW of Keighley. Hall of 17c. Medieval br across R Aire. SE 0145
Kilfinan S'clyde 63 F1 vil on E side of Loch Fyne, Argyll, 4m/7km NW of Tighnabruaich on Kyles of Bute. **K. Burn** is stream flowing past vil to **K. Bay** 1m W. NR 9378
Kilfinichen Bay S'clyde 69 C5/D5 bay on N side of Loch Scridain, Mull. See also Aird Kilfinichen. NM 4828
Kilgetty (Cilgeti) Dyfed 22 D5 vil 4m/7km N of Tenby. SN 1207
Kilham Humberside 51 E2 vil 5m/8km NE of Gt Driffield. Site of Roman villa 2km E. TA 0664
Kilham Nthmb 67 F5 loc 2m/4km NW of Kirknewton. NT 8832
Kili Holm Orkney 89 B6* small uninhabited island lying off N end of island of Egilsay. HY 4732
Kilkhampton Cornwall 6 B4 vil 4m/7km NE of Bude. SS 2511
Killamarsh Derbys 44 A3 colliery vil 4m/6km NE of Staveley. SK 4580
Killane 46 B4* stream on Isle of Man running out to sea on W coast 1km N of The Cronk. SC 3396
Killantringan Bay D & G. See Black Hd.
Killay W Glam 23 G6 loc in Swansea 3m/5km W of tn centre. **Upr Killay** loc 1m W. SS 6092
Killean S'clyde 62 D3 loc on W side of Kintyre, Argyll, 3m/5km S of Rhunahaorine Pt. Remains of medieval ch. NR 6944
Killearn Central 71 F6 vil 5m/8km NW of Strathblane. Obelisk commemorates George Buchanan, 16c reformer, and tutor to James VI of Scotland. NS 5286
Killegray W Isles 88 A4* uninhabited island in Sound of Harris 3m/5km SW of Leverburgh, W coast of Harris. Nearly 3km long NW to SE and nearly 1km wide. NF 9783
Killen H'land 81 F2 loc on Black Isle, Ross and Cromarty dist, 3m/5km W of Fortrose. NH 6758
Killerby Durham 54 B3 vil 7m/11km NW of Darlington. NZ 1919
Killerby N Yorks 54 B5* loc 2m/3km SE of Catterick. SE 2596
Killerby Halls N Yorks 55 H6* loc 1km SE of Cayton. TA 0682
Killerby, High N Yorks 55 H6* loc above Cayton Bay 3m/5km SE of Scarborough. TA 0683
Killerton Devon 7 G5* ham 5m/8km SW of Cullompton, on E side of **K. Park** (NT). Park contains garden with collection of rare trees and shrubs. SS 9700
Killeyan, Lower S'clyde 62 A4 loc on W side of The Oa, Islay, 2km N of Mull of Oa. NR 2743
Killhope Burn 53 G1* r rising on Killhope Moor, Durham, and flowing SE to join Burnhope Burn and form R Wear at Wearhead. NY 8539
Killichonan Tayside 75 F5 vil on N side of Loch Rannoch 3m/4km from head of resr. Power stn. Waterfall in burn to E. NN 5458
Killiechonate Forest H'land 74 C4, D4 deer forest in Lochaber dist NE of Ben Nevis. NN 2174
Killiecrankie Tayside 76 A4 vil on R Garry 3m/5km SE of Blair Atholl, at head of Pass of K. (NTS), wooded gorge. To NW is site of battle of 1689 in which the troops of King William III were defeated by the Jacobites under Graham of Claverhouse ('Bonnie Dundee'), who, however, was mortally wounded in the battle. NN 9162
Killilan H'land 80 A4 locality in Skye and Lochalsh dist 1m E of head of Loch Long. **K. Forest** is deer forest to E. NG 9430
Killimster H'land 86 F2 loc in Caithness dist 5m/8km NW of Wick. ND 3156
Killin Central 71 F2/G2 vil at confluence of Rs Dochart and Lochay at head of Loch Tay. NN 5732
Killinallan Point S'clyde 62 B1 headland on E side of Loch Gruinart on N coast of Islay, before loch widens out into bay enclosed by Ardnave Pt and Gortantaoid Pt. NR 3072
Killinghall N Yorks 49 E2/E3 vil 2m/4km N of Harrogate. SE 2858
Killingholme, North Humberside 51 F6 vil 3m/5km NW of Immingham. **S Killingholme** vil 1m SE. TA 1417
Killington Cumbria 53 E5 ham 3m/5km SW of Sedbergh. **Killington Resr,** large resr 2m/3km NW. SD 6189
Killington Devon 7 E1* loc 4m/6km SW of Lynton. SS 6646
Killingworth Tyne & Wear 61 G4 loc 4m/7km N of Newcastle. **K. Township** loc to W. NZ 2870
Killochan Castle S'clyde 56 C4* 16c mansion on N side of Water of Girvan 3m/5km NE of Girvan. NS 2200
Killochyett Borders 66 C4* loc on Gala Water, adjoining Stow to N. NT 4545
Killypole Loch S'clyde 62 D5* small loch or tarn in Kintyre 2m/3km S of Machrihanish. NR 6417
Kilmacolm S'clyde 64 B2 tn 6m/10km SE of Greenock. NS 3569
Kilmahog Central 72 A4 loc with woollen mill on N bank of R Leny 1m W of Callander. Site of Roman fort on S bank towards tn. NN 6108
Kilmaluag Skye, H'land 78 C2 loc near N coast 2m/3km S of Rubha na h-Aiseig. **K. Bay** 1m NE. NG 4374
Kilmannan Reservoir 64 C1* resr on borders of Central and Strathclyde regions 4m/7km W of Strathblane. NS 4978
Kilmany Fife 73 F3/G3 vil 4m/7km SW of Newport-on-Tay. NO 3821
Kilmarie Skye, H'land 79 D6 loc on E side of Strathaird peninsula 4m/7km N of Strathaird Pt. NG 5517
Kilmarnock S'clyde 64 B5 industrial tn 19m/31km SW of Glasgow. Industries include engineering, mnfre of carpets, hosiery, footwear, lace, agricultural implements, bricks, fireclay; whisky blending. Associations with Robert Burns; Burns monmt and museum. **K. Water,** r running SW through tn to confluence with R Irvine. NS 4237
Kilmartin S'clyde 70 A5 vil in Argyll 3m/5km NE of Crinan Loch. Damaged 9c cross (A.M.) in churchyard. Remains of 16c cas keep. K. Burn flows S past vil to* R Add 3m/5km S. Many prehistoric remains in vicinity. NR 8398

Kilmaurs S'clyde 64 B4 vil 2m/4km NW of Kilmarnock. NS 4141
Kilmelford S'clyde 70 A4 vil in Argyll at head of Loch Melfort. NM 8413
Kilmeny S'clyde 62 B2* loc on Islay 1km SW of Ballygrant. NR 3965
Kilmersdon Som 16 C6 vil 2m/3km S of Radstock. ST 6952
Kilmeston Hants 10 C2 vil 4m/7km S of New Alresford. SU 5926
Kilmichael Glassary S'clyde 70 B5 vil in Argyll 4m/6km N of Lochgilphead across R Add. Cup and ring marked rocks (A.M.). To NE is moorland area of **Kilmichael Forest.** NR 8593
Kilmichael of Inverlussa S'clyde 69 F8 locality on E side of Loch Sween in Knapdale, Argyll, 5m/8km S of Crinan. NR 7785
Kilmington Devon 8 D4 vil 2m/3km W of Axminster. SY 2892
Kilmington Wilts 9 E1 vil 4m/6km NW of Mere. To S and SE respectively, hams of **K. Common** and **K. Street.** ST 7736
Kilmorack H'land 81 E3 vil on R Beauly 2m/3km SW of Beauly tn in Inverness dist. NH 4944
Kilmore Skye, H'land 79 E7* loc on E coast of Sleat peninsula 2km SW of Teangue. Site of Sleat par ch. NG 6507
Kilmore S'clyde 70 B3 loc in Argyll 4m/6km SE of Oban. NM 8824
Kilmory H'land 68 D2 loc on Ardnamurchan, Lochaber dist, 4m/6km SW of Rubha Aird Druimnich. NM 5270
Kilmory S'clyde 62 D1 loc in Knapdale, Argyll, 2m/3km N of Pt of Knap. **K. Chapel,** 13c, contains collection of Celtic and later sculptured stones. Macmillan's Cross (A.M.),late 15c sculptured cross outside chapel. **K. Bay** is small bay to SW. NR 7075
Kilmory S'clyde 63 F5 loc near S coast of Arran 6m/10km W of Dippin Hd. **K. Water** is r running SW past K. to sea 1km SW. NR 9521
Kilmuir H'land 81 G1 loc on Nigg Bay, N side of Cromarty Firth, 4m/7km NE of Invergordon, Ross and Cromarty dist. NH 7573
Kilmuir Skye, H'land 78 B3 loc near N coast 5m/7km N of Uig. NG 3770
Kilmun S'clyde 70 D6 vil on N side of Holy Loch in Argyll, 2km NW of Strone Pt. NS 1781
Kilndown Kent 12 D3 vil 2m/3km SW of Goudhurst. TQ 7035
Kilneuair S'clyde 70 B4* locality with ruined ch on E side of Loch Awe in Argyll, 1m E of head of loch. NM 8803
Kiln Green Berks 18 C4 ham 2m/4km NE of Twyford. SU 8178
Kiln Green Gtr Manchester 43 E1* loc 6m/9km W of Oldham. SE 0007
Kiln Green H & W 26 B5* ham 3m/4km S of Ross-on-Wye. SO 6019
Kilnhill Cumbria 52 C2* loc 1m W of Bassenthwaite. NY 2132
Kilnhouse Ches 42 C4* loc 2km W of Winsford. SJ 6366
Kilnhurst S Yorks 43 H2 loc 4m/6km NE of Rotherham. SK 4697
Kilninian S'clyde 68 C4 vil on N side of Loch Tuath, Mull, 4m/6km S of Calgary. NM 3945
Kilninver S'clyde 70 A3 vil in Argyll 6m/9km S of Oban across Loch Feochan. NM 8221
Kiln Pit Hill Nthmb 61 E5 ham 5m/8km NW of Consett. NZ 0355
Kilnsea Humberside 51 H6 ham at N end of spit of land running out to Spurn Hd on N side of mouth of R Humber. TA 4015
Kilnsey N Yorks 48 C2 ham in Wharfedale 3m/5km NW of Grassington. **K. Crag,** overhanging limestone cliff. Rock-climbing. SD 9767
Kilnwick Humberside 51 E3 vil 7m/11km N of Beverley. SE 9949
Kilnwick Percy Humberside 50 D3 loc 2m/3km E of Pocklington. SE 8249
Kiloran S'clyde 69 C7 loc on Colonsay 2m/3km N of Scalasaig. **K. Bay** 1m N on NW coast. **K. Gardens,** containing sub-tropical plants, open to public in summer. NR 3996
Kilpatrick S'clyde 63 F5 loc on W coast of Arran at **Kilpatrick Pt,** headland at S end of Drumadoon Bay. NR 9027
Kilpatrick Hills S'clyde 64 C2 range of low hills to E of Dumbarton. Summit is Duncolm, 1316 ft or 401 metres. NS 4676
Kilpeck H & W 26 A4 vil 4m/6km NE of Pontrilas. SO 4430
Kilpheder W Isles 88 D3/E3* loc on S Uist 2km SW of Daliburgh. NF 7419
Kilpin Humberside 50 C5 vil 2m/3km SE of Howden. **K. Pike** loc on N bank of R Ouse 1m W. SE 7526
Kilravock Castle H'land 81 G3 partly 15c cas in Nairn dist 6m/10km SW of Nairn. NH 8149
Kilrenny Fife 73 H4 vil 1m NE of Anstruther. Forms part of Royal Burgh of Kilrenny, Anstruther Easter and Anstruther Wester. NO 5704
Kilrie Ches 42 C3* loc adjoining Knutsford to W. SJ 7478
Kilsby Northants 28 B1 vil 5m/7km SE of Rugby. SP 5671
Kilspindie Tayside 73 E2 vil 7m/11km E of Perth. NO 2225
Kilstay Bay D & G 57 B8* bay on E coast of Rinns of Galloway, 1m N of Drummore. NX 1338
Kilsyth S'clyde 64 D1 coal-mining tn 3m/5km NW of Cumbernauld. 2km E is site, now submerged by resr, of battle of 1645 in which Montrose defeated Covenanters. NS 7178
Kiltarlity H'land 81 E3* vil in Inverness dist 3m/5km S of Beauly. NH 5041
Kilton Cleveland 55 E3 ham 2km SE of Brotton. **K. Thorpe** ham 1km SW. NZ 7018
Kilton Notts 44 B3* E dist of Worksop. SK 5979
Kilvaxter Skye, H'land 78 B3 loc 4m/7km N of Uig. NG 3869
Kilve Som 7 H1 vil 3m/5km NW of Nether Stowey. ST 1442
Kilverstone Norfolk 38 D6 loc 2m/3km NE of Thetford. TL 8984
Kilvey W Glam 23 H6* loc in Swansea 1km NE of tn centre across R Tawe. **K. Hill** to W. SS 6693
Kilvington Notts 44 C6 vil 7m/11km S of Newark-on-Trent. SK 8042
Kilvington, North N Yorks 54 D6* loc 2m/4km N of Thirsk. SE 4285
Kilvington, South N Yorks 54 D6 vil 2km N of Thirsk. SE 4283
Kilwinning S'clyde 64 B4 tn 5m/7km E of Ardrossan, included in area of Irvine New Tn. Slight remains of **K. Abbey,** founded in 12c. NS 3043
Kilworth, North Leics 36 B5 vil 2m/3km W of Husbands Bosworth. SP 6183
Kilworth, South Leics 36 B6 vil 4m/7km SE of Lutterworth. SP 6081
Kimber, East Devon 6 D5* loc 7m/11km NW of Okehampton. SX 4998
Kimberley Norfolk 39 E4* ham with **K. Street** 3m/5km NW of Wymondham. **Kimberley Hse,** 18c hse in large park. Fragments of former hall near W end of park. TG 0704
Kimberley Notts 36 B1 urban loc 5m/9km NW of Nottingham. SK 5044
Kimber, West Devon 6 D5* loc 7m/11km NW of Okehampton. SX 4898
Kimberworth S Yorks 43 H2 dist of Rotherham 2km W of tn centre. SK 4092
Kimble, Great Bucks 18 C1 vil 2m/3km NE of Princes Risborough. SP 8206
Kimble, Little Bucks 18 C1 vil 3m/5km W of Wendover. SP 8207
Kimblesworth Durham 54 B1 vil in coal-mining dist 3m/5km N of Durham. NZ 2547
Kimble Wick Bucks 18 C1* loc 3m/4km N of Princes Risborough. SP 8007
Kimbolton Cambs 29 E1 vil 7m/11km NW of St Neots. Cas partly 16c and 17c, but mainly 18c by Vanbrugh. TL 0967
Kimbolton H & W 26 A2 vil 3m/4km NE of Leominster. SO 5261
Kimbridge Hants 10 A2* loc on R Test 3m/5km NW of Romsey. SU 3225
Kimcote Leics 36 B5 vil 4m/6km NW of Husbands Bosworth. SP 5886
Kimmeridge Dorset 9 F6 vil between Purbeck Hills and coast 5m/8km S of Wareham. To SW of vil, **K. Bay,** surrounded by dark rocks of Kimmeridge clay. SY 9179
Kimmer Lough Nthmb 67 G6* small lake 2m/3km SE of Eglingham. NU 1217
Kimmerston Nthmb 67 F5 loc 2km SE of Ford. NT 9535
Kimpton Hants 10 A1 vil 5m/9km W of Andover. SU 2846
Kimpton Herts 29 F5 vil 4m/6km NE of Harpenden. TL 1718

Kinbrace H'land 86 B4 vil in Sutherland dist 15m/24km NW of Helmsdale. NC 8631
Kinbuck Central 72 B4 vil on Allan Water 3m/4km N of Dunblane. NN 7905
Kincaple Fife 73 G3 loc 3m/5km NW of St Andrews. NO 4618
Kincardine H'land 85 F7 vil near head of Dornoch Firth, 1m S of Ardgay, Sutherland dist. NH 6089
Kincardine and Deeside 114, 115 admin dist of Grampian region.
Kincardine Castle Grampian 77 F3 ruin of former royal residence 2m/3km NE of Fettercairn. NO 6775
Kincardine Castle Tayside 72 C3 19c mansion beside Ruthven Water 1m S of Auchterarder. To SW is fragment of old cas, dismantled in 1645. NN 9411
Kincardine O'Neil Grampian 77 F1 vil on N side of R Dee 7m/11km W of Banchory. NO 5999
Kincardine-on-Forth Fife 72 C5 small port on R Forth 4m/7km SE of Alloa. Power stns up and down stream. **Kincardine Br** is swing rd br across r. NS 9387
Kinchrackine, Upper and **Lower** S'clyde 70 D2* locs in Strath of Orchy in Argyll. Upr K. adjoins Dalmally to W; Lr K. is 1m W of Dalmally. NN 1527
Kinclaven Tayside 73 E1 loc 1m SW of Meikleour across R Tay. **K. Castle,** ruined medieval cas on r bank to SE. NO 1538
Kincorth Grampian 77 H1* dist of Aberdeen 2m/3km S of city centre across R Dee. NJ 9303
Kincraig H'land 75 H1 vil on R Spey in Badenoch and Strathspey dist, 6m/9km NE of Kingussie. NH 8305
Kincraig Point Fife 73 G4 headland at E end of Largo Bay. NT 4699
Kindallachan Tayside 76 B5* vil in Strath Tay 5m/8km N of Dunkeld. NN 9949
Kinder Reservoir Derbys 43 F2/F3 resr 2km NE of Hayfield, W of Kinder Scout. SK 0588
Kinder Scout Derbys 43 F3 summit of the Peak, 2088 ft or 636 metres. SK 0887
Kindrogan Hill Tayside 76 B4 wooded crag above Kindrogan in Strath Ardle 2m/4km NW of Kirkmichael. See also Ennochdhu. NO 0462
Kineton Glos 27 E5 ham 6m/10km W of Stow-on-the-Wold. SP 0926
Kineton Warwicks 27 G3 vil 10m/15km NW of Banbury. Motte and bailey cas. Site of Battle of Edgehill, 1642, 2m/3km SE. SP 3351
Kineton Green W Midlands 35 G6 loc 2m/4km NW of Solihull tn centre. SP 1281
Kineton, Little Warwicks 27 G3 ham adjoining Kineton to S. SP 3350
Kinfare Staffs. Alternative name for Kinver, qv.
Kinfauns Tayside 73 E2, E3 vil 3m/5km E of Perth across R Tay. **K. Castle** is Gothic-style mansion. **K. Forest** is state forest in vicinity. NO 1622
Kingarth S'clyde 63 G2 vil on Bute 3m/5km N of Garroch Hd. NS 0956
Kingates Isle of Wight 10 B6* ham 1km W of Whitwell and 2m/3km E of Chale. SZ 5177
Kingcoed (Cyncoed) Gwent 16 A1 ham 2m/3km SE of Raglan. SO 4205
Kingcombe, Higher Dorset 8 D4 loc 4m/6km NW of Maiden Newton. SY 5499
Kingcombe, Lower Dorset 8 D4 loc 3m/5km NW of Maiden Newton. SY 5599
King Doniert's Stone Cornwall. See St Cleer.
King Edward Grampian 83 F2 loc 4m/7km S of Banff. Castle of K.E., medieval ruin 1m S. NJ 7157
Kingerby Lincs 45 E2 ham 4m/7km NW of Mkt Rasen. TF 0592
King George's Reservoir 20 A2* resr on border of London and Essex 3m/5km E of Enfield. One of a series of resrs in R Lea valley. TQ 3793
King George VI Reservoir Surrey 19 E4* resr 1km N of Staines. TQ 0473
Kingham Oxon 27 F5/G5 vil 4m/6km SW of Chipping Norton. SP 2624
King Harry Passage Cornwall 2 D4* reach of R Fal also known as King Harry's Reach, 3m/5km S of Truro (rd distance 5m/8km). King Harry Ferry conveys vehicles across r. SW 8439
Kingholm Quay D & G 59 E4 loc on E bank of R Nith 2m/3km S of Dumfries. NX 9773
Kinghorn Fife 73 F5 small resort on Firth of Forth 2m/3km E of Burntisland. Mnfre of glass bottles and golf-clubs. NT 2686
Kingie H'land 74 C2 r in Lochaber dist running E down Glen Kingie to R Garry 2m/3km SE of dam of Loch Quoich. **K. Pool** is widening of rs at their confluence. NH 0900
King John's House Wilts. See Tollard Royal.
Kinglass 70 C2 r in S'clyde region rising on S side of Glas Bheinn Mhór, Argyll, and running S then W down Glen K. to Loch Etive on S side of Ardmaddy Bay. NN 0737
Kinglassie Fife 73 E4 vil 2m/3km SW of Leslie. NT 2398
Kinglas Water S'clyde 70 D4 r in Argyll running W down Glen Kinglas to Loch Fyne at Cairndow, near head of loch. NN 1710
Kingmoor Cumbria 59 H5* loc 2m/3km NW of Carlisle. Large rly marshalling yards. NY 3858
Kingoodie Tayside 73 F2 loc on N side of Firth of Tay 4m/7km W of Dundee. NO 3329
King's Acre H & W 26 A3* loc 3m/4km NW of Hereford. SO 4741
Kingsand Cornwall 4 B5 on Cawsand Bay 2km SE of Millbrook. SX 4350
King's Bank E Sussex 12 D4* loc 1km S of Beckley. TQ 8523
Kingsbarns Fife 73 H3 vil near coast 3m/5km N of Crail. NO 5912
Kingsbridge Devon 4 D6 tn 11m/17km S of Totnes at head of **K. Estuary,** which runs past Salcombe and out to sea between Bolt Hd and Prawle Pt. SX 7344
Kingsbridge Som 7 G2 vil 4m/6km S of Dunster. SS 9837
King's Bromley Staffs 35 G3 vil on R Trent 5m/8km N of Lichfield. SK 1216
King's Broom Warwicks 27 E2* loc adjoining vil of Broom to S, 7m/11km W of Stratford-upon-Avon. SP 0953
Kingsbury London 19 F3 loc in borough of Brent 8m/13km NW of Charing Cross. TQ 2088
Kingsbury Warwicks 35 H4 vil 5m/8km N of Coleshill. SP 2196
Kingsbury Episcopi Som 8 C2 vil on R Parrett 4m/6km S of Langport. ST 4321
Kings Caple H & W 26 B4 vil 4m/6km NW of Ross-on-Wye across loops of r. SO 5628
Kingscavil Lothian 65 G1/G2 loc 2m/3km E of Linlithgow. NT 0276
Kingsclere Hants 18 A5 vil 8m/13km NW of Basingstoke. Site of Royal Counties Show. SU 5258
King's Cliffe Northants 37 E4 vil 5m/7km W of Wansford. TL 0097
Kingscote Glos 16 C2 vil 3m/5km SW of Nailsworth. Site of Romano-British settlement 1km SW. ST 8196
Kingscott Devon 7 D3 ham 3m/5km E of Torrington. SS 5318
King's Coughton Warwicks 27 E2* ham 1m N of Alcester. SP 0858
Kingscross S'clyde 63 G5 loc near E coast of Arran at S end of Lamlash Bay. **Kingscross Pt** is headland to E, site of Viking burial ground. NS 0428
Kingsdale Beck 47 G1* r rising W of Whernside, N Yorks, and flowing S to join R Doe at Ingleton and form R Greta. Waterfalls at Thornton Force and Pecka Falls. SD 6973
Kingsdon Som 8 C2 vil 3m/4km SE of Somerton. To E, Lyte's Cary (NT), old manor hse. ST 5126
Kingsdown Kent 13 H2 suburban coastal loc 3m/4km S of Deal. TR 3748
Kingsdown Kent 21 E5 loc 3m/5km S of Sittingbourne. TQ 9258
Kingsdown Wilts 16 C4* vil 4m/7km NE of Bath. ST 8167
Kingsdown Wilts 17 F3 NE dist of Swindon. SU 1688
Kingsdown, West Kent 20 C5 suburban loc 3m/5km SE of Farningham. TQ 5762
Kingseat Fife 73 E5 vil 3m/5km NE of Dunfermline. NT 1290
Kingsey Bucks 18 C1 vil 3m/4km E of Thame. SP 7406
Kingsferry Bridge Kent 21 E5 only br on to Isle of Sheppey, 2km NE of Iwade. TQ 9169
Kingsfold W Sussex 11 G2 ham 4m/7km N of Horsham. TQ 1636

Kingsford H & W 35 E6* loc 3m/5km N of Kidderminster. SO 8181
King's Forest of Geltsdale Cumbria. See Geltsdale.
King's Furlong Hants 18 B6* dist of Basingstoke S of tn centre. SU 6351
Kingsgate Kent 13 H1 suburban loc 2m/3km E of Margate tn centre. 18c cas on cliffs to E. TR 3870
King's Green Glos 26 C4 ham 4m/7km SE of Ledbury. SO 7633
Kingshall Green Suffolk 30 D2* loc 1km NE of Bradfield St George. TL 9160
Kingshall Street Suffolk 30 D2* vil 4m/7km E of Bury St Edmunds. TL 9161
Kingsheanton Devon 6 D2 ham 2m/4km N of Barnstaple. SS 5537
King's Heath Northants 28 C2* NW dist of Northampton. SP 7362
King's Heath W Midlands 35 G6 loc in Birmingham 4m/6km S of city centre. SP 0781
King's Hill Warwicks 35 H6* loc 3m/5km S of Coventry. SP 3274
King's Hill W Midlands 35 F4 loc 1km S of Darlaston tn centre. SO 9896
Kingshill, Great Bucks 18 D2 vil 3m/5km N of High Wycombe. SU 8798
Kingshill, Little Bucks 18 D2 vil 4m/7km NE of High Wycombe. SU 8999
Kingsholm Glos 26 D5* N dist of Gloucester. SO 8319
Kingshott Herts 29 F5* loc 2km SE of Hitchin. TL 1928
Kingshurst W Midlands 35 G5* suburb 7m/11km E of Birmingham. SP 1788
Kingside Hill Cumbria 59 F6* loc 1m NW of Abbey Tn. NY 1551
Kingskerswell Devon 5 E4 mainly residential dist between Newton Abbot and Torbay. SX 8868
Kingskettle Fife 73 F4 vil 1m S of Ladybank. NO 3008
Kingsland Gwynedd 40 A3 S dist of Holyhead, Anglesey. SH 2481
Kingsland H & W 26 A2 vil 4m/6km NW of Leominster. SO 4461
Kingsland London 19 G3* loc in borough of Islington 4m/6km NE of Charing Cross. TQ 3384
Kingsland Salop 34 B3* SW dist of Shrewsbury. SJ 4811
Kings Langley Herts 19 E2 vil 3m/5km S of Hemel Hempstead. TL 0702
Kingsley Ches 42 B4 vil 7m/11km W of Northwich. SJ 5574
Kingsley Hants 11 E1 vil 5m/8km E of Alton. SU 7838
Kingsley Staffs 43 E6 vil 2m/4km N of Cheadle. **K. Holt** 1m SE. SK 0146
Kingsley Green W Sussex 11 E2 vil 2m/3km S of Haslemere. SU 8930
Kingsley Park Northants 28 C2* dist of Northampton 2km NE of tn centre. SP 7662
Kingslow Salop 34 D4/35 E4* loc 6m/10km NE of Bridgnorth. SO 7998
King's Lynn Norfolk 38 B3* tn and port on R Ouse 39m/63km W of Norwich. Industries include canning, beet sugar refining. 17c Customs Hse. Mkt places known as Tuesday Mkt and Saturday Mkt. St George's Guildhall (NT). TF 6119
King's Meaburn Cumbria 53 E3 vil on R Lyvennet 4m/7km W of Appleby. NY 6221
Kingsmead Hants 10 C3* loc 2m/3km NE of Wickham. SU 5813
King's Men Oxon. See Rollright, Great.
Kingsmill Lake Cornwall 4 B4* mouth of creek running down from W Kingsmill N of Botusfleming into R Tamar. SX 4361
Kingsmoor Essex 19 H1* SW dist of Harlow. TL 4307
King's Moss Gtr Manchester 42 B2* loc 2m/3km NW of Billinge. SD 5001
Kings Muir Borders 65 H4* loc adjoining Peebles to S. NT 2539
Kingsmuir Fife 73 H3/H4* loc 4m/7km W of Crail. NO 5408
Kingsmuir Tayside 77 E6 vil 2m/3km SE of Forfar. NO 4749
King's Newnham Warwicks 36 A6* vil 4m/6km W of Rugby. SP 4577
King's Newton Derbys 36 A2 loc 1m NE of Melbourne. SK 3926
Kingsnorth Kent 13 F3 vil 2m/3km S of Ashford. TR 0039
Kingsnorth Power Station Kent 20 D4 situated on N bank of R Medway estuary 2m/3km E of Hoo. TQ 8172
King's Norton Leics 36 C4 vil 7m/11km SE of Leicester. SK 6800
King's Norton W Midlands 35 F6 loc in Birmingham 5m/8km S of city centre. See also Stratford-upon-Avon Canal. SP 0478
King's Nympton Devon 7 E3 vil 3m/5km N of Chulmleigh. SS 6819
King's Park S'clyde 64 D3* loc in Glasgow 3m/5km S of city centre. NS 5960
King's Pyon H & W 26 A3 vil 8m/13km NW of Hereford. SO 4350
Kings Ripton Cambs 29 G1 vil 3m/5km NE of Huntingdon. TL 2676
King's Sedgemoor Drain Som. See Cary (r).
King's Somborne Hants 10 B2 vil 3m/4km S of Stockbridge. John of Gaunt's Deer Park to W. SU 3631
King's Stag Dorset 9 E3 vil 5m/8km SW of Sturminster Newton. Here Thomas de la Lynde killed a stag of Henry III's. Sometimes spelt Kingstag. ST 7210
King's Stanley Glos 16 C1 vil 3m/4km SW of Stroud. SO 8103
King's Stone, The D & G. See Clatteringshaws Loch.
King's Sutton Northants 27 H4 vil on R Cherwell 4m/6km SE of Banbury across r. SP 4936
Kingstag Dorset. See King's Stag.
King's Tamerton Devon 4 B5* NW dist of Plymouth, 3m/5km from city centre. SX 4558
Kingstanding W Midlands 35 G5* loc 5m/8km N of Birmingham city centre. SP 0794
Kingsteignton Devon 5 E3 small industrial tn 2m/3km N of Newton Abbot. SX 8773
King Sterndale Derbys 43 F4 loc 3m/4km E of Buxton. SK 0972
Kingsthorne H & W 26 A4 vil 5m/8km S of Hereford. SO 4931
Kingsthorpe Northants 28 C2 N dist of Northampton. SP 7563
Kingsthorpe Hollow Northants 28 C2* loc in Northampton 2km N of tn centre. SP 7462
Kingston Cambs 29 G2 vil 7m/11km W of Cambridge. TL 3455
Kingston Cornwall 3 H1* loc 4m/6km N of Callington. SX 3675
Kingston Devon 4 C5 vil 3m/5km SW of Modbury. SX 6347
Kingston Devon 5 F2* loc 4m/6km N of Budleigh Salterton. SY 0687
Kingston Dorset 9 E3* vil 4m/6km SW of Sturminster Newton. ST 7509
Kingston Dorset 9 F6 vil on Isle of Purbeck 5m/8km W of Swanage. SY 9579
Kingston Grampian 82 C1 vil on Spey Bay on W side of mouth of R Spey. NJ 3365
Kingston Gtr Manchester 43 E2* loc adjoining Hyde to W. SJ 9495
Kingston Hants 9 H4 loc 2m/3km S of Ringwood. 1m NE, loc of **N Kingston.** SU 1402
Kingston Isle of Wight 10 B6 ham 2m/3km SE of Shorwell. SZ 4781
Kingston Kent 13 G2 vil 5m/8km SE of Canterbury. TR 1951
Kingston Lothian 66 C1* loc 2m/3km S of N Berwick. See also Fenton Tower. NT 5482
Kingston S'clyde 64 C3* loc in Glasgow on S side of R Clyde 1km SW of city centre. NS 5864
Kingston Suffolk 31 F3* loc 1m S of Woodbridge. TM 2647
Kingston Warwicks 27 G2* loc 6m/10km SE of Leamington. SP 3556
Kingston W Sussex 11 G4 loc near coast between E Preston and Ferring, 4m/7km W of Worthing. TQ 0802
Kingston Bagpuize Oxon 17 H2 vil 6m/9km W of Abingdon. SU 4098
Kingston Blount Oxon 18 C2 vil 3m/4km NW of Stokenchurch. SU 7399
Kingston by Sea W Sussex 11 H4 E dist of Shoreham-by-Sea. TQ 2305
Kingston Deverill Wilts 9 F1 vil 4m/6km NE of Mere. ST 8437
Kingstone H & W 26 B5* loc 2m/3km E of Ross-on-Wye. SO 6324
Kingstone H & W 26 A4 vil 6m/10km SW of Hereford. SO 4235
Kingstone Som 8 B3 vil 2km SE of Ilminster. ST 3713
Kingstone Staffs 35 F2 vil 3m/5km SW of Uttoxeter. SK 0629
Kingstone S Yorks 43 G1* dist of Barnsley 1km SW of tn centre. SE 3305
Kingstone Winslow Oxon 17 G3* loc adjoining Ashbury to N, 7m/11km E of Swindon. SU 2685
Kingston Gorse W Sussex 11 G5* loc on coast 4m/7km W of Worthing. TQ 0801
Kingston Lacy Dorset 9 G4* 17c and later hse in park 2m/4km NW of Wimborne. ST 9701
Kingston Lisle Oxon 17 G3 vil 5m/8km W of Wantage. SU 3287
Kingston Maurward Dorset 9 E5* loc 2m/3km E of Dorchester. SY 7191
Kingston near Lewes E Sussex 12 A5 vil on S Downs 2m/3km SW of Lewes. TQ 3908
Kingston on Soar Notts 36 B2 vil 6m/9km N of Loughborough. SK 5027
Kingston Russell Dorset 8 D5 ham 4m/7km S of Maiden Newton. SY 5891
Kingston St Mary Som 8 A2 vil below Quantock Hills 3m/5km N of Taunton. ST 2229
Kingston Seymour Avon 15 H4 vil 3m/5km S of Clevedon. ST 4066
Kingston Stert Oxon 18 C2* loc 3m/5km SE of Thame. SP 7201
Kingston upon Hull Humberside. Official name of Hull, qv.
Kingston upon Thames London 19 F4 tn on right bank of R Thames 10m/16km SW of Charing Cross, and a royal borough. The busy modern tn is of ancient foundation: Saxon kings were crowned there and the coronation stone can still be seen. County hall is former HQ of Surrey County Council. TQ 1769
Kingstown Cumbria 59 H5 loc in Carlisle 2m/3km N of city centre. NY 3959
Kingstreet Gtr Manchester 42 D3* loc adjoining Woodford to W. SJ 8882
King's Walden Herts 29 F5 vil 4m/6km SW of Hitchin. TL 1623
Kingsway East Tayside 73 G2* industrial estate in Dundee nearly 2m/3km NE of city centre. NO 4231
Kingswear Devon 5 E5 tn on left (E) bank of R Dart estuary opp Dartmouth. Ferries cross r. SX 8851
Kingswells Grampian 83 G6 loc 5m/7km W of Aberdeen. NJ 8606
Kingswinford W Midlands 35 E5 W dist of Dudley. SO 8888
Kingswood Avon 16 B4 tn and suburb of Bristol 4m/6km E of city centre. ST 6473
Kingswood Bucks 28 B5* ham 9m/14km NW of Aylesbury. SP 6919
Kingswood Essex 20 D3* dist of Basildon to S of tn centre. TQ 7087
Kingswood Glos 16 C2 vil 2km SW of Wotton-under-Edge. ST 7491
Kingswood Kent 12 D2* loc 2m/3km SW of Harrietsham. TQ 8450
Kingswood Northants 36 D5* SW dist of Corby. SP 8687
Kingswood Som 7 H2* ham 4m/6km SE of Watchet. ST 1037
Kingswood Surrey 19 F5 suburban loc 3m/5km S of Banstead. TQ 2455
Kingswood Warwicks 27 F1 vil 2m/4km SE of Hockley Heath. SP 1871
Kingswood Common H & W 25 G3* loc 2m/3km S of Kington. SO 2954
Kingswood, Lower Surrey 19 F6* loc 1m S of Kingswood and 2m/3km N of Reigate. TQ 2453
Kings Worthy Hants 10 C2 vil 2m/3km N of Winchester. SU 4932
Kingthorpe Lincs 45 E4 ham 2m/3km S of Wragby. TF 1275
Kingthorpe, High N Yorks 55 F6* loc 3m/5km NE of Pickering. SE 8386
Kingthorpe, Low N Yorks 55 F6* loc 3m/4km NE of Pickering. SE 8385
Kington H & W 25 G2 tn on R Arrow close to Welsh border 12m/20km W of Leominster. SO 2956
Kington H & W 27 E2 vil 6m/10km SE of Alcester. SO 9955
Kington Langley Wilts 16 D4 vil 2m/4km N of Chippenham. ST 9277
Kington Magna Dorset 9 E2* vil 4m/6km SW of Gillingham. ST 7623
Kington St Michael Wilts 16 D4 vil 3m/4km N of Chippenham. ST 9077
Kington, West Wilts 16 C4 vil 7m/12km W of Chippenham. **W Kington Wick** loc 1km SE. Site of Roman temple 1m E. ST 8077
Kingussie H'land 75 G2 small tn and tourist centre on R Spey 28m/45km S of Inverness. Highland Folk Museum. NH 7500
Kingweston Som 8 C2 vil 3m/4km NE of Somerton. ST 5230
Kinkell Grampian 83 F5 loc 2m/3km S of Inverurie. 16c ch (A.M.). NJ 7819
Kinlet Salop 34 D6 ham 4m/6km NE of Cleobury Mortimer. SO 7180
Kinloch H'land 79 C8 r on island of Rum, flowing E to vil of Kinloch at head of Loch Scresort on E coast of island. NM 4099
Kinloch H'land 84 F3 r in Caithness dist running NE into Kyle of Tongue. NC 5553
Kinloch Tayside 76 C6 vil 2m/3km W of Blairgowrie. NO 1444
Kinlochaline Castle H'land 68 E4 cas at head of Loch Aline in Lochaber dist. NM 6947
Kinlochard Central 71 F4 locality at head of Loch Ard, 4m/7km W of Aberfoyle. NN 4502
Kinlochbervie H'land 84 C2 vil on N side of Loch Inchard, W coast of Sutherland dist. NC 2256
Kinlocheil H'land 74 B3 vil in Lochaber dist near head of Loch Eil, on N shore. NM 9779
Kinlochewe H'land 80 B2 locality in Ross and Cromarty dist 2m/3km SE of head of Loch Maree. **Kinlochewe R** runs NW to Loch Maree. **K. Forest** is deer forest to N and W. NH 0261
Kinloch Hourn H'land 74 B1 locality in Lochaber dist at head of Loch Hourn. NG 9506
Kinloch Laggan H'land 75 F2* locality at NE end of Loch Laggan in Badenoch and Strathspey dist. NN 5489
Kinlochleven H'land 74 C5 small tn in Lochaber dist at head of Loch Leven. Aluminium works on R Leven to E. TV transmitting stn. NN 1861
Kinlochluichart Forest H'land 80 C1 deer forest in Ross and Cromarty dist between Loch Fannich and Loch Glascarnoch. NH 2769
Kinlochmoidart H'land 68 E2 locality at head of Loch Moidart in Lochaber dist. NM 7172
Kinlochmore H'land 74 C5 locality in Lochaber dist on E side of Kinlochleven. NN 1962
Kinlochnanuagh H'land 68 E1* locality in Lochaber dist 1km above head of Loch nan Uamh and 5m/8km E of Arisaig. NM 7384
Kinloch Rannoch Tayside 75 G5 vil at foot of Loch Rannoch. NN 6658
Kinloss Grampian 82 A1 vil near N coast 3m/4km NE of Forres. Airfield to N. Ruins of 12c abbey. NJ 0661
Kinmel Bay Clwyd 41 F3 suburb 3m/5km NE of Abergele. SH 9880
Kinmuck Grampian 83 F5* loc 3m/5km E of Inverurie. NJ 8119
Kinmundy, Nether Grampian 83 H3* loc 6m/9km W of Peterhead. NK 0443
Kinnaber Tayside 77 G4/G5* loc near E coast 3m/4km N of Montrose. 1m W is site of former rly junction famous in the days of the 'rly race to the North'. NO 7261
Kinnaird Tayside 73 E2 vil 10m/16km W of Dundee. **K. Castle,** restored 15c tower. NO 2428
Kinnaird Castle Tayside 77 F5 19c mansion surrounded by deer park 3m/5km SE of Brechin. NO 6357
Kinnairds Head Grampian 83 G1 headland with lighthouse at Fraserburgh, N of harbour. NJ 9967
Kinnairdy Castle Grampian 83 E2 castellated mansion 2m/3km SW of Aberchirder. NJ 6049
Kinneff Grampian 77 H3 loc on E coast 2m/4km NE of Inverbervie. NO 8574
Kinneil House Central 65 F1* mansion (A.M.) of 16c–17c, 1m SW of Bo'ness. NS 9880
Kinnell Tayside 77 F5 loc 1km E of Friockheim. NO 6050
Kinnel Water 59 F3 r in Dumfries & Galloway region rising N of Queensberry and running SE to R Annan 2km NE of Lochmaben. NY 0983
Kinnerley Salop 34 A2 vil 6m/10km SE of Oswestry. SJ 3320
Kinnerley Salop 34 D3. Alternative spelling for Kynnersley, qv. SJ 6716

Kinnersley H & W 25 H3 vil 2m/4km NE of Willersley. Tudor cas. SO 3449
Kinnersley H & W 26 D3 vil 7m/11km N of Tewkesbury. SO 8743
Kinnerton Ches 42 A5 ham 5m/8km SW of Chester. SJ 3462
Kinnerton Powys 25 G2 vil 3m/4km NE of New Radnor. SO 2463
Kinnerton Green Clwyd 42 A5 loc 3m/5km NW of Rossett. SJ 3361
Kinnerton, Higher Clwyd 41 H5* vil 2m/4km NE of Hope. SJ 3261
Kinnesswood Tayside 73 E4 vil 4m/6km SE of Milnathort. NO 1702
Kinning Park S'clyde 64 C3* loc in Glasgow 2km SW of city centre. NS 5664
Kinninvie Durham 54 A3 ham 3m/5km N of Barnard Castle. NZ 0521
Kinnordy Tayside 76 D5 locality 2km NW of Kirriemuir. Loch of K., marsh to SW. NO 3655
Kinnoul Hill Tayside 73 E2 hill 2km E of Perth across R Tay, at SW end of Sidlaw Hills. Noted viewpoint. Height 729 ft or 222 metres. NO 1322
Kinoulton Notts 36 C2 vil 9m/14km NW of Melton Mowbray. SK 6730
Kinross Tayside 73 E4 tn and resort on W side of Loch Leven 9m/15km N of Dunfermline. Wool spinning, linen mnfre. Angling on Loch Leven. **Kinross Hse** is late 17c hse on loch shore to E. Radio stn to W. NO 1102
Kinrossie Tayside 73 E2 vil 7m/11km NE of Perth. NO 1832
Kinsbourne Green Herts 29 E6 loc 2m/4km NW of Harpenden. TL 1015
Kinsham H & W 26 D4* vil 3m/5km NE of Tewkesbury. SO 9335
Kinsham H & W 25 H2 par containing ham of **Lr Kinsham** and loc of **Upr Kinsham** 3m/5km E of Presteigne. SO 3664
Kinsley W Yorks 49 F6 vil 1m NW of Hemsworth. SE 4114
Kinson Dorset 9 G4 N dist of Bournemouth. SZ 0696
Kintail Forest H'land 80 A5, B5 mountainous tract (NTS) in Skye and Lochalsh dist to NE of Glen Shiel. Includes Five Sisters of Kintail, and Beinn Fhada or Ben Attow. Herds of red deer and wild goats in area. NG 9917
Kintbury Berks 17 G4 vil 3m/5km E of Hungerford. Site of Roman bldg 1km E. SU 3866
Kintessack Grampian 82 A1/A2 loc on edge of Culbin Forest 3m/4km W of Forres. NJ 0060
Kinton H & W 34 B6 ham 1km NE of Leintwardine and 6m/10km W of Ludlow. SO 4074
Kinton Salop 34 B3 ham 9m/14km NW of Shrewsbury. SJ 3719
Kintore Grampian 83 F5 vil on R Don 4m/6km S of Inverurie. Site of Roman camp on W side of vil. NJ 7916
Kintyre S'clyde 62, 63 peninsula in Argyll running S to Mull of K. from narrow isthmus between E and W Loch Tarbert. Length 40m/64 km; average width 8m/13km. Chief tn is Campbeltown. Airfield at Machrihanish. NR 73
Kinuachdrach S'clyde 69 E7 loc near NE coast of Jura, 2m/3km from N end of island. **K. Harbour** is bay to SE. See also Aird of K. NR 7098
Kinveachy H'land 81 H5 loc in Badenoch and Strathspey dist 4m/6km N of Aviemore. NH 9118
Kinver Staffs 35 E5/E6 tn 4m/6km W of Stourbridge. Also known as Kinfare. To W is **K. Edge** (NT), area of heath and woodland with Iron Age fort. SO 8483
Kinwarton Warwicks 27 E2 loc adjoining Alcester to NE. 14c dovecote (NT). SP 1058
Kip Hill Durham 61 G6 loc adjoining Stanley to NE. NZ 2054
Kiplin N Yorks 54 C5 loc 1m W of Gt Langton. SE 2797
Kippax W Yorks 49 F5 vil 2m/3km SE of Garforth. SE 4130
Kippen Central 71 G5 vil 9m/15km W of Stirling. NS 6594
Kippford D & G 58 D5/D6 vil on E side of Urr Water estuary 4m/6km S of Dalbeattie. Also known as Scaur. NX 8355
Kippington Kent 20 B6* loc in SW part of Sevenoaks. TQ 5254
Kirbister Orkney 89 A6* locality on Mainland on W side of Loch of Stenness. HY 2514
Kirbister Orkney 89 B6/B7 locality on Mainland 4m/7km S of Finstown and 6m/9km W of Kirkwall, on S side of Loch of K. HY 3607
Kirby Bedon Norfolk 39 F4 ham 4m/6km SE of Norwich. TG 2705
Kirby Bellars Leics 36 C3 vil 3m/4km W of Melton Mowbray. SK 7117
Kirby Cane Norfolk 39 G5 ham 4m/6km NW of Beccles. TM 3794
Kirby Corner W Midlands 35 H6 loc in Coventry 3m/5km SW of city centre. SP 2976
Kirby Cross Essex 31 F6 suburb 2m/4km W of Walton on the Naze. TM 2120
Kirby Fields Leics 36 B4* suburb 4m/6km W of Leicester. SK 5203
Kirby Green Norfolk 39 G5* loc adjoining Kirby Cane to E. TM 3794
Kirby Grindalythe N Yorks 50 D2 vil 2m/4km NW of Sledmere. SE 9067
Kirby Hall Northants. See Gretton.
Kirby Hill N Yorks 49 F2 vil 1m N of Boroughbridge. SE 3868
Kirby Hill N Yorks 54 B4 ham 4m/6km NW of Richmond. NZ 1406
Kirby Knowle N Yorks 54 D6 vil 4m/7km NE of Thirsk. SE 4687
Kirby le Soken Essex 31 F5 vil 2m/3km W of Walton on the Naze. TM 2222
Kirby Misperton N Yorks 50 C1 vil 3m/5km S of Pickering. SE 7779
Kirby Muxloe Leics 36 B4 vil 4m/7km W of Leicester. Moated 15c brick cas (A.M.). SK 5204
Kirby Row Norfolk 39 G5* vil 3m/5km NE of Bungay. TM 3792
Kirby Sigston N Yorks 54 C5 loc 3m/5km E of Northallerton. SE 4194
Kirby Underdale Humberside 50 C3 vil in the wolds 4m/7km W of Fridaythorpe. SE 8058
Kirby, West Merseyside 41 G3 tn and resort on Wirral peninsula at seaward end of R Dee estuary. SJ 2186
Kirby Wiske N Yorks 54 C6 vil on R Wiske 4m/6km NW of Thirsk. SE 3784
Kirdford W Sussex 11 F2 vil 4m/7km NE of Petworth. TQ 0126
Kirk H'land 86 E2, F2 loc in Caithness dist 4m/6km NE of Watten. ND 2858
Kirkabister Ness Shetland 89 E8* low headland with lighthouse at SW point of island of Bressay. HU 4837
Kirkaig H'land 85 B5 r on border of Ross & Cromarty and Sutherland dists flowing NW into inlet of Loch K. on W coast. NC 0719
Kirkaig Point H'land 85 A5 headland on W coast of Sutherland dist between Lochs Inver and Kirkaig, 2m/4km SW of Lochinver. NC 0521
Kirkandrews upon Eden Cumbria 59 H5 vil 3m/5km NW of Carlisle. NY 3558
Kirkapoll Tiree, S'clyde 69 B7* loc on Gott Bay, nearly 2m/3km N of Scarinish. NM 0447
Kirkbampton Cumbria 59 G5 vil 6m/10km W of Carlisle. NY 3056
Kirkbean D & G 59 E5 vil near Solway Firth, 11m/17km S of Dumfries. NX 9759
Kirkbost W Isles 88 B2 loc on island of Gt Bernera opp Breasclete on W coast of Lewis across E Loch Roag. NB 1835
Kirk Braddan Isle of Man 46 B5 loc 2km NW of Douglas. SC 3676
Kirk Bramwith S Yorks 49 G6 vil on left bank of R Don 6m/10km NE of Doncaster. SE 6211
Kirkbride Cumbria 59 G5 vil 5m/9km N of Wigton. NY 2256
Kirkburn Borders 66 B4/B5 loc 3m/5km SE of Peebles. NT 2938
Kirkburn Humberside 51 E3 vil 3m/5km SW of Gt Driffield. SE 9855
Kirkburton W Yorks 48 D6/49 E6 tn 4m/7km SE of Huddersfield. Textiles, brick mnfre, quarrying. SE 1912
Kirkby Lincs 45 E2* ham 4m/6km NW of Mkt Rasen. TF 0692
Kirkby Merseyside 42 A2 tn 6m/10km NE of Liverpool. **K. Industrial Estate** to E. SJ 4098
Kirkby N Yorks 54 D4 vil 2m/3km SE of Stokesley. NZ 5305
Kirkby, East Lincs 45 G5 vil 5m/8km SW of Spilsby. TF 3362
Kirkby Fleetham N Yorks 54 C5 vil 4m/6km SE of Catterick. SE 2894
Kirkby Green Lincs 45 E5 vil 8m/12km N of Sleaford. TF 0857
Kirkby in Ashfield Notts tn 4m/7km SW of Mansfield. Industries include coal-mining, hosiery. SK 4956
Kirkby la Thorpe Lincs 45 E6 vil 2m/3km E of Sleaford. TF 0945
Kirkby Lonsdale Cumbria 47 F1 small tn on R Lune 14m/22km NE of Lancaster. SD 6178
Kirkby Malham N Yorks 48 B2 vil in Upper Airedale 5m/8km E of Settle. SD 8961
Kirkby Mallory Leics 36 A4 vil 5m/8km N of Hinckley. SK 4500
Kirkby Malzeard N Yorks 49 E1 vil 5m/8km NW of Ripon. SE 2374
Kirkby Mills N Yorks 55 E6* loc 1km SE of Kirkbymoorside. SE 7085
Kirkbymoorside N Yorks 55 E6 small tn below N Yorks Moors 7m/11km W of Pickering. Traces of medieval cas. SE 6986
Kirkby on Bain Lincs 45 F5 vil 3m/5km E of Woodhall Spa. TF 2462
Kirkby Overblow N Yorks 49 E3 vil 4m/6km S of Harrogate. SE 3249
Kirkby Pool 52 C6* r rising SW of Torver, Cumbria, and flowing S into R Duddon estuary at Sand Side. SD 2281
Kirkby, South W Yorks 49 F6 tn in coal-mining area adjoining S Elmsall to W. SE 4511
Kirkby Stephen Cumbria 53 G4 small tn on R Eden 9m/15km SE of Appleby. NY 7708
Kirkby Thore Cumbria 53 F2 vil on site of Roman tn of *Bravoniacum* 4m/7km NW of Appleby. NY 6325
Kirkby Underwood Lincs 37 F2 vil 5m/8km N of Bourne. TF 0727
Kirkby Wharfe N Yorks 49 G4 vil 2m/3km SE of Tadcaster. SE 5040
Kirkby Woodhouse Notts 44 A5* loc 2km S of Kirkby in Ashfield. SK 4954
Kirkcaldy Fife 73 F5 port, resort, and industrial tn 11m/17km almost due N of Edinburgh across Firth of Forth. Birthplace of Adam Smith, 1723, and Robert Adam, 1728. Industries include mnfre of linoleum, furniture, and linen; engineering. See also Ravenscraig Castle. NT 2791
Kirkcambeck Cumbria 60 B4 ham 5m/8km N of Brampton. NY 5368
Kirkcolm D & G 57 A6 vil on Rinns of Galloway, 5m/9km N of Stranraer. NX 0268
Kirkconnel D & G 58 C1 tn on R Nith 3m/5km NW of Sanquhar. NS 7312
Kirkcowan D & G 57 D6 vil 6m/10km SW of Newton Stewart. NX 3260
Kirkcudbright D & G 58 C6 small tn on R Dee estuary at head of **K. Bay.** Site of 13c cas to W beside r, known as Castledykes. Ruins of McLellan's Castle (A.M.), 16c mansion, near main square. NX 6850
Kirkdale Merseyside 42 A2* dist of Liverpool 2m/3km N of city centre. SJ 3493
Kirk Deighton N Yorks 49 F3 vil 2km N of Wetherby. SE 3950
Kirk Ella Humberside 51 E5 suburb 5m/8km W of Hull. TA 0229
Kirkfield S'clyde 64 D3* loc adjoining Bothwell to NW, 3m/4km NW of Hamilton. NS 7059
Kirkfieldbank S'clyde 65 E4 vil 1m W of Lanark across R Clyde. NS 8643
Kirkgunzeon D & G 58 D5 vil 4m/7km NE of Dalbeattie. **K. Lane** is r issuing from Lochaber Loch and flowing SW through vil and through Dalbeattie to Urr Water 1km S of Dalbeattie. NX 8666
Kirk Hallam Derbys 36 A1 suburb 1m SW of Ilkeston. SK 4540
Kirkham Lancs 47 E5 tn 8m/12km W of Preston. Textiles. Site of Roman settlement to E side. SD 4232
Kirkham N Yorks 50 C2 ham on R Derwent 5m/8km SW of Malton. Remains of priory (A.M.); 13c gatehouse. SE 7365
Kirkhamgate W Yorks 49 E5 vil 3m/4km NW of Wakefield. SE 2922
Kirk Hammerton N Yorks 50 A3 vil 9m/14km W of York. SE 4655
Kirkharle Nthmb 61 E3 ham 2m/3km SE of Kirkwhelpington. See also Littleharle Tower. NZ 0182
Kirkheaton Nthmb 61 E4 vil 5m/8km W of Belsay. NZ 0177
Kirkheaton W Yorks 48 D6 vil 3m/4km E of Huddersfield. SE 1818
Kirkhill H'land 81 E3 vil in Inverness dist 7m/11km W of Inverness. NH 5545
Kirkhill Castle S'clyde 57 B5* late 16c hse at Colmonell, qv. NX 1485
Kirkhill Forest Grampian 83 G5* state forest NW of Aberdeen and 2m/3km W of Dyce Airport. NJ 8412
Kirkhill of Kennethmont Grampian 82 D4 vil 7m/11km S of Huntly. Distillery 1m E. See also Leith Hall. NJ 5328
Kirkhill, Upper Grampian 77 H1 loc 2m/3km S of Aberdeen city centre across R Dee. WT stn. NJ 9402
Kirkhope Borders 66 B6 loc on Ettrick Water 1km SW of Ettrickbridge End. NT 3823
Kirkhouse Cumbria 60 B5* loc 3m/4km E of Brampton. NY 5659
Kirkhouse Green S Yorks 49 G6* loc 2km N of Kirk Bramwith. SE 6213
Kirkibost Skye, H'land 79 D6* loc on E side of Strathaird peninsula 4m/7km N of Strathaird Pt. NG 5517
Kirkibost Island W Isles 88 D1 low-lying uninhabited island off W coast of N Uist 5m/8km SE of Aird an Rùnair. NF 7565
Kirkinch Tayside 73 F1 loc 2m/3km E of Meigle. NO 3144
Kirkinner D & G 57 D7 vil 3m/4km S of Wigtown. NX 4251
Kirkintilloch S'clyde 64 D2 tn on line of Antonine Wall 7m/11km NE of Glasgow. Industries include iron founding, paper mnfg. NS 6573
Kirk Ireton Derbys 43 G6 vil 3m/4km SW of Wirksworth. SK 2650
Kirkland Cumbria 52 B3 ham 2km N of Ennerdale Br. NY 0718
Kirkland Cumbria 52 C1* loc 1m E of Wigton. NY 2648
Kirkland Cumbria 53 F2 loc 2m/3km E of Skirwith. NY 6432
Kirkland D & G 58 D3 vil 2m/3km E of Moniaive. NX 8090
Kirkland Fife 73 F4* N dist of Methil. NO 3700
Kirkland Guards Cumbria 52 B1* loc 1m NE of Bothel. NY 1840
Kirkland Hill D & G 58 C1* hill 3m/4km N of Kirkconnel. Height 1675 ft or 511 metres. NS 7316
Kirk Langley Derbys 35 H1 vil 4m/7km NW of Derby. SK 2838
Kirkleatham Cleveland 55 E3 vil 2m/3km S of Redcar. NZ 5921
Kirkleegreen Reservoir S'clyde 64 B3* small resr 2m/4km NE of Beith. NS 3855
Kirklees 117 admin dist of W Yorks metropolitan county.
Kirklevington Cleveland 54 D4 vil 2m/3km SE of Yarm. NZ 4309
Kirkleyditch Ches 42 D3* ham 2m/3km E of Alderley Edge. SJ 8778
Kirklington Notts 44 B5 vil 3m/4km NW of Southwell. SK 6757
Kirklington N Yorks 54 C6 vil 6m/9km SE of Bedale. Hall dates from 16c, although much altered. SE 3181
Kirklinton Cumbria 60 A4 ham 4m/6km E of Longtown. NY 4367
Kirkliston Lothian 65 G2 vil 3m/4km S of S Queensferry. NT 1274
Kirkmadrine D & G 57 B7 loc on Rinns of Galloway 2km SW of Sandhead. Inscribed stones (A.M.) of early Christian era in churchyard. NX 0848
Kirkmaiden D & G 57 B8 vil on Rinns of Galloway, nearly 1m W of Drummore. NX 1236
Kirk Merrington Durham 54 B2 vil 2km S of Spennymoor. NZ 2631
Kirk Michael Isle of Man 46 B4 vil near W coast 6m/10km NE of Peel. SC 3190
Kirkmichael S'clyde 56 D3 vil 3m/5km E of Maybole. NS 3408
Kirkmichael Tayside 76 B5 vil in Strath Ardle 9m/14km E of Pitlochry. NO 0860
Kirkmuirhill S'clyde 65 E4 vil 6m/9km W of Lanark and adjoining vil of Blackwood to S. NS 7943
Kirk Ness Shetland 89 F7* promontory on N coast of island of Whalsay, to N of Brough vil. HU 5565
Kirknewton Lothian 65 G2 vil 10m/16km SW of Edinburgh. NT 1166
Kirknewton Nthmb 67 F5 vil in R Glen valley 5m/8km W of Wooler. NT 9130
Kirkney Grampian 82 D4 loc 5m/8km S of Huntly. **K. Water** is stream running NE into R Bogie 1km NE. NJ 5133
Kirk of Mochrum D & G. See Mochrum.
Kirk of Shotts (or Kirk o' Shotts) S'clyde 65 E3 loc 4m/7km W of Harthill. TV stn 2km NW. NS 8462

Kirkoswald Cumbria 53 E1 vil 7m/11km N of Penrith. Remains of medieval cas to E. NY 5541
Kirkoswald S'clyde 56 C3 vil 4m/7km W of Maybole. Souter Johnnie's Hse (NTS), once the home of John Davidson, the original Souter Johnnie of Burns's *Tam o' Shanter*. NS 2307
Kirkpatrick Durham D & G 58 D4 vil 5m/8km N of Castle Douglas. NX 7870
Kirkpatrick-Fleming D & G 59 G4 vil 6m/10km SE of Ecclefechan. See also Bruce's Cave. NY 2770
Kirk Sandall S Yorks 44 B1 suburb 4m/6km NE of Doncaster. SE 6107
Kirksanton Cumbria 52 B6 ham 2m/3km W of Millom. SD 1480
Kirk Smeaton N Yorks 49 G6 vil 5m/8km SE of Pontefract. SE 5116
Kirkstall W Yorks 49 E4 dist of Leeds 2m/3km NW of city centre. Remains of 12c Cistercian abbey beside R Aire. SE 2635
Kirkstead Lincs 45 F5 vil on R Witham 7m/11km SW of Woodhall Spa. Slight remains of 12c abbey 1m E. TF 1762
Kirkstone Pass Cumbria 52 D4 loc and pass in Lake Dist carrying rd from Windermere to Patterdale, 5m/8km S of the latter. NY 4008
Kirkstyle D & G 60 A3 vil on Ewes Water 4m/6km N of Langholm. NY 3690
Kirkstyle H'land 86 F1* loc on Pentland Firth 4m/6km W of Duncansby Hd. ND 3472
Kirkthorpe W Yorks 49 F6* vil 2m/3km E of Wakefield. SE 3621
Kirkton Borders 60 B1 loc 3m/4km E of Hawick. NT 5413
Kirkton D & G 59 E3 vil 4m/6km N of Dumfries. Remains of Roman fort to NW. NX 9781
Kirkton Fife 73 F2* loc on Firth of Tay 2m/4km W of Wormit. NO 3625
Kirkton Grampian 83 E4 loc 2km NE of Auchleven. NJ 6425
Kirkton Grampian 83 E5* vil 3m/5km SE of Alford. NJ 6113
Kirkton H'land 79 F6 locality on N side of Loch Alsh in Skye and Lochalsh dist 4m/6km W of Dornie. NG 8227
Kirkton H'land 81 F4 locality in Inverness dist 1km N of NE end of Loch Ness. NH 6037
Kirkton Lothian 65 G2* loc in Livingston 2m/3km SW of tn centre. NT 0466
Kirkton Head Grampian 83 H2 headland on NE coast 3m/5km N of Peterhead. NK 1150
Kirktonhill S'clyde 64 B2* W dist of Dumbarton. NS 3975
Kirkton Manor Borders 65 H5* loc 3m/4km SW of Peebles. NT 2237
Kirkton of Airlie Tayside 76 D5 loc 5m/8km W of Kirriemuir. NO 3151
Kirkton of Auchterhouse Tayside 73 F1 vil 6m/10km NW of Dundee. **Auchterhouse** is loc nearly 1m W. NO 3438
Kirkton of Collace Tayside 73 E2* loc 1km SW of Collace and 7m/11km NE of Perth. NO 1931
Kirkton of Craig Tayside 77 F5* vil 2km SW of Montrose. **Craig Castle** to N is small 15c tower with 17c hse. NO 7055
Kirkton of Culsalmond Grampian 83 E4 vil 9m/14km SE of Huntly. NJ 6432
Kirkton of Durris Grampian 77 G2 vil 5m/8km E of Banchory. NO 7796
Kirkton of Glenbuchat Grampian 82 C5. See Glenbuchat.
Kirkton of Glenisla Tayside 76 C5 vil on R Isla 8m/12km N of Alyth. NO 2160
Kirkton of Kingoldrum Tayside 76 D5 vil 3m/5km W of Kirriemuir. Site of Balfour Castle to S. NO 3355
Kirkton of Largo Fife. See Largo.
Kirkton of Logie-Buchan Grampian 83 G4 vil 2m/3km E of Ellon across R Ythan. NJ 9829
Kirkton of Menmuir Tayside 77 E4 vil 5m/8km NW of Brechin. NO 5364
Kirkton of Monikie Tayside 73 G1* loc 4m/6km NW of Carnoustie. NO 5138
Kirkton of Oyne Grampian 83 E4* loc 1km E of Oyne. NJ 6825
Kirkton of Rayne Grampian 83 E4 vil 8m/12km NW of Inverurie. NJ 6930
Kirkton of Skene Grampian 77 G1 vil 9m/14km W of Aberdeen. NJ 8007
Kirkton of Slains Grampian 83 H4 loc adjoining Collieston to N, 5m/9km E of Ellon. See also Old Castle of Slains. NK 0428
Kirkton of Strathmartine Tayside 73 F1 vil 4m/6km NW of Dundee. NO 3735
Kirktown Grampian 83 G1* loc 1m S of Fraserburgh. NJ 9965
Kirktown Grampian 83 H2* S dist of Peterhead. NK 1346
Kirktown of Alvah Grampian 83 E1 vil near N coast 2m/4km S of Banff. NJ 6760
Kirktown of Auchterless Grampian 83 F3 vil 5m/8km S of Turriff. NJ 7141
Kirktown of Clatt Grampian 82 D4 vil 3m/5km E of Rhynie. Also known as Clatt. NJ 5325
Kirktown of Deskford Grampian 82 D1 vil near N coast 4m/6km S of Cullen. Ruined ch (A.M.). NJ 5061
Kirktown of Fetteresso Grampian 77 H3 vil 2km W of Stonehaven. See also Fetteresso Forest. NO 8585
Kirkwall Orkney 89 B6 chief tn and port of Mainland and capital of Orkney, situated at N end of narrow neck of land between Wide Firth to N and Scapa Flow to S, 24m/38km N of Scottish mainland at Duncansby Hd. Harbour on **Bay of K.** on N side, opening out into Wide Firth. Fishing, woollen mnfg, distilling, seaweed processing, etc. Airport (Grimsetter) 3m/4km SE. St Magnus's Cathedral dates in part from 12c. HY 4411
Kirkwhelpington Nthmb 61 E3 vil on R Wansbeck 9m/14km SE of Otterburn. NY 9984
Kirk Yetholm Borders 67 E5 vil on E side of Bowmont Water, 7m/12km SE of Kelso. N terminus of Pennine Way (see Pennines). NT 8228
Kirmington Humberside 45 E1 vil 6m/10km N of Caistor. Airport development. TA 1011
Kirmond le Mire Lincs 45 F2 vil 6m/9km NE of Mkt Rasen. TF 1892
Kirn S'clyde 70 D6 loc in Argyll adjoining Dunoon to N, on W shore of Firth of Clyde. NS 1878
Kirriemuir Tayside 76 D5 small jute mnfg tn 5m/8km NW of Forfar. The 'Thrums' of the novels of Barrie, whose birthplace here houses a museum (NTS). NO 3854
Kirriereoch Hill 56 D4 mt on border of Strathclyde and Dumfries & Galloway regions 1m NW of Merrick, in Glentrool Forest Park. Height 2565 ft or 782 metres. NX 4187
Kirroughtree Forest D & G 58 A4* state forest 4m/7km NE of Newton Stewart. NX 4473
Kirstead Green Norfolk 39 G5 vil 5m/9km NW of Bungay. Vil of **K. Lings** 1m NE. **K. Hall,** Jacbn hse 1m N. TM 2997
Kirtlebridge D & G 59 G4 vil 3m/5km SE of Ecclefechan. NY 2372
Kirtleton D & G 59 G3* loc 6m/9km NE of Ecclefechan. NY 2679
Kirtle Water 59 G4 r in Dumfries & Galloway region rising 6m/10km W of Langholm and running S to Kirtlebridge, then SE to Solway Firth 1m S of Gretna. NY 3165
Kirtling Cambs 30 B2 loc 5m/7km SE of Newmarket. Tudor gatehouse survives from former manor hse. Vil of **K. Green** 1m SW. TL 6857
Kirtlington Oxon 28 A5 vil 6m/9km W of Bicester. SP 4919
Kirtomy H'land 86 A2 vil near N coast of Caithness dist 3m/4km E of Bettyhill. **K. Bay** 1km N. **Kirtomy Pt,** headland 2km N. NC 7463
Kirton Lincs 37 G1 vil 4m/6km SW of Boston. **K. End** loc 2km NW. TF 3038
Kirton Notts 44 B4 vil 3m/4km E of Ollerton. SK 6969
Kirton Suffolk 31 F4 vil 4m/6km N of Felixstowe. TM 2739
Kirton Holme Lincs 37 G1 loc 4m/7km W of Boston. TF 2642
Kirton in Lindsey Humb 44 D2 small tn 8m/13km S of Scunthorpe. Airfield to SE. SK 9398
Kiscadale S'clyde 63 G5 two locs, **N** and **S Kiscadale,** on Whiting Bay, E coast of Arran. NS 0426
Kisdon Force N Yorks 53 G4* waterfall to E of Keld. NY 8900
Kishorn H'land 79 F5 locality in Ross and Cromarty dist at head of Loch K. **Kishorn I.** is small uninhabited island at entrance to loch. **R Kishorn** runs S to head of loch. NG 8340
Kisimul W Isles. Alternative spelling of Kiessimul, qv.
Kislingbury Northants 28 C2 vil on R Nene 4m/6km W of Northampton. SP 6959
Kitchener Memorial Orkney. See Marwick Hd.
Kite Green Warwicks 27 F1* loc 1m E of Henley-in-Arden. SP 1666
Kites Hardwick Warwicks 27 H1 loc 5m/8km SW of Rugby. SP 4768
Kit Hill Cornwall 3 H1 summit of Hingston Down above Callington to NE of tn. Height 1091 ft or 333 metres. Accessible by rd. SX 3771
Kitmere Cumbria 53 E6* small lake 4m/7km N of Kirkby Lonsdale. SD 6085
Kitnocks Hants 10 C3* loc adjoining Curdridge to S and 1m E of Botley. SU 5213
Kit's Coty Kent 20 D5 loc 1m S of Blue Bell Hill, midway between Rochester and Maidstone. To S, Kit's Coty Hse (A.M.), prehistoric monmt consisting of three upright stones and a capstone, overlooking R Medway valley. Site of Roman temple on other side of main rd. TQ 7461
Kitt Green Gtr Manchester 42 B1* loc in W part of Wigan. Food-canning factory. SD 5505
Kittisford Som 7 H3* ham 4m/6km NW of Wellington. 1km N, ham of **K. Barton.** ST 0722
Kittle W Glam 23 G6* loc on Gower peninsula between Bishopston and Pennard, 6m/10km SW of Swansea. SS 5789
Kitts End Herts 19 F2* loc 2m/3km S of Potters Bar. TQ 2498
Kitt's Green W Midlands 35 G5* loc in Birmingham 5m/9km E of city centre. SP 1487
Kitt's Moss Gtr Manchester 42 D3* dist of Bramhall to W of tn centre. SJ 8884
Kittybrewster Grampian 77 H1* dist of Aberdeen 2km NW of city centre. NJ 9207
Kitwood Hants 10 D2* loc 2km S of Four Marks and 5m/8km E of New Alresford. SU 6633
Kivernoll H & W 26 A4* ham 5m/9km SW of Hereford. SO 4632
Kiveton Park S Yorks 44 A3* loc in coal-mining and quarrying area 6m/10km W of Worksop. SK 4982
Kixley Wharf W Midlands 35 G6* loc on Grand Union Canal 3m/5km SE of Solihull. SP 1877
Knaik 72 C4 r in Tayside region running SE to Allan Water 1m S of Braco. NN 8307
Knaith Lincs 44 C3 ham 3m/5km S of Gainsborough. **K. Park** loc 1m NE. SK 8284
Knap Corner Dorset 9 E2* ham adjoining E Stour to NE and 2m/3km S of Gillingham. ST 8023
Knapdale S'clyde 63 E1, E2 area of Argyll bounded by Crinan Canal to N, and E and W Loch Tarbert to S. Largely moorland, with many small lochs. **K. Forest** is state forest at NW end of area. NR 8176
Knaphill Surrey 18 D5 suburban loc 3m/4km W of Woking. SU 9658
Knaplock Som 7 F2* ham on Exmoor 2m/3km SE of Withypool. SS 8633
Knap of Howar Orkney 89 B5* site of prehistoric stone dwellings (A.M.) on W coast of island of Papa Westray. Remains date from between 2400 and 2800 BC. HY 4851
Knapp Som 8 B2 vil 5m/8km E of Taunton. On E side of vil, ham of **Lr Knapp.** ST 3025
Knapps Loch S'clyde 64 B2* small loch 1m SE of Kilmacolm. NS 3569
Knapthorpe Notts 44 C5* loc 1m S of Caunton. SK 7458
Knaptoft Leics 36 C5* loc 4m/6km N of Husbands Bosworth. SP 6289
Knapton Norfolk 39 G2 vil 3m/5km NE of N Walsham. TG 3034
Knapton N Yorks 50 B3 vil 3m/4km W of York. SE 5652
Knapton, East N Yorks 50 D1 ham 7m/11km E of Malton. SE 8875
Knapton Green H & W 26 A2 ham 9m/15km NW of Hereford. SO 4452
Knapton, West N Yorks 50 D1 ham 6m/10km E of Malton. SE 8775
Knapwell Cambs 29 G2 vil 8m/12km NW of Cambridge. TL 3362
Knar Burn 60 C6* r rising on Northumbrian moors W of Alston, Cumbria, and flowing NE into R South Tyne 1km S of Knarsdale, Nthmb. NY 6753
Knaresborough N Yorks 49 F3 tn on escarpment above R Nidd 3m/5km NE of Harrogate. Remains of 14c cas. Petrifying well. SE 3557
Knarsdale Nthmb 60 C6 ham near confluence of Knar Burn and R South Tyne 7m/11km S of Haltwhistle. **K. Hall,** 17c, to N. NY 6753
Knarston Orkney 89 A6* loc on Mainland 1km E of Dounby. HY 3020
Knathole Derbys 43 E3 loc adjoining New Mills to SW. SJ 9985
Knatts Valley Kent 20 C5* loc 1m SW of West Kingsdown. TQ 5661
Knaves' Green Suffolk 31 F2* loc 1km S of Wetheringsett. TM 1266
Knavesmire N Yorks 49 G3* loc in York containing York Racecourse, 2m/3km S of city centre. SE 5949
Knayton N Yorks 54 D6 vil 4m/6km N of Thirsk. SE 4387
Knebworth Herts 29 F5 tn 3m/4km S of Stevenage. See also Old Knebworth. TL 2520
Knedlington Humberside 50 C5 vil 1m W of Howden. SE 7328
Kneesall Notts 44 B4 vil 4m/6m SE of Ollerton. SK 7064
Kneesworth Cambs 29 G3 vil 2m/4km N of Royston. TL 3444
Kneeton Notts 44 B6 vil 7m/12km SW of Newark-on-Trent. SK 7146
Knelhall Staffs 35 E1 loc 3m/4km NE of Stone. SJ 9237
Knelston W Glam 23 F6 vil on Gower peninsula 3m/5km N of Port Eynon Pt and 12m/19km W of Swansea. SS 4688
Kneppmill Pond W Sussex 11 G3* lake in par of Shipley 6m/9km S of Horsham. TQ 1521
Knettishall Suffolk 38 D6 loc 7m/11km E of Thetford. TL 9780
Knightacott Devon 7 E2* loc 7m/11km NE of Barnstaple. SS 6439
Knightcote Warwicks 27 H2 vil 9m/15km N of Banbury. SP 4054
Knightley Staffs 35 E2* ham 3m/5km SW of Eccleshall. **K. Dale** loc 1m S. SJ 8125
Knighton Devon 4 C5 loc at N end of Wembury 4m/6km SW of Yealmpton across R Yealm estuary. SX 5249
Knighton Dorset 8 D3* ham 2km E of Yetminster and 4m/6km SW of Sherborne. ST 6111
Knighton Dorset 9 G4* loc 4m/7km NW of Bournemouth. SZ 0497
Knighton Leics 36 B4 dist of Leicester 2m/3km SE of city centre. **S Knighton** loc adjoining to S. SK 6001
Knighton (Trefyclo) Powys 25 G1 tn on R Teme 14m/23km W of Ludlow. Livestock marketing, agricultural engineering, forestry, saw-milling, woollen mnfre. Motte and bailey cas; also remains of later cas, Bryn y Castell, to E. SO 2872
Knighton Som 15 G6 ham 3m/5km N of Nether Stowey. ST 1944
Knighton Staffs 34 D1 ham 2km S of Woore. SJ 7240
Knighton Staffs 34 D2 vil 5m/8km N of Newport. **Knighton Resr** 1m NW. SJ 7427
Knighton Wilts 17 G4* loc 3m/5km NW of Hungerford. Site of Roman villa to SE across R Kennet. SU 2971
Knighton, East Dorset 9 E5 ham 2m/3km W of Wool. SY 8185
Knighton on Teme H & W 26 B1* ham 3m/4km NE of Tenbury Wells. SO 6370
Knighton, South Devon 4 D3* loc 3m/5km W of Newton Abbot. SX 8172
Knighton, West Dorset 9 E5 vil 3m/5km SE of Dorchester. SY 7387
Knight Reservoir Surrey 19 E4* small resr to W of W Molesey. TQ 1167
Knightsbridge London 19 F4 street in West End running W from Hyde Park Corner down to site of br over Westbourne Brook, now in underground pipes. Term also applied to area surrounding K. Underground Stn. TQ 2779
Knight's End Cambs 37 H5* loc adjoining March to SE. TL 4094

Knight's Green Glos 26 C4* loc 4m/6km S of Ledbury. SO 7131
Knightsridge Lothian 65 G2* residential area of Livingston to NW of tn centre. NT 0469
Knightswood S'clyde 64 C2* dist of Glasgow 4m/7km NW of city centre. NS 5369
Knill H & W 25 G2 ham on Hindwell Brook 3m/4km N of Kington. SO 2960
Knipe, High Cumbria 53 E3* loc 4m/6km NW of Shap. **Low Knipe** loc to NW. NY 5219
Knipe Tarn Cumbria 52 D5* small lake 3m/4km S of Windermere. SD 4294
Knipton Leics 36 D2 vil 6m/10km SW of Grantham. **Knipton Resr** 1km SW. SK 8231
Knitsley Durham 61 F6* loc 2km S of Consett. NZ 1148
Kniveton Derbys 43 G6 vil 3m/5km NE of Ashbourne. SK 2050
Knochan H'land 85 C6 loc in Sutherland dist adjoining Elphin to S, 8m/12km S of Inchnadamph. NC 2110
Knock Cumbria 53 F2 ham 4m/7km N of Appleby. NY 6827
Knock Grampian 82 D2 loc with distillery 7m/12km E of Keith. **K. Hill** to N; height 1412 ft or 430 metres. NJ 5452
Knock Skye, H'land 79 E7 loc on **K. Bay** on E coast of Sleat peninsula, adjoining Teangue to E. At E end of bay is **K. Castle,** or Camus Castle, ruined cas of the Barons of Sleat. NG 6709
Knock W Isles 88 C2* vil on Eye Peninsula, Lewis, 4m/7km E of Stornoway. NB 4931
Knockaird W Isles 88 C1* loc near N end of Lewis 1km NW of Port of Ness. NB 5364
Knockandhu Grampian 82 B4 vil 4m/7km NE of Tomintoul. NJ 2123
Knockando Grampian 82 B3 loc with distillery on left bank of R Spey 7m/11km W of Craigellachie. Loc of **Upr Knockando** 1m N. NJ 1941
Knockarthur H'land 87 A6* loc in Sutherland dist 7m/11km NW of Golspie. NC 7506
Knockdolian S'clyde 57 B5 prominent hill 2m/4km NE of Ballantrae. Height 869 ft or 265 metres. NX 1184
Knockdown Wilts 16 D3 ham 5m/7km SW of Tetbury. ST 8388
Knockendon Reservoir S'clyde 64 A4* resr 4m/6km NW of Dalry. NS 2452
Knockenkelly S'clyde 63 G5* loc on E coast of Arran, towards N end of Whiting Bay.
Knockentiber S'clyde 64 B5* loc 2m/3km NW of Kilmarnock. NS 3939
Knockhall Kent 20 C4* loc 3m/5km E of Dartford. TQ 5974
Knock Head Grampian 83 E1 headland on N coast 2m/4km NW of Banff. NJ 6566
Knockholt Kent 20 B5 vil 3m/5km NE of Westerham. Vil of **K. Pound** to NE. TQ 4658
Knockin Salop 34 A2 vil 5m/8km SE of Oswestry. Mound of medieval cas E of ch. SJ 3322
Knockinlaw S'clyde 64 B5* N dist of Kilmarnock. NS 4239
Knockmill Kent 20 C5* loc 3m/5km NW of Wrotham. TQ 5761
Knocknagael Boar Stone H'land 81 F3* Pictish stone (A.M.) of 7c or 8c, bearing outline of wild boar. Situated 3m/4km S of Inverness. NH 6541
Knocknairshill Reservoir S'clyde 64 B2* small resr 3m/5km SE of Greenock. NS 3073
Knock of Crieff Tayside 72 C2 hill and viewpoint 2km N of Crieff. Height 911 ft or 278 metres. NN 8723
Knockruan Loch S'clyde 63 E5* small loch or tarn in Kintyre 2m/3km NE of Campbeltown. NR 7322
Knock Saul Grampian 83 E4 hill 5m/7km N of Alford. Surrounded by large area of conifers known as Whitehaugh Forest. NJ 5723
Knocksharry Isle of Man 46 A5 loc 2m/4km NE of Peel. SC 2785
Knocksting Loch D & G 58 C3* small loch or tarn 5m/8km W of Moniaive. NX 6988
Knock, West Tayside 77 E3 mt 3m/5km SW of Tarfside. Height 2273 ft or 693 metres. NO 4775
Knodishall Suffolk 31 H2 vil 2km W of Leiston. Loc of **K. Common** 1m SE. Loc of **K. Green** 1m NW. TM 4261
Knole Kent 20 B6 mansion (NT) of 15c–17c in large deer park on E side of Sevenoaks. Ancestral seat of the Sackvilles. TQ 5454
Knole Som 8 C2* ham 2m/4km S of Somerton.
Knollbury Gwent 16 A3* loc 1m NE of Magor. ST 4388
Knolls Green Ches 42 D3* vil 3m/4km W of Alderley Edge. SJ 8079
Knolton Clwyd 34 B1* ham 2m/3km S of Overton. Loc of **K. Bryn** 1km NW. SJ 3738
Knook Wilts 9 F1* vil on R Wylye 1m W of Heytesbury. ST 9341
Knossington Leics 36 D3 vil 4m/6km W of Oakham. SK 8608
Knottallow Tarn Cumbria 52 C6* small lake 2m/3km NW of Ulverston. SD 2780
Knott End-on-Sea Lancs 47 E3 vil on E side of mouth of R Wyre opp Fleetwood. Ferry for pedestrians across r. SD 3548
Knott Hill Reservoir Gtr Manchester 43 E1* resr 1m W of Mossley. SD 9501
Knotting Beds 29 E2 vil 4m/6km SE of Rushden. Ham of **K. Green** 1km S. TL 0063
Knottingley W Yorks 49 G5 tn on S bank of R Aire and on Aire and Calder Canal 11m/18km E of Wakefield. Various mnfres. SE 5023
Knott Lanes Gtr Manchester 43 E1* loc in Oldham 2m/4km S of tn centre. SD 9202
Knotts Lancs 48 A3* loc 4m/6km E of Slaidburn. SD 7653
Knotty Ash Merseyside 42 A2 dist of Liverpool 4m/7km E of city centre. SJ 4091
Knotty Green Bucks 18 D2 loc 2m/3km N of Beaconsfield. SU 9392
Knoutberry Hill, Great Cumbria 53 G6* summit of Whiddale Fell 5m/8km E of Dent. Height 2203 ft or 671 metres. SD 7887
Knowbury Salop 34 C6 vil 4m/7km E of Ludlow. SO 5774
Knowefield Cumbria 60 A5* loc in Carlisle 1m N of city centre. NY 4057
Knowl W Yorks 48 D6* loc adjoining Mirfield to N. SE 2020
Knowle Avon 16 B4 dist of Bristol 2m/3km SE of city centre. ST 6070
Knowle Devon 5 F3 NW outskirts of Budleigh Salterton. Between vil and tn centre is dist of **Lit Knowle.** SY 0582
Knowle Devon 6 D2 vil 5m/8km NW of Barnstaple. SS 4938
Knowle Devon 7 F5* vil 4m/6km W of Crediton. SS 7801
Knowle Salop 26 B1 ham 3m/5km N of Tenbury Wells. SO 5973
Knowle Som 7 G1* ham 2m/3km W of Dunster. SS 9643
Knowle W Midlands 35 G6 dist of Solihull 3m/4km SE of tn centre. SP 1876
Knowle Cross Devon 7 H5* loc just N of Whimple and 4m/6km NW of Ottery St Mary. SY 0497
Knowle Fold Lancs 47 G5* loc adjoining Darwen to N. SD 6923
Knowle Green Lancs 47 G4* ham 2m/3km E of Longridge. SD 6338
Knowle St Giles Som 8 B3* ham 2m/4km NE of Chard. ST 3411
Knowles Green, Great Suffolk 30 C2* loc 2km NW of Chedburgh. TL 7758
Knowles Hill Devon 5 E3* N dist of Newton Abbot. SX 8571
Knowle, The Notts 36 B1* loc 5m/8km NW of Nottingham. SK 5044
Knowle West Avon 16 B4* S dist of Bristol. ST 5970
Knowl Green Essex 30 C4* ham 3m/4km S of Clare. TL 7841
Knowl Hill Berks 18 C3 vil 3m/5km NE of Twyford. Site of Roman bldg to W. SU 8279
Knowl, The Gwent 26 A5 loc 1m N of Monmouth. SO 5014
Knowlton Kent 13 H2 ham 4m/7km SW of Sandwich. TR 2853
Knowsley Merseyside 42 A2 vil 7m/11km NE of Liverpool. Industrial estate to N. **K. Hall,** mansion in large park to E. SJ 4395
Knowsley 117 admin dist of Merseyside metropolitan county.
Knowsthorpe W Yorks 49 E5* loc in Leeds 2m/3km SE of city centre. SE 3232
Knowstone Devon 7 F3 vil 7m/11km E of S Molton. 1m E, ham of **E Knowstone.** SS 8223
Knox Bridge Kent 12 D3* ham 2m/3km S of Staplehurst. TQ 7840
Knoydart H'land 79 D7 mountainous area of Lochaber dist between Lochs Hourn and Nevis and bordering Sound of Sleat. NG 8301
Knoyle, East Wilts 9 F2 vil 5m/8km N of Shaftesbury. ST 8830
Knoyle, West Wilts 9 F1 vil 3m/5km E of Mere. ST 8632
Knucklas Powys 25 G1 ham 3m/4km NW of Knighton. Early British camp on hill to N. SO 2574
Knutsford Ches 42 C3 tn 6m/10km W of Wilmslow. Paper processing, timber. The 'Cranford' of Mrs Gaskell. SJ 7578
Knutton Staffs 42 D6* loc in Newcastle-under-Lyme 1m NW of tn centre. SJ 8346
Knuzden Brook Lancs 48 A5* loc 2m/3km E of Blackburn. SD 7127
Knypersley Staffs 42 D5 loc adjoining Biddulph to S. **Knypersley Resr** 1m SE. SJ 8856
Krumlin W Yorks 48 C6* ham 1m S of Barkisland. SE 0518
Kuggar Cornwall 2 C6* ham 4m/6km N of Lizard Pt. SW 7216
Kyle 49 G2 r rising N of Easingwold, N Yorks, and flowing circuitously southwards into R Ouse at Newton-on-Ouse. SE 5060
Kyle Akin H'land 79 E6 narrow strait between **Kyleakin,** vil on Skye, and Kyle of Lochalsh on Scottish mainland, at mouth of Loch Alsh. Vehicle ferry plies across strait. NG 7526
Kyle and Carrick 116 admin dist of S'clyde region.
Kyle Castle S'clyde 56 F2 ruined cas at confluence of Guelt Water and Glenmuir Water, 5m/8km E of Cumnock. NS 6419
Kyle Forest S'clyde 56 E3* state forest 3m/5km N of Dalmellington. NS 4911
Kyle More Skye, H'land 79 D5 sea channel between islands of Raasay and Scalpay. Also known as Caol Mór. NG 5833
Kyle of Durness H'land 84 D2 estuary of R Dionard running into Balnakeil Bay, N coast of Sutherland dist W of Durness. NC 3668
Kyle of Lochalsh H'land 79 F6 vil and port in Skye and Lochalsh dist on N side of entrance to Loch Alsh. Vehicle ferry to Kyleakin, on Skye, across narrow strait of Kyle Akin. NG 7627
Kyle of Sutherland H'land 85 F7 narrows between Invershin and Bonar Br, Sutherland dist, at head of Dornoch Firth. NH 5795
Kyle of Tongue H'land 84 E2, F2 estuarial inlet on N coast of Caithness dist running out into Tongue Bay. Vil of Tongue on E side of inlet. NC 5859
Kyle Rhea H'land 79 F6 narrow strait between E end of Skye and W coast of Scottish mainland, connecting Loch Alsh to N with Sound of Sleat to S. Vehicle ferry at S end of strait. NG 7922
Kylerhea Skye, H'land 79 F6 loc at E end of island on Kyle Rhea, 4m/7km SE of Kyleakin. Vehicle ferry across strait to Scottish mainland. NG 7820
Kyle Rona Skye, H'land 78 D4 strait separating islands of Raasay and Rona. Also known as Caol Rona. NG 6154
Kylesknoydart H'land 79 F8 locality on N shore of Loch Nevis, Lochaber dist, at S end of Knoydart. Loch narrows considerably above this point. NM 8093
Kylesku Ferry H'land 84 C4 vehicle ferry connecting Kylestrome and Unapool across head of Loch Cairnbawn, W coast of Sutherland dist. NC 2333
Kylesmorar H'land 79 F8 locality on N side of N Morar and on S shore of Loch Nevis, Lochaber dist, 1m NE of Tarbet. NM 8093
Kyles of Bute S'clyde 63 F1, G1 narrow channel surrounding N part of island of Bute and separating it from mainland of Argyll. NS 0175
Kyles Scalpay W Isles 88 B3* locality on N coast of E Loch Tarbert opp island of Scalpay. NG 2198
Kyles Stockinish W Isles 88 B3* vil on E side of entrance to Loch Stockinish on SE coast of Harris, 6m/9km S of Tarbert. NG 1391
Kylestrome H'land 84 C4 locality on N side of Loch Cairnbawn, W coast of Sutherland dist. See also Kylesku Ferry. NC 2234
Kyloe, East Nthmb 67 G4 ham 3m/5km E of Lowick. **W Kyloe** ham 1km NW. **Kyloe Hills** to W command wide views of coast. NU 0539
Kym 29 F2* r rising as R Til SE of Rushden, Northants, and flowing NE to Tilbrook, Cambs, then SE as R Kym through Kimbolton and into R Ouse on N side of St Neots. TL 1861
Kyme, North Lincs 45 F5 vil 7m/11km NE of Sleaford. **S Kyme** vil 3m/4km SE. TF 1552
Kymin Gwent 26 A6* loc 2km E of Monmouth across R Wye, on hill (partly NT) commanding views of Wye and Monnow valleys, and with 'temple' erected in 1802 in honour of Nelson's admirals. SO 5212
Kynance Cove Cornwall 2 C6 much visited cove of serpentine rock 2km NW of Lizard Pt. (See also Asparagus I. and Gull Rock.) SW 6813
Kynaston Salop 34 A3* loc 1m SE of Kinnerley. SJ 3520
Kynnersley Salop 34 D3 vil 4m/6km NE of Wellington. Sometimes spelt Kinnerley. SJ 6716
Kyo, East Durham 61 F6* loc 1km N of Annfield Plain. **W Kyo** loc to W. See also New Kyo. NZ 1752
Kype Water 64 D4 r in Strathclyde region running N through **Kype Resr** to Avon Water 1m SE of Strathaven. NS 7143
Kyre Brook 26 B2* r rising near Collington, N of Bromyard, H & W, and flowing NW into R Teme at Tenbury Wells. SO 5968
Kyre Green H & W 26 B2* loc 4m/6km S of Tenbury Wells. SO 6162
Kyrewood H & W 26 B1 ham 1km SE of Tenbury Wells. SO 6067
Kyrle Som 7 H3* loc just N of Ashbrittle. ST 0522
Kyson Hill Suffolk 31 F3* area (NT) of parkland overlooking R Deben at Kingston, S of Woodbridge. TM 2647

L

Laceby Humberside 45 F1 vil 4m/7km SW of Grimsby. TA 2106
Lacey Green Bucks 18 C2 vil 3m/4km SE of Princes Risborough. SP 8200
Lacey Green Ches 42 D3* loc adjoining Wilmslow to N. SJ 8482
Lacharn Welsh form of Laugharne, qv.
Lach Dennis Ches 42 C4 vil 4m/6km E of Northwich. SJ 7072
Lachlan Castle S'clyde. See Castle Lachlan.
Lackenby Cleveland 55 E3 loc 4m/7km E of Middlesbrough. NZ 5619
Lackford Suffolk 30 C1 vil 6m/9km NW of Bury St Edmunds. Ham of **L. Green** adjoins to NW. TL 7970
Lacock Wilts 16 D4 vil on R Avon 3m/5km S of Chippenham. **L. Abbey** (NT, together with most of vil), medieval abbey on W bank of r. ST 9168
Ladbroke Warwicks 28 A2 vil 2m/3km S of Southam. SP 4158
Ladderedge Staffs 43 E5* loc 2m/3km SW of Leek. SJ 9654
Ladder Hills Grampian 82 C5 range of hills 6m/10km E of Tomintoul. Summit at Carn Mór, 2636 ft or 804 metres. NJ 2718
Laddingford Kent 20 C6 vil on R Teise 2km S of Yalding. TQ 6948
Lade Bank Lincs 45 G5 loc 8m/13km NE of Boston. **Lade Bank Br** over Hobhole Drain 1m W. TF 3954
Ladhar Bheinn H'land 74 A2 mt in Knoydart, in Lochaber dist, 4m/7km NE of Inverie. Height 3343 ft or 1019 metres. NG 8203

Ladies Hill Lancs 47 E3* loc adjoining Pilling to N. SD 4048
Ladock Cornwall 2 D3 vil 4m/6km N of Truro. SW 8950
Ladybank Fife 73 F3 small tn 5m/8km SW of Cupar. Agriculture, engineering. NO 3009
Ladybower Reservoir Derbys 43 F3/G3 large resr 10m/16km W of Sheffield. Has two arms, one in R Derwent and one in R Ashop valley. SK 1986
Lady Brook Gtr Manchester. See Micker Brook.
Ladycross Cornwall 6 C6 loc 3m/4km N of Launceston. SX 3288
Ladyford Grampian 83 G1 loc 7m/12km SW of Fraserburgh. NJ 9060
Lady Green Merseyside 41 H1* loc adjoining Ince Blundell to NW. SD 3103
Lady Holme Cumbria 52 D5* small island (NT) on Windermere 1m SW of Windermere tn. Site of pre-Reformation chantry chapel. SD 3997
Lady House Gtr Manchester 48 C6* loc adjoining Milnrow to S. SD 9211
Lady Isle S'clyde 64 A5 small island with lighthouse in Firth of Clyde 3m/5km W of Troon. NS 2729
Ladykirk Borders 67 F4 vil on R Tweed 6m/9km NE of Coldstream. NT 8847
Lady Park Tyne & Wear 61 G5* loc 3m/5km S of Gateshead. NZ 2458
Lady's Green Suffolk 30 C2 loc 7m/11km SW of Bury St Edmunds. TL 7559
Lady's Holm Shetland 89 E8* small uninhabited island lying off S coast of Mainland 2m/4km NW of Sumburgh Hd. HU 3709
Lady's Rock S'clyde 70 A2 rock, marked by beacon, lying between Eilean Musdile and E coast of Mull. NM 7734
Ladywell London 20 A4* loc in borough of Lewisham 1m SW of Lewisham tn centre and 6m/9km SE of Charing Cross. TQ 3774
Ladywell Lothian 65 G2* residential area of Livingston near tn centre. NT 0568
Ladywood H & W 26 D2* ham 2m/4km SW of Droitwich. SO 8760
Ladywood W Midlands 35 F5* loc in Birmingham 1km W of city centre. SP 0586
Lael Forest H'land 85 C7, C8* state forest above head of Loch Broom, Ross and Cromarty dist. NH 1982
Lagavulin S'clyde 62 B3 vil on S coast of Islay 1km W of Ardbeg. Distillery. NR 4045
Lagentium W Yorks. See Castleford.
Lagg S'clyde 63 F5 loc near S coast of Arran, 7m/12km SW of Lamlash. NR 9521
Lagg S'clyde 62 D1 loc on **L. Bay** on E coast of Jura, 3m/5km S of head of Loch Tarbert. NR 5978
Laggan H'land 74 D2 locality at NE end of Loch Lochy. **S Laggan Forest** is state forest extending along both sides of loch here. NN 2997
Laggan H'land 75 F2 vil on R Spey in Badenoch and Strathspey dist 6m/10km N of Dalwhinnie. **Laggan Br** spans R Spey here. NN 6194
Laggan S'clyde 62 B3 r on Islay rising near E coast and running W to **L. Bay** 2km E of **L. Point.** Bay is 5m/8km wide and extends from L. Point southwards to Rubha Mór. L. Point is headland at entrance to Loch Indaal. NR 2955
Laggan Bay S'clyde 68 C4 small bay at SE end of Loch Tuath, W coast of Mull. NM 4540
Laggan Deer Forest S'clyde 69 E6* deer forest on E side of Loch Buie, Mull. NM 6221
Laggantalluch Head D & G 57 B8 headland on W coast of Rinns of Galloway, 3m/5km W of Drummore. NX 0836
Laid H'land 84 D2 loc in Sutherland dist 5m/8km S of Durness. NC 4159
Laide H'land 78 F1 vil in Ross and Cromarty dist 5m/8km SE of Greenstone Pt on W coast. NG 8991
Laighstonehall S'clyde 64 D3* SW dist of Hamilton. NS 7054
Laindon Essex 20 C3 W dist of Basildon. Locs of **L. Barn** and **L. Ponds** to N and NE respectively. TQ 6889
Laira Devon 4 B5* dist of Plymouth 2m/3km NE of city centre. SX 5056
Lairg H'land 85 F6 vil at SE end of Loch Shin in Sutherland dist, 17m/27km W of Golspie on E coast. NC 5806
Laisterdyke W Yorks 48 D5* dist of Bradford 2m/3km E of city centre. SE 1932
Laithe, Low N Yorks 48 D2/49 E2 loc 1m NW of Summer Br. SE 1963
Laithe Reservoir, Lower W Yorks 48 C4* resr 1m W of Haworth. SE 0237
Laithes Cumbria 52 D2 loc 4m/6km NW of Penrith. NY 4632
Laithkirk Durham 53 H3 loc 1m S of Middleton in Teesdale. NY 9524
Lake Devon loc 2km S of Barnstaple. SS 5531
Lake Devon 4 B4* ham 5m/8km SE of Tavistock. SX 5368
Lake Isle of Wight 10 C6 loc 1km SW of Sandown. SZ 5983
Lake Wilts 9 H1* ham beside R Avon 2m/3km SW of Amesbury. SU 1339
Lakeland, South 116, 117 admin dist of Cumbria.
Lake Meadows Essex 20 C2* N dist of Billericay. TQ 6795
Lakenham Norfolk 39 F4* dist of Norwich 1km S of city centre. TG 2307
Lakenheath Suffolk 38 C6 vil 5m/8km SW of Brandon. **L. Airfield** to E. TL 7182
Lake of Menteith Central 71 G4 lake to S of Menteith Hills 5m/8km SW of Callander. See also Inchmahome, Inch Talla. NN 5700
Lakesend Norfolk 38 A5 vil 2m/3km N of Welney. TL 5196
Lake Side Cumbria 52 D6 loc at S end of Windermere. SD 3787
Lake, The W Sussex 11 F2 lake 2km NE of Northchapel. SU 9631
Lake Vrynwy Powys 33 F2-G3 large resr about 7km long from NW to SE and about 1m wide at widest point. The dam, at the SE end, is 15m/24km NW of Welshpool. Built in 1880s to supply water to Liverpool. SJ 0119
Laleham Surrey 19 E4 loc on left bank of R Thames 2m/3km SE of Staines. TQ 0568
Laleston (Trelales) Mid Glam 14 D3 vil 2m/3km W of Bridgend. SS 8779
Lamachan Hill D & G 58 A4 mt in Glentrool Forest Park 2m/4km SE of Loch Trool. Height 2349 ft or 716 metres. NX 4377
Lamaload Reservoir Ches 43 E4* resr 4m/6km E of Macclesfield. SJ 9774
Lamarsh Essex 30 D4 vil 4m/6km S of Sudbury. TL 8935
Lamas Norfolk 39 F3 ham 4m/7km SE of Aylsham. TG 2423
Lamb Lothian 73 H5 islet off shore 1m W of N Berwick. Haunt of sea birds. NT 5386
Lamba Shetland 89 E6* uninhabited island in Yell Sound 2km N of entrance to Sullom Voe. Area about 120 acres or 48 hectares. HU 3981
Lamba Ness Orkney 89 C5* headland on W coast of island of Sanday 3m/5km N of Spur Ness. Vil of **Lambaness** inland. HY 6138
Lamb Corner Essex 31 E5 loc 5m/8km NE of Colchester. TM 0431
Lambden Borders 67 E4* loc 2m/3km NW of Eccles. NT 7443
Lamberal Water 6 B4* r in Cornwall rising N of Kilkhampton and running S into R Tamar 3m/4km SE thereof. SS 2808
Lamberhead Green Gtr Manchester 42 B1 dist of Wigan 2m/4km W of tn centre. SD 5404
Lamberhurst Kent 12 C3 vil on R Teise 6m/10km SE of Tunbridge Wells. Former centre of iron-working industry. Ham of **L. Down** 1km SW; loc of **L. Quarter** 2m/3km NW. See also Scotney Castle. TQ 6736
Lamberton Borders 67 F3 loc 3m/5km NW of Berwick-upon-Tweed. NT 9657
Lambert's Castle Hill Dorset. See Marshwood.
Lambert's End W Midlands 35 F5* loc on W side of W Bromwich tn centre. SO 9991
Lambeth London 19 G4* borough on S side of R Thames, here crossed by Vauxhall, Lambeth, Westminster, and Waterloo Brs. Borough extends about 7m/11km southwards from Waterloo Br. At E end of L. Br is L. Palace, official residence of Archbishop of Canterbury. TQ 3078
Lambfair Green Suffolk 30 C3* ham 6m/9km NE of Haverhill. TL 7153
Lambgarth Head Shetland 89 E7 headland on E coast of Mainland 6m/9km N of Lerwick. HU 4550
Lamb Head Orkney 89 C6 headland at SE end of island of Stronsay. HY 6921
Lambhill S'clyde 64 C2* loc in Glasgow 2m/4km N of city centre. NS 5869
Lamb Hoga Shetland 89 F6* peninsula at SW corner of Fetlar between Wick of Tresta (see Tresta) and Colgrave Sound. **Head of Lambhoga** is headland at SE end of peninsula. HU 6088
Lamb Holm Orkney 89 B7* small uninhabited island off S coast of Mainland to SE of St Mary's, joined to Mainland by causeway and rd – see Churchill Barrier. HY 4800
Lambley Notts 44 B6 vil 5m/8km NE of Nottingham. SK 6345
Lambley Nthmb 60 C5* ham 4m/6km SW of Haltwhistle. NY 6758
Lambourn Berks 17 G3 small tn 12m/19km NW of Newbury. Racehorse training centre. Vil of **Upr Lambourn** to NW. **L. Downs,** chalk uplands, to N. SU 3278
Lambourn 17 H4 r rising on Berkshire Downs above Lambourn and flowing SE into R Kennet 1m E of Newbury. SU 4867
Lambourne Essex 20 B2 loc 3m/5km E of Loughton. Ham of **L. End** 1m S. TQ 4796
Lamb Roe Lancs 48 A4* loc 1m N of Whalley. SD 7337
Lambrook Som 8 A2* E dist of Taunton. ST 2425
Lambrook, East Som 8 C3 vil 2m/3km W of Martock. 1km W, ham of **Mid Lambrook;** 2km W, ham of **W Lambrook.** ST 4318
Lambs' Green Dorset 9 G4* loc 2km SW of Wimborne. SY 9998
Lambs Green W Sussex 11 H2* ham 3m/5km W of Crawley. TQ 2136
Lambston Dyfed 22 B4 loc 3m/5km W of Haverfordwest. SM 9016
Lambton Tyne & Wear 60 G5* dist of Washington to SW of tn centre. NZ 2955
Lambton Castle Durham 61 G6 19c edifice of towers and turrets above N bank of R Wear 2m/3km E of Chester-le-Street. NZ 2952
Lamellion Cornwall 3 G2* loc in SW part of Liskeard. SX 2463
Lamerton Devon 4 B3 vil 3m/4km NW of Tavistock. SX 4576
Lamesley Tyne & Wear 61 G5 vil 3m/5km S of Gateshead. NZ 2557
Lamington S'clyde 65 F5 vil 6m/9km SW of Biggar. NS 9831
Lamlash S'clyde 63 G4 vil and small port on **L. Bay** on E coast of Arran, 3m/5km S of Brodick. NS 0231
Lammer Law Lothian 66 C3 peak on Lammermuir Hills 4m/6km S of Gifford. Height 1733 ft or 528 metres. NT 5261
Lammermuir Borders 66, 67 upland area extending westwards from St Abb's Hd and culminating in **L. Hills** on borders of Lothian and Borders regions, summit of which is Meikle Says Law, qv. NT 75
Lamonby Cumbria 52 D2 ham 2m/3km W of Skelton. NY 4035
Lamorick Cornwall 3 E2* loc 3m/5km SW of Bodmin. SX 0364
Lamorna Cornwall 2 A5 vil beside steep-sided valley running down to **L. Cove** 4m/6km S of Penzance. SW 4424
Lamorran Cornwall 2 D4 ham on inlet of R Fal 3m/5km SW of Tregony. SW 8741
Lampay Islands Skye, H'land 78 A4 two islets on E side of Loch Dunvegan 3m/5km E of Dunvegan Hd. NG 2255
Lampeter (Llanbedr Pont Steffan) Dyfed 24 B3 small mkt tn on R Teifi 20m/32km NE of Carmarthen. **St David's College,** founded 1822, is constituent college of University of Wales. SN 5748
Lampeter Velfrey (Llanbedr Felffre) Dyfed 22 D4 vil 3m/5km E of Narberth. SN 1514
Lamphey (Llandyfai) Dyfed 22 C5 vil 2m/3km E of Pembroke. Remains of medieval **L. Palace** (A.M.), formerly residence of Bishops of St David's. SN 0100
Lamplugh Cumbria 52 B3 ham 7m/11km S of Cockermouth. NY 0820
Lamport Northants 28 C1 vil 9m/14km N of Northampton. SP 7574
Lampton London 19 F4* loc in borough of Hounslow 10m/16km W of Charing Cross. TQ 1376
Lamyatt Som 8 D1 vil 2m/3km NW of Bruton. ST 6535
Lana Devon 6 B4* loc 4m/6km NW of Holsworthy. SS 3007
Lana Devon 6 C5* loc 5m/8km S of Holsworthy. SX 3496
Lanark S'clyde 65 F4 mkt tn above right bank of R Clyde 11m/18km SE of Motherwell. Industries include agricultural engineering, tanning. Racecourse to SE. NS 8843
Lanarth Cornwall 2 D6* loc 2km W of St Keverne and 8m/12km SE of Helston. SW 7621
Lancashire 116,117 north-western county of England, bounded by Cumbria, N and W Yorkshire, Gtr Manchester, Merseyside, and the Irish Sea. The inland side of the county is hilly, and includes the wild and impressive Forest of Bowland. On the other, W, side is the coastal plain, where vegetables are extensively cultivated. The S is largely urban; industries include cotton spinning and weaving, chemicals, glass, rubber, electrical goods, and motor vehicles. Chief tns are Blackburn, Blackpool, Burnley, Lancaster, Morecambe and Preston, which is also the admin centre. Fleetwood and Heysham are ports. The principal rs are the Lune and the Ribble.
Lancaster Lancs 47 E2 city and county tn on R Lune 20m/32km N of Preston. Norman cas. Georgian Old Tn Hall. University at Bailrigg, 2m/3km S. Industries include mnfre of linoleum and rayon. SD 4761
Lancaster Canal 47 F1-F5 canal navigable from Tewitfield, near Carnforth, Lancs, to Preston. There is a branch to Glasson, on R Lune estuary, providing access to Irish Sea.
Lanchester Durham 54 B1 small tn 7m/12km NW of Durham. Site of Roman fort of *Longovicium* 1km SW. NZ 1647
Lancing, North W Sussex 11 G4 urban loc in par of Lancing 3m/5km NE of Worthing. 1m NE in open country is **Lancing College,** boarding school for boys. Site of Roman temple 1km N of N Lancing. TQ 1805
Lancing, South W Sussex 11 G4 urban loc on coast in par of Lancing, 2m/4km E of Worthing. TQ 1804
Landbeach Cambs 30 A2 vil 5m/7km NE of Cambridge. TL 4765
Landcross Devon 6 D3 ham on R Torridge 2m/3km S of Bideford. SS 4623
Landerbury Grampian 77 G1* loc 1km SE of Echt. NJ 7404
Landewednack Cornwall 2 C6* vil 2km NE of Lizard Pt. SW 7112
Landford Wilts 10 A3 vil 6m/10km W of Romsey. SU 2519
Land Gate Gtr Manchester loc 2m/3km N of Ashton-in-Makerfield. SD 5701
Landguard Point Suffolk 31 F5 headland at entrance to Harwich Harbour 2m/4km SW of Felixstowe. TM 2831
Landhallow H'land 86 E4* loc near E coast of Caithness 1km W of Latheron. ND 1933
Landican Merseyside 41 H3* loc in Birkenhead 4m/6km SW of tn centre. SJ 2885
Landimor Welsh form of Landimore, qv.
Landimore (Landimor) W Glam 23 F6 ham on Gower peninsula 1m E of Cheriton and 12m/19km W of Swansea. Remains of cas. 1m E are the ruins of Weobley Castle (A.M.), fortified 13c–14c manor hse. SS 4693
Landkey Devon 6 E2 par to E and SE of Barnstaple containing vils of **Landkey Newland** and **Landkey Tn.** SS 5931
Landmark Visitor Centre H'land. See Carrbridge.
Landmoth N Yorks 54 D5* loc 4m/6km E of Northallerton. SE 4292
Land of Nod Hants 11 E2* ham 3m/5km NW of Hindhead. SU 8437
Landore W Glam 23 G5/H5 loc in Swansea 2m/3km N of tn centre. SS 6596
Landport Hants 10 D4* dist of Portsmouth 1km N of city centre. SU 6401
Landrake Cornwall 3 H2 vil 4m/6km W of Saltash. SX 3760
Landscove Devon 4 D4* loc 2m/4km SE of Ashburton. SX 7766
Land's End Cornwall 2 A5 headland 8m/13km SW of Penzance. Most westerly point of English mainland. Airport (St Just) 3m/5km NE. SW 3425
Landsend Point Essex 21 E2* headland on S bank of R Crouch estuary 4m/7km W of Burnham-on-Crouch. TQ 8896
Lands, High Durham 54 A2* ham 2km E of Butterknowle. NZ 1225

Landshipping Dyfed 22 C4 loc on E side of Daughleddau R opp confluence of Rs Eastern and Western Cleddau 10m/16km NW of Tenby. SN 0111
Land Side Gtr Manchester 42 C2* loc 2km S of Leigh. SJ 6598
Landslip, The Isle of Wight 10 C6* undercliff ravine on SE coast 2km NE of Ventnor, caused by landslip in 1818. SZ 5878
Landulph Cornwall 4 B4* vil beside R Tamar at its junction with R Tavy N of Saltash. SX 4361
Landwade Cambs 30 B1/B2* loc 3m/5km NW of Newmarket. Site of Roman villa to W. TL 6228
Land Yeo 15 H4* r rising at Barrow Gurney SW of Bristol and flowing W into mouth of R Severn 1m SW of Clevedon. ST 3970
Landywood Staffs 35 F4* loc 3m/4km S of Channock. **Upr Landywood** ham 1m SW. SJ 9906
Lane W Yorks 43 F1* loc 2km SW of Holmbridge. SE 1005
Laneast Cornwall 6 B6 vil 7m/11km W of Launceston. SX 2284
Lane Bottom Lancs 48 B4* loc 2m/3km SE of Nelson. SD 8735
Lane End Bucks 18 C2 vil 4m/6km W of High Wycombe. SU 8091
Lane End Ches 42 C2* loc 1km SW of Hollins Green. SJ 6890
Lane End Cumbria 52 B5 ham 3m/5km N of Bootle. SD 1093
Lane End Derbys 43 H5 loc 4m/6km NE of Alfreton. SK 4155
Lane End Dorset 9 F5 ham 2km S of Bere Regis. SY 8592
Lane End Gtr Manchester 42 D1* loc 1m SE of Heywood. SD 8609
Lane End Hants 10 C2* loc 2m/4km SW of Cheriton. SU 5525
Lane End H & W 26 B5* loc 4m/6km SE of Ross-on-Wye. SO 6419
Lane End Kent 20 C4* loc just E of Darenth, 2m/4km SE of Dartford. TQ 5671
Lane End Lancs 48 B3* loc adjoining Barnoldswick to N. SD 8747
Lane End S Yorks 43 G2* loc adjoining Chapeltown to NW. SK 3497
Lane End Wilts 16 C6* ham 4m/6km W of Warminster. ST 8145
Lane Ends Ches 43 E3* loc 1m SE of Disley. SJ 9883
Lane Ends Derbys 35 H1* ham 1km N of Sutton on the Hill. SK 2334
Lane Ends Durham 54 B2* loc 2km S of Willington. NZ 1833
Lane Ends Gtr Manchester 43 E2* loc 2m/3km NE of Marple. SJ 9790
Lane Ends Lancs 48 B5* loc 1km S of Hapton. SD 7930
Lane Ends N Yorks 48 C4* loc 1m NE of Cowling. SD 9743
Lane Ends Staffs 42 D5* loc 2m/4km N of Tunstall. SJ 8754
Lane Green Staffs 35 E4* loc adjoining Codsall to E. SJ 8803
Laneham Notts 44 C3 vil 7m/11km SE of E Retford. **Ch Laneham** ham with ch and inn beside R Trent 1km E. SK 8076
Lanehead Durham 53 G1* ham 2m/3km NW of Wearhead. NY 8441
Lane Head Durham 54 A2 loc 1km NW of Copley. NZ 0725
Lane Head Durham 54 A4 ham 6m/9km SE of Barnard Castle. NZ 1211
Lane Head Durham 61 E6* loc 2km E of Edmondbyers. NZ 0449
Lane Head Gtr Manchester 42 C2 loc 2km E of Golborne. SJ 6296
Lanehead Nthmb 60 D3* loc 3m/5km NW of Bellingham. Remains of Tarset Castle, perhaps late 13c. NY 7985
Lane Head W Midlands 35 F4* loc in Walsall 3m/5km NW of tn centre. SJ 9700
Lane Head W Yorks 43 F1 loc 3m/5km E of Holmfirth. SE 1908
Lane Heads Lancs 47 E4* 1m SE of Gt Eccleston. SD 4339
Lane, High Derbys 36 A1 loc 2m/3km W of Ilkeston. SK 4342
Lane, High Gtr Manchester 43 E3 loc 5m/8km SE of Stockport. SJ 9585
Lane, High H & W 26 B2 ham 4m/7km NE of Bromyard. SO 6760
Lane, High Staffs 42 D6* loc 1km SE of Alsagers Bank. SJ 8148
Lane, High Staffs 43 E5* loc 1m S of Brown Edge. SJ 9052
Lanercost Priory Cumbria 60 B5 remains of medieval priory (A.M.) on N side of R Irthing, 3m/4km NE of Brampton. NY 5563
Lanescot Cornwall 3 F3* loc 3m/5km SW of Lostwithiel. SX 0855
Lanesend Dyfed 22 C5* loc just E of Cresselly. SN 0706
Lanesfield W Midlands 35 F4/F5* S dist of Wolverhampton. SO 9295
Laneshaw Bridge Lancs 48 C4 loc 2m/4km E of Colne. SD 9240
Laneshaw Reservoir 48 C4* small resr on border of Lancs and N Yorks 4m/6km E of Colne. SD 9441
Lanes, High Cornwall 2 B4* loc on E side of Hayle. SW 5637
Lanes, High Cornwall 3 E4* loc 2m/3km SW of Mevagissey. SW 9843
Lane Side Lancs 48 B5* loc in Haslingden 1km S of tn centre. SD 7822
Laney Green Staffs 35 F4* loc 1m W of Cheslyn Hay. SJ 9606
Langaller Som 8 B2* ham 1m N of Creech St Michael. ST 2626
Langar Notts 36 C1 vil 4m/6km S of Bingham. SK 7234
Langaton Point Stroma, H'land 86 F1* headland at NW end of Island of Stroma in Pentland Firth – see Stroma. ND 3479
Langbank S'clyde 64 B2 vil on S bank of R Clyde opp Dumbarton. NS 3873
Langbar N Yorks 48 D3* ham 3m/4km NW of Ilkley. SE 0951
Langbaurgh N Yorks 54 D4* loc just N of Gt Ayton. NZ 5511
Langbaurgh 117 admin dist of Cleveland.
Langcliffe N Yorks 48 B2 vil 1m N of Settle. **L. Scar,** limestone bluff to E. SD 8265
Langdale End N Yorks 55 G5 ham 7m/11km W of Scarborough. SE 9391
Langdale, Little Cumbria 52 C4* ham 2m/3km W of Skelwith Br. To W is **Lit Langdale Tarn,** small lake in course of R Brathay. NY 3103
Langdale Pikes Cumbria 52 C4 series of jagged peaks at summit of Langdale Fell, attaining height of 2403 ft or 732 metres. NY 2807
Langden Brook 47 G3* r rising on Forest of Bowland, Lancs, and flowing E into R Hodder at Langden Br, 1km S of Dunsop Br. ST 6649
Langdon Cornwall 6 B6* loc 4m/6km N of Launceston. SX 3089
Langdon Kent 13 H3 par containing vils of **E** and **W Langdon,** respectively 3m/5km and 4m/6km N of Dover. Remains of medieval abbey at W Langdon. TR 3246
Langdon Beck Durham 53 G2* loc near confluence of stream of same name with R Tees. Loc is 7m/11km NW of Middleton in Teesdale. NY 8531
Langdon Hills Essex 20 C3* dist of Basildon S of Laindon. TQ 6787
Langdown Hants 10 B4* loc in suburban extension of Hythe. SU 4206
Langenhoe Essex 30 D6 vil 4m/7km S of Colchester. TM 0018
Langford Beds 29 F4 vil 2m/3km S of Biggleswade. TL 1841
Langford Devon 7 H4 ham with **L. Grn,** 3m/5km S of Cullompton. ST 0203
Langford Essex 21 E1 vil 2km NW of Maldon. TL 8309
Langford Norfolk 38 C5 loc on R Wissey 3m/5km NE of Mundford. TL 8396
Langford Notts 44 C5 vil 3m/5km NE of Newark-on-Trent. SK 8258
Langford Oxon 17 F2 vil 3m/5km NE of Lechlade. SP 2402
Langford Som 8 A2* ham 2m/4km NW of Taunton. ST 2027
Langford Budville Som 7 H3 vil 2m/4km NW of Wellington. ST 1122
Langford End Beds 29 F3 vil 3m/5km N of Sandy. TL 1653
Langford Green Avon 16 A5* loc 2m/3km W of Blagdon. ST 4759
Langford, Little Wilts 9 G1* ham in R Wylye valley 5m/7km NW of Wilton. SU 0436
Langford, Lower Avon 16 A5 vil 3m/4km SE of Congresbury. ST 4660
Langford, Upper Avon 16 A5* ham 2m/4km W of Blagdon. ST 4659
Langham Essex 31 E4 ham 6m/9km NE of Colchester. TM 0233
Langham Leics 36 D3 vil 2m/3km NW of Oakham. SK 8411
Langham Norfolk 39 E1 vil 5m/8km NW of Holt. TG 0041
Langham Suffolk 30 D1 vil 3m/5km E of Ixworth. TL 9769
Langham Moor Essex 31 E5 loc 4m/7km N of Colchester. TM 0131
Langham Wick Essex 31 E5* loc 4m/7km NE of Colchester. TM 0231
Langho Lancs 48 A4 vil 4m/6km N of Blackburn. SD 7034
Langholm D & G 59 H3 woollen mnfg tn on R Esk 15m/24km E of Lockerbie and 18m/29km N of Carlisle. NY 3684
Langland W Glam 23 G6* loc in Mumbles dist of Swansea 2m/3km W of Mumbles Hd. To S is **L. Bay.** SS 6087
Langley Berks 18 D4 E dist of Slough. TQ 0179
Langley Ches 42 E4 vil 2m/3km SE of Macclesfield. SJ 9471
Langley Derbys 43 H6 loc 1m E of Heanor. **L. Mill** loc 1km N. SK 4446
Langley Essex 29 H4 vil 6m/10km SE of Royston. Vil consists of **Upr** and **Lr Green.** TL 4334
Langley Glos 27 E4* loc 2km W of Winchcombe. SP 0028
Langley Gtr Manchester 42 D1* loc adjoining Middleton to NW. SD 8507
Langley Hants 10 B4 vil 2m/3km SW of Fawley. SU 4401
Langley Herts 29 F5 vil 2m/3km SW of Stevenage. TL 2122
Langley Kent 20 D6 vil 4m/6km SE of Maidstone. TQ 8051
Langley Nthmb 60 D5 vil 2m/3km SW of Haydon Br. **L. Castle,** 1m N, is 14c tower hse. NY 8261
Langley Oxon 27 G6* loc 4m/7km NE of Burford. WT stn. SP 3015
Langley Som 7 H2* ham 1km N of Wiveliscombe. ST 0828
Langley Warwicks 27 F2 vil 5m/8km N of Stratford-upon-Avon. Loc of **L. Green** 1km SE. SP 1962
Langley W Midlands 35 F5 loc in Warley 2km NW of tn centre. Loc of **L. Green** adjoins to SE. SO 9988
Langley W Sussex 11 E2* ham 3m/4km SW of Liphook. SU 8029
Langley Beck 54 B3* r rising E of Eggleston, Durham, and flowing E by Staindrop into R Tees 1m W of Gainford. NZ 1517
Langley Burrell Wilts 16 D4 vil 2km NE of Chippenham. ST 9375
Langley Chapel Salop. See Acton Burnell.
Langley Corner Bucks 19 E3* loc 4m/6km NE of Slough. TQ 0184
Langley Green Derbys 35 H1 loc 5m/8km NW of Derby. SK 2838
Langley Green Essex 30 D5* ham 2m/3km SE of Coggeshall. TL 8721
Langley Green Norfolk 39 G4* loc 3m/5km N of Loddon. TG 3503
Langley Green W Sussex 11 H2* N dist of Crawley. TQ 2638
Langley Heath Kent 20 D6* vil 4m/7km SE of Maidstone. TQ 8151
Langley Marsh Som 7 H2 vil 1m N of Wiveliscombe. ST 0729
Langley Moor Durham 54 B1 loc adjoining Brandon to E. NZ 2540
Langley Park Bromley, London. See Park Langley.
Langley Park Durham 54 B1 loc 4m/7km NW of Durham. NZ 2144
Langley Street Norfolk 39 G4* ham 2m/3km N of Loddon. TG 3601
Langmere Norfolk 31 F1* loc 2km E of Dickleburgh. TM 1881
Lang Mere Norfolk 38 D5* small lake 4m/7km NE of Thetford. TL 9088
Langness Isle of Man 46 B6 promontory on E side of Castletown Bay, running out to **Langness Pt.** SC 2765
Langney E Sussex 12 C6* NE dist of Eastbourne. **L. Point** is headland on English Channel coast 1m SE, at W end of Pevensey Bay. TQ 6302
Langold Notts 44 B2* vil 5m/8km N of Worksop. SK 5887
Langore Cornwall 6 B6 ham 2m/4km NW of Launceston. SX 2986
Langport Som 8 C2 mkt tn on R Parrett 7m/11km NW of Ilchester. ST 4226
Langrick Lincs 45 F6 ham 5m/8km NW of Boston. TF 2648
Langridge Avon 16 C4 ham 3m/5km N of Bath. ST 7469
Langridgeford Devon 6 D3 loc 7m/11km S of Barnstaple. SS 5722
Langrigg Cumbria 52 B1 vil 3m/4km NE of Aspatria. NY 1645
Langrigg Cumbria 53 G3* loc 2m/3km W of Brough. NY 7614
Langrish Hants 10 D3 vil 3m/4km W of Petersfield. SU 7023
Langriville Lincs 45 F6 ham 5m/8km NW of Boston. TF 2648
Langsett S Yorks 43 G1 ham 3m/5km SW of Penistone, on N shore of **Langsett Resr.** SE 2100
Langside S'clyde 64 C3* loc in Glasgow 3m/4km SW of city centre. NS 5761
Lang Stane o' Craigearn Grampian. See Craigearn.
Langstone Gwent 15 H3* loc 4m/7km E of Newport. ST 3989
Langstone Hants 10 D4 vil at S end of Havant and at N end of **L. Harbour,** large inlet of sea between Portsea and Hayling Is. Langstone Br connects Hayling I. to mainland. Site of Roman villa to N. SU 7105
Langstrothdale N Yorks 48 B1* valley of R Wharfe above Hubberholme. **L. Chase** moorland area astride the dale. SD 9078
Langthorne N Yorks 54 B5 vil 2m/4km N of Bedale. SE 2591
Langthorpe N Yorks 49 F2 vil opp Boroughbridge across R Ure. SE 3867
Langthwaite N Yorks 54 A4 ham in Arkengarthdale 3m/5km NW of Reeth. NZ 0002
Langtoft Humberside 51 E2 vil 6m/9km N of Gt Driffield. TA 0166
Langtoft Lincs 37 F3 vil 2m/3km NW of Mkt Deeping. TF 1212
Langton Durham 54 B3 vil 3m/4km E of Staindrop. NZ 1619
Langton Lincs 45 F4 ham 2m/3km W of Horncastle. **L. Hill** loc 1m E. TF 2368
Langton Lincs 45 G4 vil 3m/5km N of Spilsby. TF 3970
Langton N Yorks 50 C2 vil 3m/5km S of Malton. Sites of Roman bldgs 1m E. SE 7967
Langton by Wragby Lincs 45 F3 vil 2km SE of Wragby. TF 1476
Langton, East Leics 36 C5* vil 4m/6km N of Mkt Harborough. SP 7292
Langton, Great N Yorks 54 C5 vil on R Swale 5m/8km NW of Northallerton. SE 2996
Langton Green Kent 12 B3 vil suburb 3m/4km W of Tunbridge Wells. TQ 5439
Langton Green Suffolk 31 F1* loc adjoining Eye to N. TM 1474
Langton Herring Dorset 8 D6 vil 5m/7km NW of Weymouth. SY 6182
Langton Long Blandford Dorset 9 F4 ham beside R Stour 1m SE of Blandford Forum. ST 8905
Langton, Low Lincs 45 F4* loc 2m/3km SE of Wragby. TF 1576
Langton Matravers Dorset 9 G6 vil 2m/3km W of Swanage. SY 9978
Langton, West Leics 36 C5* par 4m/6km N of Mkt Harborough. **Langton Hall** dates from 17c. SP 7193
Langtree Devon 6 C4 vil 4m/6km SW of Torrington. Loc of **L. Week** 2km E. SS 4515
Langwathby Cumbria 53 E2 vil on R Eden 4m/7km NE of Penrith. NY 5633
Langwell, East H'land 87 A6 loc in Sutherland dist 8m/13km NW of Golspie on E coast. NC 7206
Langwell Forest H'land 86 C4, D4 moorland area astride Langwell Water in Caithness dist, W and NW of Berriedale. ND 02
Langwell Water H'land 86 D4/87 D5 r in Caithness dist rising on Langwell Forest and flowing E to coast at Berriedale. ND 1122
Langwith, Nether Notts 44 A4 vil 6m/10km N of Mansfield. **Langwith** (Derbys) loc adjoining to W. SK 5370
Langwith, Upper Derbys 44 A4 vil 3m/5km E of Bolsover. SK 5169
Langworth Lincs 45 E3/E4 vil 5m/7km W of Wragby. TF 0676
Lanhydrock Cornwall 3 F2* loc 2m/4km SE of Bodmin. **Lanhydrock Hse** (NT). SX 0863
Lanivet Cornwall 3 E2 vil 3m/5km SW of Bodmin. SX 0364
Lank Cornwall 3 F1 ham 5m/8km S of Camelford. SX 0975
Lanlivery Cornwall 3 F3 vil 2m/3km W of Lostwithiel. SX 0859
Lanner Cornwall 2 C4 vil 2m/3km SE of Redruth. SW 7139
Lanoy Cornwall 3 G1* loc 6m/10km NW of Callington. SX 3077
Lanreath Cornwall 3 F3 vil 5m/8km NW of Looe. SX 1856
Lanrick Castle Central 71 G4 mansion on S bank of R Teith 3m/4km NW of Doune. NN 6803
Lansallos Cornwall 3 F3 vil 3m/5km E of Fowey across r. Coast to S owned by NT. SX 1751
Lansdown Avon 16 C4 ham on hill of same name 3m/5km NW of Bath. Racecourse. Site of Roman bldg 1km E. ST 7268
Lansdown Glos 26 D5* central dist of Cheltenham. SO 9421

Lansdown Glos 27 F5* loc in N part of Bourton-on-the-Water. SP 1621
Lanshaw Dam, Higher W Yorks 48 D4* small resr on moors 2m/3km W of Burley in Wharfedale. SE 1345
Lanteglos Cornwall 3 F1 ham 2km SW of Camelford. SX 0882
Lanteglos Cornwall 3 F3 ch and farm 2km E of Fowey across r. In N part of par, which contains much NT property, lies ham of **L. Highway.** SX 1451
Lantivet Bay Cornwall 3 F3 bay on S coast 3m/4km E of Fowey, between Pencarrow Hd and Shag Rock. SX 1650
Lanton Borders 66 D6 vil 2m/3km NW of Jedburgh. NT 6221
Lanvean Cornwall 2 D2* loc 5m/8km NE of Newquay. SW 8766
Lanyon Quoit Cornwall 2 A5* cromlech (NT) 3m/5km NW of Penzance. SW 4333
Lapal W Midlands 35 F5* loc in Halesowen 2km E of tn centre. SO 9883
Lapford Devon 7 E4 vil 5m/8km SE of Chulmleigh. Vil of **L. Cross** to SW across R Taw. SS 7308
Laphroaig S'clyde 62 B3 vil on S coast of Islay 2km E of Port Ellen. Distillery. NR 3845
Lapley Staffs 35 E3 vil 3m/5km W of Penkridge. SJ 8712
Lapworth Warwicks 27 F1 vil 2km SE of Hockley Heath. See also Stratford-upon-Avon Canal. SP 1671
Larbert Central 65 E1 tn 2m/4km NW of Falkirk. Iron founding, mnfre of stoves, cookers, light castings. NS 8582
Larbreck Lancs 47 E4* loc 2km W of Gt Eccleston. SD 4240
Larches Lancs 47 F5* loc 3m/4km W of Preston. SD 4930
Larch How Cumbria 53 E5* loc on E side of Kendal. SD 5092
Larden Green Ches 42 B6 loc 4m/7km W of Nantwich. SJ 5851
Larg Hill D & G 58 A4 mt 7m/11km N of Newton Stewart. Height 2216 ft or 675 metres. NX 4275
Largie Grampian 83 E4 loc 7m/12km SE of Huntly. NJ 6131
Largo Fife 73 G4. **L. Bay** on Firth of Forth extends from Buckhaven and Methil eastwards to Kincraig Pt. **Largo** consists of two adjacent vils: **Lower L.** on the bay 2m/4km NE of Leven, and **Upper L.** or Kirkton of L. 1m farther NE. **L. Ward** (or Largoward) is vil 4m/6km NE of Upper L. **L. Law** is hill 1m N of Upper L.; height 952 ft or 290 metres. NO 40
Largs S'clyde 64 A3 tn and resort on **L. Bay,** on Firth of Clyde opp N end of island of Gt Cumbrae. NS 2059
Largybeg Point S'clyde 63 G5* headland on E coast of Arran at S end of Whiting Bay. Standing stones. NS 0523
Lark 38 A6 r rising 6m/9km S of Bury St Edmunds, Suffolk, and flowing N through that tn then NW into R Ouse 2m/3km S of Littleport, Cambs. TL 5784
Larkfield Kent 20 D5* urban development 4m/6km NW of Maidstone. TQ 7058
Larkfield S'clyde 64 A2* loc 1m S of Gourock. NS 2375
Larkhall S'clyde 65 E4 tn 4m/6km SE of Hamilton. Industries include engineering, textiles. NS 7651
Larkhill H & W 35 E6* dist of Kidderminster to N of tn centre. SO 8377
Larkhill Wilts 17 F6 military vil and camp 3m/4km NW of Amesbury. SU 1244
Larklands Derbys 36 B1* E dist of Ilkeston. SK 4741
Larling Norfolk 38 D5 ham 6m/9km SW of Attleborough. TL 9889
Larmer Tree Grounds Wilts. See Tollard Royal.
Larnog Welsh form of Lavernock, qv.
Laroch, East and **West** H'land 74 C5 adjoining vils on either side of **R Laroch,** Lochaber dist, on S side of Loch Leven. Large slate quarries at E Laroch. NN 0858
Larrick Cornwall 4 A3* loc 4m/7km SW of Launceston. SX 3078
Lartington Durham 54 A3 vil 2m/4km W of Barnard Castle. NZ 0117
Larton Merseyside 41 H3* loc 2m/3km E of W Kirby. SJ 2387
Lasborough Glos 16 C2 loc 5m/7km W of Tetbury. ST 8294
Lasham Hants 10 D1 vil 3m/5km NW of Alton. Airfield to N; gliding. SU 6742
Lashbrook, Little Devon 6 C4* ham 5m/7km NE of Holsworthy. SS 4007
Lashenden Kent 13 E3* loc 2m/3km S of Headcorn. TQ 8441
Lassodie Fife 73 E5 loc 2m/3km SW of Kelty. NT 1292
Lasswade Lothian 66 B2 tn adjoining Bonnyrigg 2m/3km SW of Dalkeith. NT 3066
Lastingham N Yorks 55 F5 vil below N Yorks Moors 6m/10km NW of Pickering. Late Norman ch incorporates part of 11c abbey. SE 7290
Latcham Som 16 A6* loc 1m SE of Wedmore. ST 4447
Latchford Ches 42 C3 dist of Warrington 2km SE of tn centre. SJ 6287
Latchford Oxon 18 B2* loc 4m/7km SW of Thame. SP 6501
Latchingdon Essex 21 E2 vil 5m/8km SE of Maldon. TL 8800
Latchley Cornwall 4 B3* vil on R Tamar 2m/3km NW of Gunnislake. SX 4073
Latchmore Brook 9 H3* upper reach of Huckles Brook in New Forest. See Huckles Brook.
Lately Common Gtr Manchester 42 C2* loc 2m/3km SE of Leigh. SJ 6798
Lathbury Bucks 28 D3 vil 1m N of Newport Pagnell. SP 8745
Latheron H'land 86 E4 vil near E coast of Caithness dist 15m/24km SW of Wick. See also Janetstown. ND 1933
Lathkill 43 G4 r rising 2km E of Monyash, Derbys, and flowing E into R Wye 1m W of Rowsley. SK 2465
Lathones Fife 73 G4 loc 1m NE of Largo Ward. NO 4607
Latimer Bucks 19 E2 vil 3m/5km SE of Chesham. TQ 0099
Latteridge Avon 16 B3 vil 4m/7km W of Chipping Sodbury. ST 6684
Lattiford Som 9 E2 ham 2m/3km SW of Wincanton. ST 6926
Latton Wilts 17 E2 vil 2km NW of Cricklade. SU 0995
Latton Bush Essex 20 B1* SE dist of Harlow. TL 4607
Lauder Borders 66 C4 small tn on Leader Water 9m/14km N of Melrose. Thirlestane Castle to NE, begun 1595, with later additions. NT 5347
Lauderdale Borders 66 C3, C4 valley of Leader Water and dist round about Lauder. NT 54
Laugharne (Lacharn) Dyfed 23 E4 vil on R Taf estuary 4m/6km S of St Clears. Burial place of Dylan Thomas. Remains of medieval cas. Army training area to S. SN 3010
Laughrigg Tarn Cumbria 52 D4* small lake 1km N of Skelwith Br, below S slope of Laughrigg Fell. NY 3404
Laughterton Lincs 44 C3/C4 vil 9m/14km S of Gainsborough. SK 8376
Laughton E Sussex 12 B5 vil 6m/9km E of Lewes. TQ 5013
Laughton Leics 36 C5 vil 5m/8km W of Mkt Harborough. SP 6689
Laughton Lincs 44 C2 vil 5m/9km NE of Gainsborough. SK 8497
Laughton en le Morthen S Yorks 44 A2 vil 2m/3km E of Thurcroft. Remains of motte and bailey cas. SK 5188
Launcells Cornwall 6 B4 ham 2m/3km E of Bude. SS 2405
Launceston Cornwall 4 A2 tn on hill above R Kensey valley 20m/32km NW of Plymouth. Officially styled 'Dunheved otherwise Launceston', Dunheved being the old Celtic name. Formerly the county capital. Remains of Norman cas (A.M.). SX 3384
Laund Lancs 48 B5* loc 1km N of Rawtenstall. SD 8023
Launde Leics 36 D4 loc 6m/9km NW of Uppingham. **L. Abbey,** remains of 12c priory. 16c–17c hse built on site. SK 7904
Laund, Far Derbys 43 H6* loc 2km NE of Belper. SK 3648
Launton Oxon 28 B5 vil 2m/3km E of Bicester. SP 6022
Laurencekirk Grampian 77 G4 small market tn 10m/16km NE of Brechin. Agricultural engineering, linen mnfre. Formerly noted for mnfre of snuff-boxes. NO 7171
Laurieston Central 65 F1 loc 2km E of Falkirk. Site of Roman fort on line of Antonine Wall to E. NS 9179
Laurieston D & G 58 C5 vil 9m/14km N of Kirkcudbright. **L. Forest** is state forest to W. NX 6864
Lauriston Castle Lothian 66 A1* cas in Edinburgh 4m/6km NW of city centre, dating in part from late 16c. Grnds overlook Firth of Forth. NT 2076
Lavan Sands (Traeth Lafan) Gwynedd 40 C4, D4 part of Conwy Bay lying between Beaumaris, Anglesey, and Welsh mainland; exposed at low tide. SH 67
Lavant, East W Sussex 11 E4 vil 2m/4km N of Chichester. Vil of **Mid Lavant** to W. SU 8608
Lavatrae Durham. See Bowes.
Lavendon Bucks 28 D2/D3 vil 2m/4km NE of Olney. Faint remains of Norman cas. SP 9153
Lavenham Suffolk 30 D3 small tn 6m/9km NE of Sudbury. Many timbered hses. Guildhall of 16c (NT), restored. Famous ch. TL 9149
Laver 49 E1 r rising on Dallowgill Moor, N of Pateley Br, N Yorks, and flowing E to join R Skell on W side of Ripon. SE 3070
Laver, High Essex 20 B1 ham 4m/6km N of Chipping Ongar. TL 5208
Laver, Little Essex 20 C1 ham 4m/7km N of Chipping Ongar. TL 5409
Lavernock (Larnog) S Glam 15 G4 ham on coast at **Lavernock Pt,** headland 2m/3km S of Penarth. ST 1868
Laversdale Cumbria 60 A5 ham 4m/6km W of Brampton. NY 4762
Laverstock Wilts 9 H2 residential dist to E of Salisbury across R Bourne. SU 1530
Laverstoke Hants 17 H6 vil on R Test 2m/3km E of Whitchurch. SU 4948
Laverton Glos 27 E4 vil 2m/3km SW of Broadway. SP 0735
Laverton N Yorks 49 E1 vil 5m/9km W of Ripon. SE 2273
Laverton Som 16 C6 ham 3m/5km N of Frome. ST 7753
Lavington, East W Sussex 11 F3 ham under S Downs 4m/7km SW of Petworth. SU 9416
Lavington, West Wilts 17 E6 vil 5m/9km S of Devizes. SU 0053
Lavington, West W Sussex 11 E3 vil 1km SE of Midhurst. SU 8920
Lavister Clwyd 42 A5 vil 1m NE of Rossett. SJ 3758
Law S'clyde 65 E3/E4 vil 2m/4km NW of Carluke. NS 8152
Law Castle S'clyde 64 A4 cas with late 15c tower at W Kilbride. NS 2148
Lawers Tayside 71 G1 vil on N side of Loch Tay 7m/11km SW of Kenmore, near mouth of **L. Burn.** NN 6739
Lawford Essex 31 E5 vil 7m/11km NE of Colchester. TM 0831
Lawford Som 7 H2* ham 6m/9km SE of Watchet. ST 1336
Lawford, Little Warwicks 36 A6 ham 3m/4km NW of Rugby. SP 4677
Lawhitton Cornwall 4 A3 vil 2m/3km SE of Launceston. SX 3582
Lawkland N Yorks 48 B2 ham 3m/5km NW of Settle. **L. Green** loc 1km SE. SD 7766
Lawley Salop 34 D3 loc in Telford 2m/4km SE of Wellington. SJ 6608
Lawling Creek Essex 21 E2 inlet of R Blackwater estuary S of Osea I. TL 9003
Lawnhead Staffs 35 E2 loc 6m/9km W of Stafford. SJ 8324
Lawns W Yorks 49 E5* loc 3m/4km N of Wakefield. SE 3124
Lawrence Castle Devon. See Dunchideock.
Lawrence Weston Avon 16 B4* NW dist of Bristol. ST 5478
Lawrenny Dyfed 22 C5 vil near R Cresswell estuary 8m/12km SW of Narberth. SN 0106
Lawshall Suffolk 30 D3 vil 5m/8km N of Long Melford. Ham of **L. Green** 1m E. TL 8654
Lawton H & W 26 A2* loc 3m/5km W of Leominster. SO 4459
Laxa Burn Shetland 89 E6* stream on island of Yell running N into head of Mid Yell Voe. HU 5091
Laxay W Isles 88 B2 vil near E coast of Lewis on N side of Loch Erisort. NB 3321
Laxdale W Isles 88 C2 vil at head of **R Laxdale** estuary 2km N of Stornoway, Lewis. The r rises 5m/8km NW and flows past vil into Broad Bay or Loch a' Tuath. NB 4234
Laxey Isle of Man 46 C5 small tn and resort on E coast 6m/10km NE of Douglas. Former lead mines. **Laxey R** rises on slopes of Snaefell and runs SE through tn into **L. Bay** on W side of **L. Head,** headland at N end of bay, which extends southwards to Clay Hd. See also Old Laxey. SC 4384
Laxfield Suffolk 31 G1 vil 6m/9km N of Framlingham. TM 2972
Lax Firth Shetland 89 E7* inlet on E coast of Mainland 5m/8km N of Lerwick. **Laxfirth** loc at head of inlet. HU 4447
Laxfirth Shetland 89 E7* loc on Mainland on S side of Dury Voe. HU 4759
Laxford 84 C3 r of Sutherland dist, H'land, running from Loch Stack NW to Loch Laxford. NC 2347
Laxford Bridge H'land 84 C3 rd junction and br over R Laxford at head of Loch Laxford near W coast of Sutherland dist. NC 2346
Laxo Shetland 89 E7 locality on E coast of Mainland at head of Dury Voe. **L. Water** is loch 1km N. HU 4463
Laxton Humberside 50 C5 vil 3m/5km SE of Howden. SE 7925
Laxton Northants 37 E4/E5 vil 6m/9km NE of Corby. SP 9596
Laxton Notts 44 C4 vil 4m/7km E of Ollerton. SK 7267
Layer Breton Essex 30 D6 vil 6m/9km SW of Colchester. TL 9418
Layer-de-la-Haye Essex 30 D6 vil 4m/7km SW of Colchester. TL 9619
Layer Marney Essex 30 D6 ham 6m/10km SW of Colchester. TL 9217
Layerthorpe N Yorks 50 B3 dist of York to E of city centre. SE 6151
Layham Suffolk 31 E4 vil 2km S of Hadleigh. TM 0340
Layland's Green Berks 17 G4* loc adjoining Kintbury to E, 4m/6km E of Hungerford. SU 3866
Laymore Dorset 8 C4* ham 4m/6km NW of Broadwindsor. ST 3804
Laysters H & W 26 B2* loc 5m/9km NE of Leominster. SO 5663
Laysters Pole H & W 26 B2 vil 5m/8km NE of Leominster. SO 5563
Layter's Green Bucks 18 D3* loc on W side of Chalfont St Peter. SU 9890
Layter's Green Essex 21 B1* loc 4m/7km E of Harlow. TL 5110
Laytham Humberside 50 C4 vil 8m/13km W of Mkt Weighton. SE 7439
Layton Lancs 46 D4 dist of Blackpool 2km NE of tn centre. **Lit Layton** adjoins to NE. SD 3236
Layton, East N Yorks 54 B4 vil 4m/7km NW of Scotch Corner. NZ 1609
Layton, West N Yorks 54 B4 ham 5m/9km NW of Scotch Corner. NZ 1409
Lazenby Cleveland 55 E3* loc 5m/8km E of Middlesbrough. NZ 5719
Lazenby N Yorks 54 C5* loc 3m/5km N of Northallerton. SE 3498
Lazonby Cumbria 53 E1 vil on R Eden 6m/10km N of Penrith. NY 5439
Lea Derbys 43 G5 vil 3m/4km SE of Matlock. SK 3257
Lea H & W 26 B5 vil 4m/7km SE of Ross-on- Wye. SO 6621
Lea Lincs 44 C3 vil and suburb 2m/3km S of Gainsborough. SK 8286
Lea Salop 34 A5/B5* ham 2m/3km E of Bishop's Castle. Remains of cas. SO 3589
Lea Salop 34 B3 loc 5m/8km SW of Shrewsbury. Site of Roman villa. SJ 4108
Lea Wilts 16 D3 vil 2m/3km E of Malmesbury. ST 9586
Lea 20 A3 r rising at Leagrave, N of Luton, Beds, and flowing SE through Luton to Hatfield, then E to Hertford and Ware, then S into R Thames at Blackwall, London. Supplies water to London through large resrs S of Waltham Abbey. Alternative spelling: Lee. TQ 3980
Leabaidh an Daimh Bhuidhe Grampian 76 B1/C1* summit of Ben Avon, qv, N of Braemar. Height 3843 ft or 1171 metres. NJ 1301
Lea Bridge Derbys 43 G5* ham 3m/5km SE of Matlock. SK 3156
Lea Bridge London 20 A3 br over R Lea and loc in vicinity, in borough of Hackney 4m/7km NE of London Br. TQ 3586
Leabrooks Derbys 43 H5* loc 2m/3km SE of Alfreton. SK 4253
Leacann Water S'clyde 70 C5* stream in Argyll running E from Loch Leacann then S to Loch Fyne at Furnace. NN 0200

Leach 17 F2 r rising near Northleach, Glos, and flowing SE into R Thames 1km SE of Lechlade. SU 2298
Leachkin H'land 81 F3 loc in Inverness dist 2m/3km W of Inverness. NH 6444
Leacon, The Kent 13 E4 loc 1m W of Ham Street. TQ 9833
Leacroft Staffs 35 F3* loc 2km SE of Cannock. SJ 9909
Lead N Yorks 49 F4* loc 1km W of Saxton. SE 4637
Leadburn 66 A3 loc on border of Lothian and Borders regions 3m/4km S of Penicuik. NT 2355
Leadenham Lincs 44 D5 vil 8m/13km NW of Sleaford. SK 9552
Leaden Roding Essex 20 C1 vil 6m/9km SW of Gt Dunmow. TL 5913
Leader Water 66 D5 r in Borders region rising on Lammermuir Hills and flowing S down Lauderdale to R Tweed at **Leaderfoot,** 2m/3km E of Melrose. NT 5734
Leadgate Cumbria 53 F1* loc 2m/3km S of Alston. NY 7043
Leadgate Durham 61 F6 suburb 2km E of Consett. NZ 1251
Leadgate 61 F5 loc on border of Nthmb and Tyne & Wear 2m/4km S of Prudhoe. NZ 1159
Leadhills S'clyde 65 F6 former lead-mining tn 6m/10km SW of Abington. NS 8815
Leadingcross Green Kent 21 E6* loc 1km SW of Lenham. TQ 8951
Leadmill Clwyd 41 H5* loc on NE side of Mold. SJ 2464
Leadon 26 C5 r rising 2km NE of Evesbatch, H & W, and flowing S past Ledbury and into R Severn 2km NW of Gloucester. SO 8119
Lea End H & W 27 E1 ham 5m/8km N of Redditch. SP 0475
Leafield Oxon 27 G5/G6 vil 4m/7km NW of Witney. SP 3115
Leagach H'land. Anglicised form of Liathach, qv.
Leagrave Beds 29 E5 NW dist of Luton. Source of R Lea between here and Sundon Park to N. TL 0523
Leagrave Marsh Beds 29 E5* NW dist of Luton. TL 0624
Leagreen Dorset 10 A5* loc 2m/3km NW of Milford on Sea. SZ 2793
Lea Green H & W 26 B2* loc 6m/9km SE of Tenbury Wells. SO 6764
Lea Green Merseyside 42 B2* loc in St Helens 2m/3km S of tn centre. SJ 5192
Lea Heath Staffs 35 F2* loc 1km W of Newton. SK 0225
Leake N Yorks 54 D5 loc 5m/8km N of Thirsk. SE 4390
Leake Common Side Lincs 45 G5/G6 vil 7m/11km NE of Boston. TF 3952
Leake, East Notts 36 B2 vil 4m/7km N of Loughborough. SK 5526
Leake Fold Hill Lincs 45 G6 loc 1m N of Old Leake. TF 4051
Leake Hurn's End Lincs 45 G6 loc 2km S of Wrangle. TF 4249
Leake, West Notts 36 B2 vil 4m/7km N of Loughborough. SK 5226
Lealholm N Yorks 55 F4 vil on R Esk 3m/5km W of Egton. **L. Side** loc up hill to NE. NZ 7607
Lealt Skye, H'land 78 C3 loc near NE coast 11m/17km N of Portree. NG 5060
Leam Derbys 43 G3* loc 2km S of Hathersage. SK 2379
Leam 27 G1 r rising at Hellidon, Northants, and flowing N then W into R Avon between Leamington and Warwick. SP 3065
Lea Marston Warwicks 35 G5 vil on R Tame 3m/4km N of Coleshill. Hams Hall Power Stn to S. SP 2093
Leamington Warwicks 27 G1 tn on R Leam 8m/13km S of Coventry. Officially styled Royal Leamington Spa since 1838. SP 3165
Leamington Hastings Warwicks 27 H1 vil 4m/7km NE of Southam. SP 4467
Leamonsley Staffs 35 G3* loc in Lichfield to W of tn centre. SK 1009
Leamoor Common Salop 34 B5* loc 3m/4km N of Craven Arms. SO 4386
Leamside Durham 54 C1* loc on W side of W Rainton. NZ 3146
Leanachan Forest H'land 74 C3, C4 state forest in Lochaber dist 4m/6km SW of Spean Br. NN 1977
Leap Moor S'clyde 64 A2 moorland area to E of Wemyss Bay. **Leapmoor Forest** is state forest on W side. NS 2369
Leargybreck S'clyde 62 C1 loc on E coast of Jura 3m/4km N of Craighouse. NR 5371
Learmouth, East Nthmb 67 E5* loc 2km S of Cornhill on Tweed. **W Learmouth** loc 1m W. NT 8637
Lease Rigg N Yorks 55 F4* loc adjoining Grosmont to SW. NZ 8204
Leasgill Cumbria 53 E6 vil 2km S of Levens. SD 4984
Leasingham Lincs 45 E6 vil 2m/3km N of Sleaford. TF 0548
Leasingthorne Durham 54 B2* vil 2m/4km S of Spennymoor. NZ 2529
Leason W Glam 23 F6* loc on Gower peninsula 1m W of Llanrhidian. SS 4892
Leasowe Merseyside 41 H2* dist of Wallasey 3m/5km W of tn centre. SJ 2791
Leat Cornwall 6 C6* loc 3m/4km NW of Launceston. SX 3087
Leathad an Taobhain 75 H3 mt on border of Highland and Tayside regions 4m/6km E of Loch an t-Seilich. Height 2991 ft or 912 metres. NN 8285
Leatherhead Surrey 19 F5 tn on R Mole 8m/13km S of Kingston. TQ 1656
Leathley N Yorks 49 E3 vil 2m/4km NE of Otley across R Wharfe. SE 2347
Leaton Salop 34 B3 vil 4m/7km NW of Shrewsbury. SJ 4618
Leaton Salop 34 C3* loc 3m/4km W of Wellington. SJ 6111
Lea Town Lancs 47 F5 loc 4m/7km W of Preston. SD 4731
Leaveland Kent 21 F6 vil 5m/8km S of Faversham. TR 0054
Leavenheath Suffolk 30 D4* ham 2m/4km NW of Nayland. TL 9537
Leavening N Yorks 50 C2 vil 5m/9km S of Malton. SE 7863
Leavesden Green Herts 19 E2 N dist of Watford. Airfield to W. TL 1000
Leaves Green London 20 B5 loc in borough of Bromley on W side of Biggin Hill airfield. TQ 4161
Lea Yeat Cumbria 53 G6 loc in Dentdale 4m/6km E of Dent. SD 7686
Leazes Durham 61 F5* vil adjoining Burnopfield to W. NZ 1656
Leazes, North Durham 54 B2* loc 2m/4km SW of Bishop Auckland. NZ 1727
Lebberston N Yorks 55 H6 vil 3m/4km NW of Filey. TA 0782
Lechlade Glos 17 F2 vil on R Thames 10m/16km NE of Swindon. Site of Roman bldg 1km N. SU 2199
Leck Lancs 47 G1 vil 2m/4km SE of Kirkby Lonsdale. SD 6476
Leck Beck 47 F1* r rising E of Kirkby Lonsdale, Cumbria, and flowing SW past Leck and Cowan Br into R Lune W of Nether Burrow, Lancs. SD 6175
Leckby N Yorks 49 F1* loc 2m/3km SE of Topcliffe across R Swale. SE 4173
Leckford Hants 10 B1 vil on R Test 2m/3km NE of Stockbridge. SU 3737
Leckfurin H'land 86 A2 loc near N coast of Caithness dist 2km S of Bettyhill. NC 7059
Leckgruinart S'clyde 62 A2 loc on Islay 4m/6km S of Ardnave Pt. NR 2769
Leckhampstead Berks 17 H4 vil 6m/9km N of Newbury. Loc of **L. Street** adjoins to N. Ham of **L. Thicket** 1m NW. SU 4376
Leckhampstead Bucks 28 C4 vil 3m/5km NE of Buckingham. SP 7237
Leckhampton Glos 26 D5* suburb 2m/3km S of Cheltenham. SO 9419
Leckmelm H'land 85 B7 locality on E shore of Loch Broom, Ross and Cromarty dist, 4m/6km SE of Ullapool. NH 1690
Leckwith (Lecwydd) S Glam 15 F4 loc 2m/3km SW of Cardiff. **L. Moors** dist of Cardiff to E across R Ely: industrial estate, wholesale fruit mkt. ST 1574
Leconfield Humberside 51 E4 vil 3m/4km N of Beverley. Airfield to E. TA 0143
Lecwydd Welsh form of Leckwith, qv.
Ledaig S'clyde 68 C3* loc with distillery at Tobermory, Mull. NM 5055
Ledaig S'clyde 70 B2 loc on Ardmucknish Bay 2m/3km N of Connel, Argyll. At S end of bay is headland of **Ledaig Pt.** on N side of entrance to Loch Etive. NM 9037
Ledburn Bucks 28 D5 ham 2m/4km SW of Leighton Buzzard. SP 9021
Ledbury H & W 26 C4 tn 12m/20km E of Hereford. Many timbered hses. SO 7137
Ledgemoor H & W 26 A3* vil 9m/14km NW of Hereford. SO 4150
Ledgowan Forest H'land 80 B2 deer forest S of Loch a' Chroisg in Ross and Cromarty dist. NH 1256
Ledicot H & W 26 A2* loc 5m/9km W of Leominster. SO 4162
Ledmore H'land 85 C5 loc in Sutherland dist 6m/10km S of Inchnadamph. NC 2412
Lednock 72 B3 r in Tayside region running SE down Glen L. to R Earn at Comrie. See also Falls of L. NN 7722
Ledsham Ches 42 A4 loc 3m/5km SW of Ellesmere Port. SJ 3574
Ledsham W Yorks 59 F5 vil 4m/6km NW of Ferrybridge. SE 4529
Ledston W Yorks 49 F5 vil 2m/3km N of Castleford. Hall dates in part from 13c, though mainly 16c-17c. SE 4328
Ledstone Devon 4 D5 loc 2m/3km N of Kingsbridge. SX 7446
Ledwell Oxon 27 H5 ham 4m/6km SW of Deddington. SP 4228
Ledwyche Brook 26 B1 r rising on S side of Brown Clee Hill, Salop, and flowing S into R Teme at Burford, W of Tenbury Wells. SO 5867
Lee Devon 6 D1 vil in coombe running down to **L. Bay** 2m/3km W of Ilfracombe. SS 4846
Lee Hants 10 B3* loc in R Test valley 2m/3km S of Romsey. SU 3617
Lee Salop 34 B2 loc 2m/3km S of Ellesmere. **L. Old Hall** is a 16c–17c hse. SJ 4032
Lee 20 A3. Alternative spelling for (R) Lea, qv.
Leebotwood Salop 34 B4 vil 4m/6km NE of Church Stretton. SO 4798
Lee Brockhurst Salop 34 C2 vil 3m/4km SE of Wem. SJ 5427
Leece Cumbria 46 D2 vil 3m/5km E of Barrow-in-Furness. SD 2469
Lee Chapel Essex 20 D3* dist of Basildon to W of tn centre. TQ 6988
Lee Clump Bucks 18 D1 vil 4m/6km NW of Chesham. SP 9004
Leeds Kent 20 D6 vil 4m/7km E of Maidstone. **L. Castle,** mainly 19c reconstruction, in park to E. TQ 8253
Leeds W Yorks 49 E5 commercial and industrial city on R Aire and on Leeds and Liverpool Canal 36m/58km NE of Manchester and 170m/274km NW of London. Various industries include clothing mnfre, engineering; coal-mining to S and SE. University (see Woodhouse). Leeds and Bradford Airport at Yeadon, 7m/11km NW. SE 2933
Leeds and Liverpool Canal 49 E4-42 A2 trans-Pennine canal from Leeds, W Yorks, to Liverpool, Merseyside, by Shipley, Skipton, Nelson, Burnley, Blackburn, Wigan, and Bootle. At Leeds it connects with the Aire and Calder Navigation to form a waterway linking the Irish Sea with the North Sea. There is a branch to Leigh from Wigan.
Leedstown Cornwall 2 B5 vil 3m/5km SE of Hayle. SW 6034
Leegomery Salop 34 D3 loc 2km NE of Wellington. SJ 6613
Lee Head Derbys 43 E2* loc adjoining Charlesworth to SW. SK 0092
Leek Staffs 43 E5 textile tn 10m/15km NE of Stoke-on-Trent. SJ 9856
Leekbrook Staffs 43 E5* loc 2m/3km S of Leek. SJ 9853
Leek Wootton Warwicks 27 G1 vil 2m/4km N of Warwick. SP 2868
Lee Mill Bridge Devon 4 C5 vil on R Yealm 2m/4km W of Ivybridge. Industrial estate to E. SX 5955
Leeming N Yorks 54 C5 vil 2m/3km NE of Bedale. Airfield to E. **L. Bar** vil 1km NW. SE 2890
Leeming W Yorks 48 C4 loc 2m/3km W of Denholme. SE 0334
Lee Moor Devon 4 C4 loc in china clay dist 5m/9km NW of Ivybridge. SX 5761
Lee Moor W Yorks 49 E5* loc 3m/5km N of Wakefield. SE 3425
Leen 44 A6* r rising near Newstead Abbey, Notts, and flowing S into R Trent on W side of Nottingham. SK 5538
Lee, North Bucks 18 C1* ham 2m/4km W of Wendover. Site of Roman bldg to SE. SP 8308
Lee-on-the-Solent Hants 10 C4 resort and residential loc 4m/6km W of Gosport. Airfield to N. SU 5133
Lees Derbys 35 H1 vil 6m/9km W of Derby. **L. Green** ham adjoining to N. SK 2637
Lees Gtr Manchester 43 E1 suburb 2m/3km E of Oldham. Textiles, light engineering. SD 9504
Lees Hill Cumbria 60 B4* loc 1m S of Askerton Castle. NY 5568
Lees, North N Yorks 49 E1 loc 2m/3km N of Ripon. SE 3073
Lees Scar Lighthouse Cumbria 59 F6 lighthouse on Solway Firth 1km SW of entrance to Silloth harbour. NY 0952
Lees, West N Yorks 54 D4* loc adjoining Swainby to W. NZ 4702
Leeswood (Coed-llai) Clwyd 41 H5* vil 3m/5km SE of Mold. SJ 2759
Lee, The Bucks 18 D1 vil 4m/7km NW of Chesham. SP 9004
Leetown Tayside 73 E3* loc 3m/4km W of Errol. NO 2121
Leftwich Green Ches 42 C4* suburb 1m S of Northwich. SJ 6672
Legbourne Lincs 45 G3 vil 3m/5km SE of Louth. TF 3684
Legburthwaite Cumbria 52 C3* loc 4m/7km SE of Keswick, near N end of Thirlmere. NY 3119
Legerwood Borders 66 D4 vil 4m/7km SE of Lauder. NT 5843
Legh, High Ches 42 C3 vil 5m/8km NW of Knutsford. SJ 7084
Legsby Lincs 45 E3 vil 3m/5km SE of Mkt Rasen. TF 1385
Leicester Leics 36 B4 city and county tn on R Soar, on site of Roman tn of *Ratae,* 89m/143km NW of London. Industries include hosiery, knitwear, footwear, engineering. University. Many Roman and medieval remains. SK 5804
Leicester Forest East Leics 36 B4 suburb 4m/6km W of Leicester. Service area on M1 motorway. SK 5303
Leicester Forest West Leics 36 B4 loc 2m/3km SE of Desford. SK 5001
Leicestershire 119 midland county of England, bounded by Northamptonshire, Warwickshire, Staffordshire, Derbyshire, Nottinghamshire, and Lincolnshire. The landscape is mostly of low, rolling hills. E and W of Leicester are areas of higher ground, notably Charnwood Forest. The W is largely industrial; industries include light engineering, hosiery, and footwear, with coal-mining in the NW. The E is rural, with large fields and scattered wds, and is noted for foxhunting. Chief tns are the city and county tn of Leicester, Ashby de la Zouch, Coalville, Loughborough, Mkt Harborough, and Melton Mowbray. R Soar traverses the county from S to N, while R Welland forms part of the boundary with Northamptonshire to the S.
Leidle Water S'clyde 69 D5 stream on Mull, rising on Beinn na Croise and running S, W, and finally NW down Glen Leidle into Loch Scridain at Pennyghael. NM 5126
Leigh Devon 7 E4* ham 3m/5km SE of Chulmleigh. **E Leigh** loc to E. SS 7212
Leigh Dorset 8 D3 vil 5m/8km S of Sherborne. ST 6108
Leigh Glos 26 D5 vil 5m/9km NE of Gloucester. SO 8726
Leigh Gtr Manchester 42 C2 tn 12m/19km W of Manchester. Coal-mining, textiles. Branch of Leeds and Liverpool Canal from Wigan connects here with Bridgewater Canal. SD 6500
Leigh H & W 26 C2 vil at confluence of L. Brook and R Teme 4m/7km W of Worcester. SO 7853
Leigh Kent 20 B6 vil with large green 3m/4km W of Tonbridge. TQ 5446
Leigh Salop 34 A4* loc 1m S of Worthen. SJ 3303
Leigh Surrey 19 F6 vil 3m/5km SW of Reigate. TQ 2296
Leigh Wilts 17 E2 vil 3m/4km W of Cricklade. SU 0692
Leigham Devon 4 B5* NE dist of Plymouth, 3m/5km from city centre. SX 5158
Leigh Beck Essex 20 D3 E dist of Canvey I. TQ 8182
Leigh Brook 26 C2* r rising SW of Gt Malvern and flowing N and then NE into R Teme at Leigh, H & W, 4m/7km W of Worcester. SO 7853
Leigh Common Som 9 E2* loc 2m/3km E of Wincanton. ST 7429
Leigh Delamere Wilts 16 D3* vil 4m/7km NW of Chippenham. Site of Roman villa to E. ST 8879
Leigh, East Devon 4 D4* ham 3m/5km SW of Totnes. 1m W, ham of **W Leigh.** SX 7658

Leigh, East Devon 4 D5* ham 2m/3km E of Modbury. To SW, ham of **W Leigh.** SX 6852
Leigh, East Devon 7 E4* ham 5m/7km SE of Winkleigh. SS 6905
Leighland Chapel Som 7 G2* loc on Brendon Hills 5m/8km SW of Watchet. ST 0336
Leigh, Little Ches 42 B4 vil 3m/5km NW of Northwich. SJ 6175
Leigh, Lower Staffs 35 F1* ham 1km W of Ch Leigh. SK 0136
Leigh, North Oxon 27 G6 vil 3m/5km NE of Witney. SP 3813
Leigh-on-Mendip Som. See Leigh upon Mendip.
Leigh-on-Sea Essex 21 E3 W dist of Southend-on-Sea. TQ 8486
Leigh Park Dorset 9 G4* residential estate in E part of Wimborne. SZ 0299
Leigh Park Hants 10 D4 N dist of Havant. SU 7108
Leigh Reservoir Som 8 A3* small resr in Blackdown Hills 4m/7km SE of Wellington. ST 1917
Leighs, Great Essex 30 C6 vil 4m/7km SW of Braintree. TL 7217
Leigh Sinton H & W 26 C3 vil 3m/5km N of Malvern. SO 7850
Leighs, Little Essex 30 B6* ham 5m/8km SW of Braintree. TL 7116
Leigh, South Oxon 17 G1 vil 3m/4km SE of Witney. SP 3908
Leighs Reservoirs Essex 30 B6* two small adjacent resrs 4m/7km SW of Braintree. TL 7018
Leighswood W Midlands 35 F4* loc 1km N of Aldridge. SK 0501
Leighterton Glos 16 D3 vil 5m/7km W of Tetbury. ST 8291
Leighton N Yorks 48 D1 loc 4m/7km W of Masham. **Leighton Resr** to S. SE 1679
Leighton Powys 34 A4 vil 2m/3km SE of Welshpool across R Severn. SJ 2405
Leighton Salop 34 C4 vil 5m/7km SW of Wellington. SJ 6105
Leighton Som 16 C6 loc 5m/9km E of Shepton Mallet. ST 7043
Leighton Bromswold Cambs 29 F1 vil 5m/7km W of Alconbury. TL 1175
Leighton Buzzard Beds 28 D5 industrial tn 11m/18km NW of Luton. SP 9225
Leighton, Low Derbys 43 E3 loc on E side of New Mills. SK 0085
Leigh upon Mendip Som 16 C6 vil 5m/8km W of Frome. Alternative form, Leigh-on-Mendip. ST 6947
Leigh, Upper Staffs 35 F1* ham 1m NW of Ch Leigh. SK 0136
Leigh, West Devon 7 E4* ham 4m/6km SE of Winkleigh. SS 6805
Leigh, West Som 7 H2* ham 3m/5km NE of Wiveliscombe. ST 1230
Leinthall Earls H & W 26 A1 vil 6m/10km NW of Leominster. SO 4467
Leinthall Starkes H & W 26 A1 vil 6m/9km SW of Ludlow. SO 4369
Leintwardine H & W 34 B6 vil at confluence of R Clun and R Teme and on site of Roman *Bravonium*, 7m/11km W of Ludlow. SO 4074
Leire Leics 36 B5 vil 4m/6km N of Lutterworth. SP 5290
Leirinmore H'land 84 D2* loc near N coast of Sutherland dist 2km SE of Durness. NC 4166
Leir Mhaodail Skye, H'land 79 D8 headland at S end of Sleat peninsula, 1km E of Pt of Sleat. NM 5799
Leiston Suffolk 31 H2 tn near coast 4m/6km E of Saxmundham. Engineering works. Ruins of 12c abbey (A.M.) 1m N. TM 4462
Leith Lothian 66 A1 dist of Edinburgh 2m/3km N of city centre. Harbour and docks on Firth of Forth. See also Water of L. NT 2676
Leith 53 E3 r rising at Shap, Cumbria, and flowing N to Melkinthorpe, then E into R Lyvennet 1m E of Cliburn. NY 6024
Leithen Water 66 B5 r in Borders region rising on Moorfoot Hills 3m/4km E of Eddleston and flowing S to R Tweed at Innerleithen. NT 3336
Leith Hall Grampian 82 D4 hse (NTS) built round central courtyard 1km NE of Kirkhill of Kennethmont, and 7m/11km S of Huntly. Home of head of Leith family since 1650. NJ 5429
Leith Hill Surrey 11 G1 wooded hill (NT) in outliers of N Downs 4m/7km SW of Dorking, standing 965 ft or 294 metres, highest point in SE England. A 64ft (20 metres) tower stands on summit. TQ 1343
Leitholm Borders 67 E4 vil 4m/7km NW of Coldstream. NT 7944
Leith, West Herts 18 D1* loc 1m SW of Tring. SP 9110
Lelant Cornwall 2 B4 loc to W of Hayle across estuary. SW 5437
Lelant Downs Cornwall 2 B5* loc 3m/5km S of St Ives. SW 5236
Lelley Humberside 51 F5 ham 3m/5km NE of Hedon. TA 2032
Lem Hill H & W 26 C1* loc 4m/7km W of Bewdley. SO 7274
Lemington Tyne & Wear 61 F5 loc on N bank of R Tyne 1m SE of Newburn. NZ 1764
Lemington, Lower Glos 27 F4* loc 2m/3km NE of Moreton-in-Marsh. SP 2134
Lemon 5 E3 Devon r rising on E slopes of Dartmoor and running E into R Teign at Newton Abbot. SX 8671
Lempitlaw Borders 67 E5 loc 3m/5km E of Kelso. NT 7832
Lemreway W Isles 88 C3 vil near E coast of Lewis on N side of Loch Shell, 3m/5km SW of Kebock Hd. NB 3711
Lemsford Herts 19 F1 vil 2km W of Welwyn Garden City. TL 2112
Len 20 D6 r rising S of Lenham in Kent and flowing W into R Medway at Maidstone. TQ 7555
Lenacre Cumbria 53 F5* loc 2m/3km SE of Sedbergh. SD 6689
Lenchwick H & W 27 E3 vil 2m/4km N of Evesham. SP 0347
Lendalfoot S'clyde 56 B4 coastal vil 6m/10km SW of Girvan. NX 1390
Lenham Kent 21 E6 vil 4m/6km NW of Charing. Loc of **L. Heath** 2m/3km SE. TQ 8952
Lenibrick Point Cumbria 47 E1* headland on E bank of R Leven estuary 2km W of Flookburgh. SD 3475
Lenie H'land 81 E4/E5 locality on NW shore of Loch Ness, 2m/3km S of Drumnadrochit, Inverness dist. NH 5126
Lenimore Arran, S'clyde. Alternative name for N Thundergay. See Thundergay.
Lennel Borders 67 E4 vil on R Tweed 1m NE of Coldstream. NT 8540
Lennox Forest S'clyde 64 D2* state forest 2km W of Lennoxtown. NS 6077
Lennoxlove Lothian 66 C2 mansion of 14c with later additions, 2km S of Haddington. NT 5172
Lennoxtown S'clyde 64 D1 small tn 8m/13km N of Glasgow. NS 6277
Lent Bucks 18 D3* loc 3m/5km W of Slough. Loc of **Lent Rise** to S. SU 9282
Lenton Lincs 37 E2 ham 8m/13km NW of Bourne. TF 0230
Lenton Notts 36 B1 loc in Nottingham 2km SW of city centre. SK 5539
Lenton Abbey Notts 36 B1* loc in Nottingham on S side of Wollaton Park 3m/5km SW of city centre. SK 5338
Lentran H'land 81 F3* loc in Inverness dist 5m/8km W of Inverness. **Lentran Pt** is headland to N on Beauly Firth. NH 5845
Lenwade Norfolk 39 E3* vil 2m/4km NW of Attlebridge. TG 0918
Leny 71 G4 r in Central region running SE from Loch Lubnaig to R Teith at Callander. See also Falls of L., Pass of L. NN 6207
Lenzie S'clyde 64 D2 loc adjoining Kirkintilloch to S. NS 6571
Lenziemill S'clyde 65 E2* loc in Cumbernauld 1km S of tn centre. NS 7673
Leochel Cushnie Grampian 82 D5 vil 5m/7km SW of Alford. NJ 5210
Leominster H & W 26 A2 tn on R Lugg 12m/19km N of Hereford. Centre of agricultural dist. SO 4959
Leonard Stanley Glos 16 C1 vil 3m/5km W of Stroud. SO 8003
Lepe Hants 10 B5* loc 3m/5km S of Fawley. SZ 4598
Leperstone Reservoir S'clyde 64 B2* small resr 1m N of Kilmacolm. NS 3571
Lephin Skye, H'land 78 A4* loc near W coast 5m/8km W of Dunvegan. NG 1749
Leppington N Yorks 50 C2 vil 5m/9km S of Malton. Site of former cas. SE 7661
Lepton W Yorks 48 D6/49 E6 vil 4m/6km E of Huddersfield. **Lit Lepton** loc to S. SE 2015
Lerags Cross S'clyde 70 B3* restored 16c cross, on a mound to E of Kilbride in Argyll 3m/4km S of Oban. NM 8625
Leri 32 D5* r rising S of Nant-y-moch Resr, Dyfed, and flowing W to within 1km of the coast at Borth, then N into R Dovey estuary opp Aberdovey. SN 6195
Lerryn Cornwall 3 F3 vil 3m/5km SE of Lostwithiel at head of creek of **R Lerryn,** which rises 4m/6km N and flows into R Fowey below St Winnow. SX 1457
Lerwick Shetland 89 E7 chief tn of Mainland and of Shetland, situated on Bressay Sound 22m/35km N of Sumburgh Hd. Fishing port, service base for North Sea oilfields, and terminus of passenger boat services from Scottish mainland. Annual festival of Up-Helly-Aa, of pagan origin, held on last Tuesday in January. Fort Charlotte (A.M.), 17c fort. HU 4741
Lesbury Nthmb 61 G1 vil 4m/6km E of Alnwick. NU 2311
Lescrow Cornwall 3 F3 loc just NW of Fowey. SX 1152
Leslie Fife 73 F4 tn 2m/3km NW of Glenrothes. Paper mnfre, textile spinning, light engineering. NO 2401
Leslie Grampian 83 E4 vil 3m/5km SW of Insch. **L. Castle** is ruined tower hse. NJ 5924
Lesmahagow S'clyde 65 E4 small tn on R Nethan 5m/8km SW of Lanark. Mnfre of knitwear and nylon hose. Also known as Abbey Green. NS 8179
Lesnes Abbey London. See Lessness Heath.
Lesnewth Devon 6 A6 vil 2m/3km E of Boscastle. SX 1390
LESSER. For names beginning with this word, see under next word. This also applies to names beginning with Great, Greater, Little; High, Low; Higher, Lower; Upper, Nether; Far, Near; Mid, Middle; Isle(s) of; North, South, East, West; The, Y, Yr.
Lessingham Norfolk 39 G2 vil 2m/3km SE of Happisburgh. TG 3928
Lessness Heath London 20 B4* loc in borough of Bexley 2km W of Erith and 12m/19km E of Charing Cross. To E, Lesnes Abbey Wds and medieval ruins of Lesnes Abbey. TQ 4978
Lessonhall Cumbria 59 G6 ham 2m/4km NW of Wigton. NY 2250
Leswalt D & G 57 A6 vil on Rinns of Galloway, 3m/5km NW of Stranraer. NX 0163
Letchmore Heath Herts 19 F2 vil 3m/5km E of Watford. TQ 1597
Letchworth Herts 29 F4 tn 5m/9km N of Stevenage. First English garden city, founded 1903. Various industries incl heavy and light engineering. TL 2132
Letcombe Bassett Oxon 17 G3 vil 2m/4km SW of Wantage. Prehistoric fort to SE. SU 3785
Letcombe Regis Oxon 17 G3 vil 2km SW of Wantage. SU 3886
Letham Central 72 C5* loc 2km S of Airth. NS 8985
Letham Fife 73 F3 vil 4m/7km W of Cupar. NO 3014
Letham Tayside 72 D2/73 E2* NW dist of Perth. NO 0924
Letham Tayside 77 E6 vil 5m/8km E of Forfar. NO 5248
Lethanhill S'clyde 56 D3 loc 2km E of Patna. NS 4310
Lethendy Tayside 73 E1 loc 2m/3km NW of Meikleour. 17c tower hse. NO 1341
Lethenty Grampian 83 F3 loc 3m/5km NE of Fyvie. NJ 8041
Letheringham Suffolk 31 G3 ham 2m/4km NW of Wickham Mkt. TM 2757
Letheringsett Norfolk 39 E1 vil 2km W of Holt. TG 0638
Letocetum Staffs. See Wall.
Lettaford Devon 4 D2* loc 4m/6km SW of Moretonhampstead. SX 7084
Letterewe H'land 85 A8 locality on NE shore of Loch Maree, Ross and Cromarty dist, 6m/10km NW of head of loch. **L. Forest** is deer forest to NE. NG 9571
Letterfearn H'land 79 F6 locality on W shore of Loch Duich, Skye and Lochalsh dist, 1m from mouth of loch. NG 8823
Lettermorar H'land 68 E1 locality on S side of Loch Morar in Lochaber dist, 4m/6km SE of vil of Morar. NM 7389
Letters H'land 85 B7 locality on W side of Loch Broom, Ross and Cromarty dist, 2m/3km from head of loch. NH 1687
Letterston (Treletert) Dyfed 22 B3 vil 5m/8km S of Fishguard. SM 9429
Letton H & W 25 H3 vil 2km SE of Willersley. SO 3346
Letton H & W 25 H1* loc 6m/10km E of Knighton. SO 3870
Letty Green Herts 19 G1* vil 3m/4km W of Hertford. TL 2810
Letwell S Yorks 44 A3 vil 4m/6km SE of Maltby. SK 5687
Leuchar Burn 77 G1 stream in Grampian region running from Loch of Skene SE to R Dee on S side of Peterculter. NJ 8400
Leuchars Fife 73 G3 vil 5m/7km S of Tayport. Airfield to SE, on N side of R Eden estuary. NO 4521
Leum Uilleim H'land 74 D5 mt in Lochaber dist 3m/5km S of head of Loch Treig. Height 2971 ft or 906 metres. NN 3364
Leurbost W Isles 88 B2 vil on Lewis 6m/9km SW of Stornoway, near head of long inlet, Loch L. NB 3725
Leusdon Devon 4 D3* ham on E edge of Dartmoor 4m/6km NW of Ashburton. SX 7073
Levedale Staffs 35 E3 ham 4m/7km SW of Stafford. SJ 8916
Level Main Drain, Middle 38 B3 fenland drainage channel running from junction of Sixteen Foot Drain and Popham's Eau at Three Holes, Norfolk, to R Ouse 1km below Wiggenhall St Germans. TF 5914
Level Main Drain, North 38 A3* drainage channel running from Thorney, Cambs, across the Fens to R Nene 1m E of Tydd Gote, Lincs. TF 4618
Level's Green Essex 29 H5* ham 2m/3km NW of Bishop's Stortford. TL 4724
Leven Fife 73 F4/G4 tn and resort on W side of Largo Bay. Industries include iron and steel founding, flax spinning, sawmilling, paper and golf-club mnfre. Docks at Methil, qv. NO 3800
Leven H'land 74 C5 r in Lochaber dist running W from Blackwater Resr to head of Loch Leven at Kinlochleven. NN 1762
Leven Humberside 51 E4 vil 6m/10km NE of Beverley. **Lit Leven** loc adjoining to W. TA 1045
Leven 52 C6 r rising in Windermere, Cumbria, and flowing SW to its estuary at Haverthwaite, then S into Morecambe Bay between Bardsea and Cowpren Pt. SD 3374
Leven 54 D3/D4 r rising on Kildale Moor, N York Moors National Park, and flowing W by Kildale, Easby, Lit Ayton, Gt Ayton, Stokesley, Hutton Rudby, and Crathorne into R Tees 1m E of Yarm, Cleveland. NZ 4312
Leven 64 B2 r in Strathclyde region running S from foot of Loch Lomond at Balloch to R Clyde at Dumbarton. NS 3974
Leven 73 F4/G4 r in Fife region issuing from Loch Leven and flowing E to Largo Bay between tns of Leven and Methil. NO 3800
Leven, High Cleveland 54 D4 ham 2m/3km E of Yarm. NZ 4412
Levenish W Isles (W of 88 A3) rock islet (NTS) in St Kilda group lying 2m/3km SE of E end of St Kilda itself. Haunt of sea birds. NF 1396
Levens Cumbria 53 E6 vil 5m/8km S of Kendal. **L. Hall,** Elizn hse with topiary gardens, 1km SE. **Nether Levens** loc 1km S. SD 4886
Levens Green Herts 29 G5* ham 2m/3km W of Puckeridge. TL 3522
Levenshulme Gtr Manchester 42 D2 dist of Manchester 3m/5km SE of city centre. SJ 8694
Leven Wick Shetland 89 E8 bay on E coast of Mainland 9m/14km N of Sumburgh Hd. Loc of **Levenwick** on W side of bay. Headland of **Levenwick Ness** to E. HU 4121
Leverburgh W Isles 88 A4 vil on SW coast of Harris 4m/6km NW of Renish Pt. Vil and harbour date from industrial development of Isle of Lewis by Lord Leverhulme in 1920s. Lighthouse. Formerly named Obbe. NG 0186
Lever Edge Gtr Manchester 42 C1* loc in Bolton 2m/3km SW of tn centre. SD 7006
Lever, Great Gtr Manchester 42 C1* dist of Bolton 2km SE of tn centre. SD 7207
Leverington Cambs 37 H3 vil 2m/3km NW of Wisbech. TF 4411
Lever, Little Gtr Manchester 42 C1* tn 3m/4km SE of Bolton. Textiles, chemicals, paper, plastics. SD 7507

Leverstock Green Herts 19 E1 E dist of Hemel Hempstead. TL 0806

Levers Water Cumbria 52 C5 mountain lake 2m/3km NW of Coniston. SD 3097

Leverton Berks 17 G4• loc 1m NW of Hungerford across R Kennet. SU 3370

Leverton Lincs 45 G6 vil 5m/8km E of Boston. **L. Lucasgate** and **L. Outgate** adjoining locs 2km E. TF 4047

Leverton, North with Habblesthorpe Notts 44 C3 vil 5m/8km E of E Retford. S Leverton vil 1km S. SK 7882

Levington Suffolk 31 F4 vil 6m/9km SE of Ipswich. TM 2339

Levisham N Yorks 55 F5 vil 5m/7km NE of Pickering. SE 8390

Lew Oxon 17 G1 vil 3m/5km SW of Witney. SP 3206

Lew 6 D4• r rising in Halwill Forest, Devon, and flowing N through Northlew into R Torridge 1m NW of Hatherleigh. SS 5306

Lew 6 D6• r in Devon rising on W side of Dartmoor 4m/6km SW of Okehampton and flowing SW into R Lyd near Marystow. SX 4483

Lewannick Cornwall 4 A3 vil 4m/7km SW of Launceston. SX 2780

Lewcombe Dorset 8 D4• loc 1m W of Melbury Osmond. ST 5507

Lewdown Devon 6 C6 vil 7m/12km E of Launceston. SX 4486

Lewes E Sussex 12 B5 county tn in gap of S Downs (R Ouse) 8m/13km NE of Brighton. Norman cas and several old hses. TQ 4110

Lewesdon Hill Dorset. See Broadwindsor.

Leweston Dorset 8 D3• loc 3m/4km S of Sherborne. ST 6312

Lewis W Isles 88 largest and most northerly island of the Outer Hebrides, measuring some 61m/99km NE to SW and a maximum of half that distance NW to SE. The name Lewis is also applied to the northern part of the island as distinct from Harris, qv. In this sense Lewis consists largely of peaty uplands containing innumerable, mostly small, lochs and streams in which salmon and trout abound. Some moorland has been reclaimed for farming, barley and potatoes being the main crops. Chief occupations of the islanders are fishing and cloth mnfre. Butt of Lewis, qv, is most northerly point. Stornoway is chief tn. NB 33

Lewis Burn 60 C3 r rising on border of Cumbria and Nthmb on W edge of Kielder Forest and flowing NE into R North Tyne 1m W of Plashetts, Nthmb. NY 6590

Lewisham London 20 A4• borough and tn 6m/10km SE of Charing Cross. Borough extends 5m/8km S from R Thames at Deptford Power Stn. Tn is situated on Ravensbourne Brook, which runs into Deptford Creek. TQ 3875

Lewiston H'land 81 E4 vil on R Coiltie 1m W of Urquhart Bay on Loch Ness, Inverness dist. NH 5129

Lewistown Mid Glam 15 E3• vil 1m E of Llangeinor. SS 9388

Lewknor Oxon 18 C2 vil 3m/5km NE of Watlington. SU 7197

Leworthy Devon 7 E2• loc 8m/13km NE of Barnstaple. SS 6738

Lewson Street Kent 21 E5• ham 3m/5km W of Faversham. TQ 9661

Lewth Lancs 47 F4• loc 2m/3km NW of Woodplumpton. SD 4836

Lewthorne Cross Devon 4 D3• loc 4m/7km N of Ashburton. SX 7776

Lewtrenchard Devon 6 D6 vil 8m/13km E of Launceston. SX 4586

Lexden Essex 30 D5• loc in W part of Colchester. TL 9725

Lexham, East Norfolk 38 D3• vil 6m/9km NE of Swaffham. **W Lexham** vil 1m W. TF 8516

Lexworthy Som 8 B1• ham 3m/4km W of Bridgwater. ST 2535

Ley Cornwall 3 F2• loc 5m/8km W of Liskeard. SX 1766

Leybourne Kent 20 C5 vil on W edge of industrial and residential development 5m/8km W of Maidstone. TQ 6858

Leyburn N Yorks 54 A5 small mkt tn 8m/12km SW of Richmond. SE 1190

Leycett Staffs 42 D6• ham 4m/6km W of Newcastle-under-Lyme. SJ 7946

Leygreen Herts 29 F5 ham 3m/5km SW of Hitchin. TL 1624

Ley Hill Bucks 19 D2• vil 2m/3km E of Chesham. SP 9802

Ley Hill W Midlands 35 G4• loc 2km N of Sutton Coldfield tn centre. SP 1298

Leyland Lancs 47 F5 tn 5m/8km S of Preston. Industries include commercial vehicles, rubber, paint, textiles. SD 5421

Leyland Green Gtr Manchester 42 B2• loc 2m/3km NW of Ashton-in-Makerfield. SD 5400

Leylodge Grampian 83 F5 loc 2m/4km SW of Kintore. NJ 7713

Ley, Lower Glos 26 C5• loc on right bank of R Severn 5m/8km NE of Newnham. SO 7516

Leymoor W Yorks 48 D6• loc 3m/4km W of Huddersfield. SE 1016

Leysdown-on-Sea Kent 21 F4 loc with holiday camps at E end of Isle of Sheppey. TR 0370

Leysmill Tayside 77 F6 vil 5m/8km NW of Arbroath. NO 6047

Leyton London 20 A3 tn in S part of borough of Waltham Forest 5m/8km NE of London Br. TQ 3886

Leytonstone London 20 A3 NE dist of Leyton in borough of Waltham Forest. TQ 3987

Ley, Upper Glos 26 C5• loc 7m/11km W of Gloucester. SO 7217

Lezant Cornwall 4 A3 vil 4m/6km S of Launceston. SX 3379

Lezayre Isle of Man 46 B4 ham 2m/3km W of Ramsey. Also known as Churchtown. SC 4294

Lezerea Cornwall 2 C5• loc 4m/6km N of Helston. SW 6833

Lhanbryde Grampian 82 B1 vil 4m/6km E of Elgin. NJ 2761

Lhen, The Isle of Man 46 B3• loc 2m/3km NW of Andreas. Also known as Ballathona. NX 3901

Lhen Trench, The 46 B3• stream on Isle of Man flowing N into sea 1km NW of Ballathona, or The Lhen. NX 3802

Liathach H'land 80 A2 mt mass in Torridon Forest, Ross and Cromarty dist, N of Torridon. Anglicised form: Leagach. Highest point is Spidean a' Choire Leith, 3456 ft or 1054 metres. NG 9257

Liath Eilean S'clyde 70 B6• offshore island in Loch Fyne, on E side of Eilean Mór and 3m/5km SE of Lochgilphead, Argyll. NR 8883

Libanus Powys 25 E5 ham 4m/6km SW of Brecon. SN 9925

Libberton S'clyde 65 F4 vil 2m/4km S of Carnwath. NS 9846

Libbery H & W 26 D2• loc 6m/10km E of Worcester. SO 9555

Liberton Lothian 66 A2 dist of Edinburgh 3m/5km SE of city centre. NT 2769

Liberty Hill S Yorks 43 G2• loc in Sheffield 3m/4km W of city centre. SK 3188

Lichfield Staffs 35 G3 tn 15m/24km N of Birmingham. Birthplace of Samuel Johnson, 1709. Cathedral 12c-15c. Industries include light engineering, iron founding. SK 1109

Lickey H & W 35 F6• vil on **L. Hills** 4m/6km NE of Bromsgrove. SO 9975

Lickey End H & W 27 E1 loc 2km NE of Bromsgrove. SO 9772

Lickfold W Sussex 11 F3 ham 4m/6km NE of Midhurst. SU 9226

Lickle 52 C6• r rising W of Torver, Cumbria, and flowing SW into R Duddon 1km W of Broughton in Furness. SD 2087

Licswm Clwyd 41 G4 ham 3m/5km S of Holywell. SJ 1671

Liddaton Green Devon 4 B3• loc 5m/9km N of Tavistock. SX 4582

Liddel Water 60 A4 r rising in Borders region, on Cheviot Hills 8m/13km SW of Carter Bar, and running SW down Liddesdale to border with England at Kershopefoot. It then continues SW along England-Scotland border to its confluence with R Esk 2m/3km S of Canonbie. NY 3973

Liddesdale Borders 60 A3-B2 valley of Liddel Water, qv. NY 48

Liddington Wilts 17 F3 vil 4m/6km SE of Swindon. 1m S on hillside, **L. Castle**, Iron Age fort. SU 2081

Lidgate Suffolk 30 C2 vil 6m/10km SE of Newmarket. Ch on site of Norman cas. TL 7257

Lidget S Yorks 44 B1• loc adjoining Auckley to S. SE 6500

Lidget Green W Yorks 48 D5• dist of Bradford 2km W of city centre. SE 1432

Lidgett Notts 44 B4• loc 1km S of Edwinstowe. SK 6365

Lidgett Park W Yorks 49 E4• dist of Leeds 3m/5km NE of city centre. SE 3238

Lidlington Beds 29 E4 vil 3m/5km W of Ampthill. SP 9939

Lidsey W Sussex 11 F4• loc 3m/4km N of Bognor Regis. SU 9303

Lidsing Kent 20 D5 loc 3m/5km S of Gillingham. TQ 7862

Liever S'clyde 70 B4 r in Argyll running S down Glen Liever to Loch Awe 2km E of head of loch. NM 8905

Liever 70 C2 r in S'clyde region running W down Glen L. into Loch Etive, Argyll, on S side of Inverliever Bay, 4m/6km NE of Bonawe. NN 0635

Liff Tayside 73 F2 vil 5m/8km NW of Dundee. NO 3333

Lifford W Midlands 35 F6• loc in Birmingham 5m/8km S of city centre. L. Hall, early 17c hse. SP 0579

Lifton Devon 6 C6 vil 4m/6km E of Launceston. SX 3885

Liftondown Devon 6 C6 ham 3m/4km E of Launceston. SX 3685

Ligger Bay Cornwall 2 C3 alternative name for Perran Bay, extending from **Ligger Pt** southwards to Perranporth, and enclosing 2m or 3km of sandy beach known as Perran Beach, backed by Penhale Sands. SW 7556

Lightbowne Gtr Manchester 42 D1• dist of Manchester 3m/4km NE of city centre. SD 8601

Lightcliffe W Yorks 48 D5• vil 2m/3km N of Brighouse. SE 1325

Lightfoot Green Lancs 47 F4• loc 3m/5km N of Preston. SD 5133

Lighthazles W Yorks 48 C6• loc 2km NW of Ripponden. SE 0220

Light Hazzles Reservoir Gtr Manchester 48 C6• resr 3m/5km NE of Littleborough. SD 9620

Lighthill W Isles 88 C2• loc adjoining vil of Back to W, near E coast of Lewis. NB 4740

Lighthorne Warwicks 27 G2 vil 6m/10km S of Leamington. SP 3355

Light Oaks Staffs 43 E6• loc 1m SW of Bagnall. SJ 9150

Lightwater Surrey 18 D5• residential loc 1m SE of Bagshot. SU 9262

Lightwood Staffs 43 E6• loc 1km E of Cheadle. SK 0143

Lightwood Green Ches 34 C1 loc 2m/3km W of Audlem. SJ 6342

Lightwood Green Clwyd 34 B1 loc 2km SE of Overton. SJ 3840

Lilbourne Northants 36 B6 vil 4m/6km E of Rugby. SP 5676

Lilburn Nthmb 67 G6 loc 3m/5km SE of Wooler. NU 0224

Lilford Northants 37 E5/E6 loc 3m/4km S of Oundle. TL 0384

Lillesdon Som 8 B2• ham 2km SW of N Curry. ST 3023

Lilleshall Salop 34 D3 vil 3m/4km SW of Newport. Monmt to Duke of Sutherland, d 1833. Ruins of 12c abbey (A.M.) 1m SE. SJ 7513

Lilley Berks 17 H4 loc 8m/12km N of Newbury. SU 4479

Lilley Herts 29 E5/F5 vil 4m/7km SW of Hitchin. TL 1126

Lilliesleaf Borders 66 C5/C6 vil 7m/11km N of Hawick. NT 5325

Lilling Green N Yorks 50 B2• loc 2m/3km NE of Strensall. SE 6463

Lillingstone Dayrell Bucks 28 C4 vil 4m/6km N of Buckingham. SP 7039

Lillingstone Lovell Bucks 28 C4 vil 4m/7km N of Buckingham. SP 7140

Lillington Dorset 8 D3 vil 3m/4km S of Sherborne. ST 6212

Lillington Warwicks 27 G1• NE dist of Leamington. SP 3267

Lilling, West N Yorks 50 B2 ham 1m S of Sheriff Hutton. Former vil of E Lilling, 1m SE, no longer exists. SE 6465

Lilly Devon 6 D2• loc 2m/3km E of Barnstaple. SS 5833

Lilly Loch S'clyde 65 E2 small loch 1km S of Caldercruix. NS 8266

Lilstock Som 15 G6• ham near coast 4m/6km NW of Nether Stowey. ST 1644

Lilybank S'clyde 64 A2/B2• loc between Greenock and Port Glasgow. Site of small Roman fort 1m SW. NS 3074

Lilyhurst Salop 34 D3• loc 4m/6km S of Newport. SJ 7413

Lily Loch S'clyde 64 C1/C2• small loch or tarn on Kilpatrick Hills 2km NE of Loch Humphrey. NS 4777

Lily Mere Cumbria 53 E5 lake 3m/5km W of Sedbergh. SD 6091

Lim 8 B5• r rising 2m/3km N of Uplyme in Devon and flowing S through Lyme Regis, partly underground, into Lyme Bay. SY 3492

Limber, Great Lincs 45 E1 vil 5m/8km N of Caistor. TA 1308

Limbourne Creek Essex 21 E2 inlet at head of R Blackwater estuary S of Northey I. and 2m/3km SE of Maldon. TL 8705

Limbrick Lancs 47 F6• loc 2m/3km N of Adlington. SD 6016

Limbury Beds 29 E5• N dist of Luton. TL 0724

Limden 12 D4 stream rising 2km SE of Wadhurst, E Sussex, and flowing SE into R Rother at Etchingham. TQ 7126

Limebrook H & W 25 H2• loc 4m/6km E of Presteigne. Remains of priory. SO 3766

Limefield Gtr Manchester 47 H6• loc in Bury 2m/3km N of tn centre. SD 8013

Lime Gate Gtr Manchester 42 D1/43 E1• loc in Oldham 2m/3km SW of tn centre. SD 9102

Limehouse London 20 A3• dist in borough of Tower Hamlets 3m/4km E of London Br. **L. Reach** is stretch of R Thames between Rotherhithe and Millwall. TQ 3681

Limehouse Reach 20 D5 stretch of R Medway on E side of Rochester, Kent. TQ 7468

Limehurst Gtr Manchester 43 E1/E2• loc in Ashton-under-Lyne 2km NW of tn centre. SD 9300

Limekilnburn S'clyde 64 D4• loc 3m/5km S of Hamilton. NS 7050

Limekiln Hill Dorset. See Bexington, West.

Limekilns Fife 65 G1 vil on N bank of Firth of Forth 3m/5km W of Inverkeithing. NT 0783

Limerigg Central 65 E2 loc 2km S of Slamannan. NS 8570

Limerstone Isle of Wight 10 B6 ham 1m W of Shorwell. SZ 4482

Limestone Brae Nthmb 53 G1 loc 2km N of Carr Shield. NY 7949

Limington Som 8 D2 vil 2km E of Ilchester. ST 5422

Limpenhoe Norfolk 39 G4 vil 2m/3km NW of Reedham. TG 3903

Limpert Bay S Glam 15 E4• bay on Bristol Channel on W side of Breaksea Pt. ST 0166

Limpley Stoke Wilts 16 C5• vil 3m/5km SE of Bath. ST 7860

Limpsfield Surrey 20 A6 vil below N Downs 3m/5km W of Westerham. TQ 4053

Linacre Reservoirs 43 G4/H4• series of three resrs in valley of Holme Brook 3m/5km W of Chesterfield, Derbys. SK 3372

Linby Notts 44 A5 vil 1m N of Hucknall. SK 5351

Linch W Sussex 11 E2• loc 3m/4km SE of Liphook. SU 8528

Linchmere W Sussex 11 E2 vil 2m/3km E of Liphook. SU 8631

Lincluden D & G 59 E4 NW dist of Dumfries. **L. College** (A.M.), remains of medieval abbey at confluence of Cluden Water and R Nith. NX 9677

Lincoln Lincs 44 D4 county tn and cathedral city on R Witham and on site of Roman *Lindum*, 120m/193km N of London. Industries include mnfre of agricultural and other machinery. Cas built by William I. 13c cathedral on hilltop dominates skyline. SK 9771

Lincolnshire 117, 119 eastern county of England, bounded by Norfolk, Cambridgeshire, Leicestershire, Nottinghamshire, Humberside, and the North Sea. It also marches briefly with Northamptonshire SW of Stamford. Much of the county is flat, and includes in the S a large area of the Fens, reclaimed marshland now richly fertile and producing large crops of peas (for canning), sugar beet, potatoes, corn, and, in the Spalding area, flower bulbs. Two ranges of hills traverse the county N and S: the narrow limestone ridge, a continuation of the Cotswolds, running from Grantham to Humberside, and the chalk Wolds, about 12m/20km wide, running N from Spilsby and Horncastle. The rs, of which the chief are the Witham and Welland, are largely incorporated into the extensive land-drainage system, and scarcely distinguishable from man-made channels. Principal tns are the cathedral city and county tn of Lincoln; Boston, Gainsborough, Grantham, Louth, Mkt Rasen, Sleaford, Spalding, and Stamford. Mablethorpe and Skegness are coastal resorts. There are some mnfres, agricultural machinery being one of the most important.

Lincomb H & W 26 C1/D1* ham 2m/3km S of Stourport. SO 8268

Lincombe Devon 4 D6* loc on W side of Kingsbridge Estuary 2km N of Salcombe. SX 7440

Lindale Cumbria 52 D6 vil 2m/3km N of Grange-over-Sands. SD 4180

Lindal in Furness Cumbria 46 D1 vil 2m/3km NE of Dalton-in-Furness. SD 2575

Linden Glos 26 D5* S dist of Gloucester. SO 8216

Lindfield W Sussex 12 A4 NE dist of Haywards Heath. TQ 3425

Lindford Hants 11 E2 vil 1km E of Bordon Camp and 5m/8km W of Hindhead. SU 8036

Lindisfarne Nthmb 67 G4. Former, and still alternative, name of Holy I., (qv). NU 1242

Lindley W Yorks 48 D6 dist of Huddersfield 2m/3km NW of tn centre. SE 1118

Lindley Green N Yorks 49 E3 ham 3m/4km NE of Otley. SE 2248

Lindley Wood Reservoir N Yorks 49 E3 resr 2m/4km N of Otley. SE 2045

Lindores Fife 73 F3 vil 2m/3km SE of Newburgh. **L. Loch** is small loch on S side. NO 2616

Lindores Abbey Fife 73 F3 scanty remains of abbey founded in 1191. Situated on E side of Newburgh. NO 2418

Lindow End Ches 42 D3* loc 2m/3km W of Alderley Edge. SJ 8178

Lindrick N Yorks 49 E2* loc 2m/3km W of Ripon. SE 2770

Lindridge H & W 26 B1* vil 5m/8km E of Tenbury Wells. SO 6769

Lindsell Essex 30 B5 vil 4m/6km N of Gt Dunmow. TL 6427

Lindsey Suffolk 30 D3 ham 4m/6km NW of Hadleigh. Ham of **L. Tye** to N. To S, near remains of motte and bailey cas, is St James's Chapel (A.M.), dating from 13c. TL 9745

Lindsey, East and **West** 117 admin dists of Lincs.

Lindum Lincs. See Lincoln.

Lineholt H & W 26 C1/D1* loc 4m/6km S of Stourport. SO 8266

Line Houses Staffs 42 D5* loc 2km NW of Tunstall. SJ 8452

Linfern Loch S'clyde 56 D4 loch 4m/7km S of Straiton. NX 3697

Linfit W Yorks 48 D6/49 E6* loc 1m NE of Kirkburton. SE 2013

Linfitts Gtr Manchester 43 E1* loc 1km NW of Delph. SD 9708

Linford Essex 20 C4* loc 3m/5km NE of Tilbury. TQ 6558

Linford Brook 9 H4* stream rising in New Forest NE of Ringwood, Hants, and flowing SW into R Avon on N side of the tn. SU 1405

Linford, Great Bucks 28 D3 vil 2m/4km E of Wolverton, within area of Milton Keynes. SP 8542

Linford, Little Bucks 28 D3 ham 2m/4km W of Newport Pagnell across R Ouse. SP 8444

Linford Wood Bucks 28 D4* area in Milton Keynes to N of the centre. SP 8440

Ling H'land 80 A4 r in Skye and Lochalsh dist running SW to head of Loch Long. NG 9330

Linga Shetland 89 D7* small uninhabited island in Vaila Sound between Vaila and vil of Walls, Mainland. HU 2348

Linga Shetland 89 E6* uninhabited island off E coast of Mainland opp Firth Ness. HU 4673

Linga Shetland 89 E7* uninhabited island of about 170 acres or 70 hectares off W coast of Mainland between Muckle Roe and the entrance to Olna Firth. HU 3563

Linga Shetland 89 F5* narrow uninhabited island, 1m long, at S end of Bluemull Sound between Yell and Unst. HU 5598

Linga, East Shetland 89 F7* small uninhabited island 2m/4km E of island of Whalsay, 3m/5km S of Skaw Taing. HU 6162

Linga Holm Orkney 89 C6 small uninhabited island off W coast of Stronsay at entrance to St Catherine's Bay. HY 6127

Linga, Little Orkney 89 C6* islet off Links Ness at NW point of island of Stronsay. HY 6030

Lingara Bay W Isles 88 A4* small bay on SE coast of Harris containing islet of **Lingarabay I.**, 4m/6km SW of Manish. NG 0684

Lingards Wood W Yorks 48 C6/D6* loc 1m NE of Marsden. SE 0612

Linga, West Shetland 89 F7* uninhabited island of 315 acres or 127 hectares lying off W coast of island of Whalsay and separated from it by **Linga Sound. Lit Linga** is much smaller island among several others to W, between W Linga and Mainland. HU 5364

Lingay W Isles 88 D4* small uninhabited island 1km N of Pabbay and 2m/3km SW of Sandray. NL 6089

Lingay W Isles 88 E3* small uninhabited island 2m/3km SW of Ludac, on S coast of S Uist. NF 7511

Lingay W Isles 88 E1* small uninhabited island off N coast of N Uist nearly 2km SE of island of Boreray. NF 8778

Lingay W Isles 88 E1* small uninhabited island at SE end of Sound of Harris 4m/7km off E coast of N Uist. NG 0179

Lingbob W Yorks 48 D4* loc adjoining Wilsden to S. SE 0935

Lingdale Cleveland 55 E3 vil 3m/5km S of Saltburn. NZ 6716

Lingen H & W 25 H2 vil 4m/6km NE of Presteigne. SO 3667

Lingfield Surrey 12 A2 vil 4m/6km N of E Grinstead. Loc of **L. Common** 1km N. Racecourse 1km S. TQ 3843

Lingley Green Ches 42 B3* loc in Warrington 3m/5km W of tn centre. SJ 5588

Lings Cross Rows Derbys 43 H4* loc 2m/3km NE of Clay Cross. SK 4165

Lings Row Derbys 43 H4* loc 2m/3km NE of Clay Cross. SK 4165

Lings, The S Yorks 44 B1* loc adjoining Hatfield to S. SE 6508

Lingwood Norfolk 39 G4 vil 3m/4km W of Acle. TG 3608

Lingwood Common Essex 20 D2* partly wooded area (NT) to N of Danbury and 4m/7km E of Chelmsford. TL 7706

Lingyclose Head Cumbria 59 H6* loc 3m/4km SW of Carlisle. NY 3752

Linhouse Water 65 G2 stream in Lothian region running N to R Almond on E side of Livingston. NT 0767

Liniclett W Isles 88 E2* vil on SW coast of Benbecula 4m/6km S of Benbecula Airfield. NF 7949

Linicro Skye, H'land 78 B3 loc 2m/4km N of Uig. NG 3966

Linkend H & W 26 D4* ham 4m/7km W of Tewkesbury across R Severn. SO 8331

Linkenholt Hants 17 G5 vil 3m/5km NW of Hurstbourne Tarrant. SU 3658

Linkhill Kent 12 D4 loc 1m E of Sandhurst. TQ 8128

Linkinhorne Cornwall 3 G1 vil 4m/6km NW of Callington. SX 3173

Linklet Bay Orkney 89 C5* wide bay on E side of N Ronaldsay, extending SW from Dennis Hd. HY 7754

Links Bay Grampian 83 E1* small bay on N coast on E side of Portsoy. NJ 5966

Linksness Orkney 89 A7* loc and headland with landing stage at N end of Hoy on Burra Sound opp Graemsay. HY 2403

Links Ness Orkney 89 C6* headland at NW end of island of Stronsay. HY 6129

Linktown Fife 73 F5 S dist of Kirkcaldy. NT 2790

Linkwood Grampian 82 B1* loc with distillery 2km SE of Elgin. NJ 2361

Linley Salop 34 A5* ham 3m/5km NE of Bishop's Castle. SO 3592

Linley Salop 34 D4* ham 4m/6km NW of Bridgnorth. SO 6898

Linley Green H & W 26 C2 ham 3m/4km E of Bromyard. SO 6953

Linlithgow Lothian 65 F1 historic tn 16m/26km W of Edinburgh. Industries include electronics, distilling, mnfre of agricultural implements, paper, pharmaceutical products. On eminence on S side of **L. Loch** to N stand ruins of **L. Palace** (A.M.), birthplace in 1542 of Mary, Queen of Scots. **L. Bridge** is loc adjoining to W, below high rly viaduct. NS 9977

Linne Mhuirich S'clyde 70 A6 western arm of Loch Sween, Argyll, running N from Taynish. NR 7284

Linne nam Beathach S'clyde 70 D1* r in Argyll running E from Loch Dochard to Loch Tulla. NN 2742

Linney Head Dyfed 22 B6 headland 3m/4km SW of Castlemartin. SR 8895

Linngeam W Isles 88 A2* islet in Loch Roag, W coast of Lewis, 1m NE of entrance to Lit Loch Roag. NB 1433

Linn of Corriemulzie Grampian 76 B2 series of small waterfalls in a ravine in course of Corriemulzie Burn, 3m/5km SW of Braemar. NO 1189

Linn of Dee Grampian 76 B2 cascades in narrow cleft in course of R Dee 2km W of Inverey. NO 0689

Linn of Muick Grampian 76 D2 waterfall in course of R Muick 4m/7km SW of Ballater. NO 3389

Linn of Quoich Grampian 76 B2 waterfall in course of Quoich Water, 1km NW of its confluence with R Dee. NO 1191

Linn of Tummel Tayside 76 A5* waterfall (NTS) in R Tummel near its confluence with R Garry 2m/3km S of Killiecrankie. NN 9060

Linnvale S'clyde 64 C2* dist of Clydebank 1m E of tn centre across canal. NS 5170

Linshiels Nthmb 60 D1 loc in Coquetdale 2m/3km W of Alwinton. **L. Lake** 1m S. NT 8906

Linsidemore H'land 85 E6 loc in Sutherland dist 6m/20km NW of Bonar Br. NH 5499

Linslade Beds 28 D5 industrial tn adjoining Leighton Buzzard to W. SP 9125

Linstead Magna Suffolk 31 G1* loc 1m N of Cratfield. TM 3176

Linstead Parva Suffolk 31 G1 ham 4m/6km W of Halesworth. TM 3377

Linstock Cumbria 60 A5* ham on N bank of R Eden 2m/4km NE of Carlisle. **L. Castle** was residence in medieval times of Bishops of Carlisle. NY 4258

Linthorpe Cleveland 54 D3 dist of Middlesbrough 2km SW of tn centre. NZ 4818

Linthurst Newtown H & W 27 E1 loc 2m/3km NE of Bromsgrove. SO 9972

Linthwaite W Yorks 48 D6 vil 3m/5km SW of Huddersfield. SE 1014

Lintlaw Borders 67 E3 vil 4m/6km NE of Duns. NT 8258

Lintmill Grampian 82 D1 vil near N coast 1m S of Cullen. NJ 5165

Linton Borders 67 E5 loc nearly 1m N of Morebattle. NT 7726

Linton Cambs 30 A3/B3 vil 7m/11km W of Haverhill. Site of Roman villa 1km SE. TL 5646

Linton Derbys 35 H3 vil 3m/4km SW of Swadlincote. **L. Heath** loc adjoining to SE. SK 2717

Linton H & W 26 B5 vil 4m/6km E of Ross-on-Wye. Vil of **L. Hill** to SE. SO 6625

Linton Kent 20 D6 vil 4m/6km S of Maidstone. TQ 7550

Linton N Yorks 48 C2 vil 1m S of Grassington. SD 9962

Linton W Yorks 49 F3 vil 2km SW of Wetherby. SE 3946

Linton Colliery Nthmb 61 G3* loc 2m/4km N of Ashington. NZ 2691

Linton, East Lothian 66 D1 small tn on R Tyne 6m/9km W of Dunbar. See also Phantassie, Preston. NT 5977

Linton, Little Cambs 30 A3* loc 1km NW of Linton, 7m/12km W of Haverhill. TL 5547

Linton-on-Ouse N Yorks 50 A2 vil 9m/14km NW of York. Airfield to N. SE 4960

Linton, West Borders 65 G3 vil on E side of Pentland Hills 7m/12km SW of Penicuik. NT 1551

Linton Woods N Yorks 50 A2* loc 2km NE of Linton-on-Ouse. SE 5062

Lintz Durham 61 F5* loc adjoining Burnopfield to SW. NZ 1656

Lintzford Tyne & Wear 61 F5 loc on R Derwent 1m SW of Rowlands Gill and 4m/7km SW of Blaydon. NZ 1457

Lintzgarth Durham 53 H1* loc 1km W of Rookhope. NY 9242

Lintz Green Durham 61 F5* loc 2m/3km W of Burnopfield. NZ 1556

Linwood Lincs 45 E3 vil 2m/3km S of Mkt Rasen. TF 1086

Linwood S'clyde 64 B3/C3 loc 2km NE of Johnstone. Car mnfg plant. NS 4464

Lionel W Isles 88 C1* vil near N end of Lewis 1km W of Port of Ness. NB 5263

Liongam W Isles 88 A2* small uninhabited island off W coast of Lewis 2m/4km NE of island of Scarp. NA 9919

Lion's Head Grampian 83 F1* headland on N coast 1m SE of Troup Hd. NJ 8366

Liphook Hants 11 E2 large vil 4m/7km W of Haslemere. SU 8331

Lipley Salop 34 D2* loc 5m/8km SE of Mkt Drayton. SJ 7431

Lipyeate Som 16 B6* loc 3m/5km S of Radstock. ST 6850

Liquo S'clyde. Alternative name for Bowhousebog, qv.

Liscard Merseyside 41 H2 dist of Wallasey 2km NW of tn centre. SJ 3092

Liscombe Som 7 F2* ham 4m/6km NW of Dulverton. SS 8732

Liskeard Cornwall 3 G2 tn 11m/18km E of Bodmin and 12m/19km W of Saltash. SX 2564

Lismore S'clyde 70 A2-B1 long, narrow, fertile island in Loch Linnhe, extending 10m/15km from Rubha Fiart north-eastwards to its NE end opp Port Appin on mainland to E. Ferry to Port Appin. NM 8440

Liss Hants 10 D2 vil 3m/5km NE of Petersfield. Includes locs of **E** and **W Liss.** SU 7727

Lissett Humberside 51 F3 vil 2m/4km NW of Skipsea. TA 1458

Liss Forest Hants 11 E2* vil 1m NE of Liss and 4m/6km SW of Liphook. SU 7828

Lissington Lincs 45 E3 vil 4m/6km S of Mkt Rasen. TF 1083

Lisson Grove London 19 F3* loc in City of Westminster 2m/3km NW of Charing Cross. TQ 2781

Listerdale S Yorks 43 H2* loc 3m/4km E of Rotherham. SK 4691

Liston Essex 30 D3 loc 2km SW of Long Melford. TL 8544

Lisvane (Llysfaen) S Glam 15 G3 vil 4m/7km N of Cardiff. **Lisvane Resr** to S, adjoining Llanishen Resr to N. ST 1983

Liswerry Gwent 15 H3 loc in Newport 2m/3km E of tn centre. Steel works to E. ST 3487

Litcham Norfolk 38 D3 vil 7m/11km NE of Swaffham. TF 8817

Litchard Mid Glam 15 E3* loc adjoining Bridgend to N. SS 9081

Litchborough Northants 28 B2 vil 6m/10km SE of Daventry. SP 6354

Litchfield Hants 17 H6 vil 4m/6km N of Whitchurch. SU 4653

Litherland Merseyside 41 H2 tn adjoining Bootle to N. Industries include engineering, tanning, rubber, clothing. SJ 3397

Litlington Cambs 29 G3 vil 3m/5km NW of Royston. TL 3142

Litlington E Sussex 12 B6 vil in valley of Cuckmere R 1m S of Alfriston. TQ 5201

LITTLE. For names beginning with this word, see under next word. This also applies to names beginning with Great, Greater, Lesser; High, Low; Higher, Lower; Upper, Nether; Far, Near; Mid, Middle; Isle(s) of; North, South, East, West; The, Y, Yr.

Littlebeck N Yorks 55 G4 loc 4m/6km S of Whitby. NZ 8704

Littleborough Devon 7 F4* loc 3m/5km SE of Witheridge and 7m/11km N of Crediton. SS 8210

Littleborough Gtr Manchester 48 C6 tn 3m/5km NE of Rochdale. Textiles, engineering, tanning. SD 9316

Littleborough Notts 44 C3 ham on W bank of R Trent on site of Roman stn of *Segelocum*, 4m/7km S of Gainsborough. SK 8282

Littlebourne Kent 13 G2 vil 4m/6km E of Canterbury. TR 2057

Littlebredy (or Little Bredy) Dorset 8 D5 vil 6m/10km W of Dorchester. SY 5889

Littlebury Essex 30 A4 vil 2m/3km NW of Saffron Walden. TL 5139

Littlebury Green Essex 29 H4* ham 3m/5km W of Saffron Walden. TL 4838

Littlecote Wilts 17 G4 Tudor manor hse with park beside R Kennet 2m/4km W of Hungerford. SU 3070

Littlecott Wilts 17 F6* loc across R Avon from Enford and 2m/3km S of Upavon. SU 1451

Littledale Lancs 47 F2* loc 6m/9km E of Lancaster. SD 5661

Littledean Glos 26 B6 vil 1m E of Cinderford. SO 6713

Littleferry H'land 87 B6 locality in Sutherland dist on N side of entrance to Loch Fleet, 3m/5km SW of Golspie. NH 8095

Littlefield Green Berks 18 D4* ham 3m/5km SW of Maidenhead. SU 8676

Littleham Devon 5 F3 vil 2m/3km E of Exmouth. 1m SE on coast, **L. Cove.** SY 0281
Littleham Devon 6 C3 vil 2m/3km S of Bideford. SS 4323
Littlehampton W Sussex 11 F4 coastal resort with sandy beach at mouth of R Arun 8m/12km W of Worthing. Site of Roman villa 1km NE of tn centre. TQ 0202
Littleharle Tower Nthmb 61 E3 modernised medieval tower on E side of Victn mansion 1km N of Kirkharle. NZ 0183
Littlehempston Devon 5 E4 vil 2m/3km NE of Totnes. SX 8162
Littlehoughton Nthmb 67 H6* loc 2km NW of Longhoughton. NU 2316
Littlemill H'land 81 H3 loc in Nairn dist 4m/7km SE of Nairn. NH 9150
Littlemill Nthmb 67 H6* loc 1m E of Rennington. NU 2218
Littlemoor Derbys 43 H4* dist of Chesterfield 2km N of tn centre. SK 3773
Littlemoor Derbys 43 H4* loc 2m/3km W of Clay Cross. SK 3662
Littlemoor Dorset 9 E5* loc 3m/5km N of Weymouth. SY 6883
Littlemore Oxon 18 A2 suburb 3m/4km SE of Oxford. SP 5302
Littlemoss Gtr Manchester 43 E2* loc 2km NW of Ashton-under-Lyne. SJ 9199
Littleover Derbys 35 H1 dist of Derby 2m/3km SW of tn centre. SK 3334
Littleport Cambs 38 A5 vil 5m/7km NE of Ely. Loc of **L. Bridge** 1m NE. TL 5686
Littler Ches 42 C4* loc 2km W of Winsford. SJ 6366
Littlestead Green Oxon 18 C4* ham 3m/4km NE of Reading. SU 7377
Littlestone-on-Sea Kent 13 F4 resort on St Mary's Bay 2km E of New Romney. TR 0824
Littlethorpe N Yorks 49 E2 vil 2m/3km S of Ripon. SE 3269
Littleton Ches 42 A4* vil 2m/4km E of Chester. SJ 4466
Littleton Durham 54 C1* vil 1km N of Sherburn Hill. NZ 3342
Littleton Hants 10 B2 vil 3m/4km NW of Winchester. SU 4532
Littleton Som 8 C2 ham 2km N of Somerton. ST 4930
Littleton Surrey 19 E4 loc on S edge of Queen Mary Resr 2m/3km NE of Chertsey. TQ 0768
Littleton Wilts 16 D5* loc 2m/4km S of Melksham. ST 9060
Littleton Drew Wilts 16 D3 vil 7m/11km NW of Chippenham. ST 8380
Littleton, High Avon 16 B5 vil 3m/5km NW of Midsomer Norton. ST 6458
Littleton, Middle H & W 27 E3 vil 3m/5km NE of Evesham. SP 0746
Littleton, North H & W 27 E3 vil 4m/6km NE of Evesham. SP 0847
Littleton-on-Severn Avon 16 B3 vil 3m/4km W of Thornbury. ST 5989
Littleton Pannell Wilts 17 E5* vil 5m/7km S of Devizes. ST 9953
Littleton, South H & W 27 E3 vil 3m/5km NE of Evesham. SP 0746
Littleton, West Avon 16 C4 vil 2m/3km NW of Marshfield. ST 7675
Littletown Devon 8 A4* S dist of Honiton. SY 1600
Littletown Isle of Wight 10 C5* loc 3m/4km NE of Newport. SZ 5390
Littletown W Yorks 48 D5/49 E5* loc 1m SE of Cleckheaton. SE 2024
Littlewick Green Berks 18 C3 vil 3m/5km W of Maidenhead. Site of Roman bldg to S. SU 8479
Littlewindsor Dorset 8 C4* loc 2km N of Broadwindsor. ST 4404
Littlewood Staffs 35 F4* loc 2m/3km S of Cannock. SJ 9807
Littleworth Beds 29 E3* loc 4m/6km SE of Bedford. TL 0744
Littleworth Glos 27 F4* loc adjoining Chipping Campden to W. SP 1439
Littleworth H & W 26 D3 vil 4m/6km SE of Worcester. SO 8850
Littleworth Oxon 17 G2 vil 2m/3km NE of Faringdon. SU 3197
Littleworth Staffs 35 F2* E dist of Stafford. SJ 9323
Littleworth Staffs 35 F3 loc 2m/4km NE of Cannock. SK 0111
Littleworth S Yorks 44 B2* loc adjoining Rossington to E. SK 6398
Littleworth End Cambs 29 F2 S end of vil of Offord Darcy, 4m/6km SW of Huntingdon. TL 2265
Littleworth End Warwicks 35 G4* loc 3m/4km NE of Sutton Coldfield. SP 1597
Littley Green Essex 30 B6 ham 5m/9km SE of Gt Dunmow. TL 6917
Litton Derbys 43 F4 vil 1m E of Tideswell. SK 1675
Litton N Yorks 48 B1 vil in Littondale 2m/3km NW of Arncliffe. SD 9074
Litton Som 16 B5 vil 6m/10km NE of Wells. ST 5954
Litton Cheney Dorset 8 D5 vil 6m/9km E of Bridport. SY 5590
Littondale N Yorks 48 B1 valley of R Skirfare. SD 97
Livermere, Great Suffolk 30 D1 vil 5m/8km NE of Bury St Edmunds. TL 8871
Liverpool Merseyside 42 A2 major port and industrial city on R Mersey estuary 178m/286km NW of London. University. Anglican and RC cathedrals. Rly tunnel and two rd tunnels under R Mersey to Birkenhead. Airport at Speke, 6m/10km SE. **L. Bay** stretches from Formby Pt to Hoylake. SJ 3490
Liversedge W Yorks 48 D5 tn 3m/5km NW of Dewsbury. SE 2024
Liverton Cleveland 55 F3 vil 2m/3km S of Loftus. **L. Mines** loc with iron ore mines 1m N. NZ 7115
Liverton Devon 4 D3 ham 4m/7km NW of Newton Abbot. SX 8075
Liverton Street Kent 21 E6 loc 2m/3km SW of Lenham. TQ 8750
Livesey Street Kent 20 D6* loc 1km N of Teston. TQ 7054
Livet Water 82 B4 r in Grampian region running NW down Glen Livet to R Avon 8m/12km N of Tomintoul. Also known as R Livet. NJ 1830
Livingston Lothian 65 G2 tn 13m/21km W of Edinburgh. New Tn designated 1962. Various light industries. Tn area includes **L. Station,** loc 2m/4km W of tn centre, and **L. Village,** 2km SW. NT 0568
Liza 52 B3/B4 r in Cumbria. See Ehen.
Lizard Cornwall 2 C6 vil on L. peninsula. To S, Lizard Pt, headland at most southerly point of English mainland. SW 7012
Lizard Point Tyne & Wear 61 H5* headland on North Sea coast at SE end of Marsden Bay. NZ 4164
Llafar 33 F2 r running SE into Bala Lake, Gwynedd. SH 8931
Llafar 40 C4/C5* r rising on W side of Carnedd Llywelyn, Gwynedd, and flowing NW into R Ogwen at Bethesda. SH 6266
Llaingarreglwyd Dyfed 24 A2* loc 2m/3km E of Newquay. SN 4158
Llaingoch Gwynedd 40 A3 loc adjoining Holyhead to W. SH 2382
Llaithddu Powys 33 G6 loc 2m/4km NW of Llanbadarn Fynydd. SO 0680
Llam Carw Gwynedd 40 B2* headland on N coast of Anglesey 1m NE of Amlwch. SH 4593
Llampha Mid Glam 15 E4* loc 3m/5km S of Bridgend. SS 9275
Llan 23 G5* r rising about 3m/5km N of Clydach, W Glam, and flowing S then W into R Lliw S of Gorseinon. SS 5897
Llanaber Gwynedd 32 D3 loc on coast 2m/3km NW of Barmouth. SH 6017
Llanaelhaearn Gwynedd 32 B1 vil on pass to E of The Rivals, 6m/10km N of Pwllheli. SH 3844
Llanafan Dyfed 24 C1 ham 9m/14km SE of Aberystwyth. Remains of Roman fort 1m W. SN 6872
Llanafan-fawr Powys 25 E3 ham 5m/9km NW of Builth Wells. SO 9655
Llanafan-fechan Powys 25 E3 loc 2km E of Garth. SN 9750
Llanallgo Gwynedd 40 C3 ham near E coast of Anglesey 6m/10km SE of Amlwch. SH 5085
Llanandras Welsh form of Presteigne, qv.
Llananno Powys 25 F1* loc 1m NW of Llanbister. SO 0974
Llanarmon Gwynedd 32 C1 loc 4m/6km NE of Pwllheli. SH 4239
Llanarmon Dyffryn Ceiriog Clwyd 33 H1/H2 vil on R Ceiriog 7m/11km SW of Llangollen. SJ 1532
Llanarmon-yn-Ial Clwyd 41 G5 vil on R Alun 4m/7km E of Ruthin. SJ 1956
Llanarth (Llannarth) Dyfed 24 A3 vil 3m/4km SE of Newquay. SN 4257
Llanarth Gwent 25 H6 vil 3m/5km NW of Raglan. SO 3710
Llanarthney (Llanarthne) Dyfed 23 G4 vil 6m/10km W of Llandeilo. SN 5320
Llanasa Clwyd 41 G3 vil 3m/4km E of Prestatyn. SJ 1081
Llanayron Dyfed 24 B2 loc 2m/3km SE of Aberaeron. SN 4760
Llanbabo Gwynedd 40 B3 loc on Anglesey 1m N of Llyn Alaw dam. SH 3786
Llanbadarn Fawr Dyfed 32 D6 suburb of Aberystwyth 2km SE of tn centre. SN 6080
Llanbadarn Fynydd Powys 33 G6 vil 9m/15km S of Newtown. SO 0977
Llanbadarn-y-garreg Powys 25 F3 ham on R Edw 5m/7km E of Builth Wells. SO 1148
Llanbadoc (Llanbadog) Gwent 15 H2 ham 1km S of Usk across r. SO 3700
Llanbadrig Gwynedd 40 B2* loc on N coast of Anglesey to E of Cemaes Bay. SH 3794
Llanbeder (Llanbedr) Gwent 15 H2/H3* vil 3m/5km NW of Magor. ST 3890
Llanbedr Gwynedd 32 D2 vil on R Artro 3m/5km S of Harlech. Royal Aircraft Establishment to W. SH 5826
Llanbedr Powys 25 F3 loc 2m/3km W of Painscastle. SO 1446
Llanbedr Powys 25 G5 vil 2m/3km NE of Crickhowell. SO 2320
Llanbedr Dyffryn Clwyd Clwyd 41 G5 vil 2km NE of Ruthin. SJ 1459
Llanbedr Felffre Welsh form of Lampeter Velfrey, qv.
Llanbedrgoch Gwynedd 40 C3 vil near E coast of Anglesey 4m/7km NE of Llangefni. SH 5180
Llanbedr Gwynllwg Welsh form of Peterstone Wentlloog, qv.
Llanbedrog Gwynedd 32 B2 vil 4m/6km SW of Pwllheli. SH 3231
Llanbedrog Point (Trwyn Llanbedrog) Gwynedd 32 B2 headland at N end of St Tudwal's Bay nearly 1m SE of Llanbedrog. SH 3330
Llanbedr Pont Steffan Welsh form of Lampeter, qv.
Llanbedr-y-cennin Gwynedd 40 D4 vil 5m/8km S of Conwy. SH 7669
Llanbedr-y-fro Welsh form of Peterston-super-Ely, qv.
Llanberis Gwynedd 40 C5 tn in slate-quarrying dist 6m/10km E of Caernarvon at foot of **Pass of Llanberis,** mt pass between Snowdon and Glyder Fawr. Tn is N terminus of Snowdon Mountain Rly. To SE, overlooking Llyn Peris, are the largely 13c remains of Dolbadarn Castle (A.M.). SH 5760
Llanbethery (Llanbydderi) S Glam 15 F4 vil 5m/8km W of Barry. ST 0369
Llanbister Powys 25 F1 vil on R Ithon 8m/12km N of Llandrindod Wells. SO 1073
Llanblethian (Llanfleiddan) S Glam 15 E4 vil adjoining Cowbridge to SW. Remains of medieval cas. SS 9874
Llanboidy Dyfed 22 D3 vil 4m/7km N of Whitland. SN 2123
Llanbradach Mid Glam 15 F3 vil 2m/4km N of Caerphilly. ST 1490
Llanbrynmair Powys 33 F4 vil 5m/8km E of Cemmaes Rd. SH 8902
Llan Bwlch-llyn Lake Powys 25 F3* small lake 3m/5km W of Painscastle. SO 1146
Llanbydderi Welsh form of Llanbethery, qv.
Llancadle (Llancatal) S Glam 15 F4* ham 5m/7km W of Barry. ST 0368
Llancaeach Welsh form of Llancaiach, qv.
Llancaeo Welsh form of Llancayo, qv.
Llancaiach (Llancaeach) Mid Glam 15 F2* loc 1m E of Treharris. ST 1196
Llancarfan S Glam 15 F4 vil 4m/7km NW of Barry. ST 0570
Llancatal Welsh form of Llancadle, qv.
Llancayo (Llancaeo) Gwent 15 H1 loc 2km N of Usk. SO 3603
Llancillo H & W 25 H5* loc 3m/4km SW of Pontrilas. SO 3625
Llancloudy H & W 26 A5* ham 5m/8km N of Monmouth. SO 4920
Llancynfelyn Dyfed 32 D5 loc 2m/3km N of Talybont. SN 6492
Llandaff (Llandaf) S Glam 15 F4 dist of Cardiff 2m/3km NW of city centre. Cathedral of 12c-13c. **Llandaff North,** dist to N across R Taff. ST 1578
Llandanwg Gwynedd 32 D2 vil on Tremadoc Bay 2m/3km S of Harlech. SH 5728
Llandarcy W Glam 14 C2* loc 3m/5km SW of Neath. Oil refinery to W. SS 7195
Llandarog Dyfed 23 F4 vil 6m/10km E of Carmarthen. SN 5016
Llandawke (Llan-dawg) Dyfed 23 E4 ham 3m/5km S of St Clears. SN 2811
Llanddaniel Fab Gwynedd 40 C4 vil on Anglesey 4m/6km W of Menai Br. SH 4970
Llanddeiniol Dyfed 24 B1 ham 6m/10km S of Aberystwyth. SN 5672
Llanddeiniolen Gwynedd 40 C5 ham 4m/7km SW of Bangor. SH 5466
Llandderfel Gwynedd 33 F1 vil in R Dee valley 4m/6km E of Bala. SH 9837
Llanddeusant Dyfed 24 D5 loc 6m/10km S of Llandovery. SN 7724
Llanddeusant Gwynedd 40 A3 vil on Anglesey 6m/9km S of Cemaes Bay. SH 3485
Llanddew Powys 25 F5 vil 2km NE of Brecon. Slight remains of former palace of Bishops of St David's. SO 0530
Llanddewi W Glam 23 F6 ham on Gower peninsula 3m/5km N of Port Eynon Pt and 12m/20km W of Swansea. SS 4689
Llanddewi Brefi Dyfed 24 C3 vil 3m/5km SW of Tregaron. SN 6655
Llanddewi Felffre Welsh form of Llanddewi Velfrey, qv.
Llanddewi Nant Hodni Welsh form of Llanthony, qv.
Llanddewi'r Cwm Powys 25 E3 loc 2m/3km S of Builth Wells. SO 0348
Llanddewi Rhydderch Gwent 25 H6 vil 3m/5km E of Abergavenny. SO 3512
Llanddewi Velfrey (Llanddewi Felffre) Dyfed 22 D4 vil 3m/5km W of Whitland. SN 1416
Llanddewi Ystradenni Powys 25 F1/F2 ham 6m/9km NE of Llandrindod Wells. SO 1068
Llanddingad Welsh form of Dingestow, qv.
Llanddinol Welsh form of Itton, qv.
Llanddoget Gwynedd 41 E5 vil 2km N of Llanrwst. SH 8063
Llanddona Gwynedd 40 C3 vil on Anglesey 3m/5km NW of Beaumaris. SH 5779
Llanddowror Dyfed 23 E4 vil 2m/3km SW of St Clears. Site of Roman fort 2km S. SN 2514
Llanddulas Clwyd 41 E4 vil 2m/4km W of Abergele. SH 9078
Llanddunwyd Welsh form of Welsh St Donats, qv.
Llanddwyn Island Gwynedd 40 B5 peninsula on SW coast of Anglesey 3m/5km SW of Newborough. **Llanddwyn Bay** to E. SH 3862
Llanddwywe Gwynedd 32 D2 ham 4m/7km N of Barmouth. SH 5822
Llandecwyn Gwynedd 32 D1* loc 3m/5km SW of Maentwrog. SH 6337
Llandefaelog Fach Powys 25 E4 loc 3m/4km N of Brecon. SO 0332
Llandefalle (Llandyfalle) Powys 25 F4 ham 3m/5km W of Talgarth. SO 1035
Llandegai Gwynedd 40 C4 vil 2km SE of Bangor. SH 5970
Llandegfan Gwynedd 40 C4 vil on Anglesey 2km NE of Menai Br. SH 5673
Llandegfedd Reservoir Gwent 15 H2 large resr 3m/5km W of Usk. See also Llandegveth. ST 3299
Llandegla Clwyd 41 G6 ham 6m/9km SE of Ruthin. SJ 1952
Llandegley Powys 25 F2 ham 2m/3km SE of Penybont. **Llandegley Rocks** to SW. SO 1362
Llandegveth (Llandegfedd) Gwent 15 H2* vil 4m/7km SW of Usk. Llandegfedd Resr, qv, is 2m/4km N. ST 3395
Llandegwning Gwynedd 32 B2 loc 3m/5km NW of Abersoch. SH 2630
Llandeilo Dyfed 23 G3 tn on R Towy near its confluence with R Cennen 14m/22km E of Carmarthen. SN 6322
Llandeilo Bertholau Welsh form of Llantilio Pertholey, qv.
Llandeilo Ferwallt Welsh form of Bishopston, qv.
Llandeilo Graban Powys 25 F3 ham 5m/8km SE of Builth Wells. SO 0944
Llandeilo Gresynni Welsh form of Llantilio Crossenny, qv.
Llandeloy (Llan-lwy) Dyfed 22 B3 vil 7m/11km E of St David's. SM 8526
Llandenny (Llandenni) Gwent 15 H1 vil 3m/5km NE of Usk. SO 4103
Llandevaud Gwent 15 H2/H3* vil 3m/4km NW of Magor. ST 4090
Llandevenny Gwent 15 H3 ham 1m W of Magor. ST 4186
Llandilo Dyfed 22 D3* ham 1m W of Llangolman. SN 1027
Llandinabo H & W 26 A4 loc 6m/10km NW of Ross-on-Wye. SO 5128
Llandinam Powys 33 G5 vil on R Severn 2m/4km S of Caersws. SO 0288
Llandissilio Dyfed 22 D4 vil 5m/7km N of Narberth. SN 1221

Llandoche Welsh form of Llandough, qv.
Llandogo Gwent 16 A1 vil on R Wye 6m/10km N of Chepstow. SO 5204
Llandough (Llandoche) S Glam 15 F4/G4 N dist of Penarth. ST 1673
Llandough S Glam 15 E4 ham 1m S of Cowbridge. SS 9972
Llandovery (Llanymddyfri) Dyfed 24 D4 small tn at confluence of Rs Bran and Gwydderig and 2km above confluence of Rs Bran and Towy, 17m/28km W of Brecon. Scanty remains of Norman cas. SN 7634
Llandow (Llandw) S Glam 15 E4 vil 4m/6km W of Cowbridge. **Llandow Industrial Estate** 2km SE in par of Llantwit Major. SS 9473
Llandre Dyfed. Alternative name of Llanfihangel Genau'r-glyn, qv.
Llandrillo Clwyd 33 G1 vil on R Ceidiog 5m/8km SW of Corwen. SJ 0337
Llandrillo-yn-Rhos Clwyd 41 E3 NW dist of Colwyn Bay. SH 8380
Llandrindod Wells Powys 25 F2 spa tn with bracing climate 30m/48km NW of Hereford. See also *Castellcollen* and Cefnllys Castle. SO 0561
Llandrinio Powys 34 A3 vil 7m/12km NE of Welshpool. SJ 2817
Llandudno Gwynedd 40 D3 coastal resort at base of peninsula running out to Gt Ormes Hd. SH 7882
Llandudno Junction Gwynedd 41 E4 rly junction and suburb 3m/5km SE of Llandudno. SJ 8077
Llandudoch Welsh form of St Dogmaels, qv.
Llandw Welsh form of Llandow, qv.
Llandwrog Gwynedd 40 B5 vil 5m/7km SW of Caernarvon. SH 4556
Llandybie Dyfed 23 G4 vil 2m/3km N of Ammanford. SN 6115
Llandyfaelog Dyfed 23 F4 vil 3m/5km N of Kidwelly. SN 4111
Llandyfaelog Tre'r-graig Powys 25 F5* loc 2km NW of Llangorse. SO 1229
Llandyfai Welsh form of Lamphey, qv.
Llandyfalle Welsh form of Llandefalle, qv.
Llandyfan Dyfed 23 G4* loc 3m/5km N of Ammanford. SN 6417
Llandyfeisant Dyfed 23 G3* par on W side of Llandeilo, with ch on edge of Dynevor Park, supposedly on site of Roman temple. SN 6222
Llandyfodwg Mid Glam 15 E3 vil 6m/9km NE of Bridgend. SS 9587
Llandyfriog Dyfed 23 E2 ham 2m/3km E of Newcastle Emlyn. SN 3341
Llandyfrydog Gwynedd 40 B3 loc on Anglesey 2m/3km NE of Llanerchymedd. SH 4485
Llandygwydd Dyfed 22 D2/23 E2 vil 4m/7km SE of Cardigan. SN 2443
Llandynan Clwyd 33 H1* loc 3m/4km NW of Llangollen. SJ 1844
Llandyrnog Clwyd 41 G5 vil 4m/6km E of Denbigh. SJ 1064
Llandysilio Powys 34 A3 ham 7m/11km S of Oswestry. SJ 2619
Llandyssul Dyfed 24 A4 small tn on R Teifi 12m/20km N of Carmarthen. Woollen mnfre. SN 4140
Llandysul Powys 33 H4/H5 vil 2m/3km W of Montgomery. SO 1995
Llanedern Welsh form of Llanedeyrn, qv.
Llanedeyrn (Llanedern) S Glam 15 G3 ham on Rhymney R 4m/6km NE of Cardiff. ST 2583
Llanedy (Llanedi) Dyfed 23 G5* loc 2m/3km N of Pontarddulais. SN 5806
Llaneglwys Powys 25 F4* loc 3m/5km NE of Lr Chapel. SO 0638
Llanegryn Gwynedd 32 D4 vil 3m/5km N of Tywyn. SH 6005
Llanegwad Dyfed 23 F3* vil 7m/11km E of Carmarthen. SN 5121
Llaneirwg Welsh form of St Mellons, qv.
Llanelen Welsh form of Llanellen, qv.
Llaneleu Welsh form of Llanelieu, qv.
Llanelian-yn-Rhos Clwyd 41 E4 vil 2m/3km SE of Colwyn Bay. SH 8676
Llanelidan Clwyd 41 G6 vil 5m/8km S of Ruthin. SJ 1050
Llanelieu (Llaneleu) Powys 25 F4/G4 ham 2m/3km E of Talgarth. SO 1834
Llanellen (Llanelen) Gwent 25 G6 vil on R Usk 2m/3km S of Abergavenny. SO 3010
Llanelli Dyfed 23 F5 industrial tn on N bank of Burry Inlet 10m/16km NW of Swansea across R Loughor. Mnfre of tinplate and sheet metal, vehicle components, radiators, rubber goods. Iron foundry. Engineering. SN 5000
Llanelltyd (Llanelltud) Gwynedd 33 E3 vil 2km NW of Dolgellau. See also Cymer Abbey. SH 7119
Llanelly Gwent 25 G6* loc 1m W of Gilwern. SO 2314
Llanelwedd Powys 25 E3/F3* vil opp Builth Wells across R Wye. Venue of annual Royal Welsh Agricultural Show. SO 0451
Llanelwy Welsh form of St Asaph, qv.
Llanenddwyn Gwynedd 32 D2 loc 5m/8km N of Barmouth. SH 5823
Llanengan Gwynedd 32 B2 vil 2km SW of Abersoch. SH 2927
Llanerchymedd Gwynedd 40 B3 vil on Anglesey 6m/9km S of Amlwch. SH 4184
Llanerfyl Powys 33 G3 vil 5m/8km NW of Llanfair Caereinion. SJ 0309
Llaneuddog Gwynedd 40 B3* loc on Anglesey 4m/6km SE of Amlwch. SH 4688
Llaneurgain Welsh form of Northop, qv.
Llanfable Welsh form of Llanvapley, qv.
Llanfach Gwent 15 G2* loc on E side of Abercarn. ST 2295
Llanfaches Welsh form of Llanvaches, qv.
Llanfachraeth Gwynedd 40 A3 vil on Anglesey 4m/7km E of Holyhead across Holyhead Bay. SH 3182
Llanfachreth Gwynedd 33 E2 ham 3m/5km NE of Dolgellau. SH 7522
Llanfadog, Lower Powys 25 E2* loc 2m/4km SW of Rhayader. SN 9365
Llanfaelog Gwynedd 40 A4 vil near W coast of Anglesey 5m/8km SE of Valley. Ty Newydd Burial-chamber (A.M.) 1km NE. SH 3373
Llanfaenor Gwent 26 A5* loc 3m/4km SW of Skenfrith. SO 4316
Llanfaes Gwynedd 40 C4 loc on Anglesey 1m N of Beaumaris. SH 6077
Llanfaes Powys 25 E5 loc adjoining Brecon to W. SO 0328
Llanfaes Welsh form of Llanmaes, qv.
Llanfaethlu Gwynedd 40 A3 vil on Anglesey 4m/6km S of Carmel Hd. SH 3186
Llanfaglan Gwynedd 40 B5 ham 2m/3km SW of Caernarvon. SH 4760
Llanfair Gwynedd 32 D2 vil 2km S of Harlech. SH 5729
Llan-fair Welsh form of St Mary Church, qv.
Llanfair Caereinion Powys 33 G4 small tn on R Banwy 8m/12km W of Welshpool. SJ 1006
Llanfair Clydogau Dyfed 24 C3 vil at confluence of Rs Clywedog and Teifi 4m/6km NE of Lampeter. Silver mines date from Roman times. SN 6251
Llanfair Dyffryn Clwyd Clwyd 41 G5 vil 2m/3km S of Ruthin. SJ 1355
Llanfairfechan Gwynedd 40 D4 small resort on Conwy Bay midway between Bangor and Conwy. SH 6874
Llanfair Isgoed (or **Llanfair Disgoed**) Welsh form of Llanvair Discoed, qv.
Llanfair Kilgeddin Gwent 15 H1* loc 4m/7km NW of Usk. SO 3407
Llanfair Llythynwg Welsh form of Gladestry, qv.
Llanfair Nant-gwyn Dyfed 22 D2 loc 5m/9km S of Cardigan. SN 1637
Llanfair-Orllwyn Dyfed 23 E2 loc 3m/5km W of Llandyssul. SN 3641
Llanfairpwllgwyngyll Gwynedd 40 C4 vil on Anglesey 2m/3km W of Menai Br. SH 5271
Llanfair Talhaiarn Clwyd 41 F4 vil on R Elwy 5m/8km S of Abergele. SH 9270
Llanfair Waterdine Salop 34 A6 vil 4m/6km NW of Knighton. SO 2476
Llanfair-ym-Muallt Welsh form of Builth Wells, qv.
Llanfairynghornwy Gwynedd 40 A3 vil near N coast of Anglesey 2m/4km SE of Carmel Hd. SH 3290
Llanfair-yn-Neubwll Gwynedd 40 A4* vil on Anglesey at N end of Valley Airfield. SH 3076
Llanfallteg Dyfed 22 D4 ham 4m/6km NW of Whitland. Ham of Llanfallteg West 1km SW. SN 1519
Llanfaredd Powys 25 F3 loc 2m/3km E of Builth Wells across R Wye. SO 0650
Llanfarian Dyfed 24 B1 vil 3m/4km S of Aberystwyth. SN 5977
Llanfarthin Welsh form of Llanmartin, qv.
Llanfechain Powys 33 H2/H3 vil on R Cain 3m/5km E of Llanfyllin. Motte and bailey cas on W side of vil. SJ 1820
Llanfechell Gwynedd 40 B3 vil near N coast of Anglesey 2m/3km S of Cemaes Bay. SH 3691
Llanferres Clwyd 41 G5 vil 4m/6km SW of Mold. SJ 1860
Llanfeuthin Welsh form of Llanvithyn, qv.
Llanfflewyn Gwynedd 40 B3* loc on Anglesey 3m/5km S of Cemaes Bay. SH 3589
Llanfigel Gwynedd 40 A3 loc on Anglesey nearly 1m E of Llanfachraeth. SH 3282
Llanfihangel Powys 33 G3 vil 4m/7km W of Llanfyllin. The full name is Llanfihangel-yng-Ngwynfa. SJ 0816
Llanfihangel Welsh form of Llanvihangel.
Llanfihangel-ar-Arth Dyfed 24 A4 vil 3m/4km E of Llandyssul. SN 4539
Llanfihangel-ar-Elai Welsh form of Michaelston-super-Ely, qv.
Llanfihangel Crucornau Welsh form of Llanvihangel Crucorney, qv.
Llanfihangel Genau'r-glyn Dyfed 32 D5 vil 4m/7km NE of Aberystwyth. Also known as Llandre. SN 6286
Llanfihangel Glyn Myfyr Clwyd 41 F6 vil 3m/4km E of Cerrigydrudion. SH 9949
Llanfihangel Nant Bran Powys 25 E4 ham 7m/11km NW of Brecon. SN 9434
Llanfihangel nant Melan Powys 25 F2 loc 3m/4km SW of New Radnor. SO 1858
Llanfihangel-Penbedw Dyfed 22 D2* loc 5m/7km SE of Cardigan. SN 2039
Llanfihangel Rhydieithon Powys 25 F2 ham 4m/6km E of Crossgates. SO 1566
Llanfihangel Tal-y-llyn Powys 25 F5 vil 4m/7km E of Brecon. SO 1128
Llanfihangel Troddi Welsh form of Mitchel Troy, qv.
Llanfihangel-uwch-Gwili Dyfed 23 F3* loc 5m/8km E of Carmarthen. SN 4822
Llanfihangel y Bont-faen Welsh form of Llanmihangel, qv.
Llanfihangel-y-Creuddyn Dyfed 24 C1 vil 5m/8km W of Devil's Br. SN 6676
Llanfihangel-y-fedw Welsh form of Michaelston-y-Vedw, qv.
Llanfihangel-y-gofion Welsh form of Llanvihangel Gobion, qv.
Llanfihangel-yng-Ngwynfa Powys 33 G3 vil 4m/7km W of Llanfyllin. SJ 0816
Llanfihangel yn Nhywyn Gwynedd 40 A4* vil 2m/3km SE of Valley, Anglesey. SH 3277
Llanfihangel-y-Pennant Gwynedd 32 C1* loc 5m/7km NW of Portmadoc. SH 5244
Llanfihangel-y-Pennant Gwynedd 32 D4 loc 8m/12km NE of Tywyn. See also Castell y Bere. SH 6708
Llanfihangel-y-pwll Welsh form of Michaelston-le-Pit.
Llanfihangel Ystum Llywern Welsh form of Llanvihangel Ystern Llewern, qv.
Llanfihangel-y-traethau Gwynedd 32 D1 ham 3m/4km N of Harlech. SH 5935
Llanfilo Powys 25 F4 vil 2m/4km W of Talgarth. SO 1133
Llanfleiddan Welsh form of Llanblethian, qv.
Llanfoist Gwent 25 G6 vil 1m SW of Abergavenny across R Usk. SO 2813
Llanfor Gwynedd 33 F1 ham 1km E of Bala. SH 9336
Llanfrechfa Gwent 15 G2 vil 2m/3km E of Cwmbran. ST 3193
Llanfrothen Gwynedd 32 D1* loc 2m/3km N of Penrhyndeudraeth. SH 6241
Llanfrynach Powys 25 F5 vil 3m/4km SE of Brecon. Site of Roman bath hse to W. SO 0725
Llanfwrog Clwyd 41 G5 loc adjoining Ruthin to W, across R Clwyd. SJ 1157
Llanfwrog Gwynedd 40 A3 ham on Anglesey 4m/6km E of Holyhead across Holyhead Bay. SH 3084
Llanfyllin Powys 33 H3 small tn on R Cain 9m/14km NW of Welshpool. SJ 1419
Llanfynydd Clwyd 41 H5 vil on line of Offa's Dyke 5m/8km NW of Wrexham. SJ 2756
Llanfynydd Dyfed 24 B5 vil 6m/9km NW of Llandeilo. SN 5527
Llanfyrnach Dyfed 22 D3 vil 3m/5km SE of Crymmych. SN 2231
Llangadfan Powys 33 G3 vil 6m/10km NW of Llanfair Caereinion. SJ 0110
Llangadog Dyfed 23 F5* loc 1m NE of Kidwelly. SN 4006
Llangadog Dyfed 24 C5 vil 5m/9km SW of Llandovery. SN 7028
Llangadwaladr Clwyd 33 H2* loc 2m/4km NW of Llansilin. SJ 1830
Llangadwaladr Gwynedd 40 B4 ham on Anglesey 2m/3km E of Aberffraw. SH 3869
Llangaffo Gwynedd 40 B4 vil on Anglesey 7m/12km W of Menai Br. SH 4468
Llangain Dyfed 23 F4* loc 3m/5km SW of Carmarthen. SN 3815
Llangammarch Wells Powys 25 E3 spa vil at confluence of Rs Cammarch and Irfon 4m/6km E of Llanwrtyd Wells. The mineral springs contain barium chloride, unique in Britain. SN 9347
Llangan S Glam 15 E4 vil 3m/5km NW of Cowbridge. SS 9577
Llangarron H & W 26 A5 vil 5m/9km N of Monmouth. SO 5221
Llangasty-Talyllyn Powys 25 f5* ch on S shore of Llangorse Lake. Par includes half of lake. SO 1326
Llangathen Dyfed 23 G3 vil 3m/5km W of Llandeilo. SN 5822
Llangattock (Llangatwg) Powys 25 G6 vil 1km SW of Crickhowell across R Usk. SO 2117
Llangattock Lingoed (Llangatwg Lingoed) Gwent 25 H5 vil 5m/9km NE of Abergavenny. SO 3620
Llangattock nigh Usk (Llangatwg Dyffryn Wysg) Gwent 15 H1 vil 3m/5km SE of Abergavenny. Also known as The Bryn. SO 3305
Llangattock Vibon Avel (Llangatwg Feibion Afel) Gwent 26 A5 loc 4m/6km NW of Monmouth. SO 4515
Llangatwg Welsh form of Cadoxton-juxta-Neath, qv.
Llangatwg Welsh form of Llangattock, qv.
Llangatwg Dyffryn Wysg Welsh form of Llangattock nigh Usk, qv.
Llangatwg Feibion Afel Welsh form of Llangattock Vibon Avel, qv.
Llangatwg Lingoed Welsh form of Llangattock Lingoed, qv.
Llangedwyn Clwyd 33 H2 ham 3m/5km S of Llansilin. SJ 1824
Llangefni Gwynedd 40 B4 mkt tn on R Cefni on Anglesey 7m/11km W of Menai Br. Mnfre of agricultural implements. SH 4575
Llangeinor (Llangeinwyr) Mid Glam 15 E3 vil 5m/8km N of Bridgend. SS 9187
Llangeitho Dyfed 24 B2/C2 vil 4m/6km W of Tregaron. SN 6159
Llangeler Dyfed 23 E2 vil 4m/7km E of Newcastle Emlyn. SN 3739
Llangelynin Gwynedd 32 D4 ham on Cardigan Bay 4m/7km N of Tywyn. SH 5707
Llangennech Dyfed 23 G5 vil 4m/6km E of Llanelli. SN 5601
Llangennith (Llangynydd) W Glam 23 F6 vil near W end of Gower peninsula 2m/3km E of Burry Holms. SS 4291
Llangenny Powys 25 G6* loc 2km E of Crickhowell. SO 2418
Llangernyw Clwyd 41 E4 vil 6m/10km NE of Llanrwst. SH 8767
Llangeview (Llangyfiw) Gwent 15 H2* loc 2km E of Usk. SO 3900
Llangian Gwynedd 32 B2 vil 2km W of Abersoch. SH 2928
Llangiwa Gwent. Alternative spelling of Llangua, qv.
Llangiwg W Glam 14 C1 loc 1m N of Pontardawe. SN 7205
Llangloffan Dyfed 22 B3* ham 2km SE of Granston. SM 9032
Llanglydwen Dyfed 22 D3 ham 6m/10km N of Whitland. SN 1826
Llangoed Gwynedd 40 C3 vil on Anglesey 2m/3km N of Beaumaris. SH 6079
Llangoedmor Dyfed 22 D2 loc 2km E of Cardigan. SN 1945
Llangofen Welsh form of Llangoven, qv.
Llangollen Clwyd 41 H6 tn on R Dee at head of Vale of Llangollen 9m/15km SW of Wrexham. Tourist centre. Industries include engineering, flannel mnfre, seed-packing, tanning. Annual International Eisteddfod. Canal connection with Shropshire Union Canal (Hurleston Junction). See also Valle Crucis Abbey. SJ 2141
Llangolman Dyfed 22 D3 vil 8m/12km N of Narberth. SN 1127

Llangorse (Llangors) Powys 25 F5 vil 4m/7km S of Talgarth. To S is **Llangorse Lake** (Llyn Syfaddan), large lake, 4m/6km in circumference. SO 1327
Llangorwen Dyfed 32 D6 loc 2m/3km NE of Aberystwyth. SN 6083
Llangovan Gwent 16 A1 alternative spelling for Llangoven, qv.
Llangoven (Llangofen) Gwent 16 A1 loc 3m/5km SE of Raglan. Also known as Llangovan. SO 4505
Llangower Gwynedd 33 F2 loc on E side of Bala Lake 3m/5km S of Bala. SH 9032
Llangrallo Welsh form of Coychurch, qv.
Llangranog (or Llangrannog) Dyfed 23 E1 vil on coast 6m/10km SW of New Quay. SN 3154
Llangristiolus Gwynedd 40 B4 vil on Anglesey 2km S of Llangefni. SH 4473
Llangrove H & W 26 A5 vil 4m/7km N of Monmouth. SO 5219
Llangua Gwent 25 H5 loc 2km SW of Pontrilas. SO 3925
Llangunllo Powys. See Llangynllo.
Llangunnor (Llangynnwr) Dyfed 23 F4 ham 2km E of Carmarthen across R Towy. SN 4220
Llangurig Powys 33 F6 vil on R Wye 4m/6km SW of Llanidloes. SN 9079
Llangwm Clwyd 33 F1 vil 7m/11km W of Corwen. SH 9644
Llangwm Dyfed 22 C4/C5 vil 3m/5km NE of Neyland, at head of creek running into Daugleddau R. SM 9909
Llangwm Gwent 15 H2 vil 3m/5km E of Usk. **Llangwm-isaf** vil nearby to NE. SO 4200
Llangwnnadl Gwynedd 32 A2 ham 3m/5km SW of Tudweiliog. SH 2033
Llangwyfan Clwyd 41 G4* loc 5m/8km N of Ruthin. N Wales Sanatorium. SJ 1266
Llangwyllog Gwynedd 40 B3 loc on Anglesey 3m/5km NW of Llangefni. SH 4379
Llangwyryfon Dyfed 24 B1 vil 7m/11km S of Aberystwyth. SN 5970
Llangybi Dyfed 24 B3 vil 4m/6km NE of Lampeter. SN 6053
Llangybi Gwent 15 H2 vil 3m/4km S of Usk. Ruined keep of Norman cas to NW. ST 3796
Llangybi Gwynedd 32 C1 ham 5m/8km NE of Pwllheli. SH 4241
Llangyfelach W Glam 23 G5 loc 4m/6km N of Swansea. SS 6498
Llangyfiw Welsh form of Llangeview, qv.
Llangyndeyrn Dyfed 23 F4 vil 5m/7km SE of Carmarthen. SN 4514
Llangynhafal Clwyd 41 G5 ham 3m/5km N of Ruthin. SJ 1263
Llangynidr Powys 25 F5 vil 4m/6km W of Crickhowell. **Llangynidr Resr** 3m/5km S. SO 1519
Llangynin Dyfed 23 E4* vil 3m/5km NW of St Clears. SN 2519
Llangynllo Dyfed 23 E2* loc 4m/6km NE of Newcastle Emlyn. SN 3543
Llangynllo (or Llangunllo) Powys 25 G1 vil in upper reaches of R Lugg valley 5m/8km W of Knighton. SO 2171
Llangynnwr Welsh form of Llangunnor, qv.
Llangynog Dyfed 23 E4 vil 5m/8km SW of Carmarthen. SN 3316
Llangynog Powys 33 G2 vil 5m/7km W of Llanrhaeadr-ym-Mochnant. Granite quarries. SJ 0526
Llangynwyd Mid Glam 14 D3 vil 2m/3km S of Maesteg. SS 8588
Llangynydd Welsh form of Llangennith, qv.
Llanhamlach Powys 25 F5 ham 3m/5km E of Brecon. SO 0926
Llanharan Mid Glam 15 E3 vil 6m/10km E of Bridgend. ST 0083
Llanharry (Llanhari) Mid Glam 15 E3 vil 3m/5km SW of Llantrisant. ST 0080
Llanhennock Gwent 15 H2 vil 2km NE of Caerleon. ST 3592
Llanhilleth (Llanhiledd) Gwent 15 G2 vil 2m/3km S of Abertillery. SO 2100
Llanidan Gwynedd 40 B4* loc on Anglesey 1km E of Brynsiencyn. To W are various antiquities, incl Bodowyr Burial-chamber, and the ancient earthworks Caer Leb and Castell Bryn-Gwyn (all A.M.). SH 4966
Llanidloes Powys 33 F5 small tn at confluence of Rs Clywedog and Severn 11m/17km SW of Newtown. Industries include leather-working. Museum of local history and industry in Tudor Old Market Hall. SN 9584
Llaniestyn Gwynedd 32 B2 ham 4m/7km NW of Abersoch. SH 2633
Llanigon Powys 25 G4 vil 2m/3km SW of Hay-on-Wye. SO 2139
Llanilar Dyfed 24 C1 vil 5m/8km SE of Aberystwyth. SN 6275
Llanilid Mid Glam 15 E3 ham 5m/8km E of Bridgend. Traces of medieval cas. SS 9781
Llanilltern Mid Glam. See Capel Llanilltern.
Llanilltud Faerdref Welsh form of Llantwit Fardre, qv.
Llanilltud Fawr Welsh form of Llantwit Major, qv.
Llanilltud Gŵyr Welsh form of Ilston, qv.
Llanishen (Llanisien) Gwent 16 A2 vil 3m/4km N of Devauden. SO 4703
Llanishen (Llanisien) S Glam 15 G3 dist of Cardiff 3m/5km N of city centre. **Llanishen Resr** to E. ST 1781
Llanismel Welsh form of St Ishmael, qv.
Llanllawddog Dyfed 24 A5 loc 6m/10km NE of Carmarthen. SN 4529
Llanllechid Gwynedd 40 C4 vil 2km N of Bethesda. SH 6268
Llanlleiana Head Gwynedd 40 B2 headland on N coast of Anglesey 2m/3km NE of Cemaes Bay. See also Dinas Gynfor. SH 3895
Llanlleonfel Powys 25 E3* loc 1m W of Garth. At Caerau, 1m W, is site of Roman fort. SN 9349
Llanllugan Powys 33 G4 ham 4m/6km SW of Llanfair Caereinion. SJ 0502
Llanllwch Dyfed 23 F4 ham 2m/3km SW of Carmarthen. SN 3818
Llanllwchaiarn Powys 33 H5* ham 2km NE of Newtown. Remains of motte and bailey cas across R Severn. SO 1292
Llanllwni Dyfed 24 B4* ham 4m/6km SW of Llanybydder. SN 4839
Llanllyfni Gwynedd 40 B6 vil on S bank of R Llyfni 7m/11km S of Caernarvon. SH 4752
Llanllywel Gwent 15 H2 ham 2m/3km S of Usk. ST 3998
Llan-lwy Welsh form of Llandeloy, qv.
Llanmadog W Glam 23 F6 vil at W end of Gower peninsula 13m/22km W of Swansea and 2m/4km S of Whitford Pt. Hill fort known as The Bulwark (mostly NT) to S. SS 4493
Llanmaes (Llanfaes) S Glam 15 E4 vil 1m NE of Llantwit Major. SS 9869
Llanmartin (Llanfarthin) Gwent 15 H3 vil 5m/9km E of Newport. ST 3989
Llanmellin Gwent 16 A2* loc 2km N of Caerwent, qv. ST 4592
Llanmerewig Powys 33 H5* loc 3m/5km E of Newtown. SO 1592
Llanmihangel (Llanfihangel y Bont-faen) S Glam 15 E4* ham 2m/3km SW of Cowbridge. SS 9871
Llan-mill Dyfed 22 D4* loc 2m/3km E of Narberth. SN 1414
Llanmiloe Dyfed 23 E5* vil 4m/6km W of Laugharne. SN 2508
Llanmorlais W Glam 23 G6 ham 8m/13km W of Swansea. SS 5294
Llannarth Welsh form of Llanarth, Dyfed, qv.
Llannefydd Clwyd 41 F4 vil 5m/8km NW of Denbigh. SH 9870
Llannerch-y-môr Clwyd 41 G3 loc 2km SE of Mostyn. SJ 1779
Llannewydd Welsh form of Newchurch, qv.
Llannon Dyfed 23 G4 vil 5m/9km N of Llanelli. SN 5308
Llannor Gwynedd 32 B1 vil 2m/3km NW of Pwllheli. SH 3537
Llanofer Fawr Welsh form of Llanover, qv.
Llanon Dyfed 24 B2 vil 4m/7km NE of Aberaeron. SN 5166
Llanover (Llanofer Fawr) Gwent 15 G1 loc 4m/6km S of Abergavenny. SO 3108
Llanpumsaint Dyfed 24 A5 ham 6m/9km N of Carmarthen. SN 4129
Llanreithan (Llanrheithan) Dyfed 22 B3 loc 8m/13km SW of Fishguard. SM 8628
Llanrhaeadr Clwyd 41 G5 vil 3m/4km SE of Denbigh. SJ 0863
Llanrhaeadr-ym-Mochnant Clwyd 33 G2 vil on Powys border (R Rhaeadr) 4m/7km N of Llanfyllin. SJ 1226
Llanrheithan Welsh form of Llanreithan, qv.
Llanrhian Welsh form of Llanrian, qv.
Llanrhidian W Glam 23 F6 vil on Gower peninsula 10m/16km W of Swansea. Llanrhidian Marshes (NT), extensive salt marshes to N, on S side of Burry Inlet. SS 4992
Llanrhos Gwynedd 41 E3 loc 2km S of Llandudno. SH 7980
Llanrhyddlad Gwynedd 40 A3 vil near NW coast of Anglesey 3m/5km SE of Carmel Hd. SH 3389
Llanrhymni Welsh form of Llanrumney, qv.
Llanrhystud Dyfed 24 B2 vil 7m/11km NE of Aberaeron. SN 5369
Llanrian (Llanrhian) Dyfed 22 B3 ham 6m/9km NE of St David's. SM 8131
Llanrug Gwynedd 40 C5 vil 4m/6km E of Caernarvon. SH 5363
Llanrumney (Llanrhymni) S Glam dist of Cardiff 4m/6km NE of city centre. ST 2280
Llanrwst Gwynedd 41 E5 small tn on R Conwy 11m/18km S of Colwyn Bay. SH 7961
Llansadurnen Dyfed 23 E4 ham 4m/6km S of St Clears. SN 2810
Llansadwrn Dyfed 24 C5 vil 5m/8km SW of Llandovery. SN 6931
Llansadwrn Gwynedd 40 C4 ham on Anglesey 3m/4km N of Menai Br. SH 5575
Llan Sain Siôr Welsh form of St George or St George's, qv.
Llansaint Dyfed 23 F5 vil 2m/3km NW of Kidwelly. SN 3808
Llansamlet W Glam 23 H5 loc in Swansea 4m/6km NE of tn centre. SS 6897
Llansanffraid Dyfed 24 B2 ham near coast 4m/7km NE of Aberaeron. SN 5167
Llansanffraid Powys 25 F5 ham on R Usk 6m/9km SE of Brecon. SO 1223
Llansanffraid-ar-Elai Welsh form of St Bride's-super-Ely, qv.
Llansanffraid Cwmteuddwr Powys 25 E2 vil opp Rhayader across R Wye. SN 9667
Llansanffraid Glan Conwy Gwynedd 41 E4 vil in R Conwy valley 4m/6km SW of Colwyn Bay. SH 8075
Llansanffraid Gwynllwg Welsh form of St Bride's Wentlloog, qv.
Llansanffraid-ym-Mechain Powys 33 H2 vil 5m/8km E of Llanfyllin. SJ 2120
Llansanffraid-yn-Elfael Welsh form of Llansantffraed-in-Elwell, qv.
Llansannan Clwyd 41 F4/F5 vil on R Aled 7m/12km W of Denbigh. SH 9365
Llansannor (Llansanwyr) S Glam 15 E4* loc 2m/3km N of Cowbridge. SS 9977
Llansantffraed-in-Elwell (Llansanffraid-yn-Elfael) Powys 25 F3 vil 4m/7km NE of Builth Wells. SO 0954
Llansanwyr Welsh form of Llansannor, qv.
Llansawel Dyfed 24 C4 vil 9m/14km N of Llandeilo. SN 6136
Llansawel Welsh form of Briton Ferry, qv.
Llansbyddyd Powys 25 E5 ham 2m/3km W of Brecon. SO 0128
Llansilin Clwyd 33 H2 vil 6m/9km E of Llanrhaeadr-ym-Mochnant. SJ 2028
Llansoy (Llan-soe) Gwent 15 H1/H2 ham 4m/7km E of Usk. SO 4402
Llanstadwell Dyfed 22 C5 vil adjoining Neyland to W. SM 9505
Llansteffan Dyfed 23 E4 vil on R Towy estuary 7m/11km SW of Carmarthen. Ruined cas (A.M.) beside r to S. St Anthony's Well, wishing well to SW of cas, said to have medicinal properties. SN 3510
Llanstephan (Llansteffan) Powys 25 F4 loc 8m/12km SE of Builth Wells. SO 1142
Llantarnam Gwent 15 G2 SE dist of Cwmbran. Biscuit factory. ST 3093
Llanteg Dyfed 22 D4* ham 4m/7km S of Whitland. SN 1810
Llanthony (Llanddewi Nant Hodni) Gwent 25 G5 ham in R Honddu valley in Black Mts 9m/14km N of Abergavenny. Remains of 12c priory (A.M.). SO 2827
Llantilio Crossenny (Llandeilo Gresynni) Gwent 25 H6 ham 6m/10km E of Abergavenny. See also Hen Gwrt. SO 3914
Llantilio Pertholey (Llandeilo Bertholau) Gwent 25 G6* ham 2m/3km N of Abergavenny. SO 3116
Llantood Dyfed 22 D2 loc 3m/5km SW of Cardigan. SN 1541
Llantriddyd S Glam 15 F4 vil 3m/5km E of Cowbridge. ST 0472
Llantrisant (Llantrisaint or Llantrissent) Gwent 15 H2 vil in valley of R Usk 3m/4km S of Usk. ST 3996
Llantrisant Gwynedd 40 B3* loc on Anglesey 2m/3km SE of Llanddeusant. Tregwhelydd Standing Stone (A.M.) 2km W. SH 3483
Llantrisant Mid Glam 15 F3 vil 4m/7km S of Pontypridd. ST 0483
Llantwit Fardre (Llanilltud Faerdref) Mid Glam 15 F3 vil 3m/5km S of Pontypridd. ST 0785
Llantwit Major (Llanilltud Fawr) S Glam 15 E4 tn near Bristol Channel coast 4m/7km SW of Cowbridge. Llandow Industrial Estate 2m/4km N. Motor-racing circuit 2m/3km N at former airfield. Site of Roman villa 1m NW. Site of Bedford Castle to NE. SS 9668
Llantydewi Welsh form of St Dogwells, qv.
Llantysilio Clwyd 41 G6 loc 2m/3km NW of Llangollen. To NW, range of hills known as **Llantysilio Mt**, rising to 1897 ft or 578 metres at Moel y Gamelin, qv. SJ 1943
Llanuwchllyn Gwynedd 33 F2 ham 5m/8km SW of Bala. SH 8730
Llanvaches (Llanfaches) Gwent 16 A2* vil 7m/11km W of Chepstow. Site of Roman bldg 1m SE. ST 4391
Llanvair Discoed (Llanfair Isgoed) Gwent 16 A2 vil 6m/9km W of Chepstow. ST 4492
Llanvapley (Llanfable) Gwent 25 H6 vil 4m/7km E of Abergavenny. SO 3614
Llanvetherine (Llanwytherin) Gwent 25 H6 ham 4m/7km E of Abergavenny. SO 3617
Llanveynoe H & W 25 G4 loc 6m/10km NW of Pontrilas. SO 3031
Llanvihangel anglicised form of the Welsh Llanfihangel.
Llanvihangel Crucorney (Llanfihangel Crucornau) Gwent 25 G5/H5 vil 4m/7km N of Abergavenny. **Llanvihangel Court** is 16c manor hse. SO 3220
Llanvihangel Gobion (Llanfihangel-y-gofion) Gwent 15 H1* ham 4m/7km SE of Abergavenny. SO 3409
Llanvihangel Pontymoel Gwent 15 G2* loc 2km E of Pontypool. SO 3001
Llanvihangel Rogiet Gwent 16 A3 ham 2m/3km W of Caldicot. ST 4587
Llanvihangel Ystern Llewern (Llanfihangel Ystum Llywern) Gwent 26 A6* loc 4m/7km W of Monmouth. SO 4313
Llanvithyn (Llanfeuthin) S Glam 15 F4* loc 1km N of Llancarfan. ST 0571
Llanwarne H & W 26 A4 vil 6m/10km NW of Ross-on-Wye. SO 5028
Llanwarw Welsh form of Wonastow, qv.
Llanwddyn Powys 33 G3* vil at SE end of Lake Vyrnwy built to replace the former vil of Llanwddyn, whose site was submerged by the construction of the resr. SJ 0219
Llanwefr Pool Powys 25 F2* tarn 2m/4km S of Llandegley. SO 1359
Llanwenarth Gwent 25 G6* loc 2km W of Abergavenny. SO 2714
Llanwenog Dyfed 24 B3 ham 6m/9km W of Lampeter. SN 4945
Llanwern Gwent 15 H3* vil 4m/6km E of Newport. ST 3688
Llanwinio Dyfed 23 E3* ham 1km NE of Cwmbach. SN 2626
Llanwnda Dyfed 22 B2 ham 2m/4km NW of Fishguard. Ancient burial-chambers in vicinity. SM 9339
Llanwnen Dyfed 24 B3 vil 3m/5km W of Lampeter. SN 5347
Llanwnog Powys 33 G5 vil 6m/9km W of Newtown. SO 0293
Llanwonno See Llanwynno.
Llanwrda Dyfed 24 C5 vil 4m/6km SW of Llandovery. SN 7131
Llanwrin Powys 33 E4 ham 3m/5km NE of Machynlleth across R Dovey. SH 7803
Llanwrthwl Powys 25 E2 ham 3m/5km S of Rhayader. SN 9763
Llanwrtyd Powys 24 D3 loc 2km NW of Llanwrtyd Wells. SN 8647
Llanwrtyd Wells Powys 24 D3 small spa on R Irfon 10m/16km NE of Llandovery. Tweed factory. SN 8746
Llanwyddelan Powys 33 G4 ham 4m/6km SW of Llanfair Caereinion. SJ 0801
Llanwynno Mid Glam 15 F2* loc in St Gwynno Forest 4m/7km NW of Pontypridd. ST 0395

Llanwytherin Welsh form of Llanvetherine, qv.
Llanyblodwel Salop 34 A2 vil 5m/8km SW of Oswestry. SJ 2422
Llanybri Dyfed 23 E4 vil 6m/10km SW of Carmarthen. SN 3312
Llanybydder (or Llanybyther) Dyfed 24 B4 vil on R Teifi 4m/7km SW of Lampeter. Ancient hill fort (Pen-y-gaer) to S. SN 5244
Llanycefn Dyfed 22 D3 ham 3m/4km S of Maenclochog. SN 0923
Llanychaer Bridge (Llanychar) Dyfed 22 C2 ham at crossing of R Gwaun 2m/3km SE of Fishguard. SM 9835
Llanycil Gwynedd 33 F1 loc on W shore of Bala Lake 2km SW of Bala. SH 9134
Llanycrwys Dyfed 24 C3* loc 5m/7km SE of Lampeter. SN 6445
Llanymawddwy Gwynedd 33 F3 ham on R Dovey 5m/8km NE of Mallwyd. SH 9019
Llanymddyfri Welsh form of Llandovery, qv.
Llanymynech Powys and Salop 34 A2 vil on English-Welsh border 6m/9km S of Oswestry. Quarries to N. SJ 2620
Llanynghenedl Gwynedd 40 A3 ham on Anglesey 2m/3km NE of Valley. SH 3181
Llanynys Clwyd 41 G5 ham 3m/5km N of Ruthin. SJ 1062
Llan-y-pwll Clwyd 42 A6 loc 2m/4km E of Wrexham. SJ 3651
Llanyrafon Gwent 15 G2* loc in Cwmbran on E bank of R Lwyd. ST 3094
Llanyre Powys 25 E2 ham 1m NE of Llandrindod Wells. SO 0462
Llanystumdwy Gwynedd 32 C1 vil on R Dwyfor 2m/3km W of Criccieth. Formerly home of David Lloyd George, 1863–1945. SH 4738
Llanywern Powys 25 F5* ham 1m W of Llanfihangel Tal-y-llyn. SO 1028
Llawhaden Dyfed 22 C4 vil 3m/5km NW of Narberth. Moated remains of medieval cas (A.M.). SN 0617
Llawndy Clwyd 41 G3* loc 1m SW of Point of Air. SJ 1183
Llawryglyn Powys 33 F5 ham 3m/4km W of Trefeglwys. SN 9790
Llech 24 D6* stream in Powys running W into R Tawe 1m SW of Pen-y-cae. See also Henrhyd Falls. SN 8312
Llechcynfarwy Gwynedd 40 B3* loc on Anglesey 3m/5km SW of Llanerchymedd. SH 3881
Llecheiddior Gwynedd 32 C1* loc 4m/6km N of Criccieth. SH 4743
Llechfaen Powys 25 F5 loc 2m/4km E of Brecon. SO 0828
Llechryd Dyfed 22 D2 vil on R Teifi 3m/5km SE of Cardigan. SN 2143
Llechryd Mid Glam 15 F1* vil 2m/3km NW of Rhymney. SO 1009
Llechwedd Gwynedd 40 D4* loc 2m/3km SW of Conwy. SH 7676
Llechwedd Quarries Gwynedd. See Blaenau Ffestiniog.
Lledr 41 E5* r rising NW of Blaenau Ffestiniog and running NE then E into R Conwy 2km S of Betws-y-coed, Gwynedd. SH 7954
Lledrod Dyfed 24 C1 vil 8m/13km SE of Aberystwyth. SN 6470
Lleiriog 33 H2* stream rising S of Llanarmon Dyffryn Ceiriog, Clwyd, and running S into R Tanat 3m/4km SE of Llanrhaeadr-ym-Mochnant. SJ 1524
Llethrid W Glam 23 G6* loc 2m/3km E of Llanrhidian. SS 5391
Lleyn Peninsula (or **The Lleyn**) Gwynedd 32 A2, B1 peninsula with rocky coastline dividing Caernarvon Bay from Cardigan Bay. SH 33
Llidiadnegog Dyfed 24 B4 loc 4m/7km S of Llanybydder. SN 5437
Llidiardau Gwynedd 33 F1* loc 4m/6km W of Bala. SH 8738
Llidiartywaen Powys 33 G6* loc 4m/6km SE of Llanidloes. SO 0081
Lliedi Reservoirs Dyfed 23 F5* two resrs (Upr and Lr) 2m/4km N of Llanelli. SN 5104
Llifior Brook 33 H4* stream running E into R Severn 2m/4km NW of Montgomery, Powys. SO 2099
Llifon 40 B6* r rising SE of Rhostryfan, Gwynedd, and flowing W into Caernarvon Bay 2m/3km SW of Llandwrog. SH 4353
Lligwy 40 B3* stream running NE into Lligwy Bay on E coast of Anglesey. SH 4987
Lligwy Bay Gwynedd 40 C3 bay on NE coast of Anglesey 5m/8km SE of Amlwch. Bronze Age burial-chamber (A.M.) 1km S. See also Capel Lligwy, Din Lligwy. SH 4987
Llithfaen Gwynedd 32 B1 vil 4m/6km NE of Nefyn. SH 3543
Lliw 23 G5 r in W Glam rising 3m/5km SE of Ammanford, Dyfed, and flowing SW through Upr and Lr Lliw Resrs into estuary of R Loughor 4m/7km NW of Swansea. SS 5697
Lliw 33 F2 r running SE into R Dee 2km W of SW end of Bala Lake, Gwynedd. SH 8730
Lliw Reservoir, Lower W Glam 23 G5* resr 2m/3km S of Upr Lliw Resr, qv. SN 6403
Lliw Reservoir, Upper W Glam 23 G5* resr in R Lliw valley 9m/14km N of Swansea. SN 6606
Lliw Valley 118 admin dist of W Glam.
Lloc Clwyd 41 G4 ham 3m/5km W of Holywell. SJ 1476
Llong Clwyd 41 H5 loc 2m/3km SE of Mold. SJ 2662
Llowes Powys 25 G4 vil 2m/4km W of Hay-on-Wye across R Wye. SO 1941
Lloyd Northants 36 D5* dist of Corby 2km NW of tn centre. SP 8889
Lluest-wen Reservoir Mid Glam 15 E2* resr near source of Lit Rhondda R (Afon Rhondda Fach) 4m/6km W of Aberdare. SN 9401
Llugwy 41 E5 r rising on S side of Carnedd Llywelyn, Gwynedd, and running S through Ffynnon Llugwy Resr then E by Capel Curig into R Conwy 1km N of Betws-y-coed. SH 7957
Llundain-fach Dyfed 24 B3* loc 1m E of Talsarn. SN 5556
Llwchwr Welsh form of Loughor (r), qv.
Llwybr-hir Clwyd 41 G4* loc 2m/3km N of Caerwys. SJ 1175
Llwyd 33 F4 r running S into R Garno 1km NW of Carno, Powys. SN 9697
Llwyd 33 F5* r running E along N edge of Hafren Forest into Clywedog Resr, Powys. SN 8890
Llwydiarth Powys 33 G3 ham on R Vyrnwy 3m/4km S of Lake Vyrnwy dam. SJ 0315
Llwydiarth 33 G3* stream running SW into R Vyrnwy 1km SE of ham of Llwydiarth, Powys. SJ 0414
Llwynbrwydrau W Glam 23 H5* loc in Swansea 4m/6km NE of tn centre. SS 6997
Llwyncelyn Dyfed 24 A2 ham 2m/4km SW of Aberaeron. SN 4459
Llwyn-croes Dyfed 24 A5* loc 2km S of Llanpumsaint. SN 4127
Llwyndafydd Dyfed 24 A3 vil 3m/5km S of New Quay. SN 3755
Llwyn-drain Dyfed 23 E2* loc 5m/8km SW of Newcastle Emlyn. SN 2634
Llwyn-du Gwent 25 G6* loc 2km N of Abergavenny. SO 2815
Llwyndyrys Gwynedd 32 B1* loc 4m/6km N of Pwllheli. SH 3741
Llwynein Clwyd 41 H6* loc 3m/4km N of Ruabon. SJ 2847
Llwyneliddon Welsh form of St Lythans, qv.
Llwyngwril Gwynedd 32 D3 coastal vil at S end of Barmouth Bay 6m/9km N of Tywyn. SH 5909
Llwynhendy Dyfed 23 G5 loc in industrial area 2m/4km E of Llanelli. SS 5499
Llwynmawr Clwyd 34 A1* ham 4m/7km W of Chirk. SJ 2237
Llwyn-on Mid Glam 15 E1* loc beside dam of **Llwyn-on Resr**, 4m/6km NW of Merthyr Tydfil. SO 0111
Llwyn-y-brain Dyfed 22 D4 loc 1m S of Whitland. SN 1915
Llwyn-y-groes Dyfed 24 B3* loc 1km E of Gartheli and 5m/9km N of Lampeter. SN 5956
Llwynypia Mid Glam 15 E2 loc in Rhondda valley 2m/3km SE of Rhondda. SS 9993
Llwytgoed Mid Glam 15 E1* loc 2km N of Aberdare. SN 9904
Llydiard-y-parc Clwyd 33 G1* loc 3m/4km E of Corwen. SJ 1143
Llyfnant 33 E4 r rising above Llyn Pen-rhaiadr, on borders of Dyfed and Powys, and flowing N to Glaspwll, Powys, then W into R Dovey S of Dovey Junction rly stn. SN 6997
Llyfni 40 B6* r running W from Llyn Nantlle Uchaf into Caernarvon Bay 2m/4km SW of Llandwrog, Gwynedd. SH 4352
Llygad Llwchwr Dyfed 23 G4* limestone cave, source of R Loughor, 4m/6km SE of Llandeilo. SN 6617
Llyn Alaw Gwynedd 40 B3 large resr on Anglesey 5m/8km S of Cemaes Bay. SH 3785
Llyn Aled Clwyd 41 E5 lake 5m/7km NE of Pentrefoelas. SH 9157
Llyn Alwen Clwyd 41 E5 lake 4m/6km NE of Pentrefoelas. SH 8956
Llyn Anafon Gwynedd 40 D4* small lake in course of R Anafon 3m/5km S of Llanfairfechan. SH 6969
Llyn Arenig Fawr Gwynedd 32 F1 lake 5m/9km W of Bala. SH 8438
Llynau Diwaunedd Gwynedd 40 D6 lake, previously two separated lakes, 4m/6km SW of Capel Curig. SH 6853
Llynau Mymbyr Gwynedd 40 D5 adjacent lakes in course of R Gwryd to W of Capel Curig. SH 7057
Llyn Barfog (Bearded Lake) Gwynedd 32 D4* small lake 4m/7km E of Tywyn. SN 6598
Llyn Berwyn Dyfed 24 C3 lake in Cwm Berwyn Plantation 4m/7km SE of Tregaron. SN 7456
Llyn Blaenmelindwr Dyfed 33 E6* small lake 4m/7km N of Devil's Br. SN 7183
Llyn Bochlwyd Gwynedd 40 D5* lake 1km S of Llyn Ogwen. SH 6559
Llyn Bodgylched Gwynedd 40 C4* lake 2km NW of Beaumaris, Anglesey. SH 5877
Llyn Bodgynydd Gwynedd 40 D5* small lake 3m/5km NW of Betws-y-coed. SH 7659
Llyn Bodlyn Gwynedd 32 D2 lake near head of R Ysgethin, 6m/10km N of Barmouth. SH 6423
Llyn Bowydd Gwynedd 40 D6* small lake 2m/3km E of Blaenau Ffestiniog. SH 7246
Llyn Bran Clwyd 41 F5 lake 3m/4km S of Bylchau. SH 9659
Llyn Brianne 24 D3 large resr in valleys of R Towy and R Camddwr, on borders of Dyfed and Powys 6m/9km W of Llanwrtyd Wells. Partly enclosed by Towy Forest. SN 7948
Llyn Bychan Gwynedd 40 D5* tarn 2m/4km E of Capel Curig. SH 7559
Llyn Caerwych Gwynedd 32 D1* tarn 2m/3km E of Talsarnau. SH 6435
Llyn Carw Powys 24 D2* tarn 2m/3km S of dam of Claerwen Resr. SN 8561
Llyn Caseg-fraith Gwynedd 40 D5* tarn 3m/5km W of Capel Curig. SH 6758
Llyn Cau Gwynedd 33 E3 tarn below Pen y Gadair, the summit of Cader Idris, on S side. SH 7112
Llyn Celyn Gwynedd 33 F1 large resr 4m/6km NW of Bala. SH 8740
Llyn Cerrigllwydion Isaf Powys 24 D1 small lake 2m/4km NE of head of Claerwen Resr. **Llyn Cerrigllwydion Uchaf** is another small lake upstream to SW. SN 8469
Llyn Clyd Gwynedd 40 C5/D5* tarn on E side of Y Garn. SH 6359
Llynclys Salop 34 A2* vil 4m/6km S of Oswestry. SJ 2824
Llyn Coch-hwyad Powys 33 F3 small lake 4m/6km E of Mallwyd. SH 9211
Llyn Conach Dyfed 33 E5* lake 5m/8km S of Machynlleth. SN 7493
Llyn Conglog Gwynedd 40 D6* small lake 2m/3km NW of Blaenau Ffestiniog. SH 6747
Llyn Conglog-mawr Gwynedd 33 E1* small lake 4m/6km NE of Trawsfynydd. SH 7538
Llyn Conwy Gwynedd 41 E6 lake 5m/9km NE of Ffestiniog. Source of R Conwy. SH 7846
Llyn Coron Gwynedd 40 B4 lake on Anglesey to W of Bodorgan rly stn. SH 3770
Llyn Cowlyd Reservoir Gwynedd 40 D5 large resr 2m/3km N of Capel Curig at upper end. SH 7363
Llyn Crafnant Reservoir Gwynedd 40 D5 resr 3m/5km W of Llanrwst. SH 7561
Llyn Craigypistyll Dyfed 33 E5 lake 6m/9km N of Devil's Br. SN 7285
Llyn Crugnant Dyfed 24 C2* small lake 5m/8km E of Tregaron. SN 7561
Llyn Cwellyn Gwynedd 40 C5 lake in course of R Gwyrfai 4m/7km N of Beddgelert. SH 5654
Llyn Cwm Bychan Gwynedd 32 D2 small lake 4m/6km E of Harlech. SH 6431
Llyn Cwm-corsiog Gwynedd 40 D6* small lake 3m/4km W of Blaenau Ffestiniog. SH 6647
Llyn Cwmdulyn Reservoir Gwynedd 40 C6* resr 2m/3km SE of Llanllyfni. SH 4949
Llyn-cwm-llwch Powys 25 E5* small tarn to NW of Brecon Beacons 1km from summit of Corn Du. SO 0022
Llyn Cwm-mynach Gwynedd 32 D2* small lake at head of R Cwm-mynach, 5m/8km NW of Dolgellau. SH 6723
Llyn Cwmorthin Gwynedd 40 D6* lake 2km W of Blaenau Ffestiniog. SH 6746
Llyn Cwm-y-ffynnon Gwynedd 40 D5* lake 1m S of Glyder Fawr. SH 6456
Llyn Cwmystradllyn Gwynedd 32 D1* lake 3m/5km N of Portmadoc. SH 5644
Llyn Cyfynwy Clwyd 41 H5 lake 1m W of Rhydtalog. SJ 2154
Llyn Cynwch Gwynedd 33 E3 small lake 2m/3km N of Dolgellau. SH 7320
Llyn Cyri Gwynedd 32 D3* tarn 4m/6km W of Cader Idris. SH 6511
Llyn Dinam Gwynedd 40 A4* lake on Anglesey 1km S of Caergeiliog. SH 3177
Llyn Dinas Gwynedd 40 C6 lake in course of R Glaslyn, 2m/3km NE of Beddgelert. SH 6149
Llyn Du Clwyd 41 F5* tarn 3m/5km S of Nantglyn. SH 9957
Llyn Du Dyfed 24 D1* tarn 2m/3km NW of head of Claerwen Resr and just S of Llyn Fyrddon-Fawr. SN 7969
Llyn Du Dyfed 24 D2* small lake on W edge of Towy Forest 6m/9km E of Tregaron. SN 7661
Llyn Du Gwynedd 32 D1* tarn 2m/4km N of Portmadoc. SH 5642
Llyn Du Gwynedd 32 D2* tarn 5m/8km E of Harlech. SH 6529
Llyn Du Powys 33 G4* small lake on S side of Llyn Mawr. SO 0096
Llyn Du Powys 33 H3 small lake 2km E of Meifod. SJ 1712
Llyn Dulyn Gwynedd 32 D2* tarn at head of R Ysgethin 1m S of Y Llethr. SH 6624
Llyn Du'r Arddu Gwynedd 40 C5* tarn 1m NW of Snowdon. SH 6055
Llyn Dwfn Dyfed 33 E5 small lake 3m/4km N of head of Nant-y-moch Resr. SN 7392
Llyn Dwythwch Gwynedd 40 C5* small lake 2km SW of Llanberis. SH 5758
Llyn Ebyr Powys 33 F5/G5 small lake 3m/4km NE of Llanidloes. SN 9788
Llyn Edno Gwynedd 40 D6* small lake 4m/6km NW of Blaenau Ffestiniog. SH 6649
Llyn Egnant Dyfed 24 D2 lake 2m/3km W of head of Claerwen Resr. SN 7967
Llyn Eiddew-mawr and **Llyn Eiddew-bach** Gwynedd 32 D2* two small lakes 2m/3km E of Eisingrug. SH 6434
Llyn Eiddwen Dyfed 24 B2 lake 2m/4km S of Llangwyryfon. SN 6066
Llyn Eigiau Reservoir Gwynedd 40 D5 resr 4m/7km N of Capel Curig. SH 7264
Llyn Elsi Reservoir Gwynedd 41 E5* resr 1m SW of Betws-y-coed. SH 7855
Llyn Fach W Glam 15 E1/E2* small lake 7m/11km NW of Rhondda. SN 9003
Llynfaes Gwynedd 40 B4 ham on Anglesey 4m/6km NW of Llangefni. SH 4178
Llyn Fanod Dyfed 24 B2* small lake 3m/5km N of Llangeitho. SN 6064
Llyn Fawr Mid Glam 15 E2* resr 6m/9km NW of Rhondda. SN 9103
Llyn Ffynhonnau Gwynedd 40 C5* tarn 2m/3km SW of Betws Garmon. SH 5255
Llynfi 15 E3* r rising N of Maesteg, Mid Glam, and flowing S through the tn and continuing S to join R Ogmore 2m/4km N of Bridgend. SS 8983
Llynfi 25 F4* r rising 1km NW of Bwlch, Powys, between Brecon and Crickhowell,

and flowing N through Llangorse Lake, and continuing N to join R Wye at Glasbury. SO 1738
Llyn Frogwy Gwynedd 40 B4* small lake 2m/4km NE of Llangefni, Anglesey. SH 4277
Llyn Frongoch Dyfed 24 C1* lake 2km SW of Devil's Br. SN 7275
Llyn Fyrddon-Fach Dyfed 24 D1* small lake on S side of Llyn Fyrddon-Fawr. SN 7970
Llyn Fyrddon-Fawr Dyfed 24 D1 lake 2m/3km S of Cwmystwyth. SN 8070
Llyn Geirionydd Gwynedd 40 D5 lake 2m/4km W of Llanrwst. SH 7661
Llyn Gelli Gain Gwynedd 33 E2* tarn 2m/4km SE of Trawsfynydd. SH 7332
Llyn Glandwgan Dyfed 24 C1* small lake 2m/4km SW of Devil's Br. SN 7075
Llyn Glas Gwynedd 40 C5* tarn 1m NE of Snowdon. SH 6155
Llyn Glasfryn Gwynedd 32 B1 small lake 2m/3km N of Four Crosses. SH 4042
Llyn Goddionduon Gwynedd 40 D5* small lake 3m/5km NW of Betws-y-coed. SH 7558
Llyn Gorast Dyfed 24 D2* small lake 1m SW of Llyn Gynon. SN 7963
Llyn Gwernan Gwynedd 33 E3 small lake 2m/3km SW of Dolgellau. SH 7016
Llyn Gweryd Clwyd 41 G5 small lake 2km SW of Llanarmon-yn-lal. SJ 1755
Llyn Gwngu Dyfed 24 D1* tarn near head of R Gwngu 3m/5km E of Cwmystwyth. SN 8372
Llyn Gwyddior Powys 33 F4 small lake in hills 6m/9km SE of Mallwyd. SH 9307
Llyn-gwyn Powys 25 E2* lake 3m/5km SE of Rhayader. SO 0164
Llyn Gwynant Gwynedd 40 D6 lake in course of R Glaslyn 4m/6km NE of Beddgelert. SH 6451
Llyn Gynon Dyfed 24 D2 lake 4m/7km E of Pontrhydfendigaid. SN 7964
Llynheilyn Powys 25 F2* small lake 3m/5km SW of Radnor to W of Llanfihangel nant Melan. SO 1658
Llyn Helyg Clwyd 41 G4 lake 5m/7km W of Holywell. SH 1177
Llyn Hendref Gwynedd 40 B4* small lake on Anglesey on E side of Gwalchmai. SH 3976
Llyn Hesgyn Gwynedd 33 F1* tarn 6m/9km NW of Bala, near head of R Hesgyn. SH 8844
Llyn Hir Dyfed 24 D2* narrow lake on E side of Llyn Teifi 2m/4km W of head of Claerwen Resr. SN 7867
Llyn Hir Powys 33 G4 small lake 3m/4km S of Llanerfyl. Source of R Einion. SJ 0309
Llyn Hiraethlyn Gwynedd 33 E1* small lake 2m/4km E of Trawsfynydd. Roman camp sites 1km NW. SH 7437
Llyn Idwal Gwynedd 40 D5* lake 1km SW of Llyn Ogwen, below N face of Glyder Fawr. SH 6459
Llyn Irddyn Gwynedd 32 D2* small lake 4m/6km N of Barmouth. SH 6322
Llyn Laethly Gwynedd 40 B3* small lake 1m S of Amlwch, Anglesey. SH 4491
Llyn Lech Owen Dyfed 23 G4* small lake 2m/3km N of Cross Hands. SN 5615
Llyn Llagi Gwynedd 40 D6* tarn 4m/6km E of Beddgelert. SH 6448
Llyn Llennyrch Gwynedd 32 D1* tarn 2m/3km S of Maentwrog. SH 6537
Llyn Lliwbran Gwynedd 33 F2* tarn 3m/5km S of Llanuwchllyn. SH 8725
Llyn Lluncaws Clwyd 33 G2* tarn below E face of Moel Sych, qv. SJ 0731
Llyn Llydaw Gwynedd 40 C5/D5 lake 1m E of summit of Snowdon. SH 6254
Llyn Llygad Rheidol Dyfed 33 E5 small lake on N side of Plynlimon near source of R Rheidol. SN 7987
Llyn Llygeirian Gwynedd 40 A3* small lake 3m/5km SW of Cemaes Bay, Anglesey. SH 3489
Llyn Llywelyn Gwynedd 40 C6* tarn in Beddgelert Forest 2m/3km NW of Beddgelert. SH 5649
Llyn Llywenan Gwynedd 40 A3 lake on Anglesey 1m NE of Bodedern. Neolithic burial-chamber (A.M.) to S. SH 3481
Llyn Login Powys 25 E3* small lake 5m/8km S of Builth Wells. SO 0044
Llyn Maelog Gwynedd 40 A4* lake near W coast of Anglesey, on E side of Rhosneigr. SH 3273
Llyn Maen Bras Gwynedd 33 F1* tarn 2m/4km N of Bala. SH 9239
Llyn Mair Gwynedd 32 D1* small lake nearly 1m NW of Maentwrog. SH 6541
Llyn Mawr Powys 33 G4 small lake 2m/4km N of Llanwnog. From it the stream **Nant-y-llyn-mawr** flows NE into R Rhiw 2m/3km W of Llanllugan. SO 0097
Llyn Moelfre Clwyd 33 H2 small lake 2m/3km W of Llansilin. SJ 1728
Llyn Morwynion Gwynedd 32 D2* tarn 5m/8km E of Harlech. SH 6530
Llyn Morynion Gwynedd 33 E1* lake 2m/3km E of Ffestiniog. SH 7342
Llyn Mynyllod 33 G1* small lake on border of Clwyd and Gwynedd 3m/5km S of Maerdy. SJ 0140
Llyn Nant-ddeiliog Powys 33 F5* small lake 2m/3km SW of Pennant. SN 8695
Llyn Nantlle Uchaf Gwynedd 40 C6 lake on SE side of Nantlle, 6m/10km S of Caernarvon. SH 5153
Llyn Nantycagl Dyfed 33 E5* small lake 2km N of head of Nant-y-moch Resr. SN 7290
Llynnau Barlwyd Gwynedd 40 D6* two small lakes 2m/3km N of Blaenau Ffestiniog. SH 7148
Llynnau Cregennen Gwynedd 32 D3* two small lakes (NT) 5m/8km W of Dolgellau. SH 6614
Llynnau Cwmsilin Gwynedd 40 C6* pair of small adjacent lakes 5m/8km W of Beddgelert, to N of Garnedd Goch. SH 5150
Llynnau Gamallt Gwynedd 33 E1* pair of lakes 3m/5km NE of Ffestiniog. SH 7444
Llyn Newydd Gwynedd 40 D6* small lake 2km NE of Blaenau Ffestiniog. SH 7247
Llynoedd Ieuan Dyfed 33 E6 small lake 4m/6km S of Plynlimon. SN 7981
Llyn Oerddwr Gwynedd 32 D1* tarn 4m/6km N of Portmadoc. SH 5744
Llyn Ogwen Gwynedd 40 D5 lake in course of R Ogwen 4m/7km W of Capel Curig. SH 6560
Llyn Padrig Gwynedd 40 B4* tarn near W coast of Anglesey 3m/5km E of Rhosneigr. SH 3672
Llyn Pendam Dyfed 33 E6* small lake 5m/7km N of Devil's Br. SN 7083
Llyn Pen-rhaiadr 33 E5 lake on borders of Dyfed and Powys 5m/8km S of Machynlleth, Powys. County boundary runs down centre of lake. SN 7593
Llyn Penrhyn Gwynedd 40 A4* lake on Anglesey 1m S of Caergeiliog. SH 3176
Llyn Perfeddau Gwynedd 32 D2* tarn 1km N of Y Llethr. SH 6626
Llyn Peris Gwynedd 40 C5 lake at foot of Pass of Llanberis 1km SE of tn of Llanberis. SH 5959
Llyn Plas-y-mynydd Dyfed 33 E5* lake 2m/4km N of head of Nant-y-moch Resr. Anglers' Retreat shelter on N shore. SN 7492
Llyn Pryfed Gwynedd 32 D2* tarn 5m/9km E of Harlech. SH 6632
Llyn Rhos-ddu Gwynedd 40 B5* small lake on Anglesey 1km S of Newborough. SH 4264
Llyn Rhosgoch Dyfed 33 E6* small lake 4m/7km N of Devil's Br. SN 7183
Llyn Rhosrhydd Dyfed 24 C1* small lake 2m/4km W of Devil's Br. SN 7075
Llyn Stwlan Gwynedd 32 D1* upper resr of Tanygrisiau Power Stn, 2m/4km N of Maentwrog. SH 6644
Llyn Syberi Gwynedd 41 E4* small narrow lake 2km S of Tal-y-cafn. SH 7869
Llyn Syfaddan Welsh form of Llangorse Lake. See Llangorse.
Llyn Syfydrin Dyfed 33 E5 lake 5m/8km N of Devil's Br. SN 7284
Llyn Tecwyn-uchaf Gwynedd 32 D1* lake 2m/3km SW of Maentwrog. SH 6438
Llyn Tegid Welsh form of Bala Lake. See Bala.
Llyn Teifi Dyfed 24 D2 lake 3m/5km E of Pontrhydfendigaid. Source of R Teifi. SN 7867
Llyn Teyrn Gwynedd 40 D5* tarn 2m/3km E of Snowdon. SH 6454
Llyn Traffwll Gwynedd 40 A4* lake on Anglesey 2km SE of Caergeiliog and on SE side of Llanfihangel yn Nhowyn. SH 3277
Llyn Trawsfynydd Gwynedd 32 D1/33 E1 large resr 2m/4km S of Ffestiniog. Nuclear power stn on N shore. SH 6936
Llyn Tryweryn Gwynedd 33 E1* small lake 4m/6km W of Llyn Celyn. SH 7838
Llyn Tyn-y-llyn Clwyd 41 E4* small lake 3m/4km NW of Llangernyw. SH 8767
Llyn y Bi Gwynedd 32 D2* tarn (NT) 1km NE of Y Llethr. SH 6726
Llyn y Cwn Gwynedd 40 C5/D5* tarn nearly 1km NW of Glyder Fawr. SH 6358
Llyn y Cwrt Clwyd 41 E6 small lake 2m/4km E of Pentrefoelas. SH 9051
Llyn y Dywarchen Gwynedd 33 E1* small lake 4m/6km E of Ffestiniog. SH 7642
Llyn-y-dywarchen Gwynedd 40 C5* lake 1km S of Llyn Cwellyn. SH 5653
Llyn y Fan fach Dyfed 24 D5 lake 3m/5km SE of Llanddeusant. SN 8021
Llyn y Fan fawr Powys 24 D5 lake 6m/9km SW of Trecastle. R Tawe rises on E side. SN 8321
Llyn y Fedw Gwynedd 32 D2* tarn 3m/5km NE of Harlech. SH 6232
Llyn-y-felin Dyfed 22 D1* loc adjoining Cardigan to N. SN 1846
Llyn y Figyn Powys 24 D1* tarn 1km E of Llyn Fyrddon-Fawr. The western corner of the tarn is in Dyfed. SN 8170
Llyn y Foel Gwynedd 40 D5* tarn 2m/4km S of Capel Curig. SH 7154
Llyn y Foel-frech Clwyd 41 E5* tarn to E of Aled Isaf Resr and 1m N of Llyn Aled. SH 9159
Llyn y Gadair Gwynedd 33 E3* tarn just below summit of Cader Idris on N side. SH 7013
Llyn-y-Gadair Gwynedd 40 C6* lake just S of Rhyd-ddu. SH 5652
Llyn y Gafr Gwynedd 33 E3* tarn on N slope of Cader Idris 3m/4km SW of Dolgellau. SH 7114
Llyn y Garn Gwynedd 33 E1* lake 4m/6km E of Trawsfynydd. SH 7637
Llyn y Gorlan Dyfed 24 D2* small lake 4m/6km E of Pontrhydfendigaid. SN 7866
Llyn y Graig-wen Gwynedd 33 E1* small lake 3m/4km SE of Ffestiniog. SH 7339
Llyn y Grinwydden Powys 33 G4* tarn 2m/3km S of Llanerfyl. SJ 0206
Llyn y Manod Gwynedd 33 E1* lake 1m SE of Blaenau Ffestiniog. SH 7144
Llyn y Mynydd Powys 33 G2* tarn 2km SW of Pennant Melangell. SJ 0025
Llyn-y-pandy Clwyd 41 G4/G5* loc 2m/4km W of Mold. SJ 2065
Llyn yr Adar Gwynedd 40 D6* tarn 3m/5km NW of Blaenau Ffestiniog. SH 6548
Llyn yr Oerfel Gwynedd 33 E1* small lake 2m/3km S of Ffestiniog. Site of Roman amphitheatre to W and Roman fort to SW. SH 7138
Llyn y Saunau Gwynedd 41 E5* tarn 2m/3km NW of Betws-y-coed. SH 7759
Llynytarw Powys 33 G4 small lake 2m/4km N of Llanwnog. SO 0297
Llyn-y-waun Powys 25 F3* tarn 2m/4km E of Hundred House. SO 1555
Llysdinam Powys 25 E2 loc to W of Newbridge on Wye across r. SO 0058
Llysfaen Welsh form of Lisvane, qv.
Llyswen Dyfed 24 A2* loc 1km S of Aberaeron. SN 4561
Llyswen Powys 25 F4 vil on R Wye 8m/13km NE of Brecon. Remains of ancient hill settlement above vil to W. SO 1337
Llysworney (Llyswyrny) S Glam 15 E4 vil 2m/3km W of Cowbridge. SS 9674
Llys-y-fran Dyfed 22 C3 vil 8m/12km NE of Haverfordwest, at S end of **Llys-y-fran Resr.** SN 0424
Llywel Powys 24 D5 ham 1m NW of Trecastle. SN 8730
Load Brook S Yorks 43 G2* loc 5m/8km W of Sheffield. SK 2788
Load, Little Som 8 C2* ham on N bank of R Yeo at N end of vil of Long Load and 3m/5km SW of Somerton. ST 4623
Loads, Nether Derbys 43 G4* loc 4m/6km W of Chesterfield. **Upr Loads** loc 1m W. SK 3369
Loam Street Suffolk 31 H1* loc 1m NW of Southwold. TM 4977
Loanend Nthmb 67 F3* loc 1m E of Horncliffe. NT 9450
Loanhead Lothian 66 A2 tn 6m/9km S of Edinburgh. Industrial estates. Engineering, coal-mining. NT 2865
Loanhead Stone Circle Grampian. See Daviot.
Loans S'clyde 64 B5 vil 2m/3km E of Troon. NS 3431
Lobb Devon 6 D2* loc 6m/10km NW of Barnstaple. Loc of **N Lobb** to N. SS 4738
Lobhillcross Devon 6 D6 ham 9m/14km E of Launceston. SX 4686
Lobscombe Corner Wilts. Alternative spelling for Lopcombe Corner, qv.
Lochaber 114 admin dist of H'land region.
Lochaber Loch D & G 59 E4 small loch 5m/8km SW of Dumfries. NX 9270
Loch a' Bhaid-luachraich H'land 78 F1/F2 loch near W coast of Ross and Cromarty dist 4m/6km NE of Poolewe. NG 8986
Loch a' Bhaile W Isles 88 B1* freshwater loch on NW coast of Lewis on N side of S Shawbost. NB 2547
Loch a' Bhaile-Mhargaidh S'clyde 62 C2* small loch on Jura 2m/3km W of Craighouse. NR 4967
Loch a' Bhand H'land 80 C4* small loch in Inverness dist immediately below dam of Loch Mullardoch. NH 2231
Loch a' Bhealaich H'land 80 B5 loch (NTS) 5m/8km E of head of Loch Duich, in Skye and Lochalsh dist. NH 0221
Loch a' Bhealaich H'land 84 F4 loch in Caithness dist running into SW end of Loch Choire. Also spelt Loch a' Vellich. NC 5926
Loch a' Bhealaich Bheithe H'land 75 F4 mt loch in Badenoch and Strathspey dist between Ben Alder and Loch Ericht. NN 5171
Loch a' Bheallaich S'clyde. See Tayvallich.
Loch a' Bhlàir H'land 74 B2 small loch in Lochaber dist 1m N of Loch Arkaig below W slopes of Meall a' Bhlàir. NN 0594
Loch a' Bhràighe Skye, H'land 78 D3 bay facing NW at N end of island of Rona. NG 6260
Loch a' Bhraoin H'land 85 B8 loch in Ross and Cromarty dist 7m/11km S of head of Loch Broom. NH 1374
Loch a' Chadh-Fi H'land 84 C3 inlet off N side of Loch Laxford, W coast of Sutherland dist. NC 2050
Loch a' Chàirn Bhàin H'land. See Loch Cairnbawn.
Loch Achall H'land 85 B7, C7 loch at foot of **Glen Achall,** Ross and Cromarty dist, 2m/4km E of Ullapool. NH 1795
Loch Achanalt H'land 80 C2 small loch in course of R Bran in Ross and Cromarty dist 3m/5km W of head of Loch Luichart. NH 2761
Loch a' Chaoruinn H'land 85 E8* small loch on Kildermorie Forest 3m/5km W of Loch Morie, Ross and Cromarty dist. NH 4678
Loch Achilty H'land 80 D2 small loch in Ross and Cromarty dist 3m/5km W of Strathpeffer. NH 4356
Loch a' Chlachain H'land 81 F5* lochan or lakelet in Inverness dist 8m/13km S of Inverness and close to NE end of Loch Duntelchaig. NH 6532
Loch a' Chnuic Bhric S'clyde 62 C1 small loch near W coast of Jura, 3m/4km W of Beinn a' Chaolais. NR 4873
Loch a' Choire H'land 81 F4 small loch in Inverness dist 4m/6km SE of Dores. NH 6229
Loch a' Choire Mhóir H'land 85 D7* small loch at head of Strath Mulzie, Sutherland dist, to E of Seana Bhraigh. NH 3088
Loch Achonachie H'land 80 D2 loch and resr of North of Scotland Hydro-Electric Board in course of R Conon, Ross and Cromarty dist, 3m/5km SW of Strathpeffer. NH 4354
Loch a' Chracaich H'land 78 E3/E4 bay on SW side of Loch Torridon, Ross and Cromarty dist, 4m/6km NW of Shieldaig. NG 7657
Loch a' Chràthaich H'land 80 D5 small loch in Inverness dist 4m/7km NW of Invermoriston. NH 3621
Loch Achray Central 71 F4 small loch in Achray Forest, within Queen Elizabeth Forest Park, 7m/11km W of Callander. NN 5106
Loch a' Chroisg H'land 80 B2 loch in Ross and Cromarty dist 1m W of Achnasheen, over 3m/5km long E to W. Also known as Loch Rosque. NH 1258
Loch a' Chuilinn H'land 80 C2 small loch in course of R Bran in Ross and

Cromarty dist 2km W of head of Loch Luichart. Also known as Loch Culen. NH 2961
Loch a' Chumhainn S'clyde 68 C4* long narrow inlet on NW coast of Mull, running up to Dervaig. NM 4252
Loch Affric H'land 80 B5, C5 loch in course of R Affric in Inverness dist 12m/19km SW of Cannich. NH 1522
Loch a' Ghille Ghobaich H'land 79 E8 loch near coast of Lochaber dist 2m/3km S of Mallaig. NM 6894
Loch a' Ghleannain S'clyde 69 E5* small loch on Mull 1m S of Lochdonhead. NM 7231
Loch a' Ghriama H'land 84 D4 loch in Sutherland dist running N to S at head of Loch Shin. NC 3926
Loch Ailort H'land 68 E1, E2 arm of Sound of Arisaig passing to S of peninsula of Ardnish in Lochaber dist. **Lochailort** is locality at head of loch. NM 7379
Loch Ailsh H'land 85 D5/D6 loch in Sutherland dist 8m/12km SE of Inchnadamph. NC 3110
Loch Ainort Skye, H'land 79 D6 inlet on E coast of island opp Scalpay. NG 5528
Loch Airdeglais S'clyde 69 E5 highest and largest of chain of small lochs in upper reaches of Lussa R, Mull, 2m/3km N of Loch Buie. Others, in order of descent, are Loch an Ellen, Loch an Eilein, and Loch Squabain. NM 6228
Lochaline H'land 68 E4 vil in Lochaber dist on W side of entrance to **Loch Aline,** which runs out into Sound of Mull. Deposits of silica sand on W shore of loch. NM 6744
Loch Allt an Fhearna H'land 86 A4 small loch in Sutherland dist between Lochs Badanloch and Rimsdale. NC 7433
Loch Alsh H'land 79 F6 arm of sea between island of Skye and mainland of Skye & Lochalsh dist, penetrating inland to Eilean Donan, where Loch Duich runs into it from SE and Loch Long from NE. NG 8125
Loch Alvie H'land 75 H1 small loch in Badenoch and Strathspey dist 2m/4km SW of Aviemore. NH 8609
Loch a' Mhuillidh H'land 80 C4 small loch in course of R Farrar in Inverness dist 4m/7km below Loch Monar. Also known as Loch a' Mhuilinn. NH 2738
Lochan a' Bhealaich Tayside 75 E4 small loch or tarn near border with Highland region 4m/6km SW of Ben Alder. NN 4568
Lochan a' Chlaidheimh 75 E5* small loch or tarn on border of Highland and Tayside regions near source of Black Water, E of Blackwater Resr. NN 4060
Lochan a' Chreachain S'clyde 71 E1* small mt loch or tarn in Argyll close to border with Tayside region, on NW side of Beinn a' Chreachain. NN 3644
Loch an Aircill S'clyde 62 C1* small loch on Jura 2km N of Beinn an Oir. NR 5077
Lochan a' Mhadaidh Riabhaich H'land 68 D3* small loch on Ardnamurchan peninsula in Lochaber dist, 1km E of Loch Mudle. NM 5565
Lochan a' Mhuilinn Tayside 72 C1* tarn 3m/5km W of Amulree. NN 8435
Lochan Balloch Central 71 G4 tarn 3m/5km SW of Callander. NN 5904
Loch an Bheallaich H'land 78 F3 loch 2m/3km in length E to W, 4m/7km N of Upr Loch Torridon, Ross and Cromarty dist. Also known as Loch Vallich. NG 8664
Lochan Breaclaich Central 71 G2 small resr 3m/5km E of Killin. NN 6231
Lochan Buidhe Grampian 76 A1* small loch or tarn 2km N of Ben Macdui. Highest lake in Britain at 3600 ft or 1097 metres. NH 9801
Lochan Coire an Lochain H'land 75 E4* small loch or tarn 1m W of Chno Dearg. NN 3674
Loch an Daimh H'land 85 C7 loch in Ross and Cromarty dist 9m/14km E of Ullapool. NH 2794
Loch an Daimh Tayside 71 F1 loch and resr of North of Scotland Hydro-Electric Board 3m/4km NE of Loch Lyon. Formed out of two smaller lochs, Loch Giorra and Loch Daimh, when water level was raised. NN 4846
Loch an Deerie H'land. See Loch an Dherue.
Loch an Dherue H'land 84 E3 loch in Caithness dist 3m/5km S of head of Kyle of Tongue. Also known as Loch an Deerie. NC 5448
Loch an Droighinn S'clyde 70 C3* small loch 1m NW of Kilchrenan, Argyll. NN 0224
Lochan Dubh H'land 74 A4 small mountain loch at head of Glen Hurich in Lochaber dist. NM 8971
Loch an Dubh-lochain H'land 79 F7 small loch in Gleann an Dubh-Lochain, qv. NG 8200
Loch an Dùin 75 G3 small deep loch on border of Highland and Tayside regions 6m/10km SE of Dalwhinnie. NN 7279
Loch an Easain Uaine H'land 84 D3 small loch in Reay Forest, Sutherland dist, 3m/4km S of Foinaven. NC 3246
Loch an Eilean H'land 81 H6 small loch in Rothiemurchus Forest, Badenoch and Strathspey dist, 3m/5km S of Aviemore. Noted for triple echo. Remains of medieval cas on islet in loch. HU 8907
Loch an Eilein Mull, S'clyde. See Loch Airdeglais.
Loch an Ellen Mull, S'clyde. See Loch Airdeglais.
Lochan Fada H'land 85 A8 loch in W part of Ross and Cromarty, 4m/6km NE of head of Loch Maree. NH 0271
Loch an Fhiarlaid H'land 80 B2 small loch in Ross and Cromarty dist 4m/6km S of Kinlochewe. NH 0556
Lochan Gaineamhach 74 D5* small loch or tarn on border of Highland and Strathclyde regions 2m/3km NW of Loch Bà. NN 3053
Lochan Gleann Astaile S'clyde 62 C1* small loch on Jura 2km SW of Beinn a' Chaolais. NR 4771
Loch an Leathaid Bhuain H'land 84 C4 loch in Sutherland dist adjoining Loch na Creige Duibhe, to W of Loch More. NC 2736
Loch an Leoid S'clyde 70 C3 small loch in Argyll 2km NW of Kilchrenan. NN 0124
Lochan Loin nan Donnlaich Tayside 75 E5 small loch 2m/4km NE of Loch Eigheach. NN 4661
Lochan Lunn Da Bhra H'land 74 C4/C5 small loch in Lochaber dist 5m/8km S of Fort William. NN 0866
Lochan Mathair Eite 74 D5* small loch or tarn on border of H'land and S'clyde regions 5m/7km SE of dam of Blackwater Resr. NN 2854
Lochan Mhic Pheadair Ruaidh S'clyde 70 D1* small loch or tarn on Black Mount, Argyll, 3m/5km N of Loch Tulla. Drains into R Bà to N. NN 2847
Lochan na Bi S'clyde 71 E2 small loch in Argyll in course of R Lochy, 2km NW of Tyndrum, Central region. NN 3031
Lochan na h-Achlaise S'clyde 71 E1 small loch on Black Mount in Argyll, 2m/3km N of Loch Tulla. NN 3148
Lochan na h-Earba H'land 75 E3 narrow loch in Badenoch and Strathspey dist running parallel to, and about 1m SE of, Loch Laggan. NN 4883
Lochan na Lairige Tayside 71 G1 resr, 2km long N to S, 4m/6km N of head of Loch Tay. NN 5940
Lochan nam Breac H'land 74 A2 small loch in Lochaber dist 1m W of head of Loch Quoich. NM 9199
Lochan nan Cat Tayside 71 F1* small mt loch or tarn on E side of Stuchd an Lochain. NN 4844
Lochan nan Cat Tayside 71 G1* small mt loch nearly 1m NE of Ben Lawers. NN 6442
Lochan na Stainge S'clyde 71 E1 small loch in Argyll in course of R Bà, between Loch Buidhe and Loch Bà. NN 3049
Loch an Nostarie H'land 79 E8 loch near coast of Lochaber dist 1m SE of Mallaig. NM 6995
Lochan Oisinneach Mór Tayside 76 B5 small loch 4m/6km NE of Ballinluig. Smaller tarn of **Lochan Oisinneach Beag** 1km NE. NO 0354
Loch an Ruathair H'land 86 B4 loch in Sutherland dist 3m/4km N of Kinbrace. NC 8636
Lochans D & G 57 B7 vil 3m/4km S of Stranraer. NX 0656
Loch An Sgòir H'land 75 E4 small mt loch 2m/3km N of Ben Alder. NN 4975
Loch an Sgoltaire S'clyde 69 C7 small loch on Colonsay 1km SW of Kiloran Bay. NR 3897
Lochan Shira S'clyde 70 D3 loch and resr of North of Scotland Hydro-Electric Board, 4m/6km S of Dalmally in Argyll. NN 1620
Lochan Spling Central 71 F4* tarn in Loch Ard Forest 2km W of Aberfoyle. NN 5000
Lochan Sròn Mór S'clyde 70 D3 loch and resr in Argyll below dam of Lochan Shira, 8m/13km NE of Inveraray. NN 1619
Lochan Sròn Smeur Tayside 75 E5 small loch 2m/3km N of Loch Eigheach. NN 4560
Lochan Thulachan H'land 86 D3 loch in Caithness dist 8m/12km NW of Latheron. ND 1041
Loch an Torr S'clyde 68 C3* small loch on Mull 2km E of Dervaig. NM 4553
Loch an t-Seilich H'land 75 G3 loch in course of R Tromie on Gaick Forest, in Badenoch and Strathspey dist, 9m/14km S of Kingussie. NN 7586
Loch a' Phuill Tiree, S'clyde 69 A8 loch near W end of island 2m/3km NE of Rinn Thorbhais. NL 9541
Locharbriggs D & G 59 E3 suburb 3m/4km NE of Dumfries. Quarries. NX 9980
Loch Ard Central 71 F4 loch 3m/5km W of Aberfoyle. Remains of medieval cas on islet near S shore. NN 4601
Loch Ard Forest Central 71 F4, F5 state forest S of Loch Ard, forming part of Queen Elizabeth Forest Park. NS 4898
Loch Ardinning Central 64 C1* small loch 1m S of Strathblane. NS 5677
Loch Ardnahoe S'clyde 62 B1 small loch 2km N of Port Askaig, Islay. NR 4271
Loch Ardvar H'land 84 B4 inlet on S side of Eddrachillis Bay to W of Loch Cairnbawn, W coast of Sutherland dist. Also spelt Loch Ardbhair. NC 1633
Loch Arienas H'land 68 E3/E4 loch in Morvern, Lochaber dist, 4m/6km N of Lochaline. NM 6851
Loch Arkaig H'land 74 B2-C3 loch in Lochaber dist running W to E from 1km below confluence of Rs Dessary and Pean to 1m NW of Bunarkaig on Loch Lochy. Length about 12m/19km. See also Achnacarry. NN 0891
Loch Arklet Central 71 E4 loch and resr between Loch Katrine and Loch Lomond 2km E of Inversnaid. NN 3709
Lochar Moss D & G 59 E4, F4 low-lying region to E and SE of Dumfries, traversed and drained by **Lochar Water,** r rising N of Dumfries and flowing into Solway Firth to SW of Cummertrees. NY 0371
Loch Arnicle S'clyde 62 D4/63 E4 small loch or tarn in Kintyre 3m/4km E of Glenbarr. NR 7135
Loch Arnish Skye, H'land 78 D4 bay on W coast of Raasay 3m/5km from N end of island. NG 5948
Loch Arnol W Isles 88 B1* loch on NW coast of Lewis 1km W of Arnol vil. R Arnol runs into loch from S and out into Port Arnol to N. NB 3048
Loch Arthur D & G 59 E4 small loch 1km E of Beeswing and 6m/10km SW of Dumfries. NX 9068
Loch Ascog S'clyde 63 G2 small loch on Bute 1m S of Rothesay. NS 0962
Loch a' Sguirr Skye, H'land 78 D4 westward-facing bay at N end of island of Raasay. NG 6052
Loch Ashie H'land 81 F4 loch in Inverness dist 6m/10km S of Inverness. Area about 390 acres or 160 hectares. NH 6234
Loch Assopol S'clyde 69 C6 loch on Ross of Mull 2km SE of Bunessan. NM 4020
Loch Assynt H'land 85 C5 loch in Sutherland dist, over 6m/10km long NW to SE and 282 ft or 86 metres at maximum depth, 5m/7km E of Lochinver. Vil of Inchnadamph at head of loch. NC 2124
Loch a' Tuath W Isles 88 C2 large bay on E coast of Lewis extending from Tolsta Hd to Tiumpan Hd on Eye Peninsula, and south-westwards to Laxdale, N of Stornoway. Also known as Broad Bay. NB 43
Loch Avail S'clyde 70 A6 small loch in Knapdale, Argyll, 2m/3km NE of Achahoish. Also known as Loch Ellen. NR 8079
Loch a' Vellich H'land. See Loch a' Bhealaich.
Loch Avich S'clyde 70 B3 loch 2m/3km NW of Dalavich on W side of Loch Awe in Argyll. NM 9314
Loch Avon Grampian 76 B1 loch below SE slope of Cairn Gorm. R Avon flows from foot of loch. NJ 0102
Loch Awe S'clyde 70 B4-C2 narrow loch 24m/39km long SW to NE in Argyll. Runs from Ford to Pass of Brander and discharges by R Awe to Loch Etive. Maximum depth over 300 ft or 90 metres. NM 9610
Lochawe S'clyde 70 C2 vil on W bank of Loch Awe in Argyll, 3m/4km W of Dalmally. NN 1227
Lochay 71 G2 r in Central region running W down Glen Lochay to join R Dochart at head of Loch Tay. NN 5733
Loch Bà S'clyde 68 D4, 69 D5 loch on Mull 3m/5km S of Salen. Length 3m/5km SE to NW. See also (R) Bà. NM 5638
Loch Bà S'clyde 74 D6 loch on Rannoch Moor in Argyll, from which R Bà flows into head of Loch Laidon. NN 3250
Loch Bad a' Bhathaich H'land 85 E8 small loch in Ross and Cromarty dist 2km N of Loch Morie. NH 5378
Loch Bad a' Ghaill H'land 85 B6 loch near NW coast of Ross and Cromarty dist 8m/12km S of Lochinver. Also known as Loch Baddagyle. NC 0710
Loch Badanloch H'land 86 A4 loch in Sutherland dist 5m/8km W of Kinbrace. N part of loch is known as Loch nan Clàr. NC 7734
Loch Bad an Sgalaig H'land 78 F3 loch near W coast of Ross and Cromarty dist 4m/7km SE of Gairloch. Upper part of loch is known as Dubh Loch. NG 8470
Loch Baddagyle H'land 85 B6 loch near NW coast of Ross and Cromarty dist 8m/12km S of Lochinver. Also known as Loch Bad a' Ghaill. NC 0710
Loch Baile Mhic Chailein S'clyde 70 C1 small loch in course of R Creran 2m/3km NW of mouth of r at head of Loch Creran, Argyll. NN 0247
Loch Bainnie (or Bainie) Tayside 76 C4 small loch or tarn 3m/5km E of Spittal of Glenshee. Also known as Loch Shechernich or Schechernich. NO 1668
Loch Ballygrant S'clyde 62 B2 small loch to E of Ballygrant vil on Islay, 3m/4km SW of Port Askaig. NR 4066
Loch Baravaig Skye, H'land 79 E7*. See Baravaig.
Loch Bay Skye, H'land 78 A4 bay on NW coast 4m/7km N of Dunvegan. NG 2655
Loch Beag H'land 68 E1 small inlet at head of Loch nan Uamh, on N side of peninsula of Ardnish in Lochaber dist. NM 7283
Loch Beannachan H'land 80 C3 small but deep loch in course of R Meig on Strathconon Forest in Ross and Cromarty dist. Also known as Loch Beannacharain. NH 2351
Loch Beannacharan H'land 80 C4, D4 small but deep loch in course of R Farrar in Inverness dist 6m/9km above Struy Br. Also known as Loch Bunacharan. NH 3038
Loch Bee W Isles 88 E2 large loch at N end of S Uist. Guided missile range in vicinity. NF 7743
Loch Beg S'clyde 69 D5 inlet at head of Loch Scridain, Mull. NM 5229
Loch Beinn a' Mheadhoin H'land. See Loch Beneveian.
Loch Belivat H'land 81 H3 lochan or lakelet in Nairn dist 7m/11km SE of Nairn. NH 9547
Loch Benachally Tayside 76 B5 small loch 4m/7km W of Br of Cally. NO 0750

Loch Beneveian H'land 80 C5 loch and resr of North of Scotland Hydro-Electricity Board in Glen Affric, Inverness dist. Length 6m/9km SW to NE. Also known as Loch Beinn a' Mheadhoin. NH 2425
Loch Beoraid H'land 74 A3 narrow but deep loch in S Morar, Lochaber dist, between Loch Morar and Loch Eilt. Length 3m/5km E to W. NM 8285
Loch Bhac Tayside 75 H5 small loch 4m/6km SW of Blair Atholl. NN 8262
Loch Bhasapoll Tiree, S'clyde 69 A7 loch near N coast 5m/8km W of Scarinish. NL 9747
Loch Bhrollum W Isles 88 B3* inlet on SE coast of Lewis 2m/4km to E of Loch Claidh. NB 3102
Loch Bhruthaich H'land 81 E4 small loch in Inverness dist 5m/8km NW of Drumnadrochit. Also known as Loch Bruicheach. NH 4536
Loch Bog Tayside 73 E1 small loch 2m/3km S of Blairgowrie. Also known as Stormont Loch. NO 1942
Lochboisdale W Isles 88 E3 vil and port on N shore of **Loch Boisdale**, inlet, containing several small islands, near S end of S Uist on the E side. **S Lochboisdale** is locality on S side of inlet. NF 7919
Loch Boltachan Tayside 71 G2* small loch or tarn 2km N of St Fillans. NN 6926
Loch Borralan H'land 85 C6 small loch in Sutherland dist 7m/11km S of Inchnadamph. NC 2610
Loch Bracadale Skye, H'land 79 B5 wide inlet on SW coast between Idrigill Pt and Rubha nan Clach. NG 2837
Loch Bradan Reservoir S'clyde 56 D4 resr within Glen Trool Forest Park 7m/11km SW of Dalmellington. NX 4297
Loch Brandy Tayside 76 D3 mt loch 2km N of Clova. NO 3375
Loch Breachacha Coll, S'clyde 68 A4 large inlet on S coast 5m/7km SW of Arinagour. See also Breachacha Castle. NM 1653
Loch Breivat W Isles 88 B1* loch near NW coast of Lewis 2m/3km SE of Arnol. NB 3345
Loch Brittle Skye, H'land. See (R) Brittle.
Loch Broom H'land 85 B7 long inlet on W coast of Ross and Cromarty dist on which small tn of Ullapool is situated. **Lit Loch Broom** to W runs parallel to it. NH 1392
Loch Broom Tayside 76 B5 small loch 4m/7km E of Pitlochry. NO 0057
Loch Brora H'land 87 B6 loch in course of R Brora, Sutherland dist, 4m/6km NW of Brora vil. NC 8507
Loch Bruicheach H'land 81 E4 small loch in Inverness dist 5m/8km NW of Drumnadrochit. Also known as Loch Bhruthaich. NH 4536
Loch Buidhe H'land 85 F6 loch in Sutherland dist 5m/8km NE of Bonar Br. NH 6698
Loch Buidhe S'clyde 71 E1* small loch in course of R Bà 5m/9km N of Br of Orchy. NN 2948
Lochbuie S'clyde 69 D5/E5 vil on S coast of Mull at head of large inlet of **Loch Buie.** Ancient stone circle to E. See also Castle Moy. NM 6025
Loch Builg Grampian 76 C1 small loch 6m/9km SW of Cock Br. See also Builg Burn. NJ 1803
Loch Bun Abhainn-eadar W Isles 88 A3/B3* inlet on N side of W Loch Tarbert, W coast of Harris. NB 1203
Loch Bunacharan H'land 80 C4, D4 small but deep loch in course of R Farrar in Inverness dist 6m/9km above Struy Br. Also known as Loch Beannacharan. NH 3038
Loch Bunachton H'land 81 F4* lochan or lakelet in Inverness dist 6m/10km S of Inverness and 2m/3km E of Loch Ashie. NH 6635
Loch Cairnbawn H'land 84 B4, C4 inlet on W coast of Sutherland dist running out into Eddrachillis Bay. Also known as Loch a' Chàirn Bhàin. NC 1934
Loch Calavie H'land 80 B4 small loch in Skye and Lochalsh dist 3m/5km SW of head of Loch Monar. NH 0538
Loch Calder H'land 86 D2 loch in Caithness dist, 2m/4km long N to S and nearly 1m wide, 5m/8km SW of Thurso. ND 0760
Loch Callater Grampian 76 C3 small loch in Glen Callater 5m/8km S of Braemar. NO 1884
Loch Càm S'clyde 62 B2 small loch on Islay 3m/4km N of Bridgend. NR 3466
Loch Caoldair H'land 75 F2 small loch in Badenoch and Strathspey dist 3m/5km NW of Dalwhinnie. NN 6189
Loch Caolisport S'clyde 62 D1, 63 E1 sea-loch in Argyll running NE from Pt of Knap to Achahoish. NR 7374
Loch Carloway W Isles 88 B2* inlet and estuary of Carloway R on W coast of Lewis W of Carloway vil. NB 1842
Loch Càrn a' Mhaoil S'clyde 62 C3* small loch on Islay 3m/4km W of Ardmore Pt. NR 4350
Loch Caroy Skye, H'land 79 B5 inlet of Loch Bracadale 4m/7km NW of Bracadale vil. NG 3043
Loch Carrie H'land 80 C4 small loch in course of R Cannich 3m/5km below dam of Loch Mullardoch in Inverness dist. NH 2633
Loch Carron H'land 79 F5, 80 A4, long inlet in Ross and Cromarty dist extending from S end of Inner Sound on N side of Kyle of Lochalsh to foot of Glen Carron. Vil of **Lochcarron** on N shore 2m/3km below head of loch. Vehicle ferry across narrows at Stromeferry. NG 8735
Loch Ceo Glais H'land 81 F4 small loch in Inverness dist nearly 1km SW of SW end of Loch Duntelchaig. Also spelt Ceo Ghlas, Ceo Glas, etc. NH 5828
Loch Chaoruinn S'clyde 63 E1 small loch in Knapdale, Argyll, 4m/7km W of W Tarbert. NR 7866
Loch Chaorunn S'clyde 63 E1 small loch in Knapdale, Argyll, 3m/4km NW of Tarbert. NR 8371
Loch Chiarain H'land 74 D5 small loch in course of Ciaran Water, Lochaber dist, 3m/5km NE of dam of Blackwater Resr. NN 2963
Loch Choire H'land 84 F4 loch in Caithness dist 6m/9km SE of Altnaharra. **Loch Choire Forest** is surrounding deer forest. NC 6328
Loch Chon Central 71 E4 loch 4m/6km E of Ben Lomond. NN 4205
Loch Ciaran S'clyde 63 E3 small loch in Kintyre, Argyll, 2km S of Clachan. NR 7754
Loch Claidh W Isles 88 B3 large inlet on S coast of Lewis to E of Loch Seaforth. NB 20
Loch Clair H'land 80 A2 small loch in Ross and Cromarty dist 3m/5km SW of Kinlochewe. NH 0057
Loch Cliad Coll, S'clyde 68 A3 largest of the numerous lochs on the island 1m S of Cliad Bay and 2km NW of Arinagour. NM 2058
Loch Cluanie H'land 74 C1 loch and resr of North of Scotland Hydro-Electric Board, partly in Skye & Lochalsh dist and partly in Inverness dist. Runs E for about 7m/11km from foot of Glen Shiel. NH 1409
Loch Cnoc an Loch S'clyde 63 F5* small loch or tarn on Arran 3m/4km E of Blackwaterfoot. NR 9328
Loch Coire Lair H'land 85 C8 small narrow loch in Ross and Cromarty dist 2m/3km N of head of Loch Glascarnoch. NH 2878
Loch Coire Mhic Fhearchair H'land 80 A2* lochan in spectacular corrie on N side of Beinn Eighe, qv, in Ross and Cromarty dist. NG 9460
Loch Coire nam Mang H'land 86 B3 loch in Sutherland dist adjacent to, and W of, Loch Druim a' Chliabhain. NC 8040
Loch Con Tayside 75 G4 small loch between Loch Errochty and Glen Garry. NN 6867
Loch Connell D & G 57 A6 small loch 1km W of Kirkcolm. NX 0168
Loch Corr S'clyde 62 A2 small loch near NW coast of Islay 2km S of Tòn Mhór. NR 2269
Loch Coruisk Skye, H'land 79 C6 loch below Cuillin Hills running into Loch na Cuilce and thence into Loch Scavaig. NG 4820
Lochcote Reservoir Lothian 65 F2* small resr 2m/4km SW of Linlithgow. NS 9773
Loch Coulin H'land 80 A2, B2 small loch in Ross and Cromarty dist 5m/7km S of Kinlochewe. NH 0155
Loch Coulter Reservoir Central 72 B5 small loch and resr 5m/8km SW of Stirling. NS 7686
Loch Coultrie H'land 78 F4 loch in Ross and Cromarty dist running into head of Loch Damh. NG 8545
Loch Craggie H'land 84 F3 loch in course of R Borgie 4m/6km SE of Tongue, in Caithness dist. NC 6152
Loch Craggie H'land 85 F6 loch in Sutherland dist 3m/5km E of Lairg. NC 6207
Lochcraig Head 65 H6 mt on border of Dumfries & Galloway and Borders regions 5m/8km SW of St Mary's Loch. Height 2625 ft or 800 metres. NT 1617
Loch Craignish S'clyde 69 F7 long inlet on coast of Argyll, on E side of peninsula comprising par of Craignish, at N end of Sound of Jura. Large standing stone and remains of two burial cairns at head of loch. NM 7901
Lochcraig Reservoir S'clyde 64 C4* resr 3m/5km W of Eaglesham. NS 5350
Loch Cravadale W Isles 88 A3* northward-facing bay on W coast of Harris 2m/3km NE of Husinish. NB 0113
Loch Creagh Tayside 76 A6* small loch or tarn 4m/7km SE of Aberfeldy. NN 9044
Loch Creran Argyll, S'clyde, 70 B1 arm of Loch Linnhe extending some 7m/11km from Lynn of Lorn to foot of Glen Creran. Width varies from nearly 2km in places to about 100 metres at Dallachoilish. NM 9442
Loch Crinan S'clyde. See Crinan.
Loch Cromore W Isles 88 C2* small loch S of Cromore, qv, near E coast of Lewis. NB 4020
Loch Crongart S'clyde 57 C5* small loch 3m/5km E of Barrhill. NX 2882
Loch Crunachdan H'land 75 F2 small loch in Badenoch and Strathspey dist 4m/7km W of Laggan Br. NN 5492
Loch Culen H'land 80 C2 small loch in course of R Bran in Ross and Cromarty dist 2km W of head of Loch Luichart. Also known as Loch a' Chuilinn. NH 2961
Loch Daimh Tayside. See Loch an Daimh.
Loch Dallas Grampian 82 A3 small loch 4m/6km SW of Dallas. NJ 0947
Loch Damh H'land 78 F4 dog-legged loch in Ross and Cromarty dist, 4m/6km long N to S, running out into S side of Upr Loch Torridon. NG 8650
Loch Davan Grampian 77 E1 small loch 2km NW of Dinnet. NJ 4400
Loch Dee D & G 58 A4/B4 loch 4m/7km W of Clatteringshaws Loch. NX 4678
Loch Derculich Tayside 75 H5 small loch 4m/6km N of Aberfeldy. NN 8655
Loch Derry D & G 57 C5* small loch or tarn 2m/4km SW of Loch Maberry. NX 2573
Loch Dhughaill H'land 80 A3 small loch in Glen Carron 5m/8km NE of head of Loch Carron. Also known as Loch Doule. NG 9947
Loch Diabaig H'land 78 F3 inlet on NE side of Loch Torridon, W coast of Ross and Cromarty dist. NG 7959
Loch Diabaigs Airde H'land 78 F3 loch in Ross and Cromarty dist 2m/3km N of mouth of Upr Loch Torridon. NG 8159
Loch Dochard S'clyde 70 D1 small loch in Argyll 4m/6km W of Loch Tulla. NN 2141
Loch Dochart Central 71 E2 small loch in course of R Fillan 1m E of Crianlarich. Ruined cas on islet in middle of loch. NN 4025
Loch Doilet H'land 74 A4 small loch in course of R Hurich in Glenhurich Forest, Lochaber dist. NM 8067
Loch Doine Central 71 F3 small loch 4m/7km W of Balquhidder. NN 4719
Loch Doir' a' Ghearrin H'land 68 E1 loch in Lochaber dist on peninsula of Ardnish. NM 7281
Loch Doire nam Mart H'land 68 E3 small loch in Morvern, Lochaber dist, 5m/8km N of Lochaline. NM 6744
Lochdonhead S'clyde 70 A2 vil at head of **Loch Don,** inlet on E coast of Mull. NM 7333
Loch Doon S'clyde 56 E4 large loch and resr at head of R Doon 4m/7km S of Dalmellington. Remains of **Loch Doon Castle** (A.M.), formerly on islet in loch, re-erected on W bank of resr. NX 4998
Loch Dornal 57 C5 loch, partly in Dumfries & Galloway region and partly in Strathclyde region, 5m/8km SE of Barrhill. NX 2976
Loch Doule H'land 80 A3 small loch in Glen Carron 5m/8km NE of head of Loch Carron. Also known as Loch Dhughaill. NG 9947
Loch Droma H'land 85 C8 small loch in Ross and Cromarty dist 1m W of head of Loch Glascarnoch. NH 2675
Loch Druidibeg W Isles 88 E2 large loch on S Uist 4m/6km N of Beinn Mhór. Nature reserve. NF 8031
Loch Druim a' Chliabhain H'land 86 B3 loch in Sutherland dist 5m/8km W of Forsinard rly stn. NC 8141
Loch Drunkie Central 71 F4 loch at E edge of Achray Forest, S of Loch Venachar. NN 5404
Loch Dùghaill H'land 84 B3 inlet on W coast of Sutherland dist 4m/6km W of Rhiconich. NC 1952
Loch Duich H'land 80 A5 loch in Skye and Lochalsh dist running NW into head of Loch Alsh. Loch Duich is 5m/8km long. NG 9022
Loch Dungeon D & G 58 B3 loch on E side of Rinns of Kells, 4m/6km N of Clatteringshaws Loch. NX 5284
Loch Duntelchaig H'land 81 F4 loch in Inverness dist 8m/13km S of Inverness and 2m/3km SE of Dores. NH 6231
Loch Earn Tayside 71 G3 loch extending over 6m/10km W to E, from Lochearnhead in Central region to St Fillans in Tayside region; width about 1km. Facilities for water sports, incl sailing and water-skiing. NN 6423
Lochearnhead Central 71 G3 vil at head, or W end, of Loch Earn, 6m/10km S of Killin. NN 5823
Loch Eatharna Coll, S'clyde 68 A3 inlet on SE coast. See also Arinagour. NM 2256
Loch Eck S'clyde 70 C5-D6 narrow loch in Argyll running 6m/10km N to S, the S end being 7m/11km N of Dunoon. **Loch Eck Forest** is state forest on E shore. Loch and forest are within Argyll Forest Park. NS 1391
Loch Ederline S'clyde 70 B4 small loch in Argyll 1m S of head of Loch Awe. NM 8602
Lochee Tayside 73 F2 dist of Dundee 2m/3km NW of city centre. NO 3731
Loch Eigheach Tayside 75 E5 loch and resr of North of Scotland Hydro-Electric Board 2km E of Rannoch rly stn. Power stn near dam at E end. NN 4556
Loch Eil H'land 74 B4 loch in Lochaber dist running 8m/13km W to E, from Kinlocheil to Corpach, where it turns S into head of Loch Linnhe. **Locheil Forest** is deer forest extending N to Loch Arkaig. NN 0277
Loch Eilde Mór H'land 74 D5 loch on E side of Mamore Forest in Lochaber dist, 3m/4km NE of Kinlochleven. **Loch Eilde Beag** is smaller loch a short distance upstream to NE. NN 2364
Loch Eilt H'land 74 A3 narrow loch in Lochaber dist between Lochailort and Glenfinnan. Length over 3m/5km E to W. NM 8182
Loch Einich H'land 76 A2 loch in Cairngorms, in Badenoch and Strathspey dist, 8m/13km S of Aviemore. NN 9199
Loch Ellen S'clyde 70 A6 small loch in Knapdale, Argyll, 2m/3km NE of Achahoish. Also known as Loch Avail. NR 8079
Lochenbreck Loch D & G 58 C5 small loch on N side of Laurieston Forest, 3m/4km W of Laurieston. NX 6465

Lochend D & G 58 D6 locality at S end of White Loch, 5m/8km SE of Dalbeattie. NX 8654
Lochend H'land 81 F4 locality at NE end of Loch Ness, Inverness dist. NH 6037
Lochend H'land 86 E1 locality in Caithness dist on E side of Loch Heilen 4m/6km SE of Dunnet. ND 2668
Lochend Lothian 66 A2* dist of Edinburgh 2m/3km E of city centre. NT 2774
Lochend Loch S'clyde 64 D2 small loch 2km W of Coatbridge. NS 7066
Loch Enoch D & G 57 E5 loch in Glentrool Forest Park 1m E of Merrick. NX 4485
Loch Eport W Isles 88 E1 long narrow inlet on E coast of N Uist 3m/5km S of Lochmaddy. Locality of **Locheport** on S shore 5m/7km from mouth. NF 8963
Loch Eriboll H'land 84 D2, E2 long inlet on N coast of Sutherland dist to E of Durness, penetrating some 9m/15km inland and varying in width from 1m to 2m/3km. NC 4360
Loch Ericht 75 F3, F4 loch partly in Highland and partly in Tayside region, running 15m/24km from near Dalwhinnie to dam at S end, whence tunnel aqueduct conveys water to power stn on Loch Rannoch. NN 5371
Loch Erisort W Isles 88 B2 inlet on E coast of Lewis penetrating 8m/13km inland. Entrance is 7m/11km S of Stornoway. NB 32
Loch Errochty Tayside 75 G4 loch and resr of North of Scotland Hydro-Electric Board at head of Glen Errochty, 10m/16km W of Blair Atholl. NN 6965
Loch Esk Tayside 76 C3 small loch or tarn near head of R South Esk 9m/15km SE of Braemar. NO 2379
Loch Etchachan Grampian 76 B1 small loch on NE side of Ben Macdui in Cairngorms. NJ 0000
Loch Etive S'clyde 70 B2-C1 sea-loch extending 18m/29km from Ledaig Pt to foot of Glen Etive, Argyll. Wild, mountainous scenery in upper reaches. Rd br spans loch at Connel, near mouth. NN 0434
Loch Ettrick D & G 59 E2 small loch 3m/5km E of Closeburn. NX 9493
Loch Ewe H'land 78 F1, F2 large inlet on W coast of Ross and Cromarty dist. Vil of Poolewe at head of loch. NG 8387
Loch Eye H'land 87 B8 loch in Ross and Cromarty dist 3m/5km SE of Tain. NH 8379
Loch Eynort Skye, H'land 79 B6 large inlet on SW coast extending inland to locality of Grula and mouth of Eynort R. NG 3724
Loch Eynort W Isles 88 E2/E3 long inlet on E coast of S Uist 5m/8km N of Lochboisdale. NF 8026
Loch Eyre Skye, H'land 78 C4 inlet at head of Loch Snizort Beag 7m/11km NW of Portree. NG 4152
Loch Fad S'clyde 63 G2 loch on Bute 2m/3km S of Rothesay. NS 0761
Loch Fada H'land 85 A7 loch near W coast of Ross and Cromarty dist 4m/7km NE of Poolewe. NG 9086
Loch Fada S'clyde 69 C7 loch on Colonsay 1m N of Scalasaig. NR 3895
Loch Fada Skye, H'land 78 C4 loch 3m/5km N of Portree. Runs into Loch Leathan, resr of North of Scotland Hydro-Electric Board. NG 4949
Loch Fannich H'land 80 C1, C2 large resr (North of Scotland Hydro-Electric Board) in Ross and Cromarty dist 18m/29km W of Dingwall. Length 7m/11km E to W. NH 2666
Loch Farr H'land 81 F4 small loch in Strathnairn Forest, Inverness dist, 2km S of Farr and 9m/15km S of Inverness. NH 6830
Loch Farroch S'clyde 57 C5* small loch 2m/4km NE of Barrhill. NX 2585
Loch Faskally Tayside 76 A5 loch and resr in course of R Tummel above Pitlochry. NN 9258
Loch Fell D & G 59 F1 mt 5m/9km E of Moffat. Height 2256 ft or 688 metres. NT 1704
Loch Fender Tayside 75 H6 small loch or tarn 5m/8km S of Aberfeldy. NN 8741
Loch Feochan S'clyde A3, B3 inlet on coast of Argyll, 4m/6km long, 4m/6km S of Oban. NM 8423
Loch Fiag H'land 84 E4 loch in Sutherland dist 8m/13km SW of Altnaharra. NC 4429
Loch Finlaggan S'clyde 62 B2 loch on Islay 3m/5km SW of Port Askaig. On islet at N end of loch are ruins of cas of the Macdonalds, Lords of the Isles. NR 3867
Loch Finlas S'clyde 56 E4 loch 5m/8km S of Dalmellington, to W of Loch Doon. NX 4598
Loch Finsbay W Isles 88 A4* inlet on SE coast of Harris 2m/3km SW of Manish. NG 0886
Loch Fithie Tayside 77 E5 tarn 2m/3km E of Forfar. NO 4951
Loch Fitty Fife 73 E5 small loch 3m/4km W of Cowdenbeath. NT 1291
Loch Fleet D & G 57 F6 loch 7m/11km SW of New Galloway. NX 5669
Loch Fleet H'land 87 B6 inlet on E coast of Sutherland dist formed by estuary of R Fleet 4m/6km N of Dornoch. NH 7896
Loch Flemington H'land 81 G2 small loch on border of Inverness and Nairn dists 5m/8km SW of Nairn. NH 8152
Loch Flodabay W Isles 88 A4* inlet on SE coast of Harris 2m/3km SW of Manish. NG 0886
Lochfoot D & G 58 D4/59 E4 vil at N end of Lochrutton Loch, 5m/8km W of Dumfries. NX 8973
Loch Freuchie Tayside 72 C1 loch in Glen Quaich nearly 2m/3km long NW to SE, and nearly 2m/3km W of Amulree. NN 8637
Loch Frisa S'clyde 68 C4, D4 loch in N part of Mull, 4m/6km S of Tobermory. NM 4848
Loch Fuar-Bheinne S'clyde 70 A6 small loch in Knapdale, Argyll, 2m/3km E of Achahoish. NR 8178
Loch Fuaron S'clyde 69 D5 loch on Mull 2m/3km NW of Lochbuie. NM 5826
Loch Fyne S'clyde 63, 70 long sea-loch in Argyll running N from Sound of Bute and penetrating inland to foot of Glen Fyne, NE of Inveraray. NR 9591
Loch Gair S'clyde 70 B5 inlet on W side of Loch Fyne in Argyll 5m/7km E of Lochgilphead. NR 9290
Loch Garasdale S'clyde 63 E3 small loch in Kintyre, Argyll, 3m/5km S of Clachan. NR 7651
Loch Garry H'land 74 C2, D2 loch and resr of North of Scotland Hydro-Electric Board in course of R Garry, Lochaber dist, 2m/4km W of Invergarry. Length 5m/7km. NH 2302
Loch Garry Tayside 75 F4 narrow, deep loch, 4km long S to N, at head of Glen Garry, Atholl. NN 6270
Loch Garten H'land 81 H5 small loch in Abernethy Forest, in Badenoch and Strathspey dist, 4m/6km E of Boat of Garten. Centre of bird reserve. Nature trail in vicinity. NJ 9718
Lochgarthside H'land 81 E5 locality in Inverness dist on NW shore of Loch Mhór. NH 5219
Loch Garve H'land 80 D2 small but deep loch in Ross and Cromarty dist 4m/7km W of Strathpeffer. NH 4159
Loch Gearach S'clyde 62 A2* small loch on Rinns of Islay 2m/3km E of Kilchiaran Bay. NR 2259
Lochgelly Fife 73 E5 coal-mining tn 7m/11km SW of Glenrothes. **Loch Gelly** is small loch to SE. NT 1893
Loch Ghuilbinn H'land 75 E4 small loch in Lochaber dist 3m/4km N of foot of Loch Ossian. Anglicised form: Loch Gulbin. NN 4174
Loch Gilp S'clyde 70 B6 inlet of Loch Fyne running up past Ardrishaig to Lochgilphead in Argyll. NR 8584
Lochgilphead S'clyde 70 B6 tn at head of Loch Gilp in Argyll. Tourist and shopping centre. NR 8687
Loch Giorra Tayside. See Loch an Daimh.
Loch Glascarnoch H'land 85 D8 resr (North of Scotland Hydro-Electric Board) in Ross and Cromarty dist 14m/23km NW of Dingwall. NH 3470
Loch Glashan S'clyde 70 B5 loch and resr of North of Scotland Hydro-Electric Board in Asknish Forest 4m/7km NE of Lochgilphead, Argyll. NR 9193
Loch Glass H'land 85 E8 loch in Ross and Cromarty dist 8m/12km W of Alness. NH 5172
Loch Glenastle S'clyde 62 B3* small loch on The Oa, Islay, 2m/3km S of Rubha Mór. NR 3044
Loch Glencoul H'land 84 C4 loch running NW to join Loch Glendhu and run past Kylesku into Loch Cairnbawn and thence into Eddrachillis Bay, W coast of Sutherland dist. NC 2531
Loch Glendhu H'land 84 C4 loch running W to join Loch Glencoul and run past Kylesku into Loch Cairnbawn and thence into Eddrachillis Bay, W coast of Sutherland dist. NC 2533
Loch Glow Fife 72 D5 small loch in Cleish Hills 3m/5km W of Kelty. NT 0895
Loch Goil S'clyde 70 D4, D5 loch in Argyll running 6m/10km N to S from Lochgoilhead to Loch Long. NS 2097
Lochgoilhead S'clyde 70 D4 vil at head of Loch Goil in Argyll. NN 1901
Lochgoin Reservoir S'clyde 64 C4 resr 4m/6km SW of Eaglesham. NS 5347
Loch Goosey S'clyde 57 C5 small loch 4m/7km E of Barrhill. NX 2982
Loch Goosie S'clyde 56 D4/E4* small loch 1km N of Loch Riecawr. NX 4494
Loch Gorm S'clyde 62 A2 loch near W coast of Islay 3m/5km NW of Bruichladdich. On islet towards E side of loch are ruins of a Macdonald stronghold. NR 2365
Loch Gowan H'land 80 B2 small loch 2km S of Achnasheen, Ross and Cromarty dist. NH 1456
Loch Grannoch (or Loch Grennoch) D & G 57 E6 loch 7m/11km SW of New Galloway. NX 5469
Loch Grennoch D & G. Alternative spelling of Loch Grannoch, qv.
Loch Greshornish Skye, H'land inlet of Loch Snizort on N coast 6m/10km NE of Dunvegan. NG 3454
Loch Grimshader W Isles 88 C2* long narrow inlet on E coast of Lewis. Vil of Grimshader at head of inlet, 5m/8km S of Stornoway. NB 4125
Loch Grosebay W Isles 88 B3* inlet on SE coast of Harris 5m/8km S of Tarbert. NG 1592
Loch Gruinart S'clyde 62 A2-B1 deep inlet on N coast of Islay. See also Gruinart. NR 2971
Loch Grunavat W Isles 88 A2* loch about 2m/4km N to S near W coast of Lewis 2m/4km W of Lit Loch Roag. NB 0827
Loch Guinach H'land 75 G1 small loch in Badenoch and Strathspey dist 2km NW of Kingussie. NH 7402
Loch Gulbin H'land 75 E4 small loch in Lochaber dist 3m/4km N of foot of Loch Ossian. Gaelic form: Loch Ghuilbinn. NN 4174
Loch Harport Skye, H'land 79 B5 long narrow inlet of Loch Bracadale running up to Drynoch, W of Sligachan. NG 3634
Loch Harrow D & G 58 B3 hill loch 2m/3km E of Corserine, summit of Rinns of Kells. NX 5866
Loch Heilen H'land 86 E1 loch in Caithness dist 3m/4km SE of Dunnet. ND 2568
Loch Hempriggs H'land 86 F3 loch in Caithness dist 2m/4km S of Wick. ND 3447
Loch Heron D & G 57 C6* small loch adjoining Loch Ronald to NE, and 4m/7km NW of Kirkcowan. NX 2764
Loch Hoil Tayside 75 H6 small loch or tarn 4m/6km S of Aberfeldy. NN 8643
Loch Hope H'land 84 E2, E3 narrow loch in Sutherland dist, some 6m/10km long N to S, 2km E of Loch Eriboll at nearest point. NC 4654
Loch Hourn H'land 74 A1 long inlet of Sound of Sleat, penetrating inland to Kinloch Hourn, 5m/8km N of head of Loch Quoich, Lochaber dist. NG 8506
Loch Howie D & G 58 C3 loch 5m/8km E of Dalry. NX 6983
Loch Humphrey S'clyde 64 C2 small loch on Kilpatrick Hills 4m/6km E of Dumbarton. NS 4576
Loch Hunish H'land 78 B2 bay on S side of Rubha Hunish at northern tip of Skye. NG 4076
Loch Inchard H'land 84 C2, C3 large inlet on W coast of Sutherland dist. R Rhiconich flows into head of loch at Rhiconich. NC 2355
Lochinch Castle D & G 57 B6 19c mansion 3m/5km E of Stranraer. Grnds contain pinetum, two lochs (White Loch and Black Loch, the latter being the more easterly), and, on isthmus between them, the ruins of Castle Kennedy, late 16c cas destroyed by fire in 1715. NX 1061
Loch Indaal S'clyde 62 A3-B2 large arm of the sea on E side of Rinns of Islay extending N to within 2m/4km of Loch Gruinart. NR 2758
Lochindorb 81 H4 loch partly in Grampian region and partly in Highland region 8m/13km N of Carrbridge and 6m/10km NW of Grantown-on-Spey. Medieval cas on island in loch. NJ 9736
Loch Insh H'land 75 H1 small loch in course of R Spey in Badenoch and Strathspey dist, 5m/8km NE of Kingussie. NH 8304
Lochinvar D & G 58 C3 loch 3m/5km NE of Dalry. Ruins of old cas on islet in loch, home of 'Young Lochinvar'. NX 6585
Lochinver H'land 85 B5 small fishing port and resort on W coast of Sutherland dist at head of **Loch Inver** 18m/29km N of Ullapool. NC 0922
Loch Iubhair Central 71 E2, F2 loch in course of R Fillan 2m/4km E of Crianlarich. NN 4226
Loch Kanaird H'land 85 B6 inlet of Loch Broom, W coast of Ross and Cromarty dist, into which R Kanaird flows, on E side of Isle Martin. NH 1099
Loch Katrine Central 71 E4, F4 loch 8m/13km long W to E, extending from Glen Gyle to the Trossachs 8m/13km W of Callander. Aqueduct conveys water to Glasgow. NN 4409
Loch Ken D & G 58 C4 long loch in course of Water of Ken, extending 4m/7km southwards from Kenmure Castle, near New Galloway. NX 6573
Loch Kennard Tayside 76 H6 small loch 4m/6km SE of Aberfeldy. NN 9046
Loch Kernsary H'land 78 F2 loch near W coast of Ross and Cromarty dist 1m E of Poolewe. NTS owns area to N and northern part of loch. NG 8780
Loch Killin H'land 81 E6 small loch in Inverness dist 9m/15km E of Fort Augustus. NH 5210
Loch Kinardochy Tayside 75 H5 small loch 3m/4km S of Tummel Br. NN 7755
Loch Kindar D & G 59 E5 loch 1m S of New Abbey. NX 9664
Loch Kinnabus S'clyde 62 B4 small loch on The Oa, Islay, 2m/3km E of Mull of Oa. NR 3042
Loch Kinord Grampian 77 E1/E2 small loch 1m W of Dinnet. NO 4499
Loch Kirkaig H'land 85 B5 inlet on W coast on border of Ross and Cromarty dist and Sutherland dist, 2m/4km SW of Lochinver. See also Kirkaig Pt. NC 0719
Loch Kishorn H'land 79 F5 wide inlet on N side of Loch Carron, Ross and Cromarty dist, opp Plockton. NG 8138
Loch Knockie H'land 75 E1 small loch in Inverness dist 5m/8km NE of Fort Augustus. NH 4513
Loch Laggan Central 71 G5 lakelet 2m/4km SW of Kippen. NS 6292
Loch Laggan H'land 75 E3, F3 loch and resr in Badenoch and Strathspey dist, NE of Loch Moy and Glen Spean. Length 7m/11km NE to SW. NN 4886
Loch Laich S'clyde 70 B1 inlet of Loch Linnhe on E shore, on SW side of Portnacroish, Argyll. See also Castle Stalker. NM 9246
Loch Laide H'land 81 E4 small loch in Inverness dist 4m/7km NE of Drumnadrochit. NH 5435
Loch Laidon 75 E5 narrow loch, 5m/8km long SW to NE, partly in Strathclyde region but mainly in Tayside region, 6m/10km W of Loch Rannoch. Rannoch rly stn near NE end. Also known as Loch Lydoch. NN 3854
Loch Laingeadail S'clyde 62 A1* small loch 3m/5km SW of Ardnave Pt on N coast of Islay. NR 2671

Loch Langavat W Isles 88 B2, B3 loch on island of Lewis midway between Loch Erisort to E and Loch Resort to W. Is 8m/13km long NE to SW, although nowhere more than 1km wide. NB 11, 22
Loch Langavat W Isles 88 A3/A4* loch, some 3m/4km in length N to S, 2m/4km NE of Leverburgh on W coast of Harris. NG 0490
Loch Larig Eala Central 71 F2 small loch 3m/5km S of Killin. NN 5527
Loch Laxford H'land 84 B3, E3 large inlet on W coast of Sutherland dist 4m/6km NE of Scourie. See also (R) Laxford. NC 1950
Loch Leacann S'clyde 70 C4 small loch in Argyll 3m/4km NW of Furnace on Loch Fyne. NN 0003
Loch Leathan Skye, H'land 78 C4 resr (North of Scotland Hydro-Electric Board) 5m/8km N of Portree. NG 5051
Loch Lednock Tayside 72 B2 loch and resr of North of Scotland Hydro-Electric Board near head of Glen Lednock, 5m/8km NW of Comrie. NN 7129
Loch Lee Tayside 77 E3 mt loch in course of Water of Lee 4m/6km W of Tarfside. NO 4279
Loch Leurbost W Isles 88 B2* long inlet on E coast of Lewis. Vil of Leurbost is near head of inlet on N side. NB 3724
Loch Leven H'land 74 B5, C5 loch in Lochaber dist running 11m/17km from Kinlochleven westwards to Loch Linnhe. NN 0859
Loch Leven Tayside 73 E4 loch, some 10m/16km in circumference, on E side of Kinross. Nature reserve. See also Castle I., St Serf's I. NO 1401
Loch Libo S'clyde 64 B3 small loch 3m/5km SW of Neilston. NS 4355
Loch Linnhe 74 C4-A6 long sea-loch, partly in Highland and partly in Strathclyde region, running 22m/35km from Fort William to Mull. NM 9354
Loch Loch Tayside 76 A3, A4 narrow, deep loch, 2km long, 9m/14km NE of Blair Atholl. NN 9874
Loch Lochy H'land 74 C3, D2 loch in Glen More in Lochaber dist, running 10m/16km from Laggan south-westwards to Gairlochy. Caledonian Canal passes through loch. NN 2390
Loch Lomond 71 E3-E6 largest stretch of inland water in Britain, on border of Central and Strathclyde regions. Extends 24m/39km from Ardlui in the N to Balloch in the S. Although generally narrow, the loch widens towards the S end, where there are a number of wooded islands. NS 3598
Loch Long H'land 80 A4, A5 narrow loch in Skye and Lochalsh dist running into Loch Alsh at Dornie. NG 8928
Loch Lossit S'clyde 62 B2 small loch on Islay 3m/5km SW of Port Askaig. NR 4065
Loch Loy H'land 81 H2* small loch in Nairn dist 3m/5km E of Nairn. NH 9358
Loch Loyal H'land 84 F3 large loch, 4m/7km N to S, in Caithness dist 4m/7km S of Tongue. NC 6247
Loch Loyne H'land 74 C1 loch and resr of North of Scotland Hydro-Electric Board, on border of Lochaber and Skye & Lochalsh dists between Lochs Cluanie and Garry. NH 1705
Loch Lubnaig Central 71 F3-G4 narrow loch, 4m/6km long N to S, 3m/5km NW of Callander. NN 5713
Loch Luichart H'land 80 D2 loch and resr of North of Scotland Hydro-Electric Board 6m/10km W of Strathpeffer, Ross and Cromarty dist. Power stn below dam. Length of loch 6m/10km NW to SE. NH 3562
Loch Lundie H'land 74 D1 loch and resr 2km N of Invergarry in Lochaber dist. NH 2903
Loch Lundie H'land 78 F4 loch in Ross and Cromarty dist 3m/5km S of Shieldaig. NG 8049
Loch Lungard H'land 80 B4 upper part of Loch Mullardoch in Skye and Lochalsh dist. NH 0929
Loch Lurgainn H'land 85 B6 loch in Ross and Cromarty dist 8m/13km N of Ullapool. NC 1108
Loch Lydoch 75 E5 alternative name for Loch Laidon, qv.
Loch Lyon Tayside 71 E1-F1 large loch and resr of North of Scotland Hydro-Electric Board at head of Glen Lyon. NN 4141
Loch Maaruig W Isles 88 B3* inlet on W side of Loch Seaforth, Harris, between Seaforth I. and the mouth of the loch. NB 1905
Lochmaben D & G 59 F3 small tn 8m/13km NE of Dumfries, surrounded by several small lochs. Remains of 14c cas on S shore of Castle Loch, to S. This loch and Hightae Mill Loch, 1km farther S, form local nature reserve. NY 0882
Loch Maberry 57 C5 loch, mainly in Dumfries & Galloway region, 5m/9km SE of Barrhill. Remains of old cas on islet in Loch. NX 2875
Loch Macaterick S'clyde 56 D4/E4 loch 4m/6km N of Merrick. NX 4491
Loch Maddy W Isles 88 E1 large inlet and anchorage on E coast of N Uist, containing innumerable islets. On W shore is vil and port of **Lochmaddy.** NF 9369
Loch Magharaidh H'land 85 E8 small loch on Kildermorie Forest, Ross and Cromarty dist, 3m/5km NW of Loch Glass. NH 4576
Loch Magillie D & G 57 B6 small loch 2m/4km E of Stranraer. Also known as Magillie Loch. NX 0959
Loch Mahaick Central 72 B4 small loch or tarn 4m/6km N of Doune. NN 7006
Loch Màma H'land 68 E1 lochan or small loch in S Morar, Lochaber dist, 2m/3km NW of Lochailort. Loch na Creige Duibhe to E runs into head of Loch Màma. NM 7585
Loch Mannoch D & G 58 C5* loch 6m/10km N of Kirkcudbright. NX 6660
Loch Maree H'land 85 A8 loch in W part of Ross and Cromarty dist extending 12m/20km from near Kinlochewe north-westwards to near Poolewe, where it runs out into Loch Ewe. For the most part the width is about 1km, although the maximum width is over 2m/3km. Maximum depth 367 ft or 112 metres. NG 9570
Loch ma Stac H'land 80 D5 small loch in Inverness dist 6m/10km NW of Invermoriston. NH 3421
Loch Meadie H'land 84 E3 loch, 3m/5km N to S, in Caithness dist 5m/8km NW to Altnaharra. NC 5040
Loch Mealt Skye, H'land 78 C3 small loch near NE coast 7m/11km E of Uig. NG 5065
Loch Meavaig W Isles 88 A3* narrow inlet on W coast of Harris 5m/8km NW of Tarbert. NB 0905
Loch Meig H'land 80 D2 loch and resr of North of Scotland Hydro-Electric Board in course of R Meig 2km above its confluence with R Conon in Ross and Cromarty dist. NH 3555
Loch Meiklie H'land 80 D4 small loch in Glen Urquhart, Inverness dist 4m/7km W of Drumnadrochit. NH 4330
Loch Melfort S'clyde 70 A4 inlet on coast of Argyll running up towards Kilmelford. NM 8112
Loch Merkland H'land 84 D4 loch in Sutherland dist 4m/6km SW of summit of Ben Hee. NC 4233
Loch Mhór H'land 81 E5 loch and resr in Inverness dist on E side of Loch Ness, 10m/16km NE of Fort Augustus. Resr used in Foyers Pump Storage Scheme (see Foyers). NH 5319
Loch Migdale H'land 85 F7 loch in Sutherland dist 1m E of Bonar Br. NH 6390
Loch Minnoch D & G 58 B3* small hill loch or tarn on E side of Rinns of Kells, 6m/10km NW of Dalry. NX 5385
Loch Moan D & G 57 D5 loch in Glentrool Forest 7m/12km E of Barrhill. NX 3485
Loch Moidart H'land 68 E2 arm of sea on W coast of Moidart, running up to Kinlochmoidart in Lochaber dist. NM 6472
Loch Monaghan Tayside 75 F5* small loch 2m/3km SE of head of Loch Rannoch. NN 5355
Loch Monar H'land 80 B3-C4 loch and resr (North of Scotland Hydro-Electric Board) at head of Glen Farrar. Level of loch artificially raised by dam at E end. Length of loch 8m/13km. Situated on borders of Inverness, Ross & Cromarty, and Skye & Lochalsh dists. NH 1440
Loch Mór Skye, H'land 78 A4 loch near W coast 7m/11km W of Dunvegan. NG 1448
Loch Moraig Tayside 76 A4 small loch 2m/4km E of Blair Atholl. NN 9066
Loch Morar H'land 79 E8, F8 long, narrow, deep loch, and resr of North of Scotland Hydro-Electricity Board, in Lochaber dist. The loch, which divides N from S Morar, runs 11m/18km E to W, and almost reaches the sea 3m/5km S of Mallaig. Reputed to be deepest loch in Scotland. NM 7790
Loch Mór Barvas W Isles 88 B1* loch to W of Barvas vil, Lewis, at foot of Glen Mór Barvas. NB 3450
Loch More H'land 84 C4, D4 loch in Sutherland dist 4m/6km long NW to SE, 6m/10km SE of Laxford Br. NC 33
Loch More H'land 86 D3 loch in course of R Thurso, Caithness dist, 9m/15km S of Halkirk. ND 0745
Loch Morie H'land 85 E8 loch in Ross and Cromarty dist 8m/13km NW of Alness. NH 5376
Loch Morlich H'land 81 H6 loch in The Queen's Forest, Glen More Forest Park, in Badenoch and Strathspey dist, 4m/6km NW of Cairn Gorm. NH 9609
Loch Moy H'land 75 E3 loch, partly in Lochaber dist and partly in Badenoch and Strathspey dist, between Loch Laggan and confluence of Rs Spean and Treig. NN 4081
Loch Moy H'land 81 G4 loch in Strathdearn Forest, Inverness dist, 9m/15km SE of Inverness. NH 7734
Loch Muck S'clyde 56 E3 small loch 4m/6km SE of Dalmellington. NS 5100
Loch Mudle H'land 68 D3 small loch on Ardnamurchan peninsula in Lochaber dist, 4m/6km NE of Kilchoan. NM 5466
Loch Muick Grampian 76 D3 loch at head of Glen Muick 9m/14km SW of Ballater. NO 2882
Loch Mullardoch H'land 80 C4 loch and resr of North of Scotland Hydro-Electricity Board, on borders of Inverness and Skye & Lochalsh dists 7m/11km W of Cannich. NH 1931
Loch na Beinne Bàine H'land 80 C5 small loch in Inverness dist 8m/13km W of Invermoriston. NH 2819
Loch na Béiste Skye, H'land 79 E6, F6 inlet of Loch Alsh 1km S of Kyleakin. NG 7525
Loch na Cairidh Skye, H'land 79 D6 strait between Scalpay and mainland of Skye. NG 5928
Loch na Caoidhe H'land 80 C3 small loch in course of R Orrin, Ross and Cromarty dist, 6m/10km W of head of Orrin Resr. NH 2246
Loch na Cille S'clyde 69 E8 inlet at S end of peninsula in Argyll situated between Loch Sween and Sound of Jura. NR 6980
Loch na Craige Tayside 75 H6 small loch or tarn 3m/5km SE of Aberfeldy. NN 8845
Loch na Creige Duibhe H'land 68 E1 lochan or small loch in S Morar, Lochaber dist, 2m/3km N of Lochailort. Runs into Loch Màma to W. NM 7685
Loch na Creige Duibhe H'land 84 C4 loch in Sutherland dist adjoining Loch an Leathaid Bhuain, to W of Loch More. NC 2836
Loch na Creitheach Skye, H'land 79 D6 loch near S coast 4m/6km N of Elgol. NG 5120
Loch na Croic H'land 80 D2* small loch in Ross and Cromarty dist in course of Black Water below Loch Garve. NH 4359
Loch na Cuaich H'land 75 G3 small loch in Badenoch and Strathspey dist 4m/6km NE of Dalwhinnie. NN 6987
Loch na Cuilce S'clyde 68 C4* small loch on Mull, on S side of Dervaig. NM 4351
Loch na Dal Skye, H'land 79 E6, E7 inlet of Sound of Sleat at head of Sleat peninsula. NG 7015
Loch na Droma Buidhe H'land 68 D3* inlet on S side of island of Oronsay. NM 5958
Loch na Fùdarlaich S'clyde 62 C1* small loch on Jura 2km NE of Beinn Shiantaidh. NR 5376
Lochnagar Grampian 76 C3 small loch or tarn below mt ridge of same name 7m/11km SE of Braemar. Summit of ridge is Cac Carn Beag, 3789 ft or 1155 metres. Distillery at foot of mt at Easter Balmoral to N. NO 2585
Loch na h-Oidhche H'land 80 A2 loch in W part of Ross and Cromarty dist 4m/7km N of head of Upr Loch Torridon. NG 8865
Loch na Keal S'clyde 69 C4/68 D4 large inlet on W coast of Mull, the head of which reaches to within 4km of E coast at Salen. NM 5038
Loch na Lap H'land 75 E4* small loch or tarn in Lochaber dist 2km NW of foot of Loch Ossian. NN 3971
Loch na Lathaich S'clyde 69 C5, C6 large bay on N coast of Ross of Mull. Vil of Bunessan is at its SE corner. NM 3623
Loch na Leitreach H'land 80 B5 small but deep loch in Skye and Lochalsh dist 6m/9km E of head of Loch Long. NH 0227
Loch nam Bonnach H'land 81 E3 small loch in Inverness dist 3m/5km NW of Beauly. NH 4848
Loch nam Breac Dearga H'land 81 E5 small loch in Inverness dist 4m/6km NE of Invermoriston. NH 4522
Loch na Mile S'clyde 62 C1 bay on E coast of Jura at mouth of Corran R, 3m/4km N of Craighouse. NR 5470
Loch nam Meur H'land 80 D5 small loch in Inverness dist 4m/7km N of Invermoriston. Another small loch of same name 1m N. NH 3923
Loch nan Ceall H'land 68 D1, E1 inlet on coast of Lochaber dist, running up to Arisaig. NM 6486
Loch nan Clach H'land 70 A1 small loch in Morvern, Lochaber dist, 5m/8km NE of Rubha an Ridire. NM 7846
Loch nan Clàr H'land 86 A4 loch in Sutherland dist 6m/10km W of Kinbrace. Southern half of loch is known as Loch Badanloch. NC 7635
Loch nan Cuinne H'land 86 A4 loch adjoining Loch nan Clàr to W, 8m/13km W of Kinbrace. Border between Caithness and Sutherland dists runs down centre of loch. Also known as Loch Rimsdale. NC 7335
Loch nan Eun H'land 80 D5 small loch in Inverness dist 7m/12km NW of Invermoriston. NH 3120
Loch nan Eun H'land 81 E3 small loch on border of Inverness and Ross & Cromarty dist 4m/6km W of Muir of Ord. NH 4648
Loch nan Eun Tayside 76 B3 small loch or tarn 6m/9km NW of Spittal of Glenshee. NO 0678
Loch nan Nighean Tayside 75 H5* small loch 3m/5km SW of Blair Atholl. NN 8461
Loch Nant S'clyde 70 C3 loch and resr of North of Scotland Hydro-Electric Board, 2m/4km NW of Kilchrenan in Argyll. NN 0024
Loch nan Torran S'clyde 63 E1 small loch in Knapdale, Argyll, 3m/4km SE of Ormsary. NR 7568
Loch nan Uamh H'land 68 E1 inlet of Sound of Arisaig on N side of peninsula of Ardnish, on coast of Lochaber dist. NM 6982
Loch na Sealga H'land 85 A7, A8 loch in W part of Ross and Cromarty dist 4m/7km SW of Lit Loch Broom. NH 0382
Loch na Tuadh H'land 84 C3 small loch in Reay Forest, Sutherland dist, 2m/3km S of Foinaven. NC 3147
Loch Naver H'land 84 F4 loch in Caithness dist extending 6m/10km eastwards from Altnaharra. NC 6136

Lochnaw Castle D & G 57 A6 mainly 17c cas, incorporating 16c tower, on S side of small loch 5m/7km W of Stranraer. Once the seat of the Agnews. NW 9962
Loch Neaty H'land 80 D4 small loch in Inverness dist 3m/5km SE of Struy Br. NH 4336
Loch Nedd H'land 84 B4 inlet on S side of Eddrachillis Bay, W coast of Sutherland dist. NC 1333
Loch Neldricken D & G 57 E5 mt loch in Glentrool Forest Park, 2m/3km SE of Merrick. NX 4482
Loch Nell S'clyde 70 B2 loch in Argyll 2m/4km SE of Oban. NM 8927
Loch Ness H'land 80 D6-81 F4 loch in Inverness dist extending NE from Fort Augustus to a point 6m/10km SW of Inverness. Length 23m/36km. Average width about 2km. Maximum depth 754 ft or 230 metres. Loch forms part of course of Caledonian Canal. NH 5023
Loch Nevis H'land 79 F8 long inlet of Sound of Sleat, between Knoydart and N Morar in Lochaber dist. Narrows considerably above Kylesknoydart. Total length about 13m/21km. NM 7695
Loch Ochiltree D & G 57 D5 loch 8m/13km NW of Newton Stewart. NX 3174
Loch of Aboyne Grampian 77 E1 small loch 1m NE of Aboyne. NO 5399
Loch of Blairs Grampian 82 A2 lochan or lakelet 2m/3km S of Forres. NJ 0255
Loch of Boardhouse Orkney 89 A6* large loch in NW Mainland 2m/3km SE of Brough Hd. Named after locality at its NW end. HY 2625
Loch of Boath H'land 81 H3 lochan or lakelet in Nairn dist 7m/11km S of Nairn. NH 8845
Loch of Bosquoy Orkney 89 A6* small loch 2km SE of Dounby, Mainland. HY 3018
Loch of Brindister Shetland. See Brindister.
Loch of Butterstone Tayside 72 D1 small loch SW of Butterstone and 2m/4km NE of Dunkeld. NO 0544
Loch of Cliff Shetland 89 F5 long narrow loch S of Burrafirth, Unst. HP 6012
Loch of Clunie Tayside 73 E1 small loch 4m/6km W of Blairgowrie. On island in loch are remains of Clunie Castle, built about 1500. NO 1144
Loch of Craiglush Tayside 72 D1 small loch 2km NE of Dunkeld. NO 0444
Loch of Drumellie Tayside 73 E1 small loch 2m/3km W of Blairgowrie. Also known as Loch of Marlee. NO 1444
Loch of Flugarth Shetland 89 E6* loch on Mainland 1km N of Burra Voe. HU 3690
Loch of Forfar Tayside 77 E5 small loch on W side of Forfar. NO 4450
Loch of Grandtully Tayside 76 A5/A6* small loch or tarn 4m/6km E of Aberfeldy. NN 9150
Loch of Harray Orkney 89 A6* large loch on Mainland, nearly 5m/8km N to S, S of Dounby. At its S end it is separated from Loch of Stenness by narrow tongue of land and a causeway. HY 2915
Loch of Hundland Orkney 89 A6* loch at N end of Mainland 3m/5km N of Dounby. HY 2925
Loch of Isbister Orkney 89 A6* small loch 3m/5km NW of Dounby. HY 2523
Loch of Kinnordy Tayside 76 D5*. See Kinnordy.
Loch of Kirbister Orkney 89 B6 loch 3m/5km S of Finstown, on N side of rd running W from Kirkwall. HY 3607
Loch of Lintrathen Tayside 76 C5/D5 loch and resr 6m/10km W of Kirriemuir. NO 2754
Loch of Lowes Tayside 72 D1 small loch 2km NE of Dunkeld. Reserve of Scottish Wildlife Trust. NO 0443
Loch of Marlee Tayside 73 E1 small loch 2m/3km W of Blairgowrie. Also known as Loch of Drumellie. NO 1444
Loch of Sabiston Orkney 89 A6* small loch 1m N of Dounby, on Mainland. Named after locality to S towards Dounby. HY 2922
Loch of Skaill Orkney 89 A6* loch near W coast of Mainland 1km E of Skara Brae. HY 2418
Loch of Skene Grampian 77 G1 small round loch 9m/15km W of Aberdeen. NJ 7807
Loch of Snarravoe Shetland 89 F5* loch near SW end of Unst 2km W of Uyeasound. HP 5701
Loch of Spiggie Shetland 89 E8* loch on Mainland 2m/4km NE of Fitful Hd. HU 3716
Loch of Stenness Orkney 89 A6* large loch on Mainland 4m/6km W of Finstown. Separated at its E end from Loch of Harray by narrow tongue of land and a causeway. HY 2812
Loch of Strathbeg Grampian 83 H1 loch near NE coast behind Strathbeg Bay, qv. Loch is 2m/3km long, NW to SE. NK 0758
Loch of Strom Shetland 89 E7* long narrow loch on Mainland in course of Burn of Sandwater and emptying into Stromness Voe, E of Weisdale Voe. HU 4048
Loch of Swannay Orkney 89 A6 large loch at N end of Mainland 5m/8km E of Brough Hd. HY 3128
Loch of Tankerness Orkney 89 B6* loch on Mainland 2m/3km SW of Rerwick Hd. HY 5109
Loch of the Lowes Borders 66 A6 small loch running into head of St Mary's Loch, qv, in Ettrick Forest. NT 2319
Loch of Tingwall Shetland 89 E7* loch on Mainland 2m/3km N of Scalloway. At N end of loch is small island traditionally held to be site of old Norse open-air parliament. HU 4142
Loch of Toftingall H'land 86 E2 loch in Caithness dist 4m/6km W of Watten. ND 1952
Loch of Trebister Shetland. See Trebister.
Loch of Watlee Shetland 89 F5 loch on Unst 2m/4km N of Uyeasound. HP 5905
Loch of Wester H'land 86 F2 loch in Caithness dist 6m/10km N of Wick. ND 3259
Loch of Yarehouse H'land 86 F3* loch in Caithness dist 5m/9km SW of Wick. Also known as Loch of Yarrows. ND 3043
Loch Oich H'land 74 D2 narrow loch in Lochaber dist between Loch Lochy and Loch Ness. Caledonian Canal passes through loch. NE end of loch is in Inverness dist. NH 3100
Loch Olginey H'land 86 D2 loch in Caithness dist 3m/5km SW of Halkirk. ND 0957
Loch Ollay W Isles 88 E2* loch on S Uist 3m/5km E of Rubha Ardvule. NF 7531
Loch Ordie Tayside 76 B5 small loch 4m/6km SE of Ballinluig. NO 0350
Lochore Fife 73 E5 tn 3m/5km N of Cowdenbeath. **Loch Ore** is loch to SW. NT 1796
Loch Osgaig H'land 85 A5/A6 loch near NW coast of Ross and Cromarty dist 1km S of Enard Bay. Also known as Loch Owskeich. NC 0412
Loch Ossian H'land 75 E4 loch in Lochaber dist between head of Loch Treig and head of Loch Ericht. Deer sanctuary to N. NN 3968
Loch o' th' Lowes S'clyde 56 F3* small loch 1m NW of New Cumnock. NS 6014
Loch Ouirn W Isles 88 C2/C3* inlet on E coast of Lewis extending from Gravir to Kebock Hd. NB 4014
Loch Owskeich H'land 85 A5/A6 loch near NW coast of Ross and Cromarty dist 1km S of Enard Bay.
Loch Park Grampian 82 C3 small loch 3m/4km NE of Dufftown. NJ 3543
Loch Pattack H'land 75 F3 small loch in Badenoch and Strathspey dist, from which R Pattack flows N then W to head of Loch Laggan. NN 5379
Loch Peallach S'clyde 68 C3* loch on Mull 2m/3km SW of Tobermory. NM 4853
Loch Pityoulish H'land 81 H5 small loch in Badenoch and Strathspey dist, 2m/3km NE of Aviemore across R Spey. NH 9213
Loch Poit na h-I S'clyde 69 B6 loch 1km E of Fionnphort, Ross of Mull. NM 3122
Loch Polly H'land 85 B5 inlet in Enard Bay, NW coast of Ross and Cromarty dist 2m/4km W of Loch Sionascaig. Also known as Polly Bay. NC 0714
Loch Pooltiel Skye, H'land 78 A4 bay on NW coast 4m/6km S of Dunvegan Hd. NG 1650
Loch Portree Skye, H'land 79 C5 bay on E coast on which tn of Portree is situated. NG 4842
Loch Poulary H'land 74 C2* narrow loch in course of R Garry in Lochaber dist, 1m below confluence of Rs Garry and Kingie. NH 1201
Loch Quien S'clyde 63 G2 small loch on Bute 1km NE of Scalpsie Bay. NS 0659
Loch Quoich H'land 74 B2 loch and resr of North of Scotland Hydro-Electric Board, in Lochaber dist at head of Glen Garry. Length about 9m/14km. NH 0102
Loch Rangag H'land 86 E3 loch in Caithness dist 5m/9km NW of Lybster. ND 1741
Loch Rannoch Tayside 75 F5 loch and resr, 10m/16km long W to E. Dam at Kinloch Rannoch at E end. See also Rannoch, Black Wood of Rannoch. NN 5957
Lochranza S'clyde 63 F3 vil and resort on W side of Loch Ranza, inlet at N end of Arran. Cas (A.M.) dates from 13c. NR 9250
Loch Recar S'clyde. Alternative spelling of Loch Riecawr, qv.
Loch Ree D & G 57 B6 small loch 5m/9km NW of New Luce. NX 1069
Loch Resort W Isles 88 A2, A3 long narrow inlet on W coast of island of Lewis, opp Scarp. NB 01
Loch Restil S'clyde 70 D4 small loch in Argyll immediately N of Rest and be Thankful. NN 2207
Loch Riddon S'clyde 63 F1 inlet in Argyll running N from Kyles of Bute opp Buttock Pt. Also known as Loch Ruel. NS 0076
Loch Riecawr S'clyde 56 D4 loch 3m/4km W of S end of Loch Doon. Alternative spelling: Loch Recar. NX 4393
Loch Righ Mór S'clyde 69 D8 loch on Jura 2m/3km N of Loch Tarbert. NR 5485
Loch Rimsdale H'land 86 A4 loch adjoining Loch nan Clar to W, 8m/13km W of Kinbrace. Border between Caithness and Sutherland dists runs down centre of loch. Also known as Loch nan Cuinne. NC 7335
Loch Roag, East W Isles 88 B2 large inlet on W coast of Lewis on E side of island of Gt Bernera. NB 1837
Loch Roag, Little W Isles 88 A2 narrow loch, 5m/8km long, opening at its N end into Loch Roag, W coast of Lewis. NB 1228
Loch Roag, West W Isles 88 A2 large inlet on W coast of Lewis on W side of island of Gt Bernera. NB 1138
Loch Roan D & G 58 C4 small loch 4m/7km N of Castle Douglas. NX 7469
Loch Ronald D & G 57 C6 loch 4m/7km NW of Kirkcowan. NX 2664
Loch Rosque H'land 80 B2 loch in Ross and Cromarty dist 1m W of Achnasheen, over 3m/5km long E to W. Also known as Loch a' Chroisg. **Lochrosque Forest** is deer forest to NE. NH 1258
Loch Ruard H'land 86 D3 loch in Caithness dist 8m/13km NW of Lybster. ND 1443
Loch Ruel S'clyde. Alternative name for Loch Riddon, qv.
Loch Rusky Central 71 G4 small loch or tarn 3m/5km S of Callander. NN 6103
Loch Ruthven H'land 81 F4 loch in Inverness dist 4m/7km S of Dores. NH 6127
Lochrutton Loch D & G 58 D4/59 E4 loch 5m/8km W of Dumfries. NX 8972
Loch Ryan D & G 57 A6, B6 large inlet and anchorage running from Milleur Pt, at N end of Rinns of Galloway, to Stranraer at head of loch. NX 0465
Loch Sand H'land 86 D3 loch in Caithness dist 8m/12km NW of Latheron. ND 0941
Loch Saugh Grampian 77 F3 small loch 4m/6km NE of Fettercairn. NO 6778
Loch Scadavay W Isles 88 E1 loch on N Uist 4m/6km W of Lochmaddy. NF 8668
Loch Scalloch S'clyde 56 C4 small loch or tarn 3m/5km S of Barr. NX 2889
Loch Scamadale S'clyde 70 B3 small but deep loch in Argyll 6m/10km S of Oban. NM 8920
Loch Scarmclate H'land 86 E2 loch in Caithness dist 7m/11km SE of Thurso. ND 1859
Loch Scavaig Skye, H'land 79 C6-D7 large inlet or bay on S coast between Elgol and island of Soay. Cuillin Hills rise steeply from N shore. NG 4916
Loch Scaven H'land 80 B3 small loch in Ross and Cromarty dist 5m/8km SW of Achnasheen. Also known as Loch Sgamhain. NH 0952
Loch Schechernich Tayside 76 C4. See Loch Shechernich.
Loch Scoly Tayside 76 A6* small loch or tarn 4m/7km E of Aberfeldy. NN 9147
Loch Scresort H'land 79 C8 inlet on E coast of island of Rum, containing the only landing place on the island. Vil of Kinloch at head of inlet. NM 4199
Loch Scridain S'clyde 69 C5, D5 long inlet on W coast of Mull penetrating to foot of Glen More. NM 4525
Loch Seaforth W Isles 88 B2, B3 narrow inlet penetrating deep into SE coast of Harris NE of Tarbert. Length 14m/23km. See also Seaforth I. NB 21, 22
Loch Sealbhanach H'land 80 C4 small loch in course of R Cannich in Inverness dist below Loch Mullardoch. NH 2331
Loch Sealg W Isles 88 B3 large inlet on E coast of Lewis SW of Kebock Hd. Also known as Loch Shell. NB 31
Loch Seil S'clyde 70 A3 small loch in Argyll 2km SW of Kilninver. NM 8020
Loch Sgamhain H'land 80 B3 small loch in Ross and Cromarty dist 5m/8km SW of Achnasheen. Also known as Loch Scaven. NH 0952
Loch Shandra Tayside 76 C4* tarn on W edge of Glenisla Forest 1m N of Kirkton of Glenisla. NO 2162
Loch Shawbost W Isles 88 B1* bay on NW coast of Lewis 1km N of S Shawbost across Loch a' Bhaile. NB 2548
Loch Shechernich (or Schechernich) Tayside 76 C4 small loch or tarn 3m/5km E of Spittal of Glenshee. Also known as Loch Bainnie or Bainie. NO 1668
Loch Sheilavaig W Isles 88 E2* inlet on E coast of S Uist 1m N of Loch Skiport. NF 8340
Loch Shell W Isles 88 B3 large inlet on E coast of Lewis SW of Kebock Hd. Also known as Loch Sealg. NB 31
Loch Shiel H'land 68 F2 narrow loch, 17m/27km long, in Lochaber dist, extending SW from Glenfinnan to Acharacle, between Moidart and Sunart. NM 8072
Loch Shieldaig H'land 78 F2 inlet of Gair Loch on W coast of Ross and Cromarty dist, 3m/4km S of Gairloch vil. NG 8072
Loch Shieldaig H'land 78 F4 arm of Loch Torridon, W coast of Ross and Cromarty dist. Vil of Shieldaig at head of loch. NG 7955
Loch Shin H'land 85 E5 loch in Sutherland dist, 17m/27km NW to SE at Lairg. Width varies from under 1km to just over 2km. Maximum depth about 195 ft or 60 metres. Water level raised by concrete dam at SE end (Shin Hydro-Electric Scheme). **Lit Loch Shin** formed by damming R Shin below Lairg. See also Shin Forest, Shin (r). NC 4816
Loch Shira S'clyde 70 C4 inlet of Loch Fyne N of Inveraray in Argyll. NN 1009
Loch Shurrery H'land 86 D2 loch in Caithness dist 9m/15km SW of Thurso. ND 0455
Lochside D & G 59 E4* NW dist of Dumfries. NX 9577
Loch Sionascaig H'land 85 B5 loch near NW coast of Ross and Cromarty dist 5m/8km S of Lochinver. NC 1213
Loch Skeen D & G 65 H6 small loch in hills NE of Moffat, 1m N of White Coomb. NT 1716
Loch Skerrow D & G 58 B4/C4 loch 7m/11km N of Gatehouse of Fleet. NX 6068
Loch Skiach Tayside 76 A6 small loch 4m/6km SW of Ballinluig. **Lit Loch Skiach** is smaller loch to S. NN 9547
Loch Skiport W Isles 88 E2 inlet on E coast of S Uist 12m/20km N of Lochboisdale. NF 8438

Loch Slapin Skye, H'land 79 D6 inlet on S coast on E side of Strathaird peninsula. NG 5717
Loch Sligachan Skye, H'land 79 C5, D5 inlet on E coast 7m/11km S of Portree. NG 5132
Loch Sloy S'clyde 70 D3-71 D4 loch and resr on W side of Ben Vorlich, 3m/5km SW of Ardlui. Tunnel aqueduct to Inveruglas on W shore of Loch Lomond. NN 2812
Loch Smigeadail S'clyde 62 B1* small loch or tarn near N coast of Islay, 2m/3km S of Rubha Bholsa. NR 3875
Loch Snizort H'land 78 B3 large bay on N coast of Skye between Trotternish and Vaternish. **Loch Snizort Beag** is long narrow inlet of bay at its SE corner, penetrating 6m/10km inland. NG 3261
Loch Spallander Reservoir S'clyde 56 D3 resr 6m/9km E of Maybole. NS 3908
Loch Spelve S'clyde 69 E5 large inlet with narrow entrance on SE coast of Mull. NM 6927
Loch Spey H'land 75 E2 small loch, or tarn, in Badenoch and Strathspey dist near source of R Spey, 10m/16km S of Fort Augustus. NN 4293
Loch Spynie Grampian 82 B1 small loch 3m/4km S of Lossiemouth. NJ 2366
Loch Squabain Mull, S'clyde. See Loch Airdeglais.
Loch Stack H'land 84 C3 loch in Sutherland dist, in course of R Laxford between Loch More and Loch Laxford. NC 2942
Loch Staoisha S'clyde 62 B1 small loch on Islay 2m/3km NW of Port Askaig. NR 4071
Loch Staosnaig S'clyde 69 C8 bay on E coast of Colonsay to S of Scalasaig. NR 3993
Loch Steisevat W Isles 88 A3* loch near SW coast of Harris on N side of Leverburgh. NG 0187
Loch Stochy S'clyde 56 D4* small loch running into Loch Riecawr from SW. NX 4292
Loch Stockinish W Isles 88 B3* inlet on SE coast of Harris 5m/8km S of Tarbert. NG 1292
Loch Stornoway S'clyde 62 D2/63 E2 bay on S coast of Knapdale, Argyll, 2m/3km N of Ardpatrick Pt. NR 7361
Loch Strandavat W Isles 88 B2* narrow loch, 2km long N to S, on Lewis 1m W of head of Loch Erisort. NB 2519
Loch Striven S'clyde 63 G1 sea-loch in Argyll running up for 8m/13km northwards from Strone Pt, Kyles of Bute. NS 0777
Loch Suainaval W Isles 88 A2 long narrow loch, nearly 4m/6km N to S, near W coast of Lewis S of Uig. NB 0629
Loch Sunart H'land 68 E3 long arm of the sea on W coast in Lochaber dist, between Ardnamurchan and Sunart to N and Morvern to S. NM 7262
Loch Sween S'clyde 69 F8 sea-loch running NE from Danna I. to Knapdale Forest, Argyll. Afforestation on banks. NR 7383
Loch Tamanavay W Isles 88 A2* inlet on W coast of Lewis 4m/7km S of Mealisval mt. Tamanavay R flows into loch from E. NB 0320
Loch Tanna S'clyde 63 F3 loch on Arran 3m/5km E of Pirnmill. NR 9242
Loch Tarbert S'clyde 69 D8 long inlet in W coast of Jura, almost bisecting the island. NR 5481
Loch Tarbert, East and **West** W Isles 88 A3, B3 large inlets on E and W coasts of Harris. Vil and port of Tarbert on isthmus between the two. NG 19, NB 10
Loch Tarbert, East S'clyde 63 E1/F1 inlet of Loch Fyne at N end of Kintyre, Argyll, running up to Tarbert, for which it provides a harbour. NR 8769
Loch Tarbert, West S'clyde sea-loch in Argyll running NE, from Ardpatrick Pt, between Knapdale and Kintyre. Isthmus of only 1m separates head of loch from E Loch Tarbert on Loch Fyne. Quay near W Tarbert at head of loch, with passenger services to Islay. NR 8062
Loch Tarff H'land 80 D6 small loch in Inverness dist 3m/5km E of Fort Augustus. NH 4210
Loch Tarsan S'clyde 70 C6 loch and resr in Argyll 1m E of head of Loch Striven. NS 0784
Loch Tay Tayside 71 G2-H1 loch 15m/24km long from Killin in the SW to Kenmore in the NE, and in places over 500 ft (over 150 metres) deep. Noted for salmon. NN 6838
Loch Teacuis H'land 68 D3, E3 long inlet on N coast of Morvern, in Lochaber dist. NM 6356
Loch Tealasavay W Isles 88 A2* inlet on W coast of Lewis between Loch Tamanavay and Loch Resort. NB 0218
Loch Teàrnait H'land 70 A1 small loch in Morvern, Lochaber dist, 4m/7km N of Rubha an Ridire. NM 7447
Loch Thom S'clyde 64 A2 loch and resr 3m/4km SW of Greenock. NS 2572
Loch Thuirnaig H'land 78 F2 inlet of Loch Ewe, on E side of loch, 2m/3km N of Poolewe, Ross and Cromarty dist. NG 8684
Loch Thulachan H'land. See Lochan Thulachan.
Loch Tinker Central 71 F4 small loch 4m/6km SE of Stronachlachar. NN 4406
Loch Tollie H'land 78 F2 loch near W coast of Ross and Cromarty dist 3m/4km E of Gairloch. Also known as **Loch Tollaidh.** NG 8478
Lochton, Upper Grampian 77 F2* loc 1m N of Banchory. NO 6997
Loch Torridon H'land 78 E3 wide inlet on W coast of Ross and Cromarty dist between Red Pt and Rubha na Fearn. Upper part of loch E of Shieldaig is known as **Upr. Loch Torridon** Distance from Rubha na Fearn to head of Upr Loch Torridon is 12m/19km NG7560
Loch Toscaig H'land 79 E5 inlet on W coast of Ross and Cromarty dist 4m/7km S of Applecross. NG 7137
Loch Tralaig S'clyde 70 B3 small loch and resr in Argyll 3m/5km NE of head of Loch Melfort. NM 8816
Loch Trealaval W Isles 88 B2* large loch of irregular shape 2m/3km NW of Balallan, Lewis. NB 2723
Loch Treaslane Skye, H'land 78 B4* inlet of Loch Snizort Beag on N coast, 8m/12km NW of Portree. NG 3952
Loch Treig H'land 74 D4 loch and resr in Lochaber dist, 5m/9km long S to N, 14m/23km E of Fort William. Supplies water to aluminium works at Fort William by tunnel under Ben Nevis. Glasgow–Fort William rly runs along E side of loch. Length of dam at N end 440 ft or 134 metres. NN 3372
Loch Triochatan H'land 74 C5 small loch in Glen Coe in Lochaber dist, 4m/7km SW of Kinlochleven. Ossian, legendary Gaelic warrior and bard, supposedly of 3c, is said to have been born beside its waters. NN 1456
Loch Trollamarig W Isles 88 B3* inlet on coast of Harris on W side of entrance to Loch Seaforth. NB 2201
Loch Tromlee S'clyde 70 C3 small loch in Argyll 2km N of Kilchrenan. NN 0425
Loch Trool D & G 58 A4 loch in Glentrool Forest Park 8m/13km N of Newton Stewart. NX 4179
Loch Truderscaig H'land 86 A4 small loch 1m SW of Loch Rimsdale. Border of Caithness and Sutherland dists runs down centre of loch. NC 7132
Loch Tuath Mull, S'clyde 68 B4, C4 arm of sea on W of island, with main island to N and Gometra and Ulva to S. NM 3943
Loch Tuill Bhearnach H'land 80 C4* small loch in Ross and Cromarty dist 1km SE of summit of Sgurr na Lapaich. NH 1634
Loch Tulla S'clyde 70 D1-71 E1 loch in Argyll 2m/3km N of Br of Orchy. See also Water of Tulla. NN 2942
Loch Tummel Tayside 75 H5 loch and resr of North of Scotland Hydro-Electric Board, 7m/11km long W to E. The dam at E end is 4m/6km NW of Pitlochry. NN 8259
Loch Turret Tayside 72 B2 loch and resr in Glen Turret 5m/8km NW of Crieff. NN 8027

Lochty Fife 73 G4 loc 4m/6km NW of Anstruther. L. Private Rly (steam). NO 5208
Loch Uigedail S'clyde 62 B3 small loch on Islay 3m/4km N of Ardbeg. NR 4050
Loch Uisg S'clyde 69 E5 loch nearly 2m/3km long between Loch Buie and Loch Spelve, Mull. NM 6425
Loch Uisge H'land 68 F3 small loch in Morvern, Lochaber dist, 3m/4km NW of Loch a' Choire. NM 8055
Loch Uraraidh S'clyde 62 B3 small loch on Islay 4m/7km N of Ardbeg. NR 4053
Loch Urigill H'land 85 C6 loch in Sutherland dist 7m/11km S of Inchnadamph. NC 2410
Loch Urr D & G 58 D3 loch 4m/7km S of Moniaive. NX 7684
Loch Urrahag W Isles 88 B1* loch 2m/3km long N to S near NW coast of Lewis, to E and SE of Arnol vil. NB 3247
Loch Uskavagh W Isles 88 E2 bay containing numerous islets on E coast of Benbecula. NF 8551
Loch Ussie H'land 81 E2 loch, roughly circular in shape, 3m/4km W of Dingwall in Ross and Cromarty dist. NH 5057
Loch Vaich H'land 85 D8 resr (North of Scotland Hydro-Electric Board) in Ross and Cromarty dist 16m/25km NW of Dingwall. NH 3475
Loch Valigan Tayside 76 A4* tarn 3m/4km S of summit of Beinn a' Ghlo. NN 9769
Loch Valley D & G 57 E5 loch in Glentrool Forest Park, 2m/3km NE of Loch Trool. NX 4481
Loch Vallich H'land 78 F3 loch 2m/3km in length E to W, 4m/7km N of Upr Loch Torridon, Ross and Cromarty dist. Also known as Loch a' Bheallaich. NG 8664
Loch Varkasaig Skye, H'land 79 A5 inlet of Loch Bracadale 3m/5km S of Dunvegan. NG 2542
Loch Venachar Central 71 F4, G4 loch extending nearly 4m/6km W to E, 2m/4km W of Callander. NN 5705
Loch Veyatie H'land 85 B5, C5 narrow loch, 4m/6km long NW to SE, 7m/11km SW of Inchnadamph. Border of Ross & Cromarty and Sutherland dists runs down centre of loch. NC 1713
Loch Voil Central 71 F3 narrow loch, nearly 4m/6km long W to E. Vil of Balquhidder at E end. NN 5019
Loch Watston Central 71 B4* lakelet 2km SW of Doune. NN 7100
Loch Wharral Tayside 76 D3 small loch or tarn 2m/3km NE of Clova. NO 3574
Loch Whinyeon D & G 58 C5 loch 3m/5km NE of Gatehouse of Fleet. NX 6260
Lochwinnoch S'clyde 64 B3 small tn 12m/19km SW of Paisley. Textiles, furniture mnfre. NS 3558
Lochy H'land 74 C4 r in Lochaber dist running SW from Loch Lochy to head of Loch Linnhe. NN 1175
Lochy S'clyde 70 D2 r in Argyll running W down Glen Lochy to R Orchy 2m/3km E of Dalmally. NN 1927
Lochy Burn 82 B4. See Burn of Lochy.
Lockengate Cornwall 3 E2 ham 4m/7km SW of Bodmin. SX 0361
Lockerbie D & G 59 F3 mkt tn 11/17km E of Dumfries. Industries include mnfre of cheese and cream; woollen goods. Livestock fairs. NY 1381
Lockeridge Wilts 17 F4 vil 3m/5km W of Marlborough. Sarsen stones known locally as Grey Wethers (NT). SU 1467
Lockerley Hants 10 A2 vil 5m/8km NW of Romsey. Adjoining vil to S, locs of **L. Green** and **Critchell's Green.** SU 2926
Lockhills Cumbria 60 B6* loc 1m N of Armathwaite. NY 5047
Locking Avon 15 H5 vil 3m/5km SE of Weston-super-Mare. ST 3659
Lockinge Oxon 17 H3 par containing hams of **E** and **W Lockinge** 2m/3km E of Wantage. SU 4287
Lockington Humberside 51 E3 vil 5m/8km NW of Beverley. SE 9947
Lockington Leics 36 A2/B2 vil 2km E of Castle Donington. SK 4627
Lockleaze Avon 16 B4* NE dist of Bristol. ST 6076
Lockleywood Salop 34 D2 ham 4m/6km S of Mkt Drayton. SJ 6928
Locksbottom London 20 B5 loc in borough of Bromley 2m/3km W of Orpington. TQ 4365
Locksgreen Isle of Wight 10 B5* loc 4m/6km W of Newport. SZ 4490
Locks Heath Hants 10 C4* suburb 1km S of Park Gate. SU 5107
Lockton N Yorks 55 F5 vil 5m/8km NE of Pickering. SE 8489
Lockwood Beck Reservoir Cleveland 55 E4* small resr 2km W of Moorsholm. NZ 6814
Lockwood Reservoir 20 A3 resr in R Lea valley W of Walthamstow and 7m/11km N of London Br. TQ 3590
Lodden 9 E2* r rising 5m/8km NE of Gillingham, Dorset, and flowing into R Stour 1m S of the tn. ST 8025
Loddington Leics 36 D4 vil 5m/8km NW of Uppingham. SK 7902
Loddington Northants 36 D6 vil 4m/6km W of Kettering. SP 8178
Loddiswell Devon 4 D5 vil 3m/4km NW of Kingsbridge, above valley of R Avon. SX 7248
Loddon Norfolk 39 G5 small tn on R Chet 6m/10km NW of Beccles. TM 3698
Loddon 18 C4 r rising E of Basingstoke, Hants, and flowing NE into R Thames W of Wargrave, Berks. SU 7778
Lode Cambs 30 A2 vil 6m/10km NE of Cambridge. Anglesey Abbey (NT), hse built *c.* 1600 on site of medieval monastery. TL 5362
Lode Heath W Midlands 35 G6* dist of Solihull 1km N of tn centre. SP 1580
Lode, High 37 G5* r rising E of Alconbury, Cambs, and flowing NE through Ramsey and thence into R Nene (old course). TL 2887
Loder Head Shetland 89 E7* headland on E coast of island of Bressay at entrance to Voe of Cullingsburgh. HU 5243
Loders Dorset 8 C5 vil 2m/3km NE of Bridport. SY 4994
Lodge Green W Midlands 35 H5* loc 6m/10km NW of Coventry. SP 2583
Lodge Island D & G 58 C5* 'island' in R Dee, connected to E bank by causeway, 2m/3km SW of Castle Douglas. NX 7361
Lodge Park H & W 27 E1* dist of Redditch S of tn centre. SP 0466
Lodge Park Northants 36 D5* W dist of Corby. SP 8689
Lodore Falls Cumbria 52 C3 cascade near mouth of Watendlath Beck, at S end of Derwent Water. NY 2618
Lodsworth W Sussex 11 F3 vil 3m/5km NE of Midhurst. SU 9223
Lofthouse N Yorks 48 D1 vil on R Nidd 6m/10km NW of Pateley Br. SE 1073
Lofthouse W Yorks 49 E5 vil in coal-mining area 3m/5km N of Wakefield. **L. Gate** vil 1m S. SE 3326
Loftus Cleveland 55 F3 iron ore mining tn 4m/6km SE of Saltburn. NZ 7218
Logan S'clyde 56 F2* vil 2km E of Cumnock. NS 5820
Logan Botanic Gardens D & G. See Port Logan.
Loganlea Lothian 65 F3* loc adjoining Addiewell to W, 4m/7km S of Bathgate. NS 9862
Loganlea Reservoir Lothian 65 H3 small resr on Pentland Hills 3m/5km NW of Penicuik. NT 1962
Logan Water 65 E5 r in Strathclyde region running E to R Nethan 2m/3km SW of Lesmahagow. **Logan Resr** in course of r near source. NS 7936
Loggerheads Staffs 34 D1 ham 4m/7km E of Mkt Drayton. SJ 7335
Loggie H'land 85 B7 locality on W shore of Loch Broom, Ross and Cromarty dist, 4m/6km from head of loch. NH 1490
Logie Fife 73 G3 vil 3m/5km W of Leuchars. NO 4020
Logie Tayside 77 F4* loc 4m/6km N of Montrose. NO 6963
Logie-Buchan Grampian. Par containing vil of Kirkton of L.-B., qv.
Logie Head Grampian 82 D1 headland on N coast 2km NE of Cullen. NJ 5268
Logie Pert Tayside 77 F4 vil 5m/8km NW of Montrose. Cottage within par, to NW of vil, is birthplace of James Mill, 1773-1836. NO 6664

Logierait Tayside 76 A5 vil 4m/7km SE of Pitlochry, near confluence of Rs Tay and Tummel. NN 9651
Login Dyfed 22 D3 vil 5m/8km NW of Whitland. SN 1623
Loin Water 71 E4* r in S'clyde region running S down Glen Loin to head of Loch Long. NN 2904
Loirston Loch Grampian 77 H1* small loch 1m W of Cove Bay and 3m/5km S of Aberdeen. NJ 9301
Lolworth Cambs 29 G2 vil 6m/10km NW of Cambridge. TL 3664
Lomond Hills 73 E4 range of hills on borders of Fife and Tayside regions NE of Loch Leven. Summit is W Lomond, 1712 ft or 522 metres. NO 2106
Lomond, West Fife 73 E4 summit of Lomond Hills 3m/4km S of Strathmiglo. Height 1712 ft or 522 metres. NO 1906
Lonan Isle of Man 46 C5 loc nearly 1m S of Laxey. SC 4383
Lonan S'clyde 70 B2 r in Argyll running W down Glen Lonan to head of Loch Nell 3m/5km E of Oban. NM 9028
Lonbain H'land 78 E4 loc in Ross and Cromarty dist 6m/9km N of Applecross. NG 6852
Londesborough Humberside 50 D4 vil 2m/4km N of Mkt Weighton. SE 8645
London 119 capital of England and conurbation of thirty-two boroughs whose central administrative authority is the Greater London Council, together with the City of London. Legislative capital of the UK. Major port (Port of London Authority). Financial, commercial, distribution and communications centre. Most industries represented except basic industries such as mining. Royal residences. University founded 1836. Airports at Heathrow and Gatwick. TQ 3079
London Apprentice Cornwall 3 E3* vil 2m/3km S of St Austell. SX 0050
London Beach Kent 13 E3* loc 2m/3km N of Tenterden. TQ 8836
London, City of 19 G3* county within Greater London, some 2m/3km E of Charing Cross. Financial centre. Small area contains St Paul's Cathedral, Guildhall, Bank of England, Stock Exchange, Mansion Hse, etc. Various Roman remains. TQ 3281
London Colney Herts 19 F2 suburb 3m/4km SE of St Albans. TL 1704
Londonderry N Yorks 54 C6 vil 2m/4km E of Bedale. SE 3087
Londonderry W Midlands 35 F5* dist of Warley 1m N of tn centre. SP 0087
London End Northants 28 D2* E end of Irchester, 3m/5km SE of Wellingborough. SP 9265
London Fields W Midlands 35 F5* loc in Dudley 1m W of tn centre. SO 9290
London (Gatwick) Airport W Sussex 11 H1 international airport 1m S of Horley and 24m/39km S of London. TQ 2841
London (Heathrow) Airport London 19 E4 major international airport, situated in borough of Hillingdon 14m/23km W of Charing Cross. TQ 0775
London, Little Bucks 18 B1* ham 6m/9km NW of Thame. SP 6412
London, Little Cambs 37 H5* loc in March to W of tn centre. TL 4196
London, Little Essex 29 H5* ham 5m/8km N of Bishop's Stortford. TL 4729
London, Little E Sussex 12 C4 ham 2km SW of Heathfield. TQ 5619
London, Little Glos 26 C5* loc 5m/8km S of Newent. SO 7018
London, Little Hants 17 G6* ham 3m/5km N of Andover. SU 3749
London, Little Hants 18 B5 vil 5m/8km N of Basingstoke. SU 6259
London, Little Isle of Man 46 B5 loc 3m/5km S of Kirk Michael. SC 3286
London, Little Lincs 37 G3 loc 1m SW of Spalding. TF 2421
London, Little Lincs 37 H2 loc adjoining Long Sutton to N. TF 4323
London, Little Lincs 45 E3* loc 3m/4km SE of Mkt Rasen. TF 1486
London, Little Lincs 45 G4 loc 6m/10km NE of Horncastle. TL 3375
London, Little Norfolk 38 B3 loc 1km E of Terrington St Clement. TF 5520
London, Little Norfolk 38 B5 E part of Southery. TL 6294
London, Little Norfolk 38 C5* loc 1km SE of Northwold. TL 7696
London, Little Norfolk 39 E2*loc adjoining Corpusty to NW. TG 1030
London, Little Norfolk 39 G2* loc 1m NE of N Walsham. TG 2931
London, Little Oxon 18 A2* suburban loc 3m/5km S of Oxford. SP 5201
London, Little Oxon 18 B3 loc at Brightwell, 2m/3km NW of Wallingford. SU 5891
London, Little Powys 33 G5* loc 2m/3km SE of Caersws. SO 0489
London, Little Som 16 B6* ham adjoining Oakhill to W, 3m/4km N of Shepton Mallet. ST 6247
London, Little Suffolk 31 E3* ham 2m/3km S of Stowmarket. TM 0555
London, Little W Yorks 48 D4/49 E4* S dist of Yeadon. SE 2039
London, Little W Yorks 49 E4* loc in Sheepscar dist of Leeds 1km NE of city centre. SE 3034
London Minstead Hants 10 A3* ham adjoining Minstead and 2m/4km NW of Lyndhurst. SU 2811
Londonthorpe Lincs 37 E1 ham 3m/5km NE of Grantham. SK 9537
Longacre Green Suffolk 30 B3* loc 6m/10km N of Haverhill. TL 6755
Longa Island H'land 78 E2 uninhabited island of about 360 acres or 145 hectares at mouth of Gair Loch, W coast of Ross and Cromarty dist 1m S of Rubha Ban. NG 7377
Longannet Fife 72 D5* power stn on N bank of R Forth 2m/4km W of Culross. NS 9585
Long Ashton Avon 16 B4 vil 3m/5km SW of Bristol. ST 5470
Longay Skye, H'land 79 E5 uninhabited island of about 150 acres or 60 hectares lying 1m E of Scalpay at S end of Inner Sound. NG 6531
Long Bank H & W 26 C1* vil 2m/3km W of Bewdley. SO 7674
Long Bennington Lincs 36 D1 vil 7m/12km NW of Grantham. SK 8344
Longbenton Tyne & Wear 61 G4 tn in N Tyneside dist 3m/4km N of Newcastle. NZ 2668
Longborough Glos 27 F4 vil 3m/4km N of Stow-on-the-Wold. SP 1729
Long Bredy Dorset 8 D5 vil 8m/12km W of Dorchester. SY 5690
Longbridge Devon 4 B5* dist of Plymouth 3m/5km NE of city centre. SX 5156
Longbridge Warwicks 27 G2 loc 2m/3km SW of Warwick. SP 2662
Longbridge W Midlands 35 F6* loc in Birmingham 7m/11km SW of city centre. Car factory. SP 0077
Longbridge Deverill Wilts 9 F1 vil 3m/4km S of Warminster. ST 8640
Longbridge Hayes Staffs 42 D6* loc 1m W of Burslem. SJ 8549
Long Buckby Northants 28 B1 vil 5m/8km NE of Daventry. SP 6267
Longburgh Cumbria 59 G5 loc 2km W of Burgh by Sands. NY 3058
Longburton Dorset 8 D3 vil 3m/4km S of Sherborne. ST 6412
Long Clawson Leics 36 C2 vil 5m/9km N of Melton Mowbray. SK 7227
Longcliffe Derbys 43 G5* ham 4m/6km W of Wirksworth. SK 2255
Longcombe Devon 5 E4* ham 2m/3km E of Totnes. SX 8359
Long Common Hants 10 C3* loc 1m N of Botley. SU 5014
Long Compton Staffs 35 E2* ham 4m/7km W of Stafford. SJ 8522
Long Compton Warwicks 27 G4 vil 4m/6km NW of Chipping Norton. SP 2832
Longcot Oxon 17 G3 vil 3m/5km SW of Faringdon. SU 2790
Long Crendon Bucks 18 B1 vil 2m/3km NW of Thame. 14c courthouse (NT). SP 6908
Long Crichel Dorset 9 G3 vil 6m/10km NE of Blandford Forum. ST 9710
Longcroft Central 65 E1 vil 3m/5km NE of Cumbernauld. NS 7979
Longcroft Cumbria 59 G5* loc 2km NW of Kirkbride across R Wampool. NY 2158
Long Cross Wilts 9 E1* ham 1m NE of Zeals and 2m/3km W of Mere. ST 7832
Longdale Cumbria 53 F4* loc 2m/3km E of Tebay. NY 6405
Long Dale Notts 44 A5* loc 4m/6km NE of Hucknall. SK 5653
Long Dean Wilts 16 D4* loc 5m/7km W of Chippenham. ST 8575
Longden Salop 34 B4 vil 5m/8km SW of Shrewsbury. **L. Common** loc 2km S. SJ 4404
Longdendale Derbys 43 E2 valley of R Etherow in Peak Dist. SK 09
Long Ditton Surrey 19 F5 suburban loc 2km SW of Surbiton. TQ 1666
Longdon H & W 26 D4 vil 4m/7km NW of Tewkesbury. SO 8336
Longdon Staffs 35 G3 vil 4m/6km SE of Rugeley. **L. Green** vil 1m SE. **Upr Longdon** vil 2km W. SK 0814
Longdon upon Tern Salop 34 C3 vil 3m/5km NW of Wellington. SJ 6215
Longdown Devon 7 F5 ham 4m/6km W of Exeter. SX 8691
Long Downs (or Longdowns) Cornwall 2 C5 vil 2m/4km W of Penryn. SW 7434
Long Drax N Yorks 50 B5* loc 1m N of Drax. SE 6728
Long Duckmanton Derbys 43 H4* vil 1km S of Duckmanton and 2m/3km W of Bolsover. SK 4471
Long Eaton Derbys 36 B1 mnfg tn 9m/14km E of Derby and 6m/10km SW of Nottingham. SK 4933
Long Eau r in Lincs. See Eau, Great.
Longfield Kent 20 C4 suburban development 4m/7km SW of Gravesend. TQ 6069
Longfield Wilts 16 D5* SE dist of Trowbridge. ST 8657
Longfield Hill Kent 20 C5* vil 4m/6km S of Gravesend. TQ 6268
Longfleet Dorset 9 H5 central dist of Poole. SZ 0191
Longford Derbys 35 H1 vil 9m/14km W of Derby. SK 2137
Longford Glos 26 D5 vil 2km N of Gloucester. SO 8320
Longford London 19 E4 loc at W end of London (Heathrow) Airport 16m/26km W of Charing Cross. TQ 0476
Longford Salop 34 D1 ham 2m/3km W of Mkt Drayton. SJ 6433
Longford Salop 34 D3* ham 2km W of Newport. SJ 7218
Longford W Midlands 35 H5 loc in Coventry 3m/5km N of city centre. SP 3583
Longford Castle Wilts. See Odstock.
Longforgan Tayside 73 F2 vil 6m/10km W of Dundee. NO 3129
Longformacus Borders 66 D3 vil on Dye Water 6m/10km W of Duns. NT 6957
Longframlington Nthmb 61 F2 vil 5m/7km E of Rothbury. NU 1301
Long Green Essex 30 D5* ham 3m/5km E of Coggeshall. TL 9023
Long Green H & W 26 D4* ham 3m/5km W of Tewkesbury. SO 8433
Long Green Suffolk 31 E1* loc adjoining Wortham to W. TM 0777
Longham Dorset 9 G4 suburb 5m/8km N of Bournemouth. SZ 0698
Longham Norfolk 38 D3 vil 4m/6km NW of E Dereham. TF 9415
Long Hanborough Oxon 27 H6 vil 5m/8km NE of Witney. SP 4114
Long Haven Grampian 83 H3 small bay on E coast 4m/6km S of Peterhead. NK 1240
Long Head Grampian 82 D1* headland at N end of Findochty on N coast. NJ 4668
Long Hermiston Lothian 65 H2 loc 5m/8km SW of Edinburgh. NT 1770
Longhill Grampian 83 G2/H2 loc just S of New Leeds and 4m/6km N of Mintlaw. NJ 9953
Longhirst Nthmb 61 G3 vil 3m/4km NE of Morpeth. NZ 2289
Longhope Glos 26 C5 vil 9m/14km W of Gloucester. SO 6818
Longhorsley Nthmb 61 F2 vil 6m/10km NW of Morpeth. Battlemented tower, probably of 16c. NZ 1494
Longhoughton Nthmb 67 H6 vil 4m/6km E of Alnwick. NU 2415
Long Island Cornwall 6 A6* island off N coast 1km NW of Trevalga. SX 0790
Long Island Dorset 9 G5* island on S side of Poole Harbour E of Arne. SY 9887
Long Island Hants 10 D4* uninhabited island at N end of Langstone Harbour 1m SW of Langstone. SU 7004
Long Itchington Warwicks 27 H1 vil 2m/4km N of Southam. Site of Roman bldg 2m/3km NW. Cement works to S. SP 4165
Long John's Hill Norfolk 39 F4* dist of Norwich 1m S of city centre. TG 2306
Longlands Cumbria 52 C2* loc 2km SE of Uldale. NY 2635
Longlands London 20 B4* loc in borough of Bexley 2km NW of Sidcup. TQ 4472
Longlane Berks 18 A4 loc 3m/5km NE of Newbury. SU 5071
Longlane Derbys 35 H1 ham 7m/11km W of Derby. SK 2538
Long Lane Salop 34 C3* loc adjoining Sleapford to S. SJ 6315
Long Lane Bottom W Yorks 48 D6* loc in Huddersfield 2m/3km E of tn centre. SE 1617
Long Lawford Warwicks 36 A6 vil 2m/4km W of Rugby. SP 4776
Longleat House Wilts 16 C6 4m/7km W of Warminster. Renaissance mansion in large park, seat of Marquess of Bath. Lion reserve; other wild animals. ST 8040
Longlevens Glos 26 D5* NE dist of Gloucester. SO 8520
Longley S Yorks 43 H2* dist of Sheffield 2m/4km N of city centre. SK 3591
Longley W Yorks 43 F1* loc 2km S of Holmfirth. SE 1405
Longley W Yorks 48 C5* loc 2km SW of Sowerby Br. SE 0521
Longley Green H & W 26 C3 loc 4m/7km NW of Gt Malvern. SO 7350
Long Load Som 8 C2 vil on S bank of R Yeo 4m/6km SE of Langport. ST 4623
Long Loch S'clyde 64 C4 loch 3m/5km S of Neilston. NS 4752
Long Loch Tayside 73 F1 small loch 2m/3km S of Newtyle. NO 2838
Longmanhill Grampian 83 F1 loc near N coast 3m/4km SE of Macduff. NJ 7362
Long Marston Herts 28 D6 vil 3m/5km NW of Tring. SP 8915
Long Marston N Yorks 50 A3 vil 7m/11km W of York. SE 5051
Long Marston Warwicks 27 F3 vil 5m/8km SW of Stratford-upon-Avon. SP 1548
Long Marton Cumbria 53 F2/F3 vil 3m/5km N of Appleby. Site of Roman camp 2km W. NY 6624
Long Meadowend Salop 34 B6* loc 2km W of Craven Arms. SO 4182
Long Meg Cumbria 53 E2 ancient stone column 6m/9km NE of Penrith, standing apart from wide circle of sixty-seven stones, the whole being known as Long Meg and her Daughters. NY 5737
Long Melford Suffolk 30 D3 small tn 3m/5km N of Sudbury. Large Perp ch. Melford Hall (NT) and Kentwell Hall are Elizn. Many other old hses. TL 8646
Longmoor Camp Hants 11 E2 military camp 3m/5km W of Liphook. SU 7931
Longmorn Grampian 82 B1 vil 3m/5km S of Elgin. Whisky distillery. NJ 2358
Longmoss Ches 42 D4* loc 2km W of Macclesfield. SJ 8974
Long Mountain Powys 34 A3, A4 hill ridge above right (E) bank of R Severn opp Welshpool. On summit, 1338 ft or 408 metres, is an ancient camp known as Beacon Ring. SJ 2605
Long Mynd, The Salop 34 B5 range of pre-Cambrian hills W of Church Stretton running 8m/13km from Plowden (SW) to Woolstaston (NE) and attaining height of 1695 ft or 517 metres. Midland Gliding Club operates from ridge above Asterton. SO 4194
Long Nab N Yorks 55 H5* headland 4m/6km N of Scarborough. TA 0394
Long Newnton Glos 16 D2 vil 2km E of Tetbury. ST 9192
Long Newton Cleveland 54 C3 vil 4m/7km W of Stockton-on-Tees. NZ 3816
Longney Glos 26 C6 vil 6m/10km SW of Gloucester. SO 7612
Longniddry Lothian 66 C1 vil 3m/4km SW of Aberlady. NT 4476
Longnor Salop 34 B4 vil 8m/12km S of Shrewsbury. SJ 4800
Longnor Staffs 43 F4 vil above R Manifold 6m/9km SE of Buxton. SK 0864
Longovicium Durham. See Lanchester. NZ 1546
Longparish Hants 10 B1 vil on R Test 3m/5km SW of Whitchurch. SU 4344
Longpark Cumbria 60 A5 loc 2m/3km SW of Scaleby. NY 4362
Long Point Dyfed 22 A5* headland (NT) 2km N of St Ann's Hd. SM 7904
Longport Staffs 42 D6* loc in Burslem dist of Stoke-on-Trent. SJ 8649
Long Preston N Yorks 48 B3 vil 4m/6km S of Settle. Site of Roman fort at SE end of vil. SD 8358
Long Reach 20 C4 stretch of R Thames extending from Crayford Ness in the London borough of Bexley to Stone Ness at S end of W Thurrock Marshes, Essex. Length over 3m/5km. Dartford rd tunnel 1m W of Stone Ness. TQ 5577
Longridge Lancs 47 F4 tn 7m/11km NE of Preston. Agriculture, textiles. **L. Fell** hill ridge to NE rising to 1148 ft or 350 metres. SD 6037
Longridge Lothian 65 F3 vil 2m/3km S of Whitburn. NS 9462
Longridge Staffs 35 E3* loc 2km NW of Penkridge. SJ 9015

Longridge End Glos 26 C5* loc 4m/6km N of Gloucester across R Severn. SO 8124
Longriggend S'clyde 65 E2 vil 5m/8km NE of Airdrie. NS 8270
Long Riston Humberside 51 F4 vil 2m/4km SE of Leven. TA 1242
Longrock Cornwall 2 B5 ham to E of Penzance. Submerged forest to E. SW 5031
Long Sandall S Yorks 44 B1* loc 2km SW of Kirk Sandall. SE 6006
Long Scar Cleveland 54 D2* large offshore rock on S side of Hartlepool Bay. NZ 5231
Longsdon Staffs 43 E5 vil 2m/3km SW of Leek. SJ 9654
Longshaw Common Gtr Manchester 42 B2* loc 1m S of Orrell. SD 5302
Longships Cornwall 2 A5* cluster of islands 2km W of Land's End. SW 3225
Longside Grampian 83 H2 vil 6m/10km W of Peterhead. NK 0347
Longsight Gtr Manchester 42 D2* dist of Manchester 2m/3km SE of city centre. SJ 8696
Long Sight Gtr Manchester 43 E1* loc 1m N of Oldham. SD 9206
Longslow Salop 34 D1 loc 2m/3km NW of Mkt Drayton. SJ 6535
Longsowerby Cumbria 59 H5* dist of Carlisle 1m S of city centre. NY 3954
Longstanton Cambs 29 G2/H2 vil 6m/10km NW of Cambridge. Airfield to SE. TL 3966
Longstock Hants 10 B1 vil on R Test 2km N of Stockbridge across r. SU 3537
Longstone Cornwall 2 B4* S suburb of St Ives. SW 5338
Longstone Cornwall 3 F1* loc 4m/6km N of Bodmin. SX 0673
Longstone Lothian 66 A2* dist of Edinburgh 3m/5km SW of city centre. NT 2170
Longstone Nthmb 67 H4 island in Farne Is. group, with lighthouse. See Farne Is. NU 2438
Longstone, Great Derbys 43 G4 vil 2m/4km NW of Bakewell. **Lit Longstone** ham 1km W. SK 2071
Longstowe Cambs 29 G2/G3 vil 9m/15km NW of Royston. TL 3054
Long Stratton Norfolk 39 F5 vil 10m/16km S of Norwich. TM 1992
Long Street Bucks 28 C3 ham 6m/9km NW of Newport Pagnell. SP 7947
Longstreet Wilts 17 F6 ham across R Avon from Enford and 2m/4km S of Upavon. SU 1451
Long Sutton Hants 11 D1 vil 5m/8km N of Alton. SU 7347
Long Sutton Lincs 37 H2 small tn 9m/13km N of Wisbech. TF 4322
Long Sutton Som 8 C2 vil 2m/4km SW of Somerton. ST 4625
Long Taing of Newark Orkney. See Newark.
Longthorpe Cambs 37 F4 loc in Peterborough 2m/3km W of city centre. **L. Tower** (A.M.), hse containing early 14c murals. TL 1698
Long Thurlow Suffolk 31 E2 ham 6m/10km NW of Stowmarket. TM 0168
Longthwaite, High Cumbria 52 C1* loc 1km S of Wigton. **Low Longthwaite** loc to NW. NY 2546
Longton Lancs 47 F5 loc 5m/7km SW of Preston. See also New Longton. SD 4725
Longton Staffs 35 E1 one of the tns of Stoke-on-Trent: Burslem, Fenton, Hanley, Longton, Stoke, Tunstall. Longton lies to SE of city centre. SJ 9043
Longtown Cumbria 59 H4 small tn 8m/13km N of Carlisle. NY 3868
Longtown H & W 25 H5 vil 5m/8km W of Pontrilas. SO 3228
Longville in the Dale Salop 34 C5 vil below W slope of Wenlock Edge 6m/9km E of Church Stretton. SO 5493
Long Waste Salop 34 C3 ham 4m/6km NW of Wellington. SJ 6115
Longwell Green Avon 16 B4* loc 2m/3km N of Keynsham. ST 6571
Long Whatton Leics 36 B2 vil 4m/6km NW of Loughborough. SK 4823
Longwick Bucks 18 C1 vil 2m/3km NW of Princes Risborough. SP 7805
Long Wittenham Oxon 18 A2 vil 3m/4km NE of Didcot. SU 5493
Longwitton Nthmb 31 F3 ham 8m/13km W of Morpeth. NZ 0788
Longwood W Yorks 48 D6* loc 3m/4km W of Huddersfield. **L. Edge** loc adjoining to N. **Longwood Resrs** three small resrs to NW. SE 1016
Longworth Oxon 17 G2 vil 7m/11km W of Abingdon. SU 3999
Lon-las W Glam 14 C2 loc 3m/5km W of Neath. SS 7097
Lonmay Grampian 83 H1 loc 5m/8km S of Fraserburgh. NK 0158
Lonmore Skye, H'land 78 A4 loc 2km SE of Dunvegan. NG 2646
Looe Cornwall 3 G3 tn on S coast 7m/11km S of Liskeard. **Looe R** divides tn into E and W Looe, connected by rd br. R rises on Bodmin Moor near St Cleer and flows past tn of Looe into **Looe Bay,** while **W Looe R** rises near Dobwalls and joins Looe R to N of tn. SX 2553
Looe Island Cornwall 3 G3 alternative name for St George's I., island off S coast 2km S of Looe. SX 2551
Looe, North Surrey 19 F5* loc 2km E of Epsom. TQ 2360
Loe Pool Cornwall 2 C5 large lake (NT), also known as The Loe, formed by R Looe, Loe, or Cober, and Looe or Loe Bar which obstructs outflow to sea. Most of coast from Porthleven to Gunwalloe also NT. SW 6425
Loose Kent 20 D6 vil on S outskirts of Maidstone. TQ 7552
Loosebeare Devon 7 E4* loc 6m/9km E of Winkleigh. SS 7105
Loosegate Lincs 37 G2 loc 1m NE of Moulton. TF 3125
Loosley Row Bucks 18 C2 vil 2m/3km S of Princes Risborough. SP 8100
Lopcombe Corner Wilts 10 A2 loc at junction of A30 and A343 rds 7m/11km W of Stockbridge. SU 2535
Lopen Som 8 C3 vil 2m/3km S of S Petherton. ST 4214
Lopham, North Norfolk 39 E6 vil 5m/9km NW of Diss. Site of Roman bldg to E. Vil of **S Lopham** 1m S. TM 0382
Lop Ness Orkney 89 C5* headland on S coast of Sanday 2m/3km W of Start Pt. **Bay of Lopness** extends westwards to Long Taing of Newark. HY 7643
Loppington Salop 34 B2 vil 3m/5km W of Wem. SJ 4729
Lopscombe Corner Wilts. Alternative spelling for Lopcombe Corner, qv.
Lorbottle Nthmb 61 E1 loc 3m/5km NW of Rothbury. NU 0306
Lord Hereford's Knob Powys 25 G4 mt on Black Mts 5m/8km S of Hay-on-Wye. Height 2263 ft or 690 metres. SO 2234
Lordington W Sussex 11 E4* loc 1km SW of Walderton and 3m/5km NE of Emsworth. SU 7809
Lord Lovat's Cave S'clyde 69 D6 cave on **Lord Lovat's Bay,** to E of entrance to Loch Buie, Mull. NM 6020
Lord Macdonald's Forest Skye, H'land 79 C6, D6 mountainous tract S of Loch Sligachan. NG 5128
Lord Macdonald's Table H'land one of a group of islets 3m/5km NW of Rubha Hunish at northern tip of Skye. See also Gaeilavore I. and Gearran I. NG 3679
Lord's Cricket Ground London. See St John's Wood.
Lord's Hill Hants 10 B3* loc in NW part of Southampton. SU 3815
Lord's Land, North Cumbria 53 F5 loc 3m/5km SE of Sedbergh. **S Lord's Land** loc 2km S. SD 6988
Loretto Lothian 66 B2* boys' public school at Musselburgh. NT 3373
Lorn S'clyde 70 B3-C1 area of Argyll lying between Loch Awe and the coast and extending northwards to Loch Leven. See also Firth of Lorn. NN 03
Lorton, High Cumbria 52 B3 vil 4m/6km SE of Cockermouth. **Low L.** ham in Lorton Vale or valley of R Cocker to W. NY 1625
Loscoe Derbys 43 H6 vil 2km NW of Heanor. SK 4247
Loscombe Dorset 8 C4* loc 3m/4km SE of Beaminster. SY 5097
Losecoat Field Leics 37 E3 site of Wars of the Roses battle, 1470, 5m/8km NW of Stamford. SK 9611
Lose Hill Derbys 43 F3 hill (NT) 2km N of Castleton. Ancient burial-chamber at summit. SK 1585
Loseley House Surrey 11 F1* Elizn manor hse in par of Artington 2m/3km N of Godalming. SU 9847
Lossie Grampian 82 B1 r rising on hills S of Dallas near border with Highland region and running N past Dallas and Elgin to North Sea at Lossiemouth. NJ 2370
Lossie Forest Grampian 82 B1, C1 state forest bordering N coast on E side of Lossiemouth. NJ 2767
Lossiemouth Grampian 82 B1 fishing port and resort on N coast of region 5m/8km N of Elgin. Ramsay MacDonald, first Labour prime minister, b here 1866. Airfield 2km W. NJ 2370
Lossit Bay S'clyde 62 A3 bay on W side of Rinns of Islay 3m/5km N of Rinns Pt. **Lossit Pt** is headland on N side of bay. NR 1756
Lostock Gtr Manchester 42 C1* loc in Bolton 4m/6km W of tn centre. Includes locs of **L. Hall Fold** and **L. Junction.** SD 6608
Lostock Gralam Ches 42 C4 vil 3m/4km E of Northwich. SJ 6573
Lostock Green Ches 42 C4 vil 3m/4km E of Northwich. SJ 6973
Lostock Hall Lancs 47 F5* loc 2m/3km N of Leyland. SD 5425
Lostwithiel Cornwall 3 F2 tn on R Fowey 5m/8km SE of Bodmin. SX 1059
Lothbeg H'land 87 C5 loc near E coast of Sutherland dist 6m/10km SW of Helmsdale. **Lothbeg Pt** is headland 1m SE. NC 9410
Lothersdale N Yorks 48 C3 vil 4m/6km SW of Skipton. SD 9545
Lotherton W Yorks 49 F4 loc 3m/5km NE of Garforth. SE 4436
Lothian 115 admin region of Scotland on S side of Firth of Forth, comprising the former counties of E and W Lothian and the greater part of Midlothian. The commercial and industrial area is centred upon Edinburgh, the capital city of Scotland, from which, however, the Pentland, Moorfoot, and Lammermuir Hills are within easy reach, whilst there is fine coastal scenery near North Berwick and Dunbar, N of the rich arable land around Haddington.
Lothianbridge Lothian 66 B2* loc on R South Esk 1km NW of Newtongrange. NT 3264
Lothian, East and **West** 115 admin dists of Lothian region. See also Midlothian.
Lothing Suffolk 39 H5* inlet of sea, known as Lake Lothing, connecting Lowestoft Harbour with Oulton Broad. TM 5392
Lothmore H'land 87 C5* loc near E coast of Sutherland dist 5m/7km SW of Helmsdale. NC 9611
Lottisham Som 8 D1* loc 1m E of Ham Street and 5m/8km SE of Glastonbury. ST 5734
Loud 47 G4 r rising on S slopes of Forest of Bowland, Lancs, and flowing E into R Hodder at Doeford Br, 2m/3km E of Chipping. SD 6443
Loudoun Hill S'clyde 64 D5 rocky knoll 3m/5km E of Darvel. To SE is site of battle of 1307 in which Robert Bruce defeated the Earl of Pembroke. NS 6037
Loudwater Bucks 18 D3 loc 3m/4km SE of High Wycombe. SU 9090
Loudwater Herts 19 E2* loc 2km NW of Rickmansworth. TQ 0496
Loughborough Leics 36 B3 hosiery and engineering tn 10m/16km N of Leicester. Bell foundry. Carillon Tower has forty-seven bells. University of Technology. SK 5319
Loughor (Casllwchwr) W Glam 23 G5 industrial loc at head of Burry Inlet 6m/10km NW of Swansea. Steel works. Remains of cas (A.M.) beside river estuary. SS 5798
Loughor (Llwchwr) 23 F5 r rising 4m/6km SE of Llandeilo, Dyfed, and flowing S to Burry Inlet and Carmarthen Bay. SS 4599
Loughton Bucks 28 D4 vil in Milton Keynes 2km SW of the centre. SP 8337
Loughton Essex 20 B2 tn on E side of Epping Forest 12m/20km NE of London. TQ 4296
Loughton Lincs 37 F2 loc 2km S of Folkingham. TF 0731
Loughton Salop 34 C5/C6 ham 6m/10km NW of Cleobury Mortimer. SO 6183
Lound Lincs 37 F3 ham 2m/3km SW of Bourne. TF 0618
Lound Notts 44 B3 vil 2m/4km N of E Retford. SK 6986
Lound Suffolk 39 H5 vil 5m/7km NW of Lowestoft. TM 5099
Lound, East Humberside 44 C2 vil 2km E of Haxey. SK 7899
Lound, The Cumbria 53 E5* loc in S part of Kendal. SD 5191
Lount Leics 36 A3* ham 3m/4km NE of Ashby de la Zouch. SK 3819
Lousie Wood Law S'clyde 65 F6* mt in Lowther Hills 2m/3km SW of Elvanfoot. Height 2028 ft or 618 metres. NS 9315
Louth Lincs 45 G3 tn 14m/23km S of Grimsby. Ch has soaring Perp spire. Industries include malting, agriculture, fruit canning, glove mnfg. TF 3287
Louther Skerry Orkney 89 B8* one of the Pentland Skerries, qv. Louther Skerry lies between Lit Skerry and Clettack Skerry. ND 4777
Lovat 28 D3.* Alternative name for R Ouzel, qv. SP 8844
Loveacott Devon 6 D3 loc 5m/7km SW of Barnstaple. Also known as Lr Loveacott. SS 5227
Love Clough Lancs 48 B5* vil adjoining Dunnockshaw to SW. SD 8127
Lovedean Hants 10 D3 suburban loc on W side of Horndean. SU 6G12
Love Green Bucks 19 E3* loc 4m/6km E of Slough. TQ 0381
Lovely Seat N Yorks 53 G5 mt 3m/5km N of Hawes. Height 2213 ft or 675 metres. SD 8795
Lover Wilts 9 H2 vil 7m/12km SE of Salisbury. SU 2120
Loversall S Yorks 44 B2 vil 3m/5km S of Doncaster. SK 5798
Loves Green Essex 20 C2* vil 3m/5km N of Ingatestone. TL 6404
Lovesome Hill N Yorks 54 C5 ham 4m/6km N of Northallerton. SE 3599
Loveston Dyfed 22 C5* ham 6m/9km NW of Tenby. SN 0808
Lovington Som 8 D2 vil 3m/5km N of Sparkford. ST 5930
LOW, LOWER. For names beginning with these words, see under next word. This also applies to names beginning with High, Higher; Upper, Nether; Far, Near; Mid, Middle; Great, Little; Greater, Lesser; Isle(s) of; North, South, East, West; The, Y, Yr.
Lowbands Glos 26 C4 loc 6m/9km SE of Ledbury. SO 7731
Lowca Cumbria 52 A3* loc 2m/4km N of Whitehaven. NX 9821
Lowcote Gate Derbys 36 A1* loc 2km W of Ilkeston. SK 4442
Lowdham Notts 44 B6 vil 7m/12km NE of Nottingham. SK 6646
Lowe Salop 34 B2/C2* loc 2km NW of Wem. SJ 5030
Low, East Durham 61 F5* ham 1km SW of Ebchester. NZ 0954
Lowe Hill Staffs 43 E5* loc 1m SE of Leek. SJ 9955
Lowerford Lancs 48 B4* loc adjoining Barrowford to W. SD 8539
Lowerhouse Lancs 48 B5* loc in Burnley 2m/3km W of tn centre. SD 8032
Lowertown Orkney 89 B7* loc on N coast of S Ronaldsay 1m NW of St Margaret's Hope. ND 4394
Lowesby Leics 36 C4 ham 9m/14km E of Leicester. Site of former vil to N. SK 7207
Lowestoft Suffolk 39 H5 tn on North Sea coast 38m/62km NE of Ipswich. Resort. Industries include fishing and canning, coach-building. **L. Ness,** headland, is most easterly point in Gt Britain. TM 5493
Lowestoft End Suffolk 39 H5* loc in N part of Lowestoft. TM 5394
Loweswater Cumbria 52 B3 one of the smaller lakes of the Lake Dist, 6m/9km S of Cockermouth. Owned by NT. Ham of Loweswater 1km E of SE end of lake, with hills of **L. Fell** to S. NY 1221
Lowfield S Yorks 43 H3* dist of Sheffield 2km S of city centre. SK 3585
Lowfield Heath W Sussex 11 H1 vil on S edge of London (Gatwick) Airport, 2m/3km N of Crawley. TQ 2740
Lowford Hants 10 B4* loc 3m/4km NW of Park Gate. SU 4810
Lowgate N Yorks 49 G6* loc 2m/3km SW of Pollington. SE 5918
Lowgill Lancs 47 G2 loc 3m/5km S of Lr Bentham. SD 6564
Lowhouse Fold Gtr Manchester 48 C6* loc adjoining Milnrow to N. SD 9313
Lowick Cumbria 52 C6 loc 5m/8km N of Ulverston. **Lowick Br** loc to N. **Lowick Green** ham 1km S. SD 2986
Lowick Northants 37 E6 vil 2m/3km NW of Thrapston. SP 9780
Lowick Nthmb 67 G4 vil 7m/12km N of Wooler. NU 0139

Lowlandman's Bay S'clyde 62 C1 bay with landing stage on E coast of Jura, 4m/6km S of Lagg. Long rocky promontory on SE side almost closes entrance. NR 5672
Lowland Point Cornwall 2 D6 headland (NT) on E coast of Lizard peninsula 2km SE of St Keverne. SW 8019
Lowlands Gwent 15 G2* loc in N part of Cwmbran. ST 2996
Lowman 7 G4 r in Devon rising near Hockworthy and flowing SW into R Exe at Tiverton. SS 9512
Lowmoor Row Cumbria 53 F2* loc 1m W of Kirkby Thore. NY 6226
Lowryhill Cumbria 59 H5* loc in Carlisle 2m/3km N of city centre. NY 3958
Lowsonford Warwicks 27 F1 vil on Stratford-upon-Avon Canal 3m/4km NE of Henley-in-Arden. SP 1867
Lowsy Point Cumbria 46 C1* sand and mud promontory on mainland opp N end of Walney I. SD 1874
Lowther Cumbria 53 E3 18c ham 4m/7km S of Penrith. To W, **L. Castle,** ruined early 19c mansion in park on E bank of R Lowther. NY 5323
Lowther 53 E2 r rising on Shap Fells, Cumbria, and flowing N into R Eamont 2m/3km SE of Penrith. NY 5329
Lowther Hill 58 D1 mt and radar stn on border of Strathclyde and Dumfries & Galloway regions 7m/11km E of Sanquhar. Height 2377 ft or 725 metres; second highest of **Lowther Hills,** mt range between Sanquhar and Moffat. See also Green Lowther. NS 8910
Lowthorpe Humberside 51 E2 vil 4m/7km NE of Gt Driffield. TA 0860
Lowthwaite Cumbria 52 D3* loc 2m/3km NE of Dockray. NY 4123
Lowton Devon 7 E4* ham 3m/5km SE of Winkleigh. SS 6604
Lowton Gtr Manchester 42 B2 loc 1km E of Golborne. **L. Common** loc 2km E. **L. St Mary's** loc 1m E. SJ 6197
Lowton Som 8 A3* ham below Blackdown Hills 4m/7km SE of Wellington. ST 1918
Loxbeare Devon 7 G3 ham 4m/6km NW of Tiverton. SS 9116
Loxford London 20 B3* S dist of Ilford in borough of Redbridge. TQ 4485
Loxhill Surrey 11 F2 ham 4m/6km W of Cranleigh. TQ 0038
Loxhore Devon 7 E2 ham 5m/8km NE of Barnstaple. To SW and S respectively, hams of **Loxhore Cott** and **Lr Loxhore.** SS 6138
Loxley S Yorks 43 G2* loc 3m/5km NW of Sheffield. SK 3089
Loxley Warwicks 27 F3/G3 vil 4m/6km SE of Stratford-upon-Avon. SP 2552
Loxley 43 H3 r rising on moors W of Bradfield, S Yorks, and flowing E into R Don in NW part of Sheffield. SK 3489
Loxley Green Staffs 35 F2* loc 3m/4km SW of Uttoxeter. SK 0630
Loxton Avon 15 H5 vil 4m/6km W of Axbridge. ST 3755
Loxwood W Sussex 11 F2 vil 5m/8km NW of Billingshurst. TQ 0331
Lox Yeo 15 H5 r rising below Mendip Hills near Winscombe, Avon, and flowing round W side of Compton Hill into R Axe 1km SE of Loxton. ST 3855
Loy H'land 74 C3 r in Lochaber dist rising on Locheil Forest and running SE down Glen Loy into R Lochy 2m/4km SW of Gairlochy. NN 1581
Lozells W Midlands 35 F5* loc in Birmingham 2m/3km N of city centre. SP 0689
Lubas Bute, S'clyde. See Standing Stones of L.
Lùb a' Sgiathain H'land 78 C2 bay on N coast of Skye to E of Rubha Hunish. NG 4176
Lubenham Leics 36 C5 vil 2m/3km W of Mkt Harborough. SP 7087
Lùb Score H'land 78 B2, B3 bay between Rubha Hunish and Ru Bornaskitaig, N coast of Skye. Also known as Score Bay. NG 3973
Lucas End Herts 19 G2* loc 2m/4km W of Cheshunt. TL 3203
Luccombe Som 7 G1 vil, largely NT, on N slopes of Exmoor 2m/3km SE of Porlock. SS 9144
Luccombe Village Isle of Wight 10 C6 vil above **L. Bay** 1m S of Shanklin. See also Landslip, The. SZ 5879
Luce Bay D & G 57 C7 large bay on S coast of Scotland, extending from Mull of Galloway eastwards to Burrow Hd, and northwards to mouth of Water of Luce. NX 2244
Lucker Nthmb 67 H5 vil 4m/6km SE of Belford. NU 1530
Luckett Cornwall 3 H1 vil by R Tamar 3m/5km NE of Callington. SX 3773
Lucking Street Essex 30 C4* ham 3m/4km N of Halstead. TL 8134
Luckington Wilts 16 D3 vil 7m/11km W of Malmesbury. ST 8383
Lucklawhill Fife 73 G3* loc below **Lucklaw Hill,** 2m/3km W of Leuchars. NO 4221
Luckwell Bridge Som 7 G2 ham on Exmoor 6m/10km SW of Dunster. SS 9038
Lucton H & W 26 A2 vil 5m/8km NW of Leominster. SO 4364
Lucy Cross N Yorks 54 B4 loc 2m/3km S of Piercebridge. NZ 2112
Ludac W Isles 88 E3 vil on S coast of S Uist 1m E of Kilbride. Ferry for pedestrians to Eriskay. NF 7714
Ludborough Lincs 45 G2 vil 6m/9km N of Louth. TF 2995
Ludbrook Devon 4 D5 ham 2m/3km N of Modbury. SX 6654
Ludchurch (Eglwys Lwyd, Yr) Dyfed 22 D4 vil 3m/5km SE of Narberth. SN 1410
Luddenden W Yorks 48 C5 vil 2m/3km E of Mytholmroyd. **L. Foot** vil at bottom of valley on R Calder 1m S. SE 0426
Luddenham Kent 21 F5* loc 2m/3km NW of Faversham. TQ 9963
Luddesdown Kent 20 C5 ham 5m/8km S of Gravesend. TQ 6766
Luddington Humberside 50 C6/D6 vil 4m/7km NE of Crowle. SE 8216
Luddington Warwicks 27 F3 vil on R Avon 3m/4km SW of Stratford-upon-Avon. SP 1652
Luddington in the Brook Northants 37 F6 vil 5m/8km SE of Oundle. TL 1083
Ludford Salop 26 A1* vil just S of Ludlow across R Teme. SO 5174
Ludford Magna Lincs 45 F2/F3 vil 6m/10km E of Mkt Rasen. **Ludford Parva** vil adjoins to W. TF 2089
Ludgershall Bucks 28 B5 vil 6m/9km SE of Bicester. SP 6617
Ludgershall Wilts 17 G6 military tn 7m/11km NW of Andover. Remains of cas (A.M.). SU 2650
Ludgvan Cornwall 2 B5 vil 2m/4km NE of Penzance. SW 5033
Ludham Norfolk 39 G3 vil 5m/8km E of Hoveton. TG 3818
Ludlow Salop 34 C6 tn on hill above R Teme 24m/38km S of Shrewsbury. 11c cas. Large parish ch mainly 15c. Some half-timbered hses, notably the 16c Feathers Inn. SO 5174
Ludstone Salop 35 E5* loc 5m/9km E of Bridgnorth. SO 8094
Ludstone, Upper Salop 35 E5 loc 6m/9km E of Bridgnorth. SO 8095
Ludwell Wilts 9 F2 vil 3m/5km E of Shaftesbury. ST 9122
Ludworth Durham 54 C1* vil 3m/4km E of Sherburn. NZ 3641
Luffenham, North Leics 37 E4 vil 6m/10km SE of Oakham. Airfield to N. **S Luffenham** vil 1m S. SK 9303
Luffincott Devon 6 C5 ham 6m/10km N of Launceston. SX 3394
Lufton Som 8 C3* ham 3m/4km W of Yeovil. ST 5116
Lugar S'clyde 56 F2 vil 2m/3km E of Cumnock. **L. Water** is r running W past Lugar and Cumnock to Ochiltree, then N to R Ayr 2km S of Mauchline. NS 5921
Lugg 26 B4 r rising some 8m/12km W of Knighton, Powys, and flowing E to Leominster then S into R Wye 4m/6km SE of Hereford. SO 5637
Luggate Lothian 66 D1/D2* loc 2m/3km S of E Linton. **L. Burn** is adjacent loc to S. NT 5974
Lugg Green H & W 26 A2* loc on R Lugg 4m/6km NW of Leominster. SO 4462
Luggiebank S'clyde 65 E2 loc in Cumbernauld 2km S of tn centre. NS 7672
Luggy Brook 33 H4* stream rising near Castell Caereinion, Powys, and flowing SE into R Severn 4m/6km S of Welshpool. SJ 2002
Lugsdale Ches 42 B3* loc 1m E of Widnes tn centre. SJ 5285
Lugton S'clyde 64 B3 vil 4m/7km N of Stewarton. NS 4152
Lugwardine H & W 26 B3 vil 3m/4km E of Hereford. SO 5541
Luing S'clyde 69 F6 island lying between Seil and Scarba, 6m/9km long N to S and about 1km wide. Formerly noted for slate-quarrying. Agriculture and cattle-breeding now chief occupations. See also Sound of L. NM 7410
Luinga Mhór H'land 68 D1 small uninhabited island off coast of Lochaber dist 3m/5km W of Arisaig. **Luinga Bheag** is smaller island to NE. NM 6085
Luinne Bheinn H'land 74 A2 mt in Knoydart, Lochaber dist, 3m/4km S of Barrisdale. Height 3083 ft or 940 metres. NG 8600
Lui Water 76 B2 r in Grampian region running SE down Glen Lui to R Dee 5m/8km W of Braemar. NO 0789
Lulham H & W 26 A3* ham 6m/10km W of Hereford. SO 4041
Lullingstone Kent. See Eynsford.
Lullington Derbys 35 H3 vil 6m/10km NE of Tamworth. SK 2513
Lullington E Sussex 12 B6 ham on S Downs across Cuckmere R from Alfriston, 4m/6km NE of Seaford. TQ 5302
Lullington Som 16 C6* vil 3m/4km N of Frome. ST 7851
Lulsgate Avon 16 A5 Bristol Airport, 7m/11km SW of city centre. 1m E, ham of **L. Bottom.** ST 5065
Lulsley H & W 26 C2* vil 7m/11km W of Worcester. SO 7455
Lulworth, East Dorset 9 F6 vil 3m/5km S of Wool. Ruined 16c cas. SY 8682
Lulworth, West Dorset 9 F6 vil on coast 4m/7km S of Wool. **L. Cove,** circular bay almost landlocked by chalk and limestone cliffs. **L. Camp,** military camp 1m NE. SY 8280
Lumb Lancs 47 H6* loc 2m/3km N of Ramsbottom. SD 7819
Lumb Lancs 48 B5* vil 2m/4km NE of Rawtenstall. SD 8324
Lumb W Yorks 48 C5* vil 2km NW of Ripponden. SE 0221
Lumburn 4 B3* r rising 3m/5km E of Milton Abbot in Devon and flowing S through vil of Lamerton into R Tavy 2m/3km S of Tavistock. SX 4671
Lumbutts W Yorks 48 C5 ham 2km SE of Todmorden. SD 9523
Lumby N Yorks 49 F5* ham 1m SW of S Milford. SE 4830
Lumley, Great Durham 61 G6 vil 2m/3km SE of Chester-le-Street. **Lit Lumley** loc 1km N. **Lumley Thicks** loc 1km NE. **Lumley Castle,** late 14c, 1m N. NZ 2949
Lumley Moor Reservoir N Yorks 49 E1/E2 resr 6m/9km W of Ripon. SE 2270
Lumphanan Grampian 77 F1 vil 9m/15km NW of Banchory. Macbeth is supposed to have died here; commemorative cairn 1km NW. Peel of L. (A.M.), 1km SW, site of medieval cas. NJ 5703
Lumphinnans Fife 73 E5 loc between Cowdenbeath and Lochgelly. NT 1792
Lumsdale Derbys 43 G5* loc 1m E of Matlock. SK 3160
Lumsden Grampian 82 D4 vil 4m/6km S of Rhynie. NJ 4721
Lunan Tayside 77 F5* small vil near mouth of L. Water, qv. NO 6851
Lunanhead Tayside 77 E5 vil 2km NE of Forfar. NO 4752
Lunan Water 77 F5 stream in Tayside region running E to **Lunan Bay** 4m/7km S of Montrose. **Lunan Castle** is ruin overlooking bay. NO 6951
Luncarty Tayside 72 D2* vil 4m/7km N of Perth. Site of battle of 990 in which Scots defeated Danes. NO 0929
Lund Humberside 51 E3 vil 7m/11km NW of Beverley. SE 9748
Lund N Yorks 50 B5 ham 2m/4km E of Selby. SE 6532
Lunda Wick Shetland 89 F5* bay on W coast of Unst, 2m/4km NW of Uyeasound. HP 5604
Lunderston Bay S'clyde 64 A2 westward-facing bay on Firth of Clyde 1m N of Inverkip. NS 2073
Lundie Tayside 73 F1 vil 3m/5km S of Newtyle. NO 2936
Lundin Links Fife 73 G4 loc on Largo Bay on W side of Lr Largo. Three large standing stones on golf-course to N of A915 rd. NO 4002
Lunds N Yorks 53 G5* loc 2km N of Moorcock Inn. SD 7994
Lundwood S Yorks 43 H1* loc in Barnsley 2km SW of Cudworth. SE 3707
Lundy Devon 6 A1 granite island at entrance to Bristol Channel 11m/18km NW of Hartland Pt. Ham at S end. Scheduled boat service from Bideford. Island is NT property. SS 1345
Lundy H'land 74 C4 r in Lochaber dist running W into R Lochy 2m/3km NE of Fort William. NN 1276
Lundy Green Norfolk 39 F5* loc 1m E of Fritton. TM 2492
Lune 47 E3 r rising on Ravenstonedale Common, Cumbria, and flowing W to Tebay, then S to Kirkby Lonsdale and SW to Lancaster and the Irish Sea at Sunderland Pt. SD 3554
Lune Forest Durham 53 G3 wild moorland area lying E of Mickle Fell and N of R Lune. NY 82
Lunga S'clyde 69 E6 uninhabited island immediately N of Scarba, and W of Luing across Sound of Luing. Area about 500 acres or 200 hectares. NM 7008
Lunga Treshnish Isles, S'clyde 68 B4 largest island in group, situated at mid point of the chain. Its summit, **Cruachan,** is also highest point of Treshnish Isles: 337 ft or 103 metres. NM 2741
Lunna Shetland 89 E6 vil on Mainland on narrow neck of land between the two small bays of **E** and **W Lunna Voe,** 4m/6km SW of headland of **L. Ness.** HU 4869
Lunna Holm Shetland 89 E6/F6* small uninhabited island off Lunna Ness on NE coast of Mainland. HU 5274
Lunnasting Shetland 89 E6, E7* dist of Mainland extending from Lunna Ness southwards to Dury Voe on E coast. HU 46
Lunning Shetland 89 E6 loc near E coast of Mainland 4m/7km NE of Laxo. **Lunning Hd** is headland to NE. **L. Sound** to S is sea passage between Mainland and island of W Linga. HU 5066
Lunnister Shetland 89 E6* locality 2km S of Sullom on W side of Sullom Voe. **Loch of L.** is small loch to W. HU 3471
Lunnon W Glam 23 G6* loc on Gower peninsula adjoining Parkmill to NE. SS 5489
Lunsford Kent 20 C5* loc 2m/3km W of Aylesford. TQ 6959
Lunsford's Cross E Sussex 12 D5 ham 2m/4km NW of Bexhill. TQ 7210
Luppitt Devon 8 A4 vil 4m/6km N of Honiton. ST 1606
Lupset W Yorks 49 E6* dist of Wakefield 2km SW of city centre. SE 3119
Lupton Cumbria 53 E6 ham 4m/6km NW of Kirkby Lonsdale. SD 5581
Lurgashall W Sussex 11 F2 vil 4m/7km NW of Petworth. SU 9327
Lusby Lincs 45 G4 vil 4m/6km W of Spilsby. TF 3367
Luskentyre W Isles 88 A3 loc on W coast of Harris 5m/8km W of Tarbert. NG 0799
Luss S'clyde 71 E5 vil on W shore of Loch Lomond 8m/12km S of Tarbet. **L. Water,** r rising on S slope of Cruach an t-Sithein, runs down Glen L. into loch on S side of vil. NS 3592
Lussa S'clyde 69 E5* r on Mull running E down Glen More to head of Loch Spelve. NM 6930
Lussa S'clyde 69 E8 r on Jura running to S to **L. Bay** on E coast. **Lussa Pt** is headland to E of bay. NR 6486
Lussa Loch S'clyde 62 D5/63 E4 large loch in Kintyre 5m/8km N of Campbeltown. NR 7130
Lusta Skye, H'land 78 A4* vil on Vaternish peninsula 4m/7km SE of Ardmore Pt. NG 2756
Lustleigh Devon 4 D3 vil 4m/6km SE of Moretonhampstead. 1m W, **L. Cleave,** deep, wooded stretch of R Bovey valley. SX 7881
Luston H & W 26 A2 vil 3m/4km N of Leominster. SO 4863
Luther Bridge Grampian 77 F4* rd br over Luther Water 2m/3km NW of Marykirk. Site of Roman camp nearly 1km E. NO 6566
Luthermuir Grampian 77 F4 vil on W side of Luther Water 3m/4km NW of Marykirk. NO 6568
Luther Water 77 F4 r in Grampian region rising in Drumtochty Forest and running S to R North Esk 2m/3km W of Marykirk. NO 6566

Luthrie Fife 73 F3 vil 4m/7km NW of Cupar. NO 3319
Luton Beds 29 E5 large industrial tn 28m/45km NW of London. Motor vehicle mnfre, brewing, precision instruments, etc. Former hat industry now much reduced. International airport 2m/3km E. **Luton Hoo,** mansion in large park 2m/3km SE. TL 0821
Luton Devon 5 E3 ham 5m/7km NE of Newton Abbot. SX 9076
Luton Devon 7 H4 ham 5m/8km SE of Cullompton. ST 0802
Luton Kent 20 D5 SE dist of Chatham. TQ 7666
Lutterworth Leics 36 B5 tn 6m/10km NE of Rugby. SP 5484
Lutton Devon 4 C4 vil 3m/5km NW of Ivybridge. SX 5959
Lutton Dorset 9 F6* loc 1km W of Steeple and 4m/7km SW of Wareham. SY 9080
Lutton Lincs 37 H2 vil 2m/3km N of Long Sutton. TF 4325
Lutton Northants 37 F5 vil 5m/8km E of Oundle. TL 1187
Lutton, East N Yorks 50 D2 ham 10m/16km E of Malton. SE 9469
Lutton, West N Yorks 50 D2 vil 9m/15km E of Malton. SE 9369
Luxborough Som 7 G2 vil on Exmoor 4m/6km S of Dunster. SS 9737
Luxted London 20 B5* loc 2km NE of Biggin Hill. TQ 4360
Luxulyan Cornwall 3 E3 vil 4m/7km NE of St Austell. SX 0558
Luzley Gtr Manchester 43 E1/E2* loc 1km SW of Mossley. SD 9601
Luzley Brook Gtr Manchester 43 E1* loc 2m/3km N of Oldham. SD 9207
Lwyd 15 H3 r rising near Blaenavon, Gwent, and flowing S by Pontypool and Cwmbran into R Usk at Caerleon. ST 3490
Lybster H'land 86 E4 vil in Caithness dist 12m/20km SW of Wick. Vil of **Upr Lybster** 1m N. ND 2435
Lyd 4 B3* r in Devon, rising on Dartmoor and running W past Lydford and through Lydford Gorge before joining R Thrushel at Lifton and flowing thence into R Tamar 3m/4km E of Launceston. SX 3985
Lydbrook, Lower Glos 26 B5 vil 4m/6km NE of Coleford. SO 5916
Lydbrook, Upper Glos 26 B5 vil 4m/6km NE of Coleford. SO 6015
Lydbrook, Upper and Lower Glos 26 B5* adjoining vils 4m/6km W of Cinderford. SO 6015
Lydbury North Salop 34 A5 vil 3m/4km SE of Bishop's Castle. SO 3585
Lydcott Devon 7 E2* loc 7m/11km N of S Molton. SS 6936
Lydd Kent 13 F5 tn 4m/7km NW of Dungeness. Airport to E. Resort of **Lydd-on-Sea** 2m/5km E. TR 0420
Lydden Kent 13 G3 vil 4m/6km NW of Dover. TR 2645
Lydden 9 E3 r rising in hills S of Mappowder in Dorset and flowing N into R Stour SW of Marnhull. ST 7617
Lyddington Leics 36 D4 vil 2m/3km S of Uppingham. **L. Bede Hse** (A.M.), 15c bishop's palace later converted into almshouses. SP 8797
Lydeard St Lawrence Som 7 H2 vil 4m/7km NE of Wiveliscombe. ST 1232
Lyde Green Avon 16 C4* loc 4m/7km SW of Chipping Sodbury. ST 6778
Lyde Green Hants 18 C5* ham 2m/3km NW of Hook. SU 7057
Lyde, Upper H & W 26 A3* loc 3m/5km N of Hereford. SO 4944
Lydford Devon 4 B2 vil 7m/11km N of Tavistock. Remains of cas (A.M.). Par includes a large part of Dartmoor. To SW, **L. Gorge** (NT), wooded ravine of R Lyd, with waterfall. SX 5184
Lydford Som 8 D2 par to E of Keinton Mandeville astride R Brue and containing vils of **E** and **W Lydford** and hams of **L. Green** and **L. Fair Place.** ST 5631
Lydgate Gtr Manchester 43 E1* loc 3m/5km E of Oldham. SD 9704
Lydgate Gtr Manchester 48 C6* loc 1m E of Littleborough. SD 9516
Lydgate W Yorks 48 C5 vil 2km NW of Todmorden. SD 9225
Lydham Salop 34 A5 vil 2m/3km NE of Bishop's Castle. SO 3391
Lydiard Green Wilts 17 E3* loc 4m/7km W of Swindon. SU 0886
Lydiard Millicent Wilts 17 E3 vil 4m/6km W of Swindon. SU 0986
Lydiard Tregoze Wilts 17 E3 ham 3m/5km W of Swindon. SU 1084
Lydiate Lancs 42 A1 loc 2km N of Maghull. SD 3604
Lydiate Ash H & W 35 F6* vil 3m/5km N of Bromsgrove. SO 9775
Lydlinch Dorset 9 E3 vil in Blackmoor Vale 3m/4km W of Sturminster Newton. ST 7413
Lydney Glos 16 B2 small tn 8m/13km NE of Chepstow. Industrial estate and harbour on R Severn estuary to S. SO 6303
Lydstep Dyfed 22 D5 ham 3m/5km SW of Tenby. 1km SE is **Lydstep Pt** (NT), headland at S end of **L. Haven,** bay extending NE to Proud Giltar. SS 0898
Lye W Midlands 35 E5 E dist of Stourbridge. SO 9284
Lye Cross Avon 16 A5* loc 2km E of Wrington. ST 4962
Lye Green Bucks 18 D2* loc 2m/3km NE of Chesham. SP 9703
Lye Green E Sussex 12 B3* ham 2m/3km N of Crowborough. TQ 5034
Lye Green Warwicks 27 F1* ham 3m/5km E of Henley-in-Arden. SP 1965
Lye Head H & W 26 C1* loc 2m/4km SW of Bewdley. SO 7573
Lye, Lower H & W 26 A1* ham 7m/12km NW of Leominster. SO 4066
Lye's Green Wilts 16 C6 ham 4m/6km W of Warminster. ST 8246
Lye, Upper H & W 25 H2* ham 8m/12km NW of Leominster. SO 3965
Lyford Oxon 17 G2 vil 4m/7km N of Wantage. SU 3994
Lymbridge Green Kent 13 F3* ham 6m/10km N of Hythe. TR 1243
Lyme Bay 5 8. Bay stretching from Start Pt in Devon to Portland Bill in Dorset, a distance of some 55 (land) miles or 88 km. Much of the coast enclosing the bay is designated as of outstanding natural beauty.
Lyme Hall Ches 43 E3 Elizn hse with later additions in large deer park (NT) 2m/3km S of Disley. SJ 9682
Lyme Regis Dorset 8 B5 small resort built into cliffs on Lyme Bay, 20m/32km SW of Yeovil. SY 3492
Lyminge Kent 13 G3 vil 4m/6km N of Hythe. **L. Forest,** large wooded area 3m/5km N. TR 1640
Lymington Hants 10 A5 residential tn and yachting centre 15m/24km E of Bournemouth. Vehicle ferry to Yarmouth, Isle of Wight. SZ 3295
Lymington 10 A5* r in Hampshire rising in the New Forest and flowing SE past the tn of Lymington and thence into the Solent. SZ 3493
Lyminster W Sussex 11 F4 vil 2m/3km N of Littlehampton. TQ 0204
Lymm Ches 42 C3 tn 5m/8kn E of Warrington. SJ 6887
Lymn 45 G4 upper reaches of Steeping R above Halton Br to E of Halton Holegate, Lincs. TF 4265
Lympne Kent 13 F3 vil 3m/4km W of Hythe. Airport. TR 1135
Lympsham Som 15 H5 vil 4m/6km NE of Burnham-on-Sea. ST 3354
Lympstone Devon 5 F2 vil on E side of R Exe estuary 2m/3km N of Exmouth. SX 9984
Lynbridge Devon 7 E1 loc 1km S of Lynton. SS 7248
Lynch Hants 17 H6* loc 1km W of Overton. SU 5049
Lynch Som 7 G1* loc adjoining Bossington, 2km NE of Porlock. SS 9047
Lynchat H'land 75 G1 loc in Badenoch and Strathspey dist 2m/3km NE of Kingussie. NH 7801
Lynch Green Norfolk 39 F4* vil adjoining Hethersett to NW. TG 1505
Lynch Hill Berks 18 D3* NW dist of Slough. SU 9482
Lyndale Point Skye, H'land 78 B4 headland on Loch Snizort, N coast, between entrances to Lochs Greshornish and Snizort Beag. NG 3657
Lyndhurst Hants 10 A4 small tn 8m/13km N of Lymington and known as 'the capital of the New Forest'. SU 2908
Lyndon Leics 37 E4 vil 4m/7km SE of Oakham. SK 9004
Lyndon Green W Midlands 35 G5* loc in Birmingham 5m/8km E of city centre. SP 1485
Lyne Borders 66 A4 loc 3m/5km W of Peebles. Site of Roman camp. NT 2041
Lyne Surrey 19 E5* vil 2m/3km W of Chertsey. TQ 0166
Lyne 60 A5 r formed by confluence of Rs Black Lyne and White Lyne 5m/7km W of Bewcastle, Cumbria, and flowing SW into R Esk 3m/5km SW of Longtown. NY 3565
Lyne 61 G3 r rising SE of Longhorsley, Nthmb, and flowing E to North Sea at Lynemouth. NZ 3090
Lyneal Salop 34 B1 ham 3m/5km SE of Ellesmere. SJ 4433
Lyn, East Devon 7 E1* loc 2km SE of Lynton. SS 7348
Lyn, East 7 E1* r of N Exmoor flowing into Bristol Channel with W Lyn R at Lynmouth. Lower reaches are NT property. SS 7249
Lyne Down H & W 26 B4* loc 5m/8km NE of Ross-on-Wye. SO 6431
Lyneham Oxon 27 G5 vil 5m/8km SW of Chipping Norton. SP 2720
Lyneham Wilts 17 E3 vil 5m/8km N of Calne. Loc of **Church End** forms E part of Lyneham. RAF stn and airfield to W. SU 0279
Lynemouth Nthmb 61 G3 coal-mining loc near North Sea coast 2m/4km NE of Ashington. Power stn to S. NZ 2991
Lyne of Gorthlick H'land 81 E5 locality on W side of Loch Mhor in Inverness dist 3m/5km E of Foyers. NH 5420
Lyne of Skene Grampian 83 F5 vil 4m/7km SW of Kintore. NJ 7610
Lyness Orkney 89 A7* loc on Hoy opp S end of island of Fara. Oil service base. ND 3094
Lyne Water 65 H4 r in Borders region rising on Pentland Hills and flowing S to R Tweed 3m/4km W of Peebles. NT 2139
Lynford Cottages Norfolk 38 C5 loc 4m/6km NE of Brandon. TL 8191
Lyng Norfolk 39 E3 vil 6m/9km NE of E Dereham. TG 0717
Lyng Som 8 B2 vil 6m/9km W of Langport. Ham of **E Lyng** adjoining; ham of **W Lyng** 2km W. ST 3329
Lyngate Norfolk 39 G2* loc 1km NE of Worstead. TG 3026
Lyngford Som 8 A2* N dist of Taunton. ST 2325
Lynher 3 H3 r in Cornwall rising on Bodmin Moor near Altarnun and flowing SE into R Tamar below Saltash. From St Germans, r is usually known as St Germans R. SX 4257
Lynmouth Devon 7 E1 small resort with harbour at foot of cliff below Lynton, on **Lynmouth Bay.** SS 7249
Lynn Salop 34 D3/35 E3* loc 3m/5km SE of Newport. SJ 7815
Lynn Staffs 35 G4* loc 2m/4km E of Brownhills. SK 0704
Lynn, North Norfolk 38 B3* loc and industrial estate adjoining King's Lynn to N. TF 6121
Lynn of Lorn S'clyde 70 B1 strait in Loch Linnhe between island of Lismore and mainland to E. NM 8741
Lynn of Morvern 70 A1 strait in Loch Linnhe running between Morvern in Lochaber dist of Highland region and island of Lismore, S'clyde. NM 84
Lynn, West Norfolk 38 B3 dist of King's Lynn on W bank of R Ouse. Ferry for pedestrians to tn centre. Rd br 1m S. TF 6120
Lynsted Kent 21 E5 vil 3m/5km SE of Sittingbourne. TQ 9460
Lynstone Cornwall 3 B4* loc in SW part of Bude. SS 2005
Lynton Devon 7 E1 clifftop resort on N coast 14m/22km NE of Barnstaple. SS 7149
Lyn, West Devon 7 E1* loc 1m SE of Lynton. SS 7248
Lyn, West 7 E1* Exmoor r flowing N into Bristol Channel with E Lyn R at Lynmouth. SS 7249
Lynworth Glos 26 D5/27 E5* NE dist of Cheltenham. SO 9623
Lyon 75 H6 r in Tayside region running from Loch Lyon eastwards down Glen Lyon to R Tay 4m/6km W of Aberfeldy. See also Pass of Lyon. NN 7947
Lyons Tyne & Wear 54 C1* loc 1km SE of Hetton-le-Hole. NZ 3546
Lyon's Green Norfolk 38 D3* loc 1m E of Lit Fransham. TF 9111
Lyonshall H & W 25 G2/H3 vil 3m/4km E of Kington. SO 3355
Lypiatt Glos 16 D1* par (Bisley-with-L.) containing locs of **Middle** and **Nether L.,** and **L. Park,** on E side of Stroud. SO 8805
Lytchett Bay Dorset 9 G5* inlet off Poole Harbour 1m SE of Lytchett Minster. SY 9791
Lytchett Matravers Dorset 9 F4 vil 5m/8km NW of Poole. SY 9495
Lytchett Minster Dorset 9 F5 vil 4m/7km NE of Wareham. SY 9692
Lyte's Cary Som 8 D2* old manor hse (NT), 1m E of Kingsdon. ST 5326
Lyth H'land 86 E2 loc in Caithness dist 6m/10km SE of Castletown. ND 2863
Lytham Lancs 47 E5* dist of Lytham St Anne's to E of tn centre. SD 3627
Lytham St Anne's Lancs 47 E5 coastal resort on N side of mouth of R Ribble estuary 12m/19km W of Preston. SD 3427
Lythbank Salop 34 B4* loc 4m/6km SW of Shrewsbury. SJ 4607
Lythe N Yorks 55 F4 vil near North Sea coast 4m/6km NW of Whitby. NZ 8413
Lythe Hill Surrey 11 E2 loc 1m E of Haslemere. SU 9132
Lythes Orkney 89 B7* loc on S Ronaldsay 2m/4km S of St Margaret's Hope. ND 4589
Lyth, Great Salop 34 B4* loc 4m/6km SW of Shrewsbury. **Lit Lyth** loc 2km E. SJ 4507
Lyveden Northants 37 E5* loc 4m/6km SW of Oundle. **L. Manor** was the home of the Tresham family from the 15c; **L. New Build** (NT) is shell of unfinished hse of early 17c built by Sir Thomas Tresham. SP 9885
Lyvennet 53 E2 r rising on Crosby Ravensworth Fell, Cumbria, and flowing N by Crosby Ravensworth, Maulds Meaburn, and King's Meaburn, into R Eden 1km S of Temple Sowerby. NY 6026

M

Maaruig W Isles 88 B3* locality on N side of Loch M., inlet on W side of Loch Seaforth, Harris. **Maaruig I.** is tiny islet to E in Loch Seaforth. NB 1906
Mabe Burnthouse Cornwall 2 C5 vil 2km W of Penryn. Two resrs to S. SW 7634
Mabie Forest D & G 59 E4* state forest 4m/7km SW of Dumfries. NX 9370
Mablethorpe Lincs 45 H3 North Sea coast resort 11m/18km E of Louth. TF 5085
Macaskin Island S'clyde. See Island Macaskin.
Macclesfield Ches 43 E4 tn 10m/17km S of Stockport. Former centre of silk mnfre; now also other textiles, clothing, pharmaceuticals. **M. Forest** ham 4m/6km E in Peak Dist National Park. **M. Canal** runs from Peak Forest Canal at Marple, past E side of tn and of Congleton to Trent and Mersey Canal at Hardings Wood Junction. SJ 9173
Macduff Grampian 83 E1 small fishing tn on E side of Banff Bay 1m E of Banff. NJ 7064
Macduff's Castle Fife 73 F4 ruin on E side of E Wemyss, supposed former stronghold of Thanes of Fife. NT 3497
Macedonia Fife 73 F4* W dist of Glenrothes. NO 2501
Macgregor's Leap Tayside 75 G6* narrowest point in Pass of Lyon in Glen Lyon 2km W of Fortingall. NN 7247
Machan S'clyde 65 E4* loc adjoining Larkhall to S. NS 7650
Machany Water 72 C3 r in Tayside region running E to R Earn 3m/4km N of Auchterarder. NN 9412
Macharioch S'clyde 63 E6 loc on Kintyre 3m/5km E of Southend. NR 7309
Machars, The D & G 57 D7, E7 dairy-farming area between Luce Bay and Wigtown Bay. NX 35
Machen Mid Glam 15 G3 small tn 4m/6km E of Caerphilly. **Lr Machen,** vil in Gwent 2km SE, on site of Roman settlement. ST 2189
Machir Bay S'clyde 62 A2 bay on W coast of Islay on S side of Coul Pt. NR 2063

Machno 41 E6 r rising 2m/4km NE of Blaenau Ffestiniog, Gwynedd, and flowing NE by Penmachno to R Conwy below **M. Falls,** 2m/3km SE of Betws-y-coed. SH 8053
Machrie S'clyde 63 F4 loc on **M. Bay** on W coast of Arran 4m/6km N of Blackwaterfoot. **M. Water** is r running W into M. Bay. NR 8934
Machrihanish S'clyde 62 D5 vil on **M. Bay,** on W coast of Kintyre 5m/8km W of Campbeltown. **M. Water** is r flowing W into bay on E side of vil. **M. Airfield** to NE beyond r. NR 6320
Machynlleth Powys 33 E4 small mkt tn and tourist centre in R Dovey valley 16m/26km NE of Aberystwyth. SH 7400
Machynys Dyfed 23 F5* loc 2km S of Llanelli tn centre. Tinplate and engineering works. SS 5098
Mackerye End Herts 29 F6* loc 2m/3km NE of Harpenden. Associations with Charles Lamb (see *Essays of Elia*). TL 1515
Mackney Oxon 18 B3* loc 2m/3km W of Wallingford. SU 5889
Mackworth Derbys 35 H1 vil 3m/5km NW of Derby. Part of 15c gatehouse of former cas survives. SK 3137
Maclean's Cross Iona, S'Clyde. See Baile Mór.
Maclean's Nose H'land 68 D3 headland on S coast of Ardnamurchan peninsula in Lochaber dist, 3m/5km SE of Kilchoan. NM 5361
Maclean's Towel H'land 74 B5* waterfall in Lochaber dist 2m/4km N of Sallachan Pt on Loch Linnhe. Also known as Tubhailt Mhic' ic Eoghain. NM 9865
Macleod's Maidens Skye H'land 79 A5 three rocks off Idrigill Pt on SW coast. NG 2436
Macleod's Table North Skye, H'land 79 A5 hill 3m/5km SW of Dunvegan. Also known as Healaval More. Height 1538 ft or 469 metres. NG 2144
Macleod's Table South Skye, H'land 79 A5 hill 4m/6km SW of Dunvegan. Also known as Healaval Beg. Height 1601 ft or 488 metres. NG 2242
Macmerry Lothian 66 B2/C2 vil 2m/3km E of Tranent. Industrial estate 1km NE. NT 4372
Macmillan's Cross S'clyde. See Kilmory.
Macringan's Point S'clyde 63 E5* headland on E coast of Kintyre on N side of entrance to Campbeltown Loch. NR 7521
Madderty Tayside 72 C3 loc 5m/9km E of Crieff. NN 9521
Maddington Wilts 17 E6* loc adjoining Shrewton to N and 6m/9km NW of Amesbury. SU 0644
Maddiston Central 65 F1/F2 vil 4m/6km W of Linlithgow. NS 9476
Madehurst W Sussex 11 F4 loc 3m/4km NW of Arundel. SU 9910
Madeley Salop 34 D4 loc 2m/3km S of Dawley, Telford. SJ 6904
Madeley Staffs 42 D6 vil 5m/8km W of Newcastle-under-Lyme. **Middle** and **Lit Madeley** locs 1km and 1m NE respectively. **Madeley Heath** loc 2km NE. SJ 7744
Madeley Heath H & W 35 F6* loc 4m/7km N of Bromsgrove. SO 9577
Madeleywood Salop 34 D4* loc adjoining Ironbridge to E. SJ 6703
Maders Cornwall 3 G1* loc 2m/3km NW of Callington. SX 3471
Madingley Cambs 29 G2 vil 4m/6km NW of Cambridge. American World War II cemetery. Hall, Tudor and later. TL 3960
Madley H & W 26 A4 vil 6m/10km W of Hereford. SO 4138
Madresfield H & W 26 C3 vil 2m/3km NE of Gt Malvern. SO 8047
Madron Cornwall 2 A5 vil 2m/3km NW of Penzance. To N, M. Well and Baptistry. SW 4531
Maen Achwyfaen Clwyd. See Whitford.
Maenaddwyn Gwynedd 40 B3* loc on Anglesey 3m/4km E of Llanerchymedd. SH 4584
Maenclochog Dyfed 22 C3 vil 9m/15km SE of Fishguard. SN 0827
Maendy S Glam 15 E4 ham 2km NE of Cowbridge. ST 0176
Maendy S Glam 15 F3/G4* loc in Cardiff 2km N of city centre. ST 1778
Maendy Welsh form of Maindee, qv.
Maenease Point Cornwall 3 E4 headland on SE side of Gorran Haven. SX 0141
Mae Ness Orkney 89 B6* headland at easternmost point of island of Egilsay. HY 4831
Maen Llia Powys 25 E6* sandstone monolith on E side of Ystradfellte–Brecon rd at top of pass 4m/6km N of Ystradfellte. SN 9219
Maen Madoc Powys 25 E6* standing stone bearing Latin inscription 2m/3km NW of Ystradfellte, beside Roman rd known as Sarn Helen. SN 9115
Maenorbyr Welsh form of Manorbier, qv.
Maentwrog Gwynedd 32 D1 vil 3m/4km W of Ffestiniog. SH 6640
Maen y Bugael Welsh form of W Mouse. See Mouse, West.
Maen-y-groes Dyfed 24 A2* ham 1m S of New Quay. SN 3858
Maer Cornwall 6 B4* loc 2km N of Bude. SS 2007
Maer Staffs 35 E1 vil 6m/9km SW of Newcastle-under-Lyme. SJ 7938
Maerdy Clwyd 33 G1 vil 4m/6km W of Corwen. SJ 0144
Maerdy Dyfed 23 G3/G4 loc 2km S of Llandeilo. SN 6220
Maerdy Gwent 15 H2* loc 2km E of Usk. SO 4001
Maerdy Mid Glam 15 E2 loc in coal-mining area 2m/3km N of Rhondda. SS 9798
Maerdy Welsh form of Mardy, qv.
Maerun Welsh form of Marshfield, qv.
Maesbrook Green Salop 34 A2 ham 5m/9km S of Oswestry. SJ 3021
Maesbury Salop 34 A2* loc 3m/4km SE of Oswestry. Vil of **M. Marsh** 1km SE on Shropshire Union Canal. SJ 3025
Maes-coed, Lower H & W 25 H4* loc 4m/7km NW of Pontrilas. SO 3430
Maes-coed, Middle H & W 25 H4* loc 3m/4km SW of Vowchurch. SO 3333
Maes-coed, Upper H & W 25 G4* loc 1m NE of Michaelchurch Escley. SO 3334
Maesgeirchen Gwynedd 40 C4* loc 1km E of Bangor. SH 5871
Maes-glas Gwent 15 G3* loc in Newport 2km S of tn centre. ST 2985
Maeshafn Clwyd 41 G5* loc 3m/5km SW of Mold. SJ 2061
Maes Howe Orkney 89 A6* Neolithic communal burial-chamber (A.M.) near S end of Loch of Harray 3m/4km W of Finstown, Mainland. HY 3112
Maesllyn Dyfed 23 E2 ham 4m/6km NW of Llandyssul. SN 3644
Maesmynis Powys 25 E3* loc 3m/4km SW of Builth Wells. SO 0147
Maesteg Mid Glam 14 D3 tn 6m/9km E of Port Talbot. Coal-mining, engineering, clothing mnfre, cosmetics. SS 8591
Maesybont Dyfed 23 G4* ham 3m/4km N of Cross Hands. SN 5616
Maesycrugiau Dyfed 24 B4* loc on R Teifi 4m/6km SW of Llanybydder. SN 4741
Maes-y-cymer Mid Glam 15 F2 vil 5m/8km N of Caerphilly. ST 1594
Maesyfed Welsh form of New Radnor, qv.
Maesyrhandir Powys 33 G5* loc adjoining Newtown to SW. SO 0990
Maesyrychen Mountain Clwyd 41 G6* range of hills N of Llangollen and E of Llantysilio Mt. SJ 14
Magdalen Laver Essex 20 B1* ham 4m/7km E of Harlow. TL 5108
Maggieknockater Grampian 82 C3 loc 2m/3km E of Craigellachie. NJ 3145
Maggots End Essex 29 H5* ham 4m/6km N of Bishop's Stortford. TL 4727
Magham Down E Sussex 12 C5 vil 2m/3km NE of Hailsham. TQ 6011
Maghull Merseyside 42 A1/A2 tn 8m/13km N of Liverpool. SD 3702
Magillie Loch D & G 57 B6 small loch 2m/4km E of Stranraer. Also known as Loch Magillie. NX 0959
Magna Carta Island Berks 19 E4 island in R Thames opp Runnymede 2km NW of Egham. Said to be actual site of sealing of Magna Carta by King John in 1215. SU 9972
Magor (Magwyr) Gwent 16 A3 vil 8m/13km SW of Chepstow. ST 4287
Magpie Green Suffolk 31 E1 loc 3m/5km W of Diss. TM 0778
Magwyr Welsh form of Magor, qv.
Maida Vale London 19 F3* loc in City of Westminster 3m/5km NW of Charing Cross. TQ 2582
Maiden Bradley Wilts 9 E1 vil 4m/6km N of Mere. ST 8038
Maiden Castle Ches 42 B5* Iron Age fort on Bickerton Hill, to NW of Bickerton and 4m/6km N of Malpas. SJ 4952
Maiden Castle Dorset 8 D5 large oval prehistoric earthworks (A.M.) 2m/3km SW of Dorchester. SY 6688
Maidencombe Devon 5 E4 loc 3m/4km N of Torquay above Babbacombe Bay. SX 9268
Maidenhall Point Dyfed 22 B4* headland on St Brides Bay 1m N of Rickets Hd. SM 8520
Maidenhayne Devon 8 B4* ham just N of Musbury and 3m/4km SW of Axminster. SY 2795
Maiden Head Avon 16 B4* ham 1km SE of Dundry and 4m/7km S of Bristol. ST 5666
Maidenhead Berks 18 D3 tn on R Thames 5m/8km W of Slough. 2m/4km W is **M. Thicket** (NT), wooded area containing Belgic farm enclosure known as Robin Hood's Arbour. SU 8881
Maidenhead Bay S'clyde 56 C3 bay between Culzean and Turnberry. NS 2108
Maiden Island S'clyde 70 A2 islet 2km N of Oban, Argyll. NM 8431
Maiden Law Durham 54 B1* loc 2km N of Lanchester. NZ 1749
Maiden Newton Dorset 8 D4 vil on R Frome 8m/13km NW of Dorchester. SY 5997
Maidens S'clyde 56 C3 fishing vil on Maidenhead Bay, 5m/9km W of Maybole. NS 2107
Maiden's Green Berks 18 D4* loc 1km W of Winkfield and 3m/4km NE of Bracknell. SU 0972
Maiden Stone, The Grampian. See Chapel of Garioch.
Maidenwell Lincs 45 G3 ham 5m/8km S of Louth. TF 3279
Maiden Wells Dyfed 22 C5 ham 2km SW of Pembroke. SR 9799
Maidford Northants 28 B3 vil 6m/9km NW of Towcester. SP 6052
Maids' Moreton Bucks 28 C4 vil 1m NE of Buckingham. SP 7035
Maids of Bute S'clyde 63 F1* two rocks at N end of island of Bute near Buttock Pt. NS 0174
Maidstone Kent 20 D6 county tn on R Medway. Industries include brewing, paper mnfg, engineering. TQ 7655
Maidwell Northants 36 C6 vil 7m/11km S of Mkt Harborough. SP 7476
Maindee (Maendy) Gwent 15 H3 dist of Newport 2km E of tn centre. ST 3288
Mainland Orkney 89 B6 largest island of Orkney group, being 26m/42km long from Brough Hd in the NW to Rose Ness in the SE, and of irregular shape. Kirkwall, chief tn of the island and of the group, is 24m/38km N of Duncansby Hd on Scottish mainland across Scapa Flow and Pentland Firth. Farming, esp rearing of beef cattle, is chief industry. Fishing, though secondary, is of some importance. Airport (Grimsetter) near Kirkwall. HY 31
Mainland 89 the largest island of Shetland, containing Lerwick, the capital, on the E coast. The island is 56m/90km long N to S, and generally narrow E to W, being much indented by inlets or *voes*. HU 35
Mains S'clyde 64 D3* dist of E Kilbride near tn centre. **M. Castle** to N is late 15c tower. NS 6354
Mains, East Grampian 77 F2* loc 2m/3km NW of Banchory. NJ 6797
Mainsforth Durham 54 C2* ham 3m/5km NW of Sedgefield. NZ 3131
Mainstone Salop 34 A5 vil 5m/8km N of Clun. SO 2787
Main Water of Luce 57 B6 r rising in Strathclyde region 4m/7km SE of Ballantrae, and flowing S into Dumfries and Galloway region to join Cross Water of Luce at New Luce, to form Water of Luce, qv. NX 1764
Maisemore Glos 26 C5 vil on right bank of R Severn 2m/3km NW of Gloucester. SO 8121
Maisgeir S'clyde 68 B4 rock island off SW coast of Gometra, Mull. NM 3439
Maison Dieu Kent. See Ospringe.
Maitland Park London 19 G3* loc in borough of Camden 3m/5km NW of Charing Cross. TQ 2884
Maize Beck 53 G2 r rising on Dufton Fell, Cumbria, and flowing E into R Tees on border of Cumbria and Durham below Caldron Snout. NY 8128
Maizebeck Force 53 G3* waterfall in Maize Beck on border of Cumbria and Durham 2km SW of Caldron Snout. NY 8027
Majorsbarn Staffs 35 F1* loc adjoining Cheadle to S. SK 0042
Major's Green H & W 35 G6* loc 3m/5km W of Solihull. SP 1077
Makeney Derbys 43 H6* vil 1m NE of Duffield. SK 3544
Makerstoun Borders 66 D5 loc 4m/6km W of Kelso. NT 6732
Maker-with-Rame Cornwall 4 B5* loc S of Millbrook. SX 4250
Malborough Devon 4 D6 vil 2m/3km W of Salcombe. SX 7039
Malcolm's Point S'clyde 69 D6 headland on S coast of Ross of Mull 3m/5km SW of Carsaig. NM 4918
Malden Rushett London 19 F5* loc in borough of Kingston 2m/4km W of Epsom. TQ 1761
Maldon Essex 21 E1 tn at head of R Blackwater estuary 9m/14km E of Chelmsford. Timber importing; flour milling. Old bldgs include 15c moot hall. TL 8507
Malham N Yorks 48 B2 vil in Upper Airedale 5m/8km E of Settle across moors. **M. Tarn,** lake on limestone moors 2m/3km N, probable source of R Aire. 1km N of vil is **M. Cove,** limestone cliff from foot of which R Aire issues. SD 9062
Malin Bridge S Yorks 43 G2* loc in Hillsborough dist of Sheffield 2m/3km NW of city centre. SK 3289
Malins Lee Salop 34 D3* loc 1km N of Dawley. SJ 6808
Mallaig H'land 79 E8 small fishing port and rly terminus on coast of Lochaber dist at entrance to Sound of Sleat, and S of entrance to Loch Inver. Vehicle ferry to Armadale, Skye. NM 6796
Mallaigvaig H'land 79 E8 loc on coast of Lochaber dist 1m NE of Mallaig. NM 6997
Mallart H'land 84 F4 r running N through Loch Choire into R Naver below Loch Naver in Caithness dist. NC 6737
Malleny Mills Lothian 65 H2* loc 1km SE of Balerno. For Malleny Hse, see Balerno. NT 1665
Mallie H'land 74 C3 r in Lochaber dist rising on Locheil Forest and running E down Glen Mallie into S side of Loch Arkaig, 2m/3km W of foot of loch. NN 1388
Malling, East Kent 20 D5 vil 4m/6km W of Maidstone. **E. Malling Heath** loc 1m S. TQ 7057
Malling, South E Sussex 12 B5 E dist of Lewes. TQ 4210
Malling, West Kent 20 C5 large vil 5m/8km W of Maidstone. To SW is St Leonard's Tower, remains of Norman keep (A.M.). TQ 6857
Mallows Green Essex 29 H5* loc 3m/5km N of Bishop's Stortford. TL 4726
Malltraeth (or **Malltraeth Yard**) Gwynedd 40 B4 vil at head of R Cefni estuary on Anglesey. **M. Sands** cover estuary at low tide. **M. Bay** at r mouth extends from Pen-y-parc to Llanddwyn I. SH 4068
Malltraeth Marsh (Cors Ddyga) Gwynedd 40 B4 marsh in valley of R Cefni, Anglesey, to S of Llangefni. SH 47
Mallwyd Gwynedd 33 F3 ham 10m/16km NE of Machynlleth. SH 8612
Mallyan Spout N Yorks 55 F5 waterfall in W Beck 1km W of Goathland. NZ 8201
Malmesbury Wilts 16 D3 country tn on R Avon 14m/22km W of Swindon. Par ch is remains of medieval abbey. Mkt cross. Electrical engineering industry. ST 9387
Malmshead Devon 7 F1 ham on Somerset border 5m/8km E of Lynton. SS 7947
Malpas Cornwall 2 D4 vil 2m/3km SE of Truro at confluence of Rs Tresillian and Truro. SW 8442
Malpas Gwent 15 G2/G3 suburb 2m/3km N of Newport. ST 3090
Maltby Cleveland 54 D3 vil 4m/6km S of Stockton-on-Tees. NZ 4613

Maltby Lincs 45 G3* loc 2m/4km SW of Louth. TF 3184
Maltby S Yorks 44 A2 tn 6m/10km E of Rotherham. Coal-mining, brick mnfre, engineering. SK 5292
Maltby le Marsh Lincs 45 H3 vil 4m/6km SW of Mablethorpe. TF 4681
Malting End Suffolk 30 C3* ham 7m/12km NE of Haverhill. TL 7454
Malting Green Essex 30 D6* vil 3m/5km S of Colchester. TL 9720
Maltman's Hill Kent 13 E3 ham 5m/8km SW of Charing. TQ 9043
Malton N Yorks 50 C1 tn on R Derwent on site of Roman stn 17m/27km NE of York. Brewing, agricultural implements. Racing stables. See also Old Malton. SE 7871
Malvern, Great H & W 26 C3 tn on steep E slope of Malvern Hills 7m/12km SW of Worcester. Developed as spa in 19c. SO 7845
Malvern Hills H & W 26 C3, C4 narrow range of limestone hills running N and S for 8m/13km. The inland resort of Gt Malvern is to the E of the N end. Highest point is Worcestershire Beacon, 1394 ft or 425 metres, near N end. SO 7641
Malvern Link H & W 26 C3 N dist of Gt Malvern. SO 7848
Malvern, Little H & W 26 C3 vil below E side of Malvern Hills 4m/6km S of Gt Malvern. SO 7740
Malvern Wells H & W 26 C3 loc under E slope of Malvern Hills and 2m/4km S of Gt Malvern tn centre. Three Counties (Agricultural) Showground to E. SO 7742
Malvern, West H & W 26 C3 vil on W side of Malvern Hills 2km W of Gt Malvern. SO 7646
Mamble H & W 26 C1 vil 3m/5km S of Cleobury Mortimer. SO 6871
Mamhead Devon 5 E3 par with ch in grnds of Mamhead Hse 3m/5km NW of Dawlish. SX 9380
Mamheilad Welsh form of Mamhilad, qv.
Mamhilad (Mamheilad) Gwent 15 G1* ham 2m/4km NE of Pontypool. SO 3003
Mamlorn See Forest of Mamlorn.
Mam na Gualainn H'land 74 C5 mt in Lochaber dist on N side of Loch Leven and 4m/7km W of Kinlochleven. Height 2611 ft or 796 metres. NN 1162
Mam nan Carn 76 B3* mt on border of Grampian and Tayside regions 7m/12km S of Inverey. Height 3235 ft or 986 metres. NO 0478
Mamore Forest H'land 74 C3-D4 mt tract in Lochaber dist between Kinlochleven and Glen Nevis. NN 1765
Mam Rattachan H'land 79 F6, 80 A5 pass with rd leading from foot of Glen Shiel in Skye and Lochalsh dist, to foot of Glen More in Lochaber dist. Also known as Mam Ratagain. See also Ratagan. NG 9019
Mam Sodhail H'land. Gaelic form of Mam Soul, qv.
Mam Soul H'land 80 B5 mt on border of Inverness and Skye & Lochalsh dists 3m/4km NW of Loch Affric. Height 3871 ft or 1180 metres. Also known as Mam Sodhail. NH 1225
Mam Tor Derbys 43 F3 hill (NT) surmounted by Iron Age fort, 2km W of Castleton. Also known as Shivering Mountain, owing to continuous crumbling of S face. SK 1283
Manaccan Cornwall 2 D5 vil 7m/11km E of Helston. SW 7625
Manacle Point Cornwall 2 D6 headland at easternmost point of Lizard peninsula, 7m/11km S of Falmouth across bay. SW 8121
Manacles, The Cornwall 2 D6* group of rocks off E coast of Lizard peninsula SE of Manacle Pt. SW 8220
Manadon Devon 4 B5* N dist of Plymouth, 2m/4km from city centre. SX 4858
Manafon Powys 33 G4 ham on R Rhiw 3m/4km S of Llanfair Caereinion. SJ 1102
Man and his Man Cornwall 2 C3* two island rocks, also known as Bawden Rocks, 2km N of St Agnes Hd. SW 7053
Manaton Devon 4 D3 vil on E edge of Dartmoor 3m/5km S of Moretonhampstead. SX 7581
Manby Lincs 45 G3 vil 5m/7km E of Louth. Airfield to W. TF 3986
Mancetter Warwicks 35 H4* vil adjoining Atherstone to SE. To E on Leics border is site of Roman settlement of *Manduessedum*. SP 3296
Manchester Gtr Manchester 42 D2 important cultural and commercial centre and port 164m/264km NW of London. Access for ships by R Mersey and Manchester Ship Canal. Industries include textiles, engineering, chemicals, clothing, rubber. University. Cathedral formerly par ch. International airport (Ringway) 9m/14km S of city centre. SJ 8398
Manchester, Greater 117 metropolitan county of NW England, comprising the urban complex which includes Manchester, Bolton, Bury, Oldham, Rochdale, Salford, Stockport, and Wigan.
Manchester Ship Canal 42 D2-A3 commercial inland waterway navigable by ocean-going ships. Runs from Manchester to R Mersey estuary at Eastham, Merseyside.
Mancot, Little Clwyd 41 H4* loc on S side of Mancot Royal and Big Mancot, between Hawarden and Queensferry. SJ 3166
Mancot Royal Clwyd 41 H4* loc 1m N of Hawarden. SJ 3165
Mandale Marshes Cleveland 54 D3* loc 2km E of Stockton-on-Tees across r. Racecourse. NZ 4618
Manduessedum Leics. See Mancetter.
Manea Cambs 37 H5 vil 6m/10km E of Chatteris. TL 4789
Maney W Midlands 35 G4* dist of Sutton Coldfield to S of tn centre. SP 1295
Manfield N Yorks 54 B3 vil 4m/7km W of Darlington. NZ 2213
Mangaster Shetland 89 E6 loc in N part of Mainland, on N side of inlet of St Magnus Bay called **M. Voe.** HU 3270
Mangerton Dorset 8 C4* loc 3m/4km NE of Bridport. SY 4895
Mangotsfield Avon 16 B4* tn 5m/8km NE of Bristol. ST 6576
Mangrove Green Herts 29 E5* ham 3m/4km NE of Luton. TL 1223
Manifold 43 F6 r rising in Staffs some 4m/7km S of Buxton, Derbys, and flowing S through the limestone country of the Peak Dist National Park into R Dove at Thorpe, NW of Ashbourne. SK 1450
Manish W Isles 88 A3/A4 loc on SE coast of Harris 8m/12km S of Tarbert. NG 1089
Manish Point Skye, H'land 78 D4 northward-facing headland on W coast of Raasay at entrance to Loch Arnish. **Manish I.** is islet to SW. NG 5648
Man, Isle of D & G 59 E4* loc on Lochar Moss 2m/4km E of Dumfries. NY 0075
Man, Isle of 46. Island 31m/50km long NE to SW, incl Calf of Man, qv, and 13m/21km wide E to W. Lies 17m/28km S of Burrow Hd, Scotland, 30m/48km W of St Bees Hd, England, and 33m/54km E of Ballyquintin Pt, N Ireland. Range of mts runs NE to SW, the highest being Snaefell, qv. Tourism, agriculture and fishing are the main industries. Douglas on E coast is chief tn and seat of government, and terminus of passenger-boat services. Ronaldsway Airport near Castletown.
Mankinholes W Yorks 48 C5* ham 2m/3km E of Todmorden. SD 9623
Manley Ches 42 B4* vil 3m/4km SE of Helsby. SJ 5071
Man, Little Cumbria 52 C2* mt in Lake Dist on S slopes of Skiddaw 3m/5km N of Keswick. Height 2837 ft or 865 metres. NY 2627
Manllegwaun Dyfed 23 E2* loc 4m/6km SE of Newcastle Emlyn. SN 3536
Manmoel Gwent 15 F1* vil 4m/6km S of Ebbw Vale. SO 1703
Mannamead Devon 4 B5* dist of Plymouth 2km N of city centre. SX 4856
Mannel Tiree, S'clyde 69 A8 loc on Hynish Bay 1km S of Balemartine. NL 9840
Manningford Wilts 17 F5 par adjoining that of Upavon to N and containing vils of **M. Abbots, M. Bohune, M. Bruce.** SU 1457
Manningham W Yorks 48 D4* dist of Bradford 1m NW of city centre. SE 1534
Mannings Heath W Sussex 11 G2 vil 2m/4km SE of Horsham. TQ 2028
Mannington Dorset 9 G4 ham 5m/8km NE of Wimborne. 1km SE, loc of **Lr Mannington.** SU 0605
Manningtree Essex 31 E5 tn at head of R Stour estuary 8m/12km NE of Colchester. TM 1031
Mannofield Grampian 77 H1* dist of Aberdeen 2m/3km SW of city centre. NJ 9104
Manor S Yorks 43 H3* dist of Sheffield 2m/4km SE of city centre. SK 3885
Manorbier (Maenorbyr) Dyfed 22 C5 vil near coast 4m/7km SW of Tenby. Remains of Norman cas. **M. Bay,** small bay to W. SS 0697
Manorbier Newton Dyfed 22 C5* ham 4m/6km E of Pembroke. SN 0400
Manordeifi Dyfed 22 D2 loc 4m/6km SE of Cardigan. SN 2243
Manordilo Dyfed 24 C5 ham 3m/5km NE of Llandeilo. SN 6726
Manorowen Dyfed 22 B2 ham 2m/3km SW of Fishguard. SM 9336
Manor Park Berks 18 D3* N dist of Slough. SU 9681
Manor Park London 20 B3* loc in borough of Newham 2km N of E Ham. TQ 4285
Manor Water 65 H4 r in Borders region rising 2m/3km SE of Dollar Law and running N to R Tweed 2m/3km W of Peebles. NT 2239
Manselfield W Glam 23 G6* loc 3m/5km NW of Mumbles Hd. SS 5988
Mansell Gamage H & W 25 H3 vil 8m/13km W of Hereford. SO 3944
Mansell Lacy H & W 26 A3 vil 6m/10km NW of Hereford. SO 4245
Manselton W Glam 23 G5/G6* dist of Swansea 2km N of tn centre. SS 6595
Mansergh Cumbria 53 E6 loc 3m/4km N of Kirkby Lonsdale. SD 6082
Mansewood S'clyde 64 C3* loc in Glasgow 3m/5km SW of city centre. NS 5560
Mansfield Notts 44 A5 mnfg and engineering tn 14m/22km N of Nottingham. SK 5361
Mansfield Woodhouse Notts 44 A4 tn adjoining Mansfield to N. Industries include coal-mining, engineering, hosiery. SK 5463
Manson Green Norfolk 39 E4* loc 1m N of Hingham. TG 0203
Mansriggs Cumbria 52 C6* loc 2m/3km N of Ulverston. SD 2980
Manston Dorset 9 E3 vil 2m/3km NE of Sturminster Newton. ST 8115
Manston Kent 13 H1 loc in W part of Ramsgate. Airport to W. TR 3466
Manston W Yorks 49 F4* loc in Seacroft dist of Leeds 4m/7km E of city centre. SE 3634
Manswood Dorset 9 G3 ham 6m/10km E of Blandford Forum. ST 9708
Manthorpe Lincs 37 E1 vil 2km N of Grantham. SK 9237
Manthorpe Lincs 37 F3 ham 3m/5km SW of Bourne. TF 0716
Manton Humberside 44 D1 ham 3m/4km N of Kirton in Lindsey. SE 9302
Manton Leics 36 D4 vil 3m/5km S of Oakham. SK 8804
Manton Notts 44 B3* coal-mining loc adjoining Worksop to SE. SK 6078
Manton Wilts 17 F4 loc 2km W of Marlborough. SU 1768
Manuden Essex 29 H5 vil 3m/5km N of Bishop's Stortford. TL 4926
Manwood Green Essex 20 C1* loc 3m/5km W of Leaden Roding. TL 5412
Manxman's Lake D & G 58 C6* arm of Kirkcudbright Bay on E side of St Mary's Isle. NX 6748
Maoile Lunndaidh H'land 80 B3 mt in Ross and Cromarty dist 3m/5km N of Loch Monar. Height 3304 ft or 1007 metres. NH 1345
Maol Chean-dearg H'land 80 A3 mt on Ben-damph Forest, Ross and Cromarty dist, 5m/8km N of head of Loch Carron. Height 3060 ft or 933 metres. NG 9249
Maol Chinn-dearg H'land 74 B1 mt ridge on border of Lochaber and Skye & Lochalsh dists between Loch Quoich and head of Loch Cluanie. See Aonach air Chrith. NH 0308
Maperton Som 8 D2* vil 3m/5km SW of Wincanton. ST 6726
Maplebeck Notts 44 B5 vil 7m/11km NW of Newark-on-Trent. SK 7160
Maple Cross Herts 19 E2* loc 2m/3km SW of Rickmansworth. TQ 0392
Mapledurham Oxon 18 B4 vil on R Thames 4m/6km NW of Reading across r. Tudor manor hse. SU 6776
Mapledurwell Hants 18 B6* vil 3m/5km E of Basingstoke. SU 6851
Maplehurst W Sussex 11 G3 ham 2m/3km NW of Cowfold. TQ 1824
Maplescombe Kent 20 C5* ham 2m/3km SE of Farningham. TQ 5664
Maplestead, Great Essex 30 C4 vil 3m/4km N of Halstead. TL 8034
Maplestead, Little Essex 30 C4 vil 2m/4km N of Halstead. TL 8234
Mapleton Derbys 43 F6 vil 2km NW of Ashbourne. Also spelt Mappleton. SK 1647
Maplin Sands 21 F3 sands off Essex coast at Foulness I. on N side of entrance to R Thames estuary. TR 0088
Mapperley Derbys 36 A1 vil 2m/3km NW of Ilkeston. **M. Park** loc 1km W. **Mapperley Resr** to N. SK 4343
Mapperley Notts 36 B1 suburb of Nottingham 2m/4km NE of city centre. SK 5843
Mapperley Park Notts 36 B1* dist of Nottingham 2km N of city centre. SK 5742
Mapperton Dorset 8 C4 ham 2m/3km SE of Beaminster. SY 5099
Mapperton Dorset 9 F4* loc 5m/8km S of Blandford Forum. SY 9098
Mappleborough Green Warwicks 27 E1 suburb 3m/5km SE of Redditch. SP 0765
Mappleton Derbys 43 F6 vil 2km NW of Ashbourne. Also spelt Mapleton. SK 1647
Mappleton Humberside 51 F4 vil on coast 3m/5km SE of Hornsea. TA 2243
Mappowder Dorset 9 E4 vil 6m/10km SW of Sturminster Newton. ST 7306
Marazion Cornwall 2 B5 small tn 3m/4km E of Penzance across Mount's Bay. Causeway to St Michael's Mount, qv. SW 5130
Marbury Ches 42 B6 vil 3m/5km NE of Whitchurch. **Big Mere** lake on S side of vil. A smaller lake on E side. SJ 5645
Marbury Ches 42 C4* loc 2m/3km N of Northwich. SJ 6576
March Cambs 37 H5 fenland tn on R Nene (old course), 14m/22km E of Peterborough. Industries include agricultural products, rly engineering; large marshalling yards to N. TL 4196
Marcham Oxon 17 H2 vil 3m/4km W of Abingdon. SU 4596
Marchamley Salop 34 C2 vil 6m/9km SW of Mkt Drayton. Loc of **M. Wood** 2km N. SJ 5929
March Ghyll Reservoir N Yorks 48 D3* small resr 2m/4km N of Ilkley. SE 1251
March Haigh Reservoir W Yorks 48 C6* small resr on moors 2m/4km NW of Marsden. SE 0112
Marchington Staffs 35 G2 vil 3m/5km SE of Uttoxeter. **M. Woodlands** loc 2m/3km SW. SK 1330
Marchlyn Bach Reservoir Gwynedd 40 C5* small resr 2m/4km NE of Llanberis. SH 6062
Marchlyn Mawr Reservoir Gwynedd 40 C5* resr 3m/4km E of Llanberis. SH 6162
Marchmont Lothian 66 A2* dist of Edinburgh 2km S of city centre. NT 2572
Marchros Gwynedd 32 B2* loc 2km S of Abersoch. SH 3126
Marchwiel Clwyd 42 A6 vil 2m/4km SE of Wrexham. SJ 3547
Marchwood Hants 10 B4 vil 3m/5km SE of Totton. 1m NE on R Test estuary, M. Power Stn. SU 3810
Marcle, Little H & W 26 B4 vil 3m/5km W of Ledbury. SO 6736
Marcroes Welsh form of Marcross, qv.
Marcross (Marcroes) S Glam 15 E4 vil 3m/4km W of Llantwit Major. SS 9269
Marden H & W 26 A3 vil on R Lugg 4m/7km N of Hereford. SO 5147
Marden Kent 12 D3 vil 7m/11km S of Maidstone. Loc of **M. Beech** 1m S. TQ 7444
Marden Tyne & Wear 61 H4* urban loc adjoining Whitley Bay to S. NZ 3570
Marden Wilts 17 E5 vil 5m/8km W of Pewsey. SU 0857
Marden 16 D4* r rising S of Calne, Wilts, and flowing into R Avon E of Chippenham. ST 9374
Marden Ash Essex 20 C2* loc adjoining Chipping Ongar to S. TL 5502
Marden, East W Sussex 11 E3 vil 5m/7km W of Singleton. SU 8014
Marden, North W Sussex 11 E3 ham 6m/10km SE of Petersfield. SU 8016
Marden's Hill E Sussex 12 B3* loc 2km NW of Crowborough. TQ 4932

Marden Thorn Kent 12 D3 ham 2km SE of Marden. TQ 7543
Marden, West W Sussex 10 D3 vil 6m/9km NE of Havant. Site of Roman villa 1km S. SU 7713
Mardington Borders 67 F3 loc 4m/6km NW of Berwick-upon-Tweed. NT 9456
Mardon Nthmb 67 F4/F5* loc 1km E of Branxton. NT 9037
Mardy (Maerdy) Gwent 25 G6 loc 2km N of Abergavenny. SO 3015
Mar Dyke 20 B4 r rising near Brentwood, Essex, and flowing S and finally W into R Thames on W side of Purfleet. TQ 5478
Marefield Leics 36 C4 loc 7m/11km S of Melton Mowbray. SK 7407
Mare Green Som 8 B2 vil 2km NE of N Curry. ST 3326
Mareham le Fen Lincs 45 F5 vil 6m/9km S of Horncastle. TF 2861
Mareham on the Hill Lincs 45 F4 vil 2m/3km SE of Horncastle. TF 2867
Marehay Derbys 43 H6* mining loc 2km S of Ripley. SK 3948
Maresfield E Sussex 12 B4 vil 2m/3km N of Uckfield. TQ 4624
Mare, The Dyfed 22 A4* island rock on E side of Green Scar, 1km W of Dinas-fawr. SM 7922
Marfleet Humberside 51 F5 dist of Hull 3m/5km E of city centre. TA 1429
Marford Clwyd 42 A5* vil 4m/6km N of Wrexham. SJ 3556
Mar Forest Grampian 76 A2, B2 deer forest astride Glen Dee on S side of Cairngorms. NO 0291
Margam W Glam 14 D3 SE dist of Port Talbot. Large steel works. **M. Burrows** and **M. Sands** on coast to SW. **M. Forest**, large wooded area to E. SS 7887
Margaret Marsh Dorset 9 F3 vil 3m/5km SW of Shaftesbury. ST 8218
Margaret Roding Essex 20 C1 loc 1m S of Leaden Roding. TL 5912
Margaretting Essex 20 C2 vil 4m/6km SW of Chelmsford. Ham of **M. Tye** 1m SE. TL 6701
Margate Kent 13 H1 N coast resort on Isle of Thanet 15m/25km NE of Canterbury. Large harbour. TR 3570
Margidunum Notts. See Bingham.
Margnaheglish S'clyde 63 G4* vil on Lamlash Bay on E coast of Arran, adjoining vil of Lamlash to NE. NS 0331
Marham Norfolk 38 C4 vil 7m/12km W of Swaffham. Remains of 13c abbey. Airfield to SE. TF 7009
Marhamchurch Cornwall 6 B5 vil 2m/3km SE of Bude. SS 2203
Marholm Cambs 37 F4 vil 4m/6km NW of Peterborough. TF 1402
Mariandyrys Gwynedd 40 C3* loc on Anglesey 3m/5km N of Beaumaris. SH 6081
Marian-glas Gwynedd 40 C3* loc near E coast of Anglesey 2km S of Moelfre. SH 5084
Mariansleigh Devon 7 F3 vil 3m/5km SE of S Molton. SS 7422
Marine Town Kent 21 E4* suburb to E of Sheerness. TQ 9274
Marishader Skye, H'land 78 C3 loc 3m/5km S of Staffin Bay. NG 4963
Marishes, High N Yorks 50 D1 ham 4m/7km N of Malton. SE 8178
Marishes, Low N Yorks 50 D1 ham 4m/7km NE of Malton. SE 8177
Maristow Devon 4 B4* ham by R Tavy 6m/10km N of Plymouth. SX 4764
Mariveg W Isles 88 C2* vil near E coast of Lewis 2m/3km S of entrance to Loch Erisort. **Loch M.** is inlet to N. NB 4119
Marjoribanks D & G 59 F3* loc 1km N of Lochmaben. NY 0883
Mark Som 15 H6 vil 5m/8km E of Burnham-on-Sea. 2km W, elongated loc of **M. Causeway.** ST 3847
Markbeech Kent 12 B3 vil 3m/5km SE of Edenbridge. TQ 4742
Markby Lincs 45 H3 vil 3m/5km NE of Alford. TF 4878
Mark Cross E Sussex 12 C3 vil 5m/8km S of Tunbridge Wells. TQ 5831
Markeaton Derbys 35 H1* loc in Derby 2m/3km NW of tn centre. SK 3337
Markenfield Hall N Yorks 49 E2* hse dating from 14c, 3m/4km S of Ripon. SE 2967
Market Bosworth Leics 36 A4 small tn 6m/10km N of Hinckley. Bosworth Field, 2m/3km S, is site of battle in 1485 in which Henry Tudor defeated Richard III. SK 4003
Market Deeping Lincs 37 F3 vil on R Welland 7m/11km E of Stamford. TF 1310
Market Drayton Salop 34 D1 tn 18m/28km NE of Shrewsbury. Important agricultural centre. SJ 6734
Market End Warwicks 36 A5* loc adjoining Bedworth to W. SP 3486
Market Harborough Leics 36 C5 tn on R Welland 14m/23km SE of Leicester. SP 7387
Market Lavington Wilts 17 E5 vil 5m/7km S of Devizes. SU 1054
Market Overton Leics 36 D3 vil 5m/8km N of Oakham. Site of Romano-British settlement 2km E. SK 8816
Market Rasen Lincs 45 E2/E3 mkt tn and agricultural centre 14m/22km NE of Lincoln. Racecourse. TF 1089
Market Stainton Lincs 45 F3 vil 6m/10km E of Wragby. TF 2279
Market Street Norfolk 39 G3* vil 3m/5km N of Wroxham. TG 2921
Market Weighton Humberside 50 D4 small tn 15m/24km NE of Goole. SE 8741
Market Weston Suffolk 31 E1 vil 6m/10km NE of Ixworth. TL 9877
Markfield Leics 36 B3 vil 7m/12km NW of Leicester. SK 4810
Mark Hall North Essex 20 B1* NE dist of Harlow. TL 4611
Mark Hall South Essex 20 B1* E dist of Harlow. TL 4610
Markham Gwent 15 F2* vil 2m/3km NE of Bargoed. SO 1601
Markham, East Notts 44 C4 vil 2km N of Tuxford. **W. Markham** vil 2km W. SK 7472
Markham Moor Notts 44 C4 ham 2m/4km NW of Tuxford. SK 7174
Markie Burn H'land 75 F2 stream in Badenoch and Strathspey dist running S into R Spey 2km W of Laggan Br. NN 5893
Markinch Fife 73 F4 small tn on E side of Glenrothes. Woollen and paper mnfre. NO 2901
Markington N Yorks 49 E2 vil 3m/4km N of Ripley. SE 2864
Markland Hill Gtr Manchester 42 C1* loc in Bolton 2m/3km W of tn centre. SD 6809
Marksbury Avon 16 B5 vil 4m/6km S of Keynsham. ST 6662
Marks Gate London 20 B3 loc in borough of Barking 5m/8km NE of Barking tn centre. TQ 4890
Marks Tey Essex 30 D5 vil 5m/8km W of Colchester. TL 9123
Markyate Herts 29 E6 vil 4m/6km SW of Luton. TL 0616
Marlais 22 D4* r rising near Narberth, Dyfed, and flowing E into R Taf 1m W of Whitland. SN 1816
Marlais 24 B5* r rising 2m/3km SE of New Inn, Dyfed, and flowing SE into R Cothi 1km E of Brechfa. SN 5330
Marlais 24 C4 r rising on Mynydd Pencarreg, Dyfed, and flowing SE to Llansawel then E into R Cothi 2km E. SN 6436
Marlais 24 C5 r rising 3m/4km NW of Llansadwrn, Dyfed, and flowing S into R Towy on W side of Llangadog. SN 6928
Marland Gtr Manchester 42 D1* loc in Rochdale 2km SW of tn centre. SD 8711
Marland, Little Devon 6 D4* loc 5m/7km S of Torrington. SS 4912
Marl Bank H & W 26 C3* loc 3m/5km S of Gt Malvern. SO 7840
Marlborough Wilts 17 F4 tn on R Kennet 10m/16km S of Swindon at foot of **M. Downs.** SU 1869
Marlbrook H & W 26 A2* loc 3m/4km S of Leominster. SO 5154
Marlbrook H & W 27 E6* loc 3m/4km NE of Bromsgrove. SO 9774
Marlcliff Warwicks 27 E3 vil 6m/9km NE of Evesham. SP 0950
Marldon Devon 5 E4 vil on W side of Torbay dist 2m/4km NW of Paignton. SX 8663
Marle Green E Sussex 12 C5* loc 1m SE of Horam. TQ 5916
Marle Hill Glos 26 D5* N dist of Cheltenham. SO 9523
Marlesford Suffolk 31 G3 vil 2m/3km NE of Wickham Mkt. TM 3258
Marley Kent 13 G2* loc 5m/9km SE of Canterbury. TR 1850
Marley Green Ches 42 B6* loc 4m/6km NE of Whitchurch. SJ 5845
Marley Hill Tyne & Wear 61 G5 vil in coal-mining area 5m/8km SW of Gateshead. NZ 2057
Marlingford Norfolk 39 E4 vil on R Yare 5m/8km W of Norwich. TG 1309
Marloes Dyfed 22 A5 vil near coast at S end of St Brides Bay 7m/11km W of Milford Haven. Par includes islands of Skomer and Grassholm and The Smalls rocks. For M. Bay see Hooper's Pt. SM 7908
Marlow Bucks 18 D3 tn on R Thames with 19c suspension br and weir 4m/7km NW of Maidenhead. SU 8586
Marlow H & W 34 B6* loc 5m/7km SW of Craven Arms. SO 3976
Marlow, Little Bucks 18 D3 vil 2m/3km NE of Marlow. SU 8787
Marlpit Hill Kent 20 B6 N suburb of Edenbridge. TQ 4447
Marlpool Derbys 43 H6 loc adjoining Heanor to SE. SK 4445
Marnham, High Notts 44 C4 vil 11m/17km N of Newark-on-Trent. Power stn to N. **Low M.** vil 1km S. SK 8070
Marnhull Dorset 9 E3 vil 3m/5km N of Sturminster Newton. ST 7818
Marnoch Grampian 83 E2 loc 2m/4km SW of Aberchirder. NJ 5950
Marple Gtr Manchester 43 E2/E3 tn 4m/7km E of Stockport. **Marple Br** loc across R Goyt 1m NE. SJ 9588
Marpleridge Gtr Manchester 43 E3* loc adjoining Marple to S. SJ 9687
Marr S Yorks 44 A1 vil 4m/6km NW of Doncaster. SE 5105
Marrel H'land 87 C5 loc in Sutherland dist 1m N of Helmsdale. ND 0117
Marrick N Yorks 54 A5 vil 3m/4km E of Reeth. SE 0798
Marron 52 B2* r rising on W side of Loweswater Fell, Cumbria, and flowing N into R Derwent 1m N of Lit Clifton. NY 0530
Marros Dyfed 22 D5 ham 2m/3km W of Pendine. SN 2008
Marsco Skye, H'land 79 C6, D6 mt 3m/4km SW of head of Loch Ainort. Height 2414 ft or 736 metres. NG 5025
Marsden Tyne & Wear 61 H5 dist of S Shields 2m/3km SE of tn centre. **M. Bay** sandy bay on North Sea coast to E. **M. Rock** stands offshore at N end of bay. NZ 3964
Marsden W Yorks 48 C6 tn on R Colne 7m/11km SW of Huddersfield. SE 0411
Marsden Hall Lancs 48 B4* loc adjoining Nelson to E. SD 8738
Marsden Height Lancs 48 B4* loc 1m S of Nelson. SD 8636
Marsden, Little Lancs 48 B4* loc in S part of Nelson. SD 8537
Marsett N Yorks 53 G6/H6 loc 3m/5km SW of Bainbridge. SD 9086
Marsh Bucks 18 C1* loc 3m/5km S of Aylesbury. SP 8109
Marsh Devon 8 B3 ham 5m/7km W of Chard. ST 2510
Marsh W Yorks 48 D6 dist of Huddersfield 2km W of tn centre. SE 1217
Marsh W Yorks 48 C4 loc 1m S of Haworth. SE 0235
Marsh W Yorks 48 D5* loc adjoining Cleckheaton to SE. SE 1925
Marshall Meadows Nthmb 67 F3 loc 3m/4km NW of Berwick-upon-Tweed. **M.M. Bay** to E. NT 9756
Marshall's Cross Merseyside 42 B2* loc in St Helens 2m/3km S of tn centre. SJ 5292
Marshall's Elm Som 8 C1* loc 2km S of Street. ST 4834
Marshall's Heath Herts 29 F6* loc 2m/3km E of Harpenden. TL 1615
Marshalswick Herts 19 F1* NE dist of St Albans. TL 1609
Marsham Norfolk 39 F3 vil 2m/3km S of Aylsham. Sites of Roman bldgs 1km NE. TG 1923
Marsh Baldon Oxon 18 B2 vil 5m/9km SE of Oxford. SU 5699
Marsh Benham Berks 17 H4* ham 3m/5km W of Newbury. SU 4267
Marshbrook Salop 34 B5 ham 3m/4km S of Church Stretton. SO 4489
Marsh Chapel Lincs 45 G2 vil 7m/11km SE of Cleethorpes. TF 3599
Marsh End H & W 26 D4* loc 5m/8km W of Tewkesbury. SO 8135
Marshfield Avon 16 C4 vil 6m/10km N of Bath. ST 7873
Marshfield (Maerun) Gwent 15 G3 vil 5m/8km SW of Newport. ST 2682
Marshgate Cornwall 6 A6* vil 4m/6km E of Boscastle. SX 1591
Marsh Gibbon Bucks 20 B5 vil 4m/7km E of Bicester. SP 6423
Marsh Green Ches 42 C5* loc 2km W of Sandbach. SJ 7461
Marsh Green Derbys 43 H4* loc 1km NW of Ashover. SK 3463
Marsh Green Devon 7 H5 ham 4m/6km W of Ottery St Mary. SY 0493
Marsh Green Gtr Manchester 42 B1 loc in Wigan 2m/3km W of tn centre. SD 5506
Marsh Green Kent 12 B2 vil 2km S of Edenbridge. TQ 4344
Marsh Green Salop 34 C3* loc 3m/5km NW of Wellington. SJ 6014
Marsh Green Staffs 42 D5* loc 2km N of Biddulph. SJ 8859
Marshlane Derbys 43 H3 vil 3m/5km E of Dronfield. SK 4079
Marshside Merseyside 47 E6 loc in Southport 2m/4km NE of tn centre. SD 3619
Marsh's Pool Powys 33 F6 small lake 2km NE of Llangurig. SN 9281
Marsh Street Som 7 G1 vil between Dunster and coast. SS 9944
Marsh, The Ches 42 D5* loc in Congleton 1m SW of tn centre. SJ 8462
Marsh, The Hants 9 G3* loc beside R Allen 1km SE of Damerham. SU 1015
Marsh, The H & W 26 A2* loc on N side of Leominster across R Lugg. SO 4959
Marsh, The Powys 34 A4* loc below NE slope of Corndon Hill 4m/6km NE of Church Stoke. SO 3197
Marsh, The Salop 34 D2* loc 1km S of Hinstock. SJ 6925
Marsh, West Humberside 45 F1 W dist of Grimsby. TA 2510
Marshwood Dorset 8 B4 vil 4m/7km SW of Broadwindsor. **M. Vale** valley 2m/3km SE, watered by R Char and tributaries. Lambert's Castle Hill (NT), hill 1m SW, commanding wide views. SY 3899
Marske N Yorks 54 A4 vil 4m/7km W of Richmond. SZ 1000
Marske-by-the-Sea Cleveland 55 E3 residential tn and resort on North Sea coast 2m/3km W of Saltburn. Wide sands. See also New Marske. NZ 6322
Marsland Green Gtr Manchester 42 C2* loc 2m/3km E of Leigh. SJ 6899
Marston Ches 42 C4 loc 1m N of Northwich. SJ 6675
Marston H & W 25 H2 ham 4m/7km E of Kington. SO 3657
Marston Lincs 36 D1 vil 5m/8km N of Grantham. SK 8943
Marston Oxon 18 A1 suburb 2m/3km NE of Oxford. SP 5208
Marston Staffs 35 E2* ham 3m/5km N of Stafford. SJ 9227
Marston Staffs 35 E3* loc 2km NW of Wheaton Aston. SJ 8314
Marston Warwicks 35 G5 loc 4m/6km N of Coleshill. SP 2094
Marston Wilts 16 D5/17 E5 vil 4m/6km SW of Devizes. ST 9656
Marston Doles Warwicks 28 A2* loc on Oxford Canal 4m/6km SE of Southam. SP 4658
Marston Gate Som 16 C6* loc in SW part of Frome. ST 7646
Marston Green W Midlands 35 G5 suburban loc 7m/11km E of Birmingham. SP 1785
Marston Jabbett Warwicks 36 A5* loc 2m/4km S of Nuneaton. SP 3788
Marston Magna Som 8 D2 vil 5m/8km NE of Yeovil. ST 5922
Marston Meysey Wilts 17 F2 vil 3m/5km NE of Cricklade. SU 1297
Marston Montgomery Derbys 35 G1 vil 4m/6km NW of Sudbury. SK 1337
Marston Moor N Yorks 50 A3 area to N of Long Marston, 7m/11km W of York. Site of Parliamentarian victory in Civil War, 1644. SE 4952
Marston Moretaine Beds 29 E4 vil 6m/10km SW of Bedford. SP 9941
Marston, North Bucks 28 C5 vil 3m/5km S of Winslow. SP 7722
Marston on Dove Derbys 35 H2 vil 4m/6km N of Burton upon Trent. SK 2329
Marston St Lawrence Northants 28 A3 vil 5m/8km E of Banbury. SP 5342
Marston, South Wilts 17 F3 vil 4m/6km NE of Swindon. SU 1987
Marston Stannett H & W 26 B2 ham 5m/9km SE of Leominster. SO 5755
Marston Trussell Northants 36 C5 vil 3m/5km W of Mkt Harborough. SP 6985
Marston, Upper H & W 25 H2* loc 4m/6km E of Kington. SO 3558
Marstow H & W 26 B5 ham 4m/7km SW of Ross-on-Wye. SO 5519

Marsworth Bucks 28 D6 vil 2m/3km N of Tring. SP 9214
Marteg 25 E1 r rising about 4m/6km N of Bwlch-y-sarnau and running SW to R Wye 3m/4km NW of Rhayader. SN 9571
Marten Wilts 17 G5 ham 6m/10km SW of Hungerford. SU 2860
Marthall Ches 42 D4* ham 4m/6km SE of Knutsford. SJ 7975
Martham Norfolk 39 H3 vil 3m/4km W of Winterton. TG 4518
Martholme Lancs 48 A4* hse with restored Tudor gatehouse 2m/3km NE of Gt Harwood. SD 7332
Marthwaite Cumbria 53 F5* loc adjoining Sedbergh to W. SD 6592
Martin Hants 9 G2 vil 4m/7km N of Cranborne. To E, ham of **E Martin.** SU 0619
Martin Kent 13 H3 vil 4m/6km NE of Dover. TR 3347
Martin Lincs 45 E5 vil 5m/8km W of Woodhall Spa. TF 1259
Martin Lincs 45 F4 ham 2m/3km SW of Horncastle. TF 2366
Martindale Cumbria 52 D3* loc 1km SE of Sandwick and SW of Howtown. NY 4319
Martin Drove End Dorset 9 G2 loc 2m/3km NW of Martin. SU 0521
Martinhoe Devon 7 E1 vil on N coast 3m/5km W of Lynton. SS 6648
Martin Hussingtree H & W 26 D2 vil 4m/6km NE of Worcester. SO 8859
Martinscroft Ches 42 C3* loc 4m/6km E of Warrington. SJ 6589
Martinstown Dorset 8 D5 vil 3m/5km W of Dorchester. SY 6488
Martin Tarn Cumbria 59 G6* small lake 2m/3km N of Wigton. NY 2551
Martlesham Suffolk 31 F3 vil 2m/3km SW of Woodbridge. To E, **M. Creek** runs down to R Deben. TM 2547
Martletwy Dyfed 22 C4 vil 8m/14km NW of Tenby. SN 0310
Martley H & W 26 C2 vil 7m/11km NW of Worcester. SO 7559
Martnaham Loch S'clyde 56 D2 loch 5m/7km SE of Ayr. Remains of cas on islet in loch. NS 3917
Martock Som 8 C3 small tn 6m/10km NW of Yeovil. Medieval Treasurer's Hse; Georgian tn hall. ST 4619
Marton Ches 42 C4* loc 2m/3km NW of Winsford. SJ 6267
Marton Ches 42 D4 vil 3m/5km N of Congleton. SJ 8568
Marton Cleveland 54 D3 vil 3m/5km SE of Middlesbrough. Birthplace of Captain Cook, explorer, in 1728. NZ 5115
Marton Humberside 51 F2* loc 2m/3km W of Flamborough. TA 2069
Marton Humberside 51 F4 ham 7m/11km N of Hedon. TA 1839
Marton Lincs 44 C3 vil 5m/8km S of Gainsborough. SK 8381
Marton N Yorks 50 A2 vil 3m/4km SE of Boroughbridge. SE 4162
Marton N Yorks 55 F6 vil 4m/7km W of Pickering. SE 7383
Marton Salop 34 A4 vil 5m/9km N of Ch Stoke. **M. Pool,** lake 1km NE. SJ 2802
Marton Salop 34 B2* ham 2m/3km NE of Baschurch. To SE is **M. Pool,** one of four small lakes in vicinity. SJ 4423
Marton Warwicks 27 H1 vil 5m/7km N of Southam. SP 4068
Marton, East N Yorks 48 B3 vil 5m/8km W of Skipton. Vil of **W Marton** 1m W. SD 9050
Marton, Great Lancs 46 D4 dist of Blackpool 2km E of tn centre. **Lit Marton** loc adjoining to E. SD 3234
Marton Grove Cleveland 54 D3* dist of Middlesbrough 2km S of tn centre. NZ 4918
Marton-in-the-Forest N Yorks 50 B2 loc 2km E of Stillington. SE 6068
Marton-le-Moor N Yorks 49 F2 vil 3m/5km NW of Boroughbridge. SE 3770
Marton Mere Lancs 47 E4* small lake 2m/4km E of Blackpool. SD 3435
Marton Moss Side Lancs 47 E4* loc in Blackpool 2m/3km SE of tn centre. **Gt Marton Moss** loc 2km S. SD 3333
Martyr's Green Surrey 19 E5 ham 2m/3km SW of Cobham. TQ 0857
Martyr Worthy Hants 10 C2 ham on R Itchen 3m/5km NE of Winchester. SU 5132
Marwick Head Orkney 89 A6 headland on NW coast of Mainland 5m/8km NW of Dounby. Kitchener Memorial commemorates death of Lord Kitchener in 1916 when *HMS Hampshire* sank after striking a mine in these waters. HY 2225
Marwood Devon 6 D2 vil 3m/4km N of Barnstaple. Ham of **Middle M.** to NW of vil. SS 5437
Marwood Durham 54 A3* loc 4m/7km W of Staindrop. NZ 0621
Mary Arden's House Warwicks. See Wilmcote.
Marybank H'land 81 E2 loc in Ross and Cromarty dist 3m/5km S of Strathpeffer. NH 4853
Maryburgh H'land 81 E2 vil in Ross and Cromarty dist 2m/3km S of Dingwall. NH 5456
Maryculter Grampian 77 G2 loc 2km SE of Peterculter across R Dee. NO 8599
Maryfield Cornwall 4 B5* vil 1m NW of Torpoint. SX 4256
Marygold Borders 67 E3* loc 4m/7km NE of Duns. NT 8160
Maryhill S'clyde 64 C2 dist of Glasgow 3m/4km NW of city centre. Aqueduct carries Forth and Clyde Canal over R Kelvin. NS 5668
Marykirk Grampian 77 F4 vil on N side of R North Esk 4m/6km SW of Laurencekirk. NO 6865
Maryland Gwent 16 A1* loc 1m E of Trelleck. SO 5105
Marylebone Gtr Manchester 42 B1* NE dist of Wigan. SD 5906
Marylebone London 19 F3 dist in City of Westminster lying S and SW of Regents Park. TQ 2881
Marypark Grampian 82 B3* loc 5m/9km SW of Charlestown of Aberlour. NJ 1938
Maryport Cumbria 52 A2 tn on Solway Firth formerly developed as coal port. Food-canning, engineering. Coal-mining in vicinity. Site of Roman fort to N. NY 0336
Maryport D & G 57 B8 loc on **M. Bay,** 3m/4km N of Mull of Galloway. NX 1434
Marystow Devon 4 B3 ham 6m/10km NW of Tavistock. SX 4382
Mary Tavy Devon 4 B3 vil on W side of Dartmoor 4m/6km NE of Tavistock. SX 5079
Maryton Tayside 77 F5 loc 2m/4km W of Montrose. NO 6856
Marywell Grampian 77 F2 vil 4m/6km SE of Aboyne. NO 5895
Marywell Tayside 73 H1 vil 2m/3km N of Arbroath. NO 6544
Mascle Bridge Dyfed 22 C5* loc 1km NW of Neyland. SM 9505
Masham N Yorks 49 E1 small tn above R Ure 8m/13km NW of Ripon. SE 2280
Mashbury Essex 20 C1 loc 5m/7km NW of Chelmsford. TL 6511
Mason Tyne & Wear 61 G4* loc adjoining Dinnington to N, 3m/4km E of Ponteland. NZ 2073
Masongill N Yorks 47 G1 ham 2m/4km NW of Ingleton. SD 6675
Massan S'clyde 70 D6 r in Argyll running SE down Glen M. to R Eachaig, 2m/4km NW of head of Holy Loch. NS 1484
Màs Sgeir W Isles 88 A1/A2* islet off W coast of Lewis 2m/4km N of island of Gt Bernera. NB 1444
Massingham, Great Norfolk 38 C3 vil 9m/14km N of Swaffham. **Lit Massingham** vil 1m N. TF 7922
Mastin Moor Derbys 43 H3 vil 6m/10km NE of Chesterfield. SK 4575
Mastrick Grampian 77 H1* dist of Aberdeen 2m/4km W of city centre. NJ 9007
Matchborough H & W 27 E1* E dist of Redditch. SP 0766
Matching Essex 20 B1 ham 3m/5km SE of Sawbridgeworth. TL 5211
Matching Green Essex 20 B1 vil 5m/8km N of Chipping Ongar. TL 5311
Matching Tye Essex 20 B1* vil 4m/7km E of Harlow. TL 5111
Matfen Nthmb 61 E4 vil 5m/8km NE of Corbridge. NZ 0371
Matfield Kent 12 C3 vil 2m/3km S of Paddock Wd. TQ 6541
Matharn Welsh form of Mathern, qv.
Mathern (Matharn) Gwent 16 A2* vil 2m/3km SW of Chepstow. ST 5291
Mathersgrave Derbys 43 H5* loc 1m W of Brackenfield. SK 3658
Mathon H & W 26 C3* vil 3m/5km W of Gt Malvern. SO 7345
Mathri Welsh form of Mathry, qv.
Mathry (Mathri) Dyfed 22 B3 vil 6m/9km SW of Fishguard. SM 8732
Matlaske Norfolk 39 F2 vil 5m/9km S of Sheringham. TG 1534
Matlock Derbys 43 G5 inland resort and spa in steep-sided limestone stretch of R Derwent valley 9m/14km SW of Chesterfield. Limestone quarries. **M. Bath, M. Bridge, M. Dale,** locs adjoining to S. **M. Forest,** wooded area on **M. Moor** to N. SK 2960
Matson Glos 26 D5* loc in S part of Gloucester. SO 8415
Matterdale Cumbria 52 D3 loc 1km N of Dockray. **M. End** loc 1km N. NY 3922
Mattersey Notts 44 B2 vil 3m/5km SE of Bawtry. Remains of medieval priory (A.M.) to E. **M. Thorpe** loc 1km NW. SK 6889
Mattingley Hants 18 C5 vil 2m/4km N of Hook. SU 7358
Mattishall Norfolk 39 E4 vil 4m/7km E of E Dereham. **M. Burgh** vil 1km N. TG 0511
Mauchline S'clyde 56 E2 small tn 8m/13km SE of Kilmarnock. Burns memorial 1km NW. NS 4927
Maud Grampian 83 G2 vil 3m/4km E of Old Deer and 13m/21km W of Peterhead. NJ 9247
Maugerhay S Yorks 43 H3* loc in Sheffield 3m/5km S of city centre. SK 3682
Maugersbury Glos 27 F5* ham 1km SE of Stow-on-the-Wold. SP 2025
Maughold Isle of Man 46 C4 vil 3m/5km SE of Ramsey. **Maughold Hd,** headland 1km SE. SC 4991
Maulden Beds 29 E4 vil 2km E of Ampthill. TL 0537
Maulds Meaburn Cumbria 53 F3 vil 1m N of Crosby Ravensworth. NY 6216
Maun 44 B4 r rising near Mansfield, Notts, and flowing through Mansfield, then NE by Edwinstowe and Ollerton to join R Meden and form R Idle 4m/6km S of E Retford. SK 7075
Maunby N Yorks 54 C6 vil on R Swale 6m/9km NW of Thirsk. SE 3586
Maund Bryan H & W 26 B3 ham 7m/11km NE of Hereford. SO 5650
Maundown Som 7 H2* ham below M. Hill 2m/3km NW of Wiveliscombe. ST 0628
Mautby Norfolk 39 H4 ham 3m/4km W of Caister-on-Sea. TG 4712
Mavesyn Ridware Staffs 35 G3* ham 3m/4km E of Rugeley. SK 0816
Mavis Enderby Lincs 45 G4 vil 2m/4km W of Spilsby. TF 4066
Mavis Grind Shetland 89 E6 narrow isthmus and former portage on Mainland between Sullom Voe and St Magnus Bay. HU 3468
Mawbray Cumbria 59 F6 vil 5m/8km S of Silloth. NY 0846
Mawddach 32 D3 r rising about 4m/6km W of Llanuwchllyn, Gwynedd, and flowing SW into Barmouth Bay on S side of Barmouth. Tidal to Llanelltyd; estuarial below Penmaenpool. SH 6014
Mawdesley Lancs 47 F6 vil 6m/10km W of Chorley. SD 4914
Mawdlam Mid Glam 14 D3 vil 3m/5km N of Porthcawl. SS 8081
Mawgan Cornwall 2 C5 vil 3m/5km SE of Helston. SW 7125
Mawgan-in-Pydar Cornwall 2 D2* par containing vil of St Mawgan, qv. SW 8765
Mawgan Porth Cornwall 2 D2 bay below vil of Trenance, 4m/7km NE of Newquay. SW 8467
Maw Green Ches 42 C5* loc in Crewe 2km N of tn centre. SJ 7157
Maw Green W Midlands 35 F4* loc 1m SE of Walsall tn centre. SP 0297
Mawla Cornwall 2 C4* ham 3m/4km N of Redruth. SW 7045
Mawnan Cornwall 2 D5 vil above mouth of Helford R 4m/6km S of Falmouth. To NW is vil of **Mawnan Smith.** SW 7827
Mawn Pools Powys 25 F3* two tarns 2km S of Glasgwm. SO 1651
Mawthorpe Lincs 45 H4* loc 2m/3km S of Alford. TF 4573
Maxey Cambs 37 F4 vil 7m/12km NW of Peterborough. TF 1208
Maxstoke Warwicks 35 H5 vil 3m/5km SE of Coleshill. Cas (2m/3km NW), priory and ch all of 14c. SP 2386
Maxted Street Kent 13 F3* ham 7m/11km N of Hythe. TR 1244
Maxton Borders 66 D5 vil 5m/8km SE of Melrose. NT 6130
Maxton Kent 13 H3 W dist of Dover. TR 3040
Maxwellhaugh Borders 67 E5 vil on S side of R Tweed opp Kelso. NT 7233
Maxwelltown D & G 59 E4 W part of Dumfries across R Nith. NX 9676
Maxwelton House D & G. See Moniaive.
Maxworthy Cornwall 6 B5 ham 7m/11km NW of Launceston. SX 2593
Mayals W Glam 23 G6* loc in Swansea 4m/6km SW of tn centre. SS 6090
Mayar Tayside 76 C4 mt 5m/9km W of Clova. Height 3043 ft or 928 metres. NO 2473
May Bank Staffs 42 D6* dist of Newcastle-under-Lyme 1m N of tn centre. SJ 8547
Maybole S'clyde 56 C3 tn 8m/12km S of Ayr. Industries include mnfre of agricultural implements, clothing, footwear. Restored cas used as offices. Remains of 15c collegiate ch (A.M.). NS 3009
Mayburgh Henge Cumbria 53 E2* ancient, roughly circular, earthwork (A.M.) on SW side of Eamont Br.
Maybury Surrey 19 E5* E dist of Woking. TQ 0158
Maybush Hants 10 B3* NW dist of Southampton. SU 3814
Mayeston Dyfed 22 C5* loc adjoining Cosheston to E. SN 0003
Mayfair London 19 G3* dist of City of Westminster in Central London, bounded by Oxford Street, Bond Street, Piccadilly, and Park Lane. TQ 2880
Mayfield E Sussex 12 C4 vil 8m/13km S of Tunbridge Wells. Convent incorporates remains of medieval palace of Archbishops of Canterbury. TQ 5826
Mayfield Staffs 43 F6 vil 2m/3km W of Ashbourne. **Ch Mayfield** and **Middle Mayfield** hams 1m S and SW respectively. SK 1546
Mayford Surrey 19 D5 S dist of Woking. SU 9956
May Hill Glos 26 C5* hill (NT) commanding wide views, 3m/5km S of Newent. Height 969 ft or 295 metres. SO 6921
May Hill Gwent 26 A6* loc on right bank of R Wye opp Monmouth. SO 5112
Mayhill W Glam 23 G6* loc in Swansea 1m NW of tn centre. SS 6493
May, Isle of Fife 73 H4 narrow island, 2km long NW to SE, lying 6m/10km SE of Anstruther at entrance to Firth of Forth. Ruins of medieval priory. Relic of first Scottish lighthouse (1636). Present lighthouse built 1816 by Robert, father of R.L., Stevenson. Bird observatory. NT 6599
Mayland Essex 21 E2* loc 3m/5km NW of Burnham-on-Crouch. Holiday settlement of **Lr Mayland** to N. TL 9200
Mayland Creek Essex 21 E2* inlet running into Lawling Creek on S side of R Blackwater estuary opp Osea I. TL 9103
Maynard's Green E Sussex 12 C5 ham 2m/3km S of Heathfield. TQ 5818
Maypole Gwent 26 A5 loc 3m/5km NW of Monmouth. SO 4716
Maypole Kent 13 G1 loc 3m/4km SE of Herne Bay. TR 2064
Maypole W Midlands 35 G6* loc in Birmingham 5m/9km S of city centre. SP 0878
Maypole End Essex 30 B4* ham 4m/6km E of Saffron Walden. TL 5937
Maypole Green Essex 30 D5* loc in S part of Colchester. TL 9822
Maypole Green Norfolk 39 G5* vil 3m/5km N of Beccles. TM 4195
Maypole Green Suffolk 30 D2* ham 1km S of Bradfield St George. TL 9159
Maypole Green Suffolk 31 G2* loc 1km W of Dennington. TM 2767
May's Green Avon 15 H5* loc 3m/5km W of Congresbury. ST 3963
Mays Green Oxon 18 C3* loc 2m/3km S of Henley-on-Thames. SU 7479
May's Green Surrey 19 E5* loc 2m/3km S of Cobham. TQ 0957
May Wick Shetland 89 E8* small northward-facing bay on W coast of Mainland 2km SE of island of S Havra. Loc of **Maywick** at head of bay. **Taing of Maywick,** headland on W side of bay. HU 3724
McArthur's Head S'clyde 62 C2 headland with lighthouse on E coast of Islay, at S end of Sound of Islay. NR 4659

McDougall's Bay S'clyde 62 C2 bay on W coast of Jura, S of Feolin Ferry. NR 4468

McLellan's Castle D & G. See Kirkcudbright.

Meachard Cornwall 6 A6* island off Penally Pt just N of Boscastle. SX 0991

Mead Devon 6 B3* loc near coast 8m/12km N of Bude. SS 2217

Mead End Hants 10 A5* loc 4m/6km SW of Brockenhurst. SZ 2698

Mead End Wilts 9 G2 loc 1km NE of Bowerchalke. SU 0223

Meadgate Avon 16 B5* ham 3m/4km N of Radstock. ST 6858

Meadle Bucks 18 C1 vil 2m/3km N of Princes Risborough. SP 8005

Meadley Reservoir Cumbria 52 B3* small resr 2km SW of Ennerdale Br. NY 0514

Meadowbank Ches 42 C4* loc 2km N of Winsford. SJ 6568

Meadowfield Durham 54 B1* loc adjoining Brandon to E. NZ 2439

Meadow Green H & W 26 C2* ham 4m/7km E of Bromyard. SO 7156

Meadow Head Lancs 47 G5* loc 3m/4km S of Blackburn. SD 6723

Meadowtown Salop 34 A4* ham 1km NE of Rorrington. SJ 3101

Meadwell Devon 4 B3* ham 5m/8km SE of Launceston. SX 4081

Meaford Staffs 35 E1* loc 2km NW of Stone. SJ 8835

Mealasta Island W Isles 88 A2* uninhabited island, 1m by 1km in extent, lying 1km off W coast of Lewis 3m/4km S of vil of Brenish. NA 9821

Meal Bank Cumbria 53 E5* loc 3m/4km NE of Kendal. SD 5495

Mealdarroch Point S'clyde 63 F1* headland on W side of Loch Fyne, Argyll, 2km E of Loch Tarbert. NR 8868

Meal Hill W Yorks 43 F1* loc 2m/3km E of Holmfirth. SE 1606

Mealisval W Isles 88 A2 mt near W coast of Lewis 3m/5km W of S end of Loch Suainaval. Height 1885 ft or 575 metres. NB 0227

Meall a' Bhealaich Tayside 75 E4 peak between Loch Ericht and Loch Ossian. Height 2827 ft or 862 metres. NN 4569

Meall a' Bhlàir H'land 74 C2 hill in Lochaber dist 2m/3km N of Loch Arkaig and 5m/7km S of dam of Loch Quoich. Height 2153 ft or 656 metres. NN 0795

Meall a' Bhuachaille H'land 82 A5 mt on N edge of Glen More Forest Park, in Badenoch and Strathspey dist, 5m/8km N of Cairn Gorm. Height 2654 ft or 809 metres. NH 9911

Meall a' Bhùirich H'land 74 D4 mt in Lochaber dist 4m/6km W of head of Loch Treig. Height 2762 ft or 842 metres. NN 2570

Meall a' Bhùiridh S'clyde 74 D6* mt in Argyll 1m NE of Clach Leathad to E of Glen Etive. Height 3636 ft or 1108 metres. NN 2550

Meall a' Chathaidh Tayside 75 G4 hill between Glen Garry and Glen Errochty. NN 7467

Meallach Mhór H'land 75 G2 mt in Badenoch and Strathspey dist 6m/10km S of Kingussie. Height 2521 ft or 768 metres. NN 7790

Meall a' Choire Chreagaich Tayside 71 H1* mt 3m/4km SE of Kenmore. Height 2182 ft or 665 metres. NN 7941

Meall a' Choire Léith Tayside 71 G1 mt 2m/3km NW of Ben Lawers. Height 3033 ft or 924 metres. NN 6143

Meall a' Chrasgaidh H'land 85 C8 mt in Ross and Cromarty dist 2km NW of Sgurr Mór. Height 3062 ft or 933 metres. NH 1873

Meall a' Churain Central 71 F2 mt 6m/10km W of Killin. Height 3007 ft or 917 metres. NN 4632

Meall a' Ghrianain H'land 85 D8* mt on Inchbae Forest, Ross and Cromarty dist, 2m/3km SE of head of Loch Vaich. Height 2531 ft or 771 metres. NH 3677

Meall a' Mheanbhchruidh H'land 75 E3 mt in Lochaber dist 5m/8km N of middle of Loch Moy. Height 2682 ft or 817 metres. NN 3989

Meall a' Mhuic Tayside 75 F6 mt 4m/6km S of Dall on S side of Loch Rannoch. Height 2444 ft or 745 metres. NN 5750

Meall an Araich S'clyde 70 D1 mt in Argyll 1m N of Loch Dochard. Height 2246 ft or 865 metres. NN 2143

Meall an Fhudair S'clyde 70 D3 mt in Argyll 7m/11km NE of head of Loch Fyne. NN 2719

Meallan Liath Coire Mhic Dhughaill H'land 84 D4* mt in Reay Forest in Sutherland dist, 2m/3km NE of Loch More. Height 2627 ft or 800 metres. NC 3539

Meall an t-Seallaidh Central 71 F3* mt 3m/5km W of Lochearnhead. Height 2794 ft or 852 metres. NN 5423

Meall an Uillt Chreagaich H'land 75 H3* mt on Glenfeshie Forest, Badenoch and Strathspey dist, 4m/7km E of Loch an t-Seilich. Height 2763 ft or 842 metres. NN 8287

Meall a' Phùbuill H'land 74 B3 mt on Locheil Forest, Lochaber dist, 5m/8km NE of Kinlocheil. Height 2533 ft or 772 metres. NN 0285

Meall a' Phuill Tayside 71 F1* mt 2km N of E end of Loch an Daimh. Height 2882 ft or 878 metres. NN 5048

Meall Buidhe H'land 79 F7/F8 mt in Knoydart, in Lochaber dist, 5m/8km E of Inverie on Loch Nevis. Height 3107 ft or 947 metres. NM 8498

Meall Buidhe S'clyde 70 D2 mt in Argyll 6m/10km N of Dalmally. Height 2043 ft or 623 metres. NN 1837

Meall Buidhe Tayside 75 F6 mt 2m/3km N of Loch an Daimh. Height 3054 ft or 931 metres. NN 4949

Meall Buidhe 75 E6 mt on border of Strathclyde and Tayside regions 2m/3km W of head of Loch an Daimh. Height 2976 ft or 907 metres. NN 4244

Meall Chuaich H'land 75 G3* mt in Badenoch and Strathspey dist 5m/9km NE of Dalwhinnie. Height 3120 ft or 951 metres. NN 7187

Meall Coire Lochain H'land 74 C2/D2 mt in Lochaber dist 2m/4km N of Clunes on NW shore of Loch Lochy. Height 2971 ft or 906 metres. NN 2192

Meall Coire nan Saobhaidh H'land 74 C2 mt in Lochaber dist 5m/8km N of Bunarkaig on Loch Lochy. Height 2695 ft or 821 metres. NN 1795

Meall Copagach S'clyde 70 D2* mt in Argyll 2km NE of Beinn Eunaich and 4m/7km N of Dalmally. Height 2656 ft or 810 metres. NN 1534

Meall Cruaidh H'land 75 F3 mt in Badenoch and Strathspey dist 4m/7km SW of Dalwhinnie. Height 2941 ft or 896 metres. NN 5780

Meall Cuanail S'clyde 70 C2* peak on S side of Ben Cruachan in Argyll, 1km from summit. Height 3004 ft or 916 metres. NN 0629

Meall Daill Tayside 71 E1 mt on N side of Loch Lyon. Height 2858 ft or 871 metres. NN 4143

Meall Dearg H'land 74 C5* peak towards E end of Aonach Eagach, N of Glen Coe. Height 3118 ft or 950 metres. NN 1658

Meall Dearg Tayside 75 H6 mt 5m/8km SE of Aberfeldy. Height 2258 ft or 688 metres. NN 8841

Meall Dhùin Croisg Central 71 F1/F2* mt 3m/5km NW of Killin. Height 2431 ft or 741 metres. NN 5437

Meall Dubh H'land 74 D1 mt on border of Inverness and Lochaber dists 3m/5km E of dam of Loch Loyne. Height 2581 ft or 787 metres. NH 2407

Meall Dubh Tayside 75 H6 mt 5m/8km S of Aberfeldy. Height 2021 ft or 616 metres. NN 8540

Meall Dubhag H'land 75 H2 mt in W part of Cairngorms, in Badenoch and Strathspey dist, 8m/13km SE of Kingussie. Height 3274 ft or 998 metres. NN 8895

Meall Garbh H'land 74 C5* a peak of Aonach Eagach in Lochaber dist, on N side of ridge towards Loch Leven. Height 2835 ft or 864 metres. NN 1558

Meall Garbh S'clyde 70 D1 mt in Argyll 5m/9km NE of head of Loch Etive. Height 2299 ft or 701 metres. NN 1948

Meall Garbh S'clyde 70 D2 mt in Argyll to E of Glen Kinglass, 6m/9km N of Dalmally. Height 2283 ft or 696 metres. NN 1636

Meall Garbh Tayside 71 G1 N shoulder of Ben Lawers. Height 3661 ft or 1116 metres. NN 6443

Meall Ghaordie 71 F1 mt on border of Central and Tayside regions 2km S of Stronwich Resr. Height 3410 ft or 1039 metres. NN 5139

Meall Glas Central 71 F2* mt 5m/8km NE of Crianlarich. Height 3150 ft or 960 metres. NN 4332

Meall Gorm H'land 80 C1 mt in Ross and Cromarty dist 2m/4km N of Fannich Lodge on N shore of Loch Fannich. Height 3174 ft or 967 metres. NH 2269

Meall Greigh Tayside 71 G1 mt 3m/5km NE of Ben Lawers. Height 3280 ft or 1000 metres. NN 6743

Meall Halm H'land 84 F2* islet off NW coast of Eilean Iosal, qv. NC 6266

Meall Luaidhe Tayside 71 G1 mt 2m/3km S of Br of Balgie. Height 2558 ft or 780 metres. NN 5843

Meall Mór and **Meall Beag** H'land 84 B4 two islets in Eddrachillis Bay off W coast of Sutherland dist, 2m/4km offshore. NC 1237

Meall Mór Central 71 E3 mt 1m N of head of Loch Katrine. Height 2451 ft or 747 metres. NN 3815

Meall Mór H'land 85 E8 mt in Ross and Cromarty dist between Loch Glass and Loch Morie. Height 2419 ft or 737 metres. NH 5174

Meall na Dige Central 71 F3* mt 5m/9km W of Balquhidder. Height 3140 ft or 957 metres. NN 4522

Meall na h-Aisre H'land 75 F2 mt on border of Inverness and Badenoch & Strathspey dists 10m/17km SE of Fort Augustus. Height 2825 ft or 861 metres. NH 5100

Meall na Leitreach Tayside 75 G4 mt on E side of Loch Garry. Height 2544 ft or 775 metres. NN 6470

Meall nam Fuaran Tayside 72 C1 mt 5m/8km W of Amulree. Height 2631 ft or 802 metres. NN 8236

Meall nan Eun S'clyde 70 D1 mt in Argyll 5m/8km E of head of Loch Etive. Height 3045 ft or 928 metres. NN 1944

Meall nan Eun Tayside 75 G5* mt 3m/5km NW of Fortingall. Height 2806 ft or 855 metres. NN 7050

Meall nan Gabhar H'land 85 A6* small island in group known as the Summer Isles, qv. Adjacent to and N of Horse I. and nearly 1m W of NW coast of Ross and Cromarty dist to S of Polglass. NC 0205

Meall nan Sùbh Tayside 71 F1 mt 2km SE of dam of Loch Lyon. Height 2638 ft or 804 metres. NN 4639

Meall nan Tarmachan Tayside 71 G1 mt 4m/6km N of Killin. Height 3421 ft or 1043 metres. NN 5839

Meall nan Tighearn 70 D3 mt on border of Central and Strathclyde regions 5m/9km SE of Dalmally. Height 2423 ft or 739 metres. NN 2323

Meall Reamhar Tayside 72 C2 mt on N side of Glen Almond 3m/5km SW of Amulree. NN 8732

Meall Tairneachan Tayside 75 H5 mt 5m/7km NW of Aberfeldy. Height 2559 ft or 780 metres. NN 8054

Meall Tarsuinn S'clyde 70 C1* mt in Argyll nearly 1m W of Meall nan Eun. Height 2871 ft or 875 metres. NN 1844

Meall Tarsuinn Tayside 72 C2 mt 5m/8km N of Crieff. Height 2124 ft or 647 metres. NN 8729

Meall Tionail Tayside 71 E1/E2* mt 1m SE of head of Loch Lyon. Height 2937 ft or 895 metres. NN 3837

Meall Tòn Eich Central 71 F1/G1* mt 4m/7km N of Killin. Height 2821 ft or 860 metres. NN 5639

Meall Uaine Tayside 76 B4 mt 2m/3km S of Spittal of Glenshee. Height 2600 ft or 792 metres. NO 1167

Mealna Letter Tayside 76 C4 mt 4m/6km SE of Spittal of Glenshee. Height 2301 ft or 701 metres. Also known as Duchray Hill. NO 1667

Meals Lincs 45 G2 loc adjoining N Somercotes to N. TF 4197

Mealsgate Cumbria 52 C1 loc 5m/8km SW of Wigton. NY 2042

Meanwood W Yorks 49 E4* dist of Leeds 2m/4km N of city centre. SE 2837

Mearbeck N Yorks 48 B2 loc 2m/3km S of Settle. SD 8160

Meare Som 8 C1 vil 4m/6km NW of Glastonbury. Abbot's Fish Hse (A.M.), 14c. ST 4541

Meare Green Som 8 B2* ham 3m/4km SW of N Curry. ST 2922

Mearley Lancs 48 B4* loc below W slope of Pendle Hill, 2m/3km E of Clitheroe. SD 7741

Mearns S'clyde 64 C3 loc adjoining Newton Mearns to SE, 3m/5km NW of Eaglesham. **M. Castle,** 1km E, dates from 15c. NS 5455

Mears Ashby Northants 28 D1 vil 4m/6km W of Wellingborough. SP 8366

Measach, Falls of H'land 85 C8 waterfall (NTS) in Abhainn Droma, headstream of R Broom in Ross and Cromarty dist, where it passes through deep gorge known as Corrieshalloch Gorge. NH 2077

Mease 35 G3 r rising E of Ashby de la Zouch, Leics, and flowing first S, then W to Harlaston, Staffs, then NW into R Trent 1km N of Croxall. SK 1914

Measham Leics 35 H3 vil 3m/5km SW of Ashby de la Zouch. SK 3312

Meath Green W Sussex 11 H1* loc adjoining Horley to NW. TQ 2744

Meathop Cumbria 52 D6 ham 2km E of Lindale. SD 4380

Meaul D & G mt towards N end of Rinns of Kells, 4m/7km W of Carsphairn. Height 2280 ft or 695 metres. NX 5090

Meaux Humberside 51 E4 loc on site of 12c abbey 4m/6km E of Beverley. TA 0939

Meavag W Isles 88 B3* loc on Harris 2m/4km S of Tarbert. NG 1596

Meavaig W Isles 88 A3* r flowing S into Loch M., Harris, on N side of W Loch Tarbert. NB 1006

Meavie Point Grampian 83 E1* headland at Banff on N coast. NJ 6864

Meavy Devon 4 C4 vil on R Meavy 6m/10km SE of Tavistock. SX 5467

Meavy 4 C4 r in Devon rising near Princetown on Dartmoor and running SW through Burrator Resr and the vil of Meavy. It then turns S and runs into R Plym at N end of Bickleigh Vale. SX 5156

Medbourne Leics 36 D5 vil 6m/10km NE of Mkt Harborough. SP 8093

Medburn Nthmb 61 F4* loc 3m/4km SW of Ponteland. NZ 1370

Meddon Devon 6 B3 loc 5m/8km SW of Clovelly. SS 2717

Meden 44 B4 r rising W of Mansfield, Notts, and flowing NE through Thoresby Park in The Dukeries to join R Maun and form R Idle 4m/6km S of E Retford. SK 7075

Medge Hall S Yorks 49 H6* loc 2m/3km W of Crowle. SE 7412

Medina 10 C5 r in Isle of Wight rising at Chale Green near S coast and flowing N into the Solent at Cowes. SZ 5096

Medina 119 admin dist of Isle of Wight.

Mediobogdum Cumbria. See Hardknott Castle.

Mediolanum Salop. See Whitchurch.

Medlam Lincs 45 G5* loc 2km S of New Bolingbroke. TF 3156

Medland Brook 6 D5* stream rising 2km NW of Okehampton, Devon, and flowing N into R Lew S of Hatherleigh. SS 5302

Medlar Lancs 47 E4* loc 2m/4km N of Kirkham. SD 4135

Medlock Vale Gtr Manchester 42 D2* loc 2m/3km W of Ashton-under-Lyne. SJ 9099

Medmenham Bucks 18 C3 vil on R Thames 3m/5km W of Marlow. SU 8084

Medomsley Durham 61 F6 vil 2m/3km N of Consett. NZ 1154

Medstead Hants 10 D2 vil 4m/6km W of Alton. SU 6537

Medway 21 E4 r rising near E Grinstead in W Sussex and flowing E into Kent, through Tonbridge and Maidstone, then N to Rochester and Chatham, where it widens into an estuary flowing E to join R Thames estuary at Sheerness. Tidal to Allington, between Maidstone and Aylesford. TQ 9075

Medwin Water 65 F4 r rising on borders of Lothian, Strathclyde, and Borders regions and flowing SW to R Clyde 2km S of Carnwath. NS 9744

Meece Brook 35 E2* r rising near Whitmore, Staffs, and flowing S into R Sow 1m SE of Chebsey. SJ 8728
Meend, Lower Glos 16 B1* loc just W of St Briavels. SO 5504
Meerbrook Staffs 43 E5 vil 3m/5km N of Leek. SJ 9860
Meer Common H & W 25 H3* loc 5m/8km SE of Kington. SO 3652
Meer End W Midlands 35 H6* ham 4m/6km NW of Kenilworth. SP 2474
Meers Bridge Lincs 45 H3* loc 2m/3km NW of Mablethorpe. TF 4886
Meersbrook S Yorks 43 H3* loc in Sheffield 2m/3km S of city centre. SK 3584
Meesden Herts 29 H4 vil 5m/7km NE of Buntingford. TL 4332
Meese 34 C2/C3 r rising in Staffs E of Newport, Salop, and flowing generally W into R Tern 1km SW of Gt Bolas. SJ 6320
Meeson Salop 34 D3 loc 1m W of Cherrington. **M. Heath** loc to SE. SJ 6520
Meeth Devon 6 D4 vil 3m/4km N of Hatherleigh. SS 5408
Meeting House Hill Norfolk 39 G2 ham 2m/3km SE of N Walsham. TG 3028
Meggat Water 59 G2 r in Dumfries & Galloway region running S to R Esk 6m/10km NW of Langholm. NY 2991
Meggernie Castle Tayside 71 F1 mansion in Glen Lyon 2m/3km W of Br of Balgie. Has a 16c tower of the Menzies. NN 5546
Megget Water 66 A6 r in Borders region running E into St Mary's Loch near Cappercleuch. NT 2422
Megginch Castle Tayside 73 E2 16c cas in Carse of Gowrie 2km N of Errol. NO 2424
Meidrim Dyfed 23 E4 vil 3m/5km N of St Clears. SN 2820
Meifod Powys 33 H3 vil 4m/7km S of Llanfyllin in valley of R Vyrnwy, here called Dyffryn Meifod. SJ 1513
Meig H'land 80 D2 r in Ross and Cromarty dist rising on W Monar Forest and running E to join R Conon 1m below Loch Luichart. NH 3956
Meigle Tayside 76 D6 vil 4m/6km SE of Alyth. See also Belmont Castle. Roman sites to N across Dean Water. NO 2844
Meigle Bay S'clyde 64 A3 bay on Firth of Clyde 2km S of Skelmorlie. NS 1965
Meikle Earnock S'clyde 64 D3 loc adjoining Hamilton to S. NS 7153
Meikle Loch Grampian 83 H4 lochan or small lake near E coast 2km N of Kirkton of Slains. NK 0230
Meikleour Tayside 73 E1 vil 4m/6km S of Blairgowrie. Beech hedge of M. Hse borders A93 rd S of here for 580 yards or 530 metres. Planted in 1746, it is now 85 ft or 26 metres high. NO 1539
Meikleross Bay S'clyde 64 A1* bay on Firth of Clyde 2m/3km E of Kilcreggan. NS 2680
Meikle Says Law Lothian 66 D3 summit of Lammermuir Hills, 5m/8km SE of Gifford. Height 1750 ft or 533 metres. NT 5861
Meikle Wartle Grampian 83 F4 loc 6m/9km NW of Oldmeldrum. NJ 7230
Meil, Bay of Orkney 89 B6* bay on coast of Mainland between Hd of Work and Hd of Holland, 2m/3km E of Kirkwall. HY 4812
Meinciau Dyfed 23 F4 ham 4m/7km NE of Kidwelly. SN 4610
Mein Water 59 F4 r in Dumfries & Galloway region, issuing from Torbeckhill Resr and flowing S then SW to R Annan 2km S of Ecclefechan. NY 1872
Meir Staffs 35 F1 loc in Stoke-on-Trent 4m/6km SE of city centre. SJ 9342
Meirchion 41 F4* r running N into R Elwy 3m/5km NW of Denbigh, Clwyd. SJ 0270
Meirheath Staffs 35 E1 loc 3m/4km SE of Longton, Stoke-on-Trent. SJ 9240
Meirionnydd 116, 118 admin dist of Gwynedd.
Meisgyn Welsh form of Miskin, qv.
Meith Bheinn H'land 74 A3 peak in S Morar, Lochaber dist, between Loch Morar and Loch Beoraid. Height 2328 ft or 710 metres. NM 8287
Melau 33 E2 r running S into R Wnion 5m/8km E of Dolgellau, Gwynedd. SH 7921
Melbost W Isles 88 C2 vil on Lewis 3m/4km E of Stornoway. **Melbost Pt** is headland to N. **M. Sands** on R Laxdale estuary to NW, covered at high tide. Stornoway Airport on W side of vil. NB 4632
Melbost Borve W Isles 88 B1/C1* loc 1km N of High Borve near NW coast of Lewis. NB 4157
Melbourn Cambs 29 G3 vil 3m/5km NE of Royston. TL 3844
Melbourne Derbys 36 A2 tn 7m/12km S of Derby. **M. Hall,** mainly 18c hse with formal gardens. SK 3825
Melbourne Humberside 50 C4 vil 4m/7km SW of Pocklington. SE 7544
Melbury Devon 6 C3 loc 6m/10km SW of Bideford. SS 3719
Melbury Abbas Dorset 9 F2 vil 2m/4km SE of Shaftesbury. ST 8820
Melbury Bubb Dorset 8 D4* vil 2m/3km NE of Evershot. ST 5906
Melbury Osmond Dorset 8 D3 vil 5m/8km S of Yeovil. ST 5707
Melbury Sampford Dorset 8 D4 loc 1m N of Evershot. Ch and 16c hse in Melbury Park. ST 5706
Melbury, West Dorset 9 F2* ham 2m/3km S of Shaftesbury. ST 8620
Melby Shetland 89 D7 loc on W coast of Mainland opp Papa Stour. **Holm of M.** is small island to N in Sound of Papa. **Ness of M.** headland to NW. HU 1957
Melchbourne Beds 29 E2 vil 5m/7km E of Rushden. TL 0265
Melcombe Bingham Dorset 9 E4* vil 5m/8km N of Puddletown. 1m W, ham of **Hr Melcombe.** ST 7602
Melcombe Horsey Dorset 9 E4* loc 5m/8km N of Puddletown. ST 7502
Melcombe Regis Dorset 9 E6 N dist of Weymouth. SY 6880
Meldon Devon 6 D5* ham 3m/4km SW of Okehampton. Extensive quarries to E. SX 5692
Meldon Nthmb 61 F3 ham 5m/8km W of Morpeth. **M. Park,** hse of 1832, 2km NW across R Wansbeck. NZ 1183
Meldreth Cambs 29 G3 vil 4m/6km NE of Royston. TL 3746
Meledor Cornwall 3 E3* loc 6m/9km W of St Austell. China clay works.
Melford Hall Suffolk. See Long Melford.
Melfort S'clyde 70 A3 locality in Argyll at head of Loch Melfort, 1m NW of Kilmelford. NM 8314
Melgund Castle Tayside 77 E5 ruined cas 4m/7km SW of Brechin. NO 5456
Meliden (Allt Melyd) Clwyd 41 F3 vil 2km S of Prestatyn. SJ 0680
Melinbyrhedyn Powys 33 E4* loc 5m/7km E of Machynlleth. SN 8198
Melin Caiach Mid Glam 15 F2* loc on E side of Treharris. ST 1097
Melincourt W Glam 14 D2* loc 6m/10km NE of Neath, where **Melin Court Brook** joins R Neath from SE. SN 8101
Melincryddan W Glam 14 C2/D2 loc in S part of Neath. SS 7596
Melinddwr 24 C4 r rising 4m/6km SE of Llanybydder, Dyfed, and flowing SE by Rhydcymerau into R Marlais at Llansawel. SN 6236
Melindwr 33 E6* r rising about 3m/5km NW of Devil's Br, Dyfed, and flowing W into R Rheidol 4m/7km E of Aberystwyth. SN 6480
Melin Ifan Ddu Welsh form of Blackmill, qv.
Melin-y-coed Gwynedd 41 E5* loc 2km SE of Llanrwst. SH 8160
Melin-y-ddol Powys 33 G4 loc in R Banwy valley 1m W of Llanfair Caereinion. SJ 0907
Melin-y-wig Clwyd 41 F6 ham 5m/9km E of Cerrigydrudion. SJ 0448
Melkinthorpe Cumbria 53 E2 ham 4m/7km SE of Penrith. NY 5525
Melkridge Nthmb 60 C5 vil 2m/3km E of Haltwhistle. NY 7363
Melksham Wilts 16 D5 tn on R Avon 6m/10km S of Chippenham. Rubber and associated factories. **M. Forest,** E dist of the tn. ST 9063
Melldalloch S'clyde 63 F1 locality in Argyll 3m/4km S of Kilfinan. **Loch M.** is small loch to E. NR 9374
Mellerstain House Borders 66 D4 18c mansion by William and Robert Adam, 6m/10km NW of Kelso. NT 6439
Mellguards Cumbria 60 A6* loc 2m/3km S of Wreay. NY 4445
Mell Head Stroma, H'land 86 F1 headland at SW end of Island of Stroma in Pentland Firth – see Stroma. ND 3376
Melling Lancs 47 F1 vil 5m/8km S of Kirkby Lonsdale. **M. Green** loc adjoining to SW. SD 5971
Melling Merseyside 42 A2* vil 2m/3km SE of Maghull. **M. Mount** 1m NE. SD 3900
Mellis Suffolk 31 E1 vil 3m/5km W of Eye. TM 1074
Mellon Charles H'land 78 F1 loc 2m/3km NW of Aultbea, W coast of Ross and Cromarty dist. NG 8591
Mellon Udrigle H'land 78 F1 loc 3m/4km SE of Greenstone Pt, W coast of Ross and Cromarty dist. NG 8895
Mellor Gtr Manchester 43 E3 vil 2m/3km E of Marple. SJ 9888
Mellor Lancs 47 G5 vil 3m/4km NW of Blackburn. **M. Brook** vil 1m W. SD 6530
Mells Som 16 C6 vil 3m/5km W of Frome. 1km SW, ham of **M. Green.** ST 7249
Mells 16 C6* r rising near Chilcompton, Som, and flowing E through vil of Mells into R Frome 2km N of Frome tn. ST 7749
Mellte 15 E1 r rising on Fforest Fawr, Powys, and flowing S by Ystradfellte into R Neath 2km E of Glyn-neath. SN 9007
Melmerby Cumbria 53 E1/E2 vil 8m/12km NE of Penrith. NY 6137
Melmerby N Yorks 49 E1 vil 4m/6km NE of Ripon. **M. Green End** loc adjoining to S. SE 3376
Melmerby N Yorks 54 A6 vil 4m/6km SW of Middleham. SE 0785
Meloch 33 F1 r running S into R Dee 2m/3km E of Bala, Gwynedd. SH 9536
Melon Green Suffolk 30 D2* loc 1m SE of Whepstead. TL 8457
Melplash Dorset 8 C4 vil 2m/3km S of Beaminster. SY 4898
Melrose Borders 66 C5 small tn on S side of R Tweed 4m/6km E of Galashiels. Ruins of 12c abbey (A.M.). See also Old M. NT 5434
Melsetter Orkney 89 A7* loc at S end of Hoy 1m NE of Tor Ness. ND 2689
Melsonby N Yorks 54 B4 vil 2m/4km NW of Scotch Corner. NZ 1908
Meltham W Yorks 48 D6 tn 5m/7km SW of Huddersfield. Textiles, engineering. 1m SW is site of ancient fort, probably dating from Iron Age. **M. Mills** loc 1km E. SE 0910
Melton Humberside 51 E5 vil 8m/12km W of Hull. SE 9726
Melton Suffolk 31 G3 vil adjoining Woodbridge to NE. TM 2850
Meltonby Humberside 50 C3 loc 2m/3km N of Pocklington. SE 7952
Melton Constable Norfolk 39 E2 vil 4m/7km SW of Holt. TG 0433
Melton, Great Norfolk 39 E4 loc 4m/6km NE of Wymondham. TG 1206
Melton, High S Yorks 44 A1 vil 4m/7km W of Doncaster. SE 5001
Melton, Little Norfolk 39 F4 vil 4m/7km W of Norwich. TG 1606
Melton Mowbray Leics 36 C3 tn on R Wreake or Eye 14m/22km NE of Leicester. Old mkt tn and hunting centre. Makes footwear, pet foods, Stilton cheese, pork pies. SK 7519
Melton Ross Humberside 45 E1 vil 5m/8km NW of Brigg. TA 0610
Melton, West S Yorks 44 A1* loc 1km W of Wath upon Dearne. SE 4200
Melvaig H'land 78 E1 vil on W coast of Ross and Cromarty dist 3m/5km S of Rubha Réidh. NG 7486
Melverley Salop 34 A3 ham 10m/16km W of Shrewsbury. **M. Green** ham 1m NW. SJ 3316
Melvich H'land 86 B2 vil near N coast of Caithness dist 15m/24km W of Thurso. **M. Bay** 1km N. NC 8864
Melville's Monument Tayside 72 B2 obelisk on a hill 1m N of Comrie, commemorating Lord Melville, 1742-1811. NN 7623
Melynllyn Gwynedd 40 D5* small mt lake 1km E of Foel-grach. SH 7065
Membury Devon 8 B4 vil 3m/5km NW of Axminster. ST 2703
Memsie Grampian 83 G1 vil 3m/5km SW of Fraserburgh. Bronze Age burial cairn (A.M.). NJ 9762
Memus Tayside 77 E5 vil 6m/9km NW of Forfar. NO 4258
Menabilly Cornwall 3 F3* loc 2m/3km W of Fowey. SX 1051
Menai Bridge Gwynedd 40 C4 tn on Anglesey at N end of rd br spanning Menai Strait 2km W of Bangor. Br designed by Telford. SH 5571
Menai Strait Gwynedd 40 B5, C4 sea channel separating Anglesey from Welsh mainland. Is some 14m/23km long from Beaumaris to Abermenai Pt, and spanned by one rd br, Menai Br, and one rly br, Britannia Br. SH 46,56,57
Men-an-Tol Cornwall 2 A5* ancient holed stone 4m/6km NW of Penzance. SW 4234
Mendham Suffolk 31 G1* vil on R Waveney 2m/3km E of Harleston. TM 2782
Mendip 118 admin dist of Som.
Mendip Hills Som 16 A5, B6 limestone ridge running WNW from a line through Bruton and Frome some 27m/42km almost to Weston-super-Mare and the Bristol Channel, and containing many potholes and caverns, the best known being at Cheddar Gorge and Wookey Hole. ST 55
Mendlesham Suffolk 31 E2 vil 6m/9km NE of Stowmarket. Vil of **M. Green** 2m/3km S. TM 1065
Menethorpe N Yorks 50 C2 loc 3m/5km S of Malton. SE 7667
Mengham Hants 10 D5* loc in S Hayling on Hayling I. SZ 7298
Menheniot Cornwall 3 G2 vil 3m/4km SE of Liskeard. SX 2862
Menial 33 G3* stream running NE into R Banwy at Llanerfyl, Powys. SJ 0309
Menithwood H & W 26 C1* loc 7m/11km E of Tenbury Wells. SO 7069
Mennock D & G 58 D1 vil 2m/3km SE of Sanquhar at confluence of R Nith and **M. Water,** which flows SW down **M. Pass.** Pass carries rd over Lowther Hills between M. and Wanlockhead. NS 8008
Men of Mey H'land 86 F1 cluster of rocks off St John's Pt on N coast of Caithness dist. ND 3175
Men Screfys Cornwall 2 A5* ancient standing stone 4m/7km NW of Penzance. SW 4235
Menston W Yorks 48 D4 vil and residential loc 6m/10km N of Bradford. County mental hospital. SE 1743
Menstrie Central 72 C5 small tn 4m/6km NE of Stirling. Furniture mnfre; large bonded whisky store. 16c cas was home of Sir William Alexander, 1567-1640, founder of Nova Scotia. NS 8496
Menteith Hills Central 71 F4 range of low hills between Aberfoyle and Callander. See also Lake of Menteith, Port of Menteith. NN 5603
Menthorpe N Yorks 50 C4* loc 2m/3km SE of N Duffield. SE 7034
Mentmore Bucks 28 D5 vil 4m/6km S of Leighton Buzzard. SP 9019
Meoble H'land 79 F8 r in S Morar, Lochaber dist, running N from foot of Loch Beoraid to Loch Morar. Locality of Meoble on right bank 2km above mouth. NM 7889
Meole Brace Salop 34 B3 S dist of Shrewsbury. SJ 4810
Meols, Great Merseyside 41 H2/H3* loc adjoining Hoylake to NE. SJ 2390
Meon 10 C4 r rising 2km S of E Meon, Hants, and flowing NW through E and W Meon, then SW through Wickham and Titchfield into the Solent 1km W of Hill Hd. SU 5302
Meon, East Hants 10 D3 vil 5m/8km W of Petersfield. SU 6722
Meonstoke Hants 10 C3 vil on R Meon 4m/7km E of Bishop's Waltham. SU 6119
Meon, West Hants 10 D3 vil 3m/5km NE of Meonstoke. 1km NW, site of Roman villa. SU 6424
Meon Woodlands, West Hants 10 D2* loc 2m/3km N of W Meon. SU 6426
Meopham Kent 20 C5 vil 5m/8km S of Gravesend. To N and S respectively, suburban locs of **M. Station** and **M. Green.** TQ 6466
Mepal Cambs 38 A6 vil 6m/10km W of Ely. TL 4480
Meppershall Beds 29 F4 vil 2m/3km S of Shefford. TL 1336
Mercaston Derbys 35 H1 loc 7m/11km NW of Derby. SK 2642
Merchant Fields W Yorks 48 D5* loc 1m N of Cleckheaton. SE 1926
Merchants Square Gtr Manchester 42 B2* loc 1km NE of Lowton. SJ 6298

Merchiston Lothian 66 A2* dist of Edinburgh 2km SW of city centre. NT 2472
Mere Ches 42 C3 vil 3m/4km NW of Knutsford. **The Mere,** lake to E. SJ 7281
Mere Wilts 9 E1 vil 7m/11km NW of Shaftesbury. ST 8132
Mere 6 D4* r rising W of Peters Marland, Devon, and flowing E into R Torridge E of Merton. SS 5512
Mere Brow Lancs 47 E6 vil 5m/9km E of Southport. SD 4118
Mere Clough Lancs 48 B5* vil 3m/5km SE of Burnley. SD 8730
Mere, East Devon 7 G3 loc 4m/6km NE of Tiverton. SS 9916
Mere Green H & W 26 D2* loc 4m/6km E of Droitwich. SO 9562
Mere Green W Midlands 35 G4 loc 2m/3km N of Sutton Coldfield. SP 1199
Mere Heath Ches 42 C4* loc 2m/3km S of Northwich. SJ 6670
Mereside Lancs 47 E4* dist of Blackpool 2m/4km SE of tn centre. SD 3434
Mere Side Lancs 47 E6* loc on S side of Holmeswood. SD 4316
Mere Tarn Cumbria 46 D1* small lake 1km SW of Scales. SD 2671
Mere, The N Yorks 55 H6 lake in Scarborough 2km S of tn centre. TA 0386
Meretown Staffs 34 D3* loc 1m NE of Newport. SJ 7520
Merevale Warwicks 36 H4 loc 2km W of Atherstone. Remains of 12c abbey. Early Victn hall in park. SP 2997
Mere, West Norfolk 38 D5* small lake to NW of Tottington. TL 8896
Mereworth Kent 20 C6 vil 6m/10km W of Maidstone. **M. Castle** to SE is 18c Palladian edifice in wooded park. TQ 6653
Meriden W Midlands 35 H6 vil 6m/10km W of Coventry. SP 2482
Merkadale Skye, H'land 79 B5* locality on S side of Loch Harport, near head of loch and 1m SE of Carbost. NG 3831
Merkinch H'land 81 F3* NW dist of Inverness. NH 6546
Merkland Point S'clyde 63 G4 headland on E coast of Arran, at N end of Brodick Bay. NS 0238
Merlin's Bridge Dyfed 22 B4 loc on Merlin's Brook 1km SW of Haverfordwest. SM 9414
Merrick D & G 57 D5 mt in Glentrool Forest Park, 4m/6km N of Loch Trool. Height 2770 ft or 844 metres. NX 4285
Merridge Som 8 A1 ham at foot of Quantock Hills 4m/6km S of Nether Stowey. To W, ham of **Lr Merridge.** ST 2034
Merrifield Devon 5 E5* loc 5m/8km SW of Dartmouth. SX 8147
Merrifield Devon 6 B5* loc 5m/8km SE of Bude. SS 2601
Merrington Salop 34 B2 loc 5m/9km N of Shrewsbury. SJ 4720
Merrion Dyfed 22 B6 loc 4m/7km SW of Pembroke. SR 9396
Merriott Som 8 C3 vil 2m/3km N of Crewkerne. ST 4412
Merrivale Devon 4 C3 loc on Dartmoor 4m/7km E of Tavistock. SX 5475
Merrow Surrey 19 E6 E dist of Guildford. TQ 0250
Merrybent Durham 54 B3* loc 3m/5km W of Darlington. NZ 2814
Merry Field Hill Dorset 9 G4* loc 2km NE of Wimborne. SU 0201
Merry Hill W Midlands 35 E4 SW dist of Wolverhampton. SO 8896
Merryhill Green Berks 18 C4* loc adjoining Winnersh to N and 2m/4km NW of Wokingham. SU 7871
Merry Lees Leics 36 A4* loc 2km S of Thornton. SK 4605
Merrymeet Cornwall 3 G2 ham 2m/3km NE of Liskeard. SX 2866
Merry Oak Hants 10 B3* dist of Southampton 2m/3km E of city centre across R Itchen. SU 4412
Mersea, East Essex 31 E6 ham on Mersea I., 8m/12km S of Colchester. TM 0514
Mersea Island Essex 31 E6 island bounded by North Sea between mouths of Rs Blackwater and Colne on the S and Pyefleet and Strood Channels on the N; joined to mainland by causeway across Strood Channel. Oyster beds. Yachting. TM 0414
Mersea, West Essex 21 F1 tn at W end of Mersea I. TM 0112
Merse, The 67 E4, F3. See Borders.
Mersey 41 H2 r whose source is at confluence of Rs Goyt and Tame at Stockport and which flows thence into Irish Sea at Liverpool. Estuary provides important shipping lane. Tidal from Warrington. SJ 3195
Merseyside 116, 117 metropolitan and maritime county of NW England, comprising the urban complex which includes Liverpool, Bootle, and St Helens; Birkenhead and the N half of the Wirral peninsula; and, in the N, the residential tn and coastal resort of Southport.
Mersham Kent 13 F3 vil 3m/5km SE of Ashford. TR 0539
Merstham Surrey 19 G6 loc 2m/3km N of Redhill. **S Merstham** loc adjoining to S. TQ 2953
Merston W Sussex 11 E4 vil 2m/3km SE of Chichester. SU 8903
Merstone Isle of Wight 10 C6 vil 3m/5km SE of Newport. SZ 5285
Merther Cornwall 2 D4* ham 2m/4km E of Truro across Tresillian R. SW 8644
Merthyr Dyfed 23 E4 loc 4m/6km W of Carmarthen. SN 3520
Merthyr Cynog Powys 25 E4 ham 7m/11km NW of Brecon. SN 9837
Merthyr Dyfan S Glam 15 F4* loc 1m N of Barry. ST 1169
Merthyr Mawr Mid Glam 15 D4 vil 2m/3km SW of Bridgend. SS 8877
Merthyr Tydfil Mid Glam 15 F1 former iron, steel, and coal tn 21m/33 km NW of Cardiff, now having also engineering and electrical works and a variety of light industries. SO 0406
Merthyr Vale (Ynysowen) Mid Glam 15 F2* vil 5m/7km S of Merthyr Tydfil. ST 0799
Merton Devon 6 D4 vil 5m/8km SE of Torrington. SS 5212
Merton London 19 F4 borough 7m/11km SW of Charing Cross. 1m S of M. High Street is Morden Hall (NT) and deer park intersected by R Wandle. TQ 2570
Merton Norfolk 38 D5 vil 2km S of Watton. TL 9098
Merton Oxon 28 B5 vil 3m/5km S of Bicester. SP 5717
Merton Abbey Wall London. See Colliers Wood.
Meshaw Devon 7 F3 vil 5m/8km SE of S Molton. SS 7519
Messing Essex 30 D6 2m/4km E of Kelvedon. Site of Roman bldg 1km NW. TL 8918
Messingham Humberside 44 D1 vil 4m/7km S of Scunthorpe. SE 8904
Mesty Croft W Midlands 35 F5 loc 3m/4km N of W Bromwich tn centre. SO 9995
Metcombe Devon 7 H5 ham 3m/4km SW of Ottery St Mary. 1m W, ham of **Hr Metcombe.** SY 0892
Metfield Suffolk 31 G1 vil 4m/6km SE of Harleston. TM 2980
Metheringham Lincs 45 E5 vil 9m/14km SE of Lincoln. TF 0661
Metherwell Cornwall 4 B4* loc 2m/3km SW of Gunnislake. SX 4069
Methil Fife 73 F4 port on N coast of Firth of Forth 8m/12km NE of Kirkcaldy. Formerly a joint burgh with Buckhaven. **Methilhill** is W dist of tn. NT 3799
Methley W Yorks 49 F5 vil in coal-mining area 5m/8km NE of Wakefield. **M. Junction** loc 1km S. **M. Lanes** loc 2km W. SE 3926
Methlick Grampian 83 G3 vil on R Ythan 6m/10km S of New Deer. NJ 8537
Methven Tayside 72 D2 vil 6m/10km W of Perth. **M. Castle,** where Queen Margaret Tudor died in 1541, is 1m E. NO 0225
Methwold Norfolk 38 C5 vil 6m/10km NW of Brandon. Vil of **M. Hythe** 2km W. TL 7394
Mettingham Suffolk 39 G5 vil 2m/3km E of Bungay. Remains of 14c cas 1m S. TM 3690
Metton Norfolk 39 F1 ham 3m/5km S of Cromer. TG 2037
Mevagissey Cornwall 3 E4 small tn on M. Bay 5m/8km S of St Austell with inner and outer harbours; fish-canning; tourism. **M. Bay** extends from Black Hd southwards to Chapel Pt. SX 0144
Mewith Head N Yorks 48 A2* loc 3m/5km SW of Clapham. SD 7067
Mew Stone, Great Devon 4 B5 large pyramidal rock island off Wembury Pt at W end of Wembury Bay, 5m/8km SE of Plymouth. SX 5047
Mexborough S Yorks 44 A1 tn 5m/8km NE of Rotherham. Coal-mining, steel, engineering, brick mnfre. SK 4799
Mey H'land 86 F1 vil near N coast of Caithness dist 6m/9km W of John o' Groats. Locs of **E** and **W Mey** to NE and NW respectively. ND 2872
Meynell Langley Derbys 35 H1 loc 5m/8km NW of Derby. SK 2839
Meysey Hampton Glos 17 F2 vil 2m/3km W of Fairford. SP 1100
Miavaig W Isles 88 A2 vil at head of inlet of Loch Roag near W coast of Lewis 4m/6km SE of Gallan Hd. NB 0834
Michael Isle of Man 46 B4* loc on coast adjoining Kirk Michael. SC 3190
Michaelchurch H & W 26 A5* ham 5m/8km W of Ross-on-Wye. SO 5225
Michaelchurch Escley H & W 25 G4 vil 7m/11km NW of Pontrilas. SO 3134
Michaelchurch-on-Arrow (Llanfihangel Dyffryn Arwy) Powys 25 G3 ham 5m/8km SW of Kington. SO 2450
Michael Muir Grampian 83 G3* loc 4m/6km NW of Ellon. NJ 9034
Michaelston-le-Pit (Llanfihangel-y-pwll) S Glam 15 F4* vil 3m/5km SW of Cardiff. ST 1573
Michaelston-super-Ely (Llanfihangel-ar-Elai) S Glam 15 F4* loc 4m/7km W of Cardiff. ST 1176
Michaelston-y-Vedw (Llanfihangel-y-fedw) Gwent 15 G3 vil 5m/8km SW of Newport. ST 2484
Michaelstow Cornwall 3 F1 vil 3m/5km SW of Camelford. SX 0878
Michelcombe Devon 4 D4* ham below Dartmoor 4m/6km W of Ashburton. SX 6968
Micheldever Hants 10 C1 vil 6m/10km N of Winchester. Some 5m/8km NE, stretch of open country known as **M. Forest.** SU 5139
Michelham Priory E Sussex 12 B5 remains of Augustinian priory founded in 1229, on an earlier moated site, 2m/3km W of Hailsham. TQ 5509
Michelmersh Hants 10 B2 vil 3m/5km N of Romsey. SU 3426
Micker Brook 42 D2* r rising as Norbury Brook near Disley, Ches, and flowing W between Hazel Grove and Poynton (where it becomes Lady Brook), then NW to Bramhall (where it becomes Micker Brook), then into R Mersey N of Cheadle, Gtr Manchester. SJ 8589
Mickfield Suffolk 31 F2 vil 3m/4km W of Debenham. TM 1361
Micklam Cumbria 52 A3* loc 3m/4km N of Whitehaven. NX 9822
Micklebring S Yorks 44 A2* vil 1m W of Braithwell. SK 5194
Mickleby N Yorks 55 F4 vil 6m/10km W of Whitby. NZ 8012
Mickle Fell Durham 53 G2/G3 mt in Pennine Range 6m/10km N of Brough. Height 2591 ft or 790 metres. **Boot of Mickle Fell,** rocky cliff below summit to S and E. NY 8024
Micklefield Bucks 18 D2* E dist of High Wycombe. SU 8993
Micklefield Green Herts 19 E2* loc 3m/4km N of Rickmansworth. TQ 0498
Mickleham Surrey 19 F6 vil in R Mole valley 2m/3km S of Leatherhead. TQ 1753
Micklehead Green Merseyside 42 B2* loc 1m E of Rainhill. SJ 5090
Micklehurst Gtr Manchester 43 E1 loc adjoining Mossley to E. SD 9702
Micklemeadow Derbys 35 H2* loc 4m/6km SW of Derby. SK 3132
Mickle Mere Norfolk 38 D5* natural lake in Wretham Park 6m/10km NE of Thetford. TL 9091
Mickle Millyea D & G 58 B3 mt in Rinns of Kells 3m/5km N of NW corner of Clatteringshaws Loch. Height 2446 ft or 746 metres. NX 5182
Mickleover Derbys 35 H1 dist of Derby 3m/5km SW of tn centre. **M. Common** suburban loc to N. SK 3034
Micklethwaite Cumbria 59 G6 loc 2m/4km NE of Wigton. NY 2850
Micklethwaite W Yorks 48 D4* loc 2m/3km N of Bingley. SE 1041
Mickleton Durham 53 H3 vil 2m/3km SE of Middleton in Teesdale. NY 9623
Mickleton Glos 27 F3 vil 3m/5km N of Chipping Campden. SP 1643
Mickletown W Yorks 49 F5 coal-mining loc 3m/4km NW of Castleford. SE 3927
Mickle Trafford Ches 42 A4 vil 3m/5km NE of Chester. SJ 4469
Mickley Derbys 43 G3* ham 2m/3km W of Dronfield. SK 3279
Mickley N Yorks 49 E1 vil 5m/8km NW of Ripon. SE 2576
Mickley Green Suffolk 30 C2/D2* ham 1km E of Whepstead. TL 8457
Mickley, High Nthmb 61 F5 vil 2m/3km SW of Prudhoe. NZ 0761
Mickley Square Nthmb 61 F5* vil 2km W of Prudhoe. NZ 0762
MID, MIDDLE. For names beginning with these words, see under next word. This also applies to names beginning with Far, Near; High, Low; Higher, Lower; Upper, Nether; Great, Little; Greater, Lesser; Isle(s) of; North, South, East, West; The, Y, Yr.
Midbea Orkney 89 B5 loc on island of Westray 3m/5km S of Pierowall. HY 4444
Middlebie D & G 59 G4 vil 2m/3km NE of Ecclefechan. Site of Roman camp to N, and Roman fort of *Blatobulgium* to S. NY 2176
Middlecave N Yorks 50 C1* loc adjoining Malton to W. SE 7772
Middlecliff S Yorks 43 H1* loc 1m S of Gt Houghton. SE 4305
Middlecott Devon 6 C4* ham 5m/8km NE of Holsworthy. SS 4105
Middlecroft Derbys 43 H4* loc adjoining Staveley to SW. SK 4273
Middlefield Grampian 77 H1* loc in Aberdeen 3m/4km NW of city centre. NJ 9008
Middleham N Yorks 54 A6 vil in Wensleydale 2m/3km SE of Leyburn. Extensive remains of 12c–15c cas (A.M.). Racing stables. See also Braithwaite Hall. SE 1287
Middlehope Salop 34 B5/C5* ham 5m/9km NE of Craven Arms. SO 4988
Middlemarsh Dorset 8 D4 ham 6m/10km SE of Sherborne. ST 6707
Middlemore Devon 4 B3* ham 2km SE of Tavistock. SX 4972
Middleport Staffs 42 D6* loc in Burslem dist of Stoke-on-Trent. SJ 8649
Middlesbrough Cleveland 54 D3 tn and port on right bank of R Tees, forming part of Teesside urban complex. Iron and steel, engineering, chemicals. NZ 4920
Middlesceugh Cumbria 52 D1 loc 2m/4km E of Sebergham. NY 3941
Middleshaw Cumbria 53 E5* ham 4m/6km SE of Kendal. SD 5589
Middlesmoor N Yorks 48 D1 vil 7m/11km NW of Pateley Br. SE 0974
Middles, The Durham 61 G6* loc 2km SE of Stanley. NZ 2051
Middlestone Durham 54 B2* ham 3m/5km NE of Bishop Auckland. NZ 2531
Middlestone Moor Durham 54 B2 loc adjoining Spennymoor to SW. NZ 2432
Middlestown W Yorks 49 E6 vil 3m/5km SE of Dewsbury. SE 2617
Middlethorpe N Yorks 49 G3 loc in York 2m/4km S of city centre. SE 5948
Middleton Cleveland 54 D2 dist of Hartlepool on E side of harbour. NZ 5233
Middleton Cumbria 53 F6 loc 5m/8km N of Kirkby Lonsdale. SD 6286
Middleton Derbys 43 G4/G5 vil 2km SW of Youlgreave. SK 1963
Middleton Derbys 43 G5 vil 2km NW of Wirksworth. SK 2756
Middleton Essex 30 D4 ham 2km S of Sudbury. TL 8739
Middleton Gtr Manchester 42 D1 tn 6m/9km N of Manchester. Textiles, chemicals, engineering. SD 8606
Middleton Hants 10 B1 vil on R Test 4m/7km E of Andover. SU 4244
Middleton H & W 26 B1* vil 3m/5km W of Tenbury Wells. SO 5469
Middleton Isle of Wight 10 A6* ham 1km SE of Totland. SZ 3386
Middleton Lancs 47 E2 loc 2m/3km SE of Heysham. SD 4258
Middleton Lothian 66 B3 loc 3m/4km SE of Gorebridge. **N Middleton** is vil 1km NW. NT 3658
Middleton Norfolk 38 B3 vil 4m/6km SE of King's Lynn. See also Tower End. TF 6616
Middleton Northants 36 D5 vil 4m/6km W of Corby. SP 8389
Middleton Nthmb 61 F3 ham 9m/14km W of Morpeth. NZ 0685
Middleton Nthmb 67 G5 loc 1m NW of Belford. **Low M.** loc 1km NE. NU 1035
Middleton N Yorks 55 F6 vil 2km NW of Pickering. SE 7885
Middleton Salop 34 A2* loc 2m/3km E of Oswestry. SJ 3129
Middleton Salop 34 C6 ham 2m/4km NE of Ludlow. SO 5377

Middleton Suffolk 31 H2 vil 3m/4km E of Yoxford. Ham of **M. Moor** 1m W. TM 4367
Middleton Tiree, S'clyde 69 A7* loc near W end of island 2m/3km SE of Rubha Chraiginis. NL 9443
Middleton Tayside 73 E4* loc 3m/5km N of Kinross. NO 1206
Middleton Warwicks 35 G4 vil 4m/6km SW of Tamworth. SP 1798
Middleton W Glam 23 F6 ham on Gower peninsula 2m/4km E of Worms Hd. SS 4287
Middleton W Yorks 49 E5 dist of Leeds 4m/6km S of city centre. SE 3027
Middleton 48 D3 loc on borders of N and W Yorks 1m N of Ilkley across R Wharfe. SE 1249
Middleton Baggot Salop 34 C5* loc 6m/10km S of Much Wenlock. SO 6290
Middleton Cheney Northants 28 A3 vil 3m/5km E of Banbury. **Lr Middleton Cheney** vil adjoining to SE. SP 4941
Middleton Green Staffs 35 F1* loc 3m/5km E of Hilderstone. SJ 9935
Middleton Hall Nthmb 67 F5 loc 2m/3km S of Wooler. NT 9825
Middleton in Teesdale Durham 53 H2 small tn 8m/13km NW of Barnard Castle. NY 9425
Middleton Junction Gtr Manchester 42 D1 loc 2m/3km SE of Middleton. SD 8804
Middleton Moat Norfolk 38 A3* loc 1m S of Terrington St Clement. TF 5418
Middleton, North Nthmb 67 F6 loc 3m/4km S of Wooler. NU 0024
Middleton One Row Durham 54 C4 ham adjoining Middleton St George to E. NZ 3512
Middleton-on-Leven N Yorks 54 D4 loc 4m/6km W of Stokesley. NZ 4609
Middleton-on-Sea W Sussex 11 F5 resort 3m/4km E of Bognor Regis. SU 9700
Middleton on the Hill H & W 26 A2/B2 vil 4m/7km NE of Leominster. SO 5464
Middleton-on-the-Wolds Humberside 50 D3 vil 7m/11km NE of Mkt Weighton. SE 9449
Middleton Priors Salop 34 C5 loc 6m/10km S of Much Wenlock. SO 6290
Middleton Quernhow N Yorks 49 E1 ham 5m/8km N of Ripon. SE 3378
Middleton St George Durham 54 C3/C4 vil on R Tees 4m/6km E of Darlington. Tees-side Airport to E. NZ 3412
Middleton Scriven Salop 34 D5 vil 4m/7km SW of Bridgnorth. SO 6887
Middleton, South Nthmb 67 F6 loc 3m/5km S of Wooler. NT 9923
Middleton Stoney Oxon 28 A5 vil 3m/5km W of Bicester. SP 5323
Middleton Tyas N Yorks 54 B4 vil 1m E of Scotch Corner. NZ 2205
Middletown Avon 16 A4* loc 3m/5km E of Clevedon. ST 4571
Middletown Cumbria 52 A4* loc 2m/3km SW of Egremont. NX 9908
Middletown Powys 34 A3 vil under S side of M. Hill, qv, in Breidden Hills, 6m/9km NE of Welshpool. SJ 3012
Middletown Hill Powys 34 A3* one of three principal peaks of Breidden Hills, qv; height 1195 ft or 364 metres. Stands on N side of Middletown vil. Remains of ancient camp, Cefn-y-Castell. SJ 3013
Middleway, The Essex 21 E3* creek running between Potton I. to W and Foulness, New England, and Havengore Is. to E. TQ 9690
Middlewich Ches 42 C4 tn 6m/9km SE of Northwich. Industries include salt and chemicals. **M. Canal** connects Trent and Mersey Canal here with Shropshire Union Canal at Barbridge Junction 4m/6km NW of Nantwich. SJ 7066
Middlewood Cornwall 4 A3* ham 7m/11km SW of Launceston. SX 2775
Middlewood S Yorks 43 G2* vil 1km S of Oughtibridge and adjoining Worrall. SK 3092
Middlewood Green Suffolk 31 E2 vil 4m/6km NE of Stowmarket. TM 0961
Middleyard Glos 16 C2* loc 3m/4km SW of Stroud. SO 8103
Middlezoy Som 8 B1 vil on Sedgemoor 6m/9km SE of Bridgwater. ST 3732
Middop Lancs 48 B4* loc 2m/4km S of Gisburn. SD 8345
Middridge Durham 54 B2 loc in NW part of Newton Aycliffe. NZ 2526
Midfield H'land 84 F2 loc on N coast of Caithness dist, on W side of entrance to Tongue Bay. NC 5864
Midford Avon 16 C5* vil 3m/4km S of Bath. ST 7660
Midford Brook 16 C5* lower reach of Wellow Brook flowing along Avon/Wilts border from Midford to confluence with R Avon 3m/4km SE of Bath. ST 7862
Midge Hall Lancs 47 F5* loc 2m/3km W of Leyland. SD 5123
Midgeholme Cumbria 60 C5 loc 7m/11km E of Brampton. NY 6359
Midgham Berks 18 A4 vil 5m/8km E of Newbury. SU 5567
Midgley W Yorks 48 C5 vil 1m E of Mytholmroyd. SE 0326
Midgley W Yorks 49 E6 ham 5m/9km SW of Wakefield. SE 2714
Midhopestones S Yorks 43 G2 vil 3m/4km S of Penistone. SK 2399
Midhope, Upper S Yorks 43 G2* loc to W of Midhope Resr and 2km W of Midhopestones. SK 2199
Midhowe Orkney 89 B6* Neolithic communal burial-chamber, and nearby *broch*, on W coast of island of Rousay. Sometimes spelt as two words, Mid Howe. HY 3730
Midhurst W Sussex 11 E3 tn in R Rother valley N of South Downs, 11m/17km N of Chichester. Ruins of Cowdray Hse, burnt in 1793. Modern hse nearby. Polo and golf in park. SU 8821
Midland Isle Dyfed 22 A5 small island between Skomer and Welsh mainland, at S end of St Brides Bay. SM 7409
Midlands Airport, East Leics 36 A2 airport 1m SE of Castle Donington. SK 4526
Midlands, West 118, 119 metropolitan county of England, comprising the urban complex around Birmingham, and including Coventry, Walsall, Wolverhampton, and W Bromwich.
Midlem Borders 66 C5 vil 4m/6km E of Selkirk. NT 5227
Midloe Cambs 29 F2* loc 3m/5km NW of St Neots. TL 1664
Midlothian 115 admin dist of Lothian region.
Midmar Grampian 77 F1 loc 6m/10km N of Banchory. 16c cas on edge of **M. Forest,** state forest to S. NJ 7005
Midsomer Norton Avon 16 B5 tn in coal-mining district, 9m/14km SW of Bath. ST 6654
Midton S'clyde 64 A2* S dist of Gourock. NS 2376
Midtown H'land 84 F2 loc in Caithness dist on W side of Kyle of Tongue. NC 5863
Midtown Brae H'land 78 F2 vil on W shore of Loch Ewe, Ross and Cromarty dist, 4m/6km NW of Poolewe. NG 8284
Midville Lincs 45 G5 loc 6m/9km S of Spilsby. TF 3857
Midway Ches 43 E3* loc adjoining Poynton to S. SJ 9282
Midway Derbys 35 H2* loc 1km N of Swadlincote. SK 3020
Migdale H'land 85 F7 locality in Sutherland dist 1m E of Bonar Br and on N side of head of Loch M. NH 6292
Migvie Grampian 77 E1 loc 3m/5km NW of Tarland. NJ 4306
Milber (or Milber Down) Devon 5 E3 SE dist of Newton Abbot. SX 8770
Milborne Port Som 9 8E small tn 3m/5km NE of Sherborne. ST 6718
Milborne St Andrew Dorset 9 E4 vil 4m/6km NE of Puddletown. SY 8097
Milborne Wick Som 8 D2 vil 2km N of Milborne Port. ST 6620
Milbourne Nthmb 61 F4 vil 3m/5km NW of Ponteland. NZ 1175
Milbourne Wilts 16 D3* ham 1m E of Malmesbury. ST 9487
Milburn Cumbria 53 F2 vil 6m/10km N of Appleby. **M. Forest** wild moorland area to NE. See also Howgill Castle. NY 6529
Milbury Heath Avon 16 B3* ham 2m/3km E of Thornbury. ST 6690
Milby N Yorks 49 F2 ham 1km NE of Boroughbridge across R Ure. SE 4067
Milcombe Oxon 27 H4 vil 5m/8km SW of Banbury. SP 4134
Milcote Warwicks 27 F3* loc 2m/3km SW of Stratford-upon-Avon. SP 1952
Milden Suffolk 30 D3 ham 5m/8km NW of Hadleigh. TL 9546
Mildenhall Suffolk 30 C1 vil on R Lark 8m/13km NE of Newmarket. Perp ch with tall tower. 'Mildenhall Treasure', horde of Roman silver found in 1942, is in British Museum. **M. Airfield** to NW. TL 7174
Mildenhall Wilts 17 F4 vil on R Kennet 2km E of Marlborough. Site of Roman tn of *Cunetio* across r. SU 2169
Milebrook Powys 25 G1* loc 2m/3km E of Knighton. SO 3172
Milebush Kent 12 D2 loc 2km NE of Marden. TQ 7545
Mile Cross Norfolk 39 F4* dist of Norwich 2m/3km NW of city centre. TG 2110
Mile Elm Wilts 17 E4* loc 2km S of Calne. ST 9969
Mile End Essex 30 D5 loc in N part of Colchester. TL 9927
Mile End Glos 26 B6 loc 1m NE of Coleford. SO 5811
Mile End London 20 A3* loc in borough of Tower Hamlets 3m/4km NE of London Br. TQ 3682
Mile End Suffolk 38 C6 loc at SW end of Brandon. TL 7785
Mile End Suffolk 39 G5* loc 1m E of Bungay. TM 3589
Mileham Norfolk 38 D3 vil 6m/10km NW of E Dereham. Remains of motte and bailey cas. TF 9219
Mile Oak E Sussex 11 H4* N dist of Portslade-by-Sea. TQ 2407
Mile Oak Kent 12 C3* loc 2km SE of Paddock Wd. TQ 6843
Miles Green Staffs 42 D6* loc 1km SE of Audley. SJ 8049
Miles Hill W Yorks 49 E4* dist of Leeds 2m/3km N of city centre. SE 2936
Miles Hope H & W 26 B2* loc 3m/5km SW of Tenbury Wells. SO 5764
Milesmark Fife 72 D5* vil 2m/3km NW of Dunfermline. NT 0688
Miles Platting Gtr Manchester 42 D2* dist of Manchester 2m/3km NE of city centre. SJ 8699
Miles's Green Berks 18 A4* loc 5m/7km E of Newbury. SU 5469
Mile Town Kent 21 E4 residential loc adjoining Sheerness to S. TQ 9174
Milfield Nthmb 67 F5 vil 5m/8km NW of Wooler. NT 9333
Milford Derbys 43 H6 vil 2km S of Belper. SK 3545
Milford Devon 6 B3 loc near coast 10m/16km N of Bude. SS 2321
Milford Powys 33 G5* loc 1m W of Newtown. SO 0991
Milford Staffs 35 F2 vil 4m/6km SE of Stafford. SJ 9721
Milford Surrey 11 F1 loc 2m/3km SW of Godalming. To S, M. Common (NT). SU 9442
Milford Haven (Aberdaugleddyf) Dyfed 22 B5 large estuary and natural harbour in SW Wales running out to sea between St Ann's Hd and Sheep I., and itself fed by many tidal estuaries. Major port for large oil tankers; oil refineries on N and S banks. Tn of Milford Haven is situated on N bank 7m/11km SW of Haverfordwest. SM 8504
Milford Heath Surrey 11 F1 loc adjoining Milford to S. SU 9441
Milford, Little Dyfed 22 C4* loc on W bank of Western Cleddau R 2m/4km S of Haverfordwest. SM 9611
Milford, North N Yorks 49 G4* loc 1m SW of Ulleskelf. SE 5039
Milford on Sea Hants 10 A5 resort and residential tn 3m/5km SW of Lymington. SZ 2891
Milford, South N Yorks 49 G5 vil 5m/8km N of Ferrybridge. SE 4931
Military Canal Kent. See Royal Military Canal.
Milkwall Glos 16 B1 vil 1m S of Coleford. SO 5809
Milkwell Wilts 9 F2* loc 4m/6km E of Shaftesbury. ST 9123
Milland W Sussex 11 E2 ham 2m/3km S of Liphook. SU 8328
Milland Marsh W Sussex 11 E2* loc 3m/5km S of Liphook. Site of Roman stn 1km SE. SU 8327
Millarston S'clyde 64 C3* W dist of Paisley. NS 4663
Mill Bank W Yorks 48 C5 vil 1m N of Ripponden. SE 0321
Mill Bay Dyfed 22 B5* small bay on NE side of St Ann's Hd at entrance to Milford Haven. Here Henry Tudor, later Henry VII, landed in 1485 at start of campaign which ended at Bosworth Field. SM 8003
Mill Bay Orkney 89 C6* wide bay on E coast of Stronsay, extending from Grice Ness (N) to Odness (S). HY 6626
Millbeck Cumbria 52 C2 loc 2m/3km N of Keswick. NY 2526
Millbreck Grampian 83 H3* loc 2m/3km S of Mintlaw. NK 0045
Millbridge Surrey 11 E1 vil on R Wey 3m/5km S of Farnham. SU 8442
Millbrook Beds 29 E4 vil 2m/3km W of Ampthill. TL 0138
Millbrook Cornwall 4 B5 vil 2m/3km S of Torpoint across St John's Lake, at head of **M. Lake,** a long inlet of R Tamar estuary. Harbour. SX 4252
Millbrook Devon 8 B4* loc on E edge of Axminster. SY 3098
Millbrook Gtr Manchester 43 E2 loc 2km NE of Stalybridge. SJ 9899
Millbrook Hants 10 B3* W dist of Southampton. SU 3813
Mill Brow Gtr Manchester 43 E2* vil 2m/3km NE of Marple. SJ 9889
Millbuie Forest H'land 81 F2 state forest on Black Isle, Ross and Cromarty dist, NW of Fortrose. NH 6960
Millcombe Devon 4 D5 loc 5m/8km W of Dartmouth. SX 8049
Mill Common Norfolk 39 F2* loc 3m/4km NE of Aylsham. TG 2229
Mill Common Norfolk 39 G4* N end of Thurton vil. TG 3201
Mill Common Suffolk 31 H1* loc 3m/5km NE of Halesworth. TM 4181
Millcorner E Sussex 12 D4* ham 1m S of Northiam. TQ 8223
Mill Cottages Humberside 50 D2* loc 1m SW of Sledmere. SE 9263
Milldale Staffs 43 F5* ham 1km SE of Alstonefield. SK 1354
Mill End Bucks 18 C3 vil on R Thames 2m/4km NE of Henley-on-Thames. Site of Roman villa to N. SU 7885
Mill End Cambs 30 B2* loc 1m S of Kirtling. TL 6956
Mill End Cambs 37 G6* E end of Warboys, 7m/11km NE of Huntingdon. TL 3180
Millend Glos 16 B1* loc 2km SW of Coleford. SO 5909
Mill End Herts 19 E2 W dist of Rickmansworth. TQ 0494
Mill End Herts 29 G4* ham 3m/5km NW of Buntingford. TL 3332
Mill End H & W 26 D4* ham 4m/6km NE of Tewkesbury on E bank of R Avon. SO 9237
Millend Oxon 27 G5* loc adjoining Chadlington to N, 3m/5km S of Chipping Norton. SP 3222
Mill End Green Essex 30 B5 ham 3m/5km N of Gt Dunmow. TL 6125
Millerhill Lothian 66 B2 vil in coal-mining area 2km N of Dalkeith. Monktonhall Colliery to N. NT 3269
Miller's Dale Derbys 43 F4 vil in R Wye valley 5m/8km E of Buxton. Also the valley itself from here down to Cressbrook. SK 1373
Millers Green Derbys 43 G5* loc 1km S of Wirksworth. SK 2852
Miller's Green Essex 20 C1* loc 4m/6km NE of Chipping Ongar. TL 5807
Millerston S'clyde 64 D2 loc 4m/6km E of Glasgow. NS 6467
Milleur Point D & G 57 A5 headland at N end of Rinns of Galloway, 3m/5km N of Kirkcolm. NX 0273
Millfield Cambs 37 G4* loc in Peterborough 1m N of city centre. TF 1900
Millfield Tyne & Wear 61 H5* dist of Sunderland 1km W of tn centre. NZ 3857
Millgate Lancs 47 H6* loc 1km N of Whitworth. SD 8819
Millgate Norfolk 39 F2* loc adjoining Aylsham to N. TG 1927
Mill Gill Force N Yorks 53 H5* waterfall 1km W of Askrigg. SD 9391
Mill Green Cambs 30 B3* ham 3m/5km W of Haverhill. TL 6245
Mill Green Essex 20 C2 ham 1m N of Ingatestone. TL 6301
Mill Green Herts 19 F1* loc 1m NE of Hatfield. TL 2409
Mill Green Norfolk 39 E6* loc 3m/5km NE of Diss. TM 1384
Millgreen Salop 34 D2* loc 2km NW of Hinstock. SJ 6827
Mill Green Staffs 35 G2* loc 1km W of Abbots Bromley. SK 0723
Mill Green Suffolk 30 D4* ham 5m/8km W of Hadleigh. TL 9542
Mill Green Suffolk 31 E2* ham 1km W of Buxhall. TL 9957
Mill Green Suffolk 31 F2* ham 1km NE of Stonham Aspal. TM 1360
Mill Green Suffolk 31 G2* loc 2km NE of Parham. TM 3161
Mill Green W Midlands 35 G4* loc 2km E of Aldridge. SK 0701

Millhalf H & W 25 G3* vil 5m/9km S of Kington. SO 2748
Millhayes Devon 7 H4* loc 4m/7km S of Wellington. ST 1414
Millhayes Devon 8 A4* loc 1m SW of Stockland. ST 2303
Millhead Lancs 47 F1 loc adjoining Carnforth to N. SD 4971
Millheugh S'clyde 65 E4 loc adjoining Larkhall to W. NS 7550
Mill Hill Cambs 29 F3* ham with disused windmill 2m/3km NE of Potton. TL 2351
Mill Hill Durham 54 D2* loc 2km E of Wingate. NZ 4237
Mill Hill E Sussex 12 C6* loc 2km W of Pevensey. TQ 6205
Mill Hill Glos 16 B1* loc 3m/4km NW of Lydney. SO 6006
Mill Hill Gtr Manchester 42 C1* dist of Bolton 1km NE of tn centre. SD 7209
Mill Hill Lancs 47 G5* loc in Blackburn 2km SW of tn centre. SD 6726
Mill Hill London 19 F3 dist in borough of Barnet 9m/14km NW of Charing Cross. TQ 2192
Mill Hill Norfolk 39 F6* loc 1km SE of Tivetshall St Mary. TM 1785
Mill Hill Suffolk 31 G2* loc adjoining Peasenhall to NW. TM 3469
Mill Hill Estate Tyne & Wear 61 H6* housing estate in Sunderland 3m/5km S of tn centre. NZ 3852
Millhouse Cumbria 52 D1/D2 loc 2m/3km E of Hesket Newmarket. NY 3637
Millhouse S'clyde 63 F1 loc in Argyll 1m SW of Kames. NR 9570
Millhouse S Yorks 43 G1* ham 2m/3km W of Penistone. SE 2203
Millhousebridge D & G 59 F3 loc on R Annan 3m/5km NW of Lockerbie. NY 1085
Mill House Brow Ches 42 C2* loc just S of Croft. SJ 6393
Millhouses S Yorks 43 G3* dist of Sheffield 3m/4km SW of city centre. SK 3383
Millhouses S Yorks 43 H1 loc adjoining Darfield to E. SE 4204
Millin Cross Dyfed 22 C4* loc at head of creek running down to Western Cleddau R, 3m/5km E of Haverfordwest. SM 9913
Millington Humberside 50 D3 vil 3m/4km NE of Pocklington. SE 8351
Millington Green Derbys 43 G6* loc 2km NE of Hulland. SK 2647
Mill, Little Gwent 15 G2* ham 3m/5km NE of Pontypool. SO 3202
Mill, Low N Yorks 55 E5* ham 6m/9km N of Kirkbymoorside. SE 6795
Mill Meads London 20 A3* loc in borough of Newham 2km W of W Ham. TQ 3883
Millmeece Staffs 35 E1 ham 3m/4km N of Eccleshall. SJ 8333
Mill, Middle Dyfed 22 A3 ham 4m/6km E of St David's. SM 8025
Millom Cumbria 52 B6 tn on W side of R Duddon estuary 5m/8km SW of Broughton in Furness. Remains of cas dating from 14c 1km N. SD 2187
Millow Beds 29 F3* ham 3m/4km E of Biggleswade. TL 2243
Mill Place Humberside 44 D1* loc 1m W of Brigg. SE 9806
Millpool Cornwall 3 F2* loc 4m/6km NE of Bodmin. SX 1270
Millport S'clyde 63 H2 resort and port on **M. Bay** at S end of island of Gt Cumbrae 3m/4km W of Fairlie across Fairlie Roads. In bay are islets known as The Eileans. NS 1655
Mills W Yorks 43 G1 loc 1km S of Shelley. SE 2010
Mills Hill Gtr Manchester 42 D1* loc 2m/3km E of Middleton. SD 8805
Mill Side Cumbria 52 D6* loc 3m/5km NE of Lindale. SD 4484
Mill Street Kent 20 C5* loc adjoining E Malling to W. TQ 6957
Mill Street Norfolk 39 E3* loc on R Wensum 4m/6km NE of E Dereham. TG 0118
Mill Street Norfolk 39 E3* loc on R Wensum 1km N of Elsing. TG 0517
Mill Street Suffolk 31 E1* ham adjoining Gislingham to W. TM 0671
Mill Street Suffolk 31 G1* loc 1m NW of Halesworth. TM 3778
Millthorpe Derbys 43 G3* loc 1m S of Holmesfield. SK 3176
Millthrop Cumbria 53 F5 ham 1km S of Sedbergh. SD 6691
Milltimber Grampian 77 G1 loc 1m E of Peterculter. NJ 8501
Milltown Cornwall 3 F3 loc 2km S of Lostwithiel. SX 1057
Milltown Derbys 43 H5* loc 3m/4km W of Clay Cross. SK 3561
Milltown Devon 6 D2 ham 4m/6km N of Barnstaple. SS 5538
Milltown Grampian 82 B1 airfield 4m/6km SE of Lossiemouth. NJ 2665
Milltown Grampian 82 B5/B6* loc just E of Cock Br. NJ 2609
Milltown Grampian 82 D2 vil 5m/9km N of Huntly. NJ 5448
Milltown Grampian 82 D5 loc 1km S of Kildrummy and 3m/5km S of Lumsden. NJ 4716
Milltown H'land 80 C2/D2 locality in Strathconon, Ross and Cromarty dist, 2m/4km above head of Loch Meig. NH 3055
Milltown of Campfield Grampian 77 F1* loc 2m/3km SE of Torphins. NJ 6400
Milltown of Edinville Grampian 82 B3* vil with nearby distillery 2m/3km S of Charlestown of Aberlour. NJ 2640
Millwall London 20 A4* dock area on Isle of Dogs, borough of Tower Hamlets, on N bank of R Thames and 5m/8km E of Charing Cross. TQ 3779
Mill, West Herts 29 F4* NW dist of Hitchin. TL 1730
Millwey Rise Devon 8 B4* loc 1km NE of Axminster. SY 3099
Milnathort Tayside 73 E4 market tn with woollen mills 2m/3km N of Kinross. See also Burleigh Castle. NO 1204
Milnbank S'clyde 64 D2* loc in Dennistoun dist of Glasgow. NS 6165
Milnefield Tayside. See Invergowrie.
Milners Heath Ches 42 A5* loc adjoining Waverton to SE. SJ 4662
Milngavie S'clyde 64 C2 tn 6m/10km N of Glasgow. Light engineering, mnfre of packaging materials. NS 5574
Milnrow Gtr Manchester 48 C6 tn 2m/4km E of Rochdale. Textiles, engineering, brick mnfre. SD 9212
Milnsbridge W Yorks 48 D6 dist of Huddersfield 2m/4km W of tn centre. SE 1116
Milnshaw Lancs 48 A5* loc adjoining Accrington to NW. SD 7429
Milnthorpe Cumbria 53 E6 vil 7m/11km S of Kendal. SD 4981
Milnthorpe W Yorks 49 E6* loc in Wakefield 2m/4km S of city centre. SE 3317
Milovaig Skye, H'land 78 A4 two locs, **Upr** and **Lr Milovaig,** 6m/10km W of Dunvegan. NG 1549
Milson Salop 26 B1* vil 4m/6km NE of Tenbury Wells. SO 6373
Milstead Kent 21 E5 vil 3m/5km S of Sittingbourne. TQ 9058
Milston Wilts 17 F6 vil on R Avon 3m/4km N of Amesbury. SU 1645
Milthorpe Northants 28 B3* loc adjoining Weedon Lois to W, 6m/10km N of Brackley. SP 5946
Milton Avon 15 H5 NE suburb of Weston-super-Mare. ST 3462
Milton Cambs 30 A2 vil 3m/5km NE of Cambridge. TL 4762
Milton Central 71 F4 loc 2km W of Aberfoyle. NN 5001
Milton Central 71 F5 vil 2m/4km NW of Drymen. NS 4490
Milton Cumbria 53 E6 loc 6m/10km S of Kendal. SD 5383
Milton Cumbria 60 B5 ham 2m/3km E of Brampton. NY 5560
Milton Derbys 35 H2 vil 1m E of Repton. SK 3226
Milton D & G 57 C7* vil 2m/4km SE of Glenluce. NX 2154
Milton D & G 58 D4 vil 2m/3km SE of Crocketford. See also Milton Loch. NX 8470
Milton Dyfed 22 C5 vil 4m/6km E of Pembroke. SN 0403
Milton Grampian 82 D1* loc near N coast 3m/4km S of Cullen. NJ 5163
Milton Gwent 15 H3 loc 4m/6km E of Newport. ST 3688
Milton Hants 10 D5 dist of Portsmouth 2km E of city centre. SZ 6699
Milton H'land 78 E4 loc on W coast of Ross and Cromarty dist, adjoining Applecross to S. NG 7043
Milton H'land 81 E3 loc in Ross and Cromarty dist on N shore of Beauly Firth 3m/5km E of Muir of Ord. NH 5749
Milton H'land 81 E4 vil in Glen Urquhart in Inverness dist, 1m W of Drumnadrochit. NH 4930
Milton H'land 87 A8/B8 vil in Ross and Cromarty dist 5m/8km NE of Invergordon. NH 7674
Milton Kent 20 C4 E dist of Gravesend. TQ 6574
Milton Notts 44 B4 vil 2m/3km NW of Tuxford. SK 7173
Milton Oxon 18 A2 vil 3m/5km NW of Didcot. SU 4892
Milton Oxon 27 H4 vil 4m/6km S of Banbury. SP 4535
Milton S'clyde 64 B2* vil 2m/3km E of Dumbarton. NS 4274
Milton S'clyde 64 D2* loc in Glasgow 3m/4km N of city centre. NS 5969
Milton Som 16 B6* locs of **Lr** and **Upr Milton** about 2km NW and N respectively of Wells. ST 5347
Milton Som 8 C2* ham 2km N of Martock. ST 4621
Milton Staffs 43 E6 loc 4m/6km NE of Stoke-on-Trent city centre. SJ 9050
Milton Surrey 19 F6* S dist of Dorking. TQ 1647
Milton W Isles 88 D3* loc near W coast of S Uist 3m/4km S of Rubha Ardvule. Birthplace of Flora MacDonald. NF 7326
Milton Abbas Dorset 9 E4 vil 6m/9km SW of Blandford Forum. 1km NW, Milton Abbey, 14c–15c, and Milton Abbey boys' school. ST 8001
Milton Abbot Devon 4 B3 vil 6m/9km NW of Tavistock. SX 4079
Milton Bridge Lothian 66 A2/A3 loc 2m/3km NE of Penicuik. NT 2562
Milton Bryan Beds 28 D4 vil 2m/3km SE of Woburn. SP 9730
Milton Clevedon Som 8 D1 vil 2m/3km NW of Bruton. ST 6637
Milton Combe Devon 4 B4* vil 6m/9km S of Tavistock. SX 4866
Milton Damerel Devon 6 C4 vil 5m/8km NE of Holsworthy. SS 3810
Milton End Glos 26 C6* loc 1km E of Arlingham. SO 7210
Milton Eonan Tayside 71 F1* loc in Glen Lyon above Br of Balgie. Waterfall in Allt Bail a' Mhuilinn, stream running into R Lyon here from S. NN 5746
Milton Ernest Beds 29 E2 vil on R Ouse 5m/7km NW of Bedford. TL 0156
Milton, Great Oxon 18 B2 vil 8m/12km SE of Oxford. SP 6202
Milton Green Ches 42 A5 ham 6m/9km SE of Chester. SJ 4658
Milton Heights Oxon 18 A3* loc 3m/4km W of Didcot. SU 4891
Milton Hill Oxon 17 H3 vil 3m/5km W of Didcot. SU 4790
Milton Keynes Bucks 28 D4 New Tn designated 1967. Includes Bletchley in the S, Stony Stratford and Wolverton in the NW, and the original vil of Milton Keynes in the E. Area about 34 sq miles or 98 sq km. SP 8539
Milton Lilbourne Wilts 17 F5 vil 2m/3km E of Pewsey. SU 1960
Milton, Little Oxon 18 B2 vil 6m/10km SW of Thame. Site of Roman villa to SE. SP 6100
Milton Loch D & G 58 D4 loch 1km SE of Crocketford. NX 8471
Milton Malsor Northants 28 C2 vil 4m/6km SW of Northampton. SP 7355
Milton Ness Grampian 77 G4 headland on E coast 6m/9km NE of Montrose. NO 7764
Milton of Auchinhove Grampian 77 E1* loc 2m/3km W of Lumphanan. NJ 5503
Milton of Balgonie Fife 73 F4 vil 2km E of Markinch. NO 3100
Milton of Campsie S'clyde 64 D2 vil 2m/3km N of Kirkintilloch. NS 6576
Milton of Cushnie Grampian 82 D5* vil 5m/7km SW of Alford. NJ 5211
Milton of Tullich Grampian 76 D2 loc on Tullich Burn, qv, 2m/3km NE of Ballater. NO 3897
Milton on Stour Dorset 9 E2 vil 2km N of Gillingham. ST 8028
Milton Regis Kent 21 E5 W suburb of Sittingbourne. TQ 8964
Milton, South Devon 4 D6 vil 3m/4km W of Kingsbridge. SX 6942
Milton Street E Sussex 12 B6* ham 1m NE of Alfriston. TQ 5304
Milton Street Kent 20 C4* loc 3m/5km W of Gravesend. TQ 6074
Milton-under-Wychwood Oxon 27 G5 vil 4m/6km N of Burford. SP 2618
Milton, Upper Oxon 27 G5* ham 3m/5km N of Burford. SP 2517
Milton, West Dorset 8 C4 vil 3m/5km NE of Bridport. SY 5096
Milverton Som 8 A2 small tn 7m/11km W of Taunton. ST 1225
Milverton Warwicks 27 G1 loc in NW part of Leamington. SP 3066
Milwich Staffs 35 F2 vil 5m/8km E of Stone. SJ 9732
Milwr Clwyd 41 G4* loc 1m SE of Holywell. SJ 1974
Mimbridge Surrey 18 D5* loc 1m SE of Chobham. SU 9861
Mimms, South Herts 19 F2 vil 2m/3km W of Potters Bar. TL 2201
Mimram 29 G6 r rising N of Whitwell, Herts, and flowing SE into R Lea at Hertford. TL 3112
Minard S'clyde 70 B5 locality in Argyll on W shore of Loch Fyne 4m/6km SW of Furnace. **M. Forest** is state forest to W. NR 9796
Minard Point S'clyde 70 A3 headland on N side of entrance to Loch Feochan in Argyll, 5m/8km SW of Oban. NM 8123
Minchington Dorset 9 G3 loc 1km SE of Farnham and 3m/4km SE of Tollard Royal. ST 9614
Minchinhampton Glos 16 D2 vil 3m/5km SE of Stroud. SO 8700
Minch, Little 88 sea passage between Western Isles and the island of Skye. NG
Minch, North 90 sea passage between Isle of Lewis and the Scottish mainland. NB
Mindrum Nthmb 67 E5 loc 4m/7km S of Cornhill on Tweed. NT 8432
Mindrummill Nthmb 67 E5 loc 5m/8km NW of Kirknewton. NT 8433
Minehead Som 7 G1 resort on Bristol Channel with extensive sands; small harbour. SS 9746
Minera Clwyd 41 H6 vil 4m/7km W of Wrexham. SJ 2751
Minety Wilts 17 E3 vil 5m/8km W of Cricklade. Vil of **Upr Minety** 2km W. Loc of **Minety Lr Moor** 1km N. SU 0290
Minffordd Gwynedd 40 C4* loc 1km S of Bangor. SH 5770
Mingary Castle H'land 68 C3 ruined 13c cas on S coast of Ardnamurchan peninsula in Lochaber dist, 1m SE of Kilchoan. NM 5063
Mingay Island Skye, H'land 78 A4 small uninhabited island in Loch Dunvegan 2km S of Ardmore Pt. NG 2257
Minginish Skye, H'land 79 B6, C6 dist lying S of a line from Sligachan to Loch Harport and W of R Sligachan. Includes Cuillin Hills. NG 42
Mingulay W Isles 88 D4 gaunt, uninhabited island of about 6 sq km, with high cliffs, 2m/3km SW of Pabbay and 6m/10km SW of Vatersay. Haunt of sea birds. NL 58
Miningsby Lincs 45 G5 ham 5m/8km SE of Horncastle. TF 3264
Minions Cornwall 3 G1 vil 4m/7km N of Liskeard. Hurlers Stone Circle (A.M.), row of three prehistoric stone circles to W. SX 2671
Minishant S'clyde 56 D3 loc 3m/5km NE of Maybole. NS 3319
Minllyn Gwynedd 33 F3 ham 1m N of Mallwyd. SH 8514
Minnigaff D & G 57 D6 vil on E side of Newton Stewart across R Cree. NX 4166
Minnis Bay Kent 13 H1 bay on N coast, W of Birchington. TR 2769
Minskip N Yorks 49 F2 vil 2km S of Boroughbridge. SE 3864
Minsmere Suffolk 31 H2* loc of meres and marsh on coast 3m/5km NE of Leiston. Nature reserve. Coast here known as **M. Haven. M. River,** rising near Ubbeston, flows E through Yoxford to E Bridge and thence by sluice to M. Haven. From source to Yoxford r is known also as R Yox. TM 4766
Minstead Hants 10 A3 vil 2m/3km NW of Lyndhurst. SU 2811
Minsted W Sussex 11 E3* ham 2m/3km W of Midhurst. SU 8520
Minster Kent 13 H1 vil on Isle of Thanet 5m/7km W of Ramsgate. TR 3064
Minster Kent 21 E4 suburb on Isle of Sheppey running down to N coast. TQ 9573
Minsteracres Nthmb 61 E5 loc 4m/6km S of Riding Mill. NZ 0255
Minsterley Salop 34 B4 vil 9m/14km SW of Shrewsbury. SJ 3705
Minster, Little Oxon 27 G6 loc 3m/5km W of Witney. SP 3111
Minster Lovell Oxon 27 G6 vil on R Windrush 3m/4km NW of Witney. Remains of moated manor hse (A.M.). SP 3111
Minsterworth Glos 26 C5* vil on right bank of R Severn 4m/6km W of Gloucester. SO 7717
Minsthorpe W Yorks 49 F6* loc between N and S Elmsall. SE 4712

Mint 53 E5 r rising W of Tebay, Cumbria, and flowing S into R Kent on N side of Kendal. SD 5194
Minterne Magna Dorset 8 D4 vil 2m/3km N of Cerne Abbas. 1km SE, loc of **Minterne Parva.** ST 6504
Minting Lincs 45 F4 vil 5m/8km NW of Horncastle. TF 1873
Mintlaw Grampian 83 H2 vil 8m/13km W of Peterhead. NK 0048
Minto Borders 66 C6 vil 5m/9km NE of Hawick. NT 5620
Minton Salop 34 B5 vil 2m/4km SW of Church Stretton. SO 4390
Minwear (Mynwar) Dyfed 22 C4 loc 9m/15km NW of Tenby. SN 0413
Minworth W Midlands 35 G5 loc 4m/6km SE of Sutton Coldfield. SP 1592
Mio Ness Shetland 89 E6* headland on Mainland at S end of Yell Sound 2km NW of Brough. HU 4279
Mirbister Orkney 89 A6* loc on Mainland 1m SE of Dounby. HY 3019
Mirehouse Cumbria 52 A3* dist of Whitehaven 2m/3km S of tn centre. NX 9815
Mireland H'land 86 F2 loc near E coast of Caithness dist 7m/11km NW of Wick. ND 3160
Mirfield W Yorks 48 D6/49 E6 tn on R Calder 3m/5km SW of Dewsbury. Textiles, chemicals, malting. See also Battye Ford. SE 2019
Mirkady Point Orkney 89 B6/B7* headland on Mainland on E side of Deer Sound, 4m/7km SW of Mull Hd. HY 5306
Miserden Glos 16 D1 vil 7m/11km NW of Cirencester. SO 9309
Mishnish S'clyde 68 C3 dist of Mull 3m/5km W of Tobermory. NM 4656
Miskin (Meisgyn) Mid Glam 15 F3 vil 2m/3km S of Llantrisant. ST 0480
Miskin Mid Glam 15 F2 loc adjoining Mountain Ash to S. ST 0498
Mislingford Hants 10 C3* loc 3m/5km SE of Bishop's Waltham. SU 5814
Misselfore Wilts 9 G2* loc 1km SW of Bowerchalke. SU 0122
Missenden, Great Bucks 18 D2 vil 4m/7km W of Chesham. SP 8901
Missenden, Little Bucks 18 D2 vil 3m/4km NW of Amersham. SU 9298
Misson Notts 44 B2 vil 3m/4km NE of Bawtry. SK 6994
Misterton Leics 36 B5* ham 1m E of Lutterworth. SP 5583
Misterton Notts 44 C2 vil 5m/8km NW of Gainsborough. **M. Soss** loc 1m E. SK 7694
Misterton Som 8 C3 vil 2km SE of Crewkerne. ST 4508
Mistley Essex 31 E5 vil on S side of R Stour estuary 1m E of Manningtree and 9m/14km W of Harwich. Vil of **New Mistley** adjoins to E. TM 1131
Mitcham London 19 F4 dist in borough of Merton 4m/6km NW of Croydon. TQ 2768
Mitcheldean Glos 26 B5 vil 3m/5km N of Cinderford. SO 6618
Mitchell Cornwall 2 D3 vil 5m/9km SE of Newquay. SW 8654
Mitchell's Fold Stone Circle Salop. See Priestweston.
Mitchell's House Reservoir Lancs 48 B5* resr 2m/3km E of Accrington. SD 7827
Mitchel Troy (Llanfihangel Troddi) Gwent 26 A6 vil 2m/3km SW of Monmouth. SO 4910
Mitchin Hole W Glam 23 G6* long cavern at foot of cliffs 1m W of Pwlldu Hd on S coast of Gower peninsula. SS 5586
Mite 52 B5 r rising in Lake Dist, Cumbria, to E of Wast Water, and flowing SW into R Esk estuary at Ravenglass. SD 0896
Mitford Nthmb 61 F3 vil on R Wansbeck 2m/3km W of Morpeth. Ruined Norman cas. NZ 1785
Mithian Cornwall 2 C3 vil 2m/3km E of St Agnes. SW 7450
Mithil Brook 25 F2* stream rising on Radnor Forest, Powys, 2m/3km E of Llandegley and flowing into R Ithon 1km S of Penybont. SO 1162
Mitton Staffs 35 E3 loc 3m/4km W of Penkridge. SJ 8815
Mitton, Great Lancs 48 A4 vil on R Ribble 3m/4km SW of Clitheroe. **M. Green** loc to N. **Lit Mitton** loc to S. SD 7139
Mitton, Upper H & W 26 C1 NE dist of Stourport. SO 8172
Miwl Welsh form of (R) Mule, qv.
Mixbury Oxon 28 B4 vil 3m/4km SE of Brackley. SP 6034
Mixenden W Yorks 48 C5/D5* loc 3m/5km NW of Halifax. **Mixenden Resr** on N side. SE 0628
Mixon Staffs 43 E5/F5* loc 2m/4km W of Butterton. SK 0457
Moat Hall Suffolk. See Parham.
Moats Tye Suffolk 31 E3* ham 2m/4km S of Stowmarket. TM 0455
Mobberley Ches 42 D3 vil 2m/4km E of Knutsford. SJ 7879
Mobberley Staffs 35 F1 ham 2km S of Cheadle. SK 0041
Moccas H & W 25 H4* ham on S side of R Wye 10m/16km W of Hereford. SO 3542
Mochdre Clwyd 41 E4 loc 2km W of Colwyn Bay. SJ 8278
Mochdre Powys 33 G5 ham on Mochdre Brook 3m/5km SW of Newtown. SO 0788
Mochdre Brook 33 G5* r rising 2m/3km SW of Pentre, Powys, and flowing NE into R Severn 2m/3km W of Newtown. SO 0890
Mochrum D & G 57 D7 vil 2m/3km N of Port William. Also known as Kirk of Mochrum. See also Mochrum Loch, Old Place of Mochrum. NX 3446
Mochrum Loch D & G 57 C7 loch 8m/13km W of Wigtown. At NE corner of loch stands the restored Old Place of Mochrum, with towers of 15c and 16c. NX 3053
Mochrum Loch S'clyde 56 C3 small loch on S side of **Mochrum Hill,** 2m/3km W of Maybole. NS 2709
Mockbeggar Hants 9 H3* loc on edge of New Forest 3m/5km NE of Ringwood. SU 1609
Mockerkin Cumbria 52 B3 ham 5m/8km SW of Cockermouth. **M. Tarn** small lake to W. NY 0923
Modbury Devon 4 C5 vil 7m/11km NW of Kingsbridge. SX 6551
Moddershall Staffs 35 E1 ham 2m/4km NE of Stone. SJ 9236
Mode Hill Ches 43 E4* loc 1m SW of Bollington. SJ 9276
Moel Eilio Gwynedd 40 C5 mt 2m/3km SW of Llanberis. Height 2382 ft or 726 metres. SH 5557
Moel Famma Clwyd 41 G5 highest point of Clwydian Range, 1820 ft or 555 metres. On summit is stump of 'Jubilee Tower' erected in 1820. SJ 1662
Moelfre Clwyd 33 H2* ham at lower end of Llyn Moelfre 2m/3km W of Llansilin. SJ 1828
Moelfre Gwynedd 40 C3 fishing vil on E coast of Anglesey 6m/10km SE of Amlwch. SH 5186
Moel Hebog Gwynedd 40 C6 mt 2m/3km W of Beddgelert. Height 2566 ft or 782 metres. SH 5646
Moel Siabod Gwynedd 40 D5 mt 2m/4km S of Capel Curig. Height 2860 ft or 872 metres. SH 7054
Moel Sych 33 G2 the highest of the Berwyn Mts 4m/6km SE of Llandrillo. The summit, 2713 ft or 827 metres, is on the border of Clwyd and Powys. SJ 0631
Moel Tryfan Gwynedd 40 C5* loc 4m/7km S of Caernarvon. SH 5156
Moel Wnion Gwynedd 40 D4 mt 4m/6km SW of Llanfairfechan. Height 1902 ft or 580 metres. SH 6469
Moel y Gaer Clwyd 41 G6* high point on Llantysilio Mt 1km W of the summit, Moel y Gamelin. Crowned by ancient British hill fort. SJ 1646
Moel y Gamelin Clwyd 41 G6 summit of Llantysilio Mt 2m/3km E of Bryneglwys. Height 1897 ft or 578 metres. SJ 1746
Moel y Golfa Powys 34 A3 highest of three principal peaks of Breidden Hills, qv. Height 1324 ft or 404 metres. Largely wooded. SJ 2812
Moffat D & G 59 F1 small tn and resort on R Annan 19m/31km NE of Dumfries. **M. Water** is r running SW to R Annan 2m/3km S. NT 0805
Mogerhanger Beds 29 F3 vil 2m/3km W of Sandy. TL 1449
Moidart H'land 68 E2, F2 that part of Lochaber dist lying W of Loch Shiel and S of Loch Eilt. Coastline indented by Lochs Ailort and M. NM 77
Moira Leics 35 H3* loc 3m/4km S of Swadlincote. **M. Baths** loc to W. SK 3115
Molash Kent 21 F6 vil 6m/9km N of Ashford. TR 0251
Mold (Yr Wyddgrug) Clwyd 41 H5 tn 11m/17km NW of Wrexham. Remains of motte and bailey cas. SJ 2364
Moldgreen W Yorks 48 D6* dist of Huddersfield 1m E of tn centre. SE 1516
Mole 19 F4 r rising at Crawley in W Sussex and flowing circuitously, past Horley, Dorking, Leatherhead, Cobham, and Esher, before running into R Thames at E Molesey in Surrey opposite Hampton Court Palace. TQ 1568
Mole 7 E3 r rising on Exmoor 2m/3km N of Twitchen, Devon, and running SW past N and S Molton into R Taw at Junction Pool, 2m/3km SW of King's Nympton. SS 6617
Molehill Green Essex 30 A5 vil 4m/7km NW of Gt Dunmow. TL 5624
Molehill Green Essex 30 B5* loc 3m/5km SW of Braintree. TL 7120
Molescroft Humberside 51 E4 suburb 1m NW of Beverley. TA 0240
Molesden Nthmb 61 F3 loc 3m/5km W of Morpeth. NZ 1484
Molesey, East Surrey 19 F4 urban loc between R Thames and R Mole 2m/3km W of Kingston. TQ 1468
Molesey, West Surrey 19 E4 urban loc between R Thames and R Mole 3m/4km NE of Walton-on-Thames. **Molesey Resrs** to W beside R Thames. TQ 1368
Molesworth Cambs 29 E1 vil 5m/8km E of Thrapston. TL 0775
Mole Valley 119 admin dist of Surrey.
Molland Devon 7 F2 vil on S slopes of Exmoor 6m/9km E of S Molton. SS 8028
Molland Cross Devon 7 E2* loc 5m/8km N of S Molton. SS 7133
Mollington Ches 42 A4 vil 3m/4km NW of Chester. SJ 3870
Mollington Oxon 27 H3 vil 4m/7km N of Banbury. SP 4447
Mollinsburn S'clyde 64 D2 loc 4m/6km SW of Cumbernauld. NS 7171
Molls Cleuch Dod Borders 65 H6 mt 5m/8km SE of Tweedsmuir. Height 2571 ft or 784 metres. NT 1518
Molton, North Devon 7 E2 vil 3m/5km NE of S Molton. SS 7329
Molton, South Devon 7 E3 mkt tn 11m/17km E of Barnstaple. SS 7125
Mon Welsh form of Anglesey, qv.
Monach Isles W Isles 88 D1 group of low-lying islands 8m/13km SW of Aird an Rùnair, W coast of N Uist. Total area about 600 acres or 240 hectares. No permanent population. Known also as Heisker. See Ceann Ear, Ceann Iar, Shillay, Stockay. NF 66
Monadhliath Mountains H'land 81 E6, F6 range of mts running NE to SW astride border between Inverness and Badenoch & Strathspey dists on W side of upper Strathspey. Summit is Carn Dearg; height 3100 ft or 945 metres. NH 60
Monadh Mór 76 A2 mt in Cairngorms, on border of Grampian and Highland regions, 4m/7km SW of Ben Macdui. Height 3651 ft or 1113 metres. NN 9394
Monar Forest, East H'land 80 C3 deer forest in Ross and Cromarty dist N of lower part of Loch Monar. NH 1042
Monar Forest, West H'land 80 B3 deer forest about head of Loch Monar, Ross and Cromarty dist. NH 0742
Monaughty Powys 25 G1* loc 4m/6km SW of Knighton. Gabled Tudor farmhouse. SO 2368
Monaughty Forest Grampian 82 A2, B2 state forest 6m/9km SW of Elgin. NJ 1358
Monboddo Grampian 77 G3 hse 2km E of Auchenblae. Formerly seat of the Burnetts, visited by Johnson and Boswell. NO 7478
Moncreiffe Tayside 73 E3* S dist of Perth. **Moncreiffe I.** (or Friarton I.) is island in R Tay to E. **M. Hill** 2m/3km SE; height 725 ft or 221 metres. NO 1121
Monewden Suffolk 31 F2 vil 4m/7km NW of Wickham Mkt. TM 2358
Money Bridge Lincs 37 G2* loc 2m/3km W of Pinchbeck. TF 2125
Moneydie Tayside 72 D2 loc 5m/8km NW of Perth. NO 0629
Moneyrow Green Berks 18 D4* loc 3m/4km S of Maidenhead. SU 8976
Mongeham, Great Kent 13 H2 vil and W suburb of Deal. TR 3451
Mongeham, Little Kent 13 H2 ham 3m/5km W of Deal. TR 3350
Moniaive D & G 58 D3 vil on Dalwhat Water 7m/11km SW of Thornhill. 3m/5km E is Maxwelton Hse, 17c; birthplace of Annie Laurie, the subject of well-known ballad. Hse incorporates parts of 14c Glencairn Castle. NX 7790
Monifieth Tayside 73 G1 suburb on Firth of Tay 6m/10km E of Dundee. NO 4932
Monikie Tayside 73 G1* vil 5m/8km NW of Carnoustie. Resr to SE. NO 5038
Monimail Fife 73 F3 vil 4m/7km W of Cupar. NO 2914
Monington (Eglwys Wythwr) Dyfed 22 D2 loc 3m/5km W of Cardigan. SN 1343
Monk Bretton S Yorks 43 H1 coal-mining loc in Barnsley 2m/3km NE of tn centre. Remains of medieval priory (A.M.) to SE. SE 3607
Monk Castle S'clyde 64 A4 remains of medieval cas 2km S of Dalry. NS 2947
Monk End N Yorks 54 C4* loc adjoining Croft to N. NZ 2809
Monken Hadley London 19 F2 loc in borough of Barnet 11m/18km N of Charing Cross. TQ 2597
Monkerton Devon 7 G5* loc at E edge of Exeter 3m/5km from city centre. SX 9693
Monkey Island Berks 18 D4* island in R Thames 1km SE of Bray. SU 9179
Monk Fryston N Yorks 49 G5 vil 7m/11km W of Selby. Hall partly medieval. SE 5029
Monk Hesleden Durham 54 D2 ham 1m SE of Hesleden and 4m/7km NW of Hartlepool. NZ 4537
Monkhide H & W 26 B3* ham 7m/11km E of Hereford. SO 6144
Monkhill Cumbria 59 H5* ham 4m/6km NW of Carlisle. NY 3458
Monkhopton Salop 34 C5 vil 6m/9km W of Bridgnorth. SO 6293
Monkland H & W 26 A2 vil on R Arrow 3m/4km W of Leominster. SO 4557
Monklands 114 admin dist of S'clyde region.
Monkleigh Devon 6 C3 vil 3m/4km NW of Torrington. SS 4520
Monknash (As Fawr, Yr) S Glam 15 E4 ham 3m/5km NW of Llantwit Major. SS 9270
Monkokehampton Devon 6 D4 vil 3m/4km E of Hatherleigh. SS 5805
Monkscross Cornwall 3 H1* loc 2m/3km NE of Callington. SX 3871
Monkseaton Tyne & Wear 61 H4 urban loc on W side of Whitley Bay. NZ 3472
Monks Eleigh Suffolk 30 D3 vil 5m/8km NW of Hadleigh. Loc of **M.E. Tye** 1m NW. TL 9647
Monk's Gate W Sussex 11 G2 ham 3m/4km SE of Horsham. TQ 2027
Monk's Green Herts 19 G1* loc 2m/4km S of Hertford. TL 3308
Monks' Heath Ches 42 D4 ham 5m/8km W of Macclesfield. SJ 8474
Monk Sherborne Hants 18 B5 vil 4m/6km NW of Basingstoke. SU 6056
Monk's Hill Kent 13 E3* loc 2m/3km NE of Biddenden. TQ 8641
Monks Horton Kent 13 F3 loc 4m/6km NW of Hythe. TR 1240
Monksilver Som 7 H2 vil on edge of Exmoor National Park 4m/6km S of Watchet. ST 0737
Monks Kirby Warwicks 36 A5 vil 6m/9km NW of Rugby. SP 4683
Monk Soham Suffolk 31 F2 vil 3m/5km NE of Debenham. Ham of **M. S. Green** 1m NE. TM 2165
Monks Orchard London 20 A5* loc in borough of Croydon 3m/4km NE of Croydon tn centre. TQ 3667
Monkspath Street W Midlands 35 G6* loc in Solihull 2m/3km SW of tn centre. SP 1376
Monks Risborough Bucks 18 C1* loc adjoining Princes Risborough to N. SP 8104
Monk's Steps Avon. See Kewstoke.
Monkstone Point Dyfed 22 D5 eastward-facing headland at SW end of Saundersfoot Bay, 2m/3km NE of Tenby. SN 1403
Monkstown Fife 73 F3* loc adjoining Ladybank to W. NO 3009
Monk Street Essex 30 B5 ham 2km S of Thaxted. TL 6128

Monkswood Gwent 15 H1/H2 ham 2m/4km NW of Usk. SO 3402
Monkswood Reservoir Avon 16 C4* small resr 4m/6km N of Bath. ST 7571
Monkton Devon 8 A4 vil 2m/4km NE of Honiton. ST 1803
Monkton Dyfed 22 C5* loc adjoining Pembroke to W. SM 9701
Monkton Kent 13 H1 vil on Isle of Thanet 6m/10km W of Ramsgate. TR 2865
Monkton S'clyde 64 B5 loc on N side of Prestwick Airport, 4m/7km N of Ayr. NS 3527
Monkton Tyne & Wear 61 G5* loc in S Tyneside dist 1km S of Hebburn. NZ 3163
Monkton 15 E4* loc on borders of Mid and S Glam 3m/5km NW of Llantwit Major. SS 9271
Monkton Combe Avon 16 C5* vil 2m/4km SE of Bath. ST 7762
Monkton Deverill Wilts 9 F1 vil 4m/7km NE of Mere. ST 8537
Monkton Farleigh Wilts 16 C5* vil 3m/5km NW of Bradford-on-Avon. ST 8065
Monktonhall Lothian 66 B2* SW part of Musselburgh. **M. Colliery** 2km SW (see Millerhill). NT 3371
Monkton Heathfield Som 8 B2* vil 3m/4km NE of Taunton. ST 2526
Monkton Up Wimborne Dorset 9 G3 loc 3m/4km W of Cranborne. SU 0113
Monkton, West Som 8 B2 vil 4m/6km NE of Taunton. ST 2628
Monkton Wyld Dorset 8 B4* ham 3m/5km N of Lyme Regis. SY 3396
Monkwearmouth Tyne & Wear 61 H5 dist of Sunderland 1m N of tn centre across R Wear. NZ 3958
Monkwood Hants 10 D2* vil 2m/3km SE of Ropley. SU 6730
Monkwood Green H & W 26 C2* loc 4m/7km NW of Worcester. SO 8060
Monmore Green W Midlands 35 F4 dist of Wolverhampton 1m SE of tn centre. SO 9297
Monmouth (Trefynwy) Gwent 16 A1 mkt tn at confluence of Rs Wye and Monnow 20m/32km NE of Newport. Remains of medieval cas (A.M.); gatehouse astride br over R Monnow. Tn is thought to be on site of Roman *Blestium*. SO 5012
Monnington on Wye H & W 25 H3 vil 9m/14km W of Hereford. SO 3743
Monnow (Mynwy) 26 A6 r rising in Black Mts on E side of Hay Bluff and flowing S through Longtown towards Pandy, then NE towards Pontrilas, then SE into R Wye at Monmouth, Gwent. SO 5116
Monreith D & G 57 D8 vil on **M. Bay,** 2m/3km SE of Port William. Ancient cross (A.M.) in grnds of **M. House** to N. NX 3541
Monsal Dale Derbys 43 F4 stretch of R Wye valley 2m/3km E of Taddington. SK 1771
Montacute Som 8 C3 estate vil built of Ham stone (see Hamdon Hill), 4m/6km W of Yeovil. M. Hse (NT), Elizn. ST 4916
Montford Salop 34 B3 vil on R Severn 5m/8km W of Shrewsbury. SJ 4114
Montford Bridge Salop 34 B3 vil on R Severn 4m/7km NW of Shrewsbury. Br by Telford. SJ 4315
Montgarrie Grampian 83 E3 vil 1m N of Alford. NJ 5717
Montgomery (Trefaldwyn) Powys 33 H4 former county tn, now vil, 7m/11km S of Welshpool. Birthplace of George Herbert, 17c poet. Site of ancient British camp on hill to NW. Motte and bailey marks probable site of original cas. Present structure (A.M.), largely demolished in 1649, dates from early 13c. SO 2296
Montgreenan S'clyde 64 B4 loc 2m/4km E of Kilwinning. NS 3343
Montpelier Avon 16 B4* dist of Bristol 1m NE of city centre. ST 5974
Montreathmont Moor Tayside 77 F5 tract, partly a state forest, 4m/6km S of Brechin. WT stn. NO 5854
Montrose Tayside 77 G5 port on E coast 26m/42km NE of Dundee. Industries include quarrying, brick mnfre, distilling, agricultural engineering, mnfre of pharmaceutical products, fruit canning, shipbuilding. **M. Basin** is large tidal lagoon to W of tn. NO 7157
Monxton Hants 10 A1 vil 3m/5km W of Andover. SU 3144
Monyash Derbys 43 F4 vil 4m/7km W of Bakewell. SK 1566
Monymusk Grampian 83 E5 vil 7m/11km SW of Inverurie. NJ 6815
Monynut Edge Lothian 66 D2 ridge and watershed in Lammermuir Hills 7m/11km S of Dunbar. **Monynut Water** is r running down W side of ridge to Whiteadder Water at Abbey St Bathans. NT 7067
Monzie Tayside 72 C2 vil 2m/4km N of Crieff. **M. Castle,** to SW of vil, is 17c cas rebuilt after fire in early 20c. See also Falls of M. NN 8725
Mooa Shetland 89 F7* small uninhabited island off E coast of island of Whalsay, 2km S of Skaw Taing. HU 6065
Moonen Bay Skye, H'land 78 A4, 79 A5 southward-facing bay on W coast 8m/12km W of Dunvegan. Headland of Neist Pt to W. NG 1346
Moon's Moat North and **South** H & W 27 E1* E dists of Redditch. SP 0768
Moonzie Fife 73 F3 loc 3m/5km NW of Cupar. NO 3417
Moor Allerton W Yorks 49 E4 dist of Leeds 4m/6km N of city centre. SE 3038
Moorbrock Hill D & G 56 F4* mt 4m/7km NE of Carsphairn. Height 2137 ft or 651 metres. NX 6298
Moorby Lincs 45 F5 vil 4m/7km SE of Horncastle. TF 2964
Moor Cliff, East Dyfed 22 C5*. See Swanlake Bay.
Moor Cliff, West Dyfed 22 C5*. See Swanlake Bay.
Moorcock Inn N Yorks 53 G5 moorland inn and rd junction 5m/8km W of Hawes. SD 7992
Moor Crichel Dorset 9 G3 vil 5m/9km N of Wimborne. ST 9908
Moordown Dorset 9 G4 dist of Bournemouth 2m/3km N of tn centre. SZ 0894
Moore Ches 42 B3 vil beside Bridgewater Canal 3m/5km SW of Warrington. SJ 5784
Moor, East W Yorks 49 E6* dist of Wakefield 1km E of city centre. SE 3421
Moor End Beds 28 D5* S end of Eaton Bray, 3m/5km W of Dunstable. SP 9720
Moor End Beds 29 E2* loc 1km N of vil of Radwell and 6m/10km NW of Bedford. TL 0058
Moor End Cambs 29 G3* ham adjoining Meldreth to NE, 4m/7km NE of Royston. TL 3847
Moorend Cumbria 59 G6* loc 1km NW of Thursby. NY 3250
Moorend Glos 16 C2* loc 1km SW of Slimbridge. SO 7302
Moor End Humberside 50 C4 loc adjoining Holme upon Spalding Moor to S. SE 8137
Moor End Lancs 47 E4* loc 2km SE of Preesall. SD 3744
Moor End N Yorks 49 G4* ham adjoining Kelfield to NE. SE 5938
Moor End N Yorks 50 B3* loc adjoining Stockton-on-the-Forest to NE. SE 6656
Moor End W Yorks 48 C5* ham 3m/5km NW of Halifax. SE 0528
Moor End, Little Lancs 48 A5* loc adjoining Oswaldtwistle to S. SD 7326
Moorends S Yorks 49 H6* coal-mining loc 2km N of Thorne. SE 6915
Moor, Far Gtr Manchester 42 B1 loc in Orrell 3m/5km W of Wigan. SD 5304
Moorfield Derbys 43 E2* loc 2km SE of Glossop. SK 0492
Moorfoot Hills 66 B3 range of hills, mainly grass-covered, running NE to SW along borders of Lothian and Borders regions between Tynehead and Eddleston. Summit is Blackhope Scar, 2136 ft or 651 metres. NT 35
Moorgreen Hants 10 B3 loc 3m/4km NW of Botley. SU 4715
Moor Green Herts 29 G5* ham 3m/5km W of Buntingford. TL 3226
Moorgreen Notts 44 A6 loc 2km E of Eastwood. **Moorgreen Resr** 1m N. SK 4847
Moor Green Wilts 16 D4* vil 2km SW of Corsham. ST 8668
Moor Green W Midlands 35 G6* loc in Birmingham 3m/5km S of city centre. SP 0682
Moorhall Derbys 43 G4* loc 5m/9km NW of Chesterfield. SK 3074
Moorhampton H & W 25 H3 loc 9m/14km NW of Hereford. SO 3847
Moor Head W Yorks 48 D4* W dist of Shipley. SE 1337
Moor Head W Yorks 49 E5* loc 2m/3km NW of Morley. SE 2329
Moor, High Derbys 44 A3* loc 1km E of Killamarsh. SK 4680
Moor, High Lancs 42 B1* loc 2km NE of Parbold. SD 5011
Moor, High Lancs 47 E4* loc 4m/6km NW of Kirkham. SD 3836
Moorhole S Yorks 43 H3* loc in Sheffield 5m/8km SE of city centre. SK 4182
Moorhouse Cumbria 59 G6* loc 2m/3km N of Wigton. NY 2551
Moorhouse Cumbria 59 H5 ham 4m/7km W of Carlisle. NY 3356
Moorhouse Notts 44 C4 ham 3m/5km SE of Tuxford. SK 7566
Moorhouse S Yorks 49 F6* loc between S Emsall and Hampole. SE 4810
Moorhouses Lincs 45 F5* loc 2m/3km W of New Bolingbroke. TF 2857
Moorland Som 8 B2 loc on R Parrett 4m/6km SE of Bridgwater. Also known as Northmoor Green. ST 3332
Moorlands W Yorks 48 D5/49 E5* loc 4m/6km SE of Bradford. SE 2029
Moorlinch Som 8 C1 vil on S side of Polden Hills 5m/9km W of Street. ST 3936
Moor, Low Lancs 48 A4* loc 1m W of Clitheroe. SD 7341
Moor, Low W Yorks 48 D5* dist of Bradford 2m/4km S of city centre. SE 1628
Moor, Lower H & W 27 E3* vil 3m/4km E of Pershore. SO 9747
Moor Monkton N Yorks 50 A3 vil on R Nidd 7m/11km NW of York. SE 5056
Moor Park Herts 19 E2 loc 2km SE of Rickmansworth. Site of Roman bldg. Golf courses. TQ 0693
Moorpark S'clyde 64 C2* S dist of Renfrew. NS 5066
Moor Row Cumbria 52 A3 loc 2m/4km N of Egremont. NY 0014
Moor Row Cumbria 52 C1* loc 3m/5km W of Wigton. NY 2049
Moor Row Durham 54 B3* loc 1m SE of Winston. NZ 1515
Moors 9 H4* r rising near Verwood in Dorset and flowing S into R Stour at Blackwater to NE of Bournemouth. SZ 1395
Moorsholm Cleveland 55 E3 vil 5m/8km S of Saltburn. NZ 6814
Moor Side Cumbria 46 D1* loc 3m/5km N of Dalton-in-Furness. SD 2278
Moorside Cumbria 52 B4* loc 2km SE of Gosforth. NY 0701
Moorside Dorset 9 E3* loc 1m E of Marnhull and 3m/5km N of Sturminster Newton. ST 7919
Moorside Gtr Manchester 42 C2* loc to SW of Swinton tn centre. SD 7701
Moorside Gtr Manchester 43 E1 loc in Oldham 2m/4km NE of tn centre. SD 9507
Moor Side Lancs 47 E4* loc 2m/3km NE of Kirkham. SD 4334
Moor Side Lancs 47 F4* loc 2km E of Catforth. SD 4935
Moor Side Lancs 47 F5* loc 1km E of Walmer Br. SD 4824
Moor Side Lincs 45 F5 loc 5m/8km SE of Woodhall Spa. TF 2457
Moor Side W Yorks 48 D5 dist of Bradford 3m/5km S of city centre. SE 1528
Moorside W Yorks 49 E5* loc 3m/4km W of Morley. SE 2228
Moorside W Yorks 49 E4* loc in Leeds 4m/6km NW of city centre. SE 2435
Moor Side, Upper W Yorks 49 E5 loc in Leeds 4m/7km SW of city centre. SE 2430
Moorsley, High Tyne & Wear 54 C1* loc 2m/3km SW of Hetton-le-Hole. NZ 3345
Moorsley, Low Tyne & Wear 54 C1* vil 1m SW of Hetton-le-Hole. NZ 3446
Moor, South Durham 61 F6 SW dist of Stanley. NZ 1851
Moor Street Kent 20 D5 loc in E part of Gillingham. TQ 8265
Moor Street W Midlands 35 F6* loc in Birmingham 5m/8km SW of city centre. SO 9982
Moors, West Dorset 9 G4 built-up area 8m/12km N of Bournemouth. SU 0703
Moor, The Cambs 29 G3* loc adjoining Melbourn to N, 4m/6km NE of Royston. TL 3845
Moor, The Cumbria 52 B6* loc adjoining Millom to SW. SD 1679
Moor, The Kent 12 D4 vil adjoining Hawkhurst to S. TQ 7529
Moorthorpe W Yorks 49 F6* W dist of S Elmsall. SE 4611
Moorthwaite Cumbria 52 C1* loc at N end of **M. Lough,** small lake 2m/4km E of Wigton. NY 2948
Moorthwaite Cumbria 60 B6* loc 2km S of Cumwhitton. NY 5050
Moor Top W Yorks 49 E5* loc in Armley dist of Leeds 2m/3km W of city centre. SE 2733
Moortown Isle of Wight 10 B6* loc adjoining Brighstone to N and 2m/3km W of Shorwell. Site of Roman villa to N. SZ 4683
Moortown Lincs 45 E2 ham 3m/5km SW of Caistor. TF 0799
Moortown Salop 34 C3* loc 2m/3km NE of High Ercall. SJ 6118
Moortown W Yorks 49 E4* dist of Leeds 4m/6km N of city centre. SE 2939
Moor, Upper H & W 27 E3* ham 2m/3km NE of Pershore. SO 9747
Moor, West Tyne & Wear 61 G4* loc adjoining Longbenton to N. NZ 2770
Morangie H'land 87 A7/B7 loc in Ross and Cromarty dist on S shore of Dornoch Firth 2km NW of Tain. Distillery. **M. Forest** is state forest to SW. NH 7683
Morar H'land 79 E8, F8 coastal area of Lochaber dist lying between Loch Nevis to N and Loch nan Uamh to S, and divided into N and S Morar by Loch Morar, qv. Vil lies on neck of N Morar between foot of loch and estuary of r. NM 78,79
Morar H'land 79 E8* estuarial r flowing W from dam of Loch Morar, Lochaber dist, to sea 3m/4km S of Mallaig. See also Loch Morar. NM 6692
Moray 115 admin dist of Grampian region.
Moray Firth H'land 81 G2-H1 arm of North Sea extending to Inverness from a line drawn from Duncansby Hd to Fraserburgh. Above the narrows between Chanonry Pt and Fort George the firth is known as Inner Moray Firth or Inverness Firth, and above Inverness as Beauly Firth, which extends to mouth of R Beauly. Other important inlets on W side of Moray Firth are Dornoch and Cromarty Firths. NH 96
Morborne Cambs 37 F5 vil 6m/9km SW of Peterborough. TL 1391
Mor Brook 34 D5 r rising S of Much Wenlock, Salop, and flowing SE into R Severn 3m/5km S of Bridgnorth. SO 7388
Morchard Bishop Devon 7 F4 vil 6m/10km NW of Crediton. SS 7707
Morcombelake (or Morecombelake) Dorset 8 C5 vil 4m/6km W of Bridport. Biscuit factory. On E side of vil, Hardown Hill (NT). SY 4094
Morcott Leics 37 E4 vil 4m/6km E of Uppingham. SK 9200
Morda Salop 34 A2 vil 2km S of Oswestry. SJ 2827
Morda 34 A3 r rising 2m/3km S of Dolywern, near Llangollen, Clwyd, and following a meandering course southwards to flow into R Vyrnwy on English-Welsh border 2m/3km E of Llanymynech. SJ 2920
Morden Dorset 9 F4 vil 4m/7km E of Bere Regis. To S and W respectively, hams of **W** and **E Morden.** SY 9195
Morden London 19 F4 dist in borough of Merton 2km S of Wimbledon. To E, M. Hall (NT) and deer park intersected by R Wandle. TQ 2568
Morden Green Cambs 29 G3/G4* loc adjoining Steeple Morden to E, 4m/6km W of Royston. TL 2942
Morden Park London 19 F4* loc in borough of Merton 3m/4km S of Wimbledon, at SW corner of the park itself. TQ 2467
Mordiford H & W 26 B4 vil on R Lugg 4m/7km SE of Hereford. SO 5737
Mordon Durham 54 C2 ham 2m/4km SW of Sedgefield. NZ 3226
More Salop 34 A5 vil 2m/4km NE of Bishop's Castle. SO 3491
Morebath Devon 7 G3 vil 2m/3km N of Bampton. SS 9524
Morebattle Borders 67 E5/E6 vil 6m/10km SE of Kelso. 1km SE is Corbet Tower, stronghold of the Kers, destroyed in 16c, restored in 19c. NT 7724
Morecambe Lancs 47 E2 coastal resort 3m/5km NW of Lancaster. **M. Bay** extends westwards to Furness region of Cumbria. SD 4364
Morecombelake Dorset. See Morcombelake.
Moredon Wilts 17 F3* NW dist of Swindon. SU 1387
Moredun Lothian 66 A2* dist of Edinburgh 3m/5km SE of city centre. NT 2869
Morefield H'land 85 B7 locality on Loch Broom, Ross and Cromarty dist, 1m NW of Ullapool. NH 1195
More Hall Reservoir S Yorks 43 G2* resr 2km S of Stocksbridge. SK 2895
More Head Grampian 83 F1 headland on N coast 5m/8km E of Macduff. NJ 7865
Moreleigh Devon 4 D5 vil 5m/9km SW of Totnes. SX 7652
Moresby Cumbria 52 A3 loc 2m/3km N of Whitehaven. NX 9921

Moresby Parks Cumbria 52 A3* loc 2m/3km NE of Whitehaven. NX 9919
Morestead Hants 10 C2 vil 3m/5km SE of Winchester. SU 5025
Moreton Dorset 9 E5 vil on R Frome 4m/7km SE of Puddletown. SY 8089
Moreton Essex 20 B1 vil 3m/4km NW of Chipping Ongar. TL 5306
Moreton H & W 26 A2 ham 3m/5km N of Leominster. SO 5064
Moreton Merseyside 41 H3 SW dist of Wallasey. SJ 2689
Moreton Oxon 18 B1 vil 1m SW of Thame. SP 6904
Moreton Staffs 35 E3* loc 3m/5km SE of Newport. SJ 7817
Moreton Staffs 35 G2* loc 2km SE of Marchington. SK 1529
Moreton Corbet Salop 34 C2 vil 8m/12km NE of Shrewsbury. Ruins of Elizn hse incorporate parts of earlier cas (A.M.). SJ 5523
Moreton Hall, Little Ches 42 D5* moated black-and-white Tudor hse (NT) 3m/5km SW of Congleton. SJ 8358
Moretonhampstead Devon 7 F6 small mkt tn on E side of Dartmoor 11m/18km W of Exeter. 17c almshouses (NT). SX 7586
Moreton-in-Marsh Glos 27 F4 small tn of Cotswold stone 8m/12km NW of Chipping Norton. SP 2032
Moreton Jeffries H & W 26 B3* vil 5m/8km SW of Bromyard. SO 6048
Moretonmill Salop 34 C2* loc 2km NE of Shawbury. SJ 5722
Moreton Morrell Warwicks 27 G2 vil 6m/10km S of Leamington. SP 3155
Moreton, North Oxon 18 B3 vil 2m/4km E of Didcot. SU 5689
Moreton on Lugg H & W 26 A3 vil 4m/6km N of Hereford. SO 5045
Moreton Paddox Warwicks 27 G2* loc 3m/5km NW of Kineton. SP 3054
Moreton Pinkney Northants 28 B3 vil 9m/15km NE of Banbury. SP 5749
Moreton Say Salop 34 C1 vil 3m/5km W of Mkt Drayton. SJ 6234
Moreton, South Oxon 18 A3 vil 3m/4km SE of Didcot. SU 5688
Moreton Valence Glos 16 C1* vil 5m/8km NW of Stroud. SO 7809
Morfa Dyfed 23 E1* loc 1m SW of Llangranog. SN 3052
Morfa Dyfed 23 G4* loc 3m/5km W of Ammanford. SN 5713
Morfa Abererch Gwynedd 32 C1* marsh to E of Abererch across R Erch. SH 4136
Morfa Bychan Gwynedd 32 C1* loc 2m/3km SW of Portmadoc. SH 5437
Morfa Camp Gwynedd 32 D4* Army Outward Bound School on N side of Tywyn. SH 5701
Morfa Dinlle Gwynedd 40 B5* marshy peninsula on W side of Foryd Bay at SW end of Menai Strait. SH 4358
Morfa Glas W Glam 14 D1* loc adjoining Glyn-neath to W. SN 8706
Morfa Harlech Gwynedd 32 D2 area of marshland formerly under the sea, to N and W of Harlech. Fringed by sand dunes on W side. SH 53
Morfa Nefyn Gwynedd 32 B1 vil 2km W of Nefyn. SH 2840
Morfil Welsh form of Morvil, qv.
Morganstown (Treforgan) S Glam 15 F3* loc 5m/8km NW of Cardiff. ST 1281
Morgan's Vale Wilts 9 H2*loc adjoining Redlynch 7m/11km SE of Salisbury. ST 1921
Morham Lothian 66 C2 loc 3m/5km E of Haddington. NT 5572
Moriah Dyfed 24 B1* loc 3m/4km SE of Aberystwyth. SN 6279
Moricambe Bay Cumbria 59 F5 bay formed by estuaries of Rs Wampool and Waver NE of Silloth. NY 1656
Moridunum Dyfed. See Carmarthen.
Moriston H'land 80 D5 r in Inverness dist running E from Loch Cluanie down Glen M. to Loch Ness. Power stn for hydro-electricity scheme at Ceannacroc Br. NH 4216
Morlais 23 G5 r rising about 2km SE of Pontyberem, Dyfed, and flowing S into R Loughor on E side of Llangennech. SN 5701
Morland Cumbria 53 E3 vil 6m/9km W of Appleby and 7m/11km SE of Penrith. NY 5922
Morlas Brook 34 A1* stream rising in Clwyd 2m/4km W of Selattyn, Salop, and flowing E then N into R Ceiriog 2km E of Chirk. SJ 3138
Morley Derbys 36 A1 vil 4m/6km NE of Derby. SK 3940
Morley Durham 54 A2 loc 4m/6km W of W Auckland. NZ 1227
Morley W Yorks 49 E5 tn 4m/7km SW of Leeds. Textiles, engineering, coal-mining. SE 2627
Morley Green Ches 42 D3* ham 2m/3km NW of Wilmslow. SJ 8282
Morley Pond S Yorks 43 H2* small lake 3m/5km NW of Rotherham. SK 4096
Morley St Botolph Norfolk 39 E4/E5 vil 3m/4km W of Wymondham. TM 0799
Mornick Cornwall 3 G1* loc 3m/5km NW of Callington. SX 3272
Morningside Lothian 66 A2* dist of Edinburgh 2km S of city centre. NT 2471
Morningthorpe Norfolk 39 F5* vil 6m/10km N of Harleston, adjoining Fritton to W. Loc of **M. Green** to S. TM 2192
Mornish Mull, S'clyde 68 B3-C4 area lying E and SE of Caliach Pt. NM 3753
Morpeth Nthmb 61 F3/G3 mkt tn on R Wansbeck, on W edge of coal-mining area 14m/23km N of Newcastle upon Tyne. Agricultural engineering, iron founding, market gardening. Remains of motte and bailey cas. NZ 1986
Morralee Wood Nthmb 60 D5* wds (NT) running down steeply to E bank of R Allen opp Ridley, qv. NY 8063
Morrey Staffs 35 G3* ham 1m W of Yoxall. SK 1218
Morridge Side Staffs 43 E5* loc 3m/5km SE of Leek. SK 0254
Morrilow Heath Staffs 35 F1* loc 2m/4km E of Hilderstone. SJ 9835
Morriston Borders 66 D4 locs of **E** and **W Morriston,** 2m/3km SE of Legerwood. NT 6041
Morriston W Glam 23 H5 dist of Swansea 3m/5km N of tn centre. SS 6798
Morristown S Glam 15 F4/G4* loc adjoining Penarth to W. ST 1771
Morsgail Forest W Isles 88 A2, B2* upland tract, broken up by innumerable streams and small lochs, to W of Loch Langavat, Lewis. NB 11, 12
Morston Norfolk 39 E1 vil 2km W of Blakeney. TG 0043
Morte Bay Devon 6 C1 westward-facing bay between Morte Pt and Baggy Pt on N coast 5m/8km SW of Ilfracombe. SS 4442
Mortehoe Devon 6 C1 vil on N coast 4m/7km W of Ilfracombe. SS 4545
Morte Point Devon 6 C1 headland (NT) at N end of Morte Bay 5m/8km W of Ilfracombe. SS 4445
Mortham Tower Durham 54 A3* hse dating partly from 14c near confluence of R Tees and R Greta 3m/5km SE of Barnard Castle. NZ 0814
Morthen S Yorks 44 A2 vil 4m/6km SE of Rotherham. SK 4789
Mortimer Common Berks 18 B5 residential loc 7m/11km SW of Reading. SU 6564
Mortimer's Cross H & W 26 A2 loc on R Lugg 5m/9km NW of Leominster. Site of Wars of the Roses battle, 1461. SO 4263
Mortimer's Deep Fife 65 H1* passage between Inchcolm and mainland of Fife. NT 1883
Mortimer West End Hants 18 B5 vil 7m/11km N of Basingstoke. SU 6363
Mortlake London 19 F4 dist on S bank of R Thames between Chiswick Br and Barnes (rly) Br, in borough of Richmond. TQ 2075
Mortomley S Yorks 43 G2* loc adjoining High Green to SE. SK 3497
Morton Avon 16 B3* loc adjoining Thornbury to N. Hams of **Lr** and **Upr Morton** to N and NW respectively. ST 6490
Morton Cleveland 54 D3* loc 4m/6km W of Guisborough. NZ 5514
Morton Cumbria 52 D1* loc 2km W of Calthwaite. NY 4439
Morton Cumbria 59 H5* dist of Carlisle 2km SW of city centre. NY 3854
Morton Derbys 43 H5 vil 3m/5km N of Alfreton. SK 4060
Morton Isle of Wight 10 C6* loc adjoining Brading to S. SZ 6086
Morton Lincs 37 F2 vil 3m/4km N of Bourne. TF 0924
Morton Lincs 44 C2 suburb 2km N of Gainsborough. SK 8091
Morton Lincs 44 D4* loc 2m/3km SW of Thorpe on the Hill. **M. Hall** is HM Borstal Institution. SK 8863
Morton Norfolk 39 E3 ham 1km NW of Attlebridge. TG 1217
Morton Notts 44 C5 vil 2m/4km SE of Southwell. SK 7251
Morton Salop 34 A2 ham 4m/6km S of Oswestry. SJ 2924
Morton Bagot Warwicks 27 F2 vil 3m/4km W of Henley-in-Arden. SP 1164
Morton Castle D & G 58 D2 ruined cas on S shore of small **Morton Loch,** 3m/4km N of Thornhill. NX 8999
Morton, East W Yorks 48 D4 vil 2m/3km N of Bingley. **W Morton** loc 1km NW. SE 0941
Morton-on-Swale N Yorks 54 C5 vil 3m/5km SW of Northallerton. SE 3291
Morton Reservoir Lothian 65 G3* small resr 3m/4km S of Mid Calder. NT 0763
Morton Tinmouth Durham 54 B3* loc 4m/6km E of Staindrop. NZ 1821
Moruisg H'land 80 B3 mt on Glencarron Forest, Ross and Cromarty dist. Height 3026 ft or 922 metres. NH 1050
Morvah Cornwall 2 A5 vil 3m/5km NE of St Just. SW 4035
Morval Cornwall 3 G3 ham 2m/3km N of Looe. SX 2656
Morven Grampian 76 D1 mt 5m/8km N of Ballater. Height 2862 ft or 872 metres. NJ 3704
Morven H'land 86 C4 mt in Caithness dist 9m/14km N of Helmsdale. ND 0028
Morvern H'land 68 D3-F4 large peninsula in Lochaber dist, bounded on N by Loch Sunart, on SW by Sound of Mull, and on SE by Loch Linnhe. NM 65
Morvich H'land 80 A5 locality in Skye and Lochalsh dist near mouth of R Croe on E side of Loch Duich. Camping site (NTS) for tents and caravans. Adventure camp. NG 9620
Morvil (Morfil) Dyfed 22 C3 loc 5m/9km S of Newport. SN 0330
Morville Salop 34 D5 vil 3m/5km W of Bridgnorth. **M. Hall** (NT), Elizn hse with 18c additions. SO 6694
Morville Heath Salop 34 D5* loc 2m/3km W of Bridgnorth. SO 6893
Morwellham Devon 4 B4* vil on R Tamar 4m/6km SW of Tavistock. Former port for copper mines. SX 4469
Morwenstow Cornwall 6 B4 vil on coast 6m/10km N of Bude. SS 2015
Morwick Nthmb 61 G2 loc 2m/3km W of Amble. NU 2604
Morwynion 41 G6 r rising on N side of Llantysilio Mt, Clwyd, and flowing SW into R Dee at Carrog, E of Corwen. SJ 1143
Mosbrough S Yorks 43 H3 dist of Sheffield 6m/10km SE of city centre. SK 4281
Moscow S'clyde 64 C4 loc 4m/7km NE of Kilmarnock. NS 4840
Mosedale Cumbria 52 D2 ham 4m/7km S of Hesket Newmarket. NY 3532
Moselden Height W Yorks 48 C6* loc 3m/4km S of Barkisland. SE 0416
Moseley H & W 26 C2 ham 4m/6km NW of Worcester. SO 8159
Moseley W Midlands 35 F4 dist of Wolverhampton 2km E of tn centre. SO 9398
Moseley W Midlands 35 G6 dist of Birmingham 3m/4km S of city centre. SP 0783
Moseley W Midlands 35 F4 loc in Wolverhampton 4m/6km N of tn centre. To N in Staffs, **M. Old Hall** (NT), hse of Elizn origin in which Charles II hid after Battle of Worcester, 1651. SJ 9304
Moses Gate Gtr Manchester 42 C1* loc in N part of Farnworth. SD 7306
Mosley Common Gtr Manchester 42 C1/C2* loc 2m/3km E of Tyldesley. SD 7201
Mosleywell Salop 34 B1/C1 loc 5m/8km SW of Whitchurch. SJ 5035
Moss Clwyd 41 H5* loc 3m/4km NW of Wrexham. SJ 3053
Moss S Yorks 49 G6 vil 6m/9km W of Thorne. SE 5914
Mossat Grampian 82 D5 loc 2m/3km S of Lumsden. NJ 4719
Moss Bank Ches 42 B3* loc 2km E of Widnes tn centre. SJ 5385
Moss Bank Merseyside 42 B2* dist of St Helens 2km N of tn centre. SJ 5198
Mossbank Shetland 89 E6 vil on NE coast of Mainland opp island of Samphrey. HU 4575
Mossbay Cumbria 52 A2* S dist of Workington on **Moss Bay.** NX 9826
Mossbrow Gtr Manchester 42 C2/C3* ham 4m/6km W of Altrincham. SJ 7089
Mossburnford Borders 66 D6* loc 3m/5km S of Jedburgh. NT 6616
Mossdale D & G 58 C4* loc at site of former rly stn 5m/8km S of New Galloway. NX 6670
Moss Eccles Tarn Cumbria 52 D5* small lake 1m N of Far Sawrey. SD 3796
Moss End Berks 18 D4* ham 2m/4km N of Bracknell. SU 8672
Mossend S'clyde 65 E3 tn 2m/4km NW of Hamilton. Steel works. NS 7360
Mosser Cumbria 52 B3 loc 4m/6km S of Cockermouth. **M. Mains** loc adjoining to N. NY 1124
Mossergate Cumbria 52 B3* loc just S of Mosser. NY 1124
Moss Force Cumbria 52 C3* waterfall in Keskadale Beck 1m E of Buttermere ham. NY 1917
Moss, Great Gtr Manchester 42 B1 loc adjoining Orrell to S. SD 5203
Moss Houses Ches 42 D4* loc 1km E of Warren. SJ 8970
Mossley Ches 42 D5* loc in Congleton 2m/3km SE of tn centre. SJ 8861
Mossley Gtr Manchester 43 E1 tn 4m/6km SE of Oldham. Textiles, light engineering. SD 9702
Mossley Staffs 35 F3 loc adjoining Rugeley to S. SK 0417
Mossley Hill Merseyside 42 A3 dist of Liverpool 3m/5km SE of city centre. SJ 3887
Moss Nook Gtr Manchester 42 D3* loc in Manchester 8m/12km S of city centre and 3m/4km N of Wilmslow. SJ 8385
Mosspark S'clyde 64 C3* loc in Glasgow 3m/5km SW of city centre. NS 5463
Moss Side Ches 42 B3* loc in SW part of Warrington between R Mersey and Manchester Ship Canal. SJ 5685
Moss Side Cumbria 59 G6* loc 2m/3km NE of Abbey Tn. NY 1952
Moss Side Gtr Manchester 42 D2* dist of Manchester 2km S of city centre. SJ 8495
Moss Side Lancs 47 E5* loc 3m/5km NE of Lytham St Anne's. SD 3830
Moss Side Merseyside 42 A1/A2* loc adjoining Maghull to E. SD 3802
Mosstown Grampian 83 H1* loc 4m/6km SE of Fraserburgh. NK 0362
Mosswood Nthmb 61 F6* loc 3m/5km E of Edmondbyers. NZ 0650
Mossy Lea Lancs 42 B1* vil 5m/8km NW of Wigan. SD 5312
Mossy Moor Reservoir N Yorks 48 C2* small resr 1m N of Hebden. SE 0364
Mosterton Dorset 8 C4 vil 3m/5km SE of Crewkerne. ST 4505
Moston Gtr Manchester 42 D1* dist of Manchester 3m/5km NE of city centre. **New M.** loc 1m E. SD 8701
Moston Salop 34 C2* loc 1m SE of Lee Brockhurst. SJ 5626
Moston Green Ches 42 C5* loc 2m/3km W of Sandbach. SJ 7261
Mostyn Clwyd 41 G3 vil with small quay on R Dee estuary 3m/5km NW of Holywell. SJ 1580
Motcombe Wilts 9 F2 vil 2m/3km NW of Shaftesbury. ST 8425
Mote of Druchtag D & G 57 D7* early medieval earthwork on NE side of vil of Mochrum. NX 3446
Mote of Mark D & G. See Rockcliffe.
Mote of Urr D & G 58 D5 remains of Saxon–early Norman fortification, on W bank of Urr Water 2m/4km N of Dalbeattie. NX 8164
Mothecombe Devon 4 C5* ham near mouth of R Erme, 5m/9km S of Ivybridge. SX 6147
Motherby Cumbria 52 D2 ham 6m/9km W of Penrith. NY 4228
Motherwell S'clyde 65 E3 tn 12m/20km SE of Glasgow. Industries include iron and steel, engineering. NS 7557
Motspur Park London 19 F4* loc on borders of Kingston and Merton boroughs 3m/5km E of Kingston tn centre. TQ 2267
Mottingham London 20 B4 loc in borough of Bromley 2m/3km N of Bromley tn centre and 9m/15km SE of Charing Cross. TQ 4272
Mottisfont Hants 10 A2 vil on R Test 4m/6km NW of Romsey. M. Abbey (NT), remains of 12c priory incorporated in 18c hse. SU 3226

Mottistone Isle of Wight 10 B6 vil 3m/5km W of Shorwell. 17c manor hse, restored after being buried by landslip. SZ 4083
Mottram in Longdendale Gtr Manchester 43 E2 loc 3m/5km E of Hyde. SJ 9995
Mott's Mill E Sussex 12 B3* loc 2m/3km SW of Groombridge. TQ 5235
Mouldsworth Ches 42 B4* vil 3m/5km SE of Helsby. SJ 5171
Moulin Tayside 76 A5 vil 1km N of Pitlochry. To SE is Caisteal Dubh (or Castle Dhu), ruined former stronghold of the Campbells. NN 9459
Moul of Eswick Shetland. See Eswick.
Moulsecoomb E Sussex 12 A5 NW dist of Brighton, with **N Moulsecoomb.** TQ 3306
Moulsford Oxon 18 B3 vil on R Thames 2m/3km N of Streatley. SU 5983
Moulsoe Bucks 28 D3 vil 3m/4km SE of Newport Pagnell. SP 9041
Mouls, The Cornwall 3 E1 island opp W end of Portquin Bay on N coast, N of Polzeath. SW 9281
Moulton Ches 42 C4 vil 3m/4km S of Northwich. SJ 6569
Moulton Lincs 37 G2 vil 4m/6km E of Spalding. **M. Seas End** vil 2m/3km NE. TF 3024
Moulton Northants 28 C1 vil 4m/7km NE of Northampton. SP 7866
Moulton N Yorks 54 B4 vil 2m/3km SE of Scotch Corner. Manor hse and hall of 17c. NZ 2303
Moulton S Glam 15 F4* ham 2m/3km NW of Barry. Site of Roman bldg to S. ST 0770
Moulton Suffolk 30 C2 vil 4m/6km E of Newmarket. TL 6964
Moulton Chapel Lincs 37 G3 vil 4m/6km SE of Spalding. TF 2918
Moulton Eaugate Lincs 37 G3* loc 1m S of Moulton Chapel. TF 3016
Moulton, Great Norfolk 39 F5 vil 7m/11km NW of Harleston. TM 1690
Moulton St Mary Norfolk 39 G4 vil 2m/3km S of Acle. TG 3907
Mount Cornwall 3 F2 vil 5m/8km E of Bodmin. SX 1468
Mount Kent 13 G3 ham 6m/9km N of Hythe. TR 1643
Mount W Yorks 48 D6* loc in Huddersfield 3m/5km W of tn centre. SE 0918
Mountain W Yorks 48 D5 vil 1m NW of Queensbury. SE 0930
Mountain Ash (Aberpennar) Mid Glam 15 F2 tn in coal-mining dist 4m/6km SE of Aberdare. ST 0499
Mountain Cross Borders 65 G4 loc 3m/5km S of W Linton. NT 1446
Mountain, Lower Clwyd 41 H5* loc 1km N of Hope. SJ 3159
Mount Ambrose Cornwall 2 C4* loc 2km NE of Redruth. SW 7043
Mount Batten Point Devon 4 B5* promontory with fort opp Plymouth, between Cattewater and Plymouth Sound. SX 4853
Mount Battock 77 E3 mt on border of Grampian and Tayside regions 5m/8km NE of Tarfside. Height 2555 ft or 779 metres. NO 5484
Mount Blair Tayside 76 C4 mt 2km SW of Forter. Height 2441 ft or 744 metres. NO 1662
Mountblow S'clyde 64 C2* loc 2m/4km NW of Clydebank. NS 4771
Mount Bures Essex 30 D4 ham 1m S of Bures. TL 9032
Mount Charles Cornwall 3 E3 E dist of St Austell. SX 0252
Mount Edgcumbe Cornwall. See Cremyll.
Mountfield E Sussex 12 D4* vil 3m/5km N of Battle. Gypsum mines 2m/3km W. TQ 7420
Mountfleurie Fife 73 F4* W dist of Leven. NO 3701
Mount Florida S'clyde 64 C3/D3* loc in Glasgow 2m/4km S of city centre. NS 5861
Mount Gould Devon 4 B5* dist of Plymouth 2km E of city centre. SX 4955
Mount Grace Priory N Yorks 54 D5* remains of 14c priory (A.M. and NT) 1m NW of Osmotherley. SE 4598
Mount Hawke Cornwall 2 C4 vil 2m/3km S of St Agnes. SW 7147
Mount Howe Devon 5 F2* loc at confluence of Rs Clyst and Exe below Topsham, 5m/7km SE of Exeter. SX 9787
Mountjoy Cornwall 2 D2* ham 3m/5km SW of St Columb Major. SW 8760
Mount Keen 76 D2 mt on border of Grampian and Tayside regions 6m/10km SE of Ballater. Height 3081 ft or 939 metres. NO 4086
Mount Misery Cornwall 2 A5* W dist of Penzance. SW 4629
Mountnessing Essex 20 C2 vil 3m/5km NE of Brentwood. TQ 6397
Mounton Gwent 16 A2* ham 2km W of Chepstow. ST 5193
Mount Pleasant Berks 18 D4* loc 2m/4km NE of Bracknell. SU 8972
Mount Pleasant Bucks 28 C4* loc on S side of Buckingham. SP 6933
Mount Pleasant Bucks 28 D3* loc adjoining Stoke Goldington to N, 4m/7km NW of Newport Pagnell. SP 8349
Mount Pleasant Ches 42 D5* loc 2m/3km NE of Kidsgrove. SJ 8456
Mount Pleasant Cleveland 54 D3* loc in Stockton-on-Tees 2km N of tn centre. NZ 4420
Mount Pleasant Clwyd 41 H4* S dist of Flint. SJ 2472
Mount Pleasant Cornwall 3 E2* loc 5m/8km SW of Bodmin. SX 0062
Mount Pleasant Derbys 35 H3* loc 2m/3km SW of Swadlincote. SK 2817
Mount Pleasant Derbys 43 H5* loc 3m/4km NE of Alfreton. SK 4358
Mount Pleasant Derbys 43 H6 NW suburb of Belper. SK 3448
Mount Pleasant Durham 54 B2* loc adjoining Spennymoor to NE. NZ 2634
Mount Pleasant Dyfed 22 C5* loc 2km N of Cosheston. SN 0105
Mount Pleasant E Sussex 12 B5* loc 4m/7km N of Lewes. TQ 4216
Mount Pleasant Gtr Manchester 47 H6* loc in Bury 3m/5km N of tn centre. SD 8015
Mount Pleasant Hants 10 A5* loc 2m/3km NW of Lymington. SZ 2997
Mount Pleasant London 19 E3* loc in R Colne valley 3m/4km SW of Rickmansworth. TQ 0490
Mount Pleasant Mid Glam 15 F2* loc on R Taff 5m/8km S of Merthyr Tydfil. ST 0798
Mount Pleasant Norfolk 38 D5* loc 4m/6km W of Attleborough. TL 9994
Mount Pleasant Staffs 35 E1 loc in Stoke-on-Trent 1m SE of city centre. SJ 8844
Mount Pleasant Suffolk 30 C3* ham 4m/7km E of Haverhill. TL 7347
Mount Pleasant Suffolk 31 H1 N suburb of Southwold. TM 5077
Mount Pleasant Tyne & Wear 61 G5* dist of Gateshead 1m SE of tn centre. NZ 2661
Mount Pleasant W Midlands 35 E5 loc in Dudley 4m/7km SW of tn centre. SO 8887
Mount Pleasant W Yorks 49 E5* loc 1km S of Batley tn centre. SE 2423
Mounts Devon 4 D5* loc 3m/5km NE of Kingsbridge. SX 7548
Mount's Bay Cornwall 2 B5 wide bay on S coast stretching from Gwennap Hd on the W to Lizard Pt on the E. SW 5423
Mount Sion Clwyd 41 H5* loc 4m/6km NW of Wrexham. SJ 2953
Mount Skippitt Oxon 27 G5* loc 4m/7km N of Witney. SP 3515
Mountsorrel Leics 36 B3 vil 4m/7km SE of Loughborough. SK 5815
Mount Sorrel Wilts 9 G2* loc 1km W of Broad Chalke. SU 0324
Mountstuart S'clyde 63 G2 Victn mansion (1877) near E coast of Bute 4m/6km SE of Rothesay. Seat of Marquess of Bute. NS 1059
Mount Tabor W Yorks 48 C5 vil 3m/5km NW of Halifax. SE 0527
Mount Vernon S'clyde 64 D3* loc 4m/7km SE of Glasgow. **N Mount Vernon** adjoins to N. NS 6563
Mousa Shetland 89 E8 uninhabited island of about 3 sq km lying 1km off E coast of Mainland in vicinity of Sandwick, across **M. Sound.** See also Broch of M. HU 4624
Mouse, East (Ynys Amlwch) Gwynedd 40 B2* island rock lying off N coast of Anglesey opp E end of Bull Bay. SH 4494
Mousehill Surrey 11 E1 loc adjoining Milford to S. SU 9441
Mousehold Heath Norfolk 39 F4* open space 2km NE of Norwich city centre, commanding extensive views. TG 2410
Mousehole Cornwall 2 A5 vil on coast 2m/3km S of Penzance across bay. SW 4626
Mouse, Middle (Ynys Badrig) Gwynedd 40 B2* island rock lying about 1km NW of Llanlleiana Hd, Anglesey. SH 3895
Mouse Water 65 E4 r in Strathclyde region rising 2m/3km SE of Forth and running SW into R Clyde 1m W of Lanark. NS 8643
Mouse, West (Maen y Bugael) Gwynedd 40 A2* island rock with beacon light about 2km N of Anglesey coast at Carmel Hd. SH 3094
Mousley End Warwicks 27 F1* loc 5m/9km NW of Warwick. SP 2169
Mouswald D & G 59 F4 vil 6m/10km E of Dumfries. NY 0672
Mow Cop 42 D5 loc on border of Ches and Staffs 2m/3km NE of Kidsgrove. On hill (NT) is artificial ruin built 1750, commanding views over Cheshire Plain. **Old Man of Mow** (NT), rock N of summit. SJ 8557
Mowhaugh Borders 67 E6 loc 4m/6km SE of Morebattle. NT 8120
Mowsley Leics 36 C5 vil 3m/5km N of Husbands Bosworth. SP 6489
Moxley W Midlands 35 F4 SW dist of Walsall. SO 9695
Moy H'land 81 G4 vil in Inverness dist on W side of Loch Moy and 9m/15km SE of Inverness. NH 7634
Moycroft Grampian 82 B1* E dist of Elgin. NJ 2262
Moylgrove (Trewyddel) Dyfed 22 D2 vil 4m/6km W of Cardigan. SN 1144
Moyse's Hall Suffolk. See Bury St Edmunds.
Muasdale S'clyde 62 D4 vil on W coast of Kintyre 3m/4km N of Glenbarr. NR 6740
Muchalls Grampian 77 H2 vil on E coast 4m/7km N of Stonehaven. Red sandstone cliffs. Bridge of M. is loc 1km S. NO 9092
Much Birch H & W 26 A4 vil 6m/10km S of Hereford. SO 5030
Much Cowarne H & W 26 B3* vil 5m/8km SW of Bromyard. SO 6247
Much Dewchurch H & W 26 A4 vil 6m/9km S of Hereford. SO 4831
Muchelney Som 8 C2 vil 2km S of Langport. Remains of medieval abbey (A.M.). Late medieval Priest's Hse (NT). 1m SE, ham of **M. Hamlet.** ST 4324
Much Hadham Herts 29 H5 vil 4m/6km W of Bishop's Stortford. TL 4219
Much Hoole Lancs 47 F5 vil 6m/10km SW of Preston. **M. H. Moss Hses** loc 2km E. **M. H. Moss Tn** loc 1km E. **Lit Hoole Moss Hses** loc 2m/3km NE. SD 4622
Muchlarnick Cornwall 3 G3* ham 3m/5km NW of Looe. SX 2156
Much Marcle H & W 26 B4 vil 7m/11km NE of Ross-on-Wye. SO 6532
Much Wenlock Salop 34 C4 small tn at NE end of Wenlock Edge 8m/12km NW of Bridgnorth. Ruined priory (A.M.). Half-timbered guildhall. SO 6299
Muck H'land 68 C2 sparsely populated island in Inner Hebrides lying 3m/5km SW of Eigg across Sound of Eigg. Area about 2 sq miles or 5 sq km. Rises to height of 451 ft or 137 metres. See also Port Mór. NM 4179
Muck Fleet 39 G4/H4* channel connecting Ormesby, Rollesby, and Filby Broads, Norfolk, with R Bure 2km E of Acle. TG 4210
Mucking Essex 20 C3 loc 1km S of Stanford le Hope. TQ 6881
Muckingford Essex 20 C4 loc 3m/5km NE of Tilbury. TQ 6779
Muckle Flugga Shetland (N of 89 F5) small rocky island 1km N of Unst. Lighthouse. HP 6019
Muckleford Dorset 8 D5* loc beside R Frome 4m/6km NW of Dorchester. SY 6493
Muckle Green Holm Orkney 89 B6* small uninhabited island 2km SW of War Ness at S end of island of Eday. Smaller island of Lit Green Holm to S. HY 5227
Muckle Holm Shetland 89 E6* small uninhabited island in Yell Sound 2m/3km E of Burra Voe. HU 4088
Muckle Ness Shetland 89 E7* headland on E coast of Mainland on S side of Dury Voe. HU 4661
Muckle Ossa Shetland 89 D6* rock off NW coast of Mainland 2m/4km W of The Faither. Lit Ossa rock is adjacent to S. HU 2285
Muckle Roe Shetland 89 E6, E7 inhabited island of some 7 sq miles or 18 sq km off W coast of Mainland in St Magnus Bay, connected to Mainland by br across Roe Sound. Has high, red cliffs. HU 3264
Muckle Skerry Orkney 89 B8* one of the Pentland Skerries, qv. Muckle Skerry is the largest of the group, with a lighthouse. ND 4678
Muckle Skerry of Neapaback Shetland 89 F6* island rock off Heoga Ness at SE end of Yell. HU 5378
Mucklestone Staffs 34 D1 vil 4m/6km NE of Mkt Drayton. SJ 7237
Muckleton Salop 34 C2* loc 2m/4km E of Shawbury. SJ 5921
Muckley Salop 34 D4* loc 3m/5km SE of Much Wenlock. SO 6495
Muckley Corner Staffs 35 G4 ham 3m/5km SW of Lichfield. SK 0806
Muckton Lincs 45 G3 vil 5m/8km SE of Louth. TF 3781
Muckwell Devon 5 E6* loc 2m/3km NW of Start Pt. SX 8039
Mudale H'land 84 F4 r running E into head of Loch Naver in Caithness dist. NC 5735
Mudd Gtr Manchester 43 E2* loc adjoining Mottram in Longdendale to S. SJ 9994
Muddiford Devon 6 D2 vil 3m/5km N of Barnstaple. Ham of **Hr Muddiford** to W. SS 5638
Muddles Green E Sussex 12 B5 ham 4m/6km NW of Hailsham. TQ 5413
Mudeford Dorset 9 H5 seaside dist of Christchurch 2m/3km E of tn centre. SZ 1892
Mudford Som 8 D2 vil on R Yeo 3m/4km NE of Yeovil. To NW, ham of **W Mudford.** To S, **Up Mudford.** To W, **Mudford Sock.** ST 5719
Mudgley Som 16 A6* loc 2km SE of Wedmore. ST 4445
Mugdock Central 64 C2 locality 2km S of Strathblane. **M. Loch** is small loch nearly 1km W. On W shore of loch are remains of **M. Castle,** formerly seat of Montrose family. **M. Resr** is small resr to S. NS 5576
Mugdrum Island Fife 73 E3 narrow low-lying island, 1m long E to W, in Firth of Tay NW of Newburgh. NO 2218
Mugginton Derbys 35 H1 vil 6m/10km NW of Derby. SK 2843
Muggintonlane End Derbys 43 G6* loc 2km N of Mugginton. SK 2844
Muggleswick Durham 61 E6 ham 4m/6km W of Consett. NZ 0450
Mugswell Surrey 19 F6* loc 3m/5km N of Reigate. TQ 2654
Muick 76 D2 r in Grampian region running NE from Loch M. down Glen M. to R Dee 1km S of Ballater. NO 3694
Muie H'land 85 F6 loc in Sutherland dist 6m/9km E of Lairg. NC 6604
Muirdrum Tayside 73 H1 vil 2m/3km N of Carnoustie. NO 5637
Muiredge Fife 73 F4* W dist of Buckhaven. NT 3598
Muirend S'clyde 64 C3* loc in Cathcart dist of Glasgow 4m/6km S of city centre. NS 5759
Muirfield Lothian. See Gullane.
Muirhead S'clyde 64 D2 vil 4m/6km NW of Coatbridge. NS 6869
Muirhead S'clyde 64 D3* loc in suburb of Baillieston, E of Glasgow. NS 6763
Muirhead Tayside 73 F1/F2 vil 5m/8km NW of Dundee. NO 3434
Muirhead Reservoir S'clyde 64 A3 resr 4m/6km SE of Largs. NS 2556
Muirhouse Lothian 66 A1* dist of Edinburgh 3m/5km NW of city centre. NT 2176
Muirhouses Central 65 F1* loc 2km SE of Bo'ness. NT 0180
Muirkirk S'clyde 56 F2 tn on R Ayr 9m/15km NE of Cumnock. Coal-mining, iron works. Cairn to S marks site of McAdam's original tar works. NS 6927
Muir of Dinnet Grampian 77 E2* flat area to W of Dinnet. NO 4397
Muir of Fowlis Grampian 82 D5 vil 3m/4km S of Alford. NJ 5612
Muir of Miltonduff Grampian 82 B1/B2 loc with distillery 3m/4km SW of Elgin. NJ 1859
Muir of Orchill Tayside 72 C3 moorland tract 3m/5km S of Muthill. NN 8612
Muir of Ord H'land 81 E3 vil in Ross and Cromarty dist 3m/4km N of Beauly. Distillery 1km NW. NH 5250

Muir of Thorn Tayside 72 D1* wooded area 4m/6km SE of Dunkeld. NO 0737
Muir Park Reservoir Central 71 F5* small resr 2m/3km N of Drymen. NS 4892
Muirshearlich H'land 74 C3 loc on NW side of Caledonian Canal in Lochaber dist, 5m/7km NE of Fort William. NN 1380
Muirton Tayside 73 E2* N dist of Perth. NO 1124
Muirton of Ardblair Tayside 73 E1 vil 2km S of Blairgowrie. NO 1743
Muirtown Grampian 82 A2* loc 3m/4km W of Forres. NH 9959
Muirtown H'land 81 F3 loc on NW side of Inverness. **M. Basin** at entrance to Caledonian Canal. NH 6546
Muirtown Tayside 72 C3 vil 2m/3km SW of Auchterarder. NN 9211
Muker N Yorks 53 H5 vil on M. Beck close to its confluence with R Swale and 8m/13km W of Reeth. SD 9097
Mulbarton Norfolk 39 F4 vil with large green 5m/8km SW of Norwich. TG 1901
Mulben Grampian 82 C2* loc 5m/8km W of Keith. Distillery 2km E. NJ 3550
Muldoanich W Isles 88 D4 uninhabited island lying 2m/3km E of SE point of Vatersay. NL 6893
Mule (Miwl) 33 H5 r rising 1m S of Dolfor, Powys, and flowing NE into R Severn at Abermule. SO 1594
Mulgrave Castle N Yorks 55 F4 remains of medieval cas in Mulgrave Wds 2km SW of Sandsend. A later, 18c-19c, Mulgrave Castle stands 1km NE. NZ 8311
Mull S'clyde 68, 69 island of Inner Hebrides lying off W coast of Scottish mainland opp entrance to Loch Linnhe, and separated from mainland by Firth of Lorne and the narrow Sound of M. Area about 350 sq miles or 910 sq km. Coastline rugged, and much indented on W side. Terrain mountainous, reaching 3169 ft or 966 metres in Ben More, qv. Chief tn is Tobermory, qv. Industries include agriculture, forestry, fishing, tourism, quarrying. See also Ross of M., Sound of M., Gometra, Iona, Ulva. NM 63
Mullach an Rathain H'land 80 A2* one of the peaks of Liathach, Ross and Cromarty dist. Height 3358 ft or 1023 metres. NG 9157
Mullach Clach a' Bhlàir H'land 76 A2 mt in Cairngorms, in Badenoch and Strathspey dist, 8m/12km SW of Ben Macdui. Height 3343 ft or 1019 metres. NN 8892
Mullach Coire Mhic Fhearchair H'land 85 B8* mt in W part of Ross and Cromarty dist 3m/5km E of head of Lochan Fada. Height 3343 ft or 1019 metres. NH 0573
Mullach Coire nan Geur-oirean H'land 74 B3 mt on Locheil Forest, Lochaber dist, 4m/7km SE of head of Loch Arkaig. Height 2373 ft or 723 metres. NN 0489
Mullach Fraoch-choire H'land 80 B5 mt on Glenaffric Forest, Inverness dist, 4m/6km SW of head of Loch Affric. Height 3614 ft or 1102 metres. NH 0917
Mullach Lochan nan Gabhar Grampian 76 C1* one of the peaks of Ben Avon, qv, N of Braemar. Height 3625 ft or 1105 metres. NJ 1402
Mullach nan Coirean H'land 74 C4 mt in Lochaber dist 5m/8km S of Fort William. Height 3077 ft or 938 metres. NN 1266
Mullacott Cross Devon 6 D1* loc 2m/3km S of Ilfracombe. SS 5144
Mull Head Orkney 89 B5 headland at N end of island of Papa Westray. HY 5055
Mull Head Orkney 89 C6 headland at E extremity of Mainland beyond Deer Sound. HY 5909
Mullion Cornwall 2 C6 vil 5m/8km S of Helston. Coast to W and SW largely NT, incl **M. Cove** and **M. Island.** SW 6719
Mull of Cara S'clyde 62 D3 headland at S end of island of Cara, qv. NR 6343
Mull of Galloway D & G 57 B8 bold headland, with high cliffs and a lighthouse, at S extremity of Rinns of Galloway. Southernmost point of Scotland. NX 1530
Mull of Kintyre S'clyde 62 D6 headland at SW end of Kintyre, 9m/14km S of Machrihanish. Mull Lighthouse to N. NR 5907
Mull of Logan D & G. See Port Logan.
Mull of Oa S'clyde 62 A4 headland at SW end of The Oa, Islay. Monmt commemorates those who died in two American troopships in 1918. NR 2641
Mullwharchar S'clyde 56 E4* mt 3m/4km W of Corserine. Height 2270 ft or 692 metres. NX 4586
Mulwith N Yorks 49 F2* loc 2m/3km W of Boroughbridge across R Ure. SE 3666
Mumbles (or **The Mumbles**) W Glam 23 G6 dist of Swansea to W and NW of Mumbles Hd. Seaside resort. SS 6188
Mumbles Head W Glam 23 G6 headland at W end of Swansea Bay consisting of two island rocks connected to mainland by causeway. Outer rock has lighthouse. SS 6387
Mumby Lincs 45 H4 vil 4m/6km E of Alford. TF 5174
Mumps Gtr Manchester 43 E1 loc in Oldham 1km E of tn centre. SD 9305
Muncaster Cumbria 52 B5 loc 2km E of Ravenglass. **M. Castle,** 19c cas by Salvin, incorporating parts of medieval bldg, incl peel tower. SD 1096
Munden, Little Herts 29 G5* loc 4m/6km W of Puckeridge. TL 3321
Munderfield Row H & W 26 B3 ham 2m/4km S of Bromyard. SO 6551
Munderfield Stocks H & W 26 B3* ham 3m/5km S of Bromyard. SO 6550
Mundesley Norfolk 39 G2 coastal resort 4m/7km NE of N Walsham. TG 3136
Mundford Norfolk 38 C5 vil 5m/8km N of Brandon. TL 8093
Mundham Norfolk 39 G5 vil 2m/4km W of Loddon. TM 3297
Mundham, North W Sussex 11 E4 vil 2m/3km SE of Chichester. SU 8702
Mundham, South W Sussex 11 E5 vil 3m/5km S of Chichester. SU 8700
Mundon Creek Essex 21 E2* inlet 4m/7km SE of Maldon, leading into Lawling Creek and thence into R Blackwater. TL 9002
Mundon Hill Essex 21 E2 vil 3m/5km SE of Maldon. TL 8602
Mu Ness Shetland 89 D7 headland on W coast of Mainland 4m/6km S of Melby. HU 1652
Mu Ness Shetland 89 F5 headland at SE end of Unst 3m/5km E of Uyeasound. **Muness Castle** (A.M.), late 16c, 1km W. HP 6301
Munga Skerries Shetland 89 E6* group of rocks off NW coast of Mainland 2m/3km NE of entrance to Ronas Voe. HU 2987
Mungrisdale Cumbria 52 D2 ham 8m/12km NE of Keswick. NY 3630
Munlochy H'land 81 F2 vil in Ross and Cromarty dist at head of **M. Bay,** inlet on W side of Inner Moray Firth or Inverness Firth. NH 6453
Munnoch Reservoir S'clyde 64 A4 resr 4m/6km N of Ardrossan. NS 2547
Munsley H & W 26 B3* ham 4m/6km NW of Ledbury. SO 6640
Munslow Salop 34 C5 vil 6m/10km NE of Craven Arms. SO 5287
Munslow Aston Salop 34 C5* ham 6m/9km NE of Craven Arms. SO 5186
Munstead Heath Surrey 11 F1 loc 2km SE of Godalming. SU 9842
Munstone H & W 26 A3* loc 2m/3km N of Hereford. SO 5142
Murch S Glam 15 F4* loc adjoining Dinas Powis to E. ST 1671
Murchington Devon 7 E6 ham 5m/7km NW of Moretonhampstead. SX 6888
Murcott Oxon 28 B6 ham 4m/7km S of Bicester. SP 5815
Murcott Wilts 16 D2* loc 3m/5km NE of Malmesbury. ST 9591
Murdishaw Ches 42 B3* E dist of Runcorn. SJ 5681
Murdoch Head Grampian 83 H3 headland on E coast 4m/7km S of Peterhead. NK 1239
Murieston Lothian 65 G2 residential area of Livingston 2m/3km S of tn centre. NT 0665
Murkle H'land 86 E1 loc near N coast of Caithness dist 3m/5km E of Thurso. ND 1668
Murraster Shetland 89 D7* locality on Mainland 2m/3km N of Gruting. **Loch of Murraster** to N. HU 2751
Murrax S'clyde 64 D3* dist of E Kilbride to S of tn centre. NS 6353
Murrayfield Lothian 66 A2* dist of Edinburgh 2m/3km W of city centre. Rugby Union football ground in S part of dist. NT 2273
Murray's Isles D & G 58 B6 two most northerly of Islands of Fleet, at entrance to Fleet Bay from Wigtown Bay. NX 5649
Murrell Green Hants 18 C5* loc 2km NE of Hook. SU 7455
Murrow Cambs 37 H4 vil 6m/9km W of Wisbech. TF 3707
Mursley Bucks 28 C4/C5 vil 3m/5km E of Winslow. SP 8128
Murthly Tayside 72 D1 vil 5m/8km SE of Dunkeld. County mental hospital. **M. Castle** stands in wooded grnds beside R Tay 2m/3km NW. NO 0938
Murton Cumbria 53 F3 vil at foot of fells 3m/5km E of Appleby. NY 7221
Murton Durham 61 H6 coal-mining tn 3m/4km SW of Seaham. NZ 3947
Murton N Yorks 50 B3 vil 3m/5km E of York. SE 6452
Murton N Yorks 54 D6 loc 5m/9km NW of Helmsley. SE 5388
Murton W Glam 23 G6* loc 3m/5km W of Mumbles Hd. SS 5889
Musbury Devon 8 B5 vil 3m/5km SW of Axminster. SY 2794
Muscliff Dorset 9 G4* N dist of Bournemouth. SZ 0995
Muscoates N Yorks 55 E6 loc 5m/8km SE of Helmsley. SE 6880
Musgrave, Great Cumbria 53 G3 vil 2m/3km SW of Brough. **Lit Musgrave** ham 1km SW. NY 7613
Mushroom Castle Berks 18 D4* loc 2m/3km NE of Bracknell. SU 8970
Mushroom Green W Midlands 35 F5* loc in Dudley 2m/4km S of tn centre. SO 9386
Muskham, North Notts 44 C5 vil on R Trent 3m/5km N of Newark-on-Trent. **S Muskham** vil 1m S. SK 7958
Mussel Brook 6 D4* stream rising 2km SW of Peters Marland and flowing S into R Torridge 1km W of Sheepwash, Devon. SS 4706
Musselburgh Lothian 66 B2 tn on Firth of Forth at mouth of R Esk, 6m/9km E of Edinburgh. Industries include fishing, mkt gardening, mnfre of nets, wire. Coal-mining to SW. Tn contains boys' public school of Loretto. Tolbooth, late 16c. Racecourse. NT 3472
Mussel End Glos 26 C5* loc between vil of Sandhurst and R Severn, 3m/5km N of Gloucester. SO 8223
Mussel Point Cornwall 2 A4* headland on N coast 1m SW of Carn Naun Pt. SW 4640
Mustard Hyrn Norfolk 39 H3* loc 1m W of Martham. TG 4418
Muston Leics 36 D1 vil 6m/9km W of Grantham. SK 8237
Muston N Yorks 51 E1 vil 2km SW of Filey. TA 0979
Mustow Green H & W 26 D1* ham 3m/5km SE of Kidderminster. SO 8874
Muswell Hill London 19 G3* loc in borough of Haringey 6m/10km N of Charing Cross. TQ 2890
Mutford Suffolk 39 H6 vil 4m/7km E of Beccles. TM 4888
Muthill Tayside 72 C3 vil 3m/5km S of Crieff. Ruined 15c ch with 12c tower (A.M.). NN 8617
Mutley Devon 4 B5* dist of Plymouth 1m N of city centre. SX 4855
Mutterton Devon 7 H4* loc 2m/3km SE of Cullompton. ST 0305
Muttonhole Lothian. Former name of Davidson's Mains, qv.
Muxton Salop 34 D3* loc 2m/4km N of Oakengates. SJ 7114
Mybster H'land 86 E2 loc in Caithness dist 5m/8km W of Watten. ND 1652
Myddfai Dyfed 24 D5 ham 3m/5km S of Llandovery. SN 7730
Myddle Salop 34 B2 vil 7m/12km N of Shrewsbury. Slender remains of medieval cas. SJ 4623
Myddlewood Salop 34 B2 loc 8m/12km NW of Shrewsbury. SJ 4523
Myddyfi 23 G3* r rising 3m/5km N of Llandeilo, Dyfed, and flowing SW into R Towy 2m/3km W thereof. SN 5922
Mydroilyn Dyfed 24 A3 vil 5m/8km S of Aberaeron. SN 4555
Mydyr 24 B2* r rising S of Mydroilyn, Dyfed, and flowing N through the vil and continuing N into R Aeron at Llanayron. SN 4760
Myerscough Lancs 47 F4* loc 2m/3km NW of Barton. SD 4939
Myerscough Smithy Lancs 47 F5* loc 4m/7km NW of Blackburn. SD 6131
Myherin 24 D1* r rising 4m/7km NE of Devil's Br, Dyfed, and flowing SW to join R Rhuddnant and form R Mynach 2m/3km E of Devil's Br. SN 7677
Mylnefield Tayside. Alternative spelling of Milnefield – see Invergowrie.
Mylor Cornwall 2 D4 vil, sometimes known as M. Churchtown, situated at mouth of **M. Creek,** 2m/3km E of Penryn. At head of creek is the large vil of **Mylor Br.** SW 8235
Mynach 24 C1* r formed by junction of Rs Myherin and Rhuddnant, qv, and flowing W to R Rheidol on N side of Devil's Br, Dyfed. SN 7477
Mynach 33 F1 stream running S into R Tryweryn 2m/4km NW of Bala, Gwynedd. SH 9039
Mynachdy S Glam 15 F3* loc in Cardiff 2m/3km NW of city centre. ST 1679
Mynach Falls Dyfed 24 C1* series of waterfalls in R Mynach near its confluence with R Rheidol at Devil's Br. SN 7477
Mynachlog-ddu Dyfed 22 D3 loc 3m/5km SW of Crymmych. SN 1430
Myndtown Salop 34 B5 ham 4m/7km E of Bishop's Castle. SO 3989
Mynwar Welsh form of Minwear, qv.
Mynwent y Crynwyr Welsh form of Quaker's Yard, qv.
Mynwy Welsh form of (R) Monnow, qv.
Mynydd Alltir-fach Gwent 16 A2* loc at S end of Wentwood Resr 2km W of Llanvair Discoed. ST 4292
Mynydd-bach Gwent 16 A2* vil just N of Shirenewton. ST 4894
Mynydd-bach W Glam 23 G5* loc on W side of Morriston, 3m/4km N of Swansea tn centre. SS 6597
Mynydd Ddu Forest 25 G5* afforested area on borders of Powys and Gwent in Black Mts, its northern edge reaching almost to the summit of Pen-y-Gader-fawr. SO 22
Mynydd Du, Y Welsh form of Black Mountain, qv.
Mynydd Epynt Powys 25 E3/E4 wild moorland area SW of Builth Wells. Artillery range. Watershed of rivers running southwards into R Usk. SN 94
Mynydd Hiraethog Clwyd 41 F5 desolate upland between Bylchau and Pentrefoelas. SH 95
Mynydd Isa Clwyd 41 H5* loc adjoining Buckley to W. SJ 2564
Mynyddislwyn Gwent 15 G2* loc 2m/3km SW of Abercarn. ST 1994
Mynydd-llan Clwyd 41 G4* loc 3m/5km SW of Holywell. SJ 1572
Mynydd Mawr Gwynedd 40 C5 mt 1m W of Llyn Cwellyn. Height 2290 ft or 698 metres. SH 5354
Mynydd Moel Gwynedd 33 E3* E peak of Cader Idris. Height 2804 ft or 855 metres. SH 7213
Mynydd Pencarreg Dyfed 24 B4 hill 3m/5km SE of Pencarreg, qv. WT stn near summit. SN 5743
Mynydd Pen-y-fal Welsh form of Sugar Loaf (Gwent), qv.
Mynydd Presely Dyfed 22 C3, D3 hill ridge running E to W for some 6m/10km, to S and SE of Newport. Also known as Mynydd Prescelly. See also Prescelly Top (Foel Cwm-cerwyn). SN 0313
Mynydd Twr Welsh form of Holyhead Mt, qv.
Mynydd y Dref Welsh form of Conwy Mt. See Conwy.
Mynydd-y-garreg Clwyd. See Whitford.
Mynyddygarreg Dyfed 23 F5* loc 2km NE of Kidwelly. SN 4208
Mynys 24 C5* r rising near Porthyrhyd, Dyfed, and flowing S into R Towy 3m/5km SW of Llandovery. SN 7231
Mynytho Gwynedd 32 B2 loc 2m/3km W of Llanbedrog. SH 3030
Myres Castle Fife 73 E3 cas on S side of Auchtermuchty, dating from 17c. NO 2411
Mytchett Surrey 18 D5* suburban loc 2km NE of Farnborough. SU 8855
Mythe, The Glos 26 D4 ham 1m N of Tewkesbury. SO 8934
Mytholm W Yorks 48 C5 vil 1km W of Hebden Br. SD 9827
Mytholmes W Yorks 48 C4* loc 1m NE of Haworth. SE 0338
Mytholmroyd W Yorks 48 C5 tn on R Calder 2m/3km SE of Hebden Br. SE 0126
Mythop Lancs 47 E4* loc 4m/6km E of Blackpool. SD 3634

Myton-on-Swale N Yorks 49 F2 vil on left bank of R Swale near its confluence with R Ure and 2m/4km S of Brafferton. SE 4366

Mytton Salop 34 B3* ham 1km SW of Fitz. SJ 4417

N

Nab Head, The Dyfed 22 A4 headland on S side of St Brides Bay 8m/13km W of Milford Haven. SM 7911

Nab's Head Lancs 47 G5* loc 2m/4km SW of Mellor. SD 6229

Naburn N Yorks 49 G4 vil on E bank of R Ouse 4m/6km S of York. 1m S is Bell Hall, hse of 1680. SE 5945

Nab Wood W Yorks 48 D4* residential dist in W part of Shipley. SE 1337

Nackington Kent 13 G2 ham 2m/3km S of Canterbury. TR 1554

Nacton Suffolk 31 F4 vil 5m/8km SE of Ipswich. TM 2240

Na Cùiltean S'clyde 62 C2 group of rocks with lighthouse about 2km SE of Rubha na Caillich on E coast of Jura. NR 5366

Nadder 9 H2* r rising to E of Shaftesbury and flowing E into R Avon at Salisbury, Wilts. SU 1429

Nadderwater Devon 7 G5* ham beside Nadder Brook 2m/3km W of Exeter. SX 8993

Nadroedd 33 F2* r rising in Gwynedd and running SE to join R Eiddew before flowing into N end of Lake Vyrnwy, Powys. SH 9624

Nafferton Humberside 51 E2/E3 vil 2m/3km NE of Gt Driffield. TA 0559

Na Glas Leacan H'land 84 D1 group of islets off N coast of Sutherland dist 3m/5km W of Faraid Hd (or Far Out Hd) across entrance to Balnakeil Bay. Also known as Eileanan nan Glas Leac. NC 3472

Na Gruagaichean H'land 74 D5* mt on Mamore Forest in Lochaber dist 2m/4km NE of Kinlochleven. Height 3460 ft or 1055 metres. NN 2065

Nail Bourne Kent 13 G1* r rising at Lyminge, Kent, and flowing N into R Lit Stour 2km N of Wingham. TR 2359

Nailbridge Glos 26 B5 vil 2m/3km N of Cinderford. SO 6416

Nailsbourne Som 8 A2* ham 3m/4km N of Taunton. ST 2128

Nailsea Avon 16 A4 small tn 7m/11km W of Bristol. ST 4770

Nailstone Leics 36 A4 vil 5m/7km S of Coalville. **Nailstone Wiggs** coal-mining loc 1m NE. SK 4107

Nailsworth Glos 16 D2 hilly tn 4m/6km S of Stroud. ST 8599

Nairn H'land 81 H2 tn and resort in Nairn dist, at mouth of r of same name, on S side of Moray Firth 7m/12km E of Fort George. Dairy products, fishing. R rises NW of Beinn Bhreac Mhor about 10m/16km E of Foyers on Loch Ness and flows NE down Strathnairn to coast at Nairn. NH 8856

Nancegollan Cornwall 2 C5* loc 3m/5km NW of Helston. SW 6332

Nancekuke Cornwall 2 C4* ham 2km NE of Portreath. SW 6745

Nancledra Cornwall 2 B5* loc 3m/5km S of St Ives. SW 4936

Nanhoron Gwynedd 32 B2* loc 6m/10km SW of Pwllheli. SH 2831

Nanmor 32 D1* stream in Gwynedd running SW into R Glaslyn 4m/6km NE of Portmadoc. SH 5943

Nannerch Clwyd 41 G4 vil 4m/7km S of Holywell. SJ 1669

Nanpantan Leics 36 B3 ham 3m/4km SW of Loughborough. SK 5017

Nanpean Cornwall 3 E3 vil in china clay dist 4m/7km NW of St Austell. SW 9656

Nanstallon Cornwall 3 E2* vil 2m/3km W of Bodmin. SX 0367

Nantaeron 24 A5* r running S into R Gwili at Llanpumsaint, Dyfed, from a point 3m/4km N thereof. SN 4129

Nant Alltwalis 24 A5* r rising 2m/3km NE of ham of Alltwalis, Dyfed, and flowing SW through it and continuing SW to join Nantaeron and run into R Gwili at Llanpumsaint. SN 4129

Nantcorrwg 24 A5* stream running into R Gwili from S side, W of Pontarsais, Dyfed. SN 4328

Nant-ddu Powys 25 E6 loc on Taf fawr R 6m/10km NW of Merthyr Tydfil. SO 0014

Nanternis Dyfed 24 A3* ham 2m/4km SW of New Quay. SN 3756

Nant Ffrancon Gwynedd 40 C5, D5 valley of R Ogwen between Bethesda and Llyn Ogwen. SH 66

Nantgaredig Dyfed 23 F3 vil 5m/8km E of Carmarthen. SN 4921

Nantgarw Mid Glam 15 F3 loc 2m/4km SW of Caerphilly. Coal mines. Coke-oven and by-products plant. ST 1185

Nant-glas Powys 25 E2 loc 3m/4km SE of Rhayader. SN 9965

Nantglyn Clwyd 41 F5 ham 4m/6km SE of Denbigh. SJ 0062

Nantgwyn Powys 25 E1* loc 5m/9km N of Rhayader. SN 9776

Nantgwynant Gwynedd 40 C6/D6 valley of R Glaslyn above Beddgelert. SH 64,65

Nantithet Cornwall 2 C6* loc 4m/6km SE of Helston. SW 6822

Nantlle Gwynedd 40 C6 loc 3m/4km E of Penygroes. SH 5053

Nant Mawr Clwyd 41 H5* loc adjoining Buckley to S. SJ 2763

Nantmawr Salop 34 A2* loc 2km NE of Llanyblodwel. SJ 2524

Nantmel Powys 25 E2 ham 4m/7km E of Rhayader. SO 0366

Nant-moel Reservoir Mid Glam 15 E1 small resr 2m/3km NE of Hirwaun. SN 9807

Nant Peris Gwynedd 40 C5 the old vil of Llanberis 2m/3km SE of the present tn. SH 6058

Nant, The Clwyd 41 H6* loc 3m/5km W of Wrexham. SJ 2850

Nantwich Ches 42 C5/C6 old tn on R Weaver 4m/7km SW of Crewe. Former centre of salt industry. Industries now include clothing, tanning. Many black-and-white hses. SJ 6552

Nant-y-Bwch Gwent 15 F1* loc adjoining Dukestown to W. SO 1210

Nant y Bwch 25 G4* stream in Black Mts, Powys, rising on S side of Lord Hereford's Knob and flowing SE into R Honddu at Capel-y-ffin. SO 2531

Nant-y-caws Dyfed 23 F4 loc 3m/4km E of Carmarthen. SN 4518

Nant-y-Caws Salop 34 A2* loc 2m/3km S of Oswestry. SJ 2826

Nant-y-derry (Nant-y-deri) Gwent 15 H1 loc 5m/9km S of Abergavenny. SO 3306

Nant-y-draenog Reservoir Gwent 15 G2* small resr 2m/3km SW of Abercarn. ST 1893

Nant-y-ffin Dyfed 24 B5* loc 2m/3km SW of Abergorlech. SN 5532

Nant y Ffrith 41 H5* r rising S of Nant-y-Ffrith Resr, Clwyd, and running N to the resr then NE into R Cegidog at Ffrith, 4m/7km NW of Wrexham. SJ 2855

Nant y Ffrith Reservoir Clwyd 41 H5* resr 2km W of Bwlch Gwyn. SJ 2453

Nantyffyllon Mid Glam 14 D2 loc 1m N of Maesteg. SS 8592

Nant-y-Flint 41 H4* stream running into R Dee estuary at Flint, Clwyd. SJ 2473

Nantyglesaid Mid Glam 15 G3* loc adjoining Machen to W. ST 2089

Nantyglo Gwent 15 G1 loc adjoining Brynmawr to S. SO 1910

Nant-y-Gollen Salop 34 A2* loc 3m/5km W of Oswestry. SJ 2428

Nant-y-moch Reservoir Dyfed 33 E5 large resr 9m/14km S of Machynlleth. SN 7586

Nant-y-Moel Mid Glam 15 E2 coal-mining vil 3m/5km SW of Treorchy. SS 9392

Nant-y-pandy Gwynedd 40 D4* loc adjoining Llanfairfechan to SE. SH 6874

Nant y Pandy. See Pandy, Y.

Naphill Bucks 18 D2 vil 3m/5km N of High Wycombe. SU 8496

Napley Heath Staffs 34 D1* loc 1km N of Mucklestone. SJ 7238

Nappa N Yorks 48 B3 loc 2m/3km S of Hellifield. SD 8553

Napton on the Hill Warwicks 28 A2 vil 3m/5km E of Southam. Series of locks on Oxford Canal to SW. SP 4661

Nar 38 B3 r rising S of Tittleshall, Norfolk, and flowing W through Narborough and finally N into R Ouse at King's Lynn. TF 6119

Narberth (Arberth) Dyfed 22 D4 small mkt tn 10m/16km E of Haverfordwest and 9m/14km N of Tenby. Remnants of 13c cas. **Narberth Br** loc adjoining to S. SN 1014

Narborough Leics 36 B4 vil 5m/9km SW of Leicester. SP 5497

Narborough Norfolk 38 C3 vil 5m/8km NW of Swaffham. TF 7413

Nare Head Cornwall 3 E4 headland (NT) on S coast of E end of Gerrans Bay. SW 9136

Nare Point Cornwall 2 D5 headland at NE corner of Meneage dist, 5m/8km S of Falmouth across bay. SW 8024

Narford Norfolk 38 C3 loc 5m/7km NW of Swaffham. **Narford Hall,** 18c–19c hse in park with lake. Of former vil only the ch remains. TF 7613

Narkurs Cornwall 3 G3* loc 7m/12km W of Torpoint. SX 3255

Narrows of Raasay Skye, H'land 79 D5 strait between Skye and Raasay at S end of Sound of Raasay. Width just over 1km. NG 5435

Narth, The Gwent 16 A1* loc 4m/7km S of Monmouth. SO 5107

Nasareth Gwynedd 40 B6* ham 2km S of Llanllyfni. SH 4750

Naseby Northants 36 C6 vil 6m/10km SW of Mkt Harborough. **Naseby Resr** to W. 1m N is site of Civil War battle, 1645. SP 6878

Nash Bucks 28 C4 vil 6m/9km E of Buckingham. SP 7834

Nash (Trefonnen) Gwent 15 H3 vil 4m/6km SE of Newport. See also Uskmouth. ST 3483

Nash H & W 25 G2* loc 2km S of Presteigne. SO 3062

Nash Kent 13 G2* loc 2m/3km NE of Wingham. TR 2658

Nash Salop 26 B1* vil 2m/4km N of Tenbury Wells. SO 6071

Nash, High Glos 26 B6* loc adjoining Coleford to S. SO 5710

Nash Lee Bucks 18 C1* loc 2m/3km W of Wendover. SP 8408

Nash, Lower Dyfed 22 C5* loc 2m/3km NE of Pembroke. SN 0103

Nash Point S Glam 15 E4 headland 3m/5km W of Llantwit Major. SS 9168

Nash's Green Hants 18 B6* ham 5m/8km SE of Basingstoke. SU 6745

Nash Street Kent 20 C4* loc 3m/5km S of Gravesend. TQ 6469

Nash, Upper Dyfed 22 C5* loc 2m/4km E of Pembroke. SN 0202

Nassington Northants 37 F5 vil 2m/3km S of Wansford. TL 0696

Nast Hyde Herts 19 F1* loc 2m/3km W of Hatfield. TL 2007

Nasty Herts 29 G5* vil 2m/3km W of Puckeridge. TL 3524

Nateby Cumbria 53 G4 vil 2km S of Kirkby Stephen. NY 7706

Nateby Lancs 47 E4 ham 2m/3km W of Garstang. SD 4644

Natland Cumbria 53 E5 vil 2m/4km S of Kendal. SD 5289

Naughton Suffolk 31 E3 ham 4m/7km N of Hadleigh. TM 0248

Naunton Glos 27 F5 vil 5m/8km W of Stow-on-the-Wold. SP 1123

Naunton H & W 26 D4 vil 4m/7km N of Tewkesbury. SO 8739

Naunton Beauchamp H & W 26 D3 vil 4m/7km N of Pershore. SO 9652

Naust H'land 78 F2 locality on W side of Loch Ewe in Ross and Cromarty dist, 3m/4km NW of Poolewe. NG 8283

Navax Point Cornwall 2 B4* headland (NT) on N coast nearly 1m E of Godrevy Pt and 4m/7km NW of Camborne. SW 5943

Nave Island S'clyde 62 A1 small island off Ardnave Pt on N coast of Islay, on W side of entrance to Loch Gruinart. NR 2875

Navenby Lincs 44 D5 vil 9m/14km S of Lincoln. SK 9857

Naver H'land 86 A2 r in Caithness dist running N from Loch Naver down Strath Naver to Torrisdale Bay on N coast. NC 6962

Navestock Essex 20 B2 ham 4m/7km NW of Brentwood. Vil of **Navestock Side** 2km E. TQ 5397

Navio Derbys. See Brough.

Naworth Castle Cumbria 60 B5 mansion in park 2m/4km E of Brampton, on site of 14c cas of which little remains. NY 5662

Nawton N Yorks 55 E6 vil 3m/4km E of Helmsley. SE 6584

Nayland Suffolk 30 D4 small tn on R Stour 6m/10km N of Colchester. Many old hses. Ch contains painting by Constable. TL 9734

Nazeing Essex 20 B1 vil 3m/5km SW of Harlow. Suburban loc of **Lr Nazeing** 2km W. Locs of **Nazeing Gate** and **Nazeing Long Green** 1m S and 2km SW respectively. TL 4106

Naze, The Essex 31 F5 North Sea headland 5m/8km S of Harwich across bay. TM 2623

Neacroft Hants 9 H4* loc 3m/5km NE of Christchurch. SZ 1896

Nealhouse Cumbria 59 H6* loc 2m/3km W of Dalston. NY 3351

Neal's Green Warwicks 35 H5* loc 4m/6km N of Coventry. SP 3384

Neap House Humberside 50 D6 loc on E bank of R Trent 3m/4km NW of Scunthorpe. SE 8613

Neaps, North Shetland 89 E5 promontory on N coast of Yell. HP 4805

NEAR. For names beginning with this word, see under next word. This also applies to names beginning with Far, Mid, Middle; High, Low; Higher, Lower; Upper, Nether; Great, Little; Greater, Lesser; Isle(s) of; North, South, East, West; The, Y, Yr.

Nearton End Bucks 28 C5* loc adjoining Swanbourne to SE, 2m/4km E of Winslow. SP 8027

Neasden London 19 F3 loc in borough of Brent 7m/11km NW of Charing Cross. TQ 2185

Neasham Durham 54 C4 vil on R Tees 4m/6km SE of Darlington. NZ 3210

Neat Enstone Oxon 27 G5* loc just E of Enstone. SP 3824

Neath (Castell-nedd) W Glam 14 D2 tn on R Neath, on site of Roman fort of *Nidum*, 8m/12km NE of Swansea. Steel, tinplate, engineering. Neath Abbey (A.M.) 2km W. SS 7597

Neath (Nedd) 14 C2 r rising in Black Mts SW of Brecon, Powys, and flowing SW down Vale of Neath to tn of Neath and into Bristol Channel at Baglan Bay, W Glam. SS 7292

Neatham Hants 10 D1 ham 2m/3km NE of Alton. SU 7440

Neatishead Norfolk 39 G3 vil 4m/6km NE of Wroxham. TG 3421

Neaton Norfolk 38 D4* loc 1km N of Watton. TF 9101

Neave Island H'land 84 F2 small uninhabited island off N coast of Caithness dist opp Skerray. Also known as Coomb I. NC 6664

Neb 46 A5* r on Isle of Man rising on central mts E of Lit London and running through that loc, then SW down Glen Helen to St John's, then NW to Peel and Peel Bay. SC 2484

Nebo Dyfed 24 B2 loc 1km N of Cross Inn. SN 5465

Nebo Gwynedd 40 B3 ham 2m/4km SE of Amlwch, Anglesey. SH 4690

Nebo Gwynedd 40 B6* ham 1m SE of Llanllyfni. SH 4750

Nebo Gwynedd 41 E5* ham 4m/7km SE of Llanrwst. SH 8356

Nechells W Midlands 35 G5* loc in Birmingham 3m/4km NE of city centre. SP 0989

Nechtansmere Tayside. See Dunnichen.

Necton Norfolk 38 D4 vil 4m/6km E of Swaffham. TF 8709

Nedd H'land 84 B4 vil at head of Loch Nedd 1m SE of Drumbeg, W coast of Sutherland dist. NC 1331

Nedd Welsh form of Neath (r), qv.

Nedderton Nthmb 61 G3 vil 2km W of Bedlington. NZ 2381

Nedging Suffolk 31 E3 ham 4m/6km NW of Hadleigh. Ham of **Nedging Tye** 2m/3km NE. TL 9948

Needham Norfolk 31 F1 vil 2m/3km SW of Harleston. TM 2281

Needham Market Suffolk 31 E3 tn on R Gipping 3m/5km SE of Stowmarket. TM 0855

Needham Street Suffolk 30 C2* loc 5m/8km E of Newmarket. TL 7265
Needingworth Cambs 29 G1 vil 2m/3km E of St Ives. TL 3472
Needle Rock Dyfed 22 C2* rock island off shore on SE side of Dinas Hd. SN 0140
Needles Eye Nthmb 67 F3 rock formation on coast 2m/3km N of Berwick-upon-Tweed. NT 9955
Needles, The Isle of Wight 10 A6 headland (NT) culminating in group of jagged, insulated chalk rocks running out into English Channel from W extremity of the island. Lighthouse at W end of series. SZ 2984
Needwood Staffs 35 G2 loc 4m/6km W of Burton upon Trent. To W, **N. Forest,** former hunting forest. SK 1724
Neen Savage Salop 34 D6 vil 1m N of Cleobury Mortimer. SO 6777
Neen Sollars Salop 26 B1 vil 5m/8km NE of Tenbury Wells. SO 6672
Neenton Salop 34 C5 vil 6m/10km SW of Bridgnorth. SO 6387
Nefyn Gwynedd 32 B1 vil and resort on cliff above Porth Nefyn, Caernarvon Bay, 6m/9km NW of Pwllheli. SH 3040
Neighbourne Som 16 B6* ham just E of Ashwick and 4m/6km NE of Shepton Mallet. ST 6448
Neilston S'clyde 64 C3 small tn 2m/3km SW of Barrhead. **Neilston Pad** is hill 2km S. NS 4757
Neist Point Skye, H'land 78 A4 headland with lighthouse on W coast 8m/13km W of Dunvegan. Most westerly point of Skye. NG 1246
Neithrop Oxon 27 H3 W dist of Banbury. SP 4440
Nell's Point S Glam 15 F4* headland on Barry I. at E end of Whitmore Bay. ST 1266
Nelly Ayre Foss N Yorks 55 F5 waterfall in W Beck 2km SW of Goathland. SE 8199
Nelly's Moss Lakes Nthmb 61 F2* two adjacent lakes 2km E of Rothbury. NU 0702
Nelson Lancs 48 B4 tn 4m/6km N of Burnley. Textiles. SD 8537
Nelson Mid Glam 15 F2 vil 2m/3km W of Ystrad Mynach. ST 1195
Nelson Village Nthmb 61 G4* loc adjoining Cramlington to NW. Industrial estate to N. NZ 2577
Nemphlar S'clyde 65 E4 loc 2m/3km W of Lanark. NS 8544
Nempnett Thrubwell Avon 16 A5 vil 2m/3km SW of Chew Stoke. ST 5360
Nene 38 A2 r rising about 3m/5km SW of Daventry, Northants, and flowing E past Northampton and Wellingborough, thence generally NE through Oundle and Peterborough, and across the Fens to Wisbech, Sutton Br, and the Wash. TF 4926
Nent 60 C6* r rising S of Nenthead, Cumbria, and flowing through Nenthead, then NW into R South Tyne on N side of Alston. NY 7146
Nenthall Cumbria 53 F1 loc 2m/3km NW of Nenthead. NY 7545
Nenthead Cumbria 53 G1 vil 4m/7km SE of Alston. NY 7843
Nenthorn Borders 66 D4/D5 vil 4m/6km NW of Kelso. NT 6837
Neopardy Devon 7 F5* loc 3m/5km W of Crediton. SX 7999
Nercwys Clwyd 41 H5 vil 2m/3km S of Mold. SJ 2360
Neroche Forest Som 8 B3* steep, partly wooded area to S of Staple Fitzpaine, running up to Staple Hill (1035 ft or 315 metres). At SE corner of area is **Neroche Castle,** ancient encampment 1m S of Curland. ST 2617
Nerston S'clyde 64 D3 loc in E Kilbride to N of tn centre. Industrial estate. NS 6456
Nesbitt Durham 54 D2* loc 2m/3km E of Hutton Henry. NZ 4536
Nesfield N Yorks 48 D3 ham 2m/3km NW of Ilkley across R Wharfe. SE 0949
Ness Ches 41 H4 loc 2km SE of Neston. SJ 3076
Nesscliff Salop 34 B3 vil 8m/13km NW of Shrewsbury. **Nesscliff Hill,** sandstone hill to E: hill forts and cave. SJ 3819
Ness, East N Yorks 50 C1 ham 2m/3km E of Nunnington. SE 6978
Ness, Great Salop 34 B3 vil 7m/11km NW of Shrewsbury. **Lit Ness** vil 1m NE. SJ 3918
Ness Head H'land 86 F1 headland on E coast of Caithness dist 5m/7km S of Duncansby Hd. 550 ND 3664 Auckingill H'land 86 F2 loc near E coast of Caithness dist 6m/9km S of John on Groats. ND 3866
Ness, Little Isle of Man 46 B6* headland 2m/3km SW of Douglas Hd. SC 3672
Ness, North Orkney 89 A7* headland and loc with pier on island of Hoy, on N side of entrance to N Bay. **S Ness** is headland and loc with pier on opp side, on peninsula of S Walls. ND 3091
Ness of Brodgar Orkney 89 A6* narrow tongue of land, carrying a rd, between Loch of Harray and Loch of Stenness; on Mainland 4m/6km W of Finstown. HY 3012
Ness of Brough Shetland 89 F6* headland at westernmost point of Fetlar, opp Hascosay. HU 5792
Ness of Burgi Shetland 89 E8* headland on W side of W Voe of Sumburgh, opp Sumburgh Hd. Ancient fort (A.M.). HU 3808
Ness of Duncansby H'land 86 F1 headland on N coast of Caithness dist 1m W of Duncansby Hd. ND 3873
Ness of Gruting Shetland. See Wick of Gruting.
Ness of Huna H'land 86 F1* headland on N coast of Caithness dist 3m/4km W of Duncansby Hd. ND 3673
Ness of Kaywick Shetland 89 F6* promontory on Yell, on N side of entrance to Mid Yell Voe. HU 5392
Ness of Litter H'land 86 D1 headland on N coast of Caithness dist 3m/5km NW of Thurso. ND 0771
Ness of Melby Shetland. See Melby.
Ness of Ork Orkney 89 B6* headland at NE end of Shapinsay. HY 5422
Ness of Ramnageo Shetland 89 F5* headland on S coast of Unst 2m/4km E of Uyeasound. HU 6299
Ness of Snabrough Shetland 89 F6* headland on W coast of Fetlar. HU 5793
Ness of Sound Shetland. See Sound.
Ness of Sound Shetland 89 E6* headland on W coast of Yell 4m/6km S of W Sandwick. Lighthouse. HU 4482
Ness of Trebister Shetland. See Trebister.
Ness Point N Yorks 55 G4* headland on North Sea coast 1m NE of Robin Hood's Bay. Also known as N Cheek. NZ 9506
Ness, West N Yorks 50 C1 ham 2km E of Nunnington. SE 6879
Nesting Shetland 89 E7* dist of Mainland consisting of **N** and **S Nesting** and enclosing **S Nesting Bay** on E coast. The bay extends from Hill of Neap southwards to N end of Moul of Eswick. HU 45
Neston Ches 41 H4 tn on Wirral peninsula 7m/11km W of Ellesmere Port. **Lit Neston** loc adjoining to SE. SJ 2977
Neston Wilts 16 D4 vil 2m/3km S of Corsham. ST 8668
Netchwood Salop 34 C5* ham 6m/9km W of Bridgnorth. Ham of **Upr Netchwood** 2km W. SO 6291
Nethan 65 E4 r in Strathclyde region rising 2m/4km N of Glenbuck and running NE into R Clyde on N side of Crossford. NS 8247
NETHER. For names beginning with this word, see under next word. This also applies to names beginning with High, Low; Higher, Upper, Lower; Far, Near; Mid, Middle; Great, Little; Greater, Lesser; Isle(s) of; North, South, East, West; The, Y, Yr.
Netheravon Wilts 17 F6 vil on R Avon 5m/7km N of Amesbury. SU 1448
Netherbrae Grampian 83 F1* loc near N coast 3m/5km S of Gardenstown. Loc of Overbrae to E. NJ 7959
Netherbrough Orkney 89 A6* loc on Mainland 4m/6km NW of Finstown. HY 3116
Netherburn S'clyde 65 E4 loc 3m/5km N of Blackwood. NS 8047
Netherbury Dorset 8 C4 vil 2km S of Beaminster. SY 4799
Netherby Cumbria 60 A4 loc in valley of R Esk 2m/3km NE of Longtown. Site of Roman fort of *Castra Exploratorum*. NY 3971
Netherby N Yorks 49 E3 ham on N bank of R Wharfe 5m/8km W of Wetherby. SE 3346
Netherby W Midlands 35 E5* loc 3m/5km NW of Dudley tn centre. SO 9193
Nethercott Devon 6 D2* loc 6m/9km NW of Barnstaple. SS 4839
Nethercott Oxon 28 A5 vil 4m/6km NE of Woodstock. SP 4820
Netherend Glos 16 B2 vil 3m/5km SW of Lydney. SO 5900
Netherfield E Sussex 12 D5 vil 3m/5km NW of Battle. TQ 7118
Netherfield Notts 36 C1 loc adjoining Carlton to SE. SK 6240
Nethergate Humberside 44 C2* loc adjoining Westwoodside to S. SK 7599
Netherhampton Wilts 9 H2 vil 2m/4km W of Salisbury across valley of R Nadder. SU 1029
Netherhay Dorset 8 C4* ham 3m/5km SW of Crewkerne. ST 4105
Netherland Green Staffs 35 G2* loc 2m/3km SE of Uttoxeter. SK 1030
Netherley Grampian 77 G2 loc 4m/7km S of Peterculter. NO 8493
Nethermill D & G 59 E3/F3 loc 1m/6km NW of Lochmaben. NY 0487
Netheroyd Hill W Yorks 48 D6* loc in Huddersfield 2m/3km N of tn centre. SE 1419
Netherseal Derbys 35 H3 vil 4m/7km S of Swadlincote. SK 2812
Netherstreet Wilts 17 E5 loc 3m/5km NW of Devizes. ST 9865
Netherthird S'clyde 56 F2* vil 1m SE of Cumnock. NS 5718
Netherthong W Yorks 43 F1 vil 1m N of Holmfirth. SE 1309
Netherthorpe Derbys 43 H4* loc 1m E of Staveley. SK 4474
Netherton Cumbria 52 A2 loc in S part of Maryport. NY 0335
Netherton Devon 5 E3 loc 2m/3km E of Newton Abbot. SX 8971
Netherton Hants 17 G5 loc 3m/5km N of Hurstbourne Tarrant. SU 3757
Netherton H & W 27 E3* loc 3m/5km SW of Evesham. SO 9941
Netherton Merseyside 42 A2* loc in NE Bootle 4m/6km from tn centre. SD 3500
Netherton Nthmb 61 E1 ham 6m/9km NW of Rothbury. Locs of **Netherton Burnfoot** and **Netherton Northside** to E and NE respectively. NT 9807
Netherton Oxon 17 H2 loc adjoining Fyfield to N, 5m/8km W of Abingdon. SU 4199
Netherton Tayside 76 C5* loc just N of Br of Cally. NO 1452
Netherton Tayside 77 E5 loc 4m/6km W of Brechin. NO 5457
Netherton W Midlands 35 F5 dist of Dudley 2km S of tn centre. SO 9388
Netherton W Yorks 48 D6* loc in Huddersfield 3m/4km SW of tn centre. SE 1213
Netherton W Yorks 49 E6 vil 2m/3km SW of Horbury. SE 2716
Netherton Colliery Nthmb 61 G3* loc 1m NW of Bedlington. NZ 2482
Netherton Green S'clyde 65 E3* loc 1m SW of Wishaw. NS 7854
Nethertown Cumbria 52 A4 coastal ham 2m/4km SW of Egremont. NX 9907
Nethertown Lancs 48 A4* loc 1m NW of Whalley. SD 7236
Nethertown Staffs 35 G3* ham 1m NW of King's Bromley. SK 1017
Nethertown Stroma, H'land 86 F1* loc near N end of Island of Stroma in Pentland Firth – see Stroma. ND 3578
Netherwitton Nthmb 61 F3 vil on R Font 7m/11km NW of Morpeth. Hall probably early 18c. NZ 1090
Nethy H'land 82 A5 r in Badenoch and Strathspey dist rising in Cairngorms and running N to R Spey 4m/7km SW of Grantown-on-Spey. Vil of **Nethy Br** on r 2km above mouth. NH 9922
Netley Hants 10 B4 vil on E bank of Southampton Water 2m/3km below mouth of R Itchen. Remains of 13c abbey (A.M.). Tudor cas converted into mansion in 19c. SU 4508
Netley Marsh Hants 10 A3 vil 2m/3km W of Totton. SU 3313
Nettlebed Oxon 18 B3 vil 5m/7km NW of Henley-on-Thames. SU 7086
Nettlebridge Som 16 B6* ham 1km E of Ashwick and 4m/6km NE of Shepton Mallet. ST 6448
Nettlecombe Dorset 8 C4 ham just S of Powerstock and 4m/6km NE of Bridport. SY 5195
Nettlecombe Isle of Wight 10 C6* loc just NE of Whitwell and 3m/4km W of Ventnor. SZ 5278
Nettlecombe Som 7 G2 ham on edge of Exmoor National Park 4m/6km S of Watchet. ST 0537
Nettleden Herts 19 E1 vil 3m/4km NE of Berkhamsted. TL 0210
Nettleham Lincs 45 E4 vil 3m/5km NE of Lincoln. TF 0075
Nettlestead Kent 20 C6 vil on R Medway 5m/7km N of Paddock Wd. Vil of **Nettlestead Green** 1m S. TQ 6852
Nettlestone Isle of Wight 10 C5 vil near NE coast 3m/4km SE of Ryde. To N on coast, **Nettlestone Pt.** SZ 6290
Nettlestone Point Isle of Wight 10 C5 headland on NE coast 3m/4km E of Ryde. SZ 6291
Nettleswell Essex 20 B1* dist of Harlow to E of tn centre. TL 4509
Nettlesworth Durham 54 B1* vil 4m/6km N of Durham. NZ 2547
Nettleton Lincs 45 E2 vil 1m SW of Caistor. TA 1000
Nettleton Wilts 16 C4 vil 7m/11km NW of Chippenham. **Nettleton Green** loc adjoining to S. **Nettleton Shrub** loc 1m SE. ST 8178
Nettleton Hill W Yorks 48 D6* loc in Huddersfield 3m/5km W of tn centre. SE 0917
Netton Wilts 9 H1 ham in R Avon valley 4m/7km N of Salisbury. SU 1336
Neuadd Reservoirs Powys 25 E6 two resrs in upr valley of Taf fechan R 2m/3km SE of Brecon Beacons. SO 0218
Neuk, The Grampian 77 G2* loc 3m/4km NE of Banchory. NO 7397
Nevendon Essex 20 D3 loc 2km S of Wickford. TQ 7391
Nevern (Nyfer) Dyfed 22 C2 vil 2m/3km E of Newport. Traces of 11c cas on hill to N. Also r rising S of Boncath and flowing W to Newport Bay. SN 0839
Nevill Holt Leics 36 D5 par with medieval hall and ch 5m/8km SW of Uppingham. SP 8193
Nevis Forest H'land 74 C4* state forest in Lochaber dist on W side of Glen Nevis, SE of Fort William. NN 1172
Nev of Stuis Shetland 89 E5 headland on Yell on W side of entrance to Whale Firth. HU 4697
New Abbey D & G 59 E4/E5 vil 6m/10km S of Dumfries. Ruins of New Abbey, or Sweetheart Abbey, (A.M.), EE-Dec. **N.A. Pow** is stream running E through vil to R Nith estuary. Monmt to W of vil commemorates Battle of Waterloo. NX 9666
New Aberdour Grampian 83 G1 vil 1m S of Aberdour Bay on N coast, and 4m/7km SW of Rosehearty. NJ 8863
New Addington London 20 A5 dist in borough of Croydon 3m/5km NW of Biggin Hill. TQ 3862
Newall W Yorks 49 E3 dist of Otley on N side of R Wharfe. SE 2046
Newall Green Gtr Manchester 42 D3* loc in Manchester 3m/5km E of Altrincham. SJ 8187
New Alresford Hants 10 C2 tn on R Alre 7m/11km E of Winchester. 'New' in the year 1200. SU 5832
New Alyth Tayside 76 C6 loc 1km S of Alyth. NO 2447
New Annesley Notts 44 A5 loc 2m/3km SE of Kirkby in Ashfield. SK 5053
Newark Cambs 37 G4 loc in Peterborough 2m/3km NE of city centre. TF 2100
Newark Orkney 89 C5* loc on Sanday at N end of **Newark Bay** 4m/7km SW of Tafts Ness. Promontory of **Long Taing of Newark** protrudes eastwards between Bay of Newark and Bay of Lopness. HY 7242
Newark Castle Borders 66 B5 ruined 15c cas beside Yarrow Water, 3m/5km W of Selkirk. NT 4229
Newark Castle S'clyde 64 B2 mansion (A.M.) of 16c–17c on E side of Port Glasgow. Incorporates 15c tower. NS 3374

Newark-on-Trent Notts 44 C5 tn 16m/25km SW of Lincoln and 17m/27km NE of Nottingham. Industries include brewing, agricultural machinery, engineering. Remains of medieval cas. Ch, EE to Perp, has lofty spire. SK 7953
New Arram Humberside 51 E4* loc adjoining Arram to NW. TA 0344
Newarthill S'clyde 65 E3 vil 3m/5km NE of Motherwell. NS 7859
New Ash Green Kent 20 C5* vil 1m S of Hartley and 6m/9km S of Northfleet. Site of Roman bldg to S. Large housing development. TQ 6065
New Balderton Notts 44 C5* loc on SE side of Newark-on-Trent and N of Balderton. SK 8152
Newbald, North Humberside 50 D4 vil 4m/6km SE of Mkt Weighton. **S Newbald** ham 1km S of N Newbald. SE 9136
Newball Lincs 45 E4 loc 4m/6km W of Wragby. TF 0776
New Barn Kent 20 C4* suburban locality 4m/6km SW of Gravesend. TQ 6168
New Barnet London 19 F2 dist in borough of Barnet 10m/16km N of Charing Cross. TQ 2695
New Barnetby Humberside 45 E1* ham 1m NE of Barnetby le Wold. TA 0710
Newbarns Cumbria 46 D1 dist of Barrow-in-Furness 2km NE of tn centre. SD 2170
New Barns Notts 36 B2* loc 1km E of Thrumpton. SK 5130
New Barton Northants 28 D2* N end of Earls Barton, 4m/6km SW of Wellingborough. SP 8564
Newbattle Lothian 66 B2 vil 1m S of Dalkeith. **Newbattle Abbey** is mansion dating mainly from 16c, on site of abbey founded in 1140. NT 3366
New Beckenham London 20 A4* loc in borough of Bromley 1km NW of Beckenham. TQ 3670
New Bedford River 38 B4 fenland drainage channel running NE from R Ouse 1km E of Earith, Cambs, to rejoin it at Denver Sluice, Norfolk. TF 5801
New Bewick Nthmb 67 G6 ham 7m/11km SE of Wooler. NU 0620
Newbiggin Cumbria 46 D2* loc on W shore of Morecambe Bay 5m/7km E of Barrow-in-Furness. SD 2669
Newbiggin Cumbria 52 B5* loc 2m/3km SE of Ravenglass across R Esk estuary. SD 0994
Newbiggin Cumbria 52 D2 vil 3m/5km W of Penrith. NY 4729
Newbiggin Cumbria 53 F2 vil 6m/10km NW of Appleby. NY 6228
Newbiggin Cumbria 60 B6 ham 8m/12km S of Brampton. NY 5549
Newbiggin Durham 53 H2 vil 2m/4km NW of Middleton in Teesdale. NY 9127
Newbiggin Nthmb 61 E6* loc 2km W of Blanchland. NY 9549
Newbiggin N Yorks 53 H5 loc to NE of Askrigg. SD 9591
Newbiggin N Yorks 54 H6 vil 2m/3km S of Aysgarth. SD 9985
Newbiggin Bay Nthmb 61 G3* bay on North Sea coast on which Newbiggin-by-the-Sea is situated. NZ 3187
Newbiggin-by-the-Sea Nthmb 61 G3 fishing tn and resort on North Sea coast in coal-mining area 2m/4km E of Ashington. NZ 3187
Newbiggin, East Durham 54 C3 loc 6m/9km NE of Darlington. NZ 3618
Newbigging S'clyde 65 F4/G4 vil 2m/4km E of Carnwath. NT 0145
Newbigging Tayside 73 G1 loc 4m/6km NE of Broughty Ferry. NO 4935
Newbigging Tayside 73 G1* loc 5m/8km N of Dundee. NO 4237
Newbiggin Hall Estate Tyne & Wear 61 G4* suburb 4m/6km NW of Newcastle. NZ 2067
Newbiggin on Lune Cumbria 53 F4 ham 5m/8km SW of Kirkby Stephen. NY 7005
Newbiggin, West Durham 54 C3 loc 5m/8km NE of Darlington. NZ 3518
Newbold Derbys 43 H4 dist of Chesterfield 1m NW of tn centre. SK 3772
Newbold Leics 36 A3* loc 3m/5km NE of Ashby de la Zouch. SK 4018
Newbold on Avon Warwicks 36 B6 loc in NW part of Rugby, on R Avon, and Oxford Canal. SP 4877
Newbold on Stour Warwicks 27 F3 vil 4m/6km N of Shipston on Stour. SP 2446
Newbold Pacey Warwicks 27 G2 vil 6m/9km S of Leamington. SP 2957
Newbold Verdon Leics 36 A4 vil 3m/4km E of Mkt Bosworth. SK 4403
New Bolingbroke Lincs 45 G5 vil 9m/14km N of Boston. TF 3058
New Bolsover Derbys 44 A4* loc adjoining Bolsover to W. SK 4670
Newborough Cambs 37 G4 vil 5m/8km N of Peterborough. TF 2006
Newborough Gwynedd 40 B5 vil on Anglesey 9m/14km SW of Menai Br. **Newborough Forest**, wooded area to SW. **Newborough Warren** to S. SH 4265
Newborough Staffs 35 G2 vil 4m/6km E of Abbots Bromley. SK 1325
New Boston Merseyside 42 B2* N part of Haydock. See also Old Boston. SJ 5697
Newbottle Northants 28 A4* loc 4m/6km W of Brackley. SP 5236
Newbottle Tyne & Wear 61 G6/H6 loc adjoining Houghton-le-Spring to N. NZ 3351
New Boultham Lincs 44 D4* SW dist of Lincoln N of Boultham. SK 9670
Newbourn Suffolk 31 F4 vil 4m/7km S of Woodbridge. TM 2743
New Bradwell 28 C3/D3 tn in Milton Keynes adjoining Wolverton to E. SP 8241
New Brampton Derbys 43 H4 dist of Chesterfield 1km SW of tn centre. SK 3770
New Brancepeth Durham 54 B1 vil 3m/5km W of Durham. NZ 2241
Newbridge Clwyd 41 H6 loc 2m/3km SW of Ruabon. SJ 2841
Newbridge Cornwall 2 A5 ham 3m/5km W of Penzance. SW 4231
New Bridge D & G 59 E3/E4 loc at rd crossing of Cluden Water, 2m/4km NW of Dumfries. NX 9479
Newbridge Dyfed 22 B3 loc 4m/6km S of Fishguard. SM 9431
Newbridge Dyfed 24 B2* loc and rd br over R Aeron 4m/6km SE of Aberaeron. SN 5059
Newbridge E Sussex 12 B3* loc below N slope of Ashdown Forest 1m S of Coleman's Hatch. TQ 4532
Newbridge Gwent 15 G2 tn on Ebbw R 8m/13km NW of Newport. ST 2197
Newbridge Hants 10 A3 ham 1m N of Cadnam. SU 2915
Newbridge Isle of Wight 10 B5 vil 4m/6km E of Yarmouth. SZ 4187
Newbridge Lancs 48 B4 loc adjoining Nelson to N. SD 8639
Newbridge Lothian 65 G2 vil 3m/5km S of Forth Rd Br. NT 1272
New Bridge N Yorks 55 F6* loc 1km N of Pickering. SE 8085
Newbridge Oxon 17 H2 loc at confluence of Rs Thames and Windrush 5m/8km S of Eynsham. SP 4001
Newbridge W Midlands 35 E4* W dist of Wolverhampton. SO 8999
Newbridge Green H & W 26 D4* ham 1m SW of Upton upon Severn. SO 8439
Newbridge-on-Usk Gwent 15 H2* loc 4m/6km S of Usk. ST 3894
Newbridge on Wye Powys 25 E2 vil 5m/8km N of Builth Wells. SO 0158
New Brighton Clwyd 41 H5* loc 2km NE of Mold. SJ 2565
New Brighton Clwyd 41 H6* loc on E slope of Esclusham Mt 4m/6km W of Wrexham. SJ 2750
New Brighton Hants 10 D4 residential development 1m N of Emsworth. SU 7407
New Brighton Merseyside 41 H2 N dist of Wallasey on R Mersey estuary. SJ 3193
New Brighton N Yorks 48 C3* loc 1m W of Gargrave. SD 9253
New Brighton W Yorks 48 D4* loc 1km SE of Cottingley. SE 1236
New Brighton W Yorks 49 E5* loc adjoining Morley to W. SE 2527
New Brimington Derbys 43 H4* loc adjoining Brimington to N, 3m/4km NE of Chesterfield. SK 4074
New Brinsley Notts 44 A5 loc 2m/3km N of Eastwood. See also Brinsley. SK 4650
New Brotton Cleveland 55 E3* loc adjoining Brotton to N. NZ 6820
Newbrough Nthmb 60 D4 vil 3m/5km NE of Haydon Br. Site of Roman fort 1km W. NY 8767
New Broughton Clwyd 41 H6 loc 2km W of Wrexham. SJ 3151
New Buckenham Norfolk 39 E5 vil 4m/7km SE of Attleborough. Remains of 12c cas. TM 0890
Newbuildings Devon 7 F4* ham 3m/5km NW of Crediton. SS 7903
Newburgh Fife 73 E3 tn with small harbour on S bank of Firth of Tay 9m/14km W of Cupar. Linoleum mnfre. NO 2318
Newburgh Grampian 83 H4 vil with quay on W side of R Ythan estuary 1m N of **Newburgh Bar** at mouth of r. Vil is 4m/7km SE of Ellon. NJ 9925
Newburgh Lancs 42 A1/B1 vil 3m/5km N of Skelmersdale. SD 4810
Newburgh Priory N Yorks 50 B1 ham and remains of monastery in grnds of 18c mansion, 1km SE of Coxwold. SE 5476
Newburn Tyne & Wear 61 F5 suburb on N side of R Tyne 5m/8km W of Newcastle. Coal-mining and mnfre of glass, steel, etc. NZ 1665
Newbury Berks 18 A4 tn on R Kennet 16m/25km W of Reading. Site of two Civil War battles. Racecourse to SE. SU 4767
New Bury Gtr Manchester 42 C1* loc adjoining Farnworth to SW. SD 7205
Newbury Som 16 C6* ham 2km NE of Coleford and 3m/5km S of Radstock. ST 6950
Newbury Wilts 16 D6* loc adjoining Horningsham to E and 4m/6km SW of Warminster. ST 8241
Newbury Park London 20 B3* loc in borough of Redbridge 2km NE of Ilford. TQ 4488
Newby Cumbria 53 E3 vil 6m/9km W of Appleby. **Newby End** and **Newby Hd** locs adjoining to E and W respectively. NY 5921
Newby Lancs 48 B3 ham 2m/3km SW of Gisburn. SD 8145
Newby N Yorks 48 A2 ham 3m/4km SE of Ingleton. **Newby Cote** loc to NE. SD 7270
Newby N Yorks 49 F2 loc 3m/5km W of Boroughbridge. Hall is 18c hse partly by Adam with garden bordering R Ure. SE 3467
Newby N Yorks 54 D4 vil 3m/4km NW of Stokesley. NZ 5012
Newby N Yorks 55 H5 loc adjoining Scarborough to NW. TA 0190
Newby Bridge Cumbria 52 D6 vil 8m/12km NE of Ulverston. SD 3786
Newby Cross Cumbria 59 H6 loc 3m/5km SW of Carlisle. NY 3653
Newby East Cumbria 60 A5* ham 4m/6km SW of Brampton. NY 4758
New Byth Grampian 83 F2 vil 7m/11km NE of Turriff. NJ 8253
Newby West Cumbria 59 H5* ham 2m/4km SW of Carlisle. NY 3653
Newby Wiske N Yorks 54 C6 vil 4m/6km S of Northallerton. SE 3687
Newcastle Fife 73 F4* W dist of Glenrothes. NO 2401
Newcastle Gwent 25 A5 ham 5m/8km NW of Monmouth. SO 4417
Newcastle (Castellnewydd, Y) Mid Glam 15 E3 dist of Bridgend on W side of R Ogmore. Ruins of 12c cas (A.M.). SS 9079
Newcastle Salop 34 A6 vil on R Clun 4m/6km W of Clun. SO 2482
Newcastle Emlyn (Castellnewydd Emlyn) Dyfed 23 E2 small tn on R Teifi 9m/14km E of Cardigan. Dairy produce, woollen mnfre. SN 3040
Newcastle, Little (Casnewydd-bach) Dyfed 22 C3 vil 5m/9km S of Fishguard. SM 9828
Newcastleton Borders 60 B3 tn on Liddel Water 17m/27km S of Hawick. Knitwear mnfre. **Newcastleton Forest** to E forms part of Border Forest Park. NY 4887
Newcastle-under-Lyme Staffs 42 D6 tn adjoining Stoke-on-Trent to W. Industries include coal-mining, engineering. SJ 8445
Newcastle upon Tyne Tyne & Wear 61 G5 city and port on R Tyne about 11m/17km upstream from r mouth and 80m/129km N of Leeds. Commercial and industrial centre: coal-mining, shipbuilding, marine engineering, chemicals, etc. Cathedral, formerly par ch. 12c cas keep, restored. 13c Black Gate. Airport 5m/8km NW; see Woolsington. NZ 2464
New Catton Norfolk 39 F4* dist of Norwich 1m N of city centre. TG 2310
Newchapel (Capel Newydd) Dyfed 22 D2 ham 5m/8km W of Newcastle Emlyn. SN 2239
Newchapel Staffs 42 D5* loc 2km E of Kidsgrove. SJ 8554
Newchapel Surrey 12 A3 ham 3m/5km NW of E Grinstead. TQ 3642
New Charlton London 20 B4* loc on S bank of R Thames at Woolwich Reach, borough of Greenwich, 7m/11km E of Charing Cross. TQ 4178
New Chesterton Cambs 29 H2* N dist of Cambridge. TL 4459
Newchurch (Eglwys Newydd, Yr) Powys 25 G3 ham 5m/9km N of Hay-on-Wye. SO 2150
Newchurch (Eglwys Newydd ar y Cefn, Yr) Gwent 16 A2 ham 2m/3km W of Devauden. ST 4597
Newchurch (Llannewydd) Dyfed 23 E3/F3 ham 3m/5km NW of Carmarthen. SN 3824
Newchurch Gwent 15 F1* loc 1m N of Ebbw Vale. SO 1710
Newchurch Isle of Wight 10 C6 vil 2m/4km NW of Sandown. SZ 5685
Newchurch Kent 13 F4 vil on Romney Marsh 4m/7km N of New Romney. TR 0531
Newchurch Lancs 48 B4 ham 3m/4km NW of Nelson. SD 8239
Newchurch Lancs 48 B5 urban loc 2m/3km E of Rawtenstall. SD 8322
Newchurch Staffs 35 G2 ham 6m/9km W of Burton upon Trent. SK 1423
New Clipstone Notts 44 B4 coal-mining loc 3m/5km NE of Mansfield. See also Clipstone. SK 5863
Newcombe, Little Devon 7 G5* loc 3m/5km E of Crediton. SX 8899
New Costessey Norfolk 39 F4* suburb 3m/5km W of Norwich. TG 1810
New Coundon Durham 54 B2* loc 2km E of Bishop Auckland. NZ 2230
New Cowper Cumbria 52 B1* loc 2km NW of Westnewton. NY 1245
Newcraighall Lothian 66 B2 colliery vil in Edinburgh 2km SE of Portobello. NT 3271
New Crofton W Yorks 49 F6* vil adjoining Crofton to SE. SE 3817
New Cross Dyfed 24 C1 loc 4m/7km SE of Aberystwyth. SN 6377
New Cross London 20 A4* dist in borough of Lewisham 5m/7km SE of Charing Cross. Includes loc of **New Cross Gate**. TQ 3676
New Cross Som 8 C3* ham 3m/5km W of Martock. ST 4119
New Cumnock S'clyde 56 F3 small tn at confluence of Afton Water and R Nith 5m/8km SE of Cumnock. Mnfre of bricks, hosiery. Coal-mining in vicinity. NS 6113
New Cut 39 H4/H5 artificial channel connecting R Yare at Reedham, Norfolk, with R Waveney near St Olaves. Length 4km. TG 4201
New Deer Grampian 83 G2 vil 14m/23km SW of Fraserburgh. NJ 8846
New Delaval Nthmb 61 G3/G4 loc adjoining Blyth to SW. NZ 2979
New Delight W Yorks 48 C5 ham 2m/3km W of Hebden Br. SD 9628
New Delph Gtr Manchester 43 E1 loc 4m/7km NE of Oldham. See also Delph. SD 9807
New Denham Bucks 19 E3* suburban loc 1km NW of Uxbridge. TQ 0484
Newdigate Surrey 11 G1 vil 5m/8km S of Dorking. TQ 1942
New Downs Cornwall 2 A5* loc on W side of St Just. SW 3631
Newdowns Head Cornwall 2 C3* headland 1km E of St Agnes Hd. SW 7051
New Duston Northants 28 C2 NW dist of Northampton. SP 7162
New Earswick N Yorks 50 B3 suburb 2m/3km N of York. SE 6055
New Edlington S Yorks 44 A2 coal-mining loc and suburb 4m/6km SW of Doncaster. See also Old Edlington. SK 5398
New Elgin Grampian 82 B1 S dist of Elgin. NJ 2261
New Ellerby Humberside 51 F4* vil 7m/11km N of Hedon. TA 1739
Newell Green Berks 18 D4 vil 2km NE of Bracknell. SU 8871
New Eltham London 20 B4* loc in borough of Greenwich 2km SE of Eltham. TQ 4372
New End H & W 27 E2 ham 3m/5km NW of Alcester. SP 0560
Newenden Kent 12 D4 vil on R Rother 5m/8km SW of Tenterden. TQ 8327
New England Cambs 37 F4/G4 dist of Peterborough 2m/3km N of city centre. TF 1801

New England Essex 30 C4* loc 3m/5km SE of Haverhill. TL 7042

New England Island Essex 21 E3/F3 island bounded by creeks 4m/6km NE of Shoeburyness. TQ 9790

Newent Glos 26 C5 small tn 8m/13km NW of Gloucester. SO 7225

Newerne Glos 16 B1 loc adjoining Lydney to NE. SO 6303

New Farnley W Yorks 49 E5 loc in Leeds 1km S of Farnley and 4m/6km SW of city centre. SE 2531

New Ferry Merseyside 41 H3 loc beside R Mersey estuary 2m/4km S of Birkenhead. SJ 3385

Newfield Durham 54 B2 vil 3m/5km W of Spennymoor. NZ 2033

Newfield Durham 61 G6 vil 2m/3km W of Chester-le-Street. NZ 2452

Newfield H'land 87 B8 loc in Ross and Cromarty dist 3m/5km S of Tain. NH 7877

New Fletton Cambs 37 G4* S dist of Peterborough. TL 1897

New Forest Hants 10 A4 area of heath and woodland extending W of Southampton to valley of R Avon at Fordingbridge and Ringwood, of nearly 150 sq miles or about 390 sq km, of which about two-thirds are Crown lands. The 'forest', or royal hunting ground, was 'new' in the 11c. SU 20

Newfound Hants 18 B6* loc 4m/6km W of Basingstoke. SU 5851

New Fryston W Yorks 49 F5* loc in coal-mining area 2m/3km NE of Castleford. SE 4527

Newgale (Niwgwl) Dyfed 22 B4 ham on St Brides Bay 3m/5km E of Solva. **Newgale Sands** stretch southwards from here to Rickets Hd. SM 8422

New Galloway D & G 58 C4 small tn on W side of Water of Ken valley 17m/27km N of Kirkcudbright. NX 6377

Newgate Lancs 42 B1* loc adjoining Up Holland to W. SD 5105

Newgate Norfolk 39 E1* loc adjoining Cley to S and containing Cley ch. TG 0443

Newgate Street Herts 19 G1 ham 4m/7km NW of Cheshunt. TL 3005

New Greens Herts 19 F1* N dist of St Albans. TL 1409

New Grimsby Isles of Scilly 2 A1* vil on W coast of island of Tresco; harbour. SV 8815

New Hadley Salop 34 D3* loc 2m/3km E of Wellington. SJ 6811

Newhailes Lothian 66 B2 loc adjoining Musselburgh to W. NT 3372

Newhall Ches 42 B6* vil 5m/8km NE of Whitchurch. SJ 6045

Newhall Derbys 35 H2 urban loc 2km NW of Swadlincote. SK 2920

New Hall Hey Bridge Lancs 48 B5* loc in S part of Rawtenstall. SD 8022

Newham London 20 A3/B3* borough on N side of R Thames bounded by R Lea on the west and R Roding on the east and containing tns of E and W Ham and the Royal Victoria, Royal Albert, and King George V Docks. TQ 4183

Newham Nthmb 67 H5 loc 4m/6km SW of Seahouses. NU 1728

Newhampton H & W 26 B2* loc 4m/7km NW of Bromyard. SO 5857

New Hartley Nthmb 61 G4 loc 3m/5km S of Blyth. NZ 3076

Newhaven E Sussex 12 B6 container and cross-Channel passenger port at mouth of R Ouse 9m/14km E of Brighton. TQ 4401

Newhaven Lothian 66 A1* dist of Edinburgh 2m/3km N of city centre. Small harbour with fish mkt on W side of Leith Harbour. NT 2577

New Haw Surrey 19 E5 loc on R Wey Navigation 3m/4km S of Chertsey. TQ 0563

New Headington Oxon 18 A1* E dist of Oxford. SP 5506

New Heaton Nthmb 67 F4* loc 2m/3km E of Cornhill on Tweed. NT 8840

New Hedges Dyfed 22 D5 loc 2km N of Tenby. SN 1202

New Herrington Tyne & Wear 61 H6* loc 2m/3km N of Houghton-le-Spring. NZ 3352

New Hey Gtr Manchester 48 C6 loc adjoining Milnrow to SE. SD 9311

Newhill S Yorks 44 A1 S dist of Wath upon Dearne. SK 4399

New Hinksey Oxon 18 A1* dist of Oxford 1m S of city centre. SP 5104

New Holland Humberside 51 E5 vil on S bank of R Humber opp Hull. Car ferry to Hull. TA 0823

Newholm N Yorks 55 G4 ham 2m/3km W of Whitby. NZ 8610

New Houghton Derbys 44 A4 vil 4m/6km NW of Mansfield. SK 4965

New Houghton Norfolk 38 C2 ham to S of Houghton Hall on edge of park. See also Houghton. TR 7927

Newhouse Industrial Estate S'clyde. See Holytown.

New Houses Durham 53 H3* loc on N side of Hury Resr 3m/5km SW of Hunderthwaite. NY 9419

New Houses Gtr Manchester 42 B1* loc 3m/4km SW of Wigan tn centre. SD 5502

New Humberstone Leics 36 C4* dist of Leicester 2m/3km E of city centre. See also Humberstone. SK 6105

New Hunstanton Norfolk 38 B1 dist of Hunstanton to N of tn centre. TF 6741

New Hunwick Durham 54 B2* loc 1km N of Hunwick. NZ 1833

New Hutton Cumbria 53 E5 ham 3m/5km E of Kendal. SD 5691

New Hythe Kent 20 D5 paper-mnfg loc on R Medway 4m/6km NW of Maidstone. TQ 7159

Newick E Sussex 12 A4 vil 4m/6km W of Uckfield. TQ 4121

Newingreen Kent 13 F3 loc 2m/4km W of Hythe. TR 1236

Newington Kent 13 G3 vil 3m/4km W of Folkestone. TR 1837

Newington Kent 13 H1* W dist of Ramsgate. TR 3666

Newington Kent 21 E5 vil 3m/5km W of Sittingbourne. Site of Roman villa 1m N. TQ 8665

Newington London 19 G4* dist in borough of Southwark N of New Kent Rd. TQ 3279

Newington Lothian 66 A2* dist of Edinburgh 2km SE of city centre. NT 2672

Newington Notts 44 B2* ham 2km NE of Bawtry. SK 6694

Newington Oxon 18 B2 vil 5m/7km N of Wallingford. SU 6096

Newington Bagpath Glos 16 C2 loc 5m/8km W of Tetbury. ST 8194

Newington, North Oxon 27 H4 vil 3m/4km W of Banbury. SP 4239

Newington, South Oxon 27 H4 vil 6m/9km SW of Banbury. SP 4033

New Inn Dyfed 24 B4 vil 6m/9km SW of Llanybydder. SN 4736

New Inn Gwent 15 G2 suburb 2km SE of Pontypool. ST 3099

New Invention Salop 34 A6 ham 3m/5km N of Knighton. SO 2976

New Invention W Midlands 35 F4 loc in Walsall 3m/5km NW of tn centre. SJ 9701

New Junction Canal 49 G6-H6 canal linking Sheffield and S Yorks Navigation at Bramwith Junction, S Yorks, with Aire and Calder Canal S of Snaith, Humberside.

New Kelso H'land 80 A3* locality in Ross and Cromarty dist 3m/5km NE of Lochcarron. NG 9342

Newkirk Grampian 77 E1 vil 4m/6km NW of Dinnet. NJ 4304

New Kyo Durham 61 F6* loc adjoining Annfield Plain to E. NZ 1751

New Lambton Durham 61 G6* loc 3m/4km E of Chester-le-Street. NZ 3150

New Lanark S'clyde 65 F4 vil 1km S of Lanark. NS 8842

Newland Cornwall 2 D1 small island 1km NW of Pentire Pt, 4m/6km N of Padstow. SX 9181

Newland Cumbria 46 D1* loc 1m NE of Ulverston. SD 3079

Newland Glos 16 B1 vil 4m/6km SE of Monmouth. SO 5509

Newland Humberside 50 C5* loc 1km SE of Eastrington. SE 8029

Newland Humberside 51 E5 dist of Hull containing university, 2m/4km NW of city centre. TA 0731

Newland H & W 26 C3* vil 2m/3km NE of Gt Malvern. SO 7948

Newland N Yorks 50 C5 ham on N bank of R Aire 7m/11km SE of Selby. SE 6924

Newland Oxon 17 G1 loc adjoining Witney to E. SP 3610

Newland Som 7 F2* ham on Exmoor 2m/3km W of Exford. SS 8238

Newland Common H & W 26 D2* loc 2m/3km S of Droitwich. SO 9060

Newland Hall W Yorks 49 F5* loc 1m W of Normanton. SE 3622

Newlands Cumbria 52 D1* loc 1m NE of Hesket Newmarket. NY 3439

Newlands Essex 20 D3* E dist of Canvey I. TQ 8183

Newlands Grampian 82 C1* loc near N coast 4m/6km SW of Buckie. NJ 3761

Newlands Nthmb 61 F5* ham 1km W of Ebchester. NZ 0955

Newlands S'clyde 64 C3* loc in Glasgow 3m/5km S of city centre. NS 5760

New Lane Lancs 42 A1* loc 1m NW of Burscough Br. SD 4212

New Lane End Ches 42 C2* loc 2m/3km W of Culcheth. SJ 6394

Newlay W Yorks 49 E4 loc on R Aire 4m/6km NW of Leeds city centre. SE 2436

New Leake Lincs 45 G5* ham 6m/10km W of Wainfleet. TF 4057

New Leeds Grampian 83 G2 vil 3m/5km E of Strichen. NJ 9954

New Lodge S Yorks 43 G1* loc in Barnsley 2m/3km N of tn centre. SE 3409

New Longton Lancs 47 F5* loc 2m/3km E of Longton. SD 5025

New Luce D & G 57 B6 vil 5m/8km N of Glenluce, at confluence of Cross Water of Luce and Main Water of Luce. NX 1764

Newlyn Cornwall 2 A5 S dist of Penzance, with harbour. Fishing, canning. SW 4628

Newlyn East Cornwall 2 D3 vil 4m/6km S of Newquay. SW 8256

Newmachar Grampian 83 G5 vil 9m/14km N of Aberdeen. NJ 8819

Newmains S'clyde 65 E3 tn 2m/3km E of Wishaw. NS 8256

New Malden London 19 F4 dist in borough of Kingston 2m/4km E of Kingston tn centre. TQ 2168

Newman's End Essex 20 B1* loc 5m/8km E of Harlow. TL 5112

Newman's Green Suffolk 30 D3/D4* ham 2m/3km NE of Sudbury. TL 8843

Newmarket Suffolk 30 B2 tn 13m/20km E of Cambridge. HQ of British horse-racing. Racecourses. TL 6463

Newmarket W Isles 88 C2* vil on Lewis 2m/3km N of Stornoway, adjoining Laxdale to N across R Laxdale. NB 4235

New Marske Cleveland 55 E3 vil 2km SW of Marske-by-the-Sea. NZ 6221

New Marston Oxon 18 A1* dist of Oxford E of R Cherwell, 2km NE of city centre. SP 5207

New Marton Salop 34 A1* loc 3m/4km N of Whittington. SJ 3334

New Micklefield W Yorks 49 F5 vil 5m/7km N of Castleford. SE 4432

Newmill Borders 60 A1 loc in Teviotdale 4m/7km SW of Hawick, at confluence of Allan Water and R Teviot. NT 4510

Newmill Cornwall 2 A5 ham 2m/4km N of Penzance. SW 4534

Newmill Grampian 82 D2 vil 1m N of Keith. NJ 4350

New Mill Herts 18 D1 loc 1km N of Tring. SP 9212

New Mill W Yorks 43 F1* vil 2km E of Holmfirth. SE 1408

Newmillerdam W Yorks 49 E6 vil 3m/5km S of Wakefield. SE 3215

New Mills Cornwall 2 D3* vil 7m/11km W of St Austell. SW 8952

New Mills Derbys 43 E3 industrial tn 8m/13km NW of Buxton. Paper mnfre, textile processing, confectionery. SK 0085

New Mills Glos 16 B1* loc 1m N of Lydney. SO 6304

Newmills Gwent 16 A1* ham 3m/5km S of Monmouth. SO 5107

Newmills H'land 81 F1 loc in Ross and Cromarty dist 2m/3km SW of Balblair on Cromarty Firth. NH 6764

Newmills Lothian 65 G2/H2* loc just N of Balerno across Water of Leith. NT 1667

New Mills Powys 33 G4* ham 4m/6km S of Llanfair Caereinion. SJ 0901

Newmilns S'clyde 64 C5 tn (with Greenholm) on R Irvine 7m/11km E of Kilmarnock. NS 5337

New Milton Hants 10 A5 urban loc 5m/8km W of Lymington. SZ 2495

New Moat Dyfed 22 C3 vil 2m/3km SW of Maenclochog. Traces of motte and bailey cas. SN 0625

New Monkland S'clyde 65 E2 vil 2m/3km NW of Airdrie. NS 7567

New Moston Gtr Manchester 42 D1* dist of Manchester 4m/7km NE of city centre. See also Moston. SD 8902

Newney Green Essex 20 C1* ham 3m/5km W of Chelmsford. TL 6506

Newnham Cambs 30 A2* SW dist of Cambridge. Women's college of Cambridge University to N. TL 4457

Newnham Glos 26 C6 vil on right bank of R Severn 10m/16km SW of Gloucester across loops of r. SO 6911

Newnham Hants 18 B5 vil 2km W of Hook. SU 7054

Newnham Herts 29 F4 vil 2m/4km N of Baldock. TL 2437

Newnham Kent 21 E5 vil 5m/8km SW of Faversham. TQ 9557

Newnham Northants 28 B2 vil 2m/3km S of Daventry. SP 5759

Newnham Bridge H & W 26 B1 vil 3m/5km E of Tenbury Wells. SO 6469

Newnham Murren Oxon 18 B3 loc across R Thames from Wallingford. SU 6189

New Normanton Derbys 36 A1* dist of Derby 2km S of city centre. SK 3534

Newnton, North Wilts 17 F5 vil 2m/3km N of Upavon. SU 1357

New Ollerton Notts 44 B4* residential loc adjoining Ollerton to N. SK 6668

New Oscott W Midlands 35 G5 loc 2m/3km SW of Sutton Coldfield. SP 0994

New Park N Yorks 49 E3 dist of Harrogate 1m N of tn centre. SE 2956

New Parks Leics 36 B4* loc in Leicester 2m/3km NW of city centre. SK 5804

New Pitsligo Grampian 83 G2 vil 10m/16km SW of Fraserburgh. See also Pitsligo Castle. NJ 8855

New Polzeath Cornwall 3 E1* loc adjoining Polzeath to N. SW 9379

Newport Devon 6 D2* SW dist of Barnstaple. SS 5632

Newport (Trefdraeth) Dyfed 22 C2 small tn at mouth of R Nyfer, 9m/14km SW of Cardigan. Remains of 13c cas. **Newport Bay** to NW extends eastwards from Dinas Hd. SN 0539

Newport Essex 30 A4 vil 3m/5km SW of Saffron Walden. TL 5234

Newport Glos 16 C2* vil 2km SE of Berkeley. ST 6997

Newport (Casnewydd-ar-Wysg) Gwent 15 G3 industrial county tn and port on R Usk 10m/16km NE of Cardiff. Ship-repairing; steel, iron, brass, and aluminium mnfre; engineering; electrical goods. Transporter br across R Usk above docks area. Cathedral, former par ch. Sparse ruins of 12c cas (A.M.). ST 3088

Newport H'land 86 D4 vil near E coast of Caithness dist 4m/6km SW of Dunbeath. ND 1324

Newport Humberside 50 D5* vil 7m/11km E of Howden. SE 8530

Newport Isle of Wight 10 B5 tn at head of R Medina estuary 4m/7km S of Cowes and midway between Yarmouth and Bembridge. SZ 4989

Newport Norfolk 39 H3* coastal loc and resort 6m/10km N of Gt Yarmouth. TG 5016

Newport Salop 34 D3 tn on Shropshire Union Canal 8m/12km NE of Wellington. SJ 7419

Newport Som 8 B2* ham 2km S of N Curry. ST 3123

Newport, High Tyne & Wear 61 H6* dist of Sunderland 2m/3km SW of tn centre. NZ 3854

Newport-on-Tay Fife 73 G2 tn on S bank of Firth of Tay opp Dundee. NO 4228

Newport Pagnell Bucks 28 D3 tn at confluence of R Ouse and R Ouzel or Lovat, 6m/10km N of Bletchley. Various mnfres. SP 8743

Newpound Common W Sussex 11 F2* loc 2m/3km NW of Billingshurst. TQ 0627

New Prestwick S'clyde 64 B6 loc at S end of Prestwick. NS 3424

Newquay Cornwall 2 D2 coastal resort with several sandy beaches, 11m/17km N of Truro. **Newquay Bay,** N of the tn, extends from Trevelgue Hd westwards to Towan Hd. SW 8161

New Quay (Ceinewydd) Dyfed 24 A2 small coastal resort 19m/30km SW of Aberystwyth across Cardigan Bay. **New Quay Hd** headland to N. SN 3859

New Quay Essex 31 E5* loc on R Colne in SE part of Colchester. TM 0223

New Quorndon Leics 36 B3* loc 2m/3km SE of Loughborough. SK 5516

New Rackheath Norfolk 39 G4* vil 4m/7km NE of Norwich. TG 2812

New Radnor (Maesyfed) Powys 25 G2 vil 6m/10km NW of Kington. Former county tn of Radnorshire. Motte and bailey earthworks mark site of Norman cas. Traces of tn walls on SW side of vil. SO 2160
New Rent Cumbria 52 D2* loc 2km NE of Skelton. NY 4536
New Ridley Nthmb 61 F5* ham 3m/5km SW of Prudhoe. NZ 0559
New River 19 G3 artificial r starting near Ware, Herts, and flowing S into two resrs N of Stoke Newington in London borough of Hackney. TQ 3287
New Road Side N Yorks 48 C4 loc adjoining Cowling to E. SD 9743
New Road Side W Yorks 48 D5* loc in Bradford 3m/5km N of Brighouse. SE 1527
New Romney Kent 13 F4 tn 9m/14km SW of Hythe, and 2km inland from Littlestone-on-Sea on St Mary's Bay. TR 0624
New Rossington S Yorks 44 B2 coal-mining loc and suburb 4m/7km SE of Doncaster. SK 6197
New Row Dyfed 24 C1* loc 1m NW of Pontrhydygroes. SN 7273
New Row Lancs 47 G4 loc 5m/9km W of Whalley. SD 6438
Newsam Green W Yorks 49 F5* loc 1m W of Swillington. SE 3630
New Sarum Wilts. Former, and still official, name of Salisbury, given to it when the tn was moved from Old Sarum.
New Sauchie Central 72 C5 loc adjoining Alloa to NE. NS 8994
New Sawley Derbys 36 B2 loc adjoining Long Eaton to SW. SK 4732
Newsbank Ches 42 D4* loc 3m/4km NW of Congleton. SJ 8366
New Scarbro' W Yorks 49 E4* dist of Leeds 3m/5km W of city centre. SE 2434
New Scone Tayside 73 E2. See Scone Palace.
Newseat Grampian 83 E4/F4* loc 2m/3km N of Kirktown of Rayne. NJ 7032
Newsells Herts 29 G4* loc 3m/5km SE of Royston. TL 3837
New Selma S'clyde 70 B1 vil on Ardmucknish Bay 3m/4km N of Connel, Argyll. NM 9038
Newsham Cleveland 54 C4 loc 6m/10km SW of Stockton-on-Tees. NZ 3811
Newsham Lancs 47 F4 ham 5m/8km N of Preston. SD 5136
Newsham Nthmb 61 G3 loc adjoining Blyth to SW. **S Newsham** loc to S. NZ 3079
Newsham N Yorks 54 A4 vil 7m/11km NW of Richmond. NZ 1010
Newsham N Yorks 54 C6 loc 4m/6km NW of Thirsk. SE 3784
Newsham, Little Durham 54 A3 vil 2m/3km S of Staindrop. NZ 1217
New Sharlston W Yorks 49 F6* coal-mining vil 2km S of Normanton. SE 3820
New Shawbost W Isles 88 B1* vil near NW coast of Lewis adjacent to N and S Shawbost and 2m/4km W of Bragar. NB 2646
Newsholme Humberside 50 C5* ham 2m/3km NW of Howden. SE 7229
Newsholme Lancs 48 B3 loc 2m/3km N of Gisburn. SD 8451
Newsholme W Yorks 48 C4* ham 3m/4km W of Keighley. SE 0239
New Shoreston Nthmb 67 H5* loc 2m/3km SE of Bamburgh. NU 1932
New Silksworth Tyne & Wear 61 H6 dist of Sunderland 3m/4km S of tn centre. NZ 3853
New Skelton Cleveland 55 E3* loc 1km E of Skelton. NZ 6618
Newsome W Yorks 48 D6* loc in Huddersfield 1m S of tn centre. SE 1414
New Somerby Lincs 37 E1* SE dist of Grantham. SK 9235
New Springs Gtr Manchester 42 B1* loc 2m/3km NE of Wigan. SD 6007
New Sprowston Norfolk 39 F4* N dist of Norwich. TG 2311
New Stapleford Notts 36 B1* loc 3m/4km W of Beeston. SK 4938
Newstead Borders 66 C5 vil 2km E of Melrose. Remains of Roman fort of *Trimontium* to E. NT 5634
Newstead Notts 44 A5 coal-mining vil 3m/5km SE of Kirkby in Ashfield. **Newstead Abbey,** in park 2km NE, given to Lord Byron's ancestors at Dissolution; Byron relics. SK 5152
Newstead W Yorks 49 F6* loc adjoining Havercroft to NE. SE 3914
New Stevenston S'clyde 65 E3* loc 2m/3km NE of Motherwell. NS 7659
New Swanage Dorset 9 G6* N dist of Swanage. SZ 0380
New Swannington Leics 36 A3* loc 1m N of Coalville. SK 4215
New Thirsk N Yorks 54 C6/D6* loc adjoining Thirsk to W. Thirsk Racecourse is here. SE 4282
Newthorpe Notts 44 A6* E dist of Eastwood. SK 4846
Newthorpe N Yorks 49 F5 ham 2m/3km SW of Sherburn in Elmet. SE 4732
New Thundersley Essex 20 D3* W dist of Thundersley, 4m/6km E of Basildon. TQ 7789
Newtimber W Sussex 11 H4 par on N slopes of S Downs to E of Poynings containing **Newtimber Hill** (NT), with views of sea and Weald, and **Newtimber Place,** moated 17c–18c hse. TQ 2613
New Tolsta W Isles 88 C1 vil near E coast of Lewis 2m/4km NW of Tolsta Hd. NB 5348
Newton Avon 16 B2 loc 2m/3km N of Thornbury. ST 6492
Newton Cambs 29 H3 vil 6m/9km S of Cambridge. TL 4349
Newton Cambs 37 H3 vil 4m/6km NW of Wisbech. TF 4314
Newton Ches 42 A4 NE dist of Chester. SJ 4268
Newton Ches 42 B4* loc 2m/3km S of Frodsham. SJ 5274
Newton Ches 42 B5 ham 2km NE of Tattenhall. SJ 5059
Newton Cumbria 46 D1 vil 2m/3km S of Dalton-in-Furness. SD 2271
Newton Derbys 43 H5 vil 3m/5km NE of Alfreton. SK 4459
Newton D & G 59 F2 vil 7m/11km S of Moffat. NY 1194
Newton Gtr Manchester 43 E2 loc 1km NE of Hyde. **Newton Moor** loc adjoining to N. SJ 9595
Newton H'land 81 G1 loc in Ross and Cromarty dist 1m SW of Cromarty. NH 7766
Newton H'land 81 G3 loc in Inverness dist near E shore of Inner Moray Firth or Inverness Firth, 2m/3km E of Alturlie Pt. NH 7448
Newton H'land 86 F3 loc in Caithness dist 2km SW of Wick. ND 3449
Newton H & W 25 H1 loc 4m/6km SW of Leintwardine. SO 3769
Newton H & W 25 H4 vil 5m/7km NW of Pontrilas. SO 3433
Newton H & W 26 A2* vil 3m/5km S of Leominster. SO 5053
Newton Lancs 47 E4* loc 2m/4km E of Blackpool. SD 3436
Newton Lancs 47 E5 vil 2m/3km SE of Kirkham. SD 4430
Newton Lancs 47 F1 ham 3m/4km S of Kirkby Lonsdale. SD 5974
Newton Lancs 47 G3 vil on R Hodder 6m/10km NW of Clitheroe. SD 6950
Newton Lincs 37 F1 vil 6m/10km S of Sleaford. TF 0436
Newton Lothian 65 G1 loc 2m/3km W of S end of Forth Rd Br. NT 0977
Newton (Drenewydd) Mid Glam 14 D4 E suburb of Porthcawl. SS 8377
Newton Norfolk 38 C3 ham 4m/7km N of Swaffham. TF 8315
Newton Northants 36 D6* vil 3m/5km N of Kettering. SP 8883
Newton Notts 36 C1 vil 2m/3km NW of Bingham. SK 6841
Newton Nthmb 61 E1 loc 2km E of Alwinton. NT 9407
Newton Nthmb 61 E5 vil 3m/5km E of Corbridge. NZ 0364
Newton N Yorks 50 D1* loc 1km SE of Wintringham. SE 8872
Newton (Drenewydd, Y) S Glam 15 G3* loc 2km E of Rumney. ST 2378
Newton Salop 34 B1* loc 2km E of Ellesmere. **Newton Mere** is a small lake. SJ 4234
Newton S'clyde 64 D3 loc 6m/9km SE of Glasgow. NS 6660
Newton S'clyde 70 C5 locality on **Newton Bay** on S shore of Loch Fyne, Argyll, opp Furnace. NS 0498
Newton Som 7 H2* ham 4m/6km SE of Watchet. ST 1038
Newton Staffs 35 F2 vil 5m/8km N of Rugeley. SK 0325
Newton Suffolk 30 D4 vil 3m/5km E of Sudbury. TL 9140
Newton S Yorks 44 B1* dist of Doncaster 1km W of tn centre. SE 5602
Newton Warwicks 36 B6 vil 3m/4km NE of Rugby. SP 5378
Newton W Glam 23 G6 loc on W side of Mumbles. SS 6088
Newton Wilts 9 H2 loc 7m/12km SE of Salisbury. SU 2322
Newton W Midlands 35 F5* loc 2m/4km NE of W Bromwich tn centre. SP 0393
Newton W Yorks 49 F5* loc 2m/3km E of Allerton Bywater. SE 4427
Newton Abbot Devon 5 E3 mkt tn at head of R Teign estuary. SX 8671
Newton Arlosh Cumbria 59 G5 vil 2m/3km SW of Kirkbride. NY 1955
Newton Aycliffe Durham 54 C3 New Tn designated 1947, 6m/10km N of Darlington. Light industry. NZ 2724
Newton Bay Dorset 9 G5* inlet on S side of Poole Harbour. SZ 0085
Newton Bewley Cleveland 54 D2 ham 1m NE of Wolviston. NZ 4626
Newton Blossomville Bucks 28 D3 vil on R Ouse 6m/9km NE of Newport Pagnell. SP 9251
Newton Bromswold Northants 29 E2 vil 3m/4km E of Rushden. SP 9965
Newton Burgoland Leics 36 A3 vil 5m/8km S of Ashby de la Zouch. SK 3609
Newton-by-the-Sea, High Nthmb 67 H5 vil 2m/3km N of Embleton. **Low Newton-by-the-Sea** ham 1km SE. NU 2325
Newton by Toft Lincs 45 E3 vil 4m/6km W of Mkt Rasen. TF 0587
Newton Common Merseyside 42 B2* suburb adjoining Newton-le-Willows to W. SJ 5695
Newton, East Humberside 51 G4* coastal loc 2km E of Aldbrough. TA 2637
Newton, East N Yorks 50 B1* loc 2km E of Oswaldkirk. SE 6479
Newton Ferrers Devon 4 C5 tn 3m/5km SW of Yealmpton, on creek running into R Yealm estuary. Yachting. SX 5448
Newton Flotman Norfolk 39 F5 vil 7m/11km S of Norwich. TM 2198
Newtongarry Croft Grampian 83 E3* loc 4m/7km SE of Huntly. NJ 5735
Newtongrange Lothian 66 B2 coal-mining tn 2m/3km S of Dalkeith. NT 3364
Newton Green Gwent 16 A2* loc 2km SW of Chepstow. ST 5191
Newton Harcourt Leics 36 C4 vil 6m/9km SE of Leicester. SP 6396
Newton Haven Nthmb 67 H5* bay (NT) on North Sea coast 1km SE of High Newton-by-the-Sea. Also known as St Mary's Haven. Newton Pt at N end. NU 2424
Newton Heath Gtr Manchester 42 D1 dist of Manchester 3m/5km NE of city centre. SD 8800
Newton, High Cumbria 52 D6 ham 2m/3km NW of Lindale. SD 4082
Newtonhill Grampian 77 H2 vil on E coast 5m/8km NE of Stonehaven. NO 9193
Newton Hill W Yorks 49 E5* loc 1m N of Wakefield. SE 3222
Newton Ketton Durham 54 C3* loc 4m/7km N of Darlington. NZ 3120
Newton Kyme N Yorks 49 F4 vil 2m/3km NW of Tadcaster. SE 4644
Newton-le-Willows Merseyside 42 B2 tn 5m/8km E of St Helens. Coal-mining, rly works. SJ 5995
Newton-le-Willows N Yorks 54 B5 vil 3m/5km W of Bedale. SE 2189
Newton Longville Bucks 28 D4 vil 2m/4km SW of Bletchley. SP 8431
Newton Mearns S'clyde 64 C3 suburb 6m/10km SW of Glasgow. NS 5355
Newtonmill Tayside 77 F4* loc 3m/4km N of Brechin. NO 6064
Newtonmore H'land 75 G2 vil on R Spey in Badenoch and Strathspey dist 3m/5km W of Kingussie. Holiday and skiing centre. Clan Macpherson Museum. NN 7199
Newton Morrell N Yorks 54 B4 ham 3m/5km NE of Scotch Corner. NZ 2309
Newton Morrell Oxon 28 B4* loc 5m/8km NE of Bicester. SP 6129
Newton Mountain Dyfed 22 C5* ham 5m/8km S of Haverfordwest. SM 9808
Newton Mulgrave N Yorks 55 F3 loc 2m/3km S of Staithes. NZ 7815
Newton, Nether Cumbria 52 D6* ham 1km SE of High Newton. SD 4082
Newton, North and **South** S'clyde 63 F3 two adjoining localities at N end of Arran, opp Lochranza across Loch Ranza. **Newton Pt** is headland to W, at entrance to loch. NR 9351
Newton, North Som 8 B2 vil 2km SE of N Petherton. ST 3031
Newton Noyes Dyfed 22 B5* loc 1m E of Milford Haven across estuary. SM 9105
Newton of Falkland Fife 73 F4 vil 1m E of Falkland. NO 2607
Newton-on-Ouse N Yorks 50 A2 vil 7m/12km NW of York. SE 5160
Newton-on-Rawcliffe N Yorks 55 F5 vil 4m/7km N of Pickering. SE 8190
Newton on the Hill Salop 34 B2* loc 2km E of Myddle. SJ 4823
Newton-on-the-Moor Nthmb 61 F1 vil 5m/8km S of Alnwick. NU 1705
Newton on Trent Lincs 44 C4 vil 9m/15km W of Lincoln. SK 8374
Newton Point Mid Glam 14 D4* headland 2km E of Porthcawl. SS 8376
Newton Point Nthmb 67 H5* headland on North Sea coast 1km E of High Newton-by-the-Sea, at N end of Newton Haven. NU 2425
Newton Poppleford Devon 5 F2 vil 3m/5km NW of Sidmouth. SY 0889
Newton Purcell Oxon 28 B4 ham 6m/9km NE of Bicester. SP 6230
Newton Regis Warwicks 35 H3/H4 vil 5m/8km NE of Tamworth. SK 2707
Newton Reigny Cumbria 52 D2/53 E2 vil 2m/4km NW of Penrith. NY 4731
Newton St Cyres Devon 7 F5 vil 3m/5km SE of Crediton. SX 8898
Newton St Faith Norfolk 39 F3 vil 5m/9km N of Norwich. TG 2117
Newton St Loe Avon 16 C5 vil 3m/5km W of Bath. ST 7064
Newton St Petrock Devon 6 C4 vil 7m/11km SW of Torrington. SS 4112
Newton Solney Derbys 35 H2 vil 3m/5km NE of Burton upon Trent, at confluence of R Dove and R Trent. SK 2825
Newton, South Wilts 9 G1 vil on R Wylye 2m/4km N of Wilton. SU 0834
Newton Stacey Hants 10 B1* ham 2km E of Chilbolton. SU 4140
Newton Stewart D & G 57 D6 small tn on R Cree 7m/11km N of Wigtown. Cattle mkt. NX 4165
Newton Tony Wilts 9 H1 vil on R Bourne 4m/7km E of Amesbury. SU 2140
Newton Tracey Devon 6 D3 vil 4m/7km SW of Barnstaple. SS 5226
Newton under Roseberry Cleveland 55 E4 ham 3m/5km SW of Guisborough. NZ 5713
Newton Underwood Nthmb 61 F3* loc 3m/5km W of Morpeth. NZ 1486
Newton upon Ayr S'clyde 64 B6* N dist of Ayr. NS 3423
Newton upon Derwent Humberside 50 C3 vil 5m/8km W of Pocklington. SE 7249
Newton Valence Hants 10 D2 vil 4m/6km S of Alton. SU 7232
Newton, West Humberside 51 F4 ham 6m/10km N of Hedon. TA 2037
Newton, West Norfolk 38 B2/C2 vil 7m/11km NE of King's Lynn. Site of Roman villa to E. TF 6927
Newton, West Som 8 B2* ham 2m/3km E of W Monkton. ST 2829
Newton Wood Gtr Manchester 43 E2* loc 1m S of Dukinfield. SJ 9496
New Town Beds 29 E5* S dist of Luton. TL 0920
New Town Beds 29 F3 N dist of Biggleswade. TL 1945
Newtown Beds 29 F4* loc 2m/3km E of Shefford. TL 1739
Newtown Bucks 18 D2 NE dist of Chesham. SP 9602
Newtown Cambs 29 F1* dist of Huntingdon 1km NE of tn centre. TL 2472
Newtown Ches 42 B3* loc 1km NE of Frodsham. SJ 5278
Newtown Ches 43 E3* loc adjoining Poynton to E. SJ 9383
Newtown Cornwall 2 B5* loc 5m/8km W of Helston. SW 5729
Newtown Cornwall 2 C5 ham 6m/9km SE of Helston. SW 7423
Newtown Cornwall 3 F3* loc 2km NW of Fowey. SX 1052
Newtown Cornwall 4 A3* loc 5m/7km SW of Launceston. SX 2978
Newtown Cumbria 52 B1* loc adjoining Aspatria to NE. NY 1542
Newtown Cumbria 52 B1* vil 1m S of Beckfoot. Site of Roman fort of *Bibra* on coast of Solway Firth to NW. NY 0948
Newtown Cumbria 53 E2 loc 4m/6km S of Penrith. NY 5224
Newtown Cumbria 59 H5* dist of Carlisle 1m W of city centre. NY 3855
Newtown Cumbria 60 B5 ham 2m/3km NW of Brampton. NY 5062
Newtown Derbys 43 E3* loc adjoining New Mills to SW. Partly also in Ches. SJ 9984
Newtown Devon 7 F3* ham 3m/5km E of S Molton. SS 7625

Newtown Devon 7 H5* ham 3m/5km NW of Ottery St Mary. SY 0699
Newtown Dorset 8 C4* loc 1km N of Beaminster. ST 4802
New Town Dorset 9 F3* ham 4m/6km NE of Sturminster Newton. ST 8318
New Town Dorset 9 G3* ham 1m NW of Sixpenny Handley. ST 9918
New Town Dorset 9 G3 loc 1km NE of Witchampton and 7m/11km E of Blandford Forum. ST 9907
Newtown Dorset 9 G5 dist of Poole 1m NE of tn centre. SZ 0393
New Town Dyfed 22 D1 E dist of Cardigan. SN 1846
New Town E Sussex 12 B4 S dist of Uckfield. TQ 4720
Newtown Glos 16 B2 vil adjoining Sharpness to S, 2m/3km N of Berkeley. SO 6701
Newtown Glos 26 D4* NE dist of Tewkesbury. SO 9033
New Town Glos 27 E4 ham 3m/5km NE of Winchcombe. SP 0432
Newtown Grampian 82 A1/B1* loc on N coast adjoining Hopeman to W, 6m/9km W of Lossiemouth. NJ 1469
Newtown Gtr Manchester 42 D1* loc 1km N of Swinton. SD 7702
Newtown Gtr Manchester 42 B1 dist of Wigan 1m W of tn centre. SD 5605
Newtown Gwent 15 F1 loc adjoining Tredegar to N. SO 1710
Newtown Gwent 15 G2* loc adjoining Crosskeys to E. ST 2291
Newtown Hants 10 A2 ham 3m/5km NW of Romsey. SU 3023
Newtown Hants 10 A4 loc in New Forest 2m/4km NW of Lyndhurst. SU 2710
Newtown Hants 10 B4* SE dist of Southampton across R Itchen. SU 4510
Newtown Hants 10 B4* loc adjoining Warsash to S; location of School of Navigation (University of Southampton). SU 4905
Newtown Hants 10 C3 vil 4m/7km S of Meonstoke. SU 6113
Newtown Hants 10 C3 loc adjoining Bishop's Waltham to W. SU 5417
Newtown Hants 11 E2* loc in S part of Liphook. SU 8430
Newtown Hants 17 H5 vil 3m/4km S of Newbury. SU 4763
Newtown H'land 80 D6 loc in Inverness dist 3m/5km SW of Fort Augustus. NH 3504
Newtown H & W 26 A2* loc 2km SW of Leominster. SO 4757
Newtown H & W 26 C1* N dist of Stourport. SO 8172
Newtown H & W 26 D2* E dist of Worcester. SO 8755
New Town H & W 26 C2* loc 6m/10km W of Worcester. SO 7557
Newtown H & W 26 C4 W dist of Ledbury. SO 7037
Newtown H & W 26 B3 vil 7m/11km E of Hereford. SO 6144
Newtown Isle of Man 46 B6* vil 4m/6km W of Douglas. SC 3273
Newtown Isle of Wight 10 B5 vil 5m/8km W of Newport. Formerly a borough; Old Tn Hall (NT), also Noah's Ark (NT), once an inn. Estuary of **Newtown R** (NT) includes nature reserve. **Newtown Bay** at r mouth; coast E and W is NT. SZ 4290
Newtown Lancs 47 F6* loc 2m/3km E of Croston. SD 5118
New Town Lothian 66 C2* vil 3m/5km SE of Tranent. NT 4470
Newtown Mid Glam 15 E3* dist of Bridgend to N of tn centre. SS 9080
Newtown Mid Glam 15 F2* loc adjoining Mountain Ash to SE. ST 0598
Newtown Northants 37 E6* W end of vil of Woodford, 2m/4km SW of Thrapston. SP 9677
Newtown Nthmb 61 E2 ham 2km SW of Rothbury. NU 0300
Newtown Nthmb 67 F5* loc 3m/4km SE of Milfield. NT 9631
Newtown Nthmb 67 G5 ham 4m/6km SE of Wooler. NU 0425
Newtown Oxon 18 C3* S dist of Henley-on-Thames. SU 7681
Newtown Salop 34 B2* ham 3m/5km NW of Wem. SJ 4731
Newtown Som 8 B1* N dist of Bridgwater. ST 2937
Newtown Som 8 B3* ham 1km SE of Buckland St Mary. ST 2612
Newtown Staffs 35 F4* loc 4m/6km N of Walsall. SJ 9904
Newtown Staffs 43 F5 ham 2m/3km SW of Longnor. SK 0663
New Town Tyne & Wear 61 H6* SE dist of Houghton-le-Spring. NZ 3449
New Town Wilts 17 G4* ham 4m/7km W of Hungerford. SU 2871
Newtown Wilts 17 G5* loc 1m W of Hungerford. SU 3063
Newtown Wilts 9 F2 ham 5m/8km NE of Shaftesbury. ST 9129
New Town W Midlands 35 F5* loc 2m/3km W of W Bromwich tn centre. SO 9791
New Town W Midlands 35 F4* loc 1km N of Brownhills. SK 0506
Newtown (Drenewydd, Y) Powys 33 G5 tn on R Severn 12m/20km SW of Welshpool. Industries include textiles, sawmills. New Tn designated 1967 extends to W. SO 1091
Newtown Linford Leics 36 B3 vil 6m/9km NW of Leicester. SK 5110
Newtown of Rockcliffe Cumbria 59 H5* loc 4m/7km N of Carlisle. NY 3862
Newtown St Boswells Borders 66 D5 vil 3m/4km SE of Melrose. NT 5731
Newtown Unthank Leics 36 B4 loc to W of Leicester 1m NE of Desford. SK 4904
New Tredegar Mid Glam 15 F1 tn 2m/4km N of Bargoed. SO 1403
Newtyle Tayside 73 F1 vil below N side of **Newtyle Hill**, 9m/15km NW of Dundee. NO 2941
Newtyle Forest Grampian 82 A2* state forest 4m/7km S of Forres. NJ 0552
New Valley W Isles 88 C2* vil on Lewis 2km NW of Stornoway. NB 4134
New Village Humberside 50 D5 E part of vil of Newport, 7m/11km E of Howden. SE 8530
New Village S Yorks 44 B1* loc adjoining Bentley to N. SE 5606
New Walsoken Cambs 38 A4* E dist of Wisbech. TF 4709
New Waltham Humberside 45 G1* suburb 3m/5km S of Grimsby. TA 2804
New Whittington Derbys 43 H3/H4 loc 3m/4km N of Chesterfield. SK 3975
New Wimpole Cambs 29 G3 vil 6m/9km N of Royston. TL 3449
New Winton Lothian 66 B2* small vil 2m/3km SE of Tranent. See also Winton Hse. NT 4271
New World Cambs 37 H5* loc 2m/3km W of Doddington. TL 3790
New Yatt Oxon 27 G6 ham 3m/4km NE of Witney. SP 3713
New Year's Bridge Reservoir Gtr Manchester 43 E1* resr 1km E of Denshaw. SD 9810
Newyears Green London 19 E3* loc in borough of Hillingdon 3m/4km NE of Uxbridge. TQ 0788
New York Lincs 45 F5 ham 3m/4km SE of Coningsby. TF 2455
New York Tyne & Wear 61 G4* loc 3m/4km W of Tynemouth. NZ 3270
New Zealand Derbys 35 H1* dist of Derby 2m/3km W of tn centre. SK 3236
Neyland Dyfed 22 C5 small tn and former port opp Pembroke Dock across estuary and 4m/6km E of Milford Haven. SM 9605
Niarbyl Island or **The Niarbyl**, Isle of Man 46 A5 small island off W coast at N end of **Niarbyl Bay** and 1km SW of Dalby. Bay extends southwards to Bradda Hill. SC 2077
Nibley Avon 16 C3* loc 2m/3km W of Chipping Sodbury. ST 6982
Nibley Glos 16 B1 loc adjoining Blakeney to SW. SO 6606
Nibley Green Glos 16 C2* loc 2m/3km SW of Dursley. ST 7396
Nibley North Glos 16 C2 vil 2m/3km SW of Dursley. Monmt on Nibley Knoll commemorates William Tyndale, translator of the Bible. ST 7495
Nibon Shetland 89 E6* loc on coast in N part of Mainland 2m/3km NW of Mangaster. Offshore is island called **Isle of Nibon.** HU 3073
Nibthwaite, High Cumbria 52 C5 ham at S end of Coniston Water. SD 2989
Nicholashayne Devon 7 H3 ham 2m/3km N of Culmstock. ST 1016
Nicholaston W Glam 23 G6 ham on Gower peninsula above E end of Oxwich Bay on S coast. SS 5288
Nickie's Hill Cumbria 60 B4* loc 2km S of Kirkambeck. NY 5264
Nick of Pendle Lancs 48 A4* pass on Pendleton Moor on SW side of Pendle Hill, carrying rd between Clitheroe and Sabden. SD 7738
Nidd N Yorks 49 E2 ham 1m E of Ripley. SE 3060
Nidd 49 G3 r rising on N slope of Gt Whernside, N Yorks, and flowing E through Angram and Scar House Resrs, then SE by Pateley Br and Knaresborough to Walshford, then E to join R Ouse at Nun Monkton. SE 5157
Niddrie Lothian 66 B2 dist of Edinburgh 3m/5km SE of city centre. NT 3071
Niddry Castle Lothian. See Winchburgh.
Nidum W Glam. See Neath.
Nigg Grampian 77 H1 loc in Aberdeen 2m/3km S of city centre across R Dee. NJ 9403
Nigg H'land 81 G1 loc in Ross and Cromarty dist near E side of **Nigg Bay**, inlet of Cromarty Firth opp Cromarty. Oil refinery authorised 1976. NH 8071
Nigg Bay Grampian 77 H1 bay on E coast between Girdle Ness and Greg Ness 2m/3km SE of centre of Aberdeen across R Dee. NJ 9604
Nightcott Som 7 G3* ham 2m/3km SW of Dulverton. SS 8925
Nilston Rigg Nthmb 60 D5* loc on shore of small resr at Langley, 2m/4km SW of Haydon Br. NY 8260
Nimble Nook Gtr Manchester 42 D1* loc 2m/3km W of Oldham. SD 9004
Nine Ashes Essex 20 C2 vil 3m/4km E of Chipping Ongar. TL 5902
Ninebanks Nthmb 60 D6* ham 4m/6km SW of Allendale Tn. NY 7853
Nine Elms London 19 G4* dist in borough of Wandsworth on S bank of R Thames. Rly goods depot. Battersea Power Stn. Fruit and vegetable mkt, removed from Covent Garden in 1974. TQ 2977
Nine Elms Wilts 17 E3 ham 3m/5km W of Swindon. SU 1085
Nine Ladies Derbys 43 G4* ancient stone circle (A.M.) on Stanton Moor 4m/6km NW of Matlock. SK 2463
Nine Mile Bar D & G. See Crocketford.
Nineveh H & W 26 B2* ham 3m/5km SE of Tenbury Wells. SO 6264
Ninfield E Sussex 12 C5 vil 4m/6km NW of Bexhill. TQ 7012
Ningwood Isle of Wight 10 B5 vil 3m/5km E of Yarmouth. SZ 4089
Nisbet Borders 66 D5 vil 4m/6km N of Jedburgh. NT 6725
Nista Shetland 89 F7* small uninhabited island off E coast of island of Whalsay, 1m S of Skaw Taing. HU 6065
Nith 59 E5 r rising in Strathclyde region 5m/7km E of Dalmellington and flowing through New Cumnock, then passing into Dumfries & Galloway region and flowing past Sanquhar and Thornhill to Dumfries and the Solway Firth. Valley of r is known as **Nithsdale.** NY 0057
Nithsdale 116 admin dist of D & G region.
Nithside D & G 59 E4* W dist of Dumfries. NX 9676
Niton Isle of Wight 10 C6 vil 4m/6km W of Ventnor. SZ 5076
Nitshill S'clyde 64 C3 dist of Glasgow 5m/8km SW of city centre. NS 5260
Niwgwl Welsh form of Newgale, qv.
Noah's Ark Kent 20 C5* loc 3m/4km NE of Sevenoaks. TQ 5557
Noah's Green H & W 27 E2* loc 6m/10km NW of Alcester. SP 0061
Noak Bridge Essex 20 C3* N dist of Basildon. TQ 6990
Noak Hill London 20 B2 loc in N part of borough of Havering 4m/6km NE of Romford. TQ 5493
Nob End Gtr Manchester 42 C1* loc 2m/3km W of Radcliffe. SD 7506
Noblehill D & G 59 E4 E dist of Dumfries. NX 9976
Noblethorpe S Yorks 43 G1* loc 4m/6km W of Barnsley. SE 2805
Nobold Salop 34 B3* loc 2m/3km SW of Shrewsbury. SJ 4710
Nobottle Northants 28 B2* loc 6m/9km NW of Northampton. Site of Roman bldg E of Nobottle Wd. SP 6763
Nob's Crook Hants 10 B3* loc 2m/3km NE of Eastleigh. SU 4821
Nobut, Upper Staffs 35 F1* ham 4m/6km NW of Uttoxeter. SK 0435
Nocton Lincs 45 E4 vil 7m/11km SE of Lincoln. TF 0564
Noctorum Merseyside 41 H3* loc in Birkenhead 2m/4km W of tn centre. SJ 2987
Node, The Herts 29 F5 loc 3m/5km SW of Stevenage. TL 2120
Noe 43 G3 r rising on S slopes of Kinder Scout in the High Peak, Derbys, and flowing generally SE past Edale into R Derwent 1km S of Bamford. SK 2082
Noe 70 C2 r in S'clyde region running NW down Glen Noe to Loch Etive, Argyll, 3m/4km E of Bonawe. NN 0434
Noel Park London 19 G3* loc in borough of Haringey 1km E of Wood Green. TQ 3190
Nogdam End Norfolk 39 G5* loc 2m/3km SW of Reedham. TG 3900
Nog Tow Lancs 47 F4* loc 1km NE of Cottam. SD 5033
Noke Oxon 28 A6 vil 5m/8km NE of Oxford. Site of Roman temple to SW. SP 5413
Noke Street Kent 20 D4* loc 2m/3km N of Rochester. TQ 7471
Noltland Orkney 89 B5* loc on island of Westray W of Pierowall. Ruins of 16c cas (A.M.). HY 4248
Nolton Dyfed 22 B4 vil near E coast of St Brides Bay 5m/9km W of Haverfordwest. SM 8618
Nolton Haven Dyfed 22 B4 ham at head of inlet of same name on E side of St Brides Bay 6m/10km W of Haverfordwest. SM 8518
No Man's Heath Ches 42 B6 ham 2m/3km E of Malpas. SJ 5148
No Man's Heath Warwicks 35 H3* ham 6m/10km NE of Tamworth. SK 2908
No Man's Land Cornwall 3 G3* loc 2m/4km NE of Looe. SX 2756
Nomansland Devon 7 F4* ham 7m/12km W of Tiverton. SS 8313
No Man's Land Hants 10 C2* loc 2m/3km E of Winchester. SU 5029
Nomansland Wilts 10 A3 vil on edge of New Forest 4m/6km NW of Cadnam. SU 2517
Noneley Salop 34 B2 loc 2m/3km W of Wem. SJ 4827
No Ness Shetland 89 E8* headland on E coast of Mainland 2km SW of island of Mousa. HU 4421
Noness Head Shetland 89 E6* headland on NE coast of Mainland between entrances to Colla Firth and Swining Voe. HU 4570
Nonington Kent 13 G2 vil 4m/6km S of Wingham. TR 2552
Nonsuch Palace site of, Surrey. See Ewell.
Nookside Tyne & Wear 61 H5* dist of Sunderland 2m/4km W of tn centre. NZ 3655
Noran Water 77 E5 r in Tayside region running S down Glen Ogil then SE to R South Esk 4m/6km W of Brechin. See also Falls of Drumly Harry. NO 5358
Norbiton London 19 F4 loc in borough of Kingston 1m E of Kingston tn centre. Norbiton Common to S. TQ 1969
Norbreck Lancs 46 E4 coastal loc in Blackpool 3m/5km N of tn centre. SD 3141
Norbury Ches 42 B6 ham 4m/6km N of Whitchurch. **Norbury Common** loc 1m NW. SJ 5547
Norbury Derbys 43 F6 vil 4m/7km SW of Ashbourne. SK 1242
Norbury London 19 G4* loc in borough of Croydon 3m/5km N of Croydon tn centre. TQ 3169
Norbury Salop 34 B5 vil 4m/6km NE of Bishop's Castle. SO 3692
Norbury Staffs 34 D2 vil 4m/6km NE of Newport. **Norbury Junction** loc and canal junction 1km SE. SJ 7823
Norbury Brook on border of Ches and Gtr Manchester. See Micker Brook.
Norbury Moor Gtr Manchester 43 E3* loc adjoining Hazel Grove to SW. SJ 9185
Norby N Yorks 54 C6/D6* loc adjoining Thirsk to N. SE 4282
Norchard Dyfed 22 C5* loc 3m/5km W of Tenby. SS 0899
Norchard H & W 26 D1 loc 3m/5km SE of Stourport. SO 8468
Norcott Brook Ches 42 B3* loc 5m/8km NW of Northwich. SJ 6080
Norcross Lancs 46 D4/47 E4* loc 2m/3km NW of Poulton-le-Fylde. SD 3341
Nordelph Norfolk 38 A4 vil 4m/6km W of Downham Mkt. TF 5500
Norden Gtr Manchester 47 H6 loc in Rochdale 3m/4km NW of tn centre. SD 8514
Nordley Salop 34 D4 ham 3m/5km NW of Bridgnorth. SO 6996
Nordley Common Salop 34 D4 loc 4m/6km NW of Bridgnorth. SO 6897

Nore, The 21 E4 sandbank at entrance to R Thames estuary between Shoeburyness, Essex and Sheerness, Kent. Its E end is marked by a revolving light (Nore Light). The name 'The Nore' also applied generally to the waters in this vicinity. TQ 9580
Norfolk 119 eastern county of England, bounded by Suffolk, Cambridgeshire, Lincolnshire, and the North Sea. Is mainly flat or gently undulating with fenland in the W, characterised by large drainage channels emptying into the Wash. In the SW is the expanse of heath and conifer forest known as Breckland, used for military training; other afforested areas are near King's Lynn and N Walsham. Otherwise the county is almost entirely agricultural. NE of Norwich are the Broads, an area of meres and rs popular for boating; reeds for thatching are grown here. Chief tns are the cathedral city and county tn of Norwich; Gt Yarmouth on the E coast, and King's Lynn near the mouth of the Gt Ouse and the Wash. Cromer is the principal resort on the N coast, while Thetford is the 'capital' of Breckland. Rs include the Gt Ouse, Bure, Nar, Wensum, Wissey, and Yare; the Lit Ouse and Waveney both enter the county briefly, but mainly form the boundary with Suffolk.
Norham Nthmb 67 F4 vil on R Tweed 7m/12km SW of Berwick-upon-Tweed. Remains of 12c cas keep (A.M.) above r. NT 8947
Nork Surrey 19 F5* loc 1m W of Banstead. TQ 2359
Norland Town W Yorks 48 D5 vil 1m SE of Sowerby Br. SE 0722
Norley Ches 42 B4 vil 6m/9km W of Northwich. SJ 5772
Norleywood Hants 10 B5 vil on S edge of Beaulieu Heath and New Forest 3m/4km NE of Lymington. SZ 3597
Norlington E Sussex 12 B5* loc adjoining Ringmer to N, 3m/5km NE of Lewes. TQ 4413
Normacot Staffs 35 E1/F1* loc in Stoke-on-Trent 4m/6km SE of city centre. SJ 9242
Normanby Cleveland 54 D3 suburb 4m/6km E of Middlesbrough. NZ 5518
Normanby Humberside 50 D6 vil 4m/6km N of Scunthorpe. SE 8816
Normanby Lincs 44 D3 vil 7m/11km W of Mkt Rasen. TF 0088
Normanby N Yorks 55 F6 vil 4m/6km SE of Kirkbymoorside. SE 7381
Normanby le Wold Lincs 45 E2 vil 4m/6km N of Mkt Rasen. TF 1295
Norman Cross Cambs 37 F5 loc and rd junction 5m/8km SW of Peterborough. TL 1590
Normandy Surrey 18 D6 vil 4m/7km E of Aldershot. SU 9251
Norman Hill Reservoir Gtr Manchester 48 C6* small resr 5m/7km E of Rochdale. SD 9613
Norman's Bay E Sussex 12 C6 loc on coast at Pevensey Sluice 4m/6km W of Bexhill. TQ 6805
Norman's Green Devon 7 H4* ham 3m/5km SE of Cullompton. ST 0503
Normanston Suffolk 39 H5* W dist of Lowestoft. TM 5393
Normanton Derbys 36 A1 dist of Derby 2m/3km S of tn centre. See also New Normanton. SK 3433
Normanton Derbys 43 H5 loc 2m/3km E of Alfreton. SK 4456
Normanton Leics 36 D1 ham 7m/12km NW of Grantham. SK 8140
Normanton Lincs 44 D6 vil 7m/11km N of Grantham. SK 9446
Normanton Notts 44 B5 ham 1m NE of Southwell. SK 7054
Normanton Wilts 9 H1* loc on R Avon 2m/3km SW of Amesbury. SU 1340
Normanton W Yorks 49 F5 coal-mining tn 4m/6km E of Wakefield. Other industries include rly engineering, textiles. SE 3822
Normanton Common Derbys 43 H5* loc 2m/3km E of Alfreton. SK 4456
Normanton le Heath Leics 36 A3 vil 3m/5km SE of Ashby de la Zouch. SK 3712
Normanton on Soar Notts 36 B2 vil 2m/4km NW of Loughborough across r. SK 5123
Normanton on the Wolds Notts 36 C2 vil 6m/9km SE of Nottingham. SK 6232
Normanton on Trent Notts 44 C4 vil 4m/6km SE of Tuxford. SK 7968
Normanton Spring S Yorks 43 H3* loc in Sheffield 4m/6km SE of city centre. SK 4084
Normoss Lancs 47 E4* loc 2km S of Poulton-le-Fylde. SD 3437
Norrington Common Wilts 16 D5* loc 2km W of Melksham. ST 8864
Norris Castle Isle of Wight 10 C5 pseudo-Norman cas by James Wyatt near coast to NE of E Cowes. SZ 5196
Norris Green Cornwall 4 B4* loc 2m/3km SW of Gunnislake. SX 4169
Norris Green Merseyside 42 A2* dist of Liverpool 4m/6km NE of city centre. SJ 3894
Norris Hill Leics 35 H3* loc 2m/3km W of Ashby de la Zouch. SK 3216
Norristhorpe W Yorks 48 D5/49 E5* loc 1km SW of Heckmondwike. SE 2022
NORTH. For names beginning with this word, see under next word. This also applies to names beginning with South, East, West; Great, Little; Greater, Lesser; High, Low; Higher, Lower; Upper, Nether; Far, Near; Mid, Middle; Isle(s) of; The, Y, Yr.
Northall Bucks 28 D5* ham 4m/6km SE of Leighton Buzzard. SP 9520
Northallerton N Yorks 54 C5 tn 14m/23km S of Darlington. Agricultural products and engineering, plastics. SE 3693
Northall Green Norfolk 39 E3 loc 2km NE of E Dereham. TF 9914
Northam Devon 6 C2 tn 2m/3km N of Bideford. To N, **Northam Burrows** extending to mouth of Rs Taw and Torridge: golf course, sheep grazing. SS 4429
Northam Hants 10 B3* dist of Southampton on W bank of R Itchen 1m E of city centre. Northam Br carries main rd over r. SU 4312
Northampton Northants 28 C2 county tn on R Nene 60m/97km NW of London. Various industries, esp footwear. New Tn designated 1968. SP 7560
Northamptonshire 119 midland county of England, bounded by Cambridgeshire, Bedfordshire, Buckinghamshire, Oxfordshire, Warwickshire and Leicestershire. It also marches briefly with Lincolnshire SW of Stamford. Consists largely of undulating agricultural country rising locally to low hills, especially along the W border. Large fields and scattered wds provide excellent terrain for foxhunting. Chief tns are Northampton, Corby, Kettering, and Wellingborough. Industries include steel, at Corby, and footwear mnfre. The principal rs are the Nene and the Welland.
Northavon 118 admin dist of Avon.
Northaw Herts 19 F2 vil 2m/3km E of Potters Bar. TL 2702
Northay Devon 8 B4* loc 2km NW of Marshwood and 5m/7km NE of Axminster. ST 3600
Northbay W Isles 88 D3 vil on Barra 4m/7km S of Scurrival Pt. **North Bay** to E contains numerous small islands. Northbay Airfield 2km N of Tràigh Mhór. Vil also known as Bayherivagh, and inlet, on which it is situated, as Bàgh Hirivagh. NF 7002
Northbeck Lincs 37 F1* loc just N of Scredington. TF 0941
Northborough Cambs 37 F4 vil 7m/11km NW of Peterborough. 14c manor hse. TF 1507
Northbourne Kent 13 H2 vil 3m/4km W of Deal. TR 3352
Northbourne Oxon 18 A3 S dist of Didcot. SU 5289
Northbridge Street E Sussex 12 D4* loc at N end of Robertsbridge. TQ 7324
Northbrook Hants 10 C1* ham 1km NW of Micheldever. SU 5139
Northbrook Oxon 28 A5 loc on E side of Oxford Canal 6m/9km W of Bicester. SP 4922
Northchapel W Sussex 11 F2 vil 4m/6km SE of Haslemere. SU 9529
Northchurch Herts 18 D1 NW dist of Berkhamsted. SP 9708
Northcoates Point Lincs 45 G1* marshy headland 2m/4km NE of N Coates, at mouth of R Humber. TA 3703
Northcott Devon 6 C5 par 5m/8km N of Launceston, containing hams of **Northcott Hamlet** and **Hr Northcott.** SX 3492
Northcott Devon 7 H4* loc 1km SW of Culmstock and 6m/9km NE of Cullompton. ST 0912
Northcourt Oxon 18 A2* NE dist of Abingdon. SU 5098
Northdown Kent 13 H1 E dist of Margate. TR 3770
Northedge Derbys 43 H4* loc 2m/4km NW of Clay Cross. SK 3565
Northend Bucks 18 C2* loc 3m/5km SE of Watlington. SU 7392
Northend Essex 21 E2* loc adjoining Southminster to N, 2m/4km N of Burnham-on-Crouch. TL 9600
Northend Warwicks 27 G3 vil 8m/13km NW of Banbury. SP 3952
Northenden Gtr Manchester 42 D2 dist of Manchester 5m/8km S of city centre. SJ 8290
Northend Woods Bucks 18 D3* loc 3m/5km SE of High Wycombe. SU 9089
Northern Common Derbys 43 G3* loc adjoining Dronfield Woodhouse to N. SK 3278
Northern Moor Gtr Manchester 42 D2 loc in Manchester 5m/8km SW of city centre. SJ 8190
Northey Island Essex 21 E2 island at head of R Blackwater estuary 2m/3km E of Maldon. TL 8806
Northfield Borders 67 F2 loc adjoining St Abbs to W. NT 9167
Northfield Grampian 77 H1* NW dist of Aberdeen. NJ 9008
Northfield Humberside 51 E5* N dist of Hessle. TA 0327
Northfield Lothian 66 B2* dist of Edinburgh 1km W of Portobello. NT 2973
Northfield Som 8 B1* W dist of Bridgwater. ST 2836
Northfield W Midlands 35 F6 dist of Birmingham 5m/9km SW of city centre. SP 0279
Northfields Lincs 37 E4* NW dist of Stamford. TF 0207
Northfleet Kent 20 C4 industrial tn on R Thames 2km W of Gravesend. Large cement works. Other industries include paper and cables. **Northfleet Hope** is stretch of r above tn. TQ 6274
Northfleet Green Kent 20 C4* loc 2m/3km S of Northfleet. TQ 6271
Northgate W Sussex 11 H2* N dist of Crawley. TQ 2737
Northiam E Sussex 12 D4 vil 7m/11km NW of Rye. TQ 8224
Northill Beds 29 F3 vil 2m/4km SW of Sandy. TL 1446
Northington Glos 16 C1* loc on R Severn estuary just N of Awre and 2m/4km NE of Blakeney. SO 7008
Northington Hants 10 C1 ham 4m/6km NW of New Alresford. SU 5637
Northlands Lincs 45 G5 vil 6m/10km N of Boston. TF 3453
Northleach Glos 27 E6/F6 vil 10m/15km NE of Cirencester. SP 1114
Northleigh Devon 6 D2 ham 3m/5km E of Barnstaple. SS 6034
Northleigh Devon 8 A4 vil 4m/6km SE of Honiton. SY 1996
Northlew Devon 6 D5 vil 6m/9km NW of Okehampton. SX 5099
Northload Bridge Som 8 C1* loc on W side of Glastonbury. ST 4939
Northmavine Shetland 89 E6* peninsular dist of Mainland lying W of Sullom Voe and Yell Sound. HU 37
Northmoor Oxon 17 H2 vil 4m/7km S of Eynsham. SP 4202
Northmoor Corner Som 8 B2* loc 1km SE of N Newton. ST 3030
Northmoor Green Som 8 B2 loc on R Parrett 4m/6km SE of Bridgwater. Also known as Moorland. ST 3332
Northmuir Tayside 76 D5 vil nearly 1m N of Kirriemuir. NO 3855
Northney Hants 10 D4 loc at N end of Hayling I. SU 7303
Northolt London 19 E3 loc in borough of Ealing 11m/18km W of Charing Cross. To W is Northolt Airfield, formerly main airport of London. TQ 1384
Northop (Llaneurgain) Clwyd 41 H4 vil 3m/4km N of Mold. SJ 2468
Northop Hall Clwyd 41 H4 vil 2m/3km E of Northop. SJ 2667
Northorpe Lincs 37 F3 loc 2m/3km S of Bourne. TF 0917
Northorpe Lincs 37 G1 ham 1km N of Donington. TF 2035
Northorpe Lincs 44 D2 vil 3m/4km W of Kirton in Lindsey. SK 8997
Northorpe W Yorks 49 E5/E6* loc adjoining Ravensthorpe to N. SE 2120
Northover Som 8 C1* loc on SW side of Glastonbury. ST 4838
Northover Som 8 C2 loc on N bank of R Yeo 1km NE of Ilchester. ST 5223
Northowram W Yorks 48 D5 vil 2m/3km NE of Halifax. SE 1127
Northport Dorset 9 F5 N dist of Wareham. SY 9288
Northrepps Norfolk 39 F1 vil 3m/4km SE of Cromer. TG 2439
Northton W Isles 88 A4* vil on W coast of Harris 4m/6km SE of Toe Hd. NF 9989
Northumberland 117 northernmost county of England, bounded by the Borders region of Scotland; the English counties of Cumbria, Durham, and Tyne & Wear; and the North Sea. In the SE coastal area there is some coal-mining and associated industry; otherwise the county is almost entirely rural, the greater part being high moorland, culminating along the Scottish border in the Cheviot Hills. The most spectacular stretches of Hadrian's Wall traverse the county N of Haltwhistle and Hexham. There is extensive afforestation in the NW, other parts of which are used for military training. The principal tns are Alnwick, Ashington, Berwick-upon-Tweed, Blyth, Hexham, and Morpeth. Rs include the Aln, Blyth, Breamish, Coquet, E and W Allen, N and S Tyne, Till, and Wansbeck. The Tweed forms part of the Scottish border and flows out to sea at Berwick.
Northumberland Heath London 20 B4* loc in borough of Bexley 1m SW of Erith and 13m/21km E of Charing Cross. TQ 5077
Northville Gwent 15 G2* loc in N part of Cwmbran. ST 2995
Northward Hill Nature Reserve Kent 20 D4 situated to N of High Halstow on edge of Cooling Marshes 6m/9km NE of Rochester. TQ 7876
Northwaterbridge 77 F4* loc on R North Esk on border of Grampian and Tayside regions 5m/8km SW of Laurencekirk. NO 6566
Northway Glos 26 D4* loc adjoining Ashchurch to N, 2m/4km E of Tewkesbury. SO 9234
Northway Som 7 H2* ham 2m/3km NE of Milverton. ST 1329
Northway W Glam 23 G6* loc on Gower peninsula 3m/5km NW of Mumbles Hd. SS 5889
Northwich Ches 42 C4 tn on site of Roman *Condate* at confluence of Rs Dane and Weaver 20m/31km SW of Manchester. Traditional salt industry still active. Other industries include chemicals, steel. SJ 6573
Northwick Avon 16 B3 loc 2m/3km NE of Severn Beach. ST 5686
Northwick H & W 26 D2* N dist of Worcester. SO 8457
Northwick Som 15 H6* loc 3m/4km E of Highbridge. ST 3548
Northwold Norfolk 38 C5 vil 4m/6km SE of Stoke Ferry. TL 7597
Northwood Derbys 43 G4* loc 4m/6km NW of Matlock. SK 3664
Northwood Devon 7 F4* loc consisting of **E** and **W Northwood,** 7m/11km SE of Chulmleigh. SS 7708
Northwood Isle of Wight 10 B5 vil 2m/3km S of Cowes. SZ 4893
Northwood Kent 13 H1 N dist of Ramsgate. TR 3767
Northwood London 19 E3 dist in borough of Hillingdon 3m/4km SE of Rickmansworth. Loc of **Northwood Hills** to S. TQ 0991
Northwood Merseyside 42 A2* NE dist of Kirkby. SJ 4299
Northwood Salop 34 B1 vil 4m/7km NW of Wem. SJ 4633
Northwood Staffs 42 D6* loc 2m/3km S of Newcastle-under-Lyme. SJ 8542
Northwood Staffs 42 D6* loc in Stoke-on-Trent 1km NE of Hanley. SJ 8948
Northwood Green Glos 26 C5 ham 4m/6km NE of Newnham. SO 7616
Norton Avon 15 H5* loc 2m/4km NE of Weston-super-Mare. ST 3463
Norton Ches 42 B3* loc in Runcorn 3m/4km E of tn centre. SJ 5581
Norton Cleveland 54 D3 dist of Stockton-on-Tees 2m/3km N of tn centre. NZ 4421
Norton Glos 26 D5 vil 4m/6km NE of Gloucester. SO 8524
Norton Gwent 25 H5* loc 1m W of Skenfrith. SO 4420
Norton Herts 29 F4 loc at N end of Letchworth. TL 2234

Norton H & W 26 D3 vil 3m/5km SE of Worcester. SO 8751
Norton H & W 27 E3 ham 3m/4km N of Evesham. SP 0448
Norton Isle of Wight 10 A5 loc 1km W of Yarmouth across R Yar. SZ 3489
Norton Kent 21 E5* loc 3m/5km W of Faversham. TQ 9661
Norton Mid Glam 14 D4* loc 1km NE of Ogmore-by-Sea. SS 8775
Norton Northants 28 B2 vil 2m/4km E of Daventry. 1km NE is site of Roman settlement of *Bannaventa*. SP 6063
Norton Notts 44 A4/B4 vil 6m/10km NW of Ollerton. SK 5771
Norton N Yorks 50 C1 tn opp Malton across R Derwent, 17m/27km NE of York. SE 7971
Norton Powys 25 G2 vil 2m/3km N of Presteigne. Remains of motte and bailey cas. SO 3067
Norton Salop 34 B6* loc 2m/3km SE of Craven Arms. SO 4681
Norton Salop 34 C3* loc 1m NE of Wroxeter. SJ 5609
Norton Salop 34 D4 vil 4m/7km N of Bridgnorth. SJ 7200
Norton Suffolk 30 D2 vil 3m/5km SE of Ixworth. Ham of **Norton Lit Green** 2km E. TL 9565
Norton S Yorks 43 H3* loc in Sheffield 3m/5km S of city centre. **Lit Norton** loc 1km SW. SK 3582
Norton S Yorks 49 G6 vil 6m/10km SE of Knottingley. SE 5415
Norton W Glam 23 G6* loc in Mumbles 4m/6km SW of Swansea tn centre across Swansea Bay. SS 6188
Norton Wilts 16 D3 vil 4m/6km SW of Malmesbury. ST 8884
Norton W Midlands 35 E6 SW dist of Stourbridge. SO 8982
Norton W Sussex 11 F4 vil 4m/7km E of Chichester. SU 9206
Norton W Sussex 11 E5* ham 2km N of Selsey. SZ 8695
Norton Bavant Wilts 16 D6 vil on R Wylye 3m/4km SE of Warminster. ST 9043
Norton Bridge Staffs 35 E2 vil 3m/5km SW of Stone. SJ 8730
Norton Bury Herts 29 F4* ham 1m NW of Baldock. TL 2334
Norton Canes Staffs 35 F3 vil 3m/5km NW of Brownhills. SK 0107
Norton Canon H & W 25 H3 vil 9m/15km NW of Hereford. SO 3847
Norton Conyers N Yorks 49 E1 hse dating from 16c or earlier, 1km S of Wath. SE 3176
Norton Corner Norfolk 39 E2* loc 3m/5km N of Reepham. TG 0928
Norton Creek Norfolk 38 C1 channel separating Scolt Hd from mainland and connecting Brancaster and Burnham Harbours. TF 8145
Norton Disney Lincs 44 D5 vil 7m/11km NE of Newark-on-Trent. Site of Roman villa 2m/3km W. SK 8859
Norton, East Leics 36 D4 vil 5m/8km W of Uppingham. SK 7800
Norton Ferris Wilts 9 E1 loc 3m/5km NW of Mere. ST 3900
Norton Fitzwarren Som 8 A2* NW suburb of Taunton. ST 1925
Norton Green Herts 29 F5* loc at W edge of Stevenage. TL 2223
Norton Green Isle of Wight 10 A5* vil 2km NE of Totland. SZ 3488
Norton Green Staffs 35 F3* loc 2m/4km NW of Brownhills. SK 0207
Norton Green Staffs 43 E5* loc 2km SW of Brown Edge. SJ 8952
Norton Hammer S Yorks 43 H3* loc in Sheffield 2m/3km S of city centre. SK 3483
Norton Hawkfield Avon 16 B5* ham 2m/3km NE of Chew Magna. ST 5964
Norton Heath Essex 20 C2 vil 3m/5km E of Chipping Ongar. TL 6004
Norton in Hales Salop 34 D1 vil 3m/5km NE of Mkt Drayton. SJ 7038
Norton in the Moors Staffs 42 D5 loc 2m/3km NE of Burslem. SJ 8951
Norton juxta Twycross Leics 35 H4 vil 6m/10km S of Ashby de la Zouch. SK 3207
Norton-le-Clay N Yorks 49 F1 vil 3m/5km N of Boroughbridge. SE 4071
Norton Lees S Yorks 43 H3* loc in Sheffield 2m/3km S of city centre. SK 3583
Norton Lindsey Warwicks 27 F2 vil 4m/6km W of Warwick. SP 2263
Norton, Little Som 8 C3* ham 1km E of Norton sub Hamdon. ST 4715
Norton, Little Staffs 35 F3* loc 2m/4km NW of Brownhills. SK 0207
Norton Malreward Avon 16 B5 vil 5m/8km S of Bristol. ST 6065
Norton Mandeville Essex 20 C2 loc 2m/4km NE of Chipping Ongar. TL 5704
Norton Mere Salop 35 E3 narrow lake to N of Tong Norton. SJ 7908
Norton St Philip Som 16 C5 vil 5m/8km N of Frome. ST 7755
Norton Street Norfolk 39 G5* loc forming part of Norton Subcourse. TM 4198
Norton Subcourse Norfolk 39 G5 vil 3m/5km E of Loddon. TM 4098
Norton sub Hamdon Som 8 C3 vil 5m/9km W of Yeovil. To E, Hamdon Hill, qv. ST 4715
Norton Wood H & W 25 H3 ham 3m/5km E of Willersley. SO 3648
Norton Woodseats S Yorks 43 H3 dist of Sheffield 3m/4km S of city centre. SK 3482
Norwell Notts 44 C5 vil 5m/8km N of Newark-on-Trent. **Norwell Woodhouse** ham 2m/3km W. SK 7761
Norwich Norfolk 39 F4 county tn and cathedral city at confluence of R Wensum and R Yare (navigable to small craft, tidal) 98m/158km NE of London. Industries include footwear, mustard and starch mnfre, engineering, printing. Notable bldgs include partly Norman cathedral, Norman cas, 15c guildhall, modern city hall, numerous chs. University of E Anglia 2m/4km W of city centre. Airport 3m/5km N. TG 2208
Nor Wick Shetland 89 F5 bay on NE coast of Unst on which loc of **Norwick** is situated. HP 6514
Norwood Derbys 44 A3* loc 1km E of Killamarsh. SK 4681
Norwood London 19 G4 dist of S London in boroughs of Croydon and Lambeth, consisting of locs of **S** and **W Norwood, Upr Norwood,** and **Norwood New Tn.** TQ 3271
Norwood S Yorks 43 H2* loc in Sheffield 2m/3km N of city centre. SK 3590
Norwood End Essex 20 C1* loc 4m/6km N of Chipping Ongar. TL 5608
Norwood Green London 19 F4 loc 10m/17km W of Charing Cross. TQ 1378
Norwood Green W Yorks 48 D5* loc 2m/4km N of Brighouse. SE 1426
Norwood Hill 11 H1 ham on border of Surrey and W Sussex 3m/5km W of Horley. TQ 2443
Norwood Park Som 8 C1* loc on E side of Glastonbury. ST 5239
Norwoodside Cambs 37 H4* loc on N side of March. TL 4198
Norwood, Upper W Sussex 11 F3 ham 4m/6km SW of Petworth. SU 9318
Noseley Leics 36 C4 18c hall 7m/11km N of Mkt Harborough. Site of former vil to W. SP 7398
Nose's Point Durham 61 H6 headland 1m S of Seaham. NZ 4347
Noss Head H'land 86 F2 headland with lighthouse on E coast of Caithness dist at S end of Sinclair's Bay. ND 3855
Noss Head Shetland 89 F7* headland on E coast of Isle of Noss, culminating in **Noup of Noss,** rising sheer from sea to 594 ft or 181 metres. HU 5539
Noss, Isle of Shetland 89 F7 uninhabited island and bird sanctuary of about 3 sq km off E coast of island of Bressay, separated from it by narrow channel of **Noss Sound.** HU 5440
Noss Mayo Devon 4 C5 vil 3m/5km SW of Yealmpton, on S side of creek running into R Yealm estuary, opp Newton Ferrers. Yachting. SX 5447
Nostell Priory W Yorks 49 F6* 18c mansion (NT) in large grnds with lake, 3m/5km NW of Hemsworth. SE 4017
Nosterfield N Yorks 54 B6 ham 3m/5km E of Masham. SE 2780
Nosterfield End Cambs 30 B3* loc 2m/4km W of Haverhill. TL 6344
Nostie H'land 79 F6 locality on N side of Loch Alsh, Skye and Lochalsh dist, 2m/3km W of Dornie. **Nostie Bay** is inlet of Loch Alsh to S. NG 8526
Notgrove Glos 27 E5 vil 4m/6km N of Northleach. SP 1020
Notley Abbey Bucks 18 C1* remains of medieval abbey 2m/3km N of Thame. SP 7109
Nottage Mid Glam 14 D4 N suburb of Porthcawl. SS 8178
Nottingham Notts 36 B1 city on R Trent 45m/72km NE of Birmingham. Cas of 17c, restored 19c, houses museum and art gallery. University. Repertory theatre. Industries include hosiery, lace, light engineering, pharmaceutical products, tobacco, bicycles and motor cycles. SK 5740
Nottinghamshire 117, 119 midland county of England, bounded by Lincolnshire, Leicestershire, Derbyshire, S Yorkshire, and Humberside. Much of the county is rural, with extensive woodlands in the central area of the Dukeries. Cattle-grazing is the chief farming activity. Around Nottingham and other large tns there is much industry, incl iron and steel, engineering, hosiery, knitwear, tobacco, pharmaceuticals, and coal-mining. Principal tns are the city and county tn of Nottingham, E Retford, Mansfield, Newark, and Worksop. The most important r is the Trent.
Notting Hill London 19 F3* loc in borough of Kensington and Chelsea 3m/5km W of Charing Cross. TQ 2480
Nottington Dorset 8 D5* loc 3m/5km N of Weymouth. SY 6682
Notton Wilts 16 D4 ham 3m/4km S of Chippenham. ST 9169
Notton W Yorks 49 E6 vil 5m/8km S of Wakefield. SE 3413
Nottswood Hill Glos 26 C5* loc 5m/8km S of Newent. SO 7018
Nounsley Essex 30 C6* loc 3m/5km SW of Witham. TL 7910
Noup Head Orkney 89 B5 headland with overhanging cliffs at NW end of island of Westray. Lighthouse. HY 3950
Nousta Ness Shetland 89 F6* headland on E coast of Fetlar 1km SE of Funzie. HU 6689
Noutard's Green H & W 26 C1 ham 4m/6km S of Stourport. SO 7966
Nover's Park Avon 16 B4* S dist of Bristol. ST 5869
Noverton Glos 27 E5* loc 2m/4km NE of Cheltenham. SO 9824
Noverton, Lower Glos 27 E5* loc 2m/3km NW of Cheltenham. SO 9723
Noviomagus W Sussex. See Chichester.
Nowton Suffolk 30 D2 ham 2m/4km S of Bury St Edmunds. TL 8660
Nox Salop 34 B3* ham 5m/9km W of Shrewsbury. SJ 4010
Nuffield Oxon 18 B3 vil 4m/6km E of Wallingford. SU 6687
Nun Appleton N Yorks 49 G4 loc on N side of R Wharfe 5m/8km SE of Tadcaster. SE 5539
Nunburnholme Humberside 50 D3 vil 3m/5km E of Pocklington. SE 8447
Nuncargate Notts 44 A5* loc 2km S of Kirkby in Ashfield. SK 5054
Nunclose Cumbria 60 B6* loc 1m SW of Armathwaite. NY 4945
Nuneaton Warwicks 36 A5 mnfg tn in coal-mining dist, 8m/13km N of Coventry. SP 3691
Nuneham Courtenay Oxon 18 A2 vil 5m/8km SE of Oxford. SU 5599
Nuney Green Oxon 18 B3* loc 5m/7km NW of Reading. SU 6779
Nunhead London 20 A4* loc in borough of Southwark 5m/7km SE of Charing Cross. TQ 3575
Nun Hills Lancs 48 B5* loc 2km SW of Bacup. SD 8521
Nun Monkton N Yorks 50 A3 vil at confluence of R Nidd and R Ouse 9m/14km SE of Boroughbridge. SE 5057
Nunney Som 16 C6 vil 3m/5km SW of Frome. Moated 14c cas (A.M.). ST 7345
Nunningham Stream 12 C5* one of the streams feeding Waller's Haven (qv) in E Sussex. TQ 6712
Nunnington H & W 26 B3* loc 3m/5km NE of Hereford. SO 5543
Nunnington N Yorks 50 B1 vil 2m/4km N of Hovingham. Hall (NT) is 16c-17c hse. SE 6679
Nunnykirk Nthmb 61 F2 loc 2m/3km NW of Netherwitton. **Nunnykirk Hall,** mansion built in 1825. NZ 0892
Nuns' Cave S'clyde 69 D6 cave at **Nuns' Pass** on S coast of Mull 2km SW of Carsaig Bay. Said to have served as shelter to nuns evicted from Iona at Reformation. NM 5220
Nunsfield Lincs 45 H3* loc 1m W of Sutton on Sea. TF 5081
Nunsthorpe Humberside 45 F1 dist of Grimsby 2km S of tn centre. TA 2607
Nunthorpe Cleveland 54 D3 loc 4m/7km SE of Middlesbrough. NZ 5314
Nunthorpe N Yorks 49 G3* dist of York 2km S of city centre. SE 5949
Nunton Wilts 9 H2 vil 3m/4km S of Salisbury. SU 1526
Nunton W Isles 88 D2* loc on W coast of Benbecula. NF 7653
Nunwick N Yorks 49 E1 loc 2m/3km N of Ripon across R Ure. SE 3274
Nup End Bucks 28 D5 loc adjoining Wingrave to NW, 5m/7km NE of Aylesbury. SP 8619
Nupend Glos 16 C1* ham 4m/6km W of Stroud. SO 7806
Nup End Glos 26 C5 loc adjoining Ashleworth to N, 5m/8km N of Gloucester. SO 8125
Nup End Herts 29 F5* loc 2m/4km N of Welwyn. TL 2219
Nuptown Berks 18 D4* loc 5m/8km S of Maidenhead. SU 8873
Nurcot, Great Som 7 G2 Exmoor ham 1m N of Winsford. SS 9036
Nursling Hants 10 B3 vil in R Test valley 3m/4km S of Romsey. Grove Place, Elizn hse. SU 3616
Nursteed Wilts 17 E5* loc 2km SE of Devizes. SU 0260
Nurston S Glam 15 F4* loc 4m/6km W of Barry. ST 0567
Nurton Staffs 35 E4 loc 5m/8km W of Wolverhampton. SO 8399
Nutberry Hill S'clyde 65 E5 hill 6m/10km SW of Lesmahagow. Height 1712 ft or 522 metres. R Nethan rises on S side. NS 7433
Nutbourne W Sussex 11 G3 vil 2m/3km E of Pulborough. TQ 0718
Nutbourne W Sussex 11 E4 vil 3m/4km E of Emsworth. SU 7805
Nutfield Surrey 19 G6 vil 2m/3km E of Redhill. TQ 3050
Nutfield, South Surrey 19 G6 loc 2m/3km E of Redhill. TQ 3049
Nuthall Notts 36 B1 loc 4m/7km NW of Nottingham. SK 5144
Nuthampstead Herts 29 G4* scattered vil 4m/7km NE of Buntingford. TL 4034
Nuthurst Warwicks 27 F1 loc 1km SW of Hockley Heath. SP 1472
Nuthurst W Sussex 11 G3 ham 3m/5km S of Horsham. TQ 1926
Nutley E Sussex 12 B4 vil 5m/7km N of Uckfield. TQ 4427
Nutley Hants 18 B6 loc 5m/8km SW of Basingstoke. SU 6044
Nutscale Reservoir Som 7 F1* small resr on Exmoor 3m/4km SW of Porlock. SS 8643
Nuttall Lane Gtr Manchester 47 H6 loc adjoining Ramsbottom to SW. SD 7816
Nutter's Platt Lancs 47 F5* loc 2m/4km SW of Preston. SD 5226
Nutwell S Yorks 44 B1* loc adjoining Armthorpe to SE. SE 6304
Nybster H'land 86 F2 loc near E coast of Caithness dist 6m/10km S of John o' Groats. ND 3663
Nyetimber W Sussex 11 E5 suburban vil 3m/5km W of Bognor Regis. SZ 8998
Nyewood W Sussex 11 E3* vil 4m/6km E of Petersfield. SU 8021
Nyfer Welsh form of Nevern, qv.
Nyland, Higher Dorset 9 E2* loc 5m/8km SW of Gillingham. ST 7322
Nyland, Lower Dorset 9 E2* loc 5m/7km SW of Gillingham. ST 7421
Nymet Rowland Devon 7 E4 vil 4m/7km SE of Chulmleigh. SS 7108
Nymet Tracey Devon 6 E5 ham 7m/11km W of Crediton. SS 7200
Nympsfield Glos 16 C2 vil 3m/5km W of Nailsworth. SO 8000
Nynehead Som 8 A2 ham 2km N of Wellington. Ham of **E Nynehead** 1m E. ST 1322
Nythe Som 8 C1 ham on Sedgemoor 4m/6km W of Street. ST 4234
Nyton W Sussex 11 F4* vil 4m/7km N of Bognor Regis. SU 9305

O

Oadby Leics 36 C4 tn adjoining Leicester to SE. SK 6200
Oad Street Kent 21 E5 ham 2m/4km SW of Sittingbourne. TQ 8662
Oakall Green H & W 26 C2* loc 4m/7km NW of Worcester. SO 8160
Oakamoor Staffs 43 F6 vil 3m/5km E of Cheadle. SK 0544
Oakbank Lothian 65 G2* loc 1km S of Mid Calder. NT 0866
Oak Beck 49 E3* stream rising on Stainburn Moor, SW of Harrogate, N Yorks, and flowing NE through Ten Acre Resr, past the W side of Harrogate, and into R Nidd 2km E of Killinghall. SE 3058
Oak Cross Devon 6 D5 ham 4m/6km NW of Okehampton. SX 5399
Oakdale Dorset 9 G5* dist of Poole to N of tn centre. SZ 0292
Oakdale Gwent 15 G2 tn 4m/7km S of Abertillery. ST 1898
Oake Som 8 A2 vil in Vale of Taunton Deane 2m/3km E of Milverton. To E, ham of **Oake Green.** To N, ham of Oake Br. ST 1525
Oaken Staffs 35 E4* vil 1m W of Codsall. SJ 8502
Oakenclough Lancs 47 F3 ham 4m/6km E of Garstang. SD 5347
Oakengates Salop 34 D3 tn 4m/6km E of Wellington, forming part of Telford. Iron-founding and coal-mining. SJ 7010
Oakenholt Clwyd 41 H4* loc 2km SE of Flint. SJ 2671
Oakenshaw Durham 54 B2* vil 2km N of Willington. NZ 2037
Oakenshaw Lancs 48 A5* loc adjoining Clayton-le-Moors to E. SD 7431
Oakenshaw W Yorks 48 D5 vil 3m/5km S of Bradford. SE 1727
Oakerthorpe Derbys 43 H5* loc 2m/3km W of Alfreton. Remains of small Roman fort 1km S. SK 3854
Oakes W Yorks 48 D6* loc in Huddersfield 2m/3km W of tn centre. SE 1117
Oakfield Fife 73 E5 loc adjoining Kelty to S. NT 1493
Oakfield Gwent 15 G2* loc in S part of Cwmbran. ST 2993
Oakfield Isle of Wight 10 C5 SE dist of Ryde. SZ 6091
Oakford Devon 7 G3 vil 3m/5km W of Bampton. 1km NE, ham of **Oakfordbridge** on R Exe. SS 9121
Oakford (Derwen-gam) Dyfed 24 A2/A3 ham 3m/5km S of Aberaeron. SN 4558
Oak Gate Gtr Manchester 42 D1* loc 1m E of Whitefield. SD 8205
Oak, Great Gwent 15 H1 ham 2m/4km NW of Raglan. SO 3809
Oakgrove Ches 43 E4* loc 3m/4km S of Macclesfield. SJ 9169
Oakham Leics 36 D3 small mkt tn in Vale of Catmose 9m/15km SE of Melton Mowbray. 12c great hall survives from former fortified manor hse. Mkt place with butter cross. SK 8608
Oakham W Midlands 35 F5* loc 2m/3km W of Oldbury. SO 9689
Oakham Ness Kent 20 D4* S point of Oakham Marsh, 'island' on saltings on N side of R Medway estuary to S of Stoke. There is a jetty reaching almost to mid-stream. TQ 8371
Oakhanger Ches 42 D5* loc 4m/6km E of Crewe. SJ 7654
Oakhanger Hants 10 D2 vil 4m/7km SE of Alton. SU 7635
Oakhill Som 16 B6 vil 3m/4km N of Shepton Mallet. ST 6347
Oak Hill Staffs 35 E1* loc in Stoke-on-Trent 2km SW of city centre. SJ 8643
Oak Hill Suffolk 31 G3/G4* loc 6m/10km SE of Woodbridge. TM 3645
Oakington Cambs 29 H2 vil 4m/7km NW of Cambridge. TL 4164
Oaklands Powys 25 F3* loc adjoining Builth Wells to E. SO 0450
Oakleigh Lancs 48 B4* loc in S part of Brierfield. SD 8435
Oakleigh Park London 19 F2 loc in borough of Barnet 9m/14km N of Charing Cross. TQ 2694
Oakle Street Glos 26 C5 ham 5m/8km W of Gloucester. SO 7517
Oakley Beds 29 E2/E3 vil 4m/6km NW of Bedford. TL 0053
Oakley Bucks 18 B1 vil 6m/9km NW of Thame. SP 6312
Oakley Dorset 9 G4* loc 1m S of Wimborne. SZ 0198
Oakley Fife 72 D5 vil 4m/7km W of Dunfermline. NT 0289
Oakley Hants 18 B6 vil 5m/7km W of Basingstoke. Also known as Church Oakley. SU 5650
Oakley Oxon 18 C2 loc adjoining Chinnor to SW. SP 7500
Oakley Suffolk 31 F1 ham 3m/5km E of Diss. TM 1677
Oakley, East Hants 18 B6* extensive loc adjoining Oakley or Church Oakley to E, 4m/6km W of Basingstoke. SU 5750
Oakley, Great Essex 31 F5 vil 5m/8km SW of Harwich. TM 1927
Oakley, Great Northants 36 D5 S dist of Corby, formerly a vil. Hall is partly Tudor. SP 8685
Oakley Green Berks 18 D4 loc 3m/4km W of Windsor. SU 9276
Oakley, Little Essex 31 F5 vil 3m/5km SW of Harwich. TM 2129
Oakley, Little Northants 36 D5 vil 2m/3km S of Corby. SP 8985
Oakley, North Hants 18 A5 loc 3m/5km S of Kingsclere. SU 5354
Oakmere Ches 42 B4 loc 4m/7km N of Tarporley. **Oak Mere** lake 1m S. SJ 5769
Oakridge Glos 16 D1 vil 4m/7km E of Stroud. Ham of **Far Oakridge** to E. SO 9103
Oakridge Hants 18 B6* N dist of Basingstoke. SU 6353
Oaks Durham 54 B2* loc adjoining Evenwood to N, 4m/7km SW of Bishop Auckland. NZ 1525
Oaks Lancs 47 G4* loc 4m/6km N of Blackburn. SD 6733
Oaks Salop 34 B4* loc 2m/3km SE of Pontesbury. SJ 4204
Oaksey Wilts 17 E2 vil 5m/9km NE of Malmesbury. ST 9993
Oaks Green Derbys 35 G1* loc 1m N of Sudbury. SK 1632
Oakshaw Ford Cumbria 60 B4 loc 7m/11km S of Newcastleton. NY 5176
Oakshott Hants 10 D2* loc 3m/5km N of Petersfield. SU 7427
Oakthorpe Leics 35 H3 vil 3m/5km SW of Ashby de la Zouch. SK 3213
Oak Tree Durham 54 C3 loc 5m/7km E of Darlington. NZ 3613
Oakwell W Yorks 49 E5* loc 1km N of Birstall. SE 2227
Oakwood London 19 G2* loc in borough of Enfield 10m/15km N of Charing Cross. TQ 2995
Oakwood Nthmb 61 E5* loc 2km NE of Hexham. NY 9465
Oakwood W Yorks 49 E4* loc in Roundhay dist of Leeds 3m/4km NE of city centre. SE 3236
Oakwoodhill Surrey 11 G2 ham 5m/8km NW of Horsham. TQ 1337
Oakworth W Yorks 48 C4 vil adjoining Keighley to SW. SE 0338
Oare Kent 21 F5 vil 2km NW of Faversham. TR 0063
Oare Som 7 F1 ham 6m/9km E of Lynton. SS 8047
Oare Wilts 17 F5 vil 2m/3km N of Pewsey. SU 1563
Oasby Lincs 37 E1 vil 6m/9km SW of Sleaford. Small Tudor manor hse. TF 0039
Oath Som 8 B2 ham 3m/4km W of Langport. ST 3827
Oa, The S'clyde 62 B3, B4 peninsula at S end of Islay, W of Port Ellen. Bold cliffs, esp to S and W. NR 3044
Oathlaw Tayside 77 E5 vil 4m/6km N of Forfar. NO 4756
Oatlands N Yorks 49 E3* dist of Harrogate 1m S of tn centre. SE 3053
Oatlands S'clyde 64 D3* loc in Glasgow 2km S of city centre. NS 5963
Oatlands Park Surrey 19 E5* loc 2km E of Weybridge. TQ 0965
Oban S'clyde 70 B2 port and resort in Argyll on **Oban Bay,** Sound of Kerrera, 60m/97km NW of Glasgow (93m/150km by rd). Ferry services to Inner and Outer Hebrides. Distillery. Glass and tweed mnfre. Annual Highland Gathering in September. See also Dunollie Castle. NM 8530
Obbe W Isles. Former name of Leverburgh, qv.
Òb Breakish Skye, H'land 79 F6* narrow inlet on which locality of Lr Breakish is situated, 2m/3km E of Broadford. NG 6723
Òb Chuaig H'land 78 E3 bay on W coast of Ross and Cromarty dist, 2m/3km SW of Rubha na Fearn and entrance to Loch Torridon. NG 7059
Òb Gauscavaig Skye, H'land 79 D7 bay on W side of Sleat peninsula, 1m N of Tarskavaig. Dunscaith, qv, at N end of bay. NG 5911
Obley Salop 34 A6 ham 3m/4km SE of Clun. SO 3277
Òb Mheallaidh H'land 78 F4* inlet on S side of Upr Loch Torridon, Ross and Cromarty dist. NG 8354
Oborne Dorset 8 D3 vil 2m/3km NE of Sherborne. ST 6518
Obridge Som 8 A2* N dist of Taunton. ST 2325
Obsdale H'land 81 F1* loc on E side of Alness, Ross and Cromarty dist. NH 6669
Obthorpe Lincs 37 F3* loc 3m/5km S of Bourne. TF 0915
Occaney N Yorks 49 F2* loc 1m SW of Staveley. SE 3561
Occold Suffolk 31 F1 vil 2m/3km SE of Eye. TM 1570
Ochil Hills 72 C4-73 E3 range of hills, partly in Central region but mainly in Tayside region, extending from Br of Allan to Firth of Tay at Newburgh. Summit is Ben Cleuch, 2363 ft or 720 metres. NO 00
Ochiltree S'clyde 56 E2 vil at confluence of Burnock Water and Lugar Water, 4m/7km W of Cumnock. NS 5021
Ochrwyth Gwent 15 G3* loc 4m/7km W of Newport. ST 2489
Ochr-y-foel Clwyd 41 F3* loc adjoining Dyserth to E. SJ 0679
Ochr-y-mynydd Mid Glam 15 E1 loc 2m/3km W of Merthyr Tydfil. SO 0206
Ock 17 H2 r rising S of Faringdon, Oxon, and flowing E into R Thames at Abingdon. SU 4996
Ockbrook Derbys 36 A1 vil 4m/7km E of Derby. Moravian settlement on W side, founded in 18c. SK 4236
Ockendon, North London 20 C3 loc in borough of Havering 2m/3km SE of Upminster. TQ 5884
Ockendon, South Essex 20 C3 suburb 3m/4km NW of Grays. TQ 5881
Ocker Hill W Midlands 35 F5* loc in W Bromwich 3m/4km NW of tn centre. SO 9793
Ockeridge H & W 26 C2* loc 7m/11km NW of Worcester. SO 7862
Ockham Surrey 19 E5 vil 5m/8km E of Woking. Airfield to N. TQ 0756
Ockle Point H'land 68 D2 headland on N coast of Ardnamurchan peninsula in Lochaber dist, 10m/16km NW of Salen. NM 5471
Ockley Surrey 11 G1 vil 6m/10km N of Horsham. TQ 1439
Ocle Pychard H & W 26 B3 vil 7m/11km NE of Hereford. SO 5946
Octon Humberside 51 E2 loc 1m W of Thwing. Former vil no longer exists. TA 0369
Odcombe Som 8 C3 vil 3m/5km W of Yeovil. ST 5015
Odda's Chapel Glos. See Deerhurst.
Odd Down Avon 16 C5* SW dist of Bath. ST 7362
Oddendale Cumbria 53 E3* loc 2m/4km SE of Shap. NY 5814
Oddingley H & W 26 D2 vil 3m/4km S of Droitwich. SO 9059
Oddington Glos 27 F5 vil 3m/4km E of Stow-on-the-Wold. SP 2325
Oddington Oxon 28 A6/B6 vil 6m/10km NE of Oxford. SP 5514
Odell Beds 28 D2/29 E2 vil 8m/12km NW of Bedford. Loc of **Lit Odell** adjoins to W. SP 9657
Odham Devon 6 D5* loc 4m/7km W of Hatherleigh. SS 4702
Odiham Hants 18 C6 vil 7m/11km E of Basingstoke. Airfield to S. SU 7451
Odin Bay Orkney 89 C6* bay on E coast of Stronsay extending N from Burgh Hd. HY 6924
Odness Orkney 89 C6* headland on E coast of Stronsay on S side of entrance to Mill Bay. HY 6926
Odsal W Yorks 48 D5* dist of Bradford 2m/3km S of city centre. Includes loc of **O. Top,** with sports stadium. SE 1529
Odsey Cambs 29 G4* ham 4m/7km W of Royston. TL 2938
Odstock Wilts 9 H2 vil on R Ebble 3m/4km S of Salisbury. To E beside R Avon, Longford Castle, triangular Tudor hse in park. SU 1426
Odstone Leics 36 A3 ham 6m/10km SE of Ashby de la Zouch. SK 3907
Offa's Dyke 34 A5 etc. Entrenchment built in 8c by Offa, King of Mercia, to mark boundary between Anglo-Saxon and Welsh territory. Runs from Prestatyn on N Wales coast to Chepstow in the S. Still visible at various points on its course.
Offchurch Warwicks 27 G1 vil 3m/4km E of Leamington. SP 3565
Offenham H & W 27 E3 vil 2m/3km NE of Evesham. SP 0546
Offenham Cross H & W 27 E3* loc 2m/3km NE of Evesham. SP 0645
Offerton Gtr Manchester 43 E3 loc in Stockport 2m/3km E of tn centre. **O. Green** loc 1km E. SJ 9288
Offerton Tyne & Wear 61 H5* loc 4m/6km W of Sunderland. NZ 3455
Offham E Sussex 12 A5 ham 2m/3km NW of Lewes. TQ 4012
Offham Kent 20 C5 vil 2m/3km W of W Malling. TQ 6557
Offham W Sussex 11 F4 ham on R Arun 2km NE of Arundel. TQ 0208
Offley, Great Herts 29 F5 vil 3m/5km SW of Hitchin. TL 1427
Offleyhay Staffs 35 E2* loc 2m/3km W of Eccleshall. SJ 7929
Offley, High Staffs 34 D2 vil 5m/8km NE of Newport. SJ 7826
Offleyhoo Herts 29 F5* loc 3m/5km SW of Hitchin. TL 1426
Offley, Little Herts 29 F5* loc 4m/6km W of Hitchin. TL 1328
Offleymarsh Staffs 34 D2/35 E2* loc 3m/5km W of Eccleshall. SJ 3429
Offord Cluny Cambs 29 F1 vil 3m/5km SW of Huntingdon. TL 2167
Offord Darcy Cambs 29 F2 vil 4m/6km SW of Huntingdon. TL 2166
Offton Suffolk 31 E3 vil 5m/8km NE of Hadleigh. TM 0649
Offwell Devon 8 A4 vil 2m/3km SE of Honiton. SY 1999
Og 17 F4 r rising near Ogbourne St George, Wilts, and flowing S into R Kennet on E side of Marlborough. SU 1969
Ogau 33 H2* r running SE into R Cynllaith 1m NE of Llansilin, Clwyd. SJ 2229
Ogbourne Maizey Wilts 17 F4* vil 2m/3km N of Marlborough. SU 1871
Ogbourne St Andrew Wilts 17 F4 vil 2m/3km N of Marlborough. SU 1872
Ogbourne St George Wilts 17 F4 vil 3m/5km N of Marlborough. SU 2074
Ogden W Yorks 48 D5 loc 2m/3km S of Denholme. **Ogden Resr** to W. SE 0630
Ogden, Higher Gtr Manchester 48 C6* loc 4m/6km E of Rochdale. **Ogden Resr** to NW. SD 9512
Ogden Reservoir Lancs 48 A5* resr 2m/3km W of Haslingden. SD 7622
Ogden Reservoirs Lancs 48 B4* two resrs on S side of Pendle Hill 3m/5km NW of Nelson. SD 8139
Ogilvie Castle Tayside 72 C4 remains of old cas on hillside 1m SE of Blackford. NN 9008
Ogle Nthmb 61 F4 ham 2m/4km E of Belsay. **O. Castle,** 14c tower hse with later manor hse added. NZ 1378
Oglet Merseyside 42 A3* loc in Liverpool S of Speke. SJ 4381
Oglethorpe W Yorks 49 F4* loc 2km NE of Bramham. SE 4444
Ogmore (Ogwr) Mid Glam 14 D4 ham 3m/4km SW of Bridgend. 12c–13c remains of cas (A.M.). SS 8876
Ogmore (Ogwr) 14 D4 r rising on S side of Craig Ogwr, W of Rhondda, Mid Glam, and flowing S to Bridgend and thence SW into sea 3m/4km E of Porthcawl. SS 8575
Ogmore-by-Sea (Aberogwr) Mid Glam 14 D4 vil 4m/6km SW of Bridgend. SS 8674
Ogmore Forest Mid Glam 15 E3* hilly wooded area to E of Ogmore Vale. SS 9489
Ogmore Vale Mid Glam 15 E3 vil 7m/11km N of Bridgend. SS 9390
Ogston Reservoir Derbys 43 H5* resr 2m/3km SW of Clay Cross. SK 3760
Ogwell Devon 5 E3 par on W side of Newton Abbot containing vil of **E Ogwell** and ham of **W Ogwell.** SX 8370

Ogwen 40 C4 r rising S of Carnedd Llywelyn, Gwynedd, and running S into Llyn Ogwen, then turning N to Bethesda and flowing into Conwy Bay 2m/3km E of Bangor. SH 6172
Ogwen Cottage Gwynedd 40 D5* loc at lower (W) end of Llyn Ogwen. Also known as Pont Pen-y-benglog. SH 6460
Ogwr Welsh form of Ogmore, qv.
Ogwr 118 admin dist of Mid Glam.
Oich H'land 80 D6 r in Inverness dist running NE from Loch Oich to Fort Augustus at head of Loch Ness. NH 3809
Oigh-sgeir H'land 79 A8 group of islets in Inner Hebrides, with lighthouse, lying 6m/10km S to SW of W end of Canna. Also known as Hyskeir. NM 1596
Oisgill Bay Skye, H'land 78 A4 bay on W coast 7m/12km W of Dunvegan. NG 1349
Okeford Fitzpaine Dorset 9 E3 vil 3m/4km SE of Sturminster Newton. ST 8010
Okehampton Devon 6 D5 mkt tn at confluence of Rs E and W Okement below N edge of Dartmoor. Remains of cas (A.M.). Artillery ranges on moors to S. SS 5895
Okement 6 D4 Devon r starting on Dartmoor as two separate streams, **E** and **W Okement,** flowing N and joining at Okehampton. The r then continues N and flows into R Torridge 2m/3km N of Hatherleigh. SS 5507
Okeover Staffs 43 F6 ham 2m/3km NW of Ashbourne. SK 1647
Olchard Devon 5 E3* loc 4m/6km N of Newton Abbot. SX 8777
Olchfa W Glam 23 G6* loc in Swansea 3m/4km W of tn centre. SS 6193
Olchon Brook 25 G5 r rising in Black Mts S of Hay Bluff and flowing SE into R Monnow S of Longtown, H & W. SO 3228
Old Northants 28 C1 vil 6m/10km SW of Kettering. Sometimes known as Wold. SP 7873
Old Aberdeen Grampian 77 H1 dist of Aberdeen 2km N of city centre. Includes the university. NJ 9408
Old Alresford Hants 10 C2 vil 1m N of New Alresford. Site of Roman bldg to SW; also 3m/5km NE. SU 5833
Oldany Island H'land 84 B4 uninhabited island of about 500 acres or 200 hectares at SW side of entrance to Eddrachillis Bay, W coast of Sutherland dist. NC 0834
Old Barns Nthmb 61 G1* loc 1km SW of Warkworth. NU 2405
Old Bedford River 38 B4 fenland drainage channel running NE from Earith, Cambs, to Salters Lode, Norfolk. TF 5801
Oldberrow Warwicks 27 F1 ham 2m/3km W of Henley-in-Arden. SP 1265
Old Bewick Nthmb 67 G6 ham 6m/10km SE of Wooler. NU 0621
Old Bexley London 20 B4 loc in borough of Bexley 3m/5km W of Dartford. TQ 4973
Old Blair Tayside 75 H4 loc with ruined ch 1m N of Blair Atholl. Burial place of 'Bonnie Dundee' – see Killiecrankie. NN 8666
Old Bolingbroke Lincs 45 G4 vil 3m/5km W of Spilsby. Earthworks mark site of cas, birthplace of Henry IV, 1367. TF 3465
Old Boston Merseyside 42 B2* loc adjoining Haydock to NE. See also New Boston. SJ 5797
Old Bradwell Bucks. See Bradwell.
Old Bramhope W Yorks 49 E4* ham 1m W of Bramhope. SE 2343
Old Brampton Derbys 43 H4 vil 3m/5km W of Chesterfield. SK 3371
Oldbridge 15 H4* r rising below N slopes of Mendip Hills to W of Churchill, Avon, and flowing NW into R Yeo 1m E of Wick St Lawrence. ST 3865
Old Bridge of Doon S'clyde. See Auld Brig o' Doon, under Alloway.
Old Bridge of Urr D & G 58 D4 loc and rd br across Urr Water, 4m/6km N of Castle Douglas. NX 7767
Old Buckenham Norfolk 39 E5 vil 3m/4km SE of Attleborough. Faint remains of cas and priory to N. TM 0691
Old Burdon Tyne & Wear 61 H6* loc 2m/3km SW of Ryhope and 1km SW of Burdon. NZ 3850
Oldbury Kent 20 C5 loc adjoining Ightham to W, 4m/6km E of Sevenoaks. To W, **O. Hill** and Styants Wd (NT), including southern half of Iron Age fort. TQ 5856
Oldbury Salop 34 D5 vil 1km S of Bridgnorth. SO 7192
Oldbury Warwicks 35 H5 ham 2m/3km S of Atherstone. Iron Age fort to N. SP 3194
Oldbury W Midlands 35 F5 dist of Warley 5m/8km W of Birmingham. Industries include mnfre of iron and steel tubes, chemical and engineering products, surgical dressings, etc. SO 9989
Oldbury Naite Avon 16 B2* loc 1m NE of Oldbury-on-Severn. ST 6293
Oldbury-on-Severn Glos 16 B2 vil near R Severn estuary 2m/3km NW of Thornbury. ST 6192
Oldbury on the Hill Glos 16 C3* ham 1km N of Didmarton. ST 8188
Old Byland N Yorks 54 D6 vil 4m/7km W of Helmsley. SE 5485
Old Carlisle Cumbria 52 C1 loc 2km S of Wigton. Site of Roman fort to W. NY 2646
Old Cassop Durham 54 C1* loc 1m NW of Cassop Colliery. NZ 3339
Oldcastle Gwent 25 G5/H5 ham 3m/4km S of Longtown. SO 3224
Oldcastle (Hengastell, Yr) Mid Glam 15 E3* loc adjoining Bridgend to E. SS 9179
Old Castle Head Dyfed 22 C6 headland 1m SE of Manorbier and 4m/7km SW of Tenby. SS 0796
Oldcastle Heath Ches 42 A6/B6 loc 2km SW of Malpas. SJ 4745
Old Castle of Slains Grampian 83 H4 remains of old cas, destroyed by James VI (James I of England), on E coast 4m/7km NE of Newburgh. See also Kirkton of Slains. NK 0530
Old Church Stoke Powys 34 A5* ham 1m NE of Church Stoke. SO 2895
Old Clee Humberside 45 G1 dist of Grimsby continuous with Cleethorpes. TA 2908
Old Cleeve Som 7 H1 vil 2m/4km SW of Watchet. Ruins of Cleeve Abbey (A.M.), 13c. ST 0341
Old Cluden Water 58 D4 stream in Dumfries & Galloway region issuing from Glenkiln Resr and joining Cairn Water to E, to form Cluden Water, 6m/10km NW of Dumfries. NX 8879
Old Colwyn Clwyd 41 E4 suburb 2km E of Colwyn Bay, incorporating original vil of Colwyn. SH 8678
Oldcotes Notts 44 B2 vil 3m/4km S of Tickhill. Site of Roman villa on E side. SK 5888
Old Craighall Lothian 66 B2* loc 2km S of Musselburgh. NT 3370
Oldcroft Glos 16 B1* loc 2m/3km W of Blakeney. SO 6406
Old Dailly S'clyde 56 C4 vil 3m/4km E of Girvan. See also Dailly. NX 2299
Old Dalby Leics 36 C2 vil 6m/9km NW of Melton Mowbray. SK 6723
Old Dam Derbys 43 F3* loc adjoining Peak Forest to N. SK 1179
Old Deer Grampian 83 G2 vil 10m/15km W of Peterhead. Ruined 13c abbey (A.M.) 1km NW. See also Forest of Deer. NJ 9747
Old Dilton Wilts 16 D6* loc on SW edge of Westbury. ST 8649
Old Dolphin W Yorks 48 D5 loc in Bradford 1m E of Queensbury. SE 1130
Old Down Avon 16 B3* loc 3m/4km SW of Thornbury. ST 6187
Old Down Som 16 B6* ham 3m/5km SW of Midsomer Norton. ST 6251
Oldeamere Cambs 37 G4/G5* loc 3m/4km E of Whittlesey. TL 3096
Old Edlington S Yorks 44 A2 vil 5m/7km SW of Doncaster. SK 5397
Old Eldon Durham 54 B2* loc 2km NE of Shildon. NZ 2427
Old Ellerby Humberside 51 F4 vil 7m/11km NE of Hull. TA 1637
Oldfallow Staffs 35 F3* loc 1km N of Cannock. SJ 9710
Old Felixstowe Suffolk 31 G4* NE dist of Felixstowe. TM 3135
Oldfield H & W 26 D1* ham 4m/6km W of Droitwich. SO 8464
Oldfield W Yorks 48 C4 loc 2km W of Haworth. SE 0037
Oldfield W Yorks 48 D6* loc 1m S of Honley. SE 1310
Oldfield Brow Gtr Manchester 42 C3* loc in Altrincham 1m NW of tn centre. SJ 7588
Old Field Carr Lancs 47 E4* loc 1km S of Poulton-le-Fylde. SD 3538
Old Fletton Cambs 37 G4 tn adjoining Peterborough to S. Numerous brick works. TL 1997
Old Ford London 20 A3* loc in borough of Tower Hamlets 3m/5km NE of London Br. TQ 3683
Oldford Som 16 C6 ham 2m/3km NE of Frome. ST 7850
Old Forge H & W 26 B5* ham on right bank of R Wye 4m/7km SW of Ross-on-Wye. SO 5518
Old Furnace Gwent 15 G2* loc 1m W of Pontypool. SO 2800
Old Glossop Derbys 43 D2 loc 2km NE of Glossop. SK 0494
Old Goginan Dyfed 32 D6/33 E6 loc 6m/10km E of Aberystwyth, to N of Goginan across R Melindwr. SN 6881
Old Goole Humberside 50 C5 S dist of Goole. SE 7422
Old Grimsbury Oxon 27 H3* loc in NE part of Banbury. SP 4641
Oldhall S'clyde 64 C3* loc 2m/3km E of Paisley. NS 5164
Old Hall Creek Essex 21 F1* marshy inlet running into Tollesbury Fleet 1m NE of Tollesbury. TL 9611
Old Hall Green Herts 29 G5* ham 2km SW of Puckeridge. TL 3722
Old Hall Street Norfolk 39 G2* loc 1km SW of Knapton. TG 3033
Oldham Gtr Manchester 43 E1 tn 7m/12km NE of Manchester. Textiles, coal-mining, aero-engineering, paper mnfre, tanning. **O. Edge** loc 1km N of tn centre. SD 9305
Oldhamstocks Lothian 67 E2 vil 6m/10km SE of Dunbar. NT 7470
Old Harlow Essex 20 B1* NE dist of Harlow. TL 4711
Old Head Orkney 89 B7 headland at SE end of S Ronaldsay. ND 4683
Old Heath Essex 31 E5 loc in SE part of Colchester. TM 0122
Old Heathfield E Sussex 12 C4* vil 2km SE of Heathfield. TQ 5920
Old Hill W Isles 88 A2* small uninhabited island off W coast of Lewis 2m/3km NW of island of Gt Bernera. NB 1143
Old Hill W Midlands 35 F5 loc in Warley 3m/5km W of tn centre. SO 9586
Oldhurst Cambs 37 G6 vil 5m/8km NE of Huntingdon. TL 3077
Old Hutton Cumbria 53 E5 ham 4m/7km SE of Kendal. SD 5688
Old Ingarsby Leics 36 C4* loc on site of former vil 6m/10km E of Leicester. SK 6805
Old Kea Cornwall 2 D4* ham above Truro R 2m/3km SE of Truro across water. SW 8441
Old Kilpatrick S'clyde 64 C2 tn on N bank of R Clyde below Erskine Br. Site of Roman fort near line of Antonine Wall. Distillery. NS 4673
Old Knebworth Herts 29 F5* vil 2m/4km S of Stevenage. **Knebworth Hse,** of 16c and 19c, in park to N. TL 2320
Oldland Avon 16 B4 suburb 6m/9km E of Bristol. ST 6771
Old Langho Lancs 48 A4* ham 2m/3km W of Whalley. See also Langho. SD 7033
Old Laund Booth Lancs 48 B4* loc adjoining Nelson to W. SD 8337
Old Laxey Isle of Man 46 C5* vil adjoining Laxey, at mouth of Laxey R. SC 4483
Old Leake Lincs 45 G6 vil 6m/10km NE of Boston. TF 4050
Old Malden London 19 F5* loc in borough of Kingston 3m/5km SE of Kingston tn centre. TQ 2166
Old Malton N Yorks 50 C1 vil adjoining Malton to NE. SE 7972
Old Man of Coniston, The Cumbria 52 C5 mountain in Lake Dist 2m/3km W of Coniston. Height 2631 ft or 802 metres. SD 2797
Old Man of Hoy Orkney 89 A7 massive column of rock rising from foot of cliffs on NW coast of Hoy 1m N of Rora Hd. Height 450 ft or 137 metres. HY 1700
Old Man of Mow. See Mow Cop.
Old Man of Storr Skye, H'land 78 C4 column of rock 160 ft or 49 metres high, on E side of The Storr 7m/11km N of Portree. NG 5053
Old Man of Wick H'land 86 F3 ruined 12c–14c tower (A.M.), also known as Castle of Old Wick, on E coast of Caithness dist, 1m S of Wick. ND 3648
Old Marton Salop 34 A1* loc 3m/4km NE of Whittington. SJ 3434
Oldmeldrum Grampian 83 F4 small tn 4m/7km NE of Inverurie. Distillery. NJ 8027
Old Melrose Borders 66 D5 site of monastery founded in 7c, in loop of R Tweed 3m/4km E of Melrose. NT 5834
Old Micklefield W Yorks 49 F4/F5 vil 5m/8km N of Castleford. SE 4433
Old Mill Creek Devon 5 E5* inlet of R Dart estuary 1km N of Dartmouth. SX 8752
Old Milton Hants 10 A5 loc 1km N of Barton on Sea. SZ 2394
Old Milverton Warwicks 27 G1 vil 2m/3km NW of Leamington. SP 2967
Old Netley Hants 10 B4 loc 3m/4km NW of Park Gate. SU 4710
Old Newton Suffolk 31 E2 vil 3m/4km N of Stowmarket. TM 0562
Oldpark Salop 34 D3* loc 2km N of Dawley. SJ 6909
Old Peak N Yorks 55 G4* headland at S end of Robin Hood's Bay on North Sea coast 1km N of Ravenscar. Also known as S Cheek. NZ 9802
Old Place of Mochrum D & G. See Mochrum Loch. NX 3054
Old Quarrington Durham 54 C1/C2* loc 1m W of Quarrington Hill. NZ 3237
Old Radnor (Pencraig) Powys 25 G2 ham 3m/4km E of New Radnor. Remains of Norman motte. SO 2559
Old Ravensworth Tyne & Wear 61 G5* loc 4m/6km S of Gateshead. NZ 2357
Old Rayne Grampian 83 E4 vil 8m/12km NW of Inverurie. NJ 6728
Oldridge Devon 7 F5 loc 3m/4km S of Crediton. SX 8296
Old Romney Kent 13 F4 vil on Romney Marsh 2m/4km W of New Romney. TR 0325
Old Sarum Wilts 9 H1 large earthwork (A.M.) 2m/3km N of Salisbury. Site of original tn, cas, and cathedral. SU 1332
Old Scone Tayside 73 E2. See Scone Palace.
Oldshore Beg H'land 84 B2* loc near W coast of Sutherland dist 3m/4km NW of Kinlochbervie. NC 1959
Oldshore More H'land 84 C2 loc near W coast of Sutherland dist 2m/3km NW of Kinlochbervie. NC 2058
Old Snydale W Yorks 49 F5 loc 2km W of Featherstone. See also Snydale. SE 4021
Old Soar Manor Kent 20 C6* solar block (NT) of late 13c knight's dwelling, 2km E of Plaxtol. TQ 6154
Old Sodbury Avon 16 C3 vil 2m/3km E of Chipping Sodbury. ST 7581
Old Somerby Lincs 37 E2 vil 3m/5km SE of Grantham. SK 9633
Oldstead N Yorks 54 D6 ham 7m/11km E of Thirsk. SE 5380
Old Stillington Durham 54 C3 ham 1km SW of Stillington. NZ 3622
Old Stratford Northants 28 C3 vil 1km NW of Stony Stratford across R Ouse. SP 7741
Old Swan Merseyside 42 A2* dist of Liverpool 3m/5km E of city centre. SJ 3891
Old Swinford W Midlands 35 E5/E6 loc in Stourbridge 1km S of tn centre. SO 9083
Old Tame Gtr Manchester 43 E1* loc 1km SW of Denshaw. SD 9609
Old Tebay Cumbria 53 E4* loc adjoining Tebay to N. NY 6105
Old Thirsk N Yorks 54 D6 E part of Thirsk. SE 4382
Old Thornville N Yorks 50 A3* loc 1km NE of Cattal. Also known as Thornville. SE 4454
Old Town Cumbria 53 E6 ham 3m/5km N of Kirkby Lonsdale. SD 5982
Old Town Cumbria 60 A6/B6* loc adjoining High Hesket to S. NY 4743
Old Town E Sussex 12 C6* W dist of Eastbourne. TV 5899
Oldtown H'land 85 F7* loc in Sutherland dist 1km S of Ardgay at head of Dornoch Firth. NH 5989
Old Town Nthmb 60 D3* loc 1m S of Otterburn. NY 8891
Old Town S Yorks 43 G1* dist of Barnsley 1m NW of tn centre. SE 3307
Old Town W Yorks 48 C5* loc 1m NE of Hebden Br. SD 9928

Oldtown of Ord Grampian 83 E1 loc 5m/8km SW of Banff. NJ 6259
Old Trafford Gtr Manchester 42 D2* dist of Salford 2m/3km SW of tn centre. Docks on Manchester Ship Canal. Cricket and football grnds. SJ 8196
Old Tree Kent 13 G1* loc 3m/5km SE of Herne Bay. TR 2064
Oldwalls W Glam 23 F6 ham 1km W of Llanrhidian. SS 4891
Old Warden Beds 29 F3 vil 4m/6km W of Biggleswade. Biggleswade (Old Warden) Airfield 2km E. TL 1343
Oldway W Glam 23 G6* loc 3m/5km W of Mumbles Hd. SS 5888
Oldways End 7 F3 ham on border of Devon and Somerset 4m/6km SW of Dulverton. SS 8624
Old Weston Cambs 37 F6 vil 6m/9km W of Alconbury. TL 0977
Oldwhat Grampian 83 G2* loc 3m/5km SW of New Pitsligo. NJ 8651
Oldwich Lane W Midlands 35 H6* loc 5m/9km W of Kenilworth. SP 2174
Old Wick H'land 86 F3 loc on S side of Wick, in Caithness dist. Also known as Pulteneytown. See also Old Man of Wick. ND 3649
Old Winchester Hill Hants 10 D3 hill 2m/3km E of Meonstoke, crowned by prehistoric fort. Nature reserve to N. SU 6420
Old Windsor Berks 18 D4 tn 2m/3km SE of Windsor across Home Park. SU 9874
Old Wingate Durham 54 C2* loc 2m/3km W of Wingate. NZ 3737
Old Wives Lees Kent 21 F6 vil 5m/8km W of Canterbury. TR 0754
Old Woking Surrey 19 E5 loc 2km SE of Woking tn centre. TQ 0156
Old Wolverton Bucks 28 C3 loc to W of Wolverton tn centre. SP 8041
Oldwood Salop 34 B3 loc 5m/9km NW of Shrewsbury. SJ 4520
Oldwood Common H & W 26 B1* loc 2km S of Tenbury Wells. SO 5966
Old Woodstock Oxon 27 H5* loc at NW end of Woodstock. SP 4417
Olicana W Yorks. See Ilkley.
Oliver's Battery Hants 10 B2 SW suburb of Winchester. So called because from here Oliver Cromwell bombarded the city. SU 4527
Oliver's Battery Hants 18 B6* loc 2m/3km NE of Basingstoke. SU 6653
Ollaberry Shetland 89 E6 loc on N side of bay of same name, on NE coast of Mainland 4m/7km N of Sullom. HU 3680
Ollach, Upper Skye, H'land 79 D5 locality on E coast 5m/7km SE of Loch Portree. **Lr Ollach** is locality nearly 1m NW. NG 5136
Ollerton Ches 42 D3 vil 2m/3km SE of Knutsford. SJ 7776
Ollerton Notts 44 B4 tn (with New Ollerton, qv) 12m/19km NW of Newark-on-Trent. SK 6567
Ollerton Salop 34 D2 ham 3m/5km SE of Hodnet. SJ 6525
Ollerton Fold Lancs 47 G5* loc 1m NW of Withnell. SD 6223
Olmarch Dyfed 24 C3* loc 4m/7km SW of Tregaron. SN 6255
Olmstead Green Cambs 30 B4* loc 4m/6km SW of Haverhill. TL 6341
Olna Firth Shetland 89 E7* inlet on W coast of Mainland with vil of Voe at its head. HU 3864
Olney Bucks 28 D3 small tn on R Ouse 5m/8km N of Newport Pagnell. Tannery, footwear mnfre. Annual pancake race on Shrove Tuesday. Site of Roman bldg to NE. SP 8851
Olney Northants 48 B3 loc adjoining Silverstone to S, 4m/6km SW of Towcester. SP 6643
Olton W Midlands 35 G6 loc in Solihull 2m/4km NW of tn centre. **Olton Resr** to SE. SP 1282
Olveston Avon 16 B3 vil 3m/5km SW of Thornbury. ST 6087
Olympia London 19 F4* exhibition hall and dist surrounding it, in borough of Hammersmith 4m/6km W of Charing Cross. TQ 2479
Ombersley H & W 26 D2 vil 4m/6km W of Droitwich. SO 8463
Ompton Notts 44 B4 vil 3m/4km SE of Ollerton. SK 6865
Onchan Isle of Man 46 B5 suburb 2m/3km NE of Douglas. To S, **Onchan Hd**, headland at NE end of Douglas Bay. SC 3978
Onecote Staffs 43 F5 vil 4m/7km E of Leek. SK 0455
Onehouse Suffolk 31 E2* vil 2m/3km W of Stowmarket. TM 0158
Onen Gwent 26 A6* loc 6m/9km W of Monmouth. SO 4314
One Tree Hill Kent 20 C6* hill (NT) 2m/3km SE of Sevenoaks. Roman cemetery on summit; view to S. TQ 5653
Ongar, High Essex 20 C2 vil 1m NE of Chipping Ongar. TL 5603
Ongar Street H & W 25 H2 loc 4m/7km S of Leintwardine. SO 3967
Onibury Salop 34 B6 vil 3m/4km SE of Craven Arms. SO 4579
Onich H'land 74 B5 vil in Lochaber dist on N side of entrance to Loch Leven, 2m/3km W of N Ballachulish. NN 0261
Onley Northants 27 H1 loc 3m/4km S of Rugby. SP 5171
Onllwyn W Glam 14 D1 vil 2m/3km NE of Seven Sisters. Brick works. SN 8410
Onneley Staffs 42 C6 vil 2km E of Woore. SJ 7543
Onn, High Staffs 35 E3* ham 2km SW of Ch Eaton. **High Onn Wharf** loc 1km NE on Shropshire Union Canal. SJ 8216
Onn, Little Staffs 35 E3* ham 1m S of Ch Eaton. SJ 8316
Onny 34 B6. River E Onny rises 3m/4km NW of Ratlinghope, Salop; river W Onny rises near Shelve, Salop. The two rivers flow S to join at Eaton, 3m/5km E of Bishop's Castle, and continue SE as R Onny until joining R Teme at Bromfield, NW of Ludlow. SO 4876
Onslow Village Surrey 18 D6* W dist of Guildford. SU 9749
Onston Orkney 89 A6* locality and chambered cairn (A.M.) on S side of Loch of Stenness, Mainland, 3m/4km NE of Stromness. HY 2811
Openshaw Gtr Manchester 42 D2* dist of Manchester 3m/4km E of city centre. Engineering and rly locomotive works. SJ 8897
Openwoodgate Derbys 43 H6* loc 2km E of Belper. SK 3647
Opinan H'land 78 E2 vil on W coast of Ross and Cromarty dist 4m/7km SW of Gairloch across Gair Loch. NG 7472
Opsay W Isles 88 E1* small uninhabited island in Sound of Harris 4m/6km off NE coast of N Uist. NF 9876
Orasay Island W Isles 88 C2* islet at entrance to Loch Leurbost, E coast of Lewis. NB 4024
Orasay Island W Isles 88 B2* small uninhabited island near head of E Loch Roag, W coast of Lewis. NB 2132
Orbliston Grampian 82 C2 loc 7m/11km SE of Elgin. NJ 3057
Orbost Skye, H'land 79 A5 loc 3m/5km S of Dunvegan. NG 2543
Orby Lincs 45 H4 vil 6m/9km NW of Skegness. TF 4967
Orchard, East Dorset 9 F3* vil 3m/5km S of Shaftesbury. ST 8317
Orchard, High Glos 26 C5* loc in SW part of Gloucester. SO 8217
Orchard-Leigh Bucks 18 D2* loc 2m/4km NE of Chesham. SP 9803
Orchard Portman Som 8 A2 vil 2m/4km SE of Taunton. ST 2421
Orchardton D & G 58 D5 12c round tower (A.M.) 1m S of Palnackie and 1m N of **O. Bay**, inlet of Auchencairn Bay. NX 8155
Orchard, West Dorset 9 F3 vil 3m/5km NE of Sturminster Newton. ST 8216
Orcheston Wilts 17 E6 vil on Salisbury Plain 7m/11km NW of Amesbury. SU 0545
Orchy S'clyde 70 C2 r in Argyll running SW from Loch Tulla down Glen Orchy to NE end of Loch Awe. NN 1327
Orcop H & W 26 A5* vil 5m/8km E of Pontrilas. SO 4726
Orcop Hill H & W 26 A4 vil 5m/9km E of Pontrilas. SO 4829
Ord Skye, H'land 79 D7 locality on S side of Loch Eishort, Sleat peninsula, 5m/8km W of Isle Ornsay. NG 6113
Ord, East Nthmb 67 F3 vil 2km SW of Berwick-upon-Tweed. NT 9851
Ordhead Grampian 83 E5 vil 7m/11km SE of Alford. NJ 6610
Ordie Grampian 77 E1 vil 2m/3km N of Dinnet. NJ 4501
Ord Point H'land 87 D5 headland on border of Caithness and Sutherland dists, on E coast 3m/4km NE of Helmsdale. ND 0617
Ordsall Gtr Manchester 42 D2* dist of Salford 2km SW of tn centre. SJ 8197
Ordsall Notts 44 B3 S dist of E Retford. SK 7079
Ore 31 G4 estuary of R Alde, Suffolk, flowing SW parallel to coast from Orford Ness into North Sea 2km E of Hollesley. TM 3743
Ore 73 F4 r issuing from Loch Ore, N of Cowdenbeath in Fife region, and flowing E to R Leven W of Windygates. NO 3300
Oreston Devon 4 B5 SE dist of Plymouth E of R Plym. SX 5053
Oreton Salop 34 D6* loc 3m/5km N of Cleobury Mortimer. SO 6580
Orfasay Shetland 89 E6* small uninhabited island off S coast of Yell, separated from it by **Sound of O.** HU 4977
Orford Ches 42 B2* dist of Warrington 2m/3km NE of tn centre. SJ 6190
Orford Suffolk 31 H3 vil on R Ore 9m/15km E of Woodbridge. Remains of Norman cas (A.M.). Headland of **Orford Ness** on coast 2m/3km E across r, marshes, and shingle. TM 4249
Orford Beach Suffolk 31 G3/H3 narrow strip of shingle extending 6m/9km from Orford Ness to mouth of R Ore. TM 4046
Organford Dorset 9 F5* ham 3m/5km N of Wareham. SY 9392
Orgreave Staffs 35 G3* loc 2km W of Alrewas. SK 1416
Orgreave S Yorks 43 H3* coal-mining loc 4m/7km E of Sheffield. SK 4286
Orielton Dyfed 22 C5 loc 3m/4km SW of Pembroke. Decoy pond of Wildfowl Inquiry Committee. SR 9598
Orinsay W Isles 88 C2* small uninhabited island off E coast of Lewis, on S side of entrance to Loch Erisort. NB 4121
Orka Voe Shetland 89 E6* inlet on coast of Mainland at S end of Yell Sound. HU 4077
Orkney 89. Group of some fifteen main islands and numerous smaller islands, islets, and rocks, for administrative purposes designated an Islands Area, lying N of the NE end of Scottish mainland across Pentland Firth; Kirkwall, the capital, on the island of Mainland, is 24m/38km N of Duncansby Hd. About twenty islands are inhabited. In general the islands are low-lying but have steep, high cliffs on W side. As in Shetland the climate is mild for the latitude but storms are frequent. Fishing and farming (mainly cattle-rearing) are the chief industries. Airport at Grimsetter, near Kirkwall. Oil terminal on island of Flotta. Oil service bases at Car Ness and Stromness, Mainland; and at Lyness, Hoy. HY 30
Orlestone Kent 13 F3 ham 5m/8km S of Ashford. TR 0034
Orleton H & W 26 A1 vil 5m/8km N of Leominster. SO 4967
Orleton H & W 26 C1* vil on R Teme 7m/11km E of Tenbury Wells. SO 6966
Orleton Common H & W 26 A1 loc 5m/7km SW of Ludlow. SO 4768
Orlingbury Northants 28 D1 vil 4m/6km NW of Wellingborough. SP 8672
Ormathwaite Cumbria 52 C3* loc 2km N of Keswick. NY 2625
Ormes Bay Gwynedd 41 E3* bay, also known as Llandudno Bay, on N Wales coast, extending from Lit Ormes Hd westwards to Pen-trwyn, N of Llandudno. SH 7982
Ormesby Cleveland 54 D3 suburb 3m/5km SE of Middlesbrough. Hall (NT) is mid-18c hse. NZ 5317
Ormesby, North Cleveland 54 D3 dist of Middlesbrough 1m E of tn centre. NZ 5019
Ormesby St Margaret Norfolk 39 H3 vil 5m/8km N of Gt Yarmouth. **O. St Michael** vil 1m W. **O. Broad** large broad or lake 2m/3km W, connected by Rollesby and Filby Broads with Muck Fleet and R Bure. TG 4914
Ormes Head, Great (Pen-y-Gogarth) Gwynedd 40 D3 limestone headland 2m/3km NW of Llandudno. SH 7584
Ormes Head, Little (Trwyn y Fuwch) Gwynedd 41 E3 headland at E end of Ormes Bay or Llandudno Bay. SH 8182
Ormiscaig H'land 78 F1 locality on E shore of Loch Ewe, Ross and Cromarty dist, 2km NW of vil of Aultbea. NG 8590
Ormiston Lothian 66 B2 vil 2m/4km S of Tranent. Mkt cross (A.M.). NT 4169
Ormsaigmore H'land 68 C3* loc on S coast of Ardnamurchan in Lochaber dist, between Kilchoan and loc of **Ormsaigbeag.** NM 4763
Ormsary S'clyde 63 E1 locality in Knapdale, Argyll, on E side of Loch Caolisport, 4m/7km SW of Achahoish. NR 7372
Ormsby, North Lincs 45 G2 vil 5m/7km NW of Louth. TF 2893
Ormsby, South Lincs 45 G4 vil 3m/5km NW of Ulceby Cross. TF 3775
Ormside, Great Cumbria 53 F3 ham 2m/4km SE of Appleby across R Eden. **Lit Ormside** loc 1km SE. NY 7017
Ormskirk Lancs 42 A1 tn 7m/12km SE of Southport. SD 4108
Ornish Island W Isles 88 E2* small uninhabited island at entrance to Loch Skiport, E coast of N Uist. NF 8538
Ornsay Skye, H'land 79 E7 small uninhabited island off E coast of Sleat peninsula opp vil of Isle Ornsay. Island forms E side of harbour. See also Eilean Sionnach. NG 7112
Ornsby Hill Durham 54 B1* loc adjoining Lanchester to N. NZ 1648
Oronsay H'land 68 D3 uninhabited island at entrance to Loch Sunart in Lochaber dist, W of island of Carna. NM 5959
Oronsay S'clyde 69 C8 barely inhabited island of about 2 sq miles or 5 sq km off S end of Colonsay, qv, to which it is connected by sands at low tide. Traces of Stone Age settlement. Remains of 14c priory near W coast. NR 3588
Oronsay Skye, H'land 79 B5 small uninhabited island off Ullinish Pt in Loch Bracadale. NG 3136
Oronsay W Isles 88 E1* low-lying uninhabited island in bay on N coast of N Uist to E of Sollas. NF 8475
Orosay W Isles 88 D3* small uninhabited island on E side of Northbay Airfield, island of Barra. NF 7106
Orosay W Isles 88 D4* islet off SE coast of Barra opp Ersary. NL 7099
Orosay W Isles 88 D4* islet off NE coast of island of Vatersay. NL 6497
Orosay W Isles 88 D4* islet on E side of entrance to Castle Bay on S coast of Barra. NL 6697
Orosay W Isles 88 D3* small uninhabited island off W coast of S Uist 3m/5km SW of Daliburgh. NF 7217
Orosay W Isles 88 B3* locality near E coast of Lewis on N side of Loch Shell 1m W of Lemreway. NB 3612
Orphir Orkney 89 B7 loc on Mainland 7m/11km SW of Kirkwall. Scant remains of 11c or 12c round ch (A.M.). HY 3406
Orpington London 20 B5 tn in borough of Bromley 14m/22km SE of Charing Cross. TQ 4665
Orrell Gtr Manchester 42 B1 tn 4m/6km W of Wigan. **O. Post** loc adjoining to N. SD 5203
Orrell Merseyside 41 H2* N dist of Bootle. SJ 3496
Orrin H'land 81 E2 r in Ross and Cromarty dist rising on E Monar Forest and running E to R Conon 4m/7km SW of Dingwall. **Orrin Resr** is resr of North of Scotland Hydro-Electricity Board, 5m/8km long and 7m/12km from confluence with R Conon. **O. Falls** are 3m/5km from confluence. NH 5153
Orrisdale Isle of Man 46 B4 ham near W coast 2km W of Ballaugh. **Orrisdale Hd,** point on coast to W. SC 3293
Orsay S'clyde 62 A3 island with lighthouse off S end of Rinns of Islay opp Port Wemyss. NR 1651
Orsedd, Yr Welsh form of Rossett, qv.
Orsett Essex 20 C3 vil 4m/6km N of Tilbury. TQ 6481
Orsett Heath Essex 20 C4* loc 3m/4km N of Tilbury. TQ 6479
Orslow Staffs 35 E3* ham 2m/3km N of Blymhill. SJ 8015
Orston Notts 36 D1 vil 4m/7km E of Bingham. SK 7641
Orthwaite Cumbria 52 C2* loc 2m/3km NE of Bassenthwaite. NY 2534
Orton Cambs 37 F4/F5 SW dist of Peterborough, including former vils of **O. Longueville** and **O. Waterville.** TL 1796
Orton Cumbria 53 F4 vil 3m/4km N of Tebay. NY 6208

Orton Northants 36 D6 vil 4m/7km W of Kettering. SP 8079
Orton, Great Cumbria 59 H5 vil 5m/8km W of Carlisle. NY 3254
Orton, Little Cumbria 59 H5* ham 3m/5km W of Carlisle. NY 3555
Orton, Little Leics 35 H4* loc 2km NE of Orton on the Hill. SK 3105
Orton on the Hill Leics 35 H4 vil 4m/6km N of Atherstone. SK 3003
Orton Rigg Cumbria 59 H6* loc 3m/5km NW of Dalston. NY 3352
Orwell Cambs 29 G3 vil 6m/10km N of Royston. TL 3650
Orwell 31 F4/F5 tidal part of R Gipping from Ipswich, Suffolk, where it forms estuary, to its confluence with R Stour at Harwich, flowing thence into Harwich Harbour and North Sea. TM 2633
Osbaldeston Lancs 47 G5 vil 3m/5km NW of Blackburn. **O. Green** loc 1km N. SD 6431
Osbaldwick N Yorks 50 B3 suburb 2m/3km E of York. SE 6351
Osbaston Leics 36 A4* ham 2m/3km NE of Mkt Bosworth. To NW, locs of **O. Hollow, O. Lount,** and **O. Toll Gate.** SK 4204
Osbaston Salop 34 A2* loc 1km NW of Knockin. SJ 3222
Osbaston Salop 34 C3 loc 6m/9km NW of Wellington. SJ 5918
Osborne Isle of Wight 10 C5 Queen Victoria's home (A.M.) designed by Prince Albert, 1m SE of E Cowes. Part now used as convalescent home. **O. Bay** to NE. SZ 5194
Osbournby Lincs 37 F1 vil 5m/8km S of Sleaford. TF 0638
Oscroft Ches 42 B4 vil 4m/7km NW of Tarporley. SJ 5066
Ose H'land 79 B5 r in Skye running SW into Loch Bracadale 3m/5km NW of Bracadale vil. NG 3140
Osea Island Essex 21 E2 island in R Blackwater estuary 4m/7km E of Maldon. TL 9106
Osgathorpe Leics 36 A3 vil 3m/5km N of Coalville. SK 4319
Osgodby Lincs 45 E2 vil 3m/5km NW of Mkt Rasen. Site of Roman settlement 1km S. TF 0792
Osgodby N Yorks 50 B4 vil 2m/3km NE of Selby. SE 6433
Osgodby N Yorks 55 H6 vil 3m/4km S of Scarborough. **Osgodby Pt** headland on North Sea coast 1km NE. TA 0584
Osgoodby N Yorks 49 F1* loc 4m/6km E of Thirsk. Osgoodby Hall dates from 17c. SE 4980
Osidge London 19 G2* loc in borough of Barnet 9m/14km N of Charing Cross. TQ 2894
Oskaig Skye, H'land 79 D5 loc on W coast of Raasay 3m/5km from S end of island. NG 5438
Osleston Derbys 35 H1* loc 7m/11km W of Derby. SK 2437
Osmaston Derbys 36 A1* loc in Derby 2m/3km SE of tn centre. SK 3633
Osmaston Derbys 43 G6 vil 2m/4km SE of Ashbourne. SK 1943
Osmington Dorset 9 E5 vil 5m/9km SE of Dorchester. 1m SE on coast, ham of **O. Mills.** SY 7783
Osmondthorpe W Yorks 49 E5* dist of Leeds 2m/4km E of city centre. SE 3333
Osmotherley N Yorks 54 D5 vil 6m/10km NE of Northallerton. SE 4597
Osnaburgh Fife. See Dairsie.
Osney Oxon 18 A1 W dist of Oxford. SP 4906
Ospringe Kent 21 F5 ham on SW side of Faversham. Maison Dieu (A.M.), 15c hse and museum. TR 0060
Ossa, Little Shetland 89 D6* rock off NW coast of Mainland 2m/4km W of The Faither. Muckle Ossa rock is adjacent to N. HU 2184
Ossett W Yorks 49 E5/E6 tn 3m/5km W of Wakefield. Textiles, engineering, coal-mining. **S Ossett** and **Ossett Spa** locs to S and SE respectively. **Ossett Street Side** loc to N. SE 2720
Ossian H'land 75 E4 r in Lochaber dist running N from Loch O. down Strath O. to Loch Ghuilbinn. NN 4174
Ossian's Cave H'land 74 C5 cleft on N face of Aonach Dubh, Lochaber dist, one of the Three Sisters of Glen Coe, qv. Ossian, legendary Gaelic warrior and bard, is said to have been born beside Loch Triochatan to W. NN 1556
Ossington Notts 44 C4 vil 7m/12km N of Newark-on-Trent. SK 7564
Oss Mere Salop 34 C1* lake 2m/3km NE of Whitchurch. SJ 5643
Ostem W Isles 88 A3* islet on W side of Kearstay, small island off N coast of Scarp. NA 9617
Ostend Essex 21 E2 loc 1m NW of Burnham-on-Crouch. TQ 9397
Ostend Norfolk 39 G2* loc on coast 2km NW of Happisburgh. TG 3632
Osterley London 19 F4 loc in borough of Hounslow 10m/16km W of Charing Cross. To N is O. Park, containing O. Hse (NT), 18c hse by Robert Adam. TQ 1477
Oswaldtwistle Lancs 48 A5 tn adjoining Accrington to SW. Textiles, chemicals. SD 7327
Oswestry Salop 34 A2 tn near Welsh border 16m/26km NW of Shrewsbury. Industries include plastics and tanning. 1m N, **Old O.,** extensive Iron Age fort (A.M.). SJ 2929
Oteley Salop 34 B1 loc on E side of The Mere at Ellesmere. SJ 4134
Otford Kent 20 B5 vil on R Darent 3m/4km N of Sevenoaks. Site of Roman villa to E. Remains of archbishop's palace. TQ 5259
Otham Kent 20 D6 vil 3m/4km SE of Maidstone. TQ 7953
Otherton Staffs 35 F3* loc 1m S of Penkridge. SJ 9212
Othery Som 8 B2 vil on Sedgemoor 6m/10km SE of Bridgwater. ST 3831
Othona Essex 21 F1* remains of Roman fort of the Saxon shore on coast 2m/3km E of Bradwell-on-Sea. Nearby are remains of St Peter's Chapel made from Roman bricks. TM 0308
Otley Suffolk 31 F3 vil 6m/9km NW of Woodbridge. Loc of **O. Green** 1km NE. TM 2055
Otley W Yorks 49 E4 tn on R Wharfe 10m/15km NW of Leeds. Engineering, textiles, tanning. SE 2045
Ot Moor Oxon 28 B6 tract lying some 6m/10km NE of Oxford. SP 5614
Otter 7 H6 r rising on S slopes of Blackdown Hills in Somerset and flowing SW through Honiton and Ottery St Mary in Devon and thence into the English Channel on E side of Budleigh Salterton. SY 0781
Otterbourne Hants 10 B3 vil 3m/5km N of Eastleigh. SU 4623
Otterburn Nthmb 60 D2 vil on R Rede 15m/24km SE of Carter Bar. Mnfre of Otterburn tweeds, although main factory is elsewhere. Site of Battle of Chevy Chase, 1388, in which Scots defeated Henry Percy. Military camp 2m/3km N. Artillery range on moors to N. NY 8893
Otterburn N Yorks 48 B3 ham on edge of Yorkshire Dales National Park 2m/3km E of Hellifield. SD 8857
Otterden Kent 21 E6 loc 3m/5km N of Charing. TQ 9454
Otter Ferry S'clyde 70 B6 locality in Argyll on E side of Loch Fyne 4m/6km N of Kilfinan. NR 9384
Otterford Som 8 A3 loc 6m/10km S of Taunton. ST 2214
Otterham Cornwall 6 B6 vil 4m/7km E of Boscastle. SX 1690
Otterhampton Som 15 G6 ham 5m/8km NW of Bridgwater. ST 2443
Otterham Quay Kent 20 D5* loc at head of **Otterham Creek** leading into R Medway estuary 3m/5km E of Gillingham. TQ 8367
Otterington N Yorks 54 C5 ham 3m/4km S of Northallerton. SE 3689
Otterington, South N Yorks 54 C6 vil 4m/6km S of Northallerton. SE 3787
Ottershaw Surrey 19 E5 vil 2m/4km SW of Chertsey. TQ 0263
Otterston Loch Fife 73 E5* small loch 2m/3km W of Aberdour. NT 1685
Otters Wick Orkney 89 C5 large inlet on N coast of island of Sanday. HY 6943
Otters Wick Shetland 89 E6/F6 bay on E coast of Yell. Loc of **Otterswick** at its head. **Ward of Otterswick** is summit of Hill of Arisdale to W - see Arisdale. HU 5285
Otterton Devon 5 F2 vil on R Otter 2m/3km NE of Budleigh Salterton. SX 0885
Otterwood Hants 10 B4* loc on edge of New Forest 2m/3km E of Beaulieu. SU 4102
Ottery 6 C6 r rising near Jacobstow, Cornwall, and flowing SE into R Tamar 2m/3km NE of Launceston. SX 3486
Ottery St Mary Devon 7 H5 tn in agricultural dist 11m/18km E of Exeter. Notable ch. Birthplace of Samuel Taylor Coleridge, 1772. SY 0995
Ottinge Kent 13 G3 ham 5m/8km N of Hythe. TR 1642
Ottringham Humberside 51 G5 vil 3m/5km W of Patrington. TA 2624
Oude S'clyde 70 A3* r in Argyll running W from Loch Tralaig then SW to head of Loch Melfort. NM 8314
Oughterby Cumbria 59 G5 loc 1m SW of Kirkbampton. NY 2955
Oughtershaw N Yorks 53 G6 loc on Oughtershaw Beck, or upper reach of R Wharfe, 5m/8km NW of Buckden. **Oughtershaw Tarn** small lake 1m E. SD 8681
Oughterside Cumbria 52 B1* vil 2m/3km SW of Aspatria. NY 1140
Oughtibridge S Yorks 43 G2 vil on R Don 5m/8km NW of Sheffield. SK 3093
Oulston N Yorks 50 B1 vil 3m/5km N of Easingwold. SE 5474
Oulton Cumbria 59 G6 vil 2m/3km N of Wigton. NY 2450
Oulton Norfolk 39 F2 ham 4m/6km NW of Aylsham. **O. Street** vil 2km SE. TG 1328
Oulton Staffs 34 D2* loc 1km S of Norbury. SJ 7822
Oulton Staffs 35 E1 vil 2km NE of Stone. **Oultoncross, O. Grange, O. Heath,** locs 1km S, W, N respectively. SJ 9135
Oulton Suffolk 39 H5 suburb 2m/3km NW of Lowestoft. **O. Broad,** loc and lake to S. TM 5294
Oulton W Yorks 49 F5 loc 5m/9km SE of Leeds. SE 3658
Oulton Park Ches 42 B5* motor-racing circuit 3m/4km NE of Tarporley. SJ 5864
Oundle Northants 37 E5 small tn on R Nene 12m/19km SW of Peterborough. Many old bldgs. Boys' public school, founded 1556. TL 0388
Ousby Cumbria 53 F2 vil 7m/11km NE of Penrith. NY 6234
Ousden Suffolk 30 C2 vil 7m/11km SE of Newmarket. TL 7459
Ouse (or **Gt Ouse**) 38 B2 r rising SW of Towcester, Northants, and flowing circuitously to the Wash by Buckingham, Newport Pagnell, Olney, Bedford, St Neots, Huntingdon, St Ives, Ely, Littleport, Downham Mkt, and King's Lynn. TF 5924
Ouse 12 B6 r rising in St Leonard's Forest E of Horsham, W Sussex, and flowing E then S through Lewes, E Sussex, and into English Channel at Newhaven. TQ 4500
Ouse 50 D5 r formed by confluence of Rs Swale and Ure E of Boroughbridge, N Yorks, and flowing generally SE by York, Cawood, Selby, and Goole, to join R Trent and form R Humber 7m/12km E of Goole. Main tributaries are Rs Swale, Ure, Nidd, Wharfe, Aire, and Don from the W, and R Derwent from the E. Tidal to within 1m of Naburn, N Yorks. SE 8623
Ouseburn, Great N Yorks 50 A2 vil 5m/7km SE of Boroughbridge. **Lit Ouseburn** vil 1km S. SE 4461
Ousefleet Humberside 50 D5 vil on S side of R Ouse 5m/9km E of Goole. SE 8223
Ouse, Little Cambs 38 B5* loc on banks of Lit Ouse R 4m/6km E of Littleport. TL 6289
Ouse, Little 38 B5 r rising on border of Norfolk and Suffolk N of Redgrave and flowing W through Thetford and Brandon and into R Ouse at Brandon Creek 4m/7km NE of Littleport. TL 6091
Ouston Durham 61 G5/G6 vil 2m/3km NW of Chester-le-Street. NZ 2554
Ouston Nthmb 61 F4 loc 1m S of Stamfordham. Airfield to SE. NZ 0770
Outcast Cumbria 46 D1* loc 2km E of Ulverston. SD 3077
Outchester Nthmb 67 G5* loc 2m/3km E of Belford. NU 1433
Out Dubs Tarn Cumbria 52 D5 small lake below S end of Esthwaite Water. SD 3694
Out Elmstead Kent 13 G2* loc 1km N of Barham. TR 2050
Outer Hebrides. See Western Isles.
Outer Holm Orkney 89 A6* islet on E side of Stromness Harbour, Mainland. HY 2508
Outer Score Shetland 89 E7* small uninhabited island off N end of island of Bressay. HU 5145
Outertown Orkney 89 A6* loc near W coast of Mainland 2km NW of Stromness. HY 2310
Outerwards Reservoir S'clyde 64 A3* small resr 4m/7km NE of Largs. NS 2365
Out Gate Cumbria 52 D5* ham 1m N of Hawkshead. SD 3599
Outhgill Cumbria 53 G4 ham 5m/8km S of Kirkby Stephen. NY 7801
Outlands Staffs 34 D2 loc 4m/6km W of Eccleshall. SJ 7730
Outlane W Yorks 48 D6 vil 4m/7km W of Huddersfield. Site of Roman fort to S. SE 0817
Out Newton Humberside 51 G6 loc near coast 4m/7km E of Patrington. TA 3821
Out Rawcliffe Lancs 47 E4* ham 4m/6km SE of Preesall. SD 4041
Outrington Ches 42 C3* loc 2km E of Lymm. SJ 6987
Outshore Point Orkney 89 A6* headland on W coast of Mainland 2m/3km S of Marwick Hd. HY 2222
Out Skerries Shetland 89 F6 group of several small islands, some no more than rocks, lying about 5m/8km NE of island of Whalsay. Housay and Bruray are inhabited and connected by a rd br. Fishing is the chief industry. The extreme eastern island, Bound Skerry, has a lighthouse. HU 67
Out Stack Shetland (N of 89 F5) island rock about 800 metres NE of Muckle Flugga and 2km NE of Herma Ness, Unst. Most northerly point of British Isles. HP 6120
Outward Gtr Manchester 42 D1* loc 1m S of Radcliffe. **Outward Gate** loc to E. SD 7705
Outwell 38 A4 vil on Cambs–Norfolk border 5m/8km SE of Wisbech. **O. Basin** loc 1m NW. TF 5103
Outwood Som 8 B2* ham 1m E of Durston. ST 3028
Outwood Surrey 19 G6 vil 3m/5km NE of Horley. TQ 3245
Outwood W Yorks 49 E5 loc 2m/3km N of Wakefield. SE 3223
Outwoods Leics 36 A3* loc 3m/5km N of Coalville. SK 4118
Outwoods Staffs 35 E3* ham 3m/4km E of Newport. SJ 7818
Outwoods, Upper Staffs 35 H2* loc 2m/3km NW of Burton upon Trent. SK 2225
Ouzel 28 D3* r rising near Dunstable, Beds, and flowing W then N past Leighton Buzzard and Bletchley into R Ouse at Newport Pagnell, Bucks. Sometimes known as R Lovat. SP 8844
Ouzlewell Green W Yorks 49 E5* vil adjoining Lofthouse to E. SE 3326
Oval, The Avon 16 C5* SW dist of Bath. ST 7363
Oval, The London. See Kennington.
Ovenden W Yorks 48 D5* loc in Halifax 2km NW of tn centre. SE 0827
Over Avon 16 B3 loc 2m/4km NW of Filton. ST 5882
Over Cambs 29 G1 vil 9m/14km NW of Cambridge. TL 3770
Over Ches 42 C4 loc adjoining Winsford to W. SJ 6466
Over Glos 26 C5* loc 2km NW of Gloucester. SO 8119
Over Alderley Ches 42 D4* loc to E of Nether Alderley. SJ 8575
Overbrae Grampian 83 F1 loc near coast 3m/5km E of Gardenstown. Loc of Netherbrae to W. NJ 8059
Over Burrows Derbys 35 H1* loc 2km S of Brailsford. SK 2541
Overbury H & W 26 D4 vil 5m/8km NE of Tewkesbury. SO 9537
Overcombe Dorset 9 E6 loc on Weymouth Bay 2m/3km NE of Weymouth. SY 6981
Over Compton Dorset 8 D3 vil 2m/4km E of Yeovil. ST 5916
Overdale Wyke N Yorks 55 G3* small rocky bay on North Sea coast 1m N of Sandsend. NZ 8514

Over Dinsdale N Yorks 54 C4* ham in loop of R Tees 4m/7km SE of Darlington across r. NZ 3411
Over End Cambs 37 F5* S part of vil of Elton, 4m/6km S of Wansford. TL 0893
Overgreen Derbys 43 G4* loc 4m/7km NW of Chesterfield. SK 3273
Over Green Warwicks 35 G5 ham 3m/5km SE of Sutton Coldfield. SP 1694
Over Haddon Derbys 43 G4 vil 2m/3km SW of Bakewell. SK 2066
Over Kellet Lancs 47 F2 vil 2km E of Carnforth. SD 5270
Over Kiddington Oxon 27 H5 ham 3m/4km SE of Enstone. SP 4022
Over Knutsford Ches 42 C3* loc adjoining Knutsford to SE. SJ 7578
Overleigh Som 8 C1 S dist of Street. ST 4835
Overley Staffs 35 G3* loc 1km NW of Alrewas. SK 1515
Over Monnow Gwent 26 A6 loc on right bank of R Monnow opp Monmouth. SO 5012
Overmoor Staffs 43 E6* loc 2km E of Werrington. SJ 9647
Over Norton Oxon 27 G4 vil 1m N of Chipping Norton. SP 3128
Overseal Derbys 35 H3 vil 3m/4km S of Swadlincote. SK 2915
Over Silton N Yorks 54 D5 ham 5m/8km E of Northallerton. See also Silton, Nether. SE 4593
Overslade Warwicks 27 H1 SW dist of Rugby. SP 4973
Oversland Kent 21 F6 ham 4m/6km SE of Faversham. TR 0557
Oversley Green Warwicks 27 E2 loc SE of Alcester across R Arrow. SP 0956
Overstone Northants 28 C1 vil 5m/8km NE of Northampton. SP 8066
Over Stowey Som 8 A1 ham on lower slopes of Quantock Hills 1m SW of Nether Stowey and 16m/25km W of Bridgwater. ST 1838
Overstrand Norfolk 39 F1 vil and coastal resort 2m/3km E of Cromer. TG 2440
Over Stratton Som 8 C3 vil 1m S of S Petherton. ST 4315
Over Street Wilts 9 G1* loc just W of Stapleford across R Till. SU 0637
Over Tabley Ches 42 C3* loc 2m/3km NW of Knutsford. SJ 7280
Overthorpe Northants 28 A3* ham 2m/3km E of Banbury. SP 4840
Overton Ches 42 B4 loc adjoining Frodsham to SE. SJ 5277
Overton Clwyd 42 A6 vil 6m/9km SE of Wrexham. **Lit Overton** loc to E. **Overton Br** ham at rd crossing of R Dee 2km W. SJ 3741
Overton Hants 17 H6 vil on R Test 4m/6km E of Whitchurch. SU 5149
Overton Lancs 47 E2/E3 vil 2m/4km SE of Heysham. SD 4358
Overton N Yorks 50 B3 ham on R Ouse 4m/6km NW of York. SE 5555
Overton Salop 26 A1 ham 2m/3km S of Ludlow. SO 5072
Overton W Glam 23 F6 ham just W of Port Eynon on Gower peninsula. **Overton Cliff** (NT) to S. SS 4685
Overton W Yorks 49 E6* vil adjoining Middlestown to SW. SE 2616
Overton Green Ches 42 D5* loc 4m/7km W of Congleton. SJ 7960
Overton, West Wilts 17 F4 vil 4m/6km W of Marlborough. SU 1368
Overtown Grampian 82 D2* loc just SE of Gordonstown, 9m/15km SW of Banff. NJ 5655
Overtown Lancs 47 G1 ham 2m/3km SE of Kirkby Lonsdale. SD 6276
Overtown S'clyde 65 E3 vil 2km S of Wishaw. NS 8052
Overtown Wilts 17 F3* loc 3m/5km S of Swindon. SU 1579
Overtown W Yorks 49 F6* loc 1km S of Walton. SE 3517
Over Wallop Hants 10 A1 vil 7m/11km SW of Andover. SU 2838
Over Water Cumbria 52 C2 lake 2km S of Uldale. NY 2535
Over Whitacre Warwicks 35 H5 vil 4m/6km E of Coleshill. SP 2491
Over Woodhouse Derbys 44 A4* loc 1m N of Bolsover. **Nether Woodhouse** loc to NW. SK 4771
Over Worton Oxon 27 H4 ham 3m/4km SW of Deddington. SP 4329
Overy Oxon 18 B2* loc across R Thame from Dorchester. SU 5893
Overy Staithe Norfolk 38 D1 vil 2m/3km NE of Burnham Mkt. TF 8444
Oving Bucks 28 C5 vil 5m/8km NW of Aylesbury. SP 7821
Oving W Sussex 11 E4 vil 3m/4km E of Chichester. SU 9005
Ovingdean E Sussex 12 A6 dist of Brighton 3m/4km E of tn centre. TQ 3503
Ovingham Nthmb 61 F5 vil 1m NW of Prudhoe across R Tyne. Rd br spans r here. NZ 0863
Ovington Durham 54 A3 vil 5m/8km E of Barnard Castle. NZ 1314
Ovington Essex 30 C4 ham 2m/3km S of Clare. TL 7642
Ovington Hants 10 C2 vil on R Itchen 2m/3km W of New Alresford. SU 5631
Ovington Norfolk 38 D4 vil 1m NE of Watton. TF 9202
Ovington Nthmb 61 F5 vil 2m/3km W of Prudhoe across R Tyne. NZ 0663
Owen's Bank Staffs 35 G2* loc adjoining Tutbury to W. SK 2028
Ower Hants 10 A3 vil 3m/4km NE of Cadnam. SU 3216
Ower Hants 10 B4 loc 2km SE of Fawley. SU 4701
Owermoigne Dorset 9 E5 vil 6m/10km SE of Dorchester. SY 7685
Owersby, North Lincs 45 E2 vil 5m/7km NW of Mkt Rasen. **S Owersby** ham 1km S. TF 0694
Owlcotes Derbys 43 H4* loc 3m/4km SW of Bolsover. SK 4467
Owl End Cambs 29 F1* NE end of vil of Gt Stukeley, 2m/4km NW of Huntingdon. TL 2275
Owler Bar Derbys 43 G3* loc 4m/6km W of Dronfield. SK 2978
Owlerton S Yorks 43 G2* dist of Sheffield 2m/3km NW of city centre. SK 3389
Owletts Kent. See Cobham.
Owletts End H & W 27 E3* loc in SE part of Evesham. SP 0443
Owlpen Glos 16 C2 loc 3m/4km E of Dursley. ST 8098
Owl's Green Suffolk 31 G2* loc 2m/3km N of Dennington. TM 2869
Owlswick Bucks 18 C1 ham 2m/3km NW of Princes Risborough. SP 7906
Owlthorpe S Yorks 43 H3* loc in Sheffield 5m/8km SE of city centre. SK 4181
Owmby Lincs 44 D3 vil 7m/11km W of Mkt Rasen. Site of Roman settlement 2m/3km W. TF 0087
Owmby Lincs 45 E1 ham 4m/6km NE of Caistor. TA 0704
Owslebury Hants 10 C3 vil 4m/7km SE of Winchester. Site of late Iron Age vil at Bottom Pond Farm. SU 5123
Owston Leics 36 D4 vil 5m/9km W of Oakham. SK 7707
Owston S Yorks 44 A1 ham 1m NE of Carcroft. SE 5511
Owston Ferry Humberside 44 C2 vil on W bank of R Trent 3m/5km SE of Epworth. Traces of medieval cas S of ch. SE 8000
Owstwick Humberside 51 G5 ham 5m/8km NW of Withernsea. TA 2732
Owthorne Humberside 51 G5* loc adjoining Withernsea to W. TA 3328
Owthorpe Notts 36 C1 vil 8m/12km SE of Nottingham. SK 6733
Oxborough Norfolk 38 C4 vil 3m/5km E of Stoke Ferry. Oxburgh Hall (NT) is moated hse dating from 15c. TF 7401
Oxcars Fife 66 A1 islet with lighthouse in Firth of Forth nearly 1m SE of Inchcolm and 2m/3km S of Hawkcraig Pt. NT 2081
Oxcliffe Hill Lancs 47 E2 loc 2m/3km SE of Morecambe on banks of R Lune. SD 4461
Oxclose Tyne & Wear 61 G5* dist of Washington to W of tn centre. NZ 2956
Oxcombe Lincs 45 G3 ham 6m/9km NE of Horncastle. TF 3177
Oxcroft Derbys 44 A4* loc 1m W of Elmton. **Oxcroft Estate** loc 1km S. SK 4873
Oxencombe Devon 5 E3* loc below Gt Haldon, 2m/3km NE of Chudleigh. SX 8882
Oxendon, Great Northants 36 C5 vil 2m/4km S of Mkt Harborough. SP 7383
Oxenhall Glos 26 C5* loc 1m NW of Newent. SO 7126
Oxenholme Cumbria 53 E5* loc and rly junction 2m/3km SE of Kendal. SD 5390
Oxenhope W Yorks 48 C4 vil 1m S of Haworth. SE 0335
Oxen Park Cumbria 52 C6 ham 3m/5km N of Greenodd. SD 3187
Oxenpill Som 8 C1* ham between Meare and Westhay, 4m/6km NW of Glastonbury. ST 4441
Oxenton Glos 26 D4 vil below W slope of O. Hill 6m/9km N of Cheltenham. SO 9531
Oxenwood Wilts 17 G5 ham 6m/10km NW of Hurstbourne Tarrant. SU 3059
Oxford Oxon 18 A1 city at confluence of Rs Thames and Cherwell 52m/84km NW of London. University dating from 13c; many notable bldgs. Cathedral. Tourist and commercial centre. Car mnfg at Cowley, qv. Airport at Kidlington, qv. **O. Canal** runs N by Banbury and Rugby to Coventry Canal at Hawkesbury Junction on N side of Coventry. SP 5106
Oxfordshire 119 south midland county of England, bounded by Berkshire, Wiltshire, Gloucestershire, Warwickshire, Northamptonshire, and Buckinghamshire. Predominantly flat or gently undulating landscape, except where the Chilterns enter the county in the SE and the Cotswolds in the NW. Chief tns are the cathedral and university city of Oxford, the county tn; Abingdon, Banbury, Bicester, Henley-on-Thames, and Witney. Burford and Chipping Norton are small Cotswold tns in the W and NW respectively. Chief rs are the Thames (or Isis), Cherwell, Ock, Thame, and Windrush. Motor vehicles are made at Cowley, a suburb of Oxford; blankets are made at Witney. Other industries are centred on the tns, but the county is largely agricultural.
Oxgangs Lothian 66 A2* dist of Edinburgh 4m/6km S of city centre. NT 2368
Oxhey Herts 19 E2 SE dist of Watford. Suburb of **S. Oxhey** 2km S. TQ 1295
Oxhill Durham 61 F6* loc adjoining Stanley to SW. NZ 1852
Oxhill Warwicks 27 G3 vil 4m/6km S of Kineton. SP 3145
Oxlease Herts 19 F1* S dist of Hatfield. TL 2207
Oxley W Midlands 35 E4 dist of Wolverhampton 2m/4km N of tn centre. SJ 9002
Oxley Green Essex 30 D6* ham 2m/3km SE of Tiptree. TL 9114
Oxley's Green E Sussex 12 C4 ham 1km NE of Brightling. TQ 6921
Oxna Shetland 89 E8* uninhabited island of about 180 acres or 73 hectares 4m/6km SE of Skelda Ness, Mainland, across The Deeps. HU 3537
Oxnam Borders 66 D6 vil on **O. Water** 4m/6km SE of Jedburgh. NT 6918
Oxnead Norfolk 39 F3 ham 3m/5km SE of Aylsham. **O. Hall** is former seat of the Pastons. One wing of original hse remains. TG 2224
Oxney Green, Great Essex 20 C1 suburb 3m/4km W of Chelmsford. Loc of **Lit Oxney Green** adjoins to W. TL 6606
Oxney, Isle of Kent 13 E4 area of higher ground surrounded by Rother Levels 5m/7km N of Rye, containing vils of Wittersham and Stone. TQ 9127
Oxshott Surrey 19 F5 suburban loc 3m/5km NW of Leatherhead. TQ 1460
Oxspring S Yorks 43 G1 vil 2m/3km SE of Penistone. SE 2602
Oxted Surrey 20 A6 tn 4m/6km W of Westerham. TQ 3852
Oxton Borders 66 C3 vil 4m/7km NW of Lauder. Site of Roman fort 1km N. NT 4953
Oxton Merseyside 41 H3 loc in Birkenhead 2m/3km W of tn centre. SJ 2987
Oxton Notts 44 B5 vil 4m/7km NW of Lowdham. SK 6251
Oxton N Yorks 49 G4* ham 2km E of Tadcaster. SE 5043
Oxwich W Glam 23 F6 vil on Gower peninsula 11m/17km W of Swansea. **Oxwich Green** ham to S. 2km SE is **Oxwich Pt**, headland (NT) from which **Oxwich Bay** extends NE to Gt Tor. The sands of the bay, with sand dunes and marshes inland, form the Oxwich Nature Reserve. SS 4986
Oxwick Norfolk 38 D2 loc 3m/5km S of Fakenham. TF 9125
Oykel H'land 85 F6 r in Sutherland dist rising S of Ben More Assynt and running SE to Oykel Br, then E down Strath Oykel to join R Shin in Kyle of Sutherland 4m/6km NW of Bonar Br. NH 5796
Oykel Bridge H'land 85 D6 rd br over R Oykel in Sutherland dist 13m/21km W of Lairg. NC 3800
Oykel Forest H'land 85 E6 state forest in Sutherland dist 7m/11km W of Lairg. NC 4802
Oyne Grampian 83 E4 vil 7m/11km NW of Inverurie. NJ 6725
Oystermouth W Glam 23 G6 chief loc in Mumbles dist of Swansea, 4m/7km SW of Swansea tn centre across bay. Cas dates from late 13c. SS 6188
Ozleworth Glos 16 C2 loc 2m/4km E of Wotton-under-Edge. ST 7993

P

Pabay Skye, H'land 79 E6 low-lying island of 360 acres or 145 hectares, sparsely inhabited, 3m/4km NE of Broadford. NG 6727
Pabay Beag W Isles 88 A2* small uninhabited island in W Loch Roag 3m/5km E of Gallan Hd, Lewis. NB 0938
Pabay Mór W Isles 88 A2* uninhabited island in W Loch Roag 3m/5km E of Gallan Hd, Lewis. NB 1038
Pabbay W Isles 88 D4 uninhabited island of about 560 acres or 225 hectares midway between Mingulay and Sandray. NL 6087
Pabbay W Isles 88 A4 uninhabited island at N end of Sound of Harris 5m/8km SW of Toe Hd. Pabbay measures 4km by nearly 3km and rises to a height of 642 ft or 196 metres. NF 8988
Pachesham Surrey 19 F5* loc 2km NW of Leatherhead. TQ 1558
Packington Leics 36 A3 vil 2km S of Ashby de la Zouch. SK 3614
Packington, Great Warwicks 35 H5* loc 4m/6km SE of Coleshill. **Old Hall**, 17c. **P. Hall**, 17c-18c, in park with lakes (by Capability Brown). 18c ch. SP 2283
Packington, Little Warwicks 35 H5* ham 3m/5km S of Coleshill. SP 2184
Packmoor Staffs 42 D5* loc 2m/3km N of Tunstall. SJ 8654
Packmores Warwicks 27 G1* N dist of Warwick. SP 2865
Packwood Warwicks 27 F1* loc 2km E of Hockley Heath. **P. Hse** (NT), Tudor hse with 17c additions. SP 1772
Padanaram Tayside 77 E5 vil 2m/3km W of Forfar. NO 4251
Padbury Bucks 28 C4 vil 3m/4km SE of Buckingham. SP 7230
Paddington Ches 42 C3* loc in E part of Warrington. SJ 6389
Paddington London 19 F3 dist in City of Westminster 3m/4km NW of Charing Cross. TQ 2681
Paddlesworth Kent 13 G3 vil 3m/5km NW of Folkestone. TR 1939
Paddock Kent 21 F6* loc 3m/4km E of Charing. TQ 9950
Paddock W Yorks 48 D6* dist of Huddersfield 1m W of tn centre. SE 1216
Paddock Wood Kent 12 C2 small tn 5m/8km E of Tonbridge. Centre of hop-growing area. TQ 6645
Paddolgreen Salop 34 C2* loc 2m/4km N of Wem. SJ 5032
Padeswood Clwyd 41 H5* loc 3m/4km E of Mold. SJ 2762
Padfield Derbys 43 E2* loc 2km N of Glossop. SK 0396
Padgate Ches 42 C2 loc 2m/3km NE of Warrington. SJ 6390
Padiham Lancs 48 B4 tn 3m/4km W of Burnley. Textiles, engineering, furniture, washing machines. See also Gawthorpe Hall. SD 7933
Padley, Nether Derbys 43 G3* vil 2m/4km SE of Hathersage. **Upr Padley** loc to N. SK 2578
Padside N Yorks 48 D2 loc 4m/6km S of Pateley Br. **P. Green** loc to NW. SE 1659
Padstow Cornwall 2 D1 tn and resort with harbour on estuary of R Camel near N coast, 5m/8km NW of Wadebridge. To N, **P. Bay** extends from Pentire Pt south-westwards to Stepper Pt. SW 9175
Padworth Berks 18 B4* vil 8m/12km SW of Reading. SU 6166
Paganhill Glos 16 D1* W dist of Stroud. SO 8405
Page Bank Durham 54 B2* loc on R Wear 2m/3km NW of Spennymoor. NZ 2335
Page Moss Merseyside 42 A2* urban loc in Roby. SJ 4291
Page's Green Suffolk 31 F2* loc 3m/5km NW of Debenham. TM 1465

Pagham W Sussex 11 E5 suburban vil 4m/6km W of Bognor Regis. **P. Harbour,** large marshy inlet of sea, to SW towards Selsey Bill. SZ 8897
Paglesham Essex 21 E3 vil 4m/6km E of Rochford. To SE, **P. Reach,** stretch of R Roach estuary. To E, **P. Pool,** inlet of R Roach separating Wallasea I. from mainland. TQ 9293
Paible W Isles 88 D1 loc near W coast of N Uist 3m/5km SE of Aird an Rùnair. NF 7367
Paignton Devon 5 E4 resort on Tor Bay with harbour and pier 3m/5km SW of Torquay. Sandy beaches. SX 8960
Pailton Warwicks 36 A6 vil 5m/7km NW of Rugby. SP 4781
Paine's Cross E Sussex 12 C4* loc 1m W of Burwash Common. TQ 6223
Paines Hill Surrey 20 A6* loc 1m S of Limpsfield. TQ 4151
Painleyhill Staffs 35 F1* loc 4m/6km W of Uttoxeter. SK 0333
Painscastle (Castell-paen)Powys 25 F3 vil 5m/7km NW of Hay-on-Wye. Site of Norman cas rebuilt in 13c. SO 1646
Painshawfield Nthmb 61 F5* suburb 3m/4km SW of Prudhoe. NZ 0660
Painsthorpe Humberside 50 C3* ham 1km E of Kirby Underdale. SE 8158
Painswick Glos 16 D1 stone-built Cotswold tn 3m/5km NE of Stroud. Site of Roman villa 1km NW. SO 8609
Painter's Forstal Kent 21 F5 ham 2m/4km SW of Faversham. TQ 9958
Painter's Green Herts 29 F5* ham adjoining Datchworth to S, 3m/5km NE of Welwyn. TL 2718
Painthorpe W Yorks 49 E6* loc adjoining Crigglestone to S. SE 3115
Paisley S'clyde 64 C3 mnfg tn 7m/11km W of Glasgow. Industries include mnfre of cotton thread, preserves, sanitary earthenware, engineering products. NS 4864
Pakefield Suffolk 39 H5 S dist of Lowestoft. TM 5390
Pakenham Suffolk 30 D2 vil 2m/3km S of Ixworth. TL 9267
Palace Fields Ches 42 B3* dist of Runcorn E of tn centre. SJ 5481
Palace of Holyroodhouse Lothian. See Edinburgh.
Pale Gwynedd 33 F1* loc 1km S of Llandderfel across R Dee. SH 9836
Palehouse Common E Sussex 12 B5* loc 2m/3km SE of Uckfield. TQ 4918
Palestine Hants 10 A1* loc 1m SW of Grateley and 7m/11km SW of Andover. SU 2640
Paley Street Berks 18 D4 vil 3m/5km S of Maidenhead. SU 8776
Palfrey W Midlands 35 F4* loc in S part of Walsall. SP 0197
Palgrave Suffolk 31 E1 vil 1m S of Diss. TM 1178
Pallion Tyne & Wear 61 H5* dist of Sunderland 2km W of tn centre. NZ 3757
Palmarsh Kent 13 G4* loc at W end of Hythe. TR 1333
Palm Bay Kent 13 H1* bay to E of Margate. TR 3771
Palmer Moor Derbys 35 G1* 2m/3km NW of Sudbury. SK 1333
Palmers Cross Surrey 11 F1* loc 4m/6km SE of Godalming. TQ 0240
Palmer's Flat Glos 16 B1* loc 1m SE of Coleford. SO 5809
Palmer's Green Kent 12 C3* loc 1km E of Brenchley. TQ 6841
Palmers Green London 19 G2 loc in borough of Enfield 2m/4km S of Enfield tn centre and 8m/13km N of Charing Cross. TQ 3913
Palmerstown S Glam 15 F4* loc 2m/3km NE of Barry. ST 1369
Palmersville Tyne & Wear 61 G4* loc adjoining Longbenton to NE. NZ 2870
Palnackie D & G 58 D5 vil 3m/5km S of Dalbeattie. NX 8256
Palnure Burn 57 E6 r in Dumfries & Galloway region running S into R Cree 3m/5km SE of Newton Stewart. NX 4562
Palterton Derbys 44 A4 vil 2km S of Bolsover. SK 4768
Pamber End Hants 18 B5 ham 4m/7km N of Basingstoke. SU 6158
Pamber Green Hants 18 B5 vil 5m/9km N of Basingstoke. SU 6059
Pamber Heath Hants 18 B5* vil 7m/11km N of Basingstoke. SU 6162
Pamington Glos 26 D4 vil 3m/5km E of Tewkesbury. SO 9433
Pamphill Dorset 9 G4 vil 2km W of Wimborne. See also Kingston Lacy. ST 9800
Pampisford Cambs 29 H3 vil 4m/6km N of Gt Chesterford. TL 4948
Panborough Som 16 A6 loc 3m/5km SE of Wedmore. ST 4745
Panbride Tayside 73 H1 vil 1km N of Carnoustie. NO 5634
Pancrasweek Devon 6 B4 ham 3m/5km NW of Holsworthy. SS 2805
Pancross S Glam 15 F4* loc 1km N of Penmark. ST 0469
Pandy Clwyd 33 H1 loc 4m/7km S of Llangollen. SJ 1935
Pandy Gwent 25 H5 vil 6m/9km N of Abergavenny. SO 3322
Pandy Gwynedd 32 D4 loc 3m/5km NE of Tywyn. SH 6203
Pandy Gwynedd 33 F2* loc adjoining Llanuwchllyn to SE. SH 8729
Pandy Powys 33 F4* loc 1m N of Llanbrynmair. SH 9004
Pandy'r Capel Clwyd 41 G6* loc 2km W of Llanelidan. SJ 0850
Pandy Tudur Clwyd 41 E5 ham 4m/6km NE of Llanrwst. SH 8564
Pandy, Y 33 H1* stream (Nant y Pandy) running NE into R Dee on N side of Glyndyfrdwy, Clwyd. SJ 1542
Panfield Essex 30 C5 vil 2m/3km NW of Braintree. TL 7325
Pang 18 B4* r rising N of Hampstead Norris, Berks, and flowing into R Thames at Pangbourne. SU 6376
Pangbourne Berks 18 B4 tn on R Thames 6m/9km NW of Reading. Nautical College 1m SW. SU 6376
Panmure Castle Tayside 73 G1* faint remains of 13c cas 2m/4km NW of Carnoustie. Monmt to W commemorates Lord Panmure of Brechin (d 1852). NO 5437
Pannal N Yorks 49 E3 residential loc 2m/4km S of Harrogate. SE 3051
Pannal Ash N Yorks 49 E3 dist of Harrogate 2km SW of tn centre. SE 2953
Panshanger Herts 19 F1* E dist of Welwyn Garden City. TL 2513
Panson, West Devon 6 C6* loc 4m/7km N of Launceston. SX 3491
Pant Clwyd 41 H6 loc 2km NW of Ruabon. SJ 2946
Pant Clwyd 42 A5* loc adjoining Gresford to NE. SJ 3555
Pant Salop 34 A2 vil 5m/7km S of Oswestry. SJ 2722
Pantasa Clwyd 41 G4 Roman Catholic model vil, with 19c Franciscan monastery, 2m/3km W of Holywell. SJ 1575
Panteg (Pant-teg) Gwent loc 2m/3km SE of Pontypool. ST 3199
Pantersbridge Cornwall 3 F2* loc 6m/9km E of Bodmin. SX 1568
Pant-glas Gwynedd 40 B6 ham 9m/15km S of Caernarvon. SH 4747
Pantgwyn Dyfed 24 B5* loc 3m/4km SE of Llanfynydd. SN 5925
Pant-lasau W Glam 23 G5 loc 5m/8km N of Swansea. SN 6500
Pant Mawr Powys 33 F6 loc on R Wye 4m/7km NW of Llangurig. SN 8482
Pantmawr S Glam 15 F3* loc 1m E of Tongwynlais. ST 1481
Panton Lincs 45 F3 ham 3m/5km E of Wragby. TF 1778
Pant-pastynog Clwyd 41 F5* loc 3m/4km S of Denbigh. SJ 0461
Pantperthog Gwynedd 33 E4* loc 2m/4km N of Machynlleth. SH 7404
Pant-teg Welsh form of Panteg, qv.
Pant-y-dwr Powys 25 E1 vil 4m/7km N of Rhayader. SN 9874
Pant-y-ffordd Clwyd 41 H5 loc 1m SW of Treuddyn. SJ 2457
Pant-y-ffridd Powys 33 H4* loc 2m/4km NW of Berriew. SJ 1502
Pantyffynnon Dyfed 23 G4 loc adjoining Ammanford to S. SN 6210
Pantygasseg Gwent 15 G2* loc 2m/3km W of Pontypool. ST 2599
Pantygelli Gwent 25 G6* ham 3m/4km N of Abergavenny. SO 3017
Pantymenyn Dyfed 22 D3* loc 2m/3km NW of Login. SN 1426
Pantymwyn Clwyd 41 G5* ham 3m/4km W of Mold. SJ 1964
Pant-yr-eos Reservoir Gwent 15 G3* resr 4m/6km NW of Newport. ST 2591
Pantyscallog Mid Glam 15 F1* loc 2m/3km NE of Merthyr Tydfil. SO 0609
Pant y Wacco Clwyd 41 G4* loc 3m/4km W of Holywell. SJ 1476
Panxworth Norfolk 39 G3 ham 4m/6km NW of Acle. TG 3413
Papa Shetland 89 E8* small uninhabited island on E side of island of Oxna and 2m/4km W of Scalloway, Mainland. HU 3637
Papa Sound Orkney 89 B5* sea channel between islands of Westray and Papa Westray. HY 4751
Papa Stour Shetland 89 D7 inhabited island 1m off W coast of Mainland at SW end of St Magnus Bay. It is roughly 3m/4km E to W and 2m/3km N to S, and is separated from Mainland by Sound of Papa, 1m wide. Coastline noted for caves. HU 1760
Papa Stronsay Orkney 89 C6 small island off NE coast of Stronsay, separated from it by **Papa Sound.** Lighthouse on far side of island. HY 6629
Papa Westray Orkney 89 B5 inhabited island N and E of Westray across Papa Sound. It is some 5km N to S and from 1km to 2km E to W. HY 4952
Papcastle Cumbria 52 B2 vil 1m NW of Cockermouth across R Derwent. Site of Roman fort of *Derventio.* NY 1031
Papil Shetland 89 E8* loc on island of W Burra 3m/4km S of Hamnavoe. HU 3731
Papil Water Shetland 89 F6* lake on Fetlar 1m W of Houbie. HU 6290
Papley Northants 37 F5* loc 4m/7km E of Oundle. TL 1089
Papley Orkney 89 B7* loc on E side of S Ronaldsay 2m/3km SE of St Margaret's Hope. ND 4691
Pap of Glencoe H'land 74 C5 mt in Lochaber dist nearly 2m/3km E of foot of Glen Coe. Height 2430 ft or 741 metres. Also known as Sgorr na Ciche. NN 1259
Papple Lothian 66 D2* loc 3m/5km S of E Linton. NT 5972
Papplewick Notts 44 A5 vil 2km NE of Hucknall. SK 5451
Paps of Jura S'clyde 62 C1 the three highest peaks of the mt ridge of Jura, situated some 5m/8km N of Craighouse. See Beinn an Oir, Beinn Shiantaidh, Beinn a' Chaolais. NR 47, 57
Papworth Everard Cambs 29 G2 vil 6m/10km SE of Huntingdon. **Papworth Vil Settlement,** originally created for tuberculosis sufferers, now available to others. TL 2862
Papworth St Agnes Cambs 29 G2 vil 5m/8km SE of Huntingdon. TL 2664
Par Cornwall 3 F3 small resort and port (for export of china clay) 4m/6km E of St Austell. SX 0753
Paradise Salop 34 D4* loc 1km N of Ironbridge. SJ 6704
Paradise Som 8 C1* loc on W side of Glastonbury. ST 4938
Paradise Staffs 35 E4* loc 1m SE of Coven. SJ 9206
Paradise Copse Devon. See Clyst Hydon.
Parallel Roads of Glen Roy H'land. See Glen Roy.
Paramour Street Kent 13 H1 loc 3m/5km NW of Sandwich. TR 2861
Parbold Lancs 42 B1 vil 7m/11km NW of Wigan. SD 4910
Parbrook Som 8 D1 vil 5m/8km SE of Glastonbury. ST 5636
Parbrook W Sussex 11 G3* loc 1km S of Billingshurst. TQ 0825
Parc Gwynedd 33 F1 ham 3m/5km SW of Bala. SH 8733
Parciau Gwynedd 40 B3/C3* loc near E coast of Anglesey 1m N of Brynteg. SH 4984
Parc le Breos W Glam 14 B3* ancient burial-chamber (A.M.) on Gower peninsula, to NW of Parkmill. SS 5389
Parcllyn Dyfed 22 D1* loc 1m W of Aberporth. SN 2451
Parc-Seymour Gwent 15 H2* ham 3m/5km N of Magor. ST 4091
Parc-y-rhos Dyfed 24 B3* loc 2km S of Lampeter. SN 5745
Pardown Hants 18 A6* loc 1m SE of Oakley or Church Oakley. SU 5749
Pardshaw Cumbria 52 B3 ham 4m/7km SW of Cockermouth. NY 0924
Parham Suffolk 31 G2 vil 2m/4km SE of Framlingham. 1km SE, Moat Hall, 15c moated manor hse. TM 3060
Parham W Sussex 11 F4 par below S Downs containing Parham Hse, Tudor hse in large park, 2m/3km W of Storrington. TQ 0614
Paris W Yorks 43 F1* loc 1m SE of Holmfirth. SE 1507
Park Grampian 77 G2 loc 4m/6km W of Peterculter. NO 7898
Park Humberside 44 C1/C2* loc adjoining Westwoodside to N. SE 7400
Park W Isles 88 B3* dist in SE Lewis between Loch Erisort and Loch Seaforth. NB 31
Park Bridge Gtr Manchester 43 E1* loc in Ashton-under-Lyne 2m/3km N of tn centre. SD 9402
Parkbroom Cumbria 60 A5* loc 3m/4km NE of Carlisle. NY 4358
Park Burn 60 C5* r formed by confluence of Coanwood Burn and Fell Burn 3m/4km S of Haltwhistle, Nthmb, and flowing NW into R South Tyne 2m/3km SW of the tn. NY 6862
Park Close Lancs 48 B4* loc 1km SW of Salterforth. SD 8844
Park Corner Avon 16 C5* loc 1km W of Freshford and 4m/6km SE of Bath. ST 7859
Park Corner Berks 18 D3* loc 2m/4km NW of Maidenhead. SU 8582
Park Corner E Sussex 12 B3* loc 1m SE of Groombridge. TQ 5336
Park Corner, High Essex 31 E6* vil 4m/6km SE of Colchester. TM 0320
Park Dam Nthmb 60 D4* small lake 2m/3km NW of Newbrough. NY 8569
Park End Beds 29 E3* loc adjoining Stevington to E, 4m/7km NW of Bedford. SP 9953
Park End Cambs 30 A2* S end of Swaffham Bulbeck. TL 5561
Park End Cleveland 54 D3* dist of Middlesbrough 2m/4km SE of tn centre. NZ 5217
Parkend Glos 16 B1 vil 4m/6km N of Lydney. SO 6108
Park End H & W 26 C1* loc 2m/3km SW of Bewdley. SO 7673
Park End Staffs 42 D6* loc 1m NW of Audley. SJ 7851
Parker's Green Kent 20 C6 ham 2m/3km NE of Tonbridge. TQ 6148
Parkeston Essex 31 F5 loc on S side of R Stour estuary 2km W of Harwich. **P. Quay** is terminal of Continental passenger and freight ferries. TM 2332
Park Farm H & W 27 E1* SE dist of Redditch. SP 0665
Parkfield Avon 16 C4* loc 4m/6km SW of Chipping Sodbury. ST 6977
Parkfield Bucks 18 C2* S part of Princes Risborough. SP 8002
Parkfield Cornwall 3 G2* loc 5m/7km NE of Liskeard. SX 3167
Parkfield H & W 26 D2* loc 2m/3km NW of Worcester. SO 8257
Parkfield W Midlands 35 F4* S dist of Wolverhampton. SO 9296
Parkgate Ches 41 H3 loc 1m NW of Neston. SJ 2778
Parkgate Ches 42 D4* loc 4m/6km SE of Knutsford. SJ 7874
Parkgate Cumbria 52 C1* loc 1km SW of Waverton. NY 2146
Parkgate D & G 59 E3 loc 5m/8km NW of Lochmaben. NY 0288
Park Gate Hants 10 C4 vil 4m/7km NW of Fareham. SU 5108
Park Gate H & W 26 D1* loc 2m/3km W of Bromsgrove. SO 9371
Parkgate Kent 13 E3* loc 2m/3km W of Tenterden. TQ 8534
Parkgate Surrey 11 H1 ham 4m/7km SE of Dorking. TQ 2043
Park Gate S Yorks 43 H2 loc 2m/3km N of Rotherham. Steel works. SK 4395
Park Gate W Yorks 43 G1 loc just N of Skelmanthorpe. SE 2310
Park Gate W Yorks 48 D4* SW dist of Guiseley. SE 1841
Parkgate Tarn Cumbria 52 B5* small lake 2km W of Eskdale Green. NY 1100
Parkgate, West Ches 43 E3* ham at W entrance to Lyme Park, 2m/3km SE of Poynton. SJ 9481
Park Green Suffolk 31 F2* loc 3m/4km NW of Debenham. TM 1364
Parkhall S'clyde 64 C2* loc 2m/3km NW of Clydebank. NS 4972
Park Hall Camp Salop 34 A2 military camp 2km NE of Oswestry. SJ 3031
Parkham Devon 6 C3 vil 5m/8km SW of Bideford. Loc of **P. Ash** in W part of par. SS 3821
Park Head Cornwall 2 D2 headland (NT) on N coast 4m/6km S of Trevose Hd. SW 8470
Parkhead Cumbria 52 D1* loc 3m/4km S of Welton. NY 3340
Park Head Cumbria 53 E1* loc 2m/3km E of Kirkoswald. NY 5841
Park Head Derbys 43 H5* loc 1m E of Crich. SK 3654
Parkhead S'clyde 64 D3* loc in Glasgow 2m/4km E of city centre. NS 6264
Parkhead S Yorks 43 G3* loc in Sheffield 3m/5km SW of city centre. SK 3183

Park Head W Yorks 43 G1* loc 2m/3km W of Denby Dale. SE 1908
Park Hill Lancs 48 B4/B5* loc in Burnley 2km NW of tn centre. SD 8133
Parkhill Notts 44 B5* loc 1km S of Southwell. SK 6952
Park Hill S Yorks 43 H3* loc in Sheffield 1m E of city centre. SK 3687
Parkhouse S'clyde 64 D2* loc in Glasgow 2m/3km N of city centre. NS 5968
Parkhouse Green Derbys 43 H4* loc 2m/3km E of Clay Cross. SK 4163
Parkhurst Isle of Wight 10 B5* vil 2m/3km N of Newport. HM Prison. SZ 4991
Parklands W Yorks 49 E4* dist of Leeds 3m/4km N of city centre. SE 2937
Park Lane Bucks 18 C2* loc 3m/5km W of High Wycombe. SU 8192
Park Langley London 20 A5 loc in borough of Bromley 2m/3km SW of Bromley tn centre. Langley Park to S, with golf course. TQ 3867
Parkmill W Glam 23 G6 vil on Gower peninsula 6m/9km W of Mumbles Hd. SS 5489
Park Mill W Yorks 43 G1 loc adjoining Clayton West to N. SE 2611
Parkneuk Fife 72 D5* loc adjoining Dunfermline to NW. NT 0788
Park Royal London 19 F3* loc in borough of Brent 7m/11km W of Charing Cross. TQ 1982
Parkside Clwyd 42 A5* loc 2m/3km E of Gresford. SJ 3755
Parkside Cumbria 52 A3* loc 1m S of Frizington. NY 0315
Parkside Durham 61 H6* S dist of Seaham. NZ 4248
Parkside S'clyde 65 E3* loc 3m/4km N of Wishaw. NS 8058
Park Side S Yorks 43 G2* loc on S side of Stannington. SK 3088
Parks, South Fife 73 F4* central dist of Glenrothes. NO 2601
Parks, The S Yorks 44 B1* loc adjoining Hatfield to W. SE 6409
Parkstone Dorset 9 G5 dist of Poole immediately E of tn centre. To SW, **P. Bay,** inlet off Poole Harbour. SZ 0391
Park Street Herts 19 F2 loc 2m/3km S of St Albans. TL 1404
Park Town Oxon 18 A1* dist of Oxford 1m N of city centre. SP 5107
Park Village W Midlands 35 F4* loc in Wolverhampton 2km NE of tn centre. SJ 9200
Parkway Som 8 D2* loc 1km S of Marston Magna. ST 5921
Parkway Suffolk 30 B3* loc at NW edge of Haverhill. TL 6646
Park, West W Yorks 49 E4* dist of Leeds 3m/5km NW of city centre. SE 2637
Parkwood Springs S Yorks 43 H2* dist of Sheffield 2km N of city centre. SK 3489
Parley Cross Dorset 9 G4* loc 1km NW of W Parley and 4m/7km N of Bournemouth. SZ 0898
Parley, East Dorset 9 G4* loc at W end of Hurn Airport 4m/7km N of Bournemouth. SZ 1097
Parley Green Dorset 9 G4* loc by N bank of R Stour 4m/6km N of Bournemouth. SZ 0997
Parley, West Dorset 9 G4 vil running down to R Stour 2m/3km S of Ferndown. SZ 0897
Parliament Hill London 19 F3* open space on high ground in borough of Camden E of Hampstead Heath, 4m/7km N of Charing Cross. See Highgate. TQ 2786
Parlington W Yorks 49 F4 loc 2m/4km NE of Garforth. SE 4236
Parlwr Du, Y Welsh form of Point of Air, qv.
Parndon, Great Essex 20 B1 SW dist of Harlow. TL 4308
Parndon, Little Essex 20 B1 W dist of Harlow. TL 4310
Parracombe Devon 7 E1 vil on Exmoor 4m/7km SW of Lynton. To E of vil is ham of **P. Churchtown.** SS 6645
Parr Brow Gtr Manchester 42 C1/C2* loc 2km E of Tyldesley. SD 7101
Parrett 15 G6 r rising near Cheddington in Dorset and flowing N to Langport and then NW through Bridgwater and into Bridgwater Bay to W of Burnham-on-Sea, Som. ST 2449
Parr Fold Gtr Manchester 42 C1* loc adjoining Walkden to S. SD 7302
Parrog Dyfed 22 C2 loc 1km NW of Newport. SN 0439
Parsonage Green Essex 20 D1* suburban loc 2m/3km N of Chelmsford. TL 7009
Parsonage Reservoir Lancs 48 A5* resr 3m/4km NE of Blackburn. SD 6931
Parson and Clerk, The Devon 5 E3* natural arch of red sandstone rock on coast below vil of Holcombe, midway between Teignmouth and Dawlish at N end of Babbacombe Bay. SX 9674
Parsonby Cumbria 52 B1/B2 loc 2m/3km S of Aspatria. NY 1438
Parson Cross S Yorks 43 H2* loc in Sheffield 3m/5km N of city centre. SK 3592
Parson Drove Cambs 37 H4 vil 6m/10km W of Wisbech. TF 3708
Parsons Tyne & Wear 61 G5* industrial estate in NW part of Washington. NZ 2957
Parsons Green London 19 F4* dist in S part of borough of Hammersmith NE of Putney Br. TQ 2476
Parson's Heath Essex 31 E5 loc in NE part of Colchester. TM 0127
Parson's Hills Derbys 35 H2* loc 1km W of Repton. SK 2926
Partick S'clyde 64 C2 dist of Glasgow 2m/3km W of city centre. **Partickhill** is loc in dist. NS 5566
Partington Gtr Manchester 42 C2 tn 4m/6km NW of Hale. SJ 7191
Partney Lincs 45 G4 vil 2m/3km NE of Spilsby. TF 4168
Parton Cumbria 52 A3 vil on **P. Bay** adjoining Whitehaven to N. Site of Roman fort to N. NX 9720
Parton D & G 58 C4 vil 7m/11km NW of Castle Douglas. NX 6970
Parton Rocks Cleveland 54 D2 rocks on North Sea coast on NE side of Hartlepool. NZ 5234
Partridge Green W Sussex 11 G3 vil 3m/4km SW of Cowfold. TQ 1919
Partrishow Powys 25 G5 loc in Black Mts 5m/8km N of Abergavenny. SO 2722
Parwich Derbys 43 G5 vil 5m/8km N of Ashbourne. SK 1854
Parys Mountain Gwynedd 40 B3 hill in Anglesey 2m/3km S of Amlwch. Earthworks mark sites of former copper mines. SH 4490
Paslow Wood Common Essex 20 C2* loc 2m/4km E of Chipping Ongar. TL 5801
Passenham Northants 28 C4 vil on R Ouse 1km SW of Stony Stratford across r. SP 7839
Passfield Hants 11 E2 ham 2m/3km NW of Liphook. SU 8234
Passingford Bridge Essex 20 B2 loc 4m/7km SE of Epping. TQ 5097
Passmores Essex 20 B1* S dist of Harlow. TL 4408
Pass of Aberglaslyn Gwynedd 40 C6 narrow part of R Glaslyn valley below Beddgelert. SH 5946
Pass of Ballater Grampian 76 D2 pass carrying E–W rd 1km N of Ballater, qv. NO 3696
Pass of Brander S'clyde 70 C2 pass traversed by R Awe running from foot of Loch Awe, on SW side of Ben Cruachan in Argyll. NN 0528
Pass of Drumochter 75 F3/F4* pass between Glen Truim in Highland region and Glen Garry in Tayside region, 6m/9km S of Dalwhinnie. Carries the A9 rd and the Perth–Inverness rly, the latter rising to 1484 ft or 452 metres, the summit of the British rly system. NN 6275
Pass of Glencoe. See Glen Coe.
Pass of Killiecrankie Tayside. See Killiecrankie.
Pass of Leny Central 71 G4 wooded defile below Loch Lubnaig, 2m/4km W of Callander. See also Falls of Leny. NN 5908
Pass of Lyon Tayside 75 G6* deep defile in Glen Lyon 2km W of Fortingall. At its narrowest point is Macgregor's Leap. NN 7247
Paston Cambs 37 G4* loc in Peterborough 2m/4km N of city centre. TF 1802
Paston Norfolk 39 G2 ham near coast 4m/6km NE of N Walsham. **P. Street** vil to NW. **P. Green** loc to SW. TG 3234
Pasturefields Staffs 35 F2* loc beside R Trent 2m/3km SE of Weston. SJ 9924
Pasture, West Durham 53 H3* loc on SE shore of Grassholme Resr, S of Middleton in Teesdale. NY 9422
Patchacott Devon 6 D5* loc 7m/12km NW of Okehampton. SX 4798
Patcham E Sussex 11 H4 N dist of Brighton. TQ 3009
Patchetts Green Herts 19 F2* loc 2m/4km E of Watford. TQ 1497
Patching W Sussex 11 G4 vil 5m/7km NW of Worthing. TQ 0806
Patchole Devon 7 E1* loc 7m/11km SE of Ilfracombe. SS 6142
Patchway Avon 16 B3 large suburb 6m/9km N of Bristol. ST 6082
Pateley Bridge N Yorks 48 D2 small tn in Nidderdale 11m/18km NW of Harrogate. Disused lead mines on surrounding moors, and remains of Bronze Age settlements. SE 1565
Paterson's Rock S'clyde 63 E6* island rock with beacon lying 1m E of Sanda I. off S coast of Kintyre. NR 7504
Pathhead Fife 73 F5 dist of Kirkcaldy in vicinity of harbour. NT 2892
Pathhead Lothian 66 B2 vil 4m/7km SE of Dalkeith. NT 3964
Pathhead S'clyde 56 F3 loc on N bank of R Nith opp New Cumnock. NS 6114
Path Head Tyne & Wear 61 F5* loc 1km W of Blaydon. NZ 1763
Pathlow Warwicks 27 F2* loc 3m/4km NW of Stratford-upon-Avon. SP 1858
Pathstruie Tayside 72 D3 loc 4m/6km SE of Dunning. NO 0711
Patmore Heath Herts 29 H5 loc 4m/6km NW of Bishop's Stortford. TL 4425
Patna S'clyde 56 D3 vil on R Doon 5m/8km NW of Dalmellington. Coal-mining in valley to SE. NS 4110
Patney Wilts 17 E5 vil 5m/8km SE of Devizes. SU 0758
Patrick Isle of Man 46 A5 vil 2km S of Peel. SC 2482
Patrick Brompton N Yorks 54 B5 vil 3m/5km W of Bedale. SE 2290
Patricroft Gtr Manchester 42 C2* dist of Eccles to W of tn centre. SJ 7698
Patrington Humberside 51 G5/G6 vil 4m/6km SW of Withernsea. Large 14c cruciform ch known as 'Queen of Holderness'. TA 3122
Patrixbourne Kent 13 G2 vil 3m/5km SE of Canterbury. TR 1855
Patshull Staffs 35 E4 loc 7m/11km W of Wolverhampton. SJ 8000
Pattack H'land 75 F2 r in Badenoch and Strathspey dist running N from Loch Pattack, then turning W to head of Loch Laggan. NN 5389
Patterdale Cumbria 52 D3 vil 1km S of SW end of Ullswater. NY 3915
Pattingham Staffs 35 E4 vil 6m/9km W of Wolverhampton. SO 8299
Pattinson Tyne & Wear 61 G5* industrial estate in E part of Washington. Wildfowl refuge to E. NZ 3255
Pattishall Northants 28 B2 vil 4m/6km N of Towcester. SP 6754
Pattiswick Green Essex 30 C5 ham 3m/4km NW of Coggeshall. TL 8124
Patton Cumbria 53 E5 loc 3m/5km NE of Kendal. SD 5496
Paul Cornwall 2 A5 vil on S side of Penzance. SW 4627
Paulerspury Northants 28 C3 vil 3m/4km SE of Towcester. SP 7145
Paull Humberside 51 F5 vil on left bank of R Humber 2m/3km SW of Hedon. **P. Holme** loc 2km SE. TA 1626
Paul's Dene Wilts 9 H1 N dist of Salisbury. SU 1431
Paul's Green Cornwall 2 B5* loc 3m/5km SE of Hayle. SW 5933
Paulsgrove Hants 10 C4* urban loc below Portsdown 4m/6km N of Portsmouth city centre. SU 6306
Paulton Avon 16 B5* vil 2m/3km NW of Midsomer Norton. ST 6556
Pauntley Glos 26 C4* loc 3m/4km NE of Newent. SO 7429
Pave Lane Salop 34 D3 loc 1m SE of Chetwynd Aston. SJ 7616
Pavenham Beds 29 E2 vil on R Ouse 5m/9km NW of Bedford. Loc of **P. Bury** to N. SP 9855
Paviland Caves W Glam 23 F6* two caves below Pitton Cliffs (NT) on Gower peninsula 2m/3km W of Port Eynon, in one of which was found, in 1823, a human skeleton now thought to be some 19,000 years old. SS 4385
Pawlett Som 15 G6 vil on flat lands near mouth of R Parrett and 4m/6km N of Bridgwater. 1km NW, ham of **P. Hill.** ST 3042
Pawston Nthmb 67 E5 loc 4m/7km S of Cornhill on Tweed. **P. Lake** 1km S on far side of **P. Hill.** NT 8532
Paxford Glos 27 F4 vil 2m/4km E of Chipping Campden. SP 1837
Paxton Borders 67 F3 vil 4m/7km W of Berwick-upon-Tweed. NT 9353
Paxton, Great Cambs 29 F2 vil 3m/5km NE of St Neots. TL 2063
Paxton, Little Cambs 29 F2 vil 2m/3km N of St Neots across R Ouse. TL 1862
Paycocke's Essex. See Coggeshall.
Payden Street Kent 21 E6* loc 2m/3km NE of Lenham. TQ 9254
Payhembury Devon 7 H7 vil 5m/8km W of Honiton. 2m/3km NE, Hembury Fort, Iron Age earthwork, 884 ft or 269 metres above sea level. ST 0801
Payne End Herts 29 G4* W part of Sandon, 5m/8km E of Baldock. TL 3134
Paynter's Lane End Cornwall 2 C4* loc 2m/3km NW of Redruth. SW 6743
Paythorne Lancs 48 B3 ham 2m/3km N of Gisburn. SD 8251
Peacehaven E Sussex 12 A6 suburb on coast 2m/3km W of Newhaven. TQ 4100
Peacemarsh Dorset 9 E2 loc adjoining Gillingham to N. ST 8027
Peachley H & W 26 C2 loc 3m/5km NW of Worcester. SO 8057
Peacock's Heath H & W 26 B2 loc 2km N of Bromyard. SO 6456
Peak Cavern Derbys 43 F3* cave at foot of crag on which Peveril Castle stands, to S of Castleton. SK 1482
Peak Dale Derbys 43 F3 ham 3m/5km NE of Buxton. SK 0976
Peak District 43 F2-F6 hill area and national park in N Derbyshire, including also part of NE Staffs and a corner of Ches. Comprises the Peak proper (also known as the High Peak), an area of millstone grit hills E of Hayfield, whose summit, Kinder Scout, attains height of 2088 ft or 636 metres; and a larger but less elevated area of limestone hills between Chapel-en-le-Frith and Ashbourne, intersected by deep valleys and criss-crossed by dry stone walls.
Peak Forest Derbys 43 F3 vil 4m/6km E of Chapel-en-le-Frith. SK 1179
Peak Forest Canal 43 E3-E2 canal running from Whaley Bridge, Derbys, to the Ashton Canal at Ashton-under-Lyne, Gtr Manchester.
Peak, High 117 admin dist of Derbys.
Peak Hill Lincs 37 G3* loc 2km S of Cowbit. TF 2616
Peakirk Cambs 37 F4 vil 5m/8km N of Peterborough. TF 1606
Pean H'land 74 B3 r in Lochaber dist running E down Glen P. to join R Dessary 1km above head of Loch Arkaig. NM 9791
Pearson Fold W Yorks 48 D5* loc in Bradford 3m/5km S of city centre. SE 1627
Pearson's Green Kent 12 D3* loc 2m/3km SE of Paddock Wd. TQ 6943
Peartree Derbys 36 A1* dist of Derby 2m/3km S of tn centre. SK 3533
Peartree Herts 19 F1* E dist of Welwyn Garden City. TL 2412
Peartree Green Essex 20 C2* loc adjoining Doddinghurst to S, 3m/5km N of Brentwood. TQ 5998
Peartree Green Hants 10 B4* dist of Southampton 2km E of city centre across R Itchen. SU 4411
Peartree Green H & W 26 B4 loc 5m/9km N of Ross-on-Wye across loops of r. SO 5932
Peasedown St John Avon 16 C5 vil 2m/3km NE of Radstock. ST 7057
Peasehill Derbys 43 H6* loc 1km SE of Ripley. SK 4049
Peaseland Green Norfolk 39 E3* loc just S of Elsing. TG 0516
Peasemore Berks 17 H4 vil 6m/10km N of Newbury. SU 4577
Peasenhall Suffolk 31 G2 vil 3m/4km W of Yoxford. TM 3569
Pease Pottage W Sussex 11 H2 ham 3m/4km S of Crawley. TQ 2533
Pease's West Durham 54 B2* loc 1km N of Crook. NZ 1636
Peas Hill Cambs 37 H4 loc in NW part of March. TL 4097
Peaslake Surrey 11 G1 vil 4m/6km N of Cranleigh. TQ 0844
Peasley Cross Merseyside 42 B2* dist of St Helens 1m SE of tn centre. SJ 5294
Peasmarsh E Sussex 13 E4 vil 3m/4km NW of Rye. TQ 8822
Peasmarsh Som 8 B3* loc 2m/3km SW of Ilminster. ST 3412
Peasmarsh Surrey 11 F1* loc 2m/3km NE of Godalming. SU 9946
Peathill Grampian 83 G1 vil 1m S of Rosehearty. NJ 9365
Peathrow Durham 54 A3* loc 1m W of Cockfield. NZ 1024

Peat Inn Fife 73 G3 vil 6m/9km SE of Cupar. NO 4509

Peatling Magna Leics 36 B5 vil 6m/10km NW of Husbands Bosworth. SP 5992

Peatling Parva Leics 36 B5 vil 4m/7km NE of Lutterworth. SP 5889

Peaton Salop 34 C5* loc 6m/10km E of Craven Arms. SO 5384

Peats Corner Suffolk 31 F2* loc 2m/3km SE of Debenham. TM 1960

Pebley Pond Derbys 44 A3* lake 2m/4km SE of Killamarsh. SK 4879

Pebmarsh Essex 30 C4 vil 3m/5km NE of Halstead. TL 8533

Pebworth H & W 27 F3 vil 6m/10km NE of Broadway. SP 1346

Pecca Falls N Yorks 47 G1* series of waterfalls on Kingsdale Beck 1m N of Ingleton. SD 6974

Pecket Well W Yorks 48 C5 vil 2km N of Hebden Br. SD 9929

Peckforton Ches 42 B5 ham 4m/6km S of Tarporley. **P. Castle** is 19c mansion 1m N on N end of wooded **P. Hills. P. Mere** is small lake to N. SJ 5356

Peckham London 19 G4* dist in borough of Southwark 4m/6km SE of Charing Cross. TQ 3476

Peckham Bush Kent 20 C6* ham 1m N of E Peckham. TQ 6650

Peckham, East Kent 20 C6 vil 2m/4km N of Paddock Wd. TQ 6648

Peckham Rye London 19 G4* loc S of Peckham. To S towards Dulwich, Peckham Rye Common and Park. TQ 3476

Peckham, West Kent 20 C6 vil 5m/8km NE of Tonbridge. TQ 6452

Peckleton Leics 36 A4 vil 8m/12km W of Leicester. SK 4700

Peckover House Cambs. See Wisbech.

Pedair-hewl Welsh form of Four Roads, qv.

Peddar's Way 38 C2 ancient trackway, traceable in part, from Ixworth, Suffolk, to the Wash at Hunstanton, Norfolk.

Pedham Norfolk 39 G4* loc 2m/3km W of S Walsham. TG 3312

Pedmore W Midlands 35 E6 SE dist of Stourbridge. SO 9182

Pednormead End Bucks 18 D2* SW dist of Chesham. SP 9501

Pedwell Som 8 C1* vil towards E end of Polden Hills 4m/6km W of Street. ST 4236

Peebles Borders 66 A4 tn and resort on R Tweed 20m/33km S of Edinburgh. Woollen mnfre. Cross Kirk (A.M.) is ruin dating from 13c. NT 2540

Peel Isle of Man 46 A5 small resort with harbour on W coast 10m/16km NW of Douglas. Kipper-curing industry. **P. Castle** on St Patrick's Isle, qv. **P. Bay,** small bay E of harbour. SC 2484

Peel Lancs 47 E5* loc 4m/6km SE of Blackpool. SD 3531

Peel Green Gtr Manchester 42 C2* loc in Eccles 2km W of tn centre. SJ 7597

Peel Island Cumbria 52 C5 small island off E shore of Coniston Water 2km from S end of lake. SD 2991

Peel of Lumphanan Grampian. See Lumphanan.

Peening Quarter Kent 13 E4* loc 2km NW of Wittersham. TQ 8828

Pegal Orkney 89 A7* headland on E coast of Hoy opp island of Rysa Little. ND 3098

Peggs Green Leics 36 A3* loc 3m/4km NW of Coalville. SK 4117

Pegsdon Beds 29 E4/F4* ham 4m/7km W of Hitchin. TL 1230

Pegswood Nthmb 61 G3 vil 2m/3km NE of Morpeth. NZ 2287

Pegwell Kent 13 H1 dist of Ramsgate on bay of same name. Hovercraft terminal. Power stn to SW. Bay is traditional site of Roman landing in AD 43, of Saxon landing in 449, and of St Augustine's in 597, the last commemorated by a cross (A.M.). TR 3664

Peinchorran Skye H'land 79 D5 locality on N side of Loch Sligachan near mouth of loch. NG 5233

Peinlich Skye, H'land 78 C4 loc 3m/5km S of Uig. NG 4158

Peinmore Skye, H'land 78 C4* loc 5m/8km NW of Portree. NG 4248

Pelaw Tyne & Wear 61 G5* E dist of Felling. NZ 2962

Pelcam Welsh form of Pelcomb, qv.

Pelcomb (Pencam) Dyfed 22 B4 loc 3m/4km NW of Haverfordwest. **P. Cross** loc to W. **Pelcomb Br** loc 1m SE. SM 9218

Peldon Essex 30 D6 vil 5m/8km S of Colchester. TL 9816

Pell Green E Sussex 12 C3* loc adjoining Wadhurst to N. TQ 6432

Pellon W Yorks 48 D5* loc in Halifax 2m/3km W of tn centre. SE 0725

Pelsall W Midlands 35 F4 loc 3m/5km N of Walsall. **Pelsall Wd** loc adjoining to N. SK 0103

Pelton Durham 61 G6 vil 2m/3km NW of Chester-le-Street. **W Pelton** vil 2km W. **Pelton Fell** loc 1m S. NZ 2553

Pelutho Cumbria 52 B1 loc 4m/6km W of Abbey Town. NY 1249

Pelynt Cornwall 3 G3 vil 3m/5km NW of Looe. SX 2055

Pemberton Dyfed 23 G5* loc in E part of Llanelli. SN 5200

Pemberton Gtr Manchester 42 B1* dist of Wigan 2m/3km W of tn centre. SD 5504

Pembrey (Pen-bre) 23 F5 vil adjoining Burry Port to W. **P. Forest,** wooded area to W. SN 4201

Pembridge H & W 25 H2 vil 6m/10km E of Kington. Many old timbered bldgs, incl mkt hall. 'New' Inn is early 16c. SO 3958

Pembroke (Penfro) Dyfed 22 C5 tn on r of same name 29m/47km SW of Carmarthen. Parts of 13c walls still remain. Ruins of 13c cas on site of earlier bldg. SM 9801

Pembroke 22 B5/C5 r rising 5m/8km E of Pembroke tn, Dyfed, and flowing W to the tn where it forms an estuary which continues W and finally N into Milford Haven on W side of tn of Pembroke Dock. SM 9402

Pembroke Dock Dyfed 22 C5 port near head of Milford Haven estuary, on S side opp Neyland. To W is estuary of Pembroke R. SM 9603

Pembroke Ferry Dyfed 22 C5 loc on S side of estuary 1m NE of Pembroke Dock, and at S end of rd br. SM 9704

Pembury Kent 12 C3 large vil 3m/5km E of Tunbridge Wells. TQ 6240

Penallt Gwent 26 A6* ham 2m/3km SE of Monmouth. SO 5210

Pen Allt-mawr Powys 25 G5* peak on Black Mts 4m/6km N of Crickhowell. Height 2360 ft or 719 metres. SO 2024

Penally Dyfed 22 D5 vil 2km SW of Tenby. SS 1199

Penalt H & W 26 B4 ham 4m/6km NW of Ross-on-Wye across loop of r. SO 5729

Pen-a-maen Cornwall 3 E4 alternative name for Maenease Pt, qv.

Penaran Powys 33 H5* loc 2km SW of Kerry. SO 1388

Penare Cornwall 3 E4* loc to N of Dodman Pt and 3m/5km S of Mevagissey. NT property to N and S. SX 0040

Penare Point Cornwall 3 E4 headland on Mevagissey Bay just N of Mevagissey. SX 0245

Penarlag Welsh form of Hawarden, qv.

Penarth S Glam 15 G4 port and resort at mouth of R Ely 3m/5km S of Cardiff. **Lr Penarth,** S dist of tn. **Penarth Hd,** headland at seaward end of combined estuaries of Rs Taff and Ely. ST 1871

Pen-bont Rhydybeddau Dyfed 32 D6 vil on Nant Silo 6m/10km E of Aberystwyth. SN 6783

Penboyr Dyfed 23 E2 loc 4m/7km SE of Newcastle Emlyn. SN 3636

Pen-bre Welsh form of Pembrey, qv.

Pen Brush Dyfed 22 B2 headland 2km SW of Strumble Hd. Group of small islands off shore. SM 8839

Penbryn Dyfed 23 E1 vil 2m/4km E of Aberporth. SN 2952

Penbryn Mid Glam 15 F2* loc in coal-mining area 2km NW of Ystrad Mynach. ST 1494

Pencader Dyfed 24 A4 vil 3m/5km SE of Llandyssul. SN 4436

Pen-cae Dyfed 24 A3* loc 1m SE of Llanarth. SN 4356

Pencaenwydd Gwynedd 32 B1* loc 4m/7km NE of Pwllheli. SH 4041

Pen Caer Dyfed 22 B2 peninsula rich in prehistoric antiquities NW of Fishguard. **Pen-caer** is headland at N end of peninsula, to E of Strumble Hd. SM 9040

Pen-cae'r-cwm Clwyd 41 F5* loc 2m/3km SW of Bylchau. SH 9461

Pen-caer-fenny W Glam 23 G6* loc to S of Salthouse Pt 4m/7km W of Gowerton. SS 5295

Pencaitland Lothian 66 C2 par containing vils of **Easter** and **Wester P.,** on either side of Tyne Water 4m/6km SE of Tranent. Distillery to S (Glenkinchie). NT 4468

Pencarnisiog Gwynedd 40 B4* ham near W coast of Anglesey 2m/4km E of Rhosneigr. SH 3573

Pencarreg Dyfed 24 B3/B4 ham 1m NE of Llanybydder. SN 5345

Pencarrow Cornwall 3 F1* loc just S of Camelford. SX 1082

Pencarrow Head Cornwall 3 F3* headland on S coast at W end of Lantivet Bay 2m/3km E of Fowey. SX 1550

Pencelli Powys 25 F5 ham 4m/6km SE of Brecon. SO 0925

Pen Cerrig-calch Powys 25 G5 peak on Black Mts 3m/4km N of Crickhowell. Height 2302 ft or 701 metres. SO 2122

Pencilan Head (Trwyn Cilan) Gwynedd 32 B2 headland on S coast of Lleyn peninsula 4m/6km S of Abersoch.

Pen-clawdd W Glam 23 G5/G6 vil 3m/5km W of Gowerton. Cockle-fishing industry. SS 5495

Pencoed Mid Glam 15 E3 vil 4m/6km E of Bridgend. SS 9681

Pen-coed Castle Gwent 15 H3* ruined mansion on an eminence adjoining Llanmartin to E. ST 4089

Pencombe H & W 26 B2 vil 4m/6km W of Bromyard. SO 6052

Pencoyd H & W 26 A5* loc 6m/9km W of Ross-on-Wye. SO 5126

Pencraig H & W 26 B5 ham 3m/5km SW of Ross-on-Wye. SO 5620

Pencraig Welsh form of Old Radnor, qv.

Pencribach Dyfed 23 E1 headland at N end of Cribach Bay 1m NW of Aberporth. SN 2552

Pendarves Point Cornwall. See St Eval.

Pendeen Cornwall 2 A5 vil 2m/3km N of St Just. SW 3834

Pendeen Watch Cornwall 2 A5* headland with lighthouse 7m/11km NW of Penzance. SW 7036

Pendennis Point Cornwall 2 D5 headland on W side of entrance to Carrick Rds. Pendennis Castle (A.M.), 16c. SW 8231

Penderyn Mid Glam 15 E1 vil 2m/3km N of Hirwaun. **Penderyn Resr,** small resr 1m SW. SN 9408

Pendeulwyn Welsh form of Pendoylan, qv.

Pendinas Dyfed 32 D6* hill 1km S of Aberystwyth across R Rheidol, crowned by Iron Age fort and 19c monument to Duke of Wellington. SN 5880

Pendinas Reservoir Clwyd 41 H6* small resr 2m/4km W of Minera. SJ 2351

Pendine Dyfed 22 D5 vil on Carmarthen Bay 5m/8km W of Laugharne. To E stretch the wide **P. Sands,** formerly used for car speed trials. SN 2308

Pendle 117 admin dist of Lancs.

Pendlebury Gtr Manchester 42 D1 tn 5m/7km NW of Manchester. Coal-mining, textiles, light engineering. SD 7802

Pendle Hill Lancs 48 B4 prominent limestone hill 4m/6km E of Clitheroe in area known as the Forest of Pendle. Height 1831 ft or 558 metres. SD 8041

Pendleton Gtr Manchester 42 D2* dist of Salford 1m NW of tn centre. SJ 8199

Pendleton Lancs 48 A4 vil 2m/3km SE of Clitheroe. SD 7539

Pendle Water 48 B4* r rising on Pendle Hill, E of Clitheroe, Lancs, and flowing into R Calder on N side of Burnley. SD 8234

Pendock H & W 26 C4 vil 7m/11km W of Tewkesbury. SO 7832

Pendogett Cornwall 3 E1* vil 5m/8km NE of Wadebridge. SX 0279

Pendomer Som 8 C3 ham 4m/7km SW of Yeovil. ST 5210

Pendoylan (Pendeulwyn) S Glam 15 F4 vil 4m/7km E of Cowbridge. ST 0676

Pendre Mid Glam 15 E3* loc in N part of Bridgend. SS 9081

Penegoes Powys 33 E4 vil 2m/3km E of Machynlleth. SH 7700

Penelewey Cornwall 2 D4* loc 3m/4km S of Truro. SW 8140

Penenden Heath Kent 20 D5* N dist of Maidstone. TQ 7657

Pen Enys Point Cornwall 2 B4* headland on N coast 2m/3km W of St Ives. SW 4941

Pen-ffordd Dyfed 22 C3 ham 3m/5km S of Maenclochog. SN 0722

Pen-fford-goch Pond Gwent 25 G6* small lake 2km N of Blaenavon. SO 2510

Penfilia W Glam 23 G5 loc in Swansea 2m/3km N of tn centre. SS 6596

Penfro Welsh form of Pembroke, qv.

Pengam Gwent 15 F2* loc 2km W of Blackwood. ST 1597

Pengam Gwent 15 G3* loc 1km W of Peterstone Wentlloog. ST 2679

Pengam S Glam 15 G3/G4* loc in Cardiff 2m/3km E of city centre. ST 2177

Penge London 19 G4 dist in borough of Bromley 1m S of Crystal Palace. TQ 3470

Pengelli-ddrain Welsh form of Grovesend, qv.

Pengenffordd. Alternative spelling of Pen-y-genffordd, qv.

Pengorffwysfa Gwynedd 40 B2* loc near N coast of Anglesey 2m/3km E of Amlwch. SH 4692

Pen-groes-oped Gwent 15 G1 loc 4m/7km S of Abergavenny. SO 3107

Penhale Jakes Cornwall 2 B5* loc 3m/5km W of Helston. SW 6028

Penhale Point Cornwall 2 C3 headland on N coast 3m/5km N of Perranporth. SW 7559

Penhale Sands Cornwall 2 C3 sand dunes behind Perran Beach N of Perranporth. SW 7656

Penhallic Point Cornwall 6 A6* headland (NT) on N coast at N end of Trebarwith Strand 1m S of Tintagel. SX 0487

Penhallow Cornwall 2 D3 ham 2m/3km S of Perranporth. SW 7651

Penhelig (Penhelyg) Gwynedd 32 D5* loc 1km E of Aberdovey. SN 6296

Penhellick Cornwall 2 C4* loc 2m/3km E of Camborne. SW 6740

Penhelyg Welsh form of Penhelig, qv.

Penhill Wilts 17 F3* N dist of Swindon. SU 1588

Penhow (or **Pen-hw**) Gwent 16 A3 ham 3m/5km W of Caerwent. Cas, now a farmhouse, is a 12c-15c fortified hse. ST 4290

Penhurst E Sussex 12 C5 loc 4m/6km W of Battle. TQ 6916

Peniarth Gwynedd 32 D4* loc 1km E of Llanegryn. SH 6105

Penicuik Lothian 66 A3 paper-mnfg tn on R North Esk 9m/14km S of Edinburgh. Other industries include electrical and photochemical engineering, mnfre of glass, plastics. NT 2359

Peniel Clwyd 41 F5* loc 2m/4km SW of Denbigh. SJ 0263

Peniel Dyfed 23 F3* ham 3m/5km NE of Carmarthen. SN 4324

Peniel Heugh Borders 66 D5 hill 4m/6km N of Jedburgh, bearing monmt raised in 1815 to commemorate Battle of Waterloo. NT 6526

Penifiler Skye, H'land 79 C5* locality 2km S of Portree across Loch Portree. NG 4841

Penilee S'clyde 64 C3* loc in Hillington dist of Glasgow. NS 5164

Peninver S'clyde 63 E5 loc on E coast of Kintyre, 4m/6km NE of Campbeltown. NR 7524

Penisa'r-waun Gwynedd 40 C5 loc 3m/5km N of Llanberis. SH 5563

Penishawain Powys 25 F4* loc 4m/6km NE of Brecon. SO 0832

Penistone S Yorks 43 G1 tn on R Don 7m/11km W of Barnsley. Sundry engineering and steel works. SE 2403

Penjerrick Cornwall 2 D5* loc 2m/3km SW of Falmouth. SW 7730

Penk 35 F2 r rising W of Codsall, Staffs, and flowing N into R Sow 2km E of Stafford. SJ 9422

Penketh Ches 42 B3 loc in W part of Warrington. SJ 5587

Penkill Castle S'clyde 56 C4 hse of 16c–17c with 19c castellations, 3m/5km E of Girvan. NX 2398

Penkiln Burn 57 D6 r in Dumfries & Galloway region rising on S slopes of Lamachan Hill and running S to R Cree at N end of Newton Stewart. NX 4166
Penkridge Staffs 35 E3 vil 6m/9km S of Stafford. SJ 9214
Penlan W Glam 23 G5* loc in Swansea 2m/3km N of tn centre. SS 6496
Penlee Point Cornwall 4 B5 headland at S end of Cawsand Bay. SX 4448
Penley Clwyd 34 B1 vil 3m/5km E of Overton. SJ 4139
Penllech Gwynedd 32 A2 loc 2m/3km SW of Tudweiliog. SH 2234
Pen Llechwen Dyfed 22 A3 headland 2km NE of St David's Hd. SM 7329
Penllergaer W Glam 23 G5 loc 5m/7km NW of Swansea. **P. Forest,** wooded area 1m NE. Industrial estate to W. SS 6198
Penllin S Glam 15 E4 vil 2m/3km NW of Cowbridge. SS 9776
Penllwyn Gwent 15 F2* loc 2km S of Blackwood. ST 1695
Pen-llyn Gwynedd 40 A3/B3* loc on Anglesey at N end of Llyn Llywenan. SH 3582
Pen-lon Gwynedd 40 B5* loc on Anglesey 1km SE of Newborough. SH 4365
Penmachno Gwynedd 41 E6 vil 4m/6km S of Betws-y-coed. SH 7950
Penmaen Gwent 15 F2/G2* loc 1km E of Blackwood across Ebbw R. ST 1897
Penmaen W Glam 23 G6 vil on Gower peninsula 6m/10km W of Mumbles Hd. SS 5388
Penmaenan Gwynedd 40 D4* loc on W side of Penmaenmawr. SH 7076
Penmaen-bach Point Gwynedd 40 D4* headland 2m/4km W of Conwy. SH 7478
Penmaen Dewi Welsh form of St David's Hd. See St David's.
Penmaenmawr Gwynedd 40 D4 resort on N Wales coast 4m/7km W of Conwy. Mt of Penmaen Mawr to SW (1550 ft or 472 metres). SH 7176
Penmaenpool Gwynedd 32 D3 ham on S bank of R Mawddach 2m/4km W of Dolgellau. SH 6918
Penmaen-rhos Clwyd 41 E4* suburb 2m/3km E of Colwyn Bay. SH 8778
Penmark (Penmarc) S Glam 15 F4 vil 3m/5km W of Barry. Remains of cas sacked by Owen Glendower. ST 0568
Penmarth Cornwall 2 C4* vil 4m/7km S of Redruth. SW 7035
Pen Mill Som 8 D3* E dist of Yeovil. ST 5616
Penmon Gwynedd 40 C3 loc on Anglesey 3m/5km NE of Beaumaris. Remains of partly Norman priory (A.M.). St Seiriol's Well (A.M.), named after 6c founder of original priory. Dovecote (A.M.) of *c.* 1600 to E. Cross (A.M.) of *c.* 1100 on hill to NW. SH 6380
Pen Morfa Dyfed 22 B3 headland 2m/3km N of Mathry. SM 8734
Penmorfa Gwynedd 32 C1 ham 2m/3km NW of Portmadoc. SH 5440
Penmynydd Gwynedd 40 C4 vil on Anglesey 3m/5km NW of Menai Br. SH 5074
Penn Bucks 18 D2 vil 3m/4km NW of Beaconsfield. Supposed ancestral home of William Penn, founder of Pennsylvania. SU 9193
Penn W Midlands, 35 E4 SW dist of Wolverhampton. SO 8995
Pennal Gwynedd 33 E4 vil 3m/5km W of Machynlleth across R Dovey. SH 6900
Pennal-isaf Gwynedd 33 E4* loc 1m N of Pennal. SH 7001
Pennan Grampian 83 F1 fishing vil on N coast, at foot of cliffs on **P. Bay,** W of **P. Head** and 2m/3km SE of Troup Hd. NJ 8465
Pennant Dyfed 24 B2 vil 4m/6km E of Aberaeron. SN 5163
Pennant Powys 33 F4 ham 4m/6km N of head of Clywedog Resr. SN 8797
Pennant Melangell Powys 33 G2 loc 2m/3km W of Llangynog. SJ 0226
Pennard W Glam 23 G6 vil on Gower peninsula 4m/7km W of Mumbles Hd. To W is **P. Castle,** ruined medieval cas on limestone rock overlooking P. Pill or Creek. SS 5688
Pennard, East Som 8 D1 vil 4m/6km SW of Shepton Mallet. ST 5937
Pennard, West Som 8 D1 vil 3m/5km E of Glastonbury. ST 5438
Pennar, East Dyfed 22 C5* loc adjoining Pembroke Dock to S. SM 9602
Pennerley Salop 34 A4/B4 ham 7m/11km N of Bishop's Castle. SO 3599
Pennines, The 117 mt range in England extending about 150m/240km from The Peak to The Cheviot; sometimes known as 'the backbone of England'. **The Pennine Way** is a footpath, largely undefined, from Edale, Derbys, to Kirk Yetholm, Borders; length about 250m/400km. SE 07
Penninghame Forest D & G 58 A4 state forest 4m/6km NW of Newton Stewart. NX 3568
Pennington Cumbria 46 D1 vil 2m/3km W of Ulverston. **Pennington Resr** 1m N. SD 2677
Pennington Gtr Manchester 42 C2* loc in Leigh 1km S of tn centre. SJ 6599
Pennington Hants 10 A5 loc 1m SW of Lymington. **Upr Pennington** loc 1km NW. **Lr Pennington** loc 1m SE. SZ 3194
Pennington Green Gtr Manchester 42 B1* loc 3m/4km E of Wigan. SD 6206
Penn, Lower Staffs 35 E4 vil 3m/5km SW of Wolverhampton. SO 8696
Pennocrucium Staffs. See Water Eaton.
Pennorth Powys 25 F5* loc 1m W of Llangorse Lake. SO 1125
Penn Street Bucks 18 D2 vil 2m/4km W of Amersham. SU 9296
Pennsylvania Avon 16 C4* loc 2m/4km W of Marshfield. ST 7473
Penny Bridge Cumbria 52 C6 vil 3m/5km NE of Ulverston. SD 3082
Pennycross Devon 4 B5* dist of Plymouth 2m/3km N of city centre. SX 4757
Pennygate Norfolk 39 G3* loc 5m/8km NE of Wroxham. TG 3422
Pennyghael S'clyde 69 D5 locality on S side of Loch Scridain, Mull, 9m/14km E of Bunessan. NM 5126
Pennygown Mull, S'clyde 68 D4 loc on Sound of Mull 2m/3km E of Salen. Ruined chapel, with decorated Celtic cross shaft, beside rd to E. NM 5942
Penny Green Derbys 44 A3* loc 1m SE of Whitwell. SK 5475
Pennyhole Bay Essex 31 F5* bay at entrance to Hamford Water 2m/3km NW of The Naze. TM 2526
Pennylands Lancs 42 A1* W dist of Skelmersdale. SD 4706
Pennymoor Devon 7 F4 ham 6m/9km W of Tiverton. SS 8611
Penny's Green Norfolk 39 F5* loc 1km NW of Wreningham. TM 1599
Pennyvenie, High S'clyde 56 E3* loc in colliery dist 2km NE of Dalmellington. NS 5007
Pennywell Tyne & Wear 61 H5* dist of Sunderland 3m/5km W of tn centre. NZ 3555
Penparc Dyfed 22 D1* ham 3m/4km NE of Cardigan. SN 2147
Penparcau Dyfed 32 D6 loc on E side of Pendinas and 1m SE of Aberystwyth across R Rheidol. SN 5980
Penpedairheol Gwent 15 H1* loc 3m/5km NW of Usk. SO 3303
Penpedairheol Mid Glam 15 F2* loc 1km NE of Gelligaer. ST 1497
Pen-Peles Dyfed 22 D1* headland 3m/4km W of Aberporth. SN 2152
Penperlleni Gwent 15 G1/H1* loc 4m/6km NE of Pontypool. SO 3204
Penpethy Cornwall 6 A6* loc 2m/3km NW of Camelford. SX 0886
Penpillick Cornwall 3 F3* loc 3m/4km SW of Lostwithiel. SX 0856
Penpol Cornwall 2 D4* loc on inlet of Restronguet Creek 4m/6km S of Truro. SW 8139
Penpoll Cornwall 3 F3* ham at head of **P. Creek** 2m/3km NE of Fowey across r. SX 1454
Penponds Cornwall 2 C4* ham 1m SW of Camborne. SW 6339
Penpont D & G 58 D2 vil on Scaur Water 2m/4km W of Thornhill. NX 8494
Penpont Powys 25 E5 loc 5m/7km W of Brecon. SN 9728
Penprysg Mid Glam 15 E3* loc 4m/7km E of Bridgend. SS 9682
Pen Pyrod Welsh form of Worms Hd, qv.
Penquit Devon 4 C5* ham 2km SE of Ivybridge. SX 6454
Penrest Cornwall 3 G1* loc 4m/7km S of Launceston. SX 3377
Penrherber Dyfed 23 E2 loc 2km SW of Newcastle Emlyn. SN 2239
Penrhiw Dyfed 23 E2* vil 4m/6km W of Newcastle Emlyn. SN 2540
Penrhiwceibr Mid Glam 15 F2 loc 1m S of Mountain Ash. ST 0597
Pen Rhiwfawr W Glam 14 C1* vil 2km S of Cwmllynfell. SN 7410
Penrhiwgarreg Gwent 15 G1* loc on E side of Abertillery. SO 2204
Penrhiwllan Dyfed 23 E2 ham 4m/6km E of Newcastle Emlyn. SN 3742
Penrhiwpal Dyfed 23 E2 ham 4m/7km NE of Newcastle Emlyn. SN 3445
Penrhiwtyn W Glam 14 C2* loc adjoining Neath to S. SS 7495
Penrhos Gwent 25 H6* ham 3m/4km N of Raglan. SO 4111
Penrhos Gwynedd 32 B2 ham on stream of same name 2m/4km W of Pwllheli. SH 3433
Penrhos Gwynedd 40 A3 loc on Holy I., Anglesey, 2m/3km SE of Holyhead. SH 2781
Penrhos Powys 14 D1 loc adjoining Ystradgynlais to NE, 2m/4km NE of Ystalyfera. SN 8011
Penrhos 32 B2* stream flowing E into Pwllheli harbour, Gwynedd, with R Rhyd-hir. SH 3634
Penrhosfeilw Standing Stones Gwynedd 40 A3* two standing stones (A.M.), about ten ft or three metres high, on Holy I., Anglesey, 2m/3km SW of Holyhead. SH 2280
Penrhos-garnedd Gwynedd 40 C4* loc 2m/3km SW of Bangor. SH 5570
Penrhyn Bay Gwynedd 41 E3 bay on E side of Lit Ormes Hd. Also the resort situated on it. SH 8281
Penrhyn Bodeilas Gwynedd 32 B1* headland on Caernarvon Bay 2km NE of Nefyn. SH 3142
Penrhyn Castle Dyfed 22 D1 cliff on W side of mouth of R Teifi 1m SE of Cemaes Hd. SN 1449
Penrhyn Castle Gwynedd 40 C4 mansion (NT) built in 19c in Norman style, 2km E of Bangor. SH 6071
Penrhyncoch Dyfed 32 D6 ham 4m/6km NE of Aberystwyth. SN 6484
Penrhyn Colmon Gwynedd 32 A2* headland at SW end of Porth Colmon 2km NW of Llangwnnadl. SH 1934
Penrhyn Cwmistir Gwynedd 32 A1* headland on N coast of Lleyn peninsula 2m/3km N of Tudweiliog. SH 2336
Penrhyndeudraeth Gwynedd 32 D1 vil 3m/5km E of Portmadoc and 6m/10km W of Ffestiniog. Slate-quarrying; explosives works. SH 6138
Penrhyn Du Gwynedd 32 B2* headland at S end of St Tudwal's Bay. SH 3226
Penrhyn Glas Gwynedd 32 B1* headland 3m/4km NE of Nefyn. SH 3343
Penrhyn Glas Gwynedd 40 B3* headland on NE coast of Anglesey 2m/3km S of Point Lynas. SH 4991
Penrhyn Mawr Gwynedd 32 A2* headland on Caernarvon Bay 4m/6km N of Aberdaron. SH 1632
Penrhyn Mawr Gwynedd 40 A3* headland on W coast of Holy I., Anglesey, 3m/5km SW of Holyhead. SH 2179
Penrhyn Melyn Gwynedd 32 A1/A2* headland 1m NW of Penllech. SH 2035
Penrhyn Nefyn Gwynedd 32 B1* headland at E end of Porth Dinllaen, W of Nefyn. SH 2941
Penrhyn Quarries. See Bethesda.
Penrhynside Gwynedd 41 E3* loc adjoining suburb of Penrhyn Bay to W. SH 8181
Penrhys Mid Glam 15 E2* loc 2m/3km E of Rhondda. ST 0094
Penrice W Glam 23 F6 ham on Gower peninsula 2m/4km NW of Oxwich Pt and 11m/17km W of Swansea. Ruins of Norman cas to N in park; annual Gower Agricultural Show held in grounds. SS 4987
Penrith Cumbria 53 E2 tn 18m/29km SE of Carlisle. Remains of 14c cas (A.M.). NY 5130
Penrose Cornwall 2 D2 vil 4m/6km SW of Padstow. SW 8770
Penrose Cornwall 6 B6* loc 5m/9km NW of Launceston. SX 2589
Penruddock Cumbria 52 D2 vil 6m/9km W of Penrith. NY 4227
Penry Bay S Glam 15 E4* small bay on Bristol Channel 3m/4km SE of Llantwit Major. ST 0066
Penryn Cornwall 2 D5 granite tn at head of inlet running down to Carrick Rds (R Fal), 2m/3km NW of Falmouth. SW 7834
Pensarn Dyfed 23 F4 loc on S side of Carmarthen across R Towy. SN 4119
Pensax H & W 26 C1 vil 6m/10km W of Stourport. SO 7269
Pensby Merseyside 41 H3* loc 2km NW of Heswall. SJ 2683
Penselwood Som 9 E2 vil 4m/6km NE of Wincanton. ST 7531
Pensford Avon 16 B5 vil 6m/10km S of Bristol. ST 6163
Penshaw Tyne & Wear 61 G6 large loc in coal-mining area 3m/4km N of Houghton-le-Spring. **Penshaw Monmt** (NT) to NE is Doric temple built in 1844 to commemorate 1st Earl of Durham. NZ 3253
Penshurst Kent 12 B3 vil on R Medway 5m/7km W of Tonbridge. **P. Place,** 14c manor hse. TQ 5243
Pensilva Cornwall 3 G2 vil 4m/7km NE of Liskeard. SX 2959
Pensnett W Midlands 35 E5 loc in Dudley 2m/4km SW of tn centre. SO 9188
Penston Lothian 66 C2* loc 1km E of Macmerry. NT 4472
Pentewan Cornwall 3 E3 vil 3m/5km S of St Austell. SX 0147
Pentir Gwynedd 40 C4 vil 3m/5km S of Bangor. SH 5767
Pentire Cornwall 2 D2*, W dist of Newquay. SW 7961
Pentire Point Cornwall 3 E1 headland (NT) on N coast at N end of Padstow Bay. SW 9280
Pentire Point, East Cornwall 2 D2* headland at N end of Crantock Beach and SW end of Fistral Bay, 2m/3km W of Newquay. SW 7861
Pentire Point, West Cornwall 2 D2* headland (NT) at W end of Crantock Beach 3m/4km W of Newquay. SW 7761
Pentire, West Cornwall 2 D2 ham near coast 3m/4km W of Newquay. SW 7760
Pentland Firth 89 A7, B7 sea area between Orkney and N coast of Scottish mainland. ND 28, 38
Pentland Hills 65 G3–H2 range of grass-covered hills, largely composed of Old Red Sandstone, running some 16m/26km from S of Edinburgh towards Carnwath. Numerous resrs. Summit is Scald Law, 1898 ft or 579 metres. NT 15
Pentland Skerries Orkney 89 B8 group of four small uninhabited islands at E end of Pentland Firth 3m/5km S of S Ronaldsay. The islands are Muckle Skerry (the largest, with a lighthouse), Lit Skerry, Louther Skerry, and Clettack Skerry. ND 47
Pentlepoir Dyfed 22 D5* loc 2km W of Saundersfoot. SN 1105
Pentlow Essex 30 C3 ham on R Stour opp Cavendish, 3m/5km W of Long Melford. Loc of **P. Street** 1km E. TL 8146
Pentney Norfolk 38 C3 vil 7m/11km NW of Swaffham. TF 7213
Penton Grafton Hants 10 A1* ham 3m/4km NW of Andover. SU 3247
Penton Mewsey Hants 10 A1 vil 3m/4km NW of Andover. SU 3347
Pentonville London 19 G3* loc in borough of Islington 2m/3km N of Charing Cross. TQ 3083
Pentraeth Gwynedd 40 C4 vil on Anglesey 5m/8km N of Menai Br. SH 5278
Pentre Clwyd 34 A1 loc 2m/3km N of Chirk. SJ 2840
Pentre Clwyd 41 G5 loc 4m/6km NW of Ruthin. SJ 0862
Pentre Clwyd 41 H4* loc on SE side of Queensferry. SJ 3267
Pentre Clwyd 41 H6* loc 2m/3km SE of Ruabon. SJ 3141
Pentre Mid Glam 15 E2 loc in Rhondda. SS 9696
Pentre Powys 33 G5 loc 4m/7km SW of Newtown. SO 0686
Pentre Powys 33 H5* loc 1m SE of Kerry. SO 1589
Pentre Salop 34 A6* loc 3m/4km S of Clun. SO 3076
Pentre Salop 34 B3 vil 9m/14km NW of Shrewsbury. SJ 3617
Pentre W Glam 23 G6* loc in Swansea 1m N of tn centre. SS 6594
Pentre Bach Clwyd 41 G4* loc 1m NW of Bagillt. SJ 2176
Pentrebach Dyfed 24 B3* loc 2m/3km W of Lampeter. SN 5547
Pentrebach Mid Glam 15 F3* loc 1m E of Pontypridd. ST 0889
Pentrebach Mid Glam 15 F1 vil 2m/3km SE of Merthyr Tydfil. SO 0603
Pentre-bach Powys 25 E4 loc 3m/5km N of Sennybridge. SN 9032
Pentrebeirdd Powys 33 H3* loc 5m/8km NW of Welshpool. SJ 1813

Pentre Berw Gwynedd 40 B4 vil on Anglesey 2m/4km S of Llangefni across Malltraeth Marsh. SH 4772
Pentre-bont Gwynedd 40 D6* loc on R Lledr opp Dolwyddelan. SH 7352
Pentre-cagal Dyfed 23 E2 loc 2m/3km E of Newcastle Emlyn. SN 3340
Pentre-celyn Clwyd 41 G5/G6 vil 4m/6km S of Ruthin. SJ 1453
Pentre-chwyth W Glam 23 H6 loc in Swansea 2km NE of tn centre across R Tawe. SS 6795
Pentre-cwrt Dyfed 23 E2 vil 2m/4km SW of Llandyssul. SN 3838
Pentre-dwr W Glam 14 C2 loc 4m/6km NE of Swansea. SS 6996
Pentrefelin Dyfed 23 G3* loc 2m/3km NW of Llandeilo. SN 5922
Pentrefelin Gwynedd 32 C1 ham 2m/3km NE of Criccieth. SH 5239
Pentrefelin Gwynedd 40 B2* loc 1km S of Amlwch, Anglesey. SH 4392
Pentrefelin Gwynedd 41 E4 vil 4m/6km SW of Colwyn Bay. Ancient burial-chamber 1km W. SH 8074
Pentre Ffwrndan Clwyd 41 H4* loc adjoining Flint to SE. SJ 2572
Pentrefoelas Clwyd 41 E6 ham 8m/12km SE of Llanrwst. SH 8751
Pentre-galar Dyfed 22 D3 loc 2m/3km S of Crymmych. SN 1731
Pentregat Dyfed 23 E1* ham 3m/5km SE of Llangranog. SN 3551
Pentre Gwenlais Dyfed 23 G4 ham 3m/4km N of Ammanford. SN 6016
Pentre Halkyn Clwyd 41 G4 loc 1m NW of Halkyn and 2m/4km SE of Holywell. SJ 2072
Pentre Ifan Dyfed 22 D2* ancient burial-chamber (A.M.) 3m/5km SE of Newport. SN 0937
Pentre-llwyn-llwyd Powys 25 E3 loc 5m/9km NW of Builth Wells. SN 9654
Pentre-llyn Dyfed 24 B1* loc just W of Llanilar. SN 6175
Pentremeurig Welsh form of Pentre Meyrick, qv.
Pentre Meyrick (Pentremeurig) S Glam 15 E4* ham 2m/3km NW of Cowbridge. SS 9675
Pentrepiod Gwent 15 G2 loc 2km NW of Pontypool. SO 2602
Pentre-poeth Gwent 15 G3 loc 3m/4km W of Newport. ST 2686
Pentre Poeth W Glam 23 H5* loc on N side of Morriston 4m/6km N of Swansea tn centre. SS 6698
Pentre'r-felin Dyfed 24 C3* loc 2m/4km E of Lampeter. SN 6148
Pentre'r Felin Gwynedd 41 E4* loc 1km S of Eglwysbach. SH 8069
Pentre'r-felin Powys 25 E5 loc 1m N of Sennybridge. SN 9230
Pentre Saron Clwyd 41 F5* loc 4m/6km S of Denbigh. SJ 0260
Pentre Tafarnyfedw Gwynedd 41 E5 ham 1m NE of Llanrwst. SH 8162
Pentre-tŷ-gwyn Gwynedd 24 D4* loc 4m/6km E of Llandovery. SN 8135
Pentrich Derbys 43 H5 vil 2km NW of Ripley. SK 3852
Pentridge Dorset 9 G3 vil 3m/4km E of Sixpenny Handley. SU 0317
Pen-trwyn Gwynedd 40 D3* headland 1m N of Llandudno. SH 7883
Pentwyn Dyfed 23 G4* loc 1km S of Cross Hands. SN 5611
Pentwyn Gwent 15 G1* loc in Abersychan 2m/3km NW of Pontypool. SO 2603
Pen-twyn Gwent 15 G2* loc 1km W of Llanhilleth. SO 2000
Pen-twyn Gwent 16 A1 vil 2m/4km S of Monmouth. SO 5209
Pentwyn Mid Glam 15 F1* ham 2m/3km S of Rhymney. SO 1004
Pentwyn Mid Glam 15 F3* loc 1km SW of Pentyrch. ST 0981
Pentwyn Berthlwyd Mid Glam 15 F2* loc 1km S of Treharris. ST 1096
Pentwyn-mawr Gwent 15 G2* loc 2km SW of Newbridge. Industrial estate to W. ST 1996
Pentyrch Mid Glam 15 F3 vil 6m/10km NW of Cardiff. ST 1081
Penuwch Dyfed 24 B2 loc 6m/9km W of Tregaron. SN 5962
Penwhapple Reservoir S'clyde 56 C4* resr 2m/4km N of Barr. NX 2697
Penwhirn Reservoir D & G 57 B6* resr 4m/7km NW of New Luce. NX 1269
Penwith 118 admin dist of Cornwall.
Penwithick Cornwall 3 E3* vil in china clay dist 2m/4km N of St Austell. SX 0256
Penwood Hants 17 H5 loc 1m NE of Highclere. SU 4461
Penwortham, Higher Lancs 47 F5 suburb 2m/3km W of Preston across R Ribble. **Lr Penwortham** loc 1m E. **P. Lane** loc 2m/3km SE. SD 5128
Penwyllt Powys 24 D6 loc 7m/11km NE of Ystalyfera. Quarries. SN 8515
Penybanc Dyfed 23 G3 ham 2km NW of Llandeilo. SN 6124
Pen-y-banc Dyfed 23 G4* loc 1m SW of Ammanford. SN 6111
Pen-y-bont Clwyd 33 H2 ham 2km E of Llangedwyn. SJ 2123
Pen-y-bont Clwyd 41 H5* loc 2km SE of Rhydtalog. SJ 2453
Pen-y-bont Clwyd 41 H6* loc 2m/3km SW of Ruabon. SJ 2841
Pen-y-bont Dyfed 23 E3* loc 8m/13km NW of Carmarthen. SN 3027
Penybont Dyfed 32 D5* loc 2m/4km SW of Talybont. SN 6288
Pen-y-bont Gwent 15 G1* loc adjoining Abertillery to N. SO 2105
Penybont Powys 25 F2 vil on R Ithon 4m/6km NE of Llandrindod Wells. SO 1164
Penybontfawr Powys 33 G2 vil on R Tanat 5m/8km NW of Llanfyllin. SJ 0824
Pen-y-bryn Clwyd 41 H6* loc 2m/4km W of Ruabon. SJ 2644
Pen-y-bryn Dyfed 22 D2* ham 2m/3km S of Cardigan. SN 1742
Penycae Clwyd 41 H6 vil 2m/3km W of Ruabon. SJ 2745
Pen-y-cae Powys 24 D6 loc 6m/9km NE of Ystalyfera. SN 8413
Pen-y-cae-mawr Gwent 15 H2* loc 2m/3km SE of Llantrisant. ST 4195
Penycaerau Gwynedd 32 A2* loc 2m/3km E of Aberdaron. SH 1927
Pen-y-cefn Clwyd 41 G4* loc 2m/4km NE of Tremeirchion. SJ 1175
Pen-y-chain Gwynedd 32 C1* headland on Tremadoc Bay 4m/6km E of Pwllheli. Large holiday camp 1m inland. SH 4335
Pen y Cil Gwynedd 32 A2 headland at W end of Aberdaron Bay. SH 1523
Pen-y-clawdd Gwent 16 A1 ham 3m/4km E of Raglan. SO 4507
Pen-y-coed Powys 34 A3* loc 5m/8km N of Welshpool. SJ 2414
Pen-y-coedcae Mid Glam 15 F3 vil 2m/3km SW of Pontypridd. ST 0687
Penycrocbren Powys 33 F5* hill and site of Roman fort 2m/4km NW of head of Clywedog Resr. SN 8593
Pen-y-crug Powys. See Brecon.
Pen-y-cwm Dyfed 22 B3 ham 6m/10km E of St David's. SM 8423
Pen-y-darren Mid Glam 15 F1 loc in Merthyr Tydfil 1km N of tn centre. SO 0507
Pen-y-fai Mid Glam 15 E3* loc 2km N of Bridgend. SS 8982
Pen y Fan Powys 25 E5 one of the two chief peaks of Brecon Beacons, qv. SO 0121
Pen-y-fan Pond Gwent 15 G2 lake 2km W of Llanhilleth. SO 1900
Pen-y-felin Clwyd 41 G4* ham 1km W of Nannerch. SJ 1569
Pen-y-ffordd Clwyd 41 G3* loc 2m/3km NW of Mostyn. SJ 1381
Pen-y-ffordd Clwyd 41 H5 vil 3m/4km S of Hawarden. SJ 3061
Penyffrid Gwynedd 40 C5* loc 4m/6km S of Caernarvon. SH 5056
Pen y Gadair Gwynedd 33 E3 central peak and summit of Cader Idris. Height 2927 ft or 893 metres. SH 7113
Pen-y-Gader-fawr Powys 25 G5 mt on Black Mts 4m/6km W of Llanthony. Height 2624 ft or 800 metres. SO 2228
Pen-y-gaer Dyfed. See Llanybydder.
Pen y Gaer Powys 25 F5* loc 2km W of Tretower. Site of Roman fort. SO 1621
Pen-y-garn Dyfed 32 D5* loc adjoining Bow Street to N. SN 6285
Penygarn Gwent 15 G2* loc 1km NE of Pontypool. SO 2801
Penygarnedd Powys 33 G2 ham 2m/3km SW of Llanrhaeadr-ym-Mochnant. SJ 1023
Pen-y-garreg Reservoir Powys 24 D2/25 E2 one of the series of large resrs in R Elan valley. It is 4m/6km W of Rhayader. SN 9167
Pen-y-genffordd Powys 25 F4 loc 3m/4km SE of Talgarth. SO 1730
Pen-y-ghent N Yorks 48 B1 mt 2m/3km NE of Horton in Ribblesdale. Height 2273 ft or 693 metres. SD 8373
Pen-y-Gogarth Welsh form of Gt Ormes Hd. See Ormes Head, Great.
Pen-y-Graig Gwynedd 32 A2* ham on W side of Llangwnnadl. SH 2033
Pen-y-graig Mid Glam 15 E2 loc 3m/5km SE of Rhondda. SS 9991
Penygroes Dyfed 22 D2* loc 2m/3km SE of Eglwyswrw. SN 1535
Penygroes Dyfed 23 G4 vil 3m/4km W of Ammanford. SN 5813
Penygroes Gwynedd 40 B6 vil 6m/10km S of Caernarvon. SH 4753
Pen-y-groes S Glam 15 G3* loc 3m/5km NE of Cardiff. ST 2181
Pen-y-gwely Reservoir Clwyd 34 A2* small resr 5m/7km NW of Oswestry. SJ 2232
Pen-y-gwryd Gwynedd 40 D5 loc 4m/7km E of Capel Curig. Site of Roman camp. SH 6655
Pen-y-lan S Glam 15 G3* loc in Cardiff 2km N of city centre. ST 1978
Pen-y-maes Clwyd 41 G4* loc adjoining Holywell to E. SJ 1975
Penymynydd Clwyd 41 H5* loc adjoining Pen-y-ffordd to N. SJ 3062
Pen-y-parc Clwyd 41 H4* loc 1m S of Halkyn. SJ 2169
Pen-y-parc Gwynedd 40 B5* headland at N end of Malltraeth Bay, W coast of Anglesey. SH 3664
Pen-y-park H & W 25 G3 loc 3m/5km NE of Hay-on-Wye. SO 2744
Pen-y-pass Gwynedd 40 D5* loc at head of Pass of Llanberis, 3m/4km E of Snowdon summit. SH 6455
Penyraber Dyfed 22 B2/C2* loc in N part of Fishguard, beside Fishguard harbour. SM 9537
Penyrenglyn Mid Glam 15 E2* loc in Rhondda valley 2m/4km NW of Rhondda. SS 9497
Pen-yr-heol Gwent 26 A6 loc 3m/4km NE of Raglan. SO 4311
Penyrheol Mid Glam 15 F3* loc 2km NW of Caerphilly. ST 1488
Penyrheol W Glam 23 G5* loc adjoining Gorseinon to N. SS 5899
Penyrheol W Glam 23 G6* loc in Swansea 3m/4km W of tn centre. SS 6192
Pen-yr-Heolgerrig Mid Glam 15 E1* loc 1m W of Merthyr Tydfil. See also Heolgerrig. SO 0306
Pen-y-rhwbyn Dyfed 22 D1* headland 4m/6km N of Cardigan. SO 1851
Pen-y-sarn Gwynedd 40 B3 vil 2m/3km SE of Amlwch, Anglesey. SH 4690
Pen-y-stryt Clwyd 41 G6 ham 6m/10km SE of Ruthin. SJ 1951
Penywaun Mid Glam 15 E1* loc 2m/4km NW of Aberdare. SN 9704
Penywern W Glam 14 D1* loc adjoining Ystalyfera to N. SN 7609
Penzance Cornwall 2 A5 resort and port 24m/39km SW of Truro. Boat and helicopter services to Isles of Scilly. SW 4730
Peopleton H & W 26 D3 vil 3m/5km N of Pershore. SO 9350
Peover Heath Ches 42 D4* ham 4m/7km NE of Holmes Chapel. SJ 7667
Peover, Lower Ches 42 C4 vil 6m/9km E of Northwich. SJ 7474
Peper Harow Surrey 11 F1 ham 2m/4km W of Godalming. SU 9344
Peplow Salop 34 C2 ham 3m/5km SE of Hodnet. Hall is of early 18c. SJ 6324
Pepper Arden N Yorks 54 C4 loc 7m/11km NW of Northallerton. NZ 2901
Peppermill Dam Fife 72 C5/D5 lake 2m/3km NE of Kincardine-on-Forth. NS 9489
Pepper's Green Essex 20 C1* loc 3m/4km SE of Leaden Roding. TL 6110
Pepperstock Beds 29 E5* ham 2m/3km S of Luton. TL 0818
Perceton S'clyde 64 B4 loc in E part of Irvine New Tn. NS 3440
Percival Hall N Yorks 48 D2* Elizn hse with hillside garden 2km NE of Appletreewick. SE 0661
Percuil River Cornwall 2 D5 r rising near Treworlas and flowing into Carrick Rds (R Fal) at St Mawes, opp Falmouth. SW 8533
Percyhorner Grampian 83 G1 loc 2m/4km SW of Fraserburgh. NJ 9665
Percy Main Tyne & Wear 61 G4 loc in N Tyneside dist 2km SW of N Shields. NZ 3367
Percy's Cross Nthmb 67 G6 shaft of cross 1m SE of Wooperton, marking spot where leader of Lancastrians was killed in Battle of Hedgeley Moor (qv), 1464. NU 0519
Perdiswell H & W 26 D2* loc in N part of Worcester. SO 8557
Pergins Island Dorset 9 G5* small uninhabited island near N end of Holes Bay W of Poole. SZ 0092
Peris 40 C5* r rising at Pen-y-Pass, at head of Pass of Llanberis, Gwynedd, and flowing NW through Llyn Peris into Llyn Padarn, whence it emerges as R Rhythallt, qv. SH 5860
Periton Som 7 G1* loc adjoining Minehead to S. SS 9645
Perivale London 19 F3 loc in borough of Ealing 9m/14km W of Charing Cross. TQ 1683
Perkin's Village Devon 7 H5* ham 7m/11km E of Exeter. SY 0291
Perkinsville Durham 61 G6* loc on N side of vil of Pelton, 2m/3km NW of Chester-le-Street. NZ 2553
Perlethorpe Notts 44 B4 ham on E edge of Thoresby Park 2m/4km N of Ollerton. SK 6471
Perranarworthal Cornwall 2 D4 vil 3m/5km N of Penryn. SW 7738
Perran Bay Cornwall 2 C3 alternative name for Ligger Bay, qv.
Perran Bay Cornwall 2 C3 bay on N coast extending from Ligger Pt in the N to Cligga Hd in the S. SW 7354
Perran Beach Cornwall. See Ligger Bay.
Perran Downs Cornwall 2 B5* loc 4m/7km S of Hayle. SW 5530
Perranporth Cornwall 2 C3 N coast resort 6m/9km SW of Newquay. SW 7554
Perranuthnoe Cornwall 2 B5 vil on S coast 4m/6km E of Penzance across Mount's Bay. SW 5329
Perranwell Station Cornwall 2 D4 loc 3m/5km N of Penryn. SW 7739
Perran Wharf Cornwall 2 D4* loc 3m/4km N of Penryn. SW 7738
Perranzabuloe Cornwall 2 D3 ham 2m/3km SE of Perranporth. SW 7752
Perrot, South Dorset 8 C4 vil 3m/5km SE of Crewkerne. ST 4706
Perrott, North Som 8 C3 vil 2m/4km E of Crewkerne. ST 4709
Perrott's Brook Glos 17 E1 loc 3m/4km N of Cirencester. SP 0106
Perry W Midlands 35 F5/G5* loc in Birmingham 3m/5km N of city centre. SP 0692
Perry 34 B3* r rising N of Oswestry, Salop, and flowing generally SE into R Severn 4m/7km NW of Shrewsbury. SJ 4416
Perry Barr W Midlands 35 G5 dist of Birmingham 3m/5km N of city centre. SP 0791
Perry Beeches W Midlands 35 F5* N dist of Birmingham. SP 0593
Perry Crofts Staffs 35 G4* loc in Tamworth to N of tn centre. SK 2004
Perry, East and **West** Cambs 29 F1 adjoining hams on S side of Grafham Water. Sailing club at E Perry. TL 1466
Perryfields H & W 26 D1* loc in N part of Bromsgrove. SO 9571
Perry Green Essex 30 C5* loc 3m/5km E of Braintree. TL 8022
Perry Green Herts 29 H6 ham 5m/8km N of Ware. TL 4317
Perry Green Wilts 16 D3* ham adjoining Charlton to E, 3m/4km NE of Malmesbury. ST 9689
Perry Hall W Midlands 35 F4* loc in Wolverhampton 3m/4km NE of tn centre. SJ 9600
Perrymead Avon 16 C5* S dist of Bath. ST 7563
Perry's Dam Cumbria 53 G1* small artificial lake 2km S of Nenthead. NY 7841
Perry Street Kent 20 C4 dist of Northfleet 1km S of R Thames. TQ 6373
Pershall Staffs 35 E2 ham 1m NW of Eccleshall. SJ 8129
Pershore H & W 26 D3 tn on R Avon and centre of a fruit-growing area. SO 9446
Persley Grampian 77 H1* loc on R Don 3m/5km NW of centre of Aberdeen. NJ 9009
Pertenhall Beds 29 E2 vil 2m/3km SW of Kimbolton. TL 0865
Perth Tayside 73 E2 ancient tn on R Tay 31m/50km N of Edinburgh. Small harbour downstream. TV and VHF radio transmitting stn. Industries include whisky distilling and blending, dyeing and dry-cleaning, glass mnfre. Centre of livestock trade. Airfield (Scone) to NE. NO 1123
Perthcelyn Mid Glam 15 F2* loc 2km S of Mountain Ash. ST 0597
Perthy Salop 34 B1 ham 2m/4km W of Ellesmere. SJ 3633

Perton Staffs 35 E4* loc 4m/6km W of Wolverhampton. SO 8598
Perwick Bay Isle of Man 46 A6 southward-facing bay on S side of Port St Mary. SC 2067
Pestalozzi Children's Village E Sussex 12 D5* situated at Sedlescombe. Founded in 1960 for refugee children. TQ 7817
Pested Kent 21 F6* loc 6m/10km S of Faversham. TR 0051
Peterborough Cambs 37 G4 industrial and cathedral city on R Nene 73m/117km N of London. New Tn designated 1967. Cathedral Norman and later. 17c guildhall. Many brick works in vicinity, esp to S. Other industries include diesel engines, rly engineering, toy mnfre, agricultural products esp sugar beet. East of England Agricultural Showground (see Alwalton). TL 1998
Peterchurch H & W 25 H4 vil 8m/12km NW of Pontrilas. SO 3438
Peterculter Grampian 77 G1 vil at confluence of Leuchar Burn and R Dee 7m/11km SW of Aberdeen. NJ 8400
Peterhead Grampian 83 H2 fishing port and oilfield supply base on NE coast 27m/44km N of Aberdeen and the most easterly tn on Scottish mainland. **P. Bay** forms large harbour to S. Electricity power stn. Industries include ammonia, petro-chemicals, and woollen mnfre, fish-canning, food-processing, boat-building, distilling, engineering. Industrial estate developments at Dales Farm and Upperton to S. See also St Fergus. NK 1346
Peterlee Durham 54 D1 New Tn designated 1948, 7m/11km NW of Hartlepool. Industries include light engineering, textiles. NZ 4240
Petersfield Hants 10 D3 tn 11m/18km NE of Portsmouth. SU 7423
Petersfinger Wilts 9 H2* loc 2km SE of Salisbury. SU 1629
Peter's Green Herts 29 F5 ham 3m/5km N of Harpenden. TL 1419
Petersham London 19 F4 loc in borough of Richmond on right bank of R Thames 9m/14km SW of Charing Cross. TQ 1873
Peters Marland Devon 6 D4 ham 4m/6km S of Torrington. SS 4713
Peterstone Wentlloog (Llanbedr Gwynllwg) Gwent 15 G3 vil near coast 6m/9km SW of Newport. ST 2680
Peterston-super-Ely (Llanbedr-y-fro) S Glam 15 F4 vil 6m/10km W of Cardiff.
Peterstow H & W 26 B5 vil 2m/4km W of Ross-on-Wye. SO 5624
Peter Tavy Devon 4 B3 vil on W side of Dartmoor 3m/5km NE of Tavistock. SX 5177
Petham Kent 13 F2 vil 4m/7km S of Canterbury. TR 1251
Petherick, Little Cornwall 2 D1 vil 4m/7km W of Wadebridge. SW 9172
Petherton, North Som 8 B1 vil 3m/4km S of Bridgwater. ST 2933
Petherton, South Som 8 C3 small tn 5m/8km E of Ilminster. ST 4316
Petherwin Gate Cornwall 6 B6* ham just S of N Petherwin and 4m/7km NW of Launceston. SX 2889
Petherwin, North Cornwall 6 B6 vil 5m/7km NW of Launceston. SX 2889
Petherwin, South Cornwall 6 C6 vil 2m/3km SW of Launceston. SX 3081
Petre Bank Ches 43 E3* loc adjoining Poynton to E. SJ 9383
Petrockstow Devon 6 D4 vil 4m/6km NW of Hatherleigh. SS 5109
Pett E Sussex 13 E5 vil 5m/7km NE of Hastings. TQ 8713
Pettaugh Suffolk 31 F2 vil 2m/4km S of Debenham. TM 1659
Petta Water Shetland. See Sand Water.
Petteridge Kent 12 C3 ham 1km SW of Brenchley. TQ 6641
Petteril 60 A5 r rising at Penruddock, Cumbria, and flowing N into R Eden on E side of Carlisle. NY 4156
Petteril Green Cumbria 52 D1* loc on R Petteril 2m/3km S of High Hesket. Site of Roman camp to N. NY 4741
Pettinain S'clyde 65 F4 vil 2m/3km S of Carstairs Junction across R Clyde. NS 9543
Pettistree Suffolk 31 G3 vil 1km SW of Wickham Mkt. TM 2954
Petton Devon 7 G3 ham 3m/5km NE of Bampton. ST 0024
Petton Salop 34 B2* loc 2km W of Burlton. SJ 4326
Pett Street Kent 13 F2* loc 2m/3km E of Wye. TR 0847
Petts Wood London 20 B5 dist in borough of Bromley 2km NW of Orpington. Named after wd (partly NT) to N. TQ 4467
Pettycur Fife 73 F5 loc with small harbour at S end of Kinghorn. NT 2686
Petty Pool Ches 42 C4 lake 3m/5km SW of Northwich. SJ 6170
Petuaria Humberside. See Brough.
Petworth W Sussex 11 F3 small tn below S Downs 13m/21km NE of Chichester. Petworth Hse (NT), 17c–19c, with large deer park. SU 9721
Pevensey E Sussex 12 C6 vil 4m/7km NE of Eastbourne. The Roman *Anderida*. Remains of Norman cas within walls of Roman fort (A.M.). 1m S is **P. Bay,** with loc of same name whose hses extend 3km along coast. To N, **P. Levels,** well-drained marshland. TQ 6404
Peverell Devon 4 B5* dist of Plymouth N of Central Park. SX 4756
Peveril Castle Derbys 43 F3* ruined Norman cas (A.M.) on rocky limestone hill to S of Castleton. SK 1482
Peveril Point Dorset 9 G6 headland at S end of Swanage Bay. SZ 0478
Pewet Island Essex 21 F1* marshy island off right bank of R Blackwater estuary. Bradwell Creek passes between island and Bradwell Waterside. TL 9907
Pewit Island Essex 31 E6* island in Pyefleet Channel on N side of Mersea I. TM 0516
Pewit Island Essex 31 F5 uninhabited marshy island 3m/5km NW of The Naze. TM 2226
Pewit Island Hants 10 C4* small uninhabited island in Portsmouth Harbour. SU 6003
Pewsey Wilts 17 F5 small tn on branch of R Avon near its source, 6m/10km S of Marlborough. 2km S, P. White Horse cut in chalk on side of P. Hill in 1937. Tn is near E end of **Vale of Pewsey,** plain surrounded on N, S, E sides by chalk hills and extending to Devizes in the W. SU 1660
Pewsey Wharf Wilts 17 F5* loc on Kennet and Avon Canal 1km N of Pewsey. SU 1561
Pewsham Wilts 16 D4* loc 3m/4km SE of Chippenham. ST 9471
Phantassie Lothian 66 D1 loc on E side of E Linton. Birthplace of Sir John Rennie, 1761-1821, engineer. Notable dovecote (NTS). NT 5977
Pharay Orkney. Alternative spelling of Faray, qv.
Pheasant's Hill Bucks 18 C3* ham 4m/7km W of Marlow. SU 7887
Philadelphia Tyne & Wear 61 G6/H6 loc 2km N of Houghton-le-Spring. NZ 3352
Philiphaugh Borders 66 C5 estate 2m/3km W of Selkirk, and site of battle of 1645 in which Montrose was defeated by Covenanters under Leslie. NT 4528
Phillack Cornwall 2 B4 loc to N of Hayle across canal. SW 5638
Philleigh Cornwall 2 D4 vil 4m/7km NE of St Mawes. SW 8739
Phillipps House Wilts. See Dinton.
Phillipstown Mid Glam 15 F1* loc 3m/4km N of Bargoed. SO 1403
Philorth Grampian 83 H1 loc 3m/4km S of Fraserburgh. Water of P. is stream on E side of loc running NE into Fraserburgh Bay. NK 0062
Philpstoun Lothian 65 G1 vil 3m/5km E of Linlithgow. **Old P.** is loc nearly 1m E. NT 0477
Phocle Green H & W 26 B5* loc 2m/4km NE of Ross-on-Wye. SO 6226
Phoenix Green Hants 18 C5 vil 2m/4km NE of Hook. SU 7555
Piall 4 C5* r in Devon rising on S Dartmoor and flowing S into R Yealm 2km SE of Sparkwell. SX 6057
Pib 24 B5* r rising 2m/4km E of Alltwalis, Dyfed, and flowing SE then E to join R Marlais at Brechfa. SN 5230
Pibsbury Som 8 C2 ham adjoining Huish Episcopi and 2km E of Langport. ST 4426
Pica Cumbria 52 A3 ham 4m/6km NE of Whitehaven. NY 0222
Picardy Stone Grampian. See Insch.
Piccadilly Corner Norfolk 39 F6 ham 3m/4km NE of Harleston. TM 2786
Piccotts End Herts 19 E1* loc in N part of Hemel Hempstead. TL 0509
Pickburn S Yorks 44 A1* loc adjoining Brodsworth to E. SE 5107
Picken End H & W 26 C3* loc 3m/5km SE of Gt Malvern. SO 8142
Pickenham, North Norfolk 38 D4 vil 3m/5km SE of Swaffham. **S Pickenham** vil 2m/3km S. TF 8606
Pickering N Yorks 55 F6 mkt tn at foot of N Yorks Moors 16m/25km W of Scarborough. Remains of Norman cas (A.M.). Pickering Vale Museum and Arts Centre. **Vale of Pickering** broad valley, formerly arm of the sea, between Pickering and Malton. SE 7984
Pickering Nook Durham 61 F5* loc adjoining vil of Hobson to S. NZ 1755
Picket Piece Hants 10 B1 loc 2m/3km NE of Andover. SU 3947
Picket Post Hants 9 H4 loc 3m/5km E of Ringwood. SU 1906
Pickford W Midlands 35 H6* ham 4m/7km NW of Coventry. Ham of **P. Green** adjoins to S. SP 2781
Pickhill N Yorks 54 C6 vil 5m/8km SE of Leeming. SE 3483
Picklecombe Point Cornwall 4 B5* headland at N end of Cawsand Bay. SX 4551
Picklescott Salop 34 B4 ham 4m/6km N of Church Stretton. SO 4399
Pickmere Ches 42 C3 vil 3m/5km NE of Northwich. **Pick Mere,** lake to W. SJ 6977
Pickney Som 8 A2* ham 4m/6km NW of Taunton. ST 1929
Pickstock Salop 34 D2* loc 3m/4km NW of Newport. SJ 7223
Picktree Durham 61 G6 loc 1m NE of Chester-le-Street. NZ 2853
Pickup Bank Lancs 48 A5* ham 2m/3km E of Darwen. SD 7222
Pickwell Devon 6 C2* loc near N coast 6m/9km SW of Ilfracombe. SS 4540
Pickwell Leics 36 D3 vil 5m/8km SE of Melton Mowbray. SK 7811
Pickworth Leics 37 E3 ham 5m/8km NW of Stamford. SK 9913
Pickworth Lincs 37 F2 vil 8m/12km S of Sleaford. TF 0433
Picton Ches 42 A4 vil 4m/6km NE of Chester. SJ 4371
Picton Clwyd 41 G3* loc 2m/3km S of Point of Air. SJ 1182
Picton N Yorks 54 C4 vil 3m/5km S of Yarm. NZ 4107
Picton Ferry Dyfed 23 E4 loc 1km N of St Clears. SN 2717
Picton Park Dyfed 22 C4 estate of **Picton Castle** (Castell Pictwn), 13c with early 19c additions, 4m/6km E of Haverfordwest. SN 0013
Picton Point Dyfed 22 C4* headland at confluence of Rs Eastern and Western Cleddau 4m/6km SE of Haverfordwest. SN 0011
Pict's Cross H & W 26 B5* loc 3m/5km NW of Ross-on-Wye. SO 5626
Piddinghoe E Sussex 12 B6 vil on R Ouse 2km NW of Newhaven. TQ 4302
Piddington Bucks 18 C2* loc 4m/6km W of High Wycombe. SU 8094
Piddington Northants 28 C2 vil 5m/8km SE of Northampton. SP 8054
Piddington Oxon 28 B5 vil 5m/8km SE of Bicester. SP 6417
Piddle 9 F5 r rising at Alton Pancras in Dorset and flowing generally SE through Puddletown and to N of Wareham into Poole Harbour. Also known as R Trent. SY 9488
Piddle Brook 26 D3* r rising E of Worcester and flowing S into R Avon between Wyre Piddle and Pershore, H & W. SO 9546
Piddlehinton Dorset 9 E4 vil 3m/5km NW of Puddletown. SY 7197
Piddle, North H & W 26 D2* vil 7m/12km E of Worcester. SO 9654
Piddletrenthide Dorset 9 E4 vil 6m/10km N of Dorchester. ST 7000
Pidley Cambs 37 G6 vil 2m/4km SE of Warboys. TL 3377
Pie Corner H & W 26 B2* loc 4m/7km N of Bromyard. SO 6461
Pield Heath London 19 E3* loc in borough of Hillingdon 2km S of Uxbridge. TQ 0681
Piel Island Cumbria 46 D2 island on S side of Piel Channel between Roa I. and the S end of Walney I. Ferry to Roa I. Remains of 14c cas. SD 2363
Piercebridge Durham 54 B3 vil on R Tees 5m/8km W of Darlington, on site of Roman fort. NZ 2115
Pierowall Orkney 89 B5 vil on **Bay of P.** on E coast of island of Westray. Lobster fishing. HY 4348
Piethorn Reservoir Gtr Manchester 48 C6* resr 4m/7km E of Rochdale. SD 9612
Piff's Elm Glos 26 D5* loc 4m/6km NW of Cheltenham. SO 8926
Pigdon Nthmb 61 F3 loc 3m/5km NW of Morpeth. NZ 1588
Pig's Bay Essex 21 E3* shallow bay at E extremity of Southend-on-Sea to NE of Shoeburyness. TQ 9585
Pikehall Derbys 43 G5 loc 8m/12km N of Ashbourne. SK 1959
Pike Hill Lancs 48 B5* loc 2m/3km E of Burnley. SD 8632
Pike of Blisco Cumbria 52 C4 Lake Dist mountain 3m/4km SE of Bow Fell and 5m/7km W of Skelwith Br. Height 2304 ft or 702 metres. NY 2704
Pikeshill Hants 10 A4* ham adjoining Lyndhurst to NW. SU 2908
Pilford Dorset 9 G4* loc 2m/3km NE of Wimborne. SU 0301
Pilgrim's Hatch Essex 20 C2 NW suburb of Brentwood. TQ 5795
Pilgrims Park Isle of Wight 10 B5 loc 3m/5km SW of Cowes. SZ 4593
Pilgrims' Way 19, 20, 21 ancient British track following S slope of N Downs, later used by pilgrims to Becket's shrine at Canterbury. SU,TQ,TR
Pilham Lincs 44 D2 ham 4m/6km NE of Gainsborough. SK 8693
Pill Avon 16 A4 loc on R Avon adjoining Easton-in-Gordano to E. ST 5275
Pillar Cumbria 52 B4 mt in Lake Dist 3m/5km N of NE end of Wast Water. Height 2927 ft or 892 metres. NY 1712
Pillar of Eliseg Clwyd. See Valle Crucis Abbey.
Pillaton Cornwall 3 H2 vil 4m/6km S of Callington. SX 3664
Pillaton Staffs 35 F3* loc 2km SE of Penkridge. SJ 9413
Pillerton Hersey Warwicks 27 G3 vil 3m/4km SW of Kineton. SP 3048
Pillerton Priors Warwicks 27 G3 vil 3m/5km SW of Kineton. SP 2947
Pilleth Powys 25 G2 loc 3m/5km SW of Knighton. SO 2568
Pilley Glos 26 D5 loc in S part of Cheltenham. SO 9519
Pilley Hants 10 A4 ham 2m/3km N of Lymington. SZ 3398
Pilley S Yorks 43 G1 vil 2m/3km W of Hoyland Nether. SE 3300
Pillgwenlly Gwent 15 G3/H3* loc in Newport on W bank of R Usk above transporter br. ST 3086
Pilling Lancs 47 E3 vil 3m/4km NE of Preesall. **P. Lane** loc 2m/3km W. SD 4048
Pillowell Glos 16 B1 vil 2m/4km N of Lydney. SO 6206
Pill, South Cornwall 4 B5* N dist of Saltash. SX 4259
Pill, The Gwent 16 A3* loc 1km SE of Caldicot. ST 4887
Pilning Avon 16 B3* vil 8m/13km N of Bristol. ST 5585
Pilrig Lothian 66 A1/A2* dist of Edinburgh 2km NE of city centre. NT 2675
Pilsdon Dorset 8 C4 ham 5m/7km W of Beaminster. SY 4199
Pilsgate Cambs 37 F4 loc 3m/4km E of Stamford. TF 0605
Pilsley Derbys 43 G4 vil 2m/4km NE of Bakewell. SK 2471
Pilsley Derbys 43 H5 vil 4m/7km N of Alfreton. **P. Green** loc adjoining to S. SK 4262
Pilson Green Norfolk 39 G3* ham 1m E of S Walsham. TG 3713
Piltanton Burn 57 B7 r in Dumfries & Galloway region, rising on Rinns of Galloway 4m/6km NW of Stranraer, and flowing SE to Water of Luce and Luce Bay, S of Glenluce. NX 1954
Piltdown E Sussex 12 B4 ham 2m/3km NW of Uckfield. TQ 4422
Pilton Devon 6 D2 N dist of Barnstaple. SS 5534
Pilton Leics 37 E3 ham 4m/6km NE of Uppingham. SK 9102
Pilton Lothian 66 A1* dist of Edinburgh 2m/3km NW of city centre. NT 2376
Pilton Northants 37 E5* vil 3m/4km SW of Oundle. TL 0284
Pilton Som 8 D1 vil 3m/4km SW of Shepton Mallet. ST 5840
Pilton W Glam 23 F6* loc on Gower peninsula 3m/5km E of Worms Hd. **P. Green** loc 1km E. SS 4387
Pilton, West Devon 6 D2* loc on N side of Barnstaple. SS 5533
Pil, Y Welsh form of Pyle, qv.

Pimbo Lancs 42 B1* industrial estate in SE part of Skelmersdale. SD 4904
Pimhole Gtr Manchester 42 D1* loc 1m E of Bury tn centre. SD 8110
Pimlico Herts 19 E1* ham 3m/5km SE of Hemel Hempstead. TL 0905
Pimlico London 19 G4* dist in City of Westminster S of Victoria Stn. TQ 2978
Pimperne Dorset 9 F3 vil 2m/4km NE of Blandford Forum. ST 9009
Pinchbeck Lincs 37 G2 vil 2m/4km N of Spalding. **P. Bars** and **P. West** locs 3m/4km and 2m/4km W respectively. TF 2425
Pincheon Green S Yorks 49 H6* loc 4m/6km NW of Thorne. SE 6517
Pinchinthorpe Cleveland 55 E3 loc 3m/4km SW of Guisborough. NZ 5714
Pinchom's Hill Derbys 43 H6* loc 1m SE of Belper. SK 3646
Pinden Kent 20 C4* loc 1km W of Longfield and 5m/8km SW of Gravesend. TQ 5969
Pindon End Bucks 28 C3* loc 6m/10km NW of Newport Pagnell. SP 7847
Pineham Kent 13 H3* loc 3m/4km N of Dover. TR 3145
Pinehurst Wilts 17 F3* N dist of Swindon. SU 1587
Pinfold Lancs 42 A1 loc 3m/4km NW of Ormskirk. SD 3911
Pinford End Suffolk 30 D2* loc 3m/5km S of Bury St Edmunds. TL 8459
Pinged Dyfed 23 F5* loc 2m/4km NW of Burry Port. SN 4203
Pin Green Herts 29 F5* NE dist of Stevenage. **P. G. Industrial Estate** to NE. TL 2425
Pinhoe Devon 7 G5 NE dist of Exeter, 3m/5km from city centre. 1m W, **P. Trading Estate.** SX 9694
Pinkery Pond Som 7 E1 small lake on Exmoor close to Devon border 4m/6km NW of Simonsbath. Also known as Pinkworthy Pond. SS 7242
Pinkett's Booth W Midlands 35 H6* loc 4m/7km NW of Coventry. SP 2781
Pink Green H & W 27 E1* loc 3m/5km NE of Redditch. SP 0869
Pinkie Lothian 66 B2* site of battle of 1547 in which English defeated Scots, 2km SE of Musselburgh. At **P. House,** Jacbn mansion on E side of tn, Prince Charles Edward spent night after battle of Prestonpans in 1745. Hse now used by Loretto School. NT 3671
Pinkneys Green Berks 18 D3 loc 2m/3km NW of Maidenhead. NT property. SU 8582
Pinkworthy Pond Som. Alternative name for Pinkery Pond, qv.
Pinley Green Warwicks 27 F1 ham 5m/8km W of Warwick. SP 2066
Pin Mill Suffolk 31 F4 ham on S bank of R Orwell 5m/8km SE of Ipswich. TM 2037
Pinmore S'clyde 56 C4 loc 5m/8km S of Girvan. NX 2090
Pinner London 19 E3 loc in borough of Harrow 12m/20km NW of Charing Cross. TQ 1289
Pin's Green H & W 26 C3* ham 3m/5km NE of Gt Malvern. SO 8049
Pinsley Green Ches 42 B6* loc 1m SW of Wrenbury. SJ 5846
Pinvin H & W 26 D3 vil 2m/3km N of Pershore. SO 9549
Pinwherry S'clyde 56 C4/57 C5* vil at confluence of R Stinchar and Duisk R, 7m/11km S of Girvan. NX 1986
Pinxton Derbys 43 H5 vil 3m/4km E of Alfreton. **P. Green** loc adjoining to E. SK 4555
Pipe and Lyde H & W 26 A3* vil 3m/4km N of Hereford. SO 5044
Pipe Gate Salop 34 D1 ham 1km SE of Woore. SJ 7340
Pipehill Staffs 35 G3* loc 2m/3km SW of Lichfield. SK 0908
Piperhill H'land 81 G2/G3 loc in Nairn dist 4m/6km S of Nairn. NH 8650
Piper Hill N Yorks 54 B5* loc on E side of Catterick Camp 2m/4km W of Catterick. SE 2098
Pipe Ridware Staffs 35 G3 ham 3m/5km E of Rugeley. SK 0917
Piper's Ash Ches 42 A4* loc 2m/3km E of Chester. SJ 4367
Pipers Pool Cornwall 6 B6 vil 5m/7km W of Launceston. SX 2684
Pipewell Northants 36 D5 ham 4m/7km SW of Corby. SP 8385
Pippacott Devon 6 D2* loc 3m/5km NW of Barnstaple. SS 5237
Pippin Street Lancs 47 F5* loc 1km W of Brindle. SD 5924
Pipps Hill Essex 20 D3* industrial estate N of Basildon tn centre. TQ 6990
Pipton Powys 25 F4 loc 5m/7km SW of Hay-on-Wye. SO 1638
Pirbright Surrey 18 D5 vil 5m/8km NW of Guildford. To NW across rly, P. Camp and firing ranges. SU 9455
Pirnmill S'clyde 63 F3 vil on W coast of Arran opp Grogport in Kintyre. NR 8744
Pirton Herts 29 F4 vil 3m/5km NW of Hitchin. TL 1431
Pirton H & W 26 D3 vil 5m/8km SE of Worcester. SO 8847
Pishill Oxon 18 C3 ham 3m/4km NE of Nettlebed. SU 7290
Pismire Hill S Yorks 43 H2* dist of Sheffield 3m/4km NE of city centre. SK 3691
Pistyll Gwynedd 32 B1* ham 2km NE of Nefyn. SH 3241
Pistyll Rhaeadr 33 G2* waterfall on border of Clwyd and Powys at head of R Rhaeadr 4m/6km NW of Llanrhaeadr-ym-Mochnant. Descends 240 ft or 73 metres. SJ 0729
Pistyll y Graig Ddu Powys 33 G3* waterfall in Nant Alan 3m/5km W of Llanfyllin. SJ 0918
Pistyll y Llyn 33 E5* waterfall on borders of Dyfed and Powys near head of R Llyfnant 4m/7km S of Machynlleth, Powys. SN 7594
Pitcairngreen Tayside 72 D2 vil with large green 4m/6km NW of Perth. NO 0627
Pitcairnie Lake Tayside 72 D3* small lake to SW of Dupplin Lake, 6m/10km SW of Perth. NO 0219
Pitcalnie H'land 81 G1* loc in Ross and Cromarty dist 2m/4km N of N side of entrance to Cromarty Firth. NH 8072
Pitcaple Grampian 83 F4 vil 4m/7km NW of Inverurie. **P. Castle** 1km NE. NJ 7225
Pitcarity Tayside 76 D4 loc in Glen Prosen 8m/13km NW of Kirriemuir. NO 3265
Pitchcombe Glos 16 D1 vil 2m/3km N of Stroud. SO 8508
Pitchcott Bucks 28 C5 vil 5m/8km NW of Aylesbury. SP 7720
Pitchford Salop 34 C4 vil 6m/10km S of Shrewsbury. SJ 5303
Pitch Green Bucks 18 C2 ham 2m/3km W of Princes Risborough. SP 7703
Pitch Place Surrey 11 E1 ham 2m/4km N of Hindhead. SU 8939
Pitch Place Surrey 18 D6 loc 2m/4km NW of Guildford. SU 9752
Pitcombe Som 8 D1* vil 2km SW of Bruton. ST 6733
Pitcot Mid Glam 15 E4 loc adjoining St Bride's Major to S, 4m/6km S of Bridgend. SS 8974
Pitcox Lothian 66 D1 loc 3m/5km SW of Dunbar. NT 6475
Pitcur Tayside 73 F1 loc 3m/4km SE of Coupar Angus. Ancient earth-house. No 2536
Pitfichie Grampian 83 E5 loc and ruined cas 7m/11km SW of Inverurie. **P. Forest** is state forest to W. NJ 6716
Pitfichie Forest Grampian 83 E5 state forest to W of Monymusk. NJ 6415
Pitfour Castle Tayside 73 E3 loc 5m/8km E of Perth. NO 1920
Pitlessie Fife 73 F3 vil 4m/6km SW of Cupar. NO 3309
Pitlochry Tayside 76 A5 summer resort on R Tummel 5m/8km NW of its confluence with R Tay and 11m/18km NW of Dunkeld. Festival Theatre. Distillery. Highland Games in August. NN 9458
Pitmachie Grampian 83 E4* loc adjoining Old Rayne to W. NJ 6728
Pitman's Corner Suffolk 31 F2* loc 1m E of Wetheringsett. TM 1466
Pitmedden Grampian 83 H4 vil 5m/9km E of Oldmeldrum. **P. Garden** (NTS), 1km NW. Remains of Tolquhon Castle (A.M.), medieval cas much enlarged in 16c, 2km NW. NJ 8927
Pitmedden Forest Tayside 73 E3* state forest to SE of Abernethy. NO 2014
Pitminster Som 8 A3 vil 4m/6km S of Taunton. ST 2219
Pitmunie Grampian 83 E5* loc 2km W of Monymusk. NJ 6615
Pitney Som 8 C2 vil 3m/4km W of Somerton. ST 4428
Pitroddie Tayside 73 E2 loc 6m/10km E of Perth. NO 2125
Pitscottie Fife 73 G3 vil 3m/5km E of Cupar. NO 4113
Pitsea Essex 20 D3 SE dist of Basildon. **P. Mount,** loc in Basildon adjoining to S. **P. Marsh** at head of Vange Creek to S. TQ 7388
Pitseahall Fleet Essex 20 D3* enclosed stretch of water in marshland 1m S of Pitsea and 2m/4km SE of Basildon. TQ 7486
Pitses Gtr Manchester 43 E1* loc in Oldham 2m/3km SE of tn centre. SD 9403
Pitsford Northants 28 C1 vil 5m/8km N of Northampton. To N is Pitsford Resr, over 3m/5km long. SP 7568
Pitsligo Grampian 83 G1 par on N coast containing ruined **Castle of P.** 1km SE of Rosehearty. See also New Pitsligo. NJ 9366
Pitsmoor S Yorks 43 H2* dist of Sheffield 2km NE of city centre. SK 3689
Pitstone Bucks 28 D6 loc 3m/4km N of Tring. Cement works. Loc of **P. Green** 1km N. SP 9315
Pitt Devon 7 H3 ham 2km N of Sampford Peverell. ST 0316
Pitt Hants 10 B2 ham 2m/3km SW of Winchester. SU 4528
Pittenheath Grampian 83 H2* loc behind Rattray Bay, 2m/3km S of Rattray Hd. NK 0955
Pittenweem Fife 73 H4 fishing port on Firth of Forth 2km W of Anstruther. NO 5402
Pitteuchar Fife 73 F4* dist and industrial estate in SE part of Glenrothes. NO 2700
Pittington Durham 54 C1 vil 4m/6km E of Durham. NZ 3244
Pitton W Glam 23 F6* loc on Gower peninsula 3m/5km E of Worms Hd. **P. Cross** loc to E. SS 4287
Pitton Wilts 9 H2 vil 5m/8km E of Salisbury. SU 2131
Pitt-Rivers Museum Dorset. See Farnham.
Pitts Hill Staffs 42 D5* loc 1m NE of Tunstall. SJ 8652
Pittulie Grampian 83 G1 loc on N coast adjoining Sandhaven to W, 2m/4km W of Fraserburgh. **P. Castle** is ruin 1m SW. NJ 9567
Pittville Glos 26 D5* N dist of Cheltenham. SO 9423
Pitwellt Pond Mid Glam 15 F1* small lake 3m/5km NE of Merthyr Tydfil. SO 0709
Pityme Cornwall 3 E1 loc 4m/6km NW of Wadebridge. SW 9576
Pity Me Durham 54 B1 vil 2m/3km N of Durham. NZ 2645
Pixey Green Suffolk 31 F1* loc 2km NE of Stradbroke. TM 2475
Pixham Surrey 19 F6* NE dist of Dorking. TQ 1750
Pixley H & W 26 B4* ham 3m/5km W of Ledbury. SO 6638
Place House Hants. See Titchfield.
Place, Lower Gtr Manchester 48 B6 loc in Rochdale 1m SE of tn centre. SD 9011
Pladda S'clyde 62 C1* one of the Small Isles, qv, off E coast of Jura. NR 5468
Pladda S'clyde 63 G5 small uninhabited island about 1km off S coast of Arran across Sound of P. NS 0219
Pladda Island S'clyde 70 A2 islet off S coast of Lismore, nearly 1km S of Eilean Dubh, and on E side of Creag I. NM 8337
Plain Dealings Dyfed 22 C4* loc 1km NW of Llawhaden. SN 0518
Plainfield Nthmb 61 E2* loc 4m/7km W of Rothbury. NT 9903
Plain, North Cumbria 59 G5* loc on coast of Solway Firth 2m/3km SW of Bowness. NY 1961
Plains S'clyde 65 E2 vil 2m/4km NE of Airdrie. NS 7966
Plains Farm Tyne & Wear 61 H5* housing estate in Sunderland 2m/3km SW of tn centre. NZ 3754
Plainsfield Som 8 A1* ham on E slopes of Quantock Hills 2m/3km S of Nether Stowey. ST 1936
Plaish Salop 34 C4* ham 6m/10km W of Much Wenlock. SO 5296
Plaistow London 20 A3* loc in borough of Newham 1km S of W Ham. TQ 4082
Plaistow London 20 A4* loc in borough of Bromley 1km N of Bromley tn centre. TQ 3970
Plaistow W Sussex 11 F2 vil 6m/10km NW of Billingshurst. TQ 0031
Plaitford Hants 10 A3 vil 5m/8km W of Romsey. To S, **P. Common** (NT), on which are round barrows of the late Bronze Age, and linear earthworks. SU 2719
Plaitford Green Hants 10 A3* ham 1m SW of Sherfield English and 4m/7km W of Romsey. SU 2821
Plank Lane Gtr Manchester 42 C2* loc 2m/3km W of Leigh. SJ 6399
Plashet London 20 B3* loc in borough of Newham 1km N of E Ham. TQ 4284
Plashett Dyfed 23 E4* loc 2m/3km SW of Laugharne. SN 2709
Plashetts Nthmb 60 C3 loc in Kielder Forest 4m/6km NW of Falstone. NY 6690
Plas Mawr Elizn hse in Conwy, Gwynedd. See Conwy.
Plasterfield W Isles 88 C2* loc on Lewis 1m E of Stornoway. NB 4433
Plastow Green Hants 18 A5* ham 2m/3km NE of Kingsclere. SU 5361
Plas-uchaf Reservoir Clwyd 41 F4* small resr 1m NW of Llannefydd. SH 9671
Plas yn Rhiw Gwynedd. See Bwlch-y-Rhiw.
Platt Kent 20 C5 vil adjoining Borough Green to E. TQ 6257
Platt Bridge Gtr Manchester 42 B1 loc 2m/3km SE of Wigan. SD 6002
Platt Lane Salop 34 C1 loc 4m/6km SW of Whitchurch. SJ 5136
Platts S Yorks 43 H1* loc adjoining Hoyland Nether to N. SE 3701
Platt's Heath Kent 21 E6* loc 2m/3km SW of Lenham. TQ 8750
Plawsworth Durham 54 B1 vil 4m/6km N of Durham. NZ 2647
Plaxtol Kent 20 C6 vil 5m/7km N of Tonbridge. TQ 6053
Playden E Sussex 13 E4 vil 1m N of Rye. TQ 9121
Playford Suffolk 31 F3 vil 4m/6km W of Woodbridge. TM 2147
Play Hatch Oxon 18 C4 ham 2m/4km NE of Reading. SU 7476
Playing Place Cornwall 2 D4* vil 2m/4km SW of Truro. SW 8141
Playley Green Glos 26 C4* ham 5m/8km SE of Ledbury. SO 7631
Plealey Salop 34 B4 ham 6m/9km SW of Shrewsbury. SJ 4206
Plean Central 72 C5 mining vil 5m/8km SE of Stirling. **E Plean** is mining vil adjoining to N. NS 8386
Pleasant Valley Essex 30 A4* loc in S part of Saffron Walden. TL 5337
Pleasant View Derbys 43 E3* loc 2km W of Hayfield. SK 0186
Pleasington Lancs 47 G5 vil 3m/5km W of Blackburn. SD 6426
Pleasley Derbys 44 A4 coal-mining vil 3m/5km NW of Mansfield. **P. Vale** loc 1m NE. SK 5064
Pleasleyhill Notts 44 A4* loc 3m/4km NW of Mansfield. SK 5064
Pleck Dorset. Alternative name for Lit Ansty (see Ansty).
Pleck Dorset 9 E3* ham 2m/3km SE of Bishop's Caundle. ST 7010
Pleck W Midlands 35 F4* dist of Walsall 2km SW of tn centre. SO 9997
Pleckgate Lancs 47 G5* loc in Blackburn 2km N of tn centre. SD 6730
Pledgdon Green Essex 30 A5* loc 5m/8km NW of Gt Dunmow. TL 5626
Pledwick W Yorks 49 E6* loc in Wakefield 3m/5km S of city centre. SE 3316
Plemstall Ches 42 A4* ham 4m/7km NE of Chester. SJ 4570
Plenmeller Nthmb 60 C5 loc 1m SE of Haltwhistle. NY 7163
Pleshey Essex 20 C1 vil 5m/9km NW of Chelmsford. Vil surrounded by Norman earthworks. Remains of cas keep. TL 6614
Plockton H'land 79 F5 vil in Skye and Lochalsh dist on S side of Loch Carron, 5m/8km NE of Kyle of Lochalsh. Airfield 1m W. NG 8033
Plocrapool Point W Isles 88 B3* headland on W side of entrance to E Loch Tarbert, Harris. NG 1893
Plomer's Hill Bucks 18 D2* NW dist of High Wycombe. SU 8494
Plompton N Yorks 49 F3* loc 2m/3km S of Knaresborough. SE 3554
Plot Gate Som 8 D1* loc adjoining Barton St David to NE, 1m N of Keinton Mandeville. ST 5432
Plot Street Som 8 D1* loc 4m/6km SE of Glastonbury. ST 5536
Ploughfield H & W 25 H4 vil 8m/13km W of Hereford. SO 3841
Plough Hill Warwicks 35 H5* loc 3m/5km W of Nuneaton. SP 3292
Ploughlands Cumbria 53 F3* loc 1m S of Warcop. NY 7513

Ploverfield Hants 10 B4* loc adjoining Bursledon to N and 2m/3km NW of Park Gate. SU 4809
Plowden Salop 34 B5 ham 4m/7km NW of Craven Arms. SO 3887
Ploxgreen Salop 34 B4 ham 10m/15km SW of Shrewsbury. SJ 3603
Pluckley Kent 13 E3 hilltop vil 3m/5km SW of Charing. Ham of **P. Thorne** 1km SW. TQ 9245
Plucks Gutter Kent 13 H1 loc on R Gt Stour 5m/8km NW of Sandwich. TR 2663
Plumbland Cumbria 52 B1 vil 2m/3km S of Aspatria. NY 1539
Plumbley S Yorks 43 H3* loc in Sheffield 1km W of Mosbrough. SK 4180
Plumgarths Cumbria 53 E5* loc 2m/3km NW of Kendal. SD 4994
Plumley Ches 42 C4* vil 3m/5km SW of Knutsford. SJ 7175
Plumpton E Sussex 12 A5 vil 4m/7km NW of Lewes below S Downs. Racecourse and rly stn 2m/3km N at vil of **P. Green.** TQ 3613
Plumpton Northants 58 B3 ham 7m/11km N of Brackley. SP 5948
Plumpton End Northants 28 C3 ham adjoining Paulerspury to E, 3m/5km SE of Towcester. SP 7245
Plumpton, Great Lancs 47 E4 ham 3m/4km W of Kirkham. **Lit Plumpton** loc 1km SW. SD 3833
Plumpton Head Cumbria 53 E2 loc 3m/5km N of Penrith. Site of Roman camp to N. NY 5035
Plumpton Wall Cumbria 53 E1 vil 4m/7km N of Penrith. Site of small Roman fort to S. NY 4937
Plumstead London 20 B4 loc in borough of Greenwich 1km SE of Woolwich and 9m/15km E of Charing Cross. To N are **P. Marshes,** on S bank of R Thames opp Barking Reach. TQ 4478
Plumstead Norfolk 39 F2 vil, with **Plumstead Green,** 4m/7km SE of Holt. TG 1334
Plumstead, Great Norfolk 39 G4 vil 5m/8km E of Norwich. **Lit Plumstead** vil 2km NE. **Plumstead Green** 1km N. TG 3010
Plumtree Notts 36 C1/C2 vil 5m/8km SE of Nottingham. SK 6133
Plungar Leics 36 D1 vil 9m/15km N of Melton Mowbray. SK 7633
Pluscarden Priory Grampian 82 A2/B2 13c priory near loc of Barnhill 5m/9km SW of Elgin. Occupied and restored by Benedictine monks since 1943. NJ 1457
Plush Dorset 9 E4 vil 2m/3km N of Piddletrenthide. ST 7102
Plusha Cornwall 4 A3* loc 6m/9km SW of Launceston. SX 2580
Plushabridge Cornwall 3 G1* loc on R Lynher 4m/6km NW of Callington. SX 3072
Plwmp Dyfed 24 A3* ham 5m/8km S of New Quay. SN 3652
Plym 4 B5 r in Devon rising at Plym Hd on Dartmoor and flowing SW into Plymouth Sound. SX 4853
Plym Forest Devon 4 B4* large woodland area 4m/7km NE of Plymouth, enclosing part of R Plym valley. A small portion is NT property. SX 5259
Plymouth Devon 4 B5 city 100m/160km SW of Bristol. Port and naval base; various industries. City centre rebuilt after World War II. *Mayflower* sailed from here to America in 1620. Airport at Roborough, to N. SX 4754
Plympton Devon 4 C5 E dist of Plymouth, 4m/7km from city centre. To S, dist of **P. St Maurice.** To W beside R Plym, hse and grnds of Saltram (NT). SX 5356
Plymstock Devon 4 C5 SE dist of Plymouth, E of R Plym and 3m/5km from city centre. SX 5153
Plymtree Devon 7 H4 vil 3m/5km SE of Cullompton. ST 0502
Plynlimon (Pumlumon) Dyfed 33 E5 mt near Powys border 10m/16km W of Llanidloes. Height 2469 ft or 752 metres. Rs Severn and Wye rise on NE and E slopes respectively, in Powys. SN 7886
Poaka Beck Reservoir Cumbria 46 D6* resr 3m/5km N of Dalton-in-Furness. SD 2478
Pochin Houses Gwent 15 F1* loc 3m/5km S of Ebbw Vale. SO 1604
Pockley N Yorks 55 E6 vil 2m/3km NE of Helmsley. SE 6386
Pocklington Humberside 50 C3 tn 7m/11km NW of Mkt Weighton. **P. Canal** between here and tidal R Derwent at E Cottingwith. SE 8048
Pockthorpe Norfolk 39 E2* loc adjoining Foulsham to S. TG 0324
Pockthorpe Norfolk 39 E3* loc 1m S of Sparham. TG 0718
Pockthorpe Norfolk 39 E4* loc 4m/7km N of Wymondham. TG 0907
Pode Hole Lincs 37 G2 loc 2m/3km W of Spalding. TF 2122
Podimore Som 8 D2 vil 2m/4km NE of Ilchester. ST 5425
Podington Beds 28 D2 vil 5m/7km SE of Wellingborough. SP 9462
Podsmead Glos 26 D5* loc in S part of Gloucester. SO 8215
Poffley End Oxon 27 G6 loc 2m/3km N of Witney. SP 3512
Pogmoor S Yorks 43 G1* dist of Barnsley 1km W of tn centre. SE 3306
Poind and his Man, The Nthmb 61 F3* standing stone, 6 ft or 2 metres high, on moorland 2m/3km S of Middleton. Second stone removed. NZ 0682
Point Clear Essex 31 E6* loc on left bank of Brightlingsea Reach at mouth of R Colne. TM 0915
Point Cranstal Isle of Man 46 C3 promontory on E coast 3m/5km S of Pt of Ayre. Also known as Shellag Pt. SC 4699
Point Lynas Gwynedd 40 B2 headland with lighthouse on N coast of Anglesey 2m/4km E of Amlwch. SH 4793
Point of Air (Y Parlwr Du) Clwyd 41 G3 promontory at W end of R Dee estuary 4m/6km E of Prestatyn. Also spelt Point of Ayr. SJ 1285
Point of Ayre Isle of Man 46 C3 northernmost point of island, with two lighthouses, 7m/11km N of Ramsey. NX 4605
Point of Ayre Orkney 89 C7 headland on E coast of Mainland 4m/6km S of Mull Hd. HY 5903
Point of Buckquoy Orkney 89 A6* headland at NW end of Mainland opp Brough of Birsay. HY 2428
Point of Bugarth Shetland 89 E6* headland on W coast of Yell 3m/5km N of W Sandwick. HU 4493
Point of Fethaland Shetland 89 E5 headland at northernmost point of Mainland. HU 3795
Point of Howana Geo Orkney 89 A6* headland on W coast of Mainland 3m/5km S of Marwick Hd. HY 2220
Point of Huro Orkney 89 B5* headland at S end of island of Westray. HY 4938
Point of Knap S'clyde 62 D1 headland in Knapdale, Argyll, on W side of entrance to Loch Caolisport. NR 6972
Point of Ness Shetland 89 F5* headland on E coast of Yell, on W side of entrance to Basta Voe. HU 5394
Point of Scaraber Orkney 89 B5* promontory at S end of island of Faray, 1km N of Fers Ness, Eday. HY 5335
Point of Sleat Skye, H'land 79 D8 headland with beacon at S end of Sleat peninsula. Most southerly point of Skye. NM 5699
Point of Stoer H'land 84 A4 headland on W coast of Sutherland dist 9m/15km NW of Lochinver. NC 0235
Point of the Graand Orkney 89 B6* headland at S end of island of Egilsay. HY 4726
Pointon Lincs 37 F2 vil 7m/12km N of Bourne. TF 0731
Point St John Dyfed 22 A3 headland (NT) at S end of Whitesand Bay 2m/4km W of St David's. SM 7125
Pokesdown Dorset 9 H5* E dist of Bournemouth. SZ 1392
Polapit Tamar Cornwall 6 C6* loc 3m/5km N of Launceston. SX 3389
Polbain H'land 85 A6 vil near NW coast of Ross and Cromarty dist 2m/3km NW of Achiltibuie. NC 0208
Polbathick Cornwall 3 H3 vil 6m/10km W of Torpoint, at head of creek running into St Germans R. SX 3456
Polbeth Lothian 65 G2 loc 3m/5km SW of Livingston. NT 0264
Polbrook Cornwall 3 E2* loc 4m/6km NW of Bodmin. SX 0169
Polden Hills Som 8 C1 ridge of low hills rising out of plain between Bridgwater and Glastonbury, and running some 10m/16km WNW to ESE. ST 33
Poldorais H'land 78 C3 strait between Eilean Flodigarry and NE coast of Skye. NG 4771
Polebrook Northants 37 F5 vil 2m/3km E of Oundle. TL 0687
Pole Elm H & W 26 D3* ham 3m/5km S of Worcester. SO 8349
Polegate E Sussex 12 C6 N suburb of Eastbourne. TQ 5804
Pole Moor W Yorks 48 D6* loc 5m/8km W of Huddersfield. SE 0616
Polesden Lacey Surrey 19 E6 Regency hse and grnds (NT) 3m/4km NW of Dorking. TQ 1352
Polesworth Warwicks 35 H4 vil 4m/7km NW of Atherstone. SK 2602
Polglass H'land 85 A6 vil on NW coast of Ross and Cromarty dist 10m/15km NW of Ullapool. NC 0307
Polgooth Cornwall 3 E3* vil 2m/3km SW of St Austell. SW 9950
Polharrow Burn 58 B3 r in Dumfries & Galloway region running E from Loch Harrow to Water of Ken, 2m/4km N of Dalry. NX 6084
Polin H'land 84 B2 loc near W coast of Sutherland dist 3m/4km NW of Kinlochbervie. NC 1959
Poling W Sussex 11 F4 vil 2m/3km NE of Littlehampton. Ham of **P. Corner** 1km N. Site of Roman villa to E. TQ 0404
Polkerris Cornwall 3 F3 coastal vil on E side of St Austell Bay 2m/4km W of Fowey. SX 0952
Poll a' Mhuineil H'land 74 A1* small bay on SW shore of Loch Hourn, Lochaber dist. Eilean a' Mhuineil is islet off E end of bay. NG 8406
Pollardras Cornwall 2 C5* loc 3m/5km NW of Helston. SW 6130
Pollard Street Norfolk 39 G2* loc 1km SW of Bacton. TG 3332
Pollicott, Lower Bucks 28 C6* loc 4m/7km N of Thame. SP 7013
Pollicott, Upper Bucks 28 C6* loc 5m/8km N of Thame. SP 7013
Pollington Humberside 49 G6 vil 3m/5km SW of Snaith. SE 6119
Polliwilline Bay S'clyde 63 E6 bay on E coast of Kintyre 3m/5km E of Southend. NR 7409
Polloch H'land 68 F2 locality in Lochaber dist on r of same name which runs NW from Loch Doilet to Loch Shiel. NM 7968
Pollok S'clyde 64 C3* dist of Glasgow 4m/7km SW of city centre. **Pollok Grnds,** to E across White Cart Water, is large open space with sports facilities. NS 5362
Pollokshaws S'clyde 64 C3 dist of Glasgow 3m/5km SW of city centre. NS 5661
Pollokshields S'clyde 64 C3* dist of Glasgow 2m/3km SW of city centre. NS 5763
Polly H'land 85 B5 r flowing W from Loch Sionascaig to Polly Bay, qv. NC 0614
Polly Bay H'land 85 B5 inlet in Enard Bay, NW coast of Ross and Cromarty dist 2m/4km W of Loch Sionascaig. Also known as Loch Polly. NC 0714
Polmaddy Burn 58 B3 r in Dumfries & Galloway region, rising on E slopes of Corserine and flowing E to Water of Ken 4m/7km SE of Carsphairn. NX 6088
Polmadie S'clyde 64 D3* loc in Govanhill dist of Glasgow. NS 5962
Polmarth Cornwall 2 C4* loc 4m/6km S of Redruth. SW 7036
Polmassick Cornwall 3 E4* vil 5m/8km SW of St Austell. SW 9745
Polmont Central 65 F1* small tn 3m/5km E of Falkirk. NS 9378
Polperro Cornwall 3 G3 S coast resort 3m/5km SW of Looe. SX 2051
Polruan Cornwall 3 F3 vil at mouth of R Fowey opp tn of Fowey. SX 1250
Polsham Som 8 C1 loc 3m/4km N of Glastonbury. ST 5142
Polstead Suffolk 30 D4/31 E4 vil 4m/6km SW of Hadleigh. TL 9938
Polstead Heath Suffolk 31 E4* loc 2m/4km SW of Hadleigh. TL 9940
Poltalloch S'clyde 70 A5 locality (hse demolished) in Argyll, 1m NE of Crinan Loch. Many prehistoric remains (A.M.) in vicinity. NR 8196
Poltesco Cornwall 2 C6* loc 3m/5km NE of Lizard Pt. SW 7215
Poltimore Devon 7 G5 vil 4m/6km NE of Exeter. SX 9696
Polton Lothian 66 A2* vil on R North Esk 1km SE of Loanhead. NT 2864
Polwarth Borders 67 E3/E4 vil 4m/6km SW of Duns. NT 7450
Polwarth Lothian 66 A2* dist of Edinburgh 2km SW of city centre. NT 2372
Polyphant Cornwall 6 B6 vil 5m/7km SW of Launceston. SX 2682
Polzeath Cornwall 3 E1 vil on E side of Padstow Bay 5m/8km NW of Wadebridge. New P. is loc adjoining to N. SW 9378
Pomona Orkney. Former name of island of Mainland, qv.
Pomphlett Devon 4 C5* SE dist of Plymouth, E of R Plym. SX 5153
Ponde Powys 25 F4* loc 4m/6km NW of Talgarth. SO 1037
Ponden Reservoir W Yorks 48 C4* resr 5m/8km SW of Keighley. SD 9937
Pondersbridge Cambs 37 G5 ham 3m/5km S of Whittlesey. TL 2692
Ponders End London 20 A2 loc in borough of Enfield 2m/3km E of Enfield tn. TQ 3595
Pond of Drummond Tayside 72 C3* small lake NE of Drummond Castle and 2m/3km S of Crieff. NN 8518
Pond Street, Lower Essex 29 H4* ham 5m/8km W of Saffron Walden. TL 4537
Pond Street, Upper Essex 29 H4 ham 5m/8km W of Saffron Walden just S of Lr Pond Street. TL 4537
Pondtail Hants 18 C6 E dist of Fleet. SU 8254
Pond Yr Oerfa Dyfed 24 C1 lake 2m/3km N of Devil's Br. SN 7279
Ponsanooth Cornwall 2 C4 vil 3m/4km NW of Penryn. SW 7537
Ponsonby Cumbria 52 B4 loc 2m/3km NW of Gosforth. NY 0505
Ponsongath Cornwall 2 C6* loc on SE edge of Goonhilly Downs 8m/13km SE of Helston. SW 7517
Ponsworthy Devon 4 D3 vil in steep valley of W Webburn R 4m/7km NW of Ashburton. SX 7073
Pont 61 F4 r rising near Lit Whittington, N of Corbridge, Nthmb, and flowing E to Ponteland, then N to R Blyth 3m/5km N of Ponteland. NZ 1777
Pont Aber Dyfed 24 C5 loc 4m/7km SE of Llangadog. SN 7322
Pontamman (Pontaman) Dyfed 23 G4 loc 1m E of Ammanford. SN 6412
Pontantwn Dyfed 23 F4 ham on R Gwendraeth Fach 5m/8km S of Carmarthen. SN 4413
Pontardawe W Glam 14 C1 tn 5m/7km NW of Neath. Coal-mining and tinplate mnfre. SN 7204
Pontarddulais W Glam 23 G5 small tn on R Loughor 8m/12km NW of Swansea. SN 5903
Pontarfynach Welsh form of Devil's Br, qv.
Pontargothi Dyfed 23 F3* ham on R Cothi 6m/9km E of Carmarthen. SN 5021
Pont ar Hydfer Powys 24 D5* loc 2m/3km SW of Trecastle. SN 8627
Pontarllechau Dyfed 24 C5* loc 3m/5km SE of Llangadog. SN 7224
Pontarsais Dyfed 24 A5 ham 5m/9km N of Carmarthen. SN 4428
Pontblyddyn Clwyd 41 H5 vil 3m/5km SE of Mold. SJ 2760
Pontbren Llwyd Mid Glam 15 E1 vil 2km N of Hirwaun. SN 9507
Pontcanna S Glam 15 F4* dist of Cardiff with large park and recreation ground on W bank of R Taff 1m W of city centre. ST 1677
Pontcysyllte Clwyd 41 H6* vil 2m/3km SW of Ruabon. High aqueduct by Telford carries Shropshire Union Canal over R Dee. SJ 2742
Pont Dolgarrog Gwynedd 40 D4 loc and br over R Ddu 1m S of Dolgarrog. SH 7766
Pontefract W Yorks 49 F5 tn 12m/19km SE of Leeds. Coal-mining, confectionery (Pomfret cakes). Racecourse to NW. Remains of Norman cas. SE 4522
Ponteland Nthmb 61 F4 tn 7m/11km NW of Newcastle upon Tyne. NZ 1672
Ponterwyd Dyfed 33 E6 vil on R Rheidol 3m/4km N of Devil's Br. SN 7480
Pontesbury Salop 34 B4 vil 7m/11km SW of Shrewsbury. **P. Hill** loc adjoining to S. SJ 3906
Pontesford Salop 34 B4 ham 6m/10km SW of Shrewsbury. SJ 4106
Pontfadog Clwyd 34 A1* vil 4m/6km W of Chirk. SJ 2338

Pontfaen (Bont-faen, Y) Dyfed 22 C3 ham on R Gwaun 4m/6km SW of Newport. SN 0234
Pont-faen Dyfed 24 B3 loc 2m/3km E of Lampeter across R Teifi. SN 6049
Pont-faen Powys 25 E4 ham 5m/7km NW of Brecon. SN 9934
Pontgarreg Dyfed 23 E1* ham 2m/3km E of Llangranog. SN 3354
Pont Henry (Pont-henri) Dyfed 23 F4 vil on R Gwendraeth Fawr 5m/8km NE of Kidwelly. SN 4709
Ponthir Gwent 15 H2 vil 2km N of Caerleon. ST 3292
Ponthirwaun Dyfed 23 E2 ham 4m/7km NW of Newcastle Emlyn. SN 2645
Pont Hwfa Gwynedd 40 A3* loc 1m W of Holyhead. SH 2382
Pont-iets Dyfed 23 F4/F5 vil 4m/6km E of Kidwelly. SN 4608
Pontllanfraith Gwent 15 G2 loc 1m S of Blackwood. ST 1895
Pontlliw W Glam 23 G5 vil 2m/3km SE of Pontarddulais. SN 6101
Pontlottyn Mid Glam 15 F1 loc 1m S of Rhymney. SO 1106
Pontlyfni Gwynedd 40 B6* vil near mouth of R Llyfni 7m/11km SW of Caernarvon. SH 4352
Pontneathvaughan (Pontneddfechan) Powys 15 E1 vil 2km NE of Glyn-neath. SN 9007
Pontnewydd Gwent 15 G2 loc in N part of Cwmbran. Tinplate mnfre. ST 2996
Pontnewynydd Gwent 15 G2 loc 1m NW of Pontypool. SO 2701
Ponton, Great Lincs 37 E2 vil 4m/6km S of Grantham. Site of Roman bldg to E. **Lit Ponton** ham 2km N. SK 9230
Pont Pen-y-benglog Gwynedd 40 D5* loc and br across R Ogwen at lower (W) end of Llyn Ogwen. Also known as Ogwen Cottage. SH 6460
Pontrhydfendigaid Dyfed 24 C2 vil on R Teifi 5m/8km NE of Tregaron. SN 7366
Pont Rhyd-sarn Gwynedd 33 F2* loc on R Dyfrdwy 2km SW of Llanuwchllyn. SH 8528
Pont-rhyd-y-cyff Mid Glam 14 D3* loc 2m/3km SE of Maesteg. SS 8789
Pontrhydyfen W Glam 14 D2 vil on R Afan 3m/5km NE of Port Talbot. SS 7994
Pontrhydygroes Dyfed 24 C1 vil 3m/5km S of Devil's Br. SN 7372
Pontrhydyrun (Pontrhydyrynn) Gwent 15 G2 loc 2m/3km N of Cwmbran. ST 2997
Pont-Rhys-Powell Gwent 25 G5* loc 5m/8km N of Abergavenny. SO 3122
Pont Rhythallt Gwynedd 40 C5* loc on R Rhythallt 3m/5km NW of Llanberis. SH 5463
Pontrilas H & W 25 H5 vil on R Dore near its confluence with R Monnow, 11m/17km SW of Hereford. SO 3927
Pontrobert Powys 33 G3 vil on R Vyrnwy 4m/6km N of Llanfair Caereinion. SJ 1012
Pont-rug Gwynedd 40 C5* loc on R Seiont 2m/3km E of Caernarvon. SH 5163
Pontsenni Welsh form of Sennybridge, qv.
Ponts Green E Sussex 12 C5 ham 5m/7km W of Battle. TQ 6715
Pontshaen Dyfed 24 A4 ham 4m/6km N of Llandyssul. SN 4346
Pontshill H & W 26 B5 vil 3m/5km SE of Ross-on-Wye. SO 6321
Pont Sion Norton Mid Glam 15 F2* loc 1m NE of Pontypridd. ST 0891
Pontsticill Mid Glam 15 F1 vil 3m/5km N of Merthyr Tydfil. SO 0511
Pont-tyweli (or Pontwelly) Dyfed 24 A4 vil just S of Llandyssul across R Teifi. SN 4140
Pont Walby Mid Glam 14 D1 loc at crossing of R Neath on E side of Glyn-neath. SN 8906
Pontwelly. Alternative spelling for Pont-tyweli, Dyfed, qv.
Pontyberem Dyfed 23 F4 vil on R Gwendraeth Fawr 8m/13km SE of Carmarthen. SN 5011
Pont-y-blew Clwyd 34 A1* loc on R Ceiriog 2km E of Chirk. SJ 3138
Pontybodkin Clwyd 41 H5 vil 4m/6km SE of Mold. SJ 2759
Pontyclun Mid Glam 15 F3 vil 2km SW of Llantrisant. ST 0381
Pontycymer Mid Glam 15 E3 coal-mining tn 7m/11km N of Bridgend. SS 9091
Pontyglazier Dyfed 22 D2* loc 2km S of Eglwyswrw. SN 1436
Pont-y-gwaith Mid Glam 15 E2* vil 3m/4km E of Rhondda. ST 0194
Pontymister Gwent 15 G3 loc on Ebbw R in Risca. ST 2490
Pontymoel Gwent 15 G2* loc in SE part of Pontypool. Glass works. SO 2900
Pont-y-pant Gwynedd 40 D5 ham on R Lledr 3m/5km SW of Betws-y-coed. SH 7553
Pontypool (Pont-y-pwl) Gwent 15 G2 tn 8m/13km N of Newport. Tinplate, glass (at Pontymoel), nylon. Steel works at Griffithstown. SO 2800
Pontypridd Mid Glam 15 F3 tn at confluence of R Rhondda and R Taff 11m/18km NW of Cardiff. Coal-mining, engineering, light industry. ST 0790
Pont-y-pwl Welsh form of Pontypool, qv.
Pont-yr-hyl Mid Glam 15 E3 loc 2km N of Llangeinor. SS 9089
Pontywaun Gwent 15 G2 vil 2km NW of Risca. ST 2292
Pooksgreen Hants 10 B4 loc 2m/3km SE of Totton. SU 3710
Pool Cornwall 2 C4 loc 2m/3km NE of Camborne. SW 6641
Pool W Yorks 49 E4 vil on S side of R Wharfe 3m/4km E of Otley. SE 2445
Pool 52 D5* r rising near Crook, Cumbria, and flowing S into R Gilpin 2m/3km NW of Levens. SD 4687
Poolcray W Isles 88 E3* loc near S end of S Uist 2m/4km N of Kilbride. NF 7717
Pool Dole Staffs 35 E1* loc in Stoke-on-Trent on E side of Fenton. SJ 9044
Poole Dorset 9 G5 port and mnfg tn on P. Harbour 4m/6km W of Bournemouth. Resort and yachting centre. **P. Harbour,** expanse of water open to sea between Sandbanks and S Haven Pt and extending thence 6m/10km to mouth of R Frome near Wareham. SZ 0291
Poole N Yorks 49 G5* loc just S of Burton Salmon. SE 4927
Poole Bay Dorset 9 G5 bay on English Channel off Poole and Bournemouth extending from The Foreland eastwards to Hengistbury Hd. SZ 1089
Poole Green Ches 42 C5* ham 3m/4km NW of Nantwich. SJ 6355
Poole Keynes Glos 17 E2 vil 4m/7km S of Cirencester. SU 0095
Poolend Staffs 43 E5* loc 2m/3km NW of Leek. SJ 9658
Poolewe H'land 78 F2 vil at head of Loch Ewe, Ross and Cromarty dist, 4m/7km NE of Gairloch. NTS property N and E, esp Inverewe gardens to N. NG 8580
Pooley Bridge Cumbria 52 D3/53 E3 vil at NE end of Ullswater, 5m/7km SW of Penrith. NY 4724
Pooley Street Norfolk 39 E6* loc 4m/6km W of Diss. TM 0580
Poolfold Staffs 42 D5* ham 2m/3km NE of Biddulph. SJ 8959
Pool Green W Midlands 35 F4 loc adjoining Aldridge to S. SK 0500
Pool Head H & W 26 B3* loc 7m/11km NE of Hereford. SO 5550
Pool Hey Lancs 47 E6* loc 2m/4km SE of Southport. SD 3615
Poolhill Glos 26 C4* ham 2m/4km N of Newent. SO 7329
Pool, North Devon 4 D6* loc in par of S Pool 4m/6km N of Prawle Pt. SX 7741
Pool of Muckhart Central 72 D4 vil 3m/5km NE of Dollar. NO 0000
Pool Quay Powys 34 A3* locality on Shropshire Union Canal 3m/5km NE of Welshpool. SJ 2511
Poolsbrook Derbys 43 H4* loc 1m SE of Staveley. SK 4473
Pools of Dee Grampian 76 A1 group of three pools in Cairngorms at source of R Dee, to NW of Ben Macdui. NH 9700
Pool, South Devon 4 D6 vil 3m/5km N of Prawle Pt, at head of **Southpool Creek,** which runs into Kingsbridge Estuary. SX 7740
Poolstock Gtr Manchester 42 B1* dist of Wigan 1km SW of tn centre. SD 5604
Pool Street Essex 30 C4* ham 5m/8km NW of Halstead. TL 7637
Poolthorne Humberside 45 E1* loc 1m E of Cadney. TA 0303
Poor's End Lincs 45 G2* loc adjoining Grainthorpe to N. TF 3897
Poorton, North Dorset 8 C4 vil 3m/5km SE of Beaminster. SY 5198
Poorton, South Dorset 8 C4* ham adjoining vil of N Poorton and 5m/7km NE of Bridport. SY 5297
Pope Hill Dyfed 22 B4 loc 2m/4km SW of Haverfordwest. SM 9312
Popeswood Berks 18 C4* vil 2m/3km W of Bracknell. SU 8469
Popham Hants 10 C1 ham 4m/7km NE of Micheldever. SU 5543
Poplar London 20 A3* dist in borough of Tower Hamlets 3m/5km E of London Br. TQ 3780
Poplar Street Suffolk 31 H2* loc 2m/3km N of Leiston. TM 4465
Poppit Sands Dyfed 22 D1* sands at end of R Teifi estuary 2m/3km NW of Cardigan. SN 1548
Poppleton, Nether N Yorks 50 B3 vil on R Ouse 3m/5km NW of York. SE 5654
Poppleton, Upper N Yorks 50 B3 vil 3m/5km NW of York. SE 5554
Popton Point Dyfed 22 B5* headland on S shore of Milford Haven opp tn of Milford Haven. Jetty terminal for oil tankers. Oil pipeline from Llandarcy, qv. SM 8903
Porchester Notts 36 B1* suburb 2m/4km NE of Nottingham. SK 5942
Porchfield Isle of Wight 10 B5 ham 4m/7km SW of Cowes. SZ 4491
Pordenack Point Cornwall 2 A6* headland to S of Land's End. SW 3424
Porin H'land 80 D2 locality in Strathconon, Ross and Cromarty dist, 2m/3km above head of Loch Meig. NH 3155
Poringland, East Norfolk 39 F4 vil 5m/8km SE of Norwich. Ham of **W Poringland** 1km SW. TG 2701
Porkellis Cornwall 2 C5 vil 4m/6km NE of Helston. SW 6933
Porlock Som 7 F1 small resort near coast at foot of steep hill. To N, **P. Bay,** with large stony beach; submarine forest visible at low tide. At W end of beach, **P. Weir,** vil with small harbour. 1m W of Porlock, vil of **W Porlock.** SS 8846
Port Appin S'clyde 70 B1 vil in Argyll on E shore of Loch Linnhe opp N end of island of Lismore. Ferry to Pt Ramsay on island. NM 9045
Port Arnol W Isles 88 B1* bay on NW coast of Lewis 1km NW of Arnol vil. NB 2949
Port Askaig S'clyde 62 B1 vil and small port on E coast of Islay. Ferry to Feolin Ferry, Jura, on opp side of Sound of Islay; car ferry service to W Loch Tarbert on mainland. NR 4369
Port Bannatyne S'clyde 63 G1 large vil and resort on S side of Kames Bay, E coast of Bute, 2m/3km N of Rothesay. NS 0767
Portbury Avon 16 A4 vil 6m/9km W of Bristol. ST 4975
Port Carlisle Cumbria 59 G5 vil on R Eden estuary 11m/17km W of Carlisle. NY 2462
Port Charlotte S'clyde 62 A2 vil on W side of Loch Indaal, Islay, 7m/11km NE of Rinns Pt. NR 2558
Portchester Hants 10 C4 tn on N shore of Portsmouth Harbour. Norman cas (A.M.) with Norman ch in precincts, built within walls of Roman fort. SU 6105
Portclair Forest H'land 80 D5, D6 state forest in Inverness dist 4m/6km N of Fort Augustus. NH 3815
Port Clarence Cleveland 54 D3 loc on N bank of R Tees. Transporter br across r to Middlesbrough. NZ 4921
Port Cornaa Isle of Man 46 C4 small bay at mouth of stream 3m/5km NE of Laxey. SC 4787
Port Dinorwic Gwynedd 40 C4 small tn on Menai Strait 4m/6km SW of Bangor. SH 5267
Port Driseach S'clyde 63 F1* loc in Argyll on W shore of Kyles of Bute, 1m NE of Tighnabruaich. NR 9873
Port Dundas S'clyde 64 C2/D2* loc in Glasgow nearly 1m N of city centre. Distillery. NS 5966
Port Einon Welsh form of Port Eynon, qv.
Port Ellen S'clyde 62 B3 small tn and chief port of Islay, on S coast. Distillery. Airport at Glenegedale, 4m/7km NW. NR 3645
Port Elphinstone Grampian 83 F5 loc 1km S of Inverurie across R Don. NJ 7720
Portencross S'clyde 64 A4 loc on Firth of Clyde 5m/9km NW of Ardrossan. Remains of medieval cas. NS 1748
Porter alternative name for Lit Don R, S Yorks. SK 2997
Port Erin Isle of Man 46 A6 small port and resort on **Port Erin Bay** 9m/15km S of Peel. SC 1969
Port Erroll Grampian 83 H3 fishing vil on E coast, at N end of Bay of Cruden and adjoining vil of Cruden Bay to SE. NK 0936
Porter's Fen Corner Norfolk 38 B4* loc 2km S of Wiggenhall St Mary Magdalen. TF 5809
Portesham Dorset 8 D5 vil 6m/10km NW of Weymouth. SY 6085
Portessie Grampian 82 D1 E dist of Buckie on N coast. NJ 4466
Port e Vullen Isle of Man 46 C4 loc and small bay on SE side of Tableland Pt or Gob ny rona. SC 4792
Port Eynon (Port Einon) W Glam 23 F6 fishing vil on S coast of Gower peninsula 13m/21km W of Swansea. **Port Eynon Pt,** rocky headland 1km S, whence **P. E. Bay** extends E towards Oxwich Pt. SS 4865
Portfield W Sussex 11 E4* loc on E side of Chichester. SU 8704
Portfield Gate Dyfed 22 B4 ham 2m/3km W of Haverfordwest. SM 9215
Portgate Devon 6 C6 ham 6m/9km E of Launceston. SX 4185
Port Gaverne Cornwall 3 E1* ham on E side of Port Isaac. SX 0080
Port Glasgow S'clyde 64 B2 industrial tn on Firth of Clyde 3m/5km E of Greenock. Industries include shipbuilding, marine engineering, rope making, mnfre of sail-cloth. See also Newark Castle. NS 3274
Portgordon Grampian 82 C1 vil on Spey Bay 2m/3km SW of Buckie. NJ 3964
Portgower H'land 87 C5 loc on E coast of Sutherland dist 2m/3km SW of Helmsdale. ND 0013
Port Grenaugh Isle of Man 46 B6 inlet 1m W of Santon Hd. SC 3170
Port Groudle Isle of Man 46 C5* inlet at foot of Groudle Glen, 2m/3km SW of Clay Hd. SC 4278
Porth Mid Glam 15 E2 tn at confluence of Rhondda and Lit Rhondda Rs 3m/5km W of Pontypridd. ST 0291
Porthallow Cornwall 2 D5 coastal vil 9m/14km E of Helston. SW 7923
Porthallow Cornwall 3 G3* ham just inland from Talland Bay on S coast 2m/3km SW of Looe. SX 2251
Porth Cadwaladr Gwynedd 40 B5* inlet on Aberffraw Bay, W coast of Anglesey. SH 3666
Porthcawl Mid Glam 14 D4 coastal resort 6m/9km W of Bridgend. **Porthcawl Pt** is headland at S end of tn. SS 8176
Porth Ceiriad Gwynedd 32 B2 bay on S coast of Lleyn peninsula 2m/4km S of Abersoch. Extends from Trwyn Llech-y-doll eastwards to Trwyn yr Wylfa. SH 3124
Porthceri S Glam 15 F4 ham near coast 2m/3km SW of Barry. ST 0866
Porth China Gwynedd 40 A4* small inlet on W coast of Anglesey 2km W of Aberffraw. SH 3368
Porth Colmon Gwynedd 32 A2 bay 1km N of Llangwnnadl, extending from Penrhyn Colmon NE to Penrhyn Melyn. Also loc at SW end of bay. SH 2034
Porthcothan Cornwall 2 D2* ham on westward-facing coast 4m/7km SW of Padstow. SW 8572
Porthcurno Cornwall 2 A6 vil 3m/5km SE of Land's End, named after bay to SE. SW 3822
Porth Cwyfan Gwynedd 40 A4* small inlet on W coast of Anglesey 2km SW of Aberffraw. SH 3368
Porth Cynfor Gwynedd 40 B2* small bay on E side of Llanlleiana Hd, Anglesey. Also known as Hell's Mouth. SH 3994
Porth Dafarch Gwynedd 40 A3* inlet on coast of Holy I., Anglesey, 2m/3km S of Holyhead. SH 2379
Porth Diana Gwynedd 40 A4* inlet on coast of Holy I., Anglesey, on S side of Trearddur Bay. SH 2578
Porth Dinllaen Gwynedd 32 B1* loc on headland of Trwyn Porth Dinllaen; and the bay extending eastwards to Penrhyn Nefyn. SH 2741

Porth Eilean Gwynedd 40 B2* bay on N coast of Anglesey on W side of Point Lynas. SH 4793
Port Henderson H'land 78 E2 vil on W coast of Ross and Cromarty dist 4m/6km SW of Gairloch across Gair Loch. NG 7573
Porthgain Dyfed 22 B3 ham at head of Porthgain inlet 4m/6km W of Mathry. SM 8132
Porth Iago Gwynedd 32 A2* small bay to S of Penrhyn Mawr, 3m/5km N of Aberdaron. SH 1631
Porthill Salop 34 B3* W dist of Shrewsbury. SJ 4712
Porthill Staffs 42 D6* loc in Newcastle-under-Lyme 2m/3km N of tn centre. SJ 8548
Porthilly Cornwall 3 E1* loc above P. Cove on E side of R Camel estuary opp Padstow. SW 9375
Porth Ledden Cornwall 2 A5* bay to N of Cape Cornwall. SW 3532
Porthleven Cornwall 2 C5 small tn with harbour 2m/3km SW of Helston. **P. Sands** to SE. SW 6225
Porth Llanllawen Gwynedd 32 A2* small bay 2m/3km W of Aberdaron. SH 1426
Porth Llanlleiana Gwynedd 40 B2* small bay on N coast of Anglesey 2km NE of Cemaes Bay. SH 3895
Porth-llwyd 40 D4* r rising on E side of Carnedd Llywelyn, Gwynedd, and flowing E into R Conwy on NE side of Dolgarrog. SH 7768
Porthlysgi Bay Dyfed 22 A3* bay on S Dyfed coast 2m/3km SW of St David's. Cliffs NT. SM 7223
Porthmadog Gwynedd 32 D1 resort on R Glaslyn estuary 12m/19km E of Pwllheli and 3m/5km W of Penrhyndeudraeth across estuary. Former port for Ffestiniog slate industry. Also known as Portmadoc. SH 5638
Porth-mawr Dyfed 22 A3 bay (also known as Whitesand Bay) extending from St David's Hd southwards to Pt St John. SM 7227
Porth Mellin Cornwall 2 C6 vil above Mullion Cove 6m/10km S of Helston. SW 6617
Porthmeor Cornwall 2 A5* loc 5m/8km NW of Penzance. **P. Cove,** bay to W. SW 4337
Porth Navas Cornwall 2 C5 vil on creek running into Helford R 5m/8km SW of Falmouth. SW 7527
Porth Nefyn Gwynedd 32 B1* bay to NW of Nefyn on E side of Penrhyn Nefyn. SH 2940
Porth Neigwl Gwynedd 32 A2, B2 bay on S side of Lleyn peninsula extending from Trwyn Talfarach eastwards to Trywn y Fulfran, S of Llanengan. Also known as Hell's Mouth. SH 22
Porth Nobla Gwynedd 40 A4* inlet on W coast of Anglesey 2km SE of Rhosneigr. SH 3271
Portholland Cornwall 3 E4 ham on Veryan Bay 4m/7km SW of Mevagissey. SW 9641
Porthoustock Cornwall 2 D6 coastal vil 1m E of St Keverne. SW 8021
Porthpean Cornwall 3 E3 vil 2m/3km SE of St Austell. Consists of Hr and Lr Porthpean, running down to St Austell Bay. SX 0350
Porth Penrhyn-mawr Gwynedd 40 A3* bay 3m/4km E of Holyhead across Holyhead Bay. SH 2883
Porth Reservoir Cornwall 2 D2* resr 4m/6km E of Newquay. SW 8662
Porth Ruffydd Gwynedd 40 A3* inlet on coast of Holy I., Anglesey, 3m/4km SW of Holyhead. SH 2179
Porthscatho Cornwall 2 D4 vil at SW end of Gerrans Bay. SW 8735
Porth Sgiwed Welsh form of Portskewett, qv.
Porth Swtan Gwynedd 40 A3* small westward-facing bay on coast of Anglesey 2m/4km S of Carmel Hd. SH 2989
Porthtowan Cornwall 2 C4 vil 4m/6km N of Redruth named after bay at its NW end. SW 6947
Porth Trecastell Gwynedd 40 A4* small bay on W coast of Anglesey 2m/3km SE of Rhosneigr. SH 3370
Porth Trefadog Gwynedd 40 A3* small bay on NW coast of Anglesey 3m/5km NE of Holyhead across Holyhead Bay. SH 2986
Porth Trwyn Gwynedd 40 A3* small bay on NW coast of Anglesey 3m/5km S of Carmel Hd. SH 2987
Porth Tywyn-mawr Gwynedd 40 A3* bay on NW coast of Anglesey 3m/5km NE of Holyhead across Holyhead Bay. SH 2885
Porth Wen Gwynedd 40 B2 bay on N coast of Anglesey 3m/4km W of Amlwch. SH 4094
Porthwgan Clwyd 42 A6* loc 4m/6km SE of Wrexham. SJ 3846
Porth-y-bribys Gwynedd 40 A3* small bay 2km S of Carmel Hd, Anglesey. SH 2991
Porth-y-felin Gwynedd 40 A3* loc adjoining Holyhead to NW, on cove of same name. SH 2483
Porth-y-garan Gwynedd 40 A4* inlet on coast of Holy I., Anglesey, 2km S of Trearddur Bay. SH 2577
Porth y Nant Gwynedd 32 B1 bay of shallow curvature on Caernarvon Bay between Trwyn y Gorlech and Penrhyn Glas, SW of Trevor. Old quarries above bay. SH 3444
Porth-y-post Gwynedd 40 A3* small inlet on coast of Holy I., Anglesey, 2m/3km S of Holyhead. SH 2479
Porthyrhyd Dyfed 23 F4 vil 3m/5km NW of Cross Hands. SN 5115
Porthyrhyd Dyfed 24 C4 ham 4m/7km NW of Llandovery. SN 7137
Porth-y-waen Salop 34 A2 loc 4m/7km SW of Oswestry. SJ 2623
Portincaple S'clyde 70 D5 locality on Loch Long 2km N of Garelochhead. NS 2393
Portington Humberside 50 C5 ham 3m/5km NE of Howden. SE 7830
Portinnisherrich S'clyde 70 B4 locality on E shore of Loch Awe in Argyll 8m/13km SW of Portsonachan. NM 9711
Portinscale Cumbria 52 C3 vil at N end of Derwent Water and 1m W of Keswick. NY 2523
Port Isaac Cornwall 3 E1 vil with harbour on N coast 5m/8km N of Wadebridge. To NE, **P. I. Bay,** extending from Varley Pt north-westwards to Penhallic Pt. SW 9980
Portishead Avon 16 A4 small port, residential tn and holiday resort 8m/12km W of Bristol. **Portishead Pt,** headland on R Severn estuary to N. ST 4676
Port Jack Isle of Man 46 B5* inlet at NE end of Douglas Bay. SC 3977
Portkil Bay S'clyde 64 A1 bay on Firth of Clyde 2km E of Kilcreggan. NS 2580
Port Kilcheran S'clyde. See Kilcheran Loch.
Portknockie Grampian 82 D1 fishing vil and resort on N coast 4m/7km NE of Buckie. NJ 4868
Port Laing Fife 65 G1* loc with landing stage on Inverkeithing Bay, to N of N Queensferry. NT 1381
Portland, Isle of Dorset 9 E6 4m/7km S of Weymouth. Limestone peninsula 4m/7km N to S and 2m/3km E to W connected with mainland by Chesil Bank, qv. Quarries of P. stone. HM prison. **P. Harbour,** 4km across and built by convict labour, lies between P. and Weymouth. **P. Bill,** or **Bill of P.,** is the S tip of the peninsula and marks the E extremity of Lyme Bay. **P. Castle** (A.M.), 16c–18c, at N end. SY 6972
Portlemouth, East Devon 4 D6 vil 1km E of Salcombe across Kingsbridge Estuary. Ferry for pedestrians. SX 7438
Portlethen Grampian 77 H2 vil on E coast 6m/10km S of Aberdeen. Inshore fishing. NO 9396
Port Lewaigue Isle of Man 46 C4* small bay 2km SE of Ramsey. SC 4693
Port Lion Dyfed 22 C5* loc 1km S of Llangwm. SM 9908
Portloe Cornwall 3 E4 vil on Veryan Bay 6m/10km SW of Mevagissey. Coast SW to Nare Hd largely NT. SW 9339
Port Logan D & G 57 B8 vil on W coast of Rinns of Galloway, 4m/6km NW of Drummore. **P.L. Bay** extends northwards to headland of Mull of Logan. **Logan Botanic Gardens** 2km N. NX 0940
Portlooe Cornwall 3 G3* loc 1m SW of Looe. SX 2452
Portmadoc Gwynedd. Alternative spelling of Porthmadog, qv.
Portmahomack H'land 87 C7 vil on S shore of Dornoch Firth 3m/5km SW of Tarbat Ness, Ross and Cromarty dist. NH 9184
Portmeirion Gwynedd 32 D1 secluded small resort on peninsula on N side of Traeth Bach, 2m/3km SW of Penrhyndeudraeth. SH 5837
Port Mhór Bragar W Isles 88 B1* bay on NW coast of Lewis 1m N of Bragar. NB 2849
Port Mór H'land 68 C2 loc with small harbour near SE end of island of Muck in Inner Hebrides. NM 4279
Port Mór S'clyde 62 D3 bay with jetty at N end of island of Gigha. NR 6654
Portmore Hants 10 A5* loc 2km NE of Lymington. SZ 3397
Portmore Loch Borders 66 A3/A4 small loch 2m/3km NE of Eddleston. NT 2650
Port Mulgrave N Yorks 55 F3 loc 1km N of Hinderwell. NZ 7917
Portnacroish S'clyde 70 B1 vil on Loch Laich, Argyll, on E side of Loch Linnhe. NM 9247
Port na Curaich S'clyde 69 B6* small bay at S end of Iona. Supposed landing-place of St Columba in 563. NM 2621
Portnaguiran W Isles 88 C2 vil at N end of Eye Peninsula, Lewis, 1m W of Tiumpan Hd. **P. New Lands** is loc 1km SW. NB 5537
Portnahaven S'clyde 62 A3 vil at S end of Rinns of Islay 1m SE of Rubha na Faing. NR 1652
Port na h-Eithar Coll, S'clyde 68 A4 bay on SE coast 3m/4km SW of Arinagour. NM 2053
Port na Long Skye, H'land 79 B5* locality between Loch Harport and Fiskavaig Bay, 3m/4km NW of Carbost. NG 3434
Portnaluchaig H'land 68 E1 loc on W coast of Lochaber dist 2m/3km N of Arisaig. NM 6589
Port na Muice Duibhe S'clyde 69 E5 small bay on SE coast of Mull 3m/4km SW of entrance to Loch Spelve. NM 6924
Portnancon H'land 84 D2 locality on W shore of Loch Eriboll, Sutherland dist, 5m/8km S of Durness. Ancient earth-house to N. NC 4260
Port Nessock D & G. Alternative name for Port Logan Bay – see Port Logan.
Portobello Lothian 66 B2 dist of Edinburgh on Firth of Forth 3m/5km E of city centre. Extensive sands. NT 3073
Portobello Tyne & Wear 61 G5* loc 1m E of Birtley. Service area on A1(M) motorway. NZ 2855
Portobello W Midlands 35 F4* E dist of Wolverhampton. SO 9598
Portobello W Yorks 49 E6* loc in Wakefield 2km S of city centre across R Calder. SE 3318
Port of Menteith Central 71 G4 vil at NE corner of Lake of Menteith, 5m/8km SW of Callander. NN 5801
Port of Ness W Isles 88 C1 vil on NE coast of Lewis 2m/3km SE of Butt of Lewis. NB 5363
Port Ohirnie S'clyde 69 E6 small bay on SE coast of Mull 2m/4km E of entrance to Loch Buie. NM 6320
Porton Wilts 9 H1 vil on R Bourne 5m/8km NE of Salisbury. SU 1936
Portontown Devon 4 B3* loc 4m/6km NW of Tavistock. SX 4276
Portpatrick D & G 57 A7 small resort with harbour on coast of Rinns of Galloway, 6m/9km SW of Stranraer, which succeeded P. as port for Ireland from mid-19c. NX 0054
Port Penrhyn Gwynedd 40 C4 dock of former port on Menai Strait 1m E of Bangor. SH 5972
Portquin Cornwall 3 E1 ham on N coast at head of inlet of **P. Bay,** which extends from Kellan Hd westwards to Rumps Pt. Cliffs round bay largely NT. SW 9780
Port Ramsay S'clyde 70 B1 locality at N end of Lismore in Loch Linnhe. Ferry to Port Appin on mainland to E. NM 8845
Portreath Cornwall 2 C4 coastal vil 4m/6km NW of Redruth. NT owns coast to W. SW 6545
Portree H'land 79 C5 port and chief tn of island of Skye, situated on Loch P. on E coast, about midway between Rubha Hunish in the N and Strathaird Pt in the S. NG 4843
Port St Mary Isle of Man 46 A6 fishing vil and resort on **Port St Mary Bay** 2m/4km NE of Spanish Hd. SC 2067
Portscatho Cornwall 2 D4 alternative spelling for Porthscatho, vil at SW end of Gerrans Bay. SW 8735
Portsdown Hants 10 C4, D4 chalk ridge running E and W above Portsmouth and Portsmouth Harbour. On ridge are six Palmerston forts built mid-19c for defence against French; also Nelson monmt, and 20c naval installations. SU 6406
Portsea Hants 10 D4 loc on Portsea I. 1km W of Portsmouth city centre. SU 6300
Portsea Island Hants 10 D4 island, on which most of Portsmouth is situated, between Portsmouth and Langstone Harbours, separated from mainland by tidal creek which, however, is spanned by four bridges. SU 6601
Port Seton Lothian. See Cockenzie and Port Seton.
Portskerra H'land 86 B2 vil near N coast of Caithness dist, adjoining Melvich to NW. NC 8765
Portskewett (Porth Sgiwed) Gwent 16 A3 vil 4m/7km SW of Chepstow. Site of Roman bldg to N. ST 4988
Port Skigersta W Isles 88 C1 small bay near N end of Lewis to NE of vil of Skigersta. NB 5462
Portslade E Sussex 11 H4 dist of Portslade-by-Sea N of tn centre. TQ 2506
Portslade-by-Sea E Sussex 11 H4 tn 3m/5km W of Brighton. Power stns and refinery. TQ 2605
Portsmouth Hants 10 D4 port and naval base (P. Harbour, on W side of city) 65m/105km SW of London. Industrial city with various industries, extending from S end of Portsea I. to S slopes of Portsdown. City airport at N end of Portsea I. Boat and hovercraft ferries to Isle of Wight. Cathedral. Nelson's flagship *HMS Victory* in harbour. SU 6400
Portsmouth W Yorks 48 B5* vil 3m/4km NW of Todmorden. SD 9026
Portsmouth Arms Devon 7 E3 loc 5m/8km NW of Chulmleigh. SS 6319
Port Soderick Isle of Man 46 B6 small bay 3m/5km SW of Douglas. SC 3472
Portsonachan (or Port Sonachan) S'clyde 70 C3 vil on E shore of Loch Awe in Argyll 8m/13km SW of Dalmally. NN 0520
Portsoy Grampian 83 E1 fishing vil on N coast 6m/10km W of Banff. NJ 5865
Port Sunlight Merseyside 41 H3 industrial loc on Wirral peninsula beside R Mersey estuary 3m/5km SE of Birkenhead. Soap mnfre. Lady Lever Art Gallery. SJ 3484
Portswood Hants 10 B3* NE dist of Southampton. SU 4314
Port Talbot W Glam 14 D3 tn and port at mouth of R Afan 8m/12km E of Swansea across Swansea Bay. Oil refinery at Baglan. Steel works at Margam. SS 7690
Port Tennant W Glam 23 H6* loc in Swansea 2km E of tn centre across R Tawe. SS 6793
Portuairk H'land 68 C2 loc near W end of Ardnamurchan peninsula in Lochaber dist, 2m/3km E of Ardnamurchan Pt. NM 4368
Portvoller W Isles 88 C2* loc on Eye Peninsula, Lewis, 1km S of Tiumpan Hd. **P. Bay** to S. NB 5636
Portway H & W 26 A4* loc 3m/5km S of Hereford. SO 4935
Portway H & W 26 A3 ham 4m/6km NW of Hereford. SO 4845

Portway H & W 25 H3 loc 9m/14km W of Hereford. SO 3844
Portway Som 8 C1* S dist of Street. ST 4836
Portway Warwicks 27 E1* ham 4m/7km NE of Redditch. SP 0872
Portway W Midlands 35 F5* loc 2m/3km NW of Warley tn centre. SO 9788
Port Wemyss S'clyde 62 A3 vil at S end of Rinns of Islay opp island of Orsay. NR 1651
Port William D & G 57 D7 small resort with quay on E shore of Luce Bay, 9m/15km SW of Wigtown. NX 3343
Portwrinkle Cornwall 3 H3* vil on Whitsand Bay 6m/10km W of Torpoint. SX 3553
Portyerrock D & G 57 E8 loc on **P. Bay** 2m/4km SE of Whithorn. NX 4738
Posbury Devon 7 F5* loc 2m/3km SW of Crediton. SX 8197
Posenhall Salop 34 D4* loc 2m/3km SW of Ironbridge. SJ 6501
Poslingford Suffolk 30 C3 vil 2m/3km N of Clare. TL 7748
Possil Park S'clyde 64 C2/D2* dist of Glasgow 2m/3km N of city centre. Iron foundry. **High Possil** is locality to N; **Possil Loch** is small loch on N side of Forth and Clyde Canal. NS 5968
Postbridge Devon 4 C3 ham on Dartmoor 8m/13km SW of Moretonhampstead. Clapper br over E Dart R. SX 6579
Postbrook, Little Hants 10 C4* loc 2km S of Titchfield and 3m/5km S of Park Gate. SU 5304
Postcombe Oxon 18 C2* vil 4m/6km N of Watlington. SU 7099
Post Green Dorset 9 F5* loc just NW of Lytchett Minster. SY 9593
Postling Kent 13 G3 vil 3m/5km N of Hythe. TR 1439
Post-mawr (or Synod Inn) Dyfed 24 A3 loc at crossroads 4m/6km S of Newquay. SN 4054
Postwick Norfolk 39 G4 vil 4m/7km E of Norwich. TG 2907
Potheridge Devon 6 D4* three locs, **Gt P., Lit P.,** and **P. Gate,** between 3m/5km and 4m/6km SE of Torrington. SS 5114
Potrail Water 59 E1 r in Strathclyde region rising on Lowther Hills and running NE to join Daer Water and form R Clyde 2m/3km S of Elvanfoot. NS 9513
Potsgrove Beds 28 D4* vil 2m/3km S of Woburn. SP 9529
Potten End Herts 19 E1 loc 2m/3km E of Berkhamsted. TL 0108
Potter Brompton N Yorks 51 E1* ham 1m SW of Ganton. SE 9777
Pottergate Street Norfolk 39 F5* loc 2km W of Wacton. TM 1591
Potterhanworth Lincs 45 E4 vil 6m/10km SE of Lincoln. **P. Booths** ham 2m/3km NE. TF 0566
Potter Heigham Norfolk 39 G3/H3 vil 10m/16km NW of Gt Yarmouth. TG 4119
Potter Hill S Yorks 43 G2* loc adjoining High Green to SW. SK 3397
Potterne Wilts 17 E5 vil 2m/3km S of Devizes. Ham of **P. Wick** on S side. ST 9958
Potternewton W Yorks 49 E4* loc in Harehills dist of Leeds 2km NE of city centre. SE 3136
Potter Row Bucks 18 D2* loc 1m NE of Gt Missenden. SP 9002
Potters Bar Herts 19 F2 tn 13m/21km N of London. TL 2501
Potters Brook Lancs 47 F3* loc 1m N of Forton. SD 4852
Potters Crouch Herts 19 E1 ham 2m/4km SW of St Albans. TL 1105
Potter's Green E Sussex 12 B4* loc on E side of Buxted. TQ 5023
Potter's Green W Midlands 36 A6* loc in Coventry 3m/5km NE of city centre. SP 3782
Pottershill Avon 16 A4* loc 1m NE of Bristol (Lulsgate) Airport and 6m/10km SW of Bristol. ST 5166
Potters Marston Leics 36 B4* ham 8m/13km SW of Leicester. SP 4996
Potter Somersal Derbys 35 G1* loc 1km NE of Somersal Herbert. SK 1435
Potterspury Northants 28 C3 vil 3m/5km NW of Stony Stratford. SP 7543
Potter Street Essex 20 B1 E dist of Harlow. TL 4709
Potter Tarn Cumbria 53 E4* small lake 4m/7km N of Kendal. SD 4998
Potterton W Yorks 49 F4* loc 1m N of Barwick in Elmet. SE 4039
Potthorpe Norfolk 38 D3* loc adjoining Brisley to NW. TF 9422
Pottle Street Wilts 9 E1* loc adjoining Horningsham to S and 2km NE of Maiden Bradley. ST 8140
Potto N Yorks 54 D4 vil 5m/8km SW of Stokesley. NZ 4703
Potton Beds 29 F3 small tn 4m/6km NE of Biggleswade, in market-gardening area. TL 2249
Potton Creek Essex 21 E3* inlet on W side of Potton I., 4m/6km N of Shoeburyness. TQ 9490
Potton Island Essex 21 E3 island on S side of R Roach estuary 4m/6km N of Shoeburyness. TQ 9591
Pott Row Norfolk 38 C3* loc 1km S of Roydon. TF 7021
Pott's Green Essex 30 D5* loc 6m/9km W of Colchester. TL 9123
Pott Shrigley Ches 43 E3* ham 1m NE of Bollington. SJ 9479
Poughill Cornwall 6 B4 vil 2km NE of Bude. SS 2207
Poughill Devon 7 F4 vil 5m/9km N of Crediton. SS 8508
Poulner Hants 9 H4 loc 2km E of Ringwood. SU 1605
Poulner, North Hants 9 H3* loc 2km NE of Ringwood. SU 1606
Poulshott Wilts 17 E5 vil 3m/4km SW of Devizes. ST 9759
Poulter 44 B4 r rising SE of Bolsover, Derbys, and flowing E through Clumber Park in The Dukeries into R Idle 4m/6km S of E Retford, Notts. SK 7075
Poulton Glos 17 E2 vil 5m/8km E of Cirencester. **P. Priory** loc and remains of medieval priory 1km SW. SP 1000
Poulton Merseyside 41 H2 loc in Wallasey 2km W of tn hall. SJ 3091
Poulton-le-Fylde Lancs 47 E4 tn 3m/5km NE of Blackpool. SD 3439
Poulton Royd Merseyside 41 H3* loc 1m S of Bebington. SJ 3282
Pound Bank H & W 26 C3* loc in E part of Gt Malvern. SO 7945
Pound Bank H & W 26 C1* loc 4m/6km W of Bewdley. SO 7373
Poundffald W Glam 23 G6 vil 6m/9km W of Swansea. SS 5694
Poundfield E Sussex 12 B4* loc on E side of Crowborough. TQ 5230
Poundgate E Sussex 12 B4 loc 2m/3km SW of Crowborough. TQ 4928
Pound Green E Sussex 12 B4 ham adjoining Buxted to E. TQ 5023
Pound Green Hants 18 B5* ham 3m/5km E of Kingsclere. SU 5759
Pound Green H & W 35 D6* loc 3m/4km NW of Bewdley. SO 7578
Pound Green Isle of Wight 10 A5* loc 1km SW of Freshwater. SZ 3386
Pound Green Norfolk 38 D4* loc adjoining Shipdham to E. TF 9607
Pound Green Suffolk 30 C3* ham 6m/10km NE of Haverhill. TL 7154
Pound Hill W Sussex 11 H2 E dist of Crawley. TQ 2937
Poundon Bucks 28 B5 vil 4m/7km NE of Bicester. Loc of **P. Hill** 1km W. SP 6425
Poundsbridge Kent 12 B3 loc 3m/5km NW of Tunbridge Wells. TQ 5341
Poundsgate Devon 4 D3 ham on E side of Dartmoor 4m/6km NW of Ashburton. SX 7072
Poundstock Cornwall 6 B5 vil 4m/7km S of Bude. SX 2099
Pound Street Hants 17 H5* loc 1m NE of Highclere. SU 4561
Powburn Nthmb 67 G6 vil 2km N of Glanton. NU 0616
Powderham Devon 5 F2 ham on right (W) bank of R Exe estuary 5m/8km N of Dawlish. Cas, home of Courtenays since 14c; present hse mainly 18c. Deer park. SX 9684
Powdermill Reservoir E Sussex 12 D5* resr in wooded area 2km E of Sedlescombe. TQ 8019
Powerstock Dorset 8 C4 vil 4m/6km NE of Bridport. SY 5196
Powfoot D & G 59 F5 vil on Solway Firth 3m/5km W of Annan. NY 1465
Powick H & W 26 D3 vil 3m/4km SW of Worcester. SO 8351
Powis Castle Powys 33 H4 medieval cas (NT) in park on S side of Welshpool. SJ 2106
Powmill Tayside 72 D4 vil 4m/6km E of Dollar. NT 0198
Powys 118 large county of central Wales, contiguous with all the other Welsh counties except S Glamorgan, and with the English counties of Salop and Hereford & Worcester. It is almost entirely rural. The terrain is mountainous, much of the country being open moorland where sheep and ponies graze. There is considerable afforestation, and a number of large resrs. N of Brecon is an extensive military training area. Tns include Brecon, Builth Wells, Llandrindod Wells, the county tn, Newtown and Welshpool. Among the many rs the largest are the Severn, Usk, and Wye.
Poxwell Dorset 9 E5 ham 5m/9km SE of Dorchester. SY 7484
Poyle Surrey 19 E4 loc with trading estate at W end of London (Heathrow) Airport 3m/5km N of Staines. TQ 0376
Poyll Vaaish Isle of Man 46 A6* inlet on E side of Bay ny Carrickey 2km W of Castletown. SC 2467
Poynders End Herts 29 F5* loc 3m/5km S of Hitchin. TL 1924
Poynings W Sussex 11 H4 vil below Devil's Dyke on S Downs 6m/10km NW of Brighton. TQ 2612
Poyntington Dorset 8 D2 vil 2m/4km N of Sherborne. ST 6520
Poynton Ches 43 E3 tn 5m/7km S of Stockport. **P. Lake** to N. SJ 9283
Poynton Salop 34 C3 loc 6m/10km NE of Shrewsbury. **P. Green** ham 1km N. SJ 5717
Poys Street Suffolk 31 G2* ham 3m/4km W of Yoxford. TM 3570
Poyston Dyfed 22 C4 loc 3m/5km NE of Haverfordwest. **P. Cross** loc 1m E. SM 9619
Poystreet Green Suffolk 30 D2* loc 1km S of Rattlesden. TL 9858
Praa Sands Cornwall 2 B5 vil 5m/8km W of Helston, named after long sandy beach to S. SW 5828
Pratling Street Kent 20 D5* loc 1m E of Aylesford. TQ 7459
Pratt's Bottom London 20 B5 loc in borough of Bromley 2m/3km SE of Orpington. TQ 4762
Prawle, East Devon 4 D6 vil 2km NE of Prawle Pt. SX 7836
Prawle Point Devon 4 D6 headland (NT) at southernmost point of Devon, 3m/5km SE of Salcombe across Kingsbridge Estuary. Cliffs along coast to NW are also NT property. SX 7735
Prawle, West Devon 4 D6* loc 2m/3km N of Prawle Pt. SX 7637
Praze-an-Beeble Cornwall 2 C5 vil 3m/4km S of Camborne. SW 6335
Predannack Head Cornwall 2 C6* headland on W side of Lizard peninsula 4m/6km NW of Lizard Pt. SW 6616
Prees Salop 34 C1 vil 5m/8km S of Whitchurch. Locs of **P. Hr Heath** and **P. Lr Heath** 2m/3km N and 2km SE respectively. SJ 5533
Preesall Lancs 47 E3 loc 3m/4km E of Fleetwood across R Wyre estuary. SD 3646
Prees Green Salop 34 C2 vil 4m/6km NE of Wem. SJ 5631
Preesgweene Salop 34 A1* loc adjoining Weston Rhyn to E. SJ 2936
Prendergast Dyfed 22 C4 loc adjoining Haverfordwest to NE. SM 9516
Prendwick Nthmb 61 E1 ham 4m/7km W of Whittingham. NU 0012
Pren-gwyn Dyfed 24 A4 ham 2m/4km N of Llandyssul. SN 4244
Prenteg Gwynedd 32 D1 ham 2m/3km NE of Portmadoc. SH 5841
Prenton Merseyside 41 H3 loc in Birkenhead 3m/4km SW of tn centre. SJ 3086
Prescelly Top (Foel Cwm-cerwyn) Dyfed 22 C3 summit of Mynydd Presely, qv, 6m/9km SE of Newport. Height 1760 ft or 537 metres. SN 0931
Prescot Merseyside 42 A2 tn 4m/6km SW of St Helens. Cable mnfre, etc. SJ 4692
Prescott Devon 7 H4* ham 6m/10km NE of Cullompton. ST 0814
Prescott Glos 27 E4* loc 2m/4km W of Winchcombe. SO 9829
Prescott Salop 34 B2 loc 7m/11km NW of Shrewsbury. SJ 4221
Preseli 118 admin dist of Dyfed.
Preshute Wilts 17 F4* loc adjoining Marlborough to W. Site of Roman bldg on Barton Down to NW. SU 1868
Press Derbys 43 H4* loc 2m/3km NW of Clay Cross. **Press Resrs,** series of three small resrs to NW. SK 3565
Pressen Nthmb 67 E5 loc 3m/4km SW of Cornhill on Tweed. NT 8335
Prestatyn Clwyd 41 F3 resort near N Wales coast 4m/6km E of Rhyl. Situated at N end of Clwydian Hills and of Offa's Dyke and Offa's Dyke Path. SJ 0682
Prestbury Ches 42 D3 vil 2m/4km NW of Macclesfield. SJ 9077
Prestbury Glos 27 E5 NE suburb of Cheltenham. SO 9723
Prestbury Park Glos 26 D5 loc with racecourse 2m/3km NE of Cheltenham. SO 9524
Presteigne (Llanandras) Powys 25 G2 small tn on R Lugg 5m/8km S of Knighton. 17c br spans r. SO 3164
Presthope Salop 34 C4* ham 3m/5km SW of Much Wenlock. SO 5897
Prestleigh Som 8 D1 ham 2m/3km SE of Shepton Mallet. Site of Agricultural Show Grnd. ST 6340
Prestolee Gtr Manchester 42 C1 loc 3m/5km SE of Bolton. SD 7505
Preston Borders 67 E3 vil 2m/4km N of Duns. NT 7957
Preston Devon 5 E3 loc 2m/3km N of Newton Abbot. SX 8574
Preston Devon 5 E4* N dist of Paignton. SX 8961
Preston Dorset 9 E5 loc 3m/5km NW of Weymouth. Site of Roman villa to S. Slight remains of Roman temple (A.M.) at Jordan Hill, to SW. SY 7083
Preston E Sussex 11 H4 dist of Brighton 2km N of tn centre. TQ 3006
Preston Glos 17 E2 vil 2km SE of Cirencester. SP 0400
Preston Glos 26 B4/C4* loc 3m/4km SW of Ledbury. SO 6734
Preston Herts 29 F5 vil 3m/5km S of Hitchin. TL 1824
Preston Humberside 51 F5 vil 2km N of Hedon. TA 1830
Preston Kent 13 G1 vil 2m/3km N of Wingham. Loc of **P. Street** adjoins to N. TR 2560
Preston Kent 21 F5 loc in SE part of Faversham. TR 0260
Preston Lancs 47 F5 large textile and engineering tn on N bank of R Ribble 27m/45km NW of Manchester. SD 5429
Preston Leics 36 D4 vil 2m/3km N of Uppingham. SK 8702
Preston London 19 F3 loc in borough of Brent 9m/14km NW of Charing Cross. TQ 1887
Preston Lothian 66 D1* vil adjoining E Linton to N. Mill (NTS) on banks of R Tyne dates from 17c; still in working order. NT 5977
Preston Nthmb 67 H5 ham 1m E of Ellingham. Medieval tower hse. NU 1725
Preston Salop 34 C3* loc 2m/3km W of Upton Magna. SJ 5211
Preston Som 7 H2* ham 5m/8km SE of Watchet. ST 1035
Preston Suffolk 30 D3 vil 2m/3km NE of Lavenham. TL 9450
Preston Wilts 17 E4 ham 4m/6km SW of Wootton Bassett. SU 0377
Preston Bagot Warwicks 27 F1* ham 2m/3km E of Henley-in-Arden. SP 1765
Preston Bissett Bucks 28 B4 vil 4m/6km SW of Buckingham. SP 6529
Preston Bowyer Som 8 A2* ham in Vale of Taunton Deane 1m E of Milverton. ST 1326
Preston Brockhurst Salop 34 C2 vil 3m/5km SE of Wem. SJ 5324
Preston Brook Ches 42 B3* ham 3m/5km E of Runcorn. Junction of Trent and Mersey Canal and Bridgewater Canal. SJ 5680
Preston Candover Hants 10 C1 vil 6m/10km N of New Alresford. SU 6041
Preston Capes Northants 28 B2 vil 5m/8km S of Daventry. SP 5754
Preston Deanery Northants 28 C2 loc 4m/6km SE of Northampton. SP 7855
Preston, East W Sussex 11 F4 coastal tn 3m/4km E of Littlehampton. TQ 0702
Prestonfield Lothian 66 A2* dist of Edinburgh 2m/3km SE of city centre. NT 2771
Preston Grange Tyne & Wear 61 H4* loc 1km NW of Preston and 2km SW of Whitley Bay. NZ 3470
Preston, Great W Yorks 49 F5 vil in coal-mining area 2m/4km S of Garforth. **Lit Preston** loc 2km NW, adjoining Swillington to E. SE 4029

Preston Green Warwicks 27 F1* ham 1m E of Henley-in-Arden. SP 1665
Preston Gubbals Salop 34 B3 vil 4m/7km N of Shrewsbury. SJ 4919
Preston-le-Skerne Durham 54 C3* loc 2m/3km E of Newton Aycliffe. NZ 3024
Preston, Little Northants 28 B2* ham 1m SE of Preston Capes and 5m/9km S of Daventry. SP 5854
Preston Montford Salop 34 B3* loc 4m/6km W of Shrewsbury. SJ 4314
Preston on Stour Warwicks 27 F3 vil 3m/5km S of Stratford-upon-Avon. SP 2049
Preston-on-Tees Cleveland 54 D3* loc 2m/3km S of Stockton-on-Tees. NZ 4315
Preston on the Hill Ches 42 B3 ham 4m/6km E of Runcorn. SJ 5780
Preston on Wye H & W 25 H4 vil on S side of R Wye 8m/13km W of Hereford. SO 3842
Prestonpans Lothian 66 B2 tn on Firth of Forth 3m/5km NE of Musselburgh. Industries include brewing, light engineering, mnfre of bricks and tiles, soap, tyres. Hamilton Hse (NTS), built 1628. On E side of tn is site of battle of 1745 in which Prince Charles Edward defeated government forces under Sir John Cope. NT 3874
Preston Patrick Cumbria 53 E6* loc 6m/10km S of Kendal. SD 5483
Preston Plucknett Som 8 D3 W dist of Yeovil. ST 5316
Preston Richard Cumbria 53 E6* loc 5m/9km S of Kendal. SD 5384
Preston-under-Scar N Yorks 54 A5 vil 3m/5km W of Leyburn. Quarries on moors to N. SE 0791
Preston upon the Weald Moors Salop 34 D3 vil 3m/5km NE of Wellington. SJ 6815
Preston, West W Sussex 11 F4 dist of Rustington 2m/3km E of Littlehampton. TQ 0502
Preston Wynne H & W 26 B3 vil 5m/8km NE of Hereford. SO 5547
Prestwich Gtr Manchester 42 D1 tn 4m/6km NW of Manchester. Textiles. SD 8203
Prestwick Nthmb 61 F4 ham 2km E of Ponteland. NZ 1872
Prestwick S'clyde 64 B6 tn and resort on Firth of Clyde adjoining Ayr to N. International airport. NS 3525
Prestwold Leics 36 B2 loc 3m/4km E of Loughborough. Consists of hall and ch. SK 5721
Prestwood Bucks 18 D2 suburban loc 2m/3km W of Gt Missenden. SP 8700
Prestwood Staffs 35 G1* loc 2m/3km N of Rocester. SK 1042
Price Town Mid Glam 15 E2 coal-mining vil 8m/13km N of Bridgend. SS 9392
Prickwillow Cambs 38 B6 vil on R Lark 4m/6km E of Ely. TL 5982
Priddy Som 16 A6 vil on Mendip Hills 4m/6km NW of Wells. ST 5251
Priestacott Devon 6 C4* loc 6m/9km NE of Holsworthy. SS 4206
Priestacott, Higher Devon 6 C5* ham 6m/9km SE of Holsworthy. SX 3996
Priestcliffe Derbys 43 F4 loc 1km N of Taddington. SK 1371
Priestfield H & W 26 D3* loc 3m/4km E of Gt Malvern. SO 8244
Priestfield W Midlands 35 F4* loc 2m/3km SE of Wolverhampton tn centre. SO 9397
Priestholm Gwynedd. Alternative name for Puffin I., qv.
Priest Hutton Lancs 47 F1 vil 3m/5km NE of Carnforth. SD 5373
Priest Island H'land 85 A6* uninhabited island, outlier of the Summer Isles group, 4m/7km NE of Greenstone Pt on W coast of Ross and Cromarty dist. Area about 500 acres or 200 hectares. Also known as Eilean a' Chleirich. NB 9202
Priestley Green W Yorks 48 D5* loc 3m/4km E of Halifax. SE 1326
Priest's Nose Dyfed 22 C5/C6* headland at SE end of Manorbier Bay. SS 0597
Priest's Tarn N Yorks 48 C2* small lake on Grassington Moor 4m/6km NE of Grassington. SE 0269
Priest Thorpe W Yorks 48 D4* E dist of Bingley. SE 1139
Priestweston Salop 34 A4 vil 2m/4km NE of Church Stoke. Mitchell's Ford Stone Circle (A.M.) 1m NE. SO 2997
Priestwood Berks 18 D4* dist of Bracknell to W of tn centre. SU 8669
Priestwood Kent 20 C5* loc 1m S of Meopham. Loc of **P. Green** adjoins to S. TQ 6564
Primethorpe Leics 36 B5 loc 5m/9km N of Lutterworth. SP 5292
Primrose Tyne & Wear 61 G5* loc in S Tyneside dist 2km S of Jarrow. NZ 3263
Primrose Green Norfolk 39 E3* loc 1m E of Elsing. TG 0616
Primrose Hill Bucks 18 D2* loc 3m/5km NE of High Wycombe. SU 8897
Primrose Hill Derbys 43 H5* loc 2m/3km NE of Alfreton. SK 4155
Primrose Hill Glos 16 B1* loc adjoining Lydney to N. SO 6303
Primrosehill Herts 19 E2* vil 3m/5km SE of Hemel Hempstead. TL 0803
Primrose Hill Lancs 42 A1* loc 2m/3km NW of Ormskirk. SD 3809
Primrose Hill London 19 G3* loc in borough of Camden N of Regents Park and 3m/4km NW of Charing Cross. Also open space to W, opp Zoological Gardens. TQ 2883
Primrosehill W Midlands 35 F5 loc in Dudley 2m/3km S of tn centre. SO 9487
Primrose Hill W Yorks 48 D4* E dist of Bingley. SE 1238
Prince Charles's (or Charlie's) **Cave.** Name given to various caves on island of Skye and in Western Highlands of Scotland which Prince Charles Edward is reputed to have occupied during and after his campaign of 1745–6.
Prince Royd W Yorks 48 D6* loc in Huddersfield 2m/3km NW of tn centre. SE 1218
Princes End W Midlands 35 F5 loc 4m/6km NW of W Bromwich tn centre. SO 9593
Princes Gate Dyfed 22 D4 loc 2m/3km SE of Narberth. SN 1312
Princes Risborough Bucks 18 C2 tn below NW edge of Chiltern Hills. Manor hse of 17c (NT) opp ch. SP 8003
Princethorpe Warwicks 27 H1 vil 6m/9km N of Southam. SP 4070
Princetown Devon 4 C3 tn on central Dartmoor 7m/11km E of Tavistock. Built beside prison originally founded to accommodate French prisoners in Napoleonic wars. SX 5873
Princetown Mid Glam 15 F1 loc 2m/3km N of Rhymney. SO 1109
Prinsted W Sussex 10 D4* loc at head of Chichester Harbour (Thorney Channel), adjoining Southbourne to S. SU 7605
Prion Clwyd 41 F5* loc 2m/4km S of Denbigh. SJ 0562
Prior's Frome H & W 26 B4 vil 4m/7km E of Hereford. SO 5739
Priors Halton Salop 34 B6 loc 2km W of Ludlow. SO 4975
Priors Hardwick Warwicks 28 A2 vil 5m/8km SE of Southam. SP 4756
Priorslee Salop 34 D3 loc 1km S of Oakengates. SJ 7010
Priors Marston Warwicks 28 A2 vil 5m/8km SE of Southam. SP 4857
Prior's Norton Glos 26 D5* ham 4m/7km NE of Gloucester. SO 8624
Priors Park Glos 26 D4* S dist of Tewkesbury. SO 8931
Priorswood Som 8 A2* N dist of Taunton. ST 2326
Priory Wood H & W 25 G3* loc 3m/5km NE of Hay-on-Wye. SO 2545
Prisk S Glam 15 F4* loc 2m/3km NE of Cowbridge. ST 0176
Priston Avon 16 C5 vil 4m/6km N of Radstock. ST 6960
Pristow Green Norfolk 39 E5* loc 1km S of Tibenham. TM 1389
Prittlewell Essex 21 E3 dist of Southend-on-Sea 1m NW of tn centre. TQ 8787
Privett Hants 10 C5* loc 2m/3km W of Gosport. SZ 5999
Privett Hants 10 D2 ham 3m/5km NE of W Meon. SU 6726
Prixford Devon 6 D2 ham 2m/3km N of Barnstaple. SS 5436
Probus Cornwall 2 D3 vil 5m/8km NE of Truro. SW 8947
Prosen Water 76 D5 r in Tayside region running SE down Glen Prosen to R South Esk 3m/5km NE of Kirriemuir. NO 4058
Proud Giltar Dyfed 22 D5* headland at NE end of Lydstep Haven. SS 1098
Provan Hall S'clyde 64 D2* 15c mansion (NTS) in Glasgow, 5m/8km E of city centre. NS 6666
Provanmill S'clyde 64 D2* loc in Glasgow 3m/4km NE of city centre. NS 6267
Provost Ross's House Grampian. See Aberdeen.
Prudhoe Nthmb 61 F5 industrial tn in coal-mining dist on S side of R Tyne 10m/16km W of Gateshead. Brick mnfre; fertilisers. 12c–14c cas. NZ 0962
Prussia Cove Cornwall 2 B5* loc on coast 6m/10km W of Helston. SW 5527
Prysor 33 E1 r rising above Llyn Conglog-mawr, Gwynedd, and running into SE end of Llyn Trawsfynydd. SH 7034
Ptarmigan Central 71 E4* mt 1km SW of Ben Lomond. Height 2398 ft or 731 metres. NN 3502
Publow Avon 16 B5* vil 3m/5km SW of Keynsham. ST 6264
Puckeridge Herts 29 G5 vil 6m/10km N of Ware. Site of Roman tn to N. TL 3823
Puckington Som 8 B3 vil 3m/4km NE of Ilminster. ST 3718
Pucklechurch Avon 16 C4* vil 4m/7km SW of Chipping Sodbury. ST 6976
Pucknall Hants 10 B2* loc 1km E of Braishfield and 3m/5km NE of Romsey. SU 3825
Puckrup Glos 26 D4* loc 3m/4km N of Tewkesbury. SO 8836
Pudding Green Essex 30 D6* loc 5m/8km SW of Colchester. TL 9419
Puddinglake Ches 42 C4* loc adjoining Byley to NE. SJ 7269
Puddington Ches 41 H4 vil 7m/11km NW of Chester. SJ 3273
Puddington Devon 7 F4 vil 7m/11km N of Crediton. SS 8310
Puddlebrook Glos 26 B5 loc 3m/5km N of Cinderford. SO 6418
Puddle Dock London 20 C3* loc 2m/4km E of Upminster in borough of Havering. TQ 5987
Puddledock Norfolk 39 E5* loc 2m/3km S of Attleborough. TM 0592
Puddletown Dorset 9 E5 vil 5m/8km NE of Dorchester. SY 7594
Pudd's Cross Herts 19 E2* loc 4m/6km E of Chesham. TL 0002
Pudleston H & W 26 B2 vil 4m/7km E of Leominster. SO 5659
Pudsey W Yorks 49 E5 tn 4m/6km E of Bradford and 6m/9km W of Leeds. Textiles, engineering, tanning. SE 2233
Puffin Island (Ynys Seiriol) Gwynedd 40 D3 island, 1km long NE to SW, lying less than 1km off E coast of Anglesey, 5m/7km NE of Beaumaris. There are remains of a monastic settlement. Also known as Priestholm. SH 6582
Pug Street Norfolk 39 G3* loc 2km NE of Thurne. TG 4117
Pulborough W Sussex 11 F3 tn on R Arun N of South Downs, 12m/19km NW of Worthing. Site of Roman bldg 1km E of tn centre. TQ 0418
Puleston Salop 34 D2 loc 2m/3km N of Newport. SJ 7322
Pulford Ches 42 A5 vil 5m/8km SW of Chester. SJ 3758
Pulford Brook 42 A5 stream rising S of Hawarden, Clwyd, and flowing SE to Pulford then E into R Dee 2m/4km E of the vil. For much of its course it marks border between England and Wales. SJ 4057
Pulham Dorset 9 E3 vil 7m/11km SE of Sherborne. To NE and SW, ham of **E** and **W Pulham.** ST 7008
Pulham 7 G2* r in Somerset rising on Brendon Hills and flowing S into R Haddeo at Hartford 3m/5km E of Dulverton. SS 9529
Pulham Market Norfolk 39 F6 vil 4m/6km NW of Harleston. TM 1986
Pulham St Mary Norfolk 39 F6 vil 3m/4km NW of Harleston. TM 2185
Pulley Salop 34 B3* loc 3m/4km SW of Shrewsbury. **Upr Pulley** loc 1km SE. SJ 4709
Pulloxhill Beds 29 E4 vil 3m/5km SE of Ampthill. TL 0533
Pulrose Isle of Man 46 B5* loc 2km W of Douglas. SC 3675
Pulteneytown H'land 86 F3 loc in Caithness dist on S side of Wick. Also known as Old Wick. ND 3649
Pulworthy Brook 6 D4* stream rising near Highampton, Devon, and flowing into R Lew 1m NW of Hatherleigh. SS 5305
Pumlumon Welsh form of Plynlimon, qv.
Pumpherston Lothian 65 G2 vil adjoining Livingston to NE. NT 0669
Pumpsaint. Alternative spelling for Pumsaint, qv.
Pumsaint (or Pumpsaint) Dyfed 24 C4 ham 7m/11km SE of Lampeter. Site of Roman bath hse to S. To NE, **Dolaucothi Estate** (NT), wooded hills astride R Cothi valley. To S of Dolaucothi across r, remains of gold mines worked intermittently since Roman times. SN 6540
Puncheston (Cas-mael) Dyfed 22 C3 vil 5m/9km SE of Fishguard. SN 0029
Puncknowle Dorset 8 D5 vil 5m/8km SE of Bridport. SY 5388
Punnett's Town E Sussex 12 C4 vil 3m/4km E of Heathfield. TQ 6220
Purbeck 118 admin dist of Dorset.
Purbeck Hills Dorset 9 F6 range of chalk hills running E and W from Ballard Down N of Swanage to W Lulworth and traversing the Isle of Purbeck, qv. SY 98
Purbeck, Isle of Dorset 9 G6 peninsula in SE Dorset bounded E and S by English Channel, N by Poole Harbour and R Frome, and extending W roughly to a line running N from Worbarrow Bay. Traversed E to W by chalk ridge of **Purbeck Hills.** Quarries for extraction of Purbeck stone. Army training area on SW part. SY 9681
Purbrook Hants 10 D4 vil adjoining Waterlooville to SW. SU 6708
Purdis Farm Suffolk 31 F4* farm 4m/6km E of Ipswich. Location of Suffolk Showground. TM 2142
Purdomstone Reservoir D & G 59 G4 small resr 2m/3km NE of Ecclefechan. NY 2177
Purewell Dorset 9 H5* dist of Christchurch 1m E of tn centre. SZ 1692
Purfleet Essex 20 C4 industrial locality on N bank of R Thames 3m/5km W of Grays. TQ 5677
Puriton Som 8 B1 vil 3m/5km NE of Bridgwater. ST 3241
Purleigh Essex 21 E2 vil 3m/5km S of Maldon. TL 8402
Purley Berks 18 B4 suburb 4m/6km NW of Reading. SU 6576
Purley London 19 G5 tn in borough of Croydon 3m/4km S of Croydon tn centre. TQ 3161
Purlogue Salop 34 A6* loc 3m/5km N of Knighton. SO 2877
Purlpit Wilts 16 D5* loc 3m/4km NW of Melksham. ST 8766
Purls Bridge Cambs 38 A5 loc 2km S of Manea. TL 4787
Purse Caundle Dorset 9 E3 vil 2km SE of Milborne Port and 4m/6km E of Sherborne. ST 6917
Purshull Green H & W 26 D1* loc 4m/6km W of Bromsgrove. SO 9071
Purslow Salop 34 B6 loc 4m/6km E of Clun. SO 3680
Purston, Great Northants 28 A4* loc 4m/7km E of Banbury. SP 5139
Purston Jaglin W Yorks 49 F6 loc 2m/3km SW of Pontefract. SE 4319
Purston, Little Northants 28 A4* loc 4m/6km E of Banbury. SP 5139
Purtington Som 8 C3* ham 3m/5km W of Crewkerne. ST 3909
Purton Glos 16 B1 loc on right bank of R Severn estuary 2m/3km S of Blakeney. SO 6704
Purton Glos 16 C1 vil on left bank of R Severn estuary 3m/5km N of Berkeley. SO 6904
Purton Wilts 17 E3 vil 5m/8km NW of Swindon. SU 0887
Purton Stoke Wilts 17 E3 vil 2m/3km S of Cricklade. SU 0990
Pury End Northants 28 C3 vil 2m/4km SE of Towcester. SP 7045
Pusey Oxon 17 G2 vil 4m/7km E of Faringdon. SU 3596
Putford, East Devon 6 C4 vil 8m/13km N of Holsworthy. SS 3616
Putford, West Devon 6 C4 vil 8m/12km N of Holsworthy. SS 3615
Putley H & W 26 B4 vil 4m/6km W of Ledbury. SO 6437
Putley Green H & W 26 B4* ham 4m/6km W of Ledbury. SO 6537
Putloe Glos 16 C1 ham 5m/8km NW of Stroud. SO 7809
Putney London 19 F4 dist S of R Thames in borough of Wandsworth 5m/8km SW of Charing Cross. P. High Street leads up from P. Br to P. Heath and Wimbledon Common. TQ 2375
Putsborough Devon 6 C2* loc near N coast 6m/10km SW of Ilfracombe. SS 4440
Puttenham Herts 28 D6 vil 3m/5km NW of Tring. SP 8814

Puttenham Surrey 11 F1 vil below S slope of Hog's Back 4m/7km W of Guildford. SU 9347
Puxton Avon 16 A5 vil 2m/3km W of Congresbury. ST 4063
Pwll Dyfed 23 F5 loc 2m/3km W of Llanelli. SN 4801
Pwllcrochan Dyfed 22 B5 loc 3m/5km N of Castlemartin. SM 9202
Pwlldu Head W Glam 23 G6 limestone headland (NT) on S coast of Gower peninsula 4m/7km W of Mumbles Hd. **Pwlldu Bay** (NT) to NE. SS 5786
Pwll-glas Clwyd 41 G5* loc 2m/3km S of Ruthin. SJ 1154
Pwllgloyw Powys 25 E4 ham 3m/5km N of Brecon. SO 0333
Pwll Gwy-rhoc Powys 25 G6* small lake 2m/4km N of Brynmawr. SO 1815
Pwllheli Gwynedd 32 B1 mkt tn with harbour, almost land-locked, on Tremadoc Bay 8m/12km W of Criccieth. Industries include boat-building. SH 3735
Pwll-Mawr S Glam 15 G3* loc adjoining Rumney to E. ST 2278
Pwllmeyric Gwent 16 A2 vil 2km SW of Chepstow. ST 5192
Pwlltrap Dyfed 23 E4 ham 1m W of St Clears. SN 2616
Pwll-y-glaw W Glam 14 D2* ham 3m/4km NE of Port Talbot. SS 7993
Pwll-y-pant Mid Glam 15 F3* loc adjoining Caerphilly to N. ST 1588
Pydew Gwynedd 41 E3* vil 1m NE of Llandudno Junction. SH 8079
Pyecombe W Sussex 11 H4 vil on S Downs 6m/9km N of Brighton. TQ 2812
Pye Corner Gwent 15 H3* loc 3m/5km SE of Newport. ST 3485
Pye Corner Herts 20 B1* ham 2km N of Harlow. TL 4412
Pye Corner Kent 13 E2* loc 3m/5km N of Headcorn. TQ 8548
Pyefleet Channel Essex 31 E6 inlet of R Colne joining with Strood Channel to W and thus separating Mersea I. from mainland. TM 0416
Pye Green Staffs 35 F3 loc 3m/4km N of Cannock. SJ 9814
Pye Hill Notts 44 A5* loc 2km SW of Selston. SK 4451
Pyewipe Humberside 45 F1* loc adjoining Grimsby to NW. TA 2511
Pykestone Hill Borders 65 H5 mt 3m/5km SE of Drumelzier. Height 2418 ft or 737 metres. NT 1731
Pyle (Pil, Y) Mid Glam 14 D3 vil 5m/8km W of Bridgend. SS 8282
Pyleigh Som 7 H2* ham 2km W of Combe Florey. ST 1230
Pylle Som 8 D1 vil 3m/5km S of Shepton Mallet. ST 6038
Pymore Cambs 38 A5* vil 4m/7km W of Littleport. TL 4986
Pymore Dorset 8 C5* ham 1m N of Bridport. SY 4794
Pyrford Surrey 19 E5 ham 2m/3km E of Woking. Ham of **P. Green** 1km NE. Rowley Bristow Orthopaedic Hospital to N. TQ 0458
Pyrland Som 8 A2* N dist of Taunton. ST 2326
Pyrton Oxon 18 B2 vil 1m N of Watlington. Elizn manor hse. SU 6895
Pytchley Northants 28 D1 vil 3m/4km S of Kettering. Gives name to famous hunt; kennels at Brixworth. SP 8574
Pyworthy Devon 6 C5 vil 2m/3km SW of Holsworthy. SS 3102

Q

Quabbs Salop 33 H6 scattered ham 3m/5km W of Newcastle. SO 2080
Quadring Lincs 37 G2 vil 7m/11km N of Spalding. **Q. Eaudyke** loc 2km E. TF 2433
Quaich 72 C1 r in Tayside region running SE down Glen Quaich through Loch Freuchie, then E by Amulree to join Cochill Burn and form R Braan. NN 9238
Quainton Bucks 28 C5 vil 6m/10km NW of Aylesbury. SP 7420
Quaker's Yard (Mynwent y Crynwyr) Mid Glam 15 F2* loc on site of former burial ground on S side of Treharris. ST 0996
Quaking Houses Durham 61 F6* loc 2km S of Stanley. NZ 1850
Quality Corner Cumbria 52 A3* loc 2km NE of Whitehaven. NX 9819
Quantock Forest Som 8 A1* wooded area on Quantock Hills between W Bagborough and Nether Stowey. ST 1736
Quantock Hills Som 8 A1 granite and limestone ridge running NW and SE, extending from Quantoxhead (NW) to Kingston (SE) and attaining height of 1260 ft or 384 metres on Bagborough Hill 1m N of W Bagborough, qv. ST 13
Quantoxhead, East Som 7 H1 vil near coast 4m/6km E of Watchet. ST 1343
Quantoxhead, West Som 7 H1 vil at N end of Quantock Hills 3m/5km E of Watchet. ST 1142
Quarff Shetland. See Easter Quarff.
Quarley Hants 17 G6 vil 6m/10km W of Andover. SU 2743
Quarmby W Yorks 48 D6* loc in Huddersfield 2m/3km W of tn centre. SE 1117
Quarme 7 G2 r in Somerset rising on Exmoor 2m/3km N of Exford and flowing E and then S into R Exe near Exton. SS 9234
Quarme, North Som 7 G2 ham above valley of R Quarme 2m/3km N of Exton. Loc of **S Quarme** to S. SS 9236
Quarndon Derbys 35 H1 vil 3m/5km N of Derby. SK 3341
Quarrelton S'clyde 64 B3* S dist of Johnstone. NS 4262
Quarrendon Bucks 28 C6* NW suburb of Aylesbury. SP 8015
Quarr Hill Isle of Wight 10 C5 loc 2km W of Ryde. To W, remains of medieval abbey; the early 20c abbey beyond. SZ 5792
Quarrington Lincs 37 F1 vil 2km SW of Sleaford. TF 0544
Quarrington Hill Durham 54 C2 coal-mining vil 5m/8km SE of Durham. See also Old Quarrington. NZ 3337
Quarrybank Ches 42 B4* loc 2m/3km N of Tarporley. SJ 5465
Quarry Bank W Midlands 35 F5* S dist of Dudley. SO 9386
Quarry Burn Durham 54 B2* loc 2m/3km SE of Crook. NZ 1833
Quarry Head Grampian 83 G1 headland on N coast 2m/3km SW of Rosehearty. NJ 9066
Quarrywood Grampian 82 B1 loc 2m/4km W of Elgin. NJ 1864
Quartalehouse Grampian 83 G2* loc adjoining Stuartfield to N, 10m/16km W of Peterhead. NJ 9746
Quarter S'clyde 64 D4 vil 3m/4km S of Hamilton. NS 7251
Quarter, Middle Kent 13 E3* loc 1km N of High Halden. 1km N again, loc of **Further Quarter.** TQ 8938
Quarter, The Kent 13 E3* loc 3m/5km E of Headcorn. TQ 8844
Quatford Salop 34 D5 vil on R Severn 2m/3km SE of Bridgnorth. SO 7390
Quatt Salop 34 D5 vil 4m/6km SE of Bridgnorth. SO 7588
Quay Bay, Little Dyfed 24 A2 small bay on coast of Cardigan Bay 1m E of Newquay. SN 4159
Quay Reach Essex 21 F3 stretch of R Roach 2km above its confluence with R Crouch to W of Foulness I. TQ 9892
Quebec Durham 54 B1 vil 3m/4km S of Lanchester. NZ 1843
Quebec House Kent. See Westerham.
Quedgeley Glos 26 C6 vil 3m/5km SW of Gloucester. SO 8014
Queen Adelaide Cambs 38 A6* vil 2m/3km NE of Ely. TL 5681
Queenborough Kent 21 E4 industrial area at W end of Isle of Sheppey 2m/3km S of Sheerness. TQ 9172
Queen Camel Som 8 D2 vil 2km SW of Sparkford. ST 5924
Queen Charlton Avon 16 B4 ham 2m/3km SW of Keynsham. ST 6367
Queen Dart Devon 7 F3* loc above Lit Dart R near its source, 3m/4km NE of Witheridge. SS 8316
Queen Elizabeth Forest Park Central 71 F4, F5* area of forest, moor, and mountainside extending from Aberfoyle to Loch Lomond and including Achray and Loch Ard Forests, Ben Lomond, and part of The Trossachs. Total area about 70 sq miles or 180 sq km. NN, NS
Queen Elizabeth II Reservoir Surrey 19 E4 resr 1m E of Walton-on-Thames. TQ 1166
Queener Point Cornwall 4 B5* headland on Whitsand Bay 1m N of Rame Hd. See Rame. SX 4148
Queenhill H & W 26 D4* loc 3m/5km NW of Tewkesbury. SO 8636
Queen Mary Reservoir Surrey 19 E4* large resr whose W edge is 2m/3km SE of Staines. TQ 0769
Queen Mary's Dubb N Yorks 49 E1* lake in Ripon Parks 2m/3km N of Ripon. SE 3074
Queen Oak Dorset 9 E2* vil between Bourton and Zeals, 3m/5km NW of Gillingham. ST 7831
Queensberry D & G 59 E2 mt in Lowther Hills 6m/10km W of Beattock. Height 2285 ft or 696 metres. Wee Q. is hill 2km S. NX 9899
Queen's Bower Isle of Wight 10 C6 ham 2m/3km W of Sandown. SZ 5784
Queensbury London 19 F3* loc in borough of Brent 2m/4km W of Hendon. TQ 1889
Queensbury W Yorks 48 D5 tn 3m/5km N of Halifax. SE 1130
Queensferry Clwyd 41 H4 tn on S bank of R Dee 6m/9km W of Chester across r, spanned by two rd brs. SJ 3168
Queensferry, North Fife 65 G1 loc at N end of Forth brs. NT 1380
Queensferry, South Lothian 65 G1 loc with harbour and lighthouse at S end of Forth brs. NT 1278
Queen's Forest, The H'land 81 H6 coniferous forest in Badenoch and Strathspey dist and mainly within the Glen More Forest Park, N of Cairn Gorm. NH 9709
Queen's Head Salop 34 A2 ham 4m/6km SE of Oswestry. SJ 3426
Queenside Muir S'clyde 64 A3 moorland tract 5m/8km NE of Largs. NS 2764
Queenslie Industrial Estate S'clyde 64 D2* loc in Glasgow 4m/7km E of city centre. NS 6565
Queen's Nympton Devon 7 E3* loc 2m/3km S of S Molton. SS 7122
Queen's Park Clwyd 42 A6* E dist of Wrexham. SJ 3550
Queen's Park Northants 28 C2* loc in Northampton 2km N of tn centre. SP 7562
Queenstown Lancs 46 D4* dist of Blackpool 2km NE of tn centre. SD 3237
Queen Street Kent 12 C2 ham 2km E of Paddock Wd. TQ 6845
Queen Street Suffolk 30 C3* ham 6m/10km NE of Haverhill. TL 7154
Queen Street Wilts 17 E3 loc 6m/10km E of Malmesbury. SU 0387
Queensville Staffs 35 F2* SE dist of Stafford. SJ 9322
Queensway Fife 73 F4* industrial estate on NE side of Glenrothes. NO 2801
Queenzieburn S'clyde 64 D1/D2 vil 2m/3km W of Kilsyth. NS 6977
Quemerford Wilts 17 E4 loc adjoining Calne to SE. SU 0069
Quendale Shetland 89 E8 loc on **Bay of Q.**, wide bay on S coast of Mainland 4m/6km NW of Sumburgh Hd. HU 3713
Quendon Essex 30 A4/A5 vil 6m/10km N of Bishop's Stortford. TL 5130
Queniborough Leics 36 C3 vil 6m/10km NE of Leicester. SK 6412
Quenington Glos 17 F1 vil 2m/3km N of Fairford. SP 1404
Quernmore Lancs 47 F2 loc 3m/4km E of Lancaster. SD 5160
Queslett W Midlands 35 G5 loc 5m/8km N of Birmingham city centre. SP 0694
Quethiock Cornwall 3 G2 vil 4m/6km E of Liskeard. SX 3164
Quey Firth Shetland 89 E6* inlet on NE coast of Mainland to S of Colla Firth and separated from it by the headland **Ness of Queyfirth.** HU 3682
Quick Edge Gtr Manchester 43 E1* loc 1km N of Mossley. SD 9703
Quick's Green Berks 18 B4* loc 3m/5km W of Pangbourne. SU 5876
Quidenham Norfolk 39 E5 ham 5m/8km S of Attleborough. TM 0287
Quidhampton Hants 17 H6* loc 1km N of Overton across R Test near its source. SU 5150
Quidhampton Wilts 9 H2 W suburb of Salisbury. SU 1131
Quies Cornwall 2 D1* group of small islands 2km W of Trevose Hd on N coast. SW 8376
Quin 29 G5* r rising NE of Barkway, Herts, and flowing S into R Rib 1km SW of Braughing. TL 3824
Quina Brook Salop 34 C2 loc 3m/4km NE of Wem. SJ 5233
Quinag H'land 84 C4 mt in Sutherland dist 2m/3km N of Loch Assynt. Height 2653 ft or 809 metres. NC 2029
Quine's Hill Isle of Man 46 B6* ham 2m/4km SW of Douglas. SC 3473
Quinish S'clyde 68 C3 dist of Mull 5m/8km W of Tobermory. **Quinish Pt** is headland at NW end. NM 4254
Quinton Northants 28 C2 vil 4m/6km S of Northampton. SP 7754
Quinton Warwicks 27 F3* par containing vil of **Lower Q.** and ham of **Upper Q.,** 5m/8km S of Stratford-upon-Avon. SP 1847
Quinton W Midlands 35 F5 loc in E part of Halesowen. SO 9984
Quinton Green Northants 28 C2* loc 4m/7km S of Northampton. SP 7853
Quinton, Lower Warwicks 27 F3 vil 5m/8km S of Stratford-upon-Avon. SP 1847
Quinton, Upper Warwicks 27 F3* ham 6m/9km S of Stratford-upon-Avon. SP 1746
Quintrell Downs Cornwall 2 D2* ham 3m/4km SE of Newquay. SW 8460
Quixhill Staffs 35 G1* loc 2km NW of Rocester. SK 1041
Quoditch Devon 6 C5 ham 6m/9km SE of Holsworthy. SX 4097
Quoich H'land 74 B1 r in Lochaber dist running S down Glen Q. to Loch Q. 4m/6km W of dam. NH 0103
Quoich Water 76 B2 r in Grampian region rising in Cairngorms and running S to R Dee 2m/3km W of Braemar. NO 1290
Quoisley Ches 42 B6* loc 1m W of Marbury. **Q. Meres** two small lakes to S. SJ 5455
Quorn Leics. Alternative name for Quorndon, qv.
Quorndon Leics 36 B3 vil 3m/4km SE of Loughborough. Also known as Quorn. The Quorn hunt was founded here. SK 5616
Quothquan S'clyde 65 F4 loc 3m/5km NW of Biggar. NS 9939
Quoyloo Orkney 89 A6* loc on Mainland 3m/5km W of Dounby. HY 2420
Quoynalonga Ness Orkney 89 B6* headland at W end of Rousay. HY 3632
Quoyness Orkney 89 C5* large chambered cairn (A.M.) on Els Ness, island of Sanday. HY 6737

R

Raasay Skye, H'land 78 D4, 79 D5 sparsely inhabited island, 13m/21km N to S and from 1km to 5km wide, lying off E coast of Skye opp Portree. NG 5640
Rabbit Islands H'land 84 F2 group of islands in Tongue Bay off N coast of Caithness dist. Inhabited by rabbits. NC 6063
Rabbit's Cross Kent 12 D2* loc 2m/4km N of Staplehurst. TQ 7847
Rableyheath Herts 29 F5* ham 2m/3km N of Welwyn. TL 2319
Raby Cumbria 59 G6* loc 2km NE of Abbey Tn. NY 1951
Raby Merseyside 41 H3 loc 2m/3km NE of Neston. SJ 3179
Raby Castle Durham 54 A3 mainly 14c hse with later additions, 1m N of Staindrop. NZ 1221
Race, Lower Gwent 15 G2* loc on W side of Pontypool. SO 2700
Race, Upper Gwent 15 G2* loc 1m SW of Pontypool. ST 2799
Rachub Gwynedd 40 C4* vil 1m N of Bethesda. SH 6268
Rackenford Devon 7 F3 vil 4m/6km NE of Witheridge. SS 8518
Rackham W Sussex 11 F4 ham below S Downs (R. Hill), 2m/4km W of Storrington. TQ 0513

Rackheath Norfolk 39 F3/G3 ham 5m/8km NE of Norwich. See also New Rackheath. TG 2814
Racks D & G 59 E4 vil on Lochar Moss 4m/6km E of Dumfries. NY 0374
Rackwick Orkney 89 A7 loc on bay of **Rack Wick** on W coast of Hoy 2m/3km E of Rora Hd. ND 2099
Rackwick Orkney 89 B5* loc on Westray 1m N of Pierowall. Bay of **Rack Wick** to W. HY 4449
Radbourne Derbys 35 H1 ham 4m/7km W of Derby. Hall, 18c hse in park. SK 2836
Radcliffe Gtr Manchester 42 D1 tn on R Irwell 2m/4km SW of Bury. Textiles, paper, engineering. SD 7807
Radcliffe Nthmb 61 G2 vil 2km S of Amble. NU 2602
Radcliffe on Trent Notts 36 C1 tn 5m/8km E of Nottingham. SK 6439
Radclive Bucks 28 B4* vil on R Ouse 2km W of Buckingham. SP 6734
Radcot Oxon 17 G2 loc on R Thames 3m/4km N of Faringdon. SU 2899
Raddington Som 7 G3* loc 4m/6km W of Wiveliscombe. ST 0226
Raddon, West Devon 7 G5* ham 4m/6km NE of Crediton. To N, **Raddon Hills,** small range attaining height of 772 ft or 235 metres. SS 8902
Radernie Fife 73 G3 loc 5m/8km SE of St Andrews. NO 4609
Radford Avon 16 B5* loc 2m/4km NW of Radstock. ST 6757
Radford Notts 36 B1* dist of Nottingham 2m/3km W of city centre. SK 5440
Radford Oxon 27 H5 ham 5m/8km NW of Woodstock. SP 4023
Radford W Midlands 35 H6 dist of Coventry 1m NW of city centre. SP 3280
Radford Semele Warwicks 27 G2 vil 2m/3km E of Leamington. SP 3464
Radipole Dorset 8 D6 N dist of Weymouth. **Radipole Lake** is an area of water and marsh formed by R Wey to S. SY 6681
Radlett Herts 19 F2 residential tn 5m/8km S of St Albans. Radlett Airfield 2m/3km N. TL 1699
Radley Oxon 18 A2 vil 2m/4km NE of Abingdon. Boys' public school in Radley Park to NW. SU 5199
Radley Green Essex 20 C2* ham 6m/9km W of Chelmsford. TL 6205
Radmore Green Ches 42 B5* loc 4m/7km NW of Nantwich. SJ 5955
Radnage Bucks 18 C2 ham 2m/3km NE of Stokenchurch. SU 7897
Radnage Common Bucks 18 C2* loc 2m/3km E of Stokenchurch. SU 7996
Radnor 118 admin dist of Powys.
Radnor Forest Powys 25 F2, G2 wild upland area (although partly afforested) between Presteigne and Penybont, with vil of New Radnor to S. Highest point is Gt Rhos, 2166 ft or 660 metres. WT stn on Black Mixen. Sheep-grazing on open hills. SO 1626
Radnor Mere Ches 42 D4* small lake on SE side of Nether Alderley. SJ 8475
Radnor Park S'clyde 64 C2* loc 2km NW of Clydebank. NS 4971
Radstock Avon 16 C5 tn 8m/12km SW of Bath. Centre of coal-mining dist. Other industries include mnfre of tools, electrical equipment, paper, gloves, prefabricated farm bldgs. ST 6854
Radstone Northants 28 B3 vil 2m/4km N of Brackley. SP 5840
Radur Welsh form of Radyr and Rhadyr, qv.
Radway Warwicks 27 G3 vil 7m/11km NW of Banbury. Site of Battle of Edgehill, 1642, 1m NW. SP 3748
Radway Green Ches 42 D5* loc 2m/3km SW of Alsager. SJ 7754
Radwell Beds 29 E2 vil 6m/9km NW of Bedford. TL 0057
Radwell Dorset 9 E6* dist of Weymouth at N end of Portland Harbour. SY 6778
Radwell Herts 29 F4* vil 2m/3km NW of Baldock. TL 2335
Radwinter Essex 30 B4 vil 4m/7km E of Saffron Walden. Loc of **Radwinter End** 2m/3km NE. TL 6037
Radworthy, North Devon 7 E2 Exmoor ham 4m/6km SW of Simonsbath. SS 7534
Radworthy, South Devon 7 E2 Exmoor ham 5m/8km NE of S Molton. SS 7432
Radyr (Radur) S Glam 15 F3 vil 4m/6km NW of Cardiff. ST 1380
Raeburnfoot D & G. See Eskdalemuir.
Raerinish Point W Isles 88 C2* headland on E coast of Lewis 2m/3km E of Crossbost. NB 3924
Rafford Grampian 82 A2 vil 2m/3km SE of Forres. NJ 0656
Ragdale Leics 36 C3 vil 6m/9km W of Melton Mowbray. SK 6619
Ragged Appleshaw Hants 17 G6* ham 1km E of Appleshaw and 4m/7km NW of Andover. SU 3148
Raggra H'land 86 F3* loc in Caithness dist 5m/8km SW of Wick. ND 3144
Raglan (Rhaglan) Gwent 16 A1 vil 7m/11km SW of Monmouth. Remains of 15c cas (A.M.) to N. SO 4107
Ragley Hall Warwicks 27 E2 large 17c-18c mansion in park, 2m/3km SW of Alcester. SP 0755
Ragnall Notts 44 C4 vil 13m/20km N of Newark-on-Trent. SK 8073
Ragwen Point Dyfed 22 D5* headland at E end of Saundersfoot Bay 1m SW of Pendine. SN 2207
Rainford Merseyside 42 A2 tn 4m/6km NW of St Helens. SD 4700
Rainham Kent 20 D5 SE dist of Gillingham. Loc of **Lr Rainham** is 1m N. TQ 8165
Rainham London 20 B3 tn in borough of Havering 5m/8km S of Romford. S of ch is **Rainham Hall** (NT), 18c hse in red brick with stone dressing. TQ 5381
Rainhill Merseyside 42 B2 tn 3m/5km SW of St Helens. **Rainhill Stoops** vil 1m SE. SJ 4991
Rainigadale W Isles 88 B3* locality in Harris on W side of entrance to Loch Seaforth. Islet of **Rainigadale I.** in Loch Trollamarig to S. NB 2201
Rainow Ches 43 E4 vil 3m/4km NE of Macclesfield. SJ 9575
Rain Shore Gtr Manchester 47 H6* loc in Rochdale on W side of Greenbooth Resr 3m/5km NW of tn centre. SD 8515
Rainsough Gtr Manchester 42 D1* loc 1m SW of Prestwich. SD 8002
Rainton N Yorks 49 F1 vil 4m/7km NE of Ripon. SE 3775
Rainton Bridge Tyne & Wear 61 H6* loc adjoining Houghton-le-Spring to S. NZ 3448
Rainton, East Tyne & Wear 61 G6* vil 2m/3km S of Houghton-le-Spring. NZ 3347
Rainton Gate Durham 54 C1* loc adjoining W Rainton to S. NZ 3146
Rainton, Middle Tyne & Wear 54 C1 loc 2m/3km SW of Houghton-le-Spring. NZ 3247
Rainton, West Durham 54 C1 vil 4m/7km NE of Durham. NZ 3246
Rainworth Notts 44 B5 coal-mining vil 4m/6km SE of Mansfield. SK 5958
Rainworth Water 44 B4 r rising near Rainworth, Notts, and flowing NE into R Maun at Ollerton. SK 6567
Raisbeck Cumbria 53 F4 loc 2m/3km SE of Orton. NY 6507
Raise Cumbria 52 D3 mt in Lake Dist 2km N of Helvellyn. Height 2889 ft or 881 metres. NY 3417
Raise Cumbria 53 F1* loc just W of Alston across R South Tyne. NY 7146
Raise, High Cumbria 52 D3 mt in Lake Dist 2m/3km W of Haweswater Resr. NY 4413
Rait Tayside 73 E2 vil 7m/12km E of Perth. NO 2226
Rait Castle H'land 81 H2 ruined medieval cas in Nairn dist 3m/4km S of Nairn. NH 8952
Raithby Lincs 45 G3 ham 2m/3km SW of Louth. TF 3184
Raithby Lincs 45 G4 vil 2m/3km W of Spilsby. TF 3767
Raithwaite N Yorks 55 G4* loc 2m/3km W of Whitby. NY 8611
Rake W Sussex 11 E2 vil 3m/5km SW of Liphook. SU 8027
Rake End Staffs 35 G3* loc adjoining Hill Ridware to NW. SK 0718
Rake Head Lancs 48 B5* loc 2m/3km SW of Bacup. SD 8421
Rakes Dale Staffs 35 F1* loc 4m/6km E of Cheadle. SK 0642
Rakeway Staffs 35 F1* loc 1m SE of Cheadle. SK 0242
Rakewood Gtr Manchester 48 C6* loc 2km S of Littleborough. SD 9414
Ram Dyfed 24 B3 loc 1m SE of Lampeter. SN 5846
Ram Alley Wilts 17 F5* loc 4m/7km NE of Pewsey. SU 2263
Ramasaig Skye, H'land 79 A5 loc near W coast 8m/13km S of Dunvegan Hd. **Ramasaig Bay** to W. **Ramasaig Cliff** to NW. NG 1644
Rame Cornwall 2 C5* vil 4m/6km W of Penryn. SW 7234
Rame Cornwall 4 B5 vil in par of Maker-with-Rame 2m/3km S of Millbrook. To S, **Rame Hd,** headland at SE end of Whitsand Bay. SX 4249
Ram Hill Avon 16 C3* loc 4m/6km SW of Chipping Sodbury. ST 6779
Ram Lane Kent 13 E3* loc 2m/3km SE of Charing. TQ 9646
Ramna Stacks Shetland 89 E5* group of island rocks some 2km N of Point of Fethaland. Nature reserve. HU 3797
Ramp Holme Cumbria 52 D5* small island (NT) on Windermere 1m S of Bowness. SD 3995
Rampisham Dorset 8 D4 vil 4m/6km NW of Maiden Newton. ST 5602
Rampside Cumbria 46 D2 vil on W shore of Morecambe Bay 3m/5km SE of Barrow-in-Furness. SD 2466
Rampton Cambs 29 H1 vil 6m/10km N of Cambridge. TL 4267
Rampton Notts 44 C3 vil 6m/10km E of E Retford. Mental hospital at Woodbeck 2m/3km W. SK 7978
Ramridge End Beds 29 E5* NE dist of Luton. TL 1023
Ramsbottom Gtr Manchester 47 H6 tn 4m/7km N of Bury. Textiles, paper. SD 7916
Ramsbury Wilts 17 G4 vil on R Kennet 6m/9km E of Marlborough. SU 2771
Ramscraigs H'land 86 D4 loc near E coast of Caithness 2m/3km SW of Dunbeath. ND 1427
Ramsdean Hants 10 D3 ham 3m/4km W of Petersfield. SU 7022
Ramsdell Hants 18 B5 vil 5m/8km NW of Basingstoke. SU 5857
Ramsden London 20 B5* loc in borough of Bromley 1m E of Orpington. TQ 4766
Ramsden Oxon 27 G6 vil 4m/6km N of Witney. SP 3515
Ramsden W Yorks 43 F1* loc on edge of Peak Dist National Park 1m S of Holmbridge. **Ramsden Resr** to W. SE 1105
Ramsden Bellhouse Essex 20 D2 vil 2m/3km W of Wickford. TQ 7194
Ramsden Clough Reservoir W Yorks 48 B5* resr 2m/4km SW of Todmorden. SD 9121
Ramsden Heath Essex 20 D2 loc 3m/4km E of Billericay. TQ 7195
Ramsey Cambs 37 G5 small Fenland tn 10m/16km SE of Peterborough. Remains of Benedictine abbey, with 15c gatehouse (NT). Vils of **Ramsey St Mary** to NW, **Ramsey Mereside** to N, **Ramsey Forby** to NE, and **Ramsey Heights** to W. TL 2885
Ramsey Essex 31 F5 vil 3m/5km W of Harwich. TM 2130
Ramsey Isle of Man 46 C4 resort on E coast 7m/11km S of Pt of Ayre. Is situated on **Ramsey Bay,** which extends from Maughold Hd northwards to Shellag Pt. Sandy beach; pier; small harbour. SC 4594
Ramsey Island (Ynys Dewi) Dyfed island 2m/3km long (N to S) and 1m wide, lying 2m/3km SW of St David's Hd, much of it protected by NT. Haunt of sea birds. Separated from mainland by **R. Sound,** narrow strait with dangerous currents. SM 7023
Ramsey Island Essex 21 E2* vil on R Blackwater estuary 6m/9km N of Burnham-on-Crouch. TL 9505
Ramsgate Kent 13 H1 resort with large harbour on Isle of Thanet 15m/24km E of Canterbury. Municipal airport; airport also at Manston. Hovercraft terminal at Pegwell Bay (cross-Channel service). TR 3865
Ramsgate Street Norfolk 39 E2 ham 4m/6km SE of Holt. TG 0933
Ramsgill N Yorks 48 D1 vil on R Nidd 4m/7km NW of Pateley Br. SE 1171
Ramsgreave Lancs 47 G5* loc 2m/3km N of Blackburn. **Top of Ramsgreave** loc 1km W. SD 6731
Ramshaw Durham 61 E6* loc 1m S of Hunstanworth. NY 9547
Ramsholt Suffolk 31 G4 loc on left bank of R Deben estuary 5m/8km SE of Woodbridge across r. TM 3042
Ramshorn Staffs 43 F6 vil 5m/8km E of Cheadle. SK 0845
Ramsley Devon 7 E5* loc 4m/6km SE of Okehampton. SX 6493
Ramsley Reservoir Derbys 43 G4* small resr 3m/4km NE of Baslow. SK 2874
Rams Ness Shetland 89 F6 headland at SW end of Fetlar. HU 6087
Ramsnest Common Surrey 11 F2 ham 3m/5km E of Haslemere. SU 9533
Ranbury Ring Glos 17 E2* prehistoric earthwork in par of Ampney St Peter 4m/7km E of Cirencester. SP 0900
Ranby Lincs 45 F3 ham 6m/10km N of Horncastle. TF 2378
Ranby Notts 44 B3 vil 4m/6km W of E Retford. SK 6480
Rand Lincs 45 E3* vil 2m/3km NW of Wragby. TF 1078
Randlawfoot Cumbria 60 B6* loc 1km W of Cumwhitton. NY 4952
Randlay Salop 34 D3/D4* dist of Telford to E of Dawley. SJ 7107
Randolph's Leap Grampian 81 H3 gorge in valley of R Findhorn, 8m/13km SE of Nairn. NH 9949
Randwick Glos 16 D1 vil 2m/3km NW of Stroud. SO 8206
Ranfurly S'clyde 64 B3* loc adjoining Br of Weir to S. NS 3865
Rangemore Staffs 35 G2 vil 4m/6km W of Burton upon Trent. SK 1822
Rangeworthy Avon 16 C3 vil 3m/5km NW of Chipping Sodbury. ST 6886
Rankinston S'clyde 56 E3 vil in colliery dist 3m/5km NE of Patna. NS 4514
Rankle Burn 66 B6 r in Borders region running N to Buccleuch, and to Ettrick Water 2m/4km farther NW. NT 3017
Rank's Green Essex 30 C6 loc 3m/5km S of Braintree. TL 7417
Ranmoor S Yorks 43 G3 dist of Sheffield 2m/4km W of city centre. SK 3185
Rann Lancs 48 A5* vil 3m/5km SE of Blackburn. SD 7124
Rannerdale Cumbria 52 B3* loc on E shore of Crummock Water. NY 1618
Rannoch H'land 68 E4 r in Lochaber dist running W to head of Loch Aline. NM 7047
Rannoch 75 F5-G5 mt area on borders of Highland, Strathclyde, and Tayside regions between Loch Rannoch and Glen Lyon. **Rannoch Moor** is upland tract to W including Loch Laidon, Loch Bà, and many small lochs or tarns, as well as a nature reserve. **Rannoch Forest** is mt area to N, on W side of foot of Loch Ericht; also state forest S of Loch Rannoch. Rannoch rly stn on Glasgow to Fort William line is near NE end of Loch Laidon. See also Loch Rannoch. NN 45, 55
Ranny Bay S Glam 15 G4* bay on N side of Lavernock Pt. ST 1868
Ranscombe Som 7 G1* ham 3m/4km W of Dunster. SS 9443
Ranskill Notts 44 B3 vil 2m/3km E of Blyth. SK 6587
Ranton Staffs 35 E2 vil 4m/7km W of Stafford. **Ranton Green** ham 1m SW. SJ 8524
Ranworth Norfolk 39 G3 vil 4m/7km NW of Acle. **Ranworth Broad** to N, broad or lake draining into R Bure. **Ranworth Marshes** to E. TG 3514
Raploch Central 72 B5* NW dist of Stirling. NS 7894
Rapness Orkney 89 B5 loc on island of Westray 6m/10km SE of Pierowall. HY 5141
Rapps Som 8 B3* ham 2m/3km NW of Ilminster. ST 3317
Rascarrel Bay D & G 58 D6 bay 4m/6km E of Dundrennan. NX 8048
Rasen, Middle Lincs 45 E2/E3 vil 2km W of Mkt Rasen. TF 0889
Rasen, West Lincs 45 E2 vil 3m/5km W of Mkt Rasen. TF 0689
Rash Cumbria 53 F5 loc 2km S of Sedbergh. SD 6689
Rashwood H & W 26 D1* vil 2m/3km NE of Droitwich. SO 9165
Raskelf N Yorks 49 G1 vil 3m/4km NW of Easingwold. SE 4971
Rassau Gwent 25 F6* loc 2m/4km W of Brynmawr. SO 1512
Rastrick W Yorks 48 D5 loc 1km SW of Brighouse. SE 1321
Ratae Leics. See Leicester.
Ratagan H'land 80 A5* locality in Skye and Lochalsh dist on SW shore of Loch

Duich, 2km NW of Shiel Br at head of loch. **Ratagan Forest** is state forest to W. See also Mam Rattachan. NG 9119
Ratby Leics 36 B4 vil 5m/8km W of Leicester. **Bury Camp** Roman earthwork 1mW. SK 5105
Ratcliff London 20 A3* loc in borough of Tower Hamlets 2m/3km E of London Br. TQ 3680
Ratcliffe Culey Leics 35 H4 vil 2m/3km NE of Atherstone. SP 3299
Ratcliffe on Soar Notts 36 B2 vil 6m/10km NW of Loughborough. Site of Roman bldg 1m to W of power stn. SK 4928
Ratcliffe on the Wreake Leics 36 C3 vil 7m/11km NE of Leicester. SK 6314
Ratfyn Wilts 17 F6 loc 1km NE of Amesbury. SU 1642
Rathen Grampian 83 G1/H1 vil 4m/6km S of Fraserburgh. NK 0060
Rathillet Fife 73 F3 loc 4m/7km N of Cupar. NO 3620
Rathmell N Yorks 48 B2 vil 2m/3km NW of Long Preston. SD 8059
Ratho Lothian 65 G2 vil 8m/12km W of Edinburgh. **Ratho Stn** is loc 1m N. NT 1370
Rathven Grampian 82 D1 vil near N coast 2km E of Buckie. Distillery. NJ 4465
Rat Island Devon 6 A1 island off SE point of Lundy, qv. SS 1443
Rat Island Essex 31 E6 island at mouth of Geedon Creek 6m/10km SE of Colchester. TM 0517
Ratley Warwicks 27 G3 vil on E side of Edge Hill 6m/10km NW of Banbury. SP 3847
Ratley, Lower Hants 10 A3* ham 2m/3km NW of Romsey. SU 3223
Ratley, Upper Hants 10 A3* ham 2m/4km NW of Romsey. SU 3223
Ratling Kent 13 G2* ham 1m N of Aylesham. TR 2453
Ratlinghope Salop 34 B4 vil 4m/6km NW of Church Stretton across Long Mynd. SO 4096
Ratsloe Devon 7 G5* loc 4m/7km NE of Exeter. SX 9597
Rattar H'land 86 E1 loc near N coast of Caithness dist 4m/6km SE of Dunnet Hd. ND 2673
Ratten Row Cumbria 52 C1* loc adjoining Caldbeck to NW. NY 3140
Ratten Row Cumbria 59 H6* loc 2m/3km E of Dalston. NY 3949
Ratten Row Lancs 47 E4* loc on N bank of R Wyre 2m/3km W of St Michael's on Wyre. SD 4241
Ratten Row Norfolk 38 A3* loc adjoining Walpole Highway to W. TF 5113
Rattery Devon 4 D4 vil 4m/6km W of Totnes. SX 7461
Rattlesden Suffolk 30 D2 vil 5m/7km W of Stowmarket. TL 9758
Ratton Village E Sussex 12 C6* suburb of Eastbourne 2m/3km NW of tn centre. TQ 5901
Rattray Tayside 73 E1 tn on R Ericht opp Blairgowrie, qv. NO 1845
Rattray Head Grampian 85 H2 headland with lighthouse on NE coast 7m/12km N of Peterhead. **Rattray Bay** extends southwards to Scotstown Hd. NK 1057
Rauceby, North Lincs 45 E6 vil 3m/5km W of Sleaford. **S Rauceby** vil 1km S. TF 0246
Raughton Cumbria 60 A6* loc 2m/3km SE of Dalston. **Raughton Hd** loc 2m/3km S. NY 3947
Raunds Northants 29 E1 small footwear-mnfg tn 6m/10km NE of Wellingborough. SP 9972
Raveley, Great Cambs 37 G6 vil 3m/5km SW of Ramsey. Vil of **Lit Raveley** 1m S. TL 2581
Ravelston Lothian 66 A2* dist of Edinburgh 2m/3km W of city centre. NT 2274
Raven Beck 53 E1* r rising on Renwick Fell, NE of Renwick, Cumbria, and flowing W into R Eden at Kirkoswald. NY 5540
Ravendale, East Humberside 45 F2 vil 4m/6km NE of Binbrook. **W Ravendale** loc 1km W: ruins of medieval chapel. TF 2399
Ravenfield S Yorks 44 A2 vil 4m/6km E of Rotherham. SK 4895
Ravenglass Cumbria 52 B5 vil on R Esk estuary 4m/7km SE of Seascale. Site of Roman fort of *Glannaventa*. SD 0896
Raveningham Norfolk 39 G5 vil 4m/7km NW of Beccles. TM 3996
Ravensbourne 20 A4* r rising at Keston in the London borough of Bromley and flowing N through Lewisham into R Thames at Deptford Creek. TQ 3777
Ravenscar N Yorks 55 G4/G5 loc above cliffs on North Sea coast 3m/5km SE of Robin Hood's Bay. NZ 9801
Ravenscraig Castle Fife 73 F5* ruined 15c cas beside sea in N part of Kirkcaldy. NT 2992
Ravensdale Isle of Man 46 B4 loc 1m S of Ballaugh. SC 3592
Ravensden Beds 29 E2 vil 4m/6km NE of Bedford. TL 0754
Raven Seat N Yorks 53 G4* loc 2m/4km NW of Keld. NY 8603
Raven's Green Essex 31 E5* ham 5m/8km W of Thorpe-le-Soken. TM 1024
Ravenshall Point D & G 58 B6 headland on Wigtown Bay, 5m/8km SE of Creetown. NX 5252
Ravenshead Notts 44 A5 loc 4m/6km NE of Hucknall. SK 5654
Ravensmoor Ches 42 C6 loc 2m/4km SW of Nantwich. SJ 6250
Ravensthorpe Cambs 37 F4* NW dist of Peterborough. Industrial area astride rly to E. TF 1700
Ravensthorpe Northants 28 B1 vil 8m/13km NW of Northampton. Ravensthorpe Resr to E. SP 6670
Ravensthorpe W Yorks 49 E6 dist of Dewsbury 2m/3km SW of tn centre. SE 2220
Ravenstone Bucks 28 D3 vil 3m/4km W of Olney. SP 8450
Ravenstone Leics 36 A3 vil 2m/3km W of Coalville. SK 4013
Ravenstonedale Cumbria 53 F4 vil 4m/7km SW of Kirkby Stephen. NY 7204
Ravenstown Cumbria 47 E1* loc adjoining Flookburgh to SW. SD 3675
Ravenstruther S'clyde 65 F4 loc 3m/5km E of Lanark. NS 9245
Ravensworth N Yorks 54 B4 vil 5m/8km NW of Richmond. Remains of medieval cas. NZ 1407
Raw N Yorks 55 G4* loc 1m W of Robin Hood's Bay. NZ 9305
Rawcliffe Humberside 50 B5/C5 vil on S bank of R Aire 4m/6km W of Goole. **Rawcliffe Br** loc 2km SE on Aire and Calder Canal. SE 6822
Rawcliffe N Yorks 50 B3* suburb 3m/4km NW of York. SE 5855
Rawdon W Yorks 49 E4 loc adjoining Yeadon to S. SE 2039
Rawfolds W Yorks 48 D5* loc 1km SE of Cleckheaton. SE 1924
Raw Green S Yorks 43 G1* loc 5m/7km W of Barnsley. SE 2707
Rawmarsh S Yorks 43 H2 tn 2m/3km N of Rotherham. Coal-mining, steel, chemicals. SK 4396
Rawnsley Staffs 35 F3* loc 3m/5km NE of Cannock. SK 0212
Rawreth Essex 20 D3 vil 2m/4km E of Wickford. TQ 7893
Rawridge Devon 8 A4* ham 4m/6km NE of Honiton. ST 2006
Rawtenstall Lancs 48 B5 tn on R Irwell 6m/10km S of Burnley. Textiles, footwear, plastics. SD 8122
Rawthey 53 F5 r rising on Baugh Fell, E of Sedbergh, Cumbria, and flowing NW to Rawthey Br then SW into R Lune 2m/4km SW of Sedbergh. SD 6289
Ray 17 F2 r rising S of Swindon, Wilts, and flowing N into R Thames 2km below Cricklade. SU 1293
Ray 28 A6 r rising SW of Winslow, Bucks, and flowing W into R Cherwell at Islip, Oxon. SP 5213
Ray Creek Essex 31 E6* inlet running into Brightlingsea Reach at mouth of R Colne opp Mersea I. TM 0913
Raydon Suffolk 31 E4 vil 3m/5km SE of Hadleigh. TM 0538
Raydon, Lower Suffolk 31 E4* ham 3m/5km S of Hadleigh. TM 0338
Raylees Nthmb 61 E3* loc 2km SW of Elsdon. nY 9291
Rayleigh Essex 20 D3 tn 6m/9km NW of Southend-on-Sea. Remains of Norman cas (NT). TQ 8090
Raymond's Hill Devon 8 B4* loc 2m/3km SE of Axminster. SY 3296
Rayne Essex 30 C5 vil 2m/3km W of Braintree. TL 7222
Rayne Grampian 83 E4* See Kirktown of Rayne.
Rayners Lane London 19 E3* loc in borough of Harrow 12m/19km NW of Charing Cross. TQ 1287
Raynes Park London 19 F4* loc in borough of Merton 3m/5km E of Kingston. TQ 2268
Raynham, East Norfolk 38 D2 vil 3m/5km SW of Fakenham. Hall of 17c. **S Raynham** vil 1m SW across R Wensum. **W Raynham** vil 1m W, with airfield to W. TF 8825
Rea Glos 26 C5* loc on left bank of R Severn in SW part of Gloucester. SO 8016
Rea 26 B1 r rising on N side of Brown Clee Hill, Salop, and flowing S through Cleobury Mortimer into R Teme near Newnham Br 3m/4km E of Tenbury Wells, H & W. SO 6368
Rea 35 G5* r rising at Longbridge, Birmingham, and flowing NE into R Tame about 3m/5km NE of city centre. SP 1089
Rea Brook 34 B3 r rising on Long Mountain, E of Welshpool, and flowing NE into R Severn at Shrewsbury. SJ 4912
Reach Cambs 30 B2 vil 5m/8km W of Newmarket. Site of Roman villa 1km SE. TL 5666
Read Lancs 48 A4 vil 2m/3km W of Padiham. SD 7634
Reading Berks 18 C4 county and industrial tn and rly centre on R Thames 36m/58km W of London. University. Remains of Norman abbey. SU 7173
Reading Green Suffolk 31 F1* loc 2m/3km W of Stradbroke. TM 2074
Readings Glos 26 B5* loc 3m/5km NW of Cinderford. SO 6116
Reading Street Kent 13 E4 ham 3m/5km SE of Tenterden. TQ 9230
Reading Street Kent 13 H1 N dist of Broadstairs. TR 3869
Read's Island Humberside 50 D5/51 E5 uninhabited island in R Humber 400 metres from right bank and 1m NW of S Ferriby. Island is about 2·6km E to W and 900 metres N to S. SE 9622
Readycon Dean Reservoir Gtr Manchester 48 C6* resr 4m/6km E of Milnrow. SD 9812
Reagill Cumbria 53 E3 ham 5m/9km W of Appleby. NY 6017
Rea Hill Devon 5 E5* dist of Brixham just E of tn centre. SX 9256
Rearquhar H'land 87 A7* loc in Sutherland dist 4m/7km NW of Dornoch. NH 7492
Rearsby Leics 36 C3 vil 7m/11km SW of Melton Mowbray. Airfield to S. SK 6514
Reasby Lincs 45 E3* loc 1m SW of Snelland. TF 0679
Rease Heath Ches 42 C5* loc 2m/3km N of Nantwich. SJ 6454
Reaster H'land 86 E2 loc in Caithness dist 4m/7km SE of Castletown. ND 2565
Reawick Shetland 89 E7 vil on Mainland on small bay of **Rea Wick** 2m/3km S of Garderhouse. HU 3244
Reay H'land 86 C2 vil near N coast of Caithness dist 10m/15km W of Thurso. Cnoc Freiceadain (A.M.), prehistoric chambered cairn 3m/5km E. NC 9664
Reay Forest H'land 84 D3, D4 mt area and deer forest in Sutherland dist extending from Foinaven south-eastwards to Ben Hee, and from Loch More north-eastwards to Glen Golly. Clan country of the Mackays. NC 34, 43
Reculver Kent 13 G1 N coast vil 3m/5km E of Herne Bay. Remains (A.M.) of Roman fort of the Saxon shore (*Regulbium*). TR 2269
Red Ball Devon 7 H3* ham 2m/3km SW of Sampford Arundel. ST 0817
Redberth Dyfed 22 C5 vil 4m/6km NW of Tenby. SN 0804
Redbourn Herts 19 E1 vil 4m/7km NW of St Albans. TL 1012
Redbourne Humberside 44 D2 vil 5m/8km SW of Brigg. Hall dates from 18c. SK 9799
Redbridge Hants 10 B3 W dist of Southampton at head of R Test estuary opp Totton. SU 3713
Redbridge London 20 B3* borough 8m/12km NE of London Br, named after loc on R Roding E of Wanstead. Tn of Ilford is in S part of borough. TQ 4288
Redbrook Clwyd 34 C1 vil 2m/3km W of Whitchurch. SJ 5041
Redbrook Glos 16 A1* vil on R Wye 3m/4km SE of Monmouth. Vil of **Lr Redbrook** 1 km S. SO 5310
Redbrook Reservoir W Yorks 43 E1* small resr 2m/3km SW of Marsden. SE 0209
Red Brow Merseyside 42 A2* loc 1m N of Kirkby. SJ 4099
Red Bull Ches 42 D5* loc 1km NW of Kidsgrove. SJ 8255
Redburn H'land 81 H3 loc in Nairn dist 7m/11km SE of Nairn. NH 9447
Redburn Nthmb 60 D5* loc just W of Bardon Mill. NY 7764
Redcar Cleveland 55 E3 tn and resort on North Sea coast 8m/12km NE of Middlesbrough. Wide sands. Racecourse. Large steel works. NZ 6025
Redcar Tarn W Yorks 48 C4 small lake 2km NW of Keighley. SE 0342
Redcastle H'land 81 E3 loc in Ross and Cromarty dist on N shore of Beauly Firth 4m/6km E of Muir of Ord. NH 5849
Red Cross Cambs 29 H2* suburban loc 3m/4km SE of Cambridge city centre. TL 4755
Red Dial Cumbria 52 C1 loc 2km S of Wigton. NY 2546
Reddicap Heath W Midlands 35 G4* loc 2km E of Sutton Coldfield. SP 1495
Redding Central 65 F1* loc 2m/4km SE of Falkirk. NS 9178
Reddingmuirhead Central 65 F1* loc 2m/4km SE of Falkirk. NS 9177
Reddings, The Glos 26 D5* W dist of Cheltenham. SO 9021
Reddish Gtr Manchester 42 D2 loc 2m/3km N of Stockport. SJ 8992
Redditch H & W 27 E1 tn 12m/19km S of Birmingham. New Tn designated 1964. SP 0467
Rede Suffolk 30 C3 vil 6m/10km SW of Bury St Edmunds. TL 8055
Rede 60 D3 r rising in Nthmb near Carter Bar on the English-Scottish border and flowing SE through Catcleugh Resr and by Rochester to Otterburn, then S into R North Tyne at Redesmouth, 2m/3km SE of Bellingham. NY 8582
Redenhall Norfolk 39 F6 vil 2km NE of Harleston. TM 2684
Redenham Hants 17 G6* loc 1km NW of Appleshaw and 5m/8km NW of Andover. SU 3049
Redesdale Camp Nthmb 60 D2* military camp 1m NW of Rochester. Site of Roman camp to E. NY 8298
Redes Mere Ches 42 D4 lake 5m/7km W of Macclesfield. SJ 8471
Redesmouth Nthmb 60 D3* ham near confluence of R Rede and R North Tyne 2m/3km SE of Bellingham. NY 8682
Redford Lothian 66 A2 dist of Edinburgh 4m/6km S of city centre. NT 2268
Redford Tayside 77 E6 vil 6m/9km NW of Arbroath. NO 5644
Redford W Sussex 11 E3 ham 3m/5km NW of Midhurst. SU 8626
Redgrave Suffolk 31 E1 vil 5m/8km W of Diss. TM 0477
Red Head Orkney 89 B5* headland at N end of island of Eday. HY 5640
Redhill Avon 16 A5 vil 4m/6km E of Congresbury. ST 4963
Red Hill Dorset 9 G4* N dist of Bournemouth. SZ 0995
Red Hill Hants 10 D4 loc adjoining Rowland's Castle to S, 3m/4km N of Havant. SU 7210
Red Hill H & W 26 D2* SE dist of Worcester. SO 8653
Redhill Surrey 19 F6 E dist of Reigate. Airfield and heliport 2m/3km SE. TQ 2750
Red Hill W Yorks 49 F5* loc 1m E of Castleford. SE 4425
Redhills Devon 7 G5* W dist of Exeter, 1m from city centre. SX 9092
Red Holm Orkney 89 B5* islet between islands of Eday and Westray at N end of Faray Sound. HY 5439
Redhythe Point Grampian 83 E1 headland on N coast 2km NW of Portsoy. NJ 5767
Redisham Suffolk 39 G6 vil 4m/6km S of Beccles. TM 4084
Redland Orkney 89 B6* loc on Mainland 1m NW of Woodwick. HY 3724
Redlingfield Suffolk 31 F1 vil 3m/5km SE of Eye. Loc of **Redlingfield Green** 1km NE. TM 1871

Redlodge Warren Suffolk 30 C1 loc 6m/9km NE of Newmarket. TL 6970
Red Lumb Gtr Manchester 47 H6* loc in Rochdale 4m/6km NW of tn centre. SD 8415
Redlynch Som 9 E1 ham 2m/3km SE of Bruton. ST 7033
Redlynch Wilts 9 H2 vil 7m/11km SE of Salisbury. SU 2021
Redmain Cumbria 52 B2* loc 1m SW of Blindcrake. NY 1333
Redmarley D'Abitot Glos 26 C4 vil 5m/8km SE of Ledbury. SO 7531
Redmarshall Cleveland 54 C3 vil 4m/6km W of Stockton-on-Tees. NZ 3821
Redmile Leics 36 D1 vil 7m/12km W of Grantham. SK 7935
Redmire N Yorks 54 A5 vil 4m/7km W of Leyburn. SE 0491
Redmires Dam W Yorks 48 C5* small resr on Stansfield Moor 2m/3km N of Todmorden. SD 9227
Redmires Reservoirs S Yorks 43 G3 three adjacent resrs on moors in W part of Sheffield 6m/9km W of city centre. SK 2685
Red Nab Lancs 47 E2* headland 1km S of Heysham harbour. SD 4059
Rednal W Midlands 35 F6 loc in Birmingham 8m/12km SW of city centre. SP 0076
Redness Point Cumbria 52 A2* headland on Solway Firth in N part of Whitehaven. NX 9719
Redpath Borders 66 D5 loc 3m/5km E of Melrose. NT 5835
Red Point H'land 78 E3 headland on W coast of Ross and Cromarty dist, on N side of entrance to Loch Torridon. NG 7267
Red Point H'land 84 B3 headland on W coast of Sutherland dist, on W side of entrance to Loch Laxford. Also known as Rubha Ruadh. NC 1651
Red Point H'land 86 C2 headland on N coast of Caithness dist 3m/4km W of Reay. NC 9366
Red Rail H & W 26 B4* loc on R Wye 4m/7km NW of Ross-on-Wye. SO 5428
Red River 2 C4 r rising 2m/4km SE of Camborne, Cornwall, and flowing into St Ives Bay 1km S of Godrevy Pt. SW 5842
Red Rock Gtr Manchester 42 B1* loc 3m/5km N of Wigan. SD 5809
Red Roses (Rhos-goch) Dyfed 22 D4 ham 3m/5km S of Whitland. SN 2011
Red Row Nthmb 61 G2 vil 3m/5km S of Amble. NZ 2599
Redruth Cornwall 2 C4 tn 8m/13km W of Truro. Developed with tin-mining industry; now mkt tn with light industry. SW 6941
Red Street Staffs 42 D6 loc 4m/6km N of Newcastle-under-Lyme. SJ 8251
Red Tarn Cumbria 52 C4* small lake below SW slope of Pike of Blisco. NY 2603
Red Tarn Cumbria 52 D3* lake below N side of Striding Edge, on E side of Helvellyn. NY 3415
Red Wharf Bay Gwynedd 40 C3 northward-facing bay with wide sands on E coast of Anglesey 6m/9km N of Menai Br. Also small resort on W side of bay. SH 58
Redwick Avon 16 B3 loc 1m NE of Severn Beach. ST 5486
Redwick Gwent 15 H3 vil near shore of R Severn estuary 7m/11km E of Newport. ST 4184
Redworth Durham 54 B3 ham 6m/10km NW of Darlington. NZ 2423
Reed Herts 29 G4 vil 3m/5km S of Royston. TL 3636
Reed End Herts 29 G4* ham 3m/5km S of Royston. TL 3436
Reedham Norfolk 39 G4 vil in Norfolk Broads 6m/9km S of Acle. Across Reedham Marshes to NE is Berney Arms Mill (A.M.), tallest marsh windmill in county. TG 4201
Reedley Lancs 48 B4* loc in S part of Brierfield. SD 8435
Reedley Hallows Lancs 48 B4* loc 2m/3km N of Burnley. SD 8335
Reedness Humberside 50 C5 vil on S bank of R Ouse 3m/5km E of Goole. **Lit Reedness** ham adjoining to E. SE 7923
Reeds Holme Lancs 48 B5* loc 1m N of Rawtenstall. SD 8024
Reekie Linn Tayside 76 C5 waterfall in R Isla below Br of Craigisla, 4m/6km N of Alyth. NO 2553
Reepham Lincs 45 E4 vil 4m/7km E of Lincoln. TF 0373
Reepham Norfolk 39 E3 vil 6m/10km SW of Aylsham. TG 1022
Reeth N Yorks 54 A5 vil in Swaledale at foot of Arkengarthdale 9m/14km W of Richmond. SE 0399
Reeves Green W Midlands 35 H6* ham 5m/8km W of Coventry. SP 2677
Refail Powys 33 H4* loc 1km SE of Berriew. SJ 1900
Regaby Isle of Man 46 C4 vil 3m/4km NW of Ramsey. SC 4397
Rèidh Eilean S'clyde 69 B5 islet 2m/3km off NW coast of Iona. NM 2426
Reiff H'land 85 A5 loc on NW coast of Ross and Cromarty dist 3m/4km S of Rubha Coigeach. NB 9614
Reigate Surrey 19 F6 tn below N Downs, 9m/14km N of Crawley. TQ 2550
Reighton N Yorks 51 F1 vil 4m/6km S of Filey. TA 1375
Rèisa an t-Sruith S'clyde 69 F7 small island midway between Craignish Pt on mainland of Argyll and Aird of Kinuachdrach on NE coast of Jura. NR 7399
Rèisa Mhic Phaidean S'clyde 69 F7 small island 2km W of Craignish Castle on mainland of Argyll. NM 7500
Reisgill Burn H'land 86 E4 stream in Caithness dist running S into Lybster Bay on E coast. ND 2434
Reiss H'land 86 F2 vil in Caithness dist 3m/5km NW of Wick. ND 3354
Rejerrah Cornwall 2 D3* loc 4m/6km S of Newquay. SW 8056
Releath Cornwall 2 C5* loc 3m/5km N of Helston. SW 6633
Relubbus Cornwall 2 B5 ham 3m/5km S of Hayle. SW 5631
Relugas Grampian 82 A2 loc in Darnaway Forest 7m/11km S of Forres. NH 9948
Remenham Berks 18 C3 vil 2km NE of Henley-on-Thames across r. Vil of **Remenham Hill** 1m SE. SU 7784
Rempstone Notts 36 B2 vil 4m/6km NE of Loughborough. SK 5724
Rendcomb Glos 17 E1 vil 5m/8km N of Cirencester. SP 0209
Rendham Suffolk 31 G2 vil 3m/4km NW of Saxmundham. Loc of **Rendham Green** adjoins to N. TM 3464
Rendlesham Suffolk 31 G3 loc 3m/4km SE of Wickham Mkt. Bentwaters Airfield to E. To S is **Rendlesham Forest**, large area planted with conifers (Forestry Commission). TM 3353
Renfrew S'clyde 64 C2 tn on S side of R Clyde 5m/9km W of Glasgow. Engineering, mnfre of boilers and cables. Car ferry across r to Yoker. Glasgow Airport to W. NS 5067
Renhold Beds 29 E3 vil 4m/6km NE of Bedford. TL 0952
Renishaw Derbys 43 H3* vil 6m/9km NE of Chesterfield. Hall, seat of the Sitwells, dates partly from early 17c. SK 4477
Renish Point W Isles 88 A4 headland at S end of Harris 7m/11km NE of N Uist across Sound of Harris. NG 0482
Rennibister Orkney 89 B6* prehistoric earth hse (A.M.) on S side of Bay of Firth, Mainland, 4m/6km W of Kirkwall. HY 3912
Rennington Nthmb 67 H6 vil 4m/6km NE of Alnwick. NU 2118
Renton S'clyde 64 B1 tn on W bank of R Leven 2m/3km N of Dumbarton. Industrial estate across r. Industries include wool-spinning, calico-processing. NS 3878
Renwick Cumbria 53 E1 vil 10m/16km NE of Penrith. NY 5943
Repps Norfolk 39 H3* ham 2m/4km W of Martham. TG 4216
Repton Derbys 35 H2 small tn 5m/8km NE of Burton upon Trent. Boys' public school. SK 3026
Rerwick Head Orkney 89 B6 headland on N coast of Mainland 6m/9km E of Kirkwall. HY 5411
Rescobie Loch Tayside 77 E5 small loch 4m/6km E of Forfar. NO 5151
Rescorla Cornwall 3 E3* loc 3m/5km N of St Austell. SX 0257
Resolis H'land 81 F1 loc on S side of Cromarty Firth, Ross and Cromarty dist, 2m/3km W of Balblair. NH 6765
Resolven W Glam 14 D2 vil 6m/9km NE of Neath. SN 8302
Restalrig Lothian 66 A2 dist of Edinburgh 2m/3km E of city centre. NT 2874
Rest and be Thankful S'clyde 70 D4 loc in Argyll at head of Glen Croe, 4m/6km NW of Ardgartan. NN 2207
Rest Bay Mid Glam 14 D4* bay extending from Sker Pt to Hutchwns Pt, NW of Porthcawl. SS 7978
Restenneth Priory Tayside 77 E5 ruined medieval priory 2m/3km E of Forfar. NO 4851
Reston Borders 67 F3 vil on Eye Water 4m/6km W of Eyemouth. NT 8862
Reston Cumbria 52 D5* loc 1m W of Staveley. SD 4598
Reston, North Lincs 45 G3 ham 4m/7km SE of Louth. **S Reston** vil 2km E. TF 3883
Restormel Cornwall 3 F2* loc on right bank of R Fowey 1m N of Lostwithiel. **Restormel Castle** (A.M.), medieval ruin. SX 1061
Restormel 118 admin dist of Cornwall.
Restronguet Cornwall 2 D4* loc 2m/4km NE of Penryn. To N, **Restronguet Creek**, running down past **Restronguet Pt** to Carrick Rds (R Fal). SW 8136
Reterth Cornwall 3 E2* loc 2m/3km E of St Columb Major. SW 9463
Retford, East Notts 44 B3 tn on R Idle, 27m/43km NE of Nottingham. Industries include engineering, wire rope mnfre, dyeing. **W Retford** loc to NW across r. SK 7080
Rettendon Essex 20 D2 vil 3m/5km NE of Wickford. TQ 7698
Reva Reservoir W Yorks 48 D4* resr on moors 2m/3km W of Menston. SE 1542
Revesby Lincs 45 G5 vil 6m/9km SE of Horncastle. To S, site of medieval abbey. To NE, **Revesby Abbey**, 19c hse in park. 1m SE, loc of **Revesby Br.** TF 2961
Rew Devon 7 F5* loc 3m/5km E of Crediton. SX 8899
Rewe Devon 7 G5 vil on R Culm 5m/8km NE of Exeter. SX 9499
Rew Street Isle of Wight 10 B5* ham 2m/3km SW of Cowes. SZ 4794
Rexon Devon 6 C6* loc 6m/9km NE of Launceston. SX 4188
Reybridge Wilts 16 D4* loc on R Avon 3m/5km S of Chippenham. ST 9169
Reydon Suffolk 31 H1 loc 2km NW of Southwold. Loc of **Reydon Smear** to E. TM 4978
Reymerston Norfolk 39 E4 vil 5m/8km S of E Dereham. TG 0106
Reynalton Dyfed 22 D5 vil 6m/9km NW of Tenby. SN 0908
Reynoldston W Glam 23 F6 vil on Gower peninsula 4m/6km NW of Oxwich Pt and 11m/18km W of Swansea. **Lit Reynoldston** loc 1km SE. SS 4889
Rezare Cornwall 3 H1* ham 5m/8km N of Callington. SX 3677
Rha H'land 78 B3 r in Skye running SW into Uig Bay. NG 3963
Rhadyr (Radur) Gwent 15 H2* loc 2km NW of Usk. Agricultural college. SO 3602
Rhaeadr 33 H2* r rising in Berwyn Mts on borders of Clwyd and Powys and running SE through Llanrhaeadr-ym-Mochnant into R Tanant 1m S of the vil. SJ 1324
Rhaeadr cwm Gwynedd 33 E1* series of six waterfalls in upper valley of R Cynfal 2m/4km E of Ffestiniog. SH 7441
Rhaeadr Cynfal Gwynedd 33 E1* two waterfalls in course of R Cynfal 1km S of Ffestiniog. SH 7041
Rhaeadr Ddu Gwynedd 33 E2* waterfall (NT) in R Gamlan just above its confluence with R Mawddach. SH 7224
Rhaeadr Du Gwynedd 32 D1 water-chute in valley 2km S of Maentwrog. SH 6638
Rhaeadr Ewynnol Welsh form of Swallow Falls, qv.
Rhaeadr Fawr Gwynedd 40 D4 high vertical waterfall in course of R Goch 2m/3km S of Aber. Also known as Aber Falls. SH 6670
Rhaeadr Fawr 40 D4* r running N past Aber, Gwynedd, into Conwy Bay 2m/3km W of Llanfairfechan. SH 6473
Rhaeadr Gwy Welsh form of Rhayader, qv.
Rhaeadr Mawddach Gwynedd 33 E2* waterfall in R Mawddach just above its confluence with R Gain in Coed y Brenin Forest. SH 7327
Rhaeadr Ogwen Gwynedd 40 D5* waterfall below Llyn Ogwen, on W side of Pont Pen-y-benglog. SH 6460
Rhaeadr y Bedd Clwyd 41 E5* waterfall in course of R Aled below Aled Isaf Resr, 4m/6km S of Llansannan. SH 9159
Rhaglan Welsh form of Raglan, qv.
Rhandirmwyn Dyfed 24 D4 vil on E side of R Towy valley 6m/9km N of Llandovery. SN 7843
Rhaslas Pond Mid Glam 15 F1* lake 2km W of Rhymney. SO 0907
Rhath, Y Welsh form of Roath, qv.
Rhayader (Rhaeadr Gwy) Powys 25 E2 small mkt tn on R Wye 11m/18km N of Builth Wells. Centre for angling and pony-trekking. SN 9768
Rhee 29 H3 r rising at Ashwell, Herts. See (R) Cam.
Rheidol 32 D6 r flowing from Nant-y-moch Resr, Dyfed, and running S through Dinas Resr to Devil's Br, then W into Cardigan Bay with R Ystwyth on S side of Aberystwyth. SN 5780
Rheidol Falls Dyfed 24 C1 waterfall in Cwm Rheidol 2m/3km NW of Devil's Br. SN 7178
Rheindown H'land 81 E3* loc in Ross and Cromarty dist 2m/3km S of Muir of Ord. NH 5247
Rhencullen Isle of Man 46 B4* loc 1m NE of Kirk Michael. SC 3291
Rheola W Glam 14 D1* loc 7m/11km NE of Neath. **Rheola Forest** is wooded area astride R Neath. SN 8304
Rhes-y-cae Clwyd 41 G4* loc 3m/5km S of Holywell. SJ 1870
Rhewl Clwyd 33 H1 ham on N bank of R Dee 3m/5km NW of Llangollen. SJ 1844
Rhewl Clwyd 41 G5 vil on R Clywedog 2m/3km NW of Ruthin. SJ 1060
Rhewl Salop 34 A1 loc 3m/5km NE of Oswestry. SJ 3034
Rhewl-fawr Clwyd 41 G3* loc 2m/3km NW of Mostyn. SJ 1281
Rhian-goll 25 G5 r rising in Black Mts on N side of Waun Fach, Powys, and flowing S into R Usk 2m/3km NW of Crickhowell. SO 1919
Rhicarn H'land 85 B5 locality in Sutherland dist 2m/3km NW of Lochinver. NC 0825
Rhiconich H'land 84 C3 locality at head of Loch Inchard, W coast of Sutherland dist. **Rhiconich R** rises on Reay Forest and runs NW into Loch Inchard here. NC 2552
Rhicullen H'land 81 F1 loc in Ross and Cromarty dist 2m/3km N of Invergordon. NH 6971
Rhidorroch H'land 85 C7 r running W into Loch Achall, Ross and Cromarty dist, E of Ullapool, through **Rhidorroch Forest**, deer forest. NH 1994
Rhigos Mid Glam 15 E1 vil 2m/4km W of Hirwaun. SN 9205
Rhilochan H'land 87 A6 loc in Sutherland dist 7m/11km NW of Golspie. NC 7407
Rhinefield Hants 10 A4* par in New Forest N of New Milton. SU 2502
Rhinns of Galloway D & G. See Rinns of Galloway.
Rhinns of Kells D & G. See Rinns of Kells.
Rhireavach H'land 85 A7 locality near E shore of Lit Loch Broom, Ross and Cromarty dist, 2km SE of Scoraig. NH 0295
Rhisga Welsh form of Risca, qv.
Rhiston Salop 34 A5* loc 1m NW of Church Stoke. SO 2595
Rhiw Gwent 15 G2* loc adjoining Newbridge to N. ST 2098
Rhiw Gwynedd. See Bwlch-y-Rhiw.
Rhiw 33 H4* r rising as several streams W of Llanllugan, Powys, which form two main streams both named R or Afon Rhiw flowing E and joining 2m/3km W of Manafon. The single r so formed continues E and runs into R Severn 1m SE of Berriew. SJ 1900
Rhiwabon Welsh form of Ruabon, qv.
Rhiwbina (Rhiwbeina) S Glam 15 F3* loc 3m/5km NW of Cardiff. Rhiwbina Garden loc 2km SE. ST 1581
Rhiwbryfdir Gwynedd 40 D6* loc adjoining Blaenau Ffestiniog to N. SH 6946
Rhiwderin (Rhiwderyn) Gwent 15 G3 ham 3m/5km W of Newport. ST 2687

Rhiwen Gwynedd 40 C5* loc below Moel Rhiwen 1km NW of Deiniolen. SH 5763
Rhiwgarn Mid Glam 15 E3* loc 3m/5km W of Pontypridd. ST 0189
Rhiwinder Mid Glam 15 E3* loc 1m E of Tonyrefail. ST 0188
Rhiwlas Clwyd 33 H2* loc 3m/4km E of Llanarmon Dyffryn Ceiriog. SJ 1932
Rhiwlas Gwynedd 40 C5 vil 4m/6km S of Bangor. SH 5765
Rhiwlech 33 F3* stream running S into R Dovey 2km N of Llanymawddwy, Gwynedd. SH 9020
Rhiwnant 24 D2* r running NE to join R Claerwen at head of Caban Coch Resr, Powys. SN 8961
Rhiwsaeson Mid Glam 15 F3* loc 2m/3km E of Llantrisant. ST 0782
Rhiw Saeson 33 F4* r running S into R Iaen at Llanbrynmair. SH 8902
Rhiw, Y Gwynedd. See Bwlch-y-Rhiw.
Rhode Som 8 B1* loc 2m/3km SW of Bridgwater. ST 2734
Rhoden Green Kent 20 C6* ham 1m E of Paddock Wd. TQ 6845
Rhodes Gtr Manchester 42 D1 loc 1m SW of Middleton. SD 8505
Rhodesia Notts 44 A3* loc 2km W of Worksop. SK 5680
Rhodes Minnis Kent 13 G3* ham 5m/8km N of Hythe. TR 1543
Rhodeswood Reservoir Derbys 43 E2* one of a chain of resrs in R Etherow valley, 3m/4km N of Glossop. SK 0498
Rhodiad Dyfed 22 A3 loc 2m/3km NE of St David's. SM 7627
Rhondda Mid Glam 15 E2 tn on R Rhondda (Afon Rhondda Fawr) 7m/11km NW of Pontypridd. Coal-mining, steel, clothing. SS 9795
Rhondda 15 E2 r whose two branches, Rhondda R (Afon Rhondda Fawr) and Lit Rhondda R (Afon Rhondda Fach) rise on high ground W of Aberdare, Mid Glam, and flow SE in roughly parallel courses until joining at Porth and flowing into R Taff at Pontypridd. ST 0789
Rhonehouse D & G. Alternative name for Kelton Hill, qv.
Rhonwydd 33 E4 r running S into R Dovey 1km S of Pennal, Gwynedd. SN 7099
Rhoose (Rhws, Y) S Glam 15 F4 loc 3m/5km W of Barry. Rhoose Airport to N. Rhoose Pt to S. ST 0666
Rhos Clwyd 41 G5* loc 2m/4km N of Ruthin. SJ 1261
Rhos Dyfed 23 E2 vil 4m/7km SW of Llandyssul. SN 3735
Rhos Powys 34 A3* loc 1km SE of Four Crosses. Loc of **Rhos Common** to N. SJ 2717
Rhos Salop 34 A1* loc 2km NE of Sellatyn. SJ 2735
Rhos W Glam 14 C2 vil 2km SE of Pontardawe. SN 7303
Rhosaman Dyfed 14 C1* loc 7m/11km E of Ammanford. SN 7313
Rhoscefnhir Gwynedd 40 C4* loc on Anglesey 2km S of Pentraeth. SH 5276
Rhoscolyn Gwynedd 40 A4 small vil and resort at S end of Holy I., Anglesey. **Rhoscolyn Hd,** headland to W. **Rhoscolyn Beacon** off shore to S marks position of island rocks, Ynysoedd Gwylanod. SH 2675
Rhoscrowther (Rhoscrowdder) Dyfed 22 B5 vil 2m/4km N of Castlemartin. Oil refinery to N. SM 9002
Rhos-ddu Clwyd 41 H6 dist of Wrexham 1km N of tn centre. SJ 3351
Rhosesmor Clwyd 41 H4 vil 2m/3km W of Northop. SJ 2168
Rhosfach Dyfed 22 D3* loc 1m N of Llangolman.
Rhosgadfan Gwynedd 40 C5* loc 4m/6km S of Caernarvon. SH 5057
Rhosgoch Gwynedd 40 B3* loc 3m/5km SW of Amlwch, Anglesey. SH 4089
Rhosgoch Powys 25 F3/G3 ham 4m/7km NW of Hay-on-Wye. SO 1847
Rhos-goch Welsh form of Red Roses, qv.
Rhos, Great Powys 25 F2 highest point on Radnor Forest, 2166 ft or 660 metres. Is 3m/4km NW of New Radnor. SO 1863
Rhos Haminiog Dyfed 24 B2* loc 1km N of Cross Inn. SN 5464
Rhos-hill (Rhos-hyl) Dyfed 22 D2 ham 4m/6km S of Cardigan. SN 1940
Rhoshirwaun Gwynedd 32 A2 ham 2m/4km NE of Aberdaron. SH 1929
Rhos-hyl Welsh form of Rhos-hill, qv.
Rhosili W Glam 23 F6 vil at W end of Gower peninsula, near S end of **Rhosili Bay,** sandy bay extending from Worms Hd northwards to Burry Holms. Inland from bay is **Rhosili Down** (NT), dominant feature of W Gower. SS 4188
Rhoslan Gwent 15 F1* loc 1m NE of Tredegar. SO 1410
Rhoslan Gwynedd 32 C1 loc 2m/3km NW of Criccieth. SH 4840
Rhoslefain Gwynedd 32 D4 ham 4m/6km N of Tywyn. SH 5705
Rhos Ligwy Gwynedd 40 B3* loc on Anglesey 5m/8km SE of Amlwch. SH 4886
Rhosllanerchrugog Clwyd 41 H6 urban loc 4m/6km SW of Wrexham. SJ 2946
Rhosmaen Dyfed 23 G3 vil 2km N of Llandeilo. SN 6222
Rhosmeirch Gwynedd 40 B4 loc on Anglesey 2km N of Llangefni. SH 4575
Rhosneigr Gwynedd 40 A4 small resort on W coast of Anglesey to SE of Valley Airfield. SH 3173
Rhosnesni Clwyd 42 A6 loc in Wrexham 2km E of tn centre. SJ 3551
Rhos-on-Sea Clwyd 41 E3 resort at E end of Penrhyn Bay, adjoining Colwyn Bay to NW. SH 8481
Rhosrobin Clwyd 41 H5/H6* loc 2km N of Wrexham. SJ 3252
Rhos, The Dyfed 22 C4 loc 4m/6km E of Haverfordwest. SN 0014
Rhostryfan Gwynedd 40 C5 vil 3m/5km S of Caernarvon. SH 4957
Rhostyllen Clwyd 41 H6 vil 2m/3km SW of Wrexham. SJ 3148
Rhosybol Gwynedd 40 B3 vil on Anglesey 3m/5km S of Amlwch. SH 4288
Rhos-y-brithdir Powys 33 H2* loc 2m/4km N of Llanfyllin. SJ 1322
Rhos-y-caerau Dyfed 22 B2* loc 2m/4km W of Fishguard. SM 9137
Rhos-y-garth Dyfed 24 C1* loc 2m/3km S of Llanilar. SN 6372
Rhosygilwen Dyfed 22 D2* loc 4m/6km SE of Cardigan. SN 2040
Rhos-y-gwaliau Gwynedd 33 F1 ham 2km SE of Bala. SH 9434
Rhos-y-llan Gwynedd 32 A1 loc 1km N of Tudweiliog. SH 2337
Rhos-y-llyn Dyfed 22 D3/23 E3* loc 6m/10km SW of Newcastle Emlyn. SN 2432
Rhos-y-meirch Powys 25 G1 loc 2m/3km S of Knighton. SO 2769
Rhu S'clyde 64 A1 vil and resort on E side of Gare Loch 2m/3km NW of Helensburgh. NS 2683
Rhuallt Clwyd 41 G4 vil 2m/4km E of St Asaph. SJ 0775
Rhubodach S'clyde 63 G1 loc on NE coast of Bute opp Colintraive, Argyll, across Kyles of Bute. Car and pedestrian ferry service to Colintraive. NS 0273
Rhuddall Heath Ches 42 B5* loc adjoining Tarporley to SE. SJ 5562
Rhuddlan Clwyd 41 F4 suburb 2m/4km SE of Rhyl. Formerly a port at mouth of R Clwyd. Remains of 13c cas (A.M.). Twt Hill (A.M.), to S, is motte of earlier Norman cas. SJ 0278
Rhuddlan 116 admin dist of Clwyd.
Rhuddnant 24 D1* r rising 6m/9km E of Devil's Br, Dyfed, and flowing W to join R Myherin and form R Mynach 2m/3km E of Devil's Br. SN 7677
Rhuddwyn Salop 34 A2* small lake 4m/6km W of Oswestry. SJ 2328
Rhulen Powys 25 F3* loc 3m/5km NW of Painscastle. SO 1349
Rhum H'land 79 B7-C8. See Rum.
Rhunahaorine Point S'clyde 62 D3 headland on W coast of Kintyre, Argyll, opp island of Gigha. NR 6849
Rhuthun Welsh form of Ruthin, qv.
Rhws, Y Welsh form of Rhoose, qv.
Rhych Point Mid Glam 14 D4* headland between Sandy Bay and Trecco Bay on E side of Porthcawl. SS 8276
Rhyd Gwynedd 32 D1 ham 2m/3km NW of Maentwrog. SH 6341
Rhydaman Welsh form of Ammanford, qv.
Rhydargaeau Dyfed 24 A5 ham 4m/7km N of Carmarthen. SN 4326
Rhydcymerau Dyfed 24 B4 ham 6m/9km S of Lampeter. SN 5738
Rhyd-ddu Gwynedd 40 C6 ham 3m/5km N of Beddgelert. SH 5652
Rhydd Green H & W 26 D3* loc on W bank of R Severn 3m/5km E of Gt Malvern. SO 8345
Rhydding W Glam 14 C2/D2* loc on N side of Neath across R Neath. SS 7498
Rhyddlan Dyfed 24 B4* loc 2m/3km W of Llanybydder. SN 4943
Rhydfelen Mid Glam 15 F3 loc 2m/3km SE of Pontypridd. ST 0988
Rhydgaled Clwyd 41 F5* loc 4m/6km W of Denbigh. SH 9964
Rhyd-hir 32 B2* stream flowing S into Pwllheli harbour, Gwynedd, with R Penrhos. SH 3634
Rhydlanfair Gwynedd 41 E6* loc 3m/5km W of Pentrefoelas. SJ 8252
Rhyd Lewis Dyfed 23 E1 ham 5m/8km NE of Newcastle Emlyn. SN 3447
Rhydlios Gwynedd 32 A2* loc 3m/4km N of Aberdaron. SH 1830
Rhyd-lydan Clwyd 41 E6* loc 2km E of Pentrefoelas. SH 8950
Rhydowen Dyfed 22 D3* loc just E of Glandwr. SN 1928
Rhydowen Dyfed 24 A4 ham 3m/5km NE of Llandyssul. SN 4445
Rhydri Welsh form of Rudry, qv.
Rhyd-ros-lan 33 G5* r running S into R Severn 2m/3km E of Caersws, Powys. SO 0592
Rhydrosser Dyfed 24 B2* loc 2m/3km SE of Llanrhystud. SN 5667
Rhydspence H & W 25 G3 loc 3m/5km N of Hay-on-Wye. SO 2447
Rhydtalog Clwyd 41 H5 loc 7m/11km NW of Wrexham. SJ 2355
Rhyd-uchaf Gwynedd 33 F1* ham 2m/3km NW of Bala. SH 9037
Rhydwaedlyd S Glam 15 F3* dist of Cardiff 3m/5km N of city centre. ST 1681
Rhyd-wen 33 F2 stream running NW to join R Glyn before flowing into Bala Lake on W side of Llangower, Gwynedd. SH 9032
Rhydwilym 33 H1 stream rising in Berwyn Mts less than 2m/3km NE of Cadair Fronwen and running E into R Ceiriog 2m/4km NW of Llanarmon Dyffryn Ceiriog, Clwyd. SJ 1335
Rhyd-y-ceirw Clwyd 41 H5* loc 2m/3km SW of Treuddyn. SJ 2356
Rhyd-y-clafdy Gwynedd 32 B2 ham 3m/5km W of Pwllheli. SH 3234
Rhydycroesau 33 H2 loc on border of Clwyd and Salop 3m/5km W of Oswestry. SJ 2430
Rhydyfelin Dyfed 24 B1 loc 2m/3km S of Aberystwyth. SN 5979
Rhyd-y-foel Clwyd 41 E4 vil 2m/4km W of Abergele. Hill fort to SE. SH 9176
Rhydyfro W Glam 14 C1 vil 2km NW of Pontardawe. SN 7105
Rhyd-y-groes Gwynedd 40 C4* ham 3m/5km S of Bangor. SH 5767
Rhyd-y-gwin W Glam 23 H5* loc 2m/3km NW of Clydach. SN 6703
Rhydymain Gwynedd 33 E2* loc 6m/9km NE of Dolgellau. SH 8022
Rhyd-y-meirch Gwent 15 G1 loc 4m/6km S of Abergavenny. SO 3107
Rhydymeudwy Clwyd 41 G6* loc 2km E of Llanelidan. SJ 1251
Rhyd-y-mwyn Clwyd 41 G4 loc 3m/4km NW of Mold. SJ 2066
Rhyd-y-pandy W Glam 23 H5* loc 2m/3km W of Clydach. SN 6602
Rhyd-yr-onnen Gwynedd 32 D4* loc 2m/3km NE of Tywyn. SH 6102
Rhyd-y-sarn Gwynedd 32 D1/33 E1* loc 1km W of Ffestiniog. SH 6942
Rhyd-y-wrach Dyfed 22 D4 loc 3m/5km NW of Whitland. SN 1619
Rhyl Clwyd 41 F3 resort on N Wales coast 8m/12km W of Point of Air. Mouth of R Clwyd on W side of tn. SJ 0081
Rhymney (Rhymni) Mid Glam 15 F1 tn on R Rhymney 4m/7km E of Merthyr Tydfil. Coal-mining, engineering, brewing. SO 1107
Rhymney (Rhymni) 15 G4 r rising on borders of Mid Glam, Gwent, and Powys, and flowing S into mouth of R Severn on E side of Cardiff. For much of its length forms boundary between Mid Glam and Gwent. ST 2275
Rhymney Valley 118 admin dist of Mid Glam.
Rhymni Welsh form of Rhymney (R), qv.
Rhynd Tayside 73 E3 vil 3m/5km SE of Perth. NO 1520
Rhynie Grampian 82 D4 vil 8m/13km S of Huntly. NJ 4927
Rhynie H'land 87 B8 loc near E coast of Ross and Cromarty dist 2km NE of Hill of Fearn. NH 8479
Rhythallt 40 C5* r running NW from Llyn Padarn, Gwynedd, to join R Seiont N of Llanrug. SH 5264
Rib 29 G6 r rising N of Buntingford, Herts, and flowing S into R Lea E of Hertford. TL 3313
Ribbesford H & W 26 C1* vil 1m S of Bewdley. SO 7874
Ribble 47 E5 r rising on Gayle Moor, N Yorks, NE of Ribblehead Viaduct, and flowing S to Settle and Long Preston, then SW to Preston and the Irish Sea between Southport, Merseyside, and Lytham St Anne's, Lancs. Tidal and navigable to seagoing vessels from Preston. SD 3025
Ribble, South 117 admin dist of Lancs.
Ribbleton Lancs 47 F5 dist of Preston 2m/4km NE of tn centre. SD 5631
Ribby Lancs 47 E5* loc adjoining Wrea Green to E. SD 4031
Ribchester Lancs 47 G4 vil on R Ribble 5m/8km N of Blackburn. Site of Roman fort of *Bremetennacum.* Museum of Roman antiquities (NT). SD 6535
Ribston, Little N Yorks 49 F3 vil 4m/6km SE of Knaresborough. Ribston Hall dates from 17c. SE 3853
Riby Lincs 45 F1 ham 6m/9km W of Grimsby. TA 1807
Riccal 55 E6 r rising on N Yorks Moors N of Helmsley and flowing SE into R Rye 3m/4km E of Nunnington. SE 7079
Riccall N Yorks 50 B4 vil 4m/6km N of Selby. SE 6237
Riccarton S'clyde 64 B5 urban loc, largely residential, on S side of Kilmarnock. NS 4236
Riccarton Junction Borders 60 B2* loc and former rly junction 2m/3km W of Saughtree. NY 5397
Richards Castle 26 A1 vil on borders of H & W and Salop, 3m/5km S of Ludlow. SO 4969
Richborough Castle Kent 13 H1 remains of Roman fort of the Saxon shore (A.M.). TR 3260
Richmond London 19 F4 tn on right bank of R Thames 8m/13km SW of Charing Cross. Also borough, **Richmond upon Thames,** on both sides of r. Richmond Park, large open space where deer roam, to SE of tn. TQ 1774
Richmond N Yorks 54 B4 tn above R Swale 11m/18km SW of Darlington. Remains of large Norman cas (A.M.). NZ 1701
Richmond S Yorks 43 H3* dist of Sheffield 3m/5km SE of city centre. SK 4085
Richmond Hill Isle of Man 46 B5* loc 3m/4km W of Douglas. SC 3374
Richmond Hill S Yorks 44 B1* suburb on W side of Doncaster across R Don. SE 5503
Richmond's Green Essex 30 B5* ham 2km SE of Thaxted. TL 6229
Richmondshire 117 admin dist of N Yorks.
Rich's Holford Som 7 H2* ham 2m/3km S of Crowcombe. ST 1434
Rickarton Grampian 77 G2 loc 4m/7km NW of Stonehaven. NO 8189
Rickerby Cumbria 60 A5* loc on N bank of R Eden 1m NE of Carlisle across r. NY 4156
Rickerscote Staffs 35 F2/F3 S dist of Stafford. SJ 9220
Rickets Head Dyfed 22 B4 headland on E side of St Brides Bay 6m/10km W of Haverfordwest. SM 8518
Rickford Avon 16 A5 vil below N slopes of Mendip Hills 1m W of Blagdon. ST 4859
Rickinghall Suffolk 31 E1 adjoining vils of **Rickinghall Superior** and **Inferior,** some 6m/9km SW of Diss. See also Botesdale. TM 0475
Rickleton Tyne & Wear 61 G6* SW dist of Washington. NZ 2853
Rickling Essex 30 A4 vil 6m/10km N of Bishop's Stortford. TL 4931
Rickling Green Essex 30 A5 ham 6m/9km N of Bishop's Stortford. TL 5029
Rickmansworth Herts 19 E2 tn on R Colne 17m/28km NW of London. TQ 0594
Riddings Cumbria 60 A4* loc 4m/7km N of Longtown. NY 4075
Riddings Derbys 43 H5 loc 2m/4km SE of Alfreton. SK 4252
Riddlecombe Devon 7 E4 vil 5m/8km W of Chulmleigh. SS 6114
Riddlesden W Yorks 48 D4 loc 2km NE of Keighley across R Aire. **E** and **W Riddlesden Halls,** 17c hses, the former NT. SE 0842
Riddlesworth Norfolk 38 D6 loc 6m/10km E of Thetford. TL 9681

Riddrie S'clyde 64 D2* dist of Glasgow 3m/4km E of city centre. HM prison (Barlinnie). NS 6368
Ridge Dorset 9 F5* ham 1m SE of Wareham. SY 9386
Ridge Herts 19 F2 vil 3m/4km W of Potters Bar. TL 2100
Ridge Wilts 9 F2 ham 2m/3km N of Tisbury. ST 9531
Ridgebourne Powys 25 F2 loc adjoining Llandrindod Wells to S. SO 0560
Ridge Green Surrey 19 G6 loc 2m/3km SE of Reigate. TQ 3048
Ridgehill Avon 16 A5 vil 2km NW of Chew Stoke. ST 5362
Ridge Hill Gtr Manchester 43 E2* loc in Stalybridge 1km N of tn centre. SJ 9699
Ridgeway Avon 16 B4* dist of Bristol 3m/5km NE of city centre. ST 6275
Ridgeway Derbys 43 H3 vil 5m/8km SE of Sheffield. **Ridgeway Moor** vil adjoining to S. SK 4081
Ridgeway Derbys 43 H5* loc 3m/5km N of Belper. SK 3651
Ridgeway Dyfed 22 D5* loc adjoining Saundersfoot to NW. SN 1305
Ridgeway Gwent 15 G3* W dist of Newport. ST 2988
Ridgeway Staffs 42 D5* ham 2m/4km S of Biddulph. SJ 8953
Ridge Way 17 F3 ancient trackway running from Vale of Pewsey along N edge of Wiltshire and Berkshire Downs to R Thames valley at Streatley. SU 38
Ridgeway Cross H & W 26 C3* loc 4m/6km W of Gt Malvern. SO 7247
Ridgewell Essex 30 C4 vil 5m/8km SE of Haverhill. Site of Roman villa to SW. TL 7340
Ridgewood E Sussex 12 B4 S dist of Uckfield. TQ 4719
Ridgmont Beds 28 D4 vil at N end of Woburn Park 3m/4km NE of Woburn. SP 9736
Ridgway Surrey 19 E5* loc 2m/3km E of Woking. TQ 0359
Riding Gate Som 9 E2* loc 2m/3km E of Wincanton. ST 7329
Riding Mill Nthmb 61 E5 vil 3m/4km SE of Corbridge. NZ 0161
Riding, The Nthmb 61 E5* loc 2km N of Hexham across R Tyne. NY 9365
Riding Wood Reservoir W Yorks 43 F1* small resr above Ramsden Resr 2km S of Holmbridge. SE 1105
Ridley Kent 20 C5 loc 3m/5km S of Longfield. TQ 6163
Ridley Nthmb 60 D5 loc 3m/5km W of Haydon Br. Wds on far side of R Allen owned by NT; see Morralee Wood. NY 7963
Ridley Green Ches 42 B5* loc 2m/3km E of Bulkeley. SJ 5554
Ridleywood Clwyd 42 A6 ham 2m/3km S of Holt. SJ 4051
Ridlington Leics 36 D4 vil 2m/4km NW of Uppingham. SK 8402
Ridlington Norfolk 39 G2 vil 2m/4km W of Happisburgh. **Ridlington Street** loc 1km S. TG 3431
Rid Reservoir, High Gtr Manchester 47 G6* small resr 3m/5km W of Bolton. SD 6610
Ridsdale Nthmb 60 D3/61 E3 ham 6m/9km S of Otterburn. NY 9084
Rienachait H'land 84 A4* loc near W coast of Sutherland dist 1m N of Stoer vil. NC 0429
Rievaulx N Yorks 55 E6 vil 2m/4km W of Helmsley. Ruins of 12c–13c Cistercian abbey (A.M.). SE 5785
Rift House Cleveland 54 D2* loc in SW dist of Hartlepool 2km SW of tn centre. NZ 4930
Rigg D & G 59 G4 vil 2m/3km SW of Gretna Green. NY 2966
Rigg Bay D & G. Alternative name for Cruggleton Bay – see Cruggleton.
Riggend S'clyde 65 E2 loc 3m/5km N of Airdrie. NS 7670
Righoul H'land 81 H2/H3* loc in Nairn dist 3m/5km S of Nairn. NH 8851
Rigifa H'land 86 F1* loc near N coast of Caithness dist 2m/3km S of St John's Pt. ND 3072
Rigsby Lincs 45 G4 ham 2m/3km W of Alford. TF 4275
Rigside S'clyde 65 F5 loc 1m S of Douglas Water. NS 8734
Rigton, East W Yorks 49 F4 vil 4m/6km SW of Wetherby. SE 3643
Rigton, North N Yorks 49 E3 vil 4m/7km SW of Harrogate. SE 2749
Riley Green Lancs 47 G5* vil 1km SE of Hoghton. SD 6225
Rileyhill Staffs 35 G3* loc 2km S of King's Bromley. SK 1115
Rilla Mill Cornwall 3 G1* vil on R Lynher 5m/7km NW of Callington. SX 2973
Rillaton Cornwall 3 G1* loc 5m/7km NW of Callington. SX 2973
Rillington N Yorks 50 D1 vil 5m/7km E of Malton. SE 8574
Rimbleton Fife 73 F4* central dist of Glenrothes. NO 2600
Rimington Lancs 48 B3 vil 3m/4km SW of Gisburn. SD 8045
Rimpton Som 8 D2 vil 3m/5km S of Sparkford. ST 6021
Rimswell Humberside 51 G5 vil 2m/3km W of Withernsea. TA 3128
Ringford D & G 58 C5 vil 4m/7km N of Kirkcudbright. NX 6857
Ringinglow S Yorks 43 G3* loc in Sheffield 4m/7km SW of city centre. SK 2983
Ringland Gwent 15 H3 loc in Newport 3m/5km E of tn centre. ST 3588
Ringland Norfolk 39 F3 vil 7m/11km NW of Norwich. TG 1314
Ringles Cross E Sussex 12 B4 loc 1m N of Uckfield. TQ 4722
Ringley Gtr Manchester 42 C1* loc 2km E of Kearsley. SD 7605
Ringmer E Sussex 12 B5 vil below S Downs 3m/4km NE of Lewes. TQ 4412
Ringmore Devon 4 C6 vil 4m/6km S of Modbury. SX 6545
Ringmore Devon 5 E3* loc on W side of Shaldon and 4m/7km E of Newton Abbot. SX 9272
Ring o' Bells Lancs 42 A1* loc 2km SE of Burscough Br. SD 4510
Ring of Brogar Orkney 89 A6* ancient stone circle (A.M.) on tongue of land between Loch of Harray and Loch of Stenness 4m/7km W of Finstown, Mainland. Twenty-seven stones are still standing out of an estimated original number of sixty. HY 2913
Ring's End Cambs 37 H4* loc 1km S of Guyhirn. TF 3902
Ringsfield Suffolk 39 G6 vil 2m/3km SW of Beccles. Ham of **Ringsfield Corner** 1m S. TM 4088
Ringshall Suffolk 31 E3 ham 4m/6km S of Stowmarket. TM 0452
Ringshall Stocks Suffolk 31 E3* ham 5m/7km S of Stowmarket. TM 0551
Ringstead Norfolk 38 C1 vil 2m/4km E of Hunstanton. TF 7040
Ringstead Northants 29 E1 vil 2m/4km S of Thrapston. SP 9875
Ringstone Edge Reservoir W Yorks 48 C6* resr on Ringstone Edge Moor 2km SE of Ripponden. SE 0416
Ringway Gtr Manchester 42 D3 vil on W side of Manchester Airport 3m/5km SE of Altrincham. SJ 8084
Ringwood Hants 9 H4 tn on E bank of R Avon with expansion eastwards, 10m/16km NE of Bournemouth. SU 1405
Ringwould Kent 13 H2 vil 3m/5km S of Deal. TR 3648
Rinnigill Orkney 89 A7* loc on E coast of Hoy 1m SW of island of Fara across strait. ND 3193
Rinns of Galloway D & G 57 A5-B8 anvil-shaped peninsula at SW extremity of Scotland, running some 28m/45km N to S. Isthmus 6m/10km wide, from Loch Ryan to Luce Bay, connects peninsula to rest of mainland. NX 0552
Rinns of Islay S'clyde 62 A2, A3 peninsula on W side of Islay, with the headland **Rinns Pt** at its S end. NR 2157
Rinns of Kells D & G 57 E5 mt range running N and S between Loch Doon and Clatteringshaws Loch. Summit is Corserine, 2669 ft or 814 metres. NX 5083
Rinn Thorbhais Tiree, S'clyde 69 A8 headland at SW end of island. NL 9340
Rinsey Croft Cornwall 2 B5* loc 4m/6km W of Helston. To SW on coast, **Rinsey Cliff** (NT), surrounding Porthcew Cove. **Rinsey Hd** is headland to W of Rinsey Cliff. SW 5927
Ripe E Sussex 12 B5 vil 5m/8km W of Hailsham. TQ 5110
Ripley Derbys 43 H5 tn 10m/15km N of Derby. Industries include coal-mining, engineering, hosiery. SK 3950
Ripley Hants 9 H4 ham 4m/6km N of Christchurch. 1m NE, loc of **N Ripley.** SZ 1698
Ripley N Yorks 49 E2 18c estate vil 3m/5km N of Harrogate. Cas rebuilt 16c-18c; gatehouse dates from 15c. SE 2860
Ripley Surrey 19 E5 vil 4m/7km SW of Cobham. Loc of **Ripley Green** to N. TQ 0556
Riplingham Humberside 50 D5* loc 3m/4km E of S Cave. SE 9231
Ripon N Yorks 49 E1 tn at confluence of Rs Laver, Skell, and Ure, 10m/16km N of Harrogate. Some light industry. Cathedral, in mixture of styles. Racecourse 2km SE. SE 3171
Rippingale Lincs 37 F2 vil 5m/8km N of Bourne. TF 0927
Ripple H & W 26 D4 vil 3m/5km N of Tewkesbury. SO 8637
Ripple Kent 13 H2 vil 2m/4km SW of Deal. TR 3550
Ripponden W Yorks 48 C6 tn on R Ryburn 5m/8km SW of Halifax. Textiles, engineering. SE 0319
Rip Row Lancs 47 F5 loc adjoining Whittle-le-Woods to N. SD 5822
Risabus S'clyde 62 b4* loc on The Oa, Islay, 3m/5km NE of Mull of Oa. NR 3143
Risay W Isles 88 C2* islet at entrance to Loch Leurbost, E coast of Lewis. NB 3923
Risbury H & W 26 B2 ham 4m/7km SE of Leominster. Prehistoric fort, **Risbury Camp,** to W. SO 5455
Risby Humberside 50 D6 loc 4m/6km NE of Scunthorpe. SE 9314
Risby Humberside 51 E4* loc 1m SW of Bentley. TA 0034
Risby Suffolk 30 C2 vil 4m/7km NW of Bury St Edmunds. TL 7966
Risca (Rhisga) Gwent 15 G2 tn 5m/7km NW of Newport. Coal-mining, steel mnfre, quarrying. ST 2391
Rise Humberside 51 F4 ham 5m/8km SW of Hornsea. TA 1542
Riseden Kent 12 D3* loc 1km NE of Kilndown. TQ 7035
Rise End Derbys 43 G5* loc 1m NW of Wirksworth. SK 2855
Risegate Lincs 37 G2 vil 5m/8km N of Spalding. TF 2129
Riseholme Lincs 44 D4 loc 2m/4km N of Lincoln. Late 18c hall enlarged in 19c. Lake in park. SK 9875
Risehow Cumbria 52 A2* loc 2km SW of Maryport. NY 0234
Riseley Beds 29 E2 vil 8m/13km N of Bedford. TL 0462
Riseley Berks 18 C5 vil 6m/10km S of Reading. SU 7263
Risga H'land 68 D3 islet in Loch Sunart in Lochaber dist, between islands of Carna and Oronsay. NM 6160
Rishangles Suffolk 31 F2 vil 4m/6km N of Debenham. TM 1668
Rishton Lancs 48 A5 tn 3m/5km NE of Blackburn. Textiles, paper, car body mnfre. **Rishton Resr** 1km W. SD 7230
Rishworth W Yorks 48 C6 vil below E slopes of Rishworth Moor 1m S of Ripponden. SE 0318
Rising Bridge Lancs 48 B5* loc 2km N of Haslingden. SD 7825
Risinghurst Oxon 18 B1* loc adjoining E outskirts of Oxford. SP 5607
Rising Sun Cornwall 3 H2* loc 3m/4km E of Callington. SX 3970
Risley Ches 42 C2* loc in NE part of Warrington. Atomic Energy Authority site. SJ 6692
Risley Derbys 36 A1 vil 2m/4km NW of Long Eaton. SK 4635
Rispain D & G 57 E8* earthworks of ancient rectangular camp (A.M.), 1m W of Whithorn. NX 4239
Risplith N Yorks 49 E2* ham 1km NW of Sawley. SE 2468
Rispond H'land 84 D2/E2 loc on **Rispond Bay,** small bay on W side of mouth of Loch Eriboll, N coast of Sutherland dist. NC 4565
Rissington, Great Glos 27 F5 vil 5m/8km NW of Burford. SP 1917
Rissington, Little Glos 27 F5 vil 4m/6km S of Stow-on-the-Wold. Airfield to SE. SP 1919
Ristol H'land 85 A6 one of the Summer Isles, qv. Lies close to NW coast of Ross and Cromarty dist 4m/7km S of Rubha Coigeach. Area about 560 acres or 225 hectares. NB 9711
Ritchings Park Bucks 19 E4 loc 4m/7km E of Slough. TQ 0379
Rivals, The (Eifl, Yr) Gwynedd 32 B1 triple-peaked mountain on Lleyn peninsula 2km S of Trevor. Height of chief, central, peak is 1849 ft or 564 metres. SH 3644
Rivar Wilts 17 G5* loc 1m S of Shalbourne. SU 3161
Rivelin 43 G2* r rising on Hallam Moors, W of Sheffield, S Yorks, and flowing E to join R Loxley on W side of Sheffield. SK 3289
Rivenhall Essex 30 C6 ham 2m/3km N of Witham. Site of Roman settlement. Loc of **Rivenhall End** to SE. TL 8217
River Kent 13 H3 suburb of Dover 2m/3km NW of tn centre. TR 2943
River W Sussex 11 F3 ham 2m/4km NW of Petworth. SU 9422
River Bank Cambs 30 A1* loc on E bank of R Cam 8m/13km NE of Cambridge. TL 5368
Riverhead Kent 20 B5 NW suburb of Sevenoaks. TQ 5156
Riverside Devon 4 B5* NW dist of Plymouth beside R Tamar, just below the rd and rly brs connecting Plymouth and Saltash. SX 4358
Riverside S Glam 15 F4* dist of Cardiff 1km SW of city centre across R Taff. ST 1776
River's Vale Derbys 43 F4* loc in Buxton 1km W of tn centre. SK 0473
Riverton Devon 7 E2* loc 6m/9km E of Barnstaple. SS 6330
Riverview Park Kent 20 C4* SE dist of Gravesend. TQ 6671
Rivington Lancs 47 G6 vil 2m/3km N of Horwich. To W, **Rivington Resrs,** 2m/3km long from N to S. SD 6214
Ro 33 H1* stream rising in Berwyn Mts and running N into R Dee 3m/4km W of Llangollen, Clwyd. SJ 1742
Roach 21 F2 r rising W of Rochford, Essex, and flowing E to the W side of Foulness I. and then N into R Crouch. TQ 9894
Roach Bridge Lancs 47 F5* loc at crossing of R Darwen 1m S of Samlesbury. SD 5928
Roade Northants 28 C3 vil 5m/9km S of Northampton. SP 7551
Road Green Norfolk 39 F5* loc 2km E of Hempnall. TM 2693
Roadhead Cumbria 60 B4 ham 9m/14km N of Brampton. NY 5174
Road Research Laboratory Berks. See Crowthorne.
Roadside H'land 86 D2 loc in Caithness dist 5m/9km SE of Thurso. ND 1560
Roadside Orkney 89 C5 loc on island of Sanday 6m/10km SW of Tafts Ness. HY 6841
Roadside of Garlogie Grampian 77 G1* loc strung out along rd leading E from Garlogie, 3m/5km E of Echt. NJ 7805
Roadside of Kinneff Grampian 77 G3 vil near E coast 3m/5km N of Inverbervie. See also Kinneff. NO 8476
Roadwater Som 7 G2 Exmoor vil 4m/6km SW of Watchet. To NE, ham of **Lr Roadwater.** ST 0338
Road Weedon Northants 28 B2* vil 4m/7km SE of Daventry. SP 6359
Roag Skye, H'land 79 A5/B5 loc 3m/4km SE of Dunvegan. NG 2744
Roa Island Cumbria 46 D2 loc at end of peninsula 3m/5km SE of Barrow-in-Furness. SD 2364
Roanheads Grampian 83 H2* coastal dist of Peterhead. NK 1346
Roan Island H'land 84 F2 fertile island of about 300 acres or 120 hectares, with rocky coast, at entrance to Tongue Bay, N coast of Caithness dist. Also known as Eilean nan Ròn. NC 6465
Roan of Craigoch S'clyde 56 C3 loc 4m/6km S of Maybole. NS 2904
Roareim W Isles (W of 88 A2) one of the Flannan Isles, qv. Roareim lies 2m/3km W of the main island, Eilean Mór, and on N side of Eilean a' Ghobha. NA 6946
Roast Green Essex 29 H4* ham 4m/7km W of Newport. TL 4532
Roath (Rhath, Y) S Glam 15 G3/G4 dist of Cardiff 1m NE of city centre. ST 1977
Robbers' Waterfall S'clyde. See Eas nam Meirleach.

Roberton Borders 66 B6/C6 vil on Borthwick Water 5m/7km W of Hawick. NT 4314
Roberton S'clyde 65 F5 vil in Upper Clydedale 4m/6km N of Abington. NS 9428
Robertsbridge E Sussex 12 D4 vil 5m/8km N of Battle. TQ 7323
Robertstown Grampian 82 B3 loc 3m/5km W of Craigellachie. NJ 2444
Robertstown Mid Glam 15 E2* loc in N part of Aberdare. SO 0003
Roberttown W Yorks 48 D5 vil 1m SW of Liversedge. SE 1922
Robeston Back Dyfed 22 C4* loc 1m W of Robeston Wathen. SN 0715
Robeston Wathen Dyfed 22 C4 vil 2m/3km NW of Narberth. SN 0815
Robeston West Dyfed 22 B5* ham 3m/5km NW of Milford Haven. SM 8809
Robin Hill Staffs 43 E5* loc 2km E of Biddulph. SJ 9057
Robin Hood Lancs 42 B1* loc 3m/5km W of Standish. SD 5211
Robin Hood W Yorks 49 E5 loc 4m/7km N of Wakefield. SE 3227
Robinhood End Essex 30 B4/C4* loc 3m/4km NE of Finchingfield. TL 7036
Robin Hood's Arbour Berks. See Maidenhead. SU 8581
Robin Hood's Bay N Yorks 55 G4 small North Sea coast resort and fishing vil on bay of same name 5m/8km SE of Whitby. NZ 9505
Robin's Brook 30 C5* stream rising N of Coggeshall, Essex, and flowing into R Blackwater there. TL 8422
Robinson's End Warwicks 35 H5* loc in W part of Nuneaton. SP 3191
Roborough Devon 4 B4 loc 5m/8km NE of Plymouth. Plymouth Airport to S. SX 5062
Roborough Devon 7 D3 vil 5m/9km SE of Torrington. SS 5717
Rob Roy's Cave Central 71 E4 crevices in rock on E shore of Loch Lomond 1km N of Inversnaid. NN 3310
Rob Roy's Prison Central 71 E4 cavern formed by rocks on E shore of Loch Lomond 2m/3km W of Ben Lomond. NN 3302
Robroyston S'clyde 64 D2* loc in Glasgow 3m/5km NE of city centre. NS 6368
Roby Merseyside 42 A2/A3 tn 6m/10km E of Liverpool. SJ 4390
Roby Mill Lancs 42 B1* loc 4m/7km W of Wigan. SD 5107
Rocester Staffs 35 G1 vil on R Dove 4m/6km N of Uttoxeter, on site of Roman settlement. SK 1139
Roch (Garn, Y) Dyfed 22 B4 vil 6m/10km NW of Haverfordwest. Restored 13c cas or tower hse. **R. Gate** loc adjoining to W. **Roch Br** ham on Brandy Brook 1m N. SM 8821
Roch 42 D1* r rising on borders of Gtr Manchester and W Yorks N of Littleborough and flowing SW through Littleborough and Rochdale into R Irwell S of Bury. SD 8007
Rochdale Gtr Manchester 42 D1 tn on R Roch 10m/16km NE of Manchester. Textiles, textile and general engineering, rubber, plastics. **Rochdale Canal** formerly extended from Bridgewater Canal at Manchester to Calder and Hebble Navigation at Sowerby Br; now only the section in Manchester is navigable. SD 8913
Roche Cornwall vil on N edge of china clay dist, 5m/8km N of St Austell. SW 9860
Roche Abbey S Yorks 44 A2* 12c Cistercian abbey (A.M.) in grnds laid out in 18c by Capability Brown, 2m/3km SE of Maltby. SK 5489
Rochester Kent 20 D5 ancient port, cathedral and commercial city on R Medway 28m/46km E of London. Ruined keep (A.M.) of Norman cas. Cathedral displays architectural styles of many periods. Airport 3m/4km S. TQ 7468
Rochester Nthmb 60 D2 ham 4m/7km NW of Otterburn. Site of Roman fort of *Bremenium* to N. NY 8398
Rochford Essex 21 E3 tn 3m/5km N of Southend-on-Sea. Par contains most of Southend Municipal Airport. TQ 8790
Rochford, Lower H & W 26 B1 vil on R Teme 2m/3km E of Tenbury Wells. SO 6268
Rochford, Upper H & W 26 B1 vil 2m/4km E of Tenbury Wells. SO 6267
Rock Cornwall 3 E1 vil opp Padstow across estuary of R Camel. SW 9476
Rock H & W 26 C1 vil 4m/7km SW of Bewdley. SO 7371
Rock Nthmb 67 H6 vil 5m/7km N of Alnwick. NU 2020
Rockall W Isles 57·6°N 13·7°W small uninhabited island lying some 186m/300km W of St Kilda. Height is about 63ft or 19 metres, the summit being surmounted by a navigation light installed in 1972.
Rockbeare Devon 7 G5 vil 5m/8km W of Ottery St Mary. SY 0195
Rockbourne Hants 9 H3 vil 3m/5km NW of Fordingbridge. SU 1118
Rockcliffe Cumbria 59 H5 vil 4m/7km NW of Carlisle. **Rockcliffe Cross** loc 2km NW. NY 3561
Rockcliffe D & G 58 D6 vil on E side of Rough Firth, 5m/8km S of Dalbeattie. NTS properties in vicinity include Mote of Mark, site of ancient hill fort, and Rough I., bird sanctuary in Rough Firth to S of vil. NX 8453
Rocken End Isle of Wight 10 B6* headland at SE end of Chale Bay. SZ 4975
Rock Ferry Merseyside 41 H3 dist of Birkenhead 2m/3km S of tn centre, on banks of R Mersey. SJ 3386
Rockfield Gwent 26 A5/A6 vil 2m/3km NW of Monmouth. SO 4814
Rockfield H'land 87 C7 loc on E coast of Ross and Cromarty dist 4m/6km SW of Tarbat Ness. NH 9282
Rockford Hants 9 H3* loc on edge of New Forest 2m/3km NE of Ringwood. SU 1608
Rockgreen Salop 34 C6* loc 1m NE of Ludlow. SO 5275
Rockham Bay Devon 6 C1* bay on N coast between Bull Pt and Morte Pt. SS 4546
Rockhampton Avon 16 B2 vil 2m/4km NE of Thornbury. ST 6593
Rockhead Cornwall 6 A6 loc 2m/3km NW of Camelford. SX 0785
Rock Hill H & W 26 D1 loc in SW part of Bromsgrove. SO 9569
Rockingham Northants 36 D5 vil above R Welland valley 3m/4km NW of Corby. Remains of Norman cas. SP 8691
Rockingham Forest Northants 36 D5/37 E5 former royal hunting preserve E of vil of Rockingham in which modern tn of Corby is situated. SP 99
Rockland All Saints Norfolk 38 D5 vil 4m/6km W of Attleborough. TL 9996
Rockland St Mary Norfolk 39 G4 vil 6m/10km SE of Norwich. **Rockland Broad** small broad or lake 2km E. TG 3104
Rockland St Peter Norfolk 38 D5 vil 4m/6km NW of Attleborough. TL 9997
Rockley Notts 44 C4* ham 3m/4km SE of Tuxford. SK 7371
Rockley Wilts 17 F4 ham 3m/4km NW of Marlborough. SU 1671
Rockliffe Lancs 48 B5* loc adjoining Bacup to SE. SD 8722
Rock Savage Ches B3* loc 2km S of Runcorn. SJ 5279
Rocks, High Kent 12 C3 loc 2m/3km SW of Tunbridge Wells. The rocks are much used for practice by climbers. TQ 5538
Rocks, The Kent 20 D5* loc on SE side of E Malling. TQ 7056
Rockvilla S'clyde 64 C2/D2* loc in Glasgow 1m N of city centre. NS 5867
Rockwell Green Som 7 H3 loc 1m W of Wellington. ST 1220
Rodborough Glos 16 D1 S dist of Stroud. SO 8404
Rodbourne Wilts 16 D3 vil 3m/4km S of Malmesbury. ST 9383
Rodbourne Wilts 17 F3 dist of Swindon 2km N of tn centre. SU 1486
Rodd H & W 25 G2* loc 2km S of Presteigne. SO 3262
Roddam Nthmb 67 G6* loc 1m W of Wooperton. NU 0220
Rodden Dorset 8 D5 ham 6m/9km NW of Weymouth. SY 6184
Roddlesworth Lancs 47 G5* loc 2m/3km E of Withnell. SD 6521
Roddymoor Durham 54 B2* loc adjoining Billy Row to W. **N Roddymoor** loc 1km E. NZ 1536
Rode Som 16 C5 vil 4m/7km NE of Frome. Loc of **Rode Hill** adjoins vil to NE. ST 8053
Rodeheath Ches 42 D4* loc 3m/5km NE of Congleton. SJ 8767
Rode Heath Ches 42 D5 vil 2km N of Alsager. SJ 8057
Rodel W Isles 88 A4* loc at S end of Harris 1m N of Renish Pt across inlet of **Loch Rodel.** NG 0481
Roden Salop 34 C3 ham 6m/9km NW of Wellington. SJ 5716
Roden 34 C3* r rising near Northwood, Salop, and flowing SE through Wem, then S into R Tern 2km SE of Withington. SJ 5912
Rode, North Ches 42 D4 ham 3m/5km NE of Congleton. SJ 8866
Rode Pool Ches 42 D5 lake extending NE from Rode Heath. SJ 8157
Rodger Law S'clyde 59 E1* mt in Lowther Hills 7m/11km S of Elvanfoot. Height 2258 ft or 688 metres. NS 9405
Rodhuish Som 7 G1 ham on edge of Exmoor National Park 3m/5km SE of Dunster. ST 0139
Roding 20 B3 r rising near Chapel End, Essex, NE of Bishop's Stortford, and flowing S into R Thames at Barking Creek, on border between boroughs of Barking and Newham, London. TQ 4581
Roding, High Essex 30 B6 vil 3m/5km SW of Gt Dunmow. TL 6017
Rodings, The Essex 20 C1 area of Essex between Chelmsford and Bishop's Stortford through which R Roding flows. Eight places here have names of two words, the second being Roding the first being Abbess, Aythorpe, Beauchamp, Berners, High, Leaden, Margaret, White. TL 51
Rodington Salop 34 C3 vil on R Roden 5m/7km NW of Wellington. **Rodington Heath** vil to NW. SJ 5814
Rodley W Yorks 49 E4 loc 5m/8km W of Leeds. SE 2236
Rodmarton Glos 16 D2 vil 5m/8km NE of Tetbury. Site of Roman villa 1km NE. ST 9498
Rodmell E Sussex 12 A6 vil 3m/4km S of Lewes. TQ 4106
Rodmersham Kent 21 E5 vil 2m/3km SE of Sittingbourne. Ham of **Rodmersham Green** 1km W. TQ 9261
Rodney's Pillar Powys 34 A3* obelisk on Breidden Hill commemorating Admiral Rodney's victory over the French off St Lucia in 1782. See also Breidden Hills. SJ 2914
Rodney Stoke Som 16 A6 vil below S slopes of Mendip Hills 3m/4km SE of Cheddar. ST 4850
Rodsley Derbys 43 G6 vil 4m/7km SE of Ashbourne. SK 2040
Rodway Som 8 B1 loc 3m/5km NW of Bridgwater. ST 2540
Rodway Hill Avon 16 B4* S dist of Mangotsfield 5m/9km E of Bristol. ST 6675
Roe 40 D4 r rising 3m/5km S of Penmaenmawr, Gwynedd, and flowing E by Roewen into R Conwy S of Caerhun. SH 7769
Roebuck Low Gtr Manchester 43 E1* loc 3m/4km NE of Oldham. SD 9607
Roeburn 47 F2 r rising on Forest of Bowland, Lancs, and flowing N into R Hindburn at Wray, 2m/3km SW of Wennington. SD 6067
Roecliffe N Yorks 49 F2 vil 2km W of Boroughbridge. SE 3765
Roe Cross Gtr Manchester 43 E2* loc 2m/3km SE of Stalybridge. SJ 9896
Roefield Lancs 48 A4* loc 1km W of Clitheroe. SD 7341
Roe Green Gtr Manchester 42 C1/C2* loc 2m/3km W of Swinton. SD 7501
Roe Green Herts 19 F1 dist of Hatfield near tn centre. TL 2208
Roe Green Herts 29 G4 ham 5m/7km E of Baldock. TL 3133
Roehampton London 19 F4 loc in borough of Wandsworth 6m/10km SW of Charing Cross. TQ 2274
Roe Lee Lancs 47 G5* loc in Blackburn 2km N of tn centre. SD 6830
Roe, Little Shetland 89 E6* uninhabited island of about 70 acres or 30 hectares at S end of Yell Sound 2m/4km E of Ollaberry, Mainland. HU 4079
Roe, North Shetland 89 E6* loc on Mainland just N of Burra Voe. HU 3689
Roestock Herts 19 F1* loc 2m/3km SW of Hatfield. TL 2106
Roffey W Sussex 11 G2 NE dist of Horsham. TQ 1932
Rogan's Seat N Yorks 53 H4 mt 3m/5km N of Muker. Height 2203 ft or 671 metres. NY 9103
Rogart H'land 87 A6 loc in Sutherland dist 4m/7km NW of head of Loch Fleet on E coast. NC 7303
Rogate W Sussex 11 E3 vil 4m/6km E of Petersfield. SU 8023
Roger Ground Cumbria 52 D5* loc just S of Hawkshead. SD 3597
Rogerstone (Ty-du) Gwent 15 G3 loc 3m/4km W of Newport. Aluminium works. ST 2688
Rogie Falls H'land 81 E2 waterfall and salmon leap in course of Black Water, Ross and Cromarty dist, 2m/4km W of Strathpeffer. NH 4458
Rogiet Gwent 16 A3 vil 2km W of Caldicot. ST 4587
Rohallion Tayside 72 D1 loc and cas 3m/4km SE of Dunkeld. NO 0439
Roinn a' Bhogha Shàmhaich H'land 79 E7* headland in Lochaber dist, on Sound of Sleat and 4m/6km N of Mallaig across entrance to Loch Nevis. NG 7002
Rois-bheinn H'land 68 E2 mt in Moidart, Lochaber dist, 3m/5km S of Lochailort. Height 2887 ft or 880 metres. NM 7577
Rokeby Durham 54 A3 loc 2m/4km SE of Barnard Castle. **Rokeby Hall** is 18c hse associated with Sir Walter Scott and painted by Turner. NZ 0713
Rokeles Hall Norfolk. See Watton.
Rokemarsh Oxon 18 B2* loc 2m/4km N of Wallingford. SU 6292
Roker Tyne & Wear 61 H5 dist of Sunderland, N of harbour. NZ 4059
Rollesby Norfolk 39 H3 vil 7m/11km NW of Gt Yarmouth. **Rollesby Broad,** broad or lake 1m SE, adjoining Ormesby Broad. TG 4415
Rolleston Leics 36 C4 vil 8m/13km N of Mkt Harborough. SK 7300
Rolleston Notts 44 vil 4m/6km W of Newark-on-Trent across r. SK 7452
Rolleston Staffs 35 H2 vil 3m/4km N of Burton upon Trent. **Rolleston on Dove** loc 1m E. SK 2327
Rollestone Wilts 17 E6* loc adjoining Shrewton to S and 5m/9km W of Amesbury. SU 0743
Rollright, Great Oxon 27 G4 vil 3m/5km N of Chipping Norton. Ham of **Lit Rollright** 2m/3km W. 'King's Men' (A.M.) is Bronze Age stone circle and 'Whispering Knights' (A.M.) is burial-chamber, respectively 1km N and 1km NE of Lit Rollright. SP 3231
Rolston Humberside 51 F4 ham near coast 2m/3km S of Hornsea. TA 2145
Rolstone Avon 15 H5 loc 5m/8km E of Weston-super-Mare. **E Rolstone** loc 1km SE. ST 3962
Rolvenden Kent 12 D4/13 E4 vil 3m/5km SW of Tenterden. Vil of **Rolvenden Layne** is 1m SE. TQ 8431
Romaldkirk Durham 54 A3 vil 5m/8km NW of Barnard Castle. NY 9922
Roman 31 E5 r (Roman R) rising 2m/3km E of Coggeshall, Essex, and flowing E into R Colne opp Wivenhoe. TM 0321
Romanby N Yorks 54 C5 suburb adjoining Northallerton to SW. SE 3693
Roman Hill Suffolk 39 H5* central dist of Lowestoft. TM 5493
Romanno Bridge Borders 65 H4 vil on Lyne Water 3m/4km S of W Linton. NT 1648
Romansleigh Devon 7 E3 vil 4m/6km SE of S Molton. SS 7220
Roman Steps Gwynedd 32 D2* staircase of unhewn rock slabs on track leading from head of Llyn Cwm Bychan towards Rhinog Fawr. Origin unknown. SH 6530
Rombalds Moor W Yorks 48 D3, D4 stretch of moorland between Wharfedale and Airedale extending from Addingham in the N to Baildon in the S and attaining height of 1321 ft or 403 metres 2km S of Ilkley. SE 1145
Romesdal Skye, H'land 78 C4 locality on E side of Loch Snizort Beag 6m/10km S of Uig. R Romesdal runs W into loch here. NG 4053
Romford London 20 B3 tn in borough of Havering 14m/23km E of Charing Cross. TQ 5189
Romiley Gtr Manchester 43 E2 tn 3m/4km E of Stockport. SJ 9390
Romney Marsh Kent 13 F4 area of well-drained marshland lying to W of Dymchurch, extensively used for sheep-grazing. TR 0430
Romney Street Kent 20 B5 loc 2m/3km NE of Otford. TQ 5561
Romsey Hants 10 B3 tn on R Test 7m/11km NW of Southampton. 10c–12c

abbey. King John's hunting box, 13c hse now museum. 1km S, Broadlands, 18c mansion formerly home of Lord Palmerston and later of Lord Mountbatten. SU 3521
Romsey Town Cambs 29 H2* E dist of Cambridge. TL 4757
Romsley H & W 35 F6 vil 3m/4km S of Halesowen. SO 9679
Romsley Salop 34 D6/35 E6* vil 5m/7km NW of Kidderminster. SO 7882
Rona Skye, H'land 78 D3, D4 uninhabited island of about 1600 acres or 650 hectares lying N of Raasay between W coast of Ross and Cromarty dist and Trotternish on mainland of Skye. Lighthouse at N end. Island is nearly 5m/8km long N to S. NG 6258
Ronachan Point S'clyde 63 E2 headland on W coast of Kintyre, Argyll, on S side of entrance to W Loch Tarbert. **Ronachan Bay** is small bay to S. NR 7455
Ronaldsay, North Orkney 89 C5 most northerly island of the group, 3m/4km N of Sanday across **N Ronaldsay Firth.** An airfield provides air link with Scottish mainland. Area of island about 3 sq miles or 8 sq km. HY 7553
Ronaldsay, South Orkney 89 B7 most southerly of main islands of Orkney group, measuring about 8m/12km N to S and 2m/4km E to W. Linked by Churchill Barrier, qv, to Burray, Glims Holm, Lamb Holm, and Mainland. ND 48
Ronaldsvoe Orkney 89 B7* loc at N end of S Ronaldsay, adjoining St Margaret's Hope to W. ND 4493
Ronaldsway Airport Isle of Man 46 B6 commercial airport for the island, 2km E of Castletown. SC 2868
Rona, North W Isles uninhabited island of about 300 acres or 120 hectares lying 46m/74km N of Butt of Lewis (88 C1) and NW of Cape Wrath (84 C1). Nature reserve; breeding-ground of grey seals. HW 8132
Ronas Hill Shetland 89 E6 hill on Mainland between Ronas Voe and Colla Firth. At 1486 ft or 453 metres it is summit of Shetland Is. HU 1486
Ronas Voe Shetland 89 D6/E6 long inlet on NW coast of Mainland on S side of Ronas Hill. HU 2882
Ronay W Isles 88 E1 barely populated island of about 2 sq miles or 5 sq km off SE coast of N Uist, on E side of Grimsay. NF 8956
Ronkswood H & W 26 D2* E dist of Worcester. SO 8655
Ron, The Grampian 83 H2* offshore rock on which lighthouse at Rattray Hd, qv, is situated. NK 1157
Rood End W Midlands 35 F5* loc in Warley 2km N of tn centre. SP 0088
Rooden Reservoir Gtr Manchester 48 C6* resr 3m/5km E of Milnrow. SD 9711
Rookery Pool Ches 42 C4* small lake 1km E of Petty Pool. SJ 6370
Rookery, The Staffs 42 D5* loc 2km NE of Kidsgrove. SJ 8555
Rookhope Durham 53 H1 vil 4m/7km NW of Stanhope. NY 9342
Rookhope Burn 53 H1 r rising on moors N of St John's Chapel, Durham, and flowing SE past Rookhope into R Wear at Eastgate. NY 9538
Rookley Isle of Wight 10 C6 vil 3m/5km S of Newport. SZ 5084
Rookleygreen Isle of Wight 10 C6* loc just S of Rookley and 4m/6km S of Newport. SZ 5083
Rooks Bridge Som 15 H6 vil 4m/7km W of Axbridge. ST 3652
Rook's Nest Som 7 H2* ham 4m/6km N of Wiveliscombe. ST 0933
Rookwith N Yorks 54 B6 loc 4m/7km W of Bedale. SE 2086
Rookwood W Sussex 10 D5* loc 2km N of W Wittering. SZ 7899
Rookwood W Yorks 49 E5* dist of Leeds 2m/3km E of city centre. SE 3233
Rookwood Farm Hants. See Denmead.
Roos Humberside 51 G5 vil 4m/6km NW of Withernsea. Site of cas near ch to S. TA 2930
Roose Cumbria 46 D2* loc in Barrow-in-Furness 2m/3km E of tn centre. SD 2269
Roosebeck Cumbria 46 D2 loc on W shore of Morecambe Bay 4m/6km E of Barrow-in-Furness. SD 2567
Roosecote Cumbria 46 D2 loc in Barrow-in-Furness 2m/3km E of tn centre. SD 2268
Roos Hall Suffolk 39 G5* Elizn hse 1km W of Beccles. TM 4190
Rootham's Green Beds 29 E2* ham 6m/10km NE of Bedford. TL 1057
Rope Ches 42 C5* loc 2m/3km S of Crewe. SJ 6952
Ropley Hants 10 D2 vil 4m/6km E of New Alresford. SU 6431
Ropley Dean Hants 10 C2 vil 3m/4km E of New Alresford. SU 6332
Ropley Soke Hants 10 D2 loc 4m/7km E of New Alresford. SU 6533
Ropsley Lincs 37 E1 vil 5m/8km E of Grantham. SK 9934
Rora Grampian 83 H2* vil on E side of Rora Moss, 5m/8km NW of Peterhead. NK 0650
Rora Hd Orkney 89 A7 headland on W coast of Hoy. ND 1799
Rorrington Salop 34 A4 ham 5m/8km NE of Ch Stoke. SJ 3000
Rosarie Forest Grampian 82 C2, C3* state forest 5m/8km N of Dufftown. NJ 3548
Rosay W Isles 88 C2* small uninhabited island on S side of entrance to Loch Erisort, E coast of Lewis. NB 4220
Roscoble Reservoir Fife 72 D5* small resr 3m/5km W of Kelty. NT 0993
Rose Cornwall 2 D3 ham 2km E of Perranporth. SW 7754
Roseacre Kent 20 D6* loc 2km/3km E of Maidstone. TQ 7955
Roseacre Lancs 47 E4 loc 3m/5km N of Kirkham. SD 4336
Rose Ash Devon 7 F3 vil 5m/9km SE of S Molton. SS 7821
Rosebank S'clyde 65 E4 loc on R Clyde 3m/5km E of Larkhall. NS 8049
Roseberry Topping 55 E4 conical hill on border of Cleveland and N Yorks 3m/5km SW of Guisborough. Height 1051 ft or 320 metres. NZ 5712
Rosebery Lothian 66 B3 loc 4m/6km SW of Gorebridge. **Rosebery Resr** 1km SE. NT 3057
Roseburn Lothian 66 A2* dist of Edinburgh 2m/3km W of city centre. NT 2273
Rosebush Dyfed 22 C3 ham 2km N of Maenclochog. **Rosebush Resr** to W. SN 0729
Rosecare Cornwall 6 B5* loc 5m/8km NE of Boscastle. SX 1695
Rosecliston Cornwall 2 D3* loc 2m/3km S of Newquay. SW 8159
Rosedale Abbey N Yorks 55 F5 vil 6m/10km N of Kirkbymoorside. Remains of 12c priory. Disused lead mines on surrounding moors. SE 7295
Roseden Nthmb 67 G6* loc 1m E of Ilderton. NU 0321
Rose Green Essex 30 D5 ham 6m/10km NW of Colchester. TL 9028
Rose Green Suffolk 30 D3/D4* ham 4m/6km W of Hadleigh. TL 9744
Rose Green W Sussex 11 E5* W dist of Bognor Regis. SZ 9099
Rose Grove Lancs 48 B5* loc in Burnley 1m W of tn centre. SD 8132
Rosehall Grampian 83 F2* loc 1m W of Turriff. NJ 7149
Rosehall H'land 85 E6 loc at foot of Glen Cassley in Sutherland dist 8m/12km W of Lairg. NC 4702
Rosehearty Grampian 83 G1 fishing vil on N coast 4m/7km W of Fraserburgh. NJ 9367
Roseheath Merseyside 42 A3* loc 1km SW of Halewood. SJ 4485
Rose Hill E Sussex 12 B5* loc 5m/8km NE of Lewes. TQ 4516
Rose Hill Lancs 48 B5* dist of Burnley 1km S of tn centre. SD 8331
Rose Hill Oxon 18 A1* S dist of Oxford. SP 5303
Rosehill Salop 34 B3* loc 2m/4km NW of Shrewsbury. SJ 4715
Rose Hill Suffolk 31 F4* SE dist of Ipswich. TM 1843
Rosehill Tyne & Wear 61 G4/G5* loc in N Tyneside dist on E side of Wallsend. NZ 3166
Roseisle Grampian 82 A1 loc 2m/3km SE of Burghead. **Roseisle Forest** is state forest bordering Burghead Bay to W. NJ 1367
Rose Lands E Sussex 12 C6* suburb of Eastbourne 1m N of tn centre. TQ 6100
Rosemarket Dyfed 22 C5 vil 2m/4km N of Neyland. Traces of ancient fort at S end. SM 9508
Rosemarkie H'land 81 G2 vil and resort on W side of Moray Firth in Ross and Cromarty dist, opp Fort George. **Rosemarkie Bay** extends southwards to Chanonry Pt. TV and radio transmitting stn. NH 7357
Rosemary Lane Devon 8 A3 ham 4m/7km SE of Wellington. ST 1514
Rosemount Tayside 73 E1 loc 1m SE of Blairgowrie. NO 1843
Rosemullion Head Cornwall 2 D5 headland (NT) at S end of Falmouth Bay 3m/5km S of Falmouth. SW 7927
Rosenannon Cornwall 3 E2* ham 3m/5km NE of St Columb Major. SW 9566
Rose Ness Orkney 89 B7 headland at SE end of Mainland 9m/14km SE of Kirkwall. Lighthouse. ND 5298
Rosenithon Cornwall 2 D6* loc to E of St Keverne, 10m/15km SE of Helston. SW 8021
Rosevean Cornwall 3 E3* loc 4m/6km N of St Austell. SX 0258
Roseville W Midlands 35 F5* loc in N part of Dudley. SO 9393
Rosevine Cornwall 2 D4* loc above W side of Gerrans Bay on N side of Porthscatho. SW 8736
Rosewarne Cornwall 2 B4 loc 3m/5km SW of Camborne. SW 6136
Rosewell Lothian 66 A3/B3 vil 4m/6km SW of Dalkeith. NT 2862
Roseworth Cleveland 54 D3* dist of Stockton-on-Tees 2m/3km NW of tn centre. NZ 4221
Roseworthy Cornwall 2 B4 loc 2m/3km W of Camborne. SW 6139
Rosgill Cumbria 53 E3 ham 2m/3km NW of Shap. NY 5316
Roshven H'land 68 E2 locality in Lochaber dist on S side of entrance to Loch Ailort. NM 7078
Roskhill Skye, H'land 78 B4/79 B5 loc 2m/4km SE of Dunvegan. NG 2745
Roskorwell Cornwall 2 D5* loc just N of Porthallow, 9m/14km E of Helston. SW 7923
Rosley Cumbria 52 C1 ham 5m/8km SE of Wigton. NY 3245
Roslin Lothian 66 A2 vil 2m/3km S of Loanhead. **Roslin Chapel,** restored 15c ch. To S above loop of R North Esk, remains of **Roslin Castle,** rebuilt 16c–17c; faint remains of original 14c cas. NT 2763
Rosliston Derbys 35 H3 vil 4m/7km S of Burton upon Trent. SK 2416
Rosneath S'clyde 64 A1 vil on W side of Gare Loch 2m/3km NE of Kilcreggan. **Rosneath Bay** to SE. **Rosneath Pt** is headland on Firth of Clyde 2m/3km SE. NS 2583
Ross Nthmb 67 G4 loc near coast 3m/4km NE of Belford. **Ross Links** sand dunes to E. NU 1337
Rossall Point Lancs 46 D3 headland 1m W of Fleetwood. SD 3147
Ross and Cromarty 114 admin dist of H'land region.
Rossay W Isles 88 B3* small uninhabited island in E Loch Tarbert, Harris, off W coast of Scalpay. NG 2095
Ross Castle Nthmb 67 G5* hill fort (NT), probably Iron Age, on E side of Chillingham Park. See Chillingham. NU 0825
Rossdhu S'clyde 71 E5 cas and seat of the Colquhouns on W shore of Loch Lomond 2m/3km S of Luss. NS 3689
Rossendale Lancs 48 B5* valley of R Irwell between Bacup and Rawtenstall, giving its name to surrounding dist. **Forest of Rossendale,** moorland area to N. SD 82
Rossendale 117 admin dist of Lancs.
Rossend Castle Fife 73 E5* ruined 17c hse overlooking shipyards at Burntisland. (Restoration proposed, 1975.) NT 2385
Rossett (Yr Orsedd) Clwyd 42 A5 vil 5m/8km N of Wrexham. 17c water-mill. SJ 3657
Rossett Green N Yorks 49 E3* dist of Harrogate 2km S of tn centre. SE 3052
Rosside Cumbria 46 D1* loc 1m W of Ulverston. SD 2778
Rossie Tayside 77 F5/G5. See Inchbraoch.
Rossington S Yorks 44 B2 vil 4m/7km SE of Doncaster. See also New Rossington. SK 6298
Rosskeen H'land 81 F1* loc in Ross and Cromarty dist 2m/3km W of Invergordon. NH 6869
Rossland S'clyde 64 B2* loc 5m/8km NW of Paisley. NS 4370
Ross, Little D & G 58 C6 island with lighthouse at entrance to Kirkcudbright Bay, at E extremity of Wigtown Bay. NX 6543
Rosslyn Lothian. See Roslin.
Rossmore Dorset 9 G5* NE dist of Poole. SZ 0593
Ross of Mull S'clyde 69 B6, C6 long granite peninsula at SW end of Mull, running out to Sound of Iona. NM 3920
Ross-on-Wye H & W 26 B5 mkt tn on R Wye 9m/14km NE of Monmouth. Old mkt hall and many old hses. SO 5924
Ross Point Central 71 E5 wooded headland on E side of Loch Lomond 2m/3km S of Rowardennan. NS 3695
Rostherne Ches 42 C3 vil 3m/5km N of Knutsford. **Rostherne Mere,** lake to N. SJ 7483
Rostholme S Yorks 44 B1* loc adjoining Bentley to N. SE 5606
Rosthwaite Cumbria 52 C3 ham in Borrowdale 3m/4km S of Derwent Water. NY 2514
Roston Derbys 43 F6 vil 5m/7km SW of Ashbourne. SK 1341
Rostrehwfa Gwynedd 40 B4* loc 2km SW of Llangefni, Anglesey. SH 4575
Rosudgeon Cornwall 2 B5* ham 6m/10km W of Helston. SW 5529
Rosyth Fife 65 G1 tn adjoining Inverkeithing to NW. Naval base on Firth of Forth to S. **Rosyth Castle** (A.M.) is 15c tower with later additions. NT 1183
Rothay 52 D4 r rising 2m/3km N of Grasmere vil, Cumbria, and flowing S through the vil to Grasmere lake, then E through Rydal Water, then SE into R Brathay 1km SW of Ambleside. SD 3703
Rothbury Nthmb 61 F2 small mkt tn on R Coquet 11m/17km SW of Alnwick. Surrounding hills known as Rothbury Forest. NU 0501
Rother 11 F3 r rising S of Selborne in Hampshire and flowing S to Sheet, near Petersfield, then E past Midhurst to join R Arun 1m W of Pulborough. TQ 0318
Rother 119 admin dist of E Sussex.
Rother 13 E5 r rising S of Rotherfield, E Sussex, and flowing into English Channel 3m/4km SE of Rye. TQ 9517
Rother 43 H2* r rising near Clay Cross, Derbys, and flowing N through Chesterfield and Staveley into R Don at Rotherham, S Yorks. SK 4292
Rotherby Leics 36 C3 vil 5m/8km W of Melton Mowbray. SK 6716
Rotherfield E Sussex 12 B4 vil 3m/5km E of Crowborough. TQ 5529
Rotherfield Greys Oxon 18 C3 vil 2m/3km W of Henley-on-Thames. SU 7282
Rotherfield Peppard Oxon 18 C3 vil 3m/5km W of Henley-on-Thames. SU 7181
Rotherham S Yorks 43 H2 industrial tn 6m/10km NE of Sheffield, at confluence of Rs Don and Rother. Coal-mining, iron and steel, glass. SK 4292
Rotherhithe London 20 A4* 4m/6km E of Charing Cross. Dock area in borough of Southwark on S bank of R Thames (Surrey Commercial Docks). Rd tunnel under r to Shadwell, borough of Tower Hamlets. TQ 3579
Rother Levels 13 E4 area of well-drained marshland N of Rye near mouth of R Rother on borders of E Sussex and Kent. TQ 82,92
Rothersthorpe Northants 28 C2 vil 4m/6km SW of Northampton. SP 7156
Rotherwick Hants 18 C5 vil 2m/3km NW of Hook. SU 7156
Rothes Grampian 82 B2 small tn with distilleries, near left bank of R Spey 9m/15km SE of Elgin. Ruined medieval cas of the Leslies. NJ 2749
Rothesay S'clyde 63 G2 chief tn and port of island of Bute, qv, situated on **Rothesay Bay** on E coast, 7m/11km W of Wemyss Bay across Firth of Clyde. Rothesay Bay extends from Bogany Pt (E) to Ardbeg Pt (N). **Rothesay Castle** (A.M.) near tn centre dates mainly from 14c, though parts are earlier. NS 0864
Rothiemay Castle Grampian 82 D2 cas on E side of Milltown, N of Huntly. NJ 5548

Rothiemurchus H'land 75 H1 loc in Badenoch and Strathspey dist 2m/3km S of Aviemore. Rothiemurchus Forest is deer forest to S. NH 8809
Rothienorman Grampian 83 F3 vil 9m/14km S of Turriff. NJ 7235
Rothiesholm Head Orkney 89 C6* headland at SW end of island of Stronsay. HY 6121
Rothley Leics 36 B3 vil on Rothley Brook 5m/8km N of Leicester. Site of Roman villa 1m W. **Rothley Temple** is a hse incorporating 13c chapel of Knights Templars. SK 5812
Rothley Nthmb 61 E3 loc 4m/6km NE of Kirkwhelpington. **Rothley Castle,** two towers built for visual effect in 18c. **Rothley Lakes,** two small lakes to N. NZ 0488
Rothley Brook 36 B3 r rising near Stanton under Bardon, Leics, and flowing in a southward loop to the E where it joins R Soar 6m/9km N of Leicester. SK 5913
Rothney Grampian 83 E4* loc adjoining Insch to S. NJ 6227
Rothwell Lincs 45 F2 vil 2m/4km SE of Caistor. TF 1599
Rothwell Northants 36 D6 small tn 4m/6km NW of Kettering. SP 8181
Rothwell W Yorks 49 E5 tn 5m/7km SE of Leeds. Coal-mining, chemicals. **Rothwell Haigh** loc 1m NW. SE 3428
Rotsea Humberside 51 E3 loc 5m/7km SE of Gt Driffield. TA 0651
Rottal Tayside 76 D4 loc in Glen Clova 6m/10km N of Dykehead. NO 3769
Rotten Calder 64 D3 r in Strathclyde region rising S of E Kilbride and running NE into R Clyde 4m/6km E of Rutherglen. Also known as Calder Water. NS 6761
Rotten Green Hants 18 C5* loc 2m/3km SE of Hartley Wintney. SU 7855
Rotten Row Bucks 18 C3* loc 3m/5km W of Marlow. SU 7986
Rotten Row Norfolk 39 E3* loc 1km NE of E Tuddenham. TG 0812
Rotten Row W Midlands 35 G6* loc in Solihull 3m/5km SE of tn centre. SP 1875
Rottingdean E Sussex 12 A6 coastal loc 4m/6km E of Brighton tn centre. TQ 3602
Rottington Cumbria 52 A4 ham 1m NW of St Bees. SX 9613
Rotton Park Reservoir W Midlands 35 F5* resr in Birmingham 2km W of city centre. SP 0486
Roud Isle of Wight 10 C6* loc 4m/6km NW of Ventnor. SZ 5180
Roudham Norfolk 38 D5 loc 6m/10km NE of Thetford. TL 9587
Rougham Norfolk 38 C3 vil 7m/12km N of Swaffham. TF 8320
Rougham Green Suffolk 30 D2* vil 4m/6km SE of Bury St Edmunds. TL 9061
Roughbirchworth S Yorks 43 G1* loc 2m/3km SE of Penistone. SE 2601
Rough Castle Central 65 E1* Roman fort on Antonine Wall 2km E of Bonnybridge. NS 8479
Rough Close Staffs 35 E1 ham 4m/6km NE of Stone. SJ 9239
Rough Common Kent 13 F1* suburban loc 2m/3km NW of Canterbury. TR 1259
Roughcote Staffs 35 F2* loc 4m/7km E of Stoke-on-Trent. SJ 9444
Rough Firth D & G 58 D6 estuary of Urr Water, 5m/8km S of Dalbeattie. See also Rockcliffe. NX 8353
Rough Hay Staffs 35 G2* loc 2m/4km W of Burton upon Trent. SK 2023
Rough Island D & G. See Rockcliffe.
Roughlee Lancs 48 B4* loc 2m/3km NW of Nelson. SD 8440
Roughley W Midlands 35 G4 loc 2m/3km NE of Sutton Coldfield. SP 1399
Roughrigg Reservoir S'clyde 65 E3* resr 3m/5km E of Airdrie. NS 8164
Roughton Lincs 45 F4 vil 3m/5km E of Woodhall Spa. TF 2464
Roughton Norfolk 39 F2 vil 3m/5km S of Cromer. TG 2137
Roughton Salop 34 D5 vil 3m/4km E of Bridgnorth. SO 7594
Rough Tor Cornwall 3 F1 granite tor (NT) on Bodmin Moor 3m/5km SE of Camelford. SX 1480
Round Bush Herts 19 F2* loc 3m/5km E of Watford. TQ 1498
Roundbush Green Essex 20 C1 ham 1m N of Leaden Roding. TL 5914
Round Green Beds 29 E5* dist of Luton 1m NE of tn centre. TL 1022
Round Green S Yorks 43 G1* loc 2m/3km SW of Barnsley. SE 3303
Roundham Som 8 C3* ham 2km W of Crewkerne. ST 4209
Roundham Head Devon 5 E4* headland on Tor Bay in S part of Paignton. SX 8960
Roundhay W Yorks 49 E4 dist of Leeds 3m/5km NE of city centre. Contains large public park with golf course and lake. SE 3337
Round Hill Devon 5 E4* N dist of Paignton. SX 8962
Round Hill Notts 44 A5* loc adjoining Sutton in Ashfield to E. SK 5158
Roundhill Reservoir N Yorks 48 D1 resr on Masham Moor 5m/8km SW of Masham. SE 1577
Round Oak Berks 18 B5 loc 8m/12km SW of Reading. SU 6265
Round Oak Salop 34 B5* ham 3m/4km NW of Craven Arms. SO 3984
Round Oak W Midlands 35 E5* loc in Dudley 2m/4km SW of tn centre. SO 9187
Round's Green W Midlands 35 F5* loc 1m W of Oldbury. SO 9789
Round Street Kent 20 C5* loc adjoining Sole Street to N, 4m/6km S of Gravesend. TQ 6568
Roundstreet Common W Sussex 11 F2 loc 3m/5km NW of Billingshurst. TQ 0528
Roundthorn Gtr Manchester 42 D3* loc in Manchester 3m/4km E of Altrincham. SJ 8088
Roundthwaite Cumbria 53 E4* loc 1m SW of Tebay. NY 6003
Roundway Wilts 17 E5 vil 2km NE of Devizes. Army barracks adjoining vil to E. SU 0163
Roundyhill Tayside 76 D5* loc 2m/4km S of Kirriemuir. NO 3750
Rounton, East N Yorks 54 D4 vil 7m/11km NE of Northallerton. NZ 4203
Rounton, West N Yorks 54 C4 vil 7m/11km NE of Northallerton. NZ 4103
Rousay Orkney 89 B6 hilly island of about 16 sq miles or 41 sq km lying 1m off N coast of island of Mainland across Eynhallow Sound. **Rousay Sound** is sea passage between E coast of Rousay and island of Egilsay. HY 33
Rousdon Devon 8 B5 ham 3m/5km W of Lyme Regis, in par of Combpyne Rousdon. SY 2991
Rousham Oxon 27 H5 ham 4m/6km W of Middleton Stoney. **Rousham Hse,** 17c-18c, with gardens laid out by William Kent. SP 4724
Rous Lench H & W 27 E2 vil 6m/10km N of Evesham. SP 0153
Routh Humberside 51 E4 vil 4m/7km NE of Beverley. TA 0942
Rout's Green Bucks 18 C2* loc 3m/4km NE of Stokenchurch. SU 7898
Row Cornwall 3 F1 vil 4m/7km S of Camelford. SX 0976
Row Cumbria 52 D5 ham 6m/10km SE of Windermere. SD 4589
Row Cumbria 53 F2* loc just E of Ousby. NY 6234
Rowallan Castle S'clyde 56 D1 cas (A.M.), mainly 16c, 3m/5km N of Kilmarnock. NS 4342
Rowanburn D & G 59 H4 vil 2km E of Canonbie. NY 4077
Rowanfield Glos 26 D5* W dist of Cheltenham. SO 9222
Rowardennan Central 71 E5 locality on E shore of Loch Lomond opp Inverbeg. Ferry for pedestrians. **Rowardennan Forest** is state forest on shore of loch to SE. NS 3598
Rowarth Derbys 43 E2* ham 2m/3km NW of Hayfield. SK 0189
Row Ash Hants 10 C3* loc between Curdridge and Shedfield, 2m/3km E of Botley. SU 5413
Rowbank Reservoir S'clyde 64 B3 eastern part of resr 2m/3km S of Howwood. Western part known as Barcraigs Resr. NS 3957
Rowbarton Som 8 A2* N dist of Taunton. ST 2225
Rowberrow Som 16 A5 ham 4m/6km S of Congresbury. ST 4558
Rowde Wilts 17 E5 vil 2m/3km NW of Devizes. ST 9762
Rowden Devon 7 E5* loc 4m/7km NE of Okehampton. SX 6498
Rowden N Yorks 49 E3* loc 1km S of Hampsthwaite. SE 2557
Row, East N Yorks 55 G4* loc on North Sea coast adjoining vil of Sandsend to SE. NZ 8612
Ro-wen Gwynedd 40 D4 vil 4m/6km S of Conwy. SH 7571
Rowe, The Staffs 35 E1 loc 6m/9km NW of Stone. SJ 8238
Rowfield Derbys 43 G6* loc 2m/3km NE of Ashbourne. SK 1949
Rowfoot Nthmb 60 C5* ham 3m/4km SW of Haltwhistle. NY 6880
Row Green Essex 30 C5* ham 2m/3km SW of Braintree. TL 7420
Rowhedge Essex 31 E5 vil on R Colne opp Wivenhoe. TM 0221
Row, High Cumbria 52 D2* loc 2m/4km SE of Hesket Newmarket. NY 3535
Rowhook W Sussex 11 G2 loc 4m/6km NW of Horsham, on course of the Roman Stane Street. Site of Roman stn 1m SW. TQ 1234
Rowington Warwicks 27 F1 vil 6m/10km NW of Warwick. Loc of **Rowington Green** to N. SP 2069
Rowland Derbys 43 G4* ham 3m/4km N of Bakewell. SK 2172
Rowland's Castle Hants 10 D4 vil 3m/5km N of Havant. Brickworks. Site of Roman bldg to S. SU 7310
Rowlands Gill Tyne & Wear 61 F5 suburb on R Derwent 3m/5km SW of Blaydon. NZ 1658
Rowledge Surrey 11 E1 SW suburb of Farnham. SU 8243
Rowley Humberside 51 E5 ham 8m/12km NW of Hull. SE 9732
Rowley Salop 34 A4 loc 5m/8km E of Welshpool. SJ 3006
Rowley Hill W Yorks 48 D6* loc 3m/5km E of Huddersfield. SE 1914
Rowley Park Staffs 35 E2* loc in Stafford 1km S of tn centre. SJ 9122
Rowley Regis W Midlands 35 F5 W dist of Warley. SO 9687
Rowley's Green W Midlands 35 H5/H6* loc in Coventry 3m/5km N of city centre. SP 3483
Row, Low Cumbria 52 B1* loc 1km S of High Scales. NY 1845
Row, Low Cumbria 52 D2* loc 2m/3km SE of Hesket Newmarket. NY 3536
Row, Low Cumbria 60 B5* ham 4m/6km E of Brampton. NY 5863
Row, Low N Yorks 53 H5 vil in Swaledale 4m/6km W of Reeth. SD 9897
Rowlstone H & W 25 H5 vil 2km W of Pontrilas. SO 3727
Rowly Surrey 11 F1 loc 2m/3km NW of Cranleigh. TQ 0440
Rownall Staffs 43 E6* loc 1m W of Wetley Rocks. SJ 9549
Rowner Hants 10 C4* dist of Gosport 2m/4km NW of tn centre. SU 5801
Row, Nether Cumbria 52 C2* loc 2km S of Caldbeck. NY 3037
Rowney Green H & W 27 E1 vil 3m/4km N of Redditch. SP 0471
Rownhams Hants 10 B3 vil 4m/6km NW of Southampton. SU 3817
Row, North Cumbria 52 C2* loc 1km W of Bassenthwaite. NY 2232
Row-of-Trees Ches 42 D3* loc 1m W of Alderley Edge. SJ 8279
Rowrah Cumbria 52 B3 ham 2m/3km NW of Ennerdale Br. NY 0518
Rowridge Isle of Wight 10 B6* loc and TV stn 4m/6km SW of Newport. SZ 4486
Rowsham Bucks 28 D5 vil 3m/5km NE of Aylesbury. SP 8518
Rowsley Derbys 43 G4 vil 3m/5km SE of Bakewell. **Lit Rowsley** loc adjoining to E. SK 2565
Rowson Green Derbys 43 H6* loc 2m/3km SE of Belper. SK 3746
Rowstock Oxon 17 H3 loc 3m/5km W of Didcot. SU 4789
Rowston Lincs 45 E5 vil 7m/11km N of Sleaford. TF 0856
Rowthorne Derbys 44 A4 loc 5m/7km NW of Mansfield. SK 4764
Rowton Ches 42 A5 vil 3m/5km SE of Chester. **Rowton Moor** loc adjoining to NW; site of Civil War battle, 1645. SJ 4564
Rowton Salop 34 B3* loc 8m/13km W of Shrewsbury. **Rowton Castle,** 1m E, is early 19c bldg on site of medieval cas. SJ 3612
Rowton Salop 34 B6* loc 2m/4km SW of Craven Arms. SO 4080
Rowton Salop 34 C3 ham 6m/9km NW of Wellington. SJ 6119
Row Town Surrey 19 E5* loc 2m/4km S of Chertsey. TQ 0363
Row, West Suffolk 38 B6 vil 2m/4km W of Mildenhall. TL 6775
Roxburgh Borders 66 D5 vil 3m/5km SW of Kelso. Remains of **Roxburghe Castle** between Rs Teviot and Tweed 1m W of Kelso. NT 7030
Roxby Humberside 50 D6 vil 4m/7km NE of Scunthorpe. SE 9116
Roxby N Yorks 54 C6* loc 2km SW of Pickhill. Site of Roman settlement to N. SE 3282
Roxby N Yorks 55 F3 vil 2m/3km SW of Staithes. NZ 7616
Roxeth London 19 F3* loc in borough of Harrow 1m W of Harrow on the Hill. TQ 1486
Roxholm Lincs 45 E6 loc 3m/4km N of Sleaford. TF 0650
Roxton Beds 29 F2 vil 4m/6km N of Sandy. TL 1554
Roxwell Essex 20 C1 vil 4m/6km W of Chelmsford. TL 6408
Roy H'land 74 D3 r in Lochaber dist rising on N side of Creag Meagaidh and running down to Loch Roy, then continuing N for 3m/5km before turning SW and running down Glen Roy to R Spean, on S side of Roy Br. NN 2780
Royal Forest S'clyde 74 C5, D5 mt area (NTS) N of Glen Etive, Argyll. Includes Buachaille Etive Mór. NN 2053
Royal Leamington Spa Warwicks 27 G1 tn on R Leam 8m/13km S of Coventry. Commonly referred to as Leamington; full style conferred on tn in 1838. SP 3165
Royal Merchant Navy School Berks. See Sindlesham.
Royal Military Canal Kent 13 E4 canal, now disused, running from Sandgate along N edge of Romney Marsh and across Rother Levels into R Rother N of Rye. TR 03
Royal Oak Durham 54 B3 loc named after public hse 4m/6km S of Bishop Auckland. NZ 2023
Royal Oak Lancs 42 A1* loc 4m/6km W of Skelmersdale. SD 4103
Royal's Green Ches 34 C1* loc 2m/4km W of Audlem. SJ 6242
Royal Tunbridge Wells Kent 12 C3 largely residential tn and shopping centre 31m/50km SE of London. Formerly a spa (chalybeate springs). Officially 'Royal' since 1909. TQ 5839
Roy Bridge H'land 74 D3 loc in Glen Spean at foot of Glen Roy in Lochaber dist, 3m/5km E of Spean Br. NN 2781
Royd S Yorks 43 G2* loc 1km SE of Stocksbridge. SK 2797
Roydhouse W Yorks 49 E6* loc 2km E of Kirkburton. SE 2112
Royd Moor S Yorks 43 G1* loc 2m/3km NW of Penistone. **Royd Moor Resr** to N. SE 2204
Roydon Essex 20 B1 vil 2m/4km W of Harlow. TL 4010
Roydon Norfolk 38 C3 vil 6m/10km E of King's Lynn. TF 7022
Roydon Norfolk 39 E6 vil 2km W of Diss. TM 0980
Roydon Hamlet Essex 20 B1* vil 2m/4km SW of Harlow. TL 4107
Royds, Far W Yorks 49 E5* loc in Leeds 2m/4km SW of city centre. SE 2731
Royds Green Upper W Yorks 49 F5* loc 1m SE of Rothwell. **Royds Green Lr** loc 1km S. SE 3526
Royd, West W Yorks 48 D4* E dist of Shipley. SE 1637
Royley Gtr Manchester 42 D1* loc adjoining Royton to W. SD 9107
Royston Herts 29 G4 tn at crossing of Icknield Way and Roman Ermine Street, 12m/20km SW of Cambridge. TL 3540
Royston S Yorks 43 H1 tn in coal-mining area 3m/5km N of Barnsley. Other industries include rly engineering. SE 3611
Royston Water Som 8 A3* loc 1m E of Churchingford. ST 2213
Royton Gtr Manchester 42 D1 tn 2m/3km N of Oldham. Textiles. SD 9207
Ruabon (Rhiwabon) Clwyd 41 H6 industrial tn 5m/7km SW of Wrexham. Coal-mining, chemicals. SJ 3043
Ruadh Meall Central 71 G2 mt on border of Central and Tayside regions 2km NW of head of Loch Lednoch. Height 2237 ft or 682 metres. NN 6731
Ruadh-phort Mór S'clyde 62 B1* vil on E coast of Islay just N of Port Askaig. Caol Ila Distillery. NR 4269
Ruadh-stac Mór H'land 80 A2 summit of Beinn Eighe, Ross and Cromarty dist. Height 3312 ft or 1010 metres. NG 9561
Ruaigh Tiree, S'clyde 69 B7 loc near E end of island, 2m/3km W of Rubha Dubh. NM 0647

Ruan Lanihorne Cornwall 2 D4 vil on Ruan R 5m/8km SE of Truro across Tresillian R. SW 8942
Ruan Major Cornwall 2 C6 ham 3m/5km N of Lizard Pt. SW 7016
Ruan Minor Cornwall 2 C6 vil 3m/5km NE of Lizard Pt. SW 7215
Ruardean Glos 26 B5 vil 3m/5km NW of Cinderford. SO 6117
Ruardean Hill Glos 26 B5* vil 2m/4km NW of Cinderford. SO 6317
Ruardean Woodside Glos 26 B5* vil 3m/4km NW of Cinderford. SO 6216
Rubery H & W 35 F6 suburb 8m/13km SW of Birmingham. SO 9877
Rubha Aird Druimnich H'land 68 D2 headland on N side of Ardnamurchan peninsula in Lochaber dist. 9m/14km NW of Salen. NM 5772
Rubha Aird Shlignich H'land 68 D3* headland on S side of Ardnamurchan peninsula in Lochaber dist. 2m/3km NE of Auliston Point across strait. NM 5660
Rubha an Dùin Bhàin H'land 68 C2* headland in Lochaber dist 3m/5km NE of Ardnamurchan Pt. NM 4470
Rubha an Ridire H'land 70 A1 headland at S end of Morvern, Lochaber dist. NM 7340
Rubha Ard Ealasaid S'clyde 68 D4* headland with pier on Sound of Mull 1km N of mouth of Aros R, Mull. NM 5645
Rubha Ardvule W Isles 88 A2 headland on W coast of S Uist 10m/16km S of Ardivachar Pt. NF 7030
Rubha Ban H'land 78 E2* headland on W coast of Ross and Cromarty dist, on N side of entrance to Gair Loch. NG 7379
Rubh' a' Bhearnaig S'clyde 70 A2 headland at N end of Kerrera, 2km NW of Oban, Argyll, across Sound of Kerrera. NM 8431
Rubh' a' Bhinnein Coll, S'clyde 68 A3 headland on NW coast 4m/6km N of Arinagour. NM 2263
Rubha Bholsa S'clyde 62 B1 headland on N coast of Islay 3m/5km W of Rubh' a' Mhàil. NR 3778
Rubh' a' Bhrocaire H'land 85 B5 small uninhabited island (a headland at low tide) off NW coast of Ross and Cromarty dist in Enard Bay, to E of Eilean Mor. NC 0717
Rubh' a' Bhuachaille H'land 84 B2 headland on NW coast of Sutherland dist 7m/11km SW of Cape Wrath. NC 2065
Rubha Bodach S'clyde 63 G1* headland on N coast of Bute 2km E of Buttock Pt. NS 0274
Rubha Buidhe H'land 79 F7 headland in Lochaber dist, on N side of entrance to Loch Hourn from Sound of Sleat. NG 7811
Rubha Carrach H'land 68 C2* headland on N side of Ardnamurchan peninsula in Lochaber dist, 4m/6km NE of Ardnamurchan Pt. NM 4670
Rubh' a' Chàirn Bhàin S'clyde 62 D3* headland on E coast of Gigha, near N end of island. NR 6653
Rubh' a' Chàirn Mhoir H'land 68 E2 headland in Lochaber dist on S side of Sound of Arisaig, 2m/3km W of Roshven. NM 6778
Rubh' a' Chaoil S'clyde 68 B4 headland on W coast of Mull, on N side of entrance to Loch Tuath. NM 3346
Rubha Chaolais H'land 68 E1 headland at W end of peninsula of Ardnish, Sound of Arisaig, on coast of Lochaber dist. NM 6980
Rubha Chàrn nan Ceare Skye, H'land 79 D7* headland on W coast of Sleat peninsula 3m/4km N of Pt of Sleat. NG 5503
Rubha Chraiginis Tiree, S'clyde 69 A7 headland at extreme W end of island. NL 9245
Rubh' a' Chrois-aoinidh S'clyde 69 D8 headland on W coast of Jura on S side of entrance to Loch Tarbert. NR 5080
Rubha Chuaig H'land 78 E3* headland on W coast of Ross and Cromarty dist, on S side of entrance to Ob Chuaig. NG 7059
Rubha Chulinish S'clyde 68 C4 headland on N coast of Ulva. NM 3942
Rubha Coigeach H'land 85 A5 headland on NW coast of Ross and Cromarty dist, at NW point of Coigach and W point of Enard Bay. NB 9818
Rubha Cruitiridh S'clyde 62 D2 headland on S coast of Knapdale, Argyll, on W side of Loch Stornoway. NR 7160
Rubha Cuilcheanna H'land 74 B5 headland on E side of Loch Linnhe in Lochaber dist, opp Sallachan Pt. NN 0161
Rubha Dubh S'clyde 63 F1* headland on NW coast of Bute opp Tighnabruaich, Argyll, across Kyles of Bute. NR 9872
Rubha Dubh S'clyde 69 C8 headland on E coast of Colonsay nearly 2m/3km S of Scalasaig. Another headland with lighthouse at Scalasaig itself has same name. NR 3991
Rubha Dubh S'clyde 69 D6 headland on S coast of Mull, on W side of entrance to Loch Buie. NM 5621
Rubha Dubh Tiree, S'clyde 69 B7 headland at E end of island. NM 0948
Rubha Dubh Ard Skye, H'land 79 D7* headland on S shore of Loch Eishort, 4m/6km NE of Tarskavaig. NG 6214
Rubha Dùin Bhàin S'clyde 62 D6 headland on W coast of Kintyre 5m/8km N of Mull of Kintyre. NR 5914
Rubha Fiart S'clyde 70 A2* headland at SW end of island of Lismore, in Loch Linnhe. NM 7835
Rubha Fiola S'clyde 69 E6* small island N of Lunga and 1km E of Eilean Dubh Mór. NM 7110
Rubha Fion-àird S'clyde 70 B2* headland in Argyll, at W extremity of Benderloch, qv. NM 8637
Rubha Garbh-àird S'clyde 70 B2 headland at W end of Ardmucknish Bay, Benderloch, Argyll. NM 8736
Rubh' a' Geadha S'clyde 69 C7 headland on NE coast of Colonsay. NR 4399
Rubha Hallagro W Isles 88 E2* headland on E coast of S Uist 2m/3km S of entrance to Loch Skiport. Lighthouse 1km S. NF 8735
Rubha Hearna Sgurr Skye, H'land 79 B6 headland on SW coast, 1m NW of entrance to Loch Brittle. NG 3619
Rubha Hunish H'land 78 B2 headland at northern end of Skye 9m/14km N of Uig. NG 4077
Rubha Lamanais S'clyde 62 A2 headland on W coast of Islay 2m/3km NW of Loch Gorm. NR 2068
Rubha Maol Skye, H'land 78 A4 headland on NW coast, on W side of entrance to Loch Bay. NG 2456
Rubh' a' Mhàil S'clyde 62 B1 headland with lighthouse at N extremity of Islay. NR 4279
Rubh' a' Mharaiche S'clyde 62 D6* headland on W coast of Kintyre 4m/6km N of Mull of Kintyre. NR 5812
Rubha Mór Coll, S'clyde 68 A3 headland on N coast, 1m W of NE end of island. NM 2464
Rubha Mór H'land 74 B5 headland on E side of Loch Linnhe in Lochaber dist, at NW end of Cuil Bay. NM 9655
Rubha Mór S'clyde 62 B3 headland on W coast of Islay at S end of Laggan Bay. NR 2948
Rubha Mór S'clyde 68 D4* headland with pier on Sound of Mull 1km NE of Salen, Mull. NM 5743
Rubha na Caillich S'clyde 62 C2 headland on E coast of Jura 1km S of Craighouse. NR 5366
Rubha na Caillich Skye, H'land 79 F6 headland at easternmost point of island at N end of Kyle Rhea. NG 8024
Rubha na Carraig-géire S'clyde 69 B6 headland at S end of Iona. NM 2621
Rubha na Cille S'clyde 69 E8* headland in Argyll to W of Loch na Cille, at S end of peninsula on W side of Loch Sween. NR 6879
Rubha na Cloiche Skye, H'land 79 D5* headland at S point of Raasay. NG 5633
Rubha na Faing S'clyde 62 A3 headland at SW point of Rinns of Islay. NR 1553
Rubha na Faoilinn S'clyde 69 D6* headland on S coast of Mull, on E side of entrance to Loch Buie. NM 5921
Rubha na Faoilinn S'clyde 70 A2 headland on SE coast of Mull, on NE side of entrance to Loch Spelve. NM 7227
Rubha na Fearn H'land 78 E3 headland on W coast of Ross and Cromarty dist, on S side of entrance to Loch Torridon. NG 7261
Rubha na Feundain S'clyde 70 A2* headland at SW end of Kerrera. NM 7826
Rubha na h-Airde Mòire S'clyde 62 A2* headland on W coast of Rinns of Islay at S end of Machir Bay. NR 1960
Rubha na h-Airde Uinnsinn H'land 74 A6 headland on W side of Loch Linnhe in Lochaber dist, 1m W of entrance to Loch a' Choire. NM 8752
Rubha na h-Aiseig H'land 78 C2 headland at northern point of Skye 9m/14km N of Uig. NG 4476
Rubha na h-Earba H'land 74 A5/B5* headland on W shore of Loch Linnhe in Lochaber dist, 3m/5km SW of Inversanda Bay. NM 9155
Rubha na h-Easgainne Skye, H'land 79 D7 headland on S coast at S end of Strathaird peninsula. Also known as Strathaird Pt. NG 5211
Rubha na h-Ordaig W Isles 88 E3 headland at SE end of S Uist 3m/5km SE of entrance to Loch Boisdale. NF 8414
Rubha na h-Uamha S'clyde 69 C5* headland (NTS) on Mull at W end of Ardmeanach. NM 4024
Rubh' an Aird Dhuirche Skye, H'land 79 D6 headland at intersection of Loch Ainort and Loch na Cairidh. NG 5729
Rubha na Lice S'clyde 70 A2 headland on NW coast of Kerrera. NM 8029
Rubha na Lice Uaine H'land. See Greenstone Pt.
Rubha nam Braithrean S'clyde 69 C6 headland on S coast of Ross of Mull 4m/7km SW of Bunessan. NM 4317
Rubha nam Brathairean Skye, H'land 78 C3/D3 headland on NE coast 8m/13km E of Uig. NG 5262
Rubha nan Cearc S'clyde 69 B5 headland at NW end of Ross of Mull. NM 3125
Rubha nan Clach Skye, H'land 79 B5 headland on W coast, on SE side of entrance to Loch Bracadale. NG 3033
Rubha nan Cùl Gheodhachan H'land 84 B2* headland on W coast of Sutherland dist 5m/8km NW of Kinlochbervie. NC 1964
Rubha nan Gall S'clyde 68 C4* headland on N coast of Ulva, 2km E of Rubha Chulinish. NM 4141
Rubha nan Gall S'clyde 68 D3 headland with lighthouse on N coast of Mull, 1m N of Tobermory. NM 5057
Rubha nan Goirteanan S'clyde 69 C5 headland on W coast of Ardmeanach dist of Mull, 4m/6km SW of Balnahard. NM 4030
Rubha nan Leacan S'clyde 62 B4 headland at S end of The Oa, Islay. Most southerly point of the island. NR 3140
Rubha nan Oirean Mull, S'clyde 68 B4 headland on W coast of island, 2m/3km W of Calgary. NM 3551
Rubha nan Sailthean S'clyde 70 A2* headland on SE coast of Mull, on SW side of entrance to Loch Spelve. NM 7227
Rubha nan Uan Coll, S'clyde 68 A3* headland on NW coast 4m/7km W of Arinagour. NM 1657
Rubh' an Dùnain Skye, H'land 79 C6 headland on SW coast, on S side of entrance to Loch Brittle. Ancient galleried chamber 1km E, on Soay Sound. NG 3816
Rubha'n Eun S'clyde 63 G3* headland with lighthouse on S coast of Bute, on E side of Glencallum Bay and 2km NE of Garroch Hd. NS 1152
Rubh' an Fheurain S'clyde 70 A2* headland on Sound of Kerrera 3m/5km SW of Oban in Argyll. NM 8226
Rubh' an Fhir Leithe H'land 84 B2 headland on W coast of Sutherland dist 5m/8km NW of Kinlochbervie. NC 1863
Rubh' an Iasgaich Skye, H'land 79 D7 headland on SW coast of Sleat peninsula 2m/3km N of Pt of Sleat. NG 5502
Rubh' an Leanachais S'clyde 62 C1* headland on E coast of Jura 1m S of Lowlandman's Bay. NR 5571
Rubh' an t-Sàilein S'clyde 69 D8 headland on W coast of Jura on N side of entrance to Loch Tarbert. NR 5082
Rubh' an t-Socaich Ghlais H'land 84 C2* headland on NW coast of Sutherland dist 4m/7km S of Cape Wrath. NC 2368
Rubha Quidnish W Isles 88 A4 headland on SE coast of Harris 2m/3km S of Manish. NG 1086
Rubha Raonuill H'land 79 E8 headland on N side of entrance to Loch Nevis, on coast of Knoydart, Lochaber dist. NM 7399
Rubh' Ardalanish Mull, S'clyde. See Ardalanish.
Rubh' Ard Eirnish S'clyde 70 A1 headland on N coast of Lismore on E side of Bernera. NM 8039
Rubh' Ard Slisneach H'land 79 E7 headland at NW point of Knoydart, Lochaber dist, on S side of entrance to Loch Hourn. NG 7409
Rubha Réidh H'land 78 E1 headland with lighthouse on W coast of Ross and Cromarty dist 10m/16km NW of Poolewe. NG 7391
Rubh' Arisaig H'land 68 D1 headland on coast of Lochaber dist 3m/5km W of vil of Arisaig. NM 6184
Rubha Ruadh H'land 84 B3 headland on W coast of Sutherland dist, on W side of entrance to Loch Laxford. Also known as Red Pt. NC 1651
Rubha Seanach S'clyde 70 A3 headland at S end of Kerrera. NM 8025
Rubha Suisnish Skye, H'land 79 D6 headland on S coast between Loch Eishort and Loch Slapin. NG 5815
Rubislaw Quarry Grampian. See Hill of Rubislaw.
Ru Bornaskitaig H'land 78 B3 headland on N coast of Skye 6m/9km N of Uig. NG 3771
Ruchazie S'clyde 64 D2* loc in Glasgow 4m/6km E of city centre. NS 6466
Ruchill S'clyde 64 C2* loc in Glasgow 2m/3km N of city centre. NS 5768
Ruchill Water 72 B3 r in Tayside region running NE down Glen Artney to R Earn at Comrie. NN 7721
Ruckcroft Cumbria 53 E1* loc 3m/4km NW of Kirkoswald. NY 5344
Ruckhall Common H & W 26 A4* loc 4m/6km W of Hereford. SO 4439
Ruckinge Kent 13 F4 vil 2m/3km E of Ham Street. TR 0233
Ruckland Lincs 45 G3 loc 6m/9km S of Louth. TF 3378
Rucklers Green Herts 19 E2* vil 2m/3km S of Hemel Hempstead. TL 0604
Ruckley Salop 34 C4 ham 6m/9km W of Much Wenlock. SJ 5300
Rudbaxton, Great Dyfed 22 C4 loc 3m/5km N of Haverfordwest. SM 9620
Rudby N Yorks 54 D4 vil opp Hutton Rudby across R Leven, 4m/6km W of Stokesley. NZ 4706
Ruddington Notts 36 B1/B2 vil 3m/5km S of W Bridgford. SK 5733
Ruddons Point Fife 73 G4 headland on E side of Largo Bay. NO 4500
Rudford Glos 26 C5* loc 4m/7km NW of Gloucester. SO 7721
Rudge Salop 35 E4* loc 6m/10km W of Wolverhampton. SO 8197
Rudge Som 16 D6 vil 3m/5km W of Westbury. ST 8251
Rudge Heath Salop 35 E4/E5 loc 5m/8km E of Bridgnorth. SO 7995
Rudgeway Avon 16 B3 vil 2m/4km S of Thornbury. ST 6286
Rudgwick W Sussex 11 G2 vil 4m/6km SE of Cranleigh. TQ 0934
Rudham, East Norfolk 38 C2 vil 6m/10km W of Fakenham. **W Rudham** vil 1km SW. TF 8228
Rudheath Ches 42 C4* loc 2m/4km NW of Holmes Chapel. SJ 7470
Rudley Green Essex 21 E2 ham 3m/5km SW of Maldon. TL 8303
Rudloe Wilts 16 D4* loc 5m/8km W of Chippenham. ST 8470
Rudry (Rhydri) Mid Glam 15 G3 ham 3m/4km E of Caerphilly. ST 1986
Rudston Humberside 51 E2 vil 5m/8km W of Bridlington. Site of Roman villa 1km SW. TA 0967

Rudyard Staffs 43 E5 vil 2m/4km NW of Leek. To N is **Rudyard Resr,** 2m/3km long. SJ 9557

Ruel S'clyde 70 C6 r in Argyll running S down Glendarvel to head of Loch Riddon. NS 0078

Rue Point Isle of Man 46 B3 promontory on N coast 2m/4km N of Andreas. NX 4003

Rueval W Isles 88 E2* hill on island of Benbecula 3m/5km SE of Benbecula Airfield. Height 408 ft or 124 metres - highest point of island. NF 8253

Rufford Lancs 47 E6 vil 6m/9km NE of Ormskirk. **Rufford Old Hall** (NT), late medieval hse with later additions. SD 4615

Rufford Notts 44 B4 loc 2m/3km S of Ollerton. **Rufford Abbey,** hse in park on site of medieval abbey. SK 6464

Rufforth N Yorks 50 A3 vil 5m/7km W of York. Airfield to SE. SE 5251

Ruffside Durham 61 E6 loc 2m/3km E of Blanchland. NY 9951

Rugby Warwicks 36 B6 tn 11m/17km E of Coventry, on R Avon. Industries include cement mnfre, electrical engineering. Boys' public school, founded 1567. Radio transmitting stn to E. SP 5075

Rugeley Staffs 35 F3 tn on R Trent 8m/13km SE of Stafford, in coal-mining area. SK 0418

Ruins Gtr Manchester 47 G6* loc 3m/4km NE of Bolton. SD 7411

Ruishton Som 8 B2 vil on R Tone 3m/4km E of Taunton. ST 2625

Ruislip London 19 E3 dist in borough of Hillingdon 3m/5km NE of Uxbridge. Locs of **Ruislip Common** to N, **Ruislip Manor** to E, **Ruislip Gardens** and **S Ruislip** to S, **W Ruislip** to SW. TQ 0987

Rule Water 66 D6 r in Borders region running N by Bonchester Br and Bedrule to confluence with R Teviot 4m/6km W of Jedburgh. NT 5920

Rum H'land 79 B7-C8 mountainous island of 42 sq miles or 109 sq km, roughly diamond-shaped, lying 7m/11km S of Rubh' an Dùnain on SW coast of Skye. Island is owned by the Nature Conservancy and provides opportunities for geological and biological research. (The spelling Rhum, although etymologically erroneous, is perhaps more usual.) See also Askival, Kinloch, Loch Scresort, Sound of Rum. NM 3798

Rumble Shetland 89 F7* rock island off island of Whalsay, 3m/5km E of Clett Hd. HU 6060

Rumble, The Shetland 89 E6* rock marked by beacon off S coast of Yell about 1km SW of island of Orfasay. HU 4876

Rumbling Bridge 72 D4 vil on R Devon, on border of Central and Tayside regions 4m/6km E of Dollar. NT 0199

Rumburgh Suffolk 31 G1 vil 4m/6km NW of Halesworth. Ham of **Rumburgh Street** 1m E. Loc of **Rumburgh Common** 1km S. TM 3481

Rumby Hill Durham 54 B2* loc 1m SE of Crook. NZ 1634

Rumer Hill Staffs 35 F3* loc 1km SE of Cannock. SJ 9809

Rumford Cornwall 2 D2* vil 4m/6km SW of Padstow. SW 8970

Rumleigh Devon 4 B4* ham by R Tamar 5m/7km SW of Tavistock. SX 4468

Rumney (Tredelerch) S Glam 15 G3 dist of Cardiff 3m/5km NE of city centre. ST 2179

Rumps Point Cornwall 3 E1* headland (NT) on N coast 4m/7km W of Port Isaac. Ruins of cliff cas. SW 9381

Rumwell Som 8 A2* ham 2m/3km SW of Taunton. ST 1923

Rumworth Lodge Reservoir Gtr Manchester 42 C1* resr in Bolton 3m/4km W of tn centre. SD 6707

Runcorn Ches 42 B3 New Tn, designated 1964, on S Bank of R Mersey 2m/3km S of Widnes to which it is connected by rly and rd brs. Chemical works, engineering, etc. **Hr Runcorn** dist of tn S of centre. SJ 5182

Runcton W Sussex 11 E4* vil 2m/3km SE of Chichester. SU 8802

Runcton Bottom Norfolk 38 B4* loc 4m/6km NE of Downham Mkt. TF 6408

Runcton Holme Norfolk 38 B4 vil 4m/6km N of Downham Mkt. TF 6109

Runcton, North Norfolk 38 B3 vil 3m/5km SE of King's Lynn. TF 6415

Runcton, South Norfolk 38 B4 ham 4m/6km N of Downham Mkt. TF 6308

Rundale Tarn, Great Cumbria 53 F2* small lake on Dufton Fell 3m/5km NE of Dufton. **Lit Rundale Tarn** 1km S. NY 7328

Runfold Surrey 11 E1 ham 2m/3km E of Farnham. SU 8747

Runhall Norfolk 39 E4* vil 5m/8km NW of Wymondham. TG 0507

Runham Norfolk 39 H4 vil 4m/6km W of Caister-on-Sea. TG 4611

Runham Norfolk 39 H4* loc in Gt Yarmouth 1km N of tn centre. TG 5208

Runie H'land 85 B6 r in Ross and Cromarty dist flowing SW to join R Kanaird 5m/7km N of Ullapool. NC 1301

Runner End Humberside 50 C4* W end of Holme upon Spalding Moor. SE 8038

Runnington Som 7 H3 ham on R Tone 2m/3km NW of Wellington. ST 1121

Running Waters Durham 54 C1* loc 4m/6km E of Durham. NZ 3340

Runnymede Surrey 19 E4 historic meadows (NT) 1m NW of Egham. Negotiations here between King John and the barons ended in the sealing of Magna Carta in 1215. Memorial to Commonwealth airmen on Cooper's Hill. John F. Kennedy Memorial opp Magna Carta I. TQ 0072

Runsell Green Essex 20 D2 loc 4m/6km W of Maldon. TL 7905

Runshaw Moor Lancs 47 F6* loc 1m W of Euxton. SD 5319

Runswick N Yorks 55 F3 holiday and fishing vil on W side of **Runswick Bay,** 6m/10km NW of Whitby. NZ 8016

Runton, East Norfolk 39 F1* resort 2km W of Cromer. TG 1942

Runton, West Norfolk 39 F1 resort 2m/3km E of Sheringham. TG 1842

Runwell Essex 20 D2 vil adjoining Wickford to NE. TQ 7594

Ruscombe Berks 18 C4 vil adjoining Twyford to E. SU 7976

Ruscombe Glos 16 D1* loc 2m/3km NW of Stroud. SO 8307

Rushall H & W 26 B4 ham 5m/8km W of Ledbury. SO 6434

Rushall Norfolk 31 F1 vil 3m/5km W of Harleston. TM 1982

Rushall Wilts 17 F5 vil 1m NW of Upavon. SU 1255

Rushall W Midlands 35 F4 loc 2m/3km NE of Walsall. SK 0201

Rushbrooke Suffolk 30 D2 vil 3m/5km SE of Bury St Edmunds. TL 8961

Rushbury Salop 34 C5 vil 4m/7km E of Church Stretton. SO 5191

Rushcliffe 119 admin dist of Notts.

Rushden Herts 29 G4 vil 4m/7km SE of Baldock. TL 3031

Rushden Northants 28 D1 footwear-mnfg tn 4m/7km E of Wellingborough. SP 9566

Rushenden Kent 21 E4 loc adjoining Queenborough to S. TQ 9071

Rushford Devon 4 B3* loc 3m/4km NW of Tavistock. SX 4476

Rushford Norfolk 38 D6 ham on Suffolk border 4m/6km E of Thetford. TL 9281

Rush Green Bucks 19 E3* loc 2m/3km NW of Uxbridge. TQ 0285

Rushgreen Ches 42 C3* loc 1m E of Lymm. SJ 6987

Rush Green Herts 29 F5* loc 2m/3km W of Stevenage. TL 2123

Rush Green London 20 B3 loc in borough of Havering 1m S of Romford. TQ 5187

Rush Hill Avon 16 C5* SW dist of Bath. ST 7362

Rushlake Green E Sussex 12 C5 vil 4m/6km SE of Heathfield. TQ 6218

Rushley Island Essex 21 E3 island bounded by creeks 3m/5km NE of Shoeburyness. TQ 9688

Rushmere Suffolk 39 H6* ham 2m/3km W of Kessingland. TM 4987

Rushmere St Andrew Suffolk 31 F3 loc 2m/4km E of Ipswich. TM 1946

Rushmere Street Suffolk 31 F3* loc adjoining Rushmere St Andrew to E, 3m/5km E of Ipswich. TM 2046

Rushmoor Surrey 11 E1 vil 3m/5km N of Hindhead. SU 8740

Rushmoor 119 admin dist of Hants.

Rushock H & W 26 D1* vil 5m/8km N of Droitwich. SO 8871

Rusholme Gtr Manchester 42 D2 dist of Manchester 2m/3km SE of city centre. SJ 8595

Rushton Northants 36 D6 vil 3m/5km NW of Kettering. Rushton Hall is 16c–17c hse with curious 'triangular lodge' (A.M.). SP 8482

Rushton Salop 34 C3 loc 4m/6km SW of Wellington. SJ 6008

Rushton Spencer Staffs 43 E5 vil 5m/8km NW of Leek. SJ 9362

Rushwick H & W 26 C2 vil 2m/3km W of Worcester. SO 8253

Rushyford Durham 54 C2 ham 3m/4km N of Newton Aycliffe. NZ 2828

Rushy Green E Sussex 12 B5* loc on SE side of Ringmer 3m/4km NE of Lewes. TQ 4512

Rusk Holm Orkney 89 B5* islet lying midway between Fers Ness, Eday and Pt of Huro, Westray. HY 5136

Ruskie Central 71 G4 loc 3m/4km W of Thornhill. NN 6200

Ruskington Lincs 45 E6 vil 4m/6km N of Sleaford. TF 0850

Rusko Castle D & G 58 B5 remains of Gordon stronghold 3m/5km N of Gatehouse of Fleet. NX 5860

Rusland Cumbria 52 D5/D6 ham 3m/4km NW of Newby Br. SD 3488

Rusper W Sussex 11 G2 vil 4m/7km W of Crawley. TQ 2037

Ruspidge Glos 26 B6 vil adjoining Cinderford to S. SO 6511

Russa Ness Shetland 89 E7* steep headland on Mainland on W side of entrance to Weisdale Voe. HU 3646

Russell Green Essex 20 D1* loc 4m/7km NE of Chelmsford. TL 7413

Russell's Green E Sussex 12 C5* loc 1m S of Ninfield. TQ 7011

Russell's Water Oxon 18 C3* vil 2m/3km N of Nettlebed. SU 7089

Russel's Green Suffolk 31 F1* loc 2m/3km SE of Stradbroke. TM 2572

Russland Orkney 89 A6* locality on E side of Loch of Harray, Mainland, 2m/3km S of Dounby. HY 3017

Ru Stafnish S'clyde 63 E6 headland on E coast of Kintyre 6m/9km SE of Campbeltown. NR 7713

Rusthall Kent 12 C3 suburban loc 2m/3km W of Tunbridge Wells. TQ 5539

Rustington W Sussex 11 F4 coastal tn 2km E of Littlehampton. TQ 0502

Ruston N Yorks 55 G6 vil 6m/10km SW of Scarborough. TA 9583

Ruston, East Norfolk 39 G2 vil 4m/7km SE of N Walsham. TG 3427

Ruston Parva Humberside 51 E2 vil 4m/6km NE of Gt Driffield. TA 0661

Rust's Green Norfolk 39 E4* loc just SW of Barnham Broom. TG 0706

Ruswarp N Yorks 55 G4 vil 2km SW of Whitby. NZ 8809

Rutherglen S'clyde 64 D3 tn on S bank of R Clyde adjoining Glasgow to SE. Industries include chemicals, paper, steel, tube and wire rope mnfre. NS 6161

Ruthernbridge Cornwall 3 E2 ham 4m/6km W of Bodmin. SX 0166

Ruthers of Howe H'land 86 F2* loc in Caithness dist 8m/13km NW of Wick. ND 3063

Ruthin (Rhuthun) Clwyd 41 G5 tn on hill above R Clwyd 14m/23km W of Wrexham. Remains of 13c cas in grnds of hotel. SJ 1258

Ruthin (Rhuthun) S Glam 15 E3* loc 4m/6km NW of Cowbridge. SS 9779

Ruthrieston Grampian 77 H1* dist of Aberdeen 2km SW of city centre. NJ 9204

Ruthven Grampian 82 D2 vil 5m/7km N of Huntly. NJ 5046

Ruthven H'land 75 G2 loc 1km S of Kingussie across R Spey. **Ruthven Barracks** (A.M.), remains of 18c military installations built to keep the Highlanders in check. NN 7699

Ruthven Tayside 76 D6 vil on R Isla 3m/5km E of Alyth. NO 2848

Ruthven Water 72 D3 r in Tayside region running NE to R Earn 4m/6km NE of Auchterarder. NN 9717

Ruthvoes Cornwall 3 E2* vil 2m/3km S of St Columb Major. SW 9260

Ruthwaite Cumbria 52 C2* loc 2km S of Ireby. NY 2336

Ruthwell D & G 59 F4 vil near shore of Solway Firth, 6m/10km W of Annan. Cross (A.M.), probably dating from early 8c, preserved in ch. NY 1067

Rutland 119 admin dist of Leics.

Rutter Force Cumbria 53 F3* waterfall in Hoff Beck 2m/3km N of Gt Asby. NY 6815

Rutupiae Kent. See Richborough Castle.

Ruxley London 20 B4* loc in borough of Bexley 2km SE of Sidcup. TQ 4870

Ruxton Green H & W 26 B5* loc 5m/7km NE of Monmouth. SO 5419

Ruyton-Eleven-Towns Salop 34 B2 vil 9m/14km NW of Shrewsbury. Remains of 14c cas keep. SJ 3922

Ryal Nthmb 61 E4 ham 6m/10km N of Corbridge. NZ 0174

Ryall Dorset 8 C4 vil on N side of Hardown Hill (see Morcombelake) and 4m/6km W of Bridport. SY 4094

Ryall H & W 26 D3* ham 1km E of Upton upon Severn across r. SO 8640

Ryarsh Kent 20 C5 vil 2m/3km N of W Malling. TQ 6759

Ryburgh, Great Norfolk 38 D2 vil 3m/5km SE of Fakenham. **Lit Ryburgh** ham 1km NE. TF 9527

Ryburn 48 C5* r rising on Rishworth Moor, W Yorks, and flowing NE through Ripponden and into R Calder at Sowerby Br. SE 0523

Ryburn Reservoir W Yorks 48 C6* resr in valley of R Ryburn near its source and 2km SW of Ripponden. SE 0218

Rycote Oxon 18 B1* loc 3m/4km W of Thame. Restored 15c chapel (A.M.). **Rycote Lake,** small lake in park to E. SP 6604

Rydal Cumbria 52 D4 ham at E end of **Rydal Water,** lake 2km NW of Ambleside. Rydal was home of Wordsworth from 1817 to 1850. NY 3606

Ryde Isle of Wight 10 C5 resort on NE coast 5m/8km SW of Portsmouth by sea. Boat and hovercraft ferries across Solent. SZ 5992

Ryde Roads 10 C5* that part of the Solent immediately N of Ryde in the Isle of Wight. SZ 5893

Ryde, The Herts 19 F1* N dist of Hatfield. TL 2309

Rye E Sussex 13 E5 tn on R Rother 9m/15km NE of Hastings. Former port, now 2m/3km from sea (**Rye Bay**). Many picturesque old bldgs. 14c Landgate. Lamb Hse (NT), 18c, once home of Henry James. 15c Mermaid Inn. **Rye Harbour** loc 2km SE near mouth of r. TQ 9220

Rye 50 D1 r rising on Cleveland Hills, N Yorks, 3m/4km E of Osmotherley, and flowing SE past Rievaulx, Helmsley, and Nunnington, into R Derwent 4m/6km NE of Malton. SE 8275

Ryebank Salop 34 C2* loc 2m/3km N of Wem. SJ 5131

Ryecroft W Yorks 48 D4* loc 2m/3km SW of Bingley. SE 0738

Ryedale 117 admin dist of N Yorks.

Ryeford Glos 16 C1* loc 2m/3km W of Stroud. SO 8104

Ryeford H & W 26 B5* loc 3m/4km E of Ross-on-Wye. SO 6422

Rye Foreign E Sussex 13 E4 vil 2m/3km NW of Rye. TQ 8922

Rye House Herts 20 A1* loc on R Lea to E of Hoddesdon. Scene of attempt to assassinate Charles II in 1683. TL 3809

Ryeish Green Berks 18 C4* loc 4m/6km S of Reading. SU 7267

Rye Street H & W 26 C4 ham 5m/8km E of Ledbury. SO 7835

Rye Water 64 A4* r in S'clyde region issuing from Camphill Resr W of Kilbirnie and flowing S to R Garnock on E side of Dalry. NS 3049

Ryhall Leics 37 E3 vil on loop of R Gwash 2m/4km N of Stamford. TF 0310

Ryhill Grampian 83 E4* loc 1km SW of Oyne. NJ 6625

Ryhill Humberside 51 F5 ham 3m/5km SE of Hedon. TA 2225

Ryhill W Yorks 49 F6 loc in coal-mining area 3m/4km NE of Royston. SE 3814

Ryhope Tyne & Wear 61 H6 dist of Sunderland 3m/5km S of tn centre. **Ryhope Colliery** loc to N. NZ 4052

Rylah Derbys 44 A4* loc 2m/3km S of Bolsover. SK 4667

Ryland Lincs 45 E3 ham adjoining Welton to E. TF 0280

Rylands Notts 36 B1 dist of Beeston 1m SE of tn centre. SK 5335

Ryle, Great Nthmb 61 E1 ham 3m/5km W of Whittingham. **Lit Ryle** loc 1m S. NU 0212

Rylstone N Yorks 48 C2 vil 5m/8km N of Skipton. SD 9758

Ryme Intrinseca Dorset 8 D3 vil 4m/6km SE of Yeovil. ST 5810

Rysa Little Orkney 89 A7* small uninhabited island off E coast of Hoy 1km NW of island of Fara. ND 3197

Ryther N Yorks 49 G4 vil on S bank of R Wharfe 2m/3km NW of Cawood. SE 5539

Ryton Glos 26 C4* loc 4m/6km N of Newent. SO 7332

Ryton N Yorks 50 C1* loc 3m/4km N of Malton. SE 7975

Ryton Salop 34 D4 vil 3m/5km S of Shifnal. SJ 7602

Ryton Tyne & Wear 61 F5 tn on S side of R Tyne 6m/10km W of Newcastle. Coal-mining; sand and gravel works. Power stn to E. **Ryton Woodside** loc 1m SW. NZ 1564

Ryton Warwicks 36 A5 loc 2m/4km E of Bedworth. SP 3986

Ryton 44 B2 r rising W of Worksop, Notts, and flowing E through Worksop to Ranby, then N past Blyth into R Idle 1km SE of Bawtry. SK 6592

Ryton, Great Salop 34 B4 ham 6m/9km S of Shrewsbury. **Lit Ryton** loc adjoining to S. SJ 4803

Ryton-on-Dunsmore Warwicks 36 A6 vil 4m/7km SE of Coventry. Car mnfg plant. SP 3874

S

Saasaig Skye, H'land 79 E7* loc on E side of Sleat peninsula to S of Teangue. NM 6608

Sabden Lancs 48 B4 vil 4m/6km SE of Clitheroe. **Sabden Fold** loc 2m/3km E. SD 7737

Sabine's Green Essex 20 C2* loc 4m/6km NW of Brentwood. TQ 5496

Sabiston, Loch of Orkney 89 A6* small loch 1m N of Dounby, on Mainland. Named after locality to S towards Dounby. HY 2922

Sacombe Herts 29 G5 vil 4m/6km NW of Ware. TL 3319

Sacombe Green Herts 29 G5* ham 4m/6km N of Ware. TL 3419

Sacquoy Head Orkney 89 B5 headland at NW end of island of Rousay. HY 3835

Sacriston Durham 54 B1 vil in coal-mining dist 3m/5km NW of Durham. NZ 2447

Sadberge Durham 54 C3 vil 4m/6km NE of Darlington. NZ 3416

Saddell S'clyde 63 E4 vil near E coast of Kintyre 8m/13km N of Campbeltown. **Saddell Water** is r running SE past vil to **Saddell Bay. Saddell Forest** is state forest astride r valley. NR 7832

Saddington Leics 36 C5 vil 6m/9km NW of Mkt Harborough. Resr 1km SE. SP 6591

Saddleback Cumbria 52 C2 mt in Lake Dist 4m/7km NE of Keswick. Height 2847 ft or 868 metres. Also known as Blencathra. NY 3227

Saddle Bow Norfolk 38 B3 ham 2km NE of Wiggenhall St Germans. TF 6015

Saddle, The H'land 80 A6 mt on border of Lochaber and Skye & Lochalsh dists 4m/6km S of Shiel Br. Height 3314 ft or 1010 metres. NG 9313

Saddleworth Gtr Manchester 43 E1 moorland loc on edge of Peak Dist National Park 6m/9km E of Oldham. SE 0006

Sadgill Cumbria 53 E4 loc 2m/3km NE of Kentmere. NY 4805

Saffron Walden Essex 30 A4 old tn 12m/19km N of Bishop's Stortford. Many pargeted hses. Remains of Norman cas. 1m W, Audley End, qv. TL 5338

Sageston Dyfed 22 C5 ham 5m/8km E of Pembroke. SN 0503

Saham Hills Norfolk 38 D4* ham adjoining Saham Toney to N. TF 9003

Saham Toney Norfolk 38 D4 vil 2km NW of Watton. TF 8902

Saighton Ches 42 A5 vil 4m/6km SE of Chester. 15c gatehouse of former **Saighton Grange.** SJ 4462

Sàil Mhór H'land 80 A2 one of the peaks of Beinn Eighe, Ross and Cromarty dist. Height 3217 ft or 981 metres. NG 9360

Sàil Mhór H'land 85 A7 mt in Ross and Cromarty dist 4m/6km W of Auchtascailt at head of Lit Loch Broom. Height 2508 ft or 764 metres. NH 0388

Sain Dunwyd Welsh form of St Donats, qv.

Sain Ffagan Welsh form of St Fagans, qv.

Sain Ffred Welsh form of St Brides, qv.

Sain Nicolas Welsh form of St Nicholas, qv.

Sain Pedrog Welsh form of St Petrox, qv.

Sain Silian Welsh form of St Julians, qv.

St Abbs Borders 67 F2 coastal vil with small harbour 3m/4km NW of Eyemouth. **St Abb's Hd,** 2km N, is rocky headland with lighthouse. NT 9167

St Aethans Grampian 82 A1 loc on N coast adjoining Burghead to E. Site of St Aethan's Well. NJ 1168

St Agnes Cornwall 2 C3 resort near N coast 6m/9km N of Redruth, with beach at Trevaunance Cove. To W, **St A. Beacon** (NT), hill of 628 ft or 191 metres commanding coastal and inland views; landmark. SW 7250

St Agnes Isles of Scilly 2 A1 the southernmost of the five inhabited islands. The island of **Gugh** is joined to it at low tide by a sand and rock bar. SV 8808

St Agnes Head Cornwall 2 C3 headland 6m/10km N of Redruth. SW 6951

St Albans Herts 19 F1 cathedral city 19m/31km NW of London, extending E from remains (A.M.) of Roman tn of *Verulamium.* Cathedral Norman and later. Various industries. TL 1407

St Alban's Head Dorset 9 F6/G6 headland at S end of Isle of Purbeck 5m/8km SW of Swanage. Also known as St Aldhelm's Hd. SY 9675

St Aldhelm's Head Dorset 9 F6/H6 headland at S end of Isle of Purbeck 5m/8km SW of Swanage. More commonly known as St Alban's Hd. SY 9675

St Allen Cornwall 2 D3 ham 4m/6km N of Truro. SW 8250

Saint Andras Welsh form of St Andrews Major, qv.

St Andrews Fife 73 G3 historic tn standing on rocky promontory on **St A. Bay,** 11m/17km SE of Dundee across Firth of Tay, and 9m/14km E of Cupar. University, founded in 1412. Royal and Ancient Golf Club is ruling authority on the game. Four golf-courses. Remains of cathedral, priory, cas (A.M.). NO 5016

St Andrews Major (Saint Andras) S Glam 15 F4* ham adjoining Dinas Powis to W, 3m/5km W of Penarth. ST 1371

St Andrew's Well Dorset 8 C5* NE dist of Bridport. SY 4793

St Anne's Lancs 46 D5* W dist of Lytham St Anne's. SD 3128

St Anne's Park Avon 16 B4* dist of Bristol on S bank of R Avon 3m/4km E of city centre. ST 6272

St Ann's D & G 59 F2 loc 6m/10km S of Beattock. NY 0793

St Ann's Chapel Cornwall 4 B4 loc 2km SW of Gunnislake. SX 4170

St Ann's Chapel Devon 4 C5* ham 3m/5km S of Modbury. SX 6647

St Ann's Head Dyfed 22 B5 headland on W side of entrance to Milford Haven, 2m/3km S of vil of Dale. SM 8002

St Anns Hill Beds 29 E5* E dist of Luton. TL 1021

St Ann's Hill Cumbria 59 H5* loc in Carlisle 1m NW of city centre across R Eden. NY 3957

St Anthony-in-Meneage Cornwall 2 D5 ham on N side of Gillan Harbour 8m/12km E of Helston. SW 7825

St Anthony-in-Roseland Cornwall 2 D5 ham on S bank of R Percuil opp St Mawes. To SW, **St Anthony Hd** (NT), at entrance to Carrick Rds. SW 8532

St Anthony's Tyne & Wear 61 G5* dist of Newcastle on N bank of R Tyne 3m/4km SE of city centre. NZ 2863

St Anthony's Hill E Sussex 12 C6 NE suburb of Eastbourne. TQ 6301

St Arvans Gwent 16 A2 vil 2m/3km NW of Chepstow. ST 5196

St Asaph (Llanelwy) Clwyd 41 F4 vil on ridge between Rs Clwyd and Elwy 5m/8km S of Rhyl. Small cathedral dating from 13c, with several later restorations. SJ 0374

St Athan (Sain Tathan) S Glam 15 E4 vil 3m/5km E of Llantwit Major. ST 0168

Sain Tathan Welsh form of St Athan, qv.

St Austell Cornwall 3 E3 tn 13m/20km NE of Truro. Centre of china clay industry. **St A. Bay,** near which tn is situated, extends from Gribbin Hd westwards to Black Hd. SX 0152

St Bees Cumbria 52 A4 vil 4m/6km S of Whitehaven. **St Bees Hd,** headland on Irish Sea close to W extremity of county 2m/3km NW. SX 9711

St Blazey Cornwall 3 F3 tn 4m/6km NE of St Austell in dist producing china clay. **St B. Gate** loc adjoins to SW. SX 0654

St Boswells Borders 66 D5 vil 4m/6km SE of Melrose. NT 5931

St Breock Cornwall 3 E2 vil just W of Wadebridge. SW 9771

St Breward Cornwall 3 F1 vil 4m/6km S of Camelford. SX 0977

St Briavels Glos 16 B1 vil 5m/7km W of Lydney. SO 5504

St Brides (Sain Ffred) Dyfed 22 A4/B4 loc on St Brides Bay 7m/11km NW of Milford Haven, at S end of small creek of **St Brides Haven.** SM 8010

St Brides Bay Dyfed 22 A4, B4 large westward-facing bay extending from Ramsey Sound in the N to Skomer in the S, and to Rickets Head in the E, and enclosed by the Pembrokeshire Coast National Park. SM 71,72,81,82

St Bride's Church S'clyde. See Douglas.

St Bride's Major (Saint-y-brid) Mid Glam 15 E4 vil 3m/4km S of Bridgend. SS 8974

St Bride's Netherwent Gwent 16 A3 loc 3m/4km W of Caerwent. ST 4289

St Bride's-super-Ely (Llansanffraid-ar-Elai) S Glam 15 F4 vil 5m/9km W of Cardiff. ST 0977

St Bride's Wentlloog (Llansanffraid Gwynllwg) Gwent 15 G3 vil near coast 4m/6km S of Newport. ST 2982

Saintbridge Glos 26 D5* loc in SE part of Gloucester. SO 8416

St Budeaux Devon 4 B5 NW dist of Plymouth, 3m/5km from city centre. SX 4458

Saintbury Glos 27 F4 vil 2m/3km NE of Broadway. SP 1139

St Buryan Cornwall 2 A5 vil 4m/7km E of Land's End. SW 4025

St Catherine Avon 16 C4 loc 4m/7km NE of Bath. ST 7770

St Catherines S'clyde 70 C4 locality on E shore of Loch Fyne in Argyll opp Inveraray (ferry for pedestrians). NN 1207

St Catherine's Bay Orkney 89 C6* wide bay on W coast of Stronsay. Island of Linga Holm is at entrance to bay. HY 6326

St Catherine's Island Dyfed 22 D5 small island off Castle Hill at Tenby. SN 1300

St Catherine's Point Isle of Wight 10 B6 headland with lighthouse at southernmost point of island. On **St Catherine's Hill,** to N, are remains of 14c lighthouse (A.M.). SZ 4975

St Clears (Sancler) Dyfed 23 E4 vil 9m/14km W of Carmarthen. Traces of motte and bailey cas. SN 2716

St Cleer Cornwall 3 G2 vil 2m/4km N of Liskeard. Doniert Stone (A.M.), 9c inscribed stone, 1m NW. (Also known as King Doniert's Stone.) SX 2468

St Clement Cornwall 2 D4 vil 2m/3km E of Truro. SW 8543

St Clement's Isle Cornwall 2 A5* rocky island off Mousehole, 2m/3km S of Penzance across bay. SW 4726

St Clement's Reach 20 C4* stretch of R Thames extending from Greenhithe, Kent to the N point of Swanscombe Marshes. Also known as Fiddler's Reach. TQ 5976

St Clether Cornwall 6 B6 vil 8m/12km W of Launceston. SX 2084

St Colmac S'clyde 63 G1* loc on Bute 2m/3km W of Port Bannatyne. NS 0467

St Columb Major Cornwall vil 6m/10km E of Newquay. SW 9163

St Columb Minor Cornwall 2 D2, E dist of Newquay. SW 8462

St Columb Road Cornwall 2 D3* vil developed beside rly 3m/4km S of St Columb Major. SW 9159

St Columb's Church W Isles. See Eilean Chaluim Chille.

St Combs Grampian 83 H1 vil on NE coast 4m/7km SE of Fraserburgh. NK 0563

St Cormac's Chapel S'clyde. See Eilean Mór, in Sound of Jura.

St Cross South Elmham Suffolk 39 G6 vil 4m/7km SW of Bungay. TM 2984

St Cyrus Grampian 77 G4 vil near coast 5m/8km NE of Montrose. NO 7464

St David's (Tyddewi) Dyfed 22 A3 vil near coast, 3m/4km SE of **St David's Hd** (Penmaen Dewi), headland at N end of Whitesand Bay. In the vil is St David's Cathedral, dating in part from 12c. SM 7525

St David's College Dyfed. See Lampeter.

St Day Cornwall 2 C4 vil 2m/3km E of Redruth. SW 7342

St Dennis Cornwall 3 E3 vil in china clay dist 5m/8km NW of St Austell. SW 9557

St Denys Hants 10 B3* dist of Southampton on W bank of R Itchen 2km NE of city centre. SU 4313

St Devereux H & W 26 A4 loc 7m/11km SW of Hereford. SO 4431

St Dials Gwent 15 G2* loc in tn of Cwmbran. ST 2894

St Dogmaels (Llandudoch) Dyfed 22 D2 vil on left bank of R Teifi estuary, 1m W of Cardigan across r. Scanty ruins of 12c abbey (A.M.). SN 1646

St Dogwells (Llantydewi) Dyfed 22 C3 loc 6m/9km S of Fishguard. SM 9627

St Dominick Cornwall 3 H2 vil 3m/5km SE of Callington. SX 3967

St Donats (Sain Dunwyd) S Glam 15 E4 vil 2m/3km W of Llantwit Major. Cas dates from 11c. To S, St Donat's Bay. SS 9368

St Edith's Marsh Wilts 17 E5* loc 3m/5km NW of Devizes. ST 9764

St Edmundsbury 119 admin dist of Suffolk.

St Endellion Cornwall 3 E1 ham 4m/6km N of Wadebridge. SW 9978

St Enoder Cornwall 2 D3* ham 4m/7km SW of St Columb Major. SW 8957

St Erme Cornwall 2 D3 vil 4m/6km NE of Truro. SW 8449

St Erney Cornwall 3 H2 vil 4m/6km W of Saltash. SX 3759

St Erth Cornwall 2 B5 vil just S of Hayle. SW 5535

St Erth Praze Cornwall 2 B5 ham 2m/3km SE of Hayle. SW 5735

St Ervan Cornwall 2 D2 vil 4m/6km SW of Padstow. SW 8970

St Eval Cornwall 2 D2 loc 6m/10km NE of Newquay. To W on coast, Pendarves Pt (NT), overlooking Bedruthan Steps, sandy beach with rocks and caves. SW 8769

St Ewe Cornwall 3 E4 vil 5m/7km SW of St Austell. SW 9746

St Fagans (Sain Ffagan) S Glam 15 F4 vil 4m/6km W of Cardiff. Welsh Folk Museum, incl the cas, an Elizn mansion with 13c curtain wall. ST 1277

St Fergus Grampian 83 H2 vil near NE coast 4m/7km N of Peterhead. Gas pipeline terminal and separation plant. NK 0952

St Fillans Tayside 71 G2/G3 vil at foot, or E end, of Loch Earn, 5m/8km W of Comrie. NN 6924

St Florence Dyfed 22 C5 vil 3m/5km W of Tenby. SN 0801

St Gabriels Tyne & Wear 61 H5* dist of Sunderland 2km W of tn centre. NZ 3756

St Gennys Cornwall 6 A5 vil 7m/11km SW of Bude across corner of Bude Bay. Some of coast is NT property. SX 1497

St George (Llan Sain Siôr) Clwyd 41 F4 ham 2m/4km SE of Abergele. Hill fort of Dinorben to W. SH 9775

St George Avon 16 B4* E dist of Bristol. ST 6373

St George's (Llan Sain Siôr) S Glam 15 F4 vil 5m/8km W of Cardiff. ST 1076

St George's Avon 15 H5* vil 4m/6km E of Weston-super-Mare. ST 3762

St George's Island Cornwall 3 G3 island off S coast 2km S of Looe. Sometimes known as Looe I. SX 2551

St Germans Cornwall 3 H3 vil 8m/13km SE of Liskeard. At SE end of vil is **St G. Quay,** loc at head of **St G. River,** alternative name for tidal part of R Lynher, qv. SX 3657

St Giles House Dorset. See Wimborne St Giles.

St Giles in the Wood Devon 6 D3 vil 3m/4km E of Torrington. SS 5319
St Giles on the Heath Devon 6 C6 ham 4m/7km NE of Launceston. SX 3590
St Giles's Hill Hants 10 C2* E dist of Winchester. SU 4929
St Govan's Head Dyfed 22 C6 headland 5m/9km S of Pembroke. SR 9792
St Gwynno Forest Mid Glam 15 F2* wooded area NW of Pontypridd. ST 09
St Harmon Powys 25 E1 vil 3m/5km N of Rhayader. SN 9872
St Helena Norfolk 39 F3 vil adjoining Horsford to NW, 6m/9km NW of Norwich. TG 1916
St Helena Warwicks 35 H4* loc 1km S of Polesworth. SK 2501
St Helens Cumbria 52 A2* loc 1m SW of Flimby. NY 0132
St Helens Isle of Wight 10 C5 vil on Brading Harbour 3m/5km SE of Ryde. To E, 1km off shore, **St H. Fort,** one of four 19c defensive forts in vicinity of Spithead (see Spithead Forts). SZ 6289
St Helens Merseyside 42 B2 industrial tn 11m/18km E of Liverpool. Glass mnfre, coal-mining, light engineering, textiles. Pilkington glass museum. SJ 5195
St Helen's S Yorks 43 H1* loc adjoining Hoyland Nether. SE 3800
St Helier London 19 F5* loc in borough of Sutton 2m/3km NE of Sutton tn centre. TQ 2666
St Hilary Cornwall 2 B5* ham 4m/6km S of Hayle. SW 5531
St Hilary S Glam 15 E4 vil 2m/3km SE of Cowbridge. ST 0173
St Ibbs Herts 29 F5* ham 2m/3km SE of Hitchin. TL 1926
St Illtyd Gwent 15 G2* ham with traces of Norman cas 2km S of Abertillery. SO 2101
St Ippollitts Herts 29 F5 vil 2m/3km SE of Hitchin. TL 1927
St Ishmael (Llanismel) Dyfed 23 E5 loc on R Towy estuary 3m/5km W of Kidwelly. SN 3608
St Ishmael's Dyfed 22 B5 vil 5m/7km W of Milford Haven across Sandyhaven Pill. SM 8307
St Issey Cornwall 3 E2 vil 4m/6km W of Wadebridge. SW 9271
St Ive Cornwall 3 G2 vil 4m/6km NE of Liskeard. SX 3067
St Ive Cross Cornwall 3 G2* vil 5m/7km NE of Liskeard. SX 3167
St Ives Cambs 29 G1 tn on R Ouse 5m/8km E of Huntingdon. TL 3171
St Ives Cornwall 2 B4 resort on N coast and on W side of **St Ives Bay,** 7m/12km NE of Penzance. To N, **St Ives Hd,** sometimes known as The Island, headland at W end of St Ives Bay. SW 5140
St Ives Dorset 9 H4 loc 2m/3km SW of Ringwood. SU 1204
St James Norfolk 39 G3* loc 1km E of Coltishall. TG 2720
St James Northants 28 C2* dist of Northampton to W of tn centre. **St James's End** loc adjoining to W. SP 7461
St James Northants 36 D5* industrial estate towards E side of Corby. SP 8988
St James's Chapel Suffolk. See Lindsey.
St James South Elmham Suffolk 31 G1 vil 5m/8km NW of Halesworth. TM 3281
St Jidgey Cornwall 3 E2* loc 4m/7km NE of St Columb Major. SW 9469
St John Cornwall 4 B5 vil 2m/3km SW of Torpoint. Stream flows into **St John's Lake,** inlet to E, on W side of R Tamar estuary. SX 4053
St Johns H & W 26 D2* SW dist of Worcester. SO 8354
St John's Isle of Man 46 B5 vil 3m/4km SE of Peel. See also Tynwald Hill. SC 2781
St John's Kent 20 B5 N dist of Sevenoaks. TQ 5356
St John's London 20 A4* loc in borough of Lewisham 1km NW of Lewisham tn centre and 5m/8km SE of Charing Cross. TQ 3776
St John's Chapel Durham 53 G1 vil on R Wear 7m/11km W of Stanhope. NY 8838
St John's Fen End Norfolk 38 A3 ham 5m/8km E of Wisbech. TF 5311
St John's Haven Nthmb 67 F3* inlet 2m/3km N of Berwick-upon-Tweed. NT 9856
St John's Head Orkney 89 A7* lofty headland on NW coast of Hoy, rising to 1140 ft or 347 metres, 3m/5km N of Rora Hd. HY 1803
St John's Highway Norfolk 38 A3 vil 6m/10km SW of King's Lynn. TF 5314
St John's Jerusalem Kent. See Sutton at Hone.
St John's Loch H'land 86 E1 loch on NE side of Dunnet vil, S of Dunnet Hd on N coast of Caithness dist.
St John's Point H'land 86 F1 headland on N coast of Caithness dist 6m/10km W of Duncansby Hd. ND 3175
St John's Town of Dalry D & G. See Dalry.
St John's Wood London 19 F3* loc in City of Westminster to W of Regents Park 3m/4km NW of Charing Cross. Includes Lord's Cricket Ground. TQ 2683
St Judes Isle of Man 46 B4 vil 4m/6km W of Ramsey. SC 3996
St Julians (Sain Silian) Gwent 15 H3* dist of Newport 2km NE of tn centre. ST 3289
St Julians Herts 19 F1* S dist of St Albans. TL 1405
St Juliot Cornwall 6 A6* loc 2m/3km E of Boscastle. SX 1291
St Just Cornwall 2 A5 small tn 4m/6km N of Land's End. Land's End Airport 2km S. SW 3731
St Just Cornwall 2 D4 vil on E side of Carrick Rds 2m/3km N of St Mawes. To E, vil of **St Just Lane.** SW 8435
St Katherines Grampian 83 F3 loc 5m/8km NW of Oldmeldrum. NJ 7834
St Keverne Cornwall 2 D6 vil near coast 9m/14km SE of Helston. SW 7921
St Kew Cornwall 3 E1 vil 4m/6km NE of Wadebridge. **St K. Highway** ham 1m SE. SX 0276
St Kew's Steps Avon. See Kewstoke.
St Keyne Cornwall 3 G2 vil 2m/4km S of Liskeard. SX 2461
St Kilda W Isles (W of 88 A3) steep rocky island, also known as Hirta, lying some 54m/86km W of Harris and 35m/56km W of N Uist. Area about 3 sq miles or 8 sq km. Uninhabited since 1930, except for Army personnel manning radar stns. Ruined vil on Village Bay at SE end. Cliffs below Conachair, qv, are highest sea cliffs in Gt Britain. Island is chief island of St Kilda group (all NTS, and collectively forming a nature reserve). See also Boreray, Dùn, Soay. NF 0999
St Lawrence Cornwall 3 E2* loc 2km W of Bodmin. SX 0466
St Lawrence Essex 21 E2 ham S of St L. Bay on S side of R Blackwater estuary. TL 9604
St Lawrence Isle of Wight 10 C6 loc near S coast 2m/3km W of Ventnor. SZ 5376
St Lawrence Kent 13 H1* W dist of Ramsgate. TR 3665
St Lawrence Bay Essex 21 E2* bay on S side of R Blackwater estuary 6m/9km N of Burnham-on-Crouch. TL 9505
St Lawrence Green Suffolk 39 G6* ham 4m/6km SE of Bungay. TM 3784
St Leonards Bucks 18 D1* vil 3m/5km E of Wendover. SP 9107
St Leonards Dorset 9 H4* loc 3m/5km SW of Ringwood. SU 1103
St Leonards E Sussex 13 D5 coastal tn adjoining Hastings to W. TQ 8009
St Leonards Lothian 66 A2* dist of Edinburgh 1m SE of city centre. NT 2672
St Leonards S'clyde 64 D3* dist of E Kilbride to SE of tn centre. NS 6453
St Leonard's Forest W Sussex 11 H2 wooded area E of Horsham. TQ 2131
St Leonard's Street Kent 20 C5 ham 1km SW of W Malling. **St Leonard's Tower,** remains of Norman keep (A.M.). TQ 6756
St Levan Cornwall 2 A6 ham 3m/5km SE of Land's End. SW 3822
St Luke's London 19 G3* loc in borough of Islington to E of Finsbury. TQ 3282
St Lythans (Llwyneliddon) S Glam 15 F4 ham 3m/5km N of Barry. Neolithic burial-chamber (A.M.) 1km SW. ST 1072
St Mabyn Cornwall 3 E1 vil 3m/5km E of Wadebridge. SX 0473
St Magnus Bay Shetland 89 D6 large bay on W coast of Mainland extending from Esha Ness (N) to Ness of Melby and Papa Stour (S), and penetrating eastwards, through Swarbacks Minn and Olna Firth, as far as Voe. HU 26
St Magnus's Church Orkney 89 B6* remains of ch (A.M.), probably of 12c, towards W side of island of Egilsay. Dedicated to Christian Norse ruler murdered on island in 1116. HY 4630
St Margarets Herts 20 A1* vil 2m/3km SE of Ware. TL 3811
St Margarets H & W 25 H4* vil 5m/8km NW of Pontrilas. SO 3533
St Margarets London 19 F4* loc to SW of Twickenham Br in borough of Richmond. TQ 1674
St Margarets Wilts 17 F4* SE dist of Marlborough. SU 1968
St Margaret's at Cliffe Kent 13 H3 small resort 4m/6km NE of Dover, on **St Margaret's Bay.** TR 3544
St Margaret's Hope Fife 65 G1* anchorage for Rosyth naval base on Firth of Forth. NT 1882
St Margaret's Hope Orkney 89 B7 vil and chief settlement on N coast of S Ronaldsay, at head of bay of same name. ND 4493
St Margaret's Island Dyfed 22 D5 small island off W end of Caldy I. SS 1297
St Margaret South Elmham Suffolk 39 G6 vil 4m/6km SW of Bungay. TM 3183
St Mark's Glos 26 D5* W dist of Cheltenham. SO 9222
St Mark's Isle of Man 46 B6 vil 5m/8km N of Castletown. SC 2974
St Martin Cornwall 3 G3 ham 1m N of Looe. SX 2655
St Martin's Isles of Scilly 2 A1 one of the five inhabited islands. SV 9315
St Martin's N Yorks 54 B4/B5* loc on S side of Richmond across R Swale. NZ 1700
St Martin's Salop 34 A1 vil 2m/3km SE of Chirk. Loc of **St M. Moor** 1km SW. SJ 3236
St Martins Tayside 73 E2 loc 5m/7km NE of Perth. NO 1530
St Martins Wilts 17 F4* NE dist of Marlborough. SU 1969
St Martin's Green Cornwall 2 C5 vil 5m/9km SE of Helston. SW 7323
St Mary Bourne Hants 17 H6 vil 3m/5km NW of Whitchurch. SU 4250
St Marychurch Devon 5 E4 N dist of Torbay, 1m N of Torquay tn centre. SX 9166
St Mary Church (Llan-fair) S Glam 15 E4 vil 2m/3km S of Cowbridge. ST 0071
St Mary Cray London 20 B5 dist in borough of Bromley 1m N of Orpington. TQ 4667
St Mary Hill (Eglwys Fair y Mynydd) S Glam 15 E4 loc 3m/5km NW of Cowbridge. SS 9678
St Mary in the Marsh Kent 13 F4 vil on Romney Marsh 2m/3km N of New Romney. TR 0627
St Marylebone London. See Marylebone. TQ 2881
St Mary's Isles of Scilly 2 A1 the largest of the islands. Terminus of air and sea services from mainland. SV 9111
St Mary's Orkney 89 B7 vil on S coast of Mainland 6m/10km S of Kirkwall. HY 4701
St Mary's Tyne & Wear 61 H4* island rock off North Sea coast, with lighthouse, 2m/3km N of Whitley Bay. Also known as Bait I. NZ 3575
St Mary's Bay Devon 5 E5* bay to E of Brixham stretching from Durl Hd (N) to Sharkham Pt (S). SX 9355
St Mary's Bay 13 F4 bay extending from Dungeness to Sandgate, Kent, and giving on to Strait of Dover. TR 0927
St Mary's Haven Nthmb 67 H5* bay (NT) on North Sea coast 1km SE of High Newton-by-the-Sea. Also known as Newton Haven. Newton Pt at N end. NU 2424
St Mary's Hoo Kent 20 D4 vil 6m/10km NE of Rochester. TQ 8076
St Mary's Isle D & G 58 C6 peninsula running out from head of Kirkcudbright Bay. NX 6749
St Mary's Loch Borders 66 A6 loch in Ettrick Forest 13m/21km W of Selkirk. Is 3m/5km long SW to NE; maximum depth over 150 ft or 45 metres. NT 2422
St Mary's Well Bay S Glam 15 G4* small bay on coast between Sully and Lavernock Pt, S of Penarth. ST 1767
St Maughan's (Llanfocha) Gwent 26 A5* loc 2m/3km S of Skenfrith. **St Maughan's Green** ham 1km E. SO 4617
St Mawes Cornwall 2 D5 tn on N bank of Percuil R at its confluence with R Fal (Carrick Rds). 16c cas (A.M.) on Castle Pt. SW 8433
St Mawgan Cornwall 2 D2 vil in par of Mawgan-in-Pydar 5m/7km NE of Newquay. SW 8765
St Mellion Cornwall 3 H2 vil 3m/5km SE of Callington. SX 3865
St Mellons (Llaneirwg) S Glam 15 G3 suburb 4m/6km NE of Cardiff. ST 2281
St Merryn Cornwall 2 D1 vil 2m/3km W of Padstow. SW 8874
St Mewan Cornwall 3 E3 vil just W of St Austell. SW 9951
St Michael Caerhays Cornwall 3 E4 ham 4m/6km SW of Mevagissey. SW 9642
St Michael Church Som 8 B2* ham 1km S of N Newton. ST 3030
St Michael Penkevil Cornwall 2 D4 vil 3m/5km SE of Truro across r. SW 8542
St Michaels H & W 26 B1 ham 2m/3km SW of Tenbury Wells. SO 5865
St Michaels Kent 13 E3 residential loc adjoining Tenterden to N. TQ 8835
St Michael's Island Isle of Man 46 B6* island connected by causeway to N end of Langness promontory at entrance to Derby Haven. SC 2967
St Michael's Mount Cornwall 2 B5 island in Mount's Bay opp Marazion. Former monastery now private residence (NT). Access on foot by causeway at low tide. SW 5129
St Michael's on Wyre Lancs 47 E4 vil 3m/5km SW of Garstang. SD 4641
St Michael South Elmham Suffolk 39 G6 ham 4m/6km S of Bungay. TM 3483
St Mildred's Bay Kent 13 H1* bay off Westgate on Sea. TR 3270
St Minver Cornwall 3 E1 vil 3m/5km NW of Wadebridge. SW 9677
St Monance (or St Monans) Fife 73 G4 small fishing and boat-building tn on Firth of Forth 3m/5km W of Anstruther. Many old hses. NO 5201
St Mungo D & G 59 F4 locality 3m/5km S of Lockerbie. NY 1476
St Neot Cornwall 3 F2 vil 5m/8km NW of Liskeard. SX 1867
St Neots Cambs 29 F2 tn on R Ouse 8m/13km SW of Huntingdon. TL 1860
St Nicholas (Sain Nicolas) Dyfed 22 B2 vil 4m/6km W of Fishguard. SM 9035
St Nicholas (Sain Nicolas) S Glam 15 F4 vil 6m/10km W of Cardiff. ST 0974
St Nicholas at Wade Kent 13 G1 vil on Isle of Thanet 6m/10km W of Margate. TR 2666
St Nicholas South Elmham Suffolk 39 G6 ham 4m/7km S of Bungay. TM 3282
St Ninians Central 72 B5 S dist of Stirling. NS 7991
St Ninian's Bay S'clyde 63 G2 southward-facing bay on W coast of Bute, 4m/6km SW of Rothesay. **St Ninian's Pt** is headland on W side of bay. Remains of ancient chapel on headland. NS 0361
St Ninian's Cave D & G. See Whithorn.
St Ninian's Chapel D & G. See Whithorn.
St Ninian's Isle Shetland 89 E8 peninsula on W coast of Mainland 9m/14km N of Sumburgh Hd. Joined to Mainland by narrow spit of land at head of **St Ninian's Bay.** HU 3620
St Olaves Norfolk 39 H5* vil 1km SW of Fritton. Remains of 13c priory. TM 4599
St Orland's Stone Tayside 76 D5* symbol stone depicting hunting and boating scenes, 4m/6km W of Forfar. NO 3950
St Osyth Essex 31 E6 vil 3m/5km W of Clacton-on-Sea. Remains of 12c abbey with late 15c flint gatehouse. **St O. Creek** runs W into Brightlingsea Creek. TM 1215
St Owen's Cross H & W 26 B5 ham 4m/6km W of Ross-on-Wye. SO 5324
St Palladius' Chapel Grampian. See Fordoun.
St Pancras London 19 G3 dist in borough of Camden in N part of Central London. TQ 3082
St Patrick's Isle Isle of Man 46 A5 island connected by causeway to W arm of Peel harbour. Peel Cas, group of ruins inside 16c walls. SC 2484
St Paul's Cray London 20 B4 dist in borough of Bromley 2km E of Chislehurst. TQ 4669

St Paul's Walden Herts 29 F5 vil 3m/5km W of Stevenage. TL 1922
St Peter's Kent 13 H1 W dist of Broadstairs (officially Broadstairs and St Peter's). TR 3868
St Petrox (Sain Pedrog) Dyfed 22 C6 loc 3m/4km S of Pembroke. SR 9797
St Philip's Marsh Avon 16 B4* dist of Bristol to E of Temple Meads rly stn. ST 6072
St Pinnock Cornwall 3 G2 ham 3m/5km W of Liskeard. SX 2063
St Piran's Round Cornwall 2 D3* ancient amphitheatre (A.M.) 2km E of Perranporth. SW 7754
St Quivox S'clyde 64 B6 loc 3m/5km NE of Ayr. Dairy Research Institute. NS 3724
St Ronan's Bay S'clyde 69 B5* small bay at Baile Mór, E coast of Iona. NM 2824
St Ruan Cornwall 2 C6* loc 3m/4km N of Lizard Pt. SW 7115
St Sampson Cornwall 3 F3 ham above right bank of R Fowey 2m/3km N of Fowey. SX 1255
St Serf's Island Tayside 73 E4 island in Loch Leven, towards SE corner. Ruins of medieval priory. NO 1600
St Stephen Cornwall 3 E3 vil 4m/7km W of St Austell. SW 9453
St Stephens Cornwall 4 B5* SW dist of Saltash. SX 4158
St Stephens Cornwall 6 C6 N dist of Launceston. SX 3285
St Stephens Herts 19 F1 SW dist of St Albans. TL 1406
St Teath Cornwall 3 E1 vil 3m/5km SW of Camelford. SX 0680
St Thomas Devon 7 G5* W dist of Exeter, on W side of R Exe. SX 9191
St Thomas W Glam 23 H6* loc in Swansea 1km E of tn centre across R Tawe. SS 6693
St Tudwal's Bay Gwynedd 32 B2 eastward-facing bay on W side of the larger Tremadoc Bay. It extends N and S of Abersoch. SH 32
St Tudwal's Island East and **St Tudwal's Island West** Gwynedd 32 B2 two small islands lying off coast of Lleyn peninsula to SE of St Tudwal's Bay. Lighthouse on St Tudwal's I. West. SH 3425
St Tudy Cornwall 3 F1 vil 5m/9km NE of Wadebridge. SX 0676
St Twynnells Dyfed 22 C6* ham 3m/5km SW of Pembroke. SR 9497
St Veep Cornwall 3 F3 ham 4m/6km SE of Lostwithiel. SX 1455
St Vigeans Tayside 73 H1 vil 2km N of Arbroath. Airfield to NW. NO 6342
St Wenn Cornwall 3 E2 vil 4m/6km E of St Columb Major. SW 9664
St Weonards H & W 26 A5 vil 7m/11km N of Monmouth. SO 4924
St Winnow Cornwall 3 F3* ham on left bank of R Fowey 2m/3km S of Lostwithiel. SX 1157
St Woollos Gwent 15 G3* dist of Newport to S of tn centre. ST 3087
Saint-y-brid Welsh form of St Bride's Major and St Bride's Netherwent, qv.
Saint-y-nyll S Glam 15 F4* loc just N of St Bride's-super-Ely, 5m/9km W of Cardiff. ST 0978
Salachan Burn 74 B6 stream in Argyll, S'clyde region, running NW down **Salachan Glen** into Loch Linnhe opp Eilean Balnagowan. NM 9653
Salcey Forest 28 C3 wooded area partly in Northants and partly in Bucks, 7m/11km NW of Newport Pagnell. SP 8052
Salcombe Devon 4 D6 resort near mouth of Kingsbridge Estuary, 3m/5km S of Kingsbridge (distance by rd 6m/10km). Yachting. SX 7439
Salcombe Regis Devon 5 G2 vil 2m/3km NE of Sidmouth. SY 1488
Salcott Essex 30 D6 vil at head of **Salcott Creek** 8m/12km SW of Colchester. TL 9513
Sale Gtr Manchester 42 D2 tn 5m/8km SW of Manchester. **Sale Ees** loc 1km NE of tn centre. SJ 7892
Saleby Lincs 45 H3 vil 2m/3km N of Alford. TF 4578
Sale Green H & W 26 D2 ham 4m/6km SE of Droitwich. SO 9358
Salehurst E Sussex 12 D4 vil 5m/8km N of Battle. Par contains the larger vil of Robertsbridge. TQ 7424
Salem Dyfed 32 D5/D6* loc 3m/5km E of Bow Street. SN 6684
Salem Gwynedd 40 C5* ham 5m/9km SE of Caernarvon. SH 5456
Salen H'land 68 E3 vil on bay of same name on N shore of Loch Sunart in Lochaber dist. NM 6864
Salen Mull, S'clyde 68 D4 vil on bay of same name on Sound of Mull, 9m/14km SE of Tobermory. NM 5743
Salendine Nook W Yorks 48 D6* loc in Huddersfield 3m/4km W of tn centre. SE 1017
Salesbury Lancs 47 G4 vil 3m/5km N of Blackburn. SD 6732
Sale, The Staffs 35 G3* loc 1km NW of Fradley. SK 1514
Saleway H & W 26 D2* loc 3m/5km SE of Droitwich. SO 9259
Salford Beds 28 D4 vil 5m/8km SE of Newport Pagnell. SP 9339
Salford Gtr Manchester 42 D2 large tn adjoining Manchester to W. Various industries include engineering, textiles, pharmaceutical products, rubber goods. Docks on Manchester Ship Canal. RC cathedral of mid-19c. SJ 8298
Salford Oxon 27 G4 vil 2m/3km NW of Chipping Norton. SP 2828
Salford Priors Warwicks 27 E3 vil 5m/8km NE of Evesham. SP 0751
Salfords Surrey 19 F6 suburban loc 3m/4km S of Redhill. TQ 2846
Salhouse Norfolk 39 G3 vil 6m/10km NE of Norwich. **Salhouse Broad** small broad or lake 1m NE. TG 3014
Saligo Bay S'clyde 62 A2 bay on W coast of Islay 2km W of Loch Gorm. NR 2066
Saline Fife 72 D5 vil 5m/8km NW of Dunfermline. NT 0292
Saling, Great Essex 30 B5 vil 4m/7km NW of Braintree. TL 7025
Salisbury Lothian 66 A2* dist of Edinburgh 2km SE of city centre. NT 2672
Salisbury Wilts 9 H2 cathedral city at confluence of Rs Avon and Nadder 21m/34km NW of Southampton. Cathedral, in EE style, has highest spire in Britain. SU 1429
Salisbury Plain Wilts 17 E6 large tract of chalk upland extending from Westbury and Warminster (W) to R Bourne valley and Tidworth (E), and from Vale of Pewsey (N) to R Wylye valley (S). Much used for military training. Ancient earthworks abound. SU 04
Salkeld Dykes Cumbria 53 E2 ham just W of Gt Salkeld. NY 5436
Salkeld, Great Cumbria 53 E2 vil 5m/8km NE of Penrith. **Lit Salkeld** ham 1m SE across R Eden. NY 5536
Sall Norfolk 39 E2 ham 2km NE of Reepham. TG 1124
Sallachan Point H'land 74 B5 low-lying promontory with beacon on W shore of Loch Linnhe in Lochaber dist. NM 9861
Sallachy H'land 80 A4 locality in Skye and Lochalsh dist on N shore of Loch Long 3m/5km NE of Dornie. NG 9130
Salmonby Lincs 45 G4 vil 5m/8km NE of Horncastle. TF 3273
Salop 118 west midland county of England, commonly called Shropshire. Is bounded by the English counties of Cheshire, Staffordshire, and Hereford & Worcester, and the Welsh counties of Powys and Clwyd. The S and W borders are hilly, with large areas of open moorland, which provide good sheep-grazing. Elsewhere the county is flat, industrial in the E (coal, iron and steel, engineering), and agricultural in the centre and N (dairy, poultry, and pig farming, and corn crops). Chief tns are Shrewsbury, the county tn; Bridgnorth, Ludlow, Oswestry, and Telford. The most important r is the Severn, which flows across the county from W to SE; others include the Clun, Corve, Perry, Rea Brook, and Teme.
Salperton Glos 27 E5 ham 4m/7km NW of Northleach. SP 0720
Salph End Beds 29 E3* loc 3m/4km NE of Bedford. TL 0752
Salsburgh S'clyde 65 E3 vil 5m/7km E of Airdrie. NS 8262
Salt Staffs 35 F2 ham 4m/6km NE of Stafford. SJ 9527
Salta Cumbria 52 B1* loc 2m/3km N of Allonby. NY 0845
Saltaire W Yorks 48 D4 W dist of Shipley on R Aire, originally built in 19c by Sir Titus Salt as model vil for workers at his worsted and alpaca mills. SE 1437
Saltash Cornwall 4 B5 tn beside narrow stretch of R Tamar estuary crossed by 19c rly br and 20c rd br. SX 4358
Saltburn H'land 81 F1 vil on N shore of Cromarty Firth, Ross and Cromarty dist, 2km NE of Invergordon. Development in connection with North Sea oil. NH 7269
Saltburn-by-the-Sea Cleveland 55 E3 North Sea coast resort 4m/7km E of Redcar. Wide sands. NZ 6621
Saltby Leics 36 D2 vil 7m/11km SW of Grantham. SK 8526
Saltcoats Cumbria 52 B5* loc 1km NW of Ravenglass across R Esk estuary. SD 0796
Saltcoats S'clyde 64 A4 tn and resort on Firth of Clyde adjoining Ardrossan to SE. NS 2441
Salt Cotes Cumbria 59 G6* loc 2m/3km NE of Abbey Tn. NY 1853
Saltcotes Lancs 47 E5 loc at E end of Lytham St Anne's. SD 3727
Saltdean E Sussex 12 A6 suburban loc on English Channel 5m/8km E of Brighton. TQ 3802
Salter Lancs 47 F2* loc in valley of R Roeburn 3m/5km S of Hornby, comprising High, Middle, and Lr Salter. SD 6063
Salterbeck Cumbria 52 A2/A3* S dist of Workington. NX 9926
Salterforth Lancs 48 B4 vil 1m SE of Barnoldswick. SD 8845
Salter Houses Cleveland 54 D2 loc 2m/4km NW of Wolviston. NZ 4227
Salters Lode Norfolk 38 B4* loc 2m/3km SW of Downham Mkt across R Ouse. TF 5801
Salter Street W Midlands 35 G6* loc 2m/4km NW of Hockley Heath. SP 1274
Salterswall Ches 42 C4* loc 2m/3km W of Winsford. SJ 6267
Saltfleet Lincs 45 H2 coastal vil 9m/14km NE of Louth. **Saltfleet Haven** outflow of R Eau to North Sea 1m E. TF 4593
Saltfleetby All Saints Lincs 45 H2 ham 5m/8km NW of Mablethorpe. **Saltfleetby St Clements** ham 1m N. **Saltfleetby St Peter** vil 2km SW. TF 4590
Saltford Avon 16 C4 vil on R Avon 2m/3km SE of Keynsham. ST 6867
Salt Hill Berks 18 D3* dist of Slough to W of tn centre. SU 9680
Salt Holme Cleveland 54 D3* loc 2m/3km N of Middlesbrough, across R Tees. NZ 5023
Salthouse Norfolk 39 E1 vil 3m/5km N of Holt. TG 0743
Salthouse Head Grampian 83 H3* headland at S end of Peterhead Bay. NK 1344
Salthouse Point W Glam 23 G6 headland on S side of Burry Inlet 4m/7km W of Gowerton. SS 5295
Saltinish W Isles 88 D3* loc on Barra 2km SE of Scurrival Pt. NF 7007
Saltley W Midlands 35 G5 loc in Birmingham 2m/3km E of city centre. SP 0987
Saltmarsh Gwent 15 H3* loc near coast 1m W of Goldcliff. ST 3582
Saltmarshe Humberside 50 C5 vil on N bank of R Ouse 4m/6km SE of Howden. SE 7824
Saltmead S Glam 15 F4/G4* dist of Cardiff 1m SW of city centre. ST 1775
Saltness Orkney 89 A7* loc at S end of Hoy 1km N of Melsetter. ND 2790
Salt Ness Orkney 89 B6* headland on W coast of Shapinsay 2m/4km N of Balfour. HY 4719
Saltney Clwyd 42 A5 suburb 2m/3km SW of Chester across R Dee. SJ 3764
Saltney, East Clwyd 41 H4* loc 2m/4km SE of Queensferry. SJ 3466
Saltney, West Clwyd 41 H4* loc adjoining Queensferry to E. SJ 3267
Salton N Yorks 55 F6 vil 4m/7km S of Kirkbymoorside. SE 7180
Salton Bay Cumbria 52 A3* bay on Irish Sea extending from Whitehaven southwards to North Hd. NX 9516
Saltoun, East Lothian 66 C2 vil 5m/8km SE of Tranent. NT 4767
Saltoun, West Lothian 66 C2 vil 5m/8km SE of Tranent and 1m W of E Saltoun. NT 4667
Saltram Devon. See Plympton.
Saltrens Devon 6 C3* ham 3m/4km S of Bideford. SS 4521
Saltwell Tyne & Wear 61 G5* dist of Gateshead 2km S of tn centre. NZ 2561
Saltwick Nthmb 61 F3* loc 4m/6km SW of Morpeth. NZ 1780
Saltwick Bay N Yorks 55 G4 bay on North Sea coast 2km E of Whitby. At N end of bay is Saltwick Nab (NT), a low, rocky headland. NZ 9110
Saltwood Kent 13 G3 N suburb of Hythe. Restored medieval cas. TR 1535
Salum Tiree, S'clyde 69 B7 loc on E side of bay of same name on N coast, 2m/3km W of Rubha Dubh. NM 0648
Salvington W Sussex 11 G4 N dist of Worthing. **High Salvington** is 1km N. TQ 1205
Salwarpe H & W 26 D2* vil on r of same name 2m/3km SW of Droitwich. SO 8761
Salwarpe 26 D2* r rising near Bromsgrove, H & W, and flowing SW into R Severn 3m/5km N of Worcester. SO 8460
Salwayash (or Salway Ash) Dorset 8 C4 ham 2m/4km N of Bridport. SY 4596
Samala W Isles 88 E1* loc on E side of island of Baleshare. NF 7962
Samalaman Island H'land 68 E2 low-lying islet on S side of Sound of Arisaig, 3m/5km W of Roshven, Lochaber dist. NM 6678
Samalan Island S'clyde 69 C5 islet at entrance to Loch Keal, W coast of Mull, lying 1km NE of Inch Kenneth. NM 4536
Sambourne Warwicks 27 E2 vil 3m/5km NW of Alcester. SP 0661
Sambrook Salop 34 D2 vil 4m/6km NW of Newport. SJ 7124
Samlesbury Lancs 47 F5 vil on R Ribble 3m/5km E of Preston. **Samlesbury Hall** dates partly from 14c and is timber-framed. **Samlesbury Bottoms** loc on R Darwen 2m/3km SE. SD 5930
Sampford Arundel Som H3 vil 2m/4km SW of Wellington. ST 1018
Sampford Brett Som 7 H1 vil 2m/3km SE of Watchet. ST 0840
Sampford Courtenay Devon 7 E5 vil 5m/8km NE of Okehampton. SS 6301
Sampford, Great Essex 30 B4 vil 4m/6km NE of Thaxted. TL 6435
Sampford, Little Essex 30 B4 vil 2m/4km W of Finchingfield. TL 6533
Sampford Peverell Devon 7 G4 vil 5m/8km E of Tiverton. ST 0314
Sampford Spiney Devon 4 C3 ham of SW Dartmoor 4m/6km E of Tavistock. SX 5372
Samphire Island Cornwall 2 B4 small island off N coast opp Carvannel Downs 2km SW of Portreath. SW 6344
Samphrey Shetland 89 E6* uninhabited island of about 200 acres or 80 hectares lying between SW end of Yell and NE coast of Mainland. HU 4676
Sampson's Creek Essex 21 F1* inlet of Thorn Fleet 7m/11km S of Colchester. TL 9914
Sampton Moor Som 7 H3* ham 1km S of Sampford Arundel and 3m/4km SW of Wellington. ST 1118
Samson Isles of Scilly 2 A1 the largest of the uninhabited islands, lying S of Bryher. SV 8712
Samson's Lane Orkney 89 C6* loc at centre of island of Stronsay. HY 6525
Samuel's Corner Essex 21 E3* loc 2m/3km NE of Shoeburyness. TQ 9587
Samuelston Lothian 66 C2* loc on R Tyne 3m/4km SW of Haddington. NT 4870
Sanaigmore Bay S'clyde 62 A1 small bay on N coast of Islay 1km SE of Tòn Mhór. NR 2371
Sancler Welsh form of St Clears, qv.
Sancreed Cornwall 2 A5 vil 3m/5km W of Penzance. SW 4229
Sancton Humberside 50 D4 vil 2m/3km SE of Mkt Weighton. SE 9039
Sanctuary, The Wilts. See Kennett, West.
Sand Som 16 A6* loc 1m S of Wedmore. ST 4346
Sandaig H'land 79 E7 locality at W end of Knoydart, Lochaber dist, on **Sandaig Bay** on N side of entrance to Loch Nevis. NG 7101
Sandaig Islands H'land 79 F6 group of islets in Sound of Sleat off N side of entrance to Loch Hourn in Lochaber dist. Lighthouse on Eilean Mór, the islet farthest from mainland shore. NG 7614

Sanda Island S'clyde 63 E6 island lying nearly 2m/3km off S coast of Kintyre across **Sanda Sound.** Measures 2km E to W and 1km N to S. Lighthouse at S point. NR 7204

Sandale Cumbria 52 C1* loc 2km E of Boltongate. NY 2440

Sandal Magna W Yorks 49 E6 dist of Wakefield 2m/3km S of city centre across R Calder. SE 3418

Sanday H'land 79 B7 island in Inner Hebrides at SE end of Canna, qv, to which it is connected at low tide. Sanday is 2m/3km E to W and has a maximum width N to S of 1km. Its N coast forms the S shore of Canna Harbour. NG 2704

Sanday Orkney 89 C5 low-lying island some 14m/23km NE to SW and of varying width, in places less than 1km, lying 4km S of N Ronaldsay and N of Stronsay at the nearest points. Spur Ness at extreme SW of island is 17m/28km NE of Kirkwall, Mainland. Airfield near centre of island. Mnfre of electronic equipment. HY 74

Sanday Sound Orkney 89 C5, C6 sea area between islands of Sanday and Stronsay. HY 63

Sanday, Upper Orkney 89 B7* loc on Mainland 8m/12km SE of Kirkwall. HY 5403

Sandbach Ches 42 C5 tn 5m/8km NE of Crewe. Industries include chemicals, motor vehicles, salt, silk, wire. Two large Saxon crosses (A.M.) in mkt place. **Sandbach Heath** loc 1m E. SJ 7760

Sandbank S'clyde 70 D6 vil on S side of Holy Loch, Argyll, 2m/4km N of Dunoon. NS 1680

Sandbanks Dorset 9 G5 dist of Poole on spit of land at entrance to Poole Harbour. SZ 0487

Sand Bay 15 B5 bay facing W on Bristol Channel and extending southwards from Sand Pt to Birnbeck I. ST 3264

Sand Beds W Midlands 35 F4* loc in W part of Walsall. SO 9799

Sandend Grampian 82 D1 vil on **Sandend Bay,** N coast, 3m/4km E of Cullen. NJ 5566

Sanderstead London 19 G5 loc in borough of Croydon 2m/3km E of Purley. TQ 3461

Sandfields Glos 26 D5* NW dist of Cheltenham. SO 9323

Sandfields W Glam 14 C3/D3* W dist of Port Talbot. SS 7490

Sandford Avon 15 H5 vil 3m/5km N of Axbridge. **Sandford Batch** loc 1km S. Quarries on sides of Sandford Hill. ST 4259

Sandford Cumbria 53 F3 vil 4m/6km SE of Appleby. NY 7216

Sandford Devon 7 F5 vil 2m/3km NW of Crediton. 1m W, ham of **W Sandford.** SS 8202

Sandford Dorset 9 F5* loc 2km N of Wareham. SY 9289

Sandford Isle of Wight 10 C6 ham 3m/4km W of Shanklin. SZ 5481

Sandford Salop 34 A2* loc 1m NE of Knockin. SJ 3423

Sandford Salop 34 C1* loc 5m/9km SE of Whitchurch. SJ 5834

Sandford S'clyde 64 D4 loc 2km SE of Strathaven. NS 7143

Sandford Bay Grampian 83 H3* bay on E coast S of Peterhead, between Burnhaven and Boddam. NK 1243

Sandfordhill Grampian 83 H3* loc near E coast 3m/5km S of Peterhead. NK 1142

Sandford Hill Staffs 35 E1* loc in Stoke-on-Trent NE of Longton. SJ 9144

Sandford-on-Thames Oxon 18 A2 vil 3m/5km SE of Oxford. **Sandford Pool** is small lake formed by diversion of main stream. SP 5301

Sandford Orcas Dorset 8 D2 vil 3m/4km N of Sherborne. ST 6220

Sandford St Martin Oxon 27 H5 vil 7m/11km E of Chipping Norton. SP 4226

Sandgate Kent 13 G3 W dist of Folkestone. TR 2035

Sandhaven Grampian 83 G1 fishing vil on N coast 2m/3km W of Fraserburgh. NJ 9667

Sandhead D & G 57 B7 coastal vil on **Sandhead Bay** on W side of Luce Bay and 7m/11km S of Stranraer. NX 0949

Sandhill S Yorks 43 H2* loc 3m/5km NE of Rotherham. SK 4497

Sandhills Dorset 8 D4* loc 2m/3km N of Maiden Newton. ST 5800

Sandhills Oxon 18 B1* loc adjoining E outskirts of Oxford. SP 5607

Sandhills Surrey 11 F2* vil 3m/5km S of Milford. SU 9337

Sandhills W Midlands 35 F4* loc 1km E of Brownhills. SK 0604

Sand Hills W Yorks 49 F4* ham 1km SW of Thorner. SE 3739

Sandhoe Nthmb 61 E5 vil 2m/3km NW of Corbridge. NY 9766

Sand Hole Humberside 50 C4 ham 1m S of Holme upon Spalding Moor. SE 8137

Sandholme Humberside 50 C5/D5 vil 5m/8km E of Howden. SE 8230

Sandholme Lincs 37 H1 loc 4m/7km S of Boston. TF 3337

Sandhurst Berks 18 C5 tn 3m/4km W of Camberley. Royal Military Academy to E. **Lit Sandhurst** loc adjoining tn to NW. SU 8361

Sandhurst Glos 26 D5 vil 3m/5km N of Gloucester. SO 8223

Sandhurst Kent 12 D4 vil 3m/4km SE of Hawkhurst. Loc of **Sandhurst Cross** 1m SW. TQ 7928

Sand Hutton N Yorks 50 C3 vil 2m/4km NW of Stamford Br. SE 6958

Sandhutton N Yorks 54 C6 vil 3m/5km W of Thirsk. SE 3882

Sandiacre Derbys 36 B1 loc 2m/3km N of Long Eaton. SK 4736

Sandihills D & G 58 D5 loc on **Sandihills Bay,** small bay 5m/9km SE of Dalbeattie. NX 8855

Sandilands Lincs 45 H3* coastal loc 1m S of Sutton on Sea. TF 5280

Sandiway Ches 42 C4* vil 4m/6km SW of Northwich. SJ 6070

Sandleheath Hants 9 H3 vil 2km W of Fordingbridge. SU 1214

Sandleigh Oxon 17 H2* vil 3m/4km N of Abingdon. SP 4701

Sandling Kent 20 D5 loc adjoining Maidstone to N. TQ 7558

Sandlow Green Ches 42 D4* loc 2m/3km SE of Holmes Chapel. SJ 7866

Sandness Shetland 89 D7 vil near W coast of Mainland adjoining Melby to E. **Sandness Hill** to S; height 817 ft or 249 metres. HU 1957

Sandon Essex 20 D2 vil 3m/5km SE of Chelmsford. TL 7404

Sandon Herts 29 G4 vil 5m/8km E of Baldock. TL 3234

Sandon Staffs 35 F2 vil 4m/7km NE of Stafford. SJ 9429

Sandown Isle of Wight 10 C6 resort on **Sandown Bay** 5m/8km S of Ryde, and 2m/3km NE of Shanklin, to which it is physically and administratively joined. Sandown Airport to W. SZ 5984

Sandown Park Surrey 19 F5 park and racecourse on N side of Esher. TQ 1365

Sandpit Hill S Yorks 44 B1* loc adjoining Branton to W. SE 6301

Sandpits Salop 34 C6* loc in NE part of Ludlow. SO 5175

Sandplace Cornwall 3 G3 ham 2m/3km N of Looe. SX 2555

Sand Point Avon 15 H4* headland at W end of Middle Hope and N end of Sand Bay on N side of Weston-super-Mare. ST 3165

Sandquoy Orkney 89 C5* loc on **Bay of Sandquoy,** on N coast of Sanday 2m/3km SW of Tafts Ness. HY 7445

Sandray W Isles 88 D4 uninhabited island of about 4 sq km, 1km S of Vatersay and 5km S of Barra. NL 6491

Sandridge Devon 5 E5* ham to N of R Dart estuary 3m/5km SW of Paignton. SX 8656

Sandridge Herts 19 F1 vil 3m/4km NE of St Albans. TL 1710

Sandridge Wilts 16 D5* loc 3m/4km NE of Melksham. ST 9465

Sandringham Norfolk 38 B2 estate vil of royal residence of Sandringham Hse, mid-19c mansion in large grnds, 7m/11km NE of King's Lynn. TF 6928

Sands End London 19 F4* loc on N bank of R Thames in borough of Hammersmith between Wandsworth and Battersea Brs. TQ 2676

Sandsend N Yorks 55 G4 vil and resort on North Sea coast 3m/4km NW of Whitby, on bay called **Sandsend Wyke. Sandsend Ness** is headland at N end of bay. NZ 8612

Sandside Cumbria 46 D1* loc 2km E of Ulverston. SD 3077

Sand Side Cumbria 52 C6 vil on E side of R Duddon estuary 5m/8km N of Dalton-in-Furness. SD 2282

Sandside Cumbria 52 D6/53 E6 loc on left bank of R Kent estuary 2km W of Milnthorpe. SD 4780

Sandside Head H'land 86 C2 headland on N coast of Caithness dist on W side of entrance to **Sandside Bay,** 2km NW of Reay. NC 9566

Sands of Forvie Grampian 83 H4 sandy waste on E coast between Collieston and Newburgh. See also Forvie Ness. NK 0227

Sandsound Voe Shetland 89 E7* narrow inlet between steep hills to W of Weisdale Voe, Mainland. Loc of **Sandsound** on E shore. HU 3549

Sands, The Surrey 11 E1* loc 3m/4km E of Farnham. SU 8846

Sandtoft Humberside 44 C1* ham 4m/6km NW of Epworth. SE 7408

Sandtop Bay Dyfed 22 D6* bay on W side of Caldy I., between W Beacon Pt and St Margaret's I. SS 1296

Sand Water Shetland 89 E7* lake on Mainland in course of **Burn of Sandwater,** which rises as Burn of Pettawater above small lake of Petta Water, 2m/4km S of Voe. The stream flows S through Petta Water, Sand Water, and Loch of Strom, into Stromness Voe to E of Weisdale Voe. HU 4154

Sandway Dorset 9 E2* loc adjoining Bourton and 4m/6km NW of Gillingham. ST 7730

Sandway Kent 21 E6 ham 2km SW of Lenham. TQ 8851

Sandwell W Midlands 35 F5* loc in NE part of Warley. SP 0289

Sandwell 118 admin dist of W Midlands metropolitan county.

Sandwich Kent 13 H2 cinque port on R Stour 2m/3km from sea **(Sandwich Bay),** 11m/18km E of Canterbury. Resort, with well-known golf courses. Power stns and factories to N. TR 3358

Sandwick Cumbria 52 D3 loc near S shore of Ullswater 3m/5km NE of Patterdale. NY 4219

Sand Wick Shetland 89 D6* bay on N shore of St Magnus Bay on W side of Hillswick. HU 2777

Sandwick Shetland 89 E8 loc at head of **Sand Wick,** southward-facing bay on E coast of Mainland 11m/18km S of Lerwick. HU 4323

Sandwick W Isles 88 C2* vil on Lewis 2km E of Stornoway. WT stn to N. NB 4432

Sand Wick, West Shetland 89 E6 small bay on W coast of Yell. Vil of **W Sandwick** 1km SE. **Holm of W Sandwick** small uninhabited island 1km offshore. **Ness of W Sandwick** headland 1m S. HU 4489

Sandwith Cumbria 52 A3 ham 2m/4km S of Whitehaven. NX 9614

Sandwood Bay H'land 84 C2 bay on NW coast of Sutherland dist between headlands of Rubh' an t-Socaich Ghlais and Rubh' a' Bhuachaille. NC 2266

Sandwood Loch H'land 84 C2 loch near NW coast of Sutherland dist at foot of Strath Shinary, draining into Sandwood Bay. NC 2264

Sandy Beds 29 F3 tn on R Ivel 8m/12km E of Bedford. Market-gardening in vicinity. TL 1749

Sandy Dyfed 23 F5* loc on W side of Llanelli, N of steel works. SN 4900

Sandy Bank Lincs 45 F5* loc 3m/5km SE of Coningsby. TF 2655

Sandy Bay Mid Glam 14 D4* bay on E side of Porthcawl Pt. SS 8276

Sandycroft Clwyd 41 H4 loc 2km SE of Queensferry. SJ 3367

Sandy Cross E Sussex 12 C4* loc in S part of Heathfield. TQ 5820

Sandy Cross H & W 26 B2* loc 2m/3km NE of Bromyard. SO 6756

Sandy Cross Surrey 11 E1* loc 3m/5km E of Farnham. SU 8847

Sandyford Staffs 42 D5* loc 1m N of Tunstall. SJ 8552

Sandygate Devon 5 E3 loc 2m/3km N of Newton Abbot. SX 8675

Sandy Gate Devon 7 G5* loc 3m/5km E of Exeter. SX 9691

Sandygate Isle of Man 46 B4 ham 2m/3km NW of Sulby. SC 3797

Sandy Gate S Yorks 43 G3* dist of Sheffield 2m/4km W of city centre. SK 3186

Sandy Haven Dyfed 22 B5 loc 2km E of St Ishmael's, on W side of **Sandyhaven Pill,** estuary running S into Milford Haven between Gt Castle Hd and S Hook Pt. SM 8507

Sandyhills S'clyde 64 D3* loc 4m/7km E of Glasgow. NS 6563

Sandylands Lancs 47 E2 SW dist of Morecambe. SD 4263

Sandy Lane Clwyd 34 B1* loc 2m/3km SE of Overton. SJ 4040

Sandylane Staffs 34 D1* loc 2m/3km NE of Mkt Drayton. SJ 7035

Sandylane W Glam 23 G6* loc on Gower peninsula adjoining Parkmill to E. SS 5588

Sandy Lane Wilts 16 D4 vil 3m/5km SW of Calne. Site of Roman tn of *Verlucio* to SE. ST 9668

Sandy Lane W Yorks 48 D4 loc in Bradford 4m/6km NW of city centre. SE 1135

Sandymoor Ches 42 B3* industrial area in NE part of Runcorn. SJ 5683

Sandypark Devon 7 E6* ham 4m/6km NW of Moretonhampstead. SX 7189

Sandyway H & W 26 A5 loc 8m/13km N of Monmouth. SO 4925

Sandy Way Isle of Wight 10 B6* loc just S of Shorwell. SZ 4582

Sangamore H'land 84 D2 loc adjoining Durness to SE, N coast of Sutherland dist. NC 4067

Sangobeg H'land 84 D2 loc in Sutherland dist 2m/3km SE of Durness. NC 4266

Sankey Bridges Ches 42 B3* loc in W part of Warrington. SJ 5887

Sankey Brook 42 B3* r rising near Orrell, Gtr Manchester, and flowing S into R Mersey 2m/3km SW of Warrington, Ches. SJ 5787

Sankey, Great Ches 42 B3 loc in W part of Warrington. SJ 5688

Sankyn's Green H & W 26 C2* ham 4m/7km S of Stourport. SO 7964

Sannan 23 G3* r rising near Llanfynydd, Dyfed, and flowing S into R Dulas 4m/7km W of Llandeilo. SN 5623

Sanna Point H'land 68 C2 headland in Lochaber dist, at N end of **Sanna Bay** and 2m/4km NE of Ardnamurchan Pt. NM 4370

Sannox, Mid S'clyde 63 G3 loc near E coast of Arran at foot of Glen Sannox. **Sannox Bay** on coast to E. NS 0145

Sanquhar D & G 58 D1 tn on R Nith 10m/16km NW of Thornhill and same distance E of New Cumnock. Industries include iron founding; mnfre of carpets, hosiery; aluminium processing; dairy farmin9 in surrounding area. Industrial estate. Remains of cas to S. Tolbooth dating from 1735. NS 7809

Santon Cumbria 52 B4* loc 1km W of Santon Br. NY 1001

Santon Bridge Cumbria 52 B4 vil on R Irt 3m/5km SE of Gosforth. NY 1101

Santon Burn 46 B6* r on Isle of Man running S into sea 2m/4km SW of Santon Hd. SC 2969

Santon Downham Suffolk 38 C5* vil 2m/4km NE of Brandon. TL 8187

Santon Head Isle of Man 46 B6 headland 4m/7km SW of Douglas. SC 3370

Sapcote Leics 36 B5 vil 4m/6km E of Hinckley. Site of Roman villa 1km E. SP 4893

Sapey Common H & W 26 C2 ham 7m/11km NE of Bromyard. SO 7063

Sapey, Lower H & W 26 C2* ham 4m/7km NE of Bromyard. SO 6960

Sapey, Upper H & W 26 B2/C2 vil 6m/10km N of Bromyard. SO 6863

Sapiston Suffolk 30 D1 vil 3m/5km N of Ixworth. TL 9175

Sapley Cambs 29 F1* loc in N part of Huntingdon. TL 2474

Sapperton Derbys 35 G1* loc 2m/3km NE of Sudbury. SK 1632

Sapperton Glos 16 D1 vil 5m/8km W of Cirencester. SO 9403

Sapperton Lincs 37 E2 ham 7m/11km E of Grantham. TF 0133

Saracen's Head Lincs 37 H2* ham 2m/3km NW of Holbeach. TF 3427

Sarclet H'land 86 F3 loc on E coast of Caithness dist 5m/8km S of Wick. **Sarclet Hd** is headland to SE. ND 3443

Sardis Mountain Dyfed 22 D5* loc 2km N of Saundersfoot. SN 1306

Saredon, Great Staffs 35 F3* loc 2m/3km SW of Cannock. **Lit Saredon** loc 1m S. SJ 9508

Sarffle 33 H1* stream running NE into R Ceiriog 1km NW of Llanarmon Dyffryn Ceiriog, Clwyd. SJ 1433

Sarisbury Hants 10 C4 vil 1m NW of Park Gate. SU 5008

Sark 59 G4 r rising in Dumfries & Galloway region and running S along border of England and Scotland to head of Solway Firth 1km SE of Gretna. NY 3266

Sarn Mid Glam 15 E3* loc 2m/4km N of Bridgend. SS 9083

Sarn Powys 33 H5 ham 6m/9km E of Newtown. SO 2090

Sarnau Dyfed 23 E1 ham 2m/3km S of Llangranog. SN 3151

Sarnau Gwynedd 33 F1* loc 3m/5km NE of Bala. SH 9739

Sarnau Powys 25 E4* loc 3m/5km N of Brecon. SO 0232

Sarnau Powys 34 A3 ham 5m/8km N of Welshpool. SJ 2315

Sarn-bach Gwynedd 32 B2 loc 2km S of Abersoch. SH 3026

Sarnesfield H & W 25 H3 vil 11m/18km NW of Hereford. SO 3750

Sarn Helen. Name (perhaps derived from the Welsh 'sarn hoelen', a paved causeway) given to several sections of Roman rd in Wales which may once have formed a continuous link between Caernarvon and Carmarthen.

Sarn Mellteyrn Gwynedd 32 A2 vil 6m/9km NE of Aberdaron. SH 2332

Saron Dyfed 23 E2* loc 3m/5km SW of Llandyssul. SN 3737

Saron Dyfed 23 G4* vil 2m/3km W of Ammanford. SN 6012

Saron Gwynedd 40 B5* loc 1m NW of Llanwnda. SH 4658

Saron Gwynedd 40 C5 vil 4m/6km NE of Caernarvon. SH 5265

Sarratt Herts 19 E2 vil 3m/5km N of Rickmansworth. Site of Roman villa 1m W. TQ 0499

Sarre Kent 13 G1 vil 4m/6km SW of Birchington. TR 2565

Sarsden Oxon 27 G5 ham 3m/5km SW of Chipping Norton. SP 2823

Sarson Hants 10 A1* loc between Amport and Monxton 4m/6km W of Andover. SU 3044

Sartfield Isle of Man 46 B3/B4 loc near coast 4m/6km NW of Sulby. SC 3599

Satley Durham 54 A1 vil 3m/5km N of Tow Law. NZ 1143

Satron N Yorks 53 H5* loc 1km SW of Gunnerside across R Swale. SD 9397

Satterleigh Devon 7 E3 ham 4m/6km SW of S Molton. SS 6622

Satterthwaite Cumbria 52 D5 vil in Grizedale Forest 4m/6km S of Hawkshead. SD 3392

Sauchar Point Fife 73 G4* headland on E side of Elie Ness and 1km SE of Elie tn. NT 4999

Sauchen Grampian 83 E5 vil 4m/6km SW of Kemnay. NJ 6911

Saughall, Great Ches 42 A4 vil 4m/6km NW of Chester. **Lit Saughall** ham 2km SE. SJ 3670

Saughall Massie Merseyside 41 H3 loc in Wallasey 5m/8km SW of tn centre. SJ 2588

Saughton Lothian 66 A2* dist of Edinburgh 2m/4km SW of city centre. **Saughtonhall** is dist to N across rly. NT 2172

Saughtree Borders 60 B2 loc 8m/12km NE of Newcastleton. NY 5696

Saul Glos 16 C1 vil 7m/11km W of Stroud. SO 7409

Saundby Notts 44 C3 vil 2m/4km SW of Gainsborough. SK 7888

Saundersfoot Dyfed 22 D5 small coastal resort with harbour 3m/4km N of Tenby and situated on **Saundersfoot Bay,** extending from Monkstone Pt NE to Ragwen Pt. SN 1304

Saunderton Bucks 18 C2 vil 2km SW of Princes Risborough. Site of Roman villa near ch. SP 7901

Saunton Devon 6 D2 at N end of Braunton Burrows 7m/11km NW of Barnstaple. To SW beyond the burrows are **Saunton Sands,** about 4km long. SS 4537

Sausthorpe Lincs 45 G4 vil 2m/3km NW of Spilsby. TF 3869

Savalmore H'land 85 F6* loc in Sutherland dist 2km N of Lairg. Loc of **Savalbeg** to SE. Numerous ancient cairns in vicinity. NC 5808

Saverley Green Staffs 35 F1* loc 1m NE of Fulford. SJ 9638

Savernake Wilts 17 F4 par lying to S and SE of Marlborough and containing most of **Savernake Forest,** wooded area extending from Marlborough 4m/6km south-eastwards. SU 2166

Savile Place W Yorks 48 D5/49 E5* loc 1m N of Mirfield. SE 2021

Savile Town W Yorks 49 E6* dist of Dewsbury S of tn centre across R Calder. SE 2420

Saviskaill Orkney 89 B5/B6* loc on N coast of Rousay, 1m S of headland of **Saviskaill Hd** and on shore of **Saviskaill Bay,** wide bay extending eastwards from the headland. HY 4033

Sawbridge Warwicks 28 A1* loc 5m/8km NW of Daventry. SP 5065

Sawbridgeworth Herts 20 B1 tn on W bank of R Stort 4m/6km NE of Harlow. TL 4814

Sawdde 24 C4 r rising in Llyn y Fan fach, Black Mt, Dyfed, and flowing NW into R Towy 1m W of Llangadog. SN 6928

Sawdde Fechan 24 C5* r rising on Black Mt, Dyfed, and flowing N into R Sawdde 1m above Pontarllechau. SN 7323

Sawdern Point Dyfed 22 B5* headland on E side of entrance to Angle Bay. SM 8803

Sawdon N Yorks 55 G6 ham 7m/11km W of Scarborough. SE 9485

Sawley Derbys 36 B2 loc adjoining Long Eaton to SW. See also New Sawley. SK 4731

Sawley Lancs 48 B3 vil on R Ribble 4m/6km NE of Clitheroe. Remains of 12c abbey (A.M.). SD 7746

Sawley N Yorks 49 E2 vil 5m/7km SW of Ripon. SE 2467

Saw Mill Powys 33 H5* loc 1km E of Kerry. SO 1589

Sawrey, Far Cumbria 52 D5 vil 2m/4km SE of Hawkshead. SD 3795

Sawrey, Near Cumbria 52 D5* vil 1km W of Far Sawrey and 2m/3km SE of Hawkshead. About half the vil is owned by the National Trust, including hse of Beatrix Potter. SD 3795

Sawston Cambs 29 H3 suburb 6m/10km SE of Cambridge. **Sawston Hall** is 16c manor hse. TL 4849

Sawtry Cambs 37 F6 vil 4m/6km S of Stilton. Site of Romano-British settlement on E side of vil. TL 1683

Saxby Leics 36 D3 vil 4m/7km E of Melton Mowbray. SK 8219

Saxby Lincs 44 D3/45 E3 vil 7m/11km W of Mkt Rasen. TF 0086

Saxby All Saints Humberside 51 E6 vil 6m/10km N of Brigg. SE 9916

Saxelby Leics 36 C2/C3 ham 4m/6km NW of Melton Mowbray. SK 7021

Saxham, Great Suffolk 30 C2* loc 4m/7km W of Bury St Edmunds. Vil of **Lit Saxham** to E. TL 7862

Saxham Street Suffolk 31 E2* loc 1km NW of Middlewood Green. TM 0862

Saxilby Lincs 44 D4 large vil on Fossdyke Navigation 6m/9km NW of Lincoln. SK 8975

Saxlingham Norfolk 39 E1 vil 3m/5km W of Holt. TG 0239

Saxlingham Nethergate Norfolk 39 F5 vil 7m/12km S of Norwich. Vils of **Saxlingham Green** and **Saxlingham Thorpe** 1km SE and 2km W respectively. TM 2297

Saxmundham Suffolk 31 G2 small tn 18m/29km NE of Ipswich. TM 3863

Saxondale Notts 36 C1 ham 7m/11km E of Nottingham. SK 6839

Saxon Street Cambs 30 B2 vil 3m/5km SE of Newmarket. TL 6759

Saxtead Suffolk 31 F2/G2 ham 2m/3km NW of Framlingham. Vils of **Saxtead Green** and **Saxtead Lit Green** 1m SW and W respectively. Former has restored 18c post-mill (A.M.). TM 2665

Saxthorpe Norfolk 39 E2 vil opp Corpusty across R Bure, 6m/9km SE of Holt. TG 1130

Saxton N Yorks 49 F4 vil 4m/6km S of Tadcaster. SE 4736

Sayers Common W Sussex 11 H3 vil 3m/5km W of Burgess Hill. TQ 2618

Sblot, Y Welsh form of Splottlands or Splott. See Splottlands.

Scackleton N Yorks 50 B1 vil 2m/3km SW of Hovingham. SE 6472

Scadabay W Isles 88 B3* locality at head of loch of same name on SE coast of Harris 5m/8km S of Tarbert. NG 1792

Scaddle H'land 74 B4 r in Ardgour, Lochaber dist, running E down Glen Scaddle to Inverscaddle Bay on Loch Linnhe. NN 0267

Scad Head Orkney 89 A7* headland on N coast of Hoy 4m/6km E of Ward Hill. HY 2900

Sca Fell Cumbria 52 C4 mt in Lake Dist 2m/3km SE of Wasdale Hd. Height 3162 ft or 964 metres. **Scafell Pike** mt 1km NE, highest in England, attains height of 3206 ft or 977 metres. NY 2006

Scaftworth Notts 44 B2 vil 2km SE of Bawtry. SK 6691

Scagglethorpe N Yorks 50 D1 vil 3m/5km E of Malton. SE 8372

Scaitcliffe Lancs 48 A5* dist of Accrington 1km SW of tn centre. SD 7427

Scaladale W Isles 88 B3* r in Harris flowing E into Loch Seaforth at Ardvourlie Castle. NB 1910

Scalasaig S'clyde 69 C8 loc on E coast of Colonsay and chief settlement on the island. Pier and lighthouse. NR 3994

Scalby Humberside 50 D5 vil 6m/9km E of Howden. SE 8329

Scalby N Yorks 55 H5 small tn and suburb 2m/4km NW of Scarborough. **Scalby Mills** loc 2km E. **Scalby Ness** headland on North Sea coast 2m/3km E. TA 0090

Scald Law Lothian 65 H3 summit of Pentland Hills, 3m/5km W of Penicuik. Height 1898 ft or 579 metres. NT 1961

Scaldwell Northants 28 C1 vil 8m/12km N of Northampton. SP 7672

Scaleber Force N Yorks 48 B2* waterfall in Scaleber Beck below Scaleber Br 2m/3km SE of Settle on rd to Kirkby Malham. SD 8462

Scaleby Cumbria 60 A5 vil 5m/9km NE of Carlisle. **Scaleby Castle,** fortified hse dating from 14c. NY 4463

Scalebyhill Cumbria 60 A5 ham 1km NW of Scaleby. NY 4463

Scale Force Cumbria 52 B3* waterfall (NT) in Scale Beck 1m W of S end of Crummock Water. NY 1517

Scale Hall Lancs 47 E2* urban loc between Lancaster and Morecambe. SD 4662

Scale Houses Cumbria 60 B6* loc 2m/3km SE of Croglin. NY 5845

Scale, North Cumbria 46 C2 loc towards N end of Walney I., 1m N of causeway to Barrow-in-Furness. SD 1870

Scales Cumbria 46 D1 vil 3m/5km E of Dalton-in-Furness. SD 2772

Scales Cumbria 52 D2 ham 5m/9km NE of Keswick. **Scales Tarn,** small lake 2km NW. NY 3426

Scales Lancs 47 E5* loc adjoining Newton to E. SD 4530

Scalesceugh Cumbria 60 A6* loc 5m/8km SE of Carlisle. NY 4449

Scales, High Cumbria 52 B1 loc 3m/5km NE of Aspatria. NY 1845

Scalford Leics 36 D2 vil 3m/5km N of Melton Mowbray. SK 7624

Scaling Cleveland 55 F4 ham up against N Yorks border 4m/7km SW of Staithes. **Scaling Dam** loc to S below dam of **Scaling Resr.** NZ 7413

Scallastle Bay Mull, S'clyde 68 E4 bay on Sound of Mull extending SE from Garmony Pt. **Scallastle R** runs NE to SE end of bay. NM 6939

Scalloway Shetland 89 E7 small tn with harbour on W coast of Mainland 5m/7km W of Lerwick. Fishing. Remains of 17c cas (A.M.), formerly residence of Earls of Shetland. HU 4039

Scalpay Skye, H'land 79 D5, D6 island of about 9 sq miles or 23 sq km and roughly circular in shape, lying off E coast of Skye mainland opp Loch Ainort. Barely inhabited. Rises to height of 1298 ft or 396 metres. NG 6030

Scalpay W Isles 88 B3 island, 4km by 2km, at entrance to E Loch Tarbert, Harris, separated from main island by the narrow Sound of Scalpay. Vil with N and S harbours at NW end; lighthouse at SE end. NG 29

Scalpsie Bay S'clyde 63 G2 southward-facing bay on W coast of Bute 3m/4km NW of Kingarth. NS 0557

Scamblesby Lincs 45 F3 vil 6m/9km N of Horncastle. TF 2778

Scammonden W Yorks 48 C6* loc 6m/10km W of Huddersfield. **Scammonden Water,** resr to N. SE 0415

Scamodale H'land 74 A4 locality in Lochaber dist halfway along SE shore of Loch Shiel. NM 8373

Scampston N Yorks 50 D1 vil 5m/8km NE of Malton. SE 8675

Scampton Lincs 44 D3 vil 5m/9km N of Lincoln. Airfield to E. Site of Roman villa 1km SE. SK 9579

Scandal Beck 53 G4* r rising on N slopes of Wild Boar Fell, Cumbria, and flowing N into R Eden 2m/3km N of Kirkby Stephen. NY 7611

Scaniport H'land 81 F3 loc in Inverness dist 4m/6km SW of Inverness. NH 6339

Scapa Bay Orkney 89 B6 bay and sheltered anchorage on S coast of Mainland at NE corner of Scapa Flow. Bay extends inland to within less than 2m/3km of Bay of Kirkwall to N, on which Kirkwall tn is situated. Pier on E side of bay provides landing facilities. Distillery at head of bay. HY 4308

Scapa Flow Orkney 89 B7 large natural anchorage surrounded by islands of Hoy, Mainland, Burra, S Ronaldsay, and Flotta, some 10m/16km E to W and 8m/13km N to S. Eastern approaches blocked by Churchill Barrier, qv. HY 30

Scapegoat Hill W Yorks 48 D6* vil 4m/6km W of Huddersfield. SE 0816

Scaraben H'land 86 D4 hill on Langwell Forest, Caithness dist, 4m/7km NW of Berriedale. Height 2054 ft or 626 metres. ND 0626

Scarastavore W Isles 88 A3* loc on W coast of Harris 4m/6km N of Leverburgh. NG 0092

Scaravay W Isles 88 E1* small uninhabited island at SE end of Sound of Harris 4m/6km off E coast of N Uist. NG 0177

Scarba S'clyde 69 E7 uninhabited island of moorland, of about 5 sq miles or 13 sq km, lying 1km N of Jura across Strait of Corryvreckan, qv. NM 7004

Scarborough N Yorks 55 H6 old North Sea fishing port built on steep cliff side, now large resort and conference tn, 35m/57km NE of York. Remains of 12c cas (A.M.) and of Roman signal stn on Castle Cliff, between North Bay and South Bay. TA 0488

Scarcewater Cornwall 3 E3 loc 6m/10km W of St Austell. SW 9154

Scarcliffe Derbys 44 A4 vil 2m/3km SE of Bolsover. SK 4968

Scarcroft W Yorks 49 F4* loc 6m/10km NE of Leeds. SE 3641

Scares D & G 57 C8 group of rocks at entrance to Luce Bay, about 7m/11km E of Mull of Galloway. NX 23

Scarfskerry H'land 86 E1 loc on N coast of Caithness dist 7m/11km W of John o' Groats. **Scarfskerry Pt** is headland to NW. ND 2674

Scargill Durham 54 A4 ham 4m/6km S of Barnard Castle. Remains of medieval cas, including 15c gatehouse. NZ 0510

Scargill Reservoir N Yorks 49 E3* resr 5m/8km W of Harrogate. SE 2353

Scargreen Cumbria 52 B4* loc 2km N of Gosforth. NY 0605

Scar House Reservoir N Yorks 48 C1/D1 resr on R Nidd below Angram Resr 9m/15km NW of Pateley Br. SD 0676

Scarinish Tiree, S'clyde 69 B7 principal vil and port of the island, situated on S coast between Hynish and Gott Bays. Lighthouse. Landing stage on Gott Bay. NM 0444

Scarisbrick Lancs 42 A1 vil 4m/6km SE of Southport. SD 3713

Scarle, North Lincs 44 C4 vil 8m/13km W of Lincoln. SK 8466

Scarle, South Notts 44 C4 vil 7m/11km NE of Newark-on-Trent. SK 8464

Scarlett Point Isle of Man 46 A6* headland at W end of Castletown Bay. SC 2566

Scarletts Berks 18 C4* loc 2m/3km NE of Twyford. SU 8178

Scarness Cumbria 52 C2* loc on E side of Bassenthwaite Lake 2km SW of Bassenthwaite vil. NY 2230

Scarning Norfolk 38 D3 vil 2m/4km W of E Dereham. TF 9512

Scar Nose Grampian 82 D1 headland on N coast on NE side of Portknockie. NJ 4968

Scarp W Isles 88 A3 rugged island, 3m/4km by 2m/3km, lying off W coast of Harris across narrow strait of Caolas and Scarp. Small vil at SE end of island on strait. Scarp rises to height of 1012 ft or 308 metres. NA 91
Scarrington Notts 36 C1 vil 2m/3km NE of Bingham. SK 7341
Scarrow Beck 39 F2* r rising near Gresham, Norfolk, and flowing S into R Bure 2m/3km N of Aylsham. TG 1730
Scarrowhill Cumbria 60 B6* loc 2km S of Cumwhitton. NY 5150
Scarr, The Glos 26 C4* loc 2km N of Newent. SO 7228
Scarth Hill Lancs 42 A1 loc 2km SE of Ormskirk. SD 4206
Scarthingwell N Yorks 49 F4/G4* loc 1km N of Barkston. SE 4937
Scartho Humberside 45 F1 dist of Grimsby 2m/3km S of tn centre. TA 2605
Scarwell Orkney 89 A6* loc near W coast of Mainland 3m/5km W of Dounby. HY 2420
Scatsta Shetland 89 E6 loc on Mainland on E side of Sullom Voe. Small inlet, **Voe of Scatsta,** to NE. **Scatsta Ness** is headland on Sullom Voe to N. HU 3972
Scatwell, Little H'land 80 D2 loc about confluence of Rs Conan and Meig below Loch Luichart, Ross and Cromarty dist. NH 3956
Scaur D & G. Alternative name for Kippford, qv.
Scaurs, The Grampian. See Skares, The.
Scaur Water 58 D2 r in Dumfries & Galloway region running SE to R Nith 2m/3km S of Thornhill. NX 8792
Scawby Humberside 44 D1 vil 2m/4km SW of Brigg. **Scawby Hall** dates in part from 17c. **Scawby Brook** loc 1m NE across park. Site of Roman bldg 1m W. SE 9605
Scaw'd Law 59 E2* mt in Lowther Hills on border of Strathclyde and Dumfries & Galloway regions 2m/3km E of Durisdeer. NS 9203
Scawsby S Yorks 44 A1* loc 2m/3km NW of Doncaster. SE 5404
Scawthorpe S Yorks 44 A1* suburb 2m/3km NW of Doncaster. SE 5505
Scawton N Yorks 54 D6 ham 4m/7km W of Helmsley. SE 5483
Scaynes Hill W Sussex 12 A4 vil 2m/4km E of Haywards Heath. TQ 3623
Scethrog (Sgethrog) Powys 25 F5 ham 4m/7km SE of Brecon. SO 1025
Schiehallion Tayside 75 G5 conical mt of quartzite 4m/7km SE of Kinloch Rannoch. Height 3547 ft or 1081 metres. NN 7154
Scholar Green Ches 42 D5 loc 2km N of Kidsgrove. SJ 8356
Scholemoor W Yorks 48 D5* loc in Bradford 2m/3km W of city centre. SE 1332
Scholes Gtr Manchester 42 B1* E dist of Wigan. SD 5905
Scholes S Yorks 43 H2* ham 3m/5km NW of Rotherham. SK 3995
Scholes W Yorks 43 F1* vil 2km E of Holmfirth. SE 1607
Scholes W Yorks 48 D5* loc 2m/3km W of Cleckheaton. SE 1625
Scholes W Yorks 49 F4 loc 5m/8km E of Leeds. SE 3736
Scholey Hill W Yorks 49 F5* loc 1m SW of Methley. SE 3825
Schoolgreen Berks 18 C4* loc adjoining Shinfield to S and 4m/6km S of Reading. SU 7367
School Green Ches 42 C5* loc 2m/3km SW of Winsford. SJ 6464
School Green Essex 30 C4* loc 3m/5km E of Finchingfield. TL 7331
School Green Isle of Wight 10 A5* loc adjoining Freshwater and 1km E of Totland. SZ 3387
School Green W Yorks 48 D5* loc in Bradford adjoining Thornton to E. SE 1132
School House Dorset 8 B4* loc 1m SW of Thorncombe. ST 3602
School Lane Lancs 47 F5* loc adjoining Bamber Br to N. SD 5626
Schoose Cumbria 52 A2 loc in Workington 2km E of tn centre. NY 0128
Scilly Isles 2 A1 group of some 140 islands 28m/45km SW of Land's End, Cornwall, of which five are inhabited: Bryher, St Agnes, St Martin's, St Mary's, Tresco. Chief industries are the growing of early flowers and vegetables, and fishing. Climate exceptionally mild. SV 91
Scissett W Yorks 43 G1 vil 2m/3km NE of Denby Dale. SE 2410
Scithwen Brook 25 F4* stream rising about 3m/4km S of Gwenddwr, Powys, and flowing E into R Wye 2km SE of Erwood. SO 1141
Scleddau Dyfed 22 B3 vil 2m/3km S of Fishguard. SM 9434
Scoat Tarn Cumbria 52 B4* small lake 1km S of Steeple. NY 1510
Scofton Notts 44 B3 ham 3m/5km E of Worksop. SK 6380
Scole Norfolk 31 F1 vil 2m/4km E of Diss. TM 1579
Scolt Head Norfolk 38 C1 island (NT) of marsh, sand dune, and shingle, off N coast at E end of Brancaster Bay. Nature reserve. Access by boat from Brancaster Staithe. TF 8046
Sconce Point Isle of Wight 10 A5 headland at W end of Solent 1m W of Yarmouth. SZ 3389
Scone Palace Tayside 73 E2 castellated early 19c mansion on site of medieval abbey and palace, 2m/3km N of Perth across R Tay. Site has historical associations dating from 8c. Loc of Old Scone to E; vil of New Scone 2m/3km to E, beyond Old Scone. Scone Airfield 2m/3km NE of New Scone. NO 1126
Sconser Skye, H'land 79 D5 locality on S side of Loch Sligachan. NG 5232
Scoonie Fife 73 F4/G4 N dist of Leven. NO 3801
Scootmore Forest Grampian 82 B3 afforested area astride Allt a' Gheallaidh immediately above its confluence with R Spey 11m/17km NE of Grantown-on-Spey. NJ 1638
Scopwick Lincs 45 E5 vil 8m/12km N of Sleaford. TF 0658
Scoraig H'land 85 A7 locality on NE side of Lit Loch Broom 2m/3km SE of Cailleach Hd on W coast of Ross and Cromarty dist. NH 0096
Scorborough Humberside 51 E4 vil 4m/6km N of Beverley. TA 0145
Score Bay H'land 78 B2, B3 bay between Rubha Hunish and Ru Bornaskitaig, N coast of Skye. Also known as Lùb Score. NG 3973
Score Head Shetland 89 E7 headland at E end of island of Outer Score off N end of large island of Bressay. HU 5145
Scorrier Cornwall 2 C4 vil 2m/3km NE of Redruth. SW 7244
Scorriton Devon 4 D4* vil on E edge of Dartmoor 3m/4km NW of Buckfastleigh. SX 7068
Scorton Lancs 47 F3 vil 3m/4km N of Garstang. SD 5048
Scorton N Yorks 54 B4 vil 2m/3km E of Catterick Br. NZ 2500
Sco Ruston Norfolk 39 G3 loc 3m/5km N of Wroxham. TG 2821
Scotasay W Isles 88 B3* island in E Loch Tarbert, Harris, 3m/4km SE of Tarbert. NG 1897
Scotby Cumbria 60 A5 suburb 3m/4km E of Carlisle. NY 4455
Scotch Corner N Yorks 54 B4 loc and rd junction 4m/6km NE of Richmond. NZ 2105
Scotch Peter's Reservoir Gwent 15 F1* small resr 1m E of Tredegar. SO 1508
Scotforth Lancs 47 F2 dist of Lancaster 2km S of city centre. SD 4859
Scot Hay Staffs 42 D6* loc 3m/5km W of Newcastle-under-Lyme. SJ 7947
Scothern Lincs 45 E3 vil 5m/9km NE of Lincoln. TF 0377
Scotland Leics 36 A2* loc 4m/6km NE of Ashby de la Zouch. SK 3822
Scotland Lincs 37 E2* loc just W of Ingoldsby. TF 0030
Scotland End Oxon 27 G4* loc adjoining Hook Norton to W, 5m/7km NE of Chipping Norton. SP 3433
Scotland Gate Nthmb 61 G3* loc 2km N of Bedlington. NZ 2584
Scotland Street Suffolk 30 D4 loc adjoining Stoke-by-Nayland to E, 4m/7km SW of Hadleigh. TL 9936
Scotlandwell Tayside 73 E4 vil 4m/6km W of Leslie. NO 1801
Scot Lane End Gtr Manchester 42 B1* loc 2km SE of Blackrod. SD 6209
Scotney Castle Kent 12 C3 moated ruins of medieval and later manor hse in grnds of 19c mansion of same name, 1m E of Lamberhurst. NT property. TQ 6835
Scotsburn Grampian 82 A1/A2* loc 3m/5km E of Forres. Distillery to E. NJ 0860
Scotscalder H'land 86 D2 loc and rly stn in Caithness dist 8m/13km S of Thurso. ND 0956
Scots' Gap Nthmb 61 E3 ham 10m/16km W of Morpeth. NZ 0386
Scotstarvit Tower Fife. See Hill of Tarvit.
Scotstoun S'clyde 64 C2* dist of Glasgow on N bank of R Clyde 3m/5km NW of city centre. Shipbuilding yards, engineering, iron and motor works. **Scotstounhill** is loc to N. NS 5367
Scotstown H'land 74 A5 vil in Sunart, Lochaber dist, 2km N of Strontian. NM 8263
Scotstown Head Grampian 83 H2 headland at S end of Rattray Bay 4m/6km N of Peterhead. NK 1151
Scotswood Tyne & Wear 61 G5* dist of Newcastle 3m/5km W of city centre. NZ 2064
Scotter Lincs 44 D1 vil on R Eau 6m/10km S of Scunthorpe. SE 8800
Scotterthorpe Lincs 44 D1* ham 1m NW of Scotter. SE 8701
Scottish Marine Biological Station S'clyde. See Keppel Pier.
Scottlethorpe Lincs 37 F3 loc 3m/4km W of Bourne. TL 0520
Scotton Lincs 44 D2 vil 7m/12km S of Scunthorpe. SK 8899
Scotton N Yorks 49 E2 vil 2m/3km NW of Knaresborough. SE 3259
Scotton N Yorks 54 B5 vil on S side of Catterick Camp 4m/6km S of Richmond. SE 1995
Scottow Norfolk 39 F3 loc 4m/6km S of N Walsham. TG 2724
Scott Willoughby Lincs 37 F1 loc 5m/8km S of Sleaford. TF 0537
Scoughall Lothian 73 H5/H6* loc on rocky coast 4m/7km SE of N Berwick. NT 6381
Scoulton Norfolk 38 D4 vil 5m/8km NW of Attleborough. To N, **Scoulton Mere,** lake with wooded island. TF 9800
Scounslow Green Staffs 35 G2* loc 3m/4km S of Uttoxeter. SK 0929
Scourie H'land 84 B3 vil on W coast of Sutherland dist at head of **Scourie Bay,** 5m/8km W of Laxford Br. NC 1544
Scour Ouran H'land 80 A5 peak on Kintail Forest (NTS) in Skye and Lochalsh dist, 3m/5km SE of Shiel Br. One of the Five Sisters of Kintail, qv. Height 3505 ft or 1068 metres. Also known as Sgurr Fhuaran. NG 9716
Scousburgh Shetland 89 E8 vil near W coast of Mainland 6m/10km N of Sumburgh Hd. **Bay of Scousburgh** to NW. **Ward of Scousburgh,** hill to NE, attains height of 862 ft or 263 metres. HU 3717
Scout Dike Reservoir S Yorks 43 G1* resr 2km NW of Penistone. SE 2304
Scouthead Gtr Manchester 43 E1* loc 3m/4km E of Oldham. SD 9605
Scowles Glos 26 B6* loc 1m W of Coleford. SO 5610
Scraada Shetland. See Holes of Scraada.
Scrabster H'land 86 D1 vil and small port on W side of Thurso Bay 2m/3km NW of Thurso, Caithness dist. ND 1070
Scrafield Lincs 45 G4* loc 3m/5km E of Horncastle. TF 3068
Scrafton, East N Yorks 54 A6* loc 3m/5km SW of Middleham. SE 0884
Scrafton, West N Yorks 54 A6 vil 3m/5km S of Wensley. SE 0783
Scrainwood Nthmb 61 E1* loc 5m/8km NE of Alwinton. NT 9909
Scrane End Lincs 37 H1 ham 4m/7km SE of Boston. TF 3841
Scraptoft Leics 36 C4 vil 4m/6km E of Leicester. SK 6405
Scratby Norfolk 39 H3* vil and coastal resort 5m/8km N of Gt Yarmouth. TG 5015
Scrayingham N Yorks 50 C2 vil 3m/5km NE of Stamford Br. SE 7360
Scredington Lincs 37 F1 vil 4m/6km SE of Sleaford. TF 0940
Scremby Lincs 45 H4 vil 3m/5km E of Spilsby. TF 4467
Scremerston Nthmb 67 F4 vil 3m/4km S of Berwick-upon-Tweed. NU 0049
Screveton Notts 36 C1 vil 3m/5km NE of Bingham. SK 7343
Scrivelsby Lincs 45 F4 loc 2m/4km S of Horncastle. TF 2666
Scriven N Yorks 49 F2 vil 1m N of Knaresborough. SE 3458
Scrooby Notts 44 B2 vil 2km S of Bawtry. SK 6590
Scropton Derbys 35 G2 vil 2m/4km SE of Sudbury. SK 1930
Scrub Hill Lincs 45 F5 ham 2m/3km S of Coningsby. TF 2355
Scruton N Yorks 54 C5 vil 4m/6km NE of Bedale. SE 3092
Scuir of Eigg H'land 68 C1 basaltic peak on island of Eigg, 1291 ft or 393 metres. Highest point on island. Also known as An Sgurr or Sgurr of Eigg. NM 4684
Scuir Vuillin H'land 80 C2 mt on Strathconon Forest, Ross and Cromarty dist. Height 2845 ft or 867 metres. Also known as Sgurr a' Mhuilinn. NH 2655
Sculcoates Humberside 51 E5* dist of Hull 1m N of city centre. TA 0930
Sculptor's Cave Grampian 82 B1* cave on N coast of region, 3m/5km W of Lossiemouth. NJ 1871
Sculthorpe Norfolk 38 D2 vil 2m/3km NW of Fakenham. Airfield to W. TF 8930
Scunthorpe Humberside 44 D1 iron and steel mnfg tn 21m/33km E of Doncaster. Other industries include mnfre of building materials, tar distilling, light engineering. SE 8910
Scurdie Ness Tayside 77 G5 headland with lighthouse on S side of mouth of R South Esk, 2km E of Montrose. NO 7356
Scurlage W Glam 23 F6* loc on Gower peninsula 2m/3km N of Port Eynon Pt. SS 4687
Scurrival Point W Isles 88 D3 headland at N extremity of island of Barra. NF 6909
Scwd Einon Gam. See Sgwd Einion Gam.
Scwd-yr-Eira 15 E1 waterfall in R Hepste on border of Powys and Mid Glam 2km NW of Penderyn. (More correctly Sgwd-yr-Eira; also known as Upr Hepste Fall.) SN 9309
Sea Som 8 B3* loc 2km SW of Ilminster. ST 3412
Seaborough Dorset 8 C4 ham 2m/4km S of Crewkerne. ST 4206
Seabridge Staffs 42 D6* loc 2km SW of Newcastle-under-Lyme. SJ 8343
Seabrights, Great Essex 20 D2* loc 2m/3km S of Chelmsford. TL 7103
Seaburn Tyne & Wear 61 H5* loc on Whitburn Bay 2m/3km N of Sunderland tn centre. NZ 4060
Seacombe Merseyside 41 H2/H3* loc in S part of Wallasey. SJ 3190
Seacroft Lincs 45 H5* loc on coast 2m/3km S of Skegness. TF 5660
Seacroft W Yorks 49 F4 dist of Leeds 4m/7km E of city centre. SE 3635
Seadyke Lincs 37 H1* loc 2m/3km SE of Kirton. TF 3236
Seafar S'clyde 65 E2* residential area of Cumbernauld near tn centre. NS 7574
Seafield Lothian 65 F2 loc 2km E of Blackburn. NT 0066
Seafield S'clyde 64 B6 S dist of Ayr. NS 3320
Seafield Bay Suffolk 31 E4* bay on N side of R Stour estuary opp Mistley. TM 1233
Seaford E Sussex 12 B6 residential tn and resort on bay of same name 3m/5km SE of Newhaven. TV 4899
Seaforth Merseyside 41 H2 S dist of Crosby. SJ 3297
Seaforth Head W Isles 88 B2* locality at head of Loch Seaforth, Isle of Lewis, 3m/4km S of Balallan across Loch Erisort. NB 2916
Seaforth Island W Isles 88 B3* uninhabited island, over 2km by over 1km, rising sheer out of Loch Seaforth, Isle of Lewis, to a height of 713 ft or 217 metres. NB 2010
Seagrave Leics 36 C3 vil 5m/9km E of Loughborough. SK 6117
Seagry Heath Wilts 16 D3* loc 6m/9km NE of Chippenham. ST 9581
Seagry, Lower Wilts 16 D3 ham 5m/9km NE of Chippenham. ST 9581
Seagry, Upper Wilts 16 D3 vil 5m/8km NE of Chippenham. ST 9480
Seaham Durham 61 H6 coal port 5m/8km S of Sunderland. NZ 4249
Seaham Grange Durham 61 H6* loc 2km NW of Seaham. NZ 4051
Seahouses Nthmb 67 H5 former fishing vil now resort on North Sea coast 3m/5km SE of Bamburgh. Sands to N (NT). NU 2132
Seal Kent 20 B5 vil 2m/3km NE of Sevenoaks. **Seal Chart** loc 2km S. TQ 5556
Sealand Clwyd 42 A4 vil 4m/6km W of Chester. SJ 3568
Seale Surrey 11 E1 vil 4m/6km E of Farnham. SU 8947

Sea, Little Dorset 9 G5 lake 2km N of Studland between Studland Heath and the marshes S of Shell Bay. SZ 0384
Sealyham Dyfed 22 C3* loc 6m/9km S of Fishguard. Gives name to breed of terriers. SM 9627
Seamer N Yorks 54 D4 vil 2m/3km NW of Stokesley. NZ 4910
Seamer N Yorks 55 H6 vil 4m/6km SW of Scarborough. Site of Mesolithic settlement 2m/3km S. TA 0183
Seamill S'clyde 64 A4 summer resort on Firth of Clyde adjoining W Kilbride to S. NS 2047
Sea Mills Avon 16 B4* NW dist of Bristol. ST 5576
Seamore Tarn Cumbria 53 F2* small lake 3m/5km NE of Dufton. NY 7327
Seana Bhraigh H'land 85 C7 mt in Sutherland dist 4m/6km S of head of Loch an Daimh. Height 3040 ft or 927 metres. NH 2887
Sea Palling Norfolk 39 H2 vil and coastal resort 4m/7km SE of Happisburgh. TG 4226
Searby Lincs 45 E1 vil 4m/7km NW of Caistor. TA 0705
Seasalter Kent 21 F5 seaside loc at W end of Whitstable. TR 0965
Seascale Cumbria 52 A5 small tn and coastal resort 12m/19km S of Whitehaven. NY 0301
Seater H'land 86 F1* loc near N coast of Caithness dist 3m/5km W of Duncansby Hd. ND 3572
Seathorne Lincs 45 H4* coastal loc and resort 2m/3km N of Skegness. TF 5766
Seathwaite Cumbria 52 C4* loc in Borrowdale 2km SW of Seatoller. NY 2312
Seathwaite Cumbria 52 C5 ham in R Duddon valley 6m/9km N of Broughton in Furness. SD 2296
Seathwaite Tarn Cumbria 52 C5 mountain lake 3m/5km W of Coniston. SD 2598
Seatle Cumbria 52 D6* loc 2m/3km S of Newby Br. SD 3783
Seatoller Cumbria 52 C3 loc in Borrowdale 3m/5km S of Derwent Water at foot of Honister Pass. NY 2413
Seaton Cornwall 3 G3 vil on S coast 3m/5km E of Looe at mouth of r of same name which rises near Darite, N of Liskeard. SX 3054
Seaton Cumbria 52 A2 suburb 2m/3km NE of Workington. **High Seaton** loc adjoining to NE. NY 0130
Seaton Devon 8 B5 small resort at mouth of R Axe 6m/10km SW of Axminster. **Seaton Bay** extends from Beer Hd (W) to Culverhole Pt (E). SY 2490
Seaton Durham 61 H6* loc 2m/3km W of Seaham. **Seaton Bank Top,** loc 1km SW. NZ 3949
Seaton Humberside 51 F4 vil 3m/5km W of Hornsea. TA 1646
Seaton Leics 36 D4/37 E4 vil 3m/4km SE of Uppingham. SP 9098
Seaton Nthmb 61 G4* ham 1m W of North Sea coast at Seaton Sluice. Here is **Seaton Delaval Hall,** 18c hse by Vanbrugh. NZ 3276
Seaton Burn Tyne & Wear 61 G4 loc in coal-mining area 6m/10km N of Newcastle. NZ 2373
Seaton Carew Cleveland 54 D2 loc on North Sea coast 2m/3km S of Hartlepool. NZ 5229
Seaton Delaval Nthmb 61 G4 tn 4m/6km S of Blyth. Coal-mining. Hall at Seaton, qv. NZ 3075
Seaton Junction Devon 8 B4* ham at former rly junction 4m/7km N of Seaton. SY 2496
Seaton, North Nthmb 61 G3 loc 2km E of Ashington. **N Seaton Colliery** loc on N bank of R Wansbeck, 1km S. NZ 2986
Seaton Point Nthmb 61 G1* headland on North Sea coast 2m/3km NE of Alnmouth. NU 2612
Seaton Ross Humberside 50 C4 vil 6m/10km W of Mkt Weighton. SE 7841
Seaton Sluice Nthmb 61 G4/H4 loc on North Sea coast at mouth of Seaton Burn 3m/5km N of Whitley Bay. NZ 3376
Seaton Terrace Nthmb 61 G4* loc between Seaton Delaval and Holywell. NZ 3175
Seatown Grampian 82 B1* harbour dist of Lossiemouth. NJ 2370
Seave Green N Yorks 54 D5* ham 6m/9km SE of Stokesley. NZ 5601
Seaview Isle of Wight 10 C5* vil on NE coast 2m/4km E of Ryde. SZ 6291
Seaville Cumbria 59 F6 ham 2m/3km NW of Abbey Tn. NY 1553
Seavington St Mary Som 8 C3 vil 3m/4km E of Ilminster. ST 4014
Seavington St Michael Som 8 C3 vil 3m/5km E of Ilminster. ST 4015
Seavy Pond N Yorks 55 F5* small lake 2m/3km N of Levisham. SE 8393
Sebastopol Gwent 15 G2 loc in S part of Griffithstown, 2km S of Pontypool. ST 2898
Sebergham Cumbria 59 H6 vil on R Caldew 8m/12km SE of Wigton. **Sebergham Castle,** 18c hse 2m/3km NW. NY 3541
Seckington Warwicks 35 H4 vil 4m/6km NE of Tamworth. SK 2607
Sedbergh Cumbria 53 F5 small tn on N slope of R Rawther valley 9m/14km E of Kendal. Boys' boarding school. SD 6592
Sedbury Glos 16 B2* vil 1m E of Chepstow across R Wye. ST 5493
Sedbusk N Yorks 53 G5 ham 1m NE of Hawes across R Ure. SD 8891
Seddington Beds 29 F3* 1m S of Sandy. TL 1747
Sedgeberrow H & W 27 E4 vil 4m/6km S of Evesham. SP 0238
Sedgebrook Lincs 36 D1 vil 4m/6km W of Grantham. SK 8537
Sedgefield Durham 54 C2 vil 8m/13km NW of Stockton-on-Tees. Racecourse to SW. NZ 3528
Sedgeford Norfolk 38 C1 vil 4m/6km SE of Hunstanton. TF 7136
Sedgehill Wilts 9 F2 vil 3m/5km N of Shaftesbury. ST 8628
Sedgeletch Tyne & Wear 61 G6* loc in NW part of Houghton-le-Spring. NZ 3350
Sedgemere W Midlands 35 H6* loc 5m/8km NW of Kenilworth. SP 2275
Sedgemoor Som 8 B1, C1 marshy tract intersected by numerous dykes or *rhines* cut for drainage purposes, extending roughly from Bridgwater (W) to a line through Street and Somerton (E), and from Polden Hills (N) to R Parrett (S). Site of battle N of Westonzoyland, 1685. ST 33, 43
Sedgley W Midlands 35 E5 NW dist of Dudley. SO 9193
Sedgley Park Gtr Manchester 42 D1* loc in S part of Prestwich. SD 8202
Sedgwick Cumbria 53 E6 vil 4m/6km S of Kendal. SD 5187
Sedlescombe E Sussex 12 D5 vil 3m/4km NE of Battle. Vil of **Sedlescombe Street** 1km SE. The name Sedlescombe is usually applied to both places, which are virtually adjoining. TQ 7718
Seed Green Lancs 47 G4* loc 3m/4km E of Longridge. SD 6437
Seedley Gtr Manchester 42 D2* dist of Salford 2km W of tn centre. SJ 8098
Seend Wilts 17 D5 vil 4m/6km W of Devizes. 1m W, vil of **Seend Cleeve.** ST 9461
Seer Green Bucks 18 D2 vil 2m/3km NE of Beaconsfield. SU 9691
Seething Norfolk 39 G5 vil 5m/9km N of Bungay. TM 3197
Sefton Merseyside 42 A2 vil 3m/5km NE of Crosby. **Sefton Town** loc 1km SW. SD 3501
Sefton 116 admin dist of Merseyside metropolitan county.
Segelocum Notts. See Littleborough.
Seghill Nthmb 61 G4 loc in coal-mining area 6m/10km NW of Tynemouth. NZ 2874
Segontium Gwynedd. See Caernarvon.
Seighford Staffs 35 E2 vil 3m/5km NW of Stafford. Airfield to W. SJ 8824
Seil S'clyde 70 A3 island on E side of Firth of Lorn connected with mainland of Argyll by Clachan Br, qv. Island is 5m/7km long N to S and 2m/3km wide. **Seil Sound** is strait between island and mainland. NM 7617
Seilebost W Isles 88 A3 loc on Harris 2km NE of Borvemore. NG 0696
Seion Gwynedd 40 C4 ham 4m/6km SW of Bangor. SH 5467
Seiont 40 B5* r rising near Llandeiniolen, Gwynedd, and flowing SW and then N into Menai Strait on W side of Caernarvon. SH 4762
Seisdon Staffs 35 E5 vil 5m/9km SW of Wolverhampton. SO 8394
Selattyn Salop 34 A1 vil 3m/5km NW of Oswestry. SJ 2633
Selborne Hants 10 D2 vil 4m/6km SE of Alton. Setting of Gilbert White's *Natural History of Selborne*, as is **Selborne Hill** (NT), 1km W. SU 7433
Selby N Yorks 50 B5 tn on R Ouse 13m/20km S of York. Abbey ch. 18c toll br. Flour mills. Coalfield in vicinity. Canal connects R Ouse here with R Aire to SW. SE 6132
Selham W Sussex 11 F3 vil 3m/5km E of Midhurst. SU 9320
Selhurst London 19 G4 loc in borough of Croydon 2km N of Croydon tn centre. TQ 3267
Selkirk Borders 66 C5 woollen-mnfg tn on hill above Ettrick Water, 9m/15km N of Hawick. Other industries include sawmilling, tanning. Tn has associations with Sir Walter Scott, and with Mungo Park, the African explorer. Centre for touring the Borders. NT 4728
Sellack H & W 26 B4* vil 3m/4km NW of Ross-on-Wye. SO 5627
Sellafirth Shetland 89 E5/F5 loc on Yell 3m/5km NW of Burra Ness. HU 5198
Sellick's Green Som 8 A3* ham 4m/6km S of Taunton. ST 2119
Sellindge Kent 13 F3 vil 5m/8km NW of Hythe. 1m E, vil of **Sellindge Lees.** TR 0938
Selling Kent 21 F6 vil 3m/5km SE of Sittingbourne. TR 0456
Sells Green Wilts 16 D5* ham 3m/5km E of Melksham. ST 9562
Selly Oak W Midlands 35 F6 dist of Birmingham 3m/5km SW of city centre. SP 0482
Selmeston E Sussex 12 B5 vil under S Downs 3m/4km N of Alfriston. TQ 5006
Selsdon London 20 A5 loc in borough of Croydon 3m/5km SE of Croydon tn centre. TQ 3562
Selset Reservoir Durham 53 H3* resr in course of R Lune 3m/5km SW of Middleton in Teesdale. NY 9121
Selsey Glos 16 D1* vil 2km SW of Stroud. SO 8303
Selsey W Sussex 11 E5 seaside resort extending along coast and inland from **Selsey Bill,** headland on English Channel 8m/13km S of Chichester. SZ 8593
Selside Cumbria 53 E5 loc 4m/7km N of Kendal. Hall dates from 14c. SD 5399
Selside N Yorks 48 B1 ham 3m/5km NW of Horton in Ribblesdale. SD 7875
Selsmore Hants 10 D5* loc in S Hayling on Hayling I. SZ 7398
Selstead Kent 13 G3 ham 6m/9km N of Folkestone. TR 2144
Selston Notts 44 A5 vil 3m/5km SW of Kirkby in Ashfield. **Selston Green** loc adjoining to W. SK 4653
Selwicks Bay Humberside 51 G2* small bay on N side of Flamborough Hd. TA 2570
Selworthy Som 7 G1 vil, largely NT, 2m/3km E of Porlock. To N, Selworthy Beacon (NT), 1013 ft or 309 metres, commanding view over Bristol Channel. SS 9146
Sem 9 F2* stream rising in Wiltshire near Dorset border to E of Shaftesbury and flowing E into R Nadder 2m/3km SW of Tisbury. ST 9227
Semer Suffolk 31 E3 ham 3m/5km NW of Hadleigh. TM 0046
Semere Green Norfolk 39 F6* loc 2km SW of Pulham Mkt. TM 1884
Semer Water N Yorks 53 H6 lake 2m/3km SW of Bainbridge. SD 9287
Semington Wilts 16 D5 vil 2m/3km S of Melksham. ST 8960
Semington Brook 16 D5* r originating in divers streams in the Devizes and Mkt Lavington areas in Wiltshire and flowing W into R Avon between Melksham and Trowbridge. ST 8861
Semley Wilts 9 F2 vil 3m/5km NE of Shaftesbury. ST 8926
Sempringham Lincs 37 F2 loc 8m/13km N of Bourne. Remains of Gilbertine monastery. Earthworks of former vil to NW. TF 1032
Sence 35 H4 r rising on W slopes of Charnwood Forest, Leics, and flowing SW into R Anker 1m NE of Atherstone. SP 3199
Sence 36 B4 r rising near Billesdon, Leics, and flowing SW then W into R Soar at Enderby, SW of Leicester. SP 5598
Send Surrey 19 E5 vil 3m/4km SE of Woking. TQ 0255
Sendmarsh Surrey 19 E5 loc 5m/8km NE of Guildford. TQ 0455
Senghennydd Mid Glam 15 F2/F3 vil in coal-mining dist 4m/6km NW of Caerphilly. ST 1190
Sennen Cornwall 2 A5 vil to E of Land's End. **Sennen Cove** vil to NW on coast. SW 3525
Senni 25 E5 r rising on Fforest Fawr, Powys, and flowing N into R Usk at Sennybridge. SN 9228
Sennybridge (Pontsenni) Powys 25 E5 vil at confluence of Rs Senni and Usk 8m/12km W of Brecon. Slight remains of Castell du, 14c stronghold, to W. SN 9228
Serlby Notts 44 B2 ham 2km NE of Blyth. SK 6389
Serpent's Mound S'clyde 70 B2 heap of large stones, supposedly a relic of pagan worship, about 300 ft or 90 metres long, near foot of Loch Nell in Argyll, 2m/4km SE of Oban. NM 8726
Serrington Wilts 9 G1 loc across R Till from Stapleford and 4m/7km NW of Wilton. SU 0637
Sessay N Yorks 49 F1 vil 4m/6km E of Topcliffe. **Lit Sessay** ham 1km SE. SE 4575
Setchey Norfolk 38 B3 ham 4m/6km S of King's Lynn. Site of Roman bldg to N. TF 6313
Setley Hants 10 A4* loc 2km S of Brockenhurst on edge of New Forest. SU 3000
Seton Mains Lothian 66 C1 loc 3m/4km E of Prestonpans. NT 4275
Settascarth Orkney 89 B6* loc on Mainland 3m/5km N of Finstown. HY 3513
Settle N Yorks 48 B2 tn on R Ribble 13m/21km NW of Skipton. SD 8163
Settrington N Yorks 50 D2 vil 3m/5km E of Malton. SE 8370
Seumas Cleite W Isles 88 C4* islet at entrance to Loch Leurbost, E coast of Lewis. NB 4123
Seven 55 F6 r rising on Cleveland Hills 5m/7km NW of Rosedale Abbey, N Yorks, and flowing S into R Rye 1km SE of Brawby. SE 7477
Seven Ash Som 8 A1* ham 1m W of W Bagborough. ST 1533
Seven Bridges Wilts 17 F2* loc 2km SE of Cricklade. Site of Roman bldg. SU 1192
Sevenhampton Glos 27 E5 vil 5m/9km E of Cheltenham. SP 0321
Sevenhampton Wilts 17 F3 vil 2km S of Highworth. SU 2090
Seven Kings London 20 B3* NE dist of Ilford in borough of Redbridge. TQ 4587
Sevenoaks Kent 20 B6 largely residential tn on outlier of N Downs 2lm/34km SE of London. TQ 5255
Sevenoaks Weald Kent 20 B6 vil 3m/4km S of Sevenoaks. TQ 5350
Seven Sisters E Sussex 12 B6* chalk cliffs on English Channel coast between Cuckmere Haven and Birling Gap, W of Beachy Hd. Cliffs and downs behind (partly NT), together with Cuckmere Haven, comprise the **Seven Sisters Country Park.** TV 5396
Seven Sisters (Blaendulais) W Glam 14 D1 vil 8m/13km NE of Neath. SN 8208
Seven Springs Glos 27 E5 loc at crossroads 4m/6km S of Cheltenham. SO 9617
Seven Star Green Essex 30 D5* loc 4m/6km W of Colchester. TL 9325
Severn (Hafren) 16 A3 r rising on Plynlimon in Cambrian Mts and flowing into Bristol Channel. Length about 180m/290km. Tidal to Maisemore, NW of Gloucester. ST 37
Severn Beach Avon 16 B3 vil on R Severn estuary 8m/13km NW of Bristol. ST 5485
Severn Stoke H & W 26 D3 vil on E side of R Severn 7m/11km S of Worcester. SO 8544
Sevick End Beds 29 E2* loc 4m/7km NE of Bedford. TL 0954

Sevington Kent 13 F3* vil 2m/3km SE of Ashford. TR 0340

Sewards End Essex 30 B4 vil 2m/3km E of Saffron Walden. TL 5738

Sewardstone Essex 20 A2 loc 2m/3km S of Waltham Abbey. TQ 3897

Sewerby Humberside 51 F2 vil adjoining Bridlington to NE. TA 1968

Seworgan Cornwall 2 C5* ham 4m/6km NE of Helston. SW 7030

Sewstern Leics 36 D2 vil 3m/5km SW of Colsterworth. SK 8821

Sexhow N Yorks 54 D4 loc 3m/5km SW of Stokesley. NZ 4706

Seymour Villas Devon 6 D1* loc just E of Woolacombe and 4m/6km SW of Ilfracombe. SS 4644

Sezincote Glos 27 F4 loc 2m/4km W of Moreton-in-Marsh. **Sezincote Hse,** early 19c hse in Indian style. SP 1730

Sgairneach Mhór Tayside 75 F4* mt 3m/5km W of Dalnaspidal Lodge. Height 3160 ft or 963 metres. NN 5972

Sgaraman nam Fiadh H'land 75 F1 mt in Monadhliath range in Inverness dist 8m/12km NW of Newtonmore. Height 2805 ft or 855 metres. NH 6106

Sgeir a' Chaisteil Treshnish Isles, S'clyde 68 B4 one of the islands of the group, lying immediately N of Lunga. NM 2742

Sgeir an Bhuic H'land 84 E2* rock island at mouth of Loch Eriboll, N coast of Sutherland dist, 2m/3km SE of Rispond. NC 4763

Sgeir an Eirionnaich Treshnish Isles, S'clyde 68 B4* island of the group lying 1km NE of Lunga and 1km W of Fladda. NM 2843

Sgeir an Fheòir Treshnish Isles, S'clyde 68 B4* small island of the group, lying between Fladda and Lunga. NM 2843

Sgeirean nan Torran H'land 74 B5* group of island rocks near W shore of Loch Linnhe, nearly 2m/3km SW of Inversanda Bay, Lochaber dist. NM 9356

Sgeir Eirin H'land 78 C3 rock island off NE coast of Skye 4m/6km SE of Rubha na h-Aiseig. NG 4872

Sgeir na Capaill H'land 78 B3* one of the Ascrib Is., qv.

Sgeir na h-Iolaire Treshnish Isles, S'clyde 68 B4 small island of the group, to W of Fladda. NM 2843

Sgeir nan Gillean H'land 74 A5* island rock near W shore of Loch Linnhe off Rubha na h-Earba, 3m/5km NE of Rubha na h-Airde Uinnsinn, Lochaber dist. NM 9054

Sgeir Shuas Skye, H'land 78 D3 rock lying off N end of island of Rona. NG 6261

Sgeir Toman W Isles (W of 88 A2) one of the Flannan Isles, qv. Sgeir Toman lies 1m S of the main island, Eilean Mór. NA 7245

Sger, Y Welsh form of Sker (Pt), qv.

Sgethrog Welsh form of Scethrog, qv.

Sgitheach H'land. R in Ross and Cromarty dist. See Skiack.

Sgiwen Welsh form of Skewen, qv.

Sgorr an Dubh Mór H'land 76 A1 mt at W end of Cairngorms in Badenoch and Strathspey dist, 6m/9km SE of Kincraig. Height 3645 ft or 1111 metres. NH 9000

Sgorr Choinnich 75 E4* peak on border of Highland and Tayside regions 2m/4km E of Loch Ossian. Height 3047 ft or 929 metres. NN 4468

Sgorr Dhearg H'land 74 B5/C5 peak of Beinn a' Bheithir in Lochaber dist 2m/4km S of Ballachulish. Height 3361 ft or 1024 metres. NN 0555

Sgorr Gaibhre 75 E4 mt on border of Highland and Tayside regions 4m/7km SW of Ben Alder. Height 3134 ft or 955 metres. NN 4467

Sgorr Gaoith H'land 75 A2 mt at W end of Cairngorms in Badenoch and Strathspey dist, 6m/10km SE of Kincraig. Height 3668 ft or 1118 metres. NN 9098

Sgorr na Ciche H'land 74 C5 mt in Lochaber dist nearly 2m/3km E of foot of Glen Coe. Height 2430 ft or 741 metres. Also known as Pap of Glencoe. NN 1259

Sgorr na h-Ulaidh H'land 74 C6 mt in Lochaber dist near border with Strathclyde region, 5m/7km S of foot of Glen Coe. Height 3258 ft or 993 metres. NN 1151

Sgorr nam Fiannaidh H'land 74 C5* summit of Aonach Eagach in Lochaber dist, at W end of ridge. Height 3173 ft or 967 metres. NN 1458

Sgorr Ruadh H'land 80 A3 mt in Ross and Cromarty dist 3m/5km NW of Achnashellach Lodge. Height 3148 ft or 960 metres. NG 9550

Sguman Coinntich H'land 80 A4 mt in Killilan Forest, Skye and Lochalsh dist. Height 2883 ft or 879 metres. NG 9730

Sgurr a' Bhac H'land 80 A6* peak on border of Lochaber and Skye & Lochalsh dists 3m/5km N of Kinloch Hourn and 1m E of Sgurr na Sgine. Height 2802 ft or 854 metres. NG 9610

Sgurr a' Bhealaich Dheirg H'land 80 B6 mt on Kintail Forest (NTS), in Skye and Lochalsh dist up against border with Inverness dist, 3m/4km NW of head of Loch Cluanie. Height 3406 ft or 1038 metres. NH 0314

Sgurr a' Choire-bheithe H'land 74 A4 peak at W end of Druim Chòsaidh, qv, in Lochaber dist. Height 2994 ft or 913 metres. NG 8901

Sgurr a' Choire Ghlais H'land 80 C3 peak on border of Inverness and Ross & Cromarty dists 4m/7km NE of dam of Loch Monar. Height 3554 ft or 1083 metres. NH 2543

Sgurr a' Ghlas Leathaid H'land 80 C2* mt on Strathconon Forest, Ross and Cromarty dist. Height 2778 ft or 847 metres. NH 2456

Sgurr a' Ghreadaidh Skye, H'land 79 C6* one of the peaks of the Cuillin Hills, to N of Sgurr Alasdair. Height 3192 ft or 973 metres. NG 4423

Sgurr Alasdair Skye, H'land 79 C6 highest peak of the Cuillin Hills, due E of mt rescue post at foot of Glen Brittle. Height 3257 ft or 993 metres. NG 4520

Sgurr a' Mhaim H'land 74 C4 mt in Lochaber dist, on Mamore Forest S of Glen Nevis. Height 3601 ft or 1098 metres. NN 1666

Sgurr a' Mhaoraich H'land 74 B1 peak in Lochaber dist 2m/3km E of Kinloch Hourn. Height 3369 ft or 1027 metres. NG 9806

Sgurr a' Mhuilinn H'land 80 C2 mt on Strathconon Forest, Ross and Cromarty dist. Height 2845 ft or 867 metres. Also known as Scuir Vuillin. NH 2655

Sgurr an Airgid H'land 80 A5 mt in Skye and Lochalsh dist 1m N of head of Loch Duich. Height 2757 ft or 840 metres. NG 9422

Sgurr an Chaorachain H'land 80 B3 peak on W Monar Forest, Ross and Cromarty dist. Height 3455 ft or 1053 metres. NH 0844

Sgurr an Fhuarail H'land 80 B6* mt on border of Inverness and Skye & Lochalsh dists 2m/3km N of head of Loch Cluanie. Height 3241 ft or 988 metres. NH 0513

Sgurr an Fhuarain H'land 74 B2 mt in Lochaber dist between Loch Quoich and head of Glen Kingie. Height 2961 ft or 903 metres. NM 9897

Sgurr an Gharaidh H'land 80 A3 peak in Ross and Cromarty dist 3m/5km N of Lochcarron. Height 2396 ft or 730 metres. NG 8844

Sgurr an Ghreadaidh Skye, H'land 79 C6* a peak of the Cuillin Hills. Height 3192 ft or 973 metres. NG 4423

Sgurr an Lochain H'land 80 B6 peak on border of Lochaber and Skye & Lochalsh dists, 4m/7km N of Loch Quoich at foot of Glen Quoich. Height 3294 ft or 1004 metres. NH 0010

Sgurr an Mhadaidh Skye, H'land 79 C6* a peak of the Cuillin Hills. Height 3014 ft or 919 metres. NG 4523

Sgurr an Utha H'land 74 A3 peak in Lochaber dist 2m/4km NW of Glenfinnan. Height 2610 ft or 796 metres. NM 8883

Sgurr Bàn H'land 80 A2* one of the peaks of Beinn Eighe, Ross and Cromarty dist. Height 3188 ft or 971 metres. NG 9759

Sgurr Ban H'land 85 B8 mt in W part of Ross and Cromarty dist 3m/4km NE of Lochan Fada. Height 3244 ft or 989 metres. NH 0574

Sgurr Beag H'land 74 B2* peak in Lochaber dist 2m/3km SE of head of Loch Quoich and 1km SW of Sgurr Mór. Height 2890 ft or 881 metres. NM 9597

Sgurr Beag H'land 80 A6* peak on border of Lochaber and Skye & Lochalsh dists 4m/7km NE of Kinloch Hourn. Height 2926 ft or 892 metres. NG 9910

Sgurr Chòinich H'land 74 C2 mt in Lochaber dist 5m/8km NW of foot of Loch Arkaig. Height 2450 ft or 747 metres. NN 1295

Sgurr Choinnich H'land 80 B3* peak on W Monar Forest, Ross and Cromarty dist. Height 3276 ft or 999 metres. NH 0744

Sgurr Chòinnich Mór H'land 74 D4 mt in Lochaber dist 4m/6km E of Ben Nevis. Height 3594 ft or 1095 metres. NN 2271

Sgurr Coire Choinnichean H'land 79 F7 mt in Knoydart, Lochaber dist, 2m/3km NE of Inverie. Height 2612 ft or 796 metres. NG 7901

Sgurr Coire nan Eun H'land 80 C3 mt in Ross and Cromarty dist 5m/8km N of lower end of Loch Monar. Height 2581 ft or 787 metres. NH 1946

Sgurr Dearg Skye, H'land 79 C6 a peak of the Cuillin Hills. Height 3234 ft or 986 metres. NG 4421

Sgurr Dhomhnuill H'land 74 A4 mt in Ardgour, Lochaber dist, 6m/10km NE of Strontian. Height 2915 ft or 888 metres. NM 8867

Sgurr Dubh H'land 80 A2 peak in Coulin Forest, Ross and Cromarty dist, 5m/8km SW of Kinlochewe. Height 2566 ft or 782 metres. NG 9755

Sgurr Dubh Mór Skye, H'land 79 C6* a peak of the Cuillin Hills. Height 3096 ft or 944 metres. NG 4520

Sgurr Eilde Mór H'land 74 D4 mt on Mamore Forest in Lochaber dist 4m/6km NE of Kinlochleven. Height 3307 ft or 1008 metres. NN 2365

Sgurr Fhuaran H'land 80 A5 peak on Kintail Forest (NTS) in Skye and Lochalsh dist, 3m/5km SE of Shiel Br. One of the Five Sisters of Kintail, qv. Height 3505 ft or 1068 metres. Also known as Scour Ouran. NG 9716

Sgurr Fhuar-thuill H'land 80 C3* mt on border of Inverness and Ross & Cromarty dists 4m/6km NE of dam of Loch Monar. Height 3439 ft or 1048 metres. NH 2343

Sgurr Fiona H'land 85 B7 one of the peaks of An Teallach, qv, in Ross and Cromarty dist. Height 3474 ft or 1059 metres. NH 0683

Sgurr Ghiubhsachain H'land 74 A4* mt in Lochaber dist 4m/6km S of Glenfinnan. Height 2784 ft or 849 metres. NM 8775

Sgurr Leac nan Each H'land 80 A6* peak on border of Lochaber and Skye & Lochalsh dists 4m/6km S of Shiel Br and 1m W of The Saddle. Height 3013 ft or 918 metres. NG 9113

Sgurr Mhic Bharraich H'land 80 A5 mt on border of Lochaber and Skye & Lochalsh dists 2m/3km SW of Shiel Br. Height 2553 ft or 778 metres. NG 9117

Sgurr Mhór H'land A peak of Beinn Alligin, qv.

Sgurr Mhurlagain H'land 74 B2 mt in Lochaber dist 3m/4km NE of head of Loch Arkaig. Height 2885 ft or 879 metres. NN 0194

Sgurr Mór H'land 74 B2 peak in Lochaber dist between Loch Quoich and head of Glen Kingie. Height 3290 ft or 1003 metres. NM 9698

Sgurr Mór H'land 85 C8 mt in Ross and Cromarty dist 4m/6km NE of head of Loch Fannich. Height 3641 ft or 110 metres. NH 2071

Sgurr na Ba Glaise H'land 68 F2 mt in Moidart, Lochaber dist, 3m/5km S of Lochailort. Height 2817 ft or 859 metres. NM 7777

Sgurr na Banachdich Skye, H'land 79 C6 a peak of the Cuillin Hills. Height 3167 ft or 965 metres. NG 4422

Sgurr na Carnach H'land 80 A5/A6* peak on Kintail Forest (NTS) in Skye and Lochalsh dist, 3m/5km SE of Shiel Br. One of the Five Sisters of Kintail, qv. Height 3287 ft or 1002 metres. NG 9715

Sgurr na Ciche H'land 74 A2 mt in Lochaber dist 3m/4km SW of head of Loch Quoich. Height 3410 ft or 1040 metres. NM 9096

Sgurr na Ciste Duibhe H'land 80 A6 peak on Kintail Forest (NTS) in Skye and Lochalsh dist, 4m/6km SE of Shiel Br. One of the Five Sisters of Kintail, qv. Height 3370 ft or 1027 metres. NG 9814

Sgurr na Coinnich Skye, H'land 79 F6 mt 3m/4km S of Kyleakin near E end of island. Height 2424 ft or 739 metres. NG 7622

Sgurr na Fearstaig H'land 80 C3* peak on border of Inverness and Ross & Cromarty dists 3m/5km N of dam of Loch Monar. Height 3326 ft or 1014 metres. NH 2243

Sgurr na Feartaig H'land 80 B3 mt ridge on Achnashellach Forest, Ross and Cromarty dist. Summit 2830 ft or 863 metres. NH 0545

Sgurr na h-Aide H'land 74 A2 mt in Lochaber dist 2m/3km NE of head of Loch Morar. Height 2818 ft or 859 metres. NM 8893

Sgurr na Lapaich H'land 80 C4 mt on border of Inverness and Ross & Cromarty dists 5m/7km NW of dam of Loch Mullardoch. Height 3775 ft or 1151 metres. NH 1635

Sgurr na Lapaich H'land 80 C5 peak in Inverness dist 1m N of Loch Affric. Height 3401 ft or 1037 metres. NH 1524

Sgurr na Moraich H'land 80 A5 peak on Kintail Forest (NTS) in Skye and Lochalsh dist, 2m/3km E of Shiel Br. One of the Five Sisters of Kintail, qv. Height 2870 ft or 875 metres. NG 9619

Sgurr na Muice H'land 80 C3 mt on border of Inverness and Ross & Cromarty dists 2m/4km NE of dam of Loch Monar. Height 2915 ft or 888 metres. NH 2241

Sgurr nan Ceanraichean H'land 80 B3* peak on Glencarron Forest, Ross and Cromarty dist. Height 2986 ft or 910 metres. NH 0848

Sgurr nan Clach Geala H'land 85 C8 mt in Ross and Cromarty dist 3m/5km NE of head of Loch Fannich. Height 3586 ft or 1093 metres. NH 1871

Sgurr nan Coireachan H'land 74 A3 mt in Lochaber dist 3m/4km SE of head of Loch Morar. Height 3136 ft or 956 metres. NM 9088

Sgurr nan Coireachan H'land 74 B2 peak in Lochaber dist 2m/4km S of head of Loch Quoich. Height 3125 ft or 953 metres. NM 9395

Sgurr nan Conbhairean H'land 80 B6 peak on border of Inverness and Skye & Lochalsh dists 4m/7km NW of dam of Loch Cluanie. Height 3642 ft or 1110 metres. NH 1213

Sgurr nan Each H'land 80 C1* mt in Ross and Cromarty dist 2m/3km NE of head of Loch Fannich. Height 3026 ft or 922 metres. NH 1869

Sgurr nan Eag Skye, H'land 79 C6* one of the peaks of the Cuillin Hills, near S end of range. Height 3031 ft or 924 metres. NG 4519

Sgurr nan Eugallt H'land 74 A2/B2* peak in Lochaber dist 2m/3km SW of Kinloch Hourn. Height 2934 ft or 894 metres. NG 9304

Sgurr nan Gillean Skye, H'land 79 C6 a peak of the Cuillin Hills. Height 3167 ft or 965 metres. NG 4725

Sgurr nan Gobhar Skye, H'land 79 C6* one of the peaks of the Cuillin Hills, at W end of range. Height 2047 ft or 624 metres. NG 4222

Sgurr nan Saighead H'land 80 A5* peak on Kintail Forest (NTS) in Skye and Lochalsh dist, 2m/4km SE of Shiel Br. One of the Five Sisters of Kintail, qv. Height 3050 ft or 929 metres. NG 9717

Sgurr na Ruaidhe H'land. See Sgurr Ruadh.

Sgurr na Sgine H'land 80 A6 peak on border of Lochaber and Skye & Lochalsh dists 3m/5km N of Kinloch Hourn. Height 3098 ft or 944 metres. NG 9411

Sgurr Ruadh H'land 80 C3 mt on border of Inverness and Ross & Cromarty dists 4m/7km SW of head of Orrin Resr. Height 3254 ft or 992 metres. Also known as Sgurr na Ruaidhe. NH 2842

Sgurr Sgiath Airigh H'land 74 A1 peak in Lochaber dist 2m/3km SW of Kinloch Hourn. Height 2890 ft or 881 metres. NG 9205

Sgurr Sgumain Skye, H'land 79 C6* a peak of the Cuillin Hills. Height 3108 ft or 947 metres. NG 4420

Sgurr Thuilm H'land 74 B3 mt in Lochaber dist 4m/6km SW of head of Loch Arkaig. Height 3160 ft or 963 metres. NM 9387

Sgurr Thuilm Skye, H'land 79 C6 a peak of the Cuillin Hills. Height 2885 ft or 879 metres. NG 4324

Sgwd Einion Gam 14 D1/15 E1* waterfall on tributary of R Neath, on border of Powys and W Glam, 1m N of Pontneathvaughan. SN 8909

Sgwd-yr-Eira. See Scwd-yr-Eira.
Shabbington Bucks 18 B1 vil 3m/4km NW of Thame. SP 6606
Shackerley Salop 35 E4 ham 4m/7km E of Shifnal. SJ 8106
Shackerstone Leics 36 A4 vil 6m/10km S of Ashby de la Zouch. SK 3706
Shackleford Surrey 11 F1 vil 3m/4km NW of Godalming. SU 9345
Shackleton W Yorks 48 C5* loc 2m/3km N of Hebden Br. SD 9829
Shacklewell London 19 G3* loc in borough of Hackney 4m/7km NE of Charing Cross. TQ 3385
Shade W Yorks 48 C5* loc adjoining Todmorden to SW. SD 9323
Shader W Isles 88 B1* r in N part of Lewis running NW into Atlantic Ocean 1km W of Lr Shader, between Barvas and Borve. NB 3754
Shader, Upper and **Lower** W Isles 88 B1* adjacent vils near NW coast of Lewis between Barvas and Borve. NB 3854
Shadforth Durham 54 C1 vil 5m/7km E of Durham. NZ 3441
Shadingfield Suffolk 39 H6 vil 4m/7km S of Beccles. TM 4384
Shadoxhurst Kent 13 E3 vil 4m/7km SW of Ashford. TQ 9737
Shadsworth Lancs 48 A5 loc in Blackburn 2m/3km E of tn centre. SD 7027
Shadwell London 20 A3* loc in borough of Tower Hamlets 2km E of Tower Br. TQ 3580
Shadwell Norfolk 38 D6 ham on S bank of R Thet 4m/7km E of Thetford. 19c hse in park with large lake to W. TL 9383
Shadwell W Yorks 49 E4 loc in Leeds 5m/8km NE of city centre. SE 3439
Shaftenhoe End Herts 29 G4* ham 4m/6km SE of Royston. TL 4037
Shaftesbury Dorset 9 F2 small tn on hillside overlooking Blackmoor Vale, 18m/29km W of Salisbury. ST 8622
Shaftholme S Yorks 44 B1* loc 1km N of Arksey. SE 5708
Shafton S Yorks 43 H1 vil 4m/7km NE of Barnsley. Includes loc of **Shafton Two Gates.** SE 3910
Shaggs Dorset 9 F5 loc 2m/4km S of Wool. SY 8583
Shakerley Gtr Manchester 42 C1* loc adjoining Tyldesley to N. SD 6903
Shakespeare Cliff Kent 13 H3 high chalk cliff on coast 2km SW of Dover. TR 3039
Shalbourne Wilts 17 G5 vil 4m/6km SW of Hungerford. SU 3163
Shalcombe Isle of Wight 10 B6* loc 4m/6km SE of Yarmouth. SZ 3985
Shalden Hants 10 D1 vil 2m/4km NW of Alton. Loc of **Shalden Green** 1m N. SU 6941
Shaldon Devon 5 E3 small resort on S side of R Teign estuary. Br connects with Teignmouth. SX 9372
Shalfleet Isle of Wight vil 4m/6km E of Yarmouth. SZ 4189
Shalford Essex 30 C5 vil 5m/7km NW of Braintree. TL 7229
Shalford Surrey 11 F1 vil adjoining Guildford to S. 18c water-mill (NT). TQ 0047
Shalford Green Essex 30 B5 ham 4m/7km NW of Braintree. TL 7127
Shalloch on Minnoch S'clyde 56 D4 mt 9m/14km S of Straiton. Height 2522 ft or 769 metres. NX 4090
Shallowford Staffs 35 E2* loc 1m S of Norton Br. SJ 8729
Shalmsford Street Kent 21 F6 vil 4m/6km SW of Canterbury. TR 0954
Shalstone Bucks 28 B4 vil 4m/6km E of Brackley. SP 6436
Shalver Gtr Manchester 43 E1* loc in Oldham 2m/3km NE of tn centre. SD 9407
Shamley Green Surrey 11 F1 vil 4m/7km SE of Guildford. TQ 0343
Shandon S'clyde locality with shipbreaking yards on E shore of Gare Loch, 3m/5km S of Garelochhead. NS 2586
Shandwick H'land 87 B8* loc on **Shandwick Bay,** E coast of Ross and Cromarty dist, 1km S of Balintore. NH 8575
Shangton Leics 36 C4 vil 6m/9km N of Mkt Harborough. SP 7196
Shankhouse Nthmb 61 G4 loc 3m/5km SW of Blyth. NZ 2778
Shanklin Isle of Wight 10 C6 resort on Sandown Bay 7m/11km SE of Newport, and 2m/3km SW of Sandown, to which it is joined physically and administratively. SZ 5881
Shap Cumbria 53 E3 small tn 9m/15km S of Penrith. **Shap Summit** highest point on London (Euston) to Carlisle rly line 3m/4km S. **Shap Abbey** (A.M.), remains of 13c–16c monastery 1m W. NY 5615
Shapinsay Orkney 89 B6 low-lying island of 10 sq miles or 26 sq km lying to N and E of Mainland, its SW corner being 1m N of Car Ness across strait known as The String, at W end of **Shapinsay Sound.** HY 51
Shapridge Glos 26 B5* loc 2m/3km NE of Cinderford. SO 6716
Shapwick Dorset 9 F4 vil on R Stour 5m/7km SE of Blandford Forum. ST 9301
Shapwick Som 8 C1 vil on N side of Polden Hills 5m/8km W of Glastonbury. ST 4138
Sharcott Wilts 17 F5* loc 2km SW of Pewsey. SU 1559
Shardeloes Bucks 18 D2 hse by Robert Adam with large park and lake 2km W of Amersham. SU 9397
Shard End W Midlands 35 G5* loc in Birmingham 6m/9km E of city centre. SP 1588
Shardlow Derbys 36 A2 vil 6m/10km SE of Derby. Situated on R Trent and on Trent & Mersey Canal. SK 4330
Shareshill Staffs 35 F4 vil 5m/9km NE of Wolverhampton. SJ 9406
Sharkham Point Devon 5 E5 headland at S end of St Mary's Bay 2km SE of Brixham. SX 9354
Sharlston W Yorks 49 F6 vil 4m/7km E of Wakefield. **Sharlston Common** loc to NW. See also New Sharlston. Coal-mining dist. SE 3918
Sharman's Cross W Midlands 35 G6* loc in Solihull 2km W of tn centre. SP 1379
Sharnal Street Kent 20 D4* loc 5m/8km NE of Strood. TQ 7974
Sharnbrook Beds 29 E2 vil 7m/12km NW of Bedford. SP 9959
Sharneyford Lancs 48 B5* loc 2km NE of Bacup. SD 8824
Sharnford Leics 36 B5 vil 4m/6km SE of Hinckley. SP 4891
Sharnhill Green Dorset 9 E4* loc 1m E of Buckland Newton and 8m/12km SW of Sturminster Newton. ST 7005
Sharoe Green Lancs 47 F4/F5* suburb 2m/3km N of Preston. SD 5332
Sharow N Yorks 49 E1 vil 1m E of Ripon across R Ure. SE 3271
Sharpenhoe Beds 29 E4 vil 6m/10km N of Luton. Viewpoint (NT) to SE. TL 0630
Sharper's Head Nthmb 67 F3 headland 1km NE of Berwick-upon-Tweed. NU 0054
Sharperton Nthmb 61 E2 ham 3m/5km SE of Alwinton. NT 9503
Sharpham Som 8 C1* loc on W side of Glastonbury. ST 4738
Sharpness Glos 16 B2 loc on R Severn estuary 11m/18km W of Stroud. Terminus of Gloucester and Sharpness Canal. Docks. SO 6702
Sharpness Point Tyne & Wear 61 H4* headland on North Sea coast at Tynemouth. NZ 3769
Sharpnose Point, Higher Cornwall 6 B4 westward-facing headland on SW side of Morwenstow and 5m/9km N of Bude. SS 1914
Sharpnose Point, Lower Cornwall 6 B4 westward-facing headland 4m/7km N of Bude, at N end of Bude Bay. SS 1912
Sharp's Green Cambs 30 B2/B3* loc 2km S of Kirtling. TL 6855
Sharpstone Avon 16 C5* loc adjoining Freshford to SW and 4m/6km SE of Bath. ST 7859
Sharp Street Norfolk 39 G3* ham 1m S of Catfield. TG 3820
Sharpthorne W Sussex 12 A3 vil on a ridge 1km E of W Hoathly. TQ 3732
Sharrington Norfolk 39 E1 vil 3m/5km W of Holt. TG 0336
Sharston Gtr Manchester 42 D3* loc in Manchester 6m/9km S of city centre. SJ 8388
Shatterford H & W 35 E6 vil 4m/6km NW of Kidderminster. SO 7981
Shatterling Kent 13 G2* loc 2km E of Wingham. TR 2658
Shaugh Prior Devon 4 C4 vil at SW corner of Dartmoor 7m/11km NE of Plymouth. SX 5463
Shave Cross Dorset 8 C4* loc in Marshwood Vale 5m/7km NW of Bridport. SY 4198
Shaver's End W Midlands 35 F5 loc 1km NW of Dudley tn centre. SO 9391
Shavington Ches 42 C6 vil 2m/4km S of Crewe. SJ 6951
Shaw Berks 17 H4 NE suburb of Newbury. SU 4768
Shaw Gtr Manchester 43 E1 tn adjoining Crompton to S, 3m/4km N of Oldham. **Shaw Side** loc adjoining to E. SD 9308
Shaw N Yorks 54 A4* loc 3m/4km NE of Reeth. NZ 0602
Shaw Wilts 16 D5 vil 2m/3km NW of Melksham. ST 8865
Shaw Wilts 17 F3 loc 2m/3km W of Swindon. SU 1285
Shawbost, North and **South** W Isles 88 B1 adjacent vils near NW coast of Lewis, respectively 2m/3km and 3m/5km W of Bragar. See also Loch Shawbost, New Shawbost. NB 2647
Shawbury Salop 34 C2 vil 7m/11km NE of Shrewsbury. Airfield to N. SJ 5521
Shawclough Gtr Manchester 47 H6 loc in Rochdale 2km NW of tn centre. SD 8814
Shawell Leics 36 B6 vil 4m/7km NE of Rugby. SP 5480
Shawfield Gtr Manchester 47 H6* loc in Rochdale 2m/3km NW of tn centre. SD 8714
Shawfield Staffs 43 F5* loc 3m/4km SW of Longnor. SK 0661
Shawford Hants 10 B2 vil on R Itchen 3m/5km S of Winchester. SU 4725
Shawford Som 16 C6* loc 1km SW of Rode and 4m/6km N of Frome. ST 7953
Shawforth Lancs 48 B6 loc 2km N of Whitworth. SD 8920
Shaw Green Herts 29 G4* loc 4m/6km E of Baldock. TL 2932
Shaw Green Lancs 47 F6* loc 4m/6km W of Chorley. SD 5218
Shaw Green N Yorks 49 E3* loc just S of Beckwithshaw. SE 2652
Shawhead D & G 58 D4 vil 6m/10km W of Dumfries. NX 8775
Shaw Heath Ches 42 D3* loc adjoining Knutsford to NE. SJ 7679
Shawlands S'clyde 64 C3* loc in Pollokshields dist of Glasgow. NS 5661
Shaw Mills N Yorks 49 E2* vil 2m/3km NW of Ripley. SE 2562
Shaws Under Loch Borders 66 B6 small loch 7m/12km NW of Hawick. Smaller loch, **Shaws Upper Loch,** nearly 1km SW. NT 3919
Shawwood S'clyde 56 E2* loc adjoining Catrine to SE. NS 5325
Sheaf 43 H3* r rising near Holmesfield, W of Dronfield, Derbys, and flowing N into R Don in central Sheffield, S Yorks. SK 3687
Shearington D & G 59 E4/E5 loc 7m/11km SE of Dumfries. NY 0366
Shearsby Leics 36 C5 vil 4m/7km N of Husbands Bosworth. SP 6290
Shebbear Devon 6 C4 vil 7m/11km NE of Holsworthy. SS 4309
Shebdon Staffs 34 D2 ham 4m/7km N of Newport. SJ 7625
Shebster H'land 86 C2 loc in Caithness dist 7m/11km SW of Thurso. ND 0164
Shedfield Hants 10 C3 vil 3m/5km E of Botley. SU 5513
Sheen Staffs 43 F5 vil 3m/5km SE of Longnor. SK 1161
Sheen, East London 19 F4* loc in borough of Richmond at N end of Richmond Park, 7m/11km SW of Charing Cross. E Sheen Common (NT). TQ 2074
Sheen, North London 19 F4 loc in borough of Richmond to W of Chiswick Br. TQ 1976
Sheepbridge Derbys 43 H4* loc in N part of Chesterfield 2m/4km N of tn centre. SK 3774
Sheep Hill Tyne & Wear 61 F5* loc 4m/6km S of Blaydon. NZ 1757
Sheep Island Dyfed 22 B5 small island on E side of entrance to Milford Haven at S end of Castles Bay. SM 8401
Sheep Island S'clyde 63 E6 small island off S coast of Kintyre across Sanda Sound, to N of Sanda I. NR 7305
Sheepridge W Yorks 48 D6* loc in Huddersfield 2m/3km N of tn centre. SE 1519
Sheepscar W Yorks 49 E4* dist of Leeds 1m NE of city centre. SE 3034
Sheepscombe Glos 26 D6 vil 2m/3km E of Painswick. SO 8910
Sheepstor Devon 4 C4 vil on SW Dartmoor 4m/7km SW of Princetown. SX 5667
Sheepwash Devon 6 D4 vil 4m/6km NW of Hatherleigh. SS 4806
Sheepwash Nthmb 61 G3 loc on R Wansbeck 2m/3km SW of Ashington. NZ 2585
Sheepway Avon 16 A4 loc 2m/3km E of Portishead. ST 4976
Sheepy Magna Leics 35 H4 vil 3m/4km NE of Atherstone. **Sheepy Parva** ham to E across R Sence. SK 3301
Sheering Essex 20 B1 vil 2m/3km E of Sawbridgeworth. Loc of **Lr Sheering** 1m W. TL 5013
Sheerness Kent 21 E4 port and resort at NW point of Isle of Sheppey. Former naval dockyard and barracks converted to industrial use. TQ 9175
Sheet Hants 10 D3 vil 1m NE of Petersfield. SU 7524
Shee Water 76 C4 upper reaches of Black Water in Tayside region. See Black Water.
Sheffield S Yorks 43 H3 city on R Don 144m/232km NW of London. Centre of steel industry. Manufactures cutlery and plate. Coal-mining in vicinity. University. SK 3587
Sheffield and South Yorkshire Navigation 43 H3-44 C1 canal linking Sheffield with R Trent at Keadby, Humberside.
Sheffield Green E Sussex 12 A4 loc 2m/3km S of Danehill. TQ 4125
Sheffield Lane Top S Yorks 43 H2* loc in Sheffield 3m/4km N of city centre. SK 3691
Sheffield Park E Sussex 12 A4 hse by James Wyatt 5m/8km E of Haywards Heath. Gardens and lakes (NT). S. P. rly stn, 1km SW, is southern terminus of Bluebell Rly (see also Horsted Keynes). TQ 4124
Shefford Beds 29 F4 small tn 9m/14km SE of Bedford. Site of Roman bldg at W end. TL 1439
Shefford, East Berks 17 G4 ham 5m/8km NE of Hungerford. SU 3875
Shefford, Great Berks 17 G4 vil 5m/8km NE of Hungerford. SU 3875
Sheigra H'land 84 B2 loc near W coast of Sutherland dist 4m/6km NW of Kinlochbervie. NC 1860
Sheinton Salop 34 C4 vil 3m/4km N of Much Wenlock. SJ 6103
Shelderton Salop 34 B6* ham 4m/6km SW of Craven Arms. SO 4077
Sheldon Derbys 43 F4 vil 3m/4km W of Bakewell. SK 1768
Sheldon Devon 7 H4 vil 6m/9km NW of Honiton. ST 1208
Sheldon W Midlands 35 G5* dist of Birmingham 6m/10km E of city centre. SP 1584
Sheldwich Kent 21 F6 vil 3m/5km S of Faversham. Loc of **Sheldwich Lees** to S. TR 0156
Shelf Mid Glam 15 E3* 2m/3km E of Bridgend. SS 9380
Shelf W Yorks 48 D5* loc 4m/6km SW of Bradford. SE 1228
Shelfanger Norfolk 39 E6 vil 3m/4km N of Diss. TM 1083
Shelfield Warwicks 27 F2* loc 3m/4km SW of Henley-in-Arden. Loc of **Shelfield Green** 1km SW. SP 1262
Shelfield W Midlands 35 F4 loc 3m/4km NE of Walsall. SK 0302
Shelford Notts 36 C1 vil 6m/10km E of Nottingham. SK 6642
Shelford Warwicks 36 A5 loc 3m/5km S of Hinckley. SP 4388
Shelford, Great Cambs 29 H3 suburb 4m/7km S of Cambridge. TL 4652
Shelford, Little Cambs 29 H3 vil 5m/8km S of Cambridge. TL 4551
Shellag Point Isle of Man 46 C3 promontory on E coast 3m/5km S of Pt of Ayre. Also known as Pt Cranstal. SC 4699
Shelland Suffolk 31 E2 loc 3m/5km W of Stowmarket. TM 0059
Shell Bay Dorset 9 G5 small bay outside entrance to Poole Harbour on S side. SZ 0386
Shell Bay Fife 73 G4* small bay on E side of Largo Bay, between Ruddons Pt and Kincraig Pt. NO 4600

Shellbrook Leics 36 A3* loc 1m W of Ashby de la Zouch. SK 3416
Shelley Essex 20 C2* loc 2km N of Chipping Ongar. TL 5505
Shelley Suffolk 31 E4 ham 3m/4km S of Hadleigh. TM 0338
Shelley W Yorks 49 E6 vil 5m/8km SE of Huddersfield. **Shelley Far Bank** loc 1km W. SE 2011
Shell Green Ches 42 B3* loc 2km NE of Widnes. SJ 5386
Shell Haven Essex 20 D3* anchorage on N side of R Thames at Coryton. Large oil refinery on shore. TQ 7481
Shellingford Oxon 17 G2 vil 2m/4km SE of Faringdon. SU 3193
Shell Island Gwynedd 32 D2* tongue of land at N end of Morfa Dyffryn almost enclosing estuary of R Artro. SH 5526
Shell Ness Kent 21 F5 headland at E extremity of Isle of Sheppey. TR 0567
Shellow Bowells Essex 20 C1 ham 4m/6km S of Leaden Roding. TL 6007
Shelsley Beauchamp H & W 26 C2 vil 7m/11km NE of Bromyard. SO 7362
Shelsley Walsh H & W 26 C2 vil 7m/11km NE of Bromyard. SO 7263
Shelswell Oxon 28 B4* loc 5m/8km NE of Bicester. SP 6030
Shelthorpe Leics 36 B3* loc in Loughborough 1m S of tn centre. SK 5317
Shelton Beds 29 E1 vil 5m/7km E of Higham Ferrers. TL 0368
Shelton Norfolk 39 F5 ham 5m/8km N of Harleston. Loc of **Shelton Green** 1m E. TM 2291
Shelton Notts 36 D1 vil 10m/16km NW of Grantham. SK 7844
Shelton Salop 34 B3 loc in W part of Shrewsbury. SJ 4513
Shelton Lock Derbys 36 A2* loc in Derby 1km N of Chellaston. SK 3731
Shelton, Lower Beds 29 E3 ham 6m/9km SW of Bedford. SP 9942
Shelton, Upper Beds 29 E3* ham 5m/9km SW of Bedford. SP 9943
Shelve Salop 34 A4 vil 7m/11km N of Bishop's Castle. SO 3399
Shelwick H & W 26 A3 ham 2m/3km N of Hereford. SO 5243
Shelwick Green H & W 26 A3* ham adjoining ham of Shelwick to E, 2m/3km NE of Hereford. SO 5243
Shenfield Essex 20 C2 E dist of Brentwood. TQ 6094
Shenington Oxon 27 G3 vil 6m/9km W of Banbury. SP 3742
Shenley Herts 19 F2 vil 5m/8km SE of St Albans. TL 1900
Shenley Brook End Bucks 28 D4 vil in Milton Keynes 3m/4km NW of Bletchley. SP 8335
Shenleybury Herts 19 F2* loc 4m/7km SE of St Albans. TL 1801
Shenley Church End Bucks 28 D4 vil in Milton Keynes 2m/3km SW of the centre. SP 8336
Shenley Fields W Midlands 35 F6* loc in Birmingham 5m/8km SW of city centre. SP 0281
Shenmore H & W 25 H4 ham 8m/12km W of Hereford. SO 3938
Shennanton D & G 57 D6 loc on R Bladnoch 2m/3km NE of Kirkcowan. NX 3463
Shenstone H & W 26 D1 vil 3m/5km SE of Kidderminster. SO 8673
Shenstone Staffs 35 G4 vil 3m/5km S of Lichfield. Site of Roman bldg 1km N: finds at museum at Wall, qv. **Shenstone Woodend** loc 2m/3km S. SK 1104
Shenton Leics 36 A4 vil 2m/4km SW of Mkt Bosworth. SK 3800
Shepeau Stow Lincs 37 G3 loc 4m/7km E of Crowland. TF 3012
Sheperdine Avon 16 B2 loc 5m/8km NE of Severn Rd Br. ST 6295
Shephall Herts 29 F5* SE dist of Stevenage. TL 2522
Shepherd's Bush London 19 F3* loc in borough of Hammersmith 5m/8km W of Charing Cross. TQ 2280
Shepherds' Gate Norfolk 38 A3/B3* loc 1m W of Tilney All Saints. TF 5518
Shepherd's Green Oxon 18 C3* ham 3m/5km W of Henley-on-Thames. SU 7183
Shepherd's Patch Glos 16 C1* loc on Gloucester and Sharpness Canal 4m/7km NE of Berkeley. SO 7204
Shepherdswell Kent 13 G2 vil 6m/9km NW of Dover. Also known as Sibertswold. TR 2548
Shepley W Yorks 43 F1 vil 3m/5km E of Holmfirth. SE 1909
Shepperton Surrey 19 E4 suburban loc on N bank of R Thames opp Walton-on-Thames. **Shepperton Green** loc 1km NW. TQ 0867
Sheppey, Isle of Kent 21 E4 island off N coast of Kent, separated from mainland by The Swale (bridged only at Kingsferry Br) and R Medway estuary. Sheppey is 9m/15km E to W and 5m/8km N to S at widest point. Nearly all the pop. is in the N half where there is high ground; the S half is mostly marshland. TQ 9770
Shepreth Cambs 29 G3 vil 5m/8km NE of Royston. TL 3947
Shepshed Leics 36 B3 hosiery tn 4m/6km W of Loughborough. SK 4719
Shepton Beauchamp Som 8 C3 vil 3m/5km NE of Ilminster. ST 4017
Shepton Mallet Som 16 B6 stone tn 18m/29km S of Bristol. Industries include glove-making, dairy produce, 'champagne perry'. ST 6143
Shepton Montague Som 9 E2 vil 2m/4km S of Bruton. ST 6731
Shepton, West Som 16 B6* SW dist of Shepton Mallet. ST 6143
Shepway Kent 20 D6* SE dist of Maidstone. TQ 7753
Shepway 119 admin dist of Kent.
Sheraton Durham 54 D2 ham 5m/7km NW of Hartlepool. NZ 4435
Sherborne Dorset 8 D3 tn 5m/8km E of Yeovil. Centre of agricultural dist. Medieval abbey and adjacent school. To E, Sherborne Old Castle (A.M.) and present cas in park beside Sherborne Lake. ST 6316
Sherborne Glos 27 F6 vil 5m/8km W of Burford. SP 1714
Sherborne Causeway Dorset 9 F2* loc 2m/3km W of Shaftesbury. ST 8323
Sherborne St John Hants 18 B5 vil 3m/5km NW of Basingstoke. 2km NE, The Vyne (NT), Tudor and later hse. SU 6255
Sherbourne Warwicks 27 G2 vil 3m/5km SW of Warwick. SP 2661
Sherbourne Street Suffolk 30 D4* ham 5m/7km W of Hadleigh. TL 9541
Sherburn Durham 54 C1 vil 3m/5km E of Durham. **Sherburn Hill** vil 1m E. NZ 3142
Sherburn N Yorks 50 D1 vil 11m/18km E of Malton. SE 9576
Sherburn in Elmet N Yorks 49 G4/G5 vil 6m/10km S of Tadcaster. SE 4933
Shere Surrey 19 E6 par and vil 5m/8km E of Guildford. TQ 0747
Shereford Norfolk 38 D2 ham 2m/3km W of Fakenham. TF 8829
Sherfield English Hants 10 A3 vil 4m/6km W of Romsey. SU 2922
Sherfield on Loddon Hants 18 B5 vil 5m/8km NE of Basingstoke. SU 6758
Sherfin Lancs 48 B5* loc 2km N of Haslingden. SD 7825
Sherford Devon 4 D6 vil 3m/5km E of Kingsbridge. SX 7744
Sherford Som 8 A2* S dist of Taunton. ST 2223
Sherford 9 G5 r rising 1m SW of Bloxworth in Dorset and flowing E into Lytchett Bay, inlet on N side of Poole Harbour. SY 9691
Sheriffhales Salop 34 D3 vil 3m/5km N of Shifnal. SJ 7512
Sheriff Hutton N Yorks 50 B2 vil 4m/6km NE of Strensall. Remains of 14c cas. SE 6566
Sheriff Muir (or Sheriffmuir) Central 72 C4 moor to E of Dunblane. Scene of indecisive battle in 1715 between government troops and those of the Old Pretender. NN 8303
Sheringham Norfolk 39 F1 coastal resort 22m/35km N of Norwich. **Sheringham Hall,** Regency hse 2km W; hse and grnds by Repton. **Upr Sheringham** vil 2km SW. TG 1543
Sherington Bucks 28 D3 vil 2m/3km NE of Newport Pagnell. SP 8846
Shermanbury W Sussex 11 H3 loc 2m/3km N of Henfield. TQ 2118
Shernal Green H & W 26 D2* loc 2m/3km SE of Droitwich. SO 9161
Shernborne Norfolk 38 C2 ham 6m/9km S of Hunstanton. TF 7132
Sherrington Wilts 9 F1 vil on R Wylye 3m/5km SE of Heytesbury. ST 9639
Sherston Wilts 16 D3 vil 5m/8km W of Malmesbury. ST 8586
Sherwood Notts 36 B1 dist of Nottingham 2m/3km N of city centre. SK 5743
Sherwood Forest Notts 44 B6-B4 ancient demesne of the Crown, lying between Nottingham and Worksop. Associated with the, perhaps legendary, exploits of Robin Hood. Still well-wooded in the N part, known as the Dukeries and consisting of the parks of Welbeck, Worksop, Clumber (NT), and Thorseby. sk 66
Sheshader W Isles 88 C2* vil on Eye Peninsula, Lewis, 3m/4km SW of Tiumpan Hd. **Sheshader Bay** on coast to E. NB 5534
Shetland 89. Group of some 100 islands, for administrative purposes designated an Islands Area, lying beyond Orkney to NE of Scottish mainland, Sumburgh Hd being about 100m/160km from Duncansby Hd. The chief islands are Mainland – on which the capital, Lerwick, is situated – Unst, and Yell. Some twenty of the islands are inhabited. Chief port is Lerwick. Airport at Sumburgh, S Mainland. Oil service bases at Lerwick and Sandwick; terminal at Sullom Voe. Industries include cattle and sheep-rearing, knitwear, fishing. The small Shetland ponies are renowned for their strength and hardiness. The islands are mainly low-lying, the highest point being Ronas Hill, qv, on Mainland. The climate is mild, considering the latitude, but severe storms are frequent. HU 36
Shettleston S'clyde 64 D2/D3 dist of Glasgow 3m/5km E of city centre. NS 6464
Shevington Gtr Manchester 42 B1 suburb 3m/5km NW of Wigan. **Shevington Moor** loc 2km N. **Shevington Vale** loc 2km NW. SD 5408
Shevington End Essex 30 B3/B4* ham 5m/8km W of Haverhill. TL 5942
Sheviock Cornwall 3 H3 vil 4m/7km W of Torpoint. SX 3755
Shewalton S'clyde 64 B5* dist of Irvine New Tn 3m/5km SE of tn centre. NS 3435
Shian Bay S'clyde 69 D8 bay on NW coast of Jura 3m/5km NW of entrance to Loch Tarbert. **Shian I.** is islet to N of bay. NR 5287
Shian, North and **South** S'clyde 70 B1 localities on N and S shores of Loch Creran in Argyll. NM 94
Shiant Islands W Isles 88 C3 uninhabited group of islands and islets 4m/6km off SE coast of Lewis. Garbh Eilean and Eilean an Tighe form one island as they are connected by a narrow neck of land. Eilean Mhuire lies 1km E. There are several islets to W. NG 49
Shiaram Mór W Isles 88 A2* islet near W shore of W Loch Roag, W coast of Lewis. NB 1036
Shibden Head W Yorks 48 D5* vil at head of **Shibden Dale** 2m/4km N of Halifax. 2m/3km down the dale is **Shibden Hall,** timber-framed hse dating probably from early 15c. SE 0929
Shide Isle of Wight 10 B5 S dist of Newport. SZ 5088
Shiel H'land 80 A5 r in Skye and Lochalsh dist running NW down Glen Shiel to Shiel Br and head of Loch Duich. Kintail Forest (NTS) rises steeply from right bank. NG 9319
Shiel Bridge H'land 80 A5 vil in Skye and Lochalsh dist at foot of Glen Shiel. NG 9318
Shieldaig H'land 78 F4 vil on E shore of Loch Shieldaig, Ross and Cromarty dist. NG 8153
Shieldaig Forest H'land 78 F3 deer forest in W part of Ross and Cromarty dist to N of Upr Loch Torridon. NG 8564
Shieldaig Island H'land 78 F4 small island (NTS) in Loch Shieldaig, Ross and Cromarty dist, almost entirely covered in Scots pine. NG 8154
Shieldhall S'clyde 64 C2* loc in Glasgow on S side of R Clyde 4m/6km W of city centre. Shipbuilding yards, saw mills. NS 5365
Shieldhill Central 65 F1/F2 vil 2m/3km S of Falkirk. NS 8976
Shieldmuir S'clyde 65 E3* loc between Motherwell and Wishaw. NS 7755
Shiel Dod S'clyde 59 E2* mt in Lowther Hills 4m/6km E of Durisdeer. Height 2191 ft or 668 metres. NS 9403
Shield Row Durham 61 G6* loc adjoining Stanley to NE. NZ 2053
Shields, North Tyne & Wear 61 H4 tn on N bank of R Tyne opp S Shields and 7m/11km E of Newcastle. Ship-repairing, fish canning. NZ 3568
Shields, South Tyne & Wear 61 H4 port with extensive docks on S bank of R Tyne 7m/12km E of Gateshead and 7m/11km N of Sunderland. Shipbuilding, engineering, electrical goods. Remains of Roman fort. Long stretch of sands on seaward side of tn. NZ 3666
Shield Water (or Black Burn) Cumbria 53 F1 r rising on N slopes of Cross Fell, Cumbria, and flowing N into R South Tyne 2m/3km S of Alston. NY 7143
Shifford Oxon 17 G2 loc 5m/8km S of Witney. SP 3701
Shifnal Salop 34 D3 small tn 7m/12km S of Newport. SJ 7407
Shilbottle Nthmb 61 F1 vil 3m/5km S of Alnwick. Medieval peel tower forms part of vicarage. **Shilbottle Grange** loc adjoining to E. NU 1908
Shildon Durham 54 B2 tn 2m/4km SE of Bishop Auckland. Coal-mining, quarrying. NZ 2226
Shillay W Isles 88 A3* small uninhabited island 5m/8km SW of Toe Hd, W coast of Harris. **Lit Shillay** is islet to SW. NF 8891
Shillay W Isles 88 D1* westernmost island of the Monach Isles, qv. Lighthouse on Shillay disused since World War II. NF 5962
Shillay More W Isles 88 E2* uninhabited island in Loch Skiport, E coast of S Uist. NF 8438
Shillingford Devon 7 G3 vil 2m/3km NE of Bampton. SS 9823
Shillingford Oxon 18 B2 vil 2m/4km N of Wallingford. SU 5992
Shillingford Abbot Devon 5 E2* ham 3m/4km S of Exeter. SX 9188
Shillingford St George Devon 5 E2 vil 3m/5km S of Exeter. SX 9087
Shillingstone Dorset 9 F3 vil in R Stour valley 3m/5km SE of Sturminster Newton. ST 8211
Shillington Beds 29 F4 vil 3m/5km SW of Shefford. TL 1234
Shilton Oxon 17 G1 vil 3m/4km SE of Burford. SP 2608
Shilton Warwicks 36 A5 vil 5m/9km NE of Coventry. SP 4084
Shilvinghampton Dorset 8 D5* loc 5m/8km NW of Weymouth. SY 6284
Shimpling Norfolk 39 F6* ham 3m/5km NE of Diss. Site of Roman bldg 2km NE. **Shimpling Place,** early 17c hse to NW. TM 1583
Shimpling Suffolk 30 D3 ham 3m/5km N of Long Melford. TL 8651
Shimpling Street Suffolk 30 D3 vil 4m/7km N of Long Melford. TL 8752
Shin H'land 85 F6 r in Sutherland dist running S from foot of Loch Shin to Invershin, 4m/6km NW of Bonar Br. **Falls of Shin,** waterfall in course of r 2m/3km above mouth. NH 5796
Shincliffe Durham 54 C1 vil 2m/3km SE of Durham. NZ 2940
Shiney Row Tyne & Wear 61 G6 loc in coal-mining area 2m/3km NW of Houghton-le-Spring. NZ 3252
Shinfield Berks 18 C4 vil 4m/6km S of Reading. SU 7268
Shin Forest H'land 85 F6* state forest 3m/5km S of Lairg in Sutherland dist. NC 5701
Shingay Cambs 29 G3 loc 5m/8km NW of Royston. TL 3046
Shingham Norfolk 38 C4* loc 1km E of Beachamwell. TF 7605
Shinglehead Point Essex 21 F1 headland 2m/4km E of Tollesbury at mouth of R Blackwater. TL 9910
Shingle Street Suffolk 31 G4 coastal loc 7m/11km SE of Woodbridge. TM 3642
Shinnel Water 58 D2 r in Dumfries & Galloway region running SE past Tynron, then NE to Scaur Water on SW side of Penpont. NX 8494
Shinness H'land 85 E5 locality on E shore of Loch Shinn, Sutherland dist, 6m/10km NW of Lairg. NC 5314
Shipbourne Kent 20 C6 vil 4m/6km N of Tonbridge. TQ 5952
Shipbrookhill Ches 42 C4* loc 2m/3km SE of Northwich. SJ 6771
Shipdham Norfolk 38 D4 vil 4m/7km SW of E Dereham. TF 9507
Shipham Som 16 A5 vil on W slope of Mendip Hills 3m/4km N of Cheddar. ST 4457
Shiphay Devon 5 E4* dist of Torbay 2m/3km NW of Torquay harbour. SX 8965
Shiplake Oxon 18 C4 vil on R Thames 3m/4km S of Henley-on-Thames. Vil of **Lr Shiplake** 1m NE; ham of **Shiplake Row** 1km W. SU 7678
Shipley Nthmb 67 H6 loc 3m/5km NW of Alnwick. NU 1416

Shipley Salop 35 E4* loc 7m/11km W of Wolverhampton. SO 8095
Shipley W Sussex 11 G3 vil 4m/7km W of Cowfold. TQ 1421
Shipley W Yorks 48 D4 industrial tn on R Aire and on Leeds and Liverpool Canal 3m/5km NW of Bradford. Textiles, engineering. SE 1437
Shipley Bridge Surrey 11 H1 ham 2m/3km SE of Horley. TQ 3040
Shipley Common Derbys 36 A1* loc 1m N of Ilkeston. SK 4543
Shipmeadow Suffolk 39 G5 vil 3m/4km W of Beccles. TM 3890
Shippea Hill Suffolk 38 B6 loc 8m/13km W of Brandon. TL 6684
Shippersea Bay Durham 54 D1 small bay on North Sea coast 2m/3km NE of Easington. NZ 4445
Shipping Dyfed 22 D5* loc adjoining Begelly to N. SN 1108
Shippon Oxon 17 H2 loc 2km NW of Abingdon. SU 4898
Shipston on Stour Warwicks 27 F3/G3 small tn 12m/20km W of Banbury. SP 2540
Shipton Glos 27 E5 vil 5m/9km NW of Northleach. SP 0318
Shipton N Yorks 50 B2 vil 5m/8km NW of York. SE 5558
Shipton Salop 34 C5 vil 6m/10km SW of Much Wenlock. SO 5691
Shipton Bellinger Hants 17 F6 vil 6m/9km NE of Amesbury. SU 2345
Shipton Gorge Dorset 8 C5 vil 2m/4km SE of Bridport. SY 4991
Shipton Green W Sussex 11 E5* vil 2m/3km NE of W Wittering. SZ 8099
Shipton Moyne Glos 16 D3 vil 2m/4km S of Tetbury. ST 8989
Shipton Oliffe Glos 27 E5* loc adjoining vil of Shipton, 5m/9km NW of Northleach. SP 0318
Shipton-on-Cherwell Oxon 27 H5 vil 7m/11km N of Oxford. SP 4716
Shipton Solers Glos 27 E5* loc adjoining Shipton to W, 5m/9km NW of Northleach. SP 0318
Shiptonthorpe Humberside 50 D4 vil 2m/3km NW of Mkt Weighton. SE 8543
Shipton-under-Wychwood Oxon 27 G5 vil 4m/6km NE of Burford. SP 2717
Shirburn Oxon 18 C2 vil 2km NE of Watlington. **Shirburn Castle,** medieval fortified hse. SU 6995
Shirdley Hill Lancs 42 A1* ham 2km W of Scarisbrick. SD 3612
Shire Cumbria 53 E2* loc adjoining Ousby to NW, 2m/3km N of Skirwith. NY 6135
Shirebrook Derbys 44 A4 tn 4m/7km N of Mansfield. Site of Roman bldg 1km N of tn centre. SK 5267
Shirecliffe S Yorks 43 H2* loc in Sheffield 2m/3km N of city centre. SK 3590
Shire Combe W Glam 23 G6* small inlet on S coast of Gower peninsula 2km S of Parkmill. SS 5487
Shiregreen S Yorks 43 H2* dist of Sheffield 3m/5km N of city centre. SK 3792
Shirehampton Avon 16 A4 NW dist of Bristol. **Shirehampton Park** (NT). Remains of Roman villa to NW. ST 5377
Shire Lodge Northants 36 D5* dist of Corby 2m/3km NW of tn centre. SP 8790
Shiremoor Tyne & Wear 61 G4* urban loc 2m/4km W of Whitley Bay. NZ 3171
Shirenewton (Drenewydd Gelli-farch) Gwent 16 A2 vil 4m/6km W of Chepstow. ST 4793
Shire Oak W Midlands 35 F4 loc 1m S of Brownhills. SK 0504
Shireoaks Notts 44 A3 coal-mining vil 2m/3km NW of Worksop. SK 5580
Shirland Derbys 43 H5 vil 3m/5km S of Clay Cross. SK 3958
Shirley Derbys 43 G6 vil 4m/7km SE of Ashbourne. SK 2141
Shirley Hants 10 B3 dist of Southampton 2km NW of city centre. To N, dists of **Old Shirley, Upr Shirley,** and **Shirley Warren.** SU 4013
Shirley Hants 9 H4 loc 4m/7km NE of Christchurch. SZ 1798
Shirley London 20 A5 loc in borough of Croydon 2m/3km E of Croydon tn centre. Loc of **Upr Shirley** is 1km SE. TQ 3565
Shirley W Midlands 35 G6 dist of Solihull 2m/4km W of tn centre. Loc of **Shirley Heath** to S. SP 1178
Shirley Moor Kent 13 E4 area of marshland forming N part of Rother Levels to E of Tenterden. TQ 9232
Shirleywich Staffs 35 F2* loc 1m SE of Weston. SJ 9825
Shirl Heath H & W 26 A2* loc 4m/6km W of Leominster. SO 4359
Shirrell Heath Hants 10 C3 vil 5m/8km N of Fareham. SU 5714
Shirwell Devon 6 D2 vil 4m/6km NE of Barnstaple. **Shirwell Cross** ham to SW. SS 5937
Shiskine S'clyde 63 F4 vil on Arran 2km NE of Blackwaterfoot. NR 9129
Shittlehope Durham 54 A1* loc 1m SE of Stanhope. NZ 0038
Shivering Mountain Derbys. See Mam Tor.
Shobdon H & W 26 A2 vil 6m/10km W of Leominster. SO 4062
Shobley Hants 9 H3* loc 3m/4km E of Ringwood. SU 1806
Shobnall Staffs 35 H2 loc in Burton upon Trent 1m W of tn centre. SK 2223
Shobrooke Devon 7 F5 vil 2m/3km NE of Crediton. SS 8601
Shocklach Ches 42 A6 vil 3m/5km NW of Malpas. **Shocklach Green** loc 1km W. SJ 4349
Shoeburyness Essex 21 E3 E dist of Southend-on-Sea, 4m/6km E of tn centre and 1km NE of **Shoebury Ness,** headland at mouth of R Thames estuary. TQ 9384
Shoebury, North Essex 21 E3 ham in E part of Southend-on-Sea 1m NW of Shoeburyness. TQ 9286
Sholden Kent 13 H2 W suburb of Deal. TR 3552
Sholing Hants 10 B4 E dist of Southampton across R Itchen. SU 4511
Shomere Pool Salop 34 C3/C4* small lake in Bomere Wd 3m/5km S of Shrewsbury. SJ 5007
Shona Beag H'land. See Eilean Shona.
Shon-Sheffrey's Reservoir Gwent 25 F6* small resr 2m/3km NW of Tredegar. SO 1211
Shooters Hill London 20 B4 loc in borough of Greenwich 2km S of Woolwich and 9m/15km E of Charing Cross. TQ 4376
Shoot Hill Salop 34 B3 loc 5m/8km W of Shrewsbury. SJ 4112
Shop Cornwall 2 D1 vil 3m/4km W of Padstow. SW 8873
Shop Cornwall 6 B4 vil 6m/9km N of Bude. SS 2214
Shopford Cumbria 60 B4 loc adjoining Bewcastle to S. NY 5674
Shopnoller Som 8 A1* ham 1km SW of W Bagborough. ST 1632
Shop Street Suffolk 31 F2* vil 1km W of Worlingworth. TM 2268
Shore Central 72 B5* dist of Stirling bordering right bank of R Forth to E and NE of tn centre. NS 8093
Shore Gtr Manchester 48 C6* loc adjoining Clough to W. SD 9217
Shoreditch London 19 G3* dist in borough of Hackney 2km N of London Br. TQ 3382
Shoreham Kent 20 B5 vil on R Darent 4m/7km N of Sevenoaks. Site of Roman bldg downstream to N. TQ 5161
Shoreham-by-Sea W Sussex 11 H4 container port at mouth of R Adur 6m/10km W of Brighton. Airport to W. Dist of **Old Shoreham** to N extends on to southern slopes of S Downs. TQ 2105
Shore, North Lancs 46 D4 dist of Blackpool to N of tn centre. SD 3038
Shoresdean Nthmb 67 F4* loc 4m/6km E of Norham. NT 9546
Shore, South Lancs 46 D4 dist of Blackpool to S of tn centre. SD 3033
Shoreston Nthmb 67 H5* loc 1m W of Seahouses. See also New Shoreston. NU 2032
Shoreswood Nthmb 67 F4 loc 3m/4km E of Norham. NT 9446
Shorley Hants 10 C2* ham 2km S of Cheriton. SU 5826
Shorncliffe Kent 13 G3 loc with military barracks in W part of Folkestone. TR 1935
Shorncote Glos 17 E2 loc 3m/5km S of Cirencester. SU 0296
Shorne Kent 20 C4 vil 4m/6km SE of Gravesend. TQ 6971
Shorne Ridgeway Kent 20 C4* vil adjoining Shorne to S, 4m/6km SE of Gravesend. TQ 6970
Shorta Cross Cornwall 3 G3* loc 4m/6km NE of Looe. SX 2957
Shortbridge E Sussex 12 B4* loc 2km W of Uckfield. TQ 4521
Shortfield Common Surrey 11 E1* loc 3m/5km S of Farnham. SU 8442
Shortflatt Tower Nthmb 61 F3 tower of 14c, much altered, with later hse attached, 2m/3km NW of Belsay. NZ 0781
Short Green Norfolk 39 E6 loc 4m/7km N of Diss. TM 1086
Shorthampton Oxon 27 G5* ham 2m/3km W of Charlbury. SP 3220
Short Heath Derbys 35 H3* loc 1km E of Overseal. SK 3015
Shortheath Hants 10 D2* loc adjoining Oakhanger to N, 4m/6km SE of Alton. SU 7736
Short Heath W Midlands 35 G5 loc 4m/7km N of Birmingham city centre. SP 0993
Short Island Cornwall 6 A6* island off N coast 1km NW of Trevalga. SX 0790
Shortlands London 20 A4* loc to W of Bromley tn centre. TQ 3968
Shortlanesend Cornwall 2 D3 vil 2m/3km NW of Truro. SW 8047
Shorton Devon 5 E4* N dist of Paignton. SX 8862
Shortroads S'clyde 64 C2/C3* N dist of Paisley. NS 4765
Shortstanding Glos 26 B6* loc 2m/3km N of Coleford. SO 5713
Shortstown Beds 29 E3* loc 2m/4km SE of Bedford. TL 0746
Shorwell Isle of Wight 10 B6 vil 5m/8km SW of Newport. SZ 4582
Shoscombe Avon 16 C5* vil 2m/3km NE of Radstock. ST 7156
Shotatton Salop 34 B2* loc 2m/3km W of Ruyton-Eleven-Towns. SJ 3622
Shotesham Norfolk 39 F5 vil 6m/10km S of Norwich. TM 2499
Shotgate Essex 20 D3* suburban loc adjoining Wickford to E. TQ 7692
Shotley Northants 37 E4* loc adjoining Harringworth to E, 6m/9km NE of Corby. SP 9297
Shotley Suffolk 31 F4 ham on W side of R Orwell estuary 7m/11km SE of Ipswich. TM 2336
Shotley Bridge Durham 61 F6 loc on R Derwent adjoining Consett to NW. NZ 0952
Shotleyfield Nthmb 61 F6 loc 3m/5km NW of Consett. NZ 0653
Shotley Gate Suffolk 31 F4 vil at mouth of R Stour opp Parkeston. Naval training establishment, HMS *Ganges,* on E side of vil opp Harwich. TM 2433
Shotley Street Suffolk 31 F4 vil 1m NW of Shotley Gate and 7m/12km SE of Ipswich. TM 2335
Shottenden Kent 21 F6 vil 7m/11km W of Canterbury. TR 0454
Shottermill Surrey 11 E2 loc 2km W of Haslemere. SU 8832
Shottery Warwicks 27 F2 loc in W part of Stratford-upon-Avon containing Anne Hathaway's Cottage, traditionally birthplace of Shakespeare's wife. SP 1854
Shottesbrooke Berks 18 D4 loc 3m/5km E of Twyford. SU 8477
Shotteswell Warwicks 27 H3 vil 4m/6km NW of Banbury. SP 4245
Shottisham Suffolk 31 G4 vil 4m/7km SE of Woodbridge across R Deben. TM 3244
Shottle Derbys 43 G6* ham 3m/4km NW of Belper. SK 3149
Shottlegate Derbys 43 G6 ham 2m/3km W of Belper. SK 3247
Shotton Clwyd 41 H4 tn adjoining Queensferry on R Dee. Steel works across r on N bank. **Hr Shotton** S dist of tn. SJ 3068
Shotton Durham 54 C1/D1 loc in SW part of Peterlee. Hall is of late 18c. Large coal-mining loc of **Shotton Colliery** 2km NW. NZ 4139
Shotton Durham 54 C2 loc 2m/4km S of Sedgefield. NZ 3625
Shotton Nthmb 61 G4* loc 2km SE of Stannington. NZ 2278
Shotton Nthmb 67 E5 loc 2m/3km NE of Kirk Yetholm. NT 8430
Shotts S'clyde 65 E3 loc 6m/9km NW of Wishaw. NS 8760
Shotwick Ches 41 H4 vil 5m/9km NW of Chester. Hall of 17c. SJ 3371
Shouldham Norfolk 38 B4 vil 6m/9km NE of Downham Mkt. **Shouldham Thorpe** vil 2km SW. TF 6708
Shoulton H & W 26 C2* ham 4m/6km NW of Worcester. SO 8158
Shover's Green E Sussex 12 C4 loc 1m SE of Wadhurst. TQ 6530
Shraleybrook Staffs 42 D6* loc 2km W of Audley. SJ 7849
Shrawardine Salop 34 B3 vil 6m/10km W of Shrewsbury. Scant remains of medieval cas. Traces of motte and bailey cas at **Lit Shrawardine** across R Severn to W. **Shrawardine Pool** is lake to N; wildfowl haunt. SJ 4015
Shrawley H & W 26 C1/C2 vil 4m/7km S of Stourport. SO 8064
Shreding Green Bucks 19 E3* loc 3m/5km E of Slough. TQ 0281
Shrewley Warwicks 27 F1 vil 5m/8km NW of Warwick. SP 2167
Shrewsbury Salop 34 B3 county, mkt, and garrison tn 39m/63km NW of Birmingham, in loop of R Severn. Cas dates from 12c. Boys' public school founded 1552. Industries include light and heavy engineering. SJ 4912
Shrewton Wilts 17 E6 vil on Salisbury Plain 6m/9km W of Amesbury. ST 0643
Shripney W Sussex 11 F4 vil 2m/3km N of Bognor Regis. SU 9302
Shrivenham Oxon 17 F3 vil 6m/10km NE of Swindon. Royal Military College of Science. SU 2489
Shropham Norfolk 38 D5 vil 4m/7km W of Attleborough. TL 9893
Shropshire See Salop.
Shropshire, North and **South** 118 admin dists of Salop.
Shropshire Union Canal 42 A3-35 E4 canal connecting R Mersey at Ellesmere Port, Ches, with Staffordshire and Worcestershire Canal at Autherley Junction, near Wolverhampton, W Midlands.
Shroton Dorset. Alternative name for Iwerne Courtney, qv.
Shrub End Essex 30 D5 loc in SW part of Colchester. TL 9723
Shrub Hill Kent 13 G1* loc in SE part of Whitstable. TR 1364
Shuckburgh, Lower Warwicks 28 A2 vil 5m/9km W of Daventry. SP 4862
Shuckburgh, Upper Warwicks 28 A2* loc 5m/8km W of Daventry. SP 4961
Shucknall H & W 26 B3* vil 5m/8km E of Hereford. SO 5842
Shudy Camps Cambs 30 B3 vil 3m/5km W of Haverhill. TL 6244
Shugborough Staffs 35 F2 17c–18c hse (NT) in park 5m/7km E of Stafford. SJ 9922
Shulishader W Isles 88 C2* vil on Eye Peninsula, Lewis, 2km NE of Garrabost. NB 5335
Shuna S'clyde 69 F6 sparsely inhabited island of about 2 sq miles or 5 sq km lying 2km SW of entrance to Loch Melfort on coast of Argyll and 1km E of Luing across **Shuna Sound. Shuna Pt** is headland at S end of island. NM 7608
Shuna Island S'clyde 70 B1 barely populated island of about 300 acres or 120 hectares in Loch Linnhe, near E shore to NW of Portnacroish. Ruined cas at S end. NM 9149
Shunner Fell, Great N Yorks 53 G5 mt 4m/6km W of Muker. Height 2340 ft or 713 metres. SD 8497
Shurdington Glos 26 D5 vil 3m/5km SW of Cheltenham. SO 9218
Shurdington, Little Glos 26 D5* loc 4m/6km SW of Cheltenham. Site of Roman villa on hillside 1m E. SO 9117
Shurlach, Higher Ches 42 C4* loc 2m/3km SE of Northwich. **Lr Shurlach** dist of Northwich 1km NW. SJ 6772
Shurlock Row Berks 18 C4 vil 3m/5km SE of Twyford. SU 8374
Shurnock H & W 27 E2* loc 4m/7km NW of Alcester. **Shurnock Court** timber-framed partly 16c farmhouse. SP 0260
Shurrery H'land 86 D2 loc in Caithness dist 8m/12km SW of Thurso. ND 0458
Shurton Som 15 G6 vil 8m/12km NW of Bridgwater. ST 2044
Shustoke Warwicks 35 H5 vil 2m/3km NE of Coleshill. Shustoke Resr N of vil. SP 2290
Shute Devon 7 G5* loc 3m/5km E of Crediton. SS 8900
Shute Devon 8 B4 vil 3m/5km W of Axminster. **Shute Barton** (NT), medieval and later manor hse. SY 2597
Shut End W Midlands 35 E5* loc 3m/5km W of Dudley tn centre. SO 9089
Shutford Oxon 27 G4 vil 5m/7km W of Banbury. SP 3840

Shut Heath Staffs 35 E2 ham 4m/6km W of Stafford. SJ 8621
Shuthonger Glos 26 D4* ham 2m/3km N of Tewkesbury. SO 8835
Shutlanehead Staffs 42 D6* loc 2km NE of Whitmore. SJ 8242
Shutlanger Northants 28 C3 vil 3m/4km E of Towcester. SP 7249
Shutt Green Staffs 35 E3* loc 1m NW of Brewood. SJ 8709
Shuttington Warwicks 35 H4 vil 3m/5km E of Tamworth. SK 2505
Shuttlewood Derbys 44 A4* vil 2m/3km N of Bolsover. **Shuttlewood Common** loc to N. SK 4672
Shuttleworth Gtr Manchester 47 H6 vil 5m/7km N of Bury. SD 8017
Shuttleworth Hall Lancs 48 B5* 17c hse 1km NW of Hapton across Leeds and Liverpool Canal. SD 7832
Sibbertoft Northants 36 C6 vil 3m/4km SE of Husbands Bosworth. Site of motte and bailey cas to NE. SP 6882
Sibdon Carwood Salop 34 B5* vil 2km W of Craven Arms. SO 4183
Sibertswold Kent 13 G2 vil 6m/9km NW of Dover. Also known as Shepherdswell. TR 2548
Sibford Ferris Oxon 27 G4 vil 7m/11km W of Banbury. SP 3537
Sibford Gower Oxon 27 G4 vil 7m/11km W of Banbury. SP 3537
Sible Hedingham Essex 30 C4 small tn 3m/5km NW of Halstead. TL 7834
Sibley's Green Essex 30 B5* ham 2m/3km S of Thaxted. TL 6128
Siblyback Reservoir Cornwall 3 G2* resr on S edge of Bodmin Moor 4m/7km NW of Liskeard. SX 2370
Sibsey Lincs 45 G6 vil 5m/7km NE of Boston. **Sibsey Fen Side** loc 1m NW of Sibsey. TF 3550
Sibson Cambs 37 F4* ham 2m/3km SE of Wansford. TL 0997
Sibson Leics 36 A4 vil 6m/9km N of Nuneaton. SK 3500
Sibster H'land 86 F2 loc in Caithness dist 3m/4km NW of Wick. ND 3252
Sibthorpe Notts 44 C6 vil 6m/9km SW of Newark-on-Trent. SK 7645
Sibton Suffolk 31 G2 loc 2m/3km W of Yoxford. Remains of 12c abbey. Loc of **Sibton Green** 2km N. TM 3669
Sicklesmere Suffolk 30 D2 vil 3m/4km SE of Bury St Edmunds. TL 8760
Sicklinghall N Yorks 49 F3 vil 3m/4km W of Wetherby. SE 3648
Sid 8 A5* r in Devon rising 6m/9km N of Sidmouth and flowing into the English Channel at that tn. SY 1287
Sidbrook Som 8 B2* loc 3m/5km NE of Taunton. ST 2527
Sidbury Devon 7 H5 vil 3m/5km N of Sidmouth. 1km W, **Sidbury Castle,** ancient camp on Castle Hill. SY 1391
Sidbury Salop 34 D5 vil 5m/8km SW of Bridgnorth. SO 6885
Sid Cop S Yorks 43 H1* loc adjoining Cudworth to N. SE 3809
Sidcot Avon 15 H5 ham 2m/3km N of Axbridge. ST 4257
Sidcup London 20 B4 dist in borough of Bexley 5m/8km W of Dartford and 12m/19km SE of Charing Cross. TQ 4671
Siddal W Yorks 48 D5* loc in Halifax 2km S of tn centre. SE 1023
Siddick Cumbria 52 A2* loc 2km N of Workington. NY 0031
Siddington Ches 42 D4 ham 5m/8km N of Congleton. **Siddington Heath** loc 1m SW. SJ 8470
Siddington Glos 17 E2 vil 2km SE of Cirencester. Loc of **Upr Siddington** to W. SU 0399
Side, East Gwent 15 G1* loc 1m N of Abertillery. SO 2105
Side, High Cumbria 52 B2* loc 3m/5km SE of Cockermouth. NY 1628
Sidemoor H & W 26 D1 loc in N part of Bromsgrove. SO 9571
Side, North Cambs 37 G4 ham on R Nene 5m/8km E of Peterborough. TL 2799
Side, North Cumbria 52 A2* dist of Workington N of R Derwent. NY 0029
Side of the Moor Gtr Manchester 47 G6* loc adjoining Bradshaw to E. SD 7412
Side, South Durham 54 A2* ham 1km N of Butterknowle. NZ 1026
Sidestrand Norfolk 39 F1 vil near coast 3m/5km SE of Cromer. TG 2639
Sideway Staffs 35 E1* loc in Stoke-on-Trent 2km S of city centre. SJ 8843
Sidford Devon 5 G2 suburb of Sidmouth, 2m/3km N of sea front. SY 1390
Sidlaw Hills Tayside 73 E2-F1 range of hills on SE side of Strathmore, extending from Perth to vicinity of Forfar. Summit is Craigowl Hill, 1492 ft or 455 metres. NO 34
Sidlesham W Sussex 11 E5 vil 4m/6km N of Selsey. Site of Roman villa 2km S. SZ 8598
Sidley E Sussex 12 D5 N dist of Bexhill. TQ 7309
Sidmouth Devon 5 G2 S coast resort at mouth of R Sid 13m/21km E of Exeter. SY 1287
Siefton Salop 34 B5* loc 3m/5km E of Craven Arms. SO 4883
Sigford Devon 4 D3* loc 3m/5km NE of Ashburton. SX 7773
Sigglesthorne Humberside 51 F4 vil 3m/5km W of Hornsea. TA 1646
Sighthill Lothian 65 H2* dist of Edinburgh 4m/7km SW of city centre. College of Commerce. **Sighthill Industrial Estate** to W. NT 1970
Sigingstone S Glam 15 E4 ham 2m/4km SW of Cowbridge. SS 9771
Signet Oxon 27 F6* loc 2km S of Burford. SP 2410
Silbury Hill Wilts 17 E4* ancient earthwork (A.M.) 1m S of Avebury. Largest artificial mound in Europe. SU 1068
Silchester Hants 18 B5 vil 7m/11km N of Basingstoke. 1m E, site of Roman tn of *Calleva.* SU 6262
Sileby Leics 36 B3 vil 5m/8km SE of Loughborough. SK 6015
Silecroft Cumbria 52 B6 vil 3m/5km W of Millom. SD 1381
Sili Welsh form of Sully, qv.
Silian Dyfed 24 B3 loc 2m/3km N of Lampeter. SN 5751
Silkstead Hants 10 B3* loc 2km SE of Hursley. SU 4424
Silkstone S Yorks 43 G1 vil 4m/6km W of Barnsley. **Silkstone Common** vil 1m S. SE 2905
Silksworth Tyne & Wear 61 H6* loc in Sunderland 3m/5km SW of tn centre. See also New Silksworth. NZ 3752
Silk Willoughby Lincs 37 F1 vil 2m/3km S of Sleaford. TF 0542
Sill Field Cumbria 53 E6* loc 5m/9km NW of Kirkby Lonsdale. SD 5585
Silloth Cumbria 59 F6 tn and small port on Solway Firth 10m/15km NW of Wigton. **Silloth Bay** to N of harbour. NY 1153
Silo 32 D5* r running W into R Stewy on W side of Penrhyncoch, Dyfed. SN 6383
Siloh Dyfed 24 C4* loc 2m/4km NW of Llandovery. SN 7437
Silpho N Yorks 55 G5 ham 5m/8km NW of Scarborough. SE 9692
Silsden W Yorks 48 C3 tn in Airedale 4m/6km N of Keighley across R Aire. Textiles. **Silsden Resr** on moors to N. SE 0446
Silsoe Beds 29 E4 vil 2km S of Clophill. TL 0835
Silstwn Welsh form of Gileston, qv.
Silton Dorset 9 E2 loc 3m/4km NW of Gillingham. ST 7829
Silton, Nether N Yorks 54 D5 vil 6m/9km E of Northallerton. See also Over Silton. SE 4592
Silton, Over N Yorks. See Over Silton.
Silverbank Grampian 77 G2* loc adjoining Banchory to E. NO 7196
Silver Bay Gwynedd 40 A4* southward-facing bay at SE end of Holy I., Anglesey. SH 2975
Silver Burn 46 B6* r on Isle of Man rising on E side of S Barrule and running S into Castletown Bay at Castletown. SC 2667
Silverdale Lancs 47 E1 vil 4m/6km NW of Carnforth. **Silverdale Green** loc adjoining to E. SD 4675
Silverdale Staffs 42 D6 dist of Newcastle-under-Lyme 2m/3km W of tn centre. Coal-mining. SJ 8146
Silver End Beds 29 E3 ham 4m/6km NW of Shefford. TL 1042
Silver End Essex 30 C6 vil 4m/6km SE of Braintree. TL 8119
Silvergate Norfolk 39 F2* loc 2km NW of Aylsham. TG 1727
Silver Green Norfolk 39 F5* loc 6m/9km NW of Bungay. TM 2593
Silverknowes Lothian 66 A1* dist of Edinburgh 3m/5km NW of city centre. NT 2075
Silverlace Green Suffolk 31 G2* loc 3m/5km SE of Framlingham. TM 3260
Silverley's Green Suffolk 31 G1* loc 2km NW of Cratfield. TM 2975
Silver, Little Devon 7 F5* ham 2m/3km NE of Crediton. SS 8601
Silver, Little Devon 7 G4* loc 3m/5km SW of Tiverton. SS 9109
Silversands Bay Fife 73 E5* bay on Firth of Forth on E side of Aberdour. NT 2085
Silverstone Northants 28 B3 vil 3m/5km SW of Towcester. Motor-racing circuit to S. SP 6744
Silver Street Kent 21 E5* loc adjoining Bredgar to W. TQ 8760
Silver Street Som 8 A2* ham 2m/4km E of Wellington. ST 1721
Silver Street Som 8 D1* loc 2km N of Keinton Mandeville. ST 5432
Silverton Devon 7 G4 vil 5m/8km SW of Cullompton. SS 9502
Silverton S'clyde 64 B2* E dist of Dumbarton. NS 4075
Silvertown London 20 A4* loc in borough of Newham on N bank of R Thames (Woolwich Reach). TQ 4079
Silverwell Cornwall 2 C3* loc 2m/4km SE of St Agnes. SW 7448
Silvington Salop 34 C6 vil 4m/7km NW of Cleobury Mortimer. SO 6279
Simister Gtr Manchester 42 D1* loc 2m/3km E of Whitefield. SD 8305
Simmondley Derbys 43 E2* 1m SW of Glossop. SK 0293
Simm's Cross Ches 42 B3* dist of Widnes to N of tn centre. SJ 5185
Simonburn Nthmb 60 D4 vil 7m/11km NW of Hexham. Slight remains of medieval cas in wd 1km W. NY 8773
Simondston Mid Glam 15 E3* loc 2km E of Bridgend. SS 9280
Simonsbath Som 7 F2 vil on Exmoor 7m/12km SE of Lynton. SS 7739
Simons Burrow Devon 7 H3* ham 2m/3km N of Hemyock. ST 1416
Simonside Tyne & Wear 61 H5* loc in S Tyneside dist 2km SE of Jarrow. NZ 3463
Simonstone Lancs 48 A4/B4* vil adjoining Read to E. SD 7734
Simonswood Merseyside 42 A2* loc 2m/3km NE of Kirkby. SD 4200
Simprim Borders 67 E4 loc 4m/6km N of Coldstream. NT 8545
Simpson Bucks 28 D4 vil in Milton Keynes 3m/4km SE of the centre. SP 8836
Simpson Green W Yorks 48 D4* loc in Bradford 3m/5km NW of city centre. SE 1837
Simpson Ground Reservoir Cumbria 52 D6* small resr 2m/3km E of Newby Br. SD 3986
Sinclair's Bay H'land 86 F2 bay on E coast of Caithness dist extending from Noss Hd northwards to Brough Hd. ND 35
Sinclairtown Fife 73 F5* N dist of Kirkcaldy. NT 2993
Sinderby N Yorks 54 C6 vil 6m/10km SE of Bedale. SE 3481
Sinderhope Nthmb 60 D6 loc 2m/4km S of Allendale Tn. NY 8452
Sinderland Gtr Manchester 42 C2* loc 2km SE of Partington. SJ 7390
Sindlesham Berks 18 C4 vil adjoining Winnersh to S. Royal Merchant Navy School at Bearwood to S of vil. SU 7769
Sinfin Derbys 36 A2* loc in Derby 3m/5km S of tn centre. SK 3431
Single Street London 20 B5* loc in borough of Bromley 2km E of Biggin Hill. TQ 4359
Singleton Lancs 47 E4 vil 2m/4km E of Poulton-le-Fylde. **Lit Singleton** 1m NW. SD 3838
Singleton W Sussex 11 E4 vil below S Downs 5m/9km N of Chichester. SU 8713
Singlewell Kent 20 C4 S dist of Gravesend, sometimes known as Ifield. TQ 6570
Singret Clwyd 41 H5* loc 3m/5km N of Wrexham. SJ 3455
Sinkhurst Green Kent 12 D3* loc 2m/3km SW of Headcorn. TQ 8142
Sinnahard Grampian 82 D5* loc 5m/9km S of Lumsden. NJ 4713
Sinnington N Yorks 55 F6 vil 4m/6km W of Pickering. SE 7485
Sinton Green H & W 26 C2 ham 4m/7km NW of Worcester. SO 8160
Sior Loch S'clyde 70 B3 small loch in Argyll 8m/13km SE of Oban. NM 0623
Sipson London 19 E4 loc in borough of Hillingdon on N side of London (Heathrow) Airport and 14m/23km W of Charing Cross. TQ 0777
Sir Edward's Lake Nthmb. See Capheaton. NZ 0379
Sirhowy Gwent 15 F1 loc 1km NE of Tredegar. SO 1410
Sirhowy (Sirhywi) 15 G2 r rising N of Tredegar, Gwent, and flowing S by Tredegar and Blackwood into Ebbw R 1m W of Risca. ST 2291
Sirhywi Welsh form of Sirhowy (R), qv.
Sisland Norfolk 39 G5 loc 1m W of Loddon. TM 3498
Sissinghurst Kent 12 D3 vil 2km NE of Cranbrook. 1m NE, **Sissinghurst Castle** (NT), Tudor hse with famous garden. TQ 7937
Sisters, The Cornwall 6 A6* two islands off N coast 1m N of Tintagel. SX 0690
Siston Avon 16 C4 vil 7m/11km E of Bristol. ST 6875
Sithney Cornwall 2 C5 vil 2m/3km NW of Helston. Ham of **Sithney Green** to E. SW 6329
Sittingbourne Kent 21 E5 industrial tn 8m/13km E of Gillingham. TQ 9063
Six Ashes 35 E5 ham on borders of Salop and Staffs 5m/9km SE of Bridgnorth. SO 7988
Six Bells Gwent 15 G1/G2 loc adjoining Abertillery to S. SO 2203
Six Hills Leics 36 C2/C3 loc and rd junction 7m/11km W of Melton Mowbray. SK 6420
Sixhills Lincs 45 F3 vil 4m/7km E of Mkt Rasen. TF 1787
Six Mile Bottom Cambs 30 B2 vil 6m/9km SW of Newmarket. TL 5756
Six Mile Cottages Kent 13 G3 loc 6m/10km N of Hythe. TR 1344
Sixpenny Handley Dorset 9 G3 vil 5m/8km NW of Cranborne. ST 9917
Six Roads End Staffs 35 G2* loc and rd junction 1km S of Draycott in the Clay. SK 1527
Sixteen Foot Drain 38 A4 fenland drainage channel connecting Forty Foot Drain NE of Chatteris, Cambs, with Middle Level Drain S of Upwell. TF 5000
Sizergh Castle Cumbria 53 E5/E6 14c cas (NT) with later additions, 3m/5km S of Kendal. SD 4987
Sizewell Suffolk 31 H2 coastal loc 2m/3km E of Leiston. Nuclear power stn to N. TM 4762
Skail H'land 86 A3 loc in Caithness dist 9m/15km S of Bettyhill. NC 7146
Skaill Orkney 89 A6* locality on W coast of Mainland between Bay of Skaill and Loch of Skaill, 4m/6km W of Dounby. HY 2318
Skaill Orkney 89 B6* loc on W side of island of Egilsay. Landing stage on **Skaill Taing** headland. HY 4630
Skaill Orkney 89 C6/C7 loc on coast at E end of Mainland 2m/3km S of Mull Hd. HY 5806
Skara Brae Orkney 89 A6 remains of Neolithic settlement (A.M.) on W coast of Mainland 4m/7km W of Dounby. HY 2218
Skares S'clyde 56 E2 vil 3m/5km SW of Cumnock. NS 5217
Skares, The Grampian 83 H3 reef of almost submerged rocks at S end of Bay of Cruden, 9m/14km S of Peterhead. Sometimes known as The Scaurs. NK 0833
Skateraw Lothian 67 E1 loc 4m/7km SE of Dunbar. **Skateraw Harbour** on rocky coast to NE. NT 7375
Skaw Shetland 89 F6* loc at head of small bay of **Skaw Voe** on N coast of island of Whalsay, 2km W of Skaw Taing, qv. HU 5866
Skaw Taing Shetland 89 F6 headland at NE end of island of Whalsay. HU 6066
Skeabost Skye, H'land 78 C4 loc 5m/8km NW of Portree. NG 4148
Skeckling Humberside 51 F5* loc adjoining Burstwick to N. TA 2228
Skeeby N Yorks 54 B4 vil 2m/3km NE of Richmond. NZ 1902
Skeffington Leics 36 C4 vil 8m/13km W of Uppingham. SK 7402
Skeffling Humberside 51 G6 vil on N side of R Humber estuary 4m/7km SE of Patrington. TA 3719
Skegby Notts 44 A5 suburb 2km N of Sutton in Ashfield. SK 5060

Skegness Lincs 45 H5 coastal resort 19m/30km NE of Boston. TF 5663

Skelberry Shetland 89 E7* loc on Mainland on N shore of Dury Voe 2m/3km E of Laxo. HU 4763

Skelberry Shetland 89 E8* loc on Mainland 1m SE of Scousburgh. HU 3916

Skelbo H'land 87 B6/B7 loc on S side of Loch Fleet near E coast of Sutherland dist 4m/6km N of Dornoch. **Skelbo Castle** is ancient seat of the Sutherlands. **Skelbo Street** is loc to SE. NH 7995

Skelbrooke S Yorks 49 G6* vil 3m/4km E of S Elmsall. SE 5112

Skelda Ness Shetland 89 E7 headland on Mainland 6m/10km W of Scalloway across The Deeps. Inlet of **Skelda Voe** to N. HU 3041

Skelding N Yorks 49 E2* loc 4m/7km NE of Pateley Br. SE 2169

Skeldyke Lincs 37 H1 ham 4m/7km S of Boston. TF 3337

Skell 49 E1 r rising on Dallow Moor, N of Pateley Br, N Yorks, and flowing E past Fountains Abbey and through Studley Park and Ripon into R Ure on E side of Ripon. SE 3270

Skellingthorpe Lincs 44 D4 vil 3m/5km W of Lincoln. SK 9272

Skellister Shetland 89 E7 locality near E coast of Mainland at head of S Nesting Bay. **Ness of Skellister** is headland to NE. **Loch of Skellister** is loch to N. HU 4654

Skellorn Green Ches 43 E3* loc 2km S of Poynton. SJ 9281

Skellow S Yorks 44 A1 loc 5m/8km NW of Doncaster. SE 5310

Skelmanthorpe W Yorks 43 G1 tn 2m/3km N of Denby Dale. SE 2310

Skelmersdale Lancs 42 A1 New Tn designated 1961, developed around former mining vil. Industries include rubber, glass, textiles. SD 4806

Skelmorlie S'clyde 64 A2 resort on Firth of Clyde adjoining Wemyss Bay to S, and 5m/9km N of Largs. **Skelmorlie Castle,** restored, dates from early 16c. **Upr Skelmorlie** is loc adjoining to E. NS 1967

Skelpick H'land 86 A2 loc in Caithness dist 4m/6km S of Bettyhill. NC 7255

Skelsmergh Cumbria 53 E5 loc 2m/4km NE of Kendal. **Skelsmergh Tarn** small lake to N. SD 5395

Skelton Cleveland 55 E3 vil 2m/3km S of Saltburn. Cas of late 18c. Locs in vicinity are **New Skelton** 1km E; **N Skelton** 1m E; **Skelton Green** 1km S, with **Skelton High Green** adjoining it to W. NZ 6518

Skelton Cumbria 52 D2 vil 6m/9km NW of Penrith. NY 4335

Skelton Humberside 50 C5 vil on left bank of R Ouse 2m/3km SE of Howden. SE 7625

Skelton N Yorks 49 F2 vil 2m/4km NW of Boroughbridge. SE 3668

Skelton N Yorks 50 B3 vil 4m/6km NW of York. SE 5656

Skelton N Yorks 54 A4 loc 5m/8km W of Richmond. NZ 0900

Skelton Wood End Cumbria 52 D1* loc 3m/4km NW of Skelton. NY 4038

Skelwick Orkney 89 B5* loc on island of Westray 4m/6km SE of Pierowall. Bay of **Skel Wick** on E coast to NE. HY 4844

Skelwith Bridge Cumbria 52 D4 ham 2m/4km W of Ambleside. **Skelwith Force** waterfall to W. NY 3403

Skendleby Lincs 45 G4/H4 vil 3m/5km NE of Spilsby. **Skendleby Psalter** loc 2km N. TF 4369

Skenfrith (Ynysgynwraidd) Gwent 26 A5 vil on R Monnow 6m/9km NW of Monmouth. Remains of small 13c cas (NT). SO 4520

Skerne Humberside 51 E3 vil 2m/3km SE of Gt Driffield. TA 0455

Skerne 54 C4* r rising N of Trimdon, Durham, and flowing E into Hurworth Burn Resr, then circuitously SW to Darlington and into R Tees at Croft. NZ 2810

Skeroblin Loch S'clyde 62 D5 small loch or tarn in Kintyre 4m/6km N of Campbeltown. NR 7026

Sker Point (Sger, Y) Mid Glam 14 D3* headland 3m/4km NW of Porthcawl. SS 7879

Skerray H'land 84 F2 loc near N coast of Caithness dist 6m/10km NE of Tongue. NC 6563

Skerries, The (Ynysoedd y Moelrhoniaidd) Gwynedd 40 A2 group of small rocky islands lying 2m/3km NW of Anglesey coast at Carmel Hd, on one of which is a lighthouse. SH 2694

Skerries, The Shetland. See Out Skerries.

Skerry, Little Orkney 89 B8* one of the Pentland Skerries, qv. Lit Skerry is the most southerly of the group. ND 4776

Skerry of Eshaness Shetland 89 D6* rock island off S end of Esha Ness on NW coast of Mainland. HU 2076

Skerton Lancs 47 E2* dist of Lancaster N of R Lune. SD 4763

Skervuile S'clyde 62 D1* island rock with lighthouse lying 2m/4km off E coast of Jura opp Lowlandman's Bay. NR 6071

Sketchley Leics 36 A5* S dist of Hinckley. SP 4292

Sketchley Hill Leics 36 A5* SE dist of Hinckley. SP 4393

Sketty W Glam 23 G6 loc in Swansea 2m/3km W of tn centre. **Lr Sketty** loc 1m SW. SS 6292

Skewen (Sgiwen) W Glam 14 C2 loc 2m/3km W of Neath. SS 7296

Skewsby N Yorks 50 B1 ham 7m/11km N of Strensall. SE 6271

Skeyton Norfolk 39 F2 loc 4m/6km E of Aylsham. **Skeyton Corner** loc 2km N. TG 2425

Skiack H'land 81 F1 r running E to Cromarty Firth, Ross and Cromarty dist, 1m SE of Evanton. Also spelt Sgitheach. NH 6165

Skiag Bridge H'land 85 C5 br and rd junction on NE side of Loch Assynt, Sutherland dist, 2m/3km NW of Inchnadamph. NC 2324

Skidbrooke Lincs 45 H2* loc 2km SW of Saltfleet. **Skidbrooke North End** loc 2m/3km N. TF 4492

Skidby Humberside 51 E5 vil 6m/10km NW of Hull. TA 0133

Skiddaw Cumbria 52 C2 mt in Lake Dist, in mountain region known as **Skiddaw Forest,** 4m/6km N of Keswick. Height 3054 ft or 931 metres. NY 2629

Skigersta W Isles 88 C1 vil near N end of Lewis 2km S of Port of Ness. Port Skigersta is small bay to NE. NB 5461

Skilgate Som 7 G3 vil on S slopes of Exmoor 4m/6km NE of Bampton. SS 9827

Skillington Lincs 36 D2/37 E2 vil 2m/4km NW of Colsterworth. SK 8925

Skinburness Cumbria 59 F5 vil on Solway Firth 2m/3km NE of Silloth. Site of small Roman fort at landward end of peninsula running out to Grune Pt. NY 1255

Skinidin Skye, H'land 78 A4 locality 2m/3km W of Dunvegan across head of loch. NG 2247

Skinners Green Berks 17 H5* loc 2m/3km SW of Newbury. SU 4465

Skinningrove Cleveland 55 F3 loc on North Sea coast 1m NW of Loftus. NZ 7119

Skinsdale H'land 87 A5 r in Sutherland dist running S from Borrobol Forest to Black Water 11m/18km NW of Brora. NC 7615

Skip Bridge Durham 54 C4* loc 3m/4km SE of Darlington. NZ 3111

Skipness S'clyde 63 F2 vil on **Skipness Bay** on E coast of Kintyre, Argyll. 1m E is **Skipness Pt,** headland at entrance to Loch Fyne. **Skipness Castle** is a ruined cas with parts dating from 13c. NR 9057

Skipper Island Essex 31 F5* uninhabited marshy island 3m/5km W of The Naze. TM 2124

Skippool Lancs 47 E4* loc adjoining Poulton-le-Fylde to NE. SD 3540

Skiprigg Cumbria 60 A6* loc 3m/5km SE of Dalston. NY 3845

Skipsea Humberside 51 F3 vil near coast 5m/8km NW of Hornsea. **Skipsea Brough** loc 1km W. Remains of motte and bailey cas (A.M.). TA 1655

Skipton N Yorks 48 C3 mkt and industrial tn on R Aire and on Leeds and Liverpool Canal 16m/26km NW of Bradford. Cas dates from 11c but is mainly of 14c-15c. SD 9851

Skipton-on-Swale N Yorks 49 F1 vil 4m/7km W of Thirsk. SE 3679

Skipwith N Yorks 50 B4 vil 5m/8km NE of Selby. **Lit Skipwith** ham adjoining Skipwith to NW. SE 6638

Skirbeck Lincs 37 H1 loc 2km SE of Boston. TF 3442

Skirbeck Quarter Lincs 37 H1 dist of Boston 1m S of tn centre. TF 3242

Skirfare 48 C2 r rising on moors N of Pen-y-ghent, N Yorks, and flowing SE through Halton Gill, Litton, and Arncliffe, into R Wharfe 2m/3km S of Kettlewell. Valley of R Skirfare is known as Littondale. SD 9769

Skirlaugh, North Humberside 51 F4 ham adjoining S Skirlaugh to N. TA 1440

Skirlaugh, South Humberside 51 F4 vil 7m/12km NE of Hull. TA 1439

Skirling Borders 65 G4 vil 2m/4km E of Biggar. NT 0739

Skirmett Bucks 18 C3 vil 5m/8km N of Henley-on-Thames. SU 7790

Skirpenbeck Humberside 50 C3 vil 2m/4km E of Stamford Br. SE 7155

Skirrid Fawr (Ysgyryd Fawr) Gwent 25 H6 hill (NT) 3m/5km NE of Abergavenny commanding views of Black Mts and R Usk valley. Height 1596 ft or 486 metres. SO 3318

Skirts of Foudland Grampian. See Hill of Foudland.

Skirwith Cumbria 53 E2 vil 7m/11km E of Penrith. NY 6132

Skirwith N Yorks 48 A1 loc 1m NE of Ingleton. To E at SW foot of Ingleborough is **Skirwith Cave,** limestone cavern. SD 7073

Skirza H'land 86 F1 loc near E coast of Caithness dist 3m/5km S of Duncansby Hd. **Skirza Hd** is headland 1km E. ND 3868

Skitby Cumbria 60 A5* loc 1km E of Smithfield. NY 4465

Skittle Green Bucks 18 C2* loc 2m/4km W of Princes Risborough. SP 7702

Skokholm Dyfed 22 A5 island off SW coast of Wales 2m/3km S of Skomer and 4m/7km W of St Ann's Hd. Bird sanctuary. SM 7305

Skomer Dyfed 22 A5 island and nature reserve at S end of St Brides Bay, opp Wooltack Pt and 11m/18km W of Milford Haven. **Skomer Hd,** headland at SW corner of island. SM 7209

Skrinkle Haven Dyfed 22 C5/C6* small bay 1m E of Manorbier. SS 0897

Skronkey Lancs 47 E3* loc 1m SE of Pilling. SD 4147

Skuda Sound Shetland 89 F5* sea passage between Uyea and S coast of Unst to E of Clivocast. HP 6000

Skulamus Skye, H'land 79 E6* loc 2km E of Broadford. NG 6622

Skullomie H'land 84 F2* loc on Tongue Bay, Caithness dist, 3m/5km NE of Tongue. NC 6161

Skutterskelfe N Yorks 54 D4 loc 3m/4km W of Stokesley. NZ 4807

Skyborry Green Salop 34 A6* loc 2m/3km NW of Knighton. SO 2674

Skyborry, Nether Salop 34 A6* loc 2km NW of Knighton. SO 2773

Skye H'land 78, 79 largest of the Hebridean islands, 535 sq miles or 1386 sq km, separated from Scottish mainland by Sound of Sleat between Kyleakin and Kyle of Lochalsh, here less than 1km in width. The coastline is much indented. The island is hilly, the Cuillin Hills rising to 3257 ft or 993 metres. The climate is moist. Industries include tourism, fishing, farming, forestry. NG 43

Skye and Lochalsh 114 admin dist of H'land region.

Skye Green Essex 30 D5* ham 2km SE of Coggeshall. TL 8722

Skye of Curr H'land 81 H5 loc in Badenoch and Strathspey dist 1km SW of Dulnain Br. NH 9924

Skyre Burn 58 B6 r in Dumfries & Galloway region running S into Fleet Bay at **Skyreburn Bay,** where there is a large caravan site. NX 5754

Skyreholme N Yorks 48 D2* loc 1m E of Appletreewick. SE 0660

Skythorns N Yorks 48 C2* loc 1km NW of Threshfield. SD 9863

Slack Derbys 43 G5* loc 3m/5km NE of Matlock. SK 3363

Slack W Yorks 48 C5 vil 2km NW of Hebden Br. Also known as Heptonstall Slack. SD 9728

Slackcote Gtr Manchester 43 E1* loc 1m S of Denshaw. SD 9709

Slack Head Cumbria 47 F1* loc 1km SW of Beetham. SD 4978

Slackholme End Lincs 45 H4* loc 1m S of Hogsthorpe. TF 5370

Slack Side W Yorks 48 D5* loc in Bradford 3m/4km SW of city centre. SE 1330

Slack, The Durham 54 A2* ham adjoining Butterknowle to SE. NZ 1125

Slad Glos 16 D1 vil 2m/3km NE of Stroud. SO 8707

Slade Devon 6 D1* vil 1m SW of Ilfracombe. **Slade Resrs** to S. SS 5046

Slade Devon 7 H4* loc 5m/9km NW of Honiton. ST 1108

Slade Dyfed 22 B4* loc 1m NW of Haverfordwest. SM 9316

Slade W Glam 23 F6 loc above Port Eynon Bay on S coast of Gower peninsula. SS 4885

Slade End Oxon 18 B3* loc 2m/3km NW of Wallingford. SU 5890

Slade Field Cambs 37 H5* loc adjoining Chatteris to N. TL 3887

Slade Green London 20 B4 loc in borough of Bexley 1m SE of Erith and 14m/23km E of Charing Cross. TQ 5276

Slade Heath Staffs 35 E4* loc 5m/8km N of Wolverhampton. SJ 9206

Slade Hooton S Yorks 44 A2* vil 2m/3km S of Maltby. SK 5289

Sladesbridge Cornwall 3 E2* loc 2m/3km SE of Wadebridge. SX 0171

Slades Green H & W 26 D4* loc 3m/5km NW of Tewkesbury. SO 8534

Slade, The Berks 18 A4* loc 4m/7km NE of Newbury. SU 5369

Slaggan Bay H'land 78 F1 westward-facing bay at entrance to Loch Ewe, Ross and Cromarty dist, 4m/6km NW of Aultbea. To E, ruined vil of Slaggan. NG 8394

Slaggyford Nthmb 60 C6 ham 5m/7km NW of Alston. NY 6752

Slaidburn Lancs 48 A3 vil at confluence of R Hodder and Croasdale Brook below Forest of Bowland 7m/11km N of Clitheroe. SD 7152

Slaid Hill W Yorks 49 E4* loc 5m/8km NE of Leeds. SE 3340

Slain Hollow Staffs 43 F6* site of battle AD 716, 4m/7km E of Cheadle. SK 0743

Slains Castle Grampian 83 H3 site of 19c cas, now demolished, on granite headland above Port Erroll, on E coast 7m/11km S of Peterhead. See also Old Castle of Slains. NK 0935

Slaithwaite W Yorks 48 D6 tn in steep-sided valley of R Colne 4m/7km W of Huddersfield. SE 0714

Slaley Derbys 43 G5* loc 3m/4km SW of Matlock. SK 2757

Slaley Nthmb 61 E5 vil 5m/7km SE of Hexham. To SW, **Slaley Forest,** area planted with conifers. NY 9757

Slamannan Central 65 E2 vil 5m/8km SW of Falkirk. NS 8573

Slapton Bucks 28 D5 vil 3m/5km S of Leighton Buzzard. SP 9320

Slapton Devon 5 E6 vil 5m/9km SW of Dartmouth. **Slapton Sands** on coast to E with raised beach backed by 1-mile long lagoon, **Slapton Ley.** SX 8245

Slapton Northants 28 B3 vil 4m/6km W of Towcester. SP 6446

Slatepit Dale Derbys 43 H4* loc 3m/5km SW of Chesterfield. SK 3468

Slatrach Bay S'clyde 70 A2 bay on N coast of Kerrera. NM 8129

Slattocks Gtr Manchester 42 D1 loc 3m/5km S of Rochdale. SD 8808

Slaugham W Sussex 11 H2 vil 1m S of Handcross. TQ 2528

Slaughden Suffolk 31 H3 loc at S end of Aldeburgh on narrow neck of land separating R Alde estuary from sea. Slaughden Quay is anchorage for small craft; sailing club. TM 4655

Slaughterford Wilts 16 D4 vil 5m/8km W of Chippenham. ST 8473

Slaughter Hill Ches 42 C5* loc adjoining Haslington to S, 2m/3km E of Crewe. SJ 7355

Slaughter, Lower Glos 27 F5 vil 3m/4km SW of Stow-on-the-Wold. SP 1622

Slaughter, Upper Glos 27 F5 vil 3m/5km SW of Stow-on-the-Wold. SP 1523

Slawston Leics 36 D5 vil 5m/9km NE of Mkt Harborough. SP 7794

Slay Pits S Yorks 44 B1* loc 1m E of Hatfield. SE 6709

Slea 45 F5 r rising on Willoughby Heath, SW of Ancaster, Lincs, and flowing E through Sleaford into R Witham 3m/4km S of Tattershall. TF 2054

Sleaford Hants 11 E2 ham 5m/9km W of Hindhead. SU 8038

Sleaford Lincs 45 E6 tn 11m/18km NE of Grantham. Agriculture, malting. TF 0645

Sleagill Cumbria 53 E3 ham 3m/5km NE of Shap. NY 5919

Sleap Salop 34 B2* loc 2m/4km SW of Wem. SJ 4826

Sleapford Salop 34 C3 ham 3m/5km N of Wellington. SJ 6315

Sleapshyde Herts 19 F1* loc 2m/4km SW of Hatfield. TL 2006
Sleat Skye, H'land 79 D7, E7 par and peninsula in SE Skye. Peninsula is connected to rest of island by isthmus between Loch Eishort and Loch na Dal and extends 14m/22km south-westwards to Pt of Sleat, most southerly point of Skye. See also Sound of Sleat. NG 6309
Slebech (Slebets) Dyfed 22 C4 loc 5m/8km E of Haverfordwest. Park contains ruined ch of the Knights Templars. SN 0314
Slebets Welsh form of Slebech, qv.
Sledge Green H & W 26 C4 loc 5m/8km W of Tewkesbury. SO 8134
Sledmere Humberside 50 D2 vil 7m/12km NW of Gt Driffield. **Sledmere Hse,** seat of Sykes family, is Ggn mansion in grnds by Capability Brown. SE 9364
Sleekburn, East Nthmb 61 G3* loc 2m/3km NE of Bedlington. NZ 2883
Sleekburn, West Nthmb 61 G3* loc 2m/3km S of Ashington across R Wansbeck. NZ 2885
Sleights N Yorks 55 G4 vil running down to R Esk 3m/5km SW of Whitby. NZ 8607
Sleningford N Yorks 49 E1* loc 1m SE of W Tanfield. Former vil no longer exists. SE 2777
Slepe Dorset 9 F5* loc 4m/6km N of Wareham. SY 9293
Slerra Devon 6 B3* loc 1km SW of Clovelly. SS 3124
Slickly H'land 86 F1 loc in Caithness dist 7m/11km SW of John o' Groats. ND 2966
Sliddery S'clyde 63 F5 loc near SW coast of Arran 4m/6km SE of Blackwaterfoot. **Sliddery Water** is r running SW out to sea 1km S of Sliddery. NR 9322
Sligachan Skye, H'land 79 C6 locality and hotel at head of Loch Sligachan, 8m/13km S of Portree. **R Sligachan** runs N from Cuillin Hills to head of loch; noted for salmon fishing. NG 4829
Sligga Skerry Shetland 89 E6* group of rocks lying off NW coast of island of Bigga at S end of Yell Sound. HU 4380
Slimbridge Glos 16 C1 vil 4m/6km N of Dursley. Wildfowl Trust nature reserve 2km NW near R Severn estuary. SO 7403
Slindon Staffs 35 E2 vil 2m/3km N of Eccleshall. SJ 8232
Slindon W Sussex 11 F4 vil 4m/6km W of Arundel. SU 9608
Slinfold W Sussex 11 G2 vil 4m/6km W of Horsham. TQ 1131
Slingley Hill Durham 61 H6* loc 3m/5km W of Seaham. NZ 3848
Slingsby N Yorks 50 C1 vil 6m/10km W of Malton. Ruins of **Slingsby Castle,** 17c hse. SE 6974
Slioch H'land 80 A1 mt in Ross and Cromarty dist 3m/5km N of head of Loch Maree. Height 3217 ft or 981 metres. NH 0068
Slip End Beds 29 E5 ham 2m/3km S of Luton. TL 0718
Slipton Northants 37 E6 vil 3m/5km W of Thrapston. SP 9579
Slitting Mill Staffs 35 F3* ham 1m SW of Rugeley. SK 0217
Slochd H'land 81 G5 loc in Badenoch and Strathspey dist 4m/6km W of Carrbridge. NH 8424
Slockavullin S'clyde 70 A5 loc in Argyll 1m SW of Kilmartin. Many prehistoric remains in vicinity. NR 8297
Sloley Norfolk 39 G3* loc 4m/6km S of N Walsham. TG 2924
Sloothby Lincs 45 H4 vil 4m/7km SE of Alford. TF 4970
Slough Berks 18 D3 industrial tn on N side of R Thames valley 21m/33km W of London. SU 9780
Slough Green Som 8 B2* ham 2m/3km W of Hatch Beauchamp. ST 2720
Slough Green W Sussex 11 H3* loc 2m/3km NW of Cuckfield. TQ 2826
Slough Trading Estate Berks 18 D3* NW dist of Slough. SU 9581
Sloyne, The Merseyside 41 H3* part of R Mersey estuary opp Birkenhead. SJ 3387
Slug of Auchrannie Tayside 76 C5/D5*. See Auchrannie.
Slumbay H'land 80 A4 two adjoining localities, **Easter** and **Wester Slumbay,** on NW shore of Loch Carron to SW of vil of Lochcarron, Ross and Cromarty dist. NG 8939
Slwch Tump Powys. See Brecon.
Slyfield Green Surrey 19 E6* loc 2m/3km N of Guildford. SU 9952
Slyne Lancs 47 E2 vil 3m/4km N of Lancaster. SD 4765
Sma' Glen Tayside 72 C2 stony defile in Glen Almond at SE edge of Highlands, 6m/9km N of Crieff. Traditional burial place of Ossian. NN 9029
Smailholm Borders 66 D5 vil 5m/8km W of Kelso. **Smailholm Tower** (A.M.), 2km SW, is 16c tower on isolated hillock, beside small loch. NT 6436
Smallbridge Gtr Manchester 48 B6 loc 2m/3km NE of Rochdale. SD 8913
Smallbrook Devon 7 F5* loc 2m/3km SE of Crediton. SX 8698
Small Brook 6 B4* r in Devon rising S of Soldon Cross and flowing SW into R Tamar 1m N of Bridgerule. SS 2704
Smallburgh Norfolk 39 G3 vil 5m/8km SE of N Walsham. TG 3324
Smalldale Derbys 43 F3* ham just NE of Peak Dale. SK 0977
Smalldale Derbys 43 F3* loc adjoining Bradwell to NW. SK 1681
Small Dole W Sussex 11 H4 vil 2m/3km S of Henfield. TQ 2112
Smalley Derbys 36 A1 vil 6m/10km NE of Derby. **Smalley Green** loc 1m S. **Smalley Common** loc 2km S. SK 4044
Smallfield Surrey 19 G6 vil 2m/3km E of Horley. TQ 3143
Smallford Herts 19 F1 loc 3m/4km E of St Albans. TL 1907
Small Heath W Midlands 35 G5* loc in Birmingham 2m/4km SE of city centre. SP 0985
Small Hythe Kent 13 E4 ham 2m/3km S of Tenterden. **Smallhythe Place** (NT), 15c half-timbered hse, formerly home of Ellen Terry. TQ 8930
Small Isles S'clyde 62 C1, C2 group of small uninhabited islands off E coast of Jura between Rubha na Caillich and Rubh' an Leanachais. From S to N they are: Eilean nan Gabhar, Eilean nan Coinein, Eilean Diomhain, Pladda, and Eilean Bhride. NR 5468
Small Isles, The H'land 68, 79 group of islands in Inner Hebrides comprising islands of Rum, Eigg, Canna, and Muck. NG, NM
Smallridge Devon 8 B4 ham 2m/3km N of Axminster. ST 3001
Smalls, The Dyfed 22 to W of sq A5. Group of rocks with lighthouse 15m/25km W of Skomer. SM 4608
Smallthorne Staffs 42 D6 loc 2km E of Burslem. SJ 8850
Small Water Cumbria 52 D4* small lake 1m SW of S end of Haweswater Resr. NY 4510
Small Way Som 8 D2* loc 1m S of Castle Cary. ST 6330
Small Wood Hey Lancs 47 E3* loc adjoining Pilling to SW. SD 3948
Smallworth Norfolk 39 E6 ham 1km S of Garboldisham. TM 0080
Smannell Hants 17 G6 ham 3m/4km N of Andover. SU 3849
Smarden Kent 13 E3 vil 7m/11km SW of Charing. TQ 8842
Smearisary H'land 68 E2 loc near coast of Lochaber dist 5m/8km NW of Kinlochmoidart. NM 6477
Smeatharpe Devon 8 A3 ham 7m/11km N of Honiton. ST 1910
Smeaton Fife 73 F5* N dist of Kirkcaldy. NT 2893
Smeaton, Great N Yorks 54 C4 vil 7m/11km N of Northallerton. NZ 3404
Smeaton, Little N Yorks 49 G6 vil 6m/9km SE of Pontefract. SE 5216
Smeaton, Little N Yorks 54 C4* loc 1km S of Gt Smeaton. NZ 3403
Smedley Gtr Manchester 42 D2* loc in Manchester 2km NE of city centre. SD 8400
Smeeth Kent 13 F3 vil 5m/7km SE of Ashford. TR 0739
Smeeton Westerby Leics 36 C5 vil 5m/8km NW of Market Harborough. SP 6792
Smelthouses N Yorks 48 D2/49 E2 loc 2m/4km E of Pateley Br. SE 1964
Smerclett W Isles 88 E3* loc near S end of S Uist, 1m NW of Kilbride. NF 7415
Smerral H'land 86 E4* loc near E coast of Caithness dist 1m NW of Janetstown. ND 1733
Smestow Staffs 35 E5* ham 6m/9km SW of Wolverhampton. SO 8591
Smethwick W Midlands 35 F5 dist of Warley 2m/3km from tn centre. SP 0288
Smethwick Green Ches 42 D5* loc 4m/6km W of Congleton. SJ 8063
Smiddy Shaw Reservoir Durham 61 E6* resr on Muggleswick Common 3m/5km SE of Edmondbyers. NZ 0446
Smisby Derbys 36 A3 vil 2m/3km N of Ashby de la Zouch. SK 3519
Smite 44 C6* r rising N of Ab Kettleby, Leics, and flowing N into R Devon 6m/9km S of Newark-on-Trent, Notts. SK 7945
Smith End Green H & W 26 C3 ham 5m/8km W of Worcester. SO 7752
Smithfield Cumbria 60 A5 ham 6m/10km NW of Brampton. NY 4465
Smith Green Lancs 47 F3* loc 4m/7km S of Lancaster. SD 4855
Smithies S Yorks 43 H1* loc in Barnsley 1m N of tn centre. SE 3508
Smithies, The Salop 34 D4* loc 4m/6km E of Much Wenlock. SO 6797
Smithill's Hall Gtr Manchester 42 C1* half-timbered 14c hse in Bolton 2m/3km NW of tn centre. SD 7011
Smithincott Devon 7 H4* ham 1m SW of Uffculme and 4m/6km NE of Cullompton. ST 0611
Smithley S Yorks 43 H1* loc 1m W of Wombwell. SE 3803
Smith's End Herts 29 G4* S end of vil of Barley, 3m/5km SE of Royston. TL 4037
Smith's Green Essex 30 A5 loc adjoining vil of Takeley to E, 4m/6km W of Gt Dunmow. TL 5621
Smith's Green Essex 30 B4* ham 4m/6km S of Haverhill. TL 6740
Smithstone S'clyde 65 E2* loc in Cumbernauld 2m/3km W of tn centre. NS 7375
Smithstown H'land 78 F2* locality on W coast of Ross and Cromarty dist 1km NW of Gairloch. NG 7977
Smithtown H'land 81 F3 loc in Inverness dist 3m/5km E of Inverness. NH 7145
Smithy Bridge Gtr Manchester 48 C6* loc on R Roch 1m SW of Littleborough. SD 9215
Smithy Brow Ches 42 C2* loc adjoining Croft to W. SJ 6293
Smithy Gate Clwyd 41 G4* loc 1km SW of Holywell. SJ 1775
Smithy Green Ches 42 C4 loc 6m/9km E of Northwich. SJ 7474
Smithy Green Cumbria 52 C6* loc adjoining Penny Br to S. SD 3082
Smithy Green Gtr Manchester 42 D3* loc 2km W of Bramhall. SJ 8785
Smithy Houses Derbys 43 H6* loc 2m/4km S of Ripley. Coal mines in vicinity. SK 3847
Smithy Lane Ends Lancs 42 A1* loc 3m/5km N of Ormskirk. SD 4012
Smockington Leics 36 A5* loc 3m/5km SE of Hinckley. SP 4589
Smoky Row Bucks 18 C1* loc 2m/3km N of Princes Risborough. SP 8106
Smoo Cave H'land 84 D2 large limestone cavern near N coast of Sutherland dist, 2km SE of Durness. NC 4167
Smug Oak Herts 19 F2 loc 4m/6km NE of Watford. TL 1303
Smyth's Green Essex 30 D6 ham 6m/10km SW of Colchester. TL 9218
Snab Point Nthmb 61 G2 headland on North Sea coast 3m/5km N of Newbiggin-by-the-Sea. NZ 3092
Snaefell Isle of Man 46 B4 mt and highest point on the island, 3m/5km NW of Laxey. Electric rly to summit. Views to England, Scotland, Wales, and Ireland, in clear weather. Height 2036 ft or 621 metres. SC 3988
Snail r rising at Snailwell, Cambs. See Soham Lode.
Snailbeach Salop 34 B4 loc 10m/16km SW of Shrewsbury. SJ 3702
Snailsden Reservoir S Yorks 43 F1* small resr 3m/4km S of Holmfirth. SE 1303
Snailswell Herts 29 F4* loc 2m/3km N of Hitchin. TL 1732
Snailwell Cambs 30 B2 vil 3m/5km N of Newmarket. TL 6467
Snainton N Yorks 55 G6 vil 8m/12km E of Pickering. SE 9282
Snaith Humberside 50 B5 vil 6m/10km W of Goole. SE 6422
Snape N Yorks 54 B6 vil 2m/4km S of Bedale. Cas, partly ruined Tudor hse. SE 2684
Snape Suffolk 31 G2 vil 3m/4km S of Saxmundham. Loc of **Snape Watering** 1km NW. Vil of **Snape Street** 1m S. **Snape Maltings,** 2km S at head of R Alde estuary, contains opera hse. TM 3959
Snape Green Lancs 42 A1 loc 1km N of Scarisbrick. SD 3814
Snape Hill S Yorks 43 H1* loc adjoining Darfield to W. SE 4004
Snaple Point W Glam 23 G6* headland at W end of Langland Bay 2m/3km W of Mumbles Hd. SS 6387
Snapper Devon 6 D2* loc 3m/4km NE of Barnstaple. SS 5934
Snap, The Shetland 89 F6* headland at SE end of Fetlar 2km S of Funzie. (See also Butsa, to NE.) HU 6587
Snaresbrook London 20 A3 loc in borough of Redbridge 1m N of Wanstead. TQ 4089
Snarestone Leics 36 A3 vil 5m/8km S of Ashby de la Zouch. SK 3409
Snarford Lincs 45 E3 ham 6m/9km SW of Mkt Rasen. TF 0582
Snargate Kent 13 E4 ham on Romney Marsh 2m/3km E of Appledore. TQ 9928
Snarra Ness Shetland 89 D7* headland on Mainland, on S shore of St Magnus Bay, 3m/5km E of Melby. **Voe of Snarraness** is inlet on W side of headland. HU 2357
Snatchwood Gwent 15 G1* loc 1km S of Abersychan. SO 2602
Snave Kent 13 F4 ham 2m/3km S of Ham Street. TR 0129
Sneachill H & W 26 D2 loc 4m/6km E of Worcester. SO 9053
Snead Powys 34 A5 loc 2m/3km N of Bishop's Castle. SO 3192
Snead's Green H & W 26 D1* loc 4m/6km NW of Droitwich. SO 8667
Sneath Common Norfolk 39 F5* loc 3m/5km NW of Pulham Market. TM 1589
Sneaton N Yorks 55 G4 vil 2m/3km S of Whitby. **Sneaton Thorpe** loc 2km SE. NZ 8907
Snelland Lincs 45 E3 vil 4m/6km NW of Wragby. TF 0780
Snelston Derbys 43 F6 vil 3m/4km SW of Ashbourne. SK 1543
Snetterton Norfolk 38 D5 ham 4m/7km SW of Attleborough. Motor-racing circuit on Snetterton Heath to S. TL 9991
Snettisham Norfolk 38 B2 vil 4m/7km S of Hunstanton. TF 6834
Sneug, The Shetland 89 D8 peak of island of Foula. Height 1372 ft or 418 metres. HT 9439
Sneyd Green Staffs 42 D6* loc 2km NE of Hanley. SJ 8949
Sneyd Park Avon 16 B4* dist of Bristol 2m/4km NW of city centre. ST 5575
Snibston Leics 36 A3 loc 1m NW of Coalville. SK 4114
Snig's End Glos 26 C4 ham adjoining Staunton to S, 7m/11km N of Gloucester. SO 7929
Snipe Point Nthmb 67 G4* headland on N coast of Holy I. NU 1244
Snipeshill Kent 21 E5* E dist of Sittingbourne. TQ 9263
Snitter Nthmb 61 E2 ham 2m/4km NW of Rothbury. NU 0203
Snitterby Lincs 44 D2 vil 4m/6km SE of Kirton in Lindsey. SK 9894
Snitterfield Warwicks 27 F2 vil 3m/5km N of Stratford-upon-Avon. SP 2159
Snitterton Derbys 43 G5* ham 2km W of Matlock. SK 2760
Snittlegarth Cumbria 52 C2 loc 3m/4km E of Bothel. NY 2137
Snizort H'land 78 C4 r in Skye running N into head of Loch Snizort Beag 6m/9km NW of Portree. NG 4148
Snodhill H & W 25 G4 loc 6m/9km E of Hay-on-Wye. SO 3140
Snodland Kent 20 D5 industrial loc on R Medway 5m/8km NW of Maidstone. Cement and paper works. TQ 7061
Snook Point Nthmb 67 H5* headland on North Sea coast at S end of Beadnell Bay. NU 2426
Snook, The Nthmb 67 G4* barren W end of Holy I. **Snook Pt,** headland at W extremity of island. NU 0943
Snoring, Great Norfolk 38 D2 vil 3m/5km NE of Fakenham. **Lit Snoring** vil 2m/3km S. TF 9434
Snowden Hill S Yorks 43 G1* loc 2m/3km SE of Penistone. SE 2600
Snowdon (Yr Wyddfa) Gwynedd 40 C5/C6 mt 4m/6km N of Beddgelert. Height

3560 ft or 1085 metres. S terminus of Snowdon Mountain Rly. The highest mt in Wales, Snowdon gives its name to the mt range of which it forms part, and to the region, **Snowdonia,** surrounding it. SH 6054
Snow End Herts 29 G4* ham 3m/5km NE of Buntingford. TL 4032
Snow Falls N Yorks 48 A1* series of waterfalls in R Doe 1m NE of Ingleton. SE 7074
Snowshill Glos 27 E4 vil 3m/4km S of Broadway. **Snowshill Manor,** Tudor hse (NT). SP 0933
Snow Street Norfolk 39 E6* loc 2m/3km NW of Diss. TM 0981
Snub, The Grampian 83 H4* spit of land on W side of R Ythan estuary, 2m/3km N of Newburgh. NK 0028
Snuff Hill H & W 26 D1* loc 3m/5km N of Bromsgrove. SO 9474
Snydale W Yorks 49 F5 loc 2m/3km SW of Featherstone. **Old Snydale** loc 1m N. SE 4020
Soa Coll, S'clyde 68 A4 small island lying off S coast of main island opp entrance to Loch Breachacha. NM 1551
Soa Tiree, S'clyde 69 B7 island lying off E end of Gott Bay on S coast. NM 0746
Soa Island S'clyde 69 B6 small island 2m/3km SW of Rubha na Carraig-géire at S end of Iona. NM 2419
Soake Hants 10 D4* ham 2km NW of Waterlooville. SU 6611
Soar Mid Glam 15 F3* loc 2m/3km W of Taff's Well. ST 0983
Soar Powys 25 E4* loc 2m/4km SE of Llanfihangel Nant Bran. SN 9732
Soay H'land 79 C7 island of about 4 sq miles or 10 sq km lying off S coast of Skye across Soay Sound. Lobster fishing. Island is mainly flat, but rises to 455 ft or 108 metres in Beinn Bhreac. NG 4514
Soay W Isles (W of 88 A3) steep, rocky, uninhabited island (NTS) in the St Kilda group about 56m/89km W of Harris and 37m/59km W of N Uist, lying off NW end of St Kilda itself. Area about 240 acres or 97 hectares. Haunt of sea birds. NA 0601
Soay Mór W Isles 88 A3* small uninhabited island in W Loch Tarbert, W coast of Harris. Adjacent to NW is smaller island of **Soay Beag.** NB 0605
Soberton Hants 10 C3 vil 2m/3km S of Meonstoke. Site of Roman bldg 2km SE. SU 6116
Soberton Heath Hants 10 C3* loc 2km S of Soberton and 4m/6km S of Meonstoke. SU 6014
Soch 32 B2* r rising S of Tudweiliog, Gwynedd, and flowing into St Tudwal's Bay at Abersoch. SH 3128
Society Lothian 65 G1 loc on S side of Firth of Forth 2m/3km W of Forth Rd Br. NT 0979
Sockbridge Cumbria 53 E2 loc 2m/4km S of Penrith. NY 5026
Sockburn Durham 54 C4 ham in loop of R Tees 6m/9km SE of Darlington. NZ 3407
Sodbury, Little Avon 16 C3 vil 2m/3km E of Chipping Sodbury. Ham of **Lit Sodbury End** 1km NW. ST 7583
Soden 24 A3* r rising 4m/7km S of Newquay, Dyfed, and flowing NW into Cardigan Bay 2m/3km SW of the tn. SN 3658
Sodom Clwyd 41 G4* loc 1m N of Bodfari. SJ 0971
Sodylt Bank Salop 34 A1 loc 2m/4km SW of Overton. SJ 3439
Softley Durham 54 A2* loc 1m NW of Butterknowle. NZ 0926
Soham Cambs 30 B1 vil 5m/8km SE of Ely. Loc of **Soham Cotes** 2m/3km NW. TL 5973
Soham Lode 30 A1* r rising as R Snail at Snailwell, Cambs, and flowing NW to Soham, thence as Soham Lode into R Ouse 3m/4km S of Ely. TL 5476
Soho London 19 G3* dist in City of Westminster bounded, roughly, by Oxford Street, Regent Street, Shaftesbury Avenue, and Charing Cross Rd. TQ 2981
Soldier's Leap, The Tayside 76 A4 narrowest part of the chasm in the Pass of Killiecrankie – see Killiecrankie. NN 9162
Soldon Devon 6 C4* loc 5m/7km N of Holsworthy. **Soldon Cross** is loc at crossroads to W. SS 3210
Soldridge Hants 10 D2* ham 5m/8km SW of Alton. SU 6534
Solent Breezes Hants 10 C4* loc on E shore of Southampton Water 4m/7km NW of Lee-on-the-Solent. SU 5003
Solent Forts See Spithead Forts.
Solent, The 10 B5, C5 sea channel separating Isle of Wight from English mainland and extending from Hurst Castle and Cliff End (W) to Portsmouth and Ryde (E). Width varies from about 2m/3km to 4m/6km. SZ 5098
Sole Street Kent 13 F2* ham 3m/5km NE of Wye. TR 0949
Sole Street Kent 20 C5 loc 4m/7km S of Gravesend. TQ 6567
Solfach Welsh form of Solva, qv.
Solihull W Midlands 35 G6 industrial tn 7m/11km SE of Birmingham. SP 1479
Solihull Lodge W Midlands 35 G6 loc in Solihull 4m/6km W of tn centre. SP 0978
Sollas W Isles 88 E1 vil near N end of N Uist 5m/8km E of Griminish Pt. NF 8074
Sollers Dilwyn H & W 26 A2* ham 5m/8km SW of Leominster. SO 4255
Sollers Hope H & W 26 B4* vil 6m/9km N of Ross-on-Wye. SO 6133
Sollom Lancs 47 E6 loc 7m/12km E of Southport. SD 4518
Solomon's Tump Glos 26 C5* loc 6m/10km W of Gloucester. SO 7319
Solsbury Hill, Little Avon 16 C4* hill (NT) with Iron Age fort, 1km W of Batheaston and 3m/4km NE of Bath. ST 7667
Solva (Solfach) Dyfed 22 A3 fishing vil near coast 3m/5km E of St David's. SM 8024
Solva 22 A3 r rising SW of Mathry, Dyfed, and flowing SW into St Brides Bay on S side of Solva vil. SM 8023
Solway Firth 59 E6, F5 arm of Irish Sea between coasts of Cumbria, England, and Dumfries and Galloway, Scotland. Receives waters of Rs Nith, Annan, Esk, Eden, Wampool, Waver, and Derwent. Largely occupied by broad sands and notorious for dangerous tides. Fish abound. NY 05
Solway Moss Cumbria 59 H4 marshy tract W of Longtown. Scene of battle in 1542 in which Scots under James V were defeated by English. NY 3469
Somborne, Little Hants 10 B2 ham 3m/4km SE of Stockbridge. SU 3832
Somerby Leics 36 D3 vil 5m/8km W of Oakham. SK 7710
Somerby Lincs 45 E1* vil 1km S of Bigby. Site of Roman bldg 1km W. TA 0606
Somercotes Derbys 43 H5 loc 2km SE of Alfreton. SK 4253
Somercotes, North Lincs 45 G2 vil near coast 3m/4km NW of Saltfleet. **Somercotes Haven** inlet 3m/4km N. **S Somercotes** vil 2m/3km S. **S Somercotes Fen Houses** loc 3m/5km SW. TF 4296
Somerford Dorset 9 H5* dist of Christchurch 2m/3km E of tn centre. SZ 1793
Somerford Staffs 35 E3 ham 2km E of Brewood. SJ 8908
Somerford, Great Wilts 16 D3 vil on R Avon 3m/5km SE of Malmesbury. ST 9682
Somerford Keynes Glos 17 E2 vil 4m/7km S of Cirencester. SU 0195
Somerford, Little Wilts 16 D3/17 E3 vil 3m/5km SE of Malmesbury. ST 9684
Somerley W Sussex 11 E5* vil 4m/7km NW of Selsey. SZ 8198
Somerleyton Suffolk 39 H5 vil 5m/8km NW of Lowestoft. **Somerleyton Hall,** 16c and 19c hse in park. TM 4897
Somersal Herbert Derbys 35 G1 vil 2m/4km NW of Sudbury. SK 1335
Somersby Lincs 45 G4 vil 6m/9km E of Horncastle. Birthplace of Lord Tennyson, 1809. TF 3472
Somerset 118 mainly agricultural county in SW England bounded by the Bristol Channel and the counties of Avon, Wiltshire, Dorset and Devon. Consists of ranges of hills – Mendips, Poldens, Quantocks, Brendons, and most of Exmoor – separated by valleys or extensive marshy flats, esp on either side of R Parrett. The chief tns are Taunton, the county tn; Bridgwater, Frome, Glastonbury, Shepton Mallet, Wellington, Wincanton, Yeovil, and the small cathedral city of Wells. The chief rs are Axe, Brue, Parrett, and Tone, draining into the Bristol Channel; and Barle and Exe, rising on Exmoor and flowing into Devon and the English Channel.
Somersham Cambs 37 H6 vil 5m/9km SW of Chatteris. TL 3677
Somersham Suffolk 31 E3 vil 5m/8km NW of Ipswich. TM 0848
Somers Town London 19 G3* loc in borough of Camden N of St Pancras in Central London. TQ 2983
Somerstown W Sussex dist of Chichester to N of tn centre. SU 8605
Somerton Gwent 15 H3* loc in Newport 2km E of tn centre. ST 3387
Somerton Oxon 28 A4 vil on R Cherwell 3m/5km S of Aynho. SP 4928
Somerton Som 8 C2 small mkt tn 4m/7km NW of Ilchester. ST 4828
Somerton Suffolk 30 C3 vil 5m/9km NW of Long Melford. TL 8153
Somerton Castle Lincs 44 D5 remains of 13c cas 2m/3km W of Boothby Graffoe. SK 9558
Somerton, East Norfolk 39 H3 vil 2km W of Winterton. **W Somerton** vil 1km W. TG 4719
Sompting W Sussex 11 G4 built-up area 2m/3km NE of Worthing. 1km NW is **Sompting Abbots** (or **Abbotts**) and Sompting ch, whose Saxon tower is only tower of 'Rhenish helm' type in Britain. TQ 1705
Sonning Berks 18 C4 vil 2m/3km W of Twyford. Ham of **Sonning Eye** across R Thames (in Oxon). SU 7575
Sonning Common Oxon 18 C3* suburban loc 4m/7km N of Reading. SU 7080
Sontley Clwyd 41 H6* loc 2m/4km S of Wrexham. **Old Sontley** loc to S. **Middle Sontley** loc to W. SJ 3346
Sooby Gill Waterfall Lancs 47 F2* waterfall 2km S of Hornby. SD 5866
Sookholme Notts 44 A4 ham 4m/6km N of Mansfield. SK 5466
Soothill, Lower W Yorks 49 E5* loc adjoining Batley to E. SE 2524
Sopley Hants 9 H4 vil in R Avon valley 3m/4km N of Christchurch. SZ 1597
Sopworth Wilts 16 D3 vil 2m/3km W of Sherston. ST 8286
Soray W Isles (W of 88 A2) one of the Flannan Isles, qv. Soray lies nearly 1m S of the main island, Eilean Mór. NA 7245
Sorbie D & G 57 E7 vil 4m/7km N of Whithorn. NX 4346
Sor Brook 28 A4* r rising NW of Banbury, Oxon. SP 4933
Sordale H'land 86 D2 loc in Caithness dist 4m/7km SE of Thurso. ND 1462
Sorisdale Coll, S'clyde 68 B3 loc on bay of same name 1km S of NE end of island. NM 2763
Sorn S'clyde 56 E2 vil on R Ayr 4m/6km E of Mauchline. **Sorn Castle** dates in part from 15c. NS 5526
Sortat H'land 86 F2 loc in Caithness dist 6m/10km SE of Castletown. ND 2863
Sotby Lincs 45 F3 ham 7m/11km NW of Horncastle. TF 2078
Sotherton Suffolk 31 H1 loc 3m/5km N of Blythburgh. TM 4479
Sots Hole Lincs 45 E4 ham 10km/6km SE of Lincoln. TF 1264
Sotterley Suffolk 39 H6 ham 4m/7km SE of Beccles. Hall is 18c hse in large undulating park. TM 4584
Sotwell Oxon 18 B3 vil 2m/3km NW of Wallingford. SU 5890
Soudley, Great Salop 34 D2 vil 5m/8km SE of Mkt Drayton. **Lit Soudley** loc 1km SW. SJ 7228
Soudley, Lower Glos 26 B6* loc 3m/4km S of Cinderford. SO 6610
Soudley, Upper Glos 26 B6 vil in Forest of Dean 2m/4km S of Cinderford. SO 6510
Soughton (Sychdyn) Clwyd 41 H4 vil 2km N of Mold. SJ 2466
Soulbury Bucks 28 D5 vil 3m/5km NW of Leighton Buzzard. SP 8827
Soulby Cumbria 52 D2/D3* loc 1km NW of Pooley Br. NY 4625
Soulby Cumbria 53 F4 vil 2m/4km NW of Kirkby Stephen. NY 7411
Souldern Oxon 28 A4 vil 7m/11km NW of Bicester. SP 5231
Souldrop Beds 29 E2 vil 4m/6km SE of Rushden. SP 9861
Soulseat Loch D & G 57 B6 loch 3m/4km SE of Stranraer. Peninsula on S shore is site of **Soulseat Abbey,** founded in 12c. NX 1058
Sound Ches 42 C6 loc 4m/6km SW of Nantwich. Contains loc of **Sound Heath.** SJ 6148
Sound Shetland 89 E7* loc on Mainland on W side of Weisdale Voe, 2km E of Tresta. HU 3850
Sound Shetland 89 E7 loc on Mainland 1m SW of Lerwick near head of large inlet, **Voe of Sound. Ness of Sound** is headland to S, on E side of inlet. Loc of **Upr Sound** to W. HU 4640
Sound Gruney Shetland 89 F5* small island 2km E of Burra Ness, Yell. HU 5796
Sound, North Orkney 89 B5, C5 sea area between islands of Sanday and Westray. HY 54
Sound of Arisaig H'land 68 D1-E2 large inlet on coast of Lochaber dist, with two arms, Loch nan Uamh and Loch Ailort, passing to N and S respectively of peninsula of Ardnish. NM 6580
Sound of Barra W Isles 88 E3 sea passage between S Uist and Barra. NF 7509
Sound of Bute S'clyde 63 F2-G3 sea area between island of Bute and N end of island of Arran. NS 05
Sound of Eigg H'land 68 C1, C2 sea passage between islands of Eigg and Muck in Inner Hebrides. NM 4382
Sound of Eriskay W Isles 88 E3 strait about 2km wide between islands of S Uist and Eriskay. NF 7913
Sound of Gigha S'clyde 62 D3 sea passage between island of Gigha and Kintyre, Argyll. NR 6749
Sound of Handa H'land 84 B3 narrow sea channel separating island of Handa from W coast of Sutherland dist. See Handa. NC 1547
Sound of Harris W Isles 88 A4 sea passage between Harris and N Uist containing innumerable small islands and rocks. The four larger islands are Berneray, Ensay, Killegray, and Pabbay, qqv. NF 97, 98
Sound of Hoxa Orkney 89 B7 sea passage between islands of Flotta and S Ronaldsay. ND 3893
Sound of Insh S'clyde 69 E6, F6 passage in Firth of Lorn between Insh I. and Seil. NM 7419
Sound of Iona S'clyde 69 B5, B6 sea strait between Iona and Ross of Mull. NM 2822
Sound of Islay S'clyde 62 B1-C2 narrow strait between islands of Islay and Jura. NR 3875
Sound of Jura S'clyde 62 C1, C2 sea passage between island of Jura and Scottish mainland. NR 6480
Sound of Kerrera S'clyde 70 A2. See Kerrera.
Sound of Luing S'clyde 69 E6, E7 sea passage to W of Luing, separating it from Scarba, Lunga, and neighbouring islands. NM 7208
Sound of Monach W Isles 88 D1 sea passage between Monach Isles, qv, and W coast of N Uist. NF 66
Sound of Mull 68 D3-E4 narrow sea passage between island of Mull, Strathclyde, and Morven, H'land, on Scottish mainland. Width varies from 2km to 5km. NM 5945
Sound of Papa Shetland 89 D7* strait 1m wide separating Papa Stour island from Mainland. See Papa Stour. HU 1758
Sound of Pladda S'clyde. See Pladda. NS 0220
Sound of Raasay H'land 78 D3, D4 sea channel between Raasay and Skye. NG 5654
Sound of Rum H'land 79 C8 sea passage between islands of Rum and Eigg, in Inner Hebrides. NM 4390
Sound of Scalpay W Isles 88 B3* narrow strait between island of Scalpay and SE coast of Harris. NG 2297
Sound of Shiant W Isles 88 B3/C3 sea passage between Shiant Is. and SE coast of Lewis. NB 30

Sound of Shuna S'clyde 70 B1 strait in Loch Linnhe between Shuna I. and mainland to E. NM 9249
Sound of Ulva S'clyde 68 C4. See Ulva.
Sound of Vatersay W Isles 88 D4* narrow, windy strait between islands of Barra and Vatersay. NL 6397
Sound, South Shetland 89 F6* sea passage between Hascosay and Ness of Vatsetter, Yell. HU 5490
Soundwell Avon 16 B4* S dist of Mangotsfield 5m/8km E of Bristol. ST 6575
Sourin Orkney 89 B6* loc at E end of island of Rousay 2m/3km N of Brinyan. HY 4330
Sourton Devon 6 D5 vil 5m/7km SW of Okehampton. SX 5390
Soutergate Cumbria 52 C6 ham 5m/8km N of Dalton-in-Furness. SD 2281
Souter Head Grampian 77 H1* headland on E coast 3m/5km SE of Aberdeen city centre. NJ 9601
Souter Johnnie's House S'clyde. See Kirkoswald.
Souter Point Tyne & Wear 61 H5 headland on North Sea coast at N end of Whitburn Bay. NZ 4162
SOUTH. For names beginning with this word, see under next word. This also applies to names beginning with North, East, West; Great, Little; Greater, Lesser; High, Low; Higher, Lower; Upper, Nether; Far, Near; Mid, Middle; Isle(s) of; The, Y, Yr.
Southall London 19 E3 dist in borough of Ealing 11m/18km W of Charing Cross. TQ 1280
Southall Green London 19 E4 loc in borough of Ealing 11m/18km W of Charing Cross. TQ 1279
Southam Glos 27 E5* vil 3m/4km NE of Cheltenham. SO 9725
Southam Warwicks 27 H2 small tn 7m/11km SE of Leamington. SP 4161
Southampton Hants 10 B3 city at confluence of Rs Itchen and Test at head of Southampton Water, 70m/113km SW of London. Container and transatlantic passenger port. Boat and helicopter ferries to Isle of Wight. Airport 2km S of Eastleigh. Divers industries. University. Remains of medieval tn walls. SU 4112
Southampton Water Hants 10 B4 arm of sea extending from Calshot Castle for 6m/10km NW to confluence of Rs Test and Itchen at Southampton. Average width at high tide about 1m or 2.5km. SU 4506
Southay Som 8 C3* ham adjoining E Lambrook 2m/3km W of Martock. ST 4319
Southborough Kent 12 C3 tn adjoining Tunbridge Wells to N. TQ 5842
Southborough London 19 F5* loc in borough of Kingston 2m/3km S of Kingston tn centre. TQ 1866
Southborough London 20 B5* loc in borough of Bromley 2m/3km SE of Bromley tn centre. TQ 4267
Southbourne Dorset 9 H5 seaside dist of Bournemouth 3m/5km E of tn centre. SZ 1391
Southbourne W Sussex 10 D4* vil 2km E of Emsworth. SU 7605
Southbrook Devon 7 G5* loc 5m/8km W of Ottery St Mary. SY 0296
Southburgh Norfolk 39 E4 vil 2m/3km NW of Hingham. TG 0004
Southburn Humberside 51 E3 vil 3m/5km SW of Gt Driffield. SE 9854
Southchurch Essex 21 E3 E dist of Southend-on-Sea. TQ 9085
Southcott Beds 28 D5* SW dist of Linslade. SP 9024
Southcott Wilts 17 F5* loc 1km SE of Pewsey. SU 1759
Southcourt Bucks 18 C1* S dist of Aylesbury. SP 8112
Southdean Borders 60 C1 loc 5m/7km NW of Carter Bar. NT 6309
Southdene Merseyside 42 A2* S dist of Kirkby. SJ 4197
Southdown Avon 16 C5* SW dist of Bath. ST 7264
Southease E Sussex 12 A6 vil in R Ouse valley 3m/5km S of Lewes. TQ 4205
Southend Bucks 18 C3* loc 5m/7km N of Henley-on-Thames. SU 7589
Southend London 20 A4 loc in borough of Lewisham 2m/4km S of Lewisham tn centre and 7m/12km SE of Charing Cross. TQ 3871
Southend Oxon 18 B2 loc adjoining Garsington to S, 5m/9km SE of Oxford. SP 5801
Southend S'clyde 62 D6 vil in Kintyre 8m/13km S of Campbeltown. NR 6908
Southend Wilts 17 F4* loc 1km SW of Ogbourne St George and 3m/4km N of Marlborough. SU 1973
Southend-on-Sea Essex 21 E3 resort on N side of Thames estuary 35m/57km E of London. Mile-long pier. Commercial centre. Radio and furniture mnfre. Municipal airport 2m/3km N. TQ 8786
Southerfield Cumbria 52 B1* loc 2m/3km SW of Abbey Town. NY 1648
Southerly Devon 6 D6* ham 6m/9km SW of Okehampton. SX 5288
Southernby Cumbria 52 D1* loc 2m/3km E of Hesket Newmarket. NY 3439
Southern Cross W Sussex 11 H4* E dist of Southwick. TQ 2405
Southerndown Mid Glam 14 D4 vil 4m/7km S of Bridgend. SS 8873
Southerness D & G 59 E5 small vil and resort with disused lighthouse at **Southerness Pt**, headland on Solway Firth 3m/5km S of Kirkbean. NX 9754
Southern Green Herts 29 G4* ham 4m/6km NW of Buntingford. TL 3131
Southerton Devon 5 F2* loc 4m/6km NW of Sidmouth. SY 0790
Southery Norfolk 38 B5 vil 5m/8km S of Downham Mkt. TL 6294
Southey Creek Essex 21 E2* channel of R Blackwater estuary running S of Northey I., 2m/4km SE of Maldon. TL 8805
Southey Green S Yorks 43 H2* loc in Sheffield 3m/4km N of city centre. SK 3491
Southfield Devon 5 E4* NW dist of Paignton. SX 8861
Southfield Fife 73 F4* dist and industrial estate on S side of Glenrothes. NT 2699
Southfield Lothian 66 B2* dist of Edinburgh 1m S of Portobello. NT 3072
Southfield Reservoir Humberside 49 H6* resr 2m/3km S of Snaith. SE 6519
Southfields London 19 F4* loc in borough of Wandsworth 2m/3km SE of Putney Br. TQ 2573
Southfleet Kent 20 C4 vil 3m/5km SW of Gravesend. TQ 6171
Southgate Ches 42 B3* dist of Runcorn SE of tn centre. SJ 5381
Southgate Dyfed 24 B1* suburb of Aberystwyth 1m S of tn centre. SN 5980
Southgate London 19 G2 dist in borough of Enfield 2m/3km SW of Enfield tn centre and 9m/14km N of Charing Cross. TQ 2994
Southgate Norfolk 38 B2* loc adjoining Snettisham to S. Site of Roman bldg to E. TF 6833
Southgate Norfolk 39 F2* loc 1km N of Cawston. TG 1324
Southgate W Glam 23 G6* loc near S coast of Gower peninsula 5m/8km W of Mumbles Hd. SS 5588
Southgate W Sussex 11 H2* S dist of Crawley. TQ 2635
Southhouse Lothian 66 A2* dist of Edinburgh 4m/7km S of city centre. NT 2767
Southill Beds 29 F3/F4 vil 2m/3km N of Shefford. TL 1542
Southington Hants 17 H6 ham 1km W of Overton. SU 5049
Southleigh Devon 8 A5 vil 3m/5km NW of Seaton. SY 2093
Southmarsh Som 9 E2* ham 2m/3km NE of Wincanton. ST 7330
Southminster Essex 21 E2 vil 2m/4km N of Burnham-on-Crouch. TQ 9599
Southmuir Tayside 76 D5 loc adjoining Kirriemuir to S. NO 3853
Southoe Cambs 29 F2 vil 3m/4km N of St Neots. TL 1864
Southolt Suffolk 31 F2 vil 4m/6km NE of Debenham. TM 1968
Southorpe Cambs 37 F4 vil 4m/7km SE of Stamford. TF 0803
Southover Dorset 8 D4* ham on S side of R Frome opp Frampton and 5m/8km NW of Dorchester. SY 6294
Southowram W Yorks 48 D5 vil 2m/3km SE of Halifax. SE 1123
Southport Merseyside 41 H1 coastal resort 16m/25km N of Liverpool. SD 3317
Southpunds Shetland 89 E8* loc on Mainland 8m/13km N of Sumburgh Hd. HU 4020
Southrepps Norfolk 39 F2 vil 4m/7km SE of Cromer. TG 2536
Southrey Lincs 45 E4 vil on R Witham 2m/3km SE of Bardney. TF 1366
Southrop Glos 17 F1 vil 3m/4km N of Lechlade. SP 2003
Southrope Hants 18 B6 ham 5m/8km SE of Basingstoke. SU 6744
Southsea Clwyd 41 H6 loc 2m/4km W of Wrexham. SJ 3051
Southsea Hants 10 D5 residential and holiday dist of Portsmouth 2km S of city centre. Hovercraft ferry for pedestrians to Isle of Wight from Clarence Pier. SZ 6498
Southtown Norfolk 39 H4 dist of Gt Yarmouth 1km S of tn centre across R Yare. TG 5206
Southtown Som 8 B3* loc 3m/4km NW of Ilminster. ST 3216
Southville Gwent 15 G2* loc near centre of Cwmbran. ST 2994
Southwaite Cumbria A6* vil 2m/3km W of High Hesket, on E side of M6 motorway service area. NY 4445
Southwark London 19 G4* borough on S side of R Thames, crossed here by Blackfriars, Southwark, London, and Tower Brs. Southwark Cathedral at S end of London Br. Surrey Commercial Docks at Rotherhithe (rd tunnel under r). Imperial War Museum (Lambeth Rd). TQ 3179
Southwater W Sussex 11 G3 vil 3m/5km S of Horsham. Loc of **Southwater Street** 1m N. TQ 1526
Southway Devon 4 B4* N dist of Plymouth, 4m/7km from city centre. SX 4860
Southway Som 8 C1* loc 2m/4km NE of Glastonbury. ST 5142
Southwell Dorset 9 E6 loc on Portland 2km N of Portland Bill. SY 6870
Southwell Notts 44 B5 tn 6m/10km W of Newark-on-Trent. Norman to Perp cathedral. SK 7053
Southwick D & G 59 E5 loc 7m/11km SE of Dalbeattie. NX 9257
Southwick Hants 10 C4 vil 3m/5km NW of Cosham. SU 6208
Southwick Northants 37 E5 vil 3m/4km NW of Oundle. Hall is Tudor and earlier. Site of Roman bldg 2m/3km W. TL 0292
Southwick Som 15 H6* loc 3m/4km E of Highbridge. ST 3546
Southwick Tyne & Wear 61 H5* dist of Sunderland 2km NW of tn centre across R Wear. NZ 3858
Southwick Wilts 16 D5 vil 2m/3km SW of Trowbridge. ST 8355
Southwick W Sussex 11 H4 tn on coast on E side of Shoreham-by-Sea. TQ 2405
Southwold Suffolk 31 H1 small coastal resort at mouth of R Blyth 8m/12km E of Halesworth. Industries include brewing. Lighthouse among hses at cliff top. TM 5076
Southwood Norfolk 39 G4* loc 1m W of Freethorpe. TG 3905
Southwood Som 8 D1* loc 2m/3km N of Keinton Mandeville. ST 5533
Sow 35 F2 r rising 1m NW of Fairoak, Staffs, and flowing SE through Stafford into R Trent 5m/8km E thereof. SJ 9922
Sowden Devon 5 F2* loc 2m/3km N of Exmouth. SX 9983
Sowe 35 H6/36 A6 r rising W of Bedworth, Warwicks, and flowing S through E parts of Coventry into R Avon 3m/4km E of Kenilworth. SP 3272
Sowerby N Yorks 54 D6 vil adjoining Thirsk to S. SE 4381
Sowerby W Yorks 48 C5 vil 2km W of **Sowerby Br**, a tn on R Calder 2m/4km SW of Halifax. Industries of Sowerby Br include textiles, carpets, engineering. SE 0423
Sowerby Row Cumbria 52 D1 ham 2m/3km E of Sebergham. NY 3940
Sower Carr Lancs 47 E4* loc 1m N of Hambleton. SD 3743
Sowerhill Som 7 G3* ham 3m/4km SW of Dulverton. SS 8924
Sowley Green Suffolk 30 C3* loc 4m/7km NE of Haverhill. TL 7050
Sowley Pond Hants 10 B5 lake to N of Sowley Hse 4m/6km E of Lymington. SZ 3796
Sow of Atholl, The Tayside 75 F4 mt of some 2500 ft or 762 metres on Dalnaspidal Forest, Atholl, 2km NW of Dalnaspidal Lodge. NN 6274
Sowood W Yorks 48 D6* ham 1km S of Stainland. **Sowood Green** ham adjoins to N. SE 0718
Sowton Devon 7 G5 vil on R Clyst 4m/6km E of Exeter. SX 9792
Soyea Island H'land 85 A5 small uninhabited island off W coast of Sutherland dist opp mouth of Loch Inver. NC 0422
Soyland Town W Yorks 48 C6* vil 1km N of Ripponden. SE 0320
Spacey Houses N Yorks 49 E3 loc adjoining Pannal to SE, 3m/4km S of Harrogate. SE 3051
Spa Common Norfolk 39 G2* loc 1m E of N Walsham. TG 2930
Spadeadam Waste Cumbria 60 B4/C4 moorland area N of Gilsland, partly afforested. Missile-testing ranges. NY 67
Spalding Lincs 37 G2 tn on R Welland 14m/23km SW of Boston. Centre of bulb-growing area; annual flower festival. Beet sugar processing. TF 2422
Spaldington Humberside 50 C5 vil 3m/5km N of Howden. SE 7633
Spaldwick Cambs 29 F1 vil 7m/11km W of Huntingdon. TL 1272
Spalford Notts 44 C4 vil 9m/14km W of Lincoln. SK 8369
Spanby Lincs 37 F1 ham 5m/8km S of Sleaford. TF 0938
Spango Water 65 E6 r in Dumfries & Galloway region running E to Crawick Water at **Spango Br**, 6m/9km NE of Sanquhar. NS 8217
Spania, High Notts 44 A6* loc adjoining Kimberley to N. SK 4945
Spaniard Rocks W Glam 23 F6* group of rocks on landward side of Burry Holms at N end of Rhosili Bay. SS 4092
Spanish Head Isle of Man 46 A6 headland (Manx NT) at SW end of island, 2m/4km SW of Port St Mary. SC 1865
Spar Cave Skye, H'land 79 D7 cave on W shore of Loch Slapin 1m N of Strathaird Pt. Also known as Uamh Altrumain. NG 5312
Sparham Norfolk 39 E3 vil 7m/11km NE of E Dereham. **Sparhamhill** loc 1km SE. TG 0719
Spark Bridge Cumbria 52 C6 ham 2km N of Greenodd. SD 3084
Sparket Cumbria 52 D3* loc 3m/4km W of Pooley Br. NY 4325
Sparkford Som 8 D2 vil 4m/7km SW of Castle Cary. ST 6026
Sparkhill W Midlands 35 G5* loc in Birmingham 3m/4km SE of city centre. SP 0983
Sparkwell Devon 4 C5 vil 4m/6km W of Ivybridge. SX 5857
Sparnon Gate Cornwall 2 C4* loc 2km NW of Redruth. SW 6843
Sparrow Green Norfolk 38 D3* loc 3m/4km NW of E Dereham. TF 9514
Sparrowpit Derbys 43 F3 ham 2m/3km E of Chapel-en-le-Frith. SK 0980
Sparrow's Green E Sussex 12 C3* N part of Wadhurst. TQ 6332
Sparsholt Hants 10 B2 vil 3m/5km NW of Winchester. Site of Roman bldg 2km SW. SU 4331
Sparsholt Oxon 17 G3 vil 3m/5km W of Wantage. SU 3587
Spartleton Edge Lothian 66 D2 ridge running NW to SE in Lammermuir Hills 6m/10km S of Stenton. NT 6565
Spartylea Nthmb 53 G1 loc 2m/4km N of Allenheads. NY 8548
Spath Staffs 35 G1 loc 2km N of Uttoxeter. SK 0835
Spaunton N Yorks 55 F5 ham 3m/5km NE of Kirkbymoorside. SE 7289
Spaxton Som 8 A1 vil 5m/7km W of Bridgwater. ST 2237
Spean H'land 74 C3 r in Lochaber dist running W down Glen Spean to R Lochy, below Loch Lochy. NN 1783
Spean Bridge H'land 74 D3 vil on R Spean in Lochaber dist 3m/5km E of foot of Loch Lochy at Gairlochy. Br built by Telford. Commandos trained hereabouts in World War II; Commando Memorial 1m W. NN 2281
Spear Head H'land 86 D1 headland on N coast of Caithness dist 2m/4km NW of Thurso. ND 0971
Spear Hill W Sussex 11 G3* loc 3m/5km N of Washington. TQ 1317
Speckington Som 8 D2* loc at E end of Yeovilton airfield 3m/4km E of Ilchester. ST 5623
Speedwell Avon 16 B4* dist of Bristol 3m/5km E of city centre. ST 6374
Speedwell Mine Derbys 43 F3* underground gallery and pothole in limestone cliff 1km W of Castleton. SK 1482

Speen Berks 17 H4 suburb 1m W of Newbury. SU 4568
Speen Bucks 18 C2 vil 3m/5km SE of Princes Risborough. SU 8499
Speeton N Yorks 51 F1 vil 4m/7km SE of Filey. TA 1474
Speke Merseyside 42 A3 dist of Liverpool 7m/11km SE of city centre. Liverpool Airport to W. **Speke Hall** (NT), half-timbered hse dating from 16c. SJ 4283
Speldhurst Kent 12 B3 vil 2m/4km NW of Tunbridge Wells. TQ 5541
Spellbrook Herts 29 H6 vil 3m/4km S of Bishop's Stortford. TL 4817
Spelsbury Oxon 27 G5 vil 2m/3km N of Charlbury. SP 3521
Spen W Yorks 48 D5* loc 1km E of Cleckheaton. SE 1925
Spencers Wood Berks 18 C4 vil 4m/7km S of Reading. SU 7166
Spen Green Ches 42 D5 ham 3m/5km SW of Congleton. SJ 8160
Spen, High Tyne & Wear 61 F5 vil 3m/5km S of Ryton. NZ 1359
Spennithorne N Yorks 54 A5 vil 2m/3km SE of Leyburn. Spennithorne Hall dates partly from 16c. SE 1389
Spennymoor Durham 54 B2 tn 4m/6km NE of Bishop Auckland. Coal-mining, electrical equipment, textiles. Trading estate 1m E. NZ 2533
Spernall Warwicks 27 E2* loc on R Arrow 3m/5km N of Alcester. SP 0862
Spetchley H & W 26 D2 vil 3m/5km E of Worcester. SO 8953
Spetisbury Dorset 9 F4 vil on R Stour 3m/5km SE of Blandford Forum. ST 9102
Spexhall Suffolk 31 G1 ham 2m/3km N of Halesworth. TM 3780
Spey 82 C1 r rising on Corrieyairack Forest in Highland region and flowing NE to Kingussie and down Strathspey by Aviemore, Grantown-on-Spey, and Rothes in Grampian region, to Spey Bay on Moray Firth at Kingston. Length 107m/172km. Noted for salmon fishing. NJ 3465
Spey Bay Grampian 82 C1 vil on bay of same name on N coast on E side of mouth of R Spey. NJ 3565
Speybridge H'land 82 A4 loc in Badenoch and Strathspey dist 1m S of Grantown-on-Spey. NJ 0326
Speymouth Forest Grampian 82 C2 state forest S of Fochabers. NJ 3657
Spidean a' Choire Leith H'land 80 A2* summit of Liathach, Ross and Cromarty dist. Height 3456 ft or 1054 metres. NG 9257
Spidean Dhomhuill Bhric H'land 80 A6 peak on border of Lochaber and Skye & Lochalsh dists 4m/6km S of Shiel Br and nearly 1m W of The Saddle. Height 3082 ft or 939 metres. NG 9212
Spidean Mialach H'land 74 B1 peak on Glenquoich Forest, Lochaber dist, 2km N of dam of Loch Quoich. Height 3268 ft or 996 metres. NH 0604
Spilsby Lincs 45 G4 small tn 11m/17km W of Skegness. Birthplace of Sir John Franklin, explorer, 1768. **New Spilsby** loc adjoining to SE. TF 4066
Spindlestone Nthmb 67 H5 loc 3m/4km E of Belford. NU 1533
Spinkhill Derbys 43 H3 vil 8m/13km SE of Sheffield. SK 4578
Spinney Hills Leics 36 B4* dist of Leicester 1m E of city centre. SK 6004
Spinningdale H'land 87 A7 vil on N shore of Dornoch Firth, Sutherland dist, 8m/12km W of Dornoch. NH 6789
Spital Berks 18 D4 S dist of Windsor. SU 9675
Spital H'land 86 E2 loc in Caithness dist 5m/8km W of Watten. ND 1654
Spital Merseyside 41 H3* loc 1m S of Bebington. SJ 3482
Spitalbrook Herts 20 A1 loc in S part of Hoddesdon. TL 3607
Spitalfields London 19 G3* loc in borough of Tower Hamlets to E of Liverpool Street rly stn, 1m NE of London Br. TQ 3381
Spital Hill S Yorks 44 B2* ham 2km E of Tickhill. SK 6193
Spital in the Street Lincs 44 D2 loc 9m/14km NW of Mkt Rasen. SK 9690
Spital Tongues Tyne & Wear 61 G5* loc in Newcastle 1m W of city centre. NZ 2365
Spithead 10 C5 roadstead off entrance to Portsmouth Harbour, Hampshire. Name often also applied to the whole of the channel separating the Isle of Wight in the vicinity of Ryde from the English mainland in the vicinity of Portsmouth and Gosport. SZ 6295
Spithead Forts 10 C5, D5* four brick and stone forts built in sea between Portsmouth and Isle of Wight in 1860s (also known as Palmerston forts after their originator) as defence against the French. The forts are Horse Sand Fort (SZ 6594), No Man's Land Fort (SZ 6393), Spit Sand Fort (SZ 6397), and St Helens Fort (SZ 6489). SZ 6489
Spithurst E Sussex 12 B5 loc 5m/8km N of Lewes. TQ 4217
Spittal Dyfed 22 C3 vil 5m/8km N of Haverfordwest. SM 9723
Spittal Humberside 50 C3 loc 4m/6km SE of Stamford Br. SE 7652
Spittal Nthmb 67 F3 dist of Berwick-upon-Tweed on S side of harbour. NU 0051
Spittalfield Tayside 73 E1 vil 5m/8km SW of Blairgowrie. Remains of Roman fortress 2km SE – see Inchtuthill. NO 1040
Spittal of Glenshee Tayside 76 B4 loc on Shee Water 13m/21km S of Braemar. NO 1169
Spixworth Norfolk 39 F3 vil 4m/7km N of Norwich. TG 2415
Splatt Cornwall 6 B6* loc 7m/12km NW of Launceston. SX 2288
Splaynens Green E Sussex 12 B4* ham 1km N of Fletching. TQ 4324
Splottlands (Sblot, Y) S Glam 15 G4* dist of Cardiff 2km E of city centre. Also known as Splott. ST 2076
Spodegreen Ches 42 C3* loc 1m SE of Bollington. SJ 7385
Spofforth N Yorks 49 F3 vil 3m/5km NW of Wetherby. Spofforth Castle (A.M.), ruined 14c fortified hse. SE 3651
Spondon Derbys 36 A1 loc in Derby 4m/6km E of tn centre. SK 4035
Spon End W Midlands 35 H6* dist of Coventry 1m W of city centre. SP 3279
Spon Green Clwyd 41 H5* loc adjoining Buckley to SE. SJ 2863
Spooner Row Norfolk 39 E5 vil 3m/4km SW of Wymondham. TM 0997
Sporle Norfolk 38 C3/D3 vil 2m/4km NE of Swaffham. TF 8411
Spotland Bridge Gtr Manchester 47 H6* dist of Rochdale 1m W of tn centre. SD 8813
Spott Lothian 66 D1 vil 2m/3km S of Dunbar. NT 6775
Spout of Ballagan Central 64 C1* series of cascades in course of Ballagan Burn 1m NE of Strathblane. NS 5780
Spratton Northants 28 C1 vil 6m/10km NW of Northampton. SP 7170
Spreakley Surrey 11 E1* vil 3m/5km S of Farnham. SU 8441
Spreyton Devon 7 E5 vil 7m/11km E of Okehampton. SX 6996
Spriddlestone Devon 4 C5* ham to SE of Plymouth, 3m/5km W of Yealmpton. SX 5351
Spridlington Lincs 45 E3 vil 9m/14km N of Lincoln. TF 0084
Springboig S'clyde 64 D2* dist of Glasgow 3m/5km E of city centre. NS 6464
Springburn S'clyde 64 D2 loc in Glasgow 2m/3km N of city centre. NS 6068
Springfield D & G 59 G4/H4 vil adjoining Gretna Green to E. NY 3268
Springfield Fife 73 F3 vil 3m/4km SW of Cupar. NO 3411
Springfield Gtr Manchester 42 C1* dist of Bolton 1m SE of tn centre. SD 7208
Springfield Gwent 15 G2* loc 2m/3km SW of Newbridge. ST 1895
Springfield Som 7 H3* W dist of Wellington. ST 1321
Springfield W Midlands 35 G6* loc in Birmingham 3m/5km SE of city centre. SP 0982
Springfield W Midlands 35 F5* loc in W part of Warley. SO 9688
Springfield Reservoir S'clyde 65 F3/F4* small resr 4m/6km E of Carluke. NS 9052
Spring Gardens Durham 54 B2* loc 1m W of W Auckland. NZ 1726
Spring Gardens Salop 34 B3/C3* loc in Shrewsbury NE of tn centre. SJ 5013
Spring Grove London 19 F4* loc in borough of Hounslow 10m/15km W of Charing Cross. TQ 1576
Spring Head Kent 20 C4* loc 1m S of Northfleet. Site of Roman settlement to W. TQ 6272
Spring Head W Yorks 48 D6 loc 4m/6km W of Huddersfield. SE 0816
Spring Hill Gtr Manchester 43 E1* loc in Oldham 2m/3km NE of tn centre. SD 9506
Springhill Staffs 35 F4* loc 4m/7km NW of Walsall. SJ 9704
Springhill Staffs 35 G4* loc 2km E of Brownhills. SK 0705
Spring Hill W Midlands 35 E4* SW dist of Wolverhampton. SO 8895
Springholm D & G 58 D4 vil 6m/9km NE of Castle Douglas. NX 8070
Spring Park London 20 A5* loc in borough of Croydon 3m/4km E of Croydon tn centre. TQ 3665
Springside S'clyde 64 B5 loc 3m/5km E of Irvine. NS 3738
Springslade Pool Staffs 35 F3* small lake 3m/5km NE of Penkridge. SJ 9616
Springs Mire W Midlands 35 F5* loc 1m W of Dudley tn centre. SO 9389
Springs Reservoir Lancs 47 G6* small resr next to Dingle Resr 4m/6km NW of Bolton. SD 6914
Springthorpe Lincs 44 D2 vil 4m/6km E of Gainsborough. SK 8789
Spring Vale Isle of Wight 10 C5* loc on NE coast 2m/3km E of Ryde. SZ 6291
Spring Vale S Yorks 43 G1* loc adjoining Penistone to E. SE 2503
Spring Valley Isle of Man 46 B5* loc 2km W of Douglas. SC 3575
Springwell Tyne & Wear 61 G5 vil 4m/6km SE of Gateshead. NZ 2858
Sprinkling Tarn Cumbria 52 C4* small lake 2km NE of Scafell Pike. NY 2209
Sprint 53 E5* r rising S of Haweswater, Cumbria, and flowing S into R Kent at Burneside. SD 5095
Sproatley Humberside 51 F4/F5 vil 4m/6km N of Hedon. TA 1934
Sproston Green Ches 42 C4* ham 2m/3km E of Middlewich. SJ 7366
Sprotbrough S Yorks 44 A1 vil 3m/4km W of Doncaster. SE 5302
Sproughton Suffolk 31 E3/E4 vil 3m/4km W of Ipswich. TM 1244
Sprouston Borders 67 E5 vil on S side of R Tweed 2m/3km NE of Kelso. NT 7535
Sprowston Norfolk 39 F4 suburb 2m/4km NE of Norwich. TG 2411
Sproxton Leics 36 D2 vil 5m/8km W of Colsterworth. SK 8524
Sproxton N Yorks 55 E6 vil 2m/3km S of Helmsley. SE 6181
Sprunston Cumbria 60 A6* loc 2m/3km SE of Dalston. NY 3948
Sprytown Devon 6 C6* ham 5m/8km E of Launceston. SX 4185
Spurlands End Bucks 18 D2* loc 4m/6km NE of High Wycombe. SU 8997
Spur Ness Orkney 89 C5/C6 headland at SW end of island of Sanday. **Holms of Spurness** are three islets to S. HY 6033
Spurn Head Humberside 51 G6 headland at end of long spit of land on N side of mouth of R Humber. Lighthouse 1km NE; lightship to SW. TA 3910
Spurstow Ches 42 B5 vil 4m/6km S of Tarporley. SJ 5557
Spynie Grampian 82 B1 loc 2m/3km NE of Elgin. To N are the ruins of Spynie Palace, formerly the cas of the Bishops of Moray. NJ 2265
Spyway Dorset 8 C5* ham above Askerswell to N, 4m/7km E of Bridport. SY 5293
Square, The Gwent 15 G2* loc in Upr Cwmbran. ST 2796
Squerryes Court Kent. See Westerham.
Sròn a' Chleirich Tayside 75 G3/H3 mt on Dail-na-mine Forest, Forest of Atholl, 9m/14km NW of Blair Atholl. Height 2670 ft or 814 metres. NN 7876
Sròn Coire na h-Iolaire H'land 75 F4* mt in Badenoch and Strathspey dist 1km SE of S end of Loch a' Bhealaich Bheithe. Height 3134 ft or 955 metres. NN 5170
Sròn na Lairig H'land 76 A1* NE peak of Braeriach, in Cairngorms. Situated in Badenoch and Strathspey dist close to border with Grampian region. Height 3885 ft or 1184 metres. NH 9601
Stableford Salop 34 D4* ham 5m/7km NE of Bridgnorth. SO 7598
Stableford Staffs 35 E1 loc 5m/8km SW of Newcastle-under-Lyme. SJ 8138
Stac an Armin W Isles (W of 88 A3) rock islet (NTS) lying off N end of Boreray, about 52m/83km W of Harris. Haunt of sea birds. NA 1506
Stacey Bank S Yorks 43 G2* ham 5m/7km NW of Sheffield. SK 2890
Stack Islands W Isles 88 E3* group of islets off S coast of Eriskay in Sound of Barra. NF 7807
Stack, North Gwynedd 40 A3 small island at NW tip of Holy I., Anglesey, 2m/3km W of Holyhead. Signal stn on mainland of Holy I. SH 2183
Stackpole Dyfed 22 C6 ham 3m/5km S of Pembroke. **Stackpole Hd,** headland 2m/3km SE. SR 9896
Stackpole Elidor Dyfed. Alternative name for Cheriton, ham 3m/4km S of Pembroke. SR 9897
Stack Rock Dyfed 22 B5* island rock in Milford Haven off S Hook Pt. Included in par of Herbrandston. SM 8604
Stack Rocks Dyfed 22 B4 group of rocks off S shore of St Brides Bay 2m/3km NE of The Nab Hd. SM 8113
Stack Skerry Orkney (W of 89 A6) islet some 40m/64km W of island of Mainland. HX 5617
Stacks of Duncansby H'land 86 F1 group of offshore rocks 1m S of Duncansby Hd. See Duncansby. ND 3971
Stack, South Gwynedd 40 A3 small island with lighthouse off W coast of Holy I., Anglesey, 3m/4km W of Holyhead. Island is connected to main island by small suspension br. SH 2082
Stacksteads Lancs 48 B5 loc 2km SW of Bacup. SD 8421
Stack, The Dyfed 22 A5 headland at NE end of island of Skokholm. SM 7405
Stac Lee W Isles (W of 88 A3) rock islet (NTS) lying off W side of Boreray, about 52m/83km W of Harris. Haunt of sea birds. NA 1404
Stac Mhic Mhurchaidh S'clyde 69 B5* islet on W side of Rèidh Eilean off NW coast of Iona. NM 2426
Stac Pollaidh H'land 85 B6 hill and well-known landmark in Ross and Cromarty dist to N of Loch Lurgainn. Height 2009 ft or 612 metres. Also known as Stac Polly. NC 1010
Staddiscombe Devon 4 B5 loc at most southerly point of Plymouth, 4m/7km W of Yealmpton. SX 5151
Staddlethorpe Humberside 50 D5 loc adjoining Gilberdyke to SE. SE 8328
Staden Derbys 43 F4* loc 2km SE of Buxton. SK 0772
Stadhampton Oxon 18 B2 vil 6m/9km N of Wallingford. SU 6098
Staffa S'clyde 69 B5 uninhabited island of basaltic rock in Inner Hebrides lying 5m/7km SE of Lunga in the Treshnish Isles and 6m/9km N of Iona. Area 70 acres or 28 hectares. Among several notable caves the best known is Fingal's Cave, qv. Various sea birds are to be seen. NM 3235
Staffield Cumbria 53 E1 ham 2km NW of Kirkoswald. NY 5541
Staffin Skye, H'land 78 C3 vil near NE coast 6m/10km E of Uig. **Staffin Bay** 1km N. **Staffin I.** is small uninhabited island opp bay. NG 4867
Stafford Staffs 35 E2 tn on R Sow 14m/23km S of Stoke-on-Trent. Industries include electrical engineering, footwear. Stafford Castle is unfinished 19c structure on site of earlier cas 2km SW of tn centre. SJ 9223
Staffordlake Surrey 18 D5* loc 1km S of Bisley. SU 9458
Stafford Park Salop 34 D3* industrial estate on SE side of Oakengates, Telford. SJ 7109

Staffordshire 117, 118, 119 midland county of England, bounded by Derbyshire, Leicestershire, Warwickshire, W Midlands, Hereford and Worcester, Salop, and Cheshire. The Trent valley is largely industrial. The Potteries and coalfields are in the N, centred on Stoke; in the S the main industries are engineering, iron and steel, rubber goods and leather production. Burton upon Trent is noted for brewing. Cannock Chase, an ancient hunting forest, is now a mining dist, although preserving tracts of moorland. The rest of the county is predominantly agricultural, and milk, wheat, and sugar beet are produced. E of Leek, moorland broken up by limestone walls extends across the Manifold valley to the Derbyshire border. Chief tns are Stafford, the county tn; Burton upon Trent, Cannock, Leek, the cathedral city of Lichfield, Newcastle-under-Lyme, Stoke-on-Trent and Tamworth. In addition to the Trent, rs include the Blithe, Manifold, Sow and Tame. R Dove forms the boundary with Derbyshire.
Staffordshire and Worcestershire Canal 35 F2-E6 an early canal by James Brindley, connecting the Trent and Mersey Canal at Gt Haywood Junction, Staffs, with R Severn at Stourport, H & W.
Staffordshire Moorlands 117 admin dist of Staffs.
Stafford, West Dorset 9 E5 vil 3m/4km E of Dorchester. SY 7789
Stagsden Beds 29 E3 vil 4m/7km W of Bedford. SP 9849
Stainborough S Yorks 43 G1* loc 3m/5km SW of Barnsley. **Stainborough Castle,** remains of early 18c folly in grnds of Wentworth Castle, qv. SE 3102
Stainburn Cumbria 52 A2 ham 2km E of Workington. NY 0129
Stainburn N Yorks 49 E3 vil 4m/6km NE of Otley. SE 2448
Stainby Lincs 37 E2 vil 2m/3km SW of Colsterworth. SK 9022
Staincliffe W Yorks 49 E5* loc 1m W of Batley. SE 2323
Staincross S Yorks 43 G1 loc 2m/4km N of Barnsley. SE 3310
Staindrop Durham 54 A3 vil 5m/9km NE of Barnard Castle. NZ 1220
Staines Surrey 19 E4 tn on R Thames 17m/28km W of London. Staines Resrs, pair of resrs separated by causeway, to N; other resrs in vicinity. London (Heathrow) Airport 4m/6km NE. TQ 0371
Staines Green Herts 19 G1* loc 2m/3km W of Hertford. TL 2911
Stainfield Lincs 37 F2* loc 3m/5km N of Bourne. TF 0825
Stainfield Lincs 45 E4 loc 2m/4km N of Bardney. TF 1173
Stainforth N Yorks 48 B2 vil on R Ribble 2m/4km N of Settle. 17c br (NT). **Lit Stainforth** loc across r. **Stainforth Force** waterfall below br. SD 8267
Stainforth S Yorks 49 H6 coal-mining tn 7m/11km NE of Doncaster. SE 6411
Staining Lancs 47 E4 vil 3m/4km E of Blackpool. SD 3436
Stainland W Yorks 48 D6 vil 2m/3km SW of Elland. SE 0719
Stainley, North N Yorks 49 E1 vil 4m/6km N of Ripon. SE 2876
Stainley, South N Yorks 49 E2 vil 2m/3km NE of Ripley. SE 3063
Stainmore, North Cumbria 53 G3 loc 2m/4km E of Brough. **S Stainmore** loc 2km SE. **Stainmore Common** and **Stainmore Forest** are moorland areas to N and SE respectively. NY 8315
Stainsacre N Yorks 55 G4 vil 2m/3km SE of Whitby. NZ 9108
Stainsby Derbys 43 H4* loc 1km S of Heath. SK 4565
Stainsby Lincs 45 G4* loc 1km E of Ashby Puerorum. TF 3371
Stainton Cleveland 54 D3 vil 4m/6km S of Middlesbrough. NZ 4814
Stainton Cumbria 52 D2/53 E2 vil 3m/4km SW of Penrith. NY 4828
Stainton Cumbria 53 E6* vil 4m/7km S of Kendal. SD 5285
Stainton Cumbria 59 H5* loc 2km W of Carlisle across R Eden. NY 3856
Stainton Durham 54 A3 vil 2m/3km NE of Barnard Castle. NZ 0718
Stainton N Yorks 54 A5 ham 4m/6km N of Leyburn. SE 1096
Stainton S Yorks 44 A2* vil 2m/3km NE of Maltby. SK 5593
Stainton by Langworth Lincs 45 E3* vil 4m/7km W of Wragby. TF 0677
Staintondale N Yorks 55 G5 vil 7m/11km NW of Scarborough. SE 9998
Stainton, Great Durham 54 C3 vil 6m/9km NE of Darlington. NZ 3322
Stainton le Vale Lincs 45 F2 vil 2m/4km W of Binbrook. TF 1794
Stainton, Little Durham 54 C3 ham 5m/8km NE of Darlington. NZ 3420
Stainton with Adgarley Cumbria 46 D1 vil 2m/3km SE of Dalton-in-Furness. SD 2472
Stair Cumbria 52 C3 loc 2m/4km SW of Keswick across Derwent Water. NY 2321
Stair S'clyde 64 C6 vil on R Ayr 7m/11km E of Ayr. NS 4323
Stairfoot S Yorks 43 H1* loc in Barnsley 2m/3km E of tn centre. SE 3705
Stair, The Kent 20 C6 loc in NE part of Tonbridge. Also known as Hadlow Stair. TQ 6047
Staith Norfolk 39 H5* loc on R Waveney 4m/6km SE of Haddiscoe. TM 4993
Staithes N Yorks 55 F3 fishing vil surrounded by high cliffs on North Sea coast 9m/14km NW of Whitby. NZ 7818
Stakeford Nthmb 61 G3 loc 2km S of Ashington. NZ 2685
Stake Hill Gtr Manchester 42 D1* loc 3m/5km S of Rochdale. SD 8908
Stake Pool Lancs 47 E3* loc 1km SE of Pilling. SD 4147
Stakes Hants 10 D4 S dist of Waterlooville. Site of Roman villa to S. SU 6808
Stakesby, High N Yorks 55 G4* W dist of Whitby. NZ 8810
Stalbridge Dorset 9 E3 vil 7m/11km S of Wincanton. 2km SW, ham of **Stalbridge Weston.** ST 7317
Stalham Norfolk 39 G2/G3 vil 7m/11km SE of N Walsham. **Stalham Green** loc adjoining to E. TG 3725
Stalisfield Green Kent 21 E6* vil 2m/3km N of Charing. TQ 9552
Stallingborough Humberside 45 F1 vil 5m/8km W of Grimsby. Chemical works to NE beside R Humber estuary. TA 1911
Stalling Busk N Yorks 53 H6 loc 3m/5km S of Bainbridge. SD 9185
Stallington Staffs 35 F1* loc 4m/6km SE of Longton, Stoke-on-Trent. SJ 9439
Stalmine Lancs 47 E3/E4 vil 1m SE of Preesall. **Stalmine Moss Side** loc adjoining to SE. SD 3745
Stalybridge Gtr Manchester 43 E2 tn 8m/12km E of Manchester. Textiles, engineering, cable mnfre, rubber. SJ 9698
Stalyhill Gtr Manchester 43 E2* loc 2m/3km SE of Stalybridge. SJ 9897
Stambourne Essex 30 C4 vil 4m/7km NE of Finchingfield. TL 7238
Stambridge, Great Essex 21 E3 vil 2m/3km E of Rochford. TQ 8991
Stamford Lincs 37 E4 ancient stone-built tn on R Welland 12m/19km NW of Peterborough. TF 0307
Stamford Nthmb 67 H6 ham 1m NE of Rennington. NU 2219
Stamford Bridge Ches 42 A4 ham 4m/7km E of Chester. SJ 4667
Stamford Bridge Humberside 50 C3 vil at crossing of R Derwent 7m/12km E of York. Site of battle in 1066 in which King Harold of England defeated Harald Hardrada of Norway. SE 7155
Stamfordham Nthmb 61 F4 vil 6m/9km N of Prudhoe. NZ 0772
Stamford Hill London 19 G3* loc in borough of Hackney 5m/8km NE of Charing Cross. TQ 3387
Stamshaw Hants 10 D4* loc in Portsmouth 2km N of city centre. SU 6402
Stanah Lancs 47 E4* loc on W side of R Wyre estuary 2m/3km N of Poulton-le-Fylde. SD 3542
Stanborough Herts 19 F1 loc 2km SW of Welwyn Garden City. TL 2211
Stanbridge Beds 28 D5 vil 3m/5km E of Leighton Buzzard. SP 9624
Stanbury W Yorks 48 C4 ham 2km W of Haworth. SE 0137
Stand Gtr Manchester 42 D1* loc adjoining Whitefield to SW. SD 7905
Standard, Battle of the. See Brompton, N Yorks.
Standburn Central 65 F2 vil 4m/7km SE of Falkirk. NS 9274
Standeford Staffs 35 E3/E4 vil 6m/9km N of Wolverhampton. SJ 9107
Standen Lancs 48 A4 loc on S side of Clitheroe, comprising **Hr** and **Lr Standen.** SD 7440
Standen Street Kent 12 D4* loc 3m/5km E of Hawkhurst. TQ 8030
Standerwick Som 16 C6* ham 3m/5km NE of Frome. ST 8250
Standford Hants 11 E2 vil 5m/8km W of Hindhead. SU 8134
Standford Bridge Salop 34 D2* loc 1km SW of Sambrook. SJ 7024
Standingstone Cumbria 52 B2* ham adjoining Broughton Moor to W. NY 0533
Standingstone Cumbria 52 C1* loc adjoining Wigton to N. NY 2549
Standing Stones of Lubas S'clyde 63 G2* group of ancient standing stones on island of Bute 1m W of Kilchattan. NS 0855
Standing Stones of Stenness Orkney. See Stenness.
Standing Tarn Cumbria 46 D1* small lake 1km E of Dalton-in-Furness. SD 2474
Standish Glos 16 C1* loc 4m/6km NW of Stroud. **Standish Moreton** loc to W. SO 8008
Standish Gtr Manchester 42 B1 tn 3m/5km NW of Wigan. Coal-mining, textiles. **Standish Lr Ground** loc 2m/3km S. SD 5610
Standlake Oxon 17 G2 vil on R Windrush 5m/8km SE of Witney. SP 3903
Standon Hants 10 B2 ham 4m/6km SW of Winchester. SU 4226
Standon Herts 29 G5 vil 6m/10km W of Bishop's Stortford. TL 3922
Standon Staffs 35 E1 vil 4m/6km N of Eccleshall. SJ 8134
Standon Green End Herts 29 G5* loc 4m/6km N of Ware. TL 3619
Standwell Green Suffolk 31 F1/F2* loc adjoining Thorndon to NW. TM 1370
Stane S'clyde 65 F3 vil 1m SE of Shotts. NS 8859
Stanecastle S'clyde 64 B5* loc adjoining Irvine to E. NS 3339
Stanely Castle S'clyde 64 C3* early 15c cas now standing in **Stanely Resr,** small resr 2m/3km SW of Paisley. NS 4661
Stanfield Norfolk 38 D3 vil 6m/9km NW of E Dereham. TF 9320
Stanfield Staffs 42 D6* loc 1km NE of Burslem. SJ 8750
Stanford Beds 29 F4 vil 2m/3km NE of Shefford. TL 1641
Stanford Kent 13 F3 vil 3m/5km NW of Hythe. TR 1238
Stanford Norfolk 38 C5/D5 loc 4m/6km E of Mundford. **Stanford Water,** natural lake NE of ch. TL 8594
Stanford Salop 34 A3* loc 1km NE of Wollaston. SJ 3312
Stanford Bishop H & W 26 C3 vil 3m/5km SE of Bromyard. SO 6851
Stanford Bridge H & W 26 C1 vil on R Teme 7m/11km SW of Stourport. SO 7165
Stanford Dingley Berks 18 B4 vil 5m/8km SW of Pangbourne. SU 5771
Stanford End Berks 18 C5* loc 1m W of Riseley. SU 7063
Stanford in the Vale Oxon 17 G2 vil 5m/8km NW of Wantage. SU 3493
Stanford le Hope Essex 20 C3 tn 5m/8km NE of Tilbury. Oil refinery to E beside R Thames. TQ 6882
Stanford on Avon Northants 36 B6 vil 6m/10km NE of Rugby. Stanford Resr to NE. SP 5878
Stanford on Soar Notts 36 B2 vil 2km N of Loughborough. SK 5422
Stanford on Teme H & W 26 C1 vil 7m/11km E of Tenbury Wells. SO 7065
Stanford Rivers Essex 20 B2 loc 2m/3km SW of Chipping Ongar. TL 5300
Stanford's End Kent 12 B2 loc 2km S of Edenbridge. TQ 4544
Stanfree Derbys 44 A4* vil 3m/4km N of Bolsover. SK 4774
Stanger Head Orkney 89 B5 headland on E coast of island of Westray, N of Rapness. HY 5142
Stanghow Cleveland 55 E3 vil 4m/6km S of Saltburn. NZ 6715
Stanground Cambs 37 G4 SE dist of Peterborough. TL 2097
Stanhill Lancs 48 A5* loc 1km NW of Oswaldtwistle. SD 7227
Stanhoe Norfolk 38 C1 vil 2m/4km E of Docking. TF 8037
Stanhope Durham 54 A1 small tn on R Wear 5m/8km W of Wolsingham. NY 9939
Stanhope Bretby Derbys 35 H2* loc 1m SW of Bretby. SK 2822
Stanion Northants 37 E5 vil 2m/3km SE of Corby. SP 9186
Stank Cumbria 46 D1* loc 2m/4km E of Barrow-in-Furness. SD 2370
Stanklyn H & W 26 D1* loc 2m/4km SE of Kidderminster. SO 8574
Stanks W Yorks 49 F4* loc in Seacroft dist of Leeds 5m/8km E of city centre. SE 3635
Stanley Derbys 36 A1 vil 5m/8km NE of Derby. **Stanley Common** loc 1m N. SK 4140
Stanley Durham 54 B1/B2 vil 2m/3km N of Crook. NZ 1637
Stanley Durham 61 G6 coal-mining tn 5m/8km W of Chester-le-Street. Includes locs of **E** and **S Stanley.** NZ 1953
Stanley Lancs 42 A1* NW dist of Skelmersdale. SD 4707
Stanley Notts 44 A4/A5* loc 3m/5km NW of Sutton in Ashfield. SK 4662
Stanley Salop 34 D5* loc in coal-mining area in R Severn valley 5m/9km NW of Bewdley. SO 7483
Stanley Staffs 43 E5 vil 6m/9km NE of Stoke-on-Trent. **Stanley Moor** loc 1km SW. **Stanley Pool** lake to S. SJ 9352
Stanley Tayside 73 E2 vil on R Tay 8m/12km SE of Dunkeld and 6m/9km N of Perth. NO 1033
Stanley Wilts 16 D4* loc 3m/4km E of Chippenham. Site of medieval abbey 1km SE. ST 9572
Stanley W Yorks 49 E5 loc 2km NE of Wakefield. Coal-mining, brick mnfre. Includes **Stanley Lane Ends,** loc to N. To E at rd crossing of Aire and Calder Canal is loc of **Stanley Ferry.** SE 3422
Stanley Downton Glos 16 C1* loc 3m/5km W of Stroud. SO 8004
Stanley Embankment Gwynedd 40 A3* rd and rly embankment 3m/4km SE of Holyhead, connecting Holy I. with main island of Anglesey. SH 2780
Stanley Force Cumbria 52 B5* waterfall on Stanley Ghyll 1m S of Boot. SD 1799
Stanley Gate Lancs 42 A1* loc 2m/3km W of Skelmersdale. SD 4405
Stanley Green Dorset 9 G5* loc at W end of Poole beside Holes Bay. SZ 0192
Stanley Green Gtr Manchester 42 D3* loc 2m/3km W of Bramhall. SJ 8684
Stanleygreen Salop 34 C1* loc 4m/7km S of Whitchurch. SJ 5235
Stanley Hill H & W 26 B3* ham 5m/8km NW of Ledbury. SO 6744
Stanley Hill Tayside. See Dunkeld.
Stanley Moor Reservoir Derbys 43 E4* small resr 2m/3km SW of Buxton. SK 0471
Stanleytown Mid Glam 15 E2* loc 3m/4km E of Rhondda. ST 0194
Stanlow Ches 42 A4* site of large oil refinery 2km E of Ellesmere Port. To N, **Stanlow Pt,** headland on R Mersey estuary to N of Manchester Ship Canal. SJ 4276
Stanlow Salop 34 D4/35 E4* loc 6m/10km NE of Bridgnorth. SO 7999
Stanmer E Sussex 12 A5 vil 4m/6km NE of Brighton tn centre. University of Sussex in Stanmer Park to SE. TQ 3309
Stanmore Berks 17 H4* loc 2m/3km SW of E Ilsley. SU 4778
Stanmore Hants 10 B2* SW dist of Winchester. SU 4628
Stanmore London 19 F3 dist in borough of Harrow 11m/17km NW of Charing Cross. TQ 9641
Stanmore Salop 34 D5* loc 2m/3km E of Bridgnorth. SO 7492
Stannergate Tayside 73 G2* dist of Dundee 2m/3km E of city centre. Shipbuilding yards. NO 4330
Stanney, Little Ches 42 A4 vil 5m/8km N of Chester. SJ 4174
Stanningfield Suffolk 30 D3 ham 5m/8km S of Bury St Edmunds. TL 8756
Stanningley W Yorks 49 E4 loc adjoining Pudsey to N. SE 2234
Stannington Nthmb 61 G4 vil 4m/7km S of Morpeth. NZ 2179
Stannington S Yorks 43 G2 suburb 3m/5km W of Sheffield. SK 3088
Stanpit Dorset 9 H5* dist of Christchurch 1m E of tn centre. To SW, **Stanpit Marsh,** nature reserve. SZ 1792
Stansbatch H & W 26 H2 ham 3m/5km SE of Presteigne. SO 3461
Stansfield Suffolk 30 C3 vil 5m/7km N of Clare. TL 7852
Stanshope Staffs 43 F5* loc 1m S of Alstonefield. SK 1254
Stansore Point Hants 10 B5 headland at SW end of Stanswood Bay 3m/5km S of Fawley. Also known as Stone Pt. SZ 4698

Stanstead Suffolk 30 D3 vil 3m/4km NW of Long Melford. Ham of **Stanstead Street** to S. TL 8449
Stanstead Abbots Herts 20 A1 vil on R Lea 3m/4km SE of Ware. TL 3911
Stanstead St Margarets Herts 20 A1* containing vil of St Margarets 2m/3km SE of Ware. TL 3811
Stansted Kent 20 C5 vil 2m/3km N of Wrotham. TQ 6062
Stansted Mountfitchet Essex 30 A5 vil (commonly known as Stansted) 3m/5km NE of Bishop's Stortford. **Stansted Airport** 2m/3km SE. **Stansted Wildlife Park** 1m NE. TL 5124
Stanswood Bay Hants 10 B4 bay in the Solent extending from Calshot to Stansore Pt. SU 4700
Stanthorne Ches 42 C4* loc 1m W of Middlewich. SJ 6865
Stantling Craig Reservoir Borders 66 B4* small resr in course of Caddon Water 4m/7km NW of Galashiels. NT 4339
Stanton Derbys 35 H2/H3 loc 2m/3km W of Swadlincote. SK 2719
Stanton Glos 27 E4 vil 3m/4km SW of Broadway. SP 0634
Stanton Gwent 25 G5* loc 1m W of Llanvihangel Crucorney. SO 3121
Stanton Staffs 43 F6 vil 4m/6km W of Ashbourne. SK 1246
Stanton Suffolk 30 D1 vil 3m/5km NE of Ixworth. Site of Roman villa 1m NW. TL 9673
Stanton Butts Cambs 29 F1* loc in NW part of Huntingdon. TL 2372
Stanton by Bridge Derbys 36 A2 vil 2m/3km NW of Melbourne. The br is Swarkestone Br (see Swarkestone). SK 3727
Stanton by Dale Derbys 36 A1/B1 vil 2m/4km S of Ilkeston. SK 4638
Stanton Drew Avon 16 B5 vil 6m/10km S of Bristol. ST 5963
Stanton Fitzwarren Wilts 17 F3 vil 2m/3km SW of Highworth. Site of Roman bldg to SW. SU 1790
Stanton Ford Derbys 43 G4* loc on R Derwent 1m N of Baslow. SK 2473
Stanton Harcourt Oxon 17 H1 vil 3m/4km SW of Eynsham. SP 4105
Stanton Hill Notts 44 A5 loc 2km NW of Sutton in Ashfield. SK 4860
Stanton in Peak Derbys 43 G4 vil 2km SW of Rowsley. SK 2464
Stanton Lacy Salop 34 B6 vil on R Corve 3m/5km N of Ludlow. SO 4978
Stanton Lees Derbys 43 G4* ham 3m/5km NW of Matlock. SK 2563
Stanton Long Salop 34 C5 vil 7m/11km SW of Much Wenlock. SO 5790
Stanton on the Wolds Notts 36 C2 vil 7m/12km SE of Nottingham. SK 6330
Stanton Prior Avon 16 B5 vil 5m/8km W of Bath. ST 6762
Stanton St Bernard Wilts 17 E5 vil 6m/9km E of Devizes. SU 0962
Stanton St John Oxon 18 B1 vil 5m/7km E of Oxford. SP 5709
Stanton St Quintin Wilts 16 D3* vil 4m/6km N of Chippenham. **Lr Stanton St Quintin** 1m NE. ST 9079
Stanton Street Suffolk 30 D2* ham 3m/4km SE of Ixworth. TL 9566
Stanton under Bardon Leics 36 A3 vil 4m/6km SE of Coalville. SK 4610
Stanton upon Hine Heath Salop 34 C2 vil 4m/7km SW of Hodnet. SJ 5624
Stanton Wick Avon 16 B5 ham 3m/4km E of Chew Magna. ST 6161
Stanwardine in the Fields Salop 34 B2 loc 9m/14km NW of Shrewsbury. SJ 4124
Stanwardine in the Wood Salop 34 B2 loc 5m/8km S of Ellesmere. SJ 4227
Stanway Essex 30 D5 vil 4m/6km W of Colchester. TL 9324
Stanway Glos 27 E4 vil 4m/6km NE of Winchcombe. SP 0632
Stanway Salop 34 C5* loc 5m/8km E of Church Stretton. SO 5391
Stanway Green Essex 30 D5* loc 3m/5km SW of Colchester. TL 9623
Stanway Green Suffolk 31 F2* loc 3m/4km S of Stradbroke. TM 2470
Stanwell Surrey 19 E4 urban loc between Staines Resr and London (Heathrow) Airport. TQ 0574
Stanwell Moor Surrey 19 E4* loc 2m/3km N of Staines. TQ 0474
Stanwick Northants 29 E1 vil 2m/4km NE of Higham Ferrers. Site of Roman bldg to W. SP 9871
Stanwick St John N Yorks 54 B4* loc 2km W of Aldbrough. **Stanwick Camp** (partly A.M.), extensive military earthworks dating from 1c and originally used in operations against the Romans. NZ 1811
Stanwix Cumbria 59 H5 dist of Carlisle 1km N of city centre. Site of Roman fort. NY 3957
Stanycliffe Gtr Manchester 42 D1* loc 1m NE of Middleton. SD 8707
Stanydale Shetland 89 D7/E7* loc on Mainland 2km N of Gruting. Neolithic remains (A.M.). HU 2851
Stape N Yorks 55 F5 ham 6m/9km N of Pickering. SE 7993
Stapehill Dorset 9 G4* loc 3m/5km E of Wimborne. SU 0500
Stapeley Ches 42 C6 ham 3m/4km SE of Nantwich. SJ 6849
Stapenhill Staffs 35 H2 dist of Burton upon Trent 2km SE of tn centre. SK 2522
Staple Kent 13 G2 vil 2m/3km E of Wingham. TR 2756
Staple Som 7 H1* ham 3m/4km E of Watchet at N end of Quantock Hills. ST 1141
Staple Cross Devon 7 H3* ham 1km NW of Hockworthy. ST 0320
Staple Cross E Sussex 12 D4 vil 5m/7km NE of Battle. TQ 7822
Staplefield W Sussex 11 H2 vil 2km SE of Handcross. TQ 2728
Staple Fitzpaine Som 8 B3 vil 5m/7km SE of Taunton. ST 2618
Stapleford Cambs 29 H3 suburb 4m/7km S of Cambridge. TL 4751
Stapleford Herts 29 G6 vil 3m/5km N of Hertford. TL 3116
Stapleford Leics 36 D3 ham 4m/6km E of Melton Mowbray. Partly 17c hall stands in park containing lion reserve and other diversions. SK 8118
Stapleford Lincs 44 D5 vil 6m/10km E of Newark-on-Trent. SK 8857
Stapleford Notts 36 B1 tn 3m/4km W of Beeston. See also New Stapleford, 1m N. SK 4837
Stapleford Wilts 9 G1 vil on R Till 4m/7km N of Wilton. SU 0737
Stapleford Abbotts Essex 20 B2 vil 4m/7km N of Romford. TQ 5096
Stapleford Tawney Essex 20 B2* loc 3m/5km SE of Epping. TQ 5099
Staplegrove Som 8 A2 NW suburb of Taunton. ST 2126
Staplehay Som 8 A2* vil adjoining Trull 3m/4km S of Taunton. ST 2121
Staple Hill Avon 16 B4* S dist of Mangotsfield 5m/8km NE of Bristol. ST 6576
Staple Hill H & W 27 E1* loc 2m/3km N of Bromsgrove SO 9773
Staple Hill Som 8 A3 eastward extension of Blackdown Hills. Height 1035 ft or 315 metres. See Neroche Forest. ST 2416
Staplehurst Kent 12 D3 vil 5m/8km N of Cranbrook. TQ 7843
Staple Lees Kent 13 F3 loc 2m/3km SE of Wye. Nature reserve to W. TR 0845
Staplers Isle of Wight 10 C5* loc 1m E of Newport. SZ 5189
Staplestreet Kent 21 F5* ham 3m/5km E of Faversham. TR 0660
Stapleton Avon 16 B4 dist of Bristol 3m/4km NE of city centre. ST 6076
Stapleton Cumbria 60 B4 loc 7m/11km N of Brampton. NY 5071
Stapleton H & W 25 G2 vil 1m NE of Presteigne. SO 3265
Stapleton Leics 36 A4 vil 3m/5km N of Hinckley. SP 4398
Stapleton N Yorks 54 B4 vil on R Tees 2m/3km SW of Darlington. NZ 2612
Stapleton Salop 34 B4 vil 5m/8km S of Shrewsbury. SJ 4704
Stapleton Som 8 C2 ham 1m N of Martock. ST 4621
Stapley Som 8 A3 ham 5m/9km SE of Wellington. ST 1813
Staploe Beds 29 F2 vil 3m/4km W of St Neots. Loc of **Upr Staploe** 1km S. TL 1460
Staplow H & W 26 C3 ham 3m/4km NW of Ledbury. SO 6941
Star Dyfed 22 D2/23 E2 ham 3m/5km SE of Boncath. SN 2435
Star Fife 73 F4 vil 2m/3km NE of Markinch. NO 3103
Starbotton N Yorks 48 C1 vil in Upper Wharfedale 2m/3km N of Kettlewell. SD 9574
Starcross Devon 5 F3 vil on W side of R Exe estuary opp Exmouth. Ferry to Exmouth (foot passengers). SX 9781
Stareton Warwicks 27 G1* loc 4m/6km N of Leamington. SP 3371
Stargate Tyne & Wear 61 F5* loc 2km W of Blaydon. NZ 1663
Starkholmes Derbys 43 G5* vil 1m S of Matlock. SK 3058
Starling Gtr Manchester 47 H6* loc 2m/3km W of Bury. SD 7710
Starling's Green Essex 29 H4 ham 4m/7km SW of Newport. TL 4531
Starr's Green E Sussex 12 D5* loc adjoining Battle to SE. TQ 7615
Starston Norfolk 39 F6 vil 1m NW of Harleston. TM 2384
Start Bay Devon 5 E6 bay on S coast extending from mouth of R Dart (N) to Start Pt (S). SX 8443
Startforth Durham 54 A3 vil on W bank of R Tees opp Barnard Castle. NZ 0416
Startley Wilts 16 D3 vil 3m/5km S of Malmesbury. ST 9482
Startop's End Bucks 28 D6* loc at Marsworth 2m/3km N of Tring. SP 9214
Start Point Devon 5 E6 E-facing headland on S coast at S end of Start Bay, qv. SX 8337
Start Point Orkney 89 C5 headland with lighthouse at E end of island of Sanday. HY 7843
Statham Ches 42 C3 loc adjoining Lymm to W. SJ 6787
Stathe Som 8 B2 vil on R Parrett 3m/5km NW of Langport. ST 3729
Stathern Leics 36 D2 vil 8m/12km N of Melton Mowbray. SK 7731
Station Hill Cumbria 52 C1* loc adjoining Wigton to N. NY 2548
Station Town Durham 54 C2* loc adjoining Wingate to S, built round former rly stn. NZ 4036
Stattio Point H'land 85 A7 headland on SW side of entrance to Lit Loch Broom, W coast of Ross and Cromarty dist. NG 9796
Staughton, Great Cambs 29 F2 vil 5m/8km NW of St Neots. To NE and E respectively, vils of **Staughton Green** and **Staughton Highway.** Site of Roman bldg 2km SE. TL 1264
Staughton, Little Beds 29 E2 vil 3m/5km S of Kimbolton. Airfield to SE. TL 1062
Staunton Glos 26 B6 vil 2m/3km NW of Coleford. SO 5412
Staunton Glos 26 C4 vil 7m/11km N of Gloucester. SO 7829
Staunton Green H & W 25 H2* ham 5m/8km NE of Presteigne. SO 3661
Staunton Harold Leics 36 A2 loc 3m/5km NE of Ashby de la Zouch. **S. H. Hall** (NT), mainly Palladian hse. To N is **S. H. Resr** (almost entirely in Derbyshire). SK 3720
Staunton in the Vale Notts 44 C6 vil 6m/10km S of Newark-on-Trent. SK 8043
Staunton on Arrow H & W 25 H2 vil 5m/8km NE of Kington. SO 3660
Staunton on Wye H & W 25 H3 vil 4m/6km SE of Willersley. SO 3745
Staupes N Yorks 49 E3* loc 2m/3km SW of Birstwith. SE 2257
Stava Ness Shetland 89 E7* headland on E coast of Mainland, on S side of entrance to Dury Voe. HU 5060
Staveley Cumbria 52 D5 vil 4m/6km E of Windermere. SD 4698
Staveley Cumbria 52 D6 vil 1km E of Newby Br. SD 3786
Staveley Derbys 43 H4 tn 4m/6km NE of Chesterfield. Industries include chemicals, coal, iron. SK 4374
Staveley N Yorks 49 F2 vil 3m/5km SW of Boroughbridge. SE 3662
Staverton Devon 4 D4 vil 2m/4km N of Totnes. 15c br over R Dart. SX 7964
Staverton Glos 26 D5 vil 4m/6km W of Cheltenham. Airport 2km S. SO 8923
Staverton Northants 28 B2 vil 2m/4km W of Daventry. SP 5361
Staverton Wilts 16 D5 vil 2m/3km N of Trowbridge. ST 8560
Staverton Bridge Glos 26 D5 loc 4m/6km W of Cheltenham. Airport to S. SO 8922
Staward Peel Nthmb 60 D5 ruined 14c tower, built partly of Roman stones, on steep wooded bank of R Allen 4m/6km SW of Haydon Br. NY 7960
Stawell Som 8 B1 vil on S side of Polden Hills 5m/7km E of Bridgwater. ST 3638
Stawley Som 7 H3 ham 5m/8km W of Wellington. ST 0622
Staxigoe H'land 86 F2 vil on E coast of Caithness dist 2m/3km NE of Wick. ND 3852
Staxton N Yorks 51 E1 vil 6m/10km W of Filey. TA 0179
Staylittle Powys 33 F5 ham at head of Clywedog Resr 7m/11km S of Llanbrynmair. SN 8892
Staynall Lancs 47 E4 ham on E bank of R Wyre estuary 2m/3km S of Preesall. SD 3643
Staythorpe Notts 44 C5 ham 3m/5km W of Newark-on-Trent. SK 7554
Steall Fall H'land 74 C4 waterfall in Glen Nevis, Lochaber dist, 2m/3km SE of Ben Nevis. NN 1768
Stean N Yorks 48 D1* ham 1km SW of Middlesmoor, on NE side of Stean Moor. SE 0873
Steane Northants 28 B4 ham 3m/4km NW of Brackley. SP 5539
Stearsby N Yorks 50 B1 ham 5m/9km E of Easingwold. SE 6171
Steart Som 15 G6 vil on W side of R Parrett estuary 2m/4km NE of Stockland Bristol. ST 2745
Stebbing Essex 30 B5 vil 3m/4km NE of Gt Dunmow. Ham of **Stebbing Green** 2km E; site of Roman bldg to E of ham. TL 6624
Stechford W Midlands 35 G5 loc in Birmingham 4m/6km E of city centre. SP 1287
Stedham W Sussex 11 E3 vil 2m/3km W of Midhurst. SU 8622
Steel Bank S Yorks 43 G2* loc in Sheffield 2km NW of city centre. SK 3388
Steel Cross E Sussex 12 B3 loc 1m E of Crowborough. TQ 5331
Steel Green Cumbria 52 B6* loc 1km E of Haverigg. SD 1679
Steel Heath Salop 34 C1* loc 3m/5km S of Whitchurch. SJ 5436
Steen's Bridge H & W 26 B2 ham 3m/5km E of Leominster. SO 5457
Steep Hants 10 D2 vil 2km N of Petersfield. Location of Bedales coeducational boarding school, founded 1893. SU 7425
Steephill Isle of Wight 10 C6* loc 1km W of Ventnor. SZ 5577
Steep Holme Avon 15 G5 island in Bristol Channel 6m/9km W of Weston-super-Mare, measuring about 1km from E to W and 300 metres from N to S. Uninhabited. ST 2260
Steeping 45 H5 r rising as R Lymm nr Salmonby, Lincs, and flowing SE through Wainfleet into North Sea on W side of Gibraltar Pt. TF 5557
Steeping, Great Lincs 45 H5 vil 3m/5km SE of Spilsby. **Lit Steeping** 1m S. TF 4364
Steep Lane W Yorks 48 C5* ham 2m/3km W of Sowerby Br. SE 0323
Steeple Cumbria 52 B4 mt in Lake Dist 3m/5km N of Wast Water. Height 2687 ft or 819 metres. NY 1511
Steeple Dorset 9 F6 ham to S of Purbeck Hills and 4m/6km S of Wareham. SY 9181
Steeple Essex 21 E2 vil 4m/7km N of Burnham-on-Crouch. TL 9302
Steeple Ashton Wilts 16 D5 vil 3m/5km E of Trowbridge. ST 9056
Steeple Aston Oxon 27 H5 vil 4m/6km S of Deddington. SP 4726
Steeple Barton Oxon 27 H5 ham 4m/7km SW of Deddington. SP 4425
Steeple Bumpstead Essex 30 B4 vil 3m/5km S of Haverhill. TL 6741
Steeplechase Terrace Suffolk 30 C3* ham 4m/7km NE of Haverhill. TL 7249
Steeple Claydon Bucks 28 C5 vil 5m/7km S of Buckingham. SP 7026
Steeple Court Hants. See Botley.
Steeple Creek Essex 21 E2* small inlet on S side of R Blackwater estuary opp E end of Osea I. TL 9304
Steeple Gidding Cambs 37 F6 vil 5m/9km SW of Stilton. TL 1381
Steeple Langford Wilts 9 G1 vil on R Wylye 5m/8km NW of Wilton. SU 0337
Steeple Morden Cambs 29 G3 vil 4m/7km W of Royston. TL 2842
Steeple View Essex 20 C3* NW dist of Basildon. TQ 6890
Steep Marsh Hants 10 D2* ham 2m/3km NE of Petersfield. SU 7526
Steeraway Salop 34 D3* loc 2km S of Wellington. SJ 6409
Steeton N Yorks 49 G4* loc 3m/5km E of Tadcaster. Hall dates partly from 14c. SE 5344
Steeton W Yorks 48 C4 vil in Airedale 4m/6km NW of Keighley. SE 0344

Steeton Hall N Yorks 49 F5* remains of medieval cas 1m W of S Milford. Gatehouse (A.M.) probably dates from 14c. SE 4831
Stein Skye, H'land 78 A4 loc on W coast of Vaternish peninsula 4m/6km SE of Ardmore Pt. NG 2656
Steinacleit W Isles 88 B1* burial cairn and stone circle (A.M.) near NW coast of Lewis, 4m/6km NE of Barvas. NB 3954
Stella Tyne & Wear 61 F5 loc 2km E of Ryton. NZ 1763
Stelling Minnis Kent 13 G2 vil 7m/11km S of Canterbury. TR 1441
Stelvio Gwent 15 G3* dist of Newport to S of tn centre. ST 3087
Stembridge Som 8 C2* ham 4m/7km S of Langport. ST 4220
Stenalees Cornwall 3 E3 vil in china clay dist 3m/5km N of St Austell. SX 0157
Stenhill Devon 7 H4* loc 3m/5km NE of Cullompton. ST 0510
Stenhouse Lothian 66 A2* dist of Edinburgh 3m/5km SW of city centre. NT 2171
Stenhousemuir Central 65 E1 tn 2m/3km NW of Falkirk. NS 8682
Stenhouse Reservoir Fife 73 E5* small resr 2m/3km NW of Burntisland. NT 2187
Stenigot Lincs 45 F3 loc 6m/10km SW of Louth. Radar stn. TF 2581
Stenness Orkney 89 A6* locality on Mainland at SE end of Loch of Stenness, 4m/6km W of Finstown. 1km N are the **Standing Stones of Stenness** (A.M.), four standing stones out of an estimated original twelve erected in Neolithic times. HY 3011
Stenness Shetland 89 D6 headland on Mainland at S end of Esha Ness. Offshore to SW is small island called **Isle of Stenness.** HU 2076
Stenscholl Skye, H'land 78 C3 loc 1m NW of Staffin. NG 4767
Stenson Derbys 35 H2* ham on Trent and Mersey Canal 4m/7km SW of Derby. SK 3230
Stenton Lothian 66 D2 vil 5m/7km SW of Dunbar. NT 6274
Stepaside Dyfed 22 D5 vil 2m/3km N of Saundersfoot. SN 1307
Stepaside Powys 33 G5* loc 2m/3km SW of Newtown. SO 0889
Stephenson Tyne & Wear 61 G5* N dist of Washington. Industrial estate. NZ 3058
Stepney London 20 A3* dist in borough of Tower Hamlets 2m/3km E of London Br. TQ 3581
Stepper Point Cornwall 2 D1* headland at SW end of Padstow Bay 2m/3km N of Padstow. SW 9178
Steppingley Beds 29 E4 vil 2m/4km SW of Ampthill. TL 0135
Stepps S'clyde 64 D2 suburb 5m/8km NE of Glasgow. NS 6568
Sternfield Suffolk 31 G2 vil 1m S of Saxmundham. TM 3961
Sterridge Devon 6 D1 loc 3m/4km SE of Ilfracombe. SS 5546
Stert Wilts 17 E5* vil 2m/3km SE of Devizes. SU 0359
Sterte Dorset 9 G5* W dist of Poole beside Holes Bay. SZ 0191
Stert Island Som 15 G6 island in Bridgwater Bay 1m SW of Burnham-on-Sea. ST 2948
Stert Point Som 15 G6* headland at mouth of R Parrett opposite Stert I. and 2m/3km SW of Burnham-on-Sea across river mouth. ST 2847
Stetchworth Cambs 30 B2 vil 3m/5km S of Newmarket. Loc of **Stetchworth Ley** 1m SE. TL 6458
Stevenage Herts 29 F3 New Tn designated 1946, 28m/45km N of London. Various industries. Old tn to N. TN 2324
Stevenston S'clyde 64 A4 tn 2m/4km E of Ardrossan. Industries include chemicals and explosives (at Ardeer), iron founding. NS 2642
Steventon Hants 18 A6 vil 6m/10km SW of Basingstoke. Birthplace of Jane Austen, 1775. SU 5448
Steventon Oxon 17 H3 vil 4m/6km W of Didcot. Priory Cottages (NT), part of former monastic bldgs. SU 4691
Stevington Beds 29 E3 vil 4m/7km NW of Bedford. SP 9853
Stewards Essex 20 B1* S dist of Harlow. TL 4407
Stewartby Beds 29 E3 vil 3m/5km N of Ampthill. TL 0142
Stewarton S'clyde 64 B4 small tn 5m/8km N of Kilmarnock. Woollen mnfre. NS 4145
Stewartry 116 admin dist of D & G region.
Stewkley Bucks 28 D5 vil 5m/7km W of Leighton Buzzard. SP 8526
Stewley Som 8 B3* ham 4m/6km NW of Ilminster. ST 3118
Stewponey Staffs 35 E5 vil at canal junction 3m/4km W of Stourbridge. SO 8684
Stewton Lincs 45 G3* loc 2m/4km E of Louth. TF 3686
Stewy 33 E5/E6* r rising N of Cwmsymlog, Dyfed, and flowing W into Cardigan Bay at Clarach Bay, N of Aberystwyth. SN 5883
Steyne Cross Isle of Wight 10 D6* loc adjoining Bembridge to S. SZ 6487
Steyning W Sussex 11 G4 tn below S Downs 5m/7km NW of Shoreham-by-Sea. TQ 1711
Steynton Dyfed 22 B5 vil 2km NE of Milford Haven. SM 9107
Stibb Cornwall 6 B4 ham 3m/5km N of Bude. SS 2210
Stibbard Norfolk 39 E2 vil 4m/7km E of Fakenham. TF 9828
Stibb Cross Devon 6 C4 ham 5m/8km SW of Torrington. SS 4214
Stibb Green Wilts 17 F5 vil 5m/8km SE of Marlborough. SU 2262
Stibbington Cambs 37 F4* vil 1m SE of Wansford. Jacbn hall. TL 0898
Stichill Borders 66 D4 vil 3m/5km N of Kelso. NT 7138
Sticker Cornwall 3 E3 vil 3m/4km SW of St Austell. SW 9850
Stickford Lincs 45 G5 vil 5m/8km SW of Spilsby. TF 3560
Sticklepath Devon 7 E5 vil 4m/6km E of Okehampton. SX 6494
Sticklepath Som 8 B3* ham 1m N of Combe St Nicholas. ST 3012
Stickle Tarn Cumbria 52 C4 small lake 3m/4km NW of Chapel Stile. NY 2807
Stickling Green Essex 29 H4* ham 3m/5km W of Newport. TL 4732
Stickney Lincs 45 G5 vil 8m/13km N of Boston. TF 3456
Stidd Lancs 47 G4* loc to NE of Ribchester. SD 6535
Stiffkey Norfolk 38 D1 vil 4m/6km E of Wells. TF 9743
Stiffkey 39 E1 r rising near Swanton Novers, Norfolk, and flowing generally W to E Barsham, then NE to vil of Stiffkey and North Sea at Blakeney Harbour. TF 9944
Stifford, North Essex 20 C4 vil 2m/3km NW of Grays. TQ 6080
Stifford's Bridge H & W 26 C3 loc at rd br over Leigh Brook 3m/5km NW of Gt Malvern. SO 7348
Stifford, South Essex 20 C4* industrial loc on N bank of R Thames 1m W of Grays. TQ 5977
Stiff Street Kent 21 E5* loc 3m/4km SW of Sittingbourne. TQ 8761
Stilamair W Isles 88 B3* islet off SW coast of Scalpay, at entrance to E Loch Tarbert, Harris. NG 2194
Stile, High Cumbria 52 B3 mt in Lake Dist 2km S of Buttermere ham. Height 2644 ft or 806 metres. NY 1614
Stileway Som 8 C1* loc 3m/5km NW of Glastonbury. ST 4641
Stilligarry W Isles 88 E2* vil on S Uist on W side of Loch Druidibeg. NF 7638
Stillingfleet N Yorks 49 G4 vil 2m/4km NE of Cawood. SE 5940
Stillington N Yorks 50 B2 vil 4m/6km E of Easingwold. SE 5867
Stillington 54 C3 vil on border of Cleveland and Durham 4m/6km S of Sedgefield. See also Old Stillington. NZ 3723
Stilton Cambs 37 F5 vil 6m/10km SW of Peterborough. The famous cheese of same name was formerly distributed from the Bell Inn here, although made in Leics. TL 1689
Stinchar S'clyde 57 B5 r in Strathclyde region rising in Glentrool Forest Park and flowing N then W through Carrick Forest, then turning SW and running by Barr, Pinwherry, and Colmonell to Ballantrae Bay on S side of Ballantrae. NX 0781
Stinchcombe Glos 16 C2 vil 2m/3km W of Dursley. Site of Roman villa 2km SE. ST 7298
Stinsford Dorset 9 E5 vil 2km E of Dorchester. SY 7191
Stiperstones, The Salop 34 B4* loc below ridge of same name, 2km SW of Snailbeach. SJ 3600
Stirchley Salop 34 D4 loc 1m SE of Dawley, Telford. SJ 6906
Stirchley W Midlands 35 F6 loc in Birmingham 4m/6km S of city centre. SP 0581
Stirling Central 72 B5 historic tn on slope of rocky eminence above S bank of R Forth 21m/34km NE of Glasgow. Medieval cas (A.M.). Industries include agricultural engineering, carpet mnfg, bacon curing and mnfre of meat products. University at Airthrey, 2m/3km N. See also Cambuskenneth, Carse of Stirling. NS 7993
Stirling Grampian 83 H3 loc adjoining Boddam to W, 3m/4km S of Peterhead. Quarry to S. NK 1242
Stirton N Yorks 48 C3* ham on edge of Yorkshire Dales National Park 2km NW of Skipton. SD 9752
Stisted Essex 30 C5 vil 3m/5km E of Braintree. TL 8024
Stitchcombe Wilts 17 F4* loc on R Kennet 3m/4km E of Marlborough. SU 2269
Stithians Cornwall 2 C4 vil 3m/5km NW of Penryn. **Stithians Resr** is 2km W of vil. SW 7336
Stiughay W Isles 88 B3* islet in E Loch Tarbert, Harris, off W coast of Scalpay. **Stiughay na Leum** is another islet on S side of Stiughay. NG 2096
Stivichall W Midlands 35 H6* S dist of Coventry. SP 3376
Stixwould Lincs 45 F4 vil 2m/4km NW of Woodhall Spa. **Stixwould Ferry** loc on R Witham 2km SW. TF 1765
Stoak Ches 42 A4 vil 4m/7km N of Chester. SJ 4273
Stob a' Bhruaich Léith S'clyde 70 D1* mt in Argyll 3m/5km SW of Clach Leathad. Height 3083 ft or 940 metres. NN 2045
Stob a' Choin Central 71 E3 mt 3m/4km NE of head of Loch Katrine. Height 2839 ft or 865 metres. NN 4116
Stob a Choire Mheadhoin H'land 74 D4* mt in Lochaber dist 1km NE of Stob Coire Easain and 2km W of Loch Treig. Height 3629 ft or 1106 metres. NN 3173
Stob a' Choire Odhair S'clyde 70 D1* mt in Argyll on NW side of Beinn Toaig and 2m/3km E of Stob Ghabhar. Height 3094 ft or 943 metres. NN 2546
Stob a' Ghrianain H'land 74 C3 summit of Druim Fada, qv. Height 2420 ft or 738 metres. NN 0882
Stob an Duine Ruaidh S'clyde 70 C1 mt 2km SW of Ben Starav, Argyll, on E side of Loch Etive. Height 2624 ft or 800 metres. NN 1140
Stob an Eas S'clyde 70 D4* mt in Argyll 4m/6km N of Lochgoilhead. Height 2402 ft or 732 metres. NN 1807
Stob Aonaich Mhóir Tayside 75 F4 mt on E side of Loch Ericht. Height 2805 ft or 855 metres. NN 5369
Stob Bac an Fhurain Grampian 76 C1* one of the peaks of Ben Avon, qv, N of Braemar. Height 3530 ft or 1076 metres. NJ 1303
Stob Bàn H'land 74 C5 mt in Lochaber dist, 3m/5km NW of Kinlochleven. Height 3274 ft or 998 metres. NN 1465
Stob Bàn H'land 74 D4 mt in Lochaber dist 4m/6km NW of head of Loch Treig. Height 3204 ft or 977 metres. NN 2672
Stob Binnein Central 71 F3 mt 1m S of Ben More and 4m/6km SE of Crianlarich. Height 3821 ft or 1165 metres. Also known as Stobinian. NN 4322
Stob Breac Central 71 F3 mt 7m/11km SE of Crianlarich. Height 2250 ft or 686 metres. NN 4416
Stob Choire Claurigh H'land 74 D4 mt in Lochaber dist 4m/7km NW of head of Loch Treig. Height 3683 ft or 1177 metres. NN 2673
Stob Coir' an Albannaich S'clyde 70 D1 mt in Argyll 4m/6km E of head of Loch Etive. Height 3431 ft or 1046 metres. NN 1644
Stob Coire an Lochain Central 71 F3* peak on SE side of summit of Stob Binnein or Stobinian. Height 3497 ft or 1066 metres. NN 4322
Stob Coire Bhuidhe Central 71 E3* peak 1m N of summit of Cruach Ardrain. Height 2806 ft or 855 metres. NN 4022
Stob Coire Easain H'land 74 D4 mt in Lochaber dist 3m/4km N of head of Loch Treig. Height 3660 ft or 1116 metres. NN 3073
Stob Coire Easain H'land 74 D4 mt in Lochaber dist 4m/7km E of Ben Nevis. Height 3545 ft or 1080 metres. NN 2372
Stob Coire nan Cearc H'land 74 B3 mt in Lochaber dist 3m/5km NE of Glenfinnan. Height 2911 ft or 887 metres. NM 9385
Stob Coire nan Lochan H'land 74 C5* mt in Lochaber dist, 1m S of Loch Triochatan in Glen Coe. Height 3657 ft or 1115 metres. NN 1454
Stob Coire Sgriodain H'land 75 E4* mt in Lochaber dist between Loch Treig and Chno Dearg. Height 3203 ft or 976 metres. NN 3574
Stob Creagach Central 71 F3* mt 5m/8km W of Balquhidder. Height 2966 ft or 904 metres. NN 4523
Stob Dearg S'clyde 74 C5* summit of Buachaille Etive Mór, qv, in Argyll. Height 3352 ft or 1022 metres. NN 2254
Stob Dubh S'clyde 70 D1* mt in Argyll on E side of Glen Etive, 4m/6km NE of head of Loch Etive. Height 2897 ft or 883 metres. NN 1648
Stob Dubh S'clyde 74 C5* summit of Buachaille Etive Beag in Argyll. Height 3142 ft or 958 metres. NN 1753
Stob Garbh Central 71 E2 peak 1km N of summit of Cruach Ardrain. Height 3148 ft or 960 metres. NN 4122
Stob Ghabhar S'clyde 70 D1 mt in Argyll 6m/9km NW of Br of Orchy. Height 3565 ft or 1087 metres. NN 2345
Stob Glas Central 71 E3* peak 1km S of summit of Cruach Ardrain. Height 2732 ft or 833 metres. NN 4020
Stobinian Central 71 F3 mt 1m S of Ben More and 4m/6km SE of Crianlarich. Height 3821 ft or 1165 metres. Also known as Stob Binnein. NN 4322
Stob na Cruaiche 75 E5* summit of A' Chruach, on border of Highland and Tayside regions between Blackwater Resr and Loch Laidon. Height 2420 ft or 738 metres. NN 3657
Stobo Borders 65 H5 vil on R Tweed 5m/8km SW of Peebles. **Stobo Castle,** early 19c, 1m SW. NT 1837
Stoborough Dorset 9 F5 vil in R Frome valley 1km S of Wareham. **Stoborough Green** ham 1km S on N edge of **Stoborough Heath.** SY 9285
Stobs Borders 60 B1 loc 4m/6km S of Hawick. NT 5009
Stock Essex 20 D2 vil 3m/5km N of Billericay. TQ 6878
Stockay W Isles 88 D1* easternmost of the Monach Isles, qv. NF 6663
Stockbridge Hants 10 B2 vil on R Test 6m/10km S of Andover. Centre for trout-fishing. To S, Common Marsh (NT). To E, **Stockbridge Down** (NT), chalk downland containing Bronze and Iron Age earthworks. SU 3535
Stockbridge Lothian 66 A2* dist of Edinburgh 1km NW of city centre. NT 2474
Stockbridge W Sussex 11 E4* suburban loc 1m S of Chichester. SU 8503
Stockbury Kent 20 D5 vil 4m/7km W of Sittingbourne. TQ 8461
Stockcross Berks 17 H4 vil 3m/4km W of Newbury. SU 4368
Stockdale Cornwall 2 D4* loc 2m/3km N of Penryn. SW 7937
Stockdalewath Cumbria 60 A6* loc 4m/6km SE of Dalston. NY 3844
Stocker's Head Kent 21 E6* loc 1m NE of Charing. TQ 9650
Stockerston Leics 36 D4 vil 2m/4km SW of Uppingham. SP 8397
Stockghyll Force Cumbria 52 D4* waterfall on Stock Ghyll 1km E of Ambleside. NY 3804
Stock Green H & W 27 E2 vil 6m/10km SE of Droitwich. SO 9758
Stockheath Hants 10 D4* N dist of Havant. SU 7107
Stockholes Turbary Humberside 44 C1* loc 3m/4km NW of Epworth. SE 7607
Stocking H & W 26 B4* ham 4m/7km NE of Ross-on-Wye. SO 6230
Stockingford Warwicks 35 H5 W dist of Nuneaton. SP 3391
Stocking Green Bucks 28 C3* loc 5m/8km NW of Stony Stratford. SP 8047
Stocking Green Essex 30 B4* loc 3m/5km E of Saffron Walden. TL 5938
Stocking Pelham Herts 29 H5 vil 5m/9km NW of Bishop's Stortford. TL 4529

Stockinish Island W Isles 88 B3* uninhabited island at entrance to Loch Stockinish, SE coast of Harris 6m/10km S of Tarbert. NG 1390
Stockland Devon 8 A4 vil 5m/8km NW of Axminster. Stockland Hill TV stn, 3m/4km SW. ST 2404
Stockland S Glam 15 F3* loc 5m/8km W of Cardiff. ST 1078
Stockland Bristol Som H G6 vil 6m/9km NW of Bridgwater. ST 2443
Stockland Green Kent 12 C3* loc 2m/4km NW of Tunbridge Wells. TQ 5642
Stockleigh English Devon 7 F4 vil 4m/7km N of Crediton. SS 8506
Stockleigh Pomeroy Devon 7 F4 vil 4m/6km NE of Crediton. SS 8703
Stockley Hill H & W 25 H4* loc 2km E of Peterchurch. SO 3638
Stocklinch Som 8 B3 vil 2m/3km NE of Ilminster. ST 3817
Stockport Gtr Manchester 42 D2 tn 6m/10km SE of Manchester where Rs Goyt and Tame unite to form R Mersey. Textiles, chemicals, engineering. SJ 8989
Stocksbridge S Yorks 43 G2 steel-mnfg tn on Lit Don R 8m/14km NW of Sheffield. SK 2798
Stocksfield Nthmb 61 F5* vil on S side of R Tyne 3m/4km W of Prudhoe. NZ 0561
Stocks Reservoir Lancs 48 A3 resr in R Hodder valley 2m/3km N of Slaidburn. SD 7255
Stocks, The Kent 13 E4 ham on Isle of Oxney 1m E of Wittersham. TQ 9127
Stock, The Wilts 16 D5* loc adjoining Seend Cleeve to SW, 3m/4km SE of Melksham. ST 9260
Stockton H & W 26 A2 vil 2m/3km NE of Leominster. SO 5161
Stockton Norfolk 39 G5 vil 3m/5km NW of Beccles. TM 3894
Stockton Salop 34 A2* loc 2m/3km SW of Marton. SJ 2601
Stockton Salop 34 D3* ham 2m/4km SE of Newport. SJ 7716
Stockton Salop 34 D4 vil 4m/7km N of Bridgnorth. SO 7299
Stockton Warwicks 27 H2 vil 2m/3km NE of Southam. 1m N, **Stockton Locks**, stair of locks on Grand Union Canal. SP 4363
Stockton Wilts 9 G1 vil on R Wylye 5m/7km SE of Heytesbury. ST 9838
Stockton Brook Staffs 43 E5* loc 1m SW of Endon. SJ 9152
Stockton Heath Ches 42 B3 suburb of Warrington 2km S of tn centre. SJ 6186
Stockton-on-Tees Cleveland 54 D3 tn mainly on left bank of R Tees forming part of Teesside urban complex. Iron and steel, light engineering, chemicals. Racecourse. NZ 4418
Stockton on Teme H & W 26 C1 vil 6m/10km SE of Cleobury Mortimer. SO 7167
Stockton-on-the-Forest N Yorks 50 B3 vil 4m/7km NE of York. SE 6556
Stockwell Glos 26 D6* loc 5m/8km S of Cheltenham. SO 9414
Stockwell London 19 G4* dist in borough of Lambeth 3m/4km S of Charing Cross. TQ 3076
Stockwell End W Midlands 35 E4* loc in Wolverhampton 2m/3km NW of tn centre. SJ 8800
Stockwell Heath Staffs 35 F2* loc 2m/4km N of Rugeley. SK 0521
Stockwitch Cross Som 8 D2* loc at NE end of Yeovilton airfield 3m/4km NE of Ilchester. ST 5524
Stockwith, East Lincs 44 C2 vil on E bank of R Trent 4m/6km NW of Gainsborough and opp vil of W Stockwith, Notts. SK 7994
Stockwith, West Notts 44 C2 vil on W bank of R Trent opp vil of E Stockwith, Lincs. Junction of Chesterfield Canal and R Trent. SK 7994
Stockwood Avon 16 B4* SE dist of Bristol. ST 6268
Stockwood Dorset 8 D4* ham 2m/3km NE of Evershot. ST 5906
Stock Wood H & W 27 E2 ham 6m/9km W of Alcester. SP 0058
Stodday Lancs 47 E2/E3 loc 2m/3km SW of Lancaster. SD 4658
Stodmarsh Kent 13 G1 vil 5m/8km E of Canterbury. TR 2160
Stody Norfolk 39 E2 ham 3m/4km SW of Holt. TG 0535
Stoer H'land 84 A4 vil on W coast of Sutherland dist 5m/8km NW of Lochinver. To N is peninsula of Stoer, culminating in the headland Pt of Stoer. Lighthouse on W point of peninsula nearly 4m/6km NW of vil. NC 0328
Stoford Som vil 2m/3km S of Yeovil. ST 5613
Stoford Wilts 9 G1* ham across R Avon from Gt Wishford 3m/4km N of Wilton. SU 0835
Stoford, Middle Som 8 A2* ham 3m/4km E of Wellington. ST 1821
Stogumber Som 7 H2 vil 4m/6km SE of Watchet. ST 0937
Stogursey Som 15 G6 vil 7m/11km NW of Bridgwater. ST 2042
Stoke Devon 4 B5* dist of Plymouth 1m NW of city centre. SX 4655
Stoke Devon 6 B3 vil 5m/8km W of Clovelly. SS 2324
Stoke Hants 10 D4 vil on Hayling I. 2km S of Langstone Br. SU 7202
Stoke Hants 17 H6 vil 2m/3km SE of Hurstbourne Tarrant. SU 4051
Stoke Kent 20 D4 vil 4m/7km W of Grain, on N side of Stoke Saltings and R Medway estuary. TQ 8275
Stoke Suffolk 31 F4* S dist of Ipswich. TM 1643
Stoke W Midlands 36 A6 E dist of Coventry. SP 3779
Stoke Abbot Dorset 8 C4 vil 2m/3km W of Beaminster. ST 4500
Stoke Albany Northants 36 D5 vil 5m/7km E of Mkt Harborough. SP 8087
Stoke Ash Suffolk 31 E1 vil 3m/5km SW of Eye. TM 1170
Stoke Bardolph Notts 36 C1 vil 5m/8km E of Nottingham. Sk 6441
Stoke Bishop Avon 16 B4* dist of Bristol 2m/4km NW of city centre. ST 5675
Stoke Bliss H & W 26 B2 ham 5m/8km N of Bromyard. SO 6562
Stoke Bruerne Northants 28 C3 vil at S end of long tunnel on Grand Union Canal 4m/6km E of Towcester. SP 7449
Stoke by Clare Suffolk 30 C3/C4 vil 5m/7km E of Haverhill. TL 7443
Stoke-by-Nayland Suffolk 30 D4 vil 5m/8km SW of Hadleigh. TL 9836
Stoke Canon Devon 7 G5 vil on R Culm 4m/6km NE of Exeter. SX 9398
Stoke Charity Hants 10 C1 vil 6m/10km N of Winchester. SU 4839
Stoke Climsland Cornwall vil 3m/5km N of Callington. SX 3674
Stoke Cross H & W 26 B3* ham 3m/5km SW of Bromyard. SO 6250
Stoke Cross H & W 27 E1* loc 2km SE of Bromsgrove. SO 9869
Stoke D'Abernon Surrey 19 E5 enlarged vil 3m/5km NW of Leatherhead. Ch contains oldest brass in Britain (1277). TQ 1259
Stoke Doyle Northants 37 E5 vil 2km SW of Oundle. TL 0286
Stoke Dry Leics 36 D4 vil on E side of Eyebrook Resr 2m/3km S of Uppingham. SP 8596
Stoke, East Dorset 9 F5 vil on R Frome 3m/5km W of Wareham. SY 8786
Stoke, East Notts 44 C6 vil 4m/6km SW of Newark-on-Trent. Site of Battle of Stoke Field, 1487 (Lambert Simnel's rebellion). SK 7549
Stoke, East Som 8 C3* ham 1km E of Stoke sub Hamdon. ST 4817
Stoke Edith H & W 26 B3* vil 6m/9km E of Hereford. SO 6040
Stoke Farthing Wilts 9 G2* ham on R Ebble 5m/7km SW of Wilton. SU 0525
Stoke Ferry Norfolk 38 B4 vil 6m/10km SE of Downham Mkt. TF 7000
Stoke Fleming Devon 5 E5 vil on S coast 2m/3km SW of Dartmouth. SX 8648
Stokeford Dorset 9 F5 ham 4m/6km W of Wareham. SY 8687
Stoke Gabriel Devon 5 E5 vil on inlet of R Dart estuary 3m/5km SW of Paignton. SX 8457
Stoke Gifford Avon 16 B3 vil 5m/8km NE of Bristol. ST 6279
Stoke Golding Leics 36 A4 vil 3m/5km NW of Hinckley. SP 3997
Stoke Goldington Bucks 28 C3 vil 4m/7km NW of Newport Pagnell. SP 8348
Stoke, Great Avon 16 B3* NE part of vil of Stoke Gifford, 5m/9km NE of Bristol. ST 6280
Stoke Green Bucks 18 D3* loc 2m/3km NE of Slough. SU 9882
Stokeham Notts 44 C3 vil 6m/9km SE of E Retford. SK 7876
Stoke Hammond Bucks 28 D4 vil 3m/4km S of Bletchley. SP 8829
Stoke Heath H & W 26 D1* loc 2km SW of Bromsgrove. SO 9468
Stoke Heath Salop 34 D2 loc 3m/5km SW of Mkt Drayton. SJ 6529
Stoke Heath W Midlands 36 A6* loc in Coventry 2m/3km NE of city centre. SP 3580
Stoke Holy Cross Norfolk 39 F4 vil 4m/7km S of Norwich. TG 2301
Stokeinteignhead Devon 5 E3 vil 4m/6km E of Newton Abbot. SX 9170
Stoke Lacy H & W 26 B3 vil 4m/7km SW of Bromyard. SO 6249
Stoke, Little Avon 16 B3* suburban loc adjoining Patchway to E. ST 6181
Stoke, Little Staffs 35 E2 loc 2km SE of Stone. SJ 9132
Stoke, Lower Kent 20 D4 vil 4m/6km W of Grain. TQ 8375
Stoke Lyne Oxon 28 B4 vil 4m/6km N of Bicester. SP 5628
Stoke Mandeville Bucks 18 C1 vil 3m/4km SE of Aylesbury. SP 8310
Stoke, Middle Kent 20 D4* ham adjoining Lr Stoke to S, 4m/6km W of Grain. TQ 8375
Stokenchurch Bucks 18 C2 vil 7m/11km W of High Wycombe. SU 7696
Stoke Newington London 19 G3* dist in borough of Hackney 4m/7km NE of Charing Cross. TQ 3386
Stokenham Devon 5 E6 vil 5m/8km E of Kingsbridge. SX 8042
Stoke, North Avon 16 C4 vil 4m/7km NW of Bath. Site of Roman bldg 1m NE. ST 8344
Stoke, North Oxon 18 B3 vil 2m/3km S of Wallingford across R Thames. SU 6186
Stoke, North W Sussex 11 F4 vil in R Arun valley 2m/4km N of Arundel. TQ 0210
Stoke-on-Trent Staffs 42 D6 city on R Trent 135m/217km NW of London. Capital of The Potteries. An amalgam of the former Stoke-upon-Trent and the tns of Burslem, Fenton, Hanley, Longton, and Tunstall. Besides pottery, industries include coal-mining, brick mnfre, engineering, iron and steel. SJ 8745
Stoke Orchard Glos 26 D4* vil 4m/7km NW of Cheltenham. SO 9228
Stoke Pero Som 7 F1* loc on Exmoor 2m/3km S of Porlock. To S, **Stoke Ridge** and **Stoke Pero Common**. SS 8743
Stoke Poges Bucks 18 D3 suburban locality 3m/4km N of Slough. SU 9883
Stoke Point Devon 4 C6 headland at NW end of Bigbury Bay, to SE of Newton Ferrers. SX 5645
Stoke Pound H & W 26 D1* loc 2m/3km S of Bromsgrove. SO 9667
Stoke Prior H & W 26 A2 vil 2m/4km SE of Leominster. SO 5256
Stoke Prior H & W 26 D1 vil 2m/4km S of Bromsgrove. SO 9567
Stoke Rivers Devon 7 E2 vil 5m/8km E of Barnstaple. SS 6335
Stoke Rochford Lincs 37 E2 vil 5m/9km S of Grantham. SK 9227
Stoke Row Oxon 18 B3 vil 5m/8km W of Henley-on-Thames. SU 6883
Stoke St Gregory Som 8 B2 vil 8m/12km E of Taunton. ST 3427
Stoke St Mary Som 8 B2 vil 3m/4km SE of Taunton. ST 2622
Stoke St Michael Som 16 B6* vil 4m/6km NE of Shepton Mallet. Quarries. ST 6646
Stoke St Milborough Salop 34 C6 vil 6m/10km NE of Ludlow. SO 5682
Stokesay Salop 34 B6 vil 1km S of Craven Arms. Stokesay Castle is 13c fortified manor hse. SO 4381
Stokes Bay Hants 10 C5* bay extending NW from Gilkicker Pt, S of Gosport. SZ 5998
Stokesby Norfolk 39 H4 vil 2m/3km E of Acle across R Bure. TG 4310
Stokesley N Yorks 54 D4 small tn 8m/12km S of Middlesbrough. NZ 5208
Stoke, South Avon 16 C5 vil 2m/4km S of Bath. ST 7461
Stoke, South Oxon 18 B3 vil 2m/3km N of Goring. SU 6083
Stoke, South W Sussex 11 F4 vil in R Arun valley 2m/3km N of Arundel. TQ 0210
Stoke sub Hamdon Som 8 C3 vil 5m/8km W of Yeovil. The Priory (NT), 15c hse. Quarries on Hamdon Hill to S, source of local building stone known as Ham stone. ST 4717
Stoke Talmage Oxon 18 B2 vil 3m/5km N of Watlington. SU 6799
Stoke Trister Som 9 E2 vil 2m/3km E of Wincanton. ST 7328
Stoke upon Tern Salop 34 C2/D2 vil 2m/3km E of Hodnet. SJ 6428
Stoke, Upper Norfolk 39 F4* ham 4m/6km S of Norwich. TG 2402
Stoke Villice Avon 16 B5* loc on W side of Chew Valley Lake 1km S of Chew Stoke. ST 5560
Stoke Wake Dorset 9 E4 ham 5m/8km S of Sturminster Newton. ST 7606
Stoke, West W Sussex 11 E4 ham 3m/5km NW of Chichester. SU 8308
Stolford Som 15 G6 vil 3m/4km NE of Stogursey. ST 2245
Stonar, Great Kent 13 H2* loc to N of Sandwich. TR 3359
Stondon, Lower Beds 29 F4 E part of Upr Stondon, 3m/4km S of Shefford. TL 1535
Stondon Massey Essex 20 C2 vil 3m/4km SE of Chipping Ongar. TL 5800
Stondon, Upper Beds 29 F4 vil 3m/4km S of Shefford. TL 1535
Stone Bucks 18 C1 vil 2m/4km W of Aylesbury. SP 7812
Stone Glos 16 B2 vil 3m/4km S of Berkeley. **Lr Stone** ham 1m SW. ST 6895
Stone H & W 35 E6* vil 2m/3km SE of Kidderminster. SO 8575
Stone Kent 13 E4 vil in par of Stone-cum-Ebony on Isle of Oxney 2m/3km SW of Appledore. TQ 9327
Stone Kent 20 C4 loc on R Thames 2m/3km E of Dartford. TQ 5774
Stone Kent 21 F5* loc 2m/3km W of Faversham. TQ 9861
Stone Som 8 D1* loc 2m/3km E of Ham Street. ST 5834
Stone Staffs 35 E1 tn on R Trent 7m/11km N of Stafford. SJ 9034
Stone S Yorks 44 A2* ham 2m/3km SE of Maltby. SK 5589
Stonea Cambs 37 H5* loc 3m/5km SE of March. TL 4593
Stone Allerton Som 15 H6 vil 3m/5km NW of Wedmore. ST 4051
Ston Easton Som 16 B6 vil 3m/4km W of Midsomer Norton. ST 6253
Stonebow H & W 26 D3* loc 2m/4km N of Pershore. SO 9349
Stonebridge Avon 15 H5* ham 5m/7km E of Weston-super-Mare. ST 3959
Stonebridge Norfolk 38 D5* loc 1km NE of E Wretham. TL 9290
Stonebridge 35 H5 loc and rd junction on border of Warwicks and W Midlands 4m/6km S of Coleshill. SP 2183
Stone Bridge Corner Cambs 37 G4* loc 2m/3km S of Thorney. TF 2700
Stonebroom Derbys 43 H5 loc 2m/4km N of Alfreton. SK 4159
Stone Chair W Yorks 48 D5* loc 2m/4km NE of Halifax. SE 1127
Stoneclough Gtr Manchester 42 C1* loc 1km NE of Kearsley. SD 7505
Stone Cross Durham 54 A3* loc 2m/4km N of Barnard Castle. NZ 0419
Stone Cross E Sussex 12 C6 loc 3m/5km N of Eastbourne. TQ 6104
Stone Cross E Sussex 12 B4 loc 2m/3km S of Crowborough. TQ 5128
Stone Cross Kent 12 B3 loc 4m/7km W of Tunbridge Wells. TQ 5239
Stone Cross Kent 13 F3 loc 4m/7km S of Ashford. TR 0236
Stone Cross Kent 13 H2* loc on S side of Sandwich. TR 3257
Stone Cross W Midlands 35 F5* loc 2m/3km N of W Bromwich tn centre. SP 0194
Stonecross Green Suffolk 30 C2* loc 1km W of Whepstead. TL 8257
Stone-edge Batch Avon 16 A4* loc 1m NW of Nailsea. ST 4671
Stoneferry Humberside 51 E5 dist of Hull 2m/3km N of city centre. TA 1031
Stonefield S'clyde 64 D3 loc 2m/4km NW of Hamilton. NS 6957
Stonefield Staffs 35 E1* loc in N part of Stone. SJ 8934
Stone Fold Lancs 48 B5* loc 2m/3km N of Haslingden. SD 7825
Stonegate E Sussex 12 C4 vil 3m/4km SE of Wadhurst. TQ 6628
Stonegate N Yorks 55 F4* loc 3m/4km NW of Egton. NZ 7709
Stonegrave N Yorks 50 B1 vil 2m/3km NW of Hovingham. SE 6577
Stoneham, North Hants 10 B3 loc in green belt between Southampton and Eastleigh, 2km SW of Eastleigh. SU 4417
Stonehaugh Nthmb 60 D4 loc 4m/7km W of Wark. NY 7976
Stonehaven Grampian 77 H3 fishing port on **Stonehaven Bay** on E coast 13m/21km S of Aberdeen. Distilling, agricultural engineering. NO 8785

Stonehenge Wilts 9 H1 Neolithic – Bronze Age earthwork and stone circle (A.M.), 2m/3km W of Amesbury. SU 1242
Stonehill Surrey 19 E5* loc 3m/5km N of Woking. SU 9963
Stone Hill S Yorks 44 B1* loc adjoining Hatfield Woodhouse to NE. SE 6808
Stonehill Green Kent 20 B4* loc 2km NW of Swanley. TQ 5070
Stonehouse Ches 42 B4* ham 1km N of Ashton. SJ 5070
Stone House Cumbria 53 G6* loc 1m SE of Lea Yeat. SD 7785
Stonehouse Devon 4 B5 dist of Plymouth 1m W of city centre. SX 4654
Stonehouse Glos 16 C1 suburb 3m/5km W of Stroud. SO 8005
Stonehouse Nthmb 60 C5* loc 4m/6km S of Haltwhistle. NY 6958
Stonehouse S'clyde 65 E4 vil 3m/5km S of Larkhall. NS 7546
Stonehouses Staffs 35 F1* loc 3m/5km SW of Cheadle. SJ 9740
Stoneleigh Surrey 19 F5 loc 1m N of Ewell. TQ 2264
Stoneleigh Warwicks 27 G1 vil 3m/5km E of Kenilworth. SP 3372
Stoneley Green Ches 42 C6* loc 2m/4km W of Nantwich. SJ 6151
Stonely Cambs 29 E1/F1 vil adjoining Kimbolton to SE. TL 1067
Stone Ness Essex 20 C4* pt on N bank of R Thames at S end of W Thurrock Marshes, marking lower end of Long Reach. TQ 5876
Stone Point Essex 31 F5 N point of **Stone Marsh**, on S side of Pennyhole Bay 2m/3km NW of The Naze. TM 2425
Stone Point Hants 10 B5 headland at SW end of Stanswood Bay 3m/5km S of Fawley. Also known as Stansore Pt. SZ 4698
Stone Rows Leics 35 H3* loc 1km NE of Donisthorpe. SK 3114
Stones W Yorks 48 C5* loc 1m SW of Todmorden. SD 9223
Stonesby Leics 36 D2 vil 6m/9km NE of Melton Mowbray. SK 8224
Stonesdale, West N Yorks 53 G4 loc 1km N of Keld. NY 8802
Stonesfield Oxon 27 G5 vil 3m/4km SE of Charlbury. Site of Roman villa to E. SP 3917
Stones Green Essex 31 F5 ham 3m/5km N of Thorpe-le-Soken. TM 1626
Stone Street Kent 20 C6 ham 3m/4km E of Sevenoaks. TQ 5754
Stone Street Suffolk 30 D4* ham 1km S of Boxford and 3m/5km N of Nayland. TL 9639
Stone Street Suffolk 31 E4* loc 1m NW of Hadleigh. TM 0143
Stone Street Suffolk 31 G1 ham 3m/5km N of Halesworth. TM 3882
Stonestreet Green Kent 13 F3 loc 5m/8km SE of Ashford. TR 0637
Stonethwaite Cumbria 52 C3/C4* loc 2km E of Seatoller. NY 2613
Stoneton Warwicks 27 H2* loc 9m/14km N of Banbury. SP 4654
Stoneybridge W Isles 88 D2 vil near W coast of S Uist 3m/5km NE of Rubha Ardvule. NF 7433
Stoneyburn Lothian 65 F3* vil 4m/6km S of Bathgate. NS 9762
Stoney Byres Linn S'clyde 65 E4 waterfall with hydro-electricity power stn on R Clyde, 2m/3km W of Lanark. NS 8544
Stoneyford Devon 5 F2* loc 4m/7km N of Budleigh Salterton. SY 0688
Stoneygate Leics 36 C4* dist of Leicester 2m/3km SE of city centre. SK 6002
Stoney Hill H & W 26 D1/27 E1* E dist of Bromsgrove. SO 9670
Stoneyhills Essex 21 E2* loc 1km N of Burnham-on-Crouch. TQ 9597
Stoneykirk D & G 57 B7 vil 5m/8km S of Stranraer. NX 0853
Stoney Middleton Derbys 43 G3/G4 vil 5m/7km N of Bakewell. SK 2375
Stoney Stanton Leics 36 B5 vil 4m/7km E of Hinckley. SP 4994
Stoney Stoke Som 9 E1 ham 2m/4km N of Wincanton. ST 7032
Stoney Stratton Som 8 D1* vil 1km E of Evercreech. ST 6539
Stoney Stretton Salop 34 B3 ham 7m/11km W of Shrewsbury. SJ 3809
Stoneywood Grampian 83 G5 vil on NW outskirts of Aberdeen. NJ 8911
Stonham Aspal Suffolk 31 F2 vil 4m/6km SW of Debenham. TM 1359
Stonham, Little Suffolk 31 E2 vil 4m/7km E of Stowmarket. TM 1160
Stonnall, Upper Staffs 35 G4 vil 2m/3km SE of Brownhills. **Lr Stonnall** loc 1m E. SK 0603
Stonor Oxon 18 C3 vil 4m/7km NW of Henley-on-Thames. SU 7388
Stonton Wyville Leics 36 C5* vil 5m/8km N of Mkt Harborough. SP 7395
Stonybridge Dyfed 22 D5* ham 2km W of Saundersfoot. SN 1104
Stony Cove Pike Cumbria 52 D4* mt in Lake Dist 2m/3km NE of Kirkstone Pass. Height 2502 ft or 762 metres. NY 4110
Stony Cross Devon 6 D3* loc 4m/6km E of Bideford. SS 5025
Stony Cross H & W 26 B1* loc 3m/5km W of Tenbury Wells. SO 5466
Stony Cross H & W 26 C3* loc 3m/5km W of Gt Malvern. SO 7247
Stony Dale Notts 36 C1* loc 1m NW of Screveton. SK 7244
Stony Gate Tyne & Wear 61 H6* loc 2km NE of Houghton-le-Spring. NZ 3551
Stony Heap Durham 61 F6* loc 2m/4km E of Consett. NZ 1451
Stony Hill Lancs 46 D5 dist of Blackpool 2m/3km S of tn centre. SD 3032
Stony Hill S'clyde 65 E6 hill 4m/7km SE of Muirkirk. Height 1843 ft or 562 metres. NS 7221
Stony Houghton Derbys 44 A4 vil 4m/7km NW of Mansfield. SK 4966
Stony Lea Staffs 35 F3* loc 1km NE of Cannock. SJ 9810
Stony Stratford Bucks 28 C4 small tn on R Ouse in NW part of Milton Keynes. SP 7140
Stony Tarn Cumbria 52 C4* small lake 2m/3km NE of Boot. NY 1902
Stoodleigh Devon 7 E2* loc 5m/9km NW of S Molton. SS 6532
Stoop, High Durham 54 A1* loc 2m/3km NW of Tow Law. NZ 1040
Stopes S Yorks 43 G2* loc 4m/7km W of Sheffield. SK 2888
Stopham W Sussex 11 F3 vil 2km W of Pulborough. Medieval br spans R Arun. TQ 0219
Stopsley Beds 29 E5 NE dist of Luton. TL 1023
Stoptide Cornwall 3 E1 loc on E side of R Camel estuary opp Padstow. SW 9475
Stores Corner Suffolk 31 G3/G4* loc 6m/9km SE of Woodbridge. TM 3545
Storeton Merseyside 41 H3 loc 2m/3km W of Bebington. SJ 3084
Stormont Loch Tayside 73 E1 small loch 2m/3km S of Blairgowrie. Also known as Loch Bog. NO 1942
Stornoway W Isles 88 C2 port and chief tn of Lewis, situated on E coast 22m/35km S of Butt of Lewis and 13m/22km E of Breasclete on W coast. **Stornoway Harbour** is large natural harbour on S side of tn. Main industries are fishing and tweed mnfre. Airport 2m/3km E towards Melbost. NB 4232
Storridge H & W 26 C3 ham 2m/4km NW of Gt Malvern. SO 7548
Storrington W Sussex 11 G3 small tn below S Downs 4m/6km SE of Pulborough. TQ 0814
Storrs S Yorks 43 G2* loc 4m/7km NW of Sheffield. **Storrs Br** loc on R Loxley 1km N. SK 2889
Storr, The Skye, H'land 78 C4 mt in Trotternish 7m/11km N of Portree. Height 2358 ft or 719 metres. See also Old Man of Storr. NG 4954
Stort 20 A1 r rising about 7m/11km W of Saffron Walden, Essex, and flowing S into R Lea 4m/6km SE of Ware, Herts. TL 3909
Storth Cumbria 47 E1 loc 2km NE of Arnside. SD 4779
Storwood Humberside 50 C4 ham 3m/4km W of Melbourne. SE 7144
Stotfield Grampian 82 B1 W dist of Lossiemouth. NJ 2270
Stotfold Beds 29 F4 suburb 3m/4km NW of Baldock. Loc of **Stotfold Green** at N end. TL 2236
Stottesdon Salop 34 D6 vil 4m/7km N of Cleobury Mortimer. SO 6782
Stoughton Leics 36 C4 vil 4m/6km E of Leicester. SK 6402
Stoughton Som 15 H6 locs of **Middle** and **W Stoughton** and **Stoughton Cross**, 2km NW of Wedmore. ST 4249
Stoughton Surrey 18 D6 NW dist of Guildford. SU 9851
Stoughton W Sussex 11 E4 vil 5m/8km NE of Emsworth. Site of Roman bldg 2km E. SU 8011
Stoul H'land 79 F8 locality on SW shore of Loch Nevis, 5m/8km E of Mallaig. NM 7594
Stoulton H & W 26 D3 vil 5m/8km SE of Worcester. SO 9049
Stour 13 H1 r running from confluence of Gt and Lit Stour Rs at Plucks Gutter into sea at Pegwell Bay, Kent. TR 3462
Stour 26 C1 r rising S of Dudley, W Midlands, and flowing SW through Stourbridge and Kidderminster into R Severn at Stourport, H & W. SO 8170
Stour 27 F2 r rising on Cotswold Hills N of Chipping Norton, Oxon, and flowing W to Burmington, then N through Shipston on Stour and into R Avon 2m/3km SW of Stratford-upon-Avon, Warwicks. SP 1815
Stour 31 F4/F5 r rising in Cambs some 4m/7km NW of Haverhill and flowing SE by Clare, Cavendish, Sudbury, Bures, Nayland, and Dedham to form estuary at Manningtree, thence E to Harwich, where it joins R Orwell to flow into Harwich Harbour and North Sea. TM 2633
Stour 9 H5 r rising near Stourhead in Wiltshire and flowing S to Sturminster Newton, then SE through Blandford and Wimborne into Christchurch Harbour, Dorset. SZ 1692
Stourbridge W Midlands 35 E5 industrial tn on R Stour 10m/17km W of Birmingham. Iron and glass works. **Stourbridge Canal** runs to N of tn from Staffordshire and Worcestershire Canal at Stourton Junction to W, and gives access to the Birmingham canal system to E. SO 9084
Stour, East Dorset 9 E2 vil 2m/4km S of Gillingham. ST 7922
Stour, East 13 F3* r rising near Brabourne, Kent, and flowing into R Gt Stour at Ashford. TR 0142
Stour, Great 13 G1 r rising near Lenham, Kent, and flowing SE to Ashford, where it is joined by the E Stour R. It then flows NE through Canterbury to Plucks Gutter where with Lit Stour R it forms R Stour. TR 2663
Stourhead Wilts 9 E1* 18c hse and pleasure grnds (NT), 3m/4km NW of Mere. ST 7734
Stour, Little 13 G1 r rising near Ash, E Kent, and flowing into R Gt Stour at Plucks Gutter, the two rs there combining to form R Stour. TR 2663
Stourmouth Kent 13 G1 par 6m/9km NW of Sandwich containing vils of **E** and **W Stourmouth.** TR 2562
Stourpaine Dorset 9 F3 vil at confluence of R Iwerne with R Stour at SW end of Cranborne Chase 3m/4km NW of Blandford Forum. ST 8609
Stourport-on-Severn H & W 26 C1 tn at confluence of R Stour and R Severn and on Staffordshire and Worcestershire Canal 3m/5km SW of Kidderminster. SO 8171
Stour Provost Dorset 9 E2 vil 3m/5km S of Gillingham. ST 7921
Stour Row Dorset 9 F2 vil 3m/5km W of Shaftesbury. ST 8221
Stour, South Kent 13 F3* loc 3m/5km SE of Ashford. TR 0338
Stourton Staffs 35 E5* ham 3m/5km W of Stourbridge. Canal junction to E (see Stourbridge). SO 8585
Stourton Warwicks 27 G4* vil adjoining Cherington to E, 6m/10km N of Chipping Norton. SP 2936
Stourton Wilts 9 E1 vil 3m/4km NW of Mere. See also Stourhead. ST 7734
Stourton W Yorks 49 E5 loc on R Aire 3m/5km SE of Leeds. SE 3230
Stourton Caundle Dorset 8 E3 vil in Blackmoor Vale 5m/8km E of Sherborne. ST 7115
Stour, West Dorset 9 E2 vil 3m/4km SW of Gillingham. ST 7822
Stout Bay S Glam 15 E4* small bay on E side of **Stout Pt**, headland on Bristol Channel coast 2km S of Llantwit Major. SS 9766
Stoven Suffolk 31 H1 vil 5m/8km NE of Halesworth. TM 4481
Stover Avon 16 C3* loc 2m/3km W of Chipping Sodbury. ST 6982
Stow Borders 66 C4 vil on Gala Water 5m/8km W of Lauder. NT 4544
Stow Lincs 44 D3 vil 4m/7km N of Saxilby. Large Saxon/Norman ch is notable landmark. **Stow Pasture** loc 1m E. SK 8881
Stow Bardolph Norfolk 38 B4 vil 2m/3km NE of Downham Mkt. TF 6205
Stow Bedon Norfolk 38 D5 vil 4m/6km SE of Watton. Mere on W side of vil. Ham of **Lr Stow Bedon** to SE. TL 9596
Stowbridge Norfolk 38 B4 ham on W bank of R Ouse 3m/4km N of Downham Mkt across r. TF 6007
Stow Creek Essex 21 E2* inlet running into R Crouch estuary from N side 1km W of N Fambridge. TQ 8496
Stow cum Quy Cambs 30 A2 vil 5m/8km E of Cambridge. TL 5260
Stowe Bucks 28 B4 par 3m/4km NW of Buckingham containing Stowe School, boys' public school housed in 18c hse in large park. SP 6737
Stowe Salop 25 G1 ham 2m/3km NE of Knighton. SO 3173
Stowe Staffs 35 F2 vil 6m/10km NE of Stafford. SK 0027
Stowe Staffs 35 G3* loc in Lichfield 1km NE of tn centre. SK 1210
Stowehill Northants 28 B2* loc 5m/8km SE of Daventry. SP 6458
Stowell Glos 27 E6 loc 2m/3km SW of Northleach. SP 0813
Stowell Som 9 E2 vil 4m/7km SW of Wincanton. ST 6822
Stowell, West Wilts 17 F5 ham 2m/3km NW of Pewsey. SU 1362
Stowe, Upper Northants 28 B2 vil 6m/9km SE of Daventry. SP 6456
Stowey Avon 16 B5 ham 3m/4km SE of Chew Magna. ST 5959
Stowey, Nether Som 8 A1 vil at foot of Quantock Hills 10m/16km W of Bridgwater. Coleridge's cottage (NT), where the poet lived from 1797 to 1800. ST 1939
Stowford Devon 5 G2* loc 2m/3km N of Sidmouth. SY 1189
Stowford Devon 6 C6* vil 7m/11km E of Launceston. SX 4386
Stowford Devon 6 E3* ham 6m/9km W of S Molton. **E Stowford** ham to E. SS 6226
Stowlangtoft Suffolk 30 D2 vil 2m/4km SE of Ixworth. TL 9568
Stow Longa Cambs 29 E1/F1 vil 8m/13km W of Huntingdon. TL 1070
Stow Maries Essex 20 D2 vil 5m/8km S of Maldon. TQ 8399
Stowmarket Suffolk 31 E2 mkt and industrial tn on R Gipping 11m/18km NW of Ipswich. Industries include iron-founding, agricultural engineering, tanning. TM 0458
Stow-on-the-Wold Glos 27 F5 small tn 8m/12km W of Chipping Norton. Site of Roman villa to NW. SP 1925
Stowting Kent 13 F3 vil 5m/8km NW of Hythe. Ham of **Stowting Common** 2km N. TR 1241
Stowupland Suffolk 31 E2 suburb 2km NE of Stowmarket. TM 0760
Stow, West Suffolk 30 C1 vil 5m/7km NW of Bury St Edmunds. TL 8170
Straad S'clyde 63 G2 loc near W coast of Bute, 3m/5km SW of Rothesay. NS 0462
Stracathro Tayside 77 F4 loc 2m/4km SE of Edzell. Site of Roman fort. NO 6165
Strachan Grampian 77 F2 vil on Water of Feugh 3m/4km SW of Banchory. NO 6792
Strachur S'clyde 70 C4 vil 1km E of **Strachur Bay** on E shore of Loch Fyne in Argyll. NN 0900
Stradbroke Suffolk 31 F1 vil 7m/12km NW of Framlingham. TM 2373
Stradbrook Wilts 16 D6* loc adjoining Bratton to W, 3m/5km E of Westbury. ST 9152
Stradishall Suffolk 30 C3 vil 7m/11km NE of Haverhill. Airfield to SW. TL 7452
Stradsett Norfolk 38 B4 ham 4m/6km E of Downham Mkt. Hall is Elizn, altered early 19c; large lake in park. TF 6605
Strae S'clyde 70 C2 r in Argyll running SW down Glen Strae to R Orchy 2m/3km W of Dalmally. NN 1328
Stragglethorpe Lincs 44 D5 ham 7m/12km E of Newark-on-Trent. SK 9152
Stragglethorpe Notts 36 C1 loc 2km S of Radcliffe on Trent. SK 6537
Strahangles Point Grampian 83 G1* headland on W side of Aberdour Bay 8m/12km W of Fraserburgh. NJ 8765
Straight Point Devon 5 F3* headland on Lyme Bay 4km E of Exmouth. Cliffs to W (NT). SY 0379

Straight Soley Wilts 17 G4* loc 2m/4km N of Hungerford. See also Crooked Soley. SU 3272
Strait of Corryvreckan S'clyde 69 E7 sea passage between islands of Scarba and Jura. Notorious for tidal races and whirlpools. NM 6902
Strait of Dover 13 H4 the narrow part of the English Channel between the coasts of England and France. TR 32
Straiton Lothian 66 A2 loc in Edinburgh 5m/8km S of city centre. NT 2766
Straiton S'clyde 56 D3 vil on Water of Girvan 6m/10km SE of Maybole. NS 3804
Straits Green W Midlands 35 E5* loc 3m/4km W of Dudley tn centre. SO 9091
Straloch Tayside 76 B2 loc in Glen Brerachan 3m/5km NW of Kirkmichael. NO 0463
Stramshall Staffs 35 G1 vil 2m/3km NW of Uttoxeter. SK 0835
Strandburgh Ness Shetland 89 F6* headland at NE point of Fetlar. HU 6793
Strands Cumbria 52 B4 ham 4m/6km E of Gosforth. NY 1204
Strands Cumbria 52 C6* loc 1km SE of The Green. SD 1884
Strang Isle of Man 46 B5 loc 2m/3km NW of Douglas. SC 3678
Strangeways Gtr Manchester 42 D2* dist of Manchester 1m N of city centre. HM prison. SJ 8399
Strangford H & W 26 B4* vil in loop of R Wye 3m/4km NW of Ross-on-Wye across r. SO 5828
Strangways Wilts 17 F6* loc 2m/3km NW of Amesbury. SU 1443
Stranraer D & G 57 B6 port and resort at head of Loch Ryan 23/37km W of Wigtown. Passenger and car ferry service to Larne in Northern Ireland (see also Cairnryan). NX 0660
Strata Florida (Ystrad-fflur) Dyfed 24 C2 loc 1m SE of Pontrhydfendigaid. Slight remains of 12c abbey (A.M.). SN 7465
Stratfield Mortimer Berks 16 B5 vil 6m/9km SW of Reading. SU 6664
Stratfield Saye Hants 18 B5 vil 8m/12km SW of Reading. SU 6861
Stratfield Turgis Hants 18 B5 vil (with Turgis Green) 6m/10km NE of Basingstoke. SU 6960
Stratford Beds 29 F3* loc 1m SE of Sandy. TL 1847
Stratford London 20 A3 tn in borough of Newham 5m/7km NE of London Br. Loc of **Stratford New Tn** 1km N, and of **Stratford Marsh** 1km W in R Lea valley. TQ 3884
Stratford-on-Avon Warwicks. See Stratford-upon-Avon. SP 2054
Stratford St Andrew Suffolk 31 G2 vil 3m/4km SW of Saxmundham. TM 3560
Stratford St Mary Suffolk 31 E4 vil 6m/10km NE of Colchester. TM 0434
Stratford sub Castle Wilts 9 H1 loc in N part of Salisbury below Old Sarum. SU 1332
Stratford Tony Wilts 9 G2 vil 3m/5km S of Wilton. SU 0926
Stratford-upon-Avon Warwicks 27 F2 tn on R Avon 8m/13km SW of Warwick. Birthplace of Shakespeare. Tourist centre. Shakespeare Memorial Theatre. Brewery. See also Shottery. SP 2054
Stratford-upon-Avon Canal 27 F2-35 F6 canal running from Stratford-upon-Avon to Worcester and Birmingham Canal at King's Norton, W Midlands. Southern section, from Stratford to Lapworth, is administered by NT.
Strathaird Skye, H'land 79 D6, D7 peninsula on S coast between Loch Scavaig and Loch Slapin. At S end is headland of **Strathaird Pt**, also known as Rubha na h-Easgainne. NG 5319
Strath Allan 72 B4, C4 valley of Allan Water in Tayside and Central regions NE of Dunblane, marking southern limit of Scottish Highlands in this area. NN 8106
Strathan H'land 74 B3* locality in Lochaber dist at head of Loch Arkaig. NM 9791
Strathan H'land 85 B5 loc near W coast of Sutherland dist 2km SW of Lochinver. NC 0821
Strath Ardle Tayside 76 B5 valley of R Ardle running SE to foot of Glen Shee below Br of Cally. NO 1054
Strathaven S'clyde 64 D4 tn 7m/11km S of Hamilton. NS 7044
Strathbeg H'land 85 B7 r in W part of Ross and Cromarty dist running N into head of Lit Loch Broom. NH 0988
Strathbeg Bay Grampian 83 H1 wide bay on NE coast extending NW from Rattray Hd to Inzie Hd. See also Loch of Strathbeg. NK 0760
Strathblane Central 64 C1 vil at head of Strath Blane 9m/14km N of Glasgow. **Strathblane Hills** on SW slopes of Campsie Fells to N. NS 5679
Strathbogie Grampian 82 D3 valley of R Bogie, S of Huntly. Name is also applied to the area E and W of the valley. NJ 5237
Strath Braan Tayside 72 C1, D1 valley of R Braan, running NE to Strath Tay at Dunkeld. NN 9840
Strath Brora H'land 87 A5, A6 valley of R Brora in Sutherland dist, running down to Brora on E coast. NC 7609
Strathbungo S'clyde 64 C3* loc in Glasgow 2m/3km S of city centre. NS 5762
Strathcarron H'land 80 A3 loc at foot of Glen Carron, Ross and Cromarty dist. NG 9442
Strath Carron H'land 85 E7 valley of R Carron running down to Kyle of Sutherland at Bonar Br, Sutherland dist. NH 5192
Strath Chuilionaich H'land 85 D7, E7 valley of **Abhainn an t-Strath Chuilionaich** in Sutherland dist, running SE into Strath Carron 8m/13km W of Bonar Br. NH 4393
Strathclyde 114,116 admin region of western Scotland, comprising the former counties of Ayr, Bute, Dunbarton, Lanark, Renfrew, and all except the extreme N of Argyll, qv. The region encloses the whole of the basin of R Clyde, commercially the most important r in Scotland, from which its name derives. The Firth of Clyde may be said to mark the division between Highlands and Lowlands. The Highland area to the N, with its islands, lochs, and mts, contains some of the finest and most spectacular scenery in Britain, although the upper basin of the Clyde and the hills and forests of the Glen Trool Forest Park to the S cannot lightly be dismissed. The lower basin of the Clyde, containing the city of Glasgow and the area generally known as Clydeside, is the commercial and industrial heart of Scotland, and contains nearly a quarter of the total population.
Strathconon H'land 80 D2, 81 E2 valley of R Conon in Ross and Cromarty dist, running E down to Conon Br at head of Cromarty Firth. **Strathconon Forest** is deer forest astride R Meig. NH 4055
Strath Dearn H'land 81 G5-H3 valley of R Findhorn, Inverness and Nairn dists. **Strathdearn Forest** is state forest 10m/16km SE of Inverness. NH 7724
Strath Dionard H'land. See Dionard.
Strathdon Grampian 82 C5 vil on R Don 12m/19km E of Tomintoul. NJ 3512
Strath Earn Tayside 72 B3-D3 valley of R Earn running E from Loch Earn to head of Firth of Tay below Perth. NN 9517
Strathenry Castle Fife 73 E4 cas 2km W of Leslie. 17c dovecote. NO 2201
Strath Errick H'land 81 E5, E6 valley in Inverness dist E of Loch Ness. Contains Loch Mhór. NH 5017
Strath Fillan Central 71 E2 valley of R Fillan above Crianlarich. NN 3627
Strath Fleet H'land 87 A6 valley of R Fleet in Sutherland dist running down to E coast N of Dornoch. NC 6702
Strath Gairloch H'land 78 F2 loc in Ross and Cromarty dist 1km NW of Gairloch. NG 7977
Strath Gartney Central 71 E4, F4 land on N shore of Loch Katrine. NN 4610
Strath Garve H'land 80 D1, D2 valley of Black Water above Garve in Ross and Cromarty dist. Strathgarve Forest is deer forest to E. NH 4064
Strathglass H'land 80 D4 valley of R Glass in Inverness dist running down to its confluence with R Farrar near Struy Br. NH 3835
Strath Gryfe S'clyde 64 B2 valley of R Gryfe, or Gryfe Water, between Gryfe Resr and Br of Weir. NS 3370
Strath Halladale H'land 86 B2, B3 valley of Halladale R in Caithness dist. See Halladale (R). NC 85
Strath Isla Grampian 82 C3-D2 valley of R Isla, qv. NJ 4250
Strathkanaird H'land 85 B6 vil in Ross and Cromarty dist on N side of Strath Kanaird, valley of R Kanaird, 5m/8km N of Ullapool. NC 1501
Strathkelvin 114 admin dist of S'clyde region.
Strathkinness Fife 73 G3 vil 3m/5km W of St Andrews. NO 4516
Strathlachlan S'clyde 70 C5 locality in Argyll on Strathlachlan R 6m/9km SW of Strachur. R flows SW to Loch Fyne 2km SW. **Strathlachlan Forest** is state forest to NE and SW. NS 0295
Strathlethan Bay Grampian 77 H3 bay on E coast 1km S of Stonehaven. NO 8884
Strathmarchin Bay Grampian 83 E1* small bay on N coast 2km E of Portsoy. NJ 6066
Strathmiglo Fife 73 E3 small tn 2m/3km SW of Auchtermuchty. Bobbin mnfre. NO 2110
Strath More H'land 85 C8 valley of R Broom above Loch Broom, Ross and Cromarty dist. Lael Forest runs down E side of valley. NH 1882
Strathmore 76, 77 great fertile valley separating Highlands of Scotland from Central Lowlands and extending from foot of Loch Lomond to Stonehaven, although term is more generally applied to part between Methven and Brechin. NO 45
Strathmore 84 E3 r of Sutherland dist, H'land, rising on Reay Forest and running N down **Strath More** into Loch Hope, whence it emerges as R Hope, qv. NC 4550
Strath Mulzie H'land 85 D7 valley of Corriemulzie R, qv, Sutherland dist. NH 3192
Strathnairn Forest H'land 81 F4* state forest in Inverness dist 9m/14km S of Inverness. NH 6930
Strath na Sealga H'land 85 B8 valley of **Abhainn Strath na Sealga,** r running NW into head of Loch na Sealga in W part of Ross and Cromarty dist. NH 0680
Strathnasheallag Forest H'land 85 A7, B8 deer forest to E of Loch na Sealga in Ross and Cromarty dist. NH 0483
Strath Naver H'land 86 A2, A3 valley of R Naver, in Caithness dist. NC 74
Strath of Appin S'clyde 70 B1 valley or pass in Argyll running across SW part of Appin, qv, from Loch Linnhe to Loch Creran. NM 9495
Strath of Appin Tayside 75 H6 broad valley of R Tay in vicinity of Dull. Also known as Appin of Dull. NN 7948
Strath of Kildonan H'land 86 B4, 87 C5 valley of R Helmsdale in Sutherland dist, between Kinbrace and Helmsdale. NC 8923
Strath of Orchy S'clyde 70 D2* valley of R Orchy in vicinity of Dalmally in Argyll. NN 1627
Strathord Forest Tayside 72 D2* state forest 2m/3km S of Bankfoot. NO 0632
Strath Ossian H'land 75 E4 valley of R Ossian between Loch Ghuilbinn and Loch Ossian. NN 4172
Strath Oykel H'land 85 D6, E6 valley of R Oykel, Sutherland dist, between Oykel Br and Invershin. NC 4300
Strathpeffer H'land 81 E2 vil in Ross and Cromarty dist 4m/7km W of Dingwall. Resort, with mineral springs. NH 4858
Strath Rannoch H'land 85 D8 valley and r in Ross and Cromarty dist running S to Black Water at Inchbae Lodge at S end of Inchbae Forest. NH 3972
Strath Rory H'land 87 A8 valley of **Strathrory R,** Ross and Cromarty dist, running E into Balnagown R 5m/7km N of Invergordon. NH 6776
Strath Rusdale H'land 85 F8 valley of Black Water in Ross and Cromarty dist running SE to R Alness 5m/8km NW of Alness. NH 5775
Strath Shinary H'land 84 C2 valley of Abhainn an t-Srathain, stream in Sutherland dist running into Sandwood Loch. NC 26
Strath Skinsdale H'land 87 A5 valley of R Skinsdale in Sutherland dist 14m/22km NW of Brora. NC 7518
Strath Tay Tayside 76 A5-B6 valley of R Tay above Dunkeld. NO 0043
Strath Vagastie H'land 84 E4 valley of Allt a' Chraisg in Caithness dist running NE down to head of Loch Naver. NC 5430
Strath Vaich H'land 85 D8 valley and r in Ross and Cromarty dist running S from Loch Vaich to join R Glascarnoch at Black Br 2m/3km W of Inchbae Lodge. NH 3573
Strathvaich Forest H'land 85 D8 deer forest in Ross and Cromarty dist to S and W of Loch Vaich. NH 3474
Strathy H'land 86 B2 vil near N coast of Caithness dist and mouth of **R Strathy** 17m/28km W of Thurso. **Strathy Bay** 1km N. **Strathy Pt** headland with lighthouse 3m/5km N. R Strathy rises about 12m/19km S and flows N on W side of vil into Strathy Bay. **Strathy Forest** is afforested area astride r 6m/9km S of vil. NC 8465
Strathyre Central 71 F3 valley of R Balvag running from Loch Voil to Loch Lubnaig, past vil of **Strathyre,** set in middle of state forest, **Strathyre Forest.** Information centre and picnic area to S of vil. NN 5617
Stratton Cornwall 6 B4 tn near N coast forming part of resort of Bude-Stratton, 15m/24km NW of Launceston. SS 2306
Stratton Dorset 8 D5 vil 3m/5km NW of Dorchester. SY 6593
Stratton Glos 17 E2 vil 1m NW of Cirencester. SP 0103
Stratton Audley Oxon 28 B5 vil 3m/5km NE of Bicester. SP 6026
Stratton, East Hants 10 C1 vil 2m/3km E of Micheldever. SU 5440
Stratton Hall Suffolk 31 F4* loc by left bank of R Orwell 5m/7km NW of Felixstowe. TM 2438
Stratton-on-the-Fosse Som 16 B6 vil on Foss Way 3m/5km SW of Radstock. On W side of vil, Downside Abbey, Benedictine monastery and boys' school. ST 6550
Stratton St Margaret Wilts 17 F3 NE suburb of Swindon. Airfield to E. SU 1787
Stratton St Michael Norfolk 39 F5 vil 9m/15km S of Norwich. TM 2093
Stratton Strawless Norfolk 39 F3 vil 8m/12km N of Norwich. TG 2220
Stratton, West Hants 10 C1 loc 2km NE of Micheldever. SU 5240
Stravanan Bay S'clyde 63 G2 bay on SW coast of Bute 2km W of Kingarth. NS 0756
Strawberry Hill London 19 F4* loc in borough of Richmond on left bank of R Thames S of Twickenham. TQ 1572
Stream Som 7 H1* ham 2m/3km S of Watchet. ST 0639
Streap H'land 74 B3 mt in Lochaber dist 4m/7km NE of Glenfinnan. Height 2988 ft or 911 metres. Peak of **Streap Comhlaidh** to SE; height 2916 ft or 889 metres. NM 9486
Street E Sussex 12 A5 vil 5m/8km NW of Lewes. TQ 3515
Streatham London 19 G4* dist in borough of Lambeth 6m/10km S of Charing Cross. **Streatham Hill** lies 2km N; **Streatham Vale** 1km SW; **Streatham Park** 1km W. TQ 2971
Streatlam Durham 54 A3 loc 3m/5km NE of Barnard Castle. **Streatlam Castle,** ruined mansion of 18c and 19c. NZ 0819
Streatley Beds 29 E5 vil 5m/8km N of Luton. TL 0728
Streatley Berks 18 B3 vil on R Thames 4m/6km NW of Pangbourne. SU 5980
Street Devon 5 G2* ham just NW of Branscombe and 4m/7km E of Sidmouth. SY 1888
Street N Yorks 55 F4* loc 3m/4km SW of Lealholm. NZ 7304
Street Som 8 B4* loc 2m/3km E of Chard. ST 3507
Street Som 8 C1 tanning and shoe-making tn 2m/3km SW of Glastonbury. ST 4836
Street Ashton Warwicks 36 A6* ham 5m/9km NW of Rugby. SP 4582
Street Dinas Salop 34 A1 ham 4m/6km SW of Overton. SJ 3338
Street, East Kent 13 H2* loc 2m/3km W of Sandwich. TR 3058
Street, East Som 8 D1* loc 3m/4km E of Glastonbury. ST 5438
Street End Kent 13 G2 ham 3m/5km S of Canterbury. TR 1453

Street End W Sussex 11 E5* ham 1km N of Sidlesham and 3m/5km S of Chichester. SZ 8599
Street Gate Tyne & Wear 61 G5* vil 4m/6km SW of Gateshead. NZ 2159
Street Green, High Suffolk 31 E3* ham 3m/5km SW of Stowmarket. TM 0055
Streethay Staffs 35 G3 vil 2m/3km E of Lichfield. SK 1410
Street, High Cambs 29 G2* loc adjoining Dry Drayton to W. TL 3762
Street, High Cumbria 52 D4 mt in Lake Dist 2m/3km W of S end of Haweswater Resr. Height 2663 ft or 812 metres. NY 4411
Street, High Kent 12 D4 loc adjoining Hawkhurst to W. TQ 7430
Street, High Norfolk 38 D3* loc 1km N of Wendling. TF 9313
Street, High Suffolk 30 D3 loc 1km N of Long Melford. TL 8647
Street, High Suffolk 31 H2* loc 1m NW of Darsham. TM 4170
Street, High Suffolk 31 H3 ham 4m/6km N of Orford. TM 4355
Street, High Suffolk 39 G6* loc 4m/6km SE of Bungay. TM 3684
Streethouse W Yorks 49 F6* loc 4m/6km W of Pontefract. SE 3920
Street Houses Cleveland 55 F3* loc 2m/3km E of Loftus. NZ 7419
Street Houses N Yorks 49 G3/G4* loc 3m/5km NE of Tadcaster. SE 5245
Streetlam N Yorks 54 C5 ham 5m/8km NW of Northallerton. SE 3199
Street Lane Derbys 43 H6* loc 2km SW of Ripley. SK 3848
Street Lane W Yorks 49 E4* loc in Leeds 4m/6km NE of city centre. SE 3238
Street, Little Cambs 38 A6* ham 1km E of Downham. TL 5383
Street, Low Norfolk 39 E4* loc 5m/8km NW of Wymondham. TG 0405
Street, Low Norfolk 39 F6* ham 2m/3km E of Harleston. TM 2784
Street, Low Norfolk 39 G3* loc 2m/3km W of Stalham. TG 3423
Street, Low Norfolk 39 H3* loc 1km E of Rollesby. TG 4515
Street, Lower Dorset 9 F4 ham just S of Winterborne Whitchurch. SY 8499
Street, Lower E Sussex 12 C5 loc adjoining Ninfield to S, 4m/6km NW of Bexhill. TQ 7012
Street, Lower Norfolk 39 F2* vil 4m/6km N of N Walsham. TG 2635
Street, Lower Norfolk 39 F2* loc 1m NW of Wickmere. TG 1634
Street, Lower Norfolk 39 G3* loc in N part of Horning. TG 3417
Street, Lower Suffolk 30 C3* ham 4m/7km N of Clare. TL 7851
Street, Lower Suffolk 31 E3* ham 6m/10km NW of Ipswich. TM 1152
Street, Lower Suffolk 31 F4* loc at Stutton, 6m/10km S of Ipswich. TM 1534
Streetly W Midlands 35 G4 loc 3m/4km NW of Sutton Coldfield. SP 0898
Streetly End Cambs 30 B3* ham 4m/7km NW of Haverhill. TL 6148
Street, Nether Essex 20 C1* loc 1m SW of Leaden Roding. TL 5812
Street, North Berks 18 B4* ham 5m/8km W of Reading. SU 6372
Street, North Cambs 30 B1/B2 N end of Burwell. TL 5867
Street, North Hants 10 D2* loc 4m/6km E of New Alresford. SU 6433
Street, North Hants 9 H3* loc 3m/5km N of Fordingbridge. SU 1518
Street, North Kent 20 D4* loc 6m/9km NE of Strood. TQ 8174
Street, North Kent 21 F5 ham 2m/3km S of Faversham. TR 0158
Street on the Fosse Som 8 D1* ham 3m/5km S of Shepton Mallet. ST 6138
Street, South E Sussex 12 A5 ham 1km S of Chailey. TQ 3918
Street, South Kent 13 F1* SE dist of Whitstable. TR 1265
Street, South Kent 20 C5 loc 2km S of Meopham. TQ 6363
Street, South Kent 20 D5* loc 5m/8km SE of Gillingham. TQ 8361
Street, South Kent 21 F5* ham 4m/6km SE of Faversham. TR 0557
Street, South London 20 B5* loc in borough of Bromley adjoining Biggin Hill to SE. TQ 4357
Street, The Norfolk 31 E1* loc adjoining vil of Blo' Norton to N. TM 0179
Street, Upper Hants 9 H3 ham 3m/4km N of Fordingbridge. SU 1518
Street, Upper Norfolk 31 F1* loc 2m/3km E of Scole. TM 1780
Street, Upper Norfolk 39 G3* vil 1m W of Horning. TG 3217
Street, Upper Norfolk 39 G3* ham 1m E of Horning. TG 3516
Street, Upper Norfolk 39 G3* loc 4m/7km N of Wroxham. TG 3024
Street, Upper Suffolk 30 C3* ham 4m/6km N of Clare. TL 7851
Street, Upper Suffolk 31 E3* ham at Baylham 6m/9km NW of Ipswich. TM 1051
Street, Upper Suffolk 31 E4/F4 loc at Stutton, 6m/10km S of Ipswich. TM 1434
Street, West Kent 20 D4* loc just W of Cliffe, 5m/8km N of Rochester. TQ 7376
Street, West Kent 21 E6* loc 2km N of Lenham. TQ 9054
Street, West Suffolk 31 E1* loc 1m E of Wattisfield. TM 0274
Street, West Suffolk 31 E1* ham 1m W of Walsham le Willows. TL 9870
Strefford Salop 34 B5* loc 2m/3km N of Craven Arms. SO 4485
Strelley Notts 36 B1 vil 4m/6km W of Nottingham. SK 5141
Strensall N Yorks 50 B2 vil 6m/9km N of York. Army camp to S. SE 6360
Strensham H & W 26 D3* loc on W bank of R Avon 5m/8km N of Tewkesbury. SO 9140
Strensham, Lower H & W 26 D3* loc 5m/8km N of Tewkesbury. SO 9040
Strensham, Upper H & W 26 D4* ham 4m/7km N of Tewkesbury. SO 9039
Stretch Down Devon 7 F4* loc 1m SE of Witheridge and 9m/14km W of Tiverton. SS 8013
Stretcholt Som 15 G6* loc on Pawlett Level 1m NW of Pawlett and 3m/4km SW of Highbridge. ST 2944
Strete Devon 5 E5 vil on S coast 4m/6km SW of Dartmouth. SX 8446
Stretford Gtr Manchester 42 D2 tn 4m/6km SW of Manchester. Engineering, chemicals, food products, textiles. SJ 7994
Stretford H & W 26 A2 loc 4m/6km SW of Leominster. SO 4455
Stretford H & W 26 A2* loc 2m/4km SE of Leominster. SO 5257
Strethall Essex 29 H4 vil 4m/6km W of Saffron Walden. TL 4839
Stretham Cambs 38 A6 vil 4m/6km SW of Ely. Site of Roman bldg 1m SE. TL 5174
Strettington W Sussex 11 E4* vil 3m/4km NE of Chichester. SU 8907
Stretton Ches 42 A5 loc 3m/4km E of Holt across R Dee. SJ 4452
Stretton Ches 42 B3/C3 vil 4m/6km S of Warrington. **Lr Stretton** loc 1km S. SJ 6182
Stretton Derbys 43 H5 vil 2km S of Clay Cross. SK 3961
Stretton Leics 37 E3 vil 8m/12km NW of Stamford. SK 9415
Stretton Staffs 35 E3 vil 6m/10km W of Cannock. Site of Roman fort 1m E. SJ 8811
Stretton Staffs 35 H2 suburb 2m/3km NE of Burton upon Trent. SK 2526
Stretton en le Field Leics 35 H3 loc 4m/7km SW of Ashby de la Zouch. SK 3011
Stretton Grandison H & W 26 B3 vil 6m/10km NW of Ledbury. SO 6344
Stretton, Little Leics 36 C4 vil 6m/9km SE of Leicester. SK 6600
Stretton, Little Salop 34 B5 vil 2km SW of Church Stretton. SO 4491
Stretton-on-Dunsmore Warwicks 27 H1 vil 6m/10km W of Rugby. SP 4072
Stretton on Fosse Warwicks 27 F4 vil 4m/6km N of Moreton-in-Marsh. SP 2238
Stretton Sugwas H & W 26 A3* vil 4m/6km NW of Hereford. SO 4642
Stretton under Fosse Warwicks 36 A6 vil 5m/8km NW of Rugby. SP 4581
Stretton Westwood Salop 34 C4* ham 2m/3km SW of Much Wenlock. SO 5998
Strichen Grampian 83 G2 vil 8m/13km S of Fraserburgh. Situated on northern branch of R Ugie known as N Ugie Water. NJ 9455
Strickland, Great Cumbria 53 E3 vil 5m/9km SE of Penrith. **Lit Strickland** vil 2m/3km S. NY 5522
Striding Edge Cumbria 52 D3 narrow ridge running up to summit of Helvellyn from E. NY 3415
Strid, The N Yorks 48 D3 fissure in channel of R Wharfe 2m/3km NW of Bolton Abbey. R narrows to about 6 ft or 2 metres. SE 0656
Strine 34 C3 r rising NW of Newport, Salop, and flowing W into R Tern at Crudgington. SJ 6217
Strines 43 E3* loc on borders of Derbys and Gtr Manchester 2m/3km NW of New Mills. SJ 9786
Strines Reservoir S Yorks 43 G2* resr below Strines Moor 3m/5km SW of Bradfield. SK 2390
Stringston Som 15 G6 vil 2m/3km NW of Nether Stowey. ST 1742
String, The Orkney 89 B6* strait between island of Shapinsay and Car Ness on island of Mainland. HY 4714
Strixton Northants 28 D2 vil 4m/6km S of Wellingborough. SP 9061
Stroan Loch D & G 58 C4 small loch in course of R Dee, 5m/8km S of New Galloway. NX 6470
Stroat Glos 16 B2 ham 4m/6km NE of Chepstow. ST 5797
Stroma H'land 86 F1 island 2m/3km N to S and 1m E to W, lying in Pentland Firth 2m/3km E of St John's Pt and 4m/6km NW of Duncansby Hd. The island is barely populated. Disused harbour on S coast. Lighthouse at N point. ND 3577
Stromay W Isles 88 E1* small uninhabited island off NE coast of N Uist 4m/6km N of Lochmaddy. NF 9374
Strome Castle H'land 79 F5 ruins of ancient cas (NTS), destroyed 1602, on N shore of Loch Carron, Ross and Cromarty dist, opp Stromeferry. NG 8635
Stromeferry H'land 79 F5 vil on S side of Loch Carron, Skye and Lochalsh dist, 8m/13km NE of Kyle of Lochalsh. Vehicle ferry to N shore. NG 8634
Stromness Orkney 89 A6 small tn and fishing port on Mainland, on an inlet of Hoy Sound 12m/20km W of Kirkwall. Oil service base. HY 2509
Strom Ness Shetland 89 E7* long narrow peninsula on Mainland some 3m/5km NW of Scalloway. To E is the parallel peninsula of White Ness, separated from Strom Ness by the long narrow inlet of **Stromness Voe.** HU 3743
Stronachlachar Central 71 E4 locality on S shore of Loch Katrine 2m/4km SE of head of loch. NN 4010
Strond W Isles 88 A4* loc on Harris 2m/3km SE of Leverburgh. NG 0383
Strone H'land 81 E4 locality on Urquhart Bay on NW shore of Loch Ness, Inverness dist. **Strone Pt** is headland on loch, to SE, with ruins of **Urquhart Castle** (A.M.). NH 5228
Strone S'clyde 70 D6 vil and resort at **Strone Pt,** Argyll, on W side of entrance to Loch Long. NS 1980
Stronenaba H'land 74 C3* locality in Lochaber dist 2m/3km NW of Spean Br. NN 2084
Strone Point S'clyde 63 G1 headland on Kyles of Bute on W side of entrance to Loch Striven, Argyll. NS 0671
Strone Water S'clyde 62 D6 r in Kintyre running SE down **Strone Glen** to Carskey Bay on S coast of the peninsula. See also Breackerie Water. NR 6507
Stronmilchan S'clyde 70 D2 vil in Argyll 1m NW of Dalmally. NN 1528
Stronsay Orkney 89 C6 irregularly shaped island 7m/11km in length from NW to SE and 12m/20km NE of Kirkwall on island of Mainland. Fishing is the main industry. **Stronsay Firth** is sea area between Stronsay and island of Shapinsay to W. HY 62
Strontian H'land 74 A5 vil on N shore of Loch Sunart, Lochaber dist, at mouth of **Strontian R,** which rises on W side of Sgurr Dhomhnuill. NM 8161
Stronuich Reservoir Tayside 71 F1 small resr in course of R Lyon 3m/5km E of Loch Lyon. NN 5041
Strood Kent 20 D4 industrial and residential dist on NW side of Rochester across R Medway. Beside r to S is Temple Manor (A.M.), 13c commandery of Knights Templars. TQ 7369
Strood Channel Essex 30 D6* sea channel at W end of Mersea I., 7m/11km S of Colchester. TM 0014
Strood Green Surrey 19 F6* loc 2m/4km SE of Dorking. TQ 2048
Strood Green W Sussex 11 F3 loc 4m/6km NE of Petworth. TQ 0224
Strood Green W Sussex 11 G2* loc 3m/4km NW of Horsham. TQ 1332
Stroodleigh Devon 7 G3 vil 5m/7km NW of Tiverton. SS 9218
Stroud Glos 16 D1 hilly tn on R Frome 8m/13km S of Gloucester. Traditionally a centre of wool cloth mnfre, but industry now much diversified. SO 8505
Stroud Hants 10 D3* vil 2km W of Petersfield. Site of Roman villa on E side of vil. SU 7223
Stroude Surrey 19 E4* loc 3m/4km SW of Staines. TQ 0068
Stroud Green Essex 21 E3* ham 1m W of Rochford. TQ 8590
Stroud Green Glos 16 C1 ham 3m/5km NW of Stroud. SO 8007
Stroud Green London 19 G3* loc in borough of Haringey 5m/8km N of Charing Cross. TQ 3188
Stroxton Lincs 37 E2 ham 3m/5km S of Grantham. Stone manor hse of 17c. SK 9031
Struan Tayside 75 H4 vil at confluence of Errochty Water and R Garry 4m/6km W of Blair Atholl. Small museum of items of historical interest associated with the Clan Donnachaidh. NN 8165
Strubby Lincs 45 F3* loc 2m/3km E of Wragby. TF 1577
Strubby Lincs 45 H3 vil 4m/6km N of Alford. Airfield to S. TF 4582
Strumble Head Dyfed 22 B2 headland 5m/8km NW of Fishguard. Lighthouse on rock island of Ynysmeicel. SM 8941
Strumpshaw Norfolk 39 G4 vil 4m/6km SW of Acle. TG 3407
Strutherhill S'clyde 65 E4* loc adjoining Larkhall to S. NS 7649
Struy Bridge H'land 80 D3 rd br over R Farrar nearly 1km above its confluence with R Glass, Inverness dist. **Struy Forest** is deer forest to SW. NH 4040
Stryd Gwynedd 40 A3* part of Holyhead to S of tn centre. SH 2482
Stryd y Facsen Gwynedd 40 A3* loc on Anglesey 2km NE of Llanfachraeth. SH 3383
Stryt-cae-rhedyn Clwyd 41 H5* loc 3m/4km SE of Mold. SJ 2660
Stryt-issa Clwyd 41 H6 loc 2km NW of Ruabon. SJ 2845
Stryt-yr-hwch Clwyd 42 A6 loc 3m/4km S of Wrexham. SJ 3346
Stuartfield Grampian 83 G2 vil 10m/16km W of Peterhead. NJ 9745
Stuarton H'land 81 G2* loc in Inverness dist adjoining Ardersier to S, on E shore of Inner Moray Firth or Inverness Firth. NH 7854
Stubb Norfolk 39 G3* loc 1km S of Hickling. TG 4122
Stubber's Green W Midlands loc 2m/4km NE of Walsall. SK 0301
Stubbin S Yorks 43 H2* loc 3m/5km N of Rotherham. SK 4297
Stubbington Hants 10 C4 suburban locality 3m/4km SW of Fareham. SU 5503
Stubbins Lancs 47 H6 vil 1km N of Ramsbottom. SD 7918
Stubb's Cross Kent 13 E3* loc 3m/5km SW of Ashford. TQ 9838
Stubb's Green Norfolk 39 F5* loc 1km SE of Shotesham. TM 2598
Stubbs Green Norfolk 39 G5* loc 1m S of Loddon. TM 3597
Stubden Reservoir W Yorks 48 D5* small resr 1km SW of Denholme. SE 0734
Stubhampton Dorset 9 F3 loc on SE side of Cranborne Chase 5m/8km NE of Blandford Forum. ST 9113
Stubley Derbys 43 H3 loc 1m W of Dronfield. SK 3478
Stubshaw Cross Gtr Manchester 42 B2* loc adjoining Ashton-in-Makerfield to NE. SD 5800
Stubton Lincs 44 D6 vil 6m/9km SE of Newark-on-Trent. SK 8748
Stùc a' Chroin 72 A3 mt on border of Central and Tayside regions 2km SW of Ben Vorlich. Height 3189 ft or 972 metres. NN 6117
Stuchd an Lochain Tayside 71 F1 mt 2m/3km SW of dam of Loch an Daimh. Height 3144 ft or 958 metres. NN 4844
Stuckton Hants 9 H3* loc 1m SE of Fordingbridge. SU 1613
Studdal, East Kent 13 H2* vil 4m/7km SW of Deal. Ham of **Studdal** adjoins to SW. TR 3149
Studd Hill Kent 13 G1* W dist of Herne Bay. TR 1567
Studfold N Yorks 48 B2 loc 2km S of Horton in Ribblesdale. **Hr Studfold** loc to N. SD 8170
Stud Green Berks 18 D4 loc 2m/4km S of Maidenhead. SU 8877
Studham Beds 29 E6 vil 6m/9km SW of Luton. TL 0115

Studland Dorset 9 G5 vil on **Studland Bay,** at SW end of Poole Bay, 3m/4km N of Swanage. SZ 0382
Studley Oxon 28 B6 vil 7m/11km NE of Oxford. SP 5912
Studley Warwicks 27 E2 suburb 4m/6km SE of Redditch. SP 0763
Studley Wilts 16 D4 vil 2m/3km W of Calne. ST 9671
Studley Green Bucks 18 C2* loc 2m/3km E of Stokenchurch. SU 7995
Studley Roger N Yorks 49 E2 ham 2m/3km SW of Ripon. SE 2970
Studley Royal N Yorks 49 E2* ham 2m/4km W of Ripon. Remains of manor hse burnt down in 1945. 18c park contains lakes, temples, statues. SE 2770
Study, The H'land 74 C5 natural terrace 3m/5km S of Kinlochleven in Lochaber dist, on N side of rd running down Glen Coe. Commands view of glen. NN 1756
Stukeley, Great Cambs 29 F1 vil 2m/4km NW of Huntingdon. **Lit Stukeley** vil 1m NW. TL 2174
Stulaval W Isles 88 E3 mt on S Uist 4m/6km N of Lochboisdale. Height 1227 ft or 374 metres. NF 8024
Stulaval W Isles 88 A3 mt in N Harris 2km W of S end of Loch Langavat. Height 1899 ft or 589 metres. NB 1312
Stuley W Isles 88 E3 uninhabited island off E coast of S Uist 4m/6km NE of Lochboisdale. Is separated from coast by the narrow **Stuley Sound.** NF 8323
Stump Cross Essex 30 A3 rd junction 1m N of Gt Chesterford. TL 5044
Stump Cross Lancs 47 F4* loc 2m/3km W of Longridge. SD 5737
Stump Cross W Yorks 48 D5* loc in Halifax 1m NE of tn centre. SE 1026
Stump Cross Caverns N Yorks 48 D2 limestone caverns 5m/7km SW of Pateley Br. SE 0863
Stuntney Cambs 38 A6 vil 2m/3km SE of Ely. TL 5578
Stunts Green E Sussex 12 C5 loc 3m/5km NE of Hailsham. TQ 6213
Sturbridge Staffs 35 E2 loc 1m N of Eccleshall. SJ 8330
Sturgate Lincs 44 D2* loc 4m/6km E of Gainsborough. SK 8789
Sturmer Essex 30 B3 vil 2m/3km SE of Haverhill. TL 6943
Sturminster Common Dorset 9 E3* vil 1m S of Sturminster Newton. ST 7812
Sturminster Marshall Dorset 9 F4 vil on R Stour 4m/6km W of Wimborne. ST 9500
Sturminster Newton Dorset 9 E3 small tn on R Stour at SE end of Blackmoor Vale, 8m/13km NW of Blandford Forum. ST 7814
Sturry Kent 13 G1 vil 3m/4km NE of Canterbury. TR 1760
Sturton Humberside 44 D1 vil 3m/4km SW of Brigg. Site of Roman villa. SE 9604
Sturton by Stow Lincs 44 D3 vil 4m/6km N of Saxilby. SK 8980
Sturton Grange W Yorks 49 F4* loc 1m E of Garforth. SE 4233
Sturton, Great Lincs 45 F4 ham 5m/9km NW of Horncastle. TF 2176
Sturton le Steeple Notts 44 C3 vil 6m/9km E of E Retford. SK 7883
Stuston Suffolk 31 F1 vil 2m/3km SE of Diss. TM 1378
Stutton N Yorks 49 F4 vil 2km S of Tadcaster. SE 4741
Stutton Suffolk 31 F4 vil 6m/10km S of Ipswich. 2km S on R Stour estuary is **Stutton Ness,** at W end of Holbrook Bay. TM 1534
Styal Ches 42 D3 vil 2km N of Wilmslow. SJ 8383
Styants Wood Kent. See Oldbury.
Stybarrow Dod Cumbria 52 D3 mt in Lake Dist 2m/3km N of Helvellyn. Height 2756 ft or 840 metres. NY 3418
Sty Head Pass Cumbria 52 C4 pass in Lake Dist between Borrowdale and Wasdale. **Sty Head Tarn** small lake on Borrowdale side of summit. NY 2109
Styrrup Notts 44 B2 vil 2m/3km SE of Tickhill. SK 6090
Suckley H & W 26 C3 vil 5m/8km NW of Gt Malvern. SO 7251
Suckley Green H & W 26 C2* loc 4m/7km E of Bromyard. SO 7153
Suckley Knowl H & W 26 C2* loc 4m/6km E of Bromyard. SO 7153
Sudborough Northants 37 E6 vil 3m/5km NW of Thrapston. SP 9682
Sudbourne Suffolk 31 G3 vil on E edge of Tunstall Forest 2m/3km N of Orford. Sudbourne Marshes to E beside R Alde estuary. TM 4153
Sudbrook Gwent 16 A3* vil on shore of R Severn estuary 4m/7km SW of Chepstow. Severn Rly Tunnel passes underneath. ST 5087
Sudbrook Lincs 37 E1 vil 6m/10km W of Sleaford. SK 9744
Sudbrooke Lincs 45 E4 vil 5m/7km NE of Lincoln. TF 0376
Sudbury Derbys 35 G2 vil 5m/7km E of Uttoxeter. **Sudbury Hall** (NT), 17c. Sudbury open prison, formerly hospital. SK 1632
Sudbury London 19 F3 loc in borough of Brent 9m/15km NW of Charing Cross. TQ 1685
Sudbury Suffolk 30 D4 tn on R Stour 13m/21km NW of Colchester. Birthplace of Gainsborough 1727. TL 8741
Sudden Gtr Manchester 42 D1 loc in Rochdale 2km SW of tn centre. SD 8811
Sudeley Glos 27 E5 loc 1km SE of Winchcombe. **Sudeley Castle** is a medieval bldg much altered and restored. Remains of Roman villa 2km S of cas. SP 0327
Sudgrove Glos 16 D1* loc 7m/11km NW of Cirencester. SO 9307
Sueno's Stone Grampian 82 A2. See Forres. NJ 0459
Suffield Norfolk 39 F2 ham 4m/6km NW of N Walsham. TG 2232
Suffield N Yorks 55 G5 ham 4m/6km NW of Scarborough. SE 9890
Suffolk 119 easternmost county of England, bounded by Essex, Cambridgeshire, Norfolk, and the North Sea. The country is low-lying and gently undulating, and almost entirely agricultural. The low coastline, behind which are areas of heath and marsh, afforested in places, is much subject to erosion, and deeply indented with river estuaries which provide good sailing. The NW corner of the county forms part of Breckland, qv. Chief tns are Ipswich, the county tn; Bury St Edmunds, Lowestoft, a fishing tn, Newmarket, the HQ of horse-racing, Stowmarket, and Sudbury. Felixstowe is a port of growing importance. R Stour forms the S boundary with Essex, and the Lit Ouse and Waveney (except near its mouth) the N boundary with Norfolk. The many other streams include the Alde, with its estuary the Ore, Deben, and Gipping, with its estuary the Orwell, in the E; and Lark in the W.
Suffolk Coastal 119 admin dist of Suffolk.
Sugar Loaf (Mynydd Pen-y-fal) Gwent 25 G5/G6 conical hill (NT) in Black Mts 3m/5km NW of Abergavenny. Height 1955 ft or 596 metres. SO 2718
Sugdon Salop 34 C3* loc 4m/6km NW of Wellington. SJ 6014
Sugnall Staffs 35 E2 ham 2m/4km NW of Eccleshall. **Lit Sugnall** ham 1km NE. SJ 7930
Sugwas Pool H & W 26 A3* ham 4m/7km W of Hereford. SO 4541
Suil Ghorm Coll, S'clyde 68 B3* islet with lighthouse, lying 2km off NE end of main island. NM 2865
Suilven H'land 85 B5 mt near W coast of Sutherland dist 5m/7km SE of Lochinver. Height 2399 ft or 731 metres. NC 1518
Suisnish Skye, H'land 79 D6* locality near coast between Loch Eishort and Loch Slapin. See also Rubha Suisnish. NG 5916
Suisnish Point Skye, H'land 79 D5 headland at SW corner of Raasay opp Balmeanach Bay on mainland of Skye. NG 5534
Sula Sgeir W Isles uninhabited island, nearly 1km long NE to SW and nowhere more than 200 metres wide, situated about 40m/64km N of Butt of Lewis (88 C1). Nature reserve. Several islets and rocks in vicinity. HW 6230
Sulby Isle of Man 46 B4 vil 4m/7km W of Ramsey. **Sulby Br** loc adjoining to E. SC 3894
Sulby Isle of Man 46 B5* loc 3m/5km N of Douglas. **Sulby R** runs into R Glass to SW. SC 3780
Sulby 46 C4* r on Isle of Man rising on central mts and running N down Sulby Glen to Sulby vil, then E into Ramsey Bay at Ramsey. SC 4594
Sulby Reservoir Northants 36 C6* resr adjoining Welford Resr 2m/4km S of Husbands Bosworth. SP 6581
Sule Skerry Orkney (W of 89 A6) islet some 37m/60km W of island of Mainland. Lighthouse. HX 6224
Sulgrave Northants 28 B3 vil 6m/9km N of Brackley. **Sulgrave Manor** was home of George Washington's great-grandfather. SP 5545
Sulgrave Tyne & Wear 61 G5* NE dist of Washington. NZ 3157
Sulham Berks 18 B4 vil 2m/3km S of Pangbourne. SU 6474
Sulhamstead Berks 18 B4 vil 6m/10km SW of Reading. Par includes locs of **Sulhamstead Abbots** and **Sulhamstead Bannister Upr End.** SU 6368
Sulhamstead Bannister Berks 18 B4* loc 5m/8km S of Reading. SU 6866
Sullington W Sussex 11 G4 loc below S Downs 2km W of Washington. TQ 0913
Sullom Shetland 89 E6 loc in N part of Mainland on W shore of **Sullom Voe,** inlet some 8m/12km long and almost separating the N part of Mainland from the rest. The voe, which runs N into Yell Sound, provides shelter for shipping. There is an oil terminal. HU 3573
Sulloniacae London. See Edgware.
Sully (Sili) S Glam 15 F4 suburb on coast 3m/4km E of Barry. Sully I., small island off shore to SE, accessible on foot at low tide. **Sully Bay** extends from Sully I. westwards to Hayes Pt. ST 1568
Sumburgh Shetland 89 E8 loc on Mainland 1m N of headland of **Sumburgh Hd** (lighthouse), at S extremity of the island. To N is **Sumburgh Airport,** the airport for Shetland. To W is the bay **W Voe of Sumburgh.** See also Jarlshof. HU 4009
Summer Bridge N Yorks 49 E2 vil in Nidderdale 3m/5km SE of Pateley Br. SE 2062
Summercourt Cornwall 2 D3 vil 6m/9km SE of Newquay. SW 8856
Summerfield H & W 26 D1* loc 2m/3km NE of Stourport. Research stn. SO 8373
Summergangs Humberside 51 F5* dist of Hull 2m/3km NE of city centre. TA 1130
Summergil Brook 25 G2* stream rising 3m/5km W of New Radnor, Powys, and flowing by New Radnor to Hindwell Brook nearly 1m W of Knill. SO 2760
Summerhill Clwyd 41 H5 loc 3m/4km NW of Wrexham. SJ 3153
Summerhill D & G 59 E4* W dist of Dumfries. NX 9576
Summerhill Grampian 77 H1* loc in Aberdeen 2m/4km W of city centre. NJ 9006
Summerhill H & W 35 E6* W dist of Kidderminster. SO 8176
Summer Hill W Midlands 35 F5* loc in W Bromwich 3m/5km NW of tn centre. SO 9693
Summerhouse Durham 54 B3 vil 6m/10km NW of Darlington. NZ 2019
Summerhouse Point S Glam 15 E4* headland on Bristol Channel coast 2m/4km SE of Llantwit Major. SS 9966
Summer Isles, The H'land 85 A6 group of uninhabited islands off NW coast of Ross and Cromarty dist between Rubha Coigeach and Greenstone Pt. NB 90
Summerlands Cumbria 53 E6* loc 4m/7km S of Kendal. SD 5386
Summerlands Som 8 D3* W dist of Yeovil. ST 5416
Summer Lodge N Yorks 53 H5 loc on stream of same name 2m/3km SW of Low Row. **S. L. Tarn,** small lake on S. L. Moor 1m SW. SD 9695
Summersdale W Sussex 11 E4* N dist of Chichester. SU 8606
Summerseat Gtr Manchester 47 H6* 3m/4km N of Bury. SD 7914
Summerstown London 19 F4* loc in borough of Wandsworth 2m/3km S of Wandsworth Br. TQ 2672
Summerville D & G 59 E4* NW dist of Dumfries. NX 9676
Summit Gtr Manchester 42 D1/43 E1* loc 2m/4km S of Rochdale. SD 9109
Summit Gtr Manchester 48 C6* loc 2km NE of Littleborough. SD 9418
Sumners Essex 19 H1* SW dist of Harlow. TL 4307
Sunart H'land 68 F2, F3 area of Lochaber dist between Loch Shiel and Loch Sunart. NM 7966
Sunbiggin Cumbria 53 F4* loc 2m/4km E of Orton. **Sunbiggin Tarn** small lake 2km SE. NY 6208
Sunbury Surrey 19 E4 tn on N bank of R Thames 4m/7km E of Chertsey. TQ 1068
Sunderland Cumbria 52 B2 ham 2m/3km S of Bothel. NY 1735
Sunderland Lancs 47 E3 vil on right bank of R Lune estuary 1km N of **Sunderland Pt.** SD 4255
Sunderland Tyne & Wear 61 H5 industrial tn and seaport at mouth of R Wear 11m/17km SE of Newcastle upon Tyne. Coal-mining, shipbuilding and repairing, engineering, glass mnfre, paper mnfre, quarrying. Airport 4m/6km W. NZ 3956
Sunderland Bridge Durham 54 B2 vil at crossing of R Wear 3m/5km S of Durham. NZ 2637
Sunderland, North Nthmb 67 H5 vil adjoining Seahouses to SW, 3m/5km SE of Bamburgh. NU 2131
Sunderlandwick Humberside 51 E3 loc 2m/3km S of Gt Driffield, containing site of former vil. TA 0155
Sundon, Lower Beds 29 E5 vil 4m/7km NW of Luton. TL 0527
Sundon Park Beds 29 E5* large housing estate at N end of Luton. TL 0525
Sundon, Upper Beds 29 E5 vil 5m/8km NW of Luton. TL 0427
Sundridge Kent 20 B6 vil 3m/5km W of Sevenoaks. TQ 4855
Sundridge London 20 B4* loc in borough of Bromley 1km NE of Bromley tn centre. **Sundridge Park** contains two golf courses. TQ 4170
Sun Green Gtr Manchester 43 E2* loc 2km NE of Stalybridge. SJ 9899
Sunken Island Essex 21 F1 island at mouth of Salcott Channel 1m W of W Mersea. TL 9912
Sunk Island Humberside 51 G6 loc on N side of R Humber estuary 4m/6km SW of Patrington. TA 2618
Sunningdale Berks 18 D4 residential dist 6m/9km SW of Staines. SU 9567
Sunninghill Berks 18 D4 residential dist 4m/7km E of Bracknell. SU 9367
Sunningwell Oxon 18 A2* vil 2m/4km N of Abingdon. SP 4900
Sunniside Durham 54 B1 vil 2km E of Tow Law. NZ 1438
Sunniside Tyne & Wear 61 G5 loc 2m/3km S of Whickham. NZ 2058
Sunny Bank Lancs 48 A5/B6* loc 2m/3km S of Haslingden. SD 7720
Sunny Brow Durham 54 B2* loc adjoining Willington to S. NZ 1934
Sunnyfields S Yorks 44 A1* suburb 2m/3km NW of Doncaster. SE 5405
Sunny Hill Derbys 36 A1/A2* dist of Derby 3m/4km SW of tn centre. SK 3332
Sunnyhurst Lancs 47 G5* loc 1m W of Darwen. SD 6722
Sunnylaw Central 72 B4 loc 3m/5km N of Stirling. NS 7998
Sunnymead Oxon 18 A1 N dist of Oxford. SP 5009
Sunnymede Essex 20 C2* E dist of Billericay. TQ 6994
Sunnyside S Yorks 44 A2* loc 4m/6km E of Rotherham. SK 4893
Sunton Wilts 17 F5* loc 1km N of Collingbourne Ducis and 3m/4km NW of Ludgershall. SU 2454
Surbiton London 19 F4 dist in borough of Kingston 2km S of Kingston tn centre. TQ 1867
Surby Isle of Man 46 A6 loc 1m NE of Port Erin. SC 2070
Surfleet Lincs 37 G2 vil 4m/6km N of Spalding. **Surfleet Seas End** loc 2km E. TF 2528
Surlingham Norfolk 39 G4 vil 6m/9km E of Norwich. **Surlingham Broad,** small broad or lake 1m NE beside R Yare. TG 3106
Surrey 119 south-eastern county of England, bounded by Kent, W Sussex, Hampshire, Berkshire, Gtr London, and briefly by Buckinghamshire and E Sussex. The chalk ridge of the N Downs, gently sloping on the N side but forming a steep escarpment on the S, traverses the county from E to W. Extensive sandy heaths in the W are much used for military training. The county is heavily wooded, with many traces of former iron industry in the S. Chief r is the Thames, into which flow the Wey and the Mole. Much of the E and N comprises residential outskirts of London. The principal tns are Guildford, with cathedral and university, Camberley, Dorking, Epsom, Leatherhead, Reigate, Redhill, and Staines. The S part of the county is predominantly rural.

Sursay W Isles 88 E1* small uninhabited island in Sound of Harris 2m/3km off NE coast of N Uist. NF 9576
Sussex, East 119 south-eastern county of England, bounded by the English Channel, W Sussex, Kent, and briefly by Surrey. In the W the coast is backed by the chalk ridge of the S Downs, ending with the white cliffs of the Seven Sisters and Beachy Hd just W of Eastbourne. E of this point are extensive areas of reclaimed marshland, which provide good sheep-grazing. Inland is the heavily wooded Weald, former centre of the iron industry, interspersed with hill ridges, the largest being the open heathland of Ashdown Forest. Rs, none large, include the Cuckmere, Ouse, Rother, and upper reaches of the Medway. The principal inland tn is the county tn of Lewes. The other tns of importance are mostly strung along the coast: Brighton and Hove in the W; the port of Newhaven; the resorts of Seaford, Eastbourne, Bexhill, St Leonards, and Hastings; and the historic tn of Rye in the E.
Sussex, West 119 south coastal county of England, bounded by Hampshire, Surrey, E Sussex, and the English Channel. N of a level coastal strip run the S Downs, a steep-sided chalk ridge, in parts thickly wooded. The remaining inland area, the Weald, is largely well-wooded farmland, although there is industrial development at Crawley, Horsham, and around Haywards Heath, as well as among the predominantly residential tns of the coast. Rs, none large, include the Adur and Arun, with its tributary the Rother; the Medway rises in the E of the county. Chief tns are the cathedral city and county tn of Chichester; Crawley, just N of which is Gatwick Airport, Horsham, Shoreham, a container port, and Worthing; E Grinstead lies in the NE corner.
Sustead Norfolk 39 F2 vil 4m/6km SW of Cromer. TG 1837
Susworth Lincs 44 C1 ham on E bank of R Trent 3m/5km W of Scotter. SE 8302
Sutcombe Devon 6 C4 vil 5m/8km N of Holsworthy. **Sutcombemill** is ham to S on R Waldon. SS 3411
Sutherland 114, 115 admin dist of H'land region.
Suther Ness Shetland 89 F7* promontory with lighthouse on N coast of island of Whalsay, NW of Brough vil. HU 5565
Suton Norfolk 39 E5* loc 2m/3km SW of Wymondham. Loc of **Suton Street** 1km S. TM 0999
Sutor, North H'land 81 G1 headland on N side of entrance to Cromarty Firth, Ross and Cromarty dist. NH 8168
Sutterby Lincs 45 G4* ham 4m/7km N of Spilsby. TF 3872
Sutterton Lincs 37 G1 vil 6m/10km SW of Boston. TF 2835
Sutton Beds 29 F3 vil 2km S of Potton. TL 2247
Sutton Bucks 19 E4* loc 4m/6km E of Slough. TQ 0278
Sutton Cambs 37 F4 vil in Peterborough 2m/3km E of Wansford. Site of Roman camp to E across Ermine Street. TL 0998
Sutton Cambs 38 A6 vil 6m/10km W of Ely. TL 4478
Sutton Devon 4 D6* ham adjacent to S Milton and 2m/4km SW of Kingsbridge. SS 7046
Sutton Devon 7 E5* loc 7m/12km W of Crediton. SS 7202
Sutton Dyfed 22 B4* loc 3m/4km W of Haverfordwest. SM 9015
Sutton Essex 21 E3 loc 2m/3km N of Southend-on-Sea. TQ 8889
Sutton E Sussex 12 B6* E dist of Seaford. TV 4999
Sutton Kent 13 H2 vil 3m/5km SW of Deal. TR 3349
Sutton Lincs 44 D5 loc 5m/8km E of Newark-on-Trent. SK 8752
Sutton London 19 F5 tn and borough 10m/17km S of Charing Cross and 4m/7km W of Croydon. TQ 2564
Sutton Merseyside 42 B2 loc in St Helens 2m/3km SE of tn centre. **Sutton Leach** loc adjoining to S. SJ 5393
Sutton Norfolk 39 G3 vil 2km SE of Stalham. To W, **Sutton Broad,** channel flanked by marsh. TG 3823
Sutton Notts 36 D1 ham 4m/6km SE of Bingham. SK 7637
Sutton Notts 44 B3 vil 3m/5km N of E Retford. SK 6884
Sutton N Yorks 49 G5* ham 1km E of Brotherton. SE 4925
Sutton Oxon 17 H1 loc adjoining Stanton Harcourt to N, 2m/4km SW of Eynsham. SP 4106
Sutton Salop 34 B2* loc 5m/7km E of Oswestry. SJ 3527
Sutton Salop 34 C3 loc in S part of Shrewsbury. SJ 5010
Sutton Salop 34 D2 loc 2m/3km S of Mkt Drayton. SJ 6631
Sutton Salop 34 D5* vil 4m/7km S of Bridgnorth. SO 7286
Sutton Staffs 34 D2 ham 2m/4km NE of Newport. SJ 7622
Sutton Suffolk 31 G3 vil 3m/5km SE of Woodbridge across R Deben. TM 3046
Sutton S Yorks 44 A1 loc 6m/10km N of Doncaster. SE 5512
Sutton W Sussex 11 F3 vil 4m/7km S of Petworth. SU 9715
Sutton at Hone Kent 20 C4 vil 3m/4km S of Dartford. On E side by R Darent is St John's Jerusalem (NT), moated 16c–18c hse with remains of Knights Hospitallers chapel. TQ 5570
Sutton Bank N Yorks 54 D6* cliff-like escarpment of Hambleton Hills 5m/9km E of Thirsk. A170 rd here has gradient of 1 in 4 and two hairpin bends. Gliding from summit. SE 5182
Sutton Bassett Northants 36 D5 vil 3m/5km NE of Mkt Harborough. SP 7790
Sutton Benger Wilts 16 D4 vil 4m/6km NE of Chippenham. ST 9478
Sutton Bingham Som 8 D3 loc 3m/5km S of Yeovil on W shore of **Sutton Bingham Resr.** ST 5411
Sutton Bonington Notts 36 B2 vil 4m/7km NW of Loughborough. SK 5025
Sutton Bridge Lincs 38 A3 tn on R Nene 9m/14km W of King's Lynn. TF 4721
Sutton Cheney Leics 36 A4 vil 2m/3km S of Mkt Bosworth. SK 4100
Sutton Coldfield W Midlands 35 G4 tn 7m/11km NE of Birmingham. To W of tn centre is **Sutton Park,** large park with wds and lakes. SP 1296
Sutton Courtenay Oxon 18 A2 vil 3m/5km NW of Didcot. SU 5093
Sutton Crosses Lincs 37 H3 loc 2km S of Long Sutton. TF 4321
Sutton Farm H & W 35 E6* SW dist of Kidderminster. SO 8175
Sutton Grange N Yorks 49 E1 ham 3m/4km NW of Ripon. SE 2874
Sutton, Great Ches 42 A4 loc in Ellesmere Port 2m/3km SW of tn centre. **Lit Sutton** loc 1m NW. SJ 3775
Sutton, Great Salop 34 C5 loc 5m/8km N of Ludlow. SO 5183
Sutton Green Clwyd 42 A6* loc 5m/8km E of Wrexham. SJ 4048
Sutton Green Oxon 17 H1* loc adjoining Stanton Harcourt to N, 2m/3km SW of Eynsham. SP 4106
Sutton Green Surrey 19 E5 ham 3m/5km S of Woking. TQ 0054
Sutton Heath Merseyside 42 B2* loc in St Helens 2m/3km S of tn centre. SJ 5092
Sutton Hill Salop 34 D4 S dist of Telford to E of Coalport. SJ 7003
Sutton Hoo Suffolk 31 G3* location of ship-burial tumuli 1m E of Woodbridge across R Deben. TM 2848
Sutton Howgrave N Yorks 49 E1 vil 5m/8km N of Ripon. SE 3179
Sutton in Ashfield Notts 44 A5 tn 3m/5km SW of Mansfield. Industries include coal-mining, engineering, hosiery, plastics. SK 5058
Sutton-in-Craven N Yorks 48 C4 loc 4m/6km NW of Keighley. SE 0044
Sutton Ings Humberside 51 F5* dist of Hull 3m/4km NE of city centre. TA 1231
Sutton in the Elms Leics 36 B5 loc 8m/13km SW of Leicester. SP 5293
Sutton Lane Ends Ches 43 E4* loc 2m/3km S of Macclesfield. SJ 9271
Sutton, Little Salop 34 C6* loc 5m/8km N of Ludlow. SO 5182
Sutton Maddock Salop 34 D4 vil 5m/9km N of Bridgnorth. SJ 7201
Sutton Mallet Som 8 B1 5m/8km E of Bridgwater. ST 3737
Sutton Mandeville Wilts 9 G2 vil 3m/4km E of Tisbury. ST 9828
Sutton Manor Merseyside 42 B2* coal-mining loc 2m/3km E of Rainhill. SJ 5190
Sutton Marsh H & W 26 B3* loc 4m/6km NE of Hereford. SO 5444
Sutton Montis Som 8 D2 vil 2m/3km SE of Sparkford. ST 6224
Sutton on Derwent Humberside. See Sutton upon Derwent.
Sutton-on-Hull Humberside 51 F5 dist of Hull 3m/5km NE of city centre. TA 1132
Sutton on Sea Lincs 45 H3 North Sea coast resort adjoining Mablethorpe to S. TF 5282
Sutton-on-the-Forest N Yorks 50 B2 vil 8m/13km N of York. SE 5864
Sutton on the Hill Derbys 35 H1 vil 8m/12km W of Derby. SK 2333
Sutton on Trent Notts 44 C4 vil 8m/12km N of Newark-on-Trent. SK 7965
Sutton Poyntz Dorset 9 E5 loc 4m/6km NE of Weymouth. SY 7083
Sutton St Edmund Lincs 37 H3 vil 7m/11km N of Guyhirn. TF 3613
Sutton St James Lincs 37 H3 vil 4m/6km SW of Long Sutton. TF 3918
Sutton St Michael H & W 26 A3* ham 4m/7km N of Hereford. SO 5246
Sutton St Nicholas H & W 26 A3 vil 4m/6km NE of Hereford. SO 5345
Sutton Scotney Hants 10 B1 vil 5m/9km S of Whitchurch. SU 4639
Sutton-under-Brailes Warwicks 27 G4 vil 3m/5km SE of Shipston on Stour. SP 3037
Sutton-under-Whitestonecliffe N Yorks 54 D6 vil below Sutton Bank 3m/5km E of Thirsk. SE 4882
Sutton upon Derwent Humberside 50 C3 vil on E side of R Derwent 7m/12km SE of York. SE 7046
Sutton Valence Kent 12 D2 vil on S edge of N Downs 4m/6km NW of Headcorn. TQ 8149
Sutton Veny Wilts 9 F1 vil 2m/3km W of Heytesbury and 3m/4km SE of Warminster. ST 9041
Sutton Waldron Dorset 9 F3 vil on W edge of Cranborne Chase 5m/8km S of Shaftesbury. ST 8615
Sutton Warblington Hants 10 D1* ham adjoining Long Sutton 5m/8km N of Alton. SU 7347
Sutton Weaver Ches 42 B3* vil 3m/4km SE of Runcorn. SJ 5479
Sutton Wick Avon 16 B5* ham on E side of Chew Valley Lake 2m/3km NE of W Harptree. ST 5758
Sutton Wick Oxon 17 H2 loc adjoining Drayton to N, 2m/3km SW of Abingdon. SU 4894
Swaby Lincs 45 G3/G4 vil 7m/12km SE of Louth. TF 3877
Swadlincote Derbys 35 H3 tn and centre of S Derbyshire coalfield, 5m/7km SE of Burton upon Trent. Industries include coal-mining, clay-working, chinaware. SK 3019
Swaffham Norfolk 38 C4 old mkt tn 14m/22km SE of King's Lynn. Palladian mkt cross. Ch has double-hammerbeam angel roof. Industries include agricultural produce, fruit canning. TF 8109
Swaffham Bulbeck Cambs 30 A2/B2 vil 6m/9km W of Newmarket. TL 5562
Swaffham Prior Cambs 30 B2 vil 5m/8km W of Newmarket. TL 5764
Swafield Norfolk 39 G2 vil 2km N of N Walsham. TG 2832
Swainby N Yorks 54 D4 vil 5m/8km SW of Stokesley. NZ 4702
Swainby N Yorks 54 C6 loc 4m/6km SE of Leeming. SE 3385
Swainshill H & W 26 A3 loc 3m/5km W of Hereford. SO 4641
Swainsthorpe Norfolk 39 F4 vil 5m/8km S of Norwich. TG 2100
Swainswick Avon 16 C4 vil 3m/4km N of Bath. ST 7568
Swaithe S Yorks 43 H1* loc 2m/4km SE of Barnsley. SE 3704
Swalcliffe Oxon 27 G4 vil 5m/8km W of Banbury. Site of ancient camp to NE. SP 3737
Swale 119 admin dist of Kent.
Swale 49 F2 r rising on moors W of Keld, N Yorks, and flowing SE down Swaledale by Reeth, Richmond, and Catterick Br, to join R Ure 2m/4km E of Boroughbridge and form R Ouse. SE 4365
Swalecliffe Kent 13 G1 E dist of Whitstable. TR 1367
Swale, The 21 F5 branch of R Medway estuary which leaves main stream at Queenborough Spit and separates Isle of Sheppey from mainland of Kent, entering Whitstable Bay opp Shell Ness. TR 0667
Swallow Lincs 45 F1 vil 4m/7km NE of Caistor. TA 1702
Swallow Beck Lincs 44 D4 dist of Lincoln 3m/4km SW of city centre. SK 9567
Swallowcliffe Wilts 9 G2 vil 2m/3km SE of Tisbury. ST 9627
Swallow Falls (Rhaeadr Ewynnol) Gwynedd 40 D5 cataract in course of R Llugwy. SH 7657
Swallowfield Berks 18 C5 vil 6m/9km S of Reading. SU 7264
Swallownest S Yorks 43 H3 loc 5m/8km S of Rotherham. SK 4585
Swallows Cross Essex 20 C2* loc 3m/4km W of Ingatestone. TQ 6198
Swalwell Tyne & Wear 61 G5* loc adjoining Whickham to N, 3m/5km W of Gateshead. NZ 2062
Swampton Hants 17 H6 loc adjoining St Mary Bourne to NW. SU 4150
Swanage Dorset 9 G6 coastal resort on **Swanage Bay** at E end of Isle of Purbeck, 9m/14km SE of Wareham. The bay extends from Ballard Pt (N) to Peveril Pt (S). SZ 0278
Swanbister Orkney 89 B7* loc on Mainland 7m/11km SW of Kirkwall. **Swanbister Bay** to SE, with landing stage on W side. HY 3505
Swanbourne Bucks 28 C5 vil 2m/3km E of Winslow. SP 8027
Swanbourne Lake W Sussex 11 F4* lake in Arundel Park. See Arundel. TQ 0108
Swanbridge S Glam 15 F4/G4* loc on coast opp Sully I. ST 1667
Swancote Salop 34 D5 loc 2m/3km E of Bridgnorth. SO 7494
Swan Green Ches 42 C4* ham 5m/8km NE of Middlewich. SJ 7373
Swan Green Suffolk 31 G1* loc 2km W of Cratfield. TM 2974
Swanibost W Isles 88 C1* vil near N end of Lewis 2m/3km SW of Port of Ness. NB 5162
Swanlake Bay Dyfed 22 C5* bay 4m/7km SE of Pembroke, between E Moor Cliff and W Moor Cliff. SS 0497
Swanland Humberside 51 E5 vil 6m/10km W of Hull. SE 9927
Swanley Kent 20 B4 tn 4m/6km S of Dartford. **Swanley Village** is 1m NE. TQ 5168
Swanmore Hants 10 C3 vil 2m/3km SE of Bishop's Waltham. SU 5716
Swanmore Isle of Wight 10 C5* S dist of Ryde. SZ 5891
Swanmore, Upper Hants 10 C3* loc 2m/3km E of Bishop's Waltham. SU 5817
Swannay Orkney 89 A6* locality at N end of island of Mainland 4m/6km E of Brough Head. Loch of Swannay is large loch to E. HY 2929
Swannies Point Orkney 89 B7* headland on N coast of W part of Burray. ND 4597
Swannington Leics 36 A3 vil 2km NW of Coalville. See also New Swannington. SK 4116
Swannington Norfolk 39 F3 vil 9m/14km NW of Norwich. TG 1319
Swanpool Garden Suburb Lincs 44 D4* SW dist of Lincoln. SK 9569
Swanscombe Kent 20 C4 industrial tn 1m from S bank of R Thames and 3m/4km W of Gravesend. **Swanscombe Marshes** lie to N between tn and r. TQ 6074
Swansea (Abertawe) W Glam 14 C2 large tn and port on Swansea Bay at mouth of R Tawe 35m/57km W of Cardiff. Iron, steel, and tinplate mnfre. Coal-mining and oil-refining in vicinity. Remains of 14c cas (A.M.) or fortified manor hse. Airport 5m/9km W at Fairwood Common. SS 6593
Swansea Bay 14 C3* bay on N side of Bristol Channel extending from Mumbles Hd, W Glam, eastwards to Sker Pt, NW of Porthcawl, Mid Glam. SS 6878
Swanston Lothian 66 A2 loc in Edinburgh 4m/7km S of city centre. Swanston Cottage was once a summer home of R. L. Stevenson. NT 2367
Swan Street Essex 30 D5 loc 7m/11km W of Colchester. TL 8927
Swanton Abbot Norfolk 39 F2 vil 3m/5km SW of N Walsham. TG 2625
Swanton Morley Norfolk 39 E3 vil 3m/5km NE of E Dereham. TG 0116
Swanton Novers Norfolk 39 E2 vil 6m/9km SW of Holt. TG 0232

Swanton Street Kent 21 E5* loc 1km S of Bredgar and 3m/5km SW of Sittingbourne. TQ 8759
Swan Village W Midlands 35 F5* loc 2m/3km N of Dudley tn centre. SO 9393
Swan Village W Midlands 35 F5* loc in W Bromwich 1m NW of tn centre. SO 9891
Swanwick Derbys 43 H5 vil 2m/3km N of Ripley. SK 4053
Swanwick Hants 10 C4 vil 1m N of Park Gate. 2km W, loc of **Lr Swanwick.** SU 5109
Swanwick Green Ches 42 B6* loc 1km NW of Norbury. SJ 5547
Swarbacks Minn Shetland 89 E7* strait between Muckle Roe and islands of Vementry and Papa Little off W coast of Mainland. HU 3161
Swarby Lincs 37 F1 vil 4m/6km S of Sleaford. TF 0440
Swardeston Norfolk 39 F4 vil 4m/7km S of Norwich. TG 2002
Swarkestone Derbys 36 A2 vil on R Trent 5m/8km S of Derby. **Swarkestone Br** to S is of 13c–14c and has seventeen arches. SK 3628
Swarland Nthmb 61 F2 ham 2m/3km NW of Felton. **Swarland Estate** loc 1m N. NU 1601
Swarraton Hants 10 C2* ham adjoining Northington to SE and 3m/5km NW of New Alresford. SU 5637
Swaton Lincs 37 F1 vil 5m/8km W of Donington. TF 1337
Swavesey Cambs 29 G1 vil 9m/14km NW of Cambridge. TL 3668
Sway Hants 10 A5 small tn 3m/4km SW of Brockenhurst. SZ 2798
Swayfield Lincs 37 E2 vil 4m/6km E of Colsterworth. SK 9922
Swaythling Hants 10 B3 NE dist of Southampton. SU 4415
Swaythorpe Humberside 51 E2 loc 1m SW of Thwing. Former vil no longer exists. TA 0368
Sweat Mere Salop 34 B2 lake 4m/6km SE of Ellesmere; the smallest of several such lakes in the dist. SJ 4330
Sweet Green H & W 26 B2* loc 5m/8km N of Bromyard. SO 6462
Sweetham Devon 7 F5* ham 3m/5km E of Crediton. SX 8898
Sweethay Som 8 A2* loc 3m/4km SW of Taunton. ST 2021
Sweetheart Abbey D & G. See New Abbey.
Sweethope Loughs Nthmb 61 E3 one large and one small lake 4m/6km W of Kirkwhelpington. NY 9482
Sweetlands Corner Kent 12 D2* loc adjoining Staplehurst to N. TQ 7845
Sweetshouse Cornwall 3 F2* ham 4m/6km S of Bodmin. SX 0861
Swefling Suffolk 31 G2 vil 3m/4km W of Saxmundham. TM 3463
Swell Som 8 B2 ham 4m/6km SW of Langport. ST 3623
Swellands Reservoir W Yorks 43 E1* small resr 2m/3km S of Marsden. SE 0309
Swell, Lower Glos 27 F5 vil 2km W of Stow-on-the-Wold. SP 1725
Swell, Upper Glos 27 F5 vil 1m NW of Stow-on-the-Wold. SP 1726
Swepstone Leics 36 A3 vil 4m/6km S of Ashby de la Zouch. SK 3610
Swere 28 A4 r rising near Hook Norton, Oxon, and flowing E into R Cherwell 5m/8km SE of Banbury. SP 4933
Swerford Oxon 27 G4 vil 5m/7km NE of Chipping Norton. SP 3731
Swettenham Ches 42 D4 vil 3m/4km E of Holmes Chapel. SJ 8067
Sweyn Holm Orkney 89 B6* small uninhabited island off NE coast of Gairsay. HY 4522
Swffryd Gwent 15 G2* loc 1m N of Newbridge. ST 2198
Swift 36 B6 r rising NW of Husbands Bosworth, Leics, and flowing SW into R Avon at Brownsover on N side of Rugby, Warwicks. SP 5077
Swift's Green Kent 13 E3* loc 2m/4km E of Headcorn. TQ 8744
Swilgate 26 D4* r rising N of Cheltenham, Glos, and flowing N into R Avon at Tewkesbury. SO 8832
Swilland Suffolk 31 F3 vil 5m/9km N of Ipswich. TM 1852
Swillbrook Lancs 47 F4 loc 5m/8km NW of Preston. SD 4834
Swillett, The Herts 19 E2* W dist of Chorleywood. TQ 0195
Swillington W Yorks 49 F5 vil 6m/10km SE of Leeds. **Swillington Common** loc 2km N. SE 3830
Swimbridge Devon 7 E2 vil 5m/8km SE of Barnstaple. **Swimbridge Newland** ham 2km along rd towards Barnstaple. SS 6230
Swinbrook Oxon 27 G6 vil 2m/3km E of Burford. SP 2812
Swinburne, Great Nthmb 61 E4 ham 7m/11km N of Hexham. **Swinburne Castle,** 17c hse beside sparse remains of earlier cas. NY 9375
Swinburne, Little Nthmb 61 E4* ham below **Lit Swinburne Resr,** small resr between Colt Crag Resr and Hallington Resrs. NY 9477
Swincliffe N Yorks 49 E3 ham 4m/6km NW of Harrogate. SE 2558
Swincliffe W Yorks 49 E5* loc 2km NW of Birstall. SE 2027
Swincombe Devon 7 E1* loc 5m/9km W of Simonsbath. SS 6941
Swincombe 4 C3* r in Devon rising S of Princetown on Dartmoor and flowing NE into W Dart R 1m SE of Hexworthy. SX 6473
Swinden N Yorks 48 B3 loc 2km S of Hellifield. SD 8654
Swinden Reservoirs Lancs 48 B4/B5* two small resrs 4m/6km E of Burnley. SD 8833
Swinderby Lincs 44 D5 vil 8m/13km SW of Lincoln. SK 8663
Swindle Beck 53 G3* r rising on Warcop Fell, N of Brough, Cumbria, and flowing S into R Eden at Gt Musgrave. NY 7713
Swindon Glos 26 D5 vil 2m/3km N of Cheltenham. SO 9325
Swindon Staffs 35 E5 vil 5m/8km W of Dudley. SO 8690
Swindon Wilts 17 F3 industrial tn 70m/113km W of London. Rly, aircraft, engineering works. SU 1584
Swine Humberside 51 F4 vil 5m/8km NE of Hull. TA 1335
Swinefleet Humberside 50 C5 vil on S bank of R Ouse 2m/3km SE of Goole across loop of r. SE 7622
Swineford Avon 16 C4* loc on R Avon, tidal to this point. ST 6969
Swineshaw Reservoirs Gtr Manchester 43 E2* two resrs 3m/5km E of Stalybridge. SK 0099
Swineshead Beds 29 E2 vil 10m/16km N of Bedford. TL 0565
Swineshead Lincs 37 G1 vil 6m/10km SW of Boston. **Swineshead Br** loc with br over S Forty Foot Drain 2m/3km NW. TF 2340
Swineside N Yorks 54 A6* loc 1m SW of W Scrafton. SE 0682
Swiney H'land 86 E4 loc in Caithness dist 1m W of Lybster. ND 2335
Swinford Leics 36 B6 vil 5m/8km NE of Rugby. SP 5679
Swinford Oxon 17 H1 loc on R Thames 1km SE of Eynsham. SP 4408
Swingate Notts 36 B1* loc 1km S of Kimberley. SK 5043
Swingfield Minnis Kent 13 G3 vil 5m/7km N of Folkestone. TR 2143
Swingfield Street Kent 13 G3* vil 5m/8km N of Folkestone. TR 2343
Swingleton Green Suffolk 30 D3* ham 5m/8km NW of Hadleigh. TL 9647
Swinhill S'clyde 65 E4* loc 2m/3km S of Larkhall. NS 7748
Swinhoe Nthmb 67 H5 ham 3m/4km S of Seahouses. NU 2128
Swinhoe Lakes Nthmb 67 G5* two small lakes 2m/3km NW of Belford. NU 0735
Swinhope Lincs 45 F2 loc 2km N of Binbrook. TF 2196
Swinhopehead Reservoir Nthmb 53 G1* small resr in course of Swinhope Burn 2m/3km NW of Allenheads. NY 8246
Swining Voe Shetland 89 E6 northward-facing inlet on E coast of Mainland 2m/3km N of Dury Voe. HU 4667
Swinithwaite N Yorks 54 A5 ham 3m/4km E of Aysgarth. SE 0489
Swinmore Common H & W 26 B3* loc 3m/5km NW of Ledbury. SO 6741
Swinnow W Yorks 49 E4* dist of Leeds 4m/6km W of city centre. SE 2334
Swinscoe Staffs 43 F6 ham 3m/5km NW of Ashbourne. SK 1348
Swinstead Lincs 37 E2 vil 5m/8km W of Bourne. TF 0122
Swinsty Reservoir N Yorks 48 D3 resr in R Washburn valley 5m/8km N of Otley. SE 1953
Swinthorpe Lincs 45 E3* loc 1m W of Snelland. TF 0680
Swinton Borders 67 E4 vil 5m/8km N of Coldstream. **Swinton Quarter** is loc 1km NE. NT 8347
Swinton Gtr Manchester 42 C1 tn 5m/7km NW of Manchester. Coal-mining, textiles, light engineering, pottery. SD 7701
Swinton N Yorks 49 E1* vil 1m SW of Masham. **Swinton Park** is early 19c mansion by Wyatt with later additions. Grnds contain early 19c copy of Stonehenge. SE 2179
Swinton N Yorks 50 C1 vil 2m/3km NW of Malton. SE 7573
Swinton S Yorks 44 A2 tn in coal-mining area 4m/6km N of Rotherham. Other industries include steel, iron, electrical goods. **Swinton Br** loc on R Don 1km E. SK 4599
Swirl How Cumbria 52 C5* mountain in Lake Dist 3m/4km NW of Coniston. Height 2630 ft or 802 metres. NY 2700
Switha Orkney 89 B7* small uninhabited island 1m E of S Walls, peninsula at SE end of Hoy. Traces of Bronze Age settlements. ND 3690
Swithland Leics 36 B3 vil 4m/7km S of Loughborough. **Swithland Resr,** large resr to NE. SK 5413
Swona Orkney 89 B7 island of about 60 acres or 25 hectares 3m/5km W of Burwick near S end of S Ronaldsay. Beacon at SW end. ND 3884
Swordale W Isles 88 C2* vil on Eye Peninsula, Lewis, 2m/3km SW of Garrabost. NB 4930
Swordland H'land 79 F8* locality in N Morar, on N shore of Loch Morar in Lochaber dist, 1km S of Tarbet. NM 7891
Swordly H'land 86 A2* loc near N coast of Caithness dist 2m/3km E of Bettyhill. NC 7363
Sworton Heath Ches 42 C3* loc 2m/3km S of Lymm. SJ 6884
Swyddffynnon Dyfed 24 C2 vil 4m/7km N of Tregaron. SN 6966
Swyncombe Oxon 18 B3 estate 2m/4km NW of Nettlebed. SU 6890
Swynnerton Staffs 31 E1 vil 3m/5km NW of Stone. SJ 8535
Swyre Dorset 8 D5 vil 5m/8km SE of Bridport. SY 5288
Sychdyn Welsh form of Soughton, qv.
Sychnant Powys 25 E1* loc 6m/9km N of Rhayader. SN 9777
Sydallt Clwyd 41 H5* loc 4m/6km N of Wrexham. SJ 3155
Syde Glos 26 D6* vil 5m/8km E of Painswick. SO 9410
Sydenham London 19 G4* dist of SE London in borough of Lewisham 7m/11km SE of Charing Cross, comprising **Upr** and **Lr Sydenham.** TQ 3671
Sydenham Oxon 18 C2 vil 3m/5km SE of Thame. SP 7301
Sydenham Som 8 B1* E dist of Bridgwater. ST 3137
Sydenham Damerel Devon 4 B3 vil 5m/8km W of Tavistock. SX 4076
Syderstone Norfolk 38 C2 vil 6m/9km W of Fakenham. TF 8332
Sydling St Nicholas Dorset 8 D4 vil 2m/4km NE of Maiden Newton. SY 6399
Sydling Water 9 D5* stream rising at Up Sydling in Dorset and flowing S, partly underground, into R Frome 1m W of Stratton. SY 6394
Sydmonton Hants 17 H5 ham 3m/4km W of Kingsclere. SU 4857
Sydnal Lane Salop 35 E4* loc 1m N of Albrighton. SJ 8005
Sydney Ches 42 C5* loc in Crewe 2km NE of tn centre. SJ 7256
Syerston Notts 44 C6 vil 5m/8km SW of Newark-on-Trent. SK 7447
Syfynwy 22 C4 r rising on Mynydd Preseli, N of Rosebush, Dyfed, and flowing S through Rosebush and Llys-y-fran Resrs into Eastern Cleddau R 3m/5km N of Canaston Br. SN 0819
Syfynwy Falls Dyfed 22 C3* waterfall below Rosebush Resr, 2m/3km NW of Maenclochog. SN 0629
Syke Gtr Manchester 47 H6* loc in Rochdale 2m/3km N of tn centre. SD 8915
Sykehouse S Yorks 49 G6 vil 4m/7km NW of Thorne. SE 6216
Sykemoor Dyfed 22 C5* loc adjoining Pembroke Dock to S. SM 9602
Syleham Suffolk 31 F1 loc 4m/6km SW of Harleston. TM 2078
Sylen Dyfed 14 B1 loc 4m/7km N of Llanelli. SN 5107
Sylfaen Powys 33 H4* loc and stn on Welshpool and Llanfair Light Rly, 3m/5km W of Welshpool. SJ 1706
Symbister Shetland 89 F7 vil and chief harbour near SW end of island of Whalsay. Lighthouse on **Symbister Ness,** headland to W. HU 5362
Symington S'clyde 64 B5 vil 4m/7km NE of Prestwick. NS 3831
Symington S'clyde 65 F5 vil 3m/5km SW of Biggar. NS 9935
Symondsbury Dorset 8 C5 vil 2km W of Bridport. SY 4493
Symonds Green Herts 29 F5* NW dist of Stevenage. TL 2224
Symonds Yat H & W 26 B5 loc and well-known beauty spot on R Wye 4m/6km NE of Monmouth across loops of r. SO 5516
Synod Inn. Alternative name of Post-mawr, Dyfed, qv.
Syon House London 19 F4 18c hse with Robert Adam interiors, in grnds on N bank of R Thames opp Royal Botanic Gardens at Kew. TQ 1776
Syre H'land 86 A3 loc in Strath Naver 11m/18km S of Bettyhill, Caithness dist. NC 6943
Syreford Glos 27 E5 ham 5m/8km E of Cheltenham. SP 0220
Syresham Northants 28 B3 vil 4m/6km NE of Brackley. SP 6341
Syston Leics 36 C3 suburb 5m/8km NE of Leicester. SK 6211
Syston Lincs 37 E1 vil 3m/5km N of Grantham. **Syston Park,** landscaped grnds and lake of former mansion to E. SK 9240
Sytchampton H & W 26 D1 vil 4m/6km SE of Stourport. SO 8466
Sywell Northants 28 D1 vil 5m/7km W of Wellingborough. SP 8267

T

Tableland Point Isle of Man 46 C4 headland (Manx NT) 2km SE of Ramsey. Also known as Gob ny rona. SC 4793
Tabley Ches 42 C3 loc 2m/3km W of Knutsford. Motorway service area (M6). **T. Mere,** lake to S. SJ 7277
Tableyhill Ches 42 C3 loc 2km NW of Knutsford. SJ 7379
Tachbrook Mallory Warwicks 27 G2* loc 2m/4km S of Leamington. SP 3162
Tackley Oxon 27 H5 vil 3m/5km NE of Woodstock. SP 4720
Tacolneston Norfolk 39 F5 vil 5m/8km S of Wymondham. TM 1495
Tadcaster N Yorks 49 F4 tn on R Wharfe 9m/15km SW of York, on site of Roman *Calcaria*. Brewing, quarrying. SE 4843
Taddington Derbys 43 F4 vil in Peak Dist 5m/8km W of Bakewell. SK 1471
Taddington Glos 27 E4* loc 4m/6km S of Broadway. SP 0831
Taddiport Devon 7 D3 loc just S of Torrington across R Torridge. SS 4818
Tadley Hants 18 B5 vil 6m/10km NW of Basingstoke. SU 6060
Tadlow Cambs 29 G3 vil 4m/6km E of Potton. TL 2847
Tadmarton Oxon 27 G4 vil 4m/7km SW of Banbury. SP 3937
Tadmarton, Lower Oxon 27 H4* loc 4m/6km SW of Banbury. SP 4037
Tadpole Bridge Oxon 17 G2 loc on R Thames 2m/3km SE of Bampton. SP 3300
Tadworth Surrey 19 F5 suburban loc 3m/4km SW of Banstead. TQ 2356
Taf Welsh form of Taff (R), qv.
Taf 23 E4 r rising at Crymmych Arms, Dyfed, and flowing by Llanfyrnach, Login, and Whitland, to S side of St Clears, where it forms an estuary which runs past Laugharne to join estuary of R Towy and flow into Carmarthen Bay. SN 3406
Tafarnaubach Gwent 15 F1* loc 2km NW of Tredegar. SO 1210
Tafarn-y-bwlch Dyfed 22 C3 loc 4m/6km SE of Newport. SN 0833
Tafarn-y-Gelyn Clwyd 41 G5 loc 6m/9km SW of Mold. SJ 1861
Taff (Taf) 15 G4 r rising as **Gt Taff** (Taf Fawr) and **Lit Taff** (Taf Fechan) on W and

S sides respectively of Brecon Beacons, Powys. The two streams follow roughly parallel courses southwards through resrs until joining on NW side of Merthyr Tydfil, Mid Glam. The r then continues S by Pontypridd to mouth of R Severn at Cardiff. ST 1972
Taf Fechan Reservoir 15 F1 large resr in valley of Taf fechan R 4m/6km N of Merthyr Tydfil. Mainly in Powys but partly in Mid Glam. SO 0611
Taff-Ely 118 admin dist of Mid Glam.
Taff Merthyr Garden Village Mid Glam 15 F2* loc 1m NE of Treharris. ST 1097
Taff's Well (Ffynnon Taf) Mid Glam vil on R Taff 6m/9km NW of Cardiff, formerly noted for medicinal springs. ST 1283
Tafolwern Powys 33 F4 loc 3m/5km E of Cemmaes Rd. SH 8902
Tafts Ness Orkney 89 C5 headland at NE end of island of Sanday. HY 7647
Tahaval W Isles 88 A2* mt near W coast of Lewis 2km E of Mealisval. Height 1688 ft or 514 metres. NB 0426
Tahay W Isles 88 E1* small uninhabited island in Sound of Harris less than 1km off NE coast of N Uist. NF 9675
Taibach W Glam 14 D3 loc 1m SE of Port Talbot. SS 7788
Tain H'land 86 E1 loc in Caithness dist 2m/3km SE of Castletown. ND 2266
Tain H'land 87 B7 small tn in Ross and Cromarty dist on S shore of Dornoch Firth 10m/15km NE of Invergordon. NH 7782
Tai'r Bull Powys 25 E5 loc 4m/6km SW of Brecon. SN 9925
Tai'r-heol Mid Glam 15 F2* loc 2km SE of Treharris. ST 1094
Tai'r-ysgol W Glam 14 C2* loc 4m/6km W of Neath. SS 6997
Takeley Essex 30 A5* vil 5m/8km E of Bishop's Stortford. Vil of **T. Street** 2km W. TL 5621
Talachddu Powys 25 F4 ham 4m/6km NE of Brecon. SO 0833
Talacre Clwyd 41 G3* loc 1km SW of Point of Air. SJ 1284
Talaton Devon 7 H5 vil 3m/5km NW of Ottery St Mary. SY 0699
Talbenny (Talbenni) Dyfed 22 B4 vil near S coast of St Brides Bay 6m/9km NW of Milford Haven. SM 8311
Talbot Green Mid Glam 15 F3* loc 1km SW of Llantrisant. ST 0382
Talbot Village Dorset 9 G5* loc on Talbot Heath 2m/3km NW of Bournemouth tn centre. SZ 0793
Tale 7 H5* r in Devon rising in par of Broadhembury and flowing S into R Otter 1km NW of Ottery St Mary. SY 0996
Taleford Devon 7 H5* ham on R Tale 2km NW of Ottery St Mary. SY 0997
Tale, Lower Devon 7 H5* loc 5m/7km NW of Ottery St Mary. ST 0601
Talerddig Powys 33 F4 ham 8m/13km NW of Caersws. SH 9300
Talgarreg Dyfed 24 A3 vil 6m/10km SE of New Quay. SN 4251
Talgarth Powys 25 F4 small tn 7m/11km SW of Hay-on-Wye. 13c fortified tower near br at tn centre. SO 1533
Taliesin Dyfed. Alternative name of Tre Taliesin, qv.
Talisker H'land 79 B6 stream in Skye running W into **T. Bay** on W coast, past loc of Talisker. **T. Point** is headland at S end of bay. NG 3130
Talisker Distillery Skye, H'land 79 B5 distillery at NW end of vil of Carbost, on SW side of Loch Harport. NG 3732
Talke Staffs 42 D5 loc adjoining Kidsgrove to SW. **T. Pits** loc 1km S. SJ 8253
Talkin Cumbria 60 B5 ham 3m/4km SE of Brampton. **T. Tarn** lake 1m N. NY 5457
Talla Bheith Forest Tayside 75 F4 mt area and game forest in Atholl E of Loch Ericht. NN 5567
Talladale H'land 85 A8 vil on SW shore of Loch Maree, Ross and Cromarty dist, 8m/13km SE of Gairloch. NG 9170
Talland Cornwall 3 G3 ham near S coast above **T. Bay,** 2m/3km SW of Looe. SX 2251
Talla Reservoir Borders 65 G6 resr 2km SE of Tweedsmuir. Length about 2m/4km SE to NW. NT 1121
Tallarn Green Clwyd 42 A6 vil 4m/6km E of Bangor Is-coed. SJ 4444
Tallentire Cumbria 52 B2 vil 3m/5km N of Cockermouth. NY 1035
Talley (Talyllychau) Dyfed 24 C4 vil 6m/10km N of Llandeilo. SN 6332
Tallington Lincs 37 F4 vil on R Welland 4m/7km E of Stamford. TF 0907
Tallistown Gwent 15 G1* loc 3m/4km S of Ebbw Vale. SO 1805
Talmine H'land 84 F2 vil in Caithness dist, on W shore of Tongue Bay. NC 5863
Talog Dyfed 23 E3 ham 6m/10km NW of Carmarthen. SN 3325
Talog 24 A4 r flowing SW into R Tyweli at Pencader, Dyfed. SN 4436
Talsarn Dyfed 24 B3 ham 6m/9km N of Lampeter. SN 5456
Talsarn Dyfed 24 D5* loc 3m/4km S of Myddfai. Site of Roman camp 2m/3km E. SN 7726
Talsarnau Gwynedd 32 D1 vil 4m/6km NE of Harlech. SH 6135
Talskiddy Cornwall 2 D2* ham 1m N of St Columb Major. SW 9165
Talwrn Clwyd 41 H6 loc 3m/5km SW of Wrexham. SJ 2948
Talwrn Clwyd 42 A6* loc 2m/3km E of Marchwiel. SJ 3847
Talwrn Gwynedd 40 B4 ham on Anglesey 2m/3km E of Llangefni. SH 4677
Talybont Dyfed 32 D5 vil 6m/10km NE of Aberystwyth. Tweed mnfre. SN 6589
Tal-y-bont Gwynedd 32 D3 ham on R Ysgethin 4m/6km N of Barmouth. SH 5821
Tal-y-bont Gwynedd 40 C4 vil 2m/3km E of Bangor. SH 6070
Tal-y-bont Gwynedd 40 D4 vil 6m/9km S of Conwy. SH 7668
Talybont Powys 25 F5 vil 6m/9km SE of Brecon. **Talybont Resr** large resr to S, in Glyn Collwn. SO 1122
Tal-y-cafn Gwynedd 41 E4 vil 4m/6km S of Conwy across r. SH 7871
Tal-y-coed Gwent 26 A5/A6* ham 5m/7km N of Raglan. SO 4115
Talyllychau Welsh form of Talley, qv.
Tal-y-llyn Gwynedd 33 E3 lake in course of R Dysynni 2m/3km S of summit of Cader Idris. Loc of same name at SW end of lake. SH 7109
Tal-y-llyn Powys 25 F5* loc 1km SW of Llanfihangel Tal-y-llyn. SO 1027
Talysarn Gwynedd 40 B6/C6 vil 6m/10km S of Caernarvon. SH 4853
Tal-y-waenydd Gwynedd 40 D6* loc 1m N of Blaenau Ffestiniog. SH 6947
Talywaun Gwent 15 G1* loc adjoining Abersychan to NW. SO 2604
Talywern Powys 33 E4* loc 5m/8km E of Machynlleth. SH 8200
Tamanaisval W Isles 88 A2* mt near W coast of Lewis 2m/4km SE of Mealisval. Height 1530 ft or 466 metres. NB 0423
Tamanavay W Isles 88 A2* r on Lewis flowing W into Loch T., qv. NB 0320
Tamar 4 B5 r rising about 4m/6km E of Morwenstow on N Cornish coast and flowing SSE into Plymouth Sound. For almost its entire length it forms boundary between Devon and Cornwall. SX 4652
Tamar Lake 6 B4 resr in R Tamar valley 4m/6km from its source and 5m/9km NW of Holsworthy, Devon. SS 2911
Tame 35 G3 r rising on the W side of Walsall, W Midlands, and flowing SE to Perry Barr, Birmingham, then E to its confluence with R Blythe NE of Coleshill, then N past Tamworth into R Trent 2km E of Alrewas, Staffs. SK 1914
Tame 42 D2 r rising on moors N of Junction, Gtr Manchester, and flowing S to join R Goyt on N side of Stockport and form R Mersey. SJ 8990
Tame 54 D4 small r rising W of Guisborough, Cleveland, and flowing SW into R Leven 2km SW of Stokesley, N Yorks. NZ 5107
Tamer Lane End Gtr Manchester 42 C1* loc 2km NW of Leigh. SD 6401
Tamerton Foliot Devon 4 B4 dist in N Plymouth, 4m/6km N of city centre. SX 4760
Tamerton, North Cornwall 6 C5 vil by R Tamar 5m/7km SW of Holsworthy. SX 3197
Tameside 117 admin dist of Gtr Manchester metropolitan county.
Tamworth Staffs 35 G4 tn on R Tame 14m/22km NE of Birmingham. Cas Norman and later. SK 2004
Tamworth Green Lincs 37 H1* loc 4m/6km E of Boston. TF 3842
Tanat 33 H2 r rising in Berwyn Mts on borders of Gwynedd and Powys and flowing E into R Vyrnwy 2km S of Llanyblodwel. SJ 2420
Tancred N Yorks 50 A2* loc 1m E of Whixley. SE 4458
Tandem W Yorks 48 D6* loc in Huddersfield 2m/3km E of tn centre. SE 1716
Tandle Hill Gtr Manchester 42 D1* loc 3m/4km S of Rochdale. SD 8909
Tandlehill S'clyde 64 B3* loc adjoining Kilbarchan to SE. NS 4062
Tandridge Surrey 20 A6 vil 2m/3km SE of Godstone. TQ 3750
Tandridge 119 admin dist of Surrey.
Tanera Beg H'land 85 A6 one of the Summer Isles, qv. Lies 3m/5km W of NW coast of Ross and Cromarty dist near Polglass. Area about 270 acres or 110 hectares. NB 9607
Tanera More H'land 85 A6 the largest of the Summer Isles, qv, being over 1 sq mile or about 3 sq km in area. Lies 1m W of NW coast of Ross and Cromarty dist across Baden Bay. NB 9807
Tanerdy Dyfed 23 F4 loc adjoining Carmarthen to N. SN 4120
Tanfield Durham 61 F5 vil 2m/3km N of Stanley. **T. Lea** vil 1m S. NZ 1855
Tanfield, East N Yorks 49 E1 loc 2km E of W Tanfield. Former vil no longer exists. SE 2877
Tanfield, West N Yorks 49 E1 vil on R Ure 5m/8km NW of Ripon. SE 2678
Tang N Yorks 49 E3* ham 1km NE of Kettlesing Bottom. SE 2357
Tang Hall N Yorks 50 B3* loc in York 2km E of city centre. SE 6252
Tangier Som 8 A2* inner dist of Taunton. ST 2224
Tangiers Dyfed 22 C4 loc 2m/3km N of Haverfordwest. SM 9518
Tangley Hants 17 G6 vil 5m/8km NW of Andover. SU 3252
Tangley, Little Surrey 11 F1* ham 3m/5km SE of Guildford. TQ 0246
Tangmere W Sussex 11 E4 vil on W side of airfield 3m/5km E of Chichester. SU 9006
Tang Wick Shetland 89 D6* bay on N shore of St Magnus Bay on Esha Ness. Loc of **Tangwick** inland. HU 2377
Tangy Loch S'clyde 62 D5 small loch in Kintyre 5m/8km N of Campbeltown. NR 6928
Tanhouse Lancs 42 B1* E dist of Skelmersdale. SD 4905
Tankerness Orkney 89 B6* locality and loch on Mainland 2m/3km SW of Rerwick Hd. HY 5109
Tankersley S Yorks 43 H2* vil 2m/3km W of Hoyland Nether. **Upr Tankersley** loc 1km S. SK 3399
Tankerton Kent 13 F1 E dist of Whitstable, on **T. Bay.** TR 1267
Tannach H'land 86 F3 loc in Caithness dist 3m/5km SW of Wick. ND 3247
Tannadice Tayside 77 E5 vil on R South Esk 8m/12km W of Brechin. NO 4758
Tanners Green H & W 27 E1 ham 5m/8km NE of Redditch. SP 0874
Tannington Suffolk 31 F2 vil 4m/6km NW of Framlingham. Loc of **T. Green** 1m N. TM 2467
Tannray W Isles 88 C2* small uninhabited island at entrance to Loch Leurbost, E coast of Lewis. NB 4023
Tan Office Green Suffolk 30 C2* ham 1m S of Chevington. TL 7858
Tan Pit Lancs 42 B1* loc in Wigan 2m/4km SW of tn centre. SD 5502
Tansey Green W Midlands 35 E5* loc 3m/4km W of Dudley tn centre. SO 9089
Tanshall Fife 73 F4* W dist of Glenrothes. NO 2500
Tanskey Rocks Merseyside 41 G3* group of rocks in R Dee estuary about 1km offshore from W Kirby. SJ 2086
Tansley Derbys 43 G5 vil 2m/3km E of Matlock. **T. Knoll** loc adjoining to N. SK 3259
Tansley Hill W Midlands 35 F5* loc 1m SE of Dudley tn centre. SO 9589
Tansor Northants 37 F5 vil 2m/3km NE of Oundle. TL 0591
Tantallon Castle Lothian 66 D1 ruined cas (A.M.) of red stone on rocky headland 3m/5km E of N Berwick, dating from 14c. NT 5985
Tantobie Durham 61 F5/F6* vil 2m/3km NW of Stanley. NZ 1754
Tanton N Yorks 54 D4 ham 2km N of Stokesley. NZ 5210
Tanwood H & W 26 D1* loc 4m/7km NW of Bromsgrove. SO 9074
Tanworth-in-Arden Warwicks 27 F1 vil 4m/6km NW of Henley-in-Arden. SP 1170
Tanyard Bay Cumbria 52 A3* small bay N of Redness Pt on N side of Whitehaven. NX 9720
Tan-y-bwlch Gwynedd 32 D1* loc on W side of Maentwrog. SH 6540
Tan-y-bwlch Gwynedd 40 C5* loc 2m/3km SW of Bethesda. SH 6065
Tan-y-coed Gwynedd 40 C5* loc 4m/6km E of Caernarvon. SH 5362
Tan-y-fron Clwyd 41 F5* loc 2m/3km SE of Llansannan. SH 9564
Tanygrisiau Gwynedd 40 D6 loc 1m SW of Blaenau Ffestiniog. To S, **Tanygrisiau Resr** in course of R Ystradau is lower resr for Tanygrisiau Power Stn situated on W bank. See also Llyn Stwlan. SH 6845
Tan-y-groes Dyfed 23 E1* ham 2m/3km SE of Aberporth. SN 2849
Tan-yr-allt Clwyd 41 F3* loc 2km S of Prestatyn. SJ 0680
Taphouse, East Cornwall 3 F2 vil 4m/7km W of Liskeard. Locs of **Middle T.** and **West T.** lie 1km and 3km W respectively. SX 1863
Taplow Bucks 18 D3 vil in R Thames valley 4m/7km W of Slough. SU 9182
Tap o' Noth Grampian 82 D4 hill surmounted by ancient fort, 2m/3km NW of Rhynie. NJ 4829
Tapton Derbys 43 H4* loc in Chesterfield 2km NE of tn centre. SK 3972
Tapton Grove Derbys 43 H4* loc 2km NE of Chesterfield. SK 4072
Taransay W Isles 88 A3 barely populated island, 4m/7km NE to SW and of varying width, lying 1m off W coast of Harris across Sound of T. **T. Glorigs** is group of rocks about 3m/5km NW. NB 0200
Tarbat Ness H'land 87 C7 headland on E coast of Ross and Cromarty dist, on S side of entrance to Dornoch Firth. Lighthouse. NH 9487
Tarbert H'land 74 B5* r in Lochaber dist running E from top of Glen T. to Loch Linnhe at Inversanda Bay. NM 9359
Tarbert S'clyde 63 E1 vil at head of E Loch Tarbert at N end of Kintyre, Argyll. Main port for Loch Fyne fishing industry. Passenger boat services to Gourock. Remains of 14c cas on S side of loch. **W Tarbert** is locality 1m SW at head of W Loch Tarbert, qv. NR 8668
Tarbert S'clyde 69 E8 loc on **T. Bay** on E coast of Jura, 5m/7km SW of Ardlussa. NR 6082
Tarbert W Isles 88 B3 vil and port of Harris, Isle of Lewis, situated on isthmus between E and W Loch Tarbert. NB 1500
Tarbert Bay, East and **West** S'clyde 62 D3 two bays on either side of Gigha, near N end of island. NR 6552
Tarbet H'land 79 F8 locality in N Morar, on S shore of Loch Nevis, Lochaber dist, at head of small inlet, **T. Bay. S Tarbet Bay** is small inlet on Loch Morar, 1km SE. NM 7992
Tarbet H'land 84 B3 loc on W coast of Sutherland dist opp island of Handa. NC 1648
Tarbet S'clyde 71 E4 vil and resort on W shore of Loch Lomond 7m/11km S of head of loch and 2km E of Arrochar at head of Loch Long. NN 3104
Tarbock Green Merseyside 42 A3 loc 2km NE of Halewood. SJ 4687
Tarbolton S'clyde 64 B6 vil 5m/8km E of Prestwick. Bachelors' Club (NTS), 17c thatched hse where Burns and friends formed club in 1780. NS 4327
Tarbrax S'clyde 65 G3* loc 6m/10km NE of Carnwath. Loc of **S Tarbrax** 1m S. NT 0255
Tardebigge H & W 27 E1 vil 3m/4km E of Bromsgrove. Flight of thirty locks on Worcester and Birmingham Canal. SO 9969
Tardy Gate Lancs 47 F5 loc 2m/4km S of Preston. SD 5425
Tarell 25 E5 r rising to W of Brecon Beacons, Powys, and flowing NE into R Usk at Brecon. SO 0328
Tarenig 33 F6 r rising on S slopes of Plynlimon and running S then SE into R Wye 1km W of Pant Mawr, Powys. SN 8482

Tarff H'land 75 E1 r in Inverness dist rising between Glendoe and Corrieyairack Forests and running generally NW down Glen Tarff to head of Loch Ness. NH 3809
Tarfside Tayside 77 E3 vil on Water of Tarf near its junction with R North Esk, 11m/17km NW of Fettercairn. NO 4979
Tarf Water 57 D6 r in Dumfries & Galloway region, rising on border with Strathclyde region S of Barrhill and running SE to R Bladnoch, 2km E of Kirkcowan. NX 3460
Tarf Water 76 A3 r in Tayside dist running E to head of Glen Tilt, 11m/17km NE of Blair Atholl. NN 9879
Tarland Grampian 77 E1 vil 9m/14km NE of Ballater. On rocky knoll 1km SE is Tomnaverie Stone Circle (A.M.). See also Culsh. NJ 4804
Tarleton Lancs 47 E6 vil 8m/12km E of Southport. SD 4520
Tarlscough Lancs 47 E6* loc 4m/6km N of Ormskirk. SD 4314
Tarlton Glos 16 D2 vil 4m/7km W of Cirencester. ST 9699
Tarn at Leaves Cumbria 52 C4* small lake 2km SE of Seatoller. NY 2512
Tarner Island Skye, H'land 79 B5 small uninhabited island in Loch Bracadale nearly 1m N of island of Wiay. NG 2938
Tarnhouse Tarn Cumbria 53 E6* small lake 4m/6km NW of Kirkby Lonsdale. SD 5783
Tarn Hows Cumbria 52 D5* lake (NT) 2m/4km NE of Coniston. NY 3300
Tarn, Low Cumbria 52 B4* small lake 2m/3km W of Wasdale Hd. NY 1609
Tarnock Som 15 H6 ham 4m/6km W of Axbridge. ST 3752
Tarns Dub Cumbria 52 B1* small lake 1km E of Holme St Cuthbert. Loc of **Tarns** to N. NY 1147
Tarnside Cumbria 52 D5* loc 5m/8km S of Windermere. SD 4390
Tarporley Ches 42 B5 vil 9m/14km NW of Nantwich. SJ 5562
Tarpots, Great Essex 20 D3* loc adjoining Thundersley to W, 4m/6km E of Basildon. TQ 7688
Tarr Som 7 H2* ham 3m/4km NE of Wiveliscombe. ST 1030
Tarrant 9 F4* r rising at T. Gunville in Dorset and flowing S into R Stour at T. Crawford 3m/5km SE of Blandford Forum. ST 9103
Tarrant Crawford Dorset 9 F4* ham 3m/5km SE of Blandford Forum. ST 9203
Tarrant Gunville Dorset 9 F3 vil 5m/8km NE of Blandford Forum. ST 9212
Tarrant Hinton Dorset 9 F3 vil 5m/7km NE of Blandford Forum. ST 9311
Tarrant Keyneston (or Tarrant Keynston) Dorset 9 F4 vil 3m/5km SE of Blandford Forum. ST 9204
Tarrant Launceston Dorset 9 F3* vil between Tarrant Hinton and Tarrant Monkton 4m/7km NE of Blandford Forum. ST 9409
Tarrant Monkton Dorset 9 F3 vil 4m/7km NE of Blandford Forum. ST 9408
Tarrant Rawston Dorset 9 F3/F4 vil adjoining Tarrant Rushton, qv, to N. ST 9306
Tarrant Rushton Dorset 9 F4 ham 3m/5km E of Blandford Forum. Airfield to E. ST 9306
Tarras Water 59 H3 r in Dumfries & Galloway region running S to R Esk 3m/4km S of Langholm. NY 3780
Tarrents Devon 7 H5* loc 4m/7km NW of Ottery St Mary. ST 0601
Tarring Neville E Sussex 12 B6 vil on E side of R Ouse valley 2m/3km N of Newhaven. Bronze Age settlement on S Downs 1m N. TQ 4403
Tarrington H & W 26 B3 vil 7m/11km E of Hereford. SO 6140
Tarrington, Little H & W 26 B3* ham 7m/11km E of Hereford. SO 6241
Tarring, West W Sussex 11 G4 dist of Worthing 1m NW of tn centre. TQ 1303
Tarr Steps Som 7 F2 ancient clapper br across R Barle, rebuilt after floods of 1952, 4m/6km NW of Dulverton. Land on left bank owned by NT. SS 8632
Tarset Burn 60 D3 r rising as Smallhope Burn on E side of Kielder Forest, Nthmb, and flowing SE into R North Tyne 4m/6km W of Bellingham. NY 7885
Tarset Castle Nthmb. See Lanehead. NY 7985
Tarskavaig Skye, H'land 79 D7 vil on **T. Bay**, on W side of Sleat peninsula 7m/11km N of Pt of Sleat. **Tarskavaig Pt** is headland on N side of entrance to bay. NG 5809
Tarty Burn 83 H4 stream in Grampian region running E into R Ythan estuary 2km N of Newburgh. NJ 9927
Tarves Grampian 83 G4 vil 4m/7km NE of Oldmeldrum. NJ 8631
Tarvie H'land 80 D2 loc in Ross and Cromarty dist 3m/4km NW of Contin. NH 4258
Tarvin Ches 42 B4 vil 5m/9km E of Chester. **T. Sands** loc to NE. SJ 4967
Tas 39 F4 r rising S of Carleton Rode, Norfolk, and flowing NE into R Yare on SE side of Norwich. TG 2407
Tasburgh Norfolk 39 F5 vil 8m/13km S of Norwich. Ham of **Upr Tasburgh** 1km E. TM 2095
Tasley Salop 34 D5* loc 2m/3km W of Bridgnorth. SO 6994
Taston Oxon 27 G5 loc 2m/3km N of Charlbury. SP 3621
Tat Bank W Midlands 35 F5* loc 1km SE of Oldbury. SO 9989
Tatenhill Staffs 35 G2 vil 2m/4km W of Burton upon Trent. **T. Common** loc 1km W. SK 2022
Tathall End Bucks 28 C3* loc 4m/6km NW of Newport Pagnell. SP 8246
Tatham Lancs 47 F2 loc 1km SW of Wennington. SD 6069
Tathwell Lincs 45 G3 vil 3m/5km S of Louth. TF 3283
Tatling End Bucks 19 E3* loc 3m/5km NW of Uxbridge. TQ 0187
Tatsfield Surrey 20 B5 suburban loc 3m/5km NW of Westerham. TQ 4157
Tattenhall Ches 42 B5 vil 7m/12km SE of Chester. SJ 4858
Tattenhoe Bucks 28 C4/D4* loc 3m/5km W of Bletchley. SP 8334
Tatterford Norfolk 38 D2 ham 4m/6km W of Fakenham. TF 8628
Tattersett Norfolk 38 D2 vil 5m/8km W of Fakenham. TF 8430
Tattershall Lincs 45 F5 vil 8m/13km SW of Horncastle. Remains of 15c cas (NT). **Tattershall Br** loc 2m/3km SW. **T. Thorpe** vil 1m NE. TF 2157
Tattingstone Suffolk 31 E4 vil 5m/8km S of Ipswich. TM 1337
Tattingstone White Horse Suffolk 31 E4* ham 4m/7km S of Ipswich. TM 1338
Tatton Park Ches 42 C3 hse and park (NT) with lake, **Tatton Mere,** to N of Knutsford. SJ 7481
Tauchers Grampian 82 C2* loc 4m/6km W of Keith. Distillery. NJ 3749
Taunton Gtr Manchester 43 E2 loc in Ashton-under-Lyne 1km NW of tn centre. SD 9300
Taunton Som 8 A2 county capital in fertile **Vale of Taunton Deane.** County museum, civic centre; remains of Norman cas. Industries include food, cider, agricultural machinery, shirts, collars. ST 2224
Tavay Mór W Isles 88 C2* small uninhabited island opp entrance to Loch Erisort, E coast of Lewis. **Tavay Beag** is smaller island on W side of Tavay Mór. NB 4222
Taverham Norfolk 39 F3 suburb 5m/9km NW of Norwich. TG 1614
Tavernspite Dyfed 22 D4 ham 3m/4km SW of Whitland. SN 1812
Taversoe Tuick Orkney 89 B6* prehistoric two-storeyed cairn (A.M.) on island of Rousay, 1km W of Brinyan. HY 4227
Tavistock Devon 4 B3 mkt tn on R Tavy on W edge of Dartmoor 13m/21km N of Plymouth. SX 4874
Tavy 4 B4 r in Devon rising in heart of Dartmoor and flowing SW through Tavistock into R Tamar opp Landulph. SX 4461
Taw 6 D2 r rising on N Dartmoor, Devon, and flowing N to Barnstaple and thence W to join R Torridge and flow out into Barnstaple or Bideford Bay. SS 4631
Tawe 23 H6 r rising in Brecon Beacons National Park on E side of Llyn y Fan Fawr, Powys, and flowing SW by Pontardawe and Clydach, W Glam, into Swansea Bay at Swansea. SS 6691
Taw Green Devon 4 C1 ham 4m/7km NE of Okehampton. SX 6597
Tawstock Devon 6 D2 vil 2m/3km S of Barnstaple. SS 5529
Tawton, North Devon 7 E5 vil 6m/10km NE of Okehampton. SS 6601
Tawton, South Devon 7 E5 vil 4m/7km E of Okehampton. SX 6594
Taxal Derbys 43 E3 ham 1m S of Whaley Br. SK 0079
Tay 73 G2 longest r in Scotland, rising on N side of Ben Lui and flowing generally E down Strath Fillan and Glen Dochart to Loch Tay, whence it issues as R Tay and flows past Aberfeldy, Dunkeld, and Perth to Firth of Tay and the E coast at Buddon Ness, E of Dundee. Total length 120m/193km. NO 5429
Tayinloan S'clyde 62 D3 vil on W side of Kintyre, Argyll, 2m/4km S of Rhunahaorine Pt. Ferry to island of Gigha. NR 6946
Taymouth Castle Tayside 71 H1 early 19c mansion on S bank of R Tay 1m NE of Kenmore. NN 7846
Taynish S'clyde 70 A6 locality in Argyll on W side of Loch Sween, just N of entrance to Linne Mhuirich. **Taynish I.** off shore to SE. NR 7283
Taynton Glos 26 C5 vil 3m/5km S of Newent. SO 7321
Taynton Oxon 27 F6 vil 2km NW of Burford. SP 2313
Taynuilt S'clyde 70 C2 vil in Argyll 1km SW of Bonawe. NN 0031
Tayport Fife 73 G2 tn with small harbour on S side of Firth of Tay opp Broughty Ferry. NO 4528
Tayside 114,115 central admin region of Scotland with coastline bordering the North Sea from 3m/5km N of Montrose to the Firth of Tay, and comprising the former counties of Angus and Kinross, and the greater part of Perth. Its northern border with Highland and Grampian regions is in the heart of the Grampian Mts, except at its eastern end, where it descends across Strathmore to the coast; while the 'Highland Line', dividing Highlands from Lowlands, passes NE through Crieff, Dunkeld, Blairgowrie, Kirriemuir, and Edzell, all within its borders. The chief r is the Tay, the longest in Scotland, running from Ben Lui through Loch Tay to Perth, the 'Fair City', and thence into the Firth of Tay, on the N bank of which the city of Dundee is situated.
Tayvallich S'clyde 69 F8 vil in Knapdale, Argyll, on Loch a' Bhealaich, an inlet on W side of Loch Sween. NR 7487
Tea Green Herts 29 F5* ham 3m/5km E of Luton. TL 1323
Tealby Lincs 45 F2 vil 3m/5km E of Mkt Rasen. TF 1590
Tealing Tayside 73 G1 loc (Kirkton of T.) 5m/7km N of Dundee. Radio stn to NW. Tealing Hse to E has unusual dovecote; also souterrain or earth-house (A.M). NO 4037
Team 61 G5 r rising N of Stanley, Durham, and flowing circuitously N into R Tyne 2km W of Gateshead, county of Tyne & Wear. Flows through Team Valley Industrial Estate in SW part of Gateshead. NZ 2362
Team, Low Tyne & Wear 61 G5* dist of Gateshead 2km SW of tn centre. NZ 2462
Teampull na Trionaid W Isles 88 E1* ruined medieval ch 1km NW of Carinish, N Uist. NF 8160
Team Valley Tyne & Wear 61 G5* trading estate in Gateshead 2m/3km SW of tn centre. NZ 2460
Tean 35 G1 r rising near Kingsley, N of Cheadle, Staffs, and flowing S then SE into R Dove 1m NE of Uttoxeter. SK 1034
Teanga Tunga W Isles 88 C2* narrow spit of land protruding into R Laxdale estuary from N, 2m/3km NE of Stornoway, Lewis. NB 4435
Teangue Skye, H'land 79 E7 vil on E coast of Sleat peninsula 4m/7km NE of Ardvasar. NG 6608
Teaninich H'land 81 F1 loc with distillery on S side of Alness in Sutherland dist. NH 6569
Tean, Upper Staffs 35 F1 vil 2m/4km S of Cheadle. **Lr Tean** vil 1m SE. SK 0139
Tebay Cumbria 53 E4 vil and former rly junction 10m/16km NE of Kendal. See also Old Tebay. NY 6104
Tebworth Beds 29 E5 vil 4m/6km NW of Dunstable. SP 9926
Tedburn St Mary Devon vil 7m/11km W of Exeter. SX 8194
Teddington Glos 26 D4/27 E4 vil 5m/7km E of Tewkesbury. SO 9633
Teddington London 19 F4 dist in borough of Richmond on left bank of R Thames, which is tidal to this point (69m/110km from its mouth). TQ 1671
Tedstone Delamere H & W 26 C2* ham 4m/6km NE of Bromyard. SO 6958
Tedstone Wafre H & W 26 B2 vil 3m/5km NE of Bromyard. SO 6759
Tees 54 D2 r rising on E slopes of Cross Fell, Cumbria, and flowing SE by Middleton in Teesdale to Barnard Castle, then E to Stockton-on-Tees and Middlesbrough, then NE into North Sea at Tees Mouth, Cleveland. Navigable to Stockton; tidal to Newsham, above Yarm. NZ 5528
Tees Bay Cleveland 54 D2/55 E2 bay at mouth of R Tees extending from Hartlepool to Redcar. NZ 5528
Teesport Cleveland 54 D3* port and oil refinery on right bank of R Tees near its mouth, 4m/6km NE of Middlesbrough. NZ 5423
Teesville Cleveland 54 D3* loc in Eston 3m/5km E of Middlesbrough. NZ 5419
Teeton Northants 28 C1 ham 7m/12km NW of Northampton. SP 6970
Teffont Wilts 9 G1 par 7m/11km W of Wilton, containing vils of **T. Evias** and **T. Magna.** ST 9932
Tegryn Dyfed 22 D3 ham 4m/6km SE of Boncath. SN 2233
Teifi 22 D1 r rising in Llyn Teifi, Dyfed, 4m/6km S of Cwmystwyth. It then flows SW by Pontrhydfendigaid and the W side of Tregaron to Lampeter, Llanybydder, and Llandyssul, then W to Newcastle Emlyn and Cardigan, then N into Cardigan Bay between Cemaes Hd and Gwbert-on-Sea. SN 1548
Teigh Leics 36 D3 vil 5m/7km N of Oakham. SK 8616
Teigl 32 D1* r running SW into R Dwyryg at Rhyd-y-sarn, 1m W of Ffestiniog, Gwynedd. SH 6842
Teign 5 E3 Devon r rising on N Dartmoor. It flows generally E past Chagford and Dunsford, then S to Newton Abbot. The tidal estuary then flows E into the English Channel at Teignmouth. SX 9472
Teignbridge 118 admin dist of Devon.
Teigngrace Devon 5 E3 vil 2m/3km NW of Newton Abbot. SX 8473
Teignmouth Devon 5 E3 resort at mouth of R Teign. Pier. Br connects with Shaldon on S side of estuary. SX 9473
Teign Village Devon 5 E3* ham above Teign valley 2m/3km NW of Chudleigh. SX 8381
Teindland Grampian B2, C2 upland tract 5m/9km SE of Elgin. **T. Forest** is state forest on E side. NJ 2655
Teinnasval W Isles 88 A2* mt near W coast of Lewis 2m/3km SE of Mealisval. Height 1626 ft or 496 metres. NB 0425
Teise 12 C2 r rising S of Tunbridge Wells, Kent, and flowing E through Lamberhurst, then N into R Beult. To SW of Marden it divides into two, the E branch joining R Beult S of Hunton, and the W branch joining it at Yalding. TQ 6950
Teith 72 B5 r in Central region issuing from Loch Venachar and running SE to R Forth 3m/4km NW of Stirling. NS 7696
Telford Salop 34 D3 New Tn designated 1963, comprising Dawley, Oakengates, and Wellington, and including the S bank of R Severn above and below Ironbridge. SJ 6807
Telham E Sussex 12 D5 loc adjoining Battle to SE. TQ 7614
Tellisford Som 16 C5* vil 5m/8km N of Frome. ST 8055
Telscombe E Sussex 12 A6 vil in S Downs 3m/5km NW of Newhaven. Romano-British settlement to NW. TQ 4003
Teme 26 D3 r rising S of Newtown, Powys, and flowing E to Ludlow, Salop, then generally SE and into R Severn 2m/3km S of Worcester. SO 8552
Templand D & G 59 F3 vil 2m/4km N of Lochmaben. NY 0886
Temple Cornwall 3 F1 ham 6m/10km NE of Bodmin. SX 1473
Temple Lothian 66 B3 vil 3m/4km SW of Gorebridge. NT 3158
Temple S'clyde 64 C2* loc in Glasgow 4m/6km NW of city centre. NS 5469
Temple Balsall W Midlands 35 G6 loc 4m/7km SE of Solihull. SP 2076
Temple Bar Dyfed 23 G4* loc 4m/6km SW of Llandeilo. SN 5917

Temple Bar Dyfed 24 B3 loc at crossroads 5m/8km NW of Lampeter. SN 5354
Temple Bar W Sussex 11 E4* loc 3m/4km NE of Chichester. SU 8907
Temple Bruer Lincs 44 D5/45 E5* loc 3m/4km E of Welbourn. TF 0054
Temple Cloud Avon 16 B5 vil 3m/5km NW of Midsomer Norton. ST 6257
Templecombe Som 9 E2 vil 4m/7km S of Wincanton. ST 7022
Temple Cowley Oxon 18 A1 SW dist of Oxford. SP 5404
Temple End Cambs 30 A2* E end of Gt Wilbraham. TL 5557
Temple End Suffolk 30 B3* loc 4m/6km N of Haverhill. TL 6650
Temple Ewell Kent 13 H3 suburb 3m/4km NW of Dover. TR 2844
Temple Fields Essex 20 B1* NE dist of Harlow. Site of Roman temple to N. TL 4611
Temple Grafton Warwicks 27 F2 vil 5m/8km W of Stratford-upon-Avon. SP 1254
Temple Guiting Glos 27 E4 vil 6m/10km W of Stow-on-the-Wold. SP 0928
Templehall Fife 73 F5* NW dist of Kirkcaldy. NT 2693
Temple Hirst N Yorks 50 B5 vil on R Aire 3m/5km NW of Snaith across r. SE 6025
Temple Manor Kent. See Strood.
Temple Mills London 20 A3* loc in borough of Waltham Forest 1km SW of Leyton. TQ 3785
Temple Newsam W Yorks 49 F5 Tudor and Jacbn hse and museum in park situated in Leeds 4m/6km E of city centre. SE 3532
Temple Normanton Derbys 43 vil in coal-mining dist 3m/5km SE of Chesterfield. SK 4167
Temple Sowerby Cumbria 53 E2 vil 6m/10km NW of Appleby. NY 6127
Templeton Devon 7 F4 vil 4m/7km W of Tiverton. 1km NW, ham of **T. Bridge.** SS 8814
Templeton Dyfed 22 D4 vil 2m/3km S of Narberth. SN 1111
Templetown Durham 61 F6* S dist of Consett. NZ 1049
Tempsford Beds 29 F3 vil 3m/4km N of Sandy. TL 1652
Ten Acre Reservoir N Yorks 49 E3* small resr 4m/6km W of Harrogate. SE 2453
Ten Acres W Midlands 35 F6* loc in Birmingham 3m/5km S of city centre. SP 0581
Tenbury Wells H & W 26 B1 small tn on R Teme. Developed as spa in 19c. SO 5968
Tenby (Dinbych-y-pysgod) Dyfed 22 D5 resort on Carmarthen Bay 9m/15km E of Pembroke. Extensive sands to N and S. Part of the old tn walls survives. Scant remains of medieval cas. Waters to N known as **Tenby Rds.** SN 1300
Tendring Essex 31 E5 vil 6m/10km NW of Clacton-on-Sea. TM 1424
Tendring 119 admin dist of Essex.
Tendring Green Essex 31 E5* ham 3m/5km NW of Thorpe-le-Soken. TM 1425
Tendring Heath Essex 31 E5* ham 4m/6km NW of Thorpe-le-Soken. TM 1326
Ten Mile Bank Norfolk 38 B5 vil on R Ouse 4m/7km S of Downham Mkt. TL 6096
Tenpenny Heath Essex 31 E6* loc 2m/4km N of Brightlingsea. TM 0820
Tenterden Kent 13 E3 country tn 10m/16km SW of Ashford. TQ 8833
Tents Muir Fife 73 G2 afforested area between Leuchars and Firth of Tay at **Tentsmuir Pt** 3m/4km E of Tayport. Nature reserve S of point, behind **Tentsmuir Sands.** NO 4825
Ter 30 C6 r rising between Gt Dunmow and Braintree, Essex, and flowing SE into R Chelmer 6m/9km E of Chelmsford. TL 7909
Terfyn Clwyd 41 E4* loc 2m/4km W of Abergele. SH 9177
Terling Essex 30 C6 vil 3m/5km W of Witham. TL 7715
Tern Salop 34 C3* loc 2m/3km E of High Ercall. SJ 6216
Tern 34 C3 r rising near Madeley, Staffs, and flowing SW through Mkt Drayton, Salop, then S into R Severn between Atcham and Wroxeter. SJ 5509
Ternhill Salop 34 C2 ham 3m/5km W of Mkt Drayton. SJ 6332
Terpersie Castle Grampian 82 D5 small ruined cas 3m/5km NW of Alford. NJ 5420
Terregles D & G 59 E4 loc 3m/4km W of Dumfries. NX 9377
Terrick Bucks 18 C1 loc 2m/3km W of Wendover. SP 8308
Terriers Bucks 18 D2* NE dist of High Wycombe. SU 8794
Terrig 41 H5* r dividing from Nant y Ffrith below Nant-y-Ffrith Resr, Clwyd, and running N into R Alun 2m/4km SE of Mold. SJ 2661
Terrington N Yorks 50 B2 vil 7m/11km W of Malton. SE 6770
Terrington St Clement Norfolk 38 A3 vil 4m/7km W of King's Lynn. TF 5520
Terrington St John Norfolk 38 A3 vil 6m/10km NE of Wisbech. TF 5315
Terrybank Tarn Cumbria 53 E6* small lake 3m/4km N of Kirkby Lonsdale. SD 5982
Terry's Green Warwicks 27 E1* loc on S side of Earlswood Lakes 3m/5km W of Hockley Heath. SP 1073
Terwick Common W Sussex 11 E3* ham 1km NE of Rogate and 4m/7km E of Petersfield. SU 8124
Test 10 B4 r rising at Ashe, near Overton in Hampshire, and flowing SW to Stockbridge, then S to Totton, and thence into Southampton Water at its confluence with R Itchen. The Test is a chalk stream famous for trout-fishing. SU 4209
Teston Kent 20 D6 vil on R Medway 4m/6km W of Maidstone. Site of Roman villa to W. TQ 7053
Testwood Hants 10 B3* suburb of Totton 1m NW of tn centre. SU 3514
Tetbury Glos 16 D2 small Cotswold tn 5m/8km NW of Malmesbury. ST 8993
Tetbury Upton Glos 16 D2 loc 2km N of Tetbury. ST 8895
Tetchill Salop 34 B1/B2 vil 2m/3km S of Ellesmere. SJ 3932
Tetcott Devon 6 C5 vil near confluence of Rs Claw and Tamar 5m/7km S of Holsworthy. SX 3396
Tetford Lincs 45 G4 vil 6m/9km NE of Horncastle. TF 3374
Tetley Humberside 50 C6* loc 1m S of Crowle. SE 7711
Tetney Lincs 45 G2 vil 5m/8km S of Cleethorpes. **T. Lock** loc on disused Louth Navigation Canal 2m/3km E. **T. Haven** at canal's outflow to mouth of R Humber. TA 3100
Tetsworth Oxon 18 B2 vil 3m/5km SW of Thame. SP 6801
Tettenhall W Midlands 35 E4 dist of Wolverhampton 3m/4km NW of tn centre. **Tettenhall Wd** loc adjoining to S. SJ 8700
Tetworth Cambs 29 F3 loc 4m/6km NE of Sandy. TL 2153
Teversal Notts 44 A5 vil 2m/3km N of Sutton in Ashfield. SK 4861
Teversham Cambs 29 H2 vil 3m/5km E of Cambridge. Cambridge Airport to W of vil. TL 4958
Teviot 67 E5 r in Borders region rising near border with Dumfries & Galloway region 6m/9km E of Eskdalemuir. R flows NE by Teviothead, Hawick, and Roxburgh, to R Tweed opp Kelso. NT 7233
Teviotdale Borders 66 C6-D5 valley of R Teviot. NT 51
Teviothead Borders 60 A1 vil in Teviotdale 8m/13km SW of Hawick. NT 4005
Tewet Tarn Cumbria 52 C3* small lake 2m/4km E of Keswick. NY 3023
Tew, Great Oxon 27 G4 vil 5m/9km E of Chipping Norton. SP 3929
Tewin Herts 19 F1 vil 4m/6km NW of Hertford. TL 2714
Tewinbury Herts 19 F1* loc 2m/3km E of Welwyn Garden City. TL 2614
Tewinwater Herts 19 F1* loc 2m/3km NE of Welwyn Garden City. TL 2514
Tewitfield Lancs 47 F1* loc 2m/4km NE of Carnforth, at N end of navigable part of Lancaster Canal. SD 5273
Tewkesbury Glos 26 D4 tn at confluence of Rs Severn and Avon 8m/12km NW of Cheltenham. Various light industries. Famous abbey ch. Site of Wars of the Roses battle, 1471, to S. SO 8932
Tew, Little Oxon 27 G4 vil 5m/7km E of Chipping Norton. SP 3828
Tewsgill Hill S'clyde 65 F6* hill 2m/3km E of Abington. Height 1868 ft or 569 metres. NS 9623

Texa S'clyde 62 B3/B4 island off S coast of Islay opp Laphroaig. NR 3943
Tey, Great Essex 30 D5 vil 7m/11km W of Colchester. TL 8925
Tey, Little Essex 30 D5 ham 2m/3km W of Marks Tey. TL 8923
Teynham Kent 21 E5 vil 3m/5km E of Sittingbourne. Loc of **T. Street** 2km NE. TQ 9562
Thackley W Yorks 48 D4 dist of Bradford 4m/6km N of city centre. **T. End** loc adjoining to W. SE 1738
Thackthwaite Cumbria 52 D3* loc 7m/11km W of Penrith and 3m/5km W of Pooley Br. NY 4225
Thakeham W Sussex 11 G3 vil 3m/5km N of Washington. TQ 1017
Thame Oxon 18 C1 tn on R Thame 9m/14km SW of Aylesbury. Airport at Haddenham 3m/4km NE. SP 7005
Thame 18 B2 r rising E of Aylesbury, Bucks, and flowing SW into R Thames 1km S of Dorchester, Oxon. SU 5793
Thames 21 E4 r rising 3m/5km SW of Cirencester, Glos, and flowing generally E through Oxford, Reading, and London, and into the North Sea at The Nore, between Shoeburyness, Essex and Sheerness, Kent. Tidal to Teddington. Forms Port of London from London Br to Blackwall. (Pool of London from London Br to Tower Br.) TQ 9580
Thames Ditton Surrey 19 F4 urban loc on S bank of R Thames 2km W of Surbiton. TQ 1667
Thamesdown 118, 119 admin dist of Wilts.
Thames Haven Essex 20 D3* loc at Coryton on N bank of R Thames. Large oil refinery. TQ 7481
Thamesmead London 20 B4 large residential development on SE edge of Erith Marshes 11m/18km E of Charing Cross. TQ 4779
Thanet 119 admin dist of Kent.
Thanet, Isle of Kent 13 H1 area bounded by North Sea, English Channel, and Rs Stour and Wantsum. Contains tns of Margate, Ramsgate, Broadstairs. TR 36
Thanington Kent 13 G2 SW dist of Canterbury. TR 1356
Thankerton S'clyde 65 F5 vil 4m/7km W of Biggar. NS 9738
Tharston Norfolk 39 F5* vil 2m/3km E of Forncett St Mary. Ham of **Low T.** 1m N. TM 1894
Thatcham Berks 18 A4 suburb 3m/5km E of Newbury. SU 5167
Thatcher Rock Devon 5 E4* island rock off N coast of Tor Bay 1km SW of Hope's Nose. SX 9462
Thatto Heath Merseyside 42 B2 loc in St Helens 2m/3km SW of tn centre. SJ 4993
Thaw (Ddawan) 15 F4* r rising 3m/5km N of Cowbridge, S Glam, and flowing circuitously S to that tn, then S again into Bristol Channel on E side of Breaksea Pt. ST 0265
Thaxted Essex 30 B4/B5 small tn 6m/10km SE of Saffron Walden. 16c guildhall. Many old hses. TL 6130
THE. For names beginning with this word, see under next word. This also applies to names beginning with Y, Yr; North, South, East, West; Great, Little; Greater, Lesser; High, Low; Higher, Lower; Upper, Nether; Far, Near; Mid, Middle; Isle(s) of.
Theakston N Yorks 54 C6* ham 1km NW of Burneston. SE 3085
Thealby Humberside 50 D6 vil 5m/7km N of Scunthorpe. SE 8917
Theale Berks 18 B4 vil 5m/8km W of Reading. Adjoining vil to W is loc of **T. Green.** SU 6471
Theale Som 16 A6 vil 2m/3km SE of Wedmore. ST 4646
Thearne Humberside 51 E4 ham 3m/5km SE of Beverley. TA 0736
Theberton Suffolk 31 H2 vil 2m/4km N of Leiston. TM 4365
Theddingworth Leics 36 C5 vil 5m/7km W of Mkt Harborough. SP 6685
Theddlethorpe All Saints Lincs 45 H3 vil 3m/5km NW of Mablethorpe. **Theddlethorpe St Helen** vil 1m NE. TF 4688
Thelbridge Devon 7 F4 ham 7m/11km E of Chulmleigh comprising **T. Barton** with ch, and **T. Cross.** SS 7812
Thelnetham Suffolk 31 E1 vil 6m/10km W of Diss. TM 0178
Thelveton Norfolk 31 F1 ham 3m/5km E of Diss. TM 1681
Thelwall Ches 42 C3 suburb 3m/5km E of Warrington. SJ 6587
Themelthorpe Norfolk 39 E3 vil 3m/5km W of Reepham. TG 0523
Thenford Northants 28 A3* vil 4m/6km E of Banbury. Site of Roman bldg to E. SP 5141
Theobald's Green Wilts 17 E4* loc 2m/3km SE of Calne. SU 0269
Therfield Herts 29 G4 vil 3m/4km S of Royston. TL 3337
Thet 38 D6* r rising near Attleborough, Norfolk, and flowing SW into Lit Ouse R at Thetford. TL8782
Thetford Lincs 37 F3* loc 1km N of Baston. TF 1114
Thetford Norfolk 38 D6 tn at confluence of R Thet and Lit Ouse R 12m/19km N of Bury St Edmunds. Remains of cas and priory (A.M.). To NW, **T. Chase,** large area of conifers planted and tended by Forestry Commission. TL 8683
Thetford, Little Cambs 38 A6 vil 3m/4km S of Ely. TL 5376
Thethwaite Cumbria 60 A6* loc 4m/6km S of Dalston. NY 3744
Theydon Bois Essex 20 B2 vil 2m/3km S of Epping. TQ 4499
Thick Hollins W Yorks 48 D6* loc 1km SE of Meltham. SE 1010
Thickwood Wilts 16 D4* ham 6m/9km W of Chippenham. Site of Roman bldg 1km E. ST 8272
Thieves Holm Orkney 89 B6* islet off Car Ness, Mainland, 3m/4km NE of Kirkwall. HY 4614
Thimbleby Lincs 45 F4 vil 2km W of Horncastle. TF 2369
Thimbleby N Yorks 54 D5 ham 5m/8km E of Northallerton. SE 4595
Thingley Wilts 16 D4* loc 3m/4km SW of Chippenham. ST 8970
Thingwall Merseyside 41 H3* loc in Birkenhead 4m/7km SW of tn centre. SJ 2784
Third Reservoir, North Central 72 B5 small resr in course of Bannock Burn 4m/6km SW of Stirling. NS 7589
Thirkleby N Yorks 49 F1 vil 4m/6km SE of Thirsk. **Lit Thirkleby** ham adjoining to S. SE 4778
Thirlby N Yorks 54 D6 vil 4m/7km E of Thirsk. SE 4884
Thirlestane Castle Borders. See Lauder.
Thirlmere Cumbria 52 C3 natural lake used as resr 4m/6km SE of Keswick. Length N to S 4m/6km. NY 3116
Thirlwall Castle Nthmb 60 C4 ruined 14c cas 1km N of Greenhead. **Thirlwall Common** is moorland tract to N and S. NY 6666
Thirn N Yorks 54 B6 ham 3m/5km N of Masham. SE 2185
Thirsk N Yorks 54 D6 tn on Cod Beck 8m/13km SE of Northallerton. Racecourse at New Thirsk, qv. See also Old Thirsk. SE 4282
Thirston, East Nthmb 61 F2/G2 ham 1m SE of Felton. NZ 1999
Thirston New Houses Nthmb 61 F2* loc 1m S of Felton. NZ 1899
Thirston, West Nthmb 61 F2 ham adjoining Felton to S. NU 1800
Thirtleby Humberside 51 F4* loc 2km E of Coniston. TA 1734
Thistleboon W Glam 23 G6* loc in Mumbles dist of Swansea 1km W of Mumbles Hd. SS 6287
Thistle Head Isle of Man 46 A5* headland 1km W of Peel. SC 2383
Thistleton Lancs 47 E4 vil 4m/6km N of Kirkham. SD 4037
Thistleton Leics 37 E3 vil 7m/11km NE of Oakham. SK 9117
Thistley Green Suffolk 38 B6* vil 3m/4km NW of Mildenhall. Site of Roman bldg to N. TL 6776
Thistly Creek Essex 21 E1* inlet of R Blackwater between mudflats 2m/3km S of Tollesbury. TL 9507
Thixendale N Yorks 50 D2 vil in the wolds 2m/4km NW of Fridaythorpe. SE 8461
Thockrington Nthmb 61 E4 ham 9m/15km N of Hexham. NY 9579
Tholomas Drove Cambs 37 H4 ham 5m/7km SW of Wisbech. TF 4006

Tholthorpe N Yorks 49 F2 vil 4m/6km SW of Easingwold. SE 4766

Thomas Chapel Dyfed 22 D5* loc 1m NW of Begelly. SN 1008

Thomas Close Cumbria 52 D1 loc 8m/12km NW of Penrith. NY 4340

Thomason Foss N Yorks 55 F4 waterfall in Eller Beck 1m NW of Goathland. NZ 8202

Thomaston Castle S'clyde 56 C3 16c keep, 4m/6km W of Maybole. NS 2309

Thomastown (Tretomas) Mid Glam 15 E3* vil 1m S of Tonyrefail. ST 0086

Thomas Town Warwicks 27 E2* loc adjoining Studley to S, 4m/6km SE of Redditch. SP 0763

Thomley Oxon 18 B1* loc 7m/12km E of Oxford. SP 6209

Thompson Norfolk 38 D5 vil 3m/4km S of Watton. **T. Water,** natural lake, 1m S. TL 9296

Thomshill Grampian 82 B2 loc with distillery 4m/6km S of Elgin. NJ 2157

Thongsbridge W Yorks 43 F1* vil on R Holme 1m N of Holmfirth. SE 1409

Thonock Lincs 44 C2 loc 2m/3km NE of Gainsborough. SK 8392

Thoralby N Yorks 53 H6 vil 1m S of Aysgarth. SE 0086

Thoresby Notts 44 B4 Victn mansion by Salvin in park laid out in 17–18c 3m/4km NW of Ollerton. SK 6371

Thoresby, North Lincs 45 G2 vil 7m/12km N of Louth. TF 2998

Thoresby, South Lincs 45 G4 vil 4m/6km W of Alford. TF 4076

Thoresthorpe Lincs 45 H3* loc 1m N of Saleby. TF 4577

Thoresway Lincs 45 F2 vil 4m/7km SE of Caistor. TF 1696

Thorganby Lincs 45 F2 vil 2m/4km N of Binbrook. TF 2097

Thorganby N Yorks 50 C4 vil 7m/12km NE of Selby. SE 6841

Thorgill N Yorks 55 E5/F5* ham 1m W of Rosedale Abbey. SE 7295

Thorington Suffolk 31 H1* ham 2km E of Bramfield. TM 4274

Thorington Street Suffolk 31 E4 ham 5m/8km S of Hadleigh. **Thorington Hall** (NT), built about 1600, with later extension. TM 0135

Thorlby N Yorks 48 C3 ham on edge of Yorkshire Dales National Park 2m/3km NW of Skipton. SD 9652

Thorley Herts 29 H6 ham 2m/3km SW of Bishop's Stortford. Ham of **T. Street** 1m E. TL 4718

Thorley Houses Herts 29 H5* loc 2m/3km SW of Bishop's Stortford. TL 4620

Thorley Street Isle of Wight 10 B5 vil 2km SE of Yarmouth. SZ 3788

Thormanby N Yorks 49 G1 vil 4m/7km NW of Easingwold. SE 4974

Thornaby-on-Tees Cleveland 54 D3 urban loc on right bank of R Tees in Stockton-on-Tees dist of county and forming part of Teesside urban complex. NZ 4517

Thornage Norfolk 39 E2 vil 2m/4km SW of Holt. **Lit Thornage** loc 2km NE. TG 0536

Thornborough Bucks 28 C4 vil 3m/5km E of Buckingham. Site of Roman temple at Thornborough Br to W. SP 7433

Thornborough N Yorks 49 E1 ham 2m/3km NE of W Tanfield. SE 2979

Thornbrough N Yorks 54 D6* loc 2m/3km N of Thirsk. SE 4284

Thornbury Avon 16 B3 tn 12m/19km N of Bristol. ST 6390

Thornbury Devon 6 C4 ham 5m/8km NE of Holsworthy. SS 4008

Thornbury H & W 26 B2 vil 4m/6km NW of Bromyard. SO 6259

Thornbury W Yorks 48 D5 dist of Bradford 2m/3km E of city centre. SE 1933

Thornby Cumbria 59 G6* loc 3m/4km NW of Thursby. NY 2852

Thornby Northants 36 C6 vil 8m/13km SW of Mkt Harborough. SP 6775

Thorncliff Staffs 43 E5 ham 2m/4km NE of Leek. SK 0158

Thorncliff W Yorks 49 E6* loc 1m NE of Kirkburton. SE 2113

Thorncombe Dorset 8 B4 vil 5m/8km SE of Chard. ST 3703

Thorncombe Street Surrey 11 F1 loc on N side of Winkworth Arboretum, 2m/4km SE of Godalming. TQ 0042

Thorncote Green Beds 29 F3 loc 2m/3km SW of Sandy. TL 1547

Thorncross Isle of Wight 10 B6* loc 2km SW of Shorwell. SZ 4381

Thorndon Suffolk 31 F1/F2 vil 3m/4km S of Eye. TM 1469

Thorndon Cross Devon 6 D5* ham 4m/6km W of Okehampton. SX 5394

Thorne S Yorks 49 H6 tn 9m/15km NE of Doncaster. SE 6813

Thorner W Yorks 49 F4 vil 7m/11km NE of Leeds. SE 3740

Thornes Staffs 35 G4 ham 2m/3km SE of Brownhills. SK 0703

Thornes W Yorks 49 E6* loc in Wakefield 1m S of city centre. SE 3219

Thorne St Margaret Som 7 H3 ham 3m/4km W of Wellington. ST 0921

Thorness Bay Isle of Wight 10 B5 bay on NW coast 3m/4km SW of Cowes. SZ 4594

Thorness, Great Isle of Wight 10 B5* loc 4m/6km SW of Cowes. **Lit Thorness** and **Thorness Bay** to N. SZ 4292

Thorney Bucks 19 E3 loc 5m/8km E of Slough. TQ 0479

Thorney Cambs 37 G4 vil 7m/11km NE of Peterborough. Remains of 12c abbey. Thorney was island stronghold of Hereward the Wake. **T. Toll** loc 4m/6km E. TF 2804

Thorney Notts 44 C4/D4 vil 7m/12km W of Lincoln. SK 8572

Thorney Som 8 C2 ham 2m/4km S of Langport. ST 4223

Thorney Bay Essex 20 D3* small bay on S coast of Canvey I. TQ 7982

Thorney Close Tyne & Wear 61 H5/H6* dist of Sunderland 3m/4km SW of tn centre. NZ 3654

Thorney Hill Hants 9 H4* vil at SW edge of New Forest 5m/8km NE of Christchurch. SZ 2099

Thorney Island W Sussex 10 D4 land area in Chichester Harbour of some 2 sq miles or 5 sq km almost separated from mainland by creek known as Great Deep; there is a narrow strip of land at each end of creek and a rd br across the centre. 'Island' contains vil of W Thorney, and an airfield. SU 7503

Thorney, West W Sussex 10 D4 vil on Thorney I. 3m/4km SE of Emsworth. SU 7602

Thorneywood Notts 36 B1* urban loc adjoining Carlton to W. SK 5941

Thornfalcon Som 8 B2 vil 4m/6km E of Taunton. ST 2823

Thornford Dorset 8 D3 vil 3m/5km SW of Sherborne. ST 6013

Thorngrafton Nthmb 60 D5 ham 1km N of Bardon Mill. NY 7865

Thorngrove Som 8 B1* loc 1km W of Middlezoy and 5m/8km SE of Bridgwater. ST 3632

Thorngumbald Humberside 51 F5 vil 2m/3km SE of Hedon. TA 2026

Thornham Norfolk 38 C1 vil 4m/7km E of Hunstanton. Site of Roman signal stn 1m SW. TF 7343

Thornham Magna Suffolk 31 E1 vil 3m/5km SW of Eye. Vil of **T. Parva** to N. TM 1071

Thornhaugh Cambs 37 F4 vil 5m/8km SE of Stamford. TF 0600

Thornhill Central 71 G4 vil 7m/12km W of Dunblane. NS 6699

Thornhill Cumbria 52 A4* loc 1m S of Egremont. NY 0108

Thornhill Derbys 43 G3* vil 3m/4km NW of Hathersage. SK 1983

Thornhill D & G 58 D2 small tn on R Nith 13m/21km NW of Dumfries. Site of Roman signal stn to S. NX 8795

Thornhill Hants 10 B3* E dist of Southampton 3m/5km E of city centre across R Itchen. To N, dist of **T. Park.** SU 4712

Thornhill Mid Glam 15 F3 loc 2km S of Caerphilly. ST 1584

Thornhill W Yorks 49 E6 loc 2m/3km S of Dewsbury. **T. Lees** loc 1km NW. **T. Edge** loc adjoining to S. SE 2518

Thornhills W Yorks 48 D5* loc 1km NE of Brighouse. SE 1523

Thorn Island Dyfed 22 B5 rock island off S shore of Milford Haven 2km NW of vil of Angle. SM 8403

Thornley Durham 54 A2* ham 1m S of Tow Law. NZ 1137

Thornley Durham 54 C1 coal-mining vil 6m/10km E of Durham. NZ 3639

Thornley Gate Nthmb 60 D5* loc on W side of R East Allen opp Allendale Tn. NY 8356

Thornlie and Pather S'clyde 65 E3* S dist of Wishaw. NS 7954

Thornliebank S'clyde 64 C3 suburb 5m/8km SW of Glasgow. NS 5559

Thornly Park S'clyde 64 C3* dist of Paisley 2km S of tn centre. NS 4862

Thornroan Grampian 83 G4* loc 1m N of Tarves. NJ 8632

Thorns N Yorks 53 G4* loc just S of Keld. NY 8900

Thorns Suffolk 30 C3* vil 8m/12km NE of Haverhill. TL 7455

Thornsett Derbys 43 E3 vil 2km W of Hayfield. SK 0186

Thorn's Flush Surrey 11 F1 loc 2km NW of Cranleigh. TQ 0440

Thorns Green Ches 42 D3* loc 3m/5km SE of Altrincham. SJ 7984

Thornship Cumbria 53 E3* loc 1m SW of Shap just SE of Keld. NY 5514

Thornthwaite Cumbria 52 C3 ham 3m/5km NW of Keswick. NY 2225

Thornthwaite N Yorks 48 D2 ham 4m/7km S of Pateley Br. SE 1759

Thornton Bucks 28 C4 vil 4m/6km E of Buckingham. SP 7536

Thornton Cleveland 54 D3 ham just S of Stainton and 4m/6km SE of Stockton-on-Tees. NZ 4713

Thornton Dyfed 22 B5* loc 2km N of Milford Haven. SM 9007

Thornton Fife 73 F4 vil 4m/7km N of Kirkcaldy. NT 2897

Thornton Humberside 50 C4 vil 4m/6km SW of Pocklington. SE 7645

Thornton Lancs 46 D4/47 E4 tn 5m/7km NE of Blackpool. SD 3442

Thornton Leics 36 A4 vil 5m/8km SE of Coalville. **Thornton Resr** to E. SK 4607

Thornton Lincs 45 F4 ham 2m/3km SW of Horncastle. TF 2467

Thornton Merseyside 41 H2 loc adjoining Crosby to NE. SD 3301

Thornton Nthmb 67 F4* loc 2m/3km SE of Horncliffe. NT 9547

Thornton W Yorks 48 D5 dist of Bradford 4m/6km W of city centre. **T. Moor Resr** 3m/5km W. SE 1032

Thornton Abbey Humberside. See Thornton Curtis.

Thornton Bridge N Yorks 49 F1* loc at crossing of R Swale 4m/6km NE of Boroughbridge. SE 4371

Thornton Castle Grampian 77 F4 cas 2m/3km W of Laurencekirk. NO 7171

Thornton Curtis Humberside 51 E6 vil 2m/4km SE of Barrow upon Humber. Thornton Abbey (A.M.), remains of medieval abbey 2m/3km E. TA 0817

Thornton Dale N Yorks 55 F6 vil 3m/4km E of Pickering. SE 8383

Thornton Force N Yorks 47 G1* waterfall over limestone cliff 2km N of Ingleton. SD 6975

Thornton Green Ches 42 A4* loc 1km S of Thornton-le-Moors. SJ 4474

Thorntonhall S'clyde 64 D3* dist of E Kilbride 3m/5km W of tn centre. NS 5955

Thornton Heath London 19 G4 loc in borough of Croydon 2m/3km N of Croydon tn centre. TQ 3168

Thornton Hough Merseyside 41 H3 vil 2m/4km NE of Neston. SJ 3080

Thornton in Craven N Yorks 48 B3 vil 2m/4km NE of Barnoldswick. SD 9048

Thornton in Lonsdale N Yorks 47 G1* ham 1km NW of Ingleton. SD 6873

Thornton-le-Beans N Yorks 54 C5 vil 3m/4km SE of Northallerton. SE 3990

Thornton-le-Clay N Yorks 50 C2 vil 4m/7km NE of Strensall. SE 6865

Thornton le Moor Lincs 45 E2 ham 6m/9km NW of Mkt Rasen. TF 0596

Thornton-le-Moor N Yorks 54 C5/C6 vil 4m/6km S of Northallerton. SE 3988

Thornton-le-Moors Ches 42 A4 vil 3m/5km SE of Ellesmere Port. SJ 4474

Thornton-le-Street N Yorks 54 C6 ham 3m/5km N of Thirsk, on site of Roman settlement. SE 4186

Thornton, Little Lancs 47 E4 loc 2km N of Poulton-le-Fylde. SD 3541

Thorntonloch Lothian 67 E2* loc on coast 5m/8km SE of Dunbar. NT 7574

Thornton Moor N Yorks 50 B2* loc 1m NW of Flaxton. SE 6763

Thornton-on-the-Hill N Yorks 50 A1/B1* loc 2m/4km N of Easingwold. SE 5373

Thornton Rust N Yorks 53 H5* ham 2m/3km W of Aysgarth. SD 9788

Thornton Steward N Yorks 54 B6 vil 5m/8km SE of Leyburn. SE 1787

Thornton Watlass N Yorks 54 B6 vil 3m/4km SW of Bedale. SE 2385

Thorntree Hill N Yorks 50 B3* loc 1km SW of Dunnington. SE 6652

Thornville N Yorks 50 A3* loc 1km NE of Cattal. Also known as Old Thornville. SE 4454

Thornwood Common Essex 20 B2 loc 2m/3km N of Epping. TL 4704

Thoroton Notts 36 D1 vil 4m/7km NE of Bingham. SK 7642

Thorp Gtr Manchester 42 D1* loc 1km NW of Royton. SD 9108

Thorp Arch W Yorks 49 F3/F4 vil 2m/4km SE of Wetherby. SE 4345

Thorpe Cumbria 53 E2* loc 3m/4km SW of Penrith. NY 4926

Thorpe Derbys 43 F6 vil 3m/4km NW of Ashbourne. SK 1550

Thorpe Humberside 51 E3 ham adjoining Lockington to S. SE 9946

Thorpe Lincs 45 H3 loc 2m/3km S of Mablethorpe. TF 4982

Thorpe Norfolk 39 H5 loc 5m/8km N of Beccles. TM 4398

Thorpe Notts 44 C6 vil 3m/5km SW of Newark-on-Trent. Site of Roman fort 1km W. SK 7650

Thorpe N Yorks 48 C2 vil 2km W of Burnsall. SE 0161

Thorpe Surrey 19 E4 vil 2m/3km SW of Staines. Sailing on gravel workings to E. TQ 0268

Thorpe Abbotts Norfolk 31 F1* vil 2km W of Brockdish. TM 1979

Thorpe Acre Leics 36 B3 loc in Loughborough 2km W of tn centre. SK 5120

Thorpe Arnold Leics 36 D3 ham 2km NE of Melton Mowbray. SK 7720

Thorpe Audlin W Yorks 49 F6* vil 4m/6km NE of Hemsworth. SE 4716

Thorpe Bassett N Yorks 50 D1 vil 5m/8km E of Malton. SE 8673

Thorpe Bay Essex 21 E3 E dist of Southend-on-Sea. TQ 9185

Thorpe by Water Leics 36 D4 vil on R Welland 3m/4km SE of Uppingham. SP 8996

Thorpe Common S Yorks 43 H2* loc just S of Thorpe Hesley. SK 3795

Thorpe Constantine Staffs 35 H3 vil 4m/7km NE of Tamworth. SK 2608

Thorpe Culvert Lincs 45 H5 loc 2m/3km NW of Wainfleet. TF 4760

Thorpe End Garden Village Norfolk 39 G4* vil 4m/6km NE of Norwich. TG 2811

Thorpe, Far Lincs 45 F4* loc 3m/5km N of Horncastle. TF 2673

Thorpefield N Yorks 49 F1 loc 2m/3km SW of Thirsk. SE 4179

Thorpe Green Essex 31 F5* ham 1m NW of Thorpe-le-Soken. TM 1723

Thorpe Green Lancs 47 F5* loc 1km NW of Brindle. SD 5923

Thorpe Green Suffolk 30 D3* ham 4m/6km N of Lavenham. TL 9354

Thorpe Green Surrey 19 E4* loc 3m/4km SW of Staines. TQ 0168

Thorpe Green, Far Essex 31 F5* loc 5m/8km N of Clacton-on-Sea. TM 1622

Thorpe Hamlet Norfolk 39 F4 loc in Norwich 2km E of city centre. TG 2408

Thorpe Hesley S Yorks 43 H2 vil 4m/6km NW of Rotherham. SK 3795

Thorpe in Balne S Yorks 44 B1 vil 5m/8km N of Doncaster. SE 5910

Thorpe in the Fallows Lincs 44 D3* ham 2m/4km W of Brattleby. SK 9180

Thorpe Langton Leics 36 C5 vil 4m/6km N of Mkt Harborough. SP 7492

Thorpe Larches 54 C2* loc on border of Cleveland and Durham 3m/4km SE of Sedgefield. NZ 3826

Thorpe Lea Surrey 19 E4* SW suburb of Staines. TQ 0270

Thorpe-le-Soken Essex 31 F5 vil 5m/7km N of Clacton-on-Sea. TM 1822

Thorpe le Street Humberside 50 D4 ham 3m/5km NW of Mkt Weighton. SE 8344

Thorpe-le-Willows N Yorks 50 B1* loc 1m S of Ampleforth. SE 5777

Thorpe, Little Durham 54 D1 ham 1km SE of Easington. NZ 4242

Thorpe, Little W Yorks 48 D5* loc 2km SW of Liversedge. SE 1822

Thorpe Malsor Northants 36 D6 vil 2m/4km W of Kettering. **T. M. Resr** to NW. SP 8379

Thorpe Mandeville Northants 28 A3 vil 6m/9km NE of Banbury. SP 5344

Thorpe Market Norfolk 39 F2 vil 4m/7km S of Cromer. TG 2436

Thorpe Marsh S Yorks 44 B1* loc on left bank of R Don 5m/7km NE of Doncaster. Power stn. SE 6009

Thorpe, Mid Lincs 45 F4* loc 2m/4km N of Horncastle. TF 2673

Thorpe Morieux Suffolk 30 D3 vil 3m/5km NE of Lavenham. TL 9453

Thorpeness Suffolk 31 H2 coastal resort 2m/4km N of Aldeburgh. Headland of **Thorpe Ness** 1km N. Nature reserve 1m inland. TM 4759

Thorpe on the Hill Lincs 44 D4 vil 6m/9km SW of Lincoln. SK 9065

Thorpe on the Hill W Yorks 49 E5 loc in coal-mining and quarrying area 5m/8km S of Leeds. SE 3126

Thorpe Row Norfolk 38 D4* loc 2km NE of Shipdham. TF 9708

Thorpe St Andrew Norfolk 39 F4* suburb 3m/4km E of Norwich. TG 2609

Thorpe St Peter Lincs 45 H5 ham 2m/3km NW of Wainfleet. TF 4860

Thorpe Salvin S Yorks 44 A3 vil 4m/7km W of Worksop. Remains of Elizn manor hse. SK 5281

Thorpe Satchville Leics 36 C3 vil 5m/8km S of Melton Mowbray. SK 7311

Thorpe, South Durham 54 A3* loc 1m S of Whorlton. NZ 1013

Thorpe Street Suffolk 31 E1* loc 1km NW of Hinderclay. TM 0277

Thorpe Thewles Cleveland 54 C3 vil 4m/6km NW of Stockton-on-Tees. NZ 4023

Thorpe Underwood Northants 36 D6* loc 2m/3km W of Rothwell. SP 7881

Thorpe Underwood N Yorks 50 A2* ham 2km SE of Lit Ouseburn. SE 4659

Thorpe Waterville Northants 37 E6 vil 3m/4km NE of Thrapston. TL 0281

Thorpe, West Notts 36 C2* ham adjoining Willoughby-on-the-Wolds to W. SK 6325

Thorpe Willoughby N Yorks 49 G5 vil 3m/4km W of Selby. SE 5731

Thorpland Norfolk 38 B4 loc 3m/5km N of Downham Mkt. TF 6108

Thorpland Hall Norfolk 38 D2* Tudor brick hse beside R Stiffkey 2m/3km NE of Fakenham. TF 9332

Thorrington Essex 31 E6 vil 2m/4km N of Brightlingsea. TM 0920

Thorverton Devon 7 G5 vil 6m/10km N of Exeter. SS 9202

Thrandeston Suffolk 31 E1 vil 2m/4km S of Diss. TM 1176

Thrapston Northants 37 E6 vil 7m/11km SW of Oundle. SP 9978

Threapland Cumbria 52 B1* loc 2m/3km S of Aspatria, adjoining Plumbland to E. NY 1539

Threapland N Yorks 48 C2 loc 2m/4km SW of Grassington. SD 9860

Threapwood Ches 42 A6 vil 3m/5km SW of Malpas. **Upr** and **Lr Threapwood** locs to E and S respectively. SJ 4345

Threapwood Head Staffs 35 F1* loc 2m/3km E of Cheadle. SK 0342

Threave D & G 58 C5. **T. Castle** (A.M.) is 14c tower of the Douglases, on **T. Island** in R Dee 2m/3km W of Castle Douglas. **T. Gardens** (NTS) and NTS School of Practical Gardening 2km SE. NX 7362

Threckingham Lincs. Alternative name for Threekingham, qv.

Three Ashes Som 16 B6* loc 3m/3km NE of Shepton Mallet. ST 6546

Three Bridges Lincs 45 H3* loc 1km S of Saltfleetby St Peter. TF 4388

Three Bridges W Sussex 11 H2 E dist of Crawley. Main-line rly stn. TQ 2837

Three Burrows Cornwall 2 C4* loc 4m/7km NE of Redruth. SW 7446

Three Chimneys Kent 12 D3 ham 2m/3km W of Biddenden. TQ 8238

Threecliff Bay W Glam 23 G6* bay on S coast of Gower peninsula S of vil of Penmaen. SS 5387

Three Cocks (Aberllynfi) Powys 25 F4 vil 3m/5km NE of Talgarth. Named after old coaching inn. SO 1737

Three Crosses (Crwys, Y) W Glam 23 G6* vil 5m/8km W of Swansea. SS 5794

Three Crossways, The Suffolk 31 F2* loc 1km E of Stonham Aspal. TM 1459

Three Cups Corner E Sussex 12 C4 ham 4m/6km E of Heathfield. TQ 6320

Three Dubs Tarn Cumbria 52 D5* small lake 2km N of Far Sawrey. SD 3797

Threehammer Common Norfolk 39 G3* loc 2m/3km N of Horning. TG 3419

Three Hammers Cornwall 6 B6* loc 7m/11km NW of Launceston. SX 2287

Three Holes Norfolk 38 A4 ham astride Middle Level Main Drain 7m/11km SE of Wisbech. TF 5000

Three Horse Shoes Devon 7 G5* ham 2m/4km N of Exeter. SX 9096

Three Households Bucks 18 D2 loc adjoining Chalfont St Giles to W. SU 9893

Threekingham Lincs 37 F1 vil 6m/10km S of Sleaford. TF 0836

Three Lane Ends Gtr Manchester 42 D1* loc 2m/4km E of Bury. SD 8309

Three Legged Cross Dorset 9 G4 vil 4m/7km W of Ringwood. SU 0805

Three Legged Cross E Sussex 12 C4* ham 1km N of Ticehurst. TQ 6831

Three Locks Bucks 28 D5* loc on Grand Union Canal 4m/6km S of Bletchley. SP 8928

Three May Poles W Midlands 35 G6* loc 3m/5km SW of Solihull. SP 1176

Three Mile Cross Berks 18 C4 vil 4m/6km S of Reading. SU 7167

Threemilestones Cornwall 2 D4 vil 3m/5km W of Truro. Sometimes known as Three Mile Stone. SW 7845

Three Oaks E Sussex 12 D5* ham 4m/6km NE of Hastings. TQ 8414

Three Rivers 119 admin dist of Herts.

Three Sisters of Glen Coe, The H'land 74 C5* three gaunt peaks overlooking Glen Coe in Lochaber dist, on S side of glen. From E to W, Beinn Fhada, Gearr Aonach, and Aonach Dubh. NN 15

Threipmuir Reservoir Lothian 65 H2/H3 resr on Pentland Hills 2m/3km SE of Balerno. NT 1763

Threlkeld Cumbria 52 C3 vil 4m/6km E of Keswick. NY 3225

Threshers Bush Essex 20 B1 loc 3m/5km E of Harlow. TL 5009

Threshfield N Yorks 48 C2 vil 1m W of Grassington. SD 9963

Thrift, The 29 G4* loc on borders of Cambs and Herts 3m/4km W of Royston. TL 3139

Thrigby Norfolk 39 H4 ham 4m/6km W of Caister-on-Sea. TG 4612

Thringstone Leics 36 A3 vil 2m/3km N of Coalville. SK 4217

Thrintoft N Yorks 54 C5 vil 3m/5km W of Northallerton. SE 3293

Thriplow Cambs 29 H3 vil 6m/10km NE of Royston. TL 4346

Throapham S Yorks 44 A3* loc adjoining Dinnington to N. SK 5387

Throckenholt Lincs 37 H3/H4* loc 1m NW of Parson Drove. TF 3509

Throcking Herts 29 G4/G5 vil 2m/3km NW of Buntingford. TL 3330

Throckley Tyne & Wear 61 F4 suburb 6m/9km W of Newcastle. NZ 1566

Throckmorton H & W 27 E3 vil on E side of Pershore Airfield and 3m/5km NE of Pershore. SO 9849

Throop Dorset 9 F5* ham 2m/3km NW of Bere Regis. SY 8293

Throphill Nthmb 61 F3 loc 4m/7km W of Morpeth. NZ 1385

Thropton Nthmb 61 E2 vil 2m/3km W of Rothbury. NU 0202

Throston, High Cleveland 54 D2 loc in Hartlepool 2m/3km NW of tn centre. NZ 4833

Througham Glos 16 D1* loc 5m/8km E of Stroud. SO 9207

Throwleigh Devon 7 E6 vil 6m/9km SE of Okehampton. SX 6690

Throwley Kent 21 E6* loc 4m/6km SW of Faversham. Ham of **T. Forstal** 1m S. TQ 9955

Throxenby N Yorks 55 H6* loc in W part of Scarborough. TA 0189

Thrumpton Notts 36 B2 vil 6m/10km SW of W Bridgford. Power stn 1km SW. SK 5131

Thrumpton Notts 44 B3* loc in S part of E Retford. SK 7080

Thrumster H'land 86 F3 vil in Caithness 4m/6km S of Wick. ND 3345

Thrunscoe Humberside 45 G1* S dist of Cleethorpes. TA 3107

Thrunton Nthmb 61 F1* loc 2km SE of Whittingham. **Thrunton Wd** large area to SW planted with conifers. Site of Roman fort 1m NE. NU 0810

Thrupp Glos 16 D1* vil 2m/3km SE of Stroud. SO 8603

Thrupp Oxon 17 G2* loc 2m/3km N of Faringdon. SU 2998

Thrupp Oxon 28 A6 ham on R Cherwell 6m/10km N of Oxford. SP 4815

Thruscross N Yorks 48 D3 loc 2m/3km N of Blubberhouses. **Thruscross Resr** in R Washburn valley to W. SE 1558

Thrushel 4 B2 r in Devon, rising on Dartmoor and flowing W, joining R Lyd at Lifton and running thence into R Tamar 3m/4km E of Launceston. SX 3985

Thrushelton Devon 6 D6 ham 8m/12km NE of Launceston. SX 4487

Thrussington Leics 36 C3 vil 7m/11km W of Melton Mowbray. SK 6415

Thruxton Hants 10 A1 vil 5m/8km W of Andover. T. Airfield to W. 1km NE, site of Roman bldg. SU 2945

Thruxton H & W 26 A4 vil 6m/9km SW of Hereford. SO 4334

Thrybergh S Yorks 44 A2 loc adjoining Rotherham to NE. **Thrybergh Resr** 1m NE. SK 4695

Thulston Derbys 36 A2 ham 4m/7km SE of Derby. SK 4031

Thunder Bridge W Yorks 48 D6* loc 4m/7km SE of Huddersfield. SE 1811

Thundergay, North, Mid, and **South** S'clyde 63 F3 three locs on NW coast of Arran, N of Pirnmill. See also Auchmore, Lenimore. NR 8846

Thundersley Essex 20 D3 tn 4m/7km E of Basildon. TQ 7888

Thundridge Herts 29 G6 vil 2m/3km N of Ware. TL 3517

Thurcaston Leics 36 B3 vil 4m/7km N of Leicester. SK 5610

Thurcroft S Yorks 44 A2 coal-mining vil 5m/8km SE of Rotherham. SK 4988

Thurdon Cornwall 6 B4* loc 6m/9km NW of Holsworthy. SS 2811

Thurgarton Norfolk 39 F2 ham adjoining Aldborough to N. TG 1834

Thurgarton Notts 44 B6 vil 3m/5km S of Southwell. SK 6949

Thurgoland S Yorks 43 G1 vil 3m/5km SE of Penistone. SE 2901

Thurlaston Leics 36 B4 vil 6m/10km SW of Leicester. SP 5099

Thurlaston Warwicks 27 H1 vil 4m/6km SW of Rugby. SP 4671

Thurlbear Som 8 B2 ham 3m/5km SE of Taunton. ST 2621

Thurlby Lincs 37 F3 vil 2m/3km S of Bourne. TF 0916

Thurlby Lincs 44 D5 vil 8m/12km SW of Lincoln. SK 9061

Thurlby Lincs 45 H4* ham 2m/4km E of Alford. TF 4975

Thurleigh Beds 29 E2 vil 6m/9km N of Bedford. Remains of motte and bailey cas. Airfield to N. TL 0558

Thurlestone Devon 4 D6 vil resort above cliffs to N of Bolt Tail and 4m/6km W of Kingsbridge. SX 6742

Thurlow, Great Suffolk 30 B3 vil 3m/5km N of Haverhill. TL 6750

Thurlow Green, Little Suffolk 30 B3 ham 4m/6km N of Haverhill. TL 6851

Thurloxton Som 8 B2 vil 2m/3km SW of N Petherton. ST 2730

Thurlstone S Yorks 43 G1 vil 1m W of Penistone. SE 2303

Thurlton Norfolk 39 G5 vil 5m/8km N of Beccles. Vil of **Low Thurlton** 1km NE. Loc of **T. Links** to S. TM 4198

Thurlwood Ches 42 D5* loc 2km N of Alsager. SJ 8057

Thurmaston Leics 36 B3/C3 suburb 4m/6km NE of Leicester. SK 6109

Thurnby Leics 36 C4 vil 4m/6km E of Leicester. SK 6403

Thurne Norfolk 39 G3 vil on R Thurne 9m/15km NW of Gt Yarmouth. TG 4015

Thurne 39 G3 r rising near Happisburgh, Norfolk, and flowing S through Horsey Mere into R Bure just S of Thurne vil. TG 4015

Thurnham Kent 20 D5 vil 3m/5km NE of Maidstone. TQ 8057

Thurnham Lancs 47 E3 loc 5m/7km S of Lancaster, comprising **Upr** and **Lr Thurnham.** SD 4654

Thurning Norfolk 39 E2 ham 6m/10km S of Holt. SG 0829

Thurning Northants 37 F6 vil 4m/7km SE of Oundle. TL 0883

Thurnscoe S Yorks 43 H1 colliery tn 7m/11km E of Barnsley. SE 4505

Thurrock 119 admin dist of Essex.

Thurrock, Little Essex 20 C4 loc on N edge of Lit Thurrock Marshes 2km NE of Tilbury. TQ 6277

Thurrock, West Essex 20 C4 industrial loc N of W Thurrock Marshes on N bank of R Thames 4m/6km W of Tilbury. TQ 5877

Thursby Cumbria 59 G6/H6 vil 6m/10km SW of Carlisle. NY 3250

Thursden Lancs 48 B4* loc 3m/5km S of Colne. SD 9035

Thursford Norfolk 38 D2 ham 5m/9km NE of Fakenham. T. Green ham 1m NW. TF 9933

Thursley Surrey 11 E1 vil 3m/4km N of Hindhead. **T. Lake** to E. Nature reserve to N. SU 9039

Thurso H'land 86 D1 tn and port on **T. Bay,** N coast of Caithness dist, at mouth of **R Thurso** 18m/30km NW of Wick. R rises in hills SE of Forsinard rly stn and flows N to T. Bay through Loch More and Halkirk. ND 1168

Thurstaston Merseyside 41 H3 vil 3m/4km SE of W Kirby. **T. Common** (NT) to N affords view across R Dee estuary. SJ 2484

Thurston Suffolk 30 D2 vil 5m/8km E of Bury St Edmunds. Loc of **T. Planch** adjoins to S. TL 9265

Thurston Clough Gtr Manchester 43 E1* loc 1km SW of Delph. SD 9707

Thurstonfield Cumbria 59 G5 vil 5m/8km W of Carlisle. **T. Lough** lake to SE. NY 3156

Thurstonland W Yorks 43 F1 vil 2m/3km NE of Holmfirth. SE 1610

Thurton Norfolk 39 G4 vil 3m/4km NW of Loddon. TG 3200

Thurvaston Derbys 35 G1* loc 1km NE of Marston Montgomery. SK 1338

Thurvaston Derbys 35 H1 ham 7m/11km W of Derby. SK 2437

Thuxton Norfolk 39 E4 ham 5m/8km SE of E Dereham. TG 0307

Thwaite N Yorks 53 G5 ham 2km W of Muker. SD 8998

Thwaite Suffolk 31 E2 vil 4m/7km SW of Eye. TM 1168

Thwaite Head Cumbria 52 D5 ham 5m/8km S of Hawkshead. SD 3490

Thwaites W Yorks 48 D4 loc 1m E of Keighley. **T. Brow** vil up hill to S. SE 0741

Thwaite St Mary Norfolk 39 G5 vil 3m/5km N of Bungay. TM 3394

Thwing Humberside 51 E2 vil 8m/13km W of Bridlington. TA 0470

Tianavaig Bay Skye, H'land 79 C5 bay on E coast 3m/5km SE of Loch Portree. NG 5138

Tibbermore Tayside 72 D2 vil 4m/7km W of Perth. To SE is site of battle of 1644 in which Montrose defeated army of Covenanters and gained control of Perth. Vil also known as Tippermuir. NO 0523

Tibbers Castle D & G 58 D2 remains of late 13c cas beside R Nith 2m/3km N of Thornhill. NX 8698

Tibberton Glos 26 C5 vil 5m/8km NW of Gloucester. SO 7621

Tibberton H & W 26 D2* vil 4m/6km NE of Worcester. SO 9057

Tibberton Salop 34 D3 vil 4m/7km W of Newport. SJ 6820

Tibenham Norfolk 39 E5 vil 6m/10km N of Diss. TM 1389

Tibshelf Derbys 43 H5 vil 3m/5km NE of Alfreton. SK 4360

Tibthorpe Humberside 50 D3 vil 4m/7km W of Gt Driffield. SE 9655

Ticehurst E Sussex 12 C4 vil 3m/5km SE of Wadhurst. TQ 6830

Tichborne Hants 10 C2 vil 2m/3km SW of New Alresford. SU 5730

Tickencote Leics 37 E3 vil 3m/5km NW of Stamford. Remarkable Norman chancel arch in ch. SK 9909

Tickenham Avon 16 A4* vil 3m/5km E of Clevedon. ST 4571

Tickford End Bucks 28 D3* loc at E end of Newport Pagnell. SP 8843

Tickhill S Yorks 44 B2 tn 6m/10km S of Doncaster. Remains of Norman cas. SK 5993

Ticklas Point Dyfed 22 B4* headland on S side of St Brides Bay 2m/3km NE of St Brides. SM 8212

Ticklerton Salop 34 B5 ham 3m/4km SE of Church Stretton. SO 4890

Ticknall Derbys 36 A2 vil 2m/4km W of Melbourne. SK 3523

Tickton Humberside 51 E4 vil 3m/4km NE of Beverley. TA 0641

Tidbury Green W Midlands 35 G6* loc 4m/7km SW of Solihull. SP 1075

Tidcombe Wilts 17 G5 ham 3m/5km SW of Shalbourne. SU 2958

Tiddington Oxon 18 B1 vil 4m/6km W of Thame. SP 6504

Tiddington Warwicks 27 F2 vil 2m/3km E of Stratford-upon-Avon. SP 2255

Tiddy 3 H3 r rising at Pensilva, Cornwall, below Caradon Hill and flowing SE into St Germans R below St Germans Quay. SX 3756

Tidebrook E Sussex 12 C4* ham 2m/3km SW of Wadhurst. TQ 6129

Tideford Cornwall 3 H2 vil 5m/8km W of Saltash. Loc of **T. Cross** 1m N. SX 3459

Tidenham Glos 16 B2 vil 2m/3km NE of Chepstow. ST 5595

Tideswell Derbys 43 F3/F4 small tn 6m/10km E of Buxton. SK 1575

Tidmarsh Berks 18 B4 vil 2km S of Pangbourne. SU 6374
Tidmington Warwicks 27 G4* vil 2km S of Shipston on Stour. SP 2638
Tidpit Hants 9 G3 loc 5m/8km NW of Fordingbridge. SU 0718
Tidworth, North Wilts 17 G6 military tn 3m/4km SW of Ludgershall. SU 2349
Tidworth, South Hants 17 F6 military tn 3m/4km SW of Ludgershall. SU 2348
Tiers Cross Dyfed 22 B4 ham 3m/5km N of Milford Haven. SM 9010
Tiffey 39 E4 r rising S of Wymondham, Norfolk, and flowing N through that tn to R Yare 1km E of Barford. TG 1207
Tiffield Northants 28 C3 vil 2m/3km N of Towcester. SP 6951
Tifty Grampian 83 F3 loc 7m/11km SE of Turriff. NJ 7740
Tigerton Tayside 77 E4 vil 5m/7km NW of Brechin. NO 5464
Tigharry W Isles 88 D1 vil on NW coast of N Uist 3m/5km S of Griminish Pt. NF 7171
Tigh Mór na Seilge H'land 80 B5 mt on Glenaffric Forest, Inverness dist, 4m/6km S of head of Loch Affric. Height 3287 ft or 1002 metres. NH 1315
Tighnabruaich S'clyde 63 F1 vil and resort in Argyll on W shore of Kyles of Bute, 3m/4km SW of entrance to Loch Riddon. State forest N and S. NR 9772
Tigley Devon 4 D4 vil 3m/5km W of Totnes. SX 7560
Til 29 E1* upper reaches of R Kym, rising SE of Rushden, Northants. See (R) Kym.
Tilbrook Cambs 29 E1 vil 7m/12km E of Higham Ferrers. TL 0769
Tilbury Essex 20 C4 industrial tn and passenger and container port on R Thames 21m/34km E of London in a straight line. Ferry for pedestrians across r to Gravesend. TQ 6476
Tilbury, East Essex 20 C4 vil 3m/5km E of Tilbury. To S are **E Tilbury Marshes** and R Thames. TQ 6877
Tilbury Green Essex 30 C4* ham 6m/9km SE of Haverhill. TL 7440
Tilbury juxta Clare Essex 30 C4 loc 3m/5km S of Clare. TL 7540
Tilbury, West Essex 20 C4 vil 2m/3km NE of Tilbury. W Tilbury Marshes to S, with Tilbury Power Stn beside R Thames. TQ 6677
Tile Cross W Midlands 35 G5 loc in Birmingham 6m/10km E of city centre. SP 1686
Tilegate Green Essex 20 B1* loc 4m/7km E of Harlow. TL 5108
Tile Hill W Midlands 35 H6 loc in Coventry 3m/5km W of city centre. SP 2878
Tilehouse Green W Midlands 35 G6* loc in Solihull 2m/3km SE of tn centre. SP 1676
Tilehurst Berks 18 B4 par on W side of Reading; also W dist of Reading. SU 6673
Tilford Surrey 11 E1 vil 3m/5km SE of Farnham. SU 8743
Tilgate W Sussex 11 H2 S dist of Crawley. TQ 2735
Tilgate Forest Row W Sussex 11 H2 loc 3m/5km S of Crawley. TQ 2532
Tilham Street Som 8 D1* ham just NE of Ham Street and 4m/7km SE of Glastonbury. ST 5535
Till 44 D4 r rising E of Gainsborough, Lincs, and flowing S into R Witham at Lincoln. SK 9771
Till 67 F4 r rising as R Breamish on S slope of the Cheviot, Nthmb, and flowing E to Bewick, then N as R Till to Chatton, then NW into R Tweed 2m/4km N of Cornhill. NT 8642
Till 9 G1* r rising on central Salisbury Plain and flowing S into R Wylye 1m NW of Gt Wishford, Wilts. SU 0636
Tillers Green Glos 26 C4 ham 5m/8km NW of Newent. SO 6932
Tilley Salop 34 C2 ham 1km SW of Wem. SJ 5027
Tillicoultry Central 72 C5 tn 3m/5km NE of Alloa. Coal-mining, woollen and paper mnfre. NS 9197
Tillingham Essex 21 F2 vil 5m/8km NE of Burnham-on-Crouch. TL 9903
Tillingham 13 E5 r rising near Staple Cross, E Sussex, and flowing E into R Brede at Rye. TQ 9119
Tillington H & W 26 A3 vil 4m/7km NW of Hereford. Vil of **T. Common** 1m NW. SO 4645
Tillington W Sussex 11 F3 vil 1m W of Petworth. SU 9622
Tillyfourie Grampian 83 E5* vil 5m/8km SE of Alford. NJ 6412
Tilmanstone Kent 13 H2 vil 5m/8km W of Deal. TR 3051
Tiln Notts 44 B3* loc 2m/3km N of E Retford. SK 7084
Tilney All Saints Norfolk 38 A3 vil 4m/6km W of King's Lynn. TF 5618
Tilney Fen Side Norfolk 38 A3* ham 2m/3km S of Tilney St Lawrence. TF 5411
Tilney High End Norfolk 38 B3 vil 4m/7km SW of King's Lynn. TF 5617
Tilney St Lawrence Norfolk 38 A3 vil 6m/9km SW of King's Lynn. TF 5414
Tilshead Wilts 17 E6 vil on Salisbury Plain 9m/14km NW of Amesbury. SU 0347
Tilstock Salop 34 C1 vil 2m/4km S of Whitchurch. SJ 5437
Tilston Ches 42 A6 vil 8m/13km NW of Whitchurch. SJ 4551
Tilstone Bank Ches 42 B5* loc 2m/3km SE of Tarporley. SJ 5659
Tilstone Fearnall Ches 42 B5* ham 2km SE of Tarporley. SJ 5660
Tilsworth Beds 28 D5/29 E5 vil 3m/5km NW of Dunstable. SP 9724
Tilt 76 A4 r in Tayside region running SW down Glen Tilt to R Garry at Blair Atholl. NN 8764
Tilton Leics 36 C4 vil 9m/14km NW of Uppingham. Also known as Tilton on the Hill. SK 7405
Tilts S Yorks 44 B1* loc 4m/6km N of Doncaster. SE 5709
Tiltups End Glos 16 D2 ham 2m/3km S of Nailsworth. ST 8497
Tilty Essex 30 B5* loc 3m/5km NW of Gt Dunmow. TL 5926
Tima Water 59 G1 r in Borders region running N to Ettrick Water at Ettrick. NT 2714
Timberland Lincs 45 E5 vil 8m/13km NE of Sleaford. TF 1258
Timbersbrook Ches 42 D5* vil 2m/4km E of Congleton. SJ 8962
Timberscombe Som 7 G1 vil below Exmoor 3m/4km W of Dunster. SS 9542
Timble N Yorks 48 D3 ham 2m/3km S of Blubberhouses. SE 1752
Timewell Devon 7 G3* loc 2m/4km N of Bampton. SS 9625
Timperley Gtr Manchester 42 D2 dist of Altrincham 2km E of tn centre. SJ 7888
Timsbury Avon 16 B5 vil 3m/5km N of Midsomer Norton. ST 6658
Timsbury Hants 10 B2* vil 2m/3km N of Romsey. SU 3424
Timworth Suffolk 30 D1 ham 4m/6km N of Bury St Edmunds. Ham of **T. Green** adjoins to S. TL 8669
Tincleton Dorset 9 E5 vil 5m/8km E of Dorchester. SY 7791
Tindale Cumbria 60 B5* ham 6m/9km E of Brampton. **T. Tarn** lake 1km SW. NY 6159
Tind, The Shetland 89 F6* headland on E coast of Fetlar nearly 1m E of Funzie. HU 6790
Tinga Skerry Shetland 89 E6* group of rocks in Yell Sound lying between islands of Brother Isle and Lit Roe. HU 4180
Tingewick Bucks 28 B4 vil 3m/4km W of Buckingham. SP 6532
Tingley W Yorks 49 E5* vil 2m/3km SE of Morley. SE 2826
Tingrith Beds 29 E4 vil 4m/6km E of Woburn. TL 0032
Tingwall Shetland. See Loch of Tingwall.
Tingwall Shetland 89 E7* dist of Mainland lying between Weisdale Voe and Lax Firth, to NW of Lerwick. HU 4148
Tinhay Devon 6 C6 vil 4m/7km E of Launceston between Rs Lyd and Thrushel at their confluence. SX 3985
Tinker's Hill Hants 10 B1* loc 3m/4km NE of Andover. SU 3947
Tinkinswood S Glam 15 F4* site of Neolithic burial-chamber (A.M.) 1km S of St Nicholas. SJ 0973
Tinnisburn Forest 60 A3 state forest on borders of Dumfries & Galloway and Borders regions 4m/6km SW of Newcastleton. NY 4382
Tinnis Castle Borders. See Drumelzier.
Tinshill W Yorks 49 E4* loc in Leeds 5m/8km NW of city centre. SE 2539
Tinsley S Yorks 43 H2 dist of Sheffield 4m/6km NE of city centre. SK 4090
Tinsley Green W Sussex 11 H2 ham 2m/3km NE of Crawley. TQ 2939
Tintagel Cornwall 6 A6 vil near N coast 4m/7km NW of Camelford. 14c Old Post Office (NT). On headland, **T. Castle** (A.M.), legendary stronghold of King Arthur. SX 0489
Tintern Abbey (Tyndyrn) Gwent 16 A2 ruined medieval abbey (A.M.) on W bank of R Wye 4m/6km N of Chepstow. SO 5300
Tintern (Tyndyrn) Parva Gwent 16 A2 vil on R Wye 4m/7km N of Chepstow. SO 5300
Tintinhull Som 8 C3 vil 4m/7km NW of Yeovil. T. Hse and garden (NT). ST 4919
Tinto S'clyde 65 F5 mt 3m/4km S of Thankerton. Height 2320 ft or 707 metres. NS 9534
Tintwistle Derbys 43 E2 vil 2m/3km N of Glossop. SK 0297
Tinwald D & G 59 E3 vil 4m/6km NE of Dumfries. NY 0081
Tinwell Leics 37 E4 vil 2m/3km W of Stamford. Site of Roman bldg 1m E. TF 0006
Tioram Castle H'land 68 E2* ruined stronghold of the Macdonalds on tidal islet in Loch Moidart in Lochaber dist, opp Dorlin, qv. Sometimes known as Tirrim Castle. NM 6672
Tiphill Head Devon 7 H5* loc on S side of Ottery St Mary. SY 1095
Tipner Hants 10 C4* loc on E shore of Portsmouth Harbour 2m/3km N of Portsmouth city centre. SU 6303
Tippermuir Tayside. See Tibbermore.
Tips Cross Essex 20 C2* loc 3m/5km SE of Chipping Ongar. TL 5800
Tips End Norfolk 38 A5* ham 2km NW of Welney. TL 5195
Tiptoe Hants 10 A5 loc 4m/6km SW of Brockenhurst. SZ 2597
Tipton W Midlands 35 F5 dist of W Bromwich 3m/5km W of tn centre. SO 9592
Tipton Cross Devon 7 H5* loc 3m/5km SW of Ottery St Mary. SY 0592
Tipton Green W Midlands 35 F5* loc 2km N of Dudley tn centre. SO 9591
Tipton St John Devon 7 H5 vil on R Otter 2m/3km S of Ottery St Mary. SY 0991
Tiptree Essex 30 D6 tn 9m/14km SW of Colchester. Jam-making; printing. TL 8916
Tipwell Cornwall 3 H2* loc 2m/4km SE of Callington. SX 3868
Tirabad Powys 24 D4 ham 3m/5km S of Llanwrtyd Wells. SN 8741
Tircanol W Glam 23 H5* loc in Morriston dist of Swansea 4m/6km N of tn centre. SS 6798
Tirdeunaw W Glam 23 G5 loc in Swansea 3m/4km N of tn centre. SS 6597
Tiree S'clyde 69 A7 island of the Inner Hebrides lying 2m/3km SW of Coll. Measures 11m/18km E to W and is of irregular shape, the total area being 29 sq miles or 75 sq km. The island is low-lying and windswept, but the climate is mild. Crofting, fishing, and bulb growing are carried on. Airfield 3m/4km W of Scarinish. NL 94
Tirga Mór W Isles 88 A3* mt in Harris 5m/8km SW of head of Loch Resort. Height 2228 ft or 679 metres. NB 0511
Tirley Glos 26 D4 vil 8m/13km NW of Cheltenham. SO 8328
Tirphil Mid Glam 15 F1/F2 vil 2m/4km NW of Bargoed. SO 1303
Tirril Cumbria 53 E2 vil 2m/4km S of Penrith. NY 5026
Tirrim Castle H'land. See Tioram Castle.
Tirry H'land 85 F5 r in Sutherland dist running S into Loch Shin 2m/3km N of Lairg. NC 5609
Tirryside H'land 85 F5* locality in Sutherland dist, on E side of Loch Shin near mouth of R Tirry. NC 5610
Tir-y-berth Mid Glam 15 F2* loc 2m/3km S of Bargoed. ST 1596
Tir-y-fron Clwyd 41 H5* loc 2m/3km W of Hope. SJ 2859
Tisbury Wilts 9 F2 vil on R Sem 10m/15km W of Wilton. ST 9429
Tisman's Common W Sussex 11 G2* loc 3m/4km SE of Alfold Crossways. TQ 0732
Tissington Derbys 43 F5 vil 4m/6km N of Ashbourne. SK 1752
Tisted, East Hants 10 D2 vil 4m/7km S of Alton. SU 7032
Tisted, West Hants 10 D2 vil 5m/8km SE of New Alresford. SU 6529
Titchberry Devon 6 B3* ham 1m E of Hartland Pt. SS 2427
Titchfield Hants 10 C4 vil 3m/4km W of Fareham. To N, T. Abbey (A.M.), 13c abbey gatehouse converted into mansion in 16c. Also known as Place Hse. SU 5305
Titchmarsh Northants 37 E6 vil 2m/3km NE of Thrapston. TL 0279
Titchwell Norfolk 38 C1 vil 5m/8km E of Hunstanton. Remains of ancient forest off shore to N. TF 7643
Tites Point Glos 16 C1* headland on left bank of R Severn estuary to N of Purton. SO 6904
Tithby Notts 36 C1 ham 2m/3km S of Bingham. SK 6936
Tithebarn Staffs 35 G1* loc 4m/7km E of Cheadle. SK 0741
Titley H & W 25 G2 vil 3m/5km NE of Kington. SO 3360
Titlington Nthmb 67 G6* loc 2m/3km E of Glanton. NU 1015
Titmore Green Herts 29 F5* ham 3m/4km SE of Hitchin. TL 2126
Titsey Surrey 20 A6 ham below S escarpment of N Downs 2km N of Limpsfield. Remains of Roman villa in T. Park. Site of Roman temple to E. TQ 4055
Titson Cornwall 6 B5 ham 4m/6km SE of Bude. Also known as Budd's Titson. SS 2401
Tittenhurst Berks 18 D4 loc at S edge of Windsor Gt Park 1km NW of Sunningdale. SU 9468
Tittensor Staffs 35 E1 vil 3m/5km NW of Stone. SJ 8738
Titterstone Clee Hill Salop 34 C6 prominent hill and landmark 5m/8km W of Cleobury Mortimer, rising to 1750 ft or 533 metres. Extensively quarried on S slope around loc known as Clee Hill, which is name more usually applied also to hill itself. SO 5977
Tittesworth Staffs 43 E5 loc 2m/4km NE of Leek. **T. Resr** 2km W. SK 0059
Tittleshall Norfolk 38 D3 vil 6m/9km SW of Fakenham. TF 8921
Tiumpan Head W Isles 88 C2 headland with lighthouse at NE end of Eye Peninsula, Lewis. NB 5737
Tiverton Ches 42 B5 vil 2km S of Tarporley. SJ 5560
Tiverton Devon 7 G4 mkt and mnfg tn on R Exe 12m/19km N of Exeter. SS 9512
Tivetshall St Margaret Norfolk 39 F6* vil 6m/9km NW of Harleston. **Tivetshall St Mary** vil 1km S. TM 1687
Tividale W Midlands 35 F5* loc in NW part of Warley, 2m/3km W of W Bromwich tn centre. SO 9790
Tivington Som 7 G1* ham, largely NT, 3m/4km W of Minehead. To S, nearby ham of T. Knowle. SS 9345
Tivy Dale S Yorks 43 G1* loc 1km SW of Cawthorne. SE 2707
Tixall Staffs 35 F2 vil 4m/6km E of Stafford. SJ 9722
Tixover Leics 37 E4* vil 5m/9km SW of Stamford. SK 9700
Toab Orkney 89 B6/B7* loc on mainland on W side of Deer Sound, 5m/8km SE of Kirkwall. HY 5006
Toad Row Suffolk 39 H6* loc 2m/3km W of Kessingland. TM 5086
Tobermory S'clyde 68 C3 resort and chief tn of island of Mull, situated on **T. Bay** near N end of Sound of Mull. Wreck of Spanish galleon, blown up in 1588, lies at bottom of bay. Distillery at Ledaig. NM 5055
Toberonochy S'clyde 69 F6 small vil on Shuna Sound on E coast of Luing. NM 7408
Tobson W Isles 88 A2* loc on W coast of Gt Bernera 2m/3km NW of Breaclete. NB 1338
Toby's Hill Lincs 45 H2* loc adjoining Saltfleet to N. TF 4594
Tocher Grampian 83 E4 loc 3m/5km E of Kirkton of Culsalmond. NJ 6932
Tockenham Wilts 17 E3 vil 3m/4km SW of Wootton Bassett. Loc of **T. Wick** 2km N. SU 0379
Tockholes Lancs 47 G5* vil 4m/6km SW of Blackburn. SD 6622
Tockington Avon 16 B3 vil 3m/5km SW of Thornbury. ST 6086

Tockwith N Yorks 50 A3 vil 5m/8km NE of Wetherby. SE 4652
Todber Dorset 9 E2 vil 4m/7km SW of Shaftesbury. ST 8020
Toddington Beds 29 E5 vil 5m/8km N of Dunstable. M1 motorway service area 2km E. TL 0028
Toddington Glos 27 E4 vil 3m/5km N of Winchcombe. SP 0333
Toddington W Sussex 11 F4 loc in N part of Littlehampton. TQ 0303
Todd's Green Herts 29 F5* ham 2m/3km NW of Stevenage. TL 2226
Todenham Glos 27 F4 vil 3m/5km NE of Moreton-in-Marsh. SP 2436
Todhead Point Grampian 77 H3 headland with lighthouse on E coast 4m/6km NE of Inverbervie. NO 8776
Todhills Cumbria 59 H5 ham 5m/8km NW of Carlisle. NY 3663
Todhills Durham 54 B2* loc 1m SE of Willington across R Wear. NZ 2134
Todmorden W Yorks 48 C5 tn on R Calder and on Rochdale Canal 8m/12km NE of Rochdale. Textiles, engineering. SD 9324
Todwick S Yorks 44 A3 vil 6m/10km NW of Worksop. SK 4984
Toe Head W Isles 88 A3 headland on W coast of Harris 6m/10km NW of Leverburgh. NF 9594
Tofshaw W Yorks 48 D5* loc 3m/4km SE of Bradford. SE 1829
Toft Cambs 29 G2 vil 6m/10km W of Cambridge. TL 3555
Toft Ches 42 C3 loc 2km S of Knutsford. SJ 7576
Toft Lincs 37 F3 ham 3m/4km SW of Bourne. TF 0617
Toft Shetland 89 E6* loc, also known as **Boath of Toft,** on NE coast of Mainland 1m NW of Mossbank across **Tofts Voe.** Vehicle ferry to Ulsta on island of Yell. HU 4376
Toft Warwicks 27 H1* loc 3m/5km SW of Rugby. SP 4770
Toft Hill Durham 54 B2 vil 3m/5km W of Bishop Auckland. NZ 1528
Toftingall H'land. See Loch of Toftingall.
Toft Monks Norfolk 39 G5/H5 vil 3m/5km N of Beccles. TM 4294
Toft next Newton Lincs 45 E3 vil 4m/7km W of Mkt Rasen. TF 0488
Toftrees Norfolk 38 D2 ham 2m/3km SW of Fakenham. TF 8927
Tofts H'land 86 F1 loc in NE corner of Caithness dist 4m/6km S of John o' Groats. ND 3668
Tofts, West Norfolk 38 C5 loc 5m/9km NE of Brandon. **W Tofts Mere** is a small lake to S. TL 8392
Toftwood Norfolk 38 D3/39 E3* loc adjoining E Dereham to S. TF 9911
Togston Nthmb 61 G2 vil adjoining Broomhill to N, 2m/3km SW of Amble. Locs of **N Togston** and **Togston Barns** to N and E respectively. NU 2401
Tokavaig Skye, H'land 79 D7 loc near W coast of Sleat peninsula, 2m/3km NE of Tarskavaig. NG 6011
Tokers Green Oxon 18 C4* vil 3m/4km N of Reading. SU 7077
Tokyngton London 19 F3* loc in borough of Brent 7m/12km NW of Charing Cross. TQ 1984
Toldish Cornwall 3 E3* loc 3m/4km S of St Columb Major. SW 9259
Tolland Som 7 H2 vil 3m/5km NE of Wiveliscombe. ST 1032
Tollard Farnham Dorset 9 F3* loc 2km S of Tollard Royal. ST 9515
Tollard Royal Wilts 9 F3 vil 6m/10km SE of Shaftesbury. King John's Hse, former royal hunting lodge. Larmer Tree Grnds, park laid out by General Pitt-Rivers in late 19c (see also Farnham, Dorset). ST 9417
Toll Bar S Yorks 44 A1* vil 3m/5km N of Doncaster. SE 5608
Tollbar End W Midlands 36 A6* loc in Coventry 3m/5km SE of city centre. SP 3675
Toll Creagach H'land 80 C4 mt in Inverness dist 3m/4km SW of dam of Loch Mullardoch. Height 3455 ft or 1053 metres. NH 1928
Tollcross S'clyde 64 D3 dist of Glasgow 3m/5km E of city centre. NS 6363
Toll End W Midlands 35 F5 loc in W Bromwich 2m/3km NW of tn centre. SO 9793
Toller Fratrum Dorset 8 D4 ham 2km W of Maiden Newton. SY 5797
Toller Porcorum Dorset 8 D4 vil 2m/4km W of Maiden Newton. SY 5698
Tollerton Notts 36 C1 vil 4m/7km SE of Nottingham. SK 6134
Tollerton N Yorks 49 G2 vil 4m/6km S of Easingwold. SE 5164
Toller Whelme Dorset 8 C4 ham 3m/4km E of Beaminster. ST 5101
Tollesbury Essex 21 E1 vil 7m/11km E of Maldon. Oyster fisheries. **T. Fleet,** inlet, 2km E. TL 9510
Tollesby Cleveland 54 D3 loc 3m/5km S of Middlesbrough. NZ 5115
Tolleshunt D'Arcy Essex 21 E1 vil 6m/9km NE of Maldon. TL 9211
Tolleshunt Major Essex 21 E1 vil 4m/7km NE of Maldon. TL 9011
Tollomuick Forest H'land 85 D8 deer forest at head of Loch Vaich. NH 3280
Tolmachan W Isles 88 A3 locality on E side of Loch Meavaig, Harris. NB 0905
Tolob Shetland 89 E8* loc on Mainland to N of Sumburgh Airport. HU 3811
Tolpuddle Dorset 9 E5 vil 4m/6km W of Bere Regis. Famous for 'Tolpuddle Martyrs', agricultural labourers transported to Australia for opposing drop in wages, 1834. SY 7994
Tolquhon Castle Grampian. See Pitmedden.
Tolstachaolais W Isles 88 B2* vil on Lewis near E shore of E Loch Roag, 2m/3km NW of Breasclete. NB 1937
Tolsta Head W Isles 88 C1 headland on E coast of Lewis 12m/20km NE of Stornoway. NB 5646
Tolsta, North W Isles 88 C1 vil near E coast of Lewis 2m/3km W of Tolsta Hd. Vil of New Tolsta 1km N. NB 5347
Tolworth London 19 F5 loc in borough of Kingston 3m/4km SE of Kingston tn centre. TQ 1965
Tom a' Chòinich H'land 80 C5 mt on border of Inverness and Ross & Cromarty dists between Loch Affric and Loch Mullardoch. Height 3646 ft or 1111 metres. NH 1627
Tomatin H'land 81 G4 vil in Inverness dist 8m/12km NW of Carrbridge. Distillery. NH 8029
Tomdoun H'land 74 C2 loc in Glen Garry, Lochaber dist, 9m/14km W of Invergarry. NH 1501
Tomich H'land 80 D4/D5 loc in Inverness dist 4m/6km SW of Cannich. NH 3027
Tomich H'land 81 E3* loc on border of Ross & Cromarty and Inverness regions 1m NE of Beauly. NH 5347
Tomintoul Grampian 82 B5 vil and resort in elevated position between R Avon and Conglass Water 10m/16km SE of Grantown-on-Spey. Distillery. NJ 1618
Tomnacross H'land 81 E3 loc in Inverness dist 3m/5km S of Beauly. NH 5141
Tom na Gruagaich H'land. A peak of Beinn Alligin, qv.
Tomnaverie Stone Circle Grampian. See Tarland.
Tomnavoulin Grampian 82 B4 vil in Glen Livet, 5m/8km NE of Tomintoul. Distillery. NJ 2126
Tompkin Staffs 43 E5/E6* loc 4m/7km SW of Leek. SJ 9451
Tonbridge Kent 20 C6 industrial and residential tn on R Medway 28m/45km SE of London. 12c cas. Boys' boarding sch. TQ 5946
Tondu Mid Glam 14 D3/15 E3 vil 3m/5km N of Bridgend. SS 8984
Tone Som 7 H3* ham on R Tone 2km NW of Wellington. ST 1221
Tone 8 B2 r rising on Brendon Hills in Somerset and flowing S to Greenham, then E through Taunton to Burrow Br, where it joins R Parrett. ST 3530
Tonedale Som 7 H3* NW dist of Wellington. ST 1221
Tone Green Som 8 A2* loc across R Tone from Bradford-on-Tone. ST 1723
Tonfanau Gwynedd 32 D4 loc on coast 3m/4km NW of Tywyn. SH 5603
Tong Kent 12 D2* loc 2m/3km N of Headcorn. TQ 8246
Tong Salop 35 E4 vil 3m/5km E of Shifnal. SJ 7907
Tong W Isles 88 C2* vil near E coast of Lewis 3m/5km NE of Stornoway across R Laxdale estuary. NB 4536
Tong W Yorks 49 E5 vil in Bradford 4m/6km SE of city centre. SE 2230
Tongdean E Sussex 11 H4* N dist of Hove. TQ 2807
Tonge Kent 21 E5* loc adjoining Sittingbourne to E. TQ 9364
Tonge Leics 36 A2 ham 5m/7km NW of Shepshed. SK 4123
Tonge Fold Gtr Manchester 42 C1* loc in Bolton 2km E of tn centre. SD 7309
Tonge Hall Gtr Manchester 42 D1 timber-framed hse of 16c, 2km SE of Middleton. SD 8805
Tonge Moor Gtr Manchester 47 G6* loc in Bolton 1m NE of tn centre. SD 7210
Tong Forge Salop 34 D3/35 E3* loc 1m NW of Tong. SJ 7808
Tongham Surrey 11 E1 vil 2m/3km SE of Aldershot. SU 8848
Tongland D & G 58 C6 vil 2m/3km NE of Kirkcudbright. Hydro-electricity power stn below resr. Early 19c rd br by Telford spans R Dee to SW. NX 6953
Tong Norton Salop 35 E3 ham 3m/5km E of Shifnal. SJ 7908
Tong Park W Yorks 48 D4* E dist of Baildon. Dyeworks. SE 1639
Tong Street W Yorks 48 D5 loc in Bradford 2m/4km SE of city centre. SE 1930
Tongue H'land 84 F2 vil near N coast of Caithness dist on E side of Kyle of Tongue. 3m/5km N is **T. Bay.** NC 5956
Tongue End Lincs 37 F3* loc 4m/7km E of Bourne. TF 1518
Tongwynlais S Glam 15 F3 vil at S entrance to narrow glen of R Taff 5m/7km NW of Cardiff. ST 1382
Tonmawr W Glam 14 D2* vil 3m/5km E of Neath. SS 8096
Tòn Mhór S'clyde 62 A1 headland on N coast of Islay 4m/7km SW of Ardnave Pt. NR 2371
Tonna W Glam 14 D2 vil 2m/3km NE of Neath. Site of Roman camp 2km E. SS 7799
Tonpentre Mid Glam 15 E2 loc in Rhondda. SS 9795
Ton-teg Mid Glam 15 F3* loc 3m/5km SE of Pontypridd. ST 0986
Tontine Lancs 42 B1* loc 1km S of Up Holland. SD 5204
Ton-ty'r-bel Gwent 15 G2* loc 2km NE of Oakdale. ST 2099
Tonwell Herts 29 G6 ham 3m/4km NW of Ware. TL 3317
Tonypandy Mid Glam 15 E2 tn in Rhondda valley 3m/4km SE of Rhondda and 5m/8km NW of Pontypridd. SS 9992
Ton-y-pistyll Gwent 15 G2* ham 2km SW of Newbridge. ST 1996
Tonyrefail Mid Glam 15 E3 vil 5m/8km S of Rhondda. ST 0188
Toot Baldon Oxon 18 B2 vil 5m/8km SE of Oxford. SP 5600
Toot Hill Essex 20 B2 vil 2m/4km W of Chipping Ongar. TL 5102
Toot Hill Hants 10 B3 loc 5m/7km NW of Southampton, below prehistoric fort. SU 3718
Toot Hill Staffs 35 F1* loc 4m/6km E of Cheadle. SK 0642
Toothill W Yorks 48 D5* loc 1m S of Brighouse. SE 1421
Tooting Bec London 19 G4* loc in borough of Wandsworth 5m/8km S of Charing Cross. Tooting Bec Common to E. TQ 2872
Tooting Graveney London 19 G4* loc in borough of Wandsworth 6m/10km S of Charing Cross. TQ 2771
Tooting, Upper London 19 G4* loc in borough of Wandsworth 5m/8km S of Charing Cross. TQ 2772
Topcliffe N Yorks 49 F1 vil on R Swale 4m/7km SW of Thirsk. Airfield to E. SE 4076
Topcliffe W Yorks 49 E5* loc 1m SE of Morley. SE 2727
Topcroft Norfolk 39 F5 vil 5m/8km NW of Bungay. Vil of **T. Street** 1m S. TM 2693
Top End Beds 29 E2 SW end of vil of Riseley, 8m/12km N of Bedford. TL 0362
Top Flash Ches 42 C5* small lake beside R Weaver 2m/3km SE of Winsford. See also Bottom Flash. SJ 6764
Topham S Yorks 49 G6* loc 1km NW of Sykehouse. SE 6217
Top of Hebers Gtr Manchester 42 D1 loc 1km N of Middleton. SD 8607
Top of Turton Lancs 47 G6* loc on border with Gtr Manchester, 3m/5km N of Bolton. SD 7214
Top o' th' Meadows Gtr Manchester 43 E1* loc 3m/4km E of Oldham. SD 9606
Toppesfield Essex 30 C4 vil 5m/7km NE of Finchingfield. TL 7337
Toppings Gtr Manchester 47 G6* loc 3m/4km N of Bolton. SD 7213
Top Pool Salop 34 C4* small lake 1km NW of Berrington. SJ 5207
Top Road Suffolk 30 D2* loc just S of Rattlesden. TL 9758
Toprow Norfolk 39 F5 ham 4m/7km SE of Wymondham. TM 1698
Topsham Devon 5 F2 SE dist of Exeter on R Exe estuary. Ancient tn and former port for Exeter. SX 9688
Top-y-rhos Clwyd 41 H5* loc adjoining Treuddyn to N. SJ 2558
Torbay Devon 5 E4 urban area on S Devon coast including tns of Torquay, Paignton, and Brixham, surrounding **Tor Bay,** which extends from Hope's Nose (N) to Berry Hd (S). SX 9184
Torbeckhill Reservoir D & G 59 G3* small resr 4m/6km NE of Ecclefechan. NY 2379
Torbeg S'clyde 63 F4 vil on Arran 1m N of Blackwaterfoot. NR 8929
Torboll H'land 87 A6 loc in Sutherland dist 5m/8km W of Golspie. NH 7598
Torbothie S'clyde 65 F3* loc 1km NE of Stane. NS 8859
Torbrex Central 72 B5* dist of Stirling 1m SW of tn centre. NS 7891
Torbryan Devon 4 D4 ham 4m/6km SW of Newton Abbot. SX 8266
Tor Castle Grampian 82 A2 ruins of cas N of Dallas, 9m/14km SW of Elgin. NJ 1252
Torcross Devon 5 E6 coastal vil 3m/5km N of Start Pt at S end of 1-mile long lagoon behind Slapton Sands. SX 8242
Torduff Point D & G 59 G5 headland on Solway Firth 2m/3km SE of Eastriggs. NY 2663
Torduff Reservoir Lothian 66 A2* small resr in Edinburgh 5m/8km SW of city centre. NT 2067
Tore H'land 81 F2 ham in Ross and Cromarty dist 5m/8km E of Muir of Ord. NH 6052
Torfaen 118 admin dist of Gwent.
Torfrey Cornwall 3 F3* loc 2m/3km N of Fowey. SX 1154
Tor, Great W Glam 23 G6* headland on S coast of Gower peninsula at E end of Oxwich Bay. SS 5287
Torhousemuir D & G 57 D6* loc 3m/5km NW of Wigtown. Ancient stone circle (A.M.). NX 3957
Torkington Gtr Manchester 43 E3* loc 1m E of Hazel Grove. SJ 9387
Torksey Lincs 44 C3 vil on R Trent 7m/11km S of Gainsborough. Site of Roman bldg by **T. Lock** on Fossdyke Navigation to S. **T. Castle,** remains of Elizn mansion. SK 8378
Torloisk S'clyde 68 C4 locality on Mull, on N side of Loch Tuath and 4m/7km S of Dervaig. NM 4145
Torlum W Isles 88 E2 loc on Benbecula 3m/5km S of Bailivanish. NF 7850
Tormarton Avon 16 C3 vil 3m/5km SE of Chipping Sodbury. ST 7678
Tormore S'clyde 63 F4 loc on W coast of Arran 3m/4km N of Blackwaterfoot. Ancient standing stones to E. NR 8932
Tornachean Forest Grampian 82 C5* tract, partly afforested, to SE of vil of Strathdon. NJ 3710
Tornagrain H'land 81 G3 loc in Inverness dist 7m/11km NE of Inverness. NH 7649
Tornaveen Grampian 77 F1 loc 3m/4km N of Torphins. NJ 6106
Torne 44 C1* r rising W of Tickhill, S Yorks, and flowing NE into R Trent at Althorpe, Humberside. SE 8309
Torness H'land 81 E4 loc in Inverness dist 5m/8km S of Dores. NH 5827
Tor Ness Orkney 89 A7 headland at S end of Hoy. Lighthouse. ND 2588
Tor Ness Orkney 89 C6* headland on S coast of Stronsay on E side of entrance to Bay of Holland. HY 6520
Torogay W Isles 88 E1* small uninhabited island off NE coast of N Uist 1km S of Berneray. NF 9278

Toronto Durham 54 B2* vil 1m NW of Bishop Auckland across R Wear. NZ 1930
Torosay Castle S'clyde 69 E5 19c cas near E coast of Mull, 1m N of Lochdonhead. NM 7235
Torpenhow Cumbria 52 C1 vil 2km NE of Bothel. NY 2039
Torphichen Lothian 65 F2 vil 2m/4km N of Bathgate. NS 9672
Torphins Grampian 77 F1 vil 6m/10km NW of Banchory. NJ 6201
Torpoint Cornwall 4 B5 tn beside part of R Tamar estuary known as the Hamoaze. Car ferry to Devonport. SX 4355
Tor Point H'land 81 F4 promontory on E shore of Loch Ness, Inverness dist, 1km NW of Dores. NH 5935
Torquay Devon 5 E4 tn 18m/30km S of Exeter. Chief tn and resort of the Torbay dist, with harbour and several beaches. Noted for mild climate. SX 9164
Torr Devon 4 C5 loc on S side of Yealmpton across R Yealm. SX 5851
Torr a' Chaisteil S'clyde 63 F5 remains of ancient fort (A.M.) at Corriecravie, Arran. NR 9223
Torrachilty Forest H'land 80 D2* state forest in Ross and Cromarty dist around Loch Achilty 4m/6km W of Strathpeffer. NH 4356
Torran H'land 78 D4 locality on N shore of Loch Arnish, Raasay. NG 5949
Torrance S'clyde 64 D2 vil 6m/9km N of Glasgow. NS 6274
Torran Rocks S'clyde 69 B6 scattered group of rocks off SW end of Mull some 5m/8km S of Iona. NM 2713
Torray W Isles 88 C2* small uninhabited island off E coast of Lewis 4m/6km N of Kebock Hd. NB 4220
Torre Devon 5 E4 dist of Torbay 1m NW of Torquay tn centre. SX 9064
Torre Som 7 H1* ham 3m/4km SW of Watchet. ST 0440
Torr, Great Devon 4 C5* ham 3m/4km SW of Modbury. SX 6348
Torridge 118 admin dist of Devon.
Torridge 6 D2 r rising on border of Devon and Cornwall S of Hartland and flowing E to Hele Br, N of Hatherleigh, then N past Torrington to Bideford, then N again to join R Taw and flow into Barnstaple or Bideford Bay. SS 4631
Torridon H'land 80 A2 vil in Ross and Cromarty dist at head of Upr Loch T. **R Torridon** runs W into head of loch, S of vil. **T. Forest** (NTS) is mountainous area to N. NG 8956
Torrie Forest Central 71 G4* state forest 3m/4km S of Callander. NN 6303
Torrin Skye, H'land 79 D6 vil 5m/7km W of Broadford. NG 5720
Torrinch S'clyde 71 E5 island in Loch Lomond 2km SW of Balmaha. Part of nature reserve comprising also Inchcailloch and Clairinch. NS 4089
Torrington Devon 6 D3 hilltop tn above R Torridge 5m/9km SE of Bideford. Also known as Gt Torrington. SS 4919
Torrington, East Lincs 45 F3 ham 5m/7km SE of Mkt Rasen. **W Torrington** vil 1m SW. TF 1382
Torrington, Little Devon 6 D3 vil 2km S of Torrington. SS 4916
Torrisdale S'clyde 63 E4 loc on **T. Bay** on E coast of Kintyre, 1m S of Dippen. **T. Castle** on banks of **T. Water**, stream running E into bay. NR 7936
Torrisdale Bay H'land 86 A2 bay on N coast of Caithness dist W of Bettyhill. NC 6962
Torrisholme Lancs 47 E2 dist of Morecambe 2km E of tn centre. SD 4564
Torry Fife 72 D5 loc on **T. Bay** on N side of R Forth, 5m/8km W of Dunfermline. Vil of **Torryburn** adjoins to E. NT 0186
Torry Grampian 77 H1* dist of Aberdeen 1m SE of city centre across R Dee. NJ 9505
Torrylin Cairn S'clyde 63 F5* ancient cairn (A.M.). on S coast of Arran, S of Kilmory. NR 9521
Torsay S'clyde 70 A4 island of slate off Luing at entrance to Seil Sound. NM 7613
Torside Reservoir Derbys 43 F2* one of a chain of resrs in R Etherow valley, 3m/5km NE of Glossop. SK 0598
Torthorwald D & G 59 E4 vil 4m/6km E of Dumfries. Tower hse dating from 14c. NY 0378
Tortington W Sussex 11 F4 ham 2m/3km SW of Arundel. TQ 0005
Torton H & W 26 D1* loc 2m/4km E of Stourport. SO 8472
Tortworth Avon 16 C2 vil 3m/5km W of Wotton-under-Edge. ST 7093
Torver Cumbria 52 C5 ham 2m/4km SW of Coniston. SD 2894
Torwood Central 65 E1 loc 4m/7km NW of Falkirk. NS 8484
Torworth Notts 44 B3 vil 2m/3km E of Blyth. SK 6287
Toryglen S'clyde 64 D3* loc in Glasgow 2m/4km S of city centre. NS 6061
Toscaig H'land 79 E5 locality at head of Loch T. near W coast of Ross and Cromarty dist, 4m/6km S of Applecross. NG 7138
Toseland Cambs 29 F2 vil 4m/6km NE of St Neots. Hall to W, red brick hse of *c.* 1600. TL 2462
Tosside 48 A3* ham on borders of Lancs and N Yorks 4m/7km W of Long Preston. SD 7656
Tosson Nthmb 61 E2* par containing ham of **Gt Tosson** and loc of **Lit Tosson,** respectively 2m/3km SW and 3m/5km W of Rothbury. NU 0200
Tostock Suffolk 30 D2 vil 6m/10km E of Bury St Edmunds. TL 9563
Totaig H'land 79 F6 locality at entrance to Loch Duich, Skye and Lochalsh dist, opp Eilean Donan. Ferry for pedestrians to Ardelve Pt, at entrance to Loch Long. NG 8725
Totaig Skye, H'land 78 A4 vil on W side of Loch Dunvegan, 4m/6km SE of Dunvegan Hd. NG 2050
Tote Skye, H'land 78 C4 vil 6m/10km NW of Portree. NG 4149
Tote Hill Hants 10 A2* loc 2m/3km S of Lockerley. SU 3024
Tote Hill W Sussex 11 E3* ham 3m/4km NW of Midhurst. SU 8624
Totham, Great Essex 21 E1 vil 3m/5km N of Maldon. **Lit Totham** vil 2m/3km E. TL 8511
Totham, Great Essex 30 D6 vil 3m/5km E of Witham. TM 8613
Totham Hill Essex 21 E1* loc 4m/6km SE of Witham. TL 8612
Totham Plains Essex 21 E1* loc 4m/7km NE of Maldon. TL 8812
Tothill Lincs 45 G3 loc 4m/7km NW of Alford. TF 4181
Totland Isle of Wight 10 A5 resort on **T. Bay** 3m/4km SW of Yarmouth. Bay extends from Warden Pt south-westwards to Hatherwood Pt. SZ 3287
Totley S Yorks 43 G3 dist of Sheffield 5m/8km SW of city centre, comprising locs of **T. Bents, T. Brook, T. Rise,** and **New T.** SK 3180
Totnes Devon 4 D4 tn at head of tidal estuary of R Dart, 7m/11km W of Torquay. Remains of cas (A.M.). SX 8060
Toton Notts 36 B1 loc 2m/4km SW of Beeston. SK 5034
Totscore Skye, H'land 78 B3* loc 2m/3km N of Uig. NG 3866
Tottenham London 19 G3 dist in borough of Haringey 7m/11km NE of Charing Cross. Locs of **S Tottenham** and **Tottenham Hale** to S and SE respectively. TQ 3389
Tottenhill Norfolk 38 B3 vil 6m/10km S of King's Lynn. Loc of **T. Row** 1m NW. TF 6311
Totteridge Bucks 18 D2* NE dist of High Wycombe. SU 8894
Totteridge London 19 F2 loc in borough of Barnet 2km S of Chipping Barnet and 9m/14km N of Charing Cross. TQ 2494
Totternhoe Beds 28 D5/29 E5 vil 2m/3km W of Dunstable. SP 9821
Totties W Yorks 43 F1* loc 1m E of Holmfirth. SE 1508
Tottiford Reservoir Devon 4 D2* horseshoe-shaped resr on E edge of Dartmoor 3m/4km N of Bovey Tracey. SX 8182
Tottington Gtr Manchester 47 H6 tn 2m/3km NW of Bury. Textiles, iron castings. SD 7712
Tottington Norfolk 38 D5 loc 4m/6km S of Watton. TL 8995
Tottleworth Lancs 48 A5* loc 1m W of Clayton-le-Moors. SD 7331
Totton Hants 10 B3 tn at head of R Test estuary 4m/6km W of Southampton. SU 3613
Touchen-end Berks 18 D4 loc 3m/5km S of Maidenhead. SU 8776
Touches Som 8 B3* NE dist of Chard. ST 3309
Touch Hills Central 72 B5 range of low hills 4m/6km W of Stirling. There are some small resrs. NS 7291
Toulston N Yorks 49 F4* loc 1km SW of Newton Kyme. SE 4544
Toulton Som 8 A2 ham at foot of Quantock Hills 5m/8km NW of Taunton. ST 1931
Toux Grampian 83 G2* loc 2m/3km N of Old Deer. NJ 9850
Tove 28 C3 r rising S of Sulgrave, Northants, and flowing generally E into R Ouse 2km NE of Stony Stratford, Bucks. SP 8042
Tovil Kent 12 D2 S dist of Maidstone. TQ 7554
Towan Cross Cornwall 2 C4* loc 2m/3km S of St Agnes Hd. SW 7048
Towan Head Cornwall 2 D2 headland at W end of Newquay Bay and N end of Fistral Bay, 2km NW of Newquay. SW 7963
Towans, The Cornwall 2 B4* loc 1km N of Hayle across harbour. SW 5538
Toward Point S'clyde 63 G1 headland in Argyll on W side of Firth of Clyde, 6m/10km S of Dunoon. **T. Castle** is medieval stronghold 2km W. **T. Quay** is loc just W of T. Castle. NS 1367
Towcester Northants 28 C3 small tn (the Roman *Lactodorum*) on A5 rd (Watling Street), 8m/13km SW of Northampton. Racecourse. SP 6948
Towednack Cornwall 2 B4 ham 2m/4km SW of St Ives. SW 4838
Tower End Norfolk 38 B3* loc 1m N of Middleton. **M. Towers,** moated late 19c hse incorporating 15c brick gatehouse. TF 6617
Tower Hamlets Kent 13 G3* W dist of Dover. TR 3041
Tower Hamlets London 20 A3* borough on N side of R Thames extending from Blackwall (E) to the Tower of London (W) and including dists of Bethnal Green and Stepney, and docks at Blackwall, Millwall, and Wapping. TQ 3582
Tower Hill Ches 43 E4* loc adjoining Rainow to SW. SJ 9475
Tower Hill Herts 19 E2* loc 4m/6km SW of Hemel Hempstead. TL 0302
Tower Hill W Sussex 11 G2* loc 1m SW of Horsham. TQ 1629
Tower Point Dyfed 22 A4 headland on St Brides Bay on S side of The Nab Hd. SM 7810
Towersey Oxon 18 C1 vil 2m/3km E of Thame. SP 7305
Towie Grampian 82 D5 vil on R Don 6m/10km SW of Lumsden. Remains of cas. NJ 4412
Towie Grampian 83 F3 loc and cas 4m/6km S of Turriff. NJ 7444
Tow Law Durham 54 A1 tn 8m/13km NW of Bishop Auckland. Coal, iron, engineering, quarrying. NZ 1238
Town, East Som 7 H2* ham 3m/5km NE of Wiveliscombe. ST 1032
Town, East Som 8 D1* loc adjoining Pilton to E and 2m/3km SW of Shepton Mallet. ST 6040
Town End Bucks 18 C2* loc at Radnage 2m/3km NE of Stokenchurch. SU 7897
Town End Cambs 37 H5 S dist of March. TL 4195
Town End Cumbria 52 D4* loc adjoining Troutbeck to S. 17c hse (NT). NY 4002
Town End Cumbria 52 D6* loc 1km NW of Newby Br. SD 3687
Town End Cumbria 52 D6 ham 2m/4km NE of Lindale. SD 4483
Town End Cumbria 53 D4* loc at NE corner of Grasmere lake, adjoining Grasmere vil to SE. Wordsworth Museum. NY 3406
Town End Cumbria 53 E2* loc adjoining Clifton to S. NY 5326
Town End Cumbria 53 F2* loc adjoining Kirkby Thore to S. NY 6325
Town End Lincs 37 E1* W end of vil of Wilsford. SK 9943
Town End Merseyside 42 B3* loc adjoining Cronton to N. SJ 4988
Townend S'clyde 64 B2* N dist of Dumbarton. NS 4076
Town End W Yorks 48 D6* loc adjoining Golcar to W. SE 0916
Town End Farm Tyne & Wear 61 H5* housing estate in NW part of Sunderland. NZ 3459
Townfield Durham 61 E6* loc just S of Hunstanworth. NY 9548
Town Fields Ches 42 C4* SW dist of Winsford. SJ 6465
Towngate Cumbria 60 B6* loc just NW of Ainstable. NY 5246
Towngate Lincs 37 F3* loc adjoining Mkt Deeping to N. TF 1310
Town Green Lancs 42 A1 loc 2m/3km S of Ormskirk. SD 4005
Town Green Norfolk 39 G4* loc adjoining S Walsham to S. TG 3612
Townhead Cumbria 52 B2* loc just E of Dearham. NY 0735
Town Head Cumbria 52 D4* loc adjoining Troutbeck to N. NY 4103
Town Head Cumbria 53 E2* loc adjoining Cliburn to NW. NY 5825
Town Head Cumbria 53 E3/F3* loc adjoining Crosby Ravensworth to S. NY 6214
Town Head Cumbria 53 F2* loc adjoining Kirkby Thore to E. NY 6425
Town Head Cumbria 53 F2* loc adjoining Dufton to SE. NY 6924
Townhead Cumbria 53 F2* loc 1m SE of Ousby. NY 6334
Town Head Cumbria 53 F3* loc at SW end of Gt Asby. NY 6712
Town Head N Yorks 48 D3* loc adjoining Askwith to N. SE 1748
Town Head N Yorks 48 A2* loc at NE end of Austwick. SD 7768
Town Head Staffs 43 E6/F6* loc adjoining Foxt to NE. SK 0349
Townhead S Yorks 43 F1* ham 1km NE of Dunford Br. SE 1602
Townhead of Greenlaw D & G 58 C5* vil 2m/4km NW of Castle Douglas. NX 7464
Town, High Cambs 30 B2* S end of Burwell. TL 5866
Town, High Staffs 35 F3* loc 2km NE of Cannock. SJ 9912
Town, Higher Cornwall 3 E2* ham 6m/9km N of St Austell. SX 0061
Town, Higher Isles of Scilly 2 A1* vil on island of St Martin's. SV 9215
Townhill Fife 73 E5 loc 2km NE of Dunfermline. NT 1089
Town Hill N Yorks 48 C2* loc adjoining Hebden to N. SE 0263
Town Hill W Glam 23 G6* loc in Swansea 1m W of tn centre. SS 6493
Town Kelloe Durham 54 C2 loc 1m E of Kelloe and 5m/8km N of Sedgefield. NZ 3536
Townland Green Kent 13 E3* loc adjoining Woodchurch to W. TQ 9434
Town Lane Gtr Manchester 42 C2* loc 2m/4km E of Leigh. SJ 6999
Town, Little Ches 42 C2* loc 1m SW of Culcheth. SJ 6494
Town, Little Cumbria 52 C3* loc 1m S of Stair. NY 2319
Town, Little Lancs 47 G4* ham 1km E of Ribchester. SD 6535
Town, Low Nthmb 61 F2* loc 1m SE of Longframlington. NU 1300
Town, Low N Yorks 54 C4* loc on R Tees 2m/4km SW of Yarm. NZ 3910
Town, Lower Cornwall 2 C5* ham on N side of Helston. SW 6529
Town, Lower Devon 4 D3* ham on E side of Dartmoor 4m/6km NW of Ashburton. SX 7172
Town, Lower Dyfed 22 C2 vil on E side of mouth of R Gwaun, opp Fishguard. SM 9637
Town, Lower H & W 26 D2* loc 3m/5km NE of Worcester. SO 8659
Town, Lower H & W 26 B3* loc 8m/13km E of Hereford. SO 6342
Town Moor Tyne & Wear 61 G5* large open space in Newcastle to N of city centre. NZ 2465
Town, North Berks 18 D3* N dist of Maidenhead. SU 8882
Town, North Devon 6 D4 ham adjoining Petrockstow, 4m/6km NW of Hatherleigh. SS 5109
Town, North Hants 18 D6 E dist of Aldershot. SU 8850
Town, North Lancs 48 B4* loc lying to N of Padiham. SD 7936
Town, North Som 16 B6* ham just N of N Wootton and 3m/4km SE of Wells. ST 5642
Town of Lowton Gtr Manchester 42 B2* loc 1m S of Golborne. SJ 6096
Town Row E Sussex 12 C4 loc adjoining Rotherfield to E. TQ 5630
Town's End Bucks 18 C1* loc at N end of Haddenham 3m/5km NE of Thame. SP 7409
Town's End Bucks 28 B5* loc at E end of Marsh Gibbon, 4m/6km E of Bicester. SP 6422

Town's End Dorset 9 G6* loc adjoining Corfe Castle to S. SY 9681
Towns End Hants 18 B5* ham 3m/4km E of Kingsclere. SU 5658
Townsend Herts 19 F1* N dist of St Albans. TL 1408
Towns Gate Gtr Manchester 42 C2* loc 2m/3km W of Urmston. SJ 7394
Towns Green Ches 42 B5* loc 3m/5km E of Tarporley. SJ 6061
Townshend Cornwall 2 B5 vil 3m/5km SE of Hayle. SW 5932
Town, South Devon 5 F3* ham adjoining Kenton to E, 4m/6km N of Dawlish. SX 9683
Town, South Hants 10 D2* loc 1km S of Medstead and 4m/6km SW of Alton. SU 6536
Town Street Suffolk 38 C6* SW dist of Brandon. TL 7785
Town, Upper Avon 16 A5* ham just E of Felton and 6m/9km SW of Bristol. ST 5265
Town, Upper Derbys 43 G5* loc 1km N of Hognaston. SK 2350
Town, Upper Derbys 43 G5* loc on S side of Birchover. SK 2461
Town, Upper Derbys 43 G5* vil 2m/3km SW of Matlock. SK 2758
Town, Upper H & W 26 B3* ham 7m/12km NE of Hereford. SO 5849
Town, Upper Suffolk 30 D2* W end of Pakenham. TL 9267
Town, West Avon 16 A4* vil 4m/6km NE of Congresbury. ST 4868
Town, West Avon 16 A5* loc on N side of Blagdon Lake or Yeo Resr. ST 5160
Town, West Devon 7 F5* ham 3m/5km SE of Crediton, on S side of Newton St Cyres. SX 8797
Town, West Hants 10 D5 loc in S Hayling on Hayling I. SZ 7199
Town, West H & W 26 A2* loc adjoining Kingsland to W, 4m/6km NW of Leominster. SO 4461
Town, West Som 8 D1* loc just N of Baltonsborough and 4m/6km SE of Glastonbury. ST 5435
Town, West W Sussex 11 H3* loc adjoining Hurstpierpoint to W. TQ 2716
Town Yetholm Borders 67 E5 vil on W side of Bowmont Water, 7m/11km SE of Kelso. NT 8228
Tows, Great Lincs 45 F2* loc 3m/4km S of Binbrook. TF 2290
Towthorpe Humberside 50 D2 loc 3m/5km NE of Fridaythorpe. Site of former vil to W. SE 9062
Towthorpe N Yorks 50 B2 vil at S end of Strensall Camp 5m/7km N of York. SE 6258
Towton N Yorks 49 F4 vil 2m/4km S of Tadcaster. To S of vil is scene of Yorkist victory in Wars of the Roses, 1461. SE 4839
Towy (Tywi) 23 E4 r rising on borders of Dyfed and Powys 1m S of Llyn Gynon, Dyfed (24 D2), and flowing S through Brianne Resr to Llandovery. It then turns SW to Llandeilo, then W to Carmarthen, then S into Carmarthen Bay with R Taf. SN 3406
Towy Forest Dyfed 24 D2* afforested area close to border with Powys 7m/11km E of Tregaron. Encloses course of Lit Towy (Tywi Fechan) R. SN 7861
Towy Forest 24 D3 afforested area on borders of Dyfed and Powys partly enclosing Llyn Brianne Resr. SN 8051
Towyn Clwyd 41 F3 loc 2m/3km NE of Abergele. SH 9779
Towyn former name of Tywyn, Gwynedd, qv.
Toy Ness Orkney 89 B7* headland on Mainland on N shore of Scapa Flow 2km S of Kirbister. Beacon. Landing stage on Swanbister Bay to NE. HY 3504
Toynton Lincs 45 F4 vil 2m/3km E of Horncastle. **Low T.** loc 1km NW. TF 2869
Toynton All Saints Lincs 45 G5 vil 2m/3km S of Spilsby. **T. St Peter** vil 1m SE. **T. Fen Side** loc 1m S. TF 3963
Toy's Hill Kent 20 B6* vil 2m/4km SE of Westerham. NT property to N, incl **Toy's Hill Beacon.** TQ 4751
Trabboch S'clyde 56 D2* loc 7m/11km E of Ayr. NS 4321
Traboe Cornwall 2 C6* loc on N edge of Goonhilly Downs 7m/11km SE of Helston. SW 7421
Tracebridge Som 7 H3* loc on R Tone 5m/8km W of Wellington. ST 0621
Tradespark H'land 81 G2 loc in Nairn dist 1m W of Nairn. NH 8656
Traeth Bach Gwynedd 32 D1 sandy combined estuary of Rs Dwyryd and Glaslyn between Harlech and Portmadoc. SH 5736
Traeth Dulas Gwynedd 40 B3* almost land-locked inlet of Dulas Bay on NE coast of Anglesey, 4m/6km SE of Amlwch. SH 4888
Traeth Lafan Welsh form of Lavan Sands, qv.
Traeth-y-mwnt Dyfed 22 D1* bay (NT) 4m/6km N of Cardigan. SN 1951
Trafalgar Merseyside 41 H3* dist of Bebington to S of tn centre. SJ 3383
Trafford 117 admin dist of Gtr Manchester metropolitan county.
Trafford Park Gtr Manchester 42 D2 dist of Stretford 2km NW of tn centre. SJ 7896
Tràigh Mhór Tiree, S'clyde 69 B7 strand of Gott Bay, qv. NM 0547
Tràigh Mhór W Isles 88 D3* strand on Barra on which Northbay Airfield is situated. NF 7005
Traligill H'land. See Inchnadamph.
Trallong Powys 25 E5 ham 3m/5km E of Sennybridge. SN 9629
Trallwn W Glam 23 H5* loc in Swansea 3m/5km NE of tn centre. SS 6996
Trallwng, Y Welsh form of Welshpool, qv.
Tranch (Transh, Y) Gwent 15 G2 loc on W side of Pontypool. SO 2700
Tranent Lothian 66 B2 tn 4m/6km E of Musselburgh. NT 4072
Tranmere Merseyside 41 H3* dist of Birkenhead 1m SW of tn centre. SJ 3187
Trannon 33 G5 r rising 2m/4km SW of Talerddig, Powys, and flowing S to Llawryglyn, then E by Trefeglwys into R Severn on W side of Caersws. SO 0291
Transh, Y Welsh form of Tranch, qv.
Trantlemore H'land 86 B2 loc in Strath Halladale in Caithness dist 7m/11km S of Melvich. Loc of **Trantlebeg** across r to E. NC 8853
Tranwell Nthmb 61 F3 loc 2m/3km SW of Morpeth. NZ 1883
Trap Welsh form of Trapp, qv.
Trapp (Trap) Dyfed 23 G4 ham 3m/4km SE of Llandeilo. SN 6518
Trap's Green Warwicks 27 E1/F1* loc 4m/6km NW of Henley-in-Arden. SP 1069
Trapshill Berks 17 G5* loc 4m/6km SE of Hungerford. SU 3763
Trap Street Ches 42 D4* loc 2m/3km W of Marton. SJ 8268
Traquair Borders 66 B5 vil 2km S of Innerleithen across R Tweed. **Traquair Hse** to N, 17c mansion, with tower of earlier date. See also Elibank and T. Forest. NT 3334
Trash Green Berks 18 B4* loc 1m NW of Burghfield and 4m/7km SW of Reading. SU 6569
Trawden Lancs 48 B4 vil 2m/3km SE of Colne. See also Forest of Trawden. SD 9138
Trawsfynydd Gwynedd 33 E1 vil on E side of Llyn Trawsfynydd 4m/7km S of Ffestiniog. SH 7035
Trawsgoed Welsh form of Crosswood, qv.
Treak Cliff Cavern Derbys 43 F3* cavern to N of Blue John Mine, qv, containing similar deposits. SK 1383
Trealaw Mid Glam 15 E2 vil opp Tonypandy across R Rhondda. SS 9992
Treales Lancs 47 E4/E5 vil 2km NE of Kirkham. SD 4432
Treamlod Welsh form of Ambleston, qv.
Trearddur Bay Gwynedd 40 A4 small resort and westward-facing bay on coast of Holy I., Anglesey, 2m/4km S of Holyhead. SH 2578
Treaslane Skye, H'land 78 B4 locality on W side of Loch Snizort Beag and entrance to Loch T., qv. **Treaslane R** runs N into head of Loch T. NG 3953
Tre-Aubrey S Glam 15 F4* loc 3m/5km SE of Cowbridge. ST 0372
Trebanog Mid Glam 15 E3 loc 2km N of Tonyrefail. ST 0190
Trebanos W Glam 14 C2* loc 1m SW of Pontardawe. SN 7103
Trebartha Cornwall 4 A3* loc 6m/10km SW of Launceston. SX 2677
Trebarvah Cornwall 2 C5* loc 4m/6km NE of Helston. SW 7030
Trebarwith Cornwall 6 A6* loc 2m/3km S of Tintagel. To NW, **T. Strand** (NT), sandy stretch of N coast. SX 0586
Trebeath Cornwall 6 B6* loc 5m/8km NW of Launceston. SX 2587
Trebefered Welsh form of Boverton, qv.
Trebetherick Cornwall 3 E1 vil on Padstow Bay 5m/8km NW of Wadebridge. SW 9378
Trebister Shetland 89 E7* locality on Mainland 2m/4km SW of Lerwick. **Loch of T,** small loch to NE. **Ness of T.**, headland to SE on E side of Gulber Wick. HU 4438
Treble's Holford Som 7 H2* loc 2km N of Combe Florey. ST 1533
Tre-boeth W Glam 23 G5* loc in Swansea 2m/3km N of tn centre. SS 6596
Treborough Som 7 G2 ham on Exmoor 5m/8km S of Dunster. ST 0136
Trebudannon Cornwall 2 D2* vil 2m/3km SW of St Columb Major. SW 8961
Trebullett Cornwall 4 A3 vil 4m/6km S of Launceston. **Lr Trebullett** loc 1km S. SX 3278
Treburley Cornwall 3 H1 vil 5m/8km N of Callington. SX 3477
Treburrick Cornwall 2 D2* loc 5m/7km SW of Padstow. SW 8670
Trebyan Cornwall 3 F2 loc 3m/4km S of Bodmin. SX 0763
Trecastle Powys 24 D5 vil 8m/13km SE of Llandovery. Early Norman motte and bailey cas. SN 8829
Trecco Bay Mid Glam 14 D4* bay between Rhych Pt and Newton Pt on E side of Porthcawl. SS 8376
Trecenydd Mid Glam 15 F3* loc in NW part of Caerphilly. ST 1487
Trecott Devon 7 E5* loc 5m/7km NE of Okehampton. SS 6300
Trecrogo Cornwall 4 A3* loc 3m/5km SW of Launceston. SX 3080
Trecwn Dyfed 22 C3 ham 3m/5km S of Fishguard. SM 9632
Trecynon Mid Glam 15 E1 loc adjoining Aberdare to NW. SN 9903
Tredaule Cornwall 6 B6* ham 6m/10km W of Launceston. SX 2381
Tredavoe Cornwall 2 A5* loc to SW of Penzance. SW 4528
Tredegar Gwent 15 F1 tn on R Sirhowy 21m/33km N of Cardiff. Coal-mining, light engineering. SO 1409
Tredelerch Welsh form of Rumney, qv.
Tredington Glos 26 D4 vil 2m/4km S of Tewkesbury. SO 9029
Tredington Warwicks 27 F3/G3 vil 2m/3km N of Shipston on Stour. SP 2543
Tredinnick Cornwall 3 E2* loc 4m/7km N of St Columb Major. SW 9270
Tredinnick Cornwall 3 G3 loc 3m/4km NW of Looe. SX 2357
Tredogan S Glam 15 F4* loc 3m/4km W of Barry. ST 0767
Tredomen Powys 25 F4 loc 3m/5km NW of Llangorse. SO 1231
Tredrissi Dyfed 22 C2 loc 2m/3km N of Newport. SN 0742
Tredrizzick Cornwall 3 E1* loc 4m/6km NW of Wadebridge. SW 9576
Tredunnock (Tredynog) Gwent 15 H2 vil 4m/6km S of Usk. ST 3794
Tredustan Powys 25 F4* loc opp Trefecca across R Llynfi 2km SW of Talgarth. SO 1332
Tredworth Glos 26 D5* S dist of Gloucester. SO 8417
Tredynog Welsh form of Tredunnock, qv.
Tree, Great Cornwall 3 G3* loc 2km NE of Looe. SX 2655
Treen Cornwall 2 A4 loc 5m/8km W of St Ives. SW 4337
Treen Cornwall 2 A6 vil 3m/5km SE of Land's End. Coast to S and SE owned by NT. SW 3923
Treesmill Cornwall 3 F3* loc 3m/5km S of Lostwithiel. SX 0855
Treeton S Yorks 43 H3 coal-mining vil 3m/5km S of Rotherham. SK 4387
Trefaldwyn Welsh form of Montgomery, qv.
Trefalun Welsh form of Trevalyn, qv.
Trefasser (Trefaser) Dyfed 22 B2 ham 2m/4km S of Strumble Hd. Hill fort to N. SM 8937
Trefdraeth Gwynedd 40 B4* loc on Anglesey at lower end of Malltraeth Marsh, 5m/7km SW of Llangefni. SH 4070
Trefdraeth Welsh form of Newport (Dyfed), qv.
Trefecca Powys 25 F4 ham 2km SW of Talgarth. SO 1432
Trefechan Dyfed 32 D6* loc in S part of Aberystwyth across R Rheidol. SN 5881
Trefechan Mid Glam 15 E1* loc 2m/3km NW of Merthyr Tydfil. SO 0308
Trefeglwys Powys 33 F5 vil 4m/6km W of Caersws. SN 9790
Trefelen Welsh form of Bletherston, qv.
Trefenter Dyfed 24 B2 loc 4m/7km E of Llanrhystud. SN 6068
Trefesgob Welsh form of Bishton, qv.
Treffgarne Owen Dyfed 22 B3* ham 2m/3km W of Hayscastle. SM 8625
Trefflemin Welsh form of Flemingston, qv.
Trefforest Welsh form of Treforest, qv.
Treffynnon Welsh form of Holywell, qv.
Trefgarn Dyfed 22 C3 vil 5m/8km N of Haverfordwest. SM 9523
Trefignath Gwynedd 40 A3* site of ancient burial-chamber (A.M.) on Holy I., Anglesey, 2km SE of Holyhead. Ty Mawr Standing Stone (A.M.) 1km W. SH 2580
Trefil Gwent 25 F6* vil 3m/4km NW of Tredegar. Quarries to N. SO 1212
Trefilan Dyfed 24 B3 ham 6m/10km N of Lampeter. SN 5457
Trefin Welsh form of Trevine, qv.
Treflach Wood Salop 34 A2 loc 3m/5km SW of Oswestry. SJ 2525
Trefnannau Powys 33 H3* loc 5m/8km N of Welshpool. SJ 2015
Trefnant Clwyd 41 F4 vil 3m/4km S of St Asaph. SJ 0570
Trefonen Salop 34 A2 vil 3m/4km SW of Oswestry. SJ 2526
Trefonnen Welsh form of Nash (Gwent), qv.
Trefor Gwynedd 40 B3 loc on Anglesey 4m/6km SW of Llanerchymedd. SH 3780
Trefor Welsh form of Trevor, qv.
Treforest (Trefforest) Mid Glam 15 F3 SE dist of Pontypridd. Industrial estate to SE. ST 0888
Treforgan Welsh form of Morganstown, qv.
Trefriw Gwynedd 40 D5/41 E5 vil on R Crafnant near its confluence with R Conwy, 2km NW of Llanrwst. Flannel mills. **T. Wells,** chalybeate spa 2km N. SH 7863
Trefwrdan Welsh form of Jordanston, qv.
Trefyclo Welsh form of Knighton, qv.
Tref-y-nant Clwyd 41 H6* loc 2m/3km W of Ruabon. SJ 2742
Trefynwy Welsh form of Monmouth, qv.
Tregadillet Cornwall 4 A3* vil 2m/3km W of Launceston. SX 2983
Tregaian Gwynedd 40 B3 loc on Anglesey 3m/4km N of Llangefni. SH 4579
Tregare (Tre'r-gaer) Gwent 26 A6 ham 2m/3km N of Raglan. SO 4110
Tregarland Cornwall 3 G3* loc 3m/4km N of Looe. SX 2557
Tregarne Cornwall 2 D5* loc in Meneage dist 8m/13km E of Helston. SW 7822
Tregaron Dyfed 24 C2 small tn 10m/15km NE of Lampeter. SN 6759
Tregarth Gwynedd 40 C4* vil 2m/3km NW of Bethesda. SH 6067
Tregaswith Cornwall 2 D2* loc 2km W of St Columb Major. SW 8962
Tregatta Cornwall 6 A6* loc 4m/6km NW of Camelford. SX 0587
Tregatwg Welsh form of Cadoxton (S Glam), qv.
Tregeare Cornwall 6 B6* ham 6m/9km W of Launceston. SX 2486
Tregeiriog Clwyd 33 H1 ham 6m/9km S of Llangollen. SJ 1733
Tregele Gwynedd 40 B2 vil near N coast of Anglesey 1m SW of Cemaes Bay. SH 3592
Tregidden Cornwall 2 C6* ham 2km SW of Manaccan. SW 7523
Tregiskey Cornwall 3 E4* loc 4m/6km S of St Austell. SX 0146
Treglemais Dyfed 22 B3 ham 8m/12km NE of St David's. SM 8128
Tregolwyn Welsh form of Colwinston, qv.
Tregonetha Cornwall 3 E2* ham 3m/4km E of St Columb Major. SW 9563
Tregonhawke Cornwall 4 B5* loc 3m/5km SW of Torpoint across St John's Lake. SX 4051
Tregony Cornwall 3 E4 vil 7m/11km SW of St Austell. SW 9245

Tregoodwell Cornwall 6 A6* loc just E of Camelford. SX 1183
Tregoss Cornwall 3 E2* loc 4m/6km SE of St Columb Major. SW 9660
Tregowris Cornwall 2 D5* loc 8m/12km SE of Helston. SW 7722
Tregrehan Mills Cornwall 3 E3* vil 2m/4km NE of St Austell. SX 0453
Tre-groes Dyfed 24 A4 ham 3m/4km N of Llandyssul. SN 4044
Tre-groes Welsh form of Whitchurch (Dyfed), qv.
Tregullon Cornwall 3 F2* loc 2m/3km S of Bodmin. SX 0664
Tregunnon Cornwall 6 B6* loc 6m/10km W of Launceston. SX 2383
Tregurrian Cornwall 2 D2 loc 3m/5km NE of Newquay. SW 8565
Tregustick Cornwall 2 D2* loc 2m/3km NE of Newquay. SW 8463
Tregwhelydd Standing Stone Gwynedd. See Llantrisant.
Tre-gŵyr Welsh form of Gowerton, qv.
Tregynon Powys 33 G4 vil 5m/8km N of Newtown. SO 0998
Trehafod Mid Glam 15 F2/F3 vil 2m/3km W of Pontypridd. ST 0490
Trehan Cornwall 4 B5* loc 2m/3km W of Saltash. SX 4058
Treharris Mid Glam 15 F2 coal-mining vil 5m/7km N of Pontypridd. ST 0996
Tre-Herbert Dyfed 24 B3* loc 1m SE of Lampeter. SN 5847
Treherbert Mid Glam 15 E2 loc in Rhondda valley 3m/4km NW of Rhondda. SS 9498
Trehill (or **Trehyl**) S Glam 15 F4* ham 6m/10km W of Cardiff. ST 0874
Trehopcyn Welsh form of Hopkinstown, qv.
Trehyl S Glam. See Trehill.
Tre-Ifor Mid Glam 15 E1* loc 2m/3km N of Aberdare. SN 9905
Treig H'land 74 D3/75 E3 r in Lochaber dist running N from Loch T. to R Spean 1m below Loch Moy. NN 3579
Trekenner Cornwall 4 A3* vil 4m/6km S of Launceston. SX 3478
Treknow Cornwall 6 A6* vil near N coast at Trebarwith Strand, 4m/6km NW of Camelford. SX 0586
Trelai Welsh form of Ely (dist of Cardiff), qv.
Trelales Welsh form of Laleston, qv.
Trelan Cornwall 2 C6* loc on Goonhilly Downs 8m/12km SE of Helston. SW 7418
Trelash Cornwall 6 B6* loc 6m/9km E of Boscastle. SX 1890
Trelawnyd Clwyd 41 G3 vil 2m/4km SE of Prestatyn. SJ 0879
Trelech Dyfed 23 E3 vil 7m/11km S of Newcastle Emlyn. SN 2830
Trelech a'r Betws Dyfed 23 E3 loc 8m/12km NW of Carmarthen. SN 3026
Treleddyd-fawr Dyfed 22 A3 ham 2m/3km N of St David's. SM 7527
Treletert Welsh form of Letterston, qv.
Trelewis Mid Glam 15 F2 vil adjoining Treharris to E. ST 1097
Treligga Cornwall 3 E1* ham 3m/5km W of Camelford. Stretch of coast to SW is NT. SX 0584
Trelights Cornwall 3 E1 vil 4m/7km N of Wadebridge. SW 9979
Trelill Cornwall 3 E1* ham 5m/8km SW of Camelford. SX 0478
Trelissick Cornwall 2 D4* hse with garden, park, farmland and wds, all NT, 4m/6km S of Truro, overlooking R Fal. SW 8339
Trelleck (Tryleg) Gwent 16 A1 vil 5m/8km S of Monmouth. To SW, three boundary stones known as Harold's Stones, Bronze Age monoliths. **T. Grange** loc 2m/4km S. SO 5005
Trelogan Clwyd 41 G3* vil 3m/4km W of Mostyn. SJ 1180
Trelowla Cornwall 3 G3* loc 3m/5km NE of Looe. SX 2956
Treludderow Cornwall 2 D3* loc 4m/6km S of Newquay. SW 8155
Trelung Ness Grampian 77 H3 headland on E coast 3m/4km S of Stonehaven. NO 8881
Trelydan Powys 34 A3* loc 2m/3km N of Welshpool. SJ 2310
Trelystan Powys 34 A4* loc 3m/5km SE of Welshpool. SJ 2603
Tremadoc Gwynedd 32 D1 vil 1m N of Portmadoc. Site of Roman bath hse at W end of vil. SH 5540
Tremadoc Bay Gwynedd 32 B2, C2 large bay on S side of Lleyn peninsula, its bow-shaped coastline extending from Pencilan Hd in the W to Morfa Dyffryn in the E. SH 5234
Tremail Cornwall 6 AC ham 4m/7km NE of Camelford. SX 1686
Tremain Dyfed 22 D1 ham 2m/4km SW of Aberporth. SN 2348
Tremaine Cornwall 6 B6 vil 7m/11km NW of Launceston. SX 2389
Tremains Mid Glam 15 E3* loc 2km E of Bridgend. SS 9279
Tremar Cornwall 3 G2 vil 3m/4km N of Liskeard. SX 2568
Trematon Cornwall 3 H2 vil 2m/4km W of Saltash. SX 3959
Trembraze Cornwall 3 G2* loc in NE part of Liskeard. SX 2565
Tremeirchion Clwyd 41 G4 vil 5m/8km N of Denbigh. SJ 0873
Tremethick Cross Cornwall 2 A5 loc 2m/3km W of Penzance. SW 4430
Tremollett Cornwall 3 G1* loc 6m/9km NW of Callington. SX 2975
Tremore Cornwall 3 E2* loc 4m/6km W of Bodmin. SX 0164
Tremorfa S Glam 15 G4* dist of Cardiff 2m/3km E of city centre. ST 2077
Tre-mostyn Clwyd 41 G3* loc 1m W of Mostyn. SJ 1580
Trenance Cornwall 2 D2* vil on coast 5m/7km NE of Newquay. SW 8567
Trenance Cornwall 3 E2* ham 4m/6km W of Wadebridge. SW 9270
Trenarren Cornwall 3 E3* ham above St Austell Bay 3m/4km SE of St Austell. SX 0348
Trench Salop 34 D3* loc 2m/3km NW of Oakengates. SJ 6913
Trench Green Oxon 18 B4* loc 3m/5km NW of Reading. SU 6877
Trencreek Cornwall 2 D2* loc on SE edge of Newquay. SW 8260
Trencrom Hill Cornwall 2 B4 hill (NT) 3m/4km S of St Ives. SW 5136
Trenear Cornwall 2 C5* ham 3m/5km N of Helston. SW 6831
Treneglos Cornwall 6 B6* vil 8m/13km NW of Launceston. SX 2088
Trenewan Cornwall 3 F3 loc 3m/5km E of Fowey across r. SX 1753
Trengune Cornwall 6 B5 loc 6m/10km NE of Boscastle. SX 1893
Trengwainton Cornwall 2 A5* hse with garden and park (NT) 2m/3km W of Penzance. SW 4431
Trent. Alternative name for Dorset r also known as Piddle, qv.
Trent Dorset 8 D3 vil 3m/5km NE of Yeovil. ST 5918
Trent 50 D5 r rising near Biddulph Moor, Staffs, and flowing by Stoke-on-Trent, Stone, Rugeley, Burton upon Trent, Nottingham, Newark-on-Trent, and Gainsborough, to join R Ouse and form R Humber 7m/12km E of Goole, Humberside. Chief tributaries are Rs Sow, Tame, Soar, Devon to right bank, and Rs Blyth, Dove, Derwent, Idle to left. Tidal to Cromwell Lock, E of Cromwell, Notts. SE 8623
Trent and Mersey Canal 36 A2-42 B3 canal linking R Trent near Shardlow, Derbys, with Bridgewater Canal at Preston Brook, Ches.
Trentham Staffs 35 E1 loc 3m/5km S of Stoke-on-Trent. R Trent flows through public park containing large lake. SJ 8641
Trentishoe Devon 7 E1 ham on N coast 5m/7km W of Lynton. SS 6448
Trent Port Lincs 44 C3* loc on E bank of R Trent SW of Marton. SK 8381
Trent Vale Staffs 35 E1* loc in Stoke-on-Trent 2km S of city centre. SJ 8643
Trenwheal Cornwall 2 B5* loc 4m/7km NW of Helston. SW 6132
Treoes S Glam 15 E4 vil 3m/4km E of Bridgend. SS 9478
Treopert Welsh form of Granston, qv.
Treorchy (Treorci) Mid Glam 15 E2 tn in Rhondda valley 8m/13km NW of Pontypridd. SS 9596
Treorci Welsh form of Treorchy, qv.
Treowen Gwent 15 G2* loc in N part of Newbridge. ST 2098
Treowman Welsh form of Brimaston, qv.
Trequite Cornwall 3 E1* ham 4m/6km NE of Wadebridge. SX 0276
Tre'r-ddol Dyfed 32 D5 loc 2m/3km N of Talybont. Museum containing local relics. SN 6592
Tre'r-gaer Welsh form of Tregare, qv.
Trerhyngyll (or **Trerhingyll**) S Glam 15 E4* ham 2km N of Cowbridge. ST 0076
Trerice Cornwall 2 D3* manor hse (NT) rebuilt in 1571, 3m/5km SE of Newquay. SW 8458
Trerule Foot Cornwall 3 G2 ham 6m/10km W of Saltash. SX 3358
Tresaith Dyfed 23 E1 coastal vil 2km E of Aberporth. SN 2751
Tresco Isles of Scilly 2 A1 second largest of the islands, and one of five which are inhabited. Nearly divided by large freshwater lake known as Great Pool. SV 8915
Trescott Staffs 35 E4 loc 4m/7km W of Wolverhampton. SO 8497
Trescowe Cornwall 2 B5 ham 4m/7km SE of Hayle. SW 5730
Tresean Cornwall 2 D3* loc 3m/4km SW of Newquay. SW 7858
Tresham Avon 16 C2 vil 3m/4km SE of Wotton-under-Edge. ST 7991
Treshnish S'clyde 68 B4 loc near W coast of Mull, 2m/4km SW of Calgary and 2km E of the headland of **Treshnish Pt.** NM 3548
Treshnish Isles S'clyde 68 B4, 69 A5 group of islands and rocks of Inner Hebrides, W of Mull and SE of Coll. Although uninhabited by man, the islands have a large population of seals, sea birds, and rabbits. See also Bac Mór and Bac Beag, Cairn na Burgh, Fladda, Lunga, Sgeir a' Chaisteil, Sgeir an Eirionnaich, Sgeir an Fheòir, Sgeir na h-Iolaire. Bac Mór is also known as Dutchman's Cap. NM 24
Tresilian Bay S Glam 15 E4* small bay on coast of Bristol Channel 2km SW of Llantwit Major. SS 9467
Tresillian Cornwall 2 D4* vil at head of creek of **R Tresillian** or Tresallian which rises some 6m/9km N and flows into R Truro. Vil is 3m/5km E of Truro. SW 8646
Tresimwn Welsh form of Bonvilston, qv.
Tresinney Cornwall 3 F1 loc 2km S of Camelford. SX 1081
Treskinnick Cross Cornwall 6 B5* loc 5m/8km S of Bude. SX 2098
Treslea Cornwall 3 F2* loc 4m/7km E of Bodmin. SX 1368
Tresmeer Cornwall 6 B6* vil 6m/11km NW of Launceston. SX 2387
Tres Ness Orkney 89 C5 headland at SE point of island of Sanday. HY 7137
Tresowes Green Cornwall 2 B5* ham 4m/7km W of Helston. SW 5929
Tresparrett Cornwall 6 A6 ham 3m/5km E of Boscastle. **T. Posts** is loc 1m NE. SX 1491
Tressait Tayside 75 H5 vil on N side of Loch Tummel, 5m/8km SW of Blair Atholl. NN 8160
Tressa Ness Shetland 89 F5* headland on N coast of Fetlar almost due N of Houbie. **Holm of Tressaness** island rock off headland. HU 6294
Tresta Shetland 89 E7 loc on Mainland at head of **T. Voe,** inlet 2m/3km E of Bixter. HU 3651
Tresta Shetland 89 F6* loc on S coast of Fetlar at head of large bay called **Wick of T.** HU 6190
Treswell Notts 44 C3 vil 5m/8km E of E Retford. SK 7879
Treswithian Cornwall 2 C4* loc 1m W of Camborne. SW 6340
Tre Taliesin Dyfed 32 D5 ham 2km N of Talybont. Also known as Taliesin. See Bedd Taliesin. SN 6591
Treteio Welsh form of Tretio, qv.
Trethevy Cornwall 6 A6* vil near N coast 4m/6km NW of Camelford. SX 0789
Trethevy Quoit Cornwall 3 G2* cromlech (A.M.) 3m/4km N of Liskeard. SX 2568
Trethewey Cornwall 2 A6* ham 3m/4km SE of Land's End. SW 3823
Trethurgy Cornwall 3 E3 vil 3m/4km NE of St Austell. SX 0355
Tretio (Treteio) Dyfed 22 A3 loc 3m/5km NE of St David's. SM 7828
Tretire H & W 26 A5* ham 5m/8km W of Ross-on-Wye. SO 5223
Tretomas Mid Glam 15 G3* loc adjoining Bedwas to E. ST 1888
Tretomas Welsh form of Thomastown, qv.
Tretower (Tretwr) Powys 25 G5 vil surrounded by orchards 3m/4km NW of Crickhowell. Ruined 12c cas (A.M.). **T. Court** (A.M.), 14c–15c manor hse, altered in 17c. SO 1821
Tretwr Welsh form of Tretower, qv.
Treuddyn Clwyd 41 H5 vil 4m/6km S of Mold. SJ 2558
Trevadlock Cornwall 4 A3* loc 6m/9km SW of Launceston. SX 2679
Trevalga Cornwall 6 A6 vil near N coast 2km SW of Boscastle. SX 0890
Trevalyn (Trefalun) Clwyd 42 A5 vil 1m E of Rossett. SJ 3856
Trevarnon Cornwall 2 B4* loc 3m/4km NE of Hayle. **T. Round** is an ancient earthwork. SW 5940
Trevarrack Cornwall 2 B5* loc just N of Penzance. SW 4731
Trevarren Cornwall 2 D2* loc 2m/3km S of St Columb Major. SW 9160
Trevarrian Cornwall 2 D2* ham 4m/6km NE of Newquay. SW 8566
Trevarrick Cornwall 3 E4* loc 2m/4km SW of Mevagissey. SW 9843
Trevaughan Dyfed 22 D4 loc on S side of Whitland across R Taf. SN 1915
Trevaughan Dyfed 23 F3/F4 loc adjoining Carmarthen to NW. SN 4021
Trevaunance Cove Cornwall 2 C3*. See St Agnes. SW 7251
Trevaylor Stream 2 A5* small r rising 4m/6km N of Penzance, Cornwall, and flowing into Mount's Bay at Chyandour. SW 4831
Treveighan Cornwall 3 F1* ham 3m/5km SW of Camelford. SX 0779
Trevelgue Head Cornwall 2 D2 headland at E end of Newquay Bay, 1m NE of Newquay. SW 8263
Trevellas Cornwall 2 C3* vil 2m/3km S of Perranporth. SX 7452
Trevella Stream 2 D4* r rising N of St Erme, Cornwall, and flowing into Tresillian or Tresallian R 1m below Tresillian vil. SW 8645
Trevelmond Cornwall 3 G2* vil 3m/5km W of Liskeard. SX 2063
Trevenen Cornwall 2 C5* loc 2m/3km NE of Helston. SW 6829
Treverbyn Cornwall 3 E3* loc 3m/5km N of St Austell. SX 0157
Treverbyn Cornwall 3 E3* loc 3m/5km NE of St Austell. SX 0356
Treverna Cornwall 2 C5* ham 3m/5km W of Falmouth. SW 7531
Trevescan Cornwall 2 A5 loc to E of Land's End. SW 3524
Trevethin Gwent 15 G2* loc 1m SE of Abersychan. SO 2702
Trevethin Gwent 15 G2* loc 1km N of Pontypool. SO 2801
Trevigro Cornwall 3 G2* loc 2km W of Callington. SX 3369
Trevilla Cornwall 2 D4 ham 4m/6km S of Truro. SW 8239
Trevine (Trefin) Dyfed 22 B3 vil near coast 7m/11km NE of St David's. SM 8332
Treviscoe Cornwall 3 E3 vil in china clay dist 5m/8km NW of St Austell. SW 9455
Trevivian Cornwall 6 B6* loc 4m/7km E of Camelford. SX 1785
Trevone Cornwall 2 D1 coastal vil 2m/3km W of Padstow. SW 8975
Trevor (Trefor) Clwyd 41 H6* loc 2m/4km W of Ruabon. SJ 2742
Trevor (Trefor) Gwynedd 40 B6 vil near coast of Caernarvon Bay 12m/19km SW of Caernarvon. SH 3746
Trevor Gardens E Sussex 12 B5* loc adjoining Glynde to S. TQ 4508
Trevose Head Cornwall 2 D1 headland with lighthouse on N coast 4m/7km W of Padstow. SW 8476
Trewalder Cornwall 3 F1 ham 2m/3km W of Camelford. SX 0782
Trewallter Welsh form of Walterston, qv.
Trewarmett Cornwall 6 A6 ham 3m/5km NW of Camelford. SX 0686
Trewarthenick Cornwall 2 D4* loc 5m/8km E of Truro. SW 9044
Trewarveneth Cornwall 2 A5* loc just S of Penzance. SW 4627
Trewassa Cornwall 6 A6* loc 4m/6km NE of Camelford. SX 1486
Trewavas Head Cornwall 2 B5 headland 4m/6km W of Helston. SW 5926
Trewellard Cornwall 2 A5 loc 2m/3km N of St Just. SW 3733
Trewen Cornwall 6 B6* vil 5m/8km W of Launceston. SX 2583
Trewen H & W 26 A5* loc 4m/7km NE of Monmouth. SO 5318
Trewennack Cornwall 2 C5* loc on NE side of Helston. SW 6828
Trewent Dyfed 22 C5/C6 loc 3m/5km SE of Pembroke. **Trewent Pt,** headland 1m E at S end of bay known as Freshwater East. SS 0197
Trewethern Cornwall 3 E1* loc 3m/5km NE of Wadebridge. SX 0076
Trewhitt Nthmb 61 E1 loc 4m/6km NW of Rothbury. NU 0005
Trewidland Cornwall 3 G2* vil 3m/5km S of Liskeard. SX 2559
Trewiliam Welsh form of Williamstown, qv.

Trewint Cornwall 6 B5 loc 6m/9km S of Bude. SX 1897
Trewint Cornwall 6 B6* ham 7m/12km SW of Launceston. SX 2280
Trewithian Cornwall 2 D4 ham 4m/6km NE of St Mawes. SW 8737
Trewoon Cornwall 3 E3* vil on W outskirts of St Austell. SW 9952
Treworga Cornwall 2 D4* ham 6m/9km SE of Truro. SW 8940
Treworlas Cornwall 2 D4* loc 5m/8km NE of St Mawes. SW 8938
Treworthal Cornwall 2 D4* loc 4m/7km NE of St Mawes. SW 8839
Trewwern Powys 34 A3 vil at S end of Breidden Hills 4m/7km NE of Welshpool. SJ 2811
Trewyddel Welsh form of Moylgrove, qv.
Tre-wyn Gwent 25 H5* loc 1km W of Pandy. SO 3222
Treyarnon Cornwall 2 D1 loc on westward-facing coast 4m/6km W of Padstow. SW 8673
Treyford W Sussex 11 E3 ham 4m/7km SW of Midhurst. SU 8218
Trezaise Cornwall 3 E3* loc 5m/7km N of St Austell. SW 9959
Triangle Staffs 35 F3/F4* loc 2km N of Brownhills. SK 0507
Triangle W Yorks 48 C5 vil 2m/3km SW of Sowerby Br. SE 0422
Trickett's Cross Dorset 9 G4 loc 6m/10km N of Bournemouth. SU 0801
Triermain Cumbria 60 B4 loc 3m/4km W of Gilsland. Fragment of 14c cas. NY 5966
Triffleton Dyfed 22 C3* loc 1km N of Spittal. SM 9724
Trimdon Durham 54 C2 vil 3m/5km N of Sedgefield. **T. Colliery** vil 2km NE. **T. Grange** vil 1m N. NZ 3634
Trimingham Norfolk 39 G1 vil on coast rd 4m/7km SE of Cromer. TG 2838
Trimley Suffolk 31 F4 vil 2m/4km NW of Felixstowe. TM 2736
Trimley Heath Suffolk 31 F4 vil 3m/5km NW of Felixstowe. TM 2737
Trimley Lower Street Suffolk 31 F4* loc 3m/5km NW of Felixstowe. TM 2636
Trimontium Borders. See Newstead. NT 5634
Trimpley H & W 35 E6 loc 3m/4km NW of Kidderminster. SO 7978
Trimsaran Dyfed 23 F5 vil 4m/7km NW of Llanelli. SN 4504
Trinafour Tayside 75 G4 locality in Glen Errochty, 1m SE of dam of Loch Errochty. NN 7264
Trinant Gwent 15 G2* loc 2km N of Newbridge. ST 2099
Tring Herts 18 D1 tn 5m/8km NW of Berkhamsted. SP 9211
Tringford Herts 28 D6* loc 2km N of Tring on W side of resr and nature reserve. SP 9113
Tring Wharf Herts 18 D1* loc on branch of Grand Union Canal 1m N of Tring. SP 9213
Trinity Lothian 66 A1* dist of Edinburgh 2m/3km N of city centre. NT 2476
Trinity Tayside 77 F4 vil 2km N of Brechin. NO 6062
Trinity College Tayside 72 D2 boys' public school on S bank of R Almond 9m/15km NW of Perth. Also known as Glenalmond. NN 9728
Trinkeld Cumbria 46 D1* loc 2km SW of Ulverston. SD 2776
Triscombe Som 7 G2* ham on Exmoor 1km S of Wheddon Cross and 6m/9km SW of Dunster. SS 9237
Triscombe Som 7 H2* ham at foot of Quantock Hills 7m/11km SE of Watchet. ST 1535
Trislaig H'land 74 C4 locality on W shore of Loch Linnhe opp Fort William. NN 0874
Trispen Cornwall 2 D3 vil 4m/6km N of Truro. SW 8450
Tritlington Nthmb 61 G2 vil 4m/7km N of Morpeth. NZ 2092
Trochrie Tayside 76 A6 vil in Strath Braan 4m/6km SW of Dunkeld. NN 9740
Troddi Welsh form of (R) Trothy, qv.
Troedrhiwfuwch Mid Glam 15 F1* ham in Rhymney Valley 3m/5km S of Tredegar. SO 1304
Troed-rhiw-gwair Gwent 15 F1* loc 2m/3km SE of Tredegar. SO 1506
Troedyraur Dyfed 23 E2 ham 3m/5km NE of Newcastle Emlyn. SN 3245
Troedyrhiw Mid Glam 15 F2 vil on R Taff 3m/5km S of Merthyr Tydfil. SO 0702
Trofarth Clwyd 41 E4* loc 3m/5km N of Llangernyw. SH 8767
Trollers Gill N Yorks 48 D2 limestone gorge above Percival Hall 2km NE of Appletreewick. SE 0661
Tromie H'land 75 G2 r in Badenoch and Strathspey dist running N from Loch an t-Seilich down Glen T. to R Spey, 2km E of Kingussie. NH 7701
Tromode Isle of Man 46 B5* loc 2km N of Douglas. SC 3777
Tronach Head Grampian 82 D1* headland on N coast between Findochty and Portknockie. NJ 4768
Trondra Shetland 89 E8* island lying S of Scalloway, Mainland. Is 4km long N to S and nowhere more than 1km wide. Rd br link with Mainland across narrow strait at N end, and with W Burra near S end. Sparsely inhabited. HU 3937
Troon Cornwall 2 C4 vil 2m/3km SE of Camborne. SW 6638
Troon S'clyde 64 B5 port and resort on Firth of Clyde at N end of Ayr Bay 6m/9km N of Ayr. Industries include shipbuilding, shipbreaking, marine engineering, hosiery mnfre, sawmilling. NS 3230
Trossachs, The Central 71 F4 area surrounding wooded gorge between Loch Achray and Loch Katrine. NN 4907
Troston Suffolk 30 D1 vil 3m/4km NW of Ixworth. TL 8972
Trostre Welsh form of Trostrey, qv.
Trostrey (Trostre) Gwent 15 H1 loc 2m/4km NW of Usk. SO 3604
Troswell Cornwall 6 B6 loc 7m/11km NW of Launceston. SX 2591
Trothy (Troddi) 26 A6 r rising E of Pandy, Gwent, and flowing S then E into R Wye 1m S of Monmouth. SO 5111
Trotternish Skye, H'land 78 C4 dist and peninsula N of isthmus between Portree and the head of Loch Snizort Beag. NG 4552
Trottick Tayside 73 G2* dist of Dundee 2m/3km N of city centre. NO 4033
Trottiscliffe Kent 20 C5 vil below S slope of N Downs 2km N of Wrotham Heath. TQ 6460
Trotton W Sussex 11 E3 ham on R Rother spanned here by 15c br, 3m/5km W of Midhurst. SU 8322
Trotton Marsh W Sussex 11 E3* loc 5m/8km E of Petersfield. SU 8225
Trough Gate Lancs 48 B5* loc adjoining Britannia to SE, 2m/3km SE of Bacup. SD 8821
Trough of Bowland Lancs. See Forest of Bowland.
Troup Head Grampian 83 F1 headland on N coast 9m/14km E of Banff and 11m/17km W of Fraserburgh. NJ 8267
Troutbeck Cumbria 52 D2 loc 8m/13km E of Keswick. Sites of Roman camps to N and W. NY 3827
Troutbeck Cumbria 52 D4 vil 3m/5km N of Windermere. See also Town End. **Troutbeck Br** ham 2m/3km S. NY 4002
Trout Beck 52 D5* r rising near Stony Cove Pike, Cumbria, and flowing S into Windermere 2km NW of Windermere tn. SD 3999
Trout Beck 53 F2* r rising S of High Cup Nick, Cumbria, and flowing W into R Eden at Kirkby Thore. NY 6325
Troway Derbys 43 H3* ham 2m/4km E of Dronfield. SK 3879
Trowbridge S Glam 15 G3* loc in Cardiff 4m/6km NE of city centre. ST 2380
Trowbridge Wilts 16 D5 tn 8m/12km SE of Bath. Administrative capital of county. Many Georgian bldgs. Industries include textiles, brewing, light engineering, dairy produce. ST 8557
Trowell Notts 36 B1 loc 5m/9km W of Nottingham. **T. Moor** loc 2km E. T. Service Area on M1 motorway 1m NE. SK 4839
Trowle Common Wilts 16 D5* loc 2km NW of Trowbridge. ST 8458
Trowley Bottom Herts 19 E1 loc adjoining Flamstead to S, 5m/7km N of Hemel Hempstead. TL 0714
Trow Point Tyne & Wear 61 H4* headland on North Sea coast at S Shields, at S end of sands. NZ 3866
Trowse Newton Norfolk 39 F4 vil 2m/3km SE of Norwich. TG 2406
Troy W Yorks 49 E4 loc in N part of Horsforth and 5m/8km NW of Leeds. SE 2438
Truckle Cornwall 3 F1* ham 1km SW of Camelford. SX 1082
Trudoxhill Som 16 C6 vil 3m/5km SW of Frome. ST 7443
Trueman's Heath H & W 35 G6* loc 6m/10km S of Birmingham. SP 0977
Truim H'land 75 G2 r in Badenoch and Strathspey dist, running N from Pass of Drumochter down Glen Truim through Dalwhinnie to R Spey, 5m/8km SW of Kingussie. **Falls of T.**, waterfall 3m/5km above mouth of r. NN 6896
Trull Som 8 A2 vil and suburb of Taunton 2m/3km S of tn centre. ST 2122
Trumfleet S Yorks 49 G6* loc 2km W of Kirk Bramwith. SE 6011
Trumisgarry W Isles 88 E1* loc on N coast of N Uist, 5m/8km NW of Lochmaddy. NF 8674
Trumpet H & W 26 B4 ham 4m/6km NW of Ledbury. SO 6539
Trumpington Cambs 29 H2 S suburb of Cambridge. TL 4454
Trumps Green Surrey 19 E4* loc adjoining that of Virginia Water to S. SU 9967
Trunch Norfolk 39 G2 vil 3m/5km N of N Walsham. Manor hse of = c. = 1600. TG 2834
Trunnah Lancs 47 E4 loc 2km E of Cleveleys. SD 3343
Truro Cornwall 2 D4 administrative capital of county. Early 20c cathedral by Pearson. Quays on **Truro R**, which rises some 5m/8km N and flows into R Fal 3m/5km SE. SW 8244
Truscott Cornwall 6 B6* loc 2m/3km NW of Launceston. SX 3085
Trusham Devon 5 E3 vil 2m/3km NW of Chudleigh. SX 8582
Trusley Derbys 35 H1 vil 6m/10km W of Derby. SK 2535
Trusthorpe Lincs 45 H3 suburb adjoining Mablethorpe to S. TF 5183
Trwyncastell Dyfed 22 A3* promontory at N end of Abereiddy Bay. SM 7931
Trwyn Cemlyn Gwynedd 40 A2* headland (NT) at N extremity of Cemlyn Bay on N coast of Anglesey 2m/4km W of Cemaes Bay. SH 3394
Trwyn Cilan Welsh form of Pencilan Hd, qv.
Trwyn Dwlban Gwynedd 40 C3* headland on E coast of Anglesey 1m SE of Benllech. SH 5382
Trwyn Llanbedrog Welsh form of Llanbedrog Pt, qv.
Trwyn Llech-y-doll Gwynedd 32 B2* headland 3m/5km S of Abersoch, at W end of Porth Ceiriad. SH 3023
Trwyn Maen Dylan Gwynedd 40 B6* headland on Caernarvon Bay 2m/3km NE of Clynnog-fawr. SH 4252
Trwyn Porth Dinllaen Gwynedd 32 B1* headland on S coast of Caernarvon Bay 2m/3km W of Nefyn. SH 2741
Trwyn Talfarach Gwynedd 32 A2* headland at W end of Porth Neigwl or Hell's Mouth. SH 2125
Trwyn y Fulfran Gwynedd 32 B2* headland at E end of Porth Neigwl or Hell's Mouth. SH 2823
Trwyn y Fuwch Welsh form of Lit Ormes Hd. See Ormes Head, Little.
Trwyn y Gader Welsh form of Carmel Hd, qv.
Trwyn y Gorlech Gwynedd 32 B1* headland 2m/3km SW of Trevor. SH 3445
Trwyn y Penrhyn Gwynedd 32 A2* point at E end of Aberdaron Bay. SH 1825
Trwyn y Penrhyn Gwynedd 40 C3* headland on Anglesey on Conwy Bay, 3m/4km NE of Beaumaris. SH 6279
Trwyn yr Wylfa Gwynedd 32 B2* headland 3m/4km S of Abersoch, at E end of Porth Ceiriad. SH 3224
Trwyn-y-Witch Mid Glam 14 D4* headland 2m/3km SE of Ogmore-by-Sea. SS 8872
Tryleg Welsh form of Trelleck, qv.
Trysull Staffs 35 E5 vil 5m/8km SW of Wolverhampton. SO 8594
Tryweryn 33 F1 r rising in Llyn Tryweryn, Gwynedd, and flowing E through Llyn Celyn, then SE into R Dee 1km SE of Bala. SH 9335
Tubhailt Mhic' ic Eoghain H'land 74 B5* waterfall in Lochaber dist 2m/4km N of Sallachan Pt on Loch Linnhe. Also known as Maclean's Towel. NM 9865
Tubney Oxon 17 H2 ham 4m/7km W of Abingdon. SU 4398
Tuckenhay Devon 5 E5* ham at head of Bow Creek 3m/4km S of Totnes. Paper mill. SX 8156
Tucker's Moor Devon 7 F3* ham 1km SW of Oldways End and 4m/7km SW of Dulverton. SS 8624
Tuckhill Salop 35 E5* ham 5m/9km SE of Bridgnorth. SO 7888
Tuckingmill Cornwall 2 C4 loc 1m NE of Camborne. SW 6641
Tuckingmill Wilts 9 F2* ham 1km W of Tisbury. ST 9329
Tuckton Dorset 9 H5* E dist of Bournemouth. SZ 1492
Tud 39 F4 r rising SW of E Dereham, Norfolk, and flowing E into R Wensum at Hellesdon, near Norwich. TG 1910
Tuddenham Norfolk 39 E4 vil 10m/16km W of Norwich. TG 0711
Tuddenham Suffolk 30 C1 vil 8m/12km NE of Newmarket. TL 7371
Tuddenham Suffolk 31 F3 vil 3m/5km NE of Ipswich. TM 1948
Tuddenham, North Norfolk 39 E3 vil 3m/5km E of E Dereham. TG 0314
Tudeley Kent 12 C2 vil 2m/3km E of Tonbridge. Loc of **T. Hale** to N. TQ 6245
Tudhoe Durham 54 B2 vil 2km NE of Spennymoor. NZ 2635
Tudhoe Grange Durham 54 B2* loc in N part of Spennymoor. NZ 2534
Tudhope Hill 60 A2 hill on border of Dumfries & Galloway and Borders regions 4m/7km SE of Teviothead. Height 1966 ft or 599 metres. NY 4399
Tudweiliog Gwynedd 32 A1 vil 3m/5km SW of Nefyn. SH 2336
Tudworth Green S Yorks 49 H6* ham 2m/3km S of Thorne. SE 6810
Tue Brook Merseyside 42 A2* dist of Liverpool 3m/5km NE of city centre. SJ 3892
Tuesley Surrey 11 F1 loc 2km E of Milford. SU 9641
Tuffley Glos 26 D5 loc in S part of Gloucester. SO 8315
Tuffley, Lower Glos 26 C6* loc in SW part of Gloucester. SO 8214
Tufnell Park London 19 G3* loc in borough of Islington 3m/5km N of Charing Cross. TQ 2985
Tufton Dyfed 22 C3 ham 9m/15km NE of Haverfordwest. SN 0428
Tufton Hants 10 B1 ham on R Test 1m SW of Whitchurch. SU 4546
Tugby Leics 36 D4 vil 7m/11km W of Uppingham. SK 7600
Tugford Salop 34 C5 vil 8m/12km N of Ludlow. SO 5587
Tughall Nthmb 67 H5 ham 3m/4km N of Embleton. NU 2126
Tulach Hill Tayside 75 H4 hill 1m SW of Blair Atholl. NN 8564
Tulchan H'land 82 A3 stream in Badenoch and Strathspey dist running SE down Glen T. to R Spey 8m/12km NE of Grantown-on-Spey. Known as Burn of Tulchan. NJ 1235
Tullibardine Tayside 72 C3 loc 2m/4km W of Auchterarder. 15c chapel (A.M.). Distillery. NN 9113
Tullibody Central 72 C5 tn 2m/3km NW of Alloa. **T. Inch** is island in R Forth to S. NS 8695
Tullibole Castle Tayside 72 D4 tower bearing the date 1608, 4m/7km W of Kinross. NO 0500
Tullich H'land 87 A8 loc 4m/6km NE of Invergordon, Ross and Cromarty dist. NH 7373
Tullich Burn 76 D2 stream in Grampian region running S into R Dee 2m/3km below Ballater. NO 3997
Tulliemet Tayside 76 B5 loc 1m E of Ballinluig. NN 9952
Tulloch H'land 85 F7 loc 1km N of Bonar Br, Sutherland dist. NH 6092
Tullynessle Grampian 82 D5 vil 3m/4km NW of Alford. NJ 5519
Tulm Island H'land 78 B2 long narrow islet in Duntulm Bay near N end of Skye 7m/11km N of Uig. NG 4074
Tulse Hill London 19 G4* loc in borough of Lambeth 1m W of Dulwich Village. TQ 3173

Tumble (Tymbl, Y)Dyfed 23 G4 vil 2km SW of Cross Hands. SN 5411
Tumby Lincs 45 F5 ham 2m/3km NE of Tattershall. **T. Woodside** ham 2m/4km SE. TF 2359
Tummel 76 A5 r in Tayside region issuing from Loch Rannoch and running E to its confluence with R Garry in Loch Faskally, then SE to R Tay S of Ballinluig. See also Linn of T., Loch T. NN 9751
Tummel Bridge Tayside 75 H5 loc on R Tummel 1m W of Loch Tummel. Hydro-electricity power stn. NN 7659
Tunbridge Wells Kent 12 C3 largely residential tn and shopping centre 31m/50km SE of London. Formerly a spa (chalybeate springs). Officially Royal Tunbridge Wells since 1909. TQ 5839
Tungate Norfolk 39 F2* loc 1m SW of N Walsham. TG 2629
Tunley Avon 16 C5* vil 3m/5km N of Radstock. ST 6959
Tunshill Gtr Manchester 48 C6* loc 1m E of Milnrow. SD 9413
Tunstall Humberside 51 G5 vil near coast 3m/5km NW of Withernsea. TA 3031
Tunstall Kent 21 E5 vil 2km SW of Sittingbourne. TQ 8961
Tunstall Lancs 47 F1 vil 3m/5km S of Kirkby Lonsdale. SD 6073
Tunstall Norfolk 39 G4 ham 2m/3km SE of Acle. TG 4108
Tunstall N Yorks 54 B5 vil 2m/3km SW of Catterick. SE 2195
Tunstall Staffs 34 D2* ham 1m NW of High Offley. SJ 7727
Tunstall Staffs 42 D6 one of the tns of Stoke-on-Trent: Burslem, Fenton, Hanley, Longton, Stoke, Tunstall. Tunstall lies 4m/6km NW of city centre. SJ 8651
Tunstall Suffolk 31 G3 vil 4m/6km E of Wickham Mkt. **T. Forest,** large area of conifers (Forestry Commission), to E. TM 3555
Tunstall Tyne & Wear 61 H6* dist of Sunderland 2m/4km S of tn centre. NZ 3853
Tunstall Reservoir Durham 54 A1* resr in course of Waskerley Beck 2m/4km N of Wolsingham. NZ 0641
Tunstead Gtr Manchester 43 E1* loc 5m/8km E of Oldham. SE 0004
Tunstead Norfolk 39 G3 ham 4m/6km N of Wroxham. TG 3022
Tunstead Milton Derbys 43 E3* ham 2m/3km W of Chapel-en-le-Frith. SK 0380
Tunworth Hants 18 B6 vil 4m/6km SE of Basingstoke. SU 6748
Tupholme Lincs 45 E4/F4 loc 2m/3km E of Bardney. Abbey remains date from 13c. TF 1468
Tupton Derbys 43 H4 loc 2km N of Clay Cross, comprising New and Old Tupton. SK 3965
Tuquoy Orkney. See Bay of Tuquoy.
Turgis Green Hants 18 B5 vil (with Stratfield Turgis) 6m/10km NE of Basingstoke. SU 6959
Turkdean Glos 27 E5 vil 2m/3km N of Northleach. SP 1017
Turkey Island Hants 10 C3* loc just E of Shedfield and 3m/5km S of Bishop's Waltham. SU 5613
Tur Langton Leics 36 C5 vil 5m/8km N of Mkt Harborough. SP 7194
Turleigh Wilts 16 C5 vil 2km W of Bradford-on-Avon. ST 8060
Turleygreen Salop 34 D5* loc 6m/9km SE of Bridgnorth. SO 7685
Turls Head Shetland 89 E6* headland on NW coast of Mainland on E side of entrance to Ronas Voe. HU 2886
Turn Lancs 47 H6* loc 1m SE of Edenfield. SD 8118
Turnastone H & W 25 H4 ham across R Dore from Vowchurch, 6m/10km NW of Pontrilas. SO 3536
Turnaware Point Cornwall 2 D4* headland (NT) at N end of Carrick Rds (R Fal) 3m/5km N of St Mawes. SW 8338
Turnberry S'clyde 56 C3 vil on **T. Bay,** 5m/8km N of Girvan. Championship golf course. Scanty remains of **T. Castle** adjoin lighthouse, 1m N. NS 2005
Turnchapel Devon 4 B5 loc in S dist of Plymouth S of R Plym estuary. SX 4952
Turnditch Derbys 45 G6 vil 3m/5km W of Belper. SK 2946
Turner Green Lancs 47 F5* loc 2km E of Samlesbury. SD 6130
Turnerheath Ches 43 E3* loc 1m SW of Bollington. SJ 9176
Turner's Green E Sussex 12 C5* loc 4m/6km E of Heathfield. TQ 6319
Turner's Green Warwicks 27 F1 loc 4m/6km SE of Hockley Heath. SP 1969
Turners Hill W Sussex 11 H2 vil 4m/6km SW of E Grinstead. TQ 3435
Turner's Pool Staffs 43 E4/E5* small lake 2m/3km SE of Wincle. SJ 9763
Turners Puddle Dorset 9 F5 ham 2km SW of Bere Regis. SY 8393
Turner Wood S Yorks 44 A3* loc 3m/5km NW of Worksop. SK 5481
Turnford Herts 20 A2 loc 2km N of Cheshunt. TL 3604
Turn Hill Som 8 C2* hill (NT) 2m/3km E of Othery, with views across Sedgemoor to Quantock Hills. ST 4131
Turnhouse Lothian 65 G2 Edinburgh Airport, 6m/10km W of city centre. NT 1573
Turnworth Dorset 9 F3 ham 4m/7km W of Blandford Forum. ST 8207
Turriff Grampian 83 F2 tn at confluence of R Deveron and Idoch Water 9m/14km S of Banff. Centre of agricultural dist. Mnfre of agricultural implements, carbon paper. NJ 7249
Turton Lancs 47 G6 moorland area N of Bolton. There are several resrs. **T. Bottoms** loc 4m/7km N of Bolton. **T. Tower,** largely Elizn hse nearby. SD 7315
Turton and Entwistle Reservoir Lancs 47 G6* resr on moors 5m/8km N of Bolton. SD 7217
Turvalds Head Shetland 89 E7* headland on W coast of Mainland 2m/3km W of Brae. HU 3268
Turves Green W Midlands 35 F6* loc in Birmingham 6m/10km SW of city centre. SP 0278
Turves, The Cambs 37 H5* loc 4m/7km E of Whittlesey. TL 3396
Turvey Beds 28 D3 vil 7m/11km W of Bedford. SP 9452
Turville Bucks 18 C3 vil 5m/9km N of Henley-on-Thames. SU 7691
Turweston Bucks 28 B4 vil 1m E of Brackley. SP 6037
Tusker Rock Mid Glam 14 D4 island rock 2km offshore opp Ogmore-by-Sea. SS 8474
Tutbury Staffs 35 G2/H2 vil 4m/6km NW of Burton upon Trent. Ruins of 14c cas. SK 2128
Tutnall H & W 27 E1* loc 2m/3km E of Bromsgrove. SO 9870
Tutshill Glos 16 B2 vil 1km NE of Chepstow across R Wye. ST 5394
Tutt Hill Kent 13 E2* loc 2m/4km SE of Charing. TQ 9746
Tuttington Norfolk 39 F2 vil 2m/3km E of Aylsham. TG 2227
Tutts Clump Berks 18 B4* ham 5m/8km SW of Pangbourne. SU 5870
Tutwell Cornwall 3 H1* ham above R Tamar 4m/7km NE of Callington. SX 3975
Tuxford Notts 44 C4 vil 7m/11km S of E Retford. Former staging post on Gt North Road. SK 7371
Twatt Orkney 89 A6 loc on Mainland 3m/4km NW of Dounby. HY 2724
Twatt Shetland 89 E7* loc on Mainland 1km N of Bixter. HU 3253
Twechar S'clyde 64 D2 vil 2m/3km SW of Kilsyth. NS 7075
Tweed 67 F3 r rising in Scotland at Tweed's Well, 6m/10km N of Moffat, and flowing by Peebles, Melrose, Kelso and Coldstream to North Sea at Berwick-upon-Tweed, England. NU 0052
Tweedale Salop 34 D4* industrial estate N of Madeley, Telford. SJ 6904
Tweedbank Borders 66 C5 loc and housing development 2m/3km W of Melrose. NT 5135
Tweeddale 116 admin dist of Borders region.
Tweedmouth Nthmb 67 F3 dist of Berwick-upon-Tweed on S bank of r. NT 9952
Tweedsmuir Borders 65 G5 loc in Upper Tweeddale 8m/12km S of Broughton. NT 0924
Tweed's Well Borders 59 F1 source of R Tweed, 6m/10km N of Moffat. NT 0514
Twelveheads Cornwall 2 C4* vil 4m/6km E of Redruth. SW 7642
Twelve Oaks E Sussex 12 C4* loc 1km SE of Brightling. TQ 6820
Twemlow Green Ches 42 D4* ham 2m/3km NE of Holmes Chapel. SJ 7868
Twenty Lincs 37 F3 ham 4m/6km E of Bourne. TF 1520
Twenty Foot River 37 H4* artificial branch of R Nene (old course) leaving old course S of Whittlesey, Cambs, and rejoining it NE of March. TL 4498
Twerton Avon 16 C5 W dist of Bath. ST 7264
Twerton, South Avon 16 C5* W dist of Bath. ST 7364
Twice Brewed Nthmb 60 C4 inn on B6318 rd to S of Hadrian's Wall and 3m/5km NE of Haltwhistle. NY 7566
Twickenham London 19 F4 dist in borough of Richmond on left bank of R Thames 10m/16km SW of Charing Cross. Rugby football ground to NW (Rugby Rd). TQ 1673
Twigworth Glos 26 D5 vil 3m/4km N of Gloucester. SO 8422
Twineham W Sussex 11 H3 ham 4m/6km W of Burgess Hill. Loc of **T. Green** to N. TQ 2519
Twinhoe Avon 16 C5* loc 3m/5km S of Bath. ST 7459
Twinstead Essex 30 D4 ham 3m/5km S of Sudbury. TL 8636
Twinstead Green Essex 30 C4/D4 ham 4m/6km SW of Sudbury. TL 8536
Twiss Green Ches 42 C2* loc adjoining Culcheth to N. SJ 6595
Twiston Lancs 48 B4* ham 2m/3km E of Downham. SD 8143
Twitchen Devon 7 F2 vil on S edge of Exmoor National Park 6m/9km NE of S Molton. SS 7830
Twitchen Salop 34 B6 loc 5m/7km SW of Craven Arms. SO 3779
Twitton Kent 20 B5* loc adjoining Otford to W. TQ 5159
Twizel Bridge Nthmb 67 F4* br, reputedly of 15c, across R Till 1m above its confluence with R Tweed. NT 8843
Twizell Burn 61 G6* stream rising S of Stanley, Durham, and flowing E into R Wear on E side of Chester-le-Street. NZ 2751
Twll Du Gwynedd 40 D5* fissure in rock face on N side of Glyder Fawr. Also known as Devil's Kitchen. SH 6358
Two Bridges Devon 4 C3 loc on W Dart R on Dartmoor 8m/13km E of Tavistock. SX 6075
Two Bridges Glos 16 B1* ham 2km N of Blakeney. SO 6609
Two Dales Derbys 43 G4/G5 vil 2m/3km NW of Matlock. SK 2762
Two Gates Staffs 35 H4 loc in Tamworth 2m/3km S of tn centre. SK 2101
Two Locks Gwent 15 G2* locality in S part of Cwmbran on Monmouthshire and Brecon Canal. ST 2994
Two Mills Ches 42 A4* loc 1m W of Capenhurst. SJ 3573
Two Tree Island Essex 20 D3* island on N side of R Thames estuary 4m/6km W of Southend-on-Sea tn centre. TQ 8285
Two Waters Herts 19 E1* loc in S part of Hemel Hempstead. TL 0505
Twrch 24 C4 r rising 3m/5km SE of Llanddewi Brefi, Dyfed, and flowing SW then S into R Cothi at Pumsaint. SN 6540
Twrch 24 D6 r rising on W side of summit of Carmarthen Van, Powys, and flowing S into R Tawe at Ystalyfera. SN 7708
Twrch 33 F2 r rising N of Llanymawddwy, Gwynedd, and flowing N into R Dee 1km W of SW end of Bala Lake. SH 8831
Twrch 33 G3 r rising in Powys close to Gwynedd border 2km E of Llanymawddwy and flowing SE into R Banwy 2km W of Llangadfan. SH 9911
Twt Hill Clwyd. See Rhuddlan.
Twycross Leics 35 H4 vil 5m/8km NE of Atherstone. **Lit Twycross** loc to N. SK 3304
Twyford Berks 18 C4 tn 5m/8km E of Reading. SU 9418
Twyford Bucks 28 B5 vil 6m/9km NE of Bicester. SP 6626
Twyford Derbys 35 H2 ham on R Trent 5m/8km SW of Derby. SK 3228
Twyford Dorset 9 F3 loc 2m/4km S of Shaftesbury. ST 8518
Twyford Hants 10 B3 vil on R Itchen 3m/5km S of Winchester. Site of Roman bldg on E side of vil. SU 4824
Twyford Leics 36 C3 vil 6m/9km S of Melton Mowbray. SK 7210
Twyford Lincs 37 E2 loc at S end of Colsterworth. SK 9323
Twyford Norfolk 39 E2 vil 5m/9km W of Reepham. TG 0124
Twyford Common H & W 26 A4 loc 3m/5km S of Hereford. SO 5135
Twymyn 33 E4 r in Powys rising to E of Glaslyn lake and running E to Dylife and 1km beyond, then N to the W side of Llanbrynmair, then W into R Dovey 1km N of Cemmaes Road. SH 8205
Twyncarno Mid Glam 15 F1* loc adjoining Rhymney to N. SO 1108
Twynholm D & G 58 C6 vil 3m/4km NW of Kirkcudbright. NX 6654
Twyning Glos 26 D4 vil 2m/3km N of Tewkesbury. SO 8936
Twyning Green Glos 26 D4 vil running down to W bank of R Avon 3m/4km N of Tewkesbury. SO 9036
Twynllanan Dyfed 24 C5/D5 ham 4m/6km SE of Llangadog. SN 7524
Twyn-mynydd Dyfed 23 G4* ham 1m NW of Glanaman and 3m/5km NE of Ammanford. SN 6614
Twyn Shon-Ifan Mid Glam 15 F2* loc 1m SE of Ystrad Mynach. Industrial estate to S. ST 1593
Twynyderyn Gwent 15 G1* loc 1km S of Brynmawr. SO 1910
Twynyrodyn Mid Glam 15 F1* loc in S part of Merthyr Tydfil. SO 0505
Twyn-yr-odyn S Glam 15 F4 loc 4m/6km N of Barry. ST 1173
Twyn-y-Sheriff Gwent 16 A1* loc 2km S of Raglan. SO 4005
Twywell Northants 37 E6 vil 3m/5km W of Thrapston. SP 9578
Tyberton H & W 25 H4 vil 8m/13km W of Hereford. SO 3839
Tybroughton Clwyd 42 B6* loc 4m/6km W of Whitchurch. SJ 4742
Tyburn W Midlands 35 G5 loc in Birmingham 5m/8km NE of city centre. SP 1391
Ty-coch Gwent 15 G2* loc on S side of Cwmbran. ST 2993
Tycroes Dyfed 23 G4 vil 2m/3km SW of Ammanford. SN 6010
Tycrwyn Powys 33 G3* ham 3m/4km W of Llanfyllin. SJ 1018
Tyddewi Welsh form of St David's, qv.
Tydd Gote Lincs 38 A3* vil 5m/8km N of Wisbech. TF 4517
Tydd St Giles Cambs 37 H3 vil 5m/8km NE of Wisbech. TF 4216
Tydd St Mary Norfolk 37 H3 vil 3m/4km S of Long Sutton. TF 4418
Ty-du Welsh form of Rogerstone, qv.
Tye Hants 10 D4* loc on Hayling I. 1km S of N Hayling. SU 7302
Tye Common Essex 20 C2 SW dist of Billericay. TQ 6693
Tyegate Green Norfolk 39 G3* loc adjoining S Walsham to W. TG 3513
Tye Green Essex 20 B1* S dist of Harlow. TL 4508
Tye Green Essex 20 C1* ham adjoining Good Easter to NE, 2m/4km E of Leaden Roding. TL 6212
Tye Green Essex 30 A5* ham to N of Stansted Airport 4m/7km NE of Bishop's Stortford. TL 5424
Tye Green Essex 30 B4* ham 3m/5km N of Thaxted. TL 5935
Tye Green Essex 30 C5 loc 2m/3km SE of Braintree. TL 7721
Tyersal W Yorks 48 D5 loc in Bradford 2m/3km E of city centre. **T. Gate** loc to S. SE 1932
Tyldesley Gtr Manchester 42 C1 tn 5m/8km SW of Bolton. Coal-mining, textiles. SD 6902
Tyle-garw Mid Glam 15 E3* loc 2m/3km SW of Llantrisant. ST 0281
Tyler Hill Kent 13 G1 vil 2m/3km N of Canterbury. TR 1461
Tylers Green Bucks 18 D2 loc 3m/4km E of High Wycombe. SU 9093
Tyler's Green Essex 20 B2 loc 3m/5km W of Chipping Ongar. TL 5005
Tyler's Green Surrey 19 G6* loc just N of Godstone. TQ 3452
Tyllgoed Welsh form of Fairwater, qv.
Ty Llwyn Gwent 15 F1* loc on E side of Ebbw Vale. SO 1708
Tylorstown Mid Glam 15 E2* vil 5m/8km NW of Pontypridd. ST 0195
Tylwch Powys 33 F6* loc 3m/5km S of Llanidloes. SN 9780
Ty-mawr Clwyd 41 E6* loc 3m/5km W of Cerrigydrudion. SJ 9047
Ty-mawr Clwyd 41 F3* loc 2m/3km NE of Abergele. SH 9679

Ty Mawr Reservoir Clwyd 41 H6* small resr 3m/5km NW of Ruabon. SJ 2747
Ty Mawr Standing Stone Gwynedd. See Trefignath.
Tymbl, Y Welsh form of Tumble, qv.
Ty-nant Clwyd 33 F1/G1* ham 6m/9km W of Corwen. SH 9844
Tynant Mid Glam 15 F3* loc 3m/5km S of Pontypridd. ST 0685
Tyndale Crescent Durham 54 B2* loc adjoining Bishop Auckland to S. NZ 1927
Tyndrum Central 71 E2 vil 4m/7km NW of Crianlarich. Has two rly stns, one on the Glasgow to Oban and one on the Glasgow to Fort William line. NN 3330
Tyndyrn Welsh form of Tintern. See Tintern Abbey, Tintern Parva.
Tyne 61 H4 r formed by confluence of Rs N and S Tyne NW of Hexham, Nthmb, and flowing E through increasingly industrial landscape to Newcastle upon Tyne, Felling, Wallsend, Jarrow, and the North Sea between S Shields and Tynemouth, county of Tyne & Wear. Tidal to Wylam. Navigable to Newcastle. NZ 3668
Tyne 66 D1 r in Lothian region known in upper reaches as **Tyne Water.** Rises on N slopes of Moorfoot Hills and runs NE through Haddington and E Linton to North Sea 3m/5km W of Dunbar. NT 6480
Tyne and Wear 117 metropolitan and maritime county of NE England, comprising the urban complex around Newcastle-upon-Tyne, S Shields, Sunderland, and Tynemouth. Named after its two important rs.
Tynedale 117 admin dist of Nthmb.
Tyne Green Nthmb 61 E5* loc adjoining Hexham to N. NY 9364
Tyneham Dorset 9 F6 vil between Purbeck Hills and coast 5m/8km SW of Wareham. Rendered derelict owing to its situation in Army firing ranges. SY 8880
Tynehead Lothian 66 B3 loc 3m/5km SE of Gorebridge. NT 3959
Tynemouth Tyne & Wear 61 H4 tn and resort N of R Tyne at its mouth 8m/13km E of Newcastle. Remains of medieval priory and cas (A.M.). NZ 3669
Tyne, North 61 E5 r rising on Kielder Forest, Nthmb, near Scottish border, and flowing SE by Falstone, Bellingham, and Wark to join R South Tyne and form R Tyne 2m/3km NW of Hexham. NY 9166
Tyneside, North and **South** 117 admin dists of Tyne & Wear metropolitan county.
Tyne, South 61 E5 r rising on Tynehead Fell, Cumbria, and flowing N by Alston to Haltwhistle, Nthmb, then E by Haydon Br to join R North Tyne and form R Tyne 2m/3km NW of Hexham. NY 9166
Tynewydd Mid Glam 15 E2 loc 3m/5km NW of Rhondda. SS 9398
Ty Newydd Burial-chamber Gwynedd. See Llanfaelog.
Tyninghame Lothian 66 D1 vil 2m/3km NE of E Linton. NT 6179
Tynings, The Glos 26 D5* loc 2m/4km SW of Cheltenham. SO 9219
Tynn-yr-eithin Dyfed 24 C2* loc 2m/3km NW of Tregaron. SN 6662
Tynribbie S'clyde 74 B6 vil in Argyll 1m SE of Portnacroish. NM 9346
Tynron D & G 58 D2 vil on Shinnel Water 2m/3km NE of Tynron. NX 8093
Tyntesfield Avon 16 A4* ham 2m/3km E of Nailsea. ST 4971
Tyntetown Mid Glam 15 F2* loc 2m/3km SE of Mountain Ash. ST 0696
Tynwald Hill Isle of Man 46 B5* artificial mound at St John's where new laws are promulgated. SC 2781
Ty'n-y-bryn Mid Glam 15 E3* loc on SW side of Tonyrefail. ST 0087
Ty'n-y-Caeau W Glam 14 D2* loc on E side of Neath. SS 7697
Ty'n-y-coedcae Mid Glam 15 G3* loc 2km SW of Machen across Rhymney R. ST 1988
Ty'n-y-garn Mid Glam 15 E3* loc 2m/3km N of Bridgend. SS 8982
Tynygongl Gwynedd 40 C3* loc on W side of Benllech, Anglesey. SH 5182
Tynygraig Dyfed 24 C2* ham 2m/3km S of Llanafan. SN 6969
Tyn-y-groes Gwynedd 40 D4 vil 4m/6km S of Conwy. SH 7771
Tyn-y-rhos 33 F4* r running SW into R Iaen at Talerddig, Powys. SH 9200
Tyrau Mawr Gwynedd 32 D3 W peak of Cader Idris. Height 2167 ft or 661 metres. SH 6713
Ty'r-bont S Glam 15 G3* loc 4m/7km NE of Cardiff. ST 2282
Tyrie Grampian 83 G1 loc near N coast 5m/8km SW of Fraserburgh. WT stn 2km SE. NJ 9262
Tyringham Bucks 28 D3* ham 2m/4km N of Newport Pagnell across loop of R Ouse. SP 8547
Tyseley W Midlands 35 G5* loc in Birmingham 3m/5km SE of city centre. SP 1083
Ty-Sign Gwent 15 G2/G3* loc on E side of Risca. ST 2490
Tysoe, Lower Warwicks 27 G3 vil 4m/6km S of Kineton. SP 3445
Tysoe, Middle Warwicks 27 G3 vil 4m/7km S of Kineton. SP 3444
Tysoe, Upper Warwicks 27 G3 vil 5m/8km S of Kineton. SP 3343
Tythe Beds 29 E5* loc at NW edge of Luton. TL 0424
Tythegston Mid Glam 14 D4 ham 3m/5km W of Bridgend. SS 8578
Tytherington Avon 16 B3 vil 2m/4km SE of Thornbury. ST 6688
Tytherington Ches 43 E4* dist of Macclesfield 1m N of tn centre. SJ 9175
Tytherington Wilts 9 F1 vil 1m SW of Heytesbury. ST 9141
Tytherleigh Devon 8 B4 ham 3m/5km S of Chard. ST 3103
Tytherley, East Hants 10 A2 ham 5m/9km SW of Stockbridge. SU 2929
Tytherley, West Hants 10 A2 vil 6m/10km SW of Stockbridge. SU 2729
Tytherton, East Wilts 16 D4 vil 3m/5km E of Chippenham. ST 9674
Tytherton, West Wilts 16 D4* vil 2m/3km E of Chippenham. ST 9474
Tyttenhanger Green Herts 19 F1* loc 2m/4km SE of St Albans. TL 1805
Tywardreath Cornwall 3 F3 vil, sometimes known as Tywardreath Highway, 5m/8km E of St Austell. SX 0854
Tywardreath Highway Cornwall 3 F3* loc 3m/5km SW of Lostwithiel. SX 0755
Tyweli 24 A4 r rising 2m/3km SW of Pencader, Dyfed, and flowing through Pencader into R Teifi at Pontwelly. SN 4140
Tywi Welsh form of Towy (r), qv.
Tywyn Gwynedd 32 D4 resort on Cardigan Bay 10m/16km W of Machynlleth. Formerly known as Towyn. SH 5800
Tywyni 24 D6* r rising on W side of Fan-Gihirych, Fforest Fawr, and flowing SW into R Tawe 2km NE of Craig-y-nos, Powys. SN 8417
Tywyn Point Dyfed 23 E5* headland at mouth of R Gwendraeth estuary, on S bank, 6m/10km NW of Burry Port. SN 3506
Tywyn Trewan Gwynedd 40 A4 extensive area of foreshore on Anglesey where Valley Airfield is situated. SH 3075

U

Uachdar W Isles 88 E1* loc at N end of Benbecula, 1km E of the airfield. NF 7955
Uamh Altrumain Skye, H'land 79 D7 cave on W shore of Loch Slapin 1m N of Strathaird Pt. Also known as Spar Cave. NG 5312
Ubberley Staffs 43 E6* dist of Stoke-on-Trent 2m/3km E of city centre. SJ 9046
Ubbeston Suffolk 31 G1 loc 5m/8km SW of Halesworth. Ham of **U. Green** 1m S. TM 3272
Ubley Avon 16 A5 vil 2m/3km E of Blagdon. ST 5258
Uckerby N Yorks 54 B4 ham 3m/4km SE of Scotch Corner. NZ 2402
Uckfield E Sussex 12 B4 tn 8m/12km NE of Lewes. TQ 4721
Uckinghall H & W 26 D4 ham 4m/6km NW of Tewkesbury. SO 8638
Uckington Glos 26 D5 vil 3m/4km NW of Cheltenham. SO 9124
Udale Bay H'land 81 F1 bay on S side of Cromarty Firth, Ross and Cromarty dist, to SE of Balblair. NH 7166
Uddingston S'clyde 64 D3 tn 4m/6km SW of Coatbridge. Ruins of 13c Bothwell Castle (A.M.) stand among wds above R Clyde 1m SW. NS 6960
Uddington S'clyde 65 E5* loc 2m/4km NE of Douglas. NS 8633
Udimore E Sussex 13 E5 vil 4m/6km W of Rye. TQ 8718
Udley Avon 16 A5* loc 2km E of Congresbury. ST 4663
Udny Green Grampian 83 G4 vil 5m/7km E of Oldmeldrum. **Udny Castle** to N. NJ 8826
Udraynian Point S'clyde 63 G1* headland on E coast of Bute, at N end of Kames Bay. NS 0768
Udston S'clyde 64 D3* loc adjoining Hamilton to W. NS 6955
Uffcott Wilts 17 F4 loc 5m/7km SW of Swindon. SU 1277
Uffculme Devon 7 H4 vil on R Culm 5m/7km NE of Cullompton. ST 0612
Uffington Lincs 37 F4 vil 2m/3km E of Stamford. TF 0607
Uffington Oxon 17 G3 vil 4m/7km S of Faringdon. **U. Castle** (A.M.), Iron Age fort 2m/3km S; on side of chalk hill below it is **U. White Horse** (A.M.), probably cut about 100 BC. SU 3089
Uffington Salop 34 C3 vil 3m/4km E of Shrewsbury across R Severn. SJ 5213
Ufford Cambs 37 F4 vil 7m/11km NW of Peterborough. TF 0904
Ufford Suffolk 31 G3 vil 3m/4km NE of Woodbridge. Vil comprises hams of **Upr** and **Lr Street.** TM 2952
Ufton Warwicks 27 G2 vil 3m/4km W of Southam. SP 3762
Ufton Green Berks 18 B4* ham 7m/11km SW of Reading. SU 6268
Ufton Nervet Berks 18 B4 vil 6m/10km SW of Reading. SU 6367
Ugadale Point S'clyde 63 E5 headland on E coast of Kintyre 2m/4km S of Saddell. NR 7828
Ugborough Devon 4 D5 vil 3m/4km E of Ivybridge. SX 6755
Ugford Wilts 9 G2 loc 1m W of Wilton. SU 0831
Uggeshall Suffolk 31 H1 ham 4m/7km NW of Southwold. TM 4480
Ugglebarnby N Yorks 55 G4* vil 3m/4km S of Whitby. NZ 8707
Ugie 83 H2 r in Grampian region running E to North Sea on N side of Peterhead. Rises as **N** and **S Ugie Water,** two branches which join 2km NE of Longside. NK 1247
Ugley Essex 30 A5 vil 5m/8km NE of Bishop's Stortford. Vil of **U. Green** 1m S. TL 5228
Ugthorpe N Yorks 55 F4 vil 6m/10km W of Whitby. NZ 7911
Uidh W Isles 88 D4* loc on NE side of island of Vatersay. Landing stage. NL 6596
Uig Skye, H'land 78 A4 locality on W side of Loch Dunvegan, 3m/4km S of Dunvegan Hd. NG 1952
Uig Skye, H'land 78 B3 vil on **U. Bay** on E shore of Loch Snizort, at foot of **Glen U.** Vehicle ferry to Lochmaddy on N Uist and to Tarbert, Harris. NG 3963
Uig W Isles 88 A2 vil near W coast of Lewis 3m/5km S of Gallan Hd. To SW are **Uig Sands,** in estuary formed by various streams and emptying into bay of Camas Uig. NB 0534
Uiginish Point Skye, H'land 78 A4* headland near head of Loch Dunvegan 2km NW of Dunvegan. Lighthouse. NG 2349
Uigshader Skye, H'land 78 C4 loc 4m/6km NW of Portree. NG 4246
Uinessan W Isles 88 D4* islet off easternmost point of Vatersay. NL 6695
Uisge Labhair H'land 75 E4 r rising to E of Aonach Beag in Badenoch and Strathspey dist and running SW into R Ossian in Lochaber dist, near foot of Loch Ossian. NN 4170
Uisken S'clyde 69 C6 loc on Mull 2m/3km S of Bunessan. NM 3819
Uisnaval More W Isles 88 A3* mt in N Harris 2m/4km W of Clisham. Height 2392 ft or 729 metres. NB 1208
Uist, North W Isles 88 D1, E1 island of about 120 sq miles or 310 sq km, between Harris and Benbecula, having innumerable lochs and offshore islands. Noted for fishing, both offshore and inland. Crofting is carried on; also bulb-growing in the comparatively mild climate. NF 87
Uist, South W Isles 88 E2, E3 island of about 140 sq miles or 365 sq km between Benbecula (causeway connection) and Barra. Contains numerous lochs, esp on W side; mts on E side rise to 2034 ft or 620 metres. Guided missile range towards N end of island. NF 72
Ulbster H'land 86 F3 vil on E coast of Caithness dist 7m/11km S of Wick. 1km NW, Cairn of Get, or Garrywhin, (A.M.), prehistoric chambered tomb. ND 3240
Ulcat Row Cumbria 52 D3 ham 1m NE of Dockray. NY 4022
Ulceby Humberside 51 E6 vil 5m/8km W of Immingham. **U. Carr** loc 2km NE. **U. Skitter** ham 2km E. TA 1014
Ulceby Lincs 45 G4 vil 3m/5km SW of Alford. **U. Cross** loc and crossroads 1m NW. TF 4272
Ulcombe Kent 13 E2 vil 3m/5km N of Headcorn. TQ 8449
Uldale Cumbria 52 C2 vil 7m/11km S of Wigton. NY 2436
Uley Glos 16 C2 vil 2m/3km E of Dursley. ST 7998
Ulfhart Point Skye, H'land 79 C6 headland on Soay Sound, on W side of entrance to Loch Scavaig. NG 4716
Ulgham Nthmb 61 G2/G3 vil 5m/7km NE of Morpeth. NZ 2392
Ulladale W Isles 88 A2* r in Harris rising in Forest of Harris and flowing NE to become R Housay and discharge its waters into head of Loch Resort. NB 1017
Ullapool H'land 85 B7 small fishing port and resort on E shore of Loch Broom, W coast of Ross and Cromarty dist. Ferry for pedestrians across loch to Allt na h-Airbhe. Vehicle ferry to Stornoway. **Ullapool R** runs from Loch Achall into Loch Broom on N side of tn. NH 1294
Ullenhall Warwicks 27 F1 vil 2m/3km NW of Henley-in-Arden. SP 1267
Ullenwood Glos 26 D5 loc 3m/5km S of Cheltenham. SO 9416
Ulleskelf N Yorks 49 G4 vil on S bank of R Wharfe 4m/6km NW of Cawood. SE 5737
Ullesthorpe Leics 36 B5 vil 3m/5km NW of Lutterworth. SP 5087
Ulley S Yorks 43 H2/H3 vil 4m/6km SE of Rotherham. **Ulley Resr** 1km W. SK 4687
Ullingswick H & W 26 B3 vil 8m/13km NE of Hereford. SO 5949
Ullinish Skye, H'land 79 B5 locality on E side of Loch Bracadale 2km W of Bracadale vil. **Ullinish Pt** is headland 1m S. NG 3238
Ullock Cumbria 52 B3 ham 5m/8km SW of Cockermouth. NY 0723
Ullswater Cumbria 52 D3 lake in Lake Dist, the largest after Windermere, running SW to NE from Patterdale to Pooley Br. NY 4220
Ulpha Cumbria 52 C5 vil 4m/6km N of Broughton in Furness. SD 1993
Ulpha Cumbria 52 D6* loc 2m/4km E of Lindale. SD 4581
Ulrome Humberside 51 F3 vil 6m/10km NW of Hornsea. TA 1656
Ulsta Shetland 89 E6* loc at SW end of Yell on small bay of same name. Vehicle ferry to Toft on Mainland. HU 4679
Ulting Essex 20 D1 loc 3m/5km NW of Maldon. TL 8009
Ulva S'clyde 68 C4 sparsely inhabited island off W coast of Mull, on S side of Loch Tuath. Measures 4m/7km E to W and 2m/4km N to S. High basalt cliffs at W end. Rd br connection with neighbouring Gometra, qv, to W. **Sound of U.** is narrow strait between U. and main island of Mull. NM 3640
Ulva Islands S'clyde 70 A6* pair of islands at entrance to Linne Mhuirich, Argyll. See Linne Mhuirich. NR 7182
Ulverley Green W Midlands 35 G6* loc in Solihull 2m/3km NW of tn centre. SP 1381
Ulverscroft Leics 36 B3* loc 2km N of Markfield. Includes nature reserve (NT). Remains of medieval priory. SK 4911
Ulverston Cumbria 46 D1 tn 8m/13km NE of Barrow-in-Furness. Light engineering, tanning, drugs mnfre. SD 2878
Ulwell Dorset 9 G6 vil 2km NW of Swanage. SZ 0280
Umaolo H'land 79 A8 island rock in Inner Hebrides lying 3m/5km S of W end of Canna. NG 1900

Umber 6 D1* r rising on W foothills of Exmoor and flowing NW through Combe Martin into Combe Martin Bay, Devon. SS 5747
Umberleigh Devon 7 E3 vil on R Taw 7m/11km SE of Barnstaple. SS 6023
Umborne Brook 8 B5 r rising 2km SE of Upottery in Devon, and flowing S into R Coly at Colyton. SY 2494
Unapool H'land 84 C4 locality on W side of mouth of Loch Glencoul, Sutherland dist, 1km SE of Kylesku Ferry. NC 2333
Uncleby Humberside 50 C2 ham in the wolds 4m/6km W of Fridaythorpe. SE 8159
Underbank Reservoir S Yorks 43 G2* resr 2m/3km W of Stocksbridge. SK 2599
Underbarrow Cumbria 52 D5 vil 3m/5km W of Kendal. SD 4692
Undercliffe W Yorks 48 D4* dist of Bradford 2m/3km NE of city centre. SE 1834
Underdale Salop 34 C3* NE dist of Shrewsbury. SJ 5113
Underhill London 19 F2* loc in borough of Barnet 1km SE of Chipping Barnet and 10m/16km N of Charing Cross. TQ 2595
Underling Green Kent 12 D2* loc 2km NE of Marden. TQ 7546
Under River Kent 20 B6* ham 3m/4km SE of Sevenoaks. TQ 5552
Under Tofts S Yorks 43 G3* loc in Sheffield 3m/5km W of city centre. SK 3087
Underwood Devon 4 C5 dist of Plymouth 4m/6km E of city centre. SX 5355
Underwood Gwent 15 H3* loc 1m NW of Bishton. ST 3888
Underwood Notts 44 A5* vil 2m/4km N of Eastwood. SK 4750
Undley Suffolk 38 B6* loc 2km SW of Lakenheath. TL 6981
Undy (Gwndy) Gwent 16 A3 vil 1km E of Magor. ST 4368
Union Bridge 67 F3 rd br across R Tweed 4m/7km W of Berwick-upon-Tweed. See Horncliffe, Nthmb. NT 9351
Union Mills Isle of Man 46 B5 vil 2m/4km NW of Douglas. SC 3577
Union Street E Sussex 12 D4* loc adjoining Flimwell to W. TQ 7131
Unk 34 A6 r rising on Clun Forest, Salop, and flowing first E then S into R Clun at Clun. SO 2981
Unst Shetland 89 F5 northernmost of main islands of Shetland Is., with much indented coastline. Is some 12m/19km N to S and from 3m to 5m (4km to 8km) E to W. Crofting, fishing. Airfield at Baltasound, qv. HP 51, 60
Unstone Derbys 43 H3 vil 2km SE of Dronfield. **U. Green** loc to S. SK 3777
Unsworth Gtr Manchester 42 D1* loc in Bury 2m/4km SE of tn centre. SD 8107
Unthank Cumbria 52 D2 loc 1m NE of Skelton. NY 4436
Unthank Cumbria 53 E1 loc 1km N of Gamblesby. NY 6140
Unthank Cumbria 59 H6* loc 2m/3km SE of Dalston. NY 3948
Unthank Derbys 43 G3* loc 2km SW of Holmesfield. SK 3076
Unthank Durham 54 B1* loc 3m/4km W of Durham. NZ 2341
Unthank End Cumbria 52 D2* loc 2km E of Skelton. NY 4535
Upavon Wilts 17 F5 vil on R Avon 4m/6km SW of Pewsey. SU 1355
Up Cerne Dorset 8 D4 ham 1m N of Cerne Abbas. ST 6502
Upchurch Kent 20 D5/21 E5 vil 4m/7km E of Gillingham. TQ 8467
Upcott Devon 6 D2* loc 4m/6km NE of Barnstaple. SS 5838
Upcott Som 7 G3* ham 2m/3km S of Dulverton. SS 9025
Upcott Som 8 A2* loc 2m/3km W of Taunton. ST 1924
Upcott, Lower Devon 5 E3* ham 2km NE of Chudleigh. SX 8880
Upend Cambs 30 C2* loc 5m/8km SE of Newmarket. TL 7058
Up Exe Devon 7 G5 vil on R Exe 6m/10km N of Exeter. SS 9402
Upgang N Yorks 55 G4 loc on North Sea coast on NW side of Whitby. NZ 8811
Upgate Norfolk 39 F3* ham 1km SE of Swannington. TG 1418
Upgate Street Norfolk 39 E5* loc 4m/6km SE of Attleborough. TM 0992
Upgate Street Norfolk 39 F5* loc 4m/6km NW of Bungay. TM 2891
Up Green Hants 18 C5* loc adjoining Eversley Cross to S. SU 7961
Uphall Dorset 8 D4 ham 1km NW of Rampisham and 4m/7km NW of Maiden Newton. ST 5502
Uphall Lothian 65 G2 loc on W side of, and par including, tn of Broxburn. **Upr Uphall** is loc adjoining Uphall to N. **Uphall Stn** is loc 1m S. NT 0671
Upham Devon 7 F4* ham 5m/8km SW of Tiverton. SS 8808
Upham Hants 10 C3 vil 2m/4km NW of Bishop's Waltham. SU 5320
Upham, Lower Hants 10 C3 vil 2m/4km NW of Bishop's Waltham. SU 5219
Uphampton H & W 26 D2 vil 4m/7km W of Droitwich. SO 8364
Uphampton H & W 25 H2* ham 5m/9km E of Presteigne. SO 3963
Upham, Upper Wilts 17 F4* loc 3m/4km NW of Aldbourne. SU 2277
Up Hatherley Glos 26 D5* SW suburb of Cheltenham. SO 9120
Uphempston Devon 5 E4* ham 2m/3km NE of Totnes. SX 8263
Uphill Avon 15 H5 S suburb of Weston-super-Mare. ST 3158
Up Holland Lancs 42 B1 urban loc 4m/6km W of Wigan. SD 5205
Uplands Glos 16 D1* NE dist of Stroud. SO 8505
Uplands W Glam 23 G6* loc in Swansea 1m W of tn centre. SS 6493
Uplawmoor S'clyde 64 B3* vil 3m/5km SW of Neilston. NS 4355
Upleadon Glos 26 C5 vil 2m/3km E of Newent. SO 7526
Upleatham Cleveland 55 E3 vil 2m/4km SW of Saltburn. NZ 6319
Uplees Kent 21 F5 loc 2m/3km NW of Faversham. TQ 9964
Uploders Dorset 8 C5 ham 3m/4km E of Bridport. SY 5093
Uplowman Devon 7 G3 vil 4m/7km NE of Tiverton. ST 0115
Uplyme Devon 8 B5 vil 2m/3km NW of Lyme Regis. SY 3293
Up Marden W Sussex 11 E3 ham 5m/8km W of Singleton. SU 7914
Upminster London 20 C3 tn in borough of Havering 3m/5km SE of Romford. TQ 5586
Up Nately Hants 18 B6 vil 4m/6km E of Basingstoke. SU 6951
Upnor, Lower Kent 20 D4 loc on N bank of R Medway 2m/3km NE of Strood. Loc of **Upr Upnor** 1km upstream; restored 16c cas (A.M.). TQ 7671
Upottery Devon 8 A3 vil on R Otter 5m/8km NE of Honiton. ST 2007
Uppark W Sussex 11 E3 17c-18c hse (NT) 4m/7km SE of Petersfield. SU 7717
UPPER. For names beginning with this word, see under next word. This also applies to names beginning with High, Low; Higher, Lower, Nether; Far, Near; Mid, Middle; Great, Little; Greater, Lesser; Isle(s) of; North, South, East, West; The, Y, Yr.
Upperby Cumbria 60 A6* dist of Carlisle 2m/3km S of city centre. NY 4053
Uppermill Gtr Manchester 43 E1 vil 5m/7km E of Oldham. SD 9905
Upperthong W Yorks 43 F1 vil 1m W of Holmfirth. SE 1208
Upperthorpe Derbys 44 A3* loc adjoining Killamarsh to S. SK 4580
Upperthorpe Humberside 44 C2* loc 1km W of Haxey. SE 7500
Upperton Grampian. See Peterhead.
Upperton W Sussex 11 F3 ham 2km NW of Petworth across Petworth Park. SU 9522
Uppertown Derbys 43 G4* loc 3m/5km NE of Matlock. SK 3265
Uppertown Orkney 89 B7* loc at NW end of S Ronaldsay, 2m/3km W of St Margaret's Hope. ND 4194
Uppertown Stroma, H'land 86 F1 loc at S end of Island of Stroma in Pentland Firth – see Stroma. ND 3576
Upperwood Derbys 43 G5* loc adjoining Matlock Bath to S. SK 2957
Uppincott Devon 7 F5* loc 3m/5km NE of Crediton. SS 8802
Uppingham Leics 36 D4 small tn 7m/12km N of Corby. Boys' boarding school. SP 8699
Uppington Salop 34 C3 vil 4m/6km SW of Wellington. SJ 5909
Upsall Cleveland 54 D3/55 E3* loc 3m/5km W of Guisborough. NZ 5615
Upsall N Yorks 54 D6 vil 4m/6km NE of Thirsk. SE 4587
Upshire Essex 20 B2 vil 2m/3km E of Waltham Abbey. TL 4101
Up Somborne Hants 10 B2 vil 3m/5km SE of Stockbridge. SU 3932
Upstreet Kent 13 G1 vil 2m/4km SW of Sarre. TR 2263
Up Sydling Dorset 8 D4* ham 3m/4km W of Cerne Abbas. ST 6101
Upthorpe Glos 16 C2* loc 2km N of Dursley. SO 7500
Upthorpe Suffolk 31 E1* loc 2km E of Stanton. TL 9872
Upton Berks 18 D4 S dist of Slough. SU 9879
Upton Bucks 18 C1* ham 3m/5km SW of Aylesbury. SP 7711
Upton Cambs 37 F4 ham 6m/9km W of Peterborough. Ailsworth Heath Nature Reserve to NE. TF 1000
Upton Cambs 37 F6 vil 6m/9km NW of Huntingdon. TL 1778
Upton Ches 42 A4 suburb 2m/3km N of Chester. **U. Heath** loc adjoining to NE. SJ 4069
Upton Ches 42 B3 loc 2m/3km N of Widnes. SJ 5087
Upton Cornwall 3 G1* ham close to vil of U. Cross, 5m/9km N of Liskeard. SX 2772
Upton Cornwall 6 B4* loc in SW part of Bude. SS 2004
Upton Cumbria 52 C1* loc adjoining Caldbeck to SW. NY 3239
Upton Devon 4 D6 loc 2m/4km W of Kingsbridge. SX 7043
Upton Devon 7 H4 ham 4m/7km NW of Honiton. ST 0902
Upton Dorset 9 E5* ham near coast 6m/10km SE of Dorchester. SY 7483
Upton Dorset 9 G5 urban loc 3m/4km NW of Poole. SY 9893
Upton Dyfed 22 C5* loc 3m/5km NE of Pembroke. Remains of medieval cas. SN 0104
Upton Hants 10 B3* ham 4m/7km NW of Southampton. SU 3716
Upton Hants 17 G5 vil 2m/3km NW of Hurstbourne Tarrant. SU 3655
Upton Humberside 51 F3* loc 1km E of Beeford. TA 1454
Upton Leics 36 A4 ham 4m/6km E of Atherstone. SP 3699
Upton Lincs 44 D3 vil 4m/6km SE of Gainsborough. SK 8686
Upton London 20 B3 N dist of W Ham in borough of Newham. TQ 4084
Upton Merseyside 41 H3 dist of Birkenhead 4m/6km W of tn centre. SJ 2788
Upton Norfolk 39 G4 vil 2km N of Acle. **U. Green** loc adjoining to E. **U. Broad** small broad or lake 1km NW. TG 3912
Upton Northants 28 C2 loc in Northampton 3m/4km W of tn centre. SP 7160
Upton Notts 44 C3 ham 4m/6km SE of E Retford. SK 7476
Upton Notts 44 C5 vil 2m/4km E of Southwell. SK 7354
Upton Oxon 18 A3 vil 2m/4km S of Didcot. SU 5186
Upton Oxon 27 F6* loc 1km W of Burford. SP 2412
Upton Som 7 G2 ham on edge of Exmoor National Park 5m/8km E of Dulverton. SS 9929
Upton Som 8 C2* ham 2m/4km E of Langport. ST 4526
Upton Warwicks 27 F2* loc 2m/3km E of Alcester. SP 1257
Upton Wilts 9 F2* ham 1m NW of E Knoyle and 6m/9km N of Shaftesbury. ST 8732
Upton W Yorks 49 F6 vil 2km N of S Elmsall. SE 4713
Upton Bishop H & W 26 B5 vil 4m/6km NE of Ross-on-Wye. SO 6527
Upton Cheyney Avon 16 C4 vil 5m/8km NW of Bath. ST 6969
Upton Cressett Salop 34 D5 vil 4m/6km W of Bridgnorth. SO 6592
Upton Crews H & W 26 B5* ham 4m/6km NE of Ross-on-Wye. SO 6427
Upton Cross Cornwall 3 G1 vil 5m/9km N of Liskeard. SX 2872
Upton End Beds 29 F4* NE part of Shillington, 3m/5km S of Shefford. TL 1234
Upton Grey Hants 10 D1 vil 4m/7km SE of Basingstoke. SU 6948
Upton Hellions Devon 7 F4 vil on R Creedy 2m/3km N of Crediton. SS 8403
Upton House Warwicks 27 G3* partly late 17c hse (NT) 6m/10km NW of Banbury. SP 3645
Upton Lovell Wilts 9 F1* vil 2m/3km SE of Heytesbury. ST 9440
Upton Magna Salop 34 C3 vil 4m/6km E of Shrewsbury. SJ 5512
Upton Noble Som 9 E1 vil 4m/6km NE of Bruton. ST 7139
Upton Park London 20 B3* loc between W and E Ham in borough of Newham, 6m/10km E of London Br. TQ 4183
Upton Pyne Devon 7 G5 vil 3m/5km N of Exeter. SX 9197
Upton St Leonards Glos 26 D6 vil 3m/5km SE of Gloucester. SO 8614
Upton Scudamore Wilts 16 D6 vil 2m/3km N of Warminster. ST 8647
Upton Snodsbury H & W 26 D2 vil 6m/9km E of Worcester. SO 9454
Upton upon Severn H & W 26 D3 vil on W bank of R Severn 6m/9km NW of Tewkesbury. SO 8540
Upton Warren H & W 26 D1 vil 3m/4km SW of Bromsgrove. SO 9267
Upwaltham W Sussex 11 F4 ham 5m/9km SW of Petworth. SU 9413
Upware Cambs 30 A1 loc on E bank of R Cam 6m/10km S of Ely. TL 5370
Upwell 38 A4 vil on Cambs-Norfolk border 5m/8km SE of Wisbech. TF 5002
Upwey Dorset 8 D5 loc 4m/6km N of Weymouth. SY 6684
Upwick Green Herts 29 H5* ham 3m/5km NW of Bishop's Stortford. TL 4524
Upwood Cambs 37 G6 vil 2m/4km SW of Ramsey. TL 2582
Ura Firth Shetland 89 E6 large inlet of St Magnus Bay on W coast of Mainland, separated from Ronas Voe to N by neck of land 1m wide. **Urafirth** locality at head of inlet, with small **Loch of Urafirth** to N. HU 2977
Urchfont Wilts 17 E5 vil 4m/6km SE of Devizes. SU 0457
Ure 49 F2 r rising on Abbotside Common 5m/8km NW of Hawes, N Yorks, and flowing SE by Hawes, Aysgarth, Middleham, Masham, Ripon, and Boroughbridge to join R Swale 2m/4km E of Boroughbridge and form R Ouse. Valley above Masham is known as Wensleydale. SE 4365
Ure 70 C1 r in Argyll, S'clyde region, with head waters to N and W of Beinn Trilleachan, running down Glen U. to R Creran. NN 0348
Ure Bank N Yorks 49 E1* loc 1m N of Ripon across R Ure. SE 3172
Urgashay Som 8 D2* loc 3m/5km E of Ilchester, beyond Yeovilton airfield. ST 5624
Urgha W Isles 88 B3* loc on Harris 2km E of Tarbert. NG 1799
Urie 83 F5 r in Grampian region running SE by Old Rayne and Pitcaple to R Don 1m SE of Inverurie. NJ 7820
Urie Lingey Shetland 89 F5* island off N coast of Fetlar 1km N of Urie Ness. HU 5995
Urie Loch S'clyde 63 G5* small loch or tarn on Arran 3m/5km NW of Whiting Bay. NS 0028
Urie Ness Shetland 89 F5* headland on N coast of Fetlar 3m/5km NW of Houbie. HU 5994
Urishay Common H & W 25 G4* loc 2m/3km N of Michaelchurch Escley. SO 3137
Urlar Burn 75 H6 stream in Tayside region running NE into R Tay at Aberfeldy. See also Falls of Moness. NN 8549
Urlay Nook Cleveland 54 C3 loc 2m/3km NW of Yarm. NZ 4014
Urmston Gtr Manchester 42 C2 tn 5m/8km SW of Manchester. Textiles, steel, rubber, soap. SJ 7694
Urpeth, High Durham 61 G6* ham 3m/5km NW of Chester-le-Street. NZ 2353
Urquhart Grampian 82 C1 vil 4m/7km E of Elgin. NJ 2862
Urquhart Bay H'land 81 E4 bay on NW shore of Loch Ness 1m E of Drumnadrochit. Rs Coiltie and Enrick run into bay. See also Strone. NH 5229
Urra N Yorks 55 E4 ham 5m/8km SE of Stokesley. NZ 5701
Urray Forest H'land 81 E3 state forest in Ross and Cromarty dist 5m/8km SW of Conon Br. NH 4850
Urr Water 58 D6 r in Dumfries & Galloway region issuing from Loch Urr and running S past Dalbeattie to Rough Firth and Solway Firth. NX 8551
Urswick, Great Cumbria 46 D1 vil ranged round three sides of **U. Tarn** 3m/4km E of Dalton-in-Furness. **Lit Urswick** vil 1km SW. SD 2674
Urvaig Tiree, S'clyde 69 B7 northernmost point of island, 2km NW of Rubha Dubh. NM 0850
Usan Tayside 77 G5 vil on E coast 2m/3km S of Montrose. Also known as Fishtown of Usan. NO 7254
Ushat Head H'land 86 C1* headland on N coast of Caithness dist 6m/9km W of Thurso. ND 0371

Ushaw Moor Durham 54 B1 vil in coal-mining dist 3m/5km W of Durham. NZ 2242
Usk (Brynbuga) Gwent 15 H2 small mkt tn on R Usk on site of Roman fort of *Burrium*. Remains of Norman cas. SO 3700
Usk (Wysg) 15 H3 r rising SW of Trecastle, Powys, on border of Powys and Dyfed, and flowing N to Usk Resr, then E to Trecastle and Brecon, then SE to Crickhowell and Abergavenny, then S by Usk and Newport to mouth of R Severn S of Newport, Gwent. River noted for salmon-fishing. ST 3281
Uskmouth Gwent 15 H3* loc 1km W of Nash near E bank of R Usk at its mouth. Power stn on river bank to W. ST 3383
Usk Reservoir 24 D5 large resr on course of R Usk on borders of Dyfed and Powys 3m/5km W of Trecastle. Afforestation on either side. SN 8328
Usselby Lincs 45 E2 ham 3m/5km N of Mkt Rasen. TF 0993
Usway Burn 60 D1* r rising on S slopes of The Cheviot and flowing S to R Coquet 1m N of Linshiels, Nthmb. NY 8807
Usworth Tyne & Wear 61 G5* N dist of Washington. NZ 3058
Utkinton Ches 42 B4 ham 2m/3km N of Tarporley. SJ 5465
Utley W Yorks 48 C4 N dist of Keighley. SE 0542
Uton Devon 7 F5 ham 2km S of Crediton. SX 8298
Utterby Lincs 45 G2 vil 4m/6km N of Louth. TF 3093
Uttlesford 119 admin dist of Essex.
Uttoxeter Staffs 35 G1 mkt tn 13m/21km NE of Stafford. Racecourse. SK 0933
Uwchmynydd Gwynedd 32 A2* loc 2m/3km W of Aberdaron. SH 1425
Uxbridge London 19 E3 tn in borough of Hillingdon 6m/10km NE of Slough and 15m/25km W of Charing Cross. TQ 0584
Uxellodunum Cumbria. See Castlesteads.
Uyea Shetland 89 E6 island off N coast of Mainland. HU 3192
Uyea Shetland 89 F5 island of about 600 acres or 240 hectares off S coast of Unst opp Uyeasound. HU 6099
Uyeasound Shetland 89 F5 vil on S coast of Unst at head of **Uyea Sound,** strait running between Unst and island of Uyea. HP 5901
Uynarey Shetland 89 E6* uninhabited island off SW coast of Yell 2km NW of Ulsta and 3m/5km W of Hamna Voe. HU 4480
Uzmaston Dyfed 22 C4 vil 2km SE of Haverfordwest. SM 9714

V

Vacasay Island W Isles 88 B2* small uninhabited island in E Loch Roag close to shore of Gt Bernera island. NB 1836
Vaceasay W Isles 88 E1* small uninhabited island in Sound of Harris 1km off NE coast of N Uist. NF 9774
Vachelich Dyfed 22 A3* loc 2m/3km E of St David's. SM 7725
Vachery Pond Surrey 11 G2 lake about 1500 metres long, 2km SE of Cranleigh. TQ 0737
Vacsay W Isles 88 A2* small uninhabited island in W Loch Roag, W coast of Lewis, 2km W of Gt Bernera. NB 1137
Vaila Shetland 89 D7 island of about 1 sq mile or 3 sq km off Mainland at entrance to **V. Sound,** inlet containing the smaller island of Linga. At head of sound is vil of Walls. HU 2346
Vaivoe Shetland 89 F6* loc at head of small bay of **Vai Voe** on N coast of island of Whalsay, 2m/3km NE of Brough. HU 5766
Valehouse Reservoir Derbys 43 E2* one of a chain of resrs in R Etherow valley, 2m/4km N of Glossop. SK 0397
Valency 6 A6* r in Cornwall rising 1m N of Davidstow and flowing N and then W into the Atlantic Ocean near Boscastle. SX 0991
Vale of Berkeley 16 B2* low-lying area between Cotswold Hills and R Severn estuary in vicinity of Berkeley, Glos. ST 69
Vale of Catmose Leics. See Catmose, Vale of. SK 8709
Vale of Edeyrnion. See Dyffryn Edeirnion.
Vale of Ewyas Gwent 25 G5* valley of R Honddu in vicinity of Llanthony. SO 22
Vale of Glamorgan 118 admin dist of S Glam.
Vale of Llangollen. See Llangollen.
Vale of Pewsey Wilts 17 E5, F5. See Pewsey.
Vale of Pickering N Yorks. See Pickering.
Vale of Taunton Deane Som 8 A2 fertile plain S of Quantock Hills extending roughly from Taunton (E) to Milverton (W), both inclusive. (Sometimes spelt without final e.) See also Taunton. ST 12,22
Vale of White Horse 119 admin dist of Oxon.
Vale of White Horse 17 G2 valley of R Ock N of Berkshire Downs. SU 3291
Vale Royal 117 admin dist of Ches.
Vale, West W Yorks 48 D6* loc 1km W of Elland. SE 0920
Valla Field Shetland 89 F5* hill ridge on Unst, extending northwards from between Lunda Wick and Loch of Watlee. HP 5807
Vallay W Isles 88 D1 island off N coast of N Uist 2m/3km E of Griminish Pt. **V. Strand,** mudflats separating island from N Uist, is fordable at low tide. Island measures 4km E to W and about 1km N to S. NF 7776
Valle Crucis Abbey Clwyd 41 G6 remains of 13c abbey (A.M.), 2km NW of Llangollen. To N is Eliseg's Pillar, remains of 9c cross (A.M.). SJ 2044
Valley Gwynedd 40 A3/A4 loc on Anglesey at convergence of rd and rly at approach to Stanley Embankment, which carries them across the strait to Holy I. Valley Airfield 3m/4km SE. SH 2979
Valley End Surrey 18 D5* ham 2m/3km NW of Chobham. SU 9563
Valleyfield Fife 72 D5 loc 2km E of Culross. NT 0086
Valley, Low S Yorks 43 H1* coal-mining loc adjoining Darfield to SW. SE 4003
Valley of Rocks, The Devon 7 E1 beauty spot just W of Lynton. SS 7049
Valley, The Dyfed 22 D5* loc 1m W of Saundersfoot. SN 1205
Valsgarth Shetland 89 F5* loc on Unst 1km N of Haroldswick. HP 6413
Valtos W Isles 88 A2* vil on W shore of W Loch Roag 3m/5km SE of Gallan Hd. NB 0936
Van Mid Glam 15 F3* loc on E side of Caerphilly. ST 1686
Van (Fan, Y) Powys 33 F5* loc 3m/5km N of Llanidloes. SN 9587
Vange Essex 20 D3 S dist of Basildon. **V. Marshes** to S beside **V. Creek.** TQ 7287
Vardre (Faedre) W Glam 14 C2 dist of Clydach, 6m/10km NE of Swansea. SN 6901
Varley Head Cornwall 3 E1* headland on N coast 1m W of Port Isaac. SW 9881
Varragill H'land 79 C5 r in Skye running N into Loch Portree. NG 4741
Varteg (Farteg, Y) Gwent 15 G1 loc 2m/3km N of Abersychan. SO 2606
Vatarsay W Isles 88 C4* islet at entrance to Loch Leurbost, E coast of Lewis. NB 4023
Vaternish H'land 78 A3-B4 peninsula on Skye, on E side of Loch Snizort, culminating in headland of **Vaternish Pt.** NG 2658
Vatersay W Isles 88 D4 irregularly shaped island of about 3 sq miles or 8 sq km off SW end of Barra across the narrow Sound of V. NL 69
Vatisker W Isles 88 C2* loc near E coast of Lewis 1km S of Back. **Vatisker Pt** is headland on coast 1km E. NB 4839
Vatsetter Shetland 89 F6* loc near E coast of Yell 2m/3km SE of Mid Yell. **Ness of V.** headland to E; **Wick of V.** small bay to NW; **Loch of V.** small loch to W, separated from bay by narrow causeway; **White Hill of V.** above cliff with lighthouse (see Gamla) to SE. HU 5389
Vatten Skye, H'land 79 B5 locality on E side of **Loch V.** at head of Loch Bracadale, 3m/5km SE of Dunvegan. NG 2843
Vaul Tiree, S'clyde 69 B7* loc on W side of bay of same name on N coast, 2m/4km N of Scarinish. See also Dùn Mór Vaul. NM 0448
Vauxhall London 19 G4* dist in borough of Lambeth between Lambeth and Vauxhall Brs. Former gardens were resort of fashion in 18c; now warehouses etc. TQ 3078
Vauxhall W Midlands 35 G5* loc in Birmingham 2km E of city centre. SP 0887
Vaynor (Faenor, Y) Mid Glam 15 F1 ham 3m/4km N of Merthyr Tydfil. SO 0410
Veantrow Bay Orkney 89 B6* wide bay on N coast of island of Shapinsay. HY 5020
Veensgarth Shetland 89 E7* loc on Mainland 4m/6km NW of Lerwick. HU 4244
Velator Devon 6 D2* loc just S of Braunton. SS 4835
Velindre (Felindre) Dyfed 22 C2/D2 ham on R Nyfer 3m/4km E of Newport. SN 1039
Velindre (Felindre) Dyfed 23 E2 vil 3m/5km SE of Newcastle Emlyn. SN 3538
Velindre (Felindre) Powys 25 G4 ham 3m/4km NE of Talgarth. SO 1836
Vellan Head Cornwall 2 C6* headland on W side of Lizard peninsula 3m/5km NW of Lizard Pt. SW 6614
Vellow Som 7 H2 loc 3m/5km SE of Watchet. ST 0938
Vementry Shetland 89 E7 uninhabited island of about 1000 acres or 400 hectares off W coast of Mainland, on S side of strait of Swarbacks Minn. Largest of the uninhabited islands of Shetland. Varied landscape with much bird life. HU 2960
Venford Reservoir Devon 4 D3 resr on Dartmoor 5m/8km W of Ashburton. SX 6871
Venn Green Devon 6 C4* ham 5m/8km NE of Holsworthy. SS 3711
Vennington Salop 34 A3* loc 2km W of Westbury. SJ 3309
Venn Ottery Devon 7 H5 vil 3m/5km SW of Ottery St Mary. SY 0791
Venny Tedburn Devon 7 F5* loc 2m/3km SW of Crediton. SX 8297
Venta Hants. See Winchester.
Venta Icenorum Norfolk. See Caistor St Edmund.
Venta Silurum Gwent. See Caerwent.
Venterdon Cornwall 3 H1* loc 3m/5km N of Callington. SX 3574
Ventnor Isle of Wight 10 C6 S coast resort and residential tn 3m/4km SW of Shanklin. **V. Bay** opp tn centre. SZ 5677
Venton Devon 4 C5* ham 3m/5km W of Ivybridge. SX 5956
Venus Hill Herts 19 E2* loc 3m/4km E of Chesham. TL 0101
Ver 19 F2 r rising at Redbourn, Herts, and flowing S past the W side of St Albans into R Colne between St Albans and Watford. TL 1401
Vercovicium Nthmb Roman fort on Hadrian's Wall. See Housesteads. NY 7968
Vernemetum Notts. See Willoughby-on-the-Wolds.
Vernham Dean Hants 17 G5 vil 3m/5km NW of Hurstbourne Tarrant. Jacbn manor hse 1km E. SU 3456
Vernham Street Hants 17 G5* ham 1km NE of Vernham Dean. SU 3557
Vernolds Common Salop 34 B6* loc 3m/5km SE of Craven Arms. SO 4780
Vernonae Leics. See Cross, High.
Verulamium Herts. See St Albans.
Verwick (Ferwig, Y) Dyfed 22 D1 ham 2m/4km N of Cardigan. SN 1849
Verwood Dorset 9 G3 scattered loc 4m/7km NW of Ringwood. SU 0808
Veryan Cornwall 3 E4 vil 7m/11km SW of Mevagissey and 2km inland from **V. Bay,** which extends from Nare Hd eastwards to Dodman Pt. Ham of **V. Green,** lies to NE of vil. SW 9139
Ve Skerries Shetland 89 D6/D7* group of rocks 3m/5km NW of Papa Stour. HU 1065
Vexford, Lower Som 7 H2 ham 6m/9km SE of Watchet. ST 1135
Vicarage Green Beds 29 E3 loc adjoining Bromham to N, 3m/5km NW of Bedford. TL 0151
Vickerstown Cumbria 46 C2 urban loc on Walney I., opp Barrow-in-Furness, connected to Barrow by causeway. SD 1868
Victoria Cornwall 3 E2 ham 6m/10km SW of Bodmin. SW 9861
Victoria Gwent 15 F1 loc adjoining Ebbw Vale to S. SO 1707
Victoria 43 F1* loc on borders of S and W Yorks 5m/7km NW of Penistone. SE 1705
Victoria Cave N Yorks 47 H2* limestone cave on Langcliffe Scar, 1m E of Langcliffe. See also Jubilee Cave. SD 8365
Victoria Park Gtr Manchester 42 D2* dist of Manchester 2m/3km SE of city centre. SJ 8595
Victoria, Upper Tayside 73 H1 loc 2m/3km NW of Carnoustie. NO 5336
Vidlin Shetland 89 E7* vil on E coast of Mainland at head of **V. Voe** 2km N of Dury Voe. HU 4765
Viewfield Fife 73 F4* dist and industrial estate in SW part of Glenrothes. NT 2599
View, South Hants 18 B6* dist of Basingstoke to N of tn centre. SU 6352
Vigo W Midlands 35 F4 loc 2m/3km S of Brownhills. SK 0502
Vigo Village Kent 20 C5* loc on N Downs 3m/4km NE of Wrotham. TQ 6461
Village, East Devon 7 F4* ham 3m/5km N of Crediton. SS 8405
Village, East S Glam 15 E4* loc on E side of Cowbridge. SS 9974
Village of Ae D & G. See Ae Village.
Village, The Berks 18 D4* loc in Windsor Gt Park 2m/4km S of Windsor. SU 9573
Village, The W Midlands 35 E5* loc 3m/5km W of Dudley tn centre. SO 8989
Village, West S Glam 15 E4* loc on W side of Cowbridge. SS 9874
Vindolanda Nthmb 60 D5 Roman fort (A.M.) 2km NW of Bardon Mill. See also Chesterholme. NY 7766
Vindomora Durham. See Ebchester.
Vindovala Nthmb 61 F4 Roman fort on Hadrian's Wall 2km W of Heddon-on-the-Wall. NZ 1167
Vinegar Hill Gwent 16 A3* loc 1km E of Magor. ST 4387
Vinegar Hill 75 G3 mt on border of Highland and Tayside regions 5m/8km SE of Dalwhinnie. Height 2584 ft or 788 metres. NN 7080
Vinehall Street E Sussex 12 D4 ham 3m/4km N of Battle. TQ 7520
Vine's Cross E Sussex 12 C5* vil 1m E of Horam. TQ 5917
Viney Hill Glos 16 B1 vil 1m W of Blakeney. SO 6506
Vinovium Durham. See Binchester.
Virginia Water Surrey 18 D4/19 E4* residential dist 3m/5km SW of Staines. Named after large lake to NW, on S edge of Windsor Gt Park. SU 9968
Virginstow Devon 6 C5* vil 6m/9km NE of Launceston. SX 3792
Virkie Shetland 89 E8 loc on Mainland at head of inlet called **Pool of V.** on N side of Sumburgh Airport. HU 3911
Virley Essex 30 D6 loc 4m/7km SE of Tiptree. TL 9414
Viroconium Salop. See Wroxeter.
Vobster Som 16 C6* ham 4m/7km W of Frome. To N, loc of **Upr Vobster.** ST 7049
Voe Shetland 89 E7 vil on Mainland at head of Olna Firth. **Loch of V.** 1km E. HU 4063
Voe of Browland Shetland. See Browland.
Voe of Cullingsburgh Shetland 89 E7* large inlet on NE coast of island of Bressay. HU 5142
Voe of Scatsta Shetland. See Scatsta.
Voe of Snarraness Shetland. See Snarra Ness.
Voe of Sound Shetland. See Sound.

Voreda Cumbria. See Castlesteads.
Vorlan (Forlan, Y) Dyfed 22 C3* loc 1m S of Maenclochog. SN 0826
Votersay W Isles 88 E1* small uninhabited island off NE coast of N Uist 3m/5km SE of Berneray. NF 9476
Vowchurch H & W 25 H4 vil in Golden Valley (R Dore) 6m/10km NW of Pontrilas. SO 3636
Vownog Clwyd 41 H4* loc adjoining Soughton to NE. SJ 2466
Vron Gate Salop 34 A3* loc 2m/3km W of Westbury. SJ 3209
Vuia Beag W Isles 88 A2* small uninhabited island in Loch Roag, W coast of Lewis 2m/4km E of Miavaig. NB 1233
Vuia Mór W Isles 88 A2* uninhabited island in Loch Roag, W coast of Lewis, close to W side of Gt Bernera. NB 1334
Vulcan Village Merseyside 42 B2* loc adjoining Newton-le-Willows to S. Rly engine works. SJ 5894
Vyne, The Hants. See Sherborne St John. SU 6357
Vyrnwy 34 A3 r originating in many streams running into Lake Vyrnwy (resr), Powys, whence it flows generally E into R Severn on English-Welsh border 8m/13km NE of Welshpool. SJ 3215

W

Waas H'land 86 D1* loc in Caithness dist 2m/3km SW of Thurso. ND 0766
Waberthwaite Cumbria 52 B5* loc 2km SE of Ravenglass across R Esk. SD 1095
Wackerfield Durham 54 B3 ham 2m/3km NE of Staindrop. NZ 1522
Wacton H & W 26 B2* loc 3m/5km NW of Bromyard. SO 6157
Wacton Norfolk 39 F5 vil 7m/11km NW of Harleston. TM 1791
Wadbister Shetland 89 E7* loc near E coast of Mainland on S side of **Wadbister Voe** and 1m W of Lambgarth Hd, headland at end of promontory of **Wadbister Ness.** HU 4349
Wadborough H & W 26 D3 vil 3m/5km NW of Pershore. SO 9047
Waddesdon Bucks 28 C5 vil 5m/8km W of Aylesbury. **Waddesdon Manor** (NT), late 19c hse in French Renaissance style. SP 7416
Waddeton Devon 5 E5* ham to N of R Dart estuary 3m/5km W of Brixham. SX 8756
Waddicar Merseyside 42 A2* loc adjoining Kirkby to NW. SJ 3999
Waddingham Lincs 44 D2 vil 4m/6km SE of Kirton in Lindsey. SK 9896
Waddington Lancs 48 A4 vil 2m/3km NW of Clitheroe. SD 7243
Waddington Lincs 44 D4 vil 5m/7km S of Lincoln. Airfield to E. SK 9764
Waddingworth Lincs 45 F4 loc 4m/7km E of Bardney. TF 1871
Waddon Devon 5 E3* loc 1m E of Chudleigh. SX 8879
Waddon London 19 G5* loc in borough of Croydon 1m W of Croydon tn centre. TQ 3164
Wadebridge Cornwall 3 E1 tn on R Camel 6m/10km NW of Bodmin. SW 9972
Wadeford Som 8 B3 2m/3km NW of Chard. ST 3110
Wade Hall Lancs 47 F5* loc 1m W of Leyland. SD 5221
Wadenhoe Northants 37 E6 vil 4m/6km SW of Oundle. TL 0183
Wadesmill Herts 29 G6 vil 2m/3km N of Ware. TL 3517
Wadhurst E Sussex 12 C4 large Wealden vil 6m/10km SE of Tunbridge Wells. TQ 6431
Wadshelf Derbys 43 G4 vil 4m/7km W of Chesterfield. SK 3170
Wadsley S Yorks 43 G2* dist of Sheffield 3m/4km NW of city centre. **Wadsley Br** loc 1m NE. SK 3290
Wadsworth W Yorks 48 C4/C5* moorland loc to N of Hebden Br. SD 9833
Wadworth S Yorks 44 B2 vil 4m/6km S of Doncaster. SK 5697
Waen Clwyd 41 F5* loc 1km NW of Nantglyn. SH 9962
Waen Clwyd 41 G4* loc 4m/6km NE of Denbigh. SJ 0969
Waen Clwyd 41 G4 ham 4m/6km E of Denbigh. SJ 1065
Waen Fach Powys 33 H3 loc 6m/10km N of Welshpool. SJ 2017
Waen-pentir Gwynedd 40 C5* loc 4m/6km S of Bangor. SH 5766
Waen-wen Gwynedd 40 C4 loc 2m/3km S of Bangor. SH 5768
Wagaford Water 6 D5* stream rising N of Halwill Junction, Devon, and flowing E into R Lew 2km N of Northlew. SS 5100
Wagg Som 8 C2* ham adjoining Huish Episcopi and 1m E of Langport. ST 4326
Wainfelin Gwent 15 G2* loc 1km NW of Pontypool. SO 2701
Wainfleet (or Wainfleet All Saints) Lincs 45 H5 tn on Steeping R 5m/8km SW of Skegness. Brewing. **Wainfleet Bank** loc 2m/3km W; **Wainfleet St Mary** par to W; **Wainfleet Tofts** loc 1m S. TF 4958
Wainford Norfolk 39 G5* loc 1m E of Bungay. TM 3490
Waingroves Derbys 43 H6* loc 1m SE of Ripley. SK 4149
Wainhouse Corner Cornwall 6 B5 ham 7m/11km SW of Bude. SX 1895
Wain Lee Staffs 42 D5* loc 1m SW of Biddulph. SJ 8655
Wainscott Kent 20 D4 loc 2m/3km N of Rochester. TQ 7471
Wainstalls W Yorks 48 C5* vil 4m/6km NW of Halifax. SD 0428
Wain Wath Force N Yorks 53 G4* waterfall 1m W of Keld. NY 8701
Waitby Cumbria 53 F4 ham 2km W of Kirkby Stephen. NY 7508
Waithwith N Yorks 54 B5* loc on W edge of Catterick Camp 2m/4km S of Richmond. SE 1597
Wakefield W Yorks 49 E6 county tn and cathedral city on R Calder 8m/13km S of Leeds. Local industries include coal-mining, textiles, brewing, engineering. Cathedral is former par ch. Toll chapel of 14c on br over R Calder. SE 3320
Wake Green W Midlands 35 G6* loc in Birmingham 3m/5km S of city centre. SP 0882
Wakering, Great Essex 21 E3 vil 2m/3km N of Shoeburyness. TQ 9487
Wakering, Little Essex 21 E3 vil 2m/4km N of Shoeburyness. TQ 9388
Wakerley Northants 37 E4 vil 7m/11km SW of Stamford. SP 9599
Wakes Colne Essex 30 D5 vil 5m/7km E of Halstead. TL 8928
Walberswick Suffolk 31 H1 vil at mouth of R Blyth 2km SW of Southwold across r. (No br or ferry.) TM 4974
Walberton W Sussex 11 F4 vil 3m/5km W of Arundel. SU 9706
Walbottle Tyne & Wear 61 F5 loc 5m/8km W of Newcastle. **N Walbottle** loc 1m N. NZ 1666
Walburn N Yorks 54 A5 loc 4m/6km N of Leyburn. Hall is fortified hse of 16c. SE 1195
Walbury Hill Berks 17 G5* hill and ancient fort 5m/8km SE of Hungerford. Highest pt on chalk downs in Britain, 964 ft or 294 metres. SU 3761
Walcot Humberside 50 D6 loc just S of Alkborough. SE 8721
Walcot Lincs 37 F1 vil 7m/11km S of Sleaford. TF 0635
Walcot Lincs 45 E5 vil 8m/13km NE of Sleaford. TF 1356
Walcot Salop 34 A5 18c hse built for Robert Clive; stands in large park 1km S of Lydbury North and 3m/5km SE of Bishop's Castle. SO 3485
Walcot Salop 34 C3* ham 4m/6km W of Wellington. SJ 5911
Walcot Warwicks 27 F2 loc 3m/4km E of Alcester. SP 1258
Walcot Wilts 17 F3* dist of Swindon 1m E of tn centre. SU 1684
Walcote Leics 36 B5 vil 2m/3km E of Lutterworth. SP 5683
Walcot Green Norfolk 39 E6* vil 1km NE of Diss. TM 1280
Walcott Norfolk 39 G2* loc on coast 2m/3km NW of Happisburgh. TG 3632
Walden N Yorks 53 H6* loc in valley of Walden Beck 3m/4km S of W Burton. SE 0082
Walden Beck 53 H5/H6 r rising on E side of Buckden Pike, N Yorks, and flowing N through W Burton into Bishopdale Beck 1m E of Aysgarth. SE 0288
Walden Head N Yorks 53 H6* loc near head of Walden Beck 5m/8km S of Aysgarth. SD 9880
Walden, Little Essex 30 A4 vil 2m/3km N of Saffron Walden. TL 5441
Walden Stubbs N Yorks 49 G6 vil 2m/3km SE of Womersley. SE 5516
Walderslade Kent 20 D5* urban loc 3m/5km S of Chatham tn centre. TQ 7663
Walderton W Sussex 11 E4 vil 4m/7km NE of Emsworth. SU 7910
Waldingfield, Great Suffolk 30 D3/D4 vil 3m/5km NE of Sudbury. TL 9143
Waldingfield, Little Suffolk 30 D3 vil 4m/7km NE of Sudbury. TL 9245
Walditch Dorset 8 C5 vil 2km E of Bridport. SY 4892
Waldley Derbys 35 G1 loc 4m/6km NW of Sudbury. SK 1237
Waldon 6 C4 tributary of R Torridge rising 2m/4km NW of Bradworthy and flowing into R Torridge 2km SW of Shebbear, Devon. SS 4207
Waldridge Durham 61 G6 vil 2m/3km SW of Chester-le-Street. NZ 2550
Waldringfield Suffolk 31 F4/G4 vil with quay on right bank of R Deben estuary 3m/5km S of Woodbridge. TM 2844
Waldron E Sussex 12 B4 vil 3m/4km SW of Heathfield. TQ 5419
Wales Som 8 D2* ham 1km W of Queen Camel. ST 5824
Wales S Yorks 44 A3 vil 7m/11km W of Worksop. **Wales Bar** loc adjoining to W. SK 4782
Walesby Lincs 45 E2 vil on edge of Wolds 3m/4km NE of Mkt Rasen. Site of Roman bldg 1km E. TF 1392
Walesby Notts 44 B4 vil 3m/4km NE of Ollerton. SK 6870
Waleswood S Yorks 44 A3* loc 2km W of Wales. SK 4583
Walford H & W 26 B5* vil 3m/4km SW of Ross-on-Wye. SO 5820
Walford H & W 25 H1 vil 7m/11km E of Knighton. SO 3972
Walford Salop 34 B2/B3 loc 6m/10km NW of Shrewsbury. **Walford Heath** ham 1m SE. SJ 4320
Walford Som 8 B2* loc 1km E of W Monkton; also loc of **Walford Cross.** ST 2728
Walford Staffs 35 E1* loc 1km SE of Standon. SJ 8133
Walgherton Ches 42 C6* ham 4m/7km S of Crewe. SJ 6948
Walgrave Northants 28 C1 vil 6m/10km NW of Wellingborough. 17c hall. SP 8072
Walham Green London 19 F4* loc in borough of Hammersmith 1m N of Wandsworth Br. TQ 2577
Walhampton Hants 10 A5 loc on E bank of Lymington R opp Lymington. SZ 3395
Walkden Gtr Manchester 42 C1 loc 4m/7km S of Bolton. SD 7303
Walker Tyne & Wear 61 G5 dist of Newcastle on N bank of R Tyne 3m/5km E of city centre. Shipbuilding. NZ 2964
Walkerburn Borders 66 B5 vil on R Tweed 2m/3km E of Innerleithen. Textile mnfre. NT 3637
Walker Fold Lancs 47 G4* loc 4m/7km W of Clitheroe. SD 6741
Walkeringham Notts 44 C2 vil 4m/6km NW of Gainsborough. SK 7792
Walkerith Lincs 44 C2 ham on E bank of R Trent 3m/5km NW of Gainsborough. SK 7893
Walkern Herts 29 G5 vil 4m/6km E of Stevenage. TL 2826
Walker's Green H & W 26 A3 vil 5m/8km N of Hereford. SO 5247
Walker's Heath W Midlands 35 F6* loc in Birmingham 5m/9km S of city centre. SP 0578
Walkerville N Yorks 54 B5* loc 2km W of Catterick Br. SE 2098
Walkerwood Reservoir Gtr Manchester 43 E2* resr 2km E of Stalybridge. SJ 9898
Walkford Dorset 10 A5 suburb 2km W of New Milton. SZ 2294
Walkham 4 B4 r in Devon rising on central Dartmoor and flowing SW into R Tavy 3m/5km S of Tavistock. SX 4769
Walkhampton Devon 4 C4 vil 5m/7km SE of Tavistock. SX 5369
Walkingham Hill N Yorks 49 F2* loc 2km W of Staveley. SE 3461
Walkington Humberside 51 E4 vil 3m/5km SW of Beverley. SE 9937
Walkley S Yorks 43 G2* dist of Sheffield 2km NW of city centre. Locs of **Walkley Bank** and **Lr Walkley** to W and NW respectively. SK 3388
Walk Mill Lancs 48 B5* ham 3m/4km SE of Burnley. SD 8629
Walkwood H & W 27 E2 S dist of Redditch. SP 0364
Wall Cornwall 2 B4* loc 3m/5km SW of Camborne. SW 6036
Wall Nthmb 61 E4 vil on S side of Hadrian's Wall 3m/5km N of Hexham. NY 9168
Wall Staffs 35 G4 vil 2m/3km SW of Lichfield. Bath hse (A.M. and NT) of Roman stn of *Letocetum.* Museum of finds. SK 1006
Wallabrook 4 B3* stream rising S of Brent Tor in Devon and flowing S into R Tavy 1m NE of Tavistock. SX 4975
Wallacetown S'clyde 56 C3 loc 1m N of Dailly across Water of Girvan. NS 2702
Wallacetown S'clyde 64 B6* E dist of Ayr. Racecourse. NS 3522
Wallacetown Shetland 89 E7* loc on Mainland 2m/3km W of Bixter. HU 3052
Walland Marsh Kent 13 E4/F4 low-lying area NW of Lydd. TQ 9823
Wallands Park E Sussex 12 A5* W dist of Lewes. TQ 4010
Wallasea Island Essex 21 E3 island bounded by R Crouch, R Roach, and Paglesham Pool. TQ 9693
Wallasey Merseyside 41 H2 industrial tn and resort at N end of Wirral peninsula beside R Mersey estuary. Food and confectionery mnfre. SJ 3291
Wallaston Green Dyfed 22 B5* loc 4m/6km W of Pembroke. SM 9200
Wallbank Lancs 47 H6* loc 1m SW of Whitworth. SD 8817
Wallbrook W Midlands 35 F5* loc in N part of Dudley. SO 9493
Wallcrouch E Sussex 12 C4* ham 2km W of Ticehurst. TQ 6330
Wall, East Salop 34 C5* ham 5m/7km E of Church Stretton. SO 5293
Wall End Cumbria 52 C6* loc 2km N of Soutergate. SD 2281
Wall End H & W 26 A2* loc 3m/5km W of Leominster. SO 4457
Wallend Kent 21 E4 loc on Isle of Grain 1m SW of Grain. TQ 8775
Waller's Green H & W 26 B4 loc 3m/4km NW of Ledbury. SO 6739
Waller's Haven 12 C6 r in E Sussex flowing into English Channel at Pevensey Sluice and fed by Nunningham Stream, Hugletts Stream, and Ash Bourne, rising on high ground S of a line from Heathfield to Battle. TQ 6805
Wall Heath W Midlands 35 E5 loc in W part of Dudley 4m/7km W of tn centre. SO 8889
Wall Hill Gtr Manchester 43 E1* loc 1m S of Delph. SD 9806
Wall Houses Nthmb 61 E4 loc on line of Hadrian's Wall 4m/7km NE of Corbridge. **E Wall Hses** loc 1km E. NZ 0368
Wallingford Oxon 18 B3 tn on R Thames 12m/19km SE of Oxford. Annual regatta. SU 6089
Wallington Clwyd 42 A6* loc nearly 1m SW of Worthenbury. SJ 4145
Wallington Hants 10 C4 loc on Wallington R 1km E of Fareham. SU 5806
Wallington Herts 29 G4 vil 3m/5km E of Baldock. TL 2933
Wallington London 19 G5 dist in borough of Sutton 2m/3km E of Sutton tn centre. TQ 2864
Wallington 10 C4 r rising in the Forest of Bere in Hampshire and flowing SW past Fareham into Portsmouth Harbour. SU 6004
Wallington Hall Nthmb 61 E3 hse (NT) of 1688 with alterations and additions of 18c and 19c, 1m S of Cambo. NZ 0284
Wallington Heath W Midlands 35 F4* loc in Walsall 3m/5km NW of tn centre. SJ 9902
Wallingwells Notts 44 B3* loc 1m W of Carlton in Lindrick. SK 5784
Wallis Dyfed 22 C3* loc between Ambleston and Woodstock Slop. SN 0125
Wallisdown Dorset 9 G5 NE dist of Poole. SZ 0693
Walliswood Surrey 11 G2 loc 4m/6km E of Cranleigh. TQ 1138

Wall, Lower Kent 13 F4* loc on Romney Marsh 3m/5km N of Dymchurch. TR 0833
Wall Mead Avon 16 B5* loc 1km N of Timsbury and 3m/5km N of Midsomer Norton. ST 6659
Wall Nook Durham 54 B1* loc adjoining Langley Park to N. NZ 2145
Wallop Brook 10 A2* stream rising at Over Wallop, Hants, and flowing SE into R Test at Bossington. SU 3331
Wallop, Middle Hants 10 A1 vil 7m/11km SW of Andover. SU 2937
Wallop, Nether Hants 10 A1 vil 4m/6km W of Stockbridge. SU 3036
Wallop, Over Hants. See Over Wallop.
Walls Shetland 89 D7 vil in W dist of Mainland known as **Walls and Sandness.** Dist also includes vil of Sandness. HU 2449
Wallsend Tyne & Wear 61 G4/G5 shipbuilding and engineering tn in N Tyneside dist 4m/6km E of Newcastle. Name derives from its situation at E end of Hadrian's Wall. NZ 3066
Walls, South Orkney 89 A7, B7* peninsula at SE end of Hoy, over 3m/5km E to W and nearly 2m/3km N to S, and joined to the rest of Hoy by narrow neck of land, The Ayre, carrying a rd. ND 3189
Wallston S Glam 15 F4* loc adjoining Wenvoe, 3m/5km N of Barry. ST 1273
Wall under Heywood Salop 34 C5 vil 4m/6km E of Church Stretton. SO 5092
Wallyford Lothian 66 B2 vil 2km E of Musselburgh. NT 3672
Walmer Kent 13 H2 S dist of Deal. **Walmer Castle** (A.M.) is official residence of Lord Warden of the Cinque Ports. TR 3750
Walmer Bridge Lancs 47 F5 vil 5m/8km SW of Preston. SD 4724
Walmersley Gtr Manchester 47 H6 loc in Bury 2m/3km N of tn centre. SD 8013
Walmley W Midlands 35 G5 loc 2m/3km SE of Sutton Coldfield tn centre. SP 1393
Walmley Ash W Midlands 35 G5 loc 3m/5km SE of Sutton Coldfield. SP 1492
Walmsgate Lincs 45 G3* loc 2km S of Burwell. TF 3677
Walney Island Cumbria 46 C2 long narrow island running N and S opp Barrow-in-Furness. Length about 8m/13km. Airfield near N end. Causeway to Barrow across the narrow **Walney Channel.** SD 1868
Walpole Suffolk 31 G1 vil 3m/4km SW of Halesworth. TM 3674
Walpole Cross Keys Norfolk 38 A3 vil 3m/4km E of Sutton Br. TF 5119
Walpole Highway Norfolk 38 A3 vil 4m/7km NE of Wisbech. TF 5113
Walpole Island Norfolk 38 A3 ham 2km W of Walpole St Peter. TF 4817
Walpole St Andrew Norfolk 38 A3 vil 6m/9km NE of Wisbech. TF 5017
Walpole St Peter Norfolk 38 A3 vil 5m/8km NE of Wisbech. TF 5016
Walrond's Park Som 8 B2* ham 4m/6km N of Ilminster. ST 3720
Walrow Som 15 H6 loc 1m E of Highbridge. ST 3347
Walsall W Midlands 35 F4 tn 8m/13km NW of Birmingham. General industry, incl metal, leather, and electrical goods, engineering, etc. SP 0198
Walsall Wood W Midlands 35 F4 loc 2km S of Brownhills. SK 0403
Walsden W Yorks 48 C5 vil 2km S of Todmorden. SD 9322
Walsgrave on Sowe W Midlands 36 A6 loc in Coventry 3m/5km NE of city centre. SP 3781
Walsham le Willows Suffolk 31 E1 vil 5m/7km E of Ixworth. TM 0071
Walsham, North Norfolk 39 G2 mkt tn 14m/22km N of Norwich. TG 2830
Walsham, South Norfolk 39 G3 vil 3m/5km NW of Acle. **S Walsham Broad** to N, broad or lake connected by Fleet Dike to R Bure. TG 3613
Walshaw Gtr Manchester 47 H6* loc 2m/3km NW of Bury. SD 7711
Walshaw Dean Reservoirs W Yorks 48 C4/C5* two resrs 4m/7km N of Hebden Br. SD 9633
Walshford N Yorks 50 A3 ham on R Nidd 3m/5km N of Wetherby. SE 4153
Walsingham, Great Norfolk 38 D1 vil 4m/7km S of Wells. **Lit Walsingham** larger vil 1m SW: formerly important place of pilgrimage. Remains of medieval priory in grnds of 18c and later abbey. TF 9336
Walsoken Cambs 38 A3 NE dist of Wisbech. See also New Walsoken. TF 4710
Walston S'clyde 65 G4 vil 5m/8km E of Carnwath. NT 0545
Walsworth Herts 29 F4 NE dist of Hitchin. TL 2030
Walter's Ash Bucks 18 C2* loc 4m/6km NW of High Wycombe. SU 8398
Walterston (Trewallter) S Glam 15 F4* loc 2km NE of Llancarfan. Site of Roman villa 1m E. ST 0671
Walterstone H & W 25 H5 loc 4m/6km SW of Pontrilas. SO 3425
Waltham Humberside 45 F1 suburb 4m/6km S of Grimsby. See also New Waltham. TA 2603
Waltham Kent 13 F2 vil 6m/10km SW of Canterbury. TR 1048
Waltham Abbey Essex 20 A2 tn in R Lea valley 7m/11km SW of Harlow. Abbey built by Henry II. TL 3800
Waltham Chase Hants 10 C3 vil 2m/3km S of Bishop's Waltham. SU 5615
Waltham Cross Herts 20 A2 S dist of Cheshunt. Eleanor cross restored, erected by Edward I; one of three extant (others at Geddington and Hardingstone). TL 3500
Waltham Forest London 20 A3* borough lying to E of R Lea valley and extending from S end of Epping Forest (N) to Hackney Marshes (S). Includes tns of Chingford, Leyton, and Walthamstow. TQ 3789
Waltham, Great Essex 20 D1 vil 4m/7km N of Chelmsford. TL 6913
Waltham, Little Essex 20 D1 vil 4m/6km N of Chelmsford. TL 7112
Waltham, North Hants 18 B6 vil 6m/9km SW of Basingstoke. SU 5646
Waltham on the Wolds Leics 36 D2 vil in elevated position 5m/8km NE of Melton Mowbray. SK 8025
Waltham St Lawrence Berks 18 C4 vil 3m/4km E of Twyford. Site of Roman temple across rly to N. SU 8276
Waltham's Cross Essex 30 B5* loc 2m/3km SE of Finchingfield. TL 6930
Walthamstow London 20 A3 tn in borough of Waltham Forest 7m/11km NE of London Br. Loc of **Upr Walthamstow** 1km E. TQ 3789
Walton Bucks 28 D4 vil in Milton Keynes 2m/3km NE of Bletchley. SP 8936
Walton Cambs 37 F4 loc in Peterborough 3m/4km NW of city centre. TF 1701
Walton Cumbria 60 B5 vil 2m/4km N of Brampton. NY 5264
Walton Derbys 43 H4 ham 2m/3km SW of Chesterfield. SK 3569
Walton Leics 36 B5 vil 4m/6km NW of Husbands Bosworth. SP 5987
Walton Powys 25 G2 ham 3m/5km E of New Radnor. SO 2559
Walton Salop 34 B6* loc 3m/5km SE of Craven Arms. SO 4679
Walton Salop 34 C3 ham 6m/10km NW of Wellington. SJ 5918
Walton Som 8 C1 vil 2km W of Street. 1m S, Walton Hill (NT) and Ivythorn Hill (NT), commanding wide views. ST 4636
Walton Staffs 35 E1 loc 1km S of Stone across R Trent. SJ 8933
Walton Suffolk 31 G4 N dist of Felixstowe. TM 2935
Walton Warwicks 27 G2* ham 6m/9km E of Stratford-upon-Avon. SP 2853
Walton W Yorks 49 F6 vil 3m/5km SE of Wakefield. SE 3517
Walton W Yorks 49 F3 vil 2m/4km E of Wetherby. SE 4447
Walton Cardiff Glos 26 D4* vil 1m E of Tewkesbury. SO 9032
Walton Castle Suffolk 31 G4* site of Roman fort offshore 2m/3km NE of Felixstowe. TM 3235
Walton Channel Essex 31 F5* stream draining marshes in vicinity of Walton on the Naze and flowing N into Pennyhole Bay 2m/3km NW of The Naze. TM 2426
Walton East (Waltwn Dwyrain) Dyfed 22 C3 vil 6m/10km NE of Haverfordwest. SN 0223
Walton, East Norfolk 38 C3 vil 6m/10km NW of Swaffham. TF 7416
Walton Elm Dorset 9 E3* ham 1km S of Marnhull and 3m/4km N of Sturminster Newton. ST 7817
Waltonferry Suffolk 31 F4* loc at mouth of R Orwell 2km W of Felixstowe. TM 2734
Walton, Higher Ches 42 B3 vil 2m/3km S of Warrington. **Lr Walton** loc 1km NE. SJ 5985
Walton, Higher Lancs 47 F5 loc 2m/3km E of Walton-le-Dale. SD 5827
Walton-in-Gordano Avon 16 A4 vil 2m/3km NE of Clevedon. ST 4273
Walton-le-Dale Lancs 47 F5 suburb 2m/3km SE of Preston across R Ribble. Site of small Roman fort 1km W. SD 5528
Walton, Lower Ches 42 B3 loc adjoining Warrington to S. SJ 6085
Walton Lower Street Suffolk 31 G4* W dist of Felixstowe. TM 2834
Walton-on-Thames Surrey 19 E5 tn on S bank of R Thames 15m/24km SW of London. TQ 1066
Walton on the Hill Merseyside 42 A2 dist of Liverpool 3m/5km NE of city centre. SJ 3795
Walton-on-the-Hill Staffs 35 F2 vil 3m/4km SE of Stafford. SJ 9521
Walton on the Hill Surrey 19 F5 vil 4m/6km SW of Banstead. Site of Roman villa 1m SE on Walton Heath golf course. TQ 2255
Walton on the Naze Essex 31 F5/F6 coastal resort 7m/11km NE of Clacton-on-Sea. TM 2521
Walton on the Wolds Leics 36 B3 vil 5m/6km E of Loughborough. SK 5919
Walton Park Avon 16 A4* N dist of Clevedon. ST 4072
Walton upon Trent Derbys 35 H3 vil 4m/6km SW of Burton upon Trent. SK 2118
Walton West (Waltwn Gorllewin) Dyfed 22 B4 vil near coast of St Brides Bay 1km S of Broad Haven. SM 8612
Walton, West Norfolk 38 A3 vil 3m/4km N of Wisbech. **W Walton Highway** vil 2km E. TF 4713
Waltwn Dwyrain Welsh form of Walton East, qv.
Waltwn Gorllewin Welsh form of Walton West, qv.
Walverden Reservoir Lancs 48 B4* small resr 2km SE of Nelson. SD 8736
Walves Reservoir Lancs 47 G6* small resr 4m/7km NE of Bolton. SD 7415
Walwen Clwyd 41 G4 loc on R Dee estuary 2km E of Holywell. SJ 2076
Walwen Clwyd 41 G4 loc 3m/5km S of Holywell. SJ 1771
Walwick Nthmb 60 D4 loc on line of Hadrian's Wall 2m/3km NE of Fourstones. NY 9070
Walworth Durham 54 B3 ham 5m/7km NW of Darlington. Cas is mansion of *c.* 1600. **Walworth Gate** loc 1km N. **Low Walworth** loc 1m SE. NZ 2318
Walworth London 19 G4* dist in borough of Southwark S of New Kent Rd. TQ 3278
Walwyn's Castle (Castell Gwalchmai) Dyfed 22 B4 ham 4m/6km NW of Milford Haven. Site of ancient fort. SM 8711
Wambrook Som 8 B3 vil 2m/3km W of Chard. 1km N, ham of **Hr Wambrook.** ST 2907
Wamphray Water 59 F2 r in Dumfries & Galloway region running S from Croft Hd to R Annan 7m/11km S of Moffat. NY 1095
Wampool Cumbria 59 G5* loc on r of same name (qv), 2km SE of Kirkbride. NY 2454
Wampool 59 F5 r rising E of Wigton, Cumbria, and flowing NW into Solway Firth W of Kirkbride between Cardurnock and Grune Pt. NY 1458
Wanborough Surrey 11 F1 ham below N slope of Hog's Back 4m/6km W of Guildford. SU 9348
Wanborough Wilts 17 F3 vil 4m/6km E of Swindon. SU 2082
Wandle 19 F4* r rising at Croydon and flowing NW and N into R Thames above Wandsworth Br in the London borough of Wandsworth. TQ 2575
Wandlebury Cambs 29 H3* ancient earthwork at summit of Gog Magog Hills 4m/6km SE of Cambridge. TL 4953
Wandon End Herts 29 F5* loc 3m/5km E of Luton. TL 1322
Wandsworth London 19 F4* borough S of R Thames 4m/7km SW of Charing Cross. R crossed here by Putney, Wandsworth, Battersea, Albert, and Chelsea Brs, and by three rly brs. TQ 2574
Wandylaw Nthmb 67 G5/H5* loc 2km W of Ellingham. NU 1525
Wangford Suffolk 31 H1 vil 3m/5km NW of Southwold. TM 4679
Wangford Suffolk 38 C6 loc 3m/5km SW of Brandon. TL 7583
Wanless Lancs 48 B4/C4* loc just E of Trawden. SD 9138
Wanlip Leics 36 B3 vil 4m/7km N of Leicester. SK 6010
Wanlockhead D & G 58 D1 vil in former lead-mining area, 6m/10km E of Sanquhar. NS 8712
Wannock E Sussex 12 C6 loc adjoining Polegate, to S. TQ 5703
Wansbeck 117 admin dist of Nthmb.
Wansbeck 61 G3 r rising near Sweethope Loughs, Nthmb, and flowing E by Morpeth to the North Sea between Blyth and Newbiggin-by-the-Sea. NZ 3085
Wansdyke 118 admin dist of Avon.
Wansdyke 16 A4* to 17 G5* ancient earthwork, possibly constructed for defence, running originally from Berkshire to the Bristol Channel at Portishead. Much of it now obliterated. ST,SU
Wansford Cambs 37 F4 vil on R Nene 7m/12km W of Peterborough. TL 0799
Wansford Humberside 51 E3 vil on R Hull 3m/4km E of Gt Driffield. TA 0656
Wanshurst Green Kent 12 D2* ham 2km E of Marden. TQ 7645
Wanstead London 20 A3 dist in borough of Redbridge 3m/4km NW of Ilford. TQ 4088
Wanstead Flats London 20 A3* open space in borough of Redbridge 1m S of Wanstead. TQ 4086
Wanstrow Som 9 E1 vil 5m/8km NE of Bruton. ST 7141
Wanswell Glos 16 C2* vil 2km N of Berkeley. SO 6801
Wantage Oxon 17 H3 tn 13m/21km SW of Oxford. Birthplace of King Alfred, 849. SU 3988
Wantisden Suffolk 31 G3 loc 4m/7km NW of Orford. Bentwaters Airfield to W. TM 3653
Wapley Avon 16 C3 ham 2m/3km SW of Chipping Sodbury. ST 7179
Wappenbury Warwicks 27 G1* vil 4m/7km NE of Leamington. SP 3769
Wappenham Northants 28 B3 vil 5m/8km SW of Towcester. SP 6245
Wapping London 19 G3* loc E of Tower Br in borough of Tower Hamlets, containing docks. TQ 3480
Wapping Warwicks 27 E2* loc 3m/5km SE of Redditch. SP 0764
Warathwaite Head Cumbria 60 A6* loc 3m/5km NW of Armathwaite. NY 4749
Warbleton E Sussex 12 C5* ham 3m/4km SE of Heathfield. TQ 6018
Warblington Hants 10 D4 ham 2km W of Emsworth. Remains of early 16c cas. SU 7205
Warborough Oxon 18 B2 vil 3m/4km N of Wallingford. SU 5993
Warboys Cambs 37 G6 vil 7m/11km NE of Huntingdon. Mid-17c manor hse. TL 3080
Warbreck Lancs 46 D4* dist of Blackpool 2m/3km NE of tn centre. SD 3238
Warbstow Cornwall 6 B6 vil 7m/11km E of Boscastle. SX 2090
Warburton Gtr Manchester 42 C2 vil 5m/7km W of Altrincham. SJ 6989
Warburton Green Gtr Manchester 42 D3* loc 3m/5km SE of Altrincham. SJ 7984
Warcop Cumbria 53 F3 vil 3m/5km W of Brough. Hall is part Elizn, part Ggn. Site of Roman camp 1m NW. NY 7415
Warden Kent 21 F4 loc on E coast of Isle of Sheppey 2km NW of Leysdown-on-Sea. TR 0271
Warden Nthmb 61 E5 ham at confluence of Rs North and South Tyne, 2m/4km NW of Hexham. **High Warden** loc to N. NY 9166
Ward End W Midlands 35 G5 loc in Birmingham 4m/6km E of city centre. SP 1288
Warden Hill Glos 26 D5* SW dist of Cheltenham. SO 9320
Warden Law Tyne & Wear 61 H6 loc 2m/3km E of Houghton-le-Spring. NZ 3649

Warden Point Isle of Wight 10 A5* headland on W coast between Totland Bay and Colwell Bay. SZ 3287
Warden Point Kent 21 F4 headland at NE end of Isle of Sheppey to N of loc of Warden. TR 0272
Warden Street Beds 29 F3* loc 4m/7km W of Biggleswade. TL 1244
Wardgate Derbys 43 G6 vil 5m/8km E of Ashbourne. SK 2547
Ward Green Suffolk 31 E2 loc 3m/5km N of Stowmarket. TM 0463
Wardhedges Beds 29 E4* loc adjoining Flitton to E, 3m/4km SE of Ampthill. TL 0635
Ward Hill Orkney 89 A7 steep hill at N end of island of Hoy, rising to 1570 ft or 479 metres. HY 2202
Ward Holm Orkney 89 C7* islet 1m W of Copinsay, qv. HY 5901
Wardie Lothian 66 A1* dist of Edinburgh 2m/3km N of city centre. NT 2476
Wardington Oxon 28 A3 vil 4m/7km NE of Banbury. SP 4946
Wardington, Upper Oxon 28 A3* vil adjoining Wardington to E, 4m/7km NE of Banbury. SP 4946
Wardle Ches 42 B5 vil 4m/6km NW of Nantwich. SJ 6157
Wardle Gtr Manchester 48 B6 tn 3m/4km NE of Rochdale. Textiles, plastics. SD 9116
Wardley Gtr Manchester 42 C1 loc 1m NW of Swinton. **Wardley Hall** dates partly from 16c. SD 7602
Wardley Leics 36 D4 vil 2m/4km W of Uppingham. SK 8300
Wardley Tyne & Wear 61 G5* E dist of Felling. NZ 2961
Wardley W Sussex 11 E2* loc 3m/4km S of Liphook. SU 8427
Wardlow Derbys 43 F4 vil 2m/3km E of Tideswell. SK 1874
Ward of Bressay Shetland. See Bressay.
Wardour Castle Wilts 9 F2 18c mansion, restored 1960, 2m/3km SW of Tisbury. **Wardour Old Castle** (A.M.), remains of 14c cas with later additions, 1m SE. ST 9226
Wardpark S'clyde 65 E1* industrial area of Cumbernauld 2m/3km NE of tn centre. Site of Roman camp. NS 7777
Wardsend Ches 43 E3* loc 1km SE of Poynton. SJ 9382
Wardy Hill Cambs 38 A6 ham 5m/7km W of Ely. TL 4782
Ware Herts 20 A1 tn on R Lea 21m/33km N of London. Maltings. R Lea Navigation forms canal link with London. TL 3514
Ware Kent 13 H1 loc 4m/6km NW of Sandwich. TR 2760
Wareham Dorset 9 F5 tn at head of R Frome estuary 6m/10km W of Poole across Poole Harbour. To N, **Wareham Forest**, area of heath, conifers, and marsh. SY 9287
Warehorne Kent 13 E4 vil 1m SW of Ham Street. TQ 9932
Warenford Nthmb 67 G5 ham 4m/6km SE of Belford. NU 1328
Waren Mill Nthmb 67 G5/H5* loc at S end of Budle Bay 2m/4km E of Belford. NU 1434
Warenton Nthmb 67 G5 loc 2m/4km S of Belford. NU 1030
Wareside Herts 29 G6 vil 3m/4km E of Ware. TL 3915
Waresley Cambs 29 F2 vil 4m/6km NE of Potton. TL 2554
Waresley H & W 26 D1* loc 2m/4km SE of Stourport. SO 8470
Ware Street Kent 20 D6* loc 2m/4km E of Maidstone. TQ 7956
Warfield Berks 18 D4 ham 2m/3km N of Bracknell. SU 8872
Warford, Great Ches 42 D3* loc 2m/3km SW of Alderley Edge. **Lit Warford** loc to S. SJ 8077
Wargate Lincs 37 G2* loc 1km S of Gosberton. TF 2330
Wargrave Berks 18 C4 vil 2m/3km N of Twyford. SU 7978
Wargrave Merseyside 42 B2* S dist of Newton-le-Willows. SJ 5894
Warham H & W 26 A4* loc 2m/3km W of Hereford. SO 4839
Warham All Saints Norfolk 38 D1 ham 2m/4km SE of Wells. TF 9441
Warham St Mary Norfolk 38 D1* ham 2m/3km SE of Wells. TF 9441
Warhill Gtr Manchester 43 E2* loc adjoining Mottram in Longdendale to S. SJ 9995
Waring's Green 35 G6* loc on borders of Warwicks and W Midlands 2m/3km NW of Hockley Heath. SP 1274
Wark Nthmb 60 D4 vil on R North Tyne 4m/7km S of Bellingham. NY 8577
Wark Nthmb 67 E4 vil on R Tweed 2m/3km W of Cornhill. NT 8238
Wark Forest Nthmb 60 C4 moorland area, partly afforested, W of Wark. NY 67, 77
Warkleigh Devon 7 E3 ham 4m/7km SW of S Molton. SS 6422
Warks Burn 60 D4 r rising near Gt Watch Hill, Wark Forest, Nthmb, near Cumbrian border, and flowing E through Wark Forest into R North Tyne just below vil of Wark. NY 8676
Warkton Northants 36 D6 vil 2m/3km NE of Kettering. SP 8979
Warkworth Northants 28 A3 ham 2m/3km E of Banbury. SP 4840
Warkworth Nthmb 61 G1 vil on R Coquet near North Sea coast 2km NW of Amble. Norman and later cas (A.M.). Medieval fortified br (A.M.). NU 2406
Warlaby N Yorks 54 C5 loc 2m/3km SW of Northallerton. SE 3491
Warland W Yorks 48 C6* loc 3m/4km S of Todmorden. **Warland Resr** to E. SD 9420
Warleggan Cornwall 3 F2 vil on S edge of Bodmin Moor 6m/9km E of Bodmin. SX 1569
Warleigh Avon 16 C5* loc on R Avon 3m/5km E of Bath. ST 7964
Warley Essex 20 C3* S dist of Brentwood. TQ 5992
Warley W Midlands 35 F5 tn 4m/6km W of Birmingham. SP 0086
Warley, Great Essex 20 C3 vil 2m/4km SW of Brentwood. TQ 5890
Warley, Little Essex 20 C3 loc 2m/4km S of Brentwood. TQ 6090
Warley Moor Reservoir W Yorks 48 C5* resr 3m/5km SW of Denholme. SE 0331
Warley Town W Yorks 48 C5 loc in Halifax 2m/4km W of tn centre. SE 0524
Warlingham Surrey 20 A5 tn 5m/8km SE of Croydon. TQ 3558
Warmbrook Derbys 43 G5* loc adjoining Wirksworth to S. SK 2853
Warmden Reservoir Lancs 48 B5* small resr 2km SE of Accrington. SD 7727
Warmfield W Yorks 49 F6 vil 1m SW of Normanton. SE 3720
Warmingham Ches 42 C5* vil 3m/5km W of Sandbach. SJ 7061
Warminghurst W Sussex 11 G3 loc 3m/4km N of Washington. TQ 1116
Warmington Northants 37 F5 vil 3m/5km NE of Oundle. TL 0791
Warmington Warwicks 27 H3 vil 5m/8km NW of Banbury. SP 4147
Warminster Som 16 B6* loc 2m/4km SE of Wells. ST 5743
Warminster Wilts 16 D6 stone tn 8m/13km S of Trowbridge. Army camps on outskirts. ST 8745
Warmley Avon 16 B4 loc 5m/9km E of Bristol. ST 6673
Warmley Hill Avon 16 B4* dist of Kingswood 5m/7km E of Bristol. ST 6573
Warmsworth S Yorks 44 A1* suburb 3m/4km SW of Doncaster. SE 5400
Warmwell Dorset 9 E5 vil 5m/8km SE of Dorchester. SY 7585
Warmwithens Reservoir Lancs 48 A5* small resr on Oswaldtwistle Moor 3m/4km SW of Accrington. SD 7324
Warnborough, North Hants 18 C6 vil on Basingstoke Canal 1km NW of Odiham. Site of Roman villa 1km N. SU 7351
Warnborough, South Hants 10 D1 vil 5m/8km N of Alton. Site of Roman bldg 1m S. SU 7247
Warndon H & W 26 D2 ham 3m/4km NE of Worcester. SO 8856
Warndon H & W 26 D2* NE dist of Worcester. SO 8756
Warners End Herts 19 E1* W dist of Hemel Hempstead. TL 0307
War Ness Orkney 89 B6* headland at S end of island of Eday. HY 5528
Warnford Hants 10 C3 vil 2m/4km NE of Meonstoke. SU 6223
Warnham W Sussex 11 G2 vil 2m/3km NW of Horsham. TQ 1533
Warningcamp W Sussex 11 F4 ham in R Arun valley 1m E of Arundel. TQ 0307
Warninglid W Sussex 11 H3 vil 2m/4km S of Handcross. TQ 2526
Warren Ches 42 D4 vil 3m/4km SW of Macclesfield. SJ 8870
Warren Dyfed 22 B6 vil 4m/7km SW of Pembroke. SR 9397
Warren London 20 B3* loc 2m/3km W of Romford, in borough of Havering. TQ 4889
Warren S Yorks 43 H2* loc 1km N of Chapeltown. SK 3597
Warrenby Cleveland 55 E3 loc 2m/3km W of Redcar. NZ 5825
Warren Corner Hants 11 E1* loc 1m E of Crondall. SU 8048
Warren, Middle Cleveland 54 D2* loc in N dist of Hartlepool. NZ 4934
Warren Mountain Clwyd 41 H5* loc 2km S of Hawarden. SJ 3163
Warren Row Berks 18 C3* vil 3m/5km NE of Twyford. SU 8180
Warren's Cross Glos 17 F2* loc 2km W of Lechlade. SU 1999
Warren's Green Herts 29 F5* loc 3m/5km NE of Stevenage. TL 2628
Warren Street Kent 21 E6* ham 2m/3km E of Lenham. TQ 9253
Warrington Bucks 28 D2 ham 2m/3km N of Olney. SP 8954
Warrington Ches 42 B3 large industrial tn on R Mersey 16m/25km SW of Manchester and same distance E of Liverpool. Wire mnfre, iron and steel, engineering, brewing, paper, etc. New Tn designated 1968. SJ 6088
Warriston Lothian 66 A1/A2* dist of Edinburgh 1m N of city centre. NT 2575
Warsash Hants 10 C4 vil on E side of R Hamble and 6m/9km W of Fareham. Strawberry-growing. School of Navigation (University of Southampton). SU 4906
Warse H'land 86 F1 loc near N coast of Caithness dist 2m/4km SE of St John's Pt. ND 3372
Warslow Staffs 43 F5 vil 7m/11km E of Leek. SK 0858
Warsop Notts 44 A4 tn 5m/7km NE of Mansfield. **Warsop Vale** loc 2km W. See also Church Warsop. SK 5667
Warter Humberside 50 D3 vil 4m/7km E of Pocklington. Site of 12c priory to N. SE 8650
Warthermaske N Yorks 49 E1* ham 2m/3km SW of Masham. SE 2078
Warthill N Yorks 50 B3 vil 5m/8km NE of York. SE 6755
Wart Holm Orkney 89 B5* island rock 1km W of Pt of Huro at S end of Westray. HY 4838
Wartling E Sussex 12 C5 vil 3m/4km N of Pevensey across Pevensey Levels. TQ 6509
Wartnaby Leics 36 C2 vil 4m/6km NW of Melton Mowbray. SK 7123
Warton Lancs 47 E5 vil 4m/7km E of Lytham St Anne's. Airfield to S. **Warton Bank** loc 1m SW. SD 4128
Warton Lancs 47 F1 vil 2km N of Carnforth. SD 5072
Warton Nthmb 61 E2* loc 2km W of Thropton. NU 0002
Warton Warwicks 35 H4 vil 4m/6km NW of Atherstone. SK 2803
Warwick Cumbria 60 A5 ham 4m/7km E of Carlisle. **Warwick Br** ham 1km E across R Eden. NY 4656
Warwick Warwicks 27 G2 tn on R Avon 9m/15km SW of Coventry. Medieval cas. Many old bldgs. SP 2865
Warwick Reservoir London 19 G3* resr in R Lea valley in borough of Waltham Forest 6m/9km NE of Charing Cross. TQ 3488
Warwickshire 118, 119 midland county of England, bounded by Oxfordshire, Gloucestershire, Hereford and Worcester, W Midlands, Staffordshire, Leicestershire, and Northamptonshire. Mostly flat or undulating farmland, with many trees, although the foothills of the Cotswolds spill over the S border. A more industrial belt extends NW from Rugby to the boundary with Staffordshire. Chief tns are Warwick, the county tn; Leamington, Nuneaton, Rugby, and Stratford-upon-Avon. The principal r is the Avon.
Warwick Wold Surrey 19 G6* loc 3m/4km NE of Redhill. TQ 3153
Wasbister Orkney 89 B6 loc on island of Rousay 2km S of Sacquoy Hd. HY 3932
Wasdale Head Cumbria 52 B4 ham 1m NE of Wast Water. NY 1808
Wash Derbys 43 F3* loc 1km N of Chapel-en-le-Frith. SK 0682
Wash 5 E5* r in Devon rising 1m NW of Halwell and flowing E into Harbourne R, or Bow Creek, at Tuckenhay. SX 8156
Washall Green Herts 29 H4* loc 5m/8km E of Buntingford. TL 4430
Washaway Cornwall 3 E2 loc 3m/4km NW of Bodmin. SX 0369
Washbourne Devon 4 D5 ham 4m/6km S of Totnes. SX 7954
Washbourne, Great Glos 27 E4 ham 4m/7km NW of Winchcombe. SO 9834
Washbourne, Little Glos 27 E4* ham 4m/6km NW of Winchcombe. SO 9933
Washbrook Som 15 H6* loc 2m/3km NW of Wedmore. ST 4250
Washbrook Suffolk 31 E4 ham 4m/6km SW of Ipswich. TM 1142
Washburn 49 E3 r rising on moors S of Greenhow Hill, N Yorks, and flowing SE through Thruscross, Fewston, Swinsty, and Lindley Wd Resrs, and into R Wharfe 2m/3km E of Otley. SE 2246
Wash Common Berks 17 H5 loc 2m/4km SW of Newbury. SU 4564
Washerwall Staffs 43 E6* loc adjoining Werrington to W. SJ 9347
Washfield Devon 7 G3 vil 2m/3km NW of Tiverton. SS 9315
Washfold N Yorks 54 A4 ham 2m/4km N of Reeth. NZ 0502
Washford H & W 27 E1* SE dist of Redditch. SP 0765
Washford Som 7 H1 vil 2m/3km SW of Watchet. ST 0441
Washford 7 H1* stream in Somerset rising in Brendon Hills and flowing N into Bridgwater Bay at Watchet. ST 0743
Washford Pyne Devon 7 F4 ham 2m/3km SE of Witheridge and 9m/14km W of Tiverton. SS 8111
Washingborough Lincs 45 E4 vil 3m/5km E of Lincoln. TF 0170
Washingley Cambs 37 F5* deserted vil 2m/3km W of Stilton. TL 1388
Washington Tyne & Wear 61 G5 New Tn, designated 1964, 6m/9km W of Sunderland. Coal-mining, iron and steel, chemicals, textiles, quarrying. **Washington Old Hall** (NT) dates mainly from 17c. NZ 2956
Washington W Sussex 11 G4 vil below S Downs 7m/11km N of Worthing. TQ 1212
Washpit W Yorks 43 F1* loc 1m S of Holmfirth. SE 1406
Wash, The 38 A1/B1 wide shallow arm of North Sea extending from coast of Lincs near Boston to coast of Norfolk at Hunstanton. It receives the waters of Rs Witham, Welland, Nene, and Gt Ouse. The ports of Boston and King's Lynn have access to the Wash by the estuaries of R Witham and R Ouse respectively. Numerous sandbanks render navigation difficult. TF 54
Washwood Heath W Midlands 35 G5* loc in Birmingham 3m/5km E of city centre. SP 1188
Wasing Berks 18 B5 loc 2km SW of Aldermaston. SU 5764
Waskerley Durham 61 F6 loc 5m/8km SW of Consett. **Waskerley Resr** 2m/3km SW. NZ 0545
Waskerley Beck 54 A2 r rising on moors N of Stanhope, Durham, and flowing through Waskerley Resr, thence SE to Tunstall Resr, thence S into R Wear at Wolsingham. NZ 0737
Wasperton Warwicks 27 G2 vil 4m/7km S of Warwick. SP 2658
Wasps Nest Lincs 45 E4* loc 2km E of Nocton. TF 0864
Wass N Yorks 50 B1 vil 2m/3km W of Ampleforth. SE 5579
Waste, North W Midlands 35 H6* loc in Coventry 3m/5km W of city centre. SP 2878
Wast Water Cumbria 52 B4 lake running NE to SW in course of R Irt 3m/4km NE of Santon Br. Steep screes on SE side of lake. NY 1606
Watchet Som 7 H1 tn with harbour on Bridgwater Bay 15m/24km NW of Bridgwater. ST 0743
Watchfield Oxon 17 F3 vil 3m/5km E of Highworth. Site of Roman bldg to E. SU 2490
Watchfield Som 15 H6* loc 2m/3km E of Highbridge. ST 3447
Watchgate Cumbria 53 E5* ham 4m/7km N of Kendal. SD 5299
Watchhill Cumbria 52 B1* loc 3m/4km E of Aspatria. NY 1842

Watch House Point Dyfed 22 B5* headland on N shore of Milford Haven 1km S of St Ishmael's. SM 8306

Watch, Middle Cambs 29 G1* loc in vil of Swavesey S of vil centre. TL 3668

Watch Water Reservoir Borders 66 D3* resr in course of **Watch Water,** 2m/3km W of Longformacus. NT 6656

Watcombe Devon 5 E4* N dist of Torbay 2m/3km N of Torquay tn centre. 1km E, **Watcombe Hd.** headland on Babbacombe Bay. SX 9167

Watendlath Cumbria 52 C3* loc at N end of small lake 3m/4km NE of Seatoller. NY 2716

Water Lancs 48 B5* loc on Forest of Rossendale 3m/4km NE of Rawtenstall. SD 8425

Waterbeach Cambs 30 A2 vil 5m/8km NE of Cambridge. Remains of medieval Denny Priory 2m/3km N beyond airfield. TL 4965

Waterbeck D & G 59 G4 vil 4m/6km NE of Ecclefechan. NY 2477

Water-break-its-neck Powys 25 G2* waterfall on small tributary of Summergil Brook 2m/3km W of New Radnor. SO 1860

Water Bridge, North. See Northwaterbridge.

Watercombe Dorset 9 E5* ham 6m/9km SE of Dorchester. SY 7584

Waterdale Herts 19 E2* loc 4m/6km N of Watford. TL 1102

Waterden Norfolk 38 D1* loc 4m/7km NW of Fakenham. TF 8835

Water Eaton Bucks 28 D4 loc in S part of Bletchley. SP 8732

Water Eaton Oxon 28 A6 ham on R Cherwell 4m/6km N of Oxford. SP 5112

Water Eaton Staffs 35 E3* loc 2m/4km SW of Penkridge. Site of Roman settlement of *Pennocrucium.* Site of Roman fort 1km NE and of Roman villa 1m SW. SJ 9011

Water End Beds 29 E3* S end of Cople, 4m/6km E of Bedford. TL 1047

Water End Beds 29 E3* loc 4m/6km E of Bedford. TL 1151

Water End Beds 29 E4* ham 2km SW of Clophill. TL 0737

Water End Beds 29 F3* S end of Wrestlingworth, 3m/4km SE of Potton. TL 2547

Waterend Bucks 18 C2* loc 2km E of Stokenchurch. SU 7896

Waterend Cumbria 52 B3* loc at NW end of Loweswater lake. NY 1122

Water End Essex 30 B4* ham 4m/6km NE of Saffron Walden. TL 5840

Water End Herts 19 E1* ham 2m/4km NW of Hemel Hempstead. TL 0310

Water End Herts 19 F2 loc 3m/4km S of Hatfield. TL 2204

Water End Humberside 50 C4 ham 6m/10km W of Mkt Weighton. SE 7838

Waterfall Staffs 43 F5 vil 7m/11km SE of Leek. SK 0851

Waterfoot Lancs 48 B5 loc 2m/3km E of Rawtenstall. SD 8321

Waterford Hants 10 A5 loc on W bank of Lymington R 1m SE of Lymington. SZ 3394

Waterford Herts 19 G1 vil 2m/3km NW of Hertford. TL 3114

Water Fryston W Yorks 49 F5 loc 2km NW of Ferrybridge. SE 4626

Watergate Cornwall 3 F1* ham 2m/3km SE of Camelford. SX 1281

Watergate Bay Cornwall 2 D2 bay on N coast, facing W and extending from Griffin's Pt opp Trevarrion southwards to Trevelgue Hd. SW 8365

Watergore Som 8 C3* ham 1km S of S Petherton. ST 4315

Watergrove Reservoir Gtr Manchester 48 B6* resr 2km E of Whitworth. SD 9017

Waterhale Essex 20 B2* loc 4m/6km W of Brentwood. TQ 5395

Waterhay, Lower Wilts 17 E2* loc on R Thames 3m/4km W of Cricklade. SU 0693

Waterhay, Upper Wilts 17 E2* loc 2m/3km W of Cricklade. SU 0693

Waterhead Cumbria 52 D4* loc 1m S of Ambleside. NY 3703

Waterheath Norfolk 39 H5* loc 3m/4km NE of Beccles. TM 4394

Waterhill of Bruxie Grampian 83 G2 loc between Maud and Old Deer. NJ 9447

Waterhouses Durham 54 B1 loc 6m/9km W of Durham. NZ 1840

Waterhouses Staffs 43 F6 vil 7m/11km SE of Leek. SK 0850

Wateringbury Kent 20 C6 vil on R Medway 5m/8km W of Maidstone. TQ 6853

Waterlane Glos 16 D1* loc 5m/8km E of Stroud. SO 9204

Waterloo Derbys 43 H4* loc 2m/3km E of Clay Cross. SK 4163

Waterloo Dyfed 22 C5 loc 1km E of Pembroke Dock. SM 9703

Waterloo Gtr Manchester 43 E2* loc in Ashton-under-Lyne 1m NW of tn centre. SD 9200

Waterloo H & W 26 D4* loc 4m/6km NE of Tewkesbury. SO 9336

Waterloo Lancs 47 G5* loc in Blackburn 2m/3km SW of tn centre. SD 6625

Waterloo Merseyside 41 H2 S dist of Crosby. SJ 3197

Waterloo Norfolk 39 F3* loc 1km NW of Hainford. TG 2219

Waterloo Norfolk 39 F3* loc adjoining Horsham St Faith to NE. TG 2215

Waterloo S'clyde 65 E3 vil adjoining Wishaw to SE. NS 8053

Waterloo Skye, H'land 79 E6* loc on coast 1m E of Broadford. NG 6623

Waterloo Tayside 72 D1 vil 4m/7km SE of Dunkeld. NO 0536

Waterloo Cross Devon 7 H4 loc 6m/10km E of Tiverton. ST 0514

Waterloo Port Gwynedd 40 B5 loc adjoining Caernarvon to NE. SH 4964

Waterlooville Hants 10 D4 tn 7m/11km NE of Portsmouth. SU 6809

Waterlow Norfolk 39 G4* loc 1km E of Blofield. TG 3409

Watermillock Cumbria 52 D3 ham near N shore of Ullswater, 2m/3km SW of Pooley Br. NY 4422

Water Newton Cambs 37 F4 vil on R Nene 3m/4km SE of Wansford. To E, site of Roman tn of *Durobrivae.* TL 1097

Water of Ae D & G. See Ae Village.

Water of Ailnack 82 B5* r in Grampian region running NE into R Avon 1m S of Tomintoul. Upper reaches on border of Grampian and Highland regions and known as Water of Caiplich. NJ 1617

Water of App 57 A5/A6* r in Strathclyde region running SW down Glenn App to Finnarts Bay, near N end of Loch Ryan. NX 0572

Water of Aven 77 F2 stream in Grampian region running NE to Water of Feugh 4m/7km SW of Banchory. NO 6392

Water of Buchat 82 C5 stream in Grampian region rising on Ladder Hills and running SE to R Don at Bridge of Buchat. NJ 4014

Water of Caiplich 82 A5. See Water of Ailnack.

Water of Charr 77 F3 stream in Grampian region running N to Water of Dye 6m/10km N of Fettercairn. NO 6182

Water of Coyle 56 D2 r in Strathclyde region rising about 3m/5km N of Dalmellington and flowing NW to R Ayr 4m/6km E of Ayr. Meanders in lower reaches. NS 3921

Water of Cruden 83 H3* stream in Grampian region running E to North Sea at N end of Cruden Bay. NK 9035

Water of Deugh 56 F4 r in Dumfries & Galloway region rising on E side of Carsphairn Forest and flowing W then S past Carsphairn vil to Kendoon Loch. NX 6090

Water of Dye 77 F2 r in Grampian region running N down Glen Dye to Water of Feugh on W side of Strachan. NO 6691

Water of Effock 77 E3 stream in Tayside region running NE down Glen Effock to R North Esk 2m/3km W of Tarfside. NO 4578

Water of Fleet 58 B6 r in Dumfries & Galloway region rising on E side of Cairnsmore of Fleet and running S past Gatehouse of Fleet into Fleet Bay and Wigtown Bay. NX 5550

Water of Fleet, Little 57 F6 stream in Dumfries & Galloway region running S from Loch Fleet into Water of Fleet 3m/5km N of Gatehouse of Fleet. NX 5860

Water of Girvan 56 B4 r in Strathclyde region running N from Loch Girvan Eye, in Glentrool Forest Park, through Loch Bradan Resr to Straiton. R then loops round the N side of Crosshill before continuing SW past Dailly to the coast at Girvan. NX 1898

Water of Glencalvie H'land. See Glen Calvie.

Water of Ken 58 C4 r in Dumfries & Galloway region rising near border with Strathclyde region, NW of Carsphairn, and flowing S through Carsfad and Earlstoun Lochs, then past Dalry and New Galloway to Loch Ken, at the foot of which it runs into R Dee. NX 6870

Water of Lee 76 D3, 77 E3 stream in Tayside region running E down Glen Lee to join Water of Mark at head of Glen Esk, 3m/4km W of Tarfside. NO 4480

Water of Leith 65 H1 r in Lothian region rising on Pentland Hills and running N through Harperrig Resr, then NE through Edinburgh to Leith Harbour and the Firth of Forth. NT 2678

Water of Luce 57 C7 r in Dumfries & Galloway region formed by confluence of Cross Water of Luce and Main Water of Luce at New Luce, and flowing S, to W of Glenluce, into Luce Bay. NX 1954

Water of Mark 76 D3, 77 E3 stream in Tayside region running first NE then SE to join Water of Lee at head of Glen Esk 3m/4km W of Tarfside. NO 4480

Water of May 72 D3 r in Tayside region running N into R Earn 5m/8km SW of Perth. NO 0418

Water of Milk 59 F4 r in Dumfries & Galloway region rising on S side of Castle O'er Forest and flowing SW then S to R Annan 3m/5km W of Ecclefechan. NY 1473

Water of Minnoch 57 D5 r in Dumfries & Galloway region running S through Glentrool Forest to R Cree 6m/10km NW of Newton Stewart. NX 3574

Water of Nevis H'land 74 C4 r in Lochaber dist rising on Mamore Forest and running first NE, then W along S side of Ben Nevis, then NW to head of Loch Linnhe at Fort William. NN 1074

Water of Nochty 82 C5 stream in Grampian region running SE to R Don at Strathdon. NJ 3512

Water of Philorth Grampian. See Philorth.

Water of Ruchill Tayside. See Ruchill Water.

Water of Tanar 77 E2 r in Grampian region running NE through Forest of Glentanar to R Dee 1m SW of Aboyne. NO 5197

Water of Tarf 77 E3 stream in Tayside region running S into R North Esk just S of vil of Tarfside. NO 4979

Water of Tig 57 B5 r in Strathclyde region rising in Arecleogh Forest and running N then W to R Stinchar 2m/3km E of Ballantrae. NX 1183

Water of Trool 58 A4 r in Dumfries & Galloway region running SW down Glen of Trool to Water of Minnoch, 8m/13km N of Newton Stewart. NX 3778

Water of Tulla S'clyde 71 E1 r in Argyll running SW to Loch Tulla. NN 3044

Water of Unich 76 D3 stream in Tayside region running E to Water of Lee 6m/10km W of Tarfside. Falls of Unich, waterfall in course of stream near its junction with Water of Lee. NO 3980

Water Orton Warwicks 35 G5 vil 2m/4km NW of Coleshill. SP 1791

Waterperry Oxon 18 B1 vil 7m/11km E of Oxford. SP 6206

Water Reservoir, West Borders 65 G3* resr on Pentland Hills 2m/3km W of W Linton. NT 1152

Waterrow Som 7 H3 vil on R Tone 3m/4km SW of Wiveliscombe. ST 0525

Watersfield W Sussex 11 F3 vil 3m/4km SW of Pulborough. TQ 0115

Waters Green Clwyd 41 H5* loc 1km N of Pen-y-ffordd. SJ 3062

Watersheddings Gtr Manchester 43 E1* loc in Oldham 2m/3km NE of tn centre. SD 9406

Water Sheddles Reservoir Lancs 48 C4* resr on S side of Colne-Haworth rd 5m/8km E of Colne. SD 9638

Waterside Cumbria 52 C1* loc 3m/4km SW of Wigton. NY 2245

Waterside Lancs 48 A5* ham 2km NE of Darwen. SD 7123

Waterside S'clyde 56 D3 vil in colliery dist in valley of R Doon, 3m/5km NW of Dalmellington. NS 4308

Waterside S'clyde 64 C4 vil 5m/8km NE of Kilmarnock. NS 4843

Waterside S'clyde 64 D2* loc 2km E of Kirkintilloch. NS 6773

Waterside S Yorks 49 H6* loc 1m NW of Thorne. SE 6714

Water's Nook Gtr Manchester 42 C1* loc 1km E of Westhoughton. SD 6605

Waterstock Oxon 18 B1 vil 5m/7km W of Thame. SP 6305

Waterston Dyfed 22 B5 vil 2m/3km E of Milford Haven. Oil refinery to S. SM 9305

Waterston, Higher Dorset 9 E4* loc 2m/4km NW of Puddletown. SY 7295

Waterston, Lower Dorset 9 E4* loc 2km NW of Puddletown. Waterston Manor is Elizn. SY 7395

Water Stratford Bucks 28 B4 vil on R Ouse 3m/5km W of Buckingham. SP 6534

Waters Upton Salop 34 C3 vil 5m/8km N of Wellington. SJ 6319

Waterton Mid Glam 15 E4* loc 2m/3km SE of Bridgend. SS 9278

Water, West 77 E4 r in Tayside region running SE to R North Esk 2m/4km SE of Edzell. NO 6266

Water Yeat Cumbria 52 C5 loc at S end of Coniston Water. SD 2889

Watford Herts 19 E2 tn on R Colne 16m/26km NW of London. Industries include brewing, paper mnfg. TQ 1096

Watford Mid Glam 15 F3 loc adjoining Caerphilly to S. ST 1486

Watford Northants 28 B1 vil 4m/7km NE of Daventry. **Watford Court,** Elizn and later. SP 6068

Watford Gap Northants 28 B1* loc 5m/8km N of Daventry. Service Area on M1 motorway 2km S. SP 5869

Wath N Yorks 48 D2 ham 2m/3km NW of Pateley Br. SE 1467

Wath N Yorks 49 E1 vil 4m/6km N of Ripon. SE 3277

Wath N Yorks 50 C1* loc 1km SE of Hovingham. SE 6775

Wath Brow Cumbria 52 A3 loc adjoining Cleator Moor to E. NY 0214

Wath upon Dearne S Yorks 43 H1 tn 5m/8km N of Rotherham. Coal-mining, bricks, glass, brewing. SE 4300

Watley's End Avon 16 B3* suburban loc adjoining Winterbourne to NE, 3m/5km N of Mangotsfield. ST 6581

Watling Street 21 F5 etc. Roman military rd, which ran from the E coast of Kent through the SE and centre of England into N Wales. Its line is still largely followed by the present A2 and A5 rds.

Watlington Norfolk 38 B3 vil 5m/8km N of Downham Mkt. TF 6110

Watlington Oxon 18 B2 small tn 7m/11km S of Thame. 1m SE on escarpment of Chiltern Hills is **Watlington Hill** (NT, together with beech wds surrounding Watlington Park to S). SU 6894

Watnall Cantelupe Notts 44 A6* loc adjoining Kimberley to N. SK 5045

Watnall Chaworth Notts 44 A6 loc 6m/9km NW of Nottingham. SK 5046

Wats Ness Shetland 89 D7 headland on W coast of Mainland 5m/7km W of Walls. HU 1750

Watten H'land 86 E2 vil in Caithness dist 8m/12km W of Wick. To N is Loch Watten, nearly 3m/5km NW to SE and up to 1km wide. ND 2454

Wattisfield Suffolk 31 E1 vil 5m/9km NE of Ixworth. TM 0174

Wattisham Suffolk 31 E3* vil 5m/9km SW of Stowmarket. Airfield to E. TM 0151

Wattle Syke W Yorks 49 F3 loc 2km SW of Wetherby. SE 3946

Watton Dorset 8 C5* ham 1km SW of Bridport. SY 4592

Watton Humberside 51 E3 vil 5m/8km S of Gt Driffield. TA 0150

Watton Norfolk 38 D4 vil 8m/13km SE of Swaffham. Loc of **Watton Green** 1m E. Rokeles Hall, hse dating from 17c, 2km E. Airfield to E. TF 9100

Watton-at-Stone Herts 29 G5 vil 5m/8km SE of Stevenage. TL 3019

Watton's Green Essex 20 B2* loc 4m/7km W of Brentwood. TQ 5295

Wattstown Mid Glam 15 E2* loc 4m/7km NW of Pontypridd. ST 0193

Wattsville Gwent 15 G2 vil 2m/3km W of Risca. ST 2091

Wauchope Forest Borders 60 B1, B2 state forest, forming part of Border Forest Park, 8m/13km SE of Hawick. **Wauchope Burn,** one of headwaters of Rule Water, flows N through W part of forest. NT 6104

Wauchope Water 59 H3 r in Dumfries & Galloway region running SE then NE to R Esk at Langholm. NY 3684

Waughtonhill Grampian 83 G2 loc below N side of Waughton Hill 3m/4km NE of Strichen. Height of hill 769 ft or 234 metres. NJ 9758
Wauldby Humberside 50 D5/51 E5 ham 8m/12km W of Hull. SE 9629
Waun Powys 33 F4* loc 1m NE of Commins-coch. SH 8504
Waun Powys 33 H3* loc 1m E of Llansanffraid-ym-Mechain. SJ 2319
Waunarlwydd W Glam 23 G6 loc in Swansea 4m/6km W of tn centre. SS 6095
Waun Fach Powys 25 G5 summit of Black Mts 5m/8km W of Llanthony. Height 2660 ft or 810 metres. SO 2129
Waun Fawr Dyfed 32 D6 suburb of Aberystwyth 2km E of tn centre. SN 6081
Waunfawr Gwynedd 40 C5 loc 4m/6km SE of Caernarvon. SH 5259
Waungilwen Dyfed 23 E2* loc 3m/4km E of Newcastle Emlyn. SN 3439
Waungron W Glam 23 G5* loc 1m S of Pontarddulais. SN 5802
Waunlwyd Gwent 15 F1/G1* loc 2m/3km S of Ebbw Vale. SO 1706
Waun, Y Welsh form of Chirk, qv.
Wavendon Bucks 28 D4 vil 4m/6km NW of Woburn. SP 9137
Waveney 119 admin dist of Suffolk.
Waveney 39 H4 r rising on Norfolk–Suffolk border near Redgrave and flowing E past Beccles then N into R Yare at W end of Breydon Water. TG 4705
Waver 59 F5 r rising E of Abbey Tn, Cumbria, and flowing in series of loops northwards into Solway Firth 1km after passing Grune Pt. NY 1357
Waverbridge Cumbria 52 C1 ham 2m/4km W of Wigton. NY 2249
Waverley Surrey 11 E1 loc 2m/3km SE of Farnham, including **Waverley Abbey**, ruins beside R Wey of oldest Cistercian house in England, from which Sir Walter Scott is said to have taken title of his first novel. SU 8645
Waverley 119 admin dist of Surrey.
Waverton Ches 42 A5 vil 4m/7km SE of Chester. SJ 4663
Waverton Cumbria 52 C1 vil 2m/4km W of Wigton. NY 2247
Wavertree Merseyside 42 A3* dist of Liverpool 3m/4km E of city centre. SJ 3889
Wawne Humberside 51 E4 vil 5m/8km N of Hull. TA 0936
Waxham Norfolk 39 H2 coastal ham 4m/7km E of Stalham. TG 4426
Waxholme Humberside 51 G5 loc on coast 2km NW of Withernsea. TA 3229
Way Kent 13 H1 loc on Isle of Thanet 1m E of Minster. TR 3265
Wayford Som 8 C4 vil 3m/5km SW of Crewkerne. ST 4006
Wayland's Smithy Oxon 17 G3* prehistoric chambered long barrow (A.M.) beside Ridge Way 1m E of Ashbury. SU 2885
Waymills Salop 34 C1* loc on E side of Whitchurch. SJ 5541
Wayne Green Gwent 26 A5* loc 3m/5km W of Skenfrith. SO 4118
Wayoh Reservoir Lancs 47 G6* resr 1km W of Edgworth. SD 7316
Waytown Dorset 8 C4 ham 3m/5km N of Bridport. SY 4797
Way Village Devon 7 F4 ham 5m/7km SW of Tiverton. SS 8810
Way Wick Avon 15 H5* loc 4m/7km E of Weston-super-Mare. ST 3862
Wdig Welsh form of Goodwick, qv.
Weacombe Som 7 H1* ham at foot of Quantock Hills 3m/5km SE of Watchet. ST 1140
Weald Cambs 29 F2* loc on site of former vil 3m/5km E of St Neots. TL 2259
Weald Kent. Alternative name for vil of Sevenoaks Weald, qv.
Weald Oxon 17 G2 loc 1km S of Bampton. SP 3002
Weald Bassett, North Essex 20 B2 vil 3m/4km NE of Epping. WT stn to E. TL 4904
Wealden 119 admin dist of E Sussex.
Weald, Lower Bucks 28 C4* loc 1m S of Stony Stratford. SP 7838
Weald, Middle Bucks 28 C4* loc 2km S of Stony Stratford. SP 7938
Weald, South Essex 20 C2 vil 2m/3km W of Brentwood. TQ 5793
Wealdstone London 19 F3 loc in borough of Harrow 11m/18km NW of Charing Cross. TQ 1589
Weald, The 11–13* region of SE England bounded by N and S Downs. TQ 63
Weald, Upper Bucks 28 C4 loc 2m/3km S of Stony Stratford. SP 8037
Wear Tyne & Wear 61 G5* industrial estate in SW part of Washington. NZ 2954
Wear 61 H5 r formed by confluence of several streams in vicinity of Wearhead, Durham, and flowing E by St John's Chapel and Stanhope to Wolsingham, then SE to Bishop Auckland, then NE by Durham and Chester-le-Street to North Sea at Sunderland, county of Tyne & Wear. NZ 4158
Wear Bay, East Kent 13 G3 bay on English Channel to E of Folkestone. TR 2537
Wear Cliffs Dorset. See Golden Cap.
Wearde Cornwall 4 B5* S dist of Saltash. SX 4258
Weardley W Yorks 49 E4* vil 7m/11km N of Leeds. SE 2944
Weare Som 15 H5 vil 2m/3km SW of Axbridge. ST 4152
Weare Giffard Devon 6 D3 vil on R Torridge 2m/3km NW of Torrington. SS 4721
Weare, Lower Som 15 H5 vil on R Axe 2m/3km W of Axbridge. ST 4053
Wearhead Durham 53 G1 vil 9m/14km W of Stanhope. NY 8539
Wear, Lower Devon 5 E2* SE dist of Exeter. SX 9489
Wearne Som 8 C2 ham 1m N of Langport. ST 4228
Wear Point Dyfed 22 B5* headland 2m/3km W of Neyland opp mouth of Pembroke R. SM 9304
Wear Valley 117 admin dist of county of Durham.
Weasdale Cumbria 53 F4* loc 2m/3km W of Ravenstonedale. NY 6903
Weasenham All Saints Norfolk 38 D3 vil 1km SW of Weasenham St Peter. TF 8521
Weasenham St Peter Norfolk 38 D3 vil 6m/10km SW of Fakenham. TF 8522
Weaste Gtr Manchester 42 D2* dist of Salford 2km W of tn centre. SJ 8098
Weathercote Cave N Yorks 47 G1* limestone cave at Chapel le Dale. SD 7377
Weather Ness Orkney 89 B5* headland at SE end of island of Westray, nearly 2m/3km SE of Stanger Hd. HY 5240
Weatheroak Hill H & W 27 E1 ham 4m/7km N of Redditch. SP 0674
Weaver 42 B3 r rising S of Peckforton, Ches, and flowing SE to its junction with R Duckow near Audlem, then N by Nantwich and Winsford to Northwich, then NW to Manchester Ship Canal and, by Weaver Sluices, to R Mersey S of Runcorn. SJ 5080
Weaverham Ches 42 B4 suburb 3m/4km W of Northwich. SJ 6174
Weavering Street Kent 20 D6* loc 2km E of Maidstone. TQ 7855
Weaver's Point W Isles 88 E1* headland with lighthouse on N side of entrance to Loch Maddy, E coast of N Uist. NF 9569
Weaverthorpe N Yorks 51 E2 vil 4m/6km NW of Langtoft. SE 9670
Webb's Green W Midlands 35 F5/F6* loc in Halesowen 1m E of tn centre. SO 9783
Webb's Heath Avon 16 C4* ham 6m/10km E of Bristol. ST 6873
Webburn 4 D3 the **E** and **W Webburn** Rs rise on Dartmoor, Devon, W of Manaton, and flow S to join at Lizwell Meet, 1m E of Ponsworthy. The Webburn then flows S in a wooded valley into R Dart, S of Buckland in the Moor. SX 7171
Webheath H & W 27 E1 W dist of Redditch. SP 0166
Webton H & W 26 A4* loc 6m/10km SW of Hereford. SO 4236
Weddell Sound Orkney 89 A7, B7 sea channel between islands of Fara and Flotta. ND 3394
Wedder Hill S'clyde 64 D5 summit of Blackside, hill ridge NE of Sorn. Height 1411 ft or 430 metres. NS 5930
Wedder Holm Shetland 89 F5* small island off SE coast of island of Uyea, S of Unst. HU 6197
Wedderlairs Grampian 83 G4* loc 2km NW of Tarves. NJ 8532
Wedder Law 59 E2 mt in Lowther Hills on border of Strathclyde and Dumfries & Galloway regions 3m/5km E of Durisdeer. Height 2185 ft or 666 metres. NS 9302
Weddicar Cumbria 52 A3* loc 3m/4km E of Whitehaven. NY 0117
Weddington Warwicks 36 A5 N dist of Nuneaton. SP 3693
Wedhampton Wilts 17 E5 vil 4m/7km SE of Devizes. SU 0657
Wedmore Som 16 A6 vil 4m/6km S of Cheddar. ST 4347
Wednesbury W Midlands 35 F5 NW dist of W Bromwich. SO 9894
Wednesbury Oak W Midlands 35 F5* loc 3m/5km NW of W Bromwich tn centre. SO 9594
Wednesfield W Midlands 35 F4 dist of Wolverhampton 2m/3km NE of tn centre. SJ 9400
Weecar Notts 44 C4* loc adjoining Girton to N. SK 8266
Weedon Bucks 28 C5 vil 3m/5km N of Aylesbury. SP 8118
Weedon Bec Northants 28 B2 vil 4m/7km SE of Daventry. SP 6259
Weedon Lois Northants 28 B3 vil 6m/10km N of Brackley. SP 6046
Weedon, Upper Northants 28 B2 vil 4m/6km SE of Daventry. SP 6258
Weeford Staffs 35 G4 vil 4m/7km W of Tamworth. SK 1403
Week Devon 4 D4* loc 2m/3km NW of Totnes. SX 7862
Week Devon 6 D3* loc 4m/6km S of Barnstaple. SS 5727
Week Devon 7 E3 loc 4m/6km NE of Chulmleigh. SS 7316
Week Som 7 G2* ham on Exmoor 1km W of Exton. SS 9133
Weeke Hants 10 B2 NW dist of Winchester. SU 4630
Weeke, Great Devon 7 E6* ham 3m/4km NW of Moretonhampstead. SX 7187
Weekley Northants 36 D6 vil 2m/3km NE of Kettering. SP 8880
Weeks Isle of Wight 10 C5* S dist of Ryde. SZ 5991
Week St Mary Cornwall 6 B5 vil 6m/9km S of Bude. SX 2397
Weel Humberside 51 E4 ham 2m/3km E of Beverley. TA 0639
Weeley Essex 31 E5 vil 5m/8km NW of Clacton-on-Sea. TM 1422
Weeley Heath Essex 31 E6/F6 vil 3m/6km NW of Clacton-on-Sea. TM 1520
Weelsby Humberside 45 G1* loc 2m/3km SE of Grimsby. TA 2806
Weem Tayside 75 H6 vil 1m NW of Aberfeldy across R Tay. NN 8449
Weeping Cross Staffs 35 F2* loc in Stafford 2m/3km SE of tn centre. SJ 9421
Wee Queensberry D & G. See Queensberry.
Weethley Warwicks 27 E2 ham 3m/4km SW of Alcester. SP 0555
Weeting Norfolk 38 C5 vil 2km N of Brandon. **Weeting Castle** (A.M.), remains of 11c fortified manor hse. TL 7788
Weeton Humberside 51 G6 ham 3m/5km SE of Patrington. TA 3520
Weeton Lancs 47 E4 vil 3m/5km NW of Kirkham. SD 3834
Weeton N Yorks 49 E3 vil 5m/8km S of Harrogate. SE 2846
Weeton Lane Heads Lancs 47 E4* loc just E of Weeton. SD 3834
Weetwood W Yorks 49 E4 dist of Leeds 3m/5km NW of city centre. SE 2737
Weighton, Little Humberside 51 E5 vil 8m/12km NW of Hull. SE 9833
Weir Lancs 48 B5 ham 2km N of Bacup. SD 8725
Weirbrook Salop 34 A2 loc 5m/8km SE of Oswestry. SJ 3524
Weir Quay Devon 4 B4* ham beside R Tamar 6m/10km SW of Yelverton. SX 4364
Weir Wood Reservoir 12 A3 large resr on border of E and W Sussex 2m/3km S of E Grinstead. TQ 3934
Weisdale Shetland 89 E7* loc on Mainland, where **Burn of Weisdale** runs into head of **Weisdale Voe**. HU 3952
Welbeck Abbey Notts 44 A4 mansion of various periods, mainly Victn, in Welbeck Park 3m/5km SW of Worksop. SK 5674
Welbeck Colliery Village Notts 44 B4 vil 6m/10km NE of Mansfield. SK 5869
Welborne Norfolk 39 E4 vil 5m/8km E of E Dereham. TG 0610
Welbourn Lincs 44 D5 vil 11m/18km S of Lincoln. SK 9654
Welburn N Yorks 50 C2 vil 5m/8km SW of Malton. SE 7267
Welburn N Yorks 55 E6 ham 4m/7km E of Helmsley. SE 6884
Welbury N Yorks 54 C4 vil 6m/9km N of Northallerton. NZ 3902
Welby Lincs 37 E1 vil 4m/7km NE of Grantham. SK 9738
Welches Dam Cambs 38 A5 ham 2m/4km S of Manea. TL 4786
Welcombe Devon 6 B3 vil near coast 8m/13km N of Bude. SS 2218
Weld Bank Lancs 47 F6* S dist of Chorley. SD 5816
Weldon Northants 37 E5 vil 2m/3km E of Corby. Iron workings and stone quarries (Weldon stone). Several Roman remains nearby. SP 9289
Welford Berks 17 H4 vil 5m/9km NW of Newbury. SU 4073
Welford Northants 36 C6 vil 3m/4km S of Husbands Bosworth. Resr to NE. SP 6480
Welford-on-Avon Warwicks 27 F3 vil in loop of r 4m/6km W of Stratford-upon-Avon. SP 1452
Welham Leics 36 D5 vil on R Welland 4m/6km NE of Mkt Harborough. SP 7692
Welham Notts 44 C3 ham 2m/3km NE of E Retford. SK 7282
Welham Green Herts 19 F1 vil 2m/3km S of Hatfield. TL 2305
Well Hants 11 D1 ham 5m/8km W of Farnham. SU 7646
Well Lincs 45 H4 ham 2km SW of Alford. TF 4473
Well N Yorks 54 C6 vil on escarpment 3m/5km E of Masham. Site of Roman bldg on hillside to W. SE 2681
Welland H & W 26 C4 vil 2m/3km SE of Malvern Wells. SO 7939
Welland 37 H1 r rising near Mowsley, W of Mkt Harborough, Leics, and flowing generally NE to Stamford, Mkt Deeping, and Spalding, Lincs, and thence into the Wash about 7m/11km N of Holbeach. TF 3635
Welland, Upper H & W 26 C3* ham 3m/5km S of Gt Malvern. SO 7740
Well Bank Lancs 48 B5* loc adjoining Haslingden to W. SD 7823
Wellbank Tayside 73 G1* loc 4m/7km N of Broughty Ferry. NO 4637
Well End Bucks 18 D3 loc adjoining Bourne End to N. SU 8888
Well End Herts 19 F2 loc 2km N of Borehamwood. TQ 2098
Wellesbourne Hastings Warwicks 27 G2 vil 5m/8km E of Stratford-upon-Avon. SP 2855
Wellesbourne Mountford Warwicks 27 G2 vil 5m/8km E of Stratford-upon-Avon. SP 2755
Wellfield Durham 54 C2* loc 1km NE of Wingate. NZ 4038
Wellgrain Dod S'clyde 65 F6 hill in Lowther Hills 3m/5km W of Elvanfoot. Height 1813 ft or 553 metres. NS 9017
Well Heads W Yorks 48 D5* loc 1m SE of Denholme. SE 0833
Well Hill Kent 20 B5 loc 3m/4km SE of Orpington. TQ 4963
Wellhouse Berks 18 A4* loc 4m/7km NE of Newbury. Site of Roman villa to E. SU 5172
Wellhouse W Yorks 48 D6* 1km S of Golcar. SE 0915
Welling London 20 B4 loc in borough of Bexley 11m/17km E of Charing Cross. TQ 4675
Wellingborough Northants 28 D1 tn 10m/16km NE of Northampton. Iron, footwear, clothing mnfre. SP 8968
Wellingham Norfolk 38 D3 vil 6m/9km SW of Fakenham. TF 8722
Wellingore Lincs 44 D5 vil 9m/15km S of Lincoln. SK 9856
Wellington Cumbria 52 B4 ham 1km NE of Gosforth. NY 0704
Wellington H & W 26 A3 vil 5m/8km N of Hereford. SO 4948
Wellington Salop 34 D3 tn 10m/16km E of Shrewsbury forming part of Telford. Various industries. SJ 6511
Wellington Som 8 A2 tn in valley of R Tone 6m/10km W of Taunton. Bedding mnfre. On Blackdown Hills to S, **Wellington Monmt** (NT), obelisk commemorating exploits of Duke of Wellington. ST 1320
Wellington College Berks. See Crowthorne.
Wellington Heath H & W 26 C3 vil 2m/3km N of Ledbury. SO 7140
Wellington Hill W Yorks 49 F4* loc in Leeds 4m/7km NE of city centre. SE 3438
Wellington Marsh H & W 26 A3 loc 5m/8km N of Hereford. SO 5047
Wellow Avon 16 C5 vil 4m/7km S of Bath. Prehistoric burial mound (A.M.) to S across Wellow Brook. ST 7458
Wellow Isle of Wight 10 B5 vil 2m/4km SE of Yarmouth. SZ 3888
Wellow Notts 44 B4 vil 2km SE of Ollerton. SK 6766
Wellow Brook 16 C5* r rising W of Midsomer Norton, Avon, and flowing E and

then NE to join R Avon 3m/4km SE of Bath. Its lower reach from Midford to its confluence with R Avon is known as Midford Brook. ST 7660
Wellow, East Hants 10 A3 ham 3m/5km W of Romsey. SU 3020
Wellow, West Hants 10 A3 vil 4m/6km N of Cadnam. SU 2819
Wellow Wood Hants 10 A3* loc just S of Sherfield English. SU 2921
Wellpond Green Herts 29 G5/H5* loc 2m/3km SE of Puckeridge. TL 4122
Wells (or Wells-next-the-Sea) Norfolk 38 D1 small commercial port and yachting centre 9m/14km N of Fakenham. TF 9143
Wells Som 16 B6 small cathedral city below S slopes of Mendip Hills, 17m/24km S of Bristol. Centre still largely medieval. Moated Bishop's Palace. Industries include cheese-making, cider, textiles, electrical instruments. ST 5445
Wellsborough Leics 36 A4* loc 3m/4km W of Mkt Bosworth. SK 3602
Wells Green Ches 42 C5* loc 2m/3km SW of Crewe. SJ 6853
Wells Green W Midlands 35 G5* loc in Solihull 3m/5km N of tn centre. SP 1483
Wells of Ythan Grampian 83 E3 vil 7m/11km E of Huntly. Here is source of R Ythan. Site of Roman camp 2km E. NJ 6338
Well Street Kent 20 C5* loc 1km SW of E Malling. TQ 6956
Wellstyle Green Essex 30 B6* ham 2m/3km S of Gt Dunmow. TL 6318
Wellswood Devon 5 E4* E dist of Torbay 1m E of Torquay tn centre. SX 9364
Wellsworth Hants 10 D4* loc adjoining Rowland's Castle to N, 3m/5km N of Havant. SU 7311
Wellwood Fife 72 D5 loc 1m N of Dunfermline. NT 0988
Welnetham, Great Suffolk 30 D2* loc 3m/5km SE of Bury St Edmunds. Loc of **Lit Welnetham** 1km E. TL 8759
Welney Norfolk 38 A5 vil 5m/8km NW of Littleport. TL 5294
Welshampton Salop 34 B1 vil 2m/4km E of Ellesmere. SJ 4335
Welsh Bicknor H & W 26 B5* loc in loop of R Wye 4m/7km S of Ross-on-Wye across r. SO 5917
Welsh Frankton Salop 34 B1* ham 3m/4km SW of Ellesmere. SJ 3633
Welsh Hook Dyfed 22 B3 loc 6m/10km S of Fishguard. SM 9327
Welsh Newton H & W 26 A5 vil 3m/5km N of Monmouth. SO 4918
Welshpool (Trallwng, Y) Powys 34 A4 mkt tn on left (W) bank of R Severn 17m/27km W of Shrewsbury. Remains of Norman motte and bailey cas near rly stn. See also Powis Castle. SJ 2207
Welsh St Donats (Llanddunwyd) S Glam 15 E4 vil 2m/4km NE of Cowbridge. ST 0276
Welson, Lower H & W 25 G3 loc 2m/3km NW of Willersley. SO 2950
Welton Cumbria 60 A6 ham 4m/6km S of Dalston. **Nether Welton** loc 1km N. NY 3544
Welton Humberside 50 D5 vil 2km E of Brough. SE 9527
Welton Lincs 45 E4 vil 6m/9km NE of Lincoln. TF 0179
Welton Northants 28 B1 vil 2m/4km N of Daventry. SP 5866
Welton le Marsh Lincs 45 H4 vil 7m/11km NW of Skegness. TF 4768
Welton le Wold Lincs 45 F3 vil 4m/6km W of Louth. TF 2787
Welton, Little Lincs 45 G3* loc 2km W of Louth. TF 3087
Welwick Humberside 51 G6 vil 2m/3km SE of Patrington. TA 3421
Welwyn Herts 29 F6 tn 5m/8km S of Stevenage. Sites of Roman bldgs beside R Mimram to E and W. TL 2316
Welwyn Garden City Herts 19 F1 New Tn designated 1948, 6m/10km NE of St Albans. Various light industries include pharmaceutical products, plastics, breakfast cereals. TL 2313
Wem Salop 34 C2 small tn on R Roden 10m/16km N of Shrewsbury. Industries include brewing. SJ 5128
Wembdon Som 8 B1, vil adjoining Bridgwater to W. ST 2837
Wembley London 19 F3 dist in borough of Brent 8m/13km NW of Charing Cross. Includes locs of **N Wembley** and **Wembley Park.** Sports stadium at Wembley Park. TQ 1885
Wembury Devon 4 B5 dist on **Wembury Bay** 5m/7km SE of Plymouth across R Plym estuary. At NE end, loc of **W Wembury.** Cliffs to E of Wembury are NT property. SX 5249
Wembworthy Devon 7 E4 vil 3m/5km SW of Chulmleigh. SS 6609
Wemyss Bay S'clyde 64 A2 vil and bay on Firth of Clyde 7m/11km SW of Greenock. Passenger boat terminus. **Wemyss Pt** is headland to N. NS 1969
Wemyss, East Fife 73 F4/F5 vil on Firth of Forth 5m/8km NE of Kirkcaldy. Linen mnfre, brewing. See also Macduff's Castle. NT 3396
Wemyss, West Fife 73 F5 vil on Firth of Forth 4m/6km NE of Kirkcaldy. **Wemyss Castle** is restored 15c-17c cas on rocky eminence to NE, towards E Wemyss. NT 3294
Wen 32 C1* stream running S into Tremadoc Bay at Afon Wen, Gwynedd. SH 4437
Wen 33 E2 r flowing SW into R Mawddach 2m/3km NE of Llanelltyd, Gwynedd. SH 7322
Wenallt Dyfed 24 C1* loc 1km W of Llanafan. SN 6771
Wendens Ambo Essex 30 A4 vil 2m/4km SW of Saffron Walden. Site of Roman villa to SW. TL 5136
Wendlebury Oxon 28 B5 vil 2m/4km SW of Bicester. SP 5619
Wendling Norfolk 38 D3 vil 4m/6km W of E Dereham. TF 9312
Wendon Lofts Essex 29 H4* loc 5m/8km W of Saffron Walden. TL 4638
Wendover Bucks 18 D1 tn at N edge of Chiltern Hills 5m/8km SE of Aylesbury. SP 8607
Wendover Dean Bucks 18 D1* loc 2m/3km S of Wendover. SP 8704
Wendron Cornwall 2 C5 ham 2m/4km N of Helston. SW 6731
Wendy Cambs 29 G3 vil 5m/7km NW of Royston. TL 3247
Wenfordbridge Cornwall 3 F1* loc on R Camel 5m/9km S of Camelford. SX 0875
Wenham, Great Suffolk 31 E4 vil 4m/7km SE of Hadleigh. TM 0738
Wenham, Little Suffolk 31 E4 ham 4m/7km SE of Hadleigh. **Lit Wenham Hall,** 13c, is oldest brick-built hse in England. TM 0839
Wenhaston Suffolk 31 H1 vil 3m/4km SE of Halesworth. TM 4275
Wenlock Edge Salop 34 B5/C5 hill ridge running from Craven Arms (SW) to Much Wenlock (NE). SO 5392
Wenlock, Little Salop 34 D4 vil 3m/5km S of Wellington. SJ 6406
Wenning 47 F2 r rising on limestone hills W of Horton-in-Ribblesdale, N Yorks, and flowing W through Wennington and into R Lune to W of Hornby, Lancs. SD 5768
Wennington Cambs 37 G6* ham 5m/8km N of Huntingdon. TL 2379
Wennington Lancs 47 F2 vil 6m/9km S of Kirkby Lonsdale. SD 6170
Wennington London 20 B3 loc in borough of Havering 2km SE of Rainham. TQ 5480
Wensley Derbys 43 G5 vil 2m/4km W of Matlock. SK 2661
Wensley N Yorks 54 A5 vil on R Ure 2km W of Leyburn. SE 0989
Wensleydale N Yorks 54 A5 valley of R Ure above Masham. SD 99, SE 08
Wensum 39 F4 r rising near Horningtoft, Norfolk, and flowing in a westward loop to Fakenham, then SE to Norwich, on the E side of which it joins R Yare. TG 2507
Wentbridge 49 F6 vil on R Went on borders of N and W Yorks 4m/6km SE of Pontefract. SE 4817
Wentnor Salop 34 B5 vil 5m/8km NE of Bishop's Castle. SO 3892
Wentwood Reservoir Gwent 16 A2* resr 2km NW of Llanvair Discoed. **Wentwood** is area of mixed woodland to N. ST 4393
Wentworth Cambs 38 A6 vil 4m/6km W of Ely. TL 4878
Wentworth Surrey 18 D4* residential dist and golf course to W of loc of Virginia Water. SU 9767
Wentworth S Yorks 43 H2 vil 4m/7km NW of Rotherham. To SE is **Wentworth Woodhouse,** large 18c mansion in park containing temples, statues, and lakes. SK 3898
Wentworth Castle S Yorks 43 G1 hse dating partly from 17c, 2m/4km SW of Barnsley. SE 3203
Wenvoe (Gwenfo) S Glam 15 F4 vil 3m/5km N of Barry. ST 1272
Weobley H & W 26 A3 vil 10m/16km NW of Hereford. Ham of **Weobley Marsh** 1m E. SO 4051
Weobley Castle W Glam. See Landimore.
Weoley Castle W Midlands 35 F6* loc in Birmingham 4m/7km SW of city centre. SP 0182
Wepham W Sussex 11 F4 ham just SE of Burpham and 4m/7km N of Littlehampton. TQ 0408
Wepre Clwyd 41 H4* S dist of Connah's Quay. SJ 2968
Wepre Brook 41 H4* stream running NE into R Dee at Wepre, Clwyd, between Connah's Quay and Shotton. SJ 3069
Wereham Norfolk 38 B4 vil 2m/3km NW of Stoke Ferry. TF 6801
Wergs W Midlands 35 E4 loc in Wolverhampton 3m/5km NW of tn centre. SJ 8600
Wern Gwynedd 32 C1* loc 3m/5km NE of Criccieth. SH 5439
Wern Powys 25 F6 loc 3m/5km SW of Llangynidr. SO 1117
Wern Powys 34 A3* locality on Shropshire Union Canal 4m/7km NE of Welshpool. SJ 2513
Wern Salop 34 A1* loc 1m NE of Sellatyn. SJ 2734
Werneth Gtr Manchester 43 E2* loc 2m/3km S of Hyde. SJ 9592
Wernffrwd W Glam 23 G6* loc 2m/3km NE of Llanrhidian. SS 5193
Wern-olau W Glam 23 G6* loc 6m/9km W of Swansea. SS 5695
Wern, The Clwyd 41 H6* loc 4m/6km W of Wrexham. SJ 2750
Wern-y-cwrt Gwent 15 H1* loc 2km NW of Raglan. SO 3908
Wern-y-gaer Clwyd 41 G4* loc 2m/4km W of Northop. SJ 2068
Wern-yr-heolydd Gwent 25 H6 loc 4m/6km N of Raglan. SO 3912
Werrington Cambs 37 F4 dist of Peterborough 4m/6km NW of city centre. TF 1603
Werrington Cornwall 6 C6* ham 2m/3km N of Launceston. SX 3287
Werrington Staffs 43 E6 loc 4m/6km E of Hanley. SJ 9447
Wervin Ches 42 A4 vil 4m/6km N of Chester. SJ 4271
Wesham Lancs 47 E4/E5 vil adjoining Kirkham to NW. SD 4132
Wessenden Reservoir W Yorks 43 F1* resr 2m/3km S of Marsden. 1m SE lies another resr, near the head of the valley (Wessenden Head, 43 F1), while farther down the valley are Blackeley and Butterley Resrs, qv. SE 0508
Wessington Derbys 43 H5* vil 3m/5km NW of Alfreton. **Wessington Green** loc adjoining to S. SK 3757
WEST. For names beginning with this word, see under next word. This also applies to names beginning with North, South, East; Great, Little; Greater, Lesser; High, Low; Higher, Lower, Upper, Nether; Far, Near; Mid, Middle; Isle(s) of; The, Y, Yr.
Westbank Derbys 43 H6* loc 2m/3km NE of Belper. SK 3649
Westbere Kent 13 G1 vil 4m/6km NE of Canterbury. TR 1961
Westborough Lincs 36 D1 vil 7m/11km NW of Grantham. SK 8544
Westbourne Dorset 9 G5* W dist of Bournemouth. SZ 0691
Westbourne Suffolk 31 F3* NW dist of Ipswich. TM 1445
Westbourne W Sussex 10 D4 vil 2m/4km E of Havant. SU 7507
Westbourne Green London 19 F3* loc in City of Westminster NW of Paddington, 3m/5km NW of Charing Cross. TQ 2582
Westbrook Berks 17 H4 ham adjoining Boxford to N, 4m/6km NW of Newbury. SU 4271
Westbrook Kent 13 H1* W dist of Margate. TR 3369
Westbrook Wilts 16 D5* ham 4m/6km NE of Melksham. ST 9565
Westbrook Green Norfolk 39 E6* loc 1m N of Diss. TM 1181
Westbury Bucks 28 B4 vil 3m/4km E of Brackley. SP 6235
Westbury Salop 34 A3/B3 vil 9m/14km W of Shrewsbury. SJ 3509
Westbury Wilts 16 D6 tn at foot of Salisbury Plain 4m/7km S of Trowbridge. Westbury White Horse (A.M.) cut in chalk on hillside to E, below Iron Age camp (see Bratton). ST 8751
Westbury Leigh Wilts 16 D6 SW dist of Westbury. ST 8650
Westbury-on-Severn Glos 26 C6 vil 4m/6km E of Cinderford. 17c-18c formal water garden (NT) at **Westbury Court.** SO 7114
Westbury on Trym Avon 16 B4 N dist of Bristol. **Westbury College** (NT), 15c gatehouse. ST 5777
Westbury Park Avon 16 B4* dist of Bristol 2m/3km N of city centre. ST 5775
Westbury-sub-Mendip Som 16 A6 vil 4m/6km NW of Wells. ST 5048
Westby Lancs 47 E5* ham 1m W of Wrea Green. SD 3831
Westby Lincs 37 E2* loc 1m W of Bitchfield. SK 9728
Westcliff-on-Sea Essex 21 E3 dist of Southend-on-Sea 1m SW of tn centre. TQ 8685
Westcombe Som 8 C2* ham 2m/3km W of Somerton. ST 4629
Westcombe Som 8 D1 ham 2m/3km E of Evercreech. ST 6739
Westcot Oxon 17 G3* ham 4m/6km W of Wantage. SU 3387
Westcote Glos 27 F5 vil 4m/6km SE of Stow-on-the-Wold. SP 2120
Westcote, Nether Glos 27 F5* ham 4m/7km SE of Stow-on-the-Wold. SP 2220
Westcott Bucks 28 C5 vil 7m/11km W of Aylesbury. SP 7117
Westcott Devon 7 G4 ham 2m/3km S of Cullompton. ST 0204
Westcott Surrey 19 F6 vil and residential loc 2km W of Dorking. TQ 1448
Westcott Barton Oxon 27 H5 vil 4m/7km SW of Deddington. SP 4325
Westcourt Wilts 17 F5* ham adjoining Burbage to W and 4m/6km E of Pewsey. SU 2261
Westdean E Sussex 12 B6 ham 2m/3km S of Alfriston. TV 5299
Westdowns Cornwall 3 E1* ham 3m/5km W of Camelford. SX 0582
Westend Glos 16 C1* loc 4m/7km W of Stroud. SO 7806
Westend 43 F2* r rising on S slope of Bleaklow Hill, Derbys, and flowing SE into Howden Resr in Derwent Dale. SK 1693
Westend Town Avon 16 C4* loc 1m W of Marshfield. ST 7674
Westend Town Nthmb 60 D5* loc 1km N of Bardon Mill. NY 7865
West-end Town S Glam 15 E4* loc on W side of Llantwit Major. SS 9668
Westenhanger Kent 13 F3 loc 3m/5km NW of Hythe. Remains of 14c fortified hse. Racecourse. TR 1237
Wester Balgedie Tayside 73 E4 vil 3m/5km E of Milnathort. NO 1604
Wester Clynekirkton H'land. See Clynekirkton.
Westerdale H'land 86 D3 loc on R Thurso 5m/8km S of Halkirk, Caithness dist. ND 1251
Westerdale N Yorks 55 E4 vil in N Yorks Moors National Park 7m/11km SE of Guisborough. NZ 6605
Wester Elchies Grampian 82 B3 mansion above left bank of R Spey 1km W of Charlestown of Aberlour across r. NJ 2543
Wester Fearn Burn H'land 85 F7 stream running E into Dornoch Firth at **Wester Fearn Pt,** Ross and Cromarty dist, low-lying promontory protruding into the firth 3m/4km SE of Ardgay. See also Easter Fearn Burn. NH 6387
Westerfield Suffolk 31 F3 vil 2m/3km N of Ipswich tn centre; vil is partly in Ipswich and partly in par of Westerfield. TM 1747
Westergate W Sussex 11 F4 vil 4m/6km N of Bognor Regis. SU 9305
Wester Greenyards H'land 85 E7* loc 7m/11km W of Bonar Br, Sutherland dist. NH 5092
Wester Hailes Lothian 66 A2* dist of Edinburgh 4m/7km SW of city centre. NT 1969
Westerham Kent 20 B6 small tn 5m/8km W of Sevenoaks. Quebec Hse (NT), once home of General Wolfe. Squerryes Court, to SW, is 17c manor hse. See also Chartwell. TQ 4454
Westerhope Tyne & Wear 61 G5* suburb 4m/6km NW of Newcastle. NZ 1967

Westerleigh Avon 16 C3* vil 2m/4km SW of Chipping Sodbury. ST 6979
Westerloch H'land 86 F2* locality in Caithness dist 5m/8km N of Wick. ND 3258
Western Bank Cumbria 52 C1* loc adjoining Wigton to W. NY 2448
Western Cleddau 22 C4 r rising about 2m/3km E of Llanrian, Dyfed, and flowing S by Haverfordwest to its confluence with Eastern Cleddau R to form Daugleddau R. SN 0011
Western Hill Durham 54 B1/C1* NW dist of Durham. NZ 2642
Western Isles 88. String of islands off W coast of Scotland, extending for some 130m/209km from Butt of Lewis (N) to Barra Hd (S), separated from Skye and the mainland by the Minch. The chief islands are Lewis, N Uist, Benbecula, S Uist, and Barra. There are airfields with scheduled passenger flights on Lewis, Benbecula, and Barra. Fishing and grazing are the main industries. Tweed mnfre on Lewis. Also known as Outer Hebrides. NF 67
Wester Pencaitland Lothian. See Pencaitland.
Wester Quarff Shetland. See Easter Quarff.
Wester Ross H'land 78, 80 rugged highland area roughly comprising W part of Ross and Cromarty dist. NH 16
Wester Skeld Shetland 89 E7* loc on W part of Mainland 2m/3km W of Reawick across Skelda Voe. HU 2943
Westerton Durham 54 B2 ham 2m/3km SW of Spennymoor. NZ 2331
Westerton W Sussex 11 E4* vil 2m/4km NE of Chichester. SU 8807
Wester Wick Shetland 89 D7* inlet on coast of Mainland 5m/7km SW of Garderhouse. Locality of **Westerwick** at head of inlet. **Loch of Westerwick** to N. HU 2842
Westfield Cleveland 55 E3* suburb adjoining Redcar to SW. NZ 5924
Westfield Cumbria 52 A2 dist of Workington 1m S of tn centre. NX 9927
Westfield E Sussex 12 D5 vil 4m/6km N of Hastings. TQ 8115
Westfield Hants 10 D5* loc in S Hayling on Hayling I. SZ 7299
Westfield H'land 86 D2* loc in Caithness dist 5m/7km SW of Thurso. ND 0564
Westfield H & W 26 C3* loc 3m/5km W of Gt Malvern. SO 7247
Westfield Lothian 65 F2* loc 3m/5km NW of Bathgate. NS 9372
Westfield Norfolk 38 D4 ham 2m/4km S of E Dereham. TF 9909
Westfield S'clyde 64 D2* loc in Cumbernauld 2m/4km W of tn centre. NS 7273
Westfield Surrey 19 E5* S dist of Woking. TQ 0056
Westfield W Yorks 48 D4/49 E4* loc adjoining to W. SE 1940
Westfield W Yorks 49 E5* loc adjoining Heckmondwike to N. SE 2124
Westfields Dorset 9 E4* ham 1km W of Mappowder and 6m/10km SW of Sturminster Newton. ST 7206
Westfields H & W 26 A3* loc with racecourse in N part of Hereford. SO 5041
Westfields of Rattray Tayside 73 E1* loc 1km N of Rattray. NO 1746
Westfield Sole Kent 20 D5* loc 4m/6km N of Maidstone. TQ 7761
Westford Som 7 H3* loc 2km W of Wellington. ST 1220
Westgate Durham 53 G1/H1 vil on R Wear 2km E of St John's Chapel. NY 9038
Westgate Humberside 44 C1 vil 2m/4km N of Epworth. SE 7707
Westgate Norfolk 38 D1 ham adjoining Binham to NW. TF 9839
Westgate Hill W Yorks 48 D5/49 E5* loc 3m/5km SE of Bradford. SE 2029
Westgate on Sea Kent 13 H1 W dist of Margate. Coastal resort. TR 3270
Westgate Street Norfolk 39 F3* W end of Hevingham. TG 1921
Westhall Suffolk 31 H1* ham 3m/5km NE of Halesworth. TM 4280
Westham Dorset 8 D6 W dist of Weymouth. SY 3255
Westham E Sussex 12 C6 vil adjoining Pevensey to W and 4m/6km NE of Eastbourne. TQ 6404
Westham Som 16 A6* ham 2m/4km SW of Wedmore. ST 4046
Westhampnett W Sussex 11 E4 vil 2m/3km NE of Chichester. SS 8806
Westhay Devon 8 B4* loc 1m E of Hawkchurch and 4m/6km NE of Axminster. ST 3500
Westhay Som 16 A6 vil 5m/7km NW of Glastonbury. ST 4342
Westhead Lancs 42 A1* loc 2m/3km E of Ormskirk. SD 4307
Westhide H & W 26 B3 vil 5m/8km NE of Hereford. SO 5844
Westholme Som 8 D1* loc 3m/5km SW of Shepton Mallet. ST 5740
Westhope H & W 26 A3 vil 8m/12km N of Hereford. SO 4651
Westhorp Northants 28 A2* loc adjoining Byfield to W, 7m/11km SW of Daventry. SP 5053
Westhorpe Derbys 44 A3* loc adjoining Killamarsh to S. SK 4579
Westhorpe Lincs 37 G2 ham 6m/9km N of Spalding. TF 2131
Westhorpe Notts 44 B5 loc adjoining Southwell to W. SK 6853
Westhorpe Suffolk 31 E2 vil 7m/11km N of Stowmarket. TM 0469
Westhoughton Gtr Manchester 42 C1 tn 5m/7km E of Wigan. Textiles, pharmaceutical products, engineering. SD 6505
Westhouse N Yorks 47 G1 ham 2m/3km NW of Ingleton. **Lr Westhouse** ham to S. SD 6774
Westhouses Derbys 43 H5 vil 2km NE of Alfreton. SK 4257
Westlake Devon 4 C5* ham 2m/3km SW of Ivybridge. SX 6253
Westlands Staffs 42 D6* S dist of Newcastle-under-Lyme. SJ 8444
Westleigh Devon 6 D3 vil above E side of R Torridge estuary 2m/3km NE of Bideford. SS 4728
Westleigh Devon 7 H3 vil 5m/8km SW of Wellington. ST 0617
Westleigh Gtr Manchester 42 C1/C2 loc in Leigh 1m NW of tn centre. SD 6401
Westleton Suffolk 31 H2 vil 3m/5km E of Yoxford. Nature reserve on Westleton Heath to E. TM 4469
Westley Essex 20 C3* SW dist of Basildon. TQ 6886
Westley Salop 34 B4 loc 9m/14km SW of Shrewsbury. SJ 3606
Westley Suffolk 30 C2 vil 2m/3km W of Bury St Edmunds. TL 8264
Westley Waterless Cambs 30 B2 vil 5m/8km S of Newmarket. TL 6256
Westlington Bucks 18 C1 vil 4m/7km SW of Aylesbury. SP 7610
Westlinton Cumbria 59 H5 ham 3m/4km S of Longtown. NY 3964
Westmancote H & W 26 D4* ham 4m/7km NE of Tewkesbury. SO 9437
Westmancote, Lower H & W 26 D4* ham 4m/7km NE of Tewkesbury. SO 9337
Westmarsh Kent 13 H1 ham 4m/7km NW of Sandwich. TR 2761
Westmeston E Sussex 12 A5 vil below Ditchling Beacon on S Downs 4m/7km SE of Burgess Hill. TQ 3313
Westmill Herts 29 G5 vil 2m/3km S of Buntingford. TL 3627
Westminster London 19 G3 dist of Central London and borough (City of Westminster), containing Westminster Abbey, Hses of Parliament, Buckingham Palace, St James's Palace, Whitehall, Trafalgar Sq, National Gallery, Tate Gallery, Royal Academy, Green Park, Hyde Park, St James's Park, Regent's Park (greater part). Westminster lies N of R Thames, here crossed by Vauxhall, Lambeth, Westminster, and Waterloo Brs. TQ 2979
Westmoor End Cumbria 52 B1* loc 3m/5km SW of Aspatria. NY 1039
Westmuir Tayside 76 D5 vil 2km SW of Kirriemuir. NO 3652
Westnewton Cumbria 52 B1 vil 2m/3km N of Aspatria. NY 1344
Westnewton Nthmb 67 F5 ham at foot of College Burn 1km W of Kirknewton. NU 9030
Westoe Tyne & Wear 61 H5* dist of S Shields 1km S of tn centre. NZ 3666
Weston Avon 16 C4 NW dist of Bath. **Upr Weston** adjoins to N. ST 7266
Weston Berks 17 H4 ham 6m/10km NW of Newbury. SU 4073
Weston Ches 42 B3 loc in Runcorn 1m S of tn centre. **Weston Pt** loc 1km NW. SJ 5080
Weston Ches 42 C5 vil 3m/5km SE of Crewe. SJ 7352
Weston Devon 5 G2* ham 3m/5km E of Sidmouth. SY 1689
Weston Devon 7 H5* ham 2km W of Honiton. ST 1400
Weston Dorset 9 E6 loc on W side of Portland. SY 6871
Weston Hants 10 B4 SE dist of Southampton beside Southampton Water beyond R Itchen. SU 4410
Weston Hants 10 D3* ham 2km SW of Petersfield. SU 7221
Weston Herts 29 F4 vil 3m/4km SE of Baldock. TL 2630
Weston H & W 25 H2* loc 4m/7km E of Kington. SO 3656
Weston Lincs 37 G2 vil 3m/5km E of Spalding. TF 2925
Weston Northants 28 B3 vil 6m/10km N of Brackley. SP 5846
Weston Notts 44 C4 vil 3m/5km SE of Tuxford. SK 7767
Weston N Yorks 48 D3 ham 2m/3km NW of Otley across R Wharfe. Hall is Elizn. SE 1746
Weston Salop 25 G1* loc 3m/5km E of Knighton. SO 3273
Weston Salop 34 C2 vil 3m/5km E of Wem. SJ 5628
Weston Salop 34 C5 ham 5m/8km S of Much Wenlock. SO 5992
Weston Staffs 35 F2 vil 4m/7km NE of Stafford. SJ 9727
Weston Bampfylde Som 8 D2* vil 1m S of Sparkford. ST 6124
Weston Bay Avon. See Weston-super-Mare.
Weston Beggard H & W 26 B3* vil 5m/7km E of Hereford. SO 5841
Westonbirt Glos 16 D3 loc 3m/5km SW of Tetbury. Girls' boarding school. ST 8589
Weston by Welland Northants 36 D5 vil 4m/6km NE of Mkt Harborough. SP 7791
Weston Colley Hants 10 C1* ham 1m W of Micheldever. SU 5039
Weston Colville Cambs 30 B3 vil 6m/10km NW of Haverhill. TL 6153
Weston Corbett Hants 10 D1 ham adjoining vil of Weston Patrick 4m/7km SE of Basingstoke. SU 6847
Weston Coton Salop 34 A2* loc 1m S of Oswestry. SJ 2928
Weston Coyney Staffs 35 F1* dist of Stoke-on-Trent 4m/6km E of city centre. SJ 9343
Weston Ditch Suffolk 38 B6* loc 3m/5km NW of Mildenhall. TL 6777
Weston Favell Northants 28 C2 E dist of Northampton. SP 7862
Weston Green Cambs 30 B3 ham 5m/8km NW of Haverhill. TL 6252
Weston Green Norfolk 39 E3 loc 9m/14km NW of Norwich. TG 1014
Weston Heath Salop 34 D3 ham 4m/7km SE of Newport. SJ 7713
Weston Hills Lincs 37 G3 loc 2m/4km SE of Spalding. TF 2821
Weston in Arden Warwicks 36 A5* loc 2m/3km E of Bedworth. SP 3887
Westoning Beds 29 E4 vil 4m/6km S of Ampthill. Loc of **Westoning Woodend** 2km W. TL 0332
Weston-in-Gordano Avon 16 A4 vil 3m/5km NE of Clevedon. ST 4474
Weston Jones Staffs 34 D2 ham 3m/5km N of Newport. SJ 7624
Weston, Little Som 8 D2* ham 1m E of Sparkford. ST 6225
Weston Longville Norfolk 39 E3 vil 9m/14km NW of Norwich. TG 1115
Weston Lullingfields Salop 34 B2 vil 9m/14km NW of Shrewsbury. SJ 4224
Weston Mill Devon 4 B5* NW dist of Plymouth, 3m/4km from city centre. SX 4557
Weston, North Oxon 18 B1* loc 2m/3km W of Thame. SP 6805
Weston-on-Avon Warwicks 27 F3* vil 4m/6km SW of Stratford-upon-Avon. SP 1551
Weston-on-the-Green Oxon 28 A5 vil 4m/6km SW of Bicester. SP 5318
Weston Patrick Hants 10 D1 vil 5m/8km SE of Basingstoke. SU 6946
Weston Rhyn Salop 34 A1 vil 4m/6km N of Oswestry. SJ 2835
Weston, South Oxon 18 C2 vil 3m/4km N of Watlington. SU 7098
Weston Subedge Glos 27 F3 vil below escarpment of Cotswold Hills 2m/3km NW of Chipping Campden. SP 1240
Weston-super-Mare Avon 15 H5 resort on Bristol Channel 18m/28km SW of Bristol, situated on Weston Bay, sandy bay extending from Birnbeck I. (N) to Howe Rock at tip of Brean Down (S). Airport to E. ST 3261
Weston Town Som 16 C6* loc 6m/9km SW of Frome. ST 7042
Weston Turville Bucks 18 D1 vil 3m/5km SE of Aylesbury. SP 8510
Weston under Lizard Staffs 35 E3 vil 7m/11km SE of Newport. SJ 8010
Weston under Penyard H & W 26 B5 vil 2m/4km E of Ross-on-Wye. Site of Roman settlement of *Ariconium* 1m E. SO 6323
Weston under Wetherley Warwicks 27 G1 vil 4m/6km NE of Leamington. SP 3669
Weston Underwood Bucks 28 D3 vil 2m/3km W of Olney. SP 8650
Weston Underwood Derbys 35 H1 vil 6m/9km NW of Derby. SK 2942
Weston upon Trent Derbys 36 A2 vil 6m/10km SE of Derby. SK 4028
Westonwharf Salop 34 B2* loc 1km NW of Weston Lullingfields. Situated on former canal. SJ 4225
Westonzoyland Som 8 B1 vil on Sedgemoor 4m/6km E of Bridgwater. 1m N, site of Battle of Sedgemoor, 1685. ST 3534
Westow N Yorks 50 C2 vil 5m/7km SW of Malton. SE 7565
Westport Som 8 B2 ham 4m/6km NE of Ilminster. ST 3819
Westquarter Central 65 F1* loc 2m/3km SE of Falkirk. NS 9178
Westra S Glam 15 F4* loc adjoining Dinas Powis to W. ST 1470
Westray Orkney 89 B5 island of 18 sq miles or 47 sq km lying 6m/9km N of island of Rousay and 18m/28km N of Kirkwall, Mainland. The western part is hilly and the W coast has high cliffs, but the eastern part is low-lying. Crab and lobster fishing and processing are carried on. HY 44
Westray Firth Orkney 89 B5 sea area bounded by Westray to N, Eday to E, Egilsay and Rousay to S, with the open sea to W. HY 43
Westridge Green Berks 18 B3* ham 2m/3km W of Streatley. SU 5679
Westrop Wilts 16 D4* ham 1m E of Corsham. ST 8870
Westrop Wilts 17 F2* loc in NE part of Highworth. SU 2092
Westruther Borders 66 D3/D4 vil 7m/11km E of Lauder. NT 6350
Westry Cambs 37 H4 vil 2m/3km NW of March. TL 3998
Westvale Merseyside 42 A2* W dist of Kirkby. SJ 4098
Westville Notts 44 A6* SW dist of Hucknall. SK 5247
Westward Cumbria 52 C1 ham 3m/4km SE of Wigton. NY 2744
Westward Ho Devon 6 C2 vil and resort on N coast 2m/3km NW of Bideford. Sands to N. Golf course on Northam Burrows. SS 4329
Westwell Kent 13 F2 vil 3m/5km N of Ashford. TQ 9947
Westwell Oxon 17 F1 vil 2m/4km SW of Burford. SP 2209
Westwell Leacon Kent 13 E2* ham 2km SE of Charing. TQ 9647
Westwick Cambs 29 H2* vil 5m/7km NW of Cambridge. TL 4265
Westwick Durham 54 A3 loc 2m/3km SE of Barnard Castle. NZ 0715
Westwick Norfolk 39 G2 loc 2m/4km S of N Walsham. **Westwick Hse** in park dates from = c. = 1800. TG 2826
Westwick N Yorks 49 F2* loc 2km E of Bishop Monkton. SE 3466
Westwick Row Herts 19 E1* loc in E part of Hemel Hempstead. TL 0906
Westwood Cambs 37 F4* W dist of Peterborough. TL 1799
Westwood Devon 7 G5 loc 5m/8km S of Cullompton. SY 0198
Westwood H & W 26 D2 loc 2m/3km W of Droitwich. **Westwood Hse** is 16c-17c. SO 8763
Westwood Kent 20 C4* loc 3m/4km S of Swanscombe. TQ 5970
Westwood Notts 44 A5* loc 1m S of Selston. SK 4551
Westwood S'clyde 64 D3* dist of E Kilbride 2km W of tn centre. NS 6154
Westwood Wilts 16 C5 vil 2km SW of Bradford-on-Avon. ST 8159
Westwood Heath W Midlands 35 H6 loc in Coventry 4m/6km SW of city centre. SP 2876
Westwood, High Durham 61 F5* ham 1m E of Ebchester. NZ 1155
Westwood, Low Durham 61 F5* ham on R Derwent 1km NE of Ebchester. NZ 1156
Westwoodside Humberside 44 C2 vil 1m W of Haxey. SK 7499
Wetham Green Kent 21 E5* loc just N of Upchurch. TQ 8468
Wetheral Cumbria 60 A6 vil 4m/7km E of Carlisle. Gatehouse of medieval priory. **Wetheral Plain** loc adjoining to N. Wooded bank of R Eden to S, NT. NY 4654

Wetherby W Yorks 49 F3 small mkt tn on R Wharfe 8m/13km SE of Harrogate. Racecourse to E. SE 4048

Wetherden Suffolk 31 E2 vil 4m/6km NW of Stowmarket. Loc of **Wetherden Upr Tn** 2km N. TM 0062

Wether Holm Shetland 89 E6* small island off NE coast of Mainland 2m/3km SE of Firth and 1km SE of Firth Ness. HU 4672

Wetheringsett Suffolk 31 F2 vil 4m/6km NW of Debenham. TM 1266

Wetherlam Cumbria 52 C4 mountain in Lake Dist 2m/4km N of Coniston. Height 2502 ft or 763 metres. NY 2801

Wethersfield Essex 30 B4 vil 2m/3km SE of Finchingfield. TL 7131

Wethersta Shetland 89 E6/E7* loc on Mainland on tongue of land between Busta Voe and Olna Firth, 2km S of Brae. HU 3665

Wetherup Street Suffolk 31 F2 vil 2m/3km NW of Debenham. TM 1464

Wetley Abbey Staffs 43 E6* loc 1km S of Wetley Rocks. SJ 9648

Wetley Rocks Staffs 43 E6 vil 5m/8km S of Leek. SJ 9649

Wetmore Staffs 35 H2* loc in Burton upon Trent 2km NE of tn centre. SK 2524

Wetreins Green Ches 42 B5* loc 2m/3km E of Holt across R Dee. SJ 4353

Wet Sleddale Reservoir Cumbria 53 E4 resr 3m/4km S of Shap. NY 5511

Wettenhall Ches 42 C5 vil 4m/6km SW of Winsford. SJ 6261

Wetton Staffs 43 F5 vil 7m/11km NW of Ashbourne. SK 1055

Wetwang Humberside 50 D3 vil 6m/9km W of Gt Driffield. SE 9359

Wetwood Staffs 34 D1/D2 ham 4m/7km NW of Eccleshall. SJ 7733

Wexcombe Wilts 17 F5 ham 5m/8km N of Ludgershall. SU 2759

Wexham Street Bucks 18 D3 loc 3m/4km NE of Slough. SU 9983

Wey 19 E5 r rising in Woolmer Forest near Liphook in Hampshire and flowing through Godalming and Guildford and into R Thames at Weybridge in Surrey. Another branch rises S of Alton in Hampshire, flows through Farnham, Surrey, and joins the former branch at Tilford 3m/5km SE of Farnham. TQ 0765

Wey 9 E6* r rising at Upwey in Dorset and flowing S into English Channel at Weymouth. SY 6878

Weybourne Norfolk 39 E1 vil 4m/6km NE of Holt. TG 1143

Weybourne Surrey 18 D6* urban loc 2km SW of Aldershot. SU 8549

Weybread Suffolk 31 F1 vil 2m/3km S of Harleston. Ham of **Weybread Street** 1km SE. Ham of **Upr Weybread** 1m SW. TM 2480

Weybridge Surrey 19 E5 largely residential tn on R Wey near its confluence with R Thames, 17m/28km SW of London. Aircraft factory. TQ 0764

Weycroft Devon 8 B4* ham on R Axe 2km NE of Axminster. SY 3099

Weydale H'land 86 D2* loc in Caithness dist 3m/5km SE of Thurso. ND 1464

Weyhill Hants 10 A1 vil 3m/5km W of Andover. SU 3146

Weymouth Dorset 9 E6 tn 26m/42km W of Bournemouth. Port for Channel Is. Resort since 18c. **Weymouth Bay** extends NE from tn to Redcliff Pt 1m E of Overcombe. SY 6778

Wgan 33 G3* stream running SE into R Banwy 1m NE of Llanerfyl, Powys. SJ 0410

Whaddon Bucks 28 C4 vil 4m/7km W of Bletchley. To S is **Whaddon Chase,** former hunting forest. SP 8034

Whaddon Cambs 29 G3 vil 4m/6km N of Royston. TL 3446

Whaddon Glos 26 D5/27 E5* NE dist of Cheltenham. SO 9622

Whaddon Glos 26 D6 vil 3m/5km S of Gloucester. SO 8313

Whaddon Wilts 16 D5* ham 3m/4km NE of Trowbridge. ST 8761

Whaddon Wilts 9 H2* ham 4m/7km SE of Salisbury. SU 1926

Whaddon Gap Cambs 29 G3* loc 4m/6km N of Royston. TL 3445

Whale Cumbria 53 E3 loc at S end of Lowther Park 5m/9km S of Penrith. NY 5221

Whalecombe Dyfed 22 C5* loc beside Daugleddau R 3m/5km NE of Pembroke. SN 0005

Whale Firth Shetland 89 E5 inlet on W coast of Yell, the head of which is 1km W of that of Mid Yell Voe on E coast. HU 4891

Whale Island Hants 10 C4* island in Portsmouth Harbour, connected by causeway to Portsea I. Naval installations. SU 6302

Whaley Derbys 44 A4 ham 3m/4km E of Bolsover. SK 5171

Whaley Bridge Derbys 43 E3 tn 6m/10km NW of Buxton. Industries include textiles, engineering. Terminus of Peak Forest Canal. SK 0181

Whaley Thorns Derbys 44 A4* coal-mining loc 6m/10km N of Mansfield. SK 5371

Whalley Lancs 48 A4 small tn 6m/10km NE of Blackburn. Remains of 13c abbey. **Whalley Banks** loc 1km S. SD 7336

Whalley Range Gtr Manchester 42 D2* loc in Manchester 2m/3km SW of city centre. SJ 8295

Whal Point Orkney 89 C5* headland at NW end of island of Sanday. HY 6545

Whalsay Shetland 89 F7 island of some 8 sq miles or 21 sq km off E coast of Mainland opp entrance to Dury Voe. Fishing is main industry. HU 56

Whalton Nthmb 61 F3 vil 5m/8km SW of Morpeth. NZ 1381

Wham, High Durham 54 A2* loc 1km NE of Butterknowle. NZ 1126

Whaplode Lincs 37 H2 vil 2m/4km W of Holbeach. TF 3224

Whaplode Drove Lincs 37 G3 vil 5m/9km E of Crowland. TF 3113

Wharf Warwicks 27 H2/H3* ham on Oxford Canal 8m/13km N of Banbury. SP 4353

Wharfe N Yorks 48 B2 ham 4m/7km NW of Settle. SD 7869

Wharfe 49 G4 r rising in Langstrothdale Chase, N Yorks, and flowing SE by Kettlewell, Burnsall, and Bolton Abbey to Ilkley, then E by Otley to Wetherby, then SE by Tadcaster to join R Ouse 1m N of Cawood. SE 5739

Wharles Lancs 47 E4 vil 3m/5km NE of Kirkham. SD 4435

Wharley End Beds 28 D3* loc to NW of Cranfield Airfield 4m/7km E of Newport Pagnell. SP 9342

Wharley Point Dyfed 23 E4 headland at confluence of estuaries of R Taf and R Towy 2km SW of Llansteffan. SN 3309

Wharmley Nthmb 60 D4 loc 4m/6km NW of Hexham. NY 8866

Wharncliffe Reservoir S Yorks 43 G2* small resr 2m/3km E of Stocksbridge. SK 3097

Wharncliffe Side S Yorks 43 G2 vil on R Don 6m/9km NW of Sheffield. SK 2994

Wharram le Street N Yorks 50 D2 vil 6m/10km SE of Malton. SE 8665

Wharram Percy N Yorks 50 D2 loc 3m/5km N of Fridaythorpe. Site of former vil to N. SE 8564

Wharton Ches 42 C4 loc adjoining Winsford to E. SJ 6666

Wharton H & W 26 A2* ham 2m/4km S of Leominster. SO 5055

Whashton N Yorks 54 B4 ham 4m/6km NW of Richmond. **Whashton Green** loc to SW. NZ 1506

Whatcombe Dorset 9 F4 locs of **Hr** and **Lr Whatcombe** on road alongside grounds of Whatcombe Hse, 4m/7km SW of Blandford Forum. ST 8301

Whatcote Warwicks 27 G3 vil 4m/6km NE of Shipston on Stour. SP 2944

Whateley Warwicks 35 H4* ham 3m/5km SE of Tamworth. SP 2299

Whatfield Suffolk 31 E3 vil 3m/4km N of Hadleigh. TM 0246

Whatley Som 16 C6 vil 3m/4km W of Frome. To E, ham of **Lr Whatley.** ST 7347

Whatlington E Sussex 12 D5 vil 2m/3km NE of Battle. TQ 7618

Whatsole Street Kent 13 F3* ham 7m/11km E of Ashford. TR 1144

Whatstandwell Derbys 43 H5* ham 4m/7km N of Belper. SK 3354

Whatton Notts 36 C1 vil 3m/4km E of Bingham. SK 7439

Whauphill D & G 57 D7 vil 4m/6km SW of Wigtown. NX 4049

Whaw N Yorks 53 H4 loc in Arkengarthdale 5m/8km NW of Reeth. NY 9804

Wheatacre Norfolk 39 H5 vil 2m/4km SE of Haddiscoe. TM 4693

Wheatcroft Derbys 43 H5* ham 4m/6km SE of Matlock. SK 3557

Wheatenhurst Glos 26 C6* ham 6m/10km NW of Stroud. SO 7609

Wheatfield Oxon 18 B2 loc 3m/5km N of Watlington. SU 6899

Wheathampstead Herts 19 F1 vil 3m/4km E of Harpenden. TL 1713

Wheathill Salop 34 C6 ham 5m/8km NW of Cleobury Mortimer. SO 6282

Wheathill Som 8 D2* loc 1m W of Lovington, and 3m/5km NW of Sparkford. ST 5830

Wheatley Hants 11 E1* ham 5m/7km E of Alton. SU 7840

Wheatley Oxon 18 B1 suburban vil 5m/8km E of Oxford. Site of Roman villa on Castle Hill to SE. SP 5905

Wheatley W Yorks 48 D3* former name of Ben Rhydding, E dist of Ilkley. SE 1347

Wheatley W Yorks 48 D5 loc in Halifax 2m/3km NW of tn centre. SE 0726

Wheatley Hill Durham 54 C1 coal-mining vil 4m/6km SW of Easington. NZ 3739

Wheatley Hills S Yorks 44 B1* dist of Doncaster 2m/3km NE of tn centre. SE 6005

Wheatley Lane Lancs 48 B4 loc 2m/3km W of Nelson. SD 8338

Wheatley, North Notts 44 C3 vil 4m/7km NE of E Retford. **S Wheatley** vil adjoins to SE. SK 7685

Wheatley Park S Yorks 44 B1* dist of Doncaster 2km NE of tn centre. SE 5804

Wheatley, South Cornwall 6 B5* vil 7m/12km NW of Launceston. SX 2492

Wheaton Aston Staffs 35 E3 vil 5m/7km W of Penkridge. SJ 8512

Wheddon Cross Som 7 G2 Exmoor vil 5m/8km SW of Dunster. SS 9238

Wheelbarrow Town Kent 13 G3* loc adjoining Stelling Minnis to S. TR 1546

Wheeler (Chwiler) 41 G4* r rising on S side of Pantasa, Clwyd, W of Holywell, and flowing S to Ddol, then W to R Clwyd 1m W of Bodfari. SJ 0869

Wheelerend Common Bucks 18 C2* loc 4m/6km W of High Wycombe. SU 8093

Wheeler's Street Kent 13 E2 loc adjoining Headcorn to E. TQ 8444

Wheelerstreet Surrey 11 F1* loc 1m S of Milford. SU 9440

Wheelock Ches 42 C5 vil on r of same name and on Trent and Mersey Canal 2km S of Sandbach. **Wheelock Heath** loc 1m S. SJ 7559

Wheelock 42 C4 r rising in Ches N of Kidsgrove, Staffs and flowing generally NW into R Dane on NW side of Middlewich, Ches. SJ 6967

Wheelton Lancs 47 F5 vil 3m/5km N of Chorley. **Hr Wheelton** vil 1m NE. SD 6021

Wheldale W Yorks 49 F5* loc 2km E of Castleford. SE 4526

Wheldrake N Yorks 50 B4 vil 7m/11km SE of York. SE 6844

Whelford Glos 17 F2 vil 2m/3km SE of Fairfield. ST 1798

Whelley Gtr Manchester 42 B1* E dist of Wigan. SD 5906

Whelpley Hill Bucks 19 E2* ham 2m/4km S of Berkhamsted. Prehistoric fort to S. SP 9904

Whelpo Cumbria 52 C1 loc 1m W of Caldbeck. NY 3039

Whelston Clwyd 41 G4* loc on R Dee estuary 1m NW of Bagillt. SJ 2076

Whenby N Yorks 50 B2 vil 6m/9km N of Strensall. SE 6369

Whepstead Suffolk 30 C2 vil 4m/7km SW of Bury St Edmunds. TL 8358

Whernside 48 A1 mt on border of Cumbria and N Yorks 6m/10km NE of Ingleton. Height 2419 ft or 737 metres. **Whernside Tarns** group of small lakes 2km N of summit. SD 7381

Whernside, Great N Yorks 48 C1 mt 2m/4km NE of Kettlewell. Height 2310 ft or 704 metres. SE 0073

Wherry Town Cornwall 2 A5* central dist of Penzance. SW 4629

Wherstead Suffolk 31 F4 vil 3m/4km S of Ipswich. TM 1540

Wherwell Hants 10 B1 vil on R Test 3m/5km SE of Andover. SU 3840

Whessoe Durham 54 C3* loc 3m/4km N of Darlington. NZ 2718

Wheston Derbys 43 F3 vil 2km W of Tideswell. SK 1575

Whetstead Kent 20 C6 ham 1m NW of Paddock Wd. TQ 6546

Whetstone Leics 36 B4 suburb 5m/8km SW of Leicester. SP 5597

Whetstone London 19 F2 loc in borough of Barnet 9m/14km N of Charing Cross. TQ 2693

Wheyrigg Cumbria 52 B1 loc 4m/6km W of Wigton. NY 1948

Whicham Cumbria 52 B6 ham 3m/5km NW of Millom. SD 1382

Whichford Warwicks 27 G4 vil 5m/8km N of Chipping Norton. SP 3134

Whickham Tyne & Wear 61 G5 tn 3m/5km W of Gateshead. Coal-mining, engineering. Power stn to NE beside R Tyne. NZ 2061

Whickham Hill Tyne & Wear 61 G5* loc adjoining Gateshead to SW. NZ 2260

Whickhope Burn 60 C3* r rising on border of Cumbria and Nthmb on W edge of Kielder Forest and flowing E into R North Tyne 2m/3km W of Falstone, Nthmb. NY 6987

Whiddon Devon 6 D2* loc 3m/5km N of Barnstaple. SS 5538

Whiddon Devon 6 D5* loc 8m/12km NW of Okehampton. SS 4700

Whiddon Down Devon 7 E5 vil 7m/11km E of Okehampton. SX 6992

Whilborough, North Devon 5 E4* ham 3m/5km NW of Torquay. SX 8766

Whilton Northants 28 B2 vil 4m/7km E of Daventry. SP 6364

Whiltonlocks Northants 28 B2* loc on Grand Union Canal 3m/5km E of Daventry. SP 6164

Whimble Devon 6 C5* loc 7km SE of Holsworthy. SS 3403

Whimple Devon 7 H5 vil in cider-making dist 4m/6km NW of Ottery St Mary. Cider factory. SY 0497

Whimpwell Green Norfolk 39 G2* vil 1m S of Happisburgh. TG 3829

Whinburgh Norfolk 39 E4 vil 3m/5km S of E Dereham. TG 0009

Whinfell Tarn Cumbria 53 E5* small lake 2km NW of Grayrigg. SD 5598

Whinhill Reservoir S'clyde 64 A2* small resr 2km S of Greenock. NS 2774

Whin Lane End Lancs 47 E4 loc 4m/6km SE of Preesall. SD 3941

Whinlatter Pass Cumbria 52 B3/C3 pass between Whinlatter to N and Grisedale Pike to S, carrying rd between Keswick and Cockermouth. NY 1924

Whinney Hill S Yorks 44 A2* loc 2m/4km NE of Rotherham. SK 4694

Whinnow, High Cumbria 59 G6* loc 2m/3km NW of Thursby. **Low Whinnow** loc to S. NY 3051

Whinnyfold Grampian 83 H3 loc on E coast opp The Skares and 2m/3km S of vil of Cruden Bay. NK 0833

Whinny Heights Lancs 47 G5* loc in Blackburn 2km SE of tn centre. SD 6926

Whinny Hill Cleveland 54 C3* loc 4m/6km W of Stockton-on-Tees. NZ 3819

Whins Pond Cumbria 53 E2* lake 3m/4km E of Penrith. NY 5530

Whippingham Isle of Wight 10 C5 ham 2km SE of E Cowes. SZ 5193

Whipsiderry Cornwall 2 D2* loc on coast 1m NE of Newquay. SW 8363

Whipsnade Beds 29 E5 vil 3m/4km S of Dunstable. **Whipsnade Park,** open zoo, to S. TL 0117

Whipton Devon 7 G5 E dist of Exeter, 2m/3km from city centre. SX 9593

Whirley Grove Ches 42 D4* loc 2m/3km NW of Macclesfield. SJ 8875

Whirlow S Yorks 43 G3* loc in Sheffield 4m/6km SW of city centre. SK 3182

Whisby Lincs 44 D4 ham 5m/9km SW of Lincoln. SK 9067

Whispering Knights Oxon. See Rollright, Great.

Whissendine Leics 36 D3 vil 4m/6km NW of Oakham. SK 8314

Whissonsett Norfolk 38 D3 vil 4m/7km S of Fakenham. TF 9123

Whisterfield Ches 42 D4* loc 1m W of Siddington. SJ 8271

Whistley Green Berks 18 C4 vil 2km S of Twyford. SU 7974

Whiston Merseyside 42 B2 tn adjoining Prescot to SE. **Whiston Cross** loc to W. **Whiston Lane Ends** loc to SW. SJ 4791

Whiston Northants 28 D2 vil 6m/10km E of Northampton. SP 8460

Whiston Staffs 35 E3 ham 2m/3km W of Penkridge. SJ 8914

Whiston Staffs 43 E6* ham 2m/3km E of Kingsley. **Whiston Eaves** loc 1km S. SK 0347

Whiston S Yorks 43 H2 suburb 2m/3km SE of Rotherham. **Upr Whiston** ham 1m SE. SK 4590

Whiston Cross Salop 35 E4* loc 1m SW of Albrighton. SJ 7903

Whitacre Fields Warwicks 35 H5* loc 4m/6km NE of Coleshill. SP 2592

Whitacre Heath Warwicks 35 H5* vil 3m/4km NE of Coleshill. SP 2192

Whitacre, Nether Warwicks 35 H5 vil 3m/5km NE of Coleshill. SP 2392
Whitaside Tarn N Yorks 53 H5* small lake on Whitaside Moor 2m/3km S of Low Row. SD 9795
Whitbeck Cumbria 52 B6 ham 3m/4km S of Bootle. SD 1184
Whitbourne H & W 26 C2 vil 5m/8km NE of Bromyard. SO 7257
Whitburn Lothian 65 F2 tn 3m/5km SW of Bathgate. NS 9465
Whitburn Tyne & Wear 61 H5 tn on North Sea coast in S Tyneside dist 4m/6km SE of S Shields. **Whitburn Bay** to S. **Whitburn Colliery** to N. NZ 4061
Whitby Ches 42 A4 loc in Ellesmere Port 1m SW of tn centre. SJ 3975
Whitby N Yorks 55 G4 resort and small port on North Sea coast 17m/27km NW of Scarborough. Fishing, boat-bldg. 13c abbey (A.M.) on site of former abbey destroyed by Danes in 867. Boyhood home of Captain Cook, navigator and explorer, is preserved. NZ 8911
Whitbyheath Ches 42 A4 loc in Ellesmere Port 2m/3km S of tn centre. SJ 3974
Whitchurch Avon 16 B4 vil 4m/6km SE of Bristol. ST 6167
Whitchurch Bucks 28 C5 vil 5m/8km N of Aylesbury. SP 8020
Whitchurch Devon 4 B3 vil adjoining Tavistock to SE. SX 4972
Whitchurch (Tre-groes) Dyfed 22 A3 vil 3m/5km E of St David's. SM 7925
Whitchurch Hants 17 H6 small tn on R Test 6m/10km E of Andover. SU 4648
Whitchurch H & W 26 B5 vil 4m/6km NE of Monmouth. SO 5517
Whitchurch Oxon 18 B4 suburb across R Thames from Pangbourne. SU 6377
Whitchurch Salop 34 C1 tn 18m/29km N of Shrewsbury, on site of Roman tn of *Mediolanum*. SJ 5441
Whitchurch S Glam 15 F3 dist of Cardiff 3m/5km NW of city centre. ST 1580
Whitchurch Warwicks 27 F3* loc 4m/7km S of Stratford-upon-Avon. SP 2248
Whitchurch Canonicorum Dorset 8 C4 vil 4m/7km NE of Lyme Regis. SY 3995
Whitchurch Heath Salop 34 C1* loc 3m/4km S of Whitchurch. SJ 5537
Whitchurch Hill Oxon 18 B4* vil 2m/3km N of Pangbourne. SU 6479
Whitcombe Dorset 9 E5 ham 3m/4km SE of Dorchester. SY 7188
Whitcott Keysett Salop 34 A6 ham 2m/3km NW of Clun. SO 2782
Whiteadder Water 67 F3 r rising in Lammermuir Hills, Scotland, 6m/10km NW of Cranshaws, and flowing SE into R Tweed in Nthmb, England, 2m/3km W of Berwick-upon-Tweed. **Whiteadder Resr** in course of r about 3m/5km from source. NT 9751
White Ball Som 7 H3* ham 1km W of Sampford Arundel. 1km SW, White Ball Tunnel on Taunton–Exeter main rly line. ST 0918
Whitebirk Lancs 48 A5* loc 2m/3km E of Blackburn. SD 7028
White Birks N Yorks 53 G5 loc 7m/11km NW of Hawes. SD 7895
White Bridge H'land 81 E5 loc in Inverness dist at confluence of R Feehlin and Allt Breinag, 3m/5km S of Foyers. NH 4815
Whitebrook Gwent 16 A1 ham 4m/7km S of Monmouth. SO 5306
Whitecairns Grampian 83 G5 loc 7m/12km N of Aberdeen. NJ 9218
White Cart Water 64 C2 r in Strathclyde region rising S of E Kilbride and running N to Cathcart, Glasgow, then NW through Paisley to join Black Cart Water 3m/4km N thereof and flow into R Clyde 1km farther N. NS 4968
White Castle Gwent 25 H6 loc and ruined 13c cas (A.M.) 5m/8km E of Abergavenny. SO 3816
White Caterthun Tayside 77 E4. See Caterthun.
White Chapel Lancs 47 F4* ham 2m/3km E of Claughton. SD 5541
Whitechapel London 19 G3* loc in borough of Tower Hamlets 1km NE of London Br. TQ 3381
Whitechurch (Eglwys Wen) Dyfed 22 D2 loc 2km SE of Eglwyswrw. SN 1536
Whitechurch Som 9 E2* loc 1km N of Henstridge and 3m/5km NE of Milborne Port. ST 7220
Whitecliff Bay Isle of Wight 10 D6 bay on SE coast NE of Culver Cliff. SZ 6486
Whiteclosegate Cumbria 60 A5* loc 2km NE of Carlisle. NY 4157
White Colne Essex 30 D5 ham 4m/7km E of Halstead. TL 8729
White Coomb D & G 59 F1 mt, partly NTS, 8m/12km NE of Moffat. Height 2696 ft or 822 metres. NT 1615
White Corries S'clyde 74 D6* skiing area in Argyll on N slope of Meall a' Bhùiridh, qv. NN 2652
Whitecote W Yorks 49 E4* loc in Leeds 4m/6km NW of city centre. SE 2435
Whitecraig Lothian 66 B2 vil 2m/3km S of Musselburgh. NT 3570
Whitecroft Glos 16 B1* loc 2m/4km NW of Lydney. SO 6106
Whitecrook S'clyde 64 C2* dist of Clydebank to E of tn centre. NS 5069
Whitecross Central 65 F1/F2* loc 2m/3km W of Linlithgow. NS 9676
Whitecross Cornwall 2 B5* loc 3m/5km SW of Hayle. SW 5234
White Cross Cornwall 2 C6* ham 4m/6km SE of Helston. SW 6821
White Cross Cornwall 2 D2 ham 3m/5km SE of St Columb Major. SW 8959
Whitecross Cornwall 3 E1* ham 2m/3km W of Wadebridge. SW 9672
White Cross Devon 5 F2* loc 7m/11km E of Exeter. SY 0290
White Cross Devon 7 F4 loc 1km E of Cheriton Fitzpaine and 5m/8km NE of Crediton. SS 8706
Whitecross Dorset 8 C4* loc adjoining Netherbury to W, 2m/3km SW of Beaminster. SY 4699
White Cross Oxon 18 A2* loc 2m/3km N of Abingdon. SP 4800
White Cross Wilts 9 E1* ham 1km NW of Zeals and 3m/4km W of Mere. ST 7732
White End Glos 26 C5 loc to E of Ashleworth, 4m/7km N of Gloucester across R Severn. SO 8125
White Esk 59 G2/G3 r in Dumfries & Galloway region running S through Eskdalemuir and Castle O'er Forest to join R Black Esk and form R Esk 8m/13km NW of Langholm. NY 2590
Whiteface H'land 87 A7 loc on N side of Dornoch Firth 6m/9km W of Dornoch, Sutherland dist. NH 7089
Whitefarland Bay S'clyde 62 C1* bay on W coast of Jura between Feolin Ferry and Carrugh an t-Sruith to N. NR 4471
Whitefarland Point S'clyde 63 F3 headland on W coast of Arran 2km S of Pirnmill. NR 8642
Whitefaulds S'clyde 56 C3* W dist of Maybole. NS 2909
Whitefield Devon 7 E2* loc 6m/10km N of S Molton. SS 7036
Whitefield Dorset 9 F5* ham 4m/6km E of Bere Regis. SY 9094
Whitefield Gtr Manchester 42 D1 tn 3m/4km S of Bury. Light industry. SD 8006
Whitefield Lane End Merseyside 42 A3* loc 5m/7km NW of Widnes. SJ 4589
Whitefield, Little Isle of Wight 10 C5* ham 2m/3km S of Ryde. SZ 5889
Whitefield Loch D & G 57 C7 small loch 3m/5km SE of Glenluce. NX 2355
Whiteford Grampian 83 F4 loc 5m/7km NW of Inverurie. NJ 7126
Whitegate Ches 42 C4 vil 3m/4km NW of Winsford. SJ 6269
Whitehall Devon 6 D2* loc 3m/5km NW of Barnstaple. SS 5337
Whitehall Devon 7 H4* loc 4m/7km S of Wellington. ST 1214
Whitehall Hants 18 C6* loc 1m NE of Odiham. SU 7452
Whitehall Orkney 89 C6 vil on N coast of Stronsay opp Papa Stronsay. Harbour and centre of island's fishing industry. Loc of **Lr Whitehall** adjoining to E. HY 6528
Whitehall W Sussex 11 G3* loc 2km SE of Coolham. TQ 1321
Whitehaugh Forest Grampian 83 E4* large wood of conifers surrounding hill of Knock Saul, 5m/7km N of Alford. NJ 5723
Whitehaven Cumbria 52 A3 port on Irish Sea 7m/11km S of Workington. Coal mines, some of which extend under sea. NX 9718
Whitehawk E Sussex 11 H4* E dist of Brighton. TV stn and site of Neolithic camp to SW. TQ 3305
Whiteheath Gate W Midlands 35 F5* loc in Warley 2m/3km NW of tn centre. SO 9887
White Hill Durham 61 G6* loc adjoining Chester-le-Street to SW. NZ 2650
White Hill E Sussex 12 D5* W dist of Bexhill. TQ 7208
Whitehill Fife 73 F4* dist and industrial estate in SW part of Glenrothes. NT 2599
Whitehill Grampian 82 D2* loc 2m/4km SW of Gordonstown. NJ 5354
Whitehill Grampian 83 G2 loc 3m/5km S of New Pitsligo. NJ 8951
Whitehill Hants 11 E2 vil 2km S of Bordon Camp and 4m/6km NW of Liphook. SU 7934
White Hill Kent 13 G2* loc 3m/4km S of Canterbury. TR 1554
Whitehill Kent 21 F5 loc 2m/3km SW of Faversham. TR 0059
Whitehill Lothian 66 B2* loc 2m/3km E of Dalkeith. NT 3566
White Hill Wilts 9 E2* loc 2km S of Mere. ST 8230
Whitehills Grampian 83 E1 fishing vil 2m/4km NE of Banff. NJ 6565
Whitehills Tayside 77 E5* loc adjoining Forfar to NE. NO 4651
White Holme Reservoir W Yorks 48 C6* resr on Soyland Moor 3m/5km NE of Littleborough. SD 9719
Whitehope Law Borders 66 B4 hill 5m/8km N of Innerleithen. Height 2038 ft or 621 metres. NT 3344
Whitehough Derbys 43 E3* loc adjoining Chinley to S. SK 0382
Whitehouse Ches 42 B3* industrial area in SE part of Runcorn. SJ 5679
Whitehouse Grampian 83 E5 vil 3m/5km E of Alford. NJ 6214
Whitehouse S'clyde 63 E2 vil in Kintyre, Argyll, 6m/9km SW of Tarbert. NR 8161
Whitehouse Common W Midlands 35 G4* loc 1m NE of Sutton Coldfield tn centre. SP 1397
Whitehouse Green Berks 18 B4* loc 1m W of Burghfield and 5m/8km SW of Reading. SU 6568
White Houses Notts 44 B3* loc adjoining E Retford to S. SK 7179
Whiteinch S'clyde 64 C2* loc on N bank of R Clyde in Scotstoun dist of Glasgow. NS 5367
Whitekirk Lothian 66 D1 vil 4m/6km SE of N Berwick. NT 5981
White Kirkley Durham 54 A2* loc 1km S of Frosterley across R Wear. NZ 0235
Whitelackington (or White Lackington) Som 8 B3 vil 2km E of Ilminster. ST 3715
White Lackington Dorset 9 E4 ham 4m/6km NW of Puddletown. SY 7198
White Ladies Salop 35 E4* remains of 12c priory (A.M.), 2m/3km E of Tong. SJ 8207
White Ladies Aston H & W vil 5m/8km E of Worcester. SO 9252
Whitelake 8 C1* r rising to S of Shepton Mallet in Somerset and cut through Sedgemoor for drainage purposes; then flows W into R Brue just E of Westhay. ST 4442
Whitelands Tyne & Wear 61 G5* loc 1m SW of Birtley. NZ 2854
Whitelane End S Yorks 43 H3* loc in Sheffield 4m/6km SE of city centre. SK 3982
Whiteleaf Bucks 18 C1* vil 1m NE of Princes Risborough. SP 8104
Whiteleas Tyne & Wear 61 H5* loc in S Tyneside dist 2m/4km S of S Shields. NZ 3663
White Lee W Yorks 49 E5* loc 2km NW of Batley. SE 2225
White-le-Head Durham 61 F6* loc at S end of Tantobie, 2m/3km NW of Stanley. NZ 1754
Whiteleigh, Higher Cornwall 6 B5* loc 8m/13km NW of Launceston. SX 2494
Whiteley Bank Isle of Wight 10 C6 ham 2m/3km W of Shanklin. SZ 5581
Whiteley Green Ches 43 E3* ham 1m NW of Bollington. SJ 9278
Whiteley Village Surrey 19 E5 small residential estate with octagonal layout 2m/3km SE of Weybridge. TQ 0962
Whitelinks Bay Grampian 83 H1 bay on NE coast 1km SE of Inverallochy. NK 0564
White Loch D & G. See Lochinch Castle.
White Loch D & G 58 D5/D6 small loch 5m/8km SE of Dalbeattie. NX 8654
White Loch of Myrton D & G 57 D7 small loch 2km E of Port William. NX 3543
White Lodge Bucks 19 E3* loc 2m/4km SW of Uxbridge. TQ 0282
White Lund Lancs 47 E2* loc 2km S of Morecambe. SD 4462
Whitelye Gwent 16 A2* loc 5m/8km N of Chepstow. SO 5101
White Lyne 60 B4 r rising on fells N of Bewcastle, Cumbria, and flowing SW to join R Black Lyne and form R Lyne 5m/7km W of Bewcastle. NY 4973
Whitemans Green W Sussex 11 H3 loc adjoining Cuckfield to N. TQ 3025
White Mere Salop 34 B1/B2 lake, one of several in dist, 2m/3km SE of Ellesmere. SJ 4133
White Mill (Felin-wen) Dyfed 23 F3* ham 3m/5km E of Carmarthen. SN 4621
Whitemill Point Orkney 89 C5* headland on N coast of Sanday, on W side of entrance to Otters Wick. HY 7046
Whitemire Grampian 81 H2 loc 5m/8km SW of Forres. NH 9754
Whitemoor Cornwall 3 E3* vil in china clay dist 4m/7km NW of St Austell. SW 9757
White Moor Derbys 43 H6 loc 1m E of Belper. SK 3647
Whitemoor Notts 36 B1* dist of Nottingham 2m/3km NW of city centre. SK 5441
White Moor Reservoir Lancs 48 B4* small resr 2m/3km N of Colne. SD 8743
White Nab N Yorks 55 H6* headland at S end of S Bay, Scarborough. TA 0586
White Ness Shetland 89 E7* long narrow peninsula on Mainland on W side of Whiteness Voe some 3m/4km NW of Scalloway. HU 3843
Whiteness Shetland 89 E7 loc on Mainland at head of **Whiteness Voe**, 4m/7km N of Scalloway. HU 3946
Whiteness Head H'land 81 G2 spit of land on Moray Firth 3m/5km E of Fort George, Inverness dist. NH 8058
Whiten Head H'land 84 E1 headland on N coast of Sutherland dist, on E side of entrance to Loch Eriboll. NC 5068
White Notley Essex 30 C6 vil 3m/5km NW of Witham. TL 7818
White Oak Kent 20 B4* loc 1km N of Swanley. TQ 5169
Whiteoak Green Oxon 27 G6* loc 3m/5km N of Witney. SP 3414
White Ox Mead Avon 16 C5* loc 2km W of Wellow. ST 7258
Whiteparish Wilts 10 A3 vil 7m/11km W of Romsey. SU 2423
White Pit Lincs 45 G3/G4 ham 7m/12km SE of Louth. TF 3777
Whiterashes Grampian 83 G4 vil 4m/6km SE of Oldmeldrum. NJ 8523
White Rocks H & W 25 H5* loc 3m/5km SE of Pontrilas. SO 4324
White Roding Essex 20 C1 vil 2m/3km W of Leaden Roding. TL 5613
Whiterow H'land 86 F3* loc in Caithness dist 2km S of Wick. ND 3548
Whitesand Bay Cornwall 2 A5 wide bay to NE of Land's End. SW 3527
Whitesand Bay Dyfed 22 A3 bay (also known as Porth-mawr) extending from St David's Hd southwards to Pt St John. SM 7227
White Scar Cave N Yorks 48 A1* limestone cavern on W side of Ingleborough 2m/3km NE of Ingleton. SD 7174
Whiteshell Point W Glam 23 G6* headland on S coast of Gower peninsula 2m/4km W of Mumbles Hd. SS 5986
Whiteshill Avon 16 B4* loc 6m/9km NE of Bristol. ST 6479
Whiteshill Glos 16 D1 vil 2km N of Stroud. SO 8407
White Sitch Staffs 35 E3* wd surrounding lake 1m W of Blymhill. SJ 7912
Whitesmith E Sussex 12 B5 ham 5m/8km NW of Hailsham. TQ 5213
Whitespout Lane 56 E4* r in Strathclyde region, running E from Loch Riecawr to join Eglin Lane and form Carrick Lane, qv. NX 4693
White Stake Lancs 47 F5* loc 3m/5km SW of Preston. SD 5125
Whitestaunton Som 8 B3 vil 3m/5km NW of Chard. ST 2810
Whitestone Devon 7 F5 vil 3m/5km W of Exeter. SX 8693
White Stone H & W 26 B3* ham 4m/6km NE of Hereford. SO 5642
White Stone Warwicks 36 A5* loc in SE part of Nuneaton. SP 3889
Whitestone Cross Devon 7 G5* ham 2m/3km W of Exeter. SX 8993
Whitestreet Green Suffolk 30 D4* ham 3m/5km N of Nayland. TL 9739
Whitewall Corner N Yorks 50 C2* loc adjoining Norton to S. SE 7970
White Walls Lancs 48 B4* loc 2km SW of Colne. SD 8739

White Waltham Berks 18 D4 vil 3m/5km SW of Maidenhead. SU 8577
Whitewater 18 C5 r rising at Spring Hd between Greywell and Upton Grey E of Basingstoke, Hants, and flowing N into Blackwater R on Berkshire and Hampshire border 2km SE of Swallowfield. SU 7463
White Water 76 D3 r in Tayside region running SE into R South Esk 3m/5km NW of Clova. NO 2875
Whitewater Dash Cumbria 52 C2* waterfall in Dash Beck 3m/4km E of Bassenthwaite. NY 2731
White Water Reservoir 37 E4* small resr on Cambs–Northants border 3m/4km S of Stamford. TF 0303
Whiteway Glos 26 D6* vil 6m/9km NE of Stroud. SO 9110
Whitewayhead Salop 34 C6* loc at S end of vil of Knowbury, 4m/7km E of Ludlow. SO 5774
Whitewell Clwyd 34 B1* loc 3m/5km W of Whitchurch. SJ 4941
Whitewell Lancs 47 G3 ham 6m/10km NW of Clitheroe. SD 6546
Whitewell Bottom Lancs 48 B5* loc 2m/3km E of Rawtenstall. SD 8323
Whitfield Avon 16 B2 ham 3m/4km E of Thornbury. ST 6791
Whitfield Kent 13 H3 N suburb of Dover. TR 3045
Whitfield Northants 28 B4 vil 2m/3km NE of Brackley. SP 6039
Whitfield Nthmb 60 D5 ham 6m/9km SW of Haydon Br. NY 7758
Whitfield Staffs 42 D5* loc 2m/4km NE of Burslem. SJ 8952
Whitfield Gill Force N Yorks 53 H5* waterfall 2km NW of Askrigg. SD 9392
Whitfield Lough Nthmb 60 C6* small lake on moors 3m/5km E of Knarsdale. NY 7254
Whitford (Chwitffordd) Clwyd 41 G4 vil 3m/5km NW of Holywell. Mynydd-y-garreg, hill to W, surmounted by a tower, possibly a Roman pharos. Maen Achwyfaen (A.M.), 2km W of vil, 10c–11c cross, tallest monmt of its type in Britain. SJ 1478
Whitford Devon 8 B4 vil running down to R Axe, 3m/5km SW of Axminster. SY 2695
Whitford Point W Glam 23 F5 headland (NT) at end of Whitford Burrows on S bank of Burry Inlet opp Burry Port. SS 4496
Whitgift Humberside 50 C5 vil on S bank of R Ouse 4m/7km E of Goole. SE 8122
Whitgreave Staffs 35 E2 vil 4m/6km N of Stafford. SJ 8928
Whithorn D & G 57 E8 small tn 9m/15km S of Wigtown. 13c remains of priory ch (A.M.), with museum. **Isle of Whithorn,** 3m/5km SE, is small port on rocky coast; St Ninian's Chapel (A.M.) dates from about 1300. St Ninian's Cave (A.M.), on coast 3m/5km SW of Whithorn, is said to have been used as oratory by St Ninian in 5c. NX 4440
Whiting Bay S'clyde 63 G5 vil and bay on E coast of Arran 3m/5km S of Lamlash. NS 0426
Whitington Norfolk 38 C4 vil on R Wissey 1m SE of Stoke Ferry. TL 7199
Whitkirk W Yorks 49 F5 dist of Leeds 4m/7km E of city centre. SE 3633
Whitland (Hendy-gwyn) Dyfed 22 D4 vil 6m/9km E of Narberth. Whitland Abbey, 2km NE, scanty ruins of 12c Cistercian hse. SN 1916
Whitletts S'clyde 64 B6 E dist of Ayr. NS 3622
Whitley Berks 18 C4* S dist of Reading. SU 7170
Whitley Gtr Manchester 42 B1* N dist of Wigan. SD 5807
Whitley N Yorks 49 G6 vil 4m/7km SE of Knottingley. SE 5621
Whitley Som 7 G2* ham 5m/8km W of Wiveliscombe. ST 0029
Whitley S Yorks 43 H2* ham 1m NE of Grenoside. SK 3494
Whitley Wilts 16 D4* vil 2m/3km NW of Melksham. ST 8866
Whitley Bay Tyne & Wear 61 H4 North Sea coast resort 2m/3km N of Tynemouth. Extensive sands to N. NZ 3572
Whitley Bridge N Yorks 49 G5* loc on Aire and Calder Canal adjoining Low Eggborough to SW. SE 5522
Whitley Castle Nthmb 53 F1 earthworks of Roman fort 2m/3km NW of Alston. NY 6948
Whitley Chapel Nthmb 61 E5* ham 4m/7km S of Hexham. NY 9257
Whitley Heath Staffs 35 E2* loc 2m/3km SW of Eccleshall. SJ 8126
Whitley, Higher Ches 42 B3 vil 5m/8km NW of Northwich. **Lr Whitley** vil 1km SW. SJ 6180
Whitley Lower W Yorks 49 E6 vil 3m/5km SW of Dewsbury. SE 2217
Whitley Reed Ches 42 C3* loc 2km S of Appleton. SJ 6481
Whitley Row Kent 20 B6* loc 2m/4km SW of Sevenoaks. TQ 5052
Whitlocks End W Midlands 35 G6* loc 4m/6km SW of Solihull. SP 1076
Whitminster Glos 16 C1 vil 5m/8km W of Stroud. SO 7708
Whitmore Staffs 35 E1 vil 4m/6km SW of Newcastle-under-Lyme. SJ 8140
Whitmore Bay S Glam 15 F4* bay on S side of Barry I. ST 1166
Whitmore Park W Midlands 36 A6* N dist of Coventry. SP 3382
Whitnage Devon 7 G3* ham 1m N of Sampford Peverell. ST 0215
Whitnash Warwicks 27 G2 S suburb of Leamington. SP 3263
Whitnell Som 8 A1* loc 2m/3km E of Nether Stowey. ST 2139
Whitney H & W 25 G3 vil on R Wye 4m/7km NE of Hay-on-Wye. SO 2647
Whitrigg Cumbria 52 C1* loc 1m S of Torpenhow. NY 2038
Whitrigg Cumbria 59 G5 loc 1m N of Kirkbride. NY 2257
Whitsand Bay Cornwall 3 H3 bay running NW from Rame Hd on S coast to The Long Stone, between Downderry and Portwrinkle. SX 3851
Whitsbury Hants 9 H3 vil 3m/5km NW of Fordingbridge. SU 1219
Whitsome Borders 67 E3/F3 vil 4m/6km S of Chirnside. NT 8650
Whitson Gwent 15 H3 vil near coast 5m/8km SE of Newport. ST 3783
Whitstable Kent 13 F1 N coast resort at E end of bay of same name, 6m/10km NW of Canterbury. Noted for oysters. TR 1166
Whitstone Cornwall 6 B5 vil 6m/10km SE of Bude. SX 2698
Whittingham Lancs 47 F4 loc 2m/4km W of Longridge. SD 5636
Whittingham Nthmb 61 F1 vil 6m/10km N of Rothbury. NU 0611
Whittingslow Salop 34 B5* ham 3m/5km S of Church Stretton. SO 4389
Whittington Derbys 43 H4 loc in Chesterfield 2m/4km N of tn centre. **New W.** loc adjoining to E. **Whittington Moor** loc 1m S. SK 3875
Whittington Glos 27 E5 vil 4m/7km E of Cheltenham. Site of Roman villa to E. SP 0120
Whittington H & W 26 D2 vil 2m/3km SE of Worcester. SO 8752
Whittington Lancs 47 F1 vil 2m/3km S of Kirkby Lonsdale. SD 6076
Whittington Salop 34 A2 vil 3m/4km NE of Oswestry. SJ 3231
Whittington Staffs 35 E6 ham 3m/5km W of Stourbridge. SO 8582
Whittington Staffs 35 G3 vil 3m/5km E of Lichfield. SK 1608
Whittington, Great Nthmb 61 E4 vil 4m/7km N of Corbridge. NZ 0070
Whittington, Little Nthmb 61 E4 loc 3m/5km N of Corbridge. NY 9969
Whittlebury Northants 28 C3 vil 3m/5km S of Towcester. SP 6944
Whittleford Warwicks 35 H5* loc in W part of Nuneaton. SP 3391
Whittle Hill Gtr Manchester 42 D1* loc 2km NW of Middleton. SD 8407
Whittle-le-Woods Lancs 47 F5 vil 2m/4km E of Leyland. SD 5821
Whittlesey Cambs 37 G4 tn 5m/8km E of Peterborough. Industries: bricks, agriculture. TL 2797
Whittlesford Cambs 29 H3 vil 7m/11km S of Cambridge. TL 4748
Whittlestone Head Lancs 47 G6 moorland loc 2m/4km NW of Edgworth. SD 7219
Whittlewood Forest 28 C3 partly wooded area on borders of Northants and Bucks some 4m/7km W of Stony Stratford. SP 7242
Whittliemuir Dam S'clyde 64 B3 resr 2km SE of Howwood. NS 4158
Whitton Cleveland 54 C3 ham 5m/7km NW of Stockton-on-Tees. NZ 3822
Whitton Humberside 50 D5 vil on S bank of R Humber 8m/13km N of Scunthorpe. **Whitton Ness** headland 1m E. SE 9024
Whitton London 19 F4 loc in borough of Richmond 1m W of Twickenham. TQ 1473
Whitton Nthmb 61 F2 ham just S of Rothbury. 14c tower hse incorporated in later bldg. NU 0501
Whitton Powys 25 G2 vil 3m/5km S of Knighton. SO 2767
Whitton Salop 26 B1 ham 3m/5km NW of Tenbury Wells. SO 5772
Whitton Suffolk 31 F3 loc in NW part of Ipswich. Also par to N. TM 1347
Whittonditch Wilts 17 G4 loc 4m/6km NW of Hungerford. SU 2872
Whittonstall Nthmb 61 F5 vil 2m/4km NW of Ebchester. NZ 0757
Whitway Hants 17 H5 ham on E side of Highclere Park 4m/7km W of Kingsclere. SU 4559
Whitwell Derbys 44 A3 vil 4m/6km SW of Worksop. Hall dates from 17c. SK 5276
Whitwell Herts 29 F5 vil 4m/7km NW of Welwyn. TL 1821
Whitwell Isle of Wight 10 C6 vil 3m/4km W of Ventnor. SZ 5277
Whitwell Leics 37 E3 vil 4m/7km E of Oakham. SK 9208
Whitwell N Yorks 54 C5 loc 6m/10km NW of Northallerton. SE 2899
Whitwell House Durham 54 C1* loc 3m/4km SE of Durham. NZ 3040
Whitwell-on-the-Hill N Yorks 50 C2 vil 5m/9km SW of Malton. SE 7265
Whitwick Leics 36 A3 loc 2km NE of Coalville. SK 4316
Whitwood W Yorks 49 F5 loc 2km SW of Castleford. SE 4024
Whitworth Lancs 47 H6 tn 4m/6km N of Rochdale. Textiles and textile machinery, light engineering. Quarries to N and W. SD 8818
Whixall Salop 34 C1 vil 4m/6km N of Wem. SJ 5134
Whixley N Yorks 50 A2 vil 6m/10km SE of Boroughbridge. SE 4458
Whoberly W Midlands 35 H6* W dist of Coventry. SP 3078
Whorlton Durham 54 A3 vil on N bank of R Tees 4m/6km E of Barnard Castle. NZ 1014
Whorlton N Yorks 54 D4 vil 5m/8km SW of Stokesley. Remains of motte and bailey cas. NZ 4802
Whyke W Sussex 11 E4* S dist of Chichester. SU 8604
Whyle H & W 26 B2* ham 4m/7km E of Leominster. SO 5560
Whyteleafe Surrey 19 G5 suburban loc 3m/4km SE of Purley. TQ 3358
Wiay Skye, H'land 79 B5 uninhabited island of about 500 acres or 200 hectares at entrance to Loch Bracadale, SW coast. Lies 2m/3km E of Idrigill Pt. NG 2936
Wiay W Isles 88 E2 uninhabited island of about 2 sq miles or 5 sq km off SE coast of Benbecula on N side of entrance to Bagh nam Faoileann. NF 8746
Wibsey W Yorks 48 D5 dist of Bradford 2m/3km SW of city centre. SE 1430
Wibtoft Warwicks 36 B5 ham 5m/7km NW of Lutterworth. SP 4787
Wichenford H & W 26 C2* vil 5m/8km NW of Worcester. SO 7860
Wichling Kent 21 E6 vil 5m/8km S of Sittingbourne. TQ 9656
Wick Avon 16 C4 vil 7m/12km E of Bristol. Quarries and works. Site of Roman villa to S. ST 7072
Wick Devon 8 A4* loc 2m/3km NE of Honiton. Iron Age fort on Dumpdon Hill (qv) to E. ST 1704
Wick Dorset 9 H5 E dist of Bournemouth. SZ 1591
Wick H'land 86 F3 fishing port on **Wick Bay,** E coast of Caithness dist, at mouth of **R Wick,** which flows SE from Loch Watten. Industries, apart from fishing, include mnfre of dairy produce, glass, leather goods and engineering tools. Distillery to S near Old Man of Wick, qv. Airport 1m N. ND 3650
Wick H & W 26 D3 vil 2km E of Pershore. SO 9645
Wick (Wig, Y) Mid Glam 15 E4 vil 5m/8km S of Bridgend. SS 9272
Wick Som 15 G6* loc 2m/3km W of Stockland Bristol. ST 2144
Wick Som 8 C1* loc on E side of Glastonbury. ST 5239
Wick Wilts 9 H2* loc 1m W of Downton. SU 1621
Wick W Sussex 11 F4 N dist of Littlehampton. TQ 0203
Wicken Cambs 30 B1 vil 2m/4km SW of Soham. To W is **Wicken Fen** (NT), nature reserve. Loc of **Wicken Lode** at E end of Wicken Fen. TL 5670
Wicken Northants 28 C4 vil 5m/8km NE of Buckingham. SP 7439
Wicken Bonhunt Essex 29 H4 vil 4m/7km SW of Saffron Walden. TL 4933
Wickenby Lincs 45 E3 vil 5m/8km S of Mkt Rasen. TF 0781
Wick Episcopi H & W 26 C2* loc 2m/3km SW of Worcester. SO 8253
Wickersley S Yorks 44 A2 suburb 3m/5km E of Rotherham. SK 4791
Wicker Street Green Suffolk 30 D4* ham 3m/5km W of Hadleigh. TL 9741
Wicketwood Hill Notts 36 C1* loc 4m/7km NE of Nottingham. SK 6244
Wickford Essex 20 D3 tn 3m/5km NE of Basildon. TQ 7493
Wickham Berks 17 G4 vil 6m/9km NW of Newbury. SU 3971
Wickham Hants 10 C4 vil 3m/5km N of Fareham. SU 5711
Wickham Bishops Essex 21 E1 vil 2m/4km SE of Witham. TL 8412
Wickhambreux Kent 13 G1/G2 vil 5m/7km E of Canterbury. Alternative spelling is Wickhambreaux. TR 2258
Wickhambrook Suffolk 30 C3 vil 6m/10km N of Clare. TL 7554
Wickham, East London 20 B4 loc in borough of Bexley 6m/9km E of Greenwich and 11m/18km E of Charing Cross. TQ 4777
Wickhamford H & W 27 E3 vil 2m/4km SE of Evesham. SP 0641
Wickham Green Berks 17 G4* loc at Wickham, 6m/9km NW of Newbury. SU 3971
Wickham Green Suffolk 31 E2* vil 4m/7km SW of Eye. See also Wickham Skeith and Wickham Street. TM 0969
Wickham Heath Berks 17 H4 loc 4m/6km NW of Newbury. SU 4169
Wickham Market Suffolk 31 G3 small tn 5m/8km NE of Woodbridge. TM 3055
Wickhampton Norfolk 39 G4/H4 vil 2m/4km N of Reedham. TG 4205
Wickham St Paul Essex 30 C4 vil 4m/7km SW of Sudbury. TL 8336
Wickham Skeith Suffolk 31 E2 vil 4m/7km SW of Eye. See also Wickham Green and Wickham Street. TM 0969
Wickham Street Suffolk 30 C3* ham 6m/9km N of Clare. TL 7554
Wickham Street Suffolk 31 E1/E2* vil 4m/7km SW of Eye. See also Wickham Green and Wickham Skeith. TM 0969
Wickham, West Cambs 30 B3 vil 4m/7km NW of Haverhill. TL 6149
Wickham, West London 20 A5 dist in borough of Bromley 3m/4km S of Bromley tn centre. TQ 3965
Wicklewood Norfolk 39 E4 vil 2m/4km W of Wymondham. TG 0702
Wick, Lower Glos 16 C2* loc 3m/4km SE of Berkeley. Loc of **Upr Wick** 1km E, on other (E) side of M5 motorway. ST 7196
Wick, Lower H & W 26 D2* loc in SW part of Worcester. SO 8352
Wickmere Norfolk 38 F2 vil 4m/7km N of Aylsham. TG 1733
Wick, North Avon 16 B5 loc 2m/3km N of Chew Magna. ST 5865
Wick of Breckin Shetland 89 E5* bay on N coast of Yell. HP 5205
Wick of Gruting Shetland 89 F6* large bay on N coast of Fetlar 2m/3km NE of Houbie. **Ness of Gruting** promontory at centre of bay. HU 6592
Wick of Shunni Shetland 89 E8* bay on W coast of Mainland on N side of Fitful Hd. HU 3515
Wick of Skaw Shetland 89 F5* bay on NE coast of Unst 2km NE of Norwick. HP 6514
Wick Rissington Glos 27 F5 vil 3m/4km S of Stow-on-the-Wold. SP 1921
Wick St Lawrence Avon 15 H4 vil 4m/6km NE of Weston-super-Mare. ST 3665
Wicks's Green Suffolk 31 E2* loc adjoining Forward Green to W. TM 0959
Wickstreet E Sussex 12 B5* loc 3m/5km W of Hailsham. TQ 5408
Wick, Upper H & W 26 C2* loc 2m/3km SW of Worcester. SO 8253
Wickwar Avon 16 C3 vil 4m/7km N of Chipping Sodbury. ST 7288
Wid 20 D2 r rising at Blackmore, E of Chipping Ongar, Essex, and flowing SE towards Billericay then NE into R Can on W side of Chelmsford. TL 6807
Widcombe Avon 16 C5* SE dist of Bath. ST 7563

Widcombe, North Avon 16 B5* loc at SE corner of Chew Valley Lake and 2km NE of W Harptree. ST 5758
Widcombe, South Avon 16 B5* ham 1m W of Hinton Blewett. ST 5856
Widdale N Yorks 53 G5/G6 valley of **Widdale Beck,** running NE to R Ure at Appersett. To W on Widdale Fell are two small lakes, **Widdale Gt Tarn** and **Widdale Lit Tarn.** SD 88
Widdington Essex 30 A4 vil 4m/7km S of Saffron Walden. Wildlife reserve 1km E. TL 5331
Widdington N Yorks 50 A2* loc 2km NW of Nun Monkton. SE 4959
Widdop W Yorks 48 C5 loc below Widdop Moor 6m/9km NW of Hebden Br. **Widdop Resr** to S. SD 9332
Widdrington Nthmb 61 G2 vil 7m/11km NE of Morpeth. **Widdrington Stn** loc 2km SW. NZ 2595
Widecombe in the Moor Devon 4 D3 vil on Dartmoor 5m/8km NW of Ashburton. Annual fair featured in popular song. SX 7176
Wide Firth Orkney 89 B6 sea channel between islands of Mainland and Shapinsay. HY 41
Wideford Hill Orkney 89 B6* hill 3m/4km W of Kirkwall, Mainland. Prehistoric chambered cairn (A.M.) on NW side of hill. HY 4111
Widegates Cornwall 3 G3 vil 3m/5km NE of Looe. SX 2857
Widemouth Bay Cornwall 3 B5* vil near coast 3m/4km S of Bude, facing W with sandy beach. SS 2002
Wide Open Tyne & Wear 61 G4 loc in coal-mining area 5m/8km N of Newcastle. NZ 2472
Widewall Orkney 89 B7* loc on S Ronaldsay 2m/3km S of St Margaret's Hope. To NW is large bay of same name on W coast of island. ND 4490
Widford Essex 20 D2 SW dist of Chelmsford. TL 6905
Widford Herts 29 H6 vil 4m/6km E of Ware. TL 4215
Widford Oxon 27 G6* loc 2km E of Burford across R Windrush. SP 2712
Widgham Green Cambs 30 B2/B3* loc 5m/8km S of Newmarket. TL 6655
Widley Hants 10 D4* suburban loc 5m/8km N of Portsmouth. SU 6606
Widmer End Bucks 18 D2* vil 2m/4km NE of High Wycombe. SU 8896
Widmerpool Notts 36 C2 vil 10m/15km NW of Melton Mowbray. SK 6328
Widmore London 20 B4 loc to E of Bromley tn centre. TQ 4169
Widnes Ches 42 B3 industrial tn on N side of R Mersey, here spanned by rly and rd brs, 6m/10km W of Warrington. Industries include chemical works, engineering, pharmaceutical products. SJ 5185
Widworthy Devon 8 A4 vil 3m/5km E of Honiton. SY 2199
Wield, Lower Hants 10 D1 ham 2m/3km SE of Preston Candover. SU 6340
Wield, Upper Hants 10 C1 vil 5m/8km NE of New Alresford. Also known as Wield. SU 6238
Wigan Gtr Manchester 42 B1 industrial tn 17m/27km NW of Manchester. Coal-mining, engineering, textiles, food-canning, etc. SD 5805
Wiganthorpe N Yorks 50 B1 loc 2m/3km S of Hovingham. SE 6672
Wigborough Som 8 C3* ham 2km SE of S Petherton. ST 4415
Wigborough, Great Essex 30 D6 vil 7m/11km S of Colchester. **Lit Wigborough** loc 1km E. TL 9614
Wigdwr Brook 33 G5* stream running SE from Llyn Ebyr, Powys, into R Severn 3m/5km E of Llanidloes. SO 0085
Wiggaton Devon 7 H5 vil 2km S of Ottery St Mary. SY 1093
Wiggenhall St Germans Norfolk 38 B3 vil 4m/6km S of King's Lynn. TF 5914
Wiggenhall St Mary Magdalen Norfolk 38 B3 vil 5m/8km N of Downham Mkt across R Ouse. TF 5911
Wiggenhall St Mary the Virgin Norfolk 38 A3 vil 4m/7km SW of King's Lynn across R Ouse. TF 5813
Wiggenhall St Peter Norfolk 38 B3 loc with ruined ch on E bank of R Ouse, 1km SE of Wiggenhall St Germans. TF 6013
Wiggens Green Essex 30 B4* ham 2m/3km S of Haverhill. TL 6642
Wigginton Herts 18 D1 vil 2km SE of Tring. Loc of **Wigginton Bottom** adjoins to S. SU 9310
Wigginton N Yorks 50 B2 vil 4m/7km N of York. SE 5958
Wigginton Oxon 27 G4 vil 6m/10km SW of Banbury. Site of Roman villa to E. SP 3833
Wigginton Salop 34 A1* loc 4m/7km W of Ellesmere. Loc of **Upr Wigginton** to N. SJ 3335
Wigginton Staffs 35 G4 vil 2m/3km N of Tamworth. SK 2006
Wigglesworth N Yorks 48 B3 vil 2m/3km SW of Long Preston. SD 8156
Wiggonby Cumbria 59 G6 ham 7m/11km W of Carlisle. NY 2953
Wiggonholt W Sussex 11 F3 loc 2km SE of Pulborough. Site of Roman bath hse 1km N. TQ 0616
Wighill N Yorks 49 F3 vil 2m/4km N of Tadcaster. SE 4746
Wight, Isle of 119 county and chalk island off S coast of English mainland, separated from Hampshire by the Solent. Area 147 sq miles or 381 sq km. Ferry and hovercraft connections at Cowes, Ryde, and Yarmouth (ferry to Lymington). Tourism flourishes owing to mild climate and the natural beauty of the island. Cowes is internationally famous for yachting. Chief tns are Newport, the capital, and Cowes, Ryde, Sandown, Shanklin, Ventnor, and Yarmouth. Chief r is the Medina.
Wighton Norfolk 38 D1 vil 3m/5km SE of Wells. See also Copy's Green. TF 9339
Wight, South 119 admin dist of Isle of Wight.
Wightwick Manor W Midlands 35 E4* late 19c hse (NT), notable example of influence of William Morris, 3m/5km W of Wolverhampton tn centre. SO 8698
Wigley Hants 10 A3 ham 3m/5km NE of Cadnam. SU 3217
Wigmore H & W 26 A1 vil 8m/13km NW of Leominster. SO 4169
Wigmore Kent 20 D5* urban loc 3m/4km SE of Gillingham tn centre. TQ 8064
Wigsley Notts 44 C4 vil 7m/12km W of Lincoln. SK 8670
Wigsthorpe Northants 37 E6* ham 4m/6km S of Oundle. TL 0482
Wigston Leics 36 B4 tn adjoining Leicester to S. SP 6099
Wigston Fields Leics 36 B4* loc 3m/4km S of Leicester city centre. SK 5900
Wigston Parva Leics 36 A5 ham 4m/6km SE of Hinckley. SP 4689
Wigston, South Leics 36 B4 suburb 4m/6km S of Leicester. SP 5898
Wig, The D & G 57 A6 SW-facing bay on W side of Loch Ryan, 4m/7km N of Stranraer. NX 0367
Wigthorpe Notts 44 B3 ham 1km S of Carlton in Lindrick. SK 5983
Wigtoft Lincs 37 G1 vil 6m/10km SW of Boston. TF 2636
Wigton Cumbria 59 G6 mkt tn 11m/17km SW of Carlisle. Clothing mnfre. NY 2548
Wigtown D & G 57 E7 small tn on hill above R Cree estuary at head of **Wigtown Bay** and on N side of R Bladnoch. Bay extends from Burrow Hd eastwards to island of Little Ross. NX 4355
Wigtwizzle S Yorks 43 G2* loc 1km W of Broomhead Resr and 2m/4km NW of Bradfield. SK 2495
Wig, Y Welsh form of Wick, qv.
Wike W Yorks 49 E4* vil 6m/10km NE of Leeds. SE 3342
Wike Well End S Yorks 49 H6* loc on Stainforth and Keadby Canal at S end of Thorne. SE 6912
Wilbarston Northants 36 D5 vil 5m/9km W of Corby. SP 8188
Wilberfoss Humberside 50 C3 vil 3m/5km SE of Stamford Br. SE 7350
Wilbraham, Great Cambs 30 A2 vil 6m/10km E of Cambridge. Vil of Lit Wilbraham to N. TL 5457
Wilburton Cambs 38 A6 vil 5m/8km SW of Ely. TL 4874
Wilby Norfolk 39 E5 ham 4m/6km SW of Attleborough. **Wilby Hall** probably early 17c. TM 0389
Wilby Northants 28 D1 vil 2m/3km SW of Wellingborough. SP 8666
Wilby Suffolk 31 F1 vil 2km SE of Stradbroke. Loc of **Wilby Green** 2km SE. TM 2472
Wilcot Wilts 17 F5 vil 2m/3km NW of Pewsey. Ham of **Wilcot Green** adjoins vil to N. SU 1460
Wilcott Salop 34 B3 vil 8m/13km NW of Shrewsbury. **Wilcott Marsh** loc 1km SE. SJ 3718
Wilcove, Upper Cornwall 4 B5* loc on R Tamar estuary 2km N of Torpoint. SX 4356
Wilcrick Gwent 16 A3 loc 2km NW of Magor. Ancient fort on Wilcrick Hill. ST 4088
Wilday Green Derbys 43 G4* loc 4m/7km NW of Chesterfield. SK 3274
Wildboarclough Ches 43 E4 vil in Peak Dist National Park 5m/8km SE of Macclesfield. SJ 9868
Wilden Beds 29 E2 vil 5m/7km NE of Bedford. TL 0955
Wilden H & W 26 D1 vil 1m NE of Stourport. SO 8272
Wilderhope Salop 34 C5 manor hse of late 16c (NT) on SE slope of Wenlock Edge 7m/11km SW of Much Wenlock. SO 5492
Wildern Hants 10 B3* loc 2m/3km W of Botley. SU 4913
Wildernesse Kent 20 B5* NE dist of Sevenoaks. TQ 5356
Wilderspool Ches 42 B3* loc in Warrington 2km SE of tn centre. SJ 6186
Wilde Street Suffolk 38 B6* loc 3m/4km N of Mildenhall. TL 7078
Wildhern Hants 17 G6 loc 4m/6km N of Andover. SU 3550
Wildhill Herts 19 F1* loc 2m/4km SE of Hatfield. TL 2606
Wildmanbridge S'clyde 65 E3* loc 2m/3km NW of Carluke. NS 8353
Wildmoor Hants 18 B5* loc 4m/6km NE of Basingstoke. SU 6856
Wildmoor H & W 35 F6* vil 3m/5km N of Bromsgrove. SO 9675
Wildridings Berks 18 D4* SW dist of Bracknell. SU 8668
Wildsworth Lincs 44 C2 vil on E bank of R Trent 5m/9km N of Gainsborough. SK 8097
Wilford Notts 36 B1 loc 1m W of W Bridgford. SK 5637
Wilkesley Ches 34 C1 ham 3m/4km SW of Audlem. SJ 6241
Wilkhaven H'land 87 C7 loc in Ross and Cromarty dist 1km SW of Tarbat Ness on E coast. NH 9486
Wilkieston Lothian 65 G2 vil 2m/3km SW of Ratho. NT 1268
Wilkins Green Herts 19 F1 loc 2m/4km W of Hatfield. TL 1907
Wilksby Lincs 45 F5 loc 4m/7km SE of Horncastle. TF 2862
Willacy Lane End Lancs 47 E4* loc 1km SW of Catforth. SD 4735
Willand Devon 7 H4 vil 3m/4km NE of Cullompton. 1km N, ham of **Willand Moor,** 1km NW, former Tiverton Junction. ST 0310
Willand Som 8 A3* ham 5m/9km SE of Wellington. ST 1913
Willaston Ches 41 H3/H4 vil 3m/4km E of Neston. SJ 3377
Willaston Ches 42 C5 vil 2m/3km E of Nantwich. SJ 6852
Willaston Isle of Man 46 B5* N dist of Douglas. SC 3878
Willaston Salop 34 C1* loc 5m/8km SE of Whitchurch. SJ 5935
Willen Bucks 28 D3/D4 vil 2m/3km NE of centre of Milton Keynes. SP 8741
Willenhall W Midlands 35 F4 W dist of Walsall. SO 9698
Willenhall W Midlands 36 A6 SE dist of Coventry. SP 3676
Willerby Humberside 51 E5 suburb 5m/8km W of Hull. TA 0230
Willerby N Yorks 51 E1 vil 7m/11km W of Filey. TA 0079
Willersey Glos 27 E4 vil 2m/3km NE of Broadway. SP 1039
Willersley H & W 25 G3 vil 6m/9km S of Kington. SO 3147
Willesborough Kent 13 F3 SE suburb of Ashford, together with **S Willesborough, Willesborough Lees** and **Willesborough Street.** TR 0341
Willesden London 19 F3 dist in borough of Brent 6m/9km NW of Charing Cross. Loc of **Willesden Green** to E. TQ 2284
Willesleigh Devon 6 D2* loc 3m/5km E of Barnstaple. SS 6033
Willesley Leics 36 A3* loc 2m/3km SW of Ashby de la Zouch. SK 3414
Willesley Wilts 16 D3* loc 2m/3km N of Sherston. ST 8588
Willett Som 7 H2 ham 4m/6km NE of Wiveliscombe. ST 1033
Willey Salop 34 D4* ham 3m/5km E of Much Wenlock. SO 6799
Willey Warwicks 36 B5 vil 3m/5km W of Lutterworth. SP 4984
Willey Green Surrey 18 D6* vil 4m/6km NW of Guildford. SU 9351
Willhays, High Devon 6 D6 summit of Dartmoor 4m/6km S of Okehampton; height 2038 ft or 621 metres. SX 5889
William Girling Reservoir, The 20 A2* resr in R Lea valley between Enfield and Chingford, London. TQ 3694
Williamsburgh S'clyde 64 C3* E dist of Paisley. NS 4964
Williamscot Oxon 28 A3 ham 4m/6km NE of Banbury. SP 4845
William's Green Suffolk 30 D4* ham 2m/4km W of Hadleigh. TL 9842
Williamston Lothian 65 G2* industrial estate 2m/3km SE of Livingston tn centre. NT 0866
Williamston, East Dyfed 22 D5 vil 4m/6km NW of Tenby. SN 0904
Williamston, West Dyfed 22 C5 ham between estuaries of Rs Carew and Cresswell 2m/3km NW of Carew. SN 0305
Williamstown (Trewiliam) Mid Glam 15 E3* loc 2m/3km N of Tonyrefail. ST 0090
Williamthorpe Derbys 43 H4 loc 3m/4km NE of Clay Cross. SK 4265
Willian Herts 29 F4* vil midway between Baldock and Hitchin. TL 2230
Willingale Essex 20 C1 vil 4m/6km NE of Chipping Ongar. TL 5907
Willingdon E Sussex 12 C6 N suburb of Eastbourne. Site of Neolithic camp 1m W on downs. TQ 5802
Willingham Cambs 29 H1 vil 8m/13km NW of Cambridge. 2km E is Belsar's Hill, large circular prehistoric earthwork. TL 4070
Willingham Lincs 44 D3 vil 5m/8km SE of Gainsborough. SK 8784
Willingham Green Cambs 30 B3* ham 6m/10km S of Newmarket. TL 6254
Willingham, North Lincs 45 F3 vil 4m/6km E of Mkt Rasen. **S Willingham** vil 4m/6km SE. TF 1688
Willington Beds 29 E3 vil 4m/6km E of Bedford. 16c stone dovecote and stables (NT). TL 1149
Willington Derbys 35 H2 vil 6m/10km SW of Derby. Power stn to E. SK 2928
Willington Durham 54 B2 tn 4m/6km N of Bishop Auckland. Coal-mining, engineering. NZ 1935
Willington Kent 20 D6 SE suburb of Maidstone. TQ 7854
Willington Tyne & Wear 61 G4 loc in N Tyneside dist 1m NE of Wallsend. **Willington Quay** loc to SE, on N bank of R Tyne. NZ 3167
Willington Warwicks 27 G4* ham 2km SE of Shipston on Stour across r. SP 2639
Willington Corner Ches 42 B4* loc 3m/5km N of Tarporley. SJ 5366
Willisham Suffolk 31 E3 loc 5m/9km S of Stowmarket. TM 0750
Willitoft Humberside 50 C4 ham 4m/7km N of Howden. SE 7435
Williton Som 7 H1 vil 2km S of Watchet. ST 0741
Willoughbridge Staffs 34 D1* loc 2m/3km SE of Woore. SJ 7440
Willoughby Lincs 45 H4 vil 3m/4km S of Alford. TF 4771
Willoughby Warwicks 28 A1 vil 5m/7km NW of Daventry. SP 5167
Willoughby-on-the-Wolds Notts 36 C2 vil 8m/13km NW of Melton Mowbray. Site of Roman settlement of *Vernemetum.* SK 6325
Willoughby Waterleys Leics 36 B5 vil 5m/9km N of Lutterworth. SP 5792
Willoughby, West Lincs 37 E1* loc 2km W of Ancaster. SK 9643
Willoughton Lincs 44 D2 vil 3m/5km S of Kirton in Lindsey. **Willoughton Cliff** loc 1m SE with site of Roman bldg to N of it. SK 9393
Willowbank Bucks 19 E3* loc in R Colne valley 1km NW of Uxbridge. TQ 0585
Willowbrae Lothian 66 A2* dist of Edinburgh 2km W of Portobello. NT 2873
Willow Brook 37 F5 r rising at Corby, Northants, and flowing circuitously E into R Nene at Elton, S of Wansford, Cambs. TL 0893
Willow Green Ches 42 B4* loc 1km W of Lit Leigh. SJ 6076

Willow Holme Cumbria 59 H5* loc in Carlisle 1km W of city centre across R Caldew. NY 3956
Willows Green Essex 30 B5* ham 3m/5km SW of Braintree. TL 7219
Willsbridge Avon 16 B4* loc 2km NE of Keynsham. ST 6670
Willslock Staffs 35 G2* loc 2m/3km SW of Uttoxeter. SK 0730
Willsworthy Devon 4 C3 loc on Dartmoor 6m/9km NE of Tavistock. SX 5381
Willtown Som 8 C2* ham adjoining Curry Rivel on S side. ST 3924
Willy Lott's Cottage Suffolk. See Bergholt, East.
Wilmcote Warwicks 27 F2 vil 3m/5km NW of Stratford-upon-Avon. Mary Arden's Hse, early 16c. SP 1658
Wilmington Avon 16 C5* loc 1m E of Stanton Prior and 4m/7km SW of Bath. ST 6962
Wilmington Devon 8 A4 vil 3m/5km E of Honiton. SY 2199
Wilmington E Sussex 12 B6 vil under S Downs 5m/8km NE of Seaford. Remains of 12c priory. To S, **Long Man of Wilmington,** figure cut in chalk of Downs; origin unknown. TQ 5404
Wilmington Kent 20 B4 suburban loc 2km S of Dartford. TQ 5371
Wilmslow Ches 42 D3 largely residential tn on R Bollin 11m/17km S of Manchester. Industries include pharmaceuticals, engineering. SJ 8481
Wilnecote Staffs 35 H4 loc in Tamworth 2m/3km SE of tn centre. SK 2201
Wilne, Great Derbys 36 A2* ham 1km NE of Shardlow. Junction of Trent and Mersey Canal and R Trent. SK 4430
Wilney Green Norfolk 39 E6* loc 4m/6km W of Diss. TM 0681
Wilpshire Lancs 47 G5 vil 3m/4km N of Blackburn. SD 6832
Wilsden W Yorks 48 D4 vil 5m/8km NW of Bradford. SE 0936
Wilsford Lincs 37 E1 vil 4m/7km SW of Sleaford. TF 0043
Wilsford Wilts 17 E5 vil 3m/4km NW of Upavon. SU 1057
Wilsford Wilts 9 H1 ham in R Avon valley 2m/3km SW of Amesbury. SU 1339
Wilsham Devon 7 E1* loc 3m/4km E of Lynton. SS 7548
Wilshamstead Beds 29 E3 vil 4m/7km S of Bedford. TL 0643
Wilshaw W Yorks 43 F1* vil 2m/3km NW of Holmfirth. SE 1109
Wilsill N Yorks 48 D2 vil 2m/3km SE of Pateley Br. SE 1864
Wilsley Green Kent 12 D3 loc 1km N of Cranbrook. TQ 7737
Wilsley Pound Kent 12 D3* loc 2km NE of Cranbrook. TQ 7837
Wilson Leics 36 A2 ham 2km E of Melbourne. SK 4024
Wilson's Row Durham 61 G6* loc 4m/6km NE of Durham. NZ 3147
Wilsthorpe Humberside 51 F2* loc 2m/3km SW of Bridlington. TA 1664
Wilsthorpe Lincs 37 F3 ham 4m/7km S of Bourne. TF 0913
Wilstone Herts 28 D6 vil 2m/3km NW of Tring. Adjoining to S is loc of **Wilstone Green,** on N side of **Wilstone Resr** (nature reserve). SP 9014
Wilstrop N Yorks 50 A3* loc 3m/4km NW of Long Marston. SE 4855
Wilton Cleveland 55 E3 ham 3m/5km NW of Guisborough. Cas of early 19c and surrounding bldgs form administrative block for nearby chemical works. NZ 5819
Wilton Cumbria 52 A4* loc 2m/3km E of Egremont. NY 0311
Wilton Borders 60 B1 W dist of Hawick. NT 4914
Wilton N Yorks 55 G6 ham 4m/6km E of Pickering. SE 8682
Wilton Som 8 A2 S dist of Taunton. ST 2223
Wilton Wilts 17 G5 vil 6m/10km SW of Hungerford. SU 2661
Wilton Wilts 9 G1 small tn 3m/5km W of Salisbury, at confluence of Rs Nadder and Wylye; formerly county tn of Wiltshire. Carpet industry dates from 17c. W. Hse is 17c and later, in park. SU 0931
Wiltown Devon 8 A3 ham in Blackdown Hills 3m/5km SE of Wellington. ST 1716
Wiltshire 118, 119 southern county of England, bounded by Dorset, Somerset, Avon, Gloucestershire, Oxfordshire, Berkshire, and Hampshire. Extensive chalk uplands scattered with prehistoric remains, notably at Avebury and Stonehenge, are interspersed with wide, well-watered valleys. The Marlborough Downs, in the N, much used for racehorse training, and Salisbury Plain, in the S, an important military training area, are separated by the Vale of Pewsey. Rs include the so-called Bristol and Wiltshire Avons, Ebble, Kennet, Nadder, Wylye, and upper reaches of the Thames. Chief tns are the cathedral city of Salisbury; Bradford-on-Avon, Chippenham, Devizes, Swindon, Trowbridge, the county tn, and Westbury. There are rly engineering and other works at Swindon; elsewhere dairy products and bacon-curing are important industries, but much of the county is deeply rural.
Wimbish Essex 30 B4 ham 4m/6km E of Saffron Walden. Ham of **Wimbish Green** 2km SE. TL 5936
Wimblebury Staffs 35 F3 loc 3m/4km E of Cannock. SK 0111
Wimbledon London 19 F4 dist in borough of Merton 7m/11km SW of Charing Cross. **S. Wimbledon** loc 1km E of tn centre. Wimbledon Common is large open space to W. Wimbledon Park is 1m N; All England Lawn Tennis Club on W side of park. TQ 2470
Wimblington Cambs 37 H5 vil 3m/5km S of March. TL 4192
Wimborne Minster Dorset 9 G4 tn, generally known as Wimborne, on R Stour 7m/11km NW of Bournemouth. Norman to Dec minster at tn centre. SZ 0199
Wimborne St Giles Dorset 9 G3 vil 2m/3km SW of Cranborne. St Giles Hse, 17c–18c; shell grotto in grnds. SU 0312
Wimbotsham Norfolk 38 B4 vil 2km NE of Downham Mkt. TF 6205
Wimpole Cambs 29 G3 par 6m/10km N of Royston. Contains **Wimpole Hall,** large 17c-18c red brick hse in park with long avenue of elms. TL 3350
Wimpson Hants 10 B3* NW dist of Southampton. SU 3814
Wimpstone Warwicks 27 F3 vil 4m/6km S of Stratford-upon-Avon. SP 2148
Wincanton Som 9 E2 small mkt tn, 12m/19km NE of Yeovil. ST 7128
Winceby Lincs 45 G4* loc 4m/6km E of Horncastle. Site of Civil War battle, 1643. TF 3168
Wincham Ches 42 C4 loc 2km NE of Northwich. SJ 6775
Winchburgh Lothian 65 G2 vil 6m/10km E of Linlithgow. Niddry Castle, 1km SE, is ruined 15c tower. NT 0974
Winchcombe Glos 27 E4 tn 6m/10km NE of Cheltenham. SP 0228
Winch, East Norfolk 38 B3 vil 5m/8km SE of King's Lynn. TF 6916
Winchelsea E Sussex 13 E5 ancient tn on hill 2m/3km SW of Rye. Loc of **Winchelsea Beach** 1m SE on coast. TQ 9017
Winchendon, Lower Bucks 18 C1 vil 4m/7km NE of Thame. SP 7312
Winchendon, Upper Bucks 28 C6 vil 5m/8km W of Aylesbury. SP 7414
Winchester Hants 10 B2 county tn on R Itchen on site of Roman tn of *Venta,* 12m/19km N of Southampton. Ancient capital of Wessex and of England. Cathedral, longest in Britain. Boys' public school founded 1382. 12c hospital of St Cross, and many other old bldgs. City Mill (NT), built over r in 18c. To S across r, St Catherine's Hill, Iron Age fort. SU 4829
Winchestown Gwent 15 G1* loc 1km S of Brynmawr. SO 1810
Winchfield Hants 18 C5 vil 2m/4km E of Hook. SU 7654
Winchmore Hill Bucks 18 D2* vil 3m/5km N of Beaconsfield. SU 9394
Winchmore Hill London 19 G2 loc in borough of Enfield 9m/14km N of Charing Cross. TQ 3194
Winch, West Norfolk 38 B3 vil 3m/4km S of King's Lynn. TF 6316
Wincle Ches 43 E4 ham 5m/9km SE of Macclesfield. SJ 9566
Wincobank S Yorks 43 H2 dist of Sheffield 3m/5km NE of city centre. Includes locs of **High** and **Low Wincobank.** SK 3791
Winder Cumbria 52 A3* loc 1km E of Frizington. NY 0417
Windermere Cumbria 52 D5 the largest of the English lakes, extending from Waterhead near Ambleside southwards for some 10m/16km to Lake Side near Newby Br. On E side of lake is tn of same name, a resort 7m/11km NW of Kendal. SD 4198
Winder Moor Cumbria 47 E1* loc just S of Flookburgh. SD 3675
Winderton Warwicks 27 G3* vil 1m S of Compton Wynyates and 4m/7km E of Shipston on Stour. SP 3240
Wind Fell 59 F1 mt on border of Dumfries & Galloway and Borders regions 6m/9km E of Moffat. Height 2180 ft or 664 metres. NT 1706
Windhill H'land 81 E3 loc in Ross and Cromarty dist 2km S of Muir of Ord. NH 5348
Windhill W Yorks 48 D4* E dist of Shipley. SE 1537
Windle Merseyside 42 B2* loc 2m/3km NW of St Helens. SJ 4897
Windle Hill Ches 41 H4* loc 2km E of Neston. SJ 3177
Windlehurst Gtr Manchester 43 E3* loc adjoining High Lane to N. SJ 9586
Windles Green Merseyside 41 H2* loc 2m/3km NE of Crosby. SD 3400
Windlesham Surrey 18 D5 vil 1m E of Bagshot. SU 9364
Windlestone Durham 54 B2 loc 3m/5km E of Bishop Auckland. NZ 2628
Windlestraw Law Borders 66 B4 hill 4m/7km NE of Innerleithen. Height 2163 ft or 659 metres. NT 3743
Windley Derbys 43 G6 vil 3m/4km NW of Duffield. **Windley Meadows** loc 1m SE. SK 3045
Windmill Derbys 43 F3* loc 1km W of Gt Hucklow. SK 1777
Windmill Hill Avon 16 B4* S dist of Bristol. ST 5971
Windmill Hill E Sussex 12 C5 vil 1m E of Herstmonceux. TQ 6412
Windmill Hill H & W 26 D3* loc 3m/5km NW of Pershore. SO 9149
Windmill Hill Lancs 47 F5* loc 1km SW of Hoghton. SD 6125
Windmill Hill Som 8 B3 ham 3m/5km NW of Ilminster. ST 3116
Windmill Hill Wilts 17 E4* Neolithic camp (NT) 2km NW of Avebury. SU 0871
Windrush Glos 27 F6 vil 4m/6km W of Burford. SP 1913
Windrush 17 H2 r rising in Cotswold Hills E of Winchcombe, Glos, and flowing SE into R Thames at Newbridge, Oxon. SP 4001
Windsor Berks 18 D4 tn on S bank of R Thames 2m/3km S of Slough and 21m/34km W of London. Cas is chief royal residence. Gt Park to S of tn is open to public; Home Park bordering r is private. SU 9676
Windsor Humberside 50 C6* loc at S end of Crowle. SE 7712
Windsor Merseyside 42 A3* dist of Liverpool 2m/3km SE of city centre. SJ 3689
Windsor Green Suffolk 30 D3 ham 4m/6km NW of Lavenham. TL 8954
Windyfields Staffs 35 F1* loc 3m/4km E of Hilderstone. SJ 9835
Windygates Fife 73 F4 vil on W side of Methil. Distillery beside R Leven. NO 3400
Windy Gyle Borders 67 E6 hill on border of England and Scotland 4m/7km SW of The Cheviot. Height 2032 ft or 619 metres. NT 8515
Windy Harbour Lancs 47 F5/G5* loc 1km W of Brinscall. SD 6121
Windy Hill Clwyd 41 H5* loc and hill 3m/5km NW of Wrexham. SJ 3054
Windy Hill S'clyde 63 G1* hill on Bute 2m/3km NW of Kames Bay. Highest point of island: 913 ft or 278 metres. NS 0469
Windy Nook Tyne & Wear 61 G5* loc adjoining Gateshead to SE. NZ 2760
Windy Standard D & G 56 F3 mt near border with Strathclyde region 6m/10km NE of Carsphairn. Height 2287 ft or 697 metres. NS 6201
Wineham W Sussex 11 H3* ham 3m/5km NE of Henfield. TQ 2320
Winestead Humberside 51 G5 vil 2m/3km NW of Patrington. TA 2924
Winewall Lancs 48 B4 loc 1km N of Trawden. SD 9139
Winfarthing Norfolk 39 E6 vil 4m/6km N of Diss. TM 1085
Winford Avon 16 B5 vil 6m/9km SW of Bristol. ST 5465
Winford Isle of Wight 10 C6* vil 2m/3km W of Sandown. SZ 5684
Winford Terrace Avon 16 B4* ham 4m/6km SW of Bristol. ST 5568
Winforton H & W 25 G3 vil 6m/10km S of Kington. SO 2947
Winfrith Heath Dorset 9 E5 site of nuclear research stn, 2m/3km W of Wool. SY 8186
Winfrith Newburgh Dorset 9 E5 vil 3m/5km SW of Wool. SY 8084
Wing Bucks 28 D5 vil 3m/5km SW of Leighton Buzzard. SP 8822
Wing Leics 36 D4 vil 4m/7km SE of Oakham. SK 8903
Wingate Durham 54 C2 coal-mining vil 4m/6km S of Easington. **S Wingate** is loc 2m/3km SE. See also Old Wingate. NZ 4037
Wingates Gtr Manchester 42 C1 loc 4m/7km W of Bolton. SD 6507
Wingates H & W 27 E1* E dist of Redditch. SP 0767
Wingates Nthmb 61 F2 loc 5m/8km SE of Rothbury. NZ 0995
Wingerworth Derbys 43 H4 vil 2m/4km S of Chesterfield. SK 3867
Wingfield Beds 29 E5* ham 3m/5km N of Dunstable. TL 0026
Wingfield Suffolk 31 F1 vil 2m/3km N of Stradbroke. 14c moated cas. Loc of Wingfield Green 1km W. TM 2276
Wingfield Wilts 16 D5 vil 2m/4km W of Trowbridge. ST 8256
Wingfield, North Derbys 43 H4 vil 2m/3km NE of Clay Cross. SK 4165
Wingfield Park Derbys 43 H5* loc 1m S of S Wingfield. SK 3753
Wingfield, South Derbys 43 H5 vil 3m/4km W of Alfreton. Ruins of medieval **Wingfield Manor** 1km S. SK 3755
Wingham Kent 13 G2 vil 6m/10km E of Canterbury. Locs of **Wingham Green** and **Wingham Well** to W and SW respectively. TR 2457
Wingmore Kent 13 G3 ham 7m/11km N of Folkestone. TR 1846
Wingrave Bucks 28 D5 vil 5m/7km NE of Aylesbury. SP 8619
Winkburn Notts 44 B5 vil 6m/10km NW of Newark-on-Trent. SK 7158
Winkfield Berks 18 D4 vil 3m/5km NE of Bracknell. Par also includes vils of **Winkfield Row** and **Winkfield Street.** SU 9072
Winkhill Staffs 43 F5 ham 6m/10km SE of Leek. SK 0651
Winklebury Hants 18 B6* industrial estate in W part of Basingstoke. SU 6152
Winkleigh Devon 7 E4 vil 9m/14km NE of Okehampton. SS 6308
Winksley N Yorks 49 E1 vil 4m/6km W of Ripon. SE 2571
Winkton Dorset 9 H4 loc beside R Avon 2m/3km N of Christchurch. SZ 1696
Winkworth Arboretum Surrey 11 F1* hillside (NT) planted with rare trees and shrubs 2m/4km SE of Godalming. Lake. Views over N Downs. SU 9941
Winlaton Tyne & Wear 61 F5 tn adjoining Blaydon to SW, 5m/8km W of Gateshead. **Winlaton Mill** loc on R Derwent 1m SE. NZ 1762
Winless H'land 86 F2 locality in Caithness dist 4m/7km NW of Wick. **Loch of Winless** is small loch to W. ND 3054
Winmarleigh Lancs 47 E3 vil 2m/4km NW of Garstang. SD 4748
Winnats Derbys 43 F3* limestone ravine (NT) 1m W of Castleton. SK 1382
Winnersh Berks 18 C4 suburb 2m/4km NW of Wokingham. SU 7870
Winnington Ches 42 C4* NW dist of Northwich. Chemical works. SJ 6474
Winnothdale Staffs 35 F1* loc 2m/4km SE of Cheadle. SK 0340
Winscales Cumbria 52 A3* loc 3m/4km SE of Workington. NY 0226
Winscombe Avon 15 H5 vil below W end of Mendip Hills 2m/3km N of Axbridge. ST 4257
Winsford Ches 42 C4 tn on R Weaver 5m/8km S of Northwich. Industries include salt, steel. Industrial estate. Central shopping precinct. SJ 6566
Winsford Som 7 G2 Exmoor vil on R Exe 5m/7km N of Dulverton. To SW, **Winsford Hill** (NT). SS 9034
Winsham Devon 6 D2* ham 5m/8km NW of Barnstaple. SS 4938
Winsham Som 8 B4 vil 4m/6km SE of Chard. ST 3706
Winshill Staffs 35 H2 dist of Burton upon Trent 2m/3km E of tn centre. SK 2623
Winsh-wen W Glam 23 H5* loc in Swansea 3m/4km NE of tn centre. SS 6896
Winskill Cumbria 53 E2 ham 5m/8km NE of Penrith. NY 5834
Winslade Hants 18 B6* ham 3m/4km S of Basingstoke. SU 6548
Winsley N Yorks 49 E2* loc 3m/5km W of Ripley. SE 2361
Winsley Wilts 16 C5 vil 2m/3km W of Bradford-on-Avon. ST 7960
Winslow Bucks 28 C5 small tn 6m/10km SE of Buckingham. SP 7627
Winson Glos 17 E1 vil 4m/6km S of Northleach. SP 0908
Winson Green W Midlands 35 F5* loc in Birmingham 2m/3km NW of city centre. SP 0488

Winsor Hants 10 A3* vil 2km E of Cadnam. SU 3114
Winstanley Hall Gtr Manchester 42 B1* Elizn hse 3m/4km SW of Wigan. SD 5403
Winster Cumbria 52 D5 vil 3m/5km S of Windermere. SD 4193
Winster Derbys 43 G5 vil 4m/6km W of Matlock. SK 2460
Winster 52 D6 r rising S of tn of Windermere, Cumbria, and flowing S into R Kent estuary 2m/3km NE of Grange-over-Sands. SD 4378
Winston Durham 54 B3 vil 6m/9km E of Barnard Castle. NZ 1416
Winston Suffolk 31 F2 ham 2km S of Debenham. Loc of **Winston Green** 1km W. TM 1861
Winstone Glos 16 D1 vil 6m/10km NW of Cirencester. WT stn to E. SO 9609
Winswell Devon 6 D4* ham 4m/6km S of Torrington. SS 4913
Winterborne 9 F4* r rising at Winterborne Houghton in Dorset and flowing E, then S, then E again into R Stour at Sturminster Marshall. ST 9400
Winterborne Came Dorset 9 E5 ham 2m/3km SE of Dorchester. SY 7088
Winterborne Clenston Dorset 9 F4 vil 4m/6km SW of Blandford Forum. ST 8303
Winterborne Herringston Dorset 9 E5* ham 2m/3km S of Dorchester. SY 6888
Winterborne Houghton Dorset vil 4m/7km W of Blandford Forum. ST 8204
Winterborne Kingston Dorset 9 F4 vil 6m/9km S of Blandford Forum. SY 8697
Winterborne Monkton Dorset 8 D5/9 E5 vil 2m/3km SW of Dorchester. SY 6787
Winterborne Muston Dorset 9 F4* loc 1km E of Winterborne Kingston and 2m/4km NE of Bere Regis. SY 8797
Winterborne, South 9 E5* stream rising at North Hill in par of Winterbourne Steepleton in Dorset and flowing E, S of Dorchester, into R Frome at W Stafford. SY 7290
Winterborne Stickland Dorset 9 F4 vil 3m/5km W of Blandford Forum. ST 8304
Winterborne Tomson Dorset 9 F4* ham just E of Anderson and 3m/5km NE of Bere Regis. SY 8897
Winterborne Whitchurch (or Winterborne Whitechurch) Dorset 9 F4 vil 5m/8km SE of Blandford Forum. ST 8300
Winterborne Zelstone Dorset 9 F4 vil 4m/6km NE of Bere Regis. SY 8997
Winterbourne Avon 16 B3 suburb 6m/10km NE of Bristol. ST 6480
Winterbourne Berks 17 H4 vil 3m/5km N of Newbury. SU 4572
Winterbourne Wilts 9 H1 par 4m/6km NE of Salisbury containing vils of **Winterbourne Dauntsey, Winterbourne Earls** and **Winterbourne Gunner,** all on R Bourne. SU 1834
Winterbourne Abbas Dorset 8 D5 vil 4m/7km W of Dorchester. SY 6190
Winterbourne Bassett Wilts 17 E4 vil 3m/5km N of Avebury. SU 1075
Winterbourne Monkton Wilts 17 E4 vil 2km N of Avebury. SU 1072
Winterbourne Steepleton Dorset 9 D5 vil 4m/6km W of Dorchester. SY 6289
Winterbourne Stoke Wilts 9 G1 vil 5m/8km W of Amesbury. SU 0741
Winterbrook Oxon 18 B3 loc adjoining Wallingford to S. SU 6088
Winterburn N Yorks 48 B3 ham 6m/9km NW of Skipton. **Winterburn Resr** 1m NE. SD 9358
Winterhope Reservoir D & G 59 G3* small resr 6m/10km W of Langholm. NY 2782
Winteringham Humberside 50 D6 vil 7m/12km N of Scunthorpe. **Winteringham Haven** inlet on R Humber 1km NE. Site of Roman settlement 1m SE. SE 9222
Winterley Ches 42 C5 vil 3m/5km NE of Crewe. SJ 7457
Wintersett W Yorks 49 F6* loc 2km S of Crofton. **Wintersett Resr** to SW. SE 3815
Winterslow Wilts 9 H1 vil 6m/9km E of Salisbury. Par also contains vils of **E, Middle,** and **W Winterslow.** SU 2332
Winterton Humberside 50 D6 vil 5m/9km NE of Scunthorpe. Sites of Roman bldgs 1km NE and 2km W. SE 9218
Winterton (or Winterton-on-Sea) Norfolk 39 H3 resort 8m/13km N of Gt Yarmouth. **Winterton Ness** headland 2m/3km NW. TG 4919
Winthorpe Lincs 45 H4* loc 2m/3km N of Skegness. TF 5665
Winthorpe Notts 44 C5 vil 2m/3km NE of Newark. SK 8156
Winton Cumbria 53 G4 vil 2km NE of Kirkby Stephen. NY 7810
Winton Dorset 9 G5 dist of Bournemouth 2km N of tn centre. SZ 0893
Winton N Yorks 54 C5 loc 3m/5km NE of Northallerton. SE 4196
Winton House Lothian 66 C2 early 17c mansion 3m/5km SE of Tranent. Formerly seat of the Earls of Winton. NT 4369
Wintringham Cambs 29 F2* loc 2m/3km E of St Neots. TL 2159
Wintringham N Yorks 50 D1 vil 6m/10km E of Malton. SE 8873
Winwick Cambs 37 F6 vil 10m/16km NW of Huntingdon. TL 1080
Winwick Ches 42 B2 vil 3m/5km N of Warrington. SJ 6092
Winwick Northants 28 B1 vil 2km N of W Haddon. SP 6273
Winyard's Gap Dorset. See Chedington.
Wirksworth Derbys 43 G5 tn 4m/7km S of Matlock. Industries include quarrying, hosiery, tape mnfre. **Wirksworth Moor** ham 1m E. SK 2854
Wirral 41 H3, H4 peninsula, some 13m/21km long and 6m/10km wide, between estuaries of R Dee to W and R Mersey to E; largely industrialised Birkenhead on the peninsula is connected to Liverpool by tunnels under R Mersey. SJ 38
Wirswall Ches 34 C1* vil 2m/3km N of Whitchurch. SJ 5444
Wisbech Cambs 38 A3/A4 fenland tn and agricultural centre on R Nene 12m/19km SW of King's Lynn. Industries include horticulture, fertilisers, canning. **Peckover Hse** (NT), 18c. TF 4609
Wisbech St Mary Cambs 37 H4 vil 3m/5km W of Wisbech. TF 4208
Wisborough Green W Sussex 11 F3 vil 2m/4km W of Billingshurst. TQ 0525
Wise Een Tarn Cumbria 52 D5* small lake 2km E of Hawkshead. SD 3797
Wiseton Notts 44 C2* vil 5m/7km SE of Bawtry. SK 7189
Wishaw S'clyde 65 E3 tn 3m/5km SE of Motherwell. NS 7954
Wishaw Warwicks 35 G5* vil 4m/6km N of Coleshill. SP 1794
Wishford, Great Wilts 9 G1 vil on R Wylye 3m/5km N of Wilton. 1km N, loc of **Lit Wishford.** SU 0735
Wiske 54 C6 r rising near Ingleby Arncliffe, N Yorks, and flowing NW to Appleton Wiske, then W to Birkby, then S by Yafforth, Newby Wiske, and Kirby Wiske into R Swale 4m/6km W of Thirsk. SE 3683
Wisley Surrey 19 E5 ham 4m/6km E of Woking. Gardens of Royal Horticultural Society 1km S. TQ 0659
Wisp Hill 60 A2 hill on border of Dumfries & Galloway and Borders regions 4m/6km S of Teviothead. Height 1953 ft or 595 metres. NY 3899
Wispington Lincs 45 F4 vil 4m/6km W of Horncastle. TF 2071
Wissett Suffolk 31 G1 vil 2m/3km NW of Halesworth. TM 3679
Wissey 38 B4 r rising 4m/6km SW of E Dereham, Norfolk, and flowing W into R Ouse 5m/8km SW of Downham Mkt. TL 5899
Wissington Suffolk 30 D4 ham by R Stour 2km W of Nayland. TL 9533
Wistanstow Salop 34 B5 vil 2m/3km N of Craven Arms. SO 4385
Wistanswick Salop 34 D2 ham 4m/6km S of Mkt Drayton. SJ 6629
Wistaston Ches 42 C5 vil 2m/3km SW of Crewe. **Wistaston Green** loc 2km W of Crewe. SJ 6853
Wistlandpound Devon 7 E1* loc on W edge of Exmoor 6m/10km SW of Lynton. **Wistlandpound Resr** to S. SS 6442
Wistman's Wood Devon 4 C3* eerie wd of stunted oaks on Dartmoor, 2km N of Two Bridges. SX 6177
Wiston (Cas-wis) Dyfed 22 C4 vil 5m/7km E of Haverfordwest. Remains of medieval cas. SM 0217
Wiston S'clyde 65 F5 vil 7m/11km SW of Biggar. NS 9531
Wiston W Sussex 11 G4* loc 2m/3km E of Washington. **Wiston Hse,** Elizn and later hse in large park. TQ 1512
Wistow Cambs 37 G6 vil 2m/3km NW of Warboys. TL 2781
Wistow Leics 36 C4* loc 6m/10km SE of Leicester. Ch and hall in park. SP 6495
Wistow N Yorks 49 G4 vil 3m/4km NW of Selby. SE 5935
Wiswell Lancs 48 A4 vil 2km NE of Whalley. SD 7437
Witcham Cambs 38 A6 vil 5m/8km W of Ely. TL 4680
Witchampton Dorset 9 G4 vil 6m/10km E of Blandford Forum. ST 9806
Witchford Cambs 38 A6 vil 3m/4km W of Ely. TL 5078
Witchingham, Great Norfolk 39 E3 loc 2m/3km S of Reepham. **Lit Witchingham** loc 1m E. TG 1020
Witcombe Som 8 C2 ham 2km NE of Martock. ST 4721
Witcombe, Great Glos 26 D6* vil 6m/9km SE of Gloucester. Remains of Roman villa (A.M.) to W. SO 9114
Witcombe, Little Glos 26 D5 ham 5m/8km SE of Gloucester. SO 9115
Witham Essex 30 C6 tn 9m/14km NE of Chelmsford. Radio equipment factory. Remains of 10c cas. TL 8215
Witham 37 H1 r rising to E of Wymondham, Leics, and flowing circuitously through Grantham to Lincoln, where it turns E then SE to Boston and the Wash. TF 3939
Witham Friary Som 9 E1 vil 6m/9km NE of Bruton. ST 7441
Witham, North Lincs 37 E2 vil 2km S of Colsterworth. **S Witham** vil 2m/3km S. SK 9221
Witham on the Hill Lincs 37 F3 vil 4m/6km SW of Bourne. TF 0516
Withcall Lincs 45 F3 ham 4m/6km SW of Louth. TF 2883
Withdean E Sussex 11 H4* N dist of Brighton. TQ 3007
Withens Clough Reservoir W Yorks 48 C5* resr 3m/5km S of Hebden Br. SD 9823
Witherenden Hill E Sussex 12 C4 ham 2m/3km NW of Burwash. TQ 6426
Withergate Norfolk 39 G2* loc 1km N of Worstead. TG 2927
Witheridge Devon 7 F4 vil 9m/16km W of Tiverton. SS 8014
Witherley Leics 36 H4 vil 2km E of Atherstone. SP 3297
Withern Lincs 45 G3/H3 vil 4m/7km N of Alford. TF 4382
Withernsea Humberside 51 G5 coastal resort 15m/24km E of Hull. TA 3428
Withernwick Humberside 51 F4 vil 5m/8km S of Hornsea. TA 1940
Withersdale Street Suffolk 31 G1 vil 2m/4km SE of Harleston. TM 2781
Withersdane Kent 13 F3* loc 1m SE of Wye. TR 0645
Withersfield Suffolk 30 B3 vil 2m/3km NW of Haverhill. TL 6547
Witherslack Cumbria 52 D6 ham 3m/4km N of Lindale. SD 4384
Witherwack Tyne & Wear 61 H5* housing estate in NW part of Sunderland. NZ 3759
Withiel Cornwall 3 E2 vil 5m/8km W of Bodmin. **Withielgoose** ham 1km E. SW 9965
Withiel Florey Som 7 G2 ham on S side of Brendon Hills 6m/9km NE of Dulverton. SS 9833
Withington Ches 42 D4 vil 4m/6km NE of Holmes Chapel. **Withington Green** loc 2km NW. SJ 8169
Withington Glos 27 E5/E6 vil 5m/8km W of Northleach. SP 0315
Withington Gtr Manchester 42 D2 dist of Manchester 3m/5km S of city centre. SJ 8492
Withington H & W 26 B3 vil 4m/7km NE of Hereford. SO 5643
Withington Salop 34 C3 vil 5m/9km E of Shrewsbury. SJ 5713
Withington Staffs 35 F1 ham 4m/7km W of Uttoxeter. SK 0335
Withington Marsh H & W 26 B3* loc 4m/6km NE of Hereford. SO 5544
Withleigh Devon 7 G4 vil 3m/5km W of Tiverton. SS 9012
Withnell Lancs 47 G5 urban loc 5m/8km SW of Blackburn. Bricks, paper, textiles. **Withnell Fold** loc 2km NW. SD 6322
Withybrook Som 16 B6* ham 1km W of Stoke St Michael and 4m/6km NE of Shepton Mallet. ST 6547
Withybrook Warwicks 36 A5 vil 7m/11km NW of Rugby. SP 4384
Withycombe Som 7 G1 vil on edge of Exmoor National Park 2m/3km SE of Dunster. ST 0141
Withycombe Raleigh Devon 5 F3 NE suburb of Exmouth. SY 0182
Withyditch Avon 16 C5* loc 1km W of Dunkerton and 3m/5km N of Radstock. ST 7059
Withyham E Sussex 12 B3 vil 6m/10km SW of Tunbridge Wells. TQ 4935
Withypool Som 7 F2 vil on Exmoor and on R Barle 2m/3km S of Exford. SS 8435
Witley Surrey 11 F1 vil 2m/4km S of Milford. 2km NW, Witley Common (NT): nature reserve. SU 9434
Witley, Great H & W 26 C1 vil 5m/8km SW of Stourport. 1m SE is **Witley Court,** ruins of 18c hse burnt down in 20c; baroque 18c ch. SO 7566
Witley, Little H & W 26 C2 vil 7m/11km NW of Worcester. SO 7863
Witnesham Suffolk 31 F3 vil 4m/6km N of Ipswich. TM 1850
Witney Oxon 17 G1* tn on R Windrush 10m/16km W of Oxford. Mnfre of blankets. SP 3510
Witney Green Essex 20 C1* loc 3m/5km NE of Chipping Ongar. TL 5806
Wittenham Clumps Oxon 18 B2* hill 3m/5km NW of Wallingford, surmounted by clump of trees within Iron Age fort. Notable landmark. SU 5692
Wittenham, Little Oxon 18 B2 vil 4m/6km NW of Wallingford. SU 5693
Wittering Cambs 37 F4 vil 3m/5km SE of Stamford. Airfield to W. TF 0502
Wittering, East W Sussex 11 E5 coastal resort 4m/7km NW of Selsey. SZ 7997
Wittering, West W Sussex 10 D5 vil 6m/9km NW of Selsey. SZ 7898
Wittersham Kent 13 E4 vil on Isle of Oxney 4m/6km S of Tenterden. TQ 8927
Wittingham Green, Little Suffolk 31 G1* loc 2km E of Fressingfield. TM 2876
Witton H & W 26 D2* S dist of Droitwich. SO 8962
Witton Norfolk 39 G4* ham 2km W of Blofield. TG 3309
Witton W Midlands 35 G5* loc in Birmingham 3m/5km NE of city centre. Electrical works. SP 0891
Witton Bridge Norfolk 39 G2* ham 4m/6km E of N Walsham. TG 3331
Witton Castle Durham 54 B2 cas dating partly from early 15c, 1km SE of Witton le Wear. NZ 1530
Witton, East N Yorks 54 B6 vil 2m/3km SE of Middleham. SE 1486
Witton Gilbert Durham 54 B1 vil 3m/5km NW of Durham. NZ 2345
Witton Green Norfolk 39 G4* loc adjoining Reedham to N. TG 4202
Witton le Wear Durham 54 B2 vil on R Wear 3m/5km SW of Crook. See also Witton Castle. NZ 1431
Witton Park Durham 54 B2* vil 2m/4km W of Bishop Auckland. NZ 1730
Witton, Upper W Midlands 35 G5* loc in Birmingham 4m/6km NE of city centre. SP 0891
Witton, West N Yorks 54 A5 vil in Wensleydale 4m/6km W of Leyburn. SE 0688
Wiveliscombe Som 7 H2 small tn 9m/15km W of Taunton. ST 0827
Wivelsfield E Sussex 12 A4 vil 2m/3km S of Haywards Heath. Vil of **Wivelsfield Green** 1m E. TQ 3420
Wivenhoe Essex 31 E5 tn on left bank of R Colne 4m/6km SE of Colchester. Loc of **Wivenhoe Cross** adjoins to N. University of Essex to NW in Wivenhoe Park. TM 0321
Wiveton Norfolk 39 E1 vil 1m SE of Blakeney. TG 0442
Wix Essex 31 F5 vil 6m/10km SW of Harwich. Loc of **Wix Green** at E end of vil. TM 1628
Wixford Warwicks 27 E2 vil 7m/11km W of Stratford-upon-Avon. SP 0854
Wixhill Salop 34 C2* loc 3m/5km E of Wem. SJ 5628
Wixoe Suffolk 30 C4* vil 3m/5km SE of Haverhill. TL 7142
Wnion 33 E3 r flowing SW into R Mawddach 2km NW of Dolgellau, Gwynedd. SH 7118
Woburn Beds 28 D4 vil 5m/9km N of Leighton Buzzard. 1m E is **Woburn Abbey,** 18c hse in large park. SP 9433
Woburn Sands Bucks 28 D4 vil 4m/6km E of Bletchley. SP 9235

Wokefield Berks 18 B5* loc 5m/8km SW of Reading. SU 6765
Woking Surrey 19 E5 residential tn 6m/9km N of Guildford. Light industry. TQ 0058
Wokingham Berks 18 C4 tn 7m/11km SE of Reading. SU 8168
Wolborough Devon 5 E3 S dist of Newton Abbot. SX 8570
Wold Northants 28 C1. Alternative name for Old, qv. SP 7873
Woldingham Surrey 20 A5 suburb 2m/3km SE of Warlingham. TQ 3755
Wold Newton Humberside 45 F2 vil 3m/5km NE of Binbrook. TF 2496
Wold Newton Humberside 51 E1 vil 7m/11km SW of Filey. TA 0473
Wolds, North 117 admin dist of Humberside.
Wolf 6 C6 r rising on Halwill Forest in Devon and flowing S into R Thrushel 1m NE of Lifton. SX 4085
Wolferlow H & W 26 B2* loc 5m/7km N of Bromyard. SO 6661
Wolferton Norfolk 38 B2 vil 6m/10km NE of King's Lynn. TF 6528
Wolfhampcote Warwicks 28 A1 loc 4m/6km NW of Daventry. SP 5265
Wolfhill Tayside 73 E2 vil 6m/10km N of Perth. NO 1533
Wolford, Great Warwicks 27 F4 vil 3m/5km NE of Moreton-in-Marsh. SP 2434
Wolford, Little Warwicks 27 G4* vil 3m/5km S of Shipston on Stour. SP 2635
Wolf's Castle (Cas-blaidd) Dyfed 22 C3 vil 7m/11km S of Fishguard. Traces of Norman cas. SM 9526
Wolfsdale Dyfed 22 B4 ham 4m/6km N of Haverfordwest. SM 9321
Wollaston Northants 28 D2 vil 4m/6km S of Wellingborough. SP 9062
Wollaston Salop 34 A3 ham 7m/11km NE of Welshpool. SJ 3212
Wollaston W Midlands 35 E5 W dist of Stourbridge. SO 8884
Wollaton Notts 36 B1 dist of Nottingham 3m/5km W of city centre. **Wollaton Hall**, Elizn mansion, now museum, in large park. Nottingham University at SE end of park. SK 5239
Wollerton Salop 34 C2 1m NE of Hodnet. SJ 6229
Wollescote W Midlands 35 E5/E6* dist of Stourbridge 2km E of tn centre. SO 9283
Wolsingham Durham 54 A2 tn at confluence of R Wear and Waskerley Beck 6m/10km NW of Bishop Auckland. NZ 0737
Wolstanton Staffs 42 D6 dist of Newcastle-under-Lyme 2m/3km N of tn centre. SJ 8548
Wolstenholme Gtr Manchester 47 H6 loc in Rochdale 3m/5km W of tn centre. SD 8514
Wolston Warwicks 36 A6 vil 5m/9km SE of Coventry. SP 4175
Wolsty Cumbria 59 F6* loc near coast of Solway Firth 2m/3km S of Silloth. Remains of cas to N. NY 1050
Wolvercote Oxon 18 A1 N dist of Oxford. SP 4909
Wolvercote, Upper Oxon 28 A6* loc in N Oxford adjoining Wolvercote to N. SP 4910
Wolverhampton W Midlands 35 E4 large industrial tn 12m/20km NW of Birmingham. Makes locks and safes, and various engineering products. SO 9198
Wolverley H & W 35 E6 vil 2m/3km N of Kidderminster. SO 8279
Wolverley Salop 34 B2* loc 3m/5km NW of Wem. SJ 4731
Wolverton Bucks 28 C3 tn in NW part of Milton Keynes and 6m/10km NW of Bletchley. SP 8141
Wolverton Hants 18 A5 ham 2m/3km E of Kingsclere. SU 5558
Wolverton Warwicks 27 F2 vil 5m/7km N of Stratford-upon-Avon. SP 2062
Wolverton Wilts 9 E2* ham just E of Zeals and 2m/3km W of Mere. ST 7831
Wolverton Common Hants 18 B5* loc 2m/4km E of Kingsclere. SU 5659
Wolvesnewton Gwent 16 A2 ham 6m/10km NW of Chepstow. ST 4599
Wolves, The S Glam 15 G4/G5* two rocks in Bristol Channel 1m NW of Flat Holm. ST 2065
Wolvey Warwicks 36 A5 vil 4m/6km S of Hinckley. Ham of **Wolvey Heath** to NE. SP 4287
Wolviston Cleveland 54 D2 vil 4m/7km N of Stockton-on-Tees. NZ 4525
Womaston Powys 25 G2* loc 4m/6km SW of Presteigne. SO 2660
Wombleton N Yorks 55 E6 vil 4m/6km E of Helmsley. SE 6683
Wombourn Staffs 35 E5 tn 4m/7km SW of Wolverhampton. SO 8793
Wombridge Salop 34 D3* loc 1m W of Oakengates. SJ 6911
Wombwell S Yorks 43 H1 tn 4m/6km SE of Barnsley. Coal-mining; also iron-founding, engineering. **Wombwell Main** loc and colliery to W. SE 3902
Womenswold Kent 13 G2 vil 7m/11km SE of Canterbury. TR 2250
Womersley N Yorks 49 G6 vil 4m/6km SE of Knottingley. SE 5319
Wonastow (Llanwarw) Gwent 26 A6 loc 2m/3km SW of Monmouth. SO 4810
Wonersh Surrey 11 F1 vil 3m/5km SE of Guildford. TQ 0145
Wonford Devon 7 G5* E dist of Exeter. SX 9392
Wonson Devon 7 E6 ham 6m/9km NW of Moretonhampstead. SX 6789
Wonston Hants 10 B1 vil 6m/10km N of Winchester. SU 4739
Wonston, South Hants 10 B2* loc 4m/7km N of Winchester. SU 4635
Wooburn Bucks 18 D3 vil 2m/4km SW of Beaconsfield. SU 9087
Wooburn Green Bucks 18 D3 suburb 4m/6km SE of High Wycombe. SU 9188
Wooburn Moor Bucks 18 D3* loc 2m/3km W of Beaconsfield. SU 9089
Woodacott Devon 6 C4* loc 4m/6km NE of Holsworthy. SS 3807
Woodall S Yorks 44 A3* vil 1km W of Harthill. Service area on M1 motorway to S. SK 4880
Woodbastwick Norfolk 39 G3 vil 8m/12km NE of Norwich. **Woodbastwick Fens and Marshes** to N between vil and R Bure. TG 3315
Woodbeck Notts 44 C3* loc 2m/3km W of Rampton. Mental hospital. SK 7777
Wood Bevington Warwicks 27 E2* ham 7m/11km N of Evesham. SP 0553
Woodbine Dyfed 22 C4 loc 2km S of Haverfordwest. SM 9513
Woodborough Notts 44 B6 vil 6m/10km NE of Nottingham. SK 6347
Woodborough Wilts 17 F5 vil 3m/5km W of Pewsey. SU 1159
Woodbridge Devon 8 A4* ham 4m/6km SE of Honiton. SY 1895
Woodbridge Dorset 9 E3* loc in Blackmoor Vale 2km SE of Bishop's Caundle and 5m/8km W of Sturminster Newton. ST 7112
Woodbridge Dorset 9 F3* loc 3m/5km S of Shaftesbury. ST 8518
Woodbridge Suffolk 31 F3 tn on R Deben 8m/12km E of Ipswich. R navigable for small craft to mouth at **Woodbridge Haven.** TM 2749
Woodbridge Hill Surrey 18 D6* NW dist of Guildford. SU 9750
Wood Burcote Northants 28 C3 loc 1m S of Towcester. SP 6946
Woodburn, East Nthmb 60 D3* ham 4m/7km S of Otterburn. NY 9085
Woodburn, West Nthmb 60 D3 ham 4m/6km S of Otterburn, and 1m W of E Woodburn. Site of Roman fort of *Habitancum* to S. NY 8986
Woodbury Beds 29 F3 loc with hall and park 4m/6km NE of Sandy. TL 2152
Woodbury Devon 5 F2 vil 4m/6km N of Exmouth. SY 0187
Woodbury Som 16 B6* E dist of Wells. ST 5646
Woodbury Salterton Devon 5 F2 vil 5m/8km N of Exmouth. SY 0189
Woodchester Glos 16 D2 vil 2m/3km S of Stroud. Site of Roman villa to N. NT properties on hills to E. SO 8402
Woodchurch Kent 13 E3 vil 4m/6km E of Tenterden. TQ 9434
Woodchurch Merseyside 41 H3 loc in Birkenhead 3m/5km SW of tn centre. SJ 2786
Woodcock Hill W Midlands 35 F6* loc in Birmingham 5m/8km SW of city centre. SP 0181
Woodcombe Som 7 G1* ham 2km W of Minehead. SS 9546
Woodcote London 19 G5* loc in borough of Croydon 1m W of Purley. TQ 2961
Woodcote Oxon 18 B3 vil 3m/5km E of Goring. SU 6482
Woodcote Salop 34 D3* ham 3m/5km SE of Newport. SJ 7615
Woodcote Green H & W 26 D1* loc 3m/5km W of Bromsgrove. SO 9172
Woodcote, Little London 19 G5* loc in borough of Sutton 2m/3km W of Purley. TQ 2861

Woodcott Hants 17 H5* loc 4m/6km E of Hurstbourne Tarrant. SU 4354
Woodcroft Glos 16 B2 vil 2km N of Chepstow. ST 5495
Woodcutts Dorset 9 G3 loc 2m/3km E of Tollard Royal. ST 9617
Wood Dalling Norfolk 39 E2 ham 3m/4km N of Reepham. TG 0827
Woodditton Cambs 30 B2 ham 3m/4km S of Newmarket. TL 6559
Woodeaton Oxon 28 A6 vil 4m/6km NE of Oxford. SP 5311
Wood Eaton Staffs 35 E3* loc just NW of Ch Eaton. SJ 8417
Wooden Dyfed 22 D5* loc 2km W of Saundersfoot. SN 1105
Wood End Beds 29 E2* loc 2km SW of Kimbolton. TL 0865
Wood End Beds 29 E3 loc 4m/6km SW of Bedford. TL 0046
Wood End Bucks 28 C4* ham adjoining Lit Horwood to E, 2m/4km NE of Winslow. SP 7930
Wood End Cambs 37 H6* NW end of vil of Bluntisham. TL 3675
Wood End Herts 29 G5 vil 3m/5km SW of Buntingford. TL 3225
Wood End Lancs 48 B4* loc 2km W of Brierfield. SD 8235
Wood End London 19 E3* loc at Hayes, borough of Hillingdon, 3m/5km SE of Uxbridge. Loc of **Wd End Green** to W. TQ 0981
Woodend Northants 28 B3 vil 5m/8km W of Towcester. SP 6149
Wood End N Yorks 50 B4* loc 2km E of Osgodby. SE 6634
Wood End Warwicks 27 E1 vil 3m/5km W of Hockley Heath. SP 1071
Wood End Warwicks 35 H4* loc 4m/7km W of Atherstone. SP 2498
Wood End Warwicks 35 H5 ham 6m/10km NW of Coventry. SP 2987
Wood End W Midlands 35 F4* loc in Wolverhampton 3m/4km NE of tn centre. SJ 9401
Wood End W Midlands 36 A5/A6* loc in Coventry 3m/5km NE of city centre. SP 3682
Wood Enderby Lincs 45 F5 vil 4m/6km S of Horncastle. TF 2763
Woodend Green Essex 30 A5* loc adjoining Henham to E, 6m/10km NE of Bishop's Stortford. TL 5528
Woodend Green Northants 28 B3* loc 5m/8km W of Towcester. SP 6148
Woodend Loch S'clyde 64 D2 small loch 2km/3km NW of Coatbridge. NS 7066
Woodend, Lower Bucks 18 C3* loc 2m/3km W of Marlow. SU 8187
Wooden Loch Borders 66 D5* small loch just S of Eckford. NT 7025
Woodfalls Wilts 9 H2 vil 7m/12km SE of Salisbury. SU 1920
Woodfield Oxon 28 B5* loc in N part of Bicester. SP 5823
Woodfield S'clyde 64 B6* N dist of Ayr. NS 3424
Woodfoot Cumbria 53 F3* loc 1km S of Crosby Ravensworth. NY 6213
Woodford Cornwall 6 B4 ham 5m/8km N of Bude. SS 2113
Woodford Devon 4 C5* E dist of Plymouth, 4m/6km from city centre. China clay works nearby. SX 5257
Woodford Devon 4 D5* ham 6m/9km NE of Kingsbridge. SX 7950
Woodford Glos 16 C2* ham 2m/3km S of Berkeley. ST 6995
Woodford Gtr Manchester 42 D3 vil 3m/5km E of Wilmslow. Airfield to E. SJ 8882
Woodford Northants 29 E1 vil 2m/3km SW of Thrapston. SP 9676
Woodford Som 7 H2* ham on edge of Exmoor National Park 3m/5km S of Watchet. ST 0638
Woodford Wilts 9 H1 par 4m/6km N of Salisbury, containing vils of **Upr, Middle, and Lr Woodford,** all on R Avon. SU 1236
Woodford Green London 20 A3 loc in borough of Redbridge 8m/13km NE of London Br. Loc of **S Woodford** to S, **Woodford Br** to E, and **Woodford Wells** to N. TQ 4091
Woodford Halse Northants 28 B2/B3 vil 6m/10km SW of Daventry. SP 5452
Woodgate Devon 7 H3* ham 1m N of Culmstock. ST 1015
Woodgate H & W 27 E1 ham 3m/5km S of Bromsgrove. SO 9666
Woodgate Norfolk 38 D3* loc 2m/3km S of Litcham. TF 8915
Woodgate Norfolk 39 E3 loc 3m/4km NE of E Dereham. TG 0216
Woodgate W Midlands 35 F6 loc in Birmingham 5m/9km SW of city centre. SO 9982
Woodgate W Sussex 11 F4* vil 3m/5km N of Bognor Regis. SU 9304
Wood Green Essex 20 B2* loc 2m/3km E of Waltham Abbey. TL 4100
Woodgreen Hants 9 H3 vil in R Avon valley on edge of New Forest, 3m/4km NE of Fordingbridge. SU 1717
Wood Green H & W 26 C1* loc 3m/4km S of Stourport. SO 8067
Wood Green London 19 G3 dist in borough of Haringey 6m/10km N of Charing Cross. To W is Alexandra Palace, TV relay stn. TQ 3090
Wood Green Norfolk 39 F5* loc 1m SE of Long Stratton. TM 2091
Woodhall Herts 19 F1* SE dist of Welwyn Garden City. TL 2411
Woodhall Lincs 45 F4* loc 3m/4km SW of Horncastle. TF 2167
Woodhall N Yorks 53 H5 ham 2m/3km E of Askrigg. SD 9790
Woodhall S'clyde 64 B2* loc 2km E of Port Glasgow. NS 3473
Woodhall W Yorks 48 D4* loc 3m/4km NE of Bradford. **Woodhall Hills** loc to N. SE 2034
Woodhall Loch D & G 58 C4, C5 narrow loch 1m N of Laurieston. NX 6667
Woodhall Spa Lincs 45 F5 19c spa tn 6m/9km SW of Horncastle. TF 1963
Woodham Bucks 28 C5* ham 8m/13km NW of Aylesbury. SP 7018
Woodham Durham 54 C2 loc 2km N of Newton Aycliffe. NZ 2826
Woodham Surrey 19 E5 urban loc 3m/5km S of Chertsey. TQ 0462
Woodham Ferrers Essex 20 D2 vil 5m/8km NE of Wickford. TQ 7999
Woodham Ferrers, South Essex 20 D2 suburban loc 5m/7km NE of Wickford. TQ 8097
Woodham Mortimer Essex 20 D2 vil 3m/4km SW of Maldon. TL 8104
Woodham Walter Essex 20 D1 vil 3m/4km W of Maldon. TL 8006
Woodhay, East Hants 17 H5 ham 2m/4km NW of Highclere. SU 4061
Wood Hayes W Midlands 35 F4* dist of Wolverhampton 3m/5km NE of tn centre. SJ 9402
Woodhay, West Berks 17 G5 ham 6m/9km SW of Newbury. SU 3963
Woodhead Derbys 43 F2 loc in valley of R Etherow beside **Woodhead Resr** 5m/8km NE of Glossop. SK 0999
Woodhead Grampian 83 F3 vil 8m/13km SE of Turriff, and 2m/3km E of Fyvie. NJ 7938
Woodhead Staffs 43 E6* loc adjoining Cheadle to N. SK 0144
Woodhenge Wilts. See Durrington.
Woodhey Merseyside 41 H3* urban loc 2m/3km S of Birkenhead. SJ 3285
Woodhey Green Ches 42 B5/B6* loc 2m/3km E of Croxley Green. SJ 5752
Woodhill Gtr Manchester 47 H6* loc in Bury 2km N of tn centre. SD 7912
Woodhill Salop 34 D5* loc 5m/9km S of Bridgnorth. SO 7384
Woodhill Som 8 B2* ham adjoining Stoke St Gregory. ST 3527
Wood Hill S Yorks 43 H2* loc in Sheffield 2m/3km NE of city centre. SK 3689
Woodhorn Nthmb 61 G3 vil 1m NW of Newbiggin-by-the-Sea. **Woodhorn Demesne** 1km S. NZ 3088
Woodhouse Humberside 44 C1* loc 3m/4km N of Epworth. SE 7808
Woodhouse Leics 36 B3* vil 3m/5km S of Loughborough. SK 5415
Woodhouse S Yorks 43 H3 dist of Sheffield 4m/7km E of city centre. **Woodhouse Mill** loc adjoining to NE. SK 4184
Woodhouse W Yorks 48 D5* loc 1km SE of Brighouse. SE 1521
Woodhouse W Yorks 49 E4* dist of Leeds 1m N of city centre. University complex on S side. SE 2835
Woodhouse W Yorks 49 F5* SE dist of Normanton. SE 3822
Woodhouse Down Avon 16 B3* loc 1m NE of Almondsbury. Site of Roman villa 1km NE. ST 6185
Woodhouse Eaves Leics 36 B3 vil 4m/6km S of Loughborough. SK 5314
Woodhouse Green Staffs 43 E5* loc 4m/6km E of Congleton. SJ 9162

Woodhouse, Nether Derbys 44 A4* loc to NW of Over Woodhouse and 2km NW of Bolsover. SK 4671
Woodhouses Cumbria 59 G6* loc 2km N of Thursby. NY 3252
Woodhouses Durham 54 B2* loc 2km SW of Bishop Auckland. NZ 1828
Woodhouses Gtr Manchester 42 D2* loc in Sale 2m/3km SW of tn centre. SJ 7690
Woodhouses Gtr Manchester 42 D1/43 E1* loc 1m SE of Failsworth. SD 9100
Woodhouses Staffs 35 G3* loc 2m/4km W of Lichfield. SK 0809
Woodhouses Staffs 35 G3 ham 1km E of Yoxall. SK 1518
Woodhurst Cambs 29 G1 vil 3m/5km N of St Ives. TL 3176
Woodingdean E Sussex 12 A6* NE dist of Brighton. TQ 3605
Woodington Hants 10 A3* loc 3m/4km W of Romsey. SU 3120
Woodkirk W Yorks 49 E5* ham 2m/3km S of Morley. SE 2725
Woodland Devon 4 D4 ham 2m/4km E of Ashburton. SX 7968
Woodland Durham 54 A2 vil 6m/10km N of Barnard Castle. NZ 0726
Woodland Kent 13 G3* ham 4m/7km N of Hythe. TR 1441
Woodland Bay S'clyde 56 B4* bay 2m/3km S of Girvan. NX 1795
Woodland Head Devon 7 F5* loc 4m/7km SW of Crediton. SX 7896
Woodlands Clwyd 41 H5* loc 2m/4km N of Wrexham. SJ 3153
Woodlands Dorset 9 G3 vil 3m/4km S of Cranborne. SU 0509
Woodlands Hants 10 A3 loc 3m/4km SW of Totton. SU 3211
Woodlands London 19 F4* loc in borough of Hounslow 10m/16km W of Charing Cross. TQ 1575
Woodlands Merseyside 42 A3* loc in Liverpool 7m/11km E of city centre. SJ 4487
Woodlands N Yorks 49 E3* dist of Harrogate 2km E of tn centre. SE 3254
Woodlands Som 16 C6 locs of **E** and **W Woodlands** 3m/4km S of Frome. ST 7844
Woodlands Som 7 H1* ham at foot of Quantock Hills 2m/3km NW of Nether Stowey. To SW on Quantocks, **Woodlands Hill** (NT). ST 1640
Woodlands S Yorks 44 A1* loc 4m/6km NW of Doncaster. SE 5307
Woodlands W Yorks 48 D5* loc in Halifax 1km N of tn centre. SE 0926
Woodlands Park Berks 18 D4* vil 2m/4km SW of Maidenhead. SU 8578
Woodlands St Mary Berks 17 G4 ham 4m/6km N of Hungerford. SU 3474
Woodland Street Som 8 D1* loc 3m/4km SE of Glastonbury. ST 5437
Woodlands Valley Derbys. See Woodland Vale.
Woodland Vale Derbys 43 F2 part of R Ashop valley immediately above Ladybower Resr. See also Peak Dist. Also known as Woodlands Valley. SK 1588
Wood Lane Salop 34 B2* loc 2m/3km SE of Ellesmere. SJ 4133
Woodlane Staffs 35 G2* loc 1m N of Yoxall. SK 1420
Wood Lane Staffs 42 D6* loc 4m/6km NW of Newcastle-under-Lyme. SJ 8150
Woodleigh Devon 4 D5 vil 3m/5km N of Kingsbridge. SX 7348
Woodlesford W Yorks 49 F5 loc on R Aire 5m/9km SE of Leeds. SE 3629
Woodley Berks 18 C4* suburb 3m/5km E of Reading. SU 7673
Woodley Gtr Manchester 43 E2 loc 2m/3km S of Hyde. SJ 9392
Wood Linkin Derbys 43 H6* loc 2m/4km SE of Ripley. SK 4348
Wood, Low Cumbria 52 D6 loc 2m/4km SW of Newby Br. SD 3483
Woodmancote Glos 16 C2* loc adjoining Dursley to E. ST 7697
Woodmancote Glos 17 E1 vil 4m/7km N of Cirencester. SP 0008
Woodmancote Glos 27 E5 vil 4m/6km NE of Cheltenham. SO 9727
Woodmancote W Sussex 10 D4 vil 2m/3km NE of Emsworth. SU 7707
Woodmancote W Sussex 11 H3 vil 2m/3km SE of Henfield. TQ 2314
Woodmancott Hants 10 C1 ham 4m/6km NE of Micheldever. SU 5642
Woodmansey Humberside 51 E4 vil 2m/3km SE of Beverley. TA 0537
Woodmansgreen W Sussex 11 E2* ham 3m/5km SE of Liphook. SU 8627
Woodmansterne Surrey 19 F5 suburban loc 2km E of Banstead. TQ 2759
Woodmanton Devon 5 F2* ham 3m/5km N of Exmouth. SY 0186
Woodmarsh Wilts 16 D5* loc 2m/3km S of Trowbridge. ST 8555
Woodmer End Beds 29 F4 loc adjoining Shillington to NW, 3m/5km SE of Clophill. TL 1234
Woodmill Staffs 35 G2* loc 2km N of Yoxall. SK 1320
Woodminton Wilts 9 G2* loc 1m SW of Bowerchalke. SU 0022
Woodnesborough Kent 13 H2 vil 2m/3km SE of Sandwich. TR 3056
Woodnewton Northants 37 E5 vil 4m/7km N of Oundle. TL 0394
Woodnook Lancs 48 A5* loc adjoining Accrington to S. SD 7527
Wood Norton Norfolk 39 H2 vil 6m/10km E of Fakenham. TG 0127
Woodperry Oxon 28 B6* loc 5m/7km NE of Oxford. Site of Roman bldg to E. SP 5710
Woodplumpton Lancs 47 F4 vil 4m/7km NW of Preston. SD 5034
Woodrising Norfolk 38 D4 ham 2m/4km NW of Hingham. Site of Roman bldg 1m W. TF 9803
Woodrow Dorset 9 E3* ham 4m/7km SW of Sturminster Newton. ST 7409
Woodrow H & W 27 E1* S dist of Redditch. SP 0565
Wood Row W Yorks 49 F5* loc just N of Methley. SE 3827
Woods Bank W Midlands 35 F4* loc 1km SW of Darlaston tn centre. SO 9796
Wood's Corner E Sussex 12 C5 ham 6m/9km NW of Battle. TQ 6619
Woodseats Derbys 43 E2* loc 3m/5km SE of Hyde. SJ 9992
Wood Seats S Yorks 43 G2* loc 1m N of Grenoside. SK 3395
Woods Eaves H & W 25 G3* loc 2m/3km NW of Willersley. SO 2849
Woodseaves Staffs 35 E2 vil 3m/5km SW of Eccleshall. SJ 7925
Woodsend Wilts 17 F4 loc 3m/5km W of Aldbourne. SU 2275
Woodsetton W Midlands 35 F5* loc in NW part of Dudley. SO 9393
Woodsetts S Yorks 44 A3 vil 3m/5km NW of Worksop. SK 5583
Woodsford Dorset 9 E5 vil on R Frome 5m/7km E of Dorchester. 1m S, loc of **Hr Woodsford.** SY 7690
Wood's Green E Sussex 12 C3* ham 1m N of Wadhurst. TQ 6433
Woodside Beds 29 E5* loc 2m/3km SW of Luton. TL 0718
Woodside Berks 18 D4 vil on W edge of Windsor Gt Park 2m/3km N of Ascot. SU 9371
Woodside Cumbria 52 A2* loc 2km SE of Maryport. NY 0434
Woodside Derbys 36 A1* loc 6m/9km NE of Derby. SK 3943
Woodside Durham 54 B2* loc 2m/3km W of Bishop Auckland. NZ 1729
Woodside Fife 73 F4* SE dist of Glenrothes. NO 2800
Woodside Grampian 77 H1 NW dist of Aberdeen, 2m/3km from city centre. NJ 9108
Woodside Hants 10 A5 loc 1m S of Lymington. SZ 3294
Woodside Herts 19 F1* loc 2m/3km SE of Hatfield. TL 2506
Woodside London 19 G5* loc in borough of Croydon 2m/3km NE of Croydon tn centre. TQ 3467
Woodside Salop 34 D4 dist of Telford to W of Madeley. SJ 6704
Woodside Tayside 73 E1 vil adjoining Burrelton to N, 2m/3km SW of Coupar Angus. NO 2037
Woodside W Midlands 35 F5* loc in Dudley 2m/3km SW of tn centre. SO 9288
Woodside Green Kent 21 E6* loc 2km NE of Lenham. TQ 9053
Woodside, West Cumbria 52 C1* loc 2km SW of Thursby. NY 3049
Woods Moor Gtr Manchester 42 D3* loc in Stockport 2km SE of tn centre. SJ 9087
Woodspring 118 admin dist of Avon.
Wood Stanway Glos 27 E4* loc 3m/5km NE of Winchcombe. SP 0631
Woodstock Dyfed 22 C3* loc 1km E of Woodstock Slop. SN 0225
Woodstock Oxon 27 H5/H6 old tn 8m/13km NW of Oxford. Glove mnfre. Oxford City and County Museum. See also Blenheim. SP 4416
Woodstock Slop Dyfed 22 C3 ham 8m/12km NE of Haverfordwest. SN 0225
Woodston Cambs 37 G4 S dist of Peterborough. TL 1897
Wood Street Norfolk 39 G3* ham 1km W of Catfield. TG 3722
Wood Street Surrey 18 D6 vil 3m/5km NW of Guildford. SU 9551
Woodthorpe Derbys 43 H4* loc 1m NW of Clay Cross. SK 3864
Woodthorpe Derbys 43 H4* loc 2km E of Staveley. SK 4574
Woodthorpe Leics 36 B3 loc 2m/3km S of Loughborough. SK 5417
Woodthorpe Lincs 45 H3* loc 3m/5km N of Alford. TF 4380
Woodthorpe S Yorks 43 H3* dist of Sheffield 3m/4km SE of city centre. SK 3985
Woodton Norfolk 39 G5 vil 4m/7km NW of Bungay. TM 2993
Wood Top Lancs 48 B5* loc 1km SW of Rawtenstall. SD 8022
Woodvale Merseyside 41 H1 loc in Southport 4m/7km SW of tn centre. Airfield to S. SD 3110
Woodville Derbys 35 H3 loc 1m E of Swadlincote. SK 3119
Woodwall Green Staffs 34 D2/35 E2* loc 3m/5km NW of Eccleshall. SJ 7831
Wood Walton Cambs 37 G6 vil 6m/9km N of Huntingdon. **Wood Walton Fen Nature Reserve** to NE. TL 2180
Woodwick Orkney 89 B6 loc on Mainland 6m/10km N of Finstown. Bay of **Wood Wick** to E. HY 3823
Woodworth Green Ches 42 B5* loc 1km SE of Bunbury. SJ 5757
Woodyates Dorset 9 G3 loc 3m/4km NE of Sixpenny Handley. SU 0219
Woody Bay Devon 7 E1 loc on N coast on edge of NT property around bay of same name, 3m/5km W of Lynton. SS 6749
Woofferton Salop 26 A1 vil 4m/6km S of Ludlow. SO 5268
Wookey Som 16 A6 vil 2m/3km W of Wells. ST 5145
Wookey Hole Som 16 A6 vil on S side of Mendip Hills 2m/3km NW of Wells. Limestone cave (floodlit) at N end of vil; source of R Axe. ST 5347
Wool Dorset 9 F5 vil on R Frome 5m/8km W of Wareham. SY 8486
Woolacombe Devon 6 C1 resort on Morte Bay 5m/7km SW of Ilfracombe. Extensive sands to S, largely NT. SS 4543
Woolage Green Kent 13 G2* ham 7m/11km NW of Dover. TR 2349
Woolage Village Kent 13 G2* loc 7m/11km NW of Dover. TR 2350
Woolaston Glos 16 B2 vil 4m/6km SW of Lydney. Locs of **High Woolaston** and **Woolaston Slade** to W. ST 5899
Woolavington Som 8 B1 vil 4m/7km NE of Bridgwater. ST 3441
Woolbeding W Sussex 11 E3 ham 2km NW of Midhurst. SU 8722
Woolcotts Som 7 G2* ham on Exmoor 1m E of Brompton Regis. SS 9631
Wooldale W Yorks 43 F1* loc 1m NE of Holmfirth. SE 1509
Wooler Nthmb 67 F5 small tn on Harthope Burn (or Wooler Water) 15m/24km NW of Alnwick. NT 9928
Wooler Water 67 F5 r rising as Harthope Burn on E side of the Cheviot, Nthmb, and flowing NE past Wooler and into R Till 2km NE thereof. NU 0030
Woolfall Heath Merseyside 42 A2* urban loc 2m/3km W of Prescot. SJ 4392
Woolfardisworthy Devon 6 C3 vil 3m/4km SE of Clovelly. Pronounced, and occasionally spelt, Woolsery. SS 3321
Woolfardisworthy Devon 7 F4 vil 5m/9km N of Crediton. SS 8208
Woolfold Gtr Manchester 47 H6* loc in Bury 2km NW of tn centre. SD 7811
Woolfords Cottages S'clyde 65 F3* loc 7m/11km N of Carnwath. NT 0057
Woolgarston Dorset 9 G6* ham 2m/3km E of Corfe Castle. 1km W, ham of **Lit Woolgarston.** SY 9881
Woolgreaves W Yorks 49 E6* loc in Wakefield 3m/4km S of city centre. SE 3416
Woolhampton Berks 18 B4 vil 6m/10km E of Newbury. Loc of **Upr Woolhampton** 1km N. SU 5766
Woolhope H & W 26 B4 vil 7m/11km SE of Hereford. SO 6135
Woolland Dorset 9 E3 vil 5m/7km S of Sturminster Newton. ST 7706
Woollard Avon 16 B5* vil 3m/5km S of Keynsham. ST 6364
Woollensbrook Herts 20 A1* loc 1m NW of Hoddesdon. TL 3609
Woolley Avon 16 C4 ham 3m/4km N of Bath. ST 7468
Woolley Cambs 29 F1 ham 6m/9km W of Huntingdon. TL 1574
Woolley Cornwall 6 B4* loc 7m/12km NE of Bude. SS 2516
Woolley Derbys 43 H5* loc on W side of Ogston Resr 2m/4km SW of Clay Cross. SK 3760
Woolley Wilts 16 D5* E dist of Bradford-on-Avon. **Woolley Green,** loc 1km NE. ST 8361
Woolley W Yorks 49 E6 vil 5m/8km S of Wakefield. SE 3213
Woolley Bridge Derbys 43 E2* loc on R Etherow adjoining Hollingworth to SE. SK 0195
Woolley Green Berks 18 D3* loc 3m/4km W of Maidenhead. SU 8580
Woolmere Green H & W 26 D2 vil 4m/7km E of Droitwich. SO 9662
Woolmer Green Herts 29 F6 vil 2m/3km NE of Welwyn. TL 2518
Woolpack Kent 13 E3 loc 1km S of Biddenden. TQ 8537
Woolpit Suffolk 30 D2 vil 5m/9km NW of Stowmarket. Hams of **Woolpit Green** and **Woolpit Heath** 1km S and 1m SE respectively. TL 9762
Woolscott Warwicks 28 A1* loc 5m/7km S of Rugby. SP 4967
Woolsgrove Devon 7 F5* loc 3m/5km NW of Crediton. SS 7902
Woolsington Tyne & Wear 61 G4* loc 5m/7km NW of Newcastle. Newcastle Airport to N. NZ 1969
Woolstaston Salop 34 B4 vil 3m/5km N of Church Stretton. SO 4598
Woolsthorpe Lincs 36 D1/D2 vil 5m/8km W of Grantham. SK 8333
Woolsthorpe Lincs 37 E2 vil adjoining Colsterworth to NW. **Woolsthorpe Manor** (NT), small early 17c hse, birthplace of Isaac Newton, 1642. SK 9224
Woolston Ches 42 C3* loc in E part of Warrington. SJ 6489
Woolston Devon 4 D6 loc 2m/3km SW of Kingsbridge. SX 7141
Woolston Hants 10 B4 SE dist of Southampton across R Itchen. SU 4310
Woolston Salop 34 A2 ham 4m/6km SE of Oswestry. SJ 3224
Woolston Salop 34 B5 ham 3m/5km N of Craven Arms. SO 4287
Woolstone Glos 26 D4 vil 5m/8km N of Cheltenham. SO 9630
Woolstone Oxon 17 G3 vil 7m/11km W of Wantage. Site of Roman villa to W. SU 2987
Woolstones Bucks 28 D4 area in E part of Milton Keynes, including vils of **Gt** and **Lit Woolstone.** SP 8739
Woolston Green Devon 4 D4 vil 3m/4km E of Buckfastleigh. SX 7766
Wooltack Point Dyfed 22 A5 headland on mainland at S end of St Brides Bay opp Midland Isle and Skomer. SM 7509
Woolton Merseyside 42 A3 dist of Liverpool 5m/9km SE of city centre. **Woolton Park** dist adjoining to N. SJ 4286
Woolton Hill Hants 17 H5* vil 2km NW of Highclere. SU 4261
Woolverstone Suffolk 31 F4 vil 4m/7km S of Ipswich. TM 1838
Woolverton Som 16 C5 vil 4m/6km N of Frome. ST 7954
Woolwich London 20 B4 dist on S bank of R Thames in borough of Greenwich 8m/14km E of Charing Cross. Ferry for vehicles to **N Woolwich,** loc on far bank in borough of Newham. **Woolwich Reach** is stretch of r W of ferry. TQ 4378
Woonton H & W 25 H3 vil 4m/7km SE of Kington. SO 3552
Wooperton Nthmb 67 G6 loc 6m/10km SE of Wooler. NU 0420
Woore Salop 34 D1 vil 6m/10km NE of Mkt Drayton. SJ 7342
Wootten Green Suffolk 31 F1* ham 1km S of Stradbroke. TM 2372
Wootton Beds 29 E3 vil 4m/7km SW of Bedford. TL 0045
Wootton Hants 10 A4 loc on S edge of New Forest 4m/7km SW of Brockenhurst. SZ 2498
Wootton Humberside 51 E6 vil 3m/5km SE of Barrow upon Humber. TA 0816
Wootton Isle of Wight 10 C5* loc 3m/5km W of Ryde. SZ 5492
Wootton Kent 13 G3 vil 6m/10km N of Folkestone. TR 2246
Wootton Northants 28 C2 S dist of Northampton. SP 7656
Wootton Oxon 17 H2 vil 3m/5km N of Abingdon. SP 4701
Wootton Oxon 27 H5 vil on R Glyme 2m/3km N of Woodstock. SP 4319
Wootton Salop 34 A2* loc 3m/5km E of Oswestry. SJ 3327

Wootton Salop 34 B6 ham 4m/7km NW of Ludlow. SO 4578
Wootton Staffs 35 E2 loc 1m S of Eccleshall. SJ 8227
Wootton Staffs 43 F6 vil 5m/8km W of Ashbourne. SK 1045
Wootton Bassett Wilts 17 E3 small tn 6m/9km W of Swindon. SU 0682
Wootton Bridge Isle of Wight 10 C5 loc 3m/5km W of Ryde. SZ 5492
Wootton Common Isle of Wight 10 C5* loc 3m/4km NE of Newport. SZ 5391
Wootton Courtenay Som 7 G1 vil on N slopes of Exmoor 3m/5km SW of Minehead. SS 9343
Wootton Fitzpaine Dorset 8 B4 vil 3m/4km NE of Lyme Regis. SY 3695
Wootton Glanville Dorset. Alternative name for Glanvilles Wootton, qv.
Wootton Green Beds 29 E3 ham 5m/8km SW of Bedford. SP 9943
Wootton, North Dorset 8 D3 vil 2m/3km SE of Sherborne. ST 6514
Wootton, North Norfolk 38 B2 vil 3m/5km NE of King's Lynn. TF 6424
Wootton, North Som 16 B6 vil 3m/4km SE of Wells. ST 5641
Wootton Rivers Wilts 17 F5 vil on Kennet and Avon Canal 3m/5km NE of Pewsey. SU 1963
Wootton St Lawrence Hants 18 B6 vil 3m/5km W of Basingstoke. SU 5953
Wootton, South Norfolk 38 B3 suburb 2m/3km NE of King's Lynn. TF 6422
Wootton, Upper Hants 18 B5 loc 4m/7km NW of Basingstoke. SU 5854
Wootton Wawen Warwicks 27 F2 vil 2m/3km S of Henley-in-Arden. SP 1563
Worbarrow Dorset 9 F6 loc at E end of **Worbarrow Bay** 6m/9km SW of Wareham. SY 8779
Worcester H & W 26 D2 cathedral city on R Severn 24m/38km SW of Birmingham. Makes gloves, porcelain, sauce. 18c guildhall. Cathedral mainly EE; Three Choirs Festival held here every third year (see also Gloucester, Hereford). SO 8555
Worcester and Birmingham Canal 26 D2-35 F5 canal connecting R Severn at Worcester with Birmingham, W Midlands. Flight of thirty locks at Tardebigge. The canal has five tunnels.
Worcester Park London 19 F5 loc in borough of Sutton 2m/3km NW of Sutton tn centre. TQ 2265
Wordsley W Midlands 35 E5 SW dist of Dudley. SO 8886
Wordwell Suffolk 30 C1 loc 5m/8km N of Bury St Edmunds. TL 8272
Worfe 34 D5 r rising near Shifnal, Salop, and flowing first S then W into R Severn 2m/3km N of Bridgnorth. SO 7295
Worfield Salop 34 D4 vil 3m/5km NE of Bridgnorth. SO 7595
Worgret Dorset 9 F5 loc 1m W of Wareham. SY 9087
Work, Bay of Orkney 89 B6* small bay on Mainland on S side of Hd of Work, opp Shapinsay and 3m/5km NE of Kirkwall. HY 4813
Workhouse Common Norfolk 39 G3* loc 4m/6km NE of Wroxham. TG 3420
Workhouse End Beds 29 E3* SE end of Renhold vil 4m/6km NE of Bedford. TL 1052
Workington Cumbria 52 A2 port on Solway Firth at mouth of R Derwent, 17m/27km W of Keswick. Industries include coal-mining, engineering, iron and steel. NX 9928
Worksop Notts 44 B3 tn on R Ryton at N end of The Dukeries 25m/40km N of Nottingham. Coal-mining, brick and glass mnfre. SK 5879
Worlaby Humberside 51 E6 vil 4m/7km N of Brigg. TA 0113
Worlaby Lincs 45 G4 loc 7m/11km S of Louth. TF 3476
Worldham, East Hants 10 D1 vil 2m/4km E of Alton. SU 7438
Worldham, West Hants 10 D2 vil 2m/3km SE of Alton. SU 7437
World's End Berks 18 A4 ham 6m/9km N of Newbury. SU 4876
World's End Bucks 18 D1* loc 1m NW of Wendover. SP 8509
World's End Hants 10 C4 ham 2m/3km SW of Hambledon. SU 6312
World's End London 19 G2* loc in borough of Enfield 1m W of Enfield tn centre and 10m/16km N of Charing Cross. TQ 3096
Worlds End W Midlands 35 G6* dist of Solihull 2km NW of tn centre. SP 1480
World's End W Sussex 11 H3 NE dist of Burgess Hill. TQ 3219
Worle Avon 15 H5 E suburb of Weston-super-Mare. ST 3562
Worlebury Avon 15 H5* NE suburb of Weston-super-Mare. To W, **Worlebury Hill,** wooded ridge to N of tn. ST 3362
Worleston Ches 42 C5 ham 3m/5km W of Crewe. SJ 6556
Worlingham Suffolk 39 H5 vil 2m/3km E of Beccles. TM 4489
Worlington Suffolk 38 B6 vil 2km SW of Mildenhall. TL 6973
Worlington, East Devon 7 F4 ham 6m/9km E of Chulmleigh. SS 7713
Worlington, West Devon 7 F4 ham 5m/8km E of Chulmleigh. SS 7713
Worlingworth Suffolk 31 F2 vil 5m/8km NW of Framlingham. TM 2368
Wormald Green N Yorks 49 E2 ham 4m/7km S of Ripon. SE 3064
Wormbridge H & W 26 A4 vil 3m/5km NE of Pontrilas. SO 4230
Wormegay Norfolk 38 B3 vil 6m/10km SE of King's Lynn. Remains of motte and bailey cas. TF 6611
Wormelow Tump H & W 26 A4 ham 6m/10km S of Hereford. SO 4930
Wormhill Derbys 43 F4 vil 4m/7km E of Buxton. SK 1274
Wormhill H & W 26 A4* loc 5m/8km W of Hereford. SO 4339
Wormingford Essex 30 D4 vil 6m/10km NW of Colchester. TL 9331
Worminghall Bucks 18 B1 vil 5m/8km NW of Thame. SP 6408
Wormington Glos 27 E4 vil 4m/6km W of Broadway. SP 0436
Wormit Fife 73 G2 loc on S side of Firth of Tay 2m/3km SW of Newport-on-Tay. **Wormit Bay** to W. NO 3926
Wormleighton Warwicks 27 H2 vil 8m/13km N of Banbury. Remains of 16c manor hse. Resr 2km S. SP 4453
Wormley Herts 20 A1 suburb 2m/3km N of Cheshunt. TL 3605
Wormley Surrey 11 F2 vil 3m/4km S of Milford. SU 9438
Wormley Hill S Yorks 49 H6* loc 2m/3km N of Fishlake. SE 6616
Worms Head (Pen Pyrod) W Glam 23 F6 headland (NT) at W extremity of Gower peninsula consisting of two connected rock ridges accessible from mainland at low tide. Blow-hole on outer ridge spouts tall column of water in rough weather. SS 3887
Wormshill Kent 21 E5 vil 3m/5km N of Harrietsham. TQ 8857
Wormsley H & W 26 A3 vil 7m/12km NW of Hereford. SO 4247
Wormwood Scrubs London 19 F3* large open space in borough of Hammersmith 5m/8km W of Charing Cross. Prison and hospital on S side. TQ 2281
Worplesdon Surrey 18 D6 vil 3m/5km NW of Guildford. SU 9753
Worrall S Yorks 43 G2* vil 1m S of Oughtibridge. SK 3092
Worsall, High N Yorks 54 C4 loc 3m/5km SW of Yarm. NZ 3809
Worsall, Low N Yorks 54 C4 ham 3m/4km SW of Yarm. NZ 3909
Worsbrough S Yorks 43 H1 coal-mining loc adjoining Barnsley to S. Includes locs of **Worsbrough Br** and **Worsbrough Dale;** also **Worsbrough Resr.** SE 3503
Worsley Gtr Manchester 42 C2 tn 6m/10km W of Manchester. Coal-mining, textiles, engineering. Bridgewater Canal begun here by Brindley in 1759. SD 7400
Worsley Mesnes Gtr Manchester 42 B1* loc in Wigan 2km SW of tn centre. SD 5703
Worstead Norfolk 39 G2 vil 3m/5km SE of N Walsham. TG 3026
Worsthorne Lancs 48 B5 vil 3m/5km E of Burnley. SD 8732
Worston Devon 4 C5* ham 2km NE of Yealmpton. SX 5952
Worston Lancs 48 A4 ham 2m/3km E of Clitheroe. SD 7642
Worth Kent 13 H2 vil 2km S of Sandwich. Site of Roman temple to S. TR 3356
Worth Som 16 A6* loc 3m/4km W of Wells. ST 5045
Worth W Sussex 11 H2 ham 2m/3km E of Crawley. To SE, Worth Abbey, Roman Catholic school for boys. TQ 3036
Worth 48 D4 r rising on borders of Lancs and W Yorks W of Haworth and flowing E to Mytholmes then NE through Keighley to R Aire. SE 0742
Wortham Suffolk 31 E1 vil 3m/4km SW of Diss. TM 0877
Worthen Salop 34 A4 vil 7m/11km E of Welshpool. SJ 3204
Worthenbury Clwyd 42 A6 vil 4m/6km NE of Overton. SJ 4246
Worthenbury Brook 42 A6* stream flowing N through vil of Worthenbury, Clwyd, and into R Dee 2m/3km N of the vil. SJ 4248
Worth Forest W Sussex 11 H2 wooded area in par of Worth to SE of Crawley. TQ 2934
Worthing Norfolk 39 E3 ham 4m/7km N of E Dereham. TF 9919
Worthing W Sussex 11 G4 residential tn and seaside resort 10m/17km W of Brighton. **W Worthing** is dist of Worthing 1m W of tn centre. TQ 1402
Worthington Leics 36 A2 vil 4m/7km NE of Ashby de la Zouch. SK 4020
Worth, Little Salop 34 D4* loc 3m/5km S of Wellington. SJ 6506
Worth Matravers Dorset 9 G6 vil near coast of Isle of Purbeck 4m/6km W of Swanage. SY 9777
Worthybrook Gwent 26 A6* loc 3m/5km W of Monmouth. SO 4711
Worting Hants 18 B6 loc 2m/4km W of Basingstoke. SU 6051
Wortley Glos 16 C2 ham 2km S of Wotton-under-Edge. ST 7691
Wortley S Yorks 43 G2 vil 2m/3km E of Stocksbridge. SK 3099
Wortley W Yorks 49 E5 dist of Leeds 2m/3km SW of city centre. SE 2732
Worton N Yorks 53 H5* ham in Wensleydale 2km E of Bainbridge. SD 9590
Worton Wilts 17 E5 vil 3m/5km SW of Devizes. 1m SE, loc of **Worton Common.** ST 9757
Worton, Nether Oxon 27 H4 ham 3m/4km W of Deddington. SP 4230
Worton, Over Oxon 27 H4 ham 3m/4km SW of Deddington. SP 4329
Wortwell Norfolk 39 F6 vil 2m/4km NE of Harleston. TM 2784
Wothersome W Yorks 49 F4 loc 4m/6km S of Wetherby. SE 3942
Wotherton Salop 34 A4* loc 1m W of Rorrington. SJ 2800
Wothorpe Cambs 37 E4* loc 1m S of Stamford. TF 0205
Wotter Devon 4 C4* loc in china clay dist 7m/11km NE of Plymouth. SX 5561
Wotton Glos 26 D5* E dist of Gloucester. SO 8418
Wotton Surrey 19 E6 ham 3m/5km W of Dorking. TQ 1247
Wotton-under-Edge Glos 16 C2 small Cotswold tn 9m/15km SW of Stroud. ST 7593
Wotton Underwood Bucks 28 B6 vil 6m/10km N of Thame. SP 6816
Woughton on the Green Bucks 28 D4* vil in Milton Keynes 2km SE of the centre. SP 8737
Wouldham Kent 20 D5 vil on E bank of R Medway 3m/5km SW of Rochester. **Wouldham Marshes** to N. TQ 7164
Wrabness Essex 31 F5 vil 5m/8km W of Harwich. TM 1831
Wrafton Devon 6 D2 vil just S of Braunton. SS 4935
Wragby Lincs 45 E3 small tn 7m/12km S of Mkt Rasen. Plastics factory and beehive works. TF 1378
Wragby W Yorks 49 F6 ham 4m/6km SW of Pontefract. SE 4117
Wramplingham Norfolk 39 E4 vil 3m/5km N of Wymondham. TG 1106
Wrangaton Devon 4 D5* vil on S edge of Dartmoor 2m/3km SW of S Brent. SX 6857
Wrangbrook W Yorks 49 G6* loc adjoining N Elmsall to E. SE 4913
Wrangle Lincs 45 G6 vil 7m/12km NE of Boston. **Wrangle Lowgate** loc adjoining to NE. TF 4251
Wrangway Som 7 H3 ham 2m/3km SW of Wellington. ST 1218
Wrantage Som 8 B2 vil 2m/3km SW of N Curry. ST 3022
Wratting, Great Suffolk 30 B3 vil 2m/3km NE of Haverhill. TL 6848
Wratting, Little Suffolk 30 B3 ham 2m/3km NE of Haverhill. TL 6947
Wratting, West Cambs 30 B3 vil 6m/10km NW of Haverhill. TL 6052
Wrawby Humberside 45 E1 vil 2m/3km NE of Brigg. TA 0108
Wraxall Avon 16 A4 vil 6m/10km W of Bristol. ST 4971
Wraxall Dorset 8 D4 two hamlets, **Hr** and **Lr Wraxall,** some 3m/4km NW of Maiden Newton. ST 5700
Wraxall Som 8 D1* vil 4m/6km NW of Castle Cary. 1km SE, loc of **Lr Wraxall.** ST 6036
Wraxall, North Wilts 16 C4 vil 6m/10km W of Chippenham. **Upr Wraxall** ham 1m W. Site of Roman villa 2km NE. ST 8175
Wraxall, South Wilts 16 D5 vil 3m/4km N of Bradford-on-Avon. ST 8364
Wray Lancs 47 F2 vil 7m/11km S of Kirkby Lonsdale. SD 6067
Wray, High Cumbria 52 D5 ham 2m/3km NE of Hawkshead. SD 3799
Wrayland Devon 4 D3* loc adjoining Lustleigh, 4m/6km SE of Moretonhampstead. SX 7881
Wray, Low Cumbria 52 D4* ham 2m/4km NE of Hawkshead. **Wray Castle** battlemented Victn mansion; grnds (NT) to W shore of Windermere. NY 3701
Wraysbury Berks 19 E4 vil among resrs 3m/4km NW of Staines. TQ 0074
Wrayton Lancs 47 F1* ham 1m S of Tunstall. SD 6172
Wrea Green Lancs 47 E5 vil 2m/3km W of Kirkham. SD 3931
Wreake 36 B3 r rising as R Eye 2km NE of Waltham on the Wolds, Leics, and flowing S then W to Melton Mowbray, whence it continues as R Wreake to its confluence with R Soar 5m/9km N of Leicester. SK 5912
Wreaks End Cumbria 52 C6* loc 1m SE of Broughton in Furness. SD 2286
Wreay Cumbria 52 D3* loc 2m/3km W of Pooley Br. NY 4423
Wreay Cumbria 60 A6 vil 5m/8km SE of Carlisle. Site of Roman signal stn 1m SE across R Petteril. NY 4348
Wrecclesham Surrey 11 E1 SW dist of Farnham. SU 8345
Wrecsam Welsh form of Wrexham, qv.
Wrekenton Tyne & Wear 61 G5* dist of Gateshead 3m/5km SE of tn centre. NZ 2759
Wrekin 118 admin dist of Salop.
Wrekin, The Salop 34 C3 craggy hill 3m/4km SW of Wellington; dominates surrounding landscape. Height 1334 ft or 407 metres. SJ 6208
Wrelton N Yorks 55 F6 vil 2m/4km NW of Pickering. SE 7686
Wrenbury Ches 42 B6 vil 5m/8km SW of Nantwich. SJ 5947
Wrench Green N Yorks 55 G6* loc 5m/8km W of Scarborough. SE 9689
Wreningham Norfolk 39 F5 vil 4m/6km SE of Wymondham. TM 1698
Wren's Egg D & G 57 D8* ancient stone circle (A.M.) 2m/3km SE of Port William. NX 3642
Wrentham Suffolk 31 H1 vil 4m/7km N of Southwold. Loc of **Wrentham West End** 2m/3km NW. TM 4982
Wrenthorpe W Yorks 49 E5 loc 2m/3km NW of Wakefield. SE 3122
Wrentnall Salop 34 B4 ham 7m/11km SW of Shrewsbury. SJ 4203
Wressle Humberside 44 D1* ham 2m/4km NW of Brigg. SE 9709
Wressle Humberside 50 C5 vil on R Derwent 3m/5km NW of Howden. SE 7031
Wrestlingworth Beds 29 F3 vil 3m/4km E of Potton. TL 2547
Wretham, East Norfolk 38 D5 vil 5m/9km NE of Thetford. TL 9190
Wretton Norfolk 38 B4 vil 2km W of Stoke Ferry. TL 6899
Wrexham (Wrecsam) Clwyd 42 A6 tn on R Gwenfro, tributary of R Clywedog, 11m/17km SW of Chester. Centre of a coal-mining area. Other industries include brewing, chemicals, tanning. **Wrexham Industrial Estate** 3m/5km E. SJ 3350
Wrexham Maelor 116, 117 admin dist of Clwyd.
Wribbenhall H & W 35 E6 loc on R Severn opp Bewdley, 3m/4km W of Kidderminster. SO 7975
Wrickton Salop 34 C5/D5* loc 7m/11km N of Cleobury Mortimer. SO 6485
Wrightington Bar Lancs 42 B1 loc 6m/10km NW of Wigan. SD 5313
Wright's Green Ches 42 C3* loc 3m/5km SE of Warrington tn centre. SJ 6384
Wright's Green Essex 30 A6* loc adjoining vil of Lit Hallingbury to S, 3m/5km S of Bishop's Stortford. TL 5017
Wrinehill Staffs 42 C6 vil 6m/10km W of Newcastle-under-Lyme. SJ 7547
Wringsdown Cornwall 6 C6* loc 2m/4km NW of Launceston. SX 3187
Wrington Avon 16 A5 vil 2m/4km E of Congresbury. ST 4762

Writhlington Avon 16 C5 coal-mining loc 1m E of Radstock. ST 7055
Writtle Essex 20 C1 suburb 2m/3km W of Chelmsford. TL 6706
Wrockwardine Salop 34 C3 vil 2m/3km W of Wellington. SJ 6212
Wroot Humberside 44 C1 vil 4m/7km NW of Haxey. SE 7103
Wrose W Yorks 48 D4* SE dist of Shipley. SE 1636
Wrotham Kent 20 C5 vil at foot of N Downs 8m/13km N of Tonbridge. TQ 6159
Wrotham Heath Kent 20 C5 2m/3km SE of Wrotham. TQ 6358
Wrottesley Staffs 35 E4* loc 4m/7km NW of Wolverhampton. Hall dates from 1696. SJ 8501
Wroughton Wilts 17 F3 vil 3m/4km S of Swindon. Suburban loc of **N Wroughton** adjoins to N. Airfield to S. SU 1480
Wroxall Isle of Wight 10 C6 vil 2m/3km N of Ventnor. SZ 5579
Wroxall Warwicks 27 F1 vil 6m/9km NW of Warwick. Remains of medieval abbey. SP 2271
Wroxeter Salop 34 C3 vil on R Severn 5m/9km SE of Shrewsbury, on site of Roman tn of *Viroconium*. Remains (A.M). SJ 5608
Wroxham Norfolk 39 G3 vil 7m/11km NE of Norwich. **Wroxham Broad,** broad or lake 1m E. TG 2917
Wroxton Oxon 27 H3 vil 3m/5km W of Banbury. Wroxton Abbey is early 17c hse. SP 4141
Wrynose Pass Cumbria 52 C4 steep pass between valleys of R Brathay and R Duddon traversed by rd from Skelwith Br to Seathwaite at height of 1281 ft or 390 metres. NY 2702
Wrythe, The London 19 F5 loc in borough of Sutton 2km NE of Sutton tn centre. TQ 2765
Wyaston Derbys 35 G1* ham 2km N of Yeaveley. SK 1842
Wyastone Leys H & W 26 A5* loc 2m/4km NE of Monmouth. SO 5315
Wyatt's Green Essex 20 C2* loc 4m/6km N of Brentwood. TQ 5999
Wyberton Lincs 37 H1 vil 2m/3km S of Boston. **Wyberton W End** loc 2m/3km NW. TF 3240
Wyboston Beds 29 F2 vil 3m/4km SW of St Neots. TL 1656
Wybourn S Yorks 43 H3* loc in Sheffield 1m E of city centre. SK 3687
Wybunbury Ches 42 C6 vil 4m/6km S of Crewe. SJ 6949
Wychavon 118 admin dist of H & W.
Wychbold H & W 26 D1 vil 2m/4km NE of Droitwich. SO 9265
Wych Cross E Sussex 12 B3 loc 2m/3km S of Forest Row. TQ 4231
Wyche, Lower H & W 26 C3* loc in Gt Malvern 1m S of tn centre. SO 7744
Wyche, Upper H & W 26 C3 loc on Malvern Hills 2km SW of Gt Malvern tn centre. SO 7643
Wych, High Herts 20 B1 vil 1m W of Sawbridgeworth. TL 4614
Wych, Higher Ches 34 B1 ham 3m/5km NW of Whitchurch. Loc of **Lr Wych** 1m NW. SJ 4943
Wychnor Staffs 35 G3* ham 1m NE of Alrewas across R Trent. **Wychnor Brs** loc 1km E. SK 1716
Wyck Hants 10 D1 ham 3m/4km E of Alton. SU 7539
Wycliffe Durham 54 A3 ham on S bank of R Tees 4m/7km E of Barnard Castle. NZ 1114
Wycoller Lancs 48 C4 ham 3m/5km E of Colne. Hall of 16c-17c. SD 9339
Wycombe 119 admin dist of Bucks.
Wycombe, High Bucks 18 D2 tn on R Wye on S side of Chiltern Hills 28m/45km NW of London. Various industries, esp furniture. Site of Roman villa 1km SE of tn centre. SU 8692
Wycombe Marsh Bucks 18 D2 E dist of High Wycombe. SU 8892
Wycombe, West Bucks 18 C2 loc in NW area of High Wycombe. W Wycombe Hse (NT), 18c, in park with lake. NT property also includes Church Hill, with Iron Age fort, and most of vil. Mausoleum and caves. SU 8294
Wyddfa, Yr Welsh form of Snowdon, qv.
Wyddgrug, Yr Welsh form of Mold, qv.
Wyddial Herts 29 G4 vil 2km NE of Buntingford. TL 3731
Wydon Som 7 G1* ham 2m/3km W of Minehead. SS 9347
Wydra N Yorks 48 D3* loc just E of Fewston. SE 1954
Wye Kent 13 F2 old mkt tn 4m/6km NE of Ashford. **Wye College** is agricultural school of London University. TR 0546
Wye (Gwy) 16 B3 r rising on Plynlimon in Cambrian Mts and flowing into R Severn at Beachley Pt near Chepstow. ST 5490
Wye 18 D3 r rising in Chiltern Hills NW of High Wycombe and flowing SE into R Thames at Bourne End, Bucks. SU 8986
Wye 43 G4 r rising near Buxton, Derbys, and flowing E through Miller's Dale, S through Monsal Dale, and SE through Bakewell into R Derwent at Rowsley. SK 2565
Wyesham Gwent 26 A6* loc 1km SE of Monmouth across R Wye. SO 5112
Wyfordby Leics 36 D3* ham 3m/4km E of Melton Mowbray. SK 7918
Wygyr 40 B2* r on Anglesey rising SW of Amlwch and flowing W then N into Cemaes Bay on N coast. SH 3793
Wyke Devon 7 F5* loc 2m/4km E of Crediton. SX 8799
Wyke Dorset 9 E2* vil adjoining Gillingham to W. ST 7926
Wyke Salop 34 D4* loc 2m/3km SW of Ironbridge. SJ 6402
Wyke Surrey 18 D6* vil 4m/6km E of Aldershot. SU 9251
Wyke W Yorks 48 D5 dist of Bradford 4m/6km S of city centre. **Lr Wyke** loc 1km S. SE 1526
Wyke Champflower Som 8 D1* ham 2km W of Bruton. ST 6634
Wyke Green Devon 8 B4* loc 2km S of Axminster. SY 2996
Wykeham N Yorks 50 D1* loc 3m/5km NE of Malton. SE 8175
Wykeham N Yorks 55 G6 vil 6m/9km SW of Scarborough. SE 9683
Wykeham Forest N Yorks 55 G6 wooded area, mainly conifers, 6m/9km W of Scarborough. SE 9488
Wyken Salop 34 D5 ham 3m/5km NE of Bridgnorth. SO 7695
Wyken W Midlands 36 A6* E dist of Coventry. SP 3680
Wyken Green W Midlands 36 A6* loc in Coventry 2m/4km NE of city centre. SP 3681
Wyke Regis Dorset 8 D6 SW dist of Weymouth. SY 6677
Wyke, The Salop 34 D4* loc 2km SW of Shifnal. SJ 7306
Wykey Salop 34 B2 ham 7m/11km SE of Oswestry. SJ 3924
Wykin Leics 36 A4 ham 2m/3km NW of Hinckley. SP 4095
Wylam Nthmb 61 F5 vil on N bank of R Tyne 8m/13km W of Newcastle. **W Wylam** loc 2km SW across R Tyne. NZ 1164
Wylde Green W Midlands 35 G5 S dist of Sutton Coldfield. SP 1294
Wylfa Head Gwynedd 40 B2* headland at W end of Cemaes Bay, on N coast of Anglesey. Power stn to SW. SH 3594
Wylye Wilts 9 G1 vil on r of same name 7m/11km NW of Wilton. R rises at Maiden Bradley, flows N towards Warminster, then SE into R Nadder at Wilton. SU 0037
Wymeswold Leics 36 B2 vil 5m/8km NE of Loughborough. SK 6023
Wymington Beds 28 D2 vil 2m/3km S of Rushden. Vil of **Lit Wymington** adjoins to N. SP 9564
Wymondham Leics 36 D3 vil 6m/10km E of Melton Mowbray. Site of Roman bldg W of ch. SK 8518
Wymondham Norfolk 39 E4 small tn 9m/14km SW of Norwich. Agricultural centre. TG 1001
Wymondley, Great Herts 29 F5 vil 2m/3km E of Hitchin. Site of Roman villa 1km NW. TL 2128
Wymondley, Little Herts 29 F5 vil 3m/4km SE of Hitchin. TL 2127
Wyndham Mid Glam 15 E2/E3* loc 4m/6km SW of Treorchy. SS 9391
Wyndhammere Cumbria 53 E6* lake 4m/7km N of Kirkby Lonsdale. SD 5985
Wyndham Park S Glam 15 F4* loc on S side of Peterston-super-Ely across R Ely. ST 0876
Wynd's Bridge Norfolk 38 B3* loc 1m NW of Wiggenhall St Mary the Virgin. TF 5715
Wynford Eagle Dorset 8 D4 ham 2m/3km SW of Maiden Newton. SY 5895
Wynn's Green H & W 26 B3* loc 6m/9km SW of Bromyard. SO 6047
Wyre Orkney 89 B6 small inhabited island, 2m/3km E to W and 1m N to S but tapering to a point at W end, lying off SE coast of Rousay across **Wyre Sound.** Remains of 12c cas - see Cobbie Row. Ruined chapel (A.M.), probably late 12c. HY 4426
Wyre 24 B2 r rising near Lledrod, Dyfed, and flowing W into Cardigan Bay less than 1m W of Llanrhystud. SN 5269
Wyre 47 E3 r rising on Forest of Bowland, Lancs, and flowing circuitously westwards into the Irish Sea at Fleetwood. SD 3448
Wyre 116, 117 admin dist of Lancs.
Wyre Fach 24 B1/B2* r rising on S side of Llangwyryfon, Dyfed, and running W into R Wyre at Llanrhystud. SN 5469
Wyre Forest 34 D6 heavily wooded area on borders of H & W and Salop to W of Bewdley. SO 7476
Wyre Piddle H & W 26 D3/27 E3 vil 2m/3km NE of Pershore. SO 9647
Wyrley, Great Staffs 35 F4 loc 2m/3km S of Cannock. **Lit Wyrley** ham 2km SE. SJ 9907
Wysall Notts 36 B2 vil 6m/10km NE of Loughborough. SK 6027
Wysg Welsh form of Usk (R), qv.
Wyson H & W 26 A1 loc adjoining vil of Brimfield to W, 4m/7km S of Ludlow. SO 5167
Wythall H & W 27 E1 vil 5m/8km NE of Redditch. SP 0774
Wytham Oxon 17 H1 vil 3m/5km NW of Oxford. SP 4708
Wythan 33 G4 r rising 3m/4km NE of Talerddig, Powys, and running N into R Gam 2m/3km S of Llangadfan. SH 9804
Wythburn Cumbria 52 C3/C4 loc on E shore of Thirlmere near S end of lake. NY 3213
Wytheford, Great Salop 34 C3* loc 2m/3km NW of High Ercall. **Lit Wytheford** loc 1km NW. SJ 5719
Wythenshawe Gtr Manchester 42 D2* residential dist of Manchester 5m/8km SW of city centre. SJ 8190
Wyther Park W Yorks 49 E4* loc in Leeds 2m/4km W of city centre. SE 2534
Wythop Mill Cumbria 52 B2* loc 4m/6km E of Cockermouth. NY 1729
Wyton Cambs 29 G1 vil 3m/4km E of Huntingdon. **Wyton Airfield** 2m/3km N. TL 2772
Wyton Humberside 51 F5 ham 3m/5km N of Hedon. TA 1733
Wyverstone Suffolk 31 E2 vil 6m/9km N of Stowmarket. Vil of **Wyverstone Street** 1km W. Loc of **Wyverstone Green** to S. TM 0467
Wyville Lincs 36 D2 loc 5m/7km SW of Grantham. SK 8829
Wyvis Forest H'land 85 E8 deer forest in Ross and Cromarty dist to W of Loch Glass. NH 4671

Y

Y, YR. For names beginning with the Welsh definite article, see under next word. This also applies to names beginning with the English definite article The, and to names beginning with the words North, South, East, West; Great, Little; Greater, Lesser; High, Low; Higher, Lower; Upper, Nether; Far, Near; Mid, Middle; Isle(s) of.
Yaddlethorpe Humberside 44 D1* vil 2m/4km S of Scunthorpe. SE 8807
Yafford Isle of Wight 10 B6* loc 1m SW of Shorwell. SZ 4481
Yafforth N Yorks 54 C5 vil 2m/3km W of Northallerton. SE 3494
Yair Hill Forest Borders 66 C5* state forest 3m/5km NW of Selkirk. NT 4333
Yalberton Devon 5 E5* loc 2m/3km SW of Paignton. SX 8658
Yalding Kent 20 C6 vil on R Beult, near its confluence with R Medway, 5m/8km SW of Maidstone. TQ 6950
Yanley Avon 16 B4* loc 3m/5km SW of Bristol. ST 5569
Yantlet Creek 21 E4 creek running into R Thames estuary on W side of Isle of Grain, Kent. TQ 8578
Yanwath Cumbria 53 E2 ham 2m/3km S of Penrith. NY 5127
Yanworth Glos 27 E6 vil 3m/4km W of Northleach. SP 0713
Yapham Humberside 50 C3 vil 2m/3km NW of Pocklington. SE 7852
Yapton W Sussex 11 F4 vil 3m/5km W of Littlehampton. SU 9703
Yar 10 A5/B5* r in Isle of Wight rising near Freshwater Bay on SW coast and flowing N into the Solent at Yarmouth. SZ 3589
Yar 10 C5 r on Isle of Wight rising at Niton near S coast and flowing N then E into Brading Harbour W of Bembridge. SZ 6489
Yarbridge Isle of Wight 10 C6* loc on R Yar adjoining Brading to S. SZ 6086
Yarburgh Lincs 45 G2 vil 4m/6km N of Louth. TF 3593
Yarcombe Devon 8 B3 vil at foot of steep hill 5m/8km W of Chard. ST 2408
Yardley W Midlands 35 G5* loc in Birmingham 4m/6km E of city centre. Loc of **S Yardley** 1m S. SP 1285
Yardley Gobion Northants 28 C3 vil 3m/5km NW of Stony Stratford. SP 7644
Yardley Hastings Northants 28 D2 vil 4m/6km NW of Olney. SP 8656
Yardley Wharf Northants 28 C3* loc on Grand Union Canal 4m/6km N of Stony Stratford. SP 7645
Yardley Wood W Midlands 35 G6* dist of Birmingham 5m/8km S of city centre. SP 0979
Yare 39 H4 r rising near Shipdham, Norfolk, and flowing E round S side of Norwich and into North Sea at Gorleston, Gt Yarmouth. TG 5303
Yarford Som 8 A2* ham 4m/6km NW of Taunton. ST 2029
Yarkhill H & W 26 B3 vil 6m/10km E of Hereford. SO 6042
Yarlet Staffs 35 E2* ham 1m E of Whitgreave. SJ 9128
Yarlington Som 8 D2 vil 4m/6km W of Wincanton. ST 6529
Yarm Cleveland 54 C3 tn in loop of R Tees 4m/7km S of Stockton-on-Tees. NZ 4112
Yarmouth Isle of Wight 10 B5 coastal resort 9m/14km W of Newport and 4m/7km SE of Lymington across Solent. Car ferry to Lymington. Cas (A.M.) built by Henry VIII for coastal defence. SZ 3589
Yarmouth, Great Norfolk 39 H4 port and resort at mouth of R Yare 18m/29km E of Norwich. Centre for herring fishing industry. Heliport 2m/3km N. Offshore anchorage known as **Y. Roads.** TG 5207
Yarnacott Devon 7 E2* loc 5m/8km E of Barnstaple. SS 6230
Yarnbury Castle Wilts 9 G1 prehistoric hill fort 3m/4km W of Winterbourne Stoke. SU 0340
Yarner Devon 4 D3* loc 5m/9km N of Ashburton. **Yarner Wd** to N is nature reserve. SX 7778
Yarnfield Staffs 35 E2 vil 3m/4km SW of Stone. SJ 8632
Yarnscombe Devon 6 D3 vil 5m/8km NE of Torrington. SS 5623
Yarnton Oxon 27 H6 vil 4m/7km NW of Oxford. SP 4712
Yarpole H & W 26 A2 vil 4m/6km NW of Leominster. SO 4764
Yarridge High Nthmb 60 D5/61 E5* loc on N side of racecourse 2m/3km SW of Hexham. NY 9162

Yarrow Borders 66 B5 loc on **Y. Water** 7m/11km W of Selkirk. **Y. Feus** is loc 2km SW, upstream. Y. Water is r issuing from St Mary's Loch and running E through Ettrick Forest to Ettrick Water 2m/3km SW of Selkirk. NT 3527
Yarrow Som 15 H6* loc 1km S of Mark and 4m/6km W of Wedmore. ST 3846
Yarrow Reservoir Lancs 47 G6* resr 1km N of Rivington. SD 6215
Yarso Orkney 89 B6* site of Neolithic communal burial-chamber (A.M.), on island of Rousay 2m/3km W of Brinyan. HY 4028
Yarsop H & W 26 A3 loc 8m/13km NW of Hereford. SO 4047
Yarty 8 B4 r rising N of Yarcombe in Devon and flowing S into R Axe 2km SW of Axminster. SY 2897
Yarwell Northants 37 F4 vil 2km S of Wansford. TL 0697
Yate Avon 16 C3 suburb adjoining Chipping Sodbury to W. ST 7182
Yateholme Reservoir W Yorks 43 F1* resr 3m/5km SW of Holmfirth. SE 1104
Yatehouse Green Ches 42 C4* loc 2m/3km N of Middlewich. SJ 7068
Yateley Hants 18 C5 residential loc 3m/5km W of Camberley. Blackbushe Airport 2km SW. SU 8160
Yatesbury Wilts 17 E4 vil 3m/4km NW of Avebury. SU 0671
Yattendon Berks 18 A4 vil 5m/9km W of Pangbourne. SU 5574
Yatton Avon 16 A5 vil 4m/7km S of Clevedon. ST 4365
Yatton H & W 26 B4* loc 5m/8km NE of Ross-on-Wye. SO 6330
Yatton H & W 26 A1* ham 6m/10km NW of Leominster. SO 4366
Yatton Keynell Wilts 16 D4 vil 4m/6km NW of Chippenham. ST 8676
Yatton, West Wilts 16 D4 loc 4m/7km W of Chippenham. ST 8575
Yaverland Isle of Wight 10 C6 vil 2km NE of Sandown. 17c manor hse. SZ 6185
Yawl Devon 8 B5* loc 2m/3km NW of Lyme Regis. SY 3194
Yawthorpe Lincs 44 D2* loc 2m/3km E of Corringham. SK 8992
Yaxham Norfolk 39 E4 vil 2m/3km SE of E Dereham. TG 0010
Yaxley Cambs 37 F5 vil 4m/7km S of Peterborough. TL 1892
Yaxley Suffolk 31 E1/F1 vil 2m/3km W of Eye. TM 1274
Yazor H & W 25 H3 vil 8m/13km NW of Hereford. SO 4046
Ydw 24 C5* r rising 2m/4km SE of Llandovery, Dyfed, and flowing SW into R Bran 2km E of Llangadog. SN 7229
Yeabridge Som 8 C3* ham 1m S of S Petherton. ST 4415
Yeading London 19 E3 loc in borough of Hillingdon 12m/19km W of Charing Cross. TQ 1181
Yeadon W Yorks 49 E4 tn 7m/11km NW of Leeds. Leeds and Bradford Airport to E. **Nether Yeadon** loc adjoining to SW. **Yeadon Tarn** small lake to E of tn centre. SE 2041
Yealand Conyers Lancs 47 F1 vil 2m/4km N of Carnforth. SD 5074
Yealand Redmayne Lancs 47 F1 vil 3m/5km N of Carnforth. SD 5075
Yealand Storrs Lancs 47 F1* loc 4m/6km N of Carnforth. SD 4976
Yealm 4 C5 r in Devon rising at Yealm Hd on Dartmoor and flowing SW through Yealmpton and into Wembury Bay. SX 5247
Yealmbridge Devon 4 C5* loc 1m E of Yealmpton. SX 5952
Yealmpton Devon 4 C5 vil on R Yealm 7m/11km E of Plymouth. SX 5751
Yearby Cleveland 55 E3 loc 3m/4km S of Redcar. NZ 6020
Yearsley N Yorks 50 B1 ham 5m/8km NE of Easingwold. SE 5874
Yeaton Salop 34 B3* ham 6m/9km NW of Shrewsbury. SJ 4319
Yeaveley Derbys 43 G6 vil 4m/7km S of Ashbourne. SK 1840
Yeavering Nthmb 67 F5* ham 4m/6km NW of Wooler under N slope of **Y. Bell**, hill crowned by ancient fort. **Old Y.** loc 1km W. NT 9330
Yedingham N Yorks 50 D1 vil on R Derwent 8m/13km NE of Malton. Scant remains of 12c priory to N. SE 8979
Yeldersley Derbys 43 G6 loc 3m/4km SE of Ashbourne. SK 2144
Yeldersley Hollies Derbys 43 G6* loc 4m/6km SE of Ashbourne. SK 2243
Yeldham, Great Essex 30 C4 vil 6m/10km NW of Halstead. TL 7638
Yeldham, Little Essex 30 C4* vil 4m/6km S of Clare. TL 7739
Yelford Oxon 17 G1 ham 3m/5km S of Witney. SP 3604
Yell Shetland 89 E6 one of the main islands of the Shetland Is., situated between Mainland and Unst, and separated from the former by **Y. Sound.** Vil of **Mid Yell** is on S side of **Mid Yell Voe,** large inlet on E coast of island opp Hascosay. HU 48
Yelland Devon 6 D2* loc 4m/7km W of Barnstaple on S side of Taw estuary. Power stn to W at water's edge. SS 4932
Yelling Cambs 29 G2 vil 6m/10km S of Huntingdon. TL 2562
Yelvertoft Northants 36 B6 vil 6m/10km E of Rugby. SP 5975
Yelverton Devon 4 B4 small tn on W edge of Dartmoor 5m/8km SE of Tavistock. SX 5267
Yelverton Norfolk 39 G4 vil 6m/9km SE of Norwich. TG 2902
Yenston Som 9 E2 vil 5m/8km S of Wincanton. ST 7121
Yeo 15 H4 r rising at Compton Martin, Avon, and flowing NW through Blagdon Lake or Yeo Resr, through Congresbury and into mouth of R Severn 4m/6km SW of Clevedon. ST 3666
Yeo 5 E2 r in Devon rising near Whiddon Down on N edge of Dartmoor and flowing generally E into R Exe below Cowley Br 2m/3km N of Exeter. SX 9095
Yeo 6 C3 r rising S of Buck's Cross, Devon and running E into R Torridge near Landcross. SS 4624
Yeo 6 D2 r rising on Berry Down, Devon, and flowing S in largely wooded valley to R Taw at Barnstaple. SS 5533
Yeo 7 E3 r rising on E Ansty Common and flowing W into R Mole 2km SE of S Molton, Devon. SS 7324
Yeo 7 E4 r in Devon rising on N foothills of Dartmoor near S Tawton and flowing generally N into R Taw 1km N of Nymet Rowland. SS 7109
Yeo 8 C2 r rising E of Sherborne in Dorset and flowing past Sherborne and Yeovil and into R Parrett S of Langport in Somerset. ST 4226
Yeoford Devon 7 F5 vil 4m/6km W of Crediton. SX 7898
Yeolmbridge Cornwall 6 C6 vil 2m/3km N of Launceston. SX 3187
Yeoman Hey Reservoir Gtr Manchester 43 E1* resr on Saddleworth Moor 6m/10km E of Oldham. SE 0204
Yeo Mill Som 7 F3* ham on R Yeo 5m/8km W of Dulverton. SS 8426
Yeo Reservoir Avon. See Blagdon Lake.
Yeovil Som 8 D3 21m/34km E of Taunton. Mnfg tn: light aircraft and helicopters, leather, gloves, agricultural goods. Airfield 1m w. ST 5515
Yeovil Marsh Som 8 D3 ham 2m/3km N of Yeovil. ST 5418
Yeovilton Som 8 D2 vil on S side of Yeovilton airfield 2m/3km E of Ilchester. ST 5423
Yerbeston Dyfed 22 C5 loc 7m/11km NW of Tenby. SN 0708
Yester House and **Castle** Lothian. See Gifford.
Yes Tor Devon 6 D6 tor on Dartmoor 3m/5km S of Okehampton. Height 2030 ft or 619 metres. See also High Willhays (Willhays, High). SX 5890
Yetholm Loch Borders 67 E5* small loch 1m W of Tn Yetholm. NT 8028
Yetholm Mains Borders 67 E5* loc 2km NE of Kirk Yetholm. NT 8329
Yetlington Nthmb 61 E1 loc 3m/5km SW of Whittingham. NT 0209
Yetminster Dorset 8 D3 vil 5m/7km SW of Sherborne. ST 5910
Yetson Devon 5 E5* loc 3m/4km S of Totnes. SX 8056
Yett S'clyde 65 E3* loc 3m/4km NE of Motherwell. NS 7759
Yettington Devon 5 F2 ham 3m/4km NW of Budleigh Salterton. SY 0585
Yetts of Muckhart Central 72 D4 vil 4m/6km NE of Dollar. NO 0001
Yew Green Warwicks 27 F1* loc 4m/6km NW of Warwick. SP 2267
Yews Green W Yorks 48 D5* loc 1m N of Queensbury. SE 0931
Yewtree Cross Kent 13 G3* loc in N part of vil of Lyminge 4m/7km N of Hythe. TR 1641
y-Ffrith Clwyd 41 F3* coastal loc 2km W of Prestatyn. SJ 0482
Yielden Beds 29 E1 vil 4m/6km E of Rushden. Remains of motte and bailey cas to E. TL 0167
Yieldingtree H & W 35 E6* loc 4m/7km E of Kidderminster. SO 8977
Yieldshields S'clyde 65 E4/F4* loc 2m/3km E of Carluke. NS 8750
Yiewsley London 19 E3 dist in borough of Hillingdon 3m/4km S of Uxbridge. TQ 0680
Yinstay Head Orkney 89 B6* headland on N coast of Mainland 2m/3km W of Rerwick Hd. HY 5110
Ynys Amlwch Welsh form of E Mouse. See Mouse, East.
Ynys Badrig Welsh form of Middle Mouse. See Mouse, Middle.
Ynys Bery Dyfed 22 A4 small island off S end of Ramsey I. SM 7022
Ynysboeth Mid Glam 15 F2 loc 3m/4km SE of Mountain Ash. ST 0796
Ynys Byr Welsh form of Caldy I., qv.
Ynys-ddu Dyfed 22 B2* small island lying off shore 2m/3km S of Strumble Hd. SM 8838
Ynysddu Gwent 15 G2 vil 3m/5km S of Blackwood. ST 1892
Ynys Deullyn Dyfed 22 B3 small island lying off shore 1km NW of Abercastle. SM 8434
Ynys Dewi Welsh form of Ramsey I., qv.
Ynys Dulas Gwynedd 40 C3 island lying 1km off NE coast of Anglesey. SH 5090
Ynys Enlli Welsh form of Bardsey I., qv.
Ynys Feirig Gwynedd 40 A4* rocky island off W coast of Anglesey, at S end of Cymyran Bay. SH 3073
Ynysforgan W Glam 23 H5* loc in Swansea 4m/7km NE of tn centre. SS 6799
Ynys Gaint Gwynedd 40 C4* island in Menai Strait on NE side of Menai Br, connected by causeways to main island of Anglesey. SH 5672
Ynys Graianog Gwynedd 32 C1* loc 3m/5km NW of Criccieth. SH 4642
Ynys Gwylan-fawr and **Ynys Gwylan-bach** Gwynedd 32 A2 two islands lying off E end of Aberdaron Bay. SH 1824
Ynys Gybi Welsh form of Holy I., Anglesey, qv.
Ynysgynwraidd Welsh form of Skenfrith, qv.
Ynyshir Mid Glam 15 E2 vil 3m/5km NW of Pontypridd. ST 0292
Ynyslas Dyfed 32 D5 loc 2m/3km N of Borth. SN 6092
Ynys-las Gwynedd 40 A4* small island in channel between Holy I. and main island of Anglesey, opp Llanfair-yn-neubwll. SH 2976
Ynys-Lochtyn Dyfed 23 E1 offshore island (NT) 1m N of Llangranog. SN 3155
Ynysmaerdy Mid Glam 15 E3/F3* loc 2km NW of Llantrisant. ST 0384
Ynys Meibion Gwynedd 40 A4* small island off W coast of Anglesey 2m/3km W of Aberffraw. SH 3268
Ynysmeicel Dyfed 22 B2* rock island on which Strumble Hd lighthouse stands. SM 8941
Ynys Melyn Dyfed 22 B2* island lying off shore 2m/3km S of Strumble Hd. SM 8838
Ynysmeudwy W Glam 14 C1 loc 2km NE of Pontardawe. SN 7305
Ynys Moelfre Gwynedd 40 C3* small island off E coast of Anglesey nearly 1km NE of Moelfre. SH 5186
Ynysoedd Gwylanod Gwynedd 40 A4* rocks lying off S coast of Holy I., Anglesey, marked by Rhoscolyn Beacon. SH 2674
Ynysoedd y Moelrhoniaidd Welsh form of The Skerries. See Skerries, The.
Ynysowen Welsh form of Merthyr Vale, qv.
Ynys Seiriol Welsh form of Puffin I., qv.
Ynys Tachwedd Dyfed 32 D5* loc 2m/3km N of Borth. SN 6093
Ynystawe W Glam 23 H5* loc in Swansea 5m/7km NE of tn centre. SN 6800
Ynys-wen Mid Glam 15 E2* loc in Rhondda valley 2m/3km NW of Rhondda. SS 9597
Ynyswen Powys 24 D6* loc 1km SW of Pen-y-cae. SN 8313
Ynysybwl Mid Glam 15 F2 vil 3m/5km N of Pontypridd. ST 0594
Ynys-y-fydlyn Gwynedd 40 A2/A3* island off coast of Anglesey 1m S of Carmel Hd. SH 2991
Ynysymwm W Glam 14 C2* loc 2km S of Pontardawe. SN 7102
Yockenthwaite N Yorks 48 B1* loc in Langstrothdale 2km W of Hubberholme. SD 9079
Yockleton Salop 34 B3 ham 6m/10km W of Shrewsbury. SJ 3910
Yokefleet Humberside 50 C5 vil on N bank of R Ouse 5m/8km SE of Howden. SE 8224
Yoker S'clyde 64 C2 loc in Glasgow 5m/8km NW of city centre. Car ferry to Renfrew across R Clyde. NS 5169
Yoke, West Kent 20 C5* loc adjoining New Ash Green to W, 2m/4km S of Longfield. TQ 6065
Yonderdown Devon 4 C5* vil 3m/5km NW of Ivybridge. SX 5959
Yondover Dorset 8 C5* loc just S of Loders and 2m/3km E of Bridport. SY 4993
Yons Nab N Yorks 55 H6* headland on North Sea coast 3m/5km NW of Filey. TA 0884
Yordas Cave N Yorks 47 G1* limestone cave in Kingsdale, 4m/6km N of Ingleton. SD 7079
Yore old name of R Ure, N Yorks. See Ure.
York Lancs 48 A4* loc adjoining Langho to S. SD 7033
York N Yorks 49 G3 ancient city and archiepiscopal see on R Ouse 22m/36km NE of Leeds. On site of Roman *Eboracum*. Medieval walls largely intact. Minster, cas; medieval guildhall. University at Heslington. Racecourse at Knavesmire. Industries include chocolate mnfre, scientific instruments, rly rolling stock. SE 6051
York Bar S Yorks 44 A1* loc 2m/3km NW of Doncaster. SE 5504
Yorkletts Kent 21 F5 vil 3m/4km SW of Whitstable. TR 0963
Yorkley Glos 16 B1 vil 3m/4km N of Lydney. Loc of **Y. Slade** to E. SO 6307
Yorkshire, North 117 large county of northern England, bounded by Humberside, S and W Yorkshire, Lancashire, Cumbria, Durham, Cleveland, and the North Sea. Apart from the wide plain around York, through which flow R Ouse and its tributaries, and the smaller Vale of Pickering, watered by the Derwent and its tributary the Rye, the county is dominated by two ranges of hills, the Pennines in the W and the Cleveland Hills in the NE. The plains are pastoral and agricultural, while the hills provide rough sheep-grazing. There is some industry round the principal tns, which include the cathedral and university city of York; Harrogate, Northallerton, the county tn, Scarborough, Selby, and Skipton. Round Selby a large coalfield was discovered in the early 1970s and is being developed. Principal rs are the Ouse and its tributaries the Derwent, Swale, Ure, Nidd and Wharfe, all draining into the Humber; the Esk, flowing into the North Sea at Whitby; and, in the W, the Ribble, passing out into Lancashire and the Irish Sea.
Yorkshire, South 117 metropolitan county of northern England, comprising the industrial and mining areas around Barnsley, Doncaster, Rotherham, and Sheffield. There is some wild moorland country to W and NW of Sheffield. The chief r is the Don.
Yorkshire, West 117 metropolitan county of northern England, comprising the industrial urban area around Bradford, Dewsbury, Halifax, Huddersfield, Keighley, Leeds, Pontefract, and Wakefield. The chief rs are the Aire and the Calder, while the Wharfe forms its N boundary below Addingham.
York Town Surrey 18 D5 W dist of Camberley. SU 8660
Yorton Salop 34 C2* loc 1m W of Clive. Loc of **Y. Heath** 1m S. SJ 5023
Youlgreave Derbys 43 G4 vil 3m/4km S of Bakewell. SK 2164
Youlstone, East Devon 6 B4 ham 7m/12km NE of Bude. SS 2715
Youlstone, West Cornwall 6 B4* ham 7m/11km NE of Bude. SS 2615

Youlthorpe Humberside 50 C3 ham 3m/5km E of Stamford Br. SE 7655
Youlton N Yorks 50 A2 ham 5m/7km SW of Easingwold. SE 4963
Young's End Essex 30 C5 ham 3m/4km SW of Braintree. TL 7319
Yox r in Suffolk. See Minsmere.
Yoxall Staffs 35 G3 vil 6m/10km N of Lichfield. SK 1418
Yoxford Suffolk 31 G2 vil 4m/6km N of Saxmundham. Loc of **Y. Lit Street** is NW part of vil. TM 3968
Ysbyty Cynfyn Dyfed 24 C1 loc 2m/3km NE of Devil's Br. SN 7579
Ysbyty Ifan Gwynedd 41 E6 vil on R Conwy 3m/4km SW of Pentrefoelas. SH 8448
Ysbyty Ystwyth Dyfed 24 C1 vil 4m/6km S of Devil's Br. SN 7371
Ysceifiog Clwyd 41 G4* vil 2m/3km SE of Caerwys. SJ 1571
Yscir 25 E5 r rising on Mynydd Epynt, Powys, as two streams, **Yscir Fawr** and **Yscir Fechan,** which follow parallel courses southwards to Pont-faen. The combined r then continues S into R Usk at Aberyscir. SO 0029
Ysgethin 32 D3 r in Gwynedd flowing W through Llyn Dulyn and Llyn Bodlyn into Cardigan Bay 5m/7km NW of Barmouth. SH 5721
Ysgubor-y-coed Dyfed 32 D5* loc between Furnace and Eglwysfach, 5m/8km SW of Machynlleth. SN 6895
Ysgyryd Fawr Welsh form of Skirrid Fawr, qv.
Yspitty Dyfed 23 G5* loc 3m/5km E of Llanelli. Chemical works. SS 5598
Ystalyfera W Glam 14 D1 vil 4m/6km NE of Pontardawe. SN 7608
Ystrad Mid Glam 15 E2 loc 1m E of Rhondda. SS 9895
Ystrad 41 G4/G5 r running NE by Nantglyn and the S side of Denbigh, Clwyd, to join R Clwyd 3m/4km E of Denbigh. SJ 0965
Ystrad Aeron Dyfed 24 B3 ham 6m/10km NW of Lampeter. SN 5256
Ystradfellte Powys 15 E1 ham 5m/8km NW of Hirwaun. **Ystradfellte Resr** 3m/4km N. SN 9213
Ystrad-fflur Welsh form of Strata Florida, qv.
Ystradgynlais Powys 14 D1 loc 2m/3km NE of Ystalyfera. SN 7810

Ystrad Meurig Dyfed 24 C2 ham 2m/3km W of Pontrhydfendigaid. SN 7067
Ystrad Mynach Mid Glam 15 F2 vil 5m/8km N of Caerphilly. ST 1494
Ystradowen S Glam 15 E3 vil 2m/4km N of Cowbridge. ST 0177
Ystumtuen Dyfed 24 C1* loc 1m N of Devil's Br. SN 7378
Ystwyth 24 B1 r rising E of Cwmystwyth, Dyfed, and flowing W by Cwmystwyth and Pontrhydygroes to the S side of Llanafan, then NW into Cardigan Bay with R Rheidol on S side of Aberystwyth. SN 5780
Ythan 83 H4 r in Grampian region rising at Wells of Ythan and running generally E to Methlick, thence SE to North Sea at Newburgh Bar 12m/19km N of Aberdeen. River is noted for fishing. NK 0023

Z

Zeal Monachorum Devon 7 E4 vil 8m/12km NW of Crediton. SS 7204
Zeals Wilts 9 E2 vil 2m/4km W of Mere. ST 7831
Zeal, South Devon 7 E5 vil on N edge of Dartmoor 4m/7km E of Okehampton. SX 6593
Zelah Cornwall 2 D3 vil 5m/7km N of Truro. SW 8151
Zennor Cornwall 2 A4 vil near coast 4m/7km W of St Ives. **Zennor Hd** (NT) is headland to N. **Zennor Quoit** is cromlech to SE. SW 4538
Zions Hill Dyfed 22 C3* loc 1km N of Spittal. SM 9723
Zone Point Cornwall 2 D5 headland at NE end of Falmouth Bay, 3m/5km SW of Porthscatho. SW 8530
Zouch Notts 36 B2* Vil. on R . Soar 3m/5km NW of Loughborough. SK 5023

Bartholomew

Road Atlas Britain

Contents
1:300 000 maps
Route planning maps
Town Plans
Index

Sommaire
Cartes au 1:300 000
Cartes de préparation d'itinéraires
Plan de villes
Index

Inhalt
Karten 1:300 000
Streckenplanungskarten
Stadtpläne
Index

Indices
Carte con scala 1:300 000
Carte programmazione tragitto
Piante delle città
Indice

Printed and Published in Scotland
Copyright © John Bartholomew & Son Ltd 1976
ISBN   0 85152 727 2
6323

1:300 000

3km to 10mm

| 0 | 1 | 2 | 3 | 4 | 5 | 6 | | 12 | | 18 | | 24 km |

10 miles to 2.1 inches

| 0 | 1 | 2 | 3 | 4 | 5 | | 10 | | 15 miles |

M11 Motorway / Autoroute / Autobahn / Autostrada	**B 1438** 'B' Road / Route secondaire 'B' / Straße Klasse 'B' / Strada secondaria	Principal Civil Airport / Aérodrome civil principal / Verkehrsflughafen / Aeroporto civile principale
25 Interchange / Echangeur / Anschlußstelle / Intercambio	**A 134 B 113** Single track road / Route à voie unique / Straße, einbahnig / Strada ad una carreggiata	LC Level Crossing · Railway (passenger) / Chemin de fer (passagers) / Eisenbahn (Personenverkehr) / Ferrovie (Passeggeri)
25 Limited Interchange / Echangeur limité / beschränkte Anschlußstelle / Intercambio limitato	Other Serviceable roads / Autres routes practicables / Nebenstraße / Altre strada utilizzabili	Canal / Canal / Kanal / Canale
Service Area / Zone de service / Tankstelle und Raststatte / Area di servizio / S.A.	2 Mileage (between circles) / Distance (entre cercles) / Entfernung in Meilen / (zwischen den Kreisen) / Distanza in miglia (tra i cerchi)	+ Church / Eglise / Kirche / Chiesa
Under Construction / En construction / im Bau / In costruzione	Track / Piste / Fahrweg / Strada non pavimentata	County boundary / Limite de comté / Grafschaftsgrenze / Confine di contea
Projected / Prévu / geplant / Progettato	Path / Chemin / Pfad / Sentiero	▲ 2450 ·167 Height (in feet) / Hauteur (en pieds) / Höhe / Altitudine (piedi)
Dual Carriageway / Route principale à voies séparées / Autostraße, zweibahnig / Doppia carreggiata	(F) Car ferry / Bac pour autos / Autofähre / Nave traghetto per automobili	75 Page Continuation / Continuation à la page / Anschlußseite / Pagina di continuazione
A 142 'A' Road / Route principale 'A' / Straße Klasse 'A' / Strada principale	Other ferries and sea routes / Autres bateaux de passage / et voies maritimes / andere Fähren und Seeverbindungen / Altri punti di traghetto e rotte	Certain built-up areas / Terrain bâti / bebaute Fläche / Agglomerati urbani

Feet
3000
2000
1000
500
100
Sea level
Below sea level
Feet

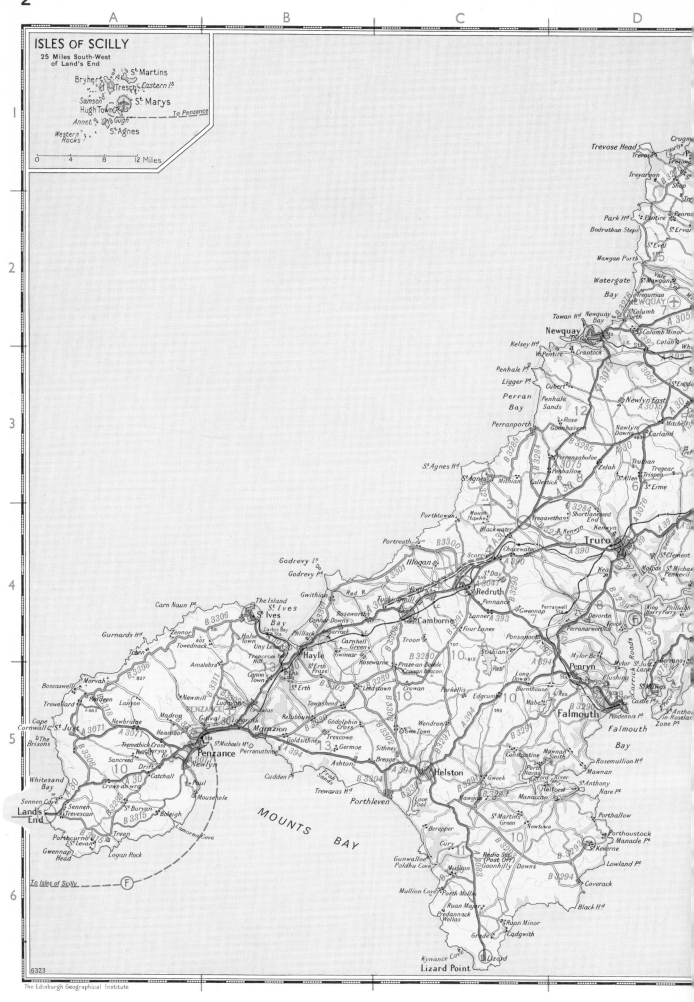

2

ISLES OF SCILLY
25 Miles South-West
of Land's End

St Martins
Bryher
Tresco
Eastern Is
Samson
Hugh Town
St Marys
Annet
Gugh
To Penzance
Western
Rocks
St Agnes

0   4   8   12 Miles

Trevose Head
Trevose
Crugmer
Harlyn
Trevone
Treyarnon
Shop
Tre
Park Hd
Pentire
Penros
St Erval
Bedruthan Steps
St Eval
Mawgan Porth
Vale
St Mawgan
Watergate
Tregurrian
Bay
NEWQUAY
Newquay
Towan Hd
Columb
Bay
Porth
Newquay
Columb Minor
Kelsey Hd
The Gannel
Colan
Wh
W Pentire
Crantock
Penhale Pt
Cubert
Newlyn East
Ligger Pt
Penhale
Perran
Sands
Bay
Rose
Newlyn
Downs
Goonhavern
Mitchel
Perranporth
Perranzabuloe
Carland
Penhallow
Zelah
Truthan
St Agnes Hd
Tregear
St Agnes
Penhallow
Trispen
St Allen
St Erme
Mithian
Callestick
Porthtowan
Mount
Hawke
Shortlanesend
Blackwater
Tregavethan
End
R Kenwyn
Portreath
Scorrier
Chacewater
R Kenwyn
Kenwyn
Truro
St Clement
Illogan
St Day
Mofods
St Michael
Godrevy Is
Redruth
Penkevil
Godrevy Pt
Boss
Kea
Red R
Pennance
Tuckingmill
Gwennap
King
The Island
Gwithian
Camborne
Perranwell
Harry Ferry
St Ives
Roseworthy
Sta
Devoran
St Ives
Connor Downs
Lanner
Bay
Carn Naun Pt
Phillack
Angarrack
Four Lanes
Restronguet
Perranarworthal
Carbis Bay
Gurnards Hd
Zennor
Halse
Troon
St Ives
Ponsanooth
Mylor Bc
Towednack
Town
Rosewarne
Mylor
Mylor
Trencrom Hill
Hayle
St Erth
Praze-an-Beeble
Sta
St Just
Treen
Amalebra
St Erth
Carnhell Green
Crowan Beacon
Rest
Flushing
Twinear
Long
St Mawes
Canon's
Sta
Downs
Town
Leedstown
Crowan
Burnthouse
Res
Castle Pt
Newmill
Ludgvan
Towednack
Godolphin
Mabe
St Just
Boscaswell
Crowlas
Cross
Edgcumbe
in-Roseland
Morvah
Lanyon
Relubbus
Zone Pt
Pendeen
PENZANCE
Penryn
Madron
Gulval
Longrock
Wendron
Falmouth
Trewellard
Newbridge
Crom Town
Heamoor
Marazion
Pendennis Pt
Cape
St Just
Towshend
Cornwall
Newlyn
St Michaels Mt
Germoe
Falmouth
The Brisons
Tremethick Cross
Goldsithney
Trescowe
Constantine
Bay
Sancreed
Perranuthnoe
Sithney
Mawnan
Drift
Ashton
Breage
Gweek
Smith
Catchall
Crows-an-wra
Paul
Helston
Rosemullion Hd
St Buryan
Cudden Pt
Porth
Mawnan
Mousehole
Trewavas Hd
Navas
Whitesand
Boleigh
Helford
Bay
Treen
Porthleven
Looe
Helford
St Anthony
Sennen Cove
Pool
Mawgan
Manaccan
Nare Pt
Sennen
Camornal Cove
St Martin's
Trevescan
Green
Porthallow
Lands
Porthcurno
Mounts Bay
Newtown
End
St Levan
Logan Rock
Berepper
Porthoustock
Gwennap Head
Manacle Pt
Gunwalloe
Radio Sta
St Keverne
To Isles of Scilly
Poldhu Cove
Post Off
Goonhilly Downs
Coverack
Mullion Cove
Mullion
Port Mellin
Ruan Major
Lowland Pt
Predannack
Ruan Minor
Wollas
Cadgwith
Grade
Black Hd
Kynance Cove
Lizard
Lizard Point

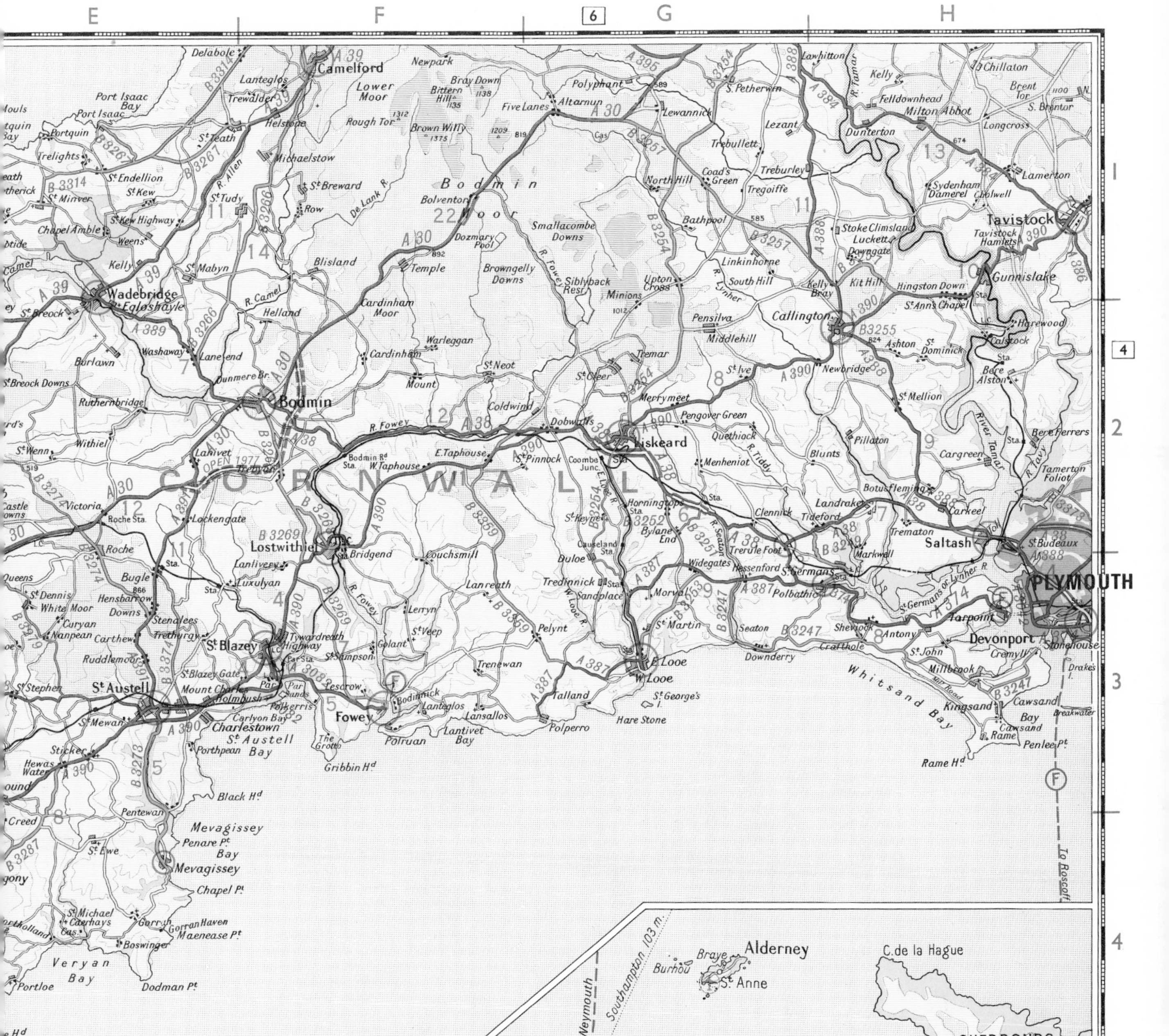

CORNWALL

Camelford
Bodmin
Bodmin Moor
Wadebridge
Eglosshayle
Lostwithiel
St Austell
Charlestown
Mevagissey
St Blazey
Fowey
Polruan
Polperro
W. Looe
E. Looe
Liskeard
Callington
Saltash
PLYMOUTH
Devonport
Tavistock
Gunnislake
Whitsand Bay
Rame Hd
Penlee Pt

CHANNEL ISLANDS

Alderney
St Anne
Burhou
Braye
GUERNSEY
St Sampson
St Peter Port
King's Mills
St Martin
Torteval
Herm
Jethou
Sark
St Martin's Pt
JERSEY
St Helier
St Aubin
Grosnez Pt
St Ouen's B.
St Mary
Trinity
St John
Rozel
St Martin
Gorey
Corbière
St Aubin's B.

C. de la Hague
CHERBOURG
FRANCE
Diélette
les Pieux
Carteret
Ecrehos
Dielette

To Weymouth
Southampton 103 m.
To Roscoff

0 4 8 12 Miles

4

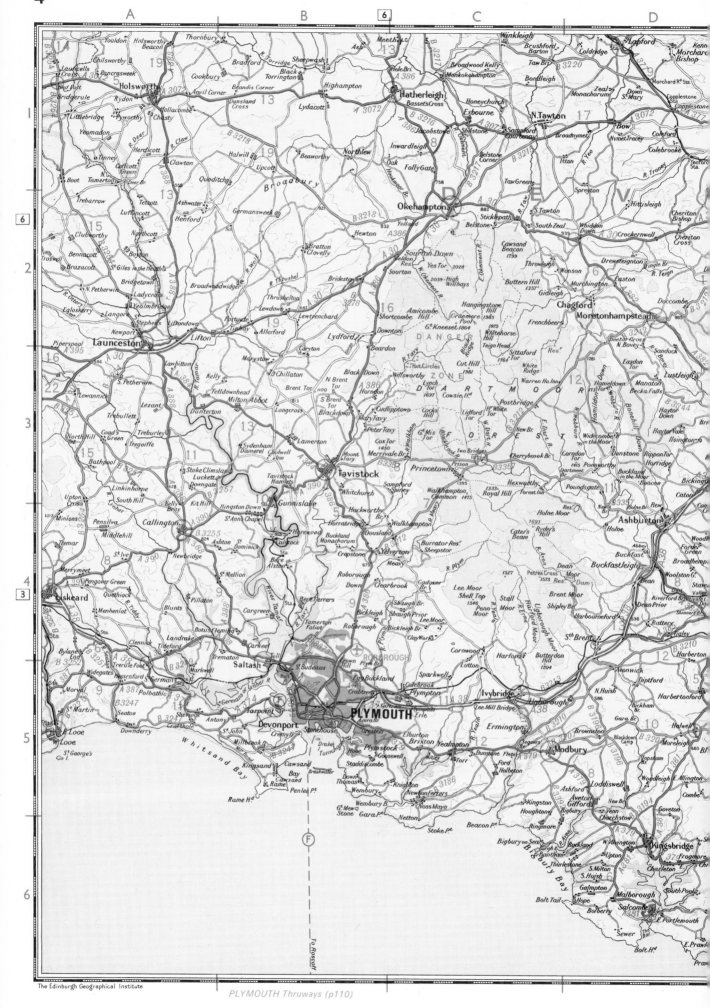

PLYMOUTH Thruways (p110)

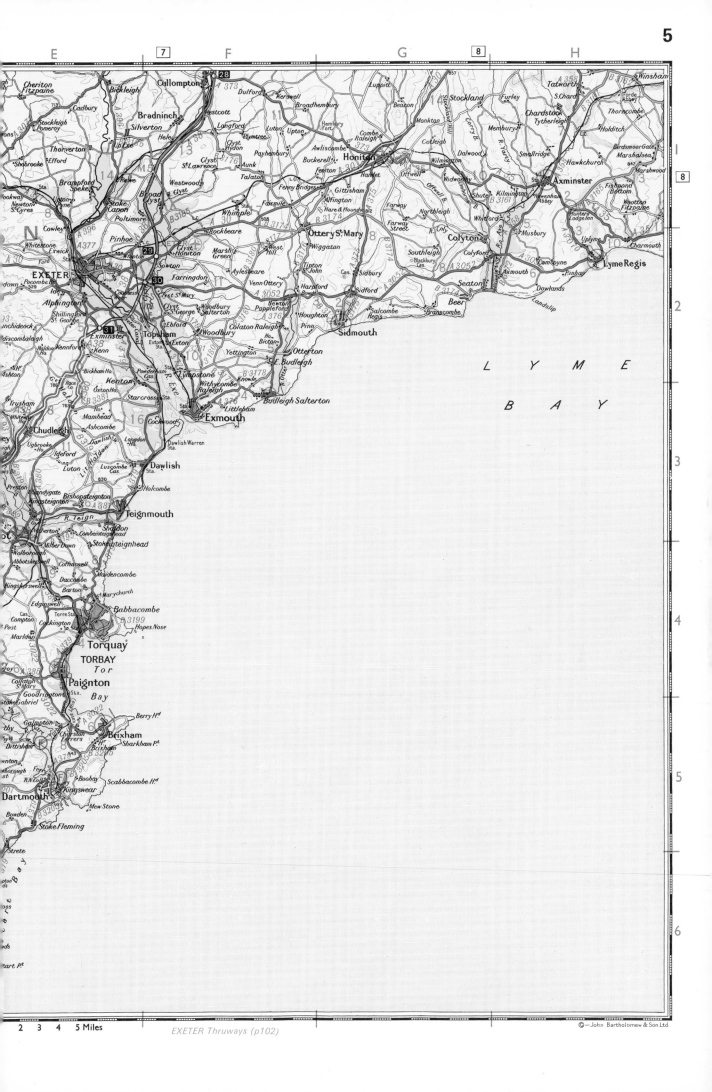

EXETER Thruways (p102)

© — John Bartholomew & Son Ltd.

A   B   C   D

1

North West Pt.
Lundy
Rat Island
Shutter Pt.

Widmouth Hd.   Combe Mart.
Ilfracombe   Bay
Bull Pt.   Lee B.   Hele   Berrynarbor
Morte Pt.   Mortehoe   Lee   Sterridge
Woolacombe   W. Down   Bittadon
Morte   Bay   10
Baggy Pt.   Croyde   Georgeham   Knowle   Milltown   Muddif...
Saunton   Marwood   Kingsheam...
Saunton Sands   Braunton   Prixford...
13   Wrafton   Ashford   Pilton
Barnstaple Burrows   Bickington   Ba
River Taw   Fremington   9
The Neck   Instow   Tawstock
Appledore   St. John's Chapel
Westward Ho!   Westleigh   Eastleigh   Newton Tracey
Northam   Loveacott   Alverdiscott   Yarnscombe   Langridge
Bideford   East-the-Water   Landcross   Huntshaw   Sherwo...
Ford   Fairy Cross   Weare Giffard   High Bullen   St. Giles in the Wood
Clovelly   Horns Cross   Goldworthy   R. Yeo   Gt. Torrington   Kingscott
Hartland Pt.   Clovelly Bay   Buck's Mills   Stevenstone Ho.
Damehole Pt.   Gallantry Bower   Parkham   Monkleigh   Taddiport   Little Torrington   Beaford
Hartland Quay   Clovelly Cross   Cranford   Buckland Brewer   Priory   13
Stoke   Buck's Cross   Almiston Cross   Frithelstock   Langtree
Milford   Eddistone   Woolfardisworthy (Woolsery)   Melbury   Frithelstock Stone   Stibb Cross   Peters Marland   Merton
Elmscott   Tosberry   Ashmansworthy   E. Putford   Bulkworthy   Newton St. Petrock   Woollaton   Heanton Sackville
Welcombe   Meddon   R. Torridge   W. Putford   17   Huish
Morwenstow   14   E. Youlstone   Brendon   Perrockstow   North Town   Meeth
Higher Sharpnose Pt.   Shop   Bradworthy   R. Tamar   Milton Damerel   Shebbear   Buckland Filleigh   Ask
Lower Sharpnose Pt.   Woodford   Suttcombe   Tamar Lake   R. Waldon   Bradford   R. Torridge   Sheepwash   Hele Bri.
Coombe   Kilkhampton   Youldonmoor Cross   Thornbury   Cookbury   Black Torrington   Highampton   Hatherle
Stibb   14   Youldon   Holsworthy Beacon   Beandis Corner   13   Lydacott   Bassets...
Poughill   Grimscott   Chilsworthy   Anvil Corner   Dunsland Cross   A 3072
Bude   Stratton   Tauncells Cross   Pancrasweek   Holsworthy   Bradford   Halwill   Beaworthy   Northlew   Inwardleigh   Okeham
Bude Bay   Launcells   Red Post   Rydon   Hollacombe   Chasty   Quoditch   Ashwater   Germansweek   Upcott   Oak   Folly Ga
Helebridge   Bude Aqueduct   Bridgerule   Pyworthy   R. Deer   Broadbury   Hewton   Bratton Clovelly   Rest...
Marhamchurch   Littlebridge   Yeomadon   Herdicott   R. Claw   Ashwater   Thrushelton   16
Budd's Titson   Week Orchard   R. Bude   Tinney   Cofcott Green   Clawton   Henford   Sourton   Shortcombe Hill
Poundstock   Whitstone   Boot   N. Tamerton   Deer Br.   Tetcott   13   Lewdown   Lydford
Crackington Haven   Week St. Mary   Trebarrow   Luffincott   Northcott   Lewtrenchard   Amicot...
St. Genneys   512   Northcott   Broadwoodwidger   Bridestow   19   Downton
Cambeak   Wainhouse Corner   15   Maxworthy   Boyton   R. Wolf   Portgate   Marystow   Black Down   Willsworthy
Crackington   Jacobstow   Caudworthy   Clubworthy   St. Giles in the Heath   Lewannick   Lifton   Chillaton   Hut Cu...
Tresparrett Posts   Higher Langdon   Bennacott   Bridgetown   Broadwoodwidger   Tinhay   Allerford   Horndon
18   Canworthy Water   Brazacott   N. Petherwin   Langore   Coryton   Beardon
Boscastle   Tresparrett   Warbstow   Troswell   Tremaine   Bridgetown   Lewannick   Felldownhead   S. Brenton
Lesnewth   Otterham   Trossell   R. Ottery   Ladycross   Newport   Lifton   Kelly   Milton Abbot
Tintagel Hd.   Trevalga   Penwenham   Egloskerry   B 3254   Yealmbridge   Brent Tor   Brent Tor
Tintagel   Hallworthy   Tremaine   Langore   Stephens   Liddondown   Lanhitton
Davidstow   R. Inny   Downhead   Piperspool   Launceston   S. Petherwin
Trewarmett   Tremail   St. Clether   Laneast   Newport   Felldownhead
Rockhead   1002   16   Bray Down   1138   Polyphant   22   S. Petherwin
Delabole   Newpark   Bittern Hills   Altarnun   Lewannick   13
Camelford   Lower Moor   Five Lanes   11
Lanteglos   Rough Tor   1312
Trewidler   Helspore   Rough Tor

The Edinburgh Geographical Institute

BARNSTAPLE OR BIDEFORD BAY

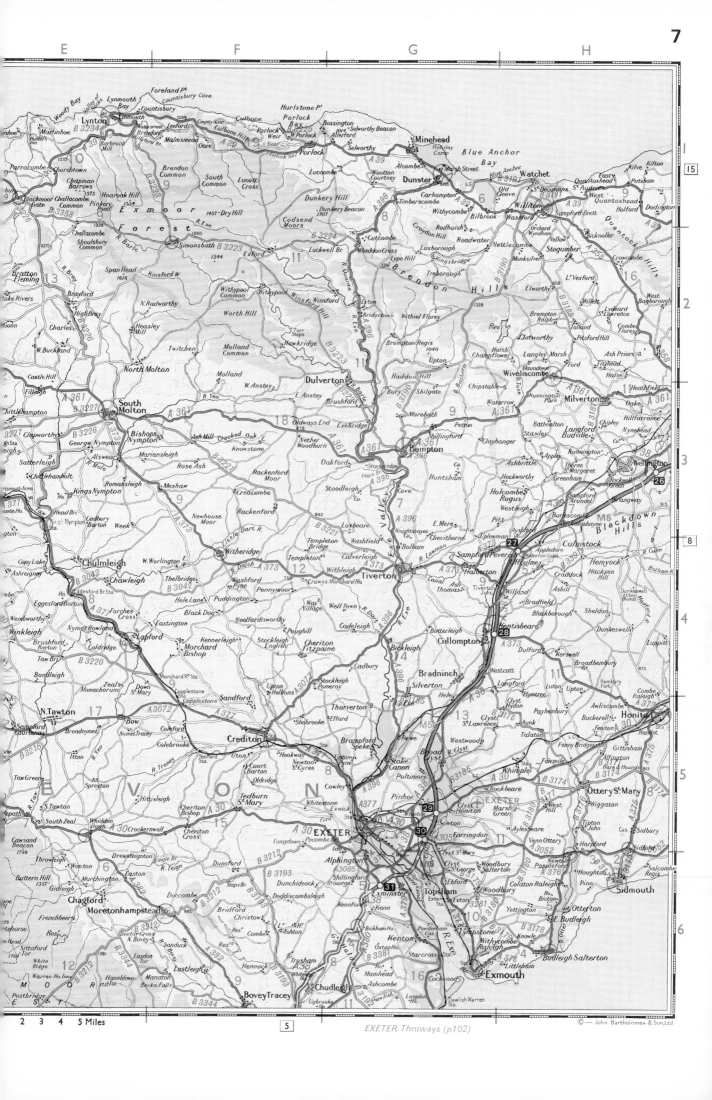

EXETER Thruways (p102)

© — John Bartholomew & Son, Ltd.

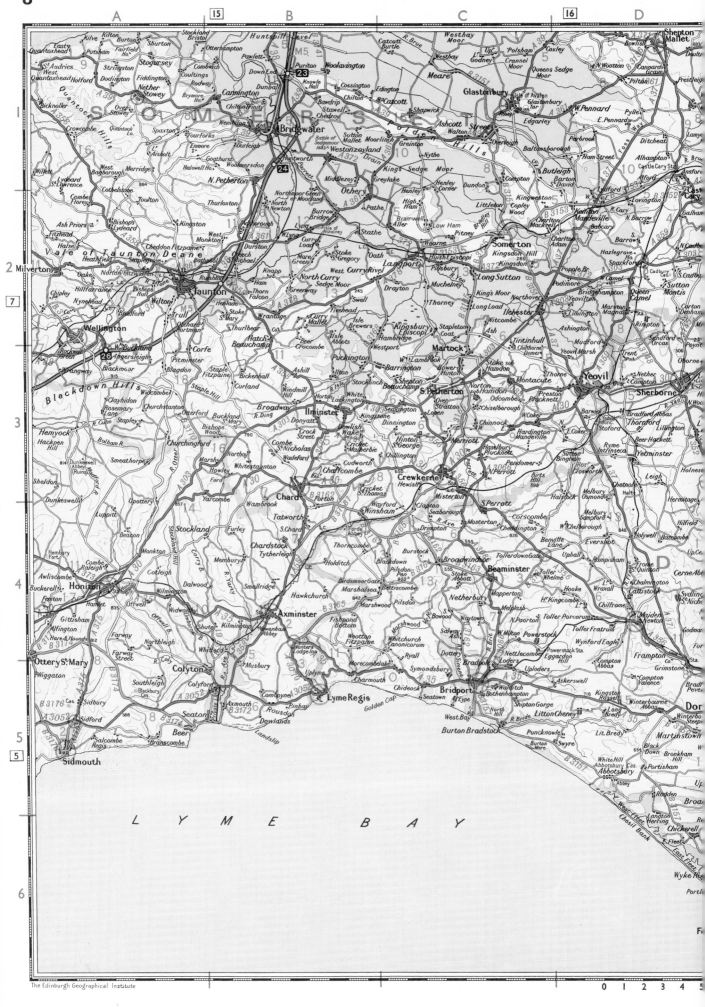

LYME BAY

E F 17 G H

WILTSHIRE · DORSET

Trudoxhill · Wanstrow · Witham Friary · Longleat Ho. · Crockerton · Horningsham · Scotland · Longbridge Deverill · Sutton Veny · Bishopstrow · Norton Bavant · Heytesbury · B390 · Winterbourne Stoke · Stonehenge · Amesbury · Bulford · Bulford Camp · Cholderton

Maiden Bradley · Long Knoll · Kilmington · Norton Ferris · Brixton Deverill · Monkton Deverill · Tytherington · Boyton · Corton · Sherrington · Codford St Mary · Fisherton de la Mere · Deptford · Steeple Langford · Berwick St James · Stapleford · Wilsford · Durnford · Up Woodford · Boscombe · Idmiston · Allington · Newton Tony

Brewham · Kilmington Common · White Sheet Cas. · Keysley Down · Chicklade · The Gt. Ridge Wood · Stockton · Wylye · Hanging Langford · Grovely Cas. · Gt. Wishford · South Newton · Woodford · Dauntsey · Winterbourne Earls · Figsbury Ring · East · Middle

Mere · Barrow · Penselwood · Bourton · Stourton · West Knoyle · Hindon · Fonthill Bishop · Ridge · Chilmark · Teffont Magna · Teffont Evias · Dinton · Baverstock · Barford St Martin · Burcombe · Wilton · Netherhampton · W. Harnham · SALISBURY · Laverstock · St Thomas's Bri · Pitton · Farley · Winterslow · West

Zeals · Huntingford · Silton · Milton on Stour · Sedgehill · East Knoyle · Newtown · Tisbury · E. Hatch · Sutton Mandeville · Fovant · Compton Chamberlayne · Chiselbury Camp · Stratford Tony · Homington · Nunton · Alderbury · W. Grimstead · Pepperbox

Wincanton · Cucklington · Gillingham · Coppleridge · Motcombe · Semley · Wardour Cas. · Anstv · Swallowcliffe · Broad Chalke · Bishopstone · Coombe Bissett · Odstock · Charlton · Trafalgar Ho. · Newton · A21

Shaftesbury · Stour Provost · Donhead St Mary · West End · Alvediston · Ebbesbourne Wake · Mead End · Bowerchalke · Marleycombe Hill · Whitsbury Down · New Court Down · Clearbury Ring · Bodenham

Temple Combe · Fifehead Magdalen · Cann · Charlton · Win Green · Tollard Royal · Sixpenny Handley · Woodyates · Martin · Tidpit · Rockbourne · Breamore Down · Whitsbury · Up. Street · Hale · Woodgreen · Deadman

Stalbridge · Marnhull · Todber · Melbury Abbas · Melbury Down · Ashmore · Chase · Woodcutts · Pentridge · Pentridge Hill · Damerham · West · Up. Burgate · Ashley Walk · Godshill · Fritham

Sturminster Newton · Lydlinch · Hinton St Mary · Fontmell Magna · Sutton Waldron · Iwerne Minster · Farnham · Minchington · Dean · Cashmoor · Monkton Up Wimborne · Gussage St Michael · Cranborne · Boveridge · Sandleheath · Ashford · Alderholt · Fordingbridge · Ibsley · Frogham

Okeford Fitzpaine · Shillingstone · Iwerne Courtney or Shroton · Steepleton Iwerne · Tarrant Gunville · Tarrant Hinton · Gussage All Saints · Knowlton · Sutton Holms · Romford · Cranborne Common · Harbridge · S. Gorley · Ellingham · Blissford

Haselbury Bryan · Droop · Woolland · Ibberton · Belchalwell · Fifehead Neville · Hod Hill · Durweston · Pimperne · Long Crichel · More Crichel · Manswood · Woodlands · Whitmore · Verwood · Blashford · Poulner · Picket Post · Burley Walk

Mappowder · Stoke Wake · Bulbarrow Hill · Turnworth · Bryanston · Blandford Forum · Blandford St Mary · Tarrant Monkton · Tarrant Rawston · New Town · Horton · Horton Common · Three Legged Cross · Ashley Heath · Ringwood · Burley Lo. · Burley

Pulham · Hartfoot Lane · Hilton · Milton Abbas · Winterborne Houghton · Winterborne Stickland · Langton Long · Charlton Marshall · Tarrant Keynston · Witchampton · British Village · Hinton Martell · South Common · H. Row · Holt Heath · St Ives · Avon · Bisterne · Kingston · Shirley · Holmsley Heath

Pleck · Plush · Dewlish · Cheselbourne · Winterborne Whitchurch · Winterborne Clenston · Spetisbury · Shapwick · Badbury Rings · Clapgate · Holt · West Moors · Uddens Pk. · Trickett's Cross · Foxbury Hill · Burley Street · Crow

White Lackington · Puddletown · Bere Regis · Winterborne Kingston · Anderson · Charborough Ho. · Corfe Mullen · Hill View · Canford Heath · Ferndown · Parley Common · Hurn · Winkton · Sopley · Bransgore · Rising Sun Inn · Bashley · New Milton

Stinsford · Affpuddle · Tolpuddle · Turner's Puddle · Bryants Puddle · Bloxworth · Morden · Lytchett Minster · Upton · New Town · Wallis Down · Branksome · Kinson · Ensbury · Moordown · Iford · Burton · Hinton Admiral · Highcliffe

Woodsford · L. Bockhampton · Hr. Bockhampton · Tincleton · Woodbury Hill · Lytchett Matravers · Wareham Sta. · Northport · Poole · Parkstone · Lilliput · Bournemouth · Boscombe · Southbourne · Hengistbury Hd. · Christchurch Bay

W. Stafford · Moreton · Bovington Camp · Wethelton · Bloxworth Heath · Gore Heath · Hamworthy · Poole Harbour · Brownsea Cas. · Sandbanks · Shell Bay · Poole Bay

W. Knighton · Galton Heath · Winfrith Heath · Stokeford · Bindon Abbey · E. Stoke · Wool · Holme · Stoborough · Wareham · Arne · Wytch Heath · Newton · Lytchett Sea · Studland Bay

Warmwell · Owermoigne · E. Knighton · Winfrith Newburgh · Coombe Keynes · Creech Heath · Creech Grange · Church Knowle · Corfe Cas. · Studland · The Foreland · Handfast Pt.

Poxwell · Chaldon Herring or East Chaldon · Chaldon Down · W. Lulworth · E. Lulworth · Lulworth Cove · Bindon Hill · Steeple · Kingston · Langton Matravers · Swanage Bay · Swanage · Peveril Pt. · Ballard Down · Ulwell · Herston · Durlston Hd.

Osmington · Osmington Mills · Ringstead B. · Abbey · Tyneham (DERELICT) · Kimmeridge · Encombe · Worth Matravers · St Albans or St Aldhelms Hd.

Isle of Portland · To Cherbourg · To Channel Islands

© — John Bartholomew & Son Ltd.

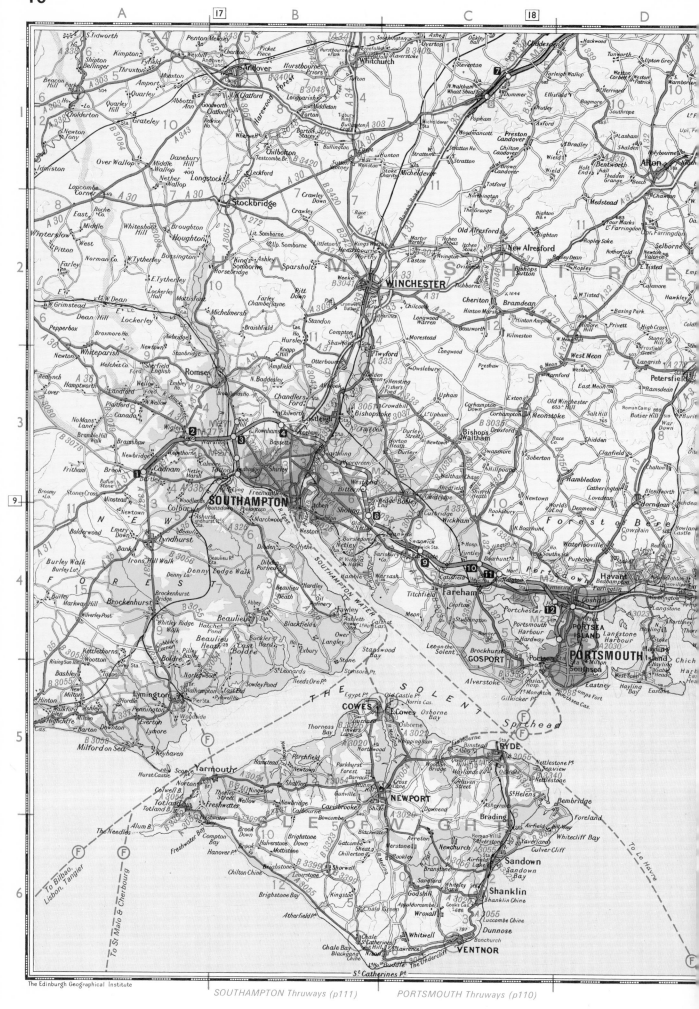

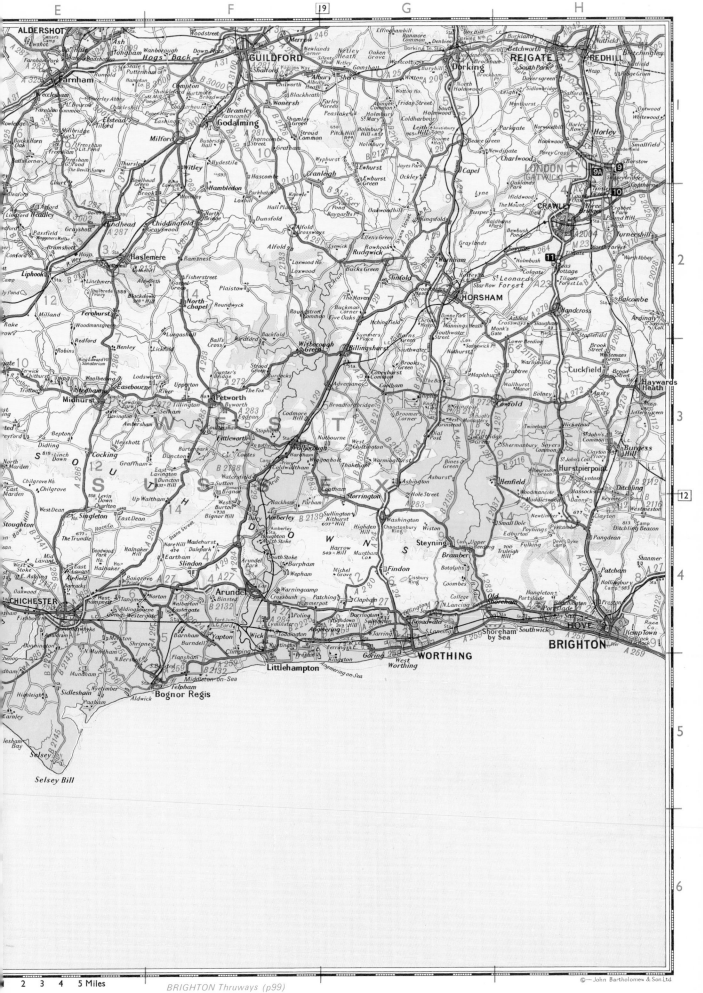

BRIGHTON Thruways (p99)

© — John Bartholomew & Son Ltd.

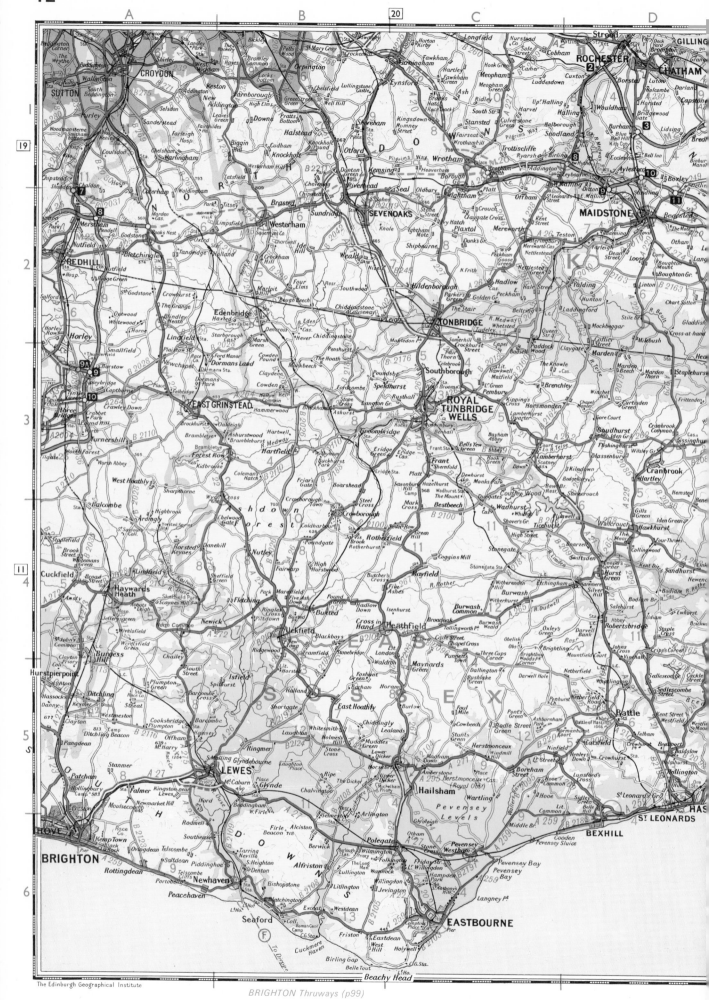

BRIGHTON Thruways (p99)

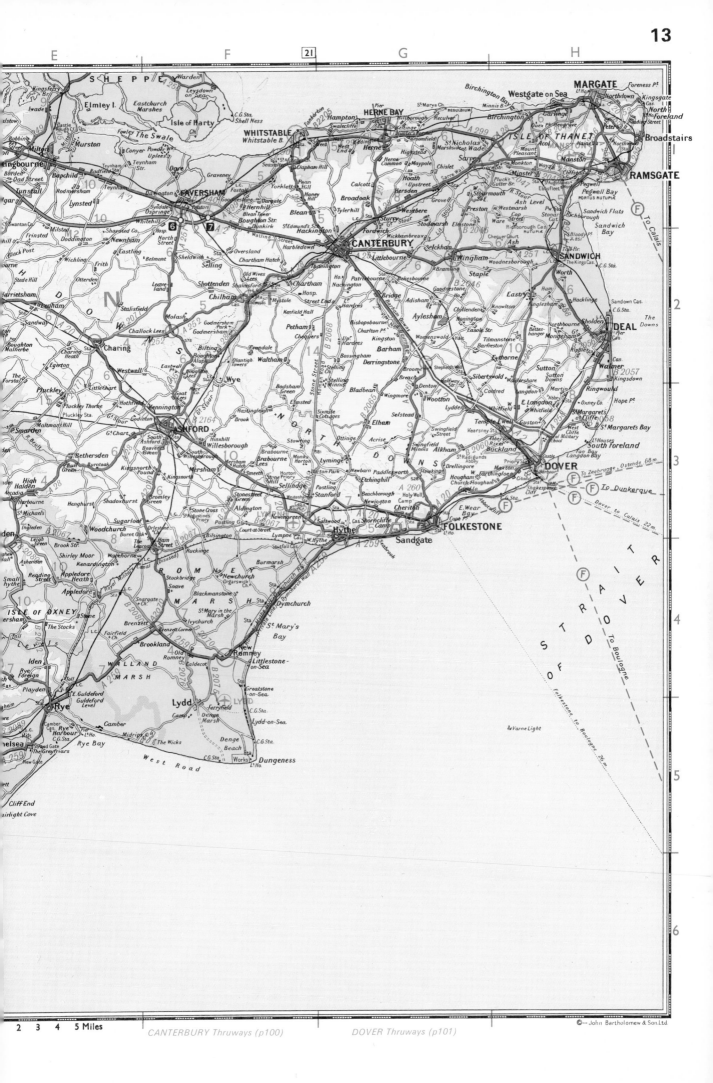

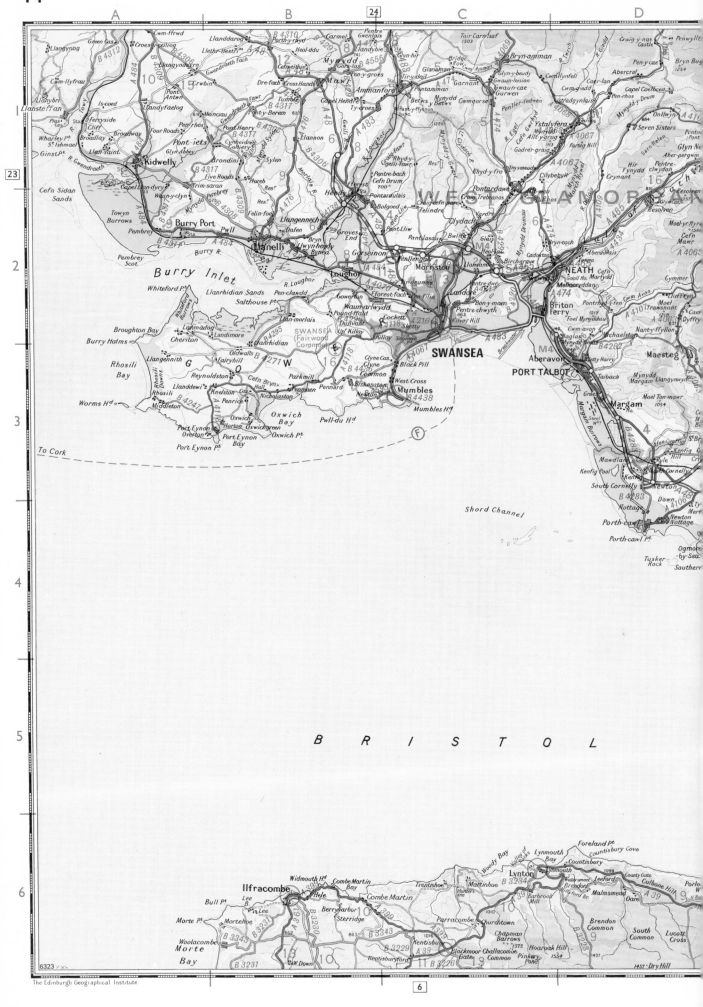

Map (Cardiff / South Wales region)

E   F   25   G   H

Abergavenny, Brynmawr, Blaenavon, Abertillery, Pontypool, Tredegar, Ebbw Vale, Rhymney, Merthyr Tydfil, Dowlais, Aberdare, Bedwellty, Newbridge, Blackwood, Gelligaer, Cwmbran, Caerleon, Risca, Cross Keys, Newport, Caerphilly, Pontypridd, Treforest, Tonyrefail, Llantrisant, Rhondda, Treorchi, Treherbert, Cowbridge, Bonvilston, Dinas Powis, Penarth, Barry, Sully, Llandaff, Whitchurch, CARDIFF (CAERDYDD), Rumney, Castleton, St Mellons, Marshfield, Michaelston, Flat Holm, Steep Holme

GWENT, WEST GLAMORGAN, SOUTH GLAMORGAN, MID GLAMORGAN

Clevedon, Walton in Gordano, Weston in Gordano, Yatton, Congresbury, Kingston Seymour, Worle, Weston super Mare, Locking, Banwell, Winscombe, Axbridge, Churchill, Sandford, Shipham, Cheddar, Bleadon, Loxton, Lympsham, Brean, Berrow, Burnham, Highbridge, Brent Knoll, East Brent, Mark, Wedmore, Meare, Blackford, West Stoughton

A N N E L   B R I D G W A T E R   B A Y

Minehead, Dunster, Alcombe, Watchet, Williton, Washford, Old Cleeve, Blue Anchor Bay, Carhampton, Timberscombe, Withycombe, Selworthy, Wootton Courtenay, Stogursey, Nether Stowey, Kilve, Holford, East Quantoxhead, West Quantoxhead, Stringston, Dodington, Fiddington, Cannington, Combwich, Pawlett, Puriton, Woolavington, Cossington, Catcott, Burtle, Westhay, Tadham Moor

20, 21, 22, 23, 24, 25, 26, 27, 28

2 3 4 5 Miles

CARDIFF Thruways (p100)

© — John Bartholomew & Son Ltd.

7   8

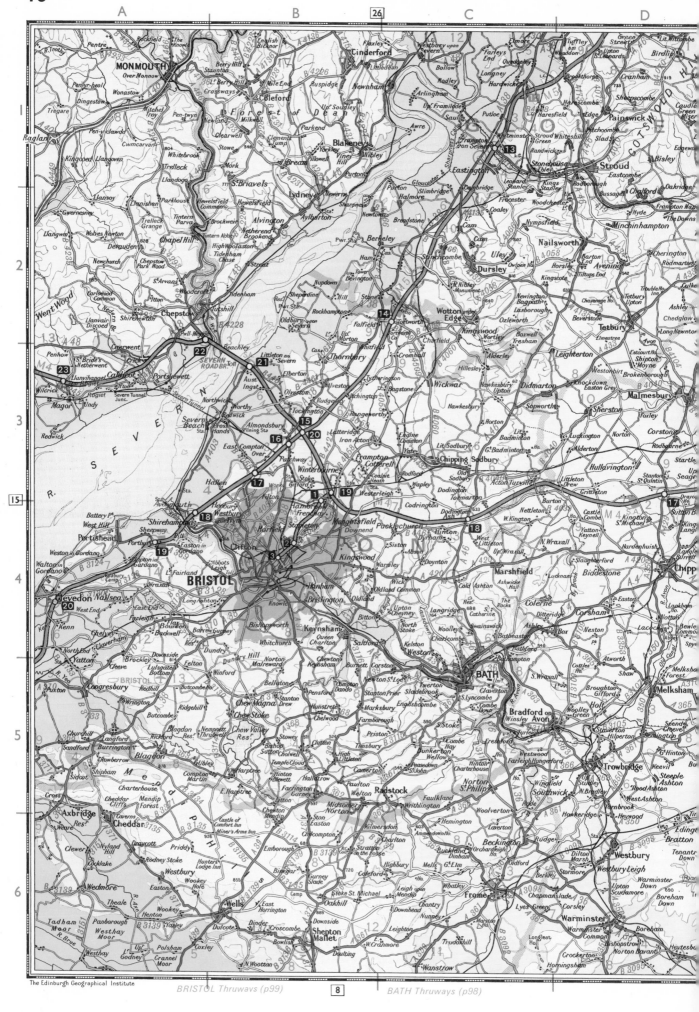

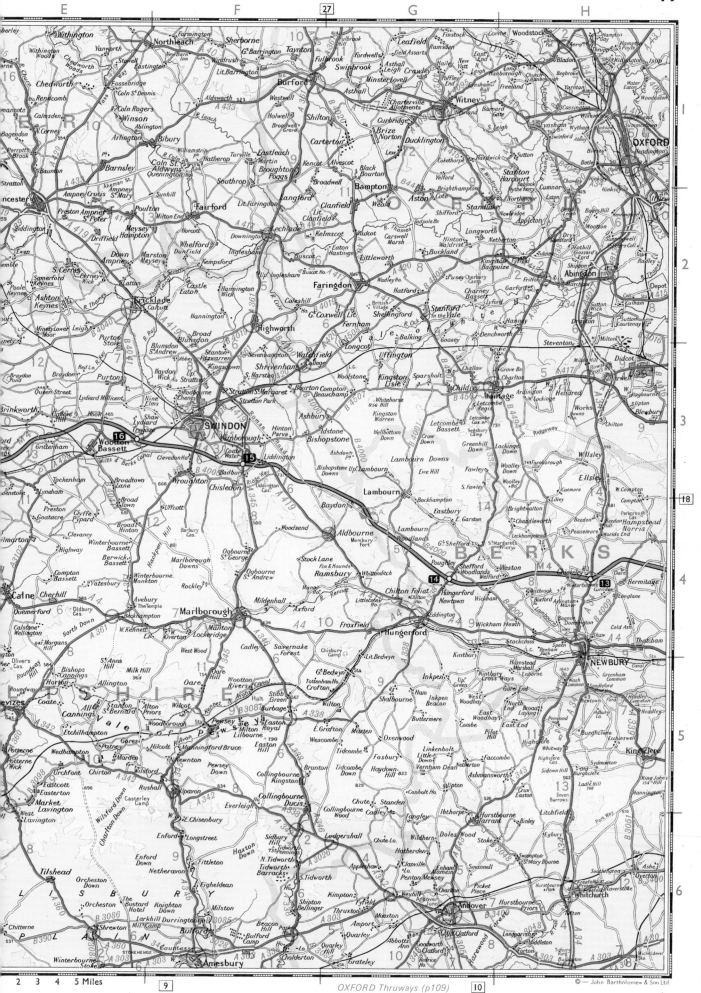

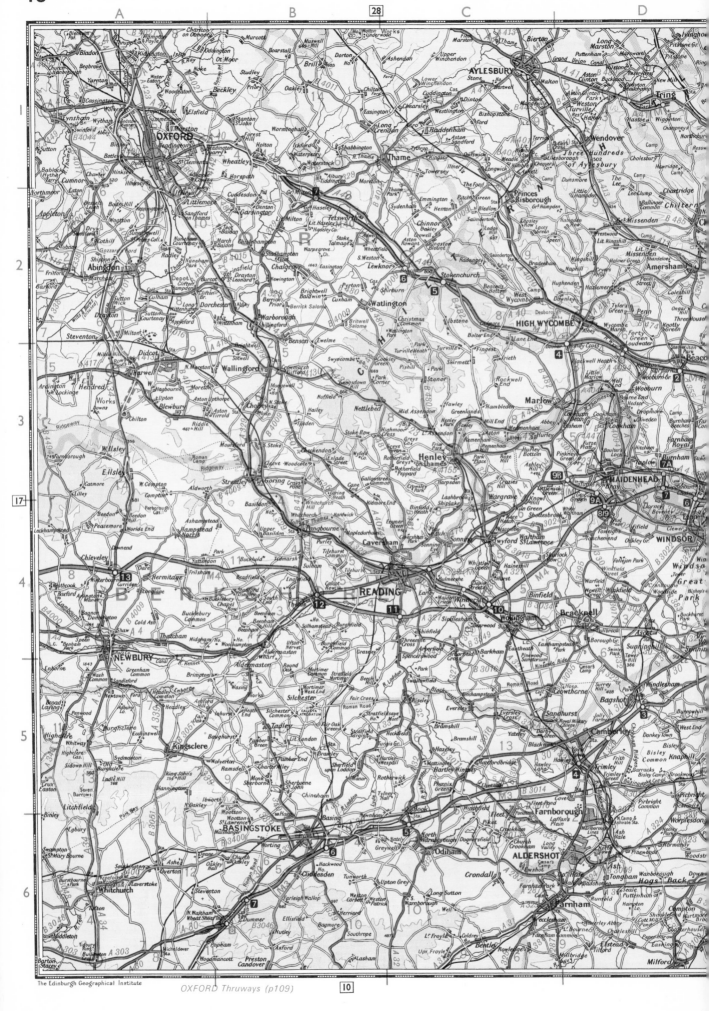

OXFORD Thruways (p109)

HERTFORD

Hemel Hempstead · Harpenden · St Albans · Welwyn Garden City · Hatfield · Hertford · Ware · Harlow · Watford · Barnet · Enfield · Waltham Abbey · Epping · Chipping Ongar · Harrow · LONDON · Romford · Ilford · Barking · Dagenham · Hounslow · Staines · Richmond · Wimbledon · Kingston · Woolwich · Greenwich · Bexley · Dartford · Bromley · Croydon · Sutton · Epsom · Leatherhead · Caterham · Sevenoaks · Westerham · Dorking · Reigate · Redhill · Edenbridge · Horley

2 3 4 5 Miles

See Pages 106-107

Signposted N. & S. Circular
Roads & Ring Road ▬▬▬

© — John Bartholomew & Son, Ltd.

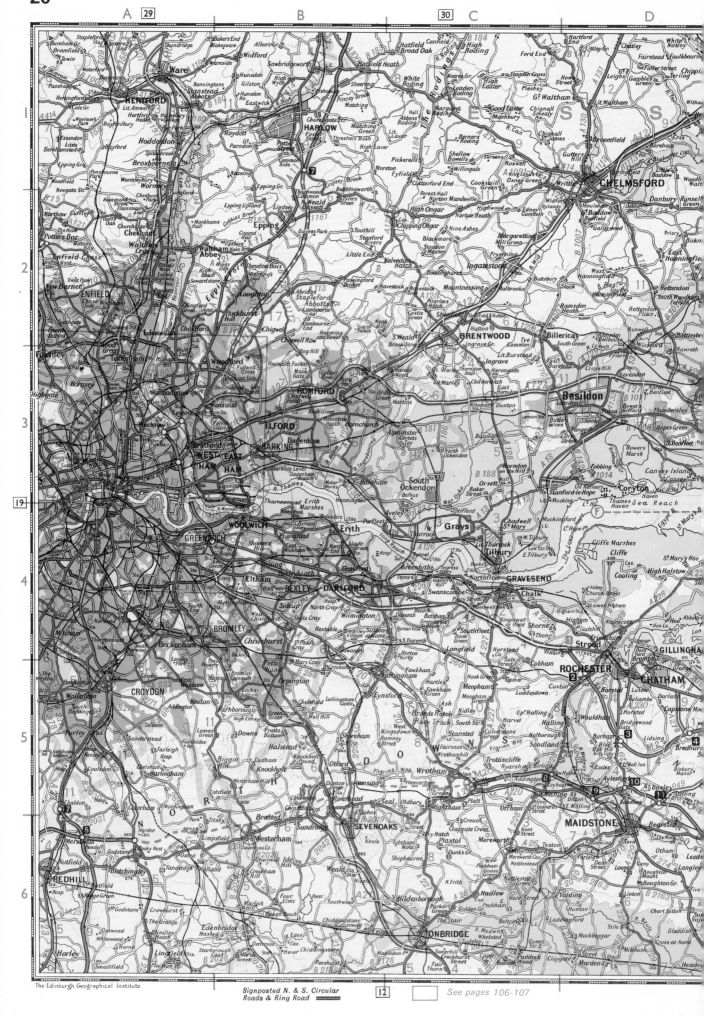

Signposted N. & S. Circular
Roads & Ring Road

See pages 106-107

2   3   4   5 Miles

© — John Bartholomew & Son,Ltd.

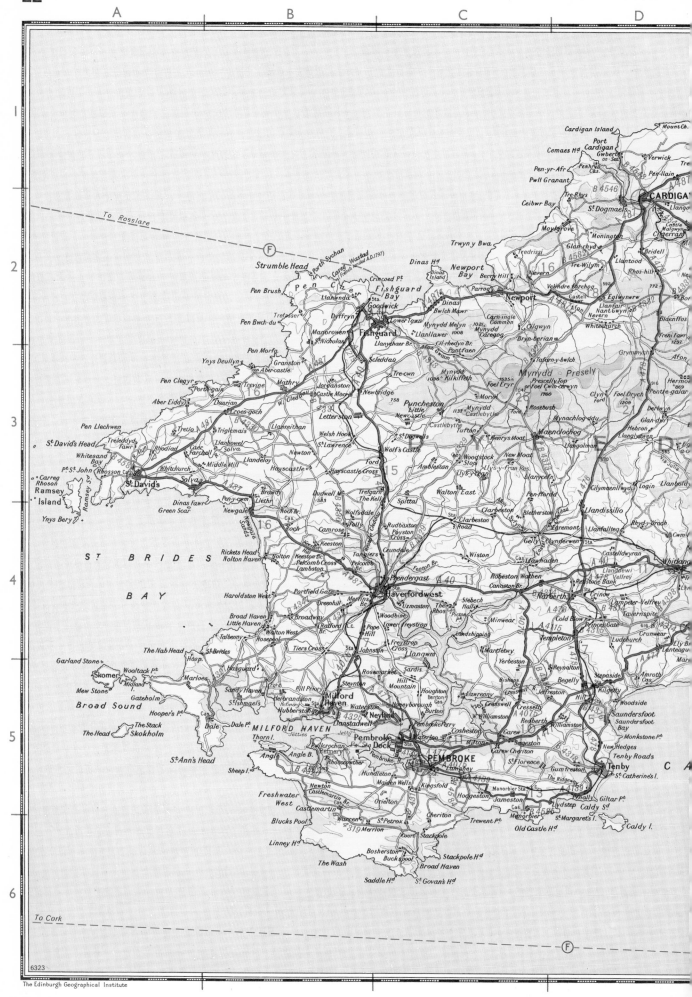

A　　　　B　　　　C　　　　D

To Rosslare

Cardigan Island
Mount Ch.
Port Cardigan
Gwbert on Sea
Verwick
Cemaes Hd
Pen-llain
Pen-yr-Afr
Pwll Granant
CARDIGAN
B 4546
Llango
Ceibwr Bay
St. Dogmaels
Castle
Malgwyn
Cilgerran
Moylgrove
Monington
Trwyn y Bwa
Glan-rhyd
Bridell
Tredrissi
Tre-Wilym
Llantood
Rhos-hill
Dinas Hd
Newport
Bay
Nevern
Berry Hill
16
Strumble Head
Porth Sychan
Carreg Wastad
(French landed A.D.1797)
Dinas
Island
Parrog
Newport
Velindre farchog
Eglwyswrw
Crincoed Pt.
Dinas Hd
Pen Caer
Fishguard
Bay
Dinas
Bwlch Mawr
Afon
Llanfair
Nant Gwyn
Nevern
772
Bldenffos
Pen Brush
Llanwnda
Goodwick
Carn-ingli
Common
Whitechurch
Freni fawr
1297
Trefasser
Dyffryn
Lower Town
Mynydd Melyn
Pen Bwch-du
1021
Manorowen
Fishguard
Llanllawer
Carn
Caregog
Cilgwyn
Bryn-berian
St. Nicholas
Mynydd
Caregog
Hermon
869
Pen Morfa
Llanychaer Br.
Cil-rhedyn Br.
Afon
Pentre-galar
Mynydd Presely
Ynys Deullyn
Aber-castle
Granston
Scleddau
Afon Gwain
Tafarn-y-bwlch
916
Pen Clegyr
Trevine
Mathry
Tre cwn
Mynydd
Kilkiffeth
Foel Eryr
1535
Prescelly Top
or Foel Cwm-cerwyn
1760
Clyn
Ford
Foel Drych
1209
Glan-dwr
Porth-gain
16
Jordanston
Castle Morris
Newbridge
758
Puncheston
Mynydd
Castleby Uss
Rosebush
Berwyn
Aber Eiddy
Llanrheithan
1135
Llanglydwen
Thurian
Croes-goch
B 4330
Letterston
Little
Newcastle
Mynachlog ddu
Hebron
Glan-dwr
Pen Llechwen
Tretio
A 487
Triglaimais
Welsh Hook
Castlebythe
Tufton
Maenclochog
Llanglynwen
St. David's Head
Treleddyd
fawr
A 487
Rhodiad
Llanhowel
Solva
St. Lawrence
Henry's Moat
Llangolman
Whitesand
Bay
Alun
Glee
Farchel
Newton
Wolf's Castle
Woodstock
Llys-y-fran Res.
Cilymaenllwyd
Login
Pt. St. John
Rhosson
Whitchurch
Middle Mill
Hayscastle
Amblestan
New Moat
Llanycefn
Llandissilio
Llanbob
Carreg
Rhoson
St. David's
Solva
Hayscastle Cross
Walton East
Pen-ffordd
Gelly
Llanfallteg
Rhyd-y-wrach
Ramsey
Island
Dinas Fawr
Pen-y-cwm
Liethr
Ford
Trefgarn
The Kell
Spittal
Clarbeston
Egremont
Clynderwen
Castelldwyran
Ynys Bery
Green Scar
Newgale
Roch Br.
Ludwell
585
Wolfsdale
Clarbeston
Road
Wiston
Cas. Llawhaden
Whitland
Roch
Cas.
Camrose
Rudbaxton
Fenton Br.
Robeston Wathen
Llanddewi
Velfrey
11
St. BRIDES
Rickets Head
Nolton Haven
Nolton
Keeston Br.
Pelcomb Cross
Lambston
Pelcomb
Br.
Poyston
Cross
Keundale
Narberth
Redstone Bank
Crinow
Lampeter Velfrey
16
Tancredston
Fenton Br.
Prendergast
Haverfordwest
A 40
Canaston
Cold Blow
Taverspite
BAY
Haroldston West
Portfield Gate
Merlins
Woodbine
Slebech
Hall
Picton
Cas.
Princes Gate
616
Crunwear
Broad Haven
Little Haven
Dreenhill
Uzmaston
Lower Freystrop
Minwear
Ludchurch
Ely Br.
Lanteague
Talbenny
Walton West
Rosepool
Ratford
Br.
Pope
Hill
Freystrop
Cross
Llangwm
Landshipping
Martletwy
Yerbeston
Reynalton
Amroth
Cas.
Garland Stone
St. Brides
Hasguard
Tiers Cross
Johnston
Rosemarket
Sardis
Templeton
Stepaside
The Nab Head
Hosp.
Steynton
Hill
Mountain
Houghton
Bishops
Begelly
Saundersfoot
Skomer
Wooltack Pt.
Marloes
Sandy Haven
Herbrandston
Milford
Haven
Waterston
Honeyborough
Lawrenny
Cresswell
Cresselly
Kilgetty
Woodside
Mew Stone
Midland
Gateholm
Broad Sound
Hooper's Pt.
St. Ishmaels
Hubberston
Neyland
Burton
W. Williamston
Redberth
Saundersfoot
Bay
The Stack
Skokholm
Dale
Llanstadwell
Pembroke
Dock
Waterloo
Coshestern
Milton
Carew
Williamston
Monkstone Pt.
The Head
Thorn I.
Jetties
Jetty
Pembroke R.
Sageston
New Hedges
Tenby Roads
St. Ann's Head
Angle
Angle B.
Rhoscrowther
Pembroke Ferry
PEMBROKE
Lamphey
Carew Cheriton
St. Florence
Gumfreston
Tenby
St. Catherine's I.
Sheep I.
Pwllcrochan
Refinery
Newton
Hundleton
Maiden Wells
Kingsford
Hoggeston
Manorbier Sta.
The Ridgeway
Penally
Giltar Pt.
Castlemartin
Orielton
Cheriton
Trewent Pt.
Jameston
Llydstep
Caldy Sd.
Freshwater
West
Warren
St. Petrox
Court
Manorbier
St. Margaret's I.
Caldy I.
Blucks Pool
Merrion
Stackpole
Old Castle Hd.
Linney Hd.
Bosherston
Buckspool
Stackpole Hd.
Broad Haven
The Wash
Saddle Hd.
St. Govan's Hd.

To Cork

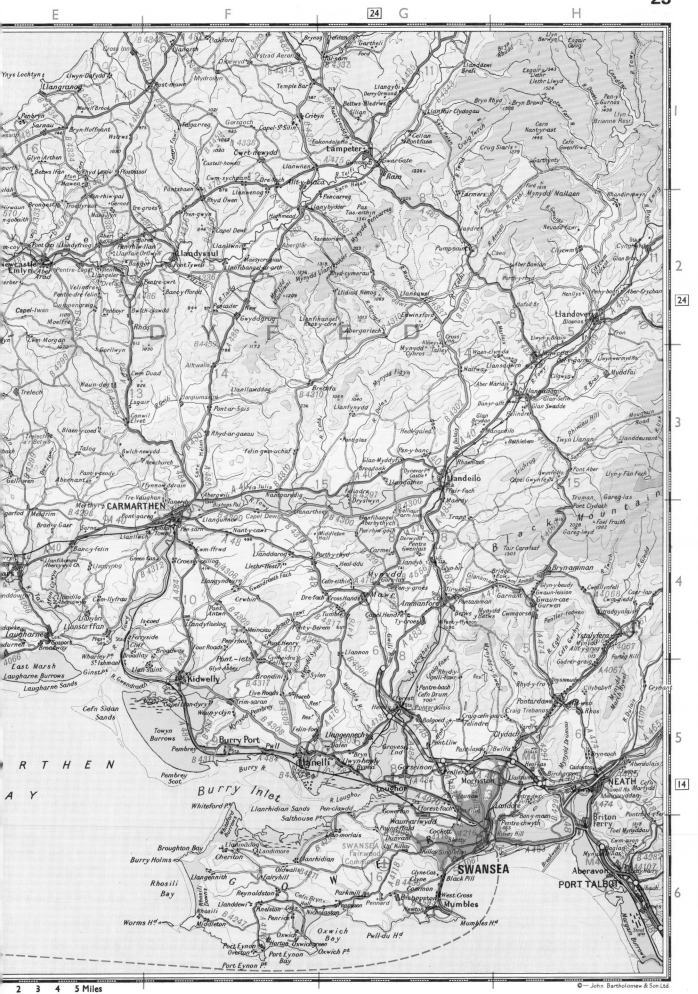

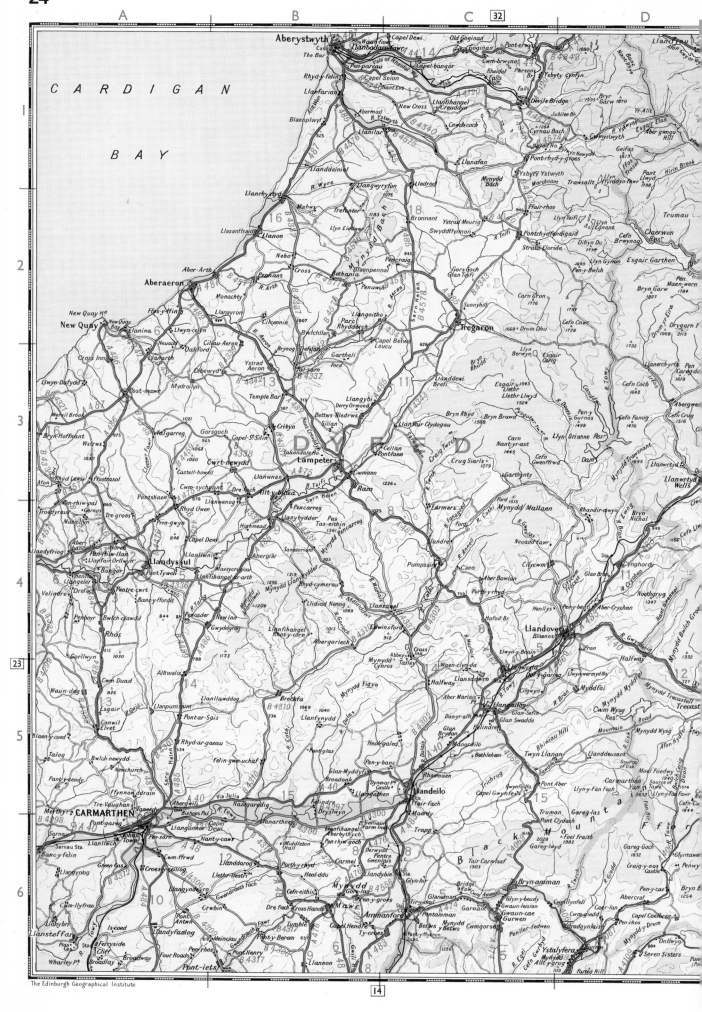

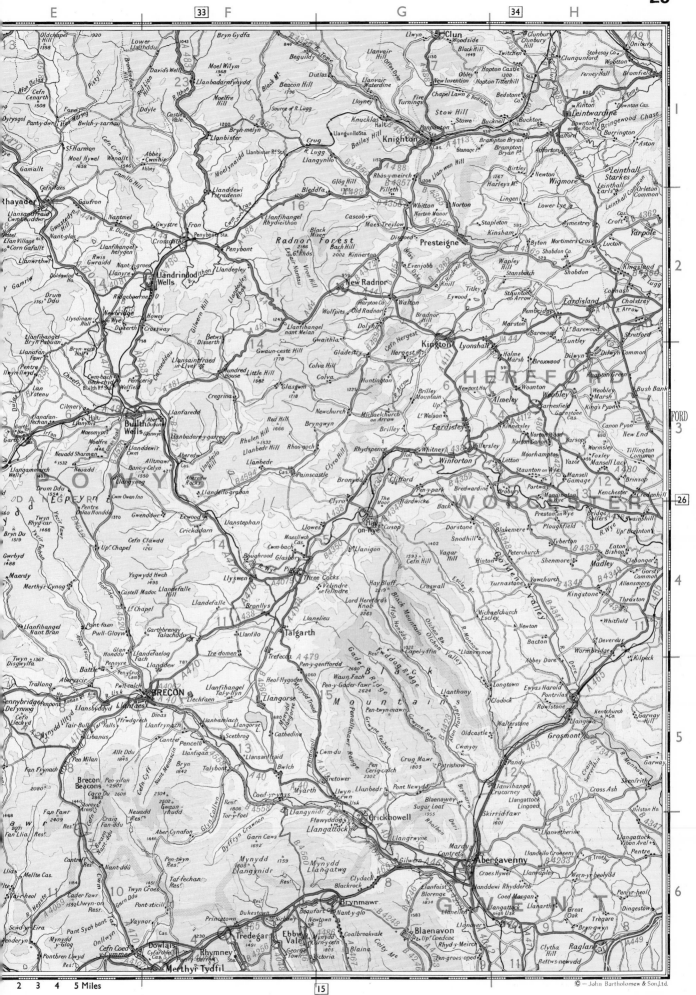

E   [33]   F   G   [34]   H

13

Oldchapel Hill 1398
Lower Llanddbu
Bryn Gydfa
Llwyn
Clun
Woodside
Clunbur
Clunbury Hill

David's Wells
1043
Moel Wilym 1568
Beguildy
R Teme
849
Llanfair Hill
Black Hill 1449
Twitchen
Clungunford
Stokesay Co
Onibury
Wootton
A 49

Cefn Cenarth 1508
Red Lion Hill
Moelfre Hill
Block Mt
Dutlas
Llanvair Waterdine
Offas Dyke
Hopton Castle
Obley
1130
New Invention
Hopton Titterhill
Ferney Hall
Bromfield

Dyrysgol
Panty-dwr
Bwlch-y-sarnau
Beacon Hill 1796
Source of R. Lugg
Five Turnings
Chapel Lawn
R Redlake
Bedstone Co
17
Downton Cas.
A 4113
Walford
R Teme

SF Harmon
Moel Hywel 1658
Cefn Crin Wenallt 1546
1200
Bryn-melyn
Llanbister
Crug
R Lugg
Knucklas Halt
LangunlloSta
Bailey Hill
Knighton
Cas.
Stanage
Brampton Bryan
Brampton Bryan Pk
Buckton
Downton on the Rock
Burrington
Aston

Rhayader
Gaufron
Abbey Cwmhir
Abbey
Llanbister Rd Sta.
1152
A 488
B 4357
Rhos-y-meirch
1208
Llan-wen Hill
539
539
Stowe
Stow Hill
Panpunton
1267
Harleys Mt
Newton
Wigmore
Leinthall Starkes

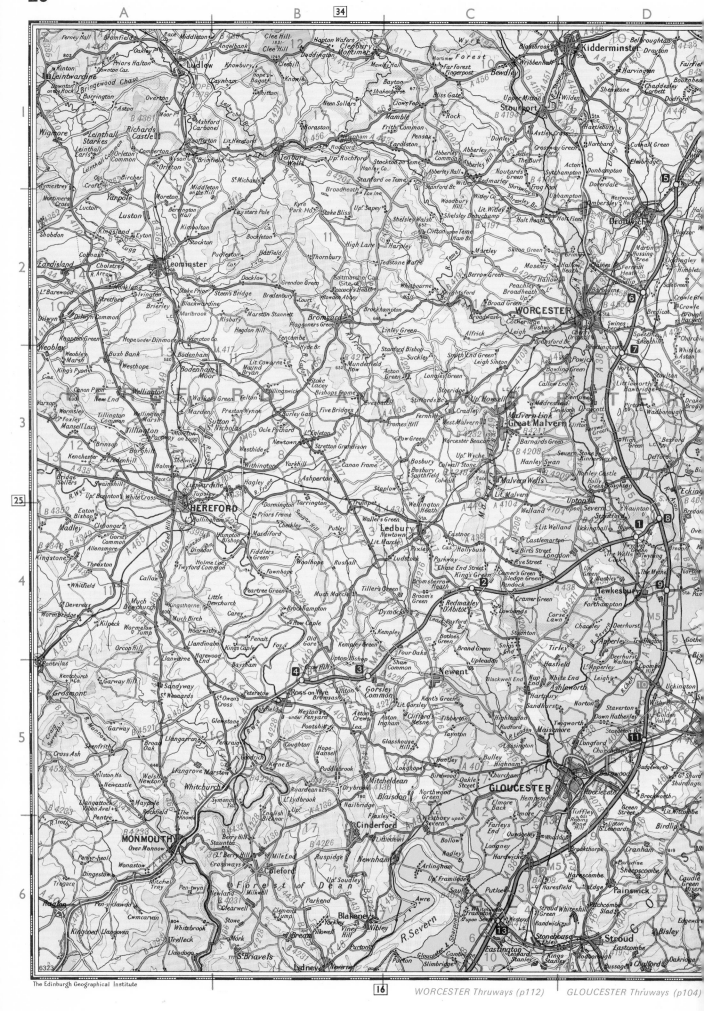

WORCESTER Thruways (p112)   GLOUCESTER Thruways (p104)

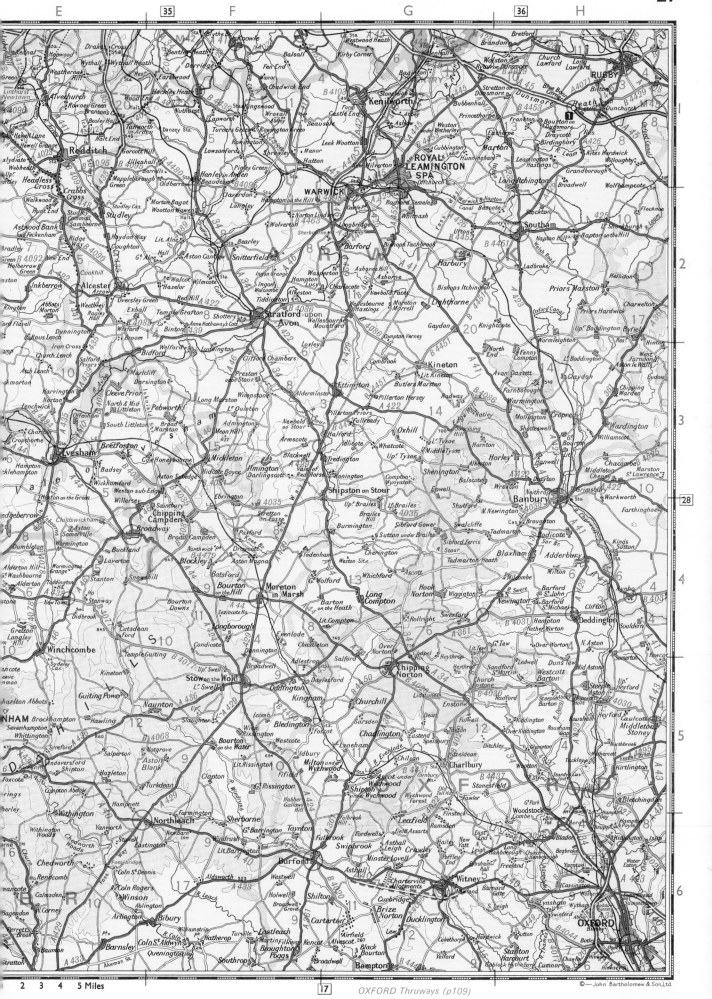

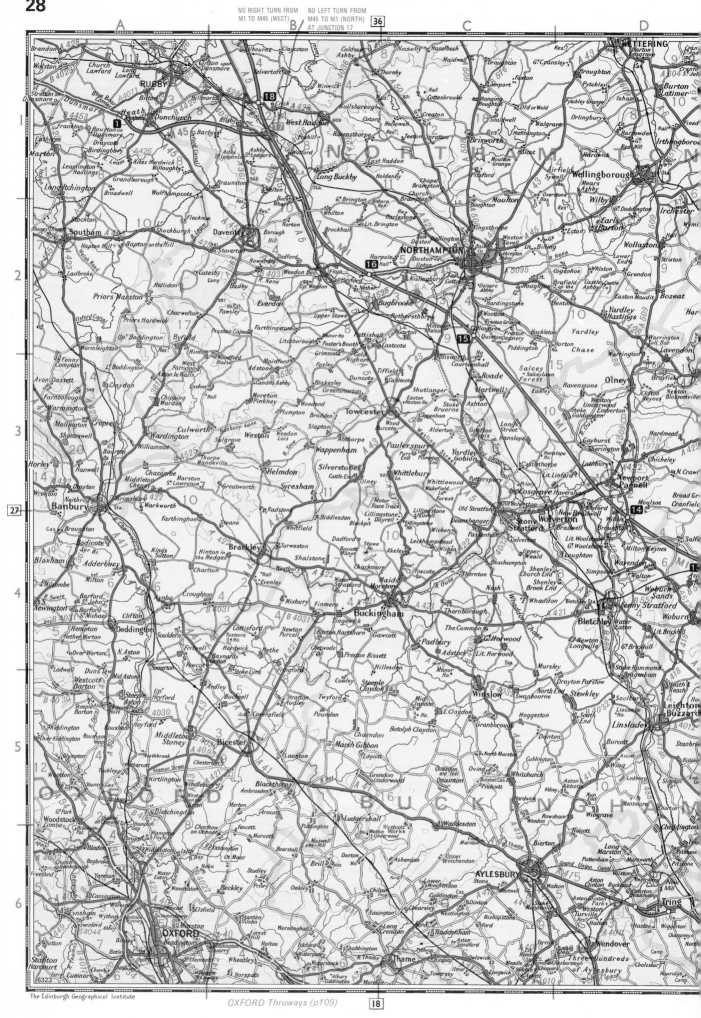

OXFORD Thruways (p109)

18

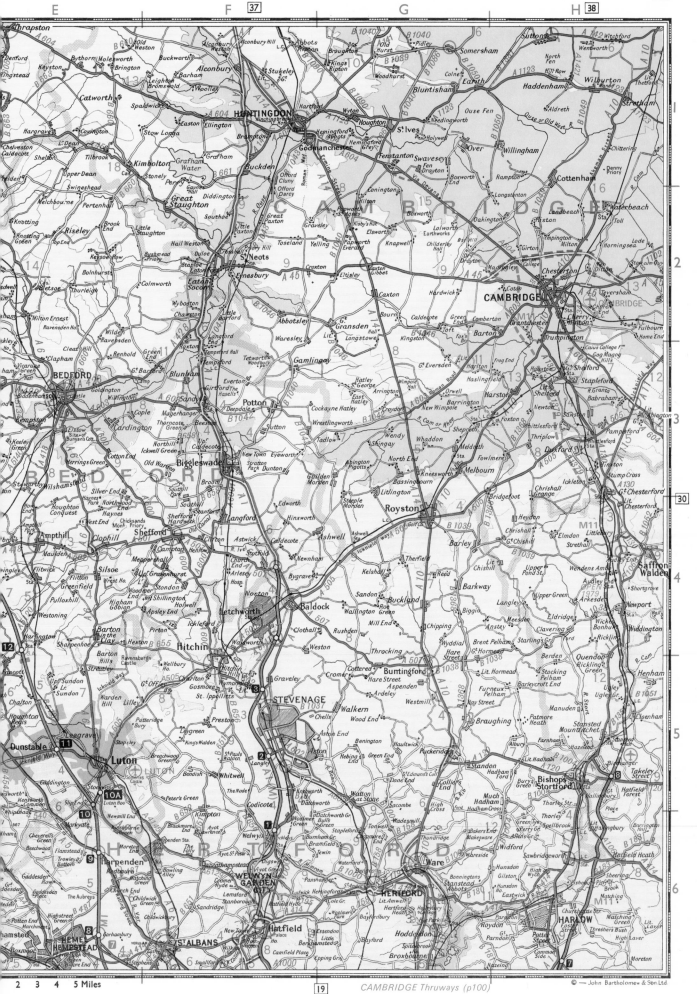

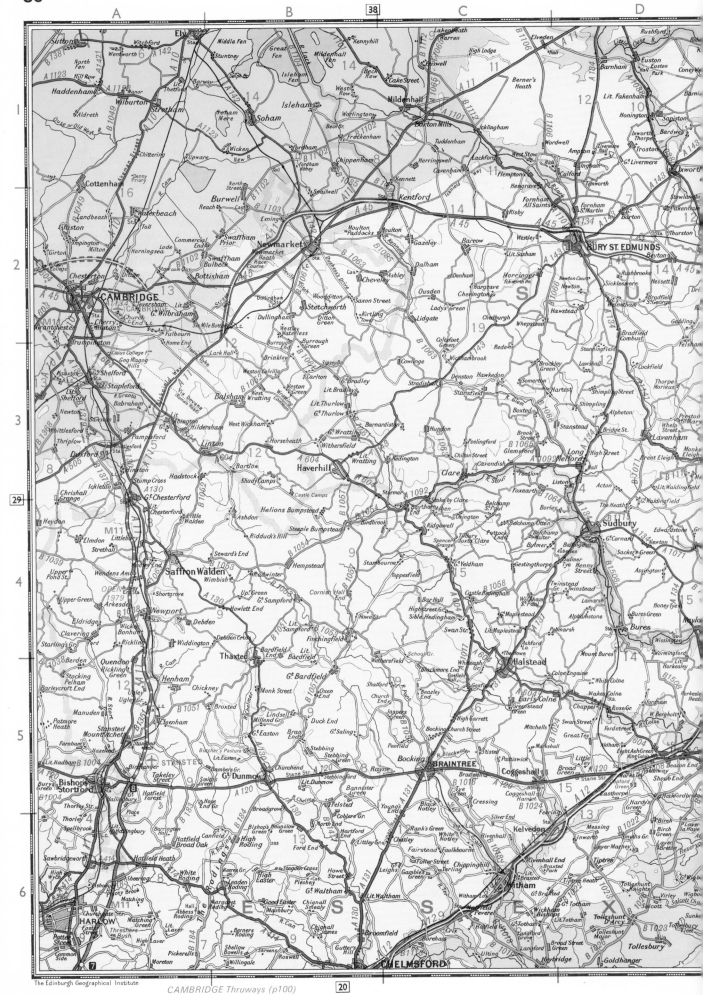

CAMBRIDGE Thruways (p100)

E   F   39   G   H

Harleston   Diss   Halesworth   Wrentham   Southwold   Walberswick

Eye   Stradbroke   Laxfield   Yoxford   Darsham   Dunwich Monastery

Stowmarket   Debenham   Framlingham   Saxmundham   Leiston   Sizewell

Needham Market   Wickham Market   Snape   Aldeburgh   Orford Ness

Ipswich   Woodbridge   Orford   Orford Beach

Hadleigh   Felixstowe   Hollesley Bay   Shingle Street

Manningtree   Harwich   Dovercourt   The Naze   Walton-on-the-Naze

Wivenhoe   Brightlingsea   Frinton-on-Sea

CLACTON-ON-SEA   Martello Tower   Gunfleet   Gunfleet Lt.

Felixstowe to Gothenburg
Harwich to Esbjerg and Kristiansand
To Bremerhaven, Hamburg
Harwich to Hoek van Holland
Harwich to Antwerp
Felixstowe to Rotterdam
Felixstowe to Zeebrugge

2   3   4   5 Miles   21

© — John Bartholomew & Son, Ltd.

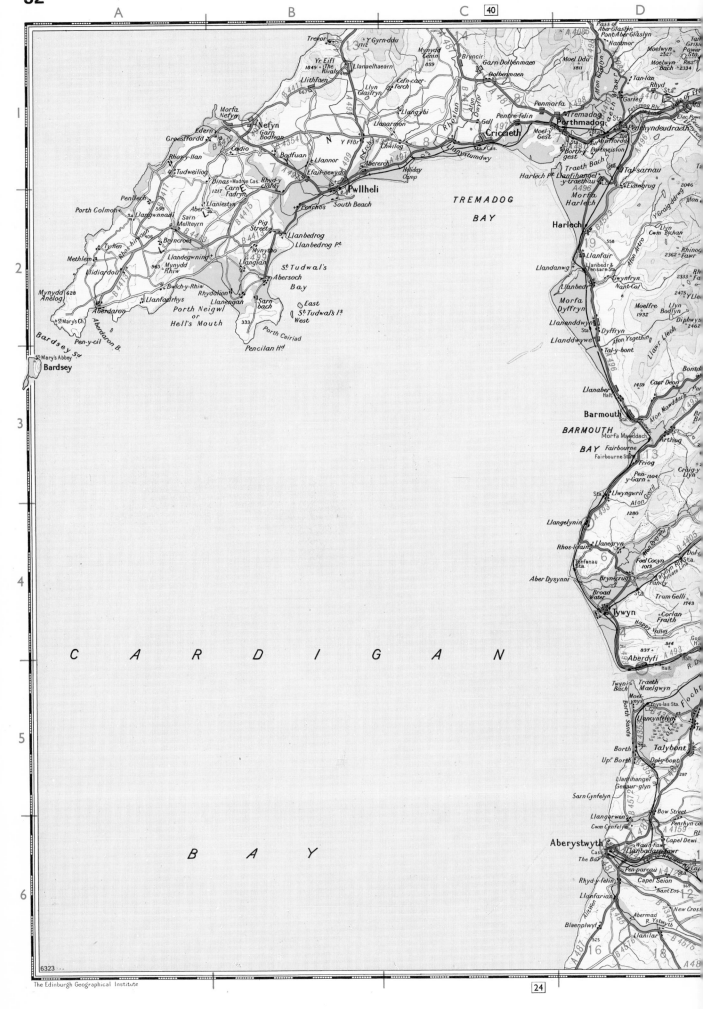

The Edinburgh Geographical Institute

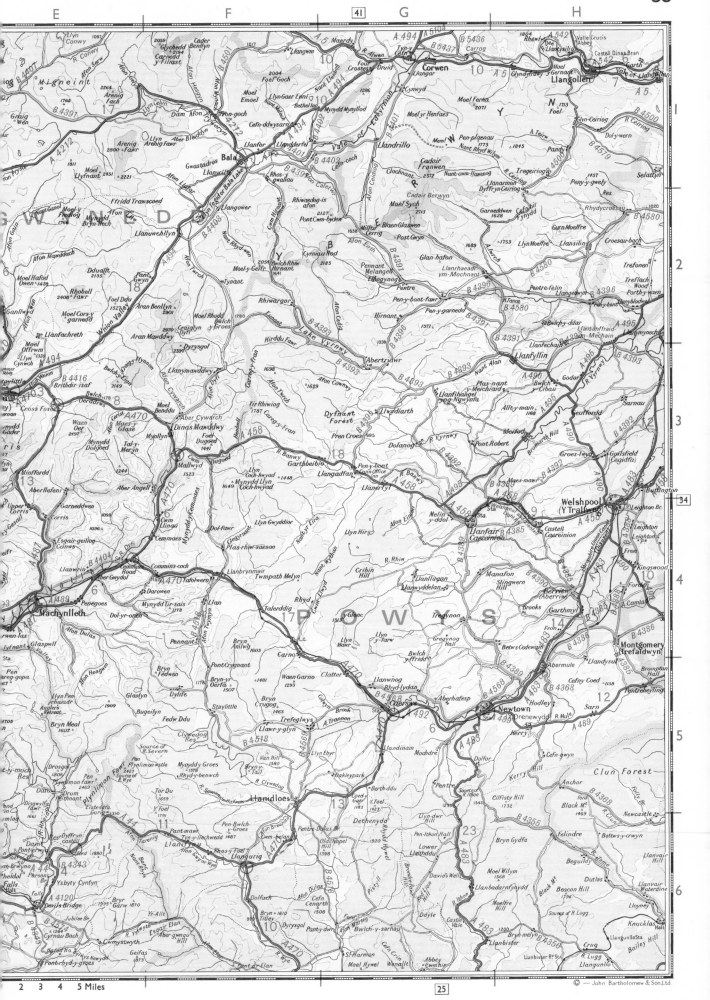

E   F   41   G   H

2   3   4   5 Miles

25

© — John Bartholomew & Son Ltd.

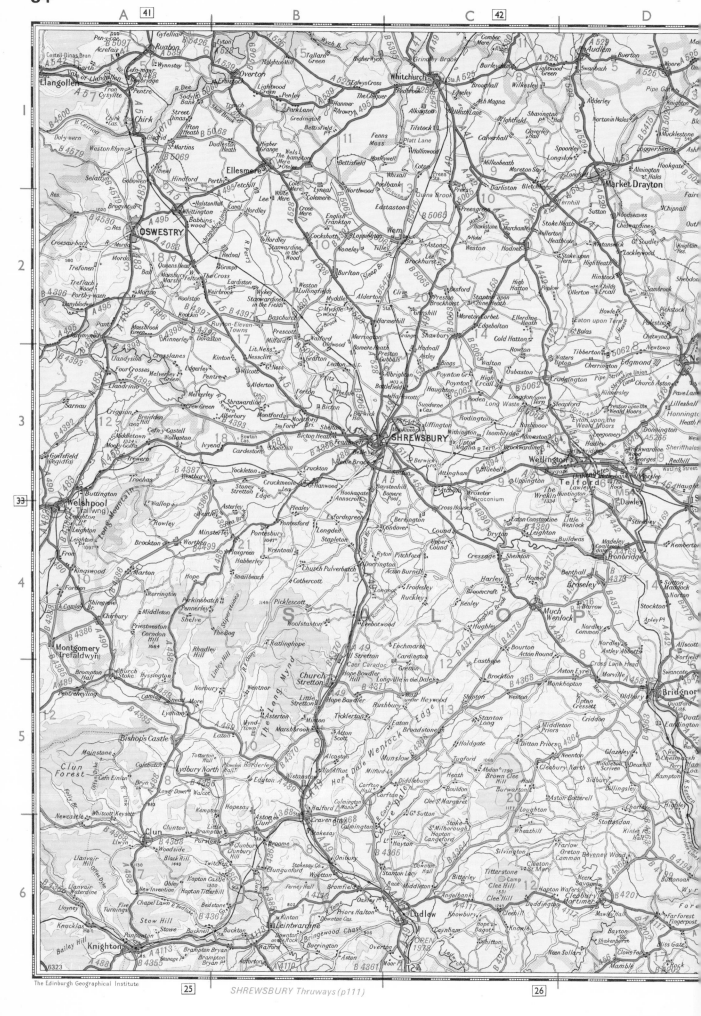

2   3   4   5 Miles

© John Bartholomew & Son Ltd.

DERBY

NOTTINGHAM

LEICESTER

COVENTRY

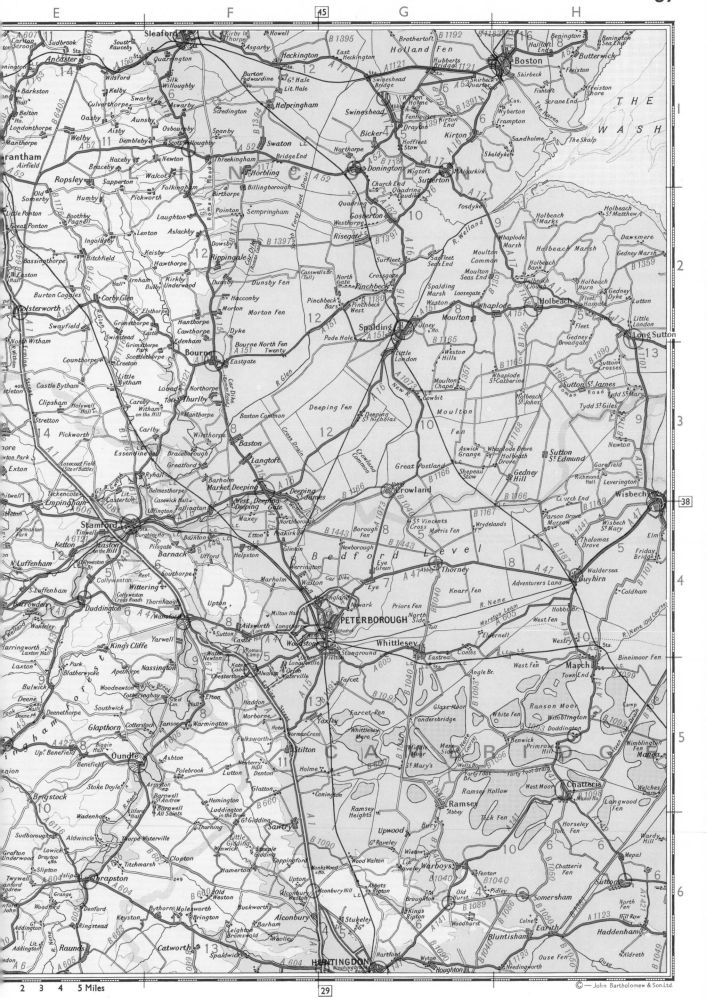

© — John Bartholomew & Son.Ltd.

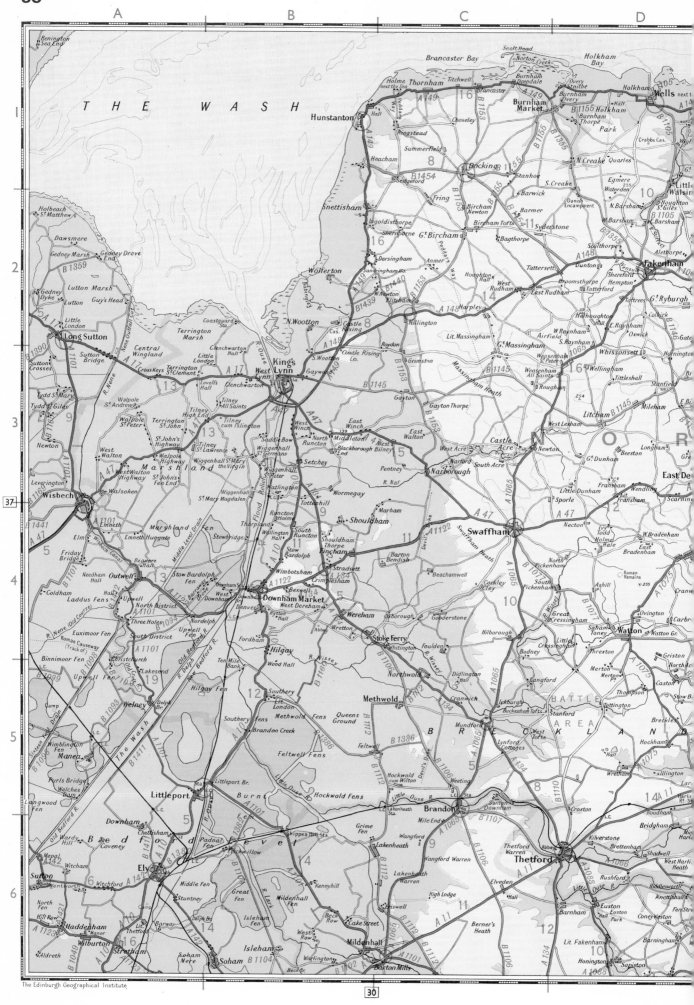

A   B   C   D

THE WASH

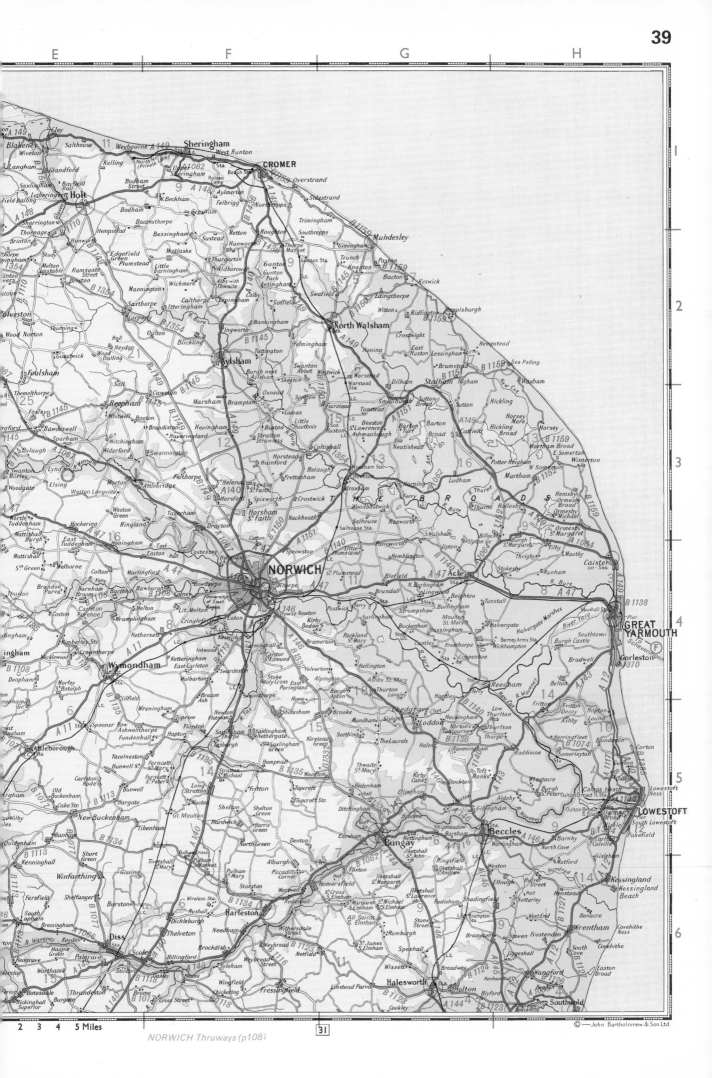

NORWICH Thruways (p108)

© —John Bartholomew & Son.Ltd.

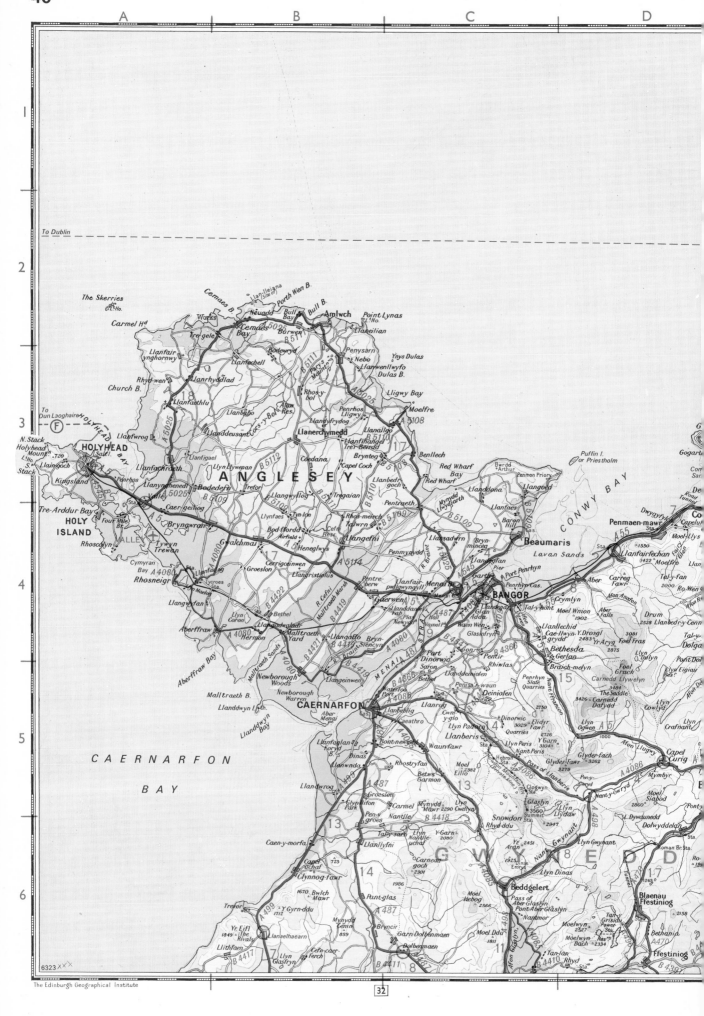

SOUTHPORT

LIVERPOOL BAY

MERSEYSIDE

LIVERPOOL

BOOTLE

WALLASEY

Birkenhead

Bebington

Hoylake

West Kirby

Point of Air

RIVER DEE

Rhyl

Prestatyn

Colwyn Bay

Old Colwyn

Abergele

Rhuddlan

St Asaph

Mostyn

Holywell

Flint

Connah's Quay

Neston

Heswall

Denbigh

Mold

Buckley

Llangernyw

Ruthin

C L W Y D

Corwen

Llangollen

WREXHAM

Rhosllannerchrugog

Ruabon

LIVERPOOL Thruways (p105)

2 3 4 5 Miles

© John Bartholomew & Son, Ltd.

To Belfast

To Douglas

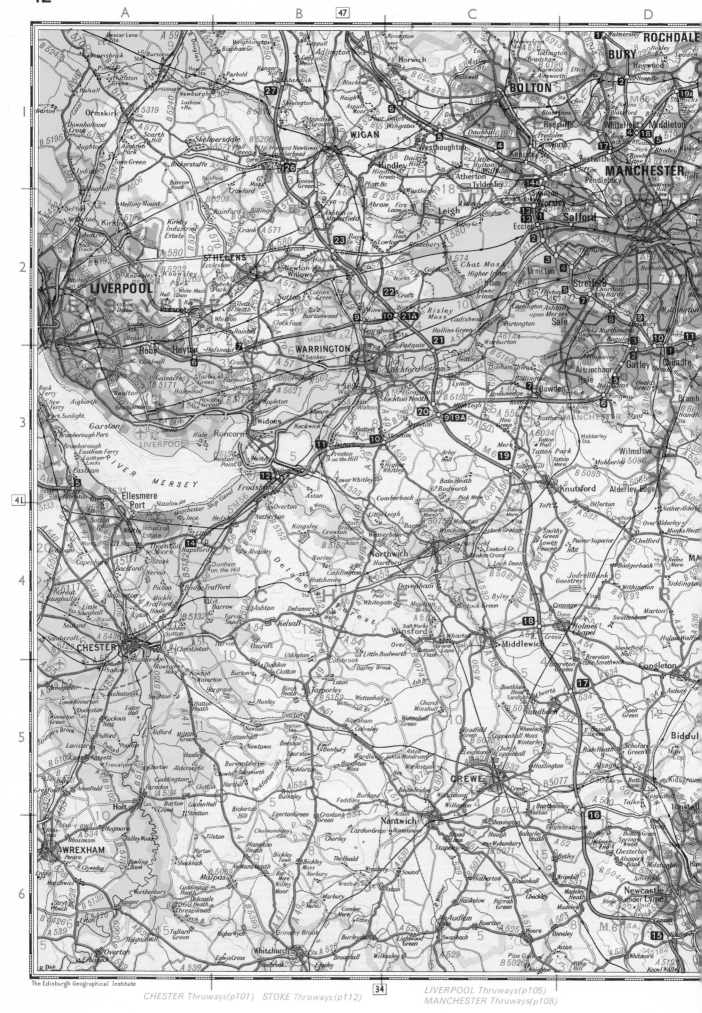

© —John Bartholomew & Son Ltd.

2 3 4 5 Miles

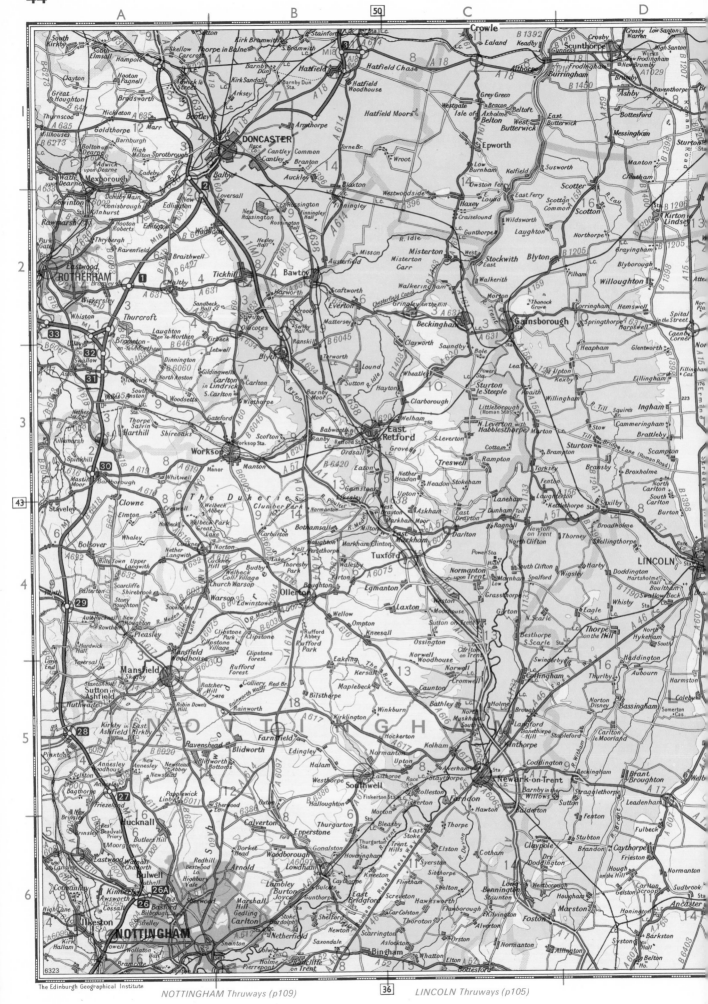

44

E   F   51   G   H

GRIMSBY
Cleethorpes
Spurn Head
Immingham to Gothenburg
Immingham to Amsterdam
Hull to Rotterdam & Zeebrugge

Elsham Croxton Ulceby Kirmington Brocklesby Stallingborough Healing Sta. Great Coates Little Coates Old Clee Beaconthorpe Pier
Wrawby Melton Ross Brocklesby Park Keelby West Marsh New Waltham Humberston Sandhaile Flats
Barnethy le Wold Barnethy Sta. Great Limber Riby Riby Grove Aylesby Bradley Scartho Low Water Mark
Bigby Searby Grasby Clixby Swallow Irby upon Humber Barnoldby le Beck Waltham Holton le Clay North Thoresby Tetney North Coates
Owmby Cabourne Beelsby Cuxwold Ashby cum Fenby Brigsley Waithe South End Marsh Chapel Somercotes Haven Donna Nook
Caistor (Roman Sta.) Rothwell Hatcliffe East Ravendale Grainsby Churchthorpe West End Wragholme Meals
Nettleton Thoresway Thorganby Swinhope Wold Newton Ludborough Fulstow Grainthorpe North Somercotes
North Owersby Normanby le Wold Stainton le Vale Canby Hall Covenham Bartholomew Rudney Conisholme Church End
Usselby Claxby Binbrook Binbrook Hall North Ormsby Covenham St Mary South Somercotes Saltfleet
Osgodby Osgodby Moor Walesby Kirmond le Mire Bayons Manor Utterby Fotherby Yarburgh Lit. Grimsby Saltfleetby St Clement Saltfleetby All Saints
Market Rasen North Willingham Ludford Parva Ludford Magna Kelstern North Elkington Alvingham North Cockerington Saltfleetby St Peter Theddlethorpe All Saints Theddlethorpe St Helen
Middle Rasen Newton by Toft Sixhills Girsby Manor Burgh on Bain Welton le Wold South Elkington Lud South Cockerington Grimoldby Manby
Faldingworth Linwood Legsby Hainton South Willingham Gayton le Wold Hallington LOUTH Little Carlton Great Carlton Mablethorpe Gibraltar
Lissington East Torrington West Torrington Benniworth Donington on Bain Raithby Withcall Castle Carlton Legbourne Trusthorpe Sutton on Sea
Wickenby Holton East Barkwith Stenigot Asterby Market Stainton Cawkwell Maidenwell Burwell Muckton South Reston Strubby Maltby le Marsh Thorpe
Snelland Panton Goulceby Scamblesby Farforth Oxcombe Ruckland Burwell Hall Authorpe Tothill Withern Beesby Hannah
Wragby Clay Br. Hatton Great Sturton Ranby Flint Hill Worlaby White Pit Swaby Claythorpe Belleau Aby Saleby Markby Salt Marsh
Langton by Wragby Baumber Hemingby Belchford Tetford Little London South Ormsby Ketsby S. Thoresby Rigsby Bilsby Huttoft Anderby Creek
Apley Kingthorpe Minting Gautby Wispington W. Ashby Low Toynton High Greetham Tetford Brinkhill Somersby Driby Ulceby Cross Alford Farlesthorpe Mumby Cumberworth Authorpe Row
Cherry Willingham Stainfield Waddingworth Edlington Salmonby Ashby Puerorum Harrington Aswardby Langton Skendleby Claxby Well Hall Willoughby Hogsthorpe Chapel St Leonards
Fiskerton Branston Bardney Bucknall Horsington Thimbleby Thornton Hagworthingham Sausthorpe Welton le Marsh Sloothby Addlethorpe
Heighington Branston Fen Southrey Langton HORNCASTLE Mareham on the Hill Hameringham Lusby R. Lymn Partney Candleby Orby Ingoldmells
Potterhanworth Nocton Stixwould Martin Asgarby Mavis Enderby Old Bolingbroke Scremby Ashby by Partney Gunby Burgh le Marsh
Potterhanworth Booths Nocton Fen Reeds Beck Daldersby Scrivelsby Court Hareby Hundleby Spilsby Halton Holegate Bratoft Skegness
Dunston Nocton Delph Roughton Claxby Pluckacre Mimingsby Toynton All Saints Gt. Steeping Irby in the Marsh Firsby
Sots Hole Woodhall Spa Moorby Res. Moorby W. Keal Toynton St Peter Lit. Steeping Thorpe St Peter Croft Croft Marsh
Metheringham Delph Kirkstead Haltham Wilksby E. Keal E. Kirkby Hagnaby Keal Cotes Thorpe Culvert Havenhouse Sta. Steeping R.
Car Dike Tattershall Thorpe Kirkby on Bain Revesby Abbey Hannah Stickford Fendike Corner Wainfleet Bank Wainfleet Keys Toft Gibraltar Point
Martin Timberland Walcot Mareham le Fen Revesby E. Kirkby Stickford Midville Eastville Friskney Gibraltar Pt.
Blankney Timberland Dales Tumby New Bolingbroke Stickney East Fen Friskney Eaudike Friskney
Scopwick Kirkby Green Thorpe Tilney Dales Coningsby Moor Side Tumby Woodside Carrington West Fen Lade Bank Wrangle Bank Wrangle Lowgate
Rowston Billinghay Hawthorn Hill Scrub Hill New York Northlands Sibsey Wrangle Leake Fold Hill
Digby Dorrington North Kyme Wildmore Fen Thornton le Fen Frithville Leake Common Side Leake Hill Leake Hurns End Old Leake
Ruskington Anwick South Kyme R. Witham West Fen Drain Langriville Fishtoft Drove Boston Long Hedges Leverton Leverton Outgate Benington Sea End
Sleaford Haverholme Priory Ewerby Ewerby Thorpe Howell Langrick Brothertoft Amber Hill Holland Fen Leverton Butterwick BOSTON DEEPS
Quarrington Kirkby la Thorpe Asgarby Heckington East Heckington Hubberts Bridge BOSTON Skirbeck Benington Halltoft Butterwick
Silk Willoughby Burton Pedwardine Lit. Hale Gt. Hale Swineshead Bridge Kirton Holme Skirbeck Quarter Fishtoft Freiston Shore
Scredington Helpringham Swineshead Kirton Fenhouses Wyberton Scrane End Cas. Freiston

2 3 4 5 Miles

37

© — John Bartholomew & Son Ltd.

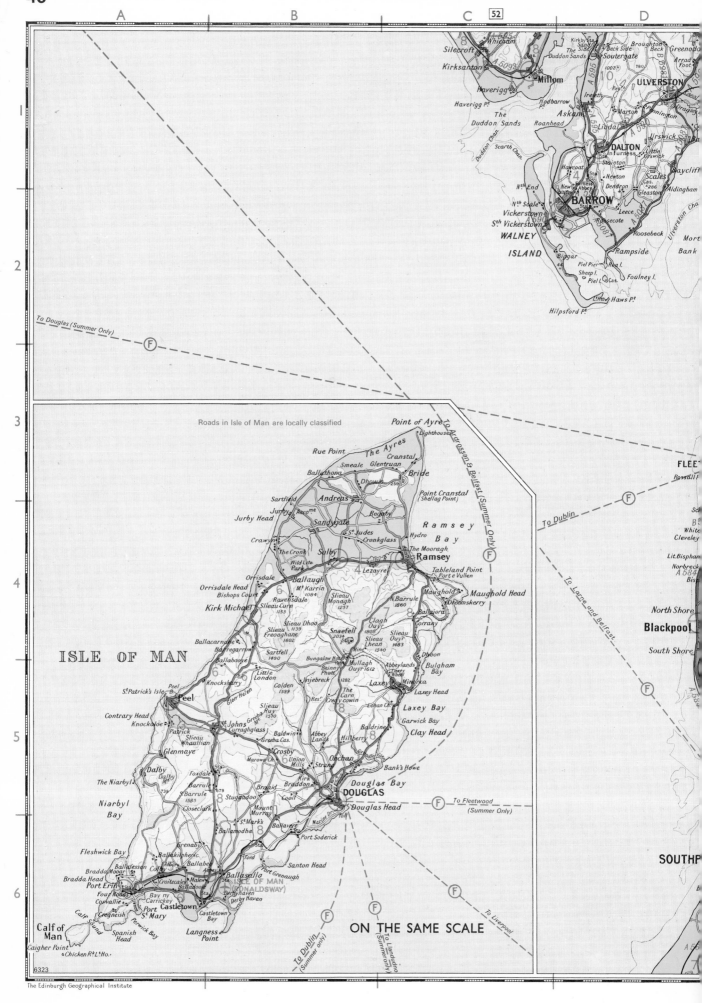

52

A   B   C   D

ULVERSTON

Silecroft
Kirksanton
Millom
Haverigg
DALTON
in Furness
BARROW
Vickerstown
Sth Vickerstown
WALNEY
ISLAND
Rampside
Hilpsford Pt

To Douglas (Summer Only)

Roads in Isle of Man are locally classified

Point of Ayre
Lighthouse
Rue Point   The Ayres
Cranstal
Smeale Glentruan
Ballathona   Bride
Dhoon
Point Cranstal
(Shellag Point)
Sartfield   Andreas
Jurby   Regaby
Jurby Head
Sandygate
Crawyn   St Judes
Cronkglass
The Cronk   Sulby
Ramsey
Bay
Hydro
Sulby R.   The Mooragh
Ramsey
Wild Life
Park
Orrisdale   Ballaugh
Orrisdale Head   Mt Karrin   Lezayre   Tableland Point
Bishops Court   1084   Port e Vullen
Ravensdale
Kirk Michael   Slieau Curn   Slieau   N Barrule
1153   Monagh   1860
Maughold   Maughold Head
1257   Ballajora   Dreemskerry
Slieau Dhoo   Corrany
Slieau   1139   Clagh
Freoaghane   1602   Ouyr   Slieau
Sartfell   1808   Ouyr   Dhoon
Ballacarnane   1490   Snaefell   Slieau   1483
Ballregarrow   2034   Lhean
Ballabooie   1540   Abbeylands
Bungalow Hotel   Mullagh   Bulgham
Little   Brainny   Ouyr 1612   Bay
Knocksharry   London   Phott.   Laxey
Colden   1282   Minorka
St Patrick's Isle   1599   Injebreck   Laxey Head
Peel   Glen Helen   Res.   The   Garwick Bay
Contrary Head   Slieau Ruy   Carn   Lohan Ch.   Laxey Bay
Knockaloe   1570   Baldwin   Creg y cowin   Clay Head
Patrick   St Johns   Greeba Cas.   Baldrine
Slieau Whuallian   Curraghglass   Abbey   Hillberry
Glenmaye   Crosby   Lands
Marown Ch.   Union   Onchan
Dalby   Mills   Strang   Bank's Howe
The Niarbyl   Dalby Mt.   Foxdale   Kirk   Douglas Bay
739   Barrule   Braddan   DOUGLAS
Niarbyl   679   Stuggadoo   Cooil   Douglas Head
Bay   S Barrule   Mount   To Fleetwood
1585   Murray   (Summer Only)
Closeclark   St Mark's   Ballavere
Grenaby   Ballamodha
Fleshwick Bay   Ballakilpheric   Ford   Port Soderick
Bradda Mooar   Ballabeg   Santon Head
Bradda Head   Balladoole   Malew   Port Grenaugh
Port Erin   Colby   Ballasalla
Four Roads   Croitecaley   ISLE OF MAN   Derbyhaven
Corvallie   (RONALDSWAY)   Derby Haven
Cregneish   Port   Castletown
St Mary   Castletown
Bay
Calf of   Perwick Bay
Man   Spanish
Caigher Point   Head   Langness
Chicken Rk Lt Ho.   Point

ISLE OF MAN

To Dublin

FLEE
Rossall P
White
Cleveley
Lit Bispham
Norbreck
North Shore
Blackpool
South Shore

To Larne and Belfast

To Dublin
(Summer only)

To Llandudno
(Summer only)

To Liverpool

ON THE SAME SCALE

SOUTHP

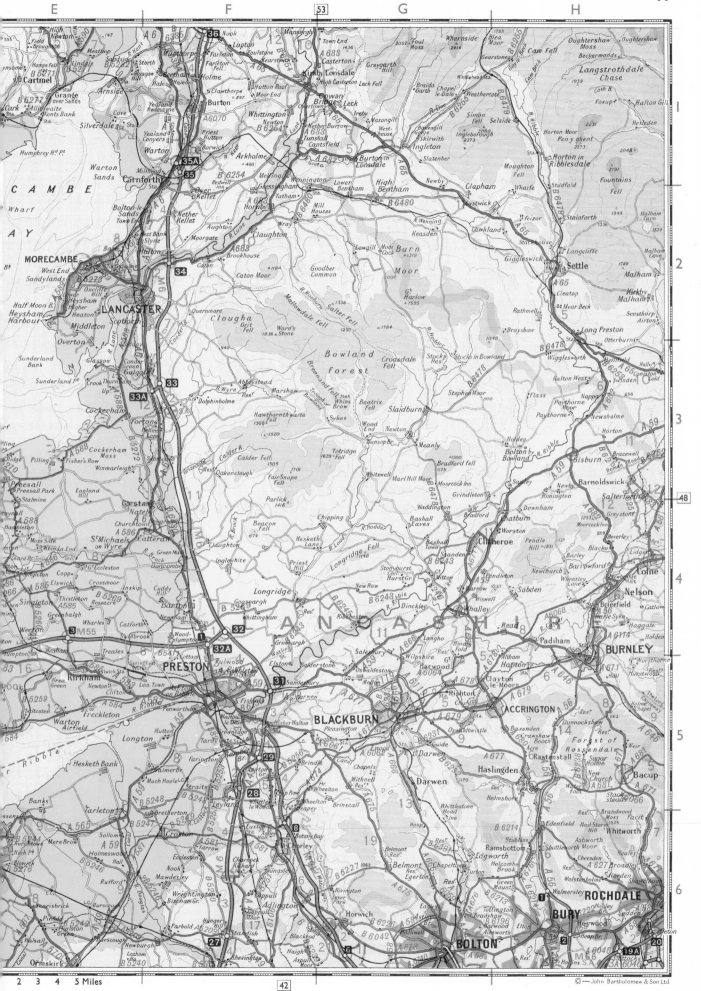

© —John Bartholomew & Son Ltd.

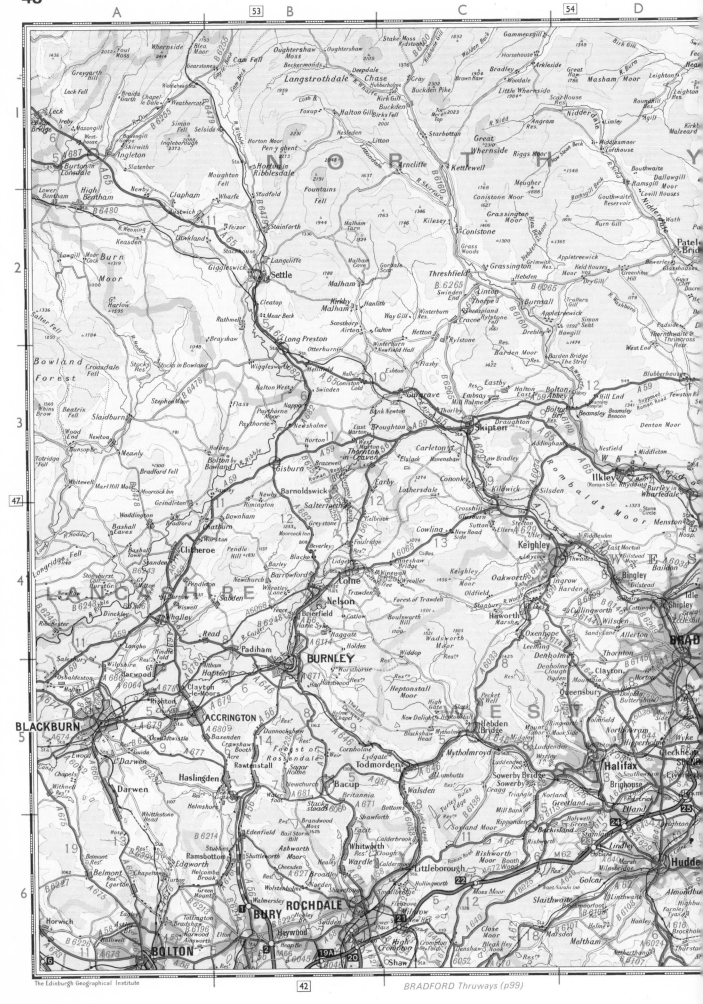

BRADFORD Thruways (p99)

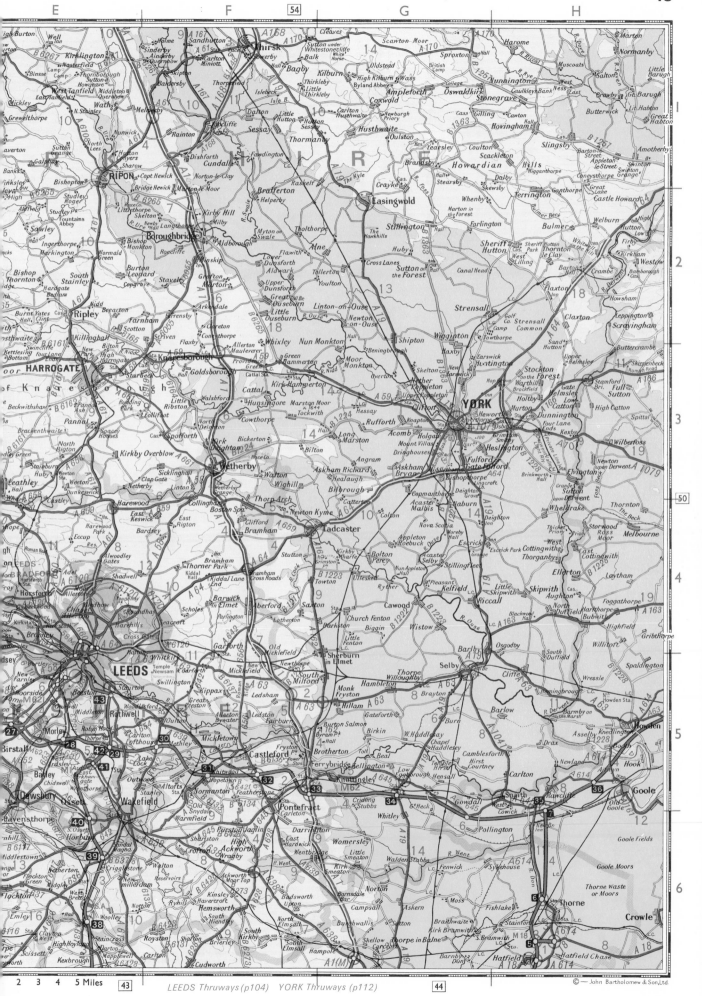

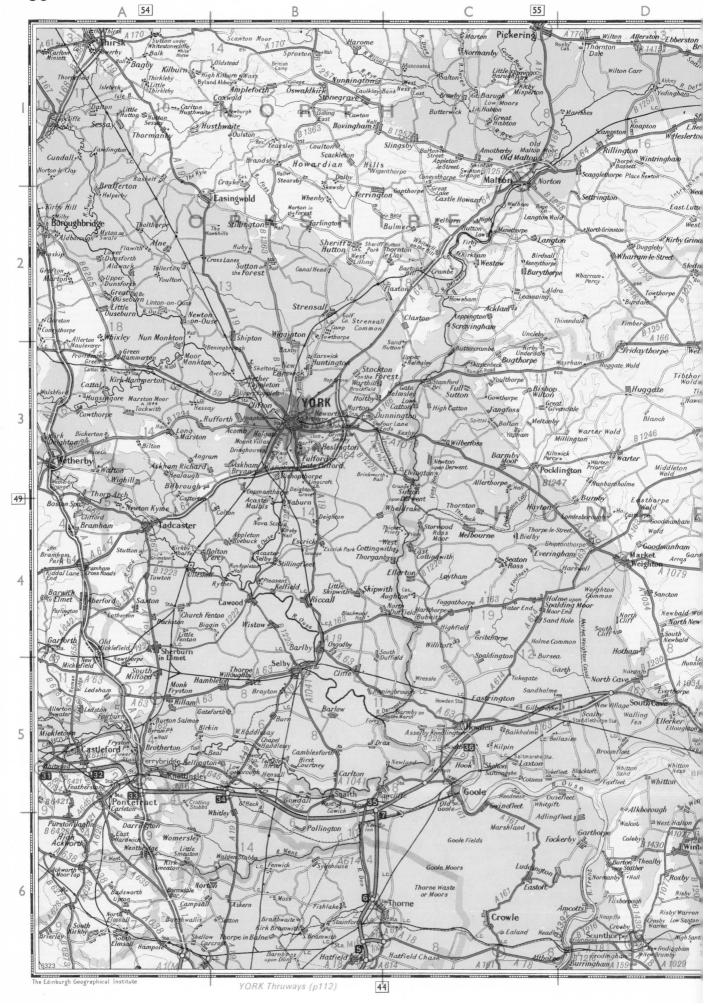

YORK Thruways (p112)

E F G H

Seamer · Cayton
Filey
Folkton
Filey Bay
Hunmanby
Reighton
Speeton
Flamborough Hd
Flamborough
Old Town
Bridlington
Hilderthorpe
Carnaby
Bessingby
Haisthorpe
Thornholme
Burton Agnes
Carnaby Moor
Fraisthorpe

B R I D L I N G T O N
B A Y

Foxholes
Thwing
Grindale
Buckton
Bempton
North Burton or Burton Fleming
Octon
Ancient Village
Swaythorpe
Boynton
Rudston
The Gypsey Race
Langtoft
West End
Kilham
Ruston Parva
Harpham
Lowthorpe
Nafferton
Great Driffield
Wansford
Skerne
Foston on the Wolds
Gransmoor
Barmston
Lissett
Gembling
Ulrome
Brigham
Church End
Beeford
Skipsea
Nth Frodingham
Dunnington
Watton
Hempholme
Bewholme
Atwick
Burshill
Brandesburton
Catfoss
Seaton
Hornsea
Leven
Catwick
Lit. Catwick
Sigglesthorne
Hornsea Mere
Golf Co.
Goxhill
Rolston
Scorborough
Aike
Arram
Routh
Long Riston
Rise
Gt. Hatfield
Mappleton
Leconfield
Tickton
Cote Bridge
Withernwick
Gt. Cowden
Beverley
Weel
Meaux
N. Skirlaugh
Marton
Aldbrough
Woodmansey
Wawne
Ellerby
Burton Constable
West. Newton
Bentley
Thearne
Swine
Flinton
Garton
Dunswell
Coniston
Sproatley
Humbleton
Grimston Hall
Hilston
Cottingham
Sutton
Bilton
Wyton
Lelley
Owstwick
Tunstall
Haltemprice
Stoneferry
Elstronwick
Willerby
Southcoates
Preston
Burton Pidsea
Roos
Waxholme
Anlaby
Marfleet
Hedon
Wadworth Hill
Rimswell
Withernsea
HULL
Paull
Thorngumbald
Burstwick
West End
Halsham
East End
Hessle
Low Water Mark
Paull Holme
Ryhill
Keyingham
Ottringham
Winestead
Hollym
Holmpton
Barrow Haven
New Holland
Goxhill Haven
East Halton Skitter
Goxhill
Sands Drain
Patrington
Haven Side
Welwick
Out Newton
Weeton
Barton upon Humber
Barrow upon Humber
Sth End
East Halton
Stone Creek Ho.
Sunk Island
Skeffling
Easington
Thornton Curtis
Burnham
Abbey Bass Garth
Nth Killingholme
South Killingholme Haven
Immingham Dock
To Amsterdam, Rotterdam & Zeebrugge
Sunk Sand
Skeffling Clays
Kilnsea
Kilnsea Clays
Wootton
Ulceby Skitter
Ulceby
Brocklesby Sta.
Habrough
Immingham
Stallingborough
R I V E R   H U M B E R
Immingham to Gothenburg
Sparn Head
Elsham
Croxton
Ulceby Chase
Kirmington
Brocklesby
Brocklesby Park
Keelby
Healing
West Marsh
GRIMSBY
New Clee Sta.
Beaconthorpe Pier
Melton Ross
Barnetby Sta.

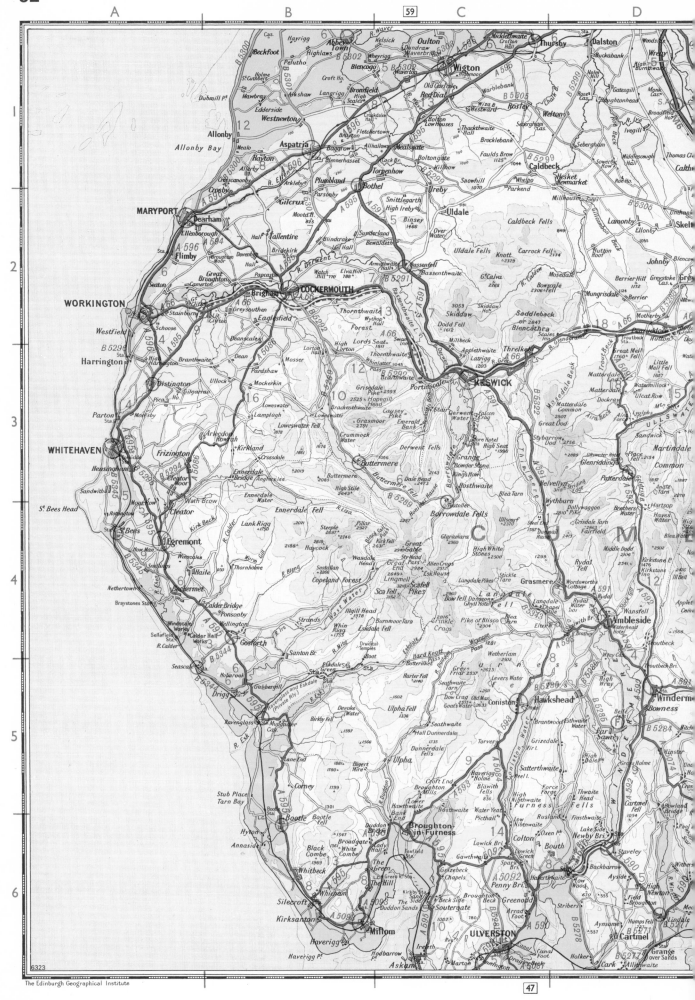

52

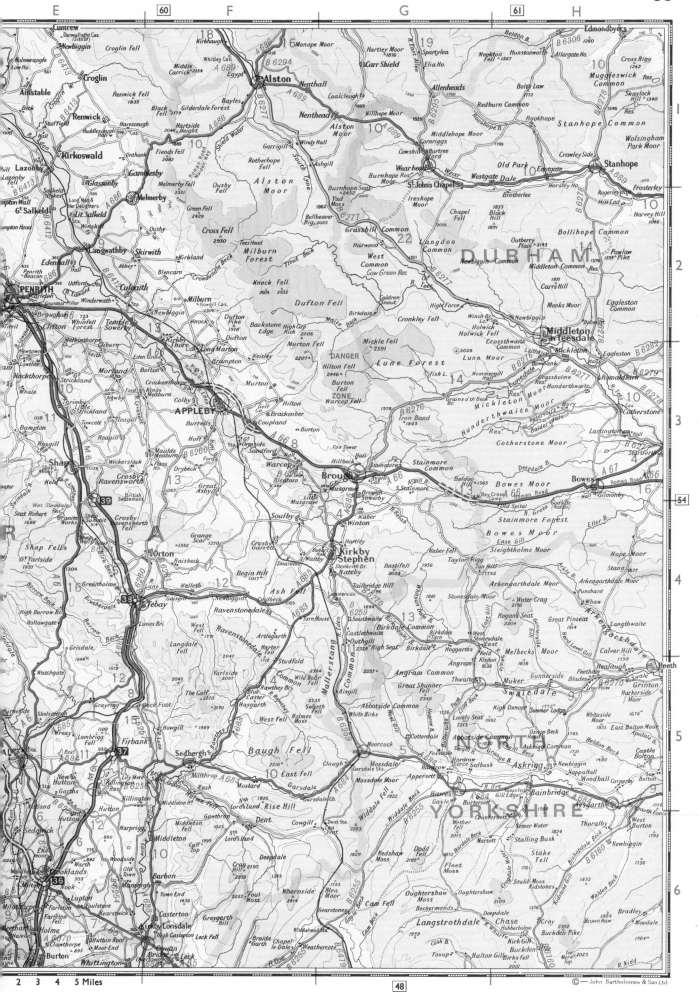

2 3 4 5 Miles

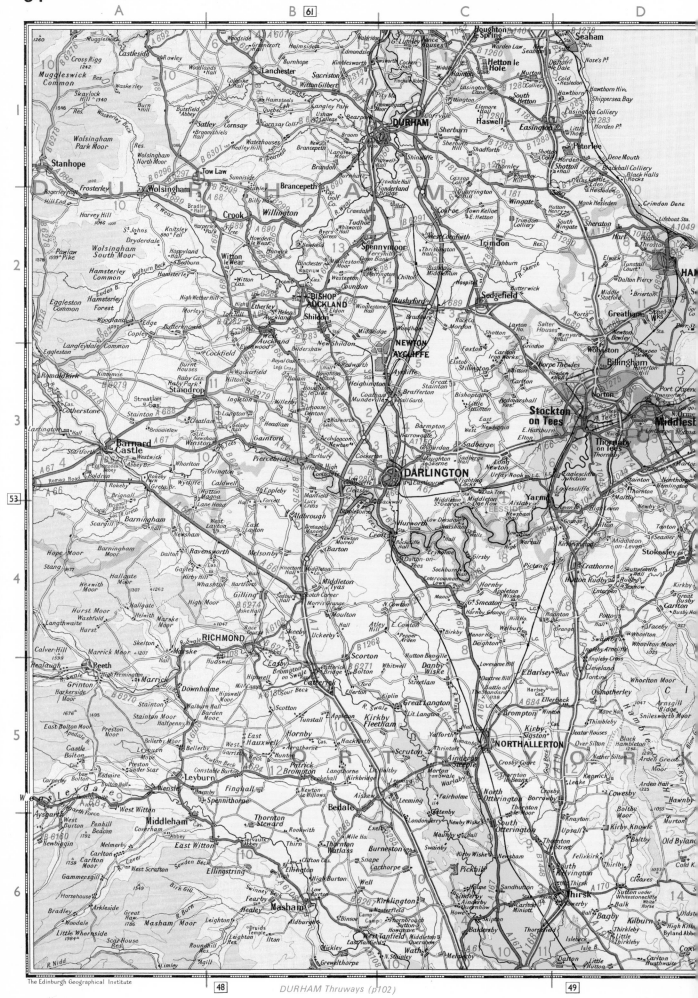

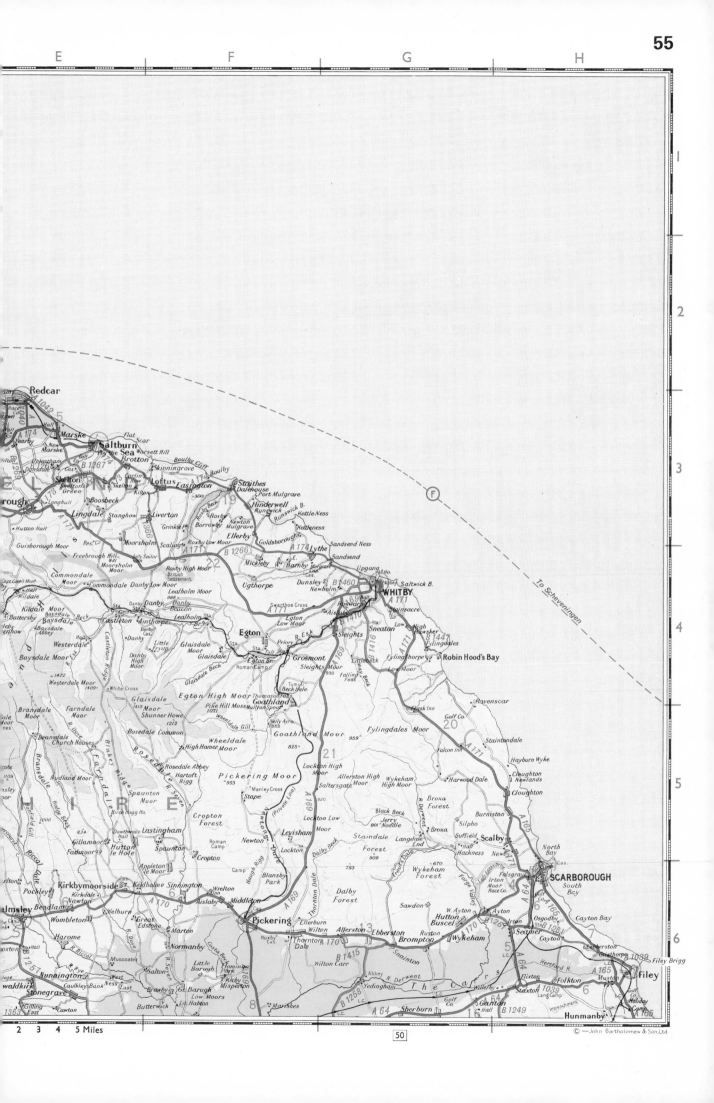

2   3   4   5 Miles

© —John Bartholomew & Son, Ltd.

STRATHCLYDE

Muirkirk · New Cumnock · Cumnock · Auchinleck · Sorn · Catrine · Mauchline · Ochiltree · Stair · Tarbolton · Galston · Newmilns · Darvel · Fenwick · Kilmarnock · Hurlford · Craigie · Dundonald · Symington · Troon · Prestwick · New Prestwick · Ayr · Maybole · Dalmellington · Straiton · Patna · Kirkmichael · Crosshill · Dalrymple · Kilwinning · Stevenston · Saltcoats · Ardrossan · New Dailly · Old Dailly · Girvan · Barr · Kirkoswald · Carsphairn

CARRICK

FIRTH OF CLYDE

Ailsa Craig 1113

ARRAN · Corrie · Brodick · Lamlash · Holy Island · Whiting Bay · Kilmory

Brodick Bay · Lamlash Bay · Irvine Bay · Ayr Bay · Culzean Bay · Maidenhead Bay · Turnberry Bay

Goat Fell 2866 · Glen Rosa · Glen Sannox · Glen Scorrodale · Benan Hill

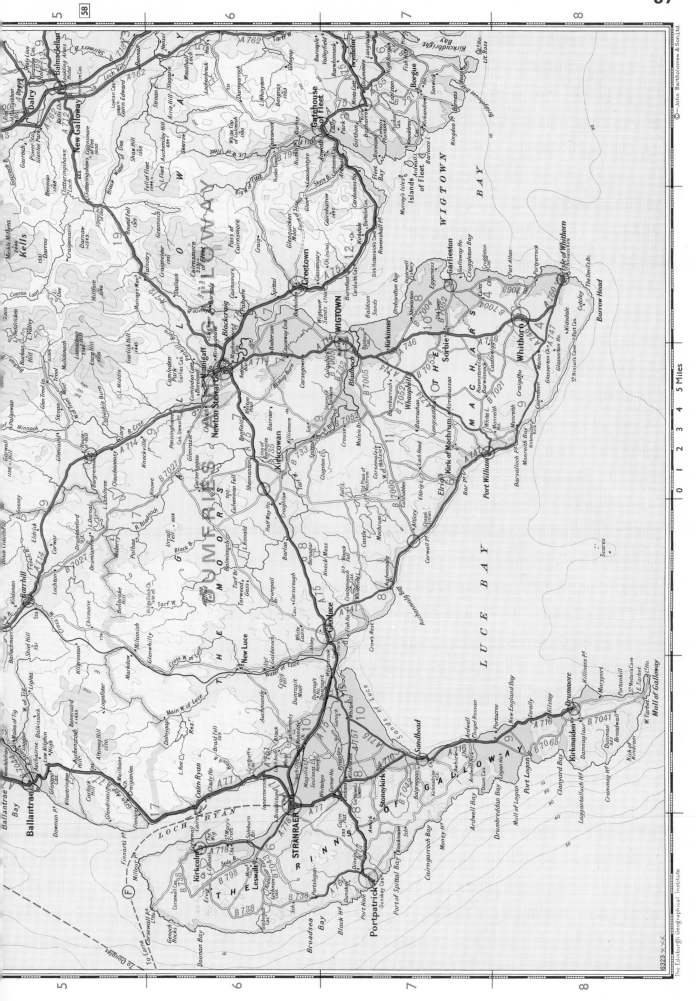

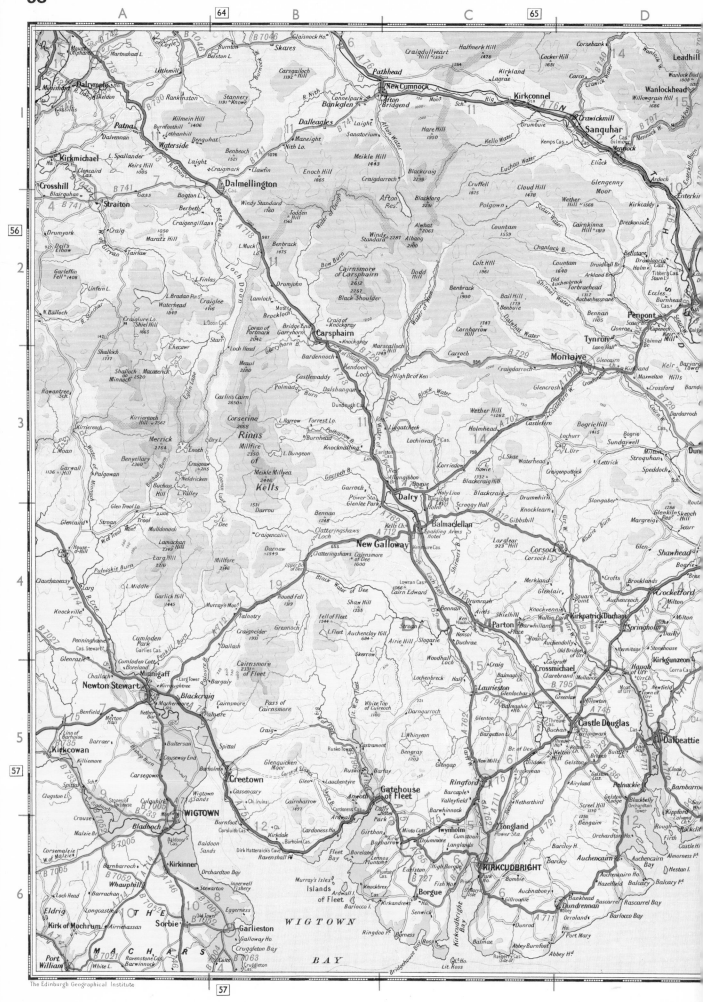

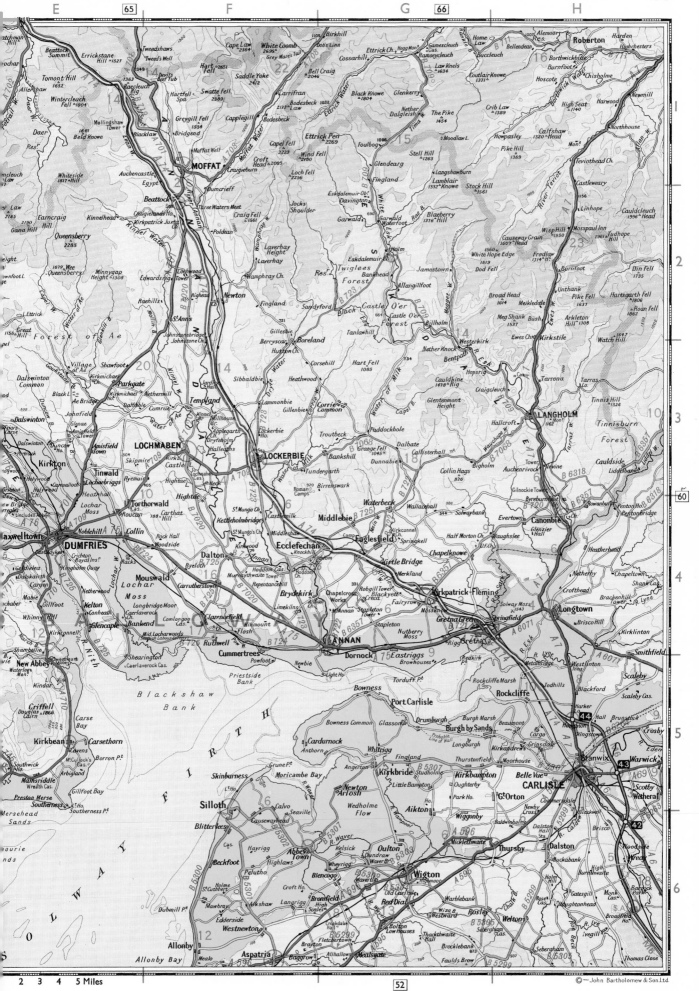

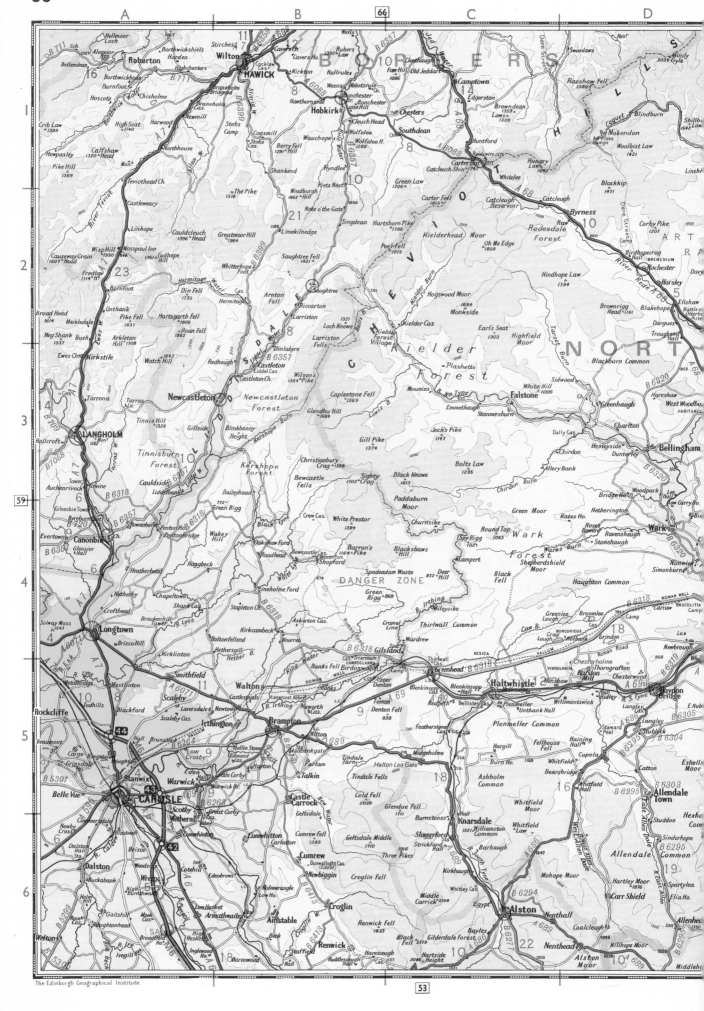

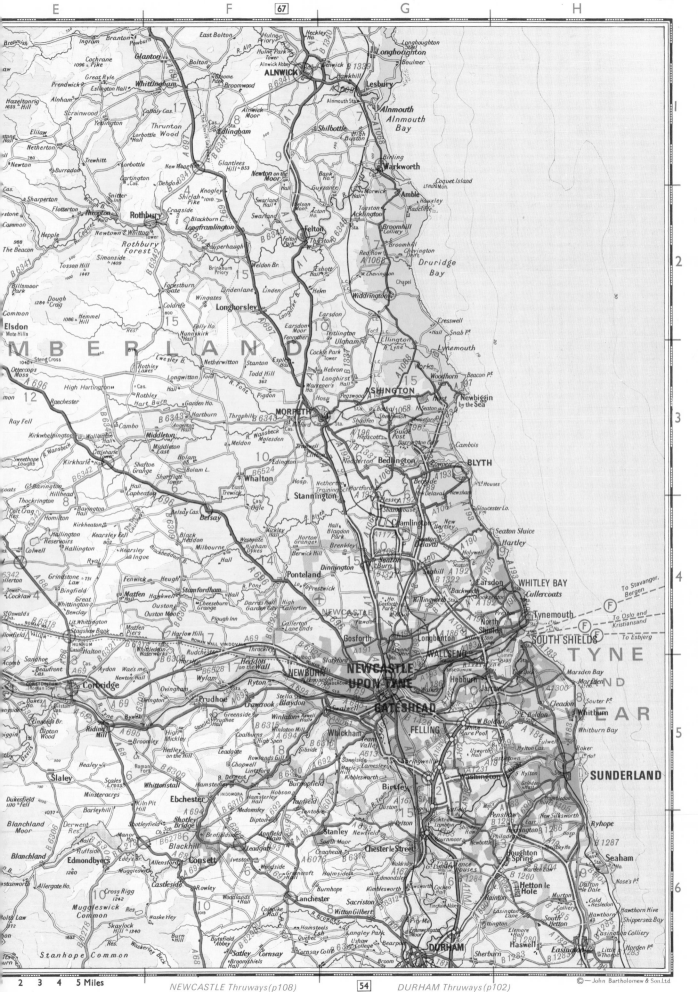

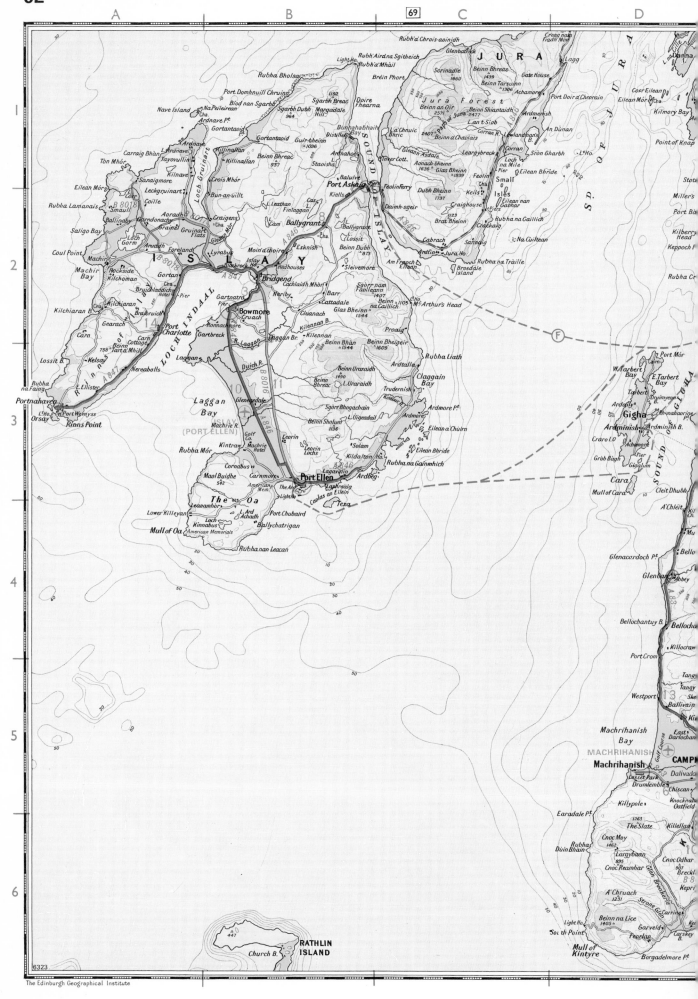

©—John Bartholomew & Son Ltd.

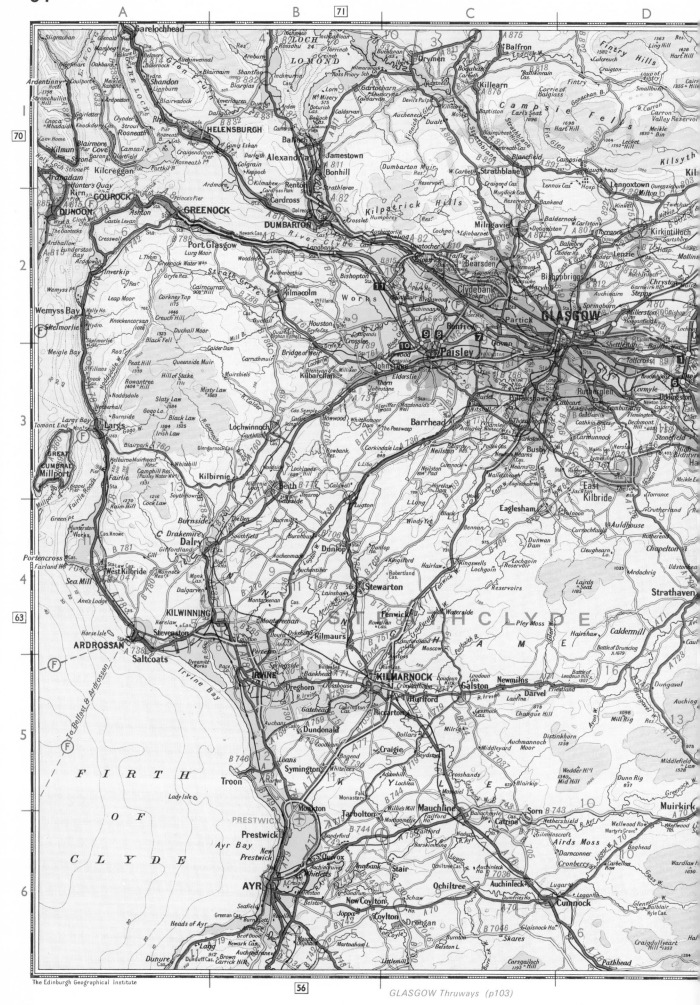

GLASGOW Thruways (p103)

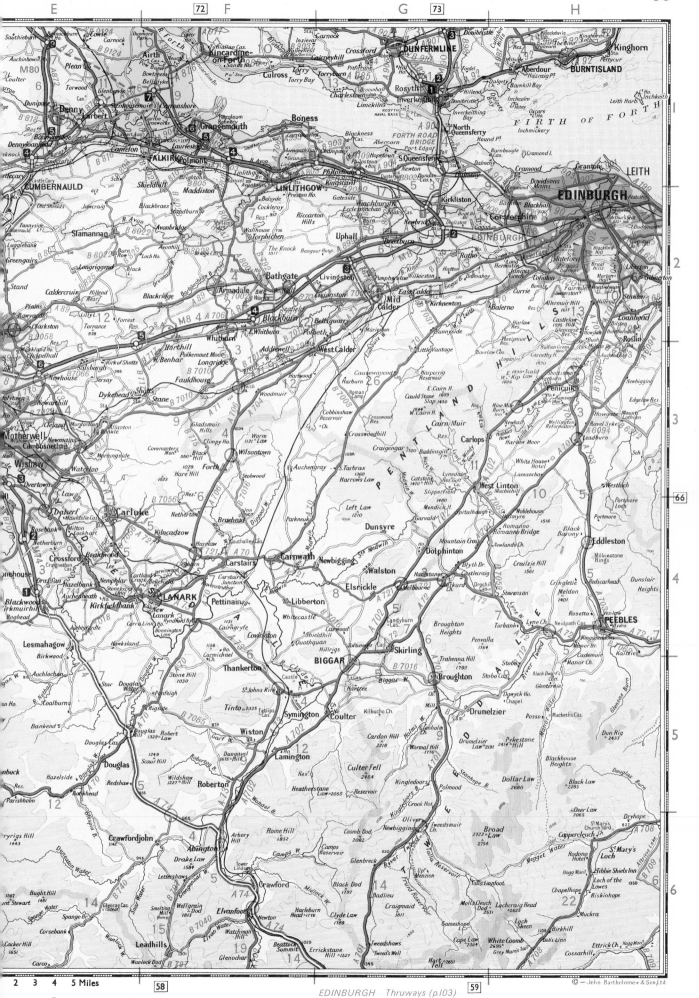

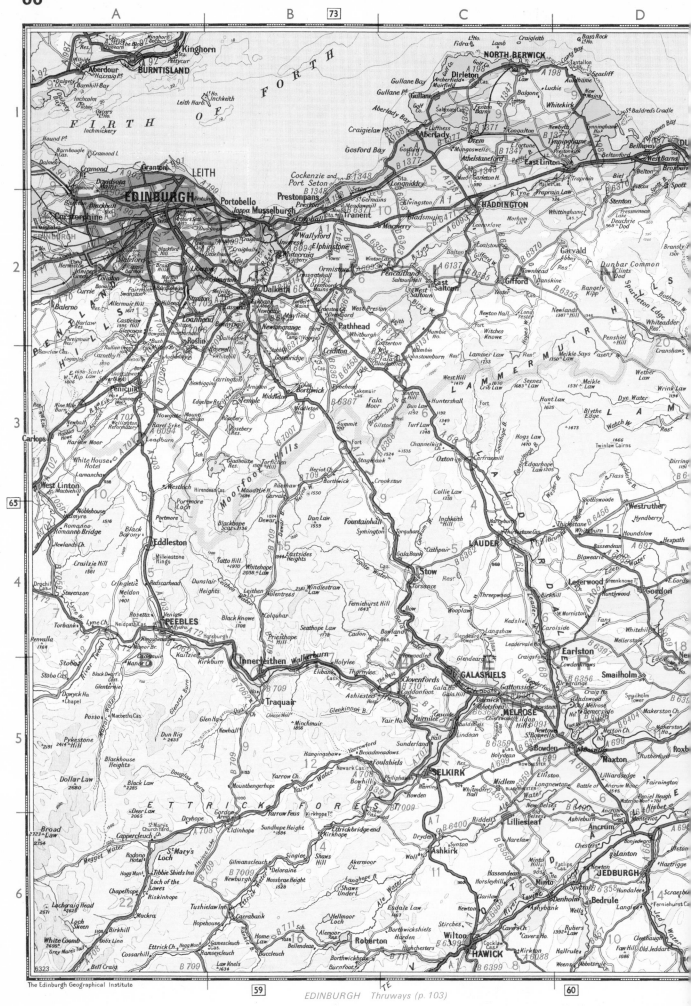

E F G H

Dateraw Harbour

Bilsdean
Reed Pt.
Cove
Pease Bay
unglass
ournspath
Craig Taw
Fast Cas.
St. Helen's Ch.
St. Abb's Head
Heriot W.
Brown Rig
Meikle
Black Law
Moorhouse
Coldingham
Loch
Northfield
St. Abb's
Ecclaw
Hill
20
Granthouse
Coldingham
Moor
Coldingham B.
Kilspindie
Cas.
Houndwood
Eyemouth
hing
Moorhouse
Drake
Mire
Horseley
Hill
Reston
Eastfield
Hallydown
Redhall
Burnmouth
Cockburn
Law
Cas.
Bonkyl Ch.
Ferney
Cas.
Ayton
Whiterig
Ayton Hill
Hilton Bay
Primrosehill
Preston
Billie Cas.
Lintlaw
Millerton
Hill
Marshall Meadows B.
DUNS
Chirnside
Edington
Lamberton
Mordington
Needles Eye
Edrom
Faulden
Halidon Hill
Sharper's Head
Dunslaw
Edrom
Newton
Whiteadder
Water
Mordington Ch.
BERWICK-
UPON-TWEED
Allanbank
Allanton
Tweedmouth
Cheeklaw
Kelloe
Blackadder
Spittal
Nisbet
Hutton
Paxton
R. Tweed
East
Ord
Mount Pleasant
Hilton
Union Br.
Longridge
Towers
Cremerston
Caldra
Fogo
Crowfoot-bank
Whitsome
Horndean
Horncliffe
Ladykirk
Swinton
Norham
W. Allerdean
Oxford
Cheswick
Ho.
Goswick
Swinton
Ho.
Upsettlington
Shoreswood
Leitholm
Ruthven
Grindon
Felkington
Ancroft
Haggerston
Beal
Lindisfarne or
(Holy Island)
Eccles
Lennel
Allington
Millfield
Park
Duddo
Bowsden
Kyloe
Cathedral
Guile Pt.
COLDSTREAM
Castle Heaton
Donaldson's
Lodge
Etal
Barmoor
Kyloe Hills
Fenwick
Fenham
Flats
Carham
Wark
Crookham
Branxton
Ford
Fordcommon
Lowick
Buckton
Ross
Elwick
Longstone
Farne Islands
Sprouston
Pressen
Flodden
Kimmerston
Brownridge
Coalshank
Detchant
Holburn
Middleton
Hall
Budle
Bay
Bamburgh
Blakelaw
Howtel
Fenton
Fenton Ho.
Cockenheugh
Belford
Easington
Gloror
Spindlestone
North Sunderland
Milfield
River Till
Doddington
Spylaw
Belford
Mains
Bradford
Lucker
Elford
Seahouses
Kilham
Coupland Cas.
Westnewton
Doddington
Br.
Bellshill
Warenton
Addershiel
Newham
Beadnell
Kirknewton
Akeld
Ewart
Park
Chatton
Park
Chatton
Swinhoe
Beadnell
Bay
Town Yetholm
Kirk Yetholm
Yeavering Bell
Wooler
Chatton
Warenford
Swinhoe
Newton
by the Sea
Dikeside
Humbleton
Haugh Head
Chillingham
Castle
Hepburn
Botany
Rosebrough
Ellingham
Preston
Brunton
Newton Seahouses
Morebattle
Corbet
Earle
Middleton
Hall
Newtown
Lilburn
Cateran
Hill
Brownyside
North
Charlton
Christon
Bank
Embleton
Embleton Bay
Gateshaws
The Curr
Attonburn
Middleton
South
Lilburn
Chillingham
Castle
Bewick Moor
South
Charlton
Rock
Dunstan
Craster
Hownam Law
Ilderton
Old
Bewick
Bewick Br.
West Ditchburn
Stamford
Cullernose Pt.
The Cheviot
Hedgehope
Hill
Wooperton
New
Bewick
Percy's
Cross
Edlingham
Rennington
Inn
Howick
Hownam
Comb Fell
Dunmoor
Hill
Brandon
Beanley
Bannamoor
East Bolton
Heckley
Ho.
Longhoughton
HILLS
Windy Gyle
Bloodybush
Edge
Cushat Law
Ingram
Branton
Pawburn
Bolton
Hulne
Priory
Denwick
Longhoughton
Boulmer
Swanlaws
Raeshaw Fell
Prendwick
Eslington Hall
Whittingham
Great Ryle
Cochrane
Pike
Glanton
Bolton
Alnwick Abbey
ALNWICK
Lesbury
Hawkhill

2 3 4 5 Miles

74

79

L. Nevis

NORTH MORAR

SOUTH MORAR

Loch Morar

RUM

Askival 2659
Ainshval 2552
Ruinsival 1802
Sgurr nan Gillean 2503

EIGG

An Sgurr 1289

MUCK

SOUND OF EIGG

SOUND OF RUM

SOUND OF ARISAIG

ARISAIG

ARDNAMURCHAN

Ardnamurchan Pt.

MOIDART

LOCH SHIEL

SUNART

LOCH SUNART

MORVERN

LOCH LINNHE

TOBERMORY

Salen

ISLE OF MULL

AROS

LOCH TUATH

COLL

SOUND OF MULL

To Lochboisdale

To Castlebay

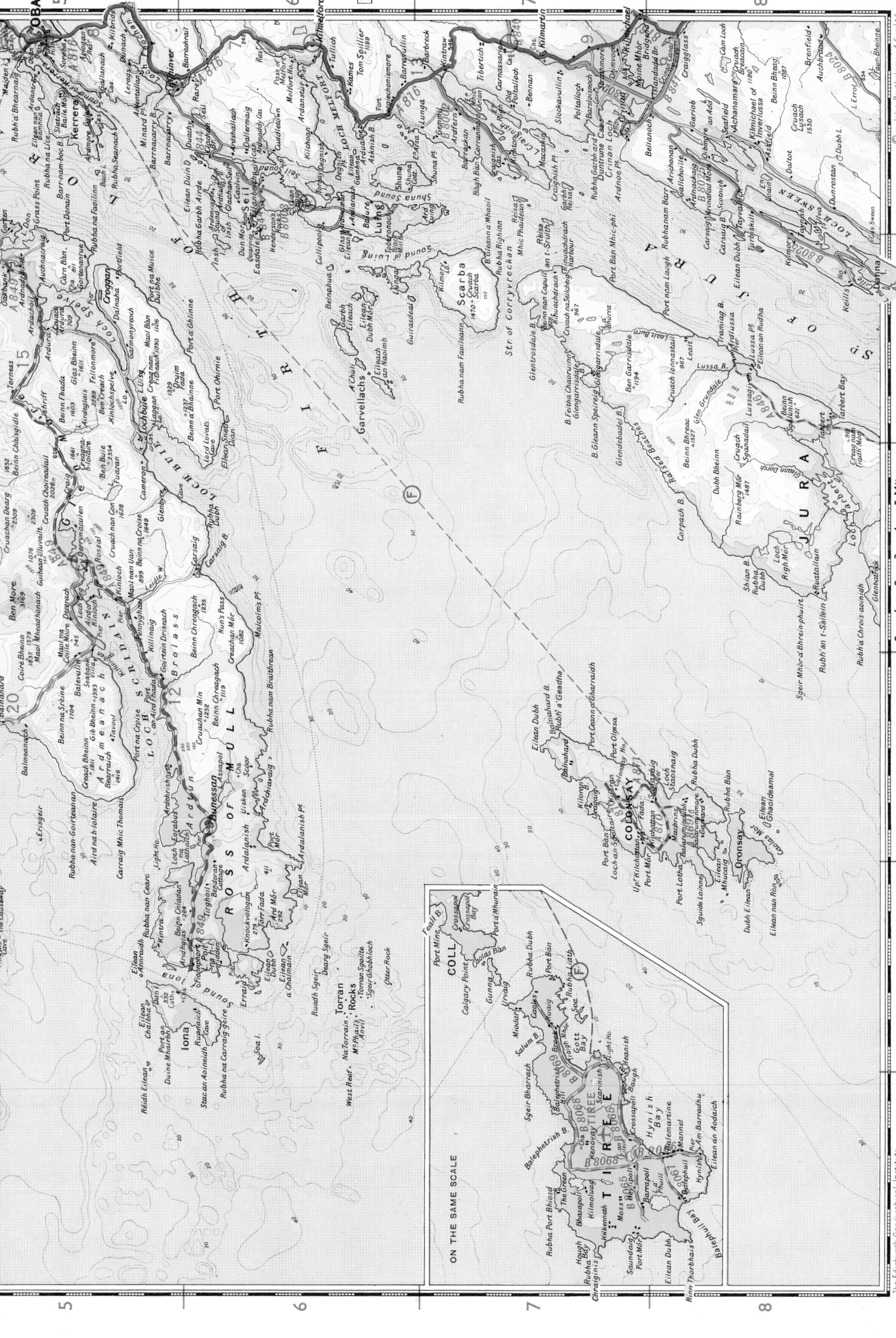

OBAN

Kerrera

LOCH LINNHE

Lismore

MORVERN

LOCH SUNART

Ben More
3169

MULL

ROSS OF MULL

Iona

Staffa
Fingal's Cave

FIRTH OF LORN

Seil

Luing

Scarba
1470

Garvellachs

Str. of Corryvreckan

JURA

SOUND OF JURA

CRINAN

LOCH SWEEN

Kilmartin

COLONSAY

Oronsay

ON THE SAME SCALE

COLL

TIREE

Gott Bay

Hynish Bay

Scarinish

0 1 2 3 4 5 Miles

The Edinburgh Geographical Institute

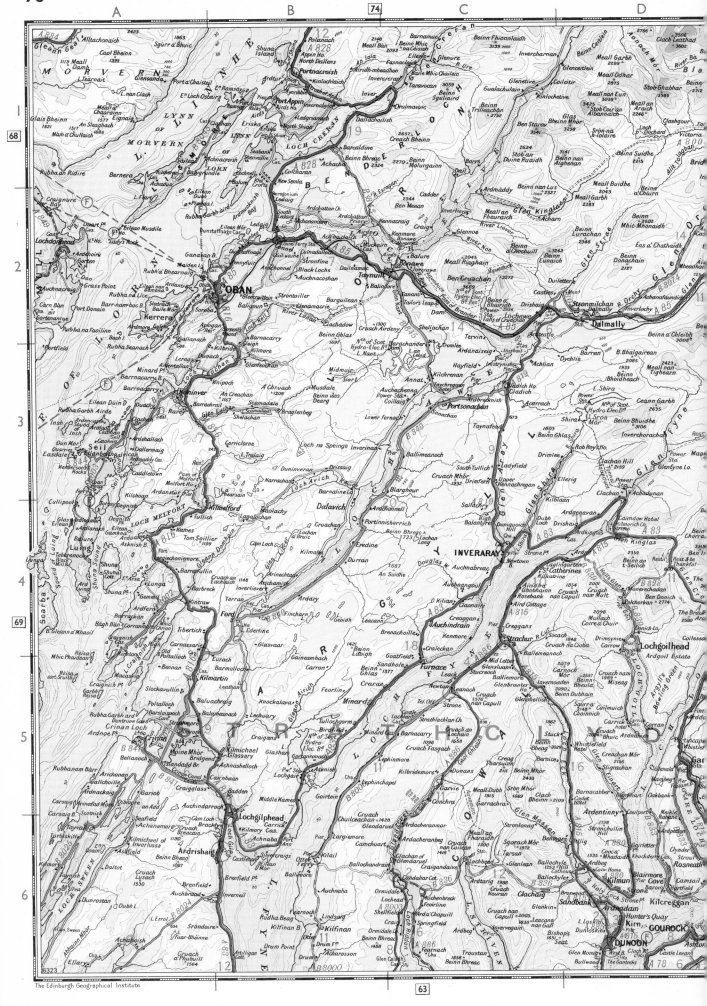

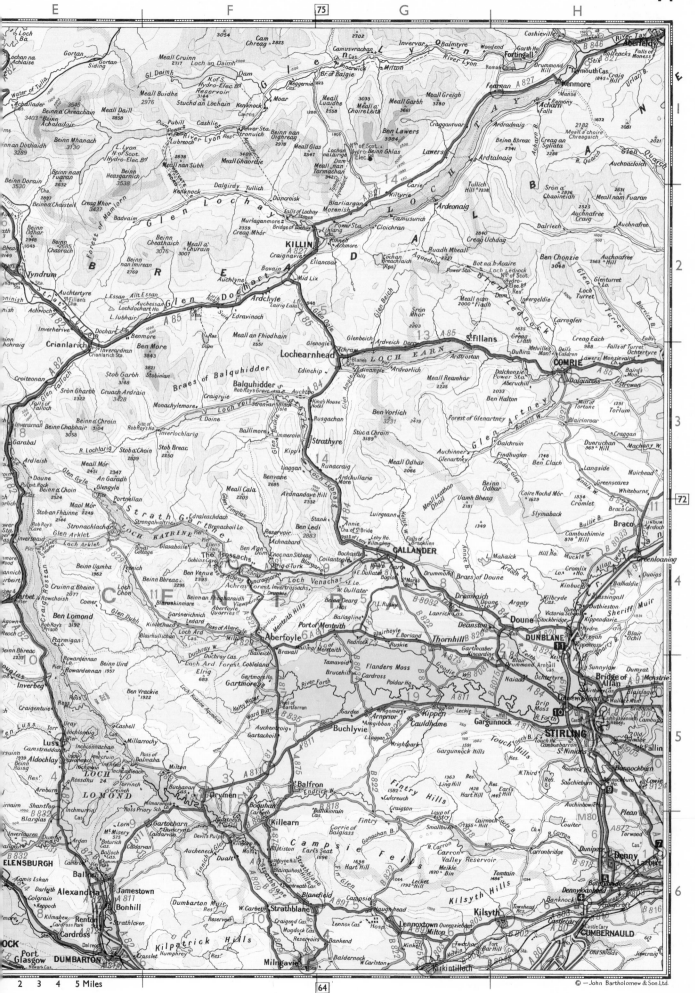

2 3 4 5 Miles

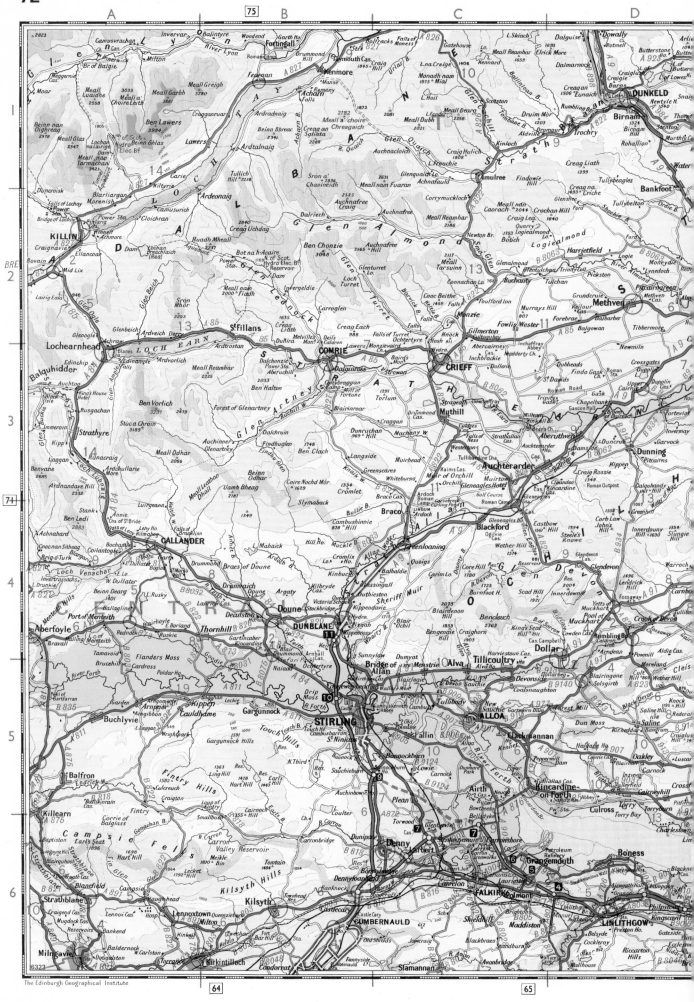

The Edinburgh Geographical Institute

© John Bartholomew & Son,Ltd.

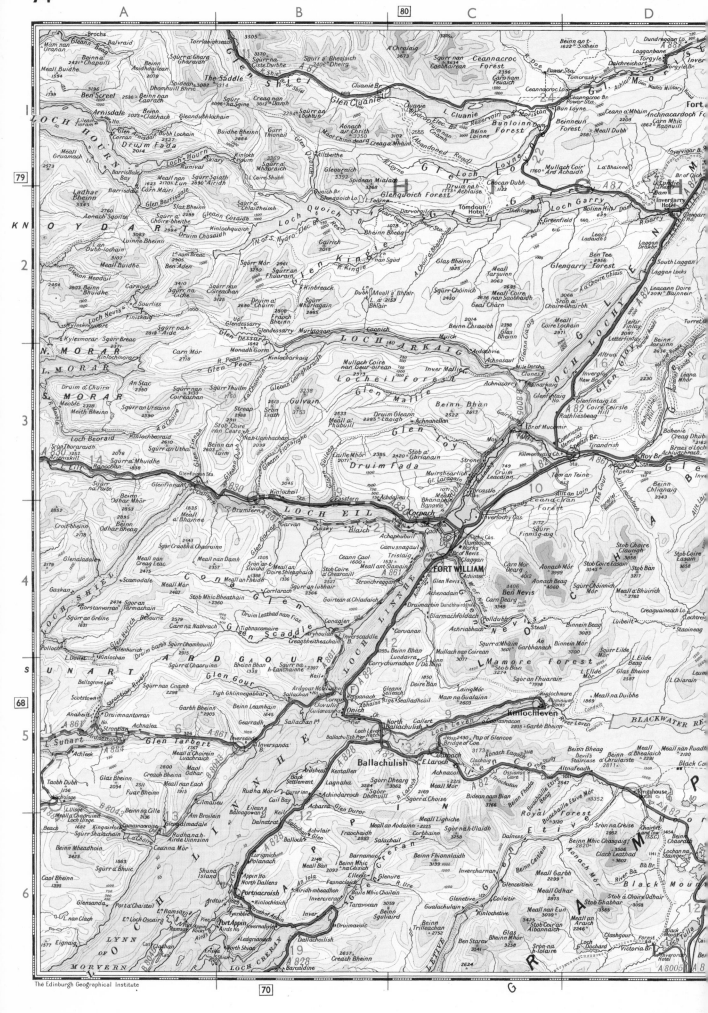

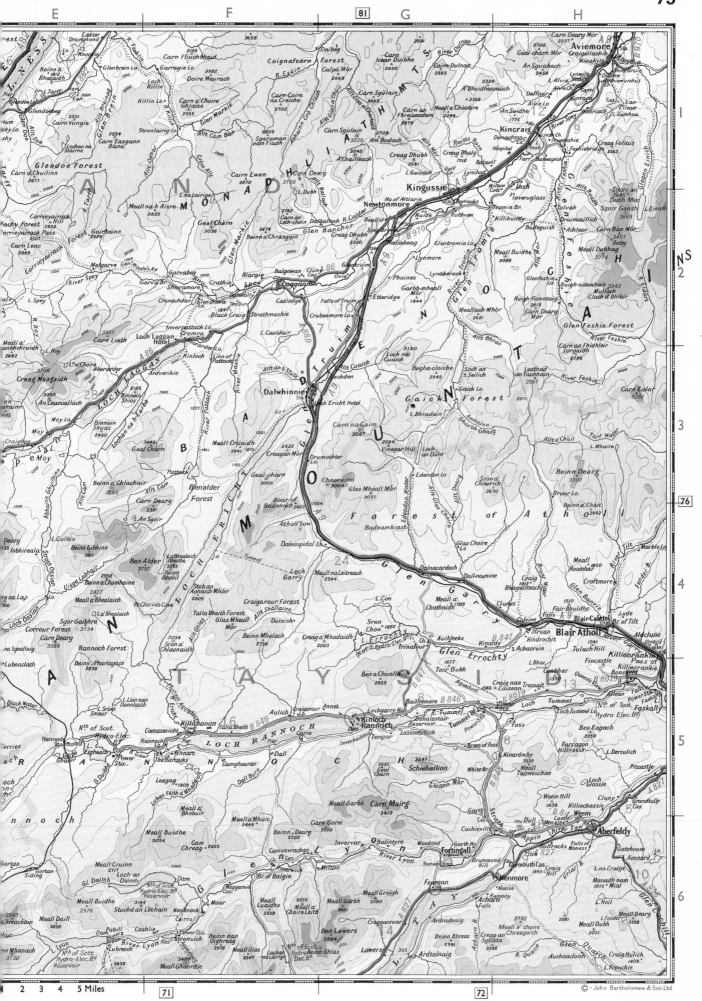

2 3 4 5 Miles

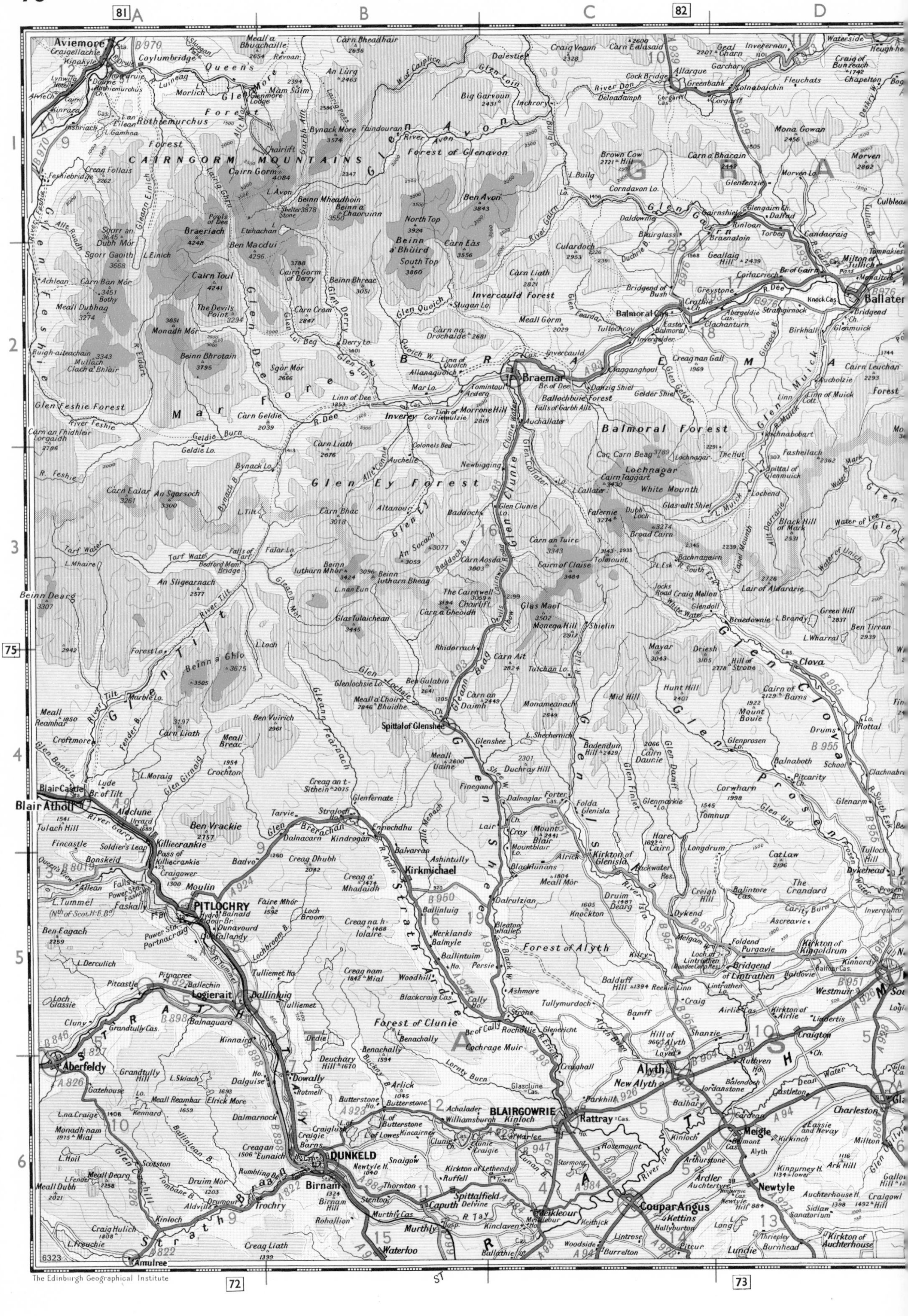

81 A 82 D

CAIRNGORM MOUNTAINS

Aviemore
Craigellachie
Kincraig
Coylumbridge
Glenmore Lodge
Queen's Forest
Glen More Forest
Rothiemurchus
Forest

Cairn Gorm 4084
Ben Macdui 4296
Braeriach 4248
Cairn Toul 4241
The Devils Point 3294
Monadh Mór 3651
Beinn Bhrotain 3795

GLEN AVON
Forest of Glenavon
Ben Avon 3843
Beinn a' Bhùird South Top 3860
North Top 3924
Càrn Làs 3556

River Don
Corgarff
Greenbank
Allargue

GAIRN
GRAMPIANS

Carn a' Bhacain
Morven 2862
Glenfenzie
Mona Gowan 2456

Corndavon Lo.
Culardoch 2953

Balmoral Cas.
Easter Balmoral
Crathie
Abergeldie Cas.
Strathgirnock
Ballater
Bridge of Gairn

River Dee
Braemar
Inverey
Morrone Hill
Inverauld Forest
Inverey
Auchallater

BALMORAL FOREST
Lochnagar
Cac Carn Beag 3789
Cairn Taggart 3430
White Mount
Broad Cairn 3274
Glas Maol 3502

Glen Ey Forest
An Socach 3077
Beinn Iutharn Mhór 3424
Beinn Iutharn Bheag
Glas Tulaichean 3445
The Cairnwell 3059
Càrn a' Gheoidh
Càrn Aosda 3003

Glen Clunie
Glen Callater
L. Callater
Càrn an Tuire 3343
Cairn of Claise 3484

Monega Hill 2917
Mayar 3043
Driesh 3105
Clova
GLEN CLOVA
GLEN PROSEN

Beinn Dearg 3307
Beinn a' Ghlo 3675
Càrn Liath 3197
Ben Vuirich 2961
Meall Reamhar

Spittal of Glenshee
Glenshee
Glen Beag
GLEN SHEE

Blair Castle
Blair Atholl
Killiecrankie
Pass of Killiecrankie
Ben Vrackie 2757
Bruar
Straloch
Kirkmichael
Kindrogan

Pitlochry
Moulin
Dunavourd
Faire Mhór 1592

Ballinluig
Logierait
Tulliemet
Forest of Clunie
Ballintuim
Persie
Woodhill
Blackcraig Cas.

Aberfeldy
Grandtully Cas.
Dalguise
Dowally
Butterstone
Loch of Lowes

Dunkeld
Birnam
Murthly
Caputh
Spittalfield
Delvine
Meikleour

Blairgowrie
Rattray
Rosemount
Kinloch
Alyth
New Alyth
Meigle
Newtyle

Coupar Angus
Kettins
Ardler
Auchterhouse H.
Kirkton of Auchterhouse

Amulree
Trochry
Waterloo
Rohallion
Strath
R. Tay

The Edinburgh Geographical Institute

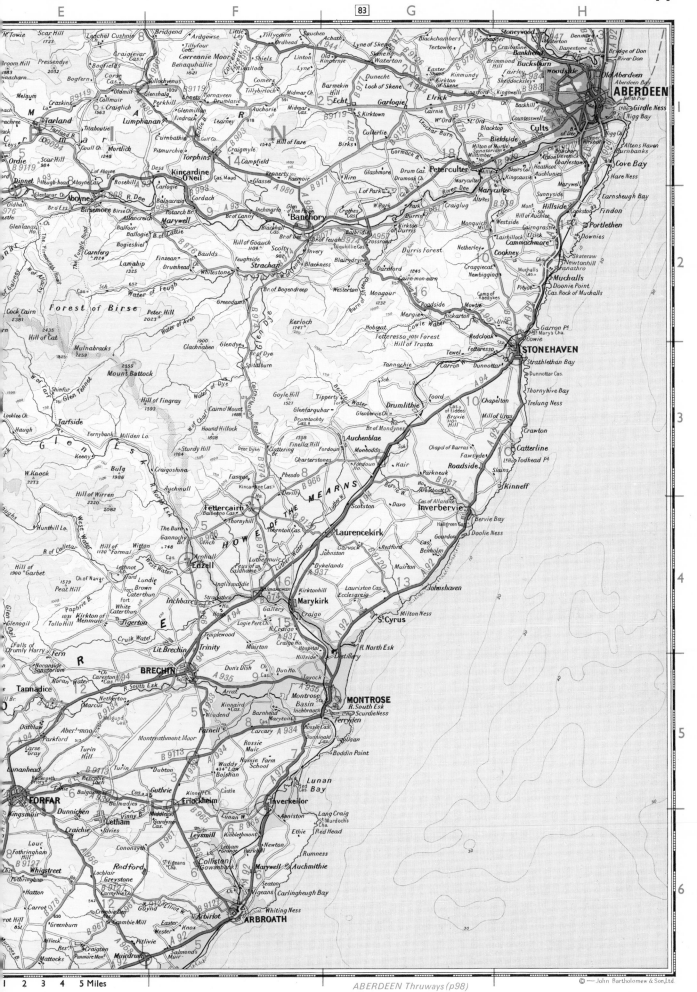

© — John Bartholomew & Son, Ltd.

1 2 3 4 5 Miles

LOCH EWE

GAIR LOCH

Gairloch

Poolewe

Inverewe

LOCH TORRIDON

UPPER LOCH TORRIDON

Shieldaig

Ben Shieldaig

Applecross Forest

Shieldaig Forest

Flowerdale Forest

Red Point

Redpoint

Port Henderson

RONA

SOUND OF RAASAY

SOUND

Portree

TROTTERNISH

Staffin

Staffin Bay

Quiraing

The Needle

Uig

Uig Bay

Kilmaluag

Rubha Hunish

Score Bay

Duntulm

Kilmuir

LOCH SNIZORT

Snizort

LOCH DUNVEGAN

Dunvegan

WATERNISH

Waternish Pt.

VATERNISH

Ascrib Islands

Greshornish

LEWIS

HARRIS

EAST LOCH TARBERT

Scalpay

Shiant Islands

Eilean Mhuire

Garbh Eilean

To Tarbert

To Lochmaddy

80 5 6 7 74 8

LOCH CARRON

Dornie
Kyle of Lochalsh
LOCH ALSH
Glenelg
Balmacara
Kyleakin

LOCH HOURN

KNOYDART
Inverie
LOCH NEVIS
Ben Screel 2586
Ladhar Bheinn 3343

NORTH MORAR
LOCH MORAR
SOUTH MORAR

Broadford
Scalpay
Raasay
Pabay
Longay
Ben Aslak 1934

SOUND OF SLEAT
Oronsay
Isle Ornsay
Knock Bay
Teangue
Tarskavaig
Ardvasar
Armadale Bay
Point of Sleat
Ard of Sleat

Mallaig
A830

A851

SKYE
Cuillin Hills
Sgurr nan Gillean 3167
Sgurr Alasdair 3257
Loch Brittle
Loch Scavaig
Loch Coruisk
Blaven 3042
Strathaird
Elgol
Loch Slapin
Loch Eishort
Torrin

MINGINISH
Glen Sligachan
Sligachan Hotel
Glen Drynoch
Carbost
Talisker
Portnalong
Glen Eynort
Glen Brittle

LOCH HARPORT
Bracadale
LOCH BRACADALE

CUILLIN SOUND

Soay
Soay Sound

RUM
Mullach Mór
Askival 2659
Ainshval 2552
Hallival
Kinloch
Kinloch Castle
Loch Scresort
Kilmory
Harris

SOUND OF RUM
SOUND OF CANNA

Canna
Sanday
Compass Hill
Tarbert

EIGG
Sgurr of Eigg
Bay of Laig
Kildonan

0 1 2 3 4 5 Miles

The Edinburgh Geographical Institute

© — John Bartholomew & Son Ltd.

68

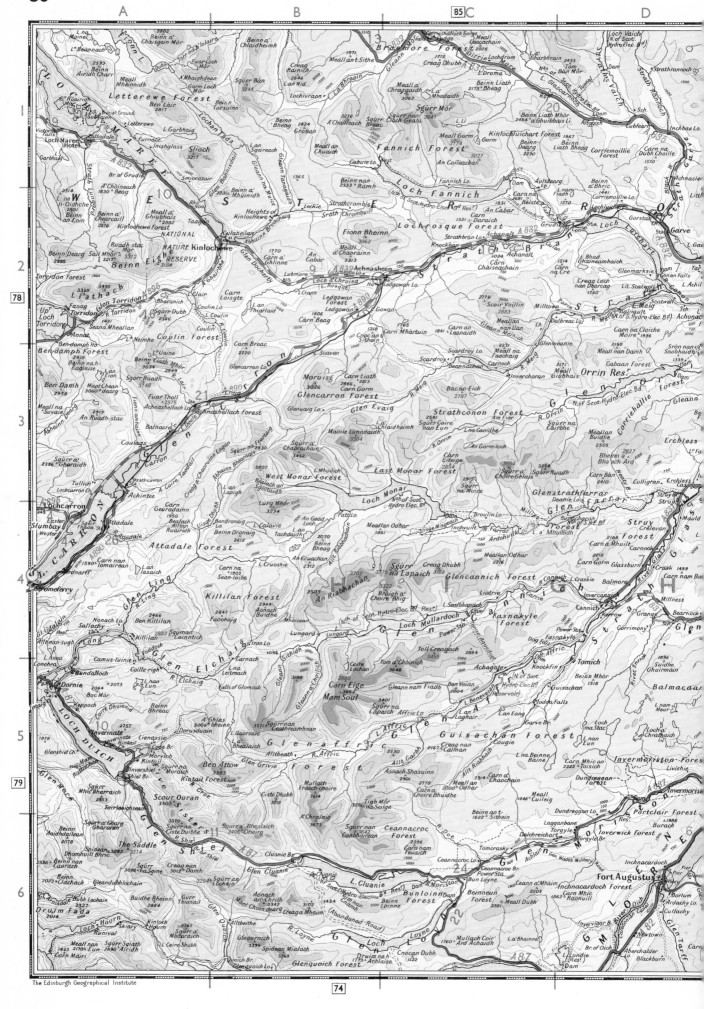

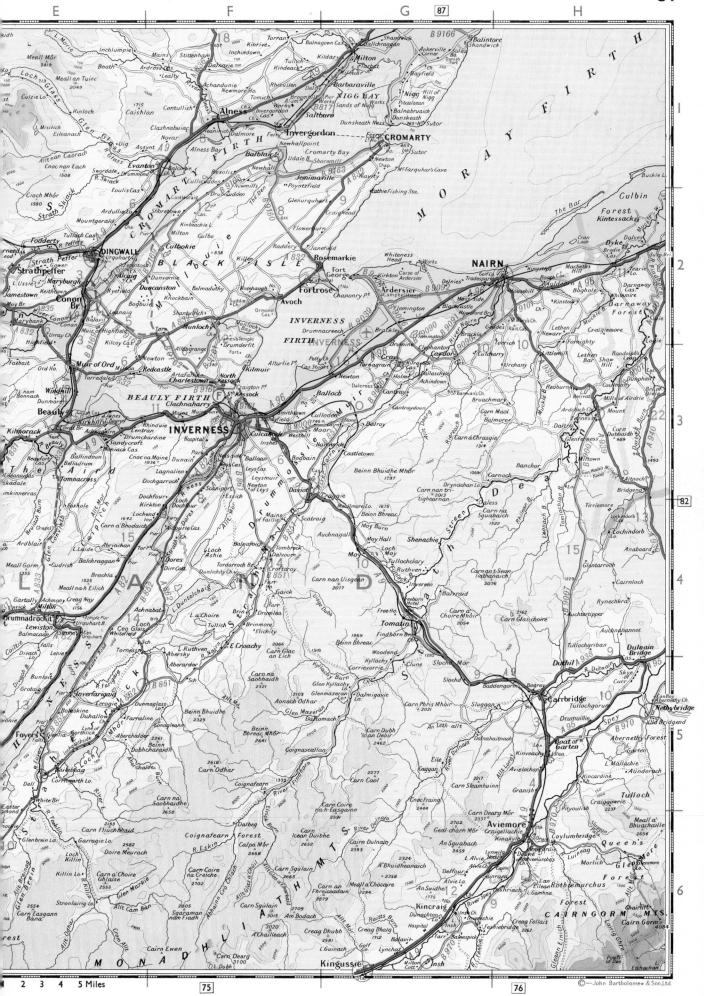

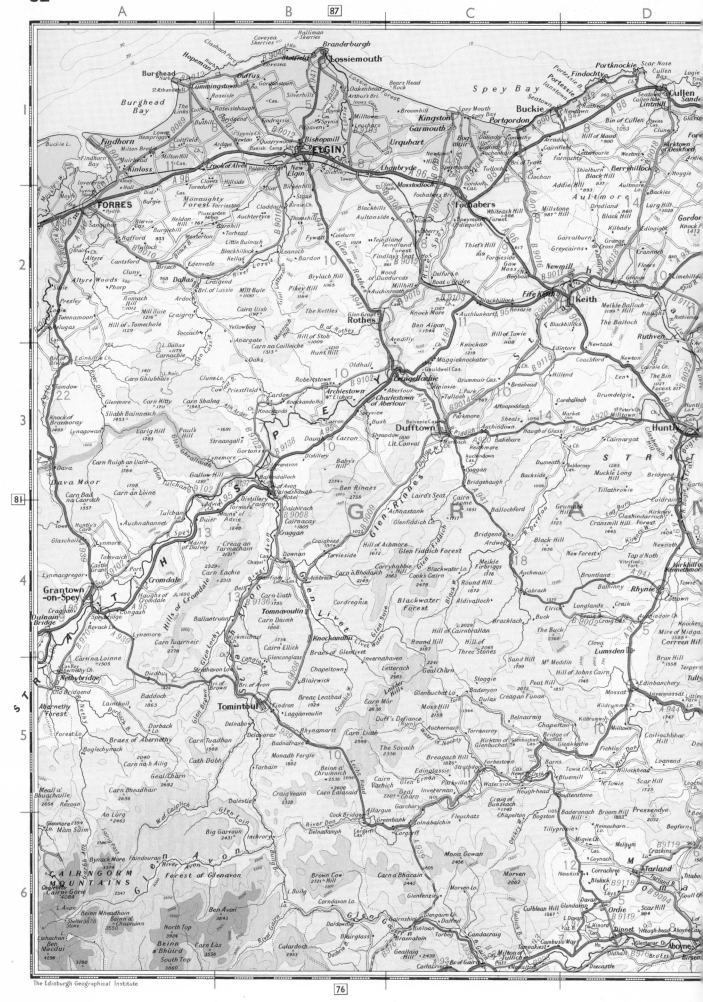

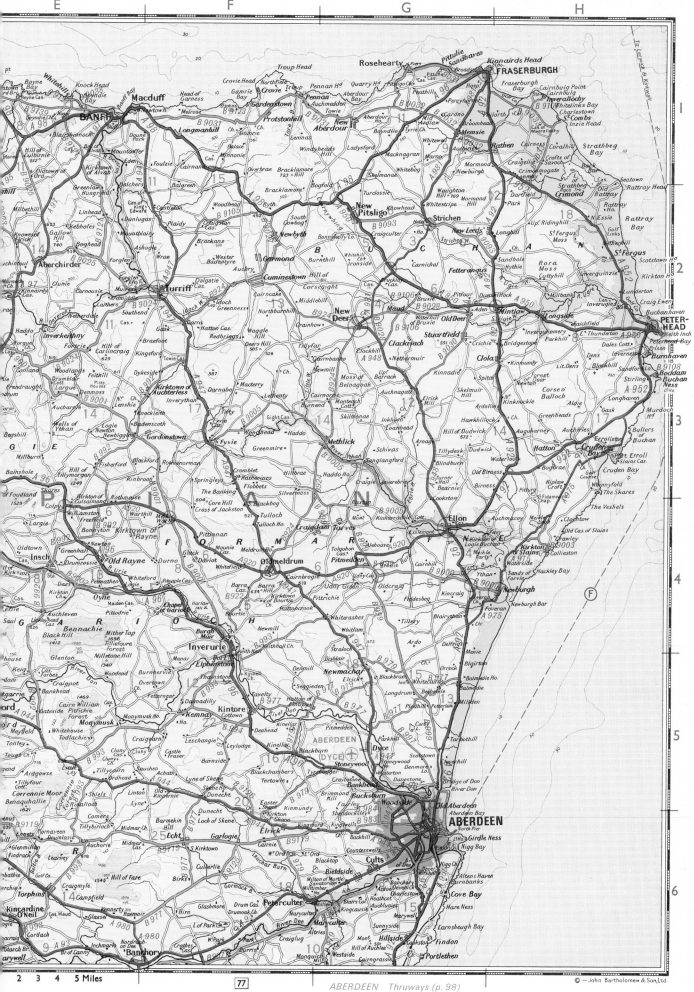

77

ABERDEEN Thruways (p. 98)

© —John Bartholomew & Son, Ltd.

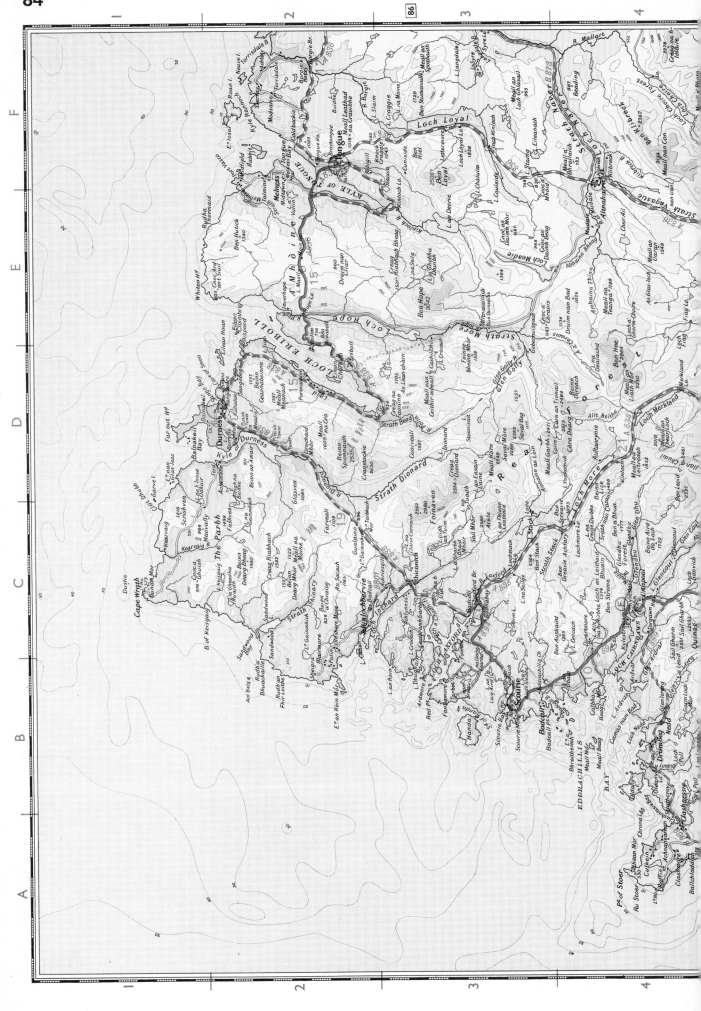

LOCH SHIN

Strath Tirry

GLEN CASSLEY

Ben Armine Forest

ROSS

Strath Carron

Strath Oykel

SEA FOREST

Inchnadamph

Ben More Assynt

Cromalt Hills

Rappach

Rhidorroch Forest

Glen Achall

Strathvaich Forest

Moravie Forest

Glen Glennie

Kildermorie Forest

Wyvis Forest

Ben Wyvis

Lochinver

ENARD BAY

Coigach

Summer Isles

LOCH BROOM

Ullapool

Braemore Forest

Inverlael Forest

Dundonnell Forest

Fannich Forest

LITTLE LOCH BROOM

Dundonnell

Fisherfield Forest

Gruinard

Strathnasheallag Forest

Letterewe Forest

LOCH MAREE

Scale: 0 1 2 3 4 5 Miles

© — John Bartholomew & Son Ltd

The Edinburgh Geographical Institute

WICK
THURSO
John o'Groats
Stroma
Dunnet
Scrabster
Halkirk
Watten
Lybster
Latheron
Dunbeath
Castletown
Freswick
Reiss
SINCLAIR'S BAY
DUNNET BAY
THURSO BAY
SINCLAIR'S BAY
Reay
Melvich Bay
Armadale Bay
Sandside Bay
Strathy
Bettyhill
Forsinard Hotel
Strath Halladale
Strath Naver
R. Naver

A9
A99
A882
A895
A836
A897
A9
B870
B874
B876
B871
B873

6323

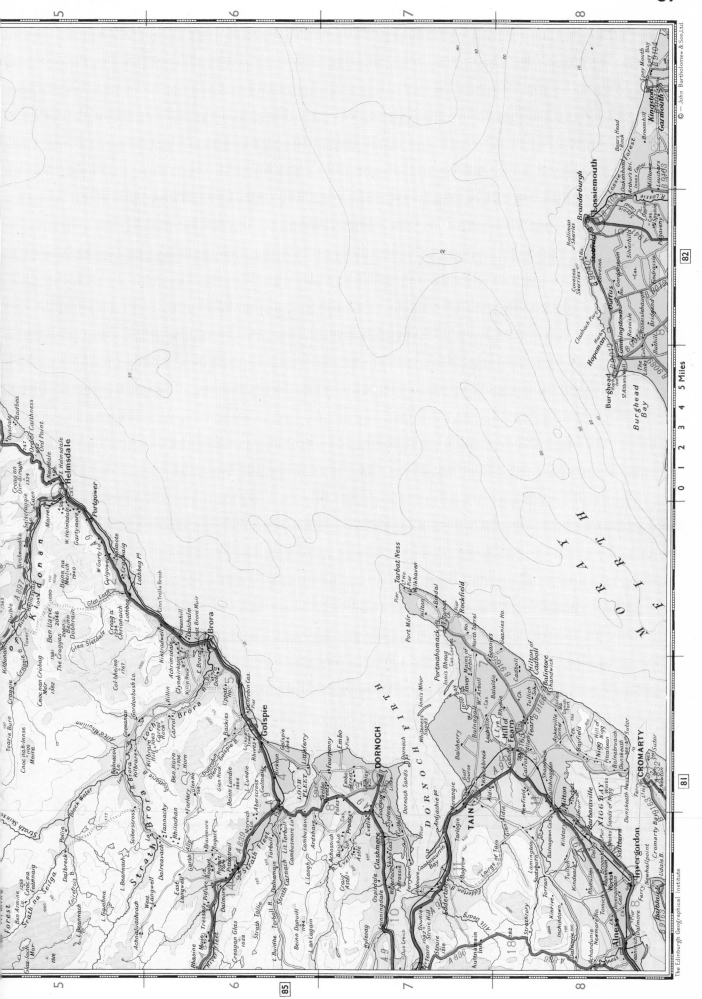

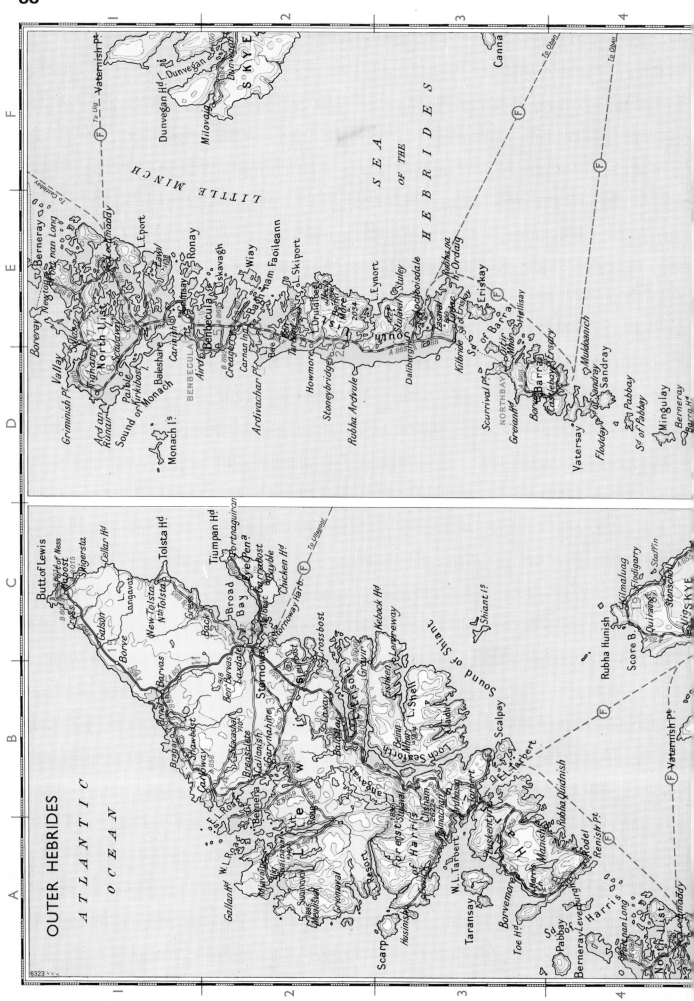

OUTER HEBRIDES

ATLANTIC OCEAN

LITTLE MINCH

SEA OF THE HEBRIDES

S K Y E

Butt of Lewis
Port of Ness
Knockaird
Skigersta
Cellar Hd
Tolsta Hd
Tiumpan Hd
Portnaguiran
Sheshader
Garrabost
Bayble
Chicken Hd
Broad Bay
Back
New Tolsta
Nth Tolsta
North Tolsta
Gress
Galson
Langivat
Borve
Barvas
Ness
Arnol
Bragar
Shawbost
Carloway
Breasclete
Callanish
Garynahine
Stornoway
Melbost
Newmarket
Sandwick
Gravir
Kershader
Crossbost
Grimshader
Lemreway
Kebock Hd
Keose
Balallan
Achmore
Laxay
L i s
W e s t
L e w i s
E a s t
Harris
H a r r i s
Scalpay
Tarbert
E.L.Tarbert
W.L.Tarbert
Rhenigidale
Maaruig
Ardvourlie
Leverburgh
Rodel
Rubha Quidnish
Renish Pt
Toe Hd
Borvemore
Luskentyre
Borve
Seilebost
Northton
Manish
Scarp
Husinish
Gheallasdal
Hushinish Pt
Gallan Hd
Scaladale
Mealista
Islivig
Brenish
Aird Uig
Hamnaway
Taransay
Pabbay
Berneray
Sd of Berneray
Sd of Pabbay
North Uist
Loch Seaforth
Sound of Shiant
Shiant Is
Rubha Hunish
Kilmaluag
Flodigarry
Staffin
Score B.
Quiraing
Stenscholl
Uist Skye
Waternish Pt

Butt of Lewis
Boreray
Berneray
Newtown
Vallay
Griminish Pt
Ard an Rùnair
Sound of Monach
Monach Is
Balranald
North Uist
Tighary
Sollas
Scabahay
L.Scadavay
Carinish
Baleshare
Lochmaddy
L.Eport
L.Portain
Ronay
Grimsay
Flodday
Wiay
Uskavagh
BENBECULA
Benbecula
Aird
Creagorry
Carnan
Bee
Nunton
Ban Faoileann
Loch Bee
Howmore
Stoneybridge
Ollay
Ben More
2034
Bornish
Ardivachar Pt
Rubha Ardvule
Dalibrog
Daliburgh
South Uist
L.Skiport
L.Eynort
Beinn Mhor
2034
Druidibeg
Stuley
Loch Boisdale
Lochboisdale
Eriskay
Sd of Eriskay
Hellisay
Eoligarry
Kilbride
Ludag
Scurrival Pt
Sd of Barra
Castlebay
NORTHBAY
Barra
Greianish
Borve
Muldoanich
Vatersay
Flodday
Sandray
Pabbay
Sd of Pabbay
Mingulay
Berneray
Barra Hd
Rubha na h-Ordaig
Usinish
Shillay

Dunvegan Hd
L.Dunvegan
Milovaig
Waternish Pt
To Uig
L.Greshornish
To Castlebay
Canna
To Oban
To Oban

6323 ×××

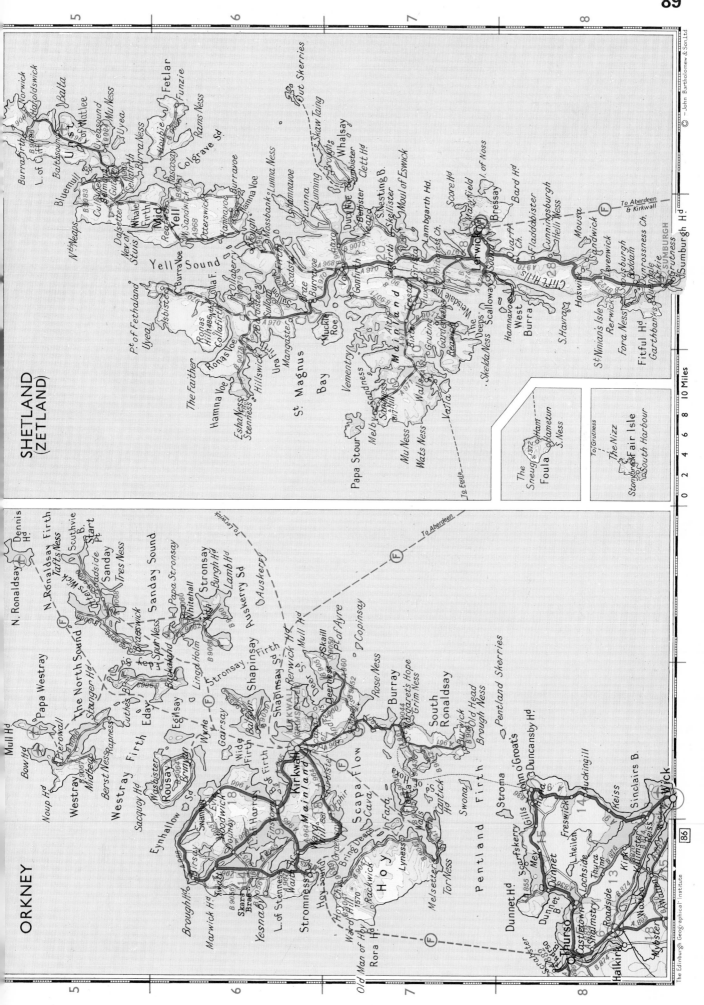

SHETLAND
(ZETLAND)

ORKNEY

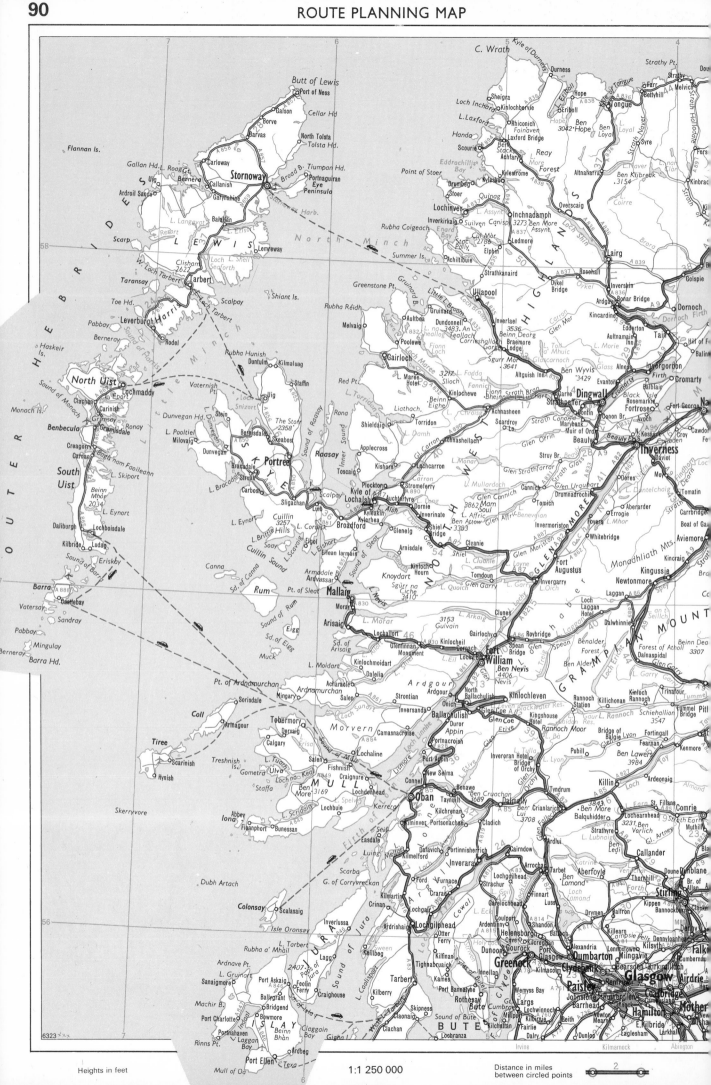

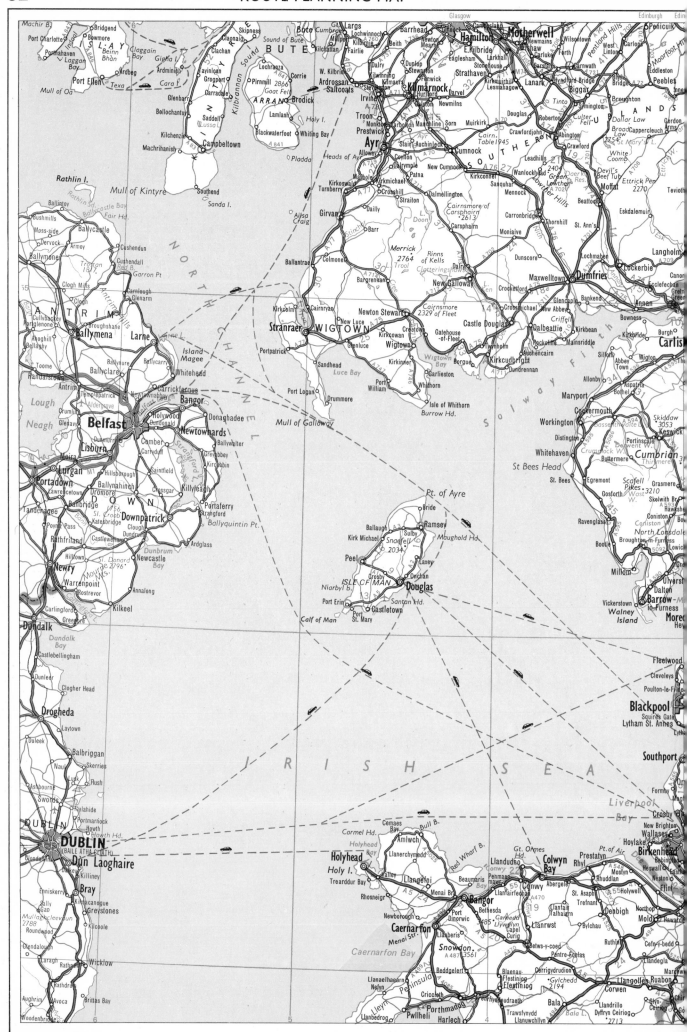

Distances in miles between circled points   11   1:1 250 000   Heights in feet

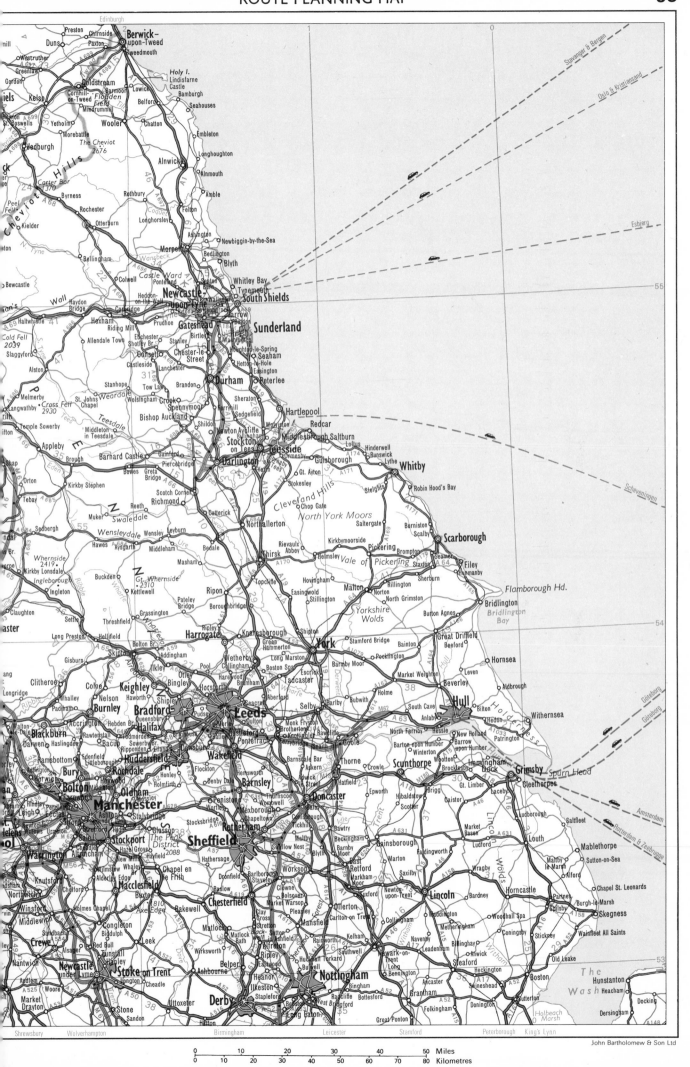

0	10	20	30	40	50 Miles
0	10 20	30	40 50	60 70	80 Kilometres

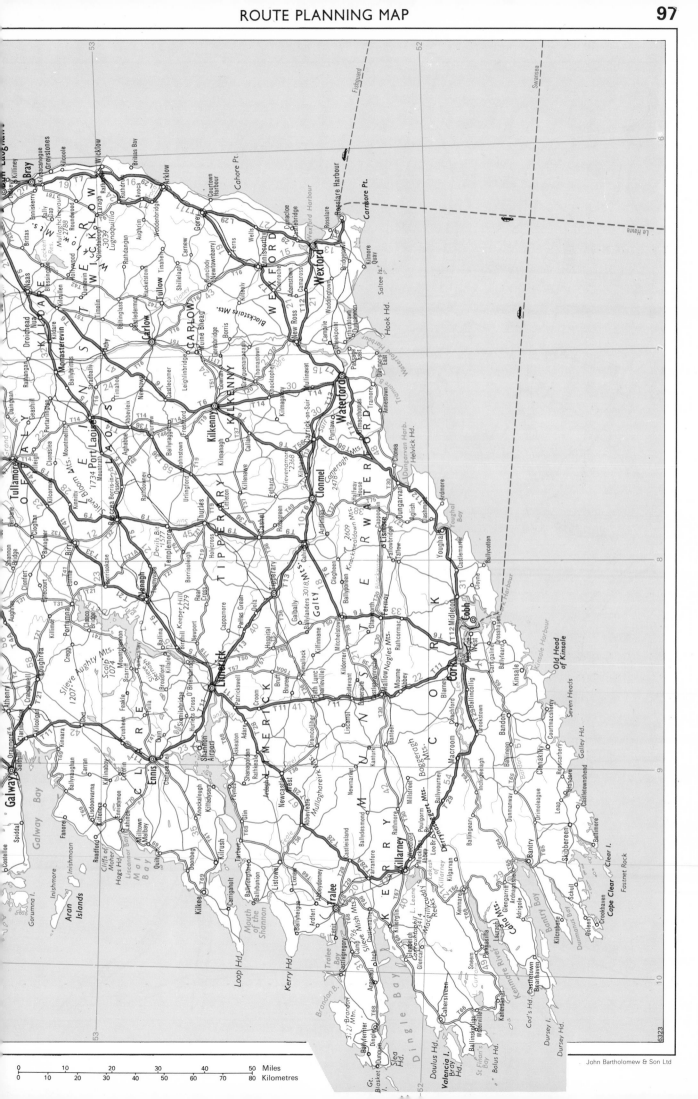

0		10		20		30		40		50 Miles
0	10	20	30	40	50	60	70	80 Kilometres

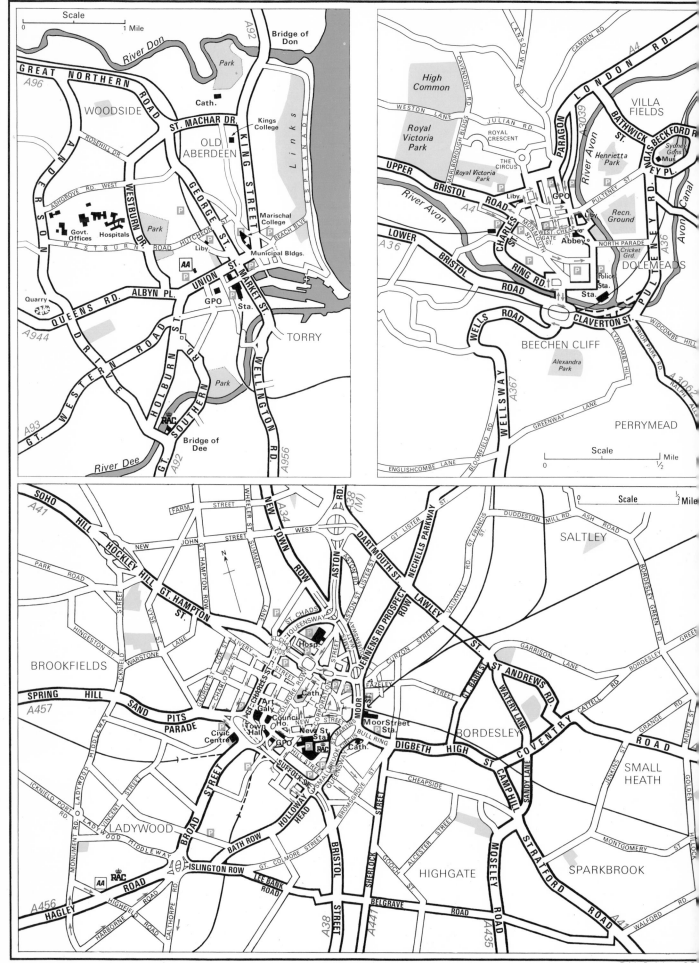

Scale
0   1 Mile

River Don

A92

Bridge of Don

Park

Cath.

GREAT NORTHERN ROAD

A96

WOODSIDE

ST. MACHAR DR.

Kings College

OLD ABERDEEN

KING STREET

Links

ESPLANADE

ROSEHILL DR.

ASHGROVE RD. WEST

WESTBURN DR.

GEORGE ST.

Marischal College

ANDERSON

Govt. Offices

Hospitals

Park

WESTBURN ROAD

HUTCHEON ST.

BEACH BLVD.

Liby.

Municipal Bldgs.

AA

UNION ST.

MARKET ST.

Quarry

QUEENS RD.

ALBYN PL.

DRIVE

HOLBURN ST.

GPO

Sta.

TORRY

A944

WESTERN ROAD

A93

GT.

SOUTHERN

RAC

Bridge of Dee

Park

WELLINGTON RD.

River Dee

A92

A956

LANSDOWN RD.

CAMDEN RD.

A4 RD.

High Common

CAVENDISH RD.

WESTON LANE

JULIAN RD.

PARAGON

A3039

VILLA FIELDS

BATHWICK ST.

BECKFORD R

Royal Victoria Park

MARLBOROUGH BLDGS.

ROYAL CRESCENT

THE CIRCUS

Royal Victoria Park

River Avon

Henrietta Park

Sydney Gdns.

Mus.

UPPER BRISTOL ROAD

River Avon

A4

Liby.

GPO

PULTENEY RD.

Recn. Ground

CHARLES ST.

LOWER

A36

BRISTOL

ROAD

RING RD.

MONMOUTH ST.

WEST CHEAP

GATE ST.

Liby.

Abbey

NORTH PARADE

Cricket Grd.

DOLEMEADS

PULTENEY RD.

A36

Avon Canal

Police Sta.

Sta.

WELLS

ROAD

CLAVERTON ST.

WIDCOMBE

PRIOR PARK RD.

LYNCOMBE HILL

RALPH ALL

A3062

BEECHEN CLIFF

Alexandra Park

WELLSWAY

A367

GREENWAY LANE

PERRYMEAD

BLOOMFIELD RD.

ENGLISHCOMBE LANE

Scale
0   ½ Mile

Scale
0   ½ Mile

SOHO

A41

HOCKLEY HILL

GT. HAMPTON ST.

FARM STREET

WHEELER ST.

NEW TOWN ROW

A34

ASTON RD.

A38 (M)

DARTMOUTH ST.

NECHELLS PARKWAY

DUDDESTON MILL RD.

ASH ROAD

SALTLEY

NEW JOHN STREET WEST

SUMMER LANE

GT. LISTER ST.

GT. FRANCIS ST.

PARK ROAD

VYSE ST.

HINGESTON ST.

ICKNIELD ST.

WARSTONE LANE

ST. CHADS QUEENSWAY

ST. CHADS CIRCUS

Hosp.

ALBION ST.

NEWTOWN ST.

WATSON ST.

ASTON ST.

JENNENS RD

LAWLEY ST.

GT. BARR ST.

ST. ANDREWS RD.

GARRISON LANE

BORDESLEY GREEN RD.

BROOKFIELDS

SPRING HILL

A457

LIVERY STREET

GEORGE ST.

CHARLOTTE ST.

ST. PAUL'S

CONSTITUTION HILL

SNOW HILL

COLMORE ROW

Cath.

Art Galy.

Council Ho.

Town Hall

MOOR STREET

PROSPECT ROW

CURZON STREET

FAZELEY ST.

COVENTRY

ST. ANDREWS RD.

CATTELL RD.

BORDESLEY

SMALL HEATH

SAND PITS PARADE

Civic Centre

NEW ST.

New St. Sta.

GPO

RAC

BULL RING

MoorStreet Sta.

DIGBETH

HIGH ST.

CAMPHILL

SANDY LANE

GRANGE RD.

STRATFORD ROAD

GOLDEN

MOSELEY ROAD

ICKNIELD PORT RD.

LADYWOOD RD.

MIDDLEWAY

VINCENT STREET

LADYWOOD

BROAD STREET

SUFFOLK ST.

HOLLOWAY HEAD

SMALLBROOK QUEENSWAY

BROMSGROVE STREET

BRISTOL STREET

CHEAPSIDE

SHERLOCK ST.

ALCESTER STREET

GOOCH ST.

HIGHGATE

MONTGOMERY ST.

HILOCK

SPARKBROOK

BATH ROW

GT. COLMORE STREET

MONUMENT RD.

LADYWOOD

AA

RAC

ISLINGTON ROW

LEE BANK ROAD

HIGHFIELD ROAD

CALTHORPE RD.

BELGRAVE ROAD

A441

A4435

A456

HAGLEY ROAD

HARBORNE ROAD

A38 STREET

WALFORD

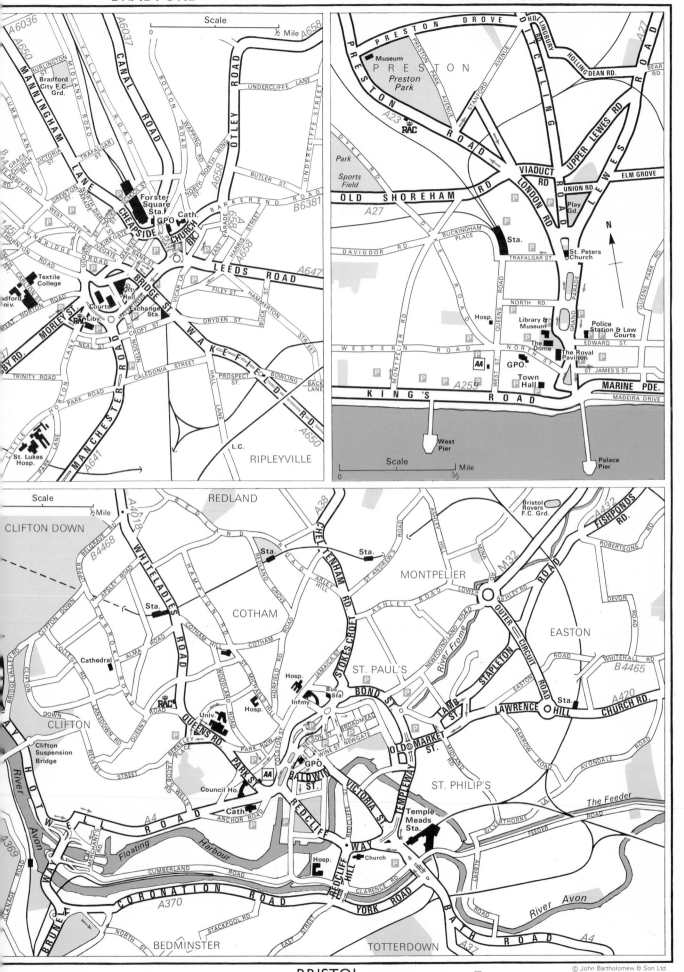

BRADFORD

BRIGHTON

Scale
0   ½ Mile

A6036 A6037 A650 A658

MANNINGHAM LANE Bradford City F.C. Grd. MIDLAND ROAD CANAL ROAD VALLEY ROAD BOLTON ROAD WAPPING ROAD NORTH WING OTLEY ROAD UNDERCLIFFE LANE BUTLER ST. UNDERCLIFFE ROAD B6381

BURLINGTON ST. TRAFALGAR ST. DREWTON NORTH PARADE DARLEY ST. BARKEREND A658 A HARRIS STREET EAST PARADE

Victoria St. Forster Square Sta. GPO Cath. CHEAPSIDE CHURCH BK. A647

West Gate IVEGATE MARKET BANK ST. Thornton Road SUNBRIDGE GODWIN ROAD City Hall BRIDGE ST. VICAR LA. LEEDS ROAD A658 FILEY ST. HAMMERTON ST. BUCK STREET

Textile College Bradford Univ. Courts RAC Liby. Exchange Sta. KING'S CROFT NESBIT ST. DRYDEN ST. PROSPECT ST. BOWLING BACK LANE

MORLEY ST. HORTON ROAD NEAL ST. CALEDONIA STREET HALL LANE WAKEFIELD RD. A650

TRINITY ROAD PARK ROAD MANCHESTER ROAD A641 L.C. RIPLEYVILLE

St. Lukes Hosp.

BRIGHTON

PRESTON DROVE HOLLINGBURY BEAR RD. DEAN RD. ITCHING HOLLINGDEAN RD.

PRESTON PARK Museum PRESTON Preston Park PRESTON PARK AVENUE STANFORD AVENUE UPPER LEWES RD. ELM GROVE

A23 RAC DYKE RD. ROAD VIADUCT LONDON RD. UNION RD. LEWES Play Gd.

OLD SHOREHAM RD. A27 Park Sports Field DAVIGDOR RD. BUCKINGHAM PLACE Sta. TRAFALGAR ST. St. Peters Church

QUEENS ROAD NORTH RD. Library & Museum Police Station & Law Courts EDWARD ST.

WESTERN ROAD MONTPELIER ROAD WEST ST. GRAND PARADE The Dome NORTH ST. The Royal Pavilion ST. JAMES'S ST.

AA GPO. Town Hall MARINE PDE. MADEIRA DRIVE

KING'S ROAD A259

Scale
0   ½ Mile

West Pier Palace Pier

N

BRISTOL

Scale
½ Mile

REDLAND A38 Bristol Rovers F.C. Grd. A432 FISHPONDS RD. DEVON ROAD

CLIFTON DOWN A4018 B4468 BELGRAVE CHELTENHAM RD. Sta. Sta. ST. ANDREWS ASHLEY HILL MINA ROAD ROBERTSONS RD.

WHITELADIES ROAD UPPER APSLEY ROAD HAMPTON REDLAND GROVE ABLEY HILL MONTPELIER LOWER M32 EASTON WHITEHALL RD. B4465

Clifton Down Sta. COTHAM COTHAM HILL ASHLEY ROAD NEWFOUNDLAND ROAD ASHLEY RD. OUTER CIRCUIT ROAD

Cathedral ALMA COTHAM WOODLAND ST. MICHAELS HILL JAMAICA ST. St. Paul's River Frome STAPLETON EASTON ROAD Sta. A420 CHURCH RD.

CLIFTON DOWN QUEENS ROAD Univ. Hosp. Infmy. Hosp. BOND ST. LAMB ST. LAWRENCE HILL BARROW ROAD AVONDALE ROAD

Clifton Suspension Bridge BERKELEY PLACE PARK ROW BROADMEAD NELSON ST. OLD MARKET ST. ST. PHILIP'S

RAC QUEENS RD. JACOB'S WELLS ROAD REGENT STREET PARK ST. AA GPO COLSTON ST. WINE ST. NEWGATE VICTORIA ST. TEMPLE WAY The Feeder SILVERTHORNE

River HOTWELL RIVER Avon A369 A4 ROAD Council Ho. BALDWIN ST. Cath. ANCHOR ROAD REDCLIFF WAY Temple Meads Sta.

Floating Harbour CUMBERLAND ROAD REDCLIFF HILL Hosp. Church YORK ROAD BATH ROAD A4

BRUNEL WAY CORONATION ROAD A370 NORTH STREET EAST STREET STACKPOOL RD. CLARENCE ROAD ALBERT ROAD FEEDER River Avon

BEDMINSTER TOTTERDOWN A37

BRISTOL

One-way Streets →   Car Parks P

© John Bartholomew & Son Ltd

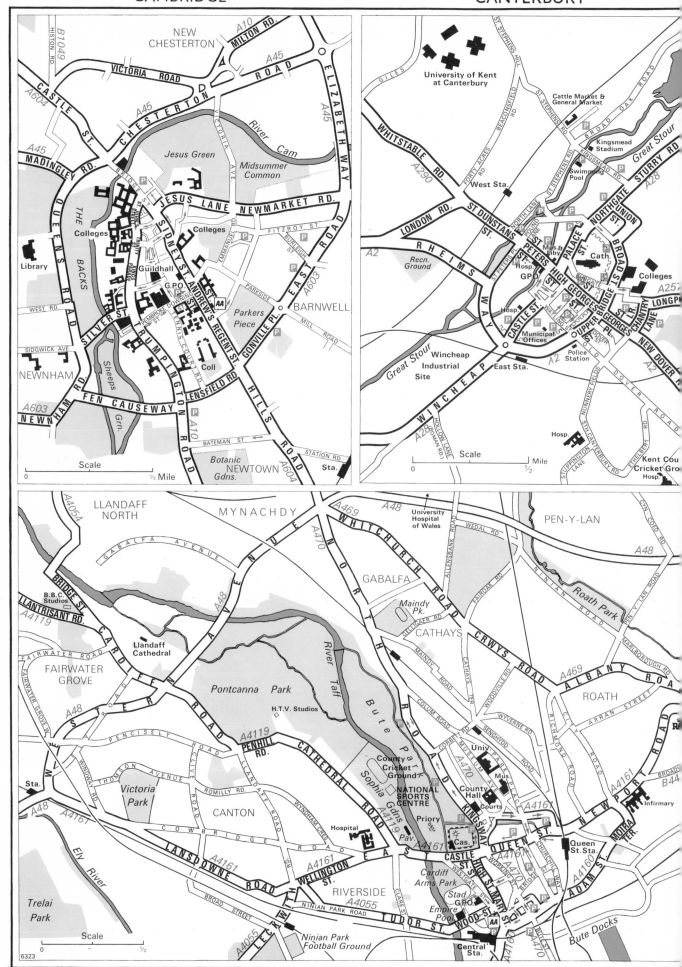

Car Parks **P**

One-way Streets →

© John Bartholomew & So

One-way Streets →   Car Parks Ⓟ

© John Bartholomew & Son Ltd

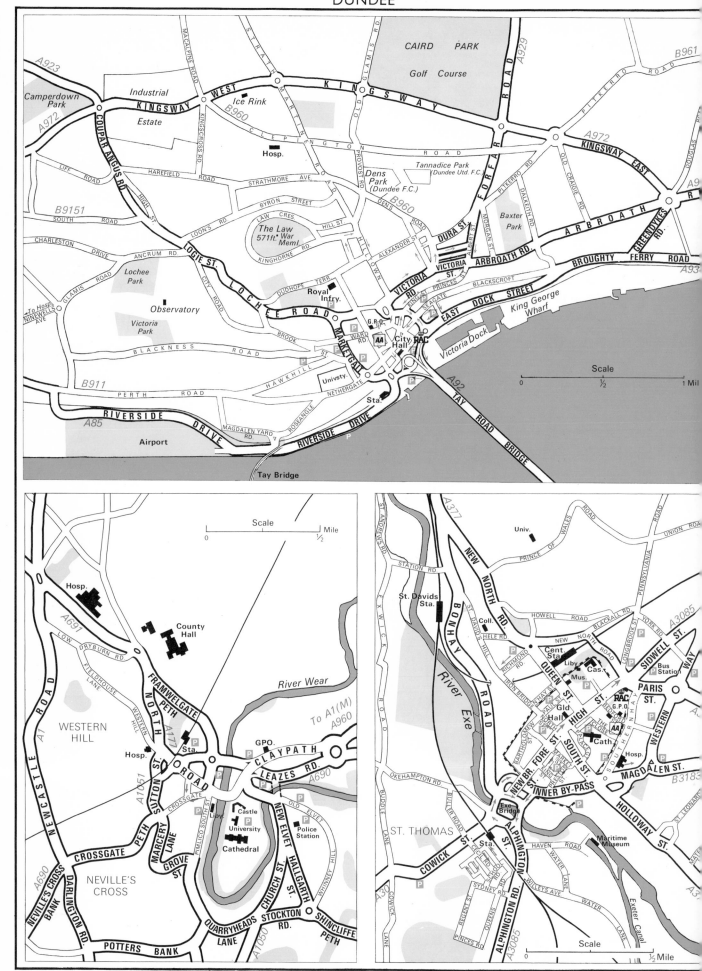

One-way Streets →   Car Parks P

© John Bartholomew & Son

EDINBURGH

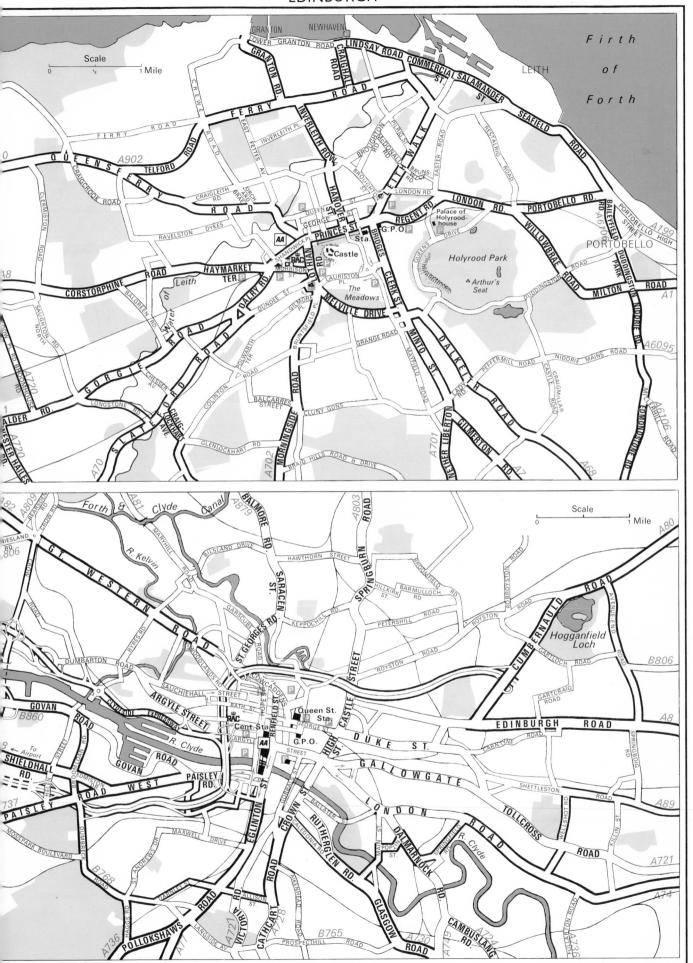

Firth

of

Forth

LEITH

PORTOBELLO

Scale
0   ½   1 Mile

Holyrood Park
△ Arthur's Seat

Palace of Holyrood-house

Castle
The Meadows

GLASGOW

Scale
0   1 Mile

Forth & Clyde Canal

Hogganfield Loch

One-way Streets →

Car Parks [P]

© John Bartholomew & Son Ltd

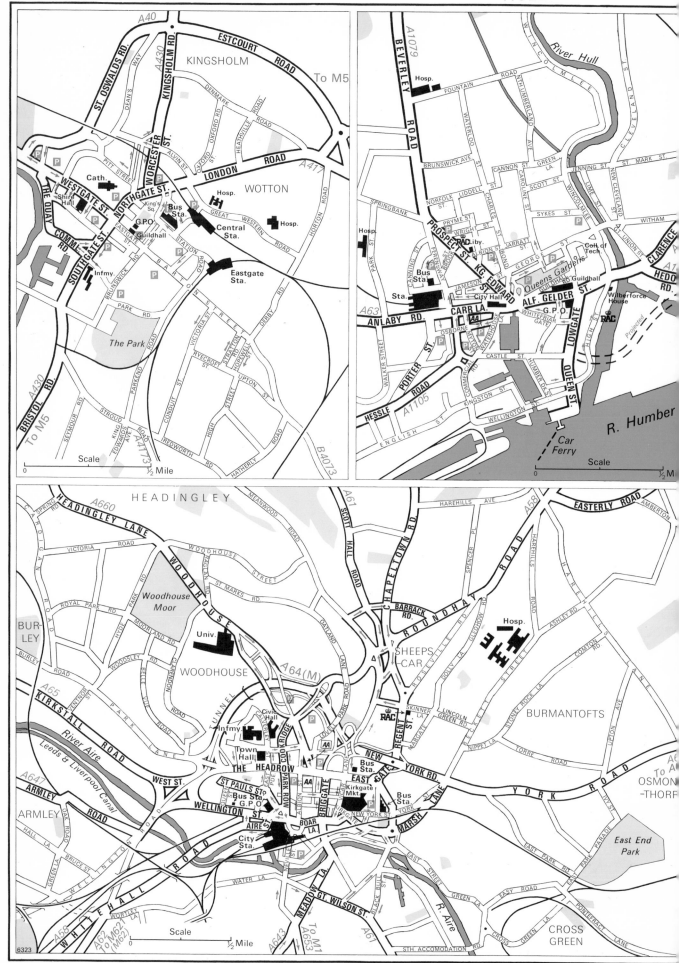

GLOUCESTER

HULL

Gloucester map:

KINGSHOLM · WOTTON

St. OSWALDS RD. · ESTCOURT ROAD · To M5 · A40 · KINGSHOLM RD. · A430 · LONDON · ROAD · A417

DENMARK · ROAD · OXFORD · HEATHVILLE · ROAD · DEAN'S WAY · PITT STREET · ALVIN ST. · WORCESTER ST. · KING'S SQ. · Hosp. · GREAT WESTERN · ROAD · HORTON · ROAD · Hosp.

THE QUAY · COMMERCIAL RD. · WESTGATE ST. · NORTHGATE ST. · Cath. · shire Hall · GPO · Guildhall · Bus Sta. · Central Sta. · SOUTHGATE ST. · Infmy. · BRUNSWICK · Eastgate Sta. · STATION RD. · BARTON · STREET · VICTORIA · DERBY · STRETTON · HOPEWELL · RD.

BRISTOL RD. · A430 · To M5 · The Park · PARK RD. · PARKEND · ROAD · RYECROFT · UPTON ST. · SEYMOUR · RD. · STROUD · CONDUIT · HIGH · ST. · KING EDWARDS AVE. · REDWORTH RD. · HATHERLY RD. · A4173 · B4073

Scale 0 — ½ Mile

Hull map:

BEVERLEY ROAD · A1079 · River Hull · WINCOLMLEE · Hosp. · FOUNTAIN · ROAD · NTH UMBERLAND · AVE · GREEN LA. · JENNING ST. · NEW CLEVELAND ST. · MARK ST. · BRUNSWICK AVE. · CANNON · CAROLINE · SCOTT ST. · SYKES · WINCOMLEE · WITHAM · CLEVELAND ST. · SPRINGBANK · NORFOLK · LIDDELL · CHARLES · PRYME ST. · WRIGHT · GEORGE · UNION ST. · Coll. of Tech. · CLARENCE ST. · Hosp. · PARK ST. · CANNING · FERENSWAY · PROSPECT ST. · K.G. EDWARD · JARRAT · BOND · P · Queens Gardens · Guildhall · HEDON RD. · Bus Sta. · Lby. · RAC · City Hall · ALF. GELDER ST. · GPO · Wilberforce House · RAC · Projected · ANLABY RD. · A63 · Sta. · JAMESON · CARR LA. · AA · WHITEFRIAR GATE · LOWGATE · HIGH ST. · WALKER STREET · OSBORNE · WATERHOUSE · COMMERCIAL · CASTLE ST. · HUMBER DK. · QUEEN ST. · PORTER ST. · ROAD · KINGSTON ST. · WELLINGTON ST. · HESSLE · ROAD · A1105 · ENGLISH ST. · Car Ferry · R. Humber

Scale 0 — ½ M

Leeds map:

HEADINGLEY · A660 · MEANWOOD ROAD · A61 · HAREHILLS AVE · A58 · EASTERLY ROAD · AMBERTON · HEADINGLEY LANE · SPRING RD. · CARDIGAN · VICTORIA · ROAD · WOODHOUSE · RAGLAN ST. · ST. MARKS · WOODHOUSE MOOR · SCOTT HALL RD. · CHAPELTOWN RD. · HAREHILLS RD. · SPENCER PL. · ROUNDHAY ROAD · ASHLEY RD. · BURLEY · ROYAL PARK RD. · HYDE PARK RD. · MOORLAND RD. · Univ. · WOODHOUSE · OATLAND LANE · BARRACK RD. · Hosp. · GLEDHOW · COMPTON RD. · SYDNEY ROCK LA. · BURMANTOFTS · BURLEY ROAD · A65 · WOODSLEY RD. · BELLE VUE RD. · A64(M) · TUNNEL · LOVELL PARK RD. · SHEEPSCAR · BOSTVILLE · DOLLY LA. · LINCOLN GREEN RD. · NIPPET LA. · TORRE ROAD · KIRKSTALL ROAD · River Aire · Leeds & Liverpool Canal · Civic Hall · Infmy. · COOKRIDGE · RAC · SKINNER LA. · REGENT ST. · OSMONDTHORPE · A647 · Town Hall · THE HEADROW · NEW YORK RD. · YORK ROAD · EAST END PARK · ARMLEY · WEST ST. · St PAULS St. · AA · BRIGGATE · Kirkgate Mkt · Bus Sta. · MARSH LANE · ARMLEY ROAD · OAK RD. · WELLINGTON ST. · Bus Sta. G.P.O. · BOAR LA. · AIRE ST. · City Sta. · NEW YORK ST. · YORK ST. · EAST PARK PARADE · WHITEHALL ROAD · A58 · WORTLEY · A62 · To M621 (M62) · WATER LA. · MEADOW LA. · GT. WILSON ST. · A643 · A61 · To M1 A653 · BLACK BULL · GREEN LA. · R. Aire · CROSS GREEN · STH. ACCOMODATION RD. · PONTEFRACT LANE · 6323

BURLEY

Scale 0 — ½ Mile

Car Parks P

LEEDS

One-way Streets

© John Bartholomew & Son

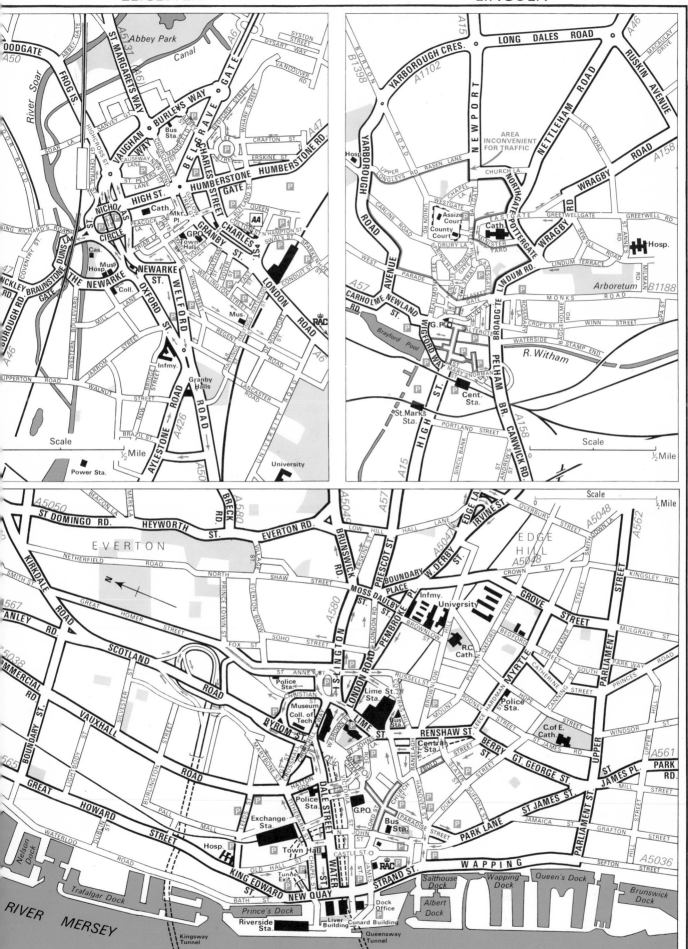

LEICESTER

LINCOLN

LIVERPOOL

One-way Streets →   Car Parks P

© John Bartholomew & Son Ltd

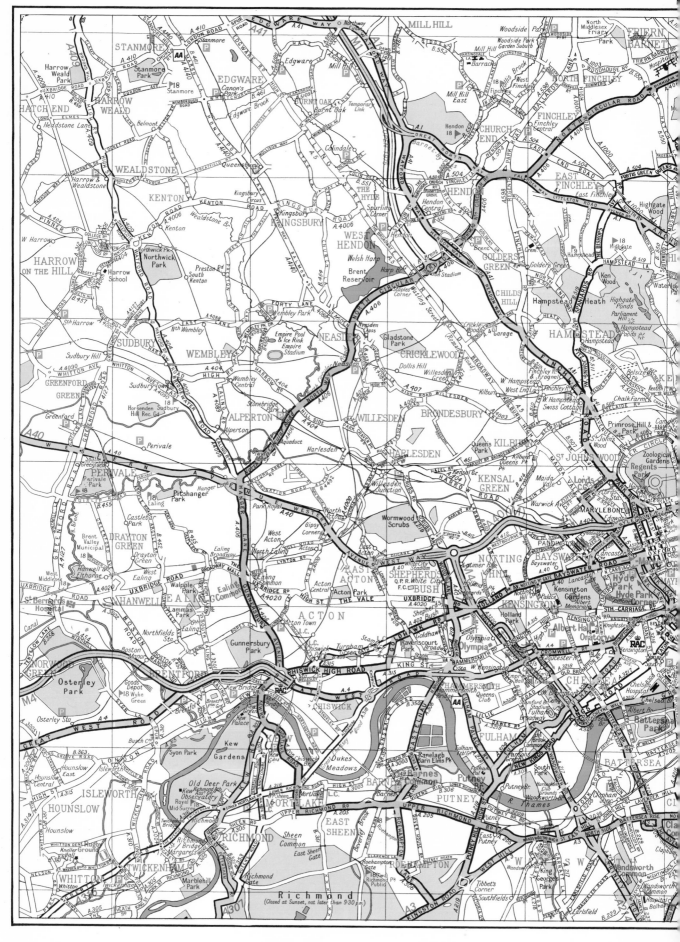

Scale

0   1   2   3 Miles

N

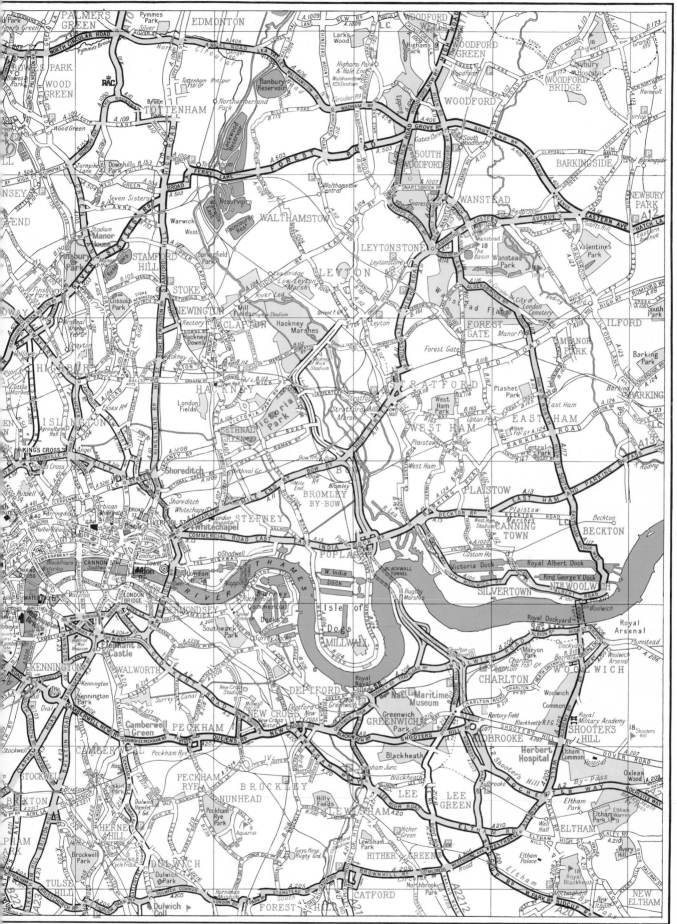

Recommended Through Routes ══════   One-way Streets ➝   Car Parks 🅿

© John Bartholomew & Son Ltd

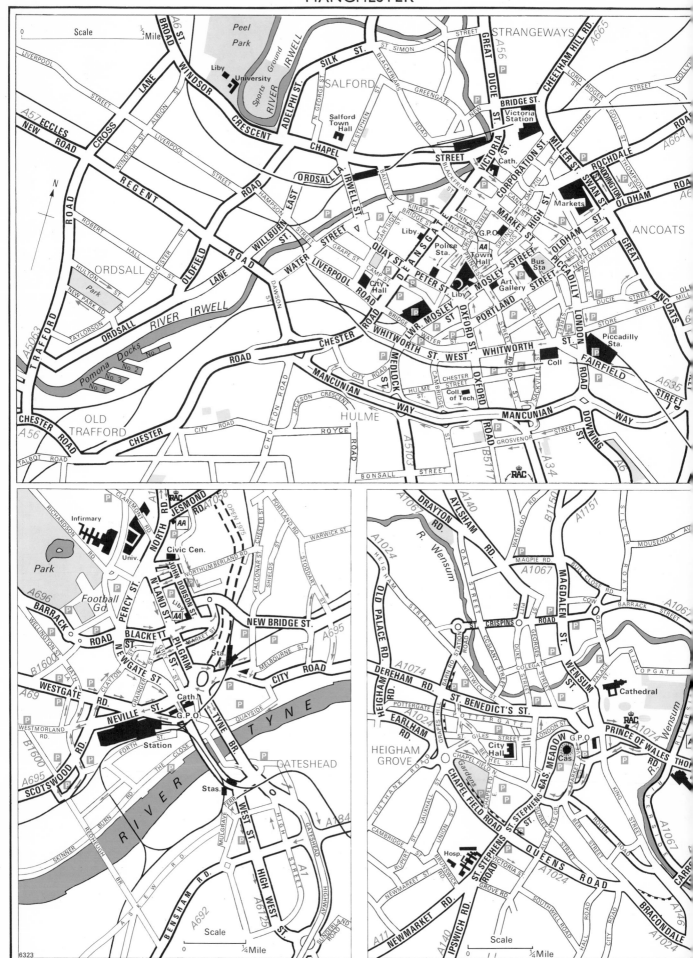

© John Bartholomew & Son

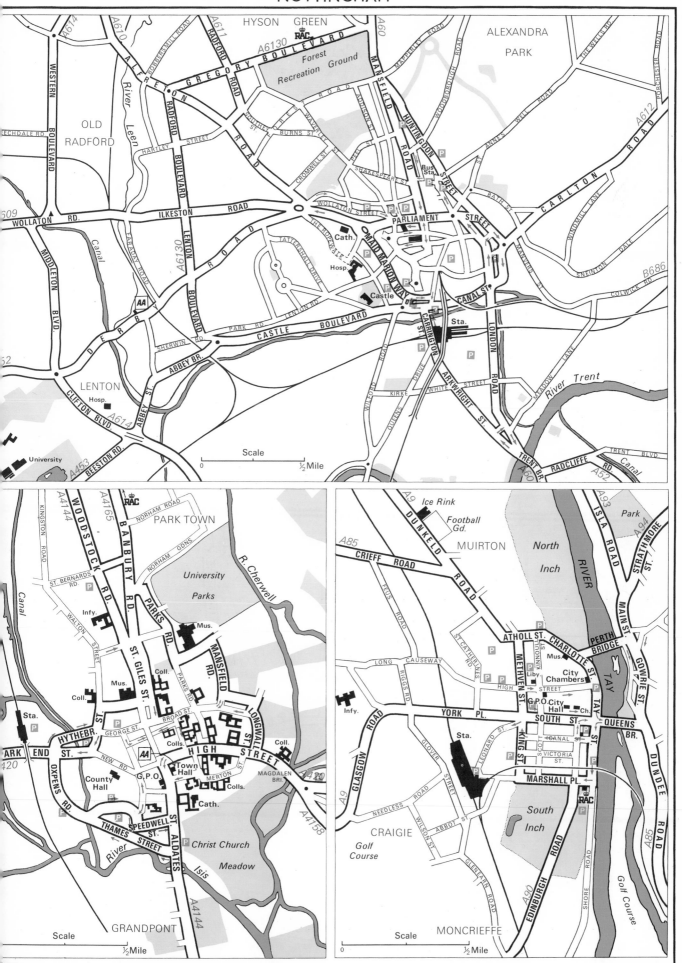

© John Bartholomew & Son Ltd

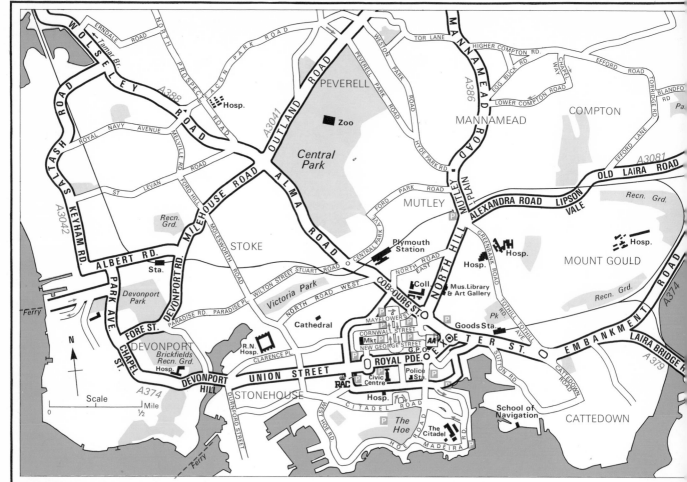

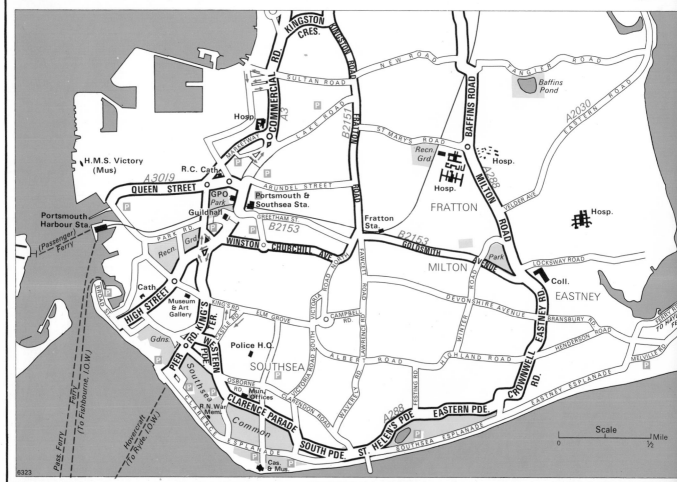

One-way Streets →   Car Parks [P]   © John Bartholomew & Son

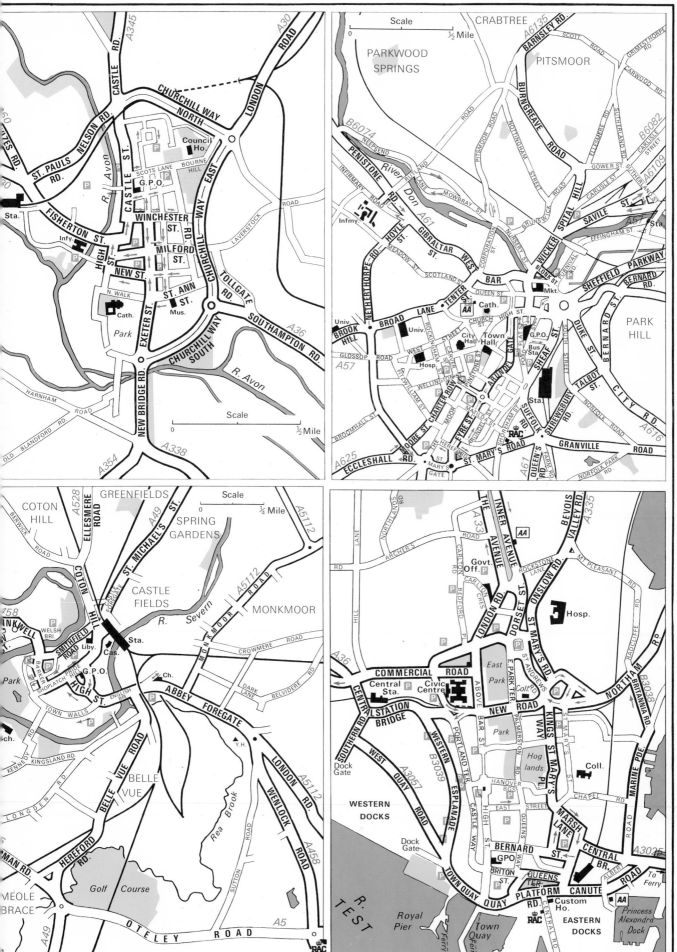

© John Bartholomew & Son Ltd

STOKE-ON-TRENT

WOLVERHAMPTON

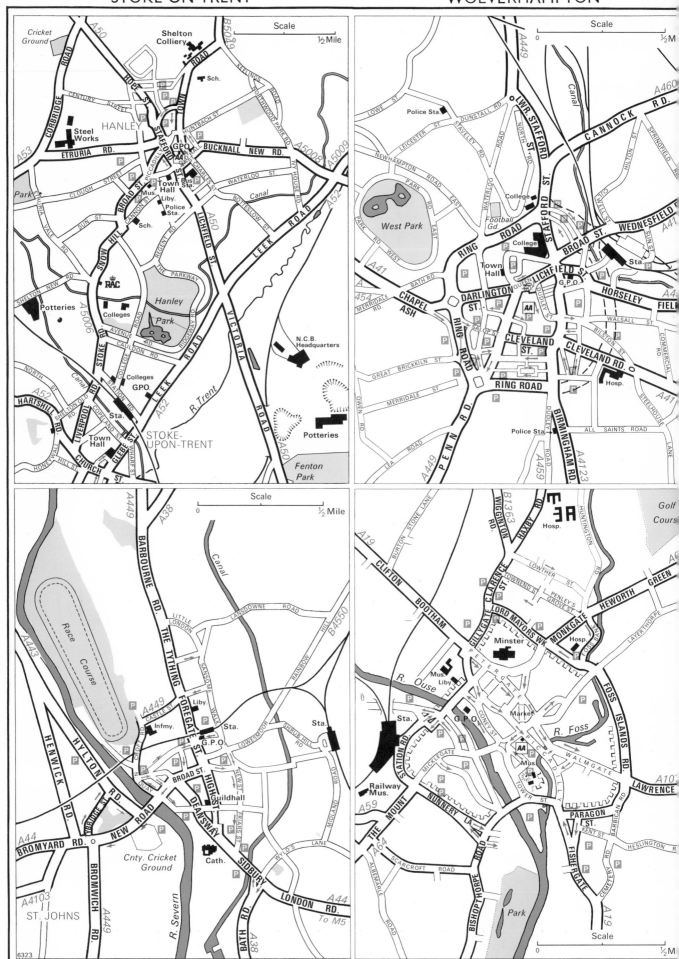

WORCESTER

One-way Streets

Car Parks P

YORK

© John Bartholomew & Son

Comparative Heights and Depths in the British Isles

Heights and depths shown in metres

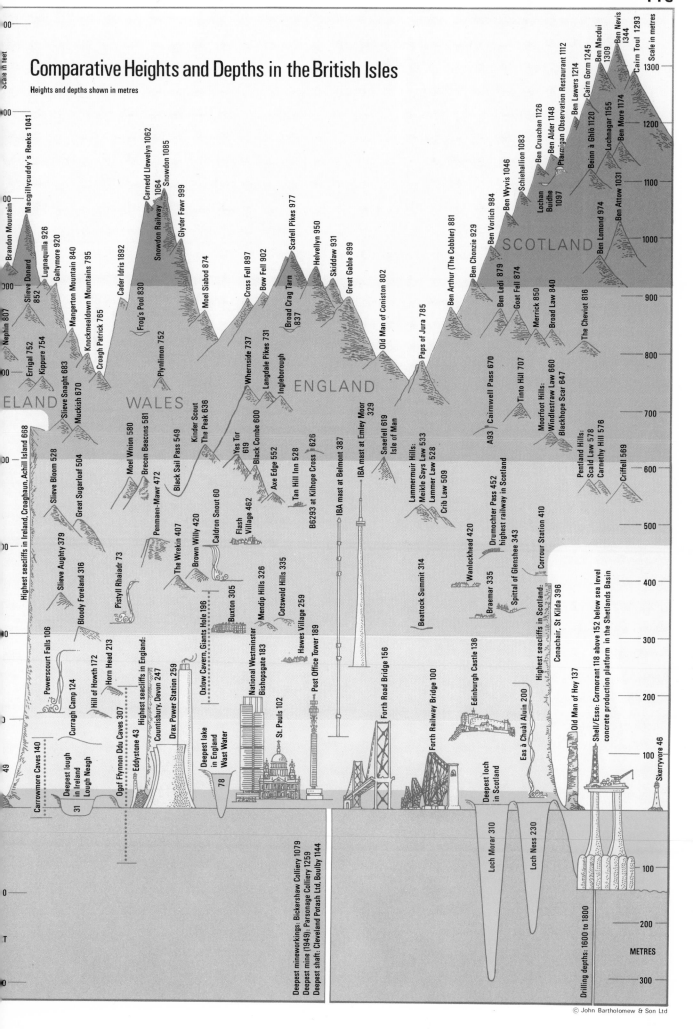

Scale in feet

Scale in metres

METRES

Deepest mineworkings: Bickershaw Colliery 1079
Deepest mine (1949): Parsonage Colliery 1259
Deepest shaft: Cleveland Potash Ltd, Boulby 1144

Drilling depths: 1600 to 1800

© John Bartholomew & Son Ltd

1:1 250 000

ORKNEY

Mull Head · North Ronaldsay · Nth. Ronaldsay Firth · The · Pierowall · Westray · North Sd. · Rapness · Overbister · Sanday · Westray Firth · Eddy · Backaland · Sanday Sd. · Rousay · Egilsay · Whitehall · Stronsay · Stronsay · Brough Hd. · Brinyan · The Barony · Marwick Hd. · Dounbay · Stenness · Shapinsay · Auskerry · Skara Brae · Balfour · Kirkwall · Stennes · Finstown · Firth · Mainland · Stromness · Graemsay · Skail · Copinsay · Ward Hill 1565' · St. Mary's · ORKNEY · Hoy · Burray · Rora Hd. · Lyness · Wateringhouse · St. Margaret's Hope · South Ronaldsay · Dunnet Head · Burwick · Brough Ness · Stroma · John o' Groats

SHETLAND

Muckle Flugga · Burra Firth · Herma Ness · Haroldswick · Baltasound · Balta · Unst · Uyeasound · Dalsetter · Belmont · Gutcher · Uyea · Isbister · Mid Yell · Fetlar · The Faither · Yell · Funzie · North Collafirth · Ollaberry · Uyeasound Sd. · Burravoe · Esha Ness · Hillswick · Mossbank · Heoga Ness · St Magnus Bay · Brae · Lunna · Out Skerries · Muckle Roe · Laxo · Whalsay · Papa Stour · Voe · Sandness · Aith · Neap · Gletness · Mainland · Walls · Tresta · Vaila · Reawick · Cliff Sd. · Foula · Ham · Scalloway · Lerwick · I. of Noss · Bressay · West Burra · Bressay Sd. · Cunningsburgh · Scousburgh · Sandwick · Mousa · Fitful Head · Tolob · Sumburgh Head · Sumburgh

John o' Groats · Mey · Dunnet · Keiss · Reiss · Sinclair's B. · Noss Hd. · Watten · Wick · Lybster · Dunbeath · Riedale

Lossiemouth · Spey Bay · Portsoy · Banff · Macduff · Fraserburgh · Elgin · Buckie · Cullen · Fochabers · Mosstodloch · Fife Keith · Keith · Cornhill · Aberchirder · Gordonstown · New Pitsligo · Rathen · Crimond · Rattray Hd. · Rothes · Craigellachie · Turriff · Mintlaw · Longside · St. Fergus · Aberlour · Dufftown · Huntly · Rothie Norman · Melie · Peterhead · Boddam · Rhynie · Insch · Oldmeldrum · Newburgh · Cruden Bay · GRAMPIAN · Lumsden · Bridge of · Inverurie · New Machar · Tomintoul · Alford · Kintore · Balmedie · Strathdon · Dunecht · Skene · Aberdeen · bridge · Aboyne · Cults · Girdle Ness · Morven 2862 · Crathie · Ballater · Banchory · Bridge of Feugh · Cove Bay · Balmoral Castle · Mr Keen 2077 · Bridge of Dye · Muchalls · Lochnagar 3786 · Baxter · Cairn o' Mount · Stonehaven · Glen Esk · Fettercairn · Catterline · Fordoun · Inverbervie · Glen Clova · Gourdon · Laurencekirk · St Cyrus · S. Esk · Brechin · Montrose · Kirriemuir · Farnell · Glenisla · Friockheim · Lunan B. · Inverkeilor · Forfar · Glamis · Arbroath · Newtyle · Muirdrum · Carnoustie · Monifieth · Buddon Ness · Dundee · Broughty Ferry · Bell Rock · New Scone · Tayport · Newport on Tay · Gleneagles · Leuchars · Newburgh · St. Andrews · Abernethy · Cupar · Dairsie · Auchtermuchty · Pitscottie · Ceres · Fife Ness · Falkland · Largoward · Crail · FIFE · Markinch · Largo · Anstruther · Leslie · Leven · I. of May · Windygates · Buckhaven and · Methil · Kirkcaldy · Lochgelly · Kinghorn · Burntisland · Bass Rock · Inchkeith · North Berwick · Aberdour · Gullane · Gullane Pt. · Dunbar · Inverkeithing · Queensferry · Preston pans · Tranent · Leith · Typne · E. Linton · Cockburnspath · St Abb's Hd. · Edinburgh · Musselburgh · Haddington · Eyemouth · LOTHIAN · Lammermuir Hills · Grantshouse · Penicuik · Newtongrange · Ayton · Cranshaws · Berwick upon Tweed · Carfraemill · Duns · Paxton · Tweedmouth · Lauder · Westruther · Swinton

BORDERS (See p.116-117)
CENTRAL
1. STIRLING
2. CLACKMANNAN
3. FALKIRK
FIFE
1. NORTH-EAST FIFE
2. KIRKCALDY
3. DUNFERMLINE
GRAMPIAN
1. MORAY
2. BANFF & BUCHAN
3. GORDON
4. ABERDEEN CITY
5. KINCARDINE & DEESIDE
HIGHLAND
1. CAITHNESS
2. SUTHERLAND
3. ROSS & CROMARTY
4. NAIRN
5. INVERNESS
6. SKYE & LOCHALSH
7. LOCHABER
8. BADENOCH & STRATHSPEY
LOTHIAN
1. WEST LOTHIAN
2. EDINBURGH CITY
3. MIDLOTHIAN
4. EAST LOTHIAN
STRATHCLYDE (See p.114-116)
1. ARGYLL & BUTE
2. DUMBARTON
3. CLYDEBANK
4. BEARSDEN & MILNGAVIE
5. STRATHKELVIN
6. CUMBERNAULD & KILSYTH
7. MONKLANDS
8. GLASGOW CITY
9. RENFREW
10. INVERCLYDE
11. CUNNINGHAME
12. KILMARNOCK & LOUDOUN
13. EASTWOOD
14. EAST KILBRIDE
15. HAMILTON
16. MOTHERWELL
17. LANARK
18. CUMNOCK & DOON VALLEY
19. KYLE & CARRICK
TAYSIDE
1. ANGUS
2. PERTH & KINROSS
3. DUNDEE CITY

© John Bartholomew & Son Ltd

0 10 20 30 40 50 Miles
0 10 20 30 40 50 60 70 80 Kilometres

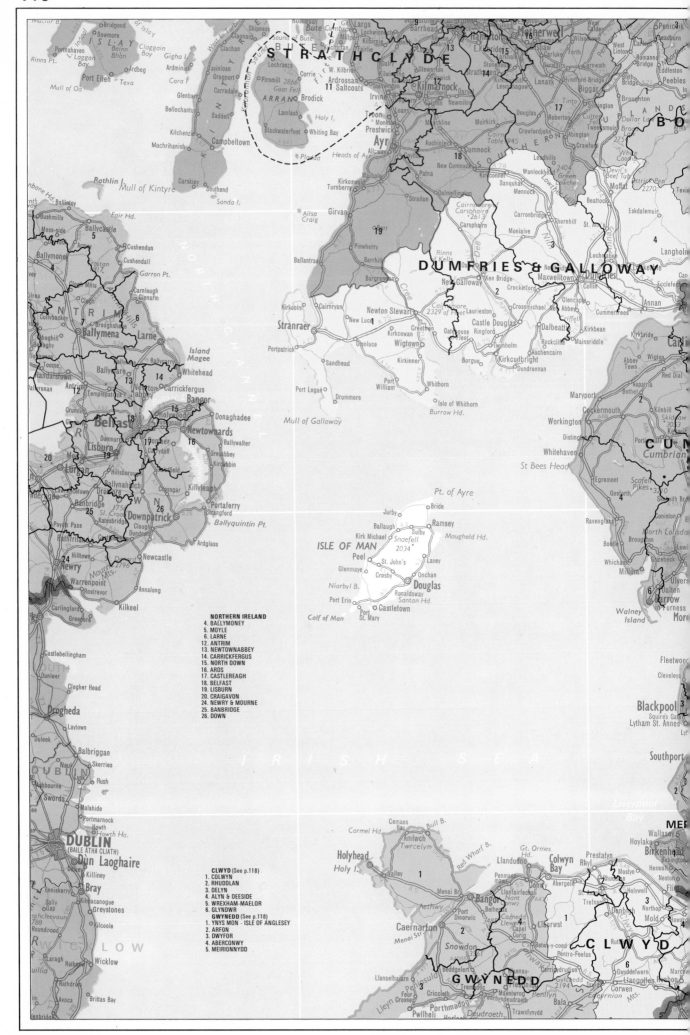

NORTHERN IRELAND
4. BALLYMONEY
5. MOYLE
6. LARNE
12. ANTRIM
13. NEWTOWNABBEY
14. CARRICKFERGUS
15. NORTH DOWN
16. ARDS
17. CASTLEREAGH
18. BELFAST
19. LISBURN
20. CRAIGAVON
24. NEWRY & MOURNE
25. BANBRIDGE
26. DOWN

CLWYD (See p.118)
1. COLWYN
2. RHUDDLAN
3. DELYN
4. ALYN & DEESIDE
5. WREXHAM-MAELOR
6. GLYNDWR
GWYNEDD (See p.118)
1. YNYS MON - ISLE OF ANGLESEY
2. ARFON
3. DWYFOR
4. ABERCONWY
5. MEIRIONNYDD

1:1 250 000

BORDERS (See p.116)
1. TWEEDDALE
2. ETTRICK & LAUDERDALE
3. BERWICKSHIRE
4. ROXBURGH
DUMFRIES & GALLOWAY
1. WIGTOWN
3. STEWARTRY
4. ANNANDALE & ESKDALE
LOTHIAN (See p.115)
STRATHCLYDE (See p.114-116)

CHESHIRE
1. WARRINGTON
2. HALTON
3. ELLESMERE PORT & NESTON
4. VALE ROYAL
5. MACCLESFIELD
6. CHESTER
7. CREWE & NANTWICH
8. CONGLETON
CLEVELAND
1. HARTLEPOOL
2. STOCKTON-ON-TEES
3. MIDDLESBROUGH
4. LANGBAURGH
CUMBRIA
1. CARLISLE
2. ALLERDALE
3. EDEN
4. COPELAND
5. SOUTH LAKELAND
6. BARROW-IN-FURNESS
DERBYSHIRE (See p.119)
1. HIGH PEAK
2. WEST DERBYSHIRE
3. NORTH EAST DERBYSHIRE
4. CHESTERFIELD
5. BOLSOVER
6. AMBER VALLEY
7. EREWASH
8. DERBY
9. SOUTH DERBYSHIRE
DURHAM
1. CHESTER-LE-STREET
2. DERWENTSIDE
3. DURHAM
4. EASINGTON
5. SEDGEFIELD
6. WEAR VALLEY
7. TEESDALE
8. DARLINGTON
HUMBERSIDE
1. NORTH WOLDS
2. HOLDERNESS
3. KINGSTON UPON HULL
4. BEVERLEY
5. BOOTHFERRY
6. SCUNTHORPE
7. GLANFORD
8. GRIMSBY
9. CLEETHORPES

LANCASHIRE
1. LANCASTER
2. WYRE
3. BLACKPOOL
4. FYLDE
5. PRESTON
6. RIBBLE VALLEY
7. PENDLE
8. BURNLEY
9. ROSSENDALE
10. HYNDBURN
11. BLACKBURN
12. CHORLEY
13. SOUTH RIBBLE
14. WEST LANCASHIRE
LINCOLNSHIRE (See p.119)
1. WEST LINDSEY
2. LINCOLN
3. EAST LINDSEY
4. NORTH KESTEVEN
5. BOSTON
6. SOUTH KESTEVEN
7. SOUTH HOLLAND
MANCHESTER, GREATER
1. WIGAN
2. BOLTON
3. BURY
4. ROCHDALE
5. OLDHAM
6. TAMESIDE
7. STOCKPORT
8. MANCHESTER
9. SALFORD
10. TRAFFORD
MERSEYSIDE
1. WIRRAL
2. SEFTON
3. LIVERPOOL
4. KNOWSLEY
5. ST. HELENS
NORTHUMBERLAND
1. BERWICK-UPON-TWEED
2. ALNWICK
3. CASTLE MORPETH
4. WANSBECK
5. BLYTH VALLEY
6. TYNEDALE
NOTTINGHAMSHIRE (See p.119)
1. BASSETLAW
2. MANSFIELD
3. NEWARK
4. ASHFIELD
5. GEDLING
6. BROXTOWE
7. NOTTINGHAM
8. RUSHCLIFFE
SALOP (See p.119)
STAFFORDSHIRE (See p.118)
1. NEWCASTLE-UNDER-LYME
2. STOKE-ON-TRENT
3. STAFFORDSHIRE MOORLANDS
4. STAFFORD
5. EAST STAFFORDSHIRE
6. SOUTH STAFFORDSHIRE
7. CANNOCK CHASE
8. LICHFIELD
9. TAMWORTH
TYNE & WEAR
1. NEWCASTLE UPON TYNE
2. NORTH TYNESIDE
3. SOUTH TYNESIDE
4. RICHMONDSHIRE
5. CRAVEN
6. HARROGATE
7. YORK
8. SELBY
YORKSHIRE, SOUTH
1. BARNSLEY
2. DONCASTER
3. ROTHERHAM
4. SHEFFIELD
YORKSHIRE, WEST
1. CALDERDALE
2. BRADFORD
3. LEEDS
4. WAKEFIELD
5. KIRKLEES

Flamborough Hd.

© John Bartholomew & Son Ltd

0   10   20   30   40   50 Miles
0 10 20 30 40 50 60 70 80 Kilometres

CLWYD (See p.116)
DYFED
1. CEREDIGION
2. PRESELI
3. SOUTH PEMBROKESHIRE
4. CARMARTHEN
5. LLANELLI
6. DINEFWR
GLAMORGAN, MID
1. OGWR
2. RHONDDA
3. CYNON VALLEY
4. MERTHYR TYDFIL
5. RHYMNEY VALLEY
6. TAFF-ELY
GLAMORGAN, SOUTH
1. VALE OF GLAMORGAN
2. CARDIFF
GLAMORGAN, WEST
1. SWANSEA
2. LLIW VALLEY
3. NEATH
4. AFAN
GWENT
1. BLAENAU GWENT
2. ISLWYN
3. TORFAEN
4. MONMOUTH
5. NEWPORT
GWYNEDD (See p.116)
POWYS
1. MONTGOMERY
2. RADNOR
3. BRECKNOCK

AVON
1. NORTHAVON
2. BRISTOL
3. KINGSWOOD
4. WOODSPRING
5. WANSDYKE
6. BATH
CORNWALL
1. NORTH CORNWALL
2. CARADON
3. RESTORMEL
4. CARRICK
5. KERRIER
6. PENWITH
DEVON
1. NORTH DEVON
2. TORRIDGE
3. TIVERTON
4. EAST DEVON
5. EXETER
6. TEIGNBRIDGE
7. WEST DEVON
8. PLYMOUTH
9. SOUTH HAMS
10. TORBAY
DORSET
1. NORTH DORSET
2. WIMBORNE
3. CHRISTCHURCH
4. BOURNEMOUTH
5. POOLE
6. PURBECK
7. WEST DORSET
8. WEYMOUTH & PORTLAND
SOMERSET
1. WEST SOMERSET
2. TAUNTON DEANE
3. SEDGEMOOR
4. MENDIP
5. YEOVIL

ISLES OF SCILLY

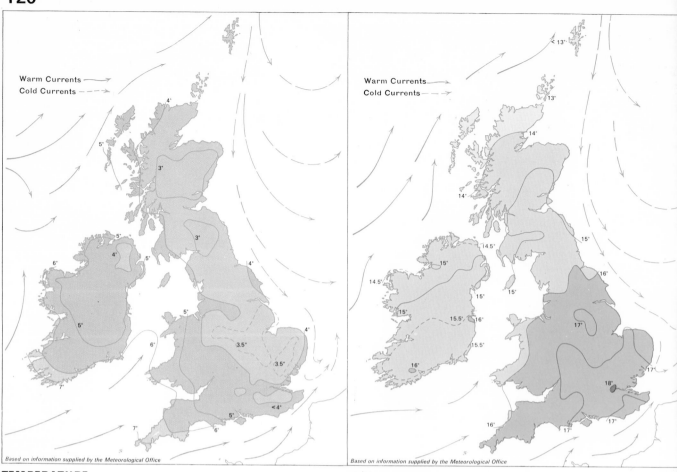

TEMPERATURE (Reduced to Sea Level)
JANUARY *The Figures indicate the Temperature in °C*

TEMPERATURE (Reduced to Sea Level)
JULY *The Figures indicate the Temperature in °C*

Based on information supplied by the Meteorological Office

Warm Currents
Cold Currents

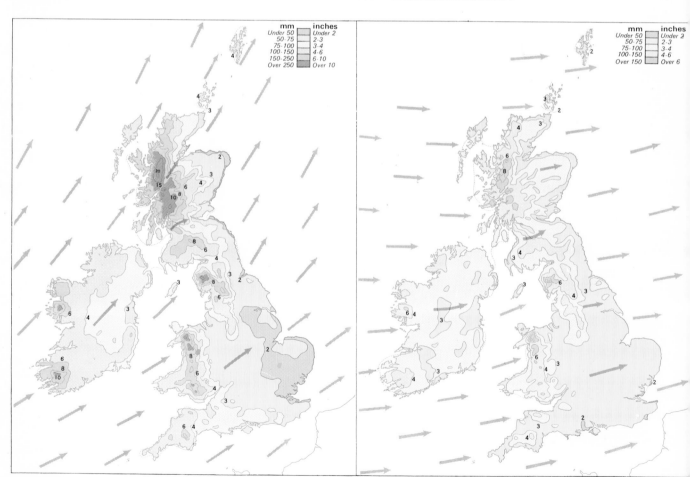

mm	inches
Under 50	Under 2
50-75	2-3
75-100	3-4
100-150	4-6
150-250	6-10
Over 250	Over 10

mm	inches
Under 50	Under 2
50-75	2-3
75-100	3-4
100-150	4-6
Over 150	Over 6

PRECIPITATION *The Figures indicate the Precipitation in Inches.*
JANUARY *The Prevailing Winds are shown by arrows*

PRECIPITATION *The Figures indicate the Precipitation in Inches.*
JULY *The Prevailing Winds are shown by arrows*

1:10 800 000

AVERAGE ANNUAL SUNSHINE
Number of days with more than
9 hours of bright sunshine

FOG
Average number of occasions of thick fog
(visibility less than 200 m at 9 a.m.)

AVERAGE ANNUAL RAINFALL *The Figures indicate the Precipitation in Inches.*

SNOW COVER
Average number of days with snow
falling on low ground (0-60m.)

1:10 800 000

© John Bartholomew & Son Ltd

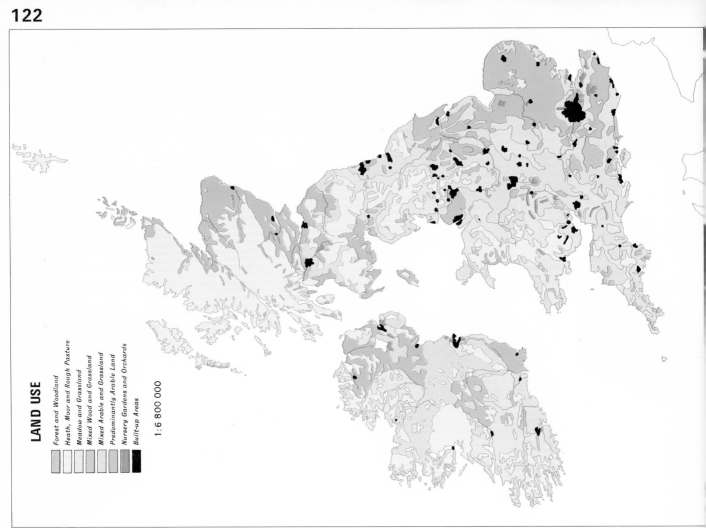

LAND USE

Forest and Woodland
Heath, Moor and Rough Pasture
Meadow and Grassland
Mixed Wood and Grassland
Mixed Arable and Grassland
Predominantly Arable Land
Nursery Gardens and Orchards
Built-up Areas

1:6 800 000

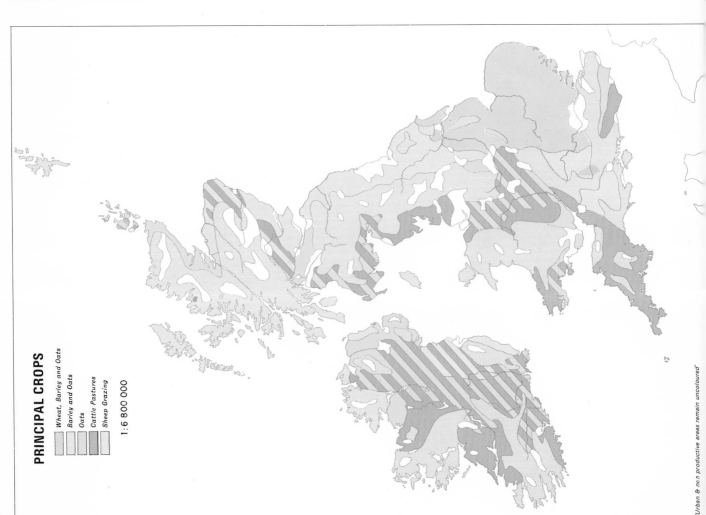

PRINCIPAL CROPS

Wheat, Barley and Oats
Barley and Oats
Oats
Cattle Pastures
Sheep Grazing

1:6 800 000

'Urban & non productive areas remain uncoloured'

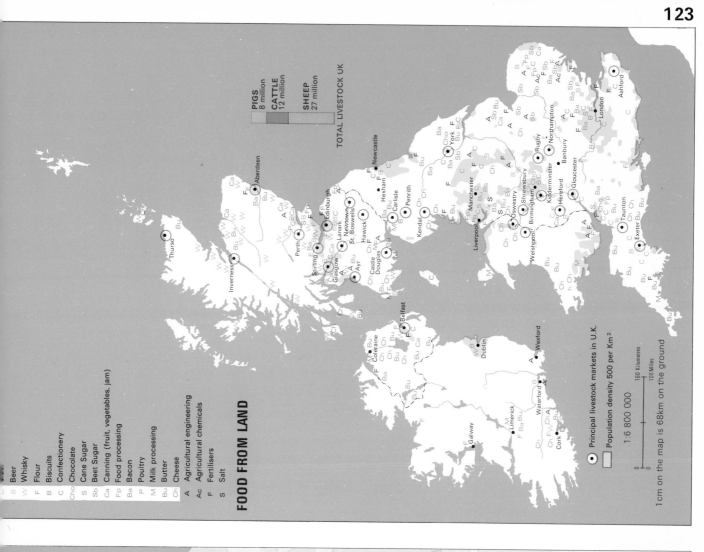

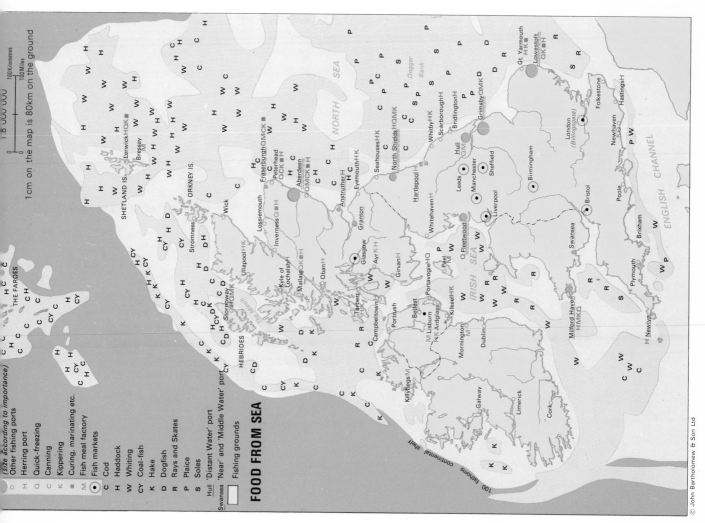

POPULATION DISTRIBUTION

KEY

CITIES AND TOWNS

over 1 Million	**LONDON**
500 000–1 Million	**GLASGOW MANCHESTER**
250 000–500 000	**Bristol**
100 000–250 000	York
50 000–100 000	Halifax
20 000–50 000	Barry
10 000–20 000	St. Andrews
Less than 10 000	Cardigan
Capital Cities	_Edinburgh_
New Towns	B=Bracknell

POPULATION

Dense
Moderate
Sparse
Few

Shetland Is.

Orkney Is.

ATLANTIC

OCEAN

NORTH SEA

GLASGOW _Edinburgh_

Belfast

DUBLIN

IRISH SEA

LEEDS

MANCHESTER

LIVERPOOL SHEFFIELD

S on T

BIRMINGHAM

LONDON

Cardiff

ENGLISH CHANNEL

0   20   40   60   80   100   120 Kilometres
0   20   40   60   80 miles

© John Bartholomew & Son Ltd

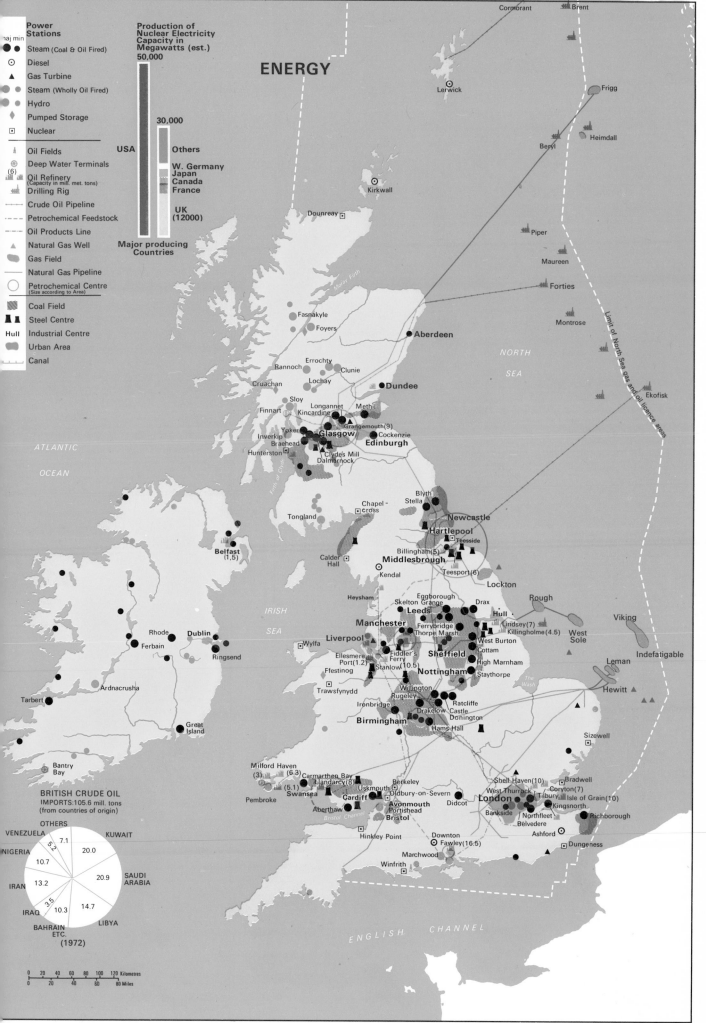

ENERGY

John Bartholomew & Son Ltd

Iron Ore, Steel and other Metals

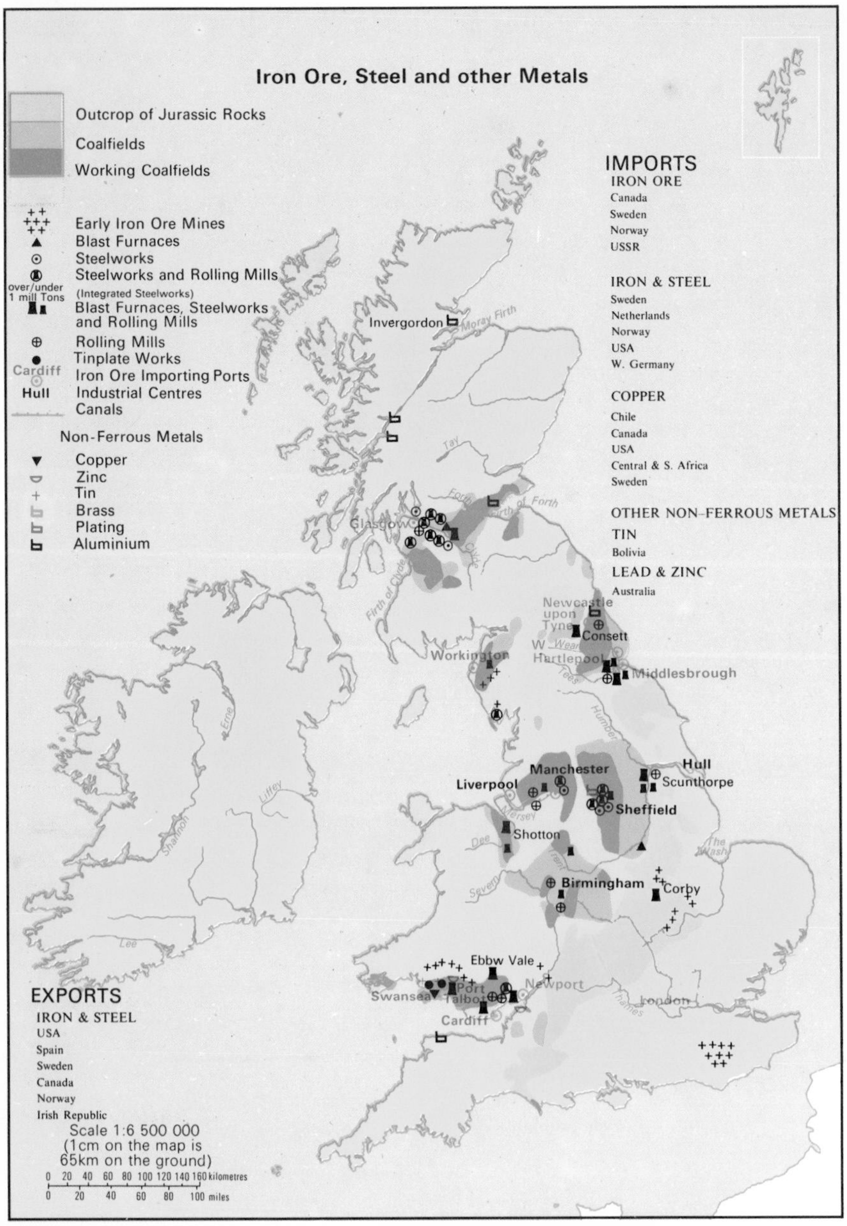
Outcrop of Jurassic Rocks
Coalfields
Working Coalfields
Early Iron Ore Mines
Blast Furnaces
Steelworks
Steelworks and Rolling Mills (Integrated Steelworks)
over/under 1 mill Tons
Blast Furnaces, Steelworks and Rolling Mills
Rolling Mills
Tinplate Works
Iron Ore Importing Ports
Industrial Centres
Canals
Non-Ferrous Metals
Copper
Zinc
Tin
Brass
Plating
Aluminium
IMPORTS
IRON ORE
Canada
Sweden
Norway
USSR
IRON & STEEL
Sweden
Netherlands
Norway
USA
W. Germany
COPPER
Chile
Canada
USA
Central & S. Africa
Sweden
OTHER NON-FERROUS METALS
TIN
Bolivia
LEAD & ZINC
Australia
EXPORTS
IRON & STEEL
USA
Spain
Sweden
Canada
Norway
Irish Republic
Scale 1:6 500 000
(1cm on the map is 65km on the ground)
0 20 40 60 80 100 120 140 160 kilometres
0 20 40 60 80 100 miles
Invergordon
Moray Firth
Tay
Forth
Firth of Forth
Glasgow
Clyde
Firth of Clyde
Newcastle upon Tyne
Consett
Workington
Wear
Hartlepool
Tees
Middlesbrough
Humber
Hull
Scunthorpe
Manchester
Liverpool
Mersey
Sheffield
Dee
Shotton
Trent
The Wash
Severn
Birmingham
Corby
Ebbw Vale
Swansea
Port Talbot
Newport
Cardiff
London
Thames
Erne
Liffey
Shannon
Lee

MANUFACTURES

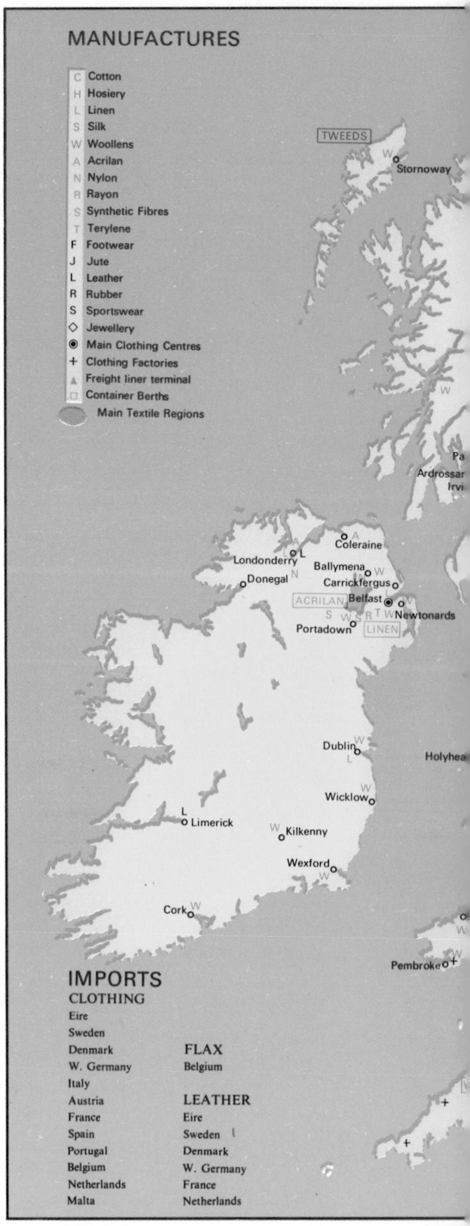
C Cotton
H Hosiery
L Linen
S Silk
W Woollens
A Acrilan
N Nylon
R Rayon
S Synthetic Fibres
T Terylene
F Footwear
J Jute
L Leather
R Rubber
S Sportswear
Jewellery
Main Clothing Centres
Clothing Factories
Freight liner terminal
Container Berths
Main Textile Regions
TWEEDS
Stornoway
Ardrossan
Irvine
Londonderry
Coleraine
Donegal
Ballymena
Carrickfergus
ACRILAN
Belfast
Newtonards
Portadown
LINEN
Dublin
Holyhead
Wicklow
Limerick
Kilkenny
Wexford
Cork
Pembroke
IMPORTS
CLOTHING
Eire
Sweden
Denmark
W. Germany
Italy
Austria
France
Spain
Portugal
Belgium
Netherlands
Malta
FLAX
Belgium
LEATHER
Eire
Sweden
Denmark
W. Germany
France
Netherlands

General and Mechanical Engineering

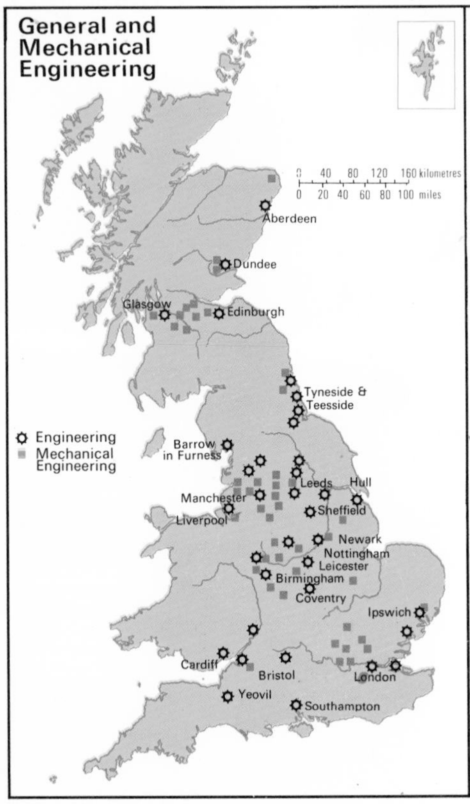
0 40 80 120 160 kilometres
0 20 40 60 80 100 miles
Engineering
Mechanical Engineering
Aberdeen
Dundee
Glasgow
Edinburgh
Tyneside & Teesside
Barrow in Furness
Leeds
Hull
Manchester
Liverpool
Sheffield
Newark
Nottingham
Leicester
Birmingham
Coventry
Ipswich
Cardiff
Bristol
London
Yeovil
Southampton

Heavy Engineering and Shipbuilding

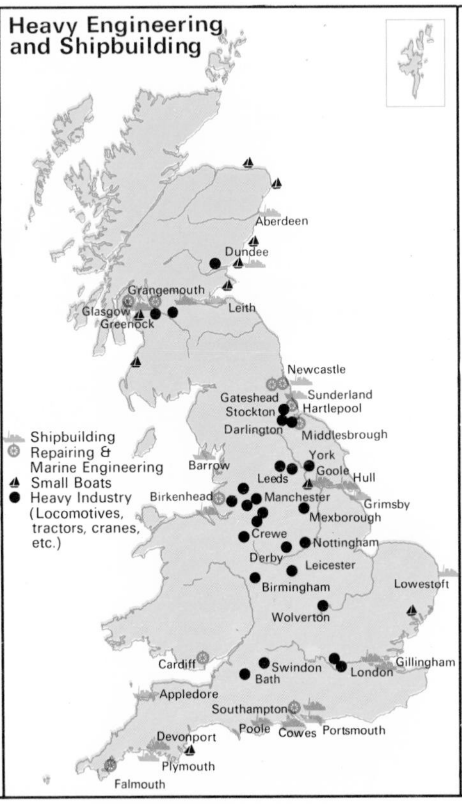
Shipbuilding
Repairing & Marine Engineering
Small Boats
Heavy Industry (Locomotives, tractors, cranes, etc.)
Aberdeen
Dundee
Grangemouth
Glasgow
Greenock
Leith
Newcastle
Gateshead
Sunderland
Stockton
Hartlepool
Darlington
Middlesbrough
York
Barrow
Leeds
Goole
Hull
Birkenhead
Manchester
Grimsby
Mexborough
Crewe
Nottingham
Derby
Leicester
Birmingham
Lowestoft
Wolverton
Cardiff
Swindon
Bath
London
Gillingham
Appledore
Southampton
Poole
Cowes
Portsmouth
Devonport
Plymouth
Falmouth

Light and Electrical Industries

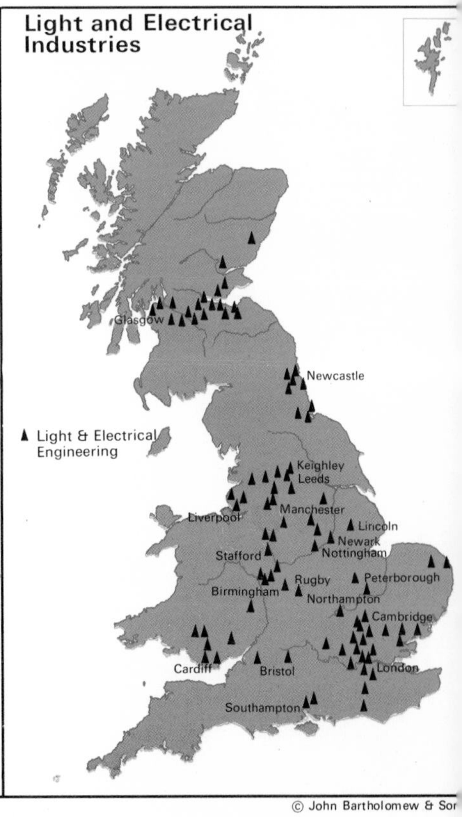
Light & Electrical Engineering
Glasgow
Newcastle
Keighley
Leeds
Liverpool
Manchester
Lincoln
Newark
Nottingham
Stafford
Rugby
Peterborough
Birmingham
Northampton
Cambridge
Cardiff
Bristol
London
Southampton

© John Bartholomew & Son

IMPORTS

FOOTWEAR
Eire
W. Germany
Poland
Czechoslovakia
France
Italy
Austria
Spain
Switzerland

TEXTILES
Eire
W. Germany
Italy
Austria
Switzerland
France
Spain
Belgium
Netherlands

HIDES, FUR & SKIN
Eire
Norway
Finland
W. Germany
Poland
France

WOOD
Finland
Sweden
Norway

TWEEDS
WOOLLENS

Inverness
Aberdeen
Dundee J
Leven J
Dunfermline J Kirkcaldy
Glasgow
W S C
Lanark Edinburgh
Kilmarnock O Galashiels
Darvel
Hawick O
Dumfries F
WORSTEDS
Carlisle J
CARPETS
Stockton
S
Kendal F
Heysham Lancaster
W York
Keighley Bradford WOOLLENS
Burnley L Leeds
Preston Halifax S
Bolton Huddersfield
Wigan Oldham Dewsbury
Liverpool Manchester Sheffield
Birkenhead Warrington
Macclesfield LACE
HOSIERY Nottingham
Derby J
Spondon Loughborough
Wolverhampton Leicester
Hinckley
Kidderminster Birmingham
Coventry
NYLON Northampton
Braintree
FOOTWEAR Harwich
Pontypool N Ipswich Felixstowe
Newport Stroud
Cardiff Bristol London
Bradford-on-Avon Camberley Croydon
WOOLLENS Yeovil Wilton
Axminster Southampton Portsmouth
Newton Abbot

Newcastle
Middlesbrough
Hull
Grimsby
Kings Lynn
Norwich F S

1:6 450 000
0   160 Kilometres
0   100 Miles
(1cm on the map is 64.5km on the ground)

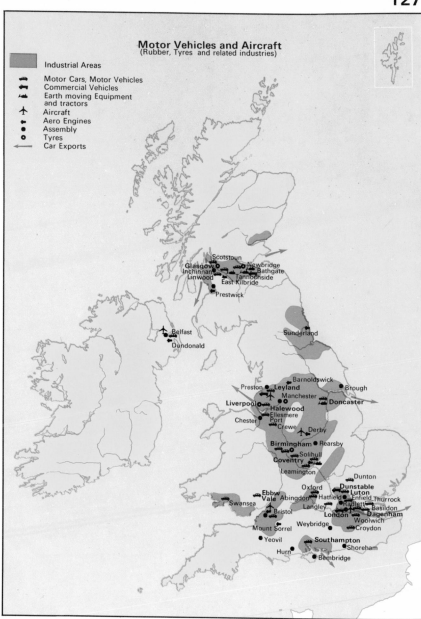

Motor Vehicles and Aircraft
(Rubber, Tyres and related industries)

Industrial Areas
🚗 Motor Cars, Motor Vehicles
🚚 Commercial Vehicles
🚜 Earth moving Equipment and tractors
✈ Aircraft
Aero Engines
● Assembly
○ Tyres
← Car Exports

Glasgow Scotstoun Newbridge
Inchinnan Bathgate
Linwood Tannochside
East Kilbride
Prestwick

Belfast
Dundonald

Sunderland

Preston Barnoldswick
Leyland Brough
Manchester
Liverpool Doncaster
Halewood
Ellesmere Chester Port
Crewe Derby
Birmingham Rearsby
Solihull
Coventry
Leamington Dunton
Oxford Dunstable
Ebbw Abingdon Hatfield Luton
Vale Langley Enfield Thurrock
Swansea Radlett Basildon
Bristol London Dagenham
Mount Sorrel Woolwich
Weybridge Croydon
Yeovil Southampton
Hurn Shoreham
Bembridge

Building and Household

Bricks
Cement
Slate
Granite
Sandstone
China
Kaolin
Saw Milling
Timber
Furniture
Hardware
Cutlery
Sewing Machines
Washing Machines
Refrigerators
Tools & Implements
Linoleum & Linotiles
Glass

Corpach
Aberdeen
Oban Tayport
Singer Kirkcaldy
Glasgow Dunbar
Penicuik
Kilmarnock
Newcastle
Creetown Hartlepool
Lancaster
Leeds Hull
Liverpool Manchester
St. Helens Sheffield
Stoke
Wolverhampton Peterborough
Birmingham Rugby
Worcester Bedford Great Yarmouth
Cardiff Harwich
Bristol London
Southampton
St. Austell

Chemicals and Plastics

GC General Chemicals
S Soap
D Detergents
Ph Pharmaceuticals
Dy Dyestuffs
○ Petrochemical Centres
R Rubber (Imported)
SR Synthetic Rubber
CP Chemical Products (Made from Rubber)
RP Rubber Plastics
RG Rubber Goods
NM Nuclear Materials
F Fertilisers

Aberdeen
Perth Dy Dundee
Dy
Glasgow Dy GC GC Leith
GC Grangemouth
Ardrossan Dy Galashiels
GC Newcastle
Durham Billingham
Barnard Castle GC Teesside
Ph
Sellafield Middlesbrough
Selwick GC Hull
Liverpool NM
Manchester
GC DPh GC Ph
Birkenhead S GC
Capenhurst Northwich
GC
Leicester Nottingham Ph
Norwich
GC Birmingham Ipswich
CP Harwich
Colchester
Swansea R GC Pontypool London
GC Slough
(Area pecked under constn.)
SR Hythe

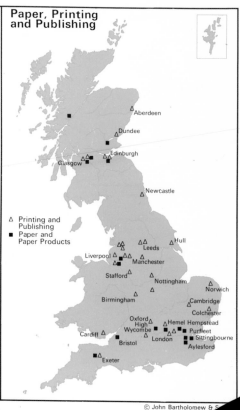

Paper, Printing and Publishing

△ Printing and Publishing
■ Paper and Paper Products

Aberdeen
Dundee
Edinburgh
Glasgow
Newcastle
Hull
Leeds
Liverpool Manchester
Stafford Nottingham
Birmingham Norwich
Cambridge
Colchester
Oxford High Hemel Hempstead
Wycombe Purfleet
Cardiff London Sittingbourne
Bristol Aylesford
Exeter

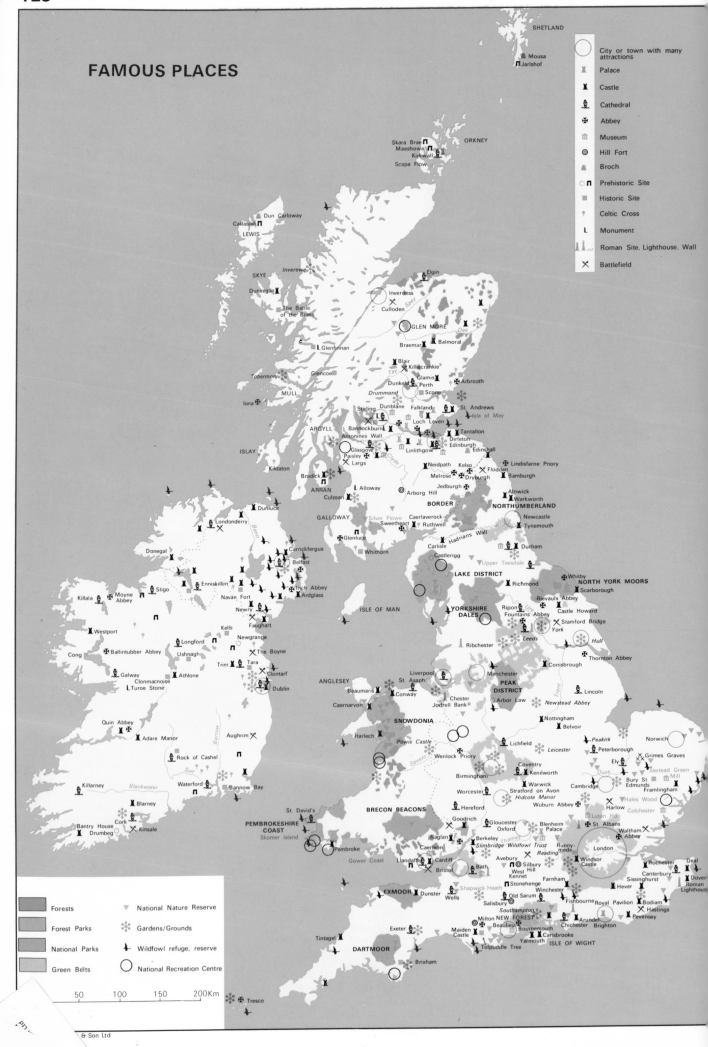

FAMOUS PLACES

Legend:
- ⭕ City or town with many attractions
- Palace
- Castle
- Cathedral
- Abbey
- Museum
- Hill Fort
- Broch
- Prehistoric Site
- Historic Site
- Celtic Cross
- Monument
- Roman Site, Lighthouse, Wall
- Battlefield

Map region labels:
SHETLAND, Mousa, Jarlshof, ORKNEY, Skara Brae, Maeshowe, Kirkwall, Scapa Flow

Callanish, Dun Carloway, LEWIS, SKYE, Inverewe, Dunvegan, The Battle of the Braes, Elgin, Inverness, Culloden, GLEN MORE, Braemar, Balmoral, Glenfinnan, Blair, Killiecrankie, Tobermory, Glencoe, Glamis, Dunkeld, Perth, Arbroath, Scone, MULL, Iona, Drummond, Dunblane, Falkland, St. Andrews, Isle of May, Stirling, Loch Leven, Tantallon, ARGYLL, Bannockburn, Antonines Wall, Dirleton, Edinburgh, Edinshall, ISLAY, Glasgow, Linlithgow, Paisley, Largs, Kildaton, Neidpath, Kelso, Flodden, Lindisfarne Priory, Brodick, Melrose, Dryburgh, Bamburgh, ARRAN, Alloway, Jedburgh, Alnwick, Culzean, Arborg Hill, Warkworth, BORDER, Newcastle, NORTHUMBERLAND, Dunluce, GALLOWAY, Caerlaverock, Tynemouth, Londonderry, Sweetheart, Ruthwell, Donegal, Carrickfergus, Carlisle, Hadrians Wall, Durham, Belfast, Castlerigg, Upper Teesdale, LAKE DISTRICT, Whitby, NORTH YORK MOORS, Enniskillen, Richmond, Scarborough, Killala, Sligo, Inch Abbey, Rievaulx Abbey, Moyne Abbey, Navan Fort, Ardglass, YORKSHIRE DALES, Ripon, Castle Howard, Westport, Newry, Fountains Abbey, Stamford Bridge, York, Longford, Kells, Newgrange, Ribchester, Leeds, Hull, Ballintubber Abbey, Ushnagh, The Boyne, Cong, ISLE OF MAN, Thornton Abbey, Galway, Trim, Tara, Clonmacnoise, Athlone, Clontarf, Conisbrough, Turoe Stone, Dublin, ANGLESEY, Liverpool, St. Asaph, Manchester, Lincoln, Quin Abbey, Beaumaris, Conway, PEAK DISTRICT, Adare Manor, Aughrim, Caernarvon, Chester, Jodrell Bank, Arbor Law, Newstead Abbey, Rock of Cashel, SNOWDONIA, Nottingham, Belvoir, Killarney, Waterford, Harlech, Powis Castle, Lichfield, Peakirk, Norwich, Blackwater, Bannow Bay, Leicester, Peterborough, Wenlock Priory, Grimes Graves, Blarney, Birmingham, Coventry, Ely, Saxtead Green Mill, Cork, Kinsale, St. David's, BRECON BEACONS, Kenilworth, Cambridge, Bury St. Edmunds, Bantry House, Drumbeg, Warwick, Stratford on Avon, Framlingham, Worcester, Hidcote Manor, Harlow, Hales Wood, Colchester, PEMBROKESHIRE COAST, Skomer Island, Hereford, Woburn Abbey, St. Albans, Goodrich, Gloucester, Oxford, Blenheim Palace, Waltham Abbey, Raglan, Berkeley, Runnymede, Caerleon, Slimbridge Wildfowl Trust, Reading, Rochester, Pembroke, Gower Coast, Llandaff, Cardiff, Avebury, Windsor Castle, Canterbury, Deal, Bristol, Bath, Silbury Hill, London, Sissinghurst, Dover Roman Lighthouse, West Kennet, Farnham, Hever, Bodiam, EXMOOR, Dunster, Stonehenge, Winchester, Fishbourne, Royal Pavilion, Wells, Old Sarum, Arundel, Brighton, Salisbury, Southampton, Chichester, Pevensey, Milton Abbas, Beaulieu, Bournemouth, ISLE OF WIGHT, Exeter, Maiden Castle, NEW FOREST, Carisbrooke, Tintagel, Tolpuddle Tree, Yarmouth, DARTMOOR, Brixham, Tresco

Bottom-left legend:
- Forests
- Forest Parks
- National Parks
- Green Belts
- ▽ National Nature Reserve
- ❋ Gardens/Grounds
- Wildfowl refuge, reserve
- ⭕ National Recreation Centre

Scale: 50 100 150 200 Km

& Son Ltd

LAYOUT OF MAP PAGES 2-89

Scale 1:4 500 000

0 20 40 60 80 100 Kilometres

0 20 40 60 Miles